W9-BVN-162

GRAPHIC NOVELS CORE COLLECTION

FIRST EDITION

CORE COLLECTION SERIES

FORMERLY
STANDARD CATALOG SERIES

MARIA HUGGER, GENERAL EDITOR

CHILDREN'S CORE COLLECTION
MIDDLE & JUNIOR HIGH CORE COLLECTION
SENIOR HIGH CORE COLLECTION
NONFICTION CORE COLLECTION
FICTION CORE COLLECTION
YOUNG ADULT FICTION CORE COLLECTION
GRAPHIC NOVELS CORE COLLECTION

GRAPHIC NOVELS CORE COLLECTION

FIRST EDITION

EDITED BY

KENDAL SPIRES

GABRIELA TOTH

AND

MARIA HUGGER

H. W. Wilson
A Division of EBSCO Information Services
Ipswich, Massachusetts
2016
GREY HOUSE PUBLISHING

ISBN 978-1-68217-070-0

Abridged Dewey Decimal Classification and Relative Index, Edition 15 is © 2004-2012 OCLC Online Computer Library Center, Inc. Used with Permission. DDC, Dewey, Dewey Decimal Classification, and WebDewey are registered trademarks of OCLC.

Graphic Novels Core Collection, 2016, published by Grey House Publishing, Inc., Amenia, NY, under exclusive license from EBSCO Infomation Systems, Inc.

Library of Congress Cataloging-in-Publication Data

Publisher's Cataloging-In-Publication Data
(Prepared by The Donohue Group, Inc.)

Names: Spires, Kendal, editor. | Toth, Gabriela, editor. | Hugger, Maria, editor.
Title: Graphic novels core collection / edited by Kendal Spires, Gabriela Toth, and Maria Hugger.
Other Titles: Core collection series.
Description: First edition. | Ipswich, Massachusetts : H. W. Wilson, a division of EBSCO Information Services ; Amenia, NY : Grey House Publishing, 2016. | Includes indexes.
Identifiers: ISBN 978-1-68217-070-0 (hardcover)
Subjects: LCSH: Graphic novels--Bibliography. | Best books.
Classification: LCC PN6710 .G73 2016 | DDC 016.7415--dc23

PRINTED IN THE UNITED STATES OF AMERICA

CONTENTS

CONTENTS

PREFACE

GRAPHIC NOVELS CORE COLLECTION is a selective list of fiction and nonfiction comics and graphic novels for all ages, together with professional aids for librarians and a selection of nonfiction prose materials about comics history and culture. This Core Collection is an abridgement of the database available via EBSCO*host* from EBSCO Information Services which has an additional two recommendation levels, Lexile® measures, book reviews, and expanded metadata, updated weekly. Contact your EBSCO sales rep for a free trial.

What's in this Edition?

This first edition includes more than 3,500 book titles at the Most Highly Recommended and Core Collection recommendation levels. A star (★) at the start of an entry indicates that a book is a "most highly recommended" title. These titles constitute a shortlist of the essential books in a given category or on a given subject. There are often a number of recommended titles on a single subject, and the star designation helps a user who wants only one or two.

History

The Collection was created as an online database in 2007 at H. W. Wilson, with original curation and annotation by librarian Katharine Kan. The initial incarnation contained 1,000 recommended titles, with more added every month after the collection's launch. After EBSCO acquired H. W. Wilson in 2011, new advisors built out the database further. This is the Collection's first time appearing in print.

Scope

All books listed are published in the United States, or published in Canada or the United Kingdom and distributed in the United States. Some out of print books (most notably manga published by TOKYOPOP) are included under the consideration that, though they are no longer available for purchase, they should not be weeded by libraries which already own them.

The Core Collection excludes non-English-language materials, with the exception of bilingual materials. It does include English-language translations of international material, including Japanese manga, Korean manhwa, Franco-Belgian comics ("bandes dessinées"), and others.

Preparation

Books included in this edition were selected by experienced collection development librarians representing public, academic, and school libraries across the United States who also act as a committee of advisors on library policy and trends. The names of participating librarians and their affiliations are listed in the Acknowledgments. To offer feedback or suggest improvements for the next edition, please contact corecollections@ebsco.com.

Organization

Organization and indexing of the records was performed by Grey House Publishing. The Core Collection is organized into multiple parts: the List of Works and separate Author, Title, and Subject Indices.

List of Works. This is arranged in groupings according to grade level (PreK through Grade 5, Grades 6 though 8, Grades 9 through 12, Adult) and by main entry (usually writer/creator, sometimes title or editor) within each section.

Author, Title, and Subject Indices. Three separate indices represent the List of Works with entries for creators, titles, and subjects. Some responsible persons (illustrators, translators, editors, etc.) may not appear in the index of this edition.

ACKNOWLEDGMENTS

H. W. Wilson and EBSCO Information Services express special gratitude to the following librarians who both advised the company in editorial matters and assisted in the selection and weeding of titles for this Core Collection:

Advisory Board

Robin Brenner
Brookline PublicLibrary
Brookline, MA

Gail de Vos
University of Alberta
Edmonton, Alberta, Canada

Brian Flota
James Madison University
Harrisonburg, VA

Leigh Anne Focareta
Carnegie Library
Pittsburgh, PA

Pam Spencer Holley
Library Consultant
Hallwood, Virginia

Steven Jablonski
Skokie Public Library
Skokie, IL

Katharine Kan
Graphic Novel Librarian
Panama City, FL

John Meier
Penn State University
University Park, PA

Rebecca Vargha
University of North Carolina
Chapel Hill, NC

Linda Ward-Callaghan
Joliet Public Library
Joliet, IL

Neal Wyatt
Library Consultant
Richmond, VA

DIRECTIONS FOR USE OF THE
CORE COLLECTION

USES OF THE COLLECTION

GRAPHIC NOVELS CORE COLLECTION is designed to serve a number of purposes:

As an aid in purchasing. The Core Collection is designed to assist in the selection and ordering of titles. Annotations are provided for each title along with information concerning the publisher, ISBN, price, and availability. In evaluating the suitability of a work each library will want to consider the special character of the patron base it serves.

As an aid to the readers' advisor. The work of the reader's advisor is furthered by the information about sequels and companion volumes and the descriptive and critical annotations in the List of Works, and by the subject access in the Index.

As an aid in verification of information. For this purpose full bibliographical data are provided in the List of Works. Entries also include recommended subject headings based upon *Sears List of Subject Headings* and a suggested classification derived from the *Abridged Dewey Decimal Classification and Relative Index*. Notes describe editions available, awards, publication history, and other titles in the series. For the most up-to-date metadata please consult the EBSCO*host* Graphic Novels Core Collection database.

As an aid in curriculum support and following Common Core standards. The subject indexing, grade levels, and annotations are helpful in identifying materials appropriate for lesson planning and classroom use and for following Common Core curricula.

As an aid in collection maintenance. Information about titles available on a subject facilitates decisions to rebind, replace, or discard items. If a book has been demoted to Supplementary or Archival recommendation level (usually because it is no longer in print but sometimes for other reasons), and therefore no longer appears in the print abridgement of the database, that demotion is not intended as a sign that the book is no longer valuable or that it should necessarily be weeded from library collections.

As an instructional aid. The Core Collection is useful in courses that deal with graphic novels & comics as literature and with graphic novel collection development.

ORGANIZATION

The Core Collection consists of two parts: a List of Works, and an Author, Title, and Subject indices.

Part 1. List of Works

The List of Works is arranged by four age groups: Pre-Kindergarten to Grade 5, Grades 6 through 8, Grades 9 through 12, and Adult. Titles repeat across sections according to the grade levels listed in their bibliographic data. The information supplied for each book includes bibliographic description, suggested subject headings, an annotation, and frequently an evaluation from a notable source. Librarians should note that many graphic works are not marketed by age as strictly as prose works, and thus, a book's presence in a juvenile age group is not necessarily indicative of a lack of appeal to adults, especially with regard to the High School and Adult categories.

Within groups, works are arranged alphabetically under main entry, usually the writer and/or creator, and sometimes the title or editor in the case of anthologies with multiple authors. For space considerations, many multi-volume series are condensed into a single entry, with full metadata for the initial volume and a note listing any subsequent volumes.

It should be noted that some titles can be listed under more than one creator. If a particular title is not found where it might be expected, the indexes should be consulted to determine if it is classified elsewhere. Librarians looking for all titles in the collection about a particular character or team (e.g. Superman or the Fantastic Four) are encouraged to consult the index for that particular character's subject heading.

Each listing consists of a full bibliographical description. Prices, which are always subject to change, have been obtained from the publisher, when available, and are as current as possible. Entries include recommended subject headings derived from the *Sears List of Subject Headings*, a suggested classification number from the *Abridged Dewey Decimal Classification and Relative Index*, a brief description of the contents, and, whenever possible, an evaluation from a quoted source. The following is an example of a typical entry and a description of its components:

Keatinge, Joe
    Shutter; Volume 1: Wanderlost. Joe Keatinge; illustrated
by Leila Del Duca, Owen Gieni, Ed Brisson. Image Comics
2014 136 p. Color illustration
Grades: 11 12 Adult   **Fic; 741.5**
    1. Explorers ; 2. Family secrets — Fiction
    1632151456; 9781632151452, $9.99
    In this graphic novel by Joe Keatinge, illustrated by Leila
Del Duca, Owen Gieni, and Ed Brisson, "Kate Kristopher,
once the most famous explorer of an Earth far more fantastic
than the one we know, is forced to return to the adventurous
life she left behind when a family secret threatens to destroy
everything she spent her life protecting." (Publisher's note)
    "Keatinge and Del Duca have created a contemporary
world that teems with casual miracles and feels all the more
real and lived in for it. Crammed with the elements of
children's storybooks, the art offers soft lines and a panoply of
almost-recognizable storybook figures that honor those
hallowed childhood recollections." Booklist
    Originally published in single magazine form as Shutter
#1-6
    Volume 1 of an ongoing series

The names of the writer and the artists are given in conformity with *Anglo-American Cataloguing Rules*, 2nd edition, 2002 revision. The title of the book is *Shutter*, the first volume. The book was published by Image Comics in 2014.

The book has 136 pages and colored illustrations. It sells for $9.99. (Prices given were current when the Collection went to press.) The book is recommended for adults and older teens.

At the end of the last line of type in the body entry is **Fic; 741.5** in bold face type. These are classification numbers derived from the fifteenth edition of the *Abridged Dewey Decimal Classification*. Most of the titles in the collection are listed under 741.5, the Dewey number for comic books and graphic novels, and many have additional numbers listed as well: "Fic" for fiction, and additional number classifications for nonfiction (e.g. graphic biographies or memoirs).

The numbered terms "1. Explorers ; 2. Family secrets — Fiction" are recommended subject headings for this book based on *Sears List of Subject Headings*.

The ISBN (International Standard Book Number) is included to facilitate ordering. The Library of Congress control number is provided when available.

Following are four notes supplying additional information about the book. The first is a description of the book's content, in this case, a description from the publisher. The second is a critical note from *Booklist*. Such annotations are useful in evaluating books for selection and in determining which of several books on the same subject is best suited for the individual reader. The third note describes the form in which the book was originally published (in this case, in single comic book issues), and the final notes that it is the initial volume in a series that is currently being published. Notes are also made to describe sequels and companion volumes, editions available, and awards.

Part 2. Author, Title, and Subject Indices

The Index is three separate alphabetical lists of all the books entered in the Core Collection. Each book is entered under author, title, and subject. The page number is the key to the location of the main entry for the book in the List of Works.

The following are examples of Index entries for the book cited above:

Author   Keatinge, Joe, 608, 980

Title   Shutter; Volume 1: Wanderlost, 608, 980

Subject   **EXPLORERS**
                    Keatinge, Joe. Shutter; Volume 1: Wanderlost, 608, 980

Standards Used

Anglo-American Cataloguing Rules, 2nd ed., 2002 revision, 2005 update. Chicago: American Library Association, 2005.

Dewey, Melvil. *Abridged Dewey Decimal Classification and Relative Index*. 15th ed. Edited by Joan S. Mitchell, et al. Dublin, Ohio: OCLC, 2012.

Bristow, Barbara A. and Christi Showman Farrar, eds. *Sears List of Subject Headings*. 21st ed. Ipswich, MA: The H. W. Wilson Company, 2014.

OUTLINE OF CLASSIFICATION

Reproduced below is the Second Summary of the Dewey Decimal Classification.* Please note, however, that the inclusion of this outline is not to be considered a substitute for consulting the Dewey Decimal Classification itself.

000 Computer science, knowledge & systems
010 Bibliographies
020 Library & information sciences
030 Encyclopedias & books of facts
040 [Unassigned]
050 Magazines, journals & serials
060 Associations, organizations & museums
070 News media, journalism & publishing
080 Quotations
090 Manuscripts & rare books

100 Philosophy
110 Metaphysics
120 Epistemology
130 Parapsychology & occultism
140 Philosophical schools of thought
150 Psychology
160 Logic
170 Ethics
180 Ancient, medieval & eastern philosophy
190 Modern western philosophy

200 Religion
210 Philosophy & theory of religion
220 The Bible
230 Christianity & Christian theology
240 Christian practice & observance
250 Christian pastoral practice & religious orders
260 Christian organization, social work & worship
270 History of Christianity
280 Christian denominations
290 Other religions

300 Social sciences, sociology & anthropology
310 Statistics
320 Political science
330 Economics
340 Law
350 Public administration & military science
360 Social problems & social services
370 Education
380 Commerce, communications & transportation
390 Customs, etiquette & folklore

400 Language
410 Linguistics
420 English & Old English languages
430 German & related languages
440 French & related languages
450 Italian, Romanian & related languages
460 Spanish & Portuguese languages
470 Latin & Italic languages
480 Classical & modern Greek languages
490 Other languages

500 Science
510 Mathematics
520 Astronomy
530 Physics
540 Chemistry
550 Earth sciences & geology
560 Fossils & prehistoric life
570 Life sciences; biology
580 Plants (Botany)
590 Animals (Zoology)

600 Technology
610 Medicine & health
620 Engineering
630 Agriculture
640 Home & family management
650 Management & public relations
660 Chemical engineering
670 Manufacturing
680 Manufacture for specific uses
690 Building & construction

700 Arts
710 Landscaping & area planning
720 Architecture
730 Sculpture, ceramics & metalwork
740 Drawing & decorative arts
750 Painting
760 Graphic arts
770 Photography & computer art
780 Music
790 Sports, games & entertainment

800 Literature, rhetoric & criticism
810 American literature in English
820 English & Old English literatures
830 German & related literatures
840 French & related literatures
850 Italian, Romanian & related literatures
860 Spanish & Portuguese literatures
870 Latin & Italian literatures
880 Classical & modern Greek literatures
890 Other literatures

900 History
910 Geography & travel
920 Biography & genealogy
930 History of ancient world (to ca. 499)
940 History of Europe
950 History of Asia
960 History of Africa
970 History of North America
980 History of South America
990 History of other areas

* Reproduced from Edition 15 of the Abridged Dewey Decimal Classification and Relative Index, published in 2012, by permission of OCLC Online Computer Library Center, Inc., owner of copyright.

GRAPHIC NOVELS CORE COLLECTION

1st Edition

Children: Pre K - 5

Abadzis, Nick
★ **Laika**. First Second Books 2007 205p. Illustration
Grades: 5 6 7 8 9 10 11 12 Adult   **741.5; Fic**
1. Soviet Union — History — 1953-1991; 2. Space flight;
3. Graphic novels
1-59643-101-6; 978-1-59643-101-0
LC 2006-51907
Laika was the abandoned puppy destined to become
Earth's first space traveler. This is her journey. Along with
Laika, there is Korolev, once a political prisoner and now a
driven engineer at the top of the Soviet space program, and
Yelena, the lab technician responsible for Laika's health and
life. The book depicts the dedication and struggles of the
scientists and technicians who worked in the Soviet space
program, based on research Abadzis did before writing this
book. The book includes a bibliography of books and
websites.
"Abadzis's tear-inducing and solidly researched
graphic novel treatment of Laika's surpassingly tragic story
is a standout." Publ Wkly

Abnett, Dan
Abraham Lincoln and the Civil War. Rosen Publishing
Group 2007 24p. Illustration

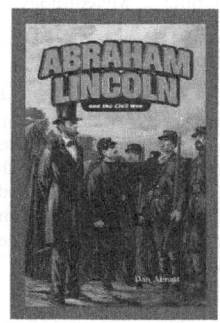
Courtesy of Rosen Publishing

Grades: 1 2 3 4 5   **741.5;
973.7; 92**
1. Biographical graphic
novels; 2. Lincoln,
Abraham, 1809-1865; 3.
United States — History —
1861-1865, Civil War
978-1-4042-3392-8, $22.50
LC 2005037160
Was honest Abe, the
man who ended slavery in
the U.S., America's first
superhero? Beginning
readers can enjoy learning
about Lincoln's life and
deeds and the Civil War in
this simplified comic format
book, which also includes a glossary and a timeline of his
life.
Part of the Jr. Graphic Biographies series.

Christopher Columbus and the Voyage of 1492. Rosen
Publishing Group 2007 24p. Illustration
Grades: 1 2 3 4 5   **741.5; 970.01; 92**
1. America — Exploration; 2. Biographical graphic
novels; 3. Columbus, Christopher, 1451-1506; 4. Graphic
novels
978-1-4042-3390-4, $22.50
LC 2005037161

Courtesy of Rosen Publishing

Readers journey along
with Columbus on his
history-making 1492 voyage to
find a water route to Asia in this
simplified graphic novel for
beginning readers. The book
includes a glossary and a
timeline of his life.
Part of the Jr. Graphic
Biographies series.

Gamble for Victory:
Battle of Gettysburg. Osprey
Publishing 2007 48p.
Illustration
Grades: 3 4 5 6 7 8 9
741.5; 973.7
1. Gettysburg (Pa), Battle of,
1863; 2. United States — History — 1861-1865, Civil
War; 3. War; 4. Graphic novels
978-1-84603-051-2, $9.95
In July 1863, after having observed a forward column
of Union General George G. Meade's cavalry, General
Robert E. Lee sent his 75,000 men of the Army of Northern
Virginia to meet the 97,000 strong Union Army of the
Potomac. Of more than 2,000 land engagements of the
American Civil War, Gettysburg ranks as one of the most
horrific and devastating battles; more men actually fought
and died on this battlefield than in any other encounter on
North American soil and the battle itself marked the
beginning of the end for the Confederacy. This full-color
comic book includes further reading, essential information
on the background, aftermath and key players of the
conflict.
Part of Osprey's Graphic History series. This book is
also available in a library binding edition from the
Rosen Publishing Group under the title The Battle of
Gettysburg: Spilled Blood on Sacred Ground.

George Washington
and the American
Revolution. Rosen
Publishing Group 2007
24p. Illustration
Grades: 1 2 3 4 5
741.5; 973.4; 92
1. Biographical graphic
novels; 2. United States
— History —
1775-1783, Revolution;
3. Washington, George,
1732-1799; 4. Graphic
novels

Courtesy of Rosen Publishing

978-1-4042-3395-9, $22.50

LC 2005037163

If the patriots hadn't won the war, Washington would have been one of the greatest traitors in history. Instead he led the rebels to victory and a great democracy was born. The simplified graphic novel introduces the story to beginning readers and includes a glossary and a timeline of his life.

Part of the Jr. Graphic Biographies series.

Harriet Tubman and the Underground Railroad. Rosen Publishing Group 2007 24p. Illustration

Grades: 1 2 3 4 5 **741.5; 973.7; 92**

1. Biographical graphic novels; 2. Slavery — United States; 3. Tubman, Harriet, 1820?-1913; 4. Underground Railroad; 5. Graphic novels

978-1-4042-3393-5, $22.50

LC 2005037162

Beginning readers can follow Tubman as she risks everything to escape to freedom, and then returns again and again to lead other Africans out of enslavement. This simplified graphic novel includes a glossary and timeline of her life.

Part of the Jr. Graphic Biographies series.

Hernan Cortes and the Fall of the Aztec Empire. Rosen Publishing Group 2007 24p. Illustration

Grades: 1 2 3 4 5

741.5; 972; 92

1. Biographical graphic novels; 2. Cortes, Hernan, 1485-1547; 3. Mexico — History — Conquest, 1519-1540; 4. Graphic novels

978-1-4042-3391-1, $22.50

LC 2006002706

Courtesy of Rosen Publishing

The ruthless explorer Cortes devastated an entire people in his search for fame and gold for himself and for his country. This simplified graphic novel retelling introduces the story for beginning readers, and includes a glossary and a time line.

Part of the Jr. Graphic Biographies series.

The **Monitor** Versus the Merrimac: Ironclads at War. Rosen Publishing Group 2007 48p. Illustration

Grades: 3 4 5 6 7 8 **741.5; 973.7**

1. Hampton Roads (Va), Battle of, 1862; 2. Merrimack (Frigate); 3. Monitor (Ironclad); 4. United States — History — 1861-1865, Civil War; 5. Virginia (Ironclad); 6. Graphic novels

978-1-4042-0778-3, $29.25; 978-1-84603-053-6 (pa)

LC 2006014843

In this historic clash in March 1862, the Union Monitor, called by many a "cheese box on a raft," exchanged cannon shot after cannon shot with the Confederate Merrimac, comically referred to as a "floating barn roof." Although an indecisive victory for either side, the spectacular event, witnessed by hundreds of people on nearby boats and shorelines, forever changed the way naval warfare was to be fought. The book also includes information on the building

Courtesy of Rosen Publishing

of the ironclads, a map showing the routes of the battle, and a list of books for further reading.

Part of the Graphic Battles of the Civil War series; the paperback edition is published by Osprey.

Wallace & Gromit: Plots in Space. Titan Books 2007 Un Illustration

Grades: 2 3 4 5 6 7 8 **741.5; Fic**

1. Humorous graphic novels; 2. Science fiction graphic novels; 3. Wallace & Gromit (Fictional characters); 4. Graphic novels

978-1-84576-362-6, $12.95

Inventor Wallace and his dog Gromit are the animated stars of a series of popular cartoons in England, and one feature film that was also a hit in the U.S. In this original story, the two travel to the orbital R.A.D.I.S.H. (Research Allotment Deployed on International Space Hub), where Wallace wants to test his new invention and eat the giant vegetables being grown in zero gravity. However, they encounter trouble when BOB the intelligent computer seems to go haywire.

Aboff, Marcie

Hurricanes!. By Marcie Aboff; illustrated by Aleksandar Sotirovski. Capstone Press 2012 24 p. Color illustration (First graphics. Wild earth)

Grades: 1 2 3 4 **551.55; 551.55/2**

1. Hurricanes — Juvenile literature; 2. Meteorology — Juvenile literature

1429676078; 1429679514; 9781429676076, $23.32; 9781429679510, $5.95

LC 2011028741

This nonfiction graphic novel, by Marcie Aboff, illustrated by Aleksandar Sotirovski, is part of the "First Graphics" series. In it the author presents information on the science and safety of hurricanes. Topics addressed include how hurricanes form, meteorology practices in naming and comparing individual hurricanes, and safety tips when preparing for a hurricane's arrival.

Includes bibliographical references (p. 23) and index

Tornadoes!. By Marcie Aboff; illustrated by Aleksandar Sotirovski; consultant, Susan L. Cutter. Capstone Press 2012 24 p. Color illustration (First graphics. Wild earth)

Grades: 1 2 3 4 **551.55/3; 551.55**

1. Tornadoes — Juvenile literature

1429679522; 1600571670; 9781429676083, $23.32; 9781429679527, $5.95

LC 2011028743

This nonfiction graphic novel, written by Marcie Aboff and illustrated by Aleksandar Sotirovski, is part of the "First Graphics" series. The book explains the science behind tornadoes, the methods used by meteorologists and other weather scientists to measure them, and advice on how to stay safe when experiencing one.

Includes bibliographical references (p. 23) and index

Abouet, Marguerite

Akissi: feline invasion. By Marguerite Abouet; illustrated by Mathieu Sapin. Flying Eye Books 2013 48 p. Illustration
Grades: 2 3 4 5
741.5; Fic
1. Conduct of life — Juvenile fiction; 2. Siblings — Juvenile fiction
190926301X;
9781909263017, $14.95

Courtesy of Flying Eye Books

This book, by Marguerite Abouet, presents "African vignettes aimed at a younger audience. All seven episodes feature young Akissi and her brother Fofana or her friends getting into trouble for less-than-exemplary . . . behavior. In 'Good Mums,' . . . she borrows a neighbor's baby and tenderly feeds it a stew concocted from discarded scraps found in the market. 'Home Cinema' has her playing lookout while Fofana sells spots in front of the television set to neighborhood children." (Kirkus Reviews)

Adamson, Heather

Charles Darwin and the Theory of Evolution. Capstone Press 2007 32p. Illustration
Grades: 3 4 5 6 7 8 9
576.8; 741.5; 92
1. Darwin, Charles, 1809-1882; 2. Evolution; 3. Naturalists; 4. Graphic novels
978-1-4296-0145-0, $25.26

LC 2007005659

This book uses the graphic novel format to tell the story of how Charles Darwin developed his controversial theory of evolution based on the research he conducted during his voyage on the HMS Beagle. The book includes additional facts and a list books for further reading.

Part of the Graphic Library Invention and Discovery series.

Adamson, Thomas K.

Lessons in Science Safety with Max Axiom, Super Scientist. Capstone/Graphic Library 2006 32p. Illustration
Grades: 5 6 7 8 9
508.2; 741.5
1. Science — Experiments; 2. Graphic novels
978-0-7368-6834-1, $18.95

Using the graphic novel format and the engaging fictional scientist character Max Axiom, a tall, muscular African American, this volume shows students conducting science experiments and demonstrates how and why to wear safety goggles, call for help when accidents occur, and safety procedures for dealing with unknown substances. This is part of the Graphic Science series.

"This will be a good choice for science classes during the opening weeks of the school year." (Booklist)

The Adventures of the Fly Volume 1
Archie Comics 2004 96p. Illustration
Grades: 3 4 5 6 7 8 9 10 11 12 Adult
741.5; Fic
1. Adventure graphic novels; 2. Superhero graphic novels
1-879794-18-7, $12.95

This book highlights one of the pioneering super-hero titles of the Silver Age: The Fly. Tommy Troy is a young boy whose world is turned upside down when he meets an emissary of the Fly World and is given a special ring that magically transforms him into the superhuman Fly. Considered an early prototype of Spider-Man, the Fly's earliest adventures were charted by some of the most legendary creative talent in comics: Jack Kirby, Joe Simon, Jack Davis, and Al Williamson. All of these artists and more are featured in this special edition that collects titanic tales from 1959 and 1960.

Aguirre, Jorge

Dragons beware!. Written by Jorge Aguirre; art by Rafael Rosado; colors by John Novak. First Second 2015 160 p. Color; Illustration (Chronicles of Claudette)
Grades: 3 4 5
741.5; Fic
1. Adventure graphic novels; 2. Dragons; 3. Fairy tales; 4. Graphic novels
1596438789; 9781596438781, $14.99

LC 2014047290

"Scrappy Claudette sets out once again with her pal Marie and her little brother Gaston to right wrongs and fight evil. And this time, it's personal. Claudette is out to get the dragon who ate her father's legs. . . and his legendary sword. But as usual, nothing is as simple as it seems, and Claudette is going to need Marie and Gaston's help more than ever." (Publisher's note)

"This volume contains many of the same elements that made its predecessor so successful. The art perfectly suits the tone and action and the story is smart and funny. The true strength of the series, however, lies in the characterization." SLJ

Sequel to: Giants beware! (2012)

★ **Giants** beware!. Written by Jorge Aguirre; illustrated by Rafael Rosado. First Second 2012 202 p.
Grades: 3 4 5
741.5/973; 741.5
1. Adventure graphic novels; 2. Fairy tales; 3. Fairy tales; 4. Giants; 5. Humorous graphic novels; 6. Graphic novels
1596435828; 9781596435827

LC 2011030471

In this children's graphic novel, "spunky Claudette is set on becoming a monster slayer like her father. . . . When she hears the story of a giant on the loose, she is determined to leave her home—accompanied by her cowardly brother, Gaston, and best friend Marie—in order to set things right. . . When Claudette discovers that not all stories are as they seem, she and her friends must fool the adults who have come to bring them home to protect an innocent monster." (Publishers Weekly)

Followed by Dragons beware! (2015)

Allan, Von

Stargazer, volume one. Von Allan Studio 2010 115p. Illustration
Grades: 4 5 6 7 8 9
741.5; Fic

1. Adventure graphic novels; 2. Friendship; 3. Science fiction graphic novels; 4. Graphic novels
978-0-9781237-2-7, $14.95

Courtesy of Von Allan Studio

Marni's grandmother has just died, and she left a strange device that the two of them played with whenever Marni had visited. No one knows how Marni's grandmother got it, and it has never done anything. Her best friends, Elora and Sophie, come over for a last backyard campout before the weather turns cold, and when they each put a hand on the device, an extremely bright light nearly blinds them. After things seem to go back to normal, the girls go outside to find Marni's house gone, the device vanished, and none of the stars look familiar. In the morning, they pack up the little food they had brought for their campout, Elora's telescope, and Sophie's pennywhistle, and hike towards a tower Elora had spotted. They know they're in a totally strange place when they come upon a statue of nonhuman, alien creatures. As they continue, they come upon a strange house, where they find food, and then a mute, boy-sized robot. Even though the three friends bicker with each other, they work together to find a way home. Allan includes extensive notes on his writing process, and an excerpt from his script. The cover art shows one interesting looking character who doesn't appear in this volume. While their age isn't specified, the girls look to be tweens, with the slightly awkward, coltish bodies and movements of pre-adolescents. The strongest language used is one instance of the word "damn."

Volume 1 of 2

Alley, Zoe B.
★ **There's** a wolf at the door. Pictures by R. W. Alley. Roaring Brook Press 2008 40p. Illustration
Grades: K 1 2 3   **398.2; 741.5; Fic**
1. Humorous graphic novels; 2. Wolves — Folklore; 3. Graphic novels
978-1-59643-275-8, $19.95; 1-59643-275-6
     LC 2007-44025
As his plans are spoiled over and over again, the wolf keeps trying to find his dinner, in this retelling of five well-known stories and fables.
This is a "hilarious romp. . . . Illustrated with softly colored pen-and-ink drawings, these five stories meld seamlessly together. The text is full of puns, alliteration, and occasional rhymes." SLJ
A Neal Porter book

Amano, Kat
The **Wonderful** Wizard of Oz. Image Comics 2006 101p. Illustration
Grades: 3 4 5 6 7 8 9   **741.5; Fic**
1. Adventure graphic novels; 2. Baum, L Frank — Adaptations; 3. Fantasy graphic novels; 4. Graphic novels

978-1-58240-715-9, $9.99
Baum's classic story gets a European treatment in this colorful adaptation of Dorothy's adventures in the land of Oz.
Originally published as Le Magicien D'Oz Volumes 1-3 by Guy Delcourt Productions, France.

Amano, Shiro
Kingdom Hearts II Vol. 1. Tokyopop 2007 204p. Illustration
Grades: 4 5 6 7 8 9 10 11 12   **741.5; Fic**
1. Fantasy graphic novels; 2. Manga; 3. Shonen manga; 4. Graphic novels
978-1-4278-0058-9, $9.99
In the quiet little hamlet of Twilight Town, there lives a boy named Roxas. He and his friends Hayner, Pence and Olette are trying to enjoy their final days of summer vacation, when strange things begin to happen. First the group is falsely accused of stealing photos from all over town. Then they are attacked by bizarre, white creatures. But the oddest occurrences are the recurring dreams Roxas has of a boy named Sora, and the presence of a girl named Namine, who has a mysterious secret to share with Roxas. What began in Kingdom Hearts and Kingdom Hearts: Chain of Memories continues in Kingdom Hearts II.

Kingdom Hearts, Chain of Memories, Vol. 1. Tokyopop 2006 198p. Illustration
Grades: 4 5 6 7 8 9   **741.5; Fic**
1. Adventure graphic novels; 2. Fantasy graphic novels; 3. Graphic novels
1-59816-637-9, $9.99
The door to Kingdom Hearts was sealed, dealing a blow to the Heartless and restoring the worlds to normal, but Riku and King Mickey were tapped inside. Now Sora, Donald, and Goofy's search for their friends leads them to the mysterious Castle Oblivion, where a hooded figure tells them, "Ahead lies something you need, but to claim it, you must lose something dear." What could be more dear than one's own memories? This is the first of two volumes, and is published in the original Japanese right-to-left page order.

Kingdom Hearts, Vol. 1. Tokyopop 2005 136p. Illustration
Grades: 4 5 6 7 8 9   **741.5; Fic**
1. Adventure graphic novels; 2. Fantasy graphic novels; 3. Manga; 4. Graphic novels
1-59816-217-9, $5.99
When a strange storm hits his island home, 14-year-old Sora is separated from his friends and swept into a mysterious new land. There he meets Court Wizard Donald and Captain Goofy, who are on a mission to find their king, Mickey, and return him to his throne at Disney Castle. When the three learn of the Heartless, ominous creatures who feed off the darkness in the hearts of others, they join forces to recover Sora's friends, return the king to his rightful position and save the universe from the Heartless. This story is based on the popular video game and is a four volume manga series.

Ambrosio, Stefan
Wizards of Mickey, vol. 1: mouse magic. Boom! Studios 2010 Un Illustration

Grades: 3 4 5 6 7 8 9   **741.5; Fic**
1. Adventure graphic novels; 2. Fantasy graphic novels; 3. Humorous graphic novels; 4. Mickey Mouse (Fictional character); 5. Graphic novels
978-1-60886-541-3, $9.99

Wizard's apprentice Mickey loses a magic talisman called the Diamagic when he and the village fall afoul of a con man who steals it from them. Mickey pursues the con man, but he learns he'll have to compete in the Great Wizard's Tournament to win it back if he can father a team to work with him. He ends up with Donald and Goofy, both misfit bunglers, but somehow they'll have to compete against Peg-Leg Pete and the Phantom Blot. This book, originally written and published in Italy, is full of fantasy adventure and fun with recognizable Disney characters.

Amend, Bill
Aaaa!: a foxtrot assortment for young readers. Bill Amend. Andrews McMeel Pub., LLC 2012 224 p.
Grades: 3 4 5   **741.5/6973; 741.5**
1. Family life — Fiction; 2. Siblings — Fiction
1449423051; 9781449423056, $9.99
LC 2012936749
This book is a compilation of "FoxTrot" comics by cartoonist Bill Amend. The family consists of Jason, "a brilliant but misguided tween" who "is a precociously too-smart-for-his-own-good little brother who enjoys wreaking havoc on the rest of his family with the help of his pet iguana, Quincy. Older sister Paige is a typical teenager, obsessed with shopping, clothes and boys. Peter, the oldest brother, does his best to dodge homework and all real responsibility." (Children's Literature)

America's 1st Patriotic Comic Book Hero: The Shield Volume 1
Archie Comics 2002 96p. Illustration
Grades: 3 4 5 6 7 8 9 10 11 12 Adult   **741.5; Fic**
1. Adventure graphic novels; 2. Superhero graphic novels
1-879794-08-X, $12.95
A hero with great power, strength and courage who donned the colors of the American flag. A hero who lived for democracy and protected the world from the foes of freedom! No, it's not who you think... it's THE SHIELD, who predated his well known counterpart by over a year. This historic full color trade paperback reprints his first 8 stories from PEP and SHIELD/WIZARD Comics. It includes his first appearance and origin, along with the covers of the comics they originally appeared in, dating from 1940.

Andersen, Hans Christian
The **Emperor's** new clothes: the graphic novel. Retold by Stephanie Peters; illustrated by Jeffrey Stewart Timmins. Stone Arch Books 2009 40p. Illustration (Graphic spin)
Grades: 4 5 6 7   **741.5; Fic**
1. Fairy tales; 2. Humorous graphic novels; 3. Graphic novels
978-1-4342-1595-6 (lib bdg), $22.65;
978-1-4342-1744-8 (pa), $4.95
LC 2009-10528
In this retelling of Andersen's tale, a vain emperor spends all his kingdom's money on clothes for himself,

neglecting the needs of the people. Then a couple of swindlers claim they can weave the most wondrous magical material for a special suit, if only they had the supplies they need. They take everything, but no one, from the emperor on down, will admit they can't see the cloth or the clothes made from it, until one honest boy pipes up. The lively adaptation features illustrations which have all the people in clown face, complete with whiteface and bulbous red noses.

Anderson, Eric A.
PX! book two: in the service of the Queen. Image Comics 2008 Un Illustration
Grades: 4 5 6 7 8 9 10 11 12   **741.5; Fic**
1. Adventure graphic novels; 2. Humorous graphic novels; 3. Science fiction graphic novels; 4. Graphic novels
978-1-60706-018-5, $16.99
In this second volume, Weatherby takes center stage. Dahlia's father is called to London to permanently shut down a super-computer, but villainous goat Pollo has already had two of his lackeys hack into the system and take over. When Weatherby, Wikkity, and Panda show up to help Dahlia and her dad, Double Aught Seven Weatherby discovers he has not been, nor ever was, a Double Aught agent in the service of the Queen. However, he soon discovers that he is the only one who can get into the system, because IT had recruited him. The book, co-written by Trembley as well as illustrated by him, includes several short stories, including one created during the 24-Hour Comic Book Day. The main story doesn't have any bad language or overt violence, but a couple of the short stories include occasional use of the word "crap," and one story involves zombies.

Anderson, Jameson
The **Z-boys** and Skateboarding. Capstone Press 2007 32p. Illustration
Grades: 3 4 5 6 7 8 9   **741.5; 796.22**
1. Skateboarding; 2. Graphic novels
978-1-4296-0150-4, $25.26
LC 2007004915
This book uses the graphic novel format to describe the birth of the Z-boys skateboarding team in Dogtown, an area of Santa Monica, in 1973, and how they influenced modern skateboarding. The book includes additional facts and a list of books for further reading.
Part of the Graphic Library Invention and Discovery series.

Anderson, Kevin J.
Grumpy old monsters. IDW Publishing 2004 96p. Illustration
Grades: 4 5 6 7 8 9   **741.5; Fic**
1. Humorous graphic novels; 2. Monsters; 3. Graphic novels
1-932382-35-6, $13.99
The old monsters Frankenstein's Monster, Dracula, the Mummy, and the Werewolf, have all retired and moved to the old monsters' home, where Nurse Wrentch terrorizes them and only little Tiffany Frankenstein, granddaughter of old Dr. F., comes to visit. But this time she comes with terrible news the Van Helsing Corporation is about to take

possession of Castle Frankenstein, tear it down, and build luxury condominiums. The monsters decide they must come out of retirement and help Tiffany stop the horror if they can escape Nurse Wrentch!

Aoi, Haruka
A **Little** Snow Fairy Sugar, Volume 1. ADV Manga 2006 168p. Illustration
Grades: 3 4 5 6 7 8   **741.5; Fic**
    1. Fairies; 2. Kodomo manga; 3. Manga; 4. Graphic novels
1-4139-0333-9, $9.99
    Eleven-year-old Saga Bergstrom lives with her grandmother and maintains a very tight, controlled schedule; in addition to school, she works part-time in a coffee shop, and every afternoon at 4:00, she goes to the music store to play her dead mother's piano. Then, one day her life becomes chaotic when she encounters Sugar, an apprentice season fairy. Saga is the only human who can see Sugar, which can be very embarrassing when she screams in frustration at Sugar. Sugar and her fellow apprentice season fairies, Salt and Pepper, need to find twinkles to make their magic seeds grow so they can become full season fairies. The problem is, no one knows what twinkles are. In the meantime, Sugar and Saga need to find a way to get along with each other. The story and the art are very sweet and cute.
    Volume 1 of 3

Aoki, Takao
Beyblade Volume 1. Viz Media/Viz Kids 2004 200p. Illustration
Grades: 3 4 5 6 7 8   **741.5; Fic**
    1. Games; 2. Manga; 3. Shonen manga; 4. Graphic novels
1-59116-621-7, $7.99
    Tyson has a passion for Beyblades and he's determined to be the best. But he's also a great guy who looks out for his friends and will never cheat to win. Even though he's one of the toughest Beybladers on the scene he still takes his share ofd knocks. Learning from these losses is what makes Tyson stronger all the time. Tyson just might have what it takes to win when he busts out with a new Beyblade given to him by a mysterious stranger. Now the Blade Sharks want his new Beyblade and they're prepared to use any dirty trick to get it.
    Volume 1 of 14

Archie & friends All-Stars: Veronica's passport
Archie Comic Publications 2009 Un Illustration
Grades: 3 4 5 6 7 8   **741.5; Fic**
    1. Humorous graphic novels; 2. Lodge, Veronica (Fictional character); 3. Travel; 4. Graphic novels
978-1-879794-43-6, $9.95
    Veronica Lodge from Riverdale has her own adventures as she travels to New York City, Paris, Rome, and Bombay in these stories originally published from 1989 to 1991. Veronica goes to New York City to stay with her cousin Whitney, and they travel all over the city to such famous landmarks as the Empire State Building and Radio City Music Hall; she even has a brief fling at being a sculptor. When Veronica accompanies her father to Paris, she doesn't realize that a notorious jewel thief has hidden the diamonds he just stole in what looks like the perfume she just bought;

as she travels all over the city with a handsome local, the thief follows everywhere, trying to recover his booty. Then Mr. Lodge decides Veronica must have a better education and sends her to what he thinks is a finishing school in Rome, but when Veronica arrives, she finds herself among obnoxious and nasty girls who act more like juvenile delinquents. Then, when they travel to Bombay, Mr. Lodge and Veronica find themselves caught up in intrigue and industrial spying. Writers include Hal Smith, Kathleen Webb, Chris Allan, Mark Waid, and George Gladir.

Archie Americana Series: Best of the Eighties
Archie Comics 2001 96p. Illustration
Grades: 3 4 5 6 7 8 9 10 11 12 Adult   **741.5; Fic**
    1. Andrews, Archie (Fictional character); 2. Humorous graphic novels; 3. Graphic novels
1-879794-06-3, $10.95
    During the 1980s pop culture ruled America; even the President was a former actor. In this volume, Archie and friends experience the punk movement, the "Urban Cowboy" craze, see the rise of MTV, get into the preppie, new wave and "Flashdance" fashions, play Trivial Pursuit, and boogie at the roller disco.
    Volume 1 of 2

Archie Americana Series: Best of the Fifties
Archie Comics 1992 96p. Illustration
Grades: 3 4 5 6 7 8 9 10 11 12 Adult   **741.5; Fic**
    1. Andrews, Archie (Fictional character); 2. Humorous graphic novels; 3. Graphic novels
1-879794-01-2, $10.95
    Readers can journey back to the days of drive-ins and hula hoops, plaid skirts and bobby sox, Elvis and beatniks, rollerskates and sock hops in this book that reprints stories from the 1950s.

Archie Americana Series: Best of the Fifties Book 2
Archie Comics 2003 96p. Illustration
Grades: 3 4 5 6 7 8 9 10 11 12 Adult   **741.5; Fic**
    1. Andrews, Archie (Fictional character); 2. Humorous graphic novels; 3. Graphic novels
1-879794-15-2, $10.95
    The '50s are a fondly remembered time for many - both those who lived during the decade as well as those who discovered it through movies like Grease and TV shows like Happy Days. They were also the perfect decade for Archie to have his misadventures - whether getting tangled up in the eternal love triangle or incurring the wrath of Mr. Weatherbee, Mr. Lodge and even his father, Archie and his friends scaled new heights of hilarity. Series editor Castiglia says in the Introduction that the 1950s was the first time the U.S. had been prosperous since the 1920s; teens could do fun things, not just work to help the family, and the Archie comics reflected the rise of popular culture.

Archie Americana Series: Best of the Forties Book 2
Archie Comics 2002 96p. Illustration
Grades: 3 4 5 6 7 8 9 10 11 12 Adult   **741.5; Fic**
    1. Andrews, Archie (Fictional character); 2. Humorous graphic novels; 3. Graphic novels
1-879794-09-8, $10.95

In 1941, Pep Comics introduced Archie Andrews, "America's newest boyfriend." Since then, Archie and his perennial teenage friends have entertained readers with their misadventures. This book includes stories from 1946 through 1949, with more slapstick and screwball comedy from Archie and the gang.

Archie Americana Series: Best of the Forties Volume 1
Archie Comics 1991 128p. Illustration
Grades: 3 4 5 6 7 8 9 10 11 12 Adult   **741.5; Fic**
1. Andrews, Archie (Fictional character); 2. Humorous graphic novels; 3. Graphic novels
1-879794-00-4, $11.95
In 1941, Pep Comics introduced Archie Andrews, "America's newest boyfriend." Since then, Archie and his perennial teenage friends have entertained readers with their misadventures. This book includes the very first Archie story, with the first appearance of Betty and Veronica, Reggie, Jughead, Mr. Weatherbee, Miss Grundy, and the rest of the Archie characters as they originally appeared.

Archie Americana Series: Best of the Seventies
Archie Comics 1998 96p. Illustration
Grades: 3 4 5 6 7 8 9 10 11 12 Adult   **741.5; Fic**
1. Andrews, Archie (Fictional character); 2. Humorous graphic novels; 3. Graphic novels
1-879794-05-5, $9.95
The decade of the 1970s was a time of transition in America, and the Archie Comics gang was right there. In this volume, Riverdale experiences the women's movement, joins in the Bicentennial celebration, sees the rise of bubble-pop, and joins the crazes for patches, pet rocks, and CB radio. Archie and the gang play "Pong" (one of the earliest video games), watch popular movies and TV shows, and go to the disco.
Volume 1 of 2

Archie Americana Series: Best of the Sixties
Archie Comics 1995 96p. Illustration
Grades: 3 4 5 6 7 8 9 10 11 12 Adult   **741.5; Fic**
1. Andrews, Archie (Fictional character); 2. Humorous graphic novels; 3. Graphic novels
1-879794-02-0, $9.95
The 1960s was a time of dreams, hopes, revolution, and social change, and the nation's youth were at the forefront. Archie and his friends came along for the ride, exploring both the fun and the mores of the times with humor. In this book readers can see the girls in slim jims, experience Beatlemania as it hits Riverdale, watch the teens become flower children, see them hit the surf, drag race, and wear mod fashions.
Volume 1 of 2

Archie Classics: The Adventures of Little Archie Volume 1
Archie Comics 2004 96p. Illustration
Grades: 3 4 5 6 7 8 9 10 11 12 Adult   **741.5; Fic**
1. Adventure graphic novels; 2. Humorous graphic novels
1-879794-17-9, $10.95
Little Archie deals with Martian invaders, secret spies, pirates, freewheeling uncles, gorillas on the loose and more!

Who knew a little boy could have so many adventures? This book collects vintage Little Archie stories originally published from 1961 through 1965.

Archie's Camp Tales
Archie Comic Publications 2007 Un Illustration
Grades: 3 4 5 6 7 8   **741.5; Fic**
1. Humorous graphic novels; 2. Graphic novels
978-1-879794-23-8, $7.49
For decades, Archie Comics have made their way into countless summer campers' backpacks... and for decades, the writers and artists at Archie have provided readers with stories of Archie and his friends' adventures at summer camp. Now, some of the best of these stories are collected in a special digest-sized edition. Will Betty and Veronica win the hearts of the cute guys they meet at camp? Will Archie lead his friends down the wrong trail again? Will camp tuition rise to keep up with Jughead's appetite?

Archie's Classic Christmas Stories Volume 1
Archie Comics 2002 96p. Illustration
Grades: 3 4 5 6 7 8 9 10 11 12 Adult   **741.5; Fic**
1. Andrews, Archie (Fictional character); 2. Humorous graphic novels; 3. Graphic novels
1-879794-10-1, $10.95
Deck the halls with smiles and laughter, fa la la la la, la la la la! Since their inception, Archie and his friends have delighted readers with scores of Yuletide tales. These stories proved so popular that in 1954 an entire series devoted to stories of Holiday Cheer and Good Will to all premiered: ARCHIE'S CHRISTMAS STOCKING. Archie and his friends show their holiday spirit in this collection of classic tales from the first decade of Santa Claus himself. This book features painstaking restorations of original stories published from 1957 through 1963.

Archie Comics Presents: The Love Showdown
Archie Comics 1994 Un Illustration
Grades: 3 4 5 6 7 8 9 10 11 12 Adult   **741.5; Fic**
1. Andrews, Archie (Fictional character); 2. Archie (Fictional character); 3. Humorous graphic novels; 4. Graphic novels
1-879794-03-9, $4.95
In the mid-1990s, Archie Comics announced that Archie might finally choose between Betty and Veronica, after the love triangle had lasted since 1941; the story was published as a crossover among the four Archie comics series. This volume reprints the stories.

Atangan, Patrick
Songs of our ancestors: The yellow jar: two tales from Japanese tradition. NBM 2003 48p. Illustration (Songs of our ancestors)
Grades: 5 6 7 8 9 10 11 12   **741.5**
1. Folklore — Japan; 2. Graphic novels
1-56163-331-3, $12.92
LC 2002-32132
"To render two magical Japanese legends, one about a fisherman who discovers a fair maiden in a big pot, the other about a monk whose fastidiously kept garden is invaded by two chrysanthemums, Atangan charmingly adopts the sharp

outlines, boldly juxtaposed color fields, and striking compositions of eighteenth-century Japanese woodblock prints." Booklist

Other titles in this series are: Silk tapestry and other Chinese folktales (2004); Tree of love (2005)

Aureliani, Franco

Billy Batson and the magic of Shazam!. DC Comics 2010 Un Illustration

Grades: 3 4 5 6 7   **741.5; Fic**
1. Captain Marvel (Fictional character); 2. Humorous graphic novels; 3. Superhero graphic novels; 4. Graphic novels

978-1-4012-2248-2, $12.99

Gifted with the power of the magic word, "Shazam!" young orphan Billy Batson transforms into the World's Mightiest Mortal, Captain Marvel. He lives in New York City with his sister Mary, who can also transform into a super powered pintsize heroine, Mary Marvel. They have found a way to live together, go to school, and battle against evil. However, one of Captain Marvel's battles has caused a rift which has allowed Theo Adam to return from banishment. Theo wants to get the magic word back so he can defeat the old wizard who mistakenly gave him the power in the first place and take over the world. This version of the Captain Marvel story is kid-friendly, with kiddie cartoon level action and lots of silly humor.

Superman Family Adventures; Volume 1. By Art Baltazar and Franco Aureliani, illustrated by Art Baltazar. DC Comics 2013 128 p. Color; Illustration (Superman Family Adventures)

Grades: 1 2 3   **741.5; Fic**
1. Superhero graphic novels; 2. Superheroes; 3. Superman (Fictional character); 4. Graphic novels
140124050X; 9781401240509, $12.99

LC 2013009138

This graphic novel, by Art Baltazar and Franco, features superheroes such as "Superman, Superboy, Supergirl [and] Krypto the Superdog. The entire Superman family is re-imagined here in this energetic all-ages graphic novel. Read on as the heroes of Metropolis fight foes such as Bizarro, Metallo, Lex Luthor and...giant monkeys." (Publisher's note)

"Adult readers will get a kick out of the clever homage to their favorite superhero, and kids will be powerless to resist the silly playfulness; colorful animated characters; and easy-to-follow, superpower-packed stories." Booklist

Followed by: Volume 2 (2014)

Originally published in single magazine form in Superman Family Adventures #1-6.

Tiny Titans. DC Comics 2010 160p. Illustration

Grades: 2 3 4 5 6 7 8   **741.5; Fic**
1. Green Lantern (Fictional character); 2. Humorous graphic novels; 3. Superhero graphic novels; 4. Tiny Titans (Fictional characters); 5. Graphic novels
978-1-4012-2892-7, $12.99

This volume collects issues 1925 of the continuing comic book series. The Tiny Titans participate in Pet Club with their super pets; Alfred has to deal with penguins and bunnies in the Bat Cave and in Wayne Manor. Then the young sidekicks get their hands on some special rings, and

the Green Lantern has to retrieve the Earth Sector's power rings. Green Lantern writer Geoff Johns co-wrote the last story. The book includes some puzzles, lots of short stories, plenty of kid-friendly silliness, and cute, colorful, cartoony art.

The comic book series won the Eisner Award for Best Publication for Kids in 2009.

Auster, Paul

Hulk: is he man or monster or . . . is he both?. ABDO/Spotlight 2008 Un Illustration

Grades: 3 4 5 6 7 8 9   **741.5; Fic**
1. Hulk (Fictional character); 2. Superhero graphic novels; 3. Graphic novels
978-1-59961-547-9, $21.35

LC 2007-52759

Dr. Bruce Banner is ready to test his new gamma ray weapon using a monkey, when his intern Rick Jones suddenly goes to Ground Zero to save the monkey. When the test won't abort, Banner races out to save Rick, only to be caught by the gamma ray blast himself. It turns him into a giant, green monster of a man, and General Ross makes him angry. The General sends troops and weapons out to capture the Hulk, but Rick and the monkey try to help him. This is the first volume of a set of comics that provide kid-friendly, action-packed Hulk stories with little in the way of graphic violence and no bad language.

This is a library bound edition of a Marvel Age: The Incredible Hulk comic book issue, with all advertising pages removed.

Hulk: Mayhem!. ABDO/Spotlight 2008 Un Illustration

Grades: 3 4 5 6 7 8 9   **741.5; Fic**
1. Hulk (Fictional character); 2. Superhero graphic novels; 3. Graphic novels
978-1-59961-548-6, $21.35

LC 2008-101

Bruce Banner, Rick Jones, and Monkey have been hanging out in a cabin near a ski resort in the Rocky Mountains, where Banner has been trying to build a nano-nuclear cellular reconfiguration matrix—or, as Rick calls it, a de-Hulkifier. However, they've been tracked by General "Thunderbolt" Ross, who has brought troops, Jamie Madrox (tricked out in an anti-Hulk armor), and Radioactive Man (former nuclear physicist Chen Lu) to capture the Hulk. Their efforts end up causing an avalanche, which only the Hulk seems interested in stopping before attacking his attackers. As with the other volumes, this book includes lots of action with no actual violence and no bad language.

This is a library bound edition of a Marvel Age: The Incredible Hulk comic book issue, with all advertising pages removed.

Hulk: Radioactive. ABDO/Spotlight 2008 Un Illustration

Grades: 3 4 5 6 7 8 9   **741.5; Fic**
1. Hulk (Fictional character); 2. Superhero graphic novels; 3. Graphic novels
978-1-59961-549-3, $21.35

LC 2008-103

When General Ross and his army of Hulkbusters (soldiers in exoskeleton armor) capture Bruce Banner, Rick Jones and Monkey break into the military compound to save their friend. Then the Hulk accidentally busts out Radioactive Man while messing up the compound. In his radioactive damper, Radioactive Man is Dr. Chen Lu, and he behaves as though he's Banner's friend, although Rick and Monkey notice Lu keeps doing things that cause Bruce to start Hulking up. This volume provides lots of action in kid-friendly mode, with little real violence and no bad language.

This is a library bound edition of a Marvel Age: The Incredible Hulk comic book issue, with all advertising pages removed.

Avery, Ben
Kingdoms Volume 1: The Coming Storm. Zondervan/Zonderkidz 2007 160p. Illustration
Grades: 5 6 7 8 9 10 **741.5; Fic**
1. Adventure graphic novels; 2. Graphic novels
978-0-310-71353-1, $9.99
LC 2007-3148
When Pharaoh Neco and his army marched across Judah, King Josiah recklessly led the attack and died. Now his faithful adviser Iddo remains loyal to his king's memory and labors to keep the nation faithful to the Lord even as he struggles to protect his own family. This story is set against the backdrop of the events in the Old Testament books, 1 & 2 Kings and 1 & 2 Chronicles.

Volume 1 of 8

Azuma, Kiyohiko
Yotsuba&!. By Kiyohiko Azuma. Yen Press 2009 224 p. Illustration
Grades: 5 6 7 8
741.5; Fic
1. Manga; 2. Moving
0316073873;
9780316073875, $13

In this book, by Kiyohiko Azuma, "Yotsuba is the charming new girl in town. . . . In seven stories, the green-haired four-year-old discovers air conditioners, doorbells, cicadas, swings and more, and does it all with the

Courtesy of Yen Press

energy of a small hurricane. Her excitement is contagious and infects her handsome young adoptive father as well as the gaggle of pretty girls next door, all of whom get tangled up in her adventures as they try to keep up with her." (Publisher's note)

"Yotsuba is the charming new girl in town in this all-ages shojo manga by the author of the popular Azumanga Daioh series. In seven stories, the green-haired four-year-old discovers air conditioners, doorbells, cicadas, swings and more, and does it all with the energy of a small hurricane." Pub Wkly

Originally published in the U.S. by ADV

Volume 1 of an ongoing series

Azuma, Naomi
Suihelibe!, vol. 1. DC Comics/CMX 2008 160p. Illustration
Grades: 3 4 5 6 7 8 **741.5; Fic**
1. Humorous graphic novels; 2. Manga; 3. Science fiction graphic novels; 4. Graphic novels
978-1-4012-1900-0, $9.99
On the cover of the manga, several chemistry elements are listed: hydrogen, helium, lithium, and belium (which probably should be beryllium). First year junior high school student Tetsu just wants to join the biology club at school, when a small flying saucer crashes into the classroom. Lan, the alien pilot who looks like a cute girl, enlists Tetsu's help to recover some escaped life forms from her planet. In order for them to accomplish this task, they need to keep the biology club going, but the student council president wants to shut down the club, so they have three months to round up three more members, even as they hunt Noids (the life forms). There's a lot of shouting and slapstick humor.

Volume 1 of 2

Bailey, Chris
Major Damage. Sky Dog Press 2004 Un Illustration
Grades: 3 4 5 6 7 8 **741.5; Fic**
1. Humorous graphic novels; 2. Superhero graphic novels; 3. Graphic novels
0-9721831-4-0, $14.95
Before The Incredibles, there was Major Damage: the tale of a little boy who is transformed into his favorite super hero, protecting the world from mutants, monsters, and alien scum. Eight-year-old Melvin was trick or treating on Halloween night, dressed as his favorite superhero, Major Damage, when he was abducted by the Mucus Men; the harmless scientists mistook Melvin for the real hero, assumed he'd had an accident, and "restored" his powers and returned him to Earth. Meanwhile, Melvin's mother thinks her son has disappeared.

Bailey, Tracey
Wonderdog, Inc. Arcana Studio Inc. 2010 Un Illustration
Grades: 5 6 7 8 9 10 **741.5; Fic**
1. Adventure graphic novels; 2. Humorous graphic novels; 3. Graphic novels
978-1-897548-87-5, $14.95
Sixteen-year-old Ryan Robertson is a typical, nerdy type of guy, except he's got a very hot-looking girlfriend, whom his best buddy Alex just doesn't trust. The two guys are looking forward to the summer break, until Ryan's history teacher parents tell him they're going to Europe on a trip and he'll have to stay with his grandfather on a pig farm. Rachel, the hot girlfriend, wants to know where he's going, so she can visit him. When he gets there, he finds a wise-cracking grandfather, lots of chores, no Internet, no television ... and then Rachel shows up to steal a little statue of a dog from his grandfather. That's when Ryan learns that his grandfather, his parents, and a lot of other people are part of a secret organization to protect the world from the likes of Rachel, err ... Dr. Sweeney, and her nefarious colleagues who are out to rule the world and get very rich with the Fountain of Youth that the little dog statue unlocks. Now he's off to Bolivia with Pappy and siblings Seth and Amie

(she's cute!), to try to stop Dr. Sweeney. Think of Indiana Jones as a grandfather who still swashbuckles, and the kind of story told in the Indiana Jones movies. Some readers may note the fairly numerous grammatical errors (using an apostrophe inappropriately), but it shouldn't distract too much from the fun story. There's a lot of action but very little actual violence.

Baker, Kyle
Through the looking-glass. By Lewis Carroll; adapted by Kyle Baker. Papercutz 2008 Un Illustration (Classics illustrated)
Grades: 3 4 5 6 7 8 9
741.5; Fic
1. Carroll, Lewis, 1832-1898 — Adaptations; 2. Fantasy graphic novels; 3. Graphic novels
978-1-59707-115-4, $9.95; 1-59707-115-3

Courtesy of Papercutz

This is Carroll's sequel to Alice's Adventures in Wonderland. This time, Alice climbs through the looking-glass in her house and finds herself in a land with talking flowers and insects, Tweedledee and Tweedledum (who recite "The Walrus and the Carpenter"), the White Queen who needs help pinning her shawl straight, Humpty Dumpty, the Red Queen, and more. The Eisner Award-winning Baker uses a different style from his usual cartoony look here, more reminiscent of Tenniel's classic illustrations of Carroll's books.

Baltazar, Art
Patrick the Wolf Boy Volume 1. Devil's Due Publishing 2004 Un Illustration
Grades: 2 3 4 5 6 7 8 9 10 11 12 Adult   **741.5; Fic**
1. Humorous graphic novels; 2. Graphic novels
1-932796-27-4, $10.95
Patrick looks at first glance like the other kids in school, but he's a werewolf. A cute werewolf. He resembles Eddie Munster (from the 1960s television comedy series "The Munsters"), and he doesn't speak, although he growls a lot and sometimes howls. He gives his teacher an apple - but with a skull biting the apple. When he goes fishing with his dad, he prefers to scare the bear into giving him his catch. He loves to play tag with the neighborhood squirrel. And when Valentine's Day comes, he makes sure that his babysitter likes him better. His utterly normal parents adore him and understand his growls; so does Neve, his classmate at school.

Patrick the Wolf Boy Volume 2. Devil's Due Publishing 2005 Un Illustration
Grades: 2 3 4 5 6 7 8 9 10 11 12 Adult   **741.5; Fic**
1. Humorous graphic novels; 2. Graphic novels
1-932796-29-0, $10.95
This volume collects previously published issues of the comic: the Super Hero Special, the Science Fiction Special,

the Wedding Special, and the After School Special. In the many short stories, Patrick the Wolf Boy attends a comic book convention with his dad, plays "Star Wars" with the neighborhood kids, meets and befriends an alien kid, Zyggie, who then crashes the wedding reception of a relative, and deals with the school bully.

Patrick the Wolf Boy Volume 3. Devil's Due Publishing 2007 Un Illustration
Grades: 2 3 4 5 6 7 8 9 10 11 12 Adult   **741.5; Fic**
1. Fantasy graphic novels; 2. Humorous graphic novels; 3. Graphic novels
978-1-932796-30-8, $12.99
The third volume of Patrick the Wolf Boy collects the Rock-n-Roll Special, the Post Father's Day Special, and the Happy Birthday Special, plus some stories written and illustrated by guest creators. Patrick meets Squatch, the baby Big Foot, accidentally bites Neve, who thinks she's turning into a werewolf, encounters various rock stars, and other adventures. In one panel, the screaming pajama lady says "crap."

Patrick the Wolf Boy Volume 4. Devil's Due Publishing 2007 Un Illustration
Grades: 3 4 5 6 7 8 9 10 11 12 Adult   **741.5; Fic**
1. Halloween; 2. Humorous graphic novels; 3. Graphic novels
978-1-932796-83-4, $12.99
This fourth collection of comics featuring Patrick the Wolf Boy focus mostly on Halloween, a natural holiday for the young wolfman ... er ... wolfboy. He plays with jack o'lanterns (he likes to wear them on his head), goes trick-or-treating with the neighbor kids, keeps trying to melt the grouchy neighbor lady after watching The Wizard of Oz, and plays with new neighbor, the Grim Reaper. The book includes a couple instances of mild language ("fricken"), and one scene in which the Grim Reaper does his thing.

Tiny Titans vs. the Fearsome Five. By Art Baltazar & Franco. Stone Arch Books 2012 25 p. Color illustration
Grades: 2 3 4 5 6 7 8   **741.5; 741.5/973**
1. Fantasy graphic novels; 2. Flash (Fictional character); 3. Playgrounds; 4. Playgrounds — Fiction; 5. Playgrounds — Juvenile fiction; 6. Superhero graphic novels; 7. Superheroes; 8. Superheroes — Fiction; 9. Superheroes — Juvenile fiction; 10. Graphic novels
1434245381; 9781434245380, $21.27
LC 2012014778
This "is the first in Stone Arch's line of 'Tiny Titans' books, reprinting DC's popular and Eisner-winning children's title. Characters like Robin, Starfire, Kid Flash, Speedy, Raven, Cyborg, and Beast Boy . . . gallivant through several fast-paced vignettes focusing on group dynamics and school life." (Booklist)

Tiny Titans: welcome to the treehouse. DC Comics 2009 144p. Illustration
Grades: K 1 2 3   **741.5; Fic**
1. Flash (Fictional character); 2. Humorous graphic novels; 3. Robin (Fictional character); 4. Superhero graphic novels; 5. Teen Titans (Fictional characters); 6. Graphic novels
978-1-4012-2078-5, $12.99

Eisner Award: Best Publication for Kids (2009)
Eisner Award: Best Publication for Kids (2011)

Here are the Teen Titans as never seen before: as little kids. They all attend Sidekick City Elementary School, where their principal and teachers are supervillains, and they get into playground showdowns with the Fearsome Five. Baltazar and Franco, who have created such characters as Patrick the Wolf Boy, present a series of short stories, most one or two pages long, featuring little kid versions of Robin, Starfire, Wonder Girl, Cassie, Speedy, Kid Flash, Cyborg, Beast Boy, Raven, and more. While these stories are written for the young readers, the humor may also appeal to teens and adults.

Other titles in this series are: Tiny Titans: adventures in awesomeness (2009); Tiny Titans: sidekickin' it (2010); Tiny Titans: the first rule of pet club (2010); Tiny Titans: field trippin' (2011); Tiny Titans: the treehouse and beyond! (2011); Tiny Titans: growing up tiny! (2012); Tiny Titans: aw yeah Titans! (2013); Tiny Titans: return to the treehouse (2015)

Balthazar, Flore

Freedom!. Frank Le Gall; illustrated by Flore Balthazar; coloring by Robin Doo. Graphic Universe 2012 40 p. Color illustration
Grades: 2 3 4   **741.5/973; 741.5**
1. Animals — Fiction; 2. Cats; 3. Freedom — Fiction; 4. Mice; 5. Graphic novels
0761378847; 9780761378846

LC 2011021726

"Miss Annie is a kitten, and she does all of the expected kitten activities—playing with pens and yarn, napping on armchairs, and begging for food. But she does the unexpected, too, like befriending a mouse she knows she's supposed to hunt. On her first adventure outside of the house, she meets two older cats, Zeno and Miss Rostropovna, who guide her through the big, new world. Annie has a wide range of expressions, from her perked ears to the tip of her pert tail." (Publishers Weekly)

"A charming balance of cartoon and natural kitty-ness in full-color, eight-panel pages, this cat's-eye view of life will induce purrs in feline fans everywhere." Kirkus

Bannister (Person)

★ The **elsewhere** chronicles book one: the shadow door. Lerner Publishing Group/Graphic Universe 2009 48p. Illustration
Grades: 4 5 6 7 8   **741.5; Fic**
1. Adventure graphic novels; 2. Fantasy graphic novels; 3. Horror graphic novels; 4. Graphic novels
978-0-7613-4459-9, $27.93; 978-0-7613-3963-2 (pa), $6.95

LC 2008-39442

Max, Noah, and Theo face a boring weekend, when they meet Rebecca, who has come to town with her family for her Grandpa Gabe's funeral. The boys tell her the house is haunted, then they decide to explore it together. Inside, they find a jumble of junk, lots of cool old books in the library, and a strange old movie projector. And something ... shadowy ... brushes against Theo and hurts his arm. The next day, Rebecca asks the guys to return to the house with her, but only Max is willing to cut school. The old projector,

when turned on, opens a portal to another world, and Rebecca disappears into it. When Max turns on the projector again, Rebecca comes back, only to be snatched by a tentacled monster, and he follows her and the creature into a strange world of shadows and menace, the land called Elsewhere.

Originally published in France under the title Les Enfants d'ailleurs. Winner of the 2007 Lyon Festival Youth Prize.

Other titles in this series are:The shadow spies (2009); The master of shadows (2009); The calling (2010); The parting (2011); The tower of shadows (2013)

Bar-el, Dan

That one spooky night. Kids Can Press 2012 80 p.
Grades: 2 3 4 5   **741.5**
1. Dracula, Count (Fictional character); 2. Dracula, Count (Fictional character) — Juvenile fiction; 3. Halloween — Juvenile fiction; 4. Witches — Juvenile fiction
1554537517; 9781554537518, $16.95

This book by Dan Bar-el presents "a graphic novel for the Halloween season. . . . In 'Broom with a View,' a girl accidentally ends up with a real witch's broom, leading to a magical experience. In '10,000 Tentacles Under the Tub,' two boys find their post-trick-or-treating bath transformed into an undersea world. The final story, 'The Fang Gang,' follows a group of friends as they end up in Dracula's mansion on the scariest night of the year." (School Library Journal)

Barba, Corey

Yam: bite-size chunks. Top Shelf Productions 2008 88p. Illustration
Grades: PreK K 1 2 3   **741.5; Fic**
1. Friendship; 2. Humorous graphic novels; 3. Stories without words; 4. Graphic novels
978-1-60309-014-8 (pa), $10; 1-60309-014-2 (pa)

Yam is a little boy who wears a hooded suit and has a magical backpack. On the island of La Leche de la Luna, Yam meets a sentient cupcake, cheers up a crying raincloud with a lollipop, plays with his friends Gato and Mary, and has a four-legged pet TV that sleeps in bed with him. Along with short stories that originally appeared as mini comics and in Nickelodeon Magazine, the book includes an original story in which Yam develops a crush on a beautiful toy seller in town. He spends so much time daydreaming about her that he neglects all his friends.

"The wordless panels are quite effective with the tenderly drawn art powerfully conveying nuanced moments." SLJ

Barberi, Carlo

Justice League Unlimited Vol. 1: United They Stand. DC Comics 2005 104p. Illustration
Grades: 4 5 6 7 8 9   **741.5; Fic**
1. Justice League (Fictional characters); 2. Superhero graphic novels; 3. Graphic novels
1401205127; 9781401205126, $6.99

Leaping straight out of their Cartoon Network show, the Worlds Greatest Heroes have their own comics series. This inaugural collection features these tales: Divide Conquer, Poker Face, Small Time, Local Hero and Monitor Duty.

Justice League Unlimited Vol. 2: World's Greatest Heroes. DC Comics 2006 104p. Illustration
Grades: 4 5 6 7 8 9   **741.5; Fic**
1. Green Lantern (Fictional character); 2. Justice League (Fictional characters); 3. Superhero graphic novels; 4. Graphic novels
1-4012-1014-7, $6.99
The JLA encounter the oldest Green Lantern as they battle the terrible Triptych, journey to deep space to thwart the malicious Darkseid and travel back in time to Camelot to battle the evil Morgaine Le Fey. Plus, the crazy Creeper helps in a battle against the Madmen, while the enigmatic Question hunts down a traitor within the League itself.

Justice League Unlimited Vol. 3: Champions of Justice. DC Comics 2006 104p. Illustration
Grades: 4 5 6 7 8 9   **741.5; Fic**
1. Flash (Fictional character); 2. Justice League (Fictional characters); 3. Superhero graphic novels; 4. Graphic novels
978-1-4012-1015-1, $6.99
The World's Greatest Heroes travel to Atlantis to confront the gigantic menace called Umbra! Plus, the two Flashes team up to battle Mirror Master, as the entire League must take on an out-of-control Red Tornado! This volume also includes a journey to Limbo and an encounter with the deadly Mr. Atom.

Barker, Clive
The **Thief** of Always. IDW Publishing 2005 144p. Illustration
Grades: 4 5 6 7 8 9 10   **741.5; Fic**
1. Fantasy graphic novels; 2. Horror graphic novels; 3. Graphic novels
1-933239-17-4, $35.00; 1-933239-38-7 (pa), $19.99
Clive Barker's fable for younger readers is adapted here into graphic novel format. Mr. Hood's Holiday House has stood for a thousand years, welcoming countless children to enjoy a blissful round of treats and holidays ... for a price. Then bored young Harvey Swick comes, and he notices disquieting little details that make him realize the place is more of a trap. Things are spooky but not terrifying, with little violence.
Originally published as The Thief of Always issues #1-3.

Barrie, J. M.
Peter Pan. Adapted by Joe Dunn; illustrated by Ben Dunn. ABDO Publishing/Magic Wagon 2008 32p.
Grades: 2 3 4 5 6
741.5; Fic
1. Adventure graphic novels; 2. Fantasy graphic novels; 3. Peter Pan (Fictional character); 4. Graphic novels

Courtesy of ABDO Publishing/Magic Wagon

978-1-60270-052-9, $27.07
LC 2007-12070
John, Michael, and Wendy love hearing their mother's stories, but they don't know that another young boy has been listening to them as well. When their protective dog Nana steals Peter Pan's shadow, the children meet him and Wendy sews his shadow back. Then the children agree to return with Peter to the magical Neverland. Can they survive in a land of pirates, Lost Boys, and Tinker Bell? The book provides a simplified adaptation that introduces young readers to Barrie's classic tale. It includes a brief biography of Barrie.
Part of the Graphic Classics series

Barry, James L.
★ The **lost** warrior. Created by Erin Hunter; written by Dan Jolley; art by James L. Barry. Tokyopop/HarperCollins Publishers 2007 96p. Illustration (Warriors)
Grades: 4 5 6 7   **741.5; Fic**
1. Adventure graphic novels; 2. Cats; 3. Graphic novels
978-0-06-124020-1, $6.99; 0-06-124020-6
LC 2006-30426
Thunderclan warrior Greystripe helps clan members escape when the twolegs destroy their forest home and capture many of them, but he himself gets captured. Now he's a kittypet and desperate to return home to his clan. He meets Millie, another kittypet who wants to learn how to become a warrior, but can Greystripe find his way out of the twolegs' land?
This series adapting Hunter's Warriors prose novel series is a co-publishing venture between Tokyopop and its book market distributor, HarperCollins.
Other titles in this series are: Warrior's refuge (2008); Warrior's return (2008); The rise of the scourge (2008)

Batman Adventures Vol. 2: Shadows & Masks
DC Comics 2004 112p. Illustration
Grades: 4 5 6 7 8 9   **741.5; Fic**
1. Batman (Fictional character); 2. Superhero graphic novels; 3. Graphic novels
978-1-4012-0330-2, $6.95
A deadly new gang is threatening Gotham City, and it's up to the Dark Knight Detective to take it down, from the inside. He goes on an undercover mission in this volume.

Baum, L. Frank
L. Frank Baum's The Wizard of Oz: the graphic novel. Puffin Books 2005 176p.
Grades: 3 4 5 6 7 8   **741.5; Fic**
1. Baum, L Frank, 1856-1919 — Adaptations; 2. Fantasy graphic novels; 3. Oz (Imaginary place)
0-14-240471-3, $9.99
LC 2006-273599
This graphic novel adaptation remains true to the story by Baum: Dorothy and her dog Toto are whisked to Oz, where they meet the Tin Woodsman, the Cowardly Lion, and the Scarecrow and they all journey to find the Wizard to grant their desires.
"The black-and-white illustrations are action packed, and the characters, with their Bazooka Joe eyes, combine classic comic touches with the popular manga style. Reluctant readers will gravitate toward the cartoon cover." SLJ

Beaulieu, Jean Francios

★ The **Wonderful** Wizard of Oz. Marvel Entertainment 2009 192p. Illustration

Grades: 3 4 5 6 7 8 9 10 11 12 Adult　　　**741.5; Fic**
　1. Adventure graphic novels; 2. Authors; 3. Baum, L Frank, 1856-1919
978-0-7851-2921-9, $29.99

A twister picks up the house Dorothy and her dog Toto are in and carries them from Kansas to the land of Oz; the house lands on top of the Wicked Witch of the East, and the Munchkins, who were her slaves, hail Dorothy as a great sorceress. All the girl wants is to get back home to Kansas, but all anyone can say is that she must go to the Emerald City and ask the Great Wizard Oz to send her home. As she travels along the Yellow Brick Road, she meets a scarecrow who wants brains so people won't think he's a dummy, a tin man who wants a heart so he can love, and a great cowardly lion who wants courage so he'll truly be king of the beasts. However, once they reach the Emerald City and each see the Wizard Oz, they learn they must do what no one, including the Wizard himself, could ever do kill the Wicked Witch of the West. Shanower's adaptation of L. Frank Baum's novel keeps all the charm of the original, while Skottie Young's art banishes any lingering images of the old Technicolor movie; Beaulieu's muted color palette works with Young's art, while Eckleberry's lettering adds to an overall effect of magic and wonder. This book will appeal to all ages

Other Oz adapations by Shanower and Young are: The Marvelous Land of Oz; Ozma of Oz; Dorothy and the Wizard in Oz; The Road to Oz; The Emerald City of Oz

Beechen, Adam

Justice League Unlimited: the ties that bind. Written by Adam Beechen and Paul Storrie; illustrated by Carlo Barberi, Rick Burchett and others. DC Comics 2008 Un Illustration (Justice league unlimited)

Grades: 3 4 5 6 7 8 9　　　**741.5; Fic**
　1. Batman (Fictional character); 2. Flash (Fictional character); 3. Green Arrow (Fictional character); 4. Green Lantern (Fictional character); 5. Justice League (Fictional characters); 6. Superhero graphic novels; 7. Superman (Fictional character); 8. Wonder Woman (Fictional character); 9. Graphic novels
978-1-4012-1691-7, $12.99; 1-4012-1691-9

This version of the Justice League was created for the Cartoon Network animated series and features such superheroes as Superman, Batman, Wonder Woman, Green Lantern, the Flash, Hawkgirl, J'onn Jonnz the Martian Manhunter, Power Girl, Green Arrow, and others. The stories collected in this volume include a clash of misunderstanding with Uncle Sam and the Freedom Fighters, a jaunt backwards in time, getting involved in a lovers' spat between super villains whose fight could destroy a city, and more. The book includes superhero vs supervillain fighting action with no bloodshed.

Another title in this series is: Justice league unlimited. Heroes (2009)

Beka

Dance Class; 3: African Folk Dance Fever. By Béka; illustrated by Crip. Papercutz 2012 47 p. Color illustration

Grades: 5 6 7 8　　　**741.5/944; Fic**

　1. Dance — Africa; 2. Dance — Juvenile fiction; 3. Folk dancing
1597073636; 9781597073639, $10.99

In this book by Béka; "Julie, Lucy, and Alia are best friends who share the same passion: dance! In addition to their regular ballet and modern dance classes, the three girls are introduced to a new style of dance ù African folk! Powered by deep percussion-based music, this style is unlike anything they've ever tried before. While the girls enjoy their new art form, problems at home and in the classroom threaten to cause them to have to stop taking their dance classes." (Publisher's note)

Bell, Cece

★ **El** deafo. Cece Bell; color by David Lasky. Abrams Books 2014 233 p. Color; Illustration

Grades: 3 4 5 6 7　　　**92; 741.5**
　1. Autobiographical graphic novels; 2. Deaf children; 3. Friendship; 4. Hearing aids for children; 5. Schools
1419710206; 9781419710209, $21.95
　　　　　　　LC 2013955590

Newbery Honor Book (2015)
Eisner Award: Best Publication for Kids (2015)

"In this . . . graphic novel memoir, author/illustrator Cece Bell chronicles her hearing loss at a young age and her subsequent experiences with the Phonic Ear, a very powerful—and very awkward—hearing aid. The Phonic Ear gives Cece the ability to hear—sometimes things she shouldn't—but also isolates her from her classmates." (Publisher's note)

"Bell's bold and blocky full-color cartoons perfectly complement her childhood stories—she often struggles to fit in and sometimes experiences bullying, but the cheerful illustrations promise a sunny future." Booklist

Bendis, Brian Michael

★ **Takio**, vol. 1. Marvel Icon 2011 Un Illustration

Grades: 5 6 7 8　　　**741.5; Fic**
　1. Sisters; 2. Superhero graphic novels; 3. Graphic novels
978-0-7851-5326-9, $9.95; 0-7851-5326-8

"This entertaining graphic novel features a crunchy and kinetic art style, quick pacing, realistic dialogue, and enough action to appeal to most middle-school readers." Booklist

Takio; vol. 2. Brian Michael Bendis, illustrated by Michael Avon Oeming. Marvel Enterprises 2013 96 p. Color illustration

Grades: 5 6 7 8　　　**741.5**
　1. Sisters — Fiction; 2. Graphic novels
0785165533; 9780785165538, $16.99

"Taki and Olivia are sisters with super-powers! In fact, they are the only ones in the world with super-powers! So obviously, they have to become super heroes! But is the world ready for real-life super heroes? Are the girls ready for the challenge? And will the accident that made them who they are reveal secrets that will change their lives forever?" (Publisher's note)

"Taki and Olivia face down danger in this bright, colorful, action-heavy series, which is unconventionally (and refreshingly) girl-focused." Booklist

Benjamin, Paul
  Hulk: the Hulks take Manhattan; Paul Benjamin, writer ; Juan Santacruz, penciler ; Raul Fernandez, inker ; Wilfredo Quintana, colorist ; Dave Sharpe, letterer. ABDO/Spotlight 2008 Un Illustration
Grades: 3 4 5 6 7 8 9   **741.5; Fic**
  1. Hulk (Fictional character); 2. Superhero graphic novels; 3. Graphic novels
  9781599615462, $21.35
                                                               LC 2008-102
  In his quest to remove the Hulk from himself, Bruce Banner hires Jamie Madrox, the Multiplying Man, to help him locate the secret laboratory of a former colleague; he hopes to use the radiation equipment there to make himself normal again. However, one of Madrox's more paranoid selves comes at just the wrong moment, and suddenly there are multiplying Hulks. As Hulk Prime tries to smash all the new Hulks, he makes more of them, and they start to take Manhattan apart. While there's a lot of smashing action and property damage, the book maintains kid-friendly dialogue and avoids graphic violence.
  This is a library bound edition of a Marvel Age: The Incredible Hulk comic book issue, with all advertising pages removed.

  Hulk: misunderstood monster, v1. Writer, Paul Benjamin; illustrated by David Nakayama and Juan Santacruz. Marvel 2007 Illustration
Grades: 5 6 7 8 9   **741.5; Fic**
  978-0-7851-2642-3, $6.99; 0-7851-2642-2
  "See how brilliant scientist Bruce Banner was cursed to transform into the rampaging Hulk! Learn why Banner's girlfriend Betty Ross left him, why her father, General 'Thunderbolt' Ross hunts him and why Rick Jones blames himself for creating the monster." (Publisher's note)

Bertozzi, Nick
  Lewis & Clark. First Second 2011 136p. Illustration
Grades: 5 6 7 8   **978; 741.5**
  978-1-59643-450-9 (pa), $16.99; 1-59643-450-3 (pa)
                                                               LC 2010-36255
  "Bertozzi offers an innovative take on Meriwether Lewis and William Clark's epic journey in this oversized graphic offering. Portraying the arduous trek through rough terrain and encounters with often unwelcoming natives, sequential panels transport readers alongside the famous duo and their equally renowned translator, Sacagawea, as they travel from St. Louis to the Pacific coast. Within a fictional framework, the narrative weaves in facets of the characters' personalities, including Lewis's tempestuous melancholy, Charbonneau's inept bumbling and Sacagawea's ability to endure this voyage surrounded by her intensely masculine cohorts." (Kirkus)

  Shackleton: Antarctic odyssey. Nick Bertozzi. First Second 2014 128 p. Illustration; Map
Grades: 5 6 7 8 9 10   **741.5; 919.89**
  1. Antarctica — Discovery and exploration — British; 2. Antarctica — Exploration; 3. Explorers — Great Britain — Biography; 4. Shackleton, Ernest Henry, Sir, 1874-1922; 5. Graphic novels
  1596434511; 9781596434516, $16.99

  This book by Nick Bertozzi describes how "Ernest Shackleton was one of the last great Antarctic explorers, and he led one of the most ambitious Antarctic expeditions ever undertaken. This is his story, and the story of the dozens of men who threw in their lot with him—many of whom nearly died in the unimaginably harsh conditions of the journey." (Publisher's note)
  "Bertozzi eschews all narrative explanation, relying solely on dialogue among the crew and the detailed black-and-white panels to tell the story. The snow- and ice-bound journey is the perfect match for Bertozzi's minimal style—vast stretches of white become gasp-worthy, desolate vistas." Booklist

Best of Josie and the Pussycats Volume 1
  Archie Comics 2001 96p. Illustration
Grades: 3 4 5 6 7 8 9 10 11 12 Adult   **741.5; Fic**
  1. Adventure graphic novels; 2. Humorous graphic novels; 3. Rock music; 4. Graphic novels
  1-879794-07-1, $10.95
  This book reprints a selection of stories about rock group Josie and the Pussycats, from their origin in 1963 to 1988. Josie, Melody, and Valerie are the Pussycats, along with their roadie Alan M., their shifty manager Alex, and his conniving sister, Alexandra. They make music, but along the way they also solve mysteries.

Bethea, Nikole Brooks
  ★ **Engineering** an awesome recycling center with Max Axiom, super scientist. By Nikole Brooks Bethea; illustrated by Pop Art Studios; consultant: Morgan Hynes, PhD, Research Assistant Professor, Education Research Program Manager, Center for Engineering Education and Outreach, Tufts University, Medford, Massachus. Capstone Press 2013 32 p. Color illustration
Grades: 2 3 4   **628.4/458; 628.4**
  1. Engineering; 2. Recycling (Waste, etc) — Juvenile literature; 3. Recycling center — Design and construction — Juvenile literature
  1429699345; 162065699X, $7.95; 9781429699341, $29.99; 9781620656990
                                                               LC 2012026438
  In this graphic novel, written by Nikole Brooks Bethea, "Max Axiom has a mission. The city mayor needs a recycling center to decrease pressure on its bulging landfill. Join Max as he uses the engineering process to design and build an awesome recycling center." (Publisher's note)
  Includes bibliographical references (page 31) and index.

Betty and Veronica in the unexpected
  ABDO Publishing Group/Spotlight 2007 Un Illustration
Grades: 3 4 5 6 7 8   **741.5; Fic**
  1. Andrews, Archie (Fictional character); 2. Cooper, Betty (Fictional character); 3. Humorous graphic novels; 4. Lodge, Veronica (Fictional character); 5. Graphic novels
  978-1599612706, $24.21
                                                               LC 2006-50265
  This volume includes 19 short comics stories featuring friends and rivals Betty and Veronica, Archie Andrews, and all the gang from Riverdale. Among the stories, Veronica decides that she doesn't want to obey signs, even if they get

other people into trouble; Betty and Veronica can't stop laughing about something they're too helpless with laughter to tell anybody else, even when it lands them in detention; Mr. Lodge tries to teach Veronica a lesson that ends up costing him lots of money; and more.

Part of the Archie digest library; this is a revision of Betty and Veronica Digest Magazine issue #120 (June 2001).

Betty and Veronica in Trendsetter
  Edited by Nelson Ribeiro & Victor Gorelick.. ABDO Publishing Group/Spotlight 2007 Un Illustration
Grades: 3 4 5 6 7 8   **741.5; Fic**
  1. Andrews, Archie (Fictional character); 2. Cooper, Betty (Fictional character); 3. Humorous graphic novels; 4. Lodge, Veronica (Fictional character); 5. Graphic novels
  978-1-59961-268-3, $24.21
                                                    LC 2006-50552
  This is a library bound edition of Betty and Veronica Digest Magazine, issue #115, originally published in March 2001, with all advertisements removed. It includes sixteen short stories about the Riverside teens, focusing mostly on Betty and Veronica, friends and rivals for the affections of Archie, but also including other favorite characters, such as Reggie and Jughead.
  Revision of issue no. 118 (March 2001) of Betty and Veronica digest magazine.

Biskup, Agnieszka
  ★ The **amazing** work of scientists with Max Axiom, super scientist. By Agnieszka Biskup; illustrated by Marcelo Baez. Capstone Press 2013 32 p. (Graphic library. Graphic science and engineering in action)
Grades: 2 3 4   **502.3**
  1. Science — Methodology; 2. Science — Methodology — Juvenile literature; 3. Scientists; 4. Scientists — Juvenile literature; 5. Graphic novels
  1429699361; 9781429699365, $29.99; 9781620657010
                                                    LC 201202842
  In this graphic novel by Agnieska Biskup and illustrated by Marcelo Baez "Max Axiom has a mission. The local university is hosting a conference to teach kids about science careers. Join Max as he meets an astronaut, an oceanographer, a virus hunter, and many other scientists that have amazing jobs to do." (Publisher's note)
  Includes bibliographical references (page 31) and index

  Exploring Ecosystems with Max Axiom, Super Scientist. Capstone Press 2007 32p. Illustration
Grades: 3 4 5 6 7 8   **577; 741.5**
  1. Ecology; 2. Science; 3. Graphic novels
  978-0-7368-6842-6 li, $25.26; 978-0-7368-7894-4 (pa)
  Max Axiom is a super-cool super-scientist who demonstrates and explains science in ways never before seen in the classroom. Whether shrinking down to the size of an ant or riding on a sound wave, Max does whatever it takes to make science super cool and accessible. This volume explores different ecosystems, from deserts to rain forests, and includes a glossary and a list of books for further reading.
  Part of the Graphic Science series.

  ★ The **incredible** work of engineers with Max Axiom, super scientist. By Agnieszka Biskup and illustrated by Marcelo Baez. Capstone Press 2013 32 p.
Grades: 2 3 4   **620.0023; 741.5; 620**
  1. Engineering — Juvenile literature; 2. Engineers; 3. Lunar bases; 4. Space colonies — Fiction; 5. Graphic novels
  142969937X; 9781429699372, $29.99
                                                    LC 2012026439
  In this graphic novel by Agnieszka Biskup "Max Axiom has a mission. The National Space Agency wants to build a lunar colony, but it needs a team of top-notch engineers to get the job done. [Readers will] join Max as he scours the globe to learn about incredible engineers and the amazing things they do." (Publisher's note)
  Includes bibliographical references and index

  A **Journey** into Adaptation with Max Axiom, Super Scientist. Capstone Press 2007 32p. Illustration
Grades: 3 4 5 6 7 8   **591.4; 741.5**
  1. Adaptation (Biology); 2. Science; 3. Graphic novels
  978-0-7368-6840-2 li, $25.26; 978-0-7368-7892-0 (pa), $7.95
  Max Axiom is a super-cool super-scientist who demonstrates and explains science in ways never before seen in the classroom. Whether shrinking down to the size of an ant or riding on a sound wave, Max does whatever it takes to make science super cool and accessible. This volume explores how animals use adaptation to blend into their environment, and includes a glossary and a list of books for further reading.
  Part of the Graphic Science series.

  The **powerful** world of energy with Max Axiom, super scientist. Capstone Press 2009 32p. Illustration
Grades: 2 3 4 5 6 7   **531; 741.5**
  1. Force and energy; 2. Motion; 3. Graphic novels
  978-1-4296-2337-7, $26.60; 978-1-4296-2337-3 (pa), $7.95
                                                    LC 2008-29651
  The cartoon super scientist Max Axiom explains energy for young readers. Energy is the ability to do work (which is motion against resistance). The book explains kinetic and potential energy, the different forms of energy, the law of conservation of energy, sources of energy, and touches on the negative aspects of burning fossil fuels for energy. It also discusses the search for other sources of energy, particularly renewable, clean sources. Back matter in the book includes more energy facts, a glossary, reading list, and an index.
  Part of the Graphic Science series

  The **solid** truth about states of matter with Max Axiom, super scientist. Capstone Press 2009 32p. Illustration
Grades: 2 3 4 5 6 7   **530.4; 741.5**
  1. Matter; 2. Graphic novels
  978-1-4296-2339-1, $26.60; 978-1-4296-3451-9 (pa), $7.95
                                                    LC 2008-28694
  The cartoon super scientist Max Axiom explains matter, which is anything that has mass and takes up space. The book progresses from the basic building blocks of matter, which are atoms, describing how movement of the atoms and molecules determine the state of matter—solid, liquid,

or gas. Back matter in the book includes more facts about the states of matter, a glossary, reading list, and an index.

Part of the Graphic Science series

Understanding Global Warming with Max Axiom, Super Scientist. Capstone Press 2007 32p. Illustration
Grades: 3 4 5 6 7 8 9   **363.7; 741.5**
  1. Greenhouse effect; 2. Graphic novels
978-1-4296-0139-9, $25.26
                    LC 2007002269
This book uses the graphic novel format to follow the adventures of super scientist Max Axiom as he explains the science behind the issue of global warming. The book includes additional facts and a list of books for further reading.

Part of the Graphic Science series.

Understanding viruses with Max Axiom, super scientist. Capstone Press 2009 32p. Illustration
Grades: 2 3 4 5 6 7   **579.2; 741.5**
  1. Bacteria; 2. Viruses; 3. Graphic novels
978-1-4296-3453-3 (pa), $7.95; 978-1-4296-2338-4, $26.60
                  LC 2008-29654
The cartoon super scientist Max Axiom explains viruses, tiny pathogenic microorganisms that cause various diseases, from colds to influenza to polio and more. Max goes submicroscopic to give readers a closer look at different viruses and how they function. The book also describes how the human body fights off infections, and how scientists and physicians have worked to develop vaccines to prevent infections. The book also talks about bacteria and how they're different from viruses. Back matter in the book includes more facts about bacteria and viruses, a glossary, reading list, and an index.

Part of the Graphic Science series

Bliss, Harry
  ★ **Luke** on the loose: a Toon Book. TOON Books 2009 32p. Illustration; Map
Grades: PreK K 1 2   **741.5; Fic**
  1. Humorous graphic novels; 2. New York (State); 3. Graphic novels
978-1-935179-00-9, $12.95; 1-935179-00-4
                  LC 2008-35699
A young boy's fascination with pigeons soon erupts into a full-blown chase around Central Park, across the Brooklyn Bridge, through a fancy restaurant, and into the sky

"The cartoon panels are so successful at engaging readers that young children do not have to be able to read the text to enjoy the story. Each drawing is filled with humorous details." SLJ

Boldman, Craig
  Archie Day by Day Volume 1. Archie Comics 2003 96p. Illustration
Grades: 3 4 5 6 7 8 9 10 11 12 Adult   **741.5; Fic**
  1. Andrews, Archie (Fictional character); 2. Humorous graphic novels; 3. Graphic novels
1-879794-16-0, $10.95
Archie and his pals have been comics' most celebrated teenage humor characters for over 60 years, since 1941. Now for the first time, selections from Archie's worldwide

syndicated newspaper strip are collected in this volume. This black and white edition includes a selection of daily strips from the mid-1990s, chronicling life in Riverdale, USA.

Bonneval, Gwen de
  William and the lost spirit. Gwen de Bonneval; illustrated by Matthieu Bonhomme; colors by Walter; translation, Anne Collins Smith and Owen M. Smith; [lettering by Dennis Pacheco]. Graphic Universe 2013 152 p.
Grades: 4 5 6 7   **Fic; 741.5/944**
  1. Families — Fiction; 2. Fantasy fiction — Juvenile fiction; 3. Folklore — Fiction; 4. Knights and knighthood — Fiction; 5. Middle Ages — Fiction; 6. Mythology — Fiction; 7. Voyages and travels — Fiction; 8. Voyages and travels — Juvenile fiction; 9. Graphic novels
1467708070; 9780761385677; 9781467708074, $9.95
                  LC 2012008115
In this book, as "William sets out to find his father (who might be dead, or lost, or both), he is joined by a knight, a troubadour, and a very unusual goat. Soon he enters a mysterious world that is populated with an amazing cast of characters, including Prester John, dog-faced men, and headless people whose faces are on their chests." (School Library Journal)

Booth, Jack
  Kazuma's Quest. Harcourt Achieve/Steck-Vaughn 2007 48p. Illustration
Grades: 3 4 5 6 7 8   **741.5; Fic**
  1. Samurai; 2. Graphic novels
978-1-4190-3215-8, $8.99
Kazuma is a young samurai who sets out to confront his father's murderer and reclaim his family's sword. The famous swordsman Matayemon offers to help him. Will they be able to outsmart their enemies? This is historical fiction in graphic novel format with facts about the samurai interspersed throughout the story in prose sections.

Part of the Timeline Graphic Novels series.

  Nomad King. Harcourt Achieve/Steck-Vaughn 2006 48p. Illustration
Grades: 3 4 5 6 7 8   **741.5; 92; Fic**
  1. Khan, Genghis, ca 1162-1227; 2. Mongolia — History; 3. Graphic novels
978-1-4190-3201-1, $8.99
In the sparse, windswept land of Mongolia in the late 12th century, Temujin becomes leader of his tribe at the age of nine. Over the years, this ruthless leader battles warring tribes for power then unites them under his rule, becoming Genghis Khan. He gradually extends his empire beyond Mongolia and China; will he be able to take over the world" This historical graphic novel includes prose intervals that provide more information about the Mongols and about Genghis Khan.

Part of the Timeline Graphic Novels series.

  Raiders of the Seas. Harcourt Achieve/Steck-Vaughn 2006 48p. Illustration
Grades: 3 4 5 6 7 8   **741.5; Fic**
  1. Adventure graphic novels; 2. Pirates; 3. Graphic novels
978-1-4190-3207-3, $8.99

Nicholas Bloom is a young sailor who lands in bad company when he joins the ship of a pirate named Blackbeard. Together they sail the seas, raiding and plundering. When Nick learns more about Blackbeard's evil ways, he must decide what to do next. This historical graphic novel includes prose intervals that give information about pirates and the differences between them and privateers.

Part of the Timeline Graphic Novels series.

Bowen, Carl

20,000 leagues under the sea. Retold by Carl Bowen ; illustrated José Alfonso Ocampo Ruiz. Stone Arch Books 2008 72p. Illustration

Grades: 4 5 6 7 8 9   **741.5; Fic**
    1. Adventure graphic novels; 2. Science fiction graphic novels; 3. Submarines
978-1-4342-0447-9, $23.93; 978-1-4342-0497-4 (pa), $9.95

Scientist Pierre Aronnax and his servant set sail to help hunt a sea monster threatening ships, but they and master harpooner Ned Land discover that the monster is actually a submarine, the Nautilus. The submarine's leader, Captain Nemo, takes the three men captive and they journey under the sea, where they see many wonders; but they must each decide whether they should trust Nemo, who bears a bitter secret, or try to escape. This graphic novel adaptation of Verne's classic adventure novel uses simple language to help reluctant and struggling readers understand the story.

Part of the Graphic Revolve series

The **strange** case of Dr. Jekyll and Mr. Hyde. By Robert L. Stevenson; retold by Carl Bowen; illustrated by Daniel Perez. Stone Arch Books 2009 72p. Illustration

Grades: 4 5 6 7 8 9 10   **741.5; Fic**
    1. Horror graphic novels; 2. Science fiction graphic novels; 3. Graphic novels
978-1-4342-0754-8, $23.93

LC 2008-6248
"Scientist Dr. Henry Jekyll believes every human has two minds: one good and one evil. He develops a potion to separate them from each other. Soon, his evil mind takes over, and Dr. Jekyll becomes a hideous fiend known as Mr. Hyde." (Publisher's note)

Part of the Graphic Revolve series

Boyd, David

Beware the Vikings. Harcourt Achieve/Steck-Vaughn 2006 48p. Illustration

Grades: 3 4 5 6 7 8   **741.5; Fic**
    1. Adventure graphic novels; 2. Vikings; 3. Graphic novels
978-1-4190-3205-9, $8.99

When Thorfinn the Viking is found guilty of murder, he is exiled as an outlaw. He says goodbye to his son, Snorri, and sets sail with his band of men. But things don't work out as he has planned when his crew discovers a stowaway, and it's Snorri. This fictional graphic novel includes intervals of prose giving information about Vikings and their customs

Part of the Timeline Graphic Novels series.

The **Hidden** Message. Harcourt Achieve/Steck-Vaughn 2007 48p. Illustration

Grades: 3 4 5 6 7 8   **741.5; Fic**

1. Great Britain — History — 1485-1603, Tudors; 2. Mystery graphic novels; 3. Graphic novels
978-1-4190-3216-5, $8.99

The famous writer Christopher Marlowe does secret work as the Queen's spy. But when the young actor Jasper Kyd decides to take revenge against this master, William Shakespeare, things become complicated and dangerous. This is historical fiction in graphic novel format with facts about Elizabethan period theater, Shakespeare, and Marlowe interspersed throughout the story in prose sections.

Part of the Timeline Graphic Novels series.

Marco Polo and the Roc. Harcourt Achieve/Steck-Vaughn 2006 48p. Illustration

Grades: 3 4 5 6 7 8   **741.5; Fic**
    1. Adventure graphic novels; 2. China — History; 3. Graphic novels
978-1-4190-3203-5, $8.99

When Marco Polo visit's the Emperor of China, Kublai Khan, he is given an impossible task. He has to find a mythical bird, the Roc, and bring one of its eggs back to the Great Khan. Can he do it? What will happen if he fails? This historical fiction graphic novel has touches of fantasy and includes facts about Marco Polo, Kublai Khan, Chinese exploration, the legend of the Roc, and speculation that Polo made up his stories.

Part of the Timeline Graphic Novels series.

Napoleon's Last Stand. Harcourt Achieve/Steck-Vaughn 2006 48p. Illustration

Grades: 3 4 5 6 7 8   **741.5; Fic**
    1. Adventure graphic novels; 2. Napoleon I, Emperor of the French; 3. Graphic novels
978-1-4190-3208-0, $8.99

Charlotte Bonaparte helps her famous uncle Napoleon escape from the island of Elba. As Napoleon prepares to go to war, Charlotte makes her own plans. This historical fiction graphic novel depicts some of the events of the Battle of Waterloo, so there is some battlefield violence. The book includes prose intervals that provide more information about Napoleon, his English opponent, the Duke of Wellington, the battle, and the death of Napoleon.

Part of the Timeline Graphic Novels series.

Pearl Harbor. Harcourt Achieve/Steck-Vaughn 2006 48p. Illustration

Grades: 3 4 5 6 7 8   **741.5; Fic**
    1. Adventure graphic novels; 2. World War, 1939-1945 — Pearl Harbor (Oahu, Hawaii), Attack on, 1941; 3. Graphic novels
978-1-4190-3220-2, $8.99

Alison is the lonely twelve-year-old daughter of a U.S. Navy captain. When she meets Jasmine, a Japanese girl her age, who is the daughter of Alison's Japanese godfather, the two become fast friends. But it is December 1941 in Pearl Harbor, Hawaii, and what happens on December 7th is the ultimate test of friendship. This historical fiction graphic novel includes scenes from the attack on Pearl Harbor; it also includes prose intervals that provide additional facts about the Japanese, Hawaii, a listing of ships lost and casualties, and information on the U.S. nuclear bombing of Hiroshima in 1945.

Part of the Timeline Graphic Novels series.

Braun, Eric

Booker T. Washington: Great American Educator. Capstone Press 2005 32p. Illustration
Grades: 3 4 5 6 7 8 9   **92; 741.5**
1. African Americans — Biography; 2. Biographical graphic novels; 3. Educators; 4. Washington, Booker T, 1856-1915; 5. 6. Graphic novels
0-7368-4630-1, $25.26
LC 2005001727

In graphic novel format, this book tells the life story of Booker T. Washington and his accomplishments toward promoting the education of African Americans. The book includes additional facts about Washington, a bibliography, and a list of books for further reading.

Part of the Graphic Biographies series.

Cesar Chavez: Fighting for Farmworkers. Capstone Press 2006 32p. Illustration
Grades: 3 4 5 6 7 8 9   **741.5; 331.8; 92**
1. Biographical graphic novels; 2. Chavez, Cesar, 1927-1993; 3. United Farm Workers of America; 4. Graphic novels
0-7368-4631-X, $25.26
LC 2005006460

This book uses the comic book format to recount the highlights of the life of labor leader Cesar Chavez and the boycotts he led to gain fair working conditions for farm workers. It includes additional information, a glossary, a list of books for further reading, and more.

Part of the Graphic Library, Graphic Biographies series.

The **Story** of Jamestown. Capstone Press 2006 32p. Illustration
Grades: 3 4 5 6 7 8 9   **741.5; 975.5**
1. Jamestown (Va) — History; 2. Graphic novels
0-7368-4967-X, $25.26
LC 2005013592

This book uses the comic book format to tell the story of Jamestown, the first permanent English settlement in North America. It includes additional information, a glossary, a list of books for further reading, and more.

Part of the Graphic Library, Graphic History series.

Bravo, Emile

★ **Beauty** and the Squat Bears. Illustrations by the author. Yen Press 2011 Un Illustration
Grades: 3 4 5 6 7 8 9   **741.5; Fic**
1. Bears; 2. Fairy tales; 3. Graphic novels
978-0-316-08362-1, $14.99
LC 2010-941434

When the queen's magic mirror declares that Snow White is the fairest in the land, the young princess flees the kingdom, and she finds herself at the cabin belonging to the seven squat bears. They don't want a princess, especially

Courtesy of Yen Press

when she refuses to earn her keep by cleaning the cabin. What to do? Well, they need to find a prince, so they send one of the squat bears out to find a suitable prince. He meets a blue bird who claims to be an enchanted prince, they cause trouble at the ball where Cinderella is supposed to captivate Prince Charming, run into the Beast, and they all run afoul of the Fairy Godmother, who is not amused. Bravo mashes up a bunch of fairy tales in a way that will amuse anyone who has a good sense of humor and sometimes loses patience with all those young girls waiting for a handsome prince to save them. While this is written for younger readers, adults will also have fun reading this book.

Originally published in France under the title, La Belle aux ours nains.

Brennan, Michael

Electric Girl. AiT/PlanetLar 2000 168p. Illustration
Grades: 5 6 7 8 9 10   **741.5; Fic**
1. Humorous graphic novels; 2. Graphic novels
0-9703555-0-5, $9.95

Virginia is an average suburban girl except for her electric powers, which cause her to zap things all the time, and except for her invisible gremlin "friend" Oogleeoog, who has been with her since she was born. The stories go back and forth in time from her early childhood to her teen years and back again as the reader learns about Virginia's powers and how they affect her life.

"Facial expressions and body postures are fluid and evocative, while the verbal text is easy to read." SLJ

Other titles is this series are: Electric Girl vol. 2 (2002); Electric Girl vol. 3 (2005)

Briggs, Raymond

★ **Ethel** & Ernest: A True Story. Pantheon 2001 104p. Illustration
Grades: 4 5 6 7 8 9 10 11 12 Adult   **741.5**
1. Biographical graphic novels; 2. Graphic novels
978-0-375-71447-4, $15.00

This is Raymond Briggs's loving depiction of his parents' lives from their chance first encounter in the 1920s until their deaths in the 1970s. Ethel and Ernest were solid members of the English working class, part of the generation that lived through the most tumultuous years of the twentieth century. They met during the Depression—she working as a maid, he as a milkman—and the reader follows them as they court and marry, make a home, raise their son, and cope with the dark days of World War II. Briggs portrays how his parents succeeded, or failed, in coming to terms with the events of their rapidly shifting world—the advent of radio, television, and telephones; the development of the atomic bomb; the moon landing; the social and political turmoil of the sixties.

Britt, Fanny

Jane, the fox & me. [written by] Fanny Britt; [illustrated by] Isabelle Arsenault; translated by Christine Morelli and Susan Ouriou. Pgw 2013 101 p.
Grades: 5 6 7 8 9   **Fic**
1. Alienation (Social psychology) — Fiction; 2. Teenage girls — Fiction
1554983606; 9781554983605, $19.95

Written by Fanny Britt, illustrated by Isabelle Arsentault, and translated by Christine Morelli and Susan Ouriou, this "graphic novel reveals the casual brutality of which children are capable, but also assures readers that redemption can be found through connecting with another, whether the other is a friend, a fictional character or even, amazingly, a fox." (Publisher's note) It "centers on Hélène, ostracized by her former friends and now a loner at school." (Horn Book Magazine)

"Britt's well-constructed narrative is achieved sensitively through Arsenault's impressionistic artwork. . . . An elegant and accessible approach to an important topic." Booklist

Brown, Don

★ The **great** American dust bowl. By Don Brown. Houghton Mifflin Harcourt 2013 80 p.

Grades: 5 6 7 8 9   **978**

1. Droughts — United States — History; 2. Dust Bowl Era, 1931-1939 — Juvenile literature; 3. Dust storms; 4. Dust storms — History

0547815506; 9780547815503, $18.99

Author Don Brown presents a "graphic novel of one of America's most catastrophic natural events: the Dust Bowl. On a clear, warm Sunday, April 14, 1935, a wild wind whipped up millions upon millions of these specks of dust to form a duster, a savage storm on America's high southern plains." (Publisher's note)

"In this bleak yet compelling graphic-novel-style glimpse at the Dirty Thirties, Brown crisply paces the narrative with fascinating glimpses of the sociological and geological causes of the Dust Bowl. The color brown is a recurring theme here, as Brown relies, aptly, almost entirely on shades of brown throughout. Primary source material is used liberally, as characters speak directly to the reader, documentary-style." (Horn Book)

Brown, Jeffrey

★ **Star** Wars: Jedi Academy. Jeffrey Brown; [edited by] Rex Ogle. Scholastic, Inc 2013 160 p. Illustration (Star Wars: Jedi Academy)

Grades: 3 4 5 6 7   **741.5; Fic**

1. Middle schools — Fiction; 2. Outer space — Fiction; 3. Star Wars

0545505178; 9780545505178, $12.99; 9780545609999

LC 2013931939

In this book, by Jeffrey Brown, "Roan Novachez thought he was destined to attend Pilot Academy Middle School, just as his older brother and father did. His dreams are crushed when he is rejected by Pilot Academy and accepted into a sketchy new school called Coruscant Jedi Academy. . . . Confused and struggling to keep up, Roan tries to fly under the radar and passes the time drawing comics of his daily life at his strange boarding school." (Booklist)

"While it might be disappointing for those familiar with this world to see scant representation of beloved characters, it makes the book an easy starting point for new fans. There are plenty of references to other elements (the T-16 Skyhopper and Jedi training remotes, for example) for diehards to get excited about." SLJ

Other titles in this series are: Return of the Padawan (2014); The Phantom Bully (2015)

Star Wars: Jedi academy 2: Return of the Padawan. Jeffrey Brown; [edited by] Rex Ogle. Scholastic 2014 176 p. Illustration (Star Wars: Jedi academy)

Grades: 3 4 5 6 7   **741.5**

1. Life on other planets — Fiction; 2. Middle schools — Fiction; 3. School stories; 4. Star Wars; 5. Star Wars fiction

0545621259; 9780545621250, $12.99

LC 2014931163

"After surviving his first year at Jedi Academy, Roan Novachez thought his second year would be a breeze. He couldn't have been more wrong. Roan feels like he's drifting apart from his friends, and it's only made worse when Roan discovers he's not the amazing pilot he thought he'd be. When the school bullies take him under their wing, he decides they aren't so bad after all—or are they?" (Publisher's note)

"Roan is a very sympathetic main character, and readers will feel his pain and laugh at his misfortune in equal measure. Roan's hand-lettered journal entries alternate with short paneled sequences and 'screenshots' of academy message boards and other ephemera." Kirkus

Star Wars: Jedi Academy; 3: The Phantom Bully. By Jeffrey Brown. Scholastic Press 2015 176 p. Illustration (Star Wars: Jedi Academy)

Grades: 3 4 5 6 7   **741.5; Fic**

1. Middle schools — Juvenile fiction; 2. School stories — Juvenile fiction; 3. Star Wars films — Juvenile fiction

0545621267; 9780545621267, $12.99

"It's hard to believe this is Roan's last year at Jedi Academy. He's been busier than ever learning to fly (and wash) starships, swimming in the Lake Country on Naboo, studying for the Jedi obstacle course exam, and tracking down dozens of vorpak clones—don't ask. But now, someone is setting him up to get in trouble with everyone at school, including Yoda. If he doesn't find out who it is, and fast, he may get kicked out of school!" (Publisher's note)

"The third graphic novel in the Jedi Academy series turns out to be a love story, although it takes the characters a while to realize it. . . . [B]y the close of this high jinks-filled year, every student at the academy gets a satisfying ending, even the bullies and troublemakers." Kirkus

Brusha, Joe

Discovery channel top 10 dangerous sharks. Silver Dragon Books 2010 120p. Illustration

Grades: 3 4 5 6 7 8 9

741.5

1. Sharks; 2. Graphic novels

978-0-9827507-2-8, $9.99

Courtesy of Discovery Channel Books

This book presents true stories about human encounters with ten of the deadliest sharks: lemon shark, blue shark, hammerhead shark, sand tiger shark, grey reef shark, mako shark, oceanic whitetip, tiger shark, great white shark, and bull shark. Anyone who watches Discovery Channel's

Shark Week programs probably knows the stories related in this book, but most middle grade students who like to read about sharks will want to read these stories anyway. Each section starts out with a two-page spread giving facts about the particular shark, including an "attack file" listing the number of recorded attacks and the number of unprovoked fatalities. Artists Anthony Spay, Shawn McCauley, Marcio Abreu, Agustin Alessio, German Nobile, HG Young, Gabriel Rearte, and Shawn Van Briesen illustrated the stories, with colors by Andrew Elder and John Hunt, and letters by Jim Campbell.

Bugs Bunny: What's Up, Doc?
DC Comics 2005 112p. Illustration
Grades: 3 4 5 6 7 8 9   741.5; Fic
1. Bugs Bunny (Fictional character); 2. Humorous graphic novels; 3. Graphic novels
1-4012-0516-X, $6.99
This volume collects stories about the wisecracking rabbit from the archives of Looney Tunes, sure to tickle the funny bones of both children and the childlike as Bugs goes up against Daffy Duck, Marvin the Martian, Elmer Fudd, and other unfortunates.

Bullock, Mike
Lions, tigers and bears volume 2: betrayal. Image Comics 2008 Un Illustration
Grades: 3 4 5 6 7 8 9   741.5; Fic
1. Adventure graphic novels; 2. Fantasy graphic novels; 3. Graphic novels
978-1-58240-930-6, $14.99
Joey and Courtney's winter wonderland is shattered when the Big Cats of the Night Pride arrive with terrible news from the Stuffed Animal Kingdom. Now all that stands between the horrible Beasties and children everywhere are Joey, Courtney, and their imaginations. For the evil Valthraax and his minions have taken over the Crystal Castle, imprisoned King Bear, and plot to capture all children who aren't being protected by the Stuffed Animal Militia. There is some fighting violence between the Night Pride and their allies against the Beasties.

Lions, tigers, and bears, vol. 1: Fear and pride. [by] Mike Bullock and Jack Lawrence. Image Comics 2006 128p. Illustration
Grades: 2 3 4 5 6   741.5; Fic
1. Adventure graphic novels; 2. Graphic novels
1-58240-657-X, $12.99
When Joey Price has to move away from his grandmother, she gives him a new set of stuffed animals that she says will guard him from nightmares. And one night, he discovers that the stuffed animals are real, and unfortunately, so are the Beasties, the nightmares in his closet

Timothy and the transgalactic towel. Silverline Books/Image Comics 2009 104p. Illustration
Grades: 3 4 5 6 7 8   741.5; Fic
1. Father-son relationship; 2. Humorous graphic novels; 3. Science fiction graphic novels; 4. Graphic novels
978-1-60706-021-5, $16.99
Timothy is having a hard time concentrating on school; his mother is gone and his father has to go away on long business trips, leaving Timothy behind. His father always

tries to bring home a special gift, but this last trip was to Hawaii and he brings home a multicolored beach towel. Timothy thinks it's totally lame, and he gets so angry with his father that he shuts himself away in his room. But, there's something different about that towel: it starts talking to him, and then it whisks him out his bedroom window and into outer space, where Timothy meets his action hero Dash Lightrider. He also finds Dash and his crew in the middle of a space war with the evil blade ships from Piratus, and they also encounter a star dragon. Timothy discovers the star dragon wants to find his son, who was kidnapped by the bad guys on Piratus, so now he leads Dash and the Zoom Rangers on a rescue mission. Bullock includes a message about father/son relationships and forgiveness along with the fun adventure. Metcalf's colorful art makes the book look like a fun television cartoon.

Burgan, Michael
The **Boston** Massacre. Capstone Press 2006 32p. Illustration
Grades: 3 4 5 6 7 8 9   741.5; 973.3
1. Boston Massacre, 1770; 2. Graphic novels
0-7368-4368-X, $25.26
LC 2005006462
This book uses the comic book format to tell the story of the Boston Massacre and its aftermath. It includes additional information, a glossary, a list of books for further reading, and more.
Part of the Graphic Library, Graphic History series.

The **Curse** of King Tut's Tomb. Capstone Press 2005 32p. Illustration
Grades: 3 4 5 6 7 8 9   741.5; 932
1. Tutankhamen, King of Egypt — Tomb; 2. Graphic novels
0-7368-3833-3, $22.60
LC 2004020452
This volume follows the discovery and excavation of King Tutankhamen's tomb and the myth of the curse that afflicted those involved in the tomb's exploration. The book includes additional information, a glossary, a list of books for further reading, and more.
Part of the Graphic Library, Graphic History series.

The **Great** San Francisco Earthquake and Fire. Capstone Press 2007 32p. Illustration
Grades: 3 4 5 6 7 8 9   741.5; 979.4
1. Earthquakes — California; 2. San Francisco Earthquake and Fire, Calif., 1906; 3. Graphic novels
978-1-4296-0155-9, $26.25
LC 2007014929
This book uses the graphic novel format to tell of the San Francisco earthquake of 1906 and the subsequent fires that nearly destroyed the city. The book includes additional facts and a list of books for further reading.
Part of the Graphic Library Disasters in History series

Muhammad Ali: American Champion. Capstone Press 2007 32p. Illustration
Grades: 3 4 5 6 7 8 9   741.5; 796.8; 92
1. Ali, Muhammad; 2. Boxing; 3. Graphic novels
978-1-4296-0153-5, $26.25
LC 2006103432

This book uses the graphic novel format to tell the life story of dynamic heavyweight boxing champion Muhammad Ali, who gained fame for his boxing skills, political views, and humanitarian efforts. The book stops short of showing Ali being rendered almost speechless by advanced Parkinson's Disease in the last couple of years. The book includes additional facts and a list of books for further reading.

Part of the Graphic Biographies series.

Burks, James

Bird & Squirrel on the run. James Burks. Graphix/Scholastic Press 2012 128 p. Illustration
Grades: 2 3 4 5   **741.5**
1. Adventure fiction — Juvenile fiction; 2. Cats — Juvenile fiction; 3. Squirrels — Juvenile fiction
0545312833; 9780545312837, $8.99
                              LC 2011934532
This children's book, by James Burks, follows "Bird and Squirrel [as they] outwit Cat and become best friends in this zany adventure. Squirrel is afraid of his own shadow. Bird doesn't have a care in the world. And Cat wants to eat Bird and Squirrel. Of course, he'll have to catch them first, and that's not going to be easy. Join this trio as they head south for the winter in a hilarious road trip. But watch out! Cat is waiting around every bend, and he's one pesky feline." (Publisher's note)

Other titles in this series are: Bird & Squirrel on ice (2014); Bird & Squirrel on the edge! (2015)

Butzer, C. M.

★ **Gettysburg:** the graphic novel. Bowen Books/HarperCollins 2009 80p. Illustration
Grades: 3 4 5 6 7 8 9 10 11 12   **741.5; 973.7**
1. American speeches; 2. Gettysburg (Pa), Battle of, 1863; 3. Gettysburg address 4. Lincoln, Abraham; 5. Lincoln, Abraham — Work — Gettysburg address; 6. Lincoln, Abraham, 1809-1865; 7. Graphic novels
978-0-06-156176-4, $16.99; 978-0-06-156175-7 (pa), $8.99
                              LC 2008-10657
In the summer of 1863, everyone knew that the Battle of Gettysburg would be an important battle that could determine the course of the War Between the States, the Civil War. What they didn't know was who would prevail. Butzer uses primary sources to play out the battle that lasted three days and caused tremendous casualties, the aftermath that nearly overwhelmed the town of Gettysburg, and the effort to build the monument to commemorate the fallen. He uses a somber blue and gray wash in his illustrations. Lincoln's famous Gettysburg Address was only 271 words long and appear in their entirety, against images of the nation's past. Some panels depicting the violence of the battles, and particularly the dead on the battlefield, could be disturbing for sensitive younger readers; but this battle was ugly and overwhelming in its violence. Butzer includes extensive end notes to explain what he depicted, and to note the sources of the dialog and narration.

Byrne, Eugene

★ **Darwin:** a graphic biography. By Eugene Byrne; illustrated by Simon Gurr. Smithsonian Books 2013 96 p. Illustration
Grades: 5 6 7 8 9 10 11 12 Adult
B; 576.8; 576.8/2092
1. Darwin, Charles, 1809-1882; 2. Evolution; 3. Evolution (Biology); 4. Natural selection; 5. Graphic novels
1588343529; 9781588343529, $9.95
                    LC 2012951786

Courtesy of Smithsonian Books

This work of graphic nonfiction by Eugene Byrne and Simon Gurr presents a "summary of [Charles] Darwin's life and achievement. . . . Darwin was an indifferent student . . .until he received an invitation to take a voyage that 'would change the course of history.' . . .The animals he encountered seemed so different . . . that he theorized that if it weren't a matter of different conditions that resulted in such 'transmutation,' they might well have had a different creator." (Kirkus Reviews)

Includes bibliographical references.

Cabarga, Leslie

Harvey Comics Classics Volume Two: Richie Rich, the Poor Little Rich Boy. Dark Horse Comics 2007 480p. Illustration
Grades: 3 4 5 6 7 8 9 10 11 12 Adult   **741.5**
1. Humorous graphic novels; 2. Richie Rich (Fictional character); 3. Graphic novels
978-1-59307-848-5, $19.95
This volume reprints 125 Richie Rich stories, taken from the comic's beginnings in 1953 through the 1960s. While most of the stories appear here in black and white, the book includes a 64-page section of color reprints. Richie Rich and his friends Gloria, Freckles, and Peewee enjoy not-so-everyday adventures, including playing "tycoon" in the new offices of Rich's father. Some stories feature rich cousin and antagonist Reggie.

Harvey comics classics voulme three: hot stuff: the little devil. Dark Horse Comics 2008 480p. Illustration
Grades: 3 4 5 6 7 8 9 10 11 12 Adult   **741.5; Fic**
1. Devil; 2. Humorous graphic novels; 3. Graphic novels
978-1-59307-914-7, $19.95
Hot Stuff: the Little Devil was created for Harvey Comics in 1957, and right away became the starring character in his own comic book series. This volume collects 110 stories from the Hot Stuff comics originally published from 1957 through 1966; the comic book actually remained in print until the 1980s. Back in 1957, having a little red hot devil as a main character caused some controversy, but most young children who read the comics had no problem with him. These stories involve Hot Stuff and his friends in comical misadventures just like any kid could get into, such as having to babysit a younger cousin, trying to outdo a

visiting ghost, going to see a doctor (of course, Hot Stuff has to see a witch doctor).

Part of the Harvey Comics Classics series

Caldwell, Ben
   Star Wars: Clone Wars Adventures Vol. 1. Dark Horse Comics 2004 Un Illustration
Grades: 5 6 7 8 9 10   **741.5; Fic**
   1. Adventure graphic novels; 2. Science fiction graphic novels; 3. Star Wars; 4. Graphic novels
   1-59307-243-0, $6.95
   On the night-world of Nivek, Obi-Wan Kenobi and Anakin Skywalker must first overcome the limitations of fighting in the dark before they can take on the dreaded Shadowmen! Meanwhile, Jedi Masters Mace Windu and Saesee Tiin discover that push can come to shove when using the Force to fight battledroids. And, fresh from leading an underwater assault against Separatist forces on the water planet of Mon Calamari, Jedi Master Kit Fisto and his remaining clone troops reach the surface to find a new threat awaiting them. These original stories use the animated style of the Cartoon Network's "Clone Wars" cartoons and are set during the time between Star Wars Episodes 2 and 3, approximately five months after the Battle of Geonosis.
   Volume 1 of 10

The **Wizard** of Oz. Written by L. Frank Baum; adapted by Ben Caldwell. Sterling Children's Books 2012 32 p. Illustration (All-Action Classics)
Grades: 4 5 6   **741.5; 741.5/973**
   1. Fantasy graphic novels; 2. Oz (Imaginary place); 3. Tornadoes — Fiction; 4. Voyages and travels; 5. Graphic novels; 6. Baum, L. Frank — Adaptations
   1402731531; 9781402731532, $7.95
                     LC 2013363513
   This book is a graphic novel adaptation of L. Frank Baum's classic tale "The Wizard of Oz." Author and illustrator Ben Caldwell "follows Baum's original novel rather than the iconic film. The heroes are pursued by the Kalidah, 'horrific beasts, with heads like tigers and bodies like bears,' and the famous path the four friends follow, as in the original, is called the 'road of golden bricks.'" (Publishers Weekly)

Cammuso, Frank
   Knights of the lunch table: the dodgeball chronicles. Graphix 2008 141p.
Grades: 3 4 5 6   **741.5; Fic**
   1. Humorous graphic novels; 2. School stories; 3. Graphic novels
   978-0-439-90322-6 (pa), $9.99; 0-439-90322-X (pa)
   Artie King's family has moved and now he has to start at a new school, Camelot Middle School. Dodgeball is the big game at Camelot, and the Horde is a champion team; the Horde members are also the worst bullies in the school. . . . Artie immediately gets into trouble with Joe, the leader of the Horde. . . . However, he manages to open the broken old locker . . . [which] provides mysterious, useful stuff, such as a lunch. Joe challenges Artie to a dodgeball game; Artie has new friends Percy and Wayne who'll help him, and then he meets Gwen. And science teacher Mr. Merlyn is also on his side.

"Arthurian legend gets an update for young readers in this outstanding graphic novel. . . . The funny, fast-paced tale of young Arthur's quest to defeat the bullies stands well on its own. The appealing illustrations are full of color, action, and life." SLJ
   Followed by: Knights of the lunch table: the dragon players (2009)

   ★ **Knights** of the lunch table: the dragon players. Scholastic/Graphix 2009 127p.
Grades: 3 4 5 6   **741.5; Fic**
   1. Arthurian romances — Adaptations; 2. Conduct of life; 3. Contests; 4. Humorous graphic novels; 5. Schools; 6. Graphic novels
   978-0-439-90323-3 (pa), $9.99; 0-439-90323-8 (pa)
                     LC 2008-51463
   Artie King may have won the dodgeball game against the school bullies, but life is not easy. The new challenge comes with the dueling robot tournament at school; it's all part of Dragon Day, and The Horde has won every year by cheating—they force the smartest kid in school to design and build their robot. This year, they've done it to Percy. Circumstances force Artie's hand and willy nilly, he has entered the tournament. Seeking an edge, they go to Evo, a mysterious techno wiz kid who can build any gadget; the problem for Artie is, is he cheating by getting help from Evo" Cammuso's bright, cartoony art and schoolyard version of Arthurian legend provides lots of fun action as well as making readers think about ethics
   Followed by: Knights of the lunch table: the battling bands (2011)
   Sequel to: Knights of the lunch table: the dodgeball chronicles (2008)

The **Misadventures** of Salem Hyde: Spelling Trouble. Harry N Abrams Inc 2013 96 p.
Grades: 2 3 4   **Fic**
   1. Occult fiction — Juvenile fiction; 2. School stories — Juvenile fiction
   1419708031; 9781419708039
   This is the first book in Frank Cammuso's Salem Hyde series. Here, "Salem Hyde just wants a friend. After a misguided attempt to use her magic lands her in the principal's office, Salem's family decides she needs an animal companion. One well-placed call later, she meets knowledgeable and talkative feline Percival J. Whamsford III, otherwise known as Whammy. Whammy isn't just a chatty kitty; he is a Magical Animal Companion and will help Salem learn how to use her magic properly." (Kirkus Reviews)
   Other titles in this series are:Big birthday bash (2014); Cookie camp catastrophe (2014); Dinosaur dilemma (2015)

Camper, Cathy
   ★ **Lowriders** in space; book 1. By Cathy Camper; illustrated by Raul Gonzalez III. Chronicle Books 2014 112 p. Color; Illustration (Lowriders)
Grades: 4 5 6 7 8   **741.5**
   1. Automobiles — Fiction; 2. Competition (Psychology) — Fiction; 3. Friendship — Fiction; 4. Lowriders; 5. Lowriders — Fiction; 6. Mechanics (Persons); 7. Mexican

Americans — Fiction; 8. Space vehicles; 9. Graphic novels
9781452121550, $22.99; 1452121559

LC 2013040709

Cathy Camper "introduces readers to Lupe Impala, Flapjack Octopus, and Elirio Malaria, three friends who love working with cars and dream of having their own garage shop. One day they see an opportunity to achieve their goal—a car competition. When they start working on a lowrider to prepare it for the competition, an out-of-this world journey begins." (School Library Journal)

"Raul's snazzy panels—impressively drawn in only red, blue, and black ballpoint pen on tea-stained paper—resemble an amped-up Mighty Mouse cartoon rendered in anarchic yet skillful doodles. It's a joyfully explosive style, and it perfectly matches the Latino characters and barrio setting." Booklist

Carre, Lilli

The **fir-tree**. It Books/HarperCollins 2009 Un Illustration

Grades: 3 4 5 6 7 8 9 10 11 12 Adult   741.5; Fic
1. Andersen, Hans Christian, 1805-1875 — Adaptations; 2. Christmas; 3. Christmas trees; Graphic novels
978-0-06-178236-7, $14.99

A young fir-tree only wants to grow tall; it's never satisfied and doesn't notice the sunlight and clean air. It never rejoices in anything, but grumbles and complains. When it sees some trees being cut down and taken away, it wonders what it's missing. The birds tell of seeing the trees inside homes, beautifully decorated, and it becomes jealous. When it does grow tall and beautiful, a woodsman comes along and cuts it down, hauling it to town to become a Christmas tree in a house. It enjoys the family playing around the tree at Christmas, but after the holiday, the family throws it into a storeroom. Will the tree ever see its forest again" Lilli Carre uses delicate coloring and illustrations to adapt Andersen's sad Christmas story. Although this is suitable for young readers, adults may better appreciate the tragedy and Carre's idiosyncratic illustrations her people have long, loopy arms.

Carroll, Lewis

New Alice in Wonderland, masterpiece edition. Antarctic Press 2007 Un Illustration

Grades: 4 5 6 7 8 9   741.5
1. Adventure graphic novels; 2. Fantasy graphic novels; 3. Humorous graphic novels; 4. Graphic novels
978-0-9787725-8-1, $14.95

Espinosa (The Courageous Princess) adapts Lewis Carroll's classic tale into a graphic novel full of pop culture references (check out the Mad Hatter, for instance). It's still the original story, which starts when the daydreaming Alice sees a rabbit checking his pocket watch and runs after him, only to find herself in a strange world with bizarre creatures.

Castellucci, Cecil

Odd Duck. By Cecil Castellucci, illustrated by Sara Varon. First Second 2013 96 p.

Grades: 1 2 3 4 5   E

1. Ducks — Juvenile fiction; 2. Eccentrics and eccentricities — Juvenile fiction; 3. Friendship — Juvenile fiction
1596435577; 9781596435575, $15.99

In this book, by Cecil Castellucci, illustrated by Sara Varon, "Theodora is a perfectly normal duck. She may swim with a teacup balanced on her head and stay north when the rest of the ducks fly south for the winter, but there's nothing so odd about that. Chad, on the other hand, is one strange bird. Theodora quite likes him, but she can't overlook his odd habits. It's a good thing Chad has a normal friend like Theodora to set a good example for him." (Publisher's note)

Cauvin, Raoul

The **bluecoats** no. 1: Robertsonville Prison. Cinebook Ltd. 2008 48p. Illustration

Grades: 5 6 7 8 9 10   741.5; Fic
1. Adventure graphic novels; 2. Humorous graphic novels; 3. United States — History — 1861-1865, Civil War — Prisoners and prisons; 4. Graphic novels
978-1-90546-071-7, $11.95

Sergeant Chesterfield and Corporal Blutch are Union soldiers during the Civil War; Blutch tends to be lazy, and Chesterfield always seems to be getting him out of trouble; but after one battle, they're both in trouble when they're captured by Confederate troops and are force-marched to Robertsonville Prison. They constantly get into trouble with a soldier and camp guard named Cockroach, and Chesterfield leads multiple attempts to escape the prison. Then when they succeed, they're wearing stolen Confederate uniforms and ultimately end up in a Union prison camp. Prison camps aren't normally subjects of humor, but the humor in this book is reminiscent of the old television series Hogan's Heroes, which was set in a German prisoner of war camp

Chad, Jon

Leo Geo and his miraculous journey through the center of the earth. Jon Chad. Roaring Brook Press 2012 40 p.

Grades: 2 3 4 5   FIC
1. Adventure graphic novels; 2. Earth — Internal structure; 3. Explorers; 4. Geology; 5. Kings, queens, rulers, etc — Fiction; 6. Magic — Fiction; 7. Scientists; 8. Graphic novels
9781596436619

LC 2011017353

In this book, "the featureless protagonist, an enthusiastic scientist named Leo, sets off on a journey to the center of the Earth through the book's tall pages, and readers are encouraged to turn the book vertically to follow his trek downward. Leo spouts real science facts, but also encounters fantastic creatures in the Earth's mantle at temperatures where nothing ought to be able to survive. Leo uses some big scientific words and even a few wicked-looking math equations, although he is careful to clarify most of what he says for younger audiences." (Publishers Weekly)

Leo Geo and the cosmic crisis: Matt Data and the cosmic crisis. Jon Chad. Roaring Brook Press 2013 40 p. Color; Illustration

Grades: 2 3 4 5   741.5

1. Adventure and adventurers — Fiction; 2. Astronauts — Fiction; 3. Astronomy; 4. Magic — Fiction; 5. Space flight — Fiction; 6. Graphic novels
1596438223; 9781596438224, $16.99

LC 2013001296

In this 2-in-1 book, "[Leo Geo] and his space-based scientist brother Matt Data trace looping paths through crowded spacescapes toward each other. Before they meet in the middle, both encounter black holes, white holes, wormholes, asteroids, space pirates and some distinctly more unusual 'space sights.'" (Kirkus Reviews)

"The bright, detailed, full-page panels are covered with strange creatures and planetary objects that will catch and hold young readers' attention, and the scientific information is simply presented and well-integrated into the dialogue. The varied layout of the pages, vertical and horizontal, and the 'search engine,' a hunt for specific objects throughout the book, encourage engagement with the story." SLJ

Sequel to Leo Geo and His Miraculous Journey through the Center of the Earth (2012)

Chantler, Scott
The **captive** prince. Scott Chantler. Kids Can Press 2012 116 p. Color illustration
Grades: 4 5 6 7   **741.5; 741.5/971; Fic**
1. Adventure fiction; 2. Thieves — Fiction; 3. Graphic novels
9781554537778, $8.95; 9781451782806, $17.95 ; 1554537762; 9781554537761, $17.95

This children's adventure book by Scott Chantler is the "third title of the . . . Three Thieves graphic novel series[.] Dessa, Topper and Fisk are still running from the Queen's Dragons and trying to find Dessa's missing twin brother. But when Dessa inadvertently rescues a prince — putting kingdoms at stake and love on the line — the adventure quickly becomes a royal mess!" (Publisher's note)

The **king's** dragon. Scott Chantler. Kids Can Press 2014 112 p. Illustration; Color (Three Thieves)
Grades: 3 4 5 6   **741.5; Fic**
1. Fantasy graphic novels; 2. Knights and knighthood
9781554537792, $8.95; 1554537797

In this graphic novel written and illustrated by Scott Chantler, "royal knight Capt. Drake . . . briefly catches up with his quarry, Dessa, a young circus acrobat hobbled (but not much) by a broken leg, and also looks back on his early days as a member of the elite but corrupt Dragons." (Kirkus Reviews)

"Black-and-white art among color signifies the flashback scenes, making the transitions easy to follow. The backstory will be satisfying to fans." Horn Book

Tower of treasure. Kids Can Press 2010 112p. Illustration (Three thieves)
Grades: 3 4 5 6   **741.5**
1. Acrobats and acrobatics — Fiction; 2. Adventure graphic novels; 3. Circus — Fiction; 4. Thieves — Fiction; 5. Graphic novels
978-1-55453-414-2, $17.99; 1-55453-414-3; 978-1-55453-415-9 (pa), $8.95; 1-55453-415-1 (pa)

"As an acrobat in a traveling circus, 14-year-old orphan Dessa Redd flies through the air with ease. Still, she is weighed down by troubling memories. But when her ragtag circus troupe pulls into the city of Kingsbridge, Dessa feels a tickle of hope. Maybe here in the royal city she will finally find her twin brother—or the mysterious man who snatched him away when they were just children. Meanwhile, Topper, the circus juggler, recruits Dessa and the circus strongman, Fisk, for the job of robbing the royal treasury." (Publisher's note)

Other titles in this series are:The sign of the black rock (2011); The captive prince (2012); The king's dragon (2014); Pirates of the silver coast (2014); The dark island (2016)

Chastain, Grant
The **Gwaii**. Arcana Comics 2009 Un Illustration
Grades: 3 4 5 6 7 8   **741.5; Fic**
1. Adventure graphic novels; 2. Sasquatch; 3. Graphic novels
978-1-897548-36-3, $14.95

In the Canadian wilderness, the young Gwaii (a Sasquatch) named Tanu seeks his mother, who was captured by loggers whose company is destroying the land. One of the men has a young son, who doesn't like what his dad and coworkers are doing. Meanwhile, Tanu's new friend Jaadaa, who saved him from the loggers, helps the young Gwaii as they venture far from home, pursuing the humans and determined to save Tanu's mother. O'Reilly has based this story on the Haida people who live in Haida Gwaii (Queen Charlotte Island), off the west coast of British Columbia in Canada; Tanu and his people are fictional, but their names are all derived from the Haida language. This colorful adventure story also carries a strong message about respecting nature.

Chen, Wei Dong
Monkey King: Birth of the Stone Monkey Vol. 01. JR Comics 2012 172 p.
Grades: 3 4 5 6   **Fic; 741.5/951**
1. Buddhism; 2. Chinese mythology; 3. Legendary characters; 4. Graphic novels
8994208690; 9788994208695, $29.27

This book "follows the adventures of Sun Wu Kong, born from a stone on Spring Mountain and given the title of Handsome Monkey King, who seeks to learn the secret of eternal life. Under the tutelage of the Buddhist Master Puti, Sun Wu Kong becomes incredibly powerful, but his hubris grows until he has run afoul of the gods, who dispatch an army to Spring Mountain to subdue the Monkey King, who has declared himself the 'Emperor of Heaven'" (Publisher's note)

Volume 1 of 20

Monkey King: Journey to the West. Created by Wei Dong Chen; illustrated by Chao Peng. JR Comics 2012 173 p. Illustration
Grades: 5 6 7   **Fic; 741.5/951**
1. Chinese mythology; 2. Graphic novels
8994208712; 9788994208718, $29.27

This is the third volume in Wei Dong Chen's Monkey King series, a graphic novel series based on the Chinese classical literature novel "Journey to the West." In "the first volume, Sun Wu Kong is born from a stone and goes on a quest of find the secret of eternal life. In succeeding volumes the Monkey King steals the heavenly peaches and is imprisoned by Buddha for 500 years." (Library Media Connection)

Monkey King: The Bane of Heaven. Created by Wei Dong Chen; illustrated by Chao Peng. Jr Comics 2012 174 p. Illustration
Grades: 5 6 7   **741.5/951; Fic**
1. Chinese mythology; 2. Graphic novels
8994208704; 9788994208701, $29.27
This is the second volume in Wei Dong Chen's Monkey King series. Here, "Sun Wu Kong is named emperor of heaven, [and] begins to make himself comfortable among the gods, and quickly wears out his welcome." The series is a retelling of the classical Chinese work "Journey to the West." (Booklist)

Chilman-Blair, Kim
What's up with Bill?: Medikidz explain epilepsy. Rosen Publishing Group, Inc. 2010 40p. Illustration (Superheroes on a medical mission)

Courtesy of Rosen Publishing

Grades: 3 4 5 6 7 8 9
616.85; 741.5
1. Epilepsy; 2. Graphic novels
978-1-4358-3533-7, $29.25; 1-4358-3533-6
LC 2009-29785
After teenage Bill suffers a seizure, he and his unnamed sister meet the Medikidz, a team of superheroes who help people with health problems. They take the two teens into the brain to explain how it works and what happens when a person has epilepsy. The book uses a lot of humor, especially with Gastro, who loves to eat and does things like pass gas. Chilman-Blair is a physician, and the book was reviewed by an expert for medical accuracy. The book includes a glossary of the medical terms used, a list of books for further reading, and contact information for some agencies that deal with epilepsy.
Includes glossary and bibliographical references
Part of the Superheroes on a Medical Mission series.

Chmakova, Svetlana
Awkward. By Svetlana Chmakova. Yen Press 2015 210 p. Illustration; Color
Grades: 5 6 7 8
741.5
1. Clubs — Fiction; 2. Clubs — Juvenile fiction; 3. Middle schools — Fiction; 4. Middle schools — Juvenile fiction; 5. Popularity — Juvenile fiction; 6. School stories; 7.

Courtesy of Yen Press

Schools — Fiction; 8. Schools — Juvenile fiction; 9. Graphic novels
0316381306; 0316381322; 9780316381307; 9780316381321, $24
LC 2015945195
In this middle grade book, by Svetlana Chmakova, "protagonist Peppi is fantastically imperfect. . . . She is the new girl at Berrybrook Middle School and is having a hard time fitting in because of her struggles with social anxiety. The work opens with the young teen pushing away the first person who tries to help her, Jaime, and it only gets more awkward from there." (School Library Journal)

Chung, Haley
Math Game 1. Youngjin Singapore 2005 196p. Illustration
Grades: 3 4 5 6 7 8   **510; 741.5**
1. Mathematics; 2. Graphic novels
981-05-2238-X, $12.95
Alice, Jimmy, Colby, and Sam are four good friends who share a common bond - they all hate math. As they complain about it on their way home from school, the King of Math appears and whisks Alice away. Jimmy, Colby, and Sam decide to rescue her, but to enter into the Math King's world they must first pass through 20 gates, guarded by 20 great mathematicians. Saving Alice hinges on the friends learning about the discovery of zero, Roman numerals, fractions, rational and irrational numbers, and more-all in the context of a puzzle-based adventure.

Cibos, Lindsay
Peach Fuzz, Vol. 1. Lindsay Cibos and Jared Hodges. Tokyopop 2005 Un Illustration
Grades: 3 4 5 6 7 8   **741.5; Fic**
1. Ferrets; 2. Pets; 3. Graphic novels
1-59532-599-9, $9.99
Amanda is a lonely little girl. Her mother means well, but doesn't have a lot of time for a 9-year-old and, after plenty of begging from Amanda, agrees to let her have a pet. Amanda chooses a ferret because ferrets aren't ordinary and neither is she. But her mother worries because ferrets are notorious for biting. Amanda wins over her mother, gets the ferret and names it Peach. The two big rules: Amanda has to care for Peach, and Peach can't ever bite Amanda. It seems like Amanda finally has the friend she needed. But Peach sees Amanda's hands as five-serpent monsters—and bites in defense. What will lonely Amanda do now?"
Volume 1 of 3

Ciencin, Scott
Point-blank paintball. Stone Arch Books 2010 56p. Illustration
Grades: 3 4 5 6 7 8   **741.5; Fic**
1. Recreation; 2. Sibling rivalry; 3. Sports; 4. Twins; 5. Graphic novels
978-1-4342-1914-5, $25.32; 978-1-4342-2293-0 (pa), $6.95
Twin brothers Noah and Peter Eccleston are great paintball players; as a team, they have beat everyone they've played. Now, a major paintball team's coach wants them to try out for a spot on his team, but there's only room for one player. Noah and Peter have to compete against each other

even as they have to beat the other members of the team. Is their father's attitude that winning is everything right, and how will this competition affect their relationship" This original graphic novel focuses on a hot sports activity and includes discussion questions and a glossary. Ciencin has written bestselling fiction, science fiction, horror, and superhero comics. Aburto, Maese, and Esparza are comics illustrators from Monterrey, Mexico.

Part of the Sports Illustrated Kids Graphic Novels series.

CLAMP

Angelic Layer. CLAMP. Dark Horse Manga 2012 426 p.

Grades: 5 6 7 8

1. Games — Fiction; 2. Japan — Fiction; 3. Manga
161655021X; 9781616550219, $19.99

"Junior high student Misaki Suzuhara has just arrived in Tokyo to live with her glamorous TV news star aunt and to attend the prestigious Eriol Academy. But what excites her above everything is Angelic Layer, the arena game where you control an 'Angel'—a miniature robot fighter whose moves depend on your mind!" (Publisher's note)

Originally published in the U.S. by Tokyopop

Volume 1 of 2

Colfer, Eoin

Artemis Fowl: the graphic novel. Adapted by Eoin Colfer and Andrew Donkin; art by Giovanni Rigano; color by Paolo Lammana. Hyperion Books for Children 2007 Un Illustration

Grades: 4 5 6 7 8 9   **741; 741.5; Fic**

1. Adventure graphic novels; 2. Fantasy graphic novels
978-0-7868-4881-2, $18.99; 0-7868-4881-2;
978-0-7868-4882-9 (pa), $9.99; 0-7868-4882-0 (pa)

Twelve-year-old genius and criminal mastermind Artemis Fowl runs his missing father's crime empire and gets his hands on a book that will give him access to the underground fairy world. This graphic novel adaptation gives the book a European lookd color palette

"Excellent use of color and shading gives the panels a tremendous sense of light with enchanting effect. Characters are expressively brought to life with fun, exaggerated style." SLJ

Other Artemis Fowl graphic novels are:Artemis Fowl: the Arctic incident (2009); Artemis Fowl: the eternity code (2013); Artemis Fowl: the opal deception (2014)

Collicutt, Paul

City in peril!. Templar Books/Candlewick Press 2009 Un Illustration (Robot City)

Grades: 3 4 5   **741.5; Fic**

1. Mystery graphic novels; 2. Robots; 3. Science fiction graphic novels; 4. Graphic novels
978-0-7636-4120-7 (pa), $8.99; 0-7636-4120-0 (pa)
LC 2009-931660

In Robot City, a metropolis of 15 million humans and 1 million robots, Curtis, the Colossal CoastGuard Robot works as part of a team of robots and humans to keep the Robot City Bay safe. In the middle of the night, the Red Star oil rig sends out a desperate distress call when something attacks it in the middle of a storm. Curtis, who looks like a light house on huge, long legs, helps to save the crew on the oil rig, but there's something out there in the ocean, and it means to attack Robot City. He has suffered damage in one of his legs, but Curtis knows he has to stop the menace. This science fiction adventure is full of action and derring-do with colorful retro-style comic book illustrations. Young readers, as well as adults, will appreciate the twist in the story.

"Curtis is a walking, talking lighthouseheaded robot who protects the coast of Robot City with his trusty human crew, Ali and Steve. When an oil rig out at sea catches fire, Curtis rushes to the rescue and then investigates the fishy mystery of the causes of this near disaster. . . . The illustrations . . . are full of retro-comicbook-style action and classic movieserial banter." Kirkus

Rust attack!: Robot City adventures. Templar Books/Candlewick Press 2009 Un Illustration

Grades: 3 4 5 6   **741.5; Fic**

1. Mystery graphic novels; 2. Robots; 3. Science fiction graphic novels; 4. Graphic novels
978-0-7636-4594-6, $8.99
LC 2009-931661

In Robot City, a metropolis of 15 million humans and 1 million robots, Mike (a human) and Rod (a robot) run Robot City Confidential Investigations, a private detective agency. A robot dancer comes to them, asking them to find out who infected her dance troupe with rust; for robots, rust is a horribly dangerous problem. When they quickly discover a disgruntled robot musician with a grudge, the detectives suspect there's more to the case and continue to investigate. The book combines noir mystery with robots, humor, and a retro-cartoon style in the colorful art.

Part of the Robot City Adventures series.

Collins, Terry

The **FBI**. Illustrated by Kelly Brown. Capstone Press 2009 32p. Illustration

Grades: 3 4 5 6 7 8   **363.2; 741.5**

1. United States — Federal Bureau of Investigation; 2. Graphic novels
978-1-4296-1982-0, $32
LC 2008-506

This graphic format book uses irreverently humorous captions and dialog and provides young readers with an introduction to the founding, history, and work of the Federal Bureau of Investigation, the FBI. The book also describes what it takes to become an agent of the FBI, what a "typical" day is like, and the top priorities of the Bureau, including national security and criminal priorities. It includes a short timeline, a glossary, and a list of books for further reading.

Part of the Graphic Library Cartoon Nation series

Comics Squad: recess!

Comics by Jarrett J. Krosoczka, Gene Yang, Eric Wight, Jennifer L. Holm and Matthew Holm, Ursula Vernon, Dan Santat, Raina Telgemeier and Dave Roman, Dav Pilkey; edited by Jennifer L. Holm, Matthew Holm, and Jarrett J. Krosoczka. Random House Inc. 2014 144 p. Illustration; Color

Grades: 2 3 4 5 6   **741.5**

1. Humorous stories; 2. Recess — Fiction; 3. School stories; 4. Schools — Fiction; 5. Short stories; 6. Graphic novels

0385370032; 9780385370035, $7.99; 9780385370042, $12.99

LC 2013035223

"An all-star lineup of graphic novel notables contributes original works to this anthology, sharing the common thread of recess." (School Library Journal)

"[T]his lively, upbeat and all-around-awesome offering is consistently convivial and laugh-out-loud funny from cover to cover." Kirkus

Another title in this series is: Lunch! (2016)

Conner, Daniel

William Shakespeare's A midsummer night's dream. Adapted by Daniel Conner; illustrated by Rod Espinosa. ABDO/Magic Wagon 2008 48p. Illustration

Grades: 5 6 7 8 9 10

741.5; Fic

1. Graphic novels; 2. Shakespeare, William, 1564-1616 — Adaptations; 3. Youths' writings

978-1-60270-191-5, $28.50

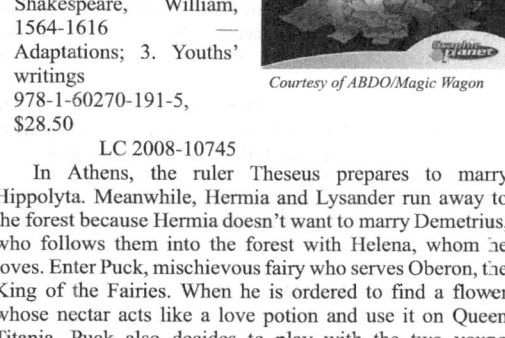

Courtesy of ABDO/Magic Wagon

LC 2008-10745

In Athens, the ruler Theseus prepares to marry Hippolyta. Meanwhile, Hermia and Lysander run away to the forest because Hermia doesn't want to marry Demetrius, who follows them into the forest with Helena, whom he loves. Enter Puck, mischievous fairy who serves Oberon, the King of the Fairies. When he is ordered to find a flower whose nectar acts like a love potion and use it on Queen Titania, Puck also decides to play with the two young couples. And meanwhile again, a group of guildsmen prepare a play for their ruler's wedding. Havoc ensues. This graphic novel adaptation retains some of the original language from Shakespeare's play, while paring down the story to appeal to struggling readers. The book includes a short biography of Shakespeare, a summary of the play, a glossary, and a short selection of famous lines and phrases from the play.

Part of the Graphic Shakespeare series

Cook, Katie

Gronk; Volume 1: a monster's story. By Katie Cook; interior color by Kevin Minor. Action Lab Entertainment 2015 64 p. Color; Illustration

Grades: 2 3 4 5

741.5; Fic

1. Friendship; 2. Monsters

9781632290885, $9.99; 163229088X

In this graphic novel by Katie Cook, "Gronk is a monster . . . and not a very good one. 'Gronk' tells the tale of a young monster who has turned her back on monsterdom (mostly because no one found her scary) and has become fascinated with humans. She moves in with her human friend Dale and her pets Kitty and Harli, a 160 lb. Newfoundland Dale wants to declare as a dependent to the IRS." (Publisher's note)

"While the humor centers on the imaginative and curious monster's mischief, there is an underlying message of acceptance and inclusion throughout. Originally published as a black-and-white webcomic, this collection adds vivid colors to Cook's strong line work and sweetly expressive characters." SLJ

Corona, Jorge

Feathers. Written & illustrated by Jorge Corona; colors by Jen Hickman; letters by Deron Bennett. Archaia 2015 160 p. Illustration

Grades: 5 6 7 8

741.5; Fic

1. Monsters; 2. Orphans

9781608867530, $24.99; 1608867536

LC 2015055238

In this graphic novel, written & illustrated by Jorge Corona, "Poe has lived his entire eleven-year-old life hidden away under the protection of his adoptive father, Gabriel. He spends his days secretly helping . . . bands of orphans who roam the slums. . . . When Bianca, an over-protected girl from the wealthy City beyond the Wall, escapes into the Maze in search of adventure, their worlds collide." (Publisher's note)

"Poe is a true underdog hero, and Bianca's wish to be set free from her restricting life is something to which middle grades readers can relate. Stunning illustrations contrast the stark white orderly city with the dark and dangerous Maze." SLJ

Cosson, M. J.

Sherlock Holmes and a scandal in Bohemia. Based on the stories of Sir Arthur Conan Doyle; adapted by Murray Shaw and M.J. Cosson; illustrated by Sophie Rohrbach.. Lerner Publishing Group/Graphic Universe 2010 48p. Illustration

Grades: 3 4 5 6 7 8

741.5; Fic

1. Authors; 2. Doyle, Arthur Conan Sir, 1859-1930 — Adaptations; 3. Mystery graphic novels; 4. Graphic novels

978-0-7613-6185-5, $26.60; 978-0-7613-6197-8 (pa), $6.95

LC 2009-51763

The King of Bohemia comes to Sherlock Holmes and asks him to retrieve a photograph from the king's former lover, Irene Adler. He wants to be married, and Miss Adler is blackmailing him with the incriminating photograph. Holmes dons a disguise in order to steal the photo from Miss Adler's house, but the singer proves to be an intelligent, formidable foe. This book adapts the story written by Sir Arthur Conan Doyle, with sepia-toned art. It includes clues to Holmes' reasoning and a list for further reading.

Coudray, Philippe

Benjamin Bear in Brain storms!. By Philippe Coudray. TOON Books 2015 40 p. Color; Illustration (Benjamin Bear)

Grades: PreK K 1 2

741.5

1. Bears; 2. Bears — Fiction; 3. Creative thinking; 4. Humorous fiction; 5. Humorous stories; 6. Graphic novels

1935179829; 9781935179825, $12.95

LC 2014028851

"Benjamin Bear can always surprise his friends, whether it's by walking on his hands during a snowstorm or by using a tree as a parachute. This unassuming bear may at first seem down-to-earth, but his ideas are always out of this world." (Publisher's note)

"Benjamin Bear returns for a third round of humorously bizarre mini-sagas. . . . Coudray uses visuals effectively to consistently get laughs (many of the strips are completely wordless)." Horn Book

★ **Benjamin** Bear in Bright ideas!. By Philippe Coudray. Toon Books 2013 32 p.

Grades: PreK K 1   **741.5/973; 741.5**
1. Animals; 2. Bears — Fiction; 3. Humorous stories; 4. Picture books for children; 5. Graphic novels
1935179225; 9781935179221, $12.95

LC 2012022895

This children's picture book is part of the Benjamin Bear series, where the bear and his animal friends appear in minimalist fables drawn . . . from French cartoonist [Philippe] Coudray's original series. . . . In 'Can I Get a Ride?' [Benjamin] picks up one woodland hitchhiker after another until, in the last panel, tables turn and they have to carry him. In 'See-Saw,' he 'helps' a fox carry a log (and demonstrates a principle of physics) not by lifting the long end, but by hopping onto the short end." (Kirkus)

Benjamin Bear in Fuzzy thinking: a Toon book. Toon Books 2011 32p. Illustration

Grades: PreK K 1 2   **741.5; 741**
1. Bears; 2. Humorous graphic novels; 3. Graphic novels
978-1-935179-12-2, $12.99; 1-935179-12-8

LC 2011000801

"The latest entry in the TOON Books line of emerging-reader comics pushes a whole new sort of envelope: outré humor for the early grade-school set. These single-page strips starring a peculiar bear and his critter pals will feel fresh to young readers not just because the jokes rely on incisive understatement rather than broad-stroke exaggeration but also because the humor requires a bit of work to arrive at the surprising, sometimes sophisticated, and yet rarely out-of-reach punch lines." (Booklist)

Other titles in this series are: Benjamin Bear in Bright Ideas (2013); Benjamin Bear in Brain Storms (2015)

Court-Kaemon, Amy

Ratatouille. Tokyopop 2007 96p. Illustration
Grades: 2 3 4 5 6 7 8 9 10 11 12 Adult   **741.5; Fic**
1. Cooking; 2. Humorous graphic novels; 3. Rats; 4. Graphic novels
978-1-4278-0087-9, $7.99

This Cine-Manga title takes stills from Pixar's popular animated film to adapt the story into a graphic novel. Remy is a rat living in Paris, who aspires to be a chef. Linguine is a hapless young man who wishes to be a chef but has no talent. When the two meet, a partnership is born.

Craddock, Erik

Robot frenzy; 8. Erik Craddock. Random House Books for Young Readers 2013 96 p. (Stone rabbit)

Grades: 2 3 4 5 6   **741.5/973; 741.5**

1. Animals — Fiction; 2. Chores — Fiction; 3. Humorous stories; 4. Rabbits — Fiction; 5. Robots — Fiction; 6. Graphic novels
0375869131; 9780375869136, $6.99; 9780375969133

LC 2012049524

In this graphic novel by Erik Craddock "Stone Rabbit and his friends create robots to help out with chores [but] a glitch in the programming sends the 'bots into a malfunctioning frenzy! Will our long-eared hero be able to shut down these mechanical maniacs before they destroy Happy Glades" Or will his systems crash—" (Publisher's note)

Stone Rabbit: Pirate Palooza. Random House Children's Books 2009 96p.

Grades: 2 3 4 5   **741.5; Fic**
1. Adventure graphic novels; 2. Humorous graphic novels; 3. Pirates; 4. Graphic novels
978-0-375-95660-7, $11.99; 978-0-375-85660-0 (pa), $5.99

Our unnamed bunny hero plays at pro wrestling with his friend Andy when they break a leg on the coffee table. On their way to buy a replacement leg, Andy gets sidetracked to the local comics store for new comics day; and the rabbit finds a wooden leg. It's the peg leg of Barnacle Bob, a legendary pirate. When the rabbit uses it to fix his coffee table, he releases the ghosts of Barnacle Bob, his crew, and his ship, the Biscotti. Andy becomes the cabin boy while our rabbit hero becomes the first mate, and there's all kinds of trouble.

"This book will give those children who love the ridiculous just what they want: a zany, mile-a-minute graphic novel. . . . The bold illustrations are bursting at the seams with energy." SLJ

Other titles in this series are: BC Mambo (2009); Deep-Space Disco (2009); Superhero stampede (2009); Ninja slice (2010)

Superhero stampede. Random House 2010 94p. Illustration

Grades: 2 3 4 5   **741; 741.5**
978-0-375-85877-2, $5.99; 0-375-85877-6

"Stone Rabbit and his friends get sucked into the world of Andy's favorite comic book, where they become the superhero characters. The villains tempt Andy to the dark side, appealing to his anger about the teasing and name-calling to which Stone Rabbit and Henri have subjected him." (Booklist)

Superhero Stampede © Erik Craddock

Crane, Jordan

The **clouds** above. Fantagraphics 2005 216p. Illustration

Grades: 3 4 5 6 7 8   **741.5; Fic**
1. Fantasy graphic novels; 2. Graphic novels
1-560976-27-6, $18.95

Courtesy of Fantagraphics

Simon and his cat Jack embark on an adventure among the clouds one day when Simon skips school and finds a rickety stairway leading skyward. They find a friendly cloud, flee thunderstorms and trick a flock of belligerent birds, only to find themselves back at school.

"Everything's exciting . . . and the dialogue is witty and bubbly. . . . The book is a joy to look at"Crane's loose, gliding lines burst with character, and his compositional gifts make every panel worth contemplating on its own." Publ Wkly

Crilley, Mark
★ **Akiko** pocket-size, vol. 1. Sirius Entertainment 2004 192p. Illustration
Grades: 3 4 5 6 7 8 9 10   **741.5; Fic**
   1. Adventure graphic novels; 2. Science fiction graphic novels
   1-579890-67-9, $11.95

Fourth-grader Akiko travels to the planet Smoo, on a mission to rescue King Froptoppit's son from the evil Alia Rellapor. Teamed up with the scruffy adventurer Spuckler, bookish Mr. Beeba, Spuckler's robot Gax, and the floating alien known as Poog, Akiko faces sea monsters, Sky Pirates, Sleeslup worms, and other dangers as they travel around the planet on their quest. Crilley also has written a series of prose fiction featuring Akiko and her friends.

Croall, Marie P.
Marwe: into the land of the dead: an East African legend. Author, Marie P. Croall; pencils by Ray Lago and inks by Craig Hamilton.. Lerner Publishing Group 2009 48p. Illustration
Grades: 3 4 5 6 7 8 9   **741.5; Fic**
   1. Fantasy graphic novels; 2. Folklore — East Africa; 3. Graphic novels
   978-0-8225-7134-6, $27.93
                      LC 2007-1828

In this story retold from the oral tradition of the Chaga people in East Africa, Marwe lives in a village where times are hard and food is scarce. When she and her brother leave the family's bean fields to cool off at the river, monkeys destroy the entire crop. When her brother goes off to ask the family's forgiveness, Marwe sees something strange in the water and dives down; she passes through a strange doorway and finds herself in another land. Soon she learns she has come to the land of the dead, where an old woman welcomes her. Too scared to go home, Marwe stays there, and despite assurances that she needn't do anything, she works in the fields. When will Marwe think it's time to return home to her anxious and mourning family?
Part of the Graphic Universe Myths and Legends series

Psyche & eros: the lady and the monster: a Greek myth. Story by Marie Croall; pencils and inks by Ron Randall. Lerner Publishing Group 2009 48p. Illustration
Grades: 3 4 5 6 7 8 9   **741.5; Fic**
   1. Fantasy graphic novels; 2. Greek mythology; 3. Graphic novels
   978-0-8225-7177-3, $27.93
                    LC 2007-43353

Psyche is a beautiful young woman, so beautiful that men start to give her gifts instead of taking them to the temple. This makes Aphrodite jealous, and she sends her son, Eros, to prick Psyche with an arrow so no man will ever fall in love with her. However, Eros falls in love with Psyche. He arranges for the Oracle to tell Psyche's father that his daughter must be taken up on a mountain to marry a monster. He only comes to her at night, and they love each other; but Psyche's sisters convince her that she should see her husband. When hot wax from her candle burns Eros and wakens him, he must leave her. Now Psyche, unable to convince any other god or goddess to help her, must go to Aphrodite, who sets impossible tasks that Psyche manages to accomplish with help from unexpected sources.
Part of the Graphic Universe Myths and Legends series

Cunningham, Scott
Scooby-Doo! hot springs, cold sweat. ABDO/Spotlight 2010 48p. Illustration
Grades: 2 3 4 5 6   **741.5; Fic**
   1. Humorous graphic novels; 2. Mystery graphic novels; 3. Scooby-Doo (Fictional character); 4. Graphic novels
   978-1-59961-695-7, $28.50
                    LC 2009-32900

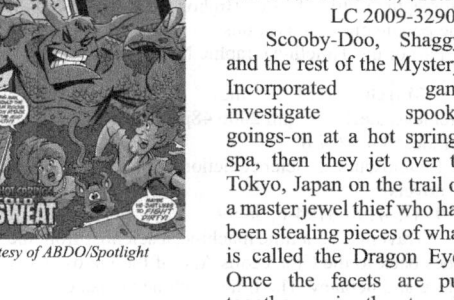
Courtesy of ABDO/Spotlight

Scooby-Doo, Shaggy, and the rest of the Mystery, Incorporated gang investigate spooky goings-on at a hot springs spa, then they jet over to Tokyo, Japan on the trail of a master jewel thief who has been stealing pieces of what is called the Dragon Eye. Once the facets are put together again, the stone is said to give its owner the power to conquer the world. These original stories were originally published in DC Comics' Scooby-Doo! comic book series.
Part of The Scooby-Doo Graphic Novels

Scooby-Doo! terror is afoot!. ABDO/Spotlight 2010 Un Illustration
Grades: 2 3 4 5 6   **741.5; Fic**
   1. Humorous graphic novels; 2. Mystery graphic novels; 3. Scooby-Doo (Fictional character); 4. Yeti; 5. Graphic novels
   978-1-59961-698-8, $22.78
                    LC 2009-32903

Shaggy and Scooby find themselves dumped in the Himalayas, right where yetis have been spotted. As the rest of the Scooby gang search for the two, man and dog meet Professor Jeffries, natives Pemba and Minga, monster hunter

Alfonse Lafleur, and Del, their friend who's now searching for the yeti.

Part of The Scooby-Doo Graphic Novel series, originally published by DC Comics.

Cutting, Robert

Cyber Patrol. Harcourt Achieve/Steck-Vaughn 2007 48p. Illustration

Grades: 3 4 5 6 7 8 **741.5; Fic**

1. Science fiction graphic novels; 2. Graphic novels

978-1-4190-3223-3, $8.99

In 2083, Mark Lewis is a twelve-year-old expert at online games. When a powerful and mysterious computer virus strikes, the authorities come asking for Mark's help. Who will win, Cyber Patrol or Cyberdoom" This science fiction graphic novel includes prose interludes that provide additional information about the Internet, computer viruses, some statistics about computer use, and speculation about what the future will hold.

Part of the Timeline Graphic Novels series.

Falling Star. Harcourt Achieve/Steck-Vaughn 2006 48p. Illustration

Grades: 3 4 5 6 7 8 **741.5; Fic**

1. Native Americans — History; 2. Graphic novels

978-1-4190-3209-7, $8.99

In 1870, a Caucasian baby is rescued by the Lakota people. They name him Falling Star and raise him as one of their own. Years later, as Chief Sitting Bull prepares for battle against the U.S. Army and one General George Armstrong Custer, Falling Star must decide which side he's on. This historical fiction graphic novel includes historical information about the Lakota people, Sitting Bull, Crazy Horse, the Battle of Little Bighorn, and the forced moves of the people onto reservations.

Part of the Timeline Graphic Novels series.

March of the Dinosaurs. Harcourt Achieve/Steck-Vaughn 2006 48p. Illustration

Grades: 3 4 5 6 7 8 **741.5; Fic**

1. Dinosaurs; 2. Science fiction graphic novels; 3. Graphic novels

978-1-4190-3194-6, $8.99

Traveling on a time machine, a scientist from the future goes back to the Cretaceous Age of the Dinosaurs with her niece and nephew. The time machine breaks down just as a giant meteor hurtles toward the Earth. Will they escape or will they share the fate of the dinosaurs" This science fiction graphic novel includes prose intervals that give facts about dinosaurs.

Part of the Timeline Graphic Novels series.

Mars Colony. Harcourt Achieve/Steck-Vaughn 2006 48p. Illustration

Grades: 3 4 5 6 7 8 **741.5; Fic**

1. Mystery graphic novels; 2. Science fiction graphic novels; 3. Graphic novels

978-1-4190-3213-4, $8.99

In the year 2130, the Chang family is one of 128 families sent to Mars to found the first human colony there. Jenny Chang and her brother Derek eagerly explore their new home; they are in for a big surprise. This science fiction story is interspersed with facts about Mars and space exploration.

Part of the Timeline Graphic Novels series.

Czekaj, Jef

Grampa & Julie: Shark hunters. Top Shelf 2004 Un Illustration

Grades: 2 3 4 5 6 **741.5; Fic**

1. Adventure graphic novels; 2. Humorous graphic novels; 3. Graphic novels

1-891830-52-X, $14.95

"In this full-color graphic novel, Julie and her grampa spend summer vacation looking for the largest shark in the world, Stephen. Meeting Stephen leads to even more exciting adventures, including a quest to find Stephen's mom. The shark hunters meet monkeys at the bottom of the ocean, pirates, and even aliens. Gramma has to rescue them from a couple of scrapes." Booklist

"Taken from the pages of Nickelodeon magazine, this charming children's comic overflows with humor, adventure and whimsy." Publ Wkly

Dabb, Andrew

G.I. Joe, Sigma 6: big time. ABDO Spotlight 2008 Un Illustration

Grades: 3 4 5 6 7 8 9 **741.5; Fic**

1. Adventure graphic novels; 2. G I Joe (Fictional character); 3. Graphic novels

978-1-59961-369-7, $21.35

LC 2006-52226

It's quiet time at R.O.C.C., the mobile headquarters of G.I. Joe, and Heavy Duty and Long Range are the only Joes there when they get a call from General Sato in Tokyo, Japan. Cobra Commander has been spotted, and Sato needs the Joes' help. Heavy Duty and Long Range are usually just the back up guys for the more well-known Joes (Duke, Scarlett, Snake Eyes . . .), but they have to take the mission. What they do is wreck havoc at a Yakuza club in Tokyo while trying to take down Cobra Commander. The book includes lots of action but no real violence.

This book is a revision of issue 5 (March 2006) of G. I. Joe Sigma 6, originally published by Devils Due Publishing.

Daffy Duck: You're Despicable!

DC Comics 2005 112p. Illustration

Grades: 3 4 5 6 7 8 9 **741.5; Fic**

1. Daffy Duck (Fictional character); 2. Humorous graphic novels; 3. Graphic novels

1-4012-0515-1, $6.99

It's duck season again. Everyone's favorite foul-tempered fowl explodes into his own collection with this first volume of Daffy Duck stories straight from the pages of Looney Tunes comics. Packed full of hilarity and anger management issues, this volume will warm the hearts of curmudgeons young and old everywhere. Of course you know this means war.

Dahl, Michael

Beauty and the beast: the graphic novel. Retold by Michael Dahl; illustrated by Luke Feldman. Stone Arch Books 2009 40p. Illustration

Grades: 2 3 4 5 6 7 **741.5; Fic**

1. Fairy tales; 2. Fantasy graphic novels; 3. Graphic novels

978-1-4342-0765-4, $21.26

LC 2008-6719

When a merchant on a journey plucks a rose to keep a promise for his daughter, Beauty, a roaring Beast demands that she come to him in payment for the rose. When she comes to the Beast's castle, he asks her to marry him; she refuses. As the days go by, the Beast asks her every evening, and every evening she refuses, despite a growing friendship. When he allows her to go home for a time, the family keeps her back beyond the time she promised the Beast, and when she returns he is dying; only one thing will save him her love. This graphic novel retells the old French folktale originally written in 1740 by Madame Gabrielle de Villeneuve in this original written version, the Beast never transformed. The book includes historical information about the versions of the story and a glossary.

Part of the Graphic Spin series

Dahl, Roald

The **Gremlins:** The Lost Walt Disney Production: A Royal Air Force Story. Dark Horse Books 2006 Un Illustration

Grades: 4 5 6 7 8 9 10 11 12 Adult **741.5; Fic**

1. Humorous graphic novels; 2. World War, 1939-1945; 3. Graphic novels

978-1-59307-496-8, $12.95

This is an illustrated novella, the first published work of RAF Flight Lieutenant Roald Dahl in his only collaboration with Walt Disney Studios. Originally published in 1943, the story was supposed to become a film combining live action with animation; the movie was never made, although the studio produced a lot of illustrations and samples. The story tells about one young Royal Air Force pilot named Gus, who first sees the little gremlins that wreak havoc on his plane. While the gremlins first cause lots of trouble, eventually Gus convinces them to work with the RAF.

Daning, Tom

African Mythology: Anansi. Rosen Publishing Group 2007 24p. Illustration

Grades: 1 2 3 4 5 **398.2; 741.5**

1. African mythology; 2. Anansi (Legendary character); 3. Graphic novels

978-1-4042-3398-0, $22.50

LC 2006002786

Anansi the spider is a trickster. In this graphic novel retelling of a West African myth, Anansi must outsmart the powerful and dangerous creatures of Africa to become the owner of all the stories in the

Courtesy of Rosen Publishing

world. Written for beginning readers, this book includes a simple family tree of the gods.

Part of the Jr. Graphic Mythologies series.

Chinese Mythology: The Four Dragons. Rosen Publishing Group 2007 24p. Illustration

Grades: 1 2 3 4 5 **398.2; 741.5**

1. Chinese mythology; 2. Folklore — China; 3. Graphic novels

978-1-4042-3400-0, $22.50

LC 2006002787

Courtesy of Rosen Publishing

The origins of the four great rivers of China are revealed in this classic myth. Against the landscapes of China, four dragons struggle against the Jade Emperor to bring water to the people of China in this simplified graphic novel for beginning readers. The book also provides a simple family tree.

Part of the Jr. Graphic Mythologies series.

Egyptian Mythology: Osiris and Isis. Rosen Publishing Group 2007 24p. Illustration

Grades: 1 2 3 4 5

299; 741.5

1. Egyptian mythology; 2. Isis (Egyptian deity); 3. Osiris (Egyptian deity); 4. Graphic novels

978-1-4042-3399-7, $22.50

LC 2006003373

Hieroglyphs reveal how Osiris, the King of Egypt, became the King of the Dead. His queen, Isis restores the body of her murdered husband and helps him become king of the underworld in this simplified graphic novel. It includes a family tree of the gods.

Courtesy of Rosen Publishing

Part of the Jr. Graphic Mythologies series.

Mesoamerican Mythology: Quetzalcoatl. Rosen Publishing Group 2007 24p. Illustration

Grades: 1 2 3 4 5 **299.7; 741.5**

1. Aztecs — Religion; 2. Quetzalcoatl (Aztec deity); 3. Graphic novels

978-1-4042-3401-7

LC 2006003371

Quetzalcoatl and Tezcatlipoca were never friends. But the two gods unite to defeat Tlatecuhtli, the demon caiman of the sea. The thrilling battle between the gods leads to the creation of the sky and land. This simplified graphic novel also includes a family tree of the gods.

Part of the Jr. Graphic Mythologies series.

Roman Mythology: Romulus and Remus. Rosen Publishing Group 2007 24p. Illustration
Grades: 1 2 3 4 5   **398.2; 292; 741.5**
1. Classical mythology; 2. Remus (Legendary character); 3. Romulus (Legendary character); 4. Graphic novels
978-1-4042-3397-3,
$22.50
  LC 2006003372
 Romulus and Remus, raised by wolves, were the twin founders of Rome. This simplified graphic novel for beginning readers recounts how the young bothers came to be cast out in the wilderness and how they avenged themselves upon their evil uncle. The book includes a simple family tree.

Courtesy of Rosen Publishing

 Part of the Jr. Graphic Mythologies series.

Dauvillier, Loïc
 Hidden: a child's story of the Holocaust. Written by Loic Dauvillier; illustrated by Marc Lizano; color by Greg Salsedo; translated by Alexis Siegel. First Second 2014 80 p. Color; Illustration
Grades: 1 2 3 4 5   **741.5**
1. France — History — German occupation, 1940-1945 — Fiction; 2. Grandmothers — Fiction; 3. Holocaust, 1939-1945 — Fiction; 4. Jews — France — Fiction; 5. Graphic novels
1596438738; 9781596438736, $16.99
  LC 2013023168
Mildred L. Batchelder Honor Book (2015)
 In this graphic novel, by Loic Dauvillier, illustrated by Greg Salsedo and Marc Lizano, and translated by Alexis Siegel, "Dounia, a grandmother, tells her granddaughter the story even her son has never heard: how, as a young Jewish girl in Paris, she was hidden away from the Nazis by a series of neighbors and friends who risked their lives to keep her alive when her parents had been taken to concentration camps." (Publisher's note)
 "Lizano's stylized illustrations depict characters with oversize heads, reminiscent of 'Peanuts' comics, giving this difficult subject an age-appropriate touch." SLJ
 Originally published in 2012 by Le Lombard under the title L'Enfant Cache?—Copyright page.

Davis, Eleanor
 Flop to the Top!. By Eleanor Davis & Drew Weing. TOON Books 2015 40 p. Color; Illustration
Grades: K 1 2 3   **741.5**
1. Dogs — Juvenile fiction; 2. Fame — Fiction; 3. Fame — Juvenile fiction; 4. Humorous fiction — Juvenile fiction; 5. Humorous stories; 6. Graphic novels
1935179896; 9781935179894, $12.95
  LC 2015003955
 In this children's book, by Eleanor Davis and Drew Weing, "Wanda calls her brother and sister 'fans,' keeps up with celebrity news, and never misses a chance to share a selfie. She's ready to show the world how Wanda-ful she really is, but all people are interested in is . . . her dog!" (Publisher's note)
 "Though centered on difficult emotions that will feel familiar to kids, the story is leavened with comedy, allowing readers to navigate comfortably even as the robust sentences and repetition massage new reading skills." Booklist

 ★ The **secret** science alliance and the copycat crook. Bloomsbury 2009 153p. Illustration
Grades: 3 4 5 6 7 8   **741.5; Fic**
1. Adventure graphic novels; 2. Humorous graphic novels; 3. Inventors — Fiction; 4. School stories; 5. Graphic novels
978-1-59990-142-8, $18.99; 1-59990-142-0;
     978-1-59990-396-5 (pa),
     $10.99; 1-59990-396-2
     (pa)
     LC 2008-45399
     Eleven-year-old Julian Calendar thought changing schools would mean leaving his "nerdy" persona behind, but instead he forms an alliance with fellow inventors Greta and Ben and works with them to prevent an adult from using one of their gadgets for nefarious purposes

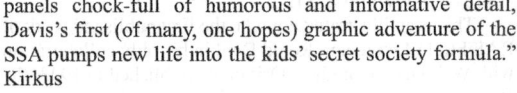
Courtesy of Bloomsbury

 "With its frenetically eye-catching, full-color panels chock-full of humorous and informative detail, Davis's first (of many, one hopes) graphic adventure of the SSA pumps new life into the kids' secret society formula." Kirkus

 Stinky: a Toon Book. RAW Junior 2008 40p. Illustration
Grades: K 1 2 3   **741.5; Fic**
1. Friendship; 2. Humorous graphic novels; 3. Monsters; 4. Graphic novels
978-0-9799238-4-5, $12.95; 0-9799238-4-0
  LC 2007-94387
A Geisel Award honor book, 2009
 Stinky the monster is sort of a young Shrek—a little grumpy, he loves pickles and likes his swamp nicely yucky and mucky, with no kids. Kids are gross, they like to take baths. When a new boy dares to build a treehouse in the middle of his swamp, Stinky takes action with all kinds of crazy plans to scare the boy away. However, every plan backfires, so what's a monster to do?
 "The charming cartoon artwork, full of humorous details, complements the text, and the muted color scheme makes Stinky endearing rather than scary. The simple vocabulary and repetition of words make the text accessible for emergent readers." SLJ

DC super heroes storybook collection
 Jerry Siegel, Joe Shuster, Bob Kane, and William Moulton Marston. Harper 2012 186 p. Illustration
Grades: 2 3 4 5   **E**

1. Batman (Fictional character); 2. Catwoman (Fictional character); 3. Joker (Fictional character); 4. Superheroes — Fiction; 5. Superman (Fictional character); 6. Wonder Woman (Fictional character)
006212398X; 9780062123985, $11.99

"This . . . collection features adventures, battles, and more, starring Superman, Batman, and Wonder Woman. These figures are the most widely recognized and, arguably, the most powerful in the DC universe. Many well-known villains are also featured, including Catwoman, The Joker, and Lex Luthor. However, all evil plans are thwarted and justice is served by our heroes, who work together well." (School Library Journal)

De Campi, Alex

Kat & Mouse. Story by Alex de Campi; art by Federica Manfredi. Tokyopop 2009 Un Illustration
Grades: 5 6 7 8 9   **741.5; Fic**
1. Mystery graphic novels; 2. Schools; 3. Graphic novels
978-1-4278-1175-2, $5.99

Kat and Mouse have pursued the thief called Artful Dodger, who has managed to elude them and the police. On the night of the Dover Academy Snow Ball, their school enemy Chloe comes to the girls for help: her diamond necklace has been stolen. They spend the evening checking clues, but an oncoming blizzard and a surprise revelation about their art teacher complicate matters. This concluding volume of the series has been long-delayed; readers might want to refresh their memory of what happened before by rereading the first three volumes before reading this one. There is no synopsis of previous events, and some characters aren't identified by name.

Kat & Mouse: Teacher torture. [by] Alex de Campi; art by Frederica Manfredi. Tokyopop 2006 96p. Illustration
Grades: 4 5 6 7 8 9   **741.5; Fic**
1. Mystery fiction; 2. Mystery graphic novels; 3. Graphic novels
1-59816-548-8, $5.99

Middle schooler Kat starts at a posh school where her father has been hired as the new science teacher, but all is not well. Accidents happen in the science lab, and an anonymous student threatens worse unless Kat's dad passes all the rich, popular students. Kat decides to investigate, aided by her one new friend, Mouse, the rebellious computer nerd and would-be CSI investigator.

Other titles in this series are: Tripped (2007); The ice storm (2007); The knave of diamonds (2009)

Kat & Mouse Vol. 2: Tripped. Tokyopop 2007 96p. Illustration
Grades: 4 5 6 7 8 9   **741.5; Fic**
1. Mystery graphic novels; 2. Graphic novels
978-1-59816-549-4, $5.99

Since her arrival at Dover Academy, the one person Kat has been able to depend on is her best friend Mee-Seen, better known as Mouse. But when Mouse gets a crush on the new art teacher, a misunderstanding comes between the two friends - and a class trip to the art museum only makes it worse. When a famous painting is stolen right under their noses, will Kat and Mouse be able to smooth things out in time to catch the thief?

De Groot, Bob

Clifton Jade. Cinebook 2008 48p.
Grades: 5 6 7 8 9   **741.5; Fic**
1. Adventure graphic novels; 2. Humorous graphic novels; 3. Spies; 4. Graphic novels
978-1-905460-52-6, $11.95

Sir Harold Wilberforce Clifton, ex-Secret Service and retired Colonel, works as a private detective, as well as leading a troop of young scouts. With the help of his housekeeper, Mrs. Partridge, who's also a dab hand at auto mechanics, he still helps the government. This time, however, he's being tailed by someone and then summoned to a retirement home where he finds his old World War II nemesis, Otto Kartoffeln, who tells him a group of neo-Nazis are searching for a long-lost Nazi treasure in order to bring about the 4th Reich. The mysterious shadow is Jade, a young agent who was trying to complete her training; now she and Clifton must stop the neo-Nazis from finding the treasure.

Part of the Clifton series, originally published in France as Clifton Jade.

DeFalco, Tom

Spider-Girl: Choices. Tom DeFalco, writer; Pat Olliffe, penciler; Al Williamson, inker; Janice Chiang, letterer; Christie Scheele, colorist; Bob Harras, chief. ABDO Spotlight 2006 Un Illustration
Grades: 5 6 7 8 9 10 11 12   **741.5; Fic**
1. Spider-Girl (Fictional character); 2. Spider-Man (Fictional character); 3. Superhero graphic novels; 4. Graphic novels
1-59961-028-0, $21.35

May, teenage daughter of Peter and Mary Jane Parker, has inherited her father's Spidey powers, but the former Spider-Man has forbidden her to use them; he doesn't want May to get crippled like him, or worse. However, May can't help but use her powers for good, so even though Peter has destroyed all the old Spider-Man equipment, May rescued some web shooters and web-cartridges. Dressed in an old gym suit and a skiing mask, she sets out to discover who has been following her father, who is working on a case involving organized crime. The book includes lots of action but little violence.

★ **Spider-Girl:** legacy . . . in black and white. ABDO Publishing Group/Spotlight 2006 Un Illustration
Grades: 5 6 7 8 9 10 11 12   **741.5; Fic**
1. Adventure graphic novels; 2. Spider-Girl (Fictional character); 3. Spider-Man (Fictional character); 4. Superhero graphic novels; 5. Graphic novels
1-59961-029-9; 978-1-59961-029-0, $21.35
                                            LC 2006-44301

In an alternate Marvel Universe, Peter and Mary Jane Parker stayed married and had a daughter, May (nicknamed Mayday). Peter's superhero career as Spider-Man ended when the Green Goblin shattered his leg, and he and Mary Jane have kept all of this secret from May. Now she's fifteen years old, popular, a star basketball player "and during a game, the powers she inherited from her father kick in. As if that isn't shock enough, a new Hobgoblin comes after Peter Parker" it's another Osborne, Norman, grandson of the original Green Goblin and May's former playmate. Does she have enough Spidey powers to take him down before he hurts her parents? This is a library-bound edition of

Spider-Girl #0, which was first Marvel What If #105, and which launched the Spider-Girl comics series.

Volume 1 of 12

Del Rio, Tania

   Sabrina the Teenage Witch: The Magic Revisited. Archie Comics 2006 Un Illustration

Grades: 4 5 6 7 8 9   **741.5; Fic**

   1. Fantasy graphic novels; 2. Humorous graphic novels; 3. Witches; 4. Graphic novels

   1-879794-19-5, $7.49

   The first four issues of Sabrina the Teenage Witch's "manga makeover" are collected in this special edition trade paperback. Writer-artist Tania del Rio presents these tales of magical flights of fancy and romantic intrigue... sprinkled with a dash of humor. Sabrina's awakening powers and the various love triangle combinations that have formed since keep her busy at school, on dates, and ... everywhere.

Delsante, Vito

   Before they were famous: Babe Ruth. Aladdin Paperbacks 2009 121p.

Grades: 3 4 5 6 7 8

741.5; 920

   1. Baseball players; 2. Baseball players; 3. Biographical graphic novels; 4. Ruth, Babe, 1895-1948; 5. Graphic novels

   978-1-4169-5071-4, $8.99

        LC 2008-929319

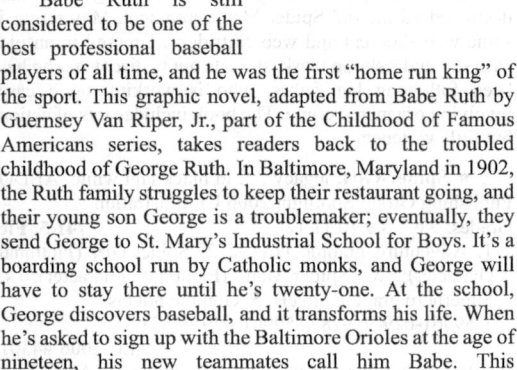

Courtesy of Aladdin Press

   Babe Ruth is still considered to be one of the best professional baseball players of all time, and he was the first "home run king" of the sport. This graphic novel, adapted from Babe Ruth by Guernsey Van Riper, Jr., part of the Childhood of Famous Americans series, takes readers back to the troubled childhood of George Ruth. In Baltimore, Maryland in 1902, the Ruth family struggles to keep their restaurant going, and their young son George is a troublemaker; eventually, they send George to St. Mary's Industrial School for Boys. It's a boarding school run by Catholic monks, and George will have to stay there until he's twenty-one. At the school, George discovers baseball, and it transforms his life. When he's asked to sign up with the Baltimore Orioles at the age of nineteen, his new teammates call him Babe. This fictionalized biography will help young readers get a sense of the person behind the legend.

DeMatteis, J. M.

   Abadazad: The Dream Thief by J.M. DeMatteis ; drawings by Mike Ploog ; colors by Nick Bell. Hyperion Books for Children 2006 Un Illustration

Grades: 5 6 7 8 9   **741.5; Fic**

   1. Adventure graphic novels; 2. Fantasy graphic novels; 3. Graphic novels

   1-4231-00646, $9.99

In the magical land of Abadazad, Kate needs all the help she can get when she encounters the Lanky Man. He's mean and heartless, and he wants to steal children's dreams. Everyone seems to be against her, which only makes her more determined to find her brother. And Matt is getting closer, isn't he? This story is a hybrid, combining prose text with pages of sequential art from the original comic books.

   Abadazad: The Road to Inconceivable. Hyperion Books for Children 2006 Un Illustration

Grades: 5 6 7 8 9   **741.5; Fic**

   1. Adventure graphic novels; 2. Fantasy graphic novels; 3. Graphic novels

   1-4231-0062-X, $9.99

   Kate's little brother Matt disappeared five years ago, and Kate thinks she will never see him again. But then she finds out that Matt is trapped in the world of Abadazad. Will Kate have the courage to look for her brother? And if she leaves home, will she ever return? This story began as comic books, but the publisher went out of business before the story was completed. Now it's published as a hybrid, combining prose sections with pages of sequential art and spot illustrations.

   ★ The **stardust** kid. Boom! created by J. M. DeMatteis, writer & Mike Ploog, illustrator ; Nick Bell & Sumi Pak, color ; Dave Lanphear, lettering. Studios 2008 Un Illustration

Grades: 3 4 5 6 7 8 9 10 11 12 Adult   **741.5; Fic**

   1. Adventure graphic novels; 2. Fantasy graphic novels; 3. Graphic novels

   978-1-934506-04-2, $14.99

   Twelve-year-old Cody's best friend is Paul Brightfield; they share a deep bond that goes far beyond mere friendship. What no one else knows is that Paul isn't human, he's one of the last Old Ones, ancient elemental beings who lived before man existed. One night, Paul disappears, and a hate-filled creature who has existed long buried beneath Wilde Park bursts out with a desire to destroy everything in the world. Only Cody, his little sister K.M., and his friend Alana and her little brother Nathaniel, remain, and somehow they must find The Stardust Kid and discover a way to stop the hate and restore their world. Some creatures might be frightening to younger readers, but anyone who likes the Harry Potter books shouldn't have a problem with this book.

DeMolay, Jack

   Atlantis: The Mystery of the Lost City. Rosen Publishing Group 2007 24p. Illustration

Grades: 1 2 3 4 5

398.2; 741.5

   1. Atlantis

   978-1-4042-3407-9

        LC 2006003854

   According to Plato, eleven thousand years ago a shining city with a marvelous civilization stood on a great island in the ocean. And then, disaster struck. Beginning readers

Courtesy of Rosen Publishing

can join the search for the lost city of Atlantis in this simplified graphic novel. The "Did You Know?" section provides more facts.

Part of the Jr. Graphic Mysteries series.

The **Bermuda** Triangle: The Disappearance of Flight 19. Rosen Publishing Group 2007 24p. Illustration
Grades: 1 2 3 4 5   741.5; 001.9
1. Bermuda Triangle; 2. Graphic novels

Courtesy of Rosen Publishing

978-1-4042-3404-8, $22.50
LC 20050337337
One day in 1945, five US Air Force bombers flew out to sea on a routine mission - and disappeared without a trace. Were they victims of a supernatural force? Beginning readers explore the mystery of the Bermuda Triangle in this simplified graphic novel. The "Did You Know?" section provides additional facts.

Part of the Jr. Graphic Mysteries series.

Bigfoot: A North American Legend. Rosen Publishing Group 2007 24p. Illustration
Grades: 1 2 3 4 5
741.5; 001.9
1. Sasquatch; 2. Graphic novels
978-1-4042-3405-5, $22.50
LC 2006003390
Beginning readers track the sightings of the mysterious creature throughout the Pacific Northwest and uncover the ongoing search for proof of Bigfoot's existence in this simplified graphic novel. The "Did You Know?" section includes more facts.

Part of the Jr. Graphic Mysteries series.

Courtesy of Rosen Publishing

Courtesy of Rosen Publishing

The **Loch** Ness Monster: Scotland's Mystery Beast. Rosen Publishing Group 2007 24p. Illustration
Grades: 1 2 3 4 5   741.5; **001.9**
1. Loch Ness Monster; 2. Graphic novels
978-1-4042-3406-2, $22.50
LC 20050337336
Beginning readers uncover evidence of Nessie's existence through historical sightings and

present-day efforts to locate this mysterious beast in this simplified graphic novel. The "Did You Know?" section provides additional facts.

Part of the Jr. Graphic Mysteries series.

Denton, Shannon Eric
Zapt!, Vol. 1. Story by Shannon Eric Denton and Keith Giffen ; art by Armand Villavert Jr. Tokyopop 2006 96p. Illustration
Grades: 4 5 6 7 8   **741.5; Fic**
1. Humorous graphic novels; 2. Science fiction graphic novels; 3. Graphic novels
1-59816-588-7, $5.99
Armand Jones is a fairly typical elementary school student who doesn't like to get up in the morning, has to deal with bullies on the school bus and on campus. As if that isn't hard enough, he finds himself zapped out of the boys' restroom into a space station full of aliens, and learns that he is now a recruit in the Pangalactic Order of Police (P.O.O.P.). Partnered with the equally young Pandekian named Paylean, Armand almost immediately gets captured by space pirates. Then, when he gets back to school, his classmate Gladys gets kidnapped by Terros, and Armand learns that she's an alien princess he now has to rescue. This first volume of an ongoing series is a global manga.

Despeyroux, Denise
Dark graphic tales by Edgar Allan Poe. Adapted by Denise Despeyroux; illustrations by Miquel Serratosa. Enslow Publishers 2012 96 p.
Grades: 3 4 5   **741.5; 741.5/946**
1. Children's stories, American; 2. Horror fiction; 3. Horror stories; 4. Horror tales, American; 5. Mental illness — Fiction; 6. Short stories; 7. Graphic novels
0766040860; 9780766040861, $30.60
LC 2011034273
"This entry in the 'Dark Graphic Novels' series adapts three [Edgar Allan] Poe stories. . . . In 'The Gold Bug,' a man becomes obsessed with a golden beetle that is the key to an ancient mystery. . . . 'The System of Doctor Tarr and Professor Fether' chronicles a man's attendance at a banquet in an insane asylum and his dawning realization of what's happened to the patients. 'The Fall of the House of Usher' . . . tells of a brother's slow decline into insanity." (Booklist)
Includes bibliographical references.

Deutsch, Barry
Hereville: how Mirka caught a fish. Barry Deutsch. Amulet Books 2015 140 p. Color; Illustration
Grades: 4 5 6 7   **741.5/973; 741.5**
1. Babysitting — Juvenile fiction; 2. Fishes — Juvenile fiction; 3. Jewish girls — Fiction
9781419708008, $17.95
LC 2015945771
In this book, by Barry Deutsch, "Welcome back to Hereville, where Mirka, the world's first time-travelling, monster-fighting Orthodox Jewish girl . . . [is] stuck babysitting her disapproving little sister, Layele. When Mirka pushes her sister into a stream, they both get in too deep with an angry magic fish. . . . When the fish kidnaps Layele, Mirka must find a way to save her little sister, and the

clues she needs are hidden in her stepmother Fruma's past." (Publisher's note)

★ **Hereville:** how Mirka got her sword. Colors by Jake Richmond. Amulet Books 2010 137p. Illustration
Grades: 4 5 6 7
741.5; Fic
1. Dragons; 2. Fantasy graphic novels; 3. Jews; 4. Graphic novels
978-0-8109-8422-6, $15.95; 0-8109-8422-9
LC 2010-924236

Courtesy of Amulet Paperbacks

Mirka and her family live in an Orthodox Jewish village called Hereville. All she really wants to do is fight dragons, but what she has to fight is a troublesome pig that talks. Then Mirka meets the witch who lives nearby, and then confronts a troll, and soon she finds she has much more adventure than she knows how to handle.

"Deutsch creates authentic characters spiced with just enough fantasy to surprise. . . . Details of Orthodox daily life are well blended into the art and given just the right touches of explanation to keep readers on track." Booklist

★ **Hereville:** How Mirka Met a Meteorite. Barry Deutsch; colors by Jake Richmond. Amulet Books 2012 123 p.
Grades: 3 4 5 6 7
741.5
1. Adventure graphic novels; 2. Jews; 3. Trolls — Fiction; 4. Witches — Fiction
1419703986; 9781419703980, $16.95
LC 2012947050

This graphic novel by Barry Deutsch features a "wisecracking, adventure-loving, sword-wielding Orthodox Jewish heroine. . . . She fearlessly stands up to local bullies. She battles a very large, very menacing pig. And she boldly accepts a challenge from a mysterious witch, a challenge that could bring Mirka her heart's desire: a dragon-slaying sword! All she has to do is find — and outwit — the giant troll who's got it!" (Publisher's note)

Dezago, Todd
Spider-Man and Storm: change the weather. ABDO Publishing Group/Spotlight 2006 Un Illustration
Grades: 3 4 5 6 7 8
741.5; Fic
1. Spider-Man (Fictional character); 2. Storm (Fictional character); 3. Superhero graphic novels; 4. X-Men (Fictional characters); 5. Graphic novels
1-59961-003-5, $21.35
LC 2006-44931

A stranger comes to New York right when Storm of the X-Men is enjoying some unscheduled free flight and Spider-Man is just swinging along for fun. Storm tries to help a helicopter whose rotor stopped working while Spidey tries to help the stranger when some toughs try to hassle her. Then he accidentally touches her bare hand after her glove tears, and he temporarily loses his power while the girl suddenly possesses them. Storm accidentally touches the girl, loses her powers, and nearly loses the helicopter, which Spider-Man saves. They both realize the girl is a mutant and try to help her.
Part of the Marvel Age Spider-Man series.

Spider-man and Thor: out of time. Todd Dezago, script ; Ron Lim, pencils ; Scott Koblish, inks ; Dave Sharpe, letters ; Digital Rainbow, colors. ABDO Publishing Company/Spotlight 2006 Un Illustration
Grades: 4 5 6 7 8 9
741.5; Fic
1. Spider-Man (Fictional character); 2. Superhero graphic novels; 3. Thor (Fictional character); 4. Graphic novels
1-59961-004-3, $21.35

It takes both Spider-Man and the Mighty Thor to deal with things when an Asgardian enemy, Kryllk, regains control of the Frostgaard Crystal; it allows him to freeze time so he and his troll hordes can conquer Midgard, er, Earth, and the gods' realm of Asgard as well. But now Kryllk faces two heroes at the same time. This is a revised, hardbound edition of the Marvel Age comic book.
Part of the Spider-Man Team Up series

Di Fiori, Lawrence
Jackie and the Shadow Snatcher. [by] Lawrence Di Fiori. Alfred A. Knopf for Young Readers 2006 Un Illustration
Grades: K 1 2 3 4
741.5; Fic
1. Adventure graphic novels; 2. Mystery graphic novels; 3. Graphic novels
0-375-87515-8; 0-375-97515-2 (lib bdg), $17.99
LC 2005-18290

"In this picture-book-size graphic novel, Di Fiori uses black-and-white illustrations to tell the story of Jackie, a boy who has lost his lunch pail, his math book, and his shadow. Wise Mr. Socrates tells Jackie that the evil Shadow Snatcher is the thief, and Jackie must confront him to get his shadow back. . . . The scenery is beautifully detailed without overwhelming the panels. Children will care less about that, however, than about the rollicking, old-fashioned adventure." Booklist

Diamond, Jeremy
Nascar heroes #2: Who is Jimmy Dash? Jeremy Diamond, writer ; Ash, layout ; Peter Habjan, artist ; Rich Duhaney ... [et al.], guest artists ; Peter Habjan ... [et al.], colorists. 2009 Un
Grades: 3 4 5 6 7 8
741.5; Fic
1. Automobile racing; 2. NASCAR; 3. Superhero graphic novels; 4. Graphic novels
978-1-59961-663-6, $22.78
LC 2009-9008

The accident that gave the Flatstock pit crew, plus Dashiell, super powers, also gave them to Jack Diesel; and he doesn't have any good intentions. When Jimmy Dash and Team Flatstock keep winning NASCAR races, Diesel resorts to dirty tricks with his laser heat vision and illegal gadgets on his cars. However, Team Flatstock owner Astor also gained powers in the accident; she sees visions of the near future. Diesel decides that the entire Flatstock team would do anything for Astor, so he kidnaps her; Dashiell reveals his identity to the guys, and they go to rescue Astor.

However, that's much easier said than done when Diesel will use any dirty trick to win.

Nascar heroes #3: Dash to the finish! Jeremy Diamond, writer ; Matt Cassan, Peter Habjan, artists. ABDO/Spotlight 2009 Un Illustration
Grades: 3 4 5 6 7 8   **741.5; Fic**
  1. Automobile racing; 2. NASCAR; 3. Superhero graphic novels; 4. Graphic novels
  978-1-59961-664-3, $22.78
                    LC 2009-9009
When Dashiell and the Flatstock pit crew went to rescue Astor from Jack Diesel, they've had to deal with car crushers, Diesel's super powers, and now his mutated dog, Lucifer, who has become a giant, drooling creature. Diesel has also managed to put their car, #76, into orbit. He takes Astor while the guys deal with Lucifer; but they still have a race to win, even as they desperately search for their boss and friend. And, even though Diesel continues to play dirty tricks, Dashiell warns the others that they must use their powers only for defense and let him win by his own driving.

Nascar heroes #4: headless stuntman. ABDO/Spotlight 2009 Un Illustration
Grades: 3 4 5 6 7 8   **741.5; Fic**
  1. Automobile racing; 2. Ghosts; 3. Motion pictures — Production and direction; 4. NASCAR; 5. Superhero graphic novels; 6. Graphic novels
  978-1-59961-665-0, $22.78
                    LC 2009-9010
During the off-season, Dashiell takes a break from racing practice to star in a racing movie. What he doesn't know is that several other actors have already quit, frightened off the set by a headless ghost. Dashiell takes on the ghost driver to save an actress, but can he do it without wrecking the set?

Nascar heroes #5: NASCAR villains!. ABDO/Spotlight 2009 Un
Grades: 3 4 5 6 7 8   **741.5; Fic**
  1. Automobile racing; 2. NASCAR; 3. Superhero graphic novels; 4. Graphic novels
  978-1-5996-666-7, $22.78
                    LC 2009-9011
Team Flatstock gains a new crew chief, the mysterious Professor N., who says he can train the crew to use their super powers. Meanwhile, Jack Diesel breaks out of prison with the help of fellow villains (including Predacar, a transforming vehicle), and they give Team Flatstock lots of trouble while using every cheat in the book to win the race.

Nascar heroes #6: Rev-Alation!. ABDO/Spotlight 2009 Un
Grades: 3 4 5 6 7 8   **741.5; Fic**
  1. Automobile racing; 2. NASCAR; 3. Superhero graphic novels; 4. Graphic novels
  978-1-59961-667-4, $22.78
                    LC 2009-9012
When Professor N. joined Team Flatstock, he brought back the car Jack Diesel had sent into orbit. Now with two cars, team owner Astor has become the second driver, and she and Jimmy Dash start a rivalry that could divide the team. Then Professor N. says he needs a sample of the material Diesel was working on in his secret laboratory at the

time of the accident that gave everyone their powers, so the pit crew decides to retrieve it for him while Astor tries to distract Diesel by going on a date with him.

Nascar heroes #3: Dash to the finish! Jeremy Diamond, writer ; Matt Cassan, Peter Habjan, artists. ABDO/Spotlight 2009 Un Illustration
Grades: 3 4 5 6 7 8   **741.5; Fic**
  1. Automobile racing; 2. NASCAR; 3. Superhero graphic novels; 4. Graphic novels
  978-1-59961-662-9, $22.78
                    LC 2009-9007
Dashiell James works as a janitor for Jack Diesel's NASCAR racing team, but on his own time he hangs out with the Team Flatstock pit crew, Zip, Gus, and Ed. Team Diesel wins a lot of races, while Team Flatstock is known on the NASCAR circuit as "Team Laughingstock." Then an explosion is a secret laboratory in Team Diesel's building affects Dashiell and the pit crew suddenly Zip has super speed, Gus has super strength, Ed can multiply himself, and Dashiell is almost indestructible. When the Flatstock driver quits, Dashiell hides his identity in a firesuit and helmet and calls himself Jimmy Dash; he becomes the new Team Flatstock driver, and wins his and Flatstock's very first race.

Dirge, Roman
  It ate Billy on Christmas; art by Steven Daily. Dark Horse Books 2007 Un Illustration
Grades: 4 5 6 7 8 9 10 11 12 Adult   **741.5; Fic**
  1. Horror graphic novels; 2. Humorous graphic novels; 3. Graphic novels
  978-1-59307-853-9, $12.95
Lumi has been bullied by her brother Billy all her life, and this Christmas would have been more of the same, but for the weird, ugly little monster that crawled up from the abandoned well and came into their house. Mistaking it for the stuffed puppy she had requested from her parents, Lumi watches in amazement as it devours the bullying Billy when he shoots it with darts from his new dart gun. She makes a cardboard Billy, which fools her unsuspecting and clueless parents. A few weeks later, back at school, Lumi has to face the bullies who have made her school life miserable, but she has her "puppy" in her backpack and it's hungry. . . . Dirge wrote the story and drew the black and white illustrations, while Daily provided the color paintings. The story shows the monster eating Billy in one gulp, but there's little actual violence on the pages. The dark humor and twisted story line will appeal to those who enjoy Coraline and The Wolves in the Walls by Neil Gaiman, and the weird humor of Edward Gorey cartoons.

Dixon, Chuck
  Transformers: Evolutions: Hearts of Steel; art by Guido Guidi IDW Publishing 2006 120p. Illustration
Grades: 4 5 6 7 8 9   **741.5; Fic**
  1. Science fiction graphic novels; 2. Transformers (Fictional characters); 3. Graphic novels
  978-1-60010-055-4, $19.99
In this new Transformers story, writer Chuck Dixon and artist Guido Guidi transplant the 'bots to the Industrial Revolution, where a charismatic hammer-man named John Henry discovers that a steam drill is really an alien robot

named Bumblebee. Before he can process this information, the pair is attacked by Decepticons disguised as tanks, trains and walking engines. Is this all part of a larger scheme by Starscream? And if so, will the other Autobots arrive in time to stop his nefarious plans? Mark Twain is among the humans who work with the Autobots.

Doeden, Matt

George Washington: Leading a New Nation; by Matt Doeden ; illustrated by Cynthia Martin. Capstone Press 2006 32p. Illustration

Grades: 3 4 5 6 7 8 9   **741.5; 973.4; 92**
1. Washington, George, 1732-1799; 2. Graphic novels
0-7368-4963-7, $25.26

                        LC 2005006530
This book uses the comic book format to recount highlights in the life of George Washington, the leader of the Continental Army during the Revolutionary War and the first President of the United States. It includes additional information, a glossary, a list of books for further reading, and more.

Part of the Graphic Library, Graphic Biographies series.

John Sutter and the California Gold Rush; by Matt Doeden ; illustrated by Ron Frenz and Charles Barnett III. Capstone Press 2006 32p. Illustration

Grades: 3 4 5 6 7 8 9   **741.5; 979.4**
1. California — Gold discoveries; 2. Sutter, John Augustus, 1803-1880; 3. Graphic novels
0-7368-4370-1, $25.26

                        LC 2005007890
This book tells the story in comic book format of the discovery of gold at John Sutter's mill and how it changed California. It includes additional information, a glossary, a list of books for further reading, and more.

Part of the Graphic Library, Graphic History series.

Winter at Valley Forge by Matt Doeden ; illustrated by Ron Frenz and Charles Barnett III ; [colorist, Bill Anderson]. Capstone Press 2006 32p. Illustration

Grades: 3 4 5 6 7 8 9   **741.5; 973.3**
1. Pennsylvania — History; 2. United States — History — 1775-1783, Revolution; 3. Valley Forge (Pa) — History; 4. Graphic novels
0-7368-4975-0, $25.26

                        LC 2005010145
This book uses the comic book format to tell the story of the American patriot troops during the Revolutionary War while wintering at Valley Forge, Pennsylvania. It includes additional information, a glossary, a list of books for further reading, and more.

Part of the Graphic Library, Graphic History series.

Dorison, Guillaume

The **planet** of music. [original screenplay] by Clélia Constantine; adapted by Guillaume Dorison; illustrated by Elyum Studio; based on the masterpiece by Antoine de Saint-Exupéry; translation, Anne Collins Smith and Owen Smith. Graphic Universe 2012 54 p.

Grades: 3 4 5   **Fic; 741.5/944**
1. Foxes — Juvenile fiction; 2. Music — Juvenile fiction; 3. Science fiction — Juvenile fiction; 4. Snakes — Juvenile fiction

9780822594246; 0822594242; 9780761387534, $7.95
                        LC 2011051352
This children's story, by Clélia Constantine, is book 3 of "The Little Prince" series. "With his wide-eyed innocence and unflappable devotion to helping others, the Little Prince works to save imperiled planets with the help of the Fox. Here, they stop the Snake from creating war between a music-loving populace and a flower-loving citizenry." (Kirkus Reviews)

Based on the animated series and an original story by Clélia Constantine.

An animated series based on the novel Le Petit Prince by Antoine de Saint Exupéry. Developed for television by Matthieu Delaporte, Alexandre de la Patelliére, and Bertrand Gatignol. Directed by Pierre-Alain Chartier—Copyright p.

Downey, Glen

Escape from East Berlin; art by Leo Lingas. Harcourt Achieve/Steck-Vaughn 2007 48p. Illustration

Grades: 3 4 5 6 7 8   **741.5; Fic**
1. Adventure graphic novels; 2. Germany (East); 3. Graphic novels
978-1-4190-3222-6, $8.99
In the summer of 1963, President Kennedy of the United States speaks in West Berlin about liberty. From the other side of the Berlin Wall, the Kappel family listens to his every word. They decide to make a bid for freedom, but at what cost? This historical fiction graphic novel includes prose intervals that describe Berlin as the divided city after World War II, the building of the Wall, the various escape attempts made by East Berliners, part of President Kennedy's speech, and the fall of the Wall in 1989. There is brief violence when a vicious East German soldier is shot.

Part of the Timeline Graphic Novels series.

Fire Mountain; art by Liam Thurston. Harcourt Achieve/Steck-Vaughn 2006 48p. Illustration

Grades: 3 4 5 6 7 8   **741.5; Fic**
1. Adventure graphic novels; 2. Pompeii (Extinct city); 3. Volcanoes; 4. Graphic novels
978-1-4190-3198-4, $8.99
Cato is a young slave boy in the bustling Roman city of Pompeii. When Mount Vesuvius erupts without warning, Cato is separated from his mother. Will they survive the terrifying day and be reunited" This historical fiction graphic novel includes prose intervals that provide additional information about what happened at Pompeii and Herculaneum, about Vesuvius and other famous volcanoes, and about the modern excavations.

Part of the Timeline Graphic Novels series.

Ice Journey; art by Glenn Brucker. Harcourt Achieve/Steck-Vaughn 2007 48p. Illustration

Grades: 3 4 5 6 7 8   **741.5; Fic**
1. Adventure graphic novels; 2. Ice age; 3. Graphic novels
978-1-4190-3204-2, $8.99
It is the Ice Age in North America, and the land is covered in ice and snow. Bruno, a young giant short-faced bear, is being hunted down by a saber-toothed cat. While his sister, Ursula, looks for him, she meets some interesting creatures of the Ice Age. This graphic novel includes prose intervals that provide information on the real animals that

lived during the Ice Age, the early people who may have lived towards the end of the Ice Age, and on the impact of global warming on the world today.

Part of the Timeline Graphic Novels series.

Rebel Prince; art by David Okum. Harcourt Achieve/Steck-Vaughn 2007 48p. Illustration

Grades: 3 4 5 6 7 8   **741.5; Fic**
1. Great Britain — Kings and Rulers; 2. Henry V, King of England, 1387-1422; 3. Graphic novels
978-1-4190-3217-2, $8.99

In 15th century London, young Will works at a tavern where Prince Hal and his companions hang out. When royal duties call, will Prince Hal be able to rise to the challenge" What is in store for young Will" This historical fiction graphic novel tells the story of how playful Prince Hal became King Henry V of England. It includes prose interludes that provide additional information about his father Henry IV, portrayals of Henry V, and about the famous battle at Agincourt.

Part of the Timeline Graphic Novels series.

Doyle, Arthur Conan

The **hound** of the Baskervilles: a Sherlock Holmes mystery. By Sir Arthur Conan Doyle; retold by Martin Powell; illustrated by Daniel Perez. Stone Arch Books 2009 63p. Illustration

Grades: 4 5 6 7 8 9 10   **741.5; Fic**
1. Holmes, Sherlock (Fictional character); 2. Mystery graphic novels; 3. Graphic novels
978-1-4342-0755-5, $23.93

LC 2008-6247

Late one night, Sir Charles Baskerville is attacked and killed outside his home in Dartmoor, England. Some say that the legendary monster, the Hound of the Baskervilles, has come back. Now Sherlock Holmes and Dr. Watson investigate the mystery, in order to protect the Baskerville heir, who has just come from America. This graphic novel adapts Doyle's one full-length mystery novel featuring his famous character.

Part of the Graphic Revolve series

Dumas, Alexandre

The **three** musketeers; adapted by Bruce Buchanan ; illustrated by Amit Tayal. Campfire 2010 104p. Illustration

Grades: 3 4 5 6 7 8 9   **741.5; Fic**
1. Adventure graphic novels; 2. Graphic novels
978-93-80028-57-6, $12.99

Young D'Artagnan comes to Paris, determined to become a king's musketeer, but runs into trouble with three musketeers in one day. When they band together to tight Cardinal Richelieu's forces, they become friends. The friends soon find themselves involved in averting a plot to discredit Queen Anne, and their efforts to help her cause them to run afoul of Richelieu. D'Artagnan, Athos, Porthos, and Aramis also must deal with Milady de Winter, a beautiful and deadly woman with her own agenda. This graphic novel adaptation features art that emphasizes the humor in the historical adventure. It also puts most of the violence off-panel, so the story is suitable for younger readers.

Dunn, Joeming W.

The **brain**: a graphic novel tour. By Joeming Dunn; illustrated by Rod Espinosa.. Magic Wagon/Graphic Planet 2009 32p. Illustration (Graphic adventures. The human body)

Grades: 2 3 4 5 6   **612.8; 741.5**
1. Brain; 2. Graphic novels
978-1-60270-683-5, $27.07

LC 2009-17650

Teacher Ms Hansen leads her Explorers class on a tour of the human brain. They learn about how the different parts control body functions through the nervous system, and how people should protect their head while participating in certain physical activities, to avoid damaging the brain. The tour is very similar to the Ms Frizzle's Magic School Bus science series by way of The Fantastic Voyage in that Ms Hansen's class shrinks to microscopic size in order to get into the brain. Back matter in the book includes a diagram of the brain, some "fun facts," a brief glossary, and information on how to use ABDO's website to find links to more information on the Internet. The author owns Antarctica Press and is also a physician; artist Espinosa has published such books as The Courageous Princess and Neotopia.

This book is part of the Graphic Adventures: The Human Body series.

The **eyes**: a graphic novel tour. Illustrated by Rod Espinosa. Magic Wagon 2009 32p. Illustration (Graphic adventures. The human body)

Grades: 2 3 4 5 6   **612.8; 741.5**
1. Eye; 2. Graphic novels
978-1-60270-684-2, $27.07

LC 2009-17651

Teacher Ms. Hansen leads her Explorers class on a tour of the human eye. They learn about how the eye functions, what purpose blinking serves, how the iris works to control the amount of light that enters the eye, and why tears are important. The tour is very similar to the Ms Frizzle's Magic School Bus science series by way of The Fantastic Voyage, in that Ms Hansen's class shrinks to microscopic size in order to get into the eye. Back matter in the book include a diagram of the eye, fun facts that include information on color blindness and vision problems, a short glossary, and information on how to use ABDO's website to find links for more information on the Internet. The author owns Antarctica Press and is also a physician; artist Espinosa has published such books as The Courageous Princess and Neotopia.

This book is part of the Graphic Adventures: The Human Body series.

H.G. Wells' The time machine. H.G. Wells; adapted by Joeming Dunn; illustrated by Ben Dunn. ABDO Publishing Group/Magic Wagon 2008 32p. Illustration

Grades: 3 4 5 6 7 8   **741.5; Fic**
1. Adventure graphic novels; 2. Authors; 3. Historians; 4. Novelists; 5. Science fiction graphic novels; 6. Science fiction writers; 7. Wells, H G (Herbert George), 1866-1946 — Adaptations; 8. Writers on politics; 9. Writers on science; 11. Graphic novels
978-1-60270-054-3, $27.07

LC 2007-6447

A gentleman hosts his friends at dinner one evening in London and then takes their leave in his time machine. When he returns, he tells them of his trip into the future, of the two peoples he encountered, the Eloi and the Morlocks, and what he learned of their relationship. When his friends refuse to believe him, the Traveler sets out again in his machine. This simplified graphic novel adaptation allows younger readers and struggling readers to get the main plot of the classic story. The book includes a brief biography of Wells and list of his other works.

Courtesy of ABDO Publishing Group/Magic Wagon

Part of the Graphic Planet Graphic Classics series.

The **heart:** a graphic novel tour. By Joeming Dunn; illustrated by Rod Espinosa.. Magic Wagon/Graphic Planet 2009 32p. Illustration (Graphic adventures. The human body)

Grades: 2 3 4 5 6   **612.8; 741.5**
1. Heart; 2. Graphic novels
978-1-60270-685-9, $27.07

              LC 2009-17851

Teacher Ms. Hansen leads her Explorers class on a tour of the human heart. They learn about how the heart functions, how it pumps blood through the circulatory system, and the functions of the major veins and arteries. The tour is very similar to the Ms Frizzle's Magic School Bus science series by way of The Fantastic Voyage, in that Ms Hansen's class shrink to microscopic size in order to get into the bloodstream. Back matter in the book include a diagram of the heart, fun facts, a short glossary, and information on how to use ABDO's website to find links for more information on the Internet. The author owns Antarctica Press and is also a physician; artist Espinosa has published such books as The Courageous Princess and Neotopia.

Includes bibliographical references

This book is part of the Graphic Adventures: The Human Body series.

Journey to the center of the earth. Adapted by Joeming Dun; illustrated by Rod Espinosa.. Magic Wagon/Graphic Planet 2009 32p. Illustration

Grades: 3 4 5 6 7   **741.5; Fic**
1. Adventure graphic novels; 2. Authors; 3. Children's authors; 4. Novelists; 5. Science fiction graphic novels; 6. Science fiction writers; 7. Verne, Jules, 1828-1905; 8. Verne, Jules, 1828-1905 — Adaptations; 9. Graphic novels
978-1-60270678-1, $27.07

              LC 2009-8588

Professor Otto Liedenbrock, his nephew Axel, and their guide Hans follow the instructions in an old note left by explorer Arne Saknussemm to descend into an old volcano in Iceland, seeking a way to the center of the Earth. This graphic novel provides an easy-reading adaptation of Jules

Verne's classic adventure story. Back matter includes a brief biography of Verne, a list of some of his novels, and a short glossary. It is a curious addition to the Graphic Planet series called Graphic Horror, since there is no horror in the book.

This is part of the Graphic Horror Series 2.

The **kidneys:** a graphic novel tour. Illustrated by Rod Espinosa. ABDO/Magic Wagon 2009 32p. (Graphic adventures. The human body)

Grades: 2 3 4 5 6
612.2; 741.5
1. Kidneys; 2. Graphic novels
978-1-60270-686-6, $27.07

      LC 2009-17852

Courtesy of ABDO Publishing Group/Magic Wagon

Ms. Hansen and her Explorers class, including the aliens Xeni and Zeno Zelman, take off on another tour inside the human body, this time into the kidneys, the body's filter to get rid of waste from the blood and to regulate the levels of water, salt, and other minerals. The tour starts in the blood system, into the left renal artery into the left kidney. Young readers might enjoy the fact that the Explorers exit the body through the urinary tract, which is where the kidneys send the waste called urea. This graphic novel series combines aspects of the Magic School Bus series and the movie Fantastic Voyage. The book includes additional facts about the kidneys, a glossary, and a link to find websites for more information. Dunn is a physician and owner of Antarctic Publishing, a comic book publishing house.

Part of the Graphic Adventures: The Human Body series.

The **liver:** a graphic novel tour. Illustrated by Rod Espinosa. ABDO/Magic Wagon 2009 32p. Illustration (Graphic adventures. The human body)

Grades: 2 3 4 5 6   **612.2; 741.5**
1. Liver; 2. Graphic novels
978-1-60270-687-3, $27.07

      LC 2009-17853

Courtesy of ABDO Publishing Group/Magic Wagon

Ms. Hansen and her Explorers class, including the aliens Xeni and Zeno Zelman, take off on another tour inside the human body, this time into the liver. The tour starts in the mouth, through the esophagus into the stomach, then through the small intestine into the liver. The liver breaks down digested proteins and medicines, and helps to convert carbohydrates to sugars; it also stores vitamins and minerals such as iron. This graphic novel series combines aspects of the Magic School Bus series and the movie Fantastic Voyage. The book includes additional facts about the liver, a glossary, and a link to find websites for more information.

Dunn is a physician and owner of Antarctic Publishing, a comic book publishing house.

Part of the Graphic Adventures: The Human Body series.

The **Lungs:** a graphic novel tour; art by Rod Espinosa. ABDO/Magic Wagon 2009 32p. Illustration
Grades: 2 3 4 5 6   **612.2; 741.5**
1. Lungs; 2. Respiratory system; 3. Graphic novels
978-1-60270-688-0, $27.07

LC 2009-17854

Ms. Hansen and her Explorers class, including the aliens Xeni and Zeno Zelman, take off on another tour inside the human body, this time into the lungs. The tour starts in the nose, through the larynx into the trachea (windpipe), then through the bronchi into the lungs. The lungs do more than help the body breathe and circulate oxygen; they help the body to speak. This graphic novel series combines aspects of the Magic School Bus series and the movie Fantastic Voyage. The book includes additional facts about the lungs, a glossary, and a link to find websites for more information. Dunn is a physician and owner of Antarctic Publishing, a comic book publishing house.

Part of the Graphic Adventures: The Human Body series.

Eaton, Maxwell

The **flying** beaver brothers and the birds vs bunnies: birds vs. bunnies. By Maxwell Eaton III. Alfred A. Knopf 2013 96 p. Illustration
Grades: 1 2 3 4 5   **Fic; 741.5/973**
1. Animals; 2. Beavers — Fiction; 3. Birds — Fiction; 4. Islands — Fiction; 5. Rabbits — Fiction; 6. Graphic novels
0449810224; 9780449810224, $6.99; 9780449810231, $12.99; 9780449810248

LC 2012034047

This graphic novel, written and illustrated by Maxwell Eaton III, presents the fourth story of his characters the Flying Beaver Brothers. They "set off in their sailboat to enjoy . . . rest and relaxation at [a] nearby island. But the birds and bunnies who live on Little Beaver Island have other ideas. Before long, Ace and Bub find themselves embroiled in an all-out war between the feathers and the fuzz [and attempt to] bring peace to Little Beaver Island." (Publisher's note)

Eisenberg, Adam

The **Creation** of Iron Man. Rosen Publishing Group 2006 48p. Illustration
Grades: 4 5 6 7 8 9 10   **741.5**
1. Iron Man (Fictional character); 2. Superhero graphic novels; 3. Graphic novels
978-1-4042-0767-7, $29.25

LC 2006000167

This volume discusses the unique character of Tony Stark, developed by Stan Lee and Jack Kirby, who was unable to live a normal life and invented a special iron suit that gave him superpowers. The book includes information about the times in which Lee and Kirby worked at Marvel Comics.

Part of the Action Heroes series.

Eisner, Will

The **Last** Knight: An Introduction to Don Quixote. NBM Publishing 2000 32p. Illustration
Grades: 3 4 5 6 7 8 9 10   **741.5; Fic**
1. Adventure graphic novels; 2. Authors; 3. Cervantes Saavedra, Miguel de, 1547-1616 — Adaptations
1-56163-251-1; 978-1-56163-251-0, $15.95

LC 2001-265049

This is Eisner's graphic novel remake of Don Quixote. Here are the adventures of a Spanish country gentleman and his companion who set out, like knights of old, to search for adventure. As the subtitle says, this book hits the highlights and serves to introduce the classic tale to younger readers.

Moby Dick. NBM Publishing 2001 32p. Illustration
Grades: 3 4 5 6 7 8 9 10   **741.5; Fic**
1. Adventure graphic novels; 2. Whaling; 3. Graphic novels
1-56163-293-7, $15.95; 1-56163-294-5 (pa)

LC 2001-032989

Ishmael, a sailor, recounts the ill-fated voyage of a whaling ship led by the fanatical Captain Ahab in search of the white whale that had crippled him. Eisner's adaptation hits the highlights of the novel.

The **Princess** and the Frog. NBM Publishing 1999 32p. Illustration
Grades: 3 4 5 6 7 8 9 10   **741.5; Fic**
1. Fairy tales; 2. Fantasy graphic novels; 3. Graphic novels
1-56163-244-9, $15.95; 1-56163-346-1 (pa)

A good prince, turned into a frog by a spiteful wizard, exacts from a princess a promise which she is reluctant to fulfill, despite his kindness and her desire not to hurt him. Comics master Will Eisner adapted the familiar tale by the Brothers Grimm.

Elder, Joshua

Mail Order Ninja, Vol. 1 written by Joshua Elder ; illustrated by Erich Owen. Tokyopop 2006 Un Illustration
Grades: 4 5 6 7 8 9   **741.5; Fic**
1. Humorous graphic novels; 2. Ninja; 3. Graphic novels
1-59816-728-6, $5.99

Timmy is a normal boy attending L. Frank Baum Elementary School in Cherry Creek, Indiana - dealing with bullies, a nasty little sister, and an even nastier super-rich girl who acts as though she owns the school. When things get really bad, Timmy decides to enter a drawing in a mail order catalog to win a ninja. Yes, a real live ninja of his very own. When Jiro arrives, Timmy soon overpowers the bullies and beats rich Felicity in the Student Body President election. But as long as Felicity's father has money, she'll find a way to get even, and she has a copy of that mail order catalog. . . . This is the first volume in a global manga series.

Ellerton, Sarah

Inverloch, Volume 1. Seven Seas 2006 Un Illustration
Grades: 4 5 6 7 8 9 10 11 12   **741.5; Fic**
1. Adventure graphic novels; 2. Fantasy graphic novels; 3. Graphic novels
1-933164-13-1, $14.99

In a world where humans, elves, and other beings coexist, albeit not altogether peacefully, Acheron is a young da'kor, a horned wolf-like race that lives in the forests. He encounters a beautiful elf and takes her quest for his own - to find another elf who went missing twelve years before. Teased by his brothers as a lousy hunter, feared by humans who think da'kor are dangerous beasts, innocent Acheron finds that the world beyond the forest is full of danger, intrigue, and betrayal.

This story began online as a webcomic.

Enz, Tammy

★ **Engineering** a totally rad skateboard with Max Axiom, super scientist. By Tammy Enz; illustrated by Pop Art Studios. Capstone Press 2013 32 p. Color illustration
Grades: 2 3 4   **688.7; 688.7/622**
1. Engineering; 2. Skateboarding — Fiction; 3. Skateboards — Design and construction; 4. Skateboards — Design and construction — Juvenile literature; 5. Graphic novels
1429699353; 9781429699358, $29.99; 9781620657034, $7.95

LC 2012026437
In this graphic novel written by Tammy Enz "Max Axiom has a mission. His nephew Nick wants to take his skateboarding skills to the next level, but he needs a new board to accomplish his dreams. Join Max as he uses the engineering process to design and build a totally rad skateboard." (Publisher's note)

Includes bibliographical references (page 31) and index.

Espinosa, Rod

Around the world in 80 days. Adapted and illustrated by Rod Espinosa. ABDO/Red Wagon 2008 32p. Illustration
Grades: 3 4 5 6 7 8 9   **741.5; Fic**
1. Adventure graphic novels; 2. Graphic novels; 3. Verne, Jules, 1828-1905 — Adaptations
978-1-60270-050-5, $27.07

LC 2007-6444
In 1872, English gentleman Phileas Fogg makes a wager that he can travel around the world in just 80 days. Unfortunately, at the time of his wager, a daring robber has made off with a fortune, and Scotland Yard detective Fix is convinced Fogg is the villain. The chase is on, around the world. This comic book adaptation has been written for younger, reluctant, and struggling readers and provides highlights of the adventures in the original novel by Verne. The book includes a brief biography of Verne, a short list of some of his other works, and a brief glossary.

★ The **courageous** princess. Dark Horse Comics 2007 240p. Illustration
Grades: 3 4 5 6 7 8 9   **741.5; Fic**
1. Fantasy graphic novels; 2. Princesses
978-1-59307-719-8, $9.95
Plain Princess Mabelrose doesn't get along with the other, prettier princesses, but her intelligence helps her when a dragon kidnaps her. Instead of waiting for rescue, Mabelrose escapes, taking a friendly hedgehog and a few useful-looking items (a pouch, a length of rope) that she doesn't know are magic.

This new edition from Dark Horse is in black and white; the previous Antarctic Press editions were in color.

Lewis and Clark. ABDO/Magic Wagon 2008 32p. Illustration (Bio-graphics)

Grades: 3 4 5 6 7 8 9   **917.8; 92; 741.5; 917**
1. Biographical graphic novels; 2. Clark, William, 1770-1838; 3. Explorers; 4. Lewis and Clark Expedition (1804-1806); 5. Lewis, Meriwether, 1774-1809; 6. Territorial governors; 7. West (US) — Exploration; 8. Graphic novels
978-1-60270-069-7, $27.07

LC 2007-5578
This graphic format book tells the story of the Lewis and Clark Expedition, which explored the land of the Louisiana Purchase, as authorized in 1803 by President Thomas Jefferson. The book includes a timeline of the Expedition, a map of the route, and a list of books for further reading.

Everheart, Chris

Recon academy: nuclear distraction; by Chris Everheart; illustrated by Arcana Studio. Stone Arch Books 2009 64p. Illustration
Grades: 3 4 5 6 7 8   **741.5; Fic**
1. Science fiction graphic novels; 2. Terrorism; 3. Graphic novels
978-1-4342-1167-5, $25.32; 978-1-4342-1381-5 (pa), $6.95

LC 2008-32457
Emmi, Jay, Ryker, and Hazmat are Recon Academy, a teenage high-tech security force based in Seaside High School. Ever since their hometown suffered a terrorist attack, they have each worked on their specialized skills to seek out and fight terrorists. Hazmat is the team's forensics expert, so what's he doing in a martial arts tournament? Emmi has been trying to train him to be able to defend himself. He loses the match, but gets a date—but only if the team can finish their investigation of the security breach at the nuclear plant in time.

Recon academy: prep squardon. Stone Arch Books 2009 64p. Illustration
Grades: 3 4 5 6 7 8   **741.5; Fic**
1. Science fiction graphic novels; 2. Terrorism; 3. Graphic novels
978-1-4342-1168-2, $25.32; 978-1-4342-1382-2 (pa), $6.95

LC 2008-32479
Emmi, Jay, Ryker, and Hazmat are Recon Academy, a teenage high-tech security force based in Seaside High School. Ever since their hometown suffered a terrorist attack, they have each worked on their specialized skills to seek out and fight terrorists. Jay is the team's gadget guru, but he feels frustrated when Ryker's drills focus on teamwork and "old-fashioned" techniques (no gadgets). Then Jay gets a message from Ryker about a special drill just for him, only it's not from Ryker, but from Shadow Cell. They're using Jay to circumvent the Navy base's security systems, but what do they want?

Recon academy: shadow cell scam. Stone Arch Books 2009 64p. Illustration
Grades: 3 4 5 6 7 8   **741.5; Fic**
1. Science fiction graphic novels; 2. Terrorism; 3. Graphic novels
978-1-4342-1166-8, $25.32; 978-1-4342-1383-9 (pa), $6.95

LC 2008-32074
Emmi, Jay, Ryker, and Hazmat are Recon Academy, a teenage high-tech security force based in Seaside High School. Ever since their hometown suffered a terrorist attack, they have each worked on their specialized skills to seek out and fight terrorists. This time, they're up against Shadow Cell operatives who have stolen some computers. Emmi goes home from school and finds a salesman from a company called PenTech who has sold a new laptop to her grandmother. All too soon, she realizes it's a trap, and she learns that the other members of Recon Academy have also received the booby-trapped laptops. They need to track down Shadow Cell and find out what the villains want to accomplish.

Recon Academy: storm surge. Stone Arch Books 2010 66p. Illustration
Grades: 3 4 5 6 7 8   741.5; Fic
  1. Adventure graphic novels; 2. Mystery graphic novels; 3. Storms; 4. Graphic novels
  978-1-4342-1918-3, $25.32
  In this volume of the Recon Academy series, Jay, Emmi and Ryker have gone mountain climbing with a school group when a storm hits. The storm also shorts out a critical communications antenna, and a Navy submarine needs it in order to transmit crucial top-secret data. Jay and Emmi set out to fix the antenna, but Ryker finds he has plenty of work when the bus crashes in the storm and knocks out Coach Kemp, the one adult with the students. Meanwhile, back at their base, Hazmat tries to maintain contact with everyone. This time, the Recon Academy team is up against nature. Arcana Studio is a Canadian comics publisher. The book includes a brief glossary, discussion questions, and writing prompts.
  Part of the Recon Academy series.

Recon academy: the hidden face of Fren-Z. Stone Arch Books 2009 64p. Illustration
Grades: 3 4 5 6 7 8   741.5; Fic
  1. Science fiction graphic novels; 2. Terrorism; 3. Graphic novels
  978-1-4342-1165-1, $25.32; 978-1-4342-1380-8 (pa), $6.95
LC 2008-32073
  Emmi, Jay, Ryker, and Hazmat are Recon Academy, a teenage high-tech security force based in Seaside High School. Ever since their hometown suffered a terrorist attack, they have each worked on their specialized skills to seek out and fight terrorists. The team, led by computer expert Ryker, goes up against a new Shadow Cell member, the hacker named Fren-Z. Shadow Cell plans to break into the Federal Reserve and shut down the world's economy, but Ryker and the others have their own plan to shut down the bad guys.

Explorer: the hidden doors
  Edited by Kazu Kibuishi. Abrams Books 2014 128 p. Color; Illustration (Explorer)
Grades: 4 5 6 7 8   741.5
  1. Bullying — Fiction; 2. Doors — Fiction; 3. Monsters — Fiction
  1419708821; 9781419708824, $19.95; 9781419708848
LC 2014938941

In this collection of comics edited by Kazu Kibuishi, "a bullied boy discovers a door guarded by a sly monster . . . A painting of a door opens in a forgotten Egyptian tomb . . . A portal in the park promises to turn you into a much cooler version 2.0 - if you can just get the bugs out." (Publisher's note)
  "Readers are once again presented with an array of stories created by a cast of comics authors and illustrators smartly assembled by Kibuishi...The range in this slim volume is expansive. From funny to deep and fantastical to refined, all of the stories have a compelling narrative arc. The colors are just as varied, and are universally dynamic and nuanced. Consider this (and previous series installments) as a necessary addition to any graphic novel collection." SLJ
  Other titles in the series are: The Mystery Boxes (2012); The Lost Islands (2013)

Explorer: the lost islands
  Kazu Kibuishi. Abrams Books 2013 128 p. (Explorer)
Grades: 4 5 6 7 8   741.5; Fic
  1. Islands; 2. Graphic novels
  1419708813; 141970883X; 9781419708817, $19.95; 9781419708831, $10.95
LC 2013935794
  In this follow-up to "Explorer: The Mystery Boxes," Kazu Kibuishi and a crew of cartoonists again take turns weaving seven tales based around a loose theme. This time the motif is islands, and the contributors are left to interpret it in illustrated shorts. Some, by using their strange and remote settings as microcosms, underscore the value of hard work . . . or finding one's niche . . ., while others examine more abstract concepts such as exploration and isolation. (Publishers Weekly)

Explorer: the mystery boxes
  Kazu Kibuishi. Abrams Books 2012 126 p. (Explorer)
Grades: 4 5 6 7 8   S C; 741.5
  1. Boxes; 2. Boxes — Fiction; 3. Mystery graphic novels; 4. Short stories; 5. Graphic novels
  1419700103; 9781419700095, $10.95; 9781419700101, $19.95
LC 2011025343
  This collection of short stories offers "[s]even . . . stories [which] answer one simple question: what's in the box" . . . [E]ach of these . . . illustrated short graphic works revolves around a central theme: a mysterious box and the marvels—or mayhem—inside. Artists include . . . Kazu Kibuishi, Raina Telgemeier ('Smile'), and Dave Roman ('Astronaut Academy'), as well as Jason Caffoe, Stuart Livingston, Johane Matte, Rad Sechrist (all contributors to the . . . comics anthology series 'Flight'), and . . . artist Emily Carroll." (Publisher's note)
  Seven graphic stories.

★ Fable Comics: Classic Tales Told by Extraordinary Cartoonists
  Edited by Chris Duffy. First Second 2015 128 p. Illustration
Grades: 1 2 3 4 5   741.5; 398.2
  1. Aesop's fables — Adaptations; 2. Fables; 3. Fairy tales
  1626721076; 9781626721074, $19.99

This collection, edited by Chris Duffy, "has something to offer every reader. Seventeen fairy tales are wonderfully adapted and illustrated in comics format by seventeen different cartoonists, including Raina Telgemeier, Brett Helquist, Cherise Harper, and more." (Publisher's note)

"Editor Duffy delivers another knockout collection of comics, this time focusing on fables. Although the majority are interpretations of different Aesop stories, other selections have their roots in Russia, India, and the U.S. Ranging from familiar to obscure, modern to traditional, this vibrant collection boasts an impressive catalog of top-name artists, who interpret the original tales with an astonishing range of creativity and originality." Booklist

Fairy Tale Comics: Classic Tales Told by Extraordinary Cartoonists

Compiled by Chris Duffy. First Second 2013 128 p. Illustration

Grades: K 1 2 3 4 5   741.5; Fic
1. Dogs; 2. Fairy tales; 3. Princesses
1596438231; 9781596438231, $19.99

In this book, editor Chris Duffy "has assembled a . . . lineup of comics versions of more than a dozen fairy tales in this . . . follow-up to 'Nursery Rhyme Comics.' Favorites like 'The Twelve Dancing Princesses' and 'Rapunzel' (whose heroines gain significant agency) join rarities like 'The Small Tooth Dog' and 'The Boy Who Drew Cats.'" (Publishers Weekly)

"Every artist here knows how to turn in an elegant, flowing story, and every tale is pitch-perfect for young readers and intimate read-alouds. Overall, the book is an ideal choice for a child's first comics experience and a new way to enjoy old favorites." Booklist

Faller, Regis

Polo: The Runaway Book. Roaring Brook Press 2006 80p. Illustration

Grades: K 1 2 3   741.5; Fic
1. Adventure graphic novels; 2. Stories without words; 3. Graphic novels
1-59643-189-X, $16.95

The little dog Polo receives a book as a gift, but a little round green alien creature steals it, and the chase is on. Polo pursues the thief up a rope into the sky onto a pink cotton candy cloud, through a funhouse mirror, and through other strange and wonderful places, making friends as he goes. The only words uttered are Polo's cry, "My book!" in several places.

Originally published in France as Polo, mon livre.

Fandel, Jennifer

Jim Thorpe: Greatest Athlete in the World. By Jennifer Fandel ; illustrated by Rod Whigham. Capstone Press 2007 32p. Illustration

Grades: 3 4 5 6 7 8 9   741.5; 796; 92
1. Athletes; 2. Thorpe, Jim; 3. Graphic novels
9781429601528, $29.99; 1429601523

LC 2007000286

This book uses the graphic novel format to tell the life story of Native American Jim Thorpe, star of the 1912 Olympic Games and member of the Pro Football Hall of

Fame. The book includes additional facts and a list of books for further reading.

Part of the Graphic Biographies series.

Farshtey, Greg

Bionicle #1: rise of the Toa Nuva. Greg Farshtey, writer; Carlos D'Anda [and] Randy Elliott, artist.. Papercutz 2008 Un Illustration

Grades: 3 4 5 6   741.5; Fic
1. Adventure graphic novels; 2. Science fiction graphic novels; 3. Graphic novels
978-1-59707-110-9, $12.95; 978-1-59707-109-3 (pa), $7.95

Six mighty heroes the Toa arrive on a tropical island to find a land under siege. The Great Spirit Mata Nui has been cast into an unending sleep by the evil Makuta. Now Makuta is attacking the island's Matoran villagers with vicious Rahi beasts.he Toa must combine their skills and elemental and mask powers to defeat Makuta and restore peace to the island.

"The art is vivid and attention grabbing, and the story line, which weaves in Polynesian mythology, is exciting and action-packed." SLJ

Other titles in this series are:Challenge of the Rahkshi (2008); City of legends (2008); Trial by fire (2008); The battle of Voya Nui (2009); The underwater city (2009); Realm of fear (2009); Legends of Bara Magna (2010); The fall of Atero (2010)

Faust, Daniel R.

Energy crisis: the future of fossil fuels. Rosen Publishing Group 2009 24p.

Grades: 2 3 4 5 6 7   333.79; 741.5
1. Energy resources — Environmental aspects; 2. Graphic novels
978-14042-4231-9, $23.95

LC 2007-49957

Using the comic book format, the book introduces young readers to the problem of finding sources of fossil fuels and dealing with the pollution resulting from their use.

Part of the Jr. Graphic Environmental Dangers series.

Courtesy of Rosen Publishing

Fein, Eric

The **Creation** of the Fantastic Four. Rosen Publishing Group 2006 48p. Illustration

Grades: 4 5 6 7 8 9 10   741.5
1. Fantastic Four (Fictional characters); 2. Superhero graphic novels; 3. Graphic novels
978-1-4042-0765-3, $29.25

LC 2005031170

Describes the history and development of the action heroes called the Fantastic Four and how they got their superpowers. Created in 1961 by the Marvel power team of

Jack Kirby and Stan Lee, the Fantastic Four was the first superhero team the men created.

Part of the Action Heroes series.

The **Creation** of the Incredible Hulk. Rosen Publishing Group 2006 48p. Illustration
Grades: 4 5 6 7 8 9 10   **741.5**
1. Hulk (Fictional character); 2. Superhero graphic novels; 3. Graphic novels
978-1-4042-0764-6, $29.25

LC 2005035267

Discusses the unique character developed in 1962 by Stan Lee and Jack Kirby who was unable to live a normal life after he was affected by a gamma bomb's blast and Dr. Bruce Banner became the huge, inarticulate, super-strong Hulk. The book also includes information on the cultural climate in the U.S. at the time, and on the way the two men worked together at Marvel Comics.

Part of the Action Heroes series.

Fillbach, Matt
Star Wars: Clone Wars Adventures Volume 8. Dark Horse Comics 2007 Un Illustration
Grades: 5 6 7 8 9 10   **741.5; Fic**
1. Adventure graphic novels; 2. Science fiction graphic novels; 3. Star Wars; 4. Graphic novels
978-1-59307-680-1, $6.95

The stories in this volume take place during the Clone Wars. Luminara Unduli battles in the Arena of Doom, Aurra Sing hunts a bounty on the Smuggler's Moon, Obi-Wan Kenobi disrupts an assassin's mission, and a battle droid makes a career change.

Fingeroth, Danny
Action Heroes: The Creation of the X-Men. Rosen Publishing Group, Inc. 2007 48p. Illustration
Grades: 3 4 5 6 7 8   **741.5**
1. X-Men (Fictional characters); 2. Graphic novels
1-4042-0762-7 (lib bdg), $29.25

Veteran Marvel Comics writer Fingeroth gives young readers a brief introduction to the creation of the Marvel superhero team, the X-Men. The book focuses on the two creators, Stan Lee and Jack Kirby, and also discusses the state of the comics industry in the early 1960s, as well as the cultural/social background that led Lee and Kirby to create a team of mutant superheroes. It includes a timeline of the X-Men creators, highlights from the long-running series, a glossary, books for further reading, and a bibliography. Photographs and color reproductions of the art highlight the book. Due to the popular series of X-Men movies, people know the characters, even if they've never read the comics.

The **U.S.** Supreme Court. Illustrated by Cynthia Martin; consultant: Michael Bailey. Capstone Press 2009 32p. Illustration (Cartoon nation)
Grades: 1 2 3 4 5 6 7 8   **347; 741.5**
1. United States — Supreme Court; 2. Graphic novels
978-1-4296-1985-1, $32

LC 2008-486

This graphic format book uses irreverently humorous captions and dialog and provides young readers with an introduction to the U. S. Supreme Court. The book covers the founding of the court, which first met on February 1,

1790, its powers, how it works, how to become a Supreme Court justice, famous cases, and its role in amending the U. S. Constitution. It includes a short timeline, a glossary, and a list of books for further reading.

Part of the Graphic Library Cartoon Nation series

Flight explorer
Edited by Kazu Kibuiski. Villard 2008 112p. Illustration
Grades: 4 5 6 7   **741.5; Fic**
1. Adventure graphic novels; 2. Fantasy graphic novels; 3. Humorous graphic novels; 4. Science fiction graphic novels; 5. Graphic novels
978-0-345-50313-8 (pa), $10; 0-345-50313-9 (pa)

This anthology includes stories that Kibuishi kept from Flight Volume 4 because they had all-ages appeal, as well as stories submitted especially for this volume. Kibuishi's own Copper and his talking dog cross a deep canyon by leaping onto mushrooms, only to discover the vegetation is intelligent. Kean Soo's Jellaby and his human friends frolic in the snow. Missile Mouse by Jake Parker defends a village on another planet, only to discover his coming was prophesied (this story includes two uses of the word "crap"). The other stories will appeal to younger readers, while some of the humor will also appeal to older readers. Other than the one bad word in "Missile Mouse" (noted above), there shouldn't be any other content that would keep this book out of most elementary and middle schools.

"Every story has a layout that promotes an acute sense of pacing and showcases the crisp, defined, full-color art." SLJ

Fogel, Rich
Transformers animated volume 3. IDW Publishing 2008 Un Illustration
Grades: 2 3 4 5 6 7 8   **741.5; Fic**
1. Adventure graphic novels; 2. Robots; 3. Science fiction graphic novels; 4. Transformers (Fictional characters); 5. Graphic novels
978-1-60010-215-8, $7.99

The Autobots have to overcome mechanical mischief orchestrated by Megatron when Sari's Allspark key wakens him and he fixes some broken pocketbots and sneaks one into Sari's backpack. Then, the Autobots have to prove their usefulness to the police force, and all of Detroit, against Prometheus Black and his biochemical makeovers. The stories have been adapted from broadcast episodes of the new animated Transformers television series and illustrated with screen captures from the programs.

Transformers animated, volume 5. IDW Publishing 2008 Un Illustration
Grades: 3 4 5 6 7 8   **741.5; Fic**
1. Adventure graphic novels; 2. Robots; 3. Science fiction; 4. Transformers (Fictional characters); 5. Graphic novels
978-1-60010-243-1, $7.99

In "Survival of the Fittest," a Dinobot kidnaps Sari, who holds the Key to the Allspark. Prowl and Bulkhead track her to the island where they let the Dinobots settle, but they are followed by New Detroit police captain Fanzone. The Dinobots had seemed to be harmless, but now they attack the Autobots, and the reason? A Decepticon named Meltdown controls them, and he wants to create transforming humans, starting with Sari. In "Lost and Found," Decepticons Blitzwing and Lugnut have come to Detroit searching for Megatron and the Allspark. Optimus Prime believes that the Autobots need to leave Earth in order to save the people from the Decepticons, but Sari doesn't want her friends to leave. The book is illustrated with screen captures from the animated television series.

Fontes, Justine
The **Trojan** Horse: The Fall of Troy; story by Justine & Ron Fontes ; pencils by Gordon Purcell ; inks by Barbara Schulz. Lerner Publishing Group/Graphic Universe 2007 48p. Illustration
Grades: 3 4 5 6 7 8 9   **398.2; 741.5**
1. Greek mythology; 2. Troy (Extinct city); 3. Graphic novels
978-0-8225-3085-5, $26.60 lib. Bdg.
This story is adapted from Virgil's Aeneid and from Smyrnacus Quintus' Posthomerica. The Trojan War has raged for ten years; then suddenly the Greek forces pull back. When the Trojans venture outside their city walls, they discover a giant wooden horse and a messenger. Should they accept this peace offering? Or is the gift horse too good to be true? This book includes a glossary and a list of books and websites for further reading.

Fontes, Ron
Atalanta: The Race Against Destiny; story by Justine & Ron Fontes ; pencils and inks by Thomas Yeates ; [coloring by Hi-Fi Design ; lettering by Bill Hauser]. Lerner Publishing Group/Graphic Universe 2007 48p. Illustration
Grades: 3 4 5 6 7 8 9
292.1; 741.5
1. Atlanta (Greek mythology); 2. Greek mythology
9780822559658, $26.60 lib bdg

Courtesy of Lerner Publishing Group

Atalanta is the best hunter and swiftest runner in the land. The Oracle at Delphi has warned her to never marry, but her father, a powerful king, insists that she choose a husband. Atalanta declares she will only marry the man who can beat her in a footrace. Can she escape her fate?

Captured by pirates. Justine & Ron Fontes ; illustrations by David Witt. Lerner Publishing Group/Graphic Universe 2007 112p. Illustration (Twisted Journeys)
Grades: 3 4 5 6 7 8 9   **741.5; Fic**
1. Adventure graphic novels; 2. Pirates; 3. Graphic novels
978-0-8225-6201-6, $27.93; 978-0-8225-6202-3 (pa), $7.95
LC 2006-101599
In the series called Twisted Journeys, readers choose how the story will progress. Pages of text alternate with comic book-style pages. In this volume, "you" are a young boy on a voyage with your father on his ship, when pirates

capture the ship. Will you fight them, or will you join them?" Readers will find many scenarios played out, depending on their choices; some end well, others not so well.

Demeter & Persephone: Spring Held Hostage; story by Justine & Ron Fontes ; pencils by Steve Kurth ; inks by Barbara Schultz. Lerner Publishing Group/Graphic Universe 2007 48p. Illustration
Grades: 3 4 5 6 7 8 9   **292.1; 741.5**
1. Demeter (Greek deity); 2. Greek mythology; 3. Persephone (Greek deity); 4. Graphic novels
978-0-8225-5966-5, $26.60 lib. Bdg.
The goddess Demeter spreads warmth and bounty throughout the world, but when her daughter Persephone disappears and Demeter learns she has been kidnapped by Hades, the god of the underworld, her sorrow causes a permanent winter to fall upon the land. Can Demeter rescue Persephone from the underworld, and can the other gods and goddesses of Mount Olympus convince Demeter to bring back spring and summer?

Ford, Michael
The **Hunchback** of Notre Dame; illustrated by Penke Gelev ; retold by Michael Ford. Barron's Educational Series, Inc. 2007 48p. Illustration
Grades: 3 4 5 6 7 8 9   **741.5**
1. Hugo, Victor, 1802-1885 — Adaptations; 2. Graphic novels
978-0-7641-3493-7 (pa); 978-0-7641-5979-4
Abandoned as a baby and raised in the cathedral of Notre Dame, the hunchback Quasimodo lives as an outcast. The arrival of the beautiful gypsy girl Esmeralda begins a tragic series of events marked by jealousy, betrayal, and murder. This volume includes a brief biography of Hugo and of Notre Dame, and information on the importance of the novel and its adaptations.

Forget, Thomas
The **Creation** of Captain America. Rosen Publishing Group 2006 48p. Illustration
Grades: 4 5 6 7 8 9 10   **741.5**
1. Captain America (Fictional character); 2. Superhero graphic novels; 3. Graphic novels
978-1-4042-0766-0, $29.25
LC 2005032024
Captain America has been a hero since 1940 and saved comic books and Marvel Comic Group. This volume discusses the times during which Cap was created and how the character has changed over the years. In light of the character's death in the aftermath of the Marvel Civil War storyline that played out in comics during 2006 and 2007, this book may have wide appeal.
Part of the Action Heroes series.

Forsythe, Matthew
Jinchalo. Matthew Forsythe. Drawn & Quarterly 2012 120 p. Illustration
Grades: 3 4 5 6 7 8   **Fic; 741.5/971**
1. Fantasy comic books, strips, etc; 2. Fantasy graphic novels; 3. Spirits — Fiction
1770460675; 9781770460676, $17.95
LC 2012379212

This graphic novel, by Matthew Forsythe, is a "companion to . . . [the author's] 'Ojingogo,' . . . [staring] the same little girl as its heroine. When the mischievous shape-shifter Jinchalo hatches from a mysterious egg, . . . magical troubles drag the pair out of the safety of her home, through the small village where she resides, up, up, and away. In the course of their flight, they visit a robot garden, follow a vine into the clouds, and leave the village far behind." (Publisher's note)

Frampton, Otis
Oddly Normal. Image 2015 128 p. Illustration
Grades: 4 5 6 7 8 9   **741.5; Fic**
1. Fantasy graphic novels; 2. Humorous graphic novels; 3. Graphic novels
978-1-63215-226-8, $9.99
Written and illustrated by Otis Frampton, this graphic novel describes how "Oddly must travel to Fignation to uncover the mystery of her parents' disappearance. Join Oddly as she navigates a strange new school, teenage angst, monstrous bullies, and Evil itself on an unforgettable fantasy adventure through the vibrant world of Fignation in Oddly Normal." (Publisher's note)
Volume 1 of 3

Oddly Normal: Family Reunion. Viper Comics 2007 Un Illustration
Grades: 4 5 6 7 8 9 10   **741.5; Fic**
1. Fantasy graphic novels; 2. Humorous graphic novels; 3. Graphic novels
978-0-9777883-9-2, $11.95
In this second volume, Oddly meets Tommy Tsunami, who is a comic book hero in the real world, and her friends Reggie and Ragnar seem a bit jealous. Then Ragnar's dad returns and claims that Oopie, the creature Ragnar created and that has bonded with Oddly, holds the secret needed to continue his experiments. And the new teacher in school is actually Mr. Gooseberry in female form, with Oddly's mother's face - and he is determined to force her to ask him to help, for a price.

Friesen, Ray
Cupcakes of doom!. Don't Eat Any Bugs Productions 2008 98p. Illustration
Grades: 3 4 5 6 7 8   **741.5; Fic**
1. Adventure graphic novels; 2. Humorous graphic novels; 3. Pirates; 4. Graphic novels
978-0-9802314-1-0 (pa), $12.95; 0-9802314-1-8 (pa)
The Pirate band led by Captain Scurvybeard must do battle with the Vikings to decide the fate of the kingdom called Pelmellia. With a decidedly shifty fellow named Flambe testing them to see if they deserve to be pirates, Yoho Joseph, Peglegless Pete (he's just a kid), Lester the parrot, Pete's sister Jamie, and the rest of the crew must find the long lost recipe for the Cupcakes of Doom, or the Deliciously-Evil Viking Pie will take over as the people's favorite baked good. The book is full of silly humor, wacky characters (including identical twin sea serpents and a Viking penguin), and a lot of action without violence or bad language. The book is suitable for younger readers, but adults will enjoy the silliness and catch more of the jokes

Furman, Simon
Transformers: Beast Wars: The Gathering; art by Don Figueroa. IDW Publishing 2007 Un Illustration
Grades: 4 5 6 7 8 9   **741.5; Fic**
1. Science fiction graphic novels; 2. Transformers (Fictional characters); 3. Graphic novels
978-1-60010-025-3, $9.99
In this story, Predacon General Magmatron is on a mission to capture the renegade Megatron, but his true intentions are fare more terrifying; he ultimately aims to bring Cybertron itself to its knees. All he need is an army, and he knows exactly where to find one. The heroic Maximals now have to battle the evil Predacons to protect their planet.

Furse, Sophie
Moby Dick; illustrated by Penko Gelev ; retold by Sophie Furse. Barron's Educational Series, Inc. 2007 48p. Illustration
Grades: 3 4 5 6 7 8 9   **741.5**
1. Melville, Herman — Adaptations; 2. Graphic novels
978-0-7641-5977-0; 978-0-7641-3492-0 (pa)
Ishmael's dream of adventure on a whaling ship becomes a nightmare as the voyage turns into a struggle for survival. Captain Ahab, maimed by a monster whale, is obsessed with revenge. As the crew discovers, he is willing to risk everything to destroy that whale. This volume includes a brief biography and timeline of Melville, and information on the legacy of his novel.

Gaff, Jackie
Christopher Columbus: The Life of a Master Navigator and Explorer by David West & Jackie Gaff ; illustrated by Ross Watton. Rosen Publishing Group 2005 48p. Illustration
Grades: 3 4 5 6 7 8   **741.5; 970.01**
1. America — Exploration; 2. Biographical graphic novels; 3. Columbus, Christopher, 1451-1506; 4. Graphic novels
1-4042-0243-9, $29.25
                    LC 2004008645
Before Christopher Columbus's voyages to the West Indies and Central and South America, Europeans knew nothing of the Americas in the New World. His four journeys, beginning in 1492 and ending in 1504, blazed a sea route west across the Atlantic Ocean that pioneered would exploration for years to come. This account captures Columbus's determination and courage as he led his crews into both unknown waters and unfamiliar native civilizations. The book includes some information on other voyages by explorers, a glossary, and a list of books for further reading.

Gagne, Michel
The **saga** of Rex. Image 2010 200p. Illustration
Grades: 4 5 6 7 8   **741.5; Fic**
978-1-60706-322-3, $17.99; 1-60706-322-0
The adorable little fox named Rex is plucked from his home world by a mysterious spaceship and transported to the arcane world of Edernia, where he meets Aven, an enigmatic biomorph with a flying saucer.

"While children may enjoy this graphic novel for its gorgeous art—especially the cute characters—its story line will more likely be appreciated by older readers. The almost wordless story isn't meant to be read on a literal level but instead on more a mystical and dreamlike level. . . . Gagné . . . offers a sensitive and intriguing graphic novel for people who like a little enigma in what they read." Publ Wkly

Gaiman, Neil

★ The **graveyard** book graphic novel Volume 1. Based on the novel by Neil Gaiman; adapted by P. Craig Russell; illustrated by Kevin Nowlan, P. Craig Russell, Tony Harris, Scott Hampton, Galen Showman, Jill Thompson, Stephen B. Scott; colorist, Lovern Kindzierski; letterer, Rick Park. HarperCollins 2014 188 p. Color; Illustration

Grades: 5 6 7 8 9 10   **741.5; Fic**
1. Cemeteries — Fiction; 2. Orphans — Fiction; 3. Graphic novels
9780062194817, $19.99; 006219481X
                          LC 2013953799

This graphic novel is an adaptation of the "Newbery Medal-winning novel, [where] Bod is an unusual boy . . ., the only living resident of a graveyard. Raised from infancy by the ghosts, werewolves, and other cemetery denizens, Bod has learned the antiquated customs of his guardians' time as well as their ghostly teachings." (Publisher's note)

"Russell brings his decades of comics know-how to this lovely, lyrical adaptation of [Gaiman's] well-loved, Newbery Medal—winning book. Not content to rely exclusively on his own distinctive talents, Russell has enlisted some of the industry's greatest contemporary illustrators as contributors, who fill the panels with appropriately gothic tones. In order to give ample room to the novel's twists and turns, the adaptation has been divided into two parts." Booklist

★ The **graveyard** book graphic novel Volume 2. Based on the novel by Neil Gaiman; adapted by P. Craig Russell; illustrated by David LaFuente, Scott Hampton, P. Craig Russell, Kevin Nowlan, Galen Showman; colorist, Lovern Kindzierski; letterer, Rick Parker. HarperCollins 2014 188 p. Color; Illustration

Grades: 5 6 7 8 9 10   **741.5; Fic**
1. Cemeteries — Fiction; 2. Dead — Fiction; 3. Orphans — Fiction; 4. Supernatural — Fiction; 5. Supernatural graphic novels; 6. Graphic novels
0062194836; 9780062194831, $19.99
                          LC 2013497350

"Russell concludes the two-part adaptation of Gaiman's Newbery Medal winner, encompassing the final three chapters of the novel. Bod, raised by the ghostly denizens of a graveyard, is a young adult now, yearning for knowledge of the world of the living. After a showdown with a pair of school bullies . . . Bod finally confronts the ancient order who murdered his family and overcomes them with his supernatural know-how and his innate courage and cleverness." (Booklist)

"Russell and his team of illustrators continue to do this amazing story justice with images that lead readers down a path into Bod's dark and magical graveyard world. Gaiman has the ability to weave beauty and intrigue into a story that has a strong potential to frighten." VOYA

Gallagher, John

Buzzboy: Trouble in paradise. Sky Dog Press 2002 144p. Illustration

Grades: 5 6 7 8 9 10 11 12   **741.5; Fic**
1. Humorous graphic novels; 2. Superhero graphic novels; 3. Graphic novels
0-8721831-0-8, $11.95

Imagine a superhero who jokes constantly, watches way too many old television shows, and loves junk food, and you have Buzzboy. Years before, he was sidekick to Captain Ultra, but the evil Dr. Schism destroyed all superheroes and their sidekicks, except for Captain Ultra. Now, Ultra has declared martial law in the city of New Paradise, and his police stomp out all rebellions. Then a mysterious superhero stops the Hoppers (police) it's Buzzboy, older and back from the dead! Aided by sarcastic teen sorceress Becca and reformed mad scientist Doc Cyber, Buzzboy is here to save the day.

Another title in this series is: Buzzboy: Monsters, dreams, & milkshakes (2003)

Ganeri, Anita

Cleopatra: The Life of an Egyptian Queen by Gary Jeffrey & Anita Ganeri ; illustrated by Ross Watton. Rosen Publishing Group 2005 48p. Illustration

Grades: 3 4 5 6 7 8   **741.5; 932; 92**
1. Biographical graphic novels; 2. Cleopatra, Queen of Egypt, d 30 BC; 3. Egypt — History; 4. Graphic novels
1-4042-0242-0, $29.25
                          LC 2004014162

Queen of Egypt, companion of Julius Caesar, and wife of Mark Antony, Cleopatra lived one of history's most fabled lives. Renowned for her great beauty and intelligence, Cleopatra was a strong ruler determined to restore the glory of Ptolemaic rule to Egypt by using her relationships with Caesar and Antony to achieve her goals. Readers will learn why the events of her life—including her tragic suicide—have inspired writers and artists for centuries. This graphic novel includes additional information and a list of books for further reading.

Part of the Graphic Nonfiction series.

Harriet Tubman: The Life of an African-American Abolitionist by Rob Shone & Anita Ganeri ; illustrated by Rob Shone. Rosen Publishing Group 2005 48p. Illustration

Grades: 3 4 5 6 7 8 9

92; 741.5
1. African American women; 2. Biographical graphic novels; 3. ss; 4. Tubman, Harriet, 1819 or 1820-1913; 5. Underground Railroad; 6. Graphic novels
1-4042-0245-5, $29.25

Courtesy of Rosen Publishing

Born a slave in the United States, Harriet Tubman escaped from bondage to risk her life and newfound liberty in becoming a leading abolitionist in the years before the

American Civil War. Tubman surreptitiously led hundreds of escaped Southern slaves to freedom in the North along the Underground Railroad, earning her the nickname as "the Moses of her people." This graphic novel format book tells her story. It includes additional information about the Underground Railroad and her legacy in the civil rights movement, and a list of books for further reading.

Part of the Graphic Nonfiction series.

Garcia, Tracy J.

Eli Whitney. By Tracy J. Garcia. PowerKids Press 2013 24 p. Color illustration

Grades: 3 4 5 6   **741**

1. Cotton gins and ginning — Juvenile literature; 2. Inventors — United States; 3. Inventors — United States — Biography — Juvenile literature; 4. Whitney, Eli, 1765-1825 — Juvenile literature

1477700757; 1477701354; 1477701362; 9781477700754, $25.25; 9781477701355, $10.60; 9781477701362

LC 2012019319

This graphic novel by Tracy J. Garcia focuses on "Eli Whitney [who] changed manufacturing with the cotton gin and helped make improvements in the area of mass production through interchangeable parts. Readers will [be exposed to] how Whitney also drastically changed farming in America with his inventions." (Publisher's note)

Includes index.

Thomas Edison. By Tracy J. Garcia. PowerKids Press 2013 24 p. (Jr. graphic American inventors)

Grades: 3 4 5 6   **621; 92**

1. Businessmen — United States — Biography — Juvenile literature; 2. Edison, Thomas A (Thomas Alva), 1847-1931; 3. Edison, Thomas A (Thomas Alva), 1847-1931 — Juvenile literature; 4. Electrical engineers — United States — Biography — Juvenile literature; 5. Inventors; 6. Inventors — United States — Biography — Juvenile literature

1477700765; 9781477700761, $25.25; 9781477701379; 9781477701386

LC 2012018690

This graphic novel by Tracy J. Garcia focuses on "Thomas Edison [who] was a prolific inventor with nearly 2,000 patents. One of his most noted inventions is the practical electrical light bulb. Readers will be [exposed to] the life of Thomas Edison, one of America's great inventors and businessmen." (Publisher's note)

Includes index.

Garland, Sarah

Azzi in Between. By Sarah Garland. Frances Lincoln Children's Books 2013 40 p.

Grades: 1 2 3 4   **Fic**

1. Immigrants — Fiction; 2. Refugees — Fiction

1847802613; 9781847802613, $17.99

In this book, illustrated by Sarah Garland, "Azzi and her parents . . . have to leave their home and escape to another country. . . In the new country they must learn to speak a new language, find a new home and Azzi must start a new school. . . . Azzi begins to learn English and understand that she is not the only one who has had to flee her home. . . . But

Grandma has been left behind and Azzi misses her more than anything. Will Azzi ever see her grandma again?" (Publisher's note)

"[T]his sensitive tale of a young war refugee slowly adapting to a new life will strike chords of sympathy and recognition almost anywhere." Kirkus

Gelatt, Philip

Indiana Jones adventures vol. 1; script, Philip Gelatt ; art, Ethen Beavers. Dark Horse Comics 2008 Un Illustration

Grades: 4 5 6 7 8 9   **741.5; Fic**

1. Adventure graphic novels; 2. Archeology; 3. Indiana Jones (Fictional character); 4. Indiana Jones (Fictional character); 5. Graphic novels

978-1-59307-905-5, $6.95

It's winter of 1930 in Sweden, and Dr. Henry Jones Jr. (Indiana Jones) finds an ancient pre-Christian temple of a religion devoted to war; he gets a scroll while Dr. Lawrence, the pretty British archeologist with him, runs with a valuable gold ring. When Indy decides to steal the ring back from the British Museum, the unscrupulous French archeologist Belloq, who works for the Nazis, steals the scroll from Marcus Brody, Indy's friend. From London, Indy and Dr. Lawrence pursue Belloq to Egypt to recover the scroll before he can sell it to the Nazis. This original graphic novel story provides adventure suitable for younger readers.

Gelev, Penko

Dr. Jekyll and Mr. Hyde; illustrated by Penko Geleve ; retold by Fiona Macdonald. Barron's Educational Series 2008 48p. Illustration

Grades: 4 5 6 7 8 9 10   **741.5; Fic**

1. Novelists; 2. Poets; 3. Science fiction graphic novels; 4. Stevenson, Robert Louis, 1850-1894 — Adaptations; 5. Graphic novels; 6. Short story writers

978-0-7641-6058-5, $15.99; 978-0-7641-3782-2 (pa), $8.99

LC 2008-923897

In Victorian London, the sinister, monstrous Mr. Hyde prowls and commits murder, and he's protected by Dr. Henry Jekyll, who is a respected member of society. Why is this? Stevenson's story of good and evil is retold in the graphic format. Words from his original text are defined on the pages, and back matter includes a brief biography of Stevenson, background information about the story, and information on the various adaptations done for film and television over the years.

Part of the Graphic Classics series.

Dracula; illustrated by Penko Gelev ; retold by Fiona MacDonald. Barron's 2007 48p.

Grades: 4 5 6 7 8 9   **741.5; Fic**

1. Authors; 2. Dracula (Fictional character); 3. Dracula, Count (Fictional character); 4. Horror graphic novels; 5. Stoker, Bram, 1847-1912 — Adaptations; 6. Vampires; 7. Graphic novels

978-0-7641-6054-7, $15.99; 978-0-7641-3778-5 (pa), $8.99

LC 2007-925724

Englishman Jonathan Harker travels to Transylvania to meet his firm's new client, Count Dracula, only to discover the horrible truth that Dracula is a vampire and seeking new hunting grounds in England. Back home, Harker's fiancee, Mina Murray, and her friend Lucy Westenra, face danger from Dracula. This graphic novel adaptation of Stoker's novel includes a biography of Stoker, information about vampires, a list of eighteenth and nineteenth century tales of mystery and horror, a list of some of the film adaptations, and more.

Part of Barron's Graphic Classics series

Frankenstein; illustrated by Penko Gelev ; retold by Fiona MacDonald. Barron's 2008 48p. Illustration
Grades: 4 5 6 7 8 9   **741.5; Fic**
1. Horror graphic novels; 2. Novelists; 3. Science fiction graphic novels; 4. Shelley, Mary Wollstonecraft, 1797-1851 — Adaptations; 5. Graphic novels
978-0-7641-6057-8, $15.99; 978-0-7641-3781-5 (pa), $8.99

LC 2006-937854

Victor Frankenstein is a brilliant medical student who has discovered the secret of bringing dead matter to life. Determined to create a living being, he gathers materials from graveyards and slaughterhouses, and creates a giant of superhuman strength, but his creature is also hideous. Horrified by what he has done, Frankenstein flees, and the creature he left behind plans his revenge. This graphic novel adaptation includes a brief biography of Shelley, a timeline of scientific and medical discoveries made during Shelley's lifetime, information on various film adaptations of her story, and more.

Part of Barron's Graphic Classics series

Gianopoulos, Andrea
The **Attractive** Story of Magnetism with Max Axiom, Super Scientist by Andrea Gianopoulos ; illustrated by Cynthia Martin and Barbara Schulz. Capstone Press 2007 32p. Illustration
Grades: 3 4 5 6 7 8 9   **538; 741.5**
1. Magnetism; 2. Magnets; 3. Graphic novels
978-1-4296-0141-2, $25.26

LC 2007002262

This book uses the graphic novel format to follow the adventures of super scientist Max Axiom as he explains the science behind magnetism. The book includes additional facts and a list of books for further reading.

Part of the Graphic Science series.

Giarrusso, Chris
G-Man, volume 1: learning to fly. Image Comics 2010 Un Illustration
Grades: 3 4 5 6   **741.5; Fic**
1. Humorous graphic novels; 2. Superhero graphic novels; 3. Graphic novels
978-1-60706-270-7 (pa), $9.99; 1-60706-270-4 (pa)

Mikey G. is G-Man, the newest superhero on the block, in a town full of superheroes (he made his cape from the family's magic blanket). His friends Billy Demon, Tan Man, Sparky, and the Suntrooper are all ready to help, but G-Man also has to deal with his older brother Great Man (aka Dave) and their superhero dad, Mr. G.

This "hits all the right notes, from its friendly cartoon figures to the occasionally hilarious one-liners." Booklist

This is a new edition, in a larger size and with a new ISBN

Other titles in this series are: Cape crisis (2010); Coming home (2013)

G-Man, volume 2: cape crisis. Image comics 2010 Un Illustration
Grades: 3 4 5 6 7 8   **741.5; Fic**
1. Humorous graphic novels; 2. Superhero graphic novels; 3. Graphic novels
978-1-60706-271-4, $9.99

The trouble starts when G-Man (aka Mikey) tells everyone that his magic cape gives him the power to fly; then everyone wants to fly. When he gives them bracelets made from the scraps of the magic blanket, everyone starts flying around and causing trouble. Then, when G-Man rounds up all the bracelets, he finds older brother Great Man (aka Dave) is selling more bracelets for $1,000 apiece. However, dividing up the magic into so many small bits is not only allowing unscrupulous people to commit crimes with their new powers, it is causing instabilities that could backfire disastrously. And that's exactly what happens. Now the brothers have to go on a quest to find the one being who can restore the magic to G-Man's cape.

Gieter, De
Papyrus: the Rameses' revenge. Cinebook 2007 48p. Illustration
Grades: 3 4 5 6 7 8   **741.5; Fic**
1. Adventure graphic novels; 2. Egypt — History; 3. Graphic novels
978-1-905460-35-9, $11.95

In ancient Egypt, Papyrus is a mischievous boy who has become a friend of the Princess Theti-Cheri, daughter of the Pharaoh, thanks to the magic sword that protects him. When Theti-Cheri insists on traveling down the Nile to see Rameses' Temple with just Papyrus, their friend Imhotep, and just a few guards, Papyrus is sure they will run into trouble. At the temple, they face two rival bands of plunderers who seek the treasure in the temple.

Part of the Papyrus series, originally published in France as Papyrus La Vengeance des Ramses.

Gilroy, Henry
Transformers animated, volume 4; Henry Gilroy and Marty Isenberg ; adapted by Zachary Rau. IDW Publishing 2008 Un Illustration
Grades: 2 3 4 5 6 7 8   **741.5; Fic**
1. Robots; 2. Science fiction graphic novels; 3. Transformers (Fictional characters); 4. Graphic novels
978-1-60010-217-2, $7.99

This volume adapts two of the animated television series' episodes. On Halloween, Blackarachnia returns to give the Autobots trouble in "Along Came a Spider." Then, in "Sound and Fury," Sumdac's birthday present to Sari causes chaos for all the robots in New Detroit, especially since Megatron helped Sumdac make Soundwave . . .

Gilson

Melusine: Halloween; illustrated by Clarke ; translated by Erica Jeffrey. Cinebook Ltd 2007 48p. Illustration

Grades: 3 4 5 6 7 8   **741.5; Fic**
1. Humorous graphic novels; 2. Witches; 3. Graphic novels

978-1-905460-34-2, $11.95

Melusine is a sorcerer's apprentice who wants to become a powerful witch. However, she's not always successful. Her friend Cancrelune can never get her potions right, and cousin Melisande is a fairy who always wants to make everything light, pretty, and fun. This volume collects stories that focus on Halloween, with pumpkin carving, monster calling, and children going trick-or-treating.

First published 2000 in France

Melusine: love potions. Cinebook 2010 48p. Illustration

Grades: 3 4 5 6 7 8

741.5; Fic
1. Humorous graphic novels; 2. Witches; 3. Graphic novels

978-1-84918-005-4, $11.95

Courtesy of Cinebook, Ltd.

Young witch in training Melusine tries to make love potions, in between encounters with her clumsy fellow student Cancrelune and various villagers who want to fall in love (or not). The full-color cartoony art keeps the witches, vampires, ghosts, dragons, and monsters more humorous looking than spooky.

Originally published in France as Melusine 5 Philtres d'amour

Melusine: The vampire's ball. Cinebook Ltd. 2008 48p. Illustration

Grades: 3 4 5 6 7 8   **741.5; Fic**
1. Humorous graphic novels; 2. Witches; 3. Graphic novels

978-1-905460-69-4, $11.95

The young witch Melusine is back for more fun with all her family, including witches Adrazelle and Cancrelune, the ghostly Madam and vampire Master of the haunted castle, and more. Melusine tries to make different potions, turns toads into dragons and vice versa, tries to avoid too many cleaning chores in the castle, and more. Some of the situations are slightly gruesome, as when a particularly nasty knight ends up eaten by a monstrous tree in the forest, or when the male vampires get too drunk to get under cover before sunrise and turn into piles of ash.

Glaser, Jason

The **Buffalo** Soldiers and the American West. Capstone Press 2005 32p. Illustration

Grades: 3 4 5 6 7 8 9   **741.5; 978**
1. African American soldiers; 2. West (US); 3. Graphic novels

0-7368-4966-1, $25.26

LC 2005006527

In graphic novel format, this book tells the story of the African American soldiers known as Buffalo Soldiers, who fought against Native Americans and protected the Western Frontier of the United States. The book includes additional information about the Buffalo Soldiers, a bibliography, and a list of books for further reading.

Part of the Graphic History series.

Jackie Robinson: Baseball's Great Pioneer. Capstone Press 2005 32p. Illustration

Grades: 3 4 5 6 7 8 9   **741.5; 796.357'092; 796.357**
1. African American athletes; 2. Baseball — Biography; 3. Biographical graphic novels; 4. Robinson, Jackie, 1919-1972; 5. Graphic novels

0-7368-463-6, $25.26

LC 2005003345

In graphic novel format, this book tells the life story of Jackie Robinson and his professional baseball career that broke the "color barrier." The book includes additional information about Robinson, including the back of a baseball card that shows his playing statistics for the 1947-1956 seasons, a bibliography, and a list of books for further reading.

Part of the Graphic Biographies series.

John Brown's raid on Harper's Ferry. Capstone Press 2005 32p. Illustration

Grades: 3 4 5 6 7 8 9   **741.5; 973.7**
1. Harpers Ferry (W Va) — History — John Brown's Raid, 1859; 2. Graphic novels

0-7368-4369-8, $25.26

LC 2004029083

This book recounts the story of John Brown's failed rebellion in Harpers Ferry in 1859, intended to start a massive slave uprising in the South and the establishment of a state in the Allegheny Mountains for freed slaves. It includes additional information, a glossary, a list of books for further reading, and more.

Part of the Graphic Library, Graphic History series.

Patrick Henry: Liberty or Death. Capstone Press 2006 32p. Illustration

Grades: 3 4 5 6 7 8 9   **741.5; 973.3; 92**
1. Biographical graphic novels; 2. Henry, Patrick, 1736-1799; 3. Graphic novels

0-7368-4970-X, $25.26

LC 2005004011

This book uses the comic book format to recount highlights of the life story of Patrick Henry, who is known as the "Voice of the American Revolution." It includes additional information, a glossary, a list of books for further reading, and more.

Part of the Graphic Library, Graphic Biographies series.

Goodwin, Vincent

Sir Arthur Conan Doyle's The adventure of the blue carbuncle. Adapted by Vincent Goodwin; illustrated by Ben Dunn. Magic Wagon 2012 48 p. Color illustration (Graphic novel adventures of Sherlock Holmes)

Grades: 2 3 4   **741.5/973; Fic**
1. Doyle, Arthur Conan, Sir,1859-1930 — Adaptations; 2. Holmes, Sherlock (Fictional character); 3. Holmes,

Sherlock (Fictional character) — Juvenile fiction; 4. Mystery and detective stories; 5. Mystery fiction — Juvenile fiction; 6. Mystery graphic novels
1616418915; 9781616418915, $29.93; 9781614788379, $20.95

LC 2011052251

This graphic novel, adapted by Vincent Goodwin, illustrated by Ben Dunn, retells a mystery story featuring Sir Arthur Conan Doyle's detective Sherlock Holmes. "Holmes must discover how the Countess of Morcar's stolen jewel came to be inside a Christmas goose! The mystery begins with a street fight and ends with a full confession. Join the wild goose chase with Sherlock Holmes in the adventure of the blue carbuncle." (Publisher's note)

Includes bibliographical references (p. 47).

Sir Arthur Conan Doyle's The adventure of the Red-Headed League. ABDO/Magic Wagon 2010 48p. Illustration
Grades: 4 5 6 7 8 9
741.5; Fic
1. Doyle, Arthur Conan Sir, 1859-1930 — Adaptations; 2. Holmes, Sherlock (Fictional character); 3. Mystery graphic novels; 4. Novelists; 5. Graphic novels
978-1-60270-726-9, $28.50; 1-60270-726-X

Courtesy of ABDO Publishing Group/Magic Wagon

LC 2009-32460

Consulting detective Sherlock Holmes and his friend Dr. John Watson take the case of Jabez Wilson, an ordinary tradesman with an extraordinary tale. His pawn shop assistant had found an advertisement in the newspaper asking for eligible men to apply for membership in The RedHeaded League, and he helped Mr. Wilson fight through a crowd of redheaded men and to be accepted into the League. Wilson was paid four pounds a week for a few hours' work copying out of an encyclopedia; then suddenly, all trace of the League disappeared. He wants Holmes to find out what has happened. This graphic novel adaptation has been done by Goodwin and Dunn, who are experienced creators with Antarctic Press (Dunn started the publishing house). The book includes a brief glossary, a short biography of Doyle, a listing of his published works, and a short sketching lesson by Dunn.

Part of The Graphic Novel Adventures of Sherlock Holmes

Sir Arthur Conan Doyle's The adventure of the speckled band. Adapted by, Vincent Goodwin; illustrated by, Ben Dunn. ABDO/Magic Wagon 2010 48p. Illustration
Grades: 4 5 6 7 8 9
741.5; Fic
1. Doyle, Arthur Conan Sir, 1859-1930 — Adaptations; 2. Holmes, Sherlock (Fictional character); 3. Mystery graphic novels; 4. Mystery writers
978-1-60270-727-6, $28.50; 1-60270-727-8

LC 2009-32461

Consulting detective Sherlock Holmes and his partner Dr. John Watson come to the aid of Miss Helen Stoner. After

moving back to England from India with their stepfather, Helen's twin sister died under mysterious circumstances. Now, two years later, Helen knows something is terribly wrong in her stepfather's house. Both men suspect the gypsies that Dr. Roylott, the stepfather, has allowed to live on his property, but Holmes soon suspects something else. This graphic novel adaptation has been done by Goodwin and Dunn, who are experienced creators with Antarctic Press (Dunn started the publishing house). The book includes a brief glossary, a short biography of Doyle, a listing of his published works, and a short sketching lesson by Dunn.

Courtesy of ABDO Publishing Group/Magic Wagon

Part of The Graphic Novel Adventures of Sherlock Holmes

Sir Arthur Conan Doyle's, The adventure of the Abbey Grange. ABDO/Magic Wagon 2010 48p. Illustration
Grades: 4 5 6 7 8 9
741.5; Fic
1. Doyle, Arthur Conan Sir, 1859-1930 — Adaptations; 2. Holmes, Sherlock (Fictional character); 3. Mystery graphic novels; 4. Mystery writers
978-1-60270-722-1, $28.50; 1-60270-722-7

A robbery and murder have occurred, and Sir Eustace Brackenstall is dead. His wife and maid say that a gang of robbers invaded their home, tied up Lady Brackenstall and killed Sir Eustace, but Holmes doesn't believe

Courtesy of ABDO Publishing Group/Magic Wagon

their story. As he investigates, he learns that Sir Eustace was a cruel man, and even though Lady Brackenstall has lied, Holmes sympathizes with her. This book adapts Doyle's short story; it includes a short glossary, a brief biography of Doyle, a short drawing lesson, and a list of Doyle's other writings. Dunn's art depicts Holmes and Dr. Watson as younger men, but continues the stereotypical portrayal of Holmes with the deerstalker cap and shoulder caped coat which Doyle never had him wear in the original stories.

Part of The Graphic Novel Adventures of Sherlock Holmes series.

Sir Arthur Conan Doyle's, The adventure of the dancing men. ABDO/Magic Wagon 2010 48p. Illustration
Grades: 4 5 6 7 8 9
1. Doyle, Arthur Conan Sir, 1859-1930 — Adaptations; 2. Holmes, Sherlock (Fictional character); 3. Mystery graphic novels; 4. Mystery writers
978-1-60270-723-8, $28.50; 1-60270-723-5

When strange writing that looks like dancing men starts appearing around the estate of Mr. Cubitt, he comes to Sherlock Holmes for help. He thinks it's the work of pranksters, but his American wife seems frightened. As he brings more of the writing samples to Holmes, the detective works on the case, but he may not be able to solve it before tragedy strikes the Cubitts. This book adapts Doyle's short story; it includes a short glossary, a brief biography of Doyle, a short drawing lesson, and a list of Doyle's other writings. Dunn's art depicts Holmes and Dr. Watson as younger men, but continues the stereotypical portrayal of Holmes with the deerstalker cap and shoulder caped coat which Doyle never had him wear in the original stories.

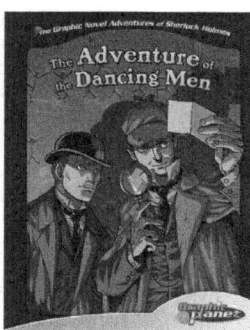

Courtesy of ABDO Publishing Group/Magic Wagon

Part of The Graphic Novel Adventures of Sherlock Holmes series

Sir Arthur Conan Doyle's, The adventure of the empty house. ABDO/Magic Wagon 2010 48p. Illustration

Courtesy of ABDO Publishing Group/Magic Wagon

Grades: 4 5 6 7 8 9   **741.5; Fic**
1. Doyle, Arthur Conan Sir, 1859-1930 — Adaptations; 2. Holmes, Sherlock (Fictional character); 3. Mystery graphic novels; 4. Mystery writers
978-1-60270-724-5, $28.50; 1-60270-724-3

Three years before, Dr. Watson witnessed the death of his friend Sherlock Holmes, who plummeted to his death along with archvillain Dr. Moriarty. Now, Inspector Lestrade asks Watson's help in a puzzling murder case, but it stumps Watson as well. Then, to his utter surprise, Holmes comes to him, explaining that he pretended to die. Together again, the two men work on the case, hoping to catch one of Moriarty's dangerous henchmen. This graphic novel adapts Doyle's original story which was the "comeback" after killing Holmes in "The Final Problem." The art depicts Watson as a fairly young man, but persists in putting Holmes into the deerstalker cap and caped overcoat which Doyle's Holmes never wore. The book includes a brief drawing lesson, a short glossary, brief biography of Doyle, and a listing of his other writings.

Part of The Graphic Novel Adventures of Sherlock Holmes

Sir Arthur Conan Doyle's, the adventure of the Norwood Builder. ABDO/Magic Wagon 2010 48p. Illustration
Grades: 4 5 6 7 8 9   **741.5; Fic**

1. Holmes, Sherlock (Fictional character); 2. Mystery graphic novels; 3. Graphic novels
978-1-60270-725-2, $28.50; 1-60270-725-1
LC 2009-32459

Courtesy of ABDO Publishing Group/Magic Wagon

Young solicitor Mr. McFarlane begs Holmes to clear his name when he's accused of the murder of Jonas Oldacre, the Norwood Builder. Inspector Lestrade thinks he has a solid case, and the evidence seems to implicate McFarlane, especially since Mr. Oldacre's new will made McFarlane his sole heir. Holmes points to the lack of a body, and digs up more clues in his quest to save McFarlane. This graphic novel adaptation of Doyle's short story retains the suspense of the original, but perpetuates the stereotypical portrayals of Holmes in the deerstalker and caped coat which he never wore in the original stories. The book includes a brief drawing lesson, a short glossary, a brief biography of Doyle, and a listing of his other writings.

Part of The Graphic Novel Adventures of Sherlock Holmes

Goosebumps: Terror Trips
Adapted by Jill Thompson, Jamie Tolagson, and Amy Kim Ganter. Scholastic/Graphix 2007 137p. Illustration
Grades: 4 5 6 7 8 9   **741.5; Fic**
1. Horror graphic novels; 2. Stine, R L — Adaptations; 3. Graphic novels
978-0-439-85780-2, $8.99

Stine's Goosebumps series was very popular years ago, and is enjoying a resurgence of popularity with new editions of the prose books. The graphic novel adaptations, all done by well-known independent comics creators, bring the stories to a new audience. Goosebumps: Creepy Creatures is also available.

This volume adapts three of Stine's Goosebumps novels into graphic novel format. Noted independent comic creator Thompson adapts One Day at Horrorland, about one family's ordeal in a very strange, all-too-realistic amusement park. Canadian artist Tolagson adapts A Shocker on Shock Street, which depicts the horrific adventures of two kids on a movie studio lot where the horror is more than just special effects. Global manga creator Ganter adapts Deep Trouble, in which a brother and sister find a real mermaid.

Gorelick, Victor
Archie in Strange change. Edited by Nelson Ribeiro & Victor Gorelick.. ABDO Publishing Group/Spotlight 2007 Un Illustration
Grades: 3 4 5 6 7 8   **741.5; Fic**
1. Andrews, Archie (Fictional character); 2. Humorous graphic novels; 3. Graphic novels
978-1-59961-262-1, $24.21

LC 2006-49671

This volume includes 10 short comics stories featuring Archie Andrews and all the gang from Riverdale. Among the stories, Archie can't find a good place to hang his hammock; Mr. Weatherbee has a wild time at the fair as he tries to hide from Archie and gets lost in the hall of mirrors, trapped on a roller coaster, and blunders into the rodeo; Mr. Lodge takes Dilton and Archie for a ride in his computerized car and loses control because of Archie's handheld electronic game; Little Archie has an adventure in "The Strange Case of the Mystery Map;" and more fun.

Part of the Archie digest library; this is a revision of Archie Digest Magazine issue #183 (Oct. 2001).

Archie in top this!. Edited by Nelson Ribeiro & Victor Gorelick. Spotlight 2007 Un Illustration
Grades: 3 4 5 6 7 8   **741.5; Fic**
1. Andrews, Archie (Fictional character); 2. Humorous graphic novels; 3. Graphic novels
978-1-59961-263-8, $24.21
                                    LC 2006-49938
This is a library bound edition of Archie digest magazine issue #178 from Archie Comics, originally published in March 2001. It includes 18 short comics stories set in Riverdale and starring all the Archie Comics characters Archie, Reggie, Jughead, Betty, Veronica, Miss Grundy, Mr. Weatherbee, and others. In one story, Archie actually dates a different girl, Melanie, who works at the local theater; he keeps trying to find fun things to do, but Melanie just loves movies.

Revision of issue no. 178 (March 2001) of Archie digest magazine.

Jughead with Archie in A day to remember. Edited by Nelson Ribeiro & Victor Gorelick. ABDO Publishing/Spotlight 2007 Un Illustration
Grades: 3 4 5 6 7 8   **741.5; Fic**
1. Andrews, Archie (Fictional character); 2. Humorous graphic novels; 3. Jones, Jughead (Fictional character)
978-1-59961-272-0, $24.21
                                    LC 2006-50551
This is a library bound edition of Jughead with Archie digest magazine issue #189 from Archie Comics, originally published in February 2004. It includes 16 short comics stories set in Riverdale and starring all the Archie Comics characters Archie, Reggie, Jughead, Betty, Veronica, Miss Grundy, Mr. Weatherbee, and others. Archie and Jughead are longtime pals who get into all kinds of trouble at school, usually together.

Revision of issue no. 189 (Feb. 2004) of Jughead with Archie digest magazine.

Laugh with fore!. Edited by Nelson Ribeiro & Victor Gorelick. ABDO Publishing Group/Spotlight 2007 Un Illustration
Grades: 3 4 5 6 7 8   **741.5; Fic**
1. Andrews, Archie (Fictional character); 2. Humorous graphic novels; 3. Graphic novels
978-1-59961-279-9, $24.21
                                    LC 2006-49180
This volume includes 18 short comics stories featuring Archie Andrews and all the gang from Riverdale. Among the stories, Archie tries to find ways to reduce stress that result in lots of trouble, including a beating from Moose; the teens try to help Mr. Weatherbee get more publicity to keep the

summer camp going; Josie and the Pussycats feature in a couple of stories; and lots more.

Part of the Archie digest library; this is a revision of Laugh Digest Magazine issue #168 (Sept. 2001).

Goscinny
The **tenderfoot**: Lucky Luke adventure, vol. 13. Cinbook Ltd. 2008 48p. Illustration
Grades: 3 4 5 6 7 8   **791.5; Fic**
1. Humorous graphic novels; 2. Western stories; 3. Graphic novels
978-1-905460-65-6, $11.95
When Rancher Baddy passes away, his heir, an Englishman, comes to town to take over the ranch. Jack Ready wants the ranch, so he plans to give the "tenderfoot" reasons to go away. When Lucky Luke, who can shoot faster than his shadow, helps Waldo get through the "welcoming ceremonies" and the phlegmatic Englishman shows he's more than a match for anything the cowboys can think to do, Jack Ready comes up with the only other plan that might work—frame Waldo for Jack's murder. The book has no real violence, but it does show drinking and gambling in the saloon. While some readers might fret over the stereotyping of the Native American characters, they should note that every single character in the book, including Lucky Luke himself, is a caricature of a "type," from rough cowboy to noble Indian, to Chinese, to hoity-toity Englishmen, to gunfighters. This is translated from the original French stories written by Rene Goscinny, who also wrote Asterix.

Goscinny, Rene
Asterix and Caesar's Gift. Orion/Sterling Publishing 2004 48p. Illustration
Grades: 4 5 6 7 8 9 10 11 12 Adult   **741.5; Fic**
1. Asterix (Fictional character); 2. Humorous graphic novels
0-75286-645-1, $12.95; 0-75286-646-X (pa)
When Legionary Tremensdelirius gets the title deeds to the little Gaulish village as a bonus, he swaps them with tavern landlord Orthopaedix for a drink. Funnily enough, Asterix and his friends aren't keen to hand over their village to anyone else. After a chieftaincy election campaign and a showdown with the Romans, both events fiercely contested, can all still end well?

Asterix and Cleopatra. Orion/Sterling Publishing 2004 48p. Illustration
Grades: 4 5 6 7 8 9 10 11 12 Adult   **741.5; Fic**
1. Asterix (Fictional character); 2. Humorous graphic novels
0-75286-606-0, $12.95; 0-75286-607-9 (pb)
How can lovely Queen Cleopatra show Julius Caesar that ancient Egypt is still a great nation" Her architect Edifis recruits his Gaulish friends to help him build a magnificent palace within three months. There are villainous saboteurs to be outwitted, but Asterix, Obelix, and Getafix still find time to go sight-seeing, and leave their mark on the Pyramids and the Sphinx's nose.

Asterix and the Banquet. Orion/Sterling Publishing 2004 48p. Illustration
Grades: 4 5 6 7 8 9 10 11 12 Adult   **741.5; Fic**

1. Asterix (Fictional character); 2. Humorous graphic novels

0-75286-608-0, $12.95; 0-75286-609-5 (pa)

When the Romans try to contain the threat from the Gaulish village by building a stockade around it, Asterix and Obelix lay a bet with them. They will break out and claim their right to travel freely all over Gaul, collecting the local delicacies and bringing them back to prove their point. Ham from Lutetia, fizzy wine from Durocortorum, fish stew from Massilia in the south ... soon their shopping bag is full. Outwitting Romans, a couple of treacherous Gauls, and the thieves Villanus and Unscrupulus, they set off for home ... but who's that little dog who has been following them all the way from Lutetia?

Asterix and the Cauldron. Orion/Sterling Publishing 2004 48p. Illustration

Grades: 4 5 6 7 8 9 10 11 12 Adult   **741.5; Fic**

1. Asterix (Fictional character); 2. Humorous graphic novels

0-75286-629-X, $9.95

There's financial skulduggery in ancient Gaul. When local Chief Whosemoralsarelastix wants a cauldron full of money kept out of Roman hands, the cash disappears while Asterix is guarding it. He and Obelix must earn enough to repay it through fairground gladiatorial contests, trendy theatrical performances, even bank robbery - they'll try anything. But whose morals are really elastic? And how to the pirates, just for once, get an unexpected bonus?

Asterix and the Class Act. Orion/Sterling Publishing 2004 56p. Illustration

Grades: 4 5 6 7 8 9 10 11 12 Adult   **741.5; Fic**

1. Asterix (Fictional character); 2. Humorous graphic novels

0-75286-068-2, $12.95; 0-75286-640-0 (pa)

This volume collects 14 stories, including the day Asterix and Obelix were born (in the middle of a fish fight); how Obelix goes back to school; fashion in ancient Gaul; how Dogmatix helps the village cockerel win a duel, and how he's adopted as a Roman mascot; Obelix's adventures under the mistletoe; the bid for the very first Gaulish Olympics, and more.

★ **Asterix** the Gaul. [by] René Goscinny and Albert Uderzo. Orion Media 2004 48p. Illustration; Map

Grades: 4 5 6 7 8 9 10 11 12   **741.5; Fic**

1. France — History; 2. Humorous graphic novels

0-7528-6604-4, $12.95; 0-7528-6605-2 (pa), $9.95

Meet Asterix, a diminutive but extremely strong Gaul living in ancient France during the time of the Roman Republic. Together with his friend Obelix, Asterix continually outwits the Roman Legionnaires sent to conquer Gaul for Julius Caesar. Full of puns and outrageous humor, the books also manage to teach a lot of history. This is the first in a long-running series of graphic novels translated from the original French.

Translated from the French

Other titles in this series are: Asterix and Caesar's Gift; Asterix and Cleopatra; Asterix and the actress; Asterix and the banquet; Asterix and the big fight; Asterix and the cauldron; Asterix and the Goths; Asterix and the Great Crossing; Asterix and the laurel wreath; Asterix the legionary; Asterix and the Normans; Asterix and the Roman Agent; Asterix and the soothsayer; Asterix at the Olympic Games; Asterix in Belgium; Asterix in Britain; Asterix in Corsica; Asterix in Spain; Asterix in Switzerland; Asterix Obelix and Co.; Asterix the gladiator; Asterix The Mansions of the Gods

Asterix and the Laurel Wreath. Orion/Sterling Publishing 2004 48p. Illustration

Grades: 4 5 6 7 8 9 10 11 12 Adult   **741.5; Fic**

1. Asterix (Fictional character); 2. Humorous graphic novels

0-75286-636-2, $12.95; 0-75286-637-0 (pa)

Chief Vitalstatistix rashly invites his brother-in-law to dine on a stew seasoned with Caesar's laurel wreath, so Asterix and Obelix must to go Rome to fetch those laurels. Hoping to get access to Caesar, they sell themselves as slaves, but can they do a deal with the corrupt Goldendelicius to swap the laurels for parsley?

Asterix in Britain. Orion/Sterling Publishing 2004 48p. Illustration

Grades: 4 5 6 7 8 9 10 11 12 Adult   **741.5; Fic**

1. Asterix (Fictional character); 2. Humorous graphic novels

0-85286-618-4, $12.95; 0-75286-619-2 (pa)

The Romans have invaded Britain, but one village still holds out. Asterix and Obelix come to help, with a barrel of magic potion in hand. But to deliver the precious brew, the Gaulish heroes must face fog, rain, bad food, warm beer, and the Romans too.

Asterix the Legionary. Orion/Sterling Publishing 2004 48p. Illustration

Grades: 4 5 6 7 8 9 10 11 12 Adult   **741.5; Fic**

1. Asterix (Fictional character); 2. Humorous graphic novels

0-75286-620-6, $12.95; 0-75286-621-4 (pa)

It's off to the wars for Asterix and Obelix: they've enlisted as legionnaires in order to rescue Tragicomix, whom the Romans forcibly conscripted. The two find Tragicomix and succeed in causing the biggest commotion ever on a battlefield.

The **Caliph's** vacation. Cinebook Ltd 2008 48p. Illustration

Grades: 3 4 5 6 7 8   **741.5; Fic**

1. Humorous graphic novels; 2. Graphic novels

978-1-905460-61-8, $11.95

Iznogoud, the Grand Vizier of Baghdad the Magnificent, wants to be Caliph, and he hatches all kinds of schemes to do in the good, kindhearted, not-too-bright Caliph, Haroun Al Plassid. First, they go to the beach, where Iznogoud and his henchman Wa'at Alahf try to drown him (the Caliph floats), send him into shark-infested waters (his suntan oil reeks), and other attempts that end up nearly doing in Iznogoud. A scheme to use a weather wizard to kill the Caliph with winter snow ends up with everyone enjoying a ski vacation. Then Iznogoud comes up with a poisoned elixir but can't get the Caliph to drink it. Goscinny is best known in the U.S. for his Asterix comics, but Iznogoud is just as filled with puns and humor, with a villain as the main character. Readers will enjoy the Wile E. Coyote type of hijinks.

First published 2000 in France

Dalton City: a Lucky Luke adventure. Cinebook 2007 48p. Illustration

Grades: 3 4 5 6 7 8   **741.5; Fic**

1. Humorous graphic novels; 2. Western stories; 3. Graphic novels

978-1-905460-13-7, $9.99

Goscinny, cocreator of Asterix, gives readers his wacky version of the American Old West in the Lucky Luke Adventures. Luke is a traveling good guy, who shoots faster than his shadow. He cleans up Fenton City, a festering sore of depravity in Texas, by capturing Dean Fenton, the boss of the town. Fenton ends up in the same prison as the Dalton brothers, a gang of not-too-smart outlaws that Luke keeps having to put away. They break out of the prison and take over Fenton City, calling it Dalton City. When Lucky Luke shows up, they ask him for advice on how to make the town a haven for outlaws, and Luke sees his chance to round up a whole lot of bad guys.

Part of the Lucky Luke Adventures series, originally published in France as Lucky Luke Dalton City.

Gould, Jane H.

George Washington Carver. By Jane Gould. PowerKids Press 2013 24 p. Color illustration

Grades: 3 4 5 6   **630.92; B**

1. African American agriculturists — Biography — Juvenile literature; 2. African American educators — Biography — Juvenile literature; 3. African American inventors; 4. African American scientists — Biography — Juvenile literature; 5. Agriculturists — United States — Biography — Juvenile literature; 6. Carver, George Washington, 1864?-1943 — Juvenile literature; 7. Peanuts — United States — History — Juvenile literature

1477700781; 9781477700785, $25.25; 9781477701416, $10.60; 9781477701423

LC 2012018689

In this biography of inventor George Washington Carver, author Jane Gould "provides the requisite biographical details, including Carver's early . . . separation from his mother, but also traces themes of his career, drawing connections between his kind masters" waste-not values and his future devotion to finding new uses for farm by-products. (Booklist)

Includes index.

Steve Jobs. By Jane Gould. PowerKids Press 2013 24 p.

Grades: 3 4 5 6

338.7/6100416092; 338.7; B

1. Apple, Inc — History — Juvenile literature; 2. Businessmen — United States — Biography — Juvenile literature; 3. Computer engineers — United States — Biography — Juvenile literature; 4. Inventors; 5. Jobs, Steve, 1955-2011 — Juvenile literature

1477700803; 9781477700808, $25.25; 9781477701454; 9781477701461

LC 2012020633

This graphic novel by Jane Gould is a biography of Steven Jobs, "best known for being a co-founder of Apple Inc. Before Apple Inc., he was a brilliant designer and inventor who approached business with an unexpected savvy and joy of discovery. Jobs created gadgets that transformed today's digital era." (Publisher's note)

Includes index.

Gownley, Jimmy

Amelia rules!: The meaning of life—and other stuff. Written and illustrated by Jimmy Gownley. Atheneum Books for Young Readers 2011 147p. Illustration

Grades: 3 4 5 6

741.5; 741

1. Friendship; 2. Humorous graphic novels

978-1-4169861-3-3, $19.99; 1-4169861-3-8; 978-1-4169861-2-6 (pa), $10.99; 1-4169861-2-X (pa)

Courtesy of Antheneum Books for Young Readers

LC 2011018407

★ **Amelia** Rules! Volume Three: Superheroes. Renaissance Press 2006 174p. Illustration

Grades: 3 4 5 6   **741.5; Fic**

1. Friendship; 2. Humorous graphic novels

9780971216969, $11.99

This third volume of Amelia Rules! contains one storyline, about the summer after fourth grade. First, Amelia faces the possibility of another move (across town); then new friends Trishia and Ninja Joan join Amelia and Rhonda, while Reggie and Pajama Man fight crime - actually, the Legion of Steves. The guys even team up with the Park Terrace Ninjas. In the middle of all the summer fun, Amelia learns Trishia's terrible secret and doesn't know how to help. Originally published as Amelia Rules! issues #11-16.

Courtesy of Antheneum Books for Young Readers

Amelia rules! True things (adults don't want kids to know). Atheneum Books for Young Readers 2010 163p.

Grades: 3 4 5 6   **741.5; 741**

1. Friendship; 2. Humorous graphic novels

978-1-4169-8609-6 (pa), $10.99; 1-4169-8609-X (pa)

Amelia rules: The tweenage guide to not being unpopular. Atheneum Books for Young Readers 2010 187p.

Grades: 3 4 5 6

741; 741.5

1. Friendship; 2. Humorous graphic novels

978-1-4169-8610-2, $18.99; 1-4169-8610-3; 978-1-4169-8608-9 (pa), $10.99; 1-4169-8608-1 (pa)

LC 2009053665

Courtesy of Antheneum Books for Young Readers

★ **Amelia** rules! when the past is a present. Renaissance Press 2008 168p. Illustration

Grades: 3 4 5 6   **741.5; Fic**
1. Friendship; 2. Humorous graphic novels
978-0-9712169-8-3, $24.95; 978-0-9712169-9-0 (pa), $11.99

The kids are now in fifth grade, and Amelia and Rhonda are officially friends and not enemies any more. Amelia is going to her first dance (with a boy no less "Kyle the ninja"), but she's not the only one with a date. Is Amelia's mom seeing someone too? Perhaps Reggie (a.k.a. Captain Amazing) can shed some light on the situation, by spying on their date. But it's not all fun for the 10-year-old spitfire. A good friend "Joan" reveals that her father will be deployed to Iraq with his job in the military, and it gets Amelia thinking about her own family, her past, and what it means for the present.

★ **Amelia** rules!: the whole world's crazy!. Renaissance Press 2003 176p.

Grades: 3 4 5 6   **741.5; Fic**
1. Family life; 2. Friendship; 3. Humorous graphic novels
0-9712169-3-2, $24.95; 0-9712169-2-4 (pa), $14.95

"Amelia . . . is getting used to life with her newly divorced mom and her hip, young aunt Tanner; settling in at a strange new school; and finding a group of friends. Amelia is no sweet innocent, nor are her three G.A.S.P (Gathering of Awesome Superpals) buddies: Reggie, superhero in the making; Rhonda, Amelia's tough bete noire with a fourth-grade "thing" for Reggie; and quiet, mysterious Pajamaman. Jealousy, meanness, sadness, and confusion, as well as surprising generosity, and love crisscross the pages in energetic, freewheeling, full-color cartoon art that unwraps a kid's-eye view of life honestly, poignantly, and with a hefty dollop of melodrama." Booklist

Other titles in this series are: Amelia rules!: What makes you happy? (2004); Amelia rules!: Superheroes (2005); Amelia rules! a very ninja Christmas (2009); Amelia rules! When the past is a present (2010); Amelia rules! The tweenage guide to not being unpopular (2010); Amelia rules! True things (adults don't want kids to know (2010); Amelia rules! The meaning of life. . . and other stuff (2011); Amelia rules! Her permanent record (2012)

★ **Her** permanent record. Written and illustrated by Jimmy Gownley. Atheneum Books for Young Readers 2012 144 p.

Grades: 3 4 5 6   **741.5**
1. Aunts — Fiction; 2. Friendship — Fiction; 3. Missing persons — Fiction; 4. School stories; 5. Schools — Fiction; 6. Voyages and travels — Fiction; 7. Graphic novels
1416986154; 9781416986140; 9781416986157, $19.99
                  LC 2011053039

This book is the eighth installment of the "Amelia Rules!" series by Jimmy Gownley. "With her new spot on the cheerleading squad, [and] Aunt Tanner's hordes of adoring fans, . . . Amelia's sailing seems remarkably smooth. Then Tanner disappears . . . sending Amelia into full panic mode. And when she boards a bus on an epic journey to find Tanner . . . it quickly becomes clear that if Amelia has learned anything in her eleven years, it's that life is never through with surprises." (Publisher's note)

Grahame, Kenneth
Classics illustrated deluxe # 1: the wind in the willows. NBM/Papercutz 2007 144p. Illustration

Grades: 3 4 5 6 7 8   **741.5; Fic**
1. Animals; 2. Fantasy graphic novels; 3. Humorous graphic novels; 4. Graphic novels
978-1-59707-095-9, $19.99; 978-1-59707-096-6 (pa), $13.95

Kenneth Grahame's classic story of the wild Mister Toad's misadventures and crazy enthusiasms that get him into great trouble from which his friends Badger, Mole, and Rat must extricate him gets a deluxe, full-color graphic novel treatment with art that looks like classic 1930s-style animation.

Gray, Harold
★ **Harold** Gray's Little Orphan Annie volume one: Will tomorrow evercome: the complete daily comics, 1924-27: Will tomorrow ever come? IDW Publishing 2008 385p. Illustration

Grades: 2 3 4 5 6 7 8 9 10 11 12 Adult   **741.5; Fic**
1. Adventure graphic novels; 2. Little Orphan Annie (Fictional character); 3. Orphans; 4. Graphic novels
978-1-60010-140-3, $39.99

Little Orphan Annie started as a daily newspaper comic strip in one newspaper, the New York Daily News, on August 5, 1924. It became a popular strip, syndicated to newspapers all over the world. It eventually became a Broadway musical, a hit movie, and Annie became an iconic character. This book is the first comprehensive collection of Gray's comic strip and is the first volume of a series planned to collect all of Gray's Little Orphan Annie strips. She is an orphan girl living in an orphanage, with an unscrupulous director who hires Annie out for work. When wealthy Mrs. Warbucks, trying to prove that she cares for the poor, takes Annie on a "trial" adoption, Annie eventually meets Oliver Warbucks, whom she calls "Daddy." As the strips go on, Annie undergoes many hardships and perils, facing everything with spunk and a positive attitude. She's no wilting girl, though "she can fight (she has a mean right hook) and will take on any bully. She rescues the dog she calls Sandy, who rewards her with a loyal friendship. This volume includes more than 1,000 comic strips, many of which haven't seen publication since their original newspaper appearance. During the first years of the strip's publication, the color Sunday comics had no connection to the weekday storylines, but a few Sunday pages are included in this book. This book may appeal most to adults who remember reading Little Orphan Annie in the "funnies" pages, but the stories will appeal to all ages. Contributing Editor Jeet Heer provides a biography of Harold Gray.

Gray-Wilburn, Renée
Earthquakes!. By Renee Gray-Wilburn; illustrated by Aleksandar Sotirovski. Capstone Press 2012 24 p. Color illustration

Grades: 1 2 3 4   **551.22**
1. Earthquakes — Juvenile literature; 2. Graphic novels
1429676051; 1429679506; 9781429676052, $23.32; 9781429679503, $5.95

                  LC 2011028740

This graphic novel, written by Renee Gray-Wilburn and illustrated by Aleksandar Sotirovski, is part of the "First Graphics: Wild Earth" series. The book explains the geophysics behind earthquakes, the methods used by earth scientists to measure them, and advice on how to stay safe when experiencing one.

Includes bibliographical references and index

Volcanoes!. By Renée Gray-Wilburn; illustrated by Aleksandar Sotirovski. Capstone Press 2012 24 p. Color illustration

Grades: 1 2 3 4   **551.21**
1. Earth sciences — Juvenile literature; 2. Volcanoes — Juvenile literature
142967606X; 9781429676069, $23.32

LC 2011028742

This graphic novel, written by Renee Gray-Wilburn and illustrated by Aleksandar Sotirovski, is part of the "First Graphics: Wild Earth" series. The book explains the geophysics behind volcanoes, the methods used by earth scientists to measure them, and advice on how to stay safe when experiencing the eruption from one.

Includes bibliographical references (p. 23) and index

Grayson, Devin
Am I blue. Udon with Long Vo, Charles Park, and Saka, art and colors ; Randy Gentile, letterer. ABDO Publishing Company/Spotlight 2006 Illustration

Grades: 4 5 6 7 8 9   **741.5; Fic**
1. Superhero graphic novels; 2. X-Men (Fictional characters); 3. Graphic novels
978-1-59961-052-8, $21.35

LC 2006-43970

The young members of the X-Men, including Kurt (Nightcrawler), Rogue, and Kitty (Shadowcat), must attend school in town as well as train at the Xavier Academy. They must conceal their identities as super powered mutants, which is difficult for Kurt since he is normally blue-skinned; he wears an image inducer that makes him appear like a normal human. When they are assigned an essay for English composition class: "What I am at home that I can't be at school," it bothers Kurt that he can't tell the truth. This book is a revised, hardbound edition of a Marvel Age comic book issue.

Part of the X-Men: Evolution series

Green, John
Phineas and Ferb: the chronicles of Meap. Disney Press 2010 32p. Illustration

Grades: 3 4 5 6   **741.5; Fic**
1. Humorous graphic novels; 2. Inventors; 3. Science fiction graphic novels; 4. Graphic novels
978-1-4231-2441-2, $4.99

It's summer vacation, and talkative Phineas and his silent brother Ferb, both super inventors, are busy having fun while their older sister Candace and her friends get their new custom-made Bango-Ru interactive dolls. Then Ferb fires a baseball into the air with his new gadget, and the ball zaps into space and knocks a spaceship out of orbit to crash into the boys' backyard. Its pilot looks adorable, like a cute Bango-Ru, in fact, and all it says is Meap. But Meap is looking for someone, who it turns out is Meap's archrival,

Mitch; and Mitch manages to capture everyone except Candace and Meap. Meanwhile the boys' pet platypus, Perry, is secretly an agent working to stop evil scientist Dr. Doofenschmirtz. This book adapts an episode of the animated series Phineas and Ferb, created by Dan Povenmire and Jeff "Swampy" Marsh, and which airs on the Disney Channel; it is illustrated with screen captures from the episode.

Phineas and Ferb: nothing but trouble. Disney Press 2010 32p. Illustration

Grades: 3 4 5 6   **741.5; Fic**
1. Humorous graphic novels; 2. Inventors; 3. Science fiction graphic novels; 4. Graphic novels
9781423124405, $4.99

Inventor brothers Phineas and Ferb and their friends take the gelatin molds made by Candace and her friends and create a swimming pool full of gelatin. Meanwhile, the boys' pet platypus Perry goes off on another secret mission to foil the latest evil plot of the evil Dr. Doofenshmirtz. This time, the mad scientist's "Turn-Everything-Evil-Nator" misses Perry, but hits the gelatin in the swimming pool, creating a gelatin monster. Then, when the family visits London, Candace and best friend Stacy decide to act like Sherlock Holmes to catch the boys in whatever plot they're hatching. And Agent P (Perry) must team up with British Agent Double 00 to stop Dr. Doofenshmirtz's latest scheme. This book adapts episodes of the animated series Phineas and Ferb, created by Dan Povenmire and Jeff "Swampy" Marsh, and which airs on the Disney Channel; it is illustrated with screen captures from the episodes.

Griffith, Saul
Howtoons: tools of mass construction. Dr. Saul Griffith, co-creator, writer & engineer; Nick Dragotta, co-creator, writer & artist; Ingrid Dragotta, project & book design; Arwen Griffith, editor; Joost Bonsen, co-creator & writer. Image Comics 2014 360 p. Illustration

Grades: 2 3 4 5 6 7   **741.5; 507.8**
1. Educational games; 2. Self-instruction
1632151014; 9781632151018, $17.99

"Follow Celine and Tucker as they learn through play with over 50 DIY projects! This brother-and-sister pair use everyday objects to invent toys that readers can build. Combining comics and real-life science and engineering principles, Howtoons are designed to encourage kids to become active participants in the world around them." (Publisher's note)

"The bright, somewhat chaotic artwork is designed to capture a kid's attention and imagination. The projects are not laid out in a staid, step-by-step manner, and several of them will require extra thought or adult assistance, but the variety is hard to beat, as the creators cover art, math, engineering, science, and more." Booklist

Grimm, Jacob
Classics illustrated delux #2: tales from the Brothers Grimm. Mazan, Philip Petit, Cecile Chicault ; [translation by Joe Johnson ; lettering by Ortho] Papercutz 2008 144p. Illustration

Grades: 3 4 5 6 7 8   **741.5; Fic**
1. Fantasy graphic novels; 2. Folklore; 3. Graphic novels

978-1-59707-101-7, $17.95

This volume of Papercutz's new Classics Illustrated Deluxe series collects French adaptations of four tales from the Brothers Grimm (Wilhelm and Jakob): Hansel and Gretel, Learning to Shudder, The Devil and the Three Golden Hairs, and The Valiant Little Tailor. These comic book adaptations don't shy away from showing scary monsters, saying rude things without using really bad language, and showing some violence.

Part of the Classics Illustrated Deluxe series

Grine, Chris.

Chickenhare. Chris Grine. Graphix / Scholastic 2013 160 p.

Grades: 4 5 6 7 8 9　　　　　　　　　　741.5

1. Animals; 2. Escapes — Juvenile fiction; 3. Taxidermy — Fiction

0545485088; 9780545485081, $10.99

LC 2012936214

Author Chris Grine presents a children's comic book. "What's a chickenhare" A cross between a chicken and a rabbit, of course. And that makes Chickenhare the rarest animal around! So when he and his turtle friend Abe are captured and sold to the evil taxidermist Klaus, they've got to find a way to escape before Klaus turns them into stuffed animals. With the help of two other strange creatures, Banjo and Meg, they might even get away. But with Klaus and his thugs hot on their trail, the adventure is only just beginning for this unlikely quartet of friends. (Publisher's note)

Gross, Allan

Cryptozoo Crew Volume 2: Call of the Thunderbird!. Jerry Carr, illustrator; NBM 2006 Un Illustration

Grades: 5 6 7 8 9 10 11 12 Adult　　　741.5; Fic

1. Humorous graphic novels; 2. Mythical animals; 3. Graphic novels

978-1-56163-466-8, $12.95

In this second volume, cryptozoologist Tork Darwyn suffers nightmares about a childhood encounter with the legendary thunderbird; it's been twenty years since that day, and he must return or be cursed. In the meantime, his teacher wife Tara has learned that her school will be shut down for lack of funding. Naturally, they travel together to Alaska to find out what is driving Tork to go there.

Guibert, Emmanuel

Ariol 2: Thunder Horse. By Emmanuel Guibert; illustrated by Marc Boutavant. Papercutz 2013 124 p.

Grades: 2 3 4 5　　　　　　　741.5/944; Fic

1. Children's literature; 2. Heroes and heroines — Fiction

1597074128; 9781597074124, $12.99

This book, written by Emmanuel Guibert and illustrated by Marc Boutavant, presents artwork and vignettes featuring the character Ariol. Ariol "[does] everything he can to grow up and become just like [his hero] the guardian of the stars." (Publisher's note)

"The author dares to depict the exclusionary, argumentative, self-centered ways children can sometimes behave." (Booklist)

Translated from the French.

Ariol: Happy as a pig. By Emmanuel Guibert; illustrated by Marc Boutavant. Papercutz 2013 124 p.

Grades: 2 3 4 5　　　　　　　　　　741.5

1. Donkeys; 2. Friendship; 3. Friendship — Juvenile fiction; 4. Pigs — Juvenile fiction; 5. Schools

159707487X; 9781597074872, $12.99

In this book, by Emmanuel Guibert and illustrated by Marc Boutavant, "Ariol's best friend, Ramono, is a pig. He's also loud, impulsive, [and] irresponsible. . . . Sneaking into a parking garage to play with fuses, carting grandpa's dog around in a wheelbarrow, wrestling matches with his sister; you may have thought Ariol was trouble enough, but you've never seen Ramono on the loose!" (Publisher's note)

"Boutavant's bright and buoyant illustrations and Guibert's pitch-perfect dialogue elevate the simple, everyday stories to illuminate something refreshingly honest about being a kid." Booklist

Ariol: Just a Donkey Like You and Me. Illustrated by Marc Boutavant; Papercutz 2013 124 p. Illustration

Grades: 2 3 4 5　　　　　　　　　　741.5

1. Animals; 2. School stories

1597073997; 9781597073998, $12.99

This book follows Ariol and his ensemble, a "cast of anthropomorphized animal children," in "10 10-page stories, originally from France, which offer . . . slice-of-life vignettes. Whether Ariol is joining his father for a trip to the ATM, arguing with a friend about sneakers, accompanying his grandmother to the movies, pursuing his great crush, or emulating his favorite superhero, the author dares to depict the exclusionary, argumentative, self-centered ways children can sometimes behave." (Booklist)

Other titles in this series are:Thunder horse (2013); Happy as a pig (2013); A beautiful cow (2014)

Ariol; 4: a beautiful cow. Emmanuel Guibert, illustrated by Marc Boutavant. Papercutz 2014 124 p. Color; Illustration

Grades: 2 3 4 5　　　　　　　　　　741.5

1. Animals — Fiction; 2. Cattle — Fiction

1597075132; 9781597075138, $12.99

In this children's book by Emmanuel Guibert, illustrated by Marc Boutavant, part of the Ariol series, "Petula is a beautiful cow who smells nice, has pretty hair, and makes Ariol tremble when she's around. And even though Ariol's story so far is almost 400 pages long, he still hasn't worked up the courage to tell Petula that he loves her! Instead, he keeps accidentally saying all the wrong things every time she turns around to talk to him in class." (Publisher's note)

"Silly situations and memorable characters make for an enjoyable, quick read. The easy-to-follow panels and colors that seem to pop from the pages make this graphic novel particularly pleasing." SLJ

Translated from the French

Sardine in outer space. [by] Emmanuel Guibert; illustrated by Joann Sfar; translated by Sasha Watson; colorist, Walter Pezzali. First Second 2006 128p. Illustration

Grades: 3 4 5 6　　　　　　　　　741.5; Fic

1. Humorous graphic novels; 2. Science fiction graphic novels; 3. Graphic novels

978-1-59643-126-3 (pa), $12.95; 1-59643-126-1 (pa)

LC 2005-21790

In this volume of twelve interconnected stories, little space pirate Sardine cruises in the spaceship Huckleberry with Uncle Yellow Shoulder and Little Louie. They do battle with Supermuscleman, who runs a tough space orphanage where children are taught "good behavior."

"Sfar's off-kilter, slightly uglified art, reminiscent of a toned-down Beavis and Butthead, gives the simple fun an unusual punch." Booklist

Other titles in this series are: Sardine in outer space 2 (2006); Sardine in outer space 3 (2007); Sardine in outer space 4 (2007); Sardine in outer space 5 (2008); Sardine in outer space 6 (2009)

Sardine in Outer Space Vol. 3. First Second Books 2007 109p. Illustration
Grades: 3 4 5 6 7 8   **741.5; Fic**
1. Adventure graphic novels; 2. Humorous graphic novels; 3. Graphic novels
978-1-59643-128-7, $12.95

Supermuscleman and Doc Krok are at it again, and it's not just the galaxy they're out to ruin, it's Sardine and Little Louie, too. Get ready for the ultimate match-up as wits battle brawn in the Space Boxing Championship. The fearless cousins must go head to head with Supermuscleman, Chief Executive Dictator of the Universe, shrunken to enter the kids' matches, but just as muscley. In another story, it's Sardine's birthday and she has a big party, but Doc Krok crashes it with his newest creation, Toxin, whose sole purpose is to destroy Sardine. There are more stories filled with adventure, space hijinks and looniness.

Sardine in Outer Space Vol. 4. First Second Books 2007 109p. Illustration
Grades: 3 4 5 6 7 8   **741.5; Fic**
1. Adventure graphic novels; 2. Humorous graphic novels; 3. Graphic novels
978-1-59643-129-4, $13.95

Sardine is back, and she's got a whole host of new problems to face even before the spaceship Huckleberry can get off the ground. In the fourth volume of this series, Sardine must tackle, among other things, monsters under the bed, flesh-eating tattoos, time machines, a flying cat, kidnapped suns, and even boredom. As always, Supermuscleman, Chief Executive Dictator of the Universe, lurks in the background, trying-unsuccessfully and incompetently-to make Sardine and her crew behave.

Another title in the author's series about Sardine in Outer Space

Sardine in outer space 5. Color by Walter Pezzali; translation by Edward Garwin. First Second Books 2008 102p. Illustration
Grades: 3 4 5 6   **741.5; 741**
978-1-59643-380-9, $14.95; 1-59643-380-9
LC 2007044126

Sardine in outer space 6. Stories by Emmanuel Guibert ; pictures by Joann Sfar ; color by Walter Pezzali ; translated by Sasha Watson. First Second Books 2008 93p. Illustration
Grades: 2 3 4 5 6   **741; 741.5; Fic**
1. Humorous graphic novels; 2. Sardine (Fictional character); 3. Science fiction graphic novels; 4. Graphic novels

978-1-59643-424-0, $14.95; 1-59643-424-4
LC 2008-23543

This latest volume of the Sardine in Outer Space series offers nine short tales featuring Sardine, Little Louie, Captain Yellow Shoulder, and villains Supermuscleman and Doc Krok. Stories include Captain Yellow Shoulder's tale of how he lost his eye (baby buggy racing against baby Supermuscleman, uh-huh); Sardine's mission to restore the merry-go-rounds in the rings of Saturn; what happens when Sardine gets a cell phone that causes big trouble; and more. There is one panel showing the newborn infant Yellow Shoulder naked); and "Robert Putto" is a Cupid in training and is therefore naked, although nothing crucial shows.

"The bouncy cartoons, wacky but well-plotted vignettes, and glowing color palette promise to reel in new readers and satisfy young fans." Booklist

Another title in the author's series about Sardine in outer space

Guojing
★ The **only** child. By Guojing. Schwartz & Wade Books 2015 112 p. Illustration
Grades: K 1 2 3 4 5   **741.5**
1. Adventure and adventurers — Fiction; 2. Adventure fiction; 3. Lost children — Fiction; 4. Stories without words; 5. Stories without words; 6. Graphic novels
9780553497045, $19.99; 9780553497052
LC 2014026977

In this wordless graphic novel, by Guojing, a "little girl—lost and alone—follows a mysterious stag deep into the woods, and, like Alice down the rabbit hole, she finds herself in a strange and wondrous world. But... home and family are very far away. How will she get back there—" (Publisher's note)

"Each arresting, softly penciled panel is surprisingly luminous in spite of its monochromatic palette, and in those gentle scenes, Guojing evokes a wide range of feeling, especially the lonesomeness of the little girl, who never quite seems at ease alone." Booklist

Hakamada, Mera
Fairy idol Kanon, volume 1. UDON Entertainment 2009 200p. Illustration
Grades: 3 4 5 6 7 8   **741.5; Fic**
1. Fairies; 2. Fantasy graphic novels; 3. Manga; 4. Music; 5. Graphic novels
978-1-897376-89-8, $7.99

Fourth grader Kanon loves to sing more than anything else, and people say her singing brings them happiness. Her friends Kodama and Marika also love to sing, although Marika wants a solo career as an idol (in Japan, young singers are often called pop idols). The three of them encounter a magical fairy princess named Alto, who tells them their singing and harmonies are needed to help her fairy kingdom. She decides to help them become pop idols in order to help her own people, and the three girls enter pop idol competitions. However, they soon encounter another very ambitious girl who seems to have a dark fairy helping her with bad magic that harms people. Some of the pages are in color.

Volume 1 of 4

Courtesy of Bloomsbury

Hale, Dean

★ **Calamity** Jack [by] Shannon and Dean Hale; illustrated by Nathan Hale. Bloomsbury 2010 144p.
Illustration
Grades: 4 5 6 7 8 9 **741.5; Fic**
1. Adventure graphic novels; 2. Fantasy graphic novels; 3. Folklore; 4. Graphic novels
9781599903736, $14.99; 9781599900766, $19.99
LC 2008-41332

In this sequel to Rapunzel's Revenge, the reader meets Jack as a child growing up in the city of Shyport; Jack has been a schemer practically since birth, but he hasn't had a whole lot of luck. His schemes usually end in unforeseen consequences. When he goes up against the giant Blunderboar, the magic beanstalk he uses to reach the giant's floating fortress destroys his neighborhood and his mother's bakery, and he just manages to leave town with a certain gold-egg-laying goose under his arm. After the events of the first book, Jack and Rapunzel come to Shyport, where Jack hopes to help his mother rebuild her bakery with the golden eggs he now has. However, they come to a city transformed Blunderboar has taken over, his security company claims to be keeping giant ants at bay, and Jack's mother is being held prisoner. Jack is still wanted for what he had done, and only Prudence, Jack's hat-loving pixie partner-in-crime, is willing to help. Then Jack and Rapunzel meet Freddie Sparksmith, newspaperman and gadget inventor, and they team up for a rescue mission. The book includes a lot of action and some non-gory violence.

Companion to: Rapunzel's Revenge

★ **Rapunzel's** revenge. [by] Shannon and Dean Hale; illustrated by Nathan Hale. Bloomsbury 2008 144p.
Illustration; Map
Grades: 5 6 7 8
741.5; Fic
1. Fairy tales; 2. Fantasy graphic novels; 3. Humorous graphic novels; 4. Graphic novels
1-59990-070-X; 1-59990-288-5 (pa); 978-1-59990-070-4, $18.99; 978-1-59990-288-3 (pa), $14.99
LC 2007-37670

Courtesy of Bloomsbury

In this graphic novel, Rapunzel escapes "from the enchanted tree where Mother Gothel imprisoned her. Rapunzel sets off alone through the ghost towns and Badlands of Gothel's Reach. She is determined to find Gothel's Villa and teach Mother Gothel a long-overdue lesson for her years of treachery and lies, and help her real mother get out of the mine camps where Mother Gothel has kept her enslaved." (Publisher's note)

"The dialogue is witty, the story is an enticing departure from the original, and the illustrations are magically fun and expressive." SLJ

Another title about these characters is: Calamity Jack (2009)

Hale, Nathan

Donner dinner party. By Nathan Hale. Harry N Abrams Inc 2013 123 p. (Nathan Hale's Hazardous Tales)
Grades: 5 6 7 8 **979.4; 741.5**
1. Donner party; 2. Sierra Nevada Mountains
1419708562; 9781419708565, $12.95

In this graphic novel, author Nathan Hale "tells the harrowing story of the ill-fated Donner party. Beginning with their departure from Springfield, Illinois, in 1846, Hale depicts the party's progress . . . and includes lots of factual details, such as a roster of everyone in the party, how they died, and a helpful map showing just how . . . close they came to California before meeting their grisly end." (Booklist)

"This informative graphic novel capitalizes on enticingly gross history to great effect, balancing raw facts with strong storytelling." Booklist

Nathan Hale's hazardous tales: big bad ironclad!. Nathan Hale. Abrams 2012 118 p.
Grades: 4 5 6 **973.7**
1. Cushing, William; 2. United States — History — 1861-1865, Civil War — Naval operations
1419703951; 9781419703959, $12.95
LC 2012947181

Author Nathan Hale "covers the history of the amazing ironclad steam warships used in the Civil War [in his book 'Big Bad Ironclad!'] From the ship's inventor, who had a history of blowing things up and only 100 days to complete his project, to the mischievous William Cushing, who pranked his way through the whole war, this book is filled with . . . facts." (Publisher's note)

Includes bibliographical references.

Map on endpapers.

Nathan Hale's hazardous tales: one dead spy. Nathan Hale. Amulet Books 2012 128 p.
Grades: 3 4 5 6 7 **741.5/973; 741.5**
1. Hale, Nathan, 1755-1776; 2. United States — History
141970396X; 9781419703966, $12.95
LC 2012947189

In this graphic novel, historical figure "[Nathan] Hale, convicted of espionage, forestalls death by telling stories from American history. In this volume, he's helped by the hangman in telling the story of the early days of the revolution. He takes readers from his college days at Yale to the Boston Massacre, the Boston Tea Party, his joining the 7th Connecticut regiment, the Battle of Bunker Hill and other pivotal scenes in New England and New York City." (Kirkus)

Nathan Hale's hazardous tales: treaties, trenches, mud, and blood (a World War I tale). By Nathan Hale. Amulet Books 2014 128 p. Color illustration; Color; Map (Nathan Hale's hazardous tales)

Grades: 4 5 6 7   **741.5; 940.3**
1. World War, 1914-1918 — Juvenile literature
1419708082; 9781419708084, $12.95
                           LC 2013049048
"Nathan Hale, Revolutionary War hero, continues to distract his executioners in this fourth volume, which tackles WWI's complex events." (Horn Book)

"Per established series formula, a frame tale finds the author's more-renowned namesake holding off the hangman, Scheherazade-like, with tales from our country's future history. In this volume, he covers the war's prelude, precipitation, major campaigns and final winding down in small but reasonably easy-to-follow two-color panels. . . . Hale cogently conveys the mind-numbing scale of it all as well as the horrors of trench warfare." Kirkus

Includes bibliographical references

The **underground** abductor: an abolitionist tale. Nathan Hale. Harry N Abrams Inc. 2015 125 p. Illustration; Color (Nathan Hale's Hazardous Tales)
Grades: 3 4 5 6 7   **741.5**
1. Biographical graphic novels; 2. Fugitive slaves — United States; 3. Tubman, Harriet, 1820?-1913 — Juvenile literature; 4. Underground Railroad
9781419715365, $12.95; 1419715364

In this graphic novel, "a fictionalized Nathan Hale (a patriot from the American Revolutionary War) tells stories about America's most extraordinary heroes and villains. In this installment, Hale tells his British captors about Harriet Tubman, the spy and nurse who helped hundreds of American slaves run away in the 1800s on the Underground Railroad." (School Library Journal)

Includes bibliographical references

Hall, M. C.
King Arthur and the Knights of the Round Table. Stone Arch Books 2006 63p. Illustration
Grades: 3 4 5 6 7 8 9   **741.5; Fic**
1. King Arthur — Adaptations; 2. Graphic novels
978-1-59889-048-8, $23.93

In a world of wizards, giants, and dragons, King Arthur and the Knights of the Round Table are the kingdom of Camelot's only defense against the threatening forces of evil. Fighting battles and saving those in need, the Knights of the Round Table can defeat every enemy but one - themselves. This adaptation focuses on how Arthur became King, on Lancelot and how Sir Galahad came to be born, the quest for the Holy Grail, and how Mordred brought about the end.

Part of the Graphic Revolve series.

Hama, Larry
The **Battle** of Antietam: The Bloodiest Day of Battle. Art by Scott Moore. Rosen Publishing Group 2007 48p. Illustration
Grades: 3 4 5 6 7 8
741.5; 973.7

Courtesy of Rosen Publishing

1. Antietam (Md), Battle of, 1862; 2. United States — History — 1861-1865, Civil War; 3. Graphic novels
978-1-4042-0775-2, $29.25; 978-1-84603-049-9 (pa)
                           LC 2006007186
The battle of Antietam on September 17, 1862 was the first major Civil War engagement on Northern soil, and it remains the bloodiest single-day battle in American history. Of the 90,000 troops that fought, over 23,000 were killed or wounded. Antietam also marked a significant turning point: General Lee's bold invasion of the North was halted, and the Union's success, though not exploited, gave President Lincoln the victory he needed to make his Emancipation Proclamation. The battle arguably sealed the fate of the Confederacy, even if the war still had nearly three years to run. This book brings to life this significant and very costly engagement in graphic novel format. It also includes eight pages of information placing Antietam in its historical context, describing the key players, the build-up to the battle and its aftermath.

Part of the Graphic Battles of the Civil War series; the paperback edition is published by Osprey.

The **Battle** of First Bull Run: The Civil War Begins. Art by Scott Moore. The Rosen Publishing Group 2007 48p. Illustration
Grades: 3 4 5 6 7 8 9 **741.5; 973.7**
1. Bull Run 1st Battle of, 1861; 2. United States — History — 1861-1865, Civil War; 3. Graphic novels
978-1-4042-0776-9, $29.25

Courtesy of Rosen Publishing

Three months after the shelling of Fort Sumter, Union and Confederate forces met for the first time in earnest combat. However, neither side was prepared at this early stage of the war, and confusion reigned on the battlefield. Finally, Confederate reinforcements forced the Union army into a panicked retreat. The intensity—and ill preparedness—of both armies convinced the nation that the conflict between the states would be a long, bloody ordeal. The book includes background information, a glossary, and a list of books for further reading.

Part of the Graphic Battles of the Civil War series. The book is also available in paperback from Osprey Publishing under the title The War is On!: Battle of First Bull Run.

The **Battle** of Guadalcanal: Land and Sea Warfare in the South Pacific. Art by Anthony Williams. The Rosen Publishing Group 2007 48p. Illustration
Grades: 3 4 5 6 7 8 9   **741.5; 940.54**
1. Guadalcanal Island (Solomon Islands), Battle of, 1942-1943; 2. World War, 1939-1945; 3. Graphic novels
978-1-4042-0784-4, $29.25
The battle of Guadalcanal shattered the myth of Japanese invincibility. August 7, 1942, marked the first American amphibious assault of World War II, and the first attempt to secure the Japanese-controlled island of

Guadalcanal. From the ranks of the units that contested this campaign a seasoned fighting force of US veterans was created that, island by island, would sweep the Japanese back across the Pacific. This full-color comic book includes further reading, essential information on the background, aftermath and key players of the conflict.

Part of the Graphic Battles of World War II series. This book is also available in a paperback edition from Osprey Publishing, under the title Fight to the Death: Battle of Guadalcanal.

The **battle** of Iwo Jima: guerilla warfare in the Pacific. By Larry Hama; illustrated by Anthony Williams. Rosen Pub. 2007 48p. Illustration; Map (Graphic battles of World War II)
Grades: 5 6 7 8 9   **940.54**
1. Iwo Jima, Battle of, 1945; 2. World War, 1939-1945; 3. Graphic novels
978-1-4042-0781-3 (lib bdg), $29.25; 1-4042-0781-3 (lib bdg)
                                                  LC 2006007645
"Using a graphic novel to introduce the battle for Iwo Jima makes it very accessible. Before the graphic-novel section of the book begins, Hama provides a short, informative background piece describing the run-up to World War II, the significance of the Japanese war machine, and the importance of the tiny island of Iwo Jima. Then the graphic novel, illustrated by Williams in camouflage colors, does a terrific job of examining the ups and downs of the battle as well as the horror of so many losses—on both sides." Booklist
Includes bibliographical references

The **Battle** of Shiloh: Surprise Attack!. Art by Scott Moore. Rosen Publishing Group 2007 48p. Illustration Grades: 3 4 5 6 7 8
741.5; 973.7
1. Shiloh (Tenn), Battle of, 1862; 2. United States — History — 1861-1865, Civil War; 3. Graphic novels
978-1-4042-0779-0, $29.25;
978-1-84603-050-5 (pb)
                LC 2006007309

Courtesy of Rosen Publishing

The first major Civil War battle in the Western theater, Shiloh came as a horrifying shock to both the American public and those in arms. On April 6, 1862, Confederate forces staged a surprise attack on the Union army encamped along the Tennessee River. Fighting was fierce as General Grant struggled to hold off the enemy until his reinforcements arrived the following day so that he could 'Whip 'em tomorrow'. Though nearly driven into the Tennessee River, the Union army could ultimately claim victory - won at a dear cost. With nearly 24,000 total casualties in two days' fighting, 'Bloody Shiloh' served as a wake-up call to the nation, announcing that the continuing fight for the Union would be devastating for both sides. This book brings to life one of the Civil War's bloodiest battles in graphic novel format. It also includes eight pages of background information placing Shiloh in its

historical context, detailing the key players, and describing the build-up to the fighting and its aftermath.

Part of the Graphic Battles of the Civil War series; the paperback edition is published by Osprey.

Courtesy of Rosen Publishing

The **Battle** of the Wilderness: Deadly Inferno. Art by Scott Moore. The Rosen Publishing Group 2007 48p. Illustration
Grades: 3 4 5 6 7 8 9 **741.5; 973.7**
1. United States — History — 1861-1865, Civil War; 2. War; 3. Wilderness, Battle of the, 1864; 4. Graphic novels
978-1-4042-0780-6, $29.25 lib. bdg.
'The Wilderness' encompassed a 70-square-mile expanse of virtually impenetrable woodland in central Virginia, so dense it made conventional warfare impossible. The first battle of Lieutenant General Ulysses S. Grant's 1864 Overland Campaign against the Army of Northern Virginia, the Wilderness witnessed some of the fiercest fighting of the Civil War. Though outnumbered, General Lee's forces posed stiff resistance to Grant's offensive. At the end of the three day battle, the outcome was uncertain, and the fight ended in a draw. Illustrating one of the American Civil War's most tactically challenging battles, this comic strip narrative brings to life a completely new type of warfare; the likes of which had never been fought before on American soil. The book includes additional information, including a map, a glossary, and a list of books for further reading.

Part of the Graphic Battles of the Civil War series; a trade paperback edition is also available from Osprey Publishing under the title Deadly Inferno: Battle of the Wilderness.

Spider-girl presents Wild Thing: crash course. Illustrated by Ron Lim. Marvel Entertainment 2007 Un Illustration
Grades: 5 6 7 8 9 10   **741.5**
1. Adventure graphic novels; 2. Superhero graphic novels; 3. Graphic novels
978-0-7851-2606-5, $7.99
A few years in the future, in the alternate Marvel Universe where Peter Parker and Mary Jane had a daughter who has become Spider-Girl, Wolverine and Elektra got together and they had a daughter, too Rina Logan, also known as Wild Thing. She has psychic claws that work pretty much like Wolverine's claws, and she has his fast healing power. She still has to deal with high school even as she fights against bad guys, demons, evil droids, and more.

Hamilton, Sue
Jack Kirby. ABDO Publishing 2007 32p. Illustration (Comic Book Creators)
Grades: 3 4 5 6 7   **92; 741.5**
1. Biographical graphic novels; 2. Captain America (Fictional character); 3. Comic books, strips, etc —

History and criticism; 4. Fantastic Four (Fictional characters); 5 Hulk (Fictional character); 6. Kirby, Jack, 1917-1994; 7. Thor (Fictional character); 8. X-Men (Fictional characters); 9. Graphic novels
978-1-59928-298-5, $25.65

LC 2006-15405

Courtesy of ABDO Publishing

Jack "King" Kirby may be one of the most famous comic book artists ever. He helped to create Captain America, The Fantastic Four, The Incredible Hulk, The X-Men, The Mighty Thor, The Silver Surfer, and other characters for Marvel Comics. A prolific artist, he also worked on westerns, romance comics, and lots of other titles. Later in his career, he also worked for DC Comics, where he created the New Gods. His struggles to regain ownership of his art sparked a movement toward creator-owned comics in the 1980s and 1990s. He passed away in 1994, but his influence is still felt today. This volume includes lots of reproductions of his comics work and photographs from his life.

Joe Simon. ABDO Publishing 2007 32p. Illustration (Comic Book Creators)

Courtesy of ABDO Publishing

Grades: 3 4 5 6 7 **92; 741.5**
1. Blue Beetle (Fictional character); 2. Captain America (Fictional character); 3. Comic book writers; 4. Comic books, strips, etc — History and criticism; 5. Simon, Joe; 6. Graphic novels
978-1-59928-300-5, $25.65

LC 2006-15408

Joe Simon may not be as much of a household name as Stan Lee or Jack Kirby, but he created Captain America (with Jack Kirby), The Blue Beetle, and other comic book characters. This volume introduces young readers to Simon's career, which included working in the Combat Art Corps during World War II and creating Sick Magazine in 1960; Sick included humor in the vein of the hugely popular Mad. This volume includes lots of reproductions of his comics and magazine work, and photographs.

Joe Sinnott. ABDO Publishing 2007 32p. Illustration (Comic Book Creators)
Grades: 3 4 5 6 7 **92; 741.5**
1. Avengers (Fictional characters); 2. Biographical graphic novels; 3. Comic books, strips, etc — History and criticism; 4. Fantastic Four (Fictional characters); 5. Sinnott, Joe, 1929-; 6. Thor (Fictional character); 7. X-Men (Fictional characters); 8. Graphic novels
978-1-59928-299-2, $25.65

LC 2006-15409

Joe Sinnott worked as an artist for Marvel Comics since 1950; he drew romance comics, westerns, super hero comics, record album covers for then-popular singers such as Bing Crosby, even covers for crossword puzzle magazines. From the early 1960s, Sinnott worked mostly as an inker, working with artists such as Jack Kirby, who would draw the pencilled art, and with writers such as Stan Lee. He worked on The Fantastic Four, The Mighty Thor, The Avengers, the X-Men, and other famous Marvel Comics titles. He officially retired in 1995, but he's still actively drawing and talking with school students. This volume includes lots of reproductions of his comics and other art work and photographs.

John Buscema. ABDO Publishing 2007 32p. Illustration (Comic Book Creators)
Grades: 3 4 5 6 7
92; 741.5
1. Biographical graphic novels; 2. Buscema, John, 1927-2002; 3. Cartoonists; 4. Comic books, strips, etc — History and criticism; 5. Thor (Fictional character); 6. Graphic novels
978-1-59928-297-8, $25.65

LC 2006-15407

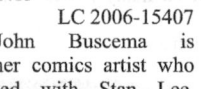

Courtesy of ABDO Publishing

John Buscema is another comics artist who worked with Stan Lee, among others. He worked on such comics as The Mighty Thor, The Silver Surfer, and Conan the Barbarian. He also worked on all kinds of comics, and in 1958 went into advertising art. He went back to Marvel in 1966, and sometimes worked with his own younger brother, Sal Buscema. In 1978, Buscema and Stan Lee created How to Draw Comics the Marvel Way, a popular how-to art book still in print now. Buscema died in 2002. This volume includes lots of reproductions of his comics work and photographs.

John Romita, Sr.. ABDO Publishing 2007 32p. Illustration (Comic Book Creators)
Grades: 3 4 5 6 7 **92; 741.5**
1. Biographical graphic novels; 2. Cartoonists; 3. Comic books, strips, etc — History and criticism; 4. Romita, John, Jr; 5. Spider-Man (Fictional character); 6. Graphic novels
978-1-59928-302-9, $25.65

Part of a biographical series discussing the lives of comic book creators and the inspirations for some of their most famous work, this book focuses on the life and work of John Romita, Sr., who is best known for his work on The Amazing Spider-Man comics.

Hamilton, Tim
Robert Louis Stevenson's Treasure Island. Penguin Young Readers Group/Puffin Books 2005 176p. Illustration
Grades: 4 5 6 7 8 9 10 **741.5; Fic**

1. Adventure graphic novels; 2. Buried treasure; 3. Pirates; 4. Stevenson, Robert Louis, 1850-1894 — Adaptations; 5. Graphic novels
0-14-240470-5, $9.99

Innkeeper's son Jim Hawkins befriends an old seaman who stays at the inn; when he dies, Jim finds a treasure map in the old man's seachest. When he takes it to the local magistrate, Jim finds himself caught up in a treasure hunt adventure with a ship's crew of pirates led by Long John Silver. This graphic novel adaptation keeps all the main action of the original novel. The book includes a gallery of the character models Hamilton used as well as sketched pages so readers can see some of the process.

Hansen, Jim

Drawing Fantasy Art: How to Draw Superheroes. Jim Hansen and John Burns. Rosen Publishing Group/PowerKids Press 2007 32p. Illustration
Grades: 2 3 4 5 6 7   741.5; 743.4
1. Drawing — Juvenile literature; 2. Graphic novels
978-1-4042-3855-8, $25.25

This introductory level art instruction book shows young artists how to draw superheroes in three different styles: cartoon, screen hero, and manga. It also includes a list of more art instruction books for those who want to learn more techniques.

Harbo, Christopher L.

The **Explosive** World of Volcanoes with Max Axiom, Super Scientist. Art by Tod Smith. Capstone Press 2007 32p. Illustration
Grades: 3 4 5 6 7 8 9   551.21; 741.5
1. Volcanoes; 2. Graphic novels
978-1-4296-0144-3, $25.26
LC 2006102361

This book uses the graphic novel format to follow the adventures of super scientist Max Axiom as he explains the science behind volcanoes, describing the different types of volcanoes found all over the world. The book includes additional facts and a list of books for further reading.

Part of the Graphic Science series.

Hardcastle, Michael

Sam's Goal. Art by Tony O'Donnell; Stone Arch Books 2007 72p. Illustration
Grades: 2 3 4 5 6 7   741.5; Fic
1. Soccer; 2. Sports; 3. Graphic novels
978-1-59889-088-4 li, $21.26; 978-1-59889-234-5 (pa)
LC 2006006071

Sam has always dreamed of playing professional soccer. When the best soccer player in the country (England) invites Sam to his next game, Sam can't believe it. The problem is, neither do his friends. Can Sam convince them that he's telling the truth? When the day of the big game arrives, Sam's goal is clearer than ever. This graphic novel is written at an easy level for reluctant and struggling readers.

Part of the Graphic Trax series.

Harper, Charise Mericle

Bean Dog and Nugget: the ball. Charise Mericle Harper. Robin Corey Books 2013 48 p. Illustration (Bean Dog and Nugget)
Grades: K 1 2 3   741.5/973; Fic
1. Friendship — Juvenile fiction; 2. Humorous fiction — Juvenile fiction; 4. Humorous stories; 3. Lost and found possessions — Juvenil Fiction; 4. Graphic novels
0307977072; 9780307977076, $4.99; 9780307977083, $12.99 ; 9780307977090, $14.97
LC 2012029373

This children's story, written and illustrated by Charise Mericle Harper, "introduces young readers to . . . Bean Dog and Nugget. . . . In . . . the first book in this series, Bean Dog and Nugget lose Bean Dog's shiny new ball in a bush. They dream up elaborate and silly ways to get it back while they argue about who is actually going to go and get it. Enter Superdog and Ninja Nugget." (Publisher's note)

Fashion Kitty. Hyperion Books for Children 2005 90p. Illustration
Grades: 3 4 5 6 7 8 9   741.5; Fic
1. Cats; 2. Humorous graphic novels; 3. Graphic novels
0-7868-5134-1, $8.99

Kiki Kittie is a very unusual cat. For one thing, she has a mouse for a pet—and that's kind of like a human having a chocolate cake for a pet. Kiki also has a natural flair for fashion, but up until a recent birthday, she was just an ordinary fashionable kitty. Then, on that day, she discovered that she had special powers: she can turn into Fashion Kitty, able to mix and match hundreds of outfits in a single second. Regular cat by day, Fashion Kitty by night, Kiki is always ready to answer a call of despair and save other cats from making fashion faux pas

Other titles about Fashion Kitty are: Fashion Kitty versus the Fashion Queen (2007); Fashion Kitty and the unlikely hero (2008); Fashion Kitty and the B.O.Y.S. (2011)

Fashion Kitty Versus the Fashion Queen. Hyperion Paperbacks for Children 2007 90p. Illustration
Grades: 3 4 5 6 7 8 9   741.5; Fic
1. Cats; 2. Humorous graphic novels; 3. Graphic novels
978-0-7868-3726-7, $8.99

After her last adventure, Fashion Kitty is truly becoming a hero. At school, she is more popular than ever. She's even been mentioned in several articles in the local newspaper, (which she clips out and saves in a scrapbook, of course). But not everyone is excited about Fashion Kitty's newfound popularity. A spoiled new kitty named Cassandra doesn't like sharing the spotlight. And when Fashion Kitty starts inspiring the other kitties at school to be more independent about their style choices, Cassandra really doesn't like it. So she hatches a plan (evil, of course) that involves lying, conniving, and outlawing bright colors and patterns. Fashion Kitty knows she must put an end to Cassandra's reign of terror. She will use her fashion sense, quick smarts, and the power of friendship to overcome fashion evil.

Harrell, Rob

Monster on the Hill. By Rob Harrell. Top Shelf Productions 2013 192 p. Color; Illustration

Grades: 4 5 6 7 8   **741.5**
1. Friendship; 2. Monsters
1603090754; 9781603090759, $19.95

This graphic novel by Rob Harrell is set in "1860s England [where] every . . . township is terrorized by a . . . monster - much to the townsfolk's delight! Each town's . . . monster is a source of local pride [and] tourism. Unfortunately, for . . . Stoker-on-Avon, their monster isn't quite as impressive. Can the morose Rayburn get a monstrous makeover and become a proper horror" It's up to the eccentric Dr. Charles Wilkie and plucky street urchin Timothy to get him up to snuff." (Publisher's note)

Hatke, Ben
★ **Legends** of Zita the spacegirl. Ben Hatke. First Second 2012 205 p. Color illustration
Grades: 4 5 6   **741.5**
1. Adventure fiction; 2. Fame — Fiction; 3. Heroes — Fiction; 4. Robots — Fiction; 5. Science fiction; 6. Science fiction graphic novels; 7. Graphic novels
1596434473; 9781596434479, $12.99; 9781596438064, $18.99

LC 2012012748
This graphic novel, by Ben Hatke, is a children's science fiction adventure story. "Zita is determined to find her way home to earth, following the events of the first book. . . . Zita's exploits from her first adventure have made her an intergalactic megastar! But she's about to find out that fame doesn't come without a price. And who can you trust when your true self is being eclipsed by your public persona, and you've got a robot doppelganger wreaking havoc . . . while wearing your face?" (Publisher's note)

"Hatke's arrestingly vibrant art commands instant adoration of its reader... Readers would be hard-pressed to not find something to like in these tales; they're a winning formula of eye-catching aesthetics, plot and creativity, adeptly executed. Imaginative and utterly bewitching." Kirkus

★ **Little** Robot. By Ben Hatke. First Second 2015 144 p. Color; Illustration
Grades: K 1 2 3 4 5   **741.5; Fic**
1. Friendship; 2. Girls; 3. Good and evil; 4. Robots
1626720800; 9781626720800, $16.99

In this graphic novel, by Ben Hatke, "when a little girl finds an adorable robot in the woods, she presses a button and accidentally activates him for the first time. Now, she finally has a friend. But the big, bad robots are coming to collect the little guy for nefarious purposes, and it's all up to a five-year-old armed only with a wrench and a fierce loyalty to her mechanical friend to save the day!" (Publisher's note)

"Unframed panel illustrations lend an expansive quality to this lively, mostly wordless graphic novel for younger readers. The absence of defined frames allows the watercolor to bleed out into the plentiful white space between panels, giving the girl and the robot space to move and even allowing the characters and dialogue to break the pattern in organic ways." Horn Book

★ The **Return** of Zita the Spacegirl. By Ben Hatke. First Second 2014 240 p.
Grades: 3 4 5 6   **741.5**

1. Good and evil — Fiction; 2. Outer space — Fiction; 3. Prisoners — Fiction; 4. Science fiction; 5. Science fiction graphic novels; 6. Graphic novels
1626720584; 9781626720589, $18.99

"Zita the Spacegirl has saved planets, battled monsters, and wrestled with interplanetary fame. But she faces her biggest challenge yet in the third and final installment of the Zita adventures. Wrongfully imprisoned on a penitentiary planet, Zita has to plot the galaxy's greatest jailbreak before the evil prison warden can execute his plan of interstellar domination!" (Publisher's note)

"The art is colorful, detailed, and child-friendly. Readers of all ages can relate to the themes of friendship and loyalty while enjoying the fantasy of a far-out sci-fi adventure." Horn Book

★ **Zita** the spacegirl. First Second 2011 182p. Illustration
Grades: 3 4 5 6   **741.5**
1. Science fiction graphic novels; 2. Graphic novels
1-59643-446-5 (pa); 1-59643-695-6; 978-1-59643-446-2 (pa), $10.99; 978-1-59643-695-4, $17.99

When her best friend is abducted by an alien doomsday cult, Zita leaps to the rescue and finds herself a stranger on a strange planet.

Hayes, Geoffrey
Benny and Penny in just pretend: a Toon Book. [by] Geoffrey Hayes. RAW Junior 2008 32p. Illustration
Grades: PreK K 1 2   **741; 741.5**
978-0-9799238-0-7, $12.95; 0-9799238-0-8

"How can Benny pretend to be a brave pirate when his pesky little sister, Penny, wants to tag along and is always asking for a hug? He tries to lose her, but when he does, he starts to feel a little lost himself. Penny proves her bravery and saves Benny from a bug. They hug as Benny explains he was only pretending she bugged him." (Publisher's note)

Other titles about Benny and Penny are: Benny and Penny in the big no-no! (2009); Benny and Penny in the toy breaker (2010);Benny and Penny in Lights out! (2012);Benny and Penny in Lost and found! (2014)

★ **Benny** and Penny in Lights out!: a Toon book. By Geoffrey Hayes. Toon Books 2012 32 p. Illustration
Grades: K 1 2   **741.5**
1. Bedtime — Fiction; 2. Brothers and sisters — Fiction; 3. Mice — Fiction; 4. Picture books for children; 5. Siblings — Fiction; 6. Graphic novels
1935179209; 9781935179207, $12.95

LC 2011050927
This children's picture book follows mouse brother and sister Benny and Penny. Penny is getting ready for bed, but "her restless big brother interrupts obnoxiously with warnings about the Boogey Mouse, loud belches and other distractions. When Benny realizes that he's left his prized pirate hat in the backyard, though, Penny braves the Boogey Mouse to follow him . . . and prod him into reclaiming it from the spooky, dark playhouse." (Kirkus)

Benny and Penny in Lost and found: a Toon book. By Geoffrey Hayes. Toon Books 2014 40 p. Color; Illustration
Grades: PreK K 1 2   **741.5; Fic**

1. Brothers and sisters — Fiction; 2. Lost and found possessions — Fiction; 3. Mice — Fiction; 4. Graphic novels
1935179640; 9781935179641, $12.95
LC 2014000649
"Benny's in a foul mood! He can't find his pirate hat, and he's been sent outside to cool his temper. When he and Penny wander away from home and realize they're lost, they must handle their emotions and put their heads together." (Publisher's note)
"The text is easily accessible to emerging readers, with simple, repeating words, while also enforcing ideas about controlling emotions and being responsible for one's actions without being overbearing. Children will easily relate to Penny and Benny as they grapple with sibling issues that are very real to this age group." SLJ

★ **Benny** and Penny in The big no-no!: a Toon Book. RAW Junior 2009 32p. Illustration
Grades: PreK K 1 2   **741; 741.5**
978-0-9799238-9-0, $12.95; 0-9799238-9-1
LC 2008-36307
"Benny and his sister Penny know it's wrong to sneak into someone else's backyard but their mysterious new neighbor – or is it a monster? – may be a thief. They go snooping and discover a lot about themselves and…a new friend." (Publisher's note)

★ **Benny** and Penny in the Toy breaker: a Toon Book. TOON Books 2010 32p. Illustration; Map
Grades: PreK K 1   **741.5; Fic**
1. Bullies; 2. Cousins; 3. Humorous graphic novels; 4. Mice; 5. Siblings; 6. Graphic novels
978-1-935179-07-8, $12.95; 1-935179-07-1
LC 2009-38066
Mouse siblings Benny and Penny unite against their bullying cousin Bo, who breaks just about everything he plays with. When they hear he's coming for a visit, they try to hide all their toys, although Penny doesn't want to give up holding her monkey. Bo wants to join in with their treasure hunt, but Benny and Penny don't want to play with him. The reader sees that much of the trouble stems from the others trying to grab their things away from Bo. Left to themselves, the children eventually work out a peaceful resolution (after poor Monkey's arm gets torn off—but Mommy will fix it).
"Hayes's cartooning is witty, expressing much with the glint of an eye or twitch of a whicker, and the neat cartoon panels carefully allow a good beginning-reader balance between information in the pictures and in the ballooned dialogue." Horn Book

Haynes, Stephen
Macbeth. Illustrated by Nick Spender ; retold by Stephen Haynes. Barron's 2008 Illustration
Grades: 4 5 6 7 8 9   **822.3; 741.5**
1. Authors; 2. Dramatists; 3. Poets; 4. Shakespeare, William, 1564-1616 — Adaptations; 5. Graphic novels
978-0-7641-6140-7, $15.99; 978-0-7641-4009-9 (pa), $8.99
LC 2007-938484
Macbeth is a loyal retainer of King Duncan of Scotland, until three witches prophesy that he will be king. Now, nothing will stop his ambition, and Macbeth and his wife kill

the king. But now that he has the throne, Macbeth is haunted by guilt and paranoia, and the murders pile up. This graphic novel adaptation of Shakespeare's play includes a brief biography of Shakespeare, background information on the real Macbeth, Scotland, and James I's campaign against witches; it also covers the superstitions about the play, and film adaptations.
Part of Barron's Graphic Classics series

Helfand, Lewis
Conquering Everest: the lives of Edmund Hillary and Tenzing Norgay. Campfire 2011 96p. Illustration
Grades: 3 4 5 6 7 8 9 10   **741.5; 796.522**
1. Hillary, Edmund Sir; 2. Mount Everest; 3. Mountaineering; 4. Mountaineers; 5. Nonfiction writers; 6. Tenzing Norgay, 1914-1986
978-93-80741-24-6, $12.99
Tenzing Norgay immigrated to Nepal with his Tibetan family when he was a boy, and he worked hard over the years to become one of the best Sherpas who helped the European, American, and other climbers who journeyed to Nepal to climb Mount Everest. Edmund Hillary was the son of a beekeeper from New Zealand, who became fascinated with mountain climbing during World War II. He came to Nepal in 1953 as part of a British expedition to reach Everest's peak, and Norgay came to be the sirdar, the head Sherpa and organizer of the expedition's support system. These two men became the first to reach Everest's summit at 11:30 a.m. on May 29, 1953. This graphic novel tells the story of the two men from such different backgrounds, and their friendship. The book notes that on May 22, 2010, Californian thirteen-year-old Jordan Romero became the youngest climber to reach Everest's peak. Tayal's panels show some of the massive scale of the mountain.

Hergé
★ The **adventures** of Tintin, vol. 1: Tintin in America, Cigars of the Pharaoh, The Blue Lotus. Little, Brown 1994 192p. Illustration
Grades: 4 5 6 7 8 9   **741.5; Fic**
1. Adventure graphic novels; 2. Tintin (Fictional character); 3. Graphic novels
0-316-35940-8, $18.99
Tintin, the heroic boy reporter from France, travels to America where he outwits gangsters in Chicago of the 1930s and adventures in the Wild West; sails the Mediterranean Sea with faithful dog Snowy and finds himself in a mystery involving a movie tycoon, drugs, and cigars in an ancient Egyptian tomb; then he travels to India to finally solve the mystery. This Little, Brown edition reprints some of the early Tintin adventures published in the 1930s in a 3-in-1 volume. This is the first in a series that reprints most of the Tintin stories by Herge. Librarians and teachers should note that the books retain some stereotypical depictions of people of other cultures and remember that these were acceptable and expected at the time of original publication.

The **secret** of the unicorn. Hergé; [translated by Leslie Lonsdale-Cooper and Michael Turner].. Joy Street Books 1991 62 p. Color illustration
Grades: 3 4 5   **741.5**

1. Adventure and adventurers — Fiction; 2. Adventure graphic novels; 3. Buried treasure; 4. Buried treasure — Fiction; 5. Cartoons and comics; 6. Tintin (Fictional character)
0316358320, $10.99; 0316359025

LC 92153472

In this graphic novel, "[t]he . . . plot revolves around young reporter Tintin, his dog Snowy, and his friend Captain Haddock, who discover a riddle left by Haddock's ancestor, the 17th century Sir Francis Haddock, which could lead them to the hidden treasure of the pirate Red Rackham. In order to unravel the riddle, Tintin and Haddock must obtain three identical models of Sir Francis' ship, the 'Unicorn,' but discover that criminals are also after these model ships, and are willing to kill in order to obtain them." (Wikipedia)

Originally published: Boston: Joy Street Books (1974)

Tintin and the Picaros. Little, Brown 1978 62p. Illustration
Grades: 4 5 6 7 8 9   **741.5; Fic**
1. Adventure graphic novels; 2. Humorous graphic novels; 3. Tintin (Fictional character); 4. Graphic novels
0-316-35849-5, $10.99

LC 77-090973

Tintin and his friends rescue prima donna Bianca Castafiore while trying to help restore their friend Alcazar to power in San Theodoros - but they'll have to defeat General Tapioca and his troops to do it.

Tintin in Tibet. Little, Brown 1978 62p. Illustration
Grades: 4 5 6 7 8 9   **741.5; Fic**
1. Adventure graphic novels; 2. Humorous graphic novels; 3. Tintin (Fictional character); 4. Graphic novels
0-316-35839-8, $10.99

LC 80-191368

Tintin, Snowy, and Captain Haddock trek through the snow-covered Himalayas to rescue their friend Chang from the hands of an abominable snowman.

Tintin: The Broken Ear. Little, Brown 1978 62p. Illustration
Grades: 4 5 6 7 8 9   **741.5; Fic**
1. Adventure graphic novels; 2. Humorous graphic novels; 3. Tintin (Fictional character); 4. Graphic novels
0-316-35850-9, $10.99

LC 77-090970

A fetish which originally belonged to the Arumbayas tribe in San Theodoros is stolen from a museum, then returned; soon Tintin discovers that the returned fetish is a forgery. When he follows the trail of the stolen fetish, it leads him and Snowy to South America and to San Theodoros, where he gets caught in the middle of a civil war. Tintin gets into all kinds of trouble even as he tries to find out why so many people want the fetish.

★ **Tintin:** The Calculus Affair. Little, Brown 1976 62p. Illustration
Grades: 4 5 6 7 8 9   **741.5; Fic**
1. Adventure graphic novels; 2. Humorous graphic novels; 3. Tintin (Fictional character); 4. Graphic novels
0-316-35847-9, $10.99

LC 76-13280

Unscrupulous Bordurians have kidnapped Professor Calculus, and Tintin, Snowy, and Captain Haddock are soon on the trail again, to rescue their friend. It's no easy task to rescue the Professor and save his fantastic invention; spies are everywhere, and Calculus lies deep in the fortress of Bakhine. But the Bordurians now have to deal with Tintin...

Tintin: The Castafiore Emerald. Little, Brown 1975 62p. Illustration
Grades: 4 5 6 7 8 9   **741.5; Fic**
1. Adventure graphic novels; 2. Humorous graphic novels; 3. Tintin (Fictional character); 4. Graphic novels
0-316-35842-8, $10.99

Tintin and Snowy investigate when prima donna Bianca Castafiore's jewels are stolen, in particular, her emerald.

Tintin: Cigars of the Pharaoh. Little, Brown 1975 62p. Illustration
Grades: 4 5 6 7 8 9   **741.5; Fic**
1. Adventure graphic novels; 2. Humorous graphic novels; 3. Tintin (Fictional character); 4. Graphic novels
0-316-35836-3, $10.99

LC 74-021620

Tintin and Snowy are on a cruise to Egypt when they happen to meet Professor Sophocles Sarcophagus (the first of Tintin's absent-minded professors) and join his expedition. But they become embroiled in a complicated scheme involving a fakir, cigars marked with an unusual brand, and Rajijah, the poison of madness. Tintin meets the detectives Thompson and Thomson as well as the movie mogul Rastapopolous. Herge wrote this book in 1932 then revised it in 1955.

Tintin: Destination Moon. Little, Brown 1976 62p. Illustration
Grades: 4 5 6 7 8 9   **741.5; Fic**
1. Adventure graphic novels; 2. Humorous graphic novels; 3. Tintin (Fictional character); 4. Graphic novels
0-316-35845-2, $10.99

LC 76-013279

Professor Calculus has designed a rocket for an expedition to the Moon. He summons Tintin and Captain Haddock (along with Snowy) to the country of Syldavia, where he's been working. Despite spies being everywhere and mysterious explosions and other problems, the rocket is soon ready to launch, and Professor Calculus wants Tintin and Captain Haddock to go with him - to the Moon.

Tintin: Explorers On the Moon. Little, Brown 1976 62p. Illustration
Grades: 4 5 6 7 8 9   **741.5; Fic**
1. Adventure graphic novels; 2. Humorous graphic novels; 3. Tintin (Fictional character); 4. Graphic novels
0-316-35846-0, $10.99

LC 76-013297

Tintin, Captain Haddock, and Prof. Calculus are headed for the Moon when they discover Thompson and Thomson, who had inadvertently stowed away on the rocket. But there's more trouble when they land on the Moon and go exploring, for Colonel Jorgen is there, another stowaway, and he wants revenge on Tintin.

Tintin: Flight 714. Little, Brown 1975 62p. Illustration
Grades: 4 5 6 7 8 9   **741.5; Fic**
1. Adventure graphic novels; 2. Humorous graphic novels; 3. Tintin (Fictional character); 4. Graphic novels

0-316-35837-1, $10.99

LC 74-021623

Tintin, Snowy, Captain Haddock, and Professor Calculus land in Djakarta and meet millionaire Mr. Carreidas, who invites them to fly to Sydney with him in his prototype jet. They find themselves in the middle of a plot to steal their new friend's fortune, and they decide to stop it.

Tintin: Land of Black Gold. Little, Brown 1975 62p. Illustration

Grades: 4 5 6 7 8 9   **741.5; Fic**
1. Adventure graphic novels; 2. Humorous graphic novels; 3. Tintin (Fictional character); 4. Graphic novels
0-316-35844-4, $10.99

LC 75-007896

The world is on the brink of a crisis when car engines begin to explode without explanation or warning; someone has been tampering with the oil supply. Tintin travels to the Middle East to investigate, and he helps Sheik Ben Kalish Ezab, whose son is kidnapped by one of Tintin's old enemies.

Tintin: Prisoners of the Sun. Little, Brown 1975 62p. Illustration

Grades: 4 5 6 7 8 9   **741.5; Fic**
1. Adventure graphic novels; 2. Humorous graphic novels; 3. Tintin (Fictional character); 4. Graphic novels
0-316-35843-6, $10.99

LC 75-007897

Tintin, Snowy, and Captain Haddock travel to Peru to rescue Professor Calculus. They meet Indian boy Zorrino, and they must travel into the jungle to the Andes to find their old friend.

Tintin: Red Rackham's Treasure. Little, Brown 1974 62p. Illustration

Grades: 4 5 6 7 8 9   **741.5; Fic**
1. Adventure graphic novels; 2. Humorous graphic novels; 3. Tintin (Fictional character); 4. Graphic novels
0-316-35834-7, $10.99

LC 73-021253

Tintin and his friends search for the pirate booty left by Captain Haddock's pirate ancestor. They're aided in their quest by the hard-of-hearing inventor, Professor Calculus.

Tintin: The Seven Crystal Balls. Little, Brown 1975 62p. Illustration

Grades: 4 5 6 7 8 9   **741.5; Fic**
1. Adventure graphic novels; 2. Humorous graphic novels; 3. Tintin (Fictional character); 4. Graphic novels
0-316-35840-1, $10.99

LC 75-007921

Tragedy strikes the members of an expedition which returned after violating Incan burial chambers; the seven men fall into comas, one by one, and fragments of crystal are found by their bodies. Tintin, Professor Calculus, Captain Haddock, and Thompson and Thomson investigate, but then Calculus disappears - he's been kidnapped.

Heuser, Randy

Land of Sokmunster. [by] Mike Kunkel and Randy Heuser. Astonish Factory 2003 60p. Illustration

Grades: 2 3 4 5 6 7 8   **741.5; Fic**
1. Adventure graphic novels; 2. Graphic novels

0-972125-92-2, $14.95

Sam dives into the family dryer's lint trap when a sock comes out and steals a rare nickel then dives back in. He finds himself in a land where the lost socks go and learns that the sokmunsters don't care much for humans. When he and a sokmunster named Spike set out to rescue King Jacque's daughter from the evil Moth King, Sam starts to learn about friendship, trust, and forgiveness.

Hicks, Faith Erin

★ The **Nameless** City. Faith Erin Hicks; color by Jordie Bellaire. First Second 2016 240 p. Color; Illustration

Grades: 5 6 7 8 9 10   **741.5; Fic**
1. Cities and towns — Fiction; 2. Fantasy graphic novels; 3. Friendship — Fiction; 4. Survival — Fiction; 5. Survival skills — Fiction
1626721564; 9781626721562, $14.99; 9781626721579

LC 2015020651

"Every nation that invades the City gives it a new name. . . . The natives don't let themselves get caught up in the unending wars. To them, their home is the Nameless City. . . . Kaidu is . . . a Dao born and bred—a member of the latest occupying nation. Rat is a native of the Nameless City. At first, she hates Kai for everything he stands for, but his love of his new home may be the one thing that can bring these two unlikely friends together." (Publisher's note)

"With comprehensive world building, well-rounded characters, and entertaining action, this expertly executed story will find a home with a wide variety of readers, all of whom will be eagerly awaiting the next installment." Booklist

Hiiragi, Aoi

Baron: The Cat Returns. Viz/Studio Ghibli Library 2005 222p. Illustration

Grades: 3 4 5 6 7 8 9   **741.5; Fic**
1. Cats; 2. Fantasy graphic novels; 3. Kodomo manga; 4. Manga; 5. Graphic novels
1-59116-956-9, $9.99

Awkward teen Haru saves a cat from being run over one afternoon, but she never expected the trouble it would cause. He is a cat prince, and his father wants to bring Haru into the kingdom of the cats to be his son's bride. A mysterious voice sends Haru to the Cat Office, where she meets Baron, a toy cat come to life, the fat cat Muta, and a magical crow. When the cats come and bear Haru to the kingdom of the cats, the three friends follow to help bring Haru back home.

This one-volume manga was the basis for the feature-length anime (Japanese animated film) called "The Cat Returns," which was produced by Studio Ghibli, the animation studio run by famed anime director Hayao Miyazaki and some partners.

Himuro, Isao

Edu-Manga: Albert Einstein. Art by Kotaro Iwasaki. Digital Manga Publishing 2006 144p. Illustration

Grades: 3 4 5 6 7 8 9   **92; 741.5**
1. Biographical graphic novels; 2. Einstein, Albert, 1879-1955; 3. Manga; 4. Graphic novels
1-56970-975-0, $9.95

At the age of 26, Einstein published his groundbreaking Theory of Relativity, revolutionizing the world of physics forever. Today, he is considered a true genius. From his boyhood quest for answers to some of science's most challenging questions, to his search to uncover the mysteries of the universe, Einstein's work led to both the formulation of his theories and his place as one of the most important scientists in history. Astro Boy and his friends introduce Einstein's story and present the Q&A that provides more information. The book also includes a timeline of Einstein's life.

Hina
Di Gi Charat Theater: Leave It to Piyoko!. Broccoli International USA, Inc. 2004 206p. Illustration
Grades: 3 4 5 6 7 8 9   **741.5; Fic**
1. Humorous graphic novels; 2. Manga; 3. Graphic novels
1-932480-17-X, $9.99
Piyoko has grand evil plans to kidnap the princess of Di Gi Charat, Dejiko, and hold her for ransom. The people of her poor Planet Analogue are all counting on her and the Black Gema Gema Gang. She and her loyal henchmen"Rik, Ky, and Coo—are scheming and plotting, but for some reason her grand plans seem to keep falling apart. Take a look into the daily lives of the Black Gema Gema Gang as they figure out their plans to kidnap Dejiko while trying to survive on the little money they have left.

Hoena, B. A.
Beyond the black hole. Illustrated by Steve Harpster.. Stone Arch Books 2009 40p. Illustration
Grades: 2 3 4 5 6 7   **741.5; Fic**
1. Humorous graphic novels; 2. Science fiction graphic novels; 3. Graphic novels
978-1-4342-0759-3, $21.26
                                            LC 2008-6709
Eek and Ack zip through space in their rocket-powered washing machine ship and find a black hole; when they get too close, they get sucked in and spat out on the other side of space. Of course, being in a new universe means they should find another planet Earth for Ack to conquer (well, that's what Ack thinks); and they do find one, but it's pink. Then they encounter two fuzzy pink creatures called Zeek and Zack, who also have a rocket-powered washing machine ship, and they defend Zearth. The book includes a short glossary (with mostly humorous definitions) and some information about black holes.
Part of the Graphic Sparks Eek and Ack series

Eek and Ack vs the Wolfman. Stone Arch Books 2009 40p. Illustration
Grades: 3 4 5 6 7 8   **741.5; Fic**
1. Humorous graphic novels; 2. Science fiction graphic novels; 3. Werewolves; 4. Graphic novels
978-1-4342-1189-1, $21.26
                                            LC 2008-32057
Eek and Ack invade Earth yet again, this time arriving on Halloween, so they blend in with the trick-or-treaters. Then they run into a strange, furry, monstrous creature that chases them and bites Ack. When they take off for space, the creature stays on their ship (that looks like a washing machine), and he changes from monster wolf to human kid and back again. The aliens land back on Earth, get rid of the Wolfman, and fly home, but something starts happening to

Ack. The book includes information about werewolves, discussion questions, and a glossary.
Part of the Graphic Sparks line, the Eek & Ack series

Jack and the beanstalk: the graphic novel. Retold by Blake A. Hoena; illustrated by Ricardo Tercio. Stone Arch Books 2009 33p. Illustration
Grades: 2 3 4 5   **741.5; 741**
1. Fairy tales; 2. Graphic novels
978-1-4342-0766-1, $21.26
                                            LC 2008-6722
When Jack sells the family cow for a handful of beans, his mother is not pleased. However, they are magic beans, and when Jack plants them, a giant beanstalk grows. Curious about where the beanstalk has gone, Jack climbs it, and finds a giant's home up there. As he brings back such things as a chicken that lays golden eggs, his mother exclaims that he is finding his father's old treasures. But sooner or later, the giant will catch Jack. This graphic novel adaptation includes information about the history of the tale, along with a short glossary and reading questions.
Part of the Graphic Spin series

Matthew Henson: Arctic Adventurer. Capstone Press 2005 32p. Illustration
Grades: 3 4 5 6 7 8 9   **741.5; 910; 92**
1. African American explorers — Biography; 2. Biographical graphic novels; 3. Henson, Matthew Alexander, 1866-1955; 4. North Pole — Discover and exploration; 5. Graphic novels
0-7368-4634-4, $25.26
                                            LC 2005005774
In graphic novel format, this book tells the life story of African American explorer Matthew Henson and his expedition to the North Pole with Robert Peary. The book includes additional facts about Henson, a bibliography, and a list of books for further reading.
Part of the Graphic Biographies series.

Perseus and Medusa. By Blake A. Hoena; illustrated by Daniel Perez. Stone Arch Books 2009 72p. Illustration (Graphic revolve)
Grades: 4 5 6 7 8 9   **741.5; Fic**
1. Greek mythology; 2. Monsters; 3. Graphic novels
978-1-4342-1170-5 (lib bdg), $23.93; 1-4342-1170-3 (lib bdg); 978-1-4342-1394-5 (pa), $6.95; 1-4342-1386-2 (pa)
                                            LC 2008-32065
Perseus is the son of Danae, daughter of the King of Argos, and of Zeus; due to a prophecy that Perseus would cause his death, the King puts his daughter and grandson into a wooden chest and has it cast out to sea. A fisherman rescues them, and Perseus grows up unaware of his royal lineage. King Polydectes wants Danae for himself and sends Perseus on what should be an impossible task that will kill him he wants Perseus to bring him the head of Medusa, whose gaze turns anyone into stone. Perseus enjoys the guidance and advice of gods and goddesses to accomplish his task
This title has a "solid awareness of how to balance visual depiction and expository captions, evident right from the striking prologue. While the artwork is cartoony and the dialogue deliberately casual and modern, the style doesn't prevent the artist from providing heroic vistas, or the author

from slipping in a couple of humorous moments, and the action is sufficiently thrilling." SLJ

The **puzzling** Pluto plot. By Blake A. Hoena; illustrated by Steve Harpster.. Stone Arch Books 2008 40p. Illustration
Grades: 3 4 5 6 7   **741.5; Fic**
1. Extraterrestrial beings; 2. Humorous graphic novels; 3. Science fiction graphic novels; 4. Graphic novels
978-1-4342-0452-3, $21.26; 978-1-4342-0502-5 (pa), $6.95

LC 2007-31255
Eek and Ack, the young aliens from the Gco Galaxy, have hatched yet another plan to zap the Earth, but they think that an ice giant is Earth. Meanwhile, Professor Hubble T. Scope has calculated that Pluto is an ice giant planet much larger than Earth. After Eek and Ack get done zapping the wrong planet, Scope sadly learns that Pluto is much, much smaller in fact, hardly a planet at all.
Part of the Graphic Sparks series, an Eek & Ack adventure.

Holm, Jennifer L.
Babymouse for president. By Jennifer L. Holm & Matthew Holm. Random House 2012 89 p.
Grades: 3 4 5 6   **741.5**
1. Elections — Fiction; 2. Mice — Fiction; 3. School stories; 4. Schools — Fiction
0375867805; 9780375867804, $6.99; 9780375967801

LC 2011024118
In this book by Jennifer L. Holm and Matt Holm, part of the Babymouse series, "it's election season and if anyone knows what . . . the student council needs, it's Babymouse. The only trouble is, everyone else is running for President, too — even Babymouse's locker! Will Felicia Furrypaws turn out the meangirl coalition" Does Babymouse have what it takes to become the voice of the people? (Publisher's note)

Babymouse: cupcake tycoon. By Jennifer L. Holm & Matthew Holm. Random House 2010 89p.
Grades: 3 4 5 6
741.5; 741
978-0-375-86573-2 (pa), $6.99; 0-375-86573-X (pa)

Babymouse: Cupcake Tycoon © Jennifer L. Holm & Matthew Holm

"It's champagne wishes and cupcake dreams for Babymouse! The school library is having a fund-raiser, and Babymouse is determined to raise the most money and WIN the GRAND PRIZE. Or . . . er, to help the school! The competition is fierce, but Babymouse will stop at nothing to get what she wants, even if it means outselling every last kid in school . . . including her nefarious nemesis, Felicia Furrypaws." (Publisher's note)

Babymouse: heartbreaker. Random House 2006 91p.
Grades: 3 4 5 6   **741; Fic; 741.5**

1. Babymouse (Fictional character); 2. Humorous graphic novels; 3. Mice; 4. Valentine's Day
0-375-93798-6 (lib bdg), $12.99; 0-375-83798-1 (pa), $5.99; 978-0-375-93798-9 (lib bdg); 978-0-375-83798-2 (pa)

LC 2006-45418
"Romantic Babymouse . . . here finds her confidence shaken by the impending Valentine's Day dance at school. . . . The text and illustrations successfully differentiate between reality and daydreams, and there's a good amount of humor injected in both." Horn Book
Another title in the author's series about Babymouse

Babymouse: mad scientist. By Jennifer L. Holm & Matthew Holm. Random House 2011 91p. Illustration
Grades: 3 4 5 6
741.5; 741
978-0-375-96574-6 (lib bdg), $12.99; 0-375-96574-2 (lib bdg); 978-0-375-86574-9 (pa), $6.99; 0-375-86574-8 (pa)

Babymouse: Mad Scientist © Jennifer L. Holm & Matthew Holm

LC 2009-47388
"Babymouse decides to enter the science fair. She daydreams about science-fiction movies and television shows (Star Trek, The Attack of the 50-Foot Woman); fantasizes about winning the Nobel Prize; learns about the scientific method in class—and then she discovers an amoeba named Squish." (Booklist)

Babymouse: monster mash. Random House 2008 93p.
Grades: 3 4 5 6   **741; 741.5; Fic**
1. Halloween; 2. Humorous graphic novels; 3. Mice; 4. Graphic novels
978-0-375-93789-7 (lib bdg), $11.99; 978-0-375-84387-7 (pa), $5.99

LC 2008-08433
It's Halloween, and Babymouse loves dressing up in spooky costumes to go trick-or-treating with best buddy Wilson. Of course, Felicia has to say that girls must be pretty "It's a rule." Then Babymouse's mother tells her she can have a Halloween party, and when Felicia finds out, she bullies Babymouse into inviting her and orders her to go trick-or-treating with them. Felicia is not a nice kid on Halloween; she leads her cronies in teepeeing and egging houses. But at Babymouse's party, she decides to do things her way after all. For this Halloween volume, the color scheme doesn't include pink, but orange. Babymouse imagines herself in classic horror movie scenarios, but they shouldn't be too scary for most young readers.
Another title in the author's series about Babymouse

Babymouse: puppy love. [by] Jennifer L. Holm and Matthew Holm. Random House 2007 91p. Illustration
Grades: 3 4 5 6   **741.5**
978-0-375-93990-7 (lib bdg), $12.99; 978-0-375-83990-0 (pa), $5.99

LC 2007-61012

"Babymouse doesn't exactly have a great history with pets—even her goldfish ran away from home. But all that's about to change. Will Babymouse get the dog of her dreams? Will she ever find her missing fish?" (Publisher's note)

Babymouse: skater girl. [by] Jennifer L. Holm & Matthew Holm. Random House 2007 91p. Illustration
Grades: 3 4 5 6   **741.5; 741**
978-0-375-93989-1 (lib bdg); 0-375-93989-X (lib bdg); 978-0-375-83989-4 (pa), $5.99; 0-375-83989-5 (pa)
LC 2006-50444

"Babymouse daydreams about being a medal-winning figure skater. She can almost hear the roar of the crowd, the fans cheering her name, the sportscasters' excitement. But when she's actually noticed by a professional coach and told she has talent, Babymouse develops a lust for glory . . . which is greatly tested by the harsh reality of before- and after-school practices, a ban on cupcakes, and no free time for friends." (Horn Book)

Babymouse: the musical. By Jennifer & Matthew Holm. Random House 2009 96p. Illustration
Grades: 3 4 5 6   **741.5; Fic**
1. Humorous graphic novels; 2. Mice; 3. School stories; 4. Graphic novels
978-0-375-93791-0, $11.99; 978-0-375-84388-4 (pa), $5.99
LC 2008-10891

The school is going to produce a musical, and Babymouse auditions. Unfortunately, she has a tendency to trip over her own two feet, and the lead role demands someone who can sing and dance. Nemesis Felicia wins the lead role, and Babymouse is her understudy, while new transfer student Henry Higgins (a British hedgehog) has the male lead role. As Babymouse gets through school days (complete with the torture of dodgeball) and rehearsals, she daydreams Broadway musicals.
Another title in the author's series about Babymouse

Camp Babymouse. Random House 2007 95p. Illustration
Grades: 2 3 4 5 6   **741.5; Fic**
1. Babymouse (Fictional character); 2. Humorous graphic novels; 3. Graphic novels
978-0-375-93988-4 (lib bdg), $12.99; 978-0-375-83988-7 (pa), $5.99

Babymouse is looking forward to Camp Wild Whiskers, and two weeks of fresh air, fun, and friendship. She can't wait for the adventures to start. All that she has to do is relax and make sure she doesn't get lost in the wilderness. What could possibly go wrong? Will camp be all that Babymouse dreams of? Problems such as losing points by spilling punch, tipping her canoe during the canoe race, accidentally starting a really big fire, and her cabin mates complaining that she'll put them in last place make her wonder if she should even be there.

Extreme Babymouse. By Jennifer L. Holm & Matthew Holm. Random House Inc. 2013 91 p. Color illustration
Grades: 2 3 4   **741.5/973; 741.5**
1. Imagination — Fiction; 2. Mice — Fiction; 3. Mice — Juvenile fiction; 4. Schools — Fiction; 5. Snowboarding — Fiction; 6. Graphic novels

0307931609, $6.99; 9780307931603
LC 2012022834

Author Matthew Holm presents the seventeenth book in his series on Babymouse, which focuses on snowboarding. "(Uh, snowboarding, Babymouse? Is that really a good idea? You don't exactly have a good history with . . . er, being outside). Will Babymouse make it off the bunny slope? Will this winter be extreme—or just extremely lame? And does locker really have a cousin? Find out in EXTREME Babymouse! Snowy Mountain will never be the same!" (Publisher's note)

★ **Sunny** side up. Jennifer L. Holm & Matthew Holm; with color by Lark Pien. Graphix 2015 224 p. Illustration
Grades: 3 4 5 6   **741.5; Fic**
1. Adventure fiction; 2. Florida — Fiction; 3. Friendship — Fiction; 4. Grandfathers — Fiction; 5. Summer — Fiction
0545741653; 9780545741651, $23.99
LC 2014957906

In this book, by Jennifer L. Holm, illustrated by Matthew Holm, "Sunny Lewin has been packed off to Florida to live with her grandfather for the summer. At first she thought Florida might be fun. . . . But the place where Gramps lives is no amusement park. It's full of . . . old people. Really old people. Luckily, Sunny isn't the only kid around. She meets Buzz, a boy who is completely obsessed with comic books, and soon they're having adventures of their own." (Publisher's note)

"Woven into the Florida frolic though, through dated flashback images, is the real reason for Sunny's last-minute visit: her older brother is struggling with addiction, and Sunny thinks she got him in trouble. Though Sunny will appeal to all kinds of readers, an authors' note shares the Holms' hope to let kids in similar situations know that it's OK to feel sad and to talk about it. Clear dialogue bubbles, plenty of wordless spreads, and Matthew's cartoons and beach-umbrella color palette keep Sunny's story an upbeat one that readers will easily stick with." Booklist

Holm, Matthew
     Babymouse #11: dragonslayer. [by] Jennifer L. Holm & Matthew Holm. Random House Childrens Books 2009 96p. Illustration
Grades: 3 4 5 6   **741.5; Fic**
1. Babymouse (Fictional character); 2. Humorous graphic novels; 3. Mathematics; 4. Mice
978-0-375-95712-3, $12.99; 978-0-375-85712-6 (pa), $5.99
LC 2008-51110

Babymouse loves to read, and to daydream about the books she reads, but she does NOT do well in math. In fact, she's just received an F on a test, and her teacher decides to have her join the Mathletes in order to make up for it. The Mathletes compete with other school teams in math competitions, and they have wanted to win the Golden Slide Rule for a long time. A competing team called the Owlgarithms have won it year after year. However, Babymouse seems to be more of a liability than a new asset for the team. She suffers through lunchtime practice sessions and much prefers to daydream of adventures with The Lion, the Witch, and the Wardrobe or The Hobbit rather than do math. Then, at the math competition, events conspire to make her the team's only hope in a final round against one of the Owlgorithms. The book is illustrated in the usual black, white and pink, and it might, just might, help some girls think of math as something they can do well (after all, if Babymouse can compete in a math tournament, maybe they can, too).

Cover title: Babymouse Dragonslayer

Babymouse burns rubber!. By Jennifer L. Holm & Matthew Holm. Random House 2010 91p. Illustration

*Babymouse Burns Rubber ©
Jennifer L. Holm & Matthew Holm*

Grades: 3 4 5 6   **741.5; 741**
978-0-375-95713-0 (lib bdg), $12.99;
0-375-95713-8 (lib bdg);
978-0-375-85713-3 (pa), $5.99; 0-375-85713-3 (pa)
LC 2009018819

"Babymouse dreams of glory in the soap box derby but doesn't put much effort into preparation. She sweet-talks best friend and fellow contestant Wilson into building (and re-building) her car, preventing him from being ready on race day." (Horn Book)

Babymouse: queen of the world. Random House Books for Young Readers 2005 91p. Illustration
Grades: 3 4 5 6   **741.5; Fic**
1. Babymouse (Fictional character); 2. Friendship; 3. Humorous graphic novels; 4. Mice; 5. Graphic novels
0-375-93229-1 (lib bdg), $12.99; 0-375-83229-7 (pa), $5.95
LC 2004-51166

"In this energetic comic . . . Babymouse, a wise-cracking rodent stand-in for your average, adventure-seeking nine-year-old, strives to capture popular Felicia's goodwill, finally achieving her end at the expense of Wilson Weasel, truest of friends. But, wouldn't you know it, Felicia's world has little to offer a smart, fun-loving mouse, after all." Booklist

Other titles in this series are: Babymouse: our hero (2005); Babymouse: beach babe (2006); Babymouse: rock star (2006); Babymouse: heartbreaker (2006); Camp Babymouse (2007); Babymouse: skater girl (2007); Babymouse: puppy love (2007); Babymouse: monster mash (2008); Babymouse the musical (2009); Babymouse: dragonslaver (2009); Babymouse burns rubber (2010); Babymouse: cupcake tycoon (2010); Babymouse: mad scientist (2011); A very Babymouse Christmas (2011); Babymouse for president (2012); Extreme Babymouse (2012); Happy birthday Babymouse (2014)

A **Very** Babymouse Christmas. By Jennifer L. Holm & Matthew Holm. Random House Childrens Books 2011 89p. Illustration (Babymouse)
Grades: 3 4 5 6   **741.5**
1. Christmas — Fiction; 2. Gifts — Fiction; 3. Humorous graphic novels; 4. Imagination — Fiction; 5. Mice —

Fiction; 6. Graphic novels; 7. Babymouse (Fictional character)
978-0-375-96779-5, $12.99;
978-0-375-86779-8 (pa), $6.99
LC 2010027988

*Very Babymouse Christmas ©
Jennifer L. Holm & Matthew Holm*

"Babymouse feels she simply cannot live without the Whiz Bang, this Christmas's must-have gift. This graphic novel's single-minded focus reflects Babymouse's all-consuming obsession, a condition with which readers are likely to be familiar. Her holiday-classic-inspired, pink-hued daydreams allow Babymouse to switch off the mania for a while." (Horn Book)

Horowitz, Anthony
Stormbreaker: the graphic novel. [by] Anthony Horowitz; adapted Antony Johnston; illustrated by Kanako Damerum & Yusuru Takasaki. Philomel Books 2006 Un Illustration (Alex Rider)
Grades: 5 6 7 8   **741; 741.5**
1. Spies; 2. Graphic novels
0-399-24633-9, $14.99

In this graphic novel version on Horowitz's novel, fourteen-year-old Alex Rider is coerced into continuing his uncle's dangerous work for Britain's intelligence agency, MI6.

"If it's possible, this is even more rapidly paced than the novel. Alex remains an appealing hero here, and the idea of a heroic teen up against insidious adults continues to be an extremely powerful draw for readers." Booklist

Other graphic novel adaptations in this series are: Point blank (2007); Skeleton key (2009); Eagle strike (2012)

Hosler, Jay
Clan Apis. Active Synapse 2000 158p. Illustration
Grades: 4 5 6 7 8 9 10 11 12   **741.5; Fic**
1. Bees; 2. Science; 3. Graphic novels
0-9677255-0-X, $15

"Opening with a creation myth . . . and working through the biological, sociological, and ecological changes affecting the life of Nyuki the bee, the text is a combination of authoritative science; appealing, detailed black-and-white drawings; and dialogue replete with humor, pubescent angst, political sloganeering, and more. Nyuki's colony undertakes migration to a new hive, is beset by a woodpecker, and hibernates through a winter that yields to a revitalizing spring." Booklist

★ The **last** of the sandwalkers. Written and illustrated by Jay Hosler. First Second 2015 312 p. Illustration
Grades: 5 6 7 8 9 10   **741.5; Fic**
1. Adventure fiction; 2. Beetles — Fiction; 3. Science fiction; 4. Scientific expeditions — Fiction; 5. Graphic novels

162672024X; 9781626720244, $16.99

LC 2014045542

This book, by Jay Hosler, is about a "civilization of beetles. In this bug's paradise, beetles write books, run restaurants, and even do scientific research. But not too much scientific research is allowed by the powerful elders, who guard a terrible secret about the world outside. . . . Lucy is not one to quietly cooperate, however. This tiny field scientist defies the law of her safe but authoritarian home and leads a team of researchers out into the desert." (Publisher's note)

"Hosler's cartooning is no less meticulous than his writing and similarly retains a sense of animated energy and humor, engaging readers with characters that are far from human, but filled with humanity." Booklist

Includes bibliographical references

The **Sandwalk** Adventures: An Adventure in Evolution Told in Five Chapters. Active Synapse 2003 160p. Illustration

Grades: 4 5 6 7 8 9 10 11 12 Adult   **576.8; 741.5**
1. Darwin, Charles; 2. Evolution; 3. Science; 4. Graphic novels
0-9677255-1-8, $20

Scientist Hosler explains Darwin's theory of evolution in a whimsical fashion. Follicle mites Mara and Willy live in Darwin's left eyebrow, and by accident they discover that Darwin, whom they call the god Flycatcher, can hear Mara. He thinks he's going crazy, but as he takes his daily walks on the Sandwalk at his home in England, Darwin does his best to convince Mara and Willy that he isn't a god and tells them about evolution. Hosler uses humor and whimsy, but also did a lot of research; the book includes explanatory notes and a long bibliography of sources.

Hotta, Yumi
★ **Hikaru** No Go, Volume 1. [by] Yumi Hotta and Takeshi Obata. Viz Media, LLC 2004 192p. Illustration
Grades: 5 6 7 8 9 10 11 12   **741.5; Fic**
1. Board games; 2. Manga; 3. Shonen manga; 4. Graphic novels
1-59116-222-X, $7.95

Sixth-grader Hikaru Shindo is not interested in intellectual pursuits, but by a twist of fate, the spirit of Fujiwara no Sai, the ghost of an ancient Go master, manages to bond with Hikaru. Now, suddenly, Hikaru can play Go, a complex board game of strategy, better than almost anyone under 18 and most adults, too. Akira, who has been raised by his Go master father, needs to know more about the upstart Hikaru, who beats him and yet seems so casual about the game. This is the first volume of an ongoing series.

Volume 1 of a 23 volume series

Huey, Debbie
Bumperboy loses his marbles. Adhouse Books 2005 96p. Illustration
Grades: 2 3 4   **741.5; Fic**
1. Graphic novels
0976661004, $7.95

Bumperboy is all set to play in the big Marble Tournament, but on his way to the park, he trips on a rock and his marbles including Grandma's prize shooter fall into a

Borp Hole! Borp Holes are short cuts through many different lands, and Bumperboy must go through the Borp Hole and search as many of the lands as he can to find his marbles in time for the tournament.

This title is currently out of print. Author is seeking a new publisher to reprint.

Another title about Bumperboy is: Bumperboy and the Loud Loud Mountain (2006)

Hughes, Susan
No girls allowed: tales of daring women dressed as men for love, freedom and adventure. Written by Susan Hughes; llustrated by Willow Dawson. Kids Can Press 2008 80p. Illustration
Grades: 3 4 5 6 7 8 9   **306.7; 741.5**
1. Biographical graphic novels; 2. Transvestites; 3. Graphic novels
978-1-55453-177-6, $16.95; 978-1-55453-178-3 (pa), $9.95

LC 2007-9060846

This book collects short biographies in graphic format of young women who dressed as and pretended to be men in order to do and be what they wanted. The real Mu Lan did pretend to be her father's son in order to serve in the Chinese Emperor's army to protect her father. Hatshepsut was an Egyptian princess who was determined to be pharaoh, although that role could only go to men. Margaret Buckley was a young Englishwoman who became Dr. James Barry in the early nineteenth century. Seven women's stories are told here, and the book includes a short list of books for further reading.

Hugo, Victor
The **Hunchback** of Notre Dame by Victor Hugo ; retold by L.L. Owens ; illustrated by Greg Rebis Stone Arch Books 2006 63p. Illustration
Grades: 3 4 5 6 7 8 9   **741.5; Fic**
1. Adventure graphic novels; 2. Hugo, Victor, 1802-1885 — Adaptations; 3. Graphic novels
978-1-59889-047-1, $23.93

Hidden away in the bell tower of the Cathedral of Notre Dame, Quasimodo is treated like a beast. Although he is gentle and kind, he has the reputation of a frightening monster because of his physical deformities. He develops affection for Esmeralda, a gypsy girl who shows him kindness in return. When the girl is sentenced to an unfair death by hanging, Quasimodo is determined to save her. But those closest to Quasimodo have other plans for the gypsy. This adaptation is written for reluctant and struggling readers, and the tragic story is handled with sensitivity.

Part of the Graphic Revolve series.

Humphreys, Jessica Dee
Child Soldier: When Boys and Girls Are Used in War. Michel Chikwanine, Jessica Dee Humphreys; illustrated by Claudia Davila. Kids Can Press 2015 48 p. Color; Illustration
Grades: 5 6 7 8   **741.5; 355**
1. Chikwanine, Michel; 2. Child soldiers
1771381264; 9781771381260, $17.95

This children's book, written by Michel Chikwanine and Jessica Dee Humphreys, and illustrated by Claudia

Davila, describes the experience of a child solder. "Michel Chikwanine was five years old when he was abducted from his schoolyard soccer game in the Democratic Republic of Congo and forced to become a soldier for a brutal rebel militia. Against the odds, Michel managed to escape . . ., but he was never the same again." (Publisher's note)

"Chikwanine's narration is matter of fact but never didactic, emphasizing less the gruesome details and more young Michel's emotional response and attempts to make sense of the world around him. Earthy hued and gentle, the images make a potentially disturbing topic accessible." SLJ

Hunter, Erin
Warriors: Tigerstar & Sasha #1: into the woods. Created by Erin Hunter; written by Dan Jolley; art by Don Hudson. HarperCollins/Tokyopop 2008 108p. Illustration
Grades: 3 4 5 6 7 8 9   **741.5; Fic**
  1. Adventure graphic novels; 2. Cats; 3. Graphic novels
  978-0-06-154792-8, $6.99; 0-06-154792-1
  Sasha was a loved, pampered kittypet, but when one of the housefolk dies and the other moves away, they leave her behind. She had always explored the woods at night, but now she has to survive on her own. Then she meets Tigerstar, leader of ShadowClan, and they spend a lot of time together as he teaches her how to improve her hunting. He even offers her membership in the clan, but he has secrets, and when Sasha discovers one of them, she has to decide if she can trust him. There are scenes of cats hunting prey such as mice and squirrels, and fighting with foxes.
  Other titles in this series are:Escape from the forest (2008); Return to the clans (2009)

Hurchalla, Elizabeth
Bakugan battle brawlers: The battle begins!. Del Rey 2008 Un Illustration
Grades: 3 4 5 6 7   **741.5; Fic**
  1. Adventure graphic novels; 2. Fantasy graphic novels; 3. Games; 4. Graphic novels
  978-0-345-51368-7, $7.99
  Dan and his online friends are Bakugan Battle Brawlers, playing a game invented when strange, magic cards fell all over the Earth and into the hands of young people. The cards contain Bakugan guardians—creatures with great powers to fight. What the young players don't know is that Bakugan isn't only a game, the Bakugan guardians come from different worlds in a dimension called Vestroia, and the games played here in this world affect the battle between good and evil there. And in Vestroia, Drago from the fire world Pyrus must save his dimension from those who would destroy it for their gain; his one hope is to join with Dan on Earth. This book is illustrated with screen captures from the animated series airing on the Cartoon Network. It contains lots of action with fighting between the various Bakugan creatures. Bakugan is also a series of games figures that people can play, similar to the Yu-Gi-Oh, Pokemon, and other game-based manga and graphic novels.

Ben 10 Alien Force: Ben 10 returns. Del Rey 2008 96p. Illustration
Grades: 3 4 5 6 7 8   **741.5; Fic**
  1. Adventure graphic novels; 2. Science fiction graphic novels; 3. Graphic novels

978-0-345-51438-7, $7.99
  Ben Tennyson had lived as Ben 10, a superhero thanks to the watch-like Omnitrix that could transform him into any of ten superpowered alien life-forms. Five years ago, he put away the Omnitrix in order to live a normal life. However, his Grandpa Max is a Plumber, a member of an intergalactic police force, and he has continued his work. Now fifteen years old and a star soccer player, Ben visits Grandpa Max's trailer only to learn that Max has disappeared, a weird and creepy alien tries to get him, and Max has left a cryptic holographic message. Ben digs out his Omnitrix, seeks out his cousin Gwen, who has super powers of her own, and then they run into another Plumber who has been searching for Max. They team up to find him and to learn why more aliens are coming to Earth and engaging in illegal transactions. This book is illustrated with screen captures from the Cartoon Network program.

Hutchison, David
Oz: The Manga. Antarctic Press 2006 Un Illustration
Grades: 4 5 6 7 8 9   **741.5; Fic**
  1. Baum, L Frank — Adaptations; 2. Fantasy graphic novels; 4. Graphic novels
  978-1-932453-69-0, $14.95
  This is Baum's classic novel, The Wizard of Oz, adapted into manga format by Hutchison. All the characters are here: Dorothy, Toto, the Cowardly Lion, the Tin Woodsman, the Scarecrow, the Wizard. And all the main plot elements are here, from the cyclone that blows Dorothy and Toto to Oz to the Flying Monkeys to dealing with the Wicked Witch. The art makes this adaptation shine, especially the Tin Woodsman, who is a steampunk wonder.

Ihara, Shigekatsu
Pokemon diamond and pearl adventure!, vol. 2. Viz Media/Viz Kids 2008 192p. Illustration
Grades: 3 4 5 6 7 8 9   **741.5; Fic**
  1. Adventure graphic novels; 2. Fantasy graphic novels; 3. Manga; 4. Graphic novels
  978-1-4215-2287-6, $7.99
  Hareta, Mitsumi, and their Pokemon friends continue on their quest to find Dialga, the Pokemon that rules time. They journey through the land of Sinnoh as Hareta and his partner Piglup grow stronger; they also keep ruining Team Galactic's nasty schemes. In Celestic Town, they find that Team Galactic's boss, Cyrus, has beat them to finding the first major clue to Dialga's whereabouts. And Hareta decides he needs help to become a better Trainer, but he and Piglup will have to pass Gym Leader Byron's test before he will accept them as students. There's lots of Pokemon fighting action.

Ikeda, Akiko
Chibikuro party. Dark Horse Books 2008 Un Illustration
Grades: 2 3 4 5 6 7   **741.5; Fic**
  1. Adventure graphic novels; 2. Animals; 3. Humorous graphic novels; 4. Graphic novels
  978-1-59582-128-7, $9.95
  One night the moon wakes up Dayan's shadow—it's the one night that the shadows are free to move about on their own. Dayan's shadow, Chip (Dayan names him) wakes him

up and wants him to go to the shadows' party, called the Chibikuro Party. The Satan of Death Forest sends Noel disguised as a shadow to kidnap all the shadows, and Noel tricks the shadows by saying they can go with him and be free forever. Dayan hears all this, and he rouses his friends to save their shadows from Death Forest.

Part of the Dayan's collection books series

Dayan's birthday. Dark Horse Books 2008 Un Illustration

Grades: 2 3 4 5 6 7   **741.5; Fic**
  1. Animals; 2. Humorous graphic novels; 3. Graphic novels
  978-1-59582-125-6, $9.95
  The cat Dayan learns that he has a birthday, but he doesn't know what it is. He goes to a trio of witches to find out when his birthday will come, and then he throws a big party for everyone. However, he forgot to invite the witches, and they come to take his birthday back. This book is done in a small picture book format and is translated from Japanese. The woodland creatures serve the witches strong liquor to help Dayan

Part of the Dayan's collection book series

Thursday rainy party. Dark Horse Boks 2008 Un Illustration

Grades: 2 3 4 5 6 7   **741.5; Fic**
  1. Animals; 2. Humorous graphic novels; 3. Graphic novels
  978-1-59582-126-3, $9.95
  One day Dayan gets caught in the rain, and he meets a friendly frog. He invites the frog to come to Willie the mouse's next rainy Thursday party, but learns the frog doesn't know anything about days of the week. Dayan creates a special calendar for his new friend, but the next rainy Thursday doesn't happen for several weeks; did the frog keep up with the calendar, and will he come to Willie's party?

Part of the Dayan's collection books series

White Eurocka. Dark Horse Books 2008 Un Illustration

Grades: 2 3 4 5 6 7   **741.5; Fic**
  1. Animals; 2. Humorous graphic novels; 3. Graphic novels
  978-1-59582-127-0, $9.95
  Winter comes to the land of Tachiel along with a strong cold wave, much colder than most winters. As the festival of Eurocka approaches, Dayan and his friends find that many other creatures have come from the North penguins, walruses, and polar bears, to participate in the festival. During the celebrations, a baby polar bear cub magically arrives.

Part of the Dayan's collection books series

Irving, Washington
  The **legend** of Sleepy Hollow. Washington Irving (retold by Blake A. Hoena); illustrated by Tod Smith.. Stone Arch Books 2008 72p. Illustration

Grades: 4 5 6 7 8 9   **741.5; Fic**
  1. Ghosts; 2. Horror graphic novels; 3. Humorous graphic novels; 4. Graphic novels
  978-1-4342-0446-2, $23.93; 978-1-4342-0496-7 (pa), $9.95

LC 2007-30807
  Tarrytown's new schoolmaster, Ichabod Crane, thinks little of the legend his students tell him about a headless horseman who haunts Sleepy Hollow. Crane must cross the Hollow in order to visit the Van Tassel home, for he fancies himself to be in love with Katrina Van Tassel. However, local strongarm man Brom wants Katrina for himself, and he plays mischief with Crane and the school. Eventually, the legendary ghost may play a role in this love triangle. This graphic novel adaptation of Irving's classic provides lots of humor and a few chills with a simple vocabulary, background notes on how Irving wrote his story, and discussion questions.

Part of the Graphic Revolve series

Isenberg, Marty
  Transformers animated volume 1. IDW Publishing 2008 Un Illustration

Grades: 2 3 4 5 6 7 8   **741.5; Fic**
  1. Adventure graphic novels; 2. Robots; 3. Science fiction graphic novels; 4. Transformers (Fictional characters); 5. Graphic novels
  978-1-60010-151-9, $7.99
  When Optimus Prime and his team of misfit Autobots accidentally unearth the Allspark, they are attacked by Megatron, leader of the Decepticons. The fight causes the Autobots' ship to travel from deep space to Earth in the twenty-second century, and to New Detroit. Now the fight between the Autobots and the Decepticons will take place on Earth, where humans live, humans who don't know what all these sentient robots are doing. This book adapts stories from the new animated television series and uses screen captures from the programs to illustrate the book.

Transformers animated volume 2. IDW Publishing 2008 Un Illustration

Grades: 2 3 4 5 6 7 8   **741.5; Fic**
  1. Adventure graphic novels; 2. Robots; 3. Science fiction graphic novels; 4. Transformers (Fictional characters); 5. Graphic novels
  978-1-60010-152-6, $7.99
  The Autobots have human allies now, one of whom, the young girl Sari, decides to give her new robotic friends a quick tour of Earth's history, starting with Dino-Drive, an old amusement park filled with animatronic dinosaurs. However, the somewhat disassembled Megatron finds a human ally, too, in the scientist named Sumdac (Sari's dad), and together they create the Dinobots. Then, someone gives the thief Nino Sexton a prototype turbo-boosting bio-armor, and he uses it to rob banks; the Autobots have to stop him and recover the armor. The stories have been adapted from broadcast episodes of the new animated Transformers television series and illustrated with screen captures from the programs.

Ishihara, Yoko
  ★ The **manga** cookbook. Presented by the Manga University Culinary Institute; illustrations by Chihiro Hattori; [with recipes by Yoko Ishihara]. Japanime Co. Ltd. 2007 158p. Illustration

Grades: 4 5 6 7 8 9 10 11 12   **641.5; 741.5**
  1. Japanese cooking; 2. Manga; 3. Graphic novels

978-4-921205-07-2, $14.95

Food appears frequently in manga and in anime, but just what are the characters eating" This book is an illustrated step-by-step guide to preparing some Japanese dishes, from onigiri (rice balls) to yakitori (skewered grilled chicken), oshinko (pickled vegetables), udon (Japanese noodles). to traditional sweets and desserts. Definitions of terms and ingredients used, basic cooking guidelines, and instructions on how to properly use chopsticks are all included. The recipes are authentic but have been simplified somewhat so older children and teens with some basic kitchen skills can prepare the foods. Adult supervision is recommended for younger children and for children who aren't very experienced with using knives, measuring spoons, and cooking on the stove.

Ita, Sam

20,000 leagues under the sea: a pop-up book. Sterling Publishing Co., Inc. 2008 Un Illustration

Grades: 1 2 3 4 5   **741.5; Fic**
1. Adventure graphic novels; 2. Pop-up books; 3. Science fiction graphic novels; 4. Verne, Jules, 1828-1905; 5. Verne, Jules, 1828-1905 — Adaptations; 6. Graphic novels
978-1-4027-5776-1, $26.95

This book combines the graphic novel format with pop-up paper engineering to provide a different kind of reading experience for this classic novel of adventure. Professor Aronnax, his servant, and harpooner Ned become captives of Captain Nemo and his submarine, the Nautilus. Intricate pop-ups provide looks at the interiors of the submarine, the lost city of Atlantis, and a gigantic squid that attacks the Nautilus. The story is presented in comic book panels with a very informal, easy-reading text suitable for younger readers.

Jacobson, Ryan

Eleanor Roosevelt: First Lady of the World by Ryan Jacobson ; illustrated by Gordon Purcell and Barbara Schulz Capstone Press 2006 32p. Illustration

Grades: 3 4 5 6 7 8 9   **741.5; 973.917; 92**
1. Biographical graphic novels; 2. Roosevelt, Eleanor, 1884-1962; 3. Graphic novels
0-7368-4969-6, $25.26

LC 2004028556

This book uses the comic book format to describe highlights in the life and work of U.S. First Lady Eleanor Roosevelt. It includes additional information, a glossary, a list of books for further reading, and more.

Part of the Graphic Library, Graphic Biographies series.

Jacques, Brian

Redwall: the graphic novel. By Brian Jacques; illustrated by Bret Blevins; adapted by Stuart Moore; lettering by Richard Starkings. Philomel Books 2007 143p. Illustration

Grades: 4 5 6 7 8 9   **741.5; Fic**
1. Adventure graphic novels; 2. Fantasy graphic novels; 3. Mice; 4. Graphic novels
978-0-399-24481-0, $12.99; 0-399-24481-6

When Cluny the rat's army attacks Redwall Abbey, young Matthias the mouse follows in the footsteps of the long-ago hero Martin the Warrior to defend his home

"The story is a page-turner, and the detailed black-and-white drawings capture both the passion and the pathos." SLJ

Jakobsen, Lars

The **mysterious** manuscript. Lars Jakobsen. Graphic Universe 2012 48 p.

Grades: 4 5 6 7 8   **741.5/9489; Fic**
1. Crime — Fiction; 2. Mystery fiction; 3. Scotland — Fiction; 4. Time travel; 5. Time travel — Fiction; 6. Graphic novels
0761378839; 9780761378839, $27.93

LC 2011027146

This graphic novel, by Lars Jakobsen, is part of the "Mortensen's Escapades" series. "A book collector shows Mortensen . . . an illuminated manuscript from 1512. When Mortensen sees a painting of an airplane on one of its pages, he knows he has a mystery to unravel. With a zap from his time gun, he travels back to medieval Scotland to look for clues. A wise scribe and a mute witch help him . . . [to] answer . . . how did an airplane crash land in the Middle Ages?" (Publisher's note)

The **Santa** Fe jail. By Lars Jakobsen; illustrated by Lars Jakobsen. Graphic Universe 2012 48 p.

Grades: 4 5 6   **741.5/9489; Fic**
1. Adventure graphic novels; 2. Kidnapping; 3. Kidnapping — Fiction; 4. Time travel; 5. Time travel — Fiction; 6. Graphic novels
0822594218; 9780761378860; 9780822594215, $6.95

LC 2011044643

This adventure graphic novel, by Lars Jakobsen, is book 2 of the "Mortensen's Escapades" series. In it "Mortensen is given a special assignment: deliver . . . [a] ransom to the Santa Fe Jail. But the kidnappers are time travelers, so nothing is as simple as it seems. . . . Mortensen . . . is drugged by a mysterious woman. He awakens to find himself packed inside a cargo plane that is about to nose dive into the jungles of Tanzania." (Publisher's note)

The **secret** mummy. Art by Lars Jakobsen; story by Lars Jakobsen; translation by Lars Jakobsen and Robyn Chapman. Graphic Universe 2013 48 p. (Mortensen's escapades)

Grades: 4 5 6 7 8   **741.5/9489**
1. Criminals — Fiction; 2. Time travel — Fiction; 3. Transplantation of organs, tissues, etc — Fiction; 4. Vampires; 6. Graphic novels
0761379150; 9780761379157, $27.93

LC 2012027015

This is the fourth Mortensen adventure from Lars Jakobsen. "Mortensen, an agent dedicated to relentlessly fighting the ever-cresting wave of nefarious time-traveling criminals, now faces vampires in 19th-century Transylvania. Jumping uneasily through time from Prague to Transylvania to Bosnia and Paris, this wayward hero follows a creepy count thought to be a villainous vampire and the shadowy sarcophagus that seems tied to him." (Kirkus)

Originally published in Danish under title: Den falske mumie, in 2012.

Jamieson, Victoria
★ **Roller** girl. By Victoria Jamieson. Dial Books 2015 240 p. Color; Illustration
Grades: 4 5 6 7 8   **741.5; Fic**
1. Friendship — Fiction; 2. Roller derby — Fiction; 3. Roller skating — Fiction; 4. Graphic novels
0803740166; 9780803740167, $12.99
                                        LC 2014011310
Newbery Honor Book (2016)
This graphic novel, by Victoria Jamieson, is "about friendship and surviving junior high through the power of roller derby. For most of her twelve years, Astrid has done everything with her best friend Nicole. But after Astrid falls in love with roller derby and signs up for derby camp, Nicole decides to go to dance camp instead. And so begins the most difficult summer of Astrid's life as she struggles to keep up with the older girls at camp." (Publisher's note)
"Jamieson captures this snapshot of preteen angst with a keenly decisive eye, brilliantly juxtaposing the nuances of roller derby with the twists and turns of adolescent girls' friendships." Kirkus

Jeffrey, Gary
Bob Marley: The Life of a Musical Legend. Art by Terry Riley. The Rosen Publishing Group 2007 48p. Illustration
Grades: 3 4 5 6 7 8 9
741.5
1. Biographical graphic novels; 2. Marley, Bob, 1945-1981; 3. Graphic novels
978-1-4042-0854-4, $29.25

This comic book format biography presents the life
Courtesy of Rosen Publishing

and musical career of legendary reggae master Marley, from his early years in Jamaica to international stardom. Additional material gives background information about Jamaica, its land and people, its music, and the Rastafarian religion. The book includes a glossary and a list of books for further reading.
Part of the Graphic Biographies

Elasmosaurus: the long-necked swimmer. Illustrated by Terry Riley. Rosen Publishing Group 2009 32p. Illustration
Grades: 2 3 4 5 6 7
567.9; 741.5
1. Dinosaurs; 2. Graphic novels
978-1-4358-2505-5, $25.25
                LC 2008-3881
This book uses comic book style art to introduce young readers to the elasmosaurus, which lived

Courtesy of Rosen Publishing

in the ancient shallow ocean that used to cover Kansas. The book provides some science-based speculation on what the dinosaur's life might have been like. Additional material includes information on fossil evidence, quick facts about the elasmosaurus, and a glossary.
Part of the Graphic Dinosaurs series.

Hurricane hunters and tornado chasers. Illustrated by Gianluca Garofalo. Rosen Publishing Group 2008 48p.
Grades: 3 4 5 6 7 8 9
551.55; 741.5
1. Meteorology; 2. Storms; 3. Vocational guidance; 4. Graphic novels
978-1-4042-1458-3, $29.25
                LC 2007-42133
After brief descriptions of what hurricane hunters and tornado chasers do (and

Courtesy of Rosen Publishing

why they do it), the book profiles hurricane hunter Jeffrey Masters and tornado chasers Roger Edwards and Tim Samaras, describing a memorable incident in each of their careers.
Part of the Graphic Careers series

Hurricanes. Art by Mike Lacey. The Rosen Publishing Group 2007 48p. Illustration
Grades: 3 4 5 6 7 8   **551.55; 741.5**
1. Hurricanes; 2. Graphic novels
978-1-4042-1991-5 (lib bdg), $29.25
After describing hurricanes and how they form, the book dramatizes three deadly hurricanes. On Labor Day in 1935, the Florida Keys were hit by a small but intense hurricane with the lowest recorded barometric reading for a landfalling U.S. storm: 26.35 inches. In 1992, Category 5 Hurricane Andrew struck South Florida, and is the second costliest storm in U.S. history. And in August 2005, the infamous Hurricane Katrina struck Louisiana and Mississippi, and the storm surge flooded almost all of New Orleans. Back material describes hurricane observation, explains the Saffir-Simpson Scale describing hurricane strengths, and includes a glossary and a list of books for further reading.
Part of the Graphic Natural Disasters series.

Martin Luther King Jr.: The Life of a Civil Rights Leader. Art by Chris Forsey. Rosen Publishing Group 2006 48p. Illustration
Grades: 3 4 5 6 7 8 9
741.5; 323.1; 92
1. African Americans — Civil rights; 2. Biographical graphic novels; 3. King, Martin

Courtesy of Rosen Publishing

Luther, Jr, 1929-1968; 4. Graphic novels
978-1-4042-0858-2, $29.25

LC 2005035525

This book uses the graphic novel format to tell of the life and career of civil rights leader King. It gives additional information about segregation in the U.S. and the civil rights movement after King's death, and a list of books for further reading.

Part of the Rosen Graphic Biographies series.

Oprah Winfrey: The Life of a Media Superstar. Rosen Publishing Group 2006 48p. Illustration
Grades: 3 4 5 6 7 8 9   **741.5; 791.4; 92**
    1. Biographical graphic novels; 2. Television personalities; 3. Winfrey, Oprah, 1954-; 4. Graphic novels
978-1-4042-0862-9, $29.25

LC 2006001559

This book uses the graphic novel format to tell of the life and career (so far) of television personality Oprah Winfrey, who has been called the queen of daytime talk shows and was the first African American billionaire. The book includes background information on the civil rights movement and on daytime television, information on Winfrey's charitable work, and a list of books for further reading.

Part of the Rosen Graphic Biographies series.

Secret agents. Art by Terry Riley. Rosen Publishing Group 2008 48p. Illustration
Grades: 3 4 5 6 7 8 9   **327.12; 741.5**
    1. Espionage; 2. Spies; 3. Graphic novels
978-14042-1464-4, $29.25

LC 2007-43334

After brief descriptions of espionage and some organizations and gadgets, the book profiles three spies. During World War II, Wulf Schmidt was airdropped into Great Britain to spy for Nazi Germany, but the British had broken the communication code and knew he was coming; he became a double agent and worked for British Intelligence for the rest of the war. Oleg Penkovsky was a Soviet Intelligence officer who started working for the British in 1961; he and his British contact were caught and tried. Penkovsky was executed for treason. Robert Baer was a career CIA case officer; this book recalls one case from 1979, in India.

Part of the Graphic Careers series

Stegosaurus: the plated dinosaur. Illustrated by James Field.. Rosen Publishing Group 2009 32p. Illustration
Grades: 2 3 4 5 6 7   **567.9; 741.5**
    1. Dinosaurs; 2. Graphic novels
978-1-4358-2503-1, $25.25

LC 2007-50587

This book uses comic book style art to introduce young readers to the stegosaurus, with some science-based speculation on what the dinosaur's life might have been like. Additional material includes information on fossil evidence, quick facts about the stegosaurus, and a glossary.

Part of the Graphic Dinosaurs series.

Tornadoes & Superstorms. Art by Terry Riley. The Rosen Publishing Group 2007 48p. Illustration
Grades: 3 4 5 6 7 8   **551.5; 741.5**
    1. Storms; 2. Tornadoes; 3. Graphic novels

978-1-4042-1993-9 (lib bdg), $29.25

After describing tornadoes and superstorms in general terms, the book covers the Tri-State Tornado that struck in Missouri, Illinois, and Indiana on March 18, 1925; the Halloween Storm of October 26, 1991, also known as the Perfect Storm, that hit the Northeast coast; and the Jarrell Killer Tornado that struck in Texas on May 27, 1997. The book includes a glossary and a list of books for further reading.

Part of the Graphic Natural Disasters series.

Tsunamis and Floods. The Rosen Publishing Group 2007 48p. Illustration
Grades: 3 4 5 6 7 8   **741.5; 904.5; 904**
    1. Floods; 2. Tsunamis; 3. Graphic novels
978-1-4042-1990-8 (lib bdg), $29.25

This volume describes tsunamis and floods, and covers a few major disasters: the Lisbon Flood of 1755, the Great Midwestern Flood of 1993, and the Asian Tsunami of 2004. Comic book style panels help young readers understand the magnitude of the destructive floods and tsunamis. The book includes a glossary and a list of books for further reading.

Part of the Graphic Natural Disasters series.

Job

Yakari and the stranger. Art by Derib. Cinebook 2007 48p. Illustration
Grades: 3 4 5 6 7 8   **741.5; Fic**
    1. Animals; 2. Fantasy graphic novels; 3. Humorous graphic novels; 4. Graphic novels
978-1-905460-27-4, $11.95

Yakari is a young Native American of undetermined nation living where beavers, otters, bears, and moose live. When a white pelican crashlands in the river, suffering from a terrible cold, Yakari and the beavers try to help him, but the loud sneezes drive them all crazy during the night. Yakari tries to get help for the pelican from the otters, too, but the pelican's huge appetite wears them out. Even when he gets annoyed at the constant loud sneezing and the big appetite, Yakari keeps helping the pelican; and when the bird finally gets well, he repays everyone's kindnesses. While the French idea of what Native Americans look like is somewhat stereotypical and seems to combine several Native nations (Yakari has a pony, lives in a tepee, but the land looks more like the Northeast), the story itself is positive. Those who prefer only authentic presentations of Native Americans may not appreciate this story.

Johns, W. E.

Biggles Spitfire parade. Cinebook Ltd. 2008 48p. Illustration
Grades: 5 6 7 8 9 10   **741.5; Fic**
    1. Adventure graphic novels; 2. World War, 1939-1945 — Aerial operations; 3. Graphic novels
978-1-905460-54-0, $11.95

James Bigglesworth, known as Biggles, takes command of 666 Fighter Squadron of the RAF during World War II. He has two flights of eccentric pilots who patrol the skies and protect England from enemy aircraft that attack from Germany. Sometimes they have to protect their own airfield from Stukas and JU88s (German bombers), and from Messerschmitts (German fighters) with their Spitfires.

Biggles also has a friendly rivalry with an acquaintance who commands a squadron of Hurricanes. The book is full of air combat action, and while there is little graphic violence, people do die. This graphic novel is adapted by a French comics creator from the novels by W. E. Johns, who was a pilot himself during WWI.

Johnson, R. Kikuo
The **Shark** King: a Toon book. By R. Kikuo Johnson. TOON Books 2012 39 p. Color illustration
Grades: 2 3 4 5   **741.5/973; Fic**
1. Father-son relationship — Juvenile fiction; 2. Folklore — Hawaii; 3. Sharks — Folklore; 4. Graphic novels
1935179160; 9781935179160, $12.95
LC 2011026592
This graphic novel written and illustrated by R. Kikuo Johnson re-tells a traditional Hawaiian folktale. "Born to a loving human woman, Nanaue is a happy child (rather than the flesh-eating monster of yore) with a huge appetite and a jagged line on his back that sometimes opens into a snapping, toothy mouth. His mischievous nature soon leads him into trouble, and he dives off a cliff to escape angry villagers from whom he had been stealing fish. This unites him with his father — a huge shark who had taken human form to marry Nanaue's mother, Kalei, but returned to the sea on the night of his birth." (Kirkus)

Jolley, Dan
Alien Incident on Planet J. By Dan Jolley; illustrated by Matt Wendt; [coloring by Hi-Fi Design; lettering by Marshall Dillon].. Lerner Publishing Group/Graphic Universe 2008 112p. Illustration
Grades: 3 4 5 6 7 8 9   **741.5; Fic**
1. Adventure graphic novels; 2. Plot-your-own stories; 3. Science fiction graphic novels
978-0-8225-6998-5, $27.93; 978-0-8225-8876-4 (pa), $7.93
LC 2007-44116
In this new take on the "Choose Your Own Adventure" type of book that combines pages of prose text with pages of comic book sequences, you are a young human stuck on Planet J; your spaceship needs a new part, and you'll never get off this planet if you don't make peace with the Makanuk, the Zirifubi, and the Frongo. Some choices will end badly, others will be better, and the choices are all up to the reader.
This is Volume 8 of the Twisted Journeys series.

Escape from Pyramid X. Art by Matt Wendt. Lerner Publishing Group/Graphic Universe 2007 112p. Illustration (Twisted Journeys)
Grades: 3 4 5 6 7 8 9   **741.5; Fic**
1. Adventure graphic novels; 2. Mummies; 3. Graphic novels
978-0-8225-6777-6, $27.93; 978-0-8225-6779-0 (pa), $7.95
LC 2006-101598
In the series called Twisted Journeys, readers choose how the story will progress. Pages of text alternate with comic book-style pages. In this volume, you the reader are a student who won an essay contest to be part of an archeological dig led by Professor Emil Snackport, at the site

of a newly discovered pyramid. In some story lines, you encounter smugglers, in others, a malevolent mummy. Readers will find many scenarios played out, depending on their choices; some end well, others not so well.

The **hero** twins: against the lords of death: a Mayan myth. Story by Dan Jolley ; pencils and inks by David Witt. Lerner Publishing Group/Graphic Universe 2008 48p. Illustration
Grades: 3 4 5 6 7 8 9   **398.2; 741.5**
1. Adventure graphic novels; 2. Mayas — Folklore; 3. Graphic novels
978-0-8225-7495-8, $26.60
LC 2007-25897
The Hero Twins, Hunahpu and Xbalanque, were blessed by the Mayan gods with special powers. However, their incredible skill at playing Pok-ta-Pok, the Mayan ball game, angers the Lords of Xibalba, rulers of the Land of the Dead. When the Lords challenge them to a Pok-ta-Pok game in Xibalba, the twins know they must use all of their powers and cunning to defeat the Lords' many challenges. Comics veteran Jolley consulted several translations of the Popol Vuh, artist Witt studied books on Mayan culture, architecture and art, and Mesoamerican folklore expert John Bierhorst reviewed the story to ensure accuracy and respect for Mayan culture.
Part of the Graphic Myths & Legends series

Pigling: a Cinderella story: a Korean tale. Art by Anne Timmons. Graphic Universe 2008 48p. Illustration (Graphic myths and legends)
Grades: 3 4 5 6 7 8 9   **741.5; Fic**
1. Fairy tales; 2. Korea — Folklore; 3. Graphic novels
978-0-8225-7174-2, $27.93; 0-8225-7174-9
LC 2007-40891
In old Korea, in a time when magic still exists, Pear Blossom lives happily with her parents. But when her mother dies, her father quickly remarries a spiteful woman and her mean daughter, and they turn Pear Blossom's life into misery. They treat her like a servant and call her Pigling. Omoni (mother in Korean) makes impossible demands of Pear Blossom, and each time magical creatures help her achieve the tasks. Then on the day of a festival, a handsome magistrate sees Pear Blossom on the road, and she runs away, frightened, leaving a sandal behind.

The **Smoking** Mountain: The Story of Popocatepetl and Iztaccihuatl: An Aztec Legend. Art by David Witt. Lerner Publishing Group 2009 48p. Illustration
Grades: 3 4 5 6 7 8 9   **741.5; Fic**
1. Aztecs — Folklore; 2. Fantasy graphic novels; 3. Graphic novels
978-0-8225-7178-0, $27.93
LC 2007-20028
Back when the Aztec Empire was at its peak, the Emperor has a favorite daughter, Iztaccihuatl (called Izta); he is troubled by an enemy nation, the Tlaxcalans, and the soldier Popocatepetl (called Popo) is the Emperor's great military leader. Popo and Izta fall in love at first sight when the Emperor honors Popo for his accomplishments, and they meet in secret. However, Cuetlachtli is a jealous soldier who wants to destroy Popo, and he finds his chance when the Emperor catches the two lovers together and tells Popo he can only marry Izta if he brings back the head of the

Tlaxcalan king. Searching for the enemy takes a long, hard time, and Cuetlachtli sends a messenger back to Tenochtitlan with word that Popo has died, which sends Izta into a decline. When victorious Popo returns, he finds his lover dead, and takes her to the top of a mountain where he stands over her until his death. Now there are two mountains in Mexico, named for the two lovers. Jolley sets the story as one told by a Mexican tour guide, using contemporary language; artist Witt conducted research to make the art look as authentic as possible. The book includes a list of books, websites, and DVDs for more information and entertainment.

Part of the Graphic Universe Myths and Legends series

The **time** travel trap. Illustrated by Matt Wendt. Graphic Universe 2008 111p. Illustration (Twisted journeys)
Grades: 3 4 5 6 7 8 9   **741.5; Fic**
1. Adventure graphic novels; 2. Plot-your-own stories; 3. Science fiction graphic novels; 4. Graphic novels
978-0-7613-9472-3 (lib bdg), $27.93; 0-7613-9472-9 (lib bdg); 978-0-8225-8874-0 (pa), $7.95; 0-8225-8874-9 (pa)
                                        LC 2007-6101
In this new take on the "Choose Your Own Adventure" type of book that combines pages of prose text with pages of comic book sequences, you are caught in a time machine a fellow student built for the school's science fair. Depending on the choices, you could end up at a medieval joust, facing woolly mammoths and "cavemen," or future aliens. Some choices will end badly, others will be better, and the choices are all up to the reader.

This is Volume 7 of the Twisted Journeys series.

Vampire hunt. Illustrated by Gregory Titus; [coloring by Hi-Fi Design; lettering by Marshall Dillon]. Lerner Publishing Group/Graphic Universe 2008 112p. Illustration
Grades: 3 4 5 6 7 8 9   **741.5; Fic**
1. Adventure graphic novels; 2. Plot-your-own stories; 3. Science fiction graphic novels; 4. Vampires; 5. Graphic novels
978-0-8225-8877-1, $27.93; 978-0-8225-8879-5 (pa), $7.95
                                        LC 2007-043732
In this new take on the "Choose Your Own Adventure" type of book that combines pages of prose text with pages of comic book sequences, you are a vampire, and you must defend yourself and your castle from vampire hunters. Some choices will end badly, others will be better, and the choices are all up to the reader.

This is Volume 7 of the Twisted Journeys series

Warriors: Ravenpaw's path: vol. 1, shattered peace. Created by Erin Hunter ; written by Dan Jolley ; art by James L. Barry. Tokyopop/HarperCollins 2009 Un Illustration
Grades: 3 4 5 6 7 8 9   **741.5; Fic**
1. Adventure graphic novels; 2. Cats; 3. Graphic novels
978-0-06-158865-2 (pa), $6.99
                                        LC 2009-920733
Ravenpaw used to be part of Thunderclan, but he left the clan and has lived on the twolegs' farm with his friend Barley, mostly to stay away from Tigerstar. Life is quiet, peaceful, with plenty of mice to hunt in the cozy barn. Then other cats come seeking shelter, because Minty, the female, is about to give birth to her kits. Barley knows there's

something bad about the cats, as he comes upon the males teaching the kits how to fight and kill other cats. Ravenpaw and Barley had always left the chickens alone and only hunted mice; after a fire damages the barn, they find the other cats have returned and plan to make the farm their territory. When the other cats kill some chicks, the farmer sees only Ravenpaw and Barley, who had tried to stop the killing, and the twoleg blames them. Now they must leave the farm, but Ravenpaw doesn't think he can return to the clan. This manga-style graphic novel is an original story featuring characters from Erin Hunter's fiction series.

Warriors: the rise of Scourge. Created by Erin Hunter ; written by Dan Jolley ; art by Bettina M. Kurkoski. Tokyopop/HarperCollins 2008 106p. Illustration
Grades: 3 4 5 6 7 8 9   **741.5; Fic**
1. Adventure graphic novels; 2. Cats; 3. Graphic novels
978-0-06-147867-3, $6.99
                                        LC 2007-935239
Scourge, leader of the Bloodclan, is a violent, fierce cat and enemy of the Thunderclan cats. This story tells of his life before he became the leader, before he became Scourge. He started life as the kittypet named Tiny, the runt of his litter, despised by his bigger litter mates. Fascinated by the woods outside the fence where he lives, he ventures out to explore, and one day runs into forest cats from Thunderclan who injure him. Convinced the twoleg family will drown him as an unwanted kitten, Tiny lives among the strays in the alleys. A series of happenstances establish a reputation for toughness and he changes his name to Scourge. What he really wants, though, is to settle things with the Thunderclan cat who almost killed him. The fights between cats might be upsetting for younger readers.

Warriors: Warrior's return. Created by Erin Hunter; written by Dan Jolley; art by James L. Barry. HarperCollins/Tokyopop 2008 111p. Illustration (Warrior's series)
Grades: 5 6 7 8   **741.5; Fic**
1. Adventure graphic novels; 2. Cats; 3. Graphic novels
978-0-06-125233-4, $6.99; 0-06-125233-6
In this third volume of the manga-style original story set in the world of the wild cat clans created by Erin Hunter, Graystripe and Millie have found Thunderclan's old territory, but it has been destroyed by Two-Legs. The forest has been stripped of its trees, human roadways and buildings are going up. Graystripe fears that his clan has been destroyed, too, but Millie won't let him give up. An old friend points out the path that the two cats must follow to find the Clan, and they continue the journey.

"The black-and-white cartoon artwork captures the cats' expressive faces, action-packed battle scenes, and familiar surroundings as these animals travel through the realm of the 'Twolegs.' This is a great choice for reluctant readers, manga fans, or 'Warriors' enthusiasts." SLJ

Jones, Christianne C.
Bella's boat surprise. Art by Mary Sullivan. Stone Arch Books 2010 32p. Illustration
Grades: K 1 2   **741.5; Fic**
1. Boats and boating; 2. Recreation; 3. Graphic novels
978-1-4342-1617-5, $21.32; 978-1-4342-2287-9 (pa), $3.95

LC 2008-53378

Bella knows that she and her family are going to go on a boat, but the rest is a surprise, so she spends the time traveling to the lake imagining what it would be like on such different boats as a cruise ship or a rowboat. Imagine her surprised chagrin when she sees the motorboat it will blow away her hat and mess up her hair. This graphic novel is geared toward beginning readers; it provides a two-page tutorial on how to read comic book panels and pages, and a brief glossary as well as discussion questions and writing prompts which are good for classroom use. Bella and her family are portrayed as African Americans.

Part of the My First Graphic Novel series.

Rah-rah Ruby! by Christianne C. Jones ; illustrated by Cori Doerrfeld Stone Arch Books 2009 32p. Illustration
Grades: K 1 2 3   **741.5; Fic**
1. Cheerleading; 2. Graphic novels
978-1-4342-1298-6, $19.93; 978-1-4342-1412-6 (pa), $3.95

LC 2008-31972

Ruby wants to be a cheerleader. She can jump, flip, tumble, kick, and yell really well, but she has a problem with spelling. She spends the summer practicing her spelling for the fall cheerleading tryouts at school. This story uses a simplified comic book layout and vocabulary for beginning readers. The book includes a two-page spread at the beginning of the book that explains how to read a graphic novel, and a glossary and discussion questions at the end of the book.

Part of the My First Graphic Novel series

Justice League Adventures Vol. 1: The Magnificent Seven
DC Comics 2004 112p. Illustration
Grades: 4 5 6 7 8 9   **741.5; Fic**
1. Batman (Fictional character); 2. Flash (Fictional character); 3. Green Lantern (Fictional character); 4. Justice League (Fictional characters); 5. Superhero graphic novels; 6. Superman (Fictional character); 7. Wonder Woman (Fictional character); 8. Graphic novels
1-4012-0179-2, $6.95

The World's Greatest Heroes: Martian Manhunter, Green Lantern, Hawkgirl, the Flash, Wonder Woman, Batman, and Superman battle against villainy from all corners of the globe, and beyond. Among other villains, they fight Chronos the Time Thief and Screamthief.

Justice League Adventures Vol. 2: Friends and Foes
DC Comics 2004 112p. Illustration
Grades: 4 5 6 7 8 9   **741.5; Fic**
1. Batman (Fictional character); 2. Flash (Fictional character); 3. Green Lantern (Fictional character); 4. Justice League (Fictional characters); 5. Superhero graphic novels; 6. Superman (Fictional character); 7. Wonder Woman (Fictional character); 8. Graphic novels
1-4012-0180-6, $6.95
The World's Greatest Heroes: Martian Manhunter, Green Lantern, Hawkgirl, the Flash, Wonder Woman, Batman, and Superman - return to thwart another round of wrongdoers, and the threats come from all sides. Brainiac and Poison Ivy are just a couple of the super villains they face.

Kanata, Konami
★ **Chi's** sweet home, volume 1. Vertical, Inc. 2010 166p. Illustration
Grades: 5 6 7 8 9 10 11 12 Adult   **741.5; Fic**
1. Cats; 2. Humorous graphic novels; 3. Manga; 4. Graphic novels
9781-934287-81-1
Young kitten Chi gets separated from her family while out on a stroll, then she meets little boy Yohei and his parents. They take her home, even though their apartment building has a strict no pets policy. While they try to find someone to take her in, they feed her, give her a cozy bed, set up a box with shredded newspaper for a litter box, and do their best to help her. Even though readers can read what she's thinking, Chi behaves just like a cat, with cat problems such as thinking the litter box is a wonderful play area instead of the place to do her business, and taking fright at Yohei's "vrooming" as he plays with his toy cars. The book is great for younger readers as well as anyone who likes cats. There is one panel where Yohei is sitting on the toilet while Chi is in her litter box in the bathroom, and a scene at the veterinarian's office where the doctor sticks a thermometer in to take Chi's temperature. And, of course, Chi tends to urinate in inappropriate places.
Also available in 3-in-1 omnibus editions
Volume 1 of 12

Kanda, Takayuki
Edu-Manga: Ludwig van Beethoven. Art by Naoko Takase. Digital Manga Publishing 2006 144p. Illustration
Grades: 3 4 5 6 7 8 9   **92; 741.5**
1. Beethoven, Ludwig van; 2. Biographical graphic novels; 3. Manga; 4. Graphic novels
1-56970-973-4, $9.95
Beethoven stands as one of the greatest musical minds the world has ever seen, with such famous works as his Symphony No. 9 ("Ode to Joy") and the classic piano piece "Fur Elise." The onset of deafness was only one of many hardships he had to face, but his strength and desire to do battle with his turbulent life led him to create the many musical pieces the world cherishes today. This manga format biography uses Astro Boy and his friends to introduce the story, present more information in a Q&A format, and provides a timeline to Beethoven's life.

Kaplan, Arie
Speed Racer: chronicles of the racer. Art by Robby Musso and German Torres. IDW Publishing 2008 Un Illustration
Grades: 5 6 7 8 9 10 11 12 Adult   **741.5; Fic**
1. Adventure graphic novels; 2. Automobile racing; 3. Racer, Speed (Fictional character); 4. Graphic novels
978-1-60010-213-4, $17.99
After a race in which something happens to Speed's Mach 5 and he's saved by Racer X, Pop Racer gives Speed a book, The Chronicles of the Racer. For thousands of years, there has been one Racer in their family, one who is destined to win. And for those thousands of years, the Racer has dealt with a villain who is associated with Mercury. From ancient Rome to medieval England to eighteenth century pirates and onward, Speed finds himself reliving his ancestors' experiences after he sneaks into Mercury Studios, and he

finds himself face-to-face with the same man who has battled his ancestors through the centuries. This book collects the four-issue miniseries of original stories based on the Speed Racer characters.

Kardy, Glenn
Manga University Presents ... Kana de Manga: A Fun, Easy Way to Learn the ABCs of Japanese!. Text by Glenn Kardy ; art by Chihiro Hattori. Japanime Co. Ltd 2004 113p. Illustration
Grades: 5 6 7 8 9 10 11 12 Adult   **495.6; 741.5**
  1. Japanese language — Teaching — Aids and devices; 2. Manga; 3. Graphic novels
4-921205-01-9, $9.99
  This book uses original manga artwork to teach students how to read, write and pronounce the Japanese hiragana and katakana alphabets, also known as "kana." Author Glenn Kardy and artist Chihiro Hattori have teamed up to create this book for manga enthusiasts who are interested in more than just pretty pictures. In addition to presenting the kana, the book illustrates stroke order in writing the characters, and each hiragana character is shown with a word, its definition, an illustration, and opportunities for practice in writing the character.

Manga University Presents ... Kanji deManga: The Comic Book That Teaches You How to Read and Write Japanese! Volume 1. Created by Glenn Kardy ; art by Chihiro Hatteri. Japanime Co. Ltd 2004 113p. Illustration
Grades: 5 6 7 8 9 10 11 12 Adult   **495.6; 741.5**
  1. Japanese language — Teaching — Aids and devices; 2. Manga; 3. Graphic novels
4-921205-02-7, $9.99
  This book uses original comic artwork to teach readers how to identify and write the most common Japanese kanji ideographs. It introduces 80 basic kanji that all Japanese schoolchildren are required to learn before entering the third grade, or for those who wish to pass Level 4 of the Japanese Language Proficiency Test for non-native speakers of Japanese. Each page features its own comic strip, kanji pronunciation guide, stroke order, and English explanations.

Keenan, Sheila
Dogs of war. By Sheila Keenan and illustrated by Nathan Fox. Graphix 2013 208 p.
Grades: 4 5 6 7   **741.5**
  1. Dogs — Fiction; 2. Dogs — War use — Fiction; 3. Vietnam War, 1961-1975 — Fiction; 4. War; 5. World War, 1914-1918 — Fiction; 6. World War, 1939-1945 — Fiction; 7. Graphic novels
0545128870; 9780545128872, $22.99; 9780545128889
                                              LC 2011006735
  This graphic novel, by Sheila Keenan, "tells the stories of the canine military heroes of World War I, World War II, and the Vietnam War. This collection of three fictional stories was inspired by historic battles and real military practice. Each story tells the remarkable adventures of a soldier and his service dog . . . bringing to life the faithful dogs who braved bombs, barrages, and battles to save the lives of countless soldiers." (Publisher's note)
  Includes bibliographical references

Kelly, Claire
Nellie in the News. Art by Faith Erin Hicks. Harcourt Achieve/Steck-Vaughn 2007 48p. Illustration
Grades: 3 4 5 6 7 8   **741.5; Fic**
  1. Adventure graphic novels; 2. Bly, Nellie, 1864-1922; 3. Graphic novels
978-1-4190-3218-9, $8.99
  Rosie Freedman is a gifted young African American girl who drops out of school when her family falls on hard times. It is only when she meets Nellie Bly, a journalist about to set out on a mission to travel around the world in 80 days, that Rosie starts to dream again. This historical fiction graphic novel includes prose intervals that provide more information on Bly's journey as well as the hard times for people in New York's Hell's Kitchen in the late 1880s.
  Part of the Timeline Graphic Novels series.

Kelly, Joe
  ★ **Captain** Stoneheart and the Truth Fairy. Image Comics 2008 Un Illustration
Grades: 5 6 7 8 9 10 11 12 Adult   **741.5; Fic**
  1. Adventure graphic novels; 2. Fairies; 3. Fantasy graphic novels; 4. Pirates; 5. Graphic novels
978-1-58240-865-1, $19.99
  The story, in rhyming text with lushly drawn and colored art, tells the tale of the pirate named Captain Stoneheart, a fierce and angry pirate who won't let people tell him what to do. After attacking a peaceful ship and killing everyone on it, his crew discovers a caged fairy in the hold, and Stoneheart knows he can wreak havoc and scourge the world with her powers. Somehow they connect even through his anger, and when she finds a way to save Stoneheart and his crew even when she is free to leave the pirates and save herself, Stoneheart starts to change. Alas, the good times can't last, and he commits one final act that destroys everything and everyone around him because he won't let anyone tell him what to do, even if he loves that one person. There is some fighting violence, and there are some monsters, so this is not a story for very young readers. Older elementary school age children who love the old fairy tales with the tragic endings will be able to handle this story.

Douglas Fredericks and the House of They. Illustrated by Ben Roman. Image Comics 2009 80p. Illustration
Grades: 3 4 5 6   **741.5; Fic**
  1. Adventure graphic novels; 2. Humorous graphic novels; 3. Graphic novels
978-1-58240-994-8, $17.99
  Douglas Fredericks just wants to give his parents a very original, unique anniversary present, but every time he comes up with an idea, someone tells him "They" say it can't happen. After many different attempts, he builds the first self-baking cake, Cake City, that will provide cake for fifteen years, because his parents (especially the Captain, his father) love cake, and then wants to just sample the first piece, people come along and tell him "No, Douglas, don't! You know what They say! You can't have your cake and eat it too!" So, Douglas decides to go find the House of They to confront the people there. After many trials, he can finally ask "WHY?" and he refuses to accept "Because They say so" as an answer. Kelly, Roman, and colorist Molina are part of The Man of Action Studios that has created the television cartoon Ben 10, as well as many comics; they have used the

deluxe picture book format for this story, with full-page color art on every other page (with quite a few double-page spreads) it even has a ribbon marker.

Kelly, Walt

Walt Kelly's Our Gang Vol. 1. Fantagraphics Books 2006 104p. Illustration

Grades: 4 5 6 7 8 9 10 11 12 Adult   **741.5; Fic**
1. Friendship; 2. Humorous graphic novels; 3. Graphic novels
978-1-56097-753-7, $12.95

Kelly's longest-running continuing comics series was based on the "real-life" characters of MGM's durable short-film series, "Our Gang" (a.k.a. "The Little Rascals"). Kelly's Our Gang harks back to the days before television, when kids spent most of their time playing outdoors, limited only by each other's imagination and ingenuity. This is the first in a series of books reprinting Walt Kelly's Our Gang stories. Suitable for both adults and children, they have been restored from their comic book appearance. These stories were originally published in 1942 and 1943.

Volume 1 of 4

Ketcham, Hank

★ **Hank** Ketcham's Complete Dennis the Menace (Volume 1): 1951-1952. Fantagraphics Books 2005 590p. Illustration

Grades: 2 3 4 5 6 7 8 9 10 11 12 Adult   **741.5; Fic**
1. Dennis the Menace (Fictional character); 2. Humorous graphic novels; 3. Graphic novels
1-56097-680-2, $24.95

This volume is the first of a series that will reprint every Dennis the Menace cartoon. The first cartoon was published in sixteen newspapers on March 12, 1951, and the cartoon was soon picked up by many more newspapers. This volume collects the daily single-panel cartoons from March 1951 through December 1952. In these cartoons, readers meet five-and-a-half-year-old Dennis Mitchell, his parents, retired neighbors George and Martha Wilson, Dennis' dog Ruff, and neighborhood pals Joey and Margaret. Every cartoon hearkens back to the positive aspects of growing up in suburban Middle America and the joys (mostly) of being a child. While older adults will catch all the references to past popular culture (i.e. Hopalong Cassidy), younger readers will enjoy the humor arising from everyday situations.

Kibuishi, Kazu

Amulet book five: prince of the elves. Kazu Kibuishi. Graphix 2012 208 p. (Amulet)

Grades: 3 4 5 6 7 8   **741.5**
1. Amulets; 2. Brothers and sisters; 3. Charms; 4. Elves; 5. Fantasy graphic novels; 6. Imaginary places; 7. Magic; 8. Magic — Juvenile fiction; 9. Single-parent families — Juvenile fiction; 10. Graphic novels
0545208890; 9780545208895, $12.99
LC 2012935527

Author Kazu Kibuishi presents book five in the graphic novel series. "Emily has survived the chaos of the Guardian Academy, but Max Griffin, who is working for the Elf King, has escaped with the Mother Stone. The Elf King has now forged new amulets, which will allow him the ability to invade Cielis and destroy it once and for all. Emily and her friends desperately make preparations to defend Cielis in what will inevitably be a brutal war, and they can only hope that it will be enough to defeat the Elf King." (Publisher's note)

"Anchored by dazzlingly lush art and a complex, character-laden plot, Kibuishi's Amulet series remains a must-have for all elementary- and middle-school graphic-novel collections. Devoted fans will appreciate that this volume begins to flesh-out the backstory of two characters while starting to tie together a few of the many plot elements." Booklist

Amulet, book four: The Last Council. Graphix 2011 207 p.

Grades: 3 4 5 6 7 8   **741.5**
978-0-545-20887-1, $10.99; 0-545-20887-4
"Emily and her friends think they'll find the help they need in Cielis, but something isn't right. Streets that were once busy are deserted, and the townspeople who are left live in crippling fear. Emily is escorted to the Academy where she's expected to compete for a spot on the Guardian Council, the most powerful Stonekeepers. But as the number of competitors gets smaller and smaller, a terrible secret is slowly uncovered—a secret that, if left buried, means certain destruction of everything Emily fights for." (Publisher's note)

Amulet, book one: The Stonekeeper. Graphix 2008 185p.

Grades: 3 4 5 6 7 8   **741; Fic; 741.5**
1. Adventure graphic novels; 2. Fantasy graphic novels; 3. Mystery graphic novels; 4. Graphic novels
978-0-439-84680-6, $21.99; 0-439-84680-3;
978-0-439-84681-3 (pa), $9.99; 0-439-84681-1 (pa)

After a family tragedy, Emily, Navin, and their mother move to an ancestral home to start a new life. When their mother is kidnapped by a tentacled creature, Em and Navin have to figure out how to set things straight and save their mother's life.

"Filled with excitement, monsters, robots, and mysteries, this fantasy adventure will appeal to many readers." SLJ
Other titles in this series are: The Stonekeeper's curse (2009); The Cloud Searchers (2010); The Last Council (2011); Prince of the elves (2012); Escape from Lucien (2014); Firelight (2016)

Amulet, book three: The Cloud Searchers. Graphix 2010 197p.

Grades: 3 4 5 6 7 8   **741.5; 741**
978-0-545-20885-7 (pa), $10.99; 0-545-20885-8 (pa)
"Emily, Navin, and their crew of resistance fighters charter an airship and set off in search of the lost city of Cielis, which is believed to be located on an island high above the clouds. The mysterious Leon Redbeard is their guide, and there's a surprising new addition to the crew: the Elf King's son, Trellis. But is he ally or enemy? And will Emily ever be able to trust the voice of the Amulet?" (Publisher's note)

Amulet, book two: The Stonekeeper's curse. Graphix 2009 217p.

Grades: 3 4 5 6 7 8   **741.5; 741**
978-0-439-84683-7, $10.99; 0-439-84683-8

"Emily and Navin's mother is still in a coma from the arachnopod's poison, and there's only one place to find help: Kanalis, the bustling, beautiful city of waterfalls. But when Em, her brother, and Miskit and the rest of the robotic crew aboard the walking house reach the city, they quickly realize that seeking help is looking for trouble, dangerous trouble." (Publisher's note)

★ **Copper.** Graphix/Scholastic 2010 94p. Illustration.
Grades: 5 6 7 8   **741; 741.5; Fic**
1. Adventure graphic novels; 2. Dogs; 3. Science fiction graphic novels; 4. Graphic novels
978-0-545-09892-2, $21.99; 0-545-09892-0;
978-0-545-09893-9 (pa), $12.99; 0-545-09893-9 (pa)

A collection of graphic novel adventures about a boy named Copper and his dog, Fred, including "navigating a dangerous forest of giant mushrooms, [and] surviving a crash landing in a homemade airplane—that run from lyrical to the downright apocalyptic. Illustrated in a deceptively simple style, its solemn tenor and deep strangeness . . . will likely inspire heavy investment from those who prefer a somewhat off-kilter read." Booklist

Escape from Lucien. Kazu Kibuishi. Scholastic / Graphix 2014 256 p. Illustration; Map (Amulet)
Grades: 3 4 5 6 7 8   **741.5; Fic**
1. Brothers and sisters — Fiction; 2. Elves — Fiction; 3. Kings and rulers — Fiction
9780545433150, $12.99

LC 2013957419
"Navin and his classmates journey to Lucien, a city ravaged by war and plagued by mysterious creatures, where they search for a beacon essential to their fight against the Elf King. Meanwhile, Emily heads back into the Void with Max, one of the Elf King's loyal followers, where she learns his darkest secrets. The stakes, for both Emily and Navin, are higher than ever." (Publisher's note)
"Most of the cleanly drawn, lushly backgrounded panels focus on faces, with occasional full-spread scenes adding dramatic visual highlights.A page-turner that gives the heroic Stonekeepers plenty of chances to show their stuff and moves the main story along an inch or two." Kirkus

Kikai, Masahide
Edu-Manga: Mother Teresa. Written by Masahide Kikai ; illustrated by Ren Kishida. Digital Manga Publishing 2007 152p. Illustration
Grades: 2 3 4 5 6 7 8   **92; 741.5**
1. Biographical graphic novels; 2. Kodomo manga; 3. Manga; 4. Teresa, Mother, 1910-1997; 5. Graphic novels
978-1-56970-972-6, $9.95

This volume in the Edu-Manga series covers the life of Mother Teresa, the nun who worked among the "poorest of the poor" in India for most of her adult life. Born to an Albanian family in Madedonia, she was named Agnes Gouxha. She chose her vocation as a nun when she was twelve years old, and when she turned eighteen she left Macedonia and her family and joined the Loreto order of nuns in Calcutta. After twenty years in the monastery there, she went into the slums to work directly among the poor. She started alone, but when she died in 1997, there were about 4,000 nuns working at 602 facilities in 125 countries throughout the world. Her story is introduced by Astro Boy

and his friends, and the book includes a "Q & A" which gives more information about Mother Teresa, nuns, her work, and a timeline of her life.

Kim, Susan
★ **City** of spies. [by] Susan Kim [and] Laurence Klavan; illustrated by Pascal Dizin. First Second 2010 172p. Illustration
Grades: 4 5 6 7   **741.5; Fic**
1. Adventure graphic novels; 2. Spies; 3. World War, 1939-1945; 4. Graphic novels
1-59643-262-4 (pa); 978-1-59643-262-8 (pa), $17

This graphic novel, set in New York City during World War II, tells the story of Kim and Klavan, who are hunting for Nazi spies. (Bull Cent Child Books)
"With her mother gone and a father who has better things to do than be bothered raising a daughter, Evelyn is sent to live with her unconventional Aunt Lia in the bohemian art world of 1942 New York City. . . . Evelyn spends much of her time in the company of imaginary superheroes, fouling up the plans of Nazi spies. Before long she finds an unlikely friend in the building superintendent's son, Tony. Together, they . . . stumble upon an actual Nazi plot. With stupefying precision, Dizin's art channels Hergé's Tintin in tone, palette, and with the remarkable expressiveness of the clean, flexible figures. . . . With villains and danger that just border on the genuinely scary, the tale is filled not only with a thrilling sense of excitement but also with a child's longing for a grown-up to believe in." Booklist

Kinney, Sarah
Nancy Drew, girl detective #14: Sleight of Dan. Stefan Petrucha & Sarah Kinney, writers ; Sho Murase, artist ; with 3D CG elements and color by Carlos Jose Guzman. Papercutz 2008 Un Illustration
Grades: 3 4 5 6 7 8 9   **741.5; Fic**
1. Adventure graphic novels; 2. Drew, Nancy (Fictional character); 3. Mystery graphic novels; 4. Graphic novels
978-1-59707-108-6, $12.95; 978-1-59707-107-9 (pa), $7.95

The assistant for magician Dan Deville has disappeared, and Nancy tries to find Tina. It all started when Nancy attended one of Dan's magic shows with buddies George and Bess, and George challenged Nancy to figure out the magician's tricks. Now, though Nancy runs into a large anaconda while trying to find Tina, and large snakes are definitely not fun.
Volume 14 of the Nancy Drew, Girl Detective series

Kipling, Rudyard
Blaise Mitildji ; illustrated by TieKo. IDW Publishing 2009 62p. Illustration
Grades: 5 6 7 8 9   **741.5; Fic**
1. Adventure graphic novels; 2. Children's authors; 3. India; 4. Kipling, Rudyard, 1865-1936 — Adaptations; 5. Wolves; 6. Graphic novels
978-1-60010-352-0, $14.99

This graphic novel adapts Kipling's tale of Mowgli, the boy who was raised by wolves, educated by Baloo the bear and Bagheera the panther, the enemy of Shere Khan the tiger. When the wolf pack overthrows the wise Akela and order

Mowgli to leave, he returns to the human village, but he never feels completely comfortable among them. When Shere Khan comes to hunt him, Mowgli fights with Akela at his side, but this causes the people to reject him. This adaptation, originally published in France, stays true to Kipling's original story; at the beginning of the tale, Mowgli is naked, although the one panel showing him from the front is a longer-distance shot. The book includes biographical information about Kipling, historical background on the British Empire and on India in the nineteenth century, and an analysis of the story.

Kishi, Daimuro
Time Guardian, Vol. 1. DC Comics/CMX 2007 198p. Illustration
Grades: 5 6 7 8 9 10 11 12   **741.5; Fic**
  1. Fantasy graphic novels; 2. Manga; 3. Shojo manga; 4. Graphic novels
1-4012-1161-5, $9.99
  High school student Miu stumbles upon a mysterious pawnshop that trades time for people's memories. Shop owner Tokiya hires Miu to be his Time Go-Between to work with his customers, but she must never speak of the shop to anyone.

Kitchen, Alexa
Drawing Comics is Easy! (Except When It's Hard). Denis Kitchen Publishing Company 2006 Un Illustration
Grades: 2 3 4 5 6 7 8 9 10 11 12 Adult   **741.5**
  1. Drawing; 2. Graphic novels
0-9710080-6-X, $19.95
  Drawing Comics is Easy! (Except When It's Hard!) is entirely the work of a seven-year-old (at the time) prodigy cartoonist, who in 2007 was ten years old. Though seemingly aimed at a peer audience of other children, this idiosyncratic How-To book will appeal to readers of any age, especially those interested in cartooning and the creative process. Kitchen is the daughter of Denis Kitchen, who's been in the comics industry as a publisher and agent for many years.

  ★ **Grown-ups** are dumb! (No offense). Hyperion Books 2009 Un Illustration
Grades: 3 4 5 6 7 8   **741.5; Fic**
  1. Family life; 2. Humorous graphic novels; 3. Graphic novels
978-1-4231-1331-7, $8.99
  Twelve-year-old Alexa Kitchen wrote the comics collected here when she was ten years old. Her characters Molly, Sharon, and Kathy navigate life in school (and piles of homework), and at home (with pesky younger brothers). In other cartoons, she depicts the frustrations of dealing with incomprehensible paper folding instructions, the joys (and despairs) of messy rooms, and of toddler Hurricane Abby's exploration of her house. Kitchen's art ranges from the heavy pencils in the cartoons about Molly to scratchy ink in most of the other stories, to highly detailed drawings of the incredibly messy bedroom, all on pink pages. She describes herself as the world's youngest professional cartoonist, has been drawing cartoons since she could hold a pencil, and already has several books published; in 2007, at the age of

ten, she was nominated for a Harvey and an Eisner Award for her book Drawing Comics is Easy! (Except When It's Hard).

Kleid, Neil
  Jack London's Call of the Wild. Art by Alex Nino. Puffin Graphics 2006 176p. Illustration
Grades: 5 6 7 8 9 10   **741.5; Fic**
  1. Adventure graphic novels; 2. Dogs; 3. London, Jack; 4. London, Jack — Adaptations; 5. Graphic novels
0-14-240571-X, $10.99
  Buck was a pampered dog on Judge Miller's estate in Santa Clara, California of 1897; then one of Judge Miller's men sold Buck to a broker selling sled dogs to the men flocking to the Yukon in the Gold Rush of that time. A strong dog, Buck manages to survive and even thrive under masters good and bad. This volume includes the artist's sketch gallery and sample script pages.

Kneece, Mark
  The **Twilight** Zone: the after hours. Adaptation by Mark Kneece; illustrated by Rebekah Isaacs. Walker & Company 2008 Un Illustration
Grades: 5 6 7 8 9 10   **741.5; Fic**
  1. Supernatural graphic novels; 2. Twilight zone (Television program); 3. Graphic novels
978-0-8027-9716-2, $16.99; 978-0-8027-9717-9 (pa), $9.99
                       LC 2008-4310
  Marsha White visits a department store to buy an advertised gold thimble, is taken by elevator to a floor with empty display cases except for one, which has the thimble, and she deals with an odd saleswoman who knows her name. When Marsha is in the elevator, she discovers the thimble is defective and tries to complain, but the manager insists there is no eighteenth floor, the store has no elevator, and the store has never carried gold thimbles. As she begins to leave, Marsha faints at the sight of a mannequin that looks exactly like the strange saleswoman, and she's put into a back room to recover. When she wakes up, the store has been closed and she's locked in. This is an actual episode of the old Twilight Zone television show.
  "Kneece's adaptation is quick and enjoyable and introduces a classic TV series to a new generation of readers. Isaacs's illustrations are clean, distinct and cinematic in scope, employing an interesting variety of angles." Kirkus

  The **Twilight** Zone: walking distance. Adaptation from Rod Serling's original script by Mark Kneece; illustrated by Dove McHargue. Walker & Company 2008 Un Illustration
Grades: 5 6 7 8 9 10   **741.5; Fic**
  1. Supernatural graphic novels; 2. Twilight zone (Television program); 3. Graphic novels
978-0-8027-9714-8, $16.99; 978-0-8027-9715-5 (pa), $9.99
                       LC 2008-4273
  Thirty-nine-year-old businessman Martin Sloan's car blows a tire as he's driving, and he realizes he is within walking distance of his hometown. Leaving his car to be repaired, he decides to walk there. However, when he reaches town, he has also gone back in time. Can he find his boyhood self and give his younger self advice? Or will

everyone think he's just crazy? This is an actual episode of the old Twilight Zone television show.

The story is "exceptionally well told and . . . [is] brilliantly adapted to a new medium." SLJ

Kochalka, James
Johnny Boo & the happy apples. Top Shelf Productions 2009 42p. Illustration
Grades: K 1 2 3
741.5; Fic
1. Apples; 2. Ghosts; 3. Humorous graphic novels; 4. Graphic novels
978-1-60309-041-4, $9.95

Johnny Boo & The Happy Apples ©
James Kochalka

Little ghost Johnny Boo has floppy, droopy, floopy muscles and wants to make them strong. Then the ice cream monster comes and says he now eats happy apples that make him strong. Johnny Boo wants to eat happy apples and get strong muscles, too, but when he eats a mushy apple he finds on the ground, his arm muscle becomes super floopy, like a long, limp noodle. What's he to do? Squiggle tries to use his squiggle power, but it only ties up Johnny Boo into a knot. Then ice cream monster returns and accidentally eats Johnny Boo and Squiggle, thinking they look like vanilla ice cream. The ghosts get out when he burps. Younger readers who are easily scared might be upset about Johnny Boo and Squiggle getting eaten, although they might think having a television in the stomach is funny.

Johnny Boo and the mean little boy. Top Shelf 2010 Illustration
Grades: K 1 2 3
741; 741.5
978-1-60309-059-9, $9.95
"When Johnny Boo announces a play date with his quiet new friend Rocky the Rock, trusty sidekick Squiggle is left to find a new friend of his own. How about this nice fellow named the Mean Little Boy? He sure is fond of his butterfly net, and he's got a great game to play with Squiggle... but, wait a minute, maybe the Mean Little Boy isn't actually so nice!" (Publisher's note)

Johnny Boo zooms to the moon!. James Kochalka. Tcp Shelf Productions 2014 40 p. Color; Illustration (Johnny Boo)
Grades: K 1 2 3
741.5
1. Skateboarding — Fiction; 2. Space flight to the moon
1603093494; 9781603093491, $9.95
In this book by James Kochalka, "Johnny Boo and Squiggle attempt to skateboard to the moon, encountering returning characters such as the friendly but not-so-bright stars and the not-so-scary ice cream monster. They also make a new friend in girl ghost Susie Boom, an enthusiastic moon resident whose powerful 'BOOM!' is equal to Johnny's signature 'BOO!'" (School Library Journal)

Johnny Boo, book two: Twinkle power!. Top Shelf Productions 2008 40p. Illustration

Grades: K 1 2 3
741.5; Fic
1. Friendship; 2. Ghosts; 3. Humorous graphic novels; 4. Graphic novels
978-1-60309-015-5, $9.95
Little ghost Johnny Boo and his pet ghost Squiggle play in the night and wonder what kind of power stars have. Then Squiggle zooms around and messes up Johnny Boo's hair; he thinks it's funny, but Johnny doesn't. Then Ice Cream Monster comes to play and wants Johnny to teach him how to boo, but the monster prefers "EEK!" over the usual "BOO!" So what power is better: Boo Power? Squiggle Power? Twinkle Power? How about Giggle Power, or even Wiggle Power?

Johnny Boo: the best little ghost in the world!. Top Shelf Productions 2008 40p.
Grades: K 1 2 3
741; 741.5; Fic
1. Friendship; 2. Ghosts; 3. Humorous graphic novels; 4. Graphic novels
978-1-60309-013-1, $9.95
"Johnny Boo may be the best little ghost in the world, with the best little ghost pet, Squiggle, but that doesn't mean he's ready to face down scary Ice Cream Monster. When the monster turns out not to be scary after all, Johnny and Squiggle take it on as a new, if unpredictable, friend. Kochalka's simple line drawings and bright crayon colors stand out in this sweet, silly graphic novel. . . . The dialogue is fairly simple but never simplistic, and the text is printed clearly enough to make the book accessible to children just beginning to pick up chapter books." Booklist
Other titles in this series are: Johnny Boo: Twinkle power (2009); Johnny Boo and the happy apples (2009); Johnny Boo and the mean little boy (2010); Johnny Boo does something! (2013); Johnny Boo zooms to the moon! (2014)

Monkey vs. Robot. Top Shelf Productions 2000 144p. Illustration
Grades: 5 6 7 8 9 10 11 12
741.5; Fic
1. Graphic novels
1-891830-15-5, $14.95
The book is almost wordless, allowing the reader to imagine one's own narrative. While there is violence, it's not graphic, and this little fable provides much food for thought.
"A very simply illustrated black and white pictorial narrative about a battle between a monkey community and a self-run robot factory encroaching on the monkeys' unspoiled forest domain." Publ Wkly
Another title in this series is: Monkey vs. Robot and the crystal of power (2003)

Peanutbutter & Jeremy's best book ever. Alternative Comics 2003 280p. Illustration
Grades: 4 5 6 7 8 9 10 11 12
741.5; Fic
1. Friendship; 2. Humorous graphic novels; 3. Graphic novels
1-891867-46-6, $14.95
Peanutbutter is a sweet cat who acts like a hardworking office cat but usually naps on top of the paperwork, and Jeremy is a troublemaking crow; and they are friends. Jeremy may seem spiteful and sometimes does very mean things to Peanutbutter, such as pretending to threaten the cat with a pistol, but most of the stories are silly and fun.

Pinky & Stinky. Top Shelf Productions 2002 208p. Illustration

Grades: 4 5 6 7 8 9 10 11 12 Adult   **741.5; Fic**
  1. Adventure graphic novels; 2. Friendship; 3. Humorous graphic novels; 4. Graphic novels
  1-891830-29-7, $17.95

Pinky & Stinky are fat little piglets, but just because they're cuties doesn't mean that they're not brave astronauts! When they embark on a daring mission to be the first pigs on Pluto, things go horribly wrong and they crash land on the moon. There they meet some not-so-friendly moon men, and end up in the middle of a conflict between the American space program and a race of alien ice creatures.

Kovalic, John
  ★ **Here** Be Snapdragons. Art by Liz Rathke. Dork Storm Press 2006 120p. Illustration

Grades: 3 4 5 6 7 8 9 10 11 12 Adult   **741.5; Fic**
  1. Children; 2. Humorous graphic novels; 3. Graphic novels
  1-930964-52-8, $12.99

'Everybody Loves Gilly,' 2003 Origins Award for Graphic Fiction (Origins International Game Expo).

The Snapdragons are fraternal twins Jake and Jody, Cooper, Benjamin, and the years-younger Mitze, along with Jake and Jody's cat Huey. They are neighbors and friends, they love role-playing games and video games. Cooper's dad is a gamer, Jake and Jody's mother is clueless (she buys years-old Halloween costumes at a discount, unaware that the characters aren't popular any more), and they all often get babysat by Goth-cute teen Gilly, who can be a very cool Dungeon Master. One of the stories has Jake and Jody sent to their room without supper and they start quoting Wild Things by Maurice Sendak as their room begins to transform . . . .

Kreie, Chris
  Lost: A Tale of Survival. Art by Marcus Smith. Stone Arch Books 2007 88p. Illustration

Grades: 3 4 5 6 7 8 9   **741.5; Fic**
  1. Adventure graphic novels; 2. Graphic novels
  978-1-59889-828-6, $22.60

LC 2007-6245

Every summer, Eric and his dad head to the Boundary Waters Canoe Area in northern Minnesota. This year, Eric has brought his friend Cris, and the boys want to explore the wilderness on their own. When they set out in their canoe, Cris and Eric promise to return before dark. But, shortly into the trip, the river becomes a violent rapids the boys can't avoid, and Cris is injured. Now Eric must race against time to find the camp and save his friend. This graphic novel is written with an easier vocabulary for struggling and reluctant readers.

Part of the Graphic Quest line of books.

Krensky, Stephen
  Comic book century: the history of American comic books. Twenty-First Century Books 2007 112p. Illustration

Grades: 5 6 7 8 9 10   **741.5; 741**
  978-0-8225-6654-0, $30.60; 0-8225-6654-0

LC 2006-20795

"Part of a series that focuses on American History, this book highlights America's love and hate relationship with comic books. Starting with the 1930s, each chapter focuses on an era of the comics. Highlighted areas include the rise of Superman and Batman in the late 1930s, comics during World War II, the creation of the Comics Code Authority, Stan Lee's Marvel superhero creations, underground comix, and more." (VOYA)

Krohn, Katherine
  The **1918** Flu Pandemic by Katherine Krohn ; illustrated by Bob Hall, Keith Williams, and Charles Barnett, III. Capstone Press 2007 32p. Illustration

Grades: 3 4 5 6 7 8 9   **614.5; 741.5**
  1. Influenza; 2. Graphic novels
  978-1-4296-0158-0, $26.25

LC 2007000004

This book uses the graphic novel format to tell of the 1918 outbreak of a mysterious influenza virus that killed millions of people worldwide, making it the deadliest pandemic in history. The book includes additional facts and a list of books for further reading.

Part of the Graphic Library Disasters in History series.

The **earth-shaking** facts about earthquakes with Max Axiom, super scientist. Illustrated by Tod Smith and Al Milgrom. Capstone Press 2008 32p. Illustration

Grades: 3 4 5 6 7 8 9   **551.2; 741.5**
  1. Earthquakes; 2. Graphic novels
  978-1-4296-1328-6, $26.26

LC 2007-25091

Young readers learn about earthquakes, how they happen, why they happen, the damage they cause, and what's being done to study them and help people be better prepared to deal with them. Back matter includes more information about earthquakes, a glossary, and a short list of books for further reading.

Part of the Graphic Science series.

Krosoczka, Jarrett J.
  Lunch Lady and the author visit vendetta. Alfred A. Knopf 2009 Un Illustration

Grades: 3 4 5 6 7 8   **741; 741.5**
  978-0-375-96094-9 (lib bdg), $12.99;
  978-0-375-86094-2 (pa), $5.99

LC 2009014886

The school lunch lady, a secret crime fighter, investigates a suspicious author after he visits the school and the gym teacher goes missing.

Lunch Lady and the bake sale bandit. Alfred A. Knopf 2010 Un Illustration

Grades: 3 4 5 6 7 8   **741.5; 741**
  978-0-375-96729-0 (lib bdg), $12.99; 0-375-96729-X (lib bdg); 978-0-375-86729-3 (pa), $6.99;
  0-375-86729-5 (pa)

LC 2010012781

Lunch Lady, Betty, and the Breakfast Bunch must figure out who is stealing the goods from the bake sale.

Lunch Lady and the cyborg substitute. Alfred A. Knopf 2009 Un Illustration

Grades: 3 4 5 6 7 8   **741.5; Fic**

1. Humorous graphic novels; 2. Robots; 3. School children — Food; 4. School stories; 5. Graphic novels
978-0-375-94683-7 (lib bdg), $11.99; 0-375-94683-7 (lib bdg); 978-0-375-84683-0 (pa), $5.99; 0-375-84683-2 (pa)

LC 2008-4709

The school lunch lady is a secret crime fighter who uncovers an evil plot to replace all the popular teachers with robots

"Yellow-highlighted pen-and-ink cartoons are as energetic and smile-provoking as Lunch Lady's epithets of "Cauliflower!" and Betty's ultimate weapon, the hairnet." Booklist

Lunch Lady and the field trip fiasco. Alfred A. Knopf 2011 Un Illustration
Grades: 3 4 5 6 7 8   **741.5**
978-0-375-96730-6, $12.99; 978-0-375-86730-9 (pa), $6.99

LC 2011005907

Lunch Lady, a secret crime fighter, accompanies the Breakfast Bunch on a class trip to an art museum, but when Dee, Hector, and Terrence begin to think there is something strange afoot, she suspects nothing.

Lunch Lady and the League of Librarians. Alfred A. Knopf 2009 Un Illustration
Grades: 3 4 5 6 7 8   **741; Fic; 741.5**
1. Games; 2. Humorous graphic novels; 3. Librarians; 4. School children — Food; 5. School stories; 6. Graphic novels
978-0-375-94684-4 (lib bdg), $11.99; 0-375-94684-5 (lib bdg); 978-0-375-84684-7 (pa), $5.99; 0-375-84684-0 (pa)

LC 2008043117

The school lunch lady, a secret crime fighter, sets out to stop a group of librarians bent on destroying a shipment of video games, while a group of students known as the Breakfast Bunch provides back-up

"The black-and-white pen-and-ink illustrations have splashes of yellow in nearly every panel. The clean layout, featuring lots of open space, is well suited for the intended audience. . . . With its appealing mix of action and humor, this clever, entertaining addition to the series should have wide appeal." SLJ

Other titles about the Lunch Lady are: Lunch lady and the cyborg substitute (2009); Lunch Lady and the author visit vendetta (2009); Lunch Lady and the summer camp shakedown (2010); Lunch Lady and the bake sale bandit (2010); Lunch Lady and the field trip fiasco (2011); Lunch Lady and the mutant mathletes (2012); Lunch Lady and the picture day peril (2012); Lunch Lady and the video game villain (2013); Lunch Lady and the schoolwide shuffle (2014)

Lunch Lady and the summer camp shakedown. Alfred A. Knopf 2010 Un Illustration
Grades: 3 4 5 6 7 8   **741; 741.5**
978-0-375-86095-9 (pa), $6.99; 0-375-86095-9 (pa)
Lunch Lady and the Breakfast Bunch kids are looking forward to a relaxing summer vacation with no funny business. What evils could befall them at summer camp?

"The two-color art is loopy and energetic, with varied, easy-to-follow page layouts. Jokes and puns are sprinkled throughout to keep the energy high until the exciting finale." SLJ

Kurosawa, Edo
50 Things We Love About Japan written by Edo Kurosawa ; illustrated by Atsuhisa Okura. Japanime Co. Ltd. 2007 112p. Illustration
Grades: 5 6 7 8 9 10 11 12 Adult   **741.5; 952**
1. Japan; 2. Graphic novels
978-4-921205-08-9, $9.99

From anime to karaoke to kaiten-zushi, this little book features manga illustrations and prose to offer the rest of the world a glimpse at what the Japanese love most about the country they call home. Manga readers and anime fans will find explanations for the some of the cultural elements found in the books and films.

Labatt, Mary
★ **Dracula** madness: A Sam & friends mystery. [illustrated by] Jo Rioux. Kids Can Press 2009 95p. Illustration (A Sam & friends mystery)
Grades: 2 3 4 5 6   **741.5; Fic**
1. Dogs; 2. Humorous graphic novels; 3. Mystery graphic novels; 4. Graphic novels
978-1-55453-418-0, $16.95; 1-55453-418-6; 978-1-55337-303-2 (pa), $7.95; 1-55337-303-0 (pa)

LC C2008-903253-5

Sam (Samantha) the sheepdog has moved to Woodford with her human family, and she's not happy about being in a small town. Next-door neighbor Jennie misses her best friend who used to live there, but when her parents send ten-year-old Jennie to deliver a housewarming gift, Joan and Bob hire her to help take care of Sam because they have no children. Soon enough, Jennie realizes she can "hear" Sam's thoughts, including Sam's wishes to eat all kinds of junk food in strange combinations (peanut butter and pickle sandwiches with ketchup, for one). Jennie takes Sam all around town, and then to the spooky old house whose owner, McIver, never comes out. Also, there are bats in the yard, and delivery people bring a suspiciously large, long box to the house. Sam is sure there's a mystery there, and they decide to investigate, along with Jennie's friend Beth. What little they see on a night investigation leads them to think McIver might be . . . Dracula.

"This graphic novel is an adaptation of Labatt's 'Spying on Dracula' (1999). There's just enough creepiness and suspense for younger readers, with simple yet expressive art that stays just on the lighter side of spooky." Booklist

Other titles in this series are: Lake monster mix-up (2009); Mummy mayhem (2010); Witches' brew (2011)

Lake Monster Mix-Up. Mary Labatt ; art by Jo-Anne Rioux. Kids Can Press 2009 96p. Illustration
Grades: 2 3 4 5 6   **741.5; Fic**
1. Humorous graphic novels; 2. Mystery graphic novels; 3. Graphic novels
978-1-55337-822-8, $16.95; 978-1-55337-302-5 (pa), $7.95

LC C2008-907085-2

When Jennie's family decides to go on a camping vacation at Lake Sagawa, Jennie brings along her best friends Beth and Sam, the next-door neighbor dog who can communicate with her. The lake seems like a very quiet place, too quiet for Sam's taste. But one of the locals has talked of a monster, and then Jennie and Beth discover the diary of a girl who lived in their cabin in 1937, and she wrote of a monster. Sam and the girls decide to investigate the glowing underwater lights, the weird cave, and the webbed footprints on the beach.

This is Book 2 in the Sam & Friends Mystery series, and it's adapted from Labatt's novel The Secret of Sagawa Lake.

★ **Mummy** mayhem: a Sam & Friends mystery, book three. Mary Labatt ; art by Jo-Anne Rioux. Kids Can Press 2010 96p. Illustration
Grades: 3 4 5 6 7 8   **741.5; Fic**
1. Dogs; 2. Humorous graphic novels; 3. Mummies; 4. Mystery graphic novels; 5. Graphic novels
978-1-55453-470-8, $16.95
                                  LC C2010-900107-9
Sam the sheepdog feels left out when her human friends Jennie and Beth go on a school field trip to the museum without her. She experiences her own mystery, though, when she finds dog treats left in the snow, hears mysterious chanting, and sees a shadowy figure following her around. The museum has brought an exhibit of Ancient Egypt to town, including the mummy of the pharaoh Menopharsib—could the mummy be searching Woolford for Sam, who resembles Akasheput, the pharaoh's pet dog, whose mummy was stolen years ago" This third book in the series has just enough spooky goings-on for younger readers.

Based on the novel The Mummy Lives! by Mary Labatt

Langridge, Roger
Jim Henson's the Musical Monsters of Turkey Hollow. Adapted from Jim Henson's screenplay by Roger Langridge. Simon & Schuster 2014 96 p. Color; Illustration
Grades: 4 5 6 7   **741.5**
1. Monsters — Juvenile fiction; 2. Music — Juvenile fiction
1608864340; 9781608864348, $24.99
"Turkey Hollow is a picturesque town where hundreds of years ago, unbeknownst to the citizens, a meteorite landed nearby a small brook on the outskirts of town. One Thanksgiving, while young Timmy Henderson practices his guitar, he's accompanied by strange, unearthly, musical sounds. That meteorite wasn't a rock at all but an egg holding seven furry, goofy monsters, each with a unique musical sound. After the initial shock, Timmy befriends the lovable creatures following him all around Turkey Hollow." (Publisher's note)

"Based on a never-produced Jim Henson screenplay, this folksy story captures the spirit of Muppet holiday specials like Emmet Otter's Jug-Band Christmas. . . . Subdued autumnal colors make up most of the palette in Langridge's clean-lined panels, while musical moments are full of big, swirling words in bright colors." Booklist

The **Muppet** Show comic book: on the road. Writer, Roger Langridge ; art, Shelli Paroline & Roger Langridge ; colors, Digikore Studios, Mickey Clausen & Eric Cobain ; letters, Shelli Paroline & Deron Bennett. Boom! Kids 2010 Un Illustration

Grades: 3 4 5 6 7 8 9 10 11 12 Adult   **741.5; Fic**
1. Humorous graphic novels; 2. Muppets (Fictional characters); 3. Travel; 4. Graphic novels
978-1-60886-516-1, $9.99
The Muppets' theater must undergo massive repairs, so the crew takes their show on the road. Standup comedian Fozzie tries to go on his own as a solo act, while Kermit and the rest of the motley group hires a caravan of buses and trailers to find small towns where they can perform. One place, Little Statwald, seems to be populated almost completely by relatives of old curmudgeons Stadler and Waldorf, who all delight in heckling the hapless performers. Langridge draws the main Muppets story, while Shelli Paroline draws the Pigs in Space episodes. The stories have been written to appeal to younger readers, while adults who remember the old Muppets television series will also enjoy the comics.

★ **Snarked!:** Forks and Hope. Roger Langridge. BOOM! Studios 2012 128 p. Illustration
Grades: 5 6 7 8   **741.5/973; Fic**
1. Adventure fiction; 2. Fantasy fiction; 3. Swindlers and swindling — Fiction
1608860957; 9781608860951, $14.99
Eisner Award: Best Publication for Kids (2011)
This graphic novel is the first in Roger Langridge's "Snarked!" series. It presents "an epic adventure featuring the Red Queen's children, Princess Scarlett and her baby brother Rusty, as they set out in search of the missing Red King. And who better to help guide the way than the Walrus and the Carpenter from [Lewis Carroll's] 'Through the Looking Glass'." (Publisher's note)
Volume 1 of 3

Larson, Hope
★ **Chiggers**. [by] Hope Larson; lettered by Jason Azzopardi. Atheneum Books for Young Readers 2008 170p. Illustration
Grades: 5 6 7 8 9   **741.5; Fic**
1. Camps — Fiction; 2. Friendship; 3. Graphic novels
978-1-4169-3584-1, $17.99; 978-1-4169-3587-2 (pa), $9.99
                                  LC 2008-09557
When Abby returns to the same summer camp she always goes to, she is dismayed to find that her old friends have changed, and the only person who wants to be her friend is the strange new girl, Shasta.

"Chiggers provides a ticket to summer fun. Larson delicately handles both the usual middle-school angst and the additional pressures that come with being somewhat different. . . . The content is perfect for upper elementary and middle school students." SLJ

A **wrinkle** in time: the graphic novel. Madeleine L'Engle; adapted and illustrated by Hope Larson. Farrar Straus Giroux 2012 392 p.
Grades: 4 5 6 7   **741.5**
1. L'Engle, Madeleine Wrinkle in time — Adaptations; 2. Science fiction; 3. Space and time — Fiction; 4. Time travel — Fiction; 5. Graphic novels
0374386153; 9780374386153, $19.99
                                  LC 2010044120

Hope Larson presents a graphic novel adaptation of Madeleine L'Engle's "allegorical fantasy in which a group of young people are guided through the universe by Mrs. Who, Mrs. Which and Mrs. What — women who possess supernatural powers. They traverse fictitious regions, meet and face evil and demonstrate courage at the right moment. Religious allusions are secondary to the philosophical struggle designed to yield the meaning of life and one's place on earth." (Kirkus Reviews)

Margaret Furguson Books.

Lash, Batton

Archie: the high school chronicles, book one: freshman year. Script, Batton Lash ; pencils, Bill Galvan ; inks, Bob Smith, Al Milgrom ; letters, Jack Morelli ; colors, Glenn Whitmore. Archie Comic Publications, Inc. 2009 120p. Illustration

Grades: 4 5 6 7 8 9 10   741.5; Fic
    1. Andrews, Archie (Fictional character); 2. High school; 3. Humorous graphic novels; 4. Graphic novels
978-1-879794-40-5, $10.95

Lash, creator of Supernatural Law, writes the story never before written about Archie Andrews and all his friends in all the decades of Archie comics (since the 1940s) what was it like for the gang to start high school" This story starts at the end of summer vacation, and everyone is looking forward to a new start at a new school especially Archie, who constantly got into trouble with his old school principal. The one bad thing is that Jughead has to leave town, because his father has got a new job. On the very first day of school, Archie already gets into trouble with the Principal and yikes! it's Mr. Weatherbee, his old nemesis. Weatherbee has more problems than just dealing with Archie, however; the superintendent doesn't like him and wants to find a way to get him fired. Top that off with Archie facing off against upper classmen bullies, and freshman year is shaping up to be interesting, in a painful way. Galvan's art shows Archie, Jughead, Betty, Veronica, and Reggie as very recognizably themselves but looking young enough to be fourteen years old. This book could be a great entry point for anyone who has never read any Archie comics before.

Lassieur, Allison

Clara Barton: Angel of the Battlefield. Illustrated by Brian Bascle. Capstone Press 2006 32p. Illustration

Grades: 3 4 5 6 7 8 9   741.5; 361.7; 92
    1. Barton, Clara, 1821-1912; 2. Biographical graphic novels; 3. Graphic novels
0-7368-4632-8, $25.26

LC 2005008122

This book uses the comic book format to describe highlights in the life and work of Clara Barton, who served as a Civil War nurse and started the American Red Cross. It includes additional information, a glossary, a list of books for further reading, and more.

Part of the Graphic Library, Graphic Biographies series.

Lords of the Sea: The Vikings Explore the North Atlantic. Illustrated by Ron Frenz and Charles Barnett III. Capstone Press 2006 32p. Illustration

Grades: 3 4 5 6 7 8 9   741.5; 948
    1. Vikings; 2. Graphic novels

0-7368-4974-2, $25.26

LC 2005007891

This book uses the comic book format to tell the story of the Vikings' exploration of the North Atlantic and their discovery of North America. It includes additional information, a glossary, a list of books for further reading, and more.

Part of the Graphic Library, Graphic History series.

Laudec

Cedric, vol. 1: High-risk class. Art by Cauvin. Cinebook Ltd. 2008 48p. Illustration

Grades: 3 4 5 6 7 8   741.5; Fic
    1. Humorous graphic novels; 2. School stories; 3. Graphic novels
978-1-905460-68-7, $11.95

Eight-year-old Cedric is the type of boy who likes to play with his chums, doesn't always get good grades, and has a crush on his teacher, Miss Nelly. Then Chen starts at his school; she's Chinese, she's cute, and Cedric falls head over heels for her. He can't just tell her, of course. Meanwhile, he gets into all kinds of mischief with his friends, including playing with a remote control car, planting stink bombs all over school, drinking champagne when his grandfather says he did so to get the courage to propose to his grandmother. Each time he does something naughty, he does face consequences for his actions. This book is translated from the French.

Le Gall, Frank

Rooftop cat. By Frank Le Gall; illustrated by Flore Balthazar; coloring by Robin Doo. Lerner/Graphic Universe 2012 40 p. Color illustration

Grades: 2 3 4   741.5; Fic; 741.5/973
    1. Animals — Infancy — Fiction; 2. Cats — Fiction; 3. Mice — Fiction; 4. Graphic novels
0761385479; 9780761385479, $6.95; 9780761378853, $29.27

LC 2011025646

The author, Frank Le Gall, presents another entry in his Miss Annie book series. "Miss Annie is just a kitten, but she loves having adventures on the rooftops outside her home. When a gang of dangerous alley cats invade her street, Miss Annie will have to prove her bravery and determination . . . and her loyalty to her very best friend, a mouse." (Publisher's note)

Lechner, John

Sticky Burr: Adventures in Burrwood Forest. Candlewick Press 2007 Un Illustration

Grades: 2 3 4 5 6   741.5; Fic
    1. Adventure graphic novels; 2. Humorous graphic novels; 3. Graphic novels
978-0-7636-3054-6, $15.99

Welcome to Burrwood Forest, where a village of seed pods leads a busy life gathering food, building stick houses, and having adventures. There are good friends like Sticky Burr and Mossy Burr, who stick together, and bad seeds like Scurvy Burr, who likes to irritate them every chance he gets. Watch out for wild dogs and maze trees, loyal insects and escapes on the fly in a graphic storybook for middle-graders and ambitious younger readers.

Leloup, Roger
 Yoko Tsuno, bk. 3: the prey and the ghost. Cinebook 2008 48p. Illustration
Grades: 3 4 5 6 7 8   **741.5; Fic**
 1. Ghosts; 2. Mystery graphic novels; 3. Graphic novels
 978-1-905460-56-4, $11.95
 Young electronics engineer Yoko Tsuno has driven to Scotland to investigate the Loch Ness Monster, when she and her companion Pol find they've taken a wrong turn. Then they encounter a distraught young woman on the road who's being chased by dogs. The young woman is Cecelia, stepdaughter of Sir William, whose parents both died. She's convinced that her mother is haunting their castle, and Yoko finds a way to investigate just what is going on.
 Part of the Yoko Tsuno series, originally published in France as Yoko Tsuno 12 La Proie et l'ombre.

Lemke, Donald B.
 Bike rider: wheelies of justice. Illustrated by Douglas Holgate. Stone Arch Books 2010 38p. Illustration
Grades: 3 4 5 6 7 8   **741.5; Fic**
 1. Adventure graphic novels; 2. Humorous graphic novels; 3. Mystery graphic novels; 4. Graphic novels
 978-1-4342-1892-6, $22.65
         LC 2009-29069
 Michael Cycle is a student at T.V. Academy, but he's also the crusading Bike Rider, with his talking BMX, C.A.T.T. In his latest case, the boy and his bike track down the latest story written by a missing school reporter and discover that the school's quarterback is cheating on his math test. Now they have to stop the team from playing a football game, or the team will be disqualified. Young readers may or may not know the television series Knight Rider, but this story spoofs that show with kid-appropriate action.
 Part of the Graphic Sparks series.

 The **Brave** Escape of Ellen and William Craft. Capstone Press 2006 32p. Illustration
Grades: 3 4 5 6 7 8 9   **741.5; 306.3; 92**
 1. Craft, Ellen, 1826-1891; 2. Craft, William, 1824-1900; 3. Fugitive slaves — United States — Biography; 4. Slavery — United States; 5. Graphic novels
 0-7368-4973-4, $25.26
         LC 2005008084
 This book uses the comic book format to tell the story of Ellen and William Craft's escape from slavery in Georgia to freedom in Pennsylvania. It includes additional information, a glossary, a list of books for further reading, and more.
 Part of the Graphic Library, Graphic History series.

 Hansel and Gretel: the graphic novel. Retold by Donald Lemke; illustrated by Sean Dietrich.. Stone Arch Books 2009 40p. Illustration
Grades: 2 3 4 5 6 7   **741.5; Fic**
 1. Fairy tales; 2. Fantasy graphic novels; 3. Graphic novels
 978-1-4342-0767-8, $21.26
         LC 2008-6721
 When things get very tough for a woodcutter's family, the man's new wife demands that they abandon his children, Hansel and Gretel, in the forest. The children try to make their way home, then find something wonderful for their empty stomachs: a house made of sweets. Unfortunately, an old witch owns the house and imprisons Hansel in a cage to fatten him up so she can eat him, while she makes Gretel do all the chores. The children must find a way to outwit the witch and save themselves. Dietrich's art is slightly creepy, with dark tones and the children's overly large eyes, which fits with the creepy atmosphere of the story. The book includes a brief history of the folktale and how it was written down and popularized by the Grimm brothers.
 Part of the Graphic Spin series

 Investigating the scientific method with Max Axiom, super scientist. Illustrated by Tod Smith and Al Milgrom. Capstone Press 2008 32p. Illustration
Grades: 3 4 5 6 7 8 9   **507; 741.5**
 1. Science — Methodology; 2. Graphic novels
 978-1-42961329-3, $26.26
         LC 2007-22792
 Super scientist Max Axiom, who has powers gained from a freak accident, takes young readers on a journey to learn about the scientific method and how scientists use it to begin their investigations into problems that need solving; readers also learn how to use it themselves in their class work. Back matter includes more historical tidbits of information, a short glossary, and a list of books for further reading.
 Part of the Graphic Science series

 The **Schoolchildren's** Blizzard. Capstone Press 2007 32p. Illustration
Grades: 3 4 5 6 7 8 9   **741.5; 977**
 1. Blizzards; 2. Middle West; 3. Graphic novels
 978-1-4296-0157-3, $26.25
         LC 2007000259
 This book uses the graphic novel format to tell of the devastating 1888 blizzard that suddenly exploded across the Great Plains and killed hundreds of children as they walked home from school. The book includes additional facts and a list of booksfor further reading.
 Part of the Graphic Library Disasters in History series.

 Zinc Alloy vs Frankenstein. Stone Arch Books 2009 40p. Illustration
Grades: 3 4 5 6 7 8   **741.5; Fic**
 1. Frankenstein (Fictional character); 2. Frankenstein's monster (Fictional character); 3. Humorous graphic novels; 4. Science fiction graphic novels; 5. Graphic novels
 978-1-4342-1188-0, $21.26
         LC 2008-32062
 Zack Allen is also superhero Zinc Alloy in his giant robot suit, but when he tries to save Metro City from a tornado, things go very wrong and he causes a lot of destruction. He has to flee from a mob ands ends up hiding in a creepy old house at the edge of town. But he's not alone—there's a robo-Frankenstein there! And there's a girl inside the robot. The book includes a glossary and notes about Mary Shelley's classic novel, Frankenstein.
 Part of the Graphic Sparks line, the Zinc Alloy series.

 Zinc Alloy: Super Zero. Illustrated by Douglas Holgate. Stone Arch Books 2009 33p. Illustration
Grades: 2 3 4 5 6 7   **741.5; Fic**
 1. Bullies; 2. Humorous graphic novels; 3. Robots; 4. Superhero graphic novels; 5. Graphic novels

978-1-4342-0762-3, $21.26

LC 2008-6712

Zack Allen loves to read comics, especially Robo Hero; unfortunately, he's the kind of kid that bullies like to pick on, and they have done so. Then Zack builds his own robot suit; he was just going to get the bullies to stop, but when he hears about a runaway train, he uses the suit to become a new superhero Zinc Alloy! He's going to have to work on controlling things a lot better, though how will he explain broken doors to his mom" The book includes a short history of comic books and the glossary includes definitions for "noogies" and "wet willies."

Part of the Graphic Sparks Zinc Alloy series

Lie, Bjorn Rune
The **wolf's** whistle. By B.R. Lie and S.J. Donaldson.. Nobrow 2012 88 p. Illustration; Color
Grades: 4 5 6 7 8 9 10   **741.5; Fic**
1. Fractured fairy tales; 2. Revenge — Fiction
1907704035; 9781907704031, $18.00

This children's book by Bjorn Rune Lie "digs into the troubled upbringing of one of storydom's most maligned figures: the house-blowing-down wolf. As a wolf cub, little Robert loved superhero comics . . . which led to much torment at the hands of three piggish brothers. Robert grows up to be not much . . . when the building owned by the Honeyroasts burns down with three of Robert's best friends trapped inside, the spark of vengeance and justice is kindled in the wolf." (Booklist)

Limke, Jeff
Isis and Osiris: To the Ends of the Earth. Story by Jeff Limke ; pencils and inks by David Witt. Lerner Publishing Group/Graphic Universe 2007 48p. Illustration
Grades: 3 4 5 6 7 8 9   **398.2; 741.5**
1. Egyptian mythology; 2. Isis (Egyptian deity); 3. Osiris (Egyptian deity); 4. Graphic novels
978-0-8225-3086-2, $26.60 lib. Bdg.

Osiris is the greatest king and god of the land of the Nile. He is a generous ruler, and the people love and worship him, along with his wife and queen, the goddess Isis. But Osiris's jealous brother Set has a terrible plan to get rid of Osiris forever and take his place on the Egyptian throne. Isis uses her magic and her love to save Osiris and conquer Set. The book includes a glossary and a list of books for further reading.

Jason: Quest for the Golden Fleece. Story by Jeff Limke ; pencils by Tim Seely ; inks by Barbara Schulz. Lerner Publishing Group/Graphic Universe 2007 48p. Illustration
Grades: 3 4 5 6 7 8 9   **292.1; 741.5**
1. Greek mythology; 2. Jason (Greek mythology); 3. Graphic novels
978-0-8225-5967-2, $26.60 lib bdg

Jason's uncle Pelias had stole the throne when Jason was a child; now a young man, Jason must prove himself by retrieving the priceless Golden Fleece from the far-off land of Colchis. He gathers a ship of heroes, the Argonauts, to aid him on his quest; but when they arrive in Colchis, the king insists that Jason prove himself in dangerous trials, and the king's daughter, Medea, has plans for Jason. This retelling is

based on the heroic poem by Apollonius of Rhodes. The book includes a glossary and a list of books and websites for further reading.

King Arthur: Excalibur Unsheathed. Story by Jeff Limke ; pencils and inks by Thomas Yeates. Lerner Publishing Group/Graphic Universe 2007 48p. Illustration
Grades: 3 4 5 6 7 8 9   **398.2; 741.5**
1. Arthurian romances; 2. Malory, Sir Thomas, 15th c — Adaptations; 3. Graphic novels
978-0-8225-3083-1, $26.60 lib. Bdg.

This story is adapted from Sir Thomas Malory's Le Morte D'Arthur. Young squire Arthur's life, and that of England, changes the day he pulls out the mysterious Sword in the Stone. Guided by Merlin the magician, Arthur takes his place as King of England. Can he win peace and freedom for his country? The book includes a glossary and a list of books for further reading.

The **treasure** of Mount Fate. Jeff Limke ; illustrated by Clint Hilinski. Lerner Publishing Group/Graphic Universe 2007 112p. Illustration (Twisted Journeys)
Grades: 3 4 5 6 7 8 9   **741.5; Fic**
1. Adventure graphic novels; 2. Graphic novels
978-0-8225-6205-4, $27.93; 978-0-8225-6206-1 (pa), $7.95

LC 2006-101596

In the series called Twisted Journeys, readers choose how the story will progress. Pages of text alternate with comic book-style pages. In this volume, you are a young knight who comes to Mount Fate in search of a treasure. In some storylines, you encounter a trapped wizard, in others a monstrous borkadrac, in yet others such hazards as fireballs, and a talking dragon. Readers will find many scenarios played out, depending on their choices; some end well, others not so well.

Lin, Yali
Hawthorne's the Scarlet letter: the Manga edition. Adapted by Adam Sexton ; illustrated by Yali Lin. Wiley Publishing 2009 186p. Illustration
Grades: 5 6 7 8 9 10 11 12   **741.5; Fic**
1. Hawthorne, Nathaniel, 1804-1864 — Adaptations; 2. Graphic novels
978-0-470-14889-1, $9.99

Hester Prynne, a young married woman in puritanical Massachusetts, stands in public shame when she bears a child long after her husband had disappeared. She refuses to identify the father of her child and instead wears the scarlet letter A always. The young minister Arthur Dimmesdale lives with his guilt in secret, but the physician, Roger Chillingworth, is actually Hester's husband, returned for vengeance. He vows to find the man who fathered Pearl, Hester's daughter, and destroy him. Meanwhile, Pearl grows up in a society that shuns her mother, and she comes to see the A as her mother's badge of honor. This book is a manga style adaptation of Hawthorne's novel.

Liniers
★ The **big** wet balloon: a Toon book. By Liniers. Toon Books 2013 32 p. Color; Illustration (Easy-to-read comics. Level 2)
Grades: PreK K 1 2   **741.5; Fic**

1. Balloons — Fiction; 2. Rain — Juvenile fiction; 3. Sisters — Juvenile fiction; 4. Graphic novels
1935179322; 9781935179320, $12.95

LC 2012047662

Eisner Nominee: Best Publication for Early Readers (2014)

This book by Ricardo Liniers "shows several tableaus of two little girls who wake up in the room they share and spend the day together. The older sister suggests fun things to do, like shouting at the top of their lungs while they run through a rain shower. Though they have one small misunderstanding, these siblings are loving and thoughtful—good companions whatever the weather." (New York Times Book Review)

"An uncommonly family-friendly tale, great for parents to share with their kids." Booklist

★ **Written** and Drawn by Henrietta. By Liniers. TOON Books 2015 64 p. Color; Illustration
Grades: 1 2 3 4 **741.5**
1. Authorship — Juvenile fiction; 2. Drawing — Fiction; 3. Drawing — Juvenile fiction; 4. Graphic novels
9781935179900, $12.95; 193517990X

LC 2015004010

Mildred L. Batchelder Honor Book (2016)

"Reading books is fun . . . but what about making them" Armed with new colored pencils, Henrietta's ready to try. Peek over her shoulder as she draws the story of a brave young girl, a three-headed monster, and an impossibly wide world of adventure." (Publisher's note)

"Argentine cartoonist Liniers presents a graphic ode to the pleasures and challenges of composition, starring his recurring character Henrietta, a young bibliophile. The little girl's cat, Fellini, looks on as she writes and illustrates 'The Monster with Three Heads and Two Hats.' Page by page, she narrates her process, her own story appearing in a childlike, colored-pencil scrawl alongside Liniers' polished panels. . . . Henrietta and her creator are kindred spirits, displaying equal knacks for the surreal and the utterly charming." Kirkus

Liu, Na
★ **Little** White Duck: a childhood in China. By Andrés Vera Martínez and Na Liu; illustrated by Andrés Vera Martínez. Graphic Universe 2012 96 p. Color illustration
Grades: 4 5 6 **741.5/973; 741.5**
1. Biographical graphic novels; 2. China — History — 1976-; 3. Liu, Na, 1973-; 4. Graphic novels
0761365877; 9780761365877, $29.27; 9780761381150, $9.95; 0761381155

LC 2011005347

This graphic novel provides a "glimpse into Chinese girlhood during the 1970s and '80s." It begins with the 3-year-old narrator trying to understand the death of Chairman Mao. "From there, her life unfolds in short sketches. . . . She explains about the four pests that plague China . . . and her stomach-turning school assignment to catch rats and deliver the severed tails to her teacher . . . [as well as] the origins of Chinese New Year, her favorite holiday." (Kirkus Reviews)

"This picturesque treasure introduces Chinese culture through a personal perspective that is both delightful and thought-provoking." SLJ

Lobdell, Scott
The **Hardy** Boys vol. 10: A Hardy day's night. Paulo H. Marcondes with Marcel Zero, artists. NBM/Papercutz 2007 Un Illustration
Grades: 3 4 5 6 7 8 **741.5; Fic**
1. Adventure graphic novels; 2. Hardy Boys (Fictional characters); 3. Mystery graphic novels; 4. Graphic novels
978-1-59707-070-6, $7.95

A rogue mentor agent within A.T.A.C. lures Frank and Joe into a deadly ambush, but they have only until dawn to rescue a kidnapped boy. But soon enough they learn there's a bigger plot afoot, and the boy is only a pawn.

Hardy Boys, undercover brothers #14: Haley Danelle's top eight. Paulo Henrique Marcondes, artist. Papercutz 2008 Un Illustration
Grades: 3 4 5 6 7 8 9 **741.5; Fic**
1. Adventure graphic novels; 2. Hardy Boys (Fictional characters); 3. Mystery graphic novels; 4. Graphic novels
978-1-59707-114-7, $12.95; 978-1-59707-113-0 (pa), $7.95

Cute little computer nerd and horse expert Haley Danelle needs the help of the Hardy Boys; she has been an ATAC operative and knows who they are. Her top friends on her MyFacePlace social network page are disappearing, one by one, and she wants Joe and Frank to help her stop it and find her friends. But things soon turn deadly, and Joe and Frank find themselves in trouble.

Volume 14 of the Hardy Boys, Undercover Brothers series

The **Hardy** boys, undercover brothers #15: Live free, die hardy!. Paulo Henrique Marcondes, artist. Papercutz 2008 Un Illustration
Grades: 3 4 5 6 7 8 9 **741.5; Fic**
1. Adventure graphic novels; 2. Hardy Boys (Fictional characters); 3. Mystery graphic novels; 4. Graphic novels
978-1-59707-124-6, $12.95; 978-1-59707-123-9 (pa), $7.95

When the guys at A.T.A.C. decide to throw Fenton Hardy a surprise party, some uninvited guests show up. The Noir Sisters, Nicolina and Shira, an evil counterpart to Frank and Joe Hardy, show up with their henchmen and get in because the security system was temporarily shut down to allow the invited guests to come in. It's going to be up to Frank and Joe to find a way to take down the bad guys without letting anyone get hurt.

Part of The Hardy Boys, Undercover Brothers series.

The **Hardy** Boys, Undercover Brothers #7: The Opposite Numbers. Daniel Rendon, Paulo Henrique, Sidney Lima, artist. NBM/Papercutz 2006 112p. Illustration
Grades: 4 5 6 7 8 9 **741.5; Fic**
1. Adventure graphic novels; 2. Mystery graphic novels; 3. Graphic novels
1-59707-035-1, $12.95; 1-59707-034-3, $7.95

Traveling across the country on the maiden voyage of a bullet train, the Hardy Boys find themselves framed for murder. But they can't depend on A.T.A.C. (American Teens Against Crime) to help them, because every indication is that it's the super secret spy organization, founded by their own father, that framed them.

The **Hardy** Boys: Undercover Brothers #1: The Ocean of Osyria. Lea Hernandez, artist. NBM/Papercutz 2005 Un Illustration
Grades: 3 4 5 6 7 8 9   **741.5; Fic**
  1. Hardy Boys (Fictional characters); 2. Mystery graphic novels; 3. Graphic novels
  1-59707-005-X, $12.95; 1-59707-001-7 (pa)
  After rescuing Jackpot, a kidnapped prize-winning racehorse, Frank and Joe are stunned to return to Bayport and discover that the Department of International Security has arrested their best friend, Chet Morton, for stealing a priceless art treasure. The Hardy Boys decide the only way to clear their friend is to journey to the Middle East and find the Ocean of Osyria themselves.

The **Hardy** Boys: Undercover Brothers #2: Identity Theft. Daniel Rendon, artist. NBM/Papercutz 2005 Un Illustration
Grades: 3 4 5 6 7 8 9   **741.5; Fic**
  1. Hardy Boys (Fictional characters); 2. Mystery graphic novels; 3. Graphic novels
  978-1-59707-007-2, $12.95; 978-1-59707-003-4 (pa)
  Joe and Frank Hardy first crack a case involving sky-diving diamond smugglers, then take on a case of stolen identity. Joy Gallagher claims another girl is now living her life, with her parents, and in her body. Is this girl insane, or can her fantastic story actually be true?

The **Hardy** Boys: Undercover Brothers #3: Mad House. Daniel Rendon, artist. NBM/Papercutz 2005 Un Illustration
Grades: 3 4 5 6 7 8 9   **741.5; Fic**
  1. Hardy Boys (Fictional characters); 2. Mystery graphic novels; 3. Graphic novels
  978-1-59707-011-9, $12.95; 978-1-59707-010-2 (pa)
  No sooner do Frank and Joe Hardy rescue a member of Her Majesty's Secret Service (who says he's shaken, not stirred), than they're off on a new top-secret ATAC (American Teens Against Crime) mission. Frank and Joe must go undercover on a new reality TV show called 'Mad House,' to discover how far the producers are willing to go risking the contestants' lives for the sake of huge ratings. The plot thickens when the producer of Mad House turns up murdered.

The **Hardy** Boys: Undercover Brothers #4: Malled. Daniel Rendon, artist. NBM/Papercutz 2005 Un Illustration
Grades: 3 4 5 6 7 8 9   **741.5; Fic**
  1. Hardy Boys (Fictional characters); 2. Mystery graphic novels; 3. Graphic novels
  978-1-59707-015-7, $12.95; 978-1-59707-014-0 (pb)
  Frank and Joe Hardy finish up a case helping a fellow ATAC (American Teens Against Crime) agent, who sharp-eyed fans may recognize despite her Alias. Things seem to quiet down when ATAC sends Frank and Joe undercover to investigate a new Mall opening in Bayport, due to several suspicious accidents there. But things get exciting when the night before the big opening, Joe, Frank, and seven others are mysteriously locked in the mall with a murderer on the loose. If that wasn't enough, everything that could go horribly wrong in a mall, does: a flood caused by water beds; an electrocution at an electronics shop; a bow and arrow used to kill in the Sporting Goods store; a

runaway elevator; a damsel in distress in the dress shop; fire in the food court; and much, much more.

The **Hardy** Boys: Undercover Brothers #5: Sea You, Sea Me. Daniel Rendon, artist. NBM/Papercutz 2006 112p. Illustration
Grades: 3 4 5 6 7 8 9   **741.5; Fic**
  1. Hardy Boys (Fictional characters); 2. Mystery graphic novels; 3. Graphic novels
  978-1-59707-023-2, $12.95; 978-1-59707-022-5 (pb)
  When a series of suspicious mishaps befall several deep sea fishing boats, the Hardy Boys are called into action by ATAC (American Teens Against Crime) before any more teen green horns can be hurt. But while in the past Frank and Joe have battled terrorists, master criminals, and multinational corporations, the undercover brothers have no experience fighting the fury of the ocean.

The **Hardy** Boys: Undercover Brothers #6: Hyde & Shriek. Art by Daniel Rendon. NBM/Papercutz 2006 112p. Illustration
Grades: 3 4 5 6 7 8 9   **741.5; Fic**
  1. Hardy Boys (Fictional characters); 2. Mystery graphic novels; 3. Graphic novels
  978-1-59707-029-4, $12.95; 978-1-59707-028-7 (pb)
  When a visiting dignitary's daughter is scheduled to attend a party at a horror-themed restaurant in New York City, ATAC agents Joe and Frank Hardy are enlisted as undercover protection. But in a building where anything can happen, where the walls literally have ears, can the Hardy Boys find and stop the assassin who has targeted Sangita before it is too late?

The **Hardy** Boys: Undercover Brothers #7: The Opposite Numbers. Daniel Rendon, Paulo Henrique, Sidney Lima, artist. NBM/Papercutz 2006 112p. Illustration
Grades: 3 4 5 6 7 8 9   **741.5; Fic**
  1. Hardy Boys (Fictional characters); 2. Mystery graphic novels; 3. Graphic novels
  978-1-59707-035-5, $12.95; 978-1-59707-034-3 (pb)
  Traveling across the country on the maiden voyage of a bullet train, the Hardy Boys find themselves framed for murder, even after their heroic efforts to save others. But they can't depend on A.T.A.C. (American Teens Against Crime) to help them, because every indication is that it's the super secret spy organization, founded by their father, that framed them.

The **Hardy** Boys: Undercover Brothers #8: Board to Death. Paulo Henrique, artist. NBM/Papercutz 2007 112p. Illustration
Grades: 3 4 5 6 7 8 9   **741.5; Fic**
  1. Hardy Boys (Fictional characters); 2. Mystery graphic novels; 3. Graphic novels
  978-1-59707-054-6, $12.95; 978-1-59707-053-9 (pb)
  Frank and Joe Hardy go undercover at a major skateboarding contest in Venice, California to find out which competitor is trying to kill off the competition, literally. The list of suspects includes Dex Thom, a skilled skateboarder whose parents wanted him to be a musical prodigy, the Pink Shadow, a girl of mystery, and her equally secretive trainer, Mr. Moto, and the Wraith, a dark and brooding young man. Will Frank and Joe solve the mystery before the killer discovers their real mission, and eliminates them?

The **Hardy** Boys: Undercover Brothers #9: To Die or Not to Die?. Paulo Henrique, artist. NBM/Papercutz 2007 112p. Illustration

Grades: 3 4 5 6 7 8 9   741.5; Fic
1. Hardy Boys (Fictional characters); 2. Mystery graphic novels; 3. Graphic novels
978-1-59707-063-8, $12.95; 978-1-59707-062-1 (pb)

At a nationwide drama competition, Frank and Joe Hardy must go undercover to discover which contestant has been knocking off the competition by any means possible - including deadly force. While Joe keeps an eye on all of the backstage drama, Frank, posing as a competing drama student, may be distracted from his mission by the romantic attentions of a beautiful acting student named Joelle. Things get further complicated when Joelle becomes the only eyewitness to the red-haired woman who is their number one suspect! Will Frank's stage debut be the Hardy Boys final bow?

Loux, Matthew
    ★ **Salt** water taffy: The legend of Old Salty. Oni Press 2008 Un Illustration

Grades: 2 3 4   741.5; Fic
1. Adventure graphic novels; 2. Humorous graphic novels; 3. Mystery graphic novels; 4. Graphic novels
978-1-932664-94-2, $5.95

Eleven-year-old Jack Putnam and his eight-year-old brother Benny aren't very happy with their parents' choice to spend a summer-long vacation in dinky little Chowder Bay, Maine. They cheer up a bit when they taste the delicious salt water taffy candy made in town, then they meet a local fisherman, old Angus O'Neil, who tells terrific stories of fishing adventures at sea. And then Jack and Benny come upon a mystery when all the salt water taffy in the local store disappears, and they try to solve the mystery

Loux "dishes up an entertaining, exciting story for young graphic-novel readers. . . . The high-contrast black-and-white art, accomplished with bold line work, is used to good effect, displaying fluidity while still remaining quirky and fun." Booklist

Other titles in this series are: A climb up Mt. Barnabas (2008); The truth about Dr. True (2009); Caldera's revenge! Part 1 (2011); Caldera's revenge! Part 2 (2011)

    ★ **Salt** water taffy: the seaside adventures of Jack and Benny, vol. 4: Caldera's revenge, part 1. Oni Press 2011 Un Illustration

Grades: 3 4 5 6 7 8 9   741.5; Fic
1. Adventure graphic novels; 2. Brothers; 3. Humorous graphic novels; 4. Whales; 5. Graphic novels
978-1-934964-62-0, $5.99

As Jack and Benny's summer vacation in Chowder Bay continues, Captain Hollister gives the boys a book called The Hidden History of Chowder Bay. The boys find it difficult to read, so they jump at the chance to investigate when a spooky whaling ship appears in the bay. The local fishermen talk about something attacking their boats in the bay, and the brothers soon discover that the culprit is the legendary whale called Caldera. But just what is that spooky whaling ship doing in the bay" This volume ends in a cliffhanger. Readers who enjoy rollicking adventure and a little whimsy (talking giant squid who like grilled hot dogs) will enjoy this book.

Love, Robert
    Shadow Rock. Jeremy and Robert Love. Dark Horse Comics 2006 80p. Illustration

Grades: 4 5 6 7 8   741.5; Fic
1. Adventure graphic novels; 2. Mystery graphic novels; 3. Supernatural graphic novels; 4. Graphic novels
1-59307-347-X, $9.95

After his mother's death, young Timothy London moves from the big city to the small New England fishing town of Shadow Rock to live with his father. His new home is up the hill from a legendary haunted lighthouse where Timothy discovers the ghost of Kendahl Fog, a boy who died under mysterious circumstances. Timothy and his new ghostly companion set out to explore the dark underbelly of Shadow Rock and the mystery of Kendahl's death. Harrowing thrills and chills ensue in this classic boy's adventure with a horror twist.

Low, Vicki
    The **First** Emperor. Art by Sarah Mayhew. Harcourt Achieve/Steck-Vaughn 2006 48p. Illustration

Grades: 3 4 5 6 7 8   741.5; Fic
1. Adventure graphic novels; 2. China — History; 3. Graphic novels
978-1-4190-3195-3, $4.88

Emperor Zheng rules over a vast empire as the first emperor of China, and he wants to live forever. He sends his son Prince Fu Su on a search for the secret of everlasting life. As the prince travels through the land, he learns about some magic herbs and much more ... This historical graphic novel includes prose intervals that provide information about Emperor Zheng and some of China's national treasures, such as the soldiers of X'ian, the Great Wall of China; and of some of the atrocities he ordered, such as the burning of all books that didn't agree with his edicts, and many deaths.

Part of the Timeline Graphic Novels series.

Luciani, Brigitte
    ★ **Mr.** Badger and Mrs. Fox #1: The meeting. Illustrated by Eve Tharlet. Graphic Universe 2010 32p. Illustration (Mr. Badger and Mrs. Fox)

Grades: 1 2 3   741.5
1. Badgers; 2. Foxes; 3. Siblings; 4. Graphic novels
0-7613-5625-8 (lib bdg); 0-7613-5631-2 (pa);
978-0-7613-5625-7 (lib bdg), $25.26;
978-0-7613-5631-8 (pa), $6.95
                            LC 2009032617

Having lost their home, a fox and her daughter move in with a badger and his three children, but when the youngsters throw a big party hoping to prove that they are incompatible, their plan backfires.

Other titles in this series are: A hubbub (2010); What a team! (2011); Peace and quiet (2012); The carnival (2014)

    Mr. Badger and Mrs. Fox #2: A hubbub. Illustrated by Eve Tharlet. Graphic Universe 2010 32p. Illustration

Grades: 1 2 3   741; 741.5
0-7613-5626-6 (lib bdg); 978-0-7613-5632-5 (pa),
$6.95; 0-7613-5632-0 (pa); 978-0-7613-5626-4 (lib bdg), $25.26
                            LC 2010005714

"Ginger Fox is having some trouble adjusting to her new life, which includes two badger stepbrothers. In the end she realizes that having a bigger family can only bring more rewards and is happy with her situation." (School Library Journal)

★ **Mr.** Badger and Mrs. Fox #3: what a team!. Lerner Publishing Group/Graphic Universe 2011 96p. Illustration (Mr. Badger and Mrs. Fox)

Grades: K 1 2 3 **741.5; Fic**
1. Boat racing; 2. Family life; 3. Sibling rivalry; 4. Graphic novels
978-0-7613-5627-1, $25.26; 978-0-7613-5633-2 (pa), $6.95

In this third book about the mixed family of badgers and foxes, badger brothers Grub and Bristle want to build a boat with their friends, but new fox sister Ginger keeps trying to take charge. They also can't decide on what type of boat they should build; Bristle wants to build a kayak, while Ginger wants a catamaran. They end up dividing into teams, with a group of the friends along with Grub building a raft, while Ginger builds a catamaran and Bristle builds his kayak, and then racing to see whose boat is better. Will the kids learn how to get along better and work together as a team after the race? This gentle story of sibling rivalry and learning about cooperation also has a more subtle message about blended families. Grub, Bristle, Ginger, and little badger sister Berry are very distinct and interesting characters that most young readers will recognize among themselves.

Originally published in France by Dargaud as Monsieur Blaireau et Madame Renard 3/Quelle equipe!

★ **Mr.** Badger and Mrs. Fox #4: Peace and quiet. Brigitte Luciani & Eve Tharlet. Graphic Universe 2012 32 p. Color illustration (Mr. Badger and Mrs. Fox)

Grades: K 1 2 3 **741.5**
1. Badgers — Juvenile fiction; 2. Brothers and sisters — Fiction; 3. Foxes — Juvenile fiction; 4. Siblings — Juvenile fiction; 5. Stepfamilies — Fiction; 6. Winter — Juvenile fiction; 7. Graphic novels
0761385207; 0822591634; 9780761385202, $25.26; 9780822591634, $6.95

LC 2011049904

This children's book by Brigitte Luciani, illustrated by Eve Tharlet, continues the "Mr. Badger and Mrs. Fox" series. "Can this family keep the peace when they're cooped up together underground?" . . . [W]inter is coming! Ginger wants to sing and play and hunt in the snow. She wishes her badger brother, Grub, would join her, but he is busy taking daylong naps. She needs a perfect plan to make the whole family happy. But what do you do with a badger who only wants peace and quiet? (Publisher's note)

Mr. Badger and Mrs. Fox #5: The carnival. By Brigitte Luciani; illustrated by Eve Tharlet; translation by Carol Klio Burrell. Graphic Universe 2014 32 p. Color; Illustration (Mr. Badger and Mrs. Fox)

Grades: K 1 2 3 **741.5**
1. Animals; 2. Badgers — Fiction; 3. Carnivals — Fiction; 4. Foxes — Fiction; 5. Grandparents — Fiction; 6. Stepfamilies — Fiction; 7. Graphic novels
1467742031; 9781467742030, $25.26

LC 2013040909

This children's graphic novel, by Brigitte Luciani, illustrated by Eve Tharlet, and translated by Carol Klio Burrell, is part of the "Mr. Badger and Mrs. Fox" series. "Can badgers and foxes get through a long, hard winter together?" . . . But Grandpa Fox also remembers an old tradition—a carnival to remind winter that it must make way for spring. A party might be just the thing to help the animals make it through a cold, dark season. (Publisher's note)

"Set against an ethereal watercolor palette, this softly told graphic offering moves slowly but lightly, like the fine snow that the animals take shelter from. The foxes and badgers are likable through and through, reminiscent of such other forest friends as Winnie the Pooh or Frog and Toad." Kirkus

Lucke, Deb

The **Lunch** Witch. By Deb Lucke. Papercutz 2015 180 p. Illustration

Grades: 3 4 5 6

741.5; Fic
1. Friendship — Fiction; 2. School children — Fiction; 3. Witches — Fiction
1629911623; 9781629911625, $14.99

Courtesy of Papercutz

In this book, by Deb Lucke, "Grunhilda inherits her famous ancestors' recipes and cauldron, but no one believes in magic anymore. Despite the fact that Grunhilda's only useful skill is cooking up potfuls of foul brew, she finds a job listing that might suit her: lunch lady. She delights in scaring the kids until she meets a timid little girl named Madison with a big set of glasses who becomes an unlikely friend." (Publisher's note)

"Lucke's splotchy, textured, quixotically paced, visual storytelling, with its mixture of crisply defined panels and sprawling full-page spreads, perfectly fits the outsider lives of both protagonists." VOYA

Lundy, Kathleen Gould

In a Class of Her Own. Art by Jeff Alward. Harcourt Achieve 2006 48p. Illustration

Grades: 3 4 5 6 7 8 **92; 741.5**
1. African Americans — Civil rights; 2. Biographical graphic novels; 3. Bridges, Ruby; 4. Graphic novels
978-1-4190-3212-7, $8.99

It is the year 1960. A six-year-old girl named Ruby Bridges makes history by being the first African American child to attend an all-white school in New Orleans. What is she up against? This graphic novel is interspersed with pages of prose giving background information about Brown v. Board of Education, Norman Rockwell's famous painting of Ruby, and about her life as an adult.

Part of the Timeline Graphic Novels series.

Lutes, Jason

★ **Houdini:** the handcuff king. Art by Nick Bertozzi. Hyperion Books for Children/Jump at the Sun 2007 90p. Illustration (Center for Cartoon Studies presents)

Grades: 4 5 6 7 8 9 10   **92; 741.5**
1. Biographical graphic novels; 2. Houdini, Harry, 1874-1926; 3. Magicians; 4. Magicians; 5. Graphic novels
978-0-7868-3902-5, $16.99; 978-0-7868-3903-2 (pa), $9.99

On May 1, 1908, magician Harry Houdini performed one of his famous handcuff escapes, this time in handcuffs and leg irons, while jumping off the Cambridge Bridge in Massachusetts into the frigid Boston River. This graphic novel takes the reader through Houdini's day, from 5:00 a.m. as he makes his preparations, makes a practice jump, coaches his wife Bess on how she's to help him, and then makes the jump.

This is a "fascinating graphic novel. . . . The format will instantly draw a lot of attention from readers and then hold on to it. Lutes and Bertozzi use grayscale comic panels to share their story about the life of Harry Houdini in a unique way. . . . The book resembles a hybrid between fiction and nonfiction, and the ingenious choice of format will appeal to a broad age range of readers." Voice Youth Advocates

Lyga, Barry
★ **Wolverine**: worst day ever. By Barry Lyga; artist, Todd Nauck. Marvel Publishing 2009 184p. Illustration
Grades: 5 6 7 8 9   **741.5; Fic**
1. Humorous graphic novels; 2. Superhero graphic novels; 3. Wolverine (Fictional character); 4. Graphic novels
978-0-7851-3757-3, $14.99; 0-7851-3757-2

Teenager Eric Mattias has just recently discovered he has mutant powers. Very sucky mutant powers: suddenly no one notices him even when he's in the same room. He's not invisible, but he might as well be, and people don't even notice him when he speaks. Eric decides to follow Wolverine around and see if he can't pick up a few pointers about living a loner-type life, as the adamantium-clawed mutant tends to do. Only when they end up in a remote forested area does Eric realize he may not have made the smartest move, because someone else has come, someone who is as strong as Wolverine, and maybe meaner: Sabretooth.

"It's a coming-of-age tale with bursts of action that's sure to appeal to its large, built-in audience." Booklist

Lynch, Jay
Mo and Jo: fighting together forever: a toon book. By [illustrator] Dean Haspiel & [writer] Jay Lynch. RAW Junior 2008 40p. Illustration
Grades: K 1 2 3   **741.5; Fic**
1. Humorous graphic novels; 2. Siblings; 3. Superhero graphic novels; 4. Graphic novels
978-0-9799238-5-2, $12.95

Mona and Joey are battling twins, and everything they do turns into a fight. They both love the same superhero, the Mighty Mojo. One day he comes to their house and says he needs to retire and gives them his costume, which has all his powers

"The text is peppered with puns and some clever idiom work, reinforced by repetition as well as what's happening in the clean panels and art." Booklist

Otto's backwards day: a Toon book. By Frank Cammuso; illustrated by Jay Lynch. Toon Books, is an imprint of Candlewick Press 2013 32 p.

Grades: K 1 2   **741.5**
1. Birthdays — Fiction; 2. Cats — Fiction; 3. Humorous fiction; 4. Humorous stories; 5. Graphic novels
1935179330; 9781935179337, $12.95
LC 2012047661
Eisner Nominee: Best Publication for Early Readers (2014)

"Someone stole Otto's birthday! When Otto and his robot sidekick, Toot, follow the crook, they discover a topsy-turvy world where rats chase cats and people wear underpants over their clothes. To get his presents back, Otto needs to solve a slew of backwards puzzles—but his greatest challenge comes at the journey's very end. On this special day, will Otto discover something even better than cake or gift?" (Publisher's note)

★ **Otto's** orange day. By Frank Cammuso & Jay Lynch.. Toon Books 2008 40p. Illustration
Grades: K 1 2 3   **741.5; Fic**
1. Color; 2. Fantasy graphic novels; 3. Humorous graphic novels; 4. Magic; 5. Graphic novels
978-0-97992382-1; 978-0-9799238-2-4, $12.95
LC 2007-40759

Otto, a young orange cat, loves the color orange. In fact, when he receives a strange little lamp as a gift from his Aunt Sally Lee, and it turns out to be a magic lamp with a genie, Otto wishes everything in the world was orange. As it turns out, though, orange isn't good for everything " orange food tastes weird, traffic lights don't work when they're all orange . . . now Otto has to fix things, but he only got one wish. Now what? This TOON book has a more detailed story line and more text, which makes it good for readers who are beyond the basic beginner level; the panel design ranges from one per page to four per page. Author Jay Lynch is one of the people responsible for Topps Chewing Gum's Wacky Packages and Garbage Pail Kids, and Frank Cammuso is the political cartoonist for the Syracuse Post-Standard and the Eisner-nominated creator of Max Hamm Fairy Tale Detective.

MacHale, D. J.
★ **Pendragon** book one: the merchant of death graphic novel. Adapted and illustrated by Carla Speed McNeil. Aladdin Paperbacks 2008 172p. Illustration
Grades: 5 6 7 8 9 10   **741.5; Fic**
1. Adventure graphic novels; 2. Fantasy graphic novels; 3. Graphic novels
978-1-4169-5080-6, $9.99; 1-4169-5080-X
LC 2007-937920

Fourteen-year-old Bobby Pendragon has had a good life with a loving family, friends, and sports, but it all changes the night his Uncle Press takes him into New York City, to a deserted subway station that contains a gate that leads them to another world. On Denduron, a peaceful tribe called the Milago face annihilation from the

Courtesy of Aladdin Paperbacks

Bedowan, and Uncle Press expects Bobby to help him stop it. Press is what he calls a Traveler, and he says Bobby is one, too, and they have a job to do. Bobby is able to write journals and send them home to his best friends Mark and Courtney. Meanwhile, he needs to learn so much, can he do it in time to help—and stay alive?

"This graphic-format adaptation streamlines the already fast-moving experience, providing satisfying interpretations of favorite characters and situations." Booklist

MacPherson, Dwight L.
Kid Houdini and the silver dollar misfits. Art by Worth Gowell and Kevin Conley. Viper Comics 2008 Un Illustration
Grades: 3 4 5 6 7 8 9   741.5; Fic
1. Houdini, Harry, 1874-1926; 2. Magicians; 3. Mystery graphic novels; 4. Nonfiction writers; 5. Supernatural graphic novels; 6. Graphic novels
978-0—9802385-2-5, $9.95

In 1886, ten-year-old Harry Houdini runs away from home, only to find himself a prisoner in Professor Murat's circus. Harry joins the "freak" children: Lydia the snake girl (and her snake Terra), Hans the legless boy, and Jacques and Joe the Siamese twins and they form a detective agency that will solve mysteries for the fee of a silver dollar. Near Kansas City, a girl named Bea hires them to find her missing father whom she fears was kidnapped. However, when the gang gets to her house, they discover that her mother has now been kidnapped, too. It all has to do with a treasure map that leads to a lost gold mine, and the gang needs to solve that mystery in order to find Bea's parents. A young Harry Houdini and his friends make a fun team and they face some supernatural elements in their cases, much like the old Scooby-Doo cartoons, and with a similar scary-fun factor.

Maeda, Shunshin
Ninja baseball Kyuma!, vol. 1. Udon Entertainment 2009 200p. Illustration
Grades: 2 3 4 5 6   741.5; Fic
1. Baseball; 2. Humorous graphic novels; 3. Manga; 4. Ninja; 5. Graphic novels
978-1-897376-86-7, $7.99

Young Kyuma Hattori, descendant of famous ninja Hanzo Hattori, is the last ninja left in the ninja compound in the mountains, and he trains with his faithful dog Inui. Kaoru is captain of the Moonstar City Club baseball team, comprised of elementary school students. When teammate Yohko says her crystal ball says they need to look to the mountains to help their team win, Kaoru goes up the mountain and finds Kyuma and asks him to join their team. Kyuma knows nothing about modern society or sports like baseball, and he thinks he's joining an army to go to battle against their enemy. Will his team ever figure out Kyuma is really a ninja, and will Kyuma ever figure out that a baseball game is just a game? The book includes some ninja-style fighting, but no violence or bad language.

Malam, John
Oliver Twist. Illustrated by Penko Gelev; retold by John Malam.. Barron's 2006 48p. Illustration
Grades: 3 4 5 6 7 8 9   741.5; Fic

1. Dickens, Charles, 1812-1870 — Adaptations; 2. Great Britain — History — 19th century; 3. Graphic novels
978-0-7641-5975-6, $15.99; 978-0-7641-3490-6 (pa), $8.99
LC 2005-936253

Born in a workhouse and immediately orphaned, Oliver Twist seems destined for a life of misery. He survives childhood years filled with neglect, hunger, and violence, but on his eighth birthday, he must start to work in the workhouse, and his troubles begin. Soon after he gets into trouble for daring to ask for more food, he's sent out to work and falls in with the evil Bill Sikes and Fagin, who run a group of raggedy young thieves. The book includes a brief biography of Dickens, a time line of world events during his life, a brief essay on the poor in London, and descriptions of some of the theatrical and motion picture adaptations of the story.

Part of the Graphic Classics series.

Mansfield, Andy
The **All-New** All-Different X-Men Pop-Up. Candlewick Press 2007 Un Illustration
Grades: K 1 2 3 4 5 6 7 8 9 10 11 12 Adult   741.5; Fic
1. Pop-up books; 2. Superhero graphic novels; 3. X-Men (Fictional characters); 4. Graphic novels
978-0-7636-3462-9, $24.99

This pop-up book uses excerpts from classic X-Men comics, paper engineering, and pull-out fact files to profile the X-Men, including Cyclops, Storm, Nightcrawler, Wolverine, Colossus, and Banshee, along with nemesis Magneto and mini-profiles of the original X-Men.

Marsh, Robert
Monster moneymaker. Art by Tom Percival. Stone Arch Books 2010 40p. Illustration
Grades: 2 3 4 5 6   741.5; Fic
1. Fantasy graphic novels; 2. Humorous graphic novels; 3. Monsters; 4. Schools; 5. Graphic novels
978-1-4342-1891-9, $21.32; 1-4342-1891-0
LC 2009-29071

Gabby and her monster friend Dwight attend a school that is suffering from funding problems. New student Bradley proposes a candy sale to raise funds that will keep the lunch program going, then he proposes a contest to see who can raise the most money. Gabby and Dwight do pretty well, but Bradley and his monster Biff are way ahead of everyone else; could they possibly be cheating? This graphic novel includes a brief glossary, discussion questions, and writing prompts.

Part of the Graphic Sparks series.

Martin, Gary
Son of Samson and the Judge of God Volume 1. Art by Sergio Cariello. Zondervan/Zonderkidz 2007 160p. Illustration
Grades: 3 4 5 6 7 8   741.5; Fic
1. Adventure graphic novels; 2. Humorous graphic novels; 3. Graphic novels
978-0-310-71279-4, $9.99
LC 2007-3157

When things get physical, Branan uses any weapon he can grab, just like his father, Samson. And like his dad, he can wield weapons other men can't even lift. The trouble is, he's not sure why God gave him such great power or what he's supposed to do with it. Trying to understand his father - and himself - Branan travels to the places where Samson did his amazing deeds. Along the way he performs some incredible heroics of his own, stirring up the anger of his father's old enemies. The book includes lots of cartoony action.

Martz, John
A **Cat** Named Tim and Other Stories. John Martz. Koyama Press 2014 52 p. Color; Illustration
Grades: PreK K 1   **741.5**
1. Animals; 2. Short stories
1927668107; 9781927668108, $19.95
This book by John Martz is set "in Tim's world, [where] a cat can paint on the ceiling and a happy pig couple can wait months for the bus. A duck and a mouse love to go flying, in a plane, of course. Every page is an adventure and each character is colorful in this collection of comics." (Publisher's note)
"In four off-kilter, virtually wordless stories, Martz . . . sketches out wild journeys, career mishaps, and unpredictable turns of events involving a small cast of amiable animals. . . . Martz's crisp, graphic forms defy readers' expectations—not to mention logic and the rules of physics—delivering pleasing absurdity with every page turn." Pub Wkly

Marunas, Nathaniel
Manga Claus, Honor, Loyalty, Tinsel: The Blade of Kringle. Penguin Group/Razorbill 2006 80p. Illustration
Grades: 4 5 6 7 8 9   **741.5; Fic**
1. Fantasy graphic novels; 2. Ninja; 3. Santa Claus; 4. Graphic novels
1-59514-134-0, $12.99
It's the night before Christmas Eve, and disgruntled elf Fritz, determined to show he belongs in Production and not Laundry, uses a dark magic spell on a ninja nutcracker. It's only supposed to cause a little damage and then he, Fritz, can use a spell to stop it. However, things go terribly wrong when elf Wallace fights back, the evil nutcracker lands in the furnace, and evil spell embers land on a pile of teddy bears. Yes, now an army of evil ninja teddy bears wreaks havoc at the North Pole, and Santa must stop them, with the help of a special pair of Japanese samurai swords.

Marvel Adventures: Spider-Man Volume One
Marvel Entertainment 2006 Un Illustration
Grades: 4 5 6 7 8 9   **741.5; Fic**
1. Spider-Man (Fictional character); 2. Superhero graphic novels; 3. Graphic novels
978-0-7851-2432-0, $19.99
This hardcover collects the first two volumes of Marvel Adventures Spider-Man. What separates the super-villains from just plain old villains" When they escape from prison, regular villains might lay low for a while and enjoy the sweetness of freedom. But not a super-villain like Doctor Octopus - the minute he's free, he's gathering up the most dangerous crew ever assembled: the Vulture, Electro, Kraven the Hunter, Sandman and Mysterio. And they've all got one thing on their minds: bringing down Spider-Man

once and for all. Also, catch the story that started it all: the origin of Spider-Man. Stories also include the return of the Human Torch, the villainy of the Scorpion, and more.

Masters, Anthony
Horror of the Heights. Art by Peter Dennis. Stone Arch Books 2006 88p. Illustration
Grades: 2 3 4 5 6 7   **741.5; Fic**
1. Mystery graphic novels; 2. Graphic novels
978-1-59889-030-3, $22.60 lib. bdg.
Dean suffers from a fear of heights, which is a problem since his older brother is a diving champion and his father runs the Wave Crest Health Club. Then someone sabotages the high diving board that Dean fears, and then they discover a problem with the water slide. Dean thinks he must find and expose the saboteur to save the club's reputation. The easy-to-read text, simple panel design, and fast-paced story make this a good choice for struggling and beginning readers.

Joker. Stone Arch Books 2006 72p. Illustration
Grades: 2 3 4 5 6 7   **741.5; Fic**
1. Adventure graphic novels; 2. Mystery graphic novels; 3. Graphic novels
978-1-59889-024-2, $21.26 lib bdg
Mel loves to do magic tricks and play practical jokes, but when his magician father gets kidnapped, no one will believe that Mel isn't trying to play a joke. He'll have to try to save his father with only his faithful dog Mutt to help him. The simple text and panel layout with a fast-paced story make this suitable for beginning and struggling readers.

The **rescue**. By Anthony Masters; illustrated by Mike Perkins. Stone Arch Books 2008 72p. Illustration
Grades: 3 4 5 6 7   **741.5; Fic**
1. Bullies; 2. Foxes; 3. Friendship; 4. Graphic novels
978-1-4342-0456-1, $21.26
                                                    LC 2007-30739
When Justin finds an injured fox that the bully brothers, Bill and Ed Baxter, plan to kill, he hides the fox in a deserted, supposedly haunted house. He takes care of it, but he knows he has to get it back into the woods and safely away from the Baxters. His friend Angie is scared of the ghost at the deserted house, but she helps Justin.
Part of the Graphic Trax series; originally published in Great Britain in 2002 under the title Freddy's Fox.

Matheny, Bill
The **Batman** Strikes! Vol. 1: Crime Time; illustrated by Terry Beatty, Christopher Jones et al. DC Comics 2005 Un Illustration
Grades: 4 5 6 7 8 9   **741.5; Fic**
1. Batman (Fictional character); 2. Joker (Fictional character); 3. Superhero graphic novels; 4. Graphic novels
1-4012-0509-7, $6.99
This book boasts five action-packed adventures of the Dark Knight Detective: Penguin Rising, City of Bats, Outlaw and Disorder, Without a Chance and Deadly Partner. Batman goes up against the Penguin, the Joker, Manbat, and other villains.

The **Batman** Strikes! Vol. 2: In Darkest Knight. DC Comics 2005 Un Illustration

Grades: 4 5 6 7 8 9   **741.5; Fic**
1. Batman (Fictional character); 2. Catwoman (Fictional character); 3. Joker (Fictional character); 4. Superhero graphic novels; 5. Graphic novels
1-4012-0510-0, $6.99
Evil can't hide, and neither can the rogues' gallery of villains who take on Gotham City's Dark Knight Detective. Catwoman, Mr. Freeze, Firefly, the Joker, and Man-Bat try their luck in this volume.

The **Batman** Strikes!: duty calls. Bill Matheny, J. Torres ; illustrated by Christopher Jones, Terry Beatty ; Colored by Heroic Age ; Lettered by Phil Balsman, Travis Lanham. DC Comics 2007 144p. Illustration
Grades: 3 4 5 6 7 8 9   **741.5; Fic**
1. Adventure graphic novels; 2. Batgirl (Fictional character); 3. Batman (Fictional character); 4. Catwoman (Fictional character); 5. Superhero graphic novels; 6. Graphic novels
978-1-4012-1548-4, $12.99
This volume of Bat-stories is based on the new WB Kids cartoon series. Batman takes on Clayface, the Penguin, the Riddler, Catwoman, and Poison Ivy; Batgirl steps in because Pamela Isley used to be Barbara Gordon's friend. The stories have lots of action, fast quips, and no foul language or actual violence.

McCann, Jim
★ **Return** of the Dapper Men. Written by Jim McCann; art by Janet Lee; lettered by Dave Lanphear; edited by Stephen Christy. Archaia Comics 2010 Un Illustration
Grades: 4 5 6 7 8   **741.5; Fic**
1. Robots; 2. Science fiction graphic novels; 3. Graphic novels
978-1-932386-90-5, $24.95; 1-932386-90-4
"In the dreamy land of Anorev, children, all under age 11, live underground among intricate gear-work mechanisms, while elegant robots live in abandoned houses aboveground. . . . All are perpetually stuck in the same day, and time has, essentially, ceased to mean anything—until 314 Dapper Men rain from the sky and set in motion the impetus for change. . . . Where this book truly stands out is how well the story works in concert with Lee's stunning artwork, which employs an art nouveau sheen. . . . A true dazzler that speaks on multiple levels for both child and adult readers and one that gets richer with each read." Booklist

McCoola, Marika
Baba Yaga's assistant. Marika McCoola; illustrated by Emily Carroll. Candlewick Press 2015 136 p. Color; Illustration
Grades: 4 5 6 7   **741.5; Fic**
1. Fairy tales; 2. Supernatural graphic novels; 3. Witches
076366961X; 9780763669614, $16.99
                       LC 2014951398
In this graphic novel, by Marika McCoola and Emily Carroll, "Russian folklore icon Baba Yaga mentors a lonely teen. . . . Most children think twice before braving a haunted wood filled with terrifying beasties to match wits with a witch, but not Masha. Her beloved grandma taught her many things: that stories are useful, that magic is fickle, that

nothing is too difficult or too dirty to clean. The fearsome witch of folklore needs an assistant, and Masha needs an adventure." (Publisher's note)
"McCoola's offering is a well-nuanced delight, satisfyingly blending fairy tale, legend, and thrills. As a perfect complement, Carroll's evocative art enthralls, capturing both the emotion and the magic of McCoola's yarn and breathing new life into an old folk tale." Kirkus

McCulloch, Derek
T. Runt!. Art by Jimmie Robinson. Image Comics 2009 Un
Grades: K 1 2   **741.5; Fic**
1. Dinosaurs; 2. Fantasy graphic novels; 3. Humorous graphic novels; 4. Graphic novels
978-1-60706-074-1, $16.99
Sometime in the late Cretaceous Period, three tyrannosaurus rex babies hatch. Magnus has big powerful jaws and sharp teeth, Maxima has huge hind feet that scares smaller animals when she stomps by, and then there's runty Vegrandis, smaller than the other two. He doesn't think it's fair that he's the smallest, but then he sees three small furry mammals picking on an even smaller mammal and he runs them off. Vegrandis makes friends with Larry, and feels better that he's not the smallest animal around; but then a funny thing happens Vegrandis grows to be bigger than both Magnus and Maxima, who now think it's unfair that he's bigger than they are. Comics writer McCulloch and artist Robinson have collaborated on a story that uses the picture book format to tell a colorful story that most young children can relate to. The book includes a word find puzzle for somewhat older readers.

McKeever, Sean
The **loyalty** thing. Art by Takeshi Miyazawa. Spotlight 2006 Un Illustration
Grades: 4 5 6 7 8 9   **741.5; Fic**
1. Romance graphic novels; 2. Spider-Man (Fictional character); 3. Superhero graphic novels; 4. Watson, Mary Jane (Fictional character); 5. Graphic novels
9781599610375, $21.35
                       LC 2006-75006
Mary Jane suffers the attention of a couple of pranksters who have targeted her for their practical jokes. Flash almost gets into trouble when he tries to "question" them with his fists, then he nearly gets into trouble with Liz when he forgets (on purpose) to register for Homecoming King. Meanwhile, Mary Jane is ready to break up with Harry, but she finally feels the magic when he kisses her. But what's going to happen when she finds Flash's notebook in her backpack?
Part of the Marvel Age: Mary Jane series. This is an edited version of an issue originally published by Marvel in 2005, with all advertisements removed.

Mary Jane Vol. 1: Circle of Friends. Art by Takeshi Miyazawa. Marvel Entertainment Group 2004 96p. Illustration
Grades: 5 6 7 8 9 10 11 12   **741.5; Fic**
1. Romance graphic novels; 2. Spider-Man (Fictional character); 3. Superhero graphic novels; 4. Graphic novels; 4. Watson, Mary Jane (Fictional character)

0-7851-1467-X, $6.99

High school student Mary Jane Watson hangs out with her friends (including nerdy Peter Parker) and starts dating old friend Harry Osborn even as she fantasizes about the new costumed superhero in town: Spider-Man. In this series, high school romance and friendships take center stage while the superhero action happens off the page and in the sidelines. This is the first of two volumes, then a new ongoing comics series called Spider-Man Loves Mary Jane continues the story.

The **money** thing. Art by Takeshi Miyazawa. ABDO/Spotlight 2006 Un Illustration
Grades: 4 5 6 7 8 9   741.5; Fic
1. Romance graphic novels; 2. Spider-Man (Fictional character); 3. Superhero graphic novels; 4. Watson, Mary Jane (Fictional character); 5. Graphic novels
978-1-59961-038-2, $21.35
LC 2006-55059

Harry Osborn is rich and loves to spend money on his dates with Mary Jane, but she's starting to feel that she should do something to get money to pay for some things on her own, such as that really beautiful prom dress she's been looking at. She tries job after job after job, and fails at each one for one reason or another, and the long hours have taken a toll on her school work and on her social life. What's going to give?

Part of the Marvel Age: Mary Jane series. This is an edited version of an issue originally published by Marvel in 2005, with all advertisements removed.

The **real** thing. Art by Takeshi Miyazawa. ABDO/Spotlight 2006 Un Illustration
Grades: 4 5 6 7 8 9   741.5; Fic
1. Mary Jane Watson (Fictional character); 2. Romance graphic novels; 3. Spider-Man (Fictional character); 4. Superhero graphic novels; 5. Watson, Mary Jane (Fictional character)
978-1-59961-039-9, $21.35
LC 2006-75007

Pressured by best friend Liz to start dating Harry Osborn so she and Harry can double date with Liz and Flash, Mary Jane has her doubts. When she sees him treat nerdy Peter Parker with affection, she decides to try a date. However, as she rides the train on the way home, a fight between Spider-Man and Electro upends the train car and she nearly falls out. Spider-Man saves her and takes her home. Uh-oh, now she's crushing on Spider-Man, how could Harry compete?

Part of the Marvel Age: Mary Jane series. This is an edited version of an issue originally published by Marvel in 2005, with all advertisements removed.

Sentinel #1: Salvage. Art by UDON. ABDO/Spotlight 2004 Un Illustration
Grades: 4 5 6 7 8 9   741.5; Fic
1. Robots; 2. Science fiction graphic novels; 3. Graphic novels
978-1-59961-316-1, $21.35
LC 2006-50623

Juston Seyfert is a teenage loner type, living with his father and younger brother at the Seyfert Salvage yard. Juston and his friends are the school misfits and face beatings and ridicule from the jocks and popular students.

One day, while fooling around in the yard, he finds a strange control chip and ends up putting it into his homemade battle 'bot, but when he turns on the remote, the toy takes off and breaks through the salvage yard fence. What Juston and his friends don't know is that there is a broken-to-pieces Sentinel out there in the woods, and the control chip belongs to it.

This book was originally published as Sentinel #1 by Marvel Comics' Marvel Age line; this book reprints the story without all the advertisements in the original comic.

Sentinel #2: Discovery. Art by UDON. ABDO/Spotlight 2004 Un Illustration
Grades: 4 5 6 7 8 9   741.5; Fic
1. Robots; 2. Science fiction graphic novels; 3. Graphic novels
978-1-59961-317-8, $21.35
LC 2006-50623

When his dad and younger brother go on an overnight trip to haul junkers to Chicago, Juston has to stay home alone, but it gives him a chance to talk with cute senior Jessie, who doesn't mind hanging out with a younger guy. Then that night, Juston finds something weird in the salvage yard's building—a half-destroyed Sentinel. Juston doesn't realize that the Sentinels were created to destroy mutants; he just knows that the one he's got is a way cool robot with artificial intelligence so he can talk with it.

This book was originally published as Sentinel #2 by Marvel Comics' Marvel Age line; this book reprints the story without all the advertisements in the original comic.

Sentinel #3: Pet project. Art by UDON. ABDO/Spotlight 2004 Un Illustration
Grades: 4 5 6 7 8 9   741.5; Fic
1. Robots; 2. Science fiction graphic novels; 3. Graphic novels
978-1-59961-318-5, $21.35
LC 2006-50623

Juston has decided to keep the giant robot he's rebuilding a secret from everyone, which causes a rift in his relationship with his younger brother, Christopher, and with his father—actually, with all his friends, too. When he does some research on the Internet, Juston discovers he's got a Sentinel. Now what's he going to do?

This book was originally published as Sentinel #3 by Marvel Comics' Marvel Age line; this book reprints the story without all the advertisements in the original comic.

Sentinel #4: Rebuilding. Art by UDON. ABDO/Spotlight 2004 Un Illustration
Grades: 4 5 6 7 8 9   741.5; Fic
1. Robots; 2. Science fiction graphic novels; 3. Graphic novels
978-1-59961-319-2, $21.35
LC 2006-50623

As Juston continues to rebuild the Sentinel, he becomes so consumed with what he's doing that he's practically abandoned all his friends. The jocks, however, haven't forgotten him. Once Juston gets the Sentinel rebuilt enough, he constructs a platform for himself to ride piggyback on the robot and they go out to the woods to test the Sentinel's weapons.

This book was originally published as Sentinel #4 by Marvel Comics' Marvel Age line; this book reprints the story without all the advertisements in the original comic.

Sentinel #6: Primary targets. Art by UDON. ABDO/Spotlight 2004 Un Illustration
Grades: 4 5 6 7 8 9   **741.5; Fic**
1. Robots; 2. Science fiction graphic novels; 3. Graphic novels
978-1-59961-321-5, $21.35

LC 2006-50623

Juston has given his Sentinel a mission, and Greg and Josh are the primary targets. The robot attacks the school in broad daylight, identifying itself as an alien machine; then Juston races in and stops the robot. He's declared a hero, even by the jocks who only the day before beat him up. However, Juston isn't sure he's done the right thing. And he doesn't know it yet, but the Sentinel has now recovered enough of its memory to get back to its primary mission—to annihilate mutants.

This book was originally published as Sentinel #6 by Marvel Comics' Marvel Age line; this book reprints the story without all the advertisements in the original comic.

Sentinel, part 5: test mission. Art by UDON. ABDO/Spotlight 2004 Un Illustration
Grades: 4 5 6 7 8 9   **741.5; Fic**
1. Robots; 2. Science fiction graphic novels; 3. Graphic novels
978-1-59961-320-8, $21.35

LC 2006-50623

Jocks Josh and Greg have beat up Juston's friend Alex, and their girlfriends have spread a false rumor about Juston guaranteed to anger Jessie. Then they beat up Juston and humiliate him in front of most of the school. Juston decides it's time to get revenge, and he's going to use the Sentinel to do it.

This book was originally published as Sentinel #5 by Marvel Comics' Marvel Age line; this book reprints the story without all the advertisements in the original comic.

The **trust** thing. Art by Takeshi Miyazawa. ABDO/Spotlight 2006 Un Illustration
Grades: 4 5 6 7 8 9   **741.5; Fic**
1. Romance graphic novels; 2. Spider-Man (Fictional character); 3. Superhero graphic novels; 4. Watson, Mary Jane (Fictional character); 5. Graphic novels
978-1-59961-040-5, $21.35

LC 2006-55061

While Mary Jane is still daydreaming about Spider-Man, her best friend Liz is having major trust issues with boyfriend Flash. Certain that he's seeing someone else, she enlists Mary Jane, even Peter Parker, to find out what's going on. Meanwhile, MJ has to figure out if she wants to keep dating rich Harry Osborn.

Part of the Marvel Age: Mary Jane series. This is an edited version of an issue originally published by Marvel in 2005, with all advertisements removed.

McLeod, Bob
★ **SuperHero** ABC. HarperCollins Pubs. 2006 40p. Illustration
Grades: PreK K 1 2   **E; 741.5**
1. Alphabet; 2. Superheroes — Fiction; 3. Graphic novels
0-06-074514-2, $15.99; 0-06-074515-0 (lib bdg), $16.89; 0-06-074516-9 (pa), $7.99

LC 2004-22180

Humorous SuperHeroes such as Goo Girl and The Volcano represent the letters of the alphabet from A to Z.

"There's strong appeal here for the youngest comic-book fans, with many doses of humor along the way. Each figure has special powers, of course, which readers learn about through alliterative captions and action-packed illustrations." SLJ

Medley, Linda
★ **Castle** waiting. Fantagraphics 2006 456p. Illustration
Grades: 5 6 7 8 9 10 11 12   **741.5; Fic**
1. Fairy tales; 2. Fantasy graphic novels; 3. Graphic novels
1-56097-747-7, $29.95

All of Medley's previously self-published comics are collected here in one volume for the first time. The titular castle was the home of Sleeping Beauty, whose story is retold from the viewpoint of the flibbertigibbet ladies in waiting. After the flighty princess awakens with the kiss of a handsome but not too bright prince, the castle becomes a sanctuary for various misfits. Readers will find references to many fairy tales, folk tales, and nursery rhymes in Medley's book, and her clean, clear black-and-white art reflects the works of classic illustrators such as Arthur Rackham.

Courtesy of Fantagraphics

Castle waiting; Volume II. By Linda Medley; [graphic design by Adam Grano; edited by Kim Thompson]. Fantagraphics Books 2013 464 p. Color; Illustration
Grades: 5 6 7 8 9 10 11 12   **741.5/973; 741.5**
1. Fairy tales
1606996339; 9781606996331, $29.99

LC 2014381744

In this graphic novel, by Linda Medley, "Lady Jain settles into her new life. . . . Unexpected visitors result in the discovery and exploration of a secret passageway, not to mention an epic bowling tournament. A quest for ladies' underpants, the identity of her baby son Pindar's father, the education of Simon, Rackham and Chess arguing about the "manly arts," and an escape-prone goat are just a few of the elements in this . . . new volume." (Publisher's note)

Meister, Cari
Dump truck day. Illustrated by Michael Emmerson. Stone Arch Books 2010 32p. Illustration

Grades: PreK K 1 2   **741.5; Fic**
  1. Trucks; 2. Graphic novels
  978-1-4342-1621-2, $21.32

                LC 2008-53376

Jacob spends the day with his uncle, who drives a dump truck; they go to the pit mine to pick up gravel and rocks that Jacob's uncle then delivers to the golf course for a new rock wall. This colorful graphic novel is aimed at beginning readers, with simple panel designs, clear art, and a repetitive text. The book includes a two-page tutorial on how to read comic book pages, a brief glossary, discussion questions, and writing prompts.
Part of the My First Graphic Novel series.

    Goalkeeper goof. Illustrated by Cori Doerrfeld. Stone Arch Books 2009 32p. Illustration
Grades: K 1 2 3   **741.5; Fic**
  1. Soccer; 2. Graphic novels
  978-1-4342-1292-4, $21.32; 978-1-4342-1409-6 (pa), $4.95

                LC 2008-31965

David loves playing soccer, but he doesn't like having to be the goalkeeper, because he can't catch the ball to prevent the other team from scoring; his teammates call him Goalkeeper Goof. But this time, he has a new strategy to help him remember that he can use his hands when he's the goalkeeper. This very simple graphic novel is aimed at new readers; it provides a sample page in the front of the book to show how to read comic book style panels, and it includes a short glossary, discussion questions, and writing prompts. This is part of the My First Graphic Novel series.

    The **kickball** kids. Stone Arch Books 2009 32p. Illustration
Grades: K 1 2 3   **741.5; Fic**
  1. Kickball; 2. Graphic novels
  978-1-4342-1294-8, $19.93; 978-1-4342-1410-2 (pa), $3.95

                LC 2008-31969

Kyle and his friends have formed a kickball team called the Kicking Kids, and they enter the Community Kickball tournament. Although they're the youngest team, they win their games and make it to the championship final, where their opponents are the Super Sharks, a team of fifth graders. This book uses a simplified comic book format and vocabulary designed for the beginning reader. The book includes a two-page spread that explains how to read a graphic novel at the beginning of the book, and a glossary and discussion questions at the end of the book.
Part of the My First Graphic Novel series

    Lily's lucky leotard. Illustrated by Jannie Ho. Stone Arch Books 2009 32p. Illustration
Grades: K 1 2 3   **741.5; Fic**
  1. Gymnastics; 2. Graphic novels
  978-1-4342-1411-9 (pa), $3.95

                LC 2008-31971

Lily is on the gymnastics team, and today she has her new leotard, and she's sure it will bring her good luck. She and the team warm up, do floor exercises, and jump the vault; Lily makes a great landing. But she wants to do a perfect star jump from the balance beam, and she hopes her new good luck leotard will help her do it today. This story uses a simplified comic book layout and vocabulary for beginning readers. The book includes a two-page spread at the beginning of the book that explains how to read a graphic novel, and a glossary and discussion questions at the end of the book.
Part of the My First Graphic Novel series

    T-ball trouble. Illustrated by Jannie Ho. Stone Arch Books 2009 32p. Illustration
Grades: K 1 2 3   **741.5; Fic**
  1. T-ball; 2. Graphic novels
  978-1-4342-1300-6, $19.93; 978-1-4342-1413-3 (pa), $3.95

                LC 2008-31973

Marco really wants to play baseball, but he's too young, so he joins a T-Ball team. He gets all the equipment: uniform, ball, bat, and a tee. He practices alone and with his team. Then they play a game, and Marco keeps hitting fouls. Can he hit the ball so it will go out onto the field" In this book, the team doesn't win the game, but everyone has tried hard and the coach has positive things to say to the children. This story uses a simplified comic book format and vocabulary for beginning readers. The book includes a two-page spread at the beginning of the book that explains how to read a graphic novel, and a glossary and discussion questions at the end of the book.
Part of the My First Graphic Novel series

Meyer, Christopher
    Adventures of Rabbit and Bear Paws: The voyageurs. Art by Chad Solomon. Little Spirit Bear Productions 2008 32p. Illustration
Grades: 3 4 5 6 7   **741.5; Fic**
  1. Adventure graphic novels; 2. Humorous graphic novels; 3. Native Americans
  978-0-9739906-2-1, $7.95

Pintsize, twelve-year-old Rabbit and giant, ten-year-old Bear Paws are brothers and members of the Ojibwa in the eighteenth century. Village medicine man Grey Stone and his wife Clover Blossom raise the brothers, who like to play and play pranks that tend to backfire. In this volume, Rabbit proves he's not a good lacrosse player; then Eagle Wing, a voyageur, stops off to visit Grey Stone on his way to this year's journey. Rabbit and Bear Paws travel with him to be carriers as Eagle Wing and the white fur traders make their trade journey. This book uses authentic details about traditions of the Ojibwa, the Mohawk, and other Nations.

Michelinie, David
    Superman Adventures Vol. 3: Last Son of Krypton. Written by Mark Millar, David Michelinie ; illustrated by Aluir Amancio, Ron Boyd, Terry Austin, Mike Manley, Neil Vokes. DC Comics 2006 112p. Illustration
Grades: 4 5 6 7 8 9   **741.5; Fic**
  1. Superhero graphic novels; 2. Superman (Fictional character); 3. Graphic novels
  978-1-4012-1037-3, $6.99

Superman confronts his own past as he encounters survivors from Krypton, including his parents, Jor-El and Lara. Plus, someone wants to expose Clark's secret to Lex Luthor and the world. Will an encounter with Dr. Fate mean the end of Superman?

The Mighty Crusaders: Origin of a Super-Team
Archie Comics 2003 96p. Illustration
Grades: 3 4 5 6 7 8 9 10 11 12 Adult   741.5; Fic
1. Humorous graphic novels; 2. Superhero graphic novels;
3. Graphic novels
1-879794-14-4, $12.95
It's a pop-art explosion as some of the wildest heroes in the history of comic books unite to form one of the most beloved super-teams of the Sixties: The Shield, The Black Hood, The Comet, The Fly, and Fly Girl. Relive the excitement as this intrepid team of heroes meet, fight super-villains as well as each other, come up with a name for their team and even recruit new members. It's all here in this colorful collection reprinting classic stories originally appearing in Fly-Man #31, #32 and #33 as well as Mighty Crusaders #1. It features restoration of all stories, and faithful recoloring.

Millar, Mark
Superman Adventures Vol. 4: The Man of Steel. Written by Mark Millar, Evan Dorkin and Sarah Dyer ; illustrated by Aluir Amancio, Terry Austin, Bret Blevins. DC Comics 2006 112p. Illustration
Grades: 4 5 6 7 8 9   741.5; Fic
1. Superhero graphic novels; 2. Superman (Fictional character); 3. Graphic novels
978-1-4012-1038-0, $6.99
The battle never ends for the Man of Steel - especially when his greatest enemies will stop at nothing in order to destroy him. Superman confronts Toyman, Multi-Face, Parasite, the mischievous Mr. Mxyzptlk, and Brainiac.

Miller, Connie Colwell
Elizabeth Cady Stanton: Women's Rights Pioneer. Illustrated by Cynthia Martin. Capstone Press 2006 32p. Illustration
Grades: 3 4 5 6 7 8 9   741.5; 305.42; 92
1. Stanton, Elizabeth Cady, 1815-1902; 2. Women — Suffrage — United States — History; 3. Graphic novels
0-7368-4971-8, $25.26
LC 2005009211
This book uses the comic book format to describe the life and career of women's suffragist Elizabeth Cady Stanton. It includes additional information, a glossary, a list of books for further reading, and more.
Part of the Graphic Library, Graphic Biographies series.

Miller, Mike S.
Lullaby: Wisdom seeker. [by] Ben Avery, Mike S. Miller, and Hector Sevilla. Alias Enterprises 2005 96p. Illustration
Grades: 4 5 6 7 8 9   741.5; Fic
1. Fantasy graphic novels; 2. Graphic novels
1-933428-62-7, $9.99
In this book, Alice never left Wonderland, she grew up to become the Queen's warrior. When dark magic threatens the world, Alice, haunted by vague memories of another life, sets out to discover the cause, and on the way she encounters the Pied Piper, Little Red Riding Hood (who is a werewolf), Jim Hawkins (from Treasure Island), and Pinocchio, as they all travel to Oz.

Millionaire, Tony
Sock Monkey: The Glass Doorknob. Dark Horse Comics 2002 Un Illustration
Grades: K 1 2 3   741.5; Fic
1. Humorous graphic novels; 2. Graphic novels
1-56971-782-6, $14.95
The Sock Monkey and the other toys in the house marvel at the prismatic spectrum shining on the parlor floor. They notice that the dazzling colors are somehow emanating from the beautiful glass doorknob on the front door. Winter turns to spring and the apple tree at the front of the house sprouts its new leaves, casting a warm green shadow on the door. But something happens to the doorknob, it seems to be broken, the magical light show has come to a disheartening end. As the leaves grow heavier, joy leaves the house, until Mr. Crow comes up with plan: to repair the doorknob using very scientifical techniques. Meanwhile outside, notions of celestial events, planetary rhythm, and farmers' almanacs are discussed by two new characters, a bug and a bird named Rickets and Scurvy.

Sock Monkey: Little and Large. Dark Horse Comics/DH Press 2005 Un Illustration
Grades: K 1 2 3   741.5; Fic
1. Humorous graphic novels; 2. Graphic novels
1-59582-010-8, $7.95
When Ann Louise's grandfather crashes through the woods to cut down a tree for use in his workshop, he never stops to think about all the creatures making their home in it. Uncle Gabby then meets a spider displaced from his tree house and begins a quest to find him a new place to live. A weathervane? A dollhouse? A goose-wagon? Sadly, no, no and no! But what is Grandfather building from the lumber? This book tells two stories, one in black and white and one in color on the facing pages.

That Darn Yarn. DH Press/Dark Horse Comics 2005 Un Illustration
Grades: K 1 2 3   741.5; Fic
1. Humorous graphic novels; 2. Toys; 3. Graphic novels
1-59582-009-4, $7.95
This book tells two stories. In the black-and-white pages, Ann-Louise decides to make a present for David's birthday; when she finds a basket full of yarn and knitting needles, she starts knitting and creates a sock monkey doll. In the facing color pages, a sock monkey doll sits on the banister at the top of some stairs and starts to slide down the banister, but the yarn at the tip of its tail has caught on a nail, and the sock monkey starts to unravel as he continues his flight down.
Millionaire has written Sock Monkey comics that are rather subversive and fairly mature, but this picture book-format book is one for children to enjoy.

Misako Rocks!
Biker girl. Story and art by Misako Rocks. Hyperion Paperbacks 2006 Un Illustration
Grades: 3 4 5 6 7 8 9   741.5; Fic
1. Adventure graphic novels; 2. Bicycles; 3. Graphic novels
0-7868-3676-8, $7.99
LC 2005-57428

"In this manga-style adventure, a young girl becomes a reluctant superhero after she inherits a bike with magical powers. . . . This fast-paced and well-executed story is . . . bound to be popular." Booklist

Rock and Roll Love. Hyperion Paperbacks 2007 Un Illustration
Grades: 5 6 7 8 9 10   **741.5; Fic**
  1. Romance graphic novels; 2. Student exchange programs; 3. Graphic novels
  978-0-7868-3685-7, $7.99

Sixteen-year-old high school student Misako comes to the U.S. as an exchange student for a year. Missouri is very different from Tokyo, but her host family and their teenage daughter, Natalie, make her welcome. Misako soon makes friends at high school, and feels comfortable enough to join a summer puppet camp in Wisconsin. There, she meets Zac, a rock and roll musician, and her dream boy. Given to strong enthusiasms, Misako falls hard for Zac, but he says he only wants to be friends. Will she ever get him to change his mind about her?

Misako Rocks! (real surname Takashima) moved to the U.S. from Japan as a teenager; this book is based on her own experiences.

Mizobuchi, Makoto
  Pokemon: Pokemon Ranger and the Temple of the Sea. Viz Media/VizKids 2008 200p. Illustration
Grades: 3 4 5 6 7 8   **741.5; Fic**
  1. Adventure graphic novels; 2. Fantasy graphic novels; 3. Manga; 4. Graphic novels
  978-1-4215-2288-3, $7.99

Ash and Pikachu learn about the legend of the Sea Temple, a mysterious floating temple that houses the Sea Crown. They meet Jackie, a Pokemon Ranger on a mission to protect a Manaphy egg and find the temple; when the egg hatches, young May bonds with Manaphy. But they aren't the only ones searching for the Sea Temple; the nefarious pirate called the Phantom wants the Sea Crown for himself to take over the world, and he also needs Manaphy to do it. Can Ash and Pikachu help Jackie protect Manaphy and stop the Phantom?

Mizuna, Tomomi
  The **big** adventures of Majoko, volume 1. Illustrated by Tomomi Mizuna. UDON Entertainment 2009 200p. Illustration
Grades: 3 4 5 6 7 8   **741; 741.5; Fic**
  1. Fantasy graphic novels; 2. Manga; 3. Witches; 4. Graphic novels
  978-1-89737-681-2 (pa), $7.99; 1-89737-681-2 (pa)

"Young witch Majoko sends her diary to the human world to find an adventuring partner and through it finds shy, quiet Nana. Together the two girls have a rollicking series of escapades. . . . Characters are simply drawn, but the backgrounds are nicely detailed and the plot elements are clearly thought out and easy to follow. . . . The content is very appropriate for the intended audience." Booklist
  Volume 1 of a 5-volume series

Morgan, Melanie J.
  Betty & Veronica: Bad Boy Trouble. Art by Steven Butler. Archie Comics 2007 112p. Illustration
Grades: 4 5 6 7 8 9 10   **741.5; Fic**
  1. Humorous graphic novels; 2. Romance graphic novels; 3. Graphic novels
  978-1-879794-25-2, $7.49

When Nick St. Clair rides into Riverdale on his motorcycle, Veronica is smitten. She likes Nick's air of assurance and his knack for getting noticed. The only problem is Nick gets noticed for all the wrong things. Nick quickly alienates all of Ronnie's friends, especially Betty, as he keeps trying to hit on her even as he dates Ronnie. Is this handsome rebel the boy of Veronica's dreams, or just plain trouble? This particular story has caused some stir among longtime Archie fans, because of the drastic artistic makeover of the Riverdale teens.

Morse, Scott
  ★ **Magic** Pickle. With color by Jose Garibaldi. Scholastic/Graphix 2008 Un Illustration
Grades: 2 3 4 5   **741.5**
  1. Humorous graphic novels; 2. Superhero graphic novels; 3. Graphic novels
  978-0-439-87995-8 (pa), $9.99; 0-439-87995-7 (pa)

"When Weapon Kosher, the Magic Pickle, erupts from the bedroom floor of little Jo Jo Wigman, she has to answer a lot of questions! What's the Magic Pickle's connection to the Brotherhood of Evil Produce? What is "Dill Justice?" How did Danny Johnson get to be so cute?" Publisher's note

"Starting with an irresistibly goofy premise, Morse layers on sly humor, astute references, and blazing action, turning in a charming, slam-bang story." Booklist
  Other titles in this series are: Magic Pickle and the Planet of the Grapes (2008); Magic Pickle vs. the Egg Poacher (2008); Magic Pickle and the Garden of Evil (2009); Magic Pickle and the Creature from the Black Legume (2009)

Mortensen, Lori
  The **end** zone. Illustrated by Mary Sullivan.. Stone Arch Books 2009 32p. Illustration
Grades: K 1 2 3   **741.5; Fic**
  1. Football; 2. Sex role; 3. Graphic novels
  978-1-4342-1289-4, $21.32; 978-1-4342-1408-9 (pa), $4.95
                                          LC 2008-31964

Olivia likes a lot of subjects in school, but she really loves to play flag football. The problem is the boys think girls should do things like jump rope. She needs to find a way to prove to the boys that she can play flag football just as well as they can. This very simple graphic novel is aimed at new readers; it provides a sample page in the front of the book to show how to read comic book style panels, and it includes a short glossary, discussion questions, and writing prompts. A nice detail is that Olivia happens to be a person of color, it's just a part of who she is; the other characters are drawn to be ethnically diverse, but it doesn't affect how they play with each other.
  This is part of the My First Graphic Novel series.

The **missing** monster card. Illustrated by Rémy Simard. Stone Arch Books 2010 25p. Illustration (My 1st graphic novel)

Grades: K 1 2   741.5; Fic
1. Mystery graphic novels; 2. Graphic novels
978-1-4342-1888-9, $21.32; 1-4342-1888-0;
978-1-4342-2284-8 (pa), $3.95; 1-4342-2284-5 (pa)

"Ethan has just found a rare Monster Card in the pack he bought, and he wants to show it to his friend Zack, but when he goes to Zack's house the next day, the card isn't in his jacket pocket. The two friends search for the card to solve the mystery. . . . The book provides a short tutorial on how to navigate the panels and uses sound effects, dialogue balloons, and brief narrative text to tell the story. . . . A brief glossary, discussion questions, and writing prompts provide teachers with easy lesson plans for classroom use. The bright colors and cartoony illustrations add to the appeal for beginning readers." Booklist

Morvan, Jean David

★ **Classics** illustrated deluxe #6: the three Musketeers. [by] Alexandre Dumas; adapted by Jean David Morvan, Michel Dufranne, Rubèn, and Marie Galopin. Papercutz 2011 Un Illustration

Grades: 5 6 7 8 9 10 11 12 Adult   741.5; Fic
1. Adventure graphic novels; 2. Dumas, Alexandre, 1802-1870 — Adaptations; 3. France — History — 1589-1789, Bourbons; 4. Graphic novels
978-1-59707-253-3, $21.99; 978-1-59707-252-6 (pa), $16.99

In seventeenth-century France, young D'Artagnan initially quarrels with, then befriends, three musketeers and joins them in trying to outwit the enemies of the king and queen. This adaptation is suitable for many readers from age ten and up, but parents, teachers, and librarians might want to consider the visual depictions of sexual tensions and situations that might go over most young readers' heads in prose (there are some heaving bosoms, perspiring men, and a couple of scenes in bed), and the violence (most of it occurs off-panel). The book's endpapers include Dumas' introduction to his novel, an Epilogue, a brief biography of Dumas, and an illustrated character guide.

This book is a 70th Anniversary Edition of Classics Illustrated

Moss, Marissa

Max disaster #1: Alien eraser to the rescue. Candlewick Press 2009 Un Illustration

Grades: 3 4 5 6 7   741.5; Fic
1. Family life; 2. Humorous graphic novels; 3. Separation; 4. Graphic novels
978-0-7636-3577-0, $15.99; 978-0-7636-4407-9 (pa), $6.99

LC 2008-937046

Max and his best friend Omar survive school together, even as they're forced to make baking soda/vinegar volcanoes in science class and hid their eraser armies from the teacher. But now Max has to deal with some problems at home, much worse than his older brother Kevin. Their parents have been fighting a lot lately, and now they call a family meeting to announce a separation. Max fills his notebook with all kinds of inventions that could stop this

from happening, but he and Kevin have to face their real life. Moss uses a mix of prose, comic book pages, and pictures of gadgets to present Max's story.

Other titles in this series are: Alien Eraser unravels the mystery of the pyramids (2009); Alien Eraser reveals the secrets of evolution (2009)

Mucci, Tim

Tom Sawyer. Adapted by Tim Mucci; illustrated by Rad Sechrist.. Sterling 2008 Un Illustration

Grades: 3 4 5 6 7 8 9   741.5; Fic
1. Adventure graphic novels; 2. Twain, Mark, 1835-1910 — Adaptations
978-1-4027-3399-4, $6.95

LC 2007-41162

Tom Sawyer lives in a small town along the Mississippi River, where he does his best to avoid Aunt Polly's list of chores and skips school so he can go fishing. When he and his friend Huckleberry Finn witness a murder, their first thought is to run away. This graphic novel adaptation includes a brief biography of Mark Twain.

Part of the All-Action Classics series.

Muir, Suzanne

Elephant Army. Art by Anthony Brennan. Harcourt Achieve/Steck-Vaughn 2007 48p. Illustration

Grades: 3 4 5 6 7 8   741.5; Fic
1. Adventure graphic novels; 2. Graphic novels
978-1-4190-3200-4, $8.99

Shaam is a very small elephant who dreams of becoming the lead elephant in the army of King Porus of India. Meanwhile, the fearsome conqueror, Alexander the Great, is planning to attack. Will Shaam and his elephant army be able to defend their homeland? This historical graphic novel includes prose intervals that provide more information about Alexander the Great and about ancient India.

Part of the Timeline Graphic Novels series.

The **Magic** Tile. Art by Anthony Brennan. Harcourt Achieve/Steck-Vaughn 2006 48p. Illustration

Grades: 3 4 5 6 7 8   741.5; Fic
1. Adventure graphic novels; 2. Islamic civilization; 3. Graphic novels
978-1-4190-3202-8, $8.99

When they find a magic tile, twins Mina and Haytham zoom back into the Middle Ages. They meet famous people such as Saladin and Ibn Battuta. But will they be able to return to their own time? The book includes prose intervals that give more information about Ibn Battuta, The Arabian Nights, and the Golden Age of Islam.

Part of the Timeline Graphic Novels series.

Naifeh, Ted

Courtney Crumrin and the night things. Oni Press 2005 128p. Illustration

Grades: 5 6 7 8 9 10 11 12   741.5; Fic
1. Fantasy graphic novels; 2. Supernatural graphic novels; 3. Graphic novels
1-929998-60-0, $11.95

Courtney's social-climber parents take her out of her comfortable city neighborhood and move into an upscale suburb to live with her creepy Great-Uncle Aloysius in her spooky old house. She has to face uppity classmates and things that go bump in the night; but she ends up making friends with the spooks! Courtney deals with magic and the supernatural, but she's no altruistic Harry Potter; in this series, magic sometimes bites hard.

Other titles in this series are: Courtney Crumrin and the coven of Mystics (2003); Courtney Crumrin in the twilight kingdom (2004); Courtney Crumrin's monstrous holiday (2009); Courtney Crumrin: the witch next door (2014); Courtney Crumrin: the final spell (2014)

Neel, Julien

Down in the dumps. Written and illustrated by Julien Neel; translation by Carol Klio Burrell. Graphic Universe 2012 48 p. (Lou!)
Grades: 4 5 6   741.5
1. Best friends — Fiction; 2. Dating (Social customs) — Fiction; 3. Friendship — Fiction; 4. Junior high schools — Fiction; 5. Mothers and daughters — Fiction; 6. School stories; 7. Schools — Fiction; 8. Graphic novels
076138779X; 9780761387794, $27.93

LC 2012003973

This book is the third in Julien Neel's Lou! series. Here, "Lou is depressed because the boy of her dreams has moved away. To make matters worse, her mother, an aspiring author, has a serious love interest that makes her even more scatterbrained than usual. Lou feels quite left out as she heads off to the first day of school, only to discover that she and her best friend are not in the same class." (School Library Journal)

The **perfect** summer. [story and art by] Julien Neel; [translation by Carol Klio Burrell]. Graphic Universe 2012 48 p. (Lou!)
Grades: 4 5 6   741.5
1. Adolescence; 2. Dating (Social customs) — Fiction; 3. Mothers and daughters — Fiction; 4. Summer — Fiction; 5. Vacations; 6. Vacations — Fiction; 7. Graphic novels
0761387803; 9780761387800, $27.93

LC 2012002988

This book is the fourth in Julien Neel's Lou! series. Here, "she vacations with a friend at an amazing beach house while her mother is on a book tour. The friendship drama [of junior high school] has settled into a nice group of girls she enjoys being with. That just leaves the boy situation, which is complicated, since Tristan is back in her life." (School Library Journal)

Nickel, Scott

Attack of the mutant lunch lady. Illustrated by Andy J Smith. Stone Arch Books 2008 40p. Illustration
Grades: 3 4 5 6 7   741.5; Fic
1. Humorous graphic novels; 2. Science fiction graphic novels; 3. Graphic novels
978-1-4342-0451-6, $21.26; 978-1-4342-0501-8 (pa), $4.95

LC 2007-31250

The cafeteria food at school is truly revolting, but that's nothing compared to what happens when the Lunch Lady falls into the vat of toxic leftovers. Now science whiz Buzz

Beaker and his best friend Larry need to find a way to deal with the Cafeteria Creature and save their school.
Part of the Graphic Sparks series, a Buzz Beaker Brainstorm.

Back to the Ice Age. By Scott Nickel; illustrated by Enrique Corts. Stone Arch Books 2008 40p. Illustration
Grades: 3 4 5 6 7   741.5; Fic
1. Humorous graphic novels; 2. Science fiction graphic novels; 3. Time travel; 4. Graphic novels
978-1-4342-0450-9, $21.26; 978-1-4342-0500-1 (pa), $6.95

LC 2007-31251

When David's parents go out, he and his buddy Ben are stuck with the worst babysitter ever. But things get really bad when she mistakes a time travel device for the TV remote and accidentally zaps herself back in time. Now David and Ben need to go back in time to save the babysitter, and they find themselves in the Ice Age, complete with mammoths and a cave dude.
Part of the Graphic Sparks series, a Time Blasters adventure.

Billions of Bats: A Buzz Beaker Brainstorm by Scott Nickel ; illustrated by Andy J. Smith. Stone Arch Books 2007 40p. Illustration
Grades: 2 3 4 5 6 7   741.5; Fic
1. Humorous graphic novels; 2. Science fiction graphic novels; 3. Graphic novels
978-1-59889-313-7 (lib bdg)

Buzz Beaker is the local science genius, but when transfer student Sarah Bellum arrives, she takes the position of top student in everything, even P.E. When she brings her newest invention, a cosmic copier, to school and puts her pet bat in to duplicate him, the machine malfunctions and keeps making multiple copies of her bat. Buzz has to work with Sarah to find a way to fix the machine and get rid of all the extra bats.

This is part of the Graphic Sparks line of easy-reading graphic novels for beginning and struggling readers.

Blast to the Past. Illustrated by Steve Harpster. Stone Arch Books 2006 40p. Illustration
Grades: 3 4 5 6 7 8   741.5; Fic
1. Adventure graphic novels; 2. Humorous graphic novels; 3. Graphic novels
978-1-59889-033-4, $21.26

David's geeky brother Darrin invents a time machine in his bedroom. Now David and his buddy Ben can zip back a few days to retake that test they flunked. But time travel is tricky; instead of zapping back to history class, the boys might just become history when they find themselves among dinosaurs.
Part of the Graphic Sparks series.

The **Boy** Who Burped Too Much. Illustrated by Steve Harpster. Stone Arch Books 2006 40p. Illustration
Grades: 2 3 4 5 6 7   741.5; Fic
1. Humorous graphic novels; 2. Graphic novels
978-1-59889-037-2, $21.26 lib bdg

Bobby Aaron is a cool kid, but not completely normal; he belches uncontrollably, at the movies, in the library, even in the principal's office. A champion speller, on paper, he enters the spelling bee, but he needs a way to control the burping if he wants to win the spelling bee. The easy-to-read text, simple panel layout, and a funny, fast-paced story make this suitable for beginning and struggling readers (and especially boys who love to burp on purpose).

Buzz Beaker vs Dracula. Illustrated by Andy J. Smith. Stone Arch Books 2009 40p.
Grades: 3 4 5 6 7 8   **741.5; Fic**
1. Dracula, Count (Fictional character); 2. Humorous graphic novels; 3. Science fiction graphic novels; 4. Graphic novels
978-1-4342-1191-0, $21.26
                                        LC 2008-32058
Dracula wants to hang out on the beach, get a tan, and go surfing, but being a vampire means he can't do these things. So, he has science genius Buzz Beaker kidnapped and brought to him. Buzz invents a super sun blocker booth, and he and Dracula hit the beach for some fun. However, a side effect of the sun blocker has taken away Dracula's super powers, and his hench fiend, Fangz, decides he wants to take over and become King of the vampires. The book includes some information about vampires, discussion questions, and a glossary.
Part of the Graphic Sparks line, the Buzz Beaker Brainstorm series

Curse of the Red Scorpion. Art by Steve Harpster. Stone Arch Books 2006 40p. Illustration
Grades: 2 3 4 5 6 7   **741.5; Fic**
1. Horror graphic novels; 2. Humorous graphic novels; 3. Graphic novels
978-1-59889-034-4, $21.26 lib bdg
Mitchell was bored at the museum during the class field trip, until he saw the amazing Red Scorpion of Manzitopia and heard about the curse. Now he thinks the creature has followed him home. Do claws click in the night? Does a stinger hide in the curtains? Will Mitchell be able to trap the scorpion before he becomes a victim of the curse? The simple text and panel layout combine with a funny story that is suitable for beginning and struggling readers.

The **Day** of the Field Trip Zombies. Illustrated by Cedric Hohnstadt. Stone Arch Books 2007 40p. Illustration
Grades: 3 4 5 6 7 8 9   **741.5; Fic**
1. Horror graphic novels; 2. Humorous graphic novels; 3. Zombies; 4. Graphic novels
978-1-59889-834-7, $21.26
                                        LC 2007-3175
Trevor is a fifth-grade expert on zombies. In fact, he's a zombie-buster. When his class takes a field trip to an aquarium, the evil scientist Dr. Brainium turns the students into radio-controlled zombies. Only Trevor can rescue them, but first he has to escape an army of psycho penguins. The book is written with an easy vocabulary for reluctant and struggling readers.
Part of the Graphic Sparks series.

Invasion of the gym class zombies. By Scott Nickel; illustrated by Matt Luxich. Stone Arch Books 2008 40p. Illustration
Grades: 3 4 5 6 7   **741.5; Fic**
1. Humorous graphic novels; 2. School stories; 3. Zombies; 4. Graphic novels

978-1-4342-0453-0, $21.26; 978-1-4342-0503-2 (pa), $6.95
                                        LC 2007-31252
Trevor, a student at Commonwealth Elementary School, has been busting zombies at school and on field trips, but now the evil scientist Dr. Brainium is in jail, so Trevor thinks his zombie-busting days are over. However, Mr. Brawnium has joined the school as the new gym teacher, and he has turned the whole gym class (except for Trevor) into zombified jocks. Only one person can help Trevor save his school, and that is Dr. Brainium.
Part of the Graphic Sparks series.

Jimmy Sniffles vs the Mummy. Illustrated by Steve Harpster. Stone Arch Books 2009 40p. Illustration
Grades: 3 4 5 6 7 8   **741.5; Fic**
1. Mummies; 2. Mystery graphic novels; 3. Graphic novels
978-1-4342-1190-3, $21.26
                                        LC 2008-32061
Jimmy Sniffles and his class go on a field trip to the museum, which has the mummy of Amun-Set and his treasured Golden Scarab of Khepera on display. However, Jimmy's superpowered nose smells trouble when he hears that the scarab and the mummy have disappeared from the museum, and he investigates. Jasper the security guard had tried to scare the class with a story of a curse on the scarab; when Jimmy hides in the museum after it closes, a mummy comes after him. But is it really the mummy of Amun-Set, or is it someone else, someone like . . . Jasper?
Part of the Graphic Sparks line, the Jimmy Sniffles series

Jimmy Sniffles: Double Trouble. Illustrated by Steve Harpster. Stone Arch Books 2007 40p. Illustration
Grades: 2 3 4 5 6 7   **741.5; Fic**
1. Humorous graphic novels; 2. Science fiction graphic novels; 3. Graphic novels
978-1-59889-314-4 (lib bdg)
This book is part of the Graphic Sparks line of graphic novels for beginning and struggling readers.
Schoolboy Jimmy Sniffles has a super-powered nose that he uses for good; but his archnemesis Dr. Von Snotenstein has decided to destroy Jimmy. During their last confrontation, he secured a nose hair from Jimmy, and he uses it to create an evil clone that also has a super-powered nose. While evil Jimmy causes all kinds of trouble at school, Jimmy finds a way to stop the evil clone.

Jimmy Sniffles: Up the President's Nose. Illustrated by Steve Harpster. Stone Arch Books 2007 40p. Illustration
Grades: 3 4 5 6 7 8 9   **741.5; Fic**
1. Humorous graphic novels; 2. Science fiction graphic novels; 3. Graphic novels
978-1-59889-837-8, $21.26
                                        LC 2007-3179
The President is suffering a strange allergic reaction, and his life could be in danger. Jimmy Sniffles, the kid with the super-powered nose, is shrunk down to microscopic size to enter the President's nose and sniff out the problem. He finds evil lurking there, but there's still more trouble in the lab, too. The book is written with an easy vocabulary for struggling and reluctant readers.
Part of the Graphic Sparks line of books.

The **Monster** of Lake Lobo. Illustrated by Enrique Corts. Stone Arch Books 2007 40p. Illustration

Grades: 3 4 5 6 7 8 9   **741.5; Fic**

1. Fantasy graphic novels; 2. Mystery graphic novels; 3. Graphic novels

978-1-59889-836-1, $21.26

LC 2007-3178

When Kevin and his dad visit Lake Lobo, their summer vacation suddenly turns creepy. Who made the claw marks outside their cabin window? What is howling in the night? Local legends say a strange creature prowls the woods. Could Kevin's new dog hold the secret to the Monster of Lake Lobo? This graphic novel is written with an easy vocabulary for reluctant and struggling readers.

Part of the Graphic Sparks line of books.

Night of the Homework Zombies. Illustrated by Steve Harpster. Stone Arch Books 2006 40p. Illustration

Grades: 2 3 4 5 6 7   **741.5; Fic**

1. Horror graphic novels; 2. Humorous graphic novels; 3. Graphic novels

978-1-59889-035-8, $21.26 lib bdg

Mr. Winklepoof, the new substitute teacher, is really a mad scientist. He plans to turn every kid in school into a brain-boggled zombie who loves homework. "Study! Study!" they chant. Only Trevor knows the truth; and only Trevor can save his friends, and himself, from this horrible fate. The simple text and panel layout, and the fast-paced humorous story make this suitable for beginning and struggling readers.

Robot Rampage: A Buzz Beaker Brainstorm. Illustrated Andy J. Smith. Stone Arch Books 2007 40p. Illustration

Grades: 2 3 4 5 6 7   **741.5; Fic**

1. Humorous graphic novels; 2. Science; 3. Graphic novels

978-1-59889-055-6 li, $21.26; 978-1-59889-227-7 (pa)

LC 2006007699

Brainy Buzz Beaker doesn't win first prize at the school science fair. The award goes to the weird new student, Elron, instead. Then Elron's homemade robot goes haywire, and Buzz gets taken on a wild, rampaging ride. This graphic novel features easy text and a controlled vocabulary for beginning and struggling readers.

Part of the Graphic Sparks series.

Secret of the summer school zombies. Illustrated by Matt Luxich. Stone Arch Books 2009 40p. Illustration

Grades: 2 3 4 5 6 7   **741.5; Fic**

1. Horror graphic novels; 2. Humorous graphic novels; 3. School stories; 4. Zombies; 5. Graphic novels

978-1-4342-0760-9, $21.26

LC 2008-6710

Trevor was having a fine summer, until his mother forced him to attend summer school. As if that isn't bad enough, all the teachers turn into zombies . . . homework and test crazed zombies. Trevor and his friend Filbert (who comes to summer school for fun) must find a way to stop the zombies, or they'll be trapped inside the classroom of doom forever. The book includes a short glossary (part of the definition of zombie: " . . . when you tell your friend to eat

worms, and he does it, he is acting like a zombie?) and information about UFOs and alien sightings.

Part of the Graphic Sparks School Zombies series

T. Rex vs Robo-Dog 3000. Illustrated by Enrique Corts. Stone Arch Books 2009 40p. Illustration

Grades: 2 3 4 5 6 7   **741.5; Fic**

1. Dinosaurs; 2. Humorous graphic novels; 3. Science fiction graphic novels; 4. Time travel; 5. Graphic novels

978-1-4342-0761-6, $21.26

LC 2008-6714

David's brother, Darrin, has just invented a radio-controlled dog that performs tricks, mixes smoothies, and grows 50 feet tall at the touch of a button. When Brendan takes David's time travel remote control from Ben and brings back a Tyrannosaurus Rex from the past, David tries to use Robo-Dog 3000 in its ultimate mode to distract the dinosaur so Darrin can zap it back to the past. The book includes some information about the Tyrannosaurus Rex, and a short glossary.

Part of the Graphic Sparks Time Blasters series

Wind power whiz kid: a Buzz Beaker brainstorm. Illustrated by Andy J. Smith. Stone Arch Books 2009 40p. Illustration

Grades: 2 3 4 5 6 7   **741.5; Fic**

1. Humorous graphic novels; 2. Science fiction graphic novels; 3. Wind power; 4. Graphic novels

978-1-4342-0758-6, $21.26

LC 2008-6713

Buzz's dad invents a supersonic windmill to provide safe power for the town, but Mr. Sludgeco, who owns the polluting energy plant now being used, wants to destroy the windmill. He installs a black box that makes the windmill go out of control; now it's up to Buzz and his friends to invent a way to stop Mr. Sludgeco. The book includes a short glossary and some information about real wind power efforts.

Part of the Graphic Sparks Buzz Beaker series

Niles, Steve

The **Cryptics**. Steve Niles and Benjamin Roman. IDW Publishing 2008 48p. Illustration

Grades: 4 5 6 7 8 9   **741.5; Fic**

978-1-60010-254-7, $17.99

The classic movie monsters: the Wolf Man, Dracula, Dr. Jekyll/Mr. Hyde, and the Creature from the Black Lagoon, have moved to the suburbs, and they have kids. Jackie Jekyll (who turns into Hyde), Wolfy (whose mother is The Bride of Frankenstein go figure), Drac, and Sea-Boy do the usual suburban going-to-school, playing in the back yard, sorts of things, except when Wolfy suddenly disappears and the rest have to go find him in the afterlife. The book collects lots of short episodes in the lives of suburban kid monsters. The stories are all humorous, but the fact that the main characters are all monsters may be too much for very sensitive young readers. On the other hand, young readers who like a touch of the scary and macabre will have fun. Roman is the coauthor as well as main artist; one story, "Front Line," is illustrated by Billy Martin, and "Identity Crisis" features art by Robert Iza, Dylan McCrae, Kris Anka, Vidar Cornelius,

Shane Long, Fabian "Monk" Schlaga, and David Igo. The book also includes pinup art by various artists.

This was originally published by Image Comics as The Cryptics Issues #13.

Niz, Xavier
Paul Revere's Ride. Illustrated by Brian Bascle. Capstone Press 2006 32p. Illustration
Grades: 3 4 5 6 7 8 9   **741.5; 973.3**
1. Concord (Mass), Battle of, 1775; 2. Lexington (Mass), Battle of, 1775; 3. Massachusetts — History; 4. United States — History — 1775-1783, Revolution; 5. Graphic novels
0-7368-4965-3, $25.26

                                           LC 200500652
This book uses the comic book format to tell the story of Paul Revere's ride to Lexington in April 1775 to warn colonists of approaching British troops. It includes additional information, a glossary, a list of books for further reading, and more.
Part of the Graphic Library, Graphic History series.

Nobleman, Marc Tyler
★ **Boys** of steel: the creators of Superman. Illustrated by Ross MacDonald. Alfred A. Knopf 2008 Un Illustration
Grades: 3 4 5 6 7 8 9   **741.5**
1. Artists; 2. Biographical graphic novels; 3. Cartoonists; 4. Cartoonists; 5. Comic book writers; 6. Illustrators; 7. Shuster, Joe, 1914-1992; 8. Siegel, Jerry, 1914-1996; 9. Superman (Fictional character); 10. Graphic novels
978-0-375-83802-6, $16.99; 978-0-375-93802-3 (lib. bdg.), $19.99

                                           LC 2007-41606
This picture book tells the story of Jerry Siegel and Joe Shuster, two teenagers living in Depression-era Cleveland, Ohio, who became friends and started writing stories together. One night they created the character who would become Superman. A text section at the back of the book tells of the struggle Siegel and Shuster had after they sold rights to Superman to the company that is now DC Comics. After Superman became wildly successful and made lots of money for DC Comics, Siegel and Shuster saw none of it. They started a legal fight that did end up with DC providing a financial settlement; Siegel's family was finally awarded half of the U.S. copyright to the material in Action Comics #1 in March 2008. Shuster's family is now asserting its right to the other half of the copyright, and negotiations are ongoing.

Nordling, Lee
BirdCatDog: a graphic novel. Lee Nordling & Meritxell Bosch. Graphic Universe 2014 32 p. Color; Illustration (Three-story books)
Grades: PreK K 1 2   **741.5**
1. Birds — Fiction; 2. Cats — Fiction; 3. Dogs — Fiction; 4. Pets; 5. Stories without words; 6. Graphic novels
1467745227; 9781467745222, $25.26

                                           LC 2013045749
This graphic novel, by Lee Nordling and illustrated by Meritxell Bosch, simultaneously describes three stories. "A bird escapes from its cage and flies out the window. A napping cat wakes up hungry and tries to catch a snack. A dog stands guard in his backyard, ready to bark at anything that comes near. Follow the tales of three animals on one wild afternoon." (Publisher's note)

"Expressive, accessible art wordlessly follows the pets' adventures, during which each animal not only interacts (badly) with the other two pets but also comes snout-to-snout (or beak-to-beak) with a wild version of itself: a hawk, a lynx, a wolf. While the consistent panel grid sacrifices the more dynamic layout and pacing afforded by a variety of panel sizes and shapes, this structure (with its protagonist-color-complementing rows) unobtrusively guides readers along." Horn Book

The **bramble**. Written by Lee Nordling; illustrated by Bruce Zick. Carolrhoda Books 2013 32 p.
Grades: K 1 2 3 4   **741.5; 741.5/973**
1. Bullies — Juvenile fiction; 2. Monsters — Juvenile fiction; 3. Picture books for children; 4. Self-confidence — Fiction; 5. Tag games — Fiction; 6. Graphic novels
0761358560; 9780761358565, $16.95

                                           LC 2013001910

Fishfishfish. By Lee Nordling; illustrated by Meritxell Bosch. Graphic Universe 2015 32 p. Color; Illustration (Three-story books)
Grades: 1 2 3 4   **741.5**
1. Fishes — Juvenile fiction; 2. Marine biology; 3. Stories without words; 4. Graphic novels
1467745766; 9781467745765, $6.95; 9781467745758

                                           LC 2014022953
"A little yellow fish swims alone in a big ocean. A hungry barracuda searches for something to eat. A school of fish band together and find strength in numbers. Under the waves, every fish is a hero in its own story. Nordling's simple storytelling engages young readers and provides a gateway into understanding multiple perspectives and points of view." (Publisher's note)

"Each story unfolds in one of three rows of panels on each page, so readers can follow one story at a time or all three at once, which sometimes requires reading the columns of panels from top to bottom in order to make sense of them chronologically. Because the book is wordless, it's accessible to early and emerging readers, who might enjoy creating their own narratives." Booklist

SheHeWe. By Lee Nordling; illustrated by Meritxell Bosch. Graphic Universe 2015 32 p.
Grades: 1 2 3 4   **741.5/973; 741.5**
1. Friendship — Juvenile fiction; 2. Games; 3. Games — Fiction; 4. Imagination — Juvenile fiction; 5. Stories without words; 6. Graphic novels
9781467745741, $25.26

                                           LC 2014021929
In this wordless graphic novel by Lee Nordling, illustrated by Meritxell Bosch, "Alex hosts a tea party and makes new friends. Drew soars through the sky, searching for adventure. Two kids play in a park, imagining they're somewhere else. In one afternoon, the worlds of imagination and reality collide." (Publisher's note)

North, Ryan
Adventure Time. Ryan North; illustrated by Braden Lamb and Shelli Paroline. Simon & Schuster 2012 128 p. Color; Illustration

Grades: 3 4 5 6 7 8 9 10   **741.5**
  1. Adventure fiction; 2. Imaginary places
  1608862801; 9781608862801, $14.99
  "The totally algebraic adventures of Finn and Jake have
come to the comic book page! The Lich, a super-lame,
SUPER-SCARY skeleton dude, has returned to the the Land
of Ooo, and he's bent on total destruction! Luckily, Finn and
Jake are on the case . . . but can they succeed against their
most destructive foe yet?" (Publisher's note)
  "The comic series has been every bit as good as the
show, with epic magic battles with an evil Lich, a multi-part
time travel story, and a host of backup strips by some of the
best indie cartoonists out there." Comics Alliance
  Volume 1 of an ongoing series

Nykko
  ★ The **elsewhere** chronicles book two: the shadow
spies. Art by Bannister ; story by Nykko ; colors by Jaffré.
Lerner Publishing Group/Graphic Universe 2009 48p.
Illustration
Grades: 4 5 6 7 8   **741.5; Fic**
  1. Adventure graphic novels; 2. Fantasy graphic novels; 3.
  Horror graphic novels; 4. Graphic novels
  978-0-7613-4460-5, $27.93; 978-0-7613-3964-9 (pa),
  $6.95
                                               LC 2008-39443
  When the Shadow Door shatters, the passageway closes
and Rebecca and Max are trapped in Elsewhere; they set out
to find another way home. The problem is that wherever
there is darkness, the Shadow Spies hunt them. Back in
Grandpa Gabe's house, Noah and Theo work to find a
replacement lens for the movie projector so they can get
through and rescue their friends. Meanwhile, the police
think Max and Rebecca have been kidnapped, and the boys
have to work around the investigation. It's clear to the kids
that Grandpa Gabe had explored Elsewhere, and his notes
have left clues for them; Max and Rebecca also meet people
who have been fighting a long war against the Shadows and
who know Grandpa Gabe. Whatever else they do, they must
keep the Shadow Spies away from Earth.
  Originally published in France as Les Enfants d'ailleurs,
winner of the 2007 Lyon Festival Youth Prize.

  ★ The **elsewhere** chronicles, book three: the master of
shadows. Art by Bannister ; story by Nykko ; colors by
Jaffré. Lerner Publishing Group/Graphic Universe 2009
48p. Illustration
Grades: 4 5 6 7 8   **741.5; Fic**
  1. Fantasy graphic novels; 2. Horror graphic novels; 3.
  Graphic novels
  978-0-7613-4461-2, $27.93; 978-0-7613-4744-6 (pa),
  $6.95
                                               LC 2008-39444
  Theo and Noah have joined Rebecca and Max in
Elsewhere, but they are on the run, pursued by the Master of
Shadows and menaced at all times by the Shadow Spies. All
they have to guide them are the strange and cryptic clues left
by Grandpa Gabe, and they see their friends in this strange
world pay the ultimate price while trying to stop the

Shadows. How far must the four friends go, and what will it
cost them, to save their own world?
  Originally published in France as Les Enfants d'ailleurs,
winner of the 2007 Lyon Festival Youth Prize.

  ★ The **tower** of shadows. By Nykko, illustrated by
Bannister; translation by Carol Klio Burrell]. Graphic
Universe 2013 48 p. (The ElseWhere chronicles)
Grades: 4 5 6 7   **741.5; Fic**
  1. Grandfathers — Fiction; 2. Horror stories; 3. Imaginary
  places; 4. Magic — Fiction; 5. Graphic novels
  1467712337; 9781467712330, $27.93
                                               LC 2013000317
  In this graphic novel by Nykko, "the time has come to
confront the Master of Shadows. Rebecca, Max, and Theo
must follow Grandpa Gabe into the heart of the Master's
realm, the Tower of Shadows. But can Grandpa Gabe be
trusted? There's a reason he's so familiar with the dark
powers that rule Elsewhere: he created them. Grandpa
Gabe's plan might just be a suicide mission, but it's their last
chance to save our world—and Rebecca's life." (Publisher's
note)
  "Bannister's atmospheric illustrations feature
expressive characters placed in finely detailed, eerily
organic landscapes or dim subterranean reaches inhabited by
menacing swirls of shadow." Kirkus

O'Brien, Anne Sibley
  The **legend** of Hong Kil Dong, the Robin Hood of
Korea. Charlesbridge 2006 Un Illustration
Grades: 3 4 5 6 7   **741.5; Fic**
  1. Hong Kil Dong (Legendary character); 2. Korea; 3.
  Graphic novels
  978-1-58089-302-2; 1-58089-302-3, $14.95
                                               LC 2005-56941
  Hong Kil Dong is the son of a powerful government
minister and one of his servants; this means the father will
not recognize his son as his own. The boy grows up with
great intelligence and wit, and leaves home to find his
fortune. He learns martial arts and magic, and when he
encounters thieves who rob only because corrupt
government officials have ruined them, he turns the thieves
into an army to right the wrongs. This story is based on a
seventeenth century Korean legend.
  Includes bibliographical references

O'Connor, George
  Ares: bringer of war. George O'Connor. First Second
Books 2015 80 p. Color; Illustration (Olympians)
Grades: 4 5 6 7 8 9   **741.5**
  1. Ares (Greek deity); 2. Greek mythology; 3. Trojan War
  1626720134; 1626720142; 9781626720138;
  9781626720145, $16.99
                                               LC 2014041225
  This graphic novel by George O'Connor "continues in
the tenth year of the fabled Trojan War where two infamous
gods of war go to battle. The spotlight is thrown on Ares, god
of war, and primarily focuses on his battle with the clever
and powerful Athena. As the battle culminates and the gods
try to one-up each other to win, the human death toll
mounts." (Publisher's note)

"In this nuanced, multilayered view of the usually vilified bringer of war, O'Connor continues his exceptional graphic novel series about the Greek gods. . . . The author's extensive notes amusingly explain connections to The Odyssey, The Aeneid, and the series' previous works." SLJ

Athena: grey-eyed goddess. First Second 2010 76p. Illustration
Grades: 5 6 7 8   **741; 741.5**
978-1-59643-649-7, $16.99; 1-59643-649-2;
978-1-59643-432-5 (pa), $9.99; 1-59643-432-5 (pa)

Hera: the goddess and her glory. First Second 2011 76p. Illustration
Grades: 5 6 7 8   **741; 741.5**
978-1-59643-433-2, $9.99; 1-59643-433-3

★ **Olympians:** Athena, grey-eyed goddess. First Second Books 2010 78p. Illustration
Grades: 4 5 6 7 8 9   **741.5; Fic**
1. Athena (Greek deity); 2. Fantasy graphic novels; 3. Gods and goddesses; 4. Greek mythology; 5. Graphic novels
978-1-59643-432-5, $9.99
The Fates retell five tales of the goddess Athena, daughter of Zeus, a warrior and also the goddess of wisdom. The first story tells of her birth, which is unlike any other, god or human; the second and third stories tell a couple of versions of how she took the name Pallas. The fourth story recounts Athena's dealings with Medusa, and how young demigod Perseus finally killed her. The events in these stories also provide Athena with her Aegis, one of her great weapons, which incorporates the impenetrable skin of the giant Pallas and the snakes from Medusa's head with the cape Zeus made from the skin of the goat Amalthea, who had nurtured him as a child. The Fates then tell of the weaving contest between Athena and the skilled but arrogant human woman, Arachne. O'Connor includes notes that provide more information about some of the historical background, discussion questions, a bibliography, and suggestions for further reading. His full-color art utilizes some of the style of super hero comics. This is the second of twelve planned volumes.

Poseidon: earth shaker. By George O'Connor. Roaring Brook Press 2012 80 p. (Olympians)
Grades: 4 5 6   **741.5/973; 741.5**
1. Greek mythology
1596437383; 1596438282; 9781596437388, $9.99; 9781596438286, $16.99
LC 2011052219
This graphic novel, by George O'Connor, is part of the "Olympians" series, featuring the mythology of the Greco-Roman gods. "The fifth installment of the Olympians series of graphic novels . . . turns the spotlight on that most mysterious and misunderstood of the Greek gods. . . . Thrill to such famous myths as Theseus and the Minotaur, Odysseus and Polyphemos, and the founding of Athens—and learn how the tempestuous Poseidon became the King of the Seas." (Publisher's note)
Includes bibliographical references and index
A Neal Porter book.

★ **Zeus:** king of the gods. First Second 2010 76p. Illustration
Grades: 5 6 7 8   **741.5**
978-1-59643-431-8, $16.99; 1-59643-625-5;
978-1-59643-432-5 (pa), $9.99; 1-59643-431-7 (pa)
"O'Connor unveils his new Olympians graphic-novel series with this story of the daddy of Greek gods. Most immediately striking about this, aside from the exciting artwork, is the care O'Connor takes to visualize the creation myth that begins with Gaea creating and taking as a husband the sky, Ouranos. Their children the Titans and other proto-Olympian entities are often neglected or at best murkily covered, but here they're vividly portrayed with all the magnificence of their beyond-good-and-evil power. After this breathtaking and lengthy sequence, Zeus enters the scene to grow from a feisty nymph-needling youth to a lightning bolt-wielding avenger." (Booklist)
Other titles in this series are:Athena: grey-eyed goddess (2010); Hera: the goddess and her glory (2011); Hades: lord of the dead (2012); Poseidon: earth shaker (2013); Aphrodite: goddess of love (2013); Ares: bringer of war (2015); Apollo: the brilliant one (2016)

O'Donnell, Liam

Food fight: a graphic guide adventure. Illustrated by Mike Deas. Orca Book Publishers 2010 Un Illustration
Grades: 3 4 5 6 7 8   **741.5; Fic**
1. Agriculture — Research; 2. Food supply; 3. Mystery graphic novels; 4. Graphic novels
978-1-55469-067-1, $9.95
LC 2009-940900
Devin and Nadia are spending their summer vacation as camp counselors for the Lil Brains Summer Camp at the university, where their mother, Dr. Chang, works in a research lab; at least Nadia is working. Devin keeps trying to escape so he can hang out with his friend Simon. Dr. Chang is working on ways to improve food crops, but someone breaks into the lab using her access code. When it happens again, her supervisors think she's trying to sabotage her own work. Nadia and Devin know their mother wouldn't do anything unethical, so they decide to investigate. When Devin goes with Dr. Chang to an experimental farm, he meets Irene, a young girl who suspects the farm is developing genetically modified corn. They work together to help Dr. Chang, but soon find there's definitely something wrong going on, and the corporation sponsoring the research is responsible. O'Donnell includes information on genetically modified foods and the controversy surrounding its use, and on the growing locavore movement (eating only locally-grown produce).
Part of the Graphic Guide Adventure series

Courtesy of Orca Book Publishers

Max Finder mystery: collected casebook, vol. 1. Illustrated by Richard Dominguez and Charles Barnett III. Owlkids Publishing 2009 96p. Illustration
Grades: 3 4 5 6 7 8   **741.5; Fic**
 1. Humorous graphic novels; 2. Mystery graphic novels; 3. Graphic novels
 978-2-89579-116-4, $9.95
                                     LC C2006-903300-5
 This book collects ten short mysteries that originally appeared in Owl Magazine. Seventh-graders Max Finder and Alison Santos live in Whispering Meadows, and they investigate mysteries that happen in their neighborhood and in school. Each story provides verbal and visual clues for the readers and invites them to try to solve the mystery themselves before turning to the back of the book to read the solution. Each story is also accompanied by a puzzle, with solutions to those in the back as well. Max and Alison's neighbors and schoolmates each take turns being victims, witnesses, and sometimes the culprits in such cases as the loss of a valuable basketball card, a vandalized brand-new CD at a slumber party, a stolen prize at the school's Halloween dance, a box of chocolate bars replaced with soap, and a werewolf at the summer camp. Anyone who has enjoyed any Encyclopedia Brown or Cam Jansen mysteries will enjoy these mystery stories.

★ **Power** play. Illustrated by Mike Deas. Orca Book Publishers 2011 64p. Illustration (Graphic guide adventure)
Grades: 3 4 5 6 7 8 9
741; 741.5; Fic
 1. Mystery graphic novels; 2. Graphic novels
 978-1-55469-069-5, $9.95; 1-55469-069-2

Courtesy of Orca Book Publishers

Siblings Devin and Nadia team up with their friend Marcus, Marcus' stepbrother Bounce, and Bounce's best friend Pema when they all attend the World Leaders Summit, where Marcus' father, Dr. Ashmore is scheduled to speak. The friends find themselves mixed up in a fight between some of the most powerful people in the world and those who want more equitable rights to clean water and other environmental concerns. They investigate when one of Dr. Ashmore's assistants is murdered at the summit, and Dr. Ashmore receives threats.
 "An enjoyable story with educational value, this strong mystery is presented along with information about world politics, power, and the benefits of political protest for social good." Booklist

Ramp rats: a graphic guide adventure. Written by Liam O'Donnell; illustrated by Mike Deas. Orca Book Publishers 2008 Un Illustration
Grades: 3 4 5 6 7 8 9   **741.5; Fic**
 1. Bullies; 2. Friendship; 3. Skateboarding; 4. Graphic novels
 978-1-55143-880-1 (pa), $9.95; 1-55143-880-1 (pa)
                                     LC 2008-928577

"Benny (nicknamed Bounce) just wants to use the cool new skate park with his friend Pema, but older bullying Crunch and his friends have taken over the park. . . . Aside from the action-packed story, great characters, and colorful artwork, this graphic-novel adventure includes an array of practical skateboarding tips for beginners. The story also delivers a deft message about standing up to bullies." Booklist

The **Shocking** World of Electricity with Max Axiom, Super Scientist. Illustrated by Richard Dominguez and Charles Barnett III. Capstone Press 2007 32p. Illustration
Grades: 3 4 5 6 7 8   **537; 741.5**
 1. Electricity; 2. Science; 3. Graphic novels
 978-0-7368-6835-8 li, $25.26; 978-0-7368-7888-3 (pa)
 Max Axiom is a super-cool super-scientist who demonstrates and explains science in ways never before seen in the classroom. Whether shrinking down to the size of an ant or riding on a sound wave, Max does whatever it takes to make science super cool and accessible. This volume explores electricity, and includes a glossary and a list of books for further reading.
 Part of the Graphic Science series.

System Shock. Art by Janet Matysiak. Stone Arch Books 2007 88p. Illustration
Grades: 4 5 6 7 8 9   **741.5; Fic**
 1. Science fiction graphic novels; 2. Video games; 3. Graphic novels
 978-1-59889-083-9 li, $22.60; 978-1-59889-214-7 (pa)
                                     LC 2006007185
 In a futuristic society, Daniel, Jack, and Jemma find themselves lost in a virtual reality game. To make matters worse, every video-game villain seems to be pursuing them. Even if they defeat the evil Cyborgs, the controllers in Realworld are working on wiping the corrupt system clean. If the friends don't find a way out soon, they are in danger of being erased forever. This graphic novel is written at an easy level for reluctant and struggling readers.
 Part of the Graphic Quest series.

Understanding Photosynthesis with Max Axiom, Super Scientist. Capstone Press 2007 32p. Illustration
Grades: 3 4 5 6 7 8   **572; 741.5**
 1. Photosynthesis; 2. Science; 3. Graphic novels
 978-0-7368-6841-9 li, $25.26; 978-0-7368-7893-7 (pa)
 Max Axiom is a super-cool super-scientist who demonstrates and explains science in ways never before seen in the classroom. Whether shrinking down to the size of an ant or riding on a sound wave, Max does whatever it takes to make science super cool and accessible. This volume explores photosynthesis, and includes a glossary and a list of books for further reading.
 Part of the Graphic Science series.

A **United** Force. Art by Mike Rooth. Harcourt Achieve/Steck-Vaughn 2006 48p. Illustration
Grades: 3 4 5 6 7 8   **741.5; Fic**
 1. Adventure graphic novels; 2. Celts; 3. Graphic novels
 978-1-4190-3206-6, $8.99
 It's 55 B.C.E. The British Isles have been home to the Celts for hundreds of years. Now, an ambitious Roman general named Julius Caesar plans to change all that. Will the Celts be able to defend their homeland? This historical

graphic novel includes prose intervals that give information about the Celts and the Romans.
Part of the Timeline Graphic Novels series.

The **World** of Food Chains with Max Axiom, Super Scientist. Art by Cynthia Martin and Bill Anderson. Capstone Press 2007 32p. Illustration
Grades: 3 4 5 6 7 8   **577; 741.5**
  1. Food chains (Ecology); 2. Science; 3. Graphic novels
978-0-7368-6839-6 li, $25.26; 978-0-7368-7891-3 (pa)

Max Axiom is a super-cool super-scientist who demonstrates and explains science in ways never before seen in the classroom. Whether shrinking down to the size of an ant or riding on a sound wave, Max does whatever it takes to make science super cool and accessible. This volume explores food chains and how they work in ecology, and includes a glossary and a list of books for further reading.
Part of the Graphic Science series.

O'Malley, Kevin
  Captain Raptor and the moon mystery. Illustrations by Patrick O'Brien. Walker & Co. 2005 Un Illustration
Grades: PreK K 1 2 3 4   **E; Fic**
  1. Dinosaurs; 2. Science fiction graphic novels; 3. Graphic novels
0-8027-8935-8, $16.95; 0-8027-8936-6 (lib bdg), $17.85
                           LC 2004-53624

When something lands on one of the moons of the planet Jurassica, Captain Raptor and his spaceship crew go to investigate

"An action-packed science-fiction romp starring a cast of dinosaur characters. . . . Presented in comic-book style, this story blends an eye-catching layout with a quick-moving plot, tongue-in-cheek humor, and an imaginative setting." SLJ
Another title about Captain Raptor is: Captain Raptor and the space pirates (2007)

Oakley, Mark
  Thieves & kings. [by Mark Oakley]. I Box Pub 1998 154p. Illustration
Grades: 4 5 6 7 8 9 10 11 12   **741.5; Fic**
  1. Adventure graphic novels; 2. Fantasy graphic novels; 3. Graphic novels
0-9681025-0-6, $18.95
                           LC 2003-446777

In a story that mixes pages of text with pages of comic book art, the reader meets the young thief Rubel, who has returned home from a long voyage to find things no longer as they were. He has to deal with soldiers and pirates, princes and princesses, a strange young wizard, and a mysterious Shadow Lady.
Originally published as individual issues of the Thieves & kings comic series, beginning in 1994
Volume 1 of 5

  Thieves & Kings Presents The Walking Mage. I Box Publishing 2006 Un Illustration
Grades: 5 6 7 8 9 10 11 12   **741.5; Fic**
  1. Fantasy graphic novels; 2. Humorous graphic novels; 3. Graphic novels
0-9681025-5-7, $9.95

In the world of Thieves & Kings, the royal wizard, Quinton Zempfester, has lost his job. Again. This time, though, his name has also been added to the top of the kingdom's list of most wanted criminals. Unfairly accused by the dark witch who has seized the throne, Quinton decides that perhaps a little treason might not be such a bad idea after all ... This book chronicles a side adventure in the series, and is done completely in comic book panels rather than the mix of prose and panels used in the main series.

Oh, Cirro
  Greek and Roman Mythology Vol. 1. Art by C.S. Chun. Youngjin Singapore 2005 188p. Illustration
Grades: 3 4 5 6 7 8   **741.5; 291**
  1. Classical mythology; 2. Graphic novels
981-05-2240-1, $12.95

This title introduces each of the 12 gods of Olympus, tells the story of the creators of the gods, Gaia and Kronos, recounts Gigantes and Typhon's battles with Zeus to rule Mt. Olympus, and more. The book includes the Greek and Roman names of the main deities and a family tree of the gods.

Olson, Kay Melchisedech
  Benjamin Franklin: An American Genius. Illustrated by Barabara Schulz and Gordon Purcell. Capstone Press 2006 32p. Illustration
Grades: 3 4 5 6 7 8 9   **741.5; 973.3; 92**
  1. Franklin, Benjamin, 1706-1790; 2. Graphic novels
0-7368-4269-8, $25.26
                           LC 2005003964

This book uses the comic book format to recount highlights in the life of American statesman and inventor Benjamin Franklin. It includes additional information, a glossary, a list of books for further reading, and more.
Part of the Graphic Library, Graphic Biographies series.

  Betsy Ross and the American Flag. Illustrated by Anna Maria Cool, Sam Delarosa, and Charles Barnett III. Capstone Press 2006 32p. Illustration
Grades: 3 4 5 6 7 8 9   **741.5; 973.3; 92**
  1. Flags; 2. Ross, Betsy, 1752-1836; 3. United States — History — 1775-1783, Revolution; 4. Graphic novels
0-7368-4962-9, $25.26
                           LC 2005006461

This book uses the comic book format to tell the story of the life of Betsy Ross and the legend of her sewing the first American flag. It includes additional information, a glossary, a list of books for further reading, and more.
Part of the Graphic Library, Graphic History series.

  Frank Zamboni and the Ice-Resurfacing Machine by Kay Melchisedech Olson ; illustrated by Richard Dominguez and Charles Barnett, III. Capstone Press 2007 32p. Illustration
Grades: 3 4 5 6 7 8 9   **688.7; 741.5; 92**
  1. Ice skating; 2. Inventors; 3. Zamboni, Frank; 4. Graphic novels
1429601477; 9781429601474, $29.99
                           LC 2007000254

This book uses the graphic novel format to tell how Frank Zamboni created the ice-resurfacing machine, and how it affected the world of ice-based sports. The book includes additional facts and a list of books for further reading.

Part of the Graphic Library Inventions and Discovery series.

Olson, Nathan

Nathan Hale: Revolutionary Spy. Illustrated by Cynthia Martin and Brent Schoonover. Capstone Press 2006 32p. Illustration

Grades: 3 4 5 6 7 8 9   **741.5; 973.3; 92**
1. Biographical graphic novels; 2. Hale, Nathan, 1755-1776; 3. Graphic novels
0-7368-4968-8, $25.26

LC 2005007894

This book uses the comic book format to recount highlights of the life story of Revolutionary War hero and spy Nathan Hale. It includes additional information, a glossary, a list of books for further reading, and more.

Part of the Graphic Library, Graphic Biographies series.

Orme, David

Billy Blaster: attack of the Rock Men. Art by Peter Richardson. Stone Arch Books 2009 40p.

Grades: 3 4 5 6 7   **741.5; Fic**
1. Adventure graphic novels; 2. Blaster, Billy (Fictional character); 3. Science fiction graphic novels; 4. Graphic novels
978-1-4342-1273-3, $22.65

LC 2008-31285

Rock Men are the hottest new toys on the market, and everyone in Zone City is getting them. However, when kids plug the Rock Men into their computers, the toys brainwash them into getting their parents' credit card information. Even General Bullet has bought a Rock Man and has been brainwashed. Billy and his ninja wizard friend Wu Hoo learn that their old enemy Red Wolf is the nefarious toymaker, and they set out to stop him. The book includes a short glossary, some facts about popular toys and games of the past, and discussion questions and writing prompts.

Originally published in the U.K. as Boffin Boy and the Rock Men. This is a volume of the Billy Blaster series.

Billy Blaster: the Cryptic code. Art by Peter Richardson. Stone Arch Books 2009 40p. Illustration

Grades: 3 4 5 6 7   **741.5; Fic**
1. Adventure graphic novels; 2. Blaster, Billy (Fictional character); 3. Science fiction graphic novels; 4. Graphic novels
978-1-4342-1265-8, $22.65

LC 2008-31286

Billy Blaster's friend Wu Hoo, the ninja wizard, always seeks more knowledge, and his quest leads him to a parchment written in a cryptic code. Before he can decipher it, a singing trio called the Big Sisters learn that Wu Hoo has the parchment and kidnap him; they want the secret wisdom on the parchment for themselves. The book includes a short glossary, some facts about codes and secret messages, and discussion questions and writing prompts.

Originally published in the U.K. as Boffin Boy and the Quest for Wisdom. This is a volume of the Billy Blaster series.

Billy Blaster: the Evil Swarm. Art by Peter Richardson. Stone Arch Books 2009 40p.

Grades: 3 4 5 6 7   **741.5; Fic**
1. Adventure graphic novels; 2. Blaster, Billy (Fictional character); 3. Science fiction graphic novels; 4. Graphic novels
978-1-4342-1274-0, $22.65

LC 2008-31287

When a swarm of giant, angry insects emerges from a volcano attacks the people of Zone City, Billy and his friend Rika enter the volcano to find out what's going on and to see if they can stop them before the swarm can spread across the world. The book includes a short glossary, some facts about real insects, and discussion questions and writing prompts.

Originally published in the U.K. as Boffin Boy and the Deadly Swarm. This is a volume of the Billy Blaster series

Courtesy of Ransom Publishing

Boffin Boy and the Invaders from Space. Art by Peter Richardson. Ransom Publishing 2007 Un Illustration

Grades: 2 3 4 5 6   **741.5; Fic**
1. Adventure graphic novels; 2. Science fiction graphic novels; 3. Superhero graphic novels; 4. Graphic novels; 5. Boffin Boy (Fictional character)
978-1-84167-613-5, $7.95

Boffin Boy and Wu Pee must fight the scaly Snurgeon space invaders and stop them from stealing all of the Earth's water. Will Boffin Boy use force, or can he find a clever way to save the planet?

Boffin Boy and the Lost City. Art by Peter Richardson. Ransom Publishing 2007 Un Illustration

Grades: 2 3 4 5 6

741.5; Fic
1. Adventure graphic novels; 2. Science fiction graphic novels; 3. Superhero graphic novels; 4. Graphic novels; 5. Boffin Boy (Fictional character)
978-1-84167-617-3, $7.95

People keep

Courtesy of Ransom Publishing

disappearing then reappearing again; but the ones that appear aren't the same as the ones that disappear. Of course, it's a door into another world, and Boffin Boy (Rick Shaw) and ninja wizard Wu Pee set off to find it. When they do, then the story really starts ...

Boffin Boy and the Monsters from the Deep. Art by Peter Richardson. Ransom Publishing 2007 Un Illustration

Grades: 2 3 4 5 6   **741.5; Fic**

Courtesy of Ransom Publishing

1. Adventure graphic novels; 2. Science fiction graphic novels; 3. Superhero graphic novels; 4. Graphic novels; 5. Boffin Boy (Fictional character)
978-1-84167-615-9, $7.95
Just when people are having a nice quiet time on the beach, some giant mutant jellyfish come along and spoil it. They're stealing all the sweets and chocolate bars they can find. But Boffin Boy and Wu Pee are soon on the case; and when Wu Pee finds a secret weapon to use against the jellyfish, they set a trap.

Boffin Boy and the Red Wolf. Art by Peter Richardson. Ransom Publishing 2007 Un Illustration
Grades: 2 3 4 5 6
741.5; Fic
1. Adventure graphic novels; 2. Science fiction graphic novels; 3. Superhero graphic novels; 4. Graphic novels; 5. Boffin Boy (Fictional character)
978-1-84167-616-6, $7.95
The evil Red Wolf is using TV to turn every wizard in the world into his slave. With their magic and money, nobody will be able to stop him. When Red Wolf captures ninja wizard Wu Pee, Boffin Boy is forced to use the same TV tricks on Red Wolf. Can Rick free the wizards and save TV?

Courtesy of Ransom Publishing

Courtesy of Ransom Publishing

Boffin Boy and the Time Warriors. Art by Peter Richardson. Ransom Publishing 2007 Un Illustration
Grades: 2 3 4 5 6 **741.5; Fic**
1. Adventure graphic novels; 2. Science fiction graphic novels; 3. Superhero graphic novels; 4. Graphic novels; 5. Boffin Boy (Fictional character)
978-1-84167-622-7, $7.95
An army of Japanese Samurai warriors travels from the past into our present. Boffin Boy must save the world from this ancient menace.

Boffin Boy and the Wizard of Edo. Art by Peter Richardson. Ransom Publishing 2006 Un Illustration
Grades: 2 3 4 5 6 **741.5; Fic**

1. Adventure graphic novels; 2. Science fiction graphic novels; 3. Superhero graphic novels; 4. Graphic novels; 5. Boffin Boy (Fictional character)
978-1-84167-614-2, $7.95
Boffin Boy and Wu Pee take on an evil wizard who has invented a camera that can steal people's minds. Then Wu Pee goes missing, too. Rick Shaw is a clever 14 year-old who is only interested in science. When his father is killed he vows to use his scientific skills to fight evil - as Boffin Boy.

Courtesy of Ransom Publishing

Mutants from the deep. Art by Peter Richardson. Stone Arch Books 2009 40p.
Grades: 2 3 4 5 6 7 **741.5; Fic**
1. Humorous graphic novels; 2. Science fiction graphic novels; 3. Graphic novels
978-1-4342-1269-6, $21.26

LC 2008-31346
Sailors dump barrels of toxic waste into the ocean, and the toxic waste causes jellyfish to mutate into giant, candy-and-ice-cream-loving monsters. Billy and his ninja master partner, Wu Hoo, must find a way to stop the mutants from grabbing all the sweets. The book includes some information about water pollution, discussion questions, and a glossary.
Originally published as Boffin Boy and the Monsters from the Deep by Ransom Publishing, 2006. Part of the Billy Blaster series.

Orr, Tamra
Manga artists. [by] Tamra Orr. Rosen Publishing Group 2009 64p. Illustration (Extreme careers)
Grades: 4 5 6 7 8 9 **741.5**
1. Graphic novels — Authorship; 2. Manga — Authorship; 3. Vocational guidance
978-1-4042-1854-3, $29.25

LC 2007-50666
This book provides an introduction to manga as a format of Japanese comics, including a brief history and mentions some famous mangaka (manga creators). It also provides information on what it's like to be a mangaka in Japan, and how to become a manga-style artist in the U.S.
Includes glossary and bibliographical references
Part of the Extreme Careers series

Otomo, Katsuhiro
Hipira. Illustrated by Shinji Kimura. Dark Horse Press 2005 Un Illustration
Grades: 2 3 4 5 6 **741.5; Fic**
1. Adventure graphic novels; 2. Fantasy graphic novels; 3. Humorous graphic novels; 4. Vampires; 5. Graphic novels
1-59582-002-7, $13.95

In the vampire city of Salta, the sun never rises and all the vampire children love to stay up late. Hipira is a precocious young vampire whose best friend is a fairy named Soul, and their games, pranks, and adventures are extraordinary even for the inhabitants of this supernatural city. All the characters, even the monsters, look cute rather than scary.

Ottaviani, Jim
    Primates: The Fearless Science of Jane Goodall, Dian Fossey, and Biruté Galdikas. Jim Ottaviani; illustrated by Maris Wicks. First Second 2013 133 p. Color; Illustration
Grades: 5 6 7 8 9 10 11 12 Adult   **741.5; 599.8**
    1. Fossey, Dian, 1932-1985; 2. Galdikas, Birute, 1946-; 3. Goodall, Jane, 1934-; 4. Primates
    1596438657; 9781596438651, $19.99
                   LC 2013427678
    This nonfiction graphic novel, by Jim Ottaviani, illustrated by Maris Wicks, presents an "account of the three greatestáprimatologists of the last century: Jane Goodall, Dian Fossey, and Birut? Galdikas. These three ground-breaking researchers were all students of the great Louis Leakey, and each made profound contributions to primatology—and to our own understanding of ourselves." (Publisher's note)
    "More story than study, the book provides an accessible introduction to Goodall's, Fossey's and Galdikas' lives and work." Kirkus
    Includes bibliographical references, page 138

    ★ **T-Minus:** the race to the moon. [illustrated by] Zander Cannon, Kevin Cannon. Aladdin 2009 124p. Illustration
Grades: 4 5 6 7 8 9 10 11 12 Adult
629.45; 741.5
    1. Apollo project; 2. Gemini project; 3. Space flight to the moon; 4. Graphic novels
    978-1-4169-8682-9, $21.99; 1-4169-8682-0; 978-1-4169-4960-2 (pa), $12.99; 1-4169-4960-7 (pa)

Courtesy of Aladdin Press

                   LC 2009-920999
    Ottaviani, Zander Cannon, and Kevin Cannon show what happened when the U.S. and the U.S.S.R. started the space race in the 1950s, and how it progressed to the NASA Apollo 11 mission which landed two men on the moon in July of 1969.
    "Organized as a countdown, making the outcome seem inevitable, the frequent, prominent sidebars list a type of rocket, the duration of its flight, and whether the mission was a success or a failure. There are more than 30 attempts chronicled, and the shift between Soviet and U.S. successes creates an interesting balance in the narrative. . . . Ottaviani is particular with facts and eager to inspire readers with regard to the scientific process." SLJ

O'Brien, John
    Look . . . look again!. John O'Brien. Boyds Mills Press 2012 63 p.
Grades: 3 4 5
741.5
    1. Cooking — Juvenile fiction; 2. Picture books for children
    159078894X; 9781590788943, $18.95
            LC 2012936283
    This book "offers a series of brief skit-like sequences that tell a visual joke or play on words in a spreadful of panel illustrations; for instance, 'The Pizza' features a pizza chef who carefully cuts and eats a slice of pizza, whereupon the now Pac-Man-shaped pie gobbles up the pizza chef. Each of the six sections follows a particular protagonist or set of protagonists ('The Dairy Farmer,' 'The Clown'), and each section offers five titled mini-stories." (Bulletin of the Center for Children's Books)

Courtesy of Boyds Mills Press

Panev, Aleksandar
    Queen Nzinga. Art by Thomas Stefflbauer. Harcourt Achieve/Steck-Vaughn 2007 48p. Illustration
Grades: 3 4 5 6 7 8   **741.5; Fic**
    1. Adventure graphic novels; 2. Africa — History; 3. Graphic novels
    978-1-4190-3214-1, $8.99
    Nzinga is a young princess in the African kingdom of Ndongo. When her friend Kakengo is kidnapped by Portuguese slave traders, she makes a vow to protect her people against slavery. Nzinga lived from 1582 to 1663 in the land now called Angola, and she fought against the slave traders. This historical fiction graphic novel includes prose intervals with information about Africa, the slave trade, and some other African leaders.
    Part of the Timeline Graphic Novels series.

Parker, Jake
    ★ **Missile** Mouse: the star crusher. Graphix 2010 172p. (Missile Mouse)
Grades: 3 4 5 6   **741; Fic; 741.5**
    1. Adventure graphic novels; 2. Mice; 3. Science fiction graphic novels; 4. Graphic novels
    978-0-545-11714-2, $21.99; 0-545-11714-3; 978-0-545-11715-9 (pa), $10.99; 0-545-11715-1 (pa)
    "When his mission to recover an ancient star compass goes wrong, intrepid Galactic Security Agent Missile Mouse finds himself saddled with a partner. . . . The two are to retrieve a missing scientist who holds the key to a horrible weapon, the Star Crusher, in his hereditary memory. . . . [This is] a gem in story and art. Bright, action-filled, at times wordless panels keep the pages turning. Intelligent space opera and a realistically rounded hero will have young fans of the future demanding the next volume." Kirkus

Parker, Jeff

The **Avengers:** finding Zemo. Art by Manuel Garcia and Scott Koblish. ABDO Publishing Company/Spotlight 2008 Un Illustration

Grades: 4 5 6 7 8 9   741.5; Fic

1. Avengers (Fictional characters); 2. Captain America (Fictional character); 3. Hulk (Fictional character); 4. Iron Man (Fictional character); 5. Spider-Man (Fictional character); 6. Storm (Fictional character); 7. Superhero graphic novels; 8. Wolverine (Fictional character); 9. Graphic novels

978-1-59961-383-3, $21.35

LC 2007-20254

A ceremony to honor Captain America is attacked by his old enemy, Baron Zemo, in a new giant attack robot. While the Avengers battle the robot, Zemo kidnaps Captain America. Now, the rest of the team must find Zemo and Cap. This Avengers team includes Storm, Spider-Man, Iron Man, Wolverine, the Hulk, and Giant-Girl. This is a revised, hardbound edition of the Marvel Adventures comic book

Part of the Avengers series

The **Avengers:** heroes assembled, v1. Artist, Manuel Garcia. Marvel 2006 Illustration

Grades: 5 6 7 8 9   741.5; Fic

1. Avengers (Fictional characters); 2. Captain America (Fictional character); 3. Spider-Man (Fictional character); 4. Storm (Fictional character); 5. Wolverine (Fictional character)

978-0-7851-2306-4, $6.99; 0-7851-2306-7

Fantastic four: law of the jungle. Manuel Garcia, pencils ; Scott Koblish, inks ; A. Crossley, colors. ABDO Publishing Company/Spotlight 2008 Un Illustration

Grades: 4 5 6 7 8 9   741.5; Fic

1. Black Panther (Fictional character); 2. Fantastic Four (Fictional characters); 3. Superhero graphic novels; 4. Graphic novels

978-1-59961-390-1, $21.35

LC 2007-20255

The Fantastic Four find themselves fighting the Black Panther and discover that the rare metal they had purchased was stolen from Wakandia, the Black Panther's home country in Africa. When they investigate, they discover the thieves plan to steal again, and the team heads to Wakandia to help the Black Panther stop the criminals. If only he'll stop and listen to them before destroying them. This is a revised, hardbound edition of the Marvel Adventures comic book issue.

Part of the Fantastic Four series

Pearson, Luke

★ **Hilda** and the Bird Parade. By Luke Pearson. Flying Eye Books 2013 44 p. Color illustration (Hildafolk)

Grades: 2 3 4 5   741.5

1. Birds — Fiction; 2. City and town life — Fiction

1909263060; 9781909263062, $24

This book, by Luke Pearson, follows "Hilda and her mother are settling into the fictional town of Trolberg. It's a far cry from their idyllic mountain home: Hilda's mother is nervous about letting her daughter roam free, and the local kids' idea of a good time is to . . . throw rocks at birds. When a large, black bird is left injured and amnesiac after being hit by one such rock, Hilda tries to help it remember how to fly as well as find her own way home." (Publishers Weekly)

"Environment being so crucial to the tale, Pearson's expressive architecture and city design are nothing short of remarkable, giving a personality to neighborhoods and even individuals doorways. His large-headed, stick-legged cartooning employs both humor and empathy and gracefully reflects the book's tone, a perfect pitch between childlike adventure, subtle mystery, and gentle lyricism." Booklist

★ **Hilda** and the Black Hound. By Luke Pearson. Flying Eye Books 2014 64 p. Color; Illustration (Hildafolk)

Grades: 3 4 5 6 7   741.5

1. City and town life — Fiction; 2. Dogs — Fiction; 3. Girls — Fiction

9781909263185, $24; 1909263184

In this graphic novel by Luke Pearson, "Hilda . . . meets the Nisse: a mischievous but charismatic bunch of misfits who occupy a world beside—but also somehow within—our own, and where the rules of physics don't quite match up. Meanwhile, on the streets of Trolberg, a dark specter looms." (Publisher's note)

"The full-size volume offers a minimum of 10 panels of varying sizes per page. Darker shades dominate when the beast lurks, and earth tones and reds and oranges when the characters go about their daily business. Touches of humor abound in both images and dialogue." SLJ

Hilda and the Midnight Giant. Luke Pearson. Nobrow Press 2012 40p Color illustration

Grades: 4 5 6 7 8   741.5

1. Forests and forestry — Fiction; 2. Giants — Fiction; 3. Girls — Fiction

1907704256; 9781907704253, $24.00

In this book, the "protagonist finds her world turned upside down as she faces the prospect of leaving her snow-capped birthplace for the hum of the megalopolis, where her mother (an architect) has been offered a prestigious job. During Hilda's daily one-and-a-half hour trek to school she looks for ways to stall her mother's decision. She conspires with the beings of the mystical Blue Forest to delay the inevitable. Will they help or hinder her? More importantly, who is this mysterious Midnight Giant?"

★ **Hilda** and the troll. Luke Pearson. Flying Eye Books 2013 40 p. Color; Illustration (Hildafolk)

Grades: 3 4 5 6   741.5

1. Adventure fiction; 2. Explorers — Fiction; 3. Trolls — Fiction

1909263141; 9781909263147, $18.95

This book, by Luke Pearson, is "about an adventurous little girl and her habit of befriending anything, no matter how curious it might seem. While on an expedition to illustrate the magical creatures of the mountains around her home, Hilda spots a mountain troll. As the blue-haired explorer sits

Courtesy of Flying Eye Books

and sketches, she slowly starts to nod off. By the time she wakes up, the troll has totally disappeared and, even worse, Hilda is lost in a snowstorm." (Publisher's note)

"The art is as whimsical as the protagonist, and the bright colors enhance this comic book's magical-realistic effect." Horn Book

Originally appearing in print in 2010 as Hildafolk

Other titles about Hilda are: Hilda and the Midnight Giant (2012); Hilda and the Bird Parade (2013); Hilda and the Black Hound (2014)

Peirce, Lincoln
Big Nate: game on!. By Lincoln Peirce. Andrews McMeel Pub., LLC 2013 224 p. Color illustration
Grades: 1 2 3 4 5 6   **Fic; 741.5/973**
1. Games — Fiction; 2. Sports — Fiction
1449427774; 9781449427771, $9.99
                  LC 2012952339

This book, written and illustrated by Lincoln Peirce, features a collection of his "Big Nate" comic strip. "To sixth-grader Nate Wright, life is one big game. From fine-tuning his trash-talking skills on the basketball court to his cocky [attitude] in the soccer goal, Nate can be a bigger challenge to his teammates than their opponents." The book features "Nate and his friends" mostly hapless sports encounters." (Publisher's note)

Peters, Stephanie True
Rapunzel: the graphic novel. By Stephanie Peters; illustrated by Jeffrey Stewart Timmins. Stone Arch Books 2009 P. cm. (Graphic spin)
Grades: 3 4 5 6 7 8   **741.5; Fic**
1. Fairy tales; 2. Folklore; 3. Graphic novels
978-1-4342-1194-1 (lib bdg), $21.26; 1-4342-1194-0 (lib bdg); 978-1-4342-1392-1 (pa), $4.95; 1-4342-1392-7 (pa)
                  LC 2008-32047

When a long-married couple finally expect a baby, the pregnant wife craves the rampion from the witch's garden next door. Her craving becomes so desperate that the husband steals the rampion for his wife, only to get caught by the witch, who demands the child when she is born, Rapunzel (another name for rampion) grows up knowing no parent but the witch, but when she accidently catches a glimpse of the outside world, the witch conjures up a tall tower with no stairs and keeps Rapunzel there. The girl's hair has grown so long over the years, that the witch uses it as her ladder. A prince wanders by, watches the witch, and uses her command to gain access to the tower. The graphic novel adaption follows the version made famous by the Brothers Grimm; the book includes information on different versions of the tale from Italy and France. The art uses a fairly dark palette and stylized figures with dark circles for eyes.

Part of the Graphic Spin series.

Storm of the century: a Hurricane Katrina story. Illustrated by Jesus Aburto. Stone Arch Books 2009 56p.
Grades: 3 4 5 6 7   **741.5; Fic**
1. Hurricane Katrina, 2005; 2. New Orleans (La); 3. Graphic novels
978-1-4342-1164-4, $23.93
                  LC 2008-32071

When Hurricane Katrina hits New Orleans, fourteen-year-old Ricky Thompson and his family try to leave the city, but their car overheats in the backed-up traffic. They end up at the Superdome, where the National Guard has set up a shelter for the thousands of people who couldn't, or didn't, leave in time. Conditions in the stadium rapidly worsen even as the city floods when the levees fail. Ricky uses his new digital camera to take as many pictures as he can of everything as he and his family cope with the horrible conditions. This book is a hybrid of prose text and comic book format pages as the story depicts the impact of Katrina on one family.

Part of the Graphic Flash line from Stone Arch Books

Petersen, David
★ **Mouse** Guard: Fall 1152. Archaia Studios Press 2007 Un Illustration
Grades: 5 6 7 8   **741.5; Fic**
1. Fantasy graphic novels; 2. Mice; 3. Graphic novels
978-1-932386-57-8, $24.95; 1-932386-57-2
Eisner Award: Best Publication for Kids (2008)

In a medieval world populated by animals, mice have their own civilization but live in constant peril from predators. They live in hidden towns protected by the Guard, who also escort travelers between towns. Three young members of the Guard, Lieam, Saxon, and Kenzie, go in search of a missing grain merchant. They find him dead in the belly of a snake who tried to eat them; but they also find evidence that the dead merchant is a traitor. Now they need to find out to whom he was betraying the Guard and why. While this story features animals and is suitable for most readers who can handle some fighting action, there's nothing cute or Disney-esque in the art. Characters die, this is a serious story, but readers who have read Bone or the Harry Potter series can handle the action in this book. This is the first in a series.

Followed by: Mouse Guard: Winter 1152 (2009)

Originally published as Mouse Guard issues #1-6.

Mouse Guard: Winter 1152. Story & art by David Petersen. Archaia Studios Press 2009 Un Illustration
Grades: 5 6 7 8   **741.5; 741**
978-1-932386-74-5, $24.95; 1-932386-74-2
Followed by: Mouse Guard: The black axe (2013)

"In the Winter of 1152, the Mouse Guard face a food and supply shortage threatening the lives of many mouse through a cold and icy season. Some of the Guard's finest—Saxon, Kenzie, Lieam, and Sadie, led by Celanawe, the legendary Black Axe—traverse the snow-blanketed territories acting as diplomats to improve relations between the mouse cities and the Guard, and find themselves on a race against time to deliver crucial medicines." (Publisher's note)

Mouse guard; 3: The Black Axe. By David Petersen. Archaia Entertainment, LLC 2013 192 p.
Grades: 5 6 7 8   **741.5; Fic**
1. Adventure fiction; 2. Fantasy fiction; 3. Mice — Fiction
1936393069; 9781936393060, $24.95
Harvey Award: Best Graphic Album of Previously Published Work (2014)

This book, by David Petersen, part of the Eisner Award-winning fantasy comic series, tells "the tale of wise oldfur and longtime Mouse Guard member Celanawe, as he fulfills the promise made to young Lieam to detail the day his paw first touched the legendary weapon, the Black Axe. The arrival of distant kin takes Celanawe on an adventure that will carry him across the sea to uncharted waters and lands, all while unraveling the legend of Farrer, the blacksmith who forged the mythical weapon." (Publisher's note)

"[N]ewcomers and fans alike will find much to explore in Petersen's finely wrought artwork, high-stakes intrigue, and derring-do tale." Booklist

Mouse guard; volume 1: legends of the guard. Jeremy Bastian, Ted Naifeh, Alex Sheikman, et al. Archaia Entertainment 2010 144 p. Color illustration
Grades: 5 6 7 8   **741.5**
1. Adventure fiction; 2. Mice — Fiction; 3. Short stories — Collections
1932386947; 9781932386943, $19.95
Eisner Award: Best Anthology (2011)

"Petersen turns to the tested and reliable bar story as a framing device to allow other writers and artists to play in his Mouse Guard universe, where heroic mice heroes are set in a world of epic fantasy. . . . One night barkeep June . . . stages a story-telling contest. What follows are thirteen tales of danger and adventure, as protagonists contend against the predators around them and the flaws that divide mouse from mouse." (Publisher's note)

"More than just supplemental material, this book broadens Petersen's magnificently imagined miniature world and is a welcome addition for any collection that values quality, all-ages graphic novels." Booklist

Mouse guard; volume 2: legends of the guard. Archaia Entertainment 2010 144 p. Color; Illustration
Grades: 5 6 7 8   **741.5**
1. Adventure fiction; 2. Mice — Fiction; 3. Short stories — Collections
1936393263; 9781936393268, $19.95
Eisner Nominee: Best Publication for Kids (2014)
Harvey Nominee: Best Anthology (2014)
Harvey Nominee: Best Continuing or Limited Series (2014)

"Inside the June Alley Inn, located in the western mouse city of Barkstone, mice gather to tell tales, each trying to outdo the other. A competition, of sorts, begins. The rules: Every story must contain one truth, one lie, and have never been told in that tavern before. With the winner getting his bar tab cleared, fantastic stories are spun throughout the evening!" (Publisher's note)

"The art styles of the ensuing stories are all over the map, from the elegant, tapestry-worthy The Battle of the Hawk's Mouse & the Fox's Mouse, by Jeremy Bastian, to the joltingly cartoony A Mouse Named Fox, from Katie Cook. In substance, the stories are equally varied, but all champion the heroism of the noble mouse warriors and even include a couple clever takes on classics." Booklist

Peterson, Christine
The **U.S.** Constitution. Illustrated by Brian Bascle. Capstone Press 2009 32p. Illustration (Graphic library)
Grades: 3 4 5 6 7 8   **342; 741.5**

1. United States — Constitution; 2. United States — Politics and government; 3. Graphic novels
978-1-4296-1984-4, $32
          LC 2008-487
This graphic format book uses irreverently humorous captions and dialog and provides young readers with an introduction to the U. S. Constitution. The book covers how and why it was written, how the Bill of Rights came to be, describes the three branches of government, how amendments are passed, and how the country protects the Constitution. It includes a short timeline, a glossary, and a list of books for further reading.
Part of the Graphic Library Cartoon Nation series

Peterson, Scott
Batman Adventures Vol. 1: Rogues' Gallery. DC Comics 2004 112p. Illustration
Grades: 4 5 6 7 8 9   **741.5; Fic**
1. Batman (Fictional character); 2. Catwoman (Fictional character); 3. Joker (Fictional character); 4. Superhero graphic novels; 5. Graphic novels
9781401203290, $6.95
Gotham City's greatest villains, including the Joker, Harley Quinn, Catwoman, the Penguin, Poison Ivy, and Ra's al Ghul, all take their turn against the World's Greatest Detective. Crime never sleeps, and neither does Batman.

Petrucha, Stefan
Nancy Drew vol. 12: dress reversal. Art by Sho Murase. NBM/Papercutz 2008 Un Illustration
Grades: 3 4 5 6 7 8   **741.5; Fic**
1. Adventure graphic novels; 2. Drew, Nancy (Fictional character); 3. Mystery graphic novels; 4. Graphic novels
978-1-59707-086-6, $7.95
Nancy buys a fancy formal dress for a charity fundraiser, but when she and her friends Bess and George arrive at Deirdre Shannon's house for the event, they discover that Deirdre and Nancy are wearing the same dress. This is bad for Deirdre, who is already jealous of Nancy. Then, when Nancy leaves the party, Bess and George watch helplessly as Nancy is kidnapped. Can they solve the mystery without Nancy?

Nancy Drew, girl detective #15: Tiger counter. Stefan Petrucha & Sarah Kinney, writers ; Sho Murase, artist. Papercutz 2008 Un Illustration
Grades: 3 4 5 6 7 8 9   **741.5; Fic**
1. Drew, Nancy (Fictional character); 2. Mystery graphic novels; 3. Tigers; 4. Graphic novels
978-1-59707-119-2, $12.95; 978-1-59707-118-5 (pa), $7.95
Due to a lack of mysteries to keep them occupied, Nancy, Bess, and George have been volunteering at the River Heights Animal Protection Center, where Jack Kingsley has been rescuing wild animals. They get a rescue call, only to find that old Mrs. Eartha has a house full of cats. Then, while driving back to town, they come upon a wrecked truck, and the driver says he was transporting a tiger that escaped. Jack hunts it with a tranquilizer gun, but Nancy soon finds more tiger tracks. Just how many tigers were in that truck, and why were they being transported to River Heights?

Nancy Drew, Girl Detective #1: The Demon of River Heights. Stefan Petrucha, writer ; Sho Murase, artist. NBM/Papercutz 2005 Un Illustration
Grades: 4 5 6 7 8 9   741.5; Fic
1. Adventure graphic novels; 2. Mystery graphic novels; 3. Graphic novels
1-59707-004-1, $12.95; 1-59707-000-9, $7.95
Everyone's favorite girl detective makes her graphic novel debut. Nancy also makes her debut in a horror film concerning a monstrous River Heights urban legend "but is it really an urban legend, or does the River Heights Demon truly exist?" And will Nancy, Bess, and George live long enough to find out? This graphic novel series updates Nancy and her friends to the twenty-first century, but she's still a klutz.

Nancy Drew: Girl Detective #2: Writ in Stone. Stefan Petrucha, writer ; Sho Murase, artist. NBM/Papercutz 2005 112p. Illustration
Grades: 3 4 5 6 7 8 9   741.5; Fic
1. Drew, Nancy (Fictional character); 2. Mystery graphic novels; 3. Graphic novels
978-1-59707-006-5, $12.95; 978-1-59707-002-7 (pb)
It's double trouble for America's favorite girl detective when Owen Zucker, a sweet young boy Nancy has often babysat, is missing and " a shore stone marker found on the coast of California, which may prove the Chinese discovered America in 1421, before Columbus, is stolen. Will Nancy, with the help of her best friends, Bess and George, be able to solve two baffling mysteries at the same time, while all of River Heights is watching?

Nancy Drew: Girl Detective #3: The Haunted Dollhouse. Sho Murase, artist. NBM/Papercutz 2005 112p. Illustration
Grades: 3 4 5 6 7 8 9   741.5; Fic
1. Drew, Nancy (Fictional character); 2. Mystery graphic novels; 3. Graphic novels
978-1-59707-009-6, $12.95; 978-1-59707-008-9 (pb)
River Heights is celebrating 'Nostalgia Week' and everyone in town is dressing up and acting like it was 1930 - including Nancy, Bess, and George. Nancy even drives a roadster (just as the original Nancy Drew did in the novels 75 years before). But when scenes of crimes displayed in Emma Blavatsky's antique dollhouse start coming true, Nancy has a full-blown mystery on her hands. Nancy's shocked when she stakes out the dollhouse, and witnesses a doll version of herself murdered. Will that scene become reality too?

Nancy Drew: Girl Detective #4: The Girl Who Wasn't There. Sho Murase, artist. NBM/Papercutz 2005 112p. Illustration
Grades: 3 4 5 6 7 8 9   741.5; Fic
1. Drew, Nancy (Fictional character); 2. Mystery graphic novels; 3. Graphic novels
978-1-59707-013-3, $12.95; 978-1-59707-012-2 (pb)
Nancy gets a call for help late one night from a girl she befriended over the phone when getting technical support to help fix her computer. When the line goes dead, Nancy is determined to get to the bottom of things. Soon, Nancy, her Dad, and friends George and Bess are on their way to India to find Kalpana, the girl who wasn't there. Then Nancy is captured by Sahadev the crime lord, who wants to sacrifice her to Kali.

Nancy Drew: Girl Detective #5: The Fake Heir. Stefan Petrucha, writer ; Daniel Vaughn Ross, artist. NBM/Papercutz 2006 112p. Illustration
Grades: 3 4 5 6 7 8 9   741.5; Fic
1. Drew, Nancy (Fictional character); 2. Mystery graphic novels; 3. Graphic novels
978-1-59707-025-6, $12.95; 978-1-59707-024-9 (pb)
Nancy, Bess and George find the wreck of an old yacht with a safe inside full of jewelry worth a small fortune. Jack and Amelia Druthers, who were clients of Nancy's dad Carson Drew, owned the yacht. Their will leaves everything to Anton Druthers, specifically excluding his wife Tanya (whom the cousins hated), but no one's seen him for ten years and the rumor is that Mrs. Druthers murdered him. Things take a surprising turn when suddenly Mr. Druthers reappears. But then Mrs. Druthers disappears. Can Nancy Drew solve the mystery of the fake heir" And what does that spider bite have to do with anything?

Nancy Drew: Girl Detective #6: Mr. Cheeters is Missing. Stefan Petrucha, writer ; Sho Murase, artist. NBM/Papercutz 2006 112p. Illustration
Grades: 3 4 5 6 7 8 9   741.5; Fic
1. Drew, Nancy (Fictional character); 2. Mystery graphic novels; 3. Graphic novels
978-1-59707-031-7, $12.95; 978-1-59707-030-0 (pb)
When the eccentric Blanche Porter reports that her beloved Mr. Cheeters has vanished, it isn't a standard missing persons case. As Nancy Drew soon discovers, Mr. Cheeters is a pet chimp. Or is he" Based on a preliminary investigation and information obtained from Blanche's brother, Lawrence, the River Heights police dismiss the case as bogus, doubting that there ever was a Mr. Cheeters to begin with. But when Nancy Drew discovers there's a missing diamond necklace as well, she's on the case. Can Nancy, along with Bess and George, recover the great ape and the necklace, or has Blanche Porter made a monkey out of Nancy Drew?

Nancy Drew: Girl Detective #7: The Charmed Bracelet. Daniel Vaughn Ross, artist. NBM/Papercutz 2006 112p. Illustration
Grades: 3 4 5 6 7 8 9   741.5; Fic
1. Drew, Nancy (Fictional character); 2. Mystery graphic novels; 3. Graphic novels
978-1-59707-037-9, $12.95; 978-1-59707-036-2 (pb)
Ned Nickerson has been arrested for shoplifting, and Nancy Drew is threatened with a lawsuit. A rare computer chip has been stolen from Rackham Industries. It all gets even more exciting when Nancy receives a mysterious charm bracelet in the mail - and soon a crime is committed for each charm. Will Nancy, even with the help of Bess and George, be able to find the real culprit and save Ned?

Nancy Drew: Girl Detective #8: Global Warning. Stefan Petrucha, writer ; Sho Murase, artist. NBM/Papercutz 2006 112p. Illustration
Grades: 3 4 5 6 7 8 9   741.5; Fic
1. Drew, Nancy (Fictional character); 2. Mystery graphic novels; 3. Graphic novels
978-1-59707-052-2, $12.95; 978-1-59707-051-5 (pb)

At a new Bio-Dome facility in River Heights, Nancy, Bess, and George get swept up in a mystery involving five different world environments encased within giant domes, animals and all. It's founded and funded by famed environmentalist billionaire, Cheri Goale. But before the Bio-Dome officially opens, a gross green substance destroys one of the domes and Sasquatch appears within the Arctic dome, creating havoc and endangering the future of the facility. Nancy Drew investigates, but is soon trapped within the dome with the legendary Bigfoot.

Nancy Drew: Girl Detective #9: Ghost in the Machinery. Sho Murase, artist. NBM/Papercutz 2007 112p. Illustration
Grades: 3 4 5 6 7 8 9   **741.5; Fic**
  1. Drew, Nancy (Fictional character); 2. Mystery graphic novels; 3. Graphic novels
  978-1-59707-061-4, $12.95; 978-1-59707-058-4 (pb), $7.95
On a mission sponsored by young, rich, and handsome Ralph Credo, Nancy teams up with eccentric scientist Roy Hinkley to find an amazing high efficiency engine able to operate at an amazing 200 miles per gallon. The experimental engine, mounted on a tank, was part of an experiment during the final days of World War II. There's just one problem, the engine and the tank are haunted. "Ghost In The Machinery" is the first in a series of three Nancy Drew adventures entitled "The High Miles Mystery."

Nancy Drew: Girl Detective Vol. 10: The Disoriented Express. Stefan Petrucha & Sarah Kinney, writers ; Sho Murase, artist. NBM/Papercutz 2007 Un Illustration
Grades: 4 5 6 7 8 9   **741.5; Fic**
  1. Drew, Nancy (Fictional character); 2. Mystery graphic novels; 3. Graphic novels
  978-1-59707-066-9, $7.95
On its journey to Professor Hinkley's research facility, Nancy Drew must protect an amazing creation that could possibly end the world's energy crisis. Unstable and dangerous, the super fuel-efficient engine must be transported by a private train. But dark forces are at work, attempting to shanghai the miracle machine - literally at every turn by using computers to jam the switches. But while Nancy, and her friend George, attempt to determine which sinister suspect is behind these despicable acts, they soon realize that if their adversaries can't succeed at stealing this miraculous machine, they'll destroy the train, along with everything, and everyone on it. "The Disoriented Express" is the second in a series of three Nancy Drew adventures entitled "The High Miles Mystery.

Petty, Kate
  Julius Caesar: The Life of a Roman General. Gary Jeffrey & Kate Petty ; illustrated by Sam Hadley. Rosen Publishing Group 2005 48p. Illustration
Grades: 3 4 5 6 7 8   **741.5; 937**
  1. Biographical graphic novels; 2. Caesar, Julius, 100 or 102 - 44 BC; 3. Rome — History — Republic, 265-30 BC; 4. Graphic novels
  1-4042-0239-0, $29.25
                                    LC 2004014392
  Ambitious, ruthless, shrewd, cruel, and intelligent are a few of the words that have been used to describe this man

who changed the course of civilization. Caesar's military conquests and political alliances altered Rome's decaying system of government, producing the greatest of all ancient empires. This graphic novel takes readers on a journey to the ancient world where political intrigue and military might gave birth not only to the rise of Caesar but also to his bloody assassination. The book includes some information on what came after his death, a glossary, and a list of books for further reading.
  Part of the Graphic Nonfiction series.

Peyo
  The **purple** smurfs. By Yvan Delporte and Peyo. Papercutz 2010 55p. Color; Illustration
Grades: 1 2 3 4
741.5
  1-59707-206-0;
  978-1-59707-206-9, $5.99;
  978-1-59707-207-6, $10.99; 1-59707-207-9
  1. Smurfs (Fictional characters)

Courtesy of Papercutz

  "[T]his previously untranslated version of the [Smurfs'] first solo collection (1963) offers three tales: A fly's contagious bite turns nearly all of the Smurfs into aggressive purple grunters. . .; one Smurf's determination to fly results in multiple crashes and calamities; another's desire to find peace and quiet away from Smurf Village runs afoul of a mosquito and other hazards. Replete with pratfalls, butt-biting and like slapstick, the neatly squared-off comic-strip-style panels look small at first glance, but coated paper and high production values make both the dialogue and the brightly colored art easy to read." (Kirkus Reviews)
  Translated from the French
  Other titles in this series are: The Smurfs and the magic flute (2010); The Smurf king (2010); The Smurfs (2011); The Smurfs and the egg (2011); The Smurfs and the howlibird (2011); Astrosmurf (2011); The smurf apprentice (2011); Gargamel and the Smurfs (2011); The return of the Smurfette (2012); The Smurf Olympics (2012); Smurf vs. Smurf (2012); Smurf soup (2012); The baby Smurf (2013); The Smurflings (2013); The Aerosmurf (2013); The Smurfs Christmas (2013)

  The **Smurfs** anthology; Vol. 1. Peyo. Papercutz 2013 190 p. Color illustration (The Smurfs graphic novels)
Grades: 4 5 6 7 8 9 10 11 12 Adult   **741.5**
  1597074179; 9781597074179, $19.99
  1. Smurfs (Fictional characters)
  "Newly remastered and presented in original publication order, along with a Smurfy collection of historical notes and photographs, the stories in this volume," by Belgian comics artist Peyo, "introduce us to Papa Smurf, Gargamel, Smurfette, and the rest of the village." (Publisher's note)

The **Smurfs** anthology; Vol. 2. Peyo. Papercutz 2013 192 p. Color illustration

Grades: 4 5 6 7 8 9 10 11 12 Adult **741.5**

1597074454; 9781597074452, $19.99

1. Smurfs (Fictional characters)

"Newly remastered and presented in original publication order, along with a Smurfy collection of historical notes and photographs, this volume," by Belgian comics artist Peyo, "introduces us to Smurfette and features a 'Johan and Peewit' story never before seen in the U.S." (Publisher's note)

"[A] delightful and instructive mix of Peyo's colorful tales. A series of essays interspersed throughout the collection provides social and historical context for the cartoons." Booklist

Translated from the French

Phelan, Matt

★ **Bluffton:** my summers with Buster Keaton. Written and illustrated by Matt Phelan. Candlewick Press 2013 240 p. Color; Illustration

Grades: 3 4 5 6 **741.5; Fic**

1. Keaton, Buster; 2. Vaudeville — Fiction

076365079X; 9780763650797, $22.99

LC 2012947260

In this graphic novel by Matt Phelan, set "in the summer of 1908, in Muskegon, Michigan, a visiting troupe of vaudeville performers is about the most exciting thing since baseball. Henry has a few months to ogle . . . a slapstick actor his own age named Buster Keaton. Henry longs to learn to take a fall like Buster . . . but Buster just wants to play ball with Henry and his friends." (Publisher's note)

"Historical detail, a rich sense of place, expert pacing—Phelan . . . keeps all the plates in the air in this fictionalized recreation of the boyhood summers of Buster Keaton. In lightly sketched, gently tinted watercolor panels, Phelan conveys the excitement a troupe of summering vaudeville actors brings to sleepy Bluffton." Pub Wkly

★ The **storm** in the barn. Candlewick Press 2009 201p. Illustration

Grades: 4 5 6 7 8 9 **741.5; Fic**

1. Adventure graphic novels; 2. Dust storms; 3. Kansas; 4. Monsters; 5. United States — History — 1933-1945; 6. Graphic novels

978-0-7636-3618-0, $24.99; 0-7636-3618-5; 978-0-7636-5290-6 (pa), $14.99; 0-7636-5290-3 (pa)

In Kansas of 1937, the land has been in the grip of the Dust Bowl for four years, and eleven-year-old Jack Carter has seen his family worn down by it. But the day Jack outruns a dust storm all the way home from town, he glimpses something odd in the abandoned Talbot barn, and he tries to find the courage to go into the barn and confront what is there.

"Children can read this as a work of historical fiction, a piece of folklore, a scary story, a graphic novel, or all four. Written with simple, direct language, it—s an almost wordless book: the illustrations" shadowy grays and blurry lines eloquently depict the haze of the dust. A complex but accessible and fascinating book." SLJ

Pien, Lark

★ **Long** Tail Kitty. By Lark Pien. Blue Apple Books 2009 51 p. Color illustration

Grades: 1 2 3 4 **741.5**

1. Cats — Fiction; 2. Humorous graphic novels; 3. Neighborhoods — Fiction

9781934706442, $17.99; 2008042448

"Long Tail Kitty narrates five episodes of his daily life. First he introduces his house and his town, including landmarks from each of his tales. He picks flowers, finds they can talk and plays chase with a bee. In winter he slides on the ice and has cocoa with Good Tall Mouse. He hosts a food fest with friends and refrains from eating all the Choco Crispy Doggy Discs. Finally, he spends an activity-filled day with buddies from outer space." (Kirkus Reviews)

"The volume's appeal lies in the tidy, thoughtfully shaded panels and the cast's playful banter and witty barbs." Horn Book

Long Tail Kitty, come out and play. Lark Pien. Blue Apple Books 2015 80 p. Color; Illustration

Grades: 1 2 3 4 **741.5; Fic**

1. Animals — Fiction; 2. Cats — Juvenile fiction; 3. Friendship — Fiction; 4. Friendship — Juvenile fiction; 5. Humorous graphic novels; 6. Jealousy — Juvenile fiction; 7. Graphic novels

9781609053949, $17.99; 160905394X

LC 2014045909

Author and illustrator "Lark Pien offers a companion book to 'Long Tail Kitty' with five new adventures featuring the eponymous feline and his whimsical gang of animal pals. Inter-friendship rivalries, woes, and jealousies fuel these gently humorous tales of the wise-beyond-his-furry-years Long Tail Kitty." (Publisher's note)

"Unfussy cartoon illustrations in a simple layout make this a good introduction to comics for young readers, and the action is comforting enough for a bedtime read. The watercolor illustrations depict a pastoral, dreamy land of rolling hills and cozy houses, in a primarily pastel palette evocative of cupcake frostings." SLJ

Piotrowski, Robert

D-Day. Art by Drew Ng. Harcourt Achieve/Steck-Vaughn 2007 48p. Illustration

Grades: 3 4 5 6 7 8 **741.5; 940.54; Fic**

1. World War, 1939-1945 — Amphibious operations; 2. Graphic novels

978-1-4190-3221-9, $8.99

On June 6, 1944, the greatest attack of World War II is about to begin; the invasion of Nazi territory by Allied forces. The battle will test the courage of young men as never before. Are they ready? The book includes battle violence and shows men dying in action. This historical graphic novel includes prose intervals that provide more information about D-Day and the various elements of the battle, including the paratrooper attack, the aerial attacks, and information about the German army.

Part of the Timeline Graphic Novels series.

Gold Rush. Art by Jeff Alward. Harcourt Achieve/Steck-Vaughn 2007 48p. Illustration

Grades: 3 4 5 6 7 8 **741.5; Fic**

1. Adventure graphic novels; 2. Klondike (Yukon) — Gold discoveries; 3. Graphic novels

978-1-4190-3210-3, $8.99

Jonathan Samuels is a young farmer whose hopes are dashed when a girl rejects him for a wealthy rival. When he hears of gold in the Klondike, Jonathan sets out with dreams of striking it rich. Does he have what it takes to succeed? This historical fiction graphic novel includes prose intervals that provide more information about the Klondike gold rush of 1896-1899 and what life was like in Dawson City at that time.

Part of the Timeline Graphic Novels series.

Piscopo, Jay

The **undersea** adventures of Capt'n Eli, vol. 2: the mystery of the Sargasso Sea. Nemo Publishing 2008 112p. Illustration

Grades: 3 4 5 6 7 8

741.5; Fic

1. Adventure graphic novels; 2. Science fiction graphic novels; 3. Graphic novels

978-0-9817132-1-2, $9.99

As Professor Wow and the Seasearchers continue their work on the ocean surface, trying to keep people away from the time anomaly, Eli, his dog Barney, and the 200-year-old parrot Jolly Roger travel with Commander X to the undersea city of Aquaria. There, Eli learns of the ancient undersea civilizations of Lemuria and Atlantis, and the origin of the Hydrons that attacked him. Then Aquaria comes under attack, and Commander X leads the defense. King Aquarius dies trying to protect his city, his son Triton is injured and in a coma, and that leaves Coral, daughter of King Aquarius, to rule. Commander X and Eli learn that the son of an old enemy has tricked Coral and the Aquarians into thinking he saved them from destruction. Now they need to sneak into Aquarius to save Coral and find a way to stop Baal's nefarious plot.

Courtesy of Nemo Publishing

The **undersea** adventures of Capt'n Eli, volume 1. Nemo Publishing 2008 104p. Illustration

Grades: 2 3 4 5 6 7

741.5; Fic

1. Adventure graphic novels; 2. Ocean; 3. Graphic novels

978-0-9817132-0-5, $9.99

Eli is a boy of mysterious origins, who surfaced from the ocean in a technologically advanced pod near the island of Eagle Rock, off the coast of Maine. The lighthouse keeper and his wife recover the pod and raise the baby they find inside, naming him Eli. The boy proves to be highly intelligent beyond his

Courtesy of Nemo Publishing

years, and able to design and build inventions, ranging from a root beer machine to a miniature submarine. While still a preteen boy, Eli saves a U.S. Navy submarine when it runs into trouble undersea (with the help of the mysterious Commander X), and then he joins the Seasearchers, a marine research group. They set out to investigate the latest disappearance of a ship in the Sargasso Sea, only to run into trouble with something that sends them back in time to around 1492. When hostile minisubs that resemble fish attack Eli in his minisub, the Dolphin, Commander X rescues him again. Cmdr X is very much like Captain Nemo from Jules Verne's 20,000 Leagues Under the Sea, although he also once was a superhero who fought alongside the Allies during World War II. Eli is the namesake of Capt'n Eli Forsley, a WWII veteran who also had his own brand of Capt'n Eli root beer in Maine; Eli's character design has been adapted from the soda's label. The book includes information about the ocean world that is incorporated into the story.

Plumeri, Arnaud

Dinosaurs 2: Bite of the Allosaurus. Bloz, art; Arnaud Plumeri, story; Maëla Cosson, colorist; Nanette McGuinness, translation. Papercutz 2014 56 p. Color; Illustration

Grades: 2 3 4 5   **567.9; 741.5**

1. Dinosaurs — Juvenile literature; 2. Paleontologists; 3. Graphic novels

1597075159; 9781597075152, $10.99

"When you're a dinosaur, there's only one thing to fear: the dinosaurs that are bigger than YOU! In the latest chapter of this thunderously funny series we find out how the giants among giants lived millions of years ago." (Publisher's note)

"For the sheer number of dinosaur names dropped, Plumeri and Bloz' series is impressive, but they deserve extra kudos for peppering the facts with jokey, sometimes crass visual humor, ensuring that the science goes down easy." Booklist

Translated from the French

Dinosaurs; 1: In the Beginning. Arnaud Plumeri, illustrated by Bloz. Papercutz 2014 56 p. Color; Illustration

Grades: 2 3 4 5   **741.5; 567.9**

1. Dinosaurs — Juvenile literature; 2. Paleontology — Juvenile literature

159707490X; 9781597074902, $10.99

In this book, by Arnaud Plumeri and illustrated by Bloz, "kid dinos show us what their lives were like in short, funny, teeth-gnashing bursts of prehistoric mayhem. DINOSAURS is your guided tour through the rough-and-tumble world of the mightiest beasts to ever walk the earth!" (Publisher's note)

"Each brief vignette is a winning combination of colorful dinosaurs, chuckle-worthy jokes, paleontology facts, and well-explained terminology." Booklist

Originally published in France

Other titles in this series are: Bite of the Albertosaurus; Jurassic smarts

Poe, Marshall

Turning points: a house divided. Illustrated by Leland Purvis. Aladdin Paperbacks 2008 122p. Illustration

Grades: 3 4 5 6 7 8
741.5; Fic
1. Abolitionists; 2. United States — History — 1815-1861; 3. Graphic novels
978-1-4169-5057-8, $8.99

LC 2008-929317

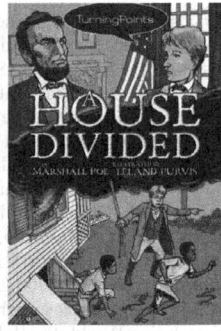

Courtesy of Aladdin Press

Owen and Amos Bennington's abolitionist parents are killed in 1856, and the brothers vow to continue their parents' quest to end slavery. However, younger brother Amos thinks the abolitionists aren't doing enough, while Owen works for a peaceful, political solution. When they move to Kansas, things don't go as planned, as proslavery people use violence to get their way. When Owen wants to move back East, Amos runs away and joins John Brown's forces, who fight against slavery with force. Owen moves to Illinois and works for Abraham Lincoln. Amos finally realizes that Brown's way is wrong and leaves just before the attempted takeover of Harper's Ferry; he makes his way across the land slowly, hoping against hope that he can find Owen again. This fictional story highlights the years leading up to the Civil War, showing a private, personal side of Lincoln and letting younger readers see the kinds of divisions suffered by many families as they debated and argued the cause of abolition or slavery, and of political action or force to end slavery.

Turning Points: Little Rock nine. Illustrated by Ellen Lindner. Simon & Schuster/Aladdin Paperbacks 2008 122p. Illustration
Grades: 3 4 5 6 7 8 9   **741.5; Fic**
1. African Americans — Civil rights; 2. African Americans — Education; 3. United States — History — 1953-1961; 4. Graphic novels
978-1-4169-5066-0, $7.99

LC 2007-937918

Sixteen-year-old William McNally and fifteen-year-old Thomas Johnson both live in Little Rock, Arkansas, in the summer of 1957. They both love baseball and teasing their little sisters. There's just one big difference: William is white, and Thomas, the son of the McNally family's maid, is black. After the U.S. Supreme Court rules in favor of desegregating public schools, Little Rock Central High School prepares to enroll its first nine African-American students, and William and Thomas are caught in the middle of a storm. William's family is divided over the issue, and Thomas' parents don't want him to get hurt and forbid him to try to enter the school. The book portrays the issues of the time and the personal beliefs of both sides to let readers see what it was like back then. William, Thomas, and their families are fictional, but what happened at Little Rock Central High School is an important part of American history.

Poon, Janice
    Claire and the water wish. Written and illustrated by Janice Poon. Kids Can Press 2009 120p. Illustration

Grades: 2 3 4 5 6   **741.5; Fic**
1. Mystery graphic novels; 2. Pollution; 3. Graphic novels
978-1-55453-381-7, $15.95; 978-1-55453-382-4 (pa), $7.95

LC C2008-903252-7

Summer is over, and Claire must start at a new school, so she's glad to have her friend Jet with her. However, Jet has become obsessed with entering a contest to win a digital camera, and when she does win it, she spends more time with the popular kids at school. Feeling a bit left out, Claire makes friends with Sky, who lives near Lovesick Lake. When they team up for a science project, Sky tells Claire that the adults in her community believe the lake is making people sick; they believe someone is dumping waste into the lake, but they haven't been able to catch anyone. Then, when Claire and Jet visit Lovesick Lake with Sky, they stumble into a bad situation. Maybe Jet's obsession with her new camera will pay off for the girls.

Powell, Martin
    Red Riding Hood: the graphic novel. Retold by Martin Powell; illustrated by Victor Rivas. Stone Arch Books 2009 40p.
Grades: 2 3 4 5 6 7   **741.5; Fic**
1. Fairy tales; 2. Graphic novels
978-1-4342-0769-2, $21.26

LC 2008-6723

In Transylvania, where many dangers lurk, a fortune teller gives Ruby's grandmother a special wool to make a garment to protect her life. Ruby receives a special red riding hood and cloak for her birthday, and she sets out through the woods to visit her grandmother. There she encounters a wolf who tricks her into telling where her grandmother lives. By the time Ruby reaches her grandmother's cottage, something else waits for her in grandmother's bed. This graphic novel adaptation of the old tale includes some different details from the most wellknown versions. The book includes a brief history of the tale, including the version by Perrault and the most famous one by the Brothers Grimm.
Part of the Graphic Spin series

    Rumpelstiltskin: the graphic novel. Retold by Martin Powell; illustrated by Erik Valdez y Alanis. Stone Arch Books 2009 40p. Illustration
Grades: 2 3 4 5 6 7   **741.5; Fic**
1. Fairy tales; 2. Graphic novels
978-1-4342-0768-5, $21.26

LC 2008-6724

When Mirabelle's father, who owes a large debt, claims that she can spin straw into gold, she haplessly goes along with the lie to save her father. An evil troll helps her accomplish the impossible task, for a price. When the king gets greedy for more gold, the troll asks for a much higher price; when a year is up, Mirabelle must guess the creature's name, or give up her child. This graphic novel adaptation provides a brief history of the tale, tracing it back much farther than the Brothers Grimm, who popularized it.
Part of the Graphic Spin series

    Sleeping Beauty: the graphic novel. Retold by Martin Powell ; illustrated by Sean Dietrich. Stone Arch Books 2009 40p. Illustration
Grades: 3 4 5 6 7 8   **741.5; Fic**

1. Fairy tales; 2. Sleeping Beauty — Adaptations; 3. Graphic novels
978-1-4342-1193-4, $21.26; 978-1-4342-1393-8 (pa), $4.95

LC 2008-32048

This graphic novel adaptation of the Sleeping Beauty story features a wise old fish who speaks to the queen before she gets pregnant with her daughter, and zombie knights who try to stop the prince from breaking the sleep spell that holds Princess Rose and everyone in the kingdom. The rest of the story follows the traditional versions—the wicked thirteenth fairy proclaims a curse that the newborn princess will die on her fifteenth birthday, the last of the good fairies mitigates the curse to a century-long sleep, the means of completing the curse is the princess pricking her finger on a spindle, everyone in the castle falls asleep, and thorny briars cover the castle. The book includes information about Perrault's original story and some of the other media adaptations. The art is very idiosyncratic, a bit dark, and the zombie knights will appeal more to boys than the girls who are the usual audience for the fairy tale.
Part of the Graphic Spin series.

Snow White: the graphic novel. Retold by Martin Powell ; illustrated by Erik Valdez y Alanis. Stone Arch Books 2009 40p. Illustration
Grades: 3 4 5 6 7 8   **741.5; Fic**
1. Fairy tales; 2. Folklore — Germany; 3. Graphic novels
978-1-4342-1192-7, $21.26; 978-1-4342-1394-5 (pa), $4.95

LC 2008-32049

In this graphic novel version of the fairy tale, the wicked Queen Mara traps Prince Marco within her magic mirror, and Snow White is a lovely young woman who lives alone. When the queen sends a wolf to kill Snow White, the girl stops the wolf, but she must find new shelter with her home destroyed. She finds a cavern, and there the dwarfs say they had a dream that they must protect her. As with the other graphic novel adaptations of fairy tales in the Graphic Spin series, the color palette is darker, the art may be spookier than most younger children would like. The book includes information about the origins of the fairy tale and why the dwarfs only have names in the Disney animated movie.
Part of the Graphic Spin series.

The **Swiss** family Robinson. By Johann D. Wyss; retold by Martin Powell; illustrated by Gerardo Sandoval.. Stone Arch Books 2009 74p. Illustration
Grades: 4 5 6 7 8 9 10   **741.5; Fic**
1. Adventure graphic novels; 2. Shipwrecks; 3. Survival after airplane accidents, shipwrecks, etc; 4. Wyss, Johann David, 1743-1818 — Adaptations
978-1-4342-0756-2, $23.93

LC 2008-6249

In the early nineteenth century, a Swiss family survives a shipwreck and land on a deserted island. They build a life for themselves there, salvaging materials from the wrecked ship and using the plants and other things they find on the island. However, some of the creatures living on the island could be deadly. This graphic novel adaptation of Wyss's classic adventure novel includes information about real-life castaways and uninhabited islands. An interesting note, the

novel has never been out of print for almost 200 years and has gone through almost 200 editions.
Part of the Graphic Revolve series

Preciado, Tony
Super grammar: learn grammar with superheroes. Written by Tony Preciado; illustrated by Rhode Montijo; colored by Jenny Hansen; inked by Joe To. Scholastic 2012 176 p. Color illustration (Illustrating the point)
Grades: 4 5 6 7 8   **428**
1. English language — Grammar — Juvenile fiction; 2. English language — Grammar — Juvenile literature; 3. Superheroes — Juvenile fiction
0545425158; 9780545425155, $8.99

LC 2012289091

In this book by Tony Preciado, illustrated by Rhode Montijo, "all of the major elements of grammar . . . [are] personified with superhero or super villain identities. . . . You'll meet the vibrant super heroine The Adverb, and you'll learn about her awesome ability to modify verbs and other adverbs. . . . You'll actually meet the sinister twin brothers, Double Negative, and you'll learn how to avoid being tricked into falling for their double talk." (Publisher's note)

Priddy, Joel
The **gift** of the Magi. It Books/HarperCollins 2009 Un Illustration
Grades: 5 6 7 8 9 10 11 12 Adult   **741.5; Fic**
1. Christmas; 2. Gifts; 3. Henry, O, 1862-1910 — Adaptations; 4. Graphic novels
978-0-06-178239-8, $14.99

Della and Jim are a young married couple, struggling to make ends meet when Jim's pay has been cut. It's Christmas time, but despite squeezing every penny, Della has managed to save only a little bit of money, and it's not enough to buy Jim a good present. He owns a gold pocket watch, and Della wants to buy him a chain for it. She has only one thing of value that she can sell her beautiful, long, long hair. Out of her love for Jim, Della sacrifices her hair. And, of course, Jim has sacrificed his gold pocket watch in order to buy beautiful hair combs for Della's gorgeous hair. As O. Henry says, they "most unwisely sacrificed for each other the greatest treasures of their house," but also that "of all who give gifts these two were the wisest." Joel Priddy's adaptation of this classic story uses black and white illustrations except when Della lets down her hair to consider her one treasure. He preserves much of O. Henry's original prose, which means that younger readers will have to look up a lot of words to understand the story. This book is suitable for younger readers but will also appeal to teens and adults.

Proimos, James
Swim! Swim!: Lerch. Scholastic Press 2010 Un Illustration
Grades: PreK K 1   **741.5; Fic**
1. Friendship; 2. Goldfish; 3. Humorous graphic novels; 4. Graphic novels
978-0-545-09419-1, $16.99

LC 2009-20520

Lerch the goldfish is lonely in his fish tank, so he sets out to find a friend. First he swims, saying "Swim! Swim!" until he comes to the pebbles at the bottom of his tank. They don't respond, so he swims around to the deep sea diver figure and to the bubbler. Just when he realizes he is all alone, there's someone outside the tank it's a cat who calls him "Lunch." Uh-oh. Or maybe not, in a cute twist ending. Proimos and Scholastic have put Lerch on the book cover and in the CIP as the author.

Pyle, Kevin C.
  Blindspot. Henry Holt & Company 2007 Un Illustration
Grades: 5 6 7 8 9 10 11 12 Adult   **741.5; Fic**
  1. Friendship; 2. Graphic novels
  978-0-8050-7998-2 (pa), $13.95; 0-8050-7998-X (pa)
                                      LC 2006041155
Dean and his friends have created an entire world in the woods behind their suburban housing development. In their army fantasy, they're at war, and Dean is the daring captain leading his troops through episodes of intrigue and danger. But no fantasy can last forever. A run-in with a homeless man in the woods snaps the boys back to reality, and little by little the real world pervades their imagined universe and drives them apart.

  Take what you can carry. Kevin C. Pyle. Henry Holt and Co. 2012 176 p. Illustration; Color
Grades: 4 5 6   **741.5**
  1. Japanese Americans — Evacuation and relocation, 1942-1945; 2. Shoplifting; 3. Teenagers
  0805082867; 9780805082869, $12.99
                                      LC 2011924430
In this graphic novel, in "1977 suburban Chicago, Kyle runs wild with his friends and learns to shoplift from the local convenience store. In 1941 Berkeley, the Himitsu family is forced to leave their home for a Japanese-American internment camp, and their teenage son must decide how to deal with his new life. But though these boys are growing up in wildly different places and times, their lives intersect in more ways than one, as they discover compassion, learn loyalty, and find renewal." (Publisher's note)

Raicht, Mike
  Hulk: big green men. Mike Raicht, writer ; Alex Sanchez, pencils ; J. Rauch, colors ; Dave Sharpe, letters ; Shane Davis & J. Rauch, cover. ABDO Publishing Company/Spotlight 2006 Un Illustration
Grades: 4 5 6 7 8 9   **741.5; Fic**
  1. Hulk (Fictional character); 2. Superhero graphic novels; 3. Graphic novels
  1-59961-042-6, $21.35
                                      LC 2005-57558
When Bruce Banner finds himself in Roswell, he finds all the inhabitants wear strange collars and act spaced out—except for a teenage girl. What they don't know is that she's really a Skrull, as are her parents, and their people have finally come to rescue them. But now her family doesn't want to leave, and when the Skrulls hurt Bruce, he becomes The Hulk and rampages against the "little green men." This

is a revised, hardbound edition of the Marvel Age comic book.
Part of the Hulk series

  Hulk: The abomination. Mike Raicht, writer; Ryan Odagawa, pencils; J. Rauch, colors; Dave Sharpe, letters; Shane Davis & J. Rauch, cover.. ABDO Spotlight 2006 Un Illustration
Grades: 3 4 5 6 7 8 9   **741.5; Fic**
  1. Hulk (Fictional character); 2. Superhero graphic novels; 3. Graphic novels
  1-59961-045-0, $21.35
                                      LC 2005-57557
  Dr. Bruce Banner was conducting research on gamma rays when he was exposed and became the Hulk. However, he can return to his human form when he's not stressed or upset or angry. Emil Blonsky worked on the project, too, and after Banner left he tried to carry on the work and experimented on himself. However, he became a monster some call the Abomination, and in his anger over not being able to change back, he takes it out on towns, and people. He rampages in Texas, and Banner travels there in hopes of stopping him; but Blonsky only succeeds in causing Banner to turn into the Hulk. Young readers who have seen the new Incredible Hulk movie that premiered in June 2008 will know the Abomination from the movie.
  This is a revision of a Dec. 2004 issue of Incredible Hulk from the Marvel Age line.

  Spider-Man in Kraven the hunter. Stan Lee & Steve Ditko, plot ; Mike Raicht, script ; Jamal Igle, pencils ; Jay Leisten, inks ; Dave Sharpe, letters ; Larry Molinar, colors. ABDO Publishing Group/Spotlight 2006 Un Illustration
Grades: 3 4 5 6 7 8   **741.5; Fic**
  1. Spider-Man (Fictional character); 2. Superhero graphic novels; 3. Graphic novels
  1-59961-009-4, $21.35
  When Spider-Man defeats the Chameleon one too many times, the criminal calls in Kraven the Hunter to hunt and kill him. As a celebrity star of his own television show, Kraven makes a big splash with his arrival, and Peter Parker must take photographs for the Daily Bugle. Somehow, he's going to have to stop the hunter and the Chameleon.
  Part of the Marvel Age Spider-Man series.

  Spider-man: Spidey strikes back Vol. 1 digest. Mike Raicht and Todd Dezago. Marvel Comics 2005 96p. Illustration
Grades: 4 5 6 7 8 9   **741.5; Fic**
  1. Spider-Man (Fictional character); 2. Superhero graphic novels; 3. Graphic novels
  0-7851-1632-X, $5.99
  Tired of saving the day and getting no respect, Spider-Man considers taking a break from his superhero duties, which leaves the city wide open for the likes of the Sandman and the Enforcers. Will Spidey let it all go to pot, or will he step up to the plate and take one for the team? This volume collects Marvel Age Spider-Man issues 17-20. Previous volumes were published under the series title Marvel Age Spider-Man. The Marvel Age titles are being collected and published in the digest size, similar to manga, and at an affordable price. The Marvel Age series are aimed at younger audiences than the other superhero titles from Marvel.

Randall, Ron

Thor and Loki: In the Land of Giants. Lerner Publishing Group/Graphic Universe 2007 48p. Illustration
Grades: 3 4 5 6 7 8 9   **741.5; 398.2**
1. Loki (Norse deity); 2. Norse mythology; 3. Thor (Norse deity); 4. Graphic novels
978-0-8225-3087-9, $26.60 lib. Bdg.

Thor the powerful god of thunder, and his brother Loki, the trickster, are eager to solve an argument: does strength always win, or do brains always beat brawn? To find an answer, they travel to the strange and forbidding land of giants. There they face a series of challenges that will prove once and for all which god is right. Or will it?The book includes a glossary and a list of books for further reading.

Realbuzz Studios

Goofyfoot Gurl vol. 1: Let There be Lighten Up!. Thomas Nelson 2007 96p. Illustration
Grades: 5 6 7 8 9   **741.5**
1. Friendship; 2. Religion; 3. Surfing; 4. Graphic novels
978-1-59554-389-9, $10.99

Surfer girl Suki, called Goofyfoot for her right-foot-forward stance on her surfboard, and her friends hang out at the beach in Orange County, California. But everyone's got their own problems: a serious lack of funds, a new young stepmother, parents who are never around, and even the possibility of an arranged marriage. But Suki finds a way to bring some happiness and good times to her friends.

Serenity #1: Bad Girl in Town. Thomas Nelson 2007 96p. Illustration
Grades: 4 5 6 7 8 9   **741.5; Fic**
1. Friendship; 2. Graphic novels
978-1-59554-383-7, $9.99

Everyone needs a little Serenity—or do they" She's only five feet tall and 98 pounds - but she's one tense bundle of attitude and anger. Serenity's life is a mess on every front. Now she's got one last shot at a fresh start . . . but her new school seems to just be adding new problems. Being the New Kid" isn't making life any easier. But her friends might have just what she's been searching for - if they don't drive her crazy first, with their Christian beliefs. Can she be like them?

Serenity #2: Stepping Out. Thomas Nelson 2007 96p. Illustration
Grades: 5 6 7 8 9 10   **741.5; Fic**
1. Christian life; 2. Friendship; 3. Graphic novels
978-1-59554-384-4, $9.99

The Prayer Club kids are nice, but that doesn't mean they can't be tough. Serenity is starting to warm up to the Christian teens who made her their project" by showing her an unconditional love she's never experienced before. But when she tries ducking responsibility for wrecking Kimberly's car, that unconditional love turns tough. Can Serenity understand it's for her own good?

Serenity #3: Basket Case. Thomas Nelson 2007 96p. Illustration
Grades: 5 6 7 8 9 10   **741.5; Fic**
1. Christian life; 2. Friendship; 3. Graphic novels
978-1-59554-385-1, $9.99

Serenity laughs at responsibility, but there's nothing funny about this job ... She disses a health class assignment that has teens caring for chicken eggs 24/7 to simulate the round-the-clock nurturing a baby requires. But when an overwhelming responsibility falls in Serenity's lap, where can she get help - from the friends she has mocked, or the God she doesn't quite believe in?

Serenity #4: Rave-n-Rant. Thomas Nelson 2007 96p. Illustration
Grades: 5 6 7 8 9 10   **741.5; Fic**
1. Christian life; 2. Friendship; 3. Graphic novels
978-1-59554-386-8, $9.99

Serenity begins to share her soul with her Prayer Club friends, and is angered to find that, while they say they love Serenity, they don't always like her. The teen with the blue hair and attitude takes her frustrations to God, but soon decides He isn't listening ... until a surprise ending makes Serenity realize there may be something to prayer after all.

Serenity #5: Snow Biz. Thomas Nelson 2007 96p. Illustration
Grades: 5 6 7 8 9 10   **741.5; Fic**
1. Christian life; 2. Friendship; 3. Graphic novels
978-1-59554-387-5, $9.99

Serenity views a Prayer Club ski trip as one more opportunity to drive a wedge between Derek and Kimberly. But while hotdogging on the slopes, Serenity takes a major tumble, breaking her leg and seriously bruising her ego. Who's going to care for her wounds - both physical and spiritual?

Serenity #6: You Shall Love. Thomas Nelson 2007 96p. Illustration
Grades: 5 6 7 8 9 10   **741.5; Fic**
1. Christian life; 2. Friendship; 3. Graphic novels
978-1-59554-388-2, $9.99

A broken bone—and heart—finds Serenity at a major crossroad. Her leg's in a cast, the power's out, and Serenity's bored stiff. Searching for answers and willing to risk everything, Serenity picks up the Bible she received when she first visited the Prayer Club. Before long, she's pestering her friends with spiritual questions and getting serious about some major life changes. There's healing for the broken—and unexpected new challenges—in this story.

Reed, Gary

Mary Shelley's Frankenstein: the graphic novel. Art by Frazer Irving. Puffin Graphics 2005 176p. Illustration
Grades: 5 6 7 8 9 10 11 12   **741.5; Fic**
1. Horror graphic novels; 2. Novelists; 3. Shelley, Mary Wollstonecraft, 1797-1851 — Adaptations; 4. Graphic novels
0-14-240407-1, $9.99

Scientist Victor Frankenstein decided to create a man, only to create something he deemed a monster.

"Reed concentrates on the emotional anguish of the story, ably capturing the rage, the hurt, and the guilt of both monster and creator. Irving . . . creates a hazy, suitably murky black-and-white backdrop, never exploiting the violence inherent in the monster's quest for vengeance." Booklist

Reilly, Chris

The **weirdly** world of strange eggs. Chris Reilly, Steve Ahlquist, and Jeremy Mann. Amaze Ink/SLG Publishing 2007 80p. Illustration

Grades: 5 6 7 8 9 10   **741.5**

1. Adventure graphic novels; 2. Fantasy graphic novels; 3. Humorous graphic novels; 4. Graphic novels

978-1-59362-085-1, $7.95

Kip and Kelly have a pretty quiet life on the farm with their father (who generally stays behind the newspaper); Kelly performs all kinds of scientific experiments while Kip always wants adventure. Then they encounter Roger Rogers, who gives them a strange egg? that hatches into a creature they name Hooper. When Roger comes with another egg, Hooper tricks him and takes it, and this time the egg hatches a creature that looks like a party hat and excretes vampire bats. As Kip and Kelly fight off the party hat, bats, and even a monster tree, they learn to protect thos they love and trust those who want to help them (such as the ex B-movie actress veterinarian).

Renier, Aaron

Spiral-bound. Top Shelf Productions 2005 144p. Illustration

Grades: 4 5 6 7 8 9

741.5; Fic

1. Mystery graphic novels; 2. Graphic novels

1-891830-50-3, $14.95

Courtesy of Top Shelf Productions

"Turnip the elephant is using the summer to find his artistic voice through sculpture, his friend Stucky the dog is building a submarine, and Ana the rabbit is working on the town's underground newspaper. Their stories all wind around the town's deep, dark secret about the monster that lives in the pond. . . . The characters seem like real children, wholesome without being too sweet, and Renier's art is light and fun, a sort of Babar meets underground comix." Booklist

★ The **Unsinkable** Walker Bean. Written and illustrated by Aaron Renier; colored by Alec Longstreth. First Second 2010 191p. Illustration

Grades: 5 6 7 8   **741.5; Fic**

978-1-59643-453-0 (pa), $13.99; 1-59643-453-8 (pa)

The story "centers around a cursed skull stolen from the lair of two deep-sea crustacean witches. Like all who look upon the skull, Walker's beloved grandpa falls deathly ill when he finds it, and the boy sets out to return the skull from whence it came. . . . The generous page size lets [the] reader dive into Renier's quavery and painstakingly detailed cartooning, and he really shows off his stuff with a bounty of full-splash dazzlers. . . . Exciting, deep, funny, and scary, with tremendous villains and valor galore." Booklist

Reynolds, Aaron

Kung Pow chicken. By Aaron Reynolds; illustrated by Erik Lervold.. Stone Arch Books 2008 40p. Illustration

Grades: 3 4 5 6 7   **741.5; Fic**

1. Humorous graphic novels; 2. Ninja; 3. Science fiction graphic novels; 4. Graphic novels

978-1-4342-0455-4, $21.26; 978-1-4342-0505-6 (pa), $6.95

LC 2007-31253

Tiger Moth, fourth grade insect ninja, has been captured by Weevil's evil minions. His fourth grade sidekick, Kung Pow, needs to rescue him, but the only person who can help him is his kid sister, first grader Amber. With his own apprentice, can Kung Pow pull off a rescue?

Part of the Graphic Sparks series, a Tiger Moth adventure.

The **pest** show on earth. By Aaron Reynolds; illustrated by Erik Lervold.. Stone Arch Books 2008 40p. Illustration

Grades: 3 4 5 6 7   **741.5; Fic**

1. Humorous graphic novels; 2. Ninja; 3. Science fiction graphic novels; 4. Graphic novels

978-1-4342-0454-7, $21.26; 978-1-4342-0504-9 (pa), $6.95

LC 2007-31254

Tiger Moth, fourth grade insect ninja, and his sidekick Kung Pow, go to the carnival that has just come to town, only to discover that the ringmaster is the evil Weevil. They learn his nefarious plan to trap the town's insect citizens with Wing Kong, a giant insect-eating bat.

Part of the Graphic Sparks series, a Tiger Moth adventure.

Tiger Moth and the Dragon Kite Contest. Illustrated by Erik Lervold. Stone Arch Books 2007 40p. Illustration

Grades: 2 3 4 5 6 7   **741.5; Fic**

1. Humorous graphic novels; 2. Mystery graphic novels; 3. Graphic novels

978-1-59889-056-3, $21.26 lib. bdg.

Fourth-grade ninjas Tiger Moth and Kung Pow have fun with their classmates celebrating the Chinese New Year. Then Tiger's rivals, the Fruit Fly Boys, enter the kite-flying contest and cheat, resulting in sky-high disaster. The easy-to-read text, simple panel layout, and fast-paced story make this suitable for beginning and struggling readers.

Tiger Moth, Insect Ninja. Illustrated by Erik Lervold. Stone Arch Books 2007 40p. Illustration

Grades: 2 3 4 5 6 7   **741.5; Fic**

1. Humorous graphic novels; 2. Ninja; 3. Graphic novels

978-1-59889-057-0 li, $21.26; 978-1-59889-228-4 (pa)

LC 2006007700

Young Tiger Moth is a ninja-in-training, a martial arts warrior who fights evil in the streets and classrooms of the bug world. With the help of his best friend, pillbug Kung Pow, he works for truth and justice, while still hoping to finish the fourth grade. This graphic novel features easy text and a controlled vocabulary for beginning and struggling readers.

Part of the Graphic Sparks series.

Tiger Moth: The Fortune Cookies of Weevil. Illustrated by Erik Lervold. Stone Arch Books 2007 40p. Illustration

Grades: 2 3 4 5 6 7   **741.5; Fic**

1. Humorous graphic novels; 2. Mystery graphic novels; 3. Graphic novels

978-1-59889-318-2, $21.26 lib. bdg.

Who is sending all the fortune cookies around the school, and why are only the bad boy bugs, such as Dragon and the Fruit Fly Boys, getting them" What messages are hidden in the cookies" Fourth-grade ninjas Tiger Moth and best buddy Kung Pow decide to investigate. The easy text, simple panel layout, and the pun-filled, fast-paced story make this suitable for beginning and struggling readers.

Riordan, Rick

Percy Jackson & the Olympians, book one: the lightning thief: the graphic novel. Adapted by Robert Venditti; art by Attila Futaki; color by José Villarrubia; layouts by Orpheus Collar; lettering by Chris Dickey. Hyperion Books for Children 2010 Un Illustration

Grades: 5 6 7 8 9 10   **741.5; Fic**

1. Adventure graphic novels; 2. Fantasy graphic novels; 3. Greek mythology; 4. Graphic novels

978-1-4231-1696-7, $19.99; 978-1-4321-1710-0 (pa), $9.99

Twelve-year-old Percy Jackson has had a hard time in school, but when a teacher transforms into a Fury and tries to kill him during a field trip to the museum, his life becomes even more complicated. He learns that he is the son of one of the Greek gods and a human woman, and then he learns that he should never have been born, and that the gods think he has stolen Zeus's master lightning bolt. Percy, his best friend Grover (a satyr), and Annabeth, daughter of Athena, have ten days to recover the lightning bolt and prevent all-out war among the Olympians. This graphic novel adapts Riordan's novel, NOT the movie. Futaki makes the water action look great in an adaptation that should make the book fans happy.

The **red** pyramid: the graphic novel. Rick Riordan; adapted by Orpheus Collar; lettered by Jared Fletcher. Disney/Hyperion Books 2012 Un Color; Illustration (The Kane chronicles)

Grades: 4 5 6 7 8 9   **741.5**

1. Brothers and sisters — Fiction; 2. Egyptian mythology — Fiction; 3. Magic — Fiction

1423150694; 1423150686; 9781423150695, $12.99; 9781423150688, $21.99

LC 2012007905

"Since their mother's death, Sadie and Carter have become near-strangers. While Sadie has lived with her grandparents in London, Carter has traveled the world with their father, the famed Egyptologist Dr. Julius Kane. One night, Dr. Kane brings the siblings to the British Museum, where he hopes to set things right for his family. Instead, he unleashes the Egyptian god Set, who banishes him to oblivion and forces the children to flee for their lives." (Publisher's note)

"Out of necessity, much of the dialogue is dedicated to explaining actions and events, but a constant stream of humor prevents the reader from getting bogged down by logistics. The colorful artwork has an almost painting-like quality, . . . and some clever visual jokes and thoughtful use of panels make good use of the format." VOYA

Rioux, Jo-Anne

The **golden** twine; Book 1. Jo Rioux. Kids Can Press 2012 111 p. Color illustration

Grades: 5 6 7 8   **741.5/971; 741.5; Fic**

1. Dragons — Fiction; 2. Magic — Fiction; 3. Monsters — Fiction; 4. Paranormal fiction

1554536367; 9781554536368, $17.95

In this book by author Jo Rioux, "parentless young storyteller Suri [buys a dragon tooth that brings her luck] . . . The ball of magical golden string that she finds . . . belongs to a trio of vicious tiger creatures called 'caitsiths' who use the string to masquerade as humans and . . . want it back . . . Suri [also] achieves her . . . desire to become a monster tamer when she meets Byron, a humongous if overly friendly dog, and the surly 500-year-old imp Caglio who . . . created him." (Kirkus)

Robbins, Trina

The **big** flush. By Trina Robbins; illustrated by Tyler Page. Graphic Universe 2012 59 p.

Grades: 3 4 5   **741.5/973; 741.5**

1. Dogs — Fiction; 2. Ghost stories; 3. Ghosts — Fiction; 4. Japanese Americans — Fiction; 5. Mystery fiction; 6. School stories; 7. Schools — Fiction; 8. Spirit possession — Fiction; 9. Graphic novels

0822591618; 9780761381655; 9780822591610, $6.95

LC 2011044490

In this mystery, a "ghost is haunting the girls' bathroom at Pine Lake Academy, but that isn't the interesting part of the story. The interesting thing is that she's singing 'Alexander's Ragtime Band.' Anyone who drinks the water ends up possessed, and even a manly young detective like Raf Hernandez finds himself saying, 'How I love the Turkey Trot! But Auntie says the Turkey Trot and the Grizzly Bear are vulgar and will corrupt today's youth.'" (Kirkus)

★ The **drained** brains caper. [by] Trina Robbins and Tyler Page. Graphic Universe 2010 64p. Illustration (Chicagoland Detective Agency)

Grades: 4 5 6 7   **Fic; 741; 741.5**

1. Brainwashing — Fiction; 2. Humorous graphic novels; 3. Japanese Americans; 4. Mystery graphic novels; 5. Schools; 6. Graphic novels

978-0-7613-4601-2 (lib bdg), $27.97; 0-7613-4601-5 (lib bdg); 978-0-7613-5635-6 (pa), $6.95; 0-7613-5635-5 (pa)

LC 2009-32620

Required to attend summer school after moving to Chicagoland, thirteen-year-old manga-love Megan Yamamura needs help from twelve-year-old computer genius Raf Hernandez to escape the maniacal principal's mind control experiment.

This tells "an entertaining story. . . . Page's black-and-white cartooning has a loose manga slant, with peppy goofiness popping out from stippled screen tones." Booklist

Other titles in this series are: The Maltese mummy (2011); Night of the living dogs (2012); The big flush (2012); The bark in space (2013); A midterm night's scheme (2014)

Go girl!. Vol. 1, The time team. Story, Trina Robbins, art, Anne Timmons. Dark Horse Comics 2004 95p. Illustration

Grades: 3 4 5 6 7 8   **741; 741.5; Fic**
1. Adventure graphic novels; 2. Go Girl! (Fictional character); 3. Superhero graphic novels; 4. Graphic novels
1-59307-230-9, $5.95

"Robbins, who has made a name for herself as a feminist in the comics world, creates a story about three stereotypical high school girls—the dismissive cheerleader, the misunderstood brain, and the daughter of a 1970s-era superheroine—who become stranded in prehistory. The girls are quick-witted, the dinosaurs are cartoony, and a late appearance by Vikings offers readers a taste of what Nordic women might have been like in a confrontation. This isn't high concept, but it's definitely good, clean fun." Booklist

Followed by:Vol. 2: Robots gone wild

Go Girl!: Robots Gone Wild!. Dark Horse Comics 2007 183p. Illustration

Grades: 4 5 6 7 8 9 10   **741.5**
1. Go Girl! (Fictional character); 2. Superhero graphic novels; 3. Graphic novels
978-1-59307-409-8

Video games can get too realistic, as the flying teenager, Go Girl! discovers in "Prisoners of the Machine," when she and her friends find themselves trapped inside a computer, menaced by giant anime-robots. And in "Double Trouble," Go Girl!'s arch-enemies create a robot that looks just like her, except that it has the mind of a master criminal. How can our heroine convince the cops that she didn't rob that bank, when everyone saw her do it? Plus, Go Girl!'s sidekick, Haseena, tired of always being rescued by the flying teen, takes up sleuthing herself in "Haseena Ross, Girl Detective."

Hedy Lamarr and a Secret Communication System. Illustrated by Cynthia Martin and Anne Timmons. Capstone Press 2007 32p. Illustration

Grades: 3 4 5 6 7 8 9   **621.384; 741.5; 92; 621.384092**
1. Biographical graphic novels; 2. Inventions; 3. Lamarr, Hedy, 1914-2000; 4. Graphic novels
978-0-7368-6479-4, $25.26
                    LC 2006004104
This volume tells the story of how gorgeous Hollywood star Hedy Lamarr came up with the idea for a secret communication system back in the early days of World War II, which would much later become the basis for wireless technology. The book provides additional information, a glossary, a list of books for further reading, and more.

Part of the Graphic Library, Inventions and Discovery series.

Lily Renée, escape artist. Illustrated by Anne Timmons and Mo Oh. Graphic Universe 2011 96p. Color illustration

Grades: 4 5 6 7 8   **92; 741.5; 940.53**
1. Artists; 2. Holocaust, 1933-1945; 3. Illustrators; 4. Jews — Biography; 5. Phillips, Lily Renee; 6. Graphic novels
978-0-7613-6010-0, $7.95; 0-7613-6010-7
                    LC 2011001084
Presents the story of Lily Ren?e Wilheim, the Jewish girl who escaped from the Nazis through the Kindertransport operation, leaving her parents behind and traveling alone to England, later becoming a comic book artist in New York.

"This comic-book biography of a Jewish girl's life under the Nazi jackboot and then as a refugee is low key and that much more profound for it. The panels are brightly lit, and the narrative is crisp, both of which serve to chillingly amplify the everyday banality of evil. . . . A fitting tribute." Kirkus

Roberts, Steven
Henry Ford. By Steven Roberts. PowerKids Press 2013 24 p. (Jr. graphic American inventors)

Grades: 3 4 5 6   **338.7/629222092; 92; B**
1. Automobile industry and trade — United States — Biography — Juvenile literature; 2. Ford, Henry, 1863-1947 — Juvenile literature; 3. Industrialists — United States — Biography — Juvenile literature; 4. Inventors
147770079X; 9781477700792, $25.25; 9781477701430; 9781477701447
                    LC 2012020485
This book, by Steven Roberts, presents a biography of inventor Henry Ford. "It looks at the man who perfected the mass market automobile. From a young age Ford tinkered with farm machines and fixed neighbors' watches. That led to jobs working with steam engines and then, under the employment of Thomas Edison, the internal combustion engine. Inspired by the work flow of other factories, Ford created the Model T,and in just a few years, he was creating a million cars per year." (Booklist)

Includes index.

Robert Fulton. By Steven Roberts. PowerKids Press 2013 24 p.

Grades: 3 4 5 6   **623.82; 623.82/4092; B**
1. Fulton, Robert, 1765-1815 — Juvenile literature; 2. Inventors — United States — Biography — Juvenile literature; 3. Marine engineers — United States — Biography — Juvenile literature; 4. Steamboats — Juvenile literature
1477700773; 9781477700778, $25.25; 9781477701393; 9781477701409
                    LC 2012020630
In this graphic novel by Steven Roberts "readers will [learn] more about [Robert] Fulton and his contributions to American society through easy to follow text and vibrant illustrations." It notes that "Robert Fulton didn't actually invent what he is most commonly associated with, yet Fulton s innovations on the steamboat changed America s trade and travel in a progressive way." (Publisher's note)

Includes bibliographical references (p. 24) and index

Robinson, Alex
★ A **kidnapped** Santa Claus. It Books/HarperCollins 2009 Un Illustration

Grades: 4 5 6 7 8 9   **741.5; Fic**
1. Adventure graphic novels; 2. Baum, L Frank, 1856-1919 — Adaptations; 3. Christmas; 4. Santa Claus; 4. Graphic novels
978-0-06-178240-4, $14.99
Santa Claus lives in the Laughing Valley, with the fairies on one side of the valley in the Forest of Burzee. On the other side of the valley stands a mountain that contains the caves of the daemons, Selfishness, Envy, Hatred, and

Repentance. On this Christmas Eve, the daemons hatch a diabolical plot to destroy Christmas. When they can't convince Santa to be selfish, envious, or to hate people, they kidnap him. Santa's helpers, led by the young fairy named Wisk, decide they need to save Christmas when the big man doesn't show up, so they set out to deliver the presents all around the world. There's one big problem Wisk can't find Santa's list; they have to improvise. Baum's story provides a different type of Christmas adventure; his Santa doesn't live at the North Pole, and his helpers aren't elves. Robinson, who's known for his adult graphic novels, makes Wisk a girl fairy with big cats-eye glasses. During the battle to rescue Santa from the daemons, one of Santa's helpers named Nuter loses his head, which might disturb some younger readers (he doesn't die).

Robinson, Fiona

★ The **3-2-3** Detective Agency: the disappearance of Dave Warthog. Amulet Books 2009 80p. Illustration
Grades: 2 3 4 5 6 **741.5; Fic**
1. Humorous graphic novels; 2. Mystery graphic novels; 3. Graphic novels
978-08109-7094-6 (pa), $9.95; 978-0-8109-8489-9, $17.95

LC 2008-37171

On the 3:23 express train to Whiska City, Jenny the donkey meets four new friends, and they decide to form a private detective agency together. Priscilla, a penguin with a penchant for drama, Slingshot, a sloth who can't sleep, very shy (but brave) rat Bluebell, and gourmet dung beetle Roger join Jenny in what they decide to call the 323 Detective Agency. When they arrive in Whiska City, they notice things aren't quite right, and they learn that animals have been disappearing almost every day. They almost immediately get new clients, all wanting their loved ones found, such as Dave Warthog, whose mother disappeared. Even the Mayor needs their help to find her police department. They notice that poodle salons have popped up around the city, and the poodles have their own exclusive, gated community. As each detective investigates, they learn that every animal who disappeared had an appointment at a poodle salon. Then Priscilla, who has gone undercover to a salon, has disappeared, and now Jenny and the others must find a way to rescue her and solve the mystery.

Robinson, James

★ **Leave** It to Chance Vol. II: Trick or Threat & Other Stories. James Robinson & Paul Smith ; with George Freeman, inks ; Jeromy Cox, color art ; and Amie Grenier, lettering. Image Comics 2003 Un Illustration
Grades: 5 6 7 8 9 10 **741.5; Fic**
1. Adventure graphic novels; 2. Fantasy graphic novels; 3. Horror graphic novels; 4. Graphic novels
1-58240-278-7, $14.95

In "Trick or Threat," Chance helps a boy save his pet monkey from being sacrificed by a gang of cultists. Then her father sends Chance away to a boarding school (to keep her out of trouble), but there she has to face the ghost of the evil pirate Captain Hitch. Back home in Devil's Echo, Chance goes to the mall with her new friends from school, but they have to confront "The Phantom of the Mall." The book includes cartoony horror violence.

★ **Leave** It to Chance Vol. III: Monster Madness & Other Stories. Image Comics 2003 Un Illustration
Grades: 5 6 7 8 9 10 **741.5; Fic**
1. Adventure graphic novels; 2. Fantasy graphic novels; 3. Horror graphic novels; 4. Graphic novels
1-58240-298-1, $14.95

Chance Falconer is the mischievous 14-year- old daughter of Lucas Falconer, who is the mystical guardian for the city of Devil's Echo and its most prominent supernatural detective. Devil's Echo faces an all-new threat, as classic matinee monsters literally come to life and walk off a movie screen to wreak havoc in the streets. It's all-out excitement as Chance and her friends try to stop them, but the most shocking secret of all is who is really behind the mayhem. Then Chance helps a zombie hockey star hunt for the men who killed him. The book includes some cartoony horror action.

Leave it to Chance: Shaman's rain. [by] James Robinson & Paul Smith. Image Comics 2002 Un Illustration
Grades: 5 6 7 8 9 10 **741.5; Fic**
1. Fantasy graphic novels; 2. Horror graphic novels; 3. Graphic novels
1-58240-253-1, $14.95

"Chance Falconer is a 14-year-old only child born into a family of municipal sorcerers that has protected the city of Devil's Echo for centuries. Chance can't wait to start training in the family business, but her father decides he doesn't want a girl joining the family's dangerous profession. Predictably, it's not long before she stumbles onto a dead body and a kidnapping in progress, and soon enough she's got a full-fledged mystery on her hands. . . . This is a girl power comic written with a younger audience in mind. The smartest cops are female, the violence is G-rated and the story is fast-paced, brightly colored and as wholesome as it gets." Publ Wkly

Other titles in this series are: Leave it to Chance, Vol. 2: Trick or treat (2003); Leave it to Chance, Vol. 3: Monster madness (2003)

Robinson, Jimmie

Evil & malice save the world!. Image Comics/Silverline Books 2009 128p. Illustration
Grades: 5 6 7 8 9 10 **741.5; Fic**
1. Humorous graphic novels; 2. Sisters; 3. Superhero graphic novels; 4. Graphic novels
978-1-60706-091-8, $14.99

Evelyn and Malinda are the twin daughters of Dooplis City's top villain, the Black Eye, but they want to go see superhero Goldie Gal at a public appearance. She has come to help unveil a new computer system, the Max2000, that will automate many city functions. However, just at the moment of the unveiling, villains Coldheart, Chef, and Drip take out Goldie Gal and try to steal the Max2000. The damage they do in town threatens Evelyn's and Malinda's only friend Cindy, so they fight the villains to save her. The local newscaster catches just enough of the action to decide that Dooplis City has two new heroes and names them Evil and Malice. The girls decide to steal a bunch of their father's gadgets, since they have no superpowers of their own, and even though Dad is a villain, they set out to be heroes. Funny that every time they try to help, they end up destroying stuff. The villainous trio pretends to team up with the Black Eye, but plan to destroy him once they get the Max2000, so the girls know they have to save their father. There's a lot of superhero-type action, with buildings getting destroyed and things blowing up, but very little actual violence. Evie and Mal are very girly girls who still manage to handle a lot of action, and they learn that their conflict between villainous and heroic impulses comes because their mother was a superhero who married her chief villainous opponent. Bright cartoony colors and action along with lots of humor make this a much lighter-hearted story than Runaways.

Rodolphe
    Scrooge:. Adapted by Rodolphe & Estelle Meyrand. Papercutz 2012 96 p. Color illustration
Grades: 3 4 5 6   **Fic; 741.5/973**
    1. Christmas — Fiction; 2. England — Fiction; 3. Ghost stories; 4. Ghosts — Fiction; 5. Supernatural — Fiction
    1597073458; 1597073466; 9781597073455, $11.99; 9781597073462, $15.00
    This book, part of the Classics Illustrated Deluxe series, presents a graphic adaptation of the Charles Dickens stories "A Christmas Carol" and "Mugby Junction." In "A Christmas Carol," miser Ebenezer Scrooge is "visited by three spirits who will show him the way to change" on Christmas Eve. (Masterplots) "Mugby Junction" also features elements of the supernatural and a protagonist to whom his future is revealed." (Publisher's note)

Rogers, Gregory
    ★ **Midsummer** knight. Roaring Brook Press 2007 Un Illustration
Grades: K 1 2 3 4 5   **E**
    1. Bears — Fiction; 2. Fairies — Fiction; 3. Heroes and heroines — Fiction; 4. Stories without words
    978-1-59643-183-6, $16.95; 1-59643-183-0
                              LC 2006-51013
    A bear is rescued by a fairy in an enchanted wood and agrees to return the favor by leading the battle against a usurper who has imprisoned the king and queen, along with their loyal subjects, in the dungeon of their castle
    "This is another wordless adventure, depicted in colorful, comics-style panels that will delight young readers." Booklist
    First published in Australia 2006
    Companion volume to: The boy, the bear, the baron, the bard (2004)

Rol, Ruud van der
    The **search**. [by] Eric Heuvel, Ruud van der Rol [and] Lies Schippers; [English translation by Lorraine T. Miller]. Farrar, Straus and Giroux 2009 61p. Illustration
Grades: 5 6 7 8 9   **741.5; Fic**
    1. Grandmothers — Fiction; 2. Holocaust survivors — Fiction; 3. Holocaust, 1933-1945; 4. Jews — Netherlands — Fiction; 5. Graphic novels
    978-0-374-36517-2, $18.99; 978-0-374-46455-4 (pa), $9.99
                              LC 2009-13603
    After recounting her experience as a Jewish girl living in Amsterdam during the Holocaust, Esther, helped by her grandson, embarks on a search to discover what happened to her parents before they died in a concentration camp.

Esther, her grandson Daniel, and her friend Helena's grandson Jeroen visit the Dutch farm where Esther hid during the Nazi occupation of the Netherlands during World War II. She tells her story, of how she managed to escape the Nazi roundup of Jews, but how her family died in a concentration camp. Daniel helps her find an old friend from the farm, now living in Israel, and he tells her what happened to her family in Auschwitz. The book depicts some of the horrendous, horrible things that happened but does it without graphic violence or gore.

Roman, Dave
    ★ **Astronaut** Academy: Zero gravity. First Second Books 2011 185p. Illustration
Grades: 4 5 6 7 8   **741; 741.5; Fic**
    1. Humorous graphic novels; 2. School life; 3. Science fiction graphic novels; 4. Graphic novels
    9781596436206, $9.99; 9781596437562, $16.99
                           LC 2010-941434
    Hakata Soy has been the leader of a futuristic superhero team, but he has given that up and just wants to be a normal student at Astronaut Academy, a school on a space station, where students take such courses as anti-gravity gymnastics and fire-throwing. Other students include Doug Hiro, who always wears his space helmet, rich girl Maribelle Mellonbelly, Miyumi San (Maribelle's rival), and egotistical Billy Lee. Hakata Soy has some trouble adjusting to school life, and things get much worse when the villainous Gotcha Birds steal a robotic twin to Hakata Soy and reprogram it to kill him. The comics originally appeared as web comics, then as mini comics that Roman took to various comic cons; this is the first trade book collection of the stories. Middle grade students, boys and girls, will enjoy this book, which is full of humor and action with little actual violence.
    "Students like the introspective Hakata Soy, the space-gymnastics-obsessed Doug Hiro, and the snooty rich girl Mirabelle Mellonbelly meet up at Astronaut Academy, a middle school where the zany mixes with the postmodern. . . . Silliness is high on the agenda, aided by minimal, cartoonish art that plays on manga tropes but also manages to build character into the simple lines of a face. . . . This is one for readers looking for more involved and complex comedy than a cursory glance at the images might lead one to expect." Booklist
    Followed by: Astronaut academy: Re-entry (2013)

Rosca, Madeleine
    Hollow Fields Omnibus collection. Seven Seas Entertainment 2009 Un Illustration
Grades: 5 6 7 8 9 10   **741.5; Fic**
    1. Adventure graphic novels; 2. Science fiction graphic novels; 3. Graphic novels
    978-1-934876-72-5, $14.99
    Rosca is an Australian global manga creator who won one of the inaugural International Manga Awards 'Shorei' awards given by the Japanese government in 2007.
    Lucy Snow was supposed to start school at a nice elementary school in town, but she manages to lose her way in a forest and finds herself at Miss Weaver's Academy for the Scientifically Gifted and Ethically Unfettered a school for archvillains in training. Lucy's fellow students are all

learning how to be mad scientists and evil geniuses, with classes such as Live Taxidermy, Cross-Species Body-Part Transplantation, and Killer Robot Construction. Hollow Fields, as the school is also called, also has a practice guaranteed to make everyone compete to do well: the student with the lowest grades at the end of the week is sent to the windmill for detention, and thus far no student has ever returned. Miss Weaver has experimented on herself, as have all the Engineers who teach; what the reader learns is that they need new, young blood to keep their stitched-together bodies going, for they are all more than a hundred years old. Befriended by a talking box that calls itself Doctor Bleak, Lucy struggles to hold her own in her classes, despite her innate niceness. She decides she needs to discover just what goes on in the windmill, and how she can make things right. The book includes some mild violence.

Rosenstiehl, Agnes
★ **Silly** Lilly and the four seasons. Toon Books 2008 36p. Illustration
Grades: PreK K 1   **741.5; 741**
1. Humorous graphic novels; 2. Seasons; 3. Graphic novels
978-0-9799238-1-4, $12.95; 0-9799238-1-6
"Rosenstiehl follows Lilly . . . as she undertakes simple, familiar activities through the seasons. . . . Lilly is bold and engaging. . . . The text is very brief, . . . the colors are warm and bright, and the panels are large enough to draw in children new to books and reading." Booklist

Ruiz, Emilio
Waluk. By Emilio Ruiz; illustrated by Ana Miralles; translated and adapted by Dan Oliverio. Graphic Universe 2013 52 p.
Grades: 3 4 5 6   **741.5; Fic**
1. Bears — Fiction; 2. Friendship — Fiction; 3. Polar bear — Fiction; 4. Tundras — Fiction; 5. Graphic novels
1467715980; 1467716065; 9781467715980, $26.60; 9781467716062, $7.95
                    LC 2012047737
"Young Waluk is all alone. His mother has abandoned him, as is the way of polar bears, and now he must fend for himself. But he doesn't know much about the world—and unfortunately, his Arctic world is changing quickly. The ice is melting, and food is hard to find." (Publisher's note)
"Marrying exemplary sequential storytelling, mythology, and science and enhanced through respectful anthropomorphizing, Waluk takes readers into a realistic world of polar bears endangered by climate change." Booklist
Originally published in Spanish in Bilbao, Spain, by Astiberri, in 2011, under the title: Wa?luk.

Runton, Andy
★ **Owly** Vol. 2: Just a Little Blue. Top Shelf Productions 2005 127p. Illustration
Grades: K 1 2 3 4 5 6 7 8 9 10 11 12 Adult   **741.5; Fic**
1. Friendship; 2. Stories without words; 3. Graphic novels
1-891830-64-3, $10
Owly is a kind, yet lonely, little owl who's always on the search for new friends and adventure. Owly learns that sometimes you have to make sacrifices and work at things that are important, especially friendship. He and Wormy try to help a stubborn bluebird by building a new home, but the bluebird rejects it and them.

★ **Owly** Vol. 3: Flying Lessons. Top Shelf Productions 2005 143p. Illustration
Grades: K 1 2 3 4 5 6 7 8 9 10 11 12 Adult   **741.5; Fic**
1. Friendship; 2. Stories without words; 3. Graphic novels
1-891830-76-7, $10
Owly figures out why he can't fly (he failed his childhood flying lessons), and helps another forest creature with his own flying problems. The flying squirrel is frightened by Owly, for he knows owls are hunters, but Owly isn't like that. How can he convince the squirrel he just wants to be friends?

★ **Owly** vol. 4: a time to be brave. Top Shelf Productions 2007 132p. Illustration
Grades: K 1 2 3 4 5 6 7 8 9 10 11 12 Adult   **741.5; Fic**
1. Fantasy graphic novels; 2. Friendship; 3. Owls; 4. Stories without words; 5. Graphic novels
978-1-891830-89-1, $10
A new visitor comes to the forest, but Wormy is scared of him because Owly had just read stories about a scary dragon, and the visitor seems to look scary. The visitor is just as scared of Owly. Things aren't just as they seem, and everyone soon finds out that a little bravery and a lot of friendship can fix just about anything. This is the latest volume in Runton's nearly wordless series about Owly and his friends.

★ **Owly** volume five: tiny tales. Top Shelf Productions 2008 175p. Illustration
Grades: K 1 2 3 4 5 6 7 8 9 10 11 12 Adult   **741.5; Fic**
1. Friendship; 2. Humorous graphic novels; 3. Graphic novels
978-1-60309-019-3, $10
This volume gathers short stories about Owly and his friends, including stories originally published for Free Comic Book Day issues from Top Shelf Productions, the first Owly mini-comics, drawings of Owly before he met Wormy, and more. Among the stories, Owly saves a friend from drowning in the cold river when the ice cracks, only to get caught in the hole himself; Owly finds a way to keep both the bees and hummingbirds happy when they get into a "turf" battle; Owly helps a friend when she falls and breaks the fancy potted plant she bought for a present; and more.

★ **Owly:** The way home and The bittersweet summer. [by] Andy Runton. Top Shelf 2004 160p. Illustration
Grades: K 1 2 3 4 5 6 7 8 9 10 11 12   **741.5; Fic**
1. Friendship; 2. Owls; 3. Graphic novels
1-891830-62-7, $10
                    LC 2005298860
Rotund little Owly befriends Wormy despite their differences, and together they help a couple of hummingbirds and learn that friendship doesn't end with separation.
"The whimsical black-and-white art is done with great facility for expressing emotion, and Runton's reliance on icons and pictures in lieu of the usual dialogue makes the

story perfect for give-and-take between children and their parents." Booklist

Other titles in this series are: Owly: Just a little blue (2005); Owly: Flying lessons (2005); Owly: A time to be brave (2007); Owly: Tiny tales (2008)

Russell, P. Craig

★ **Coraline**. Based on the novel by Neil Gaiman; adapted and illustrated by P. Craig Russell; colorist, Lovern Kindzierski; letterer, Todd Klein. HarperCollins 2008 186p. Illustration

Grades: 4 5 6 7   **741; Fic; 741.5**

1. Gaiman, Neil, 1960- — Adaptations; 2. Horror graphic novels; 3. Graphic novels

978-0-06-082543-0, $18.99; 978-0-06-082544-7 (lib bdg), $19.89

LC 2007-930658

"An adaptation of Gaiman's 2002 novel Coraline, . . . a tale of childhood nightmares. As in the original story, Coraline wanders around her new house and discovers a door leading into a mirror place, where she finds her button-eyed "other mother," who is determined to secure Coraline's love one way or another. This version is a virtuoso adaptation. . . . A master of fantastical landscapes, Russell sharpens the realism of his imagery, perserving the humanity of the characters and heightening the horror." Booklist

Fairy Tales of Oscar Wilde Vol. 4: The Devoted Friend & The Nightingale and the Rose. NBM Publishing 2004 Un Illustration

Grades: 5 6 7 8 9   **741.5; Fic**

1. Fantasy graphic novels; 2. Graphic novels

978-1-56163-391-3, $16.99

This volume adapts The Devoted Friend," on what constitutes real friendship, and The Nightingale and the Rose," a story of sacrifice to love with a cruel twist. In both stories, innocence is sacrificed to cynicism and shallowness.

Fairy tales of Oscar Wilde: 5: The Happy Prince. Illustrated by P. Craig Russell. Nantier, Beall, Minoustchine 2012 32 p. Color illustration

Grades: 3 4 5 6 7 8   **741.5/973; Fic**

1. Fairy tales; 2. Generosity — Fiction; 3. Wilde, Oscar, 1854-1900 — Adaptations

1561636266; 9781561636266, $16.99

LC 93229468

For this book, "Eisner Award-winning [P. Craig] Russell has adapted into graphic novel form" the Oscar Wilde fairy tale "The Happy Prince." In the story, "a swallow . . . befriends the statue of the Happy Prince, who was indeed happy when he lived a sheltered life. Now, however, the prince stands over the city as a statue and sees all the suffering. With the help of the swallow, he breaks down the pieces of himself, his rubies, sapphire, and gold, to feed the starving people." (Publishers Weekly)

Ruth, Greg

The **lost** boy. Greg Ruth. GRAPHIX 2013 192 p.

Grades: 3 4 5 6 7   **741.5**

1. Fantasy fiction — Juvenile fiction; 2. Historical fiction — Juvenile fiction

0439823323; 9780439823319, $24.99; 9780439823326, $12.99; 9780545576901

LC 2013937147

This book by Greg Ruth "opens as a boy named Nate moves to a new town and discovers a tape recorder hidden underneath the floorboards of his bedroom. The action shifts back several decades as Nate listens to recordings left by Walter Pidgen, an outcast boy who disappeared without a trace. Along with a neighbor, Tabitha, Nate is drawn into a supernatural battle involving the denizens of an ancient woodland kingdom, which include talking toys and insects." (Publishers Weekly)

Ryan, Michael

Transformers animated, volume 6. Michael Ryan and Casey Todd ; adapted by Zachary Rau. IDW Publishing 2008 Un Illustration

Grades: 3 4 5 6 7 8   **741.5; Fic**

1. Adventure graphic novels; 2. Robots; 3. Science fiction graphic novels; 4. Transformers (Fictional characters); 5. Graphic novels

978-1-60010-281-3, $7.99

In "Headmaster," Bulkhead's large size and strength make him destructive, even when he doesn't want to be. Meanwhile, Dr. Sumdac has just fired an engineer named Masterson for making military robots, and Masterson decides to use his technology to hold the city of Detroit for ransom. He decides that Bulkhead's body is just right for his Headmaster unit, so the Autobots now need to rescue Bulkhead's body and stop Masterson from destroying a solar fusion power plant. In "When Nature Calls," a mysterious Cybertronian energy signature starts broadcasting from the forest outside the city, and Sari goes with Prowl and Bumblebee to investigate. They find a monstrous creature that is part machine, part organic space barnacles, and it soon infects the Autobots, leaving Sari to try to figure out how to get rid of the space barnacles. The book is illustrated with screen captures from the animated television series.

Saint-Exupéry, Antoine de

★ The **little** prince by Joann Sfar. Adapted from the book by Antoine de Saint-Exupéry; translated by Sarah Ardizzone; colour by Brigitte Findakly. Houghton Mifflin Harcourt 2010 110p. Illustration

Grades: 5 6 7 8 9   **741; Fic; 741.5**

1. Extraterrestrial beings; 2. Fantasy graphic novels; 3. Saint-Exupéry, Antoine de, 1900-1944 — Adaptations; 4. Graphic novels

978-0-547-33802-6, $19.99; 0-547-33802-3

"On the surface, this is a straight graphic-novel retelling of the narrator pilot getting stranded in the desert, where he meets a curious little boy who claims to be from a wee planet very far away. . . . The ultimately tricky task is to honor the source but not sound like an adaptation (otherwise, why not just

Courtesy of Houghton Mifflin Harcourt

read the original?) and Sfar nails it on both counts. . . . Everything is handled with both reverence and ingenuity." Booklist

Sala, Richard
★ **Cat** burglar black. First Second 2009 126p. Illustration
Grades: 5 6 7 8 9 10   **741.5; Fic**
1. Mystery graphic novels; 2. Orphans; 3. Graphic novels
978-1-59643-144-7, $16.99; 1-59643-144-X
K.'s aunt, who works at the Bellsong Academy for Girls, has invited K. to attend the school. But as soon as she arrives, K. notices some strange goings-on: her aunt has suddenly taken ill; there are only three other students and no regular classes; and a statue speaks to K. when no one else is around.
"The story is structured like a lighthearted cross between a fable and a horror film, but only ever teetering on the edge of horror without depicting it. This could have resulted in a mishmash, but Sala elegantly dances through the creepy and the sweet." SLJ

Salicrup, Jim
Disney fairies: Prilla's talent. Papercutz 2010 80p. Illustration
Grades: 2 3 4 5 6   **741.5; Fic**
1. Fairies; 2. Fantasy graphic novels; 3. Graphic novels
978-1-59707-187-1, $12.99
Tinker Bell and the other fairies of Neverland live in Pixie Hollow; each fairy has a special talent Tink can fix things. New fairy Prilla seeks her special ability in "Prilla's Talent," while Vidia shows she's the fastest fairy in "Like the Wind." Tinker Bell must repair a special bell in "The Sound of Friendship," and she has to finish in time for a big festival. Then, in "Best of Friends," Tinker Bell wonders why her friend Rani won't talk to her. These stories were all originally written and published in Italy.

SAM (Special Academic Manga)
Leonardo da Vinci. Y.kids/Youngjin Singapore Pte. Ltd. 2008 152p. Illustration
Grades: 3 4 5 6 7 8 9   **92; 741.5**
1. Art; 2. Artists; 3. Biographical graphic novels; 4. Leonardo, da Vinci, 1452-1519; 5. Painters; 6. Scientists; 7. Writers on science; 8. Graphic novels
978-981-057555-7, $14.95
This graphic format biography of da Vinci uses the conceit that an adventurer from the Planet Mud seeks to learn about the great people of Earth's history in an effort to save the people of Mud, who face a disease that drains their mental powers. In the course of his search in this volume, readers learn about the life and work Leonardo da Vinci, who was a painter, scientist, mathematician, engineer, inventor, anatomist, sculptor, architect, musician, and writer. The book includes a time line of da Vinci's life, and a list of books and websites for further reading.
Part of the Great Figures in History series

Sanders, Scott
Camilla d'Errico's Burn. Art by Steve Whitmire. Simon Pulse 2009 Un Illustration

Grades: 5 6 7 8   **741.5; Fic**
1. Adventure graphic novels; 2. Robots; 3. Science fiction graphic novels; 4. Graphic novels
978-1-4169-7873-2 (pa), $9.99
In a future world, sentient robots rebel against their human makers and set out to kill humans so they can remake the world for them. One boy, Burn, encounters the sentient named Shoftiel when it destroys his neighborhood and city; the destruction damages both of them, and Shoftiel repairs itself by melding with what remains of Burn's body. Burn/Shoftiel return to the home of Dr. Anders Carnegie, the scientist who created the sentients in the first place, in order to kill him. Burn won't let Shoftiel kill Dr. Carnegie's young daughter Aeya, and the two of them join with young bikers trying to make a new home in the rubble of the destroyed city. The two natures, machine and human, battle for control of Burn, even as he must fight off Shoftiel's brother sentients who have orders to destroy their contaminated brother. The story combines post-apocalyptic adventure with mecha action using manga-influenced art. It includes quite a bit of violence (the sentients basically rip humans apart); the young people drink alcohol (there are no adults left to supervise them).

Sava, Scott Christian
★ **Cameron** and his dinosaurs. Art by Tracy Bailey. IDW Publishing 2009 174p. Illustration
Grades: 3 4 5 6 7 8   **741.5; Fic**
1. Adventure graphic novels; 2. Dinosaurs; 3. Humorous graphic novels; 4. Robots; 5. Graphic novels
978-1-60010-315-5, $12.99
The mad scientist, Professor Poindexter P. Poppycock, uses dinosaur DNA to create living dinosaurs which he plans to use for nefarious purposes. Unfortunately for him, he gave them human intelligence and the ability to speak, and the dinosaurs Charlie the tyrannosaurus rex, Dee Dee the pterodactyl, Lizzy the triceratops, and Vinnie the brachiosaurus decline to be evil and leave him. They befriend young Cameron, who helps to introduce them to the world. Professor Poppycock then creates robotic dinosaurs to do the will of the Brotherhood of Universal Revolution for Political Subterfuge (B.U.R.P.S.) to kidnap the President and take over the country. It will be up to Charlie, Dee Dee, Lizzy, Vinnie, and Cameron in his new souped-up wheelchair (with some awesome top-secret adaptations) to save the President and stop the robot dinosaurs. This book reads like an action-packed cartoon.

The **dreamland** chronicles book two. Blue Dream Studios 2007 176p. Illustration
Grades: 5 6 7 8 9 10 11 12   **741.5; Fic**
1. Adventure graphic novels; 2. Dreaming; 3. Fantasy graphic novels; 4. Graphic novels
978-0-9789168-3-1, $19.95
LC 2007-932090
Alexander Carter continues his adventures in Dreamland every night, as he and his friends escape the Dragon Lord Nicodemus' prison with the help of Felicity, a catgirl with tiger stripes, and continue their search for the King and Queen of Elves, Nastajia's parents. The problem is, Nastajia doesn't trust Felicity and thinks she could be a spy for Nicodemus. Meanwhile, the friends find themselves in

the undersea cave of the Kraken, which is a much more immediate danger to them all.

The **Dreamland** Chronicles: Book One. Blue Dream Studios 2006 Un Illustration
Grades: 5 6 7 8 9 10 11 12 Adult   **741.5; Fic**
1. Adventure graphic novels; 2. Fantasy graphic novels; 3. Graphic novels
978-0-9789168-0-0, $19.95
College student Alexander Carter has found a key that takes him back to the land of his childhood dreams. Every night he enters Dreamland, a magical world filled with dragons, fairies, and giants. Reunited with his childhood friends Paddington, Kiwi, and Nastajia, Alexander now embarks on a quest to save Dreamland from war with the Nightmare Realm. But, will his daytime life as a college student interfere" Colorful 3-D animated art makes the story look like a computer game.

Ed's terrestrials. By Scott Christian Sava; artist, Diego Jourdan. Blue Dream Studios 2006 84p. Illustration
Grades: 2 3 4 5 6   **741.5; Fic**
1. Humorous graphic novels; 2. Science fiction graphic novels; 3. Graphic novels
978-0-9789168-1-7, $19.95
Aliens have escaped from the Intergalactic Food Court, where they worked as slaves, and crashland into Ed's tree house. They all become friends, and the aliens want to help their fellow slaves come to Earth. But the Intergalactic Mall security officer, Maximus Obliterus, has come to send them back, and he has teamed up with Ed's school nemesis, Natalie
This book was originally published in 2005 by Alias Enterprises

Gary the pirate. Art by Tracy Bailey. IDW Publishing 2009 112p. Illustration
Grades: 4 5 6 7 8 9   **741.5; Fic**
1. Adventure graphic novels; 2. Humorous graphic novels; 3. Pirates; 4. Graphic novels
978-1-60010-312-4, $12.99
Gary, a teenage Sky Pirate from the secret floating city Pirate Cove, owes Stinky a lot for ruining his watch, dumping a chocolate ice cream sundae on his head, and messing up his ship all accidentally, because Gary is a klutz. Gary is also a lousy thief for a pirate. While searching for treasure, he sees thirteen-year-old Judy in the park with her grandmother. She complains to her grandmother about all the boys she knows how could she ever want to date any of them" They're either bullies, computer nerds, too cool for anyone, or just totally clueless. When klutzy Gary breaks into her bedroom in search of the brooch her grandmother just gave her (it's treasure, after all), she wants him to take her on his ship to see Pirate Cove. True to his klutzy nature, though, Gary manages to crash his ship into Stinky's ship, and now they're in big trouble. The pirates may brandish their swords, but there's no actual violence, only cartoony action.

★ **Hyperactive**. By Scott Christian Sava; artist, Joseph Bergin. IDW Publishing/Worthwhile Children's Books 2009 108p. Illustration
Grades: 3 4 5 6 7 8   **741.5; Fic**

1. Adventure graphic novels; 2. Humorous graphic novels; 3. Superhero graphic novels; 4. Graphic novels
978-1-60010-313-1, $12.99; 1-60010-313-8
"Joey Johnson learns he can move at super speed and puts his power to good use doing household chores. But when word gets out, a shady executive sees the opportunity to make big bucks off of Joey's super DNA. . . . With its surprise ending, which suggests more to come, a readership of young boys will ensure that this one flies off the shelf at the speed of light." Booklist

The **lab:** hey . . . test this!. Astonish Factory 2004 120p. Illustration
Grades: 5 6 7 8 9   **741.5; Fic**
1. Humorous graphic novels; 2. Science fiction graphic novels; 3. Graphic novels
0-9721259-3-0, $14.95
"A collection of previously published comics and original stories that highlight the working relationship between Livingston, a scientist mole, and his goofball assistant, Esteban, a weasel whose ultrasensitivity to chemicals makes him an excellent test subject for new products. With bright, colorful pictures, the stories usually consist of observing Esteban's outlandish reactions to Livingston's concoctions, such as floating to the ceiling, shrinking to microscopic size, or singing uncontrollably." SLJ

My Grandparents are Secret Agents. Art by Juan Saavedra Mourgues and Invasor Creative Art Studio. IDW Publishing 2009 104p.
Grades: 3 4 5 6   **741.5; Fic**
1. Adventure graphic novels; 2. Humorous graphic novels; 3. Mystery graphic novels; 4. Graphic novels
978-1-60010-314-8, $11.99
Secret agents The Sicilian and the Diva defeat Dr. Dementia, and after the successful mission they want to spend a weekend with their grandchildren, Nicholas and Alyssa, while the kids' parents go on a romantic trip. However, the Social Security Administration (a secret government agency working to keep the U.S. safe) needs their top two agents to go after a villain named Purple Haze, who intends to use a time machine to make everything go back to the late 1960s. Grandma and Grandpa have to take Nicholas and Alyssa with them, along with the robot security dog named S.N.A.C.K.S., to stop the whacked-out villain. Spanish illustrator Mourgues and the Invasor Creative Art Studio use a very colorful, cartoony style.

Pet Robots. Art by Diego Jourdan. Blue Dream Studios 2007 Un Illustration
Grades: 3 4 5 6 7 8 9   **741.5; Fic**
1. Humorous graphic novels; 2. Robots; 3. Science fiction graphic novels; 4. Graphic novels
978-0-9789168-2-4, $19.95
                 LC 2007902577
Four students - Jake, Chris, Tammy, and Tommy - get lost while on a field trip to the Rooty Tooty Toy Company. In their quest to find they way back to the rest of the class, the stumble upon a room inhabited only by four military robots. That night they're followed home by the robots: Skye, Rock, Aqua, and Wind. As the kids get to know their new robotic friends, they must also avoid the evil owner of the Rooty Tooty Toy Company, Vandenburger Meisterburger. He

wants his robots back and he's willing to do anything to get them.

Scalera, Buddy

   Decoy: Storm of the Century. Buddy Scalera and Courtney Huddleston. Penny-Farthing Press 2003 151p. Illustration

Grades: 5 6 7 8 9 10 11 12 Adult   **741.5; Fic**
   1. Adventure graphic novels; 2. Friendship; 3. Science fiction graphic novels; 4. Graphic novels
   0-9719012-0-1, $17.95

   He's the champion of justice and fast one-liners, a green shape-shifting alien from the planet Nacrum whose primary purpose in life is to protect the innocent and to one-up his roommate in an ongoing battle of pranks and bad jokes. All goes well until a subterranean encounter with a long-forgotten threat changes Decoy's life and threatens the friendship with his only ally on the planet: his best friend. Faced with an identity crisis of cosmic proportions, loveable alien Decoy must team up with his buddy, rookie cop Bobby Luck, to battle meteorological and psychological disaster.

Schigiel, Gregg

   X-babies: stars reborn. Written by Gregg Schigiel ; art by Jacob Chabot. Marvel Worldwide 2010 Un Illustration

Grades: 4 5 6 7 8 9 10   **741.5; Fic**
   1. Adventure graphic novels; 2. Cyclops (Fictional character); 3. Humorous graphic novels; 4. Nightcrawler (Fictional character); 5. Storm (Fictional character); 6. Superhero graphic novels; 7. Wolverine (Fictional character); 8. X-Men (Fictional characters); 9. Graphic novels
   978-0-7851-4380-2, $14.99

   In Mojoworld, where everything is televised, Mojo had created the X-Babies, child-sized versions of the X-Men, and the X-Babies have been the top-rated stars, but then Mr. Veech takes over and replaces the X-Babies with cute, safe, friendly versions who don't fight, but do such things as grow and eat! vegetables. The X-Babies know something is wrong, and they set out to find out what's happening. As they break out of their imprisonment and seek answers, they encounter lots of modified cutesy versions of other kid heroes. Younger readers will enjoy the wise-cracking kiddie versions of the X-Babies meet were stars of Marvel's mid-1980s kid-centric Star Comics line, including Top Dog, Wally the Wizard, Planet Terry, and Royal Roy. There is no bad language (Wolverine says "poot" a lot), and lots of action with little violence.

   Originally published as X-Babies issues #14

Schulz, Charles M.

   ★ The **Complete** Peanuts: 1950-1952. Fantagraphics Books 2004 330p. Illustration

Grades: 2 3 4 5 6 7 8 9 10 11 12 Adult   **741.5; Fic**
   1. Humorous graphic novels; 2. Peanuts (Comic strip); 3. Graphic novels
   1-56097-589-X, $28.95

   This is the first volume of a project to collect all of Schulz's Peanuts comic strips from 1950 to 2000. This volume includes the strips published from October 2, 1950

through all of 1952. These early strips featured characters younger readers may not recognize: Patty (not Peppermint Patty), Violet, Shermy, and a Snoopy who behaves like a normal dog. Schroeder is a baby who's already a whiz at the toy piano; Lucy is a toddler who already causes trouble for Charlie Brown; Linus shows up as a baby in September 1952. Lucy pulls the football trick on Charlie Brown for the first time in November 1952. This volume also includes a biography of Schulz and a long interview with him.

   Volume 1 of 26

Schweizer, Chris

   The **creeps;** 1: night of the frankenfrogs. By Chris Schweizer. Abrams Books 2015 128 p. Color; Illustration

Grades: 3 4 5 6   **741.5; Fic**
   1. Frogs — Juvenile fiction; 2. School stories — Juvenile fiction; 3. Scientists — Fiction
   9781419713798, $17.95; 9781419717666, $9.95
                                        LC 2014955691

   In this book, by Chris Schweizer, as "punishment for creating a giant mess in their school, Carol, Jarvis, Mitchell, and Rosario (known to their classmates as the Creeps) are being forced to perform the tasks normally completed by the janitor. When they discover that the frog specimens intended for dissection in their science class are missing, they know that they will be blamed, so they set out to discover who the real culprit might be." (School Library Journal)

   "An excellent complement to his prose, Schweizer's cleanly paneled art is bright and busy, ever ready with a gag that helps blend the ghastly with the goofy, making his gang's antics reminiscent of Scooby Doo. . . . Silly fun with a smattering of science." Kirkus

Scott, Jeremy R.

   P. T. A. night. Silverline Books/Image Comics 2009 Un Illustration

Grades: K 1 2 3 4 5   **741.5; Fic**
   1. Humorous graphic novels; 2. Schools; 3. Supernatural graphic novels; 4. Graphic novels
   978-1-60706-163-2, $12.99

   It's P.T.A. Night at Austintown Middle School, but strange things are happening. The school was built on what used to be a graveyard, and on this night, zombies come out of the ground, the lunch lady's soup comes alive with tentacles, and the janitor becomes a werewolf. Meanwhile, up in the science lab, a father and son turn on an antenna that attracts an alien in a flying saucer, the P.T.A. meeting is going on, a ghost shows up in the library, and two maintenance workers play checkers in the machine room. All of this is portrayed by Scott in a wordless book, where each room in the school is used like a comic book panel, and events progress as readers turn the pages. The youngest readers might be a little scared by the werewolf and the zombies, but all the creatures are drawn to be funny rather than scary.

Sewell, Anna

   Black Beauty. Retold by L.L. Owens ; illustrated by Jennifer Tanner. Stone Arch Books 2006 63p. Illustration

Grades: 3 4 5 6 7 8 9   **741.5; Fic**
   1. Sewell, Anna, 1820-1878 — Adaptations; 2. Graphic novels

978-1-59889-046-4, $23.93

Black Beauty, a handsome colt living in Victorian England, has a happy childhood growing up in the peaceful countryside. In his later years, he encounters cruelty, human suffering, and a tragic fire. Things go from bad to worse when his new owners begin renting him out for profit. Black Beauty endures a life of mistreatment and disrespect in a world that shows little regard for the happiness of animals. This adaptation is written for reluctant and struggling readers.

Part of the Graphic Revolve series.

Sexton, Adam

Twain's the adventure of Huckleberry Finn: the Manga edition. Art by Hyeondo Park. Wiley Publishing 2009 186p.
Grades: 5 6 7 8 9 10 11 12   **741.5; Fic**
1. Adventure graphic novels; 2. Authors; 3. Essayists; 4. Humorists; 5. Humorous graphic novels; 6. Memoirists; 7. Novelists; 8. Satirists; 9. Slaves; 10. Twain, Mark, 1835-1910; 11. Graphic novels
978-0-470-15287-4, $9.99

Huckleberry Finn, son of a ne'er-do-well, has been living with Tom Sawyer and his Aunt Polly ever since they helped solve a murder. Now, his father wants Huck's share of the reward money. When Huck gets away, he decides he has to run; he encounters Jim, a slave who has run away from his owner, and they set out on a raft down the Mississippi River, where they encounter other murderers, con artists, thieves, feuding families, and more. This is a manga-style adaptation of Twain's classic adventure. While the original novel has faced challenges because of certain language, this book does not include the inflammatory words.

Sfar, Joann

Little Vampire Does Kung Fu!. Stories and drawings by Joann Sfar ; colors by Walter. Simon & Schuster Books for Young Readers 2003 Un Illustration
Grades: 4 5 6 7 8 9   **741.5; Fic**
1. Fantasy graphic novels; 2. Humorous graphic novels; 3. Vampires; 4. Graphic novels
0-689-85769-1, $12.95

LC 2003-045770

Jeffrey the jerk is a bully and everyone knows it. Little Vampire isn't about to stand around and watch him pick on his best friend, Michael. There's only one thing to do: travel to the highest mountain and seek kung fu lessons from the master... There's an icky moment when Little Vampire's monster friends spit up bits of Jeffrey (whom they ate) and they try to put him together again.

Little Vampire goes to school. Stories and drawings by Joann Sfar; colors by Walter; translated by Mark and Alexis Siegel. Simon & Schuster Bks. for Young Readers 2003 40p. Illustration
Grades: 2 3 4 5   **741.5; Fic**
1. Vampires; 2. Graphic novels
0-689-85717-9, $12.95

LC 2002-152656

A lonely little vampire, yearning for a friend, gets permission from the other monsters to go to school and makes the acquaintance of a boy who does not believe that vampires are real

Another title about Little Vampire is: Little Vampire does kung fu! (2003)

Sardine in outer space 2. [by] Emmanuel Guibert and Joann Sfar; translated by Sasha Watson; colorist, Walter Pezzali; letterer, François Batet. First Second 2006 122p.
Grades: 3 4 5 6 7 8   **741.5**
1. Pirates — Fiction; 2. Space flight — Fiction
159643127X; 9781596431270

LC 2005021790

"The red-headed space heroine is back! This time, the evil Supermuscleman has developed a device for controlling children—a brainwashing machine! It's up to Sardine, Little Louie, and Captain Yellow Shoulder to keep him from using it. This installment of twelve more stories is filled with even more strange creatures—including a space Santa Claus, pesky flies that plant annoying music in their victim's ears, intergalactic yogurt thieves, and little monster carpet salesmen who live on a fully-carpeted comet." (Publisher's note)

Shady, Justin

The lava is a floor!. Art by Jeremy R. Scott. Silverline Books/Image Comics 2009 Un Illustration
Grades: K 1 2   **741.5; Fic**
1. Family life; 2. Humorous graphic novels; 3. Monsters; 4. Siblings; 5. Graphic novels
978-1-60706-123-6, $12.99

Monster children Clarg and Blarg live in a cave inside the crater of a live volcano, where the lava is their bedroom floor. They decide to pretend to be the weirdest creatures they can think of human children. To them, carpeted floors, television, and spaghetti with meatballs for dinner are all exotic and fantastical. The art shows Clarg and Blarg in their own home, and on the facing page what they are imagining. In an ending twist, the children are really human kids pretending to be monsters imagining that they are human. The bright, colorful art and cute monsters are fun to look at, while the dialog balloons on each single-panel page help early readers learn to read comic book panels. Wayne Chingsang, credited on the cover as co-writer, is actually also Justin Shady, according to Shady's blog.

Shakespeare, William

William Shakespeare's King Lear. Adapted by Brian Farrens; illustrated by Ben Dunn.. ABDO/Magic Wagon 2008 48p. Illustration
Grades: 5 6 7 8 9 10   **822.3; 741.5**
1. Shakespeare, William, 1564-1616 — Adaptations; 5. Graphic novels
978-1-60270-189-2, $28.50

LC 2008-10739

King Lear divides his kingdom among his three daughters but disowns Cordelia, the youngest, when she refuses to flatter him with insincerity. Then his older daughters renege on their promise to care for him, and he goes mad and roams the countryside. Meanwhile, Edmund, the illegitimate son of the Earl of Gloucester, plays political games in his quest for power. This graphic novel adaptation retains some of the original language from Shakespeare's play, while paring down the story to appeal to struggling readers. The book includes a short biography, a summary of the play, a glossary, and a short selection of famous lines and phrases from the play.

Part of the Graphic Shakespeare series

William Shakespeare's Othello. Adapted by Vincent Goodwin; illustrated by Chris Allen.. ABDO/Magic Wagon 2008 48p. Illustration
Grades: 5 6 7 8 9 10   **822.3; 741.5**
    1. Shakespeare, William, 1564-1616 — Adaptations; 5. Graphic novels
    978-1-60270-192-2, $28.50
                                LC 2008-10743
Othello the Moor is a successful general, married to the beautiful Desdemona. Life should be good, but he's incredibly jealous of anyone who looks at his wife. Iago wants Othello's position and decides that he should destroy Othello by fabricating an affair between Desdemona and Cassio. This graphic novel adaptation keeps some of the original dialog from Shakespeare's play while paring down the action to simplify it for readers who would struggle with the original. The book includes a short biography of Shakespeare, a summary of the plot, a glossary, and a sampling of famous lines and phrases.

Part of the Graphic Shakespeare series

William Shakespeare's Twelfth night. Adapted by Vincent Goodwin illustrated by Cynthia Martin. ABDO/Magic Wagon 2008 48p. Illustration
Grades: 5 6 7 8 9 10   **822.3; 741.5**
    1. Shakespeare, William, 1564-1616 — Adaptations; 5. Graphic novels
    978-1-60270-195-3, $28.50
                                LC 2008-10747
Twins Viola and Sebastian are separated in a shipwreck. Viola decides to disguise herself as a man since she's alone, and this sets the stage for mixed-up identities and a comic love triangle. This graphic novel adaptation retains some of the original language from Shakespeare's play, while paring down the story to appeal to struggling readers. The book includes a short biography, a summary of the play, a glossary, and a short selection of famous lines and phrases from the play.

Part of the Graphic Shakespeare series

Shapiro, David
    Terra Tempo: the four corners of time. David Shapiro, Christopher Herndon, Erica Melville. Craigmore Creations 2013 272 p. (Terra Tempo)
Grades: 5 6 7   **741.5**
    1. Colorado Plateau — Juvenile fiction; 2. Dinosaurs — Juvenile fiction; 3. Time travel — Juvenile fiction
    098444226X; 9780984442263, $17.99
                                LC 2012944924
This book is part of the "Terra Tiempo" series by David R. Shapiro and Erica Melville. "When Ari discovers a time map of the Colorado Plateau, he and the twins find themselves on a fast paced journey from Earth s underwater beginnings to the steamy jungles and huge creatures of the creepy Cretaceous. But this time, there is more at stake than just survival. This time, they are not alone." (Publisher's note)

Shaw, Murray
    Sherlock Holmes and the adventure of the blue gem. Adapted by Murray Shaw and M.J. Cosson ; illustrated by Sophie Rohrbach. Lerner Publishing Group/Graphic Universe 2010 48p. Illustration
Grades: 3 4 5 6 7 8
741.5; Fic
    1. Doyle, Arthur Conan Sir, 1859-1930 — Adaptations; 2. Gems; 3. Holmes, Sherlock (Fictional character); 4. Mystery graphic novels; 5. Graphic novels
    978-0-7613-6190-9, $26.60

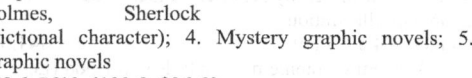

Courtesy of Lerner Publishing Group/Graphic Universe

                                LC 2009-51758
In this graphic adaptation of Doyle's "The Adventure of the Blue Carbuncle," Sherlock Holmes and Dr. Watson work on a Christmas holiday mystery when a train conductor brings them a Christmas goose and a man's hat that he found. They find a large blue gem in the throat of the goose, a famous gem that had been stolen from its owner. Holmes and Watson trace the owner of the hat, who starts them on a path to find out who stole the gem and stuffed it into the goose. This book includes discussion questions and a reading list that includes a mix of age-appropriate mysteries and nonfiction books and websites. Rohrbach's art looks almost like woodcuts; she unfortunately uses the stereotypical (and incorrect) look of the deerstalker cap and caped coat for Holmes. Her muted color palette of mostly browns matches the Victorian time period of the Holmes mysteries.

This is #3 in the On the Case with Holmes and Watson series.

Shazam!: the greatest stories ever told
    DC Comics 2008 224p. Illustration
Grades: 4 5 6 7 8 9 10 11 12 Adult   **741.5; Fic**
    1. Adventure graphic novels; 2. Captain Marvel (Fictional character); 3. Superhero graphic novels; 4. Graphic novels
    978-1-4012-1674-0, $24.99
This book collects comics stories about Captain Marvel dating from 1940 to 1998. Captain Marvel predated Superman as a comic book superhero; young newsboy Billy Batson could transform into the flying superhero by shouting the magic word "Shazam!" This gave him the wisdom of Solomon, the strength of Hercules, the stamina of Atlas, the power of Zeus, the courage of Achilles, and the speed of Mercury. In these fourteen stories, he battles against such foes as Dr. Sivana, Mr. Mind, and the Monster Society of Evil.

Shelley, Mary Wollstonecraft, 1797-1851
    Frankenstein. Retold by Michael Burgan ; illustrated by Dennis Calero. Stone Arch Books 2007 72p. Illustration
Grades: 3 4 5 6 7 8 9   **741.5; Fic**
    1. Horror graphic novels; 2. Science fiction graphic novels; 3. Graphic novels
    978-1-59889-830-9, $23.93

LC 2007-6199

The young scientist Victor Frankenstein has created something amazing and horrible at the same time, a living being out of dead flesh and bone. His creation, however, turns out to be a monster. Frankenstein's creation quickly discovers that his hideous appearance frightens away any companions. Now, Frankenstein must stop his creation before the monster's loneliness turns to violence. The book is written with an easy vocabulary for struggling and reluctant readers, and it includes facts about the novel.

Part of the Graphic Revolve series.

Shepard, Aaron

Robin Hood. Retold by Aaron Shepard and Anne L. Watson ; illustrated by Jennifer Tanner. Stone Arch Books 2006 63p. Illustration

Grades: 3 4 5 6 7 8 9   **741.5; Fic**

1. Adventure graphic novels; 2. Robin Hood (Legendary character); 3. Graphic novels

978-1-59889-049-5, $23.93

Robin Hood and his band of outlaws are the heroes of Sherwood Forest. Taking from the rich and giving to the poor, Robin Hood and his loyal followers fight for the oppressed and against the evil Sheriff of Nottingham. Among the adventures recounted are how Robin meets Little John and Friar Tuck, helping Alan-a-Dale marry his true love, Eleanor, and Robin entering the Sheriff's archery contest even though it's a trap. This adaptation is written for reluctant and struggling readers.

Part of the Graphic Revolve series.

Shiga, Jason

Meanwhile. Abrams/Amulet 2010 Un Illustration

Grades: 4 5 6 7 8 9   **741.5**

1. Science fiction graphic novels; 2. Graphic novels

0-8109-8423-7; 978-0-8109-8423-3, $15.95

LC 2009-39844

In this choose-your-own adventure graphic novel, a boy stumbles on the laboratory of a mad scientist who asks him to choose between testing a mind-reading device, a time machine, and a doomsday machine. (Bull Cent Child Books)

Shintani, Kaoru

Young Miss Holmes: casebook 1-2. By Kaoru Shintani. Seven Seas 2012 384 p.

Grades: 4 5 6 7   **741.5; 741.5952/223**

1. Detectives — Fiction; 2. Girls — Fiction

1935934864; 9781935934868, $16.99

In this book by Kaoru Shintani "Christie Holmes is a prodigy. At ten years old, she's as familiar with the sciences and classics as any older student at Cambridge or Oxford. And her facility with logic is reminiscent of her uncle, the eminent Sherlock Holmes himself. Christie's implacable curiosity leads her from one dangerous adventure to another, often joining forces with Uncle Sherlock and Doctor Watson on their famed investigations." (Publisher's note)

Young Miss Holmes: casebook 3-4. By Kaoru Shintani. Seven Seas 2012 384 p.

Grades: 4 5 6 7   **741.5**

1. Detectives — Fiction; 2. Family — Fiction

1935934945; 9781935934943, $16.99

In this graphic novel by Kaoru Shintani readers "experience classic Sherlock Holmes tales from the POV of his . . . niece. Sherlock Holmes' precocious niece Christie is back, as she helps her famous uncle solve such cases as: The Hound of the Baskervilles, The Adventure of the Six Napoleons, the Red-Headed League, and more!" (Publisher's note)

Shone, Rob

Avalanches & Landslides. The Rosen Publishing Group 2007 48p. Illustration

Grades: 3 4 5 6 7 8   **363.34; 741.5**

1. Avalanches; 2. Landslides

978-1-4042-1992-2 (lib bdg), $29.25

The book describes different kinds of landslides and avalanches, then dramatizes three major disasters. In 1910, the Wellington Avalanche in Washington swept standing trains off their tracks; in 1962, the Mount Huascaran Landslide destroyed the Peruvian town of Ranrahirca, then in 1970 the neighboring town of Yungay was destroyed by another landslide in the same area, with more than 17,000 dead. In 2006, Kan Abag Mountain on the island of Leyte in the Philippines collapsed, and the landslide buried the village of Guinsaugon. Additional information describes prevention efforts; the book includes a glossary and a list of books for further reading.

Part of the Graphic Natural Disasters series.

Earthquakes. Illustrated by Nick Spender. The Rosen Publishing Group 2007 48p. Illustration

Grades: 3 4 5 6 7 8   **551.22; 741.5**

1. Earthquakes; 2. Graphic novels

978-1-4042-1989-2, $26.25

The book describes earthquake zones and how earthquakes happen, then it dramatizes three major disasters: the San Francisco earthquake of 1906, the Great Hanshin Earthquake that devastated Kobe, Japan in 1995, and the South Asia Earthquake that struck Kashmir, Pakistan in 2005. Additional information includes an explanation of the Richter scale, a glossary, and a list of books for further reading.

Part of the Graphic Natural Disasters series.

Giganotosaurus: the giant southern lizard. Illustrated by Terry Riley. Rosen Publishing Group 2009 32p. Illustration

Grades: 3 4 5 6 7   **668; 741.5**

1. Dinosaurs; 2. Graphic novels

978-1-4358-2502-4, $25.25

LC 2008-3265

This book uses the comic book format to provide information about the Giganotosaurus, a giant meat-eating dinosaur from the Cretaceous Period. Information about its hunting habits and lifestyle are based on research and fossil records.

Part of the Graphic Dinosaur series

Muhammad Ali: The Life of a Boxing Hero. Art by Nick Spender. Rosen Publishing Group 2006 48p. Illustration

Grades: 3 4 5 6 7 8 9   **741.5; 796.8; 92**

1. African American athletes; 2. Ali, Muhammad, 1942-; 3. Biographical graphic novels; 4. Boxing — Biography; 5. Graphic novels
978-1-4042-0856-8, $29.25

LC 2005035521

This book uses the graphic novel format to tell of the life and career of boxing great Muhammad Ali. He started his career as Cassius Clay but changed his name when he converted to the Nation of Islam. He used his fame as a boxer to advocate against U.S. involvement in Vietnam, and to raise funds for charity. The book includes a list of all his boxing matches, and a list of books for further reading.

Part of the Rosen Graphic Biographies series.

Nelson Mandela: The Life of an African Statesman. Art by Neil Reed. The Rosen Publishing Group 2007 48p. Illustration

Grades: 3 4 5 6 7 8 9   **92; 741.5**

1. Biographical graphic novels; 2. Mandela, Nelson, 1918-2013; 3. Graphic novels
978-1-4042-0860-5, $29.25

After presenting information about South Africa and the apartheid system, the book presents a comic book style biography of Nelson Mandela, from his childhood through his adult life spent fighting apartheid from outside and within prison. Additional material describes the 1993 elections that brought Mandela and his political party, the ANC, to power in a new South Africa. The book includes a glossary and a list of books for further reading.

Part of the Graphic Biographies series.

Rosa Parks: The Life of a Civil Rights Heroine. Art by Nick Spender. Rosen Publishing Group 2006 48p. Illustration

Grades: 3 4 5 6 7 8 9   **741.5; 323.092; 323**

1. African American women — Alabama — Montgomery — Biography; 2. African Americans — Civil rights — Alabama — Montgomery — History — 20th century; 3. Biographical graphic novels; 4. Parks, Rosa, 1913-2005; 5. Graphic novels
978-1-4042-0864-3, $29.25

LC 2006002735

This book uses the graphic novel format to tell of the life of Rosa Parks and her act of defiance that inspired the Montgomery Bus Boycott. Additional information explains Jim Crow laws and briefly covers the civil rights movement. The book es a list of books for further reading.

Part of the Rosen Graphic Biographies series.

Triceratops: The Three Horned Dinosaur. Illustrated by Terry Riley and Geoff Ball. Rosen Publishing Group 2007 32p. Illustration

Grades: 2 3 4 5 6 7   **567.9; 741.5**

1. Dinosaurs; 2. Triceratops; 3. Graphic novels
978-1-4042-3896-1, $25.25

LC 2007-374

This volume uses colorful comic book style illustrations to explore the habitat, diet, and behavior of the triceratops. At the front of the book, facts about the triceratops are presented, while at the back of the book readers will find a picture gallery of other creatures mentioned in the book.

Part of the Graphic Dinosaurs series.

Tyrannosaurus: The Tyrant Lizard. Illustrated by James Field. Rosen Publishing Group 2007 32p. Illustration

Grades: 2 3 4 5 6 7   **567.9; 741.5**

1. Dinosaurs; 2. Tyrannosaurus; 3. Graphic novels
978-1-4042-3897-8, $25.25

LC 2007-0442

This volume uses colorful comic book style illustrations to explore the habitat, diet, and behavior of the tyrannosaurus. At the front of the book, facts about the tyrannosaurus are presented, while at the back of the book readers will find a picture gallery of other creatures mentioned in the book.

Part of the Graphic Dinosaurs series.

Volcanoes. Illustrated by Terry Riley. The Rosen Publishing Group 2007 48p. Illustration

Grades: 3 4 5 6 7 8   **551.21; 741.5**

1. Volcanoes; 2. Graphic novels
978-1-4042-1988-5, $29.25

The book first describes how volcanoes form, briefly discusses killer volcanoes, then uses comic book-style illustrations to dramatize the eruption of Vesuvius in A.D. 79, which buried Pompeii; Krakatoa, which erupted in 1883 and destroyed the island near Sumatra (a new island started growing in 1967); and Mount St. Helens in Washington, which erupted in 1980. Additional information on studying volcanoes is included, along with a glossary and a list of book for further reading.

Part of the Graphic Natural Disasters series.

War correspondents. Illustrated by Chris Forsey. Rosen Publishing Group 2008 48p. Illustration

Grades: 3 4 5 6 7 8 9   **070.4; 741.5**

1. Adie, Kate; 2. Journalists; 3. Newspaper editors; 4. Television reporters; 5. Graphic novels
978-1-4042-1449-1, $29.25

LC 2007-45936

After brief descriptions of early war reporting and the development of broadcast news from the front, the book profiles three war correspondents. Ernie Pyle made the life and wartime plight of the common soldier come alive for the folks back home; he was the first embedded journalist, staying with troops on the front. He was killed in action on Okinawa in 1945. Sydney Schanberg went to Cambodia in 1973 and witnessed the "killing fields" there. He wrote about a bombing incident in Neak Leung, when a B52 accidentally bombed the town and killed 137 people, injuring 258 more. Dith Pran, his fellow journalist from Cambodia, died on March 30, 2008. BBC journalist Kate Adie was embedded with Coalition Forces during Desert Storm, the first Gulf war, in 1990. During this war, the embedded journalists used technology to broadcast directly from the war front.

Part of the Graphic Careers series

Sias, Ryan

Zoe and Robot: let's pretend. Blue Apple 2011 Un Illustration (Balloon Toons)

Grades: K 1 2 3   **741.5; Fic**

1. Humorous graphic novels; 2. Imagination; 3. Robots; 4. Graphic novels
978-1-60905-063-4, $10.99; 1-60905-063-0

LC 2010046829

A young girl named Zoe wants Robot to play pretend with her, but she has to teach Robot how to pretend, because "Robots do not know how to pretend." From imagining a pile of pillows is a mountain to feeling the wind from a whirring fan, Zoe tries to help Robot. Finally, she draws mountains on a pair of goggles that she puts on Robot.

"The colorful art and simple panel designs make it easy to follow the story. . . . Beginning readers can easily catch the visual cues that help them interpret the simple dialogue, and they will enjoy the humor. . . . This is a fun, easy-to-read graphic novel for beginning readers." Booklist

Siegel, Elizabeth
The **Taj**. Art by Derek Toye. Harcourt Achieve/Steck-Vaughn 2007 48p. Illustration
Grades: 3 4 5 6 7 8   **741.5; Fic**
1. India — History; 2. Taj Mahal; 3. Graphic novels
978-1-4190-3197-7, $8.99
Nazma and her family move to Agra when her father gets a job as master builder of the Taj Mahal. In this new setting, Nazma discovers she has hidden talents. What lies in her future? This historical graphic novel includes prose intervals that provide more information about the Taj Mahal and about the Shah Jahan, who had it built as a shrine to his love for his dead wife, Mumtaz Mahal.
Part of the Timeline Graphic Novels series.

Siegel, Mark
To dance: a ballerina's graphic novel. [by] Siena Cherson Siegel; [illustrated by] Mark Siegel. Simon & Schuster 2006 Un Illustration
Grades: 4 5 6 7   **92; 741.5**
1. Autobiographical graphic novels; 2. Ballet; 3. Ballet dancers; 4. Puerto Ricans — Biography; 5. Siegel, Siena Cherson; 6. Graphic novels
1-4169-2687-9 (pa), $9.99
In this memoir of her youth in dance from ages six to eighteen, Siegel tells what it was like to be totally involved in dance, in ballet all the joys and the physical pain. She worked as a young dancer with George Ballanchine. Her absolute desire to be a dancer took her from her native Puerto Rico to New York City to study. Her simple but heartfelt narration is ably illustrated by her husband Mark Siegel.
Aladdin paperbacks

Simon, Kristen Koener
Bruce the little blue spruce. Penciled by Jim Valentino. Image Comics/Shadowline Press 2008 Un Illustration
Grades: PreK K 1 2   **741.5; Fic**
1. Christmas trees; 2. Graphic novels
978-1-60706-008-6, $9.99
Bruce the little blue spruce just wants to be a Christmas tree and help to make a family's holiday special, but he's blue, not green. The mice in the woods tell him he's too different, while Jack the rabbit tells him he'll be just right for the perfect family. The years go by and Bruce grows taller, but people always choose the green trees. Will he be chosen before he grows too big to fit into a house? This book is written by one of Image Comics' editors and penciled by comics veteran Jim Valentino.

Simone, Gail
The **Marvelous** adventures of Gus Beezer with Spider-Man. Jason Lethcoe, art. ABDO Publishing Company/Spotlight 2006 Un Illustration
Grades: 3 4 5 6 7 8   **741.5; Fic**
1. Humorous graphic novels; 2. Spider-Man (Fictional character); 3. Superhero graphic novels; 4. Graphic novels
978-1-59961-047-4, $21.35
                                                         LC 2006-43968
In this library bound edition of Marvel Age Spider-Man originally published in May 2003 (with all advertisements removed), super Marvel Comics fan Gus Beezer has been looking forward to the new Spider-Man movie, but his mother announces that the family will be going to the family reunion instead. With his sister waging a "Girl War" on him and the family reunion looming over him, the imaginative boy faces a miserable day. Until he meets a "distant cousin," Peter Parker, photographer for the Daily Bugle (Spider-Man fans will know who this is).

The **marvelous** adventures of Guz Beezer with the X-Men: X marks the Mutant. Jason Lethcoe, art. ABDO Spotlight 2006 Un Illustration
Grades: 3 4 5 6 7 8 9   **741.5; Fic**
1. Adventure graphic novels; 2. Humorous graphic novels; 3. Superhero graphic novels; 4. Graphic novels
1-59961-050-7, $21.35
Gus Beezer, major comics fan and collector, is convinced he's a mutant like the X-Men, even when his comic book skit at school results in major trouble and gets him grounded. What he keeps missing is that his baby sister Tillie is the one getting him into trouble at home. Another story runs on the bottom part of the page, and looks like a homemade comic written and drawn by Gus, featuring him as Marvel Boy and his baby sister as the town-consuming villain.
This book is a revision of an issue of The Marvelous Adventures of Gus Beever, originally published by Marvel's Marvel Age line.

Simpson, Dana
Phoebe and Her Unicorn. Dana Simpson. Andrews McMeel 2014 224 p. Color illustration
Grades: 3 4 5   **741.5**
1. Girls; 2. Unicorns — Fiction
1449446205; 9781449446208, $9.99
                                                     LC Bl2014039099
In this graphic novel, by Dana Simpson, "Phoebe skipped a rock across a pond and accidentally hit a unicorn in the face. Improbably, this led to Phoebe being granted one wish, and she used it to make the unicorn, Marigold Heavenly Nostrils, her obligational best friend. But can a vain mythical beast and a nine-year-old daydreamer really forge a connection?" (Publisher's note)
"A pink, bubble-gum bonbon of a tale spun of a likable, albeit self-centered, fourth-grader and her magical, self-obsessed, although sometimes-kind, unicorn." Kirkus
Other titles in this series are: Unicorn on a roll (2015); Unicorn vs. Goblins (2016)

Unicorn on a Roll: Another Phoebe and Her Unicorn Adventure. By Dana Simpson. Paw Prints 2015 Color; Illustration

Grades: 3 4 5   **741.5**
1. Friendship — Juvenile fiction; 2. Unicorns — Juvenile fiction
9781449470760, $9.99

LC 2014921935
This book, by Dana Simpson, is about the "magical friendship of Phoebe and her best friend, unicorn Marigold Heavenly Nostrils. . . . [The] reader is invited on a journey into the lives of Phoebe and Marigold as they navigate the difficulties of grade school, celebrate the winter holidays, and explore their super hero/super villain personas together." (Publisher's note)

Slade, Christian
★ **Korgi,** Book 1: Sprouting Wings. Top Shelf Productions 2007 88p. Illustration
Grades: 2 3 4 5 6 7 8 9 10 11 12 Adult   **741.5; Fic**
1. Dogs; 2. Fantasy graphic novels; 3. Stories without words; 4. Graphic novels
978-1-891830-90-7, $10
In this wordless book, a young Mollie (woodland people) named Ivy and her young Korgi companion named Sprout embark on adventures in Korgi Hollow, an enchanted place. When they wander from the Mollie village, the two fall through a hole in the ground and find nasty, monstrous creatures who want to eat them. As they deal with the danger and make their escape, Ivy and Sprout both discover new talents. Slade's extensively cross-hatched yet delicate art is highly expressive, and readers young and old will have no trouble figuring out what is going on. The Korgi are based on Welsh corgi dogs, of which Slade and his wife have two.

Korgi, book 2. Top Shelf Productions 2008 Un Illustration
Grades: 3 4 5 6 7 8 9 10 11 12 Adult   **741.5; Fic**
1. Adventure graphic novels; 2. Fantasy graphic novels; 3. Stories without words; 4. Graphic novels
978-1-60309-010-0, $10
In this second wordless volume, the young Mollie named Ivy and her Korgi cub Sprout, experience a harrowing adventure. Someone has been hunting the Mollies and cutting off their wings. Ivy and Sprout rescue one older Mollie named Art and his Korgi when they fall into a deep trap in the woods; then as Ivy flies, a barbed arrow cuts one of her wings off. She and Sprout see a strange creature carrying her wing and they follow him to his place, where he hangs all the Mollie wings like trophies. Ivy decides she wants her wing back, but she and Sprout will have to fight the creature and his automated and nasty bots.

Slavin, Bill
Big star Otto. Written by Bill Slavin with Esperança Melo; art by Bill Slavin. Kids Can Press 2015 95 p. (Elephants Never Forget)
Grades: 3 4 5 6   **741.5**
1. Chimpanzees — Juvenile fiction; 2. Elephants — Juvenile fiction; 3. Kidnapping — Juvenile fiction; 4. Parrots — Juvenile fiction; 5. Graphic novels
1894786963; 9781894786966, $16.95
"In this conclusion to the Elephants Never Forget graphic novel trilogy, [by Bill Slavin], big-hearted hero Otto and his parrot pal Crackers have landed in Hollywood, the final stop in their journey across America in search of their good friend Georgie the chimpanzee. They've been hot on Georgie's trail since he was abducted from Africa by the sinister Man with the Wooden Nose, and now they're sure they've finally found his location." (Publisher's note)

Smalley, Roger
Dolley Madison Saves History. Illustrated by Anna Maria Cool, Scott Rosema, Charles Barnett III. Capstone Press 2006 32p. Illustration
Grades: 3 4 5 6 7 8 9   **741.5; 973.5; 92**
1. Biographical graphic novels; 2. Madison, Dolley, 1768-1849; 3. War of 1812; 4. Washington (DC); 5. Graphic novels
0-7368-4972-6, $25.26

LC 2005008465
This book uses the comic book format to recount the story of First Lady Dolley Madison's actions during the War of 1812, when Washington, D.C. was invaded by British troops. It includes additional information, a glossary, a list of books for further reading, and more.
Part of the Graphic Library, Graphic History series.

Smith, Andy J.
Jeremy Kreep: Fang Fairy. Stone Arch Books 2007 40p. Illustration
Grades: 3 4 5 6 7 8 9   **741.5; Fic**
1. Fantasy graphic novels; 2. Humorous graphic novels; 3. Graphic novels
978-1-59889-835-4, $21.26

LC 2007-3176
Jeremy Kreep has a problem. Something has snagged a baby tooth from beneath his brother's pillow and left a puddle of slime. Now Jeremy and his best friend Nessy go off to find the truth behind the tooth fairy. Is the creature just a silly superstition, or a real-life collector of fangs? This graphic novel is written with an easy vocabulary for reluctant and struggling readers.
Part of the Graphic Sparks line of books.

Smith, Ian
Emily & the intergalactic lemonade stand. [by] Ian Smith and Tyson Smith. Amaze Ink/Slave Labor Graphics 2004 96p. Illustration
Grades: 4 5 6 7 8 9   **741.5; Fic**
1. Humorous graphic novels; 2. Science fiction graphic novels; 3. Graphic novels
0-943151-96-1, $12.95
Eleven-year-old Emily runs a lemonade stand with the help of her pet robot, Juicer; she wants to earn enough money to buy a pony. Complicating matters is neighborhood rival Daisy, who wants to beat Emily because cute Jace Tanner hangs around Emily (he actually only likes robots). Then aliens invade, and the military wants Juicer, because they think he's the perfect weapon. And little alien warrior Pheef wants blood, can he help it he's so cute and tiny? The defense of Earth depends on Emily; can she survive?

Smith, Jeff
★ **Bone** Book Seven: ghost circles. Scholastic/GRAPHIX 2008 152p. Illustration

Grades: 3 4 5 6 7 8 9 10 11 12 Adult   **741.5; Fic**
1. Adventure graphic novels; 2. Fantasy graphic novels; 3. Graphic novels
978-0-439-70629-2, $19.99; 978-0-439-70634-6 (pa), $9.99

LC 2007-9568403

The Bone cousins, Gran'ma Ben, Thorn, and their loyal rat creature cub Bartleby venture on a journey through the mysterious ghost circles to Atheia, the old city of the royal family. Meanwhile, the Barrelhaven villagers and the Veni Yan face enemy hordes. Steve Hamaker is the colorist for this full color version of Smith's comic epic.

★ **Bone** vol. 8: treasure hunters. Scholastic/Graphix 2008 138p. Illustration
Grades: 5 6 7 8 9 10 11 12 Adult   **741.5; Fic**
1. Adventure graphic novels; 2. Fantasy graphic novels; 3. Graphic novels
978-0-439-70630-8, $18.95; 978-0-439-70633-9 (pa), $9.99

LC 2008-9568403

The Bone cousins, Gran'ma Ben, and Thorn reach the city of Atheia, where they prepare to battle the Lord of the Locusts. Meanwhile, Thorn's visions are becoming more threatening and Phoney Bone is convinced Atheia is rich in gold, and he is determined to find it. But all is not well in Atheia, and Thorn is in great danger, not only from Briar and the Lord of the Locusts. This edition is in full color, done by Steve Hamaker.

★ **Bone:** out from Boneville. Scholastic Graphix 2005 144p. Illustration
Grades: 4 5 6 7 8 9 10 11 12   **741.5; Fic**
1. Adventure graphic novels; 2. Fantasy graphic novels; 3. Graphic novels
0-439-70623-8, $18.95; 0-439-70640-8 (pa), $9.99

"The story follows three cousins who have been thrown out of their town for cheating the citizens. Shortly thereafter, they are separated. Each Bone stumbles into a mysterious valley full of odd creatures that reveal strange happenings. The story is well paced with smooth transitions. It is dark, witty, mysterious, and exciting. The full-color art reflects that of classic comic books." SLJ

Also available Bone: one volume edition $39.95 from Cartoon Books (ISBN 1-8889-6314-X)

Other titles in this series are: Bone: the great cow race (vol. 2); Bone: eyes of the storm (vol. 3); Bone: the dragonslayer (vol. 4); Bone: Rock Jaw: master of the Eastern border (vol. 5); Bone: old man's cave (vol. 6); Bone: ghost circles (vol. 7); Bone: treasure hunters (vol. 8); Bone: crown of horns (vol. 9)

Bone: Rose. With illustrations by Charles Vess. Scholastic Graphix 2009 138p. Illustration
Grades: 4 5 6 7 8   **741.5; Fic**
978-0-545-13542-9, $21.99; 0-545-13542-7;
978-0-545-13543-6 (pa), $10.99; 0-545-13543-5 (pa)

"When a terrifying dragon attacks the small towns of the Northern Valley, a young Princess Rose (known later as Gran'ma Ben) must defeat it. The beast is actually the ancient evil, the Lord of the Locusts, and while Rose faces danger with honor, her elder sister, Princess Briar, follows a more sinister path." (Publisher's note)

Bone: tall tales. By Jeff Smith with Tom Sniegoski; color by Steve Hamaker. Graphix 2010 108p. Illustration
Grades: 4 5 6 7 8   **741; 741.5**
978-0-545-14095-9, $21.99; 0-545-14095-1;
978-0-545-14096-6 (pa), $10.99; 0-545-14096-X (pa)

"Long before the Bone cousins were ever lost in the uncharted desert on the outskirts of the Valley, Big Johnson Bone, the discoverer of the Rolling Bone River, founded Boneville. But little is known of the mighty explorer's adventures before he started his famous trading post. So when Smiley Bone sits down with a group of young campers to retell the legendary stories of Boneville's origin and its tough, no-nonsense founder, what they hear are tall tales in typical BONE fashion." (Publisher's note)

★ **Little** Mouse gets ready. TOON Books 2009 32p. Illustration
Grades: PreK K 1   **741.5; Fic**
1. Clothing and dress; 2. Humorous graphic novels; 3. Mice; 4. Graphic novels
978-1-935179-01-6, $12.95; 1-935179-01-2

LC 2008-55403

ALA ALSC Geisel Award Honor Book (2010)

"Little Mouse is eager to go to the barn with his mother. He slowly and methodically gets dressed, which is quite an accomplishment for the little guy, only to be reminded, in classic noodlehead fashion, that mice don't wear clothes. . . . The cartoon illustrations are large and uncomplicated without being babyish, and the punch line is preceded with places for knowing giggles." SLJ

Smith, Mark Andrew

The **New** Brighton Archeological Society book one: The castle of Galomar. Created by Mark Andrew Smith & Matthew Weldon. Image Comics 2009 Un Illustration
Grades: 4 5 6 7 8 9   **741.5; Fic**
1. Adventure graphic novels; 2. Fairies; 3. Fantasy graphic novels; 4. Goblins; 5. Graphic novels
978-1-58240-973-3, $17.99

When their parents die on an archeological expedition, two sets of siblings Joss and Cooper, and Brad and Becka, come to live on the estate where their parents lived as children. They first discover bottled ghosts when Becka accidentally falls through a secret door, then they find an old clubhouse connected to the estate's manor house by a tunnel. The clubhouse holds lots of books about different kinds of monsters and other creatures. And then, when they go camping, they find a society of goblins, including Mitch, who knew their parents. There, the four find themselves caught in the middle of a war between the fairies and the goblins, all for possession of powerful books. Mitch's parents tell the children about the evil Galomar, who seeks to possess all the magic books in the world. They decide to infiltrate the castle in order to try to stop Galomar. This fantasy adventure includes some action but little actual killing (the goblins use maple syrup to make the fairies' wings too sticky to fly, among other tactics).

Sohn, Emily

A **Crash** Course in Forces and Motion with Max Axiom, Super Scientist. Illustrated by Steve Erwin and Charles Barnett III. Capstone Press 2007 32p. Illustration

Grades: 3 4 5 6 7 8   **531; 741.5**
1. Motion; 2. Science; 3. Graphic novels
978-0-7368-6837-2 li, $25.26; 978-0-7368-7890-6 (pa)
Max Axiom is a super-cool super-scientist who demonstrates and explains science in ways never before seen in the classroom. Whether shrinking down to the size of an ant or riding on a sound wave, Max does whatever it takes to make science super cool and accessible. This volume explores forces such as motion and speed, and includes a glossary and a list of books for further reading.
Part of the Graphic Science series.

The **Illuminating** World of Light with Max Axiom, Super Scientist. Art by Nick Derington. Capstone Press 2007 32p. Illustration
Grades: 3 4 5 6 7 8 9   **535; 741.5**
1. Light; 2. Graphic novels
978-1-4296-0140-X, $25.26
                          LC 2007002264
This book uses the graphic novel format to follow the adventures of super scientist Max Axiom as he explains the science behind light, including how the human eye sees light. The book includes additional facts and a list of books for further reading.
Part of the Graphic Science series.

A **journey** through the digestive system with Max Axiom, super scientist. Illustrated by Cynthia Martin and Barbara Schulz. Capstone Press 2009 32p. Illustration
Grades: 2 3 4 5 6 7   **612.3; 741.5**
1. Digestion; 2. Graphic novels
978-1-4296-2336-0, $26.60; 978-1-4296-3452-6 (pa), $7.95
                          LC 2008-29650
The cartoon super scientist Max Axiom takes young readers into the human body to explore the digestive system, from the act of eating (ingestion) through the esophagus to the stomach, into the intestines. The book also explains why people get gas, and discusses the work of the large intestine without showing it. However, some very sensitive young children could get grossed out by some of the illustrations. Readers will also find facts about nutrition, including the Food Pyramid. Back matter in the book includes more digestion facts, a glossary, reading list, and an index.
Part of the Graphic Science series

Sonic the Hedgehog Archives Volume 1
Archie Comic Publications 2006 Un Illustration
Grades: 3 4 5 6 7 8   **741.5; Fic**
1. Adventure graphic novels; 2. Humorous graphic novels; 3. Sonic the Hedgehog (Fictional character); 4. Graphic novels
1-879794-20-9, $7.49
This volume collects the stories published in the first four issues of the Sonic the Hedgehog comics. In these stories, Sonic faces Robotnik's mecha-plant in the forest; he crashes the Casino Night Zone and must face the Orbinaut; he and buddy Tails have to deal with Coconuts, Scratch, and Grounder when they ruin a perfectly good day; he meets Bunnie Rabbot; and he faces the Universalamander.

Sonic the Hedgehog Archives Volume 2
Archie Comic Publications 2006 Un Illustration

Grades: 3 4 5 6 7 8   **741.5; Fic**
1. Adventure graphic novels; 2. Humorous graphic novels; 3. Sonic the Hedgehog (Fictional character); 4. Graphic novels
1-879794-21-7, $7.49
Among the stories collected in this volume, Sonic and the Freedom Fighters compete in Olympic challenges issued by Robotnik; Sonic faces the Termite-nator; Robotnik kidnaps Sally when she's dressed as a Halloween Sorceress, thinking she's a real one; and Sonic deals with ever more nasty bots created by Robotnik.

Sonic the Hedgehog Archives Volume 3
Archie Comic Publications 2007 Un Illustration
Grades: 3 4 5 6 7 8   **741.5; Fic**
1. Adventure graphic novels; 2. Humorous graphic novels; 3. Sonic the Hedgehog (Fictional character); 4. Graphic novels
1-879794-22-1, $7.49
Two of Sonic's most personal foes are introduced for the first time; the parade of robotic Sonics debuts with the evil Pseudo-Sonic; and a good hedgehog can go bad with the nasty Evil Sonic. Sonic also encounters the Nerbs, and Larry the Super-Jinx makes his first appearance.

Sonic the Hedgehog Archives Volume 4
Archie Comic Publications 2007 Un Illustration
Grades: 3 4 5 6 7 8   **741.5; Fic**
1. Adventure graphic novels; 2. Humorous graphic novels; 3. Sonic the Hedgehog (Fictional character); 4. Graphic novels
1-879794-24-5, $7.49
This volume features the debut of Sonic's first rival, Knuckles the Echidna; when Sonic and Tails meet the red warrior for the first time, they barely make it out alive. Then Tails gets too big for his britches. And Dr. Robotnik is big, but now he's huge and dwarfs the Freedom Fighters, putting them under glass.

Sonic the Hedgehog: The Beginning
Archie Comics 2003 96p. Illustration
Grades: 3 4 5 6 7 8 9 10 11 12 Adult   **741.5; Fic**
1. Adventure graphic novels; 2. Humorous graphic novels; 3. Sonic the Hedgehog (Fictional character); 4. Graphic novels
1-879794-12-8, $10.95
In 1993, Sonic the Hedgehog sped his way from video games to comic books, and has been going strong ever since. Now, readers can enjoy his earliest comic book adventures with this edition that reprints the first appearances of Tails, Princess Sally, Antoine, Rotor, Uncle Chuck, and Muttski. Fans can also marvel at Sonic's magic rings, the freedom emeralds, and King Acorn's magic crown; while booing and hissing at the villainous Robotnik, his evil Swat-Bots, and his myriad dastardly devices.

Sonishi, Kenji
     Leave it to PET!: the misadventures of a recycled super robot, vol. 1. Story & art by Kenji Sonishi; translation,

Katherine Schilling; touch-up art & lettering, John Hunt; editor, Traci N. Todd. Viz Media/VizKids 2009 192p. Illustration

Grades: 3 4 5 6   **741.5; Fic**

1. Humorous graphic novels; 2. Manga; 3. Recycling; 4. Graphic novels

978-1-4215-2649-2, $7.99

PET (polyethylene terephthalate, a type of recyclable plastic) was a simple plastic bottle until nine-year-old Noboru recycled him. Now PET is a super robot programmed to "repay" Noboru for recycling him by helping him. Unfortunately for Noboru, PET's help usually ends up causing even more trouble; being a super robot doesn't mean PET has a clue about what he is doing. The book includes lots of short stories that follow the formula of Noboru getting into a bit of a fix, calling for PET, then getting into more trouble as PET does the wrong thing. Some of the stories do include some information about recycling plastics and aluminum, which is done somewhat differently in Japan than in the U.S.

Volume 1 of a 4-volume series

Soo, Kean

★ **Jellaby:** monster in the city. Hyperion Books 2009 172p. Illustration

Grades: 4 5 6 7 8 9   **741.5; Fic**

1. Fantasy graphic novels; 2. Friendship; 3. Monsters; 4. Graphic novels

1-4231-0565-6 (pa); 978-1-4231-0565-7 (pa), $9.99

Beginning right where the first book ended, Portia, Jason, and Jellaby continue on their way to Toronto, walking after Portia panicked and they got off the train. They're searching for a way home for Jellaby, and they think a door somewhere in Exhibition Place, where the Canadian National Exhibition is taking place, holds a clue. Portia feels torn between wanting to help her friend yet not wanting to say goodbye forever, and her ambivalence causes a rift between her and Jason. When she doesn't want to trust a masked magician who seems to know too much about them and Jellaby, Portia leaves Jason. They all end up in the Automotive Building, where the masked man leads Jason and Jellaby down below the building, while Portia seems to find her long lost father. But is he really her father, and just what is waiting for Jason and Jellaby under the Automotive Building" Soo again uses a mostly purple color palette.

Another title in the author's series about Jellaby

★ **Jellaby;** Volume 1: the lost monster. By Kean Soo. Stone Arch Books 2014 160 p. Color; Illustration (Jellaby)

Grades: 4 5 6 7 8 9   **741.5**

1. Extraterrestrial beings — Fiction; 2. Friendship — Fiction; 3. Human-alien encounters; 4. Monsters — Fiction

1434291952; 9781434264206, $12.95 ; 9781434291950, $19.99

LC 2013037026

"Portia has just moved to a new neighborhood with her mom. Adjusting to life without a father is hard enough, but school is boring and her classmates are standoffish. . . . But things start to get better when Portia mounts a midnight excursion into the woods behind her house where she discovers a shy and sweet purple monster. Life with Jellaby

is exciting, but Portia's purple friend has secrets of his own." (Publisher's note)

"Soo grounds the story in a fairly gritty contemporary reality, where kids deal with bullies and well-meaning adults try to help. Clear, clean lines and easy-to-follow panel layouts round out the package." Booklist

First published 2008

Originally published: New York : Hyperion Books for Children, 2008.A Capstone imprint.

Spiegelman, Art

★ **Big** fat Little Lit. [edited by] Art Spiegelman and Francoise Mouly. Puffin 2006 144p. Illustration

Grades: 2 3 4 5 6 7 8   **741.5; Fic**

1. Folklore; 2. Graphic novels

0-14-240706-2, $14.99

This volume collects all three previously published Little Lit books: Little Lit: Once Upon a Time, Little Lit: Strange Stories for Strange Kids, and Little Lit: It Was a Dark and Silly Night. Many comics creators and children's book writers and illustrators contributed stories, including Ian Falconer, Daniel Clowes, Maurice Sendak, David Sedaris, Chris Ware, Jules Feiffer, Barbara McClintock, Crockett Johnson, J. Otto Siebold, Neil Gaiman, Art Spiegelman, and Lemony Snicket."

Spires, Ashley

★ **Binky** takes charge. By Ashley Spires. Kids Can Press 2012 64 p. Color illustration

Grades: 4 5 6   **741.5/971; Fic**

1. Cats — Fiction; 2. Picture books for children; 3. Spy stories

1554537037; 9781554537037, $16.95; 9781554537686, $8.95; 9781451765137, $17.95

"Felines of the Universe Ready for Space Travel (F.U.R.S.T.) and Captain Gracie are pleased to announce that Lt. Binky is about to get his first recruit to train [in this book by Ashley Spires.] . . . There's a new diversity program at F.U.R.S.T., and Gordon, a dog, has been assigned to Binky. Binky decides to give it his all. As expected, Gordon falls short. Then Binky discovers the unthinkable: Gordon seems to be leaving coded messages in outer space . . . If they are to prove Gordon is a double agent, Gracie and Binky will need incontrovertible proof!" (Kirkus)

★ **Binky** the space cat. Kids Can Press 2009 64p. Illustration

Grades: 2 3 4 5   **741.5; Fic**

1. Cats; 2. Humorous graphic novels; 3. Space flight; 4. Graphic novels

978-1-55453-309-1, $16.95; 1-55453-309-0; 978-1-55453-419-7 (pa), $7.95; 1-55453-419-4 (pa)

Binky the cat lives with two humans (an unnamed mother and son) in what he thinks of as a space station. He's determined to become a space cat and venture into outer space with his stuffed mousie Ted, and to that end he gets his space cat kit through the mail, complete with instructions to build a space ship.

"Spires's mix of sly, dry and slapstick humor in her first graphic novel is perfect. . . . Details in the muted watercolor illustrations, like mousie Ted covering his nose as Binky releases "space gas," will keep readers of all ages giggling, whether they're cat lovers or not." Kirkus

Other titles about Binky are: Binky to the rescue (2010); Binky under pressure (2011); Binky takes charge (2012); License to scratch (2013)

★ **Binky** to the rescue: a Binky adventure. Kids Can Press 2010 64p. Illustration

Grades: 2 3 4 5   **741.5; Fic**
1. Adventure graphic novels; 2. Cats; 3. Humorous graphic novels; 4. Graphic novels
978-1-55453-502-6, $16.95; 1-55453-502-6;
978-1-55453-597-2 (pa), $8.95; 1-55453-597-2 (pa)
LC 2009-906866-4

While in hot pursuit of an alien invader (a fly) in his space station (house), Binky, a Certified Space Cat, falls out the space station porthole (bathroom window) and lands in outer space (outside) for the first time. As he starts to explore, Binky finds his copilot Ted (his stuffed mousie), but then comes under attack by aliens (wasps). Rescued by one of his humans (Mom), Binky soon realizes Ted is still in outer space and he must get him back.

"The muted palette and variety of panel shapes, sound effects, expressive characters and deadpan humor work in perfect rib-tickling harmony." Kirkus

Companion to: Binky the Space Cat (2009)

Stanley, John

Little Lulu vol. 17: The Valentine. Writer, John Stanley ; artists, John Stanley, Irving Tripp. Dark Horse Comics 2007 228p. Illustration

Grades: 3 4 5 6 7 8 9 10 11 12 Adult   **741.5**
1. Friendship; 2. Humorous graphic novels; 3. Little Lulu (Fictional character); 4. Graphic novels
978-1-59307-686-3, $10.95

In this seventeenth volume, Lulu gets into more fun mischief, tricking Tubby into taking a sponge for a walk, rescuing a pair of pants from the tough west side gang, and defeating the clubhouse boys in a snowball war. She also tells neighborhood little terror Alvin more stories of Witch Hazel, and during a day at the beach, she tries to win a doll at the ball throwing booth where Tubby is working.

★ **Little** Lulu, vol. 1: My dinner with Lulu. [by] John Stanley and Irving Tripp. Dark Horse Comics 2005 200p. Illustration

Grades: 4 5 6 7 8 9 10 11 12 Adult   **741.5; Fic**
1. Friendship; 2. Humorous graphic novels; 3. Graphic novels
1-59307-318-6, $9.95

Lulu Moppet plays with best friend Tubby, except when he hangs out with the other neighborhood boys and tries to keep girls out of their clubhouse; she deals with terrible toddler Alvin by weaving extravagant tales featuring herself; and other everyday adventures. This is the first volume of a series that will eventually reprint every Little Lulu comic for new young readers.

Volume 1 of 29

Little Lulu, volume 21: Miss Feeny's folly and other stories. John Stanley & Irving Tripp. Dark Horse Comics 2009 200p. Illustration

Grades: 1 2 3 4 5 6 7 8 9 10 11 12 Adult   **741.5; Fic**

1. Friendship; 2. Humorous graphic novels; 3. Little Lulu (Fictional character); 4. Graphic novels
978-1-59582-365-6, $14.95

This volume collects the Little Lulu stories from issues #100 to 105 of the Dell Comics series. Lulu and Annie carry on their battle with the boys over the boys' clubhouse, Lulu tells little Alvin more stories of the poor little girl and the wicked Witch Hazel, Tubby goes to the dentist, all the neighbor kids have to attend Miss Feeny's dance party, Tubby and then Lulu each have to clean up parts of their houses and try to trick the other into helping, and more. These stories are mostly in full color, with just a few one-page stories in black and white.

Little Lulu: the alamo and other stories. John Stanley & Irving Tripp. Dark Horse Comics 2009 200p. Illustration

Grades: 1 2 3 4 5 6 7 8 9 10 11 12 Adult   **741.5; Fic**
1. Humorous graphic novels; 2. Little Lulu (Fictional character); 3. Graphic novels
978-1-59582-293-2, $14.95

With this nineteenth volume of Little Lulu reprints, the comics are in full color; this volume collects issues 88 through 93, originally published by Dell Comics in 1955 through 1956. Among the stories in this volume, Tubby and the boys try to trick Lulu and Annie into digging a well, Tubby's parents pay Lulu to keep him company while they go out, and Lulu and Annie get revenge on Tubby and the boys by dousing them with water bombs while the boys are wearing their Davy Crockett coonskin caps. These stories appeal to younger readers as well as adults who remember reading the original comic books.

★ **Nancy,** volume 1: the Johnny Stanley Library. From the comic strip by Ernie Bushmiller ; script and layout by John Stanley ; finished art by Dan Gormley. Drawn & Quarterly 2009 128p. Illustration

Grades: 2 3 4 5 6 7 8 9 10 11 12 Adult
741.5; Fic
1. Humorous graphic novels; 2. Drew, Nancy (Fictional character); 3. Graphic novels
978-1-897299-77-7, $24.95

Courtesy of Drawn & Quarterly

LC C2009-901565-X

The comic book character Nancy was created by Ernie Bushmiller; Dell Comics published the comics scripted by John Stanley with art by Dan Gormley starting with issue 146 in 1957. In these stories, Nancy meets Oona Goosepimple, a spooky girl who lives in a haunted house, has an incredible run of bad luck because of what she thinks is a four-leaf clover, and has all kinds of everyday adventures and misadventures with her friend Sluggo, their nemesis Spike, neighborhood rich kid Rollo, and her Aunt Fritzi. Always short of money yet needing some to buy ice cream sodas and other treats, many of Nancy's adventures with Sluggo involve various moneymaking schemes to get the dime needed (those were the days ...). The kinds of adventures the kids have are somewhat similar to Stanley's other work on Little Lulu, but set in an urban environment rather than the suburban neighborhood of Lulu and her friends. The book, designed by Seth, retains the soft original coloring of the old comics, with the paper even looking like old comics (but much sturdier). This book should have the same all-ages appeal as Little Lulu; the 2009 Free Comic Book Day issue featuring Nancy was a big hit with readers five years old and up to adults who remembered reading Nancy comics when they were kids.

Star Wars: Clone Wars Adventures Volume 5
Dark Horse Comics 2006 Unp. Illustration
Grades: 5 6 7 8 9 10   **741.5; Fic**
1. Adventure graphic novels; 2. Science fiction graphic novels; 3. Star Wars; 4. Graphic novels
1-59307-483-2, $6.95
As the fires of the Clone Wars burn across the galaxy, heroes on both sides of the conflict emerge, and no matter what the outcome, the galaxy will be forever changed. In this volume, the JedI Aayla Secura journeys into the heart of darkness to save an Ewok village; a clone commander learns firsthand of the sacrifices the Separatists will make for their cause; Bail Organa (Leia's adoptive father) infiltrates a dangerous world to rescue a friend; and the Padawan Joc Sah gets caught in the crosshairs of Order 66. These stories take place just before and during the events of Star Wars Episode III: The Revenge of the Sith.

Star Wars: Clone Wars Adventures Volume 6
Dark Horse Comics 2006 Un Illustration
Grades: 5 6 7 8 9 10   **741.5; Fic**
1. Adventure graphic novels; 2. Science fiction graphic novels; 3. Star Wars; 4. Graphic novels
978-1-59307-567-5, $6.95
The Clone Wars grind through the galaxy, shaking every system to its core and testing loyalties on both sides of the conflict. In this volume, Saesee Tiin steals a secret Separatist fighter, Ki-Adi-Mundi and Rivi-Anu rescue an army of clone troopers, clone commandos battle in the clouds of a gas planet, and Plo Koon and Kit Fisto get trapped in an underwater prison. These stories take place just before and during the events in Star Wars Episode III: Revenge of the Sith.

Star Wars: Clone Wars Adventures Volume 7
Dark Horse Comics 2007 Un Illustration
Grades: 5 6 7 8 9 10   **741.5; Fic**
1. Adventure graphic novels; 2. Science fiction graphic novels; 3. Star Wars; 4. Graphic novels
978-1-59307-678-8, $6.95
The fate of the galaxy hangs in the balance, the Republic and Confederacy taking their fight from the cold reaches of space to exotic alien worlds. In this volume, Obi-Wan Kenobi and Anakin Skywalker are attacked by giant monsters; Padme Naberrie becomes a spy; Bultar Swan storms an impenetrable fortress, and three friends rob a back guarded by an army of clones. These adventures take place some time during the Clone Wars.

Steinberg, David
The **adventures** of Daniel Boom AKA Loud Boy: game on!. Illustrated by Brian Smith. Grosset & Dunlap 2009 96p. Illustration
Grades: 3 4 5 6 7 8   **741.5; Fic**
1. Humorous graphic novels; 2. Superhero graphic novels; 3. Graphic novels
978-0-448-44700-1, $5.99
Loud Boy and the rest of the Freak Five thought they had helped put all the members of Kid Rid behind bars, but now "Old Fogey" Fogelman has broken out of jail. Daniel Boom, AKA Loud Boy, his sister Jeannie S., Sid, Rex, and Violet work together to help Daniel's uncle hide something called a Flooggget from Fogelman it looks like a banana, but it is a device that can digitize three-dimensional objects. Uncle Stanley warns the super powered kids that Fogelman intends to use the device on children, but he has to flee before telling them everything. Then Daniel makes a new friend, J R, who gets him hooked on the new game called Pig Planet. The other Freak Five members try to get Daniel's attention, but succeed only when it's too late, and J R has stolen the Flooggget and given it to Fogelman. It turns out J R is a robot built by Fogelman, and he uses the Flooggget to digitize the 1.7 million children playing Pig Planet. Daniel figures the only way to save the kids and stop Fogelman is to get into the game himself but can he win?

★ The **adventures** of Daniel Boom AKA Loud boy: sound off!. By D. J. Steinberg ; illustrated by Brian Smith. Grosset & Dunlap 2008 Un Illustration
Grades: 2 3 4 5 6 7   **741.5; Fic**
1. Humorous graphic novels; 2. Superhero graphic novels; 3. Graphic novels
978-0-448-44698-1, $5.99
Ten years ago, when Daniel Boom was born, he came with a very loud voice. When his family moves to a small town for his mother's work, Uncle Stanley warns them that Daniel and his sister Jeannie S. (never forget her middle initial!) are in danger from "Kid-Rid." Daniel's loud voice gets him into trouble at school, with detention, but there, he meets three other kids his exact age. They discover that a rogue scientist called Old Fogey tried to experiment on them, but something went wrong, and they each have powers of destruction, super fidgeting, temper tantrums, loud voice, and incessant chattering. And they have one hour to stop Old Fogey from silencing the entire world.
Other titles in this series are: Mac attack! (2008); Game on! (2009); Grow up! (2010)

Stevens, Eric
Skateboard sonar. Written by Eric Stevens ; illustrated by Gerardo Sandoval ; colored by Benny Fuentes. Stone Arch Books 2010 56p. Illustration
Grades: 3 4 5 6 7 8   **741.5; Fic**
1. Blind; 2. People with disabilities; 3. Skateboarding; 4. Graphic novels
978-1-4342-1910-7, $25.32; 978-1-4342-2295-4 (pa), $6.95
LC 2009-37870
Blind skateboarder Matty Lyons and his best friend Ty enter the All-City Skateboarding competition and encounter big bully Bing and his friend Clint. They try to intimidate the other boarders, but they really pick on Matty and Ty because

of Matty's blindness. However, Ty is a master of the halfpipe and Matty uses his sense of hearing like sonar to be a champion at street boarding, and they're ready to take on the bullies and show them their skills. Matty shows by his choice of sport that he doesn't consider his blindness to be any kind of handicap in his life. This graphic novel includes discussion questions and a brief glossary.

Part of the Sports Illustrated for Kids Graphic Novels series.

Stevenson, Robert Louis, 1850-1894

Kidnapped. Adapted by Mark Jones ; art by Naresh Kumar. Kalyani Navyug Media Pvt. Ltd/Campfire Classics 2010 80p. Illustration
Grades: 3 4 5 6 7 8 9   **741.5; Fic**
1. Adventure graphic novels; 2. Stevenson, Robert Louis, 1850-1894 — Adaptations
978-9-380028-52-1, $9.99

When David Balfour's father dies and he has no family left, he leaves home and goes to the house of Shaws upon the advice of his father's agent; there, he finds an uncle he had never known. However, instead of welcoming David, Ebenezer Balfour arranges for the boy to be kidnapped on a ship to be taken to the American colonies and sold into slavery. When the ship causes a smaller boat to capsize, the crew takes on the lone survivor, the adventurer Alan Breck. David befriends Breck and helps him when the crew tries to murder the man, and when the ship wrecks near the Scottish shore, David washes up alone and must find his way through the Highlands. This graphic novel adaptation was originally published in India. It includes some background information about the Jacobite Risings against the English, and some other information about the characters Stevenson created. The book does depict some sword fighting and shooting, but with little gore.

Treasure Island. Retold by Wim Coleman and Pat Perrin ; illustrated by Greg Rebis. Stone Arch Books 2007 63p. Illustration
Grades: 3 4 5 6 7 8 9   **741.5; Fic**
1. Adventure graphic novels; 2. Stevenson, Robert Louis, 1850-1894 — Adaptations; 3. Graphic novels
978-1-59889-050-1, $23.93

Young Jim Hawkins discovers an old treasure map and sets out on a harrowing voyage to a faraway island, in the company of Dr. Livesey and Mr. Trelawney. The violent sea is just the first of many obstacles, as Jim soon learns that most of the ship's crew are dangerous pirates seeking the same treasure, and they're led by Long John Silver. This adaptation is written for reluctant and struggling readers.

Part of the Graphic Revolve series.

Stine, R. L.

Goosebumps Graphix: Scary Summer. Scholastic/Graphix 2007 137p. Illustration
Grades: 4 5 6 7 8 9   **741.5; Fic**
1. Horror graphic novels; 2. Graphic novels
978-0-439-85782-6, $8.99

Someone's creeping through the garden, doing nasty things! Dean Haspiel, a veteran of Batman and Justice League comics, knows just how to portray "The Revenge of the Lawn Gnomes." In his comic series like The Bakers and

Plastic Man, Kyle Baker proves he's one funny artist, the perfect guy to draw a story about fun and games at camp—until "The Horror at Camp Jellyjam" is uncovered. And Courtney Crumrin creator Ted Naifeh adapts and illustrates "Ghost Beach," in which Terri and Jerry go on vacation with some of their father's cousins and meet other kids who dress in old-fashioned clothes and caution them about ghosts.

Slappy's tales of horror. Adapted and illustrated by Dave Roman, Jamie Tolagson, Gabriel Hernandez, and Ted Naifeh; color by Jose Garibaldi. Graphix / Scholastic 2015 176 p.
Grades: 3 4 5 6   **741.5; Fic**
1. Horror fiction — Juvenile fiction; 2. Monsters; 3. Stine, R L — Adaptations
9780545835954, $12.99; 9780545836005, $24.99
LC 2014959511

In this book "[f]our Goosebumps Graphix tales by master of horror R. L. Stine are adapted into full-color comics and feature a brand-new Slappy story by bestselling author, Dave Roman. . . . Roman [also] creates the horrifying drawings for 'The Night of the Living Dummy,' the origin story about that most evil of all ventriloquist dummies, Slappy!" Illustrators Jamie Tolagson, Gabriel Hernandez, and Ted Naifeh are also included. (Publisher's note)

"Each segment has the hallmarks of the individual artist as he balances comedy and horror, childishness and seriousness: Tolagson's deep shadows and brisk pace keep readers guessing at what is actually perilous, and Hernandez's pen and ink scratches help bridge the gap between mundane and dangerous. The more cartoony styles of Naifeh and Roman may reduce the fear factor, but Naifeh's sense of mood remains top-notch." SLJ

Stoker, Bram, 1847-1912

Bram Stoker's Dracula. Adapted by Tim Mucci, writer, Ben Caldwell, penciller/colorist, Bill Halliar, inker. Sterling 2008 Un Illustration
Grades: 5 6 7 8 9 10 11 12   **741.5; Fic**
1. Authors; 2. Horror graphic novels; 3. Novelists; 4. Stoker, Bram, 1847-1912 — Adaptations; 5. Graphic novels
978-1-4027-3152-5, $6.95
LC 2007-41554

English estate agent Jonathan Harker travels to Transylvania to meet his firm's new client, Count Dracula, but the young man discovers his host's evil secret. He escapes and returns to England, but the Count has traveled there, too, determined to settle in new land where he can find more victims, for Dracula is a vampire. Harker, his fiancee Mina Murray, and their friends are not safe from evil. This graphic novel adaptation includes background information about the real person who was the model for Stoker's villain, and a brief biography of Stoker.

Part of the All-Action Classics series.

Dracula. Retold by Michael Burgan ; illustrated by José Alfonso Ocampo Ruiz ; cover color by Benny Fuentes ; interior color by Protobunker Studio. Stone Arch Books 2008 72p. Illustration
Grades: 4 5 6 7 8 9   **741.5; Fic**

1. Horror graphic novels; 2. Vampires; 3. Graphic novels; 4. Stoker, Bram, 1847-1912 — Adaptations
978-1-4342-0448-6, $23.93; 978-1-4342-0498-1 (pa), $9.95

LC 2007-30805

Jonathan Harker and his fiancee, Mina Murray, become entangled in the affairs of the man who calls himself Count Dracula when Harker is sent by his firm to Transylvania. There, Harker learns that Dracula is a vampire. Then Dracula comes to London, where Mina's friend Lucy Westenra becomes a victim. Aided by Dr. Van Helsing, Jack Steward, and Arthur Holcombe, they hunt Dracula to stop him from killing anyone else. This graphic novel adaptation uses simple language to help reluctant and struggling readers understand the story.

Part of the Graphic Revolve series.

Storrie, Paul D.

Amaterasu: Return of the Sun. Pencils and inks by Ron Randall. Lerner Publications Company/Graphic Universe 2007 48p. Illustration
Grades: 3 4 5 6 7 8 9   299.5; 741.5
1. Amaterasu Omikami (Shinto deity); 2. Mythology, Japanese
978-0-8225-5968-9 li, $26.60

In this retelling of a Japanese myth, the Shinto goddess of the sun, Amaterasu, hides from her jealous brother Susano, the god of storms; the world plunges into cold and darkness without the sun. The other gods must find a way to lure Amaterasu out of hiding and keep Susano from harming her or anyone else. The book includes a glossary and a list of books and websites for further reading.

Hercules: The Twelve Labors. Story by Paul Storrie ; pencils by Steve Kurth ; inks by Barbara Schulz. Lerner Publishing Group/Graphic Universe 2007 48p. Illustration
Grades: 3 4 5 6 7 8 9   398.2; 741.5
1. Greek mythology; 2. Heracles (Greek mythology); 3. Graphic novels
978-0-8225-3084-8, $26.60 lib. Bdg.

Hercules was born half-god, half-man, the son of Zeus, King of the gods, and a mortal mother. Zeus's wife Hera resents her stepson, so she dupes Hercules into performing a series of twelve seemingly impossible labors that will test not only his legendary strength, but also his courage, cunning, and fighting skills. The book includes a glossary and a list of books for further reading.

Nightmare on Zombie Island. Illustrated by David Witt. Graphic Universe 2008 111p. Illustration (Twisted journeys)
Grades: 3 4 5 6 7 8 9   741.5; Fic
1. Adventure graphic novels; 2. Plot-your-own strories; 3. Science fiction graphic novels; 4. Graphic novels
978-0-8225-6198-9 (lib bdg), $27.93;
978-0-8225-6200-9 (pa), $7.95

LC 2007-10823

In this new take on the "Choose Your Own Adventure" type of book that combines pages of prose text with pages of comic book sequences, you have joined your best friend Jimmy and his famous explorer aunt, Dr. Chase, on a trip to an island with an abandoned plantation. Unfortunately, you discover only after your arrival that there are zombies on the island, undead pirates cursed by the plantation's workers. Can any of you escape? Some choices will end badly, others will be better, and the choices are all up to the reader.

This is Volume 6 of the Twisted Journeys series.

Robin Hood: Outlaw of Sherwood Forest. Pencils and inks by Thomas Yeates. Lerner Publishing Group/Graphic Universe 2007 48p. Illustration
Grades: 3 4 5 6 7 8 9   398.2; 741.5
1. Robin Hood (Legendary character); 2. Graphic novels
978-0-8225-5964-1, $26.60 lib. Bdg.

Fooled into committing a crime by the King's foresters, young Robin Hood finds himself branded an outlaw. As he takes refuge in Sherwood Forest, he meets other hideaways who also had found themselves unjustly branded outlaws. Under Robin's leadership, they form a band of "merry men" who exact justice against the unfair laws of the land by stealing from the rich and giving their loot to the poor. Robin's exploits enrage the Sheriff of Nottingham, who vows to capture his foe at any cost.

Terror in Ghost Mansion. Illustrated by Sandy Carruthers. Lerner Publishing Group/Graphic Universe 2007 112p. Illustration (Twisted Journeys)
Grades: 3 4 5 6 7 8 9   741.5; Fic
1. Ghosts; 2. Horror graphic novels; 3. Graphic novels
978-0-8225-6776-9, $27.93; 978-0-8225-6778-3 (pa), $7.95

LC 2006-101597

In the series called Twisted Journeys, readers choose how the story will progress. Pages of text alternate with comic book-style pages. In this volume, you and your friends are out on a stormy Halloween night when your car ends up in a ditch while trying not to hit a kid on the road. When the cell phone won't work, you all go up to a big house, where the butler says there is no phone or electricity, but you should stay for the night. However, the house is full of ghosts, and most of them are evil. Readers will find many scenarios played out, depending on their choices; some end well, others not so well.

William Tell: one against an Empire: a Swiss legend. Story by Paul D. Storrie; pencils and inks by Thomas Yeates.. Lerner Publishing Group 2009 48p. Illustration
Grades: 3 4 5 6 7 8 9   741.5; Fic
1. Adventure graphic novels; 2. Tell, Wilhelm; 3. Graphic novels
978-0-8225-7175-9, $27.93

LC 2007-38657

The Swiss hunter William Tell has lived a quiet life of peace, but now the free cantons have been overrun with Austrian governors and officials who threaten and punish the citizens for no reason than that they're misusing their power against the people. Tell is forced by Gessler, the governor, to shoot an apple on top of his son's head, or they will both be killed. This is when he decides he must act against the tyranny. Storrie retold the story using sources such as the 1804 play written by Friedrich Schiller and P. G. Wodehouse's William Tell Told Again (published in 1904). The book includes a list of books for further reading and websites with music from the opera by Rossini (some readers may recognize some of the music that has often been used in cartoons and one famous radio and television series, "The Lone Ranger").

Part of the Graphic Universe Myths and Legends series

Yu the Great: Conquering the Flood. Story by Paul D. Storrie ; pencils and inks by Sandy Carruthers. Lerner/Graphic Universe 2007 48p. Illustration
Grades: 4 5 6 7 8 9   **398.2; 741.5**
1. Da Yu; 2. Folklore — China; 3. Graphic novels
978-0-8225-3088-6, $26.60

When ancient China suffers from a flood caused by angry gods, the emperor begs the hero, Yu, to save the land and the people. Accompanied by a dragon and a tortoise given by his great-grandfather the Yellow Emperor, ruler of the gods, Yu sets out to save China. This story is based on the real Chinese hero, who founded the Xia Dynasty. This is a volume in the Graphic Myths and Legends series.

"The volume maintains the tone and look of an old Chinese tale (Storrie cites his sources at the end) while imbuing it with the dynamic art and feel of a contemporary comic book." (Booklist)

Sturm, James
★ **Adventures** in cartooning: Chistmas special. James Sturm, Andrew Arnold, Alexis Frederick-Frost. First Second 2012 64 p. Illustration
Grades: 2 3 4 5   **741.5/973; Fic**
1. Cartooning — Technique — Juvenile literature; 2. Christmas stories; 3. Comic books, strips, etc — Technique — Juvenile literature; 4. Elves; 5. Santa Claus
1596437308; 9781596437302, $9.99; 9781613830741, $17.45

LC 2012011299

Author James Sturm presents a children's holiday story, part of the "Adventures In Cartooning series. . . . Christmas is coming! The Magic Cartooning Elf and his friend the Knight help Santa make a Christmas comic. But will kids put away their iPads, smart phones, and video games long enough to read a book" . . . [Sturm] will inspire children to pick up a pencil and draw up a snow storm! (Publisher's note)

Adventures in cartooning: how to turn your doodles into comics. [by] James Sturm, Andrew Arnold, Alexis Frederick-Frost. First Second 2009 109p. Illustration
Grades: 2 3 4 5   **741.5; Fic**
978-1-59643-369-4 (pa), $12.95; 1-59643-369-8 (pa)

When a princess wants to draw her own comic book, the magic comic book elf shows her how to do it through the course of a story about a knight, his hungry (and easily scared) horse, and the knight's quest to find a dragon. Young aspiring cartoonists will learn about the importance of panels to convey the passage of time, how to use word balloons and different lettering to convey emotion, how to show motion, create sound effects, and lots more, even as they will giggle over the action in the story. As the magic comic book elf says, anyone who can draw simple shapes and objects can be a cartoonist.

Other titles in this series are:Adventures in cartooning activity book (2010); Christmas special (2012); Characters in action (2013); Sleepless knight (2015); Gryphons aren't so great (2015)

★ **Satchel** Paige: striking out Jim Crow by James Sturm & Rich Tommaso. Hyperion Books for Children/Jump at the Sun 2007 90p. Illustration
Grades: 4 5 6 7 8 9 10   **92; 741.5**
1. African Americans — Biography; 2. Baseball; 3. Baseball players; 4. Biographical graphic novels; 5. Paige, Satchel, 1906-1982; 6. Graphic novels
978-0-7868-3901-8, $9.99; 978-0-7868-3900-1, $16.99

Narrated by an African American who played in the Negro Leagues for a short time, this book sketches part of the career of Leroy "Satchel" Paige, a star of the Negro Leagues. Young Emmet scored a run off Paige in a game, but suffered a career-ending knee injury. Readers get a sense of the rough life African Americans faced in the south during the 1920s, 1930s, and 1940s. Then Paige and his team come to Tuckwilla, Alabama in 1944 to play an all-White team, and Emmet and his son attend the game and watch how Paige and his team take apart the home boys. There's one panel showing a man who has been lynched and hanged; most of the violence is mentioned but not depicted on the pages.

Part of The Center for Cartoon Studies Presents series

Sumerak, Marc
Big trouble at the Big Top!. GuriHiru, art; ABDO/Spotlight 2007 Un
Grades: 3 4 5 6 7 8 9   **741.5; Fic**
1. Adventure graphic novels; 2. Nightcrawler (Fictional character); 3. Power Pack (Fictional characters); 4. Superhero graphic novels; 5. X-Men (Fictional characters); 6. Graphic novels
978-1-59961-219-5, $21.35

LC 2007-130032

Marvel's youngest superheroes, the Power Pack (siblings Alex, Julie, Jack, and Katie) team up with Nightcrawler of the X-Men. The Power family has gone to the circus, but Katie is deathly afraid of clowns and won't go into the Big Top. Meanwhile, Nightcrawler has gone to visit an old friend who works in the circus, only to come under the influence of the Ringmaster and his Circus of Crime. Can the Power Pack stop the criminals and save Nightcrawler?

Part of the X-Men Power Pack series. This is a revision of the February 2006 issue of Marvel Age X-Men Power Pack, with all advertisements removed.

Costumes on!. GuriHiru, art; ABDO/Spotlight 2007 Un Illustration
Grades: 3 4 5 6 7 8 9   **741.5; Fic**
1. Adventure graphic novels; 2. Power Pack (Fictional characters); 3. Superhero graphic novels; 4. Wolverine (Fictional character); 5. X-Men (Fictional characters); 6. Graphic novels
978-1-59961-220-1, $21.35

LC 2007-130030

Marvel's youngest superheroes, the Power Pack (siblings Alex, Julie, Jack, and Katie) team up with Wolverine on Halloween. The Power family attends the big Halloween party, and Jack's convinced his Wolverine costume will win the contest until he sees that half the kids at the party are wearing Wolverine costumes. When he makes little sister Katie cry, she runs out to the woods, where she encounters the real Wolverine, who has to deal with Sabretooth with a little help from Power Pack.

Part of the X-Men Power Pack series. This is a revision of the December 2005 issue of Marvel Age X-Men Power Pack, with all advertisements removed.

Fantastic Four Presents Franklin Richards, Son of a Genius: Lab Brat. Written by Marc Sumerak ; art by Chris Eliopoulis Marvel Publishing, Inc. 2007 Un Illustration
Grades: 3 4 5 6 7 8 9   **741.5; Fic**
1. Fantastic Four (Fictional characters); 2. Humorous graphic novels; 3. Superhero graphic novels; 4. Graphic novels
0-7851-2322-9, $7.99
This book collects stories depicting the adventures of Franklin Richards, young son of Reed and Susan Richards of the Marvel superhero family, the Fantastic Four. Franklin and his robot companion H.E.R.B.I.E. keep sneaking into Reed's lab and playing with the devices they find; or, actually, Franklin does as H.E.R.B.I.E. tries to keep the boy out of trouble. In one story, Franklin accidentally turns his teacher and classmates into vegetables; in another he converts dishes of Jell-O into clones to go trick-or-treating for him; he tries to use a time machine to gather Christmas gifts for his family; he uses a device to make his comic book come to life; and he travels to another dimension where turkeys have evolved and become the dominant life form.

Originally published as Franklin Richards: Son of a Genius, Everybody Loves Franklin, Super Summer Spectacular, and Happy Franksgiving.

Franklin Richards, son of a genius: not-so-secret invasion. Art by Chris Eliopoulos. Marvel Entertainment 2009 Un Illustration
Grades: 3 4 5 6 7 8 9   **741.5; Fic**
1. Fantastic Four (Fictional characters); 2. Humorous graphic novels; 3. Superhero graphic novels; 4. Graphic novels
978-0-7851-3369-8, $9.99
This latest volume includes stories featuring Franklin Richards, son of Reed and Sue Richards of the Fantastic Four. Young Franklin, aided and abetted (albeit reluctantly) by his robot companion H.E.R.B.I.E., builds a replica of the first Iron Man robotic armor, drinks one of his dad's formulas and proceeds to belch HUGELY, de-ages his dad so they can play together, and then a multiplicity of Franklin Richards in many different timelines get into similar trouble. There are more stories, lots of silly humor and superhero action, drawn by coauthor Eliopoulos.

Hulk and Power Pack: Pack Smash!. Art by Gary Martin and David Williams. Marvel Entertainment 2007 Un Illustration
Grades: 3 4 5 6 7 8 9   **741.5; Fic**
1. Hulk (Fictional character); 2. Power Pack (Fictional characters); 3. Superhero graphic novels; 4. Graphic novels
0-7851-2490-X, $6.99
Zero-G, Lightspeed, Mass Master, and Energizer are Marvel's youngest superheroes, Power Pack. And they couldn't be more excited to meet their father's new colleague, the world-famous Dr. Bruce Banner. But when the kids find out what happens every time the good doctor becomes angry, he becomes the Hulk. Will the Pack be able

to stand by their new friend, even if it may mean fighting every other hero in the Marvel Universe?

Leader of the pack. Art by Gurihiru. ABDO/Spotlight 2007 Un Illustration
Grades: 3 4 5 6 7 8 9   **741.5; Fic**
1. Adventure graphic novels; 2. Cyclops (Fictional character); 3. Power Pack (Fictional characters); 4. Superhero graphic novels; 5. X-Men (Fictional characters); 6. Graphic novels
978-1-59961-221-8, $21.35

LC 2007-130029
Marvel's youngest superheroes, the Power Pack (siblings Alex, Julie, Jack, and Katie) team up with Cyclops of the X-Men. When the kids try to help the X-Men fight the Marauders, they end up causing enough of a distraction for the villains to get away. When Julie and Greg go to the lab where he interns, though, they discover that his boss, Dr. Essex, is actually Mr. Sinister, and the Marauders have captured Cyclops. This time, the Power Pack is determined to save Cyclops and do things right.

Part of the X-Men Power Pack series. This is a revision of the March 2006 issue of Marvel Age X-Men Power Pack, with all advertisements removed.

Mind over matter. ABDO/Spotlight 2007 Un Illustration
Grades: 3 4 5 6 7 8 9   **741.5; Fic**
1. Adventure graphic novels; 2. Beast (Fictional character); 3. Power Pack (Fictional characters); 4. Superhero graphic novels; 5. The Beast (Fictional character); 6. X-Men (Fictional characters); 7. Graphic novels
978-1-59961-222-5, $21.35

LC 2007-130026
Marvel's youngest superheroes, the Power Pack (siblings Alex, Julie, Jack, and Katie) team up with The Beast of the X-Men. The Power family has come to the Science Expo, where their father has a booth, and Dr. Hank McCoy, otherwise known as The Beast of the X-Men, is the keynote speaker. However, there's trouble when the shape-changing villain, Mystique, uses Dr. Power's appearance to steal The Beast's genetic analyzer. In order to save their father, the Power Pack teams up with The Beast to find and stop Mystique.

Part of the X-Men Power Pack series. This is a revision of the January 2006 issue of Marvel Age X-Men Power Pack, with all advertisements removed.

Power Pack: I know what we did that summer. Art by Gurihiru. ABDO Spotlight 2006 Un Illustration
Grades: 3 4 5 6 7 8 9   **741.5; Fic**
1. Adventure graphic novels; 2. Power Pack (Fictional characters); 3. Superhero graphic novels; 4. Graphic novels
1-59961-033-7, $21.35
A new school year is about to start, and Kate Power, youngest of the Power Pack siblings, has written a report about the team for her summer report. The problem is, as all her siblings point out, that public exposure will bring great risk to them. This does not sit well with Kate, and it's up to oldest brother Alex to calm her down. However, her use of her power is detected by their alien enemies, the Snark, and

one of them comes to Earth, determined to capture the Power Pack.

Power Pack: Misadventures in babysitting. Marc Sumerak, writer; Gurihiru, art. ABDO Publishing Company/Spotlight 2006 Un Illustration
Grades: 3 4 5 6 7 8 **741.5; Fic**
1. Power Pack (Fictional characters); 2. Superhero graphic novels; 3. Graphic novels
1-59961-034-5, $21.35
Power Pack is the youngest superhero team in the Marvel Universe. Alex, Jack, Julie, and Katie Power range in age from five to twelve. A peaceful alien race called the Kymellian gave the siblings superhuman powers, which they hide from their parents. Alex can defy gravity, Julie can fly fast, Katie can burn holes in things like ships, and Jack can change shape. In this volume, which reprints an issue from Marvel Comics without all the advertisements, Alex goes on a date with Caitlin even though his parents have gone out on their anniversary date. Julie is supposed to be in charge, but Jack does what he does (get into trouble a lot), and Alex comes home to pandemonium. Their inventor father just made an interdimensional teleporter, Jack turned it on, and now they have to send a squid monster back through the portal before their parents come home.

Spider-Man and Power Pack: Big-City Super Heroes. Art by Gary Martin and David Williams. Marvel Entertainment 2007 Un Illustration
Grades: 3 4 5 6 7 8 **741.5; Fic**
1. Power Pack (Fictional characters); 2. Spider-Man (Fictional character); 3. Superhero graphic novels; 4. Graphic novels
0-7851-2357-1, $6.99
When the Power family moves to New York City, Marvel's youngest superheroes, the Power Pack, have a whole new city to explore. Julie (Lightspeed), Alex (Zero-G), Jack (Mass Master), and little Katie (Energizer) meet and team up with Spider-Man and help him defeat Venom, the Sandman, and the Vulture. Katie also gets infected by the Venom symbiote, and Spidey gets dumped into a vat of liquid that turns him into a kid again. Originally published as Spider-Man and Power Pack issues #1-4.

Yo Gabba Gabba!: Gabba Ball!. Oni Press 2010 Un Illustration
Grades: PreK K **741.5; Fic**
1. Games; 2. Humorous graphic novels; 3. Yo Gabba Gabba! (television series); 4. Graphic novels
978-1-934964-55-2, $7.99
The inhabitants of Gabba Land play Gabba Ball, in which the main idea is to share; each character shares his or her name and one way he or she likes to play with the ball. This brightly colored graphic novel is a board book suitable for very young pre-readers, using the characters from the popular children's television series. Eliopoulos uses a very simple panel design, motion lines so young eyes can follow the action, and simple dialog in word balloons as well as wordless panels.

Sutton, Laurie S.
Going ape. Laurie S. Sutton, Steven E. Gordon, Eric A. Gordon; [edited by] David Linker. HarperCollins 2012 31 p. Color illustration
Grades: K 1 2 **E**
1. Adventure fiction — Juvenile fiction; 2. Batman (Fictional character); 3. Superman (Fictional character)
9780061885228, $3.99
LC 2011941961
This book, by Laurie S. Sutton, illustrated by Eric A. Gordon and Steven E. Gordon, relates an adventure of the DC Comics superheroes Batman and Superman. "The Gotham City Zoo has gone bananas! With Gorilla Grodd on the loose, Batman and Superman must join forces to put an end to the monkey business and save Gotham City." (Publisher's note)
Featuring Superman—Cover.
Batman created by Bob Zane; Superman created by Jerry Siegel and Joe Shuster.

Swift, Jonathan
Gulliver's travels. Jonathan Swift (retold by Donald B. Lemke); illustrated by Cynthia Martin.. Stone Arch Books 2008 72p. Illustration
Grades: 4 5 6 7 8 9 **741.5; Fic**
1. Adventure graphic novels; 2. Satire; 3. Graphic novels
978-1-4342-0449-3, $23.93; 978-1-4342-0499-8 (pa), $9.95
LC 2007-30806
Sailor Lemuel Gulliver finds himself shipwrecked on the island of Lilliput, where he is captured by tiny people no taller than six inches. When he leaves Lilliput and tries to go home, he ends up in the country of Blefuscu, a land of giants where he is considered to be nothing more than an intelligent animal and pet. This graphic novel adaptation includes only the first two voyages of Gulliver but does summarize the third and fourth voyages.
Part of the Graphic Revolve series.

Takamisaki, Ryo
Megaman NT Warrior Vol. 1. Viz/Viz Kids 2004 186p. Illustration
Grades: 4 5 6 7 8 9 **741.5; Fic**
1. Science fiction graphic novels; 2. Shonen manga; 3. Graphic novels
1-59116-465-6, $7.95
The year is 200X and everyone is now connected to the Cyber Network. People carry their own PET (Personal terminal) and are paired up with an artificial intelligence program called a NetNavi (or NetNavigator). Computers have turned the world into a bright and shiny utopia, but there's always trouble in paradise. While the invention of the PET and NetNavis has brought great benefits to the world, computer hacking, virus spreading, and other high-tech crimes are becoming a major problem. A sinister organization by the name of World Three has appeared, and they've vowed to destroy this technological wonderland. Enter Lan Hikari, an intensely curious and cheerful fifth grader. Synchronized with his NetNavigator, MegaMansupercharged, he becomes a super-charged dynamo. In and out of the Net, Lan and MegaMan do their best to thwart World Three's neverending quest to take over

the world. The book includes some raunchy humor and lots of action.

Pokemon: the rise of Darkrai. Viz Media/VizKids 2008
Un Illustration
Grades: 2 3 4 5 6 7 8 9   **741.5; Fic**
1. Adventure graphic novels; 2. Fantasy graphic novels; 3. Manga; 4. Graphic novels
978-1-4215-2289-0, $7.99

Ash and his friends come to Alamos Town, home of the Space-Time Towers, and while touring the town, they discover that the town's special garden has been ransacked. Some of the townspeople blame Darkrai, a sinister looking Pokemon that said to haunt the garden. However, Alamos Town faces much more peril when two powerful Pokemon that control time and space battle each other; it should be impossible for them to meet, and unless Ash and the others "and perhaps Darkrai" can stop them, Alamos Town will be destroyed. This book includes a lot of Pokemon fighting action; the panels are so filled with details that very young readers might find it difficult to follow the action.

Takeuchi, Naoko
★ **Sailor** Moon; Volume 1. [Naoko Takeuchi; translator/adapter, William Flanagan]. Kodansha Comics 2011 240 p. Illustration; Color
Grades: 5 6 7 8 9 10   **741.5**
1. Good and evil — Fiction; 2. Shojo manga; 3. Teenage girls — Fiction; 4. Teenage girls — Japan; 5. Women heroes
1935429744; 9781935429746, $10.99
LC 2012374271
"Usagi Tsukino is a normal girl until she meets up with Luna, a talking cat, who tells her that she is Sailor Moon. As Sailor Moon, Usagi must fight evils and enforce justice, in the name of the Moon and the mysterious Moon Princess. She meets other girls destined to be Sailor Senshi (Sailor Scouts), and together, they fight the forces of evil!" (Publisher's note)
First published in Japan in 2003 by Kodansha Ltd., Tokyo, as Bishoujosenshi Sailor Moon Shinsoban—End pages.
Volume 1 of 12

Tamura, Mitsuhisa
BakeGyamon, vol. 1. Viz Media/Viz Kids 2009 200p.
Grades: 3 4 5 6 7 8   **741.5; Fic**
1. Fantasy graphic novels; 2. Games; 3. Manga; 4. Shonen manga; 5. Graphic novels
978-1-4215-1793-3, $7.99

Sanshiro craves adventure, something he's not likely to find in his tiny island hometown; then a mysterious stranger invites him to play a new game. Suddenly, Sanshiro finds himself in a backwards universe to play BakeGyamon, a game that pits monster against monsters, designed by monsters. He meets other players, all of whom are there to win in order to get their one big wish the prize that only the winner can get. Sanshiro is there to experience adventure and have fun, which makes the others dismiss him. And when his first card gives him a bunch of little mud balls to play against a huge monster, how can he possibly win" The book features lots of game-playing action and hyper

dialogue (Sanshiro tends to shout in exuberance a lot), but there's no violence or bad language.

Taneja, Sweta
Krishna: Defender of Dharma. By Shweta Taneja; illustrated by Rajesh Nagulakonda. Random House Inc. 2013 152 p. Color illustration
Grades: 5 6 7   **Fic; 741.5/954**
1. Folklore; 2. Good and evil; 3. Hindu mythology
938074112X; 9789380741123, $14.99

Author Shweta Taneja presents a tale about Krishna, the Hindu diety. "To vanquish him and his horde of evil monsters, Lord Vishnu comes to Earth in his eighth avatar - Krishna, the defender of dharma. Since his birth, Krishna valiantly fights evil monsters, showing courage and valour. But as he grows up and becomes a councillor of the race of Yadavas, he observes that the real struggle in this age is not with magical monsters but with evil kings and warriors." (Publisher's note)

Taylor, G. P.
The **Tizzle** Sisters & Erik. Illustrated by Dan Boultwood. Markosia Enterprises Ltd 2006 182p. Illustration
Grades: 5 6 7 8 9 10 11 12   **741.5; Fic**
1. Adventure graphic novels; 2. Twins; 3. Graphic novels
978-1-905692-22-4, $20.01

Almost identical twins, Sadie and Saskia Tizzle have lived in St. Dunstan's School for Wayward Children ever since their actress mother left them there and never returned. When an eccentric writer decides to take Saskia to adopt her and separates the twins, she sets wild adventures into motion. Saskia finds herself in a house of intrigue with ghosts, seances, a treasure hunt, and a secret twin; while Sadie and Erik make a harrowing escape from St. Dunstan's just ahead of the police.

Noted fantasy author Taylor (Shadowmancer, 2003) teams up with British comics veterans Lee and Boultwood to create what they call an "illustronovella," which alternates pages of prose and comic book panels to tell the story.

Taylor, Sarah Stewart
Amelia Earhart: this broad ocean. [illustrations by] Ben Towle; with an introduction by Eileen Collins. Disney/Hyperion Books 2010 78p. Illustration
Grades: 5 6 7 8 9   **741.5; 741; 92**
1. Earhart, Amelia, 1898-1937
978-1-4231-1337-9 (lib bdg), $17.99; 1-4231-1337-3 (lib bdg)
LC 2009-29321
"Grace, an aspiring young journalist, is excited when Amelia Earhart arrives in her town of Trepassey, Newfoundland, on June 4, 1928. Earhart wants to become the first female passenger to cross the Atlantic Ocean by air. Grace is there to see them and to receive Earhart's telegram announcing their arrival in Ireland." (Publisher's note)
"This approach brings the legendary aviation pioneer and her fame into a manageable context. . . . Reluctant readers, adventure fans, and those who themselves yearn for the skies will be sucked right into the immediacy here." Bull Cent Child Books

Telgemeier, Raina

The **Baby-sitter's** Club: Kristy's great idea: a graphic novel. [text by Ann M. Martin; art] by Raina Telgemeier. Scholastic Graphix 2006 192p. Illustration

Grades: 3 4 5 6   **741.5; Fic**
1. Babysitting; 2. Friendship; 3. Graphic novels
0-439-80241-5, $16.99; 0-439-73933-0 (pa), $8.99
                                    LC 2005-37749

Follows the adventures of Kristy and the other members of the Baby-sitters Club as they deal with crank calls, uncontrollable two-year-olds, wild pets, and parents who do not always tell the truth. A graphic novel based on the 1988 book by the same name.

"Comics artist Telgemeier's clean-lined, black-and-white art with stark black details nicely differentiates the four personable seventh-graders who parlay their babysitting experience into a business." Booklist

Also available in full color editions
Other titles about the Baby-sitters Club are: The truth about Stacey (2006); Mary Anne saves the day (2007); Claudia and Mean Janine (2008)

★ **Drama**. Raina Telgemeier; with color by Gurihiru. Graphix 2012 233 p. Illustration

Grades: 5 6 7 8   **741.5**
1. Children's plays — Fiction; 2. Interpersonal relations — Fiction; 3. Middle schools — Fiction; 4. School stories; 5. Schools — Fiction; 6. Theater — Fiction; 7. Graphic novels
0545326982; 0545326990; 9780545326988, $23.99; 9780545326995
                                    LC 2011040748
Stonewall Honor Book (2013)

Author Raina Telgemeier's book focuses on a middle school drama production. "Callie loves theater . . . [S]he's the set designer for the stage crew, and this year she's determined to create a set worthy of Broadway on a middle-school budget. But how can she, when she doesn't know much about carpentry, ticket sales are down, and the crew members are having trouble working together?" (Publisher's note)

"In this realistic and sympathetic story, feelings and thoughts leap off the page, revealing Telgemeier's keen eye for young teen life." Booklist
Includes bibliographical references

★ **Sisters**. Raina Telgemeier; with color by Braden Lamb. Graphix 2014 197 p. Color; Illustration

Grades: 5 6 7 8   **741.5; 306.875; 92**
1. Autobiographical graphic novels; 2. Family life; 3. Interpersonal relations; 4. Siblings
9780545540599, $24.99; 9780545540605, $10.99
                                    LC 2013008700

"Raina can't wait to be a big sister. But once Amara is born, things aren't quite how she expected them to be. . . . They are sisters, after all. Raina uses her signature humor . . . in both present-day narrative and perfectly placed flashbacks to tell the story of her relationship with her sister, which unfolds during the course of a road trip from their home in San Francisco to a family reunion in Colorado." (Publisher's note)

"The author's narrative style is fresh and sharp, and the combination of well-paced and well-placed flashbacks pull the plot together, moving the story forward and helping readers understand the characters' point of view. The volume captures preadolescence in an effortless and uncanny way and turns tough subjects, such as parental marriage problems, into experiences with which readers can identify." (School Library Journal)

★ **Smile**. Scholastic/Graphix 2010 213p. Illustration

Grades: 5 6 7 8   **741; 741.5**
1. Autobiographical graphic novels; 2. Dentistry; 3. Friendship; 4. Personal appearance; 5. Graphic novels
978-0-545-13205-3, $21.99; 0-545-13205-3;
978-0-545-13206-0 (pa), $10.99; 0-545-13206-1 (pa)
                                    LC 2008-51782
Boston Globe-Horn Book Honor: Nonfiction (2010)
Eisner Award: Best Publication for Teens (2011)

Sixth grader Raina just wants to be normal, but when she falls down going home from a Girl Scout meeting, she severely injures her two front teeth, and this starts her down a long road with braces, surgery, retainers, embarrassing headgear—all sure to make her stand out from her middle school classmates for all the wrong reasons. There's also a major earthquake, then boy confusion, friends who turn out not to be good friends, sibling jealousy, all the stuff that makes life interesting, if not fun. Telgemeier wrote and drew the autobiographical Smile as a webcomic; this volume collects the story in color.

"The dental case that Telgemeier documents in this graphic memoir was extreme: a random accident led to front tooth loss when she was 12, and over the next several years, she suffered through surgery, implants, headgear, false teeth, and a rearrangement of her remaining incisors. . . . Both adults and kids . . . are vividly and rapidly portrayed. . . . Telgemeier's storytelling and full-color cartoony images form a story that will cheer and inspire any middle-schooler dealing with orthodontia." Booklist

TenNapel, Doug

Cardboard. Doug TenNapel. Graphix / Scholastic 2012 288 p.

Grades: 5 6 7 8   **741.5**
1. Boxes — Fiction; 2. Bullies; 3. Father-son relationship; 4. Gifts; 5. Magic
0545418720; 9780545418720, $24.99; 9780545418737
                                    LC 2011934533

In this graphic novel, "Cam Howerton's out-of-work father is so broke, the best he can do for Cam's birthday is an empty cardboard box purchased from a toy seller with two mysterious rules: return every unused scrap of cardboard and don't ask for any more. . . . [T]he box becomes a project. What should father and son make out of the box" 'A boxer,' Cam suggests. . . . 'Boxer Bill,' created from inanimate material, comes alive. Unfortunately, Marcus, the neighborhood bully . . . steals the scrap materials, and begins turning out a whole evil empire of cardboard monsters. . . . [A]fter losing control of them he must unite with Cam and his father to defeat the massive cardboard army. . . . [Q]uestions are raised about what it means to be a man, what makes a good man, and what forms people's character." (Horn Book)

Tommysaurus Rex. Image Comics 2005 110p. Illustration

Grades: 5 6 7 8 9 10 11 12   **741.5; Fic**
1. Dinosaurs; 2. Graphic novels
1-58240-395-3, $11.95

When Ely loses his dog, Tommy, in a car accident, his parents send him to Grandpa Joe's farm for the summer. He discovers a live, 40-foot Tyrannosaurus Rex in a cave on the farm, and soon the boy and his pet dinosaur cause a big ruckus in town. Ely promises to train the dinosaur he names Tommysaurus, but not if the town's bully, Randy, has his way.

Tetzner, Lisa
The **Black** Brothers: A Novel in Pictures. Art by Hannes Binder. Front Street 2004 144p. Illustration
Grades: 4 5 6 7 8 9   **741.5; Fic**
1. Chimney sweeps; 2. Graphic novels
1-932425-04-7, $16.95

In rural Italy, thirteen-year-old Giorgio is sold to a man who supplies chimney sweeps for Milan. After a treacherous journey in which most of the other boys die, Giorgio goes to work for a man whose wife resents another mouth to feed and starves him. He is sent up into chimneys with no training or guidance for how to do the dangerous work. After nearly dying, he is befriended by a doctor and finds the Black Brothers, a group of chimney sweeps who swear loyalty to each other.

This illustrated novel was originally published in German in 1941, and the translation's tone is similar to other children's books, such as Emil and the Detectives.

Tezuka, Osamu
Astro Boy books 1 and 2. Dark Horse Comics 2008 424p. Illustration
Grades: 3 4 5 6 7 8 9 10 11 12 Adult   **741.5; Fic**
1. Adventure graphic novels; 2. Astro Boy (Fictional character); 3. Robots; 4. Science fiction graphic novels; 5. Graphic novels
978-1-59582-153-9, $14.95

When a scientist loses his young son, he builds a robot to look exactly like the boy, but when he activates the robot, the scientist becomes repulsed and rejects him. Professor Ochanomizu (gotta love the name, it means tea water and is also a famous Tokyo neighborhood) rescues the boy robot from a circus and names him Astro Boy. He deals with aliens, with people who would use robots to commit crimes, and with adventures in outer space. This new edition collects the first two volumes of the Dark Horse manga editions.

Also available in omnibus editions

Volumes 1 and 2 of a 23 volume series

Thielbar, Melinda
The **hundred-dollar** robber: a mystery with money. Illustrated by Tintin Pantoja.. Lerner Publishing Group/Graphic Universe 2009 48p. Illustration
Grades: 1 2 3 4   **741.5; Fic**
1. Kung fu; 2. Mathematics; 3. Mystery graphic novels; 4. Graphic novels
0761352430; 9780761338543, $29.32; 9780761352433, $6.95; 0761338543

LC 2008-53709

When someone steals $100 from the soccer team's fundraiser money, Stacy asks the kung fu school students for help; the other soccer team members have accused Tom of stealing the money. Even though Tom and Stacy had played a nasty prank on the kung fu students, they decide to help anyway. First they double-check the receipts for the fundraiser, then they divide into two teams to check the stores in the neighborhood. When they take a break, Kristin and Mike from the soccer team give them a hard time, and Joy notices they're drinking coffee drinks and eating from a large bag of candy. When they visit the candy shop, the owner tells them that a soccer team member bought candy and paid with a $100 bill then asked for the change in a strange way. From this information, the kung fu students are able to solve the mystery and clear Tom.

This is #2 in the Manga Math Mysteries series

The **kung** fu puzzle: a mystery with time and temperature. Illustrated by Der-shing Helmer. Lerner Publishing Group/Graphic Universe 2009 48p. Illustration
Grades: 1 2 3 4   **741.5; Fic**
1. Kung fu; 2. Mathematics; 3. Mystery graphic novels; 4. Graphic novels
978-0-7613-3856-7, $29.27

LC 2008-55564

When Adam and Tom overhear Sifu Faiza and Sigung talking about selling, they think Sifu is planning to sell the kung fu school. When they get to her house, they learn she's actually planning to sell the house, which was also the kung fu school run by her father, and they help her pack and move things to the school. They also discover her Sifu's old kung fu journal, which is full of puzzles her father created, most dealing with time and temperature. Sifu gives the journal to Amy, who starts working with the other students to solve the puzzles, and as they work on those and the packing, they find more mysteries to do with the old house.

This is #4 in the Manga Math Mysteries series

The **lost** key: a mystery with whole numbers. Story by Melinda Thielbar; art by Tintin Pantoja. Graphic Universe/Lerner Publishing Group 2009 48p. Illustration (Manga math mysteries)
Grades: 1 2 3 4   **741.5; Fic**
1. Mathematics; 2. Mystery graphic novels; 3. Graphic novels
978-0-7613-3853-6, $29.27; 978-0-7613-5244-0 (pa), $6.95

LC 2008-53242

Joy, Adam, Sam, and Amy all take kung fu lessons at Sifu Faiza's Kung Fu School. One Friday evening, Sifu Faiza gives the school's key to Joy and asks her to open the school on Monday. They go swimming at the lake, but they also have an unpleasant encounter with Tom and Stacy from the local soccer team; the older soccer players try to bully the other four. Then, Tom steals the school's key from Joy's bag. When Joy and her friends run back to the school, they find the door unlocked and all their equipment stolen and replaced by smelly old soccer uniforms. Joy calls Sifu Faiza, who tells her to follow the clues and see if she can find the key and equipment herself. The kids use math to calculate how much of each type of equipment is gone, and to follow other clues. This story could be used in elementary math classes to show how everyone uses math in life; while the math part is rather didactic, the story's mystery pulls the reader along, and the dynamic art keeps the visual interest. Author Thielbar is a math teacher. There's nothing particularly manga-like in the format, but Philippines-born artist Pantoja shows manga influences in her art. The book features a multiethnic cast.

This is the first volume in the Manga Math Mysteries series.

The **secret** ghost: a mystery with distance and measuring (Manga math mysteries #3). Story by Melinda Thielbar; art by Yuko Ota.. Graphic Universe/Lerner Publishing Group 2009 48p. Illustration

Grades: 1 2 3 4   **741.5; Fic**
   1. Mathematics; 2. Measurement; 3. Mystery graphic novels; 4. Graphic novels
978-0-7613-3855-0, $29.27

                            LC 2008-53243

After Sifu Faiza's kung fu class, the students help to measure the class room so Sifu can purchase shelving. Then Sam tells his friends that his little sister Michelle thinks there's a ghost in the old house their father bought. Amy and Tom volunteer to help Sam figure out what's really happening in the house. When they hear a scary, loud thumping coming from the playroom, Amy realizes it's smaller than Michelle's bedroom next door, and they start using measurement to see how much smaller it is. Readers will be just as surprised by the cause of the noise as the book's characters are. Author Thielbar is a math teacher, who embeds the lessons on measurement and distance in a fun mystery; artist Ota brings a manga-influenced art style to the book, which actually uses a more American-style page and panel format.

This is the third book in the Manga Math Mysteries series.

Thompson, Bart A.
  Mummy. Adapted by Bart A. Thompson ; illustrated by Brian Miroglio ; based upon the works of Bram Stoker. ABDO/Magic Wagon 2008 Un Illustration

Grades: 4 5 6 7 8 9   **741.5**
   1. Horror graphic novels; 2. Mummies; 3. Graphic novels
978-1-60270-061-1, $27.07

                            LC 2007-16370

In ancient Egypt, Queen Tera had herself mummified and she swore she would return to life. During an expedition to Egypt in 1947, Abel Trelawney and John Corbeck uncovered her tomb. Today, all is ready for her return. This graphic novel adapts Stoker's Jewel of Seven Stars, which was the basis for the classic horror movie, The Mummy." While there is some violence, the level of horror in this adaptation has been toned down to be suitable for younger readers. Part of the Graphic Horror series

Thompson, Craig
  Space dumplins. Craig Thompson with color by Dave Stewart. Graphix / Scholastic 2015 320 p. Color; Illustration

Grades: 3 4 5 6   **741.5; Fic**
   1. Father-daughter relationship — Juvenile fiction; 2. Interplanetary voyages — Juvenile fiction; 3. Missing persons — Juvenile fiction
0545565413; 9780545565417, $24.99; 9780545565431
                            LC 2014956159

In this graphic novel by Craig Thompson, "for Violet Marlocke, family is the most important thing in the whole galaxy. So when her father goes missing while on a hazardous job, she can't just sit around and do nothing. To get him back, Violet throws caution to the stars and sets out with a group of misfit friends on a quest to find him. But space is vast and dangerous, and she soon discovers that her dad is in big, BIG trouble." (Publisher's note)

"Thompson's art is wild and busy, with overcrowded, unconventional panel structures. The worldbuilding is a strikingly imaginative pastiche that seamlessly blends biblical references, poop jokes, and social satire." Kirkus

Thompson, Jill
  ★ **Magic** Trixie. Written and illustrated by Jill Thompson; lettered by Jason Arthur. Harper Trophy 2008 93p. Illustration

Grades: 3 4 5   **741.5; Fic**
   1. Fantasy graphic novels; 2. Humorous graphic novels; 3. Magic; 4. Graphic novels
978-0-06-117045-4 (pa), $7.99

                            LC 2007-24298

Magic Trixie is feeling a bit put out; everything in her house seems to revolve around her baby sister, and she doesn't get to do anything fun. If that wasn't bad enough, Show & Tell time is coming up at Monstersorri School, and all her classmates have seen all her tricks too many times. She'll have to come up with a new one that's really special.

"Bright colors and a whimsical style make everything friendly rather than scary. Underneath the supernatural trappings lies a classical story of sibling envy to which every big sister and big brother can relate." Booklist

Other titles in this series are: Magic Trixie sleeps over (2008); Magic Trixie and the dragon (2009)

  ★ **Magic** Trixie and the dragon. HarperTrophy 2009 94p. Illustration

Grades: 3 4 5   **741.5; Fic**
   1. Dragons; 2. Fantasy graphic novels; 3. Humorous graphic novels; 4. Magic; 5. Witches; 6. Graphic novels
978-0-06-117050-8, $7.99

                            LC 2008-27473

Little witch girl Magic Trixie goes to the circus with Mimi (her grandma), and she gets to see the dragons. Mimi even gives her a real dragon scale as a souvenir, but when she meets up with her friends and shows off the scale, they think she has a pet dragon. Trixie doesn't want them to think she's lying, so she tries her transmogrification skills to make a dragon, but when she gets distracted in the middle of the spell, it changes her baby sister into a dragon. Yikes! Very soon, Trixie learns that taking care of such a pet is a lot of hard work, and she has to try to change the dragon back into her baby sister before her mother finds out. She also has to find a way to get Scratches back when she drives him away by her obsession over having a dragon pet, making him think that being a cat isn't good enough for her.

  Magic Trixie sleeps over. Written and illustrated by Jill Thompson. Harper Trophy 2008 94p. Illustration

Grades: 3 4 5   **741.5; Fic**
   1. Fantasy graphic novels; 2. Friendship; 3. Humorous graphic novels; 4. Monsters; 5. Graphic novels
978-0-06-117048-5, $7.99

                            LC 2007-33394

Magic Trixie does NOT like to take a bath, brush her teeth, and go to bed on time when there are so many more interesting things to do. At Monstersorri school, she talks with her friends, and they each invite her to a sleepover. First she stays the night with Loupi, but playing rough games and then running in the forest to howl at the moon makes Magic Trixie very tired; and their snacks are like dog food (bleah!). At Nefi's house, servants take care of her and Magic Trixie, but mummies don't eat food, they only breathe in the smell of the food that their servants eat, and Nefi gets wrapped up and put into a sarcophagus for the night. Stitch Patch has her stay the next night, but she has to take notes of all the tests he has to do to make sure all his body parts are working, and then his mother, Dr. Patch, takes him apart and puts his parts into preservation jars for the night. And Stitch snacks on batteries, which Magic Trixie can't eat. The next night she meets the twins in the cemetery, only to learn that's where they live. It's bad enough that they have to dig a hole to sleep, they also have to watch out for ghouls that scare them. There's just enough "ewww" stuff without being scary for most young readers.

★ **Scary** Godmother. Written and illustrated by Jill Thompson. Dark Horse 2010 207p. Illustration
Grades: 3 4 5 **741; 741.5; Fic**
1. Halloween; 2. Supernatural graphic novels; 3. Graphic novels
978-1-59582-589-6, $24.99; 1-59582-589-4

It's Halloween night and it's up to Scary Godmother to show one little girl just how much fun spooky can be! Meet Hannah Marie, who, with the help of Scary Godmother, stands up to her mean-spirited cousin Jimmy and her fear of monsters on her first Halloween adventure with the big kids. Later, Hannah joins forces with Orson, the vampire boy, to unravel a mystery near and dear to their hearts.

This is a "collection compiling all four of Thompson's original Scary Godmother stories plus extra goodies. Told in often-rhyming prose and word balloons on vibrant pages that balance a visually lavish picture book aesthetic with sequential-art page composition, the stories burst with complex color tones and creepy cartoon figures." Booklist

Thung, Diana
★ **Captain** Long Ears. SLG Publishing 2010 168p. Illustration
Grades: 5 6 7 8 9 10 11 12 Adult **741.5; Fic**
1. Adventure graphic novels; 2. Amusement parks; 3. Death; 4. Graphic novels
978-1-59362-187-2, $12.95

Eight-year-old Michael, aka Captain Long Ears, goes on a mission to Headquarters (an amusement park) with Captain Jam, who is actually his purple toy stuffed gorilla. They're searching for Captain Big Nose, who is Michael's father; he's been gone "on a mission" for two years. In Headquarters, Captain Long Ears and Captain Jam encounter monsters (a preschool teacher and a park attendant), then they find a large crate in a locked enclosure. When they open the crate, they find a young elephant the boy calls "Little Big Nose." They decide they must save Little Big Nose, so they hide in the park overnight. Meanwhile, Michael's mother comes home late from work and doesn't realize her son is missing until the next day. Back in the park, Michael has several dreams of his father leaving him behind.

He's so caught up in his fantasy of Captain Long Ears that he doesn't realize the dangers he faces in trying to save the young elephant from abusive handlers. Thung's art shows most of the action through Michael's imagination; readers soon realize that Michael hasn't accepted his father's death. The use of words such as "ass," "caca brain," and other childish epithets may cause more conservative schools to carefully consider their purchase. This imaginary adventure and exploration of the mourning process brings to mind such books as The Bridge to Terabithia and has a similar emotional impact. Despite Michael's young age, this book is more suited to upper elementary and middle school age readers on up.

Tolstikova, Dasha
A **Year** Without Mom. By Dasha Tolstikova. Groundwood Books 2015 176 p. Color; Illustration
Grades: 5 6 7 8 **92; 741.5**
1. Mother-daughter relationship; 2. Refugees; 3. Russia; 4. Tolstikova, Dasha
1554986923; 9781554986927, $19.95

This book, by Dasha Tolstikova, "follows 12-year-old Dasha through a year full of turmoil after her mother leaves for America. It is the early 1990s in Moscow, and political change is in the air. But Dasha is more worried about her own challenges as she negotiates family, friendships and school without her mother. Just as she begins to find her own feet, she gets word that she is to join her mother in America - a place that seems impossibly far from everything and everyone she loves." (Publisher's note)

"Scribbly, childlike pencil drawings are filled in with gray wash and accentuated with red and the occasional pop of blue. They are deceptively simple, but with great narrative sophistication, they capture both the specificity of Dasha's experience and the universality of her emotions." Kirkus

Toriyama, Akira
Cowa!. Story and art by Akira Toriyama; translation & English adaptation Alexander O. Smith, et. al.. Viz Media/Shonen Jump 2008 208p. Illustration
Grades: 5 6 7 8 9 10 11 12 **741.5; Fic**
1. Humorous graphic novels; 2. Manga; 3. Monsters; 4. Graphic novels
978-1-4215-1805-3, $7.99; 1-4215-1805-8

Mischievous Paifu is half-vampire and half-werekoala, and he's usually getting into lots of trouble with his best buddy, Jose the ghost. When the Monster Flu sweeps through town, the doctor says that without medicine, everyone will die. The only person who makes the medicine is the witch who lives hundreds of miles away, and all the adults except for the doctor are ill. Paifu and Jose team up with grumpy ex-sumo wrestler Maruyama to make the journey; will they make it before they get sick? The book includes some potty humor (Jose farts a lot) and lots of fighting scenes (Toriyama created Dragon Ball Z).
Original Japanese edition, 1997

Torres, J.
Alison Dare, Little Miss Adventures Volume 2. Illustrated by J. Bone. Oni Press 2005 Un Illustration
Grades: 4 5 6 7 8 9 **741.5; Fic**
1. Adventure graphic novels

1-932664-25-4, $11.95

Alison Dare is back in this new collection of stories, including her report about her experience at her mother's excavation site in Egypt (with the true story coming right after). Then Alison and her boarding school friends journey into the Heart of the Maiden." The costumed avenger The Blue Scarab encounters villains while gift shopping. And world renowned archaeologist Dr. Alice Dare teaches a thing or two about museum mayhem.

Into the woods. J. Torres; illustrated by Faith Erin Hicks. Kids Can Press 2012 100 p. Color illustration (Bigfoot Boy)
Grades: 3 4 5 6 7 **Fic; 741.5; 741.5/971**
1. Magic; 2. Sasquatch; 3. Totems and totemism
1554537118; 9781554537112, $17.95

In this fantasy graphic novel, "city boy Rufus is staying at his grandmother's house on the edge of a forest for a few days without his parents," and he "decides to explore the woods. He meets a girl named Penny. . . . When looking for her in the woods, Rufus finds a glowing necklace in a tree. After reading the word on the back, he turns into Bigfoot! . . . There's danger in the forest as well as magic, and when Penny disappears, Rufus . . . use[s] the totem to effect a rescue." (Kirkus Reviews)
Followed by: The unkindness of ravens (2013)

★ **Lola:** a ghost story. [by] J. Torres & [illustrated by] Elbert Or. Oni Press 2009 102p. Illustration
Grades: 4 5 6 7 8 **741.5; Fic**
1. Family life; 2. Ghosts; 3. Philippines; 4. Graphic novels
978-1-934964-33-0, $14.95; 1-934964-33-6

"Lola (—grandmother" in Tagalog) has just died, and Jesse is reluctant to visit her home in the Philippines. He was afraid of her because she was rumored to have magical abilities, and because he thinks she tried to drown him when he was a baby. Jesse listens to family members tell stories about her as he tries to adjust to their strange mix of superstitions and religion. . . . Jesse is an unusually nuanced character. . . . When he sees something extraordinary, it's unclear if he is dreaming, hallucinating, or if he has inherited his grandmother's abilities. Torres's gradual revelation of details will keep readers hanging until they learn the truth. Or's artwork uses sepia tones and smooth lines, and features characters with cute button eyes. But the sweet images can quickly turn horrific when Jesse has his visions. " SLJ

The **Sound** of Thunder. Written by J. Torres; illustrated by Faith Erin Hicks. Kids Can Press 2014 100 p. Color; Illustration (Bigfoot boy)
Grades: 3 4 5 6 7 **741.5**
1. Adventure fiction; 2. Pacific Northwest — Fiction; 3. Graphic novels
9781894786584, $17.95; 9781894786591, $9.95

"This conclusion to the Bigfoot Boy graphic novel trilogy adds a backdrop of Pacific Northwest mythology to the popular story about an ordinary boy who becomes a hero through the power of magic. As the book begins, Rufus, Penny and their squirrel friend, Sidney, are eager to recapture the magic totem they lost to the ravens in the previous book." (Publisher's note)

"Torres and Hicks conclude their woodsy trilogy with an exciting adventure dotted with humor. Rufus and Penny's attempts to understand Sidney's charades are a hoot. Rufus

has worked a bit of his city-boy out, but his bumbles and stumbles continue to round out his character." Kirkus
Sequel to: The unkindness of ravens (2013)

Teen Titans Go! Vol. 1: Truth, Justice, Pizza!. DC Comics 2004 112p. Illustration
Grades: 3 4 5 6 7 8 9 **741.5; Fic**
1. Humorous graphic novels; 2. Robin (Fictional character); 3. Superhero graphic novels; 4. Teen Titans (Fictional characters); 5. Graphic novels
1-4012-0333-7, $6.95

They're too young to drive, but not too young to save the world. The world's hottest heroes: Robin, Beast Boy, Raven, Cyborg, and Starfire, show how it's done Titan-style, as they go up against teen super villains Gizmo, Jinx, and Mammoth. Things get icky when Raven's bad dad, Trigon, comes out from a huge zit on Raven's forehead (ewwww ...).

Teen Titans Go! Vol. 2: Heroes on Patrol!. DC Comics 2004 112p. Illustration
Grades: 3 4 5 6 7 8 9 **741.5; Fic**
1. Humorous graphic novels; 2. Superhero graphic novels; 3. Teen Titans (Fictional characters); 4. Graphic novels
1-4012-0334-5, $6.95

In this volume, the Teen Titans encounter the battling brothers, Thunder and Lightning; Starfire has to deal with her naughty sister Blackfire; they encounter Aqualad; and more.

Teen Titans Go! Vol. 3: Bring It On!. Written by J. Torres, Adam Beechen. DC Comics 2005 104p. Illustration
Grades: 3 4 5 6 7 8 9 **741.5; Fic**
1. Humorous graphic novels; 2. Superhero graphic novels; 3. Teen Titans (Fictional characters); 4. Graphic novels
1-4012-0511-9, $6.99

Terra rejoins the Titans to fight Slade's robots; the teen superheroes fight Mumbo; Beast Boy tries to help a man stricken with werewolfism; Speedy joins the Titans to fight Plasmus; and they go up against Kwiz Kid, who's mad at Robin because his ex-girlfriend has a crush on Robin.

Teen Titans Go! Vol. 4: Ready for Action!. DC Comics 2005 104p. Illustration
Grades: 3 4 5 6 7 8 9 **741.5; Fic**
1. Humorous graphic novels; 2. Superhero graphic novels; 3. Teen Titans (Fictional characters); 4. Graphic novels
978-1-4012-0985-8, $6.99

In this volume, the Titans confront a rampaging Wildebeest, teach the hot-tempered Hotshot the value of patience, battle an army of zombies, find themselves trapped in a deadly video game with the Titans East and more.

Teen Titans Go! Vol. 5: On the Move!. DC Comics 2006 104p. Illustration
Grades: 3 4 5 6 7 8 9 **741.5; Fic**
1. Humorous graphic novels; 2. Robin (Fictional character); 3. Superhero graphic novels; 4. Teen Titans (Fictional characters); 5. Graphic novels
978-1-4012-0986-5, $6.95

In this collection, among other stories the Titans must stop Beast Boy, who's been turned into the terrifying vegetarian monster Garsaurus Rex; Robin is tempted to the dark side by Slade; and the Titans crash a comic book convention to discover the secret of Red X.

Teen Titans Go!: Titans Together!. DC Comics 2007 144p. Illustration
Grades: 3 4 5 6 7 8 9   741.5
  1. Robin (Fictional character); 2. Superhero graphic novels; 3. Teen Titans (Fictional characters); 4. Graphic novels
978-1-4012-1563-7, $12.99
  This volume collects eight adventures of the Teen Titans as seen in the animated series, Teen Titans Go! Robin leads the young team that includes Cyborg, Beast Boy, Raven, and Starfire. The stories have lots of action and bad puns as Beast Boy makes a movie, the Titans find themselves in an alien fighting arena, and Robin's future self, Nightwing, comes when time goes a little haywire and an evil Robin shows up.

  The **unkindness** of ravens. By J. Torres; illustrated by Faith Erin Hicks. Kids Can Press 2013 100 p. Color illustration (Bigfoot boy)
Grades: 3 4 5 6 7   741.5
  1. Magic; 2. Ravens — Fiction
9781554537136, $17.95; 9781554537143, $9.95 ; 1554537134; 1554537142
LC 2013040319
  This book, by J. Torres and illustrated by Faith Erin Hicks, tells the story of "another weekend of Rufus using his magic totem to transform himself into Bigfoot Boy! But when you're big, hairy and loud, it's hard to keep your powers a secret, especially when there are trickster ravens that want the magic for themselves." (Publisher's note)
  "Hicks's illustrations are done in bold, black lines and rich colors and are sometimes reminiscent of Native Canadian art styles. The story's adventure, magic, and characters will appeal." SLJ
Followed by: The sound of thunder (2014)
Sequel to: Into the woods (2012)

  Yo Gabba Gabba!: good night, Gabbaland. Art by Matt Loux. Oni Press 2010 Un Illustration
Grades: PreK K   741.5; Fic
  1. Bedtime; 2. Humorous graphic novels; 3. Yo Gabba Gabba! (television series); 4. Graphic novels
978-1-934964-56-9, $7.99
  DJ Lance announces it's time to get ready for bed, so the inhabitants of Gabbaland clean up and put away their toys, brush their teeth, wash their hands, shake their sillies out, listen to a bedtime story, and go to sleep. Torres and Loux use a different panel arrangement than Eliopoulos did, but this is still a board book that makes it easy for young pre-readers to follow along with the story. Torres uses a lot of repetition, which can encourage young listeners to join in the reading; the routine of getting ready for bed is something most young children will understand and enjoy. Loux makes all the characters recognizable for anyone who watches the series on Nick, Jr., while retaining his individual artistic style, long rubbery arms and all.

Townsend, Michael
  Amazing Greek myths of wonders and blunders. Dial Books for Young Readers 2010 160p. Illustration
Grades: 3 4 5 6 7   292; 741.5
  1. Greek mythology; 2. Humorous graphic novels; 3. Short stories; 4. Graphic novels
978-0-8037-3308-4, $14.99

  Townsend retells the myths of King Midas, Pandora, Pygmalion, the abduction of Persephone, Arachne, Perseus, Pyramus and Thisbe, Icarus, and Hercules and his labors all with cartoony, silly art and lots of humor. Due to the popular Percy Jackson books, young readers may be looking for more Greek myths, and this collection invites those readers to laugh and have fun. Zeus's philandering ways and wife Hera's jealousy are treated in a kid-friendly way that still manages to get the point across that neither Zeus nor Hera were very nice to humans. Despite the irreverent treatment, Townsend does tell the gist of the stories.

  Where do presidents come from?: and other presidential stuff of super great importance. Dial Books for Young Readers 2012 160 p.
Grades: 2 3 4   973.09/9; 973.09
  1. Constitutional law — United States; 2. Presidents — United States; 3. Presidents — United States — Juvenile literature; 4. United States — History — 1775-1865
0803737483; 9780803737488, $14.99
LC 2012004103
  In this book, "[Michael] Townsend introduces grade-schoolers to the lives and responsibilities of the president of the United States, as well as the constitutional separation of powers and the history of the White House. With the help of a pink bunny, some monkeys, and assorted other animals and children, he . . . walks readers through the early history of the country, from the Revolution through the Bill of Rights." (Publishers Weekly)
  Includes bibliographical references (p. [156])

★ **Trickster: Native American tales: a graphic collection**
  Edited by Matt Dembicki. Fulcrum 2010 231p. Illustration
Grades: 5 6 7 8   398.2; 398
  1. Folklore; 2. Native Americans — Folklore; 3. Graphic novels
978-1-55591-724-1 (pa), $22.95; 1-55591-724-0 (pa)
LC 2009-49668
  "More than 40 storytellers and cartoonists have contributed to this original and provocative compendium of traditional folklore presented in authentic, colorful, and engaging sequential art. The stories are drawn from a variety of Native peoples across North America, and so the trickster character appears variously as Rabbit, a raccoon, Coyote, and in other guises; landscapes, clothing and rhythms of speech and action also vary in keeping with distinct traditions. Realistic, impressionistic, painterly, and cartoon styles of art are employed to echo and announce the tone of each tale and telling style, making this a rich visual treasure as well as cultural trove." SLJ

Trondheim, Lewis
  Li'l Santa. Art by Thierry Robin. NBM Publishing 2002 Un Illustration
Grades: 3 4 5 6 7 8 9 10 11 12 Adult   741.5; Fic
  1. Fantasy graphic novels; 2. Humorous graphic novels; 3. Santa Claus; 4. Stories without words; 5. Graphic novels
1-56163-335-6, $14.95
LC 2002-32131

You have no idea what Santa must go through, all the way up there at the North Pole, until you read this fully silent graphic novel. Besides the huge yearly job that faces him, the North Pole is no friendly place, what with Impies and a Snow Dragon and the like. Santa must use all his best cunning to make all the world's kids happy.

Monster dinosaur. Lewis Trondheim; Joe Johnson, translation; Michael Petranek, lettering. Papercutz 2012 32 p.

Grades: 1 2 3   **741.594**
1. Fighting games — Fiction; 2. Monsters — Fiction; 3. Picture books for children
1597073229; 9781597073226
This book shows "two demanding children bought off with the prospect of watching fantastical creatures forced to fight to the death for the delectation of the crowd. Early victories prove terrible foreshadowing as the victor, a once-innocuous little purple monster dinosaur created from the father's own drawing, is transformed by its experiences in the ring." (Publishers Weekly)
Originally published in French as: Monstreaux dinosaure. [Paris] : Guy Delcourt Productions, c2000.
Translated from the French.

Monster turkey. Lewis Trondheim; [Joe Johnson, translation; Michael Petranek, lettering]. Papercutz 2012 32 p.

Grades: 3 4 5   **Fic**
1. Animal experimentation — Juvenile fiction; 2. Farms — Juvenile fiction; 3. Monsters — Juvenile fiction
1597073490; 9781597073493, $9.99
In this book by Lewis Trondheim, part of the Monsters book series, "Petey, Jean, their parents and their own household monster Kriss arrive as guests at a farm that seems deserted at first but soon coughs up a giant bunny, a T. Rexûsized turkey and other toothy, red-eyed horrors. . . . The family tracks a suspicious pipeline to a factory where the monsters turn out to be a . . . tomato researcher's experimental subjects." (Kirkus Reviews)

Tiny tyrant. Lewis Trondheim; translated by Alexis Siegel; illustrated by Fabrice Parme. First Second 2007 124 p. Color illustration

Grades: 4 5 6 7 8 9 10 11 12 Adult   **741.5/944; Fic**
1. Humorous graphic novels; 2. Kings and rulers — Fiction; 3. Graphic novels
9781596430945, $12.95; 159643094X
                         LC 2006021479
Translations into English of eight French stories originally published by Delacourt, 2001-2004.
"In this illustrated collection of eight translated French stories, King Ethelbert rules as much by whim as by moral or regal standards; this lack of perspective can be excused, though, since he's only six. . . . Grades three to eight." (Bull Cent Child Books)
"Tiny child-king Ethelbert is spoiled and difficult, expecting to have his every whim fulfilled-or else. . . . In the end, though, he becomes a hero. The dynamic cartoons are filled with details and riddled with humor; most pages have between six and eight small pictures. . . . This title will have wide appeal. It's young and accessible enough for elementary-grade kids, but teens will also be charmed by the rascally king." SLJ

Trumbauer, Lisa
The **three** little pigs: the graphic novel. Art by Aaron Blecha. Stone Arch Books 2009 40p.

Grades: 3 4 5 6 7 8   **741.5; Fic**
1. Fairy tales; 2. Humorous graphic novels; 3. Three little pigs — Adaptations; 4. Graphic novels
978-1-4342-1195-8, $21.26
                         LC 2008-32050
In this graphic novel retelling, the three brother pigs set out on their own, and they build their three houses, the first of straw, the second of sticks, and the third of bricks. Then the Big Bad Wolf comes into town looking for something good to eat, and decides to get the pigs. He huffs, and he puffs, and he blows down the first two houses and carries the pigs into the woods. When he can't blow down the house of bricks, he tries to trick the third pig with outings to get food. The illustrations are on the creepy side, which could appeal to older elementary age boys. The book includes information on the history of the tale, discussion questions, and a glossary.
Part of the Graphic Sparks line

Tulien, Sean
Pecos Bill: colossal cowboy: the graphic novel. Art by Lisa Weber. Stone Arch Books 2010 40p. Illustration

Grades: 3 4 5 6 7 8   **741.5; Fic**
1. Folklore — United States; 2. Pecos Bill (Legendary character); 3. Tall tales; 4. Graphic novels
978-1-4342-1896-4, $22.65; 978-1-4342-2267-1 (pa), $4.95
                         LC 2009-29100
This colorful graphic novel retells some of the legends about Pecos Bill, the Texas cowboy hero, including his childhood among the coyotes, how he invented branding to keep track of the cattle, wrestling the wild horse named Widow Maker, and his wild ride on a tornado that caused the Grand Canyon and the Rio Grande. The book includes information on other legends connected with Pecos Bill, a short glossary, discussion questions, and reading prompts.
Part of the Graphic Spin series

Twain, Mark, 1835-1910
The **Adventures** of Tom Sawyer. Retold by M.C. Hall ; illustrated by Daniel Strickland. Stone Arch Books 2006 63p. Illustration

Grades: 3 4 5 6 7 8 9   **741.5; Fic**
1. Adventure graphic novels; 2. Twain, Mark, 1835-1910 — Adaptations; 3. Graphic novels
978-1-59889-045-7, $23.93
Tom Sawyer is the cleverest of characters, constantly outwitting those around him. Then there is Huckleberry Finn, the envy of the town's schoolchildren because he has the rare gift of complete freedom, never attending school or answering to anyone but himself. After Tom and Huck witness a murder, they find themselves on a series of adventures that lead them to some seriously frightening situations. This adaptation is written for reluctant and struggling readers.
Part of the Graphic Revolve series.

Classics illustrated delux #4: the adventures of Tom Sawyer. Adapted by Jean David Morvan, Frederique

Voulyze and Severine LeFebvre. Papercutz 2009 Un Illustration

Grades: 4 5 6 7 8 9 10   **741.5; Fic**
1. Adventure graphic novels; 2. Twain, Mark, 1835-1910 — Adaptations
978-1-59707-152-9, $17.95; 978-1-59707-153-6 (pa), $13.95

Orphan Tom Sawyer lives with his half-brother Sid at Aunt Polly's house, where he messes up in school and plays hooky as often as possible; he plays practical jokes with his buddy Huckleberry Finn, crushes on Becky Thatcher, and generally has a happy life. Then Tom and Huck witness a murder, and it changes their lives. This graphic novel adaptation was originally published in France and is translated by Joe Johnson for Papercutz; artist Lefebvre's work shows strong anime influences.

Uderzo
★ **Asterix** the Gaul. [by] René Goscinny and Albert Uderzo. Orion Media 2004 48p. Illustration; Map

Grades: 4 5 6 7 8 9 10 11 12   **741.5; Fic**
1. France — History; 2. Humorous graphic novels
0-7528-6604-4, $12.95; 0-7528-6605-2 (pa), $9.95

Meet Asterix, a diminutive but extremely strong Gaul living in ancient France during the time of the Roman Republic. Together with his friend Obelix, Asterix continually outwits the Roman Legionnaires sent to conquer Gaul for Julius Caesar. Full of puns and outrageous humor, the books also manage to teach a lot of history. This is the first in a long-running series of graphic novels translated from the original French.

Translated from the French

Other titles in this series are: Asterix and Caesar's Gift; Asterix and Cleopatra; Asterix and the actress; Asterix and the banquet; Asterix and the big fight; Asterix and the cauldron; Asterix and the Goths; Asterix and the Great Crossing; Asterix and the laurel wreath; Asterix the legionary; Asterix and the Normans; Asterix and the Roman Agent; Asterix and the soothsayer; Asterix at the Olympic Games; Asterix in Belgium; Asterix in Britain; Asterix in Corsica; Asterix in Spain; Asterix in Switzerland; Asterix Obelix and Co.; Asterix the gladiator; Asterix The Mansions of the Gods

Asterix and Obelix All at Sea. Orion/Sterling Publishing 2002 48p. Illustration

Grades: 4 5 6 7 8 9 10 11 12 Adult   **741.5; Fic**
1. Asterix (Fictional character); 2. Humorous graphic novels
0-75284-778-3, $9.95

LC 2002-282560

In ancient Rome the slaves are revolting ... and not only that, they've stolen Julius Caesar's own galley, the finest warship in the Roman navy. Under their heroic leader Spartakis, the former galley slaves make for the little Gaulish village where Julius Caesar's old enemies Asterix and Obelix live - only to find the place in crisis, for Obelix, after drinking the druid Getafix's magic potions on the sly, is first turned to stone and then reverts to childhood. In search of a cure for him Asterix, Getafix and their new friends the galley slaves sail to the wonderful continent of Atlantis, ruled by its high priest Absolutlifabulos - and the ensuing sea battles against the Roman navy are fast and furious ...

Van Lente, Fred
Destructive reentry. Fred Van Lente, writer ; James Cordeiro, penciler ; Gary Erskine, inker ; Martegod Gracia, colorist ; Dave Sharpe, letterer ; Skottie Young, cover. ABDO/Spotlight 2009 Un Illustration

Grades: 4 5 6 7 8 9   **741.5; Fic**
1. Iron Man (Fictional character); 2. Superhero graphic novels; 3. Graphic novels
978-1-59961-589-9, $21.35

LC 2008-33395

Iron Man heads out to space in an attempt to prevent the Stark International lab station Delphi-1 from falling out of orbit and crashing onto Earth. When he arrives, he finds big trouble: Living Laser has taken control of the lab and is forcing the scientists to use the nanotechnology there to build him a new body. His battle with Iron Man interrupts the process, and instead of a new body for Living Laser, a new entity of ever-regenerating nanobots with LL's paranoia comes to life. Now Iron Man and Living Laser must team up to stop the entity and save Earth.

This Spotlight edition reprints the comic originally published by Marvel as part of its Marvel Age imprint, without all the advertisements. This is part of the Iron Man Set II.

Ghost of a chance. Fred Van Lente, writer ; Graham Nolan, penciler ; Victor Olazaba, inker ; Martegod Gracia, colorist ; Dave Sharpe, letterer ; Skottie Young, cover. ABDO/Spotlight 2009 Un Illustration

Grades: 4 5 6 7 8 9   **741.5; Fic**
1. Iron Man (Fictional character); 2. Superhero graphic novels; 3. Graphic novels
978-1-59961-590-5, $21.35

LC 2008-33396

Dr. Doom captures Stark International executives, including Rhodey and Pepper, claiming they invaded Latverian air space while they were flying to a mountain chalet for a conference. Stark, who had stayed behind to work on a new invention, uses his untried stealth armor to infiltrate Doom's fortress and rescue his people.

This Spotlight edition reprints the comic originally published by Marvel as part of its Marvel Age imprint, without all the advertisements. This is part of the Iron Man Set II.

Howtoons; Volume 1: (re)ignition. Writer: Fred Van Lente; artist: Tom Fowler; colors: Jordie Bellaire; letters: Rus Wooton. Image Comics 2015 160 p. Illustration; Color

Grades: 5 6 7 8   **741.5**
1. Science — Experiments; 2. Science fiction graphic novels; 3. Siblings
9781632150561, $9.99; 1632150565

In this graphic novel by Fred Van Lente and illustrated by Tom Fowler, "Celine and Tuck's parents put them to sleep for centuries to ride out the energy crisis—but when they awake in the far future and Mom and Dad are missing, it's the kids who have to save the day! Celine and Tuck must explore a strange, new Earth using their gadgeteering skills to create projects and experiments to survive hostile tribes and bizarre mechanized threats." (Publisher's note)

"Step-by-step instructions and warnings for each device are included. The materials needed for each project varies. Each example features icons denoting what kind of energy this project represents. An icon glossary provides further explanation." SLJ

Marvel Adventures: Fantastic Four: Monsters & Mysteries. Art by Clay Mann. Marvel Entertainment 2007 Un Illustration
Grades: 3 4 5 6 7 8 9   **741.5; Fic**
1. Fantastic Four (Fictional characters); 2. Superhero graphic novels; 3. Graphic novels
978-0-7851-2380-4, $6.99
Mr. Fantastic, the Invisible Woman, the Human Torch, and the Thing go for a wild ride adventures and encounter the Mole Man, the Skrulls, Rama-Tut, and the Sub-Mariner.

Pirated!. Fred Van Lente, writer ; Rafa Sandoval, penciler ; Roger Bonet, inker ; Martegod Gracia, colorist ; Dave Sharpe, letterer ; Skottie Young, cover. ABDO/Spotlight 2009 Un Illustration
Grades: 4 5 6 7 8 9   **741.5; Fic**
1. Iron Man (Fictional character); 2. Superhero graphic novels; 3. Graphic novels
978-1-59961-591-2, $21.35
                    LC 2008-33397
While using his deep-sea armor to investigate shipwrecks, Stark stumbles upon the hideout of modern pirates, led by the man who calls himself Commander Kraken. They specialize in stealing technology and strip the armor from Stark; they plan to attack Hydrobase, where Kraken used to work as a scientist before he was accused of stealing his own technological secrets. Unarmed, shot out of Kraken's submarine through its torpedo tube, Stark must find a way to survive and get his armor back.
This Spotlight edition reprints the comic originally published by Marvel as part of its Marvel Age imprint, without all the advertisements. This is part of the Iron Man Set II.

The **simple** life. Fred Van Lente, writer ; Rafa Sandoval, penciler ; Roger Bonet, inker ; Ulises Arreola, colorist ; Dave Sharpe, letterer ; Skottie Young, cover. ABDO/Spotlight 2009 Un Illustration
Grades: 4 5 6 7 8 9   **741.5; Fic**
1. Iron Man (Fictional character); 2. Superhero graphic novels; 3. Graphic novels
978-1-59961-592-9, $21.35
                    LC 2008-33398
Flying over the Alleghenies to a meeting, Stark finds himself under attack by a superpowered assassin; she shorts out his suit's power but can't finish him off when a jetliner interrupts the fight. Iron Man crash lands near a remote settlement where the people have given up on modern technology to live in peace. However, one of the women there used to work in a Stark International factory and harbors great bitterness toward Stark for closing the factory. When the assassin returns to finish him off, how will he fight her off without armor and without harming the people who saved his life?
This Spotlight edition reprints the comic originally published by Marvel as part of its Marvel Age imprint, without all the advertisements. This is part of the Iron Man Set II.

Spider-man: fashion victims. Fred Van Lente, writer ; Michael O'Hare, pencils ; Cory Hamscher, inks ; GURU

eFX, colors ; Scherberger, Paris and GURU eFX, cover ; Dave Sharpe, letterer. ABDO Publishing Company/Spotlight 2008 Un Illustration
Grades: 4 5 6 7 8 9   **741.5; Fic**
1. Spider-Man (Fictional character); 2. Superhero graphic novels; 3. Graphic novels
978-1-59961-395-6, $21.35
                    LC 2007-20239
When Spider-Man suddenly finds himself battling newbie villains in high-tech suits marked with a "T", he knows he's got to find the source who is supplying them with the means to commit crimes. But when he finds the Tinkerer, how will he be able to stop him? This is a revised, hardbound edition of the Marvel Adventures Spider-Man comic book issue #21.
Part of the Spider-Man Set III

Vanholme, Virginie
Scared to death, bk 1: the vampire from the Marshes. Illustrated by Mauricet. Cinebook 2008 48p. Illustration
Grades: 5 6 7 8 9   **741.5; Fic**
1. Horror graphic novels; 2. Mystery graphic novels; 3. Vampires; 4. Graphic novels
978-1-905460-47-2, $11.95
Young teen friends Robin and Max sneak a look into Robin's father's files. He's a forensic scientist who gets called in to investigate mysterious deaths. They read the file on the death of a man who was found in the rushes in the local park, full of little holes all over his body. Max believes the man was killed by vampires, and the two boys go to the library to do research, camp out in Robin's yard but nothing seems to happen except that they interrupt the work of a poacher. However, there are vampires out there, and now they're watching Robin and Max. There's just enough spookiness and blood for upper elementary and middle school age readers who want some horror without being grossed out by excessive gore.
Part of the Scared to Death series, originally published in France as Mort de Trouille Le vampire des marais.

Varon, Sara
Robot dreams. First Second 2007 205p. Illustration
Grades: 3 4 5 6 7 8 9 10 11 12 Adult   **741; 741.5; Fic**
1. Dogs; 2. Robots; 3. Graphic novels
978-1-59643-108-9 (pa), $16.95; 1-59643-108-3 (pa)
                    LC 2006-52640
The friendship between a dog and a robot is portrayed in this wordless graphic novel. (Bull Cent Child Books)
"Varon's drawing style is uncomplicated, and her colors are clean and refeshing. Although her story seems equally simple, it is invested with true emotion." Booklist

Sweaterweather. Alternative Comics 2006 96p. Illustration
Grades: 3 4 5 6 7 8 9   **741.5; Fic**
1. Animals; 2. Friendship; 3. Stories without words; 4. Graphic novels
1-891867-93-8, $14.95
A turtle, a rabbit, and other creatures venture out on a wordless snowy journey full of friendship and sweetness.

Varon includes interactive bits to the book, such as paper dolls, postcards, and stamps.

First published 2003

Venable, Colleen A F

★ **And** then there were gnomes. Illustrated by Stephanie Yue. Graphic Universe 2010 47p. Illustration (Guinea Pig, pet shop private eye)

Grades: 2 3 4   **741; Fic; 741.5**
1. Guinea pigs; 2. Hamsters; 3. Humorous graphic novels; 4. Mice; 5. Mystery graphic novels; 6. Graphic novels
978-0-7613-4599-2 (lib bdg), $27.93; 0-7613-4599-X (lib bdg); 978-0-7613-5480-2 (pa), $6.95; 0-7613-5480-8 (pa)

LC 2009-20896

Guinea pig detective Sasspants and her sidekick Hamisher the hamster try to solve a mystery when the mice in Mr. Venezi's pet shop are going missing and all the clues point to a ghost.

"The story is never scary. Everything about it could be described as cute, from the art to the characters' personalities." Publ Wkly

Fish you were here. Illustrated by Stephanie Yue. Graphic Universe 2011 46p. Illustration

Grades: 2 3 4   **741.5**
978-0-7613-5224-2, $27.93; 0-7613-5224-4

LC 2011001079

"Befuddled but lovable Mr. Venez"'s still advertising for an assistant to help him in his pet shop. . . . When ninth-grader Viola arrives, she seems the perfect employee. She turns a light on the lizards. She gives the ferrets tons of toys and tubes. She even puts the correct animal names on the cages; Mr. Venezi had labeled the chinchillas, 'gorillas,' among other misnomers. She does so well that guinea pig detective Sasspants becomes suspicious, and Mr. Venezi feels unneeded. When Mr. Venezi turns up missing and Viola, without supervision, starts slacking, Detective Sasspants is on the case." (Kirkus)

Hamster and cheese. Illustrated by Stephanie Yue. Graphic Universe 45p. Illustration

Grades: 2 3 4   **741.5; 741**
978-0-7613-4598-5 (lib bdg), $27.93; 0-7613-4598-1 (lib bdg); 978-0-7613-5479-6 (pa), $6.95; 0-7613-5479-4 (pa)

"There is skullduggery afoot at Mr. Venezi's Pets & Stuff: Someone keeps stealing his sandwich, which he puts outside the koala cage every day. No, he doesn't sell koalas; they're really hamsters, but Mr. Venezi is both shortsighted and incompetent (though very kind). The only cage that's correctly labeled is the one holding the guinea pig—but someone has stolen the G, so little Hamisher the koala, er, hamster has decided that guinea pig Sasspants must be a P.I. and therefore can crack the case." (Kirkus)

Other titles in this series are: And then there were gnomes (2010); The ferret's a foot (2011); Fish you were here (2011); Raining cats and detectives (2012); Going, going, dragon! (2013)

Raining cats and detectives. Colleen A.F. Venable; illustrated by Stephanie Yue. Graphic Universe 2012 46 p. Color illustration

Grades: 2 3 4   **741.5/973; Fic**
1. Animals — Fiction; 2. Cats — Fiction; 3. Detectives — Fiction; 4. Guinea pigs — Fiction; 5. Hamsters — Fiction; 6. Humorous stories; 7. Missing persons — Fiction; 8. Mystery and detective stories; 9. Pet shops — Fiction; 10. Graphic novels
0761360085; 9780761360087, $27.93

LC 2011021626

In author Colleen AF Venable's book, "[g]uinea pig Sasspants, her faithful, exuberantly enthusiastic sidekick, Hamisher the hamster, and all the denizens of Mr. Venezi's Pets & Stuff are still in the store . . . Then (human) Detective Pickles arrives and adopts Sasspants, so when Tummytickles, the bookstore cat next door, vanishes, there's no one to find him. Suddenly, everyone from the goldfish . . . to the snooty chinchillas are donning detective hats and àwell, calling themselves detectives. Will Sasspants return to save the day, or can Hamisher detect on his own?" (Kirkus)

Venditti, Robert

The **lost** hero: the graphic novel. By Rick Riordan; adapted by Robert Venditti; art by Nate Powell; color by Orpheus Collar; lettering by Chris Dickey. Disney-Hyperion Books 2014 192 p. Color; Illustration

Grades: 4 5 6 7 8   **741.5**
1. Camps — Fiction; 2. Gaia (Greek deity) — Fiction; 3. Greek mythology; 4. Hera (Greek deity) — Fiction; 5. Monsters — Fiction; 6. Mythology, Greek — Fiction; 7. Riordan, Rick Lost hero — Adaptations; 8. Graphic novels
142316279X; 9781423162797, $21.99; 9781423163251

LC 2013013559

"Jason has a problem. He doesn't remember anything before waking up on a school bus holding hands with a girl. Apparently she's his girlfriend Piper, his best friend is a kid named Leo, and they're all students in the Wilderness School, a boarding school for 'bad kids.' What he did to end up here, Jason has no idea—except that everything seems very wrong." (Publisher's note)

"Powell does an excellent job of adapting the original story into pictorial format, hitting all of the high points and representing all of the major details in the drawings, so little is lost." SLJ

The **sea** of monsters: the graphic novel. By Rick Riordan; adapted by Robert Venditti; art by Attila Futaki; colors by Tamas Gaspar; lettering by Chris Dickey. Disney-Hyperion Books 2013 128 p. Color illustration (Percy Jackson & the Olympians)

Grades: 5 6 7 8 9 10   **741.5; Fic**
1. Fathers and sons — Fiction; 2. Greek mythology; 3. Monsters — Fiction; 4. Poseidon (Greek deity) — Fiction; 5. Graphic novels
1423145291; 9781423145295, $19.99; 9781423145509

LC 2011012356

In this graphic novel, by Rick Riordan, adapted by Robert Venditti, and illustrated by Attila Futaki and Tamas Gaspar, "when an innocent game of dodgeball among Percy and his classmates turns into a death match against an ugly gang of cannibal giants, things get...well, ugly. And the unexpected arrival of his friend Annabeth brings more bad news: the magical borders that protect Camp Half-Blood have been poisoned by a mysterious enemy, and unless a cure is found, the only safe haven for demigods will be destroyed." (Publisher's note)

"This is a good summary presentation of the original novel, with active and effective art." Lib Med Con

Verne, Jules, 1828-1905
Around the world in 80 days. Adapted by Chrys Millien ; illustrated by Flo Demolis. IDW Publishing 2009 60p. Illustration
Grades: 5 6 7 8 9   **741.5; Fic**
   1. Adventure graphic novels; 2. Verne, Jules, 1828-1905 — Adaptations; 3. Graphic novels
978-1-60010-394-0, $14.99

This graphic novel Verne's globe-trotting adventures of Phileas Fogg, English gentleman, his newly-hired French manservant, Passepartout, and the English detective, Fix, who pursues Fogg, convinced he is a master bank robber. Fogg makes a bet with fellow members of the Reform Club in 1872 that he can travel around the world in eighty days, but his precipitous departure makes Scotland Yard suspect him. The three men travel through India, where Fogg saves a beautiful young Indian woman from being burned alive, to Hong Kong, then Japan and then across the United States and onward. This adaptation was originally published in France. The book includes biographical information about Verne, historical information about what the world was like in the 1870s, and an analysis of the novel.

Journey to the Center of the Earth. Retold by Davis Worth Miller and Katherine McLean Brevard ; illustrated by Greg Rebis. Stone Arch Books 2007 72p. Illustration
Grades: 3 4 5 6 7 8 9   **741.5; Fic**
   1. Adventure graphic novels; 2. Science fiction graphic novels; 3. Graphic novels
978-1-59889-832-3, $23.93

LC 2007-6202

Axel Lidenbrock and his uncle find a mysterious message inside the 300-year-old book. The dusty note describes a secret passageway to the center of the earth, and Axel reluctantly joins his uncle on a quest. Soon they are descending deeper and deeper into the heart of a volcano. With their guide, Hans, the men discover underground rivers, oceans, strange rock formations, and prehistoric monsters. They also run into danger, which threatens to trap them below the surface forever. The book is written with an easy vocabulary for reluctant and struggling readers, and it includes facts about the real center of the Earth.

Part of the Graphic Revolve series.

Vining, James
First in Space. Oni Press 2007 Un Illustration
Grades: 3 4 5 6 7 8   **629.4; 741.5; 616**
   1. Animal experimentation; 2. Space flight; 3. Graphic novels
978-1-932664-64-5, $9.95

Vining received a 2006 Xeric Grant to help him complete and publish his book.

This book tells young readers about the early years of the U.S. space program, in the late 1950s and early 1960s. After the Russians successfully sent the dog, Laika, into space in the Sputnik 2 in 1957, the U.S. successfully sent two monkeys into suborbital space and back in 1959. In 1960, NASA began training young chimpanzees to complete certain tasks; young enlisted men under Sergeant Ed Dittmer took care of the chimpanzees, one chimp per man. In 1961, one of the chimpanzees, nicknamed Ham by his young handler, Beach, became the first chimp in space when NASA sent him up in the Mercury MR-2 rocket. Vining researched this extensively, and he provides a bibliography; but for the book, he focuses on the personal interactions between Beach and Ham and on the training that Ham and the other chimpanzees went through.

Vitaliano, Fausto
Donald Duck and friends: double duck. Written by Fausto Vitaliano & Marco Bosco ; art by Alessandro Freccero ... [et al.]. Boom! Kids 2010 Un Illustration
Grades: 3 4 5 6 7 8   **741.5; Fic**
   1. Adventure graphic novels; 2. Donald Duck (Fictional character); 3. Humorous graphic novels; 4. Graphic novels
978-1-60886-551-2, $24.99

Donald Duck is having a difficult time: his relationship with Daisy is rocky due to his tendency to fall asleep during romantic movies, and he's engaged in a feud with a city employee over a parking ticket. Things take a turn for the weird when a beautiful duck who calls herself Kay K tells Donald he is also Double D, a secret agent; something he just can't remember. The Agency needs him to steal a suitcase, but won't tell him why. When it all goes wrong, Kay K bails Donald out of jail, and now he knows the suitcase contains information on all the Agency's agents. He's got to get it back, or everyone will be in danger. The book includes lots of action and comedy, but no graphic violence. The comics in this book were originally published in Italy.

Viva, Frank
A **trip** to the bottom of the world with Mouse: a Toon Book. Frank Viva. Toon Books 2012 32 p.
Grades: PreK K 1 2   **Fic; 741.5/973**
   1. Animals — Antarctica — Fiction; 2. Antarctica — Description and travel; 3. Antarctica — Fiction; 4. Mice — Juvenile fiction; 5. Picture books for children; 6. Voyages and travels — Juvenile fiction; 7. Graphic novels
1935179195; 9781935179191

LC 2011049499

This book chronicles the journey of a boy and his mouse friend to the Antarctic. The "tour features both large waves and still waters, glimpses of a killer whale and penguins of various identified sorts, and a dip in waters warmed by a half-sunken volcano. It's all in the company of a querulous mouse whose initial 'Are we there yet?' and eight-times-repeated 'Can we go home now?' inevitably turns to 'Can we go back there soon?' by the end." (Kirkus)

Waid, Mark
The **Incredibles:** revenge from below. Writers, Mark Waid and Landry Walker ; art by Marcio Takara and Ramanda Kamarga. Boom! Kids 2010 Un Illustration
Grades: 3 4 5 6 7   **741.5; Fic**
   1. Adventure graphic novels; 2. Incredibles (Fictional characters); 3. Superhero graphic novels; 4. Graphic novels

978-1-60886-518-5, $9.99

When the Incredibles encounter villainess Mesmerella, speedy Dash's impetuous actions endanger his sister Violet, so his parents ground him by taking away his powers. In his forcibly normal state (for regular folks, anyway), Dash feels sluggish and helpless; then he witnesses a couple of his teachers display alien tentacles. However, no one will believe him, so how can he get anyone to help him? This original story based on the popular movie characters will attract young readers, especially boys who will enjoy the focus on Dash. There is some action, and Dash does punch the villainess, although readers won't see Dash, just the result of the punches as Mesmerella reels from them.

Walker, Landry Q.

Little Gloomy: . . . It was a dark and stormy night. [by] Landry Q. Walker and Eric Jones. Slave Labor Graphics 2002 128p. Illustration

Grades: 4 5 6 7 **741.5; Fic**
1. Fantasy graphic novels; 2. Humorous graphic novels; 3. Graphic novels
0-943151-64-3, $12.95

In Frightsylvania, Little Gloomy is the only normal girl in a world of monsters, but that's not her problem. Mad scientist Simon, her ex-boyfriend, is her problem; he's decided to send an army of zombies against her to get revenge. Can Gloomy and her friends Larry the werewolf, Frank the lovesick monster (he's got a crush on Gloomy), and Carl Cthulhu the interdimensional octopoid demigod survive the onslaught of the undead? The monsters are all drawn to look so cute, it's hard to imagine anyone really getting scared by reading this book.

The **super** scary monster show, featuring Little Gloomy. Written by Landry Walker; drawn by Eric Jones; tones by Rikki Simons. Amaze Ink/SLG Publishing 2008 Un Illustration

Grades: 3 4 5 6 7 8 9 **741.5; Fic**
1. Horror graphic novels; 2. Humorous graphic novels; 3. Graphic novels
978-1-59362-103-2, $9.95; 1-59362-103-5

This book collects the three issues (so far) of The Super Scary Monster Show comics. Little Gloomy, her friends, and her enemies, live in the world called Frightsylvania. Gloomy deals with an alien who crashlands in her backyard and wants to take over the world (she has plenty of "pet" monsters in her house who take care of her problem). Carl the squid lies to his parents about taking over the world and enslaving all its creatures, then they come for a visit. . . . Gloomy buys a golden scorpion as a gift for her friend the Mummy, but it turns out to be cursed, and everyone around her suffers accidents. The witch Evey has come up with a new spell to torment Gloomy, but it hits werewolf buddy Larry instead and shrinks him. There are plenty more stories, all written with tongue-in-cheek humor and just a touch of horror for younger readers. Gloomy does not suffer fools gladly, so the invading alien gets eaten (off page), and other inimical creatures suffer similar fates, so this book shouldn't be given to younger readers who are sensitive and don't like any violence. There is little in the way of any gore or overt violence, except for poor Frank, whose body parts often come apart.

★ **Supergirl:** cosmic adventures in the 8th grade. DC Comics 2009 144p. Illustration

Grades: 3 4 5 6 7 8 **741.5; Fic**
1. Humorous graphic novels; 2. School life; 3. Superhero graphic novels; 4. Graphic novels
978-1-4012-2506-3, $12.99

Kara Zor-El is just an average Kryptonian girl who arrives on Earth sort of accidentally when she has an argument with her mother. Here she discovers she has super powers, just like her cousin, Superman. He tells her she can't just go home, so now she's stuck living on Earth, going to middle school, and her powers can't prevent her from being the new kid in school. She makes one friend, but Lena happens to be related to Superman's nemesis Lex Luthor; then she manages to create a mirror-image self who is evil. On top of that, weird things keep happening at school. Kara may be Supergirl, but can she survive 8th grade?

Wallace, Karen

Yikes, it's a yeti!. By Karen Wallace; illustrated by Mick Reid.. Stone Arch Books 2008 72p. Illustration

Grades: 3 4 5 6 7 **741.5; Fic**
1. Adventure graphic novels; 2. Humorous graphic novels; 3. Yeti; 4. Graphic novels
978-1-4342-0459-2, $21.26

LC 2007-30742

Norman leads a very boring life, unlike neighbor and friend Scott, who always seems to be doing something exciting. Going camping with his granny during his vacation sounds like more of the same boring stuff. However, once they hit the road, Norman's Grandma pulls off her gray wig, strips off her old-lady dress to show her cool biking leathers, and takes Norman on a trip to the Himalayas. They're off to find a yeti. Now Norman knows he's on the vacation of a lifetime, with lots of fun and excitement (and yak burgers).

Part of the Graphic Trax series; originally published in Great Britain in 2001.

Walsh, David

Shugo chara!, v1-v6. Peach-Pit; translated by June Kato; adapted by David Walsh; lettered by North Market Street Graphics. Del Rey/Ballantine Books 2007 Illustration

Grades: 5 6 7 8 9 **741.5; Fic**
978-0-345-49745-1 (v1), $10.95

LC 2007296632

"Everybody at Seiyo Elementary thinks that stylish and super cool Amu has it all: But nobody knows the real Amu, a shy girl who wishes she had the courage to truly be herself. Changing Amu's life is going to take more than wishes and dreams—it's going to take a little magic! One morning, Amu finds a surprise in her bed: three strange little eggs. Each egg contains a Guardian Character, an angel-like being who can give her the power to be someone new." (Publisher's note)

Volume 1 of 12

Watson, Andi

Princess at midnight. Image Comics 2008 Un Illustration

Grades: 4 5 6 7 8 9 10 **741.5; Fic**
1. Fantasy graphic novels; 2. Princesses; 3. War; 4. Graphic novels
978-1-58240-928-3, $5.99; 1-58240-928-5

Holly Crescent and her twin brother Henry lead sheltered lives as home-schooled children by day; their parents don't want any harm to come to their children after they were born prematurely and their early lives were so worrisome. At night, however, Holly becomes Princess of Castle Waxing, where life is good until the Horrible Horde takes over one of her favorite picnic spots. All too soon, her nights are spent in warfare against the Horde, and her days in reading books on war strategy. And when she wins, she's not satisfied with winning, she must pursue more warfare against the Horde, even as her dragon Chancellor warns her of overspending and the consequences of war on her people.

Weigel, Jeff
Dragon Girl: The Secret Valley. Jeff Weigel. Andrews McMeel Pub 2014 192 p. Illustration
Grades: 2 3 4 5 6   **741.5; Fic**
  1. Dragons — Fiction; 2. Orphans — Fiction
  1449441831; 9781449441838, $9.99
                                            LC 2013943302
"Eleven-year-old Alanna and her older brother Hamel are orphans and doing their best to take care of each other until one day Alanna stumbles upon a cave full of dragon eggs. When the eggs hatch with no mother dragon in sight, Alanna decides to take care of the babies herself, even creating a clever costume so that the babies think she, too, is a dragon." (Publisher's note)
"Weigel has created a compulsively likable heroine who seamlessly blends her strength and compassion. . . . With lovable dragons, flying ships and danger around every corner, this delightful fantasy doesn't disappoint." Kirkus

★ **Thunder** from the sea: adventure on board the HMS Defender. G. P. Putnam's Sons 2010 46p. Illustration
Grades: 3 4 5 6   **741.5; Fic**
  1. Adventure graphic novels; 2. Europe — History —
  1789-1815; 3. Great Britain — Royal Navy; 4. Naval art
  and science; 5. Graphic novels
  978-0-399-25089-7, $17.99
                                             LC 2009-32801
In 1805, during the Napoleonic Wars, twelve-year-old Jack Hoyton becomes a member of the crew of HMS Defender, a midsize ship in the British Royal Navy. The Defender patrols along a portion of the French coast to block French ships, but a major gun emplacement in Dumont hampers the ship's efforts. When some of the crew land to fill their barrels with fresh water, French gunmen fire upon them, killing an officer and wounding a crewman. The Captain assigns Jack to be part of the crew that will land and take the guns; when the men arrive, they find that there is no small village, but a major shipbuilding facility, and they're captured.
"Weigel's old-fashioned comics art shows lots of authentic details of eighteenth-century shipboard life, and there is some battle violence. . . . This picture-book-size graphic novel should find a ready audience of young adventure-loving readers." Booklist
Includes bibliographical references

Weiser, Joey
Mermin book one: out of water. Joey Weiser; [edited by] Jill Beaton. Oni Press 2013 152 p. (Mermin)

Grades: 4 5 6   **741.5**
  1. Mermaids and mermen — Fiction; 2. Science fiction
  comic books, strips, etc; 3. Graphic novels
  1934964980; 9781934964989, $19.99
                                            LC 2012953664
Author Joey Weiser presents a graphic novel about merpeople. "'MERMIN the MERMAN from MER!?' That's the question Pete and his friends ask after finding the fish-boy washed up on the beach! Mermin just escaped the undersea kingdom of Mer, and is ready to have some fun on dry land! But why would this aquatic kid be afraid to swim? Perhaps it has something to do with the fishy pursuers who have followed him from the depths below!" (Publisher's note)

Weissman, Steven
The **Kid** Firechief. Fantagraphics Books 2004 96p. Illustration
Grades: 4 5 6 7 8 9   **741.5; Fic**
  1. Adventure graphic novels; 2. Fire fighters; 3. Graphic
  novels
  1-56097-596-2, $12.95
Even though he's just a poor orphaned boy, it's a well-known fact that there's no greater firefighter than Olaf Oedwards, a.k.a. "Kid Firechief." Olaf and his assistant chief (and guardian) Smoky Joe put out fires all over the city and forests of Milltown and as far as... Ancient Rome" This adventure romp features characters including the infant rappers D.J. Diaper and M.C. Nu-Born ("This li'l piggy kept it real/while this li'l piggy was chillin'/This li'l piggy said 'Talk to the hand'/while this li'l piggy was illin'"), local school reporter "Nosy" Rosie Cheeks, Olaf's arch-nemesis Hotfoot, and Olaf's forest ranger cousin, Oella Oedwards. The book uses orange ink on light yellow paper.

White flower day. Fantagraphics 2002 112p. Illustration
Grades: 5 6 7 8 9 10 11 12 Adult   **741.5; Fic**
  1. Humorous graphic novels
  1-56097-514-8, $14.95
This book will appeal to older children who enjoy such things as "The Grim Adventures of Billy and Mandy" on Cartoon Network, with its somewhat gross and twisted humor.
"Scratch panels highlighted in ocher cast {a} jaundiced pall over three . . . twisted tales of rascaldom. They feature the Frankenstein-like Pullapart Boy, devilish L'il Bloody, and several equally weird young characters who venture forth to create mayhem, from innocent to morbid." Booklist
Another 'Yikes' book

Wells, H. G.
The **Invisible** Man. Retold by Terry Davis ; illustrated by Dennis Calero. Stone Arch Books 2007 72p. Illustration
Grades: 3 4 5 6 7 8 9   **741.5; Fic**
  1. Mystery graphic novels; 2. Science fiction graphic
  novels; 3. Graphic novels
  978-1-59889-831-6, $23.93
                                              LC 2007-6200
Late one night, a mysterious man, covered from head to toe in bandages, wanders into a tiny English village. After a series of burglaries, the villagers grow suspicious. Who is

this man? Where did he come from? When they attempt to arrest the stranger, he suddenly reveals his secret: he is invisible. How can anyone stop the Invisible Man? The book is written with an easy vocabulary for struggling and reluctant readers, and it includes facts about invisibility.
Part of the Graphic Revolve series.

The **Time** Machine. Retold by Terry Davis ; illustrated by José Alfonso Ocampo Ruiz. Stone Arch Books 2007 72p. Illustration
Grades: 3 4 5 6 7 8 9   **741.5; Fic**
1. Adventure graphic novels; 2. Science fiction graphic novels; 3. Graphic novels
978-1-59889-833-0, $23.93
             LC 2007-6201
A scientist invents a machine that he claims will travel through space, but his friends laugh at the idea. So the Time Traveler climbs aboard his machine and ends up thousands of years in the future. He meets a race of gentle humans called the Eloi, but he is soon swept up in a fight for his life against evil underground creatures known as Morlocks. Even worse, his Time Machine, his only chance to escape, is trapped deep inside the Morlock caverns. This book is written with an easy vocabulary for struggling and reluctant readers, and it includes some scientific speculations about the future.
Part of the Graphic Revolve series

The **war** of the worlds. By H.G. Wells; retold by Davis Miller and Katherine M. Brevard; illustrated by Jose Alfonso Ocampo Ruiz. Stone Arch Books 2009 72p. Illustration
Grades: 4 5 6 7 8 9 10   **741.5; Fic**
1. Science fiction graphic novels; 2. Graphic novels
978-1-4342-0757-9, $23.93
             LC 2008-6250
In 1894, a strange meteorite crashes down near London, England. When George and other residents of Woking investigate the site, they discover a large alien cylinder. Suddenly, it's activated and begins destroying everything in its path. And George finds out there are more of the things elsewhere in the country. The people eventually learn that England has been invaded by Martians, and they are definitely not friendly. This graphic novel adaptation includes information about the Halloween 1938 radio hoax in which this story was dramatized in such a way that people in the U.S. thought they were in fact being invaded by deadly aliens.
Part of the Graphic Revolve series

Wells, Zeb
    Marvel Adventures Spider-Man Vol. 4: Concrete Jungle. Pencilled by Patrick Scherberger. Marvel Entertainment 2006 Un Illustration
Grades: 3 4 5 6 7 8 9   **741.5; Fic**
1. Spider-Man (Fictional character); 2. Superhero graphic novels; 3. Graphic novels
978-0-7851-2005-6, $6.99
    Spider-Man stars in four stories featuring the Mad Thinker, the Chameleon, the Black Cat, and Doctor Octopus.

Welvaert, Scott R.
    Helen Keller: Courageous Advocate. By Scott R. Welvaert ; illustrated by Cynthia Martin and Keith Tucker. Capstone Press 2006 32p. Illustration
Grades: 3 4 5 6 7 8 9   **741.5; 362.4; 92**
1. Biographical graphic novels; 2. Keller, Helen, 1880-1968; 3. Graphic novels
0-7368-4964-5, $25.26
             LC 2005006463
    This book uses the comic book format to recount highlights of the life of Helen Keller, a blind and deaf woman who became an author and advocate for the blind and other physically handicapped people. It includes additional information, a glossary, a list of books for further reading, and more.
Part of the Graphic Library, Graphic Biographies series.

West, David
    Astronauts. Illustrated by Jim Robbins. Rosen Publishing Group 2008 48p. Illustration
Grades: 3 4 5 6 7 8 9   **629.45; 741.5**
1. Astronautics — Vocational guidance; 2. Astronauts; 3. Graphic novels
978-1-4042-1461-3, $29.25
             LC 2007-45208
    After brief descriptions of living and working conditions in space and the training one undergoes to become an astronaut, the book profiles three astronauts. Yuri Alexeyevich Gagarin was the first person to go into space; he was a Russian cosmonaut. Dr. Jerry Linenger lived and worked on the Russian space station Mir in 1997, when a fire broke out in the space station. And Thomas D. Jones flew on the space shuttle Atlantis, on its 2000 mission, STS-98.
Part of the Graphic Careers series

    Fighter pilots. Illustrated by James Field. Rosen Publishing Group 2008 48p. Illustration
Grades: 3 4 5 6 7 8 9   **358.4; 741.5**
1. Air pilots; 2. Military aeronautics; 3. Graphic novels
978-1-4042-1455-2, $29.25
             LC 2007-41458
    After brief descriptions of the rise of fighters in air combat and of the evolution of jet fighters, this book profiles three pilots. Lieutenant Edwin C. Parsons flew with the Escadrille Lafayette during World War I. Pilot Office Geoffrey Wellum piloted a Royal Air Force Spitfire during the Battle of Britain in 1940. Lieutenant Randall H. Cunningham was a Navy fighter pilot who became the first fighter ace (he shot down at least five enemy aircraft) of the Vietnam War. This is the same man who, in 2005, pleaded guilty of graft for taking bribes while serving in the U.S. Congress. His later crimes do not take away from his fighter pilot accomplishments.
Part of the Graphic Careers series

    Hernan Cortes: The Life of a Spanish Conquistador. By David West & Jackie Gaff ; illustrated by Jim Eldridge. Rosen Publishing Group 2005 48p. Illustration
Grades: 3 4 5 6 7 8   **741.5; 972; 92**
1. Biographical graphic novels; 2. Cortes, Hernan, 1485-1547; 3. Mexico — History — Conquest, 1519-1540; 4. Graphic novels
1-4042-0244-7, $29.25

LC 2004005938

Adventurous explorer or ruthless imperialist? In 1519, Spanish conquistador Hernan Cortes led a daring expedition to the heart of the Aztec Empire, in what is now central and southern Mexico. Within two years, this highly advanced civilization had fallen to the might of Cortes's Spanish conquerors, resulting in the deaths of tens of thousands of Aztecs. This graphic novel explores two cultures in conflict—and the personality of a man driven by both insatiable greed and service to his country. The book includes additional information, a glossary, and a list of books for further reading.

Part of the Graphic Nonfiction series.

Pteranodon: The Giant of the Sky. Illustrated by Terry Riley and Geoff Ball. Rosen Publishing Group 2007 32p. Illustration
Grades: 2 3 4 5 6 7   **567.9; 741.5**
1. Dinosaurs; 2. Pteranodon; 3. Graphic novels
978-1-4042-3895-4, $25.25

LC 2007-1792

This volume uses colorful comic book style illustrations to explore the habitat, diet, and behavior of the pteranodon. At the front of the book, facts about the pteranodon are presented, while at the back of the book readers will find a picture gallery of other creatures mentioned in the book.

Part of the Graphic Dinosaurs series.

Race car drivers. Illustrated by Peter Wilks and Geoff Ball. Rosen Publishing Group 2008 48p. Illustration
Grades: 3 4 5 6 7 8 9   **796.72; 741.5**
1. Automobile racing; 2. Graphic novels
978-1-4042-1452-1, $29.25

LC 2007-45174

After brief descriptions of early car racing and of the different types of car racing (NASCAR, Formula One, etc.), the book profiles three racers. Argentinian driver Juan Manuel Fangio is considered one of the best Formula One race car drivers, and he recalls the 1957 race at the Nurburgring in Germany. Dale Earnhardt, Sr. was one of the best-known NASCAR racers in the U.S. In 1996, he crashed during the Diehard 500; despite his injuries (a broken collarbone and sternum), he drove in Indianapolis, although he had to stop before finishing. The next week, he raced in Watkins Glen, New York, and finished in sixth place. He died in 2001, in a crash at the Daytona 500. The third driver profiled in this book is Formula One rookie Lewis Hamilton, who started at age seven with remote-controlled car races and spent his teen years winning Kart races in Great Britain (Karts are small racecars). He became a Formula One race driver in 2006.

Part of the Graphic Careers series

Richard the Lionheart: The Life of a King and Crusader. By David West & Jackie Gaff ; illustrated by John Cooper. Rosen Publishing Group 2005 48p. Illustration
Grades: 3 4 5 6 7 8   **741.5; 942.03; 92**
1. Biographical graphic novels; 2. Great Britain — History — 1154-1399, Plantagenets; 3. Richard, I, King of England; 4. Graphic novels
1-4042-0241-2, $29.25

LC 2004011267

Politician, military leader, crusader, and King of England, Richard the Lionheart has been the subject of Middle Ages' studies for centuries. His early years were marked by bitter rivalry with his father and brothers, but once crowned King in 1189, his primary ambition was to lead a crusade to the Holy Land to recapture the city of Jerusalem. This graphic novel treats readers to a retelling of the King's battle against Saladin for control of the Holy Land, his subsequent imprisonment, and ultimate return to the throne. It includes additional information, a glossary, and a list of books for further reading.

Part of the Graphic Nonfiction series.

Velociraptor: The Speedy Thief. Illustrated by James Field. Rosen Publishing Group 2007 32p. Illustration
Grades: 2 3 4 5 6 7
567.9; 741.5
1. Dinosaurs; 2. Velociraptor; 3. Graphic novels
978-1-4042-3898-5, $25.25

LC 2007-873

Courtesy of Rosen Publishing

This volume uses colorful comic book style illustrations to explore the habitat, diet, and behavior of the velociraptor. At the front of the book, facts about the velociraptor are presented, while at the back of the book readers will find a picture gallery of other creatures mentioned in the book.

Part of the Graphic Dinosaurs series.

Wheeler, Lisa

Seadogs: An Epic Ocean Operetta. Composed by Lisa Wheeler ; staged by Mark Siegel. Simon & Schuster/Aladdin Paperbacks 2004 Un Illustration
Grades: 2 3 4 5 6 **741.5; Fic**
1. Adventure graphic novels; 2. Dogs; 3. Humorous graphic novels; 4. Graphic novels
978-1-4169-4103-3, $7.99
2006 Texas Bluebonnet Award Winner

A young Victorian girl pup goes to sea an operetta performed, and the reader watches Seadogs performed on stage right along with the audience. Old Seadog invites his good friends Brave Beagle and Dear Dachsund along for one last sail, and they encounter pirates, storms ... and a strange little pup.

Courtesy of Aladdin Press

White, Steve

The **Battle** of Midway: the destruction of the Japanese fleet. Illustrated by Richard Elson. The Rosen Publishing Group 2007 48p. Illustration
Grades: 3 4 5 6 7 8 9   **741.5; 940.54**

1. Midway, Battle of, 1942; 2. War; 3. World War, 1939-1945; 4. Graphic novels
978-1-4042-0783-7, $29.25

Courtesy of Rosen Publishing

One of the most important naval battles in history, Midway marked a crucial turning point in the war in the Pacific. With a fleet that had dominated this theater since the attack on Pearl Harbor, the Japanese anticipated certain victory against the US forces, but the attack was not a surprise. The US Navy sank four irreplaceable aircraft carriers, and cleared the way for the island-hopping US counterattack. This book also includes eight pages of authoritative information, placing the battle in its historical context, describing the key players, and its build-up and aftermath.

Part of the Graphic Battles of World War II series. This book is also available in a paperback edition from Osprey Publishing, under the title The Empire Falls: Battle of Midway.

Pearl Harbor: A Day of Infamy. Illustrated by Jerrold Spahm. The Rosen Publishing Group 2007 48p. Illustration
Grades: 3 4 5 6 7 8 9 **741.5; 940.54**
1. Pearl Harbor (Oahu, Hawaii), Attack on, 1941; 2. War; 3. World War, 1939-1945; 4. Graphic novels
978-1-4042-0785-1, $29.25

On December 7, 1941, the Japanese Navy launched a surprise attack on American military bases in Pearl Harbor, Hawaii. Masterfully planned and executed, the attack devastated the US Pacific Fleet; in less than two hours, Japanese aircraft had sunk or damaged all eight US battleships anchored in the harbor and had destroyed 151 planes. Thrust into battle, the United States could have only one response: war. This book portrays the attack that drove the United States into World War II in full-color comic book narrative. Featuring the personal stories of front-line heroes like Ken Taylor, George Welch, and mess attendant Dorie Miller, it also provides background material - causes and consequences, key players, and a glossary of terms - as well as a list of additional resources.

Part of the Graphic Battles of World War II series. This book is also available in a paperback edition from Osprey Publishing, under the title Day of Infamy: Attack on Pearl Harbor.

Whitley, Jeremy
Princeless: Book One: Save Yourself. Jeremy Whitley; illustrated by M. Goodwin. Action Lab Entertainment 2012 116 p. Illustration
Grades: 4 5 6 7 8 **741.5; Fic**
1. Adventure graphic novels; 2. Princesses
1450798942; 9781450798945, $14.95

This graphic novel collects "the first storyline of the multiple Eisner Award-nominated and multiple Glyph Award-winning series" from Jeremy Whitley. It follows "the adventures of Princess Adrienne, a princess who's tired of

waiting to be rescued. Along with her guardian dragon, Sparky, they begin their own quest." (Publisher's note)
Volume 1 of an ongoing series

Wicks, Maris
★ **Human** Body Theater: a nonfiction revue. Maris Wicks. First Second 2015 240 p. Color; Illustration
Grades: 4 5 6 7 8 **612; 741.5**
1. Human anatomy — Juvenile literature
1626722773; 9781626722774, $19.99; 9781596439290

This book by Maris Wicks explores human anatomy on a performing stage. In it, "your master of ceremonies is going to lead you through a theatrical revue of each and every biological system of the human body! Starting out as a skeleton, the MC puts on a new layer of her costume (her body) with each 'act.'" (Publisher's note)

"Wicks' playful cartoon artwork in saturated colors makes the potentially daunting and embarrassing subject of anatomy approachable and fun, but never at the expense of accuracy or clarity. This informative, frank exploration of the body perfectly balances science and silliness." Booklist
Includes bibliographical references

Wight, Eric
★ **Frankie** Pickle and the closet of doom. Written and illustrated by Eric Wight. Simon & Schuster Books for Young Readers 2009 79p. Illustration
Grades: 2 3 4 5 **741.5; Fic**
1. Cleanliness — Fiction; 2. Family life; 3. Family life — Fiction; 4. Humorous graphic novels; 5. Imagination — Fiction; 6. Orderliness; 7. Graphic novels
978-1-4169-6484-1, $9.99; 1-4169-6484-3
LC 2008-30865

Fourth-grader Frankie Piccolini has a vivid imagination when it comes to cleaning his disastrously messy room, but eventually even he decides that it is just too dirty.

"Wight's hilarious twists of language are matched with a wicked sense of fun in the illustrations and frequent sequential-paneled episodes of pretend play." Kirkus
Other titles about Frankie Pickle are: Frankie Pickle and the Pine Run 3000 (2010); Frankie Pickle and the mathematical menace (2011); Frankie Pickle and the land of the lost recess (2012)

Williams, Aaron
PS 238, volume VI: senseless acts of tourism!. Do Gooder Press 2008 Un Illustration
Grades: 3 4 5 6 7 8 9 10 11 12 Adult **741.5; Fic**
1. Humorous graphic novels; 2. Superhero graphic novels; 3. Graphic novels
978-1-933288-49-9, $15.99

After the town had been pretty much leveled by invading aliens and repair work begins, Miss Kyle takes a vacation to Las Vegas. However, Zodon has convinced Poly and Julie that Miss Kyle is leaving for good, so they hitch a ride on the plane. They don't know that others are following and trying to kidnap Zodon. Meanwhile, Flea has hitched a ride on the bad guys' jet. Once they all get to Las Vegas, they end up helping the Masquerade Casino catch the person who has been cheating and winning too much in the casino. Meanwhile, back at PS 238, Tyler is stuck in a stasis pod because he was infected with an alien virus that could destroy the world; then Tom comes and takes Tyler, or at least a part of his soul, to make a crucial decision about whether humanity should continue to gain super powers. And then Cecil, who still sees aliens everywhere, goes with mysterious millionaire Kent Allard to scout out possible aliens. There's lots of superhero action going on, all of it at kid-friendly level.

PS 238: To the Cafeteria . . . For Justice!. Henchman Publishing/Dork Storm Press 2005 Un Illustration
Grades: 4 5 6 7 8 9 10 11 12 Adult   **741.5; Fic**
  1. Elementary schools; 2. Humorous graphic novels; 3. Superhero graphic novels; 4. Graphic novels
1-933288-13-2, $15.99
  PS 238 is the only public school for metahuman children, where the students learn how to use their powers, socialize with normal as well as super-powered classmates, and have fun adventures. In this second volume, the students learn about the importance of primary sources for history research (time traveling Tom brings a girl to the present to give them straight information about her father). Also, Tyler, son of two superheroes who hasn't yet come into his powers, spends some time training with the vigilante hero, Revenant. And in shop class, the students make some super accessories. The first volume is not available, but readers can pick up on things from this volume. This is a continuing series.

PS238 Vol. III: No Child Left Behind!. Dork Storm Press/Henchman Publishing 2006 Un Illustration
Grades: 5 6 7 8 9 10 11 12 Adult   **741.5; Fic**
  1. Adventure graphic novels; 2. Humorous graphic novels; 3. Superhero graphic novels; 4. Graphic novels
1-933288-24-8, $15.99
  In this third volume, readers meet Malphast, the child of divine and not-so-divine parents, who involves almost everyone in a cosmic game of four-square. Then Tom Davidson discovers an unusual castle floating outside of time and space. And Harold Nelson, after whom PS238's "Rainmaker Program" was named, has decided that a sizeable number of students need to be "rescued" from the school. Tyler works with the Revenant to save his friends from Nelson.

Williamson, Joshua
  Dear Dracula. Illustrated by Vicente "Vinny" Navarrette. Silverline Books/Image Comics 2008 Un Illustration
Grades: 1 2 3 4 5   **741.5; Fic**
  1. Dracula, Count (Fictional character); 2. Halloween; 3. Humorous graphic novels; 4. Graphic novels
978-1-58240-970-2, $7.99
  Sam loves scary movies, especially movies about vampires, with Dracula his favorite. He loves Dracula so much, he writes to him asking to become a real vampire on Halloween. The Count himself is so tickled to get mail, that he visits Sam on Halloween and he shares all the things that vampires do; nothing fazes Sam, until Dracula talks about drinking blood. Eeeewwww! Sam decides he doesn't need to become a vampire now, he has plenty of time yet, but he had fun with Dracula. Grandma, of course, thinks Sam just imagined everything. The book is sized like a picture book, but it uses simple panel designs to help young readers follow

along. This Dracula is not scary, and the book is a great read for Halloween.

Wilson, Britt
  Cat Dad, King of the Goblins. Britt Wilson. Koyama Press 2014 48 p. Color; Illustration
Grades: 2 3 4 5   **741.5**
  1. Cats — Juvenile fiction; 2. Fathers — Fiction; 3. Goblins — Juvenile fiction
1927668115; 9781927668115, $12
  "Miri and Luey have a dilemma. Their dad's been turned into a cat and their closet is a garden full of goblins. There is only one thing for them to do—grab their friend Phil the frog and dive headfirst into a wild, woolly, and wacky adventure." (Publisher's note)
  "It's a nonsensical story with an even more nonsensical conclusion, but it's best not to look for logic, since the off-the-wall fun and comical scenes capture kids' imaginative games perfectly." Booklist

Winick, Judd
  Hilo: the boy who crashed to Earth. By Judd Winick; with color by Guy Major. Random House Inc 2015 208 p. Color; Illustration (Hilo)
Grades: 2 3 4 5   **741.5**
  1. Amnesia — Fiction; 2. Extraterrestrial beings — Fiction; 3. Extraterrestrial beings — Juvenile fiction; 4. Friendship — Fiction; 5. Identity — Fiction; 6. Robots — Fiction; 7. Science fiction; 8. Graphic novels
0385386176; 9780385386173, $13.99; 9780385386180
                LC 2014030736
  "D.J. and his friend Gina are totally normal kids. But that was before a mysterious boy came crashing down from the sky! Hilo doesn't know where he came from, or what he's doing on Earth. . . . But what if Hilo wasn't the only thing to fall to our planet?" Can the trio unlock the secrets of his past? Can Hilo survive a day at school? And are D.J. and Gina ready to save the world? (Publisher's note)
  "Winick has concocted a universally appealing tale with bright, expressive illustrations that gently reminds readers that in this era of overscheduling and insistence on perfection, sometimes just being true to yourself is important enough." Kirkus
  Another title about Hilo is: Saving the whole wide world (2016)

Winter, Barbara
  Fight for Rights. Art by Dimitri Kostic. Harcourt Achieve/Steck-Vaughn 2006 48p. Illustration
Grades: 3 4 5 6 7 8   **741.5; Fic**
  1. Great Britain — History — 20th century; 2. Women — Suffrage; 3. Graphic novels
978-1-4190-3219-6, $8.99
  In Victorian England, a young girl named Mary is drawn into the fight for women's right to vote. She realizes that the struggle will be a long and difficult one. Could it also be dangerous? This historical graphic novel includes prose intervals that describe the women's suffrage movement and its actions, as well as the British government's actions

against the women activists. Many of the incidents described in the story really happened.

Part of the Timeline Graphic Novels series.

The **Golden** Scarab. Art by Jason Loo. Harcourt Achieve/Steck-Vaughn 2006 48p. Illustration

Grades: 3 4 5 6 7 8   **741.5; Fic**
1. Egypt — History; 2. Mystery graphic novels; 3. Graphic novels
978-1-4190-3196-0, $8.99

An Egyptian princess named Meri rescues a slave girl named Layla. When the pharaoh suddenly gets sick, Princess Meri and Layla play detective to find out what's making him ill. This historical fiction graphic novel is set during the reign of Akhenaten and Nefertiti; Meri is Meritaten, their eldest daughter. The book includes intervals of prose giving facts about Egypt, its people, and its customs.

Part of the Timeline Graphic Novels series.

Trapped in Gallipoli. Art by Scott Page. Harcourt Achieve/Steck-Vaughn 2006 48p. Illustration

Grades: 3 4 5 6 7 8   **741.5; Fic**
1. Adventure graphic novels; 2. World War, 1914-1918; 3. Graphic novels
978-1-4190-3211-0, $8.99

In the midst of the First World War, a young orphan named Duyal joins his uncle, Mustafa Kemal, commander of the Turkish forces, at Gallipoli. When the Allies attack, Duyal is captured by Australian soldiers and kept as a prisoner of war. Gallipoli was one of the bloody campaigns of the war; it ended with withdrawal by the Allied forces and huge losses on both sides. The book includes some of the battlefield violence. It also includes prose intervals that provide more information about the campaign and its legacy.

Part of the Timeline Graphic Novels series.

Witt, David

The **hero** twins: against the lords of death: a Mayan myth. Lerner Publishing Group/Graphic Universe 2008 48p. Illustration

Grades: 3 4 5 6 7 8 9   **398.2; 741.5**
1. Adventure graphic novels; 2. Mayas — Folklore; 3. Graphic novels
978-0-8225-7495-8, $26.60

LC 2007-25897

The Hero Twins, Hunahpu and Xbalanque, were blessed by the Mayan gods with special powers. However, their incredible skill at playing Pok-ta-Pok, the Mayan ball game, angers the Lords of Xibalba, rulers of the Land of the Dead. When the Lords challenge them to a Pok-ta-Pok game in Xibalba, the twins know they must use all of their powers and cunning to defeat the Lords' many challenges. Comics veteran Jolley consulted several translations of the Popol Vuh, artist Witt studied books on Mayan culture, architecture and art, and Mesoamerican folklore expert John Bierhorst reviewed the story to ensure accuracy and respect for Mayan culture.

Part of the Graphic Myths & Legends series

Wood, Don

Into the volcano: a graphic novel. Blue Sky Press 2008 174p. Illustration; Map

Grades: 2 3 4 5 6 7 8   **741.5; Fic**
1. Adventure graphic novels; 2. Brothers; 3. Graphic novels
978-0-439-72671-9, $18.99; 0-439-72671-9

LC 2007-51084

While their parents are away doing research, brothers Duffy and Sumo Pugg go with their cousin, Mister Come-and-Go, to Kokalaha Island, where they meet Aunt Lulu and become trapped in an erupting volcano.

"The visual format combined with nonstop action will keep reluctant readers and adventure fans turning pages to the very end." Voice Youth Advocates

Wooderson, Philip

Arf and the Three Dogs. Illustrated by Bridget MacKeith. Stone Arch Books 2006 72p. Illustration

Grades: 2 3 4 5 6 7   **741.5; Fic**
1. Humorous graphic novels; 2. Mystery graphic novels; 3. Graphic novels
978-1-59889-021-1, $21.26 lib. bdg.

When Arf is knocked down by three dogs held on a leash by the man known as Crazy Barney, he decides to get photos as proof of the wild behavior. Major Nimby blames the dog shelter, but Arf's sisters say the Major is playing tricks to close the shelter; will Arf's photos save the day? An easy text, simple panel layout, and fast-paced story make this suitable for beginning and struggling readers.

Guard Dog. Illustrated by David Burroughs ; cover illustrated by Nathan Lueth. Stone Arch Books 2007 80p. Illustration

Grades: 3 4 5 6 7 8 9   **741.5; Fic**
1. Mystery graphic novels; 2. Graphic novels
978-1-59889-829-3, $22.60

LC 2007-6244

Ryan would rather play his favorite video game, Guard Dog, than help his dad sell his artwork at the flea market. When the artwork is stolen, however, Ryan and his friend Steve take on the case. Soon, they're hot on the trail of the thieves, but are the clues leading them in the wrong direction" The two boys learn that a detective's work is no game. This graphic novel is written with an easy vocabulary and a simple panel layout for beginning, reluctant, and struggling readers.

Part of the Graphic Quest line.

Worley, Rob M.

Scratch 9, 1. Created and written by Rob M. Worley; illustrated by Jason T. Kruse. Ape Entertainment 2011 100p.

Grades: 3 4 5   **Fic**
1. Cats — Fiction; 2. Pets — Fiction
9781936340538

In this collection of comics, named one of the Best Comics for Kids 2010 by School Library Journal, "mad science gives an ordinary cat named Scratch the ability to summon any of his nine lives. He must use his powers to save his pet friends from the CRUEL corporation." (Publisher's note) The protagonist "can summon any of his previous or future lives and fight side-by-side with them, a handy skill when you were a saber-toothed tiger, a ninja, and a minor Egyptian deity in your previous lives!" (School Libr J)

Yamamoto, Lun Lun

Swans in space, volume 1. UDON Entertainment 2009 150p. Illustration

Grades: 2 3 4 5 6 7   741.5; Fic
    1. Humorous graphic novels; 2. Manga; 3. Science fiction graphic novels; 4. Graphic novels
    978-1-897376-93-5, $8.99

Sixth grader Corona is effectively her class's president, representing them on the Cosmos Institute student council. At home, she barely tolerates the obsessive fandom displayed by her father and younger brother for the television show, Space Patrol. Imagine her chagrin when she reaches out to an odd classmate, only to find herself recruited into ... the Space Patrol! It's a real organization that works to keep the Earth and other worlds safe, and show's episodes are edited versions of actual missions. Of course, Corona must keep her work in the Space Patrol a secret from anyone who isn't a member; and since she needs to study the old episodes to learn the history, this makes her father and brother think she has become one with them, while her classmates wonder what's wrong with her. Corona must also keep up with not only her school work, which is bad enough, because she's one of the top students, but as class president she has to take responsibility for all kinds of extra activities and work; all this makes her one tired girl. This manga for younger readers is published in full color.

Yanagawa, Sozo

Edu-manga: Helen Adams Keller. Artist, Rie Yagi. Digital Manga Publishing 2005 160p. Illustration

Grades: 3 4 5 6 7 8   92; 741.5
    1. Biographical graphic novels; 2. Keller, Helen; 3. Kodomo manga; 4. Manga; 5. Graphic novels
    1-56970-976-9, $9.95

This manga, originally written for Japanese schoolchildren, covers the life of Helen Keller and of her teacher, Anne Sullivan. It uses the Atom Boy series characters to introduce her story and to cover questions between chapters. The writer also worked with the Tokyo Helen Keller Association. Young readers can see the initial struggles between young "Teacher" Sullivan and the blind, deaf and uneducated little Helen, and how they worked together so Helen could learn to communicate, and learn to learn and get an education. As an adult, Helen traveled around the U.S. and to Europe and Japan, working to help the physically handicapped; her message was don't just pity the handicapped, but help them help themselves. The book includes a timeline of her life and short biographies of some of the important people in her life.

Yang, Gene Luen

Secret coders. Gene Yuen Lang & Mike Holmes. First Second 2015 96 p. Color; Illustration

Grades: 4 5 6 7   741.5
    1. Computer programming; 2. School stories
    9781626722767, $17.99; 9781626720756; 1626722765

In this graphic novel, by Gene Yuen Lang and Mike Holmes, "Hopper, an enthusiastic 12-year-old girl . . ., has just started school at the creepy Stately Academy. After getting in a fight . . . with Eni . . ., Hopper and Eni become friends while unraveling the secrets of the school. Robotic birds, family troubles, and sinister, child-hating school administrators lead to a story both emotionally rich and rife with learning opportunities." (School Library Journal)

Yeh, Phil

Dinosaurs Across America. NBM 2007 32p. Illustration

Grades: 2 3 4 5 6   973; 741.5
    1. United States — Geography; 2. Graphic novels
    978-1-56163-509-2, $12.95

Originally done as a comic book and sold by Cartoonists Across America, a literacy group working for decades to promote the use of comic books to teach literacy to children, this is now a graphic novel. Featuring Yeh's dinosaurs and Patrick Rabbit, the book devotes a half-page to each state in the U.S., packing in basic facts and a simple map along with fun little tidbits (for example, the largest privately owned cattle ranch in the U.S. happens to be in Hawaii, on the island of Hawaii).

YKids

Curie. Youngjin Singapore 2007 148p. Illustration

Grades: 3 4 5 6 7 8 9   92; 741.5
    1. Biographical graphic novels; 2. Curie, Marie, 1867-1934; 3. Graphic novels
    978-981-05-4946-6, $14.95

Throughout her career, Marie Curie, the renowned scientist and first woman to win the Nobel Prize, had to overcome the objections of her peers and the many obstacles facing an early female scientist. This is the story of her work in discovering radium and explaining the mysteries, benefits, and dangers of radioactivity that would ultimately lead to her own death. It also recounts the enormous time and resources she devoted to the cause of peace, having witnessed herself the horrors of war. In the fictional framing story, a boy and a robot from the future seek out Marie Curie to take one particular value from her life to help them in their time; they seek her burning passion for her work.

Part of the Great Figures in History series.

Einstein. Youngjin Singapore 2007 146p. Illustration

Grades: 3 4 5 6 7 8 9   92; 741.5
    1. Biographical graphic novels; 2. Einstein, Albert, 1879-1955; 3. Graphic novels
    978-981-05-4944-2, $14.95

A genius of enormous accomplishment, Albert Einstein overcame numerous hardships-separation from his family, religious discrimination, and the political turmoil of his day-to become one of the greatest minds of the 20th century. As a young boy, Einstein's unending curiosity and constant questioning earned him the reputation of being unfocused and inattentive. This book uses a framing story of a young boy and a robot from the future going back in time to examine the lives of great people and find the one value that will help their situation; from Einstein, they take his insatiable curiosity.

Part of the Great Figures in History series.

Gandhi. Youngjin Singapore 2007 148p. Illustration

Grades: 3 4 5 6 7 8 9   92; 741.5
    1. Biographical graphic novels; 2. Gandhi, Mahatma, 1869-1948; 3. Graphic novels
    978-981-05-4945-9, $14.95

A champion of the poor and lower classes, Mahatma Gandhi helped transform India into the democracy it is today. Young readers of this manga-style biography will learn about the key historical events during this time and how the peaceful efforts of one humble man affected enormous change. This book presents a time line of Gandhi's life-from his roots in a middle-class family in India, to his law-school education in England, his experiences with discrimination, and his key role as a leader in the Indian independence movement. Each volume in the Great Figures in History series focuses on a key value personified by the biographical subject; in Gandhi's case, it's courage.
Part of the Great Figures in History series.

Little Women: Manga Literary Classics. Youngjin Singapore 2007 145p. Illustration
Grades: 3 4 5 6 7   **741.5; Fic**
1. Alcott, Louisa May, 1832-1888 — Adaptations; 2. Graphic novels
978-981-05-4943-5, $14.95
The story of the March girls-beautiful Meg, tomboy Jo, kind and gentle Beth, and spunky Amy-is retold manga-style and in full color. With their country embroiled in war and their father far from home, the four sisters find themselves thrust into new and trying situations, and with little money and a hard winter ahead, they must learn to adapt. In the year that follows, the girls learn about compassion, sacrifice, love, and more about themselves and each other than they ever imagined.

Treasure Island: Manga Literary Classics. Youngjin Singapore 2007 148p. Illustration
Grades: 3 4 5 6 7   **741.5; Fic**
1. Stevenson, Robert Louis, 1850-1894 — Adaptations; 2. Graphic novels
978-981-05-4942-8, $14.95
Young cabin boy Jim Hawkins throws in his lot with pirates Black Dog, Blind Pew, and the unforgettable Long John Silver in this manga-style retelling of Robert Louis Stevenson's classic adventure story. Jim, overly romantic about life on the high seas, is unprepared for the frightening events ahead, including mutiny and an armed battle that poses a grim dilemma: should his loyalty lie with Captain Smollett or Long John Silver?

Yomtov, Nel
Theseus and the Minotaur. Retold by Nel Yomtov ; illustrated by Tod Smith. Stone Arch Books 2009 72p.
Grades: 4 5 6 7 8 9   **292; 741.5**
1. Greek mythology; 2. Graphic novels
978-1-4342-1171-2, $23.93
                                               LC 2008-32066
King Aegeus of Athens wants a son and ends up with Medea the sorceress; however, he had spent the night with Aethra of Troezen, and she bears a son she names Theseus. He grows up strong, and when he defeats a huge bully, Aethra tells him about his father and sends him to Athens. Along the way, Theseus defeats several evil men, and arrives in Athens. He's just in time to become part of the group of young people sent as sacrifices to appease Minos, King of Crete, who bears a grudge against Aegeus. Minos has a monstrous son, the half-bull half-human Minotaur, and the Athenian youths become the Minotaur's food. Theseus

decides to fight the creature and gets help from Ariadne. The book includes information about the Oracle at Delphi, discussion questions, and a glossary.

Yoon, Paul
Everyday Science Vol. 2: At the Amusement Park. Art by Laurence Na. Youngjin Singapore 2005 180p. Illustration
Grades: 3 4 5 6 7 8   **500; 741.5**
1. Science; 2. Graphic novels
981-05-2243-6, $12.95
In this volume, every kid is talking about a science tournament in Dreamland, the biggest amusement park in town. Four friends, Daniel, Lucy, Christine, and Sam, hope to win first prize. They soon discover that the tournament questions are linked to the park's roller coasters. Young readers can learn along with Daniel, Lucy, Christine, and Sam as they investigate Newton's Laws of Motion, acceleration, action and reaction, zero gravity, and much more. Colorful illustrations, simple text, and a storyline help to make science understandable.

Yoshizumi, Wataru
Ultra Maniac Vol. 1. Viz Media/Shojo Beat 2005 184p. Illustration
Grades: 5 6 7 8 9 10   **741.5; Fic**
1. Humorous graphic novels; 2. Romance graphic novels; 3. Shojo manga; 4. Graphic novels
1-59116-917-8, $8.99
Shy Ayu Tateishi has just made a new friend at school. But this new friend, much to her surprise, is no ordinary classmate. Nina Sakura may look like a normal middle school girl, but she's got a big secret. She's a witch. Or, rather, she's studying to be a witch. And, apparently, she's not doing her homework. Her spells are devastating in their ineffectiveness and often result in the most embarrassing situations for poor Ayu. But things wouldn't be so bad if Nina's sorcery didn't make Ayu look silly in front of the one boy she secretly adores. All she wants is a simple love potion. What she gets, however, is a new best friend who almost flunked out of witch school. This is a five-volume manga series.

Zidrou
Ducoboo: in the corner!. Godi + Zidrou ; colour work, Véronique Grobert. Cinebook 2008 48p. Illustration
Grades: 3 4 5 6 7 8   **741.5; Fic**
1. Humorous graphic novels; 2. School stories; 3. Graphic novels
978-1-905460-26-7, $9.99
Ducoboo doesn't do well in school; he hardly ever gets the right answers, and he spends a lot of time in the corner with Skelly, the classroom skeleton. Desk mate Leonie, naturally, gets very high grades and Ducoboo keeps trying out new plans to copy her work. Mr. Latouche, the teacher, has to deal with a student who seems absolutely incapable of learning. This book is translated from the French, who seem to have very similar classroom situations as those here in the U.S.
Part of the Ducoboo series, originally published in France as L'eleve Ducobu Au coin!

Zirkel, Scott

A **bit** haywire. Created & illustrated by Courtney Huddleston ; written by Scott Zirkel ; inked by Jeff Dabu and Courtney Huddleston ; colored by Mike Garcia ; lettered by Greg Gatlin. Viper 2006

Grades: 5 6 7 8 9   **741.5; Fic**

1. Humorous graphic novels; 2. Superhero graphic novels; 3. Graphic novels

978-0-9777-8835-4; 0-9777883-5-0, $11.95

Owen Brice wants more than anything to be a superhero; he lives in a city protected by the Noble Seven, a superhero team led by Captain Melee and Lady Barrage. On one memorable day, Owen discovers he does have powers, but they're . . . a bit haywire. He can run super fast—but only as long as he can hold his breath. He can fly—as long as he keps his eyes closed. He teleports when camera flashes go off (the first time, he accidentally teleports his clothes off); he burns when he sneezes; he can shoot lase beams from hiseyes when he's cold. Then he discovers his parents are Captain Melee and Lady Barrage. How does one train to be a superhero when all his powers are so weird? Owen decides to give it a try.

Middle School: 6-8

Abadzis, Nick

★ **Laika**. First Second Books 2007 205p. Illustration

Grades: 5 6 7 8 9 10 11 12 Adult **741.5; Fic**

1. Soviet Union — History — 1953-1991; 2. Space flight; 3. Graphic novels

1-59643-101-6; 978-1-59643-101-0

LC 2006-51907

Laika was the abandoned puppy destined to become Earth's first space traveler. This is her journey. Along with Laika, there is Korolev, once a political prisoner and now a driven engineer at the top of the Soviet space program, and Yelena, the lab technician responsible for Laika's health and life. The book depicts the dedication and struggles of the scientists and technicians who worked in the Soviet space program, based on research Abadzis did before writing this book. The book includes a bibliography of books and websites.

"Abadzis's tear-inducing and solidly researched graphic novel treatment of Laika's surpassingly tragic story is a standout." Publ Wkly

Abirached, Zeina

A **game** for swallows: to die, to leave, to return. Written by Zeina Abirached; art by Zeina Abirached; translation by Edward Gauvin. Graphic Universe 2012 188 p.

Grades: 7 8 9 10 11 12 **741.5**

1. Abirached, Zeina, 1981-; 2. Beirut (Lebanon); 3. Family; 4. Lebanon — History — Civil War, 1975-1990

0761385681; 9780761385684, $29.27

LC 2011038914

Mildred L. Batchelder Honor Book (2013)

This graphic novel looks at "the civil war in Lebanon in the 1980s, as seen through the eyes of a child" separated from her parents. "Young Zeina [Abirached] and her brother have been sequestered within the small foyer in their apartment," which "becomes a place for neighbors in the building to congregate and seek asylum. Though war is raging and death always seems to loom near with shells falling and snipers possibly crouching behind every wall, Zeina and her neighbors try to live the best they can." (Kirkus Reviews)

Translation of Le jeu des hirondelles.

I remember Beirut. Zeina Abirached. Graphic Universe 2014 96 p. Illustration; Map

Grades: 8 9 10 11 12 Adult **92; 741.5**

1. Abirached, Zeina, 1981-; 2. Beirut (Lebanon) — Biography — Juvenile literature; 3. Children and war; 4. Lebanon — History — 20th century — Juvenile literature

1467738220; 9781467738224, $29.27

LC 2013047112

In this graphic memoir, Zeina Abirached "reveals numerous details from her childhood in Beirut during the war from 1975 to 1990 war. 'I remember' is a recurring phrase and provides a personal frame of reference for the effect of war on kids. Some are simple childhood memories. . . . Inclusion of . . . maps and diagrams orient the reader and provide additional perspective." (Kirkus Reviews)

"The blocky, naive-style pictures quietly evoke wartime fears in ways the words simply cannot—bullet holes in the sides of cars, rubble in the streets, her father's eyebrows indicating increasing sadness at the heartbreaking state of a formerly vital market." Booklist

Abnett, Dan

Gamble for Victory: Battle of Gettysburg. Osprey Publishing 2007 48p. Illustration

Grades: 3 4 5 6 7 8 9 **741.5; 973.7**

1. Gettysburg (Pa), Battle of, 1863; 2. United States — History — 1861-1865, Civil War; 3. War; 4. Graphic novels

978-1-84603-051-2, $9.95

In July 1863, after having observed a forward column of Union General George G. Meade's cavalry, General Robert E. Lee sent his 75,000 men of the Army of Northern Virginia to meet the 97,000 strong Union Army of the Potomac. Of more than 2,000 land engagements of the American Civil War, Gettysburg ranks as one of the most horrific and devastating battles; more men actually fought and died on this battlefield than in any other encounter on North American soil and the battle itself marked the beginning of the end for the Confederacy. This full-color comic book includes further reading, essential information on the background, aftermath and key players of the conflict.

Part of Osprey's Graphic History series. This book is also available in a library binding edition from the Rosen Publishing Group under the title The Battle of Gettysburg: Spilled Blood on Sacred Ground.

The **Monitor** Versus the Merrimac: Ironclads at War. Rosen Publishing Group 2007 48p. Illustration

Grades: 3 4 5 6 7 8

741.5; 973.7

1. Hampton Roads (Va), Battle of, 1862; 2. Merrimack (Frigate); 3. Monitor (Ironclad); 4. United States — History — 1861-1865, Civil War; 5. Virginia (Ironclad); 6. Graphic novels

978-1-4042-0778-3, $29.25;

978-1-84603-053-6 (pa)

Courtesy of Rosen Publishing

LC 2006014843

In this historic clash in March 1862, the Union Monitor, called by many a "cheese box on a raft," exchanged cannon shot after cannon shot with the Confederate Merrimac, comically referred to as a "floating barn roof." Although an indecisive victory for either side, the spectacular event, witnessed by hundreds of people on nearby boats and shorelines, forever changed the way naval warfare was to be fought. The book also includes information on the building of the ironclads, a map showing the routes of the battle, and a list of books for further reading.

Part of the Graphic Battles of the Civil War series; the paperback edition is published by Osprey.

Wallace & Gromit: Plots in Space. Titan Books 2007 Un Illustration

Grades: 2 3 4 5 6 7 8   **741.5; Fic**
1. Humorous graphic novels; 2. Science fiction graphic novels; 3. Wallace & Gromit (Fictional characters); 4. Graphic novels
978-1-84576-362-6, $12.95

Inventor Wallace and his dog Gromit are the animated stars of a series of popular cartoons in England, and one feature film that was also a hit in the U.S. In this original story, the two travel to the orbital R.A.D.I.S.H. (Research Allotment Deployed on International Space Hub), where Wallace wants to test his new invention and eat the giant vegetables being grown in zero gravity. However, they encounter trouble when BOB the intelligent computer seems to go haywire.

Adamson, Heather

Charles Darwin and the Theory of Evolution. Capstone Press 2007 32p. Illustration

Grades: 3 4 5 6 7 8 9   **576.8; 741.5; 92**
1. Darwin, Charles, 1809-1882; 2. Evolution; 3. Naturalists; 4. Graphic novels
978-1-4296-0145-0, $25.26

LC 2007005659

This book uses the graphic novel format to tell the story of how Charles Darwin developed his controversial theory of evolution based on the research he conducted during his voyage on the HMS Beagle. The book includes additional facts and a list books for further reading.

Part of the Graphic Library Invention and Discovery series.

Adamson, Thomas K.

Lessons in Science Safety with Max Axiom, Super Scientist. Capstone/Graphic Library 2006 32p. Illustration

Grades: 5 6 7 8 9   **508.2; 741.5**
1. Science — Experiments; 2. Graphic novels
978-0-7368-6834-1, $18.95

Using the graphic novel format and the engaging fictional scientist character Max Axiom, a tall, muscular African American, this volume shows students conducting science experiments and demonstrates how and why to wear safety goggles, call for help when accidents occur, and safety procedures for dealing with unknown substances. This is part of the Graphic Science series.

"This will be a good choice for science classes during the opening weeks of the school year." (Booklist)

The Adventures of the Fly Volume 1

Archie Comics 2004 96p. Illustration

Grades: 3 4 5 6 7 8 9 10 11 12 Adult   **741.5; Fic**
1. Adventure graphic novels; 2. Superhero graphic novels
1-879794-18-7, $12.95

This book highlights one of the pioneering super-hero titles of the Silver Age: The Fly. Tommy Troy is a young boy whose world is turned upside down when he meets an emissary of the Fly World and is given a special ring that magically transforms him into the superhuman Fly. Considered an early prototype of Spider-Man, the Fly's earliest adventures were charted by some of the most legendary creative talent in comics: Jack Kirby, Joe Simon, Jack Davis, and Al Williamson. All of these artists and more are featured in this special edition that collects titanic tales from 1959 and 1960.

Aguirre-Sacasa, Roberto

The **Sensational** Spider-Man: Feral. Artist, Angel Medina, Clayton Crain. Marvel Entertainment 2007 Un Illustration

Grades: 7 8 9 10 11 12 Adult   **741.5; Fic**
1. Spider-Man (Fictional character); 2. Superhero graphic novels; 3. Graphic novels
978-0-7851-2126-8, $19.99

Strange changes are coming over Spidey's animalistic foes - including Dr. Curt Connors, John Jameson and Felicia Hardy - awakening the beast that dwells within them all. Spidey's beaten the Lizard, Man-Wolf and the Black Cat before, but they've never been more vicious than they are now.

Akamatsu, Ken

Mao-Chan vol. 1. Del Rey Manga 2008 394p. Illustration

Grades: 8 9 10 11 12   **741.5; Fic**
1. Humorous graphic novels; 2. Manga; 3. Graphic novels
978-0-345-50181-3, $14.95

When incredibly cute aliens invade Japan and steal its signature landmarks, Japan unleashes the Grade School Defense Corps, made up of second-grade students, such as Mao, Misora, and Sylvie. As their grandfathers, who command Ground, Air, and Marine Defense respectively, plot to make their own granddaughters the big heroes, the girls prefer to work together to defeat the aliens. Readers must love incredible cuteness along with some fan service featuring the older teenage girls. There is very little in this volume other than the mild fan service to indicate reasons for an older teen rating the publisher rates it for ages 16 and up.

Akimoto, Nami

Ultra Cute Volume 1. Tokyopop 2006 192p. Illustration

Grades: 7 8 9 10 11 12   **741.5; Fic**
1. Humorous graphic novels; 2. Romance graphic novels; 3. Shojo manga; 4. Graphic novels
1-59532-956-0, $9.99

For all 15 years of their lives, Ami and Noa have competed against each other for love with the same results: both fall for the same guy, inevitably scaring him away and leaving them boyfriend-less. But the vicious cycle is broken when the girls go to a party and each fall for two different guys! With potential love on the horizon, the sky couldn't be bluer...until Ami discovers that these two dudes are actually duds with ulterior motives. Determined to get revenge on these players, Ami vows to make her guy fall for her while she tries to protect an unsuspecting Noa.

Akino, Matsuri

Kamen Tantei Vol. 1. Tokyopop 2006 196p. Illustration

Grades: 8 9 10 11 12   **741.5; Fic**
1. Humorous graphic novels; 2. Mystery graphic novels;
3. Supernatural graphic novels; 4. Graphic novels
1-59816-499-6, $9.99

A pair of young aspiring mystery writers, Masato and Hakura, tries to crack the most bizarre, baffling, and hilarious cases around them. But when clues lead to a dead end, fortunately for this duo, the Masked Detective always seems to show up in the nick of time to help. There is some violence, mostly in the murder scenes.

Alexovich, Aaron
Kimmie66. Written & illustrated by Aaron Alexovich; lettering by Jared K. Fletcher. DC Comics/Minx 2007 176p. Illustration
Grades: 7 8 9 10 11 12 Adult   **741.5; Fic**
1. Science fiction graphic novels; 2. Graphic novels
978-1-4012-0373-3, $9.99

In the 23rd century, people spend lots of time in online VR lairs. Telly Kade is a fairly typical teen of her time, and she tends to hang out in an online vampire lair. Right now, however, she is a little creeped out, because she has received a suicide note from her best friend, Kimmie66. And now other people seem to see Kimmie66 all over the 'net, and Telly wants to know what is really going on.

A Minx graphic novel

Alice, A. (Alex)
Siegfried 1; 1. Written and illustrated by Alex Alice. Archaia Entertainment, LLC 2012 144 p.
Grades: 6 7 8 9 10 11 12   **741.5**
1. Dragons; 2. Gods and goddesses; 3. Orphans
193639345X; 9781936393459, $24.95

This graphic novel by Alex Alice presents "a three-part story inspired by [Richard] Wagner's classic opera 'The Ring of the Nibelung!' Siegfried, born of the love between a mortal man and a Valkyrie, is a young orphan being raised by Mime, one of the last of the dwarf-goblin Nibelungs. Siegfried yearns to discover who his real parents were . . ., not knowing that Odin, father of the Norse gods, has a destiny planned for him: to fight the dragon Fafnir, guardian of the Rheingold!" (Publisher's note)

All Star Comics Archives Volume 11
DC Comics 2005 273p. Illustration
Grades: 7 8 9 10 11 12 Adult   **741.5; Fic**
1. Flash (Fictional character); 2. Green Lantern (Fictional character); 3. Justice Society of America (Fictional characters); 4. Superhero graphic novels; 5. Wonder Woman (Fictional character)
1-4012-0403-1, $49.95

The adventures of the world's first super-team continue in this extra-sized final volume of the series. In Volume 11, collecting All Star Comics #50-57, the JSA face the Diamond Men, Mr. Alpha, and more. The Justice Society of America included the Golden Age Flash, Green Lantern, Dr. Mid-Nite, Hawkman, Wonder Woman, Black Canary, and Atom.

Allan, Von
Li'l kids: road to God knows . . . adventures!. Von Allan Studio 2008 86p. Illustration
Grades: 7 8 9 10 11 12 Adult   **741.5; Fic**
1. Friendship; 2. Mother-daughter relationship; 3. Graphic novels
978-0-9781237-1-0, $13.95

In three interlocked short stories, readers meet Marie, a lonely eight-year-old girl, as she meets neighbor girl Kelly. Marie has been sent outside with a little ball, told by her mother to play. Kelly has to return three late videotapes to the rental store; they're all cutesy-kiddie movies she refuses to watch, after all she is eight years old. Then Marie falls asleep at the kitchen table while drawing her own superhero comic strip and dreams that her character is real. In the last story, readers meet Betty, Marie's mother. Something about her is definitely wrong, but Marie is just confused by her mother's wonky sense of time. Allan includes concept art and the outline and completed script for each story, providing readers with a look at how he puts a comic together. While Marie and Kelly are eight years old, younger readers might not see the subtle hints at trouble that Marie will face in her teen years.

Stargazer, volume one. Von Allan Studio 2010 115p. Illustration
Grades: 4 5 6 7 8 9
741.5; Fic
1. Adventure graphic novels; 2. Friendship; 3. Science fiction graphic novels; 4. Graphic novels
978-0-9781237-2-7, $14.95

Courtesy of Von Allan Studio

Marni's grandmother has just died, and she left a strange device that the two of them played with whenever Marni had visited. No one knows how Marni's grandmother got it, and it has never done anything. Her best friends, Elora and Sophie, come over for a last backyard campout before the weather turns cold, and when they each put a hand on the device, an extremely bright light nearly blinds them. After things seem to go back to normal, the girls go outside to find Marni's house gone, the device vanished, and none of the stars look familiar. In the morning, they pack up the little food they had brought for their campout, Elora's telescope, and Sophie's pennywhistle, and hike towards a tower Elora had spotted. They know they're in a totally strange place when they come upon a statue of nonhuman, alien creatures. As they continue, they come upon a strange house, where they find food, and then a mute, boy-sized robot. Even though the three friends bicker with each other, they work together to find a way home. Allan includes extensive notes on his writing process, and an excerpt from his script. The cover art shows one interesting looking character who doesn't appear in this volume. While their age isn't specified, the girls look to be tweens, with the slightly awkward, coltish bodies and movements of pre-adolescents. The strongest language used is one instance of the word "damn."

Volume 1 of 2

Allen, Brooke A.

★ A **home** for Mr. Easter. NBM Publishing, Inc. 2010 197p. Illustration

Grades: 8 9 10 11 12 Adult   **741.5; Fic**

1. Humorous graphic novels; 2. Rabbits; 3. Graphic novels

978-1-56163-580-1, $13.99; 1-56163-580-4

High school student Tesana is large, not too bright, strong, and has always gotten into trouble. A lonely misfit, she tries to fit in better by joining a pep rally planning committee. Once she finds the white rabbits that will be used in the pep rally, she discovers one that is very different it lays colorful eggs that grant wishes. Tesana believes this is the real Easter Bunny, and she calls him Mr. Easter—and he talks to her. When the football team tries to take Mr. Easter away, Tesana takes them all down and then runs away. Soon they're pursued by cops, an unscrupulous and greedy pet shop owner, laboratory scientists, animal rights protesters, television news crews, a magician/con man, and her mom. Allen was a student at the Savannah School of Art and Design when she wrote this book.

"This is for mature readers who understand the humor, and would be a welcome addition for your multicultural section—female, robust, ethnic." Libr Media Connect

A Home for Mr. Easter © *Brooke A. Allen*

Allison, John

Bad Machinery 4: The Case of the Lonely One. By John Allison. Oni Press 2015 136 p. Color; Illustration

Grades: 7 8 9 10 11 12 Adult   **741.5**

1. Mystery fiction; 2. School stories

1620102129; 9781620102121, $19.99

LC 2012953355

In this book, by John Allison, "a new school year brings a new classmate to Griswald's Grammar School! But he's a bit strange, and he really, really likes onions. When the whole school suddenly becomes best friends with him, Shauna seems to be the only one left out. It's up to her to peel back the mystery, one onion layer at a time." (Publishers note)

Bad machinery; 1: the case of the team spirit. John Allison; [edited by] James Lucas Jones. Oni Press 2013 112 p. Color; Illustration

Grades: 7 8 9 10 11 12 Adult   **741.5**

1. Mystery graphic novels; 2. School stories

1620100843; 9781620100844, $19.99

LC 2012953355

This graphic novel, the first in John Allison's Bad Machinery series, is "set in a grammar school in a British working-class community" and follows "three earnest boys vying against three sharp-tongued girls to solve mysteries. The framing story concerns a Russian owner of a U.K. foot-ball (soccer) team trying to bully an elderly homeowner to sell her house." (Publishers Weekly)

Bad Machinery; 2: The Case of the Good Boy. By John Allison; edited by James Lucas Jones and Jill Beaton. Oni Press 2014 136 p. Color; Illustration (Bad Machinery)

Grades: 7 8 9 10 11 12 Adult   **741.5**

1. Detectives — Fiction; 2. Dogs — Fiction; 3. England — Fiction; 4. Mystery fiction

1620101149; 9781620101148, $19.99

In this book, by John Allison, "everyone's favorite pre-teen British detectives are back for another case! With toddlers disappearing and rumors of a large, beast-like creature roaming the woods, Tackleford is in serious danger. And then there's Mildred's new dog Archibald . . . if you can even call it a dog. . . . Everything comes to a head once the boys get a picture of the beast and Archibald goes missing. Is there a connection?" (Publisher's note)

"The story veers between realism and fantasy, with just a touch of absurdism to keep things fun. . . . The bright, colorful art and snarky dialogue are icing on a delightful cake." Booklist

Bad Machinery; 3: The Case of the Simple Soul. By John Allison. Oni Press 2014 136 p. Color illustration; Color; Map

Grades: 7 8 9 10 11 12 Adult   **741.5**

1. Monsters; 2. Mystery graphic novels; 3. School stories

1620101939; 9781620101933, $19.99

In this graphic novel, by John Allison, "the Tackleford gang is back with a new case that demands solving! When Tackleford's derelict barns begin going up in flames, Linton and Sonny are on the case with a moderately mysterious new friend. Paths cross, however, when Lottie and Mildred meet a terrifying yet misunderstood creature living beneath a bridge!" (Publisher's note)

"[W]hat stands out in this work is the authentic dialogue, characters' constant questioning, and the protagonists' experiences as 'new' teenagers. Allison addresses how they are coping with physical and emotional changes, balancing friendships, and romantic relationships in a humorous way." SLJ

Originally published online as a webcomic

Amano, Kat

The **Wonderful** Wizard of Oz. Image Comics 2006 101p. Illustration

Grades: 3 4 5 6 7 8 9   **741.5; Fic**

1. Adventure graphic novels; 2. Baum, L Frank — Adaptations; 3. Fantasy graphic novels; 4. Graphic novels

978-1-58240-715-9, $9.99

Baum's classic story gets a European treatment in this colorful adaptation of Dorothy's adventures in the land of Oz.

Originally published as Le Magicien D'Oz Volumes 1-3 by Guy Delcourt Productions, France.

Amano, Kozue
　　Aria, vol. 3. Tokyopop 2008 Un Illustration
Grades: 8 9 10 11 12　　　　　　　　　**741.5; Fic**
　　1. Manga; 2. Science fiction; 3. Shojo manga; 4. Graphic
novels
978-1-4278-0512-6, $9.99
　　With the coming of Spring, Akari has now been on
Neo-Venezia for one year (two Earth years). She meets a
new trainee undine named Alice, who's only fourteen years
old but has natural talent as a gondolier. Akari and Alicia go
on a hunt for Spring and find a marvelous cherry tree near an
abandoned railway track. Then Akari, Akai, and Alice go on
a treasure hunt when Akari finds a small chest in the old
gondola she has borrowed. When Akai runs away from
Himeya, Akari finally learns who Akai really is, besides
being a single undine (a journeyman). And, on the Festa del
Bocolo, Akatsuki wants Akari's help in rounding up as many
red roses as he can to give to Alicia. While Tokyopop has
rated this series for older teens, there hasn't been any content
in the first three volumes to prevent younger teens from
reading these books.
　　Aria, vol.4. Tokyopop 2008 182p.
Grades: 8 9 10 11 12　　　　　　　　　**741.5; Fic**
　　1. Manga; 2. Science fiction graphic novels; 3. Shojo
manga; 4. Graphic novels
978-1-4278-0513-3, $9.99
　　It's now summer on Neo Venezia (formerly known as
Mars), and journeyman undine (gondolier) Akari and her
friends receive invitations to a place called the Neverlands.
It turns out to be a secluded beach, and Akari swims in the
ocean for the first time in her life. She also helps a sylph an
airbike-riding deliveryman make his deliveries when he
crashes and loses his map. When Akari tries to find a street
fair where she can buy a wind chime, she gets lost and
follows President Aria (a Neo Venezian cat) to a special bar
that caters only to cats. Akari, Alice, and Aika meet the
legendary major fairy who founded Aria Company, a lady
they call Grandma; they want to learn how to become the
best undines, while she tries to help them enjoy life.
Tokyopop keeps rating this series for older teens, citing fan
service, nonsexual nudity, and alcohol use, but in four
volumes there has been very little of any of these elements in
the stories.
　　Aria, volume 1. Tokyopop 2008 Un Illustration
Grades: 8 9 10 11 12　　　　　　　　　**741.5**
　　1. Manga; 2. Science fiction graphic novels; 3. Shojo
manga; 4. Graphic novels
978-1-4278-0510-2, $9.99
　　Aria is the sequel series to Aqua, a two-volume manga.
Mars had been terraformed and is now almost completely
covered in water. Various islands have become extensions of
different nations on Manhome, and young Akari Mizunashi
lives and works in Neo-Venezia, an exact replica of old
Venice. The gondoliers of Neo-Venezia are called undines,
and Akari is a journeyman undine who loves her work. She
helps an elderly tourist find his daughter, teaches her friend
from the floating cities which maintain the climate about
Venetian history, visits an island where the Japanese have
settled and encounters a fox god, and participates in a
gondola race. The publisher rates this series for older teens,
but there's no content in this first volume to keep it from
younger teens.

Amano, Shiro
　　Kingdom Hearts II Vol. 1. Tokyopop 2007 204p.
Illustration
Grades: 4 5 6 7 8 9 10 11 12　　　　　　**741.5; Fic**
　　1. Fantasy graphic novels; 2. Manga; 3. Shonen manga; 4.
Graphic novels
978-1-4278-0058-9, $9.99
　　In the quiet little hamlet of Twilight Town, there lives a
boy named Roxas. He and his friends Hayner, Pence and
Olette are trying to enjoy their final days of summer
vacation, when strange things begin to happen. First the
group is falsely accused of stealing photos from all over
town. Then they are attacked by bizarre, white creatures. But
the oddest occurrences are the recurring dreams Roxas has
of a boy named Sora, and the presence of a girl named
Namine, who has a mysterious secret to share with Roxas.
What began in Kingdom Hearts and Kingdom Hearts: Chain
of Memories continues in Kingdom Hearts II.

　　Kingdom Hearts, Chain of Memories, Vol. 1. Tokyopop
2006 198p. Illustration
Grades: 4 5 6 7 8 9　　　　　　　　　　**741.5; Fic**
　　1. Adventure graphic novels; 2. Fantasy graphic novels; 3.
Graphic novels
1-59816-637-9, $9.99
　　The door to Kingdom Hearts was sealed, dealing a blow
to the Heartless and restoring the worlds to normal, but Riku
and King Mickey were tapped inside. Now Sora, Donald,
and Goofy's search for their friends leads them to the
mysterious Castle Oblivion, where a hooded figure tells
them, "Ahead lies something you need, but to claim it, you
must lose something dear." What could be more dear than
one's own memories? This is the first of two volumes, and is
published in the original Japanese right-to-left page order.

　　Kingdom Hearts, Vol. 1. Tokyopop 2005 136p.
Illustration
Grades: 4 5 6 7 8 9　　　　　　　　　　**741.5; Fic**
　　1. Adventure graphic novels; 2. Fantasy graphic novels; 3.
Manga; 4. Graphic novels
1-59816-217-9, $5.99
　　When a strange storm hits his island home, 14-year-old
Sora is separated from his friends and swept into a
mysterious new land. There he meets Court Wizard Donald
and Captain Goofy, who are on a mission to find their king,
Mickey, and return him to his throne at Disney Castle. When
the three learn of the Heartless, ominous creatures who feed
off the darkness in the hearts of others, they join forces to
recover Sora's friends, return the king to his rightful position
and save the universe from the Heartless. This story is based
on the popular video game and is a four volume manga
series.

The Amazing Adventures of the Escapist Vol. 3
　　Dark Horse Comics 2006 168p. Illustration
Grades: 8 9 10 11 12 Adult　　　　　　**741.5; Fic**
　　1. Adventure graphic novels; 2. Superhero graphic novels;
3. Graphic novels
978-1-59307-492-0, $14.95
　　This volume of The Escapist features the late Will
Eisner's return to the Spirit, in a crossover tale with the
Escapist. This story became Eisner's last comics work,
completed just two weeks before the death of the comics

godfather. Also in this volume is the comics writing debut of award-winning author and Guggenheim fellow Chris Offutt, illustrated by Thomas Yeates. Dan Best and Eddie Campbell contribute a fully painted story from the 1939 World's Fair in Empire City, and 2004 Russ Manning Award winner Eric Wight brings a polemic story from writer Jason Hall to life. Among the other notable contributors are Howard Chaykin, Paul Grist, Shawn Martinbrough, David Hahn, Roy Thomas, Matt Wagner and indie stalwarts Jeffrey Brown and Jason. The book includes some violence.

Ambaum, Gene

Book Club: An Unshelved Collection. by Gene Ambaum and Bill Barnes ; art by Bill Barnes. Overdue Media 2006 120p. Illustration
Grades: 7 8 9 10 11 12 Adult   **741.5**
    1. Humorous graphic novels; 2. Libraries; 3. Graphic novels
    0-9740353-3-5, $17.95
    What happens in the library stays in the library. But oh, what happens in the library! Dewey has a book club, and you do not talk about Book Club. Colleen has a blog, but she doesn't know everyone can read it. Someone gave vegan Tamara a membership to the ham-of-the-month-club. And Merv reserved every copy of the new Harry Potter for purposes nefarious. This collection also features dozens of full-page full-color comic-format book talks, plus a very special storytime zombie nursery rhyme. This is the fourth print collection of the daily web comic chronicling the shenanigans at the Mallville Public Library.

    Frequently asked questions: an Unshelved collection. By Gene Ambaum and Bill Barnes ; art by Bill Barnes. Overdue Media 2008 135p. Illustration
Grades: 7 8 9 10 11 12 Adult   **741.5**
    1. Humorous graphic novels; 2. Libraries; 3. Graphic novels
    978-0-9740353-5-2, $17.95
    This sixth collection of the Unshelved webcomics includes all daily and Sunday Book Club comic strips from February 19, 2007 through February 16, 2008. It includes "The Great Plastic Coffee Cup Lid Comic Strip Challenge," a week-long competition between Unsheleved and Dave Kellett's Sheldon, another webcomic. It also includes all the special comic strips done for ALA's Cognotes, the conference newsletter published every day of the Midwinter Meeting and Annual Conference. The Sunday Book Club strips are in color, each one is a full page, and constitutes a mini-booktalk cum reader's advisory for each title, which range from YA fiction to graphic novels to classic science fiction and more.

    ★ **Large** print: an unshelved collection. By Gene Ambaum and Bill Barnes ; art by Bill Barnes. Overdue Media 2010 128p. Illustration
Grades: 7 8 9 10 11 12 Adult   **741.5**
    1. Humorous graphic novels; 2. Libraries; 3. Graphic novels
    978-0-9740353-7-6, $11.95
    This volume collects the daily webcomic strips of Unshelved from February 16, 2009 to April 26, 2010 plus the strips that originally appeared in ALA Cognotes in June 2009 and January 2010. It introduces a change in format and

a lower price point, in that the Sunday booktalk strips are not included. The strips collected for this volume reflect the recession, as the Mallville Public Library deals with a public that now comes to the library to use the computers to apply for unemployment benefits, fill out job applications, and more. Despite the gloomy times, the strips still find humor in the everyday happenings in the public library. Librarians and people who like to use libraries will find that Mallville is not so different from their local libraries.

Courtesy of Overdue Media

    Read Responsibly: An Unshelved Collection. By Gene Ambaum and Bill Barnes ; art by Bill Barnes. Overdue Media 2007 135p. Illustration
Grades: 8 9 10 11 12 Adult   **741.5**
    1. Humorous graphic novels; 2. Libraries; 3. Graphic novels
    978-0-9740353-4-5, $17.95
    The fifth year of strips about the Mallville Public Library, its eccentric staff and even more eccentric patrons, includes the Pimp My Bookcart sequence (that sparked a nationwide contest) and a year's worth of full-color full-page Unshelved Book Clubs featuring the greatest books ever written. Probably. Plus never-before published strips, mostly those done for American Library Association conferences, and more.

Ambrosio, Stefan

    Wizards of Mickey, vol. 1: mouse magic. Boom! Studios 2010 Un Illustration
Grades: 3 4 5 6 7 8 9   **741.5; Fic**
    1. Adventure graphic novels; 2. Fantasy graphic novels; 3. Humorous graphic novels; 4. Mickey Mouse (Fictional character); 5. Graphic novels
    978-1-60886-541-3, $9.99
    Wizard's apprentice Mickey loses a magic talisman called the Diamagic when he and the village fall afoul of a con man who steals it from them. Mickey pursues the con man, but he learns he'll have to compete in the Great Wizard's Tournament to win it back if he can father a team to work with him. He ends up with Donald and Goofy, both misfit bunglers, but somehow they'll have to compete against Peg-Leg Pete and the Phantom Blot. This book, originally written and published in Italy, is full of fantasy adventure and fun with recognizable Disney characters.

America's 1st Patriotic Comic Book Hero: The Shield Volume 1

    Archie Comics 2002 96p. Illustration
Grades: 3 4 5 6 7 8 9 10 11 12 Adult   **741.5; Fic**
    1. Adventure graphic novels; 2. Superhero graphic novels
    1-879794-08-X, $12.95
    A hero with great power, strength and courage who donned the colors of the American flag. A hero who lived for democracy and protected the world from the foes of freedom! No, it's not who you think... it's THE SHIELD, who predated his well known counterpart by over a year.

This historic full color trade paperback reprints his first 8 stories from PEP and SHIELD/WIZARD Comics. It includes his first appearance and origin, along with the covers of the comics they originally appeared in, dating from 1940.

Andersen, Hans Christian
The **Emperor's** new clothes: the graphic novel. Retold by Stephanie Peters; illustrated by Jeffrey Stewart Timmins. Stone Arch Books 2009 40p. Illustration (Graphic spin)
Grades: 4 5 6 7   **741.5; Fic**
1. Fairy tales; 2. Humorous graphic novels; 3. Graphic novels
978-1-4342-1595-6 (lib bdg), $22.65;
978-1-4342-1744-8 (pa), $4.95
LC 2009-10528
In this retelling of Andersen's tale, a vain emperor spends all his kingdom's money on clothes for himself, neglecting the needs of the people. Then a couple of swindlers claim they can weave the most wondrous magical material for a special suit, if only they had the supplies they need. They take everything, but no one, from the emperor on down, will admit they can't see the cloth or the clothes made from it, until one honest boy pipes up. The lively adaptation features illustrations which have all the people in clown face, complete with whiteface and bulbous red noses.

Anderson, Eric A.
PX! Book one: a girl and her panda. Written by Eric A. Anderson and Manny Trembley; illustrated by Manny Trembley. Image Comics 2007 Un Illustration
Grades: 6 7 8 9 10 11 12 Adult   **741.5; Fic**
1. Adventure graphic novels; 2. Humorous graphic novels; 3. Science fiction graphic novels; 4. Graphic novels
978-1-58240-820-0, $16.99; 1-58240-820-3
A young girl named Dahlia and her trusty (robot) panda sidekick set off on a journey around the world to save her missing scientist father, who has been kidnapped by Pollo, an evil goat mastermind who wants to take over the world (and yes, people keep telling him his name means chicken" in Spanish). Along the way, Dahlia meets Weatherby Ian Poppington III, a Victorian English secret agent also known as Double Aught Seven," and Wikkity Jones, a rollerskating swordsman who talks like a hillbilly and stands ready to fight ninja any time. The absurd humor is punctuated by moments of intense violent action, especially in the side story about fighting zombies. This book collects the webcomic.
Followed by: PX! v.2: in the service of the Queen (2009)

PX! book two: in the service of the Queen. Image Comics 2008 Un Illustration
Grades: 4 5 6 7 8 9 10 11 12   **741.5; Fic**
1. Adventure graphic novels; 2. Humorous graphic novels; 3. Science fiction graphic novels; 4. Graphic novels
978-1-60706-018-5, $16.99
In this second volume, Weatherby takes center stage. Dahlia's father is called to London to permanently shut down a super-computer, but villainous goat Pollo has

already had two of his lackeys hack into the system and take over. When Weatherby, Wikkity, and Panda show up to help Dahlia and her dad, Double Aught Seven Weatherby discovers he has not been, nor ever was, a Double Aught agent in the service of the Queen. However, he soon discovers that he is the only one who can get into the system, because IT had recruited him. The book, co-written by Trembley as well as illustrated by him, includes several short stories, including one created during the 24-Hour Comic Book Day. The main story doesn't have any bad language or overt violence, but a couple of the short stories include occasional use of the word "crap," and one story involves zombies.

Anderson, Jameson
The **Z-boys** and Skateboarding. Capstone Press 2007 32p. Illustration
Grades: 3 4 5 6 7 8 9   **741.5; 796.22**
1. Skateboarding; 2. Graphic novels
978-1-4296-0150-4, $25.26
LC 2007004915
This book uses the graphic novel format to describe the birth of the Z-boys skateboarding team in Dogtown, an area of Santa Monica, in 1973, and how they influenced modern skateboarding. The book includes additional facts and a list of books for further reading.
Part of the Graphic Library Invention and Discovery series.

Anderson, Kevin J.
Grumpy old monsters. IDW Publishing 2004 96p. Illustration
Grades: 4 5 6 7 8 9   **741.5; Fic**
1. Humorous graphic novels; 2. Monsters; 3. Graphic novels
1-932382-35-6, $13.99
The old monsters Frankenstein's Monster, Dracula, the Mummy, and the Werewolf, have all retired and moved to the old monsters' home, where Nurse Wrentch terrorizes them and only little Tiffany Frankenstein, granddaughter of old Dr. F., comes to visit. But this time she comes with terrible news the Van Helsing Corporation is about to take possession of Castle Frankenstein, tear it down, and build luxury condominiums. The monsters decide they must come out of retirement and help Tiffany stop the horror if they can escape Nurse Wrentch!

Ando, Natsumi
Kitchen Princess, Vol. 2. Natsumi Ando ; story by Miyuki Kobayashi. Ballantine Books/ Del Rey Manga 2007 Un Illustration
Grades: 7 8 9 10 11 12   **741.5; Fic**
1. Cooking; 2. Manga; 3. Shojo manga; 4. Graphic novels
978-0-345-49659-1, $10.95
Orphaned Najika has left Hokkaido and come to the Seika Academy in Tokyo in search of the "prince" who saved her when she was a little girl. Brothers Sora and Daichi, whose parents founded the academy, discover that Najika has the gift of an absolute sense of taste; when she eats a food, she can identify all the ingredients, and she never forgets the taste. She can use this to duplicate any recipe, and she does so to win a cooking competition so she can stay at

the Academy. Then she learns that Akane, who hates Najika, wants so badly to become a supermodel like her mother that she's following an extreme diet that could lead to an eating disorder. Can Najika overcome Akane's hostility to help her? Each volume includes recipes.

This is a 10 volume series
Also available in omnibus editions

Kitchen princess, vol. 9. Natsumi Ando ; story by Miyuki Kobayashi. Del Rey Manga 2009 Un Illustration
Grades: 7 8 9 10 11 12   **741.5; Fic**
1. Cooking; 2. Manga; 3. Romance graphic novels; 4. Shojo manga; 5. Graphic novels
978-0-345-51026-6, $10.99
Najika finally discovers the true identity of her Flan Prince, but she discovers that it doesn't change how she feels about Daichi, even with Seiya trying to win her over. And Daichi starts to remember things from the past, things he had forgotten and was allowed to forget. He starts to remember the family's trip to Hokkaido when his and Sora's mother was still alive, a trip that ended tragically for the family. Now that he remembers what happened, he holes up in his room and won't let anyone see him; but Najika won't stop trying to prepare food for him and to try to cheer him up, even if Daichi's father doesn't like her. The book includes recipes for dishes mentioned throughout the story.

Aoi, Haruka
A **Little** Snow Fairy Sugar, Volume 1. ADV Manga 2006 168p. Illustration
Grades: 3 4 5 6 7 8   **741.5; Fic**
1. Fairies; 2. Kodomo manga; 3. Manga; 4. Graphic novels
1-4139-0333-9, $9.99
Eleven-year-old Saga Bergstrom lives with her grandmother and maintains a very tight, controlled schedule; in addition to school, she works part-time in a coffee shop, and every afternoon at 4:00, she goes to the music store to play her dead mother's piano. Then, one day her life becomes chaotic when she encounters Sugar, an apprentice season fairy. Saga is the only human who can see Sugar, which can be very embarrassing when she screams in frustration at Sugar. Sugar and her fellow apprentice season fairies, Salt and Pepper, need to find twinkles to make their magic seeds grow so they can become full season fairies. The problem is, no one knows what twinkles are. In the meantime, Sugar and Saga need to find a way to get along with each other. The story and the art are very sweet and cute.

Volume 1 of 3

Aoki, Takao
Beyblade Volume 1. Viz Media/Viz Kids 2004 200p. Illustration
Grades: 3 4 5 6 7 8   **741.5; Fic**
1. Games; 2. Manga; 3. Shonen manga; 4. Graphic novels
1-59116-621-7, $7.99
Tyson has a passion for Beyblades and he's determined to be the best. But he's also a great guy who looks out for his friends and will never cheat to win. Even though he's one of the toughest Beybladers on the scene he still takes his share ofd knocks. Learning from these losses is what makes Tyson stronger all the time. Tyson just might

have what it takes to win when he busts out with a new Beyblade given to him by a mysterious stranger. Now the Blade Sharks want his new Beyblade and they're prepared to use any dirty trick to get it.

Volume 1 of 14

Appignanesi, Richard
Hamlet. [Richard Appignanesi, text adaptor]; illustrated by Emma Vieceli. Harry N. Abrams/Amulet Books 2007 195p. (Manga Shakespeare)
Grades: 8 9 10 11 12 Adult   **822.3; 741.5**
1. Shakespeare, William, 1564-1616 — Adaptations
978-0-8109-9324-2, $9.95; 0-8109-9324-4
Shakespeare's classic play of murder and revenge is here adapted into a manga-style graphic novel. It's now set in 2107, after global climate change has devastated the Earth. Appignanesi uses the text of the play and abridges it to fit the pages, while Vieceli's art vigorously carries the story along. The book includes a summary of the plot and a brief biography of Shakespeare.

First published in the United Kingdom

A **midsummer** night's dream. Illustrated by Kate Brown. Abrams 2008 207p. (Manga Shakespeare)
Grades: 7 8 9 10   **822.3; 741.5**
1. Shakespeare, William, 1564-1616 — Adaptations
978-0-8109-9475-1, $9.95; 0-8109-9475-5
Shakespeare's comedy of romance, Faerie, and shenanigans in the forest is adapted into a manga-style graphic novel. Hermia is in love with Lysander, while Demetrius is in love with Hermia, and Helen loves Demetrius. When mischievous fairy Puck decides to have some fun with the powerful love potion he has fetched for Fairy King Oberon, chaos reigns. While the human foursome needs to sort itself out, Oberon seeks revenge against his wife, Queen Titania, by having Puck use the love potion on her so she falls in love with the first creature she sees—who happens to be a yokel to whom Puck gave a donkey's head. The text takes dialog from the original play. The book includes a plot summary and a brief biography of Shakespeare.

Romeo and Juliet. By William Shakespeare; adapted by Richard Appignanesi; illustrated by Sonia Leong. Amulet Books 2007 195p. (Manga Shakespeare)
Grades: 8 9 10 11 12   **822.3; 741.5**
1. Shakespeare, William, 1564-1616 — Adaptations
978-0-8109-9325-9, $9.95; 0-8109-9325-2
                                        LC 2006-100362
Shakespeare's classic play of star-crossed young lovers gets the manga treatment. The book is set in modern Tokyo with rival yakuza gangs and uses somewhat abridged text from the play for the dialogue.
"Although the richness of the language may be lost, the script keeps the spirit of the story intact, hitting all the major speeches." Booklist
First published in the United Kingdom

The **tempest**. Illustrated by Paul Duffield; [adaptor, Richard Appignanesi]. Abrams 2008 207p. Illustration (Manga Shakespeare)
Grades: 7 8 9 10   **822.3; 741.5**
1. Shakespeare, William, 1564-1616 — Adaptations

978-0-8109-9476-8, $9.95

Prospero and his daughter Miranda have lived on an isolated island for twelve years, after he had been deposed from his rule as Duke of Naples and cast out to sea to die. A powerful magician, Prospero has caused the survivors of a shipwreck to land on his island, in order to get his revenge, for these survivors are his enemies. Problems arise when Miranda falls in love with Ferdinand, the monster Caliban tries to use the survivors to kill Prospero, and Ariel the sprite is trying to set things right while still obeying Prospero. The book includes a plot summary and a brief biography of Shakespeare

"This adaptation would be useful both as an introduction to the play and as a companion piece for classroom study of it, using images to illuminate the Bard's eloquent poetry." SLJ

Aragones, Sergio

Sergio Aragones' Groo: Mightier than the Sword. Sergio Aragonés ; Mark Evanier. Dark Horse Comics 2002 Un Illustration
Grades: 7 8 9 10 11 12 Adult   **741.5; Fic**
1. Adventure graphic novels; 2. Fantasy graphic novels; 3. Humorous graphic novels; 4. Graphic novels
1-56971-612-9, $13.95

In a savage land of another era, a goodly segment of the world has long been under the heavy thumb of the evil, power-mad despot known as Pipil Khan. The tyrant wants nothing more than to name an heir and shuck his mortal coil, but one thing stands in his way: Groo. It seems Khan just can't rest easy until Groo is out of the way. He'll give his kingdom to the one of his sons who can accomplish this. One of them has a foolproof plan how to do it. Unfortunately for him, it may be that no plan is foolproof enough to thwart Groo. The book includes some comedic violence.

Sergio Aragones' Groo: The Groo Nursery. Writer/artist, Sergio Aragonés ; wordsmith, Mark Evanier ; letterer, Stan Sakai ; colorist, Tom Luth. Dark Horse Comics 2002 Un Illustration
Grades: 7 8 9 10 11 12 Adult   **741.5; Fic**
1. Adventure graphic novels; 2. Fantasy graphic novels; 3. Humorous graphic novels; 4. Graphic novels
1-56971-794-X, $11.95

In this collection, Groo visits the happy island of Felicidad and manages to stir up lots of trouble among the people. Then a minstrel sings of Groo's deeds in a country resembling Japan, only to keep finding himself in trouble. And a town that knows of Groo's dangerous reputation try to keep him out, but he's illiterate. Oy! The stories include some comic violence.

Arai, Kiyoko

Beauty Pop, Vol. 1. Story and art by Kiyoko Arai. Viz Media/Shojo Beat 2006 194p. Illustration
Grades: 7 8 9 10 11 12   **741.5; Fic**
1. Hair; 2. Shojo manga; 3. Graphic novels
978-1-4215-0575-6, $8.99

At Kiri Koshiba's high school, three popular upper classmen do occasional "Scissors Projects," working makeovers on specially selected girls. Narumi Shogo, who cuts hair, wants to become the best beautician in Japan and

has won every youth competition - except one, years ago, that a younger girl won. When girls who aren't already pretty ask Narumi for a makeover, he tells them they're too ugly. Kiri helps two of the girls, working a stylist's magic that makes the girls glow; she's not interested in competition, even though her family owns a salon. Narumi wants to know who dares to be the upstart and challenge him, and he sets up the school's cultural festival to be a haircutting duel. Will Kiri even bother to compete?

Other titles in this series are: Beauty pop, Vol. 2 (2006) (978-1-4215-0576-6); Beauty pop. Vol. 3 (2007) (978-1-4215-1009-5); Beauty pop. Vol. 4 (2007) (978-1-4215-1010-1); Beauty pop. Vol. 5 (2007) (978-1-4215-1011-8); Beauty pop. Vol. 6 (2007) (978-1-4215-1323-2); Beauty pop. Vol. 7 (2008) (978-1-4215-1784-1); Beauty pop. Vol. 8 (2008) (978-1-4215-2310-1); Beauty pop. Vol. 9 (2008) (978-1-4215-2310-1); Beauty pop. Vol. 10 (2009) (978-1-4215-2594-5)

Beauty pop, vol. 10. Viz Media/Shojo Beat 2009 200p. Illustration
Grades: 7 8 9 10 11 12   **741.5; Fic**
1. Cosmetics; 2. Hair; 3. Shojo manga; 4. Romance graphic novels; 5. Graphic novels
978-1-4215-2594-5, $8.99

The Scissors Project has been competing in the All-Japan Beauty Tournament, but for the final match, things aren't going so well. Kiri is running a high fever, Narumi has hurt his scissor hand, and his special pair of scissors has disappeared. On top of that, Narumi and Ochiai have been fighting over Kiri, so the team's harmony has gone. And Narumi's father has thrown his support behind Billy and his team. This is the final volume of the series.

Arakawa, Hiromu

★ **Fullmetal** alchemist. By Hiromu Arakawa. Viz 2005 192 p. Illustration
Grades: 8 9 10 11 12   **741.5**
1. Alchemy — Fiction; 2. Brothers — Fiction; 3. Shonen manga
1591169208; 9781591169208, $9.99

"Alchemy: the mystical power to alter the natural world. ... When two brothers, Edward and Alphonse Elric, dabbled in this power to grant their dearest wish, one of them lost an arm and a leg...and the other became nothing but a soul locked into a body of living steel. Now Edward is an agent of the government, a slave of the military-alchemical complex, using his unique powers to obey orders." (Publisher's note)
Volume 1 of 27
Also available in VIZBIG omnibus editions

Archie & friends All-Stars: Veronica's passport
Archie Comic Publications 2009 Un Illustration
Grades: 3 4 5 6 7 8   **741.5; Fic**
1. Humorous graphic novels; 2. Lodge, Veronica (Fictional character); 3. Travel; 4. Graphic novels
978-1-879794-43-6, $9.95

Veronica Lodge from Riverdale has her own adventures as she travels to New York City, Paris, Rome, and Bombay in these stories originally published from 1989 to 1991. Veronica goes to New York City to stay with her cousin Whitney, and they travel all over the city to such famous landmarks as the Empire State Building and Radio City Music Hall; she even has a brief fling at being a sculptor. When Veronica accompanies her father to Paris, she doesn't realize that a notorious jewel thief has hidden the diamonds he just stole in what looks like the perfume she just bought; as she travels all over the city with a handsome local, the thief follows everywhere, trying to recover his booty. Then Mr. Lodge decides Veronica must have a better education and sends her to what he thinks is a finishing school in Rome, but when Veronica arrives, she finds herself among obnoxious and nasty girls who act more like juvenile delinquents. Then, when they travel to Bombay, Mr. Lodge and Veronica find themselves caught up in intrigue and industrial spying. Writers include Hal Smith, Kathleen Webb, Chris Allan, Mark Waid, and George Gladir.

Archie Americana Series: Best of the Eighties
    Archie Comics 2001 96p. Illustration
Grades: 3 4 5 6 7 8 9 10 11 12 Adult   **741.5; Fic**
    1. Andrews, Archie (Fictional character); 2. Humorous graphic novels; 3. Graphic novels
1-879794-06-3, $10.95
    During the 1980s pop culture ruled America; even the President was a former actor. In this volume, Archie and friends experience the punk movement, the "Urban Cowboy" craze, see the rise of MTV, get into the preppie, new wave and "Flashdance" fashions, play Trivial Pursuit, and boogie at the roller disco.
    Volume 1 of 2

Archie Americana Series: Best of the Fifties
    Archie Comics 1992 96p. Illustration
Grades: 3 4 5 6 7 8 9 10 11 12 Adult   **741.5; Fic**
    1. Andrews, Archie (Fictional character); 2. Humorous graphic novels; 3. Graphic novels
1-879794-01-2, $10.95
    Readers can journey back to the days of drive-ins and hula hoops, plaid skirts and bobby sox, Elvis and beatniks, rollerskates and sock hops in this book that reprints stories from the 1950s.

Archie Americana Series: Best of the Fifties Book 2
    Archie Comics 2003 96p. Illustration
Grades: 3 4 5 6 7 8 9 10 11 12 Adult   **741.5; Fic**
    1. Andrews, Archie (Fictional character); 2. Humorous graphic novels; 3. Graphic novels
1-879794-15-2, $10.95
    The '50s are a fondly remembered time for many - both those who lived during the decade as well as those who discovered it through movies like Grease and TV shows like Happy Days. They were also the perfect decade for Archie to have his misadventures - whether getting tangled up in the eternal love triangle or incurring the wrath of Mr. Weatherbee, Mr. Lodge and even his father, Archie and his friends scaled new heights of hilarity. Series editor Castiglia says in the Introduction that the 1950s was the first time the U.S. had been prosperous since the 1920s; teens could do fun things, not just work to help the family, and the Archie comics reflected the rise of popular culture.

Archie Americana Series: Best of the Forties Volume 1
    Archie Comics 1991 128p. Illustration

Grades: 3 4 5 6 7 8 9 10 11 12 Adult   **741.5; Fic**
    1. Andrews, Archie (Fictional character); 2. Humorous graphic novels; 3. Graphic novels
1-879794-00-4, $11.95
    In 1941, Pep Comics introduced Archie Andrews, "America's newest boyfriend." Since then, Archie and his perennial teenage friends have entertained readers with their misadventures. This book includes the very first Archie story, with the first appearance of Betty and Veronica, Reggie, Jughead, Mr. Weatherbee, Miss Grundy, and the rest of the Archie characters as they originally appeared.

Archie Americana Series: Best of the Forties Book 2
    Archie Comics 2002 96p. Illustration
Grades: 3 4 5 6 7 8 9 10 11 12 Adult   **741.5; Fic**
    1. Andrews, Archie (Fictional character); 2. Humorous graphic novels; 3. Graphic novels
1-879794-09-8, $10.95
    In 1941, Pep Comics introduced Archie Andrews, "America's newest boyfriend." Since then, Archie and his perennial teenage friends have entertained readers with their misadventures. This book includes stories from 1946 through 1949, with more slapstick and screwball comedy from Archie and the gang.

Archie Americana Series: Best of the Seventies
    Archie Comics 1998 96p. Illustration
Grades: 3 4 5 6 7 8 9 10 11 12 Adult   **741.5; Fic**
    1. Andrews, Archie (Fictional character); 2. Humorous graphic novels; 3. Graphic novels
1-879794-05-5, $9.95
    The decade of the 1970s was a time of transition in America, and the Archie Comics gang was right there. In this volume, Riverdale experiences the women's movement, joins in the Bicentennial celebration, sees the rise of bubble-pop, and joins the crazes for patches, pet rocks, and CB radio. Archie and the gang play "Pong" (one of the earliest video games), watch popular movies and TV shows, and go to the disco.
    Volume 1 of 2

Archie Americana Series: Best of the Sixties
    Archie Comics 1995 96p. Illustration
Grades: 3 4 5 6 7 8 9 10 11 12 Adult   **741.5; Fic**
    1. Andrews, Archie (Fictional character); 2. Humorous graphic novels; 3. Graphic novels
1-879794-02-0, $9.95
    The 1960s was a time of dreams, hopes, revolution, and social change, and the nation's youth were at the forefront. Archie and his friends came along for the ride, exploring both the fun and the mores of the times with humor. In this book readers can see the girls in slim jims, experience Beatlemania as it hits Riverdale, watch the teens become flower children, see them hit the surf, drag race, and wear mod fashions.
    Volume 1 of 2

Archie Classics: The Adventures of Little Archie Volume 1
    Archie Comics 2004 96p. Illustration
Grades: 3 4 5 6 7 8 9 10 11 12 Adult   **741.5; Fic**

1. Adventure graphic novels; 2. Humorous graphic novels
1-879794-17-9, $10.95

Little Archie deals with Martian invaders, secret spies, pirates, freewheeling uncles, gorillas on the loose and more! Who knew a little boy could have so many adventures? This book collects vintage Little Archie stories originally published from 1961 through 1965.

Archie's Camp Tales

Archie Comic Publications 2007 Un Illustration
Grades: 3 4 5 6 7 8   **741.5; Fic**
1. Humorous graphic novels; 2. Graphic novels
978-1-879794-23-8, $7.49

For decades, Archie Comics have made their way into countless summer campers' backpacks... and for decades, the writers and artists at Archie have provided readers with stories of Archie and his friends' adventures at summer camp. Now, some of the best of these stories are collected in a special digest-sized edition. Will Betty and Veronica win the hearts of the cute guys they meet at camp? Will Archie lead his friends down the wrong trail again? Will camp tuition rise to keep up with Jughead's appetite?

Archie's Classic Christmas Stories Volume 1

Archie Comics 2002 96p. Illustration
Grades: 3 4 5 6 7 8 9 10 11 12 Adult   **741.5; Fic**
1. Andrews, Archie (Fictional character); 2. Humorous graphic novels; 3. Graphic novels
1-879794-10-1, $10.95

Deck the halls with smiles and laughter, fa la la la la, la la la la! Since their inception, Archie and his friends have delighted readers with scores of Yuletide tales. These stories proved so popular that in 1954 an entire series devoted to stories of Holiday Cheer and Good Will to all premiered: ARCHIE'S CHRISTMAS STOCKING. Archie and his friends show their holiday spirit in this collection of classic tales from the first decade of Santa Claus himself. This book features painstaking restorations of original stories published from 1957 through 1963.

Archie Comics Presents: The Love Showdown

Archie Comics 1994 Un Illustration
Grades: 3 4 5 6 7 8 9 10 11 12 Adult   **741.5; Fic**
1. Andrews, Archie (Fictional character); 2. Humorous graphic novels; 3. Graphic novels
1-879794-03-9, $4.95

In the mid-1990s, Archie Comics announced that Archie might finally choose between Betty and Veronica, after the love triangle had lasted since 1941; the story was published as a crossover among the four Archie comics series. This volume reprints the stories.

Arlem, Renato

Marvel Nemesis: The Imperfects. Renato Arlem and Greg Pak. Marvel Entertainment 2005 Un Illustration
Grades: 8 9 10 11 12   **741.5; Fic**
1. Spider-Man (Fictional character); 2. Superhero graphic novels; 3. Wolverine (Fictional character); 4. Graphic novels
978-0-7851-1778-0, $7.99

An evil scientist sets his cross-hairs on planet Earth, in search of test subjects for his experiments, transforming even the most timid creatures into vicious fighting machines. Thousands of years later, the Thing, Wolverine, Spider-Man, and Elektra all find themselves unwilling participants in the scientist's millennia-old trials . . . or perhaps not all of them are that unwilling. This book includes some violence and strong language.

Aso, Yusuke

The **king** of debris, volume 1. DC Comics/CMX 2009 160p. Illustration
Grades: 8 9 10 11 12   **741.5; Fic**
1. Adventure graphic novels; 2. Manga; 3. Science fiction graphic novels; 4. Graphic novels
978-1-4012-1879-9, $9.99

Young android boy Citro lives happily with his human "grandfather," an old mechanic, and the mechanic's granddaughter Corona. Then Tera zooms into their life on her flying, robotic broomstick, pursued by soldiers determined to kill her and take the device she's carrying. During the fight, Grampa is killed, and Tera drops the device which activates and bonds with Citro. The device is "The God of Destruction's Heart," and it turns little Citro into a deadly and powerful killing machine. He drives off the enemy soldiers, but now he must go with Tera and Corona, who has no other family but Citro to Altasia, where the "Heart" can be safely removed from Citro and used to defend Altasia against the enemies pursuing them. Meanwhile, word of what they have goes ahead of them, and they will have to fight to get to Altasia. This manga is full of action and fighting, but there's not too much graphic violence.

Atangan, Patrick

Songs of Our Ancestors Volume II: The Silk Tapestry and Other Chinese Folktales. NBM 2004 Un Illustration
Grades: 6 7 8 9 10   **741.5; Fic**
1. Folklore — China; 2. Graphic novels
1-56163-403-4, $12.95

In three Chinese folk tales, an old woman, a young boy and a wild spirit are all bound by a passion to create, changing the world around them forever. In "The Silk Tapestry," an impoverished elderly woman's only hope against a life of hardship lies in the completion of a magical tapestry. It is said to be the key to a paradise. Already living in squalor, how much more of herself is she willing sacrifice to see her dream come to fruition? In "Sausage-Boy and his Magic Brush," a young boy's remarkable talent for paintings that come to life attracts a greedy woman. In "The Story of Pan Gu, The First Man," a lonely but wild spirit sculpts the Earth from a cosmic egg in hopes it brings others like him to keep him company.

Songs of Our Ancestors Volume III: Tree of Love. NBM 2005 Un Illustration
Grades: 6 7 8 9 10   **741.5; Fic**
1. Folklore — India; 2. Romance graphic novels; 3. Graphic novels
1-56163-438-7, $12.95

This volume of Atangan's Asian folktale collection, Tree of Love, celebrates India's tradition of elevating romance to a work of art. Atangan adapts Rajput polyptych paintings of northern India and transforms them into a poetic comics experience. The story follows a prince's courtship of a flower peddler. The young prince is surprised by the difficulty in proving the worthiness of what everyone sees as a common woman. But she has a secret, a special gift bound in the beauty and power of nature. Each page ornaments Tree of Love's universal story about the intricacies of love. Atangan combined two Indian folktales to make this story: "The Flowering Tree" and "The Tree of Sorrow."

Songs of our ancestors: The yellow jar: two tales from Japanese tradition. NBM 2003 48p. Illustration (Songs of our ancestors)
Grades: 5 6 7 8 9 10 11 12   **741.5**
1. Folklore — Japan; 2. Graphic novels
1-56163-331-3, $12.92

LC 2002-32132

"To render two magical Japanese legends, one about a fisherman who discovers a fair maiden in a big pot, the other about a monk whose fastidiously kept garden is invaded by two chrysanthemums, Atangan charmingly adopts the sharp outlines, boldly juxtaposed color fields, and striking compositions of eighteenth-century Japanese woodblock prints." Booklist

Other titles in this series are: Silk tapestry and other Chinese folktales (2004); Tree of love (2005)

Augustyn, Brian
Gotham by Gaslight: A Tale of the Batman. Brian Augustyn, Mike Mignola, P. Craig Russell, Eduardo Barreto. DC Comics 2006 112p. Illustration
Grades: 8 9 10 11 12 Adult   **741.5; Fic**
1. Batman (Fictional character); 2. Science fiction graphic novels; 3. Superhero graphic novels; 4. Graphic novels
978-1-4012-1153-0, $12.99

In an age of mystery and superstition, how would the people of Gotham react to a weird creature of the night, a bat-garbed vigilante feared by the guilty and the innocent alike? Some would live in terror. Others would rest easier. Only one man would take no notice at all ... a man with other matters to attend to. His name? No one knows for sure. Most people know him only as Jack. Jack the Ripper. This book collects two Elseworlds adventures of Batman, Gotham by Gaslight and its sequel Master of the Future.

Aureliani, Franco
Billy Batson and the magic of Shazam!. DC Comics 2010 Un Illustration
Grades: 3 4 5 6 7   **741.5; Fic**
1. Captain Marvel (Fictional character); 2. Humorous graphic novels; 3. Superhero graphic novels; 4. Graphic novels
978-1-4012-2248-2, $12.99

Gifted with the power of the magic word, "Shazam!" young orphan Billy Batson transforms into the World's Mightiest Mortal, Captain Marvel. He lives in New York City with his sister Mary, who can also transform into a super powered pintsize heroine, Mary Marvel. They have found a way to live together, go to school, and battle against evil. However, one of Captain Marvel's battles has caused a rift which has allowed Theo Adam to return from banishment.

Theo wants to get the magic word back so he can defeat the old wizard who mistakenly gave him the power in the first place and take over the world. This version of the Captain Marvel story is kid-friendly, with kiddie cartoon level action and lots of silly humor.

Tiny Titans. DC Comics 2010 160p. Illustration
Grades: 2 3 4 5 6 7 8   **741.5; Fic**
1. Green Lantern (Fictional character); 2. Humorous graphic novels; 3. Superhero graphic novels; 4. Tiny Titans (Fictional characters); 5. Graphic novels
978-1-4012-2892-7, $12.99

This volume collects issues 1925 of the continuing comic book series. The Tiny Titans participate in Pet Club with their super pets; Alfred has to deal with penguins and bunnies in the Bat Cave and in Wayne Manor. Then the young sidekicks get their hands on some special rings, and the Green Lantern has to retrieve the Earth Sector's power rings. Green Lantern writer Geoff Johns co-wrote the last story. The book includes some puzzles, lots of short stories, plenty of kid-friendly silliness, and cute, colorful, cartoony art.

The comic book series won the Eisner Award for Best Publication for Kids in 2009.

Auster, Paul
Hulk: is he man or monster or . . . is he both?. ABDO/Spotlight 2008 Un Illustration
Grades: 3 4 5 6 7 8 9   **741.5; Fic**
1. Hulk (Fictional character); 2. Superhero graphic novels; 3. Graphic novels
978-1-59961-547-9, $21.35

LC 2007-52759

Dr. Bruce Banner is ready to test his new gamma ray weapon using a monkey, when his intern Rick Jones suddenly goes to Ground Zero to save the monkey. When the test won't abort, Banner races out to save Rick, only to be caught by the gamma ray blast himself. It turns him into a giant, green monster of a man, and General Ross makes him angry. The General sends troops and weapons out to capture the Hulk, but Rick and the monkey try to help him. This is the first volume of a set of comics that provide kid-friendly, action-packed Hulk stories with little in the way of graphic violence and no bad language.

This is a library bound edition of a Marvel Age: The Incredible Hulk comic book issue, with all advertising pages removed.

Hulk: Mayhem!. ABDO/Spotlight 2008 Un Illustration
Grades: 3 4 5 6 7 8 9   **741.5; Fic**
1. Hulk (Fictional character); 2. Superhero graphic novels; 3. Graphic novels
978-1-59961-548-6, $21.35

LC 2008-101

Bruce Banner, Rick Jones, and Monkey have been hanging out in a cabin near a ski resort in the Rocky Mountains, where Banner has been trying to build a nano-nuclear cellular reconfiguration matrix—or, as Rick calls it, a de-Hulkifier. However, they've been tracked by General "Thunderbolt" Ross, who has brought troops, Jamie Madrox (tricked out in an anti-Hulk armor), and Radioactive Man (former nuclear physicist Chen Lu) to capture the Hulk. Their efforts end up causing an avalanche, which only the

Hulk seems interested in stopping before attacking his attackers. As with the other volumes, this book includes lots of action with no actual violence and no bad language.

This is a library bound edition of a Marvel Age: The Incredible Hulk comic book issue, with all advertising pages removed.

Hulk: Radioactive. ABDO/Spotlight 2008 Un Illustration
Grades: 3 4 5 6 7 8 9 **741.5; Fic**
1. Hulk (Fictional character); 2. Superhero graphic novels; 3. Graphic novels
978-1-59961-549-3, $21.35
LC 2008-103
When General Ross and his army of Hulkbusters (soldiers in exoskeleton armor) capture Bruce Banner, Rick Jones and Monkey break into the military compound to save their friend. Then the Hulk accidentally busts out Radioactive Man while messing up the compound. In his radioactive damper, Radioactive Man is Dr. Chen Lu, and he behaves as though he's Banner's friend, although Rick and Monkey notice Lu keeps doing things that cause Bruce to start Hulking up. This volume provides lots of action in kid-friendly mode, with little real violence and no bad language.

This is a library bound edition of a Marvel Age: The Incredible Hulk comic book issue, with all advertising pages removed.

Avery, Ben
Kingdoms Volume 1: The Coming Storm. Zondervan/Zonderkidz 2007 160p. Illustration
Grades: 5 6 7 8 9 10 **741.5; Fic**
1. Adventure graphic novels; 2. Graphic novels
978-0-310-71353-1, $9.99
LC 2007-3148
When Pharaoh Neco and his army marched across Judah, King Josiah recklessly led the attack and died. Now his faithful adviser Iddo remains loyal to his king's memory and labors to keep the nation faithful to the Lord even as he struggles to protect his own family. This story is set against the backdrop of the events in the Old Testament books, 1 & 2 Kings and 1 & 2 Chronicles.

Volume 1 of 8

Avery, Fiona
Arana Vol. 1: The Heart of the Spider. Art by Roger Cruz and Mark Brooks. Marvel Entertainment 2005 Un Illustration
Grades: 8 9 10 11 12 Adult **741.5; Fic**
1. Adventure graphic novels; 2. Superhero graphic novels
0-7851-1506-4, $7.99
She's fierce, she's sassy, she sticks to walls. Anya Corazon, a.k.a. Arana, is a next-generation girl warrior. A scrappy teen from Brooklyn by day, Anya becomes the Hunter of the ancient and mystical Spider Society by night. But first, she must survive her initiation and prove herself on her first mission, all while going to high school and hiding everything from her single-parent dad. Together with her partner, the mysterious mage Miguel, Anya must fight to protect the peace of the world from the sworn enemies of the Spider Society, the evil Sisterhood of the Wasp. There's lots of super hero action here.

Arana Vol. 2: In the Beginning. Art by Roger Cruz. Marvel Entertainment 2005 Un Illustration
Grades: 8 9 10 11 12 Adult **741.5; Fic**
1. Adventure graphic novels; 2. Superhero graphic novels
0-7851-1719-9, $7.99
Anya Corazon continues her work as Arana. What seems like a routine collar turns out to be anything but when the corrupt judge Anya captured reveals a deadly new threat to the Spider Society. While her partner Miguel tangles with an old enemy, a new one appears to challenge Anya, and he's willing to kill everyone around her.

Arana Vol. 3: Night of the Hunter. Art by Roger Cruz, Jonboy Meyers, and Francis Portella. Marvel Entertainment 2006 Un Illustration
Grades: 7 8 9 10 11 12 **741.5; Fic**
1. Adventure graphic novels; 2. Superhero graphic novels
0-7851-1853-5, $7.99
Exactly what happened to Arana's mother before she disappeared all those years ago" Startling new information on her family's past spurs Anya to launch her own personal investigation. Will history be too painful to bear" Meanwhile, the evil Sisterhood of the Wasp hosts a summit of fiends, rogues and villains so big that Arana just might have to crash the party. Hopefully, she can get a few roundhouse kicks in before someone calls the cops.

Azuma, Kiyohiko
★ **Azumanga** Daioh omnibus. Translation, Stephen Paul. Yen Press 2009 675p. Illustration
Grades: 8 9 10 11 12 **741.5; Fic**
1. High school students; 2. Humorous graphic novels; 3. Manga; 4. School stories; 5. Graphic novels
978-0-316-07738-5, $24.99
An omnibus edition of a humorous four-volume manga series featuring a Japanese suburban high school class with a ditzy teacher. The adult teachers go drinking occasionally, and there's one male teacher who ogles the girls in their P.E. uniforms.

First published 2001 in Japan

Yotsuba&!. By Kiyohiko Azuma. Yen Press 2009 224 p. Illustration
Grades: 5 6 7 8
741.5; Fic
1. Manga; 2. Moving
0316073873;
9780316073875, $13
In this book, by Kiyohiko Azuma, "Yotsuba is the charming new girl in town. . . . In seven stories, the green-haired four-year-old discovers air conditioners, doorbells, cicadas, swings and more, and does it all with the

Courtesy of Yen Press

energy of a small hurricane. Her excitement is contagious and infects her handsome young adoptive father as well as the gaggle of pretty girls next door, all of whom get tangled up in her adventures as they try to keep up with her." (Publisher's note)

"Yotsuba is the charming new girl in town in this all-ages shojo manga by the author of the popular Azumanga Daioh series. In seven stories, the green-haired four-year-old discovers air conditioners, doorbells, cicadas, swings and more, and does it all with the energy of a small hurricane." Pub Wkly

Originally published in the U.S. by ADV
Volume 1 of an ongoing series

Azuma, Mayumi
Elemental Gelade Volume 1. Tokyopop 2006 192p. Illustration
Grades: 8 9 10 11 12   **741.5; Fic**
1. Adventure graphic novels; 2. Fantasy graphic novels; 3. Manga; 4. Shonen manga; 5. Graphic novels
1-59816-598-4, $9.99

During a routine raid, sky-pirate Coud Van Giruet discovers a most unusual bounty: Ren, an "Edel Raid," is a living weapon that interacts with a human to become the ultimate fighting machine. But Van Giruet soon realizes that Ren is even more prized than he first thought. When she is captured by an evil man who sells Edel Raids on the black market, Coud and the agents of Arc Aile join forces to rescue Ren. This fantasy adventure includes some violence and some mildly harsh language.

Azuma, Naomi
Suihelibe!, vol. 1. DC Comics/CMX 2008 160p. Illustration
Grades: 3 4 5 6 7 8   **741.5; Fic**
1. Humorous graphic novels; 2. Manga; 3. Science fiction graphic novels; 4. Graphic novels
978-1-4012-1900-0, $9.99

On the cover of the manga, several chemistry elements are listed: hydrogen, helium, lithium, and belium (which probably should be beryllium). First year junior high school student Tetsu just wants to join the biology club at school, when a small flying saucer crashes into the classroom. Lan, the alien pilot who looks like a cute girl, enlists Tetsu's help to recover some escaped life forms from her planet. In order for them to accomplish this task, they need to keep the biology club going, but the student council president wants to shut down the club, so they have three months to round up three more members, even as they hunt Noids (the life forms). There's a lot of shouting and slapstick humor.

Volume 1 of 2

Bailey, Chris
Major Damage. Sky Dog Press 2004 Un Illustration
Grades: 3 4 5 6 7 8   **741.5; Fic**
1. Humorous graphic novels; 2. Superhero graphic novels; 3. Graphic novels
0-9721831-4-0, $14.95

Before The Incredibles, there was Major Damage: the tale of a little boy who is transformed into his favorite super hero, protecting the world from mutants, monsters, and alien scum. Eight-year-old Melvin was trick or treating on Halloween night, dressed as his favorite superhero, Major Damage, when he was abducted by the Mucus Men; the harmless scientists mistook Melvin for the real hero, assumed he'd had an accident, and "restored" his powers and returned him to Earth. Meanwhile, Melvin's mother thinks her son has disappeared.

Bailey, Tracey
Wonderdog, Inc.. Arcana Studio Inc. 2010 Un Illustration
Grades: 5 6 7 8 9 10   **741.5; Fic**
1. Adventure graphic novels; 2. Humorous graphic novels; 3. Graphic novels
978-1-897548-87-5, $14.95

Sixteen-year-old Ryan Robertson is a typical, nerdy type of guy, except he's got a very hot-looking girlfriend, whom his best buddy Alex just doesn't trust. The two guys are looking forward to the summer break, until Ryan's history teacher parents tell him they're going to Europe on a trip and he'll have to stay with his grandfather on a pig farm. Rachel, the hot girlfriend, wants to know where he's going, so she can visit him. When he gets there, he finds a wise-cracking grandfather, lots of chores, no Internet, no television ... and then Rachel shows up to steal a little statue of a dog from his grandfather. That's when Ryan learns that his grandfather, his parents, and a lot of other people are part of a secret organization to protect the world from the likes of Rachel, err ... Dr. Sweeney, and her nefarious colleagues who are out to rule the world and get very rich with the Fountain of Youth that the little dog statue unlocks. Now he's off to Bolivia with Pappy and siblings Seth and Amie (she's cute!), to try to stop Dr. Sweeney. Think of Indiana Jones as a grandfather who still swashbuckles, and the kind of story told in the Indiana Jones movies. Some readers may note the fairly numerous grammatical errors (using an apostrophe inappropriately), but it shouldn't distract too much from the fun story. There's a lot of action but very little actual violence.

Baker, Kyle
★ **How** to draw stupid and other essentials of cartooning. Watson-Guptill 2008 110p. Illustration
Grades: 8 9 10 11 12 Adult   **741.5**
1. Cartooning — Technique; 2. Graphic novels — Drawing
978-0-8230-0143-9, $16.95

LC 2008-922161

"Baker, an award-winning cartoonist and graphic-novel illustrator, gives aspiring cartoonists irreverent advice about how to succeed in their chosen field. He offers instruction in basic drawing techniques such as choosing the right tools and discusses the importance of learning to draw shapes, exaggerating, and using references. But the author's most inspiring advice focuses on how to succeed as a cartoonist." SLJ

Plastic Man: On the Lam!. DC Comics 2004 Un Illustration
Grades: 6 7 8 9 10 11 12 Adult   **741.5; Fic**
1. Humorous graphic novels; 2. Plastic Man (Fictional character); 3. Superhero graphic novels; 4. Graphic novels
1-4012-0343-4, $14.95

2005 Eisner Award for Best Publication for a Younger Audience, also 2005 Eisner Award for Best Writer/Artists-Humor for Kyle Baker

Plastic Man has worked as a superhero, but he used to be the criminal Eel O'Brian, a fact he has hidden from the FBI. Now there's been a murder, and Eel O'Brian is the main (and only) suspect. When the FBI learns of his old identity, Plastic Man goes on the lam to clear himself.

Originally published as Plastic Man issues #1-6; this volume is bound in plastic

Through the looking-glass. By Lewis Carroll; adapted by Kyle Baker. Papercutz 2008 Un Illustration (Classics illustrated)
Grades: 3 4 5 6 7 8 9
741.5; Fic
1. Carroll, Lewis, 1832-1898 — Adaptations; 2. Fantasy graphic novels; 3. Graphic novels
978-1-59707-115-4, $9.95; 1-59707-115-3

Courtesy of Papercutz

This is Carroll's sequel to Alice's Adventures in Wonderland. This time, Alice climbs through the looking-glass in her house and finds herself in a land with talking flowers and insects, Tweedledee and Tweedledum (who recite "The Walrus and the Carpenter—), the White Queen who needs help pinning her shawl straight, Humpty Dumpty, the Red Queen, and more. The Eisner Award-winning Baker uses a different style from his usual cartoony look here, more reminiscent of Tenniel's classic illustrations of Carroll's books.

Baldwin, Stephen
Spirit Warriors Book 1. Art by Joe Simko. B & H Publishing Group 2006 Un Illustration
Grades: 7 8 9 10 11 12
741.5; Fic
1. Christian life; 2. Fantasy graphic novels; 3. Graphic novels
978-0-8054-4357-8, $9.99

Six radical young teens enter the spiritual war zone every day for classic battles of good against evil in the crumbling New City. Mia, Nano, Faith, Jon, Davy, and Hailey were all mysteriously orphaned at a young age; they each have uncommon strengths. When the Elder Seiko takes over a local church and fills it with evil, the young Spirit Warriors fight back.

Baltazar, Art
Patrick the Wolf Boy Volume 1. Devil's Due Publishing 2004 Un Illustration
Grades: 2 3 4 5 6 7 8 9 10 11 12 Adult
741.5; Fic
1. Humorous graphic novels; 2. Graphic novels
1-932796-27-4, $10.95

Patrick looks at first glance like the other kids in school, but he's a werewolf. A cute werewolf. He resembles Eddie Munster (from the 1960s television comedy series "The Munsters—), and he doesn't speak, although he growls a lot and sometimes howls. He gives his teacher an apple - but with a skull biting the apple. When he goes fishing with his dad, he prefers to scare the bear into giving him his catch. He loves to play tag with the neighborhood squirrel. And when Valentine's Day comes, he makes sure that his babysitter likes him better. His utterly normal parents adore him and understand his growls; so does Neve, his classmate at school.

Patrick the Wolf Boy Volume 2. Devil's Due Publishing 2005 Un Illustration
Grades: 2 3 4 5 6 7 8 9 10 11 12 Adult
741.5; Fic
1. Humorous graphic novels; 2. Graphic novels
1-932796-29-0, $10.95

This volume collects previously published issues of the comic: the Super Hero Special, the Science Fiction Special, the Wedding Special, and the After School Special. In the many short stories, Patrick the Wolf Boy attends a comic book convention with his dad, plays "Star Wars" with the neighborhood kids, meets and befriends an alien kid, Zyggie, who then crashes the wedding reception of a relative, and deals with the school bully.

Patrick the Wolf Boy Volume 3. Devil's Due Publishing 2007 Un Illustration
Grades: 2 3 4 5 6 7 8 9 10 11 12 Adult
741.5; Fic
1. Fantasy graphic novels; 2. Humorous graphic novels; 3. Graphic novels
978-1-932796-30-8, $12.99

The third volume of Patrick the Wolf Boy collects the Rock-n-Roll Special, the Post Father's Day Special, and the Happy Birthday Special, plus some stories written and illustrated by guest creators. Patrick meets Squatch, the baby Big Foot, accidentally bites Neve, who thinks she's turning into a werewolf, encounters various rock stars, and other adventures. In one panel, the screaming pajama lady says "crap."

Patrick the Wolf Boy Volume 4. Devil's Due Publishing 2007 Un Illustration
Grades: 3 4 5 6 7 8 9 10 11 12 Adult
741.5; Fic
1. Halloween; 2. Humorous graphic novels; 3. Graphic novels
978-1-932796-83-4, $12.99

This fourth collection of comics featuring Patrick the Wolf Boy focus mostly on Halloween, a natural holiday for the young wolfman ... er ... wolfboy. He plays with jack o'lanterns (he likes to wear them on his head), goes trick-or-treating with the neighbor kids, keeps trying to melt the grouchy neighbor lady after watching The Wizard of Oz, and plays with new neighbor, the Grim Reaper. The book includes a couple instances of mild language ("fricken"), and one scene in which the Grim Reaper does his thing.

Tiny Titans vs. the Fearsome Five. By Art Baltazar & Franco. Stone Arch Books 2012 25 p. Color illustration
Grades: 2 3 4 5 6 7 8
741.5; 741.5/973
1. Fantasy graphic novels; 2. Flash (Fictional character); 3. Playgrounds; 4. Playgrounds — Fiction; 5. Playgrounds — Juvenile fiction; 6. Superhero graphic novels; 7. Superheroes; 8. Superheroes — Fiction; 9. Superheroes — Juvenile fiction; 10. Graphic novels
1434245381; 9781434245380, $21.27

LC 2012014778

This "is the first in Stone Arch's line of 'Tiny Titans' books, reprinting DC's popular and Eisner-winning children's title. Characters like Robin, Starfire, Kid Flash, Speedy, Raven, Cyborg, and Beast Boy . . . gallivant through several fast-paced vignettes focusing on group dynamics and school life." (Booklist)

Bannister (Person)
★ The **elsewhere** chronicles book one: the shadow door. Lerner Publishing Group/Graphic Universe 2009 48p. Illustration
Grades: 4 5 6 7 8   **741.5; Fic**
1. Adventure graphic novels; 2. Fantasy graphic novels; 3. Horror graphic novels; 4. Graphic novels
978-0-7613-4459-9, $27.93; 978-0-7613-3963-2 (pa), $6.95

LC 2008-39442
Max, Noah, and Theo face a boring weekend, when they meet Rebecca, who has come to town with her family for her Grandpa Gabe's funeral. The boys tell her the house is haunted, then they decide to explore it together. Inside, they find a jumble of junk, lots of cool old books in the library, and a strange old movie projector. And something ... shadowy ... brushes against Theo and hurts his arm. The next day, Rebecca asks the guys to return to the house with her, but only Max is willing to cut school. The old projector, when turned on, opens a portal to another world, and Rebecca disappears into it. When Max turns on the projector again, Rebecca comes back, only to be snatched by a tentacled monster, and he follows her and the creature into a strange world of shadows and menace, the land called Elsewhere.

Originally published in France under the title Les Enfants d'ailleurs. Winner of the 2007 Lyon Festival Youth Prize.

Other titles in this series are:The shadow spies (2009); The master of shadows (2009); The calling (2010); The parting (2011); The tower of shadows (2013)

Barasui
Strawberry Marshmallow Volume 1. Tokyopop 2006 184p. Illustration
Grades: 8 9 10 11 12   **741.5; Fic**
1. Humorous graphic novels; 2. Manga; 3. Shonen manga; 4. Graphic novels
1-59816-494-5, $9.99

This series follows the lives of Nobue Ito, her younger sister Chika, and her friends Miu and Matsuri—these girls try to solve problems and help each other out, whether it's helping someone to quit smoking or organizing a sleepover at a friend's house. The girls all look very young, but Nobue and her friends are teenagers. The comedy is very Seinfeld-esque, with a little partial nudity and some cigarette smoking.

Barberi, Carlo
Justice League Unlimited Vol. 1: United They Stand. DC Comics 2005 104p. Illustration
Grades: 4 5 6 7 8 9   **741.5; Fic**
1. Justice League (Fictional characters); 2. Superhero graphic novels; 3. Graphic novels

1401205127; 9781401205126, $6.99

Leaping straight out of their Cartoon Network show, the Worlds Greatest Heroes have their own comics series. This inaugural collection features these tales: Divide Conquer, Poker Face, Small Time, Local Hero and Monitor Duty.

Justice League Unlimited Vol. 2: World's Greatest Heroes. DC Comics 2006 104p. Illustration
Grades: 4 5 6 7 8 9   **741.5; Fic**
1. Green Lantern (Fictional character); 2. Justice League (Fictional characters); 3. Superhero graphic novels; 4. Graphic novels
1-4012-1014-7, $6.99

The JLA encounter the oldest Green Lantern as they battle the terrible Triptych, journey to deep space to thwart the malicious Darkseid and travel back in time to Camelot to battle the evil Morgaine Le Fey. Plus, the crazy Creeper helps in a battle against the Madmen, while the enigmatic Question hunts down a traitor within the League itself.

Justice League Unlimited Vol. 3: Champions of Justice. DC Comics 2006 104p. Illustration
Grades: 4 5 6 7 8 9   **741.5; Fic**
1. Flash (Fictional character); 2. Justice League (Fictional characters); 3. Superhero graphic novels; 4. Graphic novels
978-1-4012-1015-1, $6.99

The World's Greatest Heroes travel to Atlantis to confront the gigantic menace called Umbra! Plus, the two Flashes team up to battle Mirror Master, as the entire League must take on an out-of-control Red Tornado! This volume also includes a journey to Limbo and an encounter with the deadly Mr. Atom.

Barker, Clive
The **Thief** of Always. IDW Publishing 2005 144p. Illustration
Grades: 4 5 6 7 8 9 10   **741.5; Fic**
1. Fantasy graphic novels; 2. Horror graphic novels; 3. Graphic novels
1-933239-17-4, $35.00; 1-933239-38-7 (pa), $19.99

Clive Barker's fable for younger readers is adapted here into graphic novel format. Mr. Hood's Holiday House has stood for a thousand years, welcoming countless children to enjoy a blissful round of treats and holidays ... for a price. Then bored young Harvey Swick comes, and he notices disquieting little details that make him realize the place is more of a trap. Things are spooky but not terrifying, with little violence.

Originally published as The Thief of Always issues #1-3.

Barrie, J. M.
Peter Pan. Adapted by Joe Dunn; illustrated by Ben Dunn.   ABDO Publishing/Magic   Wagon 2008 32p.
Grades: 2 3 4 5 6
741.5; Fic

Courtesy of ABDO Publishing/Magic Wagon

1. Adventure graphic novels; 2. Fantasy graphic novels; 3. Peter Pan (Fictional character); 4. Graphic novels
978-1-60270-052-9, $27.07

LC 2007-12070

John, Michael, and Wendy love hearing their mother's stories, but they don't know that another young boy has been listening to them as well. When their protective dog Nana steals Peter Pan's shadow, the children meet him and Wendy sews his shadow back. Then the children agree to return with Peter to the magical Neverland. Can they survive in a land of pirates, Lost Boys, and Tinker Bell" The book provides a simplified adaptation that introduces young readers to Barrie's classic tale. It includes a brief biography of Barrie.

Part of the Graphic Classics series

Barry, James L.
★ The **lost** warrior. Created by Erin Hunter; written by Dan Jolley; art by James L. Barry. Tokyopop/HarperCollins Publishers 2007 96p. Illustration (Warriors)
Grades: 4 5 6 7   **741.5; Fic**
1. Adventure graphic novels; 2. Cats; 3. Graphic novels
978-0-06-124020-1, $6.99; 0-06-124020-6

LC 2006-30426

Thunderclan warrior Greystripe helps clan members escape when the twolegs destroy their forest home and capture many of them, but he himself gets captured. Now he's a kittypet and desperate to return home to his clan. He meets Millie, another kittypet who wants to learn how to become a warrior, but can Greystripe find his way out of the twolegs' land?

This series adapting Hunter's Warriors prose novel series is a co-publishing venture between Tokyopop and its book market distributor, HarperCollins.

Other titles in this series are: Warrior's refuge (2008); Warrior's return (2008); The rise of the scourge (2008)

Barry, Lynda
★ **What** it is. Drawn & Quarterly 2008 209p. Illustration
Grades: 7 8 9 10 11 12 Adult   **818; 741.5**
1. Authorship; 2. Creative writing
978-1-897299-35-7, $24.95; 1-897299-35-4

LC C2007-9047319

Independent cartoonist Lynda Barry presents an unconventional book that encourages its readers to write by using her colorful art and asking questions such as "How are monsters different?" "And how are they the same?" "Can/Do images exist without thinking?" "What is the difference between lying and pretending?" Each question appears with illustrated writing prompts and Barry's own ruminations on the topics. It's a workbook of sorts, but it also exists as a book to be read for itself.

"Every so often a book comes along that surpasses expectations, taking readers on an inspirational voyage that they don't want to leave. This is one such book." SLJ

Batman Adventures Vol. 2: Shadows & Masks
DC Comics 2004 112p. Illustration
Grades: 4 5 6 7 8 9   **741.5; Fic**
1. Batman (Fictional character); 2. Superhero graphic novels; 3. Graphic novels
978-1-4012-0330-2, $6.95

A deadly new gang is threatening Gotham City, and it's up to the Dark Knight Detective to take it down, from the inside. He goes on an undercover mission in this volume.

Baum, L. Frank
L. Frank Baum's The Wizard of Oz: the graphic novel. Puffin Books 2005 176p.
Grades: 3 4 5 6 7 8   **741.5; Fic**
1. Baum, L Frank, 1856-1919 — Adaptations; 2. Fantasy graphic novels; 3. Oz (Imaginary place)
0-14-240471-3, $9.99

LC 2006-273599

This graphic novel adaptation remains true to the story by Baum: Dorothy and her dog Toto are whisked to Oz, where they meet the Tin Woodsman, the Cowardly Lion, and the Scarecrow and they all journey to find the Wizard to grant their desires.

"The black-and-white illustrations are action packed, and the characters, with their Bazooka Joe eyes, combine classic comic touches with the popular manga style. Reluctant readers will gravitate toward the cartoon cover." SLJ

Beagle, Peter
The **last** unicorn. Original story by Peter S. Beagle; adaptation by Peter B. Gillis; art by Renae De Liz. IDW 2011 167p. Illustration
Grades: 6 7 8 9 10   **741.5; Fic**
9780451450524 (rpt), $16.00; 978-1-60010-851-8, $24.99; 1-60010-851-2

"A beloved story is now a graphic novel in this excellent adaptation. . . . Much of the original novel's lyrical language has been included, and readers will be eager to find out if the unicorn will give up her quest for love, or if any of Schmendrick's spells will ever turn out right. . . . The illustrations are graceful and detailed, and inked in warm, glowing colors. This is a worthy successor to the classic novel and film." SLJ

Beatty, Scott
Nightwing: Year One. Scott Beatty & Chuck Dixon, writers ; Scott McDaniel, penciller ; Andy Owens, inker ; Gregory Wright, colorist ; Phil Balsman, letterer, DC Comics 2005 Un Illustration
Grades: 7 8 9 10 11 12 Adult   **741.5; Fic**
1. Batman (Fictional character); 2. Nightwing (Fictional character); 3. Robin (Fictional character); 4. Superhero graphic novels; 5. Teen Titans (Fictional characters); 6. Graphic novels
1-4012-0435-X, $14.99

Dick Grayson was the first Robin, the teen sidekick to the Dark Knight, Batman. Then he became Nightwing and stepped out of Batman's shadow. The story behind that transformation and how it affected Batman, the Teen Titans and Dick himself is explored in this graphic novel. When Batman fires Robin, an angry Dick Grayson is unsure of where to go. On his journey, he receives advice from Superman and aid from Deadman, and makes the decisions that lead him to become a brand new crimefighter.

Beaulieu, Jean Francios
★ The **Wonderful** Wizard of Oz. Marvel Entertainment 2009 192p. Illustration
Grades: 3 4 5 6 7 8 9 10 11 12 Adult   **741.5; Fic**
1. Adventure graphic novels; 2. Authors; 3. Baum, L Frank, 1856-1919
978-0-7851-2921-9, $29.99

A twister picks up the house Dorothy and her dog Toto are in and carries them from Kansas to the land of Oz; the house lands on top of the Wicked Witch of the East, and the Munchkins, who were her slaves, hail Dorothy as a great sorceress. All the girl wants is to get back home to Kansas, but all anyone can say is that she must go to the Emerald City and ask the Great Wizard Oz to send her home. As she travels along the Yellow Brick Road, she meets a scarecrow who wants brains so people won't think he's a dummy, a tin man who wants a heart so he can love, and a great cowardly lion who wants courage so he'll truly be king of the beasts. However, once they reach the Emerald City and each see the Wizard Oz, they learn they must do what no one, including the Wizard himself, could ever do kill the Wicked Witch of the West. Shanower's adaptation of L. Frank Baum's novel keeps all the charm of the original, while Skottie Young's art banishes any lingering images of the old Technicolor movie; Beaulieu's muted color palette works with Young's art, while Eckleberry's lettering adds to an overall effect of magic and wonder. This book will appeal to all ages

Other Oz adapations by Shanower and Young are: The Marvelous Land of Oz; Ozma of Oz; Dorothy and the Wizard in Oz; The Road to Oz; The Emerald City of Oz

Beechen, Adam
Justice League Unlimited: the ties that bind. Written by Adam Beechen and Paul Storrie; illustrated by Carlo Barberi, Rick Burchett and others. DC Comics 2008 Un Illustration (Justice league unlimited)
Grades: 3 4 5 6 7 8 9   **741.5; Fic**
1. Batman (Fictional character); 2. Flash (Fictional character); 3. Green Arrow (Fictional character); 4. Green Lantern (Fictional character); 5. Justice League (Fictional characters); 6. Superhero graphic novels; 7. Superman (Fictional character); 8. Wonder Woman (Fictional character); 9. Graphic novels
978-1-4012-1691-7, $12.99; 1-4012-1691-9

This version of the Justice League was created for the Cartoon Network animated series and features such superheroes as Superman, Batman, Wonder Woman, Green Lantern, the Flash, Hawkgirl, J'onn Jonnz the Martian Manhunter, Power Girl, Green Arrow, and others. The stories collected in this volume include a clash of misunderstanding with Uncle Sam and the Freedom Fighters, a jaunt backwards in time, getting involved in a lovers' spat between super villains whose fight could destroy a city, and more. The book includes superhero vs supervillain fighting action with no bloodshed.

Another title in this series is: Justice league unlimited. Heroes (2009)

Beimler, Hans
The **Middleman**: the Doomsday Armageddon Apocalypse. Javier Grillo-Marxuach and Hans Beimler ; art by Armando Zanker. Viper Comics 2009 68p. Illustration

Grades: 8 9 10 11 12 Adult   **741.5; Fic**
1. Humorous graphic novels; 2. Science fiction graphic novels; 3. Graphic novels
978-0-9802385-8-7, $7.95

This graphic novel picks up right where the ABC Family television series left off, tying up the loose ends left by the series cancellation. The television series is based on the graphic novels, but the art in this book bases the character designs on the television series and is in color. Wendy Watson works with the Middleman to maintain justice and goodness in the world, but right now things have become very complicated. Her boyfriend Tyler now works for Manservant Neville, whose corporation has developed a ... Umaster ... a solar powered cube that's supposed to help people, how is unclear. The Middleman discovers that Neville plans to use the Umaster to take over the world and destroy it so he can remake it the way he wants. And somehow, Neville has managed to counter everything the Middleman and Wendy do to stop him. There is only one possible way to defeat Manservant Neville, but it involves Chac-Mol, a Mayan talisman of great power that demands the ultimate sacrifice of the user. A brief introduction provides enough information for any reader who hasn't seen any of the television series; and the book includes annotations to explain the many pop culture references. It provides closure for fans of the television series, and provides a nice little diversion for fans of the comics series, and there's enough information for readers meeting Wendy Watson and the Middle Man for the first time.

Beka
Dance Class; 3: African Folk Dance Fever. By Béka; illustrated by Crip. Papercutz 2012 47 p. Color illustration
Grades: 5 6 7 8   **741.5/944; Fic**
1. Dance — Africa; 2. Dance — Juvenile fiction; 3. Folk dancing
1597073636; 9781597073639, $10.99

In this book by Béka "Julie, Lucy, and Alia are best friends who share the same passion: dance! In addition to their regular ballet and modern dance classes, the three girls are introduced to a new style of dance ù African folk! Powered by deep percussion-based music, this style is unlike anything they've ever tried before. While the girls enjoy their new art form, problems at home and in the classroom threaten to cause them to have to stop taking their dance classes." (Publisher's note)

Bell, Cece
★ El deafo. Cece Bell; color by David Lasky. Abrams Books 2014 233 p. Color; Illustration
Grades: 3 4 5 6 7   **92; 741.5**
1. Autobiographical graphic novels; 2. Deaf children; 3. Friendship; 4. Hearing aids for children; 5. Schools
1419710206; 9781419710209, $21.95

LC 2013955590
Newbery Honor Book (2015)
Eisner Award: Best Publication for Kids (2015)

"In this . . . graphic novel memoir, author/illustrator Cece Bell chronicles her hearing loss at a young age and her subsequent experiences with the Phonic Ear, a very powerful—and very awkward—hearing aid. The Phonic Ear gives Cece the ability to hear—sometimes things she shouldn't—but also isolates her from her classmates." (Publisher's note)

"Bell's bold and blocky full-color cartoons perfectly complement her childhood stories—she often struggles to fit in and sometimes experiences bullying, but the cheerful illustrations promise a sunny future." Booklist

Bendis, Brian Michael
★ **Takio,** vol. 1. Marvel Icon 2011 Un Illustration
Grades: 5 6 7 8   **741.5; Fic**
1. Sisters; 2. Superhero graphic novels; 3. Graphic novels
978-0-7851-5326-9, $9.95; 0-7851-5326-8
"This entertaining graphic novel features a crunchy and kinetic art style, quick pacing, realistic dialogue, and enough action to appeal to most middle-school readers." Booklist

Takio; vol. 2. Brian Michael Bendis, illustrated by Michael Avon Oeming. Marvel Enterprises 2013 96 p. Color illustration
Grades: 5 6 7 8   **741.5**
1. Sisters — Fiction; 2. Graphic novels
0785165533; 9780785165538, $16.99
"Taki and Olivia are sisters with super-powers! In fact, they are the only ones in the world with super-powers! So obviously, they have to become super heroes! But is the world ready for real-life super heroes? Are the girls ready for the challenge? And will the accident that made them who they are reveal secrets that will change their lives forever?" (Publisher's note)
"Taki and Olivia face down danger in this bright, colorful, action-heavy series, which is unconventionally (and refreshingly) girl-focused." Booklist

Ultimate Fantastic Four Vol. 1: The Fantastic. Writers, Brian Michael Bendis & Mark Millar ; pencils, Adam Kubert ; inks, Danny Miki and John Dell ; colors, Dave Stewart ; letters, Chris Eliopoulos/ Marvel Entertainment 2005 Un Illustration
Grades: 8 9 10 11 12 Adult   **741.5; Fic**
1. Fantastic Four (Fictional characters); 2. Superhero graphic novels; 3. Graphic novels
978-0-7851-1393-5, $12.99
The Ultimate treatment takes the Fantastic Four back to the beginning. High school genius (and bully magnet) Reed Richards suffers at school and also at home with a father who doesn't like his "troublemaking" experiments. When Reed enrolls at a secret government-sponsored school for the most gifted minds in the world, he unwittingly embarks on the journey of a lifetime. This is a story about science, adventure, and above all else, family.

Ultimate Spider-Man: Power & Responsibility. By Brian Michael Bendis (Author), Mark Bagley (Illustrator). Marvel 2009 200 p. Color illustration
Grades: 7 8 9 10 11 12 Adult   **741.5**
1. Spider-Man (Fictional character)
0785139400; 9780785139409, $19.99
In this comic book, by Brian Michael Bendis, illustrated by Mark Bagley, "Peter Parker gains super-powers after being bitten by a spider, loses his likable Uncle Ben to violent crime, and learns once again that 'with great power comes great responsibility.'" (Publisher's note)

Collected edition originally published 2001
Volume 1 of 21

Benjamin, Paul
Hulk: the Hulks take Manhattan; Paul Benjamin, writer ; Juan Santacruz, penciler ; Raul Fernandez, inker ; Wilfredo Quintana, colorist ; Dave Sharpe, letterer. ABDO/Spotlight 2008 Un Illustration
Grades: 3 4 5 6 7 8 9   **741.5; Fic**
1. Hulk (Fictional character); 2. Superhero graphic novels; 3. Hulk (Fictional character); 4. Graphic novels
9781599615462, $21.35
                                                    LC 2008-102
In his quest to remove the Hulk from himself, Bruce Banner hires Jamie Madrox, the Multiplying Man, to help him locate the secret laboratory of a former colleague; he hopes to use the radiation equipment there to make himself normal again. However, one of Madrox's more paranoid selves comes at just the wrong moment, and suddenly there are multiplying Hulks. As Hulk Prime tries to smash all the new Hulks, he makes more of them, and they start to take Manhattan apart. While there's a lot of smashing action and property damage, the book maintains kid-friendly dialogue and avoids graphic violence.
This is a library bound edition of a Marvel Age: The Incredible Hulk comic book issue, with all advertising pages removed.

Hulk: misunderstood monster, v1. Writer, Paul Benjamin; illustrated by David Nakayama and Juan Santacruz. Marvel 2007 Illustration
Grades: 5 6 7 8 9   **741.5; Fic**
978-0-7851-2642-3, $6.99; 0-7851-2642-2
"See how brilliant scientist Bruce Banner was cursed to transform into the rampaging Hulk! Learn why Banner's girlfriend Betty Ross left him, why her father, General 'Thunderbolt' Ross hunts him and why Rick Jones blames himself for creating the monster." (Publisher's note)

Bennett, Anina
Heartbreakers Meet Boilerplate. Anina Bennett and Paul Guinan. IDW Publishing 2005 100p. Illustration
Grades: 8 9 10 11 12 Adult   **741.5; Fic**
1. Adventure graphic novels; 2. Science fiction graphic novels; 3. Graphic novels
1-932382-86-0, $9.99
The pioneering female action heroes, Heartbreakers, team up with the long-lost 19th-century robot, Boilerplate (already a worldwide legend), for a science fiction adventure featuring kung fu clones and robot romance. In this world, clones have won partial human rights, and rogue researchers now race to develop androids that can serve as the new slave workers.

Bertozzi, Nick
Lewis & Clark. First Second 2011 136p. Illustration
Grades: 5 6 7 8   **978; 741.5**
978-1-59643-450-9 (pa), $16.99; 1-59643-450-3 (pa)
                                                    LC 2010-36255
"Bertozzi offers an innovative take on Meriwether Lewis and William Clark's epic journey in this oversized graphic offering. Portraying the arduous trek through rough

terrain and encounters with often unwelcoming natives, sequential panels transport readers alongside the famous duo and their equally renowned translator, Sacagawea, as they travel from St. Louis to the Pacific coast. Within a fictional framework, the narrative weaves in facets of the characters' personalities, including Lewis's tempestuous melancholy, Charbonneau's inept bumbling and Sacagawea's ability to endure this voyage surrounded by her intensely masculine cohorts." (Kirkus)

Shackleton: Antarctic odyssey. Nick Bertozzi. First Second 2014 128 p. Illustration; Map
Grades: 5 6 7 8 9 10   **741.5; 919.89**
1. Antarctica — Discovery and exploration — British; 2. Antarctica — Exploration; 3. Explorers — Great Britain — Biography; 4. Shackleton, Ernest Henry, Sir, 1874-1922; 5. Graphic novels
1596434511; 9781596434516, $16.99

This book by Nick Bertozzi describes how "Ernest Shackleton was one of the last great Antarctic explorers, and he led one of the most ambitious Antarctic expeditions ever undertaken. This is his story, and the story of the dozens of men who threw in their lot with him—many of whom nearly died in the unimaginably harsh conditions of the journey." (Publisher's note)

"Bertozzi eschews all narrative explanation, relying solely on dialogue among the crew and the detailed black-and-white panels to tell the story. The snow- and ice-bound journey is the perfect match for Bertozzi's minimal style—vast stretches of white become gasp-worthy, desolate vistas." Booklist

Best of Josie and the Pussycats Volume 1
Archie Comics 2001 96p. Illustration
Grades: 3 4 5 6 7 8 9 10 11 12 Adult   **741.5; Fic**
1. Adventure graphic novels; 2. Humorous graphic novels; 3. Rock music; 4. Graphic novels
1-879794-07-1, $10.95

This book reprints a selection of stories about rock group Josie and the Pussycats, from their origin in 1963 to 1988. Josie, Melody, and Valerie are the Pussycats, along with their roadie Alan M., their shifty manager Alex, and his conniving sister, Alexandra. They make music, but along the way they also solve mysteries.

Betty and Veronica in the unexpected
ABDO Publishing Group/Spotlight 2007 Un Illustration
Grades: 3 4 5 6 7 8   **741.5; Fic**
1. Andrews, Archie (Fictional character); 2. Cooper, Betty (Fictional character); 3. Humorous graphic novels; 4. Lodge, Veronica (Fictional character); 5. Graphic novels
978-1599612706, $24.21

LC 2006-50265

This volume includes 19 short comics stories featuring friends and rivals Betty and Veronica, Archie Andrews, and all the gang from Riverdale. Among the stories, Veronica decides that she doesn't want to obey signs, even if they get other people into trouble; Betty and Veronica can't stop laughing about something they're too helpless with laughter to tell anybody else, even when it lands them in detention;

Mr. Lodge tries to teach Veronica a lesson that ends up costing him lots of money; and more.

Part of the Archie digest library; this is a revision of Betty and Veronica Digest Magazine issue #120 (June 2001).

Betty and Veronica in Trendsetter
Edited by Nelson Ribeiro & Victor Gorelick.. ABDO Publishing Group/Spotlight 2007 Un Illustration
Grades: 3 4 5 6 7 8   **741.5; Fic**
1. Andrews, Archie (Fictional character); 2. Cooper, Betty (Fictional character); 3. Humorous graphic novels; 4. Lodge, Veronica (Fictional character); 5. Graphic novels
978-1-59961-268-3, $24.21

LC 2006-50552

This is a library bound edition of Betty and Veronica Digest Magazine, issue #115, originally published in March 2001, with all advertisements removed. It includes sixteen short stories about the Riverside teens, focusing mostly on Betty and Veronica, friends and rivals for the affections of Archie, but also including other favorite characters, such as Reggie and Jughead.

Revision of issue no. 118 (March 2001) of Betty and Veronica digest magazine.

Biggs, Gina
Red String, Vol. 1. Dark Horse Comics 2006 192p. Illustration
Grades: 7 8 9 10 11 12   **741.5; Fic**
1. High school life; 2. Romance graphic novels; 3. Graphic novels
978-1-59307-624-5, $9.95

First year high school student Miharu Ogawa can't believe it when her parents tell her they've arranged for her to marry the son of their friends, someone she has never met. They won't marry until they finish school, but the whole idea is repugnant. Then Miharu meets a cute guy and knows she has to fight her parents; but the cute guy she likes is Kazuo Fujiwara, the arranged fiance. Now Miharu just has to deal with gossip at school that hurts her friend Reika, and with her manipulative cousin Karen, who wants Kazuo for herself, and other problems and romantic obstacles. Biggs uses the manga format and manga-influenced art to tell her story of high school romance. Other than one panel of tastefully rendered partial nudity, there's no content to keep this from most middle school age readers.

Biskup, Agnieszka
Exploring Ecosystems with Max Axiom, Super Scientist. Capstone Press 2007 32p. Illustration
Grades: 3 4 5 6 7 8   **577; 741.5**
1. Ecology; 2. Science; 3. Graphic novels
978-0-7368-6842-6 li, $25.26; 978-0-7368-7894-4 (pa)

Max Axiom is a super-cool super-scientist who demonstrates and explains science in ways never before seen in the classroom. Whether shrinking down to the size of an ant or riding on a sound wave, Max does whatever it takes to make science super cool and accessible. This volume explores different ecosystems, from deserts to rain forests,

and includes a glossary and a list of books for further reading.
Part of the Graphic Science series.

A **Journey** into Adaptation with Max Axiom, Super Scientist. Capstone Press 2007 32p. Illustration
Grades: 3 4 5 6 7 8   **591.4; 741.5**
1. Adaptation (Biology); 2. Science; 3. Graphic novels
978-0-7368-6840-2 li, $25.26; 978-0-7368-7892-0 (pa), $7.95

Max Axiom is a super-cool super-scientist who demonstrates and explains science in ways never before seen in the classroom. Whether shrinking down to the size of an ant or riding on a sound wave, Max does whatever it takes to make science super cool and accessible. This volume explores how animals use adaptation to blend into their environment, and includes a glossary and a list of books for further reading.
Part of the Graphic Science series.

The **powerful** world of energy with Max Axiom, super scientist. Capstone Press 2009 32p. Illustration
Grades: 2 3 4 5 6 7   **531; 741.5**
1. Force and energy; 2. Motion; 3. Graphic novels
978-1-4296-2337-7, $26.60; 978-1-4296-2337-3 (pa), $7.95
LC 2008-29651

The cartoon super scientist Max Axiom explains energy for young readers. Energy is the ability to do work (which is motion against resistance). The book explains kinetic and potential energy, the different forms of energy, the law of conservation of energy, sources of energy, and touches on the negative aspects of burning fossil fuels for energy. It also discusses the search for other sources of energy, particularly renewable, clean sources. Back matter in the book includes more energy facts, a glossary, reading list, and an index.
Part of the Graphic Science series

The **solid** truth about states of matter with Max Axiom, super scientist. Capstone Press 2009 32p. Illustration
Grades: 2 3 4 5 6 7   **530.4; 741.5**
1. Matter; 2. Graphic novels
978-1-4296-2339-1, $26.60; 978-1-4296-3451-9 (pa), $7.95
LC 2008-28694

The cartoon super scientist Max Axiom explains matter, which is anything that has mass and takes up space. The book progresses from the basic building blocks of matter, which are atoms, describing how movement of the atoms and molecules determine the state of matter—solid, liquid, or gas. Back matter in the book includes more facts about the states of matter, a glossary, reading list, and an index.
Part of the Graphic Science series

Understanding Global Warming with Max Axiom, Super Scientist. Capstone Press 2007 32p. Illustration
Grades: 3 4 5 6 7 8 9   **363.7; 741.5**
1. Greenhouse effect; 2. Graphic novels
978-1-4296-0139-9, $25.26
LC 2007002269

This book uses the graphic novel format to follow the adventures of super scientist Max Axiom as he explains the science behind the issue of global warming. The book

includes additional facts and a list of books for further reading.
Part of the Graphic Science series.

Understanding viruses with Max Axiom, super scientist. Capstone Press 2009 32p. Illustration
Grades: 2 3 4 5 6 7   **579.2; 741.5**
1. Bacteria; 2. Viruses; 3. Graphic novels
978-1-4296-3453-3 (pa), $7.95; 978-1-4296-2338-4, $26.60
LC 2008-29654

The cartoon super scientist Max Axiom explains viruses, tiny pathogenic microorganisms that cause various diseases, from colds to influenza to polio and more. Max goes submicroscopic to give readers a closer look at different viruses and how they function. The book also describes how the human body fights off infections, and how scientists and physicians have worked to develop vaccines to prevent infections. The book also talks about bacteria and how they're different from viruses. Back matter in the book includes more facts about bacteria and viruses, a glossary, reading list, and an index.
Part of the Graphic Science series

Black, Holly
The **Good** Neighbors; book one: Kin. Art by Ted Naifeh. Graphix 2008 117p. (The Good Neighbors)
Grades: 7 8 9 10 11 12   **741.5; Fic**
1. Fairies; 2. Fantasy graphic novels; 3. Graphic novels
978-0-439-85562-4, $16.99; 0-439-85562-4
LC 2007-49008

Sixteen-year-old Rue has grown up in a world much like ours, except that the human world and the world of faerie have co-existed, as good neighbors, for a long time. When Rue's mother disappears and her professor father becomes the main suspect in the murder of a young woman, Rue's life turns strange. As she digs for information to figure out what is happening in her life, Rue discovers that her mother is a faerie and has returned to that realm because of a broken promise.

"This sophisticated tale is well served by Naifeh's stylish, angular illustrations." SLJ

Other titles in this series are: Kith (2009); Kind (2010)

Blackman, Haden
Star Wars Omnibus: X-Wing Rogue Squadron Volume 1. Haden Blackman and Michael A. Stackpole. Dark Horse Comics 2006 Un Illustration
Grades: 7 8 9 10 11 12 Adult   **741.5; Fic**
1. Adventure graphic novels; 2. Science fiction graphic novels; 3. Star Wars; 4. Graphic novels
978-1-59307-572-9, $24.95

The greatest star fighters of the Rebel Alliance become the defenders of a New Republic in this massive collection of stories featuring Wedge Antilles, hero of the Battle of Endor, and his team of ace pilots known throughout the galaxy as Rogue Squadron. Meet the Rogues for the first time and learn the fate of the galaxy immediately after the events of Return of the Jedi as the Rebellion's best pilots battle remnants of the Empire wherever its ugly agenda of fear and domination appears. Along with X-Wing Rogue Squadron: The Phantom Affair, this jam-packed volume contains never before collected material, including Star Wars X-Wing Rogue Leader #1-3, Star Wars X-Wing Rogue Squadron: The Rebel Opposition #1-4, Star Wars X-Wing Rogue Squadron: The Phantom Affair #1-4, and Star Wars Handbook: X-Wing Rogue Squadron.

Star Wars: Clone Wars Adventures Volume 2. Written by Haden Blackman, Welles Hartley ; art by the Fillbach Brothers. Dark Horse Comics 2004 Un Illustration
Grades: 5 7 8 9 10 11 12   **741.5; Fic**
1. Adventure graphic novels; 2. Science fiction graphic novels; 3. Star Wars; 4. Graphic novels
1-59307-271-6, $6.95
In the rolling asteroid rings above a remote planet, General Obi-Wan Kenobi and Anakin Skywalker play a deadly game of cat and mouse against Separatist droid fighters - and a squadron of highly skilled human pilots who have pledged their guns to Count Dooku. Also in this volume, Jedi Master Luminara Unuli and her Padawan Barriss Offee race against time to evacuate farmers and their families before the droid forces of General Grievous overrun their village. When Barriss and her squad of clone troopers are caught in the path of the enemy army, only fast thinking and steel resolve can save the day. And Jedi Master Mace Windu goes solo to foil a sinister Separatist plot. These stories take place approximately five months after the Battle of Geonosis.

Blaylock, Josh
Misplaced: Somewhere Under the Rainbow. Devil's Due Publishing 2005 Un Illustration
Grades: 7 8 9 10 11 12   **741.5; Fic**
1. Adventure graphic novels; 2. Science fiction graphic novels; 3. Graphic novels
1-932796-04-5, $10.95
Alyssa is from Realm 77, a hi-tech utopia where those who question authority aren't treated kindly. Even stranger, the only person who does is Alyssa. Ostracized from her peers since childhood, and subjected to numerous medical tests by the mysterious Elders, Alyssa grows more and more intolerant of the Realm. When it's discovered she's developing incredible powers, Alyssa escapes to Earth to live a normal life in a small college town, but the Elders won't allow it. It's only when she's forced to return to the realm that her powers truly manifest. All she wanted to do was hang out, go to some clubs, and be normal." But that's not Alyssa's destiny.

Penguin Bros.. Devil's Due Publishing 2004 Un Illustration
Grades: 7 8 9 10 11 12   **741.5; Fic**
1. Humorous graphic novels; 2. Penguins; 3. Superhero graphic novels; 4. Graphic novels
1-932796-20-7, $10.95
Three teenage penguins living in Chill City, Antarctica are the ones chosen to become their city's heroes, and granted Super Powers. There's only one problem - they'd rather go to concerts, hang with girlfriends, and play video games. It's sleigh cars, super powers and homework in the Penguin Bros. As Blaylock explains at the end of the book, he created the Penguin Bros. when he was six years old - and he has the drawings to prove it.

Bogaert, Harmen Meyndertsz van den
Journey into Mohawk Country. As written by H.M. van den Bogaert, with artwork by George O'Connor and color by Hilary Sycamore. First Second 2006 144p. Illustration
Grades: 8 9 10 11 12   **973.2**
1. New York (State) — History — 1600-1775, Colonial period; 2. United States — History — 1600-1775, Colonial period; 3. Graphic novels
1-59643-106-7, $17.95
In 1634, young Dutch trader Harmen Meyndertsz van den Bogaert, several companions, and some native guides traveled deep into what is now New York State, trading tools and weapons and trying to establish new tribal friendships to bolster Dutch trade. van den Bogaert kept a journal throughout his journeys. O'Connor has kept the original text and conducted extensive research in order to make his illustrations as authentic as possible.

Boldman, Craig
Archie Day by Day Volume 1. Archie Comics 2003 96p. Illustration
Grades: 3 4 5 6 7 8 9 10 11 12 Adult   **741.5; Fic**
1. Andrews, Archie (Fictional character); 2. Humorous graphic novels; 3. Graphic novels
1-879794-16-0, $10.95
Archie and his pals have been comics' most celebrated teenage humor characters for over 60 years, since 1941. Now for the first time, selections from Archie's worldwide syndicated newspaper strip are collected in this volume. This black and white edition includes a selection of daily strips from the mid-1990s, chronicling life in Riverdale, USA.

Bonneval, Gwen de
William and the lost spirit. Gwen de Bonneval; illustrated by Matthieu Bonhomme; colors by Walter; translation, Anne Collins Smith and Owen M. Smith; [lettering by Dennis Pacheco]. Graphic Universe 2013 152 p.
Grades: 4 5 6 7   **Fic; 741.5/944**
1. Families — Fiction; 2. Fantasy fiction — Juvenile fiction; 3. Folklore — Fiction; 4. Knights and knighthood — Fiction; 5. Middle Ages — Fiction; 6. Mythology — Fiction; 7. Voyages and travels — Fiction; 8. Voyages and travels — Juvenile fiction; 9. Graphic novels
1467708070; 9780761385677; 9781467708074, $9.95
LC 2012008115
In this book, as "William sets out to find his father (who might be dead, or lost, or both), he is joined by a knight, a troubadour, and a very unusual goat. Soon he enters a mysterious world that is populated with an amazing cast of characters, including Prester John, dog-faced men, and headless people whose faces are on their chests." (School Library Journal)

Booth, Jack
Kazuma's Quest. Harcourt Achieve/Steck-Vaughn 2007 48p. Illustration
Grades: 3 4 5 6 7 8   **741.5; Fic**
1. Samurai; 2. Graphic novels
978-1-4190-3215-8, $8.99
Kazuma is a young samurai who sets out to confront his father's murderer and reclaim his family's sword. The

famous swordsman Matayemon offers to help him. Will they be able to outsmart their enemies" This is historical fiction in graphic novel format with facts about the samurai interspersed throughout the story in prose sections.
Part of the Timeline Graphic Novels series.

Nomad King. Harcourt Achieve/Steck-Vaughn 2006 48p. Illustration
Grades: 3 4 5 6 7 8   **741.5; 92; Fic**
1. Khan, Genghis, ca 1162-1227; 2. Mongolia — History; 3. Graphic novels
978-1-4190-3201-1, $8.99
In the sparse, windswept land of Mongolia in the late 12th century, Temujin becomes leader of his tribe at the age of nine. Over the years, this ruthless leader battles warring tribes for power then unites them under his rule, becoming Genghis Khan. He gradually extends his empire beyond Mongolia and China; will he be able to take over the world" This historical graphic novel includes prose intervals that provide more information about the Mongols and about Genghis Khan.
Part of the Timeline Graphic Novels series.

Raiders of the Seas. Harcourt Achieve/Steck-Vaughn 2006 48p. Illustration
Grades: 3 4 5 6 7 8   **741.5; Fic**
1. Adventure graphic novels; 2. Pirates; 3. Graphic novels
978-1-4190-3207-3, $8.99
Nicholas Bloom is a young sailor who lands in bad company when he joins the ship of a pirate named Blackbeard. Together they sail the seas, raiding and plundering. When Nick learns more about Blackbeard's evil ways, he must decide what to do next. This historical graphic novel includes prose intervals that give information about pirates and the differences between them and privateers.
Part of the Timeline Graphic Novels series.

Bowen, Carl
20,000 leagues under the sea. Retold by Carl Bowen ; illustrated José Alfonso Ocampo Ruiz. Stone Arch Books 2008 72p. Illustration
Grades: 4 5 6 7 8 9   **741.5; Fic**
1. Adventure graphic novels; 2. Science fiction graphic novels; 3. Submarines
978-1-4342-0447-9, $23.93; 978-1-4342-0497-4 (pa), $9.95
Scientist Pierre Aronnax and his servant set sail to help hunt a sea monster threatening ships, but they and master harpooner Ned Land discover that the monster is actually a submarine, the Nautilus. The submarine's leader, Captain Nemo, takes the three men captive and they journey under the sea, where they see many wonders; but they must each decide whether they should trust Nemo, who bears a bitter secret, or try to escape. This graphic novel adaptation of Verne's classic adventure novel uses simple language to help reluctant and struggling readers understand the story.
Part of the Graphic Revolve series

The **strange** case of Dr. Jekyll and Mr. Hyde. By Robert L. Stevenson; retold by Carl Bowen; illustrated by Daniel Perez. Stone Arch Books 2009 72p. Illustration
Grades: 4 5 6 7 8 9 10   **741.5; Fic**

1. Horror graphic novels; 2. Science fiction graphic novels; 3. Graphic novels
978-1-4342-0754-8, $23.93
                                                LC 2008-6248
"Scientist Dr. Henry Jekyll believes every human has two minds: one good and one evil. He develops a potion to separate them from each other. Soon, his evil mind takes over, and Dr. Jekyll becomes a hideous fiend known as Mr. Hyde." (Publisher's note)
Part of the Graphic Revolve series

Boyd, David
Beware the Vikings. Harcourt Achieve/Steck-Vaughn 2006 48p. Illustration
Grades: 3 4 5 6 7 8   **741.5; Fic**
1. Adventure graphic novels; 2. Vikings; 3. Graphic novels
978-1-4190-3205-9, $8.99
When Thorfinn the Viking is found guilty of murder, he is exiled as an outlaw. He says goodbye to his son, Snorri, and sets sail with his band of men. But things don't work out as he has planned when his crew discovers a stowaway, and it's Snorri. This fictional graphic novel includes intervals of prose giving information about Vikings and their customs
Part of the Timeline Graphic Novels series.

The **Hidden** Message. Harcourt Achieve/Steck-Vaughn 2007 48p. Illustration
Grades: 3 4 5 6 7 8   **741.5; Fic**
1. Great Britain — History — 1485-1603, Tudors; 2. Mystery graphic novels; 3. Graphic novels
978-1-4190-3216-5, $8.99
The famous writer Christopher Marlowe does secret work as the Queen's spy. But when the young actor Jasper Kyd decides to take revenge against this master, William Shakespeare, things become complicated and dangerous. This is historical fiction in graphic novel format with facts about Elizabethan period theater, Shakespeare, and Marlowe interspersed throughout the story in prose sections.
Part of the Timeline Graphic Novels series.

Marco Polo and the Roc. Harcourt Achieve/Steck-Vaughn 2006 48p. Illustration
Grades: 3 4 5 6 7 8   **741.5; Fic**
1. Adventure graphic novels; 2. China — History; 3. Graphic novels
978-1-4190-3203-5, $8.99
When Marco Polo visit's the Emperor of China, Kublai Khan, he is given an impossible task. He has to find a mythical bird, the Roc, and bring one of its eggs back to the Great Khan. Can he do it? What will happen if he fails? This historical fiction graphic novel has touches of fantasy and includes facts about Marco Polo, Kublai Khan, Chinese exploration, the legend of the Roc, and speculation that Polo made up his stories.
Part of the Timeline Graphic Novels series.

Napoleon's Last Stand. Harcourt Achieve/Steck-Vaughn 2006 48p. Illustration
Grades: 3 4 5 6 7 8   **741.5; Fic**
1. Adventure graphic novels; 2. Napoleon I, Emperor of the French; 3. Graphic novels
978-1-4190-3208-0, $8.99

Charlotte Bonaparte helps her famous uncle Napoleon escape from the island of Elba. As Napoleon prepares to go to war, Charlotte makes her own plans. This historical fiction graphic novel depicts some of the events of the Battle of Waterloo, so there is some battlefield violence. The book includes prose intervals that provide more information about Napoleon, his English opponent, the Duke of Wellington, the battle, and the death of Napoleon.

Part of the Timeline Graphic Novels series.

Pearl Harbor. Harcourt Achieve/Steck-Vaughn 2006 48p. Illustration

Grades: 3 4 5 6 7 8   **741.5; Fic**
1. Adventure graphic novels; 2. World War, 1939-1945 — Pearl Harbor (Oahu, Hawaii), Attack on, 1941; 3. Graphic novels
978-1-4190-3220-2, $8.99

Alison is the lonely twelve-year-old daughter of a U.S. Navy captain. When she meets Jasmine, a Japanese girl her age, who is the daughter of Alison's Japanese godfather, the two become fast friends. But it is December 1941 in Pearl Harbor, Hawaii, and what happens on December 7th is the ultimate test of friendship. This historical fiction graphic novel includes scenes from the attack on Pearl Harbor; it also includes prose intervals that provide additional facts about the Japanese, Hawaii, a listing of ships lost and casualties, and information on the U.S. nuclear bombing of Hiroshima in 1945.

Part of the Timeline Graphic Novels series.

Braun, Eric
    Booker T. Washington: Great American Educator. Capstone Press 2005 32p. Illustration

Grades: 3 4 5 6 7 8 9   **92; 741.5**
1. African Americans — Biography; 2. Biographical graphic novels; 3. Educators; 4. Washington, Booker T, 1856-1915; 5. 6. Graphic novels
0-7368-4630-1, $25.26

LC 2005001727
In graphic novel format, this book tells the life story of Booker T. Washington and his accomplishments toward promoting the education of African Americans. The book includes additional facts about Washington, a bibliography, and a list of books for further reading.

Part of the Graphic Biographies series.

    Cesar Chavez: Fighting for Farmworkers. Capstone Press 2006 32p. Illustration

Grades: 3 4 5 6 7 8 9   **741.5; 331.8; 92**
1. Biographical graphic novels; 2. Chavez, Cesar, 1927-1993; 3. United Farm Workers of America; 4. Graphic novels
0-7368-4631-X, $25.26

LC 2005006460
This book uses the comic book format to recount the highlights of the life of labor leader Cesar Chavez and the boycotts he led to gain fair working conditions for farm workers. It includes additional information, a glossary, a list of books for further reading, and more.

Part of the Graphic Library, Graphic Biographies series.

The **Story** of Jamestown. Capstone Press 2006 32p. Illustration

Grades: 3 4 5 6 7 8 9   **741.5; 975.5**
1. Jamestown (Va) — History; 2. Graphic novels
0-7368-4967-X, $25.26

LC 2005013592
This book uses the comic book format to tell the story of Jamestown, the first permanent English settlement in North America. It includes additional information, a glossary, a list of books for further reading, and more.

Part of the Graphic Library, Graphic History series.

Bravo, Emile
    ★ **Beauty** and the Squat Bears. Illustrations by the author. Yen Press 2011 Un Illustration

Grades: 3 4 5 6 7 8 9   **741.5; Fic**
1. Bears; 2. Fairy tales; 3. Graphic novels
978-0-316-08362-1, $14.99

LC 2010-941434
When the queen's magic mirror declares that Snow White is the fairest in the land, the young princess flees the kingdom, and she finds herself at the cabin belonging to the seven squat bears. They don't want a princess, especially when she refuses to earn her keep by cleaning the cabin. What to do? Well, they need to find a prince, so they send one of the squat bears out to find a suitable prince. He meets a blue bird who claims to be an enchanted prince, they cause trouble at the ball where Cinderella is supposed to captivate Prince Charming, run into the Beast, and they all run afoul of the Fairy Godmother, who is not amused. Bravo mashes up a bunch of fairy tales in a way that will amuse anyone who has a good sense of humor and sometimes loses patience with all those young girls waiting for a handsome prince to save them. While this is written for younger readers, adults will also have fun reading this book.

Originally published in France under the title, La Belle aux ours nains.

Courtesy of Yen Press

Brennan, Michael
    Electric Girl. AiT/PlanetLar 2000 168p. Illustration

Grades: 5 6 7 8 9 10   **741.5; Fic**
1. Humorous graphic novels; 2. Graphic novels
0-9703555-0-5, $9.95

Virginia is an average suburban girl except for her electric powers, which cause her to zap things all the time, and except for her invisible gremlin "friend" Oogleeoog, who has been with her since she was born. The stories go back and forth in time from her early childhood to her teen years and back again as the reader learns about Virginia's powers and how they affect her life.

"Facial expressions and body postures are fluid and evocative, while the verbal text is easy to read." SLJ

Other titles is this series are: Electric Girl vol. 2 (2002); Electric Girl vol. 3 (2005)

Briggs, Raymond

★ **Ethel** & Ernest: A True Story. Pantheon 2001 104p. Illustration

Grades: 4 5 6 7 8 9 10 11 12 Adult   **741.5**

1. Biographical graphic novels; 2. Graphic novels

978-0-375-71447-4, $15.00

This is Raymond Briggs's loving depiction of his parents' lives from their chance first encounter in the 1920s until their deaths in the 1970s. Ethel and Ernest were solid members of the English working class, part of the generation that lived through the most tumultuous years of the twentieth century. They met during the Depression—she working as a maid, he as a milkman—and the reader follows them as they court and marry, make a home, raise their son, and cope with the dark days of World War II. Briggs portrays how his parents succeeded, or failed, in coming to terms with the events of their rapidly shifting world—the advent of radio, television, and telephones; the development of the atomic bomb; the moon landing; the social and political turmoil of the sixties.

Britt, Fanny

Jane, the fox & me. [written by] Fanny Britt; [illustrated by] Isabelle Arsenault; translated by Christine Morelli and Susan Ouriou. Pgw 2013 101 p.

Grades: 5 6 7 8 9   **Fic**

1. Alienation (Social psychology) — Fiction; 2. Teenage girls — Fiction

1554983606; 9781554983605, $19.95

Written by Fanny Britt, illustrated by Isabelle Arsenault, and translated by Christine Morelli and Susan Ouriou, this "graphic novel reveals the casual brutality of which children are capable, but also assures readers that redemption can be found through connecting with another, whether the other is a friend, a fictional character or even, amazingly, a fox." (Publisher's note) It "centers on Hélène, ostracized by her former friends and now a loner at school." (Horn Book Magazine)

"Britt's well-constructed narrative is achieved sensitively through Arsenault's impressionistic artwork. . . . An elegant and accessible approach to an important topic." Booklist

Broome, John

Showcase Presents: The Elongated Man Volume 1. Written by John Broome and Gardner Fox ; Art by Carmine Infantino, Neal Adams, Murphy Anderson and Gil Kane. DC Comics 2006 560p. Illustration

Grades: 6 7 8 9 10 11 12 Adult   **741.5; Fic**

1. Batman (Fictional character); 2. Elongated Man (Fictional characters); 3. Flash (Fictional character); 4. Green Lantern (Fictional character); 5. Robin (Fictional character); 6. Superhero graphic novels; 7. Graphic novels

978-1-4012-1042-7, $16.99

Ralph Dibny is the Elongated Man, a self-taught superhero who has harnessed the power of the exotic gingo fruit and attained the ability to stretch himself to fantastic lengths. As the only costumed hero whose identity has been revealed to the world, Elongated Man travels the globe with his adoring wife Sue, solving mysteries and gaining renown for his singular elastic talent. In these stories, originally published from 1960 to 1968 and reprinted here in black and white, Dibny sometimes teams up with the Flash, Batman and Robin, Green Lantern, and Zatanna. Ralph and Sue Dibny were at the heart of the Identity Crisis, so readers might want to see their early adventures.

Brown, Don

★ **Drowned** City: Hurricane Katrina and New Orleans. By Don Brown. Houghton Mifflin Harcourt 2015 96 p. Color; Illustration

Grades: 7 8 9 10

741.5; 363.34

1. Hurricane Katrina, 2005; 2. New Orleans (La) — History; 3. New Orleans (La) — History — 21st century

054415777X, $18.99; 9780544157774, $18.99

LC 2015458266

Courtesy of Houghton Mifflin Harcourt

Robert F. Sibert Honor Book (2016)

In this work of graphic nonfiction by Don Brown, "when the calamitous category five Katrina's gusty winds hurl into the city of New Orleans, most people have evacuated the city. The rest of the scared, stubborn, and simply stranded must face the dangers of what is to come—broken levees quickly swelling the city with water. Many families seek safety on their roofs or via floatation devices as a way to row to safety. However, some are not as fortunate." (Children's Literature)

"Brown's narrative is clear and precise, relying exclusively on data and statistics interspersed with quotes from residents, rescue crews, journalists, and news reports. Alone, the text might lack impact, but combined with the haunting imagery, it hits readers like a punch in the gut." Booklist

Includes bibliographical references

★ The **great** American dust bowl. By Don Brown. Houghton Mifflin Harcourt 2013 80 p.

Grades: 5 6 7 8 9   **978**

1. Droughts — United States — History; 2. Dust Bowl Era, 1931-1939 — Juvenile literature; 3. Dust storms; 4. Dust storms — History

0547815506; 9780547815503, $18.99

Author Don Brown presents a "graphic novel of one of America's most catastrophic natural events: the Dust Bowl. On a clear, warm Sunday, April 14, 1935, a wild wind whipped up millions upon millions of these specks of dust to form a duster, a savage storm on America's high southern plains." (Publisher's note)

"In this bleak yet compelling graphic-novel-style glimpse at the Dirty Thirties, Brown crisply paces the narrative with fascinating glimpses of the sociological and geological causes of the Dust Bowl. The color brown is a recurring theme here, as Brown relies, aptly, almost entirely on shades of brown throughout. Primary source material is used liberally, as characters speak directly to the reader, documentary-style." (Horn Book)

Brown, Jeffrey
Incredible Change-Bots. Top Shelf Productions 2007 Un Illustration
Grades: 8 9 10 11 12 Adult   741.5; Fic
1. Humorous graphic novels; 2. Robots; 3. Science fiction graphic novels; 4. Graphic novels
978-1-891830-91-4, $15
Far away in outer space, the Incredible Change-Bots live on the planet Electronocybercircuitron. The Awesomebots and the Fantasticons have lived in relative harmony, until Shootertron, the leader of the Fantasticons, decides to rig the election to rule the planet. The Awesomebots declare war, and over the years the Change-Bots destroy their planet. They then come to Earth, where they continue their fighting, each group gaining their own human allies. Brown has done a fun send-up of the Transformers with this story, and while there is some violence, there is very little in the way of bad language.

★ **Star** Wars: Jedi Academy. Jeffrey Brown; [edited by] Rex Ogle. Scholastic, Inc 2013 160 p. Illustration (Star Wars: Jedi Academy)
Grades: 3 4 5 6 7   741.5; Fic
1. Middle schools — Fiction; 2. Outer space — Fiction; 3. Star Wars
0545505178; 9780545505178, $12.99; 9780545609999
LC 2013931939
In this book, by Jeffrey Brown, "Roan Novachez thought he was destined to attend Pilot Academy Middle School, just as his older brother and father did. His dreams are crushed when he is rejected by Pilot Academy and accepted into a sketchy new school called Coruscant Jedi Academy.... Confused and struggling to keep up, Roan tries to fly under the radar and passes the time drawing comics of his daily life at his strange boarding school." (Booklist)
"While it might be disappointing for those familiar with this world to see scant representation of beloved characters, it makes the book an easy starting point for new fans. There are plenty of references to other elements (the T-16 Skyhopper and Jedi training remotes, for example) for diehards to get excited about." SLJ
Other titles in this series are: Return of the Padawan (2014); The Phantom Bully (2015)

Star Wars: Jedi academy 2: Return of the Padawan. Jeffrey Brown; [edited by] Rex Ogle. Scholastic 2014 176 p. Illustration (Star Wars: Jedi academy)
Grades: 3 4 5 6 7   741.5
1. Life on other planets — Fiction; 2. Middle schools — Fiction; 3. School stories; 4. Star Wars; 5. Star Wars fiction
0545621259; 9780545621250, $12.99
LC 2014931163
"After surviving his first year at Jedi Academy, Roan Novachez thought his second year would be a breeze. He couldn't have been more wrong. Roan feels like he's drifting apart from his friends, and it's only made worse when Roan discovers he's not the amazing pilot he thought he'd be. When the school bullies take him under their wing, he

decides they aren't so bad after all—or are they?" (Publisher's note)
"Roan is a very sympathetic main character, and readers will feel his pain and laugh at his misfortune in equal measure. Roan's hand-lettered journal entries alternate with short paneled sequences and 'screenshots' of academy message boards and other ephemera." Kirkus

Star Wars: Jedi Academy; 3: The Phantom Bully. By Jeffrey Brown. Scholastic Press 2015 176 p. Illustration (Star Wars: Jedi Academy)
Grades: 3 4 5 6 7   741.5; Fic
1. Middle schools — Juvenile fiction; 2. School stories — Juvenile fiction; 3. Star Wars films — Juvenile fiction
0545621267; 9780545621267, $12.99
"It's hard to believe this is Roan's last year at Jedi Academy. He's been busier than ever learning to fly (and wash) starships, swimming in the Lake Country on Naboo, studying for the Jedi obstacle course exam, and tracking down dozens of vorpak clones—don't ask. But now, someone is setting him up to get in trouble with everyone at school, including Yoda. If he doesn't find out who it is, and fast, he may get kicked out of school!" (Publisher's note)
"The third graphic novel in the Jedi Academy series turns out to be a love story, although it takes the characters a while to realize it. ... [B]y the close of this high jinks-filled year, every student at the academy gets a satisfying ending, even the bullies and troublemakers." Kirkus

Brubaker, Ed
Batman: Turning Points. By Greg Rucka, Ed Brubaker, and Chuck Dixon. DC Comics 2007 124p. Illustration
Grades: 8 9 10 11 12 Adult   741.5; Fic
1. Batgirl (Fictional character); 2. Batman (Fictional character); 3. Joker (Fictional character); 4. Robin (Fictional character); 5. Superhero graphic novels; 6. Graphic novels
978-1-4012-1360-2, $14.99
Throughout the long comic book career of Batman, Gotham policeman James Gordon has been an almost constant presence. The two men's alliance and friendship formed an important element in Batman's work. This book traces the relationship from Batman's early years, to the first time Gordon meets Robin, to the time shortly after Gordon's daughter Barbara, the Batgirl, was shot by the Joker, to the Batman who took over after Bane broke Batman's back, to come back full circle when a man Gordon and Bats stopped from killing hostages in the first story returns to Gotham City.
Originally published as Batman Turning Points issues #1-5.

Brusha, Joe
Discovery channel top 10 dangerous sharks. Silver Dragon Books 2010 120p. Illustration
Grades: 3 4 5 6 7 8 9   741.5
1. Sharks; 2. Graphic novels
978-0-9827507-2-8, $9.99
This book presents true stories about human encounters with ten of the deadliest sharks: lemon shark, blue shark, hammerhead shark, sand tiger shark, grey reef shark, mako shark, oceanic whitetip, tiger shark, great white shark, and

bull shark. Anyone who watches Discovery Channel's Shark Week programs probably knows the stories related in this book, but most middle grade students who like to read about sharks will want to read these stories anyway. Each section starts out with a two-page spread giving facts about the particular shark, including an "attack file" listing the number of recorded attacks and the number of unprovoked fatalities. Artists Anthony Spay, Shawn McCauley, Marcio Abreu, Agustin Alessio, German Nobile, HG Young, Gabriel Rearte, and Shawn Van Briesen illustrated the stories, with colors by Andrew Elder and John Hunt, and letters by Jim Campbell.

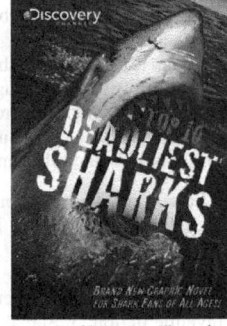

Courtesy of Discovery Channel Books

Bugs Bunny: What's Up, Doc?
DC Comics 2005 112p. Illustration
Grades: 3 4 5 6 7 8 9   **741.5; Fic**
1. Bugs Bunny (Fictional character); 2. Humorous graphic novels; 3. Graphic novels
1-4012-0516-X, $6.99
This volume collects stories about the wisecracking rabbit from the archives of Looney Tunes, sure to tickle the funny bones of both children and the childlike as Bugs goes up against Daffy Duck, Marvin the Martian, Elmer Fudd, and other unfortunates.

Bullock, Mike
Lions, tigers and bears volume 2: betrayal. Image Comics 2008 Un Illustration
Grades: 3 4 5 6 7 8 9   **741.5; Fic**
1. Adventure graphic novels; 2. Fantasy graphic novels; 3. Graphic novels
978-1-58240-930-6, $14.99
Joey and Courtney's winter wonderland is shattered when the Big Cats of the Night Pride arrive with terrible news from the Stuffed Animal Kingdom. Now all that stands between the horrible Beasties and children everywhere are Joey, Courtney, and their imaginations. For the evil Valthraax and his minions have taken over the Crystal Castle, imprisoned King Bear, and plot to capture all children who aren't being protected by the Stuffed Animal Militia. There is some fighting violence between the Night Pride and their allies against the Beasties.

Lions, tigers, and bears, vol. 1: Fear and pride. [by] Mike Bullock and Jack Lawrence. Image Comics 2006 128p. Illustration
Grades: 2 3 4 5 6   **741.5; Fic**
1. Adventure graphic novels; 2. Graphic novels
1-58240-657-X, $12.99
When Joey Price has to move away from his grandmother, she gives him a new set of stuffed animals that she says will guard him from nightmares. And one night, he

discovers that the stuffed animals are real, and unfortunately, so are the Beasties, the nightmares in his closet

Timothy and the transgalactic towel. Silverline Books/Image Comics 2009 104p. Illustration
Grades: 3 4 5 6 7 8   **741.5; Fic**
1. Father-son relationship; 2. Humorous graphic novels; 3. Science fiction graphic novels; 4. Graphic novels
978-1-60706-021-5, $16.99
Timothy is having a hard time concentrating on school; his mother is gone and his father has to go away on long business trips, leaving Timothy behind. His father always tries to bring home a special gift, but this last trip was to Hawaii and he brings home a multicolored beach towel. Timothy thinks it's totally lame, and he gets so angry with his father that he shuts himself away in his room. But, there's something different about that towel: it starts talking to him, and then it whisks him out his bedroom window and into outer space, where Timothy meets his action hero Dash Lightrider. He also finds Dash and his crew in the middle of a space war with the evil blade ships from Piratus, and they also encounter a star dragon. Timothy discovers the star dragon wants to find his son, who was kidnapped by the bad guys on Piratus, so now he leads Dash and the Zoom Rangers on a rescue mission. Bullock includes a message about father/son relationships and forgiveness along with the fun adventure. Metcalf's colorful art makes the book look like a fun television cartoon.

Burgan, Michael
The **Boston** Massacre. Capstone Press 2006 32p. Illustration
Grades: 3 4 5 6 7 8 9   **741.5; 973.3**
1. Boston Massacre, 1770; 2. Graphic novels
0-7368-4368-X, $25.26
LC 2005006462
This book uses the comic book format to tell the story of the Boston Massacre and its aftermath. It includes additional information, a glossary, a list of books for further reading, and more.
Part of the Graphic Library, Graphic History series.

The **Curse** of King Tut's Tomb. Capstone Press 2005 32p. Illustration
Grades: 3 4 5 6 7 8 9   **741.5; 932**
1. Tutankhamen, King of Egypt; 2. Tutankhamen, King of Egypt — Tomb; 3. Graphic novels
0-7368-3833-3, $22.60
LC 2004020452
This volume follows the discovery and excavation of King Tutankhamen's tomb and the myth of the curse that afflicted those involved in the tomb's exploration. The book includes additional information, a glossary, a list of books for further reading, and more.
Part of the Graphic Library, Graphic History series.

The **Great** San Francisco Earthquake and Fire. Capstone Press 2007 32p. Illustration
Grades: 3 4 5 6 7 8 9   **741.5; 979.4**
1. Earthquakes — California; 2. San Francisco Earthquake and Fire, Calif., 1906; 3. Graphic novels
978-1-4296-0155-9, $26.25
LC 2007014929

This book uses the graphic novel format to tell of the San Francisco earthquake of 1906 and the subsequent fires that nearly destroyed the city. The book includes additional facts and a list of books for further reading.
Part of the Graphic Library Disasters in History series

Muhammad Ali: American Champion. Capstone Press 2007 32p. Illustration
Grades: 3 4 5 6 7 8 9   **741.5; 796.8; 92**
1. Ali, Muhammad; 2. Boxing; 3. Graphic novels
978-1-4296-0153-5, $26.25
                                              LC 2006103432
This book uses the graphic novel format to tell the life story of dynamic heavyweight boxing champion Muhammad Ali, who gained fame for his boxing skills, political views, and humanitarian efforts. The book stops short of showing Ali being rendered almost speechless by advanced Parkinson's Disease in the last couple of years. The book includes additional facts and a list of books for further reading.
Part of the Graphic Biographies series.

Busiek, Kurt
Shockrockets: we have ignition. [by] Kurt Busiek, Stuart Immonen, and Wade Von Grawbadger. Dark Horse Comics 2004 160p. Illustration
Grades: 8 9 10 11 12   **741.5; Fic**
1. Adventure graphic novels; 2. Science fiction graphic novels; 3. Graphic novels
1-59307-129-9, $14.95
"In this graphic novel vision of 2087, Alejandro Cruz lives in a postwar world. An alien invasion has been averted but at a high cost, and people are rebuilding. Alejandro loves his family, but he doesn't want to get caught in the same dead-end jobs that his family members have had to take to survive. Then he accidentally becomes the newest pilot for the Shockrockets, the cream-of-the-crop, high-tech air squadron, and his entire life changes." Booklist
"Busiek brings the same touch of character he used in the "Astro City" series (DC Comics), making this title as much about Cruz's choices and challenges as about lasers and extreme fighter pilot moves." SLJ

The **wizard's** tale. [by] Kurt Busiek and David Wenzel. DC Comics 1998 141p. Illustration
Grades: 6 7 8 9   **741.5; Fic**
1. Graphic novels
1-56389-589-7, $19.95
Bafflerog Rumplewhisker is the most pitiful excuse for an evil wizard that ever lived, for all his evil spells end up doing good. When Lord Grimthorne, head of the Darksome Council, orders him to find the Book of Worse, the reluctant Bafflerog heads out with the toad, Gumpwort, to find it. Author Busiek and artist Wenzel have crafted a tale that honors the marks of high fantasy even while having fun with it.

Butzer, C. M.
★ **Gettysburg:** the graphic novel. Bowen Books/HarperCollins 2009 80p. Illustration
Grades: 3 4 5 6 7 8 9 10 11 12   **741.5; 973.7**
1. American speeches; 2. Gettysburg (Pa), Battle of, 1863; 3. Gettysburg address: Lincoln, Abraham; 4. Lincoln,

Abraham; 5. Lincoln, Abraham — Juvenile literature; 6. Lincoln, Abraham — Work — Gettysburg address; 7. Lincoln, Abraham, 1809-1865; 8. Graphic novels
978-0-06-156176-4, $16.99; 978-0-06-156175-7 (pa), $8.99
                                              LC 2008-10657
In the summer of 1863, everyone knew that the Battle of Gettysburg would be an important battle that could determine the course of the War Between the States, the Civil War. What they didn't know was who would prevail. Butzer uses primary sources to play out the battle that lasted three days and caused tremendous casualties, the aftermath that nearly overwhelmed the town of Gettysburg, and the effort to build the monument to commemorate the fallen. He uses a somber blue and gray wash in his illustrations. Lincoln's famous Gettysburg Address was only 271 words long and appear in their entirety, against images of the nation's past. Some panels depicting the violence of the battles, and particularly the dead on the battlefield, could be disturbing for sensitive younger readers; but this battle was ugly and overwhelming in its violence. Butzer includes extensive end notes to explain what he depicted, and to note the sources of the dialog and narration.

Byrne, Eugene
★ **Darwin:** a graphic biography. By Eugene Byrne; illustrated by Simon Gurr. Smithsonian Books 2013 96 p. Illustration
Grades: 5 6 7 8 9 10 11 12 Adult
B; 576.8; 576.8/2092
1. Darwin, Charles, 1809-1882; 2. Evolution; 3. Evolution (Biology); 4. Natural selection; 5. Graphic novels
1588343529; 9781588343529, $9.95
                    LC 2012951786

Courtesy of Smithsonian Books

This work of graphic nonfiction by Eugene Byrne and Simon Gurr presents a "summary of [Charles] Darwin's life and achievement. . . . Darwin was an indifferent student . . .until he received an invitation to take a voyage that 'would change the course of history.'. . .The animals he encountered seemed so different . . . that he theorized that if it weren't a matter of different conditions that resulted in such 'transmutation,' they might well have had a different creator." (Kirkus Reviews)
Includes bibliographical references.

Byrne, John
Alpha Flight Classics Vol. 1. Writer & artist, John Byrne ; colorist, Andy Yanchus ; letterers, Joe Rosen [and others].. Marvel Entertainment 2007 224p. Illustration
Grades: 7 8 9 10 11 12 Adult   **741.5; Fic**
1. Superhero graphic novels; 2. Graphic novels
978-0-7851-2746-8, $24.99
Guardian, Shaman, Snowbird, Aurora, Northstar, Puck, Marrina, and Sasquatch are Canada's premiere super human strike force, Alpha Flight. The team was brought together by

Department H for the greater good of humankind. They battle injustice and evil forces across the globe - including the Master of the World, Tundra, Kolomaq, Deadly Ernest and Delphine Courtney. The book features cameos by the Sub-Mariner, Invisible Woman, Wolverine and Nightcrawler.

Superman: The Man of Steel Vol. 1. Dick Giordano, illustrator. DC Comics 1991 132p. Illustration
Grades: 8 9 10 11 12 Adult   **741.5; Fic**
1. Superhero graphic novels; 2. Superman (Fictional character); 3. Graphic novels
978-0930289287, $14.99
This reprint of a 1986 book retells and reinvents the origin and early adventures of the Man of Steel. Superman begins his ascension to iconic hero as he leaves Smallville and becomes Metropolis's revered protector and guardian. Featuring the Man of Steel's legendary first encounters with Lex Luthor, Lois Lane, and Batman, this book also includes a deadly battle with Bizarro, a fateful encounter with Lana Lang, and Superman's astonishing discovery of his Kryptonian heritage.

Cabarga, Leslie
Harvey Comics Classics Volume Two: Richie Rich, the Poor Little Rich Boy. Dark Horse Comics 2007 480p. Illustration
Grades: 3 4 5 6 7 8 9 10 11 12 Adult   **741.5**
1. Humorous graphic novels; 2. Richie Rich (Fictional character); 3. Graphic novels
978-1-59307-848-5, $19.95
This volume reprints 125 Richie Rich stories, taken from the comic's beginnings in 1953 through the 1960s. While most of the stories appear here in black and white, the book includes a 64-page section of color reprints. Richie Rich and his friends Gloria, Freckles, and Peewee enjoy not-so-everyday adventures, including playing "tycoon" in the new offices of Rich's father. Some stories feature rich cousin and antagonist Reggie.

Harvey comics classics voulme three: hot stuff: the little devil. Dark Horse Comics 2008 480p. Illustration
Grades: 3 4 5 6 7 8 9 10 11 12 Adult   **741.5; Fic**
1. Devil; 2. Humorous graphic novels; 3. Graphic novels
978-1-59307-914-7, $19.95
Hot Stuff: the Little Devil was created for Harvey Comics in 1957, and right away became the starring character in his own comic book series. This volume collects 110 stories from the Hot Stuff comics originally published from 1957 through 1966; the comic book actually remained in print until the 1980s. Back in 1957, having a little red hot devil as a main character caused some controversy, but most young children who read the comics had no problem with him. These stories involve Hot Stuff and his friends in comical misadventures just like any kid could get into, such as having to babysit a younger cousin, trying to outdo a visiting ghost, going to see a doctor (of course, Hot Stuff has to see a witch doctor).
Part of the Harvey Comics Classics series

Cabot, Meg
Avalon High: Coronation Vol. 1: the Merlin prophecy. Created and written by Meg Cabot; illustrated by Jinky Coronado. Tokyopop/HarperTeen 2007 126p. Illustration
Grades: 7 8 9 10 11 12   **741.5; Fic**
1. Arthur, King; 2. Fantasy graphic novels; 3. High school students; 4. School stories; 5. Graphic novels
978-0-06-117707-1, $9.99
Being a new student at Avalon High has been exciting for Ellie, to say the least—she's an honor student, a star on the track team, and dating the super-hot class president, Will. Who also happens to be the alleged reincarnation of King Arthur. Ellie couldn't be happier to have Will in her life, but she's also worried that his estrangement from his parents is tearing him apart. To make matters worse, Will's doubt that he really is King Arthur could prevent the Merlin Prophecy—an age of enlightenment—from occurring. Can Ellie convince Will to believe in something that even she isn't sure about? And more importantly, can she get him to give his parents another chance? This global manga title continues Cabot's Avalon High story.

Avalon High: Coronation volume 2: Homecoming. Illustrated by Jinky Coronado. Tokyopop/HarperTeen 2008 Un Illustration
Grades: 7 8 9 10 11 12   **741.5; Fic**
1. Arthurian romances; 2. Fantasy graphic novels; 3. Romance graphic novels; 4. Graphic novels
978-0-06-117709-5, $9.99
At Avalon High School, football star Will is the reincarnated King Arthur, but he won't believe it. His brother Marco did, and he nearly killed Will and Ellie (who is the Lady of the Lake). Now kicked out of his house, Will has been staying with Ellie and her family, but things aren't going so great. Mr. Morton is convinced that if Will won't accept his destiny, the world will end. Marco has been released from the hospital, and he obliquely threatens Ellie to leave Will alone about the whole reincarnation thing. But she's having nightmares, and she doesn't know what to do. Except to try to reconcile Will with his parents.

Caldwell, Ben
Star Wars: Clone Wars Adventures Vol. 1. Dark Horse Comics 2004 Un Illustration
Grades: 5 6 7 8 9 10   **741.5; Fic**
1. Adventure graphic novels; 2. Science fiction graphic novels; 3. Star Wars; 4. Graphic novels
1-59307-243-0, $6.95
On the night-world of Nivek, Obi-Wan Kenobi and Anakin Skywalker must first overcome the limitations of fighting in the dark before they can take on the dreaded Shadowmen! Meanwhile, Jedi Masters Mace Windu and Saesee Tiin discover that push can come to shove when using the Force to fight battledroids. And, fresh from leading an underwater assault against Separatist forces on the water planet of Mon Calamari, Jedi Master Kit Fisto and his remaining clone troops reach the surface to find a new threat awaiting them. These original stories use the animated style of the Cartoon Network's "Clone Wars" cartoons and are set during the time between Star Wars Episodes 2 and 3, approximately five months after the Battle of Geonosis.
Volume 1 of 10

The **Wizard** of Oz. Written by L. Frank Baum; adapted by Ben Caldwell. Sterling Children's Books 2012 32 p. Illustration (All-Action Classics)
Grades: 4 5 6   **741.5; 741.5/973**
1. Fantasy graphic novels; 2. Oz (Imaginary place); 3. Tornadoes — Fiction; 4. Voyages and travels; 5. Graphic novels; 6. Baum, L. Frank — Adaptations
1402731531; 9781402731532, $7.95
LC 2013363513
This book is a graphic novel adaptation of L. Frank Baum's classic tale "The Wizard of Oz." Author and illustrator Ben Caldwell "follows Baum's original novel rather than the iconic film. The heroes are pursued by the Kalidah, 'horrific beasts, with heads like tigers and bodies like bears,' and the famous path the four friends follow, as in the original, is called the 'road of golden bricks.'" (Publishers Weekly)

Callen, Kerry
Halo and Sprocket vol. 2: Natural creatures. SLG Publishing/Amaze Ink 2008 Un Illustration
Grades: 8 9 10 11 12 Adult   **741.5; Fic**
1. Angels; 2. Humorous graphic novels; 3. Robots; 4. Graphic novels
978-1-59362-131-5, $8.95
Halo the angel and Sprocket the robot live with a young woman named Katie. Their mission: to try to figure out the human race. They are puzzled by Katie's desire for privacy when she's taking a bath; they don't understand why she'll accept being clawed and bitten by a cute little kitten but won't hold a skink; and playing a trivia game causes Halo to show anger. When Halo transforms Sprocket into a human so he can experience what eating food is all about, the temporarily human Sprocket drives Katie crazy with questions about bodily functions such as burping, sneezing, and more.

Halo and Sprocket: Welcome to Humanity. SLG Publishing/Amaze Ink 2003 Un Illustration
Grades: 7 8 9 10 11 12   **741.5; Fic**
1. Humorous graphic novels; 2. Graphic novels
0-943151-81-3, $12.95
What do an extremely powerful angel, a socially inexperienced robot, and a young, single woman have in common" Apparently, aside from the house they share, not very much! Logic, metaphysics, and human nature collide as Katie tries to educate both angel and robot about humans, philosophy, and such things as the Tooth Fairy. The book includes some slightly raunchy humor.

Cammuso, Frank
Knights of the lunch table: the dodgeball chronicles. Graphix 2008 141p.
Grades: 3 4 5 6   **741.5; Fic**
1. Humorous graphic novels; 2. School stories; 3. Graphic novels
978-0-439-90322-6 (pa), $9.99; 0-439-90322-X (pa)
Artie King's family has moved and now he has to start at a new school, Camelot Middle School. Dodgeball is the big game at Camelot, and the Horde is a champion team; the Horde members are also the worst bullies in the school. . . . Artie immediately gets into trouble with Joe, the leader of the Horde. . . . However, he manages to open the broken old locker . . . [which] provides mysterious, useful stuff, such as a lunch. Joe challenges Artie to a dodgeball game; Artie has new friends Percy and Wayne who'll help him, and then he meets Gwen. And science teacher Mr. Merlyn is also on his side.

"Arthurian legend gets an update for young readers in this outstanding graphic novel. . . . The funny, fast-paced tale of young Arthur's quest to defeat the bullies stands well on its own. The appealing illustrations are full of color, action, and life." SLJ
Followed by: Knights of the lunch table: the dragon players (2009)

★ **Knights** of the lunch table: the dragon players. Scholastic/Graphix 2009 127p.
Grades: 3 4 5 6   **741.5; Fic**
1. Arthurian romances — Adaptations; 2. Conduct of life; 3. Contests; 4. Humorous graphic novels; 5. Schools; 6. Graphic novels
978-0-439-90323-3 (pa), $9.99; 0-439-90323-8 (pa)
LC 2008-51463
Artie King may have won the dodgeball game against the school bullies, but life is not easy. The new challenge comes with the dueling robot tournament at school; it's all part of Dragon Day, and The Horde has won every year by cheating—they force the smartest kid in school to design and build their robot. This year, they've done it to Percy. Circumstances force Artie's hand and willy nilly, he has entered the tournament. Seeking an edge, they go to Evo, a mysterious techno wiz kid who can build any gadget; the problem for Artie is, is he cheating by getting help from Evo" Cammuso's bright, cartoony art and schoolyard version of Arthurian legend provides lots of fun action as well as making readers think about ethics
Followed by: Knights of the lunch table: the battling bands (2011)
Sequel to: Knights of the lunch table: the dodgeball chronicles (2008)

Camper, Cathy
★ **Lowriders** in space; book 1. By Cathy Camper; illustrated by Raul Gonzalez III. Chronicle Books 2014 112 p. Color; Illustration (Lowriders)
Grades: 4 5 6 7 8   **741.5**
1. Automobiles — Fiction; 2. Competition (Psychology) — Fiction; 3. Friendship — Fiction; 4. Lowriders; 5. Lowriders — Fiction; 6. Mechanics (Persons); 7. Mexican Americans — Fiction; 8. Space vehicles; 9. Graphic novels
9781452121550, $22.99; 1452121559
LC 2013040709
Cathy Camper "introduces readers to Lupe Impala, Flapjack Octopus, and Elirio Malaria, three friends who love working with cars and dream of having their own garage shop. One day they see an opportunity to achieve their goal—a car competition. When they start working on a lowrider to prepare it for the competition, an out-of-this world journey begins." (School Library Journal)
"Raul's snazzy panels—impressively drawn in only red, blue, and black ballpoint pen on tea-stained paper—resemble an amped-up Mighty Mouse cartoon rendered in anarchic yet skillful doodles. It's a joyfully

explosive style, and it perfectly matches the Latino characters and barrio setting." Booklist

Caniff, Milton
The **Complete** Terry and the Pirates, 1934-1936. IDW Publications 2007 368p. Illustration
Grades: 6 7 8 9 10 11 12 Adult **741.5**
1. Adventure graphic novels; 2. Graphic novels
978-1-60010-100-7, $49.99
This first volume in a projected series to collect the entire Milton Caniff run of the comic strip Terry and the Pirates covers the years 1934 through 1936. This volume includes the Sunday color comics as well as the black and white dailies. In this volume, the Sunday strips told a different story from the daily strips, so the Sunday strips come first. The Sundays and dailies were merged into one storyline sometime in 1936. Young Terry Lee, his adult pal Pat Ryan, their sidekick Connie, and such villains as Captain Judas and Captain Blade, along with the Dragon Lady, provide readers with lots of high adventure. Some racial stereotypes, common for the 1930s, occur.

Carey, Mike
★ **Re-Gifters**. Written by Mike Carey; art by Sonny Liew and Marc Hempel. DC Comics/Minx 2007 148p. Illustration
Grades: 7 8 9 10 11 12 **741.5; Fic**
1. High school students; 2. Martial arts; 3. Romance graphic novels; 4. School stories; 5. Graphic novels
978-1-4012-0371-9 (pa), $9.99; 1-4109-0371-X (pa)
"Jen Dik Seong, or Dixie, is having trouble getting her ki focused. Normally an outstanding hapkido student, she finds that her crush on classmate Adam is affecting her ability to fight. This is not good, as the national competition is fast approaching, and her parents expect her to do well.... Dixie makes a series of poor choices. She decides to spend the entry fee . . . on an elaborate birthday present for Adam. . . . This is a terrific read that features complex characters dealing with internal and external conflicts that make them believable and endearing. Lively black-and-white illustrations bring action and emotion to the story." SLJ

Spellbinders: Signs & Wonders. Writer, Mike Carey ; pencils, Mike Perkins ; inks, Drew Hennessy. Marvel Entertainment 2005 Un Illustration
Grades: 7 8 9 10 11 12 Adult **741.5; Fic**
1. Magic; 2. Mystery graphic novels; 3. Supernatural graphic novels; 4. Graphic novels
0-7851-1756-3, $7.99
Getting through high school is hard enough without having to watch your back the whole time, but magic can give you a real edge over the competition. When 15-year-old Kim Vesco moves from Chicago to Salem, MA, she finds that the local student body is divided into rival factions of witches and non-witches, with both sides bidding for her allegiance. And if that weren't enough, an unknown force seems to want her... dead. Between the tribal loyalties of the schoolyard and the brutal, fight-or-die logic of the mage-war, Kim has to steer a course that will keep her alive until she can take the fight back to her enemy and reveal the true identity of someone she thought she already knew: herself.

Carre, Lilli
The **fir-tree**. It Books/HarperCollins 2009 Un Illustration
Grades: 3 4 5 6 7 8 9 10 11 12 Adult **741.5; Fic**
1. Andersen, Hans Christian, 1805-1875 — Adaptations; 2. Christmas; 3. Christmas trees; Graphic novels
978-0-06-178236-7, $14.99
A young fir-tree only wants to grow tall; it's never satisfied and doesn't notice the sunlight and clean air. It never rejoices in anything, but grumbles and complains. When it sees some trees being cut down and taken away, it wonders what it's missing. The birds tell of seeing the trees inside homes, beautifully decorated, and it becomes jealous. When it does grow tall and beautiful, a woodsman comes along and cuts it down, hauling it to town to become a Christmas tree in a house. It enjoys the family playing around the tree at Christmas, but after the holiday, the family throws it into a storeroom. Will the tree ever see its forest again? Lilli Carre uses delicate coloring and illustrations to adapt Andersen's sad Christmas story. Although this is suitable for young readers, adults may better appreciate the tragedy and Carre's idiosyncratic illustrations her people have long, loopy arms.

Carroll, Emily
★ **Through** the woods. Emily Carroll. Margaret K. McElderry Books 2014 208 p. Color; Illustration
Grades: 8 9 10 11 12 Adult **741.5**
1. Horror fiction; 2. Short stories; 3. Graphic novels
9781442465961, $14.99; 9781442465954, $21.99
LC 2013030969
Eisner Award: Best Graphic Album—Reprint (2015)
Ignatz Award: Outstanding Artist (2015)
In this book, Emily Carroll "crafts five unsettling tales in graphic-novel format inspired by common folkloric themes—from wolves in the woods to peculiar visitors to dark possessions. In 'Our Neighbor's House,' three sisters who find themselves alone in a cabin are taken, one by one, in the middle of the night by a smiling stranger. . . . 'The Nesting Place' focus on malevolent spirit possession." (Horn Book Magazine)
"All the tales in Carroll's debut graphic novel are fairly standard ghost stories, but it is her eerie illustrations—popping with bold color on black, glossy pages—that masterfully build terrifying tension and a keep-the-lights-on atmosphere." Booklist

Carroll, Lewis
New Alice in Wonderland, masterpiece edition. Antarctic Press 2007 Un Illustration
Grades: 4 5 6 7 8 9 **741.5**
1. Adventure graphic novels; 2. Fantasy graphic novels; 3. Humorous graphic novels; 4. Graphic novels
978-0-9787725-8-1, $14.95
Espinosa (The Courageous Princess) adapts Lewis Carroll's classic tale into a graphic novel full of pop culture references (check out the Mad Hatter, for instance). It's still the original story, which starts when the daydreaming Alice sees a rabbit checking his pocket watch and runs after him, only to find herself in a strange world with bizarre creatures.

Casey, Joe
Godland Volume 1: Hello, Cosmic!. Image Comics 2006 Un Illustration
Grades: 8 9 10 11 12 Adult   **741.5; Fic**
1. Adventure graphic novels; 2. Science fiction graphic novels; 3. Superhero graphic novels; 4. Graphic novels
1-58240-712-6, $14.99
The cosmic superhero epic is back and this collection is chock-full of all the "cosmic" one could ask for. Experience the glory of Commander Adam Archer, the enigmatic alien Maxim, the wacky Basil Cronus, the evil Discordia, the confusing Freidrich Nickelhead and that's just scratching the surface. The storytelling and art bring back the kind of story that Stan Lee and Jack Kirby did, with fun superhero action and very little grim, gritty content.

Castellucci, Cecil
Janes in love. By Cecil Castellucci and Jim Rugg; with lettering by Rob Clark Jr. and gray tones by Jasen Lex. DC Comics/Minx 2008 176p. Illustration (Plain Janes)
Grades: 7 8 9 10 11 12   **741.5; Fic**
1. Art; 2. Friendship; 3. High school students; 4. Romance graphic novels; 5. School stories; 6. Graphic novels
978-1-4012-1387-9 (pa), $9.99; 1-4012-1387-1 (pa)
"The second book of the PLAIN Janes series returns to the four Janes of suburban town Kent Waters and their public art "attacks" as People Loving Art in Neighborhoods (PLAIN). This time the story line is sprinkled with bits of romance as the various Janes struggle to approach their love interests for dates to the school dance and the main Jane applies for an art grant." Publ Wkly
"Castellucci deftly deals with a number of serious issues, including anxiety and depression, mortality, body image, gay relationships, and community activism. Fortunately, they never weigh down the narrative: this is a sweet, quirky story with some uplifting (though never pedantic) messages. Rugg's clean, crisp illustrations are the perfect accompaniment." SLJ

The **Plain** Janes. [illustrated by] Jim Rugg. DC Comics/Minx 2007 Un Illustration
Grades: 7 8 9 10 11 12   **741.5; Fic**
1. Art; 2. Friendship; 3. High school students; 4. School stories; 5. Graphic novels
978-1-4012-1115-8, $9.99
After a bomb attack in Metro City, Jane's parents move to suburban Kent Waters, where Jane feels lost. Then she meets three other Janes at the "reject" table in the high school lunch room, and she convinces them to help her form their own secret club: P.L.A.I.N. "People Loving Art in Neighborhoods." However, their "art attacks" cause the authorities to think that P.L.A.I.N. is a terrorist group.
"The art, inspired by Dan Clowes' work, is absolutely engaging. Packaged like manga this is a fresh, exciting use of the graphic-novel format." Booklist
Another title about the Janes is: Janes in love (2008)

Cauvin, Raoul
The **bluecoats** no. 1: Robertsonville Prison. Cinebook Ltd. 2008 48p. Illustration
Grades: 5 6 7 8 9 10   **741.5; Fic**

1. Adventure graphic novels; 2. Humorous graphic novels; 3. United States — History — 1861-1865, Civil War — Prisoners and prisons; 4. Graphic novels
978-1-90546-071-7, $11.95
Sergeant Chesterfield and Corporal Blutch are Union soldiers during the Civil War; Blutch tends to be lazy, and Chesterfield always seems to be getting him out of trouble; but after one battle, they're both in trouble when they're captured by Confederate troops and are force-marched to Robertsonville Prison. They constantly get into trouble with a soldier and camp guard named Cockroach, and Chesterfield leads multiple attempts to escape the prison. Then when they succeed, they're wearing stolen Confederate uniforms and ultimately end up in a Union prison camp. Prison camps aren't normally subjects of humor, but the humor in this book is reminiscent of the old television series Hogan's Heroes, which was set in a German prisoner of war camp.

Chabot, Jacob
The **Mighty** Skullboy Army. Dark Horse Comics 2007 Un Illustration
Grades: 6 7 8 9 10 11 12   **741.5; Fic**
1. Humorous graphic novels; 2. Graphic novels
978-1-59307-629-0, $9.95
Skullboy may be an elementary school student, but he's already the CEO of an evil corporation (so he tells everyone), and he has the Mighty Skullboy Army. Actually, he has a robot, Unit 1, and a super-intelligent monkey, Unit 2 (who is easily distracted). He keeps trying to get out of attending school, but his efforts result in silly mayhem and sometimes backfire on him.

Chadwick, Paul
★ **Star** Wars: Empire Volume Two: Darklighter. Doug Wheatley, artist; Tomas Giorello, artist. Dark Horse Comics 2004 Un Illustration
Grades: 7 8 9 10 11 12 Adult   **741.5; Fic**
1. Adventure graphic novels; 2. Science fiction graphic novels; 3. Star Wars; 4. Graphic novels
1-56971-975-6, $17.95
Before Luke Skywalker, the Rebel Alliance had another hero: Biggs Darklighter. For the first time, the full story of Luke's boyhood friend is revealed; from his departure from Tatooine to attend the Imperial Academy, to his decision to lead a mutiny against the Empire and join the Rebellion, to the fateful attack on the Death Star.

Chantler, Scott
★ The **annotated** Northwest Passage. Oni 2007 268p. Illustration
Grades: 8 9 10 11 12 Adult   **741.5; Fic**
1. Adventure graphic novels; 2. Canada — History — 0-1763 (New France); 3. Graphic novels
978-1-932664-61-4, $19.95
It is the year 1755. Charles Lord, an acclaimed explorer and adventurer from England, has taken a desk job governing Fort Newcastle, a remote frontier trading post in Canada. On the eve of his retirement, Charles longs for a return to past glories and a second chance at his great unfulfilled quest, to find the fabled Northwest Passage. When Fort Newcastle is captured by the brutal French

privateer Guerin Montglave and his men, Charles and a few survivors flee into the Canadian wilderness. This edition includes the first three installments of Northwest Passage, along with annotations by the creator. It includes violence and some mild harsh language.

The **captive** prince. Scott Chantler. Kids Can Press 2012 116 p. Color illustration
Grades: 4 5 6 7   **741.5; 741.5/971; Fic**
1. Adventure fiction; 2. Thieves — Fiction; 3. Graphic novels
9781554537778, $8.95; 9781451782806, $17.95 ; 1554537762; 9781554537761, $17.95
This children's adventure book by Scott Chantler is the "third title of the . . . Three Thieves graphic novel series[.] Dessa, Topper and Fisk are still running from the Queen's Dragons and trying to find Dessa's missing twin brother. But when Dessa inadvertently rescues a prince — putting kingdoms at stake and love on the line — the adventure quickly becomes a royal mess!" (Publisher's note)

The **king's** dragon. Scott Chantler. Kids Can Press 2014 112 p. Illustration; Color (Three Thieves)
Grades: 3 4 5 6   **741.5; Fic**
1. Fantasy graphic novels; 2. Knights and knighthood
9781554537792, $8.95; 1554537797
In this graphic novel written and illustrated by Scott Chantler, "royal knight Capt. Drake . . . briefly catches up with his quarry, Dessa, a young circus acrobat hobbled (but not much) by a broken leg, and also looks back on his early days as a member of the elite but corrupt Dragons." (Kirkus Reviews)
"Black-and-white art among color signifies the flashback scenes, making the transitions easy to follow. The backstory will be satisfying to fans." Horn Book

Tower of treasure. Kids Can Press 2010 112p. Illustration (Three thieves)
Grades: 3 4 5 6   **741.5**
1. Acrobats and acrobatics — Fiction; 2. Adventure graphic novels; 3. Circus — Fiction; 4. Thieves — Fiction; 5. Graphic novels
978-1-55453-414-2, $17.99; 1-55453-414-3; 978-1-55453-415-9 (pa), $8.95; 1-55453-415-1 (pa)
"As an acrobat in a traveling circus, 14-year-old orphan Dessa Redd flies through the air with ease. Still, she is weighed down by troubling memories. But when her ragtag circus troupe pulls into the city of Kingsbridge, Dessa feels a tickle of hope. Maybe here in the royal city she will finally find her twin brother—or the mysterious man who snatched him away when they were just children. Meanwhile, Topper, the circus juggler, recruits Dessa and the circus strongman, Fisk, for the job of robbing the royal treasury." (Publisher's note)
Other titles in this series are:The sign of the black rock (2011); The captive prince (2012); The king's dragon (2014); Pirates of the silver coast (2014); The dark island (2016)

Chastain, Grant
The **Gwaii**. Arcana Comics 2009 Un Illustration
Grades: 3 4 5 6 7 8   **741.5; Fic**

1. Adventure graphic novels; 2. Sasquatch; 3. Graphic novels
978-1-897548-36-3, $14.95
In the Canadian wilderness, the young Gwaii (a Sasquatch) named Tanu seeks his mother, who was captured by loggers whose company is destroying the land. One of the men has a young son, who doesn't like what his dad and coworkers are doing. Meanwhile, Tanu's new friend Jaadaa, who saved him from the loggers, helps the young Gwaii as they venture far from home, pursuing the humans and determined to save Tanu's mother. O'Reilly has based this story on the Haida people who live in Haida Gwaii (Queen Charlotte Island), off the west coast of British Columbia in Canada; Tanu and his people are fictional, but their names are all derived from the Haida language. This colorful adventure story also carries a strong message about respecting nature.

Chen, Wei Dong
Monkey King: Birth of the Stone Monkey Vol. 01. JR Comics 2012 172 p.
Grades: 3 4 5 6   **Fic; 741.5/951**
1. Buddhism; 2. Chinese mythology; 3. Legendary characters; 4. Graphic novels
8994208690; 9788994208695, $29.27
This book "follows the adventures of Sun Wu Kong, born from a stone on Spring Mountain and given the title of Handsome Monkey King, who seeks to learn the secret of eternal life. Under the tutelage of the Buddhist Master Puti, Sun Wu Kong becomes incredibly powerful, but his hubris grows until he has run afoul of the gods, who dispatch an army to Spring Mountain to subdue the Monkey King, who has declared himself the 'Emperor of Heaven'" (Publisher's note)
Volume 1 of 20

Monkey King: Journey to the West. Created by Wei Dong Chen; illustrated by Chao Peng. JR Comics 2012 173 p. Illustration
Grades: 5 6 7   **Fic; 741.5/951**
1. Chinese mythology; 2. Graphic novels
8994208712; 9788994208718, $29.27
This is the third volume in Wei Dong Chen's Monkey King series, a graphic novel series based on the Chinese classical literature novel "Journey to the West." In "the first volume, Sun Wu Kong is born from a stone and goes on a quest of find the secret of eternal life. In succeeding volumes the Monkey King steals the heavenly peaches and is imprisoned by Buddha for 500 years." (Library Media Connection)

Monkey King: The Bane of Heaven. Created by Wei Dong Chen; illustrated by Chao Peng. Jr Comics 2012 174 p. Illustration
Grades: 5 6 7   **741.5/951; Fic**
1. Chinese mythology; 2. Graphic novels
8994208704; 9788994208701, $29.27
This is the second volume in Wei Dong Chen's Monkey King series. Here, "Sun Wu Kong is named emperor of heaven, [and] begins to make himself comfortable among the gods, and quickly wears out his welcome." The series is a retelling of the classical Chinese work "Journey to the West." (Booklist)

Cherrywell, Steph

★ **Pepper** Penwell and the land creature of Monster Lake. [written and drawn by Steph Cherrywell].. SLG Publishing 2011 Un Illustration
Grades: 7 8 9 10 11 12 Adult   **741.5; Fic**
1. Horror graphic novels; 2. Humorous graphic novels; 3. Monsters; 4. Mystery graphic novels; 5. Graphic novels
978-1-59362-205-3, $14.95

British teenager Pepper Penwell prefers solving mysteries over school work and wants to be a detective like her father. When the latest school boots her out, Pepper takes on the case of a missing drum majorette named Lucy. Accompanied by her brother Alex, who inexplicably (it was some kind of accident) has the body of a bird, Pepper travels to Monster Lake, a town trying to establish itself as a tourist attraction based on its local monster, which is a land creature. In the town, Pepper meets strange people, any of whom could be guilty of kidnapping the wealthy and annoying Lucy. However, after Pepper does find Lucy, there's still the matter of the land monster, which is all too real. British slang (arse, bum) provides the mildly harsh language.

Chiba, Tomohiro

Mobile Suit Gundam: Lost War Chronicles Volume 1. Art by Masato Natsumoto. Tokyopop 2006 Un Illustration
Grades: 8 9 10 11 12 Adult   **741.5; Fic**
1. Adventure graphic novels; 2. Manga; 3. Mecha manga; 4. Graphic novels
159816-213-6, $9.99

The One Year War between the Earth Federation and the Principality of Zeon has begun—and the newest Mobile Suits are tested for battle. Captain Matt Healy leads his team into dangerous territory as the leader of a Special Forces Experimental Ken Bederstadt is a Foreign Legion Lieutenant working in alliance with Zeon. These two heroes are trying to keep everyone alive...for tomorrow.

Chilman-Blair, Kim

What's up with Bill?: Medikidz explain epilepsy. Rosen Publishing Group, Inc. 2010 40p. Illustration (Superheroes on a medical mission)
Grades: 3 4 5 6 7 8 9
616.85; 741.5
1. Epilepsy; 2. Graphic novels
978-1-4358-3533-7, $29.25. 1-4358-3533-6
LC 2009-29785

Courtesy of Rosen Pubishing Group

After teenage Bill suffers a seizure, he and his unnamed sister meet the Medikidz, a team of superheroes who help people with health problems. They take the two teens into the brain to explain how it works and what happens when a person has epilepsy. The book uses a lot of humor, especially with Gastro, who loves to eat and does things like pass gas. Chilman-Blair is a physician, and the book was reviewed by an expert for medical accuracy.

The book includes a glossary of the medical terms used, a list of books for further reading, and contact information for some agencies that deal with epilepsy.

Includes glossary and bibliographical references

Part of the Superheroes on a Medical Mission series.

Chmakova, Svetlana

Awkward. By Svetlana Chmakova. Yen Press 2015 210 p. Illustration; Color
Grades: 5 6 7 8
741.5
1. Clubs — Fiction; 2. Clubs — Juvenile fiction; 3. Middle schools — Fiction; 4. Middle schools — Juvenile fiction; 5. Popularity — Fiction; 6. Popularity — Juvenile fiction; 7. School stories; 8. Schools — Fiction; 9. Schools — Juvenile fiction; 10. Graphic novels
0316381306; 0316381322; 9780316381307; 9780316381321, $24

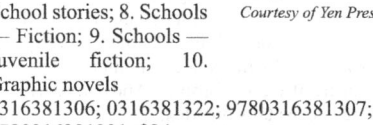

Svetlana Chmakova

Courtesy of Yen Press

LC 2015945195

In this middle grade book, by Svetlana Chmakova, "protagonist Peppi is fantastically imperfect. . . . She is the new girl at Berrybrook Middle School and is having a hard time fitting in because of her struggles with social anxiety. The work opens with the young teen pushing away the first person who tries to help her, Jaime, and it only gets more awkward from there." (School Library Journal)

★ **Nightschool:** the weirn books, volume one. [by] Svetlana Chmakova; toning artist, Dee DuPuy; lettering, JuYoun Lee. Yen Press 2009 190p. Illustration
Grades: 7 8 9 10 11 12
741.5; Fic
1. Mystery graphic novels; 2. Supernatural graphic novels; 3. Witches; 4. Graphic novels
978-0-7595-2859-8, $12.99

Courtesy of Yen Press

PS 13W is a regular public high school during the day, but after dark it is the Nightschool attended by werewolves, vampires, and weirns (a particular breed of witch). Sarah has just started her job as the new Night Keeper when she disappears from the school; when her younger sister Alex, a young weirn who's been homeschooled, discovers that Sarah's existence has been wiped out from everyone's memory but hers, she sets out to investigate. Dark forces have caused Sarah's disappearance, and they seem to be watching Alex, too. Meanwhile, Daemon, the teacher of the hunters, must try to figure out what young seer Marina has seen in her visions of a broken seal and what this has to do with his students who were severely injured while they were out on a class trip to the cemetery. This urban fantasy was first published in Yen Press's manga magazine, Yen Plus.

"Manga fans and teens looking for vampire stories will devour this one and will want to find out more about these characters." SLJ

Volume 1 of 4

★ **Nightschool:** the weirn books, volume two. Svetlana Chmakova ; toning artist, Dee DuPuy ; lettering, JuYoun Lee. Yen Press 2009 196p. Illustration

Grades: 7 8 9 10 11 12   **741.5; Fic**
1. Mystery graphic novels; 2. Supernatural graphic novels; 3. Witches; 4. Graphic novels
978-0-7595-2859-8, $10.99

Alex tries to investigate Sarah's disappearance from the Nightschool, but in order to get the Nightpass that will allow her unfettered access to the school grounds, she must enroll as a student. She soon proves to be far advanced in her astral class astrals are supernatural beings bonded to witches that help them do magic. Mr. Roi teaches an advanced astral class, but he is focused on helping Daemon investigate the broken seal and to help his student hunters who remain unconscious but are also transforming. And a mysterious girl with black wings keeps tabs on Alex.

Chrono, Nanae
Momo Tama, vol. 1. Story and art by Nanae Chrono ; [translation, Beni Axia Conrad ; English adaptation, Lorelei Laird]. Tokyopop 2009 Un

Grades: 8 9 10 11 12   **741.5; Fic**
1. Fantasy graphic novels; 2. Humorous graphic novels; 3. Manga; 4. Shonen manga; 5. Graphic novels
978-1-4278-1109-7, $9.99

Kokonose Mutsu is the 9th successor to the leadership of the Mutsu family, who lead the ogres who lost their island back when Momotaro defeated them. According to the legends, Momotaro returned home from the ogres' island with treasures, but really, he was given the island. Now the latest descendant of Momotaro runs a "school" on the island that actually trains people to be senkishi, ogre hunters. Kokonose joins the school's group of new students in order to set his plan to regain the island into motion. There are a couple of problems, one of which is that he is very small; he also doesn't have much in the way of supernatural powers (although he does possess a huge ego), and everyone knows who he is. His 20-year-old roommate smokes cigarettes, the book includes some harsh language, including several uses of the s-bomb, and there is some moderate violence.

Chung, Haley
Math Game 1. Youngjin Singapore 2005 196p. Illustration

Grades: 3 4 5 6 7 8   **510; 741.5**
1. Mathematics; 2. Graphic novels
981-05-2238-X, $12.95

Alice, Jimmy, Colby, and Sam are four good friends who share a common bond - they all hate math. As they complain about it on their way home from school, the King of Math appears and whisks Alice away. Jimmy, Colby, and

Sam decide to rescue her, but to enter into the Math King's world they must first pass through 20 gates, guarded by 20 great mathematicians. Saving Alice hinges on the friends learning about the discovery of zero, Roman numerals, fractions, rational and irrational numbers, and more-all in the context of a puzzle-based adventure.

Cibos, Lindsay
Peach Fuzz, Vol. 1. Lindsay Cibos and Jared Hodges. Tokyopop 2005 Un Illustration

Grades: 3 4 5 6 7 8   **741.5; Fic**
1. Ferrets; 2. Pets; 3. Graphic novels
1-59532-599-9, $9.99

Amanda is a lonely little girl. Her mother means well, but doesn't have a lot of time for a 9-year-old and, after plenty of begging from Amanda, agrees to let her have a pet. Amanda chooses a ferret because ferrets aren't ordinary and neither is she. But her mother worries because ferrets are notorious for biting. Amanda wins over her mother, gets the ferret and names it Peach. The two big rules: Amanda has to care for Peach, and Peach can't ever bite Amanda. It seems like Amanda finally has the friend she needed. But Peach sees Amanda's hands as five-serpent monsters—and bites in defense. What will lonely Amanda do now?"

Volume 1 of 3

Ciencin, Scott
Point-blank paintball. Stone Arch Books 2010 56p. Illustration

Grades: 3 4 5 6 7 8   **741.5; Fic**
1. Recreation; 2. Sibling rivalry; 3. Sports; 4. Twins; 5. Graphic novels
978-1-4342-1914-5, $25.32; 978-1-4342-2293-0 (pa), $6.95

Twin brothers Noah and Peter Eccleston are great paintball players; as a team, they have beat everyone they've played. Now, a major paintball team's coach wants them to try out for a spot on his team, but there's only room for one player. Noah and Peter have to compete against each other even as they have to beat the other members of the team. Is their father's attitude that winning is everything right, and how will this competition affect their relationship" This original graphic novel focuses on a hot sports activity and includes discussion questions and a glossary. Ciencin has written bestselling fiction, science fiction, horror, and superhero comics. Aburto, Maese, and Esparza are comics illustrators from Monterrey, Mexico.

Part of the Sports Illustrated Kids Graphic Novels series.

CLAMP (Mangaka group)
Angelic Layer. CLAMP. Dark Horse Manga 2012 426 p.

Grades: 5 6 7 8
1. Games — Fiction; 2. Japan — Fiction; 3. Manga
161655021X; 9781616550219, $19.99

"Junior high student Misaki Suzuhara has just arrived in Tokyo to live with her glamorous TV news star aunt and to attend the prestigious Eriol Academy. But what excites her above everything is Angelic Layer, the arena game where you control an 'Angel'—a miniature robot fighter whose moves depend on your mind!" (Publisher's note)

Originally published in the U.S. by Tokyopop

Volume 1 of 2

★ **Cardcaptor** Sakura: Book 1. Story and art by CLAMP. Dark Horse Manga 2010 576 p. Illustration; Color

Grades: 6 7 8 9 10   741.5

1. Books and reading — Juvenile fiction; 2. Fantasy fiction — Juvenile fiction; 3. Magic — Juvenile fiction; 4. Wizards — Fiction

1595825223; 9781595825223, $19.99

In this book, by CLAMP, "[f]ourth-grader Sakura Kinomoto found a strange book in her father's library—a book made by the wizard Clow to store dangerous spirits sealed within a set of magical cards. But when Sakura opened it up, there was nothing left inside but Kero-chan, the book's cute little guardian beast, who informs Sakura that since the Clow cards seem to have escaped while he was asleep, it's now her job to capture them!" (Publisher's note)

"CLAMP's classic manga series (originally published in the U.S. in a 12-volume, two-series run) is being rereleased in remastered and newly translated omnibus editions that collect three books each." Booklist

Volume 1 of 4

R. G. Veda Vol. 1. English adaptation by Christine Schilling. Tokyopop 2005 198p. Illustration

Grades: 8 9 10 11 12 Adult   741.5; Fic

1. Fantasy graphic novels; 2. Manga; 3. Shojo manga; 4. Graphic novels

1-59532-484-4, $9.99

At the dawn of creation, the world was a beautiful and tranquil place. Gods and humans lived peacefully together under the Heavenly Emperor's rule. But Taishakuten, a powerful warlord, rebelled against the King, and a violent, chaotic age began ... Three hundred years later, Kuyou, the strongest warrior in the land, hears the prophetic words of a revered stargazer: Six Stars will one day assemble and overthrow this bloody reign. Now, the quest begins to find the Six Stars and fulfill the prophecy before the heavens are torn apart. The book includes some battle violence.

Tsubasa: Reservoir Chronicle Vol. 1. Translated and adapted by Anthony Gerard ; lettered by Dana Hayward. Random House/Del Rey Manga 2004 198p. Illustration

Grades: 8 9 10 11 12   741.5; Fic

1. Fantasy graphic novels; 2. Manga; 3. Shonen manga; 4. Supernatural graphic novels; 5. Graphic novels

0-345-47057-5, $10.95

LC 2004-101711

Sakura is the princess of Clow-and possessor of a mysterious, misunderstood power that promises to change the world. Syaoran is her childhood friend and leader of the archaeological dig that took his father's life. They reside in an alternate reality . . . where whatever you least expect can happen-and does. When Sakura ventures to the dig site to declare her love for Syaoran, a puzzling symbol is uncovered-which triggers a remarkable quest. Now Syaoran embarks upon a desperate journey through other worlds-all in the name of saving Sakura. This series crosses over with xxxHolic, and both of them use characters from past CLAMP manga. The book includes some violence.

XXXHolic Vol. 1. Translated and adapted by Anthony Gerard ; lettered by Dana Hayward. Random House/Del Rey Manga 2004 Un Illustration

Grades: 8 9 10 11 12   741.5; Fic

1. Fantasy graphic novels; 2. Manga; 3. Seinen manga; 4. Supernatural graphic novels; 5. Graphic novels

0-345-47058-3, $10.95

Watanuki Kimihiro is haunted by visions of ghosts and spirits. Seemingly by chance, he encounters a mysterious witch named Yuuko, who claims she can help. In desperation, he accepts, but realizes that he's just been tricked into working for Yuuko in order to pay off the cost of her services. Soon he's employed in her little shop-a job which turns out to be nothing like his previous work experience. Most of Yuuko's customers live in Japan, but Yuuko and Watanuki are about to have some unusual visitors named Sakura and Syaoran from a land called Clow. . . The book includes some strong language and graphic violence.

Claremont, Chris

★ **X-Men:** The Dark Phoenix Saga, 2nd ed.. Penciler and co-plotter, John Byrne. Marvel Entertainment 2006 200p. Illustration

Grades: 7 8 9 10 11 12 Adult   741.5; Fic

1. Superhero graphic novels; 2. X-Men (Fictional characters); 3. Graphic novels

978-0-7851-2213-5, $24.99

Gathered together by Professor Charles Xavier to protect a world that fears and hates them, the X-Men had fought many battles, been on adventures that spanned galaxies, grappled enemies of limitless might, but none of this could prepare them for the most shocking struggle they would ever face. One of their own members, Jean Grey, has gained power beyond all comprehension, and that power has corrupted her absolutely. Now they must decide if the life of the woman they cherish is worth the existence of the entire universe.

X-Men: The End Book One: Dreamers & Demons. Writer, Chris Claremont ; pencils, Sean Chen ; inks, Sandu Florea ; colors, Avalaon's Ian Hannin ; letters, Dave Sharpe. Marvel Entertainment 2005 Un Illustration

Grades: 7 8 9 10 11 12 Adult   741.5; Fic

1. Superhero graphic novels; 2. X-Men (Fictional characters); 3. Graphic novels

978-0-7851-1690-5, $14.99

It's the epic finale to the story of the Children of the Atom as X-Men scribe Chris Claremont joins with artist Sean Chen for a trilogy in the style of the Lord of the Rings movies, one that spans the length and breadth of the X-Men canon and brings the saga of Marvel's mutants to a climax. In this volume, the unthinkable happens - attackers succeed in breaching all security at the Xavier School for the Gifted and threaten the lives of all the young mutants living there.

X-Men: The End Book Three: Men & X-Men. Sean Chen, illustrator. Marvel Entertainment 2006 Un Illustration

Grades: 7 8 9 10 11 12 Adult   741.5; Fic

1. Superhero graphic novels; 2. X-Men (Fictional characters); 3. Graphic novels

978-0-7851-1692-9, $14.99

The endgame of the last tale of Marvel's most popular mutants begins. They've suffered through sneak attacks, betrayals, and fatalities - now, Professor X and Magneto are taking the fight back to the enemy, amidst the stars.

X-Men: The End Book Two: Heroes & Martyrs. Sean Chen, illustrator. Marvel Entertainment 2005 Un Illustration
Grades: 7 8 9 10 11 12 Adult   **741.5; Fic**
1. Superhero graphic novels; 2. X-Men (Fictional characters); 3. Graphic novels
978-0-7851-1691-2, $14.99
The Xavier Academy has been reduced to a smoldering crater in a brutal sneak attack, and the casualties number in the hundreds. Now, Cyclops must mobilize the survivors to get to the bottom of who is behind these coordinated strikes on mutants in general and the X-Men in particular.

Cliff, Tony
★ **Delilah** Dirk and the king's shilling. Tony Cliff. First Second 2016 272 p.
Grades: 7 8 9 10 11 12   **741.5/973; 741.5**
1. Adventure and adventurers — Fiction; 2. Adventure graphic novels; 3. Espionage — Fiction; 4. Fantasy graphic novels; 5. Graphic novels
1626721556; 9781626721555, $17.99
                                        LC 2015020653
In this graphic novel, by Tony Cliff, "globetrotting troublemaker Delilah Dirk and her loyal friend Selim are just minding their own business, peacefully raiding castles and and traipsing across enemy lines, when they attract the unwanted attention of the English Army. Before they know it, Delilah and Selim have gotten themselves accused of espionage against the British crown!" (Publisher's note)

Cobley, Jason
Frankenstein: the graphic novel. [by] Mary Shelley; script adaptation Jason Cobley; American English adaptation: Joe Sutliff Sanders; linework: Declan Shalvey; coloring: Jason Cardy & Kat Nicholson; lettering: Terry Wiley. Classical Comics 2008 141p. Illustration
Grades: 6 7 8 9 10 11 12 Adult   **741.5; Fic**
1. Frankenstein (Fictional character); 2. Horror graphic novels; 3. Shelley, Mary Wollstonecraft, 1797-1851 — Adaptations; 4. Graphic novels
978-1-906332-49-5, $16.95
Young scientist Victor Frankenstein becomes obsessed with the idea that technology can create life, and works to prove his theories. However, his success doesn't bring him glory, but a living nightmare for himself and everyone around him. This graphic adaptation brings the entire book to the reader, using Shelley's original text for the dialog and narrative. Back matter includes a brief biography of Shelley, her family tree, a description of how she came to write the novel, and information on some of the various adaptations of the story to the stage and to film.
"More than a straightforward retelling, this edition invites readers to explore important social issues such as alienation, the consequences and ethics of scientific studies, as well as the nature of creation and destruction." SLJ
Also available quick text version $16.95 (ISBN: 978-1-906332-50-1)
Original text version

Cogan, Adam
The **Black** Coat: A Call to Arms. by Ben Lichius and Adam Cogan. Illustrated by Francesco Francavilla. APE Entertainment 2006 Un Illustration
Grades: 8 9 10 11 12 Adult   **741.5; Fic**
1. Adventure graphic novels; 2. Supernatural graphic novels; 3. Graphic novels
978-0-9741398-8-3, $12.95
In pre-Revolutionary War New York City, the masked Black Coat and his Knights of Liberty battle the British occupation forces, and the occult. Lieutenant-General Henry Savidge has accepted the help of Lord Morrow and his shadowy organization to stop the Black Coat. Morrow and his League have brought the Krauss brothers to the Colonies; Wilhelm Krauss murders people, taking their arms, as he works to perfect a serum that will make the takers immortal. The Black Coat and his people work to prevent it, even as the Krauss' butchery is blamed on the Black Coat.
This story, combining historical fiction with the occult, is the first volume; a new miniseries of comics began publication in 2007.
Originally published as The Black Coat issues #1-4.

Colfer, Eoin
Artemis Fowl: the graphic novel. Adapted by Eoin Colfer and Andrew Donkin; art by Giovanni Rigano; color by Paolo Lammana. Hyperion Books for Children 2007 Un Illustration
Grades: 4 5 6 7 8 9   **741; 741.5; Fic**
1. Adventure graphic novels; 2. Fantasy graphic novels
978-0-7868-4881-2, $18.99; 0-7868-4881-2; 978-0-7868-4882-9 (pa), $9.99; 0-7868-4882-0 (pa)
Twelve-year-old genius and criminal mastermind Artemis Fowl runs his missing father's crime empire and gets his hands on a book that will give him access to the underground fairy world. This graphic novel adaptation gives the book a European lookd color palette
"Excellent use of color and shading gives the panels a tremendous sense of light with enchanting effect. Characters are expressively brought to life with fun, exaggerated style." SLJ
Other Artemis Fowl graphic novels are: Artemis Fowl: the Arctic incident (2009); Artemis Fowl: the eternity code (2013); Artemis Fowl: the opal deception (2014)

The **supernaturalist:** the graphic novel. Eoin Colfer; Andrew Donkin; illustrated by Giovanni Rigano and Paolo Lamanna. Miramax Books/Hyperion Books for Children 2004 267 p.
Grades: 6 7 8 9   **Fic; 741.5/9415**
1. Abandoned children; 2. Friendship — Fiction; 3. Orphans — Fiction; 4. Science fiction
0786848790; 0786851481; 9780786848799, $19.99
                                        LC 2004044180
In this graphic novel by Eoin Colfer and Andrew Donkin, illustrated by Giovanni Rigano and Paolo Lamanna, "unwanted by his parents, Cosmo Hill is put to work by the state, testing highly dangerous products. Cosmo . . . escapes with the help of the Supernaturalists, a group of kids who have the same special abilities as Cosmo—they can see supernatural Parasites, creatures that feed on the life force of humans. The Supernaturalists patrol the city at night." (Publisher's note)

Collicutt, Paul

Rust attack!: Robot City adventures. Templar Books/Candlewick Press 2009 Un Illustration

Grades: 3 4 5 6   **741.5; Fic**
1. Mystery graphic novels; 2. Robots; 3. Science fiction graphic novels; 4. Graphic novels
978-0-7636-4594-6, $8.99

LC 2009-931661

In Robot City, a metropolis of 15 million humans and 1 million robots, Mike (a human) and Rod (a robot) run Robot City Confidential Investigations, a private detective agency. A robot dancer comes to them, asking them to find out who infected her dance troupe with rust; for robots, rust is a horribly dangerous problem. When they quickly discover a disgruntled robot musician with a grudge, the detectives suspect there's more to the case and continue to investigate. The book combines noir mystery with robots, humor, and a retro-cartoon style in the colorful art.

Part of the Robot City Adventures series.

Collins, Max Allan

Dick Tracy: The Collins Casefiles Volume 1. Chester Gould, artist, Rick Fletcher, artist. Checker Book Publishing Group 2003 164p. Illustration

Grades: 8 9 10 11 12 Adult   **741.5; Fic**
1. Dick Tracy (Fictional character); 2. Mystery graphic novels; 3. Graphic novels
0-9741664-2-1, $19.95

LC 2003-23068

This is the first of several volumes collecting Collins' 11-year run on the Dick Tracy comic strips. He took over scripting duties from Chester Gould in 1978, although Gould maintained his byline and consulted with Collins on plot directions. Fletcher, a longtime Gould assistant, took over the drawing and worked with Collins. This volume includes the stories "Angel Top's Last Stand," "Return of Haf-and Haf," and "Big Boy's Revenge."

Collins, Terry

The **FBI**. Illustrated by Kelly Brown. Capstone Press 2009 32p. Illustration

Grades: 3 4 5 6 7 8   **363.2; 741.5**
1. United States — Federal Bureau of Investigation; 2. Graphic novels
978-1-4296-1982-0, $32

LC 2008-506

This graphic format book uses irreverently humorous captions and dialog and provides young readers with an introduction to the founding, history, and work of the Federal Bureau of Investigation, the FBI. The book also describes what it takes to become an agent of the FBI, what a "typical" day is like, and the top priorities of the Bureau, including national security and criminal priorities. It includes a short timeline, a glossary, and a list of books for further reading.

Part of the Graphic Library Cartoon Nation series

Comics Squad: recess!

Comics by Jarrett J. Krosoczka, Gene Yang, Eric Wight, Jennifer L. Holm and Matthew Holm, Ursula Vernon, Dan Santat, Raina Telgemeier and Dave Roman, Dav Pilkey; edited by Jennifer L. Holm, Matthew Holm, and Jarrett J.

Krosoczka. Random House Inc. 2014 144 p. Illustration; Color

Grades: 2 3 4 5 6   **741.5**
1. Humorous stories; 2. Recess — Fiction; 3. School stories; 4. Schools — Fiction; 5. Short stories; 6. Graphic novels
0385370032; 9780385370035, $7.99; 9780385370042, $12.99

LC 2013035223

"An all-star lineup of graphic novel notables contributes original works to this anthology, sharing the common thread of recess." (School Library Journal)

"[T]his lively, upbeat and all-around-awesome offering is consistently convivial and laugh-out-loud funny from cover to cover." Kirkus

Another title in this series is: Lunch! (2016)

Conner, Daniel

The **picture** of Dorian Gray. Adapted by Daniel Conner; illustrated by Chris Allen.. Magic Wagon/Graphic Planet 2009 32p. Illustration

Grades: 6 7 8 9 10   **741.5; Fic**
1. Horror graphic novels; 2. Supernatural graphic novels; 3. Wilde, Oscar, 1854-1900; 10. Wilde, Oscar, 1854-1900 — Adaptations/Graphic novels; 4. Graphic novels
978-160270-680-4, $27.07

LC 2009-8597

Impossibly handsome, young Dorian Gray sits for a portrait and then impulsively wishes that he could never age and that the portrait should do so in his place. However, as life goes on, he becomes evil; he falls in love with an actress and then spurns her; he murders the portrait artist; and with every act his portrait becomes more and more grotesque while he remains a youthful, handsome fellow. This easy-reading graphic novel adaptation of Oscar Wilde's horror story makes it easier for reluctant and struggling readers to enjoy the story. Back matter includes a brief biography of Wilde, a list of some of his other works, and a short glossary. The question of morality in the story and the violence make this more suitable for somewhat older readers, despite the simplicity of language.

This is part of the Graphic Horror Series 2.

William Shakespeare's A midsummer night's dream. Adapted by Daniel Conner; illustrated by Rod Espinosa.. ABDO/Magic Wagon 2008 48p. Illustration

Grades: 5 6 7 8 9 10

741.5; Fic
1. Graphic novels; 2. Shakespeare, William, 1564-1616 — Adaptations; 3. Youths' writings
978-1-60270-191-5, $28.50

LC 2008-10745

In Athens, the ruler Theseus prepares to marry Hippolyta. Meanwhile, Hermia and Lysander run away to the forest because

Courtesy of ABDO Publishing Group/Magic Wagon

Hermia doesn't want to marry Demetrius, who follows them

into the forest with Helena, whom he loves. Enter Puck, mischievous fairy who serves Oberon, the King of the Fairies. When he is ordered to find a flower whose nectar acts like a love potion and use it on Queen Titania, Puck also decides to play with the two young couples. And meanwhile again, a group of guildsmen prepare a play for their ruler's wedding. Havoc ensues. This graphic novel adaptation retains some of the original language from Shakespeare's play, while paring down the story to appeal to struggling readers. The book includes a short biography of Shakespeare, a summary of the play, a glossary, and a short selection of famous lines and phrases from the play.

Part of the Graphic Shakespeare series

Cooke, Darwyn
★ **Will** Eisner's The Spirit. Written by Darwyn Cooke and Jeph Loeb; drawn by Darwyn Cooke; inks and finishes by J. Bone; colors by Dave Stewart. DC Comics 2007 192p. Illustration
Grades: 8 9 10 11 12 Adult   **741.5; Fic**
1. Batman (Fictional character); 2. Humorous graphic novels; 3. Spirit (Fictional character); 4. Superhero graphic novels; 5. Graphic novels
978-1-4012-1461-6; 978-1-4012-1618-4 (pa), $19.99

Will Eisner's character The Spirit was popular for decades. Eisner is gone, but Darwyn Cooke has taken up the pen to update The Spirit while maintaining the action, adventure, and humor of the original stories. Readers will meet Commissioner Dolan and his daughter Ellen, Ebony, bad girl P'Gell, and more. This volume also includes the Eisner Award winning Batman/The Spirit special, written by Jeph Loeb and drawn by Cooke. The upcoming live action movie directed by comics veteran Frank Miller will spark more interest in the comics. The book includes lots of action and some cartoony violence.

"This is fine, entertaining stuff that will satisfy any longtime comics fan; recommended for teens and adults." Libr J

Cooper, Nate
Build your own website: a comic guide to HTML, CSS, and WordPress. Nate Cooper. No Starch Press 2014 250 p. Illustration
Grades: 7 8 9 10 11 12   **006.7**
1. Web site development — Humor; 2. Web sites — Design — Humor
1593275226; 9781593275228, $19.95
      LC 2014019597
Author Nate Cooper and illustrator Kim Gee present this "illustrated introduction to the basics of creating a website. Join Kim and her little dog Tofu as she learns HTML, the language of web pages, and CSS, the language used to style web pages, from the Web Guru and Glinda, the Good Witch of CSS." (Publisher's note)

"The comic art engages the readers and gives the broad picture of what the reader will learn from Cooper's text which follows. Best suited for beginning self-learning, it is one of the few books on the topic which entertains as well as educates."

Includes index.

Corona, Jorge
Feathers. Written & illustrated by Jorge Corona; colors by Jen Hickman; letters by Deron Bennett. Archaia 2015 160 p. Illustration
Grades: 5 6 7 8   **741.5; Fic**
1. Monsters; 2. Orphans
9781608867530, $24.99; 1608867536
      LC 2015055238
In this graphic novel, written & illustrated by Jorge Corona, "Poe has lived his entire eleven-year-old life hidden away under the protection of his adoptive father, Gabriel. He spends his days secretly helping . . . bands of orphans who roam the slums. . . . When Bianca, an over-protected girl from the wealthy City beyond the Wall, escapes into the Maze in search of adventure, their worlds collide." (Publisher's note)

"Poe is a true underdog hero, and Bianca's wish to be set free from her restricting life is something to which middle grades readers can relate. Stunning illustrations contrast the stark white orderly city with the dark and dangerous Maze." SLJ

Corzine, Amy
Jane Eyre: The graphic novel original text. Charlotte Brontë ; script adaptation Amy Corzine ; American English adaptation by Joe Sutliff Sanders ; artwork by John M. Burns ; lettering by Terry Wiley. Classical Comics 2008 144p. Illustration
Grades: 6 7 8 9 10 11 12 Adult
741.5; Fic
1. Brontë, Charlotte, 1816-1855 — Adaptations; 2. Romance graphic novels; 3. Graphic novels
978-1-906332-47-1, $16.95

© Classical Comics

Orphaned as an infant and begrudgingly raised by an aunt who despises her, Jane Eyre begins to find some happiness at Lowood School, a charity school where she spends eight years of her life, as a student and then as a teacher. When she chafes for freedom and advertises for a position, Jane finds a job as governess at Thornfield Hall, where she meets Mr. Rochester. Love blooms, but his dark secret destroys what hope she ever had of happiness and she runs away. As life seems to reach its darkest, worst moments, things begin to look up for Jane, but will she ever find love again? This graphic adaptation uses Bronte's dialog and some of her narration straight from the original novel. Back matter includes a short biography of Bronte, a timeline of her life and career, and the Bronte family tree.

Also available quick text version $16.95 (ISBN: 978-1-906332-48-8)

Cosson, M. J.
Sherlock Holmes and a scandal in Bohemia. Based on the stories of Sir Arthur Conan Doyle; adapted by Murray

Shaw and M.J. Cosson; illustrated by Sophie Rohrbach.. Lerner Publishing Group/Graphic Universe 2010 48p. Illustration

Grades: 3 4 5 6 7 8   **741.5; Fic**

1. Authors; 2. Doyle, Arthur Conan Sir, 1859-1930 — Adaptations; 3. Mystery graphic novels; 4. Graphic novels

978-0-7613-6185-5, $26.60; 978-0-7613-6197-8 (pa), $6.95

LC 2009-51763

The King of Bohemia comes to Sherlock Holmes and asks him to retrieve a photograph from the king's former lover, Irene Adler. He wants to be married, and Miss Adler is blackmailing him with the incriminating photograph. Holmes dons a disguise in order to steal the photo from Miss Adler's house, but the singer proves to be an intelligent, formidable foe. This book adapts the story written by Sir Arthur Conan Doyle, with sepia-toned art. It includes clues to Holmes' reasoning and a list for further reading.

Court-Kaemon, Amy

Ratatouille. Tokyopop 2007 96p. Illustration

Grades: 2 3 4 5 6 7 8 9 10 11 12 Adult   **741.5; Fic**

1. Cooking; 2. Humorous graphic novels; 3. Rats; 4. Graphic novels

978-1-4278-0087-9, $7.99

This Cine-Manga title takes stills from Pixar's popular animated film to adapt the story into a graphic novel. Remy is a rat living in Paris, who aspires to be a chef. Linguine is a hapless young man who wishes to be a chef but has no talent. When the two meet, a partnership is born.

Craddock, Erik

Robot frenzy; 8. Erik Craddock. Random House Books for Young Readers 2013 96 p. (Stone rabbit)

Grades: 2 3 4 5 6   **741.5/973; 741.5**

1. Animals — Fiction; 2. Chores — Fiction; 3. Humorous stories; 4. Rabbits — Fiction; 5. Robots — Fiction; 6. Graphic novels

0375869131; 9780375869136, $6.99; 9780375969133

LC 2012049524

In this graphic novel by Erik Craddock "Stone Rabbit and his friends create robots to help out with chores [but] a glitch in the programming sends the 'bots into a malfunctioning frenzy! Will our long-eared hero be able to shut down these mechanical maniacs before they destroy Happy Glades? Or will his systems crash? (Publisher's note)

Crane, Jordan

The **clouds** above. Fantagraphics 2005 216p. Illustration

Grades: 3 4 5 6 7 8

741.5; Fic

1. Fantasy graphic novels; 2. Graphic novels

1-560976-27-6, $18.95

Simon and his cat Jack embark on an adventure among the clouds one day when

Courtesy of Fantagraphics

Simon skips school and finds a rickety stairway leading skyward. They find a friendly cloud, flee thunderstorms and trick a flock of belligerent birds, only to find themselves back at school.

"Everything's exciting . . . and the dialogue is witty and bubbly. . . . The book is a joy to look at"Crane's loose, gliding lines burst with character, and his compositional gifts make every panel worth contemplating on its own." Publ Wkly

Crilley, Mark

★ **Akiko** pocket-size, vol. 1. Sirius Entertainment 2004 192p. Illustration

Grades: 3 4 5 6 7 8 9 10   **741.5; Fic**

1. Adventure graphic novels; 2. Science fiction graphic novels

1-579890-67-9, $11.95

Fourth-grader Akiko travels to the planet Smoo, on a mission to rescue King Froptoppit's son from the evil Alia Rellapor. Teamed up with the scruffy adventurer Spuckler, bookish Mr. Beeba, Spuckler's robot Gax, and the floating alien known as Poog, Akiko faces sea monsters, Sky Pirates, Sleeslup worms, and other dangers as they travel around the planet on their quest. Crilley also has written a series of prose fiction featuring Akiko and her friends.

★ **Brody's** ghost: book 1. Story and art by Mark Crilley. Dark Horse Books 2010 88p. Illustration

Grades: 8 9 10 11 12 Adult   **741.5; Fic**

1. Adventure graphic novels; 2. Fantasy graphic novels; 3. Ghosts; 4. Mystery graphic novels; 5. Graphic novels

978-1-59582-521-6, $6.99

In what looks like a near-future city, Brody is down and out, eking out a living by playing guitar on the streets and working part-time as a stock clerk. Then, one day, while playing his guitar, he sees the ghost of a young woman; he thinks he's seeing things, but she won't let him alone until he talks with her. Talia, the ghost, needs to do a great deed before she can get into heaven, and she has decided to solve the mystery of a serial killer called the Penny Murderer, but she needs Brody, who is a ghostseer, to help her. First, though, he needs training to bring out his ghostseer powers, because he doesn't think he has any. Enter Kagemura, the ghost of a samurai, who decides, half-unwillingly, to train Brody. This book is much grittier than Crilley's earlier works, which were more suitable for younger readers; it is aimed more at teen and adult readers and includes some fighting violence but no graphically violent content.

"The setting—an unidentified future city partially in ruins—is a masterpiece of drawing, and Brody and the other characters are equally well crafted. . . . The story is more than a match for the art: humor, action, and mystery butt up against the reality of Brody's sad life, giving him the opportunity to change who he is." Booklist

Also available in an omnibus edition

The first in a six-volume limited series. Page 4 of cover

Book 1 of 6

Miki Falls Vol. 2: Summer. HarperTeen 2007 178p. Illustration

Grades: 7 8 9 10 11 12 Adult   **741.5; Fic**

1. Romance graphic novels; 2. Supernatural graphic novels; 3. Graphic novels

978-0-06-084617-6, $7.99

Has Miki fallen too hard" It's summer, and Miki Yoshida is learning all about love. Her senior year has blossomed with promise ever since she gained Hiro Sakurai's confidence. Now, she's resolved to keep his trust as he reveals more about his secret mission and warns: "Don't get involved." But Miki fears his work might do more harm than good, and she takes control-with disastrous results. How can trying to make things right turn out so dangerously wrong" Crilley is doing this series in manga style.

Miki Falls, Book One: Spring. HarperCollins/HarperTeen 2007 176p. Illustration
Grades: 7 8 9 10 11 12   **741.5; Fic**
  1. Friendship; 2. High school students; 3. School stories; 4. Graphic novels
978-0-06-084616-9, $7.99
"This is Miki Yoshida's final year of high school, and she's determined to make this the best year yet. Miki is in control . . . until Hiro Sakurai shows up. The tall, handsome new student is hiding something, and Miki wants to know what." Publisher's note
"Crilley uses mystery to drive the narrative and creates characters that the reader will care about. The black-and-white, manga-style art is beautiful." Voice Youth Advocates
  Other titles in this series are: Miki Falls, Book Two: Summer; Miki Falls, Book Three: Autumn; Miki Falls, Book Four: Winter

★ **Miki** Falls: Winter. HarperCollins/HarperTeen 2008 176p. Illustration
Grades: 7 8 9 10 11 12   **741.5; Fic**
  1. Adventure graphic novels; 2. Fantasy graphic novels; 3. Romance graphic novels; 4. Graphic novels
978-0-06-084619-0, $7.99
                       LC 2007-931803
Miki and Hiro have been on the run for a while now; it's now winter and they are in the far north of Japan, trying to escape from the Deliverers led by Akuzu who are determined to tear the young couple apart and punish Hiro. Miki is equally determined to stay with Hiro, whom she loves above all else. Can love conquer all? This is the final volume of the series.

Crisis on Multiple Earths Volume 1: The Team-Ups
DC Comics 2005 224p. Illustration
Grades: 8 9 10 11 12 Adult   **741.5; Fic**
  1. Flash (Fictional character); 2. Green Lantern (Fictional character); 3. Superhero graphic novels; 4. Graphic novels
1-4012-0470-8, $14.99
This collection of stories from the 1960s features team-ups of the Silver Age DC heroes with their Golden Age counterparts, with the conceit that DC Comics dreamed up, that the Golden Age heroes are from a parallel world. And along with the heroes, of course come the super-villains. The Flash, Green Lantern, and Hourman from both worlds work with each other to defeat their villains, including Solomon Grundy, the Thinker, the Trickster, and others.

Croall, Marie P.
  Marwe: into the land of the dead: an East African legend. Author, Marie P. Croall; pencils by Ray Lago and inks by Craig Hamilton.. Lerner Publishing Group 2009 48p. Illustration
Grades: 3 4 5 6 7 8 9   **741.5; Fic**
  1. Fantasy graphic novels; 2. Folklore — East Africa; 3. Graphic novels
978-0-8225-7134-6, $27.93
                       LC 2007-1828
In this story retold from the oral tradition of the Chaga people in East Africa, Marwe lives in a village where times are hard and food is scarce. When she and her brother leave the family's bean fields to cool off at the river, monkeys destroy the entire crop. When her brother goes off to ask the family's forgiveness, Marwe sees something strange in the water and dives down; she passes through a strange doorway and finds herself in another land. Soon she learns she has come to the land of the dead, where an old woman welcomes her. Too scared to go home, Marwe stays there, and despite assurances that she needn't do anything, she works in the fields. When will Marwe think it's time to return home to her anxious and mourning family?
  Part of the Graphic Universe Myths and Legends series

  Psyche & eros: the lady and the monster: a Greek myth. Story by Marie Croall; pencils and inks by Ron Randall. Lerner Publishing Group 2009 48p. Illustration
Grades: 3 4 5 6 7 8 9   **741.5; Fic**
  1. Fantasy graphic novels; 2. Greek mythology; 3. Graphic novels
978-0-8225-7177-3, $27.93
                       LC 2007-43353
Psyche is a beautiful young woman, so beautiful that men start to give her gifts instead of taking them to the temple. This makes Aphrodite jealous, and she sends her son, Eros, to prick Psyche with an arrow so no man will ever fall in love with her. However, Eros falls in love with Psyche. He arranges for the Oracle to tell Psyche's father that his daughter must be taken up on a mountain to marry a monster. He only comes to her at night, and they love each other; but Psyche's sisters convince her that she should see her husband. When hot wax from her candle burns Eros and wakens him, he must leave her. Now Psyche, unable to convince any other god or goddess to help her, must go to Aphrodite, who sets impossible tasks that Psyche manages to accomplish with help from unexpected sources.
  Part of the Graphic Universe Myths and Legends series

Cunningham, Scott
  Scooby-Doo! hot springs, cold sweat. ABDO/Spotlight 2010 48p. Illustration
Grades: 2 3 4 5 6
741.5; Fic
  1. Humorous graphic novels; 2. Mystery graphic novels; 3. Scooby-Doo (Fictional character); 4. Graphic novels

Courtesy of ABDO/Spotlight

978-1-59961-695-7, $28.50

LC 2009-32900

Scooby-Doo, Shaggy, and the rest of the Mystery, Incorporated gang investigate spooky goings-on at a hot springs spa, then they jet over to Tokyo, Japan on the trail of a master jewel thief who has been stealing pieces of what is called the Dragon Eye. Once the facets are put together again, the stone is said to give its owner the power to conquer the world. These original stories were originally published in DC Comics' Scooby-Doo! comic book series.

Part of The Scooby-Doo Graphic Novels

Scooby-Doo! terror is afoot!. ABDO/Spotlight 2010 Un Illustration

Grades: 2 3 4 5 6   **741.5; Fic**

1. Humorous graphic novels; 2. Mystery graphic novels; 3. Scooby-Doo (Fictional character); 4. Yeti; 5. Graphic novels

978-1-59961-698-8, $22.78

LC 2009-32903

Shaggy and Scooby find themselves dumped in the Himalayas, right where yetis have been spotted. As the rest of the Scooby gang search for the two, man and dog meet Professor Jeffries, natives Pemba and Minga, monster hunter Alfonse Lafleur, and Del, their friend who's now searching for the yeti.

Part of The Scooby-Doo Graphic Novel series, originally published by DC Comics.

Cutting, Robert

Cyber Patrol. Harcourt Achieve/Steck-Vaughn 2007 48p. Illustration

Grades: 3 4 5 6 7 8   **741.5; Fic**

1. Science fiction graphic novels; 2. Graphic novels

978-1-4190-3223-3, $8.99

In 2083, Mark Lewis is a twelve-year-old expert at online games. When a powerful and mysterious computer virus strikes, the authorities come asking for Mark's help. Who will win, Cyber Patrol or Cyberdoom? This science fiction graphic novel includes prose interludes that provide additional information about the Internet, computer viruses, some statistics about computer use, and speculation about what the future will hold.

Part of the Timeline Graphic Novels series.

Falling Star. Harcourt Achieve/Steck-Vaughn 2006 48p. Illustration

Grades: 3 4 5 6 7 8   **741.5; Fic**

1. Native Americans — History; 2. Graphic novels

978-1-4190-3209-7, $8.99

In 1870, a Caucasian baby is rescued by the Lakota people. They name him Falling Star and raise him as one of their own. Years later, as Chief Sitting Bull prepares for battle against the U.S. Army and one General George Armstrong Custer, Falling Star must decide which side he's on. This historical fiction graphic novel includes historical information about the Lakota people, Sitting Bull, Crazy Horse, the Battle of Little Bighorn, and the forced moves of the people onto reservations.

Part of the Timeline Graphic Novels series.

March of the Dinosaurs. Harcourt Achieve/Steck-Vaughn 2006 48p. Illustration

Grades: 3 4 5 6 7 8   **741.5; Fic**

1. Dinosaurs; 2. Science fiction graphic novels; 3. Graphic novels

978-1-4190-3194-6, $8.99

Traveling on a time machine, a scientist from the future goes back to the Cretaceous Age of the Dinosaurs with her niece and nephew. The time machine breaks down just as a giant meteor hurtles toward the Earth. Will they escape or will they share the fate of the dinosaurs? This science fiction graphic novel includes prose intervals that give facts about dinosaurs.

Part of the Timeline Graphic Novels series.

Mars Colony. Harcourt Achieve/Steck-Vaughn 2006 48p. Illustration

Grades: 3 4 5 6 7 8   **741.5; Fic**

1. Mystery graphic novels; 2. Science fiction graphic novels; 3. Graphic novels

978-1-4190-3213-4, $8.99

In the year 2130, the Chang family is one of 128 families sent to Mars to found the first human colony there. Jenny Chang and her brother Derek eagerly explore their new home; they are in for a big surprise. This science fiction story is interspersed with facts about Mars and space exploration.

Part of the Timeline Graphic Novels series.

Czekaj, Jef

Grampa & Julie: Shark hunters. Top Shelf 2004 Un Illustration

Grades: 2 3 4 5 6   **741.5; Fic**

1. Adventure graphic novels; 2. Humorous graphic novels; 3. Graphic novels

1-891830-52-X, $14.95

"In this full-color graphic novel, Julie and her grampa spend summer vacation looking for the largest shark in the world, Stephen. Meeting Stephen leads to even more exciting adventures, including a quest to find Stephen's mom. The shark hunters meet monkeys at the bottom of the ocean, pirates, and even aliens. Gramma has to rescue them from a couple of scrapes." Booklist

"Taken from the pages of Nickelodeon magazine, this charming children's comic overflows with humor, adventure and whimsy." Publ Wkly

Dabb, Andrew

G.I. Joe, Sigma 6: big time. ABDO Spotlight 2008 Un Illustration

Grades: 3 4 5 6 7 8 9   **741.5; Fic**

1. Adventure graphic novels; 2. G I Joe (Fictional character); 3. Graphic novels

978-1-59961-369-7, $21.35

LC 2006-52226

It's quiet time at R.O.C.C., the mobile headquarters of G.I. Joe, and Heavy Duty and Long Range are the only Joes there when they get a call from General Sato in Tokyo, Japan. Cobra Commander has been spotted, and Sato needs the Joes' help. Heavy Duty and Long Range are usually just the back up guys for the more well-known Joes (Duke, Scarlett, Snake Eyes . . .), but they have to take the mission. What they do is wreck havoc at a Yakuza club in Tokyo while trying to take down Cobra Commander. The book includes lots of action but no real violence.

This book is a revision of issue 5 (March 2006) of G. I. Joe Sigma 6, originally published by Devils Due Publishing.

Daffy Duck: You're Despicable!
 DC Comics 2005 112p. Illustration
Grades: 3 4 5 6 7 8 9   **741.5; Fic**
 1. Daffy Duck (Fictional character); 2. Humorous graphic novels; 3. Graphic novels
 1-4012-0515-1, $6.99
 It's duck season again. Everyone's favorite foul-tempered fowl explodes into his own collection with this first volume of Daffy Duck stories straight from the pages of Looney Tunes comics. Packed full of hilarity and anger management issues, this volume will warm the hearts of curmudgeons young and old everywhere. Of course you know this means war.

Dahl, Michael
 Beauty and the beast: the graphic novel. Retold by Michael Dahl; illustrated by Luke Feldman.. Stone Arch Books 2009 40p. Illustration
Grades: 2 3 4 5 6 7   **741.5; Fic**
 1. Fairy tales; 2. Fantasy graphic novels; 3. Graphic novels
 978-1-4342-0765-4, $21.26
                LC 2008-6719
 When a merchant on a journey plucks a rose to keep a promise for his daughter, Beauty, a roaring Beast demands that she come to him in payment for the rose. When she comes to the Beast's castle, he asks her to marry him; she refuses. As the days go by, the Beast asks her every evening, and every evening she refuses, despite a growing friendship. When he allows her to go home for a time, the family keeps her back beyond the time she promised the Beast, and when she returns he is dying; only one thing will save him her love. This graphic novel retells the old French folktale originally written in 1740 by Madame Gabrielle de Villeneuve in this original written version, the Beast never transformed. The book includes historical information about the versions of the story and a glossary.

Part of the Graphic Spin series

Dahl, Roald
 The **Gremlins:** The Lost Walt Disney Production: A Royal Air Force Story. Dark Horse Books 2006 Un Illustration
Grades: 4 5 6 7 8 9 10 11 12 Adult   **741.5; Fic**
 1. Humorous graphic novels; 2. World War, 1939-1945; 3. Graphic novels
 978-1-59307-496-8, $12.95
 This is an illustrated novella, the first published work of RAF Flight Lieutenant Roald Dahl in his only collaboration with Walt Disney Studios. Originally published in 1943, the story was supposed to become a film combining live action with animation; the movie was never made, although the studio produced a lot of illustrations and samples. The story tells about one young Royal Air Force pilot named Gus, who first sees the little gremlins that wreak havoc on his plane. While the gremlins first cause lots of trouble, eventually Gus convinces them to work with the RAF.

Dakin, Glenn
 Temptation: A Battle of Wits Through All Eternity. Active Images 2004 72p. Illustration
Grades: 8 9 10 11 12 Adult   **741.5**
 1. Humorous graphic novels; 2. Graphic novels
 0-9740567-5-8, $8.95
 It's a constant battle of wits between a hermit who lives out in the wilderness and the devil who wants his soul. While that's the main theme, there are strips in which the devil needs the hermit to babysit his little baby devils so he can see a movie, the devil tries to sell the hermit a set of encyclopedias, and more fun.

Danko, Dan
 Leonardo da Vinci: the renaissance man. Dan Danko, illustrated by Lalit Kumar Sharma. Campfire/Kalyani Navyug Media Pvt. Ltd. 2011 68 p.
Grades: 8 9 10   **709.2**
 1. Artists; 2. Artists — Italy — Biography; 3. Biographical graphic novels; 4. Inventors — Italy — Biography; 5. Leonardo, da Vinci, 1452-1519; 6. Renaissance — Italy — Biography; 7. Scientists — Italy — Biography
 9380741014; 9380741200; 9789380741017; 9789380741208, $9.99
                LC 2011294404
 This graphic novel is a biography of Leonardo da Vinci. It "opens with the theft of the 'Mona Lisa' from the Louvre in 1911, then backtracks to da Vinci's turbulent childhood in Italy during the Renaissance. Throughout the tale, the mind of da Vinci is shown to be always active, always questioning, always seeking ways to create something better." (Voice of Youth Advocates)

David, Peter
 Friendly Neighborhood Spider-Man Vol. 1: Derailed. Writer, Peter David ; pencils, Mike Wieringo & Roger Cruz ; inks, Karl Kesel ... [et al.] ; colors, Paul Mounts & Chris Sotomayor. Marvel Entertainment 2006 Un Illustration
Grades: 7 8 9 10 11 12 Adult   **741.5; Fic**
 1. Spider-Man (Fictional character); 2. Superhero graphic novels; 3. Graphic novels
 978-0-7851-2216-6, $14.99
 A major character from Peter Parker's past returns, and it looks like Hobgoblin is terrorizing the skies again. Also, a woman chronicles Spider-Man's career on her blog, convinced that he has stalked her for her entire life.

 I am Iron Man. Sean Chen, illustrator. Marvel Worldwide, Inc. 2010 Un Illustration
Grades: 7 8 9 10 11 12 Adult   **741.5; Fic**
 1. Iron Man (Fictional character); 2. Superhero graphic novels; 3. Graphic novels
 978-0-7851-4558-5, $16.99
 The first Iron Man movie, released in 2008, was a major hit, but just like the other superhero movies based on Marvel Comics properties, it wasn't based on any particular Iron Man comics. This book collects a two-issue miniseries based on the movie script, written by Peter David with pencils by Sean Chen, a one-shot written by Christos Gage with pencils by Hugo Petrus, and Iron Man #200, which was written by Denny O'Neil with pencils by Mark Bright and originally

published in 1985. David and Chen's comic adapts the movie script, hitting all the high points of the action. Gage and Petrus's one-shot, "Security Measures," looks at the action of the movie from the viewpoint of S.H.I.E.L.D. agent Coulson. Iron Man #200 features a battle between Iron Man and Iron Monger, who is Tony Stark's erstwhile partner Obadiah Stane. The book also includes an interview with Kevin Feige, producer of the Iron Man movie, and photos taken on the movie sets. The book actually cuts down on the amount of violence that was shown in the movie.

Davis, Eleanor
★ The **secret** science alliance and the copycat crook. Bloomsbury 2009 153p. Illustration
Grades: 3 4 5 6 7 8
741.5; Fic
1. Adventure graphic novels; 2. Humorous graphic novels; 3. Inventors — Fiction; 4. School stories; 5. Graphic novels
978-1-59990-142-8, $18.99; 1-59990-142-0; 978-1-59990-396-5 (pa), $10.99; 1-59990-396-2 (pa)

Courtesy of Bloomsbury

LC 2008-45399
Eleven-year-old Julian Calendar thought changing schools would mean leaving his "nerdy" persona behind, but instead he forms an alliance with fellow inventors Greta and Ben and works with them to prevent an adult from using one of their gadgets for nefarious purposes

"With its frenetically eye-catching, full-color panels chock-full of humorous and informative detail, Davis's first (of many, one hopes) graphic adventure of the SSA pumps new life into the kids' secret society formula." Kirkus

The DC Comics Rarities Archives Volume 1
Edited by Dale Crain. DC Comics 2004 348p. Illustration
Grades: 7 8 9 10 11 12 Adult   **741.5; Fic**
1. Superhero graphic novels; 2. Graphic novels
1-4012-0007-8, $75
For the first time ever, in one huge collection, three of DC Comics' most hard to find early anthology titles are reprinted in their entirety. This is a 348-page hardcover collecting New York World's Fair 1939, New York World's Fair 1940 and Big All-American Comic Book #1 (1944). The two World's Fair Comics were specially created to be distributed at the legendary New York World's Fair of 1939-40 and feature adventures revolving around the DC heroes' visits there.

The DC Encyclopedia: The Definitive Guide to the Characters of the DC Universe
Dorling Kindersley. Edited by Alastair Dougall. 2006 351p. Illustration
Grades: 6 7 8 9 10 11 12 Adult   **741.5**

1. Batman (Fictional character); 2. Comic books, strips, etc — United States — History and criticism — Encyclopedias; 3. DC Comics — Encyclopedias; 4. Joker (Fictional character); 5. Superman (Fictional character); 6. Wonder Woman (Fictional character); 7. Graphic novels
978-0-7566-0592-6, $40.00
LC 2004-3379
This one-volume encyclopedia of more than 1,000 characters created by DC Comics, features some of DC's most creative artists and heroes and villains from the world famous - such as Superman, Batman, Wonder Woman, Lex Luthor, and Joker, to lesser known characters. This guide has comic book history exploding off every page.

DC's Greatest Imaginary Stories
Otto Binder [and others], writers ; C.C. Beck [and others], pencillers and inkers. DC Comics 2005 192p. Illustration
Grades: 6 7 8 9 10 11 12 Adult   **741.5; Fic**
1. Batman (Fictional character); 2. Flash (Fictional character); 3. Superhero graphic novels; 4. Superman (Fictional character); 5. Graphic novels
1-4012-0534-8, $19.99
This volume collects eleven stories that are totally imaginary about many of DC's heroes: Superman marries Lois Lane; in another story, he marries Lana Lang; and in yet another story, he marries Lori Lemaris the mermaid. Batman abandons his millions to drive a taxi. The Flash races into action maskless. Superman and Batman are brothers. In the wedding of the century, it's Super girl and ... Jimmy Olsen" And Shazam witnesses atomic bomb and attacks and finds that even he, the World's Mightiest Mortal, can't stop the bombs.

De Campi, Alex
Kat & Mouse. Story by Alex de Campi; art by Federica Manfredi. Tokyopop 2009 Un Illustration
Grades: 5 6 7 8 9   **741.5; Fic**
1. Mystery graphic novels; 2. Schools; 3. Graphic novels
978-1-4278-1175-2, $5.99
Kat and Mouse have pursued the thief called Artful Dodger, who has managed to elude them and the police. On the night of the Dover Academy Snow Ball, their school enemy Chloe comes to the girls for help: her diamond necklace has been stolen. They spend the evening checking clues, but an oncoming blizzard and a surprise revelation about their art teacher complicate matters. This concluding volume of the series has been long-delayed; readers might want to refresh their memory of what happened before by rereading the first three volumes before reading this one. There is no synopsis of previous events, and some characters aren't identified by name.

Kat & Mouse: Teacher torture. [by] Alex de Campi; art by Frederica Manfredi. Tokyopop 2006 96p. Illustration
Grades: 4 5 6 7 8 9   **741.5; Fic**
1. Mystery fiction; 2. Mystery graphic novels; 3. Graphic novels
1-59816-548-8, $5.99
Middle schooler Kat starts at a posh school where her father has been hired as the new science teacher, but all is not well. Accidents happen in the science lab, and an anonymous student threatens worse unless Kat's dad passes

all the rich, popular students. Kat decides to investigate, aided by her one new friend, Mouse, the rebellious computer nerd and would-be CSI investigator.

Other titles in this series are: Tripped (2007); The ice storm (2007); The knave of diamonds (2009)

Kat & Mouse Vol. 2: Tripped. Tokyopop 2007 96p. Illustration
Grades: 4 5 6 7 8 9   **741.5; Fic**
  1. Mystery graphic novels; 2. Graphic novels
  978-1-59816-549-4, $5.99
Since her arrival at Dover Academy, the one person Kat has been able to depend on is her best friend Mee-Seen, better known as Mouse. But when Mouse gets a crush on the new art teacher, a misunderstanding comes between the two friends - and a class trip to the art museum only makes it worse. When a famous painting is stolen right under their noses, will Kat and Mouse be able to smooth things out in time to catch the thief?

De Groot, Bob
  Clifton Jade. Cinebook 2008 48p.
Grades: 5 6 7 8 9   **741.5; Fic**
  1. Adventure graphic novels; 2. Humorous graphic novels; 3. Spies; 4. Graphic novels
  978-1-905460-52-6, $11.95
Sir Harold Wilberforce Clifton, ex-Secret Service and retired Colonel, works as a private detective, as well as leading a troop of young scouts. With the help of his housekeeper, Mrs. Partridge, who's also a dab hand at auto mechanics, he still helps the government. This time, however, he's being tailed by someone and then summoned to a retirement home where he finds his old World War II nemesis, Otto Kartoffeln, who tells him a group of neo-Nazis are searching for a long-lost Nazi treasure in order to bring about the 4th Reich. The mysterious shadow is Jade, a young agent who was trying to complete her training; now she and Clifton must stop the neo-Nazis from finding the treasure.
Part of the Clifton series, originally published in France as Clifton Jade.

De Liz, Renae
  The **last** unicorn. Original story by Peter S. Beagle; adaptation by Peter B. Gillis; art by Renae De Liz. IDW 2011 167p. Illustration
Grades: 6 7 8 9 10   **741.5; Fic**
  9780451450524 (rpt), $16.00; 978-1-60010-851-8, $24.99; 1-60010-851-2
"A beloved story is now a graphic novel in this excellent adaptation. . . . Much of the original novel's lyrical language has been included, and readers will be eager to find out if the unicorn will give up her quest for love, or if any of Schmendrick's spells will ever turn out right. . . . The illustrations are graceful and detailed, and inked in warm, glowing colors. This is a worthy successor to the classic novel and film." SLJ

DeFalco, Tom
  The **Amazing** Spider-Girl: Whatever Happened to the Daughter of Spider-Man?. Illustrated by Ron Frenz. Marvel Entertainment 2007 Un Illustration
Grades: 7 8 9 10 11 12 Adult   **741.5; Fic**

  1. Spider-Girl (Fictional character); 2. Spider-Man (Fictional character); 3. Superhero graphic novels; 4. Graphic novels
  978-0-7851-2341-5, $14.99
After discovering she had inherited her father's incredible powers, May "Mayday" Parker donned a costume and became the amazing Spider-Girl. Recent events have forced her to hang up her webs and lead a normal life ... but how long can May keep from web-slinging when there are villains like Hobgoblin on the loose? This volume begins collecting the second run of Spider-Girl comics; the first 100 issues were published as Spider-Girl and are being collected in digest-sized trade paperbacks. This new series, The Amazing Spider-Girl, features new numbering (from #1 and on) and is being collected in regular comic book-sized trade paperbacks.

  Avengers Next: Rebirth. Written by Tom DeFalco ; pencilled by Ron Lim. Marvel Entertainment 2007 Un Illustration
Grades: 7 8 9 10 11 12   **741.5; Fic**
  1. Avengers (Fictional characters); 2. Superhero graphic novels
  978-0-7851-2518-1, $13.99
The time has come for the next generation of Avengers to choose a new lineup, but first they must battle zombie versions of themselves. Then, as Katie Power (from Power Pack) joins the team, American Dream and her friends mount a search for the missing Thunderstrike. The man called Nova guest stars when strange visitors from outer space land on Earth. And more.

  Spider-Girl Presents A-Next: Second Coming. Marvel Entertainment 2006 Un Illustration
Grades: 6 7 8 9 10 11 12   **741.5; Fic**
  1. Captain America (Fictional character); 2. Doctor Strange (Fictional character); 3. Superhero graphic novels; 4. Graphic novels
  0-7851-2131-5, $7.99
On another day unlike any other, a new collection of the World's Mightiest Heroes rocked their own remarkable reality. New heroes, such as J2 (son of Juggernaut), Thunderstrike (Kevin Masterson), Stinger (Cassie Lang), and the mysterious Mainframe, become the new Avengers. Enemies alien and Earthbound vie to end the new era of Avengerdom. This book features the heir of Captain America and the son of the Black Panther, and guest-stars Doctor Strange and the Defenders.

  Spider-Girl Presents Juggernaut, Jr.: Secrets and Lies. Written by Tom DeFalco ; art by Ron Lim. Marvel Entertainment 2006 Un Illustration
Grades: 6 7 8 9 10 11 12   **741.5; Fic**
  1. Superhero graphic novels; 2. Graphic novels
  0-7851-2047-5, $7.99
Lots of people have big shoes to fill, but how many have to fill the helmet of the Juggernaut? Teenager Zane Marko grows up fast and hits the big time head first when he inherits his father's unstoppability and joins the latest generation of Avengers. J2 squares off against villains and heroes alike, including a certain green goliath who thinks he's still the strongest one there is. This volume includes the first

appearances of the X-People and Wild Thing, daughter of Wolverine and Elektra.

Spider-girl Vol. 1: Legacy. Illustrated by Pat Olliffe. Marvel Comics 2004 144p. Illustration
Grades: 7 8 9 10 11 12   **741.5; Fic**
 1. Spider-Girl (Fictional character); 2. Spider-Man (Fictional character); 3. Superhero graphic novels; 4. Graphic novels
 0-7851-1441-6, $7.99
In an alternate future in the Marvel Universe, Peter Parker has retired from being Spider-Man after a crippling injury; but he and Mary Jane have a daughter, May. She has just turned sixteen, and suddenly discovers she has superpowers! Soon she finds out who her father used to be, and she decides to be a superhero—but Peter knows the dangers all too well and tries to stop her. Once Mayday decides to be Spider-Girl, though, no one can stop her. This is the first of an ongoing series.

Spider-Girl Vol. 2: Like Father, Like Daughter. Illustrated by Pat Olliffe. Marvel Entertainment 2004 Un Illustration
Grades: 7 8 9 10 11 12   **741.5; Fic**
 1. Spider-Girl (Fictional character); 2. Superhero graphic novels; 3. Graphic novels
 0-7851-1657-5, $7.99
Her name is May "Mayday" Parker, and she recently learned her father was the original Spider-Man. The good news is that she's having the time of her life as she hones the amazing spider-like abilities she inherited from him. The bad news is that some of her roughest, toughest battles lie ahead - against the likes of Ladyhawk, the Kingpin of Crime, Mr. Nobody, Crazy Eight...and her own parents. She also learns that it's not easy hiding such a big part of your life from all your friends in school.

Spider-Girl Vol. 3: Avenging Allies. Written by Tom DeFalco ; illustrated by Pat Olliffe. Marvel Entertainment 2005 Un. Illustration
Grades: 7 8 9 10 11 12   **741.5; Fic**
 1. Avengers (Fictional characters); 2. Spider-Girl (Fictional character); 3. Superhero graphic novels; 4. Graphic novels
 0-7851-1658-3, $7.99
The adventures of Spider-Man's daughter continue as Mayday Parker faces defeat and disgrace at the hands of Darkdevil and Kaine, then she has to prove her fighting mettle by taking on the Avengers one at a time. Plus: Beset by problems in her civilian guise, Spider-Girl teams up with Speedball to take on Mr. Abnormal, the most flexible felon of all.

Spider-Girl Vol. 4: Turning Point. Artist Pat Olliffe. Marvel Entertainment 2005 Un Illustration
Grades: 7 8 9 10 11 12   **741.5; Fic**
 1. Spider-Girl (Fictional character); 2. Spider-Man (Fictional character); 3. Superhero graphic novels; 4. Graphic novels
 0-7851-1871-3, $7.99
The adventures of Spider-Man's daughter continue as Mayday once again faces Kaine, Spider-Man swings again, and Darkdevil is . . . actually nice? Plus: Meet new heroes and villains, take a peek into the fantasies of Mayday's

friends, and witness the return of the Green Goblin. In May's life, she's caught between JJ (grandson of J. Jonah Jameson) and Brad; how is a girl to choose?

Spider-Girl Vol. 5: Endgame. Illustrated by Pat Olliffe. Marvel Entertainment 2006 Un Illustration
Grades: 7 8 9 10 11 12   **741.5; Fic**
 1. Spider-Girl (Fictional character); 2. Superhero graphic novels; 3. Graphic novels
 0-7851-2034-3, $7.99
Spider-Girl faces trouble when her deadliest enemies join forces as the Savage Six (or is it Seven?)! But even with the help of rival/critic heroes like Darkdevil and the Buzz, can she deal with the sudden loss of her super-powers? And, naturally, that's when Normie Osborn escapes from the mental institution, convinced that he, as Green Goblin, must kill Spider-Girl.

Spider-Girl Vol. 6: Too Many Spiders!. Artist Pat Olliffe. Marvel Entertainment 2006 Un Illustration
Grades: 7 8 9 10 11 12   **741.5; Fic**
 1. Spider-Girl (Fictional character); 2. Spider-Man (Fictional character); 3. Superhero graphic novels; 4. X-Men (Fictional characters); 5. Graphic novels
 0-7851-2156-0, $7.99
Sworn to follow in her father's web tracks, "May Mayday" Parker's got a lot on her plate - but an upstart imitator wants to help himself to her heritage. Who is the new Spider-Man and what role will he play in Spider-Girl's reality? This volume guest-stars the Avengers of A-Next - with looks into the legacies of the FF, the X-Men and the New Warriors.

Spider-Girl Vol. 7: Betrayed. Illustrator Pat Olliffe. Marvel Entertainment 2006 Un Illustration
Grades: 7 8 9 10 11 12   **741.5; Fic**
 1. Spider-Girl (Fictional character); 2. Spider-Man (Fictional character); 3. Superhero graphic novels; 4. Graphic novels
 0-7851-2157-9, $7.99
Who will lead the New York underworld? Will the Green Goblin go good or give grief? What secret is Mary Jane keeping? And who is the next true Spider-Man? This volume guest-stars the Fantastic Five.

Spider-Girl Vol. 8: Duty Calls. Illustrator Pat Olliffe. Marvel Entertainment 2007 Un Illustration
Grades: 7 8 9 10 11 12   **741.5; Fic**
 1. Adventure graphic novels; 2. Spider-Girl (Fictional character); 3. Spider-Man (Fictional character); 4. Superhero graphic novels; 5. Graphic novels
 07851-2495-0, $7.99
Wall-crawling gets crowded when a new Spider-Man and Scarlet Spider swing into action, and the one true web-slinger joins Spider-Girl to clear up the costumed clonery. Plus: One of Spider-Girl's longtime foes meets his doom, prompting his family into vengeful action. And this volume introduces the MC-2 incarnation of the New Warriors.

Spider-Girl: Choices. Tom DeFalco, writer; Pat Olliffe, penciler; Al Williamson, inker; Janice Chiang, letterer; Christie Scheele, colorist; Bob Harras, chief.. ABDO Spotlight 2006 Un Illustration

Grades: 5 6 7 8 9 10 11 12 **741.5; Fic**
1. Spider-Girl (Fictional character); 2. Spider-Man (Fictional character); 3. Superhero graphic novels; 4. Graphic novels
1-59961-028-0, $21.35

May, teenage daughter of Peter and Mary Jane Parker, has inherited her father's Spidey powers, but the former Spider-Man has forbidden her to use them; he doesn't want May to get crippled like him, or worse. However, May can't help but use her powers for good, so even though Peter has destroyed all the old Spider-Man equipment, May rescued some web shooters and web-cartridges. Dressed in an old gym suit and a skiing mask, she sets out to discover who has been following her father, who is working on a case involving organized crime. The book includes lots of action but little violence.

★ **Spider-Girl:** legacy . . . in black and white. ABDO Publishing Group/Spotlight 2006 Un Illustration
Grades: 5 6 7 8 9 10 11 12 **741.5; Fic**
1. Adventure graphic novels; 2. Spider-Girl (Fictional character); 3. Spider-Man (Fictional character); 4. Superhero graphic novels; 5. Graphic novels
1-59961-029-9; 978-1-59961-029-0, $21.35
LC 2006-44301

In an alternate Marvel Universe, Peter and Mary Jane Parker stayed married and had a daughter, May (nicknamed Mayday). Peter's superhero career as Spider-Man ended when the Green Goblin shattered his leg, and he and Mary Jane have kept all of this secret from May. Now she's fifteen years old, popular, a star basketball player "and during a game, the powers she inherited from her father kick in. As if that isn't shock enough, a new Hobgoblin comes after Peter Parker" it's another Osborne, Norman, grandson of the original Green Goblin and May's former playmate. Does she have enough Spidey powers to take him down before he hurts her parents? This is a library-bound edition of Spider-Girl #0, which was first Marvel What If #105, and which launched the Spider-Girl comics series.
Volume 1 of 12

DeFilippis, Nunzio
Destiny's Hand Volume 1. Written by Nunzio DeFilippis and Christina Weir ; illustrated by Melvin Calingo. Seven Seas Entertainment 2006 Un Illustration
Grades: 8 9 10 11 12 **741.5; Fic**
1. Adventure graphic novels; 2. Pirates; 3. Graphic novels
1-933164-11-5, $10.99

Destiny's Hand is a pirate ship that cannot be sunk, led by a dying Captain who will not give up. His final wish before he dies is to find the legendary Devil's Eye. And who does he appoint to lead his fearless crew in search of the lost treasure, but Olivia Soldana, a brash 16-year-old girl who can outdo any man. This is a global manga title published in the Japanese right-to-left format. There is hand-to-hand combat but no gore, and little strong language.

Once in a blue moon. Written by Nunzio DeFilippis & Christina Weir ; artwork by Jennifer Quick ; lettering by Jennie Jones ; design by Keith Wood ; edited by James Lucas Jones. Oni Press 2004 154p. Illustration
Grades: 6 7 8 9 10 11 12 **741.5; Fic**
1. Fantasy graphic novels; 2. Graphic novels

1-929998-83-X, $11.95

Aeslin had a magical childhood, with loving parents who read wonderful fables from the book, The Avalon Chronicles, about a fantastic world where a brave Dragon Knight and her Prince battled an Evil Wizard. Then, her parents left on a business trip from which only her mother returned. Her mother tried to erase any aspect of fantasy from Aeslin's life from that time. Now, she happens upon a new book, Once in a Blue Moon, and when she wishes she could go to Avalon to help the people, she finds herself magically transported there and learns she is the new Dragon Knight who must save the land.

Play ball. Written by Nunzio DeFilippis and Christina Weir ; illustrated by Jackie Lewis. Oni Press, Inc. 2012 144 p.
Grades: 6 7 8 9 **741.5/973; Fic**
1. Baseball; 2. School stories; 3. Women athletes
1934964794; 9781934964798, $19.99
LC 2011933142

This comic "traces a high school girl's struggle to join a boys' baseball team. Freckle-faced Dashiell Brody was good at softball in her private girls' school; now that she's moved to another city with her mother and older sister and they must enroll in public school, she wants to play the real game, despite stereotypical resistance from school administrators and some jocks." (Publishers Weekly)

Del Rio, Tania
Sabrina the Teenage Witch: The Magic Revisited. Archie Comics 2006 Un Illustration
Grades: 4 5 6 7 8 9 **741.5; Fic**
1. Fantasy graphic novels; 2. Humorous graphic novels; 3. Witches; 4. Graphic novels
1-879794-19-5, $7.49

The first four issues of Sabrina the Teenage Witch's "manga makeover" are collected in this special edition trade paperback. Writer-artist Tania del Rio presents these tales of magical flights of fancy and romantic intrigue... sprinkled with a dash of humor. Sabrina's awakening powers and the various love triangle combinations that have formed since keep her busy at school, on dates, and ... everywhere.

Delsante, Vito
Before they were famous: Babe Ruth. Aladdin Paperbacks 2009 121p.
Grades: 3 4 5 6 7 8
741.5; 920
1. Baseball players; 2. Baseball players; 3. Biographical graphic novels; 4. Ruth, Babe, 1895-1948; 5. Graphic novels
978-1-4169-5071-4, $8.99
LC 2008-929319

Babe Ruth is still considered to be one of the best professional baseball players of all time, and he was the first "home run

Courtesy of Aladdin Press

king" of the sport. This graphic novel, adapted from Babe Ruth by Guernsey Van Riper, Jr., part of the Childhood of Famous Americans series, takes readers back to the troubled childhood of George Ruth. In Baltimore, Maryland in 1902, the Ruth family struggles to keep their restaurant going, and their young son George is a troublemaker; eventually, they send George to St. Mary's Industrial School for Boys. It's a boarding school run by Catholic monks, and George will have to stay there until he's twenty-one. At the school, George discovers baseball, and it transforms his life. When he's asked to sign up with the Baltimore Orioles at the age of nineteen, his new teammates call him Babe. This fictionalized biography will help young readers get a sense of the person behind the legend.

DeMatteis, J. M.
   Abadazad: The Dream Thief by J.M. DeMatteis ; drawings by Mike Ploog ; colors by Nick Bell. Hyperion Books for Children 2006 Un Illustration
Grades: 5 6 7 8 9   **741.5; Fic**
   1. Adventure graphic novels; 2. Fantasy graphic novels; 3. Graphic novels
1-4231-00646, $9.99
   In the magical land of Abadazad, Kate needs all the help she can get when she encounters the Lanky Man. He's mean and heartless, and he wants to steal children's dreams. Everyone seems to be against her, which only makes her more determined to find her brother. And Matt is getting closer, isn't he? This story is a hybrid, combining prose text with pages of sequential art from the original comic books.

   Abadazad: The Road to Inconceivable. Hyperion Books for Children 2006 Un Illustration
Grades: 5 6 7 8 9   **741.5; Fic**
   1. Adventure graphic novels; 2. Fantasy graphic novels; 3. Graphic novels
1-4231-0062-X, $9.99
   Kate's little brother Matt disappeared five years ago, and Kate thinks she will never see him again. But then she finds out that Matt is trapped in the world of Abadazad. Will Kate have the courage to look for her brother? And if she leaves home, will she ever return? This story began as comic books, but the publisher went out of business before the story was completed. Now it's published as a hybrid, combining prose sections with pages of sequential art and spot illustrations.

   ★ The **stardust** kid. Boom! created by J. M. DeMatteis, writer & Mike Ploog, illustrator ; Nick Bell & Sumi Pak, color ; Dave Lanphear, lettering. Studios 2008 Un Illustration
Grades: 3 4 5 6 7 8 9 10 11 12 Adult   **741.5; Fic**
   1. Adventure graphic novels; 2. Fantasy graphic novels; 3. Graphic novels
978-1-934506-04-2, $14.99
   Twelve-year-old Cody's best friend is Paul Brightfield; they share a deep bond that goes far beyond mere friendship. What no one else knows is that Paul isn't human, he's one of the last Old Ones, ancient elemental beings who lived before man existed. One night, Paul disappears, and a hate-filled creature who has existed long buried beneath Wilde Park bursts out with a desire to destroy everything in the world. Only Cody, his little sister K.M., and his friend Alana and

her little brother Nathaniel, remain, and somehow they must find The Stardust Kid and discover a way to stop the hate and restore their world. Some creatures might be frightening to younger readers, but anyone who likes the Harry Potter books shouldn't have a problem with this book.

Denson, Abby
   Tough Love: High School Confidential. Manic D Press 2006 144p. Illustration
Grades: 8 9 10 11 12 Adult   **741.5; Fic**
   1. Homosexuality; 2. Romance graphic novels; 3. Graphic novels
978-1-933149-08-0, $12.95
   In this sweet teen romance graphic novel, shy Brian discovers he loves martial artist Chris, but also develops a supportive friendship with Julie, the first person he's ever told that he's gay. Denson was inspired by shonen-ai (boy love) manga to do an American comic depicting a positive, healthy relationship between two teen boys who accept what they are. The story was originally serialized in XY magazine. The boys are shown hugging and kissing, but that is all.

Denton, Shannon Eric
   Zapt!, Vol. 1. Story by Shannon Eric Denton and Keith Giffen ; art by Armand Villavert Jr. Tokyopop 2006 96p. Illustration
Grades: 4 5 6 7 8   **741.5; Fic**
   1. Humorous graphic novels; 2. Science fiction graphic novels; 3. Graphic novels
1-59816-588-7, $5.99
   Armand Jones is a fairly typical elementary school student who doesn't like to get up in the morning, has to deal with bullies on the school bus and on campus. As if that isn't hard enough, he finds himself zapped out of the boys' restroom into a space station full of aliens, and learns that he is now a recruit in the Pangalactic Order of Police (P.O.O.P.). Partnered with the equally young Pandekian named Paylean, Armand almost immediately gets captured by space pirates. Then, when he gets back to school, his classmate Gladys gets kidnapped by Terros, and Armand learns that she's an alien princess he now has to rescue. This first volume of an ongoing series is a global manga.

Deutsch, Barry
   Hereville: how Mirka caught a fish. Barry Deutsch. Amulet Books 2015 140 p. Color; Illustration
Grades: 4 5 6 7   **741.5/973; 741.5**
   1. Babysitting — Juvenile fiction; 2. Fishes — Juvenile fiction; 3. Jewish girls — Fiction
9781419708008, $17.95

LC 2015945771
   In this book, by Barry Deutsch, "Welcome back to Hereville, where Mirka, the world's first time-travelling, monster-fighting Orthodox Jewish girl . . . [is] stuck babysitting her disapproving little sister, Layele. When Mirka pushes her sister into a stream, they both get in too deep with an angry magic fish. . . . When the fish kidnaps Layele, Mirka must find a way to save her little sister, and the clues she needs are hidden in her stepmother Fruma's past." (Publisher's note)

★ **Hereville:** how Mirka got her sword. Colors by Jake Richmond. Amulet Books 2010 137p. Illustration
Grades: 4 5 6 7
741.5; Fic
1. Dragons; 2. Fantasy graphic novels; 3. Jews; 4. Graphic novels
978-0-8109-8422-6, $15.95; 0-8109-8422-9
LC 2010-924236

Courtesy of Amulet Paperbacks

Mirka and her family live in an Orthodox Jewish village called Hereville. All she really wants to do is fight dragons, but what she has to fight is a troublesome pig that talks. Then Mirka meets the witch who lives nearby, and then confronts a troll, and soon she finds she has much more adventure than she knows how to handle.

"Deutsch creates authentic characters spiced with just enough fantasy to surprise. . . . Details of Orthodox daily life are well blended into the art and given just the right touches of explanation to keep readers on track." Booklist

★ **Hereville:** How Mirka Met a Meteorite. Barry Deutsch; colors by Jake Richmond. Amulet Books 2012 123 p.
Grades: 3 4 5 6 7
741.5
1. Adventure graphic novels; 2. Jews; 3. Trolls — Fiction; 4. Witches — Fiction
1419703986; 9781419703980, $16.95
LC 2012947050

This graphic novel by Barry Deutsch features a "wisecracking, adventure-loving, sword-wielding Orthodox Jewish heroine. . . . She fearlessly stands up to local bullies. She battles a very large, very menacing pig. And she boldly accepts a challenge from a mysterious witch, a challenge that could bring Mirka her heart's desire: a dragon-slaying sword! All she has to do is find — and outwit — the giant troll who's got it!" (Publisher's note)

Dezago, Todd
Spider-Man and Storm: change the weather. ABDO Publishing Group/Spotlight 2006 Un Illustration
Grades: 3 4 5 6 7 8
741.5; Fic
1. Spider-Man (Fictional character); 2. Storm (Fictional character); 3. Superhero graphic novels; 4. X-Men (Fictional characters); 5. Graphic novels
1-59961-003-5, $21.35
LC 2006-44931

A stranger comes to New York right when Storm of the X-Men is enjoying some unscheduled free flight and Spider-Man is just swinging along for fun. Storm tries to help a helicopter whose rotor stopped working while Spidey tries to help the stranger when some toughs try to hassle her. Then he accidentally touches her bare hand after her glove tears, and he temporarily loses his power while the girl suddenly possesses them. Storm accidentally touches the girl, loses her powers, and nearly loses the helicopter, which

Spider-Man saves. They both realize the girl is a mutant and try to help her.
Part of the Marvel Age Spider-Man series.

Spider-man and Thor: out of time. Todd Dezago, script ; Ron Lim, pencils ; Scott Koblish, inks ; Dave Sharpe, letters ; Digital Rainbow, colors. ABDO Publishing Company/Spotlight 2006 Un Illustration
Grades: 4 5 6 7 8 9
741.5; Fic
1. Spider-Man (Fictional character); 2. Superhero graphic novels; 3. Thor (Fictional character); 4. Graphic novels
1-59961-004-3, $21.35

It takes both Spider-Man and the Mighty Thor to deal with things when an Asgardian enemy, Kryllk, regains control of the Frostgaard Crystal; it allows him to freeze time so he and his troll hordes can conquer Midgard, er, Earth, and the gods' realm of Asgard as well. But now Kryllk faces two heroes at the same time. This is a revised, hardbound edition of the Marvel Age comic book.
Part of the Spider-Man Team Up series

Diamond, Jeremy
Nascar heroes #2: Who is Jimmy Dash? Jeremy Diamond, writer ; Ash, layout ; Peter Habjan, artist ; Rich Duhaney ... [et al.], guest artists ; Peter Habjan ... [et al.], colorists. 2009 Un
Grades: 3 4 5 6 7 8
741.5; Fic
1. Automobile racing; 2. NASCAR; 3. Superhero graphic novels; 4. Graphic novels
978-1-59961-663-6, $22.78
LC 2009-9008

The accident that gave the Flatstock pit crew, plus Dashiell, super powers, also gave them to Jack Diesel; and he doesn't have any good intentions. When Jimmy Dash and Team Flatstock keep winning NASCAR races, Diesel resorts to dirty tricks with his laser heat vision and illegal gadgets on his cars. However, Team Flatstock owner Astor also gained powers in the accident; she sees visions of the near future. Diesel decides that the entire Flatstock team would do anything for Astor, so he kidnaps her; Dashiell reveals his identity to the guys, and they go to rescue Astor. However, that's much easier said than done when Diesel will use any dirty trick to win.

Nascar heroes #3: Dash to the finish! Jeremy Diamond, writer ; Matt Cassan, Peter Habjan, artists. ABDO/Spotlight 2009 Un Illustration
Grades: 3 4 5 6 7 8
741.5; Fic
1. Automobile racing; 2. NASCAR; 3. Superhero graphic novels; 4. Graphic novels
978-1-59961-664-3, $22.78
LC 2009-9009

When Dashiell and the Flatstock pit crew went to rescue Astor from Jack Diesel, they've had to deal with car crushers, Diesel's super powers, and now his mutated dog, Lucifer, who has become a giant, drooling creature. Diesel has also managed to put their car, #76, into orbit. He takes Astor while the guys deal with Lucifer; but they still have a race to win, even as they desperately search for their boss and friend. And, even though Diesel continues to play dirty tricks, Dashiell warns the others that they must use their powers only for defense and let him win by his own driving.

Nascar heroes #4: headless stuntman. ABDO/Spotlight 2009 Un Illustration
Grades: 3 4 5 6 7 8   **741.5; Fic**
1. Automobile racing; 2. Ghosts; 3. Motion pictures — Production and direction; 4. NASCAR; 5. Superhero graphic novels; 6. Graphic novels
978-1-59961-665-0, $22.78
        LC 2009-9010
During the off-season, Dashiell takes a break from racing practice to star in a racing movie. What he doesn't know is that several other actors have already quit, frightened off the set by a headless ghost. Dashiell takes on the ghost driver to save an actress, but can he do it without wrecking the set?

Nascar heroes #5: NASCAR villains!. ABDO/Spotlight 2009 Un
Grades: 3 4 5 6 7 8   **741.5; Fic**
1. Automobile racing; 2. NASCAR; 3. Superhero graphic novels; 4. Graphic novels
978-1-5996-666-7, $22.78
        LC 2009-9011
Team Flatstock gains a new crew chief, the mysterious Professor N., who says he can train the crew to use their super powers. Meanwhile, Jack Diesel breaks out of prison with the help of fellow villains (including Predacar, a transforming vehicle), and they give Team Flatstock lots of trouble while using every cheat in the book to win the race.

Nascar heroes #6: Rev-Alation!. ABDO/Spotlight 2009 Un
Grades: 3 4 5 6 7 8   **741.5; Fic**
1. Automobile racing; 2. NASCAR; 3. Superhero graphic novels; 4. Graphic novels
978-1-59961-667-4, $22.78
        LC 2009-9012
When Professor N. joined Team Flatstock, he brought back the car Jack Diesel had sent into orbit. Now with two cars, team owner Astor has become the second driver, and she and Jimmy Dash start a rivalry that could divide the team. Then Professor N. says he needs a sample of the material Diesel was working on in his secret laboratory at the time of the accident that gave everyone their powers, so the pit crew decides to retrieve it for him while Astor tries to distract Diesel by going on a date with him.

Nascar heroes #3: Dash to the finish! Jeremy Diamond, writer ; Matt Cassan, Peter Habjan, artists. ABDO/Spotlight 2009 Un Illustration
Grades: 3 4 5 6 7 8   **741.5; Fic**
1. Automobile racing; 2. NASCAR; 3. Superhero graphic novels; 4. Graphic novels
978-1-59961-662-9, $22.78
        LC 2009-9007
Dashiell James works as a janitor for Jack Diesel's NASCAR racing team, but on his own time he hangs out with the Team Flatstock pit crew, Zip, Gus, and Ed. Team Diesel wins a lot of races, while Team Flatstock is known on the NASCAR circuit as "Team Laughingstock." Then an explosion is a secret laboratory in Team Diesel's building affects Dashiell and the pit crew suddenly Zip has super speed, Gus has super strength, Ed can multiply himself, and Dashiell is almost indestructible. When the Flatstock driver quits, Dashiell hides his identity in a firesuit and helmet and

calls himself Jimmy Dash; he becomes the new Team Flatstock driver, and wins his and Flatstock's very first race.

Dickens, Charles, 1812-1870
    Classics Illustrated Deluxe #8: Oliver Twist. By Loic Dauvillier; illustrated by Olivier Deloye. Papercutz 2012 238 p.
Grades: 6 7 8 9 10 11 12   **741.5**
1. London (England) — Fiction; 2. Orphans — Fiction; 3. Graphic novels
9781597073073; 1597073075
    This graphic novel, by Charles Dickens, adapted by Loic Dauvillier, and illustrated by Olivier Deloye, is part of the "Classic Illustrated Deluxe" series. "The story is about an orphan, Oliver Twist, who endures a miserable existence in a workhouse and then is placed with an undertaker. He escapes and travels to London where he meets . . . a gang of juvenile pickpockets. Naively unaware of their unlawful activities, Oliver is led to the lair of their elderly criminal trainer Fagin." (Wikipedia)

Dini, Paul
    The **World's** Greatest Super-Heroes. Stories by Alex Ross and Paul Dini ; text by Paul Dini ; art by Alex Ross ; lettering on JLA: liberty and justice by Todd Klein. DC Comics 2005 Un Illustration
Grades: 6 7 8 9 10 11 12 Adult   **741.5; Fic**
1. Batman (Fictional character); 2. Justice League (Fictional characters); 3. Superhero graphic novels; 4. Superman (Fictional character); 5. Wonder Woman (Fictional character); 6. Graphic novels
1-4012-0254-3, $49.95
        LC 2006-159064
    This oversize hardcover volume collects the stories that DC originally published separately. Superman tries to singlehandedly end world hunger, only to face suspicion and corruption; Batman tries to stop all criminal activity; and Wonder Woman tries to free oppressed women. They each realize that, despite their super powers, they can't eradicate the problems of the world on their own. The rest of the book portrays the Justice League and highlights each member's super hero origins.

Dirge, Roman
    It ate Billy on Christmas; art by Steven Daily. Dark Horse Books 2007 Un Illustration
Grades: 4 5 6 7 8 9 10 11 12 Adult   **741.5; Fic**
1. Horror graphic novels; 2. Humorous graphic novels; 3. Graphic novels
978-1-59307-853-9, $12.95
    Lumi has been bullied by her brother Billy all her life, and this Christmas would have been more of the same, but for the weird, ugly little monster that crawled up from the abandoned well and came into their house. Mistaking it for the stuffed puppy she had requested from her parents, Lumi watches in amazement as it devours the bullying Billy when he shoots it with darts from his new dart gun. She makes a cardboard Billy, which fools her unsuspecting and clueless parents. A few weeks later, back at school, Lumi has to face the bullies who have made her school life miserable, but she has her "puppy" in her backpack and it's hungry. . . . Dirge wrote the story and drew the black and white illustrations,

while Daily provided the color paintings. The story shows the monster eating Billy in one gulp, but there's little actual violence on the pages. The dark humor and twisted story line will appeal to those who enjoy Coraline and The Wolves in the Walls by Neil Gaiman, and the weird humor of Edward Gorey cartoons.

Dixon, Chuck
Transformers: Evolutions: Hearts of Steel; art by Guido Guidi IDW Publishing 2006 120p. Illustration
Grades: 4 5 6 7 8 9   **741.5; Fic**
1. Science fiction graphic novels; 2. Transformers (Fictional characters); 3. Graphic novels
978-1-60010-055-4, $19.99
In this new Transformers story, writer Chuck Dixon and artist Guido Guidi transplant the 'bots to the Industrial Revolution, where a charismatic hammer-man named John Henry discovers that a steam drill is really an alien robot named Bumblebee. Before he can process this information, the pair is attacked by Decepticons disguised as tanks, trains and walking engines. Is this all part of a larger scheme by Starscream? And if so, will the other Autobots arrive in time to stop his nefarious plans? Mark Twain is among the humans who work with the Autobots.

The **Vanishers**. Illustrated by Andres Klacik. IDW Publishing 2002 80p. Illustration
Grades: 6 7 8 9 10 11 12 Adult   **741.5; Fic**
1. Adventure graphic novels; 2. Science fiction graphic novels; 3. Graphic novels
0-9712282-6-4, $12.99
From the turn of the 20th century, to medieval England, and into the far-flung future, Andy and Arvis must escape their pursuers, rescue their friends, and return to their own time. Andy's friends begin to disappear and only he remembers that they ever existed. When Andy discovers another student, Arvis Voltoz, has noticed that disappearances, he follows Arvis home and begins an adventure that takes him and Arvis through time.

Doctorow, Cory
In Real Life. Cory Doctorow; illustrated by Jen Wang. First Second Books 2014 192 p. Color; Illustration
Grades: 8 9 10 11 12   **741.5**
1. Computer games — Economic aspects; 2. Ethics; 3. Video games
1596436581; 9781596436589, $17.99
In this graphic novel, "online gaming and real life collide when a teen discovers the hidden economies and injustices that hide among seemingly innocent pixels. . . . Anda joins . . . a group of girls playing the game as girl avatars. . . . Another guild member named Lucy . . . asks her if she'd be interested in earning 'real cash.' . . . She's pulled into a world of real-money economies where workers 'play' the game, garnering items they can then sell for actual money to other players." (Kirkus Reviews)
"Characters come to life through Wang's . . . fluid forms and emotive faces, and her adroit shift in colors as the story moves between the physical and gaming worlds is subtle and effective." Pub Wkly

Doeden, Matt
George Washington: Leading a New Nation; by Matt Doeden ; illustrated by Cynthia Martin. Capstone Press 2006 32p. Illustration
Grades: 3 4 5 6 7 8 9   **741.5; 973.4; 92**
1. Washington, George, 1732-1799; 2. Graphic novels
0-7368-4963-7, $25.26
         LC 2005006530
This book uses the comic book format to recount highlights in the life of George Washington, the leader of the Continental Army during the Revolutionary War and the first President of the United States. It includes additional information, a glossary, a list of books for further reading, and more.
Part of the Graphic Library, Graphic Biographies series.

John Sutter and the California Gold Rush; by Matt Doeden ; illustrated by Ron Frenz and Charles Barnett III. Capstone Press 2006 32p. Illustration
Grades: 3 4 5 6 7 8 9   **741.5; 979.4**
1. California — Gold discoveries; 2. Sutter, John Augustus, 1803-1880; 3. Graphic novels
0-7368-4370-1, $25.26
         LC 2005007890
This book tells the story in comic book format of the discovery of gold at John Sutter's mill and how it changed California. It includes additional information, a glossary, a list of books for further reading, and more.
Part of the Graphic Library, Graphic History series.

Winter at Valley Forge by Matt Doeden ; illustrated by Ron Frenz and Charles Barnett III ; [colorist, Bill Anderson]. Capstone Press 2006 32p. Illustration
Grades: 3 4 5 6 7 8 9   **741.5; 973.3**
1. Pennsylvania — History; 2. United States — History — 1775-1783, Revolution; 3. Valley Forge (Pa) — History; 4. Graphic novels
0-7368-4975-0, $25.26
         LC 2005010145
This book uses the comic book format to tell the story of the American patriot troops during the Revolutionary War while wintering at Valley Forge, Pennsylvania. It includes additional information, a glossary, a list of books for further reading, and more.
Part of the Graphic Library, Graphic History series.

Donner, Rebecca
Burnout. Written by Rebecca Donner; illustrated by Inaki Miranda. DC Comics/Minx 2008 176p. Illustration
Grades: 7 8 9 10 11 12   **741.5; Fic**
1. Environmental protection; 2. Romance graphic novels; 3. Graphic novels
978-1-4012-1537-8, $9.99
Danni and her mother have made another in a long series of moves, this time moving in with her mother's boyfriend, lodge owner Hank. Danni can see that Hank is an alcoholic, and he tends to take his anger out on people, including his son Haskell (with whom Danni is forced to share a room for the time being). They live in the Pacific Northwest, in a logging town, and Haskell is a hardcore environmentalist. Danni falls for him despite herself, and she begins to go with him at night to spike trees, which is an act of ecoterrorism. As home life continues to stay rough,

Haskell starts to escalate his acts against logging, and Danni has to decide what to do. The book includes scenes of heavy petting.

"Miranda's superb illustrations complement the story well, whether they're showing landscapes of the Pacific Northwest, action sequences, or the eyes of a troubled girl." Publ Wkly

Dorkin, Evan

★ **Beasts** of Burden: animal rites. Written by Evan Dorkin; art by Jill Thompson; lettering by Jason Arthur and Jill Thompson. Dark Horse Comics 2010 184p. Illustration
Grades: 8 9 10 11 12 Adult   **741.5; Fic**
1. Cats; 2. Dogs; 3. Mystery graphic novels; 4. Supernatural graphic novels; 5. Graphic novels
978-1-59582-513-1, $19.99
2010 Eisner Award for Best Publication for Teens; 2010 Eisner Award to Jill Thompson for Best Painter/Multimedia Artist for Beasts of Burden and Magic Trixie; 2005 Eisner Award for Best Short Story for 'Unfamiliar;' 2004 Eisner Award to Jill Thompson for Best Painter/Multimedia Artist (interior art) for 'Stray.'

Burden Hill is just a nice, quiet suburban town full of houses with yards and white picket fences, demonic frogs, zombie roadkill, ghosts, etc. The humans who live in Burden Hill seem to be totally oblivious to the dangers, but the dogs, and one cat, work together to keep their town safe. Jack the beagle, Pugsley (go figure), Ace the husky, Rex the Doberman, Whitey the terrier, and Orphan the cat deal with a haunted dog house, witches, undead dogs, a werewolf, and other monsters. The book includes some mild bad language ("crap" usually from Pugs) and a fair amount of violence. This book includes the four-issue miniseries plus all of the short stories that originally appeared in The Dark Horse Book of Hauntings, The Dark Horse Book of Witchcraft, The Dark Horse Book of the Dead, and The Dark Horse Book of Monsters. Sarah Dyer co-wrote "A Dog and His Boy" with Evan Dorkin.

"Gorgeous artwork and a smart, witty script elevate this tale of household pets who unite to fight occult menaces in idyllic Burden Hill." Publ Wkly

Downey, Glen

Escape from East Berlin; art by Leo Lingas. Harcourt Achieve/Steck-Vaughn 2007 48p. Illustration
Grades: 3 4 5 6 7 8   **741.5; Fic**
1. Adventure graphic novels; 2. Germany (East); 3. Graphic novels
978-1-4190-3222-6, $8.99

In the summer of 1963, President Kennedy of the United States speaks in West Berlin about liberty. From the other side of the Berlin Wall, the Kappel family listens to his every word. They decide to make a bid for freedom, but at what cost? This historical fiction graphic novel includes prose intervals that describe Berlin as the divided city after World War II, the building of the Wall, the various escape attempts made by East Berliners, part of President Kennedy's speech, and the fall of the Wall in 1989. There is brief violence when a vicious East German soldier is shot.
Part of the Timeline Graphic Novels series.

Fire Mountain; art by Liam Thurston. Harcourt Achieve/Steck-Vaughn 2006 48p. Illustration
Grades: 3 4 5 6 7 8   **741.5; Fic**
1. Adventure graphic novels; 2. Pompeii (Extinct city); 3. Volcanoes; 4. Graphic novels
978-1-4190-3198-4, $8.99

Cato is a young slave boy in the bustling Roman city of Pompeii. When Mount Vesuvius erupts without warning, Cato is separated from his mother. Will they survive the terrifying day and be reunited? This historical fiction graphic novel includes prose intervals that provide additional information about what happened at Pompeii and Herculaneum, about Vesuvius and other famous volcanoes, and about the modern excavations.
Part of the Timeline Graphic Novels series.

Ice Journey; art by Glenn Brucker. Harcourt Achieve/Steck-Vaughn 2007 48p. Illustration
Grades: 3 4 5 6 7 8   **741.5; Fic**
1. Adventure graphic novels; 2. Ice age; 3. Graphic novels
978-1-4190-3204-2, $8.99

It is the Ice Age in North America, and the land is covered in ice and snow. Bruno, a young giant short-faced bear, is being hunted down by a saber-toothed cat. While his sister, Ursula, looks for him, she meets some interesting creatures of the Ice Age. This graphic novel includes prose intervals that provide information on the real animals that lived during the Ice Age, the early people who may have lived towards the end of the Ice Age, and on the impact of global warming on the world today.
Part of the Timeline Graphic Novels series.

Rebel Prince; art by David Okum. Harcourt Achieve/Steck-Vaughn 2007 48p. Illustration
Grades: 3 4 5 6 7 8   **741.5; Fic**
1. Great Britain — Kings and Rulers; 2. Henry V, King of England, 1387-1422; 3. Graphic novels
978-1-4190-3217-2, $8.99

In 15th century London, young Will works at a tavern where Prince Hal and his companions hang out. When royal duties call, will Prince Hal be able to rise to the challenge" What is in store for young Will" This historical fiction graphic novel tells the story of how playful Prince Hal became King Henry V of England. It includes prose interludes that provide additional information about his father Henry IV, portrayals of Henry V, and about the famous battle at Agincourt.
Part of the Timeline Graphic Novels series.

Doyle, Arthur Conan

The **hound** of the Baskervilles: a Sherlock Holmes mystery. By Sir Arthur Conan Doyle; retold by Martin Powell; illustrated by Daniel Perez. Stone Arch Books 2009 63p. Illustration
Grades: 4 5 6 7 8 9 10   **741.5; Fic**
1. Holmes, Sherlock (Fictional character); 2. Mystery graphic novels; 3. Graphic novels
978-1-4342-0755-5, $23.93

LC 2008-6247

Late one night, Sir Charles Baskerville is attacked and killed outside his home in Dartmoor, England. Some say that the legendary monster, the Hound of the Baskervilles, has come back. Now Sherlock Holmes and Dr. Watson investigate the mystery, in order to protect the Baskerville heir, who has just come from America. This graphic novel adapts Doyle's one full-length mystery novel featuring his famous character.

Part of the Graphic Revolve series

Dumas, Alexandre

The **Count** of Monte Cristo. Wordsmith, R. Jay Nudds ; illustrator, Sankha Banerjee. Campfire 2012 111 p.
Grades: 8 9 10 11 12 Adult   **741.5**
1. Literature — Adaptations; 2. Graphic novels
9380028679; 9789380028675, $12.99

This "graphic novel tells the . . . tale of revenge written by Alexandre Dumas in 1844. Set between 1815 and 1838," the book "depicts a tumultuous time in France's history when multiple powers were vying for control of the country. . . . When Edmond Dantes is unjustly arrested and placed in a prison, his anger and desire for revenge builds inside him. After his escape, he finds the means to carefully plot against his conspirators and steal away their livelihoods and happiness." (Voice of Youth Advocates)

The **three** musketeers; adapted by Bruce Buchanan ; illustrated by Amit Tayal. Campfire 2010 104p. Illustration
Grades: 3 4 5 6 7 8 9   **741.5; Fic**
1. Adventure graphic novels; 2. Graphic novels
978-93-80028-57-6, $12.99

Young D'Artagnan comes to Paris, determined to become a king's musketeer, but runs into trouble with three musketeers in one day. When they band together to tight Cardinal Richelieu's forces, they become friends. The friends soon find themselves involved in averting a plot to discredit Queen Anne, and their efforts to help her cause them to run afoul of Richelieu. D'Artagnan, Athos, Porthos, and Aramis also must deal with Milady de Winter, a beautiful and deadly woman with her own agenda. This graphic novel adaptation features art that emphasizes the humor in the historical adventure. It also puts most of the violence off-panel, so the story is suitable for younger readers.

Dunn, Joeming W.

The **brain:** a graphic novel tour. By Joeming Dunn; illustrated by Rod Espinosa.. Magic Wagon/Graphic Planet 2009 32p. Illustration (Graphic adventures. The human body)
Grades: 2 3 4 5 6   **612.8; 741.5**
1. Brain; 2. Graphic novels
978-1-60270-683-5, $27.07
LC 2009-17650

Teacher Ms Hansen leads her Explorers class on a tour of the human brain. They learn about how the brain's different parts control body functions through the nervous system, and how people should protect their head while participating in certain physical activities, to avoid damaging the brain. The tour is very similar to the Ms Frizzle's Magic School Bus science series by way of The Fantastic Voyage in that Ms Hansen's class shrinks to microscopic size in order to get into the brain. Back matter in the book includes a diagram of the brain, some "fun facts," a brief glossary, and information on how to use ABDO's website to find links to more information on the Internet. The

author owns Antarctica Press and is also a physician; artist Espinosa has published such books as The Courageous Princess and Neotopia.

This book is part of the Graphic Adventures: The Human Body series.

The **eyes:** a graphic novel tour. Illustrated by Rod Espinosa. Magic Wagon 2009 32p. Illustration (Graphic adventures. The human body)
Grades: 2 3 4 5 6   **612.8; 741.5**
1. Eye; 2. Graphic novels
978-1-60270-684-2, $27.07
LC 2009-17651

Teacher Ms. Hansen leads her Explorers class on a tour of the human eye. They learn about how the eye functions, what purpose blinking serves, how the iris works to control the amount of light that enters the eye, and why tears are important. The tour is very similar to the Ms Frizzle's Magic School Bus science series by way of The Fantastic Voyage, in that Ms Hansen's class shrinks to microscopic size in order to get into the eye. Back matter in the book include a diagram of the eye, fun facts that include information on color blindness and vision problems, a short glossary, and information on how to use ABDO's website to find links for more information on the Internet. The author owns Antarctica Press and is also a physician; artist Espinosa has published such books as The Courageous Princess and Neotopia.

This book is part of the Graphic Adventures: The Human Body series.

H.G. Wells' The time machine. H.G. Wells; adapted by Joeming Dunn; illustrated by Ben Dunn.. ABDO Publishing Group/Magic Wagon 2008 32p. Illustration
Grades: 3 4 5 6 7 8   **741.5; Fic**
1. Adventure graphic novels; 2. Authors; 3. Historians; 4. Novelists; 5. Science fiction graphic novels; 6. Science fiction writers; 7. Wells, H G (Herbert George), 1866-1946; 8. Wells, H G (Herbert George), 1866-1946 — Adaptations; 9. Writers on politics; 10. Writers on science; 11. Graphic novels
978-1-60270-054-3, $27.07
LC 2007-6447

Courtesy of ABDO Publishing Group/Magic Wagon

A gentleman hosts his friends at dinner one evening in London and then takes their leave in his time machine. When he returns, he tells them of his trip into the future, of the two peoples he encountered, the Eloi and the Morlocks, and what he learned of their relationship. When his friends refuse to believe him, the Traveler sets out again in his machine. This simplified graphic novel adaptation allows younger readers and struggling readers to get the main plot of the classic story.

The book includes a brief biography of Wells and list of his other works.

Part of the Graphic Planet Graphic Classics series.

The **heart:** a graphic novel tour. By Joeming Dunn; illustrated by Rod Espinosa.. Magic Wagon/Graphic Planet 2009 32p. Illustration (Graphic adventures. The human body)

Grades: 2 3 4 5 6   **612.8; 741.5**
   1. Heart; 2. Graphic novels
   978-1-60270-685-9, $27.07

                       LC 2009-17851

Teacher Ms. Hansen leads her Explorers class on a tour of the human heart. They learn about how the heart functions, how it pumps blood through the circulatory system, and the functions of the major veins and arteries. The tour is very similar to the Ms Frizzle's Magic School Bus science series by way of The Fantastic Voyage, in that Ms Hansen's class shrink to microscopic size in order to get into the bloodstream. Back matter in the book include a diagram of the heart, fun facts, a short glossary, and information on how to use ABDO's website to find links for more information on the Internet. The author owns Antarctica Press and is also a physician; artist Espinosa has published such books as The Courageous Princess and Neotopia.

Includes bibliographical references

This book is part of the Graphic Adventures: The Human Body series.

Journey to the center of the earth. Adapted by Joeming Dun; illustrated by Rod Espinosa. Magic Wagon/Graphic Planet 2009 32p. Illustration

Grades: 3 4 5 6 7   **741.5; Fic**
   1. Adventure graphic novels; 2. Authors; 3. Children's authors; 4. Novelists; 5. Science fiction graphic novels; 6. Science fiction writers; 7. Verne, Jules, 1828-1905; 8. Verne, Jules, 1828-1905 — Adaptations; 9. Graphic novels
   978-1-60270678-1, $27.07

                       LC 2009-8588

Professor Otto Liedenbrock, his nephew Axel, and their guide Hans follow the instructions in an old note left by explorer Arne Saknussemm to descend into an old volcano in Iceland, seeking a way to the center of the Earth. This graphic novel provides an easy-reading adaptation of Jules Verne's classic adventure story. Back matter includes a brief biography of Verne, a list of some of his novels, and a short glossary. It is a curious addition to the Graphic Planet series called Graphic Horror, since there is no horror in the book.

This is part of the Graphic Horror Series 2.

The **kidneys:** a graphic novel tour. Illustrated by Rod Espinosa.. ABDO/Magic Wagon 2009 32p. (Graphic adventures. The human body)

Grades: 2 3 4 5 6   **612.2; 741.5**
   1. Kidneys; 2. Graphic novels
   978-1-60270-686-6, $27.07

                       LC 2009-17852

Ms. Hansen and her Explorers class, including the aliens Xeni and Zeno Zelman, take off on another tour inside the human body, this time into the kidneys, the body's filter to get rid of waste from the blood and to regulate the levels of water, salt, and other minerals. The tour starts in the blood

Courtesy of ABDO Publishing Group/Magic Wagon

system, into the left renal artery into the left kidney. Young readers might enjoy the fact that the Explorers exit the body through the urinary tract, which is where the kidneys send the waste called urea. This graphic novel series combines aspects of the Magic School Bus series and the movie Fantastic Voyage. The book includes additional facts about the kidneys, a glossary, and a link to find websites for more information. Dunn is a physician and owner of Antarctic Publishing, a comic book publishing house.

Part of the Graphic Adventures: The Human Body series.

The **liver:** a graphic novel tour. Illustrated by Rod Espinosa.. ABDO/Magic Wagon 2009 32p. Illustration (Graphic adventures. The human body)

Grades: 2 3 4 5 6
612.2; 741.5
   1. Liver; 2. Graphic novels
   978-1-60270-687-3, $27.07

                       LC 2009-17853

Ms. Hansen and her Explorers class, including the aliens Xeni and Zeno Zelman, take off on another tour inside the human body, this time into the liver. The tour starts in the mouth, through the esophagus into the stomach, then through the small intestine into the liver. The liver breaks down

Courtesy of ABDO Publishing Group/Magic Wagon

digested proteins and medicines, and helps to convert carbohydrates to sugars; it also stores vitamins and minerals such as iron. This graphic novel series combines aspects of the Magic School Bus series and the movie Fantastic Voyage. The book includes additional facts about the liver, a glossary, and a link to find websites for more information. Dunn is a physician and owner of Antarctic Publishing, a comic book publishing house.

Part of the Graphic Adventures: The Human Body series.

The **Lungs:** a graphic novel tour; art by Rod Espinosa. ABDO/Magic Wagon 2009 32p. Illustration

Grades: 2 3 4 5 6   **612.2; 741.5**
   1. Lungs; 2. Respiratory system; 3. Graphic novels
   978-1-60270-688-0, $27.07

                       LC 2009-17854

Ms. Hansen and her Explorers class, including the aliens Xeni and Zeno Zelman, take off on another tour inside the human body, this time into the lungs. The tour starts in the nose, through the larynx into the trachea (windpipe), then through the bronchi into the lungs. The lungs do more than help the body breathe and circulate oxygen; they help the body to speak. This graphic novel series combines aspects of the Magic School Bus series and the movie Fantastic Voyage. The book includes additional facts about the lungs, a glossary, and a link to find websites for more information. Dunn is a physician and owner of Antarctic Publishing, a comic book publishing house.

Part of the Graphic Adventures: The Human Body series.

The **tell-tale** heart. Adapted by Joeming Dunn; illustrated by Rod Espinosa.. Magic Wagon/Graphic Planet 2009 32p. Illustration
Grades: 6 7 8 9 10   **741.5; Fic**
1. Guilt; 2. Homicide; 3. Horror graphic novels; 4. Poe, Edgar Allan, 1809-1849 — Adaptations; 5. Graphic novels
978-1-60270681-1, $27.07
             LC 2009-8589
The young narrator takes care of an old man; he tells the reader he has had no reason to do harm, he never felt any greed for the old man's wealth. However, he hates what he calls the old man's vulture eye, and his hatred of that eye makes him determined to kill the old man so he would never have to look on it again. When he finally murders the old man, however, it's not the eye, but the imagined sound of the old man's beating heart that drives the young killer insane. This easy-reading graphic novel adaptation of Edgar Allan Poe's short story provides a good introduction to Poe's work for reluctant and struggling readers; the emotional intensity of the work makes it more suitable for older readers despite the simplicity of language. Back matter includes a brief biography of Poe, a list of some of his other works, and a short glossary.

This is part of the Graphic Horror Series 2.

Dysart, Joshua
★ **Captain** Gravity and the Power of the Vril. Pencils by Sal Velluto ; inks by Bob   Almond, Joe Rubenstein & Sal Velluto ; colors by Mike Garcia. Penny-Farthing Press 2006 193p. Illustration
Grades: 8 9 10 11 12   **741.5; Fic**
1. Adventure graphic novels; 2. Superhero graphic novels; 3. Graphic novels
0-9719012-8-7, $19.95
Some years before, a young African American named Joshua Jones stumbled upon a mysterious stone at an archeological dig and became infused with an element from the stone that gave him power over gravity, including flight. He hid his identity with a helmet and became Captain Gravity. Now it's the 1930s, and Joshua Jones works in Hollywood with the two friends who know his secret. They've been making Captain Gravity movies, and no one else has figured out that the hero is Black. Now, Nazis are searching for the original source of what they call Vril, Joshua's power, and they plan to use it to conquer the Earth. Only Captain Gravity can stop them, and he has to chase them all over the world and to the lost city of Atlantis.

A young, evil Adolf Hitler, an unusual hero for the time, and a story that harks back to the Golden Age of comics storytelling all add up to a great story for this time.

Earle-Bridges, Michele
Picture This! Shakespeare: Hamlet. Barron's Educational Series, Inc. 2006 69p. Illustration
Grades: 7 8 9 10 11 12   **741.5; 822.3**
1. Drama; 2. Shakespeare, William, 1564-1616 — Adaptations; 3. Graphic novels
978-0-7641-3524-8, $7.99
This adaptation combines pages done in graphic novel format with extensive excerpts from Shakespeare's Hamlet to provide an introductory reading experience for younger and struggling students. Each scene presented in the book is preceded by a brief summary, words that modern teens would find unfamiliar are briefly defined on the page, literary terms are explained.

Picture This! Shakespeare: Hamlet Teacher's Resource Book. Barron's Educational Series, Inc. 2006 58p. Illustration
Grades: 7 8 9 10 11 12   **741.5; 371.33**
1. Drama; 2. Teaching — Aids and devices; 3. Graphic novels
978-0-7641-3523-1, $9.99
Hamlet, the Shakespearean drama that is in the curriculum of many high schools in the country, is an offering in Barron's "Picture This! Shakespeare" series. This manual supplements Barron's "Picture This: Hamlet," a book presented in graphic novel style for students' use. The manual offers teachers suggestions for classroom discussions, quizzes, and activities related to the play, including reproducible activity sheets.

Picture This! Shakespeare: Julius Caesar. Barron's Educational Series, Inc. 2006 54p. Illustration
Grades: 7 8 9 10 11 12   **741.5; 822.3**
1. Shakespeare, William, 1564-1616 — Adaptations
978-0-7641-3279-7, $7.99
This adaptation combines pages done in graphic novel format with extensive excerpts from Shakespeare's Julius Caesar to provide an introductory reading experience for younger and struggling students. Each scene presented in the book is preceded by a brief summary, words that modern teens would find unfamiliar are briefly defined on the page, literary terms are explained.

Picture This! Shakespeare: Julius Caesar Teacher's Resource Book. Barron's Educational Series, Inc. 2006 58p. Illustration
Grades: 7 8 9 10 11 12   **741.5; 371.33**
1. Drama; 2. Teaching — Aids and devices; 3. Graphic novels
978-0-7641-3280-3, $9.99
Julius Caesar, the Shakespearean drama that is in the curriculum of virtually every high school in the country, is an offering in Barron's "Picture This! Shakespeare" series. This manual supplements Barron's "Picture This: Julius Caesar," a book presented in graphic novel style for students' use. The manual offers teachers suggestions for classroom discussions, quizzes, and activities related to the play, including reproducible activity sheets.

Edginton, Ian
Kingdom of the Wicked. Illustrated by D'Israeli. Dark Horse Comics 2004 120p. Illustration

Grades: 8 9 10 11 12 Adult   **741.5; Fic**
1. Adventure graphic novels; 2. Fantasy graphic novels; 3. Graphic novels
1-59307-187-6, $15.95

Christopher Grahame is the premier children's author of the twenty-first century, a publishing phenomenon. With his work translated into everything from Aborigine to Zulu, he is the cornerstone of a multi-million dollar, franchise spewing empire. Is it any surprise then that under all this pressure something has to give? Unfortunately, it's Chris's mind. Stricken by mysterious headaches and blackouts that plagued his childhood, Chris once again finds himself walking the avenues and boulevards of Castrovalva - the fantasy realm he dreamt up as a boy, to while away his recuperation. But like Chris, Castrovalva has also changed. Deluged in mud, blood, and barbed wire, war has come to wonderland. Chris tries to tell himself it's all a bad dream. . .so why can't he wake up? The book includes violence, strong language, and brief nudity.

Eisenberg, Adam
The **Creation** of Iron Man. Rosen Publishing Group 2006 48p. Illustration
Grades: 4 5 6 7 8 9 10   **741.5**
1. Iron Man (Fictional character); 2. Superhero graphic novels; 3. Graphic novels
978-1-4042-0767-7, $29.25
                                    LC 2006000167
This volume discusses the unique character of Tony Stark, developed by Stan Lee and Jack Kirby, who was unable to live a normal life and invented a special iron suit that gave him superpowers. The book includes information about the times in which Lee and Kirby worked at Marvel Comics.
Part of the Action Heroes series.

Eisner, Will
The **Last** Knight: An Introduction to Don Quixote. NBM Publishing 2000 32p. Illustration
Grades: 3 4 5 6 7 8 9 10   **741.5; Fic**
1. Adventure graphic novels; 2. Authors; 3. Cervantes Saavedra, Miguel de, 1547-1616 — Adaptations
1-56163-251-1; 978-1-56163-251-0, $15.95
                                    LC 2001-265049
This is Eisner's graphic novel remake of Don Quixote. Here are the adventures of a Spanish country gentleman and his companion who set out, like knights of old, to search for adventure. As the subtitle says, this book hits the highlights and serves to introduce the classic tale to younger readers.

Moby Dick. NBM Publishing 2001 32p. Illustration
Grades: 3 4 5 6 7 8 9 10   **741.5; Fic**
1. Adventure graphic novels; 2. Whaling; 3. Graphic novels
1-56163-293-7, $15.95; 1-56163-294-5 (pa)
                                    LC 2001-032989
Ishmael, a sailor, recounts the ill-fated voyage of a whaling ship led by the fanatical Captain Ahab in search of the white whale that had crippled him. Eisner's adaptation hits the highlights of the novel.

The **Princess** and the Frog. NBM Publishing 1999 32p. Illustration

Grades: 3 4 5 6 7 8 9 10   **741.5; Fic**
1. Fairy tales; 2. Fantasy graphic novels; 3. Graphic novels
1-56163-244-9, $15.95; 1-56163-346-1 (pa)

A good prince, turned into a frog by a spiteful wizard, exacts from a princess a promise which she is reluctant to fulfill, despite his kindness and her desire not to hurt him. Comics master Will Eisner adapted the familiar tale by the Brothers Grimm.

Elder, Joshua
Mail Order Ninja, Vol. 1 written by Joshua Elder ; illustrated by Erich Owen. Tokyopop 2006 Un Illustration
Grades: 4 5 6 7 8 9   **741.5; Fic**
1. Humorous graphic novels; 2. Ninja; 3. Graphic novels
1-59816-728-6, $5.99

Timmy is a normal boy attending L. Frank Baum Elementary School in Cherry Creek, Indiana - dealing with bullies, a nasty little sister, and an even nastier super-rich girl who acts as though she owns the school. When things get really bad, Timmy decides to enter a drawing in a mail order catalog to win a ninja. Yes, a real live ninja of his very own. When Jiro arrives, Timmy soon overpowers the bullies and beats rich Felicity in the Student Body President election. But as long as Felicity's father has money, she'll find a way to get even, and she has a copy of that mail order catalog. . . . This is the first volume in a global manga series.

Ellerton, Sarah
Inverloch, Volume 1. Seven Seas 2006 Un Illustration
Grades: 4 5 6 7 8 9 10 11 12   **741.5; Fic**
1. Adventure graphic novels; 2. Fantasy graphic novels; 3. Graphic novels
1-933164-13-1, $14.99

In a world where humans, elves, and other beings coexist, albeit not altogether peacefully, Acheron is a young da'kor, a horned wolf-like race that lives in the forests. He encounters a beautiful elf and takes her quest for his own - to find another elf who went missing twelve years before. Teased by his brothers as a lousy hunter, feared by humans who think da'kor are dangerous beasts, innocent Acheron finds that the world beyond the forest is full of danger, intrigue, and betrayal.
This story began online as a webcomic.

Ellis, Grace
★ **Lumberjanes** 1: Beware the kitten holy. Written by Noelle Stevenson & Grace Ellis ; illustrated by Brooke Allen ; colors by Maarta Laiho. Simon & Schuster 2015 128 p. Illustration; Color (Lumberjanes)
Grades: 6 7 8 9 10 11 12 Adult   **741.5**
1. Adventure fiction; 2. Camps — Fiction; 3. Female friendship; 4. Monsters — Fiction; 5. Summer — Fiction
1608866874; 9781608866878, $14.99
Eisner Award: Best New Series (2015)
Eisner Award: Best Publication for Teens (2015)
Harvey Award: Best New Series (2015); Harvey Award: Best Original Graphic Publication For Young Readers (2015)

"[This] graphic novel begins mid-adventure as five campers are out after hours investigating a strange event that they all witnessed: a woman turning into a giant bear. This is just the first of many odd occurrences that Jo, April, Molly,

Mal, and Ripley encounter at the summer camp for 'Hardcore Lady Types.' The Lumberjanes, as the scouts are called, band together to solve puzzles, defeat three-eyed creatures, and escape the ire of their watchful counselor Jen." (School Library Journal)

"Humorously riffing on everything from scout badges to the X-Men to feminist heroes . . ., it's a sharp, smart, and most of all fun celebration of sisterhood." Pub Wkly

Volume 1 of an ongoing series

Espinosa, Rod

Around the world in 80 days. Adapted and illustrated by Rod Espinosa.. ABDO/Red Wagon 2008 32p. Illustration
Grades: 3 4 5 6 7 8 9   **741.5; Fic**
1. Adventure graphic novels; 2. Graphic novels; 3. Verne, Jules, 1828-1905 — Adaptations
978-1-60270-050-5, $27.07

                             LC 2007-6444

In 1872, English gentleman Phileas Fogg makes a wager that he can travel around the world in just 80 days. Unfortunately, at the time of his wager, a daring robber has made off with a fortune, and Scotland Yard detective Fix is convinced Fogg is the villain. The chase is on, around the world. This comic book adaptation has been written for younger, reluctant, and struggling readers and provides highlights of the adventures in the original novel by Verne. The book includes a brief biography of Verne, a short list of some of his other works, and a brief glossary.

★ The **courageous** princess. Dark Horse Comics 2007 240p. Illustration
Grades: 3 4 5 6 7 8 9   **741.5; Fic**
1. Fantasy graphic novels; 2. Princesses
978-1-59307-719-8, $9.95

Plain Princess Mabelrose doesn't get along with the other, prettier princesses, but her intelligence helps her when a dragon kidnaps her. Instead of waiting for rescue, Mabelrose escapes, taking a friendly hedgehog and a few useful-looking items (a pouch, a length of rope) that she doesn't know are magic.

This new edition from Dark Horse is in black and white; the previous Antarctic Press editions were in color.

Lewis and Clark. ABDO/Magic Wagon 2008 32p. Illustration (Bio-graphics)
Grades: 3 4 5 6 7 8 9   **917.8; 92; 741.5; 917**
1. Biographical graphic novels; 2. Clark, William, 1770-1838; 3. Explorers; 4. Lewis and Clark Expedition (1804-1806); 5. Lewis, Meriwether, 1774-1809; 6. Territorial governors; 7. West (US) — Exploration; 8. Graphic novels
978-1-60270-069-7, $27.07

                             LC 2007-5578

This graphic format book tells the story of the Lewis and Clark Expedition, which explored the land of the Louisiana Purchase, as authorized in 1803 by President Thomas Jefferson. The book includes a timeline of the Expedition, a map of the route, and a list of books for further reading.

Neotopia Color Manga, Vol. 1: The Enlightened Age. Antarctic Press 2004 161p. Illustration
Grades: 7 8 9 10 11 12   **741.5; Fic**

1. Science fiction graphic novels; 2. Graphic novels
978-1-932453-57-7, $9.99

"A young Grand Duchess who is not what she appears to be plays a role in a war to save her world . . . . The world of Neotopia with all its different races is as much of a character as the people." (VOYA)

The battle scenes are depicted with drama but aren't traumatic. This series is an example of what has been called "Amerimanga" and "Global manga."

The **prince** of heroes, chapter I. Antarctic Press 2008 Un Illustration
Grades: 8 9 10 11 12   **741.5; Fic**
1. Adventure graphic novels; 2. Science fiction graphic novels; 3. Graphic novels
978-0-9801255-0-4, $14.95

Ronen and his mother Aiymie have lived on the planet Irdne for years; now she tells him they must leave and travel to the edge of the universe to meet his father. She refuses to tell Ronen who he is, or to what Darem clan they belong, and this has made them outcasts in Darem society. Then they learn that the Nationalist Armada, a fleet of thousands of ships, is on its way to take over Irdne, and all Darem colonials must leave. Ronen must leave his friends, and his martial arts teacher, behind. During a fight with Baron Ermont Mesozora and Baroness Mazza Mesozora, Ronen strips Mazza's clothing from her; nothing really shows, but it's clear she has lost her pants.

Estes, Max

Coffee and Donuts: A Junkyard Cats Comic. Top Shelf Productions 2006 112p. Illustration
Grades: 6 7 8 9 10 11 12 Adult   **741.5; Fic**
1. Cats; 2. Humorous graphic novels; 3. Graphic novels
1-891830-80-5, $10

Dwight and Jules live in an unused dumpster and scavenge their food; every morning a mystery person leaves coffee and donuts for them. When, desperate for money, they try (and fail) to rob an armored truck, real crooks Myles and Moose try to force them into real crime.

Everheart, Chris

Recon academy: nuclear distraction; by Chris Everheart ; illustrated by Arcana Studio. Stone Arch Books 2009 64p. Illustration
Grades: 3 4 5 6 7 8   **741.5; Fic**
1. Science fiction graphic novels; 2. Terrorism; 3. Graphic novels
978-1-4342-1167-5, $25.32; 978-1-4342-1381-5 (pa), $6.95

                            LC 2008-32457

Emmi, Jay, Ryker, and Hazmat are Recon Academy, a teenage high-tech security force based in Seaside High School. Ever since their hometown suffered a terrorist attack, they have each worked on their specialized skills to seek out and fight terrorists. Hazmat is the team's forensics expert, so what's he doing in a martial arts tournament" Emmi has been trying to train him to be able to defend himself. He loses the match, but gets a date—but only if the team can finish their investigation of the security breach at the nuclear plant in time.

Recon academy: prep squardon. Stone Arch Books 2009 64p. Illustration
Grades: 3 4 5 6 7 8   **741.5; Fic**
1. Science fiction graphic novels; 2. Terrorism; 3. Graphic novels
978-1-4342-1168-2, $25.32; 978-1-4342-1382-2 (pa), $6.95

LC 2008-32479

Emmi, Jay, Ryker, and Hazmat are Recon Academy, a teenage high-tech security force based in Seaside High School. Ever since their hometown suffered a terrorist attack, they have each worked on their specialized skills to seek out and fight terrorists. Jay is the team's gadget guru, but he feels frustrated when Ryker's drills focus on teamwork and "old-fashioned" techniques (no gadgets). Then Jay gets a message from Ryker about a special drill just for him, only it's not from Ryker, but from Shadow Cell. They're using Jay to circumvent the Navy base's security systems, but what do they want?

Recon academy: shadow cell scam. Stone Arch Books 2009 64p. Illustration
Grades: 3 4 5 6 7 8   **741.5; Fic**
1. Science fiction graphic novels; 2. Terrorism; 3. Graphic novels
978-1-4342-1166-8, $25.32; 978-1-4342-1383-9 (pa), $6.95

LC 2008-32074

Emmi, Jay, Ryker, and Hazmat are Recon Academy, a teenage high-tech security force based in Seaside High School. Ever since their hometown suffered a terrorist attack, they have each worked on their specialized skills to seek out and fight terrorists. This time, they're up against Shadow Cell operatives who have stolen some computers. Emmi goes home from school and finds a salesman from a company called PenTech who has sold a new laptop to her grandmother. All too soon, she realizes it's a trap, and she learns that the other members of Recon Academy have also received the booby-trapped laptops. They need to track down Shadow Cell and find out what the villains want to accomplish.

Recon Academy: storm surge. Stone Arch Books 2010 66p. Illustration
Grades: 3 4 5 6 7 8   **741.5; Fic**
1. Adventure graphic novels; 2. Mystery graphic novels; 3. Storms; 4. Graphic novels
978-1-4342-1918-3, $25.32

In this volume of the Recon Academy series, Jay, Emmi and Ryker have gone mountain climbing with a school group when a storm hits. The storm also shorts out a critical communications antenna, and a Navy submarine needs it in order to transmit crucial top-secret data. Jay and Emmi set out to fix the antenna, but Ryker finds he has plenty of work when the bus crashes in the storm and knocks out Coach Kemp, the one adult with the students. Meanwhile, back at their base, Hazmat tries to maintain contact with everyone. This time, the Recon Academy team is up against nature. Arcana Studio is a Canadian comics publisher. The book includes a brief glossary, discussion questions, and writing prompts.
Part of the Recon Academy series.

Recon academy: the hidden face of Fren-Z. Stone Arch Books 2009 64p. Illustration
Grades: 3 4 5 6 7 8   **741.5; Fic**
1. Science fiction graphic novels; 2. Terrorism; 3. Graphic novels
978-1-4342-1165-1, $25.32; 978-1-4342-1380-8 (pa), $6.95

LC 2008-32073

Emmi, Jay, Ryker, and Hazmat are Recon Academy, a teenage high-tech security force based in Seaside High School. Ever since their hometown suffered a terrorist attack, they have each worked on their specialized skills to seek out and fight terrorists. The team, led by computer expert Ryker, goes up against a new Shadow Cell member, the hacker named Fren-Z. Shadow Cell plans to break into the Federal Reserve and shut down the world's economy, but Ryker and the others have their own plan to shut down the bad guys.

Explorer: the hidden doors
Edited by Kazu Kibuishi. Abrams Books 2014 128 p. Color; Illustration (Explorer)
Grades: 4 5 6 7 8   **741.5**
1. Bullying — Fiction; 2. Doors — Fiction; 3. Monsters — Fiction
1419708821; 9781419708824, $19.95; 9781419708848

LC 2014938941

In this collection of comics edited by Kazu Kibuishi, "a bullied boy discovers a door guarded by a sly monster . . . A painting of a door opens in a forgotten Egyptian tomb . . . A portal in the park promises to turn you into a much cooler version 2.0 - if you can just get the bugs out." (Publisher's note)

"Readers are once again presented with an array of stories created by a cast of comics authors and illustrators smartly assembled by Kibuishi...The range in this slim volume is expansive. From funny to deep and fantastical to refined, all of the stories have a compelling narrative arc. The colors are just as varied, and are universally dynamic and nuanced. Consider this (and previous series installments) as a necessary addition to any graphic novel collection." SLJ
Other titles in the series are: The Mystery Boxes (2012); The Lost Islands (2013)

Explorer: the lost islands
Kazu Kibuishi. Abrams Books 2013 128 p. (Explorer)
Grades: 4 5 6 7 8   **741.5; Fic**
1. Islands; 2. Graphic novels
1419708813; 141970883X; 9781419708817, $19.95; 9781419708831, $10.95

LC 2013935794

In this follow-up to "Explorer: The Mystery Boxes," Kazu Kibuishi and a crew of cartoonists again take turns weaving seven tales based around a loose theme. This time the motif is islands, and the contributors are left to interpret it in illustrated shorts. Some, by using their strange and remote settings as microcosms, underscore the value of hard work . . . or finding one's niche . . ., while others examine more abstract concepts such as exploration and isolation." (Publishers Weekly)

Explorer: the mystery boxes

Kazu Kibuishi. Abrams Books 2012 126 p. (Explorer)

Grades: 4 5 6 7 8   **S C; 741.5**

1. Boxes; 2. Boxes — Fiction; 3. Mystery graphic novels; 4. Short stories; 5. Graphic novels

1419700103; 9781419700095, $10.95; 9781419700101, $19.95

LC 2011025343

This collection of short stories offers "[s]even . . . stories [which] answer one simple question: what's in the box" . . . [E]ach of these . . . illustrated short graphic works revolves around a central theme: a mysterious box and the marvels—or mayhem—inside. Artists include . . . Kazu Kibuishi, Raina Telgemeier ('Smile'), and Dave Roman ('Astronaut Academy'), as well as Jason Caffoe, Stuart Livingston, Johane Matte, Rad Sechrist (all contributors to the . . . comics anthology series 'Flight'), and . . . artist Emily Carroll." (Publisher's note)

Seven graphic stories.

Fandel, Jennifer

Jim Thorpe: Greatest Athlete in the World. By Jennifer Fandel ; illustrated by Rod Whigham. Capstone Press 2007 32p. Illustration

Grades: 3 4 5 6 7 8 9   **741.5; 796; 92**

1. Athletes; 2. Thorpe, Jim; 3. Graphic novels

9781429601528, $29.99; 1429601523

LC 2007000286

This book uses the graphic novel format to tell the life story of Native American Jim Thorpe, star of the 1912 Olympic Games and member of the Pro Football Hall of Fame. The book includes additional facts and a list of books for further reading.

Part of the Graphic Biographies series.

Farshtey, Greg

Bionicle #1: rise of the Toa Nuva. Greg Farshtey, writer; Carlos D'Anda [and] Randy Elliott, artist.. Papercutz 2008 Un Illustration

Grades: 3 4 5 6   **741.5; Fic**

1. Adventure graphic novels; 2. Science fiction graphic novels; 3. Graphic novels

978-1-59707-110-9, $12.95; 978-1-59707-109-3 (pa), $7.95

Six mighty heroes the Toa arrive on a tropical island to find a land under siege. The Great Spirit Mata Nui has been cast into an unending sleep by the evil Makuta. Now Makuta is attacking the island's Matoran villagers with vicious Rahi beasts.he Toa must combine their skills and elemental and mask powers to defeat Makuta and restore peace to the island.

"The art is vivid and attention grabbing, and the story line, which weaves in Polynesian mythology, is exciting and action-packed." SLJ

Other titles in this series are:Challenge of the Rahkshi (2008); City of legends (2008); Trial by fire (2008); The battle of Voya Nui (2009); The underwater city (2009); Realm of fear (2009); Legends of Bara Magna (2010); The fall of Atero (2010)

Faust, Daniel R.

Energy crisis: the future of fossil fuels. Rosen Publishing Group 2009 24p.

Grades: 2 3 4 5 6 7

333.79; 741.5

1. Energy resources — Environmental aspects; 2. Graphic novels

978-14042-4231-9, $23.95

LC 2007-49957

Using the comic book format, the book introduces young readers to the problem of finding sources

Courtesy of Rosen Publishing

of fossil fuels and dealing with the pollution resulting from their use.

Part of the Jr. Graphic Environmental Dangers series.

Fein, Eric

The **Creation** of the Fantastic Four. Rosen Publishing Group 2006 48p. Illustration

Grades: 4 5 6 7 8 9 10   **741.5**

1. Fantastic Four (Fictional characters); 2. Superhero graphic novels; 3. Graphic novels

978-1-4042-0765-3, $29.25

LC 2005031170

Describes the history and development of the action heroes called the Fantastic Four and how they got their superpowers. Created in 1961 by the Marvel power team of Jack Kirby and Stan Lee, the Fantastic Four was the first superhero team the men created.

Part of the Action Heroes series.

The **Creation** of the Incredible Hulk. Rosen Publishing Group 2006 48p. Illustration

Grades: 4 5 6 7 8 9 10   **741.5**

1. Hulk (Fictional character); 2. Superhero graphic novels; 3. Graphic novels

978-1-4042-0764-6, $29.25

LC 2005035267

Discusses the unique character developed in 1962 by Stan Lee and Jack Kirby who was unable to live a normal life after he was affected by a gamma bomb's blast and Dr. Bruce Banner became the huge, inarticulate, super-strong Hulk. The book also includes information on the cultural climate in the U.S. at the time, and on the way the two men worked together at Marvel Comics.

Part of the Action Heroes series.

Ferraiolo, Jack D.

★ Sidekicks. Amulet 2011 309p.

Grades: 6 7 8 9   **741.5; Fic**

978-0-8109-9803-2, $16.95; 0-8109-9803-3

"By all outward appearances, Bright Boy is an average middle-school student, but at night, he becomes the sidekick to superhero Rogue Warrior. . . . Ferraiolo is delightfully unafraid to inject irreverence into the superhero formula, adding plenty of humor to the high-adventure high jinks." Booklist

Fillbach, Matt

Star Wars: Clone Wars Adventures Volume 8. Dark Horse Comics 2007 Un Illustration
Grades: 5 6 7 8 9 10   741.5; Fic
 1. Adventure graphic novels; 2. Science fiction graphic novels; 3. Star Wars; 4. Graphic novels
978-1-59307-680-1, $6.95
 The stories in this volume take place during the Clone Wars. Luminara Unduli battles in the Arena of Doom, Aurra Sing hunts a bounty on the Smuggler's Moon, Obi-Wan Kenobi disrupts an assassin's mission, and a battle droid makes a career change.

Fingeroth, Danny

Action Heroes: The Creation of the X-Men. Rosen Publishing Group, Inc. 2007 48p. Illustration
Grades: 3 4 5 6 7 8   741.5
 1. X-Men (Fictional characters); 2. Graphic novels
1-4042-0762-7 (lib bdg), $29.25
 Veteran Marvel Comics writer Fingeroth gives young readers a brief introduction to the creation of the Marvel superhero team, the X-Men. The book focuses on the two creators, Stan Lee and Jack Kirby, and also discusses the state of the comics industry in the early 1960s, as well as the cultural/social background that led Lee and Kirby to create a team of mutant superheroes. It includes a timeline of the X-Men creators, highlights from the long-running series, a glossary, books for further reading, and a bibliography. Photographs and color reproductions of the art highlight the book. Due to the popular series of X-Men movies, people know the characters, even if they've never read the comics.

The U.S. Supreme Court. Illustrated by Cynthia Martin; consultant: Michael Bailey. Capstone Press 2009 32p. Illustration (Cartoon nation)
Grades: 1 2 3 4 5 6 7 8   347; 741.5
 1. United States — Supreme Court; 2. Graphic novels
978-1-4296-1985-1, $32
                                    LC 2008-486
 This graphic format book uses irreverently humorous captions and dialog and provides young readers with an introduction to the U. S. Supreme Court. The book covers the founding of the court, which first met on February 1, 1790, its powers, how it works, how to become a Supreme Court justice, famous cases, and its role in amending the U. S. Constitution. It includes a short timeline, a glossary, and a list of books for further reading.
 Part of the Graphic Library Cartoon Nation series

Fletcher, Brenden

Gotham Academy; Volume 1: Welcome to Gotham Academy. Becky Cloonan, Brenden Fletcher; illustrated by Karl Kerschl. DC Comics 2015 160 p. Color; Illustration
Grades: 7 8 9 10 11 12   741.5
 1. Amnesia — Fiction; 2. School stories
9781401254728, $14.99
                                    LC 2015007185
 "Gotham Academy [is] the most prestigious school in Gotham City. Only the best and brightest students may enter its halls, study in its classrooms, explore its secret passages, summon its terrifying spirits. Okay, so Gotham Academy isn't like other schools. But Olive Silverlock isn't like other

students. After a mysterious incident over summer break, she's back at school with a bad case of amnesia." (Publisher's note)
 "Filled with spunky and quirky characters and unexpected plot turns, this work adds an intriguing and fresh layer to the Batman mythos. . . . Kerschl's campy art is by turns luminous and gloomy, enhancing Cloonan and Fletcher's energetic and sometimes contemplative text." SLJ
 Originally published in single magazine form as Gotham Academy 1-6
 Volume 1 of an ongoing series

Flight explorer

Edited by Kazu Kibuiski. Villard 2008 112p. Illustration
Grades: 4 5 6 7   741.5; Fic
 1. Adventure graphic novels; 2. Fantasy graphic novels; 3. Humorous graphic novels; 4. Science fiction graphic novels; 5. Graphic novels
978-0-345-50313-8 (pa), $10; 0-345-50313-9 (pa)
 This anthology includes stories that Kibuishi kept from Flight Volume 4 because they had all-ages appeal, as well as stories submitted especially for this volume. Kibuishi's own Copper and his talking dog cross a deep canyon by leaping onto mushrooms, only to discover the vegetation is intelligent. Kean Soo's Jellaby and his human friends frolic in the snow. Missile Mouse by Jake Parker defends a village on another planet, only to discover his coming was prophesied (this story includes two uses of the word "crap"). The other stories will appeal to younger readers, while some of the humor will also appeal to older readers. Other than the one bad word in "Missile Mouse" (noted above), there shouldn't be any other content that would keep this book out of most elementary and middle schools.
 "Every story has a layout that promotes an acute sense of pacing and showcases the crisp, defined, full-color art." SLJ

★ **Flight, volume six**

Edited by Kazu Kibuishi. Villard Books 2009 284p. Illustration
Grades: 8 9 10 11 12 Adult   741.5; Fic
 1. Fantasy graphic novels; 2. Short stories; 3. Graphic novels
978-0-345-50590-3, $25
 This sixth volume of the graphic anthology series includes stories by fifteen creators: J.P. Ahonen, Graham Annable, Bannister, Phil Craven, Mike Dutton, Michel Gagne, Cory Godbey, Rodolphe Guenoden, Steve Hamaker, Kazu Kibuishi, Andrea Offermann, Richard Pose, Justin Ridge, Rad Sechrist, and Kean Soo. Returning favorite characters includ Jellaby by Soo, Hamaker's Fish N Chips, Kibuishi's Daisy Kutter, and the wordless little fox Rex by Gagne. Bannister's "Cooking Duel" stands out as a lot of fun, as a couple makes a bet about which of them can make the better tasting mushroom quiche; and Justin Ridge's "Dead Bunny" shows that there is a soul mate for just about anyone, including a zombie bunny.

Fogel, Rich

Transformers animated volume 3. IDW Publishing 2008 Un Illustration

Grades: 2 3 4 5 6 7 8   **741.5; Fic**
1. Adventure graphic novels; 2. Robots; 3. Science fiction graphic novels; 4. Transformers (Fictional characters); 5. Graphic novels
978-1-60010-215-8, $7.99

The Autobots have to overcome mechanical mischief orchestrated by Megatron when Sari's Allspark key wakens him and he fixes some broken pocketbots and sneaks one into Sari's backpack. Then, the Autobots have to prove their usefulness to the police force, and all of Detroit, against Prometheus Black and his biochemical makeovers. The stories have been adapted from broadcast episodes of the new animated Transformers television series and illustrated with screen captures from the programs.

Transformers animated, volume 5. IDW Publishing 2008 Un Illustration
Grades: 3 4 5 6 7 8   **741.5; Fic**
1. Adventure graphic novels; 2. Robots; 3. Science fiction; 4. Transformers (Fictional characters); 5. Graphic novels
978-1-60010-243-1, $7.99

In "Survival of the Fittest," a Dinobot kidnaps Sari, who holds the Key to the Allspark. Prowl and Bulkhead track her to the island where they let the Dinobots settle, but they are followed by New Detroit police captain Fanzone. The Dinobots had seemed to be harmless, but now they attack the Autobots, and the reason" A Decepticon named Meltdown controls them, and he wants to create transforming humans, starting with Sari. In "Lost and Found," Decepticons Blitzwing and Lugnut have come to Detroit searching for Megatron and the Allspark. Optimus Prime believes that the Autobots need to leave Earth in order to save the people from the Decepticons, but Sari doesn't want her friends to leave. The book is illustrated with screen captures from the animated television series.

Foley, Ryan
    Don Bluth presents Dragon's Lair, volume 1. Ryan Foley and Andy Mangels ; art by Fabio Laguna. Arcana Comics, Inc. 2008 Un Illustration
Grades: 7 8 9 10 11 12   **741.5; Fic**
1. Adventure graphic novels; 2. Fantasy graphic novels; 3. Humorous graphic novels; 4. Graphic novels
978-0-9763095-5-0, $19.95

Dirk the Daring has fought against many a villain and slain many dragons, and he has won the heart of the beautiful Princess Daphne. But all is not quite well in the land, and while they travel homeward on a trip, a huge dragon attacks and takes Daphne. The dragon is Singe, father of all the dragons slain by Dirk, and he wants revenge. Now Dirk must go on a rescue mission, while Singe wants to turn Daphne into yet another fawning, scantily-clad princess slave to join the many he already has. Based on the Dragon's Lair video game, this book is full of action as Dirk faces many obstacles on his quest.

Fontes, Justine
    The **Trojan** Horse: The Fall of Troy; story by Justine & Ron Fontes ; pencils by Gordon Purcell ; inks by Barbara Schulz. Lerner Publishing Group/Graphic Universe 2007 48p. Illustration
Grades: 3 4 5 6 7 8 9   **398.2; 741.5**

1. Greek mythology; 2. Troy (Extinct city); 3. Graphic novels
978-0-8225-3085-5, $26.60 lib. Bdg.

This story is adapted from Virgil's Aeneid and from Smyrnacus Quintus' Posthomerica. The Trojan War has raged for ten years; then suddenly the Greek forces pull back. When the Trojans venture outside their city walls, they discover a giant wooden horse and a messenger. Should they accept this peace offering? Or is the gift horse too good to be true? This book includes a glossary and a list of books and websites for further reading.

Fontes, Ron
    Atalanta: The Race Against Destiny; story by Justine & Ron Fontes ; pencils and inks by Thomas Yeates ; [coloring by Hi-Fi Design ; lettering by Bill Hauser]. Lerner Publishing Group/Graphic Universe 2007 48p. Illustration
Grades: 3 4 5 6 7 8 9
292.1; 741.5
    1.   Atlanta   (Greek mythology);   2.   Greek mythology
9780822559658, $26.60 lib bdg

Courtesy of Lerner Publishing Group

Atalanta is the best hunter and swiftest runner in the land. The Oracle at Delphi has warned her to never marry, but her father, a powerful king, insists that she choose a husband. Atalanta declares she will only marry the man who can beat her in a footrace. Can she escape her fate?

Captured by pirates. Justine & Ron Fontes ; illustrations   by   David   Witt.   Lerner   Publishing Group/Graphic Universe 2007 112p. Illustration (Twisted Journeys)
Grades: 3 4 5 6 7 8 9   **741.5; Fic**
1. Adventure graphic novels; 2. Pirates; 3. Graphic novels
978-0-8225-6201-6, $27.93; 978-0-8225-6202-3 (pa), $7.95
                    LC 2006-101599

In the series called Twisted Journeys, readers choose how the story will progress. Pages of text alternate with comic book-style pages. In this volume, "you" are a young boy on a voyage with your father on his ship, when pirates capture the ship. Will you fight them, or will you join them?" Readers will find many scenarios played out, depending on their choices; some end well, others not so well.

Demeter & Persephone: Spring Held Hostage; story by Justine & Ron Fontes ; pencils by Steve Kurth ; inks by Barbara   Schultz.   Lerner   Publishing   Group/Graphic Universe 2007 48p. Illustration
Grades: 3 4 5 6 7 8 9   **292.1; 741.5**
1. Demeter (Greek deity); 2. Greek mythology; 3. Persephone (Greek deity); 4. Graphic novels
978-0-8225-5966-5, $26.60 lib. Bdg.

The goddess Demeter spreads warmth and bounty throughout the world, but when her daughter Persephone disappears and Demeter learns she has been kidnapped by Hades, the god of the underworld, her sorrow causes a permanent winter to fall upon the land. Can Demeter rescue Persephone from the underworld, and can the other gods and goddesses of Mount Olympus convince Demeter to bring back spring and summer?

Forbes, Jake

Jim Henson's Return to Labyrinth. Illustrated by Chris Lie. Tokyopop 2006 Un Illustration
Grades: 7 8 9 10 11 12 Adult   **741.5; Fic**
1. Adventure graphic novels; 2. Fantasy graphic novels; 3. Graphic novels
1-59816-725-1, $9.99

The Goblin King has kept a watchful eye on Toby, his minions secretly guiding and protecting the child. Legions of goblins work behind the scenes to ensure that Toby has whatever his heart desires, preparing him for the day when he will return to the Labyrinth and take his rightful place beside Jareth as the heir to the Goblin Kingdom. That day has come ... but no one has told Toby. This is an original story set in the world of the motion picture and is focused on Toby, who was a baby in the movie. This book is a global manga title.

Ford, Michael

The **Hunchback** of Notre Dame; illustrated by Penke Gelev ; retold by Michael Ford. Barron's Educational Series, Inc. 2007 48p. Illustration
Grades: 3 4 5 6 7 8 9   **741.5**
1. Hugo, Victor, 1802-1885 — Adaptations; 2. Graphic novels
978-0-7641-3493-7 (pa); 978-0-7641-5979-4

Abandoned as a baby and raised in the cathedral of Notre Dame, the hunchback Quasimodo lives as an outcast. The arrival of the beautiful gypsy girl Esmeralda begins a tragic series of events marked by jealousy, betrayal, and murder. This volume includes a brief biography of Hugo and of Notre Dame, and information on the importance of the novel and its adaptations.

Forget, Thomas

The **Creation** of Captain America. Rosen Publishing Group 2006 48p. Illustration
Grades: 4 5 6 7 8 9 10   **741.5**
1. Captain America (Fictional character); 2. Superhero graphic novels; 3. Graphic novels
978-1-4042-0766-0, $29.25

LC 2005032024

Captain America has been a hero since 1940 and saved comic books and Marvel Comic Group. This volume discusses the times during which Cap was created and how the character has changed over the years. In light of the character's death in the aftermath of the Marvel Civil War storyline that played out in comics during 2006 and 2007, this book may have wide appeal.

Part of the Action Heroes series.

Forsythe, Matthew

Jinchalo. Matthew Forsythe. Drawn & Quarterly 2012 120 p. Illustration

Grades: 3 4 5 6 7 8   **Fic; 741.5/971**
1. Fantasy comic books, strips, etc; 2. Fantasy graphic novels; 3. Spirits — Fiction
1770460675; 9781770460676, $17.95

LC 2012379212

This graphic novel, by Matthew Forsythe, is a "companion to . . . [the author's] 'Ojingogo,' . . . [staring] the same little girl as its heroine. When the mischievous shape-shifter Jinchalo hatches from a mysterious egg, . . . magical troubles drag the pair out of the safety of her home, through the small village where she resides, up, up, and away. In the course of their flight, they visit a robot garden, follow a vine into the clouds, and leave the village far behind." (Publisher's note)

Fox, Gardner

The **Atom** Archives Volume 2. Pencils by Gil Kane; inks by Murphy Anderson. DC Comics 2003 215p. Illustration
Grades: 7 8 9 10 11 12 Adult   **741.5; Fic**
1. Atom (Fictional character); 2. Superhero graphic novels; 3. Graphic novels
1-4012-0014-1, $49.95

This volume, reprinting The Atom issues #6-13, originally published in 1963 through 1964, features Mighty Mite's early team-ups with Hawkman and Hawkgirl, the classic villainy of Dr. Light, the return of Chronos, and much more. This Archive Edition reprints the comics in full color in a hardcover edition.

The **Green** Lantern Archives Volume 5. DC Comics 2004 239p. Illustration
Grades: 6 7 8 9 10 11 12 Adult   **741.5; Fic**
1. Green Lantern (Fictional character); 2. Superhero graphic novels; 3. Graphic novels
1-4012-0404-X, $49.95

LC 93-131923

This volume presents the further adventures of Green Lantern Hal Jordan "the Silver Age's science fiction-influenced hero. This time, the Emerald Gladiator squares off against foes such as Dr. Light, Hector Hammond, Evil Star, the Aerialist, and many more. This full-color Archive reprints nine tales from Green Lantern #30-38, originally published in 1964 and 1965. "

Showcase Presents: Adam Strange Volume One. DC Comics 2007 510p. Illustration
Grades: 6 7 8 9 10 11 12 Adult   **741.5; Fic**
1. Superhero graphic novels; 2. Graphic novels
978-1-4012-1313-8, $16.99

After being mysteriously teleported to a distant world by an alien scientist, Adam Strange went from being an Earth archaeologist to a cosmic adventurer. He soon becomes the hero of the planet Rann, shuttling between his old and new worlds via the Zeta Beam. With the love of his life, Alanna, daughter of Rann's leading scientist, they embark on a series of adventures against all types of space menaces. This black and white volume reprints stories from 1958 through 1963.

Showcase Presents: Green Lantern Volume 1. DC Comics 2005 528p. Illustration
Grades: 6 7 8 9 10 11 12 Adult   **741.5; Fic**

1. Green Lantern (Fictional character); 2. Superhero graphic novels; 3. Graphic novels
1-4012-0759-6, $9.99

A dying alien summoned test pilot Hal Jordan and gave him the most powerful weapon in the universe: a power ring. Jordan was inducted into the universe-spanning Green Lantern Corps and assigned to protect a sector of space including Earth. His sheer willpower directs the ring to create fantastic energy constructs and with it, protect the good from evil. In these earliest stories, readers meet the Guardians of the Universe, many of Jordan's intergalactic comrades, and some of his deadliest opponents, including Hector Hammond, Sonar, and Sinestro. The black and white reprints date from 1959 through 1962.

Showcase Presents: Hawkman Volume 1. DC Comics 2007 560p. Illustration
Grades: 7 8 9 10 11 12 Adult   **741.5; Fic**
1. Hawkman (Fictional character); 2. Superhero graphic novels; 3. Graphic novels
978-1-4012-1280-3, $16.99

Katar Hol and his wife Shayera, winged law officers from the planet Thanagar, visit Earth to learn about terrestrial police methods. To fit into human society, they adopt the civilian identities of Carter Hall, the curator of the Midway City Museum, and Shiera, his assistant. Dressed in their avian Thanagarian garb, Carter and Shiera patrol the skies of Midway City as Hawkman and Hawkgirl. They plunge headlong into the battle for justice against such villains as the Shadow Thief and Matter Master. With their array of alien weaponry and their scientific skill, this crime-fighting duo continue to defend Earth against nefarious threats. This book collects black and white reprints of thirty-three stories written by Fox, dating from 1961 through 1966 and featuring the work of artists such as Joe Kubert, Murphy Anderson, and Carmine Infantino.

Showcase Presents: Justice League of America Volume 1. Art by Mike Sekowsky. DC Comics 2005 544p. Illustration
Grades: 6 7 8 9 10 11 12 Adult   **741.5; Fic**
1. Justice League of America (Fictional characters); 2. Superhero graphic novels
1-4012-0761-8, $16.99

Some of the greatest super heroes in the DC Universe united to form the Justice League of America: Superman, Batman, Wonder Woman, the Flash, Green Lantern, Martian Manhunter, and Aquaman. Together, they face such foes as Dr. Light, Dr. Destiny, Starro, Felix Faust, Amos Fortune, and the Weapons Master. This volume includes the stories in which the JLS inducts new members to the team: Green Arrow and the Atom. In light of the events in Infinite Crisis, readers might be interested to see how far back the roots of the story went - all the way back to 1960. This black and white reprint volume includes stories published from 1960 through 1962.

★ **Fractured fables**
Edited by Jim Valentino and Kristen K. Simon; book design by Jim Valentino; cover illustration by Michael and Laura Allred from a sketch by Jim Valentino; cover design and graphics by Tim Daniel. Image Comics 2010 159p. Illustration

Grades: 6 7 8 9   **741.5**
978-1-60706-269-1, $29.99; 1-60706-269-0
LC 2010014838

Presents, in comic book format, thirty familiar fairy tales, songs, fables, and stories as retold by such acclaimed authors and illustrators as Ben Templesmith, Jim Di Bartolo, Scott Morse, and May Ann Licudine.

"This is a great adaptation highly worth reading or just browsing the artwork and illustrations." Voice Youth Advocates

Frampton, Otis
Oddly Normal. Image 2015 128 p. Illustration
Grades: 4 5 6 7 8 9   **741.5; Fic**
1. Fantasy graphic novels; 2. Humorous graphic novels; 3. Graphic novels
978-1-63215-226-8, $9.99

Written and illustrated by Otis Frampton, this graphic novel describes how "Oddly must travel to Fignation to uncover the mystery of her parents' disappearance. Join Oddly as she navigates a strange new school, teenage angst, monstrous bullies, and Evil itself on an unforgettable fantasy adventure through the vibrant world of Fignation in Oddly Normal." (Publisher's note)
Volume 1 of 3

Oddly Normal: Family Reunion. Viper Comics 2007 Un Illustration
Grades: 4 5 6 7 8 9 10   **741.5; Fic**
1. Fantasy graphic novels; 2. Humorous graphic novels; 3. Graphic novels
978-0-9777883-9-2, $11.95

In this second volume, Oddly meets Tommy Tsunami, who is a comic book hero in the real world, and her friends Reggie and Ragnar seem a bit jealous. Then Ragnar's dad returns and claims that Oopie, the creature Ragnar created and that has bonded with Oddly, holds the secret needed to continue his experiments. And the new teacher in school is actually Mr. Gooseberry in female form, with Oddly's mother's face - and he is determined to force her to ask him to help, for a price.

Friesen, Ray
Cupcakes of doom!. Don't Eat Any Bugs Productions 2008 98p. Illustration
Grades: 3 4 5 6 7 8   **741.5; Fic**
1. Adventure graphic novels; 2. Humorous graphic novels; 3. Pirates; 4. Graphic novels
978-0-9802314-1-0 (pa), $12.95; 0-9802314-1-8 (pa)

The Pirate band led by Captain Scurvybeard must do battle with the Vikings to decide the fate of the kingdom called Pellmellia. With a decidedly shifty fellow named Flambe testing them to see if they deserve to be pirates, Yoho Joseph, Peglegless Pete (he's just a kid), Lester the parrot, Pete's sister Jamie, and the rest of the crew must find the long lost recipe for the Cupcakes of Doom, or the Deliciously-Evil Viking Pie will take over as the people's favorite baked good. The book is full of silly humor, wacky characters (including identical twin sea serpents and a Viking penguin), and a lot of action without violence or bad language. The book is suitable for younger readers, but adults will enjoy the silliness and catch more of the jokes

Fujisaki, Ryu
Hoshin Engi Volume 1. Viz Media/Shonen Jump 2007
192p. Illustration
Grades: 8 9 10 11 12 Adult   **741.5; Fic**
1. Adventure graphic novels; 2. Fantasy graphic novels; 3.
Shonen manga; 4. Graphic novels
978-1-4215-1362-1, $7.99
When his clan is wiped out by a beautiful demon, young
Taikobo finds himself in charge of the mysterious Hoshin
Project. Its mission: find all immortals living in the human
world and seal them away forever. But who do you
trust—and whose side are you really on—when you've been
trained to hunt demons by a demon. There is demon-fighting
action.

Fujishima, Kosuke
Oh My Goddess! Volume 1. Dark Horse Comics 2005
192p. Illustration
Grades: 8 9 10 11 12   **741.5; Fic**
1. Fantasy graphic novels; 2. Humorous graphic novels; 3.
Shonen manga; 4. Graphic novels
1-59307-387-9, $10.95
Alone in his dorm on a Saturday night, Nekomi Tech
student Keiichi Morisato dials a wrong number that will
change his life forever - reaching the Goddess Technical
Help Line. Granted one wish by the charming young
goddess Belldandy - a wish for anything in the world -
Keiichi wishes she would stay with him always.
Complications are bound to ensue from this; the immediate
first being the new couple getting tossed out of the dorm - it's
males only. As the hapless student and his mysterious
"foreign beauty" ride around looking for a new place to stay
- risking the different dangers of seeking shelter with an
otaku convinced Belldandy is an imaginary woman, and a
Zen priest convinced she's a sinister witch - Keiichi's still
got his classes on Monday morning. How is his new
"exchange student" companion going to be received on the
N.I.T. campus? A little too well for normal life to ever
return... This is the beginning of the series in a new edition
that restores the original right-to-left page orientation and
includes a notes section. This classic "harem" manga has
very mild sexual innuendo and focuses more on the comedy.

Fujiyama, Kairi
Dragon Eye, Volume 1. Ballantine Books/Del Rey
Manga 2007 192p. Illustration
Grades: 8 9 10 11 12   **741.5; Fic**
1. Adventure graphic novels; 2. Science fiction graphic
novels; 3. Shonen manga; 4. Graphic novels
978-0-345-49665-2, $10.95
Ten years before, a deadly virus devastated the world,
turning its victims into bloodthirsty Dracules; human soon
learned that the only cure is death. The people who rose up to
fight the Dracules are called VIUS. Now, in the VIUS city
Mikuni, a new recruit named Leila Mikami joins VIUS;
she's determined to find a Dragon Eye, a powerful magic
weapon she plans to use to get revenge for her family's
death. To her surprise, bumbling recruit Issa Kazuma is
actually a VIUS captain, and when top-level Dracules
invade the candidates' final exam, he reveals his Dragon
Eye. Leila joins Kazuma's Squad Zero as they work to

protect Mikuni from Dracules. This first volume offers lots
of action and monster killing.

Fukuchi, Tsubasa
The **Law** of Ueki Vol. 1. Viz Media 2006 192p.
Illustration
Grades: 7 8 9 10 11 12   **741.5; Fic**
1. Humorous graphic novels; 2. Shonen manga; 3. Graphic
novels
978-1-4215-0716-3, $9.99
In a world of powerful celestial beings, an epic contest
is being conducted to select the next king. Each Celestial
selects a kid in junior high to be his champion and grants him
a special power. The kids battle it out, losers are eliminated,
and the winners are granted new talents. Seemingly ordinary
Kosuke Ueki has been chosen to be a contender in the
tournament. Granted the power to change trash into trees,
Ueki has two disadvantages to overcome: one, he doesn't
know he's a participant in the tournament, and two, how the
heck can anyone win a battle with the power to turn trash
into trees? Especially when his first opponent has power
over fire?

Furman, Simon
Transformers: Beast Wars: The Gathering; art by Don
Figueroa. IDW Publishing 2007 Un Illustration
Grades: 4 5 6 7 8 9   **741.5; Fic**
1. Science fiction graphic novels; 2. Transformers
(Fictional characters); 3. Graphic novels
978-1-60010-025-3, $9.99
In this story, Predacon General Magmatron is on a
mission to capture the renegade Megatron, but his true
intentions are fare more terrifying; he ultimately aims to
bring Cybertron itself to its knees. All he need is an army,
and he knows exactly where to find one. The heroic
Maximals now have to battle the evil Predacons to protect
their planet.

Furse, Sophie
Moby Dick; illustrated by Penko Gelev ; retold by
Sophie Furse. Barron's Educational Series, Inc. 2007 48p.
Illustration
Grades: 3 4 5 6 7 8 9   **741.5**
1. Melville, Herman — Adaptations; 2. Graphic novels
978-0-7641-5977-0; 978-0-7641-3492-0 (pa)
Ishmael's dream of adventure on a whaling ship
becomes a nightmare as the voyage turns into a struggle for
survival. Captain Ahab, maimed by a monster whale, is
obsessed with revenge. As the crew discovers, he is willing
to risk everything to destroy that whale. This volume
includes a brief biography and timeline of Melville, and
information on the legacy of his novel.

Gaff, Jackie
Christopher Columbus: The Life of a Master
Navigator and Explorer by David West & Jackie Gaff ;
illustrated by Ross Watton. Rosen Publishing Group 2005
48p. Illustration
Grades: 3 4 5 6 7 8   **741.5; 970.01**

1. America — Exploration; 2. Biographical graphic novels; 3. Columbus, Christopher, 1451-1506; 4. Graphic novels

1-4042-0243-9, $29.25

LC 2004008645

Before Christopher Columbus's voyages to the West Indies and Central and South America, Europeans knew nothing of the Americas in the New World. His four journeys, beginning in 1492 and ending in 1504, blazed a sea route west across the Atlantic Ocean that pioneered would exploration for years to come. This account captures Columbus's determination and courage as he led his crews into both unknown waters and unfamiliar native civilizations. The book includes some information on other voyages by explorers, a glossary, and a list of books for further reading.

Gagne, Michel

The **saga** of Rex. Image 2010 200p. Illustration

Grades: 4 5 6 7 8   **741.5; Fic**

978-1-60706-322-3, $17.99; 1-60706-322-0

The adorable little fox named Rex is plucked from his home world by a mysterious spaceship and transported to the arcane world of Edernia, where he meets Aven, an enigmatic biomorph with a flying saucer.

"While children may enjoy this graphic novel for its gorgeous art—especially the cute characters—its story line will more likely be appreciated by older readers. The almost wordless story isn't meant to be read on a literal level but instead on more a mystical and dreamlike level. . . . Gagné . . . offers a sensitive and intriguing graphic novel for people who like a little enigma in what they read." Publ Wkly

Gaiman, Neil

★ The **graveyard** book graphic novel Volume 1. Based on the novel by Neil Gaiman; adapted by P. Craig Russell; illustrated by Kevin Nowlan, P. Craig Russell, Tony Harris, Scott Hampton, Galen Showman, Jill Thompson, Stephen B. Scott; colorist, Lovern Kindzierski; letterer, Rick Park. HarperCollins 2014 188 p. Color; Illustration

Grades: 5 6 7 8 9 10   **741.5; Fic**

1. Cemeteries — Fiction; 2. Orphans — Fiction; 3. Graphic novels; 4. Gaiman, Neil, 1960- — Adaptations

9780062194817, $19.99; 006219481X

LC 2013953799

This graphic novel is an adaptation of the "Newbery Medal-winning novel, [where] Bod is an unusual boy . . ., the only living resident of a graveyard. Raised from infancy by the ghosts, werewolves, and other cemetery denizens, Bod has learned the antiquated customs of his guardians' time as well as their ghostly teachings." (Publisher's note)

"Russell brings his decades of comics know-how to this lovely, lyrical adaptation of [Gaiman's] well-loved, Newbery Medal—winning book. Not content to rely exclusively on his own distinctive talents, Russell has enlisted some of the industry's greatest contemporary illustrators as contributors, who fill the panels with appropriately gothic tones. In order to give ample room to the novel's twists and turns, the adaptation has been divided into two parts." Booklist

★ The **graveyard** book graphic novel Volume 2. Based on the novel by Neil Gaiman; adapted by P. Craig Russell; illustrated by David LaFuente, Scott Hampton, P. Craig Russell, Kevin Nowlan, Galen Showman; colorist, Lovern Kindzierski; letterer, Rick Parker. HarperCollins 2014 188 p. Color; Illustration

Grades: 5 6 7 8 9 10   **741.5; Fic**

1. Cemeteries — Fiction; 2. Dead — Fiction; 3. Orphans — Fiction; 4. Supernatural — Fiction; 5. Supernatural graphic novels; 6. Graphic novels

0062194836; 9780062194831, $19.99

LC 2013497350

"Russell concludes the two-part adaptation of Gaiman's Newbery Medal winner, encompassing the final three chapters of the novel. Bod, raised by the ghostly denizens of a graveyard, is a young adult now, yearning for knowledge of the world of the living. After a showdown with a pair of school bullies . . . Bod finally confronts the ancient order who murdered his family and overcomes them with his supernatural know-how and his innate courage and cleverness." (Booklist)

"Russell and his team of illustrators continue to do this amazing story justice with images that lead readers down a path into Bod's dark and magical graveyard world. Gaiman has the ability to weave beauty and intrigue into a story that has a strong potential to frighten." VOYA

Gallagher, John

Buzzboy: Trouble in paradise. Sky Dog Press 2002 144p. Illustration

Grades: 5 6 7 8 9 10 11 12   **741.5; Fic**

1. Humorous graphic novels; 2. Superhero graphic novels; 3. Graphic novels

0-8721831-0-8, $11.95

Imagine a superhero who jokes constantly, watches way too many old television shows, and loves junk food, and you have Buzzboy. Years before, he was sidekick to Captain Ultra, but the evil Dr. Schism destroyed all superheroes and their sidekicks, except for Captain Ultra. Now, Ultra has declared martial law in the city of New Paradise, and his police stomp out all rebellions. Then a mysterious superhero stops the Hoppers (police) it's Buzzboy, older and back from the dead! Aided by sarcastic teen sorceress Becca and reformed mad scientist Doc Cyber, Buzzboy is here to save the day.

Another title in this series is: Buzzboy: Monsters, dreams, & milkshakes (2003)

Ganeri, Anita

Cleopatra: The Life of an Egyptian Queen by Gary Jeffrey & Anita Ganeri ; illustrated by Ross Watton. Rosen Publishing Group 2005 48p. Illustration

Grades: 3 4 5 6 7 8   **741.5; 932; 92**

1. Biographical graphic novels; 2. Cleopatra, Queen of Egypt, d 30 BC; 3. Egypt — History; 4. Graphic novels

1-4042-0242-0, $29.25

LC 2004014162

Queen of Egypt, companion of Julius Caesar, and wife of Mark Antony, Cleopatra lived one of history's most fabled lives. Renowned for her great beauty and intelligence, Cleopatra was a strong ruler determined to restore the glory of Ptolemaic rule to Egypt by using her relationships with

Caesar and Antony to achieve her goals. Readers will learn why the events of her life—including her tragic suicide—have inspired writers and artists for centuries. This graphic novel includes additional information and a list of books for further reading.
Part of the Graphic Nonfiction series.

Harriet Tubman: The Life of an African-American Abolitionist by Rob Shone & Anita Ganeri ; illustrated by Rob Shone. Rosen Publishing Group 2005 48p. Illustration
Grades: 3 4 5 6 7 8 9   **92; 741.5**
1. African American women; 2. Biographical graphic novels; 3. ss; 4. Tubman, Harriet, 1819 or 1820-1913; 5. Underground Railroad; 6. Graphic novels
1-4042-0245-5, $29.25
Born a slave in the United States, Harriet Tubman escaped from bondage to risk her life and newfound liberty in becoming a leading abolitionist in the years before the American Civil War. Tubman surreptitiously led hundreds of escaped Southern slaves to freedom in the North along the Underground Railroad, earning her the nickname as "the Moses of her people." This graphic novel format book tells her story. It includes additional information about the Underground Railroad and her legacy in the civil rights movement, and a list of books for further reading.
Part of the Graphic Nonfiction series.

Ganter, Amy Kim
Sorcerers & Secretaries, Vol. 1. Tokyopop 2006 Un Illustration
Grades: 8 9 10 11 12   **741.5; Fic**
1. Romance graphic novels; 2. Graphic novels
1-59816-409-0, $9.99
Nicole attends university and works part-time as a receptionist, but she prefers to daydream of the fantasy characters she has created and writes about in her journal. Josh, Nicole's former neighbor, works in a bookstore; he has always liked her, but could never get her to go out with him. They reconnect, but when Nicole realizes that being with Josh prevents her from writing her fantasy stories, she has to decide what's more important to her. This is a global manga story.

Garcia, Tracy J.
Eli Whitney. By Tracy J. Garcia. PowerKids Press 2013 24 p. Color illustration
Grades: 3 4 5 6   **609.2; B**
1. Cotton gins and ginning — Juvenile literature; 2. Inventors — United States; 3. Inventors — United States — Biography — Juvenile literature; 4. Whitney, Eli, 1765-1825 — Juvenile literature
1477700757; 1477701354; 1477701362; 9781477700754, $25.25; 9781477701355, $10.60; 9781477701362
LC 2012019319
This graphic novel by Tracy J. Garcia focuses on "Eli Whitney [who] changed manufacturing with the cotton gin and helped make improvements in the area of mass production through interchangeable parts. Readers will [be exposed to] how Whitney also drastically changed farming in America with his inventions." (Publisher's note)
Includes index.

Thomas Edison. By Tracy J. Garcia. PowerKids Press 2013 24 p. (Jr. graphic American inventors)
Grades: 3 4 5 6   **621.3092; 92; 621.3**
1. Businessmen — United States — Biography — Juvenile literature; 2. Edison, Thomas A (Thomas Alva), 1847-1931; 3. Edison, Thomas A (Thomas Alva), 1847-1931 — Juvenile literature; 4. Electrical engineers — United States — Biography — Juvenile literature; 5. Inventors; 6. Inventors — United States — Biography — Juvenile literature
1477700765; 9781477700761, $25.25; 9781477701379; 9781477701386
LC 2012018690
This graphic novel by Tracy J. Garcia focuses on "Thomas Edison [who] was a prolific inventor with nearly 2,000 patents. One of his most noted inventions is the practical electrical light bulb. Readers will be [exposed to] the life of Thomas Edison, one of America's great inventors and businessmen." (Publisher's note)
Includes index.

Gauvin, Edward
Sardine in Outer Space Vol. 4. First Second Books 2007 109p. Illustration
Grades: 3 4 5 6 7 8   **741.5; Fic**
1. Adventure graphic novels; 2. Humorous graphic novels; 3. Graphic novels
978-1-59643-129-4, $13.95
Sardine is back, and she's got a whole host of new problems to face even before the spaceship Huckleberry can get off the ground. In the fourth volume of this series, Sardine must tackle, among other things, monsters under the bed, flesh-eating tattoos, time machines, a flying cat, kidnapped suns, and even boredom. As always, Supermuscleman, Chief Executive Dictator of the Universe, lurks in the background, trying-unsuccessfully and incompetently-to make Sardine and her crew behave.
Another title in the author's series about Sardine in Outer Space

Geary, Rick
★ The **Lindbergh** child: America's hero and the crime of the century. Written and illustrated by Rick Geary. NBM/ComicsLit 2008 Un Illustration; Map (Treasury of XXth century murder)
Grades: 8 9 10 11 12 Adult   **364.1; 741.5**
1. Air force officers; 2. Air pilots; 3. Generals; 4. Homicide; 5. Kidnapping; 6. Lindbergh, Charles, 1902-1974; 7. Memoirists; 8. Mystery graphic novels; 9. Graphic novels
978-1-56163-529-0, $15.95
Charles Lindbergh was an American hero following his solo crossing of the Atlantic in an airplane. He married into a wealthy family, he and his wife had a baby, they were building their dream home. Then, one night, the baby was abducted from the house. Geary's account retraces all the highly publicized events, ransom notes (false and otherwise), as well as the string of colorful characters who all claimed they could help but instead snookered the Lindberghs. While Bruno Hauptmann was arrested, tried, convicted, and executed, there remain many questions about

what really happened. Geary brings them up for readers to consider.

"A good example of the origins of modern forensics, crime-scene investigation, and celebrity hysteria, this work is an excellent choice for most collections." SLJ

Courtesy of NBM Publishing

The **murder** of Abraham Lincoln: a chronicle of 62 days in the life of the American Republic, March 4-May 4, 1865. Written and illustrated by Rick Geary. NBM ComicsLit 2005 Un Illustration; Map (A treasury of Victorian murder)

Grades: 7 8 9 10 11 12   **973.7**
1. Booth, John Wilkes, 1838-1865; 2. Lawyers; 3. Lincoln, Abraham, 1809-1865 — Assassination; 4. Murderers; 5. Presidents; 6. Graphic novels
978-1-56163-425-5; 1-56163-425-5, $15.95; 978-1-56163-426-2 (pa); 1-56163-426-3 (pa), $8.95
LC 2005-41468
This graphic novel "covers Lincoln's assassination, the events that led up to it, and the aftermath. Geary also makes a point of bringing up still-unanswered questions, like the whereabouts of the missing pages of John Wilkes Booth's journal. . . . Even teens who know nothing about the tragedy will find their heads chock-full of information when they're finished reading this book." SLJ

Includes bibliographical references

Courtesy of NBM Publishing

Gelatt, Philip
Indiana Jones adventures vol. 1; script, Philip Gelatt ; art, Ethen Beavers. Dark Horse Comics 2008 Un Illustration
Grades: 4 5 6 7 8 9   **741.5; Fic**
1. Adventure graphic novels; 2. Archeology; 3. Indiana Jones (Fictional character); 4. Indiana Jones (Fictional character); 5. Graphic novels
978-1-59307-905-5, $6.95
It's winter of 1930 in Sweden, and Dr. Henry Jones Jr. (Indiana Jones) finds an ancient pre-Christian temple of a religion devoted to war; he gets a scroll while Dr. Lawrence, the pretty British archeologist with him, runs with a valuable gold ring. When Indy decides to steal the ring back from the British Museum, the unscrupulous French archeologist Belloq, who works for the Nazis, steals the scroll from Marcus Brody, Indy's friend. From London, Indy and Dr. Lawrence pursue Belloq to Egypt to recover the scroll before he can sell it to the Nazis. This original graphic novel story provides adventure suitable for younger readers.

Gelev, Penko
Dr. Jekyll and Mr. Hyde; illustrated by Penko Gelev ; retold by Fiona Macdonald. Barron's Educational Series 2008 48p. Illustration
Grades: 4 5 6 7 8 9 10   **741.5; Fic**
1. Authors; 2. Essayists; 3. Novelists; 4. Poets; 5. Science fiction graphic novels; 6. Stevenson, Robert Louis, 1850-1894 — Adaptations; 7. Graphic novels
978-0-7641-6058-5, $15.99; 978-0-7641-3782-2 (pa), $8.99
LC 2008-923897
In Victorian London, the sinister, monstrous Mr. Hyde prowls and commits murder, and he's protected by Dr. Henry Jekyll, who is a respected member of society. Why is this? Stevenson's story of good and evil is retold in the graphic format. Words from his original text are defined on the pages, and back matter includes a brief biography of Stevenson, background information about the story, and information on the various adaptations done for film and television over the years.

Part of the Graphic Classics series.

Dracula; illustrated by Penko Gelev ; retold by Fiona MacDonald. Barron's 2007 48p.
Grades: 4 5 6 7 8 9   **741.5; Fic**
1. Authors; 2. Dracula, Count (Fictional character); 3. Horror graphic novels; 4. Stoker, Bram, 1847-1912 — Adaptations; 5. Vampires; 6. Graphic novels
978-0-7641-6054-7, $15.99; 978-0-7641-3778-5 (pa), $8.99
LC 2007-925724
Englishman Jonathan Harker travels to Transylvania to meet his firm's new client, Count Dracula, only to discover the horrible truth that Dracula is a vampire and seeking new hunting grounds in England. Back home, Harker's fiancee, Mina Murray, and her friend Lucy Westenra, face danger from Dracula. This graphic novel adaptation of Stoker's novel includes a biography of Stoker, information about vampires, a list of eighteenth and nineteenth century tales of mystery and horror, a list of some of the film adaptations, and more.

Part of Barron's Graphic Classics series

Frankenstein; illustrated by Penko Gelev ; retold by Fiona MacDonald. Barron's 2008 48p. Illustration
Grades: 4 5 6 7 8 9   741.5; Fic
1. Authors; 2. Horror graphic novels; 3. Novelists; 4. Science fiction graphic novels; 5. Shelley, Mary Wollstonecraft, 1797-1851 — Adaptations; 6. Graphic novels
978-0-7641-6057-8, $15.99; 978-0-7641-3781-5 (pa), $8.99

LC 2006-937854

Victor Frankenstein is a brilliant medical student who has discovered the secret of bringing dead matter to life. Determined to create a living being, he gathers materials from graveyards and slaughterhouses, and creates a giant of superhuman strength, but his creature is also hideous. Horrified by what he has done, Frankenstein flees, and the creature he left behind plans his revenge. This graphic novel adaptation includes a brief biography of Shelley, a timeline of scientific and medical discoveries made during Shelley's lifetime, information on various film adaptations of her story, and more.

Part of Barron's Graphic Classics series

Gerber, Steve
Guardians of the Galaxy; 1: Tomorrow's Avengers 1. By Steve Gerber, Chris Claremont, Gerry Conway, Len Wein, Arnold Drake and Roger Stern and illustrated by Gene Colan, Sal Buscema, Don Heck, and Al Milgrom. Marvel Enterprises 2013 368 p.
Grades: 7 8 9 10 11 12   741.5
1. Captain America (Fictional character); 2. Doctor Strange (Fictional character); 3. Hulk (Fictional character); 4. Outer space — Fiction; 5. Space warfare — Fiction; 6. Superheroes — Fiction
0785166874; 9780785166870, $39.99

In this graphic novel, written by Steve Gerber, Chris Claremont, Gerry Conway, Len Wien, Arnold Drake and Roger Stern, "Captain America, Doctor Strange, the Thing, the Hulk and other[s] . . . join the star-spanning heroes in the greatest war the future ever saw! As the Guardians help a planet . . . rebuild, threats rise from two other worlds: one of them living, the other gone mad!" (Publisher's note)

Gianopoulos, Andrea
The **Attractive** Story of Magnetism with Max Axiom, Super Scientist by Andrea Gianopoulos ; illustrated by Cynthia Martin and Barbara Schulz. Capstone Press 2007 32p. Illustration
Grades: 3 4 5 6 7 8 9   538; 741.5
1. Magnetism; 2. Magnets; 3. Graphic novels
978-1-4296-0141-2, $25.26

LC 2007002262

This book uses the graphic novel format to follow the adventures of super scientist Max Axiom as he explains the science behind magnetism. The book includes additional facts and a list of books for further reading.

Part of the Graphic Science series.

Giarrusso, Chris
G-Man, volume 1: learning to fly. Image Comics 2010 Un Illustration

Grades: 3 4 5 6   741.5; Fic
1. Humorous graphic novels; 2. Superhero graphic novels; 3. Graphic novels
978-1-60706-270-7 (pa), $9.99; 1-60706-270-4 (pa)

Mikey G. is G-Man, the newest superhero on the block, in a town full of superheroes (he made his cape from the family's magic blanket). His friends Billy Demon, Tan Man, Sparky, and the Suntrooper are all ready to help, but G-Man also has to deal with his older brother Great Man (aka Dave) and their superhero dad, Mr. G.

This "hits all the right notes, from its friendly cartoon figures to the occasionally hilarious one-liners." Booklist
This is a new edition, in a larger size and with a new ISBN
Other titles in this series are:Cape crisis (2010); Coming home (2013)

G-Man, volume 2: cape crisis. Image comics 2010 Un Illustration
Grades: 3 4 5 6 7 8   741.5; Fic
1. Humorous graphic novels; 2. Superhero graphic novels; 3. Graphic novels
978-1-60706-271-4, $9.99

The trouble starts when G-Man (aka Mikey) tells everyone that his magic cape gives him the power to fly; then everyone wants to fly. When he gives them bracelets made from the scraps of the magic blanket, everyone starts flying around and causing trouble. Then, when G-Man rounds up all the bracelets, he finds older brother Great Man (aka Dave) is selling more bracelets for $1,000 apiece. However, dividing up the magic into so many small bits is not only allowing unscrupulous people to commit crimes with their new powers, it is causing instabilities that could backfire disastrously. And that's exactly what happens. Now the brothers have to go on a quest to find the one being who can restore the magic to G-Man's cape.

Gieter, De
Papyrus: the Rameses' revenge. Cinebook 2007 48p. Illustration
Grades: 3 4 5 6 7 8   741.5; Fic
1. Adventure graphic novels; 2. Egypt — History; 3. Graphic novels
978-1-905460-35-9, $11.95

In ancient Egypt, Papyrus is a mischievous boy who has become a friend of the Princess Theti-Cheri, daughter of the Pharaoh, thanks to the magic sword that protects him. When Theti-Cheri insists on traveling down the Nile to see Rameses' Temple with just Papyrus, their friend Imhotep, and just a few guards, Papyrus is sure they will run into trouble. At the temple, they face two rival bands of plunderers who seek the treasure in the temple.

Part of the Papyrus series, originally published in France as Papyrus La Vengeance des Ramses.

Giffen, Keith
Blue Beetle vol. 2: road trip. John Rogers & Keith Giffen, writers; Cully Hamner . . . [et al.], artists; Guy Major, colorist; Phil Balsman, Pat Brosseau, Jared K. Fletcher, letterers. DC Comics 2007 144p. Illustration
Grades: 8 9 10 11 12 Adult   741.5; Fic

1. Adventure graphic novels; 2. Blue Beetle (Fictional character); 3. Superhero graphic novels; 4. Graphic novels
978-1-4012-1361-9, $12.99

High school teen Jaime Reyes became the latest Blue Beetle by accident, and now he needs to know more about the scarab that has bonded with his body (something it had never done with either previous Blue Beetle). He undertakes a journey with his friend Brenda and the tattooed soldier called Peacemaker to find out what is happening to him, and his journey takes him across the country and into the furthest reaches of space.

"The use of an ethnicity not often seen in comic heroes, plus engaging characters and a fast-paced, rip-snorting second half make for a divertingly lighthearted take on a young man's quest to solve the secrets of himself." Booklist

Followed by Blue Beetle vol. 3: reach for the stars (2008)

Sequel to Blue Beetle: shellshocked (2006)

Gilroy, Henry

Star Wars: The Clone wars: Shipyards of doom. Ronda Pattison, illustrator; The Fillbach Brothers, illustrators. Dark Horse Comics 2008 96p. Illustration

Grades: 6 7 8 9 10   **741.5; Fic**
1. Adventure graphic novels; 2. Science fiction graphic novels; 3. Star Wars; 4. Graphic novels
978-1-59582-207-9, $7.95

In this original story based on the Star Wars: Clone Wars animated movie and television series, Anakin Skywalker, Obi-Wan Kenobi, and Anakin's Padawan Ahsoka Tano form the nucleus of a small team whose objective is to infiltrate the Banking Clan Shipyards in order to call in a bombing strike. For now, the Separatist forces have superior numbers of ships, and destroying the shipyard could help the Republic. However, once they arrive, they learn that the shipyard is using live workers instead of being fully automated, and Anakin and Obi-Wan must find a way to save the workers while still destroying the shipyards. The workers' beaten-down attitudes and refusal to be freed hampers the Jedi Knights. This graphic novel includes the same level of action and violence as the live action Star Wars movies.

Transformers animated, volume 4; Henry Gilroy and Marty Isenberg ; adapted by Zachary Rau. IDW Publishing 2008 Un Illustration

Grades: 2 3 4 5 6 7 8   **741.5; Fic**
1. Robots; 2. Science fiction graphic novels; 3. Transformers (Fictional characters); 4. Graphic novels
978-1-60010-217-2, $7.99

This volume adapts two of the animated television series' episodes. On Halloween, Blackarachnia returns to give the Autobots trouble in "Along Came a Spider." Then, in "Sound and Fury," Sumdac's birthday present to Sari causes chaos for all the robots in New Detroit, especially since Megatron helped Sumdac make Soundwave . . .

Gilson

Melusine: Halloween; illustrated by Clarke ; translated by Erica Jeffrey. Cinebook Ltd 2007 48p. Illustration

Grades: 3 4 5 6 7 8   **741.5; Fic**

1. Humorous graphic novels; 2. Witches; 3. Graphic novels
978-1-905460-34-2, $11.95

Melusine is a sorcerer's apprentice who wants to become a powerful witch. However, she's not always successful. Her friend Cancrelune can never get her potions right, and cousin Melisande is a fairy who always wants to make everything light, pretty, and fun. This volume collects stories that focus on Halloween, with pumpkin carving, monster calling, and children going trick-or-treating.

First published 2000 in France

Melusine: love potions. Cinebook 2010 48p. Illustration
Grades: 3 4 5 6 7 8
741.5; Fic
1. Humorous graphic novels; 2. Witches; 3. Graphic novels
978-1-84918-005-4, $11.95

Young witch in training Melusine tries to make love potions, in between encounters with her clumsy fellow student Cancrelune and various villagers who want to fall in love (or not). The full-color cartoony art

Courtesy of Cinebook, Ltd.

keeps the witches, vampires, ghosts, dragons, and monsters more humorous looking than spooky.

Originally published in France as Melusine 5 Philtres d'amour

Melusine: The vampire's ball. Cinebook Ltd. 2008 48p. Illustration

Grades: 3 4 5 6 7 8   **741.5; Fic**
1. Humorous graphic novels; 2. Witches; 3. Graphic novels
978-1-905460-69-4, $11.95

The young witch Melusine is back for more fun with all her family, including witches Adrazelle and Cancrelune, the ghostly Madam and vampire Master of the haunted castle, and more. Melusine tries to make different potions, turns toads into dragons and vice versa, tries to avoid too many cleaning chores in the castle, and more. Some of the situations are slightly gruesome, as when a particularly nasty knight ends up eaten by a monstrous tree in the forest, or when the male vampires get too drunk to get under cover before sunrise and turn into piles of ash.

Gilson, Che

Dark Moon Diary Volume 1. Brett Uher, illustrator/ Tokyopop 2007 Un Illustration

Grades: 8 9 10 11 12   **741.5; Fic**
1. Fantasy graphic novels; 2. Supernatural graphic novels; 3. Graphic novels
978-1-59532-844-1, $9.99

When fifteen-year-old Priscilla's parents pass away, she has nowhere to go but to her last living" relatives in the European town of Nachtwald. Once there, she learns that not only is Nachtwald populated by ghosts, werewolves, witches, and other preternatural beings, but that her relatives are vampires. Amidst the pandemonium, she turns to her diary, and slowly learns what it takes to survive a new family, new friendships, and the anxiety of high school, all while living in an unfamiliar world.

Gipi
  Garage Band. First Second Books 2007 132p. Illustration
Grades: 8 9 10 11 12 Adult   **741.5**
  1. Friendship; 2. Rock music; 3. Graphic novels
978-1-59643-206-2
                                    LC 2006018345
  Four boys - Giuliano, Stefano, Alberto, and Alex - with turbulent home lives find refuge in the music they play together and in their friendship. When their only amp blows a fuse and the deadline to make their demo tape is pressing, they decide to steal in order to replace it. Events rapidly spiral out of control: will this be the end of everything the band has worked for?

Glaser, Jason
  The **Buffalo** Soldiers and the American West. Capstone Press 2005 32p. Illustration
Grades: 3 4 5 6 7 8 9   **741.5; 978**
  1. African American soldiers; 2. West (US); 3. Graphic novels
0-7368-4966-1, $25.00
                                    LC 2005006527
  In graphic novel format, this book tells the story of the African American soldiers known as Buffalo Soldiers, who fought against Native Americans and protected the Western Frontier of the United States. The book includes additional information about the Buffalo Soldiers, a bibliography, and a list of books for further reading.
Part of the Graphic History series.

  Jackie Robinson: Baseball's Great Pioneer. Capstone Press 2005 32p. Illustration
Grades: 3 4 5 6 7 8 9   **741.5; 796.357'092; 796.357**
  1. African American athletes; 2. Baseball — Biography; 3. Biographical graphic novels; 4. Robinson, Jackie, 1919-1972; 5. Graphic novels
0-7368-4633-6, $25.26
                                    LC 2005003345
  In graphic novel format, this book tells the life story of Jackie Robinson and his professional baseball career that broke the "color barrier." The book includes additional information about Robinson, including the back of a baseball card that shows his playing statistics for the 1947-1956 seasons, a bibliography, and a list of books for further reading.
Part of the Graphic Biographies series.

  John Brown's raid on Harper's Ferry. Capstone Press 2005 32p. Illustration
Grades: 3 4 5 6 7 8 9   **741.5; 973.7**
  1. Harpers Ferry (W Va) — History — John Brown's Raid, 1859; 2. Graphic novels
0-7368-4369-8, $25.26
                                    LC 2004029083
  This book recounts the story of John Brown's failed rebellion in Harpers Ferry in 1859, intended to start a massive slave uprising in the South and the establishment of a state in the Allegheny Mountains for freed slaves. It includes additional information, a glossary, a list of books for further reading, and more.
Part of the Graphic Library, Graphic History series.

  Patrick Henry: Liberty or Death. Capstone Press 2006 32p. Illustration
Grades: 3 4 5 6 7 8 9   **741.5; 973.3; 92**
  1. Biographical graphic novels; 2. Henry, Patrick, 1736-1799; 3. Graphic novels
0-7368-4970-X, $25.26
                                    LC 2005004011
  This book uses the comic book format to recount highlights of the life story of Patrick Henry, who is known as the "Voice of the American Revolution." It includes additional information, a glossary, a list of books for further reading, and more.
Part of the Graphic Library, Graphic Biographies series.

Glass, Bryan J. L.
  The **mice** templar, volume one: the prophecy. Created by Bryan J.L. Glass & Michael Avon Oeming. Michael Avon Oeming, illustrator. Image Comics 2008 256p. Illustration
Grades: 6 7 8 9 10 11 12 Adult   **741.5; Fic**
  1. Adventure graphic novels; 2. Fantasy graphic novels; 3. Mice; 4. Graphic novels
978-1-58240-871-2, $29.99; 1-58240-871-8
  In a land populated by animals, the Mice Templar used to protect the people of the mouse kingdom, but a civil war destroyed them; the king now employs rat soldiers, and they prey upon the mouse villages. Young Karic still idolizes the Mice Templar, but everything he knows and believes is shattered when his village is raided by rats, burned, and his family captured as slaves. He survives, saved by a mysterious mouse named Pilot, who says he was once a Templar and offers to train Karic. The salmon in the river say that Karic is the one prophesied to restore the Templar, but can he truly be the one? The book includes considerable battle violence.
  "Equal parts Norse myth, Arthurian legend, and Mrs. Frisby and the Rats of N.I.M.H., The Mice Templar series re-imagines the warrior animal tale with just enough of its own spin to make it well worth adding to the collection." Voice Youth Advocates
  The volume is a collection of the first six issues of The mice templar
  Other titles in this series are: Destiny Part One (2010) Destiny Part Two (2010) Legend (2013) A Midwinter Night's Dream (2012)

Goddard, Drew
  Buffy the Vampire Slayer season eight, volume 3: Wolves at the gate. Artist, Georges Jeanty, Jo Chen. Dark Horse Comics 2008 Un Illustration
Grades: 8 9 10 11 12 Adult   **741.5; Fic**
  1. Buffy the Vampire Slayer (Fictional character); 2. Fantasy graphic novels; 3. Horror graphic novels; 4. Vampires; 5. Graphic novels
978-1-59582-165-2, $15.95
  A band of Japanese vampires who can transform into wolves, panthers, swarms of bees, and fog, attack the Slayer

compound in Scotland, stealing Buffy's mystical scythe that she used to transform thousands of young women into Slayers. Now the only one who can help her fight these vampires is Dracula himself, and they have to travel to Japan to recover the scythe and stop the Japanese from accomplishing their plans. Meanwhile, Buffy and Satsu have one night together that seems to throw everyone else for a loop. The last panel on the last page shows Buffy and Satsu together in bed, kissing and wrapped around each other.

Goodwin, Vincent
Sir Arthur Conan Doyle's The adventure of the Red-Headed League. ABDO/Magic Wagon 2010 48p. Illustration
Grades: 4 5 6 7 8 9
741.5; Fic
1. Doyle, Arthur Conan Sir, 1859-1930 — Adaptations; 2. Holmes, Sherlock (Fictional character); 3. Mystery graphic novels; 4. Novelists; 5. Graphic novels
978-1-60270-726-9, $28.50; 1-60270-726-X

Courtesy of ABDO Publishing Group/Magic Wagon

LC 2009-32460
Consulting detective Sherlock Holmes and his friend Dr. John Watson take the case of Jabez Wilson, an ordinary tradesman with an extraordinary tale. His pawn shop assistant had found an advertisement in the newspaper asking for eligible men to apply for membership in The RedHeaded League, and he helped Mr. Wilson fight through a crowd of redheaded men and to be accepted into the League. Wilson was paid four pounds a week for a few hours' work copying out of an encyclopedia; then suddenly, all trace of the League disappeared. He wants Holmes to find out what has happened. This graphic novel adaptation has been done by Goodwin and Dunn, who are experienced creators with Antarctic Press (Dunn started the publishing house). The book includes a brief glossary, a short biography of Doyle, a listing of his published works, and a short sketching lesson by Dunn.
Part of The Graphic Novel Adventures of Sherlock Holmes

Sir Arthur Conan Doyle's The adventure of the speckled band. Adapted by, Vincent Goodwin; illustrated by, Ben Dunn. ABDO/Magic Wagon 2010 48p. Illustration
Grades: 4 5 6 7 8 9
741.5; Fic
1. Doyle, Arthur Conan Sir, 1859-1930 — Adaptations; 2. Holmes,

Courtesy of ABDO Publishing Group/Magic Wagon

Sherlock (Fictional character); 3. Mystery graphic novels; 4. Mystery writers
978-1-60270-727-6, $28.50; 1-60270-727-8
LC 2009-32461
Consulting detective Sherlock Holmes and his partner Dr. John Watson come to the aid of Miss Helen Stoner. After moving back to England from India with their stepfather, Helen's twin sister died under mysterious circumstances. Now, two years later, Helen knows something is terribly wrong in her stepfather's house. Both men suspect the gypsies that Dr. Roylott, the stepfather, has allowed to live on his property, but Holmes soon suspects something else. This graphic novel adaptation has been done by Goodwin and Dunn, who are experienced creators with Antarctic Press (Dunn started the publishing house). The book includes a brief glossary, a short biography of Doyle, a listing of his published works, and a short sketching lesson by Dunn.
Part of The Graphic Novel Adventures of Sherlock Holmes

Sir Arthur Conan Doyle's, The adventure of the Abbey Grange. ABDO/Magic Wagon 2010 48p. Illustration
Grades: 4 5 6 7 8 9
741.5; Fic
1. Doyle, Arthur Conan Sir, 1859-1930 — Adaptations; 2. Holmes, Sherlock (Fictional character); 3. Mystery graphic novels; 4. Mystery writers
978-1-60270-722-1, $28.50; 1-60270-722-7
A robbery and murder have occurred, and Sir Eustace Brackenstall is dead. His wife and maid say that a gang of robbers invaded their home, tied up Lady Brackenstall and killed Sir Eustace, but Holmes doesn't believe

Courtesy of ABDO Publishing Group/Magic Wagon

their story. As he investigates, he learns that Sir Eustace was a cruel man, and even though Lady Brackenstall has lied, Holmes sympathizes with her. This book adapts Doyle's short story; it includes a short glossary, a brief biography of Doyle, a short drawing lesson, and a list of Doyle's other writings. Dunn's art depicts Holmes and Dr. Watson as younger men, but continues the stereotypical portrayal of Holmes with the deerstalker cap and shoulder caped coat which Doyle never had him wear in the original stories.
Part of The Graphic Novel Adventures of Sherlock Holmes series.

Sir Arthur Conan Doyle's, The adventure of the dancing men. ABDO/Magic Wagon 2010 48p. Illustration
Grades: 4 5 6 7 8 9
1. Doyle, Arthur Conan Sir, 1859-1930 — Adaptations; 2. Holmes, Sherlock (Fictional character); 3. Mystery graphic novels; 4. Mystery writers
978-1-60270-723-8, $28.50; 1-60270-723-5
When strange writing that looks like dancing men starts appearing around the estate of Mr. Cubitt, he comes to Sherlock Holmes for help. He thinks it's the work of

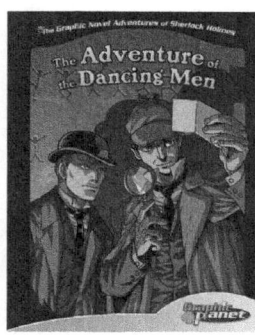

pranksters, but his American wife seems frightened. As he brings more of the writing samples to Holmes, the detective works on the case, but he may not be able to solve it before tragedy strikes the Cubitts. This book adapts Doyle's short story; it includes a short glossary, a brief biography of Doyle, a short drawing lesson, and a list of Doyle's other writings. Dunn's art depicts Holmes and Dr. Watson as younger men, but continues the stereotypical portrayal of Holmes with the deerstalker cap and shoulder caped coat which Doyle never had him wear in the original stories.

Part of The Graphic Novel Adventures of Sherlock Holmes series

Sir Arthur Conan Doyle's, The adventure of the empty house. ABDO/Magic Wagon 2010 48p. Illustration
Grades: 4 5 6 7 8 9
741.5; Fic
1. Doyle, Arthur Conan Sir, 1859-1930 — Adaptations; 2. Holmes, Sherlock (Fictional character); 3. Mystery graphic novels; 4. Mystery writers
978-1-60270-724-5, $28.50; 1-60270-724-3

Three years before, Dr. Watson witnessed the death of his friend Sherlock Holmes, who plummeted to his death along with archvillain Dr. Moriarty. Now, Inspector Lestrade asks Watson's help in a puzzling murder case, but it stumps Watson as well. Then, to his utter surprise, Holmes comes to him, explaining that he pretended to die. Together again, the two men work on the case, hoping to catch one of Moriarty's dangerous henchmen. This graphic novel adapts Doyle's original story which was the "comeback" after killing Holmes in "The Final Problem." The art depicts Watson as a fairly young man, but persists in putting Holmes into the deerstalker cap and caped overcoat which Doyle's Holmes never wore. The book includes a brief drawing lesson, a short glossary, brief biography of Doyle, and a listing of his other writings.

Part of The Graphic Novel Adventures of Sherlock Holmes

Sir Arthur Conan Doyle's, the adventure of the Norwood Builder. ABDO/Magic Wagon 2010 48p. Illustration
Grades: 4 5 6 7 8 9 **741.5; Fic**
1. Holmes, Sherlock (Fictional character); 2. Mystery graphic novels; 3. Graphic novels

978-1-60270-725-2, $28.50; 1-60270-725-1
LC 2009-32459
Young solicitor Mr. McFarlane begs Holmes to clear his name when he's accused of the murder of Jonas Oldacre, the Norwood Builder. Inspector Lestrade thinks he has a solid case, and the evidence seems to implicate McFarlane, especially since Mr. Oldacre's new will made McFarlane his sole heir. Holmes points to the lack of a body, and digs up more clues in his quest to save McFarlane. This graphic novel adaptation of Doyle's short story retains the suspense of the original, but perpetuates the stereotypical portrayals of Holmes in the deerstalker and caped coat which he never wore in the original stories. The book includes a brief drawing lesson, a short glossary, a brief biography of Doyle, and a listing of his other writings.

Part of The Graphic Novel Adventures of Sherlock Holmes

Goosebumps: Terror Trips
Adapted by Jill Thompson, Jamie Tolagson, and Amy Kim Ganter. Scholastic/Graphix 2007 137p. Illustration
Grades: 4 5 6 7 8 9 **741.5; Fic**
1. Horror graphic novels; 2. Stine, R L — Adaptations; 3. Graphic novels
978-0-439-85780-2, $8.99
Stine's Goosebumps series was very popular years ago, and is enjoying a resurgence of popularity with new editions of the prose books. The graphic novel adaptations, all done by well-known independent comics creators, bring the stories to a new audience. Goosebumps: Creepy Creatures is also available.

This volume adapts three of Stine's Goosebumps novels into graphic novel format. Noted independent comic creator Thompson adapts One Day at Horrorland, about one family's ordeal in a very strange, all-too-realistic amusement park. Canadian artist Tolagson adapts A Shocker on Shock Street, which depicts the horrific adventures of two kids on a movie studio lot where the horror is more than just special effects. Global manga creator Ganter adapts Deep Trouble, in which a brother and sister find a real mermaid.

Gorelick, Victor
Archie in Strange change. Edited by Nelson Ribeiro & Victor Gorelick.. ABDO Publishing Group/Spotlight 2007 Un Illustration
Grades: 3 4 5 6 7 8 **741.5; Fic**
1. Andrews, Archie (Fictional character); 2. Humorous graphic novels; 3. Graphic novels
978-1-59961-262-1, $24.21
LC 2006-49671
This volume includes 10 short comics stories featuring Archie Andrews and all the gang from Riverdale. Among the stories, Archie can't find a good place to hang his hammock;

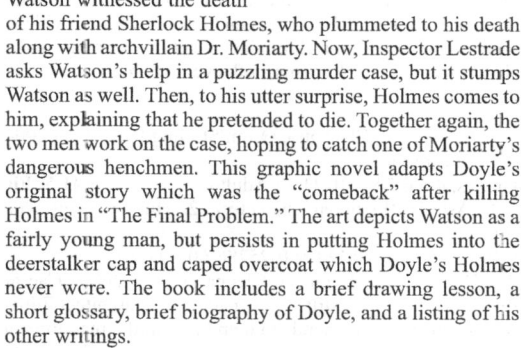

Mr. Weatherbee has a wild time at the fair as he tries to hide from Archie and gets lost in the hall of mirrors, trapped on a roller coaster, and blunders into the rodeo; Mr. Lodge takes Dilton and Archie for a ride in his computerized car and loses control because of Archie's handheld electronic game; Little Archie has an adventure in "The Strange Case of the Mystery Map;" and more fun.

Part of the Archie digest library; this is a revision of Archie Digest Magazine issue #183 (Oct. 2001).

Archie in top this!. Edited by Nelson Ribeiro & Victor Gorelick. Spotlight 2007 Un Illustration
Grades: 3 4 5 6 7 8   **741.5; Fic**
1. Andrews, Archie (Fictional character); 2. Humorous graphic novels; 3. Graphic novels
978-1-59961-263-8, $24.21

LC 2006-49938
This is a library bound edition of Archie digest magazine issue #178 from Archie Comics, originally published in March 2001. It includes 18 short comics stories set in Riverdale and starring all the Archie Comics characters Archie, Reggie, Jughead, Betty, Veronica, Miss Grundy, Mr. Weatherbee, and others. In one story, Archie actually dates a different girl, Melanie, who works at the local theater; he keeps trying to find fun things to do, but Melanie just loves movies.

Revision of issue no. 178 (March 2001) of Archie digest magazine.

Jughead with Archie in A day to remember. Edited by Nelson Ribeiro & Victor Gorelick. ABDO Publishing/Spotlight 2007 Un Illustration
Grades: 3 4 5 6 7 8   **741.5; Fic**
1. Andrews, Archie (Fictional character); 2. Humorous graphic novels; 3. Jones, Jughead (Fictional character)
978-1-59961-272-0, $24.21

LC 2006-50551
This is a library bound edition of Jughead with Archie digest magazine issue #189 from Archie Comics, originally published in February 2004. It includes 16 short comics stories set in Riverdale and starring all the Archie Comics characters Archie, Reggie, Jughead, Betty, Veronica, Miss Grundy, Mr. Weatherbee, and others. Archie and Jughead are longtime pals who get into all kinds of trouble at school, usually together.

Revision of issue no. 189 (Feb. 2004) of Jughead with Archie digest magazine.

Laugh with fore!. Edited by Nelson Ribeiro & Victor Gorelick. ABDO Publishing Group/Spotlight 2007 Un Illustration
Grades: 3 4 5 6 7 8   **741.5; Fic**
1. Andrews, Archie (Fictional character); 2. Humorous graphic novels; 3. Graphic novels
978-1-59961-279-9, $24.21

LC 2006-49180
This volume includes 18 short comics stories featuring Archie Andrews and all the gang from Riverdale. Among the stories, Archie tries to find ways to reduce stress that result in lots of trouble, including a beating from Moose; the teens try to help Mr. Weatherbee get more publicity to keep the summer camp going; Josie and the Pussycats feature in a couple of stories; and lots more.

Part of the Archie digest library; this is a revision of Laugh Digest Magazine issue #168 (Sept. 2001).

Goscinny
The **tenderfoot**: Lucky Luke adventure, vol. 13. Cinbook Ltd. 2008 48p. Illustration
Grades: 3 4 5 6 7 8   **791.5; Fic**
1. Humorous graphic novels; 2. Western stories; 3. Graphic novels
978-1-905460-65-6, $11.95

When Rancher Baddy passes away, his heir, an Englishman, comes to town to take over the ranch. Jack Ready wants the ranch, so he plans to give the "tenderfoot" reasons to go away. When Lucky Luke, who can shoot faster than his shadow, helps Waldo get through the "welcoming ceremonies" and the phlegmatic Englishman shows he's more than a match for anything the cowboys can think to do, Jack Ready comes up with the only other plan that might work—frame Waldo for Jack's murder. The book has no real violence, but it does show drinking and gambling in the saloon. While some readers might fret over the stereotyping of the Native American characters, they should note that every single character in the book, including Lucky Luke himself, is a caricature of a "type," from rough cowboy to noble Indian, to Chinese, to hoity-toity Englishmen, to gunfighters. This is translated from the original French stories written by Rene Goscinny, who also wrote Asterix.

Goscinny, Rene
Asterix and Caesar's Gift. Orion/Sterling Publishing 2004 48p. Illustration
Grades: 4 5 6 7 8 9 10 11 12 Adult   **741.5; Fic**
1. Asterix (Fictional character); 2. Humorous graphic novels
0-75286-645-1, $12.95; 0-75286-646-X (pa)

When Legionary Tremensdelirius gets the title deeds to the little Gaulish village as a bonus, he swaps them with tavern landlord Orthopaedix for a drink. Funnily enough, Asterix and his friends aren't keen to hand over their village to anyone else. After a chieftaincy election campaign and a showdown with the Romans, both events fiercely contested, can all still end well?

Asterix and Cleopatra. Orion/Sterling Publishing 2004 48p. Illustration
Grades: 4 5 6 7 8 9 10 11 12 Adult   **741.5; Fic**
1. Asterix (Fictional character); 2. Humorous graphic novels
0-75286-606-0, $12.95; 0-75286-607-9 (pb)

How can lovely Queen Cleopatra show Julius Caesar that ancient Egypt is still a great nation" Her architect Edifis recruits his Gaulish friends to help him build a magnificent palace within three months. There are villainous saboteurs to be outwitted, but Asterix, Obelix, and Getafix still find time to go sight-seeing, and leave their mark on the Pyramids and the Sphinx's nose.

Asterix and the Banquet. Orion/Sterling Publishing 2004 48p. Illustration
Grades: 4 5 6 7 8 9 10 11 12 Adult   **741.5; Fic**

1. Asterix (Fictional character); 2. Humorous graphic novels
0-75286-608-0, $12.95; 0-75286-609-5 (pa)

When the Romans try to contain the threat from the Gaulish village by building a stockade around it, Asterix and Obelix lay a bet with them. They will break out and claim their right to travel freely all over Gaul, collecting the local delicacies and bringing them back to prove their point. Ham from Lutetia, fizzy wine from Durocortorum, fish stew from Massilia in the south ... soon their shopping bag is full. Outwitting Romans, a couple of treacherous Gauls, and the thieves Villanus and Unscrupulus, they set off for home ... but who's that little dog who has been following them all the way from Lutetia?

Asterix and the Cauldron. Orion/Sterling Publishing 2004 48p. Illustration
Grades: 4 5 6 7 8 9 10 11 12 Adult   **741.5; Fic**
1. Asterix (Fictional character); 2. Humorous graphic novels
0-75286-629-X, $9.95

There's financial skulduggery in ancient Gaul. When local Chief Whosemoralsarelastix wants a cauldron full of money kept out of Roman hands, the cash disappears while Asterix is guarding it. He and Obelix must earn enough to repay it through fairground gladiatorial contests, trendy theatrical performances, even bank robbery - they'll try anything. But whose morals are really elastic? And how to the pirates, just for once, get an unexpected bonus?

Asterix and the Class Act. Orion/Sterling Publishing 2004 56p. Illustration
Grades: 4 5 6 7 8 9 10 11 12 Adult   **741.5; Fic**
1. Asterix (Fictional character); 2. Humorous graphic novels
0-75286-068-2, $12.95; 0-75286-640-0 (pa)

This volume collects 14 stories, including the day Asterix and Obelix were born (in the middle of a fish fight); how Obelix goes back to school; fashion in ancient Gaul; how Dogmatix helps the village cockerel win a duel, and how he's adopted as a Roman mascot; Obelix's adventures under the mistletoe; the bid for the very first Gaulish Olympics, and more.

★ **Asterix** the Gaul. [by] René Goscinny and Albert Uderzo. Orion Media 2004 48p. Illustration; Map
Grades: 4 5 6 7 8 9 10 11 12 Adult   **741.5; Fic**
1. France — History; 2. Humorous graphic novels
0-7528-6604-4, $12.95; 0-7528-6605-2 (pa), $9.95

Meet Asterix, a diminutive but extremely strong Gaul living in ancient France during the time of the Roman Republic. Together with his friend Obelix, Asterix continually outwits the Roman Legionnaires sent to conquer Gaul for Julius Caesar. Full of puns and outrageous humor, the books also manage to teach a lot of history. This is the first in a long-running series of graphic novels translated from the original French.

Translated from the French
Other titles in this series are: Asterix and Caesar's Gift; Asterix and Cleopatra; Asterix and the actress; Asterix and the banquet; Asterix and the big fight; Asterix and the cauldron; Asterix and the Goths; Asterix and the Great Crossing; Asterix and the laurel wreath; Asterix the legionary; Asterix and the Normans; Asterix and the Roman

Agent; Asterix and the soothsayer; Asterix at the Olympic Games; Asterix in Belgium; Asterix in Britain; Asterix in Corsica; Asterix in Spain; Asterix in Switzerland; Asterix Obelix and Co.; Asterix the gladiator; Asterix The Mansions of the Gods

Asterix and the Laurel Wreath. Orion/Sterling Publishing 2004 48p. Illustration
Grades: 4 5 6 7 8 9 10 11 12 Adult   **741.5; Fic**
1. Asterix (Fictional character); 2. Humorous graphic novels
0-75286-636-2, $12.95; 0-75286-637-0 (pa)

Chief Vitalstatistix rashly invites his brother-in-law to dine on a stew seasoned with Caesar's laurel wreath, so Asterix and Obelix must to go Rome to fetch those laurels. Hoping to get access to Caesar, they sell themselves as slaves, but can they do a deal with the corrupt Goldendelicius to swap the laurels for parsley?

Asterix in Britain. Orion/Sterling Publishing 2004 48p. Illustration
Grades: 4 5 6 7 8 9 10 11 12 Adult   **741.5; Fic**
1. Asterix (Fictional character); 2. Humorous graphic novels
0-85286-618-4, $12.95; 0-75286-619-2 (pa)

The Romans have invaded Britain, but one village still holds out. Asterix and Obelix come to help, with a barrel of magic potion in hand. But to deliver the precious brew, the Gaulish heroes must face fog, rain, bad food, warm beer, and the Romans too.

Asterix the Legionary. Orion/Sterling Publishing 2004 48p. Illustration
Grades: 4 5 6 7 8 9 10 11 12 Adult   **741.5; Fic**
1. Asterix (Fictional character); 2. Humorous graphic novels
0-75286-620-6, $12.95; 0-75286-621-4 (pa)

It's off to the wars for Asterix and Obelix: they've enlisted as legionnaires in order to rescue Tragicomix, whom the Romans forcibly conscripted. The two find Tragicomix and succeed in causing the biggest commotion ever on a battlefield.

The **Caliph's** vacation. Cinebook Ltd 2008 48p. Illustration
Grades: 3 4 5 6 7 8   **741.5; Fic**
1. Humorous graphic novels; 2. Graphic novels
978-1-905460-61-8, $11.95

Iznogoud, the Grand Vizier of Baghdad the Magnificent, wants to be Caliph, and he hatches all kinds of schemes to do in the good, kindhearted, not-too-bright Caliph, Haroun Al Plassid. First, they go to the beach, where Iznogoud and his henchman Wa'at Alahf try to drown him (the Caliph floats), send him into shark-infested waters (his suntan oil reeks), and other attempts that end up nearly doing in Iznogoud. A scheme to use a weather wizard to kill the Caliph with winter snow ends up with everyone enjoying a ski vacation. Then Iznogoud comes up with a poisoned elixir but can't get the Caliph to drink it. Goscinny is best known in the U.S. for his Asterix comics, but Iznogoud is just as filled with puns and humor, with a villain as the main character. Readers will enjoy the Wile E. Coyote type of hijinks.

First published 2000 in France

Dalton City: a Lucky Luke adventure. Cinebook 2007 48p. Illustration

Grades: 3 4 5 6 7 8   **741.5; Fic**

1. Humorous graphic novels; 2. Western stories; 3. Graphic novels

978-1-905460-13-7, $9.99

Goscinny, cocreator of Asterix, gives readers his wacky version of the American Old West in the Lucky Luke Adventures. Luke is a traveling good guy, who shoots faster than his shadow. He cleans up Fenton City, a festering sore of depravity in Texas, by capturing Dean Fenton, the boss of the town. Fenton ends up in the same prison as the Dalton brothers, a gang of not-too-smart outlaws that Luke keeps having to put away. They break out of the prison and take over Fenton City, calling it Dalton City. When Lucky Luke shows up, they ask him for advice on how to make the town a haven for outlaws, and Luke sees his chance to round up a whole lot of bad guys.

Part of the Lucky Luke Adventures series, originally published in France as Lucky Luke Dalton City.

Gossett, Christian

King Kong: The 8th Wonder of the World. Dark Horse Books 2006 Un Illustration

Grades: 7 8 9 10 11 12 Adult   **741.5; Fic**

1. King Kong (Fictional character); 2. Science fiction graphic novels; 3. Graphic novels

978-1-59307-472-2, $12.95

Director Carl Denham has one chance to make the film of his dreams - hire an unknown actress, kidnap his writer and board a tramp freighter for the mysterious Island of the Skull. But when hostile natives capture actress Ann Darrow, Denham and his crew will face horrors from giant spiders to bloodthirsty dinosaurs to get her back. Yet, nothing can prepare them for the revelation of the mighty wonder in whose clutches Ann truly remains - King Kong. This story adapts the screenplay for the motion picture directed by Peter Jackson, which is based on the original story by Merian C. Cooper and Edgar Wallace.

Gould, Jane

Steve Jobs. By Jane Gould. PowerKids Press 2013 24 p.

Grades: 3 4 5 6   **338.7/6100416092; 338.7; B**

1. Apple Computer, Inc — History — Juvenile literature; 2. Businessmen — United States — Biography — Juvenile literature; 3. Computer engineers — United States — Biography — Juvenile literature; 4. Inventors; 5. Jobs, Steve, 1955-2011; 6. Jobs, Steve, 1955-2011 — Juvenile literature

1477700803; 9781477700808, $25.25; 9781477701454; 9781477701461

LC 2012020633

This graphic novel by Jane Gould is a biography of Steven Jobs, "best known for being a co-founder of Apple Inc. Before Apple Inc., he was a brilliant designer and inventor who approached business with an unexpected savvy and joy of discovery. Jobs created gadgets that transformed today's digital era." (Publisher's note)

Includes index.

Gould, Jane H.

George Washington Carver. By Jane Gould. PowerKids Press 2013 24 p. Color illustration

Grades: 3 4 5 6   **630.92; B**

1. African American agriculturists — Biography — Juvenile literature; 2. African American educators — Biography — Juvenile literature; 3. African American inventors; 4. African American scientists — Biography — Juvenile literature; 5. Agriculturists — United States — Biography — Juvenile literature; 6. Carver, George Washington, 1864?-1943; 7. Carver, George Washington, 1864?-1943 — Juvenile literature; 8. Peanuts — United States — History — Juvenile literature

1477700781; 9781477700785, $25.25; 9781477701416, $10.60; 9781477701423

LC 2012018689

In this biography of inventor George Washington Carver, author Jane Gould "provides the requisite biographical details, including Carver—s early . . . separation from his mother, but also traces themes of his career, drawing connections between his kind masters" waste-not values and his future devotion to finding new uses for farm by-products." (Booklist)

Includes index.

Gownley, Jimmy

★ **Amelia** Rules! Volume Three: Superheroes. Renaissance Press 2006 174p. Illustration

Grades: 3 4 5 6   **741.5; Fic**

1. Friendship; 2. Humorous graphic novels

9780971216969, $11.99

This third volume of Amelia Rules! contains one storyline, about the summer after fourth grade. First, Amelia faces the possibility of another move (across town); then new friends Trishia and Ninja Joan join Amelia and Rhonda, while Reggie and Pajama Man fight crime - actually, the Legion of Steves. The guys even team up with the Park Terrace Ninjas. In the middle of all the summer fun, Amelia learns Trishia's terrible secret and doesn't know how to help.

Originally published as Amelia Rules! issues #11-16.

Amelia rules! True things (adults don't want kids to know). Atheneum Books for Young Readers 2010 163p.

Grades: 3 4 5 6

741.5; 741

1. Family life; 2. Friendship; 3. Humorous graphic novels

978-1-4169-8609-6 (pa), $10.99; 1-4169-8609-X (pa)

Amelia rules!: The meaning of life—and other stuff. Written and illustrated by Jimmy Gownley.

Courtesy of Atheneum Books for Young Readers

Atheneum Books for Young Readers 2011 147p. Illustration

Grades: 3 4 5 6   **741.5; 741**

1. Family life; 2. Friendship; 3. Humorous graphic novels

Courtesy of Antheneum Books for Young Readers

978-1-4169861-3-3, $19.99; 1-4169861-3-8; 978-1-4169861-2-6 (pa), $10.99; 1-4169861-2-X (pa)

LC 2011018407

★ **Amelia** rules!: the whole world's crazy!. Renaissance Press 2003 176p.
Grades: 3 4 5 6   **741.5; Fic**
1. Family life; 2. Friendship; 3. Humorous graphic novels
0-9712169-3-2, $24.95; 0-9712169-2-4 (pa), $14.95

"Amelia . . . is getting used to life with her newly divorced mom and her hip, young aunt Tanner; settling in at a strange new school; and finding a group of friends. Amelia is no sweet innocent, nor are her three G.A.S.P (Gathering of Awesome Superpals) buddies: Reggie, superhero in the making; Rhonda, Amelia's tough bete noire with a fourth-grade "thing" for Reggie; and quiet, mysterious Pajamaman. Jealousy, meanness, sadness, and confusion, as well as surprising generosity, and love crisscross the pages in energetic, freewheeling, full-color cartoon art that unwraps a kid's-eye view of life honestly, poignantly, and with a hefty dollop of melodrama." Booklist

Other titles in this series are: Amelia rules!: What makes you happy? (2004); Amelia rules! Superheroes (2005); Amelia rules! a very ninja Christmas (2009); Amelia rules! When the past is a present (2010); Amelia rules! The tweenage guide to not being unpopular (2010); Amelia rules! True things (adults don't want kids to know (2010); Amelia rules! The meaning of life. . . and other stuff (2011); Amelia rules! Her permanent record (2012)

Amelia rules: The tweenage guide to not being unpopular. Atheneum Books for Young Readers 2010 187p.
Grades: 3 4 5 6
741; 741.5
1. Friendship; 2. Humorous graphic novels
978-1-4169-8610-2, $18.99; 1-4169-8610-3; 978-1-4169-8608-9 (pa), $10.99, 1-4169-8608-1 (pa)

LC 2009053665

Courtesy of Antheneum Books for Young Readers

★ **Amelia** rules! when the past is a present. Renaissance Press 2008 168p. Illustration
Grades: 3 4 5 6   **741.5; Fic**
1. Friendship; 2. Humorous graphic novels
978-0-9712169-8-3, $24.95; 978-0-9712169-9-0 (pa), $11.99

The kids are now in fifth grade, and Amelia and Rhonda are officially friends and not enemies any more. Amelia is going to her first dance (with a boy no less " Kyle the ninja), but she's not the only one with a date. Is Amelia's mom

seeing someone too? Perhaps Reggie (a.k.a. Captain Amazing) can shed some light on the situation, by spying on their date. But it's not all fun for the 10-year-old spitfire. A good friend " Joan" reveals that her father will be deployed to Iraq with his job in the military, and it gets Amelia thinking about her own family, her past, and what it means for the present.

★ **Her** permanent record. Written and illustrated by Jimmy Gownley. Atheneum Books for Young Readers 2012 144 p.
Grades: 3 4 5 6   **741.5**
1. Aunts — Fiction; 2. Friendship — Fiction; 3. Missing persons — Fiction; 4. School stories; 5. Schools — Fiction; 6. Voyages and travels — Fiction; 7. Graphic novels
1416986154; 9781416986140; 9781416986157, $19.99

LC 2011053039

This book is the eighth installment of the "Amelia Rules!" series by Jimmy Gownley. "With her new spot on the cheerleading squad, [and] Aunt Tanner's hordes of adoring fans, . . . Amelia's sailing seems remarkably smooth. Then Tanner disappears . . . sending Amelia into full panic mode. And when she boards a bus on an epic journey to find Tanner . . . it quickly becomes clear that if Amelia has learned anything in her eleven years, it's that life is never through with surprises." (Publisher's note)

Grahame, Kenneth

Classics illustrated deluxe # 1: the wind in the willows. NBM/Papercutz 2007 144p. Illustration
Grades: 3 4 5 6 7 8   **741.5; Fic**
1. Animals; 2. Fantasy graphic novels; 3. Humorous graphic novels; 4. Graphic novels
978-1-59707-095-9, $19.99; 978-1-59707-096-6 (pa), $13.95

Kenneth Grahame's classic story of the wild Mister Toad's misadventures and crazy enthusiasms that get him into great trouble from which his friends Badger, Mole, and Rat must extricate him gets a deluxe, full-color graphic novel treatment with art that looks like classic 1930s-style animation.

Grant, Alan

Robert Louis Stevenson's Kidnapped. Adaptation by Alan Grant; illustrator, Cam Kennedy. Tundra Books 2007 Un Illustration
Grades: 6 7 8 9 10   **741.5; Fic**
1. Adventure graphic novels; 2. Stevenson, Robert Louis, 1850-1894 — Adaptations; 3. Graphic novels
978-0-88776-843-9 (pa), $11.95; 0-88776-843-1 (pa)

LC 2007921350

Kidnapped is set in 1751, during the time of the Jacobite rebellion " a tumultuous and tragic period in Scottish history. When David Balfour sets out to find his uncle, he never dreamed that he would be kidnapped " but saved from a life of slavery " and thrown from one escapade to another in the company of the fugitive, masterful swordsman Alan Breck Stewart.

"This is an engaging adaptation, aided by Kennedy's vibrant illustrations in a palette dominated by blues, greens, and sepia tones. The action scenes are exciting." SLJ

Robert Louis Stevenson's Strange case of Dr. Jekyll and Mr. Hyde. Adapted by Alan Grant; illustrated by Cam Kennedy; colored and lettered by Jamie Grant. Tundra Books 2008 40p. Illustration
Grades: 6 7 8 9 10   **741.5; Fic**
978-0-88776-882-8 (pa), $11.95; 0-88776-882-2 (pa)

The graphic canon of children's literature: the world's great kids' lit as comics and visuals
Edited by Russ Kick. Seven Stories Press 2014 480 p. Color; Illustration
Grades: 6 7 8 9 10 11 12 Adult   **741.5**
1. Children's literature; 2. Graphic novels in education; 3. Literature — Adaptations
1609805305; 9781609805302, $38.95
                      LC 2014010178
Edited by Russ Kick, "the original three-volume anthology 'The Graphic Canon' presented the world's classic literature—from ancient times to the late twentieth century—as eye-popping comics, illustrations, and other visual forms. In this follow-up volume, young people's literature through the ages is given new life by the best comics artists and illustrators." (Publisher's note)
"These dazzlingly varied renderings run the gamut from haunting to comical while offering visceral reminders that children's stories are often densely layered, infinitely transposable, and peddle in imagery both macabre and whimsical. It is the unfettered imagination of these stories that make them not only wildly entertaining, but also vessels of forgotten truths." Pub Wkly

Graphic Classics volume eleven: O. Henry
Edited by Tom Pomplun. Eureka Productions 2005 144p. Illustration
Grades: 7 8 9 10 11 12 Adult   **741.5; Fic**
1. Henry, O, 1862-1910 — Adaptations; 2. Short stories; 3. Graphic novels
978-0-9746648-2-0, $11.95
This volume of Graphics Classics adapts some of the short stories by O. Henry, the master of the surprise ending. Stories include "The Ransom of Red Chief," illustrated by Johnny Ryan, "The Gift of the Magi," illustrated by Lisa Weber, "The Caballero's Way" (the original story of the Cisco Kid), illustrated by Mark A. Nelson, and more.

Graphic Classics volume fifteen: Fantasy classics
Edited by Tom Pomplun. Eureka Productions 2008 144p. Illustration
Grades: 8 9 10 11 12 Adult   **741.5; Fic**
1. Fantasy graphic novels; 2. Horror graphic novels; 3. Short stories; 4. Graphic novels
978-0-9787919-3-3, $11.95
This volume provides graphic novel adaptations of Mary Shelley's Frankenstein, "Rappaccini's Daughter" by Nathaniel Hawthorne, "The Glass Dog" by L. Frank Baum, "The Dream Quest of Unknown Kadath" by H. P. Lovecraft, and poems "After the Fire" by Lord Dunsany and "The Dream-Bridge" by Clark Ashton Smith. There are a few instances of mild violence and mild language in some of the stories. Illustrators include Skot Olsen, Lance Tooks, Brad Teare, and Leong Wan Kok; adapters include Rod Lott, Lance Tooks, Antonella Caputo, and Ben Avery.

Graphic Classics volume four: H. P. Lovecraft
Edited by Tom Pomplun. Eureka Productions 2007 144p. Illustration
Grades: 7 8 9 10 11 12 Adult   **741.5; Fic**
1. Horror graphic novels; 2. Lovecraft, H P (Howard Phillips), 1890-1937 — Adaptations; 3. Mystery writers; 4. Short stories
978-0-9746648-9-7, $11.95
Here are comic book adaptations of stories by Lovecraft, master of the macabre and creator of the Cthulhu Mythos. It includes adaptations of "The Shadow Over Innsmouth," illustrated by Simon Gane and "Dreams in the Witch House," by Pedro Lopez. Plus: "Sweet Ermengarde," a rare comedy by Lovecraft. Returning from the previous edition are "Reanimator," "The Shadow Out of Time," "The Terrible Old Man" and "The Cats of Ulthar." Illustrations of headless corpses and monstrous beings might disturb more tender sensibilities.
First published 2002

★ **Graphic Classics volume fourteen: Gothic classics**
Edited by Tom Pomplun. Eureka Productions 2007 144p. Illustration
Grades: 7 8 9 10 11 12 Adult   **741.5; Fic**
1. Horror graphic novels; 2. Short stories; 3. Graphic novels
978-0-9787919-0-2, $11.95
This volume includes graphic adaptations of classic novels Carmilla by Joseph Sheridan Le Fanu, The Mysteries of Udolpho by Ann Radcliffe, and Northanger Abbey by Jane Austen, along with shorter works "The Oval Portrait" by Edgar Allan Poe, "At the Gate" by Myla Jo Closser, and "I've a Pain in My Head" by Jane Austen. Radcliffe's novel is one mentioned by Austen in Northanger Abbey and is a famous gothic novel from the late eighteenth century, considered to be the world's first best-seller. Le Fanu's vampire novel was published twenty-five years before Stoker's Dracula. Austen wrote Northanger Abbey as a satire of the popular gothic genre.

Graphic Classics volume seven: Bram Stoker
Edited by Tom Pomplun. Eureka Productions 2007 144p. Illustration
Grades: 7 8 9 10 11 12 Adult   **741.5; Fic**
1. Fantasy graphic novels; 2. Horror graphic novels; 3. Short stories; 4. Stoker, Bram, 1847-1912 — Adaptations; 5. Graphic novels
978-0-9787919-1-9, $11.95
This collection includes a comics adaptation of Dracula by Rich Rainey and Joe Ollmann, "The Judge's House" by Gerry Alanguilan, "Torture Tower" by Onsmith Jeremi, and "The Lair of the White Worm" by South African artist Rico Schacherl. Also "The Bridal of Death," an excerpt from "The Jewel of Seven Stars" by J.B. Bonivert and "The Wondrous Child" illustrated by Evert Geradts. The book includes some violence, and one panel of partial nudity.
"A must-read for fans of horror comics, this collection also works as a good introduction to Stoker's contributions to the traditions of Gothic horror." SLJ
First published 2003

Graphic Classics Volume Twelve: Adventure Classics
Eureka Productions 2005 144p. Illustration
Grades: 8 9 10 11 12   **741.5; 808.3**
  1. Adventure graphic novels; 2. Short stories; 3. Graphic novels
978-0-9746648-4-7, $11.95

This volume of the Graphic Classics series includes a selection of poems and short stories that more or less fit the adventure genre. Rudyard Kipling's poem "Gunga Din" is here, as is Robert Service's "The Shooting of Dan McGrew." Short stories include "In the Valley of the Sorceress" by Sax Rohmer. "Tigre" by Zane Grey, "Blood Money" (a Captain Blood story) by Rafael Sabatini, "The Crime of the Brigadier" (a Brigadier Gerard adventure) by Sir Arthur Conan Doyle, "The Roads We Take" by O. Henry, and more. "The Mystery of the Semi-Detached" by Edith Nesbit may surprise readers who only know her as a children's fantasy author.

Gray, Harold
  ★ **Harold** Gray's Little Orphan Annie volume one: Will tomorrow evercome: the complete daily comics, 1924-27: Will tomorrow ever come? IDW Publishing 2008 385p. Illustration
Grades: 2 3 4 5 6 7 8 9 10 11 12 Adult   **741.5; Fic**
  1. Adventure graphic novels; 2. Little Orphan Annie (Fictional character); 3. Orphans; 4. Graphic novels
978-1-60010-140-3, $39.99

Little Orphan Annie started as a daily newspaper comic strip in one newspaper, the New York Daily News, on August 5, 1924. It became a popular strip, syndicated to newspapers all over the world. It eventually became a Broadway musical, a hit movie, and Annie became an iconic character. This book is the first comprehensive collection of Gray's comic strip and is the first volume of a series planned to collect all of Gray's Little Orphan Annie strips. She is an orphan girl living in an orphanage, with an unscrupulous director who hires Annie out for work. When wealthy Mrs. Warbucks, trying to prove that she cares for the poor, takes Annie on a "trial" adoption, Annie eventually meets Oliver Warbucks, whom she calls "Daddy." As the strips go on, Annie undergoes many hardships and perils, facing everything with spunk and a positive attitude. She's no wilting girl, though "she can fight (she has a mean right hook) and will take on any bully. She rescues the dog she calls Sandy, who rewards her with a loyal friendship. This volume includes more than 1,000 comic strips, many of which haven't seen publication since their original newspaper appearance. During the first years of the strip's publication, the color Sunday comics had no connection to the weekday storylines, but a few Sunday pages are included in this book. This book may appeal most to adults who remember reading Little Orphan Annie in the "funnies" pages, but the stories will appeal to all ages. Contributing Editor Jeet Heer provides a biography of Harold Gray.

Grayson, Devin
  Am I blue. Udon with Long Vo, Charles Park, and Saka, art and colors ; Randy Gentile, letterer. ABDO Publishing Company/Spotlight 2006 Illustration
Grades: 4 5 6 7 8 9   **741.5; Fic**

  1. Superhero graphic novels; 2. X-Men (Fictional characters); 3. Graphic novels
978-1-59961-052-8, $21.35
                  LC 2006-43970

The young members of the X-Men, including Kurt (Nightcrawler), Rogue, and Kitty (Shadowcat), must attend school in town as well as train at the Xavier Academy. They must conceal their identities as super powered mutants, which is difficult for Kurt since he is normally blue-skinned; he wears an image inducer that makes him appear like a normal human. When they are assigned an essay for English composition class: "What I am at home that I can't be at school," it bothers Kurt that he can't tell the truth. This book is a revised, hardbound edition of a Marvel Age comic book issue.

Part of the X-Men: Evolution series

Grecian, Alexander
  Seven Sons. Riley Rossmo, artist. AiT/Planet Lar 2006 120p. Illustration
Grades: 7 8 9 10 11 12 Adult   **741.5; Fic**
  1. China — Folklore; 2. Graphic novels
978-1-932051-46-9, $12.95

Seven identical Chinese brothers come to America during the Gold Rush of the 1850s. When two children fall through an iced-over river, Brother Number One tries to save them by breathing the entire river into his mouth. But he can't hold it long enough for them to get to safety and lets the water go, accidentally drowning the children. When a mob of angry townspeople tries to retaliate, each of Number One's brothers takes his place, using their remarkable abilities each time to save his life. This retelling doesn't have the happy ending usually found in the children's picture books, and by moving the story to the U.S., Grecian infuses a message about intolerance and prejudice in the story.

Green, Jen
  Great expectations: the graphic novel. Script by Jen Green ; adapted by Brigit Viney. Lucent Books 2010 160p. Illustration (Classic graphic novels)
Grades: 7 8 9 10 11 12   **741.5; Fic**
  1. Dickens, Charles, 1812-1870 — Adaptations; 2. Great Britain — History — 19th century; 3. Social classes; 4. Graphic novels
978-1-4205-0372-2, $32.45
                LC 2010-924002

In 1812, young orphaned Pip encounters an escaped convict in the graveyard near his home; that encounter changes his life. He had helped the man by stealing food and a file from his older sister's home. When the convict is recaptured, he keeps Pip's secret and claims he was the thief. As time goes by, Pip becomes his brother-inlaw's apprentice as a blacksmith, but then the eccentric Miss Havisham wants Pip to attend to her. Miss Havisham's adopted niece, Estella, calls Pip coarse and rough, which makes him determined to improve himself and become a gentleman. His wish comes true when a mysterious benefactor has Miss Havisham's solicitor, Mr. Jaggers, set Pip up in London, with expenses paid. Pip has only to keep using his nickname, to learn how to be a gentleman, and have "great expectations." Getting his wish doesn't make him happy, however, for he wants Estella, whom he adores, to love him; Miss Havisham has raised

Estella to break men's hearts as her heart was once broken by a man. Pip must also learn what is most important to him improving his social standing or standing loyal to family and friends. This graphic novel adaptation includes every chapter in Dickens' original novel; this library bound edition uses a more colloquial American adaptation, which was done by arrangement with Classical Comics, the original publisher. This adaptation is meant for reluctant and struggling readers. The artist, John Stokes, is not credited anywhere in this edition. The back matter includes a biography of Dickens, a glossary, illustrated character summaries, notes on the historical context of the novel, and a brief discussion of the different ending Dickens originally wrote.

Great expectations: the graphic novel: original text version. Joe Sutliff Sanders ; character designs & original artwork, John Stokes ; coloring. Classical Comics 2009 160p. Illustration
Grades: 7 8 9 10 11 12
741.5; Fic
1. Dickens, Charles, 1812-1870 — Adaptations; 2. Great Britain — History — 19th century; 3. Social classes; 4. Graphic novels
978-1-906332-59-4, $16.95

©Classical Comics

In 1812, young orphaned Pip encounters an escaped convict in the graveyard near his home; that encounter changes his life. He had helped the man by stealing food and a file from his older sister's home. When the convict is recaptured, he keeps Pip's secret and claims he was the thief. As time goes by, Pip becomes his brother-in-law's apprentice as a blacksmith, but then the eccentric Miss Havisham wants Pip to attend to her. Miss Havisham's adopted niece, Estella, calls Pip coarse and rough, which makes him determined to improve himself and become a gentleman. His wish comes true when a mysterious benefactor has Miss Havisham's solicitor, Mr. Jaggers, set Pip up in London, with expenses paid. Pip has only to keep using his nickname, to learn how to be a gentleman, and have "great expectations." Getting his wish doesn't make him happy, however, for he wants Estella, whom he adores, to love him; Miss Havisham has raised Estella to break men's hearts as her heart was once broken by a man. Pip must also learn what is most important to him improving his social standing or standing loyal to family and friends. This graphic novel adaptation includes every chapter in Dickens' original novel; the Original Text Version uses excerpts from Dickens' dialog and narration. The book includes biographical information about Dickens and information about the English justice system and Newgate prison.
Also available Quick Text edition pa $16.95 (ISBN: 978-1-906332-60-0)

Green, John
Phineas and Ferb: nothing but trouble. Disney Press 2010 32p. Illustration
Grades: 3 4 5 6
741.5; Fic
1. Humorous graphic novels; 2. Inventors; 3. Science fiction graphic novels; 4. Graphic novels
9781423124405, $4.99
Inventor brothers Phineas and Ferb and their friends take the gelatin molds made by Candace and her friends and create a swimming pool full of gelatin, the boys' pet platypus Perry goes off on another secret mission to foil the latest evil plot of the evil Dr. Doofenshmirtz. This time, the mad scientist's "Turn-Everything-Evil-Nator" misses Perry, but hits the gelatin in the swimming pool, creating a gelatin monster. Then, when the family visits London, Candace and best friend Stacy decide to act like Sherlock Holmes to catch the boys in whatever plot they're hatching. And Agent P (Perry) must team up with British Agent Double 00 to stop Dr. Doofenshmirtz's latest scheme. This book adapts episodes of the animated series Phineas and Ferb, created by Dan Povenmire and Jeff "Swampy" Marsh, and which airs on the Disney Channel; it is illustrated with screen captures from the episodes.

Phineas and Ferb: the chronicles of Meap. Disney Press 2010 32p. Illustration
Grades: 3 4 5 6
741.5; Fic
1. Humorous graphic novels; 2. Inventors; 3. Science fiction graphic novels; 4. Graphic novels
978-1-4231-2441-2, $4.99
It's summer vacation, and talkative Phineas and his silent brother Ferb, both super inventors, are busy having fun while their older sister Candace and her friends get their new custom-made Bango-Ru interactive dolls. Then Ferb fires a baseball into the air with his new gadget, and the ball zaps into space and knocks a spaceship out of orbit to crash into the boys' backyard. Its pilot looks adorable, like a cute Bango-Ru, in fact, and all it says is Meap. But Meap is looking for someone, who it turns out is Meap's archrival, Mitch; and Mitch manages to capture everyone except Candace and Meap. Meanwhile the boys' pet platypus, Perry, is secretly an agent working to stop evil scientist Dr. Doofenschmirtz. This book adapts an episode of the animated series Phineas and Ferb, created by Dan Povenmire and Jeff "Swampy" Marsh, and which airs on the Disney Channel; it is illustrated with screen captures from the episode.

Greenberger, Robert
Will Eisner. Rosen Publishing Group 2005 112p. Illustration
Grades: 8 9 10 11 12 Adult
92; 741.5
1. Cartoonists — Biography; 2. Graphic novels
1-4042-0286-2, $31.95
LC 2004016656
Veteran comics insider Greenberger has written this biography of Eisner, covering his long career in comics, from the 1930s through the early

Courtesy of Rosen Publishing

2000s. Eisner created the groundbreaking comic series The Spirit, and in the 1970s started writing original graphic novels set in New York City. The Eisner Awards for comics are named after him, due to his strong influence on the industry over the decades. This volume includes a list of books for further reading and a bibliography.

Part of the Library of Graphic Novelists

Griffith, Saul

Howtoons: tools of mass construction. Dr. Saul Griffith, co-creator, writer & engineer; Nick Dragotta, co-creator, writer & artist; Ingrid Dragotta, project & book design; Arwen Griffith, editor; Joost Bonsen, co-creator & writer. Image Comics 2014 360 p. Illustration
Grades: 2 3 4 5 6 7   **741.5; 507.8**
1. Educational games; 2. Self-instruction
1632151014; 9781632151018, $17.99
"Follow Celine and Tucker as they learn through play with over 50 DIY projects! This brother-and-sister pair use everyday objects to invent toys that readers can build. Combining comics and real-life science and engineering principles, Howtoons are designed to encourage kids to become active participants in the world around them." (Publisher's note)
"The bright, somewhat chaotic artwork is designed to capture a kid's attention and imagination. The projects are not laid out in a staid, step-by-step manner, and several of them will require extra thought or adult assistance, but the variety is hard to beat, as the creators cover art, math, engineering, science, and more." Booklist

Grimm, Jacob

Classics illustrated delux #2: tales from the Brothers Grimm. Mazan, Philip Petit, Cecile Chicault ; [translation by Joe Johnson ; lettering by Ortho] Papercutz 2008 144p. Illustration
Grades: 3 4 5 6 7 8   **741.5; Fic**
1. Fantasy graphic novels; 2. Folklore; 3. Graphic novels
978-1-59707-101-7, $17.95
This volume of Papercutz's new Classics Illustrated Deluxe series collects French adaptations of four tales from the Brothers Grimm (Wilhelm and Jakob): Hansel and Gretel, Learning to Shudder, The Devil and the Three Golden Hairs, and The Valiant Little Tailor. These comic book adaptations don't shy away from showing scary monsters, saying rude things without using really bad language, and showing some violence.
Part of the Classics Illustrated Deluxe series

Grine, Chris

Chickenhare: The House of Klaus. Dark Horse Comics 2006 160p. Illustration
Grades: 7 8 9 10 11 12   **741.5**
1. Adventure graphic novels; 2. Fantasy graphic novels; 3. Graphic novels
978-1-59307-574-3, $9.95
Friends Chickenhare (who is exactly that, a cross between a chicken and a hare) and bearded turtle Abe are captives being taken to the mad taxidermist Klaus, who looks like an evil Santa. Chickenhare and Abe escape, along with obnoxious monkey Banjo and horned girl Meg; Chickenhare finds the dead goat Mr. Buttons, and the others

encounter the warlike, cave-dwelling Shromph, who have a bone to pick with Klaus. A few harsh words, some violence, and implied cannibalism may be disturbing for younger readers.

Chickenhare: fire in the hole. Dark Horse Comics 2008 200p. Illustration
Grades: 7 8 9 10 11 12 Adult   **741.5; Fic**
1. Adventure graphic novels; 2. Fantasy graphic novels; 3. Graphic novels
978-1-59307-907-9, $10.95
Chickenhare, his friend Abe, and their new friends Scabby, Meg and Banjo managed to escape the evil Taxidermist Klaus, but they have gone from one dangerous situation into . . . something worse. While at sea in a small boat about to be swamped by rain and waves, Banjo's brother and some warriors from the Underworld pop up, they zap the soul out of Abe and take Banjo and Meg. Chickenhare is left with Scabby and Abe's body. He must venture into the Underworld to recover Abe's soul. Meanwhile, Banjo and Meg face punishment for deserting the Underworld. And just why do the Sea Folk call Chickenhare "Your Majesty?"

Grine, Chris.

Chickenhare. Chris Grine. Graphix / Scholastic 2013 160 p.
Grades: 4 5 6 7 8 9   **741.5**
1. Animals; 2. Escapes — Juvenile fiction; 3. Taxidermy — Fiction
0545485088; 9780545485081, $10.99
                              LC 2012936214
Author Chris Grine presents a children's comic book. "What's a chickenhare" A cross between a chicken and a rabbit, of course. And that makes Chickenhare the rarest animal around! So when he and his turtle friend Abe are captured and sold to the evil taxidermist Klaus, they've got to find a way to escape before Klaus turns them into stuffed animals. With the help of two other strange creatures, Banjo and Meg, they might even get away. But with Klaus and his thugs hot on their trail, the adventure is only just beginning for this unlikely quartet of friends." (Publisher's note)

Gross, Allan

Cryptozoo Crew Volume 2: Call of the Thunderbird!. Jerry Carr, illustrator; NBM 2006 Un Illustration
Grades: 5 6 7 8 9 10 11 12 Adult   **741.5; Fic**
1. Humorous graphic novels; 2. Mythical animals; 3. Graphic novels
978-1-56163-466-8, $12.95
In this second volume, cryptozoologist Tork Darwyn suffers nightmares about a childhood encounter with the legendary thunderbird; it's been twenty years since that day, and he must return or be cursed. In the meantime, his teacher wife Tara has learned that her school will be shut down for lack of funding. Naturally, they travel together to Alaska to find out what is driving Tork to go there.

Cryptozoo Crew, Vol. 1. Art and lettering by Jerry Carr. NBM 2005 Un Illustration
Grades: 6 7 8 9 10 11 12   **741.5; Fic**
1. Adventure graphic novels; 2. Humorous graphic novels; 3. Monsters; 4. Graphic novels

1-56163-437-9, $9.99

"Preteens will enjoy the humor and adventure, while older teens will appreciate the banter between Tork and Tara along with everything else. The black-and-white art makes the cryptids look more funny than scary, so even the squeamish can read this one without getting grossed out." (VOYA)

Intrepid cryptozoologist Tork Darwyn hunts for cryptids, those legendary creatures such as the Loch Ness Monster, the Yeti, and others. His beautiful wife Tara works as a science teacher but often accompanies Tork on his expeditions; it's a good thing, too, because she's much smarter and gets him out of trouble a lot. There is a second volume, published in 2006.

Guibert, Emmanuel
Sardine in outer space. [by] Emmanuel Guibert; illustrated by Joann Sfar; translated by Sasha Watson; colorist, Walter Pezzali. First Second 2006 128p. Illustration

Grades: 3 4 5 6   741.5; Fic
1. Humorous graphic novels; 2. Science fiction graphic novels; 3. Graphic novels
978-1-59643-126-3 (pa), $12.95; 1-59643-126-1 (pa)
LC 2005-21790

In this volume of twelve interconnected stories, little space pirate Sardine cruises in the spaceship Huckleberry with Uncle Yellow Shoulder and Little Louie. They do battle with Supermuscleman, who runs a tough space orphanage where children are taught "good behavior."

"Sfar's off-kilter, slightly uglified art, reminiscent of a toned-down Beavis and Butthead, gives the simple fun an unusual punch." Booklist

Other titles in this series are: Sardine in outer space 2 (2006); Sardine in outer space 3 (2007); Sardine in outer space 4 (2007); Sardine in outer space 5 (2008); Sardine in outer space 6 (2009)

Sardine in Outer Space Vol. 3. First Second Books 2007 109p. Illustration
Grades: 3 4 5 6 7 8   741.5; Fic
1. Adventure graphic novels; 2. Humorous graphic novels; 3. Graphic novels
978-1-59643-128-7, $12.95

Supermuscleman and Doc Krok are at it again, and it's not just the galaxy they're out to ruin, it's Sardine and Little Louie, too. Get ready for the ultimate match-up as wits battle brawn in the Space Boxing Championship. The fearless cousins must go head to head with Supermuscleman, Chief Executive Dictator of the Universe, shrunken to enter the kids' matches, but just as muscley. In another story, it's Sardine's birthday and she has a big party, but Doc Krok crashes it with his newest creation, Toxin, whose sole purpose is to destroy Sardine. There are more stories filled with adventure, space hijinks and looniness.

Sardine in Outer Space Vol. 4. First Second Books 2007 109p. Illustration
Grades: 3 4 5 6 7 8   741.5; Fic
1. Adventure graphic novels; 2. Humorous graphic novels; 3. Graphic novels
978-1-59643-129-4, $13.95

Sardine is back, and she's got a whole host of new problems to face even before the spaceship Huckleberry can get off the ground. In the fourth volume of this series, Sardine must tackle, among other things, monsters under the bed, flesh-eating tattoos, time machines, a flying cat, kidnapped suns, and even boredom. As always, Supermuscleman, Chief Executive Dictator of the Universe, lurks in the background, trying-unsuccessfully and incompetently-to make Sardine and her crew behave.

Another title in the author's series about Sardine in Outer Space

Sardine in outer space 5. Color by Walter Pezzali; translation by Edward Garwin. First Second Books 2008 102p. Illustration
Grades: 3 4 5 6   741.5; 741
978-1-59643-380-9, $14.95; 1-59643-380-9
LC 2007044126

Sardine in outer space 6. Stories by Emmanuel Guibert ; pictures by Joann Sfar ; color by Walter Pezzali ; translated by Sasha Watson. First Second Books 2008 93p. Illustration
Grades: 2 3 4 5 6   741; 741.5; Fic
1. Humorous graphic novels; 2. Sardine (Fictional character); 3. Science fiction graphic novels; 4. Graphic novels
978-1-59643-424-0, $14.95; 1-59643-424-4
LC 2008-23543

This latest volume of the Sardine in Outer Space series offers nine short tales featuring Sardine, Little Louie, Captain Yellow Shoulder, and villains Supermuscleman and Doc Krok. Stories include Captain Yellow Shoulder's tale of how he lost his eye (baby buggy racing against baby Supermuscleman, uh-huh); Sardine's mission to restore the merry-go-rounds in the rings of Saturn; what happens when Sardine gets a cell phone that causes big trouble; and more. There is one panel showing the newborn infant Yellow Shoulder naked); and "Robert Putto" is a Cupid in training and is therefore naked, although nothing crucial shows.

"The bouncy cartoons, wacky but well-plotted vignettes, and glowing color palette promise to reel in new readers and satisfy young fans." Booklist
Another title in the author's series about Sardine in outer space

Gulledge, Laura Lee
★ **Page** by Paige. Amulet Books 2011 Un Illustration
Grades: 7 8 9 10 11 12   741.5; Fic
1. Artists; 2. Friendship; 3. Humorous graphic novels; 4. New York (NY); 5. Graphic novels
0-8109-9721-5; 0-8109-9722-3 (pa);
978-0-8109-9721-9, $18.95; 978-0-8109-9722-6 (pa), $9.95

Teenage Paige Turner (blame her writer parents) moves to New York City from Virginia, and she finds the big city rather overwhelming. She decides to buy a sketchbook and sort out her thoughts and feelings in drawings. Soon she does make some friends, and she explores more of the city, but as she begins to feel happier, she clashes with her parents. All of this goes into her sketchbook journal, which she starts to show to her new friends"Jules, Longo, and Gabe. The book is organized by Paige's "rules," which she uses to try to change herself, such as "Rule #2: Draw what you know. If you feel it or see it . . . DRAW IT!

"Gulledge's b&w illustrations are simple but well-suited to their subject matter; the work as a whole is a good-natured, optimistic portrait of a young woman evolving toward adulthood." Publ Wkly

Hadley, Amy Reeder
Fool's gold vol. 1. Tokyopop 2006 192p. Illustration
Grades: 7 8 9 10 11 12   741.5; Fic
1. Humorous graphic novels; 2. Romance graphic novels; 3. Graphic novels
978-1-59816-585-2, $9.99
Penny observes that, with rare exceptions, most of the girls in her high school are fatally drawn to jerks. She starts out trying to save her best friend Katie from just such a relationship, when she decides to form her own underground club (using the geology club as a decoy) to help girls identify the jerks and avoid them. She calls such jerks Pyrites (fool's gold). She's also a dress designer and works in her young aunt's shop, even though her father objects and wants her to do better in school. She really wants to just design cool, fun and funky clothes, but her crusade against jerks takes a lot of her time. And what's going to happen when she finds a nice, cool, creative, nonjerk boy she can like? This is a global manga series.

Hage, Anika
Gothic sports vol. 3. Tokyopop 2008 196p. Illustration
Grades: 8 9 10 11 12   741.5; Fic
1. Friendship; 2. Soccer; 3. Graphic novels
978-1-59816-994-2, $9.99
Anya's quest to start the Gothic-Lolita soccer team at her school has been officially approved by the school principal. The team is excited, but when summer vacation starts, everyone has different plans that don't include soccer practice. Delia comes up with a solution: she invites the whole team to come to a cabin in the Bavarian mountains for a training camp to work on their skills. The book includes one scene with incidental and nonsexual partial nudity. This is a global manga series, translated from German.

Gothic sports, Vol. 1. Tokyopop 2007 176p. Illustration
Grades: 8 9 10 11 12   741.5; Fic
1. High school students; 2. Manga; 3. School stories; 4. Soccer
978-1-59816-992-8, $9.99
When Anya starts at Lucrece High, she wants to join one of the sports teams for which the school is famed. Since she's never played on a school's team before, she gets rejected. But this time, she's determined to succeed, so she joins with some of the other school misfits and they form their own soccer team. And with the help of a Goth-Lolita classmate, they have fantastically fashionable Goth-Lolita uniforms (even for the boys!). This is the first volume of a series translated from German, making it a global manga title.

Hakamada, Mera
Fairy idol Kanon, volume 1. UDON Entertainment 2009 200p. Illustration
Grades: 3 4 5 6 7 8   741.5; Fic
1. Fairies; 2. Fantasy graphic novels; 3. Manga; 4. Music; 5. Graphic novels
978-1-897376-89-8, $7.99
Fourth grader Kanon loves to sing more than anything else, and people say her singing brings them happiness. Her friends Kodama and Marika also love to sing, although Marika wants a solo career as an idol (in Japan, young singers are often called pop idols). The three of them encounter a magical fairy princess named Alto, who tells them their singing and harmonies are needed to help her fairy kingdom. She decides to help them become pop idols in order to help her own people, and the three girls enter pop idol competitions. However, they soon encounter another very ambitious girl who seems to have a dark fairy helping her with bad magic that harms people. Some of the pages are in color.

Hale, Dean
★ **Calamity** Jack [by] Shannon and Dean Hale; illustrated by Nathan Hale. Bloomsbury 2010 144p. Illustration
Grades: 4 5 6 7 8 9
741.5; Fic
1. Adventure graphic novels; 2. Fantasy graphic novels; 3. Folklore; 4. Graphic novels
9781599903736, $14.99; 9781599900766, $19.99
LC 2008-41332

Courtesy of Bloomsbury

In this sequel to Rapunzel's Revenge, the reader meets Jack as a child growing up in the city of Shyport; Jack has been a schemer practically since birth, but he hasn't had a whole lot of luck. His schemes usually end in unforeseen consequences. When he goes up against the giant Blunderboar, the magic beanstalk he uses to reach the giant's floating fortress destroys his neighborhood and his mother's bakery, and he just manages to leave town with a certain gold-egg-laying goose under his arm. After the events of the first book, Jack and Rapunzel come to Shyport, where Jack hopes to help his mother rebuild her bakery with the golden eggs he now has. However, they come to a city transformed Blunderboar has taken over, his security company claims to be keeping giant ants at bay, and Jack's mother is being held prisoner. Jack is still wanted for what he had done, and only Prudence, Jack's hat-loving pixie partner-in-crime, is willing to help. Then Jack and Rapunzel meet Freddie Sparksmith, newspaperman and gadget inventor, and they team up for a rescue mission. The book includes a lot of action and some non-gory violence.
Companion to: Rapunzel's Revenge

★ **Rapunzel's revenge.** [by] Shannon and Dean Hale; illustrated by Nathan Hale. Bloomsbury 2008 144p. Illustration; Map
Grades: 5 6 7 8   741.5; Fic
1. Fairy tales; 2. Fantasy graphic novels; 3. Humorous graphic novels; 4. Graphic novels

1-59990-070-X;
1-59990-288-5 (pa);
978-1-59990-070-4,
$18.99;
978-1-59990-288-3 (pa),
$14.99
LC 2007-37670
In this graphic novel,
Rapunzel escapes "from the
enchanted tree where
Mother Gothel imprisoned
her. Rapunzel sets off alone
through the ghost towns and
Badlands of Gothel's
Reach. She is determined to

Courtesy of Bloomsbury

find Gothel's Villa and teach
Mother Gothel a long-overdue lesson for her years of
treachery and lies, and help her real mother get out of the
mine camps where Mother Gothel has kept her enslaved."
(Publisher's note)
"The dialogue is witty, the story is an enticing departure
from the original, and the illustrations are magically fun and
expressive." SLJ
Another title about these characters is: Calamity Jack
(2009)

Hale, Nathan
Donner dinner party. By Nathan Hale. Harry N Abrams
Inc 2013 123 p. (Nathan Hale's Hazardous Tales)
Grades: 5 6 7 8   **979.4; 741.5**
1. Donner party; 2. Sierra Nevada Mountains
1419708562; 9781419708565, $12.95
In this graphic novel, author Nathan Hale "tells the
harrowing story of the ill-fated Donner party. Beginning
with their departure from Springfield, Illinois, in 1846, Hale
depicts the party's progress . . . and includes lots of factual
details, such as a roster of everyone in the party, how they
died, and a helpful map showing just how . . . close they
came to California before meeting their grisly end."
(Booklist)
"This informative graphic novel capitalizes on
enticingly gross history to great effect, balancing raw facts
with strong storytelling." Booklist

Nathan Hale's hazardous tales: big bad ironclad!.
Nathan Hale. Abrams 2012 118 p.
Grades: 4 5 6   **973.7**
1. Cushing, William; 2. United States — History —
1861-1865, Civil War — Naval operations
1419703951; 9781419703959, $12.95
LC 2012947181
Author Nathan Hale "covers the history of the amazing
ironclad steam warships used in the Civil War [in his book
'Big Bad Ironclad!'] From the ship's inventor, who had a
history of blowing things up and only 100 days to complete
his project, to the mischievous William Cushing, who
pranked his way through the whole war, this book is filled
with . . . facts." (Publisher's note)
Includes bibliographical references.
Map on endpapers.

Nathan Hale's hazardous tales: one dead spy. Nathan
Hale. Amulet Books 2012 128 p.

Grades: 3 4 5 6 7   **741.5/973; 741.5**
1. Hale, Nathan, 1755-1776; 2. United States — History
141970396X; 9781419703966, $12.95
LC 2012947189
In this graphic novel, historical figure "[Nathan] Hale,
convicted of espionage, forestalls death by telling stories
from American history. In this volume, he's helped by the
hangman in telling the story of the early days of the
revolution. He takes readers from his college days at Yale to
the Boston Massacre, the Boston Tea Party, his joining the
7th Connecticut regiment, the Battle of Bunker Hill and
other pivotal scenes in New England and New York City."
(Kirkus)

Nathan Hale's hazardous tales: treaties, trenches, mud,
and blood (a World War I tale). By Nathan Hale. Amulet
Books 2014 128 p. Color illustration; Color; Map (Nathan
Hale's hazardous tales)
Grades: 4 5 6 7   **741.5; 940.3**
1. World War, 1914-1918 — Juvenile literature
1419708082; 9781419708084, $12.95
LC 2013049048
"Nathan Hale, Revolutionary War hero, continues to
distract his executioners in this fourth volume, which tackles
WWI's complex events." (Horn Book)
"Per established series formula, a frame tale finds the
author's more-renowned namesake holding off the
hangman, Scheherazade-like, with tales from our country's
future history. In this volume, he covers the war's prelude,
precipitation, major campaigns and final winding down in
small but reasonably easy-to-follow two-color panels. . . .
Hale cogently conveys the mind-numbing scale of it all as
well as the horrors of trench warfare." Kirkus
Includes bibliographical references

The **underground** abductor: an abolitionist tale.
Nathan Hale. Harry N Abrams Inc. 2015 125 p. Illustration;
Color (Nathan Hale's Hazardous Tales)
Grades: 3 4 5 6 7   **741.5**
1. Biographical graphic novels; 2. Fugitive slaves —
United States; 3. Tubman, Harriet, 1820?-1913 —
Juvenile literature; 4. Underground Railroad
9781419715365, $12.95; 1419715364
In this graphic novel, "a fictionalized Nathan Hale (a
patriot from the American Revolutionary War) tells stories
about America's most extraordinary heroes and villains. In
this installment, Hale tells his British captors about Harriet
Tubman, the spy and nurse who helped hundreds of
American slaves run away in the 1800s on the Underground
Railroad." (School Library Journal)
Includes bibliographical references

Hale, Tricia Riley
Grand Theft Galaxy, Vol. 1. Illustrated by Jim Jimenez.
Tokyopop 2007 Un Illustration
Grades: 8 9 10 11 12   **741.5; Fic**
1. Humorous graphic novels; 2. Science fiction graphic
novels; 3. Graphic novels
978-1-59816-713-9, $9.99
College freshman Samantha Beagley has her life all
figured out. She's a pre-law student, and she lives by her
charts and planners. On her eighteenth birthday, Sam loses
control of her life. She receives a very strange present from

her parents, and learns to her horror that they are alien thieves. Some years ago they stole a certain object, the Evo Cube, and they hid it away so well they can't remember where it is. And now the Galactic Order Directorate has found Sam's parents, and they will destroy the Earth in three days if the Evo Cube isn't returned. When her parents grab her and go off-planet to save themselves, Sam decides to find the Evo Cube herself; and that leads her to find the master thief Jackal. He turns out to be her former pet cat, Mr. Fluffy. This is the first of a global manga series.

Hall, M. C.
King Arthur and the Knights of the Round Table. Stone Arch Books 2006 63p. Illustration
Grades: 3 4 5 6 7 8 9   741.5; Fic
1. King Arthur — Adaptations; 2. Graphic novels
978-1-59889-048-8, $23.93
In a world of wizards, giants, and dragons, King Arthur and the Knights of the Round Table are the kingdom of Camelot's only defense against the threatening forces of evil. Fighting battles and saving those in need, the Knights of the Round Table can defeat every enemy but one - themselves. This adaptation focuses on how Arthur became King, on Lancelot and how Sir Galahad came to be born, the quest for the Holy Grail, and how Mordred brought about the end.
Part of the Graphic Revolve series.

Halliday, Ayun
Peanut. Ayun Halliday; illustrated by Paul Hoppe. Schwartz & Wade Books 2012 216 p. Color illustration
Grades: 6 7 8 9 10   741.5
1. Food allergy — Fiction; 2. High schools — Fiction; 3. Mothers and daughters — Fiction; 4. Moving, Household — Fiction; 5. Peanut allergy; 6. Popularity — Fiction; 7. School stories; 8. Graphic novels
037586590X, $15.99; 0375965904, $18.99; 9780375865909, $15.99; 9780375965906, $18.99
LC 2009047168
In this graphic novel by Ayun Halliday, illustrated by Paul Hoppe, "Sadie has the perfect plan to snag some friends when she transfers to Plainfield High—pretend to have a peanut allergy. But what happens when you have to hand in that student health form your unsuspecting mom was supposed to fill out" And what if your new friends want to come over and your mom serves them snacks? (Peanut butter sandwich, anyone?)" (Publisher's note)

Hama, Larry
The **Battle** of Antietam: The Bloodiest Day of Battle. Art by Scott Moore. Rosen Publishing Group 2007 48p. Illustration
Grades: 3 4 5 6 7 8   741.5; 973.7
1. Antietam (Md), Battle of, 1862; 2. United States — History — 1861-1865, Civil War; 3. Graphic novels
978-1-4042-0775-2, $29.25; 978-1-84603-049-9 (pa)
LC 2006007186
The battle of Antietam on September 17, 1862 was the first major Civil War engagement on Northern soil, and it remains the bloodiest single-day battle in American history. Of the 90,000 troops that fought, over 23,000 were killed or wounded. Antietam also marked a significant turning point:

Courtesy of Rosen Publishing

General Lee's bold invasion of the North was halted, and the Union's success, though not exploited, gave President Lincoln the victory he needed to make his Emancipation Proclamation. The battle arguably sealed the fate of the Confederacy, even if the war still had nearly three years to run. This book brings to life this significant and very costly engagement in graphic novel format. It also includes eight pages of information placing Antietam in its historical context, describing the key players, the build-up to the battle and its aftermath.
Part of the Graphic Battles of the Civil War series; the paperback edition is published by Osprey.

The **Battle** of First Bull Run: The Civil War Begins. The Rosen Publishing Group 2007 48p. Illustration
Grades: 3 4 5 6 7 8 9   741.5; 973.7
1. Bull Run 1st Battle of, 1861; 2. United States — History — 1861-1865, Civil War; 3. War; 4. Graphic novels
978-1-4042-0776-9, $29.25

Courtesy of Rosen Publishing

Three months after the shelling of Fort Sumter, Union and Confederate forces met for the first time in earnest combat. However, neither side was prepared at this early stage of the war, and confusion reigned on the battlefield. Finally, Confederate reinforcements forced the Union army into a panicked retreat. The intensity—and ill preparedness—of both armies convinced the nation that the conflict between the states would be a long, bloody ordeal. The book includes background information, a glossary, and a list of books for further reading.
Part of the Graphic Battles of the Civil War series. The book is also available in paperback from Osprey Publishing under the title The War is On!: Battle of First Bull Run.

The **Battle** of Guadalcanal: Land and Sea Warfare in the South Pacific. The Rosen Publishing Group 2007 48p. Illustration
Grades: 3 4 5 6 7 8 9   741.5; 940.54
1. Guadalcanal Island (Solomon Islands), Battle of, 1942-1943; 2. World War, 1939-1945; 3. Graphic novels
978-1-4042-0784-4, $29.25
The battle of Guadalcanal shattered the myth of Japanese invincibility. August 7, 1942, marked the first American amphibious assault of World War II, and the first attempt to secure the Japanese-controlled island of Guadalcanal. From the ranks of the units that contested this

campaign a seasoned fighting force of US veterans was created that, island by island, would sweep the Japanese back across the Pacific. This full-color comic book includes further reading, essential information on the background, aftermath and key players of the conflict.

Part of the Graphic Battles of World War II series. This book is also available in a paperback edition from Osprey Publishing, under the title Fight to the Death: Battle of Guadalcanal.

The **battle** of Iwo Jima: guerilla warfare in the Pacific. By Larry Hama; illustrated by Anthony Williams. Rosen Pub. 2007 48p. Illustration; Map (Graphic battles of World War II)

Grades: 5 6 7 8 9   **940.54**

1. Iwo Jima, Battle of, 1945; 2. World War, 1939-1945; 3. Graphic novels

978-1-4042-0781-3 (lib bdg), $29.25; 1-4042-0781-3 (lib bdg)

      LC 2006007645

"Using a graphic novel to introduce the battle for Iwo Jima makes it very accessible. Before the graphic-novel section of the book begins, Hama provides a short, informative background piece describing the run-up to World War II, the significance of the Japanese war machine, and the importance of the tiny island of Iwo Jima. Then the graphic novel, illustrated by Williams in camouflage colors, does a terrific job of examining the ups and downs of the battle as well as the horror of so many losses—on both sides." Booklist

Includes bibliographical references

The **Battle** of Shiloh: Surprise Attack!. Rosen Publishing Group 2007 48p. Illustration

Grades: 3 4 5 6 7 8

741.5; 973.7

1. Shiloh (Tenn), Battle of, 1862; 2. United States — History — 1861-1865, Civil War; 3. Graphic novels

978-1-4042-0779-0, $29.25;

978-1-84603-050-5 (pb)

      LC 2006007309

Courtesy of Rosen Publishing

The first major Civil War battle in the Western theater, Shiloh came as a horrifying shock to both the American public and those in arms. On April 6, 1862, Confederate forces staged a surprise attack on the Union army encamped along the Tennessee River. Fighting was fierce as General Grant struggled to hold off the enemy until his reinforcements arrived the following day so that he could 'Whip 'em tomorrow'. Though nearly driven into the Tennessee River, the Union army could ultimately claim victory - won at a dear cost. With nearly 24,000 total casualties in two days' fighting, 'Bloody Shiloh' served as a wake-up call to the nation, announcing that the continuing fight for the Union would be devastating for both sides. This book brings to life one of the Civil War's bloodiest battles in graphic novel format. It also includes eight pages of background information placing Shiloh in its

historical context, detailing the key players, and describing the build-up to the fighting and its aftermath.

Part of the Graphic Battles of the Civil War series; the paperback edition is published by Osprey.

The **Battle** of the Wilderness: Deadly Inferno. The Rosen Publishing Group 2007 48p. Illustration

Grades: 3 4 5 6 7 8 9   **741.5; 973.7**

Courtesy of Rosen Publishing

1. United States — History — 1861-1865, Civil War; 2. War; 3. Wilderness, Battle of the, 1864; 4. Graphic novels

978-1-4042-0780-6, $29.25 lib. bdg.

'The Wilderness' encompassed a 70-square-mile expanse of virtually impenetrable woodland in central Virginia, so dense it made conventional warfare impossible. The first battle of Lieutenant General Ulysses S. Grant's 1864 Overland Campaign against the Army of Northern Virginia, the Wilderness witnessed some of the fiercest fighting of the Civil War. Though outnumbered, General Lee's forces posed stiff resistance to Grant's offensive. At the end of the three day battle, the outcome was uncertain, and the fight ended in a draw. Illustrating one of the American Civil War's most tactically challenging battles, this comic strip narrative brings to life a completely new type of warfare; the likes of which had never been fought before on American soil. The book includes additional information, including a map, a glossary, and a list of books for further reading.

Part of the Graphic Battles of the Civil War series; a trade paperback edition is also available from Osprey Publishing under the title Deadly Inferno: Battle of the Wilderness.

Spider-girl presents Wild Thing: crash course. Illustrated by Ron Lim. Marvel Entertainment 2007 Un Illustration

Grades: 5 6 7 8 9 10   **741.5**

1. Adventure graphic novels; 2. Superhero graphic novels; 3. Graphic novels

978-0-7851-2606-5, $7.99

A few years in the future, in the alternate Marvel Universe where Peter Parker and Mary Jane had a daughter who has become Spider-Girl, Wolverine and Elektra got together and they had a daughter, too Rina Logan, also known as Wild Thing. She has psychic claws that work pretty much like Wolverine's claws, and she has his fast healing power. She still has to deal with high school even as she fights against bad guys, demons, evil droids, and more.

Hamilton, Sue

   Jack Kirby. ABDO Publishing 2007 32p. Illustration (Comic Book Creators)

Grades: 3 4 5 6 7   **92; 741.5**

1. Biographical graphic novels; 2. Captain America (Fictional character); 3. Comic books, strips, etc —

History and criticism; 4. Fantastic Four (Fictional characters); 5. Hulk (Fictional character); 6. Kirby, Jack, 1917-1994; 7. Thor (Fictional character); 8. X-Men (Fictional characters); 9. Graphic novels
978-1-59928-298-5, $25.65

LC 2006-15405

Courtesy of ABDO Publishing

Jack "King" Kirby may be one of the most famous comic book artists ever. He helped to create Captain America, The Fantastic Four, The Incredible Hulk, The X-Men, The Mighty Thor, The Silver Surfer, and other characters for Marvel Comics. A prolific artist, he also worked on westerns, romance comics, and lots of other titles. Later in his career, he also worked for DC Comics, where he created the New Gods. His struggles to regain ownership of his art sparked a movement toward creator-owned comics in the 1980s and 1990s. He passed away in 1994, but his influence is still felt today. This volume includes lots of reproductions of his comics work and photographs from his life.

Joe Simon. ABDO Publishing 2007 32p. Illustration (Comic Book Creators)
Grades: 3 4 5 6 7
92; 741.5
1. Blue Beetle (Fictional character); 2. Captain America (Fictional character); 3. Comic book writers; 4. Comic books, strips, etc — History and criticism; 5. Simon, Joe; 6. Graphic novels
978-1-59928-300-5, $25.65

LC 2006-15408

Courtesy of ABDO Publishing

Joe Simon may not be as much of a household name as Stan Lee or Jack Kirby, but he created Captain America (with Jack Kirby), The Blue Beetle, and other comic book characters. This volume introduces young readers to Simon's career, which included working in the Combat Art Corps during World War II and creating Sick Magazine in 1960; Sick included humor in the vein of the hugely popular Mad. This volume includes lots of reproductions of his comics and magazine work, and photographs.

Joe Sinnott. ABDO Publishing 2007 32p. Illustration (Comic Book Creators)
Grades: 3 4 5 6 7 **92; 741.5**
1. Avengers (Fictional characters); 2. Biographical graphic novels; 3. Comic books, strips, etc — History and criticism; 4. Fantastic Four (Fictional characters); 5. Sinnott, Joe, 1929-; 6. Thor (Fictional character); 7. X-Men (Fictional characters); 8. Graphic novels

978-1-59928-299-2, $25.65

LC 2006-15409

Joe Sinnott worked as an artist for Marvel Comics since 1950; he drew romance comics, westerns, super hero comics, record album covers for then-popular singers such as Bing Crosby, even covers for crossword puzzle magazines. From the early 1960s, Sinnott worked mostly as an inker, working with artists such as Jack Kirby, who would draw the pencilled art, and with writers such as Stan Lee. He worked on The Fantastic Four, The Mighty Thor, The Avengers, the X-Men, and other famous Marvel Comics titles. He officially retired in 1995, but he's still actively drawing and talking with school students. This volume includes lots of reproductions of his comics and other art work and photographs.

John Buscema. ABDO Publishing 2007 32p. Illustration (Comic Book Creators)
Grades: 3 4 5 6 7
92; 741.5
1. Biographical graphic novels; 2. Buscema, John, 1927-2002; 3. Cartoonists; 4. Comic books, strips, etc — History and criticism; 5. Thor (Fictional character); 6. Graphic novels
978-1-59928-297-8, $25.65

LC 2006-15407

John Buscema is

Courtesy of ABDO Publishing

another comics artist who worked with Stan Lee, among others. He worked on such comics as The Mighty Thor, The Silver Surfer, and Conan the Barbarian. He also worked on all kinds of comics, and in 1958 went into advertising art. He went back to Marvel in 1966, and sometimes worked with his own younger brother, Sal Buscema. In 1978, Buscema and Stan Lee created How to Draw Comics the Marvel Way, a popular how-to art book still in print now. Buscema died in 2002. This volume includes lots of reproductions of his comics work and photographs.

John Romita, Sr.. ABDO Publishing 2007 32p. Illustration (Comic Book Creators)
Grades: 3 4 5 6 7 **92; 741.5**
1. Biographical graphic novels; 2. Cartoonists; 3. Comic books, strips, etc — History and criticism; 4. Romita, John, Jr; 5. Spider-Man (Fictional character); 6. Graphic novels
978-1-59928-302-9, $25.65

Part of a biographical series discussing the lives of comic book creators and the inspirations for some of their most famous work, this book focuses on the life and work of John Romita, Sr., who is best known for his work on The Amazing Spider-Man comics.

Hamilton, Tim
Robert Louis Stevenson's Treasure Island. Penguin Young Readers Group/Puffin Books 2005 176p. Illustration
Grades: 4 5 6 7 8 9 10 **741.5; Fic**

1. Adventure graphic novels; 2. Buried treasure; 3. Pirates; 4. Stevenson, Robert Louis, 1850-1894 — Adaptations; 5. Graphic novels
0-14-240470-5, $9.99

Innkeeper's son Jim Hawkins befriends an old seaman who stays at the inn; when he dies, Jim finds a treasure map in the old man's seachest. When he takes it to the local magistrate, Jim finds himself caught up in a treasure hunt adventure with a ship's crew of pirates led by Long John Silver. This graphic novel adaptation keeps all the main action of the original novel. The book includes a gallery of the character models Hamilton used as well as sketched pages so readers can see some of the process.

Hansen, Jim
Drawing Fantasy Art: How to Draw Superheroes. Jim Hansen and John Burns. Rosen Publishing Group/PowerKids Press 2007 32p. Illustration
Grades: 2 3 4 5 6 7   **741.5; 743.4**
1. Drawing — Juvenile literature; 2. Graphic novels
978-1-4042-3855-8, $25.25

This introductory level art instruction book shows young artists how to draw superheroes in three different styles: cartoon, screen hero, and manga. It also includes a list of more art instruction books for those who want to learn more techniques.

Harbo, Christopher L.
The **Explosive** World of Volcanoes with Max Axiom, Super Scientist. Art by Tod Smith. Capstone Press 2007 32p. Illustration
Grades: 3 4 5 6 7 8 9   **551.21; 741.5**
1. Volcanoes; 2. Graphic novels
978-1-4296-0144-3, $25.26
                 LC 2006102361

This book uses the graphic novel format to follow the adventures of super scientist Max Axiom as he explains the science behind volcanoes, describing the different types of volcanoes found all over the world. The book includes additional facts and a list of books for further reading.
Part of the Graphic Science series.

Hardcastle, Michael
Sam's Goal. Art by Tony O'Donnell; Stone Arch Books 2007 72p. Illustration
Grades: 2 3 4 5 6 7   **741.5; Fic**
1. Soccer; 2. Sports; 3. Graphic novels
978-1-59889-088-4 li, $21.26; 978-1-59889-234-5 (pa)
                 LC 2006006071

Sam has always dreamed of playing professional soccer. When the best soccer player in the country (England) invites Sam to his next game, Sam can't believe it. The problem is, neither do his friends. Can Sam convince them that he's telling the truth" When the day of the big game arrives, Sam's goal is clearer than ever. This graphic novel is written at an easy level for reluctant and struggling readers.
Part of the Graphic Trax series.

Harper, Charise Mericle
Fashion Kitty. Hyperion Books for Children 2005 90p. Illustration

Grades: 3 4 5 6 7 8 9   **741.5; Fic**
1. Cats; 2. Humorous graphic novels; 3. Graphic novels
0-7868-5134-1, $8.99

Kiki Kittie is a very unusual cat. For one thing, she has a mouse for a pet—and that's kind of like a human having a chocolate cake for a pet. Kiki also has a natural flair for fashion, but up until a recent birthday, she was just an ordinary fashionable kitty. Then, on that day, she discovered that she had special powers: she can turn into Fashion Kitty, able to mix and match hundreds of outfits in a single second. Regular cat by day, Fashion Kitty by night, Kiki is always ready to answer a call of despair and save other cats from making fashion faux pas

Other titles about Fashion Kitty are: Fashion Kitty versus the Fashion Queen (2007); Fashion Kitty and the unlikely hero (2008); Fashion Kitty and the B.O.Y.S. (2011)

Fashion Kitty Versus the Fashion Queen. Hyperion Paperbacks for Children 2007 90p. Illustration
Grades: 3 4 5 6 7 8 9   **741.5; Fic**
1. Cats; 2. Humorous graphic novels; 3. Graphic novels
978-0-7868-3726-7, $8.99

After her last adventure, Fashion Kitty is truly becoming a hero. At school, she is more popular than ever. She's even been mentioned in several articles in the local newspaper, (which she clips out and saves in a scrapbook, of course). But not everyone is excited about Fashion Kitty's newfound popularity. A spoiled new kitty named Cassandra doesn't like sharing the spotlight. And when Fashion Kitty starts inspiring the other kitties at school to be more independent about their style choices, Cassandra really doesn't like it. So she hatches a plan (evil, of course) that involves lying, conniving, and outlawing bright colors and patterns. Fashion Kitty knows she must put an end to Cassandra's reign of terror. She will use her fashion sense, quick smarts, and the power of friendship to overcome fashion evil.

Harrell, Rob
Monster on the Hill. By Rob Harrell. Top Shelf Productions 2013 192 p. Color; Illustration
Grades: 4 5 6 7 8   **741.5**
1. Friendship; 2. Monsters
1603090754; 9781603090759, $19.95

This graphic novel by Rob Harrell is set in "1860s England [where] every . . . township is terrorized by a . . . monster - much to the townsfolk's delight! Each town's . . . monster is a source of local pride [and] tourism. Unfortunately, for . . . Stoker-on-Avon, their monster isn't quite as impressive. Can the morose Rayburn get a monstrous makeover and become a proper horror? It's up to the eccentric Dr. Charles Wilkie and plucky street urchin Timothy to get him up to snuff." (Publisher's note)

Harris, James S.
Shades of blue, Volume 1. Art by Rachel Nacion. D3 Digest/Devil's Due Publishing 2005 144p. Illustration
Grades: 7 8 9 10 11 12   **741.5; Fic**
1. Superhero graphic novels; 2. Graphic novels
1-932796-26-6, $10.95

Heidi Page's "life takes an odd turn after she awakens with blue hair and the power to control electricity. Although she tries to keep her powers from getting in the way of her normal life, weird situations pop up, and her best friend, K. T., and Marcus (who calls himself her sidekick) insist that she's the superhero for the job. This sarcastic, funny send-up of superhero comics hinges on great characterizations and an immensely likable, believable cast." Booklist

The series changed artists after the second issue. This is the first volume of a series.

Hartley, Welles
Star Wars: Empire Volume Seven: The Wrong Side of the War. Writers, Welles Hartley, John Jackson Miller ; pencillers, Davidé Fabbri ; colorists, Davidé Fabbri, Neziti Domenico, Michael Atiyeh ; letterer, Michael David Thomas Dark Horse Comics 2007 Un Illustration
Grades: 7 8 9 10 11 12 Adult   **741.5; Fic**
1. Adventure graphic novels; 2. Science fiction graphic novels; 3. Star Wars; 4. Graphic novels
978-1-59307-709-9, $17.95
Fresh from the killing fields of Jabiim, where the Empire has virtually wiped out the populace of that world, Imperial Lieutenant Janek Sunber is sent to the quiet prison base on Kalist VI. But, unbeknownst to the Empire, the Rebels have designs on Kalist Base both for its desirable fuel supplies and for the presence of a very important prisoner - one of their own who has already attracted the interest of Darth Vader. Sunber doesn't know it, but he's on a collision course with an old friend who is with the Rebels, and he finds himself wondering which of them is on the wrong side of the war. The book includes battle violence.

Hashimoto, Kyoko
Love master A, vol.1. Go! Comi 2008 Un Illustration
Grades: 7 8 9 10 11 12   **741.5; Fic**
1. Humorous graphic novels; 2. Romance graphic novels; 3. Shojo manga; 4. Graphic novels
978-1933617-60-2, $10.99
Aria starts at a new high school, hoping to have a normal school experience. Since elementary school, when she confessed her love to a classmate and was summarily rejected, she has suffered rejection all through school and earned the ironic nickname "Love Master." Now, she has renounced love. However, on her first day at school, she discovers the school's strange way of selecting Student Council members, and not only is she as a first year student a Student Council member, she is the President! And her reputation has been twisted so everyone thinks she's a real "Love Master" and wants her advice. Tonohashi High School is in for a very interesting year.

Hatke, Ben
★ Legends of Zita the spacegirl. Ben Hatke. First Second 2012 205 p. Color illustration
Grades: 4 5 6   **741.5**
1. Adventure fiction; 2. Fame — Fiction; 3. Heroes — Fiction; 4. Robots — Fiction; 5. Science fiction; 6. Science fiction graphic novels; 7. Graphic novels
1596434473; 9781596434479, $12.99; 9781596438064, $18.99
LC 2012012748

This graphic novel, by Ben Hatke, is a children's science fiction adventure story. "Zita is determined to find her way home to earth, following the events of the first book. . . . Zita's exploits from her first adventure have made her an intergalactic megastar! But she's about to find out that fame doesn't come without a price. And who can you trust when your true self is being eclipsed by your public persona, and you've got a robot doppelganger wreaking havoc . . . while wearing your face—" (Publisher's note)

"Hatke's arrestingly vibrant art commands instant adoration of its reader... Readers would be hard-pressed to not find something to like in these tales, they're a winning formula of eye-catching aesthetics, plot and creativity, adeptly executed. Imaginative and utterly bewitching." Kirkus

★ The Return of Zita the Spacegirl. By Ben Hatke. First Second 2014 240 p.
Grades: 3 4 5 6   **741.5**
1. Good and evil — Fiction; 2. Outer space — Fiction; 3. Prisoners — Fiction; 4. Science fiction; 5. Science fiction graphic novels; 6. Graphic novels
1626720584; 9781626720589, $18.99
"Zita the Spacegirl has saved planets, battled monsters, and wrestled with interplanetary fame. But she faces her biggest challenge yet in the third and final installment of the Zita adventures. Wrongfully imprisoned on a penitentiary planet, Zita has to plot the galaxy's greatest jailbreak before the evil prison warden can execute his plan of interstellar domination!" (Publisher's note)

"The art is colorful, detailed, and child-friendly. Readers of all ages can relate to the themes of friendship and loyalty while enjoying the fantasy of a far-out sci-fi adventure." Horn Book

★ Zita the spacegirl. First Second 2011 182p. Illustration
Grades: 3 4 5 6   **741.5**
1. Science fiction graphic novels; 2. Graphic novels
1-59643-446-5 (pa); 1-59643-695-6; 978-1-59643-446-2 (pa), $10.99; 978-1-59643-695-4, $17.99
When her best friend is abducted by an alien doomsday cult, Zita leaps to the rescue and finds herself a stranger on a strange planet.

Hatori, Bisco
Millennium Snow Vol. 1. Viz Media/Shojo Beat 2007 200p. Illustration
Grades: 8 9 10 11 12   **741.5; Fic**
1. Romance graphic novels; 2. Shojo manga; 3. Vampires; 4. Graphic novels
978-1-4215-1202-0, $8.99
17-year-old Chiyuki Matsuoka was born with heart problems, and her doctors say she won't live to see the next snow. Toya is an 18-year-old vampire who hates blood and refuses to make the traditional partnership with a human, whose life-giving blood would keep them both alive for a thousand years. Can Chiyuki teach Toya to feel a passion for life, even as her own is ending? The book has some mildly strong language, and romance without graphic depictions of vampiric action.
Volume 1 of 4

Hayashi, Mikase

    March on earth, volume one. DC Comics/CMX 2009 Un Illustration

Grades: 7 8 9 10 11 12   **741.5; Fic**

    1. Family life; 2. Romance graphic novels; 3. Shojo manga; 4. Graphic novels

    978-1-4012-1594-1, $9.99

    When Yuzu was a young girl, her older sister Tsubaki raised her after their parents died. Then a few years ago, Tsubaki got pregnant and decided to have the baby and raise him as a single parent; she would never tell Yuzu who the father was. Just a few months ago, Tsubaki died in a car accident, and Yuzu, now a 10th grader in high school, has decided she will raise her nephew Shou herself. She and Shou live in an apartment in the building owned by Mrs. Kusano, who lives there with her two sons, Seita and Keita. They help her take care of Shou, even with their help it's difficult to focus on her studies. She reads her sister's picture books to Shou, especially the last one Tsubaki wrote, called March on Earth. Yuzu wants to become a lawyer to help people, but will there be enough money from what her parents left to pay for college, after paying for rent and all the other expenses? Other teens worry about boyfriends, and whether they should go sing karaoke, but Yuzu has to take care of a two-year-old boy and worry about having enough money to buy him one Christmas present. She doesn't seem to see that Seita has fallen for her, and she seems to be oblivious to his efforts to appear before her half naked (wearing only an apron to cook curry, claiming to have just come out of the bath with only a towel around his waist, ...).

Haynes, Stephen

    Macbeth. Barron's 2008 Illustration

Grades: 4 5 6 7 8 9   **822.3; 741.5**

    1. Authors; 2. Dramatists; 3. Poets; 4. Shakespeare, William, 1564-1616 — Adaptations; 5. Graphic novels

    978-0-7641-6140-7, $15.99; 978-0-7641-4009-9 (pa), $8.99

                   LC 2007-938484

    Macbeth is a loyal retainer of King Duncan of Scotland, until three witches prophesy that he will be king. Now, nothing will stop his ambition, and Macbeth and his wife kill the king. But now that he has the throne, Macbeth is haunted by guilt and paranoia, and the murders pile up. This graphic novel adaptation of Shakespeare's play includes a brief biography of Shakespeare, background information on the real Macbeth, Scotland, and James I's campaign against witches; it also covers the superstitions about the play, and film adaptations.

Part of Barron's Graphic Classics series

Helfand, Lewis

    Conquering Everest: the lives of Edmund Hillary and Tenzing Norgay. Campfire 2011 96p. Illustration

Grades: 3 4 5 6 7 8 9 10   **741.5; 796.522**

    1. Hillary, Edmund Sir; 2. Mount Everest; 3. Mountaineering; 4. Mountaineers; 5. Nonfiction writers; 6. Tenzing Norgay, 1914-1986

    978-93-80741-24-6, $12.99

    Tenzing Norgay immigrated to Nepal with his Tibetan family when he was a boy, and he worked hard over the years to become one of the best Sherpas who helped the European, American, and other climbers who journeyed to Nepal to climb Mount Everest. Edmund Hillary was the son of a beekeeper from New Zealand, who became fascinated with mountain climbing during World War II. He came to Nepal in 1953 as part of a British expedition to reach Everest's peak, and Norgay came to be the sirdar, the head Sherpa and organizer of the expedition's support system. These two men became the first to reach Everest's summit at 11:30 a.m. on May 29, 1953. This graphic novel tells the story of the two men from such different backgrounds, and their friendship. The book notes that on May 22, 2010, Californian thirteen-year-old Jordan Romero became the youngest climber to reach Everest's peak. Tayal's panels show some of the massive scale of the mountain.

    Mother Teresa: Angel of the Slums. By Lewis Helfand and illustrated by Sachin Nagar. Random House Inc 2013 88 p.

Grades: 6 7 8 9   **271.9**

    1. Teresa, Mother, 1910-1997

    9380028709; 9789380028705, $11.99

    This illustrated biography written by Lewis Helfand and illustrated by Sachin Nagar "presents the facts about Mother Teresa, born Agnes Gonxha Bojaxhiu in Macedonia in 1910. The book describes her decision to become a nun, her early work in Europe, and her path to teaching at a convent in India. From there it covers, in greater detail, her life among the poor and sick in Calcutta, and the foundation of Mother Teresa's worldwide charitable order." (Publisher's Weekly)

    Nelson Mandela: the unconquerable soul. Lewis Helfand. Kalyani Navyug Media Pvt LTD 2011 115 p.

Grades: 8 9 10

    1. Biographical graphic novels; 2. Mandela, Nelson, 1918-2013; 3. South Africa — History

    9380741162; 9789380741161, $12.99

                   LC 2012374765

    This book is a graphic novel biography of Nelson Mandela. It "includes a brief history of 20th-century South Africa along with a full account of Mandela's full life. . . . [B]lack, white, and gray illustrations are" included. "Endnotes include a glossary and additional facts about South Africa." (School Library Journal)

Herge

    ★ The **adventures** of Tintin, vol. 1: Tintin in America, Cigars of the Pharaoh, The Blue Lotus. Little, Brown 1994 192p. Illustration

Grades: 4 5 6 7 8 9   **741.5; Fic**

    1. Adventure graphic novels; 2. Tintin (Fictional character); 3. Graphic novels

    0-316-35940-8, $18.99

    Tintin, the heroic boy reporter from France, travels to America where he outwits gangsters in Chicago of the 1930s and adventures in the Wild West; sails the Mediterranean Sea with faithful dog Snowy and finds himself in a mystery involving a movie tycoon, drugs, and cigars in an ancient Egyptian tomb; then he travels to India to finally solve the mystery. This Little, Brown edition reprints some of the early Tintin adventures published in the 1930s in a 3-in-1 volume. This is the first in a series that reprints most of the Tintin stories by Herge. Librarians and teachers should note that the books retain some stereotypical depictions of people of other cultures and remember that these were acceptable and expected at the time of original publication.

Tintin and the Picaros. Little, Brown 1978 62p. Illustration
Grades: 4 5 6 7 8 9   **741.5; Fic**
1. Adventure graphic novels; 2. Humorous graphic novels; 3. Tintin (Fictional character); 4. Graphic novels
0-316-35849-5, $10.99
LC 77-090973
Tintin and his friends rescue prima donna Bianca Castafiore while trying to help restore their friend Alcazar to power in San Theodoros - but they'll have to defeat General Tapioca and his troops to do it.

Tintin in Tibet. Little, Brown 1978 62p. Illustration
Grades: 4 5 6 7 8 9   **741.5; Fic**
1. Adventure graphic novels; 2. Humorous graphic novels; 3. Tintin (Fictional character); 4. Graphic novels
0-316-35839-8, $10.99
LC 80-191368
Tintin, Snowy, and Captain Haddock trek through the snow-covered Himalayas to rescue their friend Chang from the hands of an abominable snowman.

Tintin: The Broken Ear. Little, Brown 1978 62p. Illustration
Grades: 4 5 6 7 8 9   **741.5; Fic**
1. Adventure graphic novels; 2. Humorous graphic novels; 3. Tintin (Fictional character); 4. Graphic novels
0-316-35850-9, $10.99
LC 77-090970
A fetish which originally belonged to the Arumbayas tribe in San Theodoros is stolen from a museum, then returned; soon Tintin discovers that the returned fetish is a forgery. When he follows the trail of the stolen fetish, it leads him and Snowy to South America and to San Theodoros, where he gets caught in the middle of a civil war. Tintin gets into all kinds of trouble even as he tries to find out why so many people want the fetish.

★ **Tintin:** The Calculus Affair. Little, Brown 1976 62p. Illustration
Grades: 4 5 6 7 8 9   **741.5; Fic**
1. Adventure graphic novels; 2. Humorous graphic novels; 3. Tintin (Fictional character); 4. Graphic novels
0-316-35847-9, $10.99
LC 76-13280
Unscrupulous Bordurians have kidnapped Professor Calculus, and Tintin, Snowy, and Captain Haddock are soon on the trail again, to rescue their friend. It's no easy task to rescue the Professor and save his fantastic invention; spies are everywhere, and Calculus lies deep in the fortress of Bakhine. But the Bordurians now have to deal with Tintin ...

Tintin: Cigars of the Pharaoh. Little, Brown 1975 62p. Illustration
Grades: 4 5 6 7 8 9   **741.5; Fic**
1. Adventure graphic novels; 2. Humorous graphic novels; 3. Tintin (Fictional character); 4. Graphic novels
0-316-35836-3, $10.99
LC 74-021620
Tintin and Snowy are on a cruise to Egypt when they happen to meet Professor Sophocles Sarcophagus (the first

of Tintin's absent-minded professors) and join his expedition. But they become embroiled in a complicated scheme involving a fakir, cigars marked with an unusual brand, and Rajijah, the poison of madness. Tintin meets the detectives Thompson and Thomson as well as the movie mogul Rastapopolous. Herge wrote this book in 1932 then revised it in 1955.

Tintin: Destination Moon. Little, Brown 1976 62p. Illustration
Grades: 4 5 6 7 8 9   **741.5; Fic**
1. Adventure graphic novels; 2. Humorous graphic novels; 3. Tintin (Fictional character); 4. Graphic novels
0-316-35845-2, $10.99
LC 76-013279
Professor Calculus has designed a rocket for an expedition to the Moon. He summons Tintin and Captain Haddock (along with Snowy) to the country of Syldavia, where he's been working. Despite spies being everywhere and mysterious explosions and other problems, the rocket is soon ready to launch, and Professor Calculus wants Tintin and Captain Haddock to go with him - to the Moon.

Tintin: Explorers On the Moon. Little, Brown 1976 62p. Illustration
Grades: 4 5 6 7 8 9   **741.5; Fic**
1. Adventure graphic novels; 2. Humorous graphic novels; 3. Tintin (Fictional character); 4. Graphic novels
0-316-35846-0, $10.99
LC 76-013297
Tintin, Captain Haddock, and Prof. Calculus are headed for the Moon when they discover Thompson and Thomson, who had inadvertently stowed away on the rocket. But there's more trouble when they land on the Moon and go exploring, for Colonel Jorgen is there, another stowaway, and he wants revenge on Tintin.

Tintin: Flight 714. Little, Brown 1975 62p. Illustration
Grades: 4 5 6 7 8 9   **741.5; Fic**
1. Adventure graphic novels; 2. Humorous graphic novels; 3. Tintin (Fictional character); 4. Graphic novels
0-316-35837-1, $10.99
LC 74-021623
Tintin, Snowy, Captain Haddock, and Professor Calculus land in Djakarta and meet millionaire Mr. Carreidas, who invites them to fly to Sydney with him in his prototype jet. They find themselves in the middle of a plot to steal their new friend's fortune, and they decide to stop it.

Tintin: Land of Black Gold. Little, Brown 1975 62p. Illustration
Grades: 4 5 6 7 8 9   **741.5; Fic**
1. Adventure graphic novels; 2. Humorous graphic novels; 3. Tintin (Fictional character); 4. Graphic novels
0-316-35844-4, $10.99
LC 75-007896
The world is on the brink of a crisis when car engines begin to explode without explanation or warning; someone has been tampering with the oil supply. Tintin travels to the Middle East to investigate, and he helps Sheik Ben Kalish Ezab, whose son is kidnapped by one of Tintin's old enemies.

Tintin: Prisoners of the Sun. Little, Brown 1975 62p. Illustration

Grades: 4 5 6 7 8 9   **741.5; Fic**
1. Adventure graphic novels; 2. Humorous graphic novels; 3. Tintin (Fictional character); 4. Graphic novels
0-316-35843-6, $10.99

LC 75-007897

Tintin, Snowy, and Captain Haddock travel to Peru to rescue Professor Calculus. They meet Indian boy Zorrino, and they must travel into the jungle to the Andes to find their old friend.

Tintin: Red Rackham's Treasure. Little, Brown 1974 62p. Illustration

Grades: 4 5 6 7 8 9   **741.5; Fic**
1. Adventure graphic novels; 2. Humorous graphic novels; 3. Tintin (Fictional character); 4. Graphic novels
0-316-35834-7, $10.99

LC 73-021253

Tintin and his friends search for the pirate booty left by Captain Haddock's pirate ancestor. They're aided in their quest by the hard-of-hearing inventor, Professor Calculus.

Tintin: The Castafiore Emerald. Little, Brown 1975 62p. Illustration

Grades: 4 5 6 7 8 9   **741.5; Fic**
1. Adventure graphic novels; 2. Humorous graphic novels; 3. Tintin (Fictional character); 4. Graphic novels
0-316-35842-8, $10.99

Tintin and Snowy investigate when prima donna Bianca Castafiore's jewels are stolen, in particular, her emerald.

Tintin: The Seven Crystal Balls. Little, Brown 1975 62p. Illustration

Grades: 4 5 6 7 8 9   **741.5; Fic**
1. Adventure graphic novels; 2. Humorous graphic novels; 3. Tintin (Fictional character); 4. Graphic novels
0-316-35840-1, $10.99

LC 75-007921

Tragedy strikes the members of an expedition which returned after violating Incan burial chambers; the seven men fall into comas, one by one, and fragments of crystal are found by their bodies. Tintin, Professor Calculus, Captain Haddock, and Thompson and Thomson investigate, but then Calculus disappears - he's been kidnapped.

Herriman, George
★ **Krazy** & Ignatz, 1937-1938: Shifting Sands Dusts its Cheeks in Powdered Beauty. Fantagraphics Books 2006 176p. Illustration

Grades: 7 8 9 10 11 12 Adult   **741.5; Fic**
1. Humor graphic novels; 2. Krazy Kat (Fictional character); 3. Graphic novels
978-1-56097-734-6, $19.95

Krazy Kat is a love story, focusing on the relationships of its three main characters. Krazy Kat adored Ignatz Mouse. Ignatz Mouse simply tolerated Krazy Kat, except for recurrent onsets of targeted tumescence, which found expression in the fast delivery of bricks to Krazy's cranium. Offisa Pup loved Krazy and sought to protect "her" (Herriman always maintained that Krazy was genderless) by throwing Ignatz in jail. Each of the characters was ignorant of the others' true motivations, and this simple structure

allowed Herriman to build entire worlds of meaning into the actions, building thematic depth and sweeping his readers up by the looping verbal rhythms of Krazy & Co.'s unique dialogue. Most of these strips in this volume have not seen print since originally running in Hearst newspapers over 70 years ago. This seventh volume collecting all of the comic strips, is the second one to be published in color; Herriman started doing the strip in color in 1935. Other than the brick-throwing, this book has no violence, foul language, or any other usual objectionable content. Krazy Kat cartoons were made for children in the mid-1930s, and there was a Krazy Kat animated series which aired on television in the mid-1960s.

Heuser, Randy
Land of Sokmunster. [by] Mike Kunkel and Randy Heuser. Astonish Factory 2003 60p. Illustration

Grades: 2 3 4 5 6 7 8   **741.5; Fic**
1. Adventure graphic novels; 2. Graphic novels
0-972125-92-2, $14.95

Sam dives into the family dryer's lint trap when a sock comes out and steals a rare nickel then dives back in. He finds himself in a land where the lost socks go and learns that the sokmunsters don't care much for humans. When he and a sokmunster named Spike set out to rescue King Jacque's daughter from the evil Moth King, Sam starts to learn about friendship, trust, and forgiveness.

Heuvel, Eric
A **family** secret. [English translation, Lorraine T. Miller]. Farrar, Straus and Giroux 2009 62p. Illustration

Grades: 7 8 9 10 11 12   **741.5; Fic**
1. Grandmothers; 2. Holocaust, 1933-1945; 3. Jews; 4. Graphic novels
0-374-32271-6; 978-0-374-42265-3 (pa), $9.99; 0-374-42265-6 (pa); 978-0-374-32271-7, $18.99

LC 2009-13943

While searching his Dutch grandmother's attic for yard sale items, Jeroen finds a scrapbook which leads Gran to tell of her experiences as a girl living in Amsterdam during the Holocaust, when her father was a Nazi sympathizer and Esther, her Jewish best friend, disappeared

This is a "moving graphic novel. . . . The art is in ink and watercolor, with very clear, highly detailed panels. . . . [A] gripping story." Booklist

Original Dutch edition, 2003

Anne Frank House

Hicks, Faith Erin
Friends with boys. Faith Erin Hicks. First Second 2012 Un Illustration

Grades: 6 7 8 9 10   **741.5**
1. Ghost stories; 2. Teenagers — Fiction; 3. Graphic novels
9781596435568, $16.99

LC 2011030470

In this graphic novel, "[the] youngest of four siblings and the only girl, Maggie is both excited and worried about starting high school after being home-schooled her whole life. . . . As Maggie makes friends with a perky indie girl named Lucy and her mysterious brother, Alistair, she broods over the loss of her mother, who recently left the family without much of an explanation, and tries to figure out what the ghost wants from her." (Bulletin of the Center for Children's Books)

★ The **Nameless** City. Faith Erin Hicks; color by Jordie Bellaire. First Second 2016 240 p. Color; Illustration
Grades: 5 6 7 8 9 10   741.5; Fic
1. Cities and towns — Fiction; 2. Fantasy graphic novels; 3. Friendship — Fiction; 4. Survival — Fiction; 5. Survival skills — Fiction
1626721564; 9781626721562, $14.99; 9781626721579
                                                      LC 2015020651
"Every nation that invades the City gives it a new name. . . . The natives don't let themselves get caught up in the unending wars. To them, their home is the Nameless City. . . . Kaidu is . . . a Dao born and bred—a member of the latest occupying nation. Rat is a native of the Nameless City. At first, she hates Kai for everything he stands for, but his love of his new home may be the one thing that can bring these two unlikely friends together." (Publisher's note)

"With comprehensive world building, well-rounded characters, and entertaining action, this expertly executed story will find a home with a wide variety of readers, all of whom will be eagerly awaiting the next installment." Booklist

★ The **war** at Ellsmere. Slave Labor Graphics 2008 156p. Illustration
Grades: 5 7 8 9 10 11   741.5; Fic
1. Friendship; 2. Humorous graphic novels; 3. School stories; 4. Graphic novels
1-59362-140-X; 978-1-59362-140-7, $12.95
Juniper is the newest scholarship student at the prestigious Ellsmere Academy; she wanted to attend there in order to increase her chances of getting into a good medical school. She's on scholarship because her mom has had to raise her alone since her father died when she was young. Jun makes one friend at Ellsmere, Cassie, who calls herself the cliche of the poor little rich girl. Wealthy Emily calls Cassie "Orphan" because her parents ignore her, and chooses to call Jun "Project," as in Headmistress Ms. Bishop's latest project. Emily is also determined to get rid of Jun, especially when Jun encourages Cassie to work harder and even win the extra credit essay contest. Now it's war, or as Jun puts it, "It's like Upstairs Downstairs meets Lord of the Flies. In plaid skirts. And sweater vests." There's one incident when Jun punches Emily in the face.

"Hicks gives readers enough tension and quirky turns to satisfy and pleasantly surprise." Booklist

Zombies calling. SLG Publishing 2007 104p. Illustration
Grades: 8 9 10 11 12 Adult   741.5; Fic
1. Horror graphic novels; 2. Humorous graphic novels; 3. Zombies; 4. Graphic novels
978-1-59362-079-0, $9.95
Anglophile/zombie movie fan/college student Joss is going crazy in the middle of exams week, but when her college campus is overrun with actual zombies, she knows what to do. With her roommate Sonnet and their buddy Robyn, Joss uses the Rules gleaned from years of watching zombie movies to fight the undead hordes. When the first rule is that the ordinary person suddenly becomes a total ass-kicking cool fighter able to beat off zombies with no

fighting lessons, yeah, it's cool. Except the zombies just keep coming and coming. . . . The book has some harsh language and lots of black and white zombie fighting action without gore.

Hidaka, Banri
I Hate You More than Anyone! Volume 1. DC Comics/CMX 2007 192p. Illustration
Grades: 7 8 9 10 11 12   741.5; Fic
1. Humorous graphic novels; 2. Romance graphic novels; 3. Shojo manga; 4. Graphic novels
978-1-4012-1310-7, $9.99
Kazuha Akiyoshi is the eldest of six children. She's very responsible and also irresistibly cute, but she is something of a tomboy who has never allowed her romantic side to show throught. Then she meets Mizushima, the first guy to treat her like a girl. He's Kazuha's first crush, but does Mizushima feel the same way about her" And then there's Sugimoto, an older guy who's determined to make himself an important part of her life, only he's the one she hates more than anyone.

Higashiyama, Kazuko
Tactics Vol. 1. Tokyopop 2007 Un Illustration
Grades: 7 8 9 10 11 12   741.5; Fic
1. Fantasy graphic novels; 2. Manga; 3. Supernatural graphic novels; 4. Graphic novels
978-1-59816-960-7, $9.99
Ever since Kantarou was a child, he has been able to see and talk to various spirits. But now that Kantarou's all grown up and a folklore scholar living in the Taisho period (1912-1926), he moonlights as an exorcist solving the problems of ghosts and demons...all with the help of Haruka, the legendary demon-eating tengu. Throw in some supernatural elements, a bit of Japanese mythology, and plenty of pretty boys... There's some harsh language, but very little violence. This first volume includes language and culture notes.
The first two volumes of this series were originally published by ADV Manga in 2004-2005.

Hiiragi, Aoi
Baron: The Cat Returns. Viz/Studio Ghibli Library 2005 222p. Illustration
Grades: 3 4 5 6 7 8 9   741.5; Fic
1. Cats; 2. Fantasy graphic novels; 3. Kodomo manga; 4. Manga; 5. Graphic novels
1-59116-956-9, $9.99
Awkward teen Haru saves a cat from being run over one afternoon, but she never expected the trouble it would cause. He is a cat prince, and his father wants to bring Haru into the kingdom of the cats to be his son's bride. A mysterious voice sends Haru to the Cat Office, where she meets Baron, a toy cat come to life, the fat cat Muta, and a magical crow. When the cats come and bear Haru to the kingdom of the cats, the three friends follow to help bring Haru back home.
This one-volume manga was the basis for the feature-length anime (Japanese animated film) called "The Cat Returns," which was produced by Studio Ghibli, the animation studio run by famed anime director Hayao Miyazaki and some partners.

Himuro, Isao
★ **Edu-Manga:** Albert Einstein. Art by Kotaro Iwasaki. Digital Manga Publishing 2006 144p. Illustration
Grades: 3 4 5 6 7 8 9 **92; 741.5**
1. Biographical graphic novels; 2. Einstein, Albert, 1879-1955; 3. Manga; 4. Graphic novels
1-56970-975-0, $9.95
At the age of 26, Einstein published his groundbreaking Theory of Relativity, revolutionizing the world of physics forever. Today, he is considered a true genius. From his boyhood quest for answers to some of science's most challenging questions, to his search to uncover the mysteries of the universe, Einstein's work led to both the formulation of his theories and his place as one of the most important scientists in history. Astro Boy and his friends introduce Einstein's story and present the Q&A that provides more information. The book also includes a timeline of Einstein's life.

Hina
Di Gi Charat Theater: Leave It to Piyoko!. Broccoli International USA, Inc. 2004 206p. Illustration
Grades: 3 4 5 6 7 8 9 **741.5; Fic**
1. Humorous graphic novels; 2. Manga; 3. Graphic novels
1-932480-17-X, $9.99
Piyoko has grand evil plans to kidnap the princess of Di Gi Charat, Dejiko, and hold her for ransom. The people of her poor Planet Analogue are all counting on her and the Black Gema Gema Gang. She and her loyal henchmen"Rik, Ky, and Coo—are scheming and plotting, but for some reason her grand plans seem to keep falling apart. Take a look into the daily lives of the Black Gema Gema Gang as they figure out their plans to kidnap Dejiko while trying to survive on the little money they have left.

Hinds, Gareth
★ **Beowulf**. Adapted and illustrated by Gareth Hinds. Candlewick Press 2007 Un Illustration
Grades: 8 9 10 11 12 Adult **741.5; Fic**
1. Adventure graphic novels; 2. Beowulf; 3. Monsters; 4. Graphic novels
978-0-7636-3022-5, $21.99; 0-7636-3022-5; 978-0-7636-3023-2 (pa); 0-7636-3023-3 (pa), $9.99
LC 2006-49023
Graphic novel adaptation of the Old English epic poem, Beowulf
"For fantasy fans both young and old, this makes an ideal introduction to a story without which the entire fantasy genre would look very different; many scenes may be too intense for very young readers." Publ Wkly

King Lear. A play by William Shakespeare; adapted and illustrated by Gareth Hinds. Candlewick Press 2009 123p. Illustration
Grades: 7 8 9 10 11 12 **741.5; 822.3**
978-0-7636-4343-0, $22.99; 0-7636-4343-2; 978-0-7636-4344-7 (pa), $11.99; 0-7636-4344-0 (pa)
"Employing a range of artistic styles that convey dramatic mood, the artist begins the play almost as a fairy tale, featuring bright, softly washed drawings. Once Cordelia is cast out and things sour, the images become darker and more compact. As the king descends into madness, the art becomes downright menacing, with Lear appearing as a jagged, ghostly figure drawn with white pencil on a dark background." (Kirkus)

Macbeth. Adapted and illustrated by Gareth Hinds. Candlewick Press 2015 152 p. Color illustration; Color; Map
Grades: 8 9 10 11 12 **741.5**
1. Kings and rulers — Fiction; 2. Murder — Fiction; 3. Scotland — Fiction; 4. Graphic novels; 5. Shakespeare, William, 1564-1616 — Adaptations
0763678023; 9780763669430; 9780763678029, $12.99
LC 2014939338
"Set against the moody backdrop of eleventh-century Scotland, [illustrator] Gareth Hinds's . . . interpretation takes readers into the claustrophobic mind of a man driven mad by ambition. An evil seed takes root in the mind of Macbeth, a general in the king's army, when three witches tell him he will one day be king." (Publisher's note)
"Though many lines of the original are intact, Hinds does undertake some changes to make this version more accessible to contemporary readers, and a closing note addresses those alterations. Students struggling to find an entry point into the Scottish play should look no further than this entertaining and elucidating volume." Booklist

The **merchant** of Venice: a play. By William Shakespeare; adapted and illustrated by Gareth Hinds. Candlewick Press 2008 68p. Illustration
Grades: 8 9 10 11 12 Adult **822.3; 741.5**
1. Shakespeare, William, 1564-1616 — Adaptations
978-0-7636-3024-9, $21.99; 978-0-7636-3025-6 (pa), $11.99
LC 2007-938349
Hinds uses a sketchy art style and blue and gray tones to illustrate his graphic adaptation of Shakespeare's controversial play. He sets the play in modern Venice and uses more modern language, including prose, at the beginning of the play and then gradually returns to Shakespeare's original language for the courtroom scenes. The play tells the story of a debt owed to a Jewish merchant of Venice, of a strong-willed young woman who is determined to choose her own husband, and of the quest to save a young man from the fate of having a pound of flesh cut from him.
"Fans of the play will find this an intriguing adaptation." Publ Wkly

The **most** excellent and lamentable tragedy of Romeo & Juliet: a play by William Shakespeare. By William Shakespeare, adapted and illustrated by Gareth Hinds. Candlewick Press 2013 128 p.
Grades: 7 8 9 10 **741.5**
1. Shakespeare, William, 1564-1616 — Adaptations; 2. Shakespeare, William, 1564-1616 — Tragedies; 3. Graphic novels
0763659487; 0763668079; 9780763659486, $21.99; 9780763668075, $12.99
LC 2012950561
This book by Gareth Hinds presents a graphic novel adaptation of William Shakespeare's play "Romeo and Juliet." "The most notable change between this story and Shakespeare's original is the creative license that Hinds takes with ethnicity—he makes the characters of African,

Indian, and Caucasian descent in order to promote the universality of the story. The Shakespearean language is abridged but not adapted into contemporary English." (School Library Journal)

"Cleaving to Shakespeare's words and dramatic arc, Hinds (The Merchant of Venice) creates another splendid graphic novel, tracing each scene in taut, coherent dialogue. The characters, in period dress modified by a few more contemporary touches, are poignantly specific yet universal. Hinds delivers the play's essence and beauty, its glorious language, furious conflict, yearning love, and wrenching tragedy." (Horn Book)

The **Odyssey:** a graphic novel. By Gareth Hinds. Candlewick Press 2010 248 p. Color illustration
Grades: 7 8 9 10 11 12 Adult $\qquad$ **741.5**
1. Greek mythology; 2. Homer; 3. Mythology, Greek — Juvenile literature; 4. Odyssey; 5. Graphic novels
0763642665; 0763642681; 9780763642662, $24.99; 9780763642686
$\qquad$ LC 2010007512
"Retells, in graphic novel format, Homer's epic tale of Odysseus, the ancient Greek hero who encounters witches and other obstacles on his journey home after fighting in the Trojan War." (Publisher's note)

Hino, Matsuri
Captive hearts, vol. 1. Viz Media/Shojo Beat 2008 200p. Illustration
Grades: 7 8 9 10 11 12 $\qquad$ **741.5; Fic**
1. Manga; 2. Romance graphic novels; 3. Shojo manga; 4. Graphic novels
978-1-4215-1932-6, $8.99
Carefree college student Megumi Kuroishi finds his life turned upside down when the last surviving member of the Kogami family, teenage Suzuka, is found in China. That's when Megumi learns of the curse against his family, that they will serve the Kogami family for 100 generations. Whenever he looks into Suzuka's eyes, the curse overwhelms him and he becomes far too subservient; complicating matters is the fact that he does indeed find Suzuka captivating. She likes him, too, but can't trust his feelings because of the curse. The book includes two short romance stories. In "Real Storm," shy high school student Io Ayase has a huge crush on Kuji-sensei, who only wants to help her learn to deal with a pervy stalker. In "Let Time Freeze," Ayu and Yuji are childhood friends now in their senior year of high school, and she doesn't want the year to end; when it does, Yuji will go to university in Tokyo while Ayu must remain behind. Now that she loves him, the impending separation already hurts.

MeruPuri: Marchen Prince Vol. 1. Viz Media/Shojo Beat 2005 Un Illustration
Grades: 8 9 10 11 12 $\qquad$ **741.5; Fic**
1. Fantasy graphic novels; 2. Manga; 3. Romance graphic novels; 4. Shojo manga; 5. Graphic novels
1-4215-0120-1, $8.99
All high-school freshman Airi Hoshina ever wanted was to someday live in a cozy home with a loving husband, and find joy in the little things in life. As a result, she makes it her daily mission to get to school on time because school legend has it that the longer one's non-tardy streak is, the

better boyfriend one will find. But, on the way to school one morning, Airi drops her mirror, one that had been passed down to her through generations, and suddenly finds herself in a bizarre situation. Never in her wildest dreams did she expect to meet Aram, a little boy from a magical kingdom, to have emerged from the mirror in the short time it took her to track it down. The series includes some mild sexual situations.

Hitch, Bryan
Bryan Hitch's Ultimate Comics Studio. Impact 2010 128p. Illustration
Grades: 7 8 9 10 $\qquad$ **741.5; 741**
1. Captain America (Fictional character); 2. Fantastic Four (Fictional characters)
978-1-6006-1327-2, $24.99; 1-6006-1327-6
"The book is a skillful blend of text, photos of the artist at work, annotated sketches, and finished illustrations. It is a visual treat in its own right, with well-organized subject matter complemented by thoughtful composition and lavish photography and art. Hitch considers himself to be primarily a storyteller, and he delves into the philosophy and technique of visual storytelling. He gives a glimpse into his thought processes, offering 'guided tours' of sketches by walking readers through his work, starting with analyzing script to making decisions regarding action, panels, rhythm, and sample initial sketches." (School Library Journal)

Hiwatari, Saki
Tower of the Future, Vol. 1. DC Comics/CMX 2005 192p. Illustration
Grades: 8 9 10 11 12 $\qquad$ **741.5; Fic**
1. Fantasy graphic novels; 2. Romance graphic novels; 3. Shojo manga; 4. Graphic novels
978-1-4012-0814-1, $9.99
Takeru's mother has died, and then he finds out that his half-English father has a daughter in England; on her deathbed, Takeru's mother asked that Hyoju be allowed to move to Japan and live with them. Shocked and upset, Takeru's first reaction is anger and disgust. He then meets Ichigo, a girl his age upon whom he immediately has a crush, and a strange little boy named Zen who knows way too much about Takeru. As the series progresses, Takeru learns a little more about Zen and why he knows so much. Also, a fantasy element comes in as Takeru learns about a parasitic being called Noize, and Ichigo's adult older brother has an unhealthy fixation on her.

Hoena, B. A.
Beyond the black hole. Illustrated by Steve Harpster.. Stone Arch Books 2009 40p. Illustration
Grades: 2 3 4 5 6 7 $\qquad$ **741.5; Fic**
1. Humorous graphic novels; 2. Science fiction graphic novels; 3. Graphic novels
978-1-4342-0759-3, $21.26
$\qquad$ LC 2008-6709
Eek and Ack zip through space in their rocket-powered washing machine ship and find a black hole; when they get too close, they get sucked in and spat out on the other side of space. Of course, being in a new universe means they should find another planet Earth for Ack to conquer (well, that's what Ack thinks); and they do find one, but it's pink. Then

they encounter two fuzzy pink creatures called Zeek and Zack, who also have a rocket-powered washing machine ship, and they defend Zearth. The book includes a short glossary (with mostly humorous definitions) and some information about black holes.

Part of the Graphic Sparks Eek and Ack series

Eek and Ack vs the Wolfman. Stone Arch Books 2009 40p. Illustration
Grades: 3 4 5 6 7 8   **741.5; Fic**
1. Humorous graphic novels; 2. Science fiction graphic novels; 3. Werewolves; 4. Graphic novels
978-1-4342-1189-1, $21.26
LC 2008-32057

Eek and Ack invade Earth yet again, this time arriving on Halloween, so they blend in with the trick-or-treaters. Then they run into a strange, furry, monstrous creature that chases them and bites Ack. When they take off for space, the creature stays on their ship (that looks like a washing machine), and he changes from monster wolf to human kid and back again. The aliens land back on Earth, get rid of the Wolfman, and fly home, but something starts happening to Ack. The book includes information about werewolves, discussion questions, and a glossary.

Part of the Graphic Sparks line, the Eek & Ack series

Matthew Henson: Arctic Adventurer. Capstone Press 2005 32p. Illustration
Grades: 3 4 5 6 7 8 9   **741.5; 910; 92**
1. African American explorers — Biography; 2. Biographical graphic novels; 3. Henson, Matthew Alexander, 1866-1955; 4. North Pole — Discover and exploration; 5. Graphic novels
0-7368-4634-4, $25.26
LC 2005005774

In graphic novel format, this book tells the life story of African American explorer Matthew Henson and his expedition to the North Pole with Robert Peary. The book includes additional facts about Henson, a bibliography, and a list of books for further reading.

Part of the Graphic Biographies series.

Perseus and Medusa. By Blake A. Hoena; illustrated by Daniel Perez. Stone Arch Books 2009 72p. Illustration
(Graphic revolve)
Grades: 4 5 6 7 8 9   **741.5; Fic**
1. Greek mythology; 2. Monsters; 3. Graphic novels
978-1-4342-1170-5 (lib bdg), $23.93; 1-4342-1170-3 (lib bdg); 978-1-4342-1394-5 (pa), $6.95; 1-4342-1386-2 (pa)
LC 2008-32065

Perseus is the son of Danae, daughter of the King of Argos, and of Zeus; due to a prophecy that Perseus would cause his death, the King puts his daughter and grandson into a wooden chest and has it cast out to sea. A fisherman rescues them, and Perseus grows up unaware of his royal lineage. King Polydectes wants Danae for himself and sends Perseus on what should be an impossible task that will kill him he wants Perseus to bring him the head of Medusa, whose gaze turns anyone into stone. Perseus enjoys the guidance and advice of gods and goddesses to accomplish his task

This title has a "solid awareness of how to balance visual depiction and expository captions, evident right from the striking prologue. While the artwork is cartoony and the dialogue deliberately casual and modern, the style doesn't prevent the artist from providing heroic vistas, or the author from slipping in a couple of humorous moments, and the action is sufficiently thrilling." SLJ

The **puzzling** Pluto plot. By Blake A. Hoena; illustrated by Steve Harpster.. Stone Arch Books 2008 40p. Illustration
Grades: 3 4 5 6 7   **741.5; Fic**
1. Extraterrestrial beings; 2. Humorous graphic novels; 3. Science fiction graphic novels; 4. Graphic novels
978-1-4342-0452-3, $21.26; 978-1-4342-0502-5 (pa), $6.95
LC 2007-31255

Eek and Ack, the young aliens from the Goo Galaxy, have hatched yet another plan to zap the Earth, but they think that an ice giant is Earth. Meanwhile, Professor Hubble T. Scope has calculated that Pluto is an ice giant planet much larger than Earth. After Eek and Ack get done zapping the wrong planet, Scope sadly learns that Pluto is much, much smaller in fact, hardly a planet at all.

Part of the Graphic Sparks series, an Eek & Ack adventure.

Holm, Jennifer L.
Babymouse for president. By Jennifer L. Holm & Matthew Holm. Random House 2012 89 p.
Grades: 3 4 5 6   **741.5**
1. Elections — Fiction; 2. Mice — Fiction; 3. School stories; 4. Schools — Fiction
0375867805; 9780375867804, $6.99; 9780375967801
LC 2011024118

In this book by Jennifer L. Holm and Matt Holm, part of the Babymouse series, "it's election season and if anyone knows what . . . the student council needs, it's Babymouse. The only trouble is, everyone else is running for President, too — even Babymouse's locker! Will Felicia Furrypaws turn out the meangirl coalition? Does Babymouse have what it takes to become the voice of the people? (Publisher's note)

Babymouse: cupcake tycoon. By Jennifer L. Holm & Matthew Holm. Random House 2010 89p.
Grades: 3 4 5 6   **741.5; 741**
978-0-375-86573-2 (pa), $6.99; 0-375-86573-X (pa)
"It's champagne wishes and cupcake dreams for Babymouse! The school library is having a fund-raiser, and

Babymouse is determined to raise the most money and WIN the GRAND PRIZE. Or . . . er, to help the school! The competition is fierce, but Babymouse will stop at nothing to get what she wants, even if it means outselling every last kid in school . . . including her nefarious nemesis, Felicia Furrypaws." (Publisher's note)

Babymouse: Cupcake Tycoon ©
Jennifer L. Holm & Matthew Holm

Babymouse: heartbreaker. Random House 2006 91p.
Grades: 3 4 5 6 **741; Fic; 741.5**
1. Babymouse (Fictional character); 2. Humorous graphic novels; 3. Mice; 4. Valentine's Day
0-375-93798-6 (lib bdg), \$12.99; 0-375-83798-1 (pa), \$5.99; 978-0-375-93798-9 (lib bdg); 978-0-375-83798-2 (pa)

LC 2006-45418

"Romantic Babymouse . . . here finds her confidence shaken by the impending Valentine's Day dance at school. . . . The text and illustrations successfully differentiate between reality and daydreams, and there's a good amount of humor injected in both." Horn Book
Another title in the author's series about Babymouse

Babymouse: mad scientist. By Jennifer L. Holm & Matthew Holm. Random House 2011 91p. Illustration
Grades: 3 4 5 6
741.5; 741
978-0-375-96574-6 (lib bdg), \$12.99;
0-375-96574-2 (lib bdg);
978-0-375-86574-9 (pa), \$6.99; 0-375-86574-8 (pa)

LC 2009-47388

Babymouse: Mad Scientist ©
Jennifer L. Holm & Matthew Holm

"Babymouse decides to enter the science fair. She daydreams about science-fiction movies and television shows (Star Trek, The Attack of the 50-Foot Woman); fantasizes about winning the Nobel Prize; learns about the scientific method in class—and then she discovers an amoeba named Squish." (Booklist)

Babymouse: monster mash. Random House 2008 93p.
Grades: 3 4 5 6 **741; 741.5; Fic**
1. Halloween; 2. Humorous graphic novels; 3. Mice; 4. Graphic novels
978-0-375-93789-7 (lib bdg), \$11.99;
978-0-375-84387-7 (pa), \$5.99

LC 2008-08433

It's Halloween, and Babymouse loves dressing up in spooky costumes to go trick-or-treating with best buddy Wilson. Of course, Felicia has to say that girls must be pretty "It's a rule." Then Babymouse's mother tells her she can have a Halloween party, and when Felicia finds out, she bullies Babymouse into inviting her and orders her to go trick-or-treating with them. Felicia is not a nice kid on Halloween; she leads her cronies in teepeeing and egging houses. But at Babymouse's party, she decides to do things her way after all. For this Halloween volume, the color scheme doesn't include pink, but orange. Babymouse imagines herself in classic horror movie scenarios, but they shouldn't be too scary for most young readers.
Another title in the author's series about Babymouse

Babymouse: puppy love. [by] Jennifer L. Holm and Matthew Holm. Random House 2007 91p. Illustration
Grades: 3 4 5 6 **741.5**

978-0-375-93990-7 (lib bdg), \$12.99;
978-0-375-83990-0 (pa), \$5.99

LC 2007-61012

"Babymouse doesn't exactly have a great history with pets—even her goldfish ran away from home. But all that's about to change. Will Babymouse get the dog of her dreams? Will she ever find her missing fish?" (Publisher's note)

Babymouse: skater girl. [by] Jennifer L. Holm & Matthew Holm. Random House 2007 91p. Illustration
Grades: 3 4 5 6 **741.5; 741**
978-0-375-93989-1 (lib bdg); 0-375-93989-X (lib bdg); 978-0-375-83989-4 (pa), \$5.99; 0-375-83989-5 (pa)

LC 2006-50444

"Babymouse daydreams about being a medal-winning figure skater. She can almost hear the roar of the crowd, the fans cheering her name, the sportscasters' excitement. But when she's actually noticed by a professional coach and told she has talent, Babymouse develops a lust for glory . . . which is greatly tested by the harsh reality of before- and after-school practices, a ban on cupcakes, and no free time for friends." (Horn Book)

Babymouse: the musical. By Jennifer & Matthew Holm. Random House 2009 96p. Illustration
Grades: 3 4 5 6 **741.5; Fic**
1. Humorous graphic novels; 2. Mice; 3. School stories; 4. Graphic novels
978-0-375-93791-0, \$11.99; 978-0-375-84388-4 (pa), \$5.99

LC 2008-10891

The school is going to produce a musical, and Babymouse auditions. Unfortunately, she has a tendency to trip over her own two feet, and the lead role demands someone who can sing and dance. Nemesis Felicia wins the lead role, and Babymouse is her understudy, while new transfer student Henry Higgins (a British hedgehog) has the male lead role. As Babymouse gets through school days (complete with the torture of dodgeball) and rehearsals, she daydreams Broadway musicals.
Another title in the author's series about Babymouse

Camp Babymouse. Random House 2007 95p. Illustration
Grades: 2 3 4 5 6 **741.5; Fic**
1. Babymouse (Fictional character); 2. Humorous graphic novels; 3. Graphic novels
978-0-375-93988-4 (lib bdg), \$12.99;
978-0-375-83988-7 (pa), \$5.99

Babymouse is looking forward to Camp Wild Whiskers, and two weeks of fresh air, fun, and friendship. She can't wait for the adventures to start. All that she has to do is relax and make sure she doesn't get lost in the wilderness. What could possibly go wrong? Will camp be all that Babymouse dreams of" Problems such as losing points by spilling punch, tipping her canoe during the canoe race, accidentally starting a really big fire, and her cabin mates complaining that she'll put them in last place make her wonder if she should even be there.

★ **Sunny** side up. Jennifer L. Holm & Matthew Holm; with color by Lark Pien. Graphix 2015 224 p. Illustration
Grades: 3 4 5 6 **741.5; Fic**

1. Adventure fiction; 2. Florida — Fiction; 3. Friendship — Fiction; 4. Grandfathers — Fiction; 5. Summer — Fiction
0545741653; 9780545741651, $23.99

LC 2014957906

In this book, by Jennifer L. Holm, illustrated by Matthew Holm, "Sunny Lewin has been packed off to Florida to live with her grandfather for the summer. At first she thought Florida might be fun. . . . But the place where Gramps lives is no amusement park. It's full of . . . old people. Really old people. Luckily, Sunny isn't the only kid around. She meets Buzz, a boy who is completely obsessed with comic books, and soon they're having adventures of their own." (Publisher's note)

"Woven into the Florida frolic though, through dated flashback images, is the real reason for Sunny's last-minute visit: her older brother is struggling with addiction, and Sunny thinks she got him in trouble. Though Sunny will appeal to all kinds of readers, an authors' note shares the Holms' hope to let kids in similar situations know that it's OK to feel sad and to talk about it. Clear dialogue bubbles, plenty of wordless spreads, and Matthew's cartoons and beach-umbrella color palette keep Sunny's story an upbeat one that readers will easily stick with." Booklist

Holm, Matthew

Babymouse #11: dragonslayer. [by] Jennifer L. Holm & Matthew Holm. Random House Childrens Books 2009 96p. Illustration
Grades: 3 4 5 6   **741.5; Fic**
1. Babymouse (Fictional character); 2. Humorous graphic novels; 3. Mathematics; 4. Mice
978-0-375-95712-3, $12.99; 978-0-375-85712-6 (pa), $5.99

LC 2008-51110

Babymouse loves to read, and to daydream about the books she reads, but she does NOT do well in math. In fact, she's just received an F on a test, and her teacher decides to have her join the Mathletes in order to make up for it. The Mathletes compete with other school teams in math competitions, and they have wanted to win the Golden Slide Rule for a long time. A competing team called the Owlgarithms have won it year after year. However, Babymouse seems to be more of a liability than a new asset for the team. She suffers through lunchtime practice sessions and much prefers to daydream of adventures with The Lion, the Witch, and the Wardrobe or The Hobbit rather than do math. Then, at the math competition, events conspire to make her the team's only hope in a final round against one of the Owlgorithms. The book is illustrated in the usual black, white and pink, and it might, just might, help some girls think of math as something they can do well (after all, if Babymouse can compete in a math tournament, maybe they can, too).

Cover title: Babymouse Dragonslayer

Babymouse burns rubber!. By Jennifer L. Holm & Matthew Holm. Random House 2010 91p. Illustration
Grades: 3 4 5 6   **741.5; 741**
978-0-375-95713-0 (lib bdg), $12.99; 0-375-95713-8 (lib bdg); 978-0-375-85713-3 (pa), $5.99; 0-375-85713-3 (pa)

LC 2009018819

*Babymouse Burns Rubber ©
Jennifer L. Holm & Matthew Holm*

"Babymouse dreams of glory in the soap box derby but doesn't put much effort into preparation. She sweet-talks best friend and fellow contestant Wilson into building (and re-building) her car, preventing him from being ready on race day." (Horn Book)

Babymouse: queen of the world. Random House Books for Young Readers 2005 91p. Illustration
Grades: 3 4 5 6   **741.5; Fic**
1. Babymouse (Fictional character); 2. Friendship; 3. Humorous graphic novels; 4. Mice; 5. Graphic novels
0-375-93229-1 (lib bdg), $12.99; 0-375-83229-7 (pa), $5.95

LC 2004-51166

"In this energetic comic . . . Babymouse, a wise-cracking rodent stand-in for your average, adventure-seeking nine-year-old, strives to capture popular Felicia's goodwill, finally achieving her end at the expense of Wilson Weasel, truest of friends. But, wouldn't you know it, Felicia's world has little to offer a smart, fun-loving mouse, after all." Booklist

Other titles in this series are: Babymouse: our hero (2005); Babymouse: beach babe (2006); Babymouse: rock star (2006); Babymouse: heartbreaker (2006); Camp Babymouse (2007); Babymouse: skater girl (2007); Babymouse: puppy love (2007); Babymouse: monster mash (2008); Babymouse the musical (2009); Babymouse: dragonslayer (2009); Babymouse burns rubber (2010); Babymouse: cupcake tycoon (2010); Babymouse: mad scientist (2011); A very Babymouse Christmas (2011); Babymouse for president (2012); Extreme Babymouse (2012); Happy birthday Babymouse (2014)

A **very** Babymouse Christmas. By Jennifer L. Holm & Matthew Holm. Random House Childrens Books 2011 89p. Illustration (Babymouse)
Grades: 3 4 5 6
741.5
1. Christmas — Fiction; 2. Gifts — Fiction; 3. Humorous graphic novels; 4. Imagination — Fiction; 5. Mice — Fiction; 6. Graphic novels
978-0-375-96779-5, $12.99; 978-0-375-86779-8 (pa), $6.99

*A Very Babymouse Christmas ©
Jennifer L. Holm & Matthew Holm*

LC 2010027988

"Babymouse feels she simply cannot live without the Whiz Bang, this Christmas's must-have gift. This graphic novel's single-minded focus reflects Babymouse's all-consuming obsession, a condition with which readers are likely to be familiar. Her holiday-classic-inspired, pink-hued daydreams allow Babymouse to switch off the mania for a while." (Horn Book)

Hopkins, David
   Emily Edison. David Hopkins, illustrated by Brock Rizy. Viper Comics 2006 144p. Illustration
Grades: 7 8 9 10 11 12 Adult   **741.5; Fic**
   1. Humorous graphic novels; 2. Science fiction graphic novels; 3. Graphic novels
0-9777883-2-6, $12.95
   High schooler Emily has more than her share of problems; along with trying to keep up in school and survive such things as parties and boys, she has to deal with her parents' very mixed marriage. Her father is human, but her mother came from another dimension. Since their divorce, Emily has had to split her time between Earth and elsewhere; and now her grandfather wants her to live permanently in his dimension, and he's prepared to destroy Earth to force her hand. What's a girl to do?

Horowitz, Anthony
   Stormbreaker: the graphic novel. [by] Anthony Horowitz; adapted Antony Johnston; illustrated by Kanako Damerum & Yusuru Takasaki. Philomel Books 2006 Un Illustration (Alex Rider)
Grades: 5 6 7 8   **741; 741.5**
   1. Spies; 2. Graphic novels
0-399-24633-9, $14.99
   In this graphic novel version on Horowitz's novel, fourteen-year-old Alex Rider is coerced into continuing his uncle's dangerous work for Britain's intelligence agency, MI6.
   "If it's possible, this is even more rapidly paced than the novel. Alex remains an appealing hero here, and the idea of a heroic teen up against insidious adults continues to be an extremely powerful draw for readers." Booklist
   Other graphic novel adaptations in this series are: Point blank (2007); Skeleton key (2009); Eagle strike (2012)

Hosler, Jay
   Clan Apis. Active Synapse 2000 158p. Illustration
Grades: 4 5 6 7 8 9 10 11 12   **741.5; Fic**
   1. Bees; 2. Science; 3. Graphic novels
0-9677255-0-X, $15
   "Opening with a creation myth . . . and working through the biological, sociological, and ecological changes affecting the life of Nyuki the bee, the text is a combination of authoritative science; appealing, detailed black-and-white drawings; and dialogue replete with humor, pubescent angst, political sloganeering, and more. Nyuki's colony undertakes migration to a new hive, is beset by a woodpecker, and hibernates through a winter that yields to a revitalizing spring." Booklist

★ The **last** of the sandwalkers. Written and illustrated by Jay Hosler. First Second 2015 312 p. Illustration
Grades: 5 6 7 8 9 10   **741.5; Fic**

   1. Adventure fiction; 2. Beetles — Fiction; 3. Science fiction; 4. Scientific expeditions — Fiction; 5. Graphic novels
162672024X; 9781626720244, $16.99
                                       LC 2014045542
   This book, by Jay Hosler, is about a "civilization of beetles. In this bug's paradise, beetles write books, run restaurants, and even do scientific research. But not too much scientific research is allowed by the powerful elders, who guard a terrible secret about the world outside. . . . Lucy is not one to quietly cooperate, however. This tiny field scientist defies the law of her safe but authoritarian home and leads a team of researchers out into the desert." (Publisher's note)
   "Hosler's cartooning is no less meticulous than his writing and similarly retains a sense of animated energy and humor, engaging readers with characters that are far from human, but filled with humanity." Booklist
   Includes bibliographical references

   The **Sandwalk** Adventures: An Adventure in Evolution Told in Five Chapters. Active Synapse 2003 160p. Illustration
Grades: 4 5 6 7 8 9 10 11 12 Adult   **576.8; 741.5**
   1. Darwin, Charles; 2. Evolution; 3. Science; 4. Graphic novels
0-9677255-1-8, $20
   Scientist Hosler explains Darwin's theory of evolution in a whimsical fashion. Follicle mites Mara and Willy live in Darwin's left eyebrow, and by accident they discover that Darwin, whom they call the god Flycatcher, can hear Mara. He thinks he's going crazy, but as he takes his daily walks on the Sandwalk at his home in England, Darwin does his best to convince Mara and Willy that he isn't a god and tells them about evolution. Hosler uses humor and whimsy, but also did a lot of research; the book includes explanatory notes and a long bibliography of sources.

Hotta, Yumi
   ★ **Hikaru** No Go, Volume 1. [by] Yumi Hotta and Takeshi Obata. Viz Media, LLC 2004 192p. Illustration
Grades: 5 6 7 8 9 10 11 12   **741.5; Fic**
   1. Board games; 2. Manga; 3. Shonen manga; 4. Graphic novels
1-59116-222-X, $7.95
   Sixth-grader Hikaru Shindo is not interested in intellectual pursuits, but by a twist of fate, the spirit of Fujiwara no Sai, the ghost of an ancient Go master, manages to bond with Hikaru. Now, suddenly, Hikaru can play Go, a complex board game of strategy, better than almost anyone under 18 and most adults, too. Akira, who has been raised by his Go master father, needs to know more about the upstart Hikaru, who beats him and yet seems so casual about the game. This is the first volume of an ongoing series.
   Volume 1 of a 23 volume series

Hughes, Susan
   No girls allowed: tales of daring women dressed as men for love, freedom and adventure. Written by Susan Hughes; llustrated by Willow Dawson. Kids Can Press 2008 80p. Illustration
Grades: 3 4 5 6 7 8 9   **306.7; 741.5**

1. Biographical graphic novels; 2. Transvestites; 3. Graphic novels
978-1-55453-177-6, $16.95; 978-1-55453-178-3 (pa), $9.95

LC 2007-9060846

This book collects short biographies in graphic format of young women who dressed as and pretended to be men in order to do and be what they wanted. The real Mu Lan did pretend to be her father's son in order to serve in the Chinese Emperor's army to protect her father. Hatshepsut was an Egyptian princess who was determined to be pharaoh, although that role could only go to men. Margaret Buckley was a young Englishwoman who became Dr. James Barry in the early nineteenth century. Seven women's stories are told here, and the book includes a short list of books for further reading.

Hugo, Victor

The **Hunchback** of Notre Dame by Victor Hugo ; retold by L.L. Owens ; illustrated by Greg Rebis Stone Arch Books 2006 63p. Illustration
Grades: 3 4 5 6 7 8 9   **741.5; Fic**
1. Adventure graphic novels; 2. Hugo, Victor, 1802-1885 — Adaptations; 3. Graphic novels
978-1-59889-047-1, $23.93

Hidden away in the bell tower of the Cathedral of Notre Dame, Quasimodo is treated like a beast. Although he is gentle and kind, he has the reputation of a frightening monster because of his physical deformities. He develops affection for Esmeralda, a gypsy girl who shows him kindness in return. When the girl is sentenced to an unfair death by hanging, Quasimodo is determined to save her. But those closest to Quasimodo have other plans for the gypsy. This adaptation is written for reluctant and struggling readers, and the tragic story is handled with sensitivity.

Part of the Graphic Revolve series.

Humphreys, Jessica Dee

Child Soldier: When Boys and Girls Are Used in War. Michel Chikwanine, Jessica Dee Humphreys; illustrated by Claudia Davila. Kids Can Press 2015 48 p. Color; Illustration
Grades: 5 6 7 8   **741.5; 355**
1. Chikwanine, Michel; 2. Child soldiers
1771381264; 9781771381260, $17.95

This children's book, written by Michel Chikwanine and Jessica Dee Humphreys, and illustrated by Claudia Davila, describes the experience of a child solder. "Michel Chikwanine was five years old when he was abducted from his schoolyard soccer game in the Democratic Republic of Congo and forced to become a soldier for a brutal rebel militia. Against the odds, Michel managed to escape . . ., but he was never the same again." (Publisher's note)

"Chikwanine's narration is matter of fact but never didactic, emphasizing less the gruesome details and more young Michel's emotional response and attempts to make sense of the world around him. Earthy hued and gentle, the images make a potentially disturbing topic accessible." SLJ

Hunter, Erin

Warriors: Tigerstar & Sasha #1: into the woods. Created by Erin Hunter; written by Dan Jolley; art by Don Hudson. HarperCollins/Tokyopop 2008 108p. Illustration
Grades: 3 4 5 6 7 8 9   **741.5; Fic**
1. Adventure graphic novels; 2. Cats; 3. Graphic novels
978-0-06-154792-8, $6.99; 0-06-154792-1

Sasha was a loved, pampered kittypet, but when one of the housefolk dies and the other moves away, they leave her behind. She had always explored the woods at night, but now she has to survive on her own. Then she meets Tigerstar, leader of ShadowClan, and they spend a lot of time together as he teaches her how to improve her hunting. He even offers her membership in the clan, but he has secrets, and when Sasha discovers one of them, she has to decide if she can trust him. There are scenes of cats hunting prey such as mice and squirrels, and fighting with foxes.

Other titles in this series are:Escape from the forest (2008); Return to the clans (2009)

Hurchalla, Elizabeth

Bakugan battle brawlers: The battle begins!. Del Rey 2008 Un Illustration
Grades: 3 4 5 6 7   **741.5; Fic**
1. Adventure graphic novels; 2. Fantasy graphic novels; 3. Games; 4. Graphic novels
978-0-345-51368-7, $7.99

Dan and his online friends are Bakugan Battle Brawlers, playing a game invented when strange, magic cards fell all over the Earth and into the hands of young people. The cards contain Bakugan guardians—creatures with great powers to fight. What the young players don't know is that Bakugan isn't only a game, the Bakugan guardians come from different worlds in a dimension called Vestroia, and the games played here in this world affect the battle between good and evil there. And in Vestroia, Drago from the fire world Pyrus must save his dimension from those who would destroy it for their gain; his one hope is to join with Dan on Earth. This book is illustrated with screen captures from the animated series airing on the Cartoon Network. It contains lots of action with fighting between the various Bakugan creatures. Bakugan is also a series of games figures that people can play, similar to the Yu-Gi-Oh, Pokemon, and other game-based manga and graphic novels.

Ben 10 Alien Force: Ben 10 returns. Del Rey 2008 96p. Illustration
Grades: 3 4 5 6 7 8   **741.5; Fic**
1. Adventure graphic novels; 2. Science fiction graphic novels; 3. Graphic novels
978-0-345-51438-7, $7.99

Ben Tennyson had lived as Ben 10, a superhero thanks to the watch-like Omnitrix that could transform him into any of ten superpowered alien life-forms. Five years ago, he put away the Omnitrix in order to live a normal life. However, his Grandpa Max is a Plumber, a member of an intergalactic police force, and he has continued his work. Now fifteen years old and a star soccer player, Ben visits Grandpa Max's trailer only to learn that Max has disappeared, a weird and creepy alien tries to get him, and Max has left a cryptic holographic message. Ben digs out his Omnitrix, seeks out his cousin Gwen, who has super powers of her own, and then they run into another Plumber who has been searching for

Max. They team up to find him and to learn why more aliens are coming to Earth and engaging in illegal transactions. This book is illustrated with screen captures from the Cartoon Network program.

Hutchison, David
Oz: The Manga. Antarctic Press 2006 Un Illustration
Grades: 4 5 6 7 8 9   **741.5; Fic**
1. Baum, L Frank — Adaptations; 2. Fantasy graphic novels; 4. Graphic novels
978-1-932453-69-0, $14.95
This is Baum's classic novel, The Wizard of Oz, adapted into manga format by Hutchison. All the characters are here: Dorothy, Toto, the Cowardly Lion, the Tin Woodsman, the Scarecrow, the Wizard. And all the main plot elements are here, from the cyclone that blows Dorothy and Toto to Oz to the Flying Monkeys to dealing with the Wicked Witch. The art makes this adaptation shine, especially the Tin Woodsman, who is a steampunk wonder.

I-Huan
Real/Fake Princess, Vol. 1. DrMaster Publications 2006 176p. Illustration
Grades: 6 7 8 9 10 11 12   **741.5; Fic**
1. Adventure graphic novels; 2. Manhua; 3. Romance graphic novels; 4. Graphic novels
978-1-59796-079-3, $9.95
In Tang Dynasty China, the country is in great chaos due to the infamous Jin Kang Rebellion. Fearing the possible destruction that might eventually result, Concubine Liu tearfully entrusts the care of her baby daughter, Princess Yi Fu, to a common citizen named Tang Hui. Tang Hui immediately escapes with the princess to the South. A decade passes, and Emperor Gao Zon of Tang has decided he wants to find all of his long-lost relatives and has appointed Zhong Lu to the task. From there an adventure begins as Zhong Lu discovers and takes a special interest in Princess Yi Fu (renamed Zi Li), who is happily living in a quiet fishing village with her childhood crush and savior - Tang Hui. Returning with Zhong Lu to a life of royalty means leaving behind the humble life she has come to know with the commoners.

Igarashi, Daisuke
★ **Children** of the sea, vol. 1. Viz Media/Viz Signature 2009 320p. Illustration
Grades: 7 8 9 10 11 12
741; Fic; 741.5
1. Adventure graphic novels; 2. Fantasy graphic novels; 3. Manga; 4. Mystery graphic novels; 5. Ocean; 6. Graphic novels
978-1-4215-2914-1, $14.99; 1-4215-2914-9
"As a young girl, Ruka sees a fish turn into light and disappear at the aquarium where her father works, but no one believes her. Years later,

Courtesy of VIZ Media LLC

the mystery of the ghost of the sea unfolds before Ruka and a pair of mysterious young boys, Umi and Sora." Publ Wkly
"Igarashi's storytelling is quiet, thoughtful, and thought provoking, but it is his drawings that make this manga so amazing. Extremely detailed settings turn panels into mini-masterpieces." Booklist
Volume 1 of a 5-volume series

Ihara, Shigekatsu
Pokemon diamond and pearl adventure!, vol. 2. Viz Media/Viz Kids 2008 192p. Illustration
Grades: 3 4 5 6 7 8 9   **741.5; Fic**
1. Adventure graphic novels; 2. Fantasy graphic novels; 3. Manga; 4. Graphic novels
978-1-4215-2287-6, $7.99
Hareta, Mitsumi, and their Pokemon friends continue on their quest to find Dialga, the Pokemon that rules time. They journey through the land of Sinnoh as Hareta and his partner Piglup grow stronger; they also keep ruining Team Galactic's nasty schemes. In Celestic Town, they find that Team Galactic's boss, Cyrus, has beat them to finding the first major clue to Dialga's whereabouts. And Hareta decides he needs help to become a better Trainer, but he and Piglup will have to pass Gym Leader Byron's test before he will accept them as students. There's lots of Pokemon fighting action.

Ikeda, Akiko
Chibikuro party. Dark Horse Books 2008 Un Illustration
Grades: 2 3 4 5 6 7   **741.5; Fic**
1. Adventure graphic novels; 2. Animals; 3. Humorous graphic novels; 4. Graphic novels
978-1-59582-128-7, $9.95
One night the moon wakes up Dayan's shadow—it's the one night that the shadows are free to move about on their own. Dayan's shadow, Chip (Dayan names him), wakes him up and wants him to go to the shadows' party, called the Chibikuro Party. The Satan of Death Forest sends Noel disguised as a shadow to kidnap all the shadows, and Noel tricks the shadows by saying they can go with him and be free forever. Dayan hears all this, and he rouses his friends to save their shadows from Death Forest.
Part of the Dayan's collection books series

Dayan's birthday. Dark Horse Books 2008 Un Illustration
Grades: 2 3 4 5 6 7   **741.5; Fic**
1. Animals; 2. Humorous graphic novels; 3. Graphic novels
978-1-59582-125-6, $9.95
The cat Dayan learns that he has a birthday, but he doesn't know what it is. He goes to a trio of witches to find out when his birthday will come, and then he throws a big party for everyone. However, he forgot to invite the witches, and they come to take his birthday back. This book is done in a small picture book format and is translated from Japanese. The woodland creatures serve the witches strong liquor to help Dayan
Part of the Dayan's collection book series

Thursday rainy party. Dark Horse Boks 2008 Un Illustration

Grades: 2 3 4 5 6 7 **741.5; Fic**
1. Animals; 2. Humorous graphic novels; 3. Graphic novels
978-1-59582-126-3, $9.95

One day Dayan gets caught in the rain, and he meets a friendly frog. He invites the frog to come to Willie the mouse's next rainy Thursday party, but learns the frog doesn't know anything about days of the week. Dayan creates a special calendar for his new friend, but the next rainy Thursday doesn't happen for several weeks; did the frog keep up with the calendar, and will he come to Willie's party?
Part of the Dayan's collection books series

White Eurocka. Dark Horse Books 2008 Un Illustration
Grades: 2 3 4 5 6 7 **741.5; Fic**
1. Animals; 2. Humorous graphic novels; 3. Graphic novels
978-1-59582-127-0, $9.95

Winter comes to the land of Tachiel along with a strong cold wave, much colder than most winters. As the festival of Eurocka approaches, Dayan and his friends find that many other creatures have come from the North penguins, walruses, and polar bears, to participate in the festival. During the celebrations, a baby polar bear cub magically arrives.
Part of the Dayan's collection books series

Ikeda, Miyoko
Fairy navigator Runa, vol.1. Del Rey Manga 2010 186p. Illustration
Grades: 7 8 9 10 11 12 **741.5; Fic**
1. Adventure graphic novels; 2. Fairies; 3. Fantasy graphic novels; 4. Magic; 5. Manga; 6. Shojo manga; 7. Graphic novels
978-0-345-52226-9, $10.99

Fourth grader Runa Rindo has lived in the Children of the Stars School ever since she was very young, it's the only home she has ever really known. All she has from her parents is a ring pendant and a small wooden box. Then two young strangers ask Runa "Are you the Legendary Girl?" And with that, her life changes. Suneri and Mokke are Fairies who can change shape to a cat (Suneri) and an owl (Mokke), and they tell Runa that she is a princess from the Fairy world. When another fairy, Kamachi, kidnaps Runa's best friend, Chae ("my name is Sae!"), Runa finds she must accept her destiny as the one who can control passage between the human and fairy worlds to save Chae.

Inada, Shiho
Ghost hunt, Vol. 1. Manga by Shiho Inada; story by Fuyumi Ono; translated by Akira Tsubasa; adapted by David Walsh; lettered by Foltz Design. Del Rey Manga 2005 216p. Illustration
Grades: 8 9 10 11 12 Adult **741.5; Fic**
1. Horror graphic novels; 2. Shojo manga; 3. Graphic novels
0-345-48624-2, $10.95

A decrepit old building stands on the campus of Mai's high school; every time the school tries to demolish it, unexplained accidents occur. Finally, the school hires a psychic researcher, and when Mai accidentally injures his assistant and damages an expensive camera, Shibuya (the researcher) insists she work off her debt by helping him. A miko (Shinto priestess), a Buddhist monk, and a Roman Catholic exorcist also come—but none of their methods work to stop the strange occurrences. Despite herself, Mai gets drawn into the investigation. This is the first of an ongoing manga series that provides some ghostly thrills without graphic violence, bad language, or sexual innuendo.

Indiana Jones Omnibus: the further adventures, volume 1
Edited by Katie Moody. Dark Horse Comics 2009 366p. Illustration
Grades: 7 8 9 10 11 12 **741.5; Fic**
1. Adventure graphic novels; 2. Archeology; 3. Indiana Jones (Fictional character); 4. Graphic novels
978-1-59582-246-8, $24.95

This volume collects the Marvel Comics adaptation of "Raiders of the Lost Ark" and the first twelve issues of Marvel Comics' "The Further Adventures of Indiana Jones," which were originally published in the 1980s. Artists on the comics include John Byrne, Ron Frenz, Terry Austin, John Buscema, Howard Chaykin, Kerry Gammill, and a lot more. Marion Ravenwood appears in many of the further adventures, sometimes working with Indy and sometimes needing rescue by him. When she tries to open a nightclub, a gangster tries to force her into partnership with him so he can use the club as a front. In other stories, Indy travels to Africa and finds (as he has done so in the movies) that sometimes the damsel is the villain. The book includes the same level of action and violence that can be found in the movies.

Indiana Jones Omnibus, Volume 1
Dark Horse Comics 2008 352p.
Grades: 7 8 9 10 11 12 Adult **741.5; Fic**
1. Adventure graphic novels; 2. Archeology; 3. Indiana Jones (Fictional character); 4. Graphic novels
978-1-59307-887-4, $24.95

This volume collects original comics stories starring movie hero Indiana Jones that were originally published by Dark Horse Comics in the early 1990s. Stories include Indiana Jones and the Fate of Atlantis, Indiana Jones: Thunder in the Orient, and Indiana Jones and the Arms of Gold. All of the stories predate the movies, as Indy races against the Nazis to recover and secure ancient treasures that could give great power to the owners. The book includes some violence.

Inoue, Takehiko
★ **Slam** dunk, volume 1: Sakuragi. Story and art by Takehiko Inoue; English adaptation Kelly Sue DeConnick. Viz Media/Shonen Jump 2008 197p. Illustration
Grades: 8 9 10 11 12 **741.5; Fic**
1. Basketball; 2. Shonen manga; 3. Graphic novels
978-1-4215-0679-1, $7.99

Hanamichi Sakuragi is a first year student at Shohoku Prefecture High School; he's got a reputation as a bruising fighter and has suffered 50 rejections from girls who were scared of his fighting. He's looked down on sports all his life, but on this first day of high school, he meets Haruko Akagi; she's not scared of him, and she loves basketball. He falls for her completely, enough to try to play basketball.

But, he has competition"Kaeda Rukawa is another first year student; he's a star basketball player, and Haruko has a huge crush on him. Then Sakuragi gets on the bad side of the basketball team captain, who happens to be Haruko's older brother. Sakuragi does everything he can to convince Takenori Akagi to let him join the team. However, he has a long way to go before he can build the fundamental skills to play basketball effectively; will he stick it out" There's some fighting, one male student's buttocks get exposed accidentally, but there's no bad language.

Original Japanese edition, 1991

Volume 1 of a 31-volume series

Inzana, Ryan

Ichiro. Written & illustrated by Ryan Inzana. Houghton Mifflin/Houghton Mifflin Harcourt 2012 288 p. Illustration; Color

Grades: 7 8 9 10   **741.5/973; 741.5**
1. Fantasy graphic novels; 2. Folklore — Japan; 3. Gods and goddesses — Fiction; 4. Grandfathers — Fiction; 5. Japan — Fiction; 6. Japan — History; 7. Japanese Americans; 8. Monsters — Fiction; 9. Supernatural — Fiction; 10. Supernatural graphic novels; 11. Graphic novels

0547252692; 9780547252698

                                    LC 2011277558

This graphic novel depicts the story of Ichiro, "a young American teen, son of a Japanese immigrant and an American soldier killed in combat, [who] goes to Japan with his mother for an extended visit and begins to grapple with sophisticated cultural complexities.... After his mother and Japanese grandfather tell him stories of Japanese history and folklore, Ichiro has a fantastical adventure involving the Japanese myth of the shape-shifting tanuki spirit." (Kirkus Reviews)

Irving, Washington

The **legend** of Sleepy Hollow. Washington Irving (retold by Blake A. Hoena); illustrated by Tod Smith.. Stone Arch Books 2008 72p. Illustration

Grades: 4 5 6 7 8 9   **741.5; Fic**
1. Ghosts; 2. Horror graphic novels; 3. Humorous graphic novels; 4. Graphic novels

978-1-4342-0446-2, $23.93; 978-1-4342-0496-7 (pa), $9.95

                                  LC 2007-30807

Tarrytown's new schoolmaster, Ichabod Crane, thinks little of the legend his students tell him about a headless horseman who haunts Sleepy Hollow. Crane must cross the Hollow in order to visit the Van Tassel home, for he fancies himself to be in love with Katrina Van Tassel. However, local strongarm man Brom wants Katrina for himself, and he plays mischief with Crane and the school. Eventually, the legendary ghost may play a role in this love triangle. This graphic novel adaptation of Irving's classic provides lots of humor and a few chills with a simple vocabulary, background notes on how Irving wrote his story, and discussion questions.

Part of the Graphic Revolve series

Irwin, Jane

   Vogelein: clockwork faerie. [by] Jane Irwin with Jeff Berndt; foreword by Jennifer M. Contino. Fiery Studios 2003 167p. Illustration

Grades: 6 7 8 9 10 11 12

741.5; Fic
1. Fairies; 2. Fantasy graphic novels; 3. Graphic novels

0-9743110-06, $12.95

Courtesy of Fiery Studios

This is a "graphic novel about Vogelein, a beautiful mechanical fairy created in the seventeenth century. Although she is immortal, she must be wound every 36 hours. After her old friend and caretaker dies, she must find someone new to take care of her. . . . This modern fable is a rare treasure that weaves fanciful imagination into themes of individuality, diversity, and independence. The art is beautifully shaded black and white, and it carries the narrative impeccably." Booklist

Most of the material contained within was originally printed in issues 15 of the magazine

   Vogelein: Old Ghosts. Fiery Studios 2007 168p. Illustration

Grades: 7 8 9 10 11 12 Adult   **741.5; Fic**
1. Fantasy graphic novels; 2. Graphic novels

0-9743110-1-4, $12.95

Though three hundred years have passed since Alexi's death, Vogelein finds herself still haunted by the unkept promise she made to her first Guardian. Now the clockwork faerie must confront her past with the help of Mason, an itinerant musician whose spirit bears a striking resemblance to the one she desperately wants to lay to rest. As she struggles to find peace for both herself and Alexi, Vogelein discovers that centuries-old questions rarely have easy answers, intended paths reveal themselves in mysterious ways, and present-day threats strike just as suddenly as those from long ago.

Isayama, Hajime

   ★ **Attack** on Titan 1. Hajime Isayama. Kodansha 2012 186 p. Illustration (Attack on Titan)

Grades: 8 9 10 11 12   **741.5**
1. Giants; 2. Good and evil; 3. Horror graphic novels; 4. Shonen manga

1612620248; 9781612620244, $10.99

"Humanity has been devastated by the bizarre, giant humanoids known as the Titans. Little is known about . . . why they are bent on consuming mankind. . . . People believe their 100-meter-high walls will protect them from the Titans, but the sudden appearance of an immense Titan is about to change everything." (Publisher's note)

"Along with the setting and intricate, twisting plot, Attack on Titan derives its appeal from its willingness to bend the conventions of shounen manga. Here, friendship and burning spirit do not conquer all, and your favorite character stands a good chance of getting eaten without the opportunity to give a cool speech first." LJ

Volume 1 of an ongoing series

Isenberg, Marty

Transformers animated volume 1. IDW Publishing 2008 Un Illustration

Grades: 2 3 4 5 6 7 8   **741.5; Fic**
1. Adventure graphic novels; 2. Robots; 3. Science fiction graphic novels; 4. Transformers (Fictional characters); 5. Graphic novels

978-1-60010-151-9, $7.99

When Optimus Prime and his team of misfit Autobots accidentally unearth the Allspark, they are attacked by Megatron, leader of the Decepticons. The fight causes the Autobots' ship to travel from deep space to Earth in the twenty-second century, and to New Detroit. Now the fight between the Autobots and the Decepticons will take place on Earth, where humans live, humans who don't know what all these sentient robots are doing. This book adapts stories from the new animated television series and uses screen captures from the programs to illustrate the book.

Transformers animated volume 2. IDW Publishing 2008 Un Illustration

Grades: 2 3 4 5 6 7 8   **741.5; Fic**
1. Adventure graphic novels; 2. Robots; 3. Science fiction graphic novels; 4. Transformers (Fictional characters); 5. Graphic novels

978-1-60010-152-6, $7.99

The Autobots have human allies now, one of whom, the young girl Sari, decides to give her new robotic friends a quick tour of Earth's history, starting with Dino-Drive, an old amusement park filled with animatronic dinosaurs. However, the somewhat disassembled Megatron finds a human ally, too, in the scientist named Sumdac (Sari's dad), and together they create the Dinobots. Then, someone gives the thief Nino Sexton a prototype turbo-boosting bio-armor, and he uses it to rob banks; the Autobots have to stop him and recover the armor. The stories have been adapted from broadcast episodes of the new animated Transformers television series and illustrated with screen captures from the programs.

Ishihara, Yoko

★ The **manga** cookbook. Presented by the Manga University Culinary Institute; illustrations by Chihiro Hattori; [with recipes by Yoko Ishihara]. Japanime Co. Ltd. 2007 158p. Illustration

Grades: 4 5 6 7 8 9 10 11 12   **641.5; 741.5**
1. Japanese cooking; 2. Manga; 3. Graphic novels

978-4-921205-07-2, $14.95

Food appears frequently in manga and in anime, but just what are the characters eating" This book is an illustrated step-by-step guide to preparing some Japanese dishes, from onigiri (rice balls) to yakitori (skewered grilled chicken), oshinko (pickled vegetables), udon (Japanese noodles), to traditional sweets and desserts. Definitions of terms and ingredients used, basic cooking guidelines, and instructions on how to properly use chopsticks are all included. The recipes are authentic but have been simplified somewhat so older children and teens with some basic kitchen skills can

prepare the foods. Adult supervision is recommended for younger children and for children who aren't very experienced with using knives, measuring spoons, and cooking on the stove.

Iwaoka, Hisae

★ **Saturn** apartments, volume 1. [translation, Matt Thorn]. Viz Signature 2010 184p. Illustration

Grades: 7 8 9 10

741; 741.5; Fic
1. Manga; 2. Science fiction graphic novels; 3. Graphic novels

978-1-4215-3364-3, $12.99; 1-4215-3364-2

Courtesy of VIZ Media LLC

Far in the future, humankind has left Earth to live in a gigantic ringlike structure that circles the planet. In this structure, humans have developed a class structure based on where one lives: the higher the floor on which you live, the greater your status. Mitsu has just graduated from junior high and is now expected to work as a window washer, just like his father before him. The thing is, his father disappeared while washing windows and is presumed dead. Window washing means one must get into a space suit and go out of the structure into outer space, 35 kilometers above the Earth's surface; space winds and other hazards make the work dangerous and expensive. Even as he wonders still, five years after his father's disappearance, what happened to him, Mitsu finds his job gives him a unique perspective on the lives of those who live in the Saturn Apartments. This is science fiction from the viewpoint of the mundane service work rather than heroics of space action.

"This story of a young teen struggling to live alone will appeal to YAs, and the introspective nature of the narrative will have plenty of crossover appeal for adult readers as well." Booklist

Reads from right to left

Volume 1 of a 7-volume series

Jablonski, Carla

Defiance. Written by Carla Jablonski; art by Leland Purvis; color by Hilary Sycamore. First Second 2011 126p. Illustration

Grades: 7 8 9 10 11 12   **741.5; Fic**
978-1-59643-292-5, $16.99; 1-59643-292-6

LC 2010036253

"World War II has taken its toll on the French countryside. German soldiers patrol the towns, searching for any challenge to their rule. The Tessier siblings, Paul, Marie, and Sophie, keep their noses clean and their faces blank as the French military police tighten their grip on their small country town. But all three are secretly doing their part for the Resistance: the men and women working hard to undermine the Germans and win back France's freedom . . . even if it ends up costing them their lives." (Publisher's note)

★ **Resistance,** book 1. Art by Leland Purvis; color by Hilary Sycamore. First Second Books 2010 121p. Illustration (Resistance)
Grades: 6 7 8 9 10 11 12   **741.5; Fic**
1. Adventure graphic novels; 2. France — History — 1940-1945, German occupation; 3. World War, 1939-1945 — Jews — Rescue; 4. World War, 1939-1945 — Underground movements; 5. Graphic novels
978-1-59643-291-8, $16.99; 1-59643-291-8

Paul and his younger sister Marie live in a small village in Vichy France during World War II. Thus far, the war hasn't really touched them, but now Nazi soldiers come, and Paul's friend, Henri, and his parents are Jews and therefore in danger. When Paul and Marie try to protect Henri, their secret leaks out to members of the Resistance. Although they are young, they soon become recruits in the Resistance. Paul's incessant sketching in his book turns out to be a valuable talent, but he and Marie, and then their older sister, Sylvie, don't quite realize just how dangerous things can get. The cover is very striking, with Paul aiming a slingshot at a Nazi soldier. The Author's Note at the end of the book talks about history, the Resistance, and why the events in France during World War II should not be depicted as black and white, heroic Resistance versus villainous Vichy.

Followed by: Defiance (2011)

★ **Victory.** Written by Carla Jablonski; art by Leland Purvis; color by Hilary Sycamore.. First Second 2012 123 p. Color illustration
Grades: 6 7 8 9 10 11 12   **741.5/973; 741.5**
1. France — History; 2. France — History — German occupation, 1940-1945 — Fiction; 3. France — History — German occupation, 1940-1945 — Juvenile fiction; 4. Resistance to government — Fiction; 5. World War, 1939-1945 — France — Fiction; 6. World War, 1939-1945 — France — Juvenile fiction; 7. World War, 1939-1945 — Underground movements — France — Fiction; 8. Graphic novels
1596432934; 9781596432932

                                                LC 2011030504
"In this third volume in the graphic novel trilogy about the Tessier family," set during the French Resistance, "Sylvie relays information she gathers from her unwitting German boyfriend, Marie hides a man she discovers after a plane crash in the woods, and Paul is the ears of the Resistance in town.... At the end of the book, Paul travels to Paris to pass along information. He's on the scene for the city's liberation." (Horn Book Magazine)

"The storyline is brisk and edgy, complementing the worn nerves of people who have lived through war... Fans of graphic art and WWII will appreciate this book, as well as reluctant readers who are interested in historical fiction." VOYA

Jackson, B. Albers
Rama: The legend. Art by Ashok Bhadana. Arcana Studio 2008 Un Illustration
Grades: 6 7 8 9 10 11 12   **398.2; 741.5**
1. Adventure graphic novels; 2. Fantasy graphic novels; 3. Hindu mythology; 4. Ramayana; 5. Graphic novels
978-0-9809204-0-6, $14.95

The Hindu legend, The Ramayana, is retold in comic book form, adapted for Western readers. Jackson created two original characters, Rarecrow (a crow, of course) and Raj the mongoose; they tend to speak in contemporary slang. Rama is the oldest son of King Dasaratha, one of several brothers born after Vishnu blesses Dasaratha and his wives. The heavens have been wracked by war between the gods, and the evil god Ravana leads the thus-far victorious forces; Brahman had granted him a boon that he could not be defeated by anyone from the heavens or the underworld, but the gods had dismissed the humans as insignificant. As Rama and his brothers grow up, they become mighty warriors and begin to defeat the evil Ragasthas warriors, and as adults they must face Ravana himself when he kidnaps Rama's beautiful and faithful wife Sita. This graphic novel adaptation makes the famous Hindu legend approachable for younger teen readers.

Jacobs, Edgar P.
The **mystery** of the Great Pyramid part 1. Cinebook Ltd 2007 56p. Illustration
Grades: 7 8 9 10 11 12 Adult   **741.5; Fic**
1. Adventure graphic novels; 2. Egypt — Antiquities; 3. Graphic novels
978-1-905460-37-3, $13.95

Professor Mortimer has come to Egypt on vacation with his servant, Nasir; his old friend, Professor Ahmed Rassim Bey has offered him an opportunity to satsify his passion for Egyptology by inviting him to take part in deciphering his latest discoveries. Mortimer and Bey soon realize that one of the fragments of papyrus deals with the "Chamber of Horus," a fabled crypt that could hold priceless treasures. However, Bey's assistant has been in league with villainous adventurers with their own plans to grab the treasures. . . . Jacobs was a close relative of Herge, creator of Tintin, and his adventures of Blake and Mortimer follow a similar pattern and style.

This is a part of The Adventures of Blake and Mortimer.

Jacobson, Ryan
Eleanor Roosevelt: First Lady of the World by Ryan Jacobson ; illustrated by Gordon Purcell and Barbara Schulz Capstone Press 2006 32p. Illustration
Grades: 3 4 5 6 7 8 9   **741.5; 973.917; 92**
1. Biographical graphic novels; 2. Roosevelt, Eleanor, 1884-1962; 3. Graphic novels
0-7368-4969-6, $25.26

                                                LC 2004028556
This book uses the comic book format to describe highlights in the life and work of U.S. First Lady Eleanor Roosevelt. It includes additional information, a glossary, a list of books for further reading, and more.

Part of the Graphic Library, Graphic Biographies series.

Jacques, Brian
Redwall: the graphic novel. By Brian Jacques; illustrated by Bret Blevins; adapted by Stuart Moore; lettering by Richard Starkings. Philomel Books 2007 143p. Illustration
Grades: 4 5 6 7 8 9   **741.5; Fic**
1. Adventure graphic novels; 2. Fantasy graphic novels; 3. Mice; 4. Graphic novels
978-0-399-24481-0, $12.99; 0-399-24481-6

When Cluny the rat's army attacks Redwall Abbey, young Matthias the mouse follows in the footsteps of the long-ago hero Martin the Warrior to defend his home

"The story is a page-turner, and the detailed black-and-white drawings capture both the passion and the pathos." SLJ

Jaffe, Michele

Bad kitty volume 1: catnipped. Art by Lince. HarperCollins/Tokyopop 2008 176p. Illustration

Grades: 7 8 9 10 11 12   **741.5; Fic**

1. Humorous graphic novels; 2. Mystery graphic novels; 3. Graphic novels

978-0-06-135162-4, $9.99; 0-06-135162-8

Teenage aspiring detective Jasmine Callihan just wants to hang out with her boyfriend, rock star Jack, but while they're at the mall, trouble strikes. First, Jas finds a schoolmate's purse, then there's a jewelry store heist and the cops arrest the store owner whom she believes is innocent, then she says exactly the wrong thing to Jack, and her cousin Alyson with her Evil Hench Twin Veronique decided to join the investigation along with Jas and her best friends Roxy, Polly, and Tom. This global manga is an original story using the same characters as Jaffe's prose teen novels Bad Kitty and Kitty Kitty.

"Catnipped will be especially appreciated by fans of Jaffe's novels, but it is not necessary to have read them to enjoy this rollicking, fast-paced, and funny mystery." SLJ

Jakobsen, Lars

The **mysterious** manuscript. Lars Jakobsen. Graphic Universe 2012 48 p.

Grades: 4 5 6 7 8   **741.5/9489; Fic**

1. Crime — Fiction; 2. Mystery fiction; 3. Scotland — Fiction; 4. Time travel; 5. Time travel — Fiction; 6. Graphic novels

0761378839; 9780761378839, $27.93

LC 2011027146

This graphic novel, by Lars Jakobsen, is part of the "Mortensen's Escapades" series. "A book collector shows Mortensen . . . an illuminated manuscript from 1512. When Mortensen sees a painting of an airplane on one of its pages, he knows he has a mystery to unravel. With a zap from his time gun, he travels back to medieval Scotland to look for clues. A wise scribe and a mute witch help him . . . [to] answer . . . how did an airplane crash land in the Middle Ages?" (Publisher's note)

The **Santa** Fe jail. By Lars Jakobsen; illustrated by Lars Jakobsen. Graphic Universe 2012 48 p.

Grades: 4 5 6   **741.5/9489; Fic**

1. Adventure graphic novels; 2. Kidnapping; 3. Kidnapping — Fiction; 4. Time travel; 5. Time travel — Fiction; 6. Graphic novels

0822594218; 9780761378860; 9780822594215, $6.95

LC 2011044643

This adventure graphic novel, by Lars Jakobsen, is book 2 of the "Mortensen's Escapades" series. In it "Mortensen is given a special assignment: deliver . . . [a] ransom to the Santa Fe Jail. But the kidnappers are time travelers, so nothing is as simple as it seems. . . . Mortensen . . . is drugged by a mysterious woman. He awakens to find himself packed

inside a cargo plane that is about to nose dive into the jungles of Tanzania." (Publisher's note)

The **secret** mummy. Art by Lars Jakobsen; story by Lars Jakobsen; translation by Lars Jakobsen and Robyn Chapman. Graphic Universe 2013 48 p. (Mortensen's escapades)

Grades: 4 5 6 7 8   **741.5/9489**

1. Criminals — Fiction; 2. Time travel — Fiction; 3. Transplantation of organs, tissues, etc — Fiction; 4. Vampires; 6. Graphic novels

0761379150; 9780761379157, $27.93

LC 2012027015

This is the fourth Mortensen adventure from Lars Jakobsen. "Mortensen, an agent dedicated to relentlessly fighting the ever-cresting wave of nefarious time-traveling criminals, now faces vampires in 19th-century Transylvania. Jumping uneasily through time from Prague to Transylvania to Bosnia and Paris, this wayward hero follows a creepy count thought to be a villainous vampire and the shadowy sarcophagus that seems tied to him." (Kirkus)

Originally published in Danish under title: Den falske mumie, in 2012.

Jamieson, Victoria

★ **Roller** girl. By Victoria Jamieson. Dial Books 2015 240 p. Color; Illustration

Grades: 4 5 6 7 8   **741.5; Fic**

1. Friendship — Fiction; 2. Roller derby — Fiction; 3. Roller skating — Fiction; 4. Graphic novels

0803740166; 9780803740167, $12.99

LC 2014011310

Newbery Honor Book (2016)

This graphic novel, by Victoria Jamieson, is "about friendship and surviving junior high through the power of roller derby. For most of her twelve years, Astrid has done everything with her best friend Nicole. But after Astrid falls in love with roller derby and signs up for derby camp, Nicole decides to go to dance camp instead. And so begins the most difficult summer of Astrid's life as she struggles to keep up with the older girls at camp." (Publisher's note)

"Jamieson captures this snapshot of preteen angst with a keenly decisive eye, brilliantly juxtaposing the nuances of roller derby with the twists and turns of adolescent girls' friendships." Kirkus

Jansson, Tove

Moomin Book One. Drawn & Quarterly 2006 96p. Illustration

Grades: 8 9 10 11 12 Adult   **741.5; Fic**

1. Humorous graphic novels; 2. Moomins (Fictional characters); 3. Graphic novels

1-894937-80-5, $19.95

Jansson is best known in the U.S. for her children's books featuring the Moomins, hippo-shaped creatures. Her comic strips have a more mature outlook. Moomin needs help getting rid of unwanted guests, but the only solution that works costs him his house. Then his scheming friend Sniff involves him in all sorts of shady get-rich-quick schemes. And when Moomin finds his long-lost parents, his father's craving for adventure causes more trouble. Snorkmaiden, Moomin's girlfriend, is just as bad as

Moominpapa, and they spark a boat trip south to a resort, where the naive Moomins think they're houseguests and everyone else, including the hotel staff, assumes they're wealthy eccentrics. The childlike look of the strips belie the goings-on; this book is not really for young readers, although teens and adults will enjoy the whimsy overlaying sharp satire.

Moomin's winter follies. Trove Jansson. Enfant 2012 45 p.
Grades: 8 9 10 11 12 Adult   **741.5**
  1. Moomins (Fictional characters)
  1770460985; 9781770460980, $9.95
    Author Tove Jansson presents a graphic novel. "Moomin wakes up one morning to find the pond frozen over, and rather than hibernate, the family decides to brave the winter weather. At first, their wintry adventure seems to be going swimmingly, until Mr. Brisk of the Great Outdoors Club takes over and forces everyone to embrace the winter sports, whether they want to or not." (Comic Vine)

Jeffrey, Gary
  Bob Marley: The Life of a Musical Legend. Art by Terry Riley. The Rosen Publishing Group 2007 48p. Illustration
Grades: 3 4 5 6 7 8 9
741.5
  1. Biographical graphic novels; 2. Marley, Bob, 1945-1981; 3. Graphic novels
  978-1-4042-0854-4, $29.25

Courtesy of Rosen Publishing

  This comic book format biography presents the life and musical career of legendary reggae master Marley, from his early years in Jamaica to international stardom. Additional material gives background information about Jamaica, its land and people, its music, and the Rastafarian religion. The book includes a glossary and a list of books for further reading.
  Part of the Graphic Biographies

  Elasmosaurus: the long-necked swimmer. Illustrated by Terry Riley. Rosen Publishing Group 2009 32p. Illustration

Courtesy of Rosen Publishing

Grades: 2 3 4 5 6 7   **567.9; 741.5**
  1. Dinosaurs; 2. Graphic novels
  978-1-4358-2505-5, $25.25
               LC 2008-3881
    This book uses comic book style art to introduce young readers to the elasmosaurus, which lived in the ancient shallow ocean that used to cover Kansas. The book provides some science-based speculation on what the dinosaur's life

might have been like. Additional material includes information on fossil evidence, quick facts about the elasmosaurus, and a glossary.
  Part of the Graphic Dinosaurs series.

  Hurricane hunters and tornado chasers. Illustrated by Gianluca Garofalo. Rosen Publishing Group 2008 48p.
Grades: 3 4 5 6 7 8 9
551.55; 741.5
  1. Meteorology; 2. Storms; 3. Vocational guidance; 4. Graphic novels
  978-1-4042-1458-3, $29.25
             LC 2007-42133
  After brief descriptions of what hurricane hunters and tornado chasers do (and why they do it), the book profiles hurricane hunter Jeffrey Masters and tornado chasers Roger Edwards and Tim Samaras, describing a memorable incident in each of their careers.
  Part of the Graphic Careers series

Courtesy of Rosen Publishing

  Hurricanes. Art by Mike Lacey. The Rosen Publishing Group 2007 48p. Illustration
Grades: 3 4 5 6 7 8   **551.55; 741.5**
  1. Hurricanes; 2. Graphic novels
  978-1-4042-1991-5 (lib bdg), $29.25
    After describing hurricanes and how they form, the book dramatizes three deadly hurricanes. On Labor Day in 1935, the Florida Keys were hit by a small but intense hurricane with the lowest recorded barometric reading for a landfalling U.S. storm: 26.35 inches. In 1992, Category 5 Hurricane Andrew struck South Florida, and is the second costliest storm in U.S. history. And in August 2005, the infamous Hurricane Katrina struck Louisiana and Mississippi, and the storm surge flooded almost all of New Orleans. Back material describes hurricane observation, explains the Saffir-Simpson Scale describing hurricane strengths, and includes a glossary and a list of books for further reading.
  Part of the Graphic Natural Disasters series.

  Martin Luther King Jr.: The Life of a Civil Rights Leader. Art by Chris Forsey. Rosen Publishing Group 2006 48p. Illustration
Grades: 3 4 5 6 7 8 9
741.5; 323.1; 92
  1. African Americans — Civil rights; 2. Biographical graphic novels; 3. King, Martin Luther, Jr, 1929-1968; 4. Graphic novels
  978-1-4042-0858-2, $29.25

Courtesy of Rosen Publishing

LC 2005035525

This book uses the graphic novel format to tell of the life and career of civil rights leader King. It gives additional information about segregation in the U.S. and the civil rights movement after King's death, and a list of books for further reading.

Part of the Rosen Graphic Biographies series.

Oprah Winfrey: The Life of a Media Superstar. Rosen Publishing Group 2006 48p. Illustration
Grades: 3 4 5 6 7 8 9   **741.5; 791.4; 92**
1. Biographical graphic novels; 2. Television personalities; 3. Winfrey, Oprah, 1954-; 4. Graphic novels
978-1-4042-0862-9, $29.25

LC 2006001559

This book uses the graphic novel format to tell of the life and career (so far) of television personality Oprah Winfrey, who has been called the queen of daytime talk shows and was the first African American billionaire. The book includes background information on the civil rights movement and on daytime television, information on Winfrey's charitable work, and a list of books for further reading.

Part of the Rosen Graphic Biographies series.

Secret agents. Art by Terry Riley. Rosen Publishing Group 2008 48p. Illustration
Grades: 3 4 5 6 7 8 9   **327.12; 741.5**
1. Espionage; 2. Spies; 3. Graphic novels
978-14042-1464-4, $29.25

LC 2007-43334

After brief descriptions of espionage and some organizations and gadgets, the book profiles three spies. During World War II, Wulf Schmidt was airdropped into Great Britain to spy for Nazi Germany, but the British had broken the communication code and knew he was coming; he became a double agent and worked for British Intelligence for the rest of the war. Oleg Penkovsky was a Soviet Intelligence officer who started working for the British in 1961; he and his British contact were caught and tried. Penkovsky was executed for treason. Robert Baer was a career CIA case officer; this book recalls one case from 1979, in India.

Part of the Graphic Careers series

Stegosaurus: the plated dinosaur. Illustrated by James Field.. Rosen Publishing Group 2009 32p. Illustration
Grades: 2 3 4 5 6 7   **567.9; 741.5**
1. Dinosaurs; 2. Graphic novels
978-1-4358-2503-1, $25.25

LC 2007-50587

This book uses comic book style art to introduce young readers to the stegosaurus, with some science-based speculation on what the dinosaur's life might have been like. Additional material includes information on fossil evidence, quick facts about the stegosaurus, and a glossary.

Part of the Graphic Dinosaurs series.

Tornadoes & Superstorms. Art by Terry Riley. The Rosen Publishing Group 2007 48p. Illustration
Grades: 3 4 5 6 7 8   **551.5; 741.5**
1. Storms; 2. Tornadoes; 3. Graphic novels
978-1-4042-1993-9 (lib bdg), $29.25

After describing tornadoes and superstorms in general terms, the book covers the Tri-State Tornado that struck in Missouri, Illinois, and Indiana on March 18, 1925; the Halloween Storm of October 26, 1991, also known as the Perfect Storm, that hit the Northeast coast; and the Jarrell Killer Tornado that struck in Texas on May 27, 1997. The book includes a glossary and a list of books for further reading.

Part of the Graphic Natural Disasters series.

Tsunamis and Floods. The Rosen Publishing Group 2007 48p. Illustration
Grades: 3 4 5 6 7 8   **741.5; 904.5; 904**
1. Floods; 2. Tsunamis; 3. Graphic novels
978-1-4042-1990-8 (lib bdg), $29.25

This volume describes tsunamis and floods, and covers a few major disasters: the Lisbon Flood of 1755, the Great Midwestern Flood of 1993, and the Asian Tsunami of 2004. Comic book style panels help young readers understand the magnitude of the destructive floods and tsunamis. The book includes a glossary and a list of books for further reading.

Part of the Graphic Natural Disasters series.

Jerwa, Brandon
    G. I. Joe Vol. 6: Players & Pawns. Illustrated by Tim Seeley. Devil's Due Publishing 2004 Un Illustration
Grades: 7 8 9 10 11 12 Adult   **741.5; Fic**
1. Adventure graphic novels; 2. G I Joe (Fictional character); 3. Graphic novels
1-932796-18-5, $12.95

Cobra has re-established its island base, but the organization is crumbling; Destro and Zartan have both resigned, and the Baroness is caught between love and duty. While the Joes infiltrate Cobra Island, Cobra Commander makes a violent attempt on General Hawk's life and the South American nation of Sierra Gordo is invaded by a mysterious new high-tech commando unit. As the players enact their strategies, the pawns move into place. The book includes fighting action.

Job
    Yakari and the stranger. Art by Derib. Cinebook 2007 48p. Illustration
Grades: 3 4 5 6 7 8   **741.5; Fic**
1. Animals; 2. Fantasy graphic novels; 3. Humorous graphic novels; 4. Graphic novels
978-1-905460-27-4, $11.95

Yakari is a young Native American of undetermined nation living where beavers, otters, bears, and moose live. When a white pelican crashlands in the river, suffering from a terrible cold, Yakari and the beavers try to help him, but the loud sneezes drive them all crazy during the night. Yakari tries to get help for the pelican from the otters, too, but the pelican's huge appetite wears them out. Even when he gets annoyed at the constant loud sneezing and the big appetite, Yakari keeps helping the pelican; and when the bird finally gets well, he repays everyone's kindnesses. While the French idea of what Native Americans look like is somewhat stereotypical and seems to combine several Native nations (Yakari has a pony, lives in a tepee, but the land looks more like the Northeast), the story itself is positive. Those who prefer only authentic presentations of Native Americans may not appreciate this story.

Johns, Geoff

JSA Presents Stars and S.T.R.I.P.E.. writer, Geoff Johns ; penciller, Lee Moder ; inker, Dan Davis ; colorist, Tom McCraw ; letterer, Bill Oakely. DC Comics 2007 192p. Illustration
Grades: 8 9 10 11 12 Adult   **741.5; Fic**
   1. Superhero graphic novels; 2. Graphic novels
   978-1-4012-1390-9, $17.99

Courtney Whitmore is just your typical teenage girl trying to make it through high school, but she's about to stumble upon a secret that will make her life a lot more complicated. Her new stepfather, Pat Dugan, was once Stripesy, sidekick of the Golden Age hero The Star-Spangled Kid. Finding the Kid's old costume, Courtney modifies it for herself and becomes the new Star-Spangled Kid, aiming to fight crime and annoy the heck out of her stepfather. But Dugan isn't about to let his new daughter get into any danger. Putting his mechanical skills to work, he creates a robotic suit called S.T.R.I.P.E., and joins Courtney's battle for justice. They fight side-by-side - and sometimes with each other - taking on aliens, cults, new villains, and more. These stories are the first that Johns wrote in comics, back in 1999.

Superman: Up, Up and Away!. Geoff Johns and Kurt Busiek ; art by Pete Woods and Renato Guedes. DC Comics 2006 192p. Illustration
Grades: 8 9 10 11 12 Adult   **741.5; Fic**
   1. Green Lantern (Fictional character); 2. Superhero graphic novels; 3. Superman (Fictional character); 4. Graphic novels
   978-1-4012-0954-4, $14.99

In the wake of Infinite Crisis, Superman had lost his powers. For the past year, as Clark Kent he has worked with the help of his super-powered allies, Green Lantern, Supergirl, and Hawkgirl, to keep Metropolis safe. Now, Lex Luthor has been acquitted of his past crimes, and he has managed to get his hands on a powerful and ancient Kryptonian artifact and plans to use it to destroy Superman once and for all. What can a powerless Superman do?

Teen Titans Vol. 4: The Future is Now. writers, Geoff Johns and Mark Waid ; pencillers, Mike McKone ... [et al.]. DC Comics 2005 Un Illustration
Grades: 8 9 10 11 12 Adult   **741.5; Fic**
   1. Science fiction graphic novels; 2. Superhero graphic novels; 3. Teen Titans (Fictional characters); 4. Graphic novels
   1-4012-0475-9, $9.99

The Titans' weekends are usually a chance to get away from it all, but this time they've gone to the 31st century, where they must help the Legion of Super-Heroes stop a threat known as the Fatal Five Hundred. Their return trip drops them off ten years into their future, and they don't like what they see. And when they finally get back home, they meet Speedy, who has arrived just in time to help them fight Dr. Light

Johns, W. E.

Biggles Spitfire parade. Cinebook Ltd. 2008 48p. Illustration
Grades: 5 6 7 8 9 10   **741.5; Fic**
   1. Adventure graphic novels; 2. World War, 1939-1945 — Aerial operations; 3. Graphic novels
   978-1-905460-54-0, $11.95

James Bigglesworth, known as Biggles, takes command of 666 Fighter Squadron of the RAF during World War II. He has two flights of eccentric pilots who patrol the skies and protect England from enemy aircraft that attack from Germany. Sometimes they have to protect their own airfield from Stukas and JU88s (German bombers), and from Messerschmitts (German fighters) with their Spitfires. Biggles also has a friendly rivalry with an acquaintance who commands a squadron of Hurricanes. The book is full of air combat action, and while there is little graphic violence, people do die. This graphic novel is adapted by a French comics creator from the novels by W. E. Johns, who was a pilot himself during WWI.

Johnson, Dan

Sinbad: The legacy. Wordsmith, Dan Johnson; illustrator, Naresh Kumar; colorist, Ajo Kurian; letterer, Laxmi Chand Gupta. Campfire 2011 86 p. Color illustration
Grades: 7 8 9 10   **813.6; Fic**
   1. Historical fiction; 2. Sea stories; 3. Sinbad the Sailor (Legendary character); 4. Graphic novels
   8190751557; 9788190751551, $12.99
                       LC 2011287737

In this graphic novel, "[w]hen King Haakim sends his teenage son Habib on a voyage to teach him" maturity, "the spoiled brat makes enemies of Sinbad's crew and is responsible for the ship being blown off course and forced to anchor near islands full of dangerous giant animals, beautiful cannibal women, and [a] . . . death-obsessed kingdom. Despite this, Sinbad rescues the prince from his blunders, while relating the tale of his own . . . adventures that helped him grow up." (Publishers Weekly)

Jolley, Dan

Alien Incident on Planet J. By Dan Jolley; illustrated by Matt Wendt; [coloring by Hi-Fi Design; lettering by Marshall Dillon].. Lerner Publishing Group/Graphic Universe 2008 112p. Illustration
Grades: 3 4 5 6 7 8 9   **741.5; Fic**
   1. Adventure graphic novels; 2. Plot-your-own stories; 3. Science fiction graphic novels
   978-0-8225-6998-5, $27.93; 978-0-8225-8876-4 (pa), $7.93
                       LC 2007-44116

In this new take on the "Choose Your Own Adventure" type of book that combines pages of prose text with pages of comic book sequences, you are a young human stuck on Planet J; your spaceship needs a new part, and you'll never get off this planet if you don't make peace with the Makanuk, the Zirifubi, and the Frongo. Some choices will end badly, others will be better, and the choices are all up to the reader.

This is Volume 8 of the Twisted Journeys series.

Escape from Pyramid X. Art by Matt Wendt. Lerner Publishing Group/Graphic Universe 2007 112p. Illustration (Twisted Journeys)
Grades: 3 4 5 6 7 8 9   **741.5; Fic**
1. Adventure graphic novels; 2. Mummies; 3. Graphic novels
978-0-8225-6777-6, $27.93; 978-0-8225-6779-0 (pa), $7.95
                                        LC 2006-101598
In the series called Twisted Journeys, readers choose how the story will progress. Pages of text alternate with comic book-style pages. In this volume, the reader are a student who won an essay contest to be part of an archeological dig led by Professor Emil Snackport, at the site of a newly discovered pyramid. In some story lines, you encounter smugglers, in others, a malevolent mummy. Readers will find many scenarios played out, depending on their choices; some end well, others not so well.

The **girl** who owned a city. By O.T. Nelson; adapted by Dan Jolley; illustrated by Joe?lle Jones; coloring by Jenn Manley Lee. Graphic Universe 2012 125 p.
Grades: 6 7 8 9 10   **741.5**
1. Adventure graphic novels; 2. Apocalyptic fiction; 3. Children; 4. Dystopian juvenile fiction; 5. Science fiction; 6. Survival — Fiction; 7. Graphic novels
9780761349037; 9780761356349; 0761356347
                                        LC 2009033270
This graphic novel, by Dan Jolley, O.T. Nelson, and illustrated by Joelle Jones, describes a post-apocalyptic world. "A deadly virus killed every adult on Earth, leaving only us kids behind. . . . I have to make sure we stay alive. . . . I figured out how to give the kids on Grand Avenue food, homes, and protection against the gangs. But Tom Logan and his army are determined to take away what we've built and rule the streets themselves." (Publisher's note)

The **hero** twins: against the lords of death: a Mayan myth. Story by Dan Jolley ; pencils and inks by David Witt. Lerner Publishing Group/Graphic Universe 2008 48p. Illustration
Grades: 3 4 5 6 7 8 9   **398.2; 741.5**
1. Adventure graphic novels; 2. Mayas — Folklore; 3. Graphic novels
978-0-8225-7495-8, $26.60
                                        LC 2007-25897
The Hero Twins, Hunahpu and Xbalanque, were blessed by the Mayan gods with special powers. However, their incredible skill at playing Pok-ta-Pok, the Mayan ball game, angers the Lords of Xibalba, rulers of the Land of the Dead. When the Lords challenge them to a Pok-ta-Pok game in Xibalba, the twins know they must use all of their powers and cunning to defeat the Lords' many challenges. Comics veteran Jolley consulted several translations of the Popol Vuh, artist Witt studied books on Mayan culture, architecture and art, and Mesoamerican folklore expert John Bierhorst reviewed the story to ensure accuracy and respect for Mayan culture.
Part of the Graphic Myths & Legends series

Pigling: a Cinderella story: a Korean tale. Art by Anne Timmons. Graphic Universe 2008 48p. Illustration (Graphic myths and legends)
Grades: 3 4 5 6 7 8 9   **741.5; Fic**

1. Fairy tales; 2. Korea — Folklore; 3. Graphic novels
978-0-8225-7174-2, $27.93; 0-8225-7174-9
                                        LC 2007-40891
In old Korea, in a time when magic still exists, Pear Blossom lives happily with her parents. But when her mother dies, her father quickly remarries a spiteful woman and her mean daughter, and they turn Pear Blossom's life into misery. They treat her like a servant and call her Pigling. Omoni (mother in Korean) makes impossible demands of Pear Blossom, and each time magical creatures help her achieve the tasks. Then on the day of a festival, a handsome magistrate sees Pear Blossom on the road, and she runs away, frightened, leaving a sandal behind.

The **Smoking** Mountain: The Story of Popocatepetl and Iztaccihuatl: An Aztec Legend. Art by David Witt. Lerner Publishing Group 2009 48p. Illustration
Grades: 3 4 5 6 7 8 9   **741.5; Fic**
1. Aztecs — Folklore; 2. Fantasy graphic novels; 3. Graphic novels
978-0-8225-7178-0, $27.93
                                        LC 2007-20028
Back when the Aztec Empire was at its peak, the Emperor has a favorite daughter, Iztaccihuatl (called Izta); he is troubled by an enemy nation, the Tlaxcalans, and the soldier Popocatepetl (called Popo) is the Emperor's great military leader. Popo and Izta fall in love at first sight when the Emperor honors Popo for his accomplishments, and they meet in secret. However, Cuetlachtli is a jealous soldier who wants to destroy Popo, and he finds his chance when the Emperor catches the two lovers together and tells Popo he can only marry Izta if he brings back the head of the Tlaxcalan king. Searching for the enemy takes a long, hard time, and Cuetlachtli sends a messenger back to Tenochtitlan with word that Popo has died, which sends Izta into a decline. When victorious Popo returns, he finds his lover dead, and takes her to the top of a mountain where he stands over her until his death. Now there are two mountains in Mexico, named for the two lovers. Jolley sets the story as one told by a Mexican tour guide, using contemporary language; artist Witt conducted research to make the art look as authentic as possible. The book includes a list of books, websites, and DVDs for more information and entertainment.
Part of the Graphic Universe Myths and Legends series

The **time** travel trap. Illustrated by Matt Wendt. Graphic Universe 2008 111p. Illustration (Twisted journeys)
Grades: 3 4 5 6 7 8 9   **741.5; Fic**
1. Adventure graphic novels; 2. Plot-your-own stories; 3. Science fiction graphic novels; 4. Graphic novels
978-0-7613-9472-3 (lib bdg), $27.93; 0-7613-9472-9 (lib bdg); 978-0-8225-8874-0 (pa), $7.95; 0-8225-8874-9 (pa)
                                        LC 2007-6101
In this new take on the "Choose Your Own Adventure" type of book that combines pages of prose text with pages of comic book sequences, you are caught in a time machine a fellow student built for the school's science fair. Depending on the choices, you could end up at a medieval joust, facing woolly mammoths and "cavemen," or future aliens. Some

choices will end badly, others will be better, and the choices are all up to the reader.

This is Volume 7 of the Twisted Journeys series.

Vampire hunt. Illustrated by Gregory Titus; [coloring by Hi-Fi Design; lettering by Marshall Dillon]. Lerner Publishing Group/Graphic Universe 2008 112p. Illustration
Grades: 3 4 5 6 7 8 9   **741.5; Fic**
1. Adventure graphic novels; 2. Plot-your-own stories; 3. Science fiction graphic novels; 4. Vampires; 5. Graphic novels
978-0-8225-8877-1, $27.93; 978-0-8225-8879-5 (pa), $7.95

LC 2007-043732

In this new take on the "Choose Your Own Adventure" type of book that combines pages of prose text with pages of comic book sequences, you are a vampire, and you must defend yourself and your castle from vampire hunters. Some choices will end badly, others will be better, and the choices are all up to the reader.

This is Volume 7 of the Twisted Journeys series

Warriors: Ravenpaw's path: vol. 1, shattered peace. Created by Erin Hunter ; written by Dan Jolley ; art by James L. Barry Tokyopop/HarperCollins 2009 Un Illustration
Grades: 3 4 5 6 7 8 9   **741.5; Fic**
1. Adventure graphic novels; 2. Cats; 3. Graphic novels
978-0-06-158865-2 (pa), $6.99

LC 2009-920733

Ravenpaw used to be part of Thunderclan, but he left the clan and has lived on the twolegs' farm with his friend Barley, mostly to stay away from Tigerstar. Life is quiet, peaceful, with plenty of mice to hunt in the cozy barn. Then other cats come seeking shelter, because Minty, the female, is about to give birth to her kits. Barley knows there's something bad about the cats, as he comes upon the males teaching the kits how to fight and kill other cats. Ravenpaw and Barley had always left the chickens alone and only hunted mice; after a fire damages the barn, they find the other cats have returned and plan to make the farm their territory. When the other cats kill some chicks, the farmer sees only Ravenpaw and Barley, who had tried to stop the killing, and the twoleg blames them. Now they must leave the farm, but Ravenpaw doesn't think he can return to the clan. This manga-style graphic novel is an original story featuring characters from Erin Hunter's fiction series.

Warriors: the Created by Erin Hunter ; written by Dan Jolley ; art by Bettina M. Kurkoski. Tokyopop/HarperCollins 2008 106p. Illustration
Grades: 3 4 5 6 7 8 9   **741.5; Fic**
1. Adventure graphic novels; 2. Cats; 3. Graphic novels
978-0-06-147867-3, $6.99

LC 2007-935239

Scourge, leader of the Bloodclan, is a violent, fierce cat and enemy of the Thunderclan cats. This story tells of his life before he became the leader, before he became Scourge. He started life as the kittypet named Tiny, the runt of his litter, despised by his bigger litter mates. Fascinated by the woods outside the fence where he lives, he ventures out to explore, and one day runs into forest cats from Thunderclan who injure him. Convinced the twoleg family will drown him as an unwanted kitten, Tiny lives among the strays in the alleys. A series of happenstances establish a reputation for

toughness and he changes his name to Scourge. What he really wants, though, is to settle things with the Thunderclan cat who almost killed him. The fights between cats might be upsetting for younger readers.

Warriors: Warrior's return. Created by Erin Hunter; written by Dan Jolley; art by James L. Barry. HarperCollins/Tokyopop 2008 111p. Illustration (Warrior's series)
Grades: 5 6 7 8   **741.5; Fic**
1. Adventure graphic novels; 2. Cats; 3. Graphic novels
978-0-06-125233-4, $6.99; 0-06-125233-6

In this third volume of the manga-style original story set in the world of the wild cat clans created by Erin Hunter, Graystripe and Millie have found Thunderclan's old territory, but it has been destroyed by Two-Legs. The forest has been stripped of its trees, human roadways and buildings are going up. Graystripe fears that his clan has been destroyed, too, but Millie won't let him give up. An old friend points out the path that the two cats must follow to find the Clan, and they continue the journey.

"The black-and-white cartoon artwork captures the cats' expressive faces, action-packed battle scenes, and familiar surroundings as these animals travel through the realm of the 'Twolegs.' This is a great choice for reluctant readers, manga fans, or 'Warriors' enthusiasts." SLJ

Wrapped up in you. By Dan Jolley; illustrated by Natalie Nourigat. Graphic Universe 2012 127 p.
Grades: 6 7 8 9 10 11 12   **741.5; Fic**
1. Horror graphic novels; 2. Horror stories; 3. Love stories; 4. Mummies; 5. Mummies — Fiction; 6. North Carolina — Fiction; 7. Supernatural graphic novels; 8. Witches — Fiction; 9. Graphic novels
0761368566; 9780761368564, $29.27

LC 2011044655

This graphic novel, by Dan Jolley, illustrated by Natalie Nourigat, is book 6 in the "My Boyfriend Is a Monster" series. "Prince Pachacutec—or 'Chuck'—is a man with a past. He died tragically five hundred years ago, but that's all ancient history as far as Staci is concerned. He is everything she could want. . . . But the witches aren't willing to live and let live. Will Staci fight for Chuck? Or do the witches have a point when they say reanimated corpses make bad boyfriends?" (Publisher's note)

Jones, Gerard
Dragon Ball Z (vizbig edition vol. 1). Viz Media/Shonen Jump 2008 528p. Illustration
Grades: 7 8 9 10 11 12   **741.5; Fic**
1. Adventure graphic novels; 2. Manga; 3. Martial arts; 4. Shonen manga; 5. Graphic novels
978-1-4215-2064-3, $17.99

The first three volumes of DragonBall Z are now collected in a larger size volume. The Saiyans are an alien race of deadly warriors who wipe out entire planets for their own profit and gain. When the Saiyans set their sights on Earth, it's up to Son Goku to fight off the invaders with his superhuman strength. This series is an almost nonstop series of martial arts action scenes, so there's lots of fighting and yelling, but no harsh language.

Also available in 26 individual volumes

Volume 1 of 9

Joy, Bob

Batman: The Greatest Stories Ever Told Volume Two. DC Comics 2007 208p. Illustration

Grades: 7 8 9 10 11 12 Adult   741.5; Fic

1. Batgirl (Fictional character); 2. Batman (Fictional character); 3. Joker (Fictional character); 4. Superhero graphic novels; 5. Graphic novels
978-1-4012-1214.8, $19.99

This volume includes stories from different periods in the nearly seventy-year career of Batman, from 1940 to 2003. He goes up against classic villains - the Joker, Killer Croc, the Penguin; he meets Batgirl (Barbara Gordon); deals with crooked businessmen and other criminals.

Flash: The Greatest Stories Ever Told. DC Comics 2007 208p. Illustration

Grades: 6 7 8 9 10 11 12 Adult   741.5; Fic

1. Flash (Fictional character); 2. Superhero graphic novels; 3. Graphic novels
978-1-4012-1372-5, $19.99

Jay Garrick, Barry Allen, and Wally West are all men who have donned the symbol of the yellow lightning bolt to combat evil as the Flash. Each hero with his own unique style of commanding a mastery over momentum, they have fought separately and together over the years. This volume collects stories that see them pitted against such villains as Gorilla Grodd, the Reverse Flash, the Fiddler, and many others. This volume also includes the story of Barry and Iris' wedding.

The **Helmet** of fate. DC Comics 2007 128p. Illustration

Grades: 8 9 10 11 12 Adult   741.5

1. Superhero graphic novels; 2. Supernatural graphic novels; 3. Graphic novels
978-1-4012-1470-8, $14.99

The tenth age of magic is about to begin, but it needs a new champion, a new Dr. Fate. The Helmet of Fate seeks a new master and encounters some of the most powerful beings of the supernatural world on its quest. Candidates include Zauriel from JLA, Black Alice from Birds of Prey, Shadowpact's Detective Chimp (what!—), as well as Sargon the Sorcerer and Ibis the Invincible. Who will become the successor to Dr. Fate" The book includes some violence and some mild harsh language.

Showcase Presents: Batgirl Volume 1. DC Comics 2007 552p. Illustration

Grades: 6 7 8 9 10 11 12 Adult   741.5; Fic

1. Batgirl (Fictional character); 2. Superhero graphic novels; 3. Graphic novels
978-1-4012-1367-1, $16.99

In the late 1960s, DC Comics added a new character to the world of Batman and Robin: Batgirl. Daughter of Commissioner Jim Gordon, Barbara Gordon is a librarian who relocates to Gotham City and soon dons her costume as the crime fighting Batgirl. This volume of black and white reprints includes her early adventures, from 1967 through 1975. The cover art notwithstanding, Batgirl is a woman of action.

Showcase Presents: Batman Vol. 1. DC Comics 2006 552p. Illustration

Grades: 6 7 8 9 10 11 12 Adult   741.5; Fic

1. Batman (Fictional character); 2. Superhero graphic novels; 3. Graphic novels
1-4012-1086-4, $16.99

The spotlight's on Batman in this volume featuring Detective Comics #327-342 and Batman #164-174. The Dynamic Duo take on some of their most enduring Rogues Gallery members, including Penguin, the Riddler, and the Outsider in these classic Silver Age stories from the era of famed editor Julius Schwartz. This Showcase edition reprints the comics in black and white.

Showcase Presents: Batman Vol. 2. DC Comics 2007 510p. Illustration

Grades: 6 7 8 9 10 11 12 Adult   741.5; Fic

1. Batgirl (Fictional character); 2. Batman (Fictional character); 3. Joker (Fictional character); 4. Riddler (Fictional character); 5. Robin (Fictional character); 6. Superhero graphic novels; 7. Graphic novels
978-1-4012-1362-6, $16.99

Over 500 pages of classic adventures are included in this volume collecting Silver Age tales of Batman and Robin as they face their most enduring enemies, including the Joker, Poison Ivy, the Riddler, Blockbuster, and many others. These are the stories that inspired the Dynamic Duo's 1960s TV series, which featured Batman's astonishing detective skills and impressive array of Bat-gadgets. The stories, reprinted in black and white, date from 1965 and 1966.

Superman: The Amazing Transformations of Jimmy Olsen. DC Comics 2007 192p. Illustration

Grades: 6 7 8 9 10 11 12 Adult   741.5; Fic

1. Humorous graphic novels; 2. Superhero graphic novels; 3. Superman (Fictional character); 4. Graphic novels
978-1-4012-1369-5, $14.99

Cub reporter Jimmy Olsen stars in this light-hearted volume collecting some of his most memorable adventures from the late 1950s and 1960s, all of which guest-star Superman. While investigating crime for The Daily Planet, Jimmy undergoes one startling transformation after another, gaining temporary super-powers as Elastic Lad and becoming a Giant Turtle Man, The Wolf-Man of Metropolis, The Human Porcupine and much more. At times like these, Superman finds that he must not only protect Metropolis from Jimmy, but Jimmy from himself.

Judal

Vampire Game Vol.1. Tokyopop 2003 193p. Illustration

Grades: 8 9 10 11 12   741.5; Fic

1. Fantasy graphic novels; 2. Humorous graphic novels; 3. Shojo manga; 4. Graphic novels
1-59182-369-2, $9.99

In an epic battle, valiant King Phelios defeats the evil vampire King Duzell, but both monarchs are mortally wounded. As the two lay dying, Duzell prophesies that they will meet again, in another place and another time, and vows that he will be triumphant. Hundreds of years later, Duzell comes back as a menacing baby wildcat who is rescued from the wild and adopted by Ishtar, the great-granddaughter of his nemesis, King Phelios. Ishtar is a playful girl with an iron will and a penchant for pranks, a trait that distresses her caretaker, Sir Keld, and a dashing imperial guard, Captain

Dales. Ishtar is not, however, the reincarnation of Phelios, leaving the now-feline Duzell to continue his quest for revenge - without letting his new owner know that he is hell-bent on destroying her family ... but would Ishtar even care about that if she knew" The book includes some strong language, some violence, and some brief sexual situations.

Jurgens, Dan
DC Showcase presents Booster Gold volume 1. DC Comics 2008 624p. Illustration
Grades: 8 9 10 11 12 Adult   **741.5; Fic**
  1. Booster Gold (Fictional character); 2. Superhero graphic novels; 3. Graphic novels
  978-1-4012-1655-9, $16.99
This volume collects the entire run of the Booster Gold comics series written and drawn by Dan Jurgens and published from 1986 through 1988. Michael Jon Carter lives in the 25th century, and he wants thrills, wealth, and fame. He "borrows" items from the Space Museum and travels back in time to the twentieth century, where he uses his knowledge of things to come to build an empire and become the super hero, Booster Gold. His constant self-promotion annoys and offends the heroic community, and eventually he will have to learn that fame and fortune come at a price. DC brought Booster Gold back for its 2007 crossover event, 52, but here readers can find the original "anti-superhero."

Justice League Adventures Vol. 1: The Magnificent Seven
DC Comics 2004 112p. Illustration
Grades: 4 5 6 7 8 9   **741.5; Fic**
  1. Batman (Fictional character); 2. Flash (Fictional character); 3. Green Lantern (Fictional character); 4. Justice League (Fictional characters); 5. Superhero graphic novels; 6. Superman (Fictional character); 7. Wonder Woman (Fictional character); 8. Graphic novels
  1-4012-0179-2, $6.95
The World's Greatest Heroes: Martian Manhunter, Green Lantern, Hawkgirl, the Flash, Wonder Woman, Batman, and Superman battle against villainy from all corners of the globe, and beyond. Among other villains, they fight Chronos the Time Thief and Screamthief.

Justice League Adventures Vol. 2: Friends and Foes
DC Comics 2004 112p. Illustration
Grades: 4 5 6 7 8 9   **741.5; Fic**
  1. Batman (Fictional character); 2. Flash (Fictional character); 3. Green Lantern (Fictional character); 4. Justice League (Fictional characters); 5. Superhero graphic novels; 6. Superman (Fictional character); 7. Wonder Woman (Fictional character); 8. Graphic novels
  1-4012-0180-6, $6.95
The World's Greatest Heroes: Martian Manhunter, Green Lantern, Hawkgirl, the Flash, Wonder Woman, Batman, and Superman - return to thwart another round of wrongdoers, and the threats come from all sides. Brainiac and Poison Ivy are just a couple of the super villains they face.

Kanari, Yozaburo
The **Kindaichi** case files vol. 17: the undying butterflies. Tokyopop 2008 Un Illustration
Grades: 8 9 10 11 12 Adult   **741.5; Fic**
  1. Manga; 2. Mystery graphic novels; 3. Graphic novels
  978-1-59532-701-7, $9.99
The article about the discoverer of a rediscovered species of butterfly is not the sort of thing that teenage detective Hajime Kindaichi would care about, but the photograph included with the article catches his eye; the assistant to Madarame, the butterfly expert, looks identical to Eiji Touno, a killer Kindaichi had uncovered and whom he thought had died in a massive fire. Kindaichi, best friend Miyuki, and their detective buddy Itsuki, travel to Madarame's impressive estate to uncover the mystery about Touno. However, while they are there, murders begin to occur, starting tragically with Madarame's youngest daughter Ruri, who is only twelve years old. Can Kindaichi match wits with the murderer and stop him? There is little bloodshed or overt violence in this murder mystery, and one instance of nonsexual partial nudity.

Kindaichi Case Files Volume 1: The Opera House Murders. Tokyopop 2003 186p. Illustration
Grades: 8 9 10 11 12 Adult   **741.5; Fic**
  1. Manga; 2. Mystery graphic novels; 3. Shonen manga; 4. Graphic novels
  1-59182-354-4, $9.99
Teenager Hajime Kindaichi is a slacker, but a genius at solving mysteries, which is needed when the Fudo High drama club travels to a hotel on an isolated island to rehearse the play, 'Phantom of the Opera.' People start turning up dead, murdered in ways appearing in the play, and with no way off the island, Hajime better find the killer before everyone dies. The book includesgraphic violence, some strong language, and some nudity (usually the dead bodies).

Kanata, Konami
★ **Chi's** sweet home, volume 1. Vertical, Inc. 2010 166p. Illustration
Grades: 5 6 7 8 9 10 11 12 Adult   **741.5; Fic**
  1. Cats; 2. Humorous graphic novels; 3. Manga; 4. Graphic novels
  9781-934287-81-1
Young kitten Chi gets separated from her family while out on a stroll, then she meets little boy Yohei and his parents. They take her home, even though their apartment building has a strict no pets policy. While they try to find someone to take her in, they feed her, give her a cozy bed, set up a box with shredded newspaper for a litter box, and do their best to help her. Even though readers can read what she's thinking, Chi behaves just like a cat, with cat problems such as thinking the litter box is a wonderful play area instead of the place to do her business, and taking fright at Yohei's "vrooming" as he plays with his toy cars. The book is great for younger readers as well as anyone who likes cats. There is one panel where Yohei is sitting on the toilet while Chi is in her litter box in the bathroom, and a scene at the veterinarian's office where the doctor sticks a thermometer in to take Chi's temperature. And, of course, Chi tends to urinate in inappropriate places.
Also available in 3-in-1 omnibus editions
Volume 1 of 12

Kanda, Takayuki
Edu-Manga: Ludwig van Beethoven. Art by Naoko Takase. Digital Manga Publishing 2006 144p. Illustration
Grades: 3 4 5 6 7 8 9   **92; 741.5**
1. Beethoven, Ludwig van; 2. Biographical graphic novels; 3. Manga; 4. Graphic novels
1-56970-973-4, $9.95
Beethoven stands as one of the greatest musical minds the world has ever seen, with such famous works as his Symphony No. 9 ("Ode to Joy") and the classic piano piece "Fur Elise." The onset of deafness was only one of many hardships he had to face, but his strength and desire to do battle with his turbulent life led him to create the many musical pieces the world cherishes today. This manga format biography uses Astro Boy and his friends to introduce the story, present more information in a Q&A format, and provides a timeline to Beethoven's life.

Kane, Bob
Batman Archives Volume 1. Bob Kane and Bill Finger. DC Comics 1990 304p. Illustration
Grades: 7 8 9 10 11 12 Adult   **741.5; Fic**
1. Batman (Fictional character); 2. Robin (Fictional character); 3. Superhero graphic novels; 4. Graphic novels
978-0-930289-60-7, $39.95
When a young Bruce Wayne watched in horror as his parents were murdered, the legend of the Batman was born. Collected here are the first stories of the masked vigilante as they were originally printed in 1939. These stories include the classic first appearance of the Batman and the introduction of his teenage ally, Robin. These early adventures show how a dark and grim character and his humorous and light sidekick were masterfully combined to create one of the most enduring partnerships of all time.

The **Batman** Chronicles Volume Two. Bob Kane and Bill Finger. DC Comics 2006 224p. Illustration
Grades: 7 8 9 10 11 12 Adult   **741.5; Fic**
1. Batman (Fictional character); 2. Catwoman (Fictional character); 3. Joker (Fictional character); 4. Robin (Fictional character); 5. Superhero graphic novels; 6. Graphic novels
978-1-4012-0790-8, $14.99
This series reprints the Batman comics in chronological order; this second volume includes stories originally published in 1940. Batman is becoming more of a father figure to Robin; the villains become more colorful, the scientists get madder; the Dynamic Duo take on the Joker, Catwoman, Clayface, and more classic Bat-villains.

Kang, E-Jin
Good Luck Volume 1. Tokyopop 2007 Un Illustration
Grades: 8 9 10 11 12   **741.5; Fic**
1. Manwha; 2. Romance graphic novels; 3. Graphic novels
978-1-59816-761-0, $9.99
Shi-Hyun is pure bad luck. That's what everyone says ... and in some ways, she believes it. So for their protection and her own, she's developed a hard shell that keeps people at bay. But when Shi-Hyun transfers to a new school, an array of new characters comes into her life. The Queen Bee has a cool personality and the fighting skills to match. The Cold

Prince has the looks and demeanor to make all the girls swoon. And what about the nice girl, Hee-Soo, the only one who'll come near Shi-Hyun? Well, she has an agenda of her own ...

Kanigher, Robert
Showcase Presents: The Haunted Tank Volume 1. Art by Joe Kubert and Russ Heath. DC Comics 2006 560p. Illustration
Grades: 7 8 9 10 11 12 Adult   **741.5; Fic**
1. Ghosts; 2. World War, 1939-1945; 3. Graphic novels
1-4012-0789-8, $16.99
What happens when the ghost of General J. E. B. Stuart, a long-deceased Confederate general, returns to act as a protector to his namesake, Sgt. Jeb Stuart, commander of a tank in North Africa during World War II" These stories combine the fast-paced action of war with a supernatural bent. This black and white volume reprints the first thirty-three tales of the Haunted Tank, dating from 1961 to 1966. Writer Kanigher was just voted into the Eisner Awards Hall of Fame as a Judges' Choice in 2007.

Showcase Presents: Wonder Woman Vol. 1. DC Comics 2007 528p. Illustration
Grades: 6 7 8 9 10 11 12 Adult   **741.5; Fic**
1. Superhero graphic novels; 2. Wonder Woman (Fictional character); 3. Graphic novels
978-1-4012-1373-2, $16.99
Wonder Woman faces some of her deadliest challenges as she battles a variety of aliens and robots, and confronts the evil menaces of the Time Master, the Gadget Maker, Dike of Deception, and one of her most incessant foes, the Angle Man. This volume also includes the re-done origin of Wonder Woman, and some of her teenage adventures as Wonder Girl. Created by William Moulton Marston as a strong, liberated warrior in 1941, these adventures published in the late 1950s and early 1960s cast Wonder Woman in a more "traditional" female superhero role.

Kanno, Aya
Otomen; Volume 1. Story & art by Aya Kanno. Viz Media 2010 208 p. Illustration
Grades: 8 9 10 11 12   **741.5; Fic**
1. Dating (Social customs) — Fiction; 2. Shojo manga; 3. Teenagers — Fiction
1421521865; 9781421521862, $9.99
"Asuka Masamune is a guy who loves girly things—sewing, knitting, making cute stuffed animals and reading shojo comics. But in a world where boys are expected to act manly, Asuka must hide his beloved hobbies and play the part of a masculine jock instead. Ryo Miyakozuka, on the other hand, is a girl who can't sew or bake a cake to save her life. Asuka finds himself drawn to Ryo, but she likes only the manliest of men! Can Asuka ever show his true self to anyone, much less to the girl that he's falling for?" (Publisher's note)
"Although the art is as sugary and cute as Asuka himself, with lots of sparkling and glitter in the periphery, hidden among all the prettiness are important themes of individuality and being true to yourself, making this an empowering read for teenage girls." Booklist
Volume 1 of 18

Soul Rescue Volume 1. Tokyopop 2006 Un Illustration
Grades: 8 9 10 11 12   **741.5; Fic**
1. Adventure graphic novels; 2. Fantasy graphic novels; 3. Shonen manga; 4. Graphic novels
1-59816-672-7, $9.99
    When Angels are supposed to epitomize all that is perfect in love and mercy, where does a rogue angel fit into it all? Renji is one of heaven's most powerful but overly violent angels. As punishment for going too far in the last great battle against the demons, Renji is banished to Earth. His mission? Saving 10,000 souls. But for an angel who's never known anything outside of fighting, there may be nothing in Heaven or Hell that can help him. Where bad boy angels must learn to love humanity, it's all in the Soul Rescue. The series includes some fighting action.

Kaplan, Arie
    Speed Racer: chronicles of the racer. Art by Robby Musso and German Torres. IDW Publishing 2008 Un Illustration
Grades: 5 6 7 8 9 10 11 12 Adult   **741.5; Fic**
1. Adventure graphic novels; 2. Automobile racing; 3. Racer, Speed (Fictional character); 4. Graphic novels
978-1-60010-213-4, $17.99
    After a race in which something happens to Speed's Mach 5 and he's saved by Racer X, Pop Racer gives Speed a book, The Chronicles of the Racer. For thousands of years, there has been one Racer in their family, one who is destined to win. And for those thousands of years, the Racer has dealt with a villain who is associated with Mercury. From ancient Rome to medieval England to eighteenth century pirates and onward, Speed finds himself reliving his ancestors' experiences after he sneaks into Mercury Studios, and he finds himself face-to-face with the same man who has battled his ancestors through the centuries. This book collects the four-issue miniseries of original stories based on the Speed Racer characters.

Kardy, Glenn
    Manga University Presents . . . Kana de Manga Special Edition: Japanese Sound FX!. Writer, Glenn Kardy; artist, Chihiro Hattori. Japanime Co. Ltd./Manga University 2007 110p. Illustration
Grades: 6 7 8 9 10 11 12 Adult   **495.6; 741.5**
1. Japanese language; 2. Manga; 3. Graphic novels
978-4-921205-12-6, $9.99
    What does a cat's meow sound like in Japanese? How about the grumble of an empty stomach, the wail of a police car's siren or the crash of an ocean wave? Japanese manga artists rely heavily upon onomatopoeia—sound-effect words—and this entry in the Kana de Manga / Kanji de Manga language-learning series includes illustrated examples of those sounds in action. It features more than 100 Japanese onomatopoeia and their English equivalents in categories such as "Humans," "Animals," "Machines" and "Nature." The text is written in both English and Japanese hiragana.

    Manga University Presents ... Kana de Manga: A Fun, Easy Way to Learn the ABCs of Japanese!. Text by Glenn Kardy ; art by Chihiro Hattori. Japanime Co. Ltd 2004 113p. Illustration

Grades: 5 6 7 8 9 10 11 12 Adult   **495.6; 741.5**
1. Japanese language — Teaching — Aids and devices; 2. Manga; 3. Graphic novels
4-921205-01-9, $9.99
    This book uses original manga artwork to teach students how to read, write and pronounce the Japanese hiragana and katakana alphabets, also known as "kana." Author Glenn Kardy and artist Chihiro Hattori have teamed up to create this book for manga enthusiasts who are interested in more than just pretty pictures. In addition to presenting the kana, the book illustrates stroke order in writing the characters, and each hiragana character is shown with a word, its definition, an illustration, and opportunities for practice in writing the character.

    Manga University Presents ... Kanji deManga: The Comic Book That Teaches You How to Read and Write Japanese! Volume 1. Created by Glenn Kardy ; art by Chihiro Hattori. Japanime Co. Ltd 2004 113p. Illustration
Grades: 5 6 7 8 9 10 11 12 Adult   **495.6; 741.5**
1. Japanese language — Teaching — Aids and devices; 2. Manga; 3. Graphic novels
4-921205-02-7, $9.99
    This book uses original comic artwork to teach readers how to identify and write the most common Japanese kanji ideographs. It introduces 80 basic kanji that all Japanese schoolchildren are required to learn before entering the third grade, or for those who wish to pass Level 4 of the Japanese Language Proficiency Test for non-native speakers of Japanese. Each page features its own comic strip, kanji pronunciation guide, stroke order, and English explanations.

    Manga University Presents ... Kanji deManga: The Comic Book That Teaches You How to Read and Write Japanese! Volume 2. Japanime Co. Ltd 2005 113p. Illustration
Grades: 7 8 9 10 11 12 Adult   **495.6; 741.5**
1. Japanese language — Teaching — Aids and devices; 2. Manga; 3. Graphic novels
4-921205-03-5, $9.99
    The second volume in this series - using original comic artwork to teach readers how to identify and write the most common Japanese kanji ideographs - introduces 80 kanji that all Japanese school children are required to learn by the time they graduate from sixth grade, or for those who wish to pass Level 3 of the Japanese Language Proficiency Test for non-native speakers of Japanese. Each page features its own comic strip, kanji pronunciation guide, stroke order, and English explanations.

    Manga University Presents ... Kanji deManga: The Comic Book That Teaches You How to Read and Write Japanese! Volume 3. Japanime Co. Ltd 2005 113p. Illustration
Grades: 7 8 9 10 11 12 Adult   **495.6; 741.5**
1. Japanese language — Teaching — Aids and devices; 2. Manga; 3. Graphic novels
4-921205-04-3, $9.99
    The third volume in this series - using original comic artwork to teach readers how to identify and write the most common Japanese kanji ideographs - introduces 80 more kanji that all Japanese school children are required to learn by the time they graduate from sixth grade, or for those who wish to pass Level 3 of the Japanese Language Proficiency

Test for non-native speakers of Japanese. Each page features its own comic strip, kanji pronunciation guide, stroke order, and English explanations.

Manga University Presents ... Kanji deManga: The Comic Book That Teaches You How to Read and Write Japanese! Volume 4. Japanime Co. Ltd 2006 144p. Illustration
Grades: 7 8 9 10 11 12 Adult   **495.6; 741.5**
1. Japanese language — Teaching — Aids and devices; 2. Manga; 3. Graphic novels
4-921205-09-4, $9.99
The fourth volume in this series - using original comic artwork to teach readers how to identify and write the most common Japanese kanji ideographs - introduces 80 more kanji that all Japanese school children are required to learn by the time they graduate from sixth grade, or for those who wish to pass Level 3 of the Japanese Language Proficiency Test for non-native speakers of Japanese. Each page features its own comic strip, kanji pronunciation guide, stroke order, and English explanations.

Kari, Erika
Vampire Doll: Guilt-na-Zan Vol. 1. Tokyopop 2006 196p. Illustration
Grades: 8 9 10 11 12 Adult   **741.5; Fic**
1. Horror graphic novels; 2. Humorous graphic novels; 3. Manga; 4. Graphic novels
1-59816-519-4, $9.99
Guilt-na-Zan is a vampire aristocrat who has been sealed into a cross for more than 100 years. When he is released by Kyoji, a powerful exorcist from the family that first banished the vampire, Guilt-na-Zan is resurrected as a female doll and can only transform into his real form when he sucks blood from Kyoji's sister Tonae. Kyoji uses Guilt-na-Zan and his old servant Vincent as Tonae's bodyguards at school. They also have to deal with black sheep brother Kyoichi, who constantly tries to steal old family artifacts, trying to gain occult power. The series includes some mild sexual encounters.

Kariya, Tetsu
Oishinbo a la carte: the joy of rice. Story by Tetsu Kariya ; art by Akira Hanasaki. Viz Signature Edition 2009 268p. Illustration
Grades: 8 9 10 11 12 Adult   **741.5; Fic**
1. Cooking; 2. Manga; 3. Rice; 4. Graphic novels
978-1-4215-2144-2, $12.99
This volume collects the Oishinbo stories centering on rice, the supreme staple of the Japanese diet. As Yamaoka continues, with the help of other Tozai News staffers, to work on the newspaper's Ultimate Menu to celebrate its 100th anniversary, they examine rice. Among other stories, Yamaoka rails against the importing of rice from other countries; he shows that organic rice farming could be unhealthy depending on the farm's location; and he helps the company cafeteria chef attract more business by focusing on homestyle rice dishes. The big competition between the Ultimate Menu and the Supreme Menu is rice balls (omusubi). The stories here may help American readers understand a little more about how important rice is to Japanese culture, and they may want to try some of the

dishes. The book includes a recipe for scallop rice, which is published in color with photos. As with the other volumes, this book includes stories that originally appeared throughout the original manga series, so the characters' lives and relationships change abruptly from story to story.

Oishinbo a la carte: vegetables. Story by Tetsu Kariya ; art by Akira Hanasaki. Viz Media/Viz Signature 2009 268p. Illustration
Grades: 8 9 10 11 12 Adult **741.5; Fic**
1. Cooking — Vegetables; 2. Manga; 3. Graphic novels
978-1-4215-2143-5, $12.99

Courtesy of VIZ Media LLC

Tozai News reporter Yamaoka Shiro and his colleagues continue their quest for the Ultimate Menu. In this volume, he competes against his father Kaibara, who represents rival newspaper Teito Times and their Supreme Menu, in a competition involving the vegetables cabbage and turnip. In other stories, Yamaoka and his friends use asparagus as a way to reunite a culinary specialist and a pottery artist who broke up years ago; and they help Tomii's son get over his hatred of eggplant. A number of the stories discuss the debate between organic cultivation and the use of pesticides and imported vegetable types. Since the stories are selected from the Oishinbo series to fit into themes, they skip around in time and lack a real narrative flow. The book is suitable for teens, but the main appeal may be to adults, especially to those who want to read about food. The artist's focus on presenting all the vegetables so realistically and in great detail may just make the reader hungry.

Kate Petty
Julius Caesar: The Life of a Roman General. Gary Jeffrey & Kate Petty ; illustrated by Sam Hadley. Rosen Publishing Group 2005 48p. Illustration
Grades: 3 4 5 6 7 8   **741.5; 937**
1. Biographical graphic novels; 2. Caesar, Julius, 100 or 102 - 44 BC; 3. Rome — History — Republic, 265-30 BC; 4. Graphic novels
1-4042-0239-0, $29.25
                LC 2004014392
Ambitious, ruthless, shrewd, cruel, and intelligent are a few of the words that have been used to describe this man who changed the course of civilization. Caesar's military conquests and political alliances altered Rome's decaying system of government, producing the greatest of all ancient empires. This graphic novel takes readers on a journey to the ancient world where political intrigue and military might gave birth not only to the rise of Caesar but also to his bloody assassination. The book includes some information on what came after his death, a glossary, and a list of books for further reading.
Part of the Graphic Nonfiction series.

Kawahara, Kazune

High school debut vol. 1. VizMedia/Shojo Beat 2008 184p. Illustration

Grades: 7 8 9 10 11 12   **741.5; Fic**
1. Manga; 2. Romance graphic novels; 3. Shojo manga; 4. Graphic novels
978-1-4215-1481-9, $8.99

Haruna used to be interested only in softball and manga, but now that she's starting in high school, she wants to change her focus, to find a boyfriend and have a fun romance. The problem is, no boy will hit on her. She's done her research in magazines, but nothing is working. Then a friend's comment causes her to decide to find a coach who will help her attract boys. Upperclassman Yoh Komiyama agrees to help her, but only if Haruna promises to not fall in love with him. It's a struggle, though, for Yoh's sister and his friends decide to tag along for fun. There's one scary moment when a guy tries to abduct Haruna.

Volume 1 of 13

★ **My** Love Story!!; Volume 1. Story, Kazune Kawahara; art, Aruko; English adaptations, Ysabet Reinhardt MacFarlane; translation, JN Productions. Viz 2014 184 p. Illustration

Grades: 8 9 10 11 12   **741.5**
1. Man-woman relationship — Fiction; 2. Shojo manga
1421571447; 9781421571447, $9.99

In this graphic novel, by Kazune Kawahara, "Takeo is big and manly in a macho kind of way. His best friend, Sunakawa, is handsome in a pretty/pointy-haired way, which means that girls always find him attractive. One day Takeo rescues a girl named Yamato from a groper on the train, and she starts falling in love with him. Unfortunately for Takeo, he is too dense to realize this and spends most of the story convinced that Yamato is really in love with Sunakawa." (School Library Journal)

Volume 1 of an ongoing series

Kawase, Natsuna

The **Lapis** Lazuli crown, vol. 1. DC Comics/CMX 2009 Un Illustration

Grades: 6 7 8 9 10 11 12   **741.5; Fic**
1. Magic; 2. Manga; 3. Romance graphic novels; 4. Shojo manga; 5. Graphic novels
978-1-4012-2120-1, $9.99

Teenage Miel is a member of the Violette family, which once was influential due to having so many important magicians who protected the kingdom of Savarin. Now, her older sister Sara is a strong magician, but Miel won't use her talent. The problem is Miel has talent but no control, which tends to get her into trouble. Then she meets a handsome young man on the street, and after he eggs her into using her magic, she learns he is really the reclusive Prince Radian. Will her desire to be his friend and work in the palace be enough to motivate her to practice using her magical powers? Can she be the one who will protect the kingdom again? The book includes a short backup story, "Daisy Romance," in which Hinagiku tries to protect her house from the thief who calls himself New Moon, only to get help from the thief to catch an impostor using his name. All the romance in both stories is very innocent and sweet.

Kazumi, Yuana

Million Tears Vol. 1. Tokyopop 2007 Un Illustration

Grades: 8 9 10 11 12   **741.5; Fic**
1. Family life; 2. Mystery graphic novels; 3. Shojo manga; 4. Graphic novels
978-1-4278-0056-5, $9.99

When friends and loved ones begin to disappear and no one else remembers them, Hiromu's sense of reality begins to crumble—until the day he runs into a mysterious figure who can erase a person's very existence, and tells Hiromu he's another "destiny thief." This is the first of two volumes.

Keenan, Sheila

Dogs of war. By Sheila Keenan and illustrated by Nathan Fox. Graphix 2013 208 p.

Grades: 4 5 6 7   **741.5**
1. Dogs — Fiction; 2. Dogs — War use — Fiction; 3. Vietnam War, 1961-1975 — Fiction; 4. War; 5. World War, 1914-1918 — Fiction; 6. World War, 1939-1945 — Fiction; 7. Graphic novels
0545128870; 9780545128872, $22.99; 9780545128889
LC 2011006735

This graphic novel, by Sheila Keenan, "tells the stories of the canine military heroes of World War I, World War II, and the Vietnam War. This collection of three fictional stories was inspired by historic battles and real military practice. Each story tells the remarkable adventures of a soldier and his service dog . . . bringing to life the faithful dogs who braved bombs, barrages, and battles to save the lives of countless soldiers." (Publisher's note)

Includes bibliographical references

Kelly, Claire

Nellie in the News. Art by Faith Erin Hicks. Harcourt Achieve/Steck-Vaughn 2007 48p. Illustration

Grades: 3 4 5 6 7 8   **741.5; Fic**
1. Adventure graphic novels; 2. Bly, Nellie, 1864-1922; 3. Graphic novels
978-1-4190-3218-9, $8.99

Rosie Freedman is a gifted young African American girl who drops out of school when her family falls on hard times. It is only when she meets Nellie Bly, a journalist about to set out on a mission to travel around the world in 80 days, that Rosie starts to dream again. This historical fiction graphic novel includes prose intervals that provide more information on Bly's journey as well as the hard times for people in New York's Hell's Kitchen in the late 1880s.

Part of the Timeline Graphic Novels series.

Kelly, Joe

★ **Captain** Stoneheart and the Truth Fairy. Image Comics 2008 Un Illustration

Grades: 5 6 7 8 9 10 11 12 Adult   **741.5; Fic**
1. Adventure graphic novels; 2. Fairies; 3. Fantasy graphic novels; 4. Pirates; 5. Graphic novels
978-1-58240-865-1, $19.99

The story, in rhyming text with lushly drawn and colored art, tells the tale of the pirate named Captain Stoneheart, a fierce and angry pirate who won't let people tell him what to do. After attacking a peaceful ship and killing everyone on it, his crew discovers a caged fairy in the hold, and Stoneheart knows he can wreak havoc and scourge the world with her powers. Somehow they connect even through his anger, and when she finds a way to save Stoneheart and his crew even when she is free to leave the pirates and save herself, Stoneheart starts to change. Alas, the good times can't last, and he commits one final act that destroys everything and everyone around him because he won't let anyone tell him what to do, even if he loves that one person. There is some fighting violence, and there are some monsters, so this is not a story for very young readers. Older elementary school age children who love the old fairy tales with the tragic endings will be able to handle this story.

Douglas Fredericks and the House of They. Illustrated by Ben Roman. Image Comics 2009 80p. Illustration
Grades: 3 4 5 6   **741.5; Fic**
1. Adventure graphic novels; 2. Humorous graphic novels; 3. Graphic novels
978-1-58240-994-8, $17.99
   Douglas Fredericks just wants to give his parents a very original, unique anniversary present, but every time he comes up with an idea, someone tells him "They" say it can't happen. After many different attempts, he builds the first self-baking cake, Cake City, that will provide cake for fifteen years, because his parents (especially the Captain, his father) love cake, and then wants to just sample the first piece, people come along and tell him "No, Douglas, don't! You know what They say! You can't have your cake and eat it too!" So, Douglas decides to go find the House of They to confront the people there. After many trials, he can finally ask "WHY?" and he refuses to accept "Because They say so" as an answer. Kelly, Roman, and colorist Molina are part of The Man of Action Studios that has created the television cartoon Ben 10, as well as many comics; they have used the deluxe picture book format for this story, with full-page color art on every other page (with quite a few double-page spreads) it even has a ribbon marker.

★ **I** kill giants. Image Comics 2009 Un Illustration
Grades: 8 9 10 11 12   **741.5; Fic**
1. Family life; 2. Fantasy graphic novels; 3. Giants; 4. Graphic novels
978-1-60706-092-5, $15.99
   Fifth-grader Barbara Thorson appears to be a smart-aleck troublemaker, and she does get into trouble at school, with great regularity. She has no friends, she has to deal with teachers and a principal who don't understand her, with the bully Taylor, with Sophie, the new girl who wants to be her friend, and now with a school psychologist. She has no time for this nonsense, she is a giant killer, with her mighty weapon she calls Coveleski (after Stanley Coveleski, a baseball player in the early twentieth century). What writer Kelly reveals slowly to the reader is Barbara's real family situation: her mother is dying, her older sister is trying to keep the family together, and Barbara is convinced that if she can slay the Titan, a huge giant, she can keep her mother alive. While Barbara is young, the story has an emotional intensity better suited for older teens.

Space Ghost. Joe Kelly, writer ; Ariel Olivetti, illustrator ; Richard Starkings, letterer. DC Comics 2005 Un Illustration
Grades: 8 9 10 11 12 Adult   **741.5; Fic**
1. Superhero graphic novels; 2. Graphic novels
1-4012-0721-9, $14.99

The masked avenger of the cartoon spaceways has been a popular character since his introduction to television in 1966. Since then, people have wondered who he is, how he got those power bands and why he protects the galaxy from evil. Now his story is told for the first time ever, and readers will learn the tragic circumstances that led to his donning a cowl and his first battle with arch nemesis Zorak. This is not the funny character from Cartoon Network.

Kelly, Walt
   Walt Kelly's Our Gang Vol. 1. Fantagraphics Books 2006 104p. Illustration
Grades: 4 5 6 7 8 9 10 11 12 Adult   **741.5; Fic**
1. Friendship; 2. Humorous graphic novels; 3. Graphic novels
978-1-56097-753-7, $12.95
   Kelly's longest-running continuing comics series was based on the "real-life" characters of MGM's durable short-film series, "Our Gang" (a.k.a. "The Little Rascals"). Kelly's Our Gang harks back to the days before television, when kids spent most of their time playing outdoors, limited only by each other's imagination and ingenuity. This is the first in a series of books reprinting Walt Kelly's Our Gang stories. Suitable for both adults and children, they have been restored from their comic book appearance. These stories were originally published in 1942 and 1943.
   Volume 1 of 4

Kennedy, Mike
   Superman: Infinite City. Art by Carlos Meglia. DC Comics 2005 96p. Illustration
Grades: 8 9 10 11 12 Adult   **741.5; Fic**
1. Superhero graphic novels; 2. Superman (Fictional character); 3. Graphic novels
978-1-4012-0066-4, $17.99
   When a villain uses a very powerful weapon in Metropolis, Clark and Lois trace him back to an old town called Infinite City. They find the town abandoned, except for a doorway that leads to another amazing world.... the true Infinite City, where magic and science happily coexist. Superman and Lois step through the magic portal and become embroiled in a war for power on the other side. One faction wants to stay in its dimension, and another wants to branch out to our world. Superman will meet a doppelganger called the Warden, who shares the Kryptonian's might but not his intellect. He will also come across the architect of this world, a robot leader who claims to be what remains of his father Jor-El.

Kesel, Barbara
   Legends of the Dark Crystal, vol. 1: The Garthim Wars. Written by Barbara Randall Kesel ; illustrated by Heidi Arnhold and Max Kim. Tokyopop 2007 192p. Illustration
Grades: 8 9 10 11 12 Adult   **741.5**
1. Adventure graphic novels; 2. Fantasy graphic novels; 3. Graphic novels
978-1-59816-701-6, $9.99
   Lahr and Neffi are gentle and fun-loving Gelflings who enjoy the simple pleasures of life. Their world is turned upside down when the violent Garthim attack their villages, and after a narrow escape, the two Gelflings must join forces and learn how to become leaders to help another Gelfling

village defend themselves against the Garthim. This story is a prequel to the Jim Henson film, The Dark Crystal. It includes some violence.

Ketcham, Hank

★ **Hank** Ketcham's Complete Dennis the Menace (Volume 1): 1951-1952. Fantagraphics Books 2005 590p. Illustration
Grades: 2 3 4 5 6 7 8 9 10 11 12 Adult   **741.5; Fic**
1. Dennis the Menace (Fictional character); 2. Humorous graphic novels; 3. Graphic novels
1-56097-680-2, $24.95

This volume is the first of a series that will reprint every Dennis the Menace cartoon. The first cartoon was published in sixteen newspapers on March 12, 1951, and the cartoon was soon picked up by many more newspapers. This volume collects the daily single-panel cartoons from March 1951 through December 1952. In these cartoons, readers meet five-and-a-half-year-old Dennis Mitchell, his parents, retired neighbors George and Martha Wilson, Dennis' dog Ruff, and neighborhood pals Joey and Margaret. Every cartoon hearkens back to the positive aspects of growing up in suburban Middle America and the joys (mostly) of being a child. While older adults will catch all the references to past popular culture (i.e. Hopalong Cassidy), younger readers will enjoy the humor arising from everyday situations.

Kibuishi, Kazu

Amulet book five: prince of the elves. Kazu Kibuishi. Graphix 2012 208 p. (Amulet)
Grades: 3 4 5 6 7 8   **741.5**
1. Amulets; 2. Brothers and sisters; 3. Charms; 4. Elves; 5. Fantasy graphic novels; 6. Imaginary places; 7. Magic; 8. Magic — Juvenile fiction; 9. Single-parent families — Juvenile fiction; 10. Graphic novels
0545208890; 9780545208895, $12.99
LC 2012935527
Author Kazu Kibuishi presents book five in the graphic novel series. "Emily has survived the chaos of the Guardian Academy, but Max Griffin, who is working for the Elf King, has escaped with the Mother Stone. The Elf King has now forged new amulets, which will allow him the ability to invade Cielis and destroy it once and for all. Emily and her friends desperately make preparations to defend Cielis in what will inevitably be a brutal war, and they can only hope that it will be enough to defeat the Elf King." (Publisher's note)

"Anchored by dazzlingly lush art and a complex, character-laden plot, Kibuishi's Amulet series remains a must-have for all elementary- and middle-school graphic-novel collections. Devoted fans will appreciate that this volume begins to flesh-out the backstory of two characters while starting to tie together a few of the many plot elements." Booklist

Amulet, book four: The Last Council. Graphix 2011 207 p.
Grades: 3 4 5 6 7 8   **741.5**
978-0-545-20887-1, $10.99; 0-545-20887-4
"Emily and her friends think they'll find the help they need in Cielis, but something isn't right. Streets that were once busy are deserted, and the townspeople who are left

live in crippling fear. Emily is escorted to the Academy where she's expected to compete for a spot on the Guardian Council, the most powerful Stonekeepers. But as the number of competitors gets smaller and smaller, a terrible secret is slowly uncovered—a secret that, if left buried, means certain destruction of everything Emily fights for." (Publisher's note)

Amulet, book one: The Stonekeeper. Graphix 2008 185p.
Grades: 3 4 5 6 7 8   **741; Fic; 741.5**
1. Adventure graphic novels; 2. Fantasy graphic novels; 3. Mystery graphic novels; 4. Graphic novels
978-0-439-84680-6, $21.99; 0-439-84680-3; 978-0-439-84681-3 (pa), $9.99; 0-439-84681-1 (pa)
After a family tragedy, Emily, Navin, and their mother move to an ancestral home to start a new life. When their mother is kidnapped by a tentacled creature, Em and Navin have to figure out how to set things straight and save their mother's life.

"Filled with excitement, monsters, robots, and mysteries, this fantasy adventure will appeal to many readers." SLJ
Other titles in this series are: The Stonekeeper's curse (2009); The Cloud Searchers (2010); The Last Council (2011); Prince of the elves (2012); Escape from Lucien (2014); Firelight (2016)

Amulet, book three: The Cloud Searchers. Graphix 2010 197p.
Grades: 3 4 5 6 7 8   **741.5; 741**
978-0-545-20885-7 (pa), $10.99; 0-545-20885-8 (pa)
"Emily, Navin, and their crew of resistance fighters charter an airship and set off in search of the lost city of Cielis, which is believed to be located on an island high above the clouds. The mysterious Leon Redbeard is their guide, and there's a surprising new addition to the crew: the Elf King's son, Trellis. But is he ally or enemy? And will Emily ever be able to trust the voice of the Amulet?" (Publisher's note)

Amulet, book two: The Stonekeeper's curse. Graphix 2009 217p.
Grades: 3 4 5 6 7 8   **741.5; 741**
978-0-439-84683-7, $10.99; 0-439-84683-8
"Emily and Navin's mother is still in a coma from the arachnopod's poison, and there's only one place to find help: Kanalis, the bustling, beautiful city of waterfalls. But when Em, her brother, and Miskit and the rest of the robotic crew aboard the walking house reach the city, they quickly realize that seeking help is looking for trouble, dangerous trouble." (Publisher's note)

★ **Copper.** Graphix/Scholastic 2010 94p. Illustration
Grades: 5 6 7 8   **741; 741.5; Fic**
1. Adventure graphic novels; 2. Dogs; 3. Science fiction graphic novels; 4. Graphic novels
978-0-545-09892-2, $21.99; 0-545-09892-0; 978-0-545-09893-9 (pa), $12.99; 0-545-09893-9 (pa)
A collection of graphic novel adventures about a boy named Copper and his dog, Fred, including "navigating a dangerous forest of giant mushrooms, [and] surviving a crash landing in a homemade airplane—that run from lyrical to the downright apocalyptic. Illustrated in a deceptively

simple style, its solemn tenor and deep strangeness . . . will likely inspire heavy investment from those who prefer a somewhat off-kilter read." Booklist

Escape from Lucien. Kazu Kibuishi. Scholastic / Graphix 2014 256 p. Illustration; Map (Amulet)
Grades: 3 4 5 6 7 8   **741.5; Fic**
  1. Brothers and sisters — Fiction; 2. Elves — Fiction; 3. Kings and rulers — Fiction
9780545433150, $12.99
                                    LC 2013957419
  "Navin and his classmates journey to Lucien, a city ravaged by war and plagued by mysterious creatures, where they search for a beacon essential to their fight against the Elf King. Meanwhile, Emily heads back into the Void with Max, one of the Elf King's loyal followers, where she learns his darkest secrets. The stakes, for both Emily and Navin, are higher than ever." (Publisher's note)
  "Most of the cleanly drawn, lushly backgrounded panels focus on faces, with occasional full-spread scenes adding dramatic visual highlights.A page-turner that gives the heroic Stonekeepers plenty of chances to show their stuff and moves the main story along an inch or two." Kirkus

Explorer: the hidden doors. Edited by Kazu Kibuishi. Abrams Books 2014 128 p. Color; Illustration (Explorer)
Grades: 4 5 6 7 8   **741.5**
  1. Bullying — Fiction; 2. Doors — Fiction; 3. Monsters — Fiction
1419708821; 9781419708824, $19.95; 9781419708848
                                    LC 2014938941
  In this collection of comics edited by Kazu Kibuishi, "a bullied boy discovers a door guarded by a sly monster . . . A painting of a door opens in a forgotten Egyptian tomb . . . A portal in the park promises to turn you into a much cooler version 2.0 - if you can just get the bugs out." (Publisher's note)
  "Readers are once again presented with an array of stories created by a cast of comics authors and illustrators smartly assembled by Kibuishi...The range in this slim volume is expansive. From funny to deep and fantastical to refined, all of the stories have a compelling narrative arc. The colors are just as varied, and are universally dynamic and nuanced. Consider this (and previous series installments) as a necessary addition to any graphic novel collection." SLJ
  Other titles in the series are: The Mystery Boxes (2012); The Lost Islands (2013)

Explorer: the lost islands. Kazu Kibuishi. Abrams Books 2013 128 p. (Explorer)
Grades: 4 5 6 7 8   **741.5; Fic**
  1. Islands; 2. Graphic novels
1419708813; 141970883X; 9781419708817, $19.95; 9781419708831, $10.95
                                    LC 2013935794
  In this follow-up to "Explorer: The Mystery Boxes," Kazu Kibuishi and a crew of cartoonists again take turns weaving seven tales based around a loose theme. This time the motif is islands, and the contributors are left to interpret it in illustrated shorts. Some, by using their strange and remote settings as microcosms, underscore the value of hard work . . . or finding one's niche . . ., while others examine more

abstract concepts such as exploration and isolation." (Publishers Weekly)

Explorer: the mystery boxes. Kazu Kibuishi. Abrams Books 2012 126 p. (Explorer)
Grades: 4 5 6 7 8   **S C; 741.5**
  1. Boxes; 2. Boxes — Fiction; 3. Mystery graphic novels; 4. Short stories; 5. Graphic novels
1419700103; 9781419700095, $10.95; 9781419700101, $19.95
                                    LC 2011025343
  This collection of short stories offers "[s]even . . . stories [which] answer one simple question: what's in the box" . . . [E]ach of these . . . illustrated short graphic works revolves around a central theme: a mysterious box and the marvels—or mayhem—inside. Artists include . . . Kazu Kibuishi, Raina Telgemeier ('Smile'), and Dave Roman ('Astronaut Academy'), as well as Jason Caffoe, Stuart Livingston, Johane Matte, Rad Sechrist (all contributors to the . . . comics anthology series 'Flight'), and . . . artist Emily Carroll." (Publisher's note)
  Seven graphic stories.

Kikai, Masahide

Edu-Manga: Mother Teresa. Written by Masahide Kikai ; illustrated by Ren Kishida. Digital Manga Publishing 2007 152p. Illustration
Grades: 2 3 4 5 6 7 8   **92; 741.5**
  1. Biographical graphic novels; 2. Kodomo manga; 3. Manga; 4. Teresa, Mother, 1910-1997; 5. Graphic novels
978-1-56970-972-6, $9.95
  This volume in the Edu-Manga series covers the life of Mother Teresa, the nun who worked among the "poorest of the poor" in India for most of her adult life. Born to an Albanian family in Madedonia, she was named Agnes Gouxha. She chose her vocation as a nun when she was twelve years old, and when she turned eighteen she left Macedonia and her family and joined the Loreto order of nuns in Calcutta. After twenty years in the monastery there, she went into the slums to work directly among the poor. She started alone, but when she died in 1997, there were about 4,000 nuns working at 602 facilities in 125 countries throughout the world. Her story is introduced by Astro Boy and his friends, and the book includes a "Q & A" which gives more information about Mother Teresa, nuns, her work, and a timeline of her life.

Kikuta, Michiyo

Mamotte! Lollipop Vol. 1. Random House/Del Rey Manga 2007 224p. Illustration
Grades: 8 9 10 11 12 Adult   **741.5; Fic**
  1. Fantasy graphic novels; 2. Shojo manga; 3. Graphic novels
978-0-345-49623-2, $10.95
  Junior high schooler Nina is ready to fall in love. She's looking for a boy who's cute and sweet-and strong enough to support her when the chips are down. But what happens when Nina's dream comes true . . . twice? One day, two cute boys literally fall from the sky: they're both wizards and they've come to the Human World to take the Magic Exam. The boys' success on this test depends on protecting Nina from evil, so now Nina has a pair of cute magical boys

chasing her everywhere she goes. But, because Nina accidentally swallowed a magic "crystal pearl" that is part of the Magic Exam, Zero and Ichi aren't the only wizards around her, and some are willing to do just about anything to get their hands on the magic pearl.

Kim, Derek Kirk
★ **Good** as Lily. Written by Derek Kirk Kim; illustrated by Jesse Hamm; lettering by Jared K. Fletcher. DC Comics/Minx 2007 Un Illustration
Grades: 7 8 9 10 11 12   **741.5; Fic**
1. Fantasy graphic novels; 2. Humorous graphic novels; 3. Graphic novels
978-1-4012-1381-7, $9.99
"On her eighteenth birthday, Korean American Grace suddenly finds herself surrounded by three very corporeal essences of herself: as a small child, as a 30-year-old woman, and as "a cranky old fart." Each of these incarnations is at an emotional precipice, which teenage Grace helps resolve, allowing the other self to quietly disappear. . . . Kim's pacing and plotting are excellent, and Hamm's black, white, and gray artwork is lively, witty, and full of appropriate comedy and melodrama." Booklist

Kim, Susan
★ **City** of spies. [by] Susan Kim [and] Laurence Klavan; illustrated by Pascal Dizin. First Second 2010 172p. Illustration
Grades: 4 5 6 7   **741.5; Fic**
1. Adventure graphic novels; 2. Spies; 3. World War, 1939-1945; 4. Graphic novels
1-59643-262-4 (pa); 978-1-59643-262-8 (pa), $17
This graphic novel, set in New York City during World War II, tells the story of Kim and Klavan, who are hunting for Nazi spies. (Bull Cent Child Books)
"With her mother gone and a father who has better things to do than be bothered raising a daughter, Evelyn is sent to live with her unconventional Aunt Lia in the bohemian art world of 1942 New York City. . . . Evelyn spends much of her time in the company of imaginary superheroes, fouling up the plans of Nazi spies. Before long she finds an unlikely friend in the building superintendent's son, Tony. Together, they . . . stumble upon an actual Nazi plot. With stupefying precision, Dizin's art channels Hergé's Tintin in tone, palette, and with the remarkable expressiveness of the clean, flexible figures. . . . With villains and danger that just border on the genuinely scary, the tale is filled not only with a thrilling sense of excitement but also with a child's longing for a grown-up to believe in." Booklist

Kinney, Sarah
Nancy Drew, girl detective #14: Sleight of Dan. Stefan Petrucha & Sarah Kinney, writers ; Sho Murase, artist ; with 3D CG elements and color by Carlos Jose Guzman. Papercutz 2008 Un Illustration
Grades: 3 4 5 6 7 8 9   **741.5; Fic**
1. Adventure graphic novels; 2. Drew, Nancy (Fictional character); 3. Mystery graphic novels; 4. Graphic novels
978-1-59707-108-6, $12.95; 978-1-59707-107-9 (pa), $7.95

The assistant for magician Dan Deville has disappeared, and Nancy tries to find Tina. It all started when Nancy attended one of Dan's magic shows with buddies George and Bess, and George challenged Nancy to figure out the magician's tricks. Now, though Nancy runs into a large anaconda while trying to find Tina, and large snakes are definitely not fun.
Volume 14 of the Nancy Drew, Girl Detective series

Kipling, Rudyard
Jungle book adapted by Jean-Blaise Mitildji ; illustrated by TieKo. IDW Publishing 2009 62p. Illustration
Grades: 5 6 7 8 9   **741.5; Fic**
1. Adventure graphic novels; 2. Children's authors; 3. India; 4. Kipling, Rudyard, 1865-1936 — Adaptations; 5. Wolves; 6. Graphic novels
978-1-60010-352-0, $14.99
This graphic novel adapts Kipling's tale of Mowgli, the boy who was raised by wolves, educated by Baloo the bear and Bagheera the panther, the enemy of Shere Khan the tiger. When the wolf pack overthrows the wise Akela and order Mowgli to leave, he returns to the human village, but he never feels completely comfortable among them. When Shere Khan comes to hunt him, Mowgli fights with Akela at his side, but this causes the people to reject him. This adaptation, originally published in France, stays true to Kipling's original story; at the beginning of the tale, Mowgli is naked, although the one panel showing him from the front is a longer-distance shot. The book includes biographical information about Kipling, historical background on the British Empire and on India in the nineteenth century, and an analysis of the story.

Kirby, Jack
Jack Kirby's Fourth World Omnibus Volume Two. Image Comics 2007 396p. Illustration
Grades: 7 8 9 10 11 12 Adult   **741.5; Fic**
1. Superhero graphic novels; 2. Graphic novels
978-1-4012-1357-2, $49.99
DC collects four series by Kirby — The New Gods, The Forever People, Mister Miracle, and Superman's Pal Jimmy Olsen — in chronological order as they originally appeared. These comics spanned galaxies, from the streets of Metropolis to the far-flung worlds of New Genesis and Apokolips, as cosmic-powered heroes and villains struggled for supremacy. In this second volume, the evil Darkseid's schemes continue to unfold while the New Gods, the Forever People, Mr. Miracle and other heroes battle his many minions.

Jack Kirby's Fourth World Omnibus, Volume One. DC Comics 2007 396p. Illustration
Grades: 8 9 10 11 12 Adult   **741.5; Fic**
1. Science fiction graphic novels; 2. Superhero graphic novels; 3. Graphic novels
978-1-4012-1344-2, $49.99
In the 1970s, legendary comics creator Kirby left Marvel Comics to work for DC Comics, writing and drawing several new series and also taking over Superman's Pal Jimmy Olsen. This volume collects the first three issues of his new series, plus the start of his run on Jimmy Olsen, from issue #133. With the Fourth World storylines in Kirby's New

Gods, Forever People, and Mister Miracle, he created new mythologies and epic storylines. This hardcover edition uses a flat paper that shows off the inks and colors brilliantly.

Jack Kirby's Omac: one man army corps. Jack Kirby, writer/penciller ; D. Bruce Berry, Mike Royer, inkers and letterers. DC Comics 2008 176p. Illustration
Grades: 7 8 9 10 11 12 Adult   **741.5; Fic**
1. Superhero graphic novels; 2. Graphic novels
978-1-4012-1790-7, $24.99
In the 1970s, comics master creator Jack Kirby shocked the comics industry when he left Marvel Comics to work for the opposition DC Comics. He created new characters and new worlds. Among them was an unusual science fiction concept: OMAC, One Man Army Corps. Corporate nobody Buddy Blank is changed by the artificial intelligence "Brother Eye" into a superpowered agent of the Global Peace Agency, fighting bizarre menaces in a disturbing, near-future world. This book collects the complete 8-issue saga as published by DC; readers will note it ends in a cliffhanger that was never resolved.

Silver Star. Image Comics 2007 152p. Illustration
Grades: 8 9 10 11 12 Adult   **741.5; Fic**
1. Superhero graphic novels; 2. Graphic novels
978-1-58240-764-7, $34.99
Chronicling the rise of Homo-Geneticus, the New Breed of humanity that spawns both Silver Star (Morgan Miller) and the nefarious Darius Brumm. Silver Star was Kirby's final creation and one of only two creator-owned projects published by Pacific Comics in the early '80s. This volume also includes the original screenplay, written by Kirby and Steve Sherman, upon which Kirby based the comic.

Silver Star: Graphite Edition. Twomorrows Publishing 2006 Un Illustration
Grades: 8 9 10 11 12 Adult   **741.5; Fic**
1. Adventure graphic novels; 2. Science fiction graphic novels; 3. Graphic novels
1-893905-55-1, $19.95
Jack Kirby first conceptualized Silver Star in the mid-1970s as a movie screenplay, complete with illustrations to sell the idea to Hollywood. Too far ahead of its time for Tinseltown, Jack instead adapted his Visual Novel" as a six-issue mini-series for Pacific Comics in the early 1980s, making it the last original creation of his career. Now, in Silver Star: Graphite Edition, King" Kirby's final series is collected at last, this time reproduced from his un-inked pencil art. This is the complete story of Homo-Geneticus, the New Breed of humanity that spawns both hero (Silver Star) and villain (the nefarious Darius Drumm). The book includes Kirby's screenplay, including illustrations and never-published character sketches. Plus there are pin-ups and other rare Kirby art, and an historical overview to put it all in perspective.

Kishi, Daimuro
Time Guardian, Vol. 1. DC Comics/CMX 2007 198p. Illustration
Grades: 5 6 7 8 9 10 11 12   **741.5; Fic**
1. Fantasy graphic novels; 2. Manga; 3. Shojo manga; 4. Graphic novels

1-4012-1161-5, $9.99
High school student Miu stumbles upon a mysterious pawnshop that trades time for people's memories. Shop owner Tokiya hires Miu to be his Time Go-Between to work with his customers, but she must never speak of the shop to anyone.

Kishimoto, Masashi
★ **Naruto.** vol. 1, The tests of the Ninja. Story and art by Masashi Kishimoto; [English adaptation by Jo Duffy]. Viz 2003 186p. Illustration
Grades: 7 8 9 10 11 12   **741.5; Fic**
1. Manga; 2. Martial arts; 3. Shonen manga; 4. Graphic novels
1-56931-900-6; 978-1-56931-900-0, $7.95
"Teen orphan Naruto wants to become the greatest ninja of all, despite the fact that most people in his village have despised him from birth because a terrible demon has been imprisoned in his body. . . . Teens love this series." Voice Youth Advocates
Volume 1 of 72

Kita, Naoe
The **Empty** Empire Volume 1. DC Comics/CMX 2006 192p. Illustration
Grades: 7 8 9 10 11 12   **741.5; Fic**
1. Science fiction graphic novels; 2. Shojo manga; 3. Graphic novels
1-4012-1121-6, $9.99
Long ago, the Emperor possessed great mystical powers. Now, a young boy wonders if he will have them as well. With no memories and only a rose-shaped scar on his forehead as a clue, he ponders his legacy while on the run with the girl who rescued him from a group of armed warriors. She takes him to a scientist who identifies Rose as the Emperor's clone and believes that this young boy must assume the mantle of leadership. But opposing forces with their own agenda have created another clone from the Emperor's DNA...and now the struggle for power begins. The book includes some mildly strong language and some violence.

Kitchen, Alexa
Drawing Comics is Easy! (Except When It's Hard). Denis Kitchen Publishing Company 2006 Un Illustration
Grades: 2 3 4 5 6 7 8 9 10 11 12 Adult   **741.5**
1. Drawing; 2. Graphic novels
0-9710080-6-X, $19.95
Drawing Comics is Easy! (Except When It's Hard!) is entirely the work of a seven-year-old (at the time) prodigy cartoonist, who in 2007 was ten years old. Though seemingly aimed at a peer audience of other children, this idiosyncratic How-To book will appeal to readers of any age, especially those interested in cartooning and the creative process. Kitchen is the daughter of Denis Kitchen, who's been in the comics industry as a publisher and agent for many years.

★ **Grown-ups** are dumb! (No offense). Hyperion Books 2009 Un Illustration
Grades: 3 4 5 6 7 8   **741.5; Fic**

1. Family life; 2. Humorous graphic novels; 3. Graphic novels

978-1-4231-1331-7, $8.99

Twelve-year-old Alexa Kitchen wrote the comics collected here when she was ten years old. Her characters Molly, Sharon, and Kathy navigate life in school (and piles of homework), and at home (with pesky younger brothers). In other cartoons, she depicts the frustrations of dealing with incomprehensible paper folding instructions, the joys (and despairs) of messy rooms, and of toddler Hurricane Abby's exploration of her house. Kitchen's art ranges from the heavy pencils in the cartoons about Molly to scratchy ink in most of the other stories, to highly detailed drawings of the incredibly messy bedroom, all on pink pages. She describes herself as the world's youngest professional cartoonist," has been drawing cartoons since she could hold a pencil, and already has several books published; in 2007, at the age of ten, she was nominated for a Harvey and an Eisner Award for her book Drawing Comics is Easy! (Except When It's Hard).

Klavan, Laurence

★ **Brain** camp. By Susan Kim and Laurence Klavan; illustrated by Faith Erin Hicks. First Second 2010 151p. Illustration

Grades: 7 8 9 10   **741.5; Fic**
  1. Camps; 2. Horror graphic novels; 3. Mystery graphic novels; 4. Science fiction graphic novels; 5. Graphic novels

978-1-59643-366-3, $16.99; 1-59643-366-3

Jenna and Lucas are both under-achieving young teens who suddenly receive invitations to join the Fielding Camp for the summer. Pressed by their respective parents to attend, Jenna and Lucas both notice some strange things at the camp, and neither feels like eating the nasty slop served at every meal. The other campers are either intellectually challenged bullies, misfits, or supersmart zombies. At first Dwayne, a self-described spaz, befriends them, but when his cabin "wins" ice cream treats at dinner, Lucas sees the camp counselors sneaking in that night to "inoculate" all his cabin mates. Lucas and Jenna work against time to escape the camp and develop an antidote.

The authors present a "well-rounded adventure here, as the far-out (and kind of gross) climax mixes with genuine insight into dealing with parents, fitting into a new crowd, and handling the pressures of performance. Hicks' line work is cool enough to assuage older readers who might be suspicious of the summer-camp setting." Booklist

Kleid, Neil

Jack London's Call of the Wild. Art by Alex Nino. Puffin Graphics 2006 176p. Illustration

Grades: 5 6 7 8 9 10   **741.5; Fic**
  1. Adventure graphic novels; 2. Dogs; 3. London, Jack; 4. London, Jack — Adaptations; 5. Graphic novels

0-14-240571-X, $10.99

Buck was a pampered dog on Judge Miller's estate in Santa Clara, California of 1897; then one of Judge Miller's men sold Buck to a broker selling sled dogs to the men flocking to the Yukon in the Gold Rush of that time. A strong dog, Buck manages to survive and even thrive under masters good and bad. This volume includes the artist's sketch gallery and sample script pages.

Klein, Grady

The **cartoon** introduction to statistics. By Grady Klein and Alan Dabney, Ph.D. Hill and Wang, a Division of Farrar, Straus and Giroux 2013 240 p.

Grades: 7 8 9 10 11 12   **519.5**
  1. Mathematical statistics; 2. Statistics; 3. Graphic novels

0809033593; 9780809033591, $17.95

LC 2012030027

This book, by Grady Klien and Alan Dabney, explores statistics in humorous cartoon illustrations. "Separating the book into two main parts (hunting statistics and gathering parameters) for readers both in and outside the classroom, they explore the key foundational concepts of statistics and the perils of improper methods. They round out the book with the 'Math Cave,' which provides easy access to the formulas every student will want to have close at hand." (Publisher's note)

Klimowski, Andrzej

Dr. Jekyll and Mr. Hyde: a graphic novel. Illustrated and adapted by Andrzej Klimowski and Danusia Schejbal. Sterling 2009 122p. Illustration

Grades: 6 7 8 9   **741; 741.5**
  1. Graphic novels; 2. Horror graphic novels; 3. Stevenson, Robert Louis, 1850-1894 — Adaptations

978-1-4114-1595-9 (pa), $14.95; 1-4114-1595-7 (pa)

This graphic novel adaptation of Robert Louis Stevenson's story "is the story of a respectable London doctor who ends up leading a dreadful double life—as a doctor, and as a cold-blooded murderer." Publisher's note

"Klimowski captures a . . . formal air with a literal but still quick-moving adaptation, and Schejbal's grainy art displays a Richard Sala-like sense of both grit and unease. . . . Overall, this will have the most appeal for readers with an eye for the moody and strange." Booklist

Kneece, Mark

The **Twilight** Zone: the after hours. Adaptation by Mark Kneece; illustrated by Rebekah Isaacs. Walker & Company 2008 Un Illustration

Grades: 5 6 7 8 9 10   **741.5; Fic**
  1. Supernatural graphic novels; 2. Twilight zone (Television program); 3. Graphic novels

978-0-8027-9716-2, $16.99; 978-0-8027-9717-9 (pa), $9.99

LC 2008-4310

Marsha White visits a department store to buy an advertised gold thimble, is taken by elevator to a floor with empty display cases except for one, which has the thimble, and she deals with an odd saleswoman who knows her name. When Marsha is in the elevator, she discovers the thimble is defective and tries to complain, but the manager insists there is no eighteenth floor, the store has no elevator, and the store has never carried gold thimbles. As she begins to leave, Marsha faints at the sight of a mannequin that looks exactly like the strange saleswoman, and she's put into a back room to recover. When she wakes up, the store has been closed and she's locked in. This is an actual episode of the old Twilight Zone television show.

"Kneece's adaptation is quick and enjoyable and introduces a classic TV series to a new generation of readers.

Isaacs's illustrations are clean, distinct and cinematic in scope, employing an interesting variety of angles." Kirkus

The **Twilight** Zone: walking distance. Adaptation from Rod Serling's original script by Mark Kneece; illustrated by Dove McHargue. Walker & Company 2008 Un Illustration
Grades: 5 6 7 8 9 10   **741.5; Fic**
  1. Supernatural graphic novels; 2. Twilight zone (Television program); 3. Graphic novels
978-0-8027-9714-8, $16.99; 978-0-8027-9715-5 (pa), $9.99
                              LC 2008-4273
Thirty-nine-year-old businessman Martin Sloan's car blows a tire as he's driving, and he realizes he is within walking distance of his hometown. Leaving his car to be repaired, he decides to walk there. However, when he reaches town, he has also gone back in time. Can he find his boyhood self and give his younger self advice? Or will everyone think he's just crazy? This is an actual episode of the old Twilight Zone television show.
  The story is "exceptionally well told and . . . [is] brilliantly adapted to a new medium." SLJ

Kobayashi, Miyuki
  Kitchen princess vol. 6. Del Rey Manga 2008 Un Illustration
Grades: 8 9 10 11 12   **741.5; Fic**
  1. Cooking; 2. Shojo manga; 3. Graphic novels
978-0-345-50194-3, $10.95
  On the eve of the dessert contest finals, Sora is hit by a truck. In the hospital, he tells Najika that he isn't her Flan Prince, then dies. Stunned by his death, and by his confession, Najika loses her sense of taste. She loses the competition, and the Director, Sora's father, orders her to leave the academy minutes before the memorial service. However, Daichi offers to take Sora's place at the academy and give up on his own dreams, if Najika can stay. She loses her scholarship, is forced into the regular classes, and almost everyone at the academy shuns her, blaming her for Sora's death.

Kochalka, James
  Monkey vs. Robot. Top Shelf Productions 2000 144p. Illustration
Grades: 5 6 7 8 9 10 11 12   **741.5; Fic**
  1. Graphic novels
1-891830-15-5, $14.95
  The book is almost wordless, allowing the reader to imagine one's own narrative. While there is violence, it's not graphic, and this little fable provides much food for thought.
  "A very simply illustrated black and white pictorial narrative about a battle between a monkey community and a self-run robot factory encroaching on the monkeys' unspoiled forest domain." Publ Wkly
  Another title in this series is: Monkey vs. Robot and the crystal of power (2003)

  Peanutbutter & Jeremy's best book ever. Alternative Comics 2003 280p. Illustration
Grades: 4 5 6 7 8 9 10 11 12   **741.5; Fic**
  1. Friendship; 2. Humorous graphic novels; 3. Graphic novels
1-891867-46-6, $14.95

Peanutbutter is a sweet cat who acts like a hardworking office cat but usually naps on top of the paperwork, and Jeremy is a troublemaking crow; and they are friends. Jeremy may seem spiteful and sometimes does very mean things to Peanutbutter, such as pretending to threaten the cat with a pistol, but most of the stories are silly and fun.

  Pinky & Stinky. Top Shelf Productions 2002 208p. Illustration
Grades: 4 5 6 7 8 9 10 11 12 Adult   **741.5; Fic**
  1. Adventure graphic novels; 2. Friendship; 3. Humorous graphic novels; 4. Graphic novels
1-891830-29-7, $17.95
  Pinky & Stinky are fat little piglets, but just because they're cuties doesn't mean that they're not brave astronauts! When they embark on a daring mission to be the first pigs on Pluto, things go horribly wrong and they crash land on the moon. There they meet some not-so-friendly moon men, and end up in the middle of a conflict between the American space program and a race of alien ice creatures.

Komura, Ayumi
  Mixed vegetables, vol. 1. Viz Media/Shojo Beat 2008 Un Illustration
Grades: 7 8 9 10 11 12   **741.5; Fic**
  1. Cooking; 2. Romance graphic novels; 3. Shojo manga; 4. Graphic novels
978-1-4215-1967-8, $8.99
  Hanayu Ashitaba is the daughter of the Patisserie Ashitaba, a famous pastry shop, but ever since she was a little girl she has wanted to become a sushi chef. Hayato Hyuga is the son of the famed Sushi Hyuga, but all he's ever wanted to be is a pastry chef, even though he's got mad skills with the knives. Both of them are students at the Oikawa High School Cooking Department, where Hanayu has decided she needs to make Hayato fall for her and marry her. However, Hayato wants Hanayu to teach him more about pastry making.
  Volume 1 of 8

Konomi, Takeshi
  The **Prince** of Tennis, Vol. 1. Viz Media, LLC 2004 192p. Illustration
Grades: 6 7 8 9 10   **741.5; Fic**
  1. Shonen manga; 2. Tennis; 3. Graphic novels
1-59116-435-4, $7.95
  "Ryoma is a former U.S. junior tennis champion who attends a Japanese academy, where his skill and natural talent make him nearly unbeatable. The younger students are inspired by him, but he's ruffling the feathers of the older tennis team members. Then the journalists appear, trying to discover the next champion, adding to the pressure. There's lots of tennis action, dramatically illustrated, and the characters, already pretty boys, are made even more attractive with their intensity." Publ Wkly
  Volume 1 of 42

Kovalic, John
  ★ **Here** Be Snapdragons. Art by Liz Rathke. Dork Storm Press 2006 120p. Illustration
Grades: 3 4 5 6 7 8 9 10 11 12 Adult   **741.5; Fic**

1. Children; 2. Humorous graphic novels; 3. Graphic novels
1-930964-52-8, $12.99
'Everybody Loves Gilly,' 2003 Origins Award for Graphic Fiction (Origins International Game Expo).

The Snapdragons are fraternal twins Jake and Jody, Cooper, Benjamin, and the years-younger Mitze, along with Jake and Jody's cat Huey. They are neighbors and friends, they love role-playing games and video games. Cooper's dad is a gamer, Jake and Jody's mother is clueless (she buys years-old Halloween costumes at a discount, unaware that the characters aren't popular any more), and they all often get babysat by Goth-cute teen Gilly, who can be a very cool Dungeon Master. One of the stories has Jake and Jody sent to their room without supper and they start quoting Wild Things by Maurice Sendak as their room begins to transform . . .

Kreie, Chris
Lost: A Tale of Survival. Art by Marcus Smith. Stone Arch Books 2007 88p. Illustration
Grades: 3 4 5 6 7 8 9   **741.5; Fic**
1. Adventure graphic novels; 2. Graphic novels
978-1-59889-828-6, $22.60
LC 2007-6245
Every summer, Eric and his dad head to the Boundary Waters Canoe Area in northern Minnesota. This year, Eric has brought his friend Cris, and the boys want to explore the wilderness on their own. When they set out in their canoe, Cris and Eric promise to return before dark. But, shortly into the trip, the river becomes a violent rapids the boys can't avoid, and Cris is injured. Now Eric must race against time to find the camp and save his friend. This graphic novel is written with an easier vocabulary for struggling and reluctant readers.
Part of the Graphic Quest line of books.

Krensky, Stephen
Comic book century: the history of American comic books. Twenty-First Century Books 2007 112p. Illustration
Grades: 5 6 7 8 9 10   **741.5; 741**
978-0-8225-6654-0, $30.60; 0-8225-6654-0
LC 2006-20795
"Part of a series that focuses on American History, this book highlights America's love and hate relationship with comic books. Starting with the 1930s, each chapter focuses on an era of the comics. Highlighted areas include the rise of Superman and Batman in the late 1930s, comics during World War II, the creation of the Comics Code Authority, Stan Lee's Marvel superhero creations, underground comix, and more." (VOYA)

Kris
A **bag** of marbles. Based on the memoir by Joseph Joffo; adapted by Kris; illustrated by Vincent Bailly; translated by Edward Gauvin. Graphic Universe 2013 126 p. Color; Illustration
Grades: 6 7 8 9 10   **940.53; 741.5; B**
1. Children and war — Fiction; 2. France — History — German occupation, 1940-1945 — Fiction; 3. Holocaust, 1939-1945; 4. Holocaust, Jewish (1939-1945) — France — Fiction; 5. Jews — France — Fiction; 7. Joffo, Joseph

— Fiction; 8. Joffo, Maurice — Fiction; 10. World War, 1939-1945 — France; 12. Graphic novels
1467715166; 9781467707008; 9781467715164, $9.95; 9781467716512
LC 2013002284
In this book by Joseph Joffo, set "in 1941 in occupied Paris, brothers Maurice and Joseph play a last game of marbles before running home to their father's barbershop. With the German occupation threatening their family's safety, the boys' parents decide Maurice and Joseph must disguise themselves and flee to their older brothers in the free zone. Surviving the long journey will take every scrap of ingenuity and courage they can muster. And if they hope to elude the Nazis, they must never, under any circumstances, admit to being Jewish."
"This graphic-novel adaptation of Joffo's 1973 memoir of the same name succeeds in melding sensitive and accurate imagery with the original narrative flow of a young secular Jewish boy's experiences in occupied France." Booklist

Krohn, Katherine
The **1918** Flu Pandemic by Katherine Krohn ; illustrated by Bob Hall, Keith Williams, and Charles Barnett, III. Capstone Press 2007 32p. Illustration
Grades: 3 4 5 6 7 8 9   **614.5; 741.5**
1. Influenza; 2. Graphic novels
978-1-4296-0158-0, $26.25
LC 2007000004
This book uses the graphic novel format to tell of the 1918 outbreak of a mysterious influenza virus that killed millions of people worldwide, making it the deadliest pandemic in history. The book includes additional facts and a list of books for further reading.
Part of the Graphic Library Disasters in History series.

The **earth-shaking** facts about earthquakes with Max Axiom, super scientist. Illustrated by Tod Smith and Al Milgrom. Capstone Press 2008 32p. Illustration
Grades: 3 4 5 6 7 8 9   **551.2; 741.5**
1. Earthquakes; 2. Graphic novels
978-1-4296-1328-6, $26.26
LC 2007-25091
Young readers learn about earthquakes, how they happen, why they happen, the damage they cause, and what's being done to study them and help people be better prepared to deal with them. Back matter includes more information about earthquakes, a glossary, and a short list of books for further reading.
Part of the Graphic Science series.

Krosoczka, Jarrett J.
Lunch Lady and the author visit vendetta. Alfred A. Knopf 2009 Un Illustration
Grades: 3 4 5 6 7 8   **741; 741.5**
978-0-375-96094-9 (lib bdg), $12.99; 978-0-375-86094-2 (pa), $5.99
LC 2009014886
The school lunch lady, a secret crime fighter, investigates a suspicious author after he visits the school and the gym teacher goes missing.

Lunch Lady and the bake sale bandit. Alfred A. Knopf 2010 Un Illustration

Grades: 3 4 5 6 7 8   **741.5; 741**
978-0-375-96729-0 (lib bdg), $12.99; 0-375-96729-X
(lib bdg); 978-0-375-86729-3 (pa), $6.99;
0-375-86729-5 (pa)
                                                LC 2010012781
Lunch Lady, Betty, and the Breakfast Bunch must figure
out who is stealing the goods from the bake sale.

Lunch Lady and the cyborg substitute. Alfred A. Knopf
2009 Un Illustration
Grades: 3 4 5 6 7 8   **741.5; Fic**
1. Humorous graphic novels; 2. Robots; 3. School
children — Food; 4. School stories; 5. Graphic novels
978-0-375-94683-7 (lib bdg), $11.99; 0-375-94683-7
(lib bdg); 978-0-375-84683-0 (pa), $5.99;
0-375-84683-2 (pa)
                                                LC 2008-4709
The school lunch lady is a secret crime fighter who
uncovers an evil plot to replace all the popular teachers with
robots
    "Yellow-highlighted pen-and-ink cartoons are as
energetic and smile-provoking as Lunch Lady's epithets of
"Cauliflower!" and Betty's ultimate weapon, the hairnet."
Booklist

Lunch Lady and the field trip fiasco. Alfred A. Knopf
2011 Un Illustration
Grades: 3 4 5 6 7 8   **741.5**
978-0-375-96730-6, $12.99; 978-0-375-86730-9 (pa),
$6.99
                                                LC 2011005907
Lunch Lady, a secret crime fighter, accompanies the
Breakfast Bunch on a class trip to an art museum, but when
Dee, Hector, and Terrence begin to think there is something
strange afoot, she suspects nothing.

Lunch Lady and the League of Librarians. Alfred A.
Knopf 2009 Un Illustration
Grades: 3 4 5 6 7 8   **741; Fic; 741.5**
1. Games; 2. Humorous graphic novels; 3. Librarians; 4.
School children — Food; 5. School stories; 6. Graphic
novels
978-0-375-94684-4 (lib bdg), $11.99; 0-375-94684-5
(lib bdg); 978-0-375-84684-7 (pa), $5.99;
0-375-84684-0 (pa)
                                                LC 2008043117
The school lunch lady, a secret crime fighter, sets out to
stop a group of librarians bent on destroying a shipment of
video games, while a group of students known as the
Breakfast Bunch provides back-up
    "The black-and-white pen-and-ink illustrations have
splashes of yellow in nearly every panel. The clean layout,
featuring lots of open space, is well suited for the intended
audience. . . . With its appealing mix of action and humor,
this clever, entertaining addition to the series should have
wide appeal." SLJ
    Other titles about the Lunch Lady are: Lunch lady and
the cyborg substitute (2009); Lunch Lady and the author
visit vendetta (2009); Lunch Lady and the summer camp
shakedown (2010); Lunch Lady and the bake sale bandit
(2010); Lunch Lady and the field trip fiasco (2011);
Lunch Lady and the mutant mathletes (2012); Lunch
Lady and the picture day peril (2012); Lunch Lady and

the video game villain (2013); Lunch Lady and the
schoolwide shuffle (2014)

Lunch Lady and the summer camp shakedown. Alfred
A. Knopf 2010 Un Illustration
Grades: 3 4 5 6 7 8   **741; 741.5**
978-0-375-86095-9 (pa), $6.99; 0-375-86095-9 (pa)
Lunch Lady and the Breakfast Bunch kids are looking
forward to a relaxing summer vacation with no funny
business. What evils could befall them at summer camp?
    "The two-color art is loopy and energetic, with varied,
easy-to-follow page layouts. Jokes and puns are
sprinkled throughout to keep the energy high until the
exciting finale." SLJ

Krueger, Jim
    Justice Volume One. Jim Krueger and Alex Ross, story
; Doug Braithwaite and Alex Ross, art. DC Comics 2006
160p. Illustration
Grades: 8 9 10 11 12 Adult   **741.5; Fic**
1. Justice League of America (Fictional characters); 2.
Superhero graphic novels; 3. Graphic novels
978-1-4012-0969-8, $19.99
    The Justice League of America are the World's Greatest
Super-Heroes, but now villains - the Riddler, Lex Luthor,
Poison Ivy, Captain Cold, and others are banding together
and making sweeping, worldwide changes that appear to be
noble acts. But, one by one the members of the JLA are being
taken down; will anyone be left to truly protect the people of
Earth?

Kuper, Peter
    The **metamorphosis**. [based on the story by] Franz
Kafka; adapted by Peter Kuper. Crown 2003 77p.
Illustration
Grades: 8 9 10 11 12   **741.5; Fic**
1. Kafka, Franz, 1883-1924 — Adaptations
1-4000-4795-1; 1-4000-5299-8 (pa), $10.95;
9781400052998
                                                LC 2003-273589
    "Gregor Samsa wakes up and discovers he has been
changed into a giant cockroach. Thus begins "The
Metamorphosis," and Kuper translates this story masterfully
with his scratchboard illustrations. The text is more spare,
but the visuals are so strongly rendered that little of the
original is changed or omitted." SLJ

Kurata, Hideyuki
    Train + Train, Vol. 1. Original story by Hideyuki Kurata
; art by Tomomasa Takuma. Go! Comi 2007 196p.
Illustration
Grades: 8 9 10 11 12 Adult   **741.5; Fic**
1. Adventure graphic novels; 2. High school students; 3.
Manga; 4. Graphic novels
978-1-933617-18-3, $10.99
    Reiichi and Liae have come to the planet Deloca to
board the high school train. On Deloca, different schools run
on special trains, with stops where students complete certain
assignments; they live in dorms on the trains. Reiichi and
Liae are registered to board the "General" school train.
Arena Pendleton, on the other hand, has determined to board
the Special Train, and she won't let anyone stop her, not even

the men her wealthy grandfather has hired to capture her and bring her home. In Ideo City, where the students must board their respective trains, Reiichi accidentally gets involved in a run-in between Arena and Kong Seeval, who intends to take Arena home. Reiichi and Arena become handcuffed together, and he has no choice but to board the Special Train. There's lots of action but little in the way of violence or bad language in this first of a manga series.

Kure, Yuki
La Corda D'Oro, Volume 1. Viz Media/Shojo Beat 2006 Un Illustration
Grades: 7 8 9 10 11 12   **741.5; Fic**
   1. Music; 2. Shojo manga; 3. Violinists; 4. Graphic novels
   978-1-4215-0583-1, $8.99
   Kahoko is a second-year (junior) general education student at Seison Academy, which also has a famous music school. Every few years, the Academy holds a music competition in which only the best students are selected to participate. However, this year the director selects Kahoko. She has just encountered a "fata," a music fairy, whom very few can see. The fairy gives her a magical violin and tells Kahoko she must participate in the competition. While some of the music students consider Kahoko to be an interloper, several of the boys find her intriguing and help her. Even with a magical violin, Kahoko still needs to learn to find the right connection with the music in order to play well.

Kurkoski, Bettina
My Cat Loki Vol. 1. Tokyopop 2006 Un Illustration
Grades: 8 9 10 11 12   **741.5; Fic**
   1. Cats; 2. Fantasy graphic novels; 3. Graphic novels
   978-1-59816-731-3, $9.99
   As a child, Ameya had always considered his cat more a sibling than a pet. As the years went by, their bond grew ever tighter. But the day his feline "brother" died was the day Ameya withdrew from the world. Several years later, Ameya encounters a drenched stray cat in the park. Little does he know what fate has in store for him... Most of the time, the cats in this global manga look like cats, but sometimes they're drawn as catboys and catgirls.

My Cat Loki Vol. 2. Tokyopop 2007 Un Illustration
Grades: 8 9 10 11 12   **741.5; Fic**
   1. Cats; 2. Fantasy graphic novels; 3. Graphic novels
   978-1-59816-732-0, $9.99
   It's a warm and sunny day when Ameya makes his way to his favorite cafe and fate rears its strange and beautiful head. When a young woman named Luci literally stumbles into Ameya's life, will the encounter lead to something more? She is just like him—a struggling artist who has a strong relationship with her pet, and she's more than a little clumsy, in a totally adorable way. But neither Loki nor Miss Chacha find Ameya's growing interest in the newcomer to be even the least bit cute; Loki doesn't care for Luci's cat Calli at all. What's a lonely cat and a heartsick agent to do?

Kurosawa, Edo
50 Things We Love About Japan written by Edo Kurosawa ; illustrated by Atsuhisa Okura. Japanime Co. Ltd. 2007 112p. Illustration
Grades: 5 6 7 8 9 10 11 12 Adult   **741.5; 952**

1. Japan; 2. Graphic novels
978-4-921205-08-9, $9.99
   From anime to karaoke to kaiten-zushi, this little book features manga illustrations and prose to offer the rest of the world a glimpse at what the Japanese love most about the country they call home. Manga readers and anime fans will find explanations for the some of the cultural elements found in the books and films.

Kurtz, Scott
Truth, Justin, and the American Way. Written by Aaron Williams and Scott Kurtz ; illustrated by Giuseppe Ferrario. Image Comics 2007 Un Illustration
Grades: 8 9 10 11 12 Adult   **741.5; Fic**
   1. Humorous graphic novels; 2. Superhero graphic novels; 3. Graphic novels
   978-1-58240-705-0, $14.99
   1980s-era slacker Justin is supposed to get married this weekend, but due to a colossal mix-up, the silly t-shirt his friends got him for his bachelor party has been switched with an alien suit. When clueless Justin puts it on, the suit molds to his body, and when an FBI agent after the suit crashes the party, Justin learns what the suit can do. Before the weekend is over, Justin will have to fight not only FBI, but also aliens who want their property back. Filled with references to television shows and movies from the 1980s, the wacky story will appeal to younger teens even if they don't catch all the references.

Kusakawa, Nari
Recipe for Gertrude. DC Comics/CMX 2006 200p. Illustration
Grades: 6 7 8 9 10 11 12   **741.5; Fic**
   1. Humorous graphic novels; 2. Manga; 3. Shojo manga; 4. Supernatural graphic novels; 5. Graphic novels
   978-1-4012-1110-3, $9.99
   Sahara is a normal high school girl whose life gets turned upside down when she meets "Gertrude," a 100-year-old demon who looks like a teen-age boy. Gertrude is a man-made demon, constructed from the parts of various other demons and brought to life through a "recipe" from an ancient spell book. Gertrude searches for the recipe, in order to learn more about his origin and destroy the formula so that it can never be repeated. Sahara becomes his resourceful ally in Gertrude's quest and they are aided by some very comical and non-threatening demons. There's a little bit of violence as Gertrude and Sahara fight with various demons and other creepy enemies. This is a five-volume manga series that was completed in 2007.

Kwitney, Alisa
Token. Illustrated by Joelle Jones. DC Comics/Minx 2008 176p. Illustration
Grades: 7 8 9 10 11 12   **741.5; Fic**
   1. Shoplifting; 2. Graphic novels
   978-1-4012-1538-5, $9.99
   Almost-sixteen Shira lives in Miami's South Beach in the mid-1980s, in a hotel with her attorney father, her grandmother, and elderly friend Minerva. She's sort of a spaz at sports, the popular girls at her Jewish high school think she's weird, and her father has started dating his new secretary. Life isn't good. She impulsively starts shoplifting

just to feel something, and then she meets Rafael, a streetwise boy who decides to teach her the finer points of stealing. And more.

Kye, Seung-Hui
 ★ **Recast** Volume 1. Tokyopop 2006 192p. Illustration
Grades: 8 9 10 11 12   741.5; Fic
 1. Adventure graphic novels; 2. Fantasy graphic novels; 3. Manwha; 4. Graphic novels
 1-59816-664-6, $9.99
 JD has grown up in a country village with his magician grandfather; they live in a world divided into different realms, and suddenly a "puppet" from the fourth realm attacks JD. He defeats it, but now his grandfather knows that time is running out; he used much of his power and sacrificed his immortality to recast his magic into JD, but bounty hunters from the fourth realm and the church's warriors from the fifth realm are now coming to find JD before the recast spell is complete. JD is destined for greatness, but only if he can survive. This manwha, Korean comics, series, is full of fighting action, with martial arts and monsters.

Labatt, Mary
 ★ **Dracula** madness: A Sam & friends mystery. [illustrated by] Jo Rioux. Kids Can Press 2009 95p. Illustration (A Sam & friends mystery)
Grades: 2 3 4 5 6   741.5; Fic
 1. Dogs; 2. Humorous graphic novels; 3. Mystery graphic novels; 4. Graphic novels
 978-1-55453-418-0, $16.95; 1-55453-418-6;
 978-1-55337-303-2 (pa), $7.95; 1-55337-303-0 (pa)
                        LC C2008-903253-5
 Sam (Samantha) the sheepdog has moved to Woodford with her human family, and she's not happy about being in a small town. Next-door neighbor Jennie misses her best friend who used to live there, but when her parents send ten-year-old Jennie to deliver a housewarming gift, Joan and Bob hire her to help take care of Sam because they have no children. Soon enough, Jennie realizes she can "hear" Sam's thoughts, including Sam's wishes to eat all kinds of junk food in strange combinations (peanut butter and pickle sandwiches with ketchup, for one). Jennie takes Sam all around town, and then to the spooky old house whose owner, McIver, never comes out. Also, there are bats in the yard, and delivery people bring a suspiciously large, long box to the house. Sam is sure there's a mystery there, and they decide to investigate, along with Jennie's friend Beth. What little they see on a night investigation leads them to think McIver might be . . . Dracula.
 "This graphic novel is an adaptation of Labatt's 'Spying on Dracula' (1999). There's just enough creepiness and suspense for younger readers, with simple yet expressive art that stays just on the lighter side of spooky." Booklist
 Other titles in this series are: Lake monster mix-up (2009); Mummy mayhem (2010); Witches' brew (2011)

 Lake Monster Mix-Up. Kids Can Press 2009 96p. Illustration
Grades: 2 3 4 5 6   741.5; Fic
 1. Humorous graphic novels; 2. Mystery graphic novels; 3. Graphic novels

 978-1-55337-822-8, $16.95; 978-1-55337-302-5 (pa), $7.95
                        LC C2008-907085-2
 When Jennie's family decides to go on a camping vacation at Lake Sagawa, Jennie brings along her best friends Beth and Sam, the next-door neighbor dog who can communicate with her. The lake seems like a very quiet place, too quiet for Sam's taste. But one of the locals has talked of a monster, and then Jennie and Beth discover the diary of a girl who lived in their cabin in 1937, and she wrote of a monster. Sam and the girls decide to investigate the glowing underwater lights, the weird cave, and the webbed footprints on the beach.
 This is Book 2 in the Sam & Friends Mystery series, and it's adapted from Labatt's novel The Secret of Sagawa Lake.

 ★ **Mummy** mayhem: a Sam & Friends mystery, book three. Mary Labatt ; art by Jo-Anne Rioux. Kids Can Press 2010 96p. Illustration
Grades: 3 4 5 6 7 8   741.5; Fic
 1. Dogs; 2. Humorous graphic novels; 3. Mummies; 4. Mystery graphic novels; 5. Graphic novels
 978-1-55453-470-8, $16.95
                        LC C2010-900107-9
 Sam the sheepdog feels left out when her human friends Jennie and Beth go on a school field trip to the museum without her. She experiences her own mystery, though, when she finds dog treats left in the snow, hears mysterious chanting, and sees a shadowy figure following her around. The museum has brought an exhibit of Ancient Egypt to town, including the mummy of the pharaoh Menopharsib—could the mummy be searching Woolford for Sam, who resembles Akasheput, the pharaoh's pet dog, whose mummy was stolen years ago" This third book in the series has just enough spooky goings-on for younger readers.
 Based on the novel The Mummy Lives! by Mary Labatt

Lagos, Alexander
 The **sons** of liberty. Created and written by Alexander Lagos and Joseph Lagos; art by Steve Walker; color by Oren Kramek; letters by Chris Dickey. Random House 2010 Un Illustration
Grades: 6 7 8 9 10 11 12   741.5; Fic
 1. Adventure graphic novels; 2. African Americans; 3. Superhero graphic novels; 4. United States — History — 1600-1775, Colonial period; 5. Graphic novels
 978-0-375-85670-9, $18.99; 0-375-85670-6;
 978-0-375-95667-6 (lib bdg), $21.99; 0-375-95667-6 (lib bdg); 978-0-375-85667-9 (pa), $12.99;
 0-375-85667-9 (pa)
 In the mid-eighteenth century American colonies, Graham and Brody work as slaves on a tobacco plantation not far from Philadelphia. When they run away after injuring the plantation owner's son for threatening another slave, they seek Benjamin Lay, an eccentric abolitionist who might give them shelter. Instead, William Franklin, son of Benjamin Franklin, finds them and conducts unknown experiments on them.
 "History offers few villains as vile as slaveholders, but this graphic novel is far from being a simple revenge thriller. The use of historical figures and well-researched (but

embellished) history, and a willingness to flesh out characters and set up situations to pay off in future installments, makes for an uncommonly complex, literate, and satisfying adventure." Booklist

The **sons** of liberty 2: death and taxes. Created and written by Alexander Lagos and Joseph Lagos; art by Steve Walker; color by Oren Kramek; letters by Chris Dickey. Random House Children's Books 2011 Un Illustration
Grades: 6 7 8 9 10 11 12   **741.5; Fic**
1. Adventure graphic novels; 2. African Americans; 3. Superhero graphic novels; 4. United States — History — 1600-1775, Colonial period
978-0-375-85671-6, $18.99; 978-0-375-85668-6 (pa), $12.99

"Graham and Brody, escaped slaves gifted with superpowers, remain at the center of this continuing pre-Revolutionary War saga of political intrigue and reimagined history. As Benjamin Franklin seeks to stop the stamp tax from falling on the colonies and enemies attack his good name, Graham attempts to arrange an escape back to Africa along with his love, the slave girl Isabel. . . . The embellishments, literate dialogue, and several historical truths—effectively counterpointed with glossy contemporary art—keep things fun and suspenseful." Booklist

Lane, Miles
Star Wars: Clone Wars Volume 7: When They Were Brothers. Written by Haden Blackman and Miles Lane ; art by Brian Ching and Nicola Scott. Dark Horse Comics 2005 Un. Illustration
Grades: 7 8 9 10 11 12 Adult   **741.5; Fic**
1. Adventure graphic novels; 2. Science fiction graphic novels; 3. Star Wars; 4. Graphic novels
1-59307-396-8, $17.95

Consumed by the belief that the Dark Jedi Asajj Ventress still lives, Obi-Wan Kenobi has temporarily forsaken his duties and recruited Anakin Skywalker in his desperate hunt for Ventress. But Anakin believes that Obi-Wan is chasing a ghost-because he himself killed Ventress. And Anakin's doubts about his former Master's quest are not assuaged when, following the trail of the rumors of Ventress' existence, they walk into a trap set by their old enemies, the bounty hunter Durge and Count Dooku. The book includes battle violence.

Langridge, Roger
Jim Henson's the Musical Monsters of Turkey Hollow. Adapted from Jim Henson's screenplay by Roger Langridge. Simon & Schuster 2014 96 p. Color; Illustration
Grades: 4 5 6 7   **741.5**
1. Monsters — Juvenile fiction; 2. Music — Juvenile fiction
1608864340; 9781608864348, $24.99

"Turkey Hollow is a picturesque town where hundreds of years ago, unbeknownst to the citizens, a meteorite landed nearby a small brook on the outskirts of town. One Thanksgiving, while young Timmy Henderson practices his guitar, he's accompanied by strange, unearthly, musical sounds. That meteorite wasn't a rock at all but an egg holding seven furry, goofy monsters, each with a unique musical sound. After the initial shock, Timmy befriends the lovable creatures following him all around Turkey Hollow." (Publisher's note)

"Based on a never-produced Jim Henson screenplay, this folksy story captures the spirit of Muppet holiday specials like Emmet Otter's Jug-Band Christmas. . . . Subdued autumnal colors make up most of the palette in Langridge's clean-lined panels, while musical moments are full of big, swirling words in bright colors." Booklist

The **Muppet** Show comic book: on the road. Writer, Roger Langridge ; art, Shelli Paroline & Roger Langridge ; colors, Digikore Studios, Mickey Clausen & Eric Cobain ; letters, Shelli Paroline & Deron Bennett. Boom! Kids 2010 Un Illustration
Grades: 3 4 5 6 7 8 9 10 11 12 Adult   **741.5; Fic**
1. Humorous graphic novels; 2. Muppets (Fictional characters); 3. Travel; 4. Graphic novels
978-1-60886-516-1, $9.99

The Muppets' theater must undergo massive repairs, so the crew takes their show on the road. Standup comedian Fozzie tries to go on his own as a solo act, while Kermit and the rest of the motley group hires a caravan of buses and trailers to find small towns where they can perform. One place, Little Statwald, seems to be populated almost completely by relatives of old curmudgeons Stadler and Waldorf, who all delight in heckling the hapless performers. Langridge draws the main Muppets story, while Shelli Paroline draws the Pigs in Space episodes. The stories have been written to appeal to younger readers, while adults who remember the old Muppets television series will also enjoy the comics.

★ Snarked!: Forks and Hope. Roger Langridge. BOOM! Studios 2012 128 p. Illustration
Grades: 5 6 7 8   **741.5/973; Fic**
1. Adventure fiction; 2. Fantasy fiction; 3. Swindlers and swindling — Fiction
1608860957; 9781608860951, $14.99
Eisner Award: Best Publication for Kids (2011)

This graphic novel is the first in Roger Langridge's "Snarked!" series. It presents "an epic adventure featuring the Red Queen's children, Princess Scarlett and her baby brother Rusty, as they set out in search of the missing Red King. And who better to help guide the way than the Walrus and the Carpenter from [Lewis Carroll's] 'Through the Looking Glass'." (Publisher's note)
Volume 1 of 3

★ Thor, the mighty avenger, v.1.. Illustrated by Chris Samnee. Marvel 2011 Un Illustration
Grades: 8 9 10 11 12   **741.5; 741**
1. Thor (Fictional character)
978-0-7851-4121-1, $14.99; 0-7851-4121-9

"Readers meet the mysterious blond-haired God of Thunder with no memory when historian Jane Foster watches him get tossed out of a Norse exhibition one day. After the gallant fellow helps her out and she takes him in, an utterly charming romance ensues. . . . Langridge deserves top marks for taking a character whose story possibilities might seem limited and imbuing him with a fresh and highly entertaining life. . . . Samnee's art grounds the vigorous superhero action with expressive faces, subtle lighting tones, and an individual style that makes the drama sing." Booklist

Larson, Hope

★ **Chiggers**. [by] Hope Larson; lettered by Jason Azzopardi. Atheneum Books for Young Readers 2008 170p. Illustration

Grades: 5 6 7 8 9   **741.5; Fic**
1. Camps — Fiction; 2. Friendship; 3. Graphic novels
978-1-4169-3584-1, $17.99; 978-1-4169-3587-2 (pa), $9.99

LC 2008-09557

When Abby returns to the same summer camp she always goes to, she is dismayed to find that her old friends have changed, and the only person who wants to be her friend is the strange new girl, Shasta.

"Chiggers provides a ticket to summer fun. Larson delicately handles both the usual middle-school angst and the additional pressures that come with being somewhat different. . . . The content is perfect for upper elementary and middle school students." SLJ

Who is AC?. Hope Larson; iIllustrated by Tintin Pantoja. Atheneum Books for Young Readers 2013 176 p.
Grades: 7 8 9 10 11 12   **741.5/973; Fic**
1. Female superhero graphic novels; 2. Superheroes — Fiction; 3. Graphic novels
1442426500; 9781442426504, $14.99; 9781442465404, $21.99

LC 2011052616

In this book, "Lin, a zine-writing 15-year-old who's just moved to a small town, becomes an unwitting Sailor Moon-style superhero, activated by mysterious cellphone messages and visited by a 'dispatcher' who nags her until she suits up. Her nemesis is a shadowy villain who possesses a glamorous rich girl in order to snare a boy named Trace." (Publishers Weekly)

A **wrinkle** in time: the graphic novel. Madeleine L'Engle; adapted and illustrated by Hope Larson. Farrar Straus Giroux 2012 392 p.
Grades: 4 5 6 7   **741.5**
1. L'Engle, Madeleine Wrinkle in time — Adaptations; 2. Science fiction; 3. Space and time — Fiction; 4. Time travel — Fiction; 5. Graphic novels
0374386153; 9780374386153, $19.99

LC 2010044120

Hope Larson presents a graphic novel adaptation of Madeleine L'Engle's "allegorical fantasy in which a group of young people are guided through the universe by Mrs. Who, Mrs. Which and Mrs. What — women who possess supernatural powers. They traverse fictitious regions, meet and face evil and demonstrate courage at the right moment. Religious allusions are secondary to the philosophical struggle designed to yield the meaning of life and one's place on earth." (Kirkus Reviews)

Margaret Furguson Books.

Lash, Batton

Archie: the high school chronicles, book one: freshman year. Script, Batton Lash ; pencils, Bill Galvan ; inks, Bob Smith, Al Milgrom ; letters, Jack Morelli ; colors, Glenn Whitmore. Archie Comic Publications, Inc. 2009 120p. Illustration

Grades: 4 5 6 7 8 9 10   **741.5; Fic**
1. Andrews, Archie (Fictional character); 2. High school; 3. Humorous graphic novels; 4. Graphic novels
978-1-879794-40-5, $10.95

Lash, creator of Supernatural Law, writes the story never before written about Archie Andrews and all his friends in all the decades of Archie comics (since the 1940s) what was it like for the gang to start high school" This story starts at the end of summer vacation, and everyone is looking forward to a new start at a new school especially Archie, who constantly got into trouble with his old school principal. The one bad thing is that Jughead has to leave town, because his father has got a new job. On the very first day of school, Archie already gets into trouble with the Principal and yikes! it's Mr. Weatherbee, his old nemesis. Weatherbee has more problems than just dealing with Archie, however; the superintendent doesn't like him and wants to find a way to get him fired. Top that off with Archie facing off against upper classmen bullies, and freshman year is shaping up to be interesting, in a painful way. Galvan's art shows Archie, Jughead, Betty, Veronica, and Reggie as very recognizably themselves but looking young enough to be fourteen years old. This book could be a great entry point for anyone who has never read any Archie comics before.

Mister Negativity and Other Tales of Supernatural Law. Exhibit A Press 2004 170p. Illustration
Grades: 8 9 10 11 12 Adult   **741.5; Fic**
1. Humorous graphic novels; 2. Supernatural graphic novels; 3. Graphic novels
0-9633954-8-3, $15.95

LC 2003113227

Attorneys Wolff & Byrd represent clients that include Nagy D'Viti, a fellow with such a negative attitude that he physically repels people, Huberis the Dybbuk, a born again demon seeking church membership, Nicky Gorillo, a gangster who has literally become a gorilla mob boss, Steven Gink, a horror novelist in a coma who summons them through their dreams, Susann, the Muse of Potboilers, who sues the author she has "inspired," and Perry Otter, a boy magician with an unusual affliction.

Lassieur, Allison

Clara Barton: Angel of the Battlefield. Illustrated by Brian Bascle. Capstone Press 2006 32p. Illustration
Grades: 3 4 5 6 7 8 9   **741.5; 361.7; 92**
1. Barton, Clara, 1821-1912; 2. Biographical graphic novels; 3. Graphic novels
0-7368-4632-8, $25.26

LC 2005008122

This book uses the comic book format to describe highlights in the life and work of Clara Barton, who served as a Civil War nurse and started the American Red Cross. It includes additional information, a glossary, a list of books for further reading, and more.

Part of the Graphic Library, Graphic Biographies series.

Lords of the Sea: The Vikings Explore the North Atlantic. Illustrated by Ron Frenz and Charles Barnett III. Capstone Press 2006 32p. Illustration
Grades: 3 4 5 6 7 8 9   **741.5; 948**
  1. Vikings; 2. Graphic novels
0-7368-4974-2, $25.26
                                                                LC 2005007891
This book uses the comic book format to tell the story of the Vikings' exploration of the North Atlantic and their discovery of North America. It includes additional information, a glossary, a list of books for further reading, and more.

Part of the Graphic Library, Graphic History series.

Lat
  Kampung boy. First Second 2006 141p. Illustration
Grades: 7 8 9 10 11 12 Adult   **741.5; Fic**
  1. Family life; 2. Malaysia; 3. Muslims; 4. Graphic novels
1-59643-121-0, $16.95
                                                                LC 2005-34135
"Malaysian cartoonist Lat uses the graphic novel format to share the story of his childhood in a small village, or kampung. From his birth and adventures as a toddler to the enlargement of his world as he attends classes in the village, makes friends, and, finally, departs for a prestigious city boarding school, this autobiography is warm, authentic, and wholly engaging." Booklist

First published 1979 in Malaysia with title: Lat, the kampung boy

  ★ **Town** boy. First Second Books 2007 191p. Illustration
Grades: 7 8 9 10 11 12 Adult   **741.5; Fic**
  1. Bildungsromans; 2. Humorous graphic novels; 3. Malaysia; 4. Graphic novels
978-1-59643-331-1, $16.95; 1-59643-331-0
                                                                LC 2006-102857
In this sequel to Kampung Boy, it's the late 1960s and Mat is now a teenager attending a boarding school in the town of Ipoh, far from his kampung. He discovers bustling streets, hip music, heady literature, budding romance, and through it all his growing passion for art.

Laudec
  Cedric, vol. 1: High-risk class. Art by Cauvin. Cinebook Ltd. 2008 48p. Illustration
Grades: 3 4 5 6 7 8   **741.5; Fic**
  1. Humorous graphic novels; 2. School stories; 3. Graphic novels
978-1-905460-68-7, $11.95
Eight-year-old Cedric is the type of boy who likes to play with his chums, doesn't always get good grades, and has a crush on his teacher, Miss Nelly. Then Chen starts at his school; she's Chinese, she's cute, and Cedric falls head over heels for her. He can't just tell her, of course. Meanwhile, he gets into all kinds of mischief with his friends, including playing with a remote control car, planting stink bombs all over school, drinking champagne when his grandfather says he did so to get the courage to propose to

his grandmother. Each time he does something naughty, he does face consequences for his actions. This book is translated from the French.

Lechner, John
  Sticky Burr: Adventures in Burrwood Forest. Candlewick Press 2007 Un Illustration
Grades: 2 3 4 5 6   **741.5; Fic**
  1. Adventure graphic novels; 2. Humorous graphic novels; 3. Graphic novels
978-0-7636-3054-6, $15.99
Welcome to Burrwood Forest, where a village of seed pods leads a busy life gathering food, building stick houses, and having adventures. There are good friends like Sticky Burr and Mossy Burr, who stick together, and bad seeds like Scurvy Burr, who likes to irritate them every chance he gets. Watch out for wild dogs and maze trees, loyal insects and escapes on the fly in a graphic storybook for middle-graders and ambitious younger readers.

Lee, Stan
  Essential Fantastic Four Vol. 1, 2nd ed.. Art by Jack Kirby. Marvel Entertainment 2005 Un Illustration
Grades: 7 8 9 10 11 12 Adult   **741.5; Fic**
  1. Fantastic Four (Fictional characters); 2. Hulk (Fictional character); 3. Superhero graphic novels; 4. Graphic novels
978-0-7851-1828-2, $16.99
This massive trade paperback collects the first 20 issues of The Fantastic Four plus the Annual #1. Reprinted in black and white, this volume lets readers get the origin and early stories as originally written by Lee and drawn by Kirby. The Fantastic Four fights against Skrulls, Sub-Mariner, The Impossible Man, The Hulk, the Red Ghost, The Thinker, Doctor Doom (who first appeared in issue #5), the Puppet Master, and many more super villains.

Lee, Tony
  ★ **Outlaw:** the legend of Robin Hood: a graphic novel. Written by Tony Lee; illustrated by Sam Hart; colored by Artur Fujita. Candlewick Press 2009 Un Illustration
Grades: 7 8 9 10 11 12   **741.5; Fic**
  1. Adventure graphic novels; 2. Great Britain — History — 1154-1399, Plantagenets; 3. Robin Hood (Legendary character); 4. Graphic novels
978-0-7636-4399-7, $21.99; 0-7636-4399-8;
978-0-7636-4400-0 (pa), $11.99; 0-7636-4400-5 (pa)
                                                                LC 2008-943331
In this retelling of the Robin Hood legend, it's the year 1192, and Robin of Loxley has returned home from the Crusades after receiving news of his father's death. The Sheriff of Nottingham and Sir Guy of Gisburn govern Nottingham at the pleasure of Prince John. When Gisburn treacherously stabs Robin in a murder attempt, Robin escapes to Sherwood Forest, where the outlaws befriend him. With the help of such men as Little John and Friar Tuck, he organizes the outlaws and they start hurting Prince John where it matters—in his moneybags.

"Lee's excellent rendition of the famed selfless hero goes hand-in-hand with Hart's expressive illustrations, featuring lots of closeups and dramatic lighting and a beautiful jewel-toned palette. Teens will get caught up in this exciting page-turner." SLJ

Leloup, Roger
Yoko Tsuno, bk. 3: the prey and the ghost. Cinebook 2008 48p. Illustration
Grades: 3 4 5 6 7 8   **741.5; Fic**
1. Ghosts; 2. Mystery graphic novels; 3. Graphic novels
978-1-905460-56-4, $11.95

Young electronics engineer Yoko Tsuno has driven to Scotland to investigate the Loch Ness Monster, when she and her companion Pol find they've taken a wrong turn. Then they encounter a distraught young woman on the road who's being chased by dogs. The young woman is Cecelia, stepdaughter of Sir William, whose parents both died. She's convinced that her mother is haunting their castle, and Yoko finds a way to investigate just what is going on.

Part of the Yoko Tsuno series, originally published in France as Yoko Tsuno 12 La Proie et l'ombre.

Lemke, Donald B.
Bike rider: wheelies of justice. Illustrated by Douglas Holgate. Stone Arch Books 2010 38p. Illustration
Grades: 3 4 5 6 7 8   **741.5; Fic**
1. Adventure graphic novels; 2. Humorous graphic novels; 3. Mystery graphic novels; 4. Graphic novels
978-1-4342-1892-6, $22.65
LC 2009-29069

Michael Cycle is a student at T.V. Academy, but he's also the crusading Bike Rider, with his talking BMX, C.A.T.T. In his latest case, the boy and his bike track down the latest story written by a missing school reporter and discover that the school's quarterback is cheating on his math test. Now they have to stop the team from playing a football game, or the team will be disqualified. Young readers may or may not know the television series Knight Rider, but this story spoofs that show with kid-appropriate action.

Part of the Graphic Sparks series.

The **Brave** Escape of Ellen and William Craft. Capstone Press 2006 32p. Illustration
Grades: 3 4 5 6 7 8 9   **741.5; 306.3; 92**
1. Craft, Ellen, 1826-1891; 2. Craft, William, 1824-1900; 3. Fugitive slaves — United States — Biography; 4. Slavery — United States; 5. Graphic novels
0-7368-4973-4, $25.26
LC 2005008084

This book uses the comic book format to tell the story of Ellen and William Craft's escape from slavery in Georgia to freedom in Pennsylvania. It includes additional information, a glossary, a list of books for further reading, and more.

Part of the Graphic Library, Graphic History series.

Hansel and Gretel: the graphic novel. Retold by Donald Lemke; illustrated by Sean Dietrich.. Stone Arch Books 2009 40p. Illustration
Grades: 2 3 4 5 6 7   **741.5; Fic**
1. Fairy tales; 2. Fantasy graphic novels; 3. Graphic novels
978-1-4342-0767-8, $21.26
LC 2008-6721

When things get very tough for a woodcutter's family, the man's new wife demands that they abandon his children, Hansel and Gretel, in the forest. The children try to make their way home, then find something wonderful for their empty stomachs: a house made of sweets. Unfortunately, an old witch owns the house and imprisons Hansel in a cage to fatten him up so she can eat him, while she makes Gretel do all the chores. The children must find a way to outwit the witch and save themselves. Dietrich's art is slightly creepy, with dark tones and the children's overly large eyes, which fits with the creepy atmosphere of the story. The book includes a brief history of the folktale and how it was written down and popularized by the Grimm brothers.

Part of the Graphic Spin series

Investigating the scientific method with Max Axiom, super scientist. Illustrated by Tod Smith and Al Milgrom. Capstone Press 2008 32p. Illustration
Grades: 3 4 5 6 7 8 9   **507; 741.5**
1. Science — Methodology; 2. Graphic novels
978-1-42961329-3, $26.26
LC 2007-22792

Super scientist Max Axiom, who has powers gained from a freak accident, takes young readers on a journey to learn about the scientific method and how scientists use it to begin their investigations into problems that need solving; readers also learn how to use it themselves in their class work. Back matter includes more historical tidbits of information, a short glossary, and a list of books for further reading.

Part of the Graphic Science series

The **Schoolchildren's** Blizzard. Capstone Press 2007 32p. Illustration
Grades: 3 4 5 6 7 8 9   **741.5; 977**
1. Blizzards; 2. Middle West; 3. Graphic novels
978-1-4296-0157-3, $26.25
LC 2007000259

This book uses the graphic novel format to tell of the devastating 1888 blizzard that suddenly exploded across the Great Plains and killed hundreds of children as they walked home from school. The book includes additional facts and a list of booksfor further reading.

Part of the Graphic Library Disasters in History series.

Zinc Alloy vs Frankenstein. Stone Arch Books 2009 40p. Illustration
Grades: 3 4 5 6 7 8   **741.5; Fic**
1. Frankenstein (Fictional character); 2. Frankenstein's monster (Fictional character); 3. Humorous graphic novels; 4. Science fiction graphic novels; 5. Graphic novels
978-1-4342-1188-0, $21.26
LC 2008-32062

Zack Allen is also superhero Zinc Alloy in his giant robot suit, but when he tries to save Metro City from a tornado, things go very wrong and he causes a lot of destruction. He has to flee from a mob ands ends up hiding in a creepy old house at the edge of town. But he's not alone—there's a robo-Frankenstein there! And there's a girl inside the robot. The book includes a glossary and notes about Mary Shelley's classic novel, Frankenstein.

Part of the Graphic Sparks line, the Zinc Alloy series.

Zinc Alloy: Super Zero. Illustrated by Douglas Holgate. Stone Arch Books 2009 33p. Illustration
Grades: 2 3 4 5 6 7   **741.5; Fic**
1. Bullies; 2. Humorous graphic novels; 3. Robots; 4. Superhero graphic novels; 5. Graphic novels

978-1-4342-0762-3, $21.26

LC 2008-6712

Zack Allen loves to read comics, especially Robo Hero; unfortunately, he's the kind of kid that bullies like to pick on, and they have done so. Then Zack builds his own robot suit; he was just going to get the bullies to stop, but when he hears about a runaway train, he uses the suit to become a new superhero Zinc Alloy! He's going to have to work on controlling things a lot better, though how will he explain broken doors to his mom" The book includes a short history of comic books and the glossary includes definitions for "noogies" and "wet willies."

Part of the Graphic Sparks Zinc Alloy series

Lent, Michael

P.R.E.Y.: Origin of the Species. Written by Michael Lent ; adapted by Mike Raicht ; art by Bong Dazo and Alex Sanchez, Marvel Entertainment/Dabel Brothers 2007 Un Illustration

Grades: 7 8 9 10 11 12 Adult   741.5; Fic
1. Horror graphic novels; 2. Science fiction graphic novels; 3. Graphic novels
978-0-7851-2658-4, $10.99

The Prometheus Corporation has unearthed something ancient and dangerous in its underwater excavations, and now it's come to the surface to make humanity its prey. Their solution" To lure the thing back in the sea and kill everything within a five mile radius, effectively covering the corporation's tracks. And so a disgraced marine biologist must race against the clock and find a way to keep the ocean from being destroyed by the corporation before something even more dangerous is unleashed on mankind. The book includes some strong language and some violence.

Levitz, Paul

The **Huntress:** Darknight Daughter. Paul Levitz and Joe Staton. DC Comics 2006 224p. Illustration

Grades: 8 9 10 11 12 Adult   741.5; Fic
1. Batman (Fictional character); 2. Catwoman (Fictional character); 3. Superhero graphic novels; 4. Graphic novels
978-1-4012-09131, $19.99

She is unique in comics, the daughter of a hero and a villain: the Earth-Two Batman and Catwoman. Helena Wayne was trained by her parents to become a superb athlete, and she studied law with the hope of bringing criminals to justice. But after Catwoman is blackmailed to resume her life of crime, leading to her death, Helena dons a costume and crossbow to become the Huntress to avenge her mother. This volume collects the stories originally published in the 1970s and 1980s.

Justice Society Volume One. Paul Levitz and Gerry Conway. DC Comics 2006 224p. Illustration

Grades: 7 8 9 10 11 12 Adult   741.5; Fic
1. Flash (Fictional character); 2. Green Lantern (Fictional character); 3. Justice Society of America (Fictional characters); 4. Robin (Fictional character); 5. Superhero graphic novels; 6. Graphic novels
978-1-4012-0970-4, $14.99

The volume collects stories originally published in the 1970s, when DC revived the very first superhero team that was originally created in 1940: the Justice Society of America. This incarnation of the Justice Society includes the Golden Age Flash and Green Lantern, Hawkman, Dr. Fate, Wildcat, Dr. Mid-Nite, Robin, Power Girl, and the Star-Spangled Kid. Artists on this run include Wally Wood, Joe Staton, Keith Giffen, and Ric Estrada.

Justice Society Vol. 2. Written by Paul Levitz ; art by Joe Staton, Bob Layton, Joe Giella, Dave Hunt. DC Comics 2007 224p. Illustration

Grades: 8 9 10 11 12 Adult   741.5; Fic
1. Batman (Fictional character); 2. Flash (Fictional character); 3. Green Lantern (Fictional character); 4. Justice Society of America (Fictional characters); 5. Robin (Fictional character); 6. Superhero graphic novels; 7. Superman (Fictional character); 8. Graphic novels
978-1-4012-1194-3, $14.99

The Justice Society of America was the first comic book super-team, created in All Star Comics in the 1940s. They faded into obscurity until they were revived in the 1970s. This volume includes stories from the 1970s, featuring Superman, the Flash, Green Lantern, Hawkman, Dr. Fate, Wildcat, Robin, Power Girl, Star-Spangled Kid, and the Huntress. Among other stories in this volume, Batman dies, and Huntress is his daughter.

Lewis, Corey Sutherland

Sharknife Volume 1. Oni Press 2006 Un Illustration

Grades: 8 9 10 11 12 Adult   741.5; Fic
1. Humorous graphic novels; 2. Martial arts; 3. Graphic novels
1-932664-17-3, $9.95

The Guandong Factory isn't like other restaurants. It's five stories tall, produces more peach dumplings per day than most eateries do in a decade, and it's the home of Sharknife - a mystical protector charged with protecting the establishment from those who would do it harm. But who is this mysterious yet colorful being? Once just a simple busboy, now Caesar Ives is something more - a crazy red rocket hero destined for greatness. But can Caesar juggle both lives - nabbing the girl (the super-sexy Chieko Momuza), and stopping the wide assortment of bizarre baddies that would love to do his precious eatery harm? There's lots of martial arts action.

Lewis, John

★ **March:** Book One. John Lewis; [co-written by] Andrew Aydin; [art by] Nate Powell. Top Shelf Productions 2013 121 p. Illustration

Grades: 8 9 10 11 12 Adult   92; 741.5
1. African Americans — Civil rights; 2. Civil rights movements — United States; 3. Lewis, John, 1940 February 21-
9781603093002, $14.95

LC 2013218903

Coretta Scott King (Author) Honor Book (2014)

This graphic novel, by U.S. congressman John Lewis, "in collaboration with co-writer Andrew Aydin and New York Times best-selling artist Nate Powell . . . spans John Lewis' youth in rural Alabama, his life-changing meeting with Martin Luther King, Jr., the birth of the Nashville Student Movement, and their battle to tear down segregation through nonviolent lunch counter sit-ins, building to a . . . climax on the steps of City Hall." (Publisher's note)

"This is superb visual storytelling that establishes a convincing, definitive record of a key eyewitness to significant social change." SLJ

★ **March:** Book Two. By John Lewis and Andrew Aydin; illustrated by Nate Powell. Top Shelf Productions 2015 192 p. Illustration
Grades: 8 9 10 11 12 Adult   **92; 741.5**
1. African American civil rights workers; 2. African American legislators; 3. African Americans — Civil rights; 4. Civil rights movements; 5. Civil rights workers — United States; 6. Legislators — United States
9781603094009, $19.95; 1603094008
                                    LC Bl2015004150
This graphic novel, by John Lewis and Andrew Aydin, illustrated by Nate Powell, "takes us behind the scenes of some of the most pivotal moments of the Civil Rights Movement. . . . After the success of the Nashville sit-in campaign, John Lewis is more committed than ever to changing the world through nonviolence — but as he and his fellow Freedom Riders board a bus into the vicious heart of the deep south, they will be tested like never before." (Publisher's note)

"Heroism and steadiness of purpose continue to light up Lewis' frank, harrowing account of the civil rights movement's climactic days. . . . The contrast between the dignified marchers and the vicious, hate-filled actions and expressions of their tormentors will leave a deep impression on readers." Kirkus

Lie, Bjorn Rune
The **wolf's** whistle. By B.R. Lie and S.J. Donaldson.. Nobrow 2012 88 p. Illustration; Color
Grades: 4 5 6 7 8 9 10   **741.5; Fic**
1. Fractured fairy tales; 2. Revenge — Fiction
1907704035; 9781907704031, $18.00
This children's book by Bjorn Rune Lie "digs into the troubled upbringing of one of storydom's most maligned figures: the house-blowing-down wolf. As a wolf cub, little Robert loved superhero comics . . . which led to much torment at the hands of three piggish brothers. Robert grows up to be not much . . . when the building owned by the Honeyroasts burns down with three of Robert's best friends trapped inside, the spark of vengeance and justice is kindled in the wolf." (Booklist)

Lim, Ron
Spider-Girl Presents Juggernaut, Jr.: Secrets and Lies. Marvel Entertainment 2006 Un Illustration
Grades: 6 7 8 9 10 11 12   **741.5; Fic**
1. Superhero graphic novels; 2. Graphic novels
0-7851-2047-5, $7.99
Lots of people have big shoes to fill, but how many have to fill the helmet of the Juggernaut? Teenager Zane Marko grows up fast and hits the big time head first when he inherits his father's unstoppability and joins the latest generation of Avengers. J2 squares off against villains and heroes alike, including a certain green goliath who thinks he's still the strongest one there is. This volume includes the first

appearances of the X-People and Wild Thing, daughter of Wolverine and Elektra.

Limke, Jeff
Isis and Osiris: To the Ends of the Earth. Story by Jeff Limke ; pencils and inks by David Witt. Lerner Publishing Group/Graphic Universe 2007 48p. Illustration
Grades: 3 4 5 6 7 8 9   **398.2; 741.5**
1. Egyptian mythology; 2. Isis (Egyptian deity); 3. Osiris (Egyptian deity); 4. Graphic novels
978-0-8225-3086-2, $26.60 lib. Bdg.
Osiris is the greatest king and god of the land of the Nile. He is a generous ruler, and the people love and worship him, along with his wife and queen, the goddess Isis. But Osiris's jealous brother Set has a terrible plan to get rid of Osiris forever and take his place on the Egyptian throne. Isis uses her magic and her love to save Osiris and conquer Set. The book includes a glossary and a list of books for further reading.

Jason: Quest for the Golden Fleece. Story by Jeff Limke ; pencils by Tim Seely ; inks by Barbara Schulz. Lerner Publishing Group/Graphic Universe 2007 48p. Illustration
Grades: 3 4 5 6 7 8 9   **292.1; 741.5**
1. Greek mythology; 2. Jason (Greek mythology); 3. Graphic novels
978-0-8225-5967-2, $26.60 lib bdg
Jason's uncle Pelias had stole the throne when Jason was a child; now a young man, Jason must prove himself by retrieving the priceless Golden Fleece from the far-off land of Colchis. He gathers a ship of heroes, the Argonauts, to aid him on his quest; but when they arrive in Colchis, the king insists that Jason prove himself in dangerous trials, and the king's daughter, Medea, has plans for Jason. This retelling is based on the heroic poem by Apollonius of Rhodes. The book includes a glossary and a list of books and websites for further reading.

King Arthur: Excalibur Unsheathed. Story by Jeff Limke ; pencils and inks by Thomas Yeates. Lerner Publishing Group/Graphic Universe 2007 48p. Illustration
Grades: 3 4 5 6 7 8 9   **398.2; 741.5**
1. Arthurian romances; 2. Malory, Sir Thomas, 15th c — Adaptations; 3. Graphic novels
978-0-8225-3083-1, $26.60 lib. Bdg.
This story is adapted from Sir Thomas Malory's Le Morte D'Arthur. Young squire Arthur's life, and that of England, changes the day he pulls out the mysterious Sword in the Stone. Guided by Merlin the magician, Arthur takes his place as King of England. Can he win peace and freedom for his country? The book includes a glossary and a list of books for further reading.

The **treasure** of Mount Fate. Jeff Limke ; illustrated by Clint Hilinski. Lerner Publishing Group/Graphic Universe 2007 112p. Illustration (Twisted Journeys)
Grades: 3 4 5 6 7 8 9   **741.5; Fic**
1. Adventure graphic novels; 2. Graphic novels
978-0-8225-6205-4, $27.93; 978-0-8225-6206-1 (pa), $7.95
                                    LC 2006-101596

In the series called Twisted Journeys, readers choose how the story will progress. Pages of text alternate with comic book-style pages. In this volume, you are a young knight who comes to Mount Fate in search of a treasure. In some storylines, you encounter a trapped wizard, in others a monstrous borkadrac, in yet others such hazards as fireballs, and a talking dragon. Readers will find many scenarios played out, depending on their choices; some end well, others not so well.

Lin, Yali
Hawthorne's the Scarlet letter: the Manga edition. Adapted by Adam Sexton ; illustrated by Yali Lin. Wiley Publishing 2009 186p. Illustration
Grades: 5 6 7 8 9 10 11 12　　　**741.5; Fic**
1. Hawthorne, Nathaniel, 1804-1864 — Adaptations; 2. Graphic novels
978-0-470-14889-1, $9.99
Hester Prynne, a young married woman in puritanical Massachusetts, stands in public shame when she bears a child long after her husband had disappeared. She refuses to identify the father of her child and instead wears the scarlet letter A always. The young minister Arthur Dimmesdale lives with his guilt in secret, but the physician, Roger Chillingworth, is actually Hester's husband, returned for vengeance. He vows to find the man who fathered Pearl, Hester's daughter, and destroy him. Meanwhile, Pearl grows up in a society that shuns her mother, and she comes to see the A as her mother's badge of honor. This book is a manga style adaptation of Hawthorne's novel.

Liu, Na
★ **Little** White Duck: a childhood in China. By Andrés Vera Martínez and Na Liu; illustrated by Andrés Vera Martínez. Graphic Universe 2012 96 p. Color illustration
Grades: 4 5 6　　　**741.5/973; 741.5**
1. Biographical graphic novels; 2. China — History — 1976-; 3. Liu, Na, 1973-; 4. Graphic novels
0761365877; 9780761365877, $29.27; 9780761381150, $9.95; 0761381155
　　　　　　　　　　　　　　LC 2011005347
This graphic novel provides a "glimpse into Chinese girlhood during the 1970s and '80s." It begins with the 3-year-old narrator trying to understand the death of Chairman Mao. "From there, her life unfolds in short sketches. . . . She explains about the four pests that plague China . . . and her stomach-turning school assignment to catch rats and deliver the severed tails to her teacher . . . [as well as] the origins of Chinese New Year, her favorite holiday." (Kirkus Reviews)
"This picturesque treasure introduces Chinese culture through a personal perspective that is both delightful and thought-provoking." SLJ

Lobdell, Scott
The **Hardy** Boys vol. 10: A Hardy day's night. Paulo H. Marcondes with Marcel Zero, artists. NBM/Papercutz 2007 Un Illustration
Grades: 3 4 5 6 7 8　　　**741.5; Fic**
1. Adventure graphic novels; 2. Hardy Boys (Fictional characters); 3. Mystery graphic novels; 4. Graphic novels
978-1-59707-070-6, $7.95

A rogue mentor agent within A.T.A.C. lures Frank and Joe into a deadly ambush, but they have only until dawn to rescue a kidnapped boy. But soon enough they learn there's a bigger plot afoot, and the boy is only a pawn.

Hardy Boys, undercover brothers #14: Haley Danelle's top eight. Paulo Henrique Marcondes, artist. Papercutz 2008 Un Illustration
Grades: 3 4 5 6 7 8 9　　　**741.5; Fic**
1. Adventure graphic novels; 2. Hardy Boys (Fictional characters); 3. Mystery graphic novels; 4. Graphic novels
978-1-59707-114-7, $12.95; 978-1-59707-113-0 (pa), $7.95
Cute little computer nerd and horse expert Haley Danelle needs the help of the Hardy Boys; she has been an ATAC operative and knows who they are. Her top friends on her MyFacePlace social network page are disappearing, one by one, and she wants Joe and Frank to help stop it and find her friends. But things soon turn deadly, and Joe and Frank find themselves in trouble.
Volume 14 of the Hardy Boys, Undercover Brothers series

The **Hardy** boys, undercover brothers #15: Live free, die hardy!. Paulo Henrique Marcondes, artist. Papercutz 2008 Un Illustration
Grades: 3 4 5 6 7 8 9　　　**741.5; Fic**
1. Adventure graphic novels; 2. Hardy Boys (Fictional characters); 3. Mystery graphic novels; 4. Graphic novels
978-1-59707-124-6, $12.95; 978-1-59707-123-9 (pa), $7.95
When the guys at A.T.A.C. decide to throw Fenton Hardy a surprise party, some uninvited guests show up. The Noir Sisters, Nicolina and Shira, an evil counterpart to Frank and Joe Hardy, show up with their henchmen and get in because the security system was temporarily shut down to allow the invited guests to come in. It's going to be up to Frank and Joe to find a way to take down the bad guys without letting anyone get hurt.
Part of The Hardy Boys, Undercover Brothers series.

The **Hardy** Boys, Undercover Brothers #7: The Opposite Numbers. Daniel Rendon, Paulo Henrique, Sidney Lima, artist. NBM/Papercutz 2006 112p. Illustration
Grades: 4 5 6 7 8 9　　　**741.5; Fic**
1. Adventure graphic novels; 2. Mystery graphic novels; 3. Graphic novels
1-59707-035-1, $12.95; 1-59707-034-3, $7.95
Traveling across the country on the maiden voyage of a bullet train, the Hardy Boys find themselves framed for murder. But they can't depend on A.T.A.C. (American Teens Against Crime) to help them, because every indication is that it's the super secret spy organization, founded by their own father, that framed them.

The **Hardy** Boys: Undercover Brothers #1: The Ocean of Osyria. Lea Hernandez, artist. NBM/Papercutz 2005 Un Illustration
Grades: 3 4 5 6 7 8 9　　　**741.5; Fic**
1. Hardy Boys (Fictional characters); 2. Mystery graphic novels; 3. Graphic novels
1-59707-005-X, $12.95; 1-59707-001-7 (pa)
After rescuing Jackpot, a kidnapped prize-winning racehorse, Frank and Joe are stunned to return to Bayport

and discover that the Department of International Security has arrested their best friend, Chet Morton, for stealing a priceless art treasure. The Hardy Boys decide the only way to clear their friend is to journey to the Middle East and find the Ocean of Osyria themselves.

The **Hardy** Boys: Undercover Brothers #2: Identity Theft. Daniel Rendon, artist. NBM/Papercutz 2005 Un Illustration
Grades: 3 4 5 6 7 8 9   **741.5; Fic**
 1. Hardy Boys (Fictional characters); 2. Mystery graphic novels; 3. Graphic novels
 978-1-59707-007-2, $12.95; 978-1-59707-003-4 (pa)
 Joe and Frank Hardy first crack a case involving sky-diving diamond smugglers, then take on a case of stolen identity. Joy Gallagher claims another girl is now living her life, with her parents, and in her body. Is this girl insane, or can her fantastic story actually be true?

The **Hardy** Boys: Undercover Brothers #3: Mad House. Daniel Rendon, artist. NBM/Papercutz 2005 Un Illustration
Grades: 3 4 5 6 7 8 9   **741.5; Fic**
 1. Hardy Boys (Fictional characters); 2. Mystery graphic novels; 3. Graphic novels
 978-1-59707-011-9, $12.95; 978-1-59707-010-2 (pa)
 No sooner do Frank and Joe Hardy rescue a member of Her Majesty's Secret Service (who says he's shaken, not stirred), than they're off on a new top-secret ATAC (American Teens Against Crime) mission. Frank and Joe must go undercover on a new reality TV show called 'Mad House,' to discover how far the producers are willing to go risking the contestants' lives for the sake of huge ratings. The plot thickens when the producer of Mad House turns up murdered.

The **Hardy** Boys: Undercover Brothers #4: Malled. Daniel Rendon, artist. NBM/Papercutz 2005 Un Illustration
Grades: 3 4 5 6 7 8 9   **741.5; Fic**
 1. Hardy Boys (Fictional characters); 2. Mystery graphic novels; 3. Graphic novels
 978-1-59707-015-7, $12.95; 978-1-59707-014-0 (pb)
 Frank and Joe Hardy finish up a case helping a fellow ATAC (American Teens Against Crime) agent, who sharp-eyed fans may recognize despite her Alias. Things seem to quiet down when ATAC sends Frank and Joe undercover to investigate a new Mall opening in Bayport, due to several suspicious accidents there. But things get exciting when the night before the big opening, Joe, Frank, and seven others are mysteriously locked in the mall with a murderer on the loose. If that wasn't enough, everything that could go horribly wrong in a mall, does: a flood caused by water beds; an electrocution at an electronics shop; a bow and arrow used to kill in the Sporting Goods store; a runaway elevator; a damsel in distress in the dress shop; fire in the food court; and much, much more.

The **Hardy** Boys: Undercover Brothers #5: Sea You, Sea Me. Daniel Rendon, artist. NBM/Papercutz 2006 112p. Illustration
Grades: 3 4 5 6 7 8 9   **741.5; Fic**
 1. Hardy Boys (Fictional characters); 2. Mystery graphic novels; 3. Graphic novels
 978-1-59707-023-2, $12.95; 978-1-59707-022-5 (pb)

When a series of suspicious mishaps befall several deep sea fishing boats, the Hardy Boys are called into action by ATAC (American Teens Against Crime) before any more teen green horns can be hurt. But while in the past Frank and Joe have battled terrorists, master criminals, and multinational corporations, the undercover brothers have no experience fighting the fury of the ocean.

The **Hardy** Boys: Undercover Brothers #6: Hyde & Shriek. Art by Daniel Rendon. NBM/Papercutz 2006 112p. Illustration
Grades: 3 4 5 6 7 8 9   **741.5; Fic**
 1. Hardy Boys (Fictional characters); 2. Mystery graphic novels; 3. Graphic novels
 978-1-59707-029-4, $12.95; 978-1-59707-028-7 (pb)
 When a visiting dignitary's daughter is scheduled to attend a party at a horror-themed restaurant in New York City, ATAC agents Joe and Frank Hardy are enlisted as undercover protection. But in a building where anything can happen, where the walls literally have ears, can the Hardy Boys find and stop the assassin who has targeted Sangita before it is too late?

The **Hardy** Boys: Undercover Brothers #7: The Opposite Numbers. Daniel Rendon, Paulo Henrique, Sidney Lima, artist. NBM/Papercutz 2006 112p. Illustration
Grades: 3 4 5 6 7 8 9   **741.5; Fic**
 1. Hardy Boys (Fictional characters); 2. Mystery graphic novels; 3. Graphic novels
 978-1-59707-035-5, $12.95; 978-1-59707-034-3 (pb)
 Traveling across the country on the maiden voyage of a bullet train, the Hardy Boys find themselves framed for murder, even after their heroic efforts to save others. But they can't depend on A.T.A.C. (American Teens Against Crime) to help them, because every indication is that it's the super secret spy organization, founded by their father, that framed them.

The **Hardy** Boys: Undercover Brothers #8: Board to Death. Paulo Henrique, artist. NBM/Papercutz 2007 112p. Illustration
Grades: 3 4 5 6 7 8 9   **741.5; Fic**
 1. Hardy Boys (Fictional characters); 2. Mystery graphic novels; 3. Graphic novels
 978-1-59707-054-6, $12.95; 978-1-59707-053-9 (pb)
 Frank and Joe Hardy go undercover at a major skateboarding contest in Venice, California to find out which competitor is trying to kill off the competition, literally. The list of suspects includes Dex Thom, a skilled skateboarder whose parents wanted him to be a musical prodigy, the Pink Shadow, a girl of mystery, and her equally secretive trainer, Mr. Moto, and the Wraith, a dark and brooding young man. Will Frank and Joe solve the mystery before the killer discovers their real mission, and eliminates them?

The **Hardy** Boys: Undercover Brothers #9: To Die or Not to Die?. Paulo Henrique, artist. NBM/Papercutz 2007 112p. Illustration
Grades: 3 4 5 6 7 8 9   **741.5; Fic**
 1. Hardy Boys (Fictional characters); 2. Mystery graphic novels; 3. Graphic novels
 978-1-59707-063-8, $12.95; 978-1-59707-062-1 (pb)
 At a nationwide drama competition, Frank and Joe Hardy must go undercover to discover which contestant has

been knocking off the competition by any means possible - including deadly force. While Joe keeps an eye on all of the backstage drama, Frank, posing as a competing drama student, may be distracted from his mission by the romantic attentions of a beautiful acting student named Joelle. Things get further complicated when Joelle becomes the only eyewitness to the red-haired woman who is their number one suspect! Will Frank's stage debut be the Hardy Boys final bow?

Loux, Matthew
★ **Salt** water taffy: the seaside adventures of Jack and Benny, vol. 4: Caldera's revenge, part 1. Oni Press 2011 Un Illustration
Grades: 3 4 5 6 7 8 9   **741.5; Fic**
1. Adventure graphic novels; 2. Brothers; 3. Humorous graphic novels; 4. Whales; 5. Graphic novels
978-1-934964-62-0, $5.99
As Jack and Benny's summer vacation in Chowder Bay continues, Captain Hollister gives the boys a book called The Hidden History of Chowder Bay. The boys find it difficult to read, so they jump at the chance to investigate when a spooky whaling ship appears in the bay. The local fishermen talk about something attacking their boats in the bay, and the brothers soon discover that the culprit is the legendary whale called Caldera. But just what is that spooky whaling ship doing in the bay" This volume ends in a cliffhanger. Readers who enjoy rollicking adventure and a little whimsy (talking giant squid who like grilled hot dogs) will enjoy this book.

Love, Robert
Shadow Rock. Jeremy and Robert Love. Dark Horse Comics 2006 80p. Illustration
Grades: 4 5 6 7 8   **741.5; Fic**
1. Adventure graphic novels; 2. Mystery graphic novels; 3. Supernatural graphic novels; 4. Graphic novels
1-59307-347-X, $9.95
After his mother's death, young Timothy London moves from the big city to the small New England fishing town of Shadow Rock to live with his father. His new home is up the hill from a legendary haunted lighthouse where Timothy discovers the ghost of Kendahl Fog, a boy who died under mysterious circumstances. Timothy and his new ghostly companion set out to explore the dark underbelly of Shadow Rock and the mystery of Kendahl's death. Harrowing thrills and chills ensue in this classic boy's adventure with a horror twist.

Low, Vicki
The **First** Emperor. Art by Sarah Mayhew. Harcourt Achieve/Steck-Vaughn 2006 48p. Illustration
Grades: 3 4 5 6 7 8   **741.5; Fic**
1. Adventure graphic novels; 2. China — History; 3. Graphic novels
978-1-4190-3195-3, $4.88
Emperor Zheng rules over a vast empire as the first emperor of China, and he wants to live forever. He sends his son Prince Fu Su on a search for the secret of everlasting life. As the prince travels through the land, he learns about some magic herbs and much more ... This historical graphic novel includes prose intervals that provide information about

Emperor Zheng and some of China's national treasures, such as the soldiers of X'ian, the Great Wall of China; and of some of the atrocities he ordered, such as the burning of all books that didn't agree with his edicts, and many deaths.
Part of the Timeline Graphic Novels series.

Lucke, Deb
The **Lunch** Witch. By Deb Lucke. Papercutz 2015 180 p. Illustration
Grades: 3 4 5 6
741.5; Fic
1. Friendship — Fiction; 2. School children — Fiction; 3. Witches Fiction
1629911623;
9781629911625, $14.99
In this book, by Deb Lucke, "Grunhilda inherits her famous ancestors'

Courtesy of Papercutz

recipes and cauldron, but no one believes in magic anymore. Despite the fact that Grunhilda's only useful skill is cooking up potfuls of foul brew, she finds a job listing that might suit her: lunch lady. She delights in scaring the kids until she meets a timid little girl named Madison with a big set of glasses who becomes an unlikely friend." (Publisher's note)
"Lucke's splotchy, textured, quixotically paced, visual storytelling, with its mixture of crisply defined panels and sprawling full-page spreads, perfectly fits the outsider lives of both protagonists." VOYA

Lundy, Kathleen Gould
In a Class of Her Own. Art by Jeff Alward. Harcourt Achieve 2006 48p. Illustration
Grades: 3 4 5 6 7 8   **92; 741.5**
1. African Americans — Civil rights; 2. Biographical graphic novels; 3. Bridges, Ruby; 4. Graphic novels
978-1-4190-3212-7, $8.99
It is the year 1960. A six-year-old girl named Ruby Bridges makes history by being the first African American child to attend an all-white school in New Orleans. What is she up against" This graphic novel is interspersed with pages of prose giving background information about Brown v. Board of Education, Norman Rockwell's famous painting of Ruby, and about her life as an adult.
Part of the Timeline Graphic Novels series.

Lung, Khoo Fuk
Ultraman Tiga, Vol. 1: Return of the warrior. [by] Tony Wong and Khoo Fuk Lung. Dark Horse Comics 2004 128p. Illustration
Grades: 7 8 9 10   **741.5; Fic**
1. Monsters; 2. Science fiction graphic novels; 3. Superhero graphic novels; 4. Ultraman (Fictional character); 5. Graphic novels
1-59307-119-1, $15.95
A cultural icon in Hong Kong and Japan, Ultraman has punched, kicked and karate-chopped in TV shows and movies for nearly four decades. Now this incarnation of Ultraman, called Tiga, finds the 100-foot-tall hero revived in the year 2049 and finding a world ill-equipped to handle the

onslaught of gigantic beasts that are attacking all over the world. There is a second volume: Past Sins, Future Dangers.

"Wong's script moves briskly from one fight scene to the next, and Lung's art effectively uses line work and color. The duo is capable of winking knowingly at readers while still taking the story seriously enough to be compelling." Publ Wkly

Lutes, Jason

★ **Houdini:** the handcuff king. Art by Nick Bertozzi. Hyperion Books for Children/Jump at the Sun 2007 90p. Illustration (Center for Cartoon Studies presents)

Grades: 4 5 6 7 8 9 10   **92; 741.5**

1. Biographical graphic novels; 2. Houdini, Harry, 1874-1926; 3. Magicians; 4. Magicians; 5. Graphic novels
978-0-7868-3902-5, $16.99; 978-0-7868-3903-2 (pa), $9.99

On May 1, 1908, magician Harry Houdini performed one of his famous handcuff escapes, this time in handcuffs and leg irons, while jumping off the Cambridge Bridge in Massachusetts into the frigid Boston River. This graphic novel takes the reader through Houdini's day, from 5:00 a.m. as he makes his preparations, makes a practice jump, coaches his wife Bess on how she's to help him, and then makes the jump.

This is a "fascinating graphic novel. . . . The format will instantly draw a lot of attention from readers and then hold on to it. Lutes and Bertozzi use grayscale comic panels to share their story about the life of Harry Houdini in a unique way. . . . The book resembles a hybrid between fiction and nonfiction, and the ingenious choice of format will appeal to a broad age range of readers." Voice Youth Advocates

Lyga, Barry

★ **Wolverine:** worst day ever. By Barry Lyga; artist, Todd Nauck. Marvel Publishing 2009 184p. Illustration

Grades: 5 6 7 8 9   **741.5; Fic**

1. Humorous graphic novels; 2. Superhero graphic novels; 3. Wolverine (Fictional character); 4. Graphic novels
978-0-7851-3757-3, $14.99; 0-7851-3757-2

Teenager Eric Mattias has just recently discovered he has mutant powers. Very sucky mutant powers: suddenly no one notices him even when he's in the same room. He's not invisible, but he might as well be, and people don't even notice him when he speaks. Eric decides to follow Wolverine around and see if he can't pick up a few pointers about living a loner-type life, as the adamantium-clawed mutant tends to do. Only when they end up in a remote forested area does Eric realize he may not have made the smartest move, because someone else has come, someone who is as strong as Wolverine, and maybe meaner: Sabretooth.

"It's a coming-of-age tale with bursts of action that's sure to appeal to its large, built-in audience." Booklist

Ma, Wing Shing

Chinese Hero, Tales of the Blood Sword, Vol. 1. DrMaster Publications, Inc. 2007 270p. Illustration

Grades: 8 9 10 11 12 Adult   **741.5; Fic**

1. Adventure graphic novels; 2. Martial arts; 3. Graphic novels
978-1-59796-041-1, $19.95

When he was a child, Hero's family was attacked and killed by a practitioner of Northern Mantis kung fu. This assassin was tasked, by the affluent head of a local triad, to retrieve Hero's family heirloom - the legendary Blood Sword. Barely escaping with his life, Hero has now reached adulthood, having mastered several forms of kung fu to aid him in his lifelong endeavor to safeguard the family treasure. But now his enemies turn their gaze to his newborn son. This series is full of full-color kung fu action. This is a Chinese manhua.

MacHale, D. J.

★ **Pendragon** book one: the merchant of death graphic novel. Adapted and illustrated by Carla Speed McNeil.   Aladdin Paperbacks 2008 172p. Illustration

Grades: 5 6 7 8 9 10

741.5; Fic

1. Adventure graphic novels; 2. Fantasy graphic novels; 3. Graphic novels
978-1-4169-5080-6, $9.99; 1-4169-5080-X

LC 2007-937920

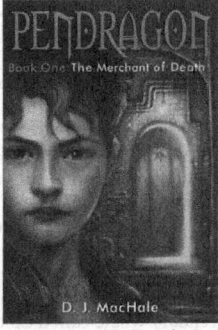

Courtesy of Aladdin Paperbacks

Fourteen-year-old Bobby Pendragon has had a good life with a loving family, friends, and sports, but it all changes the night his Uncle Press takes him into New York City, to a deserted subway station that contains a gate that leads them to another world. On Denduron, a peaceful tribe called the Milago face annihilation from the Bedowan, and Uncle Press expects Bobby to help him stop it. Press is what he calls a Traveler, and he says Bobby is one, too, and they have a job to do. Bobby is able to write journals and send them home to his best friends Mark and Courtney. Meanwhile, he needs to learn so much, can he do it in time to help—and stay alive?

"This graphic-format adaptation streamlines the already fast-moving experience, providing satisfying interpretations of favorite characters and situations." Booklist

Macklin, Ken

The **weasel** patrol. Illustrated by Lela Dowling. About Comics/About Infinity 2009 104p. Illustration

Grades: 7 8 9 10 11 12 Adult   **741.5; Fic**

1. Humorous graphic novels; 2. Science fiction graphic novels; 3. Weasels; 4. Graphic novels
978-0-9790750-8-7, $9.99

When criminals strike, the intergalactic troopers called the Weasel Patrol will ferret out the bad guys every time. Despite their utter lack of planning, attentiveness, cohesion, or competence, they always succeed, even if their favorite tactic when faced with danger is to run away. This book includes twelve comedic adventures, in which the weasels face mythical monsters (Big Foot), aliens, kidnapped cattle in disguise, and the ever-ready bad guy Reefer Rick. Willy, Leroy, Biff, Roscoe, and Bob are the genetically uplifted Weasel Patrol. The book includes mild, cartoony violence and no bad language and no nudity. Villainous Reefer Rick smokes. Artist Dowling includes fun little details, such as the Acme name on some of the gadgets.

MacPherson, Dwight L.
   Kid Houdini and the silver dollar misfits. Art by Worth Gowell and Kevin Conley. Viper Comics 2008 Un Illustration
Grades: 3 4 5 6 7 8 9   **741.5; Fic**
   1. Houdini, Harry, 1874-1926; 2. Magicians; 3. Mystery graphic novels; 4. Nonfiction writers; 5. Supernatural graphic novels; 6. Graphic novels
978-0—9802385-2-5, $9.95
   In 1886, ten-year-old Harry Houdini runs away from home, only to find himself a prisoner in Professor Murat's circus. Harry joins the "freak" children: Lydia the snake girl (and her snake Terra), Hans the legless boy, and Jacques and Joe the Siamese twins and they form a detective agency that will solve mysteries for the fee of a silver dollar. Near Kansas City, a girl named Bea hires them to find her missing father whom she fears was kidnapped. However, when the gang gets to her house, they discover that her mother has now been kidnapped, too. It all has to do with a treasure map that leads to a lost gold mine, and the gang needs to solve that mystery in order to find Bea's parents. A young Harry Houdini and his friends make a fun team and they face some supernatural elements in their cases, much like the old Scooby-Doo cartoons and with a similar scary-fun factor.

Mad About the Fifties
   Grant Geissman, editor. E.C. Publications/MAD Books 2005 Un. Illustration
Grades: 8 9 10 11 12 Adult   **741.5**
   1. Humorous graphic novels; 2. Satire; 3. Graphic novels
1-4012-0753-7, $12.99
   MAD Magazine was founded in 1952 as a ten-cent comic book that parodied other comic books; three years later it became a twenty-five cent (cheap!) magazine. This volume collects some of the regular features and parodies of television programs and movies of the decade. Some of the advertising parodies feature tobacco and alcohol products, and some parodies portray the imbibing of alcohol products.

Mad About the Sixties: The Best of the Decade
   Grant Geissman, editor. Mad Books/E.C. Publications 1997 Un Illustration
Grades: 7 8 9 10 11 12 Adult   **741.5; Fic**
   1. Humorous graphic novels; 2. Satire; 3. Graphic novels
1-4012-0754-5, $9.99
   Alfred E. Newman as a flower child" Ecch! Here is a look back at the Sixties from the satire magazine, full of send-ups, takeoffs, and put-ons from the decade that gave the world Timothy Leary and Tiny Tim. Along with Spy vs. Spy, Sergio Aragones' "Mad Marginals," Don Martin's lunacies, and Snappy Answers to Stupid Questions, this volume includes TV satires such as Star Blecch, Bats-Man, and The Phewgitive, and movie takeoffs 201 Min. of a Space Idiocy, East Side Story, and Flawrence of Arabia. Back in the 1960s, preteens read the magazine and most of them turned out okay ...

Madara, Sai
   Mamoru the shadow protector volume 1. DrMaster Publications 2008 168p. Illustration
Grades: 7 8 9 10 11 12   **741.5; Fic**
   1. Humorous graphic novels; 2. Manga; 3. Ninja; 4. Graphic novels
978-1-59796-183-7, $9.95
                                          LC 2008-249015
   Mamoru Kagemori seems to be just an ordinary, boring high school boy, but he's really the eldest son of a ninja clan that has been charged with guarding their neighbors, the Konnyakus, for four hundred years. Mamoru must secretly guard Yuna Konnyaku, his classmate; she's a total klutz and rather ditzy, and gets into all kinds of trouble. Take, for example, the fact that she witnessed a drug deal without even realizing what went on; now, the criminals want her dead, and Mamoru has to stop them all. The book includes some minor fan service and some mild violence.

Maeda, Jun
   Hibiki's magic, vol. 1. Art by Rei Izumi. Tokyopop 2007 234p. Illustration
Grades: 7 8 9 10 11 12   **741.5; Fic**
   1. Fantasy graphic novels; 2. Magic; 3. Manga; 4. Graphic novels
978-1-59816-766-5, $9.99
   Hibiki works as a sorcerer's assistant, but she's lousy at magic; her best talent is making tea. When criminal ruffians interrupt an experiment, her master's soul becomes trapped in a squirrellike gusk and his body is destroyed when the house's magical defenses are triggered by the intrusion. Bereft of her master, Hibiki comes to the big city, Kamigusk, where she is taken to Kamisaid Academy and welcomed as an expert magic user, but what can she do? The story includes some mild bad language, minor fan service, and mild violence.

Maeda, Shunshin
   Ninja baseball Kyuma!, vol. 1. Udon Entertainment 2009 200p. Illustration
Grades: 2 3 4 5 6   **741.5; Fic**
   1. Baseball; 2. Humorous graphic novels; 3. Manga; 4. Ninja; 5. Graphic novels
978-1-897376-86-7, $7.99
   Young Kyuma Hattori, descendant of famous ninja Hanzo Hattori, is the last ninja left in the ninja compound in the mountains, and he trains with his faithful dog Inui. Kaoru is captain of the Moonstar City Club baseball team, comprised of elementary school students. When teammate Yohko says her crystal ball says they need to look to the mountains to help their team win, Kaoru goes up the mountain and finds Kyuma and asks him to join their team. Kyuma knows nothing about modern society or sports like baseball, and he thinks he's joining an army to go to battle against their enemy. Will his team ever figure out Kyuma is really a ninja, and will Kyuma ever figure out that a baseball game is just a game" The book includes some ninja-style fighting, but no violence or bad language.

Majiko!
   St. Lunatic High School Volume 1. Tokyopop 2007 Un Illustration

Grades: 8 9 10 11 12   **741.5; Fic**
1. Horror graphic novels; 2. Humorous graphic novels; 3. Manga; 4. Graphic novels
978-1-59816-944-7, $9.99

Forced to attend the prestigious St. Lunatic School when her brother gets a needed teaching job there, Niko Kanzaki discovers a haunting secret in her demon-filled night-classes. She applies higher learning to find out the differences between humans and demons, but the handsome and mysterious Ren shows her that the races also share some things in common... High school—filled with cute boys, delicious secrets, and debonair demons...oh, my.

Maki, Yoko
    Aishiteruze Baby Vol. 1. Viz Media/Shojo Beat 2006 Un Illustration
Grades: 8 9 10 11 12 Adult   **741.5; Fic**
1. Shojo manga; 2. Graphic novels
978-1-4215-0711-8, $19.95

Kippei Katakura is a 17-year-old playboy who spends his time chasing girls, careless of their feelings. But when his 5-year-old cousin Yuzuyu comes to live with his family after her mother's sudden disappearance, Kippei is put in charge of taking care of her. As Kippei gets to know Yuzuyu and starts to understand how she feels, he also begins to realize that all girls were like Yuzuyu once... Kippei has a lot to figure out, like what to make for Yuzuyu's lunch and how to drop her off at kindergarten while still getting to high school on time. Kippei is enjoying his time with Yuzuyu, but not everyone is happy about it. The girls at school miss their quality time with Kippei, and one decides to play dirty to get him back.

Malam, John
    Oliver Twist. Illustrated by Penko Gelev; retold by John Malam.. Barron's 2006 48p. Illustration
Grades: 3 4 5 6 7 8 9   **741.5; Fic**
1. Dickens, Charles, 1812-1870 — Adaptations; 2. Great Britain — History — 19th century; 3. Graphic novels
978-0-7641-5975-6, $15.99; 978-0-7641-3490-6 (pa), $8.99
                      LC 2005-936253

Born in a workhouse and immediately orphaned, Oliver Twist seems destined for a life of misery. He survives childhood years filled with neglect, hunger, and violence, but on his eighth birthday, he must start to work in the workhouse, and his troubles begin. Soon after he gets into trouble for daring to ask for more food, he's sent out to work and falls in with the evil Bill Sikes and Fagin, who run a group of raggedy young thieves. The book includes a brief biography of Dickens, a time line of world events during his life, a brief essay on the poor in London, and descriptions of some of the theatrical and motion picture adaptations of the story.

Part of the Graphic Classics series.

Mangels, Andy
    Iron man: beneath the armor. Del Rey Books 2008 216p. Illustration
Grades: 8 9 10 11 12 Adult   **741.5**
1. Iron Man (Fictional character); 2. Graphic novels
978-0-345-50615-3, $19.95

This book gives readers lots of information about Marvel Comics' hero, Iron Man. Millionaire industrialist and genius Tony Stark creates the armor and together, human and machine become Iron Man. Readers will find the history of Iron Man, from his debut in the 1960s to the movie which opened on May 2, 2008. They will see an overview of the armor's design evolution through the decades, and also find profiles of the characters who have appeared in Iron Man comics, from Tony Stark himself to Virginia "Pepper" Potts, James Rhodes, villains such as Mandarin, Crimson Dynamo, Fin Fang Foom, and many more.

Manglobe
    Samurai Champloo Vol. 1. Iillustrated by Masaru Gotsubo. Tokyopop 2005 177p. Illustration
Grades: 8 9 10 11 12 Adult   **741.5; Fic**
1. Adventure graphic novels; 2. Humorous graphic novels; 3. Manga; 4. Samurai; 5. Shonen manga; 6. Graphic novels
1-59182-282-3, $9.99

In a world full of evil, a hardworking waitress, an arrogant mercenary and a mysterious samurai meet. Through a series of misunderstandings, Fuu, Mugen and Jin find themselves running from officials and wanted by the law. Together they form an uneasy alliance to search for the enigmatic Sunflower Samurai. Along the way they come across misleading characters, ninjas, assassins and a prince in disguise. Their journey proves to be nothing less than a roller coaster ride of battles, danger, desperation and companionship. The book includes some strong language and some fighting violence.

Manning, Matthew K.
    Wolverine: inside the world of the living weapon. Written by Matthew K. Manning. DK 2009 199p. Illustration
Grades: 6 7 8 9   **741.5**
1. X-Men (Fictional characters)
978-0-7566-4547-2, $24.95; 0-7566-4547-6
                      LC 2009284799

"Super-fans can learn about Wolverine's comic book debut (a cameo in a Hulk comic in 1974), and the development of his character, his story, the X-Men, and more." (Publisher's note)

Mansfield, Andy
    The **All-New** All-Different X-Men Pop-Up. Candlewick Press 2007 Un Illustration
Grades: K 1 2 3 4 5 6 7 8 9 10 11 12 Adult   **741.5; Fic**
1. Pop-up books; 2. Superhero graphic novels; 3. X-Men (Fictional characters); 4. Graphic novels
978-0-7636-3462-9, $24.99

This pop-up book uses excerpts from classic X-Men comics, paper engineering, and pull-out fact files to profile the X-Men, including Cyclops, Storm, Nightcrawler, Wolverine, Colossus, and Banshee, along with nemesis Magneto and mini-profiles of the original X-Men.

Marsh, Robert
    Monster moneymaker. Art by Tom Percival. Stone Arch Books 2010 40p. Illustration

Grades: 2 3 4 5 6   **741.5; Fic**
1. Fantasy graphic novels; 2. Humorous graphic novels; 3. Monsters; 4. Schools; 5. Graphic novels
978-1-4342-1891-9, $21.32; 1-4342-1891-0
      LC 2009-29071
Gabby and her monster friend Dwight attend a school that is suffering from funding problems. New student Bradley proposes a candy sale to raise funds that will keep the lunch program going, then he proposes a contest to see who can raise the most money. Gabby and Dwight do pretty well, but Bradley and his monster Biff are way ahead of everyone else; could they possibly be cheating? This graphic novel includes a brief glossary, discussion questions, and writing prompts.
Part of the Graphic Sparks series.

Martin, Gary
Son of Samson and the Judge of God Volume 1. Art by Sergio Cariello. Zondervan/Zonderkidz 2007 160p. Illustration
Grades: 3 4 5 6 7 8   **741.5; Fic**
1. Adventure graphic novels; 2. Humorous graphic novels; 3. Graphic novels
978-0-310-71279-4, $9.99
      LC 2007-3157
When things get physical, Branan uses any weapon he can grab, just like his father, Samson. And like his dad, he can wield weapons other men can't even lift. The trouble is, he's not sure why God gave him such great power or what he's supposed to do with it. Trying to understand his father - and himself - Branan travels to the places where Samson did his amazing deeds. Along the way he performs some incredible heroics of his own, stirring up the anger of his father's old enemies. The book includes lots of cartoony action.

Martin, George R. R.
The **Hedge** Knight II: sworn sword. George R.R. Martin and Ben Avery ; artist, Mike Miller. Marvel Entertainment 2008 Un Illustration
Grades: 8 9 10 11 12 Adult   **741.5; Fic**
1. Adventure graphic novels; 2. Fantasy graphic novels; 3. Knights and knighthood; 4. Graphic novels
978-0-7851-2650-8, $19.99
Dunk, who is now Ser Duncan the Tall, has roamed Westeros as a hedge knight, accompanied by his squire, Egg. Now they're employed by Ser Eustace of Standfast, whose land suffers a severe drought because of his dispute with Lady Rohanna, whom many call the "Red Widow." Dunk tries to find a peaceful settlement to the feud, even as he deals with his strong attraction to Lady Rohanna. The book includes some fighting violence and mild sexual innuendo, and one scene of partial nudity.

Marunas, Nathaniel
Manga Claus, Honor, Loyalty, Tinsel: The Blade of Kringle. Penguin Group/Razorbill 2006 80p. Illustration
Grades: 4 5 6 7 8 9   **741.5; Fic**
1. Fantasy graphic novels; 2. Ninja; 3. Santa Claus; 4. Graphic novels
1-59514-134-0, $12.99

It's the night before Christmas Eve, and disgruntled elf Fritz, determined to show he belongs in Production and not Laundry, uses a dark magic spell on a ninja nutcracker. It's only supposed to cause a little damage and then he, Fritz, can use a spell to stop it. However, things go terribly wrong when elf Wallace fights back, the evil nutcracker lands in the furnace, and evil spell embers land on a pile of teddy bears. Yes, now an army of evil ninja teddy bears wreaks havoc at the North Pole, and Santa must stop them, with the help of a special pair of Japanese samurai swords.

Marvel Adventures: Spider-Man Volume One
Marvel Entertainment 2006 Un Illustration
Grades: 4 5 6 7 8 9   **741.5; Fic**
1. Spider-Man (Fictional character); 2. Superhero graphic novels; 3. Graphic novels
978-0-7851-2432-0, $19.99
This hardcover collects the first two volumes of Marvel Adventures Spider-Man. What separates the super-villains from just plain old villains? When they escape from prison, regular villains might lay low for a while and enjoy the sweetness of freedom. But not a super-villain like Doctor Octopus - the minute he's free, he's gathering up the most dangerous crew ever assembled: the Vulture, Electro, Kraven the Hunter, Sandman and Mysterio. And they've all got one thing on their minds: bringing down Spider-Man once and for all. Also, catch the story that started it all: the origin of Spider-Man. Stories also include the return of the Human Torch, the villainy of the Scorpion, and more.

Masters, Anthony
Horror of the Heights. Art by Peter Dennis. Stone Arch Books 2006 88p. Illustration
Grades: 2 3 4 5 6 7   **741.5; Fic**
1. Mystery graphic novels; 2. Graphic novels
978-1-59889-030-3, $22.60 lib. bdg.
Dean suffers from a fear of heights, which is a problem since his older brother is a diving champion and his father runs the Wave Crest Health Club. Then someone sabotages the high diving board that Dean fears, and then they discover a problem with the water slide. Dean thinks he must find and expose the saboteur to save the club's reputation. The easy-to-read text, simple panel design, and fast-paced story make this a good choice for struggling and beginning readers.

Joker. Stone Arch Books 2006 72p. Illustration
Grades: 2 3 4 5 6 7   **741.5; Fic**
1. Adventure graphic novels; 2. Mystery graphic novels; 3. Graphic novels
978-1-59889-024-2, $21.26 lib bdg
Mel loves to do magic tricks and play practical jokes, but when his magician father gets kidnapped, no one will believe that Mel isn't trying to play a joke. He'll have to try to save his father with only his faithful dog Mutt to help him. The simple text and panel layout with a fast-paced story make this suitable for beginning and struggling readers.

The **rescue**. By Anthony Masters; illustrated by Mike Perkins.. Stone Arch Books 2008 72p. Illustration
Grades: 3 4 5 6 7   **741.5; Fic**
1. Bullies; 2. Foxes; 3. Friendship; 4. Graphic novels
978-1-4342-0456-1, $21.26

LC 2007-30739

When Justin finds an injured fox that the bully brothers, Bill and Ed Baxter, plan to kill, he hides the fox in a deserted, supposedly haunted house. He takes care of it, but he knows he has to get it back into the woods and safely away from the Baxters. His friend Angie is scared of the ghost at the deserted house, but she helps Justin.

Part of the Graphic Trax series; originally published in Great Britain in 2002 under the title Freddy's Fox.

Matheny, Bill
The **Batman** Strikes! Vol. 1: Crime Time; illustrated by Terry Beatty, Christopher Jones et al. DC Comics 2005 Un Illustration
Grades: 4 5 6 7 8 9   **741.5; Fic**
1. Batman (Fictional character); 2. Joker (Fictional character); 3. Superhero graphic novels; 4. Graphic novels
1-4012-0509-7, $6.99
This book boasts five action-packed adventures of the Dark Knight Detective: Penguin Rising, City of Bats, Outlaw and Disorder, Without a Chance and Deadly Partner. Batman goes up against the Penguin, the Joker, Manbat, and other villains.

The **Batman** Strikes! Vol. 2: In Darkest Knight. DC Comics 2005 Un Illustration
Grades: 4 5 6 7 8 9   **741.5; Fic**
1. Batman (Fictional character); 2. Catwoman (Fictional character); 3. Joker (Fictional character); 4. Superhero graphic novels; 5. Graphic novels
1-4012-0510-0, $6.99
Evil can't hide, and neither can the rogues' gallery of villains who take on Gotham City's Dark Knight Detective. Catwoman, Mr. Freeze, Firefly, the Joker, and Man-Bat try their luck in this volume.

The **Batman** Strikes!: duty calls. Bill Matheny, J. Torres ; illustrated by Christopher Jones, Terry Beatty ; Colored by Heroic Age ; Lettered by Phil Balsman, Travis Lanham. DC Comics 2007 144p. Illustration
Grades: 3 4 5 6 7 8 9   **741.5; Fic**
1. Adventure graphic novels; 2. Batgirl (Fictional character); 3. Batman (Fictional character); 4. Catwoman (Fictional character); 5. Superhero graphic novels; 6. Graphic novels
978-1-4012-1548-4, $12.99
This volume of Bat-stories is based on the new WB Kids cartoon series. Batman takes on Clayface, the Penguin, the Riddler, Catwoman, and Poison Ivy; Batgirl steps in because Pamela Isley used to be Barbara Gordon's friend. The stories have lots of action, fast quips, and no foul language or actual violence.

Matoh, Sanami
Ra-I. Tokyopop 2006 196p. Illustration
Grades: 7 8 9 10 11 12   **741.5; Fic**
1. Manga; 2. Mystery graphic novels; 3. Romance graphic novels; 4. Shojo manga; 5. Graphic novels
1-59816-663-8, $9.99
Al Foster is a private detective whose workaday life suddenly shakes up with the arrival of thirteen-year-old Rai Spencer, youngest son of the billionaire Spencer family, genius child prodigy, and unrepentant smart aleck. Rai also has telekinetic powers that can knock out anyone who stands in his path. His older sister Rei sports a mean left hook. What Rai desperately needs is someone to figure out who has been trying to kill him for the past month. This is a standalone manga.

Matsumoto, Nina
Yokaiden, volume 1. Del Rey Manga 2008 Un Illustration
Grades: 6 7 8 9 10 11 12   **741.5; Fic**
1. Fantasy graphic novels; 2. Folklore — Japan; 3. Monsters; 4. Graphic novels
978-0-345-50327-5, $10.95
In what looks like 18th or 19th-century Japan, young Hamachi Uramaki lives with his crotchety old grandmother (his parents died years before); he's obsessed with yokai, Japan's legendary monsters and other supernatural creatures, and he desperately wants to meet one. He does encounter a kappa who fell into a trap, and Hamachi saves the creature he names Madkap. When Hamachi returns home after selling bamboo in town, he finds his grandmother dead and thinks Madkap did it (grandmother had set the kappa trap). He decides to enter the yokai realm to find Madkap and get revenge; but once Hamachi enters, the trick is to survive, for the yokai realm is not meant for humans. This is a global manga story that uses Western page order (left to right). Matsumoto features lesser-known yokai, such as the chochin obake, the paper lantern ghost, and the namahage, an ogre who disciplines naughty children by crippling them for a while. The book includes some violence and mild bad language.
"Matsumoto's manga is silly fun, anchored by a clueless but plucky hero and a dry sense of humor. Taking place in a fantasy setting close to historical Japan, Hamachi's adventures read like lighthearted folktales centered on the wide variety of yokai and the various means of dealing with them." Booklist

Matsumoto, Tomo
Beauty is the Beast Volume 1. Viz Media/Shojo Beat 2005 184p. Illustration
Grades: 7 8 9 10 11 12   **741.5; Fic**
1. Humorous graphic novels; 2. Romance graphic novels; 3. Shojo manga; 4. Graphic novels
1-4215-0289-5, $8.99
When bubbly eleventh-grader Eimi Yamashita finds out that her parents are relocating for work, she decides to strike out on her own and move into a dormitory for girls. Little does Eimi suspect the exciting romantic adventures that await her there. Eimi's fellow residents are a little bit crazy, but a whole lot of fun. They've got a secret mission planned for Eimi's new resident initiation...and it has something to do with sneaking into the boys dormitory across the street and returning with a special keepsake! Can Eimi pull it off without getting caught by one of the handsomest (and cruelest) boys in the dorm?

Matsumuto, Natsumi
St. [heart] dragon girl, vol. 1. Viz Media/Shojo Beat 2008 Un Illustration
Grades: 7 8 9 10 11 12   **741.5; Fic**

1. Fantasy graphic novels; 2. Manga; 3. Romance graphic novels; 4. Shojo manga; 5. Graphic novels
978-1-4215-2010-0, $8.99

High schooler Momoka Sendou, nicknamed Dragon Girl, is a martial artist; her childhood friend Ryuga Kou is a Chinese sorcerer who banishes demons. They have helped each other over the years, but now the Serpent King has threatened to take Ryuga's cousin Shunran as his bride. Ryuga knows he needs more strength, so he tries to summon the clan's dragon spirit to possess him, but Momoka sees only a threat to her friend and pushes him out of the way; the dragon enters her instead. Ryuga does possess the power to seal or unseal the dragon within Momoka, so now they really have to work together to fight the demons, especially the Serpent King. Complicating matters is the little fact that Momoka loves Ryuga but won't tell him, even though everyone around them knows it.

St. Dragon Girl, vol. 2. Viz Media/Shojo Beat 2009 Un Illustration
Grades: 7 8 9 10 11 12   **741.5; Fic**
1. Magic; 2. Manga; 3. Martial arts; 4. Romance graphic novels; 5. Shojo manga; 6. Graphic novels
978-1-4215-2011-7, $8.99

Childhood friends, Momoka is a martial artist and Ryuga is a Chinese magic master; Momoka is possessed by a dragon spirit that only Ryuga can unseal whenever its strength is needed. When the Kenpo class goes on a training camp in the old school building, Momoka finds "her" peach tree; but now she learns that a demon that had been trapped beneath the tree is trying to get free, and it possesses her classmates then Ryuga. Somehow she's going to have to defeat it. One would think she wouldn't need the dragon during the school's festival. Momoka stars in the Kenpo class's play, but when she takes a break to enjoy the festival with Ryuga, thieves steal the sword she was using it belongs to Ryuga's family, and she must get it back. Then a new transfer student comes to school, and it's Ryuga's cousin, Raika. She says they're promised to each other and wants Momoka's help to make sure Ryuga will fall in love with her; the problem is Momoka loves Ryuga herself. The book includes martial arts action and a few chaste kisses.

Matsuzuki, Kou
Happy Cafe, vol. 1. Tokyopop 2010 194p. Illustration
Grades: 7 8 9 10 11 12   **741.5; Fic**
1. Humorous graphic novels; 2. Manga; 3. Restaurants; 4. Romance graphic novels; 5. Shojo manga; 6. Graphic novels
978-1-4278-1730-3, $10.99

Sixteen-year-old Uru lives by herself because her mother has married a younger man (stepfather is 29) and she wants to give them privacy. She decides she has to help pay her bills, so she gets a part time job as a waitress at the Cafe Bonheur (which means Happy Cafe), where she meets Shindo and Ichiro, two very handsome but rather grumpy young men. Uru is a major klutz, which is a liability for a waitress, but Shindo and Ichiro manage to save her most of the time. Shindo is especially cranky, and Ichiro seems to be eating all the time" he tends to fall asleep when he's hungry. Despite all that, Uru enjoys working at the cafe, but she's under pressure to get good scores on her school exams, or her mother has threatened to make her move back home.

When Uru helps another teenager live her dream of being a model, Mitsuka texts her a question that puts Uru in a fluster. "Is that dark haired crank your crush or something?" The romance is light, with very little suggestiveness. Instead of the usual chibi characters to express deep emotions, Matsuzuki uses very simple round-headed figures.

Matthews, Brett
The **Lone** Ranger. Brett Matthews, writer ; Sergio Cariello, artist ; Dean White, colorist ; Simon Bowland, lettering ; John Cassaday, cover artist & art direction. Dynamite Entertainment 2007 160p. Illustration
Grades: 8 9 10 11 12 Adult
741.5; Fic
1. Adventure graphic novels; 2. Lone Ranger (Fictional character); 3. Western stories; 4. Graphic novels

Courtesy of Dynamite Entertainment

978-1-933305-39-4, $24.99; 978-1-933305-40-0 (pa), $19.99

"A fiery horse with the speed of light, a cloud of dust, and a hearty "Hi Yo Silver!" The Lone Ranger ..." A popular radio show starting in the 1930s that became a popular television show that ran from 1949 through 1957, a few film serials (extremely hard to find), some paperback novels, and a movie in 1981, The Lone Ranger became an iconic figure. In March 2008, Disney Studios announced it's planning to make a new Lone Ranger movie. In the meantime, Dynamite Entertainment started publishing Lone Ranger comics in 2006. This Lone Ranger is different from the old radio and television shows, and so is Tonto. These aren't the squeaky clean heroes one might expect, although they are heroic. This volume shows the origin of the Lone Ranger, from a young Texas Ranger who has just joined his father and brother. They are ambushed and all killed, except for John. Tonto, a Native American of unknown tribal nation, takes care of John; he has killed all of the killers. When John recovers from his wounds, they set off to find out who ordered the killing, while the reader knows that another killer is murdering all the dead Rangers' families. This book includes some graphic violence.

Texas Ranger John Reid seeks revenge for the murders of his family and friends, only to find justice . . . and that he's something greater than he ever thought he could be. Together with Tonto, he rides against rich criminals like Cavendish and the politicians Cavendish backs. This new version of the Lone Ranger includes more violence than some might remember from the old television show and books.

Serenity: Those Left Behind. Story by Joss Whedon & Brett Matthews ; script by Brett Matthews ; art by Will Conrad ; colors by Laura Martin ; letters by Michael Heisler ; front cover art by Adam Hughes ; back cover art by Sean Phillips. Dark Horse Comics 2006 Un Illustration
Grades: 8 9 10 11 12 Adult   **741.5; Fic**

1. Adventure graphic novels; 2. Science fiction graphic novels; 3. Graphic novels
1-59307-449-2, $9.95

Penned by Firefly creator Whedon and Brett Matthews, who wrote several episodes of the show, this book follows a ship full of mercenaries, fugitives and one law-abiding prostitute in their pursuit for fast cash and a little peace along the fringes of space. The ragtag crew of Serenity take on a scavenger mission with the hopes of earning enough dough to disappear for a while. Only too late do they realize the whole gig is orchestrated by an old enemy eager remake their acquaintance with the help of some covert-operatives known only as the Blue Gloves. The book includes some violence; most of the strong language is written in Chinese characters so most readers won't know what is being said.

Serenity: Better days. Script by Joss Whedon and Brett Matthews ; art by Will Conrad ; colors by Michelle Madsen ; letters by Michael Heisler. Dark Horse Books 2008 Un Illustration
Grades: 8 9 10 11 12 Adult   **741.5; Fic**
1. Adventure graphic novels; 2. Science fiction graphic novels; 3. Graphic novels
978-1-59582-162-1, $9.95

Mal Reynolds and his ragtag crew take their ship Serenity to the far frontiers of space, as far from the Alliance as they can get. They have actually succeeded in pulling off a heist, and got a much larger than expected payoff from the guy who hired them. However, while the crew members fantasize about what each will do with the newfound wealth, the Alliance is hunting for whoever stole their high-tech weapon and will do whatever it takes to get it back. The book includes some mild sexual innuendo and some violence. This is an original story based on the "Firefly" television series and characters that Joss Whedon created.

McCann, Jim
★ **Return** of the Dapper Men. Written by Jim McCann; art by Janet Lee; lettered by Dave Lanphear; edited by Stephen Christy. Archaia Comics 2010 Un Illustration
Grades: 4 5 6 7 8   **741.5; Fic**
1. Robots; 2. Science fiction graphic novels; 3. Graphic novels
978-1-932386-90-5, $24.95; 1-932386-90-4

"In the dreamy land of Anorev, children, all under age 11, live underground among intricate gear-work mechanisms, while elegant robots live in abandoned houses aboveground. . . . All are perpetually stuck in the same day, and time has, essentially, ceased to mean anything—until 314 Dapper Men rain from the sky and set in motion the impetus for change. . . . Where this book truly stands out is how well the story works in concert with Lee's stunning artwork, which employs an art nouveau sheen. . . . A true dazzler that speaks on multiple levels for both child and adult readers and one that gets richer with each read." Booklist

McClintock, Norah
I, witness. Norah McClintock, Mike Deas. Orca Book Publishers 2012 144 p.
Grades: 6 7 8   **741.5/971; Fic**
1. Gangs; 2. Witnesses; 3. Graphic novels

1554697891; 9781459803220; 9781554697892, $16.95; 9781554697908
LC 2012938210

In this book, "teenager David Boone and his friend Robbie witness a brutal murder. Boone talks Robbie out of going to the cops, and a few days later, Robbie's killed in a drive-by. . . . When Boone is wounded and [his friend] Andre killed at Robbie's funeral, Boone is well and truly scared. Boone's classmates call him coward; his dad sends him to a therapist. Detective Rylander practically begs him for help, but it takes another, unrelated murder to prompt Boone to come forward as a witness." (Kirkus)

McCoola, Marika
Baba Yaga's assistant. Marika McCoola; illustrated by Emily Carroll. Candlewick Press 2015 136 p. Color; Illustration
Grades: 4 5 6 7   **741.5; Fic**
1. Fairy tales; 2. Supernatural graphic novels; 3. Witches
076366961X; 9780763669614, $16.99
LC 2014951398

In this graphic novel, by Marika McCoola and Emily Carroll, "Russian folklore icon Baba Yaga mentors a lonely teen. . . . Most children think twice before braving a haunted wood filled with terrifying beasties to match wits with a witch, but not Masha. Her beloved grandma taught her many things: that stories are useful, that magic is fickle, that nothing is too difficult or too dirty to clean. The fearsome witch of folklore needs an assistant, and Masha needs an adventure." (Publisher's note)

"McCoola's offering is a well-nuanced delight, satisfyingly blending fairy tale, legend, and thrills. As a perfect complement, Carroll's evocative art enthralls, capturing both the emotion and the magic of McCoola's yarn and breathing new life into an old folk tale." Kirkus

McDonald, John
Henry V: the graphic novel: original text version. [by] William Shakespeare; script adaptation, John McDonald; pencils, Neill Cameron ...; editor in chief, Clive Bryant. Classical Comics 2008 143p. Illustration
Grades: 8 9 10 11 12 Adult   **822.3; 741.5**
1. Shakespeare, William, 1564-1616 — Adaptations
978-1-906332-41-9, $16.95

This graphic novel adaptation of Shakespeare's play uses a full and unabridged text combined with full color comic book style illustrations. Young King Henry V goes to war against France when he learns he has a legitimate claim to the French

Also available plain text version (ISBN: 978-1-906332-42-6) and quick text version (ISBN: 978-1-906332-43-3) ea $16.95

First published 2007 in the United Kingdom

McKay, Sharon E.
War brothers: the graphic novel. Sharon E. McKay, Daniel Lafrance ; art by Daniel Lafrance. Annick Press 2013 176 p. Illustration
Grades: 8 9 10 11 12   **741.5/971; Fic**
1. Kidnapping; 2. Lord's Resistance Army
1554514894; 9781554514892, $27.95

In this graphic novel, "14-year-old Jacob and his friends are just starting school at George Jones Seminary for Boys. The story tells of their subsequent kidnapping and near induction into the Lord's Resistance Army (LRA). Complete innocents at first, the boys endure near starvation, grueling conditions, and physical violence as they travel out of northern Uganda and into Sudan." (School Library Journal)

McKeever, Sean
The **loyalty** thing. Art by Takeshi Miyazawa. Spotlight 2006 Un Illustration
Grades: 4 5 6 7 8 9   **741.5; Fic**
1. Romance graphic novels; 2. Spider-Man (Fictional character); 3. Superhero graphic novels; 4. Watson, Mary Jane (Fictional character); 5. Graphic novels
9781599610375, $21.35
LC 2006-75006
Mary Jane suffers the attention of a couple of pranksters who have targeted her for their practical jokes. Flash almost gets into trouble when he tries to "question" them with his fists, then he nearly gets into trouble with Liz when he forgets (on purpose) to register for Homecoming King. Meanwhile, Mary Jane is ready to break up with Harry, but she finally feels the magic when he kisses her. But what's going to happen when she finds Flash's notebook in her backpack?
Part of the Marvel Age: Mary Jane series. This is an edited version of an issue originally published by Marvel in 2005, with all advertisements removed.

Mary Jane Vol. 1: Circle of Friends. Art by Takeshi Miyazawa. Marvel Entertainment Group 2004 96p. Illustration
Grades: 5 6 7 8 9 10 11 12   **741.5; Fic**
1. Romance graphic novels; 2. Spider-Man (Fictional character); 3. Superhero graphic novels; 4. Graphic novels; 4. Watson, Mary Jane (Fictional character)
0-7851-1467-X, $6.99
High school student Mary Jane Watson hangs out with her friends (including nerdy Peter Parker) and starts dating old friend Harry Osborn even as she fantasizes about the new costumed superhero in town: Spider-Man. In this series, high school romance and friendships take center stage while the superhero action happens off the page and in the sidelines. This is the first of two volumes, then a new ongoing comics series called Spider-Man Loves Mary Jane continues the story.

The **money** thing. Art by Takeshi Miyazawa. ABDO/Spotlight 2006 Un Illustration
Grades: 4 5 6 7 8 9   **741.5; Fic**
1. Romance graphic novels; 2. Spider-Man (Fictional character); 3. Superhero graphic novels; 4. Watson, Mary Jane (Fictional character); 5. Graphic novels
978-1-59961-038-2, $21.35
LC 2006-55059
Harry Osborn is rich and loves to spend money on his dates with Mary Jane, but she's starting to feel that she should do something to get money to pay for some things on her own, such as that really beautiful prom dress she's been looking at. She tries job after job after job, and fails at each one for one reason or another, and the long hours have taken a toll on her school work and on her social life. What's going to give?
Part of the Marvel Age: Mary Jane series. This is an edited version of an issue originally published by Marvel in 2005, with all advertisements removed.

The **real** thing. Art by Takeshi Miyazawa. ABDO/Spotlight 2006 Un Illustration
Grades: 4 5 6 7 8 9   **741.5; Fic**
1. Mary Jane Watson (Fictional character); 2. Romance graphic novels; 3. Spider-Man (Fictional character); 4. Superhero graphic novels; 5. Watson, Mary Jane (Fictional character)
978-1-59961-039-9, $21.35
LC 2006-75007
Pressured by best friend Liz to start dating Harry Osborn so she and Harry can double date with Liz and Flash, Mary Jane has her doubts. When she sees him treat nerdy Peter Parker with affection, she decides to try a date. However, as she rides the train on the way home, a fight between Spider-Man and Electro upends the train car and she nearly falls out. Spider-Man saves her and takes her home. Uh-oh, now she's crushing on Spider-Man, how could Harry compete?
Part of the Marvel Age: Mary Jane series. This is an edited version of an issue originally published by Marvel in 2005, with all advertisements removed.

Sentinel #1: Salvage. Art by UDON. ABDO/Spotlight 2004 Un Illustration
Grades: 4 5 6 7 8 9   **741.5; Fic**
1. Robots; 2. Science fiction graphic novels; 3. Graphic novels
978-1-59961-316-1, $21.35
LC 2006-50623
Juston Seyfert is a teenage loner type, living with his father and younger brother at the Seyfert Salvage yard. Juston and his friends are the school misfits and face beatings and ridicule from the jocks and popular students. One day, while fooling around in the yard, he finds a strange control chip and ends up putting it into his homemade battle 'bot, but when he turns on the remote, the toy takes off and breaks through the salvage yard fence. What Juston and his friends don't know is that there is a broken-to-pieces Sentinel out there in the woods, and the control chip belongs to it.
This book was originally published as Sentinel #1 by Marvel Comics' Marvel Age line; this book reprints the story without all the advertisements in the original comic.

Sentinel #2: Discovery. Art by UDON. ABDO/Spotlight 2004 Un Illustration
Grades: 4 5 6 7 8 9   **741.5; Fic**
1. Robots; 2. Science fiction graphic novels; 3. Graphic novels
978-1-59961-317-8, $21.35
LC 2006-50623
When his dad and younger brother go on an overnight trip to haul junkers to Chicago, Juston has to stay home alone, but it gives him a chance to talk with cute senior Jessie, who doesn't mind hanging out with a younger guy. Then that night, Juston finds something weird in the salvage yard's building—a half-destroyed Sentinel. Juston doesn't

realize that the Sentinels were created to destroy mutants; he just knows that the one he's got is a way cool robot with artificial intelligence so he can talk with it.

This book was originally published as Sentinel #2 by Marvel Comics' Marvel Age line; this book reprints the story without all the advertisements in the original comic.

Sentinel #3: Pet project. Art by UDON. ABDO/Spotlight 2004 Un Illustration
Grades: 4 5 6 7 8 9   **741.5; Fic**
1. Robots; 2. Science fiction graphic novels; 3. Graphic novels
978-1-59961-318-5, $21.35

LC 2006-50623

Juston has decided to keep the giant robot he's rebuilding a secret from everyone, which causes a rift in his relationship with his younger brother, Christopher, and with his father—actually, with all his friends, too. When he does some research on the Internet, Juston discovers he's got a Sentinel. Now what's he going to do?

This book was originally published as Sentinel #3 by Marvel Comics' Marvel Age line; this book reprints the story without all the advertisements in the original comic.

Sentinel #4: Rebuilding. Art by UDON. ABDO/Spotlight 2004 Un Illustration
Grades: 4 5 6 7 8 9   **741.5; Fic**
1. Robots; 2. Science fiction graphic novels; 3. Graphic novels
978-1-59961-319-2, $21.35

LC 2006-50623

As Juston continues to rebuild the Sentinel, he becomes so consumed with what he's doing that he's practically abandoned all his friends. The jocks, however, haven't forgotten him. Once Juston gets the Sentinel rebuilt enough, he constructs a platform for himself to ride piggyback on the robot and they go out to the woods to test the Sentinel's weapons.

This book was originally published as Sentinel #4 by Marvel Comics' Marvel Age line; this book reprints the story without all the advertisements in the original comic.

Sentinel #6: Primary targets. Art by UDON. ABDO/Spotlight 2004 Un Illustration
Grades: 4 5 6 7 8 9   **741.5; Fic**
1. Robots; 2. Science fiction graphic novels; 3. Graphic novels
978-1-59961-321-5, $21.35

LC 2006-50623

Juston has given his Sentinel a mission, and Greg and Josh are the primary targets. The robot attacks the school in broad daylight, identifying itself as an alien machine; then Juston races in and stops the robot. He's declared a hero, even by the jocks who only the day before beat him up. However, Juston isn't sure he's done the right thing. And he doesn't know it yet, but the Sentinel has now recovered enough of its memory to get back to its primary mission—to annihilate mutants.

This book was originally published as Sentinel #6 by Marvel Comics' Marvel Age line; this book reprints the

story without all the advertisements in the original comic.

Sentinel, part 5: test mission. Art by UDON. ABDO/Spotlight 2004 Un Illustration
Grades: 4 5 6 7 8 9   **741.5; Fic**
1. Robots; 2. Science fiction graphic novels; 3. Graphic novels
978-1-59961-320-8, $21.35

LC 2006-50623

Jocks Josh and Greg have beat up Juston's friend Alex, and their girlfriends have spread a false rumor about Juston guaranteed to anger Jessie. Then they beat up Juston and humiliate him in front of most of the school. Juston decides it's time to get revenge, and he's going to use the Sentinel to do it.

This book was originally published as Sentinel #5 by Marvel Comics' Marvel Age line; this book reprints the story without all the advertisements in the original comic.

Sentinel Vol. 3: Past Imperfect. Art by Scott Hepburn and Joe Vriens. Marvel Entertainment 2006 Un Illustration
Grades: 8 9 10 11 12   **741.5; Fic**
1. Adventure graphic novels; 2. Robots; 3. Graphic novels
0-7851-1914-0, $7.99

After using his refurbished government weapon of mutant destruction to make himself popular, one would think Juston Seyfert would be on top of the world. Instead, he's run away from home, torn up inside by the guilt brought on by his selfish acts. Now in search of his mother, who left his family at an early age, Juston must figure out what to do with his life. And if he doesn't figure it out soon, there are a couple government types who would be more than happy to figure it out for him.

Spider-Man Loves Mary Jane, Vol. 2: The New Girl. Art by Takeshi Miyazawa and Valentine de Landro. Marvel Entertainment 2006 Un Illustration
Grades: 6 7 8 9 10   **741.5; Fic**
1. Romance graphic novels; 2. Spider-Man (Fictional character); 3. Superhero graphic novels; 4. Graphic novels
0-7851-2265-6, $7.99

This is the second trade paperback collection of the continuing comic book series that focuses on Mary Jane Watson and everyone in the high school rather than on Spider-Man. Mary Jane gets dumped by football player Ned Leeds and spirals into despair, almost missing the fact that her friend Peter Parker has just lost his Uncle Ben. As Liz, Flash, and Harry try to cheer her up, Mary Jane also has afterschool conversations with Spider-Man, who has his own problems trying to catch a villain named The Looter. Mary Jane discovers she really likes Peter, but new girl Gwen Stacy has latched onto him. Meanwhile, Spider-Man/Peter thinks Mary Jane likes Harry. . . .

Originally published as Spider-man Loves Mary Jane issues #6-10.

The **trust** thing. Art by Takeshi Miyazawa. ABDO/Spotlight 2006 Un Illustration
Grades: 4 5 6 7 8 9   **741.5; Fic**
1. Romance graphic novels; 2. Spider-Man (Fictional character); 3. Superhero graphic novels; 4. Watson, Mary Jane (Fictional character); 5. Graphic novels

978-1-59961-040-5, $21.35

LC 2006-55061

While Mary Jane is still daydreaming about Spider-Man, her best friend Liz is having major trust issues with boyfriend Flash. Certain that he's seeing someone else, she enlists Mary Jane, even Peter Parker, to find out what's going on. Meanwhile, MJ has to figure out if she wants to keep dating rich Harry Osborn.

Part of the Marvel Age: Mary Jane series. This is an edited version of an issue originally published by Marvel in 2005, with all advertisements removed.

Mechner, Jordan

Solomon's thieves. Artwork by LeUyen Pham & Alex Puvilland. First Second 2010 139p. Illustration

Grades: 6 7 8 9 10 **741.5; Fic**
1. France — History — 0-1328; 2. Knights and knighthood; 3. Middle Ages; 4. Graphic novels
978-1-59643-391-5, $12.99; 1-59643-391-4

LC 2010-282641

Life as a Templar Knight returning from the Crusades is dull- bread, beans, and lots and lots of walking. But after Martin stumbles upon his lost love (now married—to someone else), things begin to get more interesting very quickly. There's a vast conspiracy afoot to destroy the Templar Order and steal their treasure. Soon, Martin finds himself one of the only Templars out of prison—and out for revenge!

"Pham and Puvilland . . . are again in top form, balancing grainy, hatched textures and clean spaces to lend a weighty historical feel as a vibrant sense of kineticism brings the action sequences to life." Booklist

Includes bibliographical references

Medley, Linda

★ **Castle** waiting. Fantagraphics 2006 456p. Illustration

Grades: 5 6 7 8 9 10 11 12 **741.5; Fic**
1. Fairy tales; 2. Fantasy graphic novels; 3. Graphic novels
1-56097-747-7, $29.95

All of Medley's previously self-published comics are collected here in one volume for the first time. The titular castle was the home of Sleeping Beauty, whose story is retold from the viewpoint of the flibbertigibbet ladies in waiting. After the flighty princess awakens with the kiss of a handsome but not too bright prince, the castle

Courtesy of Fantagraphics

becomes a sanctuary for various misfits. Readers will find references to many fairy tales, folk tales, and nursery rhymes in Medley's book, and her clean, clear black-and-white art reflects the works of classic illustrators such as Arthur Rackham.

Castle waiting; Volume II. By Linda Medley; [graphic design by Adam Grano; edited by Kim Thompson]. Fantagraphics Books 2013 464 p. Color; Illustration

Grades: 5 6 7 8 9 10 11 12 **741.5/973; 741.5**
1. Fairy tales
1606996339; 9781606996331, $29.99

LC 2014381744

In this graphic novel, by Linda Medley, "Lady Jain settles into her new life. . . . Unexpected visitors result in the discovery and exploration of a secret passageway, not to mention an epic bowling tournament. A quest for ladies' underpants, the identity of her baby son Pindar's father, the education of Simon, Rackham and Chess arguing about the ômanly arts,ö and an escape-prone goat are just a few of the elements in this . . . new volume." (Publisher's note)

Melchior-Durand, Stéphane

The **golden** compass; volume 1: the graphic novel. Adapted and illustrated by Stéphane Melchior-Durand and Clément Oubrerie; coloring by Clément Oubrerie with Philippe Bruno. Alfred A. Knopf 2015 80 p. Color; Illustration

Grades: 6 7 8 9 10 **741.5; 741.5/973**
1. Fantasy; 2. Fantasy graphic novels; 3. Pullman, Philip, 1946- Golden compass — Adaptations; 4. Graphic novels
9780553523713, $18.99; 9780553523720; 9780553523867

LC 2015005828

In this graphic novel adaptation of the young adult fantasy by Philip Pullman, adapted and illustrated by Stéphane Melchior-Durand and Clément Oubrerie, "Lyra Belacqua is content to run wild among the scholars of Jordan College, with her daemon familiar always by her side. But the arrival of her fearsome uncle, Lord Asriel, draws her to the heart of a terrible struggle-a struggle born of Gobblers and stolen children, and a mysterious substance known as Dust." (Publisher's note)

Originally published by Gallimard Jeunesse, Paris, France, in 2014—Copyright page.

Meyer, Christopher

Adventures of Rabbit and Bear Paws: The voyageurs. Art by Chad Solomon. Little Spirit Bear Productions 2008 32p. Illustration

Grades: 3 4 5 6 7 **741.5; Fic**
1. Adventure graphic novels; 2. Humorous graphic novels; 3. Native Americans
978-0-9739906-2-1, $7.95

Pintsize, twelve-year-old Rabbit and giant, ten-year-old Bear Paws are brothers and members of the Ojibwa in the eighteenth century. Village medicine man Grey Stone and his wife Clover Blossom raise the brothers, who like to play and play pranks that tend to backfire. In this volume, Rabbit proves he's not a good lacrosse player; then Eagle Wing, a voyageur, stops off to visit Grey Stone on his way to this year's journey. Rabbit and Bear Paws travel with him to be carriers as Eagle Wing and the white fur traders make their trade journey. This book uses authentic details about traditions of the Ojibwa, the Mohawk, and other Nations.

Michelinie, David

Superman Adventures Vol. 3: Last Son of Krypton. Written by Mark Millar, David Michelinie ; illustrated by Aluir Amancio, Ron Boyd, Terry Austin, Mike Manley, Neil Vokes. DC Comics 2006 112p. Illustration

Grades: 4 5 6 7 8 9   **741.5; Fic**
1. Superhero graphic novels; 2. Superman (Fictional character); 3. Graphic novels
978-1-4012-1037-3, $6.99

Superman confronts his own past as he encounters survivors from Krypton, including his parents, Jor-El and Lara. Plus, someone wants to expose Clark's secret to Lex Luthor and the world. Will an encounter with Dr. Fate mean the end of Superman?

Midorikawa, Shin

Aventura vol. 1. Del Rey Manga 2007 188p. Illustration

Grades: 8 9 10 11 12   **741.5; Fic**
1. Adventure graphic novels; 2. Fantasy graphic novels; 3. Magic; 4. Manga; 5. Graphic novels
978-0-345-49744-4, $10.95

Since ancient days, the Gaius School of Witchcraft and Wizardry has trained the fiercest swordsmen and the most powerful wizards. Now one boy could become the greatest of them all. If he studies hard. If he is true to his friends. If he believes. And if he survives. The book includes some mild violence.

The Mighty Crusaders: Origin of a Super-Team

Archie Comics 2003 96p. Illustration

Grades: 3 4 5 6 7 8 9 10 11 12 Adult   **741.5; Fic**
1. Humorous graphic novels; 2. Superhero graphic novels; 3. Graphic novels
1-879794-14-4, $12.95

It's a pop-art explosion as some of the wildest heroes in the history of comic books unite to form one of the most beloved super-teams of the Sixties: The Shield, The Black Hood, The Comet, The Fly, and Fly Girl. Relive the excitement as this intrepid team of heroes meet, fight super-villains as well as each other, come up with a name for their team and even recruit new members. It's all here in this colorful collection reprinting classic stories originally appearing in Fly-Man #31, #32 and #33 as well as Mighty Crusaders #1. It features restoration of all stories, and faithful recoloring.

Mikimoto, Haruhiko

Mobile Suit Gundam Ecole du Ciel Vol. 1. Tokyopop 2005 Un Illustration

Grades: 8 9 10 11 12 Adult   **741.5; Fic**
1. Mecha manga; 2. Science fiction graphic novels; 3. Graphic novels
1-59532-851-3, $9.99

Ecole du Ciel is where aspiring pilots train to become Top Gundam. The year is 0085 of the Universal Century. Daughter of a brilliant professor, Asuna is a below-average student at Ecole du Ciel. But with the world spiraling toward war, Asuna is headed for a crash course in danger, battle, and most of all, love. This story is set in the original Gundam universe, and is full of mecha (giant battle robot) battles.

Milky, D. J.

Princess Ai Volume 1. Created by Courtney Love & D.J. Milky ; illustrated by Misaho Kujiradou ; written by Misaho Kujiradou and D.J. Milky. Tokyopop 2004 192p. Illustration

Grades: 7 8 9 10 11 12   **741.5; Fic**
1. Fantasy graphic novels; 2. Manga; 3. Romance graphic novels; 4. Shojo manga; 5. Graphic novels
1-59182-669-1, $9.99

Ai finds herself lost, alone and penniless on the cold, hard streets of Tokyo. With flickers of memory, she must piece together clues about who she is, how she ended up on Earth and the secret of the ornate heart-shaped box she carries with her. Sparks fly when Kent, a complicated young college student, offers his help...and possibly more. But time is running out, as the clashing forces of love and chaos close in around her... This is the first of a three-volume series created by rocker Courtney Love and co-written and illustrated by Misaho Kujiradou.

Millar, Mark

Superman Adventures Vol. 4: The Man of Steel. Written by Mark Millar, Evan Dorkin and Sarah Dyer ; illustrated by Aluir Amancio, Terry Austin, Bret Blevins. DC Comics 2006 112p. Illustration

Grades: 4 5 6 7 8 9   **741.5; Fic**
1. Superhero graphic novels; 2. Superman (Fictional character); 3. Graphic novels
978-1-4012-1038-0, $6.99

The battle never ends for the Man of Steel - especially when his greatest enemies will stop at nothing in order to destroy him. Superman confronts Toyman, Multi-Face, Parasite, the mischievous Mr. Mxyzptlk, and Brainiac.

Miller, Connie Colwell

Elizabeth Cady Stanton: Women's Rights Pioneer. Illustrated by Cynthia Martin. Capstone Press 2006 32p. Illustration

Grades: 3 4 5 6 7 8 9   **741.5; 305.42; 92**
1. Stanton, Elizabeth Cady, 1815-1902; 2. Women — Suffrage — United States — History; 3. Graphic novels
0-7368-4971-8, $25.26

LC 2005009211

This book uses the comic book format to describe the life and career of women's suffragist Elizabeth Cady Stanton. It includes additional information, a glossary, a list of books for further reading, and more.

Part of the Graphic Library, Graphic Biographies series.

Miller, Frank

Batman: Year One. DC Comics 2005 168p. Illustration

Grades: 8 9 10 11 12 Adult   **741.5; Fic**
1. Batman (Fictional character); 2. Catwoman (Fictional character); 3. Superhero graphic novels; 4. Graphic novels
978-1-4012-0752-6, $14.99

In the late-1980s, after publishing Miller's Batman: The Dark Knight Returns, DC realized they should remain faithful to the original roots of Batman. Miller then wrote this book, which reinvents the very early years of Batman as a superhero. In this book, Jim Gordon arrives in Gotham City to work in the police department and discovers the high level of corruption there; Batman encounters Selina, who becomes Catwoman, for the first time; and he develops some of the weapons he uses to fight crime. This new edition includes preliminary sketches and other extras.

Miller, John Jackson
Star Wars: Knights of the Old Republic Volume One: Commencement. Script, John Jackson Miller ; art, Brian Ching and Travel Foreman, ; colors, Michael Atiyeh ; lettering, Michael Heisler ; cover art, Travis Charest. Dark Horse Comics 2006 Un Illustration
Grades: 8 9 10 11 12 Adult   741.5; Fic
    1. Adventure graphic novels; 2. Science fiction graphic novels; 3. Graphic novels
    978-1-59307-640-5, $18.95
    Thousands of years before Luke Skywalker would destroy the Death Star in that fateful battle above Yavin 4, one lone Padawan would become a fugitive hunted by his own Masters, charged with murdering every one of his fellow Jedi-in-training. From criminals hiding out in the treacherous under-city of the planet Taris, to a burly, mysterious droid recovered from the desolate landscape of a cratered moon, Padawan Zayne Carrick will find unexpected allies in his desperate race to clear his name before the unmerciful authorities enact swift retribution upon him.

Miller, Mike S.
Lullaby: Wisdom seeker. [by] Ben Avery, Mike S. Miller, and Hector Sevilla. Alias Enterprises 2005 96p. Illustration
Grades: 4 5 6 7 8 9   741.5; Fic
    1. Fantasy graphic novels; 2. Graphic novels
    1-933428-62-7, $9.99
    In this book, Alice never left Wonderland, she grew up to become the Queen's warrior. When dark magic threatens the world, Alice, haunted by vague memories of another life, sets out to discover the cause, and on the way she encounters the Pied Piper, Little Red Riding Hood (who is a werewolf), Jim Hawkins (from Treasure Island), and Pinocchio, as they all travel to Oz.

Millionaire, Tony
Sock Monkey: The Inches Incident. Dark Horse Comics 2007 88p. Illustration
Grades: 7 8 9 10 11 12 Adult   741.5; Fic
    1. Fantasy graphic novels; 2. Toys; 3. Graphic novels
    978-1-59307-842-3, $12.95
    Inches the doll was the cutest in the whole house. Loved by everyone, the world was Inches' oyster. Then one day something happened... The Sock Monkey and Mr. Crow became concerned for their diminutive friend, but by then it was too late. The truth sent the terrified Sock Monkey and Crow fleeing for their lives, for Inches had been invaded by a colony of evil ants. The sight of ants swarming over Inches and other things might be too creepy-crawly for some readers; the violence is aimed at toys rather than people, however, this is not a book for younger readers.

Sock Monkey: Uncle Gabby. Dark Horse Comics 2004 Un Illustration
Grades: 8 9 10 11 12 Adult   741.5; Fic

    1. Adventure graphic novels; 2. Humorous graphic novels; 3. Graphic novels
    1-59307-026-8, $14.95
    Uncle Gabby, the Sock Monkey, and Drinky the crow set off on a journey to solve the mystery of unremembered memories. This looks like a children's book, but the underlying bitter sweetness of a lost past and longing is more suited to teens and adults.

Misako Rocks!
Biker girl. Story and art by Misako Rocks. Hyperion Paperbacks 2006 Un Illustration
Grades: 3 4 5 6 7 8 9   741.5; Fic
    1. Adventure graphic novels; 2. Bicycles; 3. Graphic novels
    0-7868-3676-8, $7.99

                                LC 2005-57428
    "In this manga-style adventure, a young girl becomes a reluctant superhero after she inherits a bike with magical powers. . . . This fast-paced and well-executed story is . . . bound to be popular." Booklist

Rock and Roll Love. Hyperion Paperbacks 2007 Un Illustration
Grades: 5 6 7 8 9 10   741.5; Fic
    1. Romance graphic novels; 2. Student exchange programs; 3. Graphic novels
    978-0-7868-3685-7, $7.99
    Sixteen-year-old high school student Misako comes to the U.S. as an exchange student for a year. Missouri is very different from Tokyo, but her host family and their teenage daughter, Natalie, make her welcome. Misako soon makes friends at high school, and feels comfortable enough to join a summer puppet show in Wisconsin. There, she meets Zac, a rock and roll musician, and her dream boy. Given to strong enthusiasms, Misako falls hard for Zac, but he says he only wants to be friends. Will she ever get him to change his mind about her?
    Misako Rocks! (real surname Takashima) moved to the U.S. from Japan as a teenager; this book is based on her own experiences.

Miyazaki, Hayao
★ **Nausicaa** of the Valley of the Wind, Vol. 1. Viz Media 2004 136p. Illustration
Grades: 7 8 9 10 11 12   741.5; Fic
    1. Manga; 2. Science fiction graphic novels; 3. Graphic novels
    978-1-59116-408-1, $9.95
    In a world devastated by ecological disaster and war, pockets of humanity exist in the vast wastelands. When some begin another war that could totally destroy the world, hope rests upon one young girl, Nausicaa, who can communicate with the strange creatures of the wasteland.
    "Miyazaki is best known for his anime features . . . This tale contains all the classic elements of Miyazaki's films . . ." (VOYA)
    This is a seven-volume series.

Mizobuchi, Makoto
Pokemon: Pokemon Ranger and the Temple of the Sea. Viz Media/VizKids 2008 200p. Illustration

Grades: 3 4 5 6 7 8   **741.5; Fic**
1. Adventure graphic novels; 2. Fantasy graphic novels; 3. Manga; 4. Graphic novels
978-1-4215-2288-3, $7.99

Ash and Pikachu learn about the legend of the Sea Temple, a mysterious floating temple that houses the Sea Crown. They meet Jackie, a Pokemon Ranger on a mission to protect a Manaphy egg and find the temple; when the egg hatches, young May bonds with Manaphy. But they aren't the only ones searching for the Sea Temple; the nefarious pirate called the Phantom wants the Sea Crown for himself to take over the world, and he also needs Manaphy to do it. Can Ash and Pikachu help Jackie protect Manaphy and stop the Phantom?

Mizukami, Wataru
Four-eyed prince, v1. Del Rey Manga 2009 184p. Illustration
Grades: 8 9 10 11 12   **741.5; Fic**
1. Manga; 2. Romance graphic novels; 3. Shojo manga; 4. Graphic novels
978-0-345-51624-4, $10.99

High school student Sachiko has a huge crush on upper classman Akihiko, but he claims to have absolutely no interest in her. He's quiet, studious, wears glasses, but something about him attracts Sachiko. Then, to her horror, when her long-gone mother summons Sachiko to live with her and her new family, Sachiko discovers Akihiko is her mother's stepson. She will have to live in the same home with the boy who rejected her and who objected to her moving in. When he leaves the house at night, Sachiko follows him, gets caught in a downpour in a strange neighborhood, and a handsome young bartender named Akira helps her. Except he's not Akira, he's Akihiko, a warm, friendly, confident guy that all the girls want. Akihiko wants Sachiko to keep his secret, but she's torn between his two personalities. This volume includes another short story. There are a few "beefcake" shots of Akihiko/Akira shirtless, and one panel in the short story showing Sakamoto (the girl) lying down naked and face down while being massaged.

Mizuki, Shigeru
NonNonBa. Shigeru Mizuki; translation by Jocelyne Allen. Drawn & Quarterly 2012 408 p. Illustration; Color
Grades: 7 8 9 10 11 12 Adult   **741.5/952; 741.5**
1. Autobiographical graphic novels; 2. Cartoonists — Japan — Biography; 3. Folklore — Japan; 4. Grandmothers; 5. Grandparent- grandchild relationship; 6. Mizuki, Shigeru, 1922-2015 — Childhood and youth; 7. Yokai (Japanese folklore)
1770460721; 9781770460720, $26.95
                            LC 2012427667

This graphic novel, by Shigeru Mizuki, translated by Jocelyne Allen, is "a poetic memoir detailing his interest in yokai (spirit monsters). Mizuki's childhood experiences with yokai influenced the course of his life and oeuvre; he is now known as the forefather of yokai manga. . . . Mizuki explores the legacy left him by his childhood explorations of the spirit world, explorations encouraged by his grandmother, a grumpy old woman named NonNonBa." (Publisher's note)
Includes bibliographical references

Mizuna, Tomomi
The **big** adventures of Majoko, volume 1. Illustrated by Tomomi Mizuna. UDON Entertainment 2009 200p. Illustration
Grades: 3 4 5 6 7 8   **741; 741.5; Fic**
1. Fantasy graphic novels; 2. Manga; 3. Witches; 4. Graphic novels
978-1-89737-681-2 (pa), $7.99; 1-89737-681-2 (pa)

"Young witch Majoko sends her diary to the human world to find an adventuring partner and through it finds shy, quiet Nana. Together the two girls have a rollicking series of escapades. . . . Characters are simply drawn, but the backgrounds are nicely detailed and the plot elements are clearly thought out and easy to follow. . . . The content is very appropriate for the intended audience." Booklist
Volume 1 of a 5-volume series

Mizuto, Aqua
Yume Kira Dream Shoppe. Viz Media/Shojo Beat 2007 186p. Illustration
Grades: 7 8 9 10 11 12   **741.5; Fic**
1. Fantasy graphic novels; 2. Romance graphic novels; 3. Shojo manga; 4. Graphic novels
978-1-4215-1173-3, $8.99

They say that any dream can be made true in exchange for something dear to you. The Yume Kira Dream Shoppe flies through the dusk sky as Rin the shopkeeper listens for wishes that travel on the wind. With the help of his assistant Alpha (a stuffed rabbit), Rin uses the magical wares of the Dream Shoppe to make desires a reality ... But it costs the wisher something dear to the person. In the first story, a tree that has never bloomed falls in love with the music played by a young man, then the tree falls in love with the young man; she wishes for a human form so she can tell him how much his music means to her. Then she finds out he suffers from a disease that will take away the use of his hands, and she wants to change her wish ... In the second story, Alpha is the one who makes the wish, and at the end of the story, he leaps off a bridge so the young girl who owned him won't be dependent on him; it's so much like a suicide that it might disturb younger readers who might otherwise enjoy this book.

Mochizuki, Jun
Pandora hearts; Volume 1. Jun Mochizuki; [translation, Tomo Kimura; lettering, Tania Biswas]. Yen Press 2013 187 p. Illustration
Grades: 8 9 10 11 12   **741.5; Fic**
1. False imprisonment; 2. Nobility — Fiction
0316076074; 9780316076074, $13

"The air of celebration surrounding fifteen-year-old Oz Vessalius's coming-of-age ceremony quickly turns to horror when he is condemned for a sin about which he knows nothing. He is thrown into an eternal, inescapable prison known as the Abyss from which there is no escape. There, he meets a young girl named Alice, who is not what she seems. Now that the relentless cogs of fate have begun to turn, do they lead only to crushing despair for Oz, or is there some shred of hope for him to grasp on to?" (Publisher's note)
Volume 1 of 24

MOONSHOT: The Indigenous Comics Collection
Edited by Hope Nicholson. Alternate History Comics
Inc 2015 176 p. Illustration
Grades: 6 7 8 9 10 11 12 Adult   **741.5**

Courtesy of Alternate History

1. American literature —
Native American authors; 2.
Graphic novels
0987715259;
9780987715258, $17.99
This comic anthology,
edited by Hope Nicholson,
"from traditional stories to
exciting new visions of the
future, . . . presents some of
the finest comic book and
graphic novel work in North
America. The traditional
stories presented in the book
are with the permission from
the elders in their respective
communities, making this a
truly genuine, never-before-seen publication." (Publisher's
note)
"This collection of folklore from a powerhouse team of
Native authors, including Buffy Sainte-Marie and Richard
Van Camp, will wow readers with traditional and futuristic
tales based on tribal-specific cultural teachings. . . . The
full-page illustrations in some selections and the bright
colors in others add depth and understanding to the
narratives. The artwork is as diverse as the stories collected."
SLJ

Moore, Alan
Terra Obscura Vol. Two. Alan Moore and Peter Hogan,
co-plotters ; Peter Hogan, scripts ; Yanick Paquette, pencils ;
Karl Story, inks ; Jeremy Cox, colors. DC
Comics/Wildstorm 2005 Un Illustration
Grades: 8 9 10 11 12 Adult   **741.5; Fic**
1. Science fiction graphic novels; 2. Superhero graphic
novels; 3. Graphic novels
1-4012-0622-0, $14.99
Just as things have returned to normal for everyone on
Terra Obscura, including the members of S.M.A.S.H., a
mysterious object appears on the edge of their galaxy, and
it's on a collision course with the planet. Even more
distressing is that the object appears to be the spacecraft of
long-lost hero Captain Future. As the ship nears, time
anomalies crop up over the entire planet, wreaking terrible
havoc the closer the ship gets. Can Tom Strange and the
other heroes unravel this mystery before it spells doom for
the entire planet?

Morgan, Melanie J.
Betty & Veronica: Bad Boy Trouble. Art by Steven
Butler. Archie Comics 2007 112p. Illustration
Grades: 4 5 6 7 8 9 10   **741.5; Fic**
1. Humorous graphic novels; 2. Romance graphic novels;
3. Graphic novels
978-1-879794-25-2, $7.49
When Nick St. Clair rides into Riverdale on his
motorcycle, Veronica is smitten. She likes Nick's air of
assurance and his knack for getting noticed. The only

problem is Nick gets noticed for all the wrong things. Nick
quickly alienates all of Ronnie's friends, especially Betty, as
he keeps trying to hit on her even as he dates Ronnie. Is this
handsome rebel the boy of Veronica's dreams, or just plain
trouble" This particular story has caused some stir among
longtime Archie fans, because of the drastic artistic
makeover of the Riverdale teens.

Mori, Kaoru
Shirley volume 1. Del Rey Manga 2008 200p.
Illustration
Grades: 8 9 10 11 12 Adult   **741.5; Fic**
1. Household employees; 2. Manga; 3. Graphic novels
978-1-4012-1777-8, $9.99
In Edwardian England, the independent Miss Bennett
runs a cafe, but finds she has no time to take care of her
house, so she advertises for a house maid. Young Shirley
Madison answers the advertisement, and despite her very
young age—she's only 13—she proves to be a competent
maid and a good companion. In other stories, two maids take
care of their young master, a five-year-old boy, but they
don't know how to relieve his loneliness; and an experienced
maid must deal with her bored master's pranks that have
driven away most of the household help.

Morinaga, Ai
My Heavenly Hockey Club Vol. 1. Ballantine
Books/Del Rey Manga 2007 212p. Illustration
Grades: 8 9 10 11 12 Adult   **741.5; Fic**
1. Hockey; 2. Humorous graphic novels; 3. Shojo manga;
4. Graphic novels
978-0-345-49904-2, $10.95
Hana Suzuki loves only two things in life: eating and
sleeping. So when handsome classmate Izumi Oda asks
Hana, his major crush, to join the school hockey club,
persuading her proves to be a difficult task. True, the Grand
Hockey Club is full of boys, and all the boys are super-cute,
but given a choice, Hana prefers a sizzling steak to a hot
date. Then Izumi mentions the field trips to fancy resorts.
Now Hana can't wait for the first away game, with its
promise of delicious food and luxurious linens. Of course
there's also the getting up early, working hard, and playing
well with others. How will Hana survive?

Morrison, Grant
All-Star Superman, Volume One. Written by Grant
Morrison; pencilled by Frank Quitely. DC Comics 2007
160p. Illustration
Grades: 8 9 10 11 12 Adult   **741.5; Fic**
1. Superhero graphic novels; 2. Superman (Fictional
character); 3. Graphic novels
978-1-4012-0914-8; 978-1-4012-1102-8 (pa), $12.99
Eisner Award: Best New Series (2006)
Writer Morrison and artist Quitely present several
episodes in the life of the iconic superhero, Superman. When
he saves a group of scientists from burning up in the sun,
what no one realizes is that uber-villain Lex Luthor set up
everything in order to kill Superman, who absorbed so much
solar radiation that it is now slowly killing him. Once
Superman learns that he is dying, he sets out to give Lois
Lane a birthday she will never forget, by giving her his
powers for one day. Then, when Jimmy Olsen takes charge

of the science think tank P.R.O.J.E.C.T. for one day, they discover black kryptonite, which makes Superman turn evil. And, in his guise as Clark Kent, he interviews Lex Luthor in prison, but super-villain Parasite is taken from his shielded cell and begins to absorb Superman's powers, causing chaos.

Also available as a single volume collecting all 12 issues
Originally published as All-Star Superman issues #1-6
Volume 1 of 2

Superman - Action Comics; Volume 1. Grant Morrison, Rags Morales, Andy Kubert. DC Comics 2012 256 p.
Grades: 7 8 9 10 11 12 Adult   **Fic; 741.5/9411**
1. Adventure fiction; 2. Superhero comic books, strips, etc; 3. Superman (Fictional character)
1401235468; 9781401235468, $24.99
     LC 2012010313
This comic book anthology, by Grant Morrison, illustrated by Rags Morales, presents volume one of "The New 52" re-launch of the DC Comics Superman series. This collection includes the first eight issues of the series, depicting "humanity's first encounters with Superman, before he became one of the world's greatest super heroes." (Publisher's note)

Morrow, John
Kirby five-oh!: celebrating 50 years of the king of comics. [edited by John Morrow]. Twomorrows Publishing 2008 165p. Illustration
Grades: 7 8 9 10 11 12 Adult   **741.5**
1. Cartoonists; 2. Comic books, strips, etc — History and criticism; 3. Kirby, Jack, 1917-1994
978-1-893905-89-4, $19.95
     LC 2008-299709
In celebration of Jack Kirby's 50-year career in comics, this book features lists of such things as the best Kirby story published each year from 1938 through 1987, the best covers from each decade, Kirby's best 50 character designs, and more. The book includes a color section of photographs and art from his career.

Morvan, Jean David
★ **Classics** illustrated deluxe #6: the three Musketeers. [by] Alexandre Dumas; adapted by Jean David Morvan, Michel Dufranne, Rubèn, and Marie Galopin. Papercutz 2011 Un Illustration
Grades: 5 6 7 8 9 10 11 12 Adult   **741.5; Fic**
1. Adventure graphic novels; 2. Dumas, Alexandre, 1802-1870 — Adaptations; 3. France — History — 1589-1789, Bourbons; 4. Graphic novels
978-1-59707-253-3, $21.99; 978-1-59707-252-6 (pa), $16.99
In seventeenth-century France, young D'Artagnan initially quarrels with, then befriends, three musketeers and joins them in trying to outwit the enemies of the king and queen. This adaptation is suitable for many readers from age ten and up, but parents, teachers, and librarians might want to consider the visual depictions of sexual tensions and situations that might go over most young readers' heads in prose (there are some heaving bosoms, perspiring men, and a couple of scenes in bed), and the violence (most of it occurs off-panel). The book's endpapers include Dumas'

introduction to his novel, an Epilogue, a brief biography of Dumas, and an illustrated character guide.

This book is a 70th Anniversary Edition of Classics Illustrated

Moss, Marissa
Max disaster #1: Alien eraser to the rescue. Candlewick Press 2009 Un Illustration
Grades: 3 4 5 6 7   **741.5; Fic**
1. Family life; 2. Humorous graphic novels; 3. Separation; 4. Graphic novels
978-0-7636-3577-0, $15.99; 978-0-7636-4407-9 (pa), $6.99
     LC 2008-937046
Max and his best friend Omar survive school together, even as they're forced to make baking soda/vinegar volcanoes in science class and hid their eraser armies from the teacher. But now Max has to deal with some problems at home, much worse than his older brother Kevin. Their parents have been fighting a lot lately, and now they call a family meeting to announce a separation. Max fills his notebook with all kinds of inventions that could stop this from happening, but he and Kevin have to face their real life. Moss uses a mix of prose, comic book pages, and pictures of gadgets to present Max's story.
Other titles in this series are: Alien Eraser unravels the mystery of the pyramids (2009); Alien Eraser reveals the secrets of evolution (2009)

Mucci, Tim
Tom Sawyer. Adapted by Tim Mucci; illustrated by Rad Sechrist.. Sterling 2008 Un Illustration
Grades: 3 4 5 6 7 8 9   **741.5; Fic**
1. Adventure graphic novels; 2. Twain, Mark, 1835-1910 — Adaptations
978-1-4027-3399-4, $6.95
     LC 2007-41162
Tom Sawyer lives in a small town along the Mississippi River, where he does his best to avoid Aunt Polly's list of chores and skips school so he can go fishing. When he and his friend Huckleberry Finn witness a murder, their first thought is to run away. This graphic novel adaptation includes a brief biography of Mark Twain.
Part of the All-Action Classics series.

Muir, Suzanne
Elephant Army. Art by Anthony Brennan. Harcourt Achieve/Steck-Vaughn 2007 48p. Illustration
Grades: 3 4 5 6 7 8   **741.5; Fic**
1. Adventure graphic novels; 2. Graphic novels
978-1-4190-3200-4, $8.99
Shaam is a very small elephant who dreams of becoming the lead elephant in the army of King Porus of India. Meanwhile, the fearsome conqueror, Alexander the Great, is planning to attack. Will Shaam and his elephant army be able to defend their homeland? This historical graphic novel includes prose intervals that provide more information about Alexander the Great and about ancient India.
Part of the Timeline Graphic Novels series.

The **Magic** Tile. Art by Anthony Brennan. Harcourt Achieve/Steck-Vaughn 2006 48p. Illustration
Grades: 3 4 5 6 7 8   **741.5; Fic**
   1. Adventure graphic novels; 2. Islamic civilization; 3. Graphic novels
978-1-4190-3202-8, $8.99
   When they find a magic tile, twins Mina and Haytham zoom back into the Middle Ages. They meet famous people such as Saladin and Ibn Battuta. But will they be able to return to their own time? The book includes prose intervals that give more information about Ibn Battuta, The Arabian Nights, and the Golden Age of Islam.
   Part of the Timeline Graphic Novels series.

Mukai, Natsumi
   +Anima, Vol. 1. Tokyopop 2006 194p. Illustration
Grades: 7 8 9 10 11 12   **741.5; Fic**
   1. Adventure graphic novels; 2. Fantasy graphic novels; 3. Manga; 4. Shonen manga; 5. Graphic novels
1-59816-347-7, $9.99
   In an alternate world, +Anima are people who possess animal-like powers. Cooro, who has the black wings of a crow, befriends a boy named Husky who can live and breathe underwater. The two boys escape the circus and meet Senri, who has the powers of a bear. They just want to find a place where they can live in peace, but normal humans fear and shun them, or try to use them as the circus did. In the city called Octopus they encounter Nana, a bat-winged +Anima who has been stealing to live.
   Volume 1 of 10

Myers, Walter Dean, 1937-2014
   Monster: a graphic novel. By Walter Dean Myers; adapted for graphic novel by Guy A. Sims; illustrated by Dawud Anyabwile. HarperTeen, an imprint of HarperCollinsPublishers 2015 160 p. Illustration
Grades: 8 9 10 11 12   **741.5; Fic**
   1. African Americans — Fiction; 2. Bildungsromans; 3. Myers, Walter Dean, 1937-2014 Monster — Adaptations; 4. Prisons — Fiction; 5. Self-perception — Fiction; 6. Teenagers; 7. Trials (Murder) — Fiction; 8. Graphic novels
0062275003; 9780062274991; 9780062275004, $17.99
                   LC 2013043138
   This graphic novel by Guy Sims, illustrated by Dawud Anyabwile, and adapted from the novel by Walter Dean Myers, is a "coming-of-age story about Steve Harmon, a teenager awaiting trial for a murder and robbery. As Steve acclimates to juvenile detention and goes to trial, he envisions the ordeal as a movie." (Publisher's note)
   "Using panels like a filmstrip, Sims and Anyabwile achieve several remarkably cinematic effects: alternating grids and splash pages captures the tension between close-up and long shots; the use of jittery lettering and uneven word balloons injects deeper anxiety into the sound design; having a jury view the events recounted in testimony as a movie audience creates incisive visual metaphors." Booklist

Nagatomo, Haruno
   Draw your own Manga: beyond the basics. Translated by Françoise White. Kodansha International 2005 111p. Illustration

Grades: 7 8 9 10 11 12   **741.5; 741**
   1. Graphic novels — Drawing; 2. Manga — Drawing
4-7700-2304-9, $19.95; 978-4-7700-2304-9
   "This advanced manual looks at how to enhance manga with a range of special effects as well as how to use various types of color ink, markers, and airbrushes to reach more creative levels. Supplemented by an interview with the immensely popular Japanese sports manga artist Shinji Mizushima, this book is recommended for any cartoon or animation library." Libr J
   Also available: Draw your own Manga; all the basics (2003)

Naifeh, Ted
   Courtney Crumrin & the Coven of Mystics. Oni Press 2003 Un Illustration
Grades: 7 8 9 10 11 12   **741.5; Fic**
   1. Fantasy graphic novels; 2. Magic; 3. Supernatural graphic novels; 4. Graphic novels
1-929998-59-3, $11.95
   When the night things of Courtney's community start causing trouble, it's up to the girl to find out why. The Coven of Mystics blames the hobgoblin initially but quickly turns its ire to Skarrow, a night thing in service to the town's most reclusive witch. Uncle Aloysius doesn't believe the disturbances are that easy to explain. His dismissal of the Coven's alleged culprit starts Courtney down a twisted path that leads to the true mastermind behind all the horror. But does Courtney stand a chance against a being that powerful and manipulative? This is a darker book than the first volume.

   Courtney Crumrin and the fire thief's tale. Oni Press 2007 62p. Illustration
Grades: 7 8 9 10 11 12 Adult   **741.5; Fic**
   1. Fantasy graphic novels; 2. Horror graphic novels; 3. Werewolves; 4. Graphic novels
978-1-932664-85-0, $5.95
   Courtney travels with Uncle Aloysius to Romania, where they stay with Alexi Markovic, an old friend of Uncle Aloysius. Things aren't quite right there, though; the townspeople hunt wolves at night unnatural wolves, werewolves. Markovic's daughter has fallen in love with a Roman man even though her father has arranged her betrothal to an influential man in town. Courtney gets involved against Uncle Aloysius' wishes, and learns more than she wanted about werewolf origins and thwarted love.

   Courtney Crumrin and the night things. Oni Press 2005 128p. Illustration
Grades: 5 6 7 8 9 10 11 12   **741.5; Fic**
   1. Fantasy graphic novels; 2. Supernatural graphic novels; 3. Graphic novels
1-929998-60-0, $11.95
   Courtney's social-climber parents take her out of her comfortable city neighborhood and move into an upscale suburb to live with her creepy Great-Uncle Aloysius in her spooky old house. She has to face uppity classmates and things that go bump in the night; but she ends up making friends with the spooks! Courtney deals with magic and the

supernatural, but she's no altruistic Harry Potter; in this series, magic sometimes bites hard.

Other titles in this series are: Courtney Crumrin and the coven of Mystics (2003); Courtney Crumrin in the twilight kingdom (2004); Courtney Crumrin's monstrous holiday (2009); Courtney Crumrin: the witch next door (2014); Courtney Crumrin: the final spell (2014)

Courtney Crumrin in the Twilight Kingdom. Oni Press 2004 Un Illustration

Grades: 7 8 9 10 11 12   **741.5; Fic**
1. Fantasy graphic novels; 2. Magic; 3. Supernatural graphic novels; 4. Graphic novels
1-932664-01-7, $11.95

Courtney has changed schools yet again, but this time she's in the Coven's special class for magical studies. But when a student spell goes wrong and leaves one of her classmates cursed, can Courtney lead the kids into Goblin Town and find a cure, or will misfortune follow the group straight to the Twilight Kingdom? And the law keeper, Templeton, intends to stop Courtney from what he considers her most terrible crime yet.

Courtney Crumrin's monstrous holiday. Oni Press, Inc. 2009 192p. Illustration

Grades: 7 8 9 10 11 12   **741.5; Fic**
1. Fantasy graphic novels; 2. Horror graphic novels; 3. Graphic novels
978-1-934964-11-8, $11.95

Courtney accompanies Uncle Aloysius on his trip through Europe, and their first stop is in Romania. He has come to visit with an old friend, Professor Alexi Markovic, but they soon find they have stumbled into a family turmoil. Markovic's daughter Magda loves a young Gypsy, but the local bully and noble (even if he has denounced his title), Petru has claimed Magda as his betrothed. Courtney learns that some of the wolves in the woods surrounding Markovic's house are werewolves, and Petru and his men hunt them, convinced that they are members of the Gypsy group in town. Courtney thinks she's helping a romantic young couple only to be disillusioned by Magda's attitude. Then, in Krumrhein, Germany, she meets a handsome young man named Wolfgang and maybe falls a little in love with him. Which turns out to be a bad thing, for Wolfgang is a vampire. Aloysius had come there for he has learned he has cancer and doesn't want to die; but when he discovers that something is draining the life blood from Courtney, he knows he needs to save her.

Nakahara, Aya
Love*Com Vol. 1. Story and art by Aya Nakahara; [translation & English adaptation, Pookie Rolf]. Viz Media/Shojo Beat 2007 Un Illustration

Grades: 8 9 10 11 12   **741.5; Fic**
1. Humorous graphic novels; 2. Manga; 3. Romance graphic novels; 4. Shojo manga; 5. Graphic novels
978-1-4215-1343-0, $8.99

Risa Koizumi is the tallest girl in class, and the last thing she wants is the humiliation of standing next to Atsushi Otoni, the shortest guy. Fate and the whole school have other ideas, and the two find themselves cast as the unwilling stars of a bizarre romantic comedy duo. Rather than bow to the inevitable, Risa and Atsushi join forces to pursue their true

objects of affection. But in the quest for love, will their budding friendship become something more complex?

First published 2001 in Japan
Volume 1 of a 17-volume series

Nakajo, Hisaya
Sugar Princess volume 1: skating to win. Story & art by Hisaya Nakajo. Viz Media/Shojo Beat 2008 184p. Illustration

Grades: 7 8 9 10 11 12   **741.5; Fic**
1. Ice skating; 2. Manga; 3. Romance graphic novels; 4. Shojo manga; 5. Graphic novels
978-1-4215-1930-2, $8.99; 1-4215-1930-5

Maya Kurinoko takes her little brother to the local ice-skating rink with free tickets, but he won't skate unless she does a jump just like they saw on television the night before. So, she attempts a double axel, and lands it. Skating coach Eishi Todo sees her make the jump and scouts her as an ice skater. He wants famous skater Shun Kano (who attends Maya's high school she's in junior high) to coach and then partner with her, but Shun doesn't want it. However, Maya loves ice skating and realizes it may be the one thing she can be good at doing, and she's willing to persevere.

Followed by: Sugar pincess. Vol. 2 : skating to win (2008)
Orginal Japanese editon, 2005

Nakamura, Yoshiki
Skip Beat! Vol. 1. Viz Media/Shojo Beat 2006 Un Illustration

Grades: 8 9 10 11 12   **741.5; Fic**
1. Entertainers; 2. Humorous graphic novels; 3. Shojo manga; 4. Graphic novels
978-1-4215-0585-5, $8.99

Kyoko Mogami has followed her true love, Sho, to Tokyo, where he wants to become an idol, a pop star. Idols can be pop singers or actors, and young hopefuls audition at talent agencies hoping to become the next big star. Sho succeeds, then he tosses Kyoko aside, saying that she's boring. Now Kyoko wants revenge, and thinks the best way to get it is to become an idol and eclipse Sho; but the talent agency rejects her audition. Is revenge an appropriate motivation? Kyoko doesn't care.

Nakamura uses different visual techniques to show characters' feelings, and with Kyoko's emotions in particular, especially her anger.

Volume 1 of 36

Nakano, Hitori
Densha Otoko: The Story of the Train Man Who Fell in Love with a Girl, Vol. 1. Written by Hitori Nakano ; illustrated by Wataru Watanabe. DC Comics/CMX 2006 182p. Illustration

Grades: 8 9 10 11 12   **741.5; Fic**
1. Romance graphic novels; 2. Shonen manga; 3. Graphic novels
978-1-4012-1141-7, $9.99

In Tokyo, a hapless otaku (nerdy anime fanatic) saves a pretty young woman from a harasser on the train. She sends him an expensive thank you gift, and members of the 2channel online forum encourage him and advise him as he first wants to ask her on a date, and then realizes he really likes her and wants a relationship. This off-beat romance is supposedly based on actual events; this series is one of several versions of manga adapted from Nakano's original novel.

Naruse, Kaori
Pretear, Volume 1. ADV Manga 2004 188p. Illustration
Grades: 6 7 8 9 10 11 12   **741.5; Fic**
1. Fantasy graphic novels; 2. Manga; 3. Shojo manga; 4. Graphic novels
1-4139-0144-1, $9.99

Naruse combines elements of fairy tales such as Cinderella and Snow White with fantasy adventure in this four-volume series.

"Himeno's alcoholic novelist father marries a rich businesswoman with two snobby daughters. They treat [Himeno] terribly, of course, but she . . . is goodhearted, virtuous, and patient. Himeno. . . [meets] seven knights who use leafe, a substance emitted by everything in the natural world. The Princess of Disaster wants to destroy all the leafe so the world will die. The knights need Himeno to become the Pretear so they can combine with her and combat the princess." SLJ

Neel, Julien
Down in the dumps. Written and illustrated by Julien Neel; translation by Carol Klio Burrell. Graphic Universe 2012 48 p. (Lou!)
Grades: 4 5 6   **741.5**
1. Best friends — Fiction; 2. Dating (Social customs) — Fiction; 3. Friendship — Fiction; 4. Junior high schools — Fiction; 5. Mothers and daughters — Fiction; 6. School stories; 7. Schools — Fiction; 8. Graphic novels
076133779X; 9780761387794, $27.93
                                                   LC 2012003973
This book is the third in Julien Neel's Lou! series. Here, "Lou is depressed because the boy of her dreams has moved away. To make matters worse, her mother, an aspiring author, has a serious love interest that makes her even more scatterbrained than usual. Lou feels quite left out as she heads off to the first day of school, only to discover that she and her best friend are not in the same class." (School Library Journal)

The **perfect** summer. [story and art by] Julien Neel; [translation by Carol Klio Burrell]. Graphic Universe 2012 48 p. (Lou!)
Grades: 4 5 6   **741.5**
1. Adolescence; 2. Dating (Social customs) — Fiction; 3. Mothers and daughters — Fiction; 4. Summer — Fiction; 5. Vacations; 6. Vacations — Fiction; 7. Graphic novels
0761387803; 9780761387800, $27.93
                                                   LC 2012002988
This book is the fourth in Julien Neel's Lou! series. Here, "she vacations with a friend at an amazing beach house while her mother is on a book tour. The friendship drama [of junior high school] has settled into a nice group of girls she enjoys being with. That just leaves the boy situation, which is complicated, since Tristan is back in her life." (School Library Journal)

Nickel, Scott
Attack of the mutant lunch lady. Illustrated by Andy J Smith. Stone Arch Books 2008 40p. Illustration
Grades: 3 4 5 6 7   **741.5; Fic**
1. Humorous graphic novels; 2. Science fiction graphic novels; 3. Graphic novels
978-1-4342-0451-6, $21.26; 978-1-4342-0501-8 (pa), $4.95
                                                   LC 2007-31250
The cafeteria food at school is truly revolting, but that's nothing compared to what happens when the Lunch Lady falls into the vat of toxic leftovers. Now science whiz Buzz Beaker and his best friend Larry need to find a way to deal with the Cafeteria Creature and save their school.
Part of the Graphic Sparks series, a Buzz Beaker Brainstorm.

Back to the Ice Age. By Scott Nickel; illustrated by Enrique Corts. Stone Arch Books 2008 40p. Illustration
Grades: 3 4 5 6 7   **741.5; Fic**
1. Humorous graphic novels; 2. Science fiction graphic novels; 3. Time travel; 4. Graphic novels
978-1-4342-0450-9, $21.26; 978-1-4342-0500-1 (pa), $6.95
                                                   LC 2007-31251
When David's parents go out, he and his buddy Ben are stuck with the worst babysitter ever. But things get really bad when she mistakes a time travel device for the TV remote and accidentally zaps herself back in time. Now David and Ben need to go back in time to save the babysitter, and they find themselves in the Ice Age, complete with mammoths and a cave dude.
Part of the Graphic Sparks series, a Time Blasters adventure.

Billions of Bats: A Buzz Beaker Brainstorm by Scott Nickel ; illustrated by Andy J. Smith. Stone Arch Books 2007 40p. Illustration
Grades: 2 3 4 5 6 7   **741.5; Fic**
1. Humorous graphic novels; 2. Science fiction graphic novels; 3. Graphic novels
978-1-59889-313-7 (lib bdg)
Buzz Beaker is the local science genius, but when transfer student Sarah Bellum arrives, she takes the position of top student in everything, even P.E. When she brings her newest invention, a cosmic copier, to school and puts her pet bat in to duplicate him, the machine malfunctions and keeps making multiple copies of her bat. Buzz has to work with Sarah to find a way to fix the machine and get rid of all the extra bats.
This is part of the Graphic Sparks line of easy-reading graphic novels for beginning and struggling readers.

Blast to the Past. Illustrated by Steve Harpster. Stone Arch Books 2006 40p. Illustration
Grades: 3 4 5 6 7 8   **741.5; Fic**
1. Adventure graphic novels; 2. Humorous graphic novels; 3. Graphic novels
978-1-59889-033-4, $21.26
David's geeky brother Darrin invents a time machine in his bedroom. Now David and his buddy Ben can zip back a few days to retake that test they flunked. But time travel is tricky; instead of zapping back to history class, the boys

might just become history when they find themselves among dinosaurs.

Part of the Graphic Sparks series.

The **Boy** Who Burped Too Much. Illustrated by Steve Harpster. Stone Arch Books 2006 40p. Illustration
Grades: 2 3 4 5 6 7   **741.5; Fic**
1. Humorous graphic novels; 2. Graphic novels
978-1-59889-037-2, $21.26 lib bdg

Bobby Aaron is a cool kid, but not completely normal; he belches uncontrollably, at the movies, in the library, even in the principal's office. A champion speller, on paper, he enters the spelling bee, but he needs a way to control the burping if he wants to win the spelling bee. The easy-to-read text, simple panel layout, and a funny, fast-paced story make this suitable for beginning and struggling readers (and especially boys who love to burp on purpose).

Buzz Beaker vs Dracula. Illustrated by Andy J. Smith. Stone Arch Books 2009 40p.
Grades: 3 4 5 6 7 8   **741.5; Fic**
1. Dracula, Count (Fictional character); 2. Humorous graphic novels; 3. Science fiction graphic novels; 4. Graphic novels
978-1-4342-1191-0, $21.26

                    LC 2008-32058

Dracula wants to hang out on the beach, get a tan, and go surfing, but being a vampire means he can't do these things. So, he has science genius Buzz Beaker kidnapped and brought to him. Buzz invents a super sun blocker booth, and he and Dracula hit the beach for some fun. However, a side effect of the sun blocker has taken away Dracula's super powers, and his hench fiend, Fangz, decides he wants to take over and become King of the vampires. The book includes some information about vampires, discussion questions, and a glossary.

Part of the Graphic Sparks line, the Buzz Beaker Brainstorm series

Curse of the Red Scorpion. Art by Steve Harpster. Stone Arch Books 2006 40p. Illustration
Grades: 2 3 4 5 6 7   **741.5; Fic**
1. Horror graphic novels; 2. Humorous graphic novels; 3. Graphic novels
978-1-59889-034-4, $21.26 lib bdg

Mitchell was bored at the museum during the class field trip, until he saw the amazing Red Scorpion of Manzitopia and heard about the curse. Now he thinks the creature has followed him home. Do claws click in the night? Does a stinger hide in the curtains? Will Mitchell be able to trap the scorpion before he becomes a victim of the curse? The simple text and panel layout combine with a funny story that is suitable for beginning and struggling readers.

The **Day** of the Field Trip Zombies. Illustrated by Cedric Hohnstadt. Stone Arch Books 2007 40p. Illustration
Grades: 3 4 5 6 7 8 9   **741.5; Fic**
1. Horror graphic novels; 2. Humorous graphic novels; 3. Zombies; 4. Graphic novels
978-1-59889-834-7, $21.26

                    LC 2007-3175

Trevor is a fifth-grade expert on zombies. In fact, he's a zombie-buster. When his class takes a field trip to an aquarium, the evil scientist Dr. Brainium turns the students into radio-controlled zombies. Only Trevor can rescue them, but first he has to escape an army of psycho penguins. The book is written with an easy vocabulary for reluctant and struggling readers.

Part of the Graphic Sparks series.

Invasion of the gym class zombies. By Scott Nickel; illustrated by Matt Luxich. Stone Arch Books 2008 40p. Illustration
Grades: 3 4 5 6 7   **741.5; Fic**
1. Humorous graphic novels; 2. School stories; 3. Zombies; 4. Graphic novels
978-1-4342-0453-0, $21.26; 978-1-4342-0503-2 (pa), $6.95

                    LC 2007-31252

Trevor, a student at Commonwealth Elementary School, has been busting zombies at school and on field trips, but now the evil scientist Dr. Brainium is in jail, so Trevor thinks his zombie-busting days are over. However, Mr. Brawnium has joined the school as the new gym teacher, and he has turned the whole gym class (except for Trevor) into zombified jocks. Only one person can help Trevor save his school, and that is Dr. Brainium.

Part of the Graphic Sparks series.

Jimmy Sniffles vs the Mummy. Illustrated by Steve Harpster. Stone Arch Books 2009 40p. Illustration
Grades: 3 4 5 6 7 8   **741.5; Fic**
1. Mummies; 2. Mystery graphic novels; 3. Graphic novels
978-1-4342-1190-3, $21.26

                    LC 2008-32061

Jimmy Sniffles and his class go on a field trip to the museum, which has the mummy of Amun-Set and his treasured Golden Scarab of Khepera on display. However, Jimmy's superpowered nose smells trouble when he hears that the scarab and the mummy have disappeared from the museum, and he investigates. Jasper the security guard had tried to scare the class with a story of a curse on the scarab; when Jimmy hides in the museum after it closes, a mummy comes after him. But is it really the mummy of Amun-Set, or is it someone else, someone like . . . Jasper?

Part of the Graphic Sparks line, the Jimmy Sniffles series

Jimmy Sniffles: Double Trouble. Illustrated by Steve Harpster. Stone Arch Books 2007 40p. Illustration
Grades: 2 3 4 5 6 7   **741.5; Fic**
1. Humorous graphic novels; 2. Science fiction graphic novels; 3. Graphic novels
978-1-59889-314-4 (lib bdg)

This book is part of the Graphic Sparks line of graphic novels for beginning and struggling readers.

Schoolboy Jimmy Sniffles has a super-powered nose that he uses for good; but his archnemesis Dr. Von Snotenstein has decided to destroy Jimmy. During their last confrontation, he secured a nose hair from Jimmy, and he uses it to create an evil clone that also has a super-powered nose. While evil Jimmy causes all kinds of trouble at school, Jimmy finds a way to stop the evil clone.

Jimmy Sniffles: Up the President's Nose. Illustrated by Steve Harpster. Stone Arch Books 2007 40p. Illustration
Grades: 3 4 5 6 7 8 9   **741.5; Fic**

1. Humorous graphic novels; 2. Science fiction graphic novels; 3. Graphic novels
978-1-59889-837-8, $21.26

LC 2007-3179

The President is suffering a strange allergic reaction, and his life could be in danger. Jimmy Sniffles, the kid with the super-powered nose, is shrunk down to microscopic size to enter the President's nose and sniff out the problem. He finds evil lurking there, but there's still more trouble in the lab, too. The book is written with an easy vocabulary for struggling and reluctant readers.
Part of the Graphic Sparks line of books.

The **Monster** of Lake Lobo. Illustrated by Enrique Corts. Stone Arch Books 2007 40p. Illustration
Grades: 3 4 5 6 7 8 9   **741.5; Fic**
1. Fantasy graphic novels; 2. Mystery graphic novels; 3. Graphic novels
978-1-59889-836-1, $21.26

LC 2007-3178

When Kevin and his dad visit Lake Lobo, their summer vacation suddenly turns creepy. Who made the claw marks outside their cabin window? What is howling in the night? Local legends say a strange creature prowls the woods. Could Kevin's new dog hold the secret to the Monster of Lake Lobo? This graphic novel is written with an easy vocabulary for reluctant and struggling readers.
Part of the Graphic Sparks line of books.

Night of the Homework Zombies. Illustrated by Steve Harpster. Stone Arch Books 2006 40p. Illustration
Grades: 2 3 4 5 6 7   **741.5; Fic**
1. Horror graphic novels; 2. Humorous graphic novels; 3. Graphic novels
978-1-59889-035-8, $21.26 lib bdg

Mr. Winklepoof, the new substitute teacher, is really a mad scientist. He plans to turn every kid in school into a brain-boggled zombie who loves homework. "Study! Study!" they chant. Only Trevor knows the truth; and only Trevor can save his friends, and himself, from this horrible fate. The simple text and panel layout, and the fast-paced humorous story make this suitable for beginning and struggling readers.

Robot Rampage: A Buzz Beaker Brainstorm. Illustrated Andy J. Smith. Stone Arch Books 2007 40p. Illustration
Grades: 2 3 4 5 6 7   **741.5; Fic**
1. Humorous graphic novels; 2. Science; 3. Graphic novels
978-1-59889-055-6 li, $21.26; 978-1-59889-227-7 (pa)
LC 2006007699

Brainy Buzz Beaker doesn't win first prize at the school science fair. The award goes to the weird new student, Elron, instead. Then Elron's homemade robot goes haywire, and Buzz gets taken on a wild, rampaging ride. This graphic novel features easy text and a controlled vocabulary for beginning and struggling readers.
Part of the Graphic Sparks series.

Secret of the summer school zombies. Illustrated by Matt Luxich. Stone Arch Books 2009 40p. Illustration
Grades: 2 3 4 5 6 7   **741.5; Fic**

1. Horror graphic novels; 2. Humorous graphic novels; 3. School stories; 4. Zombies; 5. Graphic novels
978-1-4342-0760-9, $21.26

LC 2008-6710

Trevor was having a fine summer, until his mother forced him to attend summer school. As if that isn't bad enough, all the teachers turn into zombies . . . homework and test crazed zombies. Trevor and his friend Filbert (who comes to summer school for fun) must find a way to stop the zombies, or they'll be trapped inside the classroom of doom forever. The book includes a short glossary (part of the definition of zombie: " . . . when you tell your friend to eat worms, and he does it, he is acting like a zombie?) and information about UFOs and alien sightings.
Part of the Graphic Sparks School Zombies series

T. Rex vs Robo-Dog 3000. Illustrated by Enrique Corts. Stone Arch Books 2009 40p. Illustration
Grades: 2 3 4 5 6 7   **741.5; Fic**
1. Dinosaurs; 2. Humorous graphic novels; 3. Science fiction graphic novels; 4. Time travel; 5. Graphic novels
978-1-4342-0761-6, $21.26

LC 2008-6714

David's brother, Darrin, has just invented a radio-controlled dog that performs tricks, mixes smoothies, and grows 50 feet tall at the touch of a button. When Brendan takes David's time travel remote control from Ben and brings back a Tyrannosaurus Rex from the past, David tries to use Robo-Dog 3000 in its ultimate mode to distract the dinosaur so Darrin can zap it back to the past. The book includes some information about the Tyrannosaurus Rex, and a short glossary.
Part of the Graphic Sparks Time Blasters series

Wind power whiz kid: a Buzz Beaker brainstorm. Illustrated by Andy J. Smith. Stone Arch Books 2009 40p. Illustration
Grades: 2 3 4 5 6 7   **741.5; Fic**
1. Humorous graphic novels; 2. Science fiction graphic novels; 3. Wind power; 4. Graphic novels
978-1-4342-0758-6, $21.26

LC 2008-6713

Buzz's dad invents a supersonic windmill to provide safe power for the town, but Mr. Sludgeco, who owns the polluting energy plant now being used, wants to destroy the windmill. He installs a black box that makes the windmill go out of control; now it's up to Buzz and his friends to invent a way to stop Mr. Sludgeco. The book includes a short glossary and some information about real wind power efforts.
Part of the Graphic Sparks Buzz Beaker series

Niles, Steve
Checkmate: Big Book of Horror. IDW Publishing 2006 Un Illustration
Grades: 6 7 8 9 10 11 12 Adult   **741.5; Fic**
1. Horror graphic novels; 2. Shelley, Mary Wollstonecraft, 1797-1851 — Adaptations; 3. Stoker, Bram, 1847-1912 — Adaptations; 4. Wells, H G — Adaptations; 5. Graphic novels
978-1-600100-14-7, $19.99

Modern horror master Niles (30 Days of Night) retells three classic tales: Frankenstein, War of the Worlds, and

Dracula. This book is not so much an adaptation of the stories as it is a telling inspired by the original novels. Scott Morse illustrates Frankenstein, Ted McKeever paints War of the Worlds, and Richard Sala does the honors for Dracula. Each artist paints full-page and double-page spreads in full color, with Niles' prose appearing on each page. Niles focuses on the main plot of each story; for example, in Dracula, the entire section dealing with Lucy Westenra and her suitors is omitted, so the reader only meets Jonathan Harker, Mina Murray, and Dr. Van Helsing. This book serves best as a brief introduction or as an accompaniment to the original novels.

Originally published as three separate volumes under the series title Little Book of Horror.

The **Cryptics**. Steve Niles and Benjamin Roman. IDW Publishing 2008 48p. Illustration
Grades: 4 5 6 7 8 9   **741.5; Fic**
978-1-60010-254-7, $17.99

The classic movie monsters: the Wolf Man, Dracula, Dr. Jekyll/Mr. Hyde, and the Creature from the Black Lagoon, have moved to the suburbs, and they have kids. Jackie Jekyll (who turns into Hyde), Wolfy (whose mother is The Bride of Frankenstein go figure), Drac, and Sea-Boy do the usual suburban going-to-school, playing in the back yard, sorts of things, except when Wolfy suddenly disappears and the rest have to go find him in the afterlife. The book collects lots of short episodes in the lives of suburban kid monsters. The stories are all humorous, but the fact that the main characters are all monsters may be too much for very sensitive young readers. On the other hand, young readers who like a touch of the scary and macabre will have fun. Roman is the coauthor as well as main artist; one story, "Front Line," is illustrated by Billy Martin, and "Identity Crisis" features art by Robert Iza, Dylan McCrae, Kris Anka, Vidar Cornelius, Shane Long, Fabian "Monk" Schlaga, and David Igo. The book also includes pinup art by various artists.

This was originally published by Image Comics as The Cryptics Issues #13.

Niz, Xavier

Paul Revere's Ride. Illustrated by Brian Bascle. Capstone Press 2006 32p. Illustration
Grades: 3 4 5 6 7 8 9   **741.5; 973.3**
1. Concord (Mass), Battle of, 1775; 2. Lexington (Mass), Battle of, 1775; 3. Massachusetts — History; 4. United States — History — 1775-1783, Revolution; 5. Graphic novels
0-7368-4965-3, $25.26
               LC 200500652
This book uses the comic book format to tell the story of Paul Revere's ride to Lexington in April 1775 to warn colonists of approaching British troops. It includes additional information, a glossary, a list of books for further reading, and more.

Part of the Graphic Library, Graphic History series.

Nobleman, Marc Tyler

Bill the boy wonder: the secret co-creator of Batman. Marc Tyler Nobleman; illustrated by Ty Templeton. Charlesbridge 2012 48 p.
Grades: 6 7 8   **741.5; 741.5/973; B**

1. Batman (Comic strip) — Juvenile literature; 2. Batman (Fictional character); 3. Cartoonists — United States — Biography — Juvenile literature; 4. Finger, Bill, 1914-1974 — Juvenile literature; 5. Superhero comic books, strips, etc
1580892892; 9781580892896, $17.95
               LC 2011025695
Author Marc Tyler Nobleman discusses the creation of Batman, credited to Bob Kane. "A struggling writer named Bill Finger . . . helped invent Batman, from concept to costume to character. He dreamed up Batman's haunting origins and his colorful nemeses. Despite his brilliance, Bill worked in obscurity. It was only after his death that fans went to bat for Bill, calling for acknowledgment that he was co-creator of Batman." (Publisher's note)

★ **Boys** of steel: the creators of Superman. Illustrated by Ross MacDonald. Alfred A. Knopf 2008 Un Illustration
Grades: 3 4 5 6 7 8 9   **741.5**
1. Artists; 2. Biographical graphic novels; 3. Cartoonists; 4. Cartoonists; 5. Comic book writers; 6. Illustrators; 7. Shuster, Joe, 1914-1992; 8. Siegel, Jerry, 1914-1996; 9. Superman (Fictional character); 10. Graphic novels
978-0-375-83802-6, $16.99; 978-0-375-93802-3 (lib. bdg.), $19.99
               LC 2007-41606
This picture book tells the story of Jerry Siegel and Joe Shuster, two teenagers living in Depression-era Cleveland, Ohio, who became friends and started writing stories together. One night they created the character who would become Superman. A text section at the back of the book tells of the struggle Siegel and Shuster had after they sold rights to Superman to the company that is now DC Comics. After Superman became wildly successful and made lots of money for DC Comics, Siegel and Shuster saw none of it. They started a legal fight that did end up with DC providing a financial settlement; Siegel's family was finally awarded half of the U.S. copyright to the material in Action Comics #1 in March 2008. Shuster's family is now asserting its right to the other half of the copyright, and negotiations are ongoing.

Nolen-Weathington, Eric

★ **Modern** Masters volume twenty-five: Jeff Smith. TwoMorrows Publishing 2011 117p. Illustration
Grades: 6 7 8 9 10 11 12 Adult   **741.5**
1. Artists; 2. Authors; 3. Cartoonists; 4. Comic books, strips, etc — History and criticism; 5. Graphic novels — History and criticism; 6. Smith, Jeff
978-1-60549-024-3, $15.95

This volume in the Modern Masters series focuses on Jeff Smith, creator of Bone. In an interview that covers his childhood, college career, and early work before becoming a cartoonist, Smith talks about how he created Fone Bone when he

Courtesy of TwoMorrows Publishing

was just five years old. The artwork in the book includes young Smith's hand-created comics from his childhood. Only a couple of "craps" slip out. The book includes mostly black and white art and photographs, with a few color illustrations from the Bone comics.

North, Ryan
Adventure Time. Ryan North; illustrated by Braden Lamb and Shelli Paroline. Simon & Schuster 2012 128 p. Color; Illustration
Grades: 3 4 5 6 7 8 9 10   **741.5**
1. Adventure fiction; 2. Imaginary places
1608862801; 9781608862801, $14.99

"The totally algebraic adventures of Finn and Jake have come to the comic book page! The Lich, a super-lame, SUPER-SCARY skeleton dude, has returned to the the Land of Ooo, and he's bent on total destruction! Luckily, Finn and Jake are on the case . . . but can they succeed against their most destructive foe yet?" (Publisher's note)

"The comic series has been every bit as good as the show, with epic magic battles with an evil Lich, a multi-part time travel story, and a host of backup strips by some of the best indie cartoonists out there." Comics Alliance
Volume 1 of an ongoing series

★ The **unbeatable** Squirrel Girl; Volume 1: Squirrel power!. Ryan North; illustrated by Erica Henderson. Marvel Enterprises 2015 136 p. Color; Illustration
Grades: 7 8 9 10 11 12 Adult   **741.5**
1. Female superhero graphic novels; 2. Squirrel Girl (Fictional character); 3. Squirrels — Fiction; 4. Superheroes — Fiction
0785197028; 9780785197027, $15.99

In this comic by Ryan North, illustrated by Erica Henderson, "supervillains and criminals meet their match . . . Squirrel Girl, aka Doreen Green, a college freshman with the appearance, speed, and agility of a squirrel. When Galactus threatens Earth, the heroine must rely on more than strength to defeat the Devourer of Worlds. She may have extraordinary strength . . . but it is her ability to form connections with people that proves to be her most powerful asset." (School Library Journal)

Contains material originally published in magazine form as The Unbeatable Squirrel Girl #1-4 and Marvel Super-Heroes #8
Volume 1 of an ongoing series

Nykko
★ The **elsewhere** chronicles book two: the shadow spies. Art by Bannister ; story by Nykko ; colors by Jaffré. Lerner Publishing Group/Graphic Universe 2009 48p. Illustration
Grades: 4 5 6 7 8   **741.5; Fic**
1. Adventure graphic novels; 2. Fantasy graphic novels; 3. Horror graphic novels; 4. Graphic novels
978-0-7613-4460-5, $27.93; 978-0-7613-3964-9 (pa), $6.95

LC 2008-39443
When the Shadow Door shatters, the passageway closes and Rebecca and Max are trapped in Elsewhere; they set out to find another way home. The problem is that wherever there is darkness, the Shadow Spies hunt them. Back in

Grandpa Gabe's house, Noah and Theo work to find a replacement lens for the movie projector so they can get through and rescue their friends. Meanwhile, the police think Max and Rebecca have been kidnapped, and the boys have to work around the investigation. It's clear to the kids that Grandpa Gabe had explored Elsewhere, and his notes have left clues for them; Max and Rebecca also meet people who have been fighting a long war against the Shadows and who know Grandpa Gabe. Whatever else they do, they must keep the Shadow Spies away from Earth.

Originally published in France as Les Enfants d'ailleurs, winner of the 2007 Lyon Festival Youth Prize.

★ The **elsewhere** chronicles, book three: the master of shadows. Art by Bannister ; story by Nykko ; colors by Jaffré. Lerner Publishing Group/Graphic Universe 2009 48p. Illustration
Grades: 4 5 6 7 8   **741.5; Fic**
1. Fantasy graphic novels; 2. Horror graphic novels; 3. Graphic novels
978-0-7613-4461-2, $27.93; 978-0-7613-4744-6 (pa), $6.95

LC 2008-39444
Theo and Noah have joined Rebecca and Max in Elsewhere, but they are on the run, pursued by the Master of Shadows and menaced at all times by the Shadow Spies. All they have to guide them are the strange and cryptic clues left by Grandpa Gabe, and they see their friends in this strange world pay the ultimate price while trying to stop the Shadows. How far must the four friends go, and what will it cost them, to save their own world?

Originally published in France as Les Enfants d'ailleurs, winner of the 2007 Lyon Festival Youth Prize.

★ The **tower** of shadows. By Nykko, illustrated by Bannister; translation by Carol Klio Burrell]. Graphic Universe 2013 48 p. (The ElseWhere chronicles)
Grades: 4 5 6 7   **741.5; Fic**
1. Grandfathers — Fiction; 2. Horror stories; 3. Imaginary places; 4. Magic — Fiction; 5. Graphic novels
1467712337; 9781467712330, $27.93

LC 2013000317
In this graphic novel by Nykko, "the time has come to confront the Master of Shadows. Rebecca, Max, and Theo must follow Grandpa Gabe into the heart of the Master's realm, the Tower of Shadows. But can Grandpa Gabe be trusted? There's a reason he's so familiar with the dark powers that rule Elsewhere: he created them. Grandpa Gabe's plan might just be a suicide mission, but it's their last chance to save our world—and Rebecca's life." (Publisher's note)

"Bannister's atmospheric illustrations feature expressive characters placed in finely detailed, eerily organic landscapes or dim subterranean reaches inhabited by menacing swirls of shadow." Kirkus

O'Brien, Anne Sibley
The **legend** of Hong Kil Dong, the Robin Hood of Korea. Charlesbridge 2006 Un Illustration
Grades: 3 4 5 6 7   **741.5; Fic**
1. Hong Kil Dong (Legendary character); 2. Korea; 3. Graphic novels
978-1-58089-302-2; 1-58089-302-3, $14.95

LC 2005-56941

Hong Kil Dong is the son of a powerful government minister and one of his servants; this means the father will not recognize his son as his own. The boy grows up with great intelligence and wit, and leaves home to find his fortune. He learns martial arts and magic, and when he encounters thieves who rob only because corrupt government officials have ruined them, he turns the thieves into an army to right the wrongs. This story is based on a seventeenth century Korean legend.

Includes bibliographical references

O'Connor, George

Aphrodite: Goddess of love. George O'Connor. First Second 2014 76 p. Color; Illustration (Olympians)

Grades: 6 7 8 9 **741.5**

1. Aphrodite (Greek deity); 2. Gods and goddesses — Fiction; 3. Graphic novels

1596437391; 1596439475; 9781596437395, $9.99; 9781596439474, $16.99

This graphic novel, volume six of the Olympians series on Greek mythology, by George O'Connor, "turns the spotlight on Aphrodite, the goddess of love. . . . O'Connor tackles the story of the Aphrodite from her dramatic birth (emerging from sea-foam) to her role in the Trojan War." (Publisher's note)

"Like the prior volumes, this book injects the mythology with an accessible modern sensibility through its colorful, action-packed graphic storytelling." Horn Book

Includes bibliographical references

Other titles in this series are:Zeus (2010); Athena (2010); Hera (2011); Hades (2012); Poseidon (2013); Ares (2015)

Ares: bringer of war. George O'Connor. First Second Books 2015 80 p. Color; Illustration (Olympians)

Grades: 4 5 6 7 8 9 **741.5**

1. Ares (Greek deity); 2. Greek mythology; 3. Trojan War

1626720134; 1626720142; 9781626720138; 9781626720145, $16.99

LC 2014041225

This graphic novel by George O'Connor "continues in the tenth year of the fabled Trojan War where two infamous gods of war go to battle. The spotlight is thrown on Ares, god of war, and primarily focuses on his battle with the clever and powerful Athena. As the battle culminates and the gods try to one-up each other to win, the human death toll mounts." (Publisher's note)

"In this nuanced, multilayered view of the usually vilified bringer of war, O'Connor continues his exceptional graphic novel series about the Greek gods. . . . The author's extensive notes amusingly explain connections to The Odyssey, The Aeneid, and the series' previous works." SLJ

A Neal Porter Book.

Other titles in this series are: Athena: Grey-eyed Goddess (2010); Zeus: King of the Gods (2010); Hera: The Goddess and her Glory (2011); Hades: Lord of the Dead (2012); Poseidon: Earth Shaker (2013); Aphrodite: Goddess of Love (2014)

Athena: grey-eyed goddess. First Second 2010 76p. Illustration

Grades: 5 6 7 8 **741; 741.5**

978-1-59643-649-7, $16.99; 1-59643-649-2; 978-1-59643-432-5 (pa), $9.99; 1-59643-432-5 (pa)

Hera: the goddess and her glory. First Second 2011 76p. Illustration

Grades: 5 6 7 8 **741; 741.5**

978-1-59643-433-2, $9.99; 1-59643-433-3

★ **Olympians:** Athena, grey-eyed goddess. First Second Books 2010 78p. Illustration

Grades: 4 5 6 7 8 9 **741.5; Fic**

1. Athena (Greek deity); 2. Fantasy graphic novels; 3. Gods and goddesses; 4. Greek mythology; 5. Graphic novels

978-1-59643-432-5, $9.99

The Fates retell five tales of the goddess Athena, daughter of Zeus, a warrior and also the goddess of wisdom. The first story tells of her birth, which is unlike any other, god or human; the second and third stories tell a couple of versions of how she took the name Pallas. The fourth story recounts Athena's dealings with Medusa, and how young demigod Perseus finally killed her. The events in these stories also provide Athena with her Aegis, one of her great weapons, which incorporates the impenetrable skin of the giant Pallas and the snakes from Medusa's head with the cape Zeus made from the skin of the goat Amalthea, who had nurtured him as a child. The Fates then tell of the weaving contest between Athena and the skilled but arrogant human woman, Arachne. O'Connor includes notes that provide more information about some of the historical background, discussion questions, a bibliography, and suggestions for further reading. His full-color art utilizes some of the style of super hero comics. This is the second of twelve planned volumes.

Poseidon: earth shaker. By George O'Connor. Roaring Brook Press 2012 80 p. (Olympians)

Grades: 4 5 6 **741.5/973; 741.5**

1. Greek mythology

1596437383; 1596438282; 9781596437388, $9.99; 9781596438286, $16.99

LC 2011052219

This graphic novel, by George O'Connor, is part of the "Olympians" series, featuring the mythology of the Greco-Roman gods. "The fifth installment of the Olympians series of graphic novels . . . turns the spotlight on that most mysterious and misunderstood of the Greek gods. . . . Thrill to such famous myths as Theseus and the Minotaur, Odysseus and Polyphemos, and the founding of Athens—and learn how the tempestuous Poseidon became the King of the Seas." (Publisher's note)

Includes bibliographical references and index

A Neal Porter book.

★ **Zeus:** king of the gods. First Second 2010 76p. Illustration

Grades: 5 6 7 8 **741.5**

978-1-59643-431-8, $16.99; 1-59643-625-5; 978-1-59643-432-5 (pa), $9.99; 1-59643-431-7 (pa)

"O'Connor unveils his new Olympians graphic-novel series with this story of the daddy of Greek gods. Most immediately striking about this, aside from the exciting artwork, is the care O'Connor takes to visualize the creation myth that begins with Gaea creating and taking as a husband the sky, Ouranos. Their children the Titans and other proto-Olympian entities are often neglected or at best murkily covered, but here they're vividly portrayed with all the magnificence of their beyond-good-and-evil power. After this breathtaking and lengthy sequence, Zeus enters the scene to grow from a feisty nymph-needling youth to a lightning bolt-wielding avenger." (Booklist)

Other titles in this series are: Athena: grey-eyed goddess (2010); Hera: the goddess and her glory (2011); Hades: lord of the dead (2012); Poseidon: earth shaker (2013); Aphrodite: goddess of love (2013); Ares: bringer of war (2015); Apollo: the brilliant one (2016)

O'Donnell, Liam

Food fight: a graphic guide adventure. Illustrated by Mike Deas. Orca Book Publishers 2010 Un Illustration
Grades: 3 4 5 6 7 8   **741.5; Fic**
  1. Agriculture — Research; 2. Food supply; 3. Mystery graphic novels; 4. Graphic novels
978-1-55469-067-1, $9.95

LC 2009-940900

Devin and Nadia are spending their summer vacation as camp counselors for the Lil Brains Summer Camp at the university, where their mother, Dr. Chang, works in a research lab; at least Nadia is working "Devin keeps trying to escape so he can hang out with his friend Simon. Dr. Chang is working on ways to improve food crops, but someone breaks into the lab using her access code. When it happens again, her supervisors think she's trying to sabotage her own work. Nadia and Devin know their mother wouldn't do anything unethical, so they decide to investigate.

Courtesy of Orca Book Publishers

When Devin goes with Dr. Chang to an experimental farm, he meets Irene, a young girl who suspects the farm is developing genetically modified corn. They work together to help Dr. Chang, but soon find there's definitely something wrong going on, and the corporation sponsoring the research is responsible. O'Donnell includes information on genetically modified foods and the controversy surrounding its use, and on the growing locavore movement (eating only locally-grown produce).
Part of the Graphic Guide Adventure series

Max Finder mystery: collected casebook, vol. 1. Illustrated by Richard Dominguez and Charles Barnett III. Owlkids Publishing 2009 96p. Illustration
Grades: 3 4 5 6 7 8   **741.5; Fic**
  1. Humorous graphic novels; 2. Mystery graphic novels; 3. Graphic novels
978-2-89579-116-4, $9.95

LC C2006-903300-5

This book collects ten short mysteries that originally appeared in Owl Magazine. Seventh-graders Max Finder and Alison Santos live in Whispering Meadows, and they investigate mysteries that happen in their neighborhood and in school. Each story provides verbal and visual clues for the readers and invites them to try to solve the mystery themselves before turning to the back of the book to read the solution. Each story is also accompanied by a puzzle, with solutions to those in the back as well. Max and Alison's neighbors and schoolmates each take turns being victims, witnesses, and sometimes the culprits in such cases as the loss of a valuable basketball card, a vandalized brand-new CD at a slumber party, a stolen prize at the school's Halloween dance, a box of chocolate bars replaced with soap, and a werewolf at the summer camp. Anyone who has enjoyed any Encyclopedia Brown or Cam Jansen mysteries will enjoy these mystery stories.

Media meltdown: a graphic guide adventure. Written by Liam O'Donnell; illustrated by Mike Deas. Orca Book Publishers 2009 Un Illustration
Grades: 6 7 8 9 10
741.5; Fic
  1. Media literacy; 2. Mystery graphic novels; 3. Graphic novels
978-1-55469-065-7 (pa), $9.95; 1-55469-065-X (pa)

LC 2009-927573

Courtesy of Orca Book Publishers

Pema and Bounce find a new housing development going up in the middle of what used to be their favorite biking trail, and then they learn that the developer is trying to force Jagroop's farmer father to sell his land. Pema's older sister Nima has been working as an intern at the local TV station, and she tries to help the teens put together a news story about what's happening. Then they learn that the developer buys a lot of advertising on the station, and he gets the station owner to pressure the producer to kill their story. They need to get their story out, but since traditional media won't help them, they turn to alternate media on the internet and a little guerilla newscasting by Nima to stop the developer and preserve their land.

This "is an excellent choice for developing media literacy. . . . The design and layout are colorful and fast paced. The text is well written and paired with useful imagery." SLJ

★ **Power** play. Illustrated by Mike Deas. Orca Book Publishers 2011 64p. Illustration (Graphic guide adventure)
Grades: 3 4 5 6 7 8 9   **741; 741.5; Fic**
  1. Mystery graphic novels; 2. Graphic novels
978-1-55469-069-5, $9.95; 1-55469-069-2

Siblings Devin and Nadia team up with their friend Marcus, Marcus' stepbrother Bounce, and

Courtesy of Orca Book Publishers

Bounce's best friend Pema when they all attend the World Leaders Summit, where Marcus' father, Dr. Ashmore is scheduled to speak. The friends find themselves mixed up in a fight between some of the most powerful people in the world and those who want more equitable rights to clean water and other environmental concerns. They investigate when one of Dr. Ashmore's assistants is murdered at the summit, and Dr. Ashmore receives threats.

"An enjoyable story with educational value, this strong mystery is presented along with information about world politics, power, and the benefits of political protest for social good." Booklist

Ramp rats: a graphic guide adventure. Written by Liam O'Donnell; illustrated by Mike Deas. Orca Book Publishers 2008 Un Illustration
Grades: 3 4 5 6 7 8 9   **741.5; Fic**
1. Bullies; 2. Friendship; 3. Skateboarding; 4. Graphic novels
978-1-55143-880-1 (pa), $9.95; 1-55143-880-1 (pa)
LC 2008-928577
"Benny (nicknamed Bounce) just wants to use the cool new skate park with his friend Pema, but older bullying Crunch and his friends have taken over the park. . . . Aside from the action-packed story, great characters, and colorful artwork, this graphic-novel adventure includes an array of practical skateboarding tips for beginners. The story also delivers a deft message about standing up to bullies." Booklist

The **Shocking** World of Electricity with Max Axiom, Super Scientist. Illustrated by Richard Dominguez and Charles Barnett III. Capstone Press 2007 32p. Illustration
Grades: 3 4 5 6 7 8   **537; 741.5**
1. Electricity; 2. Science; 3. Graphic novels
978-0-7368-6835-8 li, $25.26; 978-0-7368-7888-3 (pa)
Max Axiom is a super-cool super-scientist who demonstrates and explains science in ways never before seen in the classroom. Whether shrinking down to the size of an ant or riding on a sound wave, Max does whatever it takes to make science super cool and accessible. This volume explores electricity, and includes a glossary and a list of books for further reading.
Part of the Graphic Science series.

System Shock. Art by Janet Matysiak. Stone Arch Books 2007 88p. Illustration
Grades: 4 5 6 7 8 9   **741.5; Fic**
1. Science fiction graphic novels; 2. Video games; 3. Graphic novels
978-1-59889-083-9 li, $22.60; 978-1-59889-214-7 (pa)
LC 2006007185
In a futuristic society, Daniel, Jack, and Jemma find themselves lost in a virtual reality game. To make matters worse, every video-game villain seems to be pursuing them. Even if they defeat the evil Cyborgs, the controllers in Realworld are working on wiping the corrupt system clean. If the friends don't find a way out soon, they are in danger of being erased forever. This graphic novel is written at an easy level for reluctant and struggling readers.
Part of the Graphic Quest series.

Understanding Photosynthesis with Max Axiom, Super Scientist. Capstone Press 2007 32p. Illustration

Grades: 3 4 5 6 7 8   **572; 741.5**
1. Photosynthesis; 2. Science; 3. Graphic novels
978-0-7368-6841-9 li, $25.26; 978-0-7368-7893-7 (pa)
Max Axiom is a super-cool super-scientist who demonstrates and explains science in ways never before seen in the classroom. Whether shrinking down to the size of an ant or riding on a sound wave, Max does whatever it takes to make science super cool and accessible. This volume explores photosynthesis, and includes a glossary and a list of books for further reading.
Part of the Graphic Science series.

A **United** Force. Art by Mike Rooth. Harcourt Achieve/Steck-Vaughn 2006 48p. Illustration
Grades: 3 4 5 6 7 8   **741.5; Fic**
1. Adventure graphic novels; 2. Celts; 3. Graphic novels
978-1-4190-3206-6, $8.99
It's 55 B.C.E. The British Isles have been home to the Celts for hundreds of years. Now, an ambitious Roman general named Julius Caesar plans to change all that. Will the Celts be able to defend their homeland? This historical graphic novel includes prose intervals that give information about the Celts and the Romans.
Part of the Timeline Graphic Novels series.

The **World** of Food Chains with Max Axiom, Super Scientist. Art by Cynthia Martin and Bill Anderson. Capstone Press 2007 32p. Illustration
Grades: 3 4 5 6 7 8   **577; 741.5**
1. Food chains (Ecology); 2. Science; 3. Graphic novels
978-0-7368-6839-6 li, $25.26; 978-0-7368-7891-3 (pa)
Max Axiom is a super-cool super-scientist who demonstrates and explains science in ways never before seen in the classroom. Whether shrinking down to the size of an ant or riding on a sound wave, Max does whatever it takes to make science super cool and accessible. This volume explores food chains and how they work in ecology, and includes a glossary and a list of books for further reading.
Part of the Graphic Science series.

Oakley, Mark
Thieves & kings. [by Mark Oakley]. I Box Pub 1998 154p. Illustration
Grades: 4 5 6 7 8 9 10 11 12   **741.5; Fic**
1. Adventure graphic novels; 2. Fantasy graphic novels; 3. Graphic novels
0-9681025-0-6, $18.95
LC 2003-446777
In a story that mixes pages of text with pages of comic book art, the reader meets the young thief Rubel, who has returned home from a long voyage to find things no longer as they were. He has to deal with soldiers and pirates, princes and princesses, a strange young wizard, and a mysterious Shadow Lady.
Originally published as individual issues of the Thieves & kings comic series, beginning in 1994
Volume 1 of 5

Thieves & Kings Presents The Walking Mage. I Box Publishing 2006 Un Illustration
Grades: 5 6 7 8 9 10 11 12   **741.5; Fic**
1. Fantasy graphic novels; 2. Humorous graphic novels; 3. Graphic novels

0-9681025-5-7, $9.95

In the world of Thieves & Kings, the royal wizard, Quinton Zempfester, has lost his job. Again. This time, though, his name has also been added to the top of the kingdom's list of most wanted criminals. Unfairly accused by the dark witch who has seized the throne, Quinton decides that perhaps a little treason might not be such a bad idea after all ... This book chronicles a side adventure in the series, and is done completely in comic book panels rather than the mix of prose and panels used in the main series.

Ochi, Yoshihiko

Atelier Marie and Elie, Zarlburg Alchemist. Tokyopop 2008 159p. Illustration
Grades: 8 9 10 11 12   **741.5; Fic**
  1. Adventure graphic novels; 2. Fantasy graphic novels; 3. Humorous graphic novels; 4. Manga; 5. Graphic novels
978-1-59816-528-9, $9.99

Millie accidentally puts a tadpole into a magical barrel in her workshop, and now Ingrid, Marie, and Elie need to find a watery home for the creature before it does too much damage to the town. Then, along with demon Strafe, they go on a journey to deliver medicines and such, only to encounter troublesome magical beasts. The book includes some minor fan service with a few skimpy women's tops.

Atelier Marie and Elie, Zarlburg Alchemist Vol. 2. Tokyopop 2007 Un Illustration
Grades: 8 9 10 11 12   **741.5; Fic**
  1. Adventure graphic novels; 2. Fantasy graphic novels; 3. Manga; 4. Graphic novels
978-1-59816-526-5, $9.99

Alchemists Marie and Elie run their shop, teach two young elves, build a better flying broom, take down some thieves, and help a half-demon half-human warrior friend. Now if they can just manage to do all that without blowing up Zarlburg around them ... The book includes some mild violence.

Atelier Marie and Elie: Zarlburg Alchemist Volume 1. Tokyopop 2007 162p. Illustration
Grades: 7 8 9 10 11 12 Adult   **741.5; Fic**
  1. Fantasy graphic novels; 2. Manga
978-1-59816-525-8, $9.99

Welcome to the Zarlburg Royal Magic Academy" producers of the best alchemists in the world. When Marie, Zalburg's prodigal daughter and premier alchemist, returns to her alma mater after thrilling journeys in many foreign lands, she suddenly realizes things are not too exciting at home. But all that changes after running into fellow alchemist Elie, who has plans to open an alchemy workshop and become famous. Now, adventure comes to them in all shapes and sizes—curious elves, flying broomsticks, giant monsters, and explosive bombs. It's all inside Yoshihiko Ochi's new manga series based on the popular video game franchise. There's lots of monster fighting action.

Oda, Eiichiro

★ **One** Piece Volume 1. Viz Media/Shonen Jump 2003 216p. Illustration
Grades: 8 9 10 11 12 Adult   **741.5; Fic**
  1. Adventure graphic novels; 2. Fantasy graphic novels; 3. Manga; 4. Shonen manga; 5. Graphic novels

1-56931-901-4, $7.95

Monkey D. Luffy's main ambition is to become a pirate, inspired by listening to the tales of the buccaneer "Red-Haired" Shanks. When he accidentally eats the Gum-Gum Fruit, it gives him strange powers to stretch like rubber, but doing so also invokes the fruit's curse: anybody who consumes it can never learn to swim. Nevertheless, Monkey and his crewmate Roronoa Zoro, master of the three-sword fighting style, sail the Seven Seas of swashbuckling adventure in search of the elusive treasure "One Piece." As the series goes on, Luffy gains more crew and they encounter sea monsters, far away kingdoms, cloud island, and super powered pirates of every shape, size, and description - which means lots of epic and comical fight scenes.

Volume 1 of an ongoing series

Oh, Cirro

Greek and Roman Mythology Vol. 1. Art by C.S. Chun. Youngjin Singapore 2005 188p. Illustration
Grades: 3 4 5 6 7 8   **741.5; 291**
  1. Classical mythology; 2. Graphic novels
981-05-2240-1, $12.95

This title introduces each of the 12 gods of Olympus, tells the story of the creators of the gods. Gaia and Kronos, recounts Gigantes and Typhon's battles with Zeus to rule Mt. Olympus, and more. The book includes the Greek and Roman names of the main deities and a family tree of the gods.

Oima, Yoshitoki

A silent voice; Volume 1. Yoshitoki Oima; translation, lettering, Steven LeCroy. Kodansha 2015 186 p. Illustration
Grades: 7 8 9 10   **741.5; Fic**
  1. Bullies; 2. Deaf children; 3. School stories
163236056X; 9781632360564, $10.99

"Shoya is a bully. When Shoko, a girl who can't hear, enters his elementary school class, she becomes their favorite target. . . . But the children's cruelty goes too far. Shoko is forced to leave the school, and Shoya ends up shouldering all the blame. Six years later, the two meet again. Can Shoya make up for his past mistakes, or is it too late?" (Publisher's note)

Volume 1 of 7

Okamoto, Kazuhiro

Translucent Volume One. Dark Horse Comics 2007 192p. Illustration
Grades: 7 8 9 10 11 12   **741.5; Fic**
  1. Humorous graphic novels; 2. Manga; 3. Romance graphic novels; 4. Graphic novels
978-1-59307-647-4, $9.95

Eighth grader Shizuka is an introverted girl, dealing with schoolwork, boys, and a medical condition - the Translucent Syndrome - that begins to turn her invisible. She finds support with Mamoru, a hyperactive boy who is falling for Shizuka despite her condition, and with Keiko, another girl who suffers from this illness and has finally turned completely invisible. The mysterious disease that these teens struggle with becomes a metaphor in the ordinary lives of the students in their classes, as they try to work their way through their friendships and romances. There are brief moments of partial nudity.

Okuda, Hitoshi

No Need for Tenchi! Vol. 1 (2nd edition). Viz Media 2004 184p. Illustration
Grades: 8 9 10 11 12 Adult   **741.5; Fic**
1. Adventure graphic novels; 2. Humorous graphic novels; 3. Shonen manga; 4. Graphic novels
1-59116-610-1, $9.99

The trouble and fun began when ordinary teenager Tenchi Masaki inadvertently released the legendary demon Ryoko from his grandfather's shrine. Turned out Ryoko was actually a marooned space pirate; since then, she's become Tenchi's unwanted houseguest, attracting a host of other troublemaking alien women: Ayeka, a haughty alien priess; Sasami, her mischievous little sister; and Washu, Ryoko's mad-scientist "mother." Add Ryo-oh-Ki, an adorable little carrot-eating spaceship, and you've got one full Shinto shrine. Now Tenchi's troubles double—in the form of Minagi, a dead-ringer for Ryoko who attacks our hapless friends and then conveniently develops amnesia. But Minagi is just a pawn of the alien warrior Yakage, who plans to steal Tenchi's miraculous sword and abduct Ayeka. And the only hero who has what it takes to rescue the kidnapped princess is...Ryoko. The series includes some sexual innuendo, raunchy humor, comic violence, and a little strong language.

Olson, Kay Melchisedech

Benjamin Franklin: An American Genius. Illustrated by Barabara Schulz and Gordon Purcell. Capstone Press 2006 32p. Illustration
Grades: 3 4 5 6 7 8 9   **741.5; 973.3; 92**
1. Franklin, Benjamin, 1706-1790; 2. Graphic novels
0-7368-4269-8, $25.26

LC 2005003964

This book uses the comic book format to recount highlights in the life of American statesman and inventor Benjamin Franklin. It includes additional information, a glossary, a list of books for further reading, and more.

Part of the Graphic Library, Graphic Biographies series.

Betsy Ross and the American Flag. Illustrated by Anna Maria Cool, Sam Delarosa, and Charles Barnett III. Capstone Press 2006 32p. Illustration
Grades: 3 4 5 6 7 8 9   **741.5; 973.3; 92**
1. Flags; 2. Ross, Betsy, 1752-1836; 3. United States — History — 1775-1783, Revolution; 4. Graphic novels
0-7368-4962-9, $25.26

LC 2005006461

This book uses the comic book format to tell the story of the life of Betsy Ross and the legend of her sewing the first American flag. It includes additional information, a glossary, a list of books for further reading, and more.

Part of the Graphic Library, Graphic History series.

Frank Zamboni and the Ice-Resurfacing Machine by Kay Melchisedech Olson ; illustrated by Richard Dominguez and Charles Barnett, III. Capstone Press 2007 32p. Illustration
Grades: 3 4 5 6 7 8 9   **688.7; 741.5; 92**
1. Ice skating; 2. Inventors; 3. Zamboni, Frank; 4. Graphic novels

1429601477; 9781429601474, $29.99

LC 2007000254

This book uses the graphic novel format to tell how Frank Zamboni created the ice-resurfacing machine, and how it affected the world of ice-based sports. The book includes additional facts and a list of books for further reading.

Part of the Graphic Library Inventions and Discovery series.

Olson, Nathan

Nathan Hale: Revolutionary Spy. Illustrated by Cynthia Martin and Brent Schoonover. Capstone Press 2006 32p. Illustration
Grades: 3 4 5 6 7 8 9   **741.5; 973.3; 92**
1. Biographical graphic novels; 2. Hale, Nathan, 1755-1776; 3. Graphic novels
0-7368-4968-8, $25.26

LC 2005007894

This book uses the comic book format to recount highlights of the life story of Revolutionary War hero and spy Nathan Hale. It includes additional information, a glossary, a list of books for further reading, and more.

Part of the Graphic Library, Graphic Biographies series.

One (Manga author)

★ One-punch man; Volume 1. Story by One; art by Yusuke Murata. Viz 2015 189 p. Illustration
Grades: 8 9 10 11 12 Adult   **741.5; Fic**
1. Manga; 2. Superheroes; 3. Graphic novels
1421585642; 9781421585642, $9.99
Eisner Nominee: Best U.S. Edition of International Material—Asia (2015)

"Nothing about Saitama passes the eyeball test when it comes to superheroes, from his lifeless expression to his bald head to his unimpressive physique. However, this average-looking guy has a not-so-average problem—he just can't seem to find an opponent strong enough to take on! Every time a promising villain appears, he beats the snot out of 'em with one punch!" (Publisher's note)

"The story is fast-paced, humorous, and entertaining in a way that looks and feels like an action movie." SLJ

Volume 1 of an ongoing series

Blaster, Billy (Fictional character);

Billy Blaster: attack of the Rock Men. Art by Peter Richardson. Stone Arch Books 2009 40p.
Grades: 3 4 5 6 7   **741.5; Fic**
1. Adventure graphic novels; 2. Blaster, Billy (Fictional character); 3. Science fiction graphic novels; 4. Graphic novels
978-1-4342-1273-3, $22.65

LC 2008-31285

Rock Men are the hottest new toys on the market, and everyone in Zone City is getting them. However, when kids plug the Rock Men into their computers, the toys brainwash them into getting their parents' credit card information. Even General Bullet has bought a Rock Man and has been brainwashed. Billy and his ninja wizard friend Wu Hoo learn that their old enemy Red Wolf is the nefarious toymaker, and they set out to stop him. The book includes a short glossary, some facts about popular toys and games of the past, and discussion questions and writing prompts.

Originally published in the U.K. as Boffin Boy and the Rock Men. This is a volume of the Billy Blaster series.

Billy Blaster: the Cryptic code. Art by Peter Richardson. Stone Arch Books 2009 40p. Illustration
Grades: 3 4 5 6 7   **741.5; Fic**
1. Adventure graphic novels; 2. Blaster, Billy (Fictional character); 3. Science fiction graphic novels; 4. Graphic novels
978-1-4342-1265-8, $22.65

LC 2008-31286

Billy Blaster's friend Wu Hoo, the ninja wizard, always seeks more knowledge, and his quest leads him to a parchment written in a cryptic code. Before he can decipher it, a singing trio called the Big Sisters learn that Wu Hoo has the parchment and kidnap him; they want the secret wisdom on the parchment for themselves. The book includes a short glossary, some facts about codes and secret messages, and discussion questions and writing prompts.

Originally published in the U.K. as Boffin Boy and the Quest for Wisdom. This is a volume of the Billy Blaster series.

Billy Blaster: the Evil Swarm. Art by Peter Richardson. Stone Arch Books 2009 40p.
Grades: 3 4 5 6 7   **741.5; Fic**
1. Adventure graphic novels; 2. Blaster, Billy (Fictional character); 3. Science fiction graphic novels; 4. Graphic novels
978-1-4342-1274-0, $22.65

LC 2008-31287

When a swarm of giant, angry insects emerges from a volcano attacks the people of Zone City, Billy and his friend Rika enter the volcano to find out what's going on and to see if they can stop them before the swarm can spread across the world. The book includes a short glossary, some facts about real insects, and discussion questions and writing prompts.

Originally published in the U.K. as Boffin Boy and the Deadly Swarm. This is a volume of the Billy Blaster series

Boffin Boy and the Invaders from Space. Art by Peter Richardson. Ransom Publishing 2007 Un Illustration
Grades: 2 3 4 5 6
741.5; Fic
1. Adventure graphic novels; 2. Science fiction graphic novels; 3. Superhero graphic novels; 4. Graphic novels; 5. Boffin Boy (Fictional character)
978-1-84167-613-5, $7.95

Courtesy of Ransom Publishing

Boffin Boy and Wu Pee must fight the scaly Snurgeon space invaders and stop them from stealing all of the Earth's water. Will Boffin Boy use force, or can he find a clever way to save the planet?

Boffin Boy and the Lost City. Art by Peter Richardson. Ransom Publishing 2007 Un Illustration

Courtesy of Ransom Publishing

Grades: 2 3 4 5 6 **741.5; Fic**
1. Adventure graphic novels; 2. Science fiction graphic novels; 3. Superhero graphic novels; 4. Graphic novels; 5. Boffin Boy (Fictional character)
978-1-84167-617-3, $7.95

People keep disappearing then reappearing again; but the ones that appear aren't the same as the ones that disappear. Of course, it's a door into another world, and Boffin Boy (Rick Shaw) and ninja wizard Wu Pee set off to find it. When they do, then the story really starts ...

Boffin Boy and the Monsters from the Deep. Art by Peter Richardson. Ransom Publishing 2007 Un Illustration
Grades: 2 3 4 5 6
741.5; Fic
1. Adventure graphic novels; 2. Science fiction graphic novels; 3. Superhero graphic novels; 4. Graphic novels; 5. Boffin Boy (Fictional character)
978-1-84167-615-9, $7.95

Just when people are having a nice quiet time on the beach, some giant mutant jellyfish come along and spoil it. They're stealing all the sweets and chocolate bars they can find. But

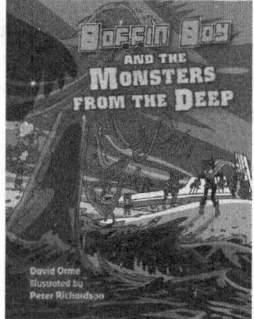

Courtesy of Ransom Publishing

Boffin Boy and Wu Pee are soon on the case; and when Wu Pee finds a secret weapon to use against the jellyfish, they set a trap.

Boffin Boy and the Red Wolf. Art by Peter Richardson. Ransom Publishing 2007 Un Illustration

Courtesy of Ransom Publishing

Grades: 2 3 4 5 6 **741.5; Fic**
1. Adventure graphic novels; 2. Science fiction graphic novels; 3. Superhero graphic novels; 4. Graphic novels; 5. Boffin Boy (Fictional character)
978-1-84167-616-6, $7.95

The evil Red Wolf is using TV to turn every wizard in the world into his slave. With their magic and money, nobody will be able to stop him. When Red Wolf captures ninja wizard Wu Pee, Boffin Boy is forced to use the same TV tricks on Red Wolf. Can Rick free the wizards and save TV?

Boffin Boy and the Time Warriors. Art by Peter Richardson. Ransom Publishing 2007 Un Illustration
Grades: 2 3 4 5 6
741.5; Fic

1. Adventure graphic novels; 2. Science fiction graphic novels; 3. Superhero graphic novels; 4. Graphic novels; 5. Boffin Boy (Fictional character)
978-1-84167-622-7, $7.95

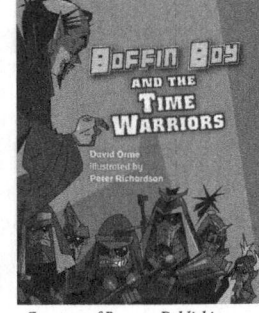

Courtesy of Ransom Publishing

An army of Japanese Samurai warriors travels from the past into our present. Boffin Boy must save the world from this ancient menace.

Boffin Boy and the Wizard of Edo. Art by Peter Richardson. Ransom Publishing 2006 Un Illustration
Grades: 2 3 4 5 6 **741.5; Fic**

1. Adventure graphic novels; 2. Science fiction graphic novels; 3. Superhero graphic novels; 4. Graphic novels; 5. Boffin Boy (Fictional character)
978-1-84167-614-2, $7.95

Boffin Boy and Wu Pee take on an evil wizard who has invented a camera that can steal people's minds. Then Wu Pee goes missing, too. Rick Shaw is a clever 14 year-old who is only interested in science. When his father is killed he vows to use his scientific skills to fight evil - as Boffin Boy.

Courtesy of Ransom Publishing

Mutants from the deep. Art by Peter Richardson. Stone Arch Books 2009 40p.
Grades: 2 3 4 5 6 7 **741.5; Fic**
1. Humorous graphic novels; 2. Science fiction graphic novels; 3. Graphic novels
978-1-4342-1269-6, $21.26

LC 2008-31346

Sailors dump barrels of toxic waste into the ocean, and the toxic waste causes jellyfish to mutate into giant, candy-and-ice-cream-loving monsters. Billy and his ninja master partner, Wu Hoo, must find a way to stop the mutants from grabbing all the sweets. The book includes some information about water pollution, discussion questions, and a glossary.

Originally published as Boffin Boy and the Monsters from the Deep by Ransom Publishing, 2006. Part of the Billy Blaster series.

Orr, Tamra
Manga artists. [by] Tamra Orr. Rosen Publishing Group 2009 64p. Illustration (Extreme careers)
Grades: 4 5 6 7 8 9 **741.5**
1. Graphic novels — Authorship; 2. Manga — Authorship; 3. Vocational guidance
978-1-4042-1854-3, $29.25

LC 2007-50666

This book provides an introduction to manga as a format of Japanese comics, including a brief history and mentions some famous mangaka (manga creators). It also provides information on what it's like to be a mangaka in Japan, and how to become a manga-style artist in the U.S.

Includes glossary and bibliographical references
Part of the Extreme Careers series

Osada, Yuko
Toto! the wonderful adventure vol.1. Del Rey Manga 2008 204p. Illustration
Grades: 7 8 9 10 11 12 **741.5; Fic**
1. Adventure graphic novels; 2. Dogs; 3. Humorous graphic novels; 4. Shonen manga; 5. Graphic novels
978-0-345-50147-9, $10.95

Orphaned Kakashi is a small-town boy with a big dream, to travel around the world like his long-lost explorer father. He's so determined to leave his little island home that he stows away on board a zeppelin. What he doesn't know is that the Man Chicken crime family has hijacked the zeppelin. What they don't know is that the zeppelin carries a cargo that the military wants back at any cost. Could it possibly be the cute little puppy Kakashi befriends in the cargo hold? When the military attacks the zeppelin, the Boss of the Man Chicken family straps the last parachute onto Kakashi and kicks him out of the burning aircraft. On the ground, Kakashi meets Dorothy, a girl about his age who names the puppy Toto. Neither of them knows why the military wants the dog so badly. Just what is Toto? The book includes some violence and Kakashi shouts a lot.

Toto! the wonderful adventure vol.2. Del Rey Manga 2008 202p. Illustration
Grades: 7 8 9 10 11 12 Adult **741.5; Fic**
1. Adventure graphic novels; 2. Manga; 3. Science fiction graphic novels; 4. Graphic novels
978-0-345-50555-2, $10.95

In this second volume, Dorothy and Kakashi have been trapped in a burning building by the Nassau Imperial Army, who are there to recover Toto, their "test subject." The cute little dog had turned into a gigantic monster, but Toto saves Dorothy and Kakashi. When the Army then tries to destroy Toto and Kakashi gets to him first, they merge, and the dog bracelet that had been around Toto's neck is now on Kakashi's right wrist. When danger threatens, Toto the monstrous weapon emerges from Kakashi's hand. The two kids flee to Dego City, hoping to catch a train to Emerald, but the Nassau Army has occupied the city and destroyed all the trains to use the metal for weapons. Kakashi and Dorothy meet Millica, an older girl who saves them, and the soldier Noil, who would much rather become a standup comedian. The book includes some violence and mild fan service.

Osborne, Wayne
FX. Art by John Byrne. IDW Publishing 2008 160p. Illustration
Grades: 7 8 9 10 11 12 Adult   **741.5; Fic**
1. Adventure graphic novels; 2. Humorous graphic novels; 3. Superhero graphic novels; 4. Graphic novels
978-1-60010-274-5, $19.99
Teenager Tom Talbot was playing with his best friend when Jack accidentally hit Tom so hard he went into a coma. When Tom recovers, he discovers that he's got the power to make what he imagines be real; he discovers this when they're playing around in an alley and Tom imagines he's got a bazooka and really destroys a dumpster. He cobbles together a masked costume, and finds himself fighting superpowered giant talking apes, nasty weapons-bearing lizards, and more. But someone notices him and decides he wants Tom's powers Lord Everos, the Father of Death. And it's not just Tom, either; Vicki, the class weirdo, does really talk with the dead, and Lord Everos wants her, too. And that's not the worst of it, for apparently Tom was never supposed to get the power of the thunderbolt, and a whole pantheon of heroes has just arrived to stop him. Oops again.

Ostrander, John
Star Wars: Clone Wars Volume 1: The Defense of Kamino. John Ostrander and Haden Blackman. Dark Horse Comics 2003 Un Illustration
Grades: 7 8 9 10 11 12 Adult   **741.5; Fic**
1. Adventure graphic novels; 2. Science fiction graphic novels; 3. Star Wars; 4. Graphic novels
1-56971-962-4, $14.95
Two undercover Jedi discover a Separatist plan to destroy the cloning facility on the watery world of Kamino, thus crippling the Republic's ability to maintain their clone army. Obi-Wan Kenobi and Anakin Skywalker are part of a Jedi fighter squadron sent to protect the installation. Meanwhile, Mace Windu, the leader of the Jedi Council, must deal with a rift in the Jedi ranks—a matter that reveals a Jedi traitor and a new Dark Jedi working in league with Dooku. Mace is considered one of the best swordsmen in the galaxy, but can he stand up to the sword master who taught him everything he knows—including the mysterious technique known as Vaapad. The book includes battle violence.
Volume 1 of 9

Star Wars: Clone Wars Volume 2: Victories and Sacrifices. Written by Haden Blackman and John Ostrander; Pencillers Tomás Giorello, Brian Ching, and Jan Duursema; Inkers Dan Parsons, Joe Weems, Curtis Arnold. Dark Horse Comics 2003 Un Illustration
Grades: 7 8 9 10 11 12 Adult   **741.5; Fic**
1. Adventure graphic novels; 2. Science fiction graphic novels; 3. Star Wars; 4. Graphic novels
1-56971-969-1, $14.95
From one of the swamp moons of Naboo, to the war-torn cityscapes of Brentaal IV, the battles of the Clone Wars have thrown the galaxy into turmoil. New Separatist threats, ranging from deadly biological weapons, to dark Jedi, to unkillable alien bounty hunters, have the loyalist Jedi and their clone troops pushed to their limits. This graphic

novel collection contains three separate, yet linked stories of heroism and sacrifice. The book includes battle violence.

Star Wars: Clone Wars Volume 3: Last Stand on Jabiim. Written by Haden Blackman and John Ostrander; Pencillers Brian Ching and Jan Duursema; Inkers Dan Parsons and Victor Llamas. Dark Horse Comics 2004 Un Illustration
Grades: 7 8 9 10 11 12 Adult   **741.5; Fic**
1. Adventure graphic novels; 2. Science fiction graphic novels; 3. Star Wars; 4. Graphic novels
1-59307-006-3, $14.95
General Obi-Wan Kenobi and his Padawan Anakin Skywalker find themselves in command of a regiment of Clone Troopers on the muddy battlefields of the rain world of Jabiim. With their supply lines stretched thin and reinforcements unable to land due to the perpetual storms, the Jedi and their army have become easy targets for the rebel Alto Stratus and his elite Nimbus warriors. The situation goes from bad to worse when General Kenobi is listed missing in action, and Anakin is teamed with a group of other masterless young Jedi on a doomed mission to hold the last line in the Republic's defense.

Star Wars: Clone Wars Volume 6: On the Fields of Battle. Written by John Ostrander; pencilled by Jan Duursema; inked by Dan Parsons; colored by Brad Anderson. Dark Horse Comics 2005 Un Illustration
Grades: 7 8 9 10 11 12 Adult   **741.5; Fic**
1. Adventure graphic novels; 2. Science fiction graphic novels; 3. Star Wars; 4. Graphic novels
1-59307-352-6, $17.95
Mace Windu leads an elite Jedi strike force against an army of trained killers in a demonstration of Jedi power and resolve... Aayla Secura must confront her former Master in an effort to retrieve the plans for a weapon that has already destroyedne world... Obi-Wan Kenobi and Anakin Skywalker must joins forces with a renegade Jedi to prevent a fleet of warships from falling into the hands of the enemy...

Star Wars: Clone Wars Volume 8: The Last Siege, the Final Truth. Written by John Ostrander; pencilled by Jan Duursema; inked by Dan Parsons; colored by Brad Anderson. Dark Horse Comics 2006 Un Illustration
Grades: 7 8 9 10 11 12 Adult   **741.5; Fic**
1. Adventure graphic novels; 2. Science fiction graphic novels; 3. Star Wars; 4. Graphic novels
1-59307-482-4, $17.95
Beneath the surface of this Outer Rim planet, the Dark Jedi Sora Bulq has begun cloning an army of Morgukai assassins. Unwilling to leave this grave new threat unchecked, the Jedi and their armies soon find themselves entrenched in a five-month siege. Now, time and resources have run out, and it's up to a crack team of Jedi, led by Quinlan Vos and Aayla Secura, to infiltrate the Separatist base. The book includes battle violence.

Star Wars: Clone Wars Volume 9: Endgame. Written by John Ostrander and Welles Hartley; art by Jan Duursema and Douglas Wheatley. Dark Horse Comics 2006 Un Illustration
Grades: 7 8 9 10 11 12 Adult   **741.5; Fic**
1. Adventure graphic novels; 2. Science fiction graphic novels; 3. Star Wars; 4. Graphic novels
978-1-59307-553-8, $17.95

Suddenly, clone troopers are turning on the Jedi and killing them; it's Order 66. In the jungles of the Wookiee homeworld Kashyyyk, Quinlan Vos wages a battle of impossible odds against his own troops to protect his loved ones. On the icy Outer Rim world of Toola, Jedi Master Kai Huddora takes a terrified Padawan into his charge after her own master falls to Order 66. Amidst the forests of New Plymto, Dass Jennir finds himself in league with a band of rebels he'd led attacks against only days before. And Darth Vader hunts for Obi Wan Kenobi.

Star Wars: Empire Volume One: Betrayal. Scott Allie and Ryan Benjamin. Dark Horse Comics 2003 Un Illustration
Grades: 7 8 9 10 11 12 Adult   **741.5; Fic**
1. Adventure graphic novels; 2. Science fiction graphic novels; 3. Star Wars; 4. Graphic novels
1-56971-964-0, $12.95
In the weeks before the events in Star Wars: A New Hope, as the Death Star is readied for its fateful first mission, a power-hungry cabal of Grand Moffs and Imperial Officers embark on a dangerous plan to kill Emperor Palpatine and Darth Vader and seize control of the Empire. When word that a Jedi has made an appearance on a backwater world lures Vader away from his master, the cabal makes its move. But even the galaxy isn't enough of a prize to sate the ambitions of some of the conspirators, and before long the would-be assassins are turning on one another. Their plans are further complicated by the actions of bounty hunter Boba Fett. And, of course, they may have fatally underestimated the cunning of their primary target: Emperor Palpatine.

Star Wars: Empire Volume Six: In the Shadows of Their Fathers. writers, Thomas Andrews, Scott Allie ; artists, Adriana Melo, Joe Corroney, Michel LaCombe. Dark Horse Comics 2006 Un Illustration
Grades: 7 8 9 10 11 12 Adult   **741.5; Fic**
1. Adventure graphic novels; 2. Science fiction graphic novels; 3. Star Wars; 4. Graphic novels
978-1-59307-627-6, $17.95
Luke Skywalker confronts the legacy of the Jedi father he never knew in an epic story involving Princess Leia, Darth Vader and the fate of an entire planet! When Luke and Leia travel to Jabiim recruiting allies for the fledgling Rebellion, they unwittingly set into motion events that will ignite one man's betrayal of his people, pit rebel hero against rebel hero and attract the attention of the Empire's deadliest enforcer - Darth Vader. The book includes battle violence.

Star Wars: Legacy, Volume One: Broken. Story, John Ostrander and Jan Duuresma ; script, John Ostrander ; pencils, Jan Duuresma ; inks, Dan Parsons ; colors, Brad Anderson ; lettering, Michael David Thomas ; cover art, Adam Hughes. Dark Horse Comics 2007 Un Illustration
Grades: 7 8 9 10 11 12   **741.5; Fic**
1. Adventure graphic novels; 2. Science fiction graphic novels; 3. Star Wars; 4. Graphic novels
978-1-59307-716-7, $17.95
125 years have passed since the events in Return of the Jedi and the days of the New Jedi Order. There is a new evil gripping the galaxy, shattering a resurgent Empire and seeking to destroy the last of the Jedi. Even as their power is failing, the Jedi hold onto one final hope, the last remaining heir to the Skywalker legacy: Cade, who has rejected the

way of the Jedi. The book's fighting action is at the same level as the motion picture series.

Otomo, Katsuhiro
    Hipira. Illustrated by Shinji Kimura. Dark Horse Press 2005 Un Illustration
Grades: 2 3 4 5 6   **741.5; Fic**
1. Adventure graphic novels; 2. Fantasy graphic novels; 3. Humorous graphic novels; 4. Vampires; 5. Graphic novels
1-59582-002-7, $13.95
In the vampire city of Salta, the sun never rises and all the vampire children love to stay up late. Hipira is a precocious young vampire whose best friend is a fairy named Soul, and their games, pranks, and adventures are extraordinary even for the inhabitants of this supernatural city. All the characters, even the monsters, look cute rather than scary.

Ottaviani, Jim
    Dignifying science: stories about women scientists. Written by Jim Ottaviani and illustrated by Donna Barr . . . [et al.]. G.T. Labs 2009 142p. Illustration
Grades: 6 7 8 9 10 11 12
920
1. Biographical graphic novels; 2. Women scientists; 3. Graphic novels
978-0-9788037-3-5, $16.95; 0-9788037-3-5

Courtesy Jim Ottaviani and G.T. Labs; art by Ramona Fradon and Linda Medley

    Ottaviani provides biographical sketches of women scientists such as Lise Meitner, Rosalind Franklin, Barbara McClintock, and Hedy Lamarr (yes, the actress was also an inventor); all the stories are illustrated by women comics artists, including Lea Hernandez, Linda Medley, Anne Timmons, and others.
    First published 1999

    Levitation: physics and psychology in the service of deception. [by] Jim Ottaviani and Janine Johnston; lettering by Tom Orzechowski. G. T. Labs 2007 71p. Illustration
Grades: 6 7 8 9 10 11 12 Adult   **793.8; 741.5**
1. Magic tricks; 2. Graphic novels
978-0-9788037-0-4, $12.95
    This book tells the story of how John Neville Maskelyne developed the stage magic trick of levitation, of the American Harry Kellar, who acquired the trick through devious means, of the old school engineer Guy Jarrett, who perfected the magicians' tricks, and of stage performer Howard Thurston, who inherited the levitation trick from Kellar and ruined it. Or did he" The book includes notes and reprints of old posters and other information on the magicians.
    Includes bibliographical references
    A General Tektronics Labs book

Primates: The Fearless Science of Jane Goodall, Dian Fossey, and Biruté Galdikas. Jim Ottaviani; illustrated by Maris Wicks. First Second 2013 133 p. Color; Illustration
Grades: 5 6 7 8 9 10 11 12 Adult   **741.5; 599.8**
1. Fossey, Dian, 1932-1985; 2. Galdikas, Birute, 1946-; 3. Goodall, Jane, 1934-; 4. Primates
1596438657; 9781596438651, $19.99
LC 2013427678

This nonfiction graphic novel, by Jim Ottaviani, illustrated by Maris Wicks, presents an "account of the three greatest primatologists of the last century: Jane Goodall, Dian Fossey, and Birut? Galdikas. These three ground-breaking researchers were all students of the great Louis Leakey, and each made profound contributions to primatology—and to our own understanding of ourselves." (Publisher's note)

"More story than study, the book provides an accessible introduction to Goodall's, Fossey's and Galdikas' lives and work." Kirkus

Includes bibliographical references, page 138

★ **T-Minus:** the race to the moon. [illustrated by] Zander Cannon, Kevin Cannon. Aladdin 2009 124p. Illustration
Grades: 4 5 6 7 8 9 10 11 12 Adult
629.45; 741.5
1. Apollo project; 2. Gemini project; 3. Space flight to the moon; 4. Graphic novels
978-1-4169-8682-9, $21.99; 1-4169-8682-0; 978-1-4169-4960-2 (pa), $12.99; 1-4169-4960-7 (pa)

Courtesy of Aladdin Press

LC 2009-920999

Ottaviani, Zander Cannon, and Kevin Cannon show what happened when the U.S. and the U.S.S.R. started the space race in the 1950s, and how it progressed to the NASA Apollo 11 mission which landed two men on the moon in July of 1969.

"Organized as a countdown, making the outcome seem inevitable, the frequent, prominent sidebars list a type of rocket, the duration of its flight, and whether the mission was a success or a failure. There are more than 30 attempts chronicled, and the shift between Soviet and U.S. successes creates an interesting balance in the narrative. . . . Ottaviani is particular with facts and eager to inspire readers with regard to the scientific process." SLJ

Page, Philip
Picture This! Shakespeare: A Midsummer Night's Dream. Barron's Educational Series, Inc. 2002 58p. Illustration
Grades: 7 8 9 10 11 12   **741.5; 822.3**
1. Drama; 2. Shakespeare, William, 1564-1616 — Adaptations
0-7641-3142-7, $7.95

This adaptation combines pages done in graphic novel format with extensive excerpts from Shakespeare's A Midsummer Night's Dream to provide an introductory reading experience for younger and struggling students. Each scene presented in the book is preceded by a brief summary, words that modern teens would find unfamiliar are briefly defined on the page, literary terms are explained.

Picture This! Shakespeare: Macbeth. Barron's Educational Series, Inc. 2002 56p. Illustration
Grades: 7 8 9 10 11 12   **741.5; 822.3**
1. Drama; 2. Shakespeare, William, 1564-1616 — Adaptations
978-0-7641-3140-0, $7.99

This adaptation combines pages done in graphic novel format with extensive excerpts from Shakespeare's Macbeth to provide an introductory reading experience for younger and struggling students. Each scene presented in the book is preceded by a brief summary, words that modern teens would find unfamiliar are briefly defined on the page, literary terms are explained.

Picture This! Shakespeare: Romeo and Juliet. Barron's Educational Series, Inc. 2005 58p. Illustration
Grades: 7 8 9 10 11 12   **741.5; 822.3**
1. Drama; 2. Shakespeare, William, 1564-1616 — Adaptations
978-0-7641-3144-8, $7.99

This adaptation combines pages done in graphic novel format with extensive excerpts from Shakespeare's Romeo and Juliet to provide an introductory reading experience. Each scene presented in the book is preceded by a brief summary, words that modern teens would find unfamiliar are briefly defined on the page, literary terms are explained.

Picture This! Shakespeare: Twelfth Night or, What You Will. Barron's Educational Series, Inc. 2005 58p. Illustration
Grades: 7 8 9 10 11 12   **822.3; 741.5**
1. Shakespeare, William, 1564-1616 — Adaptations
978-0-7641-3147-9, $7.95

This adaptation combines pages done in graphic novel format with extensive excerpts from Shakespeare's Twelfth Night to provide an introductory reading experience for younger and struggling students. Each scene presented in the book is preceded by a brief summary, words that modern teens would find unfamiliar are briefly defined on the page, literary terms are explained.

Picture This! Shakespeare: Twelfth Night Teacher's Resource Book. Barron's Educational Series, Inc. 2005 59p. Illustration
Grades: 7 8 9 10 11 12   **741.5; 371.33**
1. Drama; 2. Teaching — Aids and devices; 3. Graphic novels
0-7641-3148-6, $9.95

Twelfth Night, the Shakespearean drama that is in the curriculum of many high schools in the country, is an offering in Barron's "Picture This! Shakespeare" series. This manual supplements Barron's "Picture This: Twelfth Night," a book presented in graphic novel style for students' use. The manual offers teachers suggestions for classroom discussions, quizzes, and activities related to the play, including reproducible activity sheets.

Panev, Aleksandar
 Queen Nzinga. Art by Thomas Stefflbauer. Harcourt Achieve/Steck-Vaughn 2007 48p. Illustration
Grades: 3 4 5 6 7 8   **741.5; Fic**
 1. Adventure graphic novels; 2. Africa — History; 3. Graphic novels
 978-1-4190-3214-1, $8.99
 Nzinga is a young princess in the African kingdom of Ndongo. When her friend Kakengo is kidnapped by Portuguese slave traders, she makes a vow to protect her people against slavery. Nzinga lived from 1582 to 1663 in the land now called Angola, and she fought against the slave traders. This historical fiction graphic novel includes prose intervals with information about Africa, the slave trade, and some other African leaders.
 Part of the Timeline Graphic Novels series.

Park, Eun Ah
 Bird Kiss Vol. 1. Tokyopop 2006 Un Illustration
Grades: 8 9 10 11 12 Adult   **741.5; Fic**
 1. Humorous graphic novels; 2. Manwha; 3. Romance graphic novels; 4. Graphic novels
 1-59816-491-0, $9.99
 Miyoul is a feisty, boy-crazed girl who is in love with Guelin, a talk, dark, and handsome high school boy. But Heerack—short, scrawny, and too dorky to be given the time of day—has the hots for Miyoul, and worships her every move. Of course, Miyoul is awfully embarrassed by him and tries to avoid him like the plague. And of course, it doesn't work. This Korean manwha is filled with the trials and tribulations of high school—and some wacky, slapstick moments.

Park, Min-Seo
 Blazin' Barrels Volume 1. Tokyopop 2005 186p. Illustration
Grades: 8 9 10 11 12 Adult   **741.5; Fic**
 1. Adventure graphic novels; 2. Science fiction graphic novels; 3. Western graphic novels; 4. Graphic novels
 1-59532-559-X, $9.99
 Sting may look harmless and naive, but he's really an excellent fighter and a wannabe bounty hunter in the futuristic Wild West. When he comes across a notice that advertises a reward for the criminal outfit named Gold Romany, he decides that capturing the all-girl gang of bad guys is his ticket to fame and fortune. The book includes some strong language and sexual suggestiveness, along with some violence.

Parker, Jake
 ★ **Missile** Mouse: the star crusher. Graphix 2010 172p. (Missile Mouse)
Grades: 3 4 5 6   **741; Fic; 741.5**
 1. Adventure graphic novels; 2. Mice; 3. Science fiction graphic novels; 4. Graphic novels
 978-0-545-11714-2, $21.99; 0-545-11714-3;
 978-0-545-11715-9 (pa), $10.99; 0-545-11715-1 (pa)
 "When his mission to recover an ancient star compass goes wrong, intrepid Galactic Security Agent Missile Mouse finds himself saddled with a partner. . . . The two are to retrieve a missing scientist who holds the key to a horrible weapon, the Star Crusher, in his hereditary memory. . . . [This

is] a gem in story and art. Bright, action-filled, at times wordless panels keep the pages turning. Intelligent space opera and a realistically rounded hero will have young fans of the future demanding the next volume." Kirkus

Parker, Jeff
 The **Avengers:** finding Zemo. Art by Manuel Garcia and Scott Koblish. ABDO Publishing Company/Spotlight 2008 Un Illustration
Grades: 4 5 6 7 8 9   **741.5; Fic**
 1. Avengers (Fictional characters); 2. Captain America (Fictional character); 3. Hulk (Fictional character); 4. Iron Man (Fictional character); 5. Spider-Man (Fictional character); 6. Storm (Fictional character); 7. Superhero graphic novels; 8. Wolverine (Fictional character); 9. Graphic novels
 978-1-59961-383-3, $21.35
                    LC 2007-20254
 A ceremony to honor Captain America is attacked by his old enemy, Baron Zemo, in a new giant attack robot. While the Avengers battle the robot, Zemo kidnaps Captain America. Now, the rest of the team must find Zemo and Cap. This Avengers team includes Storm, Spider-Man, Iron Man, Wolverine, the Hulk, and Giant-Girl. This is a revised, hardbound edition of the Marvel Adventures comic book.
 Part of the Avengers series

 The **Avengers:** heroes assembled, v1. Artist, Manuel Garcia. Marvel 2006 Illustration
Grades: 5 6 7 8 9   **741.5; Fic**
 1. Avengers (Fictional characters); 2. Captain America (Fictional character); 3. Spider-Man (Fictional character); 4. Storm (Fictional character); 5. Wolverine (Fictional character)
 978-0-7851-2306-4, $6.99; 0-7851-2306-7

 Fantastic four: law of the jungle. Manuel Garcia, pencils ; Scott Koblish, inks ; A. Crossley, colors. ABDO Publishing Company/Spotlight 2008 Un Illustration
Grades: 4 5 6 7 8 9   **741.5; Fic**
 1. Black Panther (Fictional character); 2. Fantastic Four (Fictional characters); 3. Superhero graphic novels; 4. Graphic novels
 978-1-59961-390-1, $21.35
                    LC 2007-20255
 The Fantastic Four find themselves fighting the Black Panther and discover that the rare metal they had purchased was stolen from Wakandia, the Black Panther's home country in Africa. When they investigate, they discover the thieves plan to steal again, and the team heads to Wakandia to help the Black Panther stop the criminals. If only he'll stop and listen to them before destroying them. This is a revised, hardbound edition of the Marvel Adventures comic book issue.
 Part of the Fantastic Four series

 Meteor men. Written by Jeff Parker; illustrated by Sandy Jarrell; colored by Kevin Volo; lettered by Crank!. Oni Press 2014 133 p. Color; Illustration
Grades: 8 9 10 11   **741.5; Fic**
 1. Extraterrestrial beings; 2. Human-alien encounters — Fiction; 3. Science fiction graphic novels
 1620101513; 9781620101513, $19.99

Eisner Nominee: Best Publication for Teens (2015)

"On a summer night, Alden Baylor sits in a field watching the largest meteor shower in human history. What begins as teenage adventure becomes something more—the celestial event brings travelers who will change the world completely, and Alden discovers a connection to one of them. How does a young man who had to grow up fast handle the invasion of his planet? Can Alden keep humanity from oblivion?" (Publisher's note)

"Parker combines the familiar concept with gentle domesticity and deliberate humanism, thus circumventing clich? and providing an accessible perspective to the logical and realistic extensions of such an event." SLJ

Pascoe, Jim

Hellboy Animated Vol. 2: The Judgment Bell. Written by Jim Pascoe, art by Ricky Lacy. Dark Horse Comics 2007 Un Illustration
Grades: 7 8 9 10 11 12   **741.5; Fic**
1. Fantasy graphic novels; 2. Hellboy (Fictional character); 3. Horror graphic novels; 4. Graphic novels
978-1-59307-799-0, $6.25

In "The Judgment Bell," written by Jim Pascoe and drawn by Rick Lacy a figure from Dr. Broom's past wreaks havoc on the children of a small Polish village. And in a backup story written and drawn by Hellboy Animated creator Tad Stones, a young Hellboy is once again stirred to heroism by the radio adventures of Lobster Johnson, only to cause chaos.

Undertown Volume 1. Art by Jake Myler. Tokyopop 2007 Un Illustration
Grades: 7 8 9 10 11 12   **741.5; Fic**
1. Adventure graphic novels; 2. Fantasy graphic novels; 3. Graphic novels
978-1-4278-0103-6, $9.99

Sama is so sad that tears have literally stained his cheeks. His father has congestive heart failure, and doctors only give him a month to live. With nowhere to turn, Sama grabs his teddy bear and crawls under his bed...magically entering a portal to a fantastic realm called Undertown, where his teddy bear comes to life. Sama looks for the Sugar Stone: a "secret something" that might be able to heal his dad. But The Cloud—the wicked leader of the Insect Insurgents—hunts for the Stone, as well ... This global manga has some violence and darker moments that could disturb younger readers.

Patterson, James

Daniel X: alien hunter: a graphic novel. James Patterson & Leopoldo Gout ; art by Klaus Lyngeled, Jon Girin & Joseph McLamb. Little, Brown and Company 2008 128p. Illustration
Grades: 6 7 8 9 10 11 12   **741.5; Fic**
1. Extraterrestrial beings; 2. Science fiction graphic novels; 3. Graphic novels
978-0-316004-25-1, $9.99; 0-31600-425-1

When his parents were murdered, young Daniel inherited the List of Alien Outlaws and took over his father's job as Alien Hunter; his family were also aliens, and Daniel possesses the ability to shape-shift and to conjure up anybody and anything out of thin air. He's been hunting aliens on the list for years, and now he's in Tokyo, going after Number 7. That alien has been running a "game" in which he releases an alien creature for alien bounty hunters to hunt, and the more destruction they cause in the process, the better. This time is different, however, when Daniel learns that Number 7 has a teenage son, and that son is somewhat alienated from his father. This graphic novel is a companion to the novel The Dangerous Days of Daniel X, which is the first of a series of novels.

Pearson, Luke

★ **Hilda** and the Black Hound. By Luke Pearson. Flying Eye Books 2014 64 p. Color; Illustration (Hildafolk)
Grades: 3 4 5 6 7   **741.5**
1. City and town life — Fiction; 2. Dogs — Fiction; 3. Girls — Fiction
9781909263185, $24; 1909263184

In this graphic novel by Luke Pearson, "Hilda . . . meets the Nisse: a mischievous but charismatic bunch of misfits who occupy a world beside—but also somehow within—our own, and where the rules of physics don't quite match up. Meanwhile, on the streets of Trolberg, a dark specter looms." (Publisher's note)

"The full-size volume offers a minimum of 10 panels of varying sizes per page. Darker shades dominate when the beast lurks, and earth tones and reds and oranges when the characters go about their daily business. Touches of humor abound in both images and dialogue." SLJ

Hilda and the Midnight Giant. Luke Pearson. Nobrow Press 2012 40p Color illustration
Grades: 4 5 6 7 8   **741.5**
1. Forests and forestry — Fiction; 2. Giants — Fiction; 3. Girls — Fiction
1907704256; 9781907704253, $24.00

In this book, the "protagonist finds her world turned upside down as she faces the prospect of leaving her snow-capped birthplace for the hum of the megalopolis, where her mother (an architect) has been offered a prestigious job. During Hilda's daily one-and-a-half hour trek to school she looks for ways to stall her mother's decision. She conspires with the beings of the mystical Blue Forest to delay the inevitable. Will they help or hinder her? More importantly, who is this mysterious Midnight Giant?

★ **Hilda** and the troll. Luke Pearson. Flying Eye Books 2013 40 p. Color; Illustration (Hildafolk)
Grades: 3 4 5 6
74.5
1. Adventure fiction; 2. Explorers — Fiction; 3. Trolls — Fiction
1909263141; 9781909263147, $18.95

This book, by Luke Pearson, is "about an adventurous little girl and her habit of befriending anything, no matter how curious it might seem. While on an expedition to illustrate the magical creatures of

Courtesy of Flying Eye Books

the mountains around her home, Hilda spots a mountain troll. As the blue-haired explorer sits and sketches, she slowly starts to nod off. By the time she wakes up, the troll has totally disappeared and, even worse, Hilda is lost in a snowstorm." (Publisher's note)

"The art is as whimsical as the protagonist, and the bright colors enhance this comic book's magical-realistic effect." Horn Book

Originally appearing in print in 2010 as Hildafolk
Other titles about Hilda are: Hilda and the Midnight Giant (2012); Hilda and the Bird Parade (2013); Hilda and the Black Hound (2014)

Peirce, Lincoln
Big Nate: game on!. By Lincoln Peirce. Andrews McMeel Pub., LLC 2013 224 p. Color illustration
Grades: 1 2 3 4 5 6 **Fic; 741.5/973**
1. Games — Fiction; 2. Sports — Fiction
1449427774; 9781449427771, $9.99
LC 2012952339
This book, written and illustrated by Lincoln Peirce, features a collection of his "Big Nate" comic strip. "To sixth-grader Nate Wright, life is one big game. From fine-tuning his trash-talking skills on the basketball court to his cocky [attitude] in the soccer goal, Nate can be a bigger challenge to his teammates than their opponents." The book features "Nate and his friends" mostly hapless sports encounters." (Publisher's note)

Pet avengers classic
Marvel Entertainment 2009 208p. Illustration
Grades: 7 8 9 10 11 12 Adult **741.5; Fic**
1. Adventure graphic novels; 2. Pets; 3. Superhero graphic novels; 4. Graphic novels
9780785139669, $24.99
This volume collects the various Marvel Pets stories, from 1960 to 2007, with each story featuring a different pet, from Lockjaw the teleporting dog to Kitty Pryde's dragon Lockheed to Brightwind the winged horse, and many more. Lockjaw, Lockheed, Redwing the falcon, the cat named Niels, and Zabu the saber tooth tiger all starred in th 2009 mini series titled Pet Avengers. Some of the stories in this collection include violence.

Peters, Stephanie True
Rapunzel: the graphic novel. By Stephanie Peters; illustrated by Jeffrey Stewart Timmins. Stone Arch Books 2009 P. cm. (Graphic spin)
Grades: 3 4 5 6 7 8 **741.5; Fic**
1. Fairy tales; 2. Folklore; 3. Graphic novels
978-1-4342-1194-1 (lib bdg), $21.26; 1-4342-1194-0 (lib bdg); 978-1-4342-1392-1 (pa), $4.95; 1-4342-1392-7 (pa)
LC 2008-32047
When a long-married couple finally expect a baby, the pregnant wife craves the rampion from the witch's garden next door. Her craving becomes so desperate that the husband steals the rampion for his wife, only to get caught by the witch, who demands the child when she is born, Rapunzel (another name for rampion) grows up knowing no parent but the witch, but when she accidently catches a glimpse of the outside world, the witch conjures up a tall

tower with no stairs and keeps Rapunzel there. The girl's hair has grown so long over the years, that the witch uses it as her ladder. A prince wanders by, watches the witch, and uses her command to gain access to the tower. The graphic novel adaption follows the version made famous by the Brothers Grimm; the book includes information on different versions of the tale from Italy and France. The art uses a fairly dark palette and stylized figures with dark circles for eyes.
Part of the Graphic Spin series.

Storm of the century: a Hurricane Katrina story. Illustrated by Jesus Aburto. Stone Arch Books 2009 56p.
Grades: 3 4 5 6 7 **741.5; Fic**
1. Hurricane Katrina, 2005; 2. New Orleans (La); 3. Graphic novels
978-1-4342-1164-4, $23.93
LC 2008-32071
When Hurricane Katrina hits New Orleans, fourteen-year-old Ricky Thompson and his family try to leave the city, but their car overheats in the backed-up traffic. They end up at the Superdome, where the National Guard has set up a shelter for the thousands of people who couldn't, or didn't, leave in time. Conditions in the stadium rapidly worsen even as the city floods when the levees fail. Ricky uses his new digital camera to take as many pictures as he can of everything as he and his family cope with the horrible conditions. This book is a hybrid of prose text and comic book format pages as the story depicts the impact of Katrina on one family.
Part of the Graphic Flash line from Stone Arch Books

Petersen, David
★ **Mouse** Guard: Fall 1152. Archaia Studios Press 2007 Un Illustration
Grades: 5 6 7 8 **741.5; Fic**
1. Fantasy graphic novels; 2. Mice; 3. Graphic novels
978-1-932386-57-8, $24.95; 1-932386-57-2
Eisner Award: Best Publication for Kids (2008)
In a medieval world populated by animals, mice have their own civilization but live in constant peril from predators. They live in hidden towns protected by the Guard, who also escort travelers between towns. Three young members of the Guard, Lieam, Saxon, and Kenzie, go in search of a missing grain merchant. They find him dead in the belly of a snake who tried to eat them; but they also find evidence that the dead merchant is a traitor. Now they need to find out to whom he was betraying the Guard and why. While this story features animals and is suitable for most readers who can handle some fighting action, there's nothing cute or Disney-esque in the art. Characters die, this is a serious story, but readers who have read Bone or the Harry Potter series can handle the action in this book. This is the first in a series.
Followed by: Mouse Guard: Winter 1152 (2009)
Originally published as Mouse Guard issues #1-6.

Mouse Guard: Winter 1152. Story & art by David Petersen. Archaia Studios Press 2009 Un Illustration
Grades: 5 6 7 8 **741.5; 741**
978-1-932386-74-5, $24.95; 1-932386-74-2
Followed by: Mouse Guard: The black axe (2013)
"In the Winter of 1152, the Mouse Guard face a food and supply shortage threatening the lives of many mouse

through a cold and icy season. Some of the Guard's finest—Saxon, Kenzie, Lieam, and Sadie, led by Celanawe, the legendary Black Axe—traverse the snow-blanketed territories acting as diplomats to improve relations between the mouse cities and the Guard, and find themselves on a race against time to deliver crucial medicines." (Publisher's note)

Mouse guard; 3: The Black Axe. By David Petersen. Archaia Entertainment, LLC 2013 192 p.

Grades: 5 6 7 8   **741.5; Fic**
1. Adventure fiction; 2. Fantasy fiction; 3. Mice — Fiction
1936393069; 9781936393060, $24.95
Harvey Award: Best Graphic Album of Previously Published Work (2014)

This book, by David Petersen, part of the Eisner Award-winning fantasy comic series, tells "the tale of wise oldfur and longtime Mouse Guard member Celanawe, as he fulfills the promise made to young Lieam to detail the day his paw first touched the legendary weapon, the Black Axe. The arrival of distant kin takes Celanawe on an adventure that will carry him across the sea to uncharted waters and lands, all while unraveling the legend of Farrer, the blacksmith who forged the mythical weapon." (Publisher's note)

"[N]ewcomers and fans alike will find much to explore in Petersen's finely wrought artwork, high-stakes intrigue, and derring-do tale." Booklist

Mouse guard; volume 1: legends of the guard. Jeremy Bastian, Ted Naifeh, Alex Sheikman, et al. Archaia Entertainment 2010 144 p. Color illustration

Grades: 5 6 7 8   **741.5**
1. Adventure fiction; 2. Mice — Fiction; 3. Short stories — Collections
1932386947; 9781932386943, $19.95
Eisner Award: Best Anthology (2011)

"Petersen turns to the tested and reliable bar story as a framing device to allow other writers and artists to play in his Mouse Guard universe, where heroic mice heroes are set in a world of epic fantasy.... One night barkeep June ... stages a story-telling contest. What follows are thirteen tales of danger and adventure, as protagonists contend against the predators around them and the flaws that divide mouse from mouse." (Publisher's note)

"More than just supplemental material, this book broadens Petersen's magnificently imagined miniature world and is a welcome addition for any collection that values quality, all-ages graphic novels." Booklist

Mouse guard; volume 2: legends of the guard. Archaia Entertainment 2010 144 p. Color; Illustration

Grades: 5 6 7 8   **741.5**
1. Adventure fiction; 2. Mice — Fiction; 3. Short stories — Collections
1936393263; 9781936393268, $19.95
Eisner Nominee: Best Publication for Kids (2014)
Harvey Nominee: Best Anthology (2014)
Harvey Nominee: Best Continuing or Limited Series (2014)

"Inside the June Alley Inn, located in the western mouse city of Barkstone, mice gather to tell tales, each trying to outdo the other. A competition, of sorts, begins. The rules: Every story must contain one truth, one lie, and have never

been told in that tavern before. With the winner getting his bar tab cleared, fantastic stories are spun throughout the evening!" (Publisher's note)

"The art styles of the ensuing stories are all over the map, from the elegant, tapestry-worthy The Battle of the Hawk's Mouse & the Fox's Mouse, by Jeremy Bastian, to the joltingly cartoony A Mouse Named Fox, from Katie Cook. In substance, the stories are equally varied, but all champion the heroism of the noble mouse warriors and even include a couple clever takes on classics." Booklist

Peterson, Christine
The **U.S.** Constitution. Illustrated by Brian Bascle. Capstone Press 2009 32p. Illustration (Graphic library)

Grades: 3 4 5 6 7 8   **342; 741.5**
1. United States — Constitution; 2. United States — Politics and government; 3. Graphic novels
978-1-4296-1984-4, $32
                                    LC 2008-487

This graphic format book uses irreverently humorous captions and dialog and provides young readers with an introduction to the U. S. Constitution. The book covers how and why it was written, how the Bill of Rights came to be, describes the three branches of government, how amendments are passed, and how the country protects the Constitution. It includes a short timeline, a glossary, and a list of books for further reading.

Part of the Graphic Library Cartoon Nation series

Peterson, Scott
Batman Adventures Vol. 1: Rogues' Gallery. DC Comics 2004 112p. Illustration

Grades: 4 5 6 7 8 9   **741.5; Fic**
1. Batman (Fictional character); 2. Catwoman (Fictional character); 3. Joker (Fictional character); 4. Superhero graphic novels; 5. Graphic novels
9781401203290, $6.95

Gotham City's greatest villains, including the Joker, Harley Quinn, Catwoman, the Penguin, Poison Ivy, and Ra's al Ghul, all take their turn against the World's Greatest Detective. Crime never sleeps, and neither does Batman.

Petrucha, Stefan
Nancy Drew vol. 12: dress reversal. Art by Sho Murase. NBM/Papercutz 2008 Un Illustration

Grades: 3 4 5 6 7 8   **741.5; Fic**
1. Adventure graphic novels; 2. Drew, Nancy (Fictional character); 3. Mystery graphic novels; 4. Graphic novels
978-1-59707-086-6, $7.95

Nancy buys a fancy formal dress for a charity fundraiser, but when she and her friends Bess and George arrive at Deirdre Shannon's house for the event, they discover that Deirdre and Nancy are wearing the same dress. This is bad for Deirdre, who is already jealous of Nancy. Then, when Nancy leaves the party, Bess and George watch helplessly as Nancy is kidnapped. Can they solve the mystery without Nancy?

Nancy Drew, girl detective #15: Tiger counter. Stefan Petrucha & Sarah Kinney, writers ; Sho Murase, artist. Papercutz 2008 Un Illustration

Grades: 3 4 5 6 7 8 9   **741.5; Fic**

1. Drew, Nancy (Fictional character); 2. Mystery graphic novels; 3. Tigers; 4. Graphic novels
978-1-59707-119-2, $12.95; 978-1-59707-118-5 (pa), $7.95

Due to a lack of mysteries to keep them occupied, Nancy, Bess, and George have been volunteering at the River Heights Animal Protection Center, where Jack Kingsley has been rescuing wild animals. They get a rescue call, only to find that old Mrs. Eartha has a house full of cats. Then, while driving back to town, they come upon a wrecked truck, and the driver says he was transporting a tiger that escaped. Jack hunts it with a tranquilizer gun, but Nancy soon finds more tiger tracks. Just how many tigers were in that truck, and why were they being transported to River Heights?

Nancy Drew, Girl Detective #1: The Demon of River Heights. Stefan Petrucha, writer ; Sho Murase, artist. NBM/Papercutz 2005 Un Illustration
Grades: 4 5 6 7 8 9   **741.5; Fic**
  1. Adventure graphic novels; 2. Mystery graphic novels; 3. Graphic novels
  1-59707-004-1, $12.95; 1-59707-000-9, $7.95

Everyone's favorite girl detective makes her graphic novel debut. Nancy also makes her debut in a horror film concerning a monstrous River Heights urban legend " but is it really an urban legend, or does the River Heights Demon truly exist" And will Nancy, Bess, and George live long enough to find out? This graphic novel series updates Nancy and her friends to the twenty-first century, but she's still a klutz.

Nancy Drew: Girl Detective #2: Writ in Stone. Stefan Petrucha, writer ; Sho Murase, artist. NBM/Papercutz 2005 112p. Illustration
Grades: 3 4 5 6 7 8 9   **741.5; Fic**
  1. Drew, Nancy (Fictional character); 2. Mystery graphic novels; 3. Graphic novels
  978-1-59707-006-5, $12.95; 978-1-59707-002-7 (pb)

It's double trouble for America's favorite girl detective when Owen Zucker, a sweet young boy Nancy has often babysat, is missing and " a shore stone marker found on the coast of California, which may prove the Chinese discovered America in 1421, before Columbus, is stolen. Will Nancy, with the help of her best friends, Bess and George, be able to solve two baffling mysteries at the same time, while all of River Heights is watching?

Nancy Drew: Girl Detective #3: The Haunted Dollhouse. Sho Murase, artist. NBM/Papercutz 2005 112p. Illustration
Grades: 3 4 5 6 7 8 9   **741.5; Fic**
  1. Drew, Nancy (Fictional character); 2. Mystery graphic novels; 3. Graphic novels
  978-1-59707-009-6, $12.95; 978-1-59707-008-9 (pb)

River Heights is celebrating 'Nostalgia Week' and everyone in town is dressing up and acting like it was 1930 - including Nancy, Bess, and George. Nancy even drives a roadster (just as the original Nancy Drew did in the novels 75 years before). But when scenes of crimes displayed in Emma Blavatsky's antique dollhouse start coming true, Nancy has a full-blown mystery on her hands. Nancy's shocked when she stakes out the dollhouse, and witnesses a doll version of herself murdered. Will that scene become reality too?

Nancy Drew: Girl Detective #4: The Girl Who Wasn't There. Sho Murase, artist. NBM/Papercutz 2005 112p. Illustration
Grades: 3 4 5 6 7 8 9   **741.5; Fic**
  1. Drew, Nancy (Fictional character); 2. Mystery graphic novels; 3. Graphic novels
  978-1-59707-013-3, $12.95; 978-1-59707-012-2 (pb)

Nancy gets a call for help late one night from a girl she befriended over the phone when getting technical support to help fix her computer. When the line goes dead, Nancy is determined to get to the bottom of things. Soon, Nancy, her Dad, and friends George and Bess are on their way to India to find Kalpana, the girl who wasn't there. Then Nancy is captured by Sahadev the crime lord, who wants to sacrifice her to Kali.

Nancy Drew: Girl Detective #5: The Fake Heir. Stefan Petrucha, writer ; Daniel Vaughn Ross, artist. NBM/Papercutz 2006 112p. Illustration
Grades: 3 4 5 6 7 8 9   **741.5; Fic**
  1. Drew, Nancy (Fictional character); 2. Mystery graphic novels; 3. Graphic novels
  978-1-59707-025-6, $12.95; 978-1-59707-024-9 (pb)

Nancy, Bess and George find the wreck of an old yacht with a safe inside full of jewelry worth a small fortune. Jack and Amelia Druthers, who were clients of Nancy's dad Carson Drew, owned the yacht. Their will leaves everything to Anton Druthers, specifically excluding his wife Tanya (whom the cousins hated), but no one's seen him for ten years and the rumor is that Mrs. Druthers murdered him. Things take a surprising turn when suddenly Mr. Druthers reappears. But then Mrs. Druthers disappears. Can Nancy Drew solve the mystery of the fake heir? And what does that spider bite have to do with anything?

Nancy Drew: Girl Detective #6: Mr. Cheeters is Missing. Stefan Petrucha, writer ; Sho Murase, artist. NBM/Papercutz 2006 112p. Illustration
Grades: 3 4 5 6 7 8 9   **741.5; Fic**
  1. Drew, Nancy (Fictional character); 2. Mystery graphic novels; 3. Graphic novels
  978-1-59707-031-7, $12.95; 978-1-59707-030-0 (pb)

When the eccentric Blanche Porter reports that her beloved Mr. Cheeters has vanished, it isn't a standard missing persons case. As Nancy Drew soon discovers, Mr. Cheeters is a pet chimp. Or is he" Based on a preliminary investigation and information obtained from Blanche's brother, Lawrence, the River Heights police dismiss the case as bogus, doubting that there ever was a Mr. Cheeters to begin with. But when Nancy Drew discovers there's a missing diamond necklace as well, she's on the case. Can Nancy, along with Bess and George, recover the great ape and the necklace, or has Blanche Porter made a monkey out of Nancy Drew?

Nancy Drew: Girl Detective #7: The Charmed Bracelet. Daniel Vaughn Ross, artist. NBM/Papercutz 2006 112p. Illustration
Grades: 3 4 5 6 7 8 9   **741.5; Fic**
  1. Drew, Nancy (Fictional character); 2. Mystery graphic novels; 3. Graphic novels

978-1-59707-037-9, $12.95; 978-1-59707-036-2 (pb)

Ned Nickerson has been arrested for shoplifting, and Nancy Drew is threatened with a lawsuit. A rare computer chip has been stolen from Rackham Industries. It all gets even more exciting when Nancy receives a mysterious charm bracelet in the mail - and soon a crime is committed for each charm. Will Nancy, even with the help of Bess and George, be able to find the real culprit and save Ned?

Nancy Drew: Girl Detective #8: Global Warning. Stefan Petrucha, writer ; Sho Murase, artist. NBM/Papercutz 2006 112p. Illustration

Grades: 3 4 5 6 7 8 9   741.5; Fic
1. Drew, Nancy (Fictional character); 2. Mystery graphic novels; 3. Graphic novels
978-1-59707-052-2, $12.95; 978-1-59707-051-5 (pb)

At a new Bio-Dome facility in River Heights, Nancy, Bess, and George get swept up in a mystery involving five different world environments encased within giant domes, animals and all. It's founded and funded by famed environmentalist billionaire, Cheri Goale. But before the Bio-Dome officially opens, a gross green substance destroys one of the domes and Sasquatch appears within the Arctic dome, creating havoc and endangering the future of the facility. Nancy Drew investigates, but is soon trapped within the dome with the legendary Bigfoot.

Nancy Drew: Girl Detective #9: Ghost in the Machinery. Sho Murase, artist. NBM/Papercutz 2007 112p. Illustration

Grades: 3 4 5 6 7 8 9   741.5; Fic
1. Drew, Nancy (Fictional character); 2. Mystery graphic novels; 3. Graphic novels
978-1-59707-061-4, $12.95; 978-1-59707-058-4 (pb), $7.95

On a mission sponsored by young, rich, and handsome Ralph Credo, Nancy teams up with eccentric scientist Roy Hinkley to find an amazing high efficiency engine able to operate at an amazing 200 miles per gallon. The experimental engine, mounted on a tank, was part of an experiment during the final days of World War II. There's just one problem, the engine and the tank are haunted. "Ghost In The Machinery" is the first in a series of three Nancy Drew adventures entitled "The High Miles Mystery."

Nancy Drew: Girl Detective Vol. 10: The Disoriented Express. Stefan Petrucha & Sarah Kinney, writers ; Sho Murase, artist. NBM/Papercutz 2007 Un Illustration

Grades: 4 5 6 7 8 9   741.5; Fic
1. Drew, Nancy (Fictional character); 2. Mystery graphic novels; 3. Graphic novels
978-1-59707-066-9, $7.95

On its journey to Professor Hinkley's research facility, Nancy Drew must protect an amazing creation that could possibly end the world's energy crisis. Unstable and dangerous, the super fuel-efficient engine must be transported by a private train. But dark forces are at work, attempting to shanghai the miracle machine - literally at every turn by using computers to jam the switches. But while Nancy, and her friend George, attempt to determine which sinister suspect is behind these despicable acts, they soon realize that if their adversaries can't succeed at stealing this miraculous machine, they'll destroy the train, along with everything, and everyone on it. "The Disoriented Express" is

the second in a series of three Nancy Drew adventures entitled "The High Miles Mystery."

Petty, J. T. (John T.)

The **Fall** of the House of West. By Paul Pope and J. T. Petty; illustrated by David Rubín. First Second 2015 160 p. Illustration (Battling Boy)

Grades: 7 8 9 10 11 12   741.5; Fic
1. Father-daughter relationship — Fiction; 2. Gods; 3. Monsters; 4. Mothers — Fiction; 5. Secrets — Fiction; 6. Graphic novels
162672010X; 9781626720107, $9.99

In this graphic novel, by Paul Pope and J. T. Petty, illustrated by David Rubín, "Aurora West is on the verge of solving the mystery of her mother's death, but it's hard keeping her efforts a secret from her grieving father, the legendary monster-hunter Haggard West. Between her school work and her hours training and hunting with her dad, Aurora is hard-pressed to find time to be a secret sleuth. But she's nothing if not persistent." (Publisher's note)

"Rubín's frenetic black-and-white illustrations stylistically complement Pope and Petty's breakneck-paced plotting. True to the genre, the story explores notions of good and evil but provides no easy answers." Kirkus

The **Rise** of Aurora West. By Paul Pope, J. T. Petty, illustrated by David Rubín. First Second Books 2014 160 p. Illustration (Battling Boy)

Grades: 7 8 9 10 11 12   741.5
1. Adventure graphic novels; 2. Female superhero graphic novels
1626722684; 9781626722682, $17.99

In this graphic novel, by Paul Pope and J. T. Petty, illustrated by David Rubín, the "world introduced in . . . 'Battling Boy' is rife with monsters and short on heroes. . . . But in this action-driven extension of the Battling Boy universe, we see it through a new pair of eyes: Aurora West, daughter of Arcopolis's last great hero, Haggard West." (Publisher's note)

"Since Aurora and her father were only briefly mentioned in the previous installment, this volume does a wonderful job of fleshing out their characters further; readers see an Aurora that's not as confident in her abilities, and a slightly jaded and darker side to her heroic father. Pope's gritty, experimental art from the original Battling Boy has been replaced by Rubín's more traditional style, giving a '60s 'Silver Age' appearance to the work." SLJ

Petty, Kate

Julius Caesar: The Life of a Roman General. Gary Jeffrey & Kate Petty ; illustrated by Sam Hadley. Rosen Publishing Group 2005 48p. Illustration

Grades: 3 4 5 6 7 8   741.5; 937
1. Biographical graphic novels; 2. Caesar, Julius, 100 or 102 - 44 BC; 3. Rome — History — Republic, 265-30 BC; 4. Graphic novels
1-4042-0239-0, $29.25

LC 2004014392

Ambitious, ruthless, shrewd, cruel, and intelligent are a few of the words that have been used to describe this man who changed the course of civilization. Caesar's military conquests and political alliances altered Rome's decaying system of government, producing the greatest of all ancient empires. This graphic novel takes readers on a journey to the ancient world where political intrigue and military might gave birth not only to the rise of Caesar but also to his bloody assassination. The book includes some information on what came after his death, a glossary, and a list of books for further reading.

Part of the Graphic Nonfiction series.

Peyer, Tom

Go boy 7, Vol. 1: Ready set go!. [by] Tom Peyer and Jon Sommariva. Rocket Comics/Dark Horse Comics 2004 96p. Illustration

Grades: 6 7 8 9 10 11 12   **741.5; Fic**
1. Science fiction graphic novels; 2. Graphic novels
1-56971-937-3, $12.95

When Jonny Zero's family jet is shot down, he survives only because his uncle uses his experimental nanotech plasm to save his life. Now Jonny is more than human, which is a good thing, because Uncle Noah and his Go Base are under attack by the forces of The Cultist, an evil madman out to destroy all thinking life. The problem is, he's still just a young teen and a wee bit impulsive when taking action. The action and violence level is similar to what preteens might see in a PG rated movie.

Another title in this series is: Go boy 7 Vol 2: The human factor, written by Brian Augustyn (2004)

Peyo

The **Smurfs** anthology; Vol. 1. Peyo. Papercutz 2013 190 p. Color illustration (The Smurfs graphic novels)
Grades: 4 5 6 7 8 9 10 11 12 Adult   **741.5**
1597074179; 9781597074179, $19.99
1. Smurfs (Fictional characters)

"Newly remastered and presented in original publication order, along with a Smurfy collection of historical notes and photographs, the stories in this volume," by Belgian comics artist Peyo, "introduce us to Papa Smurf, Gargamel, Smurfette, and the rest of the village." (Publisher's note)

The **Smurfs** anthology; Vol. 2. Peyo. Papercutz 2013 192 p. Color illustration
Grades: 4 5 6 7 8 9 10 11 12 Adult   **741.5**
1597074454; 9781597074452, $19.99
1. Smurfs (Fictional characters)

"Newly remastered and presented in original publication order, along with a Smurfy collection of historical notes and photographs, this volume," by Belgian comics artist Peyo, "introduces us to Smurfette and features a 'Johan and Peewit' story never before seen in the U.S." (Publisher's note)

"[A] delightful and instructive mix of Peyo's colorful tales. A series of essays interspersed throughout the collection provides social and historical context for the cartoons." Booklist

Translated from the French

Phelan, Matt

★ **Bluffton:** my summers with Buster Keaton. Written and illustrated by Matt Phelan. Candlewick Press 2013 240 p. Color; Illustration

Grades: 3 4 5 6   **741.5; Fic**
1. Keaton, Buster; 2. Vaudeville — Fiction
076365079X; 9780763650797, $22.99
                                    LC 2012947260

In this graphic novel by Matt Phelan, set "in the summer of 1908, in Muskegon, Michigan, a visiting troupe of vaudeville performers is about the most exciting thing since baseball. Henry has a few months to ogle . . . a slapstick actor his own age named Buster Keaton. Henry longs to learn to take a fall like Buster . . . but Buster just wants to play ball with Henry and his friends." (Publisher's note)

"Historical detail, a rich sense of place, expert pacing—Phelan . . . keeps all the plates in the air in this fictionalized recreation of the boyhood summers of Buster Keaton. In lightly sketched, gently tinted watercolor panels, Phelan conveys the excitement a troupe of summering vaudeville actors brings to sleepy Bluffton." Pub Wkly

★ The **storm** in the barn. Candlewick Press 2009 201p. Illustration

Grades: 4 5 6 7 8 9   **741.5; Fic**
1. Adventure graphic novels; 2. Dust storms; 3. Kansas; 4. Monsters; 5. United States — History — 1933-1945; 6. Graphic novels
978-0-7636-3618-0, $24.99; 0-7636-3618-5; 978-0-7636-5290-6 (pa), $14.99; 0-7636-5290-3 (pa)

In Kansas of 1937, the land has been in the grip of the Dust Bowl for four years, and eleven-year-old Jack Carter has seen his family worn down by it. But the day Jack outruns a dust storm all the way home from town, he glimpses something odd in the abandoned Talbot barn, and he tries to find the courage to go into the barn and confront what is there.

"Children can read this as a work of historical fiction, a piece of folklore, a scary story, a graphic novel, or all four. Written with simple, direct language, it's an almost wordless book: the illustrations" shadowy grays and blurry lines eloquently depict the haze of the dust. A complex but accessible and fascinating book." SLJ

Pini, Wendy

Elfquest: The Discovery. Written by Wendy & Richard Pini ; script, art, letters, and colors by Wendy Pini. DC Comics 2006 128p. Illustration

Grades: 8 9 10 11 12 Adult   **741.5; Fic**
1. Adventure graphic novels; 2. Fantasy graphic novels; 3. Graphic novels
1-4012-0958-0, $14.99

Wonder and danger mount as the Wolfrider chief's son Sunstream finds romance in the form of the lovely sea elf Brill and fierce hostility whe he exposes her long-hidden tribe, the Wave Dancers. Rule by fear of the "Landers" who hunt and slay his folk, the mighty mer-chief Surge will do anything, even destroy Sunstream and Brill's happiness, to keep his tribe secret and safe. This full-color story is the first new Elfquest story in years.

Piotrowski, Robert

D-Day. Art by Drew Ng. Harcourt Achieve/Steck-Vaughn 2007 48p. Illustration

Grades: 3 4 5 6 7 8   **741.5; 940.54; Fic**

1. World War, 1939-1945 — Amphibious operations; 2. Graphic novels
978-1-4190-3221-9, $8.99

On June 6, 1944, the greatest attack of World War II is about to begin; the invasion of Nazi territory by Allied forces. The battle will test the courage of young men as never before. Are they ready? The book includes battle violence and shows men dying in action. This historical graphic novel includes prose intervals that provide more information about D-Day and the various elements of the battle, including the paratrooper attack, the aerial attacks, and information about the German army.

Part of the Timeline Graphic Novels series.

Gold Rush. Art by Jeff Alward. Harcourt Achieve/Steck-Vaughn 2007 48p. Illustration
Grades: 3 4 5 6 7 8   **741.5; Fic**
1. Adventure graphic novels; 2. Klondike (Yukon) — Gold discoveries; 3. Graphic novels
978-1-4190-3210-3, $8.99

Jonathan Samuels is a young farmer whose hopes are dashed when a girl rejects him for a wealthy rival. When he hears of gold in the Klondike, Jonathan sets out with dreams of striking it rich. Does he have what it takes to succeed? This historical fiction graphic novel includes prose intervals that provide more information about the Klondike gold rush of 1896-1899 and what life was like in Dawson City at that time.

Part of the Timeline Graphic Novels series.

Piscopo, Jay
The **undersea** adventures of Capt'n Eli, vol. 2: the mystery of the Sargasso Sea. Nemo Publishing 2008 112p. Illustration
Grades: 3 4 5 6 7 8   **741.5; Fic**
1. Adventure graphic novels; 2. Science fiction graphic novels; 3. Graphic novels
978-0-9817132-1-2, $9.99

As Professor Wow and the Seasearchers continue their work on the ocean surface, trying to keep people away from the time anomaly, Eli, his dog Barney, and the 200-year-old parrot Jolly Roger travel with Commander X to the undersea city of Aquaria. There, Eli learns of the ancient undersea civilizations of Lemuria and Atlantis, and the origin of the Hydrons that attacked him. Then Aquaria comes under attack, and Commander X leads the defense. King Aquarius dies trying to protect his city, his son Triton is injured and in a coma, and that leaves Coral, daughter of King Aquarius, to rule. Commander X and Eli learn that the son of an old enemy has tricked Coral and the Aquarians into thinking he saved them from destruction. Now they need to sneak into Aquarius to save Coral and find a way to stop Baal's nefarious plot.

Courtesy of Nemo Publishing

The **undersea** adventures of Capt'n Eli, volume 1. Nemo Publishing 2008 104p. Illustration
Grades: 2 3 4 5 6 7
741.5; Fic
1. Adventure graphic novels; 2. Ocean; 3. Graphic novels
978-0-9817132-0-5, $9.99

Eli is a boy of mysterious origins, who surfaced from the ocean in a technologically advanced pod near the island of Eagle

Courtesy of Nemo Publishing

Rock, off the coast of Maine. The lighthouse keeper and his wife recover the pod and raise the baby they find inside, naming him Eli. The boy proves to be highly intelligent beyond his years, and able to design and build inventions, ranging from a root beer machine to a miniature submarine. While still a preteen boy, Eli saves a U.S. Navy submarine when it runs into trouble undersea (with the help of the mysterious Commander X), and then he joins the Seasearchers, a marine research group. They set out to investigate the latest disappearance of a ship in the Sargasso Sea, only to run into trouble with something that sends them back in time to around 1492. When hostile minisubs that resemble fish attack Eli in his minisub, the Dolphin, Commander X rescues him again. Cmdr X is very much like Captain Nemo from Jules Verne's 20,000 Leagues Under the Sea, although he also once was a superhero who fought alongside the Allies during World War II. Eli is the namesake of Capt'n Eli Forsley, a WWII veteran who also had his own brand of Capt'n Eli root beer in Maine; Eli's character design has been adapted from the soda's label. The book includes information about the ocean world that is incorporated into the story.

Poe, Marshall
Turning points: a house divided. Illustrated by Leland Purvis. Aladdin Paperbacks 2008 122p. Illustration
Grades: 3 4 5 6 7 8   **741.5; Fic**
1. Abolitionists; 2. United States — History — 1815-1861; 3. Graphic novels
978-1-4169-5057-8, $8.99

LC 2008-929317

Owen and Amos Bennington's abolitionist parents are killed in 1856, and the brothers vow to continue their parents' quest to end slavery. However, younger brother Amos thinks the abolitionists aren't doing enough, while Owen works for a peaceful, political solution. When they move to Kansas, things don't go as planned, as proslavery people use violence to get their way. When Owen wants to move back East, Amos runs away and joins John Brown's

Courtesy of Aladding Paperbacks

forces, who fight against slavery with force. Owen moves to Illinois and works for Abraham Lincoln. Amos finally realizes that Brown's way is wrong and leaves just before the attempted takeover of Harper's Ferry; he makes his way across the land slowly, hoping against hope that he can find Owen again. This fictional story highlights the years leading up to the Civil War, showing a private, personal side of Lincoln and letting younger readers see the kinds of divisions suffered by many families as they debated and argued the cause of abolition or slavery, and of political action or force to end slavery.

Turning Points: Little Rock nine. Illustrated by Ellen Lindner. Simon & Schuster/Aladdin Paperbacks 2008 122p. Illustration

Grades: 3 4 5 6 7 8 9   **741.5; Fic**
1. African Americans — Civil rights; 2. African Americans — Education; 3. United States — History — 1953-1961; 4. Graphic novels
978-1-4169-5066-0, $7.99

LC 2007-937918

Sixteen-year-old William McNally and fifteen-year-old Thomas Johnson both live in Little Rock, Arkansas, in the summer of 1957. They both love baseball and teasing their little sisters. There's just one big difference: William is white, and Thomas, the son of the McNally family's maid, is black. After the U.S. Supreme Court rules in favor of desegregating public schools, Little Rock Central High School prepares to enroll its first nine African-American students, and William and Thomas are caught in the middle of a storm. William's family has divided over the issue, and Thomas' parents don't want him to get hurt and forbid him to try to enter the school. The book portrays the issues of the time and the personal beliefs of both sides to let readers see what it was like back then. William, Thomas, and their families are fictional, but what happened at Little Rock Central High School is an important part of American history.

Poon, Janice
Claire and the water wish. Written and illustrated by Janice Poon. Kids Can Press 2009 120p. Illustration

Grades: 2 3 4 5 6   **741.5; Fic**
1. Mystery graphic novels; 2. Pollution; 3. Graphic novels
978-1-55453-381-7, $15.95; 978-1-55453-382-4 (pa), $7.95

LC C2008-903252-7

Summer is over, and Claire must start at a new school, so she's glad to have her friend Jet with her. However, Jet has become obsessed with entering a contest to win a digital camera, and when she does win it, she spends more time with the popular kids at school. Feeling a bit left out, Claire makes friends with Sky, who lives near Lovesick Lake. When they team up for a science project, Sky tells Claire that the adults in her community believe the lake is making people sick; they believe someone is dumping waste into the lake, but they haven't been able to catch anyone. Then, when Claire and Jet visit Lovesick Lake with Sky, they stumble into a bad situation. Maybe Jet's obsession with her new camera will pay off for the girls.

Pope, Paul
★ **Battling** Boy. Paul Pope; colors by Hilary Sycamore. First Second 2013 208 p. Illustration

Grades: 7 8 9 10 11 12   **741.5; Fic**
1. Fantasy graphic novels; 2. Superhero graphic novels
1596438053; 9781596431454, $15.99; 9781596438057, $24.99

LC 2013030815

Eisner Award: Best Publication for Teens (2014)

In this book, "the hero Haggard West helps battle the evil forces of Sadisto and his hooded ghouls. However, in a shocking turn of events, evil triumphs over good, and the metropolis is left without protection. In a world far, far away, a 13-year-old son of a god has been chosen to help Earth fight the onslaught of monsters as a rite of passage. Sent with only a few possessions, including an array of magical T-shirts, Battling Boy helps the cityùbut he finds he cannot do it alone." (Kirkus Reviews)

"This is a sophisticated tale for younger readers, but Pope manages to both grant full-scale wish fulfillment and acknowledge the limitations of young boys with equal aplomb. His art, meanwhile, looks like nothing else in comics, with ropy, sinewy figures, dynamic action, and gritty urban design all captured in panels that have the rough, subversive tone of classic punk album covers." Booklist

Porcellino, John
Thoreau at Walden. By John Porcellino, from the writings of Henry David Thoreau; introduction by D.B. Johnson. Hyperion 2008 Viii, 99 p. Illustration; Map (Center for Cartoon Studies presents)

Grades: 8 9 10 11 12 Adult   **818/.303; 741.5**
1. American authors; 2. Thoreau, Henry David, 1817-1862; 3. Walden Woods (Mass) — Social life and customs; 4. Graphic novels
1423100387; 1423100395; 9781423100386, $16.99; 9781423100393

LC 2007061358

This graphic novel, by John Porcellino, "introduces . . . Henry David Thoreau. . . . Thoreau's writings, excerpted out of chronological order, are recast into a narrative that moves from the philosopher's self-ostracism from society and his time at Walden and into the feeling of calm reverie he took from his experiences." (Booklist)

"Presents in graphic novel format an account of the two years that Thoreau spent at Walden Pond, excerpted from Thoreau's writings." Publisher's note

Includes bibliographical references (p. 99)

Powell, Martin
Red Riding Hood: the graphic novel. Retold by Martin Powell; illustrated by Victor Rivas. Stone Arch Books 2009 40p.

Grades: 2 3 4 5 6 7   **741.5; Fic**
1. Fairy tales; 2. Graphic novels
978-1-4342-0769-2, $21.26

LC 2008-6723

In Transylvania, where many dangers lurk, a fortune teller gives Ruby's grandmother a special wool to make a garment to protect her life. Ruby receives a special red riding hood and cloak for her birthday, and she sets out through the woods to visit her grandmother. There she encounters a wolf

who tricks her into telling where her grandmother lives. By the time Ruby reaches her grandmother's cottage, something else waits for her in grandmother's bed. This graphic novel adaptation of the old tale includes some different details from the most wellknown versions. The book includes a brief history of the tale, including the version by Perrault and the most famous one by the Brothers Grimm.
Part of the Graphic Spin series

Rumpelstiltskin: the graphic novel. Retold by Martin Powell; illustrated by Erik Valdez y Alanis. Stone Arch Books 2009 40p. Illustration
Grades: 2 3 4 5 6 7   **741.5; Fic**
1. Fairy tales; 2. Graphic novels
978-1-4342-0768-5, $21.26
LC 2008-6724
When Mirabelle's father, who owes a large debt, claims that she can spin straw into gold, she haplessly goes along with the lie to save her father. An evil troll helps her accomplish the impossible task, for a price. When the king gets greedy for more gold, the troll asks for a much higher price; when a year is up, Mirabelle must guess the creature's name, or give up her child. This graphic novel adaptation provides a brief history of the tale, tracing it back much farther than the Brothers Grimm, who popularized it.
Part of the Graphic Spin series

Sleeping Beauty: the graphic novel. Retold by Martin Powell ; illustrated by Sean Dietrich. Stone Arch Books 2009 40p. Illustration
Grades: 3 4 5 6 7 8   **741.5; Fic**
1. Fairy tales; 2. Sleeping Beauty — Adaptations; 3. Graphic novels
978-1-4342-1193-4, $21.26; 978-1-4342-1393-8 (pa), $4.95
LC 2008-32048
This graphic novel adaptation of the Sleeping Beauty story features a wise old fish who speaks to the queen before she gets pregnant with her daughter, and zombie knights who try to stop the prince from breaking the sleep spell that holds Princess Rose and everyone in the kingdom. The rest of the story follows the traditional versions—the wicked thirteenth fairy proclaims a curse that the newborn princess will die on her fifteenth birthday, the last of the good fairies mitigates the curse to a century-long sleep, the means of completing the curse is the princess pricking her finger on a spindle, everyone in the castle falls asleep, and thorny briars cover the castle. The book includes information about Perrault's original story and some of the other media adaptations. The art is very idiosyncratic, a bit dark, and the zombie knights will appeal more to boys than the girls who are the usual audience for the fairy tale.
Part of the Graphic Spin series.

Snow White: the graphic novel. Retold by Martin Powell ; illustrated by Erik Valdez y Alanis. Stone Arch Books 2009 40p. Illustration
Grades: 3 4 5 6 7 8   **741.5; Fic**
1. Fairy tales; 2. Folklore — Germany; 3. Graphic novels
978-1-4342-1192-7, $21.26; 978-1-4342-1394-5 (pa), $4.95
LC 2008-32049
In this graphic novel version of the fairy tale, the wicked Queen Mara traps Prince Marco within her magic mirror,

and Snow White is a lovely young woman who lives alone. When the queen sends a wolf to kill Snow White, the girl stops the wolf, but she must find new shelter with her home destroyed. She finds a cavern, and there the dwarfs say they had a dream that they must protect her. As with the other graphic novel adaptations of fairy tales in the Graphic Spin series, the color palette is darker, the art may be spookier than most younger children would like. The book includes information about the origins of the fairy tale and why the dwarfs only have names in the Disney animated movie.
Part of the Graphic Spin series.

The **Swiss** family Robinson. By Johann D. Wyss; retold by Martin Powell; illustrated by Gerardo Sandoval.. Stone Arch Books 2009 74p. Illustration
Grades: 4 5 6 7 8 9 10   **741.5; Fic**
1. Adventure graphic novels; 2. Shipwrecks; 3. Survival after airplane accidents, shipwrecks, etc; 4. Wyss, Johann David, 1743-1818 — Adaptations
978-1-4342-0756-2, $23.93
LC 2008-6249
In the early nineteenth century, a Swiss family survives a shipwreck and land on a deserted island. They build a life for themselves there, salvaging materials from the wrecked ship and using the plants and other things they find on the island. However, some of the creatures living on the island could be deadly. This graphic novel adaptation of Wyss's classic adventure novel includes information about real-life castaways and uninhabited islands. An interesting note, the novel has never been out of print for almost 200 years and has gone through almost 200 editions.
Part of the Graphic Revolve series

Preciado, Tony
Super grammar: learn grammar with superheroes. Written by Tony Preciado; illustrated by Rhode Montijo; colored by Jenny Hansen; inked by Joe To. Scholastic 2012 176 p. Color illustration (Illustrating the point)
Grades: 4 5 6 7 8   **428**
1. English language — Grammar — Juvenile fiction; 2. English language — Grammar — Juvenile literature; 3. Superheroes — Juvenile fiction
0545425158; 9780545425155, $8.99
LC 2012289091
In this book by Tony Preciado, illustrated by Rhode Montijo, "all of the major elements of grammar . . . [are] personified with superhero or super villain identities. . . . You'll meet the vibrant super heroine The Adverb, and you'll learn about her awesome ability to modify verbs and other adverbs. . . . You'll actually meet the sinister twin brothers, Double Negative, and you'll learn how to avoid being tricked into falling for their double talk." (Publisher's note)

Priddy, Joel
The **gift** of the Magi. It Books/HarperCollins 2009 Un Illustration
Grades: 5 6 7 8 9 10 11 12 Adult   **741.5; Fic**
1. Christmas; 2. Gifts; 3. Henry, O, 1862-1910 — Adaptations; 4. Graphic novels
978-0-06-178239-8, $14.99

Della and Jim are a young married couple, struggling to make ends meet when Jim's pay has been cut. It's Christmas time, but despite squeezing every penny, Della has managed to save only a little bit of money, and it's not enough to buy Jim a good present. He owns a gold pocket watch, and Della wants to buy him a chain for it. She has only one thing of value that she can sell her beautiful, long, long hair. Out of her love for Jim, Della sacrifices her hair. And, of course, Jim has sacrificed his gold pocket watch in order to buy beautiful hair combs for Della's gorgeous hair. As O. Henry says, they "most unwisely sacrificed for each other the greatest treasures of their house," but also that "of all who give gifts these two were the wisest." Joel Priddy's adaptation of this classic story uses black and white illustrations except when Della lets down her hair to consider her one treasure. He preserves much of O. Henry's original prose, which means that younger readers will have to look up a lot of words to understand the story. This book is suitable for younger readers but will also appeal to teens and adults.

Prince, Liz
★ **Tomboy:** A Graphic Memoir. By Liz Prince. Zest Books 2014 256 p. Illustration
Grades: 7 8 9 10 11 12 Adult
741.5; 305.309; 92
1. Cartoonists — Caricatures and cartoons; 2. Cartoonists — United States — Biography; 3. Gender identity; 4. Gender role; 5. Prince, Liz; 6. Sex differences (Psychology); 7. Sex role; 8. Stereotype (Social psychology); 9. Graphic novels
1936976552; 9781936976553, $15.99
LC 2014034070

Courtesy of Zest Books

This memoir, by Liz Prince, "is a graphic novel about refusing gender boundaries, yet unwittingly embracing gender stereotypes at the same time, and realizing later in life that you can be just as much of a girl in jeans and a T-shirt as you can in a pink tutu." (Publisher's note)

"Prince's honest voice and self-deprecating humor help make young Liz a sympathetic and relatable character. The simply rendered black-and-white panel drawings have an unpretentious quality, in keeping with the narrative tone." Horn Book

Pyle, Kevin C.
Blindspot. Henry Holt & Company 2007 Un Illustration
Grades: 5 6 7 8 9 10 11 12 Adult **741.5; Fic**
1. Friendship; 2. Graphic novels
978-0-8050-7998-2 (pa), $13.95; 0-8050-7998-X (pa)
LC 2006041155
Dean and his friends have created an entire world in the woods behind their suburban housing development. In their

army fantasy, they're at war, and Dean is the daring captain leading his troops through episodes of intrigue and danger. But no fantasy can last forever. A run-in with a homeless man in the woods snaps the boys back to reality, and little by little the real world pervades their imagined universe and drives them apart.

★ **Katman.** Henry Holt and Co. 2009 Un Illustration
Grades: 7 8 9 10 11 12 **741.5; Fic**
1. Cats; 2. Friendship; 3. Graphic novels
978-0-8050-8285-2, $12.99; 0-8050-8285-9
LC 2008-937398
Kit is a bored sixteen-year-old with nothing to do one summer when he starts feeding stray cats. He loves it when cool, artistic Jess helps him out, even though he has to endure constant taunting by her disaffected metalhead friends. They make fun of him for being like the local cat lady, but Kit doesn't care—especially after Jess draws him an anime-style avatar named Katman.
"Beautifully simple and straightforward." Voice Youth Advocates

Take what you can carry. Kevin C. Pyle. Henry Holt and Co. 2012 176 p. Illustration; Color
Grades: 4 5 6 **741.5**
1. Japanese Americans — Evacuation and relocation, 1942-1945; 2. Shoplifting; 3. Teenagers
0805082867; 9780805082869, $12.99
LC 2011924430
In this graphic novel, in "1977 suburban Chicago, Kyle runs wild with his friends and learns to shoplift from the local convenience store. In 1941 Berkeley, the Himitsu family is forced to leave their home for a Japanese-American internment camp, and their teenage son must decide how to deal with his new life. But though these boys are growing up in wildly different places and times, their lives intersect in more ways than one, as they discover compassion, learn loyalty, and find renewal." (Publisher's note)

Quinn, Jason
Gandhi: My Life is My Message. By Jason Quinn; illustrated by Naresh Kumar. Random House Inc 2014 212 p. Color; Illustration
Grades: 8 9 10 11 12 Adult **92; 741.5**
1. Gandhi, Mahatma, 1869-1948
9380741227; 9789380741222, $16.99
This book by Jason Quinn, illustrated by Naresh Kumar, focuses on the life of "Mohandas Karamchand Gandhi, better known as the Mahatma or Great Soul. . . . We discover the man behind the legend, following him from his birth in the Indian coastal town of Porbandar in 1869, to the moment of his tragic death at the hands of an assassin in January 1948, just months after the Independence of India." (Publisher's note)
"Just as the writing eloquently intertwines explication with reenactments of dramatic, poignant events, the panels are meticulously arranged to move the reader's attention from broad and busy scenes to intimate close-ups." Booklist

Steve Jobs: genius by design. By Jason Quinn; illustrated by Amit Tayal. Random House Inc 2012 104 p. Illustration; Color
Grades: 7 8 9 10 11 12 Adult **92; 741.5**

1. Apple Inc — Officials & employees; 2. Biographical graphic novels; 3. Computer industry; 4. Jobs, Steve, 1955-2011
9380028768; 9789380028767, $12.99

This graphic novel, by Jason Quinn, illustrated by Amit Tayal, presents a biography of the 20th-century technology entrepreneur and Apple Inc. founder Steve Jobs. "Steve Jobs and his inventions changed the world we live in." The book ranges "from his birth and his adoption, through the advent of the computer age and on into the digital age. Forced out of the company he created, his indomitable vision allowed him to change the world of computers, movies, music and telecommunications." (Publisher's note)

"This cleverly designed volume provides a concise but well-balanced view of Steve Jobs the wunderkind, including his difficult personality and complex genius." Booklist

Ragawa, Marimo
   Baby & Me, Vol. 1. Viz Media/Shojo Beat 2006 200p. Illustration
Grades: 6 7 8 9 10 11 12 Adult   **741.5; Fic**
   1. Family; 2. Humorous graphic novels; 3. Shojo manga
1-4215-0234-8, $8.99

Young Takuya has it tough. After his mother passed away it has been his job to take care of his baby brother, Minoru while their father, Harumi, works the long hours of a Japanese "salaryman." Takuya must sacrifice the playtime usually associated with childhood for the responsibilities of an adult. Cooking, cleaning, sewing and scolding are all now an integral part of the sixth-grader's life. "All work and no play" has Takuya incredibly frustrated and resentful of his little brother. Will Takuya find it in his heart to love the brother who is causing him so much grief" This isn't so much a soap opera drama as it is a comedy with dramatic moments.

Raicht, Mike
   Hulk: big green men. Mike Raicht, writer ; Alex Sanchez, pencils ; J. Rauch, colors ; Dave Sharpe, letters ; Shane Davis & J. Rauch, cover. ABDO Publishing Company/Spotlight 2006 Un Illustration
Grades: 4 5 6 7 8 9   **741.5; Fic**
   1. Hulk (Fictional character); 2. Superhero graphic novels; 3. Graphic novels
1-59961-042-6, $21.35

                                LC 2005-57558
   When Bruce Banner finds himself in Roswell, he finds all the inhabitants wear strange collars and act spaced out—except for a teenage girl. What they don't know is that she's really a Skrull, as are her parents, and their people have finally come to rescue them. But now her family doesn't want to leave, and when the Skrulls hurt Bruce, he becomes The Hulk and rampages against the "little green men." This is a revised, hardbound edition of the Marvel Age comic book.
   Part of the Hulk series

   Hulk: The abomination. Mike Raicht, writer; Ryan Odagawa, pencils; J. Rauch, colors; Dave Sharpe, letters; Shane Davis & J. Rauch, cover.. ABDO Spotlight 2006 Un Illustration
Grades: 3 4 5 6 7 8 9   **741.5; Fic**

1. Hulk (Fictional character); 2. Superhero graphic novels; 3. Graphic novels
1-59961-045-0, $21.35

                                LC 2005-57557
   Dr. Bruce Banner was conducting research on gamma rays when he was exposed and became the Hulk. However, he can return to his human form when he's not stressed or upset or angry. Emil Blonsky worked on the project, too, and after Banner left he tried to carry on the work and experimented on himself. However, he became a monster some call the Abomination, and in his anger over not being able to change back, he takes it out on towns, and people. He rampages in Texas, and Banner travels there in hopes of stopping him; but Blonsky only succeeds in causing Banner to turn into the Hulk. Young readers who have seen the new Incredible Hulk movie that premiered in June 2008 will know the Abomination from the movie.
   This is a revision of a Dec. 2004 issue of Incredible Hulk from the Marvel Age line.

   Spider-Man in Kraven the hunter. Stan Lee & Steve Ditko, plot ; Mike Raicht, script ; Jamal Igle, pencils ; Jay Leisten, inks ; Dave Sharpe, letters ; Larry Molinar, colors. ABDO Publishing Group/Spotlight 2006 Un Illustration
Grades: 3 4 5 6 7 8   **741.5; Fic**
   1. Spider-Man (Fictional character); 2. Superhero graphic novels; 3. Graphic novels
1-59961-009-4, $21.35

   When Spider-Man defeats the Chameleon one too many times, the criminal calls in Kraven the Hunter to hunt and kill him. As a celebrity star of his own television show, Kraven makes a big splash with his arrival, and Peter Parker must take photographs for the Daily Bugle. Somehow, he's going to have to stop the hunter and the Chameleon.
   Part of the Marvel Age Spider-Man series.

   Spider-man: Spidey strikes back Vol. 1 digest. Mike Raicht and Todd Dezago. Marvel Comics 2005 96p. Illustration
Grades: 4 5 6 7 8 9   **741.5; Fic**
   1. Spider-Man (Fictional character); 2. Superhero graphic novels; 3. Graphic novels
0-7851-1632-X, $5.99

   Tired of saving the day and getting no respect, Spider-Man considers taking a break from his superhero duties, which leaves the city wide open for the likes of the Sandman and the Enforcers. Will Spidey let it all go to pot, or will he step up to the plate and take one for the team? This volume collects Marvel Age Spider-Man issues 17-20. Previous volumes were published under the series title Marvel Age Spider-Man. The Marvel Age titles are being collected and published in the digest size, similar to manga, and at an affordable price. The Marvel Age series are aimed at younger audiences than the other superhero titles from Marvel.

   ★ The **Stuff** of Legend; Omnibus one. By Mike Raicht and Brian Smith; illustrated by Charles Paul Wilson III. Th3rd World Studios 2014 284 p. Color illustration (The Stuff of Legend)
Grades: 8 9 10 11 12 Adult   **741.5**
   1. Kidnapping; 2. Rescues; 3. Toys; 4. Graphic novels
9780983216193; 0989574482; 9780989574488, $29.99

"This hardcover collection brings together the first two volumes. . . . As Allied forces fight the enemy on Europe's war-torn beaches, another battle begins in a child's bedroom in Brooklyn when the nightmarish Boogeyman snatches a boy and takes him to the realm of the Dark. The child's playthings, led by the toy soldier known as the Colonel, band together to stage a daring rescue. On their perilous mission they will confront the boy's bitter and forgotten toys, as well as betrayal in their own ranks." (Publisher's note)

"Wilson renders the harrowing closet netherworld with full-fleshed detailing and sepia tones that nail both the 1940s time frame and the classicism of children's stories. But don't mistake this for a kids' comic‐the violence is often explicit, and the Boogeyman creepy enough to slither his way right back onto grownups' most-terrifying lists." Booklist

★ The **stuff** of legend; Omnibus two. By Mike Raicht and Brian Smith; illustrated by Charles Paul Wilson III. Th3rd World Studios 2014 270 p. Color illustration (The Stuff of Legend)

Grades: 8 9 10 11 12 Adult   741.5
    1. Horror comic books, strips, etc; 2. Kidnapping; 3. Toys; 4. Graphic novels
    0989574490; 9780989574495, $34.99

The second omnibus edition "finds our toys at a crossroads. Unable to find their boy, our loyal toys' bonds have been tested and broken. Now scattered across The Dark, the toys must decide whether to continue their search or admit defeat and return home." (Publisher's note)

Randall, Ron
    Thor and Loki: In the Land of Giants. Lerner Publishing Group/Graphic Universe 2007 48p. Illustration

Grades: 3 4 5 6 7 8 9   741.5; 398.2
    1. Loki (Norse deity); 2. Norse mythology; 3. Thor (Norse deity); 4. Graphic novels
    978-0-8225-3087-9, $26.60 lib. Bdg.

Thor the powerful god of thunder, and his brother Loki, the trickster, are eager to solve an argument: does strength always win, or do brains always beat brawn? To find an answer, they travel to the strange and forbidding land of giants. There they face a series of challenges that will prove once and for all which god is right. Or will it? The book includes a glossary and a list of books for further reading.

Randolph, Grace
    Marvel her-oes. Art by Craig Rousseau. Marvel Worldwide, Inc. 2010 Un Illustration

Grades: 7 8 9 10 11 12   741.5; Fic
    1. High schools; 2. Superhero graphic novels; 3. Teenagers; 4. Graphic novels
    978-0-7851-4842-5, $14.99

Janet Van Dyne has to deal with the perils of high school while keeping a major secret: she can shrink to the size of a wasp, and she can shoot energy blasts from her hands. Then she discovers that snooty Namora also has superpowers, and then she discovers that her best friend Jenny Walters also has powers. The school definitely has secrets, so do Janet's parents, and now she, Namora, and Jenny have to figure out what's going on. This book collects the four-issue miniseries that re-imagines the origins of some of Marvel's female superheroes in a manner that doesn't require the reader to

know much about the Marvel Universe. The book also includes the first issue of Savage She-Hulk #1 from 1980.

Realbuzz Studios
    Goofyfoot Gurl vol. 1: Let There be Lighten Up!. Thomas Nelson 2007 96p. Illustration

Grades: 5 6 7 8 9   741.5
    1. Friendship; 2. Religion; 3. Surfing; 4. Graphic novels
    978-1-59554-389-9, $10.99

Surfer girl Suki, called Goofyfoot for her right-foot-forward stance on her surfboard, and her friends hang out at the beach in Orange County, California. But everyone's got their own problems: a serious lack of funds, a new young stepmother, parents who are never around, and even the possibility of an arranged marriage. But Suki finds a way to bring some happiness and good times to her friends.

Serenity #2: Stepping Out. Thomas Nelson 2007 96p. Illustration

Grades: 5 6 7 8 9 10   741.5; Fic
    1. Christian life; 2. Friendship; 3. Graphic novels
    978-1-59554-384-4, $9.99

The Prayer Club kids are nice, but that doesn't mean they can't be tough. Serenity is starting to warm up to the Christian teens who made her their project "by showing her an unconditional love she's never experienced before." But when she tries ducking responsibility for wrecking Kimberly's car, that unconditional love turns tough. Can Serenity understand it's for her own good?

Serenity #3: Basket Case. Thomas Nelson 2007 96p. Illustration

Grades: 5 6 7 8 9 10   741.5; Fic
    1. Christian life; 2. Friendship; 3. Graphic novels
    978-1-59554-385-1, $9.99

Serenity laughs at responsibility, but there's nothing funny about this job ... She disses a health class assignment that has teens caring for chicken eggs 24/7 to simulate the round-the-clock nurturing a baby requires. But when an overwhelming responsibility falls in Serenity's lap, where can she get help - from the friends she has mocked, or the God she doesn't quite believe in?

Serenity #4: Rave-n-Rant. Thomas Nelson 2007 96p. Illustration

Grades: 5 6 7 8 9 10   741.5; Fic
    1. Christian life; 2. Friendship; 3. Graphic novels
    978-1-59554-386-8, $9.99

Serenity begins to share her soul with her Prayer Club friends, and is angered to find that, while they say they love Serenity, they don't always like her. The teen with the blue hair and attitude takes her frustrations to God, but soon decides He isn't listening ... until a surprise ending makes Serenity realize there may be something to prayer after all.

Serenity #5: Snow Biz. Thomas Nelson 2007 96p. Illustration

Grades: 5 6 7 8 9 10   741.5; Fic
    1. Christian life; 2. Friendship; 3. Graphic novels
    978-1-59554-387-5, $9.99

Serenity views a Prayer Club ski trip as one more opportunity to drive a wedge between Derek and Kimberly. But while hotdogging on the slopes, Serenity takes a major tumble, breaking her leg and seriously bruising her ego.

Who's going to care for her wounds - both physical and spiritual?

Serenity #6: You Shall Love. Thomas Nelson 2007 96p. Illustration
Grades: 5 6 7 8 9 10   **741.5; Fic**
  1. Christian life; 2. Friendship; 3. Graphic novels
978-1-59554-388-2, $9.99

A broken bone—and heart—finds Serenity at a major crossroad. Her leg's in a cast, the power's out, and Serenity's bored stiff. Searching for answers and willing to risk everything, Serenity picks up the Bible she received when she first visited the Prayer Club. Before long, she's pestering her friends with spiritual questions and getting serious about some major life changes. There's healing for the broken—and unexpected new challenges—in this story.

Serenity Vol. 1: Bad Girl in Town. Thomas Nelson 2007 96p. Illustration
Grades: 4 5 6 7 8 9   **741.5; Fic**
  1. Friendship; 2. Graphic novels
978-1-59554-383-7, $9.99

Everyone needs a little Serenity—or do they? She's only five feet tall and 98 pounds - but she's one tense bundle of attitude and anger. Serenity's life is a mess on every front. Now she's got one last shot at a fresh start . . . but her new school seems to just be adding new problems. Being the New Kid isn't making life any easier. But her friends might have just what she's been searching for - if they don't drive her crazy first, with their Christian beliefs. Can she be like them?

Reed, Gary
Bram Stoker's Dracula: The Graphic Novel. Illustrated by Becky Cloonan. Puffin Graphics 2006 176p. Illustration
Grades: 5 6 7 8 9 10 11 12   **741.5; Fic**
  1. Dracula, Count (Fictional character); 2. Horror graphic novels; 3. Stoker, Bram, 1847-1912 — Adaptations; 4. Vampires; 5. Graphic novels
0-14-240572-8, $10.99

When Jonathan Harker travels to Transylvania to meet his firm's client, Count Dracula, he discovers his host's terrifying secret: Dracula is a vampire. The monster moves to England and targets young Lucy Westenra, and then Harker's fiancee, Mina Murray. Harker joins with Dr. Van Helsing and several other men who have pledged to destroy the vampire. This volume includes notes by Reed and Cloonan, some of Cloonan's sketches, and pages that show her early art for the book.

Mary Shelley's Frankenstein: the graphic novel. Art by Frazer Irving. Puffin Graphics 2005 176p. Illustration
Grades: 5 6 7 8 9 10 11 12   **741.5; Fic**
  1. Horror graphic novels; 2. Novelists; 3. Shelley, Mary Wollstonecraft, 1797-1851 — Adaptations; 4. Graphic novels
0-14-240407-1, $9.99

Scientist Victor Frankenstein decided to create a man, only to create something he deemed a monster.

"Reed concentrates on the emotional anguish of the story, ably capturing the rage, the hurt, and the guilt of both monster and creator. Irving . . . creates a hazy, suitably murky black-and-white backdrop, never exploiting the violence inherent in the monster's quest for vengeance." Booklist

Regnaud, Jean
  ★ **My** mommy is in America and she met Buffalo Bill. Jean Regnaud & Émile Bravo (artist). Fanfare/Ponent Mon 2009 120p. Illustration
Grades: 6 7 8 9 10 11 12 Adult   **741.5; Fic**
  1. Family life; 2. Mother; 3. School life; 4. Graphic novels
978-84-96427-85-3, $25
Essentials Award winner at the 35th Festival of Angouleme,n France, 2008; Tam Tam Literary Award 2009 from Salon du Livres et de la Presse Jeunesse, for Comic Album, age group eight to thirteen years old.

Narrator Jean has just started first grade and has a younger brother, Paul, in kindergarten. They live with their factory boss father and nanny Yvette; Jean says his mother is on a trip. As he talks about his first day at school, meeting a new friend, Alain, and fighting with Paul, he mentions his mother has been away so long he can't quite remember her. Next door neighbor Michelle claims to be receiving postcards from Jean's mother and reads them to him; they come from places such as Switzerland and the United States. As the reader sees Jean and Paul spend a day with their mother's parents and interact with their grandparents' friends, the reader understands what Jean does not: his mother is dead. This book, translated from its original French, won an award for best comic album for ages eight to thirteen; however, with the essential fact never stated and Jean deciding that he's getting to old to believe in his mother, just as he's too old to believe in Father Christmas, makes this more suitable for the upper age range, teens, and adults.

Reilly, Chris
The **weirdly** world of strange eggs. Chris Reilly, Steve Ahlquist, and Jeremy Mann. Amaze Ink/SLG Publishing 2007 80p. Illustration
Grades: 5 6 7 8 9 10   **741.5**
  1. Adventure graphic novels; 2. Fantasy graphic novels; 3. Humorous graphic novels; 4. Graphic novels
978-1-59362-085-1, $7.95

Kip and Kelly have a pretty quiet life on the farm with their father (who generally stays behind the newspaper); Kelly performs all kinds of scientific experiments while Kip always wants adventure. Then they encounter Roger Rogers, who gives them a strange egg that hatches into a creature they name Hooper. When Roger comes with another egg, Hooper tricks him and takes it, and this time the egg hatches a creature that looks like a party hat and excretes vampire bats. As Kip and Kelly fight off the party hat, bats, and even a monster tree, they learn to protect thos they love and trust those who want to help them (such as the ex B-movie actress veterinarian).

Renier, Aaron
Spiral-bound. Top Shelf Productions 2005 144p. Illustration
Grades: 4 5 6 7 8 9
741.5; Fic
  1. Mystery graphic novels; 2. Graphic novels

Courtesy of Top Shelf Productions

1-891830-50-3, $14.95

"Turnip the elephant is using the summer to find his artistic voice through sculpture, his friend Stucky the dog is building a submarine, and Ana the rabbit is working on the town's underground newspaper. Their stories all wind around the town's deep, dark secret about the monster that lives in the pond. . . . The characters seem like real children, wholesome without being too sweet, and Renier's art is light and fun, a sort of Babar meets underground comix." Booklist

★ The **Unsinkable** Walker Bean. Written and illustrated by Aaron Renier; colored by Alec Longstreth. First Second 2010 191p. Illustration
Grades: 5 6 7 8   **741.5; Fic**
978-1-59643-453-0 (pa), $13.99; 1-59643-453-8 (pa)
The story "centers around a cursed skull stolen from the lair of two deep-sea crustacean witches. Like all who look upon the skull, Walker's beloved grandpa falls deathly ill when he finds it, and the boy sets out to return the skull from whence it came. . . . The generous page size lets [the] reader dive into Renier's quavery and painstakingly detailed cartooning, and he really shows off his stuff with a bounty of full-splash dazzlers. . . . Exciting, deep, funny, and scary, with tremendous villains and valor galore." Booklist

Reynolds, Aaron
Kung Pow chicken. By Aaron Reynolds; illustrated by Erik Lervold.. Stone Arch Books 2008 40p. Illustration
Grades: 3 4 5 6 7   **741.5; Fic**
1. Humorous graphic novels; 2. Ninja; 3. Science fiction graphic novels; 4. Graphic novels
978-1-4342-0455-4, $21.26; 978-1-4342-0505-6 (pa), $6.95
LC 2007-31253
Tiger Moth, fourth grade insect ninja, has been captured by Weevil's evil minions. His fourth grade sidekick, Kung Pow, needs to rescue him, but the only person who can help him is his kid sister, first grader Amber. With his own apprentice, can Kung Pow pull off a rescue?
Part of the Graphic Sparks series, a Tiger Moth adventure.

The **pest** show on earth. By Aaron Reynolds; illustrated by Erik Lervold.. Stone Arch Books 2008 40p. Illustration
Grades: 3 4 5 6 7   **741.5; Fic**
1. Humorous graphic novels; 2. Ninja; 3. Science fiction graphic novels; 4. Graphic novels
978-1-4342-0454-7, $21.26; 978-1-4342-0504-9 (pa), $6.95
LC 2007-31254
Tiger Moth, fourth grade insect ninja, and his sidekick Kung Pow, go to the carnival that has just come to town, only to discover that the ringmaster is the evil Weevil. They learn his nefarious plan to trap the town's insect citizens with Wing Kong, a giant insect-eating bat.
Part of the Graphic Sparks series, a Tiger Moth adventure.

Tiger Moth and the Dragon Kite Contest. Illustrated by Erik Lervold. Stone Arch Books 2007 40p. Illustration
Grades: 2 3 4 5 6 7   **741.5; Fic**
1. Humorous graphic novels; 2. Mystery graphic novels; 3. Graphic novels

978-1-59889-056-3, $21.26 lib. bdg.
Fourth-grade ninjas Tiger Moth and Kung Pow have fun with their classmates celebrating the Chinese New Year. Then Tiger's rivals, the Fruit Fly Boys, enter the kite-flying contest and cheat, resulting in sky-high disaster. The easy-to-read text, simple panel layout, and fast-paced story make this suitable for beginning and struggling readers.

Tiger Moth, Insect Ninja. Illustrated by Erik Lervold. Stone Arch Books 2007 40p. Illustration
Grades: 2 3 4 5 6 7   **741.5; Fic**
1. Humorous graphic novels; 2. Ninja; 3. Graphic novels
978-1-59889-057-0 li, $21.26; 978-1-59889-228-4 (pa)
LC 2006007700
Young Tiger Moth is a ninja-in-training, a martial arts warrior who fights evil in the streets and classrooms of the bug world. With the help of his best friend, pillbug Kung Pow, he works for truth and justice, while still hoping to finish the fourth grade. This graphic novel features easy text and a controlled vocabulary for beginning and struggling readers.
Part of the Graphic Sparks series.

Tiger Moth: The Fortune Cookies of Weevil. Illustrated by Erik Lervold. Stone Arch Books 2007 40p. Illustration
Grades: 2 3 4 5 6 7   **741.5; Fic**
1. Humorous graphic novels; 2. Mystery graphic novels; 3. Graphic novels
978-1-59889-318-2, $21.26 lib. bdg.
Who is sending all the fortune cookies around the school, and why are only the bad boy bugs, such as Dragon and the Fruit Fly Boys, getting them? What messages are hidden in the cookies? Fourth-grade ninjas Tiger Moth and best buddy Kung Pow decide to investigate. The easy text, simple panel layout, and the pun-filled, fast-paced story make this suitable for beginning and struggling readers.

Rieber, John Ney
G. I. Joe Reloaded Vol. 1: In the Name of Patriotism. Devil's Due Publishing 2004 Un Illustration
Grades: 7 8 9 10 11 12 Adult   **741.5; Fic**
1. Adventure graphic novels; 2. G I Joe (Fictional character); 3. Graphic novels
1-932796-23-1, $12.95
The Threat: Unknown. The Mission: Critical. The Team: G.I. Joe. United by the twisted strategic genius of a madman, a deadly cabal of conspirators unleashes a savage assault on the very heart of America. The nation is defenseless against these faceless paramilitary hordes whose dread insignia is a striking cobra... Until a rogue Lieutenant Colonel forges a handful of hard-hitting soldiers into the ultimate elite fighting force: G.I. Joe. The book includes fighting action.

Riordan, Rick
Percy Jackson & the Olympians, book one: the lightning thief: the graphic novel. Adapted by Robert Venditti; art by Attila Futaki; color by José Villarrubia; layouts by Orpheus Collar; lettering by Chris Dickey. Hyperion Books for Children 2010 Un Illustration
Grades: 5 6 7 8 9 10   **741.5; Fic**
1. Adventure graphic novels; 2. Fantasy graphic novels; 3. Greek mythology; 4. Graphic novels

978-1-4231-1696-7, $19.99; 978-1-4321-1710-0 (pa), $9.99

Twelve-year-old Percy Jackson has had a hard time in school, but when a teacher transforms into a Fury and tries to kill him during a field trip to the museum, his life becomes even more complicated. He learns that he is the son of one of the Greek gods and a human woman, and then he learns that he should never have been born, and that the gods think he has stolen Zeus's master lightning bolt. Percy, his best friend Grover (a satyr), and Annabeth, daughter of Athena, have ten days to recover the lightning bolt and prevent all-out war among the Olympians. This graphic novel adapts Riordan's novel, NOT the movie. Futaki makes the water action look great in an adaptation that should make the book fans happy.

The **red** pyramid: the graphic novel. Rick Riordan; adapted by Orpheus Collar; lettered by Jared Fletcher. Disney/Hyperion Books 2012 Un Color; Illustration (The Kane chronicles)
Grades: 4 5 6 7 8 9   **741.5**
1. Brothers and sisters — Fiction; 2. Egyptian mythology — Fiction; 3. Magic — Fiction
1423150694; 1423150686; 9781423150695, $12.99; 9781423150688, $21.99
       LC 2012007905
"Since their mother's death, Sadie and Carter have become near-strangers. While Sadie has lived with her grandparents in London, Carter has traveled the world with their father, the famed Egyptologist Dr. Julius Kane. One night, Dr. Kane brings the siblings to the British Museum, where he hopes to set things right for his family. Instead, he unleashes the Egyptian god Set, who banishes him to oblivion and forces the children to flee for their lives." (Publisher's note)
"Out of necessity, much of the dialogue is dedicated to explaining actions and events, but a constant stream of humor prevents the reader from getting bogged down by logistics. The colorful artwork has an almost painting-like quality, . . . and some clever visual jokes and thoughtful use of panels make good use of the format." VOYA

Rioux, Jo-Anne
The **golden** twine; Book 1. Jo Rioux. Kids Can Press 2012 111 p. Color illustration
Grades: 5 6 7 8   **741.5/971; 741.5; Fic**
1. Dragons — Fiction; 2. Magic — Fiction; 3. Monsters — Fiction; 4. Paranormal fiction
1554536367; 9781554536368, $17.95
In this book by author Jo Rioux, "parentless young storyteller Suri [buys a dragon tooth that brings her luck] . . .The ball of magical golden string that she finds . . belongs to a trio of vicious tiger creatures called 'caitsiths' who use the string to masquerade as humans and . . . want it back . . . Suri [also] achieves her . . . desire to become a monster tamer when she meets Byron, a humongous if overly friendly dog, and the surly 500-year-old imp Caglio who . . . created him." (Kirkus)

Rivkah
Steady Beat, Vol. 1. Tokyopop 2005 Un Illustration
Grades: 8 9 10 11 12   **741.5; Fic**

1. Homosexuality; 2. Lesbians; 3. Romance graphic novels; 4. Graphic novels
1-59816-135-0, $9.99
Sixteen-year-old Leah finds a love letter in her older sister's things; it's signed "Jessica." That wouldn't really be a problem, except that their single mother is a conservative Republican politician and they live in a conservative Texas town. And someone wants to blackmail Sarai through Leah. While she's trying to keep Sarai's secret, Leah meets Elijah, who has a gay father. This is a global manga series.

Robbins, Trina
★ The **drained** brains caper. [by] Trina Robbins and Tyler Page. Graphic Universe 2010 64p. Illustration (Chicagoland Detective Agency)
Grades: 4 5 6 7   **Fic; 741; 741.5**
1. Brainwashing — Fiction; 2. Humorous graphic novels; 3. Japanese Americans; 4. Mystery graphic novels; 5. Schools; 6. Graphic novels
978-0-7613-4601-2 (lib bdg), $27.97; 0-7613-4601-5 (lib bdg); 978-0-7613-5635-6 (pa), $6.95; 0-7613-5635-5 (pa)
       LC 2009-32620
Required to attend summer school after moving to Chicagoland, thirteen-year-old manga-love Megan Yamamura needs help from twelve-year-old computer genius Raf Hernandez to escape the maniacal principal's mind control experiment.
This tells "an entertaining story. . . . Page's black-and-white cartooning has a loose manga slant, with peppy goofiness popping out from stippled screen tones." Booklist
Other titles in this series are: The Maltese mummy (2011); Night of the living dogs (2012); The big flush (2012); The bark in space (2013); A midterm night's scheme (2014)

Go girl!. Vol. 1, The time team. Story, Trina Robbins, art, Anne Timmons. Dark Horse Comics 2004 95p. Illustration
Grades: 3 4 5 6 7 8   **741; 741.5; Fic**
1. Adventure graphic novels; 2. Go Girl! (Fictional character); 3. Superhero graphic novels; 4. Graphic novels
1-59307-230-9, $5.95
"Robbins, who has made a name for herself as a feminist in the comics world, creates a story about three stereotypical high school girls—the dismissive cheerleader, the misunderstood brain, and the daughter of a 1970s-era superheroine—who become stranded in prehistory. The girls are quick-witted, the dinosaurs are cartoony, and a late appearance by Vikings offers readers a taste of what Nordic women might have been like in a confrontation. This isn't high concept, but it's definitely good, clean fun." Booklist
Followed by:Vol. 2: Robots gone wild

Go Girl!: Robots Gone Wild!. Dark Horse Comics 2007 183p. Illustration
Grades: 4 5 6 7 8 9 10   **741.5**
1. Go Girl! (Fictional character); 2. Superhero graphic novels; 3. Graphic novels
978-1-59307-409-8
Video games can get too realistic, as the flying teenager, Go Girl! discovers in "Prisoners of the Machine," when she

and her friends find themselves trapped inside a computer, menaced by giant anime-robots. And in "Double Trouble," Go Girl!'s arch-enemies create a robot that looks just like her, except that it has the mind of a master criminal. How can our heroine convince the cops that she didn't rob that bank, when everyone saw her do it? Plus, Go Girl!'s sidekick, Haseena, tired of always being rescued by the flying teen, takes up sleuthing herself in "Haseena Ross, Girl Detective."

Hedy Lamarr and a Secret Communication System. Illustrated by Cynthia Martin and Anne Timmons. Capstone Press 2007 32p. Illustration
Grades: 3 4 5 6 7 8 9   **621.384; 741.5; 92; 621.384092**
1. Biographical graphic novels; 2. Inventions; 3. Lamarr, Hedy, 1914-2000; 4. Graphic novels
978-0-7368-6479-4, $25.26
                                LC 2006004104
This volume tells the story of how gorgeous Hollywood star Hedy Lamarr came up with the idea for a secret communication system back in the early days of World War II, which would much later become the basis for wireless technology. The book provides additional information, a glossary, a list of books for further reading, and more.
Part of the Graphic Library, Inventions and Discovery series.

Lily Renée, escape artist. Illustrated by Anne Timmons and Mo Oh. Graphic Universe 2011 96p. Color illustration
Grades: 4 5 6 7 8   **92; 741.5; 940.53**
1. Artists; 2. Holocaust, 1933-1945; 3. Illustrators; 4. Jews — Biography; 5. Phillips, Lily Renee; 6. Graphic novels
978-0-7613-6010-0, $7.95; 0-7613-6010-7
                                LC 2011001084
Presents the story of Lily Ren?e Wilheim, the Jewish girl who escaped from the Nazis through the Kindertransport operation, leaving her parents behind and traveling alone to England, later becoming a comic book artist in New York.
"This comic-book biography of a Jewish girl's life under the Nazi jackboot and then as a refugee is low key and that much more profound for it. The panels are brightly lit, and the narrative is crisp, both of which serve to chillingly amplify the everyday banality of evil. . . . A fitting tribute." Kirkus

Roberts, Steven
Henry Ford. By Steven Roberts. PowerKids Press 2013 24 p. (Jr. graphic American inventors)
Grades: 3 4 5 6   **338.7/629222092; 92; B**
1. Automobile industry and trade — United States — Biography — Juvenile literature; 2. Ford, Henry, 1863-1947 — Juvenile literature; 3. Industrialists — United States — Biography — Juvenile literature; 4. Inventors
147770079X; 9781477700792, $25.25; 9781477701430; 9781477701447
                                LC 2012020485
This book, by Steven Roberts, presents a biography of inventor Henry Ford. "It looks at the man who perfected the mass market automobile. From a young age Ford tinkered with farm machines and fixed neighbors' watches. That led to jobs working with steam engines and then, under the employment of Thomas Edison, the internal combustion engine. Inspired by the work flow of other factories, Ford

created the Model T, and in just a few years, he was creating a million cars per year." (Booklist)
Includes index.

Robert Fulton. By Steven Roberts. PowerKids Press 2013 24 p.
Grades: 3 4 5 6   **623.82; 623.82/4092; B**
1. Fulton, Robert, 1765-1815 — Juvenile literature; 2. Inventors — United States — Biography — Juvenile literature; 3. Marine engineers — United States — Biography — Juvenile literature; 4. Steamboats — Juvenile literature
1477700773; 9781477700778, $25.25; 9781477701393; 9781477701409
                                LC 2012020630
In this graphic novel by Steven Roberts "readers will [learn] more about [Robert] Fulton and his contributions to American society through easy to follow text and vibrant illustrations." It notes that "Robert Fulton didn't actually invent what he is most commonly associated with, yet Fulton s innovations on the steamboat changed America s trade and travel in a progressive way." (Publisher's note)
Includes bibliographical references (p. 24) and index

Robinson, Alex
★ A **kidnapped** Santa Claus. It Books/HarperCollins 2009 Un Illustration
Grades: 4 5 6 7 8 9   **741.5; Fic**
1. Adventure graphic novels; 2. Baum, L Frank, 1856-1919 — Adaptations; 3. Christmas; 4. Santa Claus; 4. Graphic novels
978-0-06-178240-4, $14.99
Santa Claus lives in the Laughing Valley, with the fairies on one side of the valley in the Forest of Burzee. On the other side of the valley stands a mountain that contains the caves of the daemons, Selfishness, Envy, Hatred, and Repentance. On this Christmas Eve, the daemons hatch a diabolical plot to destroy Christmas. When they can't convince Santa to be selfish, envious, or to hate people, they kidnap him. Santa's helpers, led by the young fairy named Wisk, decide they need to save Christmas when the big man doesn't show up, so they set out to deliver the presents all around the world. There's one big problem Wisk can't find Santa's list; they have to improvise. Baum's story provides a different type of Christmas adventure; his Santa doesn't live at the North Pole, and his helpers aren't elves. Robinson, who's known for his adult graphic novels, makes Wisk a girl fairy with big cats-eye glasses. During the battle to rescue Santa from the daemons, one of Santa's helpers named Nuter loses his head, which might disturb some younger readers (he doesn't die).

Robinson, Fiona
★ The **3-2-3** Detective Agency: the disappearance of Dave Warthog. Amulet Books 2009 80p. Illustration
Grades: 2 3 4 5 6   **741.5; Fic**
1. Humorous graphic novels; 2. Mystery graphic novels; 3. Graphic novels
978-08109-7094-6 (pa), $9.95; 978-0-8109-8489-9, $17.95
                                LC 2008-37171

On the 3:23 express train to Whiska City, Jenny the donkey meets four new friends, and they decide to form a private detective agency together. Priscilla, a penguin with a penchant for drama, Slingshot, a sloth who can't sleep, very shy (but brave) rat Bluebell, and gourmet dung beetle Roger join Jenny in what they decide to call the 323 Detective Agency. When they arrive in Whiska City, they notice things aren't quite right, and they learn that animals have been disappearing almost every day. They almost immediately get new clients, all wanting their loved ones found, such as Dave Warthog, whose mother disappeared. Even the Mayor needs their help to find her police department. They notice that poodle salons have popped up around the city, and the poodles have their own exclusive, gated community. As each detective investigates, they learn that every animal who disappeared had an appointment at a poodle salon. Then Priscilla, who has gone undercover to a salon, has disappeared, and now Jenny and the others must find a way to rescue her and solve the mystery.

Robinson, James

★ **Leave** It to Chance Vol. II: Trick or Threat & Other Stories. James Robinson & Paul Smith ; with George Freeman, inks ; Jeromy Cox, color art ; and Amie Grenier, lettering. Image Comics 2003 Un Illustration
Grades: 5 6 7 8 9 10   **741.5; Fic**
1. Adventure graphic novels; 2. Fantasy graphic novels; 3. Horror graphic novels; 4. Graphic novels
1-58240-278-7, $14.95

In "Trick or Threat," Chance helps a boy save his pet monkey from being sacrificed by a gang of cultists. Then her father sends Chance away to a boarding school (to keep her out of trouble), but there she has to face the ghost of the evil pirate Captain Hitch. Back home in Devil's Echo, Chance goes to the mall with her new friends from school, but they have to confront "The Phantom of the Mall." The book includes cartoony horror violence.

★ **Leave** It to Chance Vol. III: Monster Madness & Other Stories. Image Comics 2003 Un Illustration
Grades: 5 6 7 8 9 10   **741.5; Fic**
1. Adventure graphic novels; 2. Fantasy graphic novels; 3. Horror graphic novels; 4. Graphic novels
1-58240-298-1, $14.95

Chance Falconer is the mischievous 14-year- old daughter of Lucas Falconer, who is the mystical guardian for the city of Devil's Echo and its most prominent supernatural detective. Devil's Echo faces an all-new threat, as classic matinee monsters literally come to life and walk off a movie screen to wreak havoc in the streets. It's all-out excitement as Chance and her friends try to stop them, but the most shocking secret of all is who is really behind the mayhem. Then Chance helps a zombie hockey star hunt for the men who killed him. The book includes some cartoony horror action.

Leave it to Chance: Shaman's rain. [by] James Robinson & Paul Smith. Image Comics 2002 Un Illustration
Grades: 5 6 7 8 9 10   **741.5; Fic**
1. Fantasy graphic novels; 2. Horror graphic novels; 3. Graphic novels
1-58240-253-1, $14.95

"Chance Falconer is a 14-year-old only child born into a family of municipal sorcerers that has protected the city of Devil's Echo for centuries. Chance can't wait to start training in the family business, but her father decides he doesn't want a girl joining the family's dangerous profession. Predictably, it's not long before she stumbles onto a dead body and a kidnapping in progress, and soon enough she's got a full-fledged mystery on her hands. . . . This is a girl power comic written with a younger audience in mind. The smartest cops are female, the violence is G-rated and the story is fast-paced, brightly colored and as wholesome as it gets." Publ Wkly

Other titles in this series are: Leave it to Chance, Vol. 2: Trick or treat (2003); Leave it to Chance, Vol. 3: Monster madness (2003)

Robinson, Jimmie

Evil & malice save the world!. Image Comics/Silverline Books 2009 128p. Illustration
Grades: 5 6 7 8 9 10   **741.5; Fic**
1. Humorous graphic novels; 2. Sisters; 3. Superhero graphic novels; 4. Graphic novels
978-1-60706-091-8, $14.99

Evelyn and Malinda are the twin daughters of Dooplis City's top villain, the Black Eye, but they want to go see superhero Goldie Gal at a public appearance. She has come to help unveil a new computer system, the Max2000, that will automate many city functions. However, just at the moment of the unveiling, villains Coldheart, Chef, and Drip take out Goldie Gal and try to steal the Max2000. The damage they do in town threatens Evelyn's and Malinda's only friend Cindy, so they fight the villains to save her. The local newscaster catches just enough of the action to decide that Dooplis City has two new heroes and names them Evil and Malice. The girls decide to steal a bunch of their father's gadgets, since they have no superpowers of their own, and even though Dad is a villain, they set out to be heroes. Funny that every time they try to help, they end up destroying stuff. The villainous trio pretends to team up with the Black Eye, but plan to destroy him once they get the Max2000, so the girls know they have to save their father. There's a lot of superhero-type action, with buildings getting destroyed and things blowing up, but very little actual violence. Evie and Mal are very girly girls who still manage to handle a lot of action, and they learn that their conflict between villainous and heroic impulses comes because their mother was a superhero who married her chief villainous opponent. Bright cartoony colors and action along with lots of humor make this a much lighter-hearted story than Runaways.

Rodolphe

Scrooge:. Adapted by Rodolphe & Estelle Meyrand. Papercutz 2012 96 p. Color illustration
Grades: 3 4 5 6   **Fic; 741.5/973**
1. Christmas — Fiction; 2. England — Fiction; 3. Ghost stories; 4. Ghosts — Fiction; 5. Supernatural — Fiction
1597073458; 1597073466; 9781597073455, $11.99; 9781597073462, $15.00

This book, part of the Classics Illustrated Deluxe series, presents a graphic adaptation of the Charles Dickens stories "A Christmas Carol" and "Mugby Junction." In "A Christmas Carol," miser Ebenezer Scrooge is "visited by three spirits who will show him the way to change" on Christmas Eve. (Masterplots) "Mugby Junction" also features elements of the supernatural and a protagonist to whom his future is revealed." (Publisher's note)

Rogers, John

Blue Beetle: Shellshocked. Writers, Keith Giffen & John Rogers; Cully Hamner . . . [et al], pencillers; Phil Balsman, Pat Brosseau, letterers; David Self, Guy Major, colorists; Cully Hamner, Phil Moy, Duncan Rouleau, Jack Purcell, inkers. DC Comics 2006 144p. Illustration

Grades: 8 9 10 11 12 Adult   **741.5; Fic**
1. Adventure graphic novels; 2. Blue Beetle (Fictional character); 3. Superhero graphic novels; 4. Graphic novels
978-1-4012-0965-0, $12.99

Ted Kord, the Blue Beetle, is dead; but the Blue Beetle scarab has chosen a new guardian, El Paso teenager Jaime Reyes. Supernatural powers can be a blessing or a curse, and when it comes to the powers of the Scarab, you don't get one without the other. The new hero will now have to deal with increasingly strange and dangerous days ahead, as he learns to handle his new skills while intergalactic trouble comes looking for him.

Rol, Ruud van der

The **search**. [by] Eric Heuvel, Ruud van der Rol [and] Lies Schippers; [English translation by Lorraine T. Miller]. Farrar, Straus and Giroux 2009 61p. Illustration

Grades: 5 6 7 8 9   **741.5; Fic**
1. Grandmothers — Fiction; 2. Holocaust survivors — Fiction; 3. Holocaust, 1933-1945; 4. Jews — Netherlands — Fiction; 5. Graphic novels
978-0-374-36517-2, $18.99; 978-0-374-46455-4 (pa), $9.99

LC 2009-13603

After recounting her experience as a Jewish girl living in Amsterdam during the Holocaust, Esther, helped by her grandson, embarks on a search to discover what happened to her parents before they died in a concentration camp.

Esther, her grandson Daniel, and her friend Helena's grandson Jeroen visit the Dutch farm where Esther hid during the Nazi occupation of the Netherlands during World War II. She tells her story, of how she managed to escape the Nazi roundup of Jews, but how her family died in a concentration camp. Daniel helps her find an old friend from the farm, now living in Israel, and he tells her what happened to her family in Auschwitz. The book depicts some of the horrendous, horrible things that happened but does it without graphic violence or gore.

Roman, Dave

Agnes Quill: an anthology of mystery. All transcripts written by Dave Roman; illustrated by Jason Ho, Raina Telgemeier, Jeff Zornow and Dave Roman. SLG Publishing 2006 130p. Illustration

Grades: 7 8 9 10 11 12   **741.5**
1. Horror graphic novels; 2. Mystery graphic novels; 3. Graphic novels
978-1-59362-052-3, $10.95

Orphaned teen Agnes Quill lives in the city of Legerdemain and carries on a family tradition; she can see and communicate with ghosts, and she works as a detective

to help them. Her cases range from recovering the mummified head of a ghost's old body in order to save the valuable necklace hidden there, to helping a little girl ghost find her doll, to helping a man find his legs, and more. Roman works with artists including Raina Telgemeier, and their styles range from childlike cartoons to gloomy, atmospheric art full of shadows.

"The variety of drawing styles and Agnes' story of being a teenage detective who can see the dead among the living combine in an interesting read that will likely keep readers' attention." Voice Youth Advocates

★ **Astronaut** Academy: Zero gravity. First Second Books 2011 185p. Illustration

Grades: 4 5 6 7 8   **741; 741.5; Fic**
1. Humorous graphic novels; 2. School life; 3. Science fiction graphic novels; 4. Graphic novels
9781596436206, $9.99; 9781596437562, $16.99

LC 2010-941434

Hakata Soy has been the leader of a futuristic superhero team, but he has given that up and just wants to be a normal student at Astronaut Academy, a school on a space station, where students take such courses as anti-gravity gymnastics and fire-throwing. Other students include Doug Hiro, who always wears his space helmet, rich girl Maribelle Mellonbelly, Miyumi San (Maribelle's rival), and egotistical Billy Lee. Hakata Soy has some trouble adjusting to school life, and things get much worse when the villainous Gotcha Birds steal a robotic twin to Hakata Soy and reprogram it to kill him. The comics originally appeared as web comics, then as mini comics that Roman took to various comic cons; this is the first trade book collection of the stories. Middle grade students, boys and girls, will enjoy this book, which is full of humor and action with little actual violence.

"Students like the introspective Hakata Soy, the space-gymnastics-obsessed Doug Hiro, and the snooty rich girl Mirabelle Mellonbelly meet up at Astronaut Academy, a middle school where the zany mixes with the postmodern... . Silliness is high on the agenda, aided by minimal, cartoonish art that plays on manga tropes but also manages to build character into the simple lines of a face.... This is one for readers looking for more involved and complex comedy than a cursory glance at the images might lead one to expect." Booklist

Followed by: Astronaut academy: Re-entry (2013)

Jax Epoch and the Quicken Forbidden: Borrowed Magic. John Green, illustrator. AiT/PlanetLar 2003 152p. Illustration

Grades: 7 8 9 10 11 12 Adult   **741.5; Fic**
1. Science fiction graphic novels; 2. Graphic novels
1-932051-11-2, $14.95

When teenager Jax stumbles into an interdimensional portal, she "borrows" several items: an ancient book, a pair of gloves, and a pair of boots. When she returns home through the portal, things are a bit . . . off. Her little escapade has caused magic to leak into her world, and now she's deep in trouble, unstuck in time and on trial for the crime of crossing dimensions. The story continues in Volume 2: Separation Anxiety.

"Jax is a great character - quite real but with flaws that get her into deep trouble while possessing the aplomb to get herself out." (VOYA)

Followed by Volume 2: Separation Anxiety

Romance Without Tears

Edited by John Benson. Fantagraphics Books 2004 160p. Illustration
Grades: 8 9 10 11 12 Adult   **741.5; Fic**
1. Romance graphic novels; 2. Graphic novels
1-56097-558-X, $22.95

This revisionist collection of romance comics stories from the '50s challenges the cliché of the "tear-stained face" that later dominated the genre and became widely known and vilified as a tiresome icon of moral uplift. Editor Benson has picked stories that portray stron young women who learn from their mistakes and choose their guys, and get themselves out of trouble. The stories were all originally published by Archer St. John in the late-1940s to mid-1950s.

Rosa, Don

Walt Disney's Uncle Scrooge and Donald Duck: the Son of the sun. [written and drawn by Don Rosa; lettered by John Clark]. Fantagraphics Books 2014 207 p. Color; Illustration
Grades: 7 8 9 10 11 12 Adult   **741.5**
1. Ducks — Fiction; 2. Fictional characters
1606997424; 9781606997420, $29.99

LC 2012287668

This collection by Don Rosa, featuring Disney's Donald Duck and Scrooge McDuck, is "filled with epic adventures, like hunting for buried treasure or recovering stolen money. . . . At the end of each volume are whole pages of reference notes, explaining each comic in depth and addressing Rosa's process and nods to previous works." (School Library Journal)

"When Rosa began creating Uncle Scrooge comics in 1987, his work instilled childish wonder in readers. Disney comics had entirely disappeared from circulation, and those that had just preceded the fall had become completely hackneyedùrife with repeating storylines and drab artwork. But under Rosa's creative flair, a zippy, glamorous franchise suddenly appeared, with riveting stories and detailed yet kinetic artwork. While remaining totally true to Scrooge McDuck's ornery persona, Rosa turned the moody miser into a plucky adventurer worthy of Tintin." Pub Wkly

Other titles in this series are: Return to plain awful (2014); Treasure under glass (2015)

Rosca, Madeleine

Hollow Fields Omnibus collection. Seven Seas Entertainment 2009 Un Illustration
Grades: 5 6 7 8 9 10   **741.5; Fic**
1. Adventure graphic novels; 2. Science fiction graphic novels; 3. Graphic novels
978-1-934876-72-5, $14.99

Rosca is an Australian global manga creator who won one of the inaugural International Manga Awards 'Shorei' awards given by the Japanese government in 2007.

Lucy Snow was supposed to start school at a nice elementary school in town, but she manages to lose her way in a forest and finds herself at Miss Weaver's Academy for the Scientifically Gifted and Ethically Unfettered a school for archvillains in training. Lucy's fellow students are all learning how to be mad scientists and evil geniuses, with classes such as Live Taxidermy, Cross-Species Body-Part Transplantation, and Killer Robot Construction. Hollow Fields, as the school is also called, also has a practice guaranteed to make everyone compete to do well: the student with the lowest grades at the end of the week is sent to the windmill for detention, and thus far no student has ever returned. Miss Weaver has experimented on herself, as have all the Engineers who teach; what the reader learns is that they need new, young blood to keep their stitched-together bodies going, for they are all more than a hundred years old. Befriended by a talking box that calls itself Doctor Bleak, Lucy struggles to hold her own in her classes, despite her innate niceness. She decides she needs to discover just what goes on in the windmill, and how she can make things right. The book includes some mild violence.

Rubio, Kevin

Star Wars: Tag & Bink Were Here. Pencils by Lucas Marangon. Dark Horse Comics 2006 Un Illustration
Grades: 7 8 9 10 11 12 Adult   **741.5; Fic**
1. Adventure graphic novels; 2. Humorous graphic novels; 3. Science fiction graphic novels; 4. Star Wars; 5. Graphic novels
978-1-59307-641-2, $14.95

Rebel officers Tag Greenley and Bink Otauna were minding their own business aboard a familiar, princess-harboring freighter when they suddenly found themselves under siege. Now under attack by the Empire, they will choose life over a noble death and "borrow" the armor off a pair of deceased stormtroopers. Their new disguises might get them off the freighter alive, but they'll also lead Tag and Bink on an adventure neither could have predicted. Chock-full of appearances by everyone's favorite Star Wars characters, Tag & Bink weaves the pair's misadventures into the movies themselves. No setting is safe as they traverse the galaxy from the Death Star to the Sarlacc pit to Cloud City to Endor.

Ruiz, Emilio

Waluk. By Emilio Ruiz; illustrated by Ana Miralles; translated and adapted by Dan Oliverio. Graphic Universe 2013 52 p.
Grades: 3 4 5 6   **741.5; Fic**
1. Bears — Fiction; 2. Friendship — Fiction; 3. Polar bear — Fiction; 4. Tundras — Fiction; 5. Graphic novels
1467715980; 1467716065; 9781467715980, $26.60; 9781467716062, $7.95

LC 2012047787

"Young Waluk is all alone. His mother has abandoned him, as is the way of polar bears, and now he must fend for himself. But he doesn't know much about the world—and unfortunately, his Arctic world is changing quickly. The ice is melting, and food is hard to find." (Publisher's note)

"Marrying exemplary sequential storytelling, mythology, and science and enhanced through respectful anthropomorphizing, Waluk takes readers into a realistic world of polar bears endangered by climate change." Booklist

Originally published in Spanish in Bilbao, Spain, by Astiberri, in 2011, under the title: Wa?luk.

Runton, Andy

★ **Owly** Vol. 2: Just a Little Blue. Top Shelf Productions 2005 127p. Illustration
Grades: K 1 2 3 4 5 6 7 8 9 10 11 12 Adult   741.5; Fic
1. Friendship; 2. Stories without words; 3. Graphic novels
1-891830-64-3, $10

Owly is a kind, yet lonely, little owl who's always on the search for new friends and adventure. Owly learns that sometimes you have to make sacrifices and work at things that are important, especially friendship. He and Wormy try to help a stubborn bluebird by building a new home, but the bluebird rejects it and them.

★ **Owly** Vol. 3: Flying Lessons. Top Shelf Productions 2005 143p. Illustration
Grades: K 1 2 3 4 5 6 7 8 9 10 11 12 Adult   741.5; Fic
1. Friendship; 2. Stories without words; 3. Graphic novels
1-891830-76-7, $10

Owly figures out why he can't fly (he failed his childhood flying lessons), and helps another forest creature with his own flying problems. The flying squirrel is frightened by Owly, for he knows owls are hunters, but Owly isn't like that. How can he convince the squirrel he just wants to be friends?

★ **Owly** vol. 4: a time to be brave. Top Shelf Productions 2007 132p. Illustration
Grades: K 1 2 3 4 5 6 7 8 9 10 11 12 Adult   741.5; Fic
1. Fantasy graphic novels; 2. Friendship; 3. Owls; 4. Stories without words; 5. Graphic novels
978-1-891830-89-1, $10

A new visitor comes to the forest, but Wormy is scared of him because Owly had just read stories about a scary dragon, and the visitor seems to look scary. The visitor is just as scared of Owly. Things aren't just as they seem, and everyone soon finds out that a little bravery and a lot of friendship can fix just about anything. This is the latest volume in Runton's nearly wordless series about Owly and his friends.

★ **Owly** volume five: tiny tales. Top Shelf Productions 2008 175p. Illustration
Grades: K 1 2 3 4 5 6 7 8 9 10 11 12 Adult   741.5; Fic
1. Friendship; 2. Humorous graphic novels; 3. Graphic novels
978-1-60309-019-3, $10

This volume gathers short stories about Owly and his friends, including stories originally published for Free Comic Book Day issues from Top Shelf Productions, the first Owly mini-comics, drawings of Owly before he met Wormy, and more. Among the stories, Owly saves a friend from drowning in the cold river when the ice cracks, only to get caught in the hole himself; Owly finds a way to keep both the bees and hummingbirds happy when they get into a "turf" battle; Owly helps a friend when she falls and breaks the fancy potted plant she bought for a present; and more.

★ **Owly**: The way home and The bittersweet summer. [by] Andy Runton. Top Shelf 2004 160p. Illustration
Grades: K 1 2 3 4 5 6 7 8 9 10 11 12   741.5; Fic
1. Friendship; 2. Owls; 3. Graphic novels
1-891830-62-7, $10

LC 2005298860

Rotund little Owly befriends Wormy despite their differences, and together they help a couple of hummingbirds and learn that friendship doesn't end with separation.

"The whimsical black-and-white art is done with great facility for expressing emotion, and Runton's reliance on icons and pictures in lieu of the usual dialogue makes the story perfect for give-and-take between children and their parents." Booklist

Other titles in this series are: Owly: Just a little blue (2005); Owly: Flying lessons (2005); Owly: A time to be brave (2007); Owly: Tiny tales (2008)

Russell, P. Craig

★ **Coraline**. Based on the novel by Neil Gaiman; adapted and illustrated by P. Craig Russell; colorist, Lovern Kindzierski; letterer, Todd Klein. HarperCollins 2008 186p. Illustration
Grades: 4 5 6 7   741; Fic; 741.5
1. Gaiman, Neil, 1960- — Adaptations; 2. Horror graphic novels; 3. Graphic novels
978-0-06-082543-0, $18.99; 978-0-06-082544-7 (lib bdg), $19.89

LC 2007-930658

"An adaptation of Gaiman's 2002 novel Coraline, . . . a tale of childhood nightmares. As in the original story, Coraline wanders around her new house and discovers a door leading into a mirror place, where she finds her button-eyed "other mother," who is determined to secure Coraline's love one way or another. This version is a virtuoso adaptation. . . . A master of fantastical landscapes, Russell sharpens the realism of his imagery, perserving the humanity of the characters and heightening the horror." Booklist

Fairy Tales of Oscar Wilde Vol. 4: The Devoted Friend & The Nightingale and the Rose. NBM Publishing 2004 Un Illustration
Grades: 5 6 7 8 9   741.5; Fic
1. Fantasy graphic novels; 2. Graphic novels
978-1-56163-391-3, $16.99

This volume adapts The Devoted Friend," on what constitutes real friendship, and The Nightingale and the Rose," a story of sacrifice to love with a cruel twist. In both stories, innocence is sacrificed to cynicism and shallowness.

Fairy tales of Oscar Wilde: 5: The Happy Prince. Illustrated by P. Craig Russell. Nantier, Beall, Minoustchine 2012 32 p. Color illustration
Grades: 3 4 5 6 7 8   741.5/973; Fic
1. Fairy tales; 2. Generosity — Fiction; 3. Wilde, Oscar, 1854-1900 — Adaptations
1561636266; 9781561636266, $16.99

LC 93229468

For this book, "Eisner Award-winning [P. Craig] Russell has adapted into graphic novel form" the Oscar Wilde fairy tale "The Happy Prince." In the story, "a swallow . . . befriends the statue of the Happy Prince, who was indeed happy when he lived a sheltered life. Now, however, the prince stands over the city as a statue and sees all the suffering. With the help of the swallow, he breaks down the pieces of himself, his rubies, sapphire, and gold, to feed the starving people." (Publishers Weekly)

Ruth, Greg

The **lost** boy. Greg Ruth. GRAPHIX 2013 192 p.
Grades: 3 4 5 6 7   **741.5**
1. Fantasy fiction — Juvenile fiction; 2. Historical fiction
— Juvenile fiction
0439823323; 9780439823319, $24.99; 9780439823326,
$12.99; 9780545576901

LC 2013937147

This book by Greg Ruth "opens as a boy named Nate
moves to a new town and discovers a tape recorder hidden
underneath the floorboards of his bedroom. The action shifts
back several decades as Nate listens to recordings left by
Walter Pidgen, an outcast boy who disappeared without a
trace. Along with a neighbor, Tabitha, Nate is drawn into a
supernatural battle involving the denizens of an ancient
woodland kingdom, which include talking toys and insects."
(Publishers Weekly)

Ryan, Michael

Transformers animated, volume 6. Michael Ryan and
Casey Todd ; adapted by Zachary Rau. IDW Publishing
2008 Un Illustration
Grades: 3 4 5 6 7 8   **741.5; Fic**
1. Adventure graphic novels; 2. Robots; 3. Science fiction
graphic novels; 4. Transformers (Fictional characters); 5.
Graphic novels
978-1-60010-281-3, $7.99

In "Headmaster," Bulkhead's large size and strength
make him destructive, even when he doesn't want to be.
Meanwhile, Dr. Sumdac has just fired an engineer named
Masterson for making military robots, and Masterson
decides to use his technology to hold the city of Detroit for
ransom. He decides that Bulkhead's body is just right for his
Headmaster unit, so the Autobots now need to rescue
Bulkhead's body and stop Masterson from destroying a solar
fusion power plant. In "When Nature Calls," a mysterious
Cybertronian energy signature starts broadcasting from the
forest outside the city, and Sari goes with Prowl and
Bumblebee to investigate. They find a monstrous creature
that is part machine, part organic space barnacles, and it soon
infects the Autobots, leaving Sari to try to figure out how to
get rid of the space barnacles. The book is illustrated with
screen captures from the animated television series.

Saavedra, Scott

Dr. Radium Battles Phill, King of the Pill Bugs!. Amaze
Ink/SLG Publishing 2004 112p. Illustration
Grades: 7 8 9 10 11 12 Adult   **741.5; Fic**
1. Humorous graphic novels; 2. Science fiction graphic
novels; 3. Graphic novels
0-943151-84-8, $9.95

Before "Dexter's Laboratory" and before "Jimmy
Neutron," there was Dr. Radium, the last scientist left
standing in the "perfect" world of tomorrow. Ignored by
society and feared by his assistant, Dr. Radium pursues
Science with happy disregard for knowledge, progress, or
safety. Stuck with Penny, a girl from the present presently
trapped in the future, Dr. Radium suffers distractions from
giant scientist rats, screaming dinosaurs, and Phill, one very
mad King of the Pill Bugs.

Saint-Exupéry, Antoine de

★ The **little** prince by
Joann Sfar. Adapted from
the book by Antoine de
Saint-Exupéry; translated
by Sarah Ardizzone; colour
by Brigitte Findakly.
Houghton Mifflin Harcourt
2010 110p. Illustration
Grades: 5 6 7 8 9
741; Fic; 741.5
1. Extraterrestrial beings;
2. Fantasy graphic
novels; 3. Saint-Exupéry,
Antoine de, 1900-1944
— Adaptations; 4.
Graphic novels
978-0-547-33802-6,
$19.99; 0-547-33802-3

Courtesy of Houghton Mifflin Harcourt

"On the surface, this is a straight graphic-novel retelling
of the narrator pilot getting stranded in the desert, where he
meets a curious little boy who claims to be from a wee planet
very far away. . . . The ultimately tricky task is to honor the
source but not sound like an adaptation (otherwise, why not
just read the original?) and Sfar nails it on both counts. . . .
Everything is handled with both reverence and ingenuity."
Booklist

Sakai, Stan

★ **Usagi** Yojimbo, book one: The Ronin. Fantagraphics
Books 1999 144p. Illustration
Grades: 7 8 9 10 11 12   **741.5;**
Fic
1. Adventure graphic novels; 2.
Japan; 3. Rabbits; 4. Samurai;
5. Usagi Yojimbo (Fictional
character); 6. Graphic novels
0-930193-35-0;
978-0-930193-35-5, $15.95

LC 93-239124

This series contains the
adventures of Miyamoto Usagi,
a ronin samurai rabbit in
17th-century Japan.
First published 1987
Vol. 1 of an ongoing series;
Vols. 1-7 published by
Fantagraphics; Vols. 8-25 published by Dark Horse
Comics

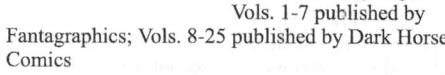

Courtesy of Fantagraphics

★ **Usagi** Yojimbo: Yokai. Created, written, and
illustrated by Stan Sakai. Dark Horse Books 2009 62p.
Illustration
Grades: 6 7 8 9 10 11 12 Adult   **741.5; Fic**
1. Adventure graphic novels; 2. Japan; 3. Monsters; 4.
Samurai; 5. Usagi Yojimbo (Fictional character); 6.
Graphic novels
978-1-59582-362-5, $14.95

LC 2009-20024

As he walks through a spooky forest at night, samurai
rabbit Usagi Yojimbo encounters a woman who begs him to
find her daughter, who was kidnapped and dragged into the
forest. That night, the yokai—monsters, demons, and spirits

from Japanese folklore—are amassing for a once-a-century attempt to take over the living world. Armed only with his swords and his wit, Usagi can't hope to win against so many supernatural beings, but luckily Sasuke the Demon Queller has come, knowing about the yokais' plan, and together they fight the gathered monsters. The fighting is not graphic or bloody, and the monsters and demons aren't too scary looking for most younger readers.

"Sakai's art deftly demonstrates that comics can be simultaneously cartoony and scary. . . . Usagi Yojimbo is a genuine pleasure for readers of all ages." Publ Wkly

Sakura, Kenichi

Dragon drive. Vol. 1, D-break. Story & art by Ken-ichi Sakura. Viz Media/Shonen Jump 2007 195p. Illustration
Grades: 6 7 8 9 10   **741.5; Fic**
1. Manga; 2. Shonen manga; 3. Video games; 4. Graphic novels
978-1-4215-1187-0, $7.99; 1-4215-1187-8

Reiji Ozora knows that he's no good at anything, people keep telling him that. Then best friend Maiko takes him to a secret center where people play a virtual reality game, Dragon Drive. Reiji signs up and finds that, despite the fact that his virtual dragon, Chibi, is small and weak, together they have more power than meets the eye. While they play the game, they're in a world called Rikyu, where everything feels all too real; can Reiji, Chibi, and their friends be in real danger?

Other titles in the Dragon Drive series are: Dragon drive. Vol. 2 : another world (2007); Dragon drive. Vol. 3: believe (2007); Dragon drive. Vol. 4: hero (2007); Dragon drive. Vol. 5: mission (2007); Dragon drive. Vol. 6: hope (2008); Dragon drive. Vol. 7: decisive battle (2008); Dragon drive. Vol. 8: excitement (2008); Dragon drive. Vol. 9: reshuffle (2008); Dragon drive. Vol. 10: departure (2008); Dragon drive. Vol. 11: trust (2008); Dragon drive. Vol. 12: promise (2009); Dragon drive. Vol. 13: reunion (2009); Dragon drive. Vol. 14: wait (2009)

Sakurakoji, Kanoko

Backstage Prince, Vol. 1. Viz Media/Shojo Beat 2007 188p. Illustration
Grades: 8 9 10 11 12 Adult   **741.5; Fic**
1. Kabuki; 2. Romance graphic novels; 3. Shojo manga; 4. Graphic novels
978-1-4215-1172-6, $8.99

High school freshman Akari stumbles into hottie Ryusei Horiuchi and hurts him with her school bag. That evening, she stumbles upon the kabuki theater where he, as famous kabuki actor Shonosuke Ichimura, is performing, and becomes his backstage assistant. Ryusei is very shy and aloof, and he's only opened up to his cat, Mr. Ken, and now to Akari; and she, despite herself, has fallen hard for Ryusei. Can an ordinary girl and a handsome, famous actor be together?

Sala, Richard

★ **Cat** burglar black. First Second 2009 126p. Illustration
Grades: 5 6 7 8 9 10   **741.5; Fic**
1. Mystery graphic novels; 2. Orphans; 3. Graphic novels

978-1-59643-144-7, $16.99; 1-59643-144-X

K.'s aunt, who works at the Bellsong Academy for Girls, has invited K. to attend the school. But as soon as she arrives, K. notices some strange goings-on: her aunt has suddenly taken ill; there are only three other students and no regular classes; and a statue speaks to K. when no one else is around.

"The story is structured like a lighthearted cross between a fable and a horror film, but only ever teetering on the edge of horror without depicting it. This could have resulted in a mishmash, but Sala elegantly dances through the creepy and the sweet." SLJ

Salicrup, Jim

Disney fairies: Prilla's talent. Papercutz 2010 80p. Illustration
Grades: 2 3 4 5 6   **741.5; Fic**
1. Fairies; 2. Fantasy graphic novels; 3. Graphic novels
978-1-59707-187-1, $12.99

Tinker Bell and the other fairies of Neverland live in Pixie Hollow; each fairy has a special talent Tink can fix things. New fairy Prilla seeks her special ability in "Prilla's Talent," while Vidia shows she's the fastest fairy in "Like the Wind." Tinker Bell must repair a special bell in "The Sound of Friendship," and she has to finish in time for a big festival. Then, in "Best of Friends," Tinker Bell wonders why her friend Rani won't talk to her. These stories were all originally written and published in Italy.

Salvatore, R. A.

DemonWars Vol. 1: The Demon Awakens. Art by Tim Seeley. Devil's Due Publishing 2007 Un Illustration
Grades: 8 9 10 11 12 Adult   **741.5; Fic**
1. Adventure graphic novels; 2. Fantasy graphic novels; 3. Graphic novels
978-1-932796-89-6, $18.99

A fearsome evil has awakened in the land of Corona. A demon determined to spread death and misery has unleashed his goblins and giants to ravage the settlements of the frontier. Two orphans, Pony and Elbryan, have survived the attacks. Taken in by elves, Elbryan grows up to be a formidable ranger. Meanwhile, on a far-off island, a shower of gemstones falls onto the black sand shores; these heaven-sent stones carry power for both good and evil. One young monk must liberate them from the corrupt monastery that harvests them. The book includes some violence.

SAM (Special Academic Manga)

Leonardo da Vinci. Y.kids/Youngjin Singapore Pte. Ltd. 2008 152p. Illustration
Grades: 3 4 5 6 7 8 9   **92; 741.5**
1. Art; 2. Artists; 3. Biographical graphic novels; 4. Leonardo, da Vinci, 1452-1519; 5. Painters; 6. Scientists; 7. Writers on science; 8. Graphic novels
978-981-057555-7, $14.95

This graphic format biography of da Vinci uses the conceit that an adventurer from the Planet Mud seeks to learn about the great people of Earth's history in an effort to save the people of Mud, who face a disease that drains their mental powers. In the course of his search in this volume, readers learn about the life and work Leonardo da Vinci, who was a painter, scientist, mathematician, engineer, inventor, anatomist, sculptor, architect, musician, and writer. The book includes a time line of da Vinci's life, and a list of books and websites for further reading.

Part of the Great Figures in History series

Sanders, Scott
   Camilla d'Errico's Burn. Art by Steve Whitmire. Simon Pulse 2009 Un Illustration
Grades: 5 6 7 8   **741.5; Fic**
   1. Adventure graphic novels; 2. Robots; 3. Science fiction graphic novels; 4. Graphic novels
   978-1-4169-7873-2 (pa), $9.99
   In a future world, sentient robots rebel against their human makers and set out to kill humans so they can remake the world for them. One boy, Burn, encounters the sentient named Shoftiel when it destroys his neighborhood and city; the destruction damages both of them, and Shoftiel repairs itself by melding with what remains of Burn's body. Burn/Shoftiel return to the home of Dr. Anders Carnegie, the scientist who created the sentients in the first place, in order to kill him. Burn won't let Shoftiel kill Dr. Carnegie's young daughter Aeya, and the two of them join with young bikers trying to make a new home in the rubble of the destroyed city. The two natures, machine and human, battle for control of Burn, even as he must fight off Shoftiel's brother sentients who have orders to destroy their contaminated brother. The story combines post-apocalyptic adventure with mecha action using manga-influenced art. It includes quite a bit of violence (the sentients basically rip humans apart); the young people drink alcohol (there are no adults left to supervise them).

Sanjo, Riku
   Beet the Vandel Buster Vol. 1. Viz Media/Shonen Jump 2004 178p. Illustration
Grades: 6 7 8 9 10 11 12   **741.5; Fic**
   1. Adventure graphic novels; 2. Fantasy graphic novels; 3. Manga; 4. Shonen manga; 5. Graphic novels
   1-59116-690-X, $7.99
   The Vandel Busters are a roving band of certified monster destroyers. Beet's biggest ambition in life is to become a Buster, but what can you say about a monster hunter who can barely stand the pain when he receives the mystical brand of a Level 1 Vandel Buster"" Still, Beet is ready for action, and when a nearby town is invaded by demons, he rushes to help—without a clue as to how to trounce even a single member of the rampaging horde. But not knowing how formidable the Vandels are might work to his advantage because he doesn't know enough to be scared. Beet is about to learn that being a hero may be more than he bargained for... The book includes monster fighting action.

Sava, Scott Christian
   ★ **Cameron** and his dinosaurs. Art by Tracy Bailey. IDW Publishing 2009 174p. Illustration
Grades: 3 4 5 6 7 8   **741.5; Fic**
   1. Adventure graphic novels; 2. Dinosaurs; 3. Humorous graphic novels; 4. Robots; 5. Graphic novels
   978-1-60010-315-5, $12.99
   The mad scientist, Professor Poindexter P. Poppycock, uses dinosaur DNA to create living dinosaurs which he plans to use for nefarious purposes. Unfortunately for him, he gave

them human intelligence and the ability to speak, and the dinosaurs Charlie the tyrannosaurus rex, Dee Dee the pterodactyl, Lizzy the triceratops, and Vinnie the brachiosaurus decline to be evil and leave him. They befriend young Cameron, who helps to introduce them to the world. Professor Poppycock then creates robotic dinosaurs to do the will of the Brotherhood of Universal Revolution for Political Subterfuge (B.U.R.P.S.) to kidnap the President and take over the country. It will be up to Charlie, Dee Dee, Lizzy, Vinnie, and Cameron in his new souped-up wheelchair (with some awesome top-secret adaptations) to save the President and stop the robot dinosaurs. This book reads like an action-packed cartoon.

   The **dreamland** chronicles book two. Blue Dream Studios 2007 176p. Illustration
Grades: 5 6 7 8 9 10 11 12   **741.5; Fic**
   1. Adventure graphic novels; 2. Dreaming; 3. Fantasy graphic novels; 4. Graphic novels
   978-0-9789168-3-1, $19.95

                                                       LC 2007-932090
   Alexander Carter continues his adventures in Dreamland every night, as he and his friends escape the Dragon Lord Nicodemus' prison with the help of Felicity, a catgirl with tiger stripes, and continue their search for the King and Queen of Elves, Nastajia's parents. The problem is, Nastajia doesn't trust Felicity and thinks she could be a spy for Nicodemus. Meanwhile, the friends find themselves in the undersea cave of the Kraken, which is a much more immediate danger to them all.

   The **Dreamland** Chronicles: Book One. Blue Dream Studios 2006 Un Illustration
Grades: 5 6 7 8 9 10 11 12 Adult   **741.5; Fic**
   1. Adventure graphic novels; 2. Fantasy graphic novels; 3. Graphic novels
   978-0-9789168-0-0, $19.95
   College student Alexander Carter has found a key that takes him back to the land of his childhood dreams. Every night he enters Dreamland, a magical world filled with dragons, fairies, and giants. Reunited with his childhood friends Paddington, Kiwi, and Nastajia, Alexander now embarks on a quest to save Dreamland from war with the Nightmare Realm. But, will his daytime life as a college student interfere" Colorful 3-D animated art makes the story look like a computer game.

   Ed's terrestrials. By Scott Christian Sava; artist, Diego Jourdan. Blue Dream Studios 2006 84p. Illustration
Grades: 2 3 4 5 6   **741.5; Fic**
   1. Humorous graphic novels; 2. Science fiction graphic novels; 3. Graphic novels
   978-0-9789168-1-7, $19.95
   Aliens have escaped from the Intergalactic Food Court, where they worked as slaves, and crashland into Ed's tree house. They all become friends, and the aliens want to help their fellow slaves come to Earth. But the Intergalactic Mall security officer, Maximus Obliterus, has come to send them back, and he has teamed up with Ed's school nemesis, Natalie
   This book was originally published in 2005 by Alias Enterprises

Gary the pirate. Art by Tracy Bailey. IDW Publishing 2009 112p. Illustration

Grades: 4 5 6 7 8 9   **741.5; Fic**
   1. Adventure graphic novels; 2. Humorous graphic novels; 3. Pirates; 4. Graphic novels
   978-1-60010-312-4, $12.99

Gary, a teenage Sky Pirate from the secret floating city Pirate Cove, owes Stinky a lot for ruining his watch, dumping a chocolate ice cream sundae on his head, and messing up his ship all accidentally, because Gary is a klutz. Gary is also a lousy thief for a pirate. While searching for treasure, he sees thirteen-year-old Judy in the park with her grandmother. She complains to her grandmother about all the boys she knows how could she ever want to date any of them" They're either bullies, computer nerds, too cool for anyone, or just totally clueless. When klutzy Gary breaks into her bedroom in search of the brooch her grandmother just gave her (it's treasure, after all), she wants him to take her on his ship to see Pirate Cove. True to his klutzy nature, though, Gary manages to crash his ship into Stinky's ship, and now they're in big trouble. The pirates may brandish their swords, but there's no actual violence, only cartoony action.

★ **Hyperactive**. By Scott Christian Sava; artist, Joseph Bergin. IDW Publishing/Worthwhile Children's Books 2009 108p. Illustration

Grades: 3 4 5 6 7 8   **741.5; Fic**
   1. Adventure graphic novels; 2. Humorous graphic novels; 3. Superhero graphic novels; 4. Graphic novels
   978-1-60010-313-1, $12.99; 1-60010-313-8

"Joey Johnson learns he can move at super speed and puts his power to good use doing household chores. But when word gets out, a shady executive sees the opportunity to make big bucks off of Joey's super DNA. . . . With its surprise ending, which suggests more to come, a readership of young boys will ensure that this one flies off the shelf at the speed of light." Booklist

The **lab**: hey . . . test this!. Astonish Factory 2004 120p. Illustration

Grades: 5 6 7 8 9   **741.5; Fic**
   1. Humorous graphic novels; 2. Science fiction graphic novels; 3. Graphic novels
   0-9721259-3-0, $14.95

"A collection of previously published comics and original stories that highlight the working relationship between Livingston, a scientist mole, and his goofball assistant, Esteban, a weasel whose ultrasensitivity to chemicals makes him an excellent test subject for new products. With bright, colorful pictures, the stories usually consist of observing Esteban's outlandish reactions to Livingston's concoctions, such as floating to the ceiling, shrinking to microscopic size, or singing uncontrollably." SLJ

My Grandparents are Secret Agents. Art by Juan Saavedra Mourgues and Invasor Creative Art Studio. IDW Publishing 2009 104p.

Grades: 3 4 5 6   **741.5; Fic**
   1. Adventure graphic novels; 2. Humorous graphic novels; 3. Mystery graphic novels; 4. Graphic novels
   978-1-60010-314-8, $11.99

Secret agents The Sicilian and the Diva defeat Dr. Dementia, and after the successful mission they want to spend a weekend with their grandchildren, Nicholas and Alyssa, while the kids' parents go on a romantic trip. However, the Social Security Administration (a secret government agency working to keep the U.S. safe) needs their top two agents to go after a villain named Purple Haze, who intends to use a time machine to make everything go back to the late 1960s. Grandma and Grandpa have to take Nicholas and Alyssa with them, along with the robot security dog named S.N.A.C.K.S., to stop the whacked-out villain. Spanish illustrator Mourgues and the Invasor Creative Art Studio use a very colorful, cartoony style.

Pet Robots. Art by Diego Jourdan. Blue Dream Studios 2007 Un Illustration

Grades: 3 4 5 6 7 8 9   **741.5; Fic**
   1. Humorous graphic novels; 2. Robots; 3. Science fiction graphic novels; 4. Graphic novels
   978-0-9789168-2-4, $19.95

                          LC 2007902577

Four students - Jake, Chris, Tammy, and Tommy - get lost while on a field trip to the Rooty Tooty Toy Company. In their quest to find they way back to the rest of the class, the stumble upon a room inhabited only by four military robots. That night they're followed home by the robots: Skye, Rock, Aqua, and Wind. As the kids get to know their new robotic friends, they must also avoid the evil owner of the Rooty Tooty Toy Company, Vandenburger Meisterburger. He wants his robots back and he's willing to do anything to get them.

Scalera, Buddy

Decoy: Storm of the Century. Buddy Scalera and Courtney Huddleston. Penny-Farthing Press 2003 151p. Illustration

Grades: 5 6 7 8 9 10 11 12 Adult   **741.5; Fic**
   1. Adventure graphic novels; 2. Friendship; 3. Science fiction graphic novels; 4. Graphic novels
   0-9719012-0-1, $17.95

He's the champion of justice and fast one-liners, a green shape-shifting alien from the planet Nacrum whose primary purpose in life is to protect the innocent and to one-up his roommate in an ongoing battle of pranks and bad jokes. All goes well until a subterranean encounter with a long-forgotten threat changes Decoy's life and threatens the friendship with his only ally on the planet: his best friend. Faced with an identity crisis of cosmic proportions, loveable alien Decoy must team up with his buddy, rookie cop Bobby Luck, to battle meteorological and psychological disaster.

Schigiel, Gregg

X-babies: stars reborn. Written by Gregg Schigiel ; art by Jacob Chabot. Marvel Worldwide 2010 Un Illustration

Grades: 4 5 6 7 8 9 10   **741.5; Fic**
   1. Adventure graphic novels; 2. Cyclops (Fictional character); 3. Humorous graphic novels; 4. Nightcrawler (Fictional character); 5. Storm (Fictional character); 6. Superhero graphic novels; 7. Wolverine (Fictional character); 8. X-Men (Fictional characters); 9. Graphic novels
   978-0-7851-4380-2, $14.99

In Mojoworld, where everything is televised, Mojo had created the X-Babies, child-sized versions of the X-Men, and the X-Babies have been the top-rated stars, but then Mr. Veech takes over and replaces the X-Babies with cute, safe, friendly versions who don't fight, but do such things as grow and eat! vegetables. The X-Babies know something is wrong, and they set out to find out what's happening. As they break out of their imprisonment and seek answers, they encounter lots of modified cutesy versions of other kid heroes. Younger readers will enjoy the wise-cracking kiddie versions of Wolverine, Storm, Cyclops, Rogue, Colossus, Kitty Pryde, and Nightcrawler. The other kid heroes whom the X-Babies meet were stars of Marvel's mid-1980s kid-centric Star Comics line, including Top Dog, Wally the Wizard, Planet Terry, and Royal Roy. There is no bad language (Wolverine says "poot" a lot), and lots of action with little violence.

Originally published as X-Babies issues #14

Schreiber, Ellen

Vampire kisses: blood relatives volume 2. Art by Rem. HarperCollins/Tokyopop 2008 Un Illustration
Grades: 7 8 9 10 11 12   **741.5; Fic**
1. Horror graphic novels; 2. Romance graphic novels; 3. Vampires; 4. Graphic novels
978-0-06-134082-6, $9.99

Raven and Alexander face enough challenges about their relationship—she's human, he's a vampire—but things get really complicated when Alexander's half-vampire cousin Claude shows up with his gang. They're looking for a stash of vials filled with blood that will turn them into pure vampires. Since that would mean disastrous trouble, Raven and Alexander must come up with a plan to outwit Claude. This is the second volume of Schreiber's global manga story based on her vampire romance novels for teens.

Schulz, Charles M.

★ The **Complete** Peanuts: 1950-1952. Fantagraphics Books 2004 330p. Illustration
Grades: 2 3 4 5 6 7 8 9 10 11 12 Adult   **741.5; Fic**
1. Humorous graphic novels; 2. Peanuts (Comic strip); 3. Graphic novels
1-56097-589-X, $28.95

This is the first volume of a project to collect all of Schulz's Peanuts comic strips from 1950 to 2000. This volume includes the strips published from October 2, 1950 through all of 1952. These early strips featured characters younger readers may not recognize: Patty (not Peppermint Patty), Violet, Shermy, and a Snoopy who behaves like a normal dog. Schroeder is a baby who's already a whiz at the toy piano; Lucy is a toddler who already causes trouble for Charlie Brown; Linus shows up as a baby in September 1952. Lucy pulls the football trick on Charlie Brown for the first time in November 1952. This volume also includes a biography of Schulz and a long interview with him.

Volume 1 of 26

Schultz, Brandon

Blokhedz, Vol. 1: Genesis. Created by Mark & Mike Davis ; written by Mark & Mike Davis, Brandon Schultz. Pocket Books 2007 Un Illustration
Grades: 8 9 10 11 12   **741.5; Fic**

1. Fantasy graphic novels; 2. Rap music; 3. Graphic novels
978-1-4165-4073-1, $12.95

In the decaying Monarch projects of Empire City, teenage Blak aspires to become a big rap star, while his older brother Konzaquenz, who recently got out of prison for gang activity, wants to unite all the Monarch neighborhoods. Old friend Bloko, who runs the local recording industry, and the gangs, sees Konz as a problem. When gang members kill Konz, Blak gets drawn into Bloko's schemes. What no one realizes, yet, is that Blak's rhymes have a mystical power, fed by the Original People upon whose burial grounds Monarch was built. Soon Blak will have to choose his path. Bad words are present but not completely spelled out ("sh*t" for example), so the content is appropriate for older middle school and high school readers.

"This is urban fiction mixed with the supernatural and depicted in a colorful, dynamic, animated style." (VOYA - upcoming, Aug 07 issue)

Schweizer, Chris

The **creeps**; 1: night of the frankenfrogs. By Chris Schweizer. Abrams Books 2015 128 p. Color; Illustration
Grades: 3 4 5 6   **741.5; Fic**
1. Frogs — Juvenile fiction; 2. School stories — Juvenile fiction; 3. Scientists — Fiction
9781419713798, $17.95; 9781419717666, $9.95
LC 2014955691

In this book, by Chris Schweizer, as "punishment for creating a giant mess in their school, Carol, Jarvis, Mitchell, and Rosario (known to their classmates as the Creeps) are being forced to perform the tasks normally completed by the janitor. When they discover that the frog specimens intended for dissection in their science class are missing, they know that they will be blamed, so they set out to discover who the real culprit might be." (School Library Journal)

"An excellent complement to his prose, Schweizer's cleanly paneled art is bright and busy, ever ready with a gag that helps blend the ghastly with the goofy, making his gang's antics reminiscent of Scooby Doo. . . . Silly fun with a smattering of science." Kirkus

★ **Crogan's** loyalty. Chris Schweizer; [edited by] James Lucas Jones. Oni Press, Inc. 2012 150 p. Color; Illustration
Grades: 8 9 10 11 12 Adult   **741.5**
1. Adventure graphic novels; 2. United States — History — 1775-1783, Revolution
9781934964408, $14.99; 1934964409
LC 2011943514

"Schweizer takes another bite out of history in this story of two brothers divided by the American Revolution. Charlie, the elder Crogan and a Loyalist ranger, is infuriated that his younger brother would turn rebel, stating 'There's a passion that makes most young men wanna tear society down because they ain't in charge of it.' Meanwhile, Will, a colonial scout, is no less incensed that his older brother would stand for a tyrant against his own country." (Booklist)

★ **Crogan's** march. Oni Press 2009 212p. Illustration
Grades: 8 9 10 11 12 Adult   **741.5; Fic**

1. Adventure graphic novels; 2. Imperialism; 3. North Africa — World history — 20th century; 4. Graphic novels

978-1-934964-24-8, $14.95

When brothers Eric and Cory squabble at the dinner table, their father tells them the story of Peter Crogan, one of their ancestors, who fought in the French Foreign Legion in 1912. Crogan's five-year term of service is one month from completion when he's asked to stay and become an officer. His unit is stationed in North Africa, where the French hold territory and depend on the French Foreign Legion to police the territory, putting down the rebellious attacks of the Tuaregs. He finds himself torn between the heroic Captain Poitelet (who tends to be the sole survivor of various battles) and the grizzled sergeant who actually cares about the people the Legion polices. When Crogan's unit escorts a caravan that endures an attack by Tuaregs, the captain's reckless actions endanger everyone, and Crogan must find help. Schweizer's story includes the kind of violence military actions cause, but very little in the way of bad language. Some may wince at the heavily French-accented English of some of the characters ("zee Daughters of France send zem out to all of zee units," etc.). This action-packed historical fiction graphic novel will appeal to teens, but adults who remember such novels as Beau Geste by Percival Christopher Wren (and the movies, of course) will also enjoy reading Schweizer's tale.

This book is part of The Crogan Adventures series

Sequel to: Crogan's vengeance (2008)

★ **Crogan's** vengeance. Book design by Keith Wood; edited by James Lucas Jones with Jill Beaton. Oni Press 2008 185p. Illustration

Grades: 8 9 10 11 12 Adult   **741.5; Fic**
1. Adventure graphic novels; 2. Pirates; 3. Graphic novels

978-1-934964-06-4, $14.95

Catfoot Crogan serves as an honest and honorable sailor on a ship commanded by an unjust captain when the ship is taken over by pirates. In order to save their lives, the sailors all take the oath to become pirates, but Crogan immediately runs afoul of D'Or, a brutal man who enjoys torturing others. Catfoot is a pirate, but he's determined to remain as honest and honorable as he can be, which continually puts him in danger. This swashbuckling tale shows a less romantic story than Rafael Sabatini's Captain Blood, with more violence, but it is more action-oriented than merely violent.

"Filled with mutiny, ferocious storms, shark-infested waters, commandeering of ships, and—of course—swashbuckling sword fights, this book has high teen appeal." SLJ

Part of the Crogan Adventures series

Scott, Jerry
★ **Chillax**. By Jerry Scott; illustrated by Jim Borgman. HarperTeen 2013 256 p. Illustration

Grades: 7 8 9 10   **Fic**
1. Concerts — Fiction; 2. Teenagers — Fiction

9780062228512, $9.99; 006222851X

LC 2013931374

"Jeremy Duncan, high school sophomore and future rock god, offers up a comedic outlook on teenage life, including school, parents, chores, bands, and friends. Jeremy and his best friend, Hector Garcia, are planning to [go] to a

rock concert without parental supervision. But the . . . concert falls on the same night their friend Tim is donating bone marrow for his mom, a cancer patient. Jeremy and Hector are determined to go to the showàfor Tim." (Publisher's note)

Segami, Akira
Kagetora, volume 1. Del Rey Manga 2008 202p. Illustration

Grades: 8 9 10 11 12   **741.5; Fic**
1. Humorous graphic novels; 2. Manga; 3. Martial arts; 4. Romance graphic novels; 5. Graphic novels

978-0-345-49141-6, $10.95

Young ninja Kagetora arrives at the Toudou family dojo on assignment, and he learns that he must teach martial arts to the family hime (princess), Yuki. The problem is, Yuki is a total, absolute klutz; she's also tiny and absolutely cute and charming. As he tries his best to train her, Kagetora finds himself doing the forbidden—he's falling for Yuki. How can he perform his duty? On top of that, Yuki's best friend Aki, one of the Toudou's top students, has been protecting Yuki for years and resents Kagetora's presence. The book includes a lot of fan service, which actually ties into the plot as Kagetora can't help but look at Yuki, even though he knows that his feelings are not appropriate.

Seo, Eun-Jin
Fantamir Volume 1. Tokyopop 2007 Un Illustration
Grades: 8 9 10 11 12   **741.5; Fic**
1. Fantasy graphic novels; 2. Manwha; 3. Graphic novels

978-1-4278-0290-3, $9.99

When a mysterious incident causes Mir to lose her magical abilities, she decides to retire as successor to the Sorceress and become a student in a normal school. To her surprise, she enrolls in a school with a special connection to her family, and before she knows it, she's in trouble with the uber-popular Ba-ri, who has challenged her to a duel.

Peppermint Volume 1. Tokyopop 2006 Un Illustration
Grades: 8 9 10 11 12   **741.5; Fic**
1. Humorous graphic novels; 2. Manwha; 3. Romance graphic novels; 4. Graphic novels

1-59816-681-6, $9.99

What do you do when true love is just beyond your reach? Hey is a normal high school girl who has a crush on the hot teen singer EZ. But whenever she tries to work up the nerve to confess her feeling toward him, middle schooler Eo always gets in the middle of things. Pop star EZ may never think of Hey as anything more than a fan ... But dealing with people thinking Eo is her boyfriend may get Hey in big trouble.

The Seven Soldiers of Victory Archives Volume 1
Edited by Dale Crain. DC Comics 2005 237p. Illustration

Grades: 6 7 8 9 10 11 12 Adult   **741.5; Fic**
1. Green Arrow (Fictional character); 2. Superhero graphic novels; 3. Graphic novels

1-4012-0401-5, $49.95

Collecting Leading Comics #1-4, featuring the adventures of The Seven Soldiers of Victory: The Crimson Avenger, Green Arrow, the Shining Knight, The Vigilante, the Star-Spangled Kid, and their sidekicks Speedy, Stripesy, and Wing (yes, there were eight of them). In 1941, one year after DC Comics launched the Justice Society of America in All-Star Comics, sister company All-American Comics released Leading Comics #1 featuring its very own super-team; in these early stories they take on various criminals and villains who possess super-senses.

Sewell, Anna

Black Beauty. Retold by L.L. Owens ; illustrated by Jennifer Tanner. Stone Arch Books 2006 63p. Illustration
Grades: 3 4 5 6 7 8 9   **741.5; Fic**
1. Sewell, Anna, 1820-1878 — Adaptations; 2. Graphic novels
978-1-59889-046-4, $23.93

Black Beauty, a handsome colt living in Victorian England, has a happy childhood growing up in the peaceful countryside. In his later years, he encounters cruelty, human suffering, and a tragic fire. Things go from bad to worse when his new owners begin renting him out for profit. Black Beauty endures a life of mistreatment and disrespect in a world that shows little regard for the happiness of animals. This adaptation is written for reluctant and struggling readers.

Part of the Graphic Revolve series.

Sexton, Adam

Twain's the adventure of Huckleberry Finn: the Manga edition. Art by Hyeondo Park. Wiley Publishing 2009 186p.
Grades: 5 6 7 8 9 10 11 12   **741.5; Fic**
1. Adventure graphic novels; 2. Authors; 3. Essayists; 4. Humorists; 5. Humorous graphic novels; 6. Memoirists; 7. Novelists; 8. Satirists; 9. Slaves; 10. Twain, Mark, 1835-1910; 11. Graphic novels
978-0-470-15287-4, $9.99

Huckleberry Finn, son of a ne'er-do-well, has been living with Tom Sawyer and his Aunt Polly ever since they helped solve a murder. Now, his father wants Huck's share of the reward money. When Huck gets away, he decides he has to run; he encounters Jim, a slave who has run away from his owner, and they set out on a raft down the Mississippi River, where they encounter other murderers, con artists, thieves, feuding families, and more. This is a manga-style adaptation of Twain's classic adventure. While the original novel has faced challenges because of certain language, this book does not include the inflammatory words.

Sfar, Joann

Dungeon Vol. 1: Duck Heart. [by] Joann Sfar & Lewis Trondheim. NBM 2003 96p. Illustration
Grades: 7 8 9 10 11 12   **741.5; Fic**
1. Fantasy graphic novels; 2. Humorous graphic novels; 3. Graphic novels
1-56163-401-8, $14.95

"As a result of some unfortunate accidents, Herbert, usually a lowly messenger in the great Dungeon, is called upon to defend it from all manner of beasties. In his endeavors to become a warrior, he is helped by his friend Marvin the vegetarian dragon and by the Dungeon Keeper. Although there's a solid dose of cartoon-style violence and gore, teens will appreciate Herbert's pseudo-slacker attitude,

which turns him into an accidental hero time and time again." Booklist

Other titles in this series are: Dungeon, the early years: the night shirt (2005); Zenith: the barbarian princess (2005)

Dungeon: Parade Vol. 1: A Dungeon Too Many. By Joann Sfar, Lewis Trondheim & Manu Larcenet. NBM 2007 Un Illustration
Grades: 6 7 8 9 10 11 12 Adult   **741.5; Fic**
1. Adventure graphic novels; 2. Fantasy graphic novels; 3. Humorous graphic novels; 4. Graphic novels
978-1-56163-495-8, $9.95

Marvin the Vegetarian Dragon and Herbert the Duck do battle with the new, rival dungeon next door that is actually a theme park. Then, Herbert finds a magic lamp that has one wish left, and he and Marvin set out on a quest to find a dying sage to get advice on the best wish.

Little Vampire Does Kung Fu!. Stories and drawings by Joann Sfar ; colors by Walter. Simon & Schuster Books for Young Readers 2003 Un Illustration
Grades: 4 5 6 7 8 9   **741.5; Fic**
1. Fantasy graphic novels; 2. Humorous graphic novels; 3. Vampires; 4. Graphic novels
0-689-85769-1, $12.95
                                           LC 2003-045770

Jeffrey the jerk is a bully and everyone knows it. Little Vampire isn't about to stand around and watch him pick on his best friend, Michael. There's only one thing to do: travel to the highest mountain and seek kung fu lessons from the master... There's an icky moment when Little Vampire's monster friends spit up bits of Jeffrey (whom they ate) and they try to put him together again.

The **professor's** daughter. [story by] Joann Sfar & [illustrated by] Emmanuel Guibert; translated by Alexis Siegel. First Second Books 2007 63p. Illustration
Grades: 7 8 9 10 11 12 Adult   **741.5**
1. Humorous graphic novels; 2. Mummies; 3. Romance graphic novels; 4. Graphic novels
978-1-59643-130-0; 1-59643-130-X, $16.95
                                           LC 2006-22177

In Victorian London, Lillian, the daughter of a famed archeologist, has fallen in love with the mummy of Imhotep IV; he thinks that Lillian bears a strong resemblance to this long-dead wife. Their love faces many obstacles, from Lillian's father, the police, a pirate who is actually Imhotep III (yes, the father and another mummy), even Queen Victoria herself. Dainty Victorian manners mix with broad farce and black comedy in a beautifully illustrated book with muted colors and sepia tones.

Sardine in outer space 2. [by] Emmanuel Guibert and Joann Sfar; translated by Sasha Watson; colorist, Walter Pezzali; letterer, François Batet. First Second 2006 122p.
Grades: 3 4 5 6 7 8   **741.5**
1. Pirates — Fiction; 2. Space flight — Fiction
159643127X; 9781596431270
                                           LC 2005021790

"The red-headed space heroine is back! This time, the evil Supermuscleman has developed a device for controlling children—a brainwashing machine! It's up to Sardine, Little Louie, and Captain Yellow Shoulder to keep him from using it. This installment of twelve more stories is filled with even more strange creatures—including a space Santa Claus, pesky flies that plant annoying music in their victim's ears, intergalactic yogurt thieves, and little monster carpet salesmen who live on a fully-carpeted comet." (Publisher's note)

Shakespeare, William

William Shakespeare's King Lear. Illustrated by Ian Pollock. Black Dog & Leventhal/Workman Publishing 2006 148p. Illustration

Grades: 7 8 9 10 11 12 Adult   **741.5; 822.3**
  1. Shakespeare, William, 1564-1616 — Adaptations; 2. Graphic novels
978-1-57912-617-9, $12.95

This graphic novel adaptation of King Lear, originally published in 1984, uses excerpted text from the play together with full-color illustrations to tell the story of the king whose ill-fated attempts to learn which of his daughters loves him best causes loss and madness.

Part of the Shakespeare Graphic Library.

William Shakespeare's King Lear. Adapted by Brian Farrens; illustrated by Ben Dunn.. ABDO/Magic Wagon 2008 48p. Illustration

Grades: 5 6 7 8 9 10   **822.3; 741.5**
  1. Shakespeare, William, 1564-1616 — Adaptations; 2. Graphic novels
978-1-60270-189-2, $28.50

              LC 2008-10739

King Lear divides his kingdom among his three daughters but disowns Cordelia, the youngest, when she refuses to flatter him with insincerity. Then his older daughters renege on their promise to care for him, and he goes mad and roams the countryside. Meanwhile, Edmund, the illegitimate son of the Earl of Gloucester, plays political games in his quest for power. This graphic novel adaptation retains some of the original language from Shakespeare's play, while paring down the story to appeal to struggling readers. The book includes a short biography, a summary of the play, a glossary, and a short selection of famous lines and phrases from the play.

Part of the Graphic Shakespeare series

William Shakespeare's Macbeth. Illustrated by Von. Black Dog & Leventhal/Workman Publishing 1982 92p. Illustration

Grades: 7 8 9 10 11 12 Adult   **741.5; 822.3**
· 1. Shakespeare, William, 1564-1616 — Adaptations; 2. Tragedy; 3. Graphic novels
978-1-57912-621-6, $12.95

This graphic novel adaptation of Macbeth, originally published in 1982, uses excerpted text from the play together with full-color illustrations to tell the story of the Thane of Cawdor who listens to a trio of witches and slays the King of Scotland to take his throne.

Part of the Shakespeare Graphic Library

William Shakespeare's Othello. Adapted by Vincent Goodwin; illustrated by Chris Allen.. ABDO/Magic Wagon 2008 48p. Illustration

Grades: 5 6 7 8 9 10   **822.3; 741.5**

  1. Shakespeare, William, 1564-1616 — Adaptations; 2. Graphic novels
978-1-60270-192-2, $28.50

              LC 2008-10743

Othello the Moor is a successful general, married to the beautiful Desdemona. Life should be good, but he's incredibly jealous of anyone who looks at his wife. Iago wants Othello's position and decides that he should destroy Othello by fabricating an affair between Desdemona and Cassio. This graphic novel adaptation keeps some of the original dialog from Shakespeare's play while paring down the action to simplify it for readers who would struggle with the original. The book includes a short biography of Shakespeare, a summary of the plot, a glossary, and a sampling of famous lines and phrases.

Part of the Graphic Shakespeare series

William Shakespeare's Twelfth night. Adapted by Vincent Goodwin illustrated by Cynthia Martin. ABDO/Magic Wagon 2008 48p. Illustration

Grades: 5 6 7 8 9 10   **822.3; 741.5**
  1. Shakespeare, William, 1564-1616 — Adaptations; 2. Graphic novels
978-1-60270-195-3, $28.50

              LC 2008-10747

Twins Viola and Sebastian are separated in a shipwreck. Viola decides to disguise herself as a man since she's alone, and this sets the stage for mixed-up identities and a comic love triangle. This graphic novel adaptation retains some of the original language from Shakespeare's play, while paring down the story to appeal to struggling readers. The book includes a short biography, a summary of the play, a glossary, and a short selection of famous lines and phrases from the play.

Part of the Graphic Shakespeare series

Shan, Darren

Cirque du Freak, vol. 1. Art by Takahiro Arai. Yen Press 2009 Un Illustration

Grades: 6 7 8 9 10   **741.5; Fic**
  1. Authors; 2. Horror graphic novels; 3. Manga; 4. Novelists; 5. Shan, Darren, 1972- — Adaptations; 6. Vampires; 7. Graphic novels
978-0-7595-3041-6, $10.99

Middle schoolers Darren and Steve hustle soccer games against older players for money; Steve obsesses over horror movies, while Darren has a huge fascination with spiders. When a mysterious stranger hands Darren a flyer advertising a Cirque du Freak, he and Steve decide they must attend. At the circus, they discover that the freaks in the show are true monsters, not the usual hokey hoaxes, and Darren loves the monstrous spider. Then Steve decides that Mr. Crepsley, the spider handler, is a vampire, and Steve wants

Courtesy of Yen Press

more than anything to become a vampire. However, Mr. Crepsley rejects him after tasting his blood Steve is too bloodthirsty. Then Darren steals Madame Octa, the spider, only to lose control of her while she's out of her cage and she bites Steve. Crepsley comes for his pet and tells Darren he'll save Steve, but only if Darren will become his assistant and become a vampire. This book is the English translation of the original Japanese manga that is based on Shan's novel.

Shapiro, David
    Terra Tempo: the four corners of time. David Shapiro, Christopher Herndon, Erica Melville. Craigmore Creations 2013 272 p. (Terra Tempo)
Grades: 5 6 7   **741.5**
    1. Colorado Plateau — Juvenile fiction; 2. Dinosaurs — Juvenile fiction; 3. Time travel — Juvenile fiction
098444226X; 9780984442263, $17.99
                            LC 2012944924
    This book is part of the "Terra Tiempo" series by David R. Shapiro and Erica Melville. "When Ari discovers a time map of the Colorado Plateau, he and the twins find themselves on a fast paced journey from Earth s underwater beginnings to the steamy jungles and huge creatures of the creepy Cretaceous. But this time, there is more at stake than just survival. This time, they are not alone." (Publisher's note)

Shaw, Murray
    Sherlock Holmes and the adventure of the blue gem. Adapted by Murray Shaw and M.J. Cosson ; illustrated by Sophie Rohrbach. Lerner Publishing Group/Graphic Universe 2010 48p. Illustration
Grades: 3 4 5 6 7 8
741.5; Fic
    1. Doyle, Arthur Conan Sir, 1859-1930 — Adaptations; 2. Gems; 3. Holmes, Sherlock (Fictional character); 4. Mystery graphic novels; 5. Graphic novels

Courtesy of Lerner Publishing Group

978-0-7613-6190-9, $26.60
                            LC 2009-51758
    In this graphic adaptation of Doyle's "The Adventure of the Blue Carbuncle," Sherlock Holmes and Dr. Watson work on a Christmas holiday mystery when a train conductor brings them a Christmas goose and a man's hat that he found. They find a large blue gem in the throat of the goose, a famous gem that had been stolen from its owner. Holmes and Watson trace the owner of the hat, who starts them on a path to find out who stole the gem and stuffed it into the goose. This book includes discussion questions and a reading list that includes a mix of age-appropriate mysteries and nonfiction books and websites. Rohrbach's art looks almost like woodcuts; she unfortunately uses the stereotypical (and incorrect) look of the deerstalker cap and caped coat for Holmes. Her muted color palette of mostly browns matches the Victorian time period of the Holmes mysteries.
    This is #3 in the On the Case with Holmes and Watson series.

Shazam!: the greatest stories ever told
    DC Comics 2008 224p. Illustration
Grades: 4 5 6 7 8 9 10 11 12 Adult   **741.5; Fic**
    1. Adventure graphic novels; 2. Captain Marvel (Fictional character); 3. Superhero graphic novels; 4. Graphic novels
978-1-4012-1674-0, $24.99
    This book collects comics stories about Captain Marvel dating from 1940 to 1998. Captain Marvel predated Superman as a comic book superhero; young newsboy Billy Batson could transform into the flying superhero by shouting the magic word "Shazam!" This gave him the wisdom of Solomon, the strength of Hercules, the stamina of Atlas, the power of Zeus, the courage of Achilles, and the speed of Mercury. In these fourteen stories, he battles against such foes as Dr. Sivana, Mr. Mind, and the Monster Society of Evil.

Shelley, Mary Wollstonecraft, 1797-1851
    Frankenstein. Retold by Michael Burgan ; illustrated by Dennis Calero. Stone Arch Books 2007 72p. Illustration
Grades: 3 4 5 6 7 8 9   **741.5; Fic**
    1. Horror graphic novels; 2. Science fiction graphic novels; 3. Graphic novels
978-1-59889-830-9, $23.93
                              LC 2007-6199
    The young scientist Victor Frankenstein has created something amazing and horrible at the same time, a living being out of dead flesh and bone. His creation, however, turns out to be a monster. Frankenstein's creation quickly discovers that his hideous appearance frightens away any companions. Now, Frankenstein must stop his creation before the monster's loneliness turns to violence. The book is written with an easy vocabulary for struggling and reluctant readers, and it includes facts about the novel.
    Part of the Graphic Revolve series.

Shen, Prudence
    ★ **Nothing** Can Possibly Go Wrong. By Prudence Shen, illustrated by Faith Erin Hicks. First Second 2013 288 p.
Grades: 7 8 9 10   **741.5/973; Fic**
    1. Cheerleading — Juvenile fiction; 2. Robots — Juvenile fiction; 3. School stories
159643659X; 9781596436596, $16.99
    In this juvenile graphic novel, by Prudence Shen, illustrated by Faith Erin Hicks, "you wouldn't expect Nate and Charlie to be friends. Charlie's the laid-back captain of the basketball team, and Nate is the neurotic, scheming president of the robotics club. But they are friends, however unlikely—until Nate declares war on the cheerleaders. At stake is funding that will either cover a robotics competition or new cheerleading uniforms—but not both." (Publisher's note)
    "Shen's plot ably balances drama, humor, angst, and robotic geekery, giving the book an immediate YA appeal, but one that's broad enough to be enjoyable to older readers, as well. Visually, Hicks's wide-eyed, inky b&w panels

infuse the characters with real emotion and personality, capturing the book's heartfelt youthfulness." Pub Wkly

Shepard, Aaron
Robin Hood. Retold by Aaron Shepard and Anne L. Watson ; illustrated by Jennifer Tanner. Stone Arch Books 2006 63p. Illustration
Grades: 3 4 5 6 7 8 9   **741.5; Fic**
    1. Adventure graphic novels; 2. Robin Hood (Legendary character); 3. Graphic novels
    978-1-59889-049-5, $23.93

Robin Hood and his band of outlaws are the heroes of Sherwood Forest. Taking from the rich and giving to the poor, Robin Hood and his loyal followers fight for the oppressed and against the evil Sheriff of Nottingham. Among the adventures recounted are how Robin meets Little John and Friar Tuck, helping Alan-a-Dale marry his true love, Eleanor, and Robin entering the Sheriff's archery contest even though it's a trap. This adaptation is written for reluctant and struggling readers.

Part of the Graphic Revolve series.

Shiga, Jason
Meanwhile. Abrams/Amulet 2010 Un Illustration
Grades: 4 5 6 7 8 9   **741.5**
    1. Science fiction graphic novels; 2. Graphic novels
    0-8109-8423-7; 978-0-8109-8423-3, $15.95
                                                        LC 2009-39844
In this choose-your-own adventure graphic novel, a boy stumbles on the laboratory of a mad scientist who asks him to choose between testing a mind-reading device, a time machine, and a doomsday machine. (Bull Cent Child Books)

Shigeno, Shuichi
Initial D Volume 1. Tokyopop 2002 229p. Illustration
Grades: 8 9 10 11 12 Adult   **741.5; Fic**
    1. Automobile racing; 2. Seinen manga; 3. Graphic novels
    1-931514-98-4, $9.99
Tak Fujiwara spends a lot of time behind the wheel, delivering tofu for his dad's shop. He races down the treacherous roads of Mount Akina all the time, and without even realizing it, he has mastered racing techniques that take most drivers a lifetime to learn. None of his friends realize this, because they're too busy watching the local street racing team. When the Red Suns, an outside team, shows up to challenge the Akina Speed Stars, it doesn't look good for the local team; then a mysterious Trueno Eight Six shows up and the driver exhibits great skill. Who is the driver? The book includes some strong language and some sexual situations (the girl Tak likes is dating older men for money).

Shimabukuro, Mitsutoshi
Toriko, vol. 1. Viz Media/Shonen Jump 2010 208p. Illustration
Grades: 8 9 10 11 12 Adult   **741.5; Fic**
    1. Adventure graphic novels; 2. Food; 3. Humorous graphic novels; 4. Hunting; 5. Manga; 6. Graphic novels
    978-1-4215-3509-8, $9.99
Toriko is a Gourmet Hunter, who earns huge bounties for finding ferocious, delicious foods. We're not talking salmon fishing or deer hunting here, but eight-legged

alligators and rare fruit guarded by four-armed, bloodthirsty gorilla-type creatures. Toriko himself has a huge appetite for the rare foods, and sometimes eats most of what he's supposed to bring to the fancy restaurants that hire him. Komatsu, the head chef at Igo, a restaurant that caters to those wealthy enough to afford the rare foods, tags along with Toriko, who is a muscular giant of a man. This odd

Courtesy of VIZ Media LLC

couple forms a friendship born in their mutual love of fine foods. The book is full of crazy action, lots of bugeyed, drop-jawed, slapstick moments, and some potty humor.

Shinkai, Makoto
    ★ **Hoshi** No Koe: The Voices of a Distant Star. Original concept by Makaoto Shinkai; manga adaptation by Mizu Sahara. Tokyopop 2006 232p. Illustration
Grades: 8 9 10 11 12 Adult   **741.5; Fic**
    1. Manga; 2. Romance graphic novels; 3. Science fiction graphic novels; 4. Graphic novels
    1-59816-529-1, $9.99
In the mid-twenty-first century, high school student Mikako joins a research team heading out to space on a U.N. ship, to explore recent contact with aliens called the Tarsians. Her friend Noboru stays behind on Earth. While he continues with school, he receives cell-phone text messages, his only contact with Mikako. As her ship travels farther away, the low-priority messages take longer to reach Noboru, and he grows older while Mikako remains a teenager. Even as he considers moving on with his life, Noboru learns that love will find a way. This one-volume manga adapts the anime film; however, it stands alone as a story.

Shintani, Kaoru
Young Miss Holmes: casebook 1-2. By Kaoru Shintani. Seven Seas 2012 384 p.
Grades: 4 5 6 7   **741.5; 741.5952/223**
    1. Detectives — Fiction; 2. Girls — Fiction
    1935934864; 9781935934868, $16.99
In this book by Kaoru Shintani "Christie Holmes is a prodigy. At ten years old, she's as familiar with the sciences and classics as any older student at Cambridge or Oxford. And her facility with logic is reminiscent of her uncle, the eminent Sherlock Holmes himself. Christie's implacable curiosity leads her from one dangerous adventure to another, often joining forces with Uncle Sherlock and Doctor Watson on their famed investigations." (Publisher's note)

Young Miss Holmes: casebook 3-4. By Kaoru Shintani. Seven Seas 2012 384 p.
Grades: 4 5 6 7   **741.5**
    1. Detectives — Fiction; 2. Family — Fiction
    1935934945; 9781935934943, $16.99

In this graphic novel by Kaoru Shintani readers "experience classic Sherlock Holmes tales from the POV of his . . . niece. Sherlock Holmes' precocious niece Christie is back, as she helps her famous uncle solve such cases as: The Hound of the Baskervilles, The Adventure of the Six Napoleons, the Red-Headed League, and more!" (Publisher's note)

Shiomi, Chika
Canon Vol. 1. DC Comics/CMX 2007 200p. Illustration
Grades: 8 9 10 11 12 Adult   **741.5; Fic**
1. Horror graphic novels; 2. Shojo manga; 3. Vampires; 4. Graphic novels
978-1-4012-1163-9, $9.99

Suspense and the supernatural collide in the tale of Canon—the only student to escape the bloody vampire attack that takes the lives of her fellow classmates. But she doesn't get very far before she is captured, bitten and turned into a vampire herself. Struggling against the terrible needs that compel the undead, Canon commits herself to using her powers for good. She'll do whatever she can to avenge the death of her friends and her own unfortunate fate. Joining forces with Fuui—a talking vampire crow—she begins her quest to find Rodd, Lord of the Vampires. There's some mildly harsh language and lots of fighting vampire attacks, but nothing more than has been seen in most Buffy the Vampire Slayer or Angel episodes on television.

Shone, Rob
Avalanches & Landslides. The Rosen Publishing Group 2007 48p. Illustration
Grades: 3 4 5 6 7 8   **363.34; 741.5**
1. Avalanches; 2. Landslides
978-1-4042-1992-2 (lib bdg), $29.25

The book describes different kinds of landslides and avalanches, then dramatizes three major disasters. In 1910, the Wellington Avalanche in Washington swept standing trains off their tracks; in 1962, the Mount Huascaran Landslide destroyed the Peruvian town of Ranrahirca, then in 1970 the neighboring town of Yungay was destroyed by another landslide in the same area, with more than 17,000 dead. In 2006, Kan Abag Mountain on the island of Leyte in the Philippines collapsed, and the landslide buried the village of Guinsaugon. Additional information describes prevention efforts; the book includes a glossary and a list of books for further reading.
Part of the Graphic Natural Disasters series.

Earthquakes. Illustrated by Nick Spender. The Rosen Publishing Group 2007 48p. Illustration
Grades: 3 4 5 6 7 8   **551.22; 741.5**
1. Earthquakes; 2. Graphic novels
978-1-4042-1989-2, $26.25

The book describes earthquake zones and how earthquakes happen, then it dramatizes three major disasters: the San Francisco earthquake of 1906, the Great Hanshin Earthquake that devastated Kobe, Japan in 1995, and the South Asia Earthquake that struck Kashmir, Pakistan in 2005. Additional information includes an explanation of the

Richter scale, a glossary, and a list of books for further reading.
Part of the Graphic Natural Disasters series.

Giganotosaurus: the giant southern lizard. Illustrated by Terry Riley. Rosen Publishing Group 2009 32p. Illustration
Grades: 3 4 5 6 7   **668; 741.5**
1. Dinosaurs; 2. Graphic novels
978-1-4358-2502-4, $25.25
                                            LC 2008-3265

This book uses the comic book format to provide information about the Giganotosaurus, a giant meat-eating dinosaur from the Cretaceous Period. Information about its hunting habits and lifestyle are based on research and fossil records.
Part of the Graphic Dinosaur series

Muhammad Ali: The Life of a Boxing Hero. Art by Nick Spender. Rosen Publishing Group 2006 48p. Illustration
Grades: 3 4 5 6 7 8 9   **741.5; 796.8; 92**
1. African American athletes; 2. Ali, Muhammad, 1942-; 3. Biographical graphic novels; 4. Boxing — Biography; 5. Graphic novels
978-1-4042-0856-8, $29.25
                                            LC 2005035521

This book uses the graphic novel format to tell of the life and career of boxing great Muhammad Ali. He started his career as Cassius Clay but changed his name when he converted to the Nation of Islam. He used his fame as a boxer to advocate against U.S. involvement in Vietnam, and to raise funds for charity. The book includes a list of all his boxing matches, and a list of books for further reading.
Part of the Rosen Graphic Biographies series.

Nelson Mandela: The Life of an African Statesman. Art by Neil Reed. The Rosen Publishing Group 2007 48p. Illustration
Grades: 3 4 5 6 7 8 9   **92; 741.5**
1. Biographical graphic novels; 2. Mandela, Nelson, 1918-2013; 3. Graphic novels
978-1-4042-0860-5, $29.25

After presenting information about South Africa and the apartheid system, the book presents a comic book style biography of Nelson Mandela, from his childhood through his adult life spent fighting apartheid from outside and within prison. Additional material describes the 1993 elections that brought Mandela and his political party, the ANC, to power in a new South Africa. The book includes a glossary and a list of books for further reading.
Part of the Graphic Biographies series.

Rosa Parks: The Life of a Civil Rights Heroine. Art by Nick Spender. Rosen Publishing Group 2006 48p. Illustration
Grades: 3 4 5 6 7 8 9   **741.5; 323.092; 323**
1. African American women — Alabama — Montgomery — Biography; 2. African Americans — Civil rights — Alabama — Montgomery — History — 20th century; 3. Biographical graphic novels; 4. Parks, Rosa, 1913-2005; 5. Graphic novels
978-1-4042-0864-3, $29.25
                                            LC 2006002735

This book uses the graphic novel format to tell of the life of Rosa Parks and her act of defiance that inspired the Montgomery Bus Boycott. Additional information explains Jim Crow laws and briefly covers the civil rights movement. The bookes a list of books for further reading.
Part of the Rosen Graphic Biographies series.

Triceratops: The Three Horned Dinosaur. Illustrated by Terry Riley and Geoff Ball. Rosen Publishing Group 2007 32p. Illustration
Grades: 2 3 4 5 6 7   **567.9; 741.5**
1. Dinosaurs; 2. Triceratops; 3. Graphic novels
978-1-4042-3896-1, $25.25
                                       LC 2007-374
This volume uses colorful comic book style illustrations to explore the habitat, diet, and behavior of the triceratops. At the front of the book, facts about the triceratops are presented, while at the back of the book readers will find a picture gallery of other creatures mentioned in the book.
Part of the Graphic Dinosaurs series.

Tyrannosaurus: The Tyrant Lizard. Illustrated by James Field. Rosen Publishing Group 2007 32p. Illustration
Grades: 2 3 4 5 6 7   **567.9; 741.5**
1. Dinosaurs; 2. Tyrannosaurus; 3. Graphic novels
978-1-4042-3897-8, $25.25
                                       LC 2007-0442
This volume uses colorful comic book style illustrations to explore the habitat, diet, and behavior of the tyrannosaurus. At the front of the book, facts about the tyrannosaurus are presented, while at the back of the book readers will find a picture gallery of other creatures mentioned in the book.
Part of the Graphic Dinosaurs series.

Volcanoes. Illustrated by Terry Riley. The Rosen Publishing Group 2007 48p. Illustration
Grades: 3 4 5 6 7 8   **551.21; 741.5**
1. Volcanoes; 2. Graphic novels
978-1-4042-1988-5, $29.25
The book first describes how volcanoes form, briefly discusses killer volcanoes, then uses comic book-style illustrations to dramatize the eruption of Vesuvius in A.D. 79, which buried Pompeii; Krakatoa, which erupted in 1883 and destroyed the island near Sumatra (a new island started growing in 1967); and Mount St. Helens in Washington, which erupted in 1980. Additional information on studying volcanoes is included, along with a glossary and a list of book for further reading.
Part of the Graphic Natural Disasters series.

War correspondents. Illustrated by Chris Forsey. Rosen Publishing Group 2008 48p. Illustration
Grades: 3 4 5 6 7 8 9   **070.4; 741.5**
1. Adie, Kate; 2. Journalists; 3. Newspaper editors; 4. Television reporters; 5. Graphic novels
978-1-4042-1449-1, $29.25
                                       LC 2007-45936
After brief descriptions of early war reporting and the development of broadcast news from the front, the book profiles three war correspondents. Ernie Pyle made the life and wartime plight of the common soldier come alive for the folks back home; he was the first embedded journalist, staying with troops on the front. He was killed in action on

Okinawa in 1945. Sydney Schanberg went to Cambodia in 1973 and witnessed the "killing fields" there. He wrote about a bombing incident in Neak Leung, when a B52 accidentally bombed the town and killed 137 people, injuring 258 more. Dith Pran, his fellow journalist from Cambodia, died on March 30, 2008. BBC journalist Kate Adie was embedded with Coalition Forces during Desert Storm, the first Gulf war, in 1990. During this war, the embedded journalists used technology to broadcast directly from the war front.
Part of the Graphic Careers series

Showcase Presents The Flash, Volume One
DC Comics 2007 509p. Illustration
Grades: 7 8 9 10 11 12 Adult   **741.5; Fic**
1. Flash (Fictional character); 2. Superhero graphic novels; 3. Graphic novels
978-1-4012-1327-5, $16.99
A freak accident gives Central City police scientist Barry Allen fantastic super-speed abilities. Inspired by his favorite childhood comic book hero, Allen uses the name the Flash and uses his powers to help humanity. He soon finds himself facing such villains as Captain Cold, Mirror Master, Gorilla Grodd, the Pied Piper, Weather Wizard, and more. This volume collects 39 stories from the 1950s and 1960s in black and white.

Showcase Presents Superman Family Volume One
Otto Binder [and others], writers ; C.C. Beck [and others], pencillers and inkers. DC Comics 2006 572p. Illustration
Grades: 6 7 8 9 10 11 12 Adult   **741.5; Fic**
1. Jimmy Olsen (Fictional character); 2. Lois Lane (Fictional character); 3. Superhero graphic novels; 4. Superman (Fictional character); 5. Graphic novels
978-1-4012-0787-8, $16.99
This volume spotlights Superman's girlfriend Lois Lane and his pal Jimmy Olsen. Learn more about these two dynamic personalities in their solo stories as each braves danger for the latest scoop. These stories from the 1950s also introduceing elements such as the Daily Planet's Flying Newsroom and Jimmy's penchant for disguises. The Showcase series reprints the older comics stories in black and white collections.

Showcase Presents The Unknown Soldier Volume 1
DC Comics 2006 552p. Illustration
Grades: 8 9 10 11 12 Adult   **741.5; Fic**
1. Adventure graphic novels; 2. Unknown Soldier (Fictional character); 3. Graphic novels
978-1-4012-1090-8, $16.99
His face hideously disfigured by a grenade explosion in the early days of World War II, the young man who would become the Unknown Soldier was determined to continue fighting for his country. His true identity kept top secret, he became the perfect covert operative, using a multitude of disguises to carry out his exploits against the Axis powers. The first 38 adventures of the Unknown Soldier are collected in this black and white reprint volume, with stories dating from 1970 through 1975.

Showcase Presents: Green Arrow Volume 1
Otto Binder [and others], writers ; C.C. Beck [and others], pencillers and inkers. DC Comics 2006 528p. Illustration
Grades: 7 8 9 10 11 12 Adult   **741.5; Fic**
1. Green Arrow (Fictional character); 2. Superhero graph:c novels; 3. Graphic novels
1-4012-0785-5, $16.99
Millionaire Oliver Queen mastered the bow and arrow as a matter of survival when he was trapped on a desert island. Back home in Star City, he chose to use his newfound skills as the costumed champion Green Arrow. With his sidekick, Speedy, he tackled crooks and solved mysteries with energy, style, and the occasional boxing glove arrow. The stories collected in this black and white volume were originally published from 1958 through 1969

Showcase Presents: The House of Mystery Volume 1
DC Comics 2006 552p. Illustration
Grades: 7 8 9 10 11 12 Adult   **741.5; Fic**
1. Horror graphic novels; 2. Supernatural graphic novels; 3. Graphic novels
978-1-4012-0786-1, $16.99
Just beyond the door of the House of Mystery await spine-chilling (and some rib-tickling) stories of the supernatural, tales of ghosts and witches, ghouls and gargoyles, all hosted by Cain, the caretaker of the House. This black and white volume reprints House of Mystery issues 174-194, dating from 1968 through 1971. Some of the stories have a "Twilight Zone" feel, others are a little more gruesome.

Showcase Presents: Legion of Super-Heroes Volume 1
DC Comics 2007 552p. Illustration
Grades: 7 8 9 10 11 12 Adult   **741.5; Fic**
1. Legion of Super-Heroes (Fictional characters); 2. Superhero graphic novels; 3. Graphic novels
978-1-4012-1382-4, $16.99
The Legion of Super-Heroes, teenagers from across the cosmos, each with a unique ability, are the sworn protectors of the galaxy. Headquartered in their Super-Hero Club House, Lightning Lad, Saturn Girl, and Cosmic Boy have high standards for young hopeful champions wishing to join their ranks. With the largest roster of any super-team of the 2960s, they patrol all sectors of the universe to ensure peace and justice for all sentient beings. This volume collects black and white reprints of stories originally published from 1958 through 1964.

Showcase Presents: Martian Manhunter Volume 1
DC Comics 2007 544p. Illustration
Grades: 7 8 9 10 11 12 Adult   **741.5; Fic**
1. Martian Man hunter (Fictional character); 2. Superhero graphic novels; 3. Graphic novels
978-1-4012-1368-8, $16.99
After being accidentally teleported to Earth, Martian J'onn J'onzz finds himself stranded in a strange new world, with no way home. Using his powers to disguise his appearance, J'onn J'onzz adopts the name of deceased Denver police detective John Jones. With this new identity, he joins the Middleton Police force, secretly using his powers to help the inhabitants of Earth. Jack Miller and Joe

Samachson were principal writers on the series in the early years, and artist Joe Certa did all the pencils; this black and white volume reprints stories originally published from 1953 through 1962.

Showcase Presents: Metamorpho, the Element Man Volume 1
DC Comics 2005 560p. Illustration
Grades: 7 8 9 10 11 12 Adult   **741.5; Fic**
1. Science fiction graphic novels; 2. Superhero graphic novels; 3. Graphic novels
1-4012-0762-6, $16.99
Adventurer Rex Mason would do almost anything for the right price, but he ended up paying with his own humanity for stealing the legendary Orb of Ra for millionaire industrialist Simon Stagg. The mysterious relic transformed Rex into a freakish "element" man, with the ability to transform his body into hundreds of different substances. Calling himself Metamorpho, Rex considered his life cursed and sought a way to reverse the Orb's powers. Along the way, Stagg used Metamorpho's unique skills for his own purposes, and the Element Man would go along, since it meant more time with Stagg's gorgeous daughter Sapphire. The stories in this black and white volume date from 1964 through 1966.

Showcase Presents: Sgt. Rock
DC Comics 2007 543p. Illustration
Grades: 8 9 10 11 12 Adult   **741.5**
1. Adventure graphic novels; 2. Sgt Rock (Fictional character); 3. World War, 1939-1945; 4. Graphic novels
978-1-4012-1713-6, $16.99
Sgt. Rock, created by Robert Kanigher, was an ordinary soldier fighting in World War II. The stories collected in this volume, published from 1959 through 1962, depict Rock and his Easy Company fighting against evil during the war. Even today, Sgt. Rock is a symbol of patriotism and of America's fighting spirit. The stories include battle action.

Showcase Presents: Superman Volume 1
Otto Binder [and others], writers ; C.C. Beck [and others], pencillers and inkers. DC Comics 2005 560p. Illustration
Grades: 6 7 8 9 10 11 12 Adult   **741.5; Fic**
1. Superhero graphic novels; 2. Superman (Fictional character); 3. Graphic novels
1-4012-0758-8, $9.99
This first volume in the Showcase Presents Library of Classics features stories about Superman dating from 1958 through 1959. The adventure collected here have influenced the history of Superman and his extended family. From the introduction of his first love, the mermaid Lori Lemaris, to the introduction of his cousin Supergirl, Superman faces his most dangerous opponents, including Bizarro, Metallo, and Brainiac.

Showcase Presents: Superman Volume 2
DC Comics 2006 576p. Illustration
Grades: 7 8 9 10 11 12 Adult   **741.5; Fic**
1. Superhero graphic novels; 2. Superman (Fictional character); 3. Graphic novels

978-1-4012-1041-0, $16.99

The beginning of the 1960s ushered in a new era for Superman. These Silver Age exploits see Superman confront a wide array of villains, explore the planet Krypton, and overcome Kryptonite exposure, become a Bizarro, and more. The stories, reprinted here in black and white, date from December 1959 through May 1961.

Showcase Presents: Teen Titans Volume 1
DC Comics 2006 528p. Illustration
Grades: 6 7 8 9 10 11 12 Adult   **741.5; Fic**
1. Flash (Fictional character); 2. Robin (Fictional character); 3. Superhero graphic novels; 4. Teen Titans (Fictional characters); 5. Graphic novels
978-1-4012-0788-5, $16.99

The Teen Titans were all sidekicks to such heroes as Batman, Wonder Woman, Aquaman, and the Flash. When teen heroes Robin, Aqualad, and Kid Flash joined together, they became a forced to be reckoned with. Wonder Girl quickly joined them, and occasionally Speedy would come, and they all proved they were just as capable of defeating the bad guys and saving the world as their mentors, while still being teens and having fun. The black and white reprinted stories originally appeared from 1964 through 1968. Today's teens will get a kick out of what the writers thought was cool "teen speak" back then.

Showcase Presents: The War That Time Forgot
DC Comics 2007 560p. Illustration
Grades: 6 7 8 9 10 11 12 Adult   **741.5; Fic**
1. Adventure graphic novels; 2. Dinosaurs; 3. World War, 1939-1945; 4. Graphic novels
978-1-4012-1253-7, $16.99

On an unnamed, uncharted Pacific island, dinosaurs continued to thrive while World War II raged across the globe. It is on this island that members of the U.S. Armed Forces found themselves " armed only with standard issue weapons against the deadliest predators ever to roam the Earth. This volume collects Star Spangled War Stories issues #90-128, from 1960 through 1966. There's a lot of war action and dinosaur-fighting action. The stories here have been reprinted in black and white.

Siddell, Thomas
Gunnerkrigg Court: orientation. [by] Tom Siddell. Archaia Studios Press 2009 296p. Illustration
Grades: 6 7 8 9 10 11 12   **741; Fic; 741.5**
978-1-932386-34-9, $26.95; 1-932386-34-3

"Antimony Carver is a precocious and preternaturally self-possessed young girl starting her first year of school at gloomy Gunnerkrigg Court, a very British boarding school that has robots running around along side body-snatching demons, forest gods, and the odd mythical creature. The opening volume in the series follows Antimony through her orientation year: the people she meets, the strange things that happen, and the things she causes to happen as she and her new friend, Kat, unravel the mysteries of the Court and deal with the everyday adventures of growing up." (Publisher's note)

Other titles in this series are: Vol. 2: Research (2009); Vol. 3: Reason (2011); Vol. 4: Materia (2013); Vol. 5: Refine (2015)

Siegel, Elizabeth
The **Taj**. Art by Derek Toye. Harcourt Achieve/Steck-Vaughn 2007 48p.
Illustration
Grades: 3 4 5 6 7 8   **741.5; Fic**
1. India — History; 2. Taj Mahal; 3. Graphic novels
978-1-4190-3197-7, $8.99

Nazma and her family move to Agra when her father gets a job as master builder of the Taj Mahal. In this new setting, Nazma discovers she has hidden talents. What lies in her future? This historical graphic novel includes prose intervals that provide more information about the Taj Mahal and about the Shah Jahan, who had it built as a shrine to his love for his dead wife, Mumtaz Mahal.

Part of the Timeline Graphic Novels series.

Siegel, Jerry
The **Superman** Chronicles Volume Three. Superman created by Jerry Siegel & Joe Shuster ; all stories written by Jerry Siegel and illustrated by Joe Shuster. DC Comics 2007 190p. Illustration
Grades: 6 7 8 9 10 11 12 Adult   **741.5; Fic**
1. Superhero graphic novels; 2. Superman (Fictional character); 3. Graphic novels
978-1-4012-1374-9, $14.99

In this third volume of the adventures of Superman presented in chronological order, the Man of Steel faces the villain who would plague him ever since: Lex Luthor. Clark Kent and Lois Lane become European war correspondents covering the conflicts that will eventually become World War II. And Superman maintains his reputation as the champion of the oppressed by battling jewel thieves, blackmailers, and predatory monsters.

The **Superman** Chronicles Volume Two. Superman created by Jerry Siegel & Joe Shuster ; all stories written by Jerry Siegel and illustrated by Joe Shuster. DC Comics 2007 192p. Illustration
Grades: 7 8 9 10 11 12 Adult   **741.5; Fic**
1. Superhero graphic novels; 2. Superman (Fictional character); 3. Graphic novels
978-1-4012-1215-5, $14.99

Experience the history of Superman with this series that reprints the early adventures of the Man of Tomorrow in chronological order. This volume features classic tales from 1939 and 1940 written and illustrated by Superman co-creators Jerry Siegel and Joe Shuster, in which the Man of Tomorrow battles crooked politicians and slumlords as he brings justice to the downtrodden masses.

Superman: The World's Finest Comics Archives Volume 1. Jerry Siegel & Joe Shuster. DC Comics 2004 240p. Illustration
Grades: 7 8 9 10 11 12 Adult   **741.5; Fic**
1. Superhero graphic novels; 2. Superman (Fictional character); 3. Graphic novels
1-4012-0151-2, $49.99

This Archives volume collects Superman stories from World's Finest Comics, dating from 1939 through 1944, with stories by the original creators, Siegel and Schuster, in these early adventures, Superman battled "regular" criminals, and his super powers were but a fraction of what they are in current Superman comics. These full-color reprints are bound in a sturdy hardcover edition.

Siegel, Mark
   To dance: a ballerina's graphic novel. [by] Siena Cherson Siegel; [illustrated by] Mark Siegel. Simon & Schuster 2006 Un Illustration
Grades: 4 5 6 7   **92; 741.5**
   1. Autobiographical graphic novels; 2. Ballet; 3. Ballet dancers; 4. Puerto Ricans — Biography; 5. Siegel, Siena Cherson; 6. Graphic novels
   1-4169-2687-9 (pa), $9.99
   In this memoir of her youth in dance from ages six to eighteen, Siegel tells what it was like to be totally involved in dance, in ballet-all the joys and the physical pain. She worked as a young dancer with George Ballanchine. Her absolute desire to be a dancer took her from her native Puerto Rico to New York City to study. Her simple but heartfelt narration is ably illustrated by her husband Mark Siegel.
   Aladdin paperbacks

Sierra, Sergio A.
   Frankenstein by Mary Shelley: a Dark graphic novel. Adaptation Sergio A. Sierra; illustration Meritxell Ribas. Enslow Publishers 2013 95 p.
Grades: 6 7 8 9 10 11 12 Adult   **741.5**
   1. Horror stories; 2. Monsters — Fiction; 3. Graphic novels; 4. Frankenstein (Fictional character)
   0766040844; 9780766040847, $25.26
                                            LC 2011035826
   This book is a black-and-white graphic novel adaptation of Mary Shelley's 19th-century gothic novel "Frankenstein." The plot tells the "tale of a monster, assembled by a scientist from parts of dead bodies, who develops a mind of his own as he learns to loathe himself and hate his creator." (WorldCat)
   Includes bibliographical references.

Siku
   The **manga** Bible: from Genesis to Revelation. [by] Siku ; concept and art, Siku ; script, Akinsiku. Doubleday 2008 218p. Illustration
Grades: 8 9 10 11 12   **220.9; 741.5**
   1. Bible; 2. Graphic novels
   978-0-385-52431-5, $12.95
                                            LC 2007-42413
   This graphic novel with some manga influences hits the highlights of the Bible, all the way from Genesis to Revelation, with stops for the story of Adam and Eve's fall into sin, the story of Abraham and Sarah, Joseph's fall into slavery and rise to power in Egypt, Moses and the Exodus of the Israelites to Canaan, on to the story of Ruth the Moabite, her descendant David who became King, to the Babylonian Captivity and the prophet Daniel, to John the Baptist, the three-year journey of Jesus who was crucified, died, and rose from the dead to show that He was the Son of God, to the work of Paul, who started as an enemy of the new Christians but became one of the great apostles, to John's writing of the Revelation. The angular, almost sketchy art combines with casual, slangy dialogue to make the stories more accessible to those who may have never read the Bible, but even with

some violence and partial nudity, the stories are still faithful to the original text.

Silvermoon, Crystal
   Les misérables. Victor Hugo; adapted by Crystal Silvermoon; illustrated by SunNeko Lee. Udon Entertainment 2014 337 p. Illustration; Color (Manga Classics)
Grades: 8 9 10 11 12   **741.5; Fic**
   1. France — History — 1789-1799, Revolution; 2. Manga
   1927925169; 9781927925164, $19.99
   In this graphic novel adaptation by Crystal Silvermoon, illustrated by SunNeko Lee, "Victor Hugo's classic novel of love & tragedy during the French Revolution is reborn in this fantastic new manga edition! The gorgeous art of TseMei Lee brings to life the tragic stories of Jean Valjean, Inspector Javert, and the beautiful Fantine, in this epic adaptation of Les Miserables!" (Publisher's note)
   "All major plot points and iconic scenes are included in the text and art, and both work seamlessly to tell the story. . . . The characters, for the most part, are instantly recognizable. It is clear that research has gone into making this adaptation." VOYA

Simone, Gail
   The **Marvelous** adventures of Gus Beezer with Spider-Man. Jason Lethcoe, art. ABDO Publishing Company/Spotlight 2006 Un Illustration
Grades: 3 4 5 6 7 8   **741.5; Fic**
   1. Humorous graphic novels; 2. Spider-Man (Fictional character); 3. Superhero graphic novels; 4. Graphic novels
   978-1-59961-047-4, $21.35
                                            LC 2006-43968
   In this library bound edition of Marvel Age Spider-Man originally published in May 2003 (with all advertisements removed), super Marvel Comics fan Gus Beezer has been looking forward to the new Spider-Man movie, but his mother announces that the family will be going to the family reunion instead. With his sister waging a "Girl War" on him and the family reunion looming over him, the imaginative boy faces a miserable day. Until he meets a "distant cousin," Peter Parker, photographer for the Daily Bugle (Spider-Man fans will know who this is).

   The **marvelous** adventures of Guz Beezer with the X-Men: X marks the Mutant. Jason Lethcoe, art. ABDO Spotlight 2006 Un Illustration
Grades: 3 4 5 6 7 8 9   **741.5; Fic**
   1. Adventure graphic novels; 2. Humorous graphic novels; 3. Superhero graphic novels; 4. Graphic novels
   1-59961-050-7, $21.35
   Gus Beezer, major comics fan and collector, is convinced he's a mutant like the X-Men, even when his comic book skit at school results in major trouble and gets him grounded. What he keeps missing is that his baby sister Tillie is the one getting him into trouble at home. Another story runs on the bottom part of the page, and looks like a homemade comic written and drawn by Gus, featuring him

as Marvel Boy and his baby sister as the town-consuming villain.

This book is a revision of an issue of The Marvelous Adventures of Gus Beever, originally published by Marvel's Marvel Age line.

Sizer, Paul
★ **Little** White Mouse Omnibus Edition. Cafe Digital Studios 2006 447p. Illustration
Grades: 6 7 8 9 10 11 12   **741.5; Fic**
1. Science fiction graphic novels; 2. Graphic novels
978-0-9768565-5-9, $24.95
"In a far future universe, teenaged Loo is the lone survivor of the mysterious destruction of a luxury space liner. She finds an abandoned space mining station, where she must evade a security system that seeks to destroy an intruder such as her, and find a way home before the automated life systems fail. With its strong and appealing young female protagonist, Sizer's story is science fiction that girls will love." (VOYA)
Originally published in serial form, and then as a four-volume series from Blue Line Pro.

Slade, Christian
★ **Korgi,** Book 1: Sprouting Wings. Top Shelf Productions 2007 88p. Illustration
Grades: 2 3 4 5 6 7 8 9 10 11 12 Adult   **741.5; Fic**
1. Dogs; 2. Fantasy graphic novels; 3. Stories without words; 4. Graphic novels
978-1-891830-90-7, $10
In this wordless book, a young Mollie (woodland people) named Ivy and her young Korgi companion named Sprout embark on adventures in Korgi Hollow, an enchanted place. When they wander from the Mollie village, the two fall through a hole in the ground and find nasty, monstrous creatures who want to eat them. As they deal with the danger and make their escape, Ivy and Sprout both discover new talents. Slade's extensively cross-hatched yet delicate art is highly expressive, and readers young and old will have no trouble figuring out what is going on. The Korgi are based on Welsh corgi dogs, of which Slade and his wife have two.

Korgi, book 2. Top Shelf Productions 2008 Un Illustration
Grades: 3 4 5 6 7 8 9 10 11 12 Adult   **741.5; Fic**
1. Adventure graphic novels; 2. Fantasy graphic novels; 3. Stories without words; 4. Graphic novels
978-1-60309-010-0, $10
In this second wordless volume, the young Mollie named Ivy and her Korgi cub Sprout, experience a harrowing adventure. Someone has been hunting the Mollies and cutting off their wings. Ivy and Sprout rescue one older Mollie named Art and his Korgi when they fall into a deep trap in the woods; then as Ivy flies, a barbed arrow cuts one of her wings off. She and Sprout see a strange creature carrying her wing and they follow him to his place, where he hangs all the Mollie wings like trophies. Ivy decides she wants her wing back, but she and Sprout will have to fight the creature and his automated and nasty bots.

Slavin, Bill
Big star Otto. Written by Bill Slavin with Esperança Melo; art by Bill Slavin. Kids Can Press 2015 95 p. (Elephants Never Forget)
Grades: 3 4 5 6   **741.5**
1. Chimpanzees — Juvenile fiction; 2. Elephants — Juvenile fiction; 3. Kidnapping — Juvenile fiction; 4. Parrots — Juvenile fiction; 5. Graphic novels
1894786963; 9781894786966, $16.95
"In this conclusion to the Elephants Never Forget graphic novel trilogy, [by Bill Slavin], big-hearted hero Otto and his parrot pal Crackers have landed in Hollywood, the final stop in their journey across America in search of their good friend Georgie the chimpanzee. They've been hot on Georgie's trail since he was abducted from Africa by the sinister Man with the Wooden Nose, and now they're sure they've finally found his location." (Publisher's note)

Smalley, Roger
Dolley Madison Saves History. Illustrated by Anna Maria Cool, Scott Rosema, Charles Barnett III. Capstone Press 2006 32p. Illustration
Grades: 3 4 5 6 7 8 9   **741.5; 973.5; 92**
1. Biographical graphic novels; 2. Madison, Dolley, 1768-1849; 3. War of 1812; 4. Washington (DC); 5. Graphic novels
0-7368-4972-6, $25.26
LC 2005008465
This book uses the comic book format to recount the story of First Lady Dolley Madison's actions during the War of 1812, when Washington, D.C. was invaded by British troops. It includes additional information, a glossary, a list of books for further reading, and more.
Part of the Graphic Library, Graphic History series.

Smith, Andy J.
Jeremy Kreep: Fang Fairy. Stone Arch Books 2007 40p. Illustration
Grades: 3 4 5 6 7 8 9   **741.5; Fic**
1. Fantasy graphic novels; 2. Humorous graphic novels; 3. Graphic novels
978-1-59889-835-4, $21.26
LC 2007-3176
Jeremy Kreep has a problem. Something has snagged a baby tooth from beneath his brother's pillow and left a puddle of slime. Now Jeremy and his best friend Nessy go off to find the truth behind the tooth fairy. Is the creature just a silly superstition, or a real-life collector of fangs? This graphic novel is written with an easy vocabulary for reluctant and struggling readers.
Part of the Graphic Sparks line of books.

Smith, Dwayne Alexander
Speed Racer. Art by Dwayne Alexander Smith. Seven Seas Entertainment 2007 Un Illustration
Grades: 8 9 10 11 12 Adult   **741.5; Fic**
1. Adventure graphic novels; 2. Automobile racing; 3. Racer, Speed (Fictional character); 4. Graphic novels
978-1-933164-33-5, $9.99
The popular cartoon character Speed Racer is back in an original global manga story. Speed comes from a family with racing in its blood; his older brother Rex presumably died in

an accident. Speed drives the Mach 5 and, in this book, he's participating in a grueling three-day, 900 mile race. His main opponent, Adam Matic, determines to win at any cost and tries to sabotage the Mach 5, but on the second day of the race, he's the one who dies. His father, the mad scientist Otto Matic, takes Adam's heart and builds a cyborg version of his son to carry on; but Adam 2 also retains the original man's hatred and tries to kill Speed. Several publishers are bringing Speed Racer back to the U.S. in book form, and a new live-action movie is scheduled for a May 2008 release. This one has lots of action and some violence that makes it more suitable for teen readers.

Smith, Ian

Emily & the intergalactic lemonade stand. [by] Ian Smith and Tyson Smith. Amaze Ink/Slave Labor Graphics 2004 96p. Illustration

Grades: 4 5 6 7 8 9   **741.5; Fic**
1. Humorous graphic novels; 2. Science fiction graphic novels; 3. Graphic novels
0-943151-96-1, $12.95

Eleven-year-old Emily runs a lemonade stand with the help of her pet robot, Juicer; she wants to earn enough money to buy a pony. Complicating matters is neighborhood rival Daisy, who wants to beat Emily because cute Jace Tanner hangs around Emily (he actually only likes robots). Then aliens invade, and the military wants Juicer, because they think he's the perfect weapon. And little alien warrior Pheef wants blood, can he help it he's so cute and tiny" The defense of Earth depends on Emily; can it survive?

Smith, Jeff

★ **Bone** Book Seven: ghost circles. Scholastic/GRAPHIX 2008 152p. Illustration

Grades: 3 4 5 6 7 8 9 10 11 12 Adult   **741.5; Fic**
1. Adventure graphic novels; 2. Fantasy graphic novels; 3. Graphic novels
978-0-439-70629-2, $19.99; 978-0-439-70634-6 (pa), $9.99

                                  LC 2007-9568403

The Bone cousins, Gran'ma Ben, Thorn, and their loyal rat creature cub Bartleby venture on a journey through the mysterious ghost circles to Atheia, the old city of the royal family. Meanwhile, the Barrelhaven villagers and the Veni Yan face enemy hordes. Steve Hamaker is the colorist for this full color version of Smith's comic epic.

★ **Bone** vol. 8: treasure hunters. Scholastic/Graphix 2008 138p. Illustration

Grades: 5 6 7 8 9 10 11 12 Adult   **741.5; Fic**
1. Adventure graphic novels; 2. Fantasy graphic novels; 3. Graphic novels
978-0-439-70630-8, $18.95; 978-0-439-70633-9 (pa), $9.99

                                  LC 2008-9568403

The Bone cousins, Gran'ma Ben, and Thorn reach the city of Atheia, where they prepare to battle the Lord of the Locusts. Meanwhile, Thorn's visions are becoming more threatening and Phoney Bone is convinced Atheia is rich in gold, and he is determined to find it. But all is not well in Atheia, and Thorn is in great danger, not only from Briar and the Lord of the Locusts. This edition is in full color, done by Steve Hamaker.

★ **Bone**: out from Boneville. Scholastic Graphix 2005 144p. Illustration

Grades: 4 5 6 7 8 9 10 11 12   **741.5; Fic**
1. Adventure graphic novels; 2. Fantasy graphic novels; 3. Graphic novels
0-439-70623-8, $18.95; 0-439-70640-8 (pa), $9.99

"The story follows three cousins who have been thrown out of their town for cheating the citizens. Shortly thereafter, they are separated. Each Bone stumbles into a mysterious valley full of odd creatures that reveal strange happenings. The story is well paced with smooth transitions. It is dark, witty, mysterious, and exciting. The full-color art reflects that of classic comic books." SLJ

Also available Bone: one volume edition $39.95 from Cartoon Books (ISBN 1-8889-6314-X)

Other titles in this series are: Bone: the great cow race (vol. 2); Bone: eyes of the storm (vol. 3); Bone: the dragonslayer (vol. 4); Bone: Rock Jaw: master of the Eastern border (vol. 5); Bone: old man's cave (vol. 6); Bone: ghost circles (vol. 7); Bone: treasure hunters (vol. 8); Bone: crown of horns (vol. 9)

Bone: Rose. With illustrations by Charles Vess. Scholastic Graphix 2009 138p. Illustration

Grades: 4 5 6 7 8   **741.5; Fic**
978-0-545-13542-9, $21.99; 0-545-13542-7;
978-0-545-13543-6 (pa), $10.99; 0-545-13543-5 (pa)

"When a terrifying dragon attacks the small towns of the Northern Valley, a young Princess Rose (known later as Gran'ma Ben) must defeat it. The beast is actually the ancient evil, the Lord of the Locusts, and while Rose faces danger with honor, her elder sister, Princess Briar, follows a more sinister path." (Publisher's note)

Bone: tall tales. By Jeff Smith with Tom Sniegoski; color by Steve Hamaker. Graphix 2010 108p. Illustration

Grades: 4 5 6 7 8   **741; 741.5**
978-0-545-14095-9, $21.99; 0-545-14095-1;
978-0-545-14096-6 (pa), $10.99; 0-545-14096-X (pa)

"Long before the Bone cousins were ever lost in the uncharted desert on the outskirts of the Valley, Big Johnson Bone, the discoverer of the Rolling Bone River, founded Boneville. But little is known of the mighty explorer's adventures before he started his famous trading post. So when Smiley Bone sits down with a group of young campers to retell the legendary stories of Boneville's origin and its tough, no-nonsense founder, what they hear are tall tales in typical BONE fashion." (Publisher's note)

Smith, Mark Andrew

The **New** Brighton Archeological Society book one: The castle of Galomar. Created by Mark Andrew Smith & Matthew Weldon. Image Comics 2009 Un Illustration

Grades: 4 5 6 7 8 9   **741.5; Fic**
1. Adventure graphic novels; 2. Fairies; 3. Fantasy graphic novels; 4. Goblins; 5. Graphic novels
978-1-58240-973-3, $17.99

When their parents die on an archeological expedition, two sets of siblings Joss and Cooper, and Brad and Becka, come to live on the estate where their parents lived as children. They first discover bottled ghosts when Becka accidentally falls through a secret door, then they find an old clubhouse connected to the estate's manor house by a tunnel. The clubhouse holds lots of books about different kinds of monsters and other creatures. And then, when they go camping, they find a society of goblins, including Mitch, who knew their parents. There, the four find themselves caught in the middle of a war between the fairies and the goblins, all for possession of powerful books. Mitch's parents tell the children about the evil Galomar, who seeks to possess all the magic books in the world. They decide to infiltrate the castle in order to try to stop Galomar. This fantasy adventure includes some action but little actual killing (the goblins use maple syrup to make the fairies' wings too sticky to fly, among other tactics).

Smith, Tyson
Dream Maiden Megan. Tyson Smith and Ian Smith ; Art by Ian Smith. SLG Publishing/Amaze Ink 2008 93p. Illustration
Grades: 8 9 10 11 12   **741.5; Fic**
1. Fantasy graphic novels; 2. Humorous graphic novels; 3. Graphic novels
978-1-59362-129-2, $8.95
High school student Jef is a good student who now works as a manager at a coffee bar. He has no time for sleep, which causes a problem for Dream Maiden Megan, who needs to get Jef to sleep and dream. However, once he finds out she can't leave until he sleeps, he refuses to do so because she's beautiful and he isn't lucky with girls. Megan decides to set up shop in his closet and brings in her friends, such as a monster in the closet and some other dream maidens. And they plot to make Jef fall asleep even as he does everything in his power to stay awake. Megan finally figures out she needs to set up Jef on a date, but no one will go out with him. . . . There's some violence, especially with Maiden-in-Training Tulip, who likes to bash Jef in the head.

Sohn, Emily
A **Crash** Course in Forces and Motion with Max Axiom, Super Scientist. Illustrated by Steve Erwin and Charles Barnett III. Capstone Press 2007 32p. Illustration
Grades: 3 4 5 6 7 8   **531; 741.5**
1. Motion; 2. Science; 3. Graphic novels
978-0-7368-6837-2 li, $25.26; 978-0-7368-7890-6 (pa)
Max Axiom is a super-cool super-scientist who demonstrates and explains science in ways never before seen in the classroom. Whether shrinking down to the size of an ant or riding on a sound wave, Max does whatever it takes to make science super cool and accessible. This volume explores forces such as motion and speed, and includes a glossary and a list of books for further reading.
Part of the Graphic Science series.

The **Illuminating** World of Light with Max Axiom, Super Scientist. Art by Nick Derington. Capstone Press 2007 32p. Illustration
Grades: 3 4 5 6 7 8 9   **535; 741.5**
1. Light; 2. Graphic novels
978-1-4296-0140-X, $25.26
LC 2007002264

This book uses the graphic novel format to follow the adventures of super scientist Max Axiom as he explains the science behind light, including how the human eye sees light. The book includes additional facts and a list of books for further reading.
Part of the Graphic Science series.

A **journey** through the digestive system with Max Axiom, super scientist. Illustrated by Cynthia Martin and Barbara Schulz. Capstone Press 2009 32p. Illustration
Grades: 2 3 4 5 6 7   **612.3; 741.5**
1. Digestion; 2. Graphic novels
978-1-4296-2336-0, $26.60; 978-1-4296-3452-6 (pa), $7.95
LC 2008-29650
The cartoon super scientist Max Axiom takes young readers into the human body to explore the digestive system, from the act of eating (ingestion) through the esophagus to the stomach, into the intestines. The book also explains why people get gas, and discusses the work of the large intestine without showing it. However, some very sensitive young children could get grossed out by some of the illustrations. Readers will also find facts about nutrition, including the Food Pyramid. Back matter in the book includes more digestion facts, a glossary, reading list, and an index.
Part of the Graphic Science series

Sonic the Hedgehog Archives Volume 1
Archie Comic Publications 2006 Un Illustration
Grades: 3 4 5 6 7 8   **741.5; Fic**
1. Adventure graphic novels; 2. Humorous graphic novels; 3. Sonic the Hedgehog (Fictional character); 4. Graphic novels
1-879794-20-9, $7.49
This volume collects the stories published in the first four issues of the Sonic the Hedgehog comics. In these stories, Sonic faces Robotnik's mecha-plant in the forest; he crashes the Casino Night Zone and must face the Orbinaut; he and buddy Tails have to deal with Coconuts, Scratch, and Grounder when they ruin a perfectly good day; he meets Bunnie Rabbot; and he faces the Universalamander.

Sonic the Hedgehog Archives Volume 2
Archie Comic Publications 2006 Un Illustration
Grades: 3 4 5 6 7 8   **741.5; Fic**
1. Adventure graphic novels; 2. Humorous graphic novels; 3. Sonic the Hedgehog (Fictional character); 4. Graphic novels
1-879794-21-7, $7.49
Among the stories collected in this volume, Sonic and the Freedom Fighters compete in Olympic challenges issued by Robotnik; Sonic faces the Termite-nator; Robotnik kidnaps Sally when she's dressed as a Halloween Sorceress, thinking she's a real one; and Sonic deals with ever more nasty bots created by Robotnik.

Sonic the Hedgehog Archives Volume 3
Archie Comic Publications 2007 Un Illustration
Grades: 3 4 5 6 7 8   **741.5; Fic**

1. Adventure graphic novels; 2. Humorous graphic novels; 3. Sonic the Hedgehog (Fictional character); 4. Graphic novels
1-879794-22-1, $7.49

Two of Sonic's most personal foes are introduced for the first time; the parade of robotic Sonics debuts with the evil Pseudo-Sonic; and a good hedgehog can go bad with the nasty Evil Sonic. Sonic also encounters the Nerbs, and Larry the Super-Jinx makes his first appearance.

Sonic the Hedgehog Archives Volume 4
Archie Comic Publications 2007 Un Illustration
Grades: 3 4 5 6 7 8   **741.5; Fic**
1. Adventure graphic novels; 2. Humorous graphic novels; 3. Sonic the Hedgehog (Fictional character); 4. Graphic novels
1-879794-24-5, $7.49

This volume features the debut of Sonic's first rival, Knuckles the Echidna; when Sonic and Tails meet the red warrior for the first time, they barely make it out alive. Then Tails gets too big for his britches. And Dr. Robotnik is big, but now he's huge and dwarfs the Freedom Fighters, putting them under glass.

Sonic the Hedgehog: The Beginning
Archie Comics 2003 96p. Illustration
Grades: 3 4 5 6 7 8 9 10 11 12 Adult   **741.5; Fic**
1. Adventure graphic novels; 2. Humorous graphic novels; 3. Sonic the Hedgehog (Fictional character); 4. Graphic novels
1-879794-12-8, $10.95

In 1993, Sonic the Hedgehog sped his way from video games to comic books, and has been going strong ever since. Now, readers can enjoy his earliest comic book adventures with this edition that reprints the first appearances of Tails, Princess Sally, Antoine, Rotor, Uncle Chuck, and Muttski. Fans can also marvel at Sonic's magic rings, the freedom emeralds, and King Acorn's magic crown; while booing and hissing at the villainous Robotnik, his evil Swat-Bots, and his myriad dastardly devices.

Sonishi, Kenji
Leave it to PET!: the misadventures of a recycled super robot, vol. 1. Story & art by Kenji Sonishi; translation, Katherine Schilling; touch-up art & lettering, John Hunt; editor, Traci N. Todd. Viz Media/VizKids 2009 192p. Illustration
Grades: 3 4 5 6   **741.5; Fic**
1. Humorous graphic novels; 2. Manga; 3. Recycling; 4. Graphic novels
978-1-4215-2649-2, $7.99

PET (polyethylene terephthalate, a type of recyclable plastic) was a simple plastic bottle until nine-year-old Noboru recycled him. Now PET is a super robot programmed to "repay" Noboru for recycling him by helping him. Unfortunately for Noboru, PET's help usually ends up causing even more trouble; being a super robot doesn't mean PET has a clue about what he is doing. The book includes lots of short stories that follow the formula of Noboru getting into a bit of a fix, calling for PET, then getting into more trouble as PET does the wrong thing. Some of the stories do include some information about recycling plastics and aluminum, which is done somewhat differently in Japan than in the U.S.

Volume 1 of a 4-volume series

Soo, Kean
★ **Jellaby:** monster in the city. Hyperion Books 2009 172p. Illustration
Grades: 4 5 6 7 8 9   **741.5; Fic**
1. Fantasy graphic novels; 2. Friendship; 3. Monsters; 4. Graphic novels
1-4231-0565-6 (pa); 978-1-4231-0565-7 (pa), $9.99

Beginning right where the first book ended, Portia, Jason, and Jellaby continue on their way to Toronto, walking after Portia panicked and they got off the train. They're searching for a way home for Jellaby, and they think a door somewhere in Exhibition Place, where the Canadian National Exhibition is taking place, holds a clue. Portia feels torn between wanting to help her friend yet not wanting to say goodbye forever, and her ambivalence causes a rift between her and Jason. When she doesn't want to trust a masked magician who seems to know too much about them and Jellaby, Portia leaves Jason. They all end up in the Automotive Building, where the masked man leads Jason and Jellaby down below the building, while Portia seems to find her long lost father. But is he really her father, and just what is waiting for Jason and Jellaby under the Automotive Building?" Soo again uses a mostly purple color palette.

Another title in the author's series about Jellaby

★ **Jellaby;** Volume 1: the lost monster. By Kean Soo. Stone Arch Books 2014 160 p. Color; Illustration (Jellaby)
Grades: 4 5 6 7 8 9   **741.5**
1. Extraterrestrial beings — Fiction; 2. Friendship — Fiction; 3. Human-alien encounters; 4. Monsters — Fiction
1434291952; 9781434264206, $12.95 ; 9781434291950, $19.99

LC 2013037026

"Portia has just moved to a new neighborhood with her mom. Adjusting to life without a father is hard enough, but school is boring and her classmates are standoffish. . . . But things start to get better when Portia mounts a midnight excursion into the woods behind her house where she discovers a shy and sweet purple monster. Life with Jellaby is exciting, but Portia's purple friend has secrets of his own." (Publisher's note)

"Soo grounds the story in a fairly gritty contemporary reality, where kids deal with bullies and well-meaning adults try to help. Clear, clean lines and easy-to-follow panel layouts round out the package." Booklist

First published 2008

Originally published: New York : Hyperion Books for Children, 2008.A Capstone imprint.

Sorano, Kaili
Monochrome factor, volume 1. Tokyopop 2007 182p. Illustration
Grades: 8 9 10 11 12   **741.5**
1. Manga; 2. Shonen manga; 3. Supernatural graphic novels; 4. Graphic novels
978-1-4278-0069-5, $9.99

Akira Nikaido is the ultimate slacker, able to skip entire days of school with relative impunity. Then, one day a mysterious man named Shirogane confronts him and when Akira refuses to listen to him, he tells him to meet him at the school that night. Due to circumstances beyond his control, Akira finds himself at the school and a shadow monster attacks. When Akira ignores Shirogane's warning and runs past a psychic barrier, he becomes caught in the shadow world, and now the only way to live is for Akira to become a shin, a creature of the shadow world just like Shirogane, and work to restore the balance between the human and shadow worlds. The book includes some minor incidental partial nudity, some mildly harsh language and some violence.

Spangler, Bill
Tom Corbett: space cadet. Art by John DaCosta and Wilson Ramos Jr.. Bluewater Productions 2010 96p. Illustration
Grades: 7 8 9 10 11 12 Adult   **741.5; Fic**
1. Adventure graphic novels; 2. Science fiction graphic novels; 3. Tom Corbett, Space Cadet (Television series); 4. Graphic novels
978-1-4507-0014-6, $15.95
In the year 2251 A.D., Solar Guard Cadets Tom Corbett, Roger Manning, and Astro Deaver come to Rescue Station RSA-4 to conduct routine maintenance, but instead they find big trouble when the fully automated station doesn't respond to their computers, and the robots attack them. When the cadets manage to stop an alien robot that had taken over the station, they take it back to the Academy, where Solar Guard scientists discover that it isn't alien, but based on the old designs of Dr. Sanderson Dale of Earth. Then robot-run ships attack every planet of the Solar System except Earth, with a demand that humans leave space and return to Earth or face destruction. The Solar Alliance's only hope is to find Dr. Dale's original software, in order to reboot the robots of the One State. This space adventure is an original story set in the universe created for the Tom Corbett, Space Cadet television series that aired in the 1950s, as well as the novels and comics that were spun off the series. Spangler wrote some of the comics published in the 1990s. DaCosta's full-color art uses a retro/epic look for the outer space architecture and ships. This book was originally published as a four-issue miniseries of comic books.

Spider-Man: The Birth of Venom
Marvel Entertainment 2007 Un Illustration
Grades: 8 9 10 11 12 Adult   **741.5; Fic**
1. Fantastic Four (Fictional characters); 2. Spider-Man (Fictional character); 3. Superhero graphic novels; 4. Graphic novels
978-0-7851-2498-6, $29.99
The Beyonder's Battleworld might seem a strange place to get new threads, but it's Spider-Man who becomes unraveled when his new symbiotic, shape-changing costume attempts to darken his life as well as his fashion sense. But ridding himself of his black costume proves an even greater mistake when its alien enmity bonds with mortal madness to form our hero's most dedicated enemy, Venom. Other stories include the first appearances of Puma and the Rose, Mary Jane Watson's startling secret, and the debut of the battling . .

. Bag-Man? The Black Cat, the Fantastic Four and other Marvel characters appear.

Spider-Man: Saga of the Sandman
Marvel Entertainment 2007 176p. Illustration
Grades: 7 8 9 10 11 12 Adult   **741.5; Fic**
1. Fantastic Four (Fictional characters); 2. Hulk (Fictional character); 3. Spider-Man (Fictional character); 4. Superhero graphic novels; 5. Graphic novels
978-0-7851-2497-9, $19.99
It was no day at the beach when criminal Flint Marko was mutated into one of Marveldom's most versatile villains. This book recounts his origins and some of the best battles between Sandman, Spider-Man, the Fantastic Four and the Hulk.

Spiegelman, Art
★ **Big** fat Little Lit. [edited by] Art Spiegelman and Francoise Mouly. Puffin 2006 144p. Illustration
Grades: 2 3 4 5 6 7 8   **741.5; Fic**
1. Folklore; 2. Graphic novels
0-14-240706-2, $14.99
This volume collects all three previously published Little Lit books: Little Lit: Once Upon a Time, Little Lit: Strange Stories for Strange Kids, and Little Lit: It Was a Dark and Silly Night. Many comics creators and children's book writers and illustrators contributed stories, including Ian Falconer, Daniel Clowes, Maurice Sendak, David Sedaris, Chris Ware, Jules Feiffer, Barbara McClintock, Crockett Johnson, J. Otto Siebold, Neil Gaiman, Art Spiegelman, and Lemony Snicket."

★ **Maus:** a survivor's tale, 2v in 1. Art Spiegelman.. Pantheon Bks. 1996 295 p. Illustration; Map; Color
Grades: 7 8 9 10 11 12 Adult   **741.5; 92; 940.53**
1. Biographical graphic novels; 2. Holocaust, 1933-1945; 3. Spiegelman, Vladek; 4. Graphic novels
0-679-40641-7, $35

LC 96-32796
Awards: 1992 Pulitzer Prize Special Award; Eisner Award for Best Graphic Album: Reprint for Maus II; Harvey Award for Best Graphic Album of Previously Published Work (for Maus II); 1993 Los Angeles Times Book Prize for Fiction (for Maus II)
"An undisputed classic and award-winning title (including a Pulitzer Prize in 1992) in which renowned cartoonist Spiegelman depicts his father's experiences as a World War II Nazi concentration camp survivor. The memoir is also a chronicle of Spiegelman's relationship with his father as we witness their visits and disagreements. The black-and-white drawings are straightforward, but with an interesting twist: all of the Jews are depicted as mice and the Nazis as cats." LJ
Also available: paperback boxed set edition $23.25 (ISBN 0141014083)
A combined edition of Maus I : My father bleeds history (1986) and Maus II : And here my troubles began (1991)

Spires, Ashley
★ **Binky** takes charge. By Ashley Spires. Kids Can Press 2012 64 p. Color illustration
Grades: 4 5 6   **741.5/971; Fic**

1. Cats — Fiction; 2. Picture books for children; 3. Spy stories

1554537037; 9781554537037, $16.95; 9781554537686, $8.95; 9781451765137, $17.95

"Felines of the Universe Ready for Space Travel (F.U.R.S.T.) and Captain Gracie are pleased to announce that Lt. Binky is about to get his first recruit to train [in this book by Ashley Spires.] . . . There's a new diversity program at F.U.R.S.T., and Gordon, a dog, has been assigned to Binky. Binky decides to give it his all. As expected, Gordon falls short. Then Binky discovers the unthinkable: Gordon seems to be leaving coded messages in outer space . . . If they are to prove Gordon is a double agent, Gracie and Binky will need incontrovertible proof!" (Kirkus)

Spradlin, Michael P.

Spy goddess volume 1: the chase for the chalice. Created by Michael P. Spradlin ; script by Rachel Manija Brown ; illustrated by Rainbow Buddy. HarperCollins/Tokyopop 2008 Un Illustration

Grades: 7 8 9 10 11 12   **741.5; Fic**

1. Adventure graphic novels; 2. Spies; 3. Graphic novels

978-0-06-136299-6, $9.99

Rachel Buchanan and her fellow Blackthorn Academy spy students travel with Headmaster Mr. Kim to Japan, where Simon Blankenship and his Mithrian followers have stolen another Mithrian artifact. In between the shopping (by both guys and gals), Pilar and Rachel suspect that their local police contacts are actually Mithrians. Then Rachel gets kidnapped, for Blankenship is convinced she is the goddess Etherea, his mortal enemy, and sacrificing her will awaken the god Mithras within him. This graphic novel is a sequel to the prose Spy Goddess novels and has been put into manga format. It includes some martial arts fighting violence.

Stanley, John

Little Lulu vol. 17: The Valentine. Writer, John Stanley ; artists, John Stanley, Irving Tripp. Dark Horse Comics 2007 228p. Illustration

Grades: 3 4 5 6 7 8 9 10 11 12 Adult   **741.5**

1. Friendship; 2. Humorous graphic novels; 3. Little Lulu (Fictional character); 4. Graphic novels

978-1-59307-686-3, $10.95

In this seventeenth volume, Lulu gets into more fun mischief, tricking Tubby into taking a sponge for a walk, rescuing a pair of pants from the tough west side gang, and defeating the clubhouse boys in a snowball war. She also tells neighborhood little terror Alvin more stories of Witch Hazel, and during a day at the beach, she tries to win a doll at the ball throwing booth where Tubby is working.

★ **Little** Lulu, vol. 1: My dinner with Lulu. [by] John Stanley and Irving Tripp. Dark Horse Comics 2005 200p. Illustration

Grades: 4 5 6 7 8 9 10 11 12 Adult   **741.5; Fic**

1. Friendship; 2. Humorous graphic novels; 3. Graphic novels

1-59307-318-6, $9.95

Lulu Moppet plays with best friend Tubby, except when he hangs out with the other neighborhood boys and tries to keep girls out of their clubhouse; she deals with terrible toddler Alvin by weaving extravagant tales featuring

herself; and other everyday adventures. This is the first volume of a series that will eventually reprint every Little Lulu comic for new young readers.

Volume 1 of 29

Little Lulu, volume 21: Miss Feeny's folly and other stories. John Stanley & Irving Tripp. Dark Horse Comics 2009 200p. Illustration

Grades: 1 2 3 4 5 6 7 8 9 10 11 12 Adult   **741.5; Fic**

1. Friendship; 2. Humorous graphic novels; 3. Little Lulu (Fictional character); 4. Graphic novels

978-1-59582-365-6, $14.95

This volume collects the Little Lulu stories from issues #100 to 105 of the Dell Comics series. Lulu and Annie carry on their battle with the boys over the boys' clubhouse, Lulu tells little Alvin more stories of the poor little girl and the wicked Witch Hazel, Tubby goes to the dentist, all the neighbor kids have to attend Miss Feeny's dance party, Tubby and then Lulu each have to clean up parts of their houses and try to trick the other into helping, and more. These stories are mostly in full color, with just a few one-page stories in black and white.

Little Lulu: the alamo and other stories. John Stanley & Irving Tripp. Dark Horse Comics 2009 200p. Illustration

Grades: 1 2 3 4 5 6 7 8 9 10 11 12 Adult   **741.5; Fic**

1. Humorous graphic novels; 2. Little Lulu (Fictional character); 3. Graphic novels

978-1-59582-293-2, $14.95

With this nineteenth volume of Little Lulu reprints, the comics are in full color; this volume collects issues 88 through 93, originally published by Dell Comics in 1955 through 1956. Among the stories in this volume, Tubby and the boys try to trick Lulu and Annie into digging a well, Tubby's parents pay Lulu to keep him company while they go out, and Lulu and Annie get revenge on Tubby and the boys by dousing them with water bombs while the boys are wearing their Davy Crockett coonskin caps. These stories appeal to younger readers as well as adults who remember reading the original comic books.

★ **Nancy,** volume 1: the Johnny Stanley Library. From the comic strip by Ernie Bushmiller ; script and layout by John Stanley ; finished art by Dan Gormley. Drawn & Quarterly 2009 128p. Illustration

Grades: 2 3 4 5 6 7 8 9 10 11 12 Adult

741.5; Fic

1. Humorous graphic novels; 2. Drew, Nancy (Fictional character); 3. Graphic novels

978-1-897299-77-7, $24.95

LC C2009-901565-X

The comic book character Nancy was created by Ernie Bushmiller; Dell Comics published the comics scripted by John Stanley with art by Dan Gormley starting with issue 146 in 1957. In these stories, Nancy meets Oona Goosepimple, a spooky girl who lives in

Courtesy of Drawn & Quarterly

a haunted house, has an incredible run of bad luck because of what she thinks is a four-leaf clover, and has all kinds of everyday adventures and misadventures with her friend Sluggo, their nemesis Spike, neighborhood rich kid Rollo, and her Aunt Fritzi. Always short of money yet needing some to buy ice cream sodas and other treats, many of Nancy's adventures with Sluggo involve various moneymaking schemes to get the dime needed (those were the days ...). The kinds of adventures the kids have are somewhat similar to Stanley's other work on Little Lulu, but set in an urban environment rather than the suburban neighborhood of Lulu and her friends. The book, designed by Seth, retains the soft original coloring of the old comics, with the paper even looking like old comics (but much sturdier). This book should have the same all-ages appeal as Little Lulu; the 2009 Free Comic Book Day issue featuring Nancy was a big hit with readers five years old and up to adults who remembered reading Nancy comics when they were kids.

Star Trek the Manga Volume 1: Shinsei Shinsei
Tokyopop 2006 Un Illustration
Grades: 7 8 9 10 11 12 Adult   **741.5; Fic**
1. Adventure graphic novels; 2. Science fiction graphic novels; 3. Star Trek; 4. Graphic novels
1-59816-744-8, $9.99
Ten writers and artists deliver tales of triumph aboard the original NCC-1701, the starship Enterprise, featuring the characters from the original television series. These new stories venture into the terrain of social politics, personal reflection ... and bare-knuckled brawls between Captain Kirk and various alien creatures, Spock's unflappable logic, Dr. McCoy's flare for drama, Scotty's perpetual struggle to keep the engines running smoothly, and more. The stories are written and illustrated as global manga.

Star Trek the Manga: Uchu
Tokyopop 2008 Un Illustration
Grades: 7 8 9 10 11 12 Adult   **741.5; Fic**
1. Science fiction graphic novels; 2. Star trek (Television program); 3. Graphic novels
978-1-4278-0787-8, $10.99
This third collection of manga-style stories set in the original Star Trek universe includes "Art of War" by Star Trek: The Next Generation actor Wil Wheaton and artist E. J. Su, "Bandi" by The Trouble with Tribbles writer David Gerrold and artist Don Hudson, "Inalienable Rights" by Nathaniel Bowden and artist Heidi Arnhold, and "The Humanitarian" by Luis Reyes and artist Nate Watson. Kirk has an encounter with a Klingon that makes both men rethink their hatred; the Bandi is yet another alien creature that has invaded the Enterprise, this one is highly empathic and can influence peoples' emotions; Kirk and his command team visit a planet and find a society in which bureaucracy runs wild; and Spock has command of the Enterprise during a very difficult situation, when a huge explosion causes major casualties of the Enterprise crew. People who like Star Trek's original series and characters will find stories in keeping with the philosophy of that series.

Star Wars Adventures: Han Solo and the Hollow Moon of Khorya
Dark Horse Books 2009 80p. Illustration
Grades: 5 6 7 8 9   **741.5; Fic**
1. Adventure graphic novels; 2. Science fiction graphic novels; 3. Star Wars; 4. Graphic novels
978-1-58582-198-0, $7.95
Approximately one year before they meet Luke Skywalker and Obi-Wan Kenobi, Han Solo and his first mate Chewbacca get into major trouble with the gangster Sollima. Han must team up with his treacherous former partner, Billal Batross, to retrieve an accounting droid currently in the hands of the Empire; meanwhile, Chewie is supposed to be held as a hostage, but Sollima orders him into the gladiatorial games. Han discovers that Billal is just as shady and treacherous as ever when his "partner" betrays him to the Imperial forces on Khorya. And Chewie, who was supposed to be killed, defeats one opponent after another and becomes the champion of the games. The book provides lots of action without showing graphic violence.

Star Wars: Clone Wars Adventures Volume 3
Dark Horse Comics 2005 Un Illustration
Grades: 6 7 8 9 10 11 12   **741.5; Fic**
1. Adventure graphic novels; 2. Science fiction graphic novels; 3. Star Wars; 4. Graphic novels
1-59307-307-0, $6.95
Asajj Ventress and Durge pit themselves against General Grievous; Republic commandos battle through the streets of Ord Mantell to recover a most precious cargo; and Jedi Master Yoda brings law to a lawless town, whether they want it or not. These stories take place approximately six months after the Battle of Geonosis.

Star Wars: Clone Wars Adventures Volume 4
Dark Horse Comics 2005 Un Illustration
Grades: 6 7 8 9 10 11 12   **741.5; Fic**
1. Adventure graphic novels; 2. Science fiction graphic novels; 3. Star Wars; 4. Graphic novels
1-59307-402-6, $6.95
As the Clone Wars burn across the galaxy and the true intentions of the Sith are revealed, the true heroes of the conflict emerge. Chewbacca leads the Wookiees against the Republic invaders on the jungle world of Kashyyyk; R2-D2 and C-3PO uncover a plot to assassinate Padme; an orphaned refugee witnesses the rough life of a Clone Trooper firsthand, and Anakin Skywalker fights alongside Serra Keto, a young Jedi who will play a part in his descent into the dark side.

Star Wars: Clone Wars Adventures Volume 5
Dark Horse Comics 2006 Unp. Illustration
Grades: 5 6 7 8 9 10   **741.5; Fic**
1. Adventure graphic novels; 2. Science fiction graphic novels; 3. Star Wars; 4. Graphic novels
1-59307-483-2, $6.95
As the fires of the Clone Wars burn across the galaxy, heroes on both sides of the conflict emerge, and no matter what the outcome, the galaxy will be forever changed. In this volume, the Jedi Aayla Secura journeys into the heart of darkness to save an Ewok village; a clone commander learns firsthand of the sacrifices the Separatists will make for their

cause; Bail Organa (Leia's adoptive father) infiltrates a dangerous world to rescue a friend; and the Padawan Joc Sah gets caught in the crosshairs of Order 66. These stories take place just before and during the events of Star Wars Episode III: The Revenge of the Sith.

Star Wars: Clone Wars Adventures Volume 6
Dark Horse Comics 2006 Un Illustration
Grades: 5 6 7 8 9 10   **741.5; Fic**
1. Adventure graphic novels; 2. Science fiction graphic novels; 3. Star Wars; 4. Graphic novels
978-1-59307-567-5, $6.95
The Clone Wars grind through the galaxy, shaking every system to its core and testing loyalties on both sides of the conflict. In this volume, Saesee Tiin steals a secret Separatist fighter, Ki-Adi-Mundi and Rivi-Anu rescue an army of clone troopers, clone commandos battle in the clouds of a gas planet, and Plo Koon and Kit Fisto get trapped in an underwater prison. These stories take place just before and during the events in Star Wars Episode III: Revenge of the Sith.

Star Wars: Clone Wars Adventures Volume 7
Dark Horse Comics 2007 Un Illustration
Grades: 5 6 7 8 9 10   **741.5; Fic**
1. Adventure graphic novels; 2. Science fiction graphic novels; 3. Star Wars; 4. Graphic novels
978-1-59307-678-8, $6.95
The fate of the galaxy hangs in the balance, the Republic and Confederacy taking their fight from the cold reaches of space to exotic alien worlds. In this volume, Obi-Wan Kenobi and Anakin Skywalker are attacked by giant monsters; Padme Naberrie becomes a spy; Bultar Swan storms an impenetrable fortress, and three friends rob a bank guarded by an army of clones. These adventures take place some time during the Clone Wars.

Star Wars: Clone Wars Volume 5: The Best Blades
Dark Horse Comics 2004 Un Illustration
Grades: 7 8 9 10 11 12 Adult   **741.5; Fic**
1. Adventure graphic novels; 2. Science fiction graphic novels; 3. Star Wars; 4. Graphic novels
1-59307-273-2, $17.95
The darkest days of the Clone Wars have arrived, when even victories are cause for abiding sorrow; when the hopes for a brighter future are lost in the turmoil of a divided galaxy; and when friendships are tools of convenience and the reason for betrayals. From political intrigue within the Senate to bloody battlefields on exotic worlds, the war has left its mark on the bystanders as well as the combatants. Obi-Wan Kenobi and Anakin Skywalker battle for survival, Senator Bail Organa struggles to preserve freedom within the Republic, and Master Yoda strives to prevent an old friend from plunging a system into war in four stories from the Clone Wars. The book includes battle violence.

Star Wars: Empire Volume Five: Allies and Adversaries
Written by Jeremy Barlow and Ron Marz ; art by Brandon Badeaux, Jeff Johnson, et al. Dark Horse Comics 2006 Un Illustration
Grades: 7 8 9 10 11 12 Adult   **741.5; Fic**

1. Adventure graphic novels; 2. Science fiction graphic novels; 3. Star Wars; 4. Graphic novels
1-59307-466-2, $14.95
Luke Skywalker fights side-by-side with a shipwrecked veteran from the Clone Wars, Han Solo's flirtations with an old flame land him in the fire, and BoShek (the galaxy's second-coolest smuggler) attracts a whole lot of blaster fire from Rebels and Imperials alike in this collection featuring some of the most unexpected stories in the era of the Empire. Whether it's BoShek transporting an innocent-enough looking girl, Han making a supply run for the resource-strapped Alliance or Luke flying escort for a Rebel Intelligence team on a supposedly deserted planet, these adventures may start as routine missions, but their endings are anything but predictable. The book includes battle violence.

Star Wars: Empire Volume Four: The Heart of the Rebellion
Dark Horse Comics 2005 Un Illustration
Grades: 7 8 9 10 11 12 Adult   **741.5; Fic**
1. Adventure graphic novels; 2. Science fiction graphic novels; 3. Star Wars; 4. Graphic novels
1-59307-308-9, $17.95
She was the catalyst that helped to turn a rag-tag rebellion into the Rebel Alliance. She provided the impetus for the 'Heroes of Yavin' in their attack on the Death Star. And she was the spark that ignited the flames of passion in one of the galaxy's most notorious rogues. 'She,' of course, is Princess Leia, the leader—and heart—of the Rebellion against Palpatine's galactic Empire. The four stories in this volume follow Leia from the weeks just before the events in A New Hope, to the time just before The Empire Strikes Back—from her first transforming experience with armed rebellion, to facing the ramifications of consequences of the destruction of her home planet, to the beginnings of true love. The book includes some battle violence.

Star Wars: Empire Volume Three: The Imperial Perspective
Dark Horse Comics 2004 Un Illustration
Grades: 7 8 9 10 11 12 Adult   **741.5; Fic**
1. Adventure graphic novels; 2. Science fiction graphic novels; 3. Star Wars; 4. Graphic novels
1-59307-128-0, $17.95
A loyal Stormtrooper, thwarted by the very bureaucracy which he serves, struggles to track down a Rebel saboteur on board the Death Star in the days and hours before the fateful Rebel attack. Darth Vader, the sole survivor of the explosion of the Death Star, crash lands on a primitive world where savagery is the key to survival. A young Imperial lieutenant learns all service comes at a price when his small company of Stormtroopers is attacked by thousands of angry aliens. Assassins vow revenge on the man responsible for killing their families - the Dark Lord, Darth Vader. These four tales are all told from the point of view of the major villains of the Star Wars galaxy - the Imperials. But, as these stories show, even the bad guys are no strangers to loyalty, honor, and sacrifice. The book includes battle violence.

Star Wars: Tales Volume 6
Dark Horse Comics 2006 232p. Illustration

Grades: 7 8 9 10 11 12 Adult   **741.5; Fic**
1. Adventure graphic novels; 2. Science fiction graphic novels; 3. Star Wars; 4. Graphic novels
1-59307-447-6, $19.95

The vastness of the Star Wars galaxy hosts an ever-unfolding mythology, filled with character-driven stories of loss and tragedy, of heroism and redemption. Collected here are ten such tales - adventures that traverse and illuminate every era in the Star Wars mythos. From the life-affirming lessons of the Force to the moral and emotional fall-out that comes with giving oneself over to the ways of the Sith, these stories will change the way readers see that galaxy far, far away.

Steinbach, Hans Hanzo
Midnight Opera Vol. 1. Tokyopop 2005 Un Illustration
Grades: 8 9 10 11 12 Adult   **741.5; Fic**
1. Fantasy graphic novels; 2. Horror graphic novels; 3. Graphic novels
1-59816-265-9, $9.99

For nearly a millennium, undead creatures have blended into a Europe driven by religious dogma... Ein DeLaLune is an underground Goth metal sensation on the Paris music scene, tragic and beautiful. He has the edge on other Goth music powerhouses...he's undead, a fact he's kept hidden for centuries. But his newfound fame might just bring out the very phantoms of his past from whom he has been hiding for centuries, including his powerful brother, Leroux. And if the two don't reconcile, the entire undead nation could rise up from the depths of modern society to lay waste to mankind. There's fighting action between the two undead brothers.

Steinberg, David
The **adventures** of Daniel Boom AKA Loud Boy: game on!. Illustrated by Brian Smith. Grosset & Dunlap 2009 96p. Illustration
Grades: 3 4 5 6 7 8   **741.5; Fic**
1. Humorous graphic novels; 2. Superhero graphic novels; 3. Graphic novels
978-0-448-44700-1, $5.99

Loud Boy and the rest of the Freak Five thought they had helped put all the members of Kid Rid behind bars, but now "Old Fogey" Fogelman has broken out of jail. Daniel Boom, AKA Loud Boy, his sister Jeannie S., Sid, Rex, and Violet work together to help Daniel's uncle hide something called a Flooggget from Fogelman it looks like a banana, but it is a device that can digitize three-dimensional objects. Uncle Stanley warns the super powered kids that Fogelman intends to use the device on children, but he has to flee before telling them everything. Then Daniel makes a new friend, J R, who gets him hooked on the new game called Pig Planet. The other Freak Five members try to get Daniel's attention, but succeed only when it's too late, and J R has stolen the Flooggget and given it to Fogelman. It turns out J R is a robot built by Fogelman, and he uses the Flooggget to digitize the 1.7 million children playing Pig Planet. Daniel figures the only way to save the kids and stop Fogelman is to get into the game himself but can he win?

★ The **adventures** of Daniel Boom AKA Loud boy: sound off!. By D. J. Steinberg ; illustrated by Brian Smith. Grosset & Dunlap 2008 Un Illustration

Grades: 2 3 4 5 6 7   **741.5; Fic**
1. Humorous graphic novels; 2. Superhero graphic novels; 3. Graphic novels
978-0-448-44698-1, $5.99

Ten years ago, when Daniel Boom was born, he came with a very loud voice. When his family moves to a small town for his mother's work, Uncle Stanley warns them that Daniel and his sister Jeannie S. (never forget her middle initial!) are in danger from "Kid-Rid." Daniel's loud voice gets him into trouble at school, with detention, but there, he meets three other kids his exact age. They discover that a rogue scientist called Old Fogey tried to experiment on them, but something went wrong, and they each have powers of destruction, super fidgeting, temper tantrums, loud voice, and incessant chattering. And they have one hour to stop Old Fogey from silencing the entire world.

Other titles in this series are: Mac attack! (2008); Game on! (2009); Grow up! (2010)

Stern, Roger
Captain America: War & Remembrance 2nd ed.. Artist, John Byrne ; inker, Rubinstein, Joe. Marvel Entertainment 2007 207p. Illustration
Grades: 8 9 10 11 12 Adult   **741.5; Fic**
1. Avengers (Fictional characters); 2. Captain America (Fictional character); 3. Superhero graphic novels; 4. Graphic novels
978-0-7851-2693-5, $24.99

Captain America's endless war on crime and tyranny sets him against new enemies and old, from an army of robot replicas to the black deeds of Baron Blood. Plus: "Cap for president." This book guest-stars the Avengers, S.H.I.E.L.D. and Union Jack, and features Cobra, Mister Hyde and Batroc the Leaper. This is the complete Stern/Byrne run, culminating with the standard-setting version of Cap's origin. Byrne co-scripted as well as pencilled the art.

Spider-Man Visionaries: Roger Stern Vol. 1. Marvel Entertainment 2007 256p. Illustration
Grades: 7 8 9 10 11 12 Adult   **741.5; Fic**
1. Spider-Man (Fictional character); 2. Superhero graphic novels; 3. Graphic novels
978-0-7851-2710-9, $24.99

Roger Stern sets his stamp on Spider-Man and his supporting cast with a collection of costumed criminals, would-be alien abductors, and gangsters both local and imported. Spidey is up against Belladonna, the Vulture, the Prowler, the Smuggler, Mysterio, a roomful of aliens, and an abundance of gas. These stories were originally published in the 1980s, and Stern worked with a number of different artists, including Steve Leialoha and Marie Severin.

Stevens, Eric
Skateboard sonar. Written by Eric Stevens ; illustrated by Gerardo Sandoval ; colored by Benny Fuentes. Stone Arch Books 2010 56p. Illustration
Grades: 3 4 5 6 7 8   **741.5; Fic**
1. Blind; 2. People with disabilities; 3. Skateboarding; 4. Graphic novels
978-1-4342-1910-7, $25.32; 978-1-4342-2295-4 (pa), $6.95
LC 2009-37870

Blind skateboarder Matty Lyons and his best friend Ty enter the All-City Skateboarding competition and encounter big bully Bing and his friend Clint. They try to intimidate the other boarders, but they really pick on Matty and Ty because of Matty's blindness. However, Ty is a master of the halfpipe and Matty uses his sense of hearing like sonar to be a champion at street boarding, and they're ready to take on the bullies and show them their skills. Matty shows by his choice of sport that he doesn't consider his blindness to be any kind of handicap in his life. This graphic novel includes discussion questions and a brief glossary.

Part of the Sports Illustrated for Kids Graphic Novels series.

Stevenson, Noelle

★ **Nimona**. By Noelle Stevenson. HarperCollins Childrens Books 2015 272 p.
Grades: 7 8 9 10 11 12   **741.5**
1. Fantasy graphic novels; 2. Good and evil — Fiction; 3. Heroes and heroines; 4. Magic; 5. Shapeshifting
0062278231; 9780062278234, $17.99
Eisner Nominee: Best Digital/Web Comic (2015)
National Book Award Finalist: Young People's Literature (2015)

In this graphic novel, by Noelle Stevenson, "Nimona is an impulsive young shapeshifter with a knack for villainy. Lord Ballister Blackheart is a villain with a vendetta. As sidekick and supervillain, Nimona and Lord Blackheart are about to wreak some serious havoc. Their mission: prove to the kingdom that Sir Ambrosius Goldenloin and his buddies at the Institution of Law Enforcement and Heroics aren't the heroes everyone thinks they are." (Publisher's note)

"This celebrated webcomic, a mash-up of medieval culture with modern science and technology, is now available in print. . . . Action scenes dominate as Nimona shifts with Hulk-like ferocity from frightful creatures such as a fire-breathing dragon to a docile cat or a timid child. Dialogue is fresh and witty with an abundance of clever lines." SLJ

Stevenson, Robert Louis, 1850-1894

Kidnapped. Adapted by Mark Jones ; art by Naresh Kumar. Kalyani Navyug Media Pvt. Ltd/Campfire Classics 2010 80p. Illustration
Grades: 3 4 5 6 7 8 9   **741.5; Fic**
1. Adventure graphic novels; 2. Stevenson, Robert Louis, 1850-1894 — Adaptations
978-9-380028-52-1, $9.99

When David Balfour's father dies and he has no family left, he leaves home and goes to the house of Shaws upon the advice of his father's agent; there, he finds an uncle he had never known. However, instead of welcoming David, Ebenezer Balfour arranges for the boy to be kidnapped on a ship to be taken to the American colonies and sold into slavery. When the ship causes a smaller boat to capsize, the crew takes on the lone survivor, the adventurer Alan Breck. David befriends Breck and helps him when the crew tries to murder the man, and when the ship wrecks near the Scottish shore, David washes up alone and must find his way through the Highlands. This graphic novel adaptation was originally published in India. It includes some background information about the Jacobite Risings against the English, and some

other information about the characters Stevenson created. The book does depict some sword fighting and shooting, but with little gore.

Treasure Island. Retold by Wim Coleman and Pat Perrin ; illustrated by Greg Rebis. Stone Arch Books 2007 63p. Illustration
Grades: 3 4 5 6 7 8 9   **741.5; Fic**
1. Adventure graphic novels; 2. Stevenson, Robert Louis, 1850-1894 — Adaptations
978-1-59889-050-1, $23.93

Young Jim Hawkins discovers an old treasure map and sets out on a harrowing voyage to a faraway island, in the company of Dr. Livesey and Mr. Trelawney. The violent sea is just the first of many obstacles, as Jim soon learns that most of the ship's crew are dangerous pirates seeking the same treasure, and they're led by Long John Silver. This adaptation is written for reluctant and struggling readers.

Part of the Graphic Revolve series.

Stine, R. L.

Goosebumps Graphix: Scary Summer. Scholastic/Graphix 2007 137p. Illustration
Grades: 4 5 6 7 8 9   **741.5; Fic**
1. Horror graphic novels; 2. Graphic novels
978-0-439-85782-6, $8.99

Someone's creeping through the garden, doing nasty things! Dean Haspiel, a veteran of Batman and Justice League comics, knows just how to portray "The Revenge of the Lawn Gnomes." In his comic series like The Bakers and Plastic Man, Kyle Baker proves he's one funny artist, the perfect guy to draw a story about fun and games at camp—until "The Horror at Camp Jellyjam" is uncovered. And Courtney Crumrin creator Ted Naifeh adapts and illustrates "Ghost Beach," in which Terri and Jerry go on vacation with some of their father's cousins and meet other kids who dress in old-fashioned clothes and caution them about ghosts.

Slappy's tales of horror. Adapted and illustrated by Dave Roman, Jamie Tolagson, Gabriel Hernandez, and Ted Naifeh; color by Jose Garibaldi. Graphix / Scholastic 2015 176 p.
Grades: 3 4 5 6   **741.5; Fic**
1. Horror fiction — Juvenile fiction; 2. Monsters; 3. Stine, R L — Adaptations
9780545835954, $12.99; 9780545836005, $24.99
LC 2014959511

In this book "[f]our Goosebumps Graphix tales by master of horror R. L. Stine are adapted into full-color comics and feature a brand-new Slappy story by bestselling author, Dave Roman. . . . Roman [also] creates the horrifying drawings for 'The Night of the Living Dummy,' the origin story about that most evil of all ventriloquist dummies, Slappy!" Illustrators Jamie Tolagson, Gabriel Hernandez, and Ted Naifeh are also included. (Publisher's note)

"Each segment has the hallmarks of the individual artist as he balances comedy and horror, childishness and seriousness: Tolagson's deep shadows and brisk pace keep readers guessing at what is actually perilous, and Hernandez's pen and ink scratches help bridge the gap between mundane and dangerous. The more cartoony styles of Naifeh and Roman may reduce the fear factor, but Naifeh's sense of mood remains top-notch." SLJ

Stoker, Bram, 1847-1912
   Bram Stoker's Dracula. Adapted by Tim Mucci, writer, Ben Caldwell, penciller/colorist, Bill Halliar, inker. Sterling 2008 Un Illustration
Grades: 5 6 7 8 9 10 11 12   **741.5; Fic**
   1. Authors; 2. Horror graphic novels; 3. Novelists; 4. Stoker, Bram, 1847-1912 — Adaptations; 5. Graphic novels
978-1-4027-3152-5, $6.95
                                                    LC 2007-41554
English estate agent Jonathan Harker travels to Transylvania to meet his firm's new client, Count Dracula, but the young man discovers his host's evil secret. He escapes and returns to England, but the Count has traveled there, too, determined to settle in new land where he can find more victims, for Dracula is a vampire. Harker, his fiancee Mina Murray, and their friends are not safe from evil. This graphic novel adaptation includes background information about the real person who was the model for Stoker's villain, and a brief biography of Stoker.
   Part of the All-Action Classics series.

   Dracula. Retold by Michael Burgan ; illustrated by José Alfonso Ocampo Ruiz ; cover color by Benny Fuentes ; interior color by Protobunker Studio. Stone Arch Books 2008 72p. Illustration
Grades: 4 5 6 7 8 9   **741.5; Fic**
   1. Horror graphic novels; 2. Vampires; 3. Graphic novels; 4. Stoker, Bram, 1847-1912 — Adaptations
978-1-4342-0448-6, $23.93; 978-1-4342-0498-1 (pa), $9.95
                                                    LC 2007-30805
Jonathan Harker and his fiancee, Mina Murray, become entangled in the affairs of the man who calls himself Count Dracula when Harker is sent by his firm to Transylvania. There, Harker learns that Dracula is a vampire. Then Dracula comes to London, where Mina's friend Lucy Westenra becomes a victim. Aided by Dr. Van Helsing, Jack Steward, and Arthur Holcombe, they hunt Dracula to stop him from killing anyone else. This graphic novel adaptation uses simple language to help reluctant and struggling readers understand the story.
   Part of the Graphic Revolve series.

Stolarz, Laurie Faria
   Black is for beginnings. Adaptation by Barbara Randall Kesel; artwork by Janina Gørrissen. Llewellyn Publications/Flux 2009 160p. Illustration
Grades: 8 9 10 11 12   **741.5; Fic**
   1. Dreams; 2. Romance graphic novels; 3. Supernatural graphic novels; 4. Graphic novels
978-0-7387-1438-7, $9.95; 0-7387-1438-0
   When Stacey, a college student and hereditary witch, again begins to have disturbing dreams about her former boyfriend and a little girl who was murdered years earlier, she knows that the dreams are trying to tell her something important, but she does not know what
   "The story's weirdo flashes of humor make the darkness bearable, as do the everyday settings of a pizza parlor and

dorm room. A unique and somewhat unhinged blend of realism and fantasy." Booklist

Stones, Tad
   Hellboy Animated Volume 1: The Black Wedding. Jim Pasco and Tad Stones ; Pencils by Fabio Laguna and Rick Lacy. Dark Horse Comics 2007 Un Illustration
Grades: 7 8 9 10 11 12 Adult   **741.5; Fic**
   1. Fantasy graphic novels; 2. Hellboy (Fictional character); 3. Horror graphic novels; 4. Graphic novels
978-1-59307-700-6, $6.95
   In the lead feature, "The Black Wedding," written by Jim Pascoe and drawn by Rick Lacy, Liz Sherman is kidnapped by an ancient cult, dragging the entire Bureau for Paranormal Research and Defense into a horrifying tale of witchcraft and possession. Tad Stones and Fabio Laguna team up in "Pyramid of Death," in which radio hero Lobster Johnson inspires a young Hellboy to inflict some imaginary justice of his own, causing havoc on the military base where he lives. The art matches the style used in the Hellboy Animated features shown on Cartoon Network, and the horror is kept to a level suitable for younger teen readers.

Storrie, Paul D.
   Amaterasu: Return of the Sun. Pencils and inks by Ron Randall. Lerner Publications Company/Graphic Universe 2007 48p. Illustration
Grades: 3 4 5 6 7 8 9   **299.5; 741.5**
   1. Amaterasu Omikami (Shinto deity); 2. Mythology, Japanese
978-0-8225-5968-9 li, $26.60
   In this retelling of a Japanese myth, the Shinto goddess of the sun, Amaterasu, hides from her jealous brother Susano, the god of storms; the world plunges into cold and darkness without the sun. The other gods must find a way to lure Amaterasu out of hiding and keep Susano from harming her or anyone else. The book includes a glossary and a list of books and websites for further reading.

   Hercules: The Twelve Labors. Story by Paul Storrie ; pencils by Steve Kurth ; inks by Barbara Schulz. Lerner Publishing Group/Graphic Universe 2007 48p. Illustration
Grades: 3 4 5 6 7 8 9   **398.2; 741.5**
   1. Greek mythology; 2. Heracles (Greek mythology); 3. Graphic novels
978-0-8225-3084-8, $26.60 lib. Bdg.
   Hercules was born half-god, half-man, the son of Zeus, King of the gods, and a mortal mother. Zeus's wife Hera resents her stepson, so she dupes Hercules into performing a series of twelve seemingly impossible labors that will test not only his legendary strength, but also his courage, cunning, and fighting skills. The book includes a glossary and a list of books for further reading.

   Nightmare on Zombie Island. Illustrated by David Witt. Graphic Universe 2008 111p. Illustration (Twisted journeys)
Grades: 3 4 5 6 7 8 9   **741.5; Fic**
   1. Adventure graphic novels; 2. Plot-your-own strories; 3. Science fiction graphic novels; 4. Graphic novels
978-0-8225-6198-9 (lib bdg), $27.93; 978-0-8225-6200-9 (pa), $7.95
                                                    LC 2007-10823

In this new take on the "Choose Your Own Adventure" type of book that combines pages of prose text with pages of comic book sequences, you have joined your best friend Jimmy and his famous explorer aunt, Dr. Chase, on a trip to an island with an abandoned plantation. Unfortunately, you discover only after your arrival that there are zombies on the island, undead pirates cursed by the plantation's workers. Can any of you escape? Some choices will end badly, others will be better, and the choices are all up to the reader.

This is Volume 6 of the Twisted Journeys series.

Robin Hood: Outlaw of Sherwood Forest. Pencils and inks by Thomas Yeates. Lerner Publishing Group/Graphic Universe 2007 48p. Illustration
Grades: 3 4 5 6 7 8 9   398.2; 741.5
1. Robin Hood (Legendary character); 2. Graphic novels
978-0-8225-5964-1, $26.60 lib. Bdg.

Fooled into committing a crime by the King's foresters, young Robin Hood finds himself branded an outlaw. As he takes refuge in Sherwood Forest, he meets other hideaways who also had found themselves unjustly branded outlaws. Under Robin's leadership, they form a band of "merry men" who exact justice against the unfair laws of the land by stealing from the rich and giving their loot to the poor. Robin's exploits enrage the Sheriff of Nottingham, who vows to capture his foe at any cost.

Terror in Ghost Mansion. Illustrated by Sandy Carruthers. Lerner Publishing Group/Graphic Universe 2007 112p. Illustration (Twisted Journeys)
Grades: 3 4 5 6 7 8 9   741.5; Fic
1. Ghosts; 2. Horror graphic novels; 3. Graphic novels
978-0-8225-6776-9, $27.93; 978-0-8225-6778-3 (pa), $7.95
                                            LC 2006-101597
In the series called Twisted Journeys, readers choose how the story will progress. Pages of text alternate with comic book-style pages. In this volume, you and your friends are out on a stormy Halloween night when your car ends up in a ditch while trying not to hit a kid on the road. When the cell phone won't work, you all go up to a big house, where the butler says there is no phone or electricity, but you should stay for the night. However, the house is full of ghosts, and most of them are evil. Readers will find many scenarios played out, depending on their choices; some end well, others not so well.

William Tell: one against an Empire: a Swiss legend. Story by Paul D. Storrie; pencils and inks by Thomas Yeates.. Lerner Publishing Group 2009 48p. Illustration
Grades: 3 4 5 6 7 8 9   741.5; Fic
1. Adventure graphic novels; 2. Tell, Wilhelm; 3. Graphic novels
978-0-8225-7175-9, $27.93
                                            LC 2007-38657
The Swiss hunter William Tell has lived a quiet life of peace, but now the free cantons have been overrun with Austrian governors and officials who threaten and punish the citizens for no reason than that they're misusing their power against the people. Tell is forced by Gessler, the governor, to shoot an apple on top of his son's head, or they will both be killed. This is when he decides he must act against the tyranny. Storrie retold the story using sources such as the 1804 play written by Friedrich Schiller and P. G.

Wodehouse's William Tell Told Again (published in 1904). The book includes a list of books for further reading and websites with music from the opera by Rossini (some readers may recognize some of the music that has often been used in cartoons and one famous radio and television series, "The Lone Ranger").
Part of the Graphic Universe Myths and Legends series

Yu the Great: Conquering the Flood. Story by Paul D. Storrie ; pencils and inks by Sandy Carruthers. Lerner/Graphic Universe 2007 48p. Illustration
Grades: 4 5 6 7 8 9   398.2; 741.5
1. Da Yu; 2. Folklore — China; 3. Graphic novels
978-0-8225-3088-6, $26.60

When ancient China suffers from a flood caused by angry gods, the emperor begs the hero, Yu, to save the land and the people. Accompanied by a dragon and a tortoise given by his great-grandfather the Yellow Emperor, ruler of the gods, Yu sets out to save China. This story is based on the real Chinese hero, who founded the Xia Dynasty. This is a volume in the Graphic Myths and Legends series.

"The volume maintains the tone and look of an old Chinese tale (Storrie cites his sources at the end) while imbuing it with the dynamic art and feel of a contemporary comic book." (Booklist)

Strait, Sonny
We Shadows Vol. 1. Tokyopop 2007 188p. Illustration
Grades: 7 8 9 10 11 12   741.5; Fic
1. Fantasy graphic novels; 2. Humorous graphic novels; 3. Graphic novels
978-1-4278-0104-3, $9.99

There is a song—it is a key to unlocking a gateway into a world of Shadows. A dark yet magical place where faeries, ogres and hobgoblins co-exist. One such creature is Goat, a homely being considered insane by the others. Her only friend is a talking mushroom who assures her she is a "fairy princess in training." However the truth of Goat's destiny is far more interesting ... And then there's poor Tucker, an accountant who blacks out for hours at a time, and who may just be someone, or something, other than merely human. This global manga has some nudity that doesn't show any crucial parts.

Strazewski, Len
Speed Racer volume 1. Len Strazewski and Brian Thomas ; illustrated by Gary Washington and Jill Thompson. IDW Publishing 2008 120p. Illustration
Grades: 7 8 9 10 11 12   741.5; Fic
1. Adventure graphic novels; 2. Automobile racing; 3. Racer, Speed (Fictional character); 4. Graphic novels
978-1-60010-174-8, $19.99

This book collects the first five issues of the Speed Racer comic originally published by Now Comics. In these stories the reader sees the origin of Speed Racer and the Mach 5, the first encounter with Racer X, and a very strange situation with a racing team called The V-Team that participates in a demolition derby as well as in Speed's next race. The book includes some minimal fan service and some violence with crashes during the races.

Stuck in the middle: seventeen comics from an unpleasant age
Edited by Ariel Schrag. Viking 2007 210p. Illustration
Grades: 7 8 9 10 11 12   741.5; Fic
1. Middle schools; 2. Teenagers; 3. Graphic novels
978-0-670-06221-8, $18.99

LC 2006-52581

This book collects seventeen short stories about the perils of middle school, each by independent comics creators, including editor Schrag, her younger sister Tania Schrag, Aaron Renier, Daniel Clowes, Gabrielle Bell, and others. Stories include the experience of being the new kid in school, getting betrayed by your best friend, being a Jewish nonathlete at a Christian sports summer camp, finding a creative outlet despite having attention deficit disorder, and more of the everyday bad situations and joys of being twelve and thirteen years old. Some harsh language (one story is also called "Shit") reflects the reality of young teen life.

Sturm, James
★ **Satchel** Paige: striking out Jim Crow by James Sturm & Rich Tommaso. Hyperion Books for Children/Jump at the Sun 2007 90p. Illustration
Grades: 4 5 6 7 8 9 10   92; 741.5
1. African Americans — Biography; 2. Baseball; 3. Baseball players; 4. Biographical graphic novels; 5. Paige, Satchel, 1906-1982; 6. Graphic novels
978-0-7868-3901-8, $9.99; 978-0-7868-3900-1, $16.99

Narrated by an African American who played in the Negro Leagues for a short time, this book sketches part of the career of Leroy "Satchel" Paige, a star of the Negro Leagues. Young Emmet scored a run off Paige in a game, but suffered a career-ending knee injury. Readers get a sense of the rough life African Americans faced in the south during the 1920s, 1930s, and 1940s. Then Paige and his team come to Tuckwilla, Alabama in 1944 to play an all-White team, and Emmet and his son attend the game and watch how Paige and his team take apart the home boys. There's one panel showing a man who has been lynched and hanged; most of the violence is mentioned but not depicted on the pages.
Part of The Center for Cartoon Studies Presents series

Sumerak, Marc
Big trouble at the Big Top!. GuriHiru, art; ABDO/Spotlight 2007 Un
Grades: 3 4 5 6 7 8 9   741.5; Fic
1. Adventure graphic novels; 2. Nightcrawler (Fictional character); 3. Power Pack (Fictional characters); 4. Superhero graphic novels; 5. X-Men (Fictional characters); 6. Graphic novels
978-1-59961-219-5, $21.35

LC 2007-130032

Marvel's youngest superheroes, the Power Pack (siblings Alex, Julie, Jack, and Katie) team up with Nightcrawler of the X-Men. The Power family has gone to the circus, but Katie is deathly afraid of clowns and won't go into the Big Top. Meanwhile, Nightcrawler has gone to visit an old friend who works in the circus, only to come under the influence of the Ringmaster and his Circus of Crime. Can the Power Pack stop the criminals and save Nightcrawler?
Part of the X-Men Power Pack series. This is a revision of the February 2006 issue of Marvel Age X-Men Power Pack, with all advertisements removed.

Costumes on!. GuriHiru, art; ABDO/Spotlight 2007 Un Illustration
Grades: 3 4 5 6 7 8 9   741.5; Fic
1. Adventure graphic novels; 2. Power Pack (Fictional characters); 3. Superhero graphic novels; 4. Wolverine (Fictional character); 5. X-Men (Fictional characters); 6. Graphic novels
978-1-59961-220-1, $21.35

LC 2007-130030

Marvel's youngest superheroes, the Power Pack (siblings Alex, Julie, Jack, and Katie) team up with Wolverine on Halloween. The Power family attends the big Halloween party, and Jack's convinced his Wolverine costume will win the contest until he sees that half the kids at the party are wearing Wolverine costumes. When he makes little sister Katie cry, she runs out to the woods, where she encounters the real Wolverine, who has to deal with Sabretooth with a little help from Power Pack.
Part of the X-Men Power Pack series. This is a revision of the December 2005 issue of Marvel Age X-Men Power Pack, with all advertisements removed.

Fantastic Four Presents Franklin Richards, Son of a Genius: Lab Brat. Written by Marc Sumerak ; art by Chris Eliopoulis Marvel Publishing, Inc. 2007 Un Illustration
Grades: 3 4 5 6 7 8 9   741.5; Fic
1. Fantastic Four (Fictional characters); 2. Humorous graphic novels; 3. Superhero graphic novels; 4. Graphic novels
0-7851-2322-9, $7.99

This book collects stories depicting the adventures of Franklin Richards, young son of Reed and Susan Richards of the Marvel superhero family, the Fantastic Four. Franklin and his robot companion H.E.R.B.I.E. keep sneaking into Reed's lab and playing with the devices they find; or, actually, Franklin does as H.E.R.B.I.E. tries to keep the boy out of trouble. In one story, Franklin accidentally turns his teacher and classmates into vegetables; in another he converts dishes of Jell-O into clones to go trick-or-treating for him; he tries to use a time machine to gather Christmas gifts for his family; he uses a device to make his comic book come to life; and he travels to another dimension where turkeys have evolved and become the dominant life form.
Originally published as Franklin Richards: Son of a Genius, Everybody Loves Franklin, Super Summer Spectacular, and Happy Franksgiving.

Franklin Richards, son of a genius: not-so-secret invasion. Art by Chris Eliopoulos. Marvel Entertainment 2009 Un Illustration
Grades: 3 4 5 6 7 8 9   741.5; Fic
1. Fantastic Four (Fictional characters); 2. Humorous graphic novels; 3. Superhero graphic novels; 4. Graphic novels
978-0-7851-3369-8, $9.99

This latest volume includes stories featuring Franklin Richards, son of Reed and Sue Richards of the Fantastic Four. Young Franklin, aided and abetted (albeit reluctantly) by his robot companion H.E.R.B.I.E., builds a replica of the first Iron Man robotic armor, drinks one of his dad's formulas and proceeds to belch HUGELY, de-ages his dad so they can play together, and then a multiplicity of Franklin Richards in many different timelines get into similar trouble. There are more stories, lots of silly humor and superhero action, drawn by coauthor Eliopoulos.

Hulk and Power Pack: Pack Smash!. Art by Gary Martin and David Williams. Marvel Entertainment 2007 Un Illustration
Grades: 3 4 5 6 7 8 9   **741.5; Fic**
1. Hulk (Fictional character); 2. Power Pack (Fictional characters); 3. Superhero graphic novels; 4. Graphic novels
0-7851-2490-X, $6.99
Zero-G, Lightspeed, Mass Master, and Energizer are Marvel's youngest superheroes, Power Pack. And they couldn't be more excited to meet their father's new colleague, the world-famous Dr. Bruce Banner. But when the kids find out what happens every time the good doctor becomes angry, he becomes the Hulk. Will the Pack be able to stand by their new friend, even if it may mean fighting every other hero in the Marvel Universe?

Leader of the pack. Art by Gurihiru. ABDO/Spotlight 2007 Un Illustration
Grades: 3 4 5 6 7 8 9   **741.5; Fic**
1. Adventure graphic novels; 2. Cyclops (Fictional character); 3. Power Pack (Fictional characters); 4. Superhero graphic novels; 5. X-Men (Fictional characters); 6. Graphic novels
978-1-59961-221-8, $21.35
LC 2007-130029
Marvel's youngest superheroes, the Power Pack (siblings Alex, Julie, Jack, and Katie) team up with Cyclops of the X-Men. When the kids try to help the X-Men fight the Marauders, they end up causing enough of a distraction for the villains to get away. When Julie and Greg go to the lab where he interns, though, they discover that his boss, Dr. Essex, is actually Mr. Sinister, and the Marauders have captured Cyclops. This time, the Power Pack is determined to save Cyclops and do things right.
Part of the X-Men Power Pack series. This is a revision of the March 2006 issue of Marvel Age X-Men Power Pack, with all advertisements removed.

Mind over matter. ABDO/Spotlight 2007 Un Illustration
Grades: 3 4 5 6 7 8 9   **741.5; Fic**
1. Adventure graphic novels; 2. Beast (Fictional character); 3. Power Pack (Fictional characters); 4. Superhero graphic novels; 5. The Beast (Fictional character); 6. X-Men (Fictional characters); 7. Graphic novels
978-1-59961-222-5, $21.35
LC 2007-130026
Marvel's youngest superheroes, the Power Pack (siblings Alex, Julie, Jack, and Katie) team up with The Beast of the X-Men. The Power family has come to the Science Expo, where their father has a booth, and Dr. Hank McCoy, otherwise known as The Beast of the X-Men, is the keynote speaker. However, there's trouble when the shape-changing villain, Mystique, uses Dr. Power's appearance to steal The Beast's genetic analyzer. In order to save their father, the Power Pack teams up with The Beast to find and stop Mystique.
Part of the X-Men Power Pack series. This is a revision of the January 2006 issue of Marvel Age X-Men Power Pack, with all advertisements removed.

Machine Teen: History 101001. Illustrated by Mike Hawthorne. Marvel Entertainment 2005 Un Illustration
Grades: 8 9 10 11 12   **741.5; Fic**
1. Adventure graphic novels; 2. Science fiction graphic novels; 3. Graphic novels
0-7851-1799-7, $7.99
Adam Aaronson is the ideal teenager. Straight "A" student, Captain of the West Tech football team, smart, handsome, charismatic. Every boy wants to be him. Every girl wants to be with him. But after a series of debilitating seizures, Adam makes a discovery that will shake his very reality to the core - the fact that he isn't real at all, but a sophisticated android created by a rogue scientist. Adam must now begin to decrypt the truth about his origins and what it truly means to be human. It's not easy being the perfect teen ... even when you're built that way.

Power pack: I know what we did that summer. Art by Gurihiru. ABDO Spotlight 2006 Un Illustration
Grades: 3 4 5 6 7 8 9   **741.5; Fic**
1. Adventure graphic novels; 2. Power Pack (Fictional characters); 3. Superhero graphic novels; 4. Graphic novels
1-59961-033-7, $21.35
A new school year is about to start, and Kate Power, youngest of the Power Pack siblings, has written a report about the team for her summer report. The problem is, as all her siblings point out, that public exposure will bring great risk to them. This does not sit well with Kate, and it's up to oldest brother Alex to calm her down. However, her use of her power is detected by their alien enemies, the Snark, and one of them comes to Earth, determined to capture the Power Pack.

Power Pack: Misadventures in babysitting. Marc Sumerak, writer; Gurihiru, art. ABDO Publishing Company/Spotlight 2006 Un Illustration
Grades: 3 4 5 6 7 8   **741.5; Fic**
1. Power Pack (Fictional characters); 2. Superhero graphic novels; 3. Graphic novels
1-59961-034-5, $21.35
Power Pack is the youngest superhero team in the Marvel Universe. Alex, Jack, Julie, and Katie Power range in age from five to twelve. A peaceful alien race called the Kymellian gave the siblings superhuman powers, which they hide from their parents. Alex can defy gravity, Julie can fly fast, Katie can burn holes in things like ships, and Jack can change shape. In this volume, which reprints an issue from Marvel Comics without all the advertisements, Alex goes on a date with Caitlin even though his parents have gone out on their anniversary date. Julie is supposed to be in charge, but Jack does what he does (get into trouble a lot), and Alex comes home to pandemonium. Their inventor father just made an interdimensional teleportal, Jack turned it on, and now they have to send a squid monster back through the portal before their parents come home.

Spider-Man and Power Pack: Big-City Super Heroes. Art by Gary Martin and David Williams. Marvel Entertainment 2007 Un Illustration
Grades: 3 4 5 6 7 8   **741.5; Fic**
1. Power Pack (Fictional characters); 2. Spider-Man (Fictional character); 3. Superhero graphic novels; 4. Graphic novels
0-7851-2357-1, $6.99

When the Power family moves to New York City, Marvel's youngest superheroes, the Power Pack, have a whole new city to explore. Julie (Lightspeed), Alex (Zero-G), Jack (Mass Master), and little Katie (Energizer) meet and team up with Spider-Man and help him defeat Venom, the Sandman, and the Vulture. Katie also gets infected by the Venom symbiote, and Spidey gets dumped into a vat of liquid that turns him into a kid again.
Originally published as Spider-Man and Power Pack issues #1-4.

Superman Archives Volume 7
Edited by Dale Crain. DC Comics 2006 237p. Illustration
Grades: 8 9 10 11 12 Adult   **741.5; Fic**
1. Superhero graphic novels; 2. Superman (Fictional character); 3. Graphic novels
978-1-4012-1051-9, $49.99

This seventh volume of the Superman Archive Editions collects issues 25-29 of Superman, with tales featuring the Man of Steel fighting subversion and sabotage on the home front during World War II, meeting mythic figures like Paul Bunyan and Hercules and foiling villains including the Toyman and the Prankster. This volume also features the first episodes of "Lois Lane, Girl Reporter." These stories were originally published in 1943 and 1944.

Superman in the Eighties
Otto Binder [and others], writers ; C.C. Beck [and others], pencillers and inkers. DC Comics 2006 192p. Illustration
Grades: 8 9 10 11 12 Adult   **741.5; Fic**
1. Superhero graphic novels; 2. Superman (Fictional character); 3. Graphic novels
1-4012-0952-1, $19.99

The '80s were a decade that forever redefined the world's first super-hero. The first half of the decade brought the story of Superman to a close, while the latter half of the decade brought a revamped Man of Steel to an all-new audience. This volume includes ten stories by such creators as John Byrne, Curt Swan, Gil Kane, George Perez, Marv Wolfman, Jim Starlin, and Len Wein. Writer/artist Jerry Ordway provides historical and personal perspectives to these stories.

Superman in the Forties
Otto Binder [and others], writers ; C.C. Beck [and others], pencillers and inkers. DC Comics 2005 192p. Illustration
Grades: 6 7 8 9 10 11 12 Adult   **741.5; Fic**
1. Superhero graphic novels; 2. Superman (Fictional character); 3. Graphic novels
1-4012-0457-0, $19.99

At the end of the 1930s, comics saw a new breed of hero. The man could withstand bullets, leap over tall buildings in a single bound, and bend steel in his bare hands. Fighting for the oppressed, this man of steel captured the imagination of the readers. He was, of course, Superman. This volume reprints stories originally published from 1938 through 1949. The reader sees Superman first fighting "regular" criminals, but as the years go by, super-powered villains start to menace Metropolis, along with such villains as Lex Luthor and troublemakers such as the mischievous Mr. Mxyztplk.

Superman: Back in Action
DC Comics 2007 144p. Illustration
Grades: 8 9 10 11 12 Adult   **741.5; Fic**
1. Superhero graphic novels; 2. Superman (Fictional character); 3. Graphic novels
978-1-4012-1263-6, $14.99

This book collects several stories. When Superman returns after the events of Infinite Crisis, he faces skepticism from the people and then gets kidnapped and put up for an intergalactic auction. In stories from the past, he encounters the Metal Men, Firestorm, and Deadman.

Superman: The Greatest Stories Ever Told Volume Two
DC Comics 2006 192p. Illustration
Grades: 7 8 9 10 11 12 Adult   **741.5; Fic**
1. Superhero graphic novels; 2. Superman (Fictional character); 3. Graphic novels
978-1-4012-0956-8, $19.99

This volume includes nine stories from different times in Superman's career. Readers can experience Superman's first meeting with the other dimensional imp Mr. Mxyztplk, his return to Krypton, a deadly battle against the team of Lex Luthor and Brainiac, an after-life adventure with Pa Kent, his greatest secret revealed, and more.

Suzumi, Atsushi
Haridama magic cram school. Translated and adapted by Kaya Laterman.. Del Rey Manga 2008 202p. Illustration
Grades: 7 8 9 10 11 12   **741.5; Fic**
1. Fantasy graphic novels; 2. Magic; 3. Manga; 4. Graphic novels
978-0-345-50136-3, $10.95

LC 2008-299354
Kokuyo and Harika are sorcery students, but they're Obsidians, wizards who must use special stones set in swords to help them cast spells. Other sorcery students think they're inferior because they lack both yin and yang. But Kokuyo and Harika do have something no one else has: the power of friendship. They'll have to figure it out, but when they work together, they don't need their swords. This is a one-volume manga.

Swift, Jonathan
Gulliver's travels. Jonathan Swift (retold by Donald B. Lemke); illustrated by Cynthia Martin.. Stone Arch Books 2008 72p. Illustration
Grades: 4 5 6 7 8 9   **741.5; Fic**
1. Adventure graphic novels; 2. Satire; 3. Graphic novels

978-1-4342-0449-3, $23.93; 978-1-4342-0499-8 (pa), $9.95

LC 2007-30806

Sailor Lemuel Gulliver finds himself shipwrecked on the island of Lilliput, where he is captured by tiny people no taller than six inches. When he leaves Lilliput and tries to go home, he ends up in the country of Blefuscu, a land of giants where he is considered to be nothing more than an intelligent animal and pet. This graphic novel adaptation includes only the first two voyages of Gulliver but does summarize the third and fourth voyages.

Part of the Graphic Revolve series.

Tachibana, Yutaka
Gatcha Gacha Vol. 1. Tokyopop 2006 204p. Illustration
Grades: 8 9 10 11 12   **741.5; Fic**
1. Humorous graphic novels; 2. Romance graphic novels; 3. Shojo manga; 4. Graphic novels
978-1-59816-153-9, $9.99

Yuri has a big crush on Yabe, but Yabe has decided the only girl he will ever seriously date is Motoko. So what's the problem? Yuri and Motoko are friends, and Motoko doesn't want to have anything to do with Yabe. But is she secretly harboring a crush on him, too? Will they ever get this mess straightened out? Only time will tell if love will tear these best friends apart in this love triangle—that may get another member. Yuri has a bad reputation from having so many skeevy boyfriends who have dumped her; Motoko is a tough girl. The book includes some strong language and some school fight scenes. This series is not to be confused with the shonen manga series, Gacha Gacha by Tamakoshi.

Taira, Shino
Bogle, vol. 2. by Shino Taira & Yuko Ichiju. Go! Comi 2008 200p. Illustration
Grades: 7 8 9 10 11 12   **741.5; Fic**
1. Mystery graphic novels; 2. Romance graphic novels; 3. Shojo manga; 4. Graphic novels
978-1-933617-97-8, $10.99

The secret organization called Bogle operates as "chivalrous thieves," helping people recover items taken from them. High school student Asuka Hamuro is their newest recruit, and she's been doing well, until the night they steal a statue and she drops it while they're escaping from the house from which they stole it. Worse, she dropped it right in front of a dog, and the house belongs to a schoolmate who has shown interest in Asuko. Later, Asuko's police detective brother arrests fellow Bogle member Masato's older brother, a physician whose patient has died under suspicious circumstances. Can Bogle find out what's really happening" The book includes romantic moments but no sexual content or actual violence.

Takabayashi, Tomo
Kyo Kara Maoh, volume 1. Tokyopop 2008 Un Illustration
Grades: 8 9 10 11 12   **741.5; Fic**
1. Fantasy graphic novels; 2. Shojo manga; 3. Graphic novels
978-1-4278-1099-1, $9.99

Teenager Yuri Shibuya tries to stop a student mugging, only to be beaten and dragged to a restroom where the bullies dunk his head in the toilet; except, instead of just getting dunked, Yuri gets sucked into and through the toilet and comes out into a strange world. There, he learns that he is the King of the Mazoku, who are magic working demons hated by the humans who also inhabit the world. As King, Yuri is supposed to possess magic skills and powers, too, but he doesn't yet know how to access or use them. And since he doesn't know the customs of the land, he also finds himself engaged to a young man who hates him and must also fight a duel. With all the bishonen (beautiful young men) and the fact that same sex relationships are considered to be normal, this manga has some boy love manga aspects, although there's very little in the way of sexual content in this first volume.

Takada, Rie
Gaba Kawa. Viz Media/Shojo Beat 2008 Un Illustration
Grades: 7 8 9 10 11 12   **741.5; Fic**
1. Fantasy graphic novels; 2. Manga; 3. Romance graphic novels; 4. Shojo manga; 5. Supernatural graphic novels; 6. Graphic novels
978-1-4215-2259-3, $8.99

Young demon Rara has come to Earth to attend high school and draw human souls to darkness. She's had a crush on a master demon she has been calling Aku, and she already has a rival, the ruthless demon Bibi. Then Rara does the unthinkable—she falls for a human boy named Retsu Aku. Despite the fact that she'll lose a power when she uses it to help a human, she does so, she can't help it. And Retsu is different from other boys, he can sense ghosts and supernatural beings; he likes Rara because she's so open in her affection for him. However, as Rara continues to lose her powers, the other demons decide to punish her and offer her only one recourse—she must kill Retsu in order to regain her powers, or disappear forever. There's very little in the way of fan service or violence; Rara and Bibi often appear in chibi (super-cute miniaturized) form when they get excited or upset. This is a standalone, one volume manga story.

Takahashi, Kazuki
Yu-Gi-Oh! Duelist Volume 1. Viz Media/Shonen Jump 2005 216p. Illustration
Grades: 7 8 9 10 11 12 Adult   **741.5; Fic**
1. Adventure graphic novels; 2. Games; 3. Shonen manga; 4. Graphic novels
1-59116-614-4, $7.95

In the second saga of the Yu-Gi-Oh! epic, Duel Monsters is the world's most popular collectible card game-but to Yugi, it's the most dangerous game of all. Entering the Duel Monsters world championship, Yugi fights ruthless opponents like game designer Maximillion Pegasus and teenage multimillionaire Kaiba Seto, hoping to discover the origin of the game...and his own powers. When Yugi beat Kaiba, little did he know the consequences: a trip through Kaiba's "Death T" - a theme park of death - and a series of evil spells against Yugi's family. It doesn't help that Kaiba's little brother also has a score to settle. There's more gaming violence in the manga series compared to what has been shown on American television; this is not a book for younger children.

Yu-Gi-Oh! Millenium World Volume 1. Viz Media/Shonen Jump 2005 200p. Illustration
Grades: 7 8 9 10 11 12 Adult   **741.5; Fic**
1. Adventure graphic novels; 2. Games; 3. Shonen manga; 4. Graphic novels
1-59116-878-3, $7.95
This is the final Yu-Gi-Oh! story. After hundreds of battles, Yugi has finally gathered all the Egyptian God Cards... the key to unlocking his memories of his past life as an Egyptian pharaoh. When Ryo Bakura gives him the Millennium Eye, Yugi opens the door to the "world of memory," and his mind travels back in time to ancient Egypt, when the magic and monsters were real. Now Yugi and his friends must explore the world of Yugi's forgotten past...and fight an enemy who has been waiting for them for 3,000 years. The manga contains more action and violence in the gaming action than has been shown in the animated series that has aired on American television; this series is not for younger children.

Takahashi, Rumiko
★ **InuYasha:** Volume One. By Rumiko Takahashi. Viz 2009 562 p.
Grades: 7 8 9 10 11 12   **741.5; 741.5/952**
1. Japanese mythology; 2. Manga
1421532808; 9781421532806, $19.99
                         LC Bl2009031710
In this book, by Rumiko Takahashi, "Kagome is a modern Japanese high school girl. Never the type to believe in myths and legends, her world view dramatically changes when, one day, she's pulled out of her own time and into another! There, in Japan's ancient past, Kagome discovers more than a few of those dusty old legends are true, and that her destiny is linked to one legendary creature in particular—the dog like half-demon called Inuyasha!" (Publisher's note)
Originally published in 56 individual volumes
Volume 1 of 18

Takako, Shimura
Wandering son: Volume One. Shimura Takako; translated by Matt Thorn. Fantagraphics 2011 192 p. Illustration
Grades: 7 8 9 10   **Fic**
1. Bildungsromans; 2. Manga; 3. Puberty; 4. Sex role; 5. Transgender people; 6. Graphic novels
1606994166; 9781606994160, $19.99
This manga "tells the story of a friendship between Shuichi, a young boy who wishes he were a girl, and Yoshino, a young girl who wishes she were a boy. . . . Shuichi's impulses toward a female identity feel confusing and shameful to him, and it's the girls in his life-first Yoshino, and then Saori-who point out his difference and encourage it. . . . Both children are teased mercilessly by their classmates, whose sexual development, while perhaps more socially normative, is just as confusing to them." (Publishers Weekly)

Wandering son: Volume Three. Shimura Takako; translated by Matt Thorn. Fantagraphics Books 2012 200 p.
Grades: 7 8 9 10   **741.5; Fic**
1. Friendship; 2. Secrets — Fiction; 3. Transgender people

1606995332; 9781606995334, $19.99
In this graphic novel, by Shimura Takako, "Shuichi and his friend Yoshino have a secret: Shuichi is a boy who wants to be a girl, and Yoshino is a girl who wants to be a boy. But one day . . . their secret is exposed, and the two find themselves the target of sixth-grade cruelty. Their friendship is strained, . . . and their mentor, Yuki, reveals the harder reality of being transgendered. Meanwhile, Shuichi's sister, Maho, realizes her dream of becoming a model, and drags Shuichi along." (Publisher's note)

Wandering son: Volume Two. Shimura Takako; translated by Matt Thorn. Fantagraphics Books 2012 200 p.
Grades: 7 8 9 10   **741.5; Fic**
1. Bildungsromans; 2. Middle schools — Fiction; 3. Transgender people
1606994565; 9781606994566, $19.99
"In the second volume of Shimura Takako's [Wandering Son series], . . . transgendered protagonists, Shuichi and Yoshino, have entered the sixth grade. Shuichi spends a precious gift of cash from his grandmother on a special present for himself, a purchase that triggers a chain of events in which his sister Maho learns his secret, and Shuichi inadvertently steals the heart of a boy Maho in interested in." (Publisher's note)
"While the first volume served as an introduction to Shuichi and Yoshino's lives, their stories and identities really begin to evolve in this lovely, exciting, and surprising follow-up." Booklist

Wandering son; Volume four. Shimura Takako; [translation: Matt Thorn]. Fantagraphics Books 2013 219 p.
Grades: 7 8 9 10   **741.5; Fic**
1. Friendship; 2. Gender identity; 3. Gender role; 4. Middle schools — Juvenile fiction
1606996053; 9781606996058, $19.99
                         LC 2013363244
This book, by Shimura Takako, the fourth in the series, "continues the story of Nitori Shuichi, a girl who wants to be a boy named Takatsuki Yoshino. . . . The story is filled with mixed signals, rumors, unrequited love, boys and girls fighting over one another, and love-hate relationships. . . . And as the characters get ready to enter middle school, with its gender-specific uniforms, each one is being pushed to conform to society's standards." (School Library Journal)

Takamisaki, Ryo
Megaman NT Warrior Vol. 1. Viz/Viz Kids 2004 186p. Illustration
Grades: 4 5 6 7 8 9   **741.5; Fic**
1. Science fiction graphic novels; 2. Shonen manga; 3. Graphic novels
1-59116-465-6, $7.95
The year is 200X and everyone is now connected to the Cyber Network. People carry their own PET (Personal terminal) and are paired up with an artificial intelligence program called a NetNavi (or NetNavigator). Computers have turned the world into a bright and shiny utopia, but there's always trouble in paradise. While the invention of the PET and NetNavis has brought great benefits to the world, computer hacking, virus spreading, and other high-tech crimes are becoming a major problem. A sinister organization by the name of World Three has appeared, and

they've vowed to destroy this technological wonderland. Enter Lan Hikari, an intensely curious and cheerful fifth grader. Synchronized with his NetNavigator, MegaMansupercharged, he becomes a super-charged dynamo. In and out of the Net, Lan and MegaMan do their best to thwart World Three's neverending quest to take over the world. The book includes some raunchy humor and lots of action.

Pokemon: the rise of Darkrai. Viz Media/VizKids 2008 Un Illustration
Grades: 2 3 4 5 6 7 8 9   **741.5; Fic**
1. Adventure graphic novels; 2. Fantasy graphic novels; 3. Manga; 4. Graphic novels
978-1-4215-2289-0, $7.99
Ash and his friends come to Alamos Town, home of the Space-Time Towers, and while touring the town, they discover that the town's special garden has been ransacked. Some of the townspeople blame Darkrai, a sinister looking Pokemon that said to haunt the garden. However, Alamos Town faces much more peril when two powerful Pokemon that control time and space battle each other; it should be impossible for them to meet, and unless Ash and the others "and perhaps Darkrai" can stop them, Alamos Town will be destroyed. This book includes a lot of Pokemon fighting action; the panels are so filled with details that very young readers might find it difficult to follow the action.

Takanashi, Mitsuba
    Crimson Hero, Vol. 1. Viz Media/Shojo Beat 2005 Un Illustration
Grades: 8 9 10 11 12   **741.5; Fic**
1. High school students; 2. Shojo manga; 3. Volleyball; 4. Graphic novels
978-1-4215-0140-6, $8.99
First year high school student Nobara wants more than anything to play volleyball, and she enrolled in Crimson Field High School to do so. However, her mother, who runs the high class ryotei restaurant called Seiryu, has used her wealth and position to eliminate the girls' volleyball club in order to force Nobara to be her successor in running the restaurant. Incensed at her mother's actions, Nobara runs away from home; she ends up in the dorm with the boys on volleyball scholarships and works for them as cook and clean-up maid for room and board. And she works to start a new girls' volleyball club at school.

The **Devil** Does Exist Volume 1. DC Comics/CMX 2005 192p. Illustration
Grades: 7 8 9 10 11 12   **741.5; Fic**
1. Romance graphic novels; 2. Shojo manga; 3. Graphic novels
1-4012-0545-3, $9.99
High school is difficult for most kids. But for Kayano, a shy girl whose single mother seems to work all the time, it's even worse than usual. She's so afraid of drawing attention to herself, in fact, that she can't tell the handsome Kamijo how much she loves him-until one day she finally gets up the courage to write him a letter confessing her feelings. But her plans go awry when the letter falls into the hands of the school's most notorious student, Edogawa Takeru. To Kayano, Takeru seems to be Satan himself. Not only is he devilishly handsome, he is the son of the school's principal.

Even the teachers dare not stand up to him. Kayano, appalled by how badly her first attempt at a social life has gone, thinks she can struggle through, and get her letter back. But, Takeru enjoys watching her suffer. Just when she thinks she's solved the problem, her mother comes home to announce she's getting married-to principal Edogawa. Now Kayano will have to live with this devil Takeru 24/7. How will she cope with this literal living hell? The book includes some mild strong language, mild violence, and some brief sexual situations.

Takarai, Saori
    Manga Moods: 40 Faces + 80 Phrases. Japanime Co. Ltd./Manga University 2006 96p. Illustration
Grades: 6 7 8 9 10 11 12 Adult   **741.5**
1. Manga; 2. Graphic novels
978-4-921205-13-3, $12.95
A raised eyebrow, a curled lip, a wink of the eye. All it takes is a single stroke of the pen to instantly change a manga character's mood from one extreme to the other: glad to sad, sassy to shy, angry to embarrassed. In addition, each of the facial expressions is labeled with the Japanese word for the mood being depicted, along with common Japanese conversational phrases and English translations, making this book fun for aspiring artists, language enthusiasts and manga fans. As a bonus, the 46 basic hiragana, as well as contracted hiragana and two-dash and one-circle hiragana characters are shown for those who want to start learning to write Japanese.

Takaya, Natsuki
    ★ **Fruits** Basket Collector's Edition, Vol. 1. Natsuki Takaya. Yen Press 2016 400 p. Illustration
Grades: 7 8 9 10 11 12   **Fic**
1. Family — Fiction; 2. Secrets — Fiction
0316360163; 9780316360166, $20
"After a family tragedy turns her life upside down, plucky high schooler Tohru Honda takes matters into her own hands and moves out...into a tent! Unfortunately for her, she pitches her new home on private land belonging to the mysterious Sohma clan, and it isn't long before the owners discover her secret." (Publisher's note)
Originally published in the U.S. by Tokyopop

Takei, Hiroyuki
    Shaman King Volume 1. Viz Media/Shonen Jump 2003 204p. Illustration
Grades: 8 9 10 11 12 Adult   **741.5; Fic**
1. Adventure graphic novels; 2. Shonen manga; 3. Supernatural graphic novels; 4. Graphic novels
1-56931-902-2, $7.95
When he takes a shortcut through a cemetery, Manta Oyamada meets a strange kid with headphones - surrounded by ghosts. The kid is the teenage shaman Yoh Asakura. Tapping the supernatural swordfighting powers of samurai ghost Admidamaru, Yoh fights Bokuto no Ryu, a sword-wielding gang member. But an even more dangerous opponent is stalking Yoh and Manta - a Chinese shaman who wants to possess Amidamaru.

Takeuchi, Naoko
★ **Sailor** Moon; Volume 1. [Naoko Takeuchi; translator/adapter, William Flanagan]. Kodansha Comics 2011 240 p. Illustration; Color
Grades: 5 6 7 8 9 10   **741.5**
1. Good and evil — Fiction; 2. Shojo manga; 3. Teenage girls — Fiction; 4. Teenage girls — Japan; 5. Women heroes
1935429744; 9781935429746, $10.99
LC 2012374271
"Usagi Tsukino is a normal girl until she meets up with Luna, a talking cat, who tells her that she is Sailor Moon. As Sailor Moon, Usagi must fight evils and enforce justice, in the name of the Moon and the mysterious Moon Princess. She meets other girls destined to be Sailor Senshi (Sailor Scouts), and together, they fight the forces of evil!" (Publisher's note)
First published in Japan in 2003 by Kodansha Ltd., Tokyo, as Bishoujosenshi Sailor Moon Shinsoban—End pages.
Volume 1 of 12

Tamaki, Mariko
★ **Emiko** superstar. Written by Mariko Tamaki; illustrated by Steve Rolston. DC Comics/Minx 2008 149p. Illustration
Grades: 7 8 9 10 11 12   **741.5; Fic**
1. Performance art; 2. Racially mixed people; 3. Graphic novels
978-1-4012-1536-1, $9.99
"Emiko, a half-Japanese, half-Caucasian Canadian, is a self-described geek facing a summer of babysitting and isolation. Things change when she stumbles upon an underground performing art scene inspired by Andy Warhol's Factory. She eventually takes to the stage . . . and achieves minor celebrity. Soon, though, Emiko must face the troubling complexities in the lives of her new friends and the consequences of her own questionable actions. . . . Rolston's playful, vibrant b&w illustrations bring the characters to life." Publ Wkly

★ **Skim**. Words by Mariko Tamaki; drawings by Jillian Tamaki. Groundwood Books 2008 144p. Illustration
Grades: 7 8 9 10 11 12   **741; 741.5; Fic**
1. Friendship; 2. Humorous graphic novels; 3. School stories; 4. Graphic novels
088899964X; 0-88899-753-1; 9780888999641, 12.95; 978-0-88899-753-1, $18.95
Ignatz Award: Outstanding Graphic Novel (2008)
Skim is Kimberly Keiko Cameron, a not-slim half-Japanese would-be Wiccan goth who attends a private school. When classmate Katie Matthews' ex-boyfriend commits suicide, concerned guidance counselors descend upon the school because so many of the student body goes into mourning overdrive. The popular clique starts a new club, Girls Celebrate Life, and make Katie their project, especially after she falls off her roof and breaks both arms. Kim and her best friend Lisa observe all this, but counselors target Kim for her goth tendencies and are convinced she'll become suicidal any moment. All she is, is in love with her English teacher, Ms. Archer, who seems to reciprocate and then leaves the school. As Lisa starts to get sucked into the GLC, Kim and Katie tentatively begin a new friendship.

There is only one rather chaste kiss between Kim and Ms. Archer. Artist Jillian Tamaki draws Kim to look like a classical Heian period Japanese woman.

★ **This** One Summer. Mariko Tamaki, Jillian Tamaki. First Second 2014 320 p. Illustration
Grades: 7 8 9 10 11 12 Adult   **741.5; Fic**
1. Friendship — Fiction; 2. Vacations — Fiction; 3. Graphic novels
159643774X, 17.99; 1626720940, 21.99; 9781626720947, $21.99; 9781596437746, 17.99
Caldecott Honor Book (2015)
Printz Honor Book (2015)
Eisner Award: Best Graphic Album—New (2015)
Ignatz Award: Outstanding Graphic Novel (2014)
Harvey Nominee: Best Artist (2015)
Harvey Nominee: Best Graphic Album of Original Work (2015)
Harvey Nominee: Best Original Graphic Publication For Young Readers (2015)
In this young adult graphic novel written by Mariko Tamaki and illustrated by Jillian Tamaki, "Every summer, Rose goes with her mom and dad to a lake house in Awago Beach. . . . Rosie's friend Windy is always there, too, like the little sister she never had. But this summer is different. . . . It's a summer of secrets, and sorrow, and growing up, and it's a good thing Rose and Windy have each other." (Publisher's note)
"This captivating graphic novel presents a fully realized picture of a particular time in a young girl's life, an in-between summer filled with yearning and a sense of ephemerality." SLJ

Tamura, Mitsuhisa
BakeGyamon, vol. 1. Viz Media/Viz Kids 2009 200p.
Grades: 3 4 5 6 7 8   **741.5; Fic**
1. Fantasy graphic novels; 2. Games; 3. Manga; 4. Shonen manga; 5. Graphic novels
978-1-4215-1793-3, $7.99
Sanshiro craves adventure, something he's not likely to find in his tiny island hometown; then a mysterious stranger invites him to play a new game. Suddenly, Sanshiro finds himself in a backwards universe to play BakeGyamon, a game that pits monster against monsters, designed by monsters. He meets other players, all of whom are there to win in order to get their one big wish the prize that only the winner can get. Sanshiro is there to experience adventure and have fun, which makes the others dismiss him. And when his first card gives him a bunch of little mud balls to play against a huge monster, how can he possibly win" The book features lots of game-playing action and hyper dialogue (Sanshiro tends to shout in exuberance a lot), but there's no violence or bad language.

Tan, Shaun
★ The **arrival**. Arthur A. Levine Books 2007 Un Illustration
Grades: 6 7 8 9 10   **741.5; Fic**
1. Immigrants; 2. Stories without words; 3. Graphic novels
0-439-89529-4, $19.99; 9780439895293
LC 2006-21706
Boston Globe-Horn Book Award special citation (2008)

In this wordless graphic novel, a man leaves his homeland and sets off for a new country, where he must build a new life for himself and his family.

"Young readers will be fascinated by the strange new world the artist creates. . . . They will linger over the details in the beautiful sepia pictures and will likely pick up the book to pore over it again and again." SLJ

Tanaka, Masashi
Gon Volume 1. DC Comics/CMX 2007 Un Illustration
Grades: 6 7 8 9 10 11 12 Adult   **741.5; Fic**
1. Humorous graphic novels; 2. Manga; 3. Stories without words; 4. Graphic novels
978-1-4012-1273-5, $5.99
Volume 1 of 7
A tiny dinosaur with a feisty attitude marches across the wilderness defending the friendly and furry from the mean and hungry. Told entirely without words, the stories highlight the detailed art and visual storytelling ability of creator Masashi Tanaka. This new edition from CMX restores the book to its original right-to-left orientation.

Gon volume 4. DC Comics/CMX 2008 Un Illustration
Grades: 7 8 9 10 11 12 Adult   **741.5; Fic**
1. Adventure graphic novels; 2. Dinosaurs; 3. Gon (Fictional character); 4. Manga; 5. Graphic novels
978-1-4012-1275-6, $5.99
Gon, the little dinosaur living in the time of mammals, is back for more wordless adventures. First, he finds a turtle shell and decides to try it on, only to find he can't get out of it. He ends up doing his best to protect the newly hatched sea turtles as they face a gauntlet of hungry predators in their journey to the sea. Then Gon finds himself in the desert with several savannah animals after a tornado dumps them there, and has to save them. The book includes predator/prey animal violence; some readers might get upset to see the baby turtles being eaten by so many other animals.

Gon volume 5. DC Comics/CMX 2008 Un Illustration
Grades: 7 8 9 10 11 12 Adult   **741.5; Fic**
1. Animals; 2. Gon (Fictional character); 3. Manga; 4. Graphic novels
978-1-4012-1277-3, $5.99
In this book-length episode, Gon starts out by exploring an anthill, then defending prairie dogs against a coyote. When an earthquake sends Gon, a prairie dog and the adult coyote and its pup underground, they unite against a giant spider that traps the pup. They must deal with various giant insects (ants, pillbugs, mayflies), bats, and the deadly huge spider. People who don't like to see so many creepy crawlies on the page may want to skip this book.

Gon volume 6. DC Comics/CMX 2008 Un Illustration
Grades: 6 7 8 9 10 11 12 Adult   **741.5; Fic**
1. Gon (Fictional character); 2. Manga; 3. Stories without words; 4. Graphic novels
978-1-4012-1278-0, $5.99
In this volume, Gon acquires headgear—a bird's nest with three orphaned chicks falls onto his head when he headbutts a tree, and the three young birds are in for the ride of their life as Gon goes his way. Then he and a band of ragtag creatures make their way through a forest and a fire. And he befriends an old elephant as they make their way to a

goal only the old elephant knows. The book includes animal-on-animal violence.

Taneja, Sweta
Krishna: Defender of Dharma. By Shweta Taneja; illustrated by Rajesh Nagulakonda. Random House Inc. 2013 152 p. Color illustration
Grades: 5 6 7   **Fic; 741.5/954**
1. Folklore; 2. Good and evil; 3. Hindu mythology
938074112X; 9789380741123, $14.99
Author Shweta Taneja presents a tale about Krishna, the Hindu diety. "To vanquish him and his horde of evil monsters, Lord Vishnu comes to Earth in his eighth avatar - Krishna, the defender of dharma. Since his birth, Krishna valiantly fights evil monsters, showing courage and valour. But as he grows up and becomes a councillor of the race of Yadavas, he observes that the real struggle in this age is not with magical monsters but with evil kings and warriors." (Publisher's note)

Tanemura, Arina
Full Moon Vol. 1: O Sagashite. Viz Media/Shojo Beat 2005 200p. Illustration
Grades: 7 8 9 10   **741.5; Fic**
1. Fantasy graphic novels; 2. Manga; 3. Romance graphic novels; 4. Shojo manga; 5. Graphic novels
1-59116-928-3, $8.99
Young Mitsuki loves singing and dreams of becoming a pop star. Unfortunately, a malignant tumor in her throat prevents her from pursuing her passion. However, her life turns around when two surprisingly fun-loving harbingers of death appear to grant Mitsuki a temporary reprieve from her illness and give her singing career a magical push start. They transform her into a 16-year-old, and she becomes a sensation, but when one of the spirits falls in love with Mitsuki, complications abound.

I-O-N. Viz Media/Shojo Beat 2008 208p. Illustration
Grades: 7 8 9 10 11 12   **741.5; Fic**
1. Humorous graphic novels; 2. Psychokinesis; 3. Romance graphic novels; 4. Shojo manga; 5. Graphic novels
978-1-4215-1800-8, $8.99
Ion Tsuburagi chants the letters of her first name as a charm to bring good luck when she needs it; in school, she uses it to get away from Kouki Shiraishi, the Student Council President, who has vowed to make Ion his girlfriend. Then she meets Mikado Horai, the president of the Psychic Powers Research Society at school, and she touches a mysterious substance he's been developing. Now, chanting "ION" gives her telekinetic powers. This is a one-volume manga by the creator of Kamikaze Kaito Jeanne, Full Moon, and The Gentlemen's Alliance.

Kamikaze Kaito Jeanne, Vol. 1. DC Comics/CMX 2006 176p. Illustration
Grades: 6 7 8 9 10   **741.5; Fic**
1. Fantasy graphic novels; 2. Shojo manga; 3. Supernatural graphic novels; 4. Graphic novels
978-1-4012-0555-3, $9.99
Sixteen-year-old Maron Kusakabe is a high school student, but she's also the reincarnation of Joan of Arc (called here by her French name, Jeanne d'Arc). At night,

Maron takes the magical form of Kamikaze Kaito Jeanne, and with the help of angel-in-training Finn, she steals paintings that have been possessed by demons in order to save the paintings' owners from the demons' enchantments. Jeanne soon has a rival, Kaito Sinbad; coincidentally, in school Maron meets a transfer student, Chiaki. She also has to deal with the determined investigations of her friend Miyako, daughter of a police detective. This seven-volume manga series finished publication in 2007.

Short-tempered Melancholic and other stories. Viz Media/Shojo Beat 2008 192p. Illustration
Grades: 7 8 9 10 11 12   **741.5; Fic**
1. Humorous graphic novels; 2. Manga; 3. Romance graphic novels; 4. Shojo manga; 5. Graphic novels
978-1-4215-1801-5, $8.99
This manga collects some of Tanemura's early, shorter manga works, including her debut story, "The Style of the Second Love." In this story, Mana secretly like's her friend's boyfriend, but the younger Nakamura is determined to win Mana's heart. In "Short Tempered Melancholic," female ninja Kajika Yamano's job is to protect her family's legendary weapon, but when Fujisaki, an older boy she likes, tells her she should act more ladylike, Kajika tries to give up all ninja deeds. Minori falls in love with Takato, who shared his umbrella with her one rainy afternoon. Now, she thinks "Rainy Afternoons are for Romantic Heroines" and "forgets" her umbrella every time it rains. Then Yuri sends her penpal Ryo a picture of her best friend Karin instead of one of herself, because Karin is prettier. But "This Love is Nonfiction," and now Ryo wants to meet her. Now she has to send Karin, but Yuri can't help but follow, then she meets up with a weird guy.

Taylor, G. P.
The **Tizzle** Sisters & Erik. Illustrated by Dan Boultwood. Markosia Enterprises Ltd 2006 182p. Illustration
Grades: 5 6 7 8 9 10 11 12   **741.5; Fic**
1. Adventure graphic novels; 2. Twins; 3. Graphic novels
978-1-905692-22-4, $20.01
Almost identical twins, Sadie and Saskia Tizzle have lived in St. Dunstan's School for Wayward Children ever since their actress mother left them there and never returned. When an eccentric writer decides to take Saskia to adopt her and separates the twins, she sets wild adventures into motion. Saskia finds herself in a house of intrigue with ghosts, seances, a treasure hunt, and a secret twin; while Sadie and Erik make a harrowing escape from St. Dunstan's just ahead of the police.
Noted fantasy author Taylor (Shadowmancer, 2003) teams up with British comics veterans Lee and Boultwood to create what they call an "illustronovella," which alternates pages of prose and comic book panels to tell the story.

Taylor, Sarah Stewart
Amelia Earhart: this broad ocean. [illustrations by] Ben Towle; with an introduction by Eileen Collins. Disney/Hyperion Books 2010 78p. Illustration
Grades: 5 6 7 8 9   **741.5; 741; 92**
1. Earhart, Amelia, 1898-1937

978-1-4231-1337-9 (lib bdg), $17.99; 1-4231-1337-3 (lib bdg)
LC 2009-29321
"Grace, an aspiring young journalist, is excited when Amelia Earhart arrives in her town of Trepassey, Newfoundland, on June 4, 1928. Earhart wants to become the first female passenger to cross the Atlantic Ocean by air. Grace is there to see themùand to receive Earhart's telegram announcing their arrival in Ireland." (Publisher's note)
"This approach brings the legendary aviation pioneer and her fame into a manageable context. . . . Reluctant readers, adventure fans, and those who themselves yearn for the skies will be sucked right into the immediacy here." Bull Cent Child Books

Telgemeier, Raina
The **Baby-sitter's** Club: Kristy's great idea: a graphic novel. [text by Ann M. Martin; art] by Raina Telgemeier. Scholastic Graphix 2006 192p. Illustration
Grades: 3 4 5 6   **741.5; Fic**
1. Babysitting; 2. Friendship; 3. Graphic novels
0-439-80241-5, $16.99; 0-439-73933-0 (pa), $8.99
LC 2005-37749
Follows the adventures of Kristy and the other members of the Baby-sitters Club as they deal with crank calls, uncontrollable two-year-olds, wild pets, and parents who do not always tell the truth. A graphic novel based on the 1988 book by the same name.
"Comics artist Telgemeier's clean-lined, black-and-white art with stark black details nicely differentiates the four personable seventh-graders who parlay their babysitting experience into a business." Booklist
Also available in full color editions
Other titles about the Baby-sitters Club are: The truth about Stacey (2006); Mary Anne saves the day (2007); Claudia and Mean Janine (2008)

★ **Drama**. Raina Telgemeier; with color by Gurihiru. Graphix 2012 233 p. Illustration
Grades: 5 6 7 8   **741.5**
1. Children's plays — Fiction; 2. Interpersonal relations — Fiction; 3. Middle schools — Fiction; 4. School stories; 5. Schools — Fiction; 6. Theater — Fiction; 7. Graphic novels
0545326982; 0545326990; 9780545326988, $23.99; 9780545326995
LC 2011040748
Stonewall Honor Book (2013)
Author Raina Telgemeier's book focuses on a middle school drama production. "Callie loves theater . . . [S]he's the set designer for the stage crew, and this year she's determined to create a set worthy of Broadway on a middle-school budget. But how can she, when she doesn't know much about carpentry, ticket sales are down, and the crew members are having trouble working together?" (Publisher's note)
"In this realistic and sympathetic story, feelings and thoughts leap off the page, revealing Telgemeier's keen eye for young teen life." Booklist
Includes bibliographical references

★ **Sisters**. Raina Telgemeier; with color by Braden Lamb. Graphix 2014 197 p. Color; Illustration
Grades: 5 6 7 8   **741.5; 306.875; 92**
1. Autobiographical graphic novels; 2. Family life; 3. Interpersonal relations; 4. Siblings
9780545540599, $24.99; 9780545540605, $10.99
LC 2013008700

"Raina can't wait to be a big sister. But once Amara is born, things aren't quite how she expected them to be. . . . They are sisters, after all. Raina uses her signature humor . . . in both present-day narrative and perfectly placed flashbacks to tell the story of her relationship with her sister, which unfolds during the course of a road trip from their home in San Francisco to a family reunion in Colorado." (Publisher's note)

"The author's narrative style is fresh and sharp, and the combination of well-paced and well-placed flashbacks pull the plot together, moving the story forward and helping readers understand the characters' point of view. The volume captures preadolescence in an effortless and uncanny way and turns tough subjects, such as parental marriage problems, into experiences with which readers can identify." (School Library Journal)

★ **Smile**. Scholastic/Graphix 2010 213p. Illustration
Grades: 5 6 7 8   **741; 741.5**
1. Autobiographical graphic novels; 2. Dentistry; 3. Friendship; 4. Personal appearance; 5. Graphic novels
978-0-545-13205-3, $21.99; 0-545-13205-3;
978-0-545-13206-0 (pa), $10.99; 0-545-13206-1 (pa)
LC 2008-51782
Boston Globe-Horn Book Honor: Nonfiction (2010)
Eisner Award: Best Publication for Teens (2011)

Sixth grader Raina just wants to be normal, but when she falls down going home from a Girl Scout meeting, she severely injures her two front teeth, and this starts her down a long road with braces, surgery, retainers, embarrassing headgear—all sure to make her stand out from her middle school classmates for all the wrong reasons. There's also a major earthquake, then boy confusion, friends who turn out not to be good friends, sibling jealousy, all the stuff that makes life interesting, if not fun. Telgemeier wrote and drew the autobiographical Smile as a webcomic; this volume collects the story in color.

"The dental case that Telgemeier documents in this graphic memoir was extreme: a random accident led to front tooth loss when she was 12, and over the next several years, she suffered through surgery, implants, headgear, false teeth, and a rearrangement of her remaining incisors. . . . Both adults and kids . . . are vividly and rapidly portrayed. . . . Telgemeier's storytelling and full-color cartoony images form a story that will cheer and inspire any middle-schooler dealing with orthodontia." Booklist

TenNapel, Doug
Bad Island. Created, written, and drawn by Doug TenNapel. Graphix 2011 218p. Illustration
Grades: 6 7 8 9 10   **741.5**
1. Adventure graphic novels; 2. Extraterrestrial beings; 3. Family life; 4. Father-son relationship; 5. Survival after airplane accidents, shipwrecks, etc
0545314798; 0545314801 (pa); 9780545314794, $24.99; 9780545314800 (pa)

LC 2011276008

"Dad has decided to take Reese, who is too cool for family outings, and his sister, Janine, on a fishing trip. The vacation takes an unexpected turn when their boat capsizes during a storm and they find themselves marooned on a strange island. To their horror, the family slowly realizes that the island is the submerged body of a giant creature, escaped from another world. The story alternates between the shipwreck survivors and the faraway world that created this "island." Both stories feature conflict between an adolescent son and his father. . . . Ultimately, both rebellious adolescents grow up and find their place as young men." (School Libr J)

"Though father, mother, teenage son, and tween daughter face the various dangers like a gang of Indiana Joneses, their family stresses are believable. . . . A clever, old-fashioned adventure with some modern twists and a lighthearted tone." Booklist

Cardboard. Doug TenNapel. Graphix / Scholastic 2012 288 p.
Grades: 5 6 7 8   **741.5**
1. Boxes — Fiction; 2. Bullies; 3. Father-son relationship; 4. Gifts; 5. Magic
0545418720; 9780545418720, $24.99; 9780545418737
LC 2011934533

In this graphic novel, "Cam Howerton's out-of-work father is so broke, the best he can do for Cam's birthday is an empty cardboard box purchased from a toy seller with two mysterious rules: return every unused scrap of cardboard and don't ask for any more. . . . [T]he box becomes a project. What should father and son make out of the box" 'A boxer,' Cam suggests. . . . 'Boxer Bill,' created from inanimate material, comes alive. Unfortunately, Marcus, the neighborhood bully . . . steals the scrap materials, and begins turning out a whole evil empire of cardboard monsters. . . . [A]fter losing control of them he must unite with Cam and his father to defeat the massive cardboard army. . . . [Q]uestions are raised about what it means to be a man, what makes a good man, and what forms people's character." (Horn Book)

Creature Tech. Top Shelf Productions 2002 208p. Illustration
Grades: 8 9 10 11 12 Adult   **741.5; Fic**
1. Science fiction graphic novels; 2. Graphic novels
978-1-891830-34-1, $17.95

Resurrected by the Shroud of Turin, the zombified Dr. Jameson intends to finish what he started 150 years ago—destroying the earth with a giant space eel. Standing in his way is Dr. Ong, a would-be pastor turned scientist who now works in a government research facility infamously known as "Creature Tech." Aided by an unlikely cast of rednecks, symbiotic aliens, and a CIA-trained mantid, Dr. Ong embarks on a journey of faith, love, and self-discovery. All in a day's work at Creature Tech. There's some mild violence and language.

Earthboy Jacobus. Image Comics 2005 272p. Illustration
Grades: 7 8 9 10 11 12 Adult   **741.5; Fic**
1. Science fiction graphic novels; 2. Graphic novels
1-58240-492-5, $17.95

"The alien settings are vivid, weird, and even bordering on goofy, but this story's very human characters provide a grounding that keeps the reader involved and believing. The heavily inked black-and-white panels serve well for quiet scenes as well as those bursting with action or bathroom jokes." (VOYA)

Ex-Marine and Chief of Police "Chief" Edwards hits a whale while driving home; he rescues a boy from the inside and becomes an "instant" father. Jacobus comes from a rather nasty parallel world, and Chief has to teach the boy to defend himself against the enemies who inevitably come. When they end up in Jacobus' world, the values "Chief" had instilled comprise the well from which Jacobus can draw strength.

Flink. Image Comics 2007 122p. Illustration
Grades: 6 7 8 9 10 11 12 Adult   **741.5; Fic**
1. Adventure graphic novels; 2. Sasquatch; 3. Graphic novels
978-1-58240-891-0, $13.99; 1-58240-891-2

Conrad is flying with his father on his first hunting trip when the plane crashes in the wilderness. When Conrad comes to after the crash, he's completely alone, with only the clothes on his back, a handheld game player, and a pocketknife his father had just given him. When he wakes up from a sleep, he finds a deerskin wrapped around him and follows a trail of berries; a Bigfoot named Flink has saved him. Now they have to deal with a rabid she-bear that injures Flink; he needs his brother's medicine to heal, but the Bigfoot community hates humans who hunt them. How can Flink convince them that Conrad is harmless? The book includes some violence and one scene where Conrad pees on a tree.

Gear. Image Comics 2007 Un Illustration
Grades: 7 8 9 10 11 12   **741.5; Fic**
1. Adventure graphic novels; 2. Animals; 3. Fantasy graphic novels; 4. War; 5. Graphic novels
978-1-58240-680-0, $14.99

In a world populated only with animals, the cats of Newton need to find a way to defend themselves against the dogs and the bugs. The dogs and cats have metal guardians that they ride and operate like walking armored robots, and other technology. What the dogs want, especially crime boss Big Tomato, is the Forbidden Mechanism that dog scientist Dr. Pilk has hidden in Newton. This graphic novel started as a black and white comic series, then a graphic novel in 1998. Nickelodeon hired TenNapel to do a cartoon series, Catscratch, based on Gear; it went on the air in 2005. Then Image Comics published Gear in color. TenNapel used Japanese bamboo brushes and sumi ink to draw the art. The book includes considerable violence; characters die, a war is raging.

Ghostopolis. Created, written, and drawn by Doug TenNapel. Graphix 2010 266 p. Illustration
Grades: 7 8 9 10   **741.5**
1. Ghosts; 2. Graphic novels
9780545210287, $12.99; 9780545210270, $24.99; 0545210275

LC 20090942984

This graphic novel tells the story of an "agent for the Supernatural Immigration Task Force, . . . Frank Gallows[, whose] . . . job [is] to catch ghosts on Earth and send them back to the afterlife. However, during one particularly tricky deportation, he accidentally zaps a youngùlivingùboy. Garth

Hale suddenly finds himself surrounded by mummies and goblins in a crumbling, ghastly city, with a skeleton horse and his long-departed grandfather as his only friends. Gallows comes crashing into the afterlife, as well, on a daring rescue mission. As this bumbling team tries to find a way home, they end up face to face with the evil ruler of Ghostopolis, who doesn't look too kindly upon mortals in his city." (Kirkus)

Iron West. Image Comics 2006 160p. Illustration
Grades: 8 9 10 11 12 Adult   **741.5; Fic**
1. Science fiction graphic novels; 2. Western stories; 3. Graphic novels
978-1-58240-630-5, $14.99

Preston Struck has worked as a con artist and crooked gambler, but when he encounters a horde of technological killers while escaping bounty hunters, he discovers an unfortunate streak of responsibility. Awakened by greedy miners, an alien artifact has begun manufacturing humanoid form robots to kill every human, starting with the town of Twain Harte. Aided by a wizened shaman, a Sasquatch, and the not-too-trusting sheriff, Struck reluctantly sets out to stop the killer robots.

TenNapel uses well-worn cliches of American Westerns and turns them on their heads, including Native American stereotypes, the saloon gal with a heart of gold. The level of violence is similar to that seen in any classic Western movie (think John Wayne films). "This finely balanced piece of work is polished with style." Voice Youth Advocates

Tommysaurus Rex. Image Comics 2005 110p. Illustration
Grades: 5 6 7 8 9 10 11 12   **741.5; Fic**
1. Dinosaurs; 2. Graphic novels
1-58240-395-3, $11.95

When Ely loses his dog, Tommy, in a car accident, his parents send him to Grandpa Joe's farm for the summer. He discovers a live, 40-foot Tyrannosaurus Rex in a cave on the farm, and soon the boy and his pet dinosaur cause a big ruckus in town. Ely promises to train the dinosaur he names Tommysaurus, but not if the town's bully, Randy, has his way.

Tetzner, Lisa
The **Black** Brothers: A Novel in Pictures. Art by Hannes Binder. Front Street 2004 144p. Illustration
Grades: 4 5 6 7 8 9   **741.5; Fic**
1. Chimney sweeps; 2. Graphic novels
1-932425-04-7, $16.95

In rural Italy, thirteen-year-old Giorgio is sold to a man who supplies chimney sweeps for Milan. After a treacherous journey in which most of the other boys die, Giorgio goes to work for a man whose wife resents another mouth to feed and starves him. He is sent up into chimneys with no training or guidance for how to do the dangerous work. After nearly dying, he is befriended by a doctor and finds the Black Brothers, a group of chimney sweeps who swear loyalty to each other.

This illustrated novel was originally published in German in 1941, and the translation's tone is similar to other children's books, such as Emil and the Detectives.

Tezuka, Osamu

Astro Boy books 1 and 2. Dark Horse Comics 2008 424p. Illustration
Grades: 3 4 5 6 7 8 9 10 11 12 Adult   741.5; Fic
1. Adventure graphic novels; 2. Astro Boy (Fictional character); 3. Robots; 4. Science fiction graphic novels; 5. Graphic novels
978-1-59582-153-9, $14.95

When a scientist loses his young son, he builds a robot to look exactly like the boy, but when he activates the robot, the scientist becomes repulsed and rejects him. Professor Ochanomizu (gotta love the name, it means tea water and is also a famous Tokyo neighborhood) rescues the boy robot from a circus and names him Astro Boy. He deals with aliens, with people who would use robots to commit crimes, and with adventures in outer space. This new edition collects the first two volumes of the Dark Horse manga editions.

Also available in omnibus editions

Volumes 1 and 2 of a 23 volume series

Thomas, Roy

The **man** in the iron mask, volume 1: The three Musketeers. Writer, Roy Thomas ; penciler, Hugo Petrus ; inker, Tom Palmer ; letterer, Joe Caramagna ; colorist, June Chung ; editors, Ralph Macchio, Nicole Boose. L. ABDO/Spotlight 2009 Un
Grades: 6 7 8 9 10 11 12   741.5; Fic
1. Adventure graphic novels; 2. Dumas, Alexandre, 1802-1870 — Adaptations; 3. France — History — 1589-1789, Bourbons; 4. Graphic novels
978-1-59961-594-3, $21.35

LC 2008-35321

In this Marvel Comics adaptation of Alexandre Dumas' Man in the Iron Mask, the reader first receives a summary of The Three Musketeers, then this story gets rolling. Aramis, now a Bishop, is still scheming; this time, he's determined to finagle the release of a young man named Philippe from the Bastille. Philippe is the younger twin brother of Louis XIV, and the new King has made enemies of the former Musketeers. This book is part of the Marvel Illustrated line of classics adaptations.

This is a library bound edition that doesn't include any of the advertisements from the original Marvel Illustrated comic book issue.

Thompson, Bart A.

Mummy. Adapted by Bart A. Thompson ; illustrated by Brian Miroglio ; based upon the works of Bram Stoker. ABDO/Magic Wagon 2008 Un Illustration
Grades: 4 5 6 7 8 9   741.5
1. Horror graphic novels; 2. Mummies; 3. Graphic novels
978-1-60270-061-1, $27.07

LC 2007-16370

In ancient Egypt, Queen Tera had herself mummified and she swore she would return to life. During an expedition to Egypt in 1947, Abel Trelawney and John Corbeck uncovered her tomb. Today, all is ready for her return. This graphic novel adapts Stoker's Jewel of Seven Stars, which was the basis for the classic horror movie, The Mummy." While there is some violence, the level of horror in this adaptation has been toned down to be suitable for younger readers. Part of the Graphic Horror series

Thompson, Craig

Space dumplins. Craig Thompson with color by Dave Stewart. Graphix / Scholastic 2015 320 p. Color; Illustration
Grades: 3 4 5 6   741.5; Fic
1. Father-daughter relationship — Juvenile fiction; 2. Interplanetary voyages — Juvenile fiction; 3. Missing persons — Juvenile fiction
0545565413; 9780545565417, $24.99; 9780545565431

LC 2014956159

In this graphic novel by Craig Thompson, "for Violet Marlocke, family is the most important thing in the whole galaxy. So when her father goes missing while on a hazardous job, she can't just sit around and do nothing. To get him back, Violet throws caution to the stars and sets out with a group of misfit friends on a quest to find him. But space is vast and dangerous, and she soon discovers that her dad is in big, BIG trouble." (Publisher's note)

"Thompson's art is wild and busy, with overcrowded, unconventional panel structures. The worldbuilding is a strikingly imaginative pastiche that seamlessly blends biblical references, poop jokes, and social satire." Kirkus

Thompson, Jill

Scary Godmother: Wild About Harry. Sirius Entertainment 2001 Un Illustration
Grades: 6 7 8 9 10 11 12   741.5; Fic
1. Humorous graphic novels; 2. Monsters; 3. Supernatural graphic novels; 4. Graphic novels
1-57989-046-6, $9.95

Obnoxiously lazy, selfish, boorish, gluttonous Harry the Werewolf has worn out his mother, Irene the fortune teller. Encouraged by Scary Godmother and her other Fright Side friends, Irene orders Harry out of her house to earn his own living and find his own place to stay. Of course Harry first tries freeloading off his friends, but eventually he has to get a job, working for the Fright Brothers.

This story is for older audiences than the picture book format Scary Godmother books, and is in regular comic book format with black-and-white art. Another title in this format is Scary Godmother: Ghoul's Out for Summer.

Originally published as Scary Godmother: Wild About Harry issues #1-3

Thung, Diana

★ **Captain** Long Ears. SLG Publishing 2010 168p. Illustration
Grades: 5 6 7 8 9 10 11 12 Adult   741.5; Fic
1. Adventure graphic novels; 2. Amusement parks; 3. Death; 4. Graphic novels
978-1-59362-187-2, $12.95

Eight-year-old Michael, aka Captain Long Ears, goes on a mission to Headquarters (an amusement park) with Captain Jam, who is actually his purple toy stuffed gorilla. They're searching for Captain Big Nose, who is Michael's father; he's been gone "on a mission" for two years. In Headquarters, Captain Long Ears and Captain Jam encounter monsters (a preschool teacher and a park attendant), then they find a large crate in a locked enclosure. When they open the crate, they find a young elephant the boy calls "Little Big Nose." They decide they must save Little Big Nose, so they hide in the park overnight. Meanwhile, Michael's mother comes home late from work and doesn't realize her son is missing until the next day. Back in the park, Michael has several dreams of his father leaving him behind. He's so caught up in his fantasy of Captain Long Ears that he doesn't realize the dangers he faces in trying to save the young elephant from abusive handlers. Thung's art shows most of the action through Michael's imagination; readers soon realize that Michael hasn't accepted his father's death. The use of words such as "ass," "caca brain," and other childish epithets may cause more conservative schools to carefully consider their purchase. This imaginary adventure and exploration of the mourning process brings to mind such books as The Bridge to Terabithia and has a similar emotional impact. Despite Michael's young age, this book is more suited to upper elementary and middle school age readers on up.

Tipton, David
Star Trek: miror images. David and Scott Tipton ; art by Sara Pichelli and David Messina. IDW Publishing 2010 128p. Illustration
Grades: 7 8 9 10 11 12 Adult   **741.5; Fic**
    1. Adventure graphic novels; 2. Science fiction graphic novels; 3. Star Trek (Television series); 4. Graphic novels
978-1-60010-293-6, $19.99
    In Star Trek, the original television series, the second-season episode called "Mirror, Mirror" put Captain Kirk, Dr. McCoy, Lieutenant Uhura, and Commander Scott into an alternate universe where the Federation had never been. In that universe, Captain Kirk commanded the I.S.S. Enterprise for the Terran Empire, where promotions occurred by assassination. That Mirror-Kirk was evil. This book shows how Mirror-Kirk seized command of the Enterprise from Captain Pike. One doesn't have to know the television episode in order to enjoy the story, but that knowledge will help readers know right away just what device Mirror-Kirk has Mirror-Scotty building for him. The book also includes an incident in a young Lieutenant Jean-Luc Picard's career; it's about seventy years since the "Mirror, Mirror" incident. At the end of the episode, Captain Kirk encouraged Mirror-Spock to seize command of the Mirror-Enterprise and find a way to gain control of the Empire so he can try to change the Empire to be more like the Federation. As far as Mirror-Picard is concerned, those changes made by Emperor Spock have weakened the Empire. Things come to a head when the I.S.S. Starbreaker encounters a force of Klingon-Cardassian Alliance ships. Captain Sorek, a Vulcan, refuses to fight back and is ready to surrender the ship, so Picard decides to take action. "Mirror, Mirror" ended with Kirk's hope that Mirror-Spock would bring about a change for the better; Mirror-Picard's story show that such change didn't do much good for the Terran Empire. Picard utters the word "merde" once, one will have to know at least a little French to know he said a bad word. The book's cover is somewhat misleading, since it shows Spock and Mirror-Spock instead of Kirk and Mirror-Kirk.

Tipton, Scott
Star Trek: Alien spotlight volume 1. Written by Scott Tipton; Art by David Messina. IDW Publishing 2008 152p. Illustration
Grades: 6 7 8 9 10 11 12 Adult   **741.5; Fic**

    1. Adventure graphic novels; 2. Science fiction graphic novels; 3. Star Trek; 4. Graphic novels
978-1-60010-179-3, $19.99
    This volume collects a series of one-shots (standalone comics issues), each devoted to one of the alien races featured in the Star Trek series. Readers meet the Gorns, Vulcans, Andorians, Orions, the Borg, and the Romulans in stories that also give the aliens' point of view. The stories are set in the various time periods of the Star Trek universe; for example, Captain Clark Terrell and Pavel Chekov (before they were captured by Khan in "The Wrath of Khan") and their landing party encounter the Gorns on a planet designed to train Gorn warriors, while Captain Picard encounters the Borg.

Star Trek: Klingons: blood will tell. David and Scott Tipton ; art by David Messina. IDW Publishing 2007 168p. Illustration
Grades: 7 8 9 10 11 12 Adult   **741.5; Fic**
    1. Science fiction graphic novels; 2. Star Trek; 3. Graphic novels
978-1-60010-108-3, $24.99
    In this volume, readers look back at some of the most famous encounters between the United Federation of Planets and the Klingon Empire, from the Klingon perspective. Kahnrah must decide if he will side with Gorkon and ask the Federation for aid in a time of crisis for all Klingons, and he seeks enlightenment from the actions of his relatives who encountered such Federation officers as Captain James T. Kirk of the starship Enterprise. The book includes the Klingon language variant of the first comic book issue.

Tobe, Keiko
With the Light: Raising an Autistic Child (Hikari to Tomoni). Yen Press 2007 528p. Illustration
Grades: 8 9 10 11 12 Adult
741.5; Fic
    1. Autism; 2. Manga; 3. Graphic novels
978-0-7595-2356-2, $14.99
    Born during the sunrise - an auspicious beginning - the Azumas' newborn son is named Hikaru, which means "light." But during one play date, his mother notices that

Courtesy of Yen Press

her son is slightly different from the other children. In this alternately heartwarming and bittersweet tale, a young mother tries to cope with both the overwhelming discovery of her child's autism and the trials of raising him while keeping her family together. This fictional story is based on true accounts; and the book includes notes about how parents can deal with certain situations depicted in the story.
    Volume 1 of 8

Tobin, Paul
Bandette: Presto!. By Paul Tobin, illustrated by Collen Coover, edited by Brendan Wright. Dark Horse Books 2013 144 p. (Bandette)

Grades: 7 8 9 10 11 12 Adult   **741.5**
1. Burglars; 2. Organized crime — Fiction; 3. Paris (France); 4. Teenage girls — Fiction; 5. Thieves
1616552794; 9781616552794, $14.99
                       LC 2013024226
Eisner Award: Best Digital Comic (2013)
In this graphic novel by Paul Tobin and Colleen Coover, "the world's greatest thief is a costumed teen burglar in swinging Paris by the nome d'arte of Bandette! But it's not all breaking hearts and purloining masterpieces when a rival thief discovers that an international criminal organization wants Bandette dead!" (Publisher's note)
"[O]ne of the brightest, and most fun, comics of the year." Pub Wkly
Another title about Bandette is: Stealers keepers! (2015)

Togashi, Yoshihiro
YuYu Hakusho Vol. 1. Viz Media/Shonen Jump 2003 208p. Illustration
Grades: 8 9 10 11 12 Adult   **741.5; Fic**
1. Fantasy graphic novels; 2. Shonen manga; 3. Supernatural graphic novels; 4. Graphic novels
1-56931-904-9, $7.95
Yusuke Urameshi was a tough teen delinquent until one selfless act changed his life...by ending it. When he died saving a little kid from a speeding car, the afterlife didn't know what to do with him, so it gave him a second chance at life. Now, Yusuke is a ghost with a mission, performing good deeds at the behest of Botan, the spirit guide of the dead, and Koenma, her pacifier-sucking boss from the other side. But what strange things await him on the borderline between life and death? It's going to include a lot of battles against supernatural creatures. The series includes some strong language, lots of supernatural martial arts fighting action, and some mildly suggestive humor.

Tokeino, Hari
Me and My Brothers Vol. 1. Tokyopop 2007 Un Illustration
Grades: 8 9 10 11 12   **741.5; Fic**
1. Family life; 2. Humorous graphic novels; 3. Shojo manga; 4. Graphic novels
978-1-4278-0071-8, $9.99
When Sakura, a fourteen-year-old orphaned girl, discovers she has four half-brothers, her world is turned upside down as they're all forced to live under one roof ... Masashi, the eldest at 25, is a romance novelist; Takashi is a teacher now working as a substitute in Sakura's school; Tsuyoshi works several part-time jobs; and Takeshi is in 11th grade. Sakura has been so used to living quietly with her grandmother that adjusting to the controlled chaos of having four brothers in the house isn't so easy.

Tolstikova, Dasha
A Year Without Mom. By Dasha Tolstikova. Groundwood Books 2015 176 p. Color; Illustration
Grades: 5 6 7 8   **92; 741.5**
1. Mother-daughter relationship; 2. Refugees; 3. Russia; 4. Tolstikova, Dasha
1554986923; 9781554986927, $19.95
This book, by Dasha Tolstikova, "follows 12-year-old Dasha through a year full of turmoil after her mother leaves

for America. It is the early 1990s in Moscow, and political change is in the air. But Dasha is more worried about her own challenges as she negotiates family, friendships and school without her mother. Just as she begins to find her own feet, she gets word that she is to join her mother in America ù a place that seems impossibly far from everything and everyone she loves." (Publisher's note)
"Scribbly, childlike pencil drawings are filled in with gray wash and accentuated with red and the occasional pop of blue. They are deceptively simple, but with great narrative sophistication, they capture both the specificity of Dasha's experience and the universality of her emotions." Kirkus

Toriyama, Akira
Cowa!. Story and art by Akira Toriyama; translation & English adaptation Alexander O. Smith, et. al.. Viz Media/Shonen Jump 2008 208p. Illustration
Grades: 5 6 7 8 9 10 11 12   **741.5; Fic**
1. Humorous graphic novels; 2. Manga; 3. Monsters; 4. Graphic novels
978-1-4215-1805-3, $7.99; 1-4215-1805-8
Mischievous Paifu is half-vampire and half-werekoala, and he's usually getting into lots of trouble with his best buddy, Jose the ghost. When the Monster Flu sweeps through town, the doctor says that without medicine, everyone will die. The only person who makes the medicine is the witch who lives hundreds of miles away, and all the adults except for the doctor are ill. Paifu and Jose team up with grumpy ex-sumo wrestler Maruyama to make the journey; will they make it before they get sick" The book includes some potty humor (Jose farts a lot) and lots of fighting scenes (Toriyama created Dragon Ball Z).
Original Japanese edition, 1997

Jaco the galactic patrolman. Story and art, Akira Toriyama; translation, Tetsuichiro Miyaki; touch-up art and lettering, James Gaubatz. Viz 2015 245 p. Illustration
Grades: 7 8 9 10 11 12   **741.5**
1. Interplanetary voyages; 2. Manga; 3. Police — Fiction
1421566303; 9781421566306, $9.99
"Retired scientist Omori lives alone on a deserted island while continuing his research into time-travel. His quiet life is interrupted when galactic patrolman Jaco crash-lands and decided to move in with him. Can Jaco get along with the old man long enough to save the earth from a dangerous threat?" (Publisher's note)
"Dragon Ball creator Toriyama returns to comedic serials with the story of an eccentric alien who befriends a grumpy old man. . . . Toriyama's punchy dialogue and waggish spirit are still intact, and his art, although pared down, remains sharp in its sense of movement and pace in this back-to-basics one-off from one of the industry's giants." Pub Wkly

Torres, J.
Alison Dare, Little Miss Adventures Volume 2. Illustrated by J. Bone. Oni Press 2005 Un Illustration
Grades: 4 5 6 7 8 9   **741.5; Fic**
1. Adventure graphic novels
1-932664-25-4, $11.95
Alison Dare is back in this new collection of stories, including her report about her experience at her mother's

excavation site in Egypt (with the true story coming right after). Then Alison and her boarding school friends journey into the Heart of the Maiden." The costumed avenger The Blue Scarab encounters villains while gift shopping. And world renowned archaeologist Dr. Alice Dare teaches a thing or two about museum mayhem.

Blue Beetle: reach for the stars. John Rogers, J. Torres, Keith Giffen, writers ; Rafael Albuquerque, David Baldeon, Freddie Williams II, pencillers ; Rafael Albuquerque, Steve Bird, Dan Davis, inkers ; Guy Major, colorist ; Phil Balsman, Pat Brosseau, letterers. DC Comics 2008 168p. Illustration
Grades: 8 9 10 11 12 Adult   **741.5; Fic**
1. Adventure graphic novels; 2. Green Lantern (Fictional character); 3. Superhero graphic novels; 4. Teen Titans (Fictional characters); 5. Graphic novels
978-1-4012-1642-9, $14.99
In the previous volume, teenager Jaime Reyes discovered that the scarab fused to his spine that turns him into the Blue Beetle was created by aliens. Now he learns that those aliens are invading Earth, but they're doing it so insidiously that humans are welcoming the Reach and no one will believe one boy from Texas. It's up to Jaime, his friends, and some other superheroes, such as Green Lantern Guy Gardner and the Teen Titans, to try to stop them. The book includes some violence.

Days Like This. Written by J. Torres ; illustrated by Scott Chantler. Oni Press 2003 Un Illustration
Grades: 6 7 8 9 10 11 12 Adult   **741.5; Fic**
1. Rock music; 2. Graphic novels
1-929998-48-1, $8.95
It's the early 1960s, and rock'n'roll and r&b are ushering in a new golden age of pop music. Tina & the Tiaras, three teenage girl singers, songwriter Karen Prince, and new music mogul Anna Solomon team to create a new girl group sound and move up the charts.

Degrassi the Next Generation Extra Credit Vol. 1: Turning Japanese. Art by Ed Northcott. Pocket Books 2006 Un Illustration
Grades: 8 9 10 11 12   **741.5; Fic**
1. Graphic novels
978-1-4165-3076-3, $9.95
It's the end of Ellie's senior year, and as though final exams aren't enough to worry about, she's been placed in a compromising position by one of her bosses at a comic book company. Is quitting her only option? J.T. turns to the Internet to help cope with the recent troubles in his life. But now he spends most of his time locked in his room, and he can't seem to move on. Is his new habit just making his problems worse? This original story follows the sixth season of the popular television series.

Degrassi the Next Generation Extra Credit Vol. 2: Suddenly Last Summer. Art by Ramon Perez. Pocket Books 2007 Un Illustration
Grades: 8 9 10 11 12   **741.5; Fic**
1. Graphic novels
978-1-4165-3077-0, $9.95
Emma gets her groove back with the help of group therapy and a family trip to New York City. But as she returns to her old self, her relationship with Peter begins to suffer. Is he helping Emma recover, or holding her back? In

the meantime, while coaching at basketball camp, Jimmy finds himself dealing with the fallout of a hazing incident. Was the initiation just a prank, or did it cross the line? When the police get involved, Jimmy is faced with a tough decision. This is another original story set during the summer vacation following the sixth season of the popular television series.

Into the woods. J. Torres; illustrated by Faith Erin Hicks. Kids Can Press 2012 100 p. Color illustration (Bigfoot Boy)
Grades: 3 4 5 6 7   **Fic; 741.5; 741.5/971**
1. Magic; 2. Sasquatch; 3. Totems and totemism
1554537118; 9781554537112, $17.95
In this fantasy graphic novel, "city boy Rufus is staying at his grandmother's house on the edge of a forest for a few days without his parents," and he "decides to explore the woods. He meets a girl named Penny. . . . When looking for her in the woods, Rufus finds a glowing necklace in a tree. After reading the word on the back, he turns into Bigfoot! . . . There's danger in the forest as well as magic, and when Penny disappears, Rufus . . . use[s] the totem to effect a rescue." (Kirkus Reviews)
Followed by: The unkindness of ravens (2013)

★ **Lola:** a ghost story. [by] J. Torres & [illustrated by] Elbert Or. Oni Press 2009 102p. Illustration
Grades: 4 5 6 7 8   **741.5; Fic**
1. Family life; 2. Ghosts; 3. Philippines; 4. Graphic novels
978-1-934964-33-0, $14.95; 1-934964-33-6
"Lola ("grandmother" in Tagalog) has just died, and Jesse is reluctant to visit her home in the Philippines. He was afraid of her because she was rumored to have magical abilities, and because he thinks she tried to drown him when he was a baby. Jesse listens to family members tell stories about her as he tries to adjust to their strange mix of superstitions and religion. . . . Jesse is an unusually nuanced character. . . . When he sees something extraordinary, it's unclear if he is dreaming, hallucinating, or if he has inherited his grandmother's abilities. Torres's gradual revelation of details will keep readers hanging until they learn the truth. Or's artwork uses sepia tones and smooth lines, and features characters with cute button eyes. But the sweet images can quickly turn horrific when Jesse has his visions. " SLJ

The **Sound** of Thunder. Written by J. Torres; illustrated by Faith Erin Hicks. Kids Can Press 2014 100 p. Color; Illustration (Bigfoot boy)
Grades: 3 4 5 6 7   **741.5**
1. Adventure fiction; 2. Pacific Northwest — Fiction; 3. Graphic novels
9781894786584, $17.95; 9781894786591, $9.95
"This conclusion to the Bigfoot Boy graphic novel trilogy adds a backdrop of Pacific Northwest mythology to the popular story about an ordinary boy who becomes a hero through the power of magic. As the book begins, Rufus, Penny and their squirrel friend, Sidney, are eager to recapture the magic totem they lost to the ravens in the previous book." (Publisher's note)
"Torres and Hicks conclude their woodsy trilogy with an exciting adventure dotted with humor. Rufus and Penny's attempts to understand Sidney's charades are a hoot. Rufus

has worked a bit of his city-boy out, but his bumbles and stumbles continue to round out his character." Kirkus

Sequel to: The unkindness of ravens (2013)

Teen Titans Go! Vol. 1: Truth, Justice, Pizza!. DC Comics 2004 112p. Illustration

Grades: 3 4 5 6 7 8 9   **741.5; Fic**
1. Humorous graphic novels; 2. Robin (Fictional character); 3. Superhero graphic novels; 4. Teen Titans (Fictional characters); 5. Graphic novels
1-4012-0333-7, $6.95

They're too young to drive, but not too young to save the world. The world's hottest heroes: Robin, Beast Boy, Raven, Cyborg, and Starfire, show how it's done Titan-style, as they go up against teen super villains Gizmo, Jinx, and Mammoth. Things get icky when Raven's bad dad, Trigon, comes out from a huge zit on Raven's forehead (ewwww ...).

Teen Titans Go! Vol. 2: Heroes on Patrol!. DC Comics 2004 112p. Illustration

Grades: 3 4 5 6 7 8 9   **741.5; Fic**
1. Humorous graphic novels; 2. Superhero graphic novels; 3. Teen Titans (Fictional characters); 4. Graphic novels
1-4012-0334-5, $6.95

In this volume, the Teen Titans encounter the battling brothers, Thunder and Lightning; Starfire has to deal with her naughty sister Blackfire; they encounter Aqualad; and more.

Teen Titans Go! Vol. 3: Bring It On!. Written by J. Torres, Adam Beechen. DC Comics 2005 104p. Illustration

Grades: 3 4 5 6 7 8 9   **741.5; Fic**
1. Humorous graphic novels; 2. Superhero graphic novels; 3. Teen Titans (Fictional characters); 4. Graphic novels
1-4012-0511-9, $6.99

Terra rejoins the Titans to fight Slade's robots; the teen superheroes fight Mumbo; Beast Boy tries to help a man stricken with werewolfism; Speedy joins the Titans to fight Plasmus; and they go up against Kwiz Kid, who's mad at Robin because his ex-girlfriend has a crush on Robin.

Teen Titans Go! Vol. 4: Ready for Action!. DC Comics 2005 104p. Illustration

Grades: 3 4 5 6 7 8 9   **741.5; Fic**
1. Humorous graphic novels; 2. Superhero graphic novels; 3. Teen Titans (Fictional characters); 4. Graphic novels
978-1-4012-0985-8, $6.99

In this volume, the Titans confront a rampaging Wildebeest, teach the hot-tempered Hotshot the value of patience, battle an army of zombies, find themselves trapped in a deadly video game with the Titans East and more.

Teen Titans Go! Vol. 5: On the Move!. DC Comics 2006 104p. Illustration

Grades: 3 4 5 6 7 8 9   **741.5; Fic**
1. Humorous graphic novels; 2. Robin (Fictional character); 3. Superhero graphic novels; 4. Teen Titans (Fictional characters); 5. Graphic novels
978-1-4012-0986-5, $6.99

In this collection, among other stories the Titans must stop Beast Boy, who's been turned into the terrifying vegetarian monster Garsaurus Rex; Robin is tempted to the dark side by Slade; and the Titans crash a comic book convention to discover the secret of Red X.

Teen Titans Go!: Titans Together!. DC Comics 2007 144p. Illustration

Grades: 3 4 5 6 7 8 9   **741.5**
1. Robin (Fictional character); 2. Superhero graphic novels; 3. Teen Titans (Fictional characters); 4. Graphic novels
978-1-4012-1563-7, $12.99

This volume collects eight adventures of the Teen Titans as seen in the animated series, Teen Titans Go! Robin leads the young team that includes Cyborg, Beast Boy, Raven, and Starfire. The stories have lots of action and bad puns as Beast Boy makes a movie, the Titans find themselves in an alien fighting arena, and Robin's future self, Nightwing, comes when time goes a little haywire and an evil Robin shows up.

The **unkindness** of ravens. By J. Torres; illustrated by Faith Erin Hicks. Kids Can Press 2013 100 p. Color illustration (Bigfoot boy)

Grades: 3 4 5 6 7   **741.5**
1. Magic; 2. Ravens — Fiction
9781554537136, $17.95; 9781554537143, $9.95 ; 1554537134; 1554537142

LC 2013040319

This book, by J. Torres and illustrated by Faith Erin Hicks, tells the story of "another weekend of Rufus using his magic totem to transform himself into Bigfoot Boy! But when you're big, hairy and loud, it's hard to keep your powers a secret, especially when there are trickster ravens that want the magic for themselves." (Publisher's note)

"Hicks's illustrations are done in bold, black lines and rich colors and are sometimes reminiscent of Native Canadian art styles. The story's adventure, magic, and characters will appeal." SLJ

Followed by: The sound of thunder (2014)

Sequel to: Into the woods (2012)

Townsend, Michael

Amazing Greek myths of wonders and blunders. Dial Books for Young Readers 2010 160p. Illustration

Grades: 3 4 5 6 7   **292; 741.5**
1. Greek mythology; 2. Humorous graphic novels; 3. Short stories; 4. Graphic novels
978-0-8037-3308-4, $14.99

Townsend retells the myths of King Midas, Pandora, Pygmalion, the abduction of Persephone, Arachne, Perseus, Pyramus and Thisbe, Icarus, and Hercules and his labors all with cartoony, silly art and lots of humor. Due to the popular Percy Jackson books, young readers may be looking for more Greek myths, and this collection invites those readers to laugh and have fun. Zeus's philandering ways and wife Hera's jealousy are treated in a kid-friendly way that still manages to get the point across that neither Zeus nor Hera were very nice to humans. Despite the irreverent treatment, Townsend does tell the gist of the stories.

Toyama, Ema

Pixie Pop: Gokkun Pucho Vol. 1. Tokyopop 2007 Un Illustration

Grades: 7 8 9 10 11 12   **741.5; Fic**
1. Humorous graphic novels; 2. Manga; 3. Romance graphic novels; 4. Shojo manga; 5. Graphic novels
978-1-59816-813-6, $9.99

Mayu, the daughter of a cafe owner, is down-in-the-dumps and unlucky in love...until she meets Pucho, the magical fairy of beverages. Now, whenever Mayu drinks something, she transforms! But there's a catch—milk makes her grow (into a giant), water turns her invisible, and pork soup turns her into a cute little piglet. Only Pucho can reverse the transformations. But what will help her win the man of her dreams?

★ **Trickster: Native American tales: a graphic collection**
Edited by Matt Dembicki. Fulcrum 2010 231p. Illustration Grades: 5 6 7 8
398.2; 398
1. Folklore; 2. Native Americans — Folklore; 3. Graphic novels
978-1-55591-724-1 (pa), $22.95; 1-55591-724-0 (pa)
LC 2009-49668
"More than 40 storytellers and cartoonists have contributed to this original and provocative compendium of traditional folklore presented in authentic, colorful, and engaging sequential art. The stories are drawn from a variety of Native peoples across North America, and so the trickster character appears variously as Rabbit, a raccoon, Coyote, and in other guises; landscapes, clothing and rhythms of speech and action also vary in keeping with distinct traditions. Realistic, impressionistic, painterly, and cartoon styles of art are employed to echo and announce the tone of each tale and telling style, making this a rich visual treasure as well as cultural trove." SLJ

Trondheim, Lewis
A.L.I.E.E.E.N.. First Second Books 2006 Un Illustration
Grades: 8 9 10 11 12   **741.5; Fic**
1. Humorous graphic novels; 2. Science fiction graphic novels; 3. Stories without words; 4. Graphic novels
978-1-59643-095-2, $12.95
According to the title page, the full title is Archives of Lost Issues and Earthly Editions of Extraterrestrial Novelties. The book purports to be an alien comic book, and all dialog is in an alien script, rendering it basically wordless for human readers. In several separate stories, little creatures suffer injuries, perpetrate bullying violence on others, suffer extreme pooping, and other bizarre and weird experiences. The dark humor in this book will appeal to teens who enjoy snarky attitudes and macabre humor.
Originally published in France in 2004 by Editions Breal.

Astronauts of the future. [by] Lewis Trondheim, Manu Larcenet. NBM 2004 96p. Illustration
Grades: 7 8 9 10 11 12   **741.5; Fic**
1. Science fiction graphic novels; 2. Graphic novels
1-561-63407-7, $14.95
LC 2004-49960
This story "begins as a witty, gentle tale of two precocious youngsters, Gil and Martina, whose estrangement from their classmates and parents leads them to conclude that others are either, as Martina insists, aliens, or, according to Gil, robots. Initially wryly depicting the loneliness and alienation of brainy children and their joy at discovering simpatico souls—think Calvin and Hobbes

meets To Be and to Have—the story suddenly swirls into an outrageous but compelling science-fiction epic." Booklist

Li'l Santa. NBM Publishing 2002 Un Illustration
Grades: 3 4 5 6 7 8 9 10 11 12 Adult   **741.5; Fic**
1. Fantasy graphic novels; 2. Humorous graphic novels; 3. Santa Claus; 4. Stories without words; 5. Graphic novels
1-56163-335-6, $14.95
LC 2002-32131
You have no idea what Santa must go through, all the way up there at the North Pole, until you read this fully silent graphic novel. Besides the huge yearly job that faces him, the North Pole is no friendly place, what with Impies and a Snow Dragon and the like. Santa must use all his best cunning to make all the world's kids happy.

The **Spiffy** Adventures of McConey: Harum Scarum. Fantagraphics Books 1998 48p. Illustration
Grades: 8 9 10 11 12 Adult   **741.5; Fic**
1. Humorous graphic novels; 2. Mystery graphic novels; 3. Science fiction graphic novels; 4. Graphic novels
1-56097-288-2, $10.95
This is a story about horrible monsters and science gone awry ... about kidnappings, murder, arson, and pitiless beatings ... about fairy dust, time machines, and the teleportation cap ... about sinister commies, double agents, and corrupt commissioners ... about the niceties of tipping and the precise location of the jugular vein. McConey the bunny and his friends blunder and wisecrack their way through a monstrous mystery.

Tiny tyrant. Lewis Trondheim; translated by Alexis Siegel; illustrated by Fabrice Parme. First Second 2007 124 p. Color illustration
Grades: 4 5 6 7 8 9 10 11 12 Adult   **741.5/944; Fic**
1. Humorous graphic novels; 2. Kings and rulers — Fiction; 3. Graphic novels
9781596430945, $12.95; 159643094X
LC 2006021479
Translations into English of eight French stories originally published by Delacourt, 2001-2004.
"In this illustrated collection of eight translated French stories, King Ethelbert rules as much by whim as by moral or regal standards; this lack of perspective can be excused, though, since he's only six. . . . Grades three to eight." (Bull Cent Child Books)
"Tiny child-king Ethelbert is spoiled and difficult, expecting to have his every whim fulfilled-or else. . . . In the end, though, he becomes a hero. The dynamic cartoons are filled with details and riddled with humor; most pages have between six and eight small pictures. . . . This title will have wide appeal. It's young and accessible enough for elementary-grade kids, but teens will also be charmed by the rascally king." SLJ

Trumbauer, Lisa
The **three** little pigs: the graphic novel. Art by Aaron Blecha. Stone Arch Books 2009 40p.
Grades: 3 4 5 6 7 8   **741.5; Fic**
1. Fairy tales; 2. Humorous graphic novels; 3. Three little pigs — Adaptations; 4. Graphic novels
978-1-4342-1195-8, $21.26
LC 2008-32050

In this graphic novel retelling, the three brother pigs set out on their own, and they build their three houses, the first of straw, the second of sticks, and the third of bricks. Then the Big Bad Wolf comes into town looking for something good to eat, and decides to get the pigs. He huffs, and he puffs, and he blows down the first two houses and carries the pigs into the woods. When he can't blow down the house of bricks, he tries to trick the third pig with outings to get food. The illustrations are on the creepy side, which could appeal to older elementary age boys. The book includes information on the history of the tale, discussion questions, and a glossary.
Part of the Graphic Sparks line

Tsang, Evonne
    I love him to pieces: or my date is dead weight or he only loves me for my brains. Illustrated by Janina Gorrissen. Graphic Universe 2011 123p. Illustration (My boyfriend is a monster)
Grades: 6 7 8 9 10 11 12   **741.5; Fic**
    1. Horror graphic novels; 2. Humorous graphic novels; 3. Romance graphic novels; 4. Zombies; 5. Graphic novels
    978-0-7613-6004-9 (lib bdg), $29.27; 0-7613-6004-2 (lib bdg); 978-0-7613-7079-6 (pa), $9.95; 0-7613-7079-X (pa)
                                            LC 2010-30774
    Dicey Bell, star of her high school baseball team in St. Petersburg, Florida, falls for Jack Chen, the star of the science program, and she wangles her way into partnering with Jack on a school project. They work together well, like each other a lot, and things look good for a romance, when a weird infection hits the city. The infection attacks the brain and turns the infected people into human flesh-craving monsters. Dicey and Jack try to get to safety, but find themselves surrounded by zombie-like monsters. This story combines romance with zombie fighting in a story that works like a lighter version of The Walking Dead; the extra subtitles on the title page indicate the humor: "My Date is Dead Weight, or He Only Loves Me For My Brains." Gorrissen's black and white art makes the teens look like teens, and the zombies look yucky and scary without being too icky for most teen readers. This is the first volume in a series of standalone stories, each taking on a different kind of monster.

Tulien, Sean
    Pecos Bill: colossal cowboy: the graphic novel. Art by Lisa Weber. Stone Arch Books 2010 40p. Illustration
Grades: 3 4 5 6 7 8   **741.5; Fic**
    1. Folklore — United States; 2. Pecos Bill (Legendary character); 3. Tall tales; 4. Graphic novels
    978-1-4342-1896-4, $22.65; 978-1-4342-2267-1 (pa), $4.95
                                            LC 2009-29100
    This colorful graphic novel retells some of the legends about Pecos Bill, the Texas cowboy hero, including his childhood among the coyotes, how he invented branding to keep track of the cattle, wrestling the wild horse named Widow Maker, and his wild ride on a tornado that caused the Grand Canyon and the Rio Grande. The book includes

information on other legends connected with Pecos Bill, a short glossary, discussion questions, and reading prompts.
    Part of the Graphic Spin series

Twain, Mark, 1835-1910
    The **Adventures** of Tom Sawyer. Retold by M.C. Hall ; illustrated by Daniel Strickland. Stone Arch Books 2006 63p. Illustration
Grades: 3 4 5 6 7 8 9   **741.5; Fic**
    1. Adventure graphic novels; 2. Twain, Mark, 1835-1910 — Adaptations; 3. Graphic novels
    978-1-59889-045-7, $23.93
    Tom Sawyer is the cleverest of characters, constantly outwitting those around him. Then there is Huckleberry Finn, the envy of the town's schoolchildren because he has the rare gift of complete freedom, never attending school or answering to anyone but himself. After Tom and Huck witness a murder, they find themselves on a series of adventures that lead them to some seriously frightening situations. This adaptation is written for reluctant and struggling readers.
    Part of the Graphic Revolve series.

    Classics illustrated delux #4: the adventures of Tom Sawyer. Adapted by Jean David Morvan, Frederique Voulyze and Severine LeFebvre. Papercutz 2009 Un Illustration
Grades: 4 5 6 7 8 9 10   **741.5; Fic**
    1. Adventure graphic novels; 2. Twain, Mark, 1835-1910 — Adaptations
    978-1-59707-152-9, $17.95; 978-1-59707-153-6 (pa), $13.95
    Orphan Tom Sawyer lives with his half-brother Sid at Aunt Polly's house, where he messes up in school and plays hooky as often as possible; he plays practical jokes with his buddy Huckleberry Finn, crushes on Becky Thatcher, and generally has a happy life. Then Tom and Huck witness a murder, and it changes their lives. This graphic novel adaptation was originally published in France and is translated by Joe Johnson for Papercutz; artist Lefebvre's work shows strong anime influences.

Type-Moon
    Fate stay night, volume 1. Art by Nishiwaki. Tokyopop 2008 196p. Illustration
Grades: 8 9 10 11 12   **741.5; Fic**
    1. Fantasy graphic novels; 2. Grail; 3. Magic; 4. Shonen manga; 5. Graphic novels
    978-1-4278-1037-3, $9.99
    When he was still a little boy, Shirou Emiya was the lone survivor of a devastating fire that destroyed his entire village; a magus saved him and raised him. Now in high school, Shirou helps the various school clubs with minor mechanical repairs, but he really wants to follow his stepfather's footsteps and become a hero of justice. Then one afternoon he stumbles upon two men fighting with swords and causing major magical havoc. That day he discovers he's a magus, and he's now in the middle of a new war between the Seven Magi to win the Holy Grail, and he has a magical servant, the Saber (who looks like a young woman). If he refuses to join in the war, many innocent lives will be lost, just like his home village. The book includes considerable

fighting violence, some strong language; any moderate sexuality mentioned in the book's rating hasn't appeared in the first volume.

Uderzo
★ **Asterix** the Gaul. [by] René Goscinny and Albert Uderzo. Orion Media 2004 48p. Illustration; Map
Grades: 4 5 6 7 8 9 10 11 12   741.5; Fic
1. France — History; 2. Humorous graphic novels
0-7528-6604-4, $12.95; 0-7528-6605-2 (pa), $9.95
Meet Asterix, a diminutive but extremely strong Gaul living in ancient France during the time of the Roman Republic. Together with his friend Obelix, Asterix continually outwits the Roman Legionnaires sent to conquer Gaul for Julius Caesar. Full of puns and outrageous humor, the books also manage to teach a lot of history. This is the first in a long-running series of graphic novels translated from the original French.
Translated from the French
Other titles in this series are: Asterix and Caesar's Gift; Asterix and Cleopatra; Asterix and the actress; Asterix and the banquet; Asterix and the big fight; Asterix and the cauldron; Asterix and the Goths; Asterix and the Great Crossing; Asterix and the laurel wreath; Asterix the legionary; Asterix and the Normans; Asterix and the Roman Agent; Asterix and the soothsayer; Asterix at the Olympic Games; Asterix in Belgium; Asterix in Britain; Asterix in Corsica; Asterix in Spain; Asterix in Switzerland; Asterix Obelix and Co.; Asterix the gladiator; Asterix The Mansions of the Gods

Asterix and Obelix All at Sea. Orion/Sterling Publishing 2002 48p. Illustration
Grades: 4 5 6 7 8 9 10 11 12 Adult   741.5; Fic
1. Asterix (Fictional character); 2. Humorous graphic novels
0-75284-778-3, $9.95
LC 2002-282560
In ancient Rome the slaves are revolting ... and not only that, they've stolen Julius Caesar's own galley, the finest warship in the Roman navy. Under their heroic leader Spartakis, the former galley slaves make for the little Gaulish village where Julius Caesar's old enemies Asterix and Obelix live - only to find the place in crisis, for Obelix, after drinking the druid Getafix's magic potions on the sly, is first turned to stone and then reverts to childhood. In search of a cure for him Asterix, Getafix and their new friends the galley slaves sail to the wonderful continent of Atlantis, ruled by its high priest Absolutlifabulos - and the ensuing sea battles against the Roman navy are fast and furious ...

Ueda, Miwa
Papillon, vol. 1. Del Rey Manga 2008 184p. Illustration
Grades: 8 9 10 11 12   741.5; Fic
1. Manga; 2. Romance graphic novels; 3. Shojo manga; 4. Graphic novels
978-0-345-50519-4, $10.05
Hana and Ageha are twins, but they were raised separately for years. Now they're in high school, and Hana is totally glamorous and popular, while Ageha is quiet, and shy and everyone thinks of her as plain. Ageha has a crush on Ryuhei, a classmate who was her childhood play buddy

while she lived in the country, but Hana decides to date him. A college student who works as the school's counselor tries to get Ageha to open up and strive for what she wants, but his first scheme results in making her a laughingstock of her class. He calls her a chrysallis, but can she break out and become the butterfly?

Papillon, vol. 2. Del Rey Manga 2009 186p. Illustration
Grades: 8 9 10 11 12   741.5; Fic
1. Manga; 2. Romance graphic novels; 3. Shojo manga; 4. Graphic novels
978-0-345-50592-7, $10.99
Ichijiku-sensei has been trying to help Ageha get out from twin sister Hana's shadow and get her friend Ryusei see her as girlfriend material, but when Ageha sees Ryuseia and Hana kissing when he's supposed to pick her up to visit her grandmother in the hospital, Ageha goes alone. Ageha has felt for so many years that her mother didn't want her, that it comes as a shock when her mother follows her as Ichijiku-sensei seems to be leading her into a love hotel. Then, when Ageha runs into the street, her mother saves her from being run over and suffers a head injury. Ageha is able to tell her mother how she feels, and the healing process begins. Hana isn't sure she wants this. But now, Ageha no longer wants Ryusei; she's falling for Ichijiku-sensei. The book includes some mildly suggestive scenes.

Umezu, Kazuo
Scary Book Volume 3: Faces. Dark Horse Manga 2006 232p. Illustration
Grades: 8 9 10 11 12   741.5; Fic
1. Horror graphic novels; 2. Manga; 3. Shojo manga; 4. Graphic novels
978-1-59307-487-6, $13.95
This is the third volume of the anthology series. In "Fear," Aiko is always ignored and neglected when compared to her beautiful older sister, Momoko. But when Momoko is horribly disfigured in an accident and goes mad, it's up to Aiko to bring home young girls her sister can use... to make a new face. And in "The Coincidental Letter," a young girl named Yoko, in a fit of mischief, sends an insulting letter to a made-up girl at a made-up address warning her of a horrible fate. However, by incredible coincidence, both the girl and the address are real, and everything in the letter starts coming true. Both stories rely on psychological suspense rather than violent horror, although there is some mildly strong language and a little violence in the first story.

Unita, Yumi
★ **Bunny** drop vol. 1. [translation, Kaori Inoue; lettering, Alexis Eckerman]. Yen Press 2010 196p. Illustration
Grades: 8 9 10 11 12 Adult
741.5; Fic
1. Josei manga; 2. Unmarried fathers; 3. Graphic novels
978-0-7595-3122-2, $12.99

Courtesy of Yen Press

Thirty-year-old bachelor Daikichi is a salaryman, a junior executive, living on his own in Tokyo. When he goes home for his grandfather's funeral, he discovers that his grandfather had a younger lover who left him with a little girl, Rin (which makes her his aunt). The lover is nowhere to be found, and none of Daikichi's relatives will have anything to do with Rin, who won't talk to anyone but sticks close to Daikichi, who closely resembles his grandfather. When no one will step forward to take care of the six-year-old, Daikichi impulsively decides he will. Once he brings Rin home, the reality of his new situation finally dawns on him; Daikichi is now a single father and has to provide care for Rin. There's one scene with Rin and Daikichi together in their furo bath (a very typical Japanese family scene), and a few panels with Rin and Daikichi in their underwear. In one chapter, Daikichi has to deal with Rin's night time bedwetting, and Rin is shown changing her clothes.

"This sweet-natured manga shows the joys, frustrations, and quirks of family life; and while it is aimed at teens, it would also be more than welcome in the hands of adult readers." Booklist

First published 2006 in Japan

★ **Bunny** drop, vol. 2. Yen Press 2010 206p. Illustration
Grades: 8 9 10 11 12 Adult **741.5; Fic**
1. Humorous graphic novels; 2. Single-parent families; 3. Graphic novels
978-0-7595-3119-2, $12.99

Courtesy of Yen Press

Thirty-year-old bachelor Daikichi Kawachi had impulsively decided to become the guardian of his dead grandfather's illegitimate child, six-year-old Rin, when all the other relatives refused to help her. The reality of the responsibilities he's taken on have hit, and he makes a risky job transfer in order to have more time for Rin. Now, he has to navigate the choices for school as he must enroll Rin in elementary school, and he continues to search for Rin's mother. Being a parent is not easy, and being a male single parent is even harder. And just how is he supposed to help when Rin says her classmates tell her she is not cute? Picture a bachelor trying to brush a little girl's hair into pigtails.

Urrea, Luis Alberto

★ **Mr.** Mendoza's paintbrush. Artwork by Christopher Cardinale; color masking and compositing, Anthony Cardinale; design, Anne M. Giangiulio. Cinco Puntos Press 2010 Un Illustration
Grades: 7 8 9 10 11 12 Adult **741.5; Fic**
1. Artists; 2. Humorous graphic novels; 3. Mexico; 4. Young adult literature — Works; 5. Graphic novels
978-1-933693-23-1, $17.95

LC 2008-11636

Rosario is a small town in the Sinaloa region of Mexico, nestled into a wet, green, mango-sweet subtropical landscape. There, Mr. Mendoza wields his paintbrush to write graffiti with a purpose. When Mr. Mendoza catches the young narrator and his best friend Jaime spying on the girls who are swimming, he strips them, writes graffiti all over their bodies, and chases the naked boys down the street through town. He also appoints himself as the town's conscience and angers the authorities with his graffiti on the town's whorehouse, bridge, and other places. Then, one day, he takes his paint and paintbrush to the center square and paints steps into the sky and walks up until he disappears. Women and girls are shown in their underwear, and the naked boys are shown only from the back. The talk of sex, the way the boys sneak peeks at the girls and one of the town's women, make this book suitable for teens even though the format resembles a picture book.

"Not only does the art perfectly capture the mood of the piece—from the blocky woodcuts to the muted earth tones—but it also reinforces the lucid dreamlike quality of its magical realism, serving as an enticing invitation to further explore the genre." Horn Book Guide

Van Lente, Fred

Destructive reentry. Fred Van Lente, writer ; James Cordeiro, penciler ; Gary Erskine, inker ; Martegod Gracia, colorist ; Dave Sharpe, letterer ; Skottie Young, cover. ABDO/Spotlight 2009 Un Illustration
Grades: 4 5 6 7 8 9 **741.5; Fic**
1. Iron Man (Fictional character); 2. Superhero graphic novels; 3. Graphic novels
978-1-59961-589-9, $21.35

LC 2008-33395

Iron Man heads out to space in an attempt to prevent the Stark International lab station Delphi-1 from falling out of orbit and crashing onto Earth. When he arrives, he finds big trouble: Living Laser has taken control of the lab and is forcing the scientists to use the nanotechnology there to build him a new body. His battle with Iron Man interrupts the process, and instead of a new body for Living Laser, a new entity of ever-regenerating nanobots with LL's paranoia comes to life. Now Iron Man and Living Laser must team up to stop the entity and save Earth.

This Spotlight edition reprints the comic originally published by Marvel as part of its Marvel Age imprint, without all the advertisements. This is part of the Iron Man Set II.

Ghost of a chance. Fred Van Lente, writer ; Graham Nolan, penciler ; Victor Olazaba, inker ; Martegod Gracia, colorist ; Dave Sharpe, letterer ; Skottie Young, cover. ABDO/Spotlight 2009 Un Illustration
Grades: 4 5 6 7 8 9 **741.5; Fic**
1. Iron Man (Fictional character); 2. Superhero graphic novels; 3. Graphic novels
978-1-59961-590-5, $21.35

LC 2008-33396

Dr. Doom captures Stark International executives, including Rhodey and Pepper, claiming they invaded Latverian air space while they were flying to a mountain chalet for a conference. Stark, who had stayed behind to work on a new invention, uses his untried stealth armor to infiltrate Doom's fortress and rescue his people.

This Spotlight edition reprints the comic originally published by Marvel as part of its Marvel Age imprint, without all the advertisements. This is part of the Iron Man Set II.

Howtoons; Volume 1: (re)ignition. Writer: Fred Van Lente; artist: Tom Fowler; colors: Jordie Bellaire; letters: Rus Wooton. Image Comics 2015 160 p. Illustration; Color
Grades: 5 6 7 8   **741.5**
1. Science — Experiments; 2. Science fiction graphic novels; 3. Siblings
9781632150561, $9.99; 1632150565
In this graphic novel by Fred Van Lente and illustrated by Tom Fowler, "Celine and Tuck's parents put them to sleep for centuries to ride out the energy crisis—but when they awake in the far future and Mom and Dad are missing, it's the kids who have to save the day! Celine and Tuck must explore a strange, new Earth using their gadgeteering skills to create projects and experiments to survive hostile tribes and bizarre mechanized threats." (Publisher's note)
"Step-by-step instructions and warnings for each device are included. The materials needed for each project varies. Each example features icons denoting what kind of energy this project represents. An icon glossary provides further explanation." SLJ

Marvel Adventures: Fantastic Four: Monsters & Mysteries. Art by Clay Mann. Marvel Entertainment 2007 Un Illustration
Grades: 3 4 5 6 7 8 9   **741.5; Fic**
1. Fantastic Four (Fictional characters); 2. Superhero graphic novels; 3. Graphic novels
978-0-7851-2380-4, $6.99
Mr. Fantastic, the Invisible Woman, the Human Torch, and the Thing go for a wild ride adventures and encounter the Mole Man, the Skrulls, Rama-Tut, and the Sub-Mariner.

Pirated!. Fred Van Lente, writer ; Rafa Sandoval, penciler ; Roger Bonet, inker ; Martegod Gracia, colorist ; Dave Sharpe, letterer ; Skottie Young, cover. ABDO/Spotlight 2009 Un Illustration
Grades: 4 5 6 7 8 9   **741.5; Fic**
1. Iron Man (Fictional character); 2. Superhero graphic novels; 3. Graphic novels
978-1-59961-591-2, $21.35
                                              LC 2008-33397
While using his deep-sea armor to investigate shipwrecks, Stark stumbles upon the hideout of modern pirates, led by the man who calls himself Commander Kraken. They specialize in stealing technology and strip the armor from Stark; they plan to attack Hydrobase, where Kraken used to work as a scientist before he was accused of stealing his own technological secrets. Unarmed, shot out of Kraken's submarine through its torpedo tube, Stark must find a way to survive and get his armor back.
This Spotlight edition reprints the comic originally published by Marvel as part of its Marvel Age imprint, without all the advertisements. This is part of the Iron Man Set II.

The **simple** life. Fred Van Lente, writer ; Rafa Sandoval, penciler ; Roger Bonet, inker ; Ulises Arreola, colorist ; Dave Sharpe, letterer ; Skottie Young, cover. ABDO/Spotlight 2009 Un Illustration
Grades: 4 5 6 7 8 9   **741.5; Fic**

1. Iron Man (Fictional character); 2. Superhero graphic novels; 3. Graphic novels
978-1-59961-592-9, $21.35
                                              LC 2008-33398
Flying over the Alleghenies to a meeting, Stark finds himself under attack by a superpowered assassin; she shorts out his suit's power but can't finish him off when a jetliner interrupts the fight. Iron Man crash lands near a remote settlement where the people have given up on modern technology to live in peace. However, one of the women there used to work in a Stark International factory and harbors great bitterness toward Stark for closing the factory. When the assassin returns to finish him off, how will he fight her off without armor and without harming the people who saved his life?
This Spotlight edition reprints the comic originally published by Marvel as part of its Marvel Age imprint, without all the advertisements. This is part of the Iron Man Set II.

Spider-man: fashion victims. Fred Van Lente, writer ; Michael O'Hare, pencils ; Cory Hamscher, inks ; GURU eFX, colors ; Scherberger, Paris and GURU eFX, cover ; Dave Sharpe, letterer. ABDO Publishing Company/Spotlight 2008 Un Illustration
Grades: 4 5 6 7 8 9   **741.5; Fic**
1. Spider-Man (Fictional character); 2. Superhero graphic novels; 3. Graphic novels
978-1-59961-395-6, $21.35
                                              LC 2007-20239
When Spider-Man suddenly finds himself battling newbie villains in high-tech suits marked with a "T" he knows he's got to find the source who is supplying them with the means to commit crimes. But when he finds the Tinkerer, how will he be able to stop him? This is a revised, hardbound edition of the Marvel Adventures Spider-Man comic book issue #21.
Part of the Spider-Man Set III

Van Meter, Jen
Hopeless Savages. Art by Christine Norrie and Chynna Clugston-Major. Oni Press 2002 128p. Illustration
Grades: 7 8 9 10 11 12 Adult   **741.5; Fic**
1. Family; 2. Humorous graphic novels; 3. Rock music; 4. Graphic novels
1-929998-24-4, $13.95
Family ties are the earliest ties that bind, setting the tone for the paths we will take in our future. So what if your father is Dirk Hopeless and your mother Nikki Savage, a superstar couple from the days of punk rock? When you're born a rebel, what can you possibly do to make yourself stand apart? For Rat Hopeless-Savage, the answer is to leave home and become a normal citizen with a nine-to-five job.

Hopeless Savages Vol. 2: Ground Zero. Art by Christine Norrie, Chynna Clugston-Major, Andi Watson, and Bryan Lee O'Malley. Oni Press 2004 128p. Illustration
Grades: 7 8 9 10 11 12 Adult   **741.5; Fic**
1. Family; 2. Humorous graphic novels; 3. Rock music; 4. Romance graphic novels; 5. Graphic novels
1-929998-99-6, $11.95
When you're sixteen, the world is a different place. When you're Zero Hopeless-Savage, the youngest daughter

of rock stars Dirk Hopeless and Nikki Savage, the world is practically unrecognizable. Imagine you're in the midst of high school, you have your first band, and WHAMMO! Some boy comes along who doesn't think you're a total freak, and you think he's pretty swell, too. But before you can do anything about it, there's a TV crew outside your house that wants to chronicle the gossip and scandals of your parents' careers, and a massive misunderstanding has gotten you grounded. How's a self-respecting young lady supposed to handle all that?

Hopeless Savages Vol. 3: Too Much Hopeless. Art, Christine Norrie and Ross Campbell. Oni Press 2004 Un Illustration
Grades: 7 8 9 10 11 12 Adult   **741.5; Fic**
1. Family; 2. Humorous graphic novels; 3. Martial arts; 4. Romance graphic novels; 5. Graphic novels
1-929998-85-6, $11.95
This was supposed to be a leisurely vacation. Arsenal Hopeless-Savage has a rematch with an old high school rival in a kung-fu tournament in Hong Kong. She and her brother Twitch figured they could turn it into a nice jaunt with their boyfriends to meet their aging grandmother, a renowned Chinese fortune teller. Too bad Grandma Shi didn't phone ahead to tell them that it was going to be the trip from Hell. It begins at the airport when a shady character slips something into Arsenal's bag, putting the quartet on the radar of the local bad guys, the British secret service, and the Hong Kong police. It becomes even more complicated when the rest of the Hopeless-Savage clan decides to join the middle children in Asia, getting caught up in the international intrigue themselves. Arsenal is the only person that can get them all out of the jam they're in, and for her it's all too much. Twitch's gay relationship is treated matter-of-factly.

Vance, Steve
★ **Bad** girls. Steve Vance, writer ; Jennifer Graves, Christine Norrie, pencillers ; Jennifer Graves, J. Bone, Daniel Krall, inkers ; Kurt Hathaway, letterer. DC Comics 2009 128p. Illustration
Grades: 8 9 10 11 12   **741.5; Fic**
1. Humorous graphic novels; 2. Schools; 3. Superhero graphic novels; 4. Graphic novels
978-1-4012-2359-5, $14.99
Lauren's first day at San Narciso High becomes a disaster when she collides with the school's uber-nerd Ronald and gets on the wrong side of the school's queen bee cheerleaders led by Tiffany. Things only get worse as the days go by, then Lauren unknowingly helps to create even more trouble when Tiffany, Brittany, Ashley, and Destinee all drink from Ronald's thermos that Lauren had been holding. That thermos held Ronald's secret science project, a potion that gives the drinker super powers. Oh, and all that stuff about "with great power comes great responsibility?" Pfftt! These girls decide to have their own kind of fun at the expense of everyone else. So how is Lauren supposed to stop them? Ronald decides to give her a dose of his potion, and now suddenly she can read minds. How is that supposed to help? Meanwhile, a couple of sinister government agents come to town, and the science teacher wants to find out just what Ronald has been doing ...

Vanholme, Virginie
Scared to death, bk 1: the vampire from the Marshes. Illustrated by Mauricet. Cinebook 2008 48p. Illustration
Grades: 5 6 7 8 9   **741.5; Fic**
1. Horror graphic novels; 2. Mystery graphic novels; 3. Vampires; 4. Graphic novels
978-1-905460-47-2, $11.95
Young teen friends Robin and Max sneak a look into Robin's father's files. He's a forensic scientist who gets called in to investigate mysterious deaths. They read the file on the death of a man who was found in the rushes in the local park, full of little holes all over his body. Max believes the man was killed by vampires, and the two boys go to the library to do research, camp out in Robin's yard but nothing seems to happen except that they interrupt the work of a poacher. However, there are vampires out there, and now they're watching Robin and Max. There's just enough spookiness and blood for upper elementary and middle school age readers who want some horror without being grossed out by excessive gore.
Part of the Scared to Death series, originally published in France as Mort de Trouille Le vampire des marais.

Vankin, Deborah
Poseurs. [written by Deborah Vankin; illustrated by Rick Mays; lettering by Robert Clark, Jr., Clem Robins and Drew Gill].. Image Comics 2011 149p. Illustration
Grades: 8 9 10 11 12   **741.5; Fic**
1. Friendship; 2. Kidnapping; 3. Mystery graphic novels; 4. Graphic novels
978-1-60706-358-2, $16.99
Jenna's friendship with Mac, a busboy, and Pouri, a Taiwanese partygoer, is tested when Pouri suggests that Jenna and Mac help her stage her own kidnapping in order to avoid flunking out of school and being sent back to Taiwan. This book was originally meant to be part of DC Comics' Minx line; Mays' black and white art looks clear and spare in the larger size pages of this Image Comics publication. One page shows a nude young woman whose naughty parts are covered by sushi, and on another page, Pouri throws a drink into a man's lap; other than these, there's no overt violence, no bad language (just a lot of Mac-isms), and the one time Jenna and Mac are in bed together, they are fully clothed. The cover copy states "Gossip Girl meets Bret Easton Ellis for the comic book crowd," but the book stays teen friendly throughout.

Varon, Sara
Robot dreams. First Second 2007 205p. Illustration
Grades: 3 4 5 6 7 8 9 10 11 12 Adult   **741; 741.5; Fic**
1. Dogs; 2. Robots; 3. Graphic novels
978-1-59643-108-9 (pa), $16.95; 1-59643-108-3 (pa)
                                           LC 2006-52640
The friendship between a dog and a robot is portrayed in this wordless graphic novel. (Bull Cent Child Books)
"Varon's drawing style is uncomplicated, and her colors are clean and refeshing. Although her story seems equally simple, it is invested with true emotion." Booklist

Sweaterweather. Alternative Comics 2006 96p. Illustration
Grades: 3 4 5 6 7 8 9   **741.5; Fic**

1. Animals; 2. Friendship; 3. Stories without words; 4. Graphic novels

1-891867-93-8, $14.95

A turtle, a rabbit, and other creatures venture out on a wordless snowy journey full of friendship and sweetness. Varon includes interactive bits to the book, such as paper dolls, postcards, and stamps.

First published 2003

Vaughan, Brian K.

Buffy the Vampire Slayer season eight volume 2: No future for you. Writers, Brian K. Vaughan and Joss Whedon ; art by Georges Jeanty. Dark Horse Comics 2008 Un Illustration

Grades: 8 9 10 11 12 Adult   **741.5; Fic**
1. Buffy the Vampire Slayer (Fictional character); 2. Fantasy graphic novels; 3. Horror graphic novels; 4. Graphic novels

978-1-59307-963-5, $15.95

While Buffy is busy trying to uncover just who or what "Twilight" is, Giles recruits Faith to carry out an undercover mission. A Slayer in Great Britain has gone rogue, and she must be stopped. Since she's the daughter of a Peer, Faith has to make like Eliza Doolittle and learn how to become a "lady" in order to infiltrate into the upper crust world to carry out her mission. It's only when she's in the middle of the job that she learns this rogue Slayer is messing around with evil magic and wants to slay Buffy. The book includes brief partial nudity and some violence.

Runaways Vol. 2: Teenage Wasteland. Pencils, Adrian Alphona and Takeshi Miyazawa. Marvel Entertainment 2004 Un Illustration

Grades: 8 9 10 11 12   **741.5; Fic**
1. Adventure graphic novels; 2. Runaways (Fictional characters); 3. Superhero graphic novels; 4. Graphic novels

0-7851-1415-7, $7.99

Still on the run from their super-villain parents, the motley crew of super-powered kids finds a kindred spirit in a daring young stranger and welcomes him into their fold. But will this dashing young man help the teens defeat their villainous parents, or tear them apart. Then Marvel's original teen runaway crime fighters, Cloak and Dagger, are sent to catch the runaways.

Runaways Vol. 3: The Good Die Young. Writer, Brian K. Vaughan ; penciler, Adrian Alphona ; inks, Craig Yeung ; colors, UDON's Christina Strain. Marvel Entertainment 2005 Un Illustration

Grades: 8 9 10 11 12   **741.5; Fic**
1. Adventure graphic novels; 2. Runaways (Fictional characters); 3. Superhero graphic novels; 4. Graphic novels

0-7851-1684-2, $7.99

The world as people know it is about to end and the Runaways are the only hope to prevent it. But if the fledgling teenage heroes are going to succeed, they may have to become just as evil as their villainous parents. The Runaways have learned how their parents' criminal organization began, and now they must decide how it should end. As the Runaways' epic battle against their evil parents reaches its shocking conclusion, the team's mole stands

revealed, and blood must be shed. Which kids will still be standing when the smoke finally clears?

Runaways Vol. 4: True Believers. Writer, Brian K. Vaughan ; penciler, Adrian Alphona ; inker, Craig Yeung ; colorist, UDON's Christina Strain ; letterer, Virtual Calligraphy's Randy Gentile & Dave Sharpe. Marvel Entertainment 2005 Un Illustration

Grades: 8 9 10 11 12   **741.5; Fic**
1. Adventure graphic novels; 2. Runaways (Fictional characters); 3. Superhero graphic novels; 4. Graphic novels

0-7851-1705-9, $7.99

Now that the evil Pride is gone, nearly every bad guy in the Marvel Universe is trying to fill the power vacuum in Los Angeles, and the Runaways are the only heroes who can stop them. Plus: What does a mysterious new team of young heroes want with the Runaways, and which fan-favorite Marvel characters are part of this group?

Runaways Vol. 5: Escape to New York. Writer, Brian K. Vaughan ; penciler, Adrian Alphona ; inks, Craig Yeung ; colors, UDON's Christina Strain. Marvel Entertainment 2006 Un Illustration

Grades: 8 9 10 11 12   **741.5; Fic**
1. Adventure graphic novels; 2. Runaways (Fictional characters); 3. Superhero graphic novels; 4. Graphic novels

0-7851-1901-9, $7.99

When a dangerous alien invades Los Angeles, the Runaways' own Karolina Dean may be the only hero in the Marvel Universe who can stop him ... but at what cost" Then, the Runaways embark on a coast-to-coast adventure. When Clock is accused of a crime he didn't commit, the vigilante is forced to turn to the teenage Runaways for help. They go on a road trip to New York City. Meanwhile, back in LA, someone is tracking the teens, and it can't be good.

Runaways Vol. 6: Parental Guidance. Writer, Brian K. Vaughan ; penciler, Adrian Alphona ; inker, Craig Yeung. Marvel Entertainment 2006 Un Illustration

Grades: 8 9 10 11 12   **741.5; Fic**
1. Adventure graphic novels; 2. Runaways (Fictional characters); 3. Superhero graphic novels; 4. Graphic novels

0-7851-1952-3, $7.99

The Pride is back as an all-new group, and they have it in for the Runaways. And when Molly is separated from her teammates, she must survive a night alone on the mean streets of Los Angeles. The eleven-year-old mutant girl soon hooks up with a new group of runaways, but is their mysterious leader a hero or a villain" In this volume, a member of the team dies.

Runaways Vol. 7: Live Fast. Brian K. Vaughan, writer ; Adrian Alphona, Mike Norton, pencilers. Marvel Entertainment 2007 Un Illustration

Grades: 8 9 10 11 12   **741.5; Fic**
1. Adventure graphic novels; 2. Runaways (Fictional characters); 3. Superhero graphic novels; 4. Graphic novels

978-0-7851-2267-8, $7.99

The Runaways say good-bye to the past, and make hard decisions about their future. Plus: Still reeling from the events of Young Avengers/Runaways (part of Marvel's Civil War), the teenage heroes must now confront a horrific enemy who threatens to tear the team apart.

★ **Runaways,** Vol. 1: Pride & Joy. Writer, Brian K. Vaughan ; pencils, Adrian Alphona ; inks, David Newbold and Craig Yeung ; colors, Brian Reber. Marvel Entertainment 2004 Un Illustration
Grades: 7 8 9 10 11 12   **741.5; Fic**
1. Runaways (Fictional characters); 2. Science fiction graphic novels; 3. Superhero graphic novels; 4. Graphic novels
0-7851-1379-7, $7.99

All young people believe their parents are evil ... but what if they really are? Meet Alex, Karolina, Gert, Chase, Molly and Nico - whose lives are about to take an unexpected turn. When these six young friends discover their parents are all secretly super-powered villains, the shocked teens find strength in one another. Together, they run away from home and straight into the adventure of their lives - vowing to turn the tables on their evil legacy. This is the first volume of an ongoing series.

Originally published as Runaways issues #1-6. Other Runaways volumes are: 2: Teenage Wasteland; 3: The Good Die Young; 4: True Believers; 5: Escape to New York; 6: Parental Guidance; 7: Live Fast; 8: Dead End Kids; 9: Dead Wrong; 10: Rock Zombies; 11: Homeschooling

Venditti, Robert
Blue Bloods: the graphic novel. By Melissa de la Cruz; adapted by Robert Venditti; art by Alina Urusov; illustrations by Disney Enterprises, Inc.. Hyperion 2013 112 p. Color illustration
Grades: 8 9 10 11 12   **741.5/973; Fic**
1. New York (NY) — Fiction; 2. Secrets — Fiction; 3. Supernatural graphic novels; 4. Teenagers; 5. Vampires — Fiction; 6. Wealth — Fiction; 7. Graphic novels
9781423134466, $19.99; 9781423134473, $11.99; 142313446X
                                LC 2011053237

In this graphic novel, written by Melissa de la Cruz, adapted by Robert Venditti, and illustrated by Alina Urusov, the focus is on a group of New York teenagers. "Schuyler Van Alen is a loner, and happy that way. But when she turns fifteen, her life dramatically changes. A mosaic of blue veins appears on her arms, and she begins to have memories of another time and place. When a classmate is found dead at a night club, the mystery deepens." (Publisher's note)

The **lost** hero: the graphic novel. By Rick Riordan; adapted by Robert Venditti; art by Nate Powell; color by Orpheus Collar; lettering by Chris Dickey. Disney-Hyperion Books 2014 192 p. Color; Illustration
Grades: 4 5 6 7 8   **741.5**
1. Camps — Fiction; 2. Gaia (Greek deity) — Fiction; 3. Greek mythology; 4. Hera (Greek deity) — Fiction; 5. Monsters — Fiction; 6. Mythology, Greek — Fiction; 7. Riordan, Rick Lost hero — Adaptations; 8. Graphic novels
142316279X; 9781423162797, $21.99; 9781423163251
                                LC 2013013559

"Jason has a problem. He doesn't remember anything before waking up on a school bus holding hands with a girl. Apparently she's his girlfriend Piper, his best friend is a kid named Leo, and they're all students in the Wilderness School, a boarding school for 'bad kids.' What he did to end up here, Jason has no idea—except that everything seems very wrong." (Publisher's note)

"Powell does an excellent job of adapting the original story into pictorial format, hitting all of the high points and representing all of the major details in the drawings, so little is lost." SLJ

The **sea** of monsters: the graphic novel. By Rick Riordan; adapted by Robert Venditti; art by Attila Futaki; colors by Tamas Gaspar; lettering by Chris Dickey. Disney-Hyperion Books 2013 128 p. Color illustration (Percy Jackson & the Olympians)
Grades: 5 6 7 8 9 10   **741.5; Fic**
1. Fathers and sons — Fiction; 2. Greek mythology; 3. Monsters — Fiction; 4. Poseidon (Greek deity) — Fiction; 5. Graphic novels
1423145291; 9781423145295, $19.99; 9781423145509
                                LC 2011012356

In this graphic novel, by Rick Riordan, adapted by Robert Venditti, and illustrated by Attila Futaki and Tamas Gaspar, "when an innocent game of dodgeball among Percy and his classmates turns into a death match against an ugly gang of cannibal giants, things get...well, ugly. And the unexpected arrival of his friend Annabeth brings more bad news: the magical borders that protect Camp Half-Blood have been poisoned by a mysterious enemy, and unless a cure is found, the only safe haven for demigods will be destroyed." (Publisher's note)

"This is a good summary presentation of the original novel, with active and effective art." Lib Med Con

Verne, Jules, 1828-1905
Around the world in 80 days. Adapted by Chrys Millien ; illustrated by Flo Demolis. IDW Publishing 2009 60p. Illustration
Grades: 5 6 7 8 9   **741.5; Fic**
1. Adventure graphic novels; 2. Verne, Jules, 1828-1905 — Adaptations; 3. Graphic novels
978-1-60010-394-0, $14.99

This graphic novel Verne's globe-trotting adventures of Phileas Fogg, English gentleman, his newly-hired French manservant, Passepartout, and the English detective, Fix, who pursues Fogg, convinced he is a master bank robber. Fogg makes a bet with fellow members of the Reform Club in 1872 that he can travel around the world in eighty days, but his precipitous departure makes Scotland Yard suspect him. The three men travel through India, where Fogg saves a beautiful young Indian woman from being burned alive, to Hong Kong, then Japan and then across the United States and onward. This adaptation was originally published in France. The book includes biographical information about Verne, historical information about what the world was like in the 1870s, and an analysis of the novel.

Journey to the Center of the Earth. Retold by Davis Worth Miller and Katherine McLean Brevard ; illustrated by Greg Rebis. Stone Arch Books 2007 72p. Illustration
Grades: 3 4 5 6 7 8 9   **741.5; Fic**

1. Adventure graphic novels; 2. Science fiction graphic novels; 3. Graphic novels

978-1-59889-832-3, $23.93

LC 2007-6202

Axel Lidenbrock and his uncle find a mysterious message inside the 300-year-old book. The dusty note describes a secret passageway to the center of the earth, and Axel reluctantly joins his uncle on a quest. Soon they are descending deeper and deeper into the heart of a volcano. With their guide, Hans, the men discover underground rivers, oceans, strange rock formations, and prehistoric monsters. They also run into danger, which threatens to trap them below the surface forever. The book is written with an easy vocabulary for reluctant and struggling readers, and it includes facts about the real center of the Earth.

Part of the Graphic Revolve series.

Vining, James

First in Space. Oni Press 2007 Un Illustration

Grades: 3 4 5 6 7 8   **629.4; 741.5; 616**

1. Animal experimentation; 2. Space flight; 3. Graphic novels

978-1-932664-64-5, $9.95

Vining received a 2006 Xeric Grant to help him complete and publish his book.

This book tells young readers about the early years of the U.S. space program, in the late 1950s and early 1960s. After the Russians successfully sent the dog, Laika, into space in the Sputnik 2 in 1957, the U.S. successfully sent two monkeys into suborbital space and back in 1959. In 1960, NASA began training young chimpanzees to complete certain tasks; young enlisted men under Sergeant Ed Dittmer took care of the chimpanzees, one chimp per man. In 1961, one of the chimpanzees, nicknamed Ham by his young handler, Beach, became the first chimp in space when NASA sent him up in the Mercury MR-2 rocket. Vining researched this extensively, and he provides a bibliography; but for the book, he focuses on the personal interactions between Beach and Ham and on the training that Ham and the other chimpanzees went through.

Vitaliano, Fausto

Donald Duck and friends: double duck. Written by Fausto Vitaliano & Marco Bosco ; art by Alessandro Freccero ... [et al.]. Boom! Kids 2010 Un Illustration

Grades: 3 4 5 6 7 8   **741.5; Fic**

1. Adventure graphic novels; 2. Donald Duck (Fictional character); 3. Humorous graphic novels; 4. Graphic novels

978-1-60886-551-2, $24.99

Donald Duck is having a difficult time: his relationship with Daisy is rocky due to his tendency to fall asleep during romantic movies, and he's engaged in a feud with a city employee over a parking ticket. Things take a turn for the weird when a beautiful duck who calls herself Kay K tells Donald he is also Double D, a secret agent; something he just can't remember. The Agency needs him to steal a suitcase, but won't tell him why. When it all goes wrong, Kay K bails Donald out of jail, and now he knows the suitcase contains information on all the Agency's agents. He's got to get it back, or everyone will be in danger. The book includes lots

of action and comedy, but no graphic violence. The comics in this book were originally published in Italy.

Vollmar, Rob

The castaways. Illustrated by Pablo G. Callejo. NBM/ComicsLit 2007 64p. Illustration

Grades: 6 7 8 9 10 11 12   **741.5; Fic**

1. United States — History — 1919-1933; 2. Graphic novels

978-1-56163-492-7, $17.95

"Afraid that he's just a burden on his family, 13-year-old Tucker Freeman lets himself be driven away from home and jumps on a freight train heading west. His inexperience makes him vulnerable to all the angry, desperate people looking for any way they can survive during America's economic collapse, but fortunately he's taken under the wing of Elijah Hopkins, an elderly colored man who introduces him to the cooperative hobo subculture. . . . Vollmer's script, based on family reminiscences, rings true; his dialogue has the vocabulary and the rhythms of real people talking. . . . Callejo's art creates a solid setting in which Tucker's experience can reveal squalor or grace." Publ Wkly

An expanded and newly illustrated edition of the title first published 2002 by Absence of Ink Comic Press

Wagahara, Satoshi

The devil is a part-timer!; Volume One. Satoshi Wagahara; illustrated by Akio Hiiragi. Yen Press 2015 176 p.

Grades: 7 8 9 10 11 12

1. Demonology — Fiction; 2. Devil — Fiction; 3. Fantasy; 4. Fast food restaurants — Fiction; 5. Manga

9780316383134; 0316383139 $13

LC 2015028390

"This comical tale of a demon-lord-turned-fry-slinger follows the daily travails of (former) Devil King Sadao Maou and his general Shiro Ashiya as they navigate the complexities of life in modern-day Tokyo. Having suffered utter defeat at the hands of a plucky hero, they've been banished to earth and stripped of magical power. And if that wasn't enough, that pesky hero is still hell bent on finishing the job. Artist Akio Hiiragi brings Satoshi Wagahara's story to hilarious life in this manga adaptation of the hit light novel series." (Publisher's note)

Volume 1 of an ongoing series

Wagner, Josh

Sky pirates of Neo Terra. Art by Camilla D'Errico. Image Comics 2010 Un Illustration

Grades: 7 8 9 10 11 12   **741.5; Fic**

1. Adventure graphic novels; 2. Fantasy graphic novels; 3. Science fiction graphic novels; 4. Graphic novels

978-1-60706-324-7, $17.99

The world of Neo Terra blends forgotten technology with natural magic, and glide-wing racing is its major sport. Reckless young glide-wing pilot Billy Boom Boom wants to help his friend Ricket, a young master mechanic whose father was taken by the Pirate King. Sky Pirates have been trying to take over everything, including the glide-wing races. After a race that Billy wins, a huge monstrous creature crashes in among the spectators, but he's actually got word of Ricket's father; Wurl tells the young racers that Ricket's father is on the Forgotten Isle, captive of the Pirate King and the Witch Queen. Billy and his main rival, Rena, set out on their glide-wings to rescue Ricket's father. However, the Witch Queen has her own plans; she's using the master mechanic to improve "Mother," a machine that finds a person's Dark Side and magnifies it to overcome one's better nature. And Mother has corrupted Ricket's father. This book is based on the video game co-created by D'Errico and Sean Megaw, Tyler Sigman, and Jeff Simpson. D'Errico's manga-influenced art blazes with brightly saturated colors in this story of adventure that also explores the meaning of heroism and of friendships. There is some violent action, but nothing excessive for most younger teens.

Waid, Mark
The **Incredibles**: revenge from below. Boom! Kids 2010 Un Illustration
Grades: 3 4 5 6 7   **741.5; Fic**
  1. Adventure graphic novels; 2. Incredibles (Fictional characters); 3. Superhero graphic novels; 4. Graphic novels
  978-1-60886-518-5, $9.99
    When the Incredibles encounter villainess Mesmerella, speedy Dash's impetuous actions endanger his sister Violet, so his parents ground him by taking away his powers. In his forcibly normal state (for regular folks, anyway), Dash feels sluggish and helpless; then he witnesses a couple of his teachers display alien tentacles. However, no one will believe him, so how can he get anyone to help him?" This original story based on the popular movie characters will attract young readers, especially boys who will enjoy the focus on Dash. There is some action, and Dash does punch the villainess, although readers won't see Dash, just the result of the punches as Mesmerella reels from them.

Legion of Super-Heroes Vol. 1: Teenage Revolution. Mark Waid, writer ; Barry Kitson, penciller. DC Comics 2005 Un Illustration
Grades: 8 9 10 11 12 Adult   **741.5; Fic**
  1. Science fiction graphic novels; 2. Superhero graphic novels; 3. Graphic novels
  1-4012-0482-1, $14.99
    Poverty, famine, war, and disease have been eliminated in the early days of the 31st century. The Dawning Millenium is utopian: shining, optimistic, hopeful ... and deadly dull. Dull, that is, until a team of bright, defiant, super-powered teenagers from different worlds assemble. The come together as activists and fierce dreamers, crusading to make a difference in a society that has forgotten how to change. Cosmic Boy, Lightning Lad, Saturn Girl, and the rest of the Legion of Super-Heroes fight for freedom and justice while learning from, and learning to tolerate, one another.

Walker, Landry Q.
Little Gloomy: . . . It was a dark and stormy night. [by] Landry Q. Walker and Eric Jones. Slave Labor Graphics 2002 128p. Illustration
Grades: 4 5 6 7   **741.5; Fic**
  1. Fantasy graphic novels; 2. Humorous graphic novels; 3. Graphic novels
  0-943151-64-3, $12.95

In Frightsylvania, Little Gloomy is the only normal girl in a world of monsters, but that's not her problem. Mad scientist Simon, her ex-boyfriend, is her problem; he's decided to send an army of zombies against her to get revenge. Can Gloomy and her friends Larry the werewolf, Frank the lovesick monster (he's got a crush on Gloomy), and Carl Cthulhu the interdimensional octopoid demigod survive the onslaught of the undead?" The monsters are all drawn to look so cute, it's hard to imagine anyone really getting scared by reading this book.

The **super** scary monster show, featuring Little Gloomy. Written by Landry Walker; drawn by Eric Jones; tones by Rikki Simons. Amaze Ink/SLG Publishing 2008 Un Illustration
Grades: 3 4 5 6 7 8 9   **741.5; Fic**
  1. Horror graphic novels; 2. Humorous graphic novels; 3. Graphic novels
  978-1-59362-103-2, $9.95; 1-59362-103-5
    This book collects the three issues (so far) of The Super Scary Monster Show comics. Little Gloomy, her friends, and her enemies, live in the world called Frightsylvania. Gloomy deals with an alien who crashlands in her backyard and wants to take over the world (she has plenty of "pet" monsters in her house who take care of her problem). Carl the squid lies to his parents about taking over the world and enslaving all its creatures, then they come for a visit. . . . Gloomy buys a golden scorpion as a gift for her friend the Mummy, but it turns out to be cursed, and everyone around her suffers accidents. The witch Evey has come up with a new spell to torment Gloomy, but it hits werewolf buddy Larry instead and shrinks him. There are plenty more stories, all written with tongue-in-cheek humor and just a touch of horror for younger readers. Gloomy does not suffer fools gladly, so the invading alien gets eaten (off page), and other inimical creatures suffer similar fates, so this book shouldn't be given to younger readers who are sensitive and don't like any violence. There is little in the way of any gore or overt violence, except for poor Frank, whose body parts often come apart.

★ **Supergirl**: cosmic adventures in the 8th grade. DC Comics 2009 144p. Illustration
Grades: 3 4 5 6 7 8   **741.5; Fic**
  1. Humorous graphic novels; 2. School life; 3. Superhero graphic novels; 4. Graphic novels
  978-1-4012-2506-3, $12.99
    Kara Zor-El is just an average Kryptonian girl who arrives on Earth sort of accidentally when she has an argument with her mother. Here she discovers she has super powers, just like her cousin, Superman. He tells her she can't just go home, so now she's stuck living on Earth, going to middle school, and her powers can't prevent her from being the new kid in school. She makes one friend, but Lena happens to be related to Superman's nemesis Lex Luthor; then she manages to create a mirror-image self who is evil. On top of that, weird things keep happening at school. Kara may be Supergirl, but can she survive 8th grade?

Wallace, Karen
Yikes, it's a yeti!. By Karen Wallace; illustrated by Mick Reid.. Stone Arch Books 2008 72p. Illustration
Grades: 3 4 5 6 7   **741.5; Fic**

1. Adventure graphic novels; 2. Humorous graphic novels; 3. Yeti; 4. Graphic novels

978-1-4342-0459-2, $21.26

LC 2007-30742

Norman leads a very boring life, unlike neighbor and friend Scott, who always seems to be doing something exciting. Going camping with his granny during his vacation sounds like more of the same boring stuff. However, once they hit the road, Norman's Grandma pulls off her gray wig, strips off her old-lady dress to show her cool biking leathers, and takes Norman on a trip to the Himalayas. They're off to find a yeti. Now Norman knows he's on the vacation of a lifetime, with lots of fun and excitement (and yak burgers).

Part of the Graphic Trax series; originally published in Great Britain in 2001.

Walsh, David

Shugo chara!, v1-v6. Peach-Pit; translated by June Kato; adapted by David Walsh; lettered by North Market Street Graphics. Del Rey/Ballantine Books 2007 Illustration

Grades: 5 6 7 8 9   **741.5; Fic**

978-0-345-49745-1 (v1), $10.95

LC 2007296632

Volume 1 of 12

"Everybody at Seiyo Elementary thinks that stylish and super cool Amu has it all: But nobody knows the real Amu, a shy girl who wishes she had the courage to truly be herself. Changing Amu's life is going to take more than wishes and dreams—it's going to take a little magic! One morning, Amu finds a surprise in her bed: three strange little eggs. Each egg contains a Guardian Character, an angel-like being who can give her the power to be someone new." (Publisher's note)

Wang, Sean

Runners, Book 1: Bad Goods. Serve Man Press 2005 168p. Illustration

Grades: 8 9 10 11 12

741.5; Fic

1. Adventure graphic novels; 2. Science fiction graphic novels; 3. Graphic novels

0-9768517-0-9, $14.95

Courtesy of Serve Man Press

Reluctant smuggler Roka Nostaco and the crew of his ship, the Khoruysa Brimia, were just trying to complete a job for the mob, but they find themselves fighting space pirates, bounty hunters, and just about everyone in Oniaka City Station. And it's all over some cargo they retrieved from another ship, the Tique Amara. Or is it because of the mysterious young woman they found unconscious in the Amara's cargo hold? Wang has taken a chance by making almost all of his characters nonhumanoid aliens. This story is everything Star Wars should have been.

Watanabe, Yoshitomo

Beyond the Beyond Volume 1. Tokyopop 2006 194p. Illustration

Grades: 6 7 8 9 10 11 12   **741.5; Fic**

1. Adventure graphic novels; 2. Fantasy graphic novels; 3. Manga; 4. Graphic novels

1-59816-371-X, $9.99

Sixth-grader Futaba feels smothered by his older siblings' overprotective actions, so when Kiara literally falls from the sky and a mysterious, sinister warrior immediately comes to threaten her, Futaba decides to take action. Kiara then transports herself and Futaba to a magical realm, where she must find her master in order to join with him and become powerful; in the meantime, almost everyone hunts her, calling her the Amaranthine. The two encounter Lady Belbel, a powerful wizard who looks like a cute bunny, and a mysterious prince named Virid, who has a twin brother also named Virid.

Most of the time, the story feels like a children's fantasy, but every so often it's punctuated by violence that would bother younger readers. It combines shojo and shonen elements.

Watson, Andi

Clubbing. Written by Andi Watson ; illustrated by Josh Howard. DC Comics/Minx 2007 176p. Illustration

Grades: 7 8 9 10 11 12   **741.5**

1. Mystery graphic novels; 2. Teenagers; 3. Graphic novels

978-1-4012-0370-2, $9.99

Spoiled, rebellious Charlotte "Lottie" Brook lives in London, but her parents send her to Yorkshire to work at her grandparents' country club, and Lottie has to trade her trendy platform boots for Wellies to walk around the muck outside, and she has to learn all about golf clubs. But something's not quite right out there, and Lottie discovers the body of another employee. Along with Howard, the only other young person at the club, Lottie uncovers bizarre evidence and begins to suspect her own grandfather of murder. The book includes a short glossary of English slang.

Princess at midnight. Image Comics 2008 Un Illustration

Grades: 4 5 6 7 8 9 10   **741.5; Fic**

1. Fantasy graphic novels; 2. Princesses; 3. War; 4. Graphic novels

978-1-58240-928-3, $5.99; 1-58240-928-5

Holly Crescent and her twin brother Henry lead sheltered lives as home-schooled children by day; their parents don't want any harm to come to their children after they were born prematurely and their early lives were so worrisome. At night, however, Holly becomes Princess of Castle Waxing, where life is good until the Horrible Horde takes over one of her favorite picnic spots. All too soon, her nights are spent in warfare against the Horde, and her days in reading books on war strategy. And when she wins, she's not satisfied with winning, she must pursue more warfare against the Horde, even as her dragon Chancellor warns her of overspending and the consequences of war on her people.

Weigel, Jeff

Dragon Girl: The Secret Valley. Jeff Weigel. Andrews McMeel Pub 2014 192 p. Illustration

Grades: 2 3 4 5 6   **741.5; Fic**

1. Dragons — Fiction; 2. Orphans — Fiction

1449441831; 9781449441838, $9.99

LC 2013943302

"Eleven-year-old Alanna and her older brother Hamel are orphans and doing their best to take care of each other until one day Alanna stumbles upon a cave full of dragon eggs. When the eggs hatch with no mother dragon in sight, Alanna decides to take care of the babies herself, even creating a clever costume so that the babies think she, too, is a dragon." (Publisher's note)

"Weigel has created a compulsively likable heroine who seamlessly blends her strength and compassion. . . . With lovable dragons, flying ships and danger around every corner, this delightful fantasy doesn't disappoint." Kirkus

★ **Thunder** from the sea: adventure on board the HMS Defender. G. P. Putnam's Sons 2010 46p. Illustration
Grades: 3 4 5 6   **741.5; Fic**
1. Adventure graphic novels; 2. Europe — History — 1789-1815; 3. Great Britain — Royal Navy; 4. Naval art and science; 5. Graphic novels
978-0-399-25089-7, $17.99

LC 2009-32801

In 1805, during the Napoleonic Wars, twelve-year-old Jack Hoyton becomes a member of the crew of HMS Defender, a midsize ship in the British Royal Navy. The Defender patrols along a portion of the French coast to block French ships, but a major gun emplacement in Dumont hampers the ship's efforts. When some of the crew land to fill their barrels with fresh water, French gunmen fire upon them, killing an officer and wounding a crewman. The Captain assigns Jack to be part of the crew that will land and take the guns; when the men arrive, they find that there is no small village, but a major shipbuilding facility, and they're captured.

"Weigel's old-fashioned comics art shows lots of authentic details of eighteenth-century shipboard life, and there is some battle violence. . . . This picture-book-size graphic novel should find a ready audience of young adventure-loving readers." Booklist
Includes bibliographical references

Weing, Drew
Set to sea. Fantagraphics 2010 Un Illustration
Grades: 8 9 10 11 12   **Fic; 741; 741.5**
978-1-60699-368-2, $16.99; 1-60699-368-2
"The unnamed hero is a poet who writes overblown verse about the wonders of sea life, while trying to pay his bar bill with promises of book dedications. That attitude quickly changes when he's shanghaied aboard a clipper bound for Hong Kong." Publ Wkly

The author "has produced a beautiful gem here, with minimal dialogue, one jolting battle scene, and each small page owned by a single panel filled with art whose figures have a comfortable roundness dredged up from the cartoon landscapes of our childhood unconscious, even as the intensely crosshatched shadings suggest the darkness that sometimes traces the edges of our lives. . . . [This book] is playful, atmospheric, dark, wistful, and wise." Booklist

Weinstein, Lauren
Girl stories. By Lauren R. Weinstein. Henry Holt 2006 237p. Illustration
Grades: 7 8 9 10 11 12 Adult   **741.5; Fic**
1. Friendship; 2. Girls; 3. Humorous graphic novels; 4. Graphic novels
978-0-8050-7863-3, $16.95; 0-8050-7863-0

LC 2005-46205

"Smart, creative Lauren sheds her geeky rep in high school in Weinstein's collection of comic strips, which have to intimacy of a teen's diary. The color-washed sketches have an edgy quality." Booklist

Weir, Christina
Amazing Agent Luna Volume 1. Nunzio Defilippis and Christina Weir ; artist, Shiei. Seven Seas Entertainment 2005 184p. Illustration
Grades: 8 9 10 11 12 Adult   **741.5; Fic**
1. Adventure graphic novels; 2. Science fiction graphic novels
193316400X; 9781933164007, $10.99

This is the story of Luna, the perfect secret agent. A girl grown in a lab from the finest genetic material, she has been trained since her birth fifteen years ago to be the U.S. government's ultimate espionage weapon. But now she is given an assignment that will test her abilities to the utmost - high school. In order to uncover an evil plot, the government sends Luna to a prominent high school to pose as a student. But the one thing Luna has not been trained to handle is her own feelings. They are powerful and out of control, like your average teen, but without parents or the usual interaction with her peers to guide her. Putting her in high school is lighting the fuse on an emotional bomb of adolescent confusion, especially when she starts making friends, creating rivals, and having her first big crush on bad boy Jonah, the son of her arch-nemesis, Count Von Brucken.
Volume 1 of 11

Maria's Wedding. Nunzio Defilippis and Christina Weir ; art by Jose Garibaldi. Oni Press 2003 88p. Illustration
Grades: 8 9 10 11 12 Adult   **741.5; Fic**
1. Family; 2. Weddings; 3. Graphic novels
1-929998-57-0, $10.95

Few events exude as much joy, happiness, and hope as a wedding, and for the Pirellis these ceremonies mean even more. Pirelli weddings are about tradition and family as much as they're about the happy couple, or at least they used to be. When Joseph Pirelli married Matthew it rocked the clan to its knees. Now a year later, the tension and downright animosity between different factions of the family have turned Maria's special day into a powder keg. And poor Frankie, Joseph's outspoken brother, is holding the match. But while some fear the fuse being lit, others in the family are ready and secretly looking forward to the blow-up. Frankie, on the other hand, thinks his reputation for speaking his mind is undeserved. He just wants to see his favorite cousin get married and maybe rekindle his childhood romance with Maria's maid of honor, Brenna. Can Frankie balance the Pirellis expectations of him with his own or will the scales tip and bring the whole ceremony crashing down?

Weiser, Joey
Mermin book one: out of water. Joey Weiser; [edited by] Jill Beaton. Oni Press 2013 152 p. (Mermin)
Grades: 4 5 6   **741.5**

1. Mermaids and mermen — Fiction; 2. Science fiction comic books, strips, etc; 3. Graphic novels
1934964980; 9781934964989, $19.99

LC 2012953664

Author Joey Weiser presents a graphic novel about merpeople. "'MERMIN the MERMAN from MER!?' That's the question Pete and his friends ask after finding the fish-boy washed up on the beach! Mermin just escaped the undersea kingdome of Mer, and is ready to have some fun on dry land! But why would this aquatic kid be afraid to swim" Perhaps it has something to do with the fishy pursuers who have followed him from the depths below!" (Publisher's note)

Weissman, Steven

The **Kid** Firechief. Fantagraphics Books 2004 96p. Illustration

Grades: 4 5 6 7 8 9   **741.5; Fic**

1. Adventure graphic novels; 2. Fire fighters; 3. Graphic novels
1-56097-596-2, $12.95

Even though he's just a poor orphaned boy, it's a well-known fact that there's no greater firefighter than Olaf Oedwards, a.k.a. "Kid Firechief." Olaf and his assistant chief (and guardian) Smoky Joe put out fires all over the city and forests of Milltown and as far as... Ancient Rome" This adventure romp features characters including the infant rappers D.J. Diaper and M.C. Nu-Born ("This li'l piggy kept it real/while this li'l piggy was chillin'/This li'l piggy said 'Talk to the hand'/while this li'l piggy was illin'"), local school reporter "Nosy" Rosie Cheeks, Olaf's arch-nemesis Hotfoot, and Olaf's forest ranger cousin, Oella Oedwards. The book uses orange ink on light yellow paper.

White flower day. Fantagraphics 2002 112p. Illustration

Grades: 5 6 7 8 9 10 11 12 Adult   **741.5; Fic**

1. Humorous graphic novels
1-56097-514-8, $14.95

This book will appeal to older children who enjoy such things as "The Grim Adventures of Billy and Mandy" on Cartoon Network, with its somewhat gross and twisted humor.

"Scratch panels highlighted in ocher cast {a} jaundiced pall over three . . . twisted tales of rascaldom. They feature the Frankenstein-like Pullapart Boy, devilish L'il Bloody, and several equally weird young characters who venture forth to create mayhem, from innocent to morbid." Booklist

Another 'Yikes' book

Wells, H. G. (Herbert George), 1866-1946

Classics illustrated #12: The Island of Dr. Moreau. Adapted by Steven Grant ; Illustrated by Eric Vincent. Papercutz 2011 Un Illustration

Grades: 7 8 9 10 11 12 Adult   **741.5; Fic**

1. Horror graphic novels; 2. Novelists; 3. Wells, H G (Herbert George), 1866-1946 — Adaptations
978-1-59707-235-9, $9.99

Edward Prendick is the sole survivor of a shipwreck when a passing ship picks him up. It carries a strange cargo of animals, a doctor, who takes care of Prendick, and an odd man who looks more like an ape. Montgomery, the doctor, is

taking the animals to a small island he won't name, and Prendick ends up with them when the drunken ship's captain casts him off. On that island, Prendick discovers half-human, half-beast creatures, all created by the arrogant Dr. Moreau. This book adapts Wells' classic story; it was originally published in 1990 as part of the Classics Illustrated line published by First Comics. This edition includes an interview with Steven Grant, who wrote the adaptation.

The **Invisible** Man. Retold by Terry Davis ; illustrated by Dennis Calero. Stone Arch Books 2007 72p. Illustration

Grades: 3 4 5 6 7 8 9   **741.5; Fic**

1. Mystery graphic novels; 2. Science fiction graphic novels; 3. Graphic novels
978-1-59889-831-6, $23.93

LC 2007-6200

Late one night, a mysterious man, covered from head to toe in bandages, wanders into a tiny English village. After a series of burglaries, the villagers grow suspicious. Who is this man? Where did he come from? When they attempt to arrest the stranger, he suddenly reveals his secret: he is invisible. How can anyone stop the Invisible Man? The book is written with an easy vocabulary for struggling and reluctant readers, and it includes facts about invisibility.

Part of the Graphic Revolve series.

The **Time** Machine. Retold by Terry Davis ; illustrated by José Alfonso Ocampo Ruiz. Stone Arch Books 2007 72p. Illustration

Grades: 3 4 5 6 7 8 9   **741.5; Fic**

1. Adventure graphic novels; 2. Science fiction graphic novels; 3. Graphic novels
978-1-59889-833-0, $23.93

LC 2007-6201

A scientist invents a machine that he claims will travel through time, but his friends laugh at the idea. So the Time Traveler climbs aboard his machine and ends up thousands of years in the future. He meets a race of gentle humans called the Eloi, but he is soon swept up in a fight for his life against evil underground creatures known as Morlocks. Even worse, his Time Machine, his only chance to escape, is trapped deep inside the Morlock caverns. This book is written with an easy vocabulary for struggling and reluctant readers, and it includes some scientific speculations about the future.

Part of the Graphic Revolve series

The **war** of the worlds. By H.G. Wells; retold by Davis Miller and Katherine M. Brevard; illustrated by Jose Alfonso Ocampo Ruiz. Stone Arch Books 2009 72p. Illustration

Grades: 4 5 6 7 8 9 10   **741.5; Fic**

1. Science fiction graphic novels; 2. Graphic novels
978-1-4342-0757-9, $23.93

LC 2008-6250

In 1894, a strange meteorite crashes down near London, England. When George and other residents of Woking investigate the site, they discover a large alien cylinder. Suddenly, it's activated and begins destroying everything in its path. And George finds out there are more of the things elsewhere in the country. The people eventually learn that England has been invaded by Martians, and they are definitely not friendly. This graphic novel adaptation includes information about the Halloween 1938 radio hoax in which this story was dramatized in such a way that people in the U.S. thought they were in fact being invaded by deadly aliens.

Part of the Graphic Revolve series

Wells, Zeb

Civil War: Young Avengers & Runaways. Writer, Zeb Wells ; artist, Stefano Caseli ; color art, Daniele Rundoni ; letterer, Virtual Calligraphy's Cory Petit. Marvel Entertainment 2007 Un Illustration

Grades: 8 9 10 11 12 Adult   **741.5; Fic**
1. Runaways (Fictional characters); 2. Superhero graphic novels; 3. Graphic novels
0-7851-2317-2, $11.99

As the Civil War goes on between the two super hero camps, the public turns against their heroes, and the teen Runaways get caught up in the struggle despite their best efforts to stay out of the fight. When the Young Avengers offer their assistance, how can the Runaways believe they're on the same side?

Marvel Adventures Spider-Man Vol. 4: Concrete Jungle. Pencilled by Patrick Scherberger. Marvel Entertainment 2006 Un Illustration

Grades: 3 4 5 6 7 8 9   **741.5; Fic**
1. Spider-Man (Fictional character); 2. Superhero graphic novels; 3. Graphic novels
978-0-7851-2005-6, $6.99

Spider-Man stars in four stories featuring the Mad Thinker, the Chameleon, the Black Cat, and Doctor Octopus.

Welvaert, Scott R.

Helen Keller: Courageous Advocate. By Scott R. Welvaert ; illustrated by Cynthia Martin and Keith Tucker. Capstone Press 2006 32p. Illustration

Grades: 3 4 5 6 7 8 9   **741.5; 362.4; 92**
1. Biographical graphic novels; 2. Keller, Helen, 1880-1968; 3. Graphic novels
0-7368-4964-5, $25.26

LC 2005006463

This book uses the comic book format to recount highlights of the life of Helen Keller, a blind and deaf woman who became an author and advocate for the blind and other physically handicapped people. It includes additional information, a glossary, a list of books for further reading, and more.

Part of the Graphic Library, Graphic Biographies series.

West, David

Astronauts. Illustrated by Jim Robbins. Rosen Publishing Group 2008 48p. Illustration

Grades: 3 4 5 6 7 8 9   **629.45; 741.5**
1. Astronautics — Vocational guidance; 2. Astronauts; 3. Graphic novels
978-1-4042-1461-3, $29.25

LC 2007-45208

After brief descriptions of living and working conditions in space and the training one undergoes to become an astronaut, the book profiles three astronauts. Yuri Alexeyevich Gagarin was the first person to go into space; he was a Russian cosmonaut. Dr. Jerry Linenger lived and worked on the Russian space station Mir in 1997, when a fire broke out in the space station. And Thomas D. Jones flew on the space shuttle Atlantis, on its 2000 mission, STS-98.

Part of the Graphic Careers series

Fighter pilots. Illustrated by James Field. Rosen Publishing Group 2008 48p. Illustration

Grades: 3 4 5 6 7 8 9   **358.4; 741.5**
1. Air pilots; 2. Military aeronautics; 3. Graphic novels
978-1-4042-1455-2, $29.25

LC 2007-41458

After brief descriptions of the rise of fighters in air combat and of the evolution of jet fighters, this book profiles three pilots. Lieutenant Edwin C. Parsons flew with the Escadrille Lafayette during World War I. Pilot Office Geoffrey Wellum piloted a Royal Air Force Spitfire during the Battle of Britain in 1940. Lieutenant Randall H. Cunningham was a Navy fighter pilot who became the first fighter ace (he shot down at least five enemy aircraft) of the Vietnam War. This is the same man who, in 2005, pleaded guilty of graft for taking bribes while serving in the U.S. Congress. His later crimes do not take away from his fighter pilot accomplishments.

Part of the Graphic Careers series

Hernan Cortes: The Life of a Spanish Conquistador. By David West & Jackie Gaff ; illustrated by Jim Eldridge. Rosen Publishing Group 2005 48p. Illustration

Grades: 3 4 5 6 7 8

741.5; 972; 92
1. Biographical graphic novels; 2. Cortes, Hernan, 1485-1547; 3. Mexico — History — Conquest, 1519-1540; 4. Graphic novels
1-4042-0244-7, $29.25

Courtesy of Rosen Publishing

LC 2004005938

Adventurous explorer or ruthless imperialist? In 1519, Spanish conquistador Hernan Cortes led a daring expedition to the heart of the Aztec Empire, in what is now central and southern Mexico. Within two years, this highly advanced civilization had fallen to the might of Cortes's Spanish conquerors, resulting in the deaths of tens of thousands of Aztecs. This graphic novel explores two cultures in conflict—and the personality of a man driven by both insatiable greed and service to his country. The book includes additional information, a glossary, and a list of books for further reading.

Part of the Graphic Nonfiction series.

Pteranodon: The Giant of the Sky. Illustrated by Terry Riley and Geoff Ball. Rosen Publishing Group 2007 32p. Illustration

Grades: 2 3 4 5 6 7   **567.9; 741.5**
1. Dinosaurs; 2. Pteranodon; 3. Graphic novels
978-1-4042-3895-4, $25.25

LC 2007-1792

This volume uses colorful comic book style illustrations to explore the habitat, diet, and behavior of the pteranodon.

At the front of the book, facts about the pteranodon are presented, while at the back of the book readers will find a picture gallery of other creatures mentioned in the book.

Part of the Graphic Dinosaurs series.

Race car drivers. Illustrated by Peter Wilks and Geoff Ball. Rosen Publishing Group 2008 48p. Illustration
Grades: 3 4 5 6 7 8 9   **796.72; 741.5**
1. Automobile racing; 2. Graphic novels
978-1-4042-1452-1, $29.25

LC 2007-45174

After brief descriptions of early car racing and of the different types of car racing (NASCAR, Formula One, etc.), the book profiles three racers. Argentinian driver Juan Manuel Fangio is considered one of the best Formula One race car drivers, and he recalls the 1957 race at the Nurburgring in Germany. Dale Earnhardt, Sr. was one of the best-known NASCAR racers in the U.S. In 1996, he crashed during the Diehard 500; despite his injuries (a broken collarbone and sternum), he drove in Indianapolis, although he had to stop before finishing. The next week, he raced in Watkins Glen, New York, and finished in sixth place. He died in 2001, in a crash at the Daytona 500. The third driver profiled in this book is Formula One rookie Lewis Hamilton, who started at age seven with remote-controlled car races and spent his teen years winning Kart races in Great Britain (Karts are small racecars). He became a Formula One race driver in 2006.

Part of the Graphic Careers series

Richard the Lionheart: The Life of a King and Crusader. By David West & Jackie Gaff ; illustrated by John Cooper. Rosen Publishing Group 2005 48p. Illustration
Grades: 3 4 5 6 7 8   **741.5; 942.03; 92**
1. Biographical graphic novels; 2. Great Britain — History — 1154-1399, Plantagenets; 3. Richard, I, King of England; 4. Graphic novels
1-4042-0241-2, $29.25

LC 2004011267

Politician, military leader, crusader, and King of England, Richard the Lionheart has been the subject of Middle Ages' studies for centuries. His early years were marked by bitter rivalry with his father and brothers, but once crowned King in 1189, his primary ambition was to lead a crusade to the Holy Land to recapture the city of Jerusalem. This graphic novel treats readers to a retelling of the King's battle against Saladin for control of the Holy Land, his subsequent imprisonment, and ultimate return to the throne. It includes additional information, a glossary, and a list of books for further reading.

Part of the Graphic Nonfiction series.

Velociraptor: The Speedy Thief. Illustrated by James Field. Rosen Publishing Group 2007 32p. Illustration
Grades: 2 3 4 5 6 7
567.9; 741.5

Courtesy of Rosen Publishing

1. Dinosaurs; 2. Velociraptor; 3. Graphic novels
978-1-4042-3898-5, $25.25

LC 2007-873

This volume uses colorful comic book style illustrations to explore the habitat, diet, and behavior of the velociraptor. At the front of the book, facts about the velociraptor are presented, while at the back of the book readers will find a picture gallery of other creatures mentioned in the book.

Part of the Graphic Dinosaurs series.

Westerfeld, Scott
Uglies: Shay's story. Created by Scott Westerfeld; written by Scott Westerfeld and Devin Grayson; illustrations by Steven Cummings. Del Rey 2012 160 p. Illustration
Grades: 7 8 9 10   **741.5**
1. Beauty, Personal — Fiction; 2. Conformity; 3. Dystopian graphic novels; 4. Friendship — Fiction; 5. Plastic surgery; 6. Science fiction
9780606264754, $22.10; 0345527224; 9780345527226, $10.99

LC 2012374898

This young adult graphic novel retells the story of author Scott Westerfeld's dystopia "Uglies" from "the point of view of recurring frenemy Shay." It is "set in a . . . future time when discord is suppressed through ruthlessly enforced conformity and obligatory plastic surgery at age 16. . . . Shay yearns for freedom. An encounter with the flawed and alluring David, a covert envoy from the Smoke, a secret community of nonconformists, may offer Shay the escape she craves." (Publishers Weekly)

Followed by:Uglies: Cutters (2012)

Whedon, Joss
Buffy the Vampire Slayer season eight, volume 1: the long way home. Writer, Joss Whedon ; artists, Georges Jeanty, Andy Owens, Jo Chen. Dark Horse Comics 2007 136p. Illustration
Grades: 8 9 10 11 12 Adult   **741.5**
1. Adventure graphic novels; 2. Buffy the Vampire Slayer (Fictional character); 3. Horror graphic novels; 4. Graphic novels
978-1-59307-822-5, $15.95

The television series of Buffy the Vampire Slayer lasted seven seasons; this volume begins the comics-only eighth season. Buffy and her friends may have destroyed the Hellmouth, but all is not fun and games, as an old enemy returns, younger sister Dawn experiences some "growing pains," and a former decoy Slayer has her own troubles. There is a considerable amount of monster fighting.

Runaways: dead end kids. Writer, Joss Whedon ; artist, Michael Ryan. Marvel Entertainment 2008 Un Illustration
Grades: 7 8 9 10 11 12 Adult   **741.5; Fic**
1. Adventure graphic novels; 2. Runaways (Fictional characters); 3. Superhero graphic novels; 4. Graphic novels
978-0-7851-2853-3, $19.99

When the team's Los Angeles hideout is compromised, they flee to New York, where they become mixed up with Kingpin, and he pressures them to pull a "minor" heist. When the Punisher shows up, with more killers behind him, the Runaways make a desperate escape and find themselves a hundred years in the past. They find that there are other "specials" in that time, too, and more danger, even as they try to find a way back home.

Wheeler, Lisa
    Seadogs: An Epic Ocean Operetta. Composed by Lisa Wheeler ; staged by Mark Siegel. Simon & Schuster/Aladdin Paperbacks 2004 Un Illustration
Grades: 2 3 4 5 6
741.5; Fic
    1. Adventure graphic novels; 2. Dogs; 3. Humorous graphic novels; 4. Graphic novels
978-1-4169-4103-3, $7.99
2006 Texas Bluebonnet Award Winner

Courtesy of Simon & Schuster/ Aladdin Paperbacks

    A young Victorian girl pup goes to sea an operetta performed, and the reader watches Seadogs performed on stage right along with the audience. Old Seadog invites his good friends Brave Beagle and Dear Dachsund along for one last sail, and they encounter pirates, storms ... and a strange little pup.

White, Steve
    The **Battle** of Midway: the destruction of the Japanese fleet. Illustrated by Richard Elson.The Rosen Publishing Group 2007 48p. Illustration
Grades: 3 4 5 6 7 8 9 **741.5; 940.54**
    1. Midway, Battle of, 1942; 2. War; 3. World War, 1939-1945; 4. Graphic novels
978-1-4042-0783-7, $29.25

Courtesy of Rosen Publishing

    One of the most important naval battles in history, Midway marked a crucial turning point in the war in the Pacific. With a fleet that had dominated this theater since the attack on Pearl Harbor, the Japanese anticipated certain victory against the US forces, but the attack was not a surprise. The US Navy sank four irreplaceable aircraft carriers, and cleared the way for the island-hopping US counterattack. This book also includes eight pages of authoritative information, placing the battle in its historical context, describing the key players, and its build-up and aftermath.
    Part of the Graphic Battles of World War II series. This book is also available in a paperback edition from Osprey Publishing, under the title The Empire Falls: Battle of Midway.

    Pearl Harbor: A Day of Infamy. Illustrated by Jerrold Spahm. The Rosen Publishing Group 2007 48p. Illustration
Grades: 3 4 5 6 7 8 9 **741.5; 940.54**
    1. Pearl Harbor (Oahu, Hawaii), Attack on, 1941; 2. War; 3. World War, 1939-1945; 4. Graphic novels
978-1-4042-0785-1, $29.25
    On December 7, 1941, the Japanese Navy launched a surprise attack on American military bases in Pearl Harbor, Hawaii. Masterfully planned and executed, the attack devastated the US Pacific Fleet; in less than two hours, Japanese aircraft had sunk or damaged all eight US battleships anchored in the harbor and had destroyed 151 planes. Thrust into battle, the United States could have only one response: war. This book portrays the attack that drove the United States into World War II in full-color comic book narrative. Featuring the personal stories of front-line heroes like Ken Taylor, George Welch, and mess attendant Dorie Miller, it also provides background material - causes and consequences, key players, and a glossary of terms - as well as a list of additional resources.
    Part of the Graphic Battles of World War II series. This book is also available in a paperback edition from Osprey Publishing, under the title Day of Infamy: Attack on Pearl Harbor.

Whitley, Jeremy
    Princeless: Book One: Save Yourself. Jeremy Whitley; illustrated by M. Goodwin. Action Lab Entertainment 2012 116 p. Illustration
Grades: 4 5 6 7 8   **741.5; Fic**
    1. Adventure graphic novels; 2. Princesses
1450798942; 9781450798945, $14.95
    This graphic novel collects "the first storyline of the multiple Eisner Award-nominated and multiple Glyph Award-winning series" from Jeremy Whitley. It follows "the adventures of Princess Adrienne, a princess who's tired of waiting to be rescued. Along with her guardian dragon, Sparky, they begin their own quest." (Publisher's note)
    Volume 1 of an ongoing series

Whitta, Gary
    Death Jr. Vol. 1. Gary Whitta & Ted Naifeh. Image Comics 2005 Un Illustration
Grades: 8 9 10 11 12 Adult   **741.5; Fic**
    1. Adventure graphic novels; 2. Fantasy graphic novels; 3. Horror graphic novels; 4. Graphic novels
1-58240-526-3, $14.99
    When a school field trip to the local museum coincides with coming-of-age angst and an overly inquisitive friend (a cute goth girl named Pandora), Junior releases an ancient evil into the world... and it's up to him to fix it. He's helped by his friends Stigmartha, whose hands bleed when she gets nervous; Smith & Weston, two twins conjoined at the head and The Seep, a foul-mouthed, armless, legless fetus in a tube. He's your average, everyday, happy-go-lucky middle-school student... who just happens to be the son of the grim reaper.

    Death Jr. Vol. 2. Gary Whitta & Ted Naifeh. Image Comics 2007 Un Illustration
Grades: 7 8 9 10 11 12   **741.5; Fic**

1. Horror graphic novels; 2. Humorous graphic novels; 3. Graphic novels
978-1-58240-682-4, $14.99

Death Jr. returns with all of his friends in a new adventure that finds him filling a summer internship with his father at Terminal Industries, while the rest of the gang heads off to summer camp. Can they manage to survive the summer unscathed? And what is DJ going to do when he causes his father, the Grim Reaper, to be fired and his mom has to get a job?

Wicks, Maris
★ **Human** Body Theater: a nonfiction revue. Maris Wicks. First Second 2015 240 p. Color; Illustration
Grades: 4 5 6 7 8   **612; 741.5**
1. Human anatomy — Juvenile literature
1626722773; 9781626722774, $19.99; 9781596439290

This book by Maris Wicks explores human anatomy on a performing stage. In it, "your master of ceremonies is going to lead you through a theatrical revue of each and every biological system of the human body! Starting out as a skeleton, the MC puts on a new layer of her costume (her body) with each 'act.'" (Publisher's note)

"Wicks' playful cartoon artwork in saturated colors makes the potentially daunting and embarrassing subject of anatomy approachable and fun, but never at the expense of accuracy or clarity. This informative, frank exploration of the body perfectly balances science and silliness." Booklist
Includes bibliographical references

Wight, Eric
My dead girlfriend, Vol. 1. Tokyopop 2007 Un Illustration
Grades: 8 9 10 11 12 Adult   **741.5; Fic**
1. High school students; 2. Romance graphic novels; 3. School stories; 4. Supernatural graphic novels; 5. Graphic novels
978-1-59816-996-6, $9.99

As a perfectly normal boy, Finney Bleak stands out among the monsters and ghosts of his town and in school, Mephisto Prep. He's the youngest in a family known for the many weird and wacky ways everyone has died. In school, Finney must deal with bullies such as Karl the Frankenstein-type monster, teen vampire Drake, and others. He had one memorable night at the carnival with the perfect girl, Jenny, months ago, but she never made it to the meeting they had arranged for the next day. Now, as he's chased in the woods by Karl and company, somebody comes to his aid—it's Jenny, who's now a ghost. So, nobody's ever perfect, right? This is another global manga title, the first of a projected series.

Williams, Aaron
PS 238, volume VI: senseless acts of tourism!. Do Gooder Press 2008 Un Illustration
Grades: 3 4 5 6 7 8 9 10 11 12 Adult   **741.5; Fic**
1. Humorous graphic novels; 2. Superhero graphic novels; 3. Graphic novels
978-1-933288-49-9, $15.99

After the town had been pretty much leveled by invading aliens and repair work begins, Miss Kyle takes a vacation to Las Vegas. However, Zodon has convinced Poly and Julie that Miss Kyle is leaving for good, so they hitch a ride on the plane. They don't know that others are following and trying to kidnap Zodon. Meanwhile, Flea has hitched a ride on the bad guys' jet. Once they all get to Las Vegas, they end up helping the Masquerade Casino catch the person who has been cheating and winning too much in the casino. Meanwhile, back at PS 238, Tyler is stuck in a stasis pod because he was infected with an alien virus that could destroy the world; then Tom comes and takes Tyler, or at least a part of his soul, to make a crucial decision about whether humanity should continue to gain super powers. And then Cecil, who still sees aliens everywhere, goes with mysterious millionaire Kent Allard to scout out possible aliens. There's lots of superhero action going on, all of it at kid-friendly level.

PS 238: To the Cafeteria . . . For Justice!. Henchman Publishing/Dork Storm Press 2005 Un Illustration
Grades: 4 5 6 7 8 9 10 11 12 Adult   **741.5; Fic**
1. Elementary schools; 2. Humorous graphic novels; 3. Superhero graphic novels; 4. Graphic novels
1-933288-13-2, $15.95

PS 238 is the only public school for metahuman children, where the students learn how to use their powers, socialize with normal as well as super-powered classmates, and have fun adventures. In this second volume, the students learn about the importance of primary sources for history research (time traveling Tom brings a girl to the present to give them straight information about her father). Also, Tyler, son of two superheroes who hasn't yet come into his powers, spends some time training with the vigilante hero, Revenant. And in shop class, the students make some super accessories. The first volume is not available, but readers can pick up on things from this volume. This is a continuing series.

PS238 Vol. III: No Child Left Behind!. Dork Storm Press/Henchman Publishing 2006 Un Illustration
Grades: 5 6 7 8 9 10 11 12 Adult   **741.5; Fic**
1. Adventure graphic novels; 2. Humorous graphic novels; 3. Superhero graphic novels; 4. Graphic novels
1-933288-24-8, $15.99

In this third volume, readers meet Malphast, the child of divine and not-so-divine parents, who involves almost everyone in a cosmic game of four-square. Then Tom Davidson discovers an unusual castle floating outside of time and space. And Harold Nelson, after whom PS238's "Rainmaker Program" was named, has decided that a sizeable number of students need to be "rescued" from the school. Tyler works with the Revenant to save his friends from Nelson.

Williams, Rob
Star Wars: Rebellion Volume 1: My Brother, My Enemy. Script, Rob Williams ; "Crossroads" script, Thomas Andrews ; art, Brandon Badeaux and Michel Lacombe ; colors, Wil Glass ; lettering, Michael Heisler. Dark Horse Comics 2007 Un Illustration
Grades: 8 9 10 11 12 Adult   **741.5; Fic**
1. Adventure graphic novels; 2. Science fiction graphic novels; 3. Graphic novels
9781593077112, $14.95; 1593077114

Having rescued Rebel strategist Jorin Sol from the Empire, Luke Skywalker now leads X-Wing attack runs on Imperial convoys to rustle up much needed supplies for the Rebel fleet. Little does he know that within Sol lies a secret that will put the entire Alliance in danger. What's worse, when Luke receives a coded message from Lt. Sunber, who wants to defect to the Rebel Alliance, he must decide whether to trust his old friend or obey the orders of Princess Leia who believes Tank may be part of an Imperial plot to capture the Rebellion's greatest hero.

Willingham, Bill

Robin: To Kill a Bird. Bill Willingham, writer ; Damion Scott, Giusseppe Camuncoli, Scott McDaniel, Pop Mhan, pencillers ; Sandra Hope, Damion Scott, Andy Owens, inkers ; Guy Major, colorist ; Phil Balsam, Jared K. Fletcher, Rob Leigh, letterers. DC Comics 2006 Un Illustration
Grades: 8 9 10 11 12 Adult   **741.5; Fic**
   1. Robin (Fictional character); 2. Superhero graphic novels; 3. Graphic novels
978-1-4012-0909-4, $14.99
It's a brand-new start for Batman's sidekick, Robin: a new town (Bludhaven), a new school, new adventures and new problems. Before our hero can fully recover from the recent deaths of his father and girlfriend Spoiler, he must come face to face with his enemies: the Penguin, the Dark Rider, the Veteran, and a mysterious archer who seems to want the Boy Wonder dead. There's lots of superhero fighting action.

Wilson, Sean Michael

A **Christmas** Carol: The graphic novel original text by Charles Dickens. Illustrated by Mike Collins. Classical Comics 2008 144p. Illustration
Grades: 5 7 8 9 10 11 12 Adult   **741.5; Fic**
   1. Christmas; 2. Dickens, Charles, 1812-1870 — Adaptations; 3. Ghosts; 4. Graphic novels
978-1-906332-51-8, $16.95
Miserly Ebenezer Scrooge has pronounced "Bah, humbug!" against Christmas, but on this Christmas Eve night, the ghost of his dead partner Jacob Marley visits him and proclaims his only hope to escape Marley's fate is to endure the visits of the Ghosts of Christmas Past, Present, and Future. Scrooge sees his past as a hopeful young man who slowly becomes bitter and obsessed with money as a means to avoid poverty, sees how his relatives and employees view him in the present, and how his future death is a matter of joy. This graphic adaptation uses dialog and narration taken directly from Dickens' novel. Back matter includes a short biography of Dickens, a description of a typical Victorian period Christmas celebration, a description of the harsh poverty in London of the mid-nineteenth century, and more.
Also available quick text version $16.95 (ISBN: 978-1-906332-52-5)

Winick, Judd

★ **Pedro** & me: friendship, loss, & what I learned. Henry Holt and Co. 2009 187p. Illustration
Grades: 7 8 9 10 11 12   **362.1**
   1. AIDS (Disease); 2. AIDS activists; 3. AIDS patients; 4. Biographical graphic novels; 5. Friendship; 6. Real world (Television program); 7. Television personalities; 8. Graphic novels
978-0-8050-8964-6, $16.99
2001 Robert F. Sibert Honor Book
In this "volume—part graphic novel, part memoir—professional cartoonist Winick pays tribute to his Real World housemate and friend Pedro Zamora, an AIDS activist who died of the disease in 1994." Publ Wkly
First published 2000

Superman/Shazam/First Thunder. Judd Winick, writer ; Joshua Middleton, artist ; Nick J. Napolitano, letterer. DC Comics 2006 128p. Illustration
Grades: 8 9 10 11 12 Adult   **741.5; Fic**
   1. Shazam (Fictional character); 2. Superhero graphic novels; 3. Superman (Fictional character); 4. Graphic novels
978-1-4012-0923-0, $12.99
With one word, young orphan Billy Batson transforms into a man imbued with the powers of the gods, but even one gifted with the Wisdom of Solomon can learn from a Superman. While Superman must stop members of a cult from stealing ancient artifacts from the Metropolis Natural History Museum, Billy must battle giant robots rampaging through Fawcett City. These separate events lead the heroes to cross paths, and a mighty friendship is formed as Earth's most powerful defenders team up to stop such menaces as Lex Luthor, Dr. Sivana, Eclipso, and the monstrous Lord Sabbac. There's some violence, and the climax is heartbreaking.

Winter, Barbara

Fight for Rights. Art by Dimitri Kostic. Harcourt Achieve/Steck-Vaughn 2006 48p. Illustration
Grades: 3 4 5 6 7 8   **741.5; Fic**
   1. Great Britain — History — 20th century; 2. Women — Suffrage; 3. Graphic novels
978-1-4190-3219-6, $8.99
In Victorian England, a young girl named Mary is drawn into the fight for women's right to vote. She realizes that the struggle will be a long and difficult one. Could it also be dangerous" This historical graphic novel includes prose intervals that describe the women's suffrage movement and its actions, as well as the British government's actions against the women activists. Many of the incidents described in the story really happened.
Part of the Timeline Graphic Novels series.

The **Golden** Scarab. Art by Jason Loo. Harcourt Achieve/Steck-Vaughn 2006 48p. Illustration
Grades: 3 4 5 6 7 8   **741.5; Fic**
   1. Egypt — History; 2. Mystery graphic novels; 3. Graphic novels
978-1-4190-3196-0, $8.99
An Egyptian princess named Meri rescues a slave girl named Layla. When the pharaoh suddenly gets sick, Princess Meri and Layla play detective to find out what's making him ill. This historical fiction graphic novel is set during the reign of Akhenaten and Nefertiti; Meri is Meritaten, their eldest daughter. The book includes intervals of prose giving facts about Egypt, its people, and its customs.
Part of the Timeline Graphic Novels series.

Trapped in Gallipoli. Art by Scott Page. Harcourt Achieve/Steck-Vaughn 2006 48p. Illustration
Grades: 3 4 5 6 7 8   741.5; Fic
1. Adventure graphic novels; 2. World War, 1914-1918; 3. Graphic novels
978-1-4190-3211-0, $8.99
In the midst of the First World War, a young orphan named Duyal joins his uncle, Mustafa Kemal, commander of the Turkish forces, at Gallipoli. When the Allies attack, Duyal is captured by Australian soldiers and kept as a prisoner of war. Gallipoli was one of the bloody campaigns of the war; it ended with withdrawal by the Allied forces and huge losses on both sides. The book includes some of the battlefield violence. It also includes prose intervals that provide more information about the campaign and its legacy. Part of the Timeline Graphic Novels series.

Wisna, Chris
Doris Danger, volume one: Giant monster adventures. SLG Publishing 2009 96p. Illustration
Grades: 8 9 10 11 12 Adult   741.5; Fic
1. Humorous graphic novels; 2. Monsters; 3. Graphic novels
978-1-59362-180-3, $9.95
Intrepid ace photo-journalist Doris Danger seeks out the truth about giant alien monsters, and her quest takes her to isolated islands, jungles in Africa, rural Kansas, the Niagara Falls, and many other places where mysterious military officials cover up the existence of creatures such as Splazoo, Kockh, and Spoosh. Also, everywhere she goes in search of the giant alien monsters, the Monster Liberation Army shows up. The book reads like a collection of stories from a magazine, and Wisna's black and white art resembles the old Jack Kirby monster comics of the 1950s and 1960s.

Wolfman, Marv
The **New** Teen Titans: Terra Incognito. Marv Wolfman, writer ; George Pérez, penciller ; Romeo Tanghal, Pablo Markos, inkers ; Adrienne Roy, colorist. DC Comics 2006 224p. Illustration
Grades: 7 8 9 10 11 12 Adult   741.5; Fic
1. Robin (Fictional character); 2. Superhero graphic novels; 3. Teen Titans (Fictional characters); 4. Graphic novels
978-1-4012-0972-8, $19.99
Tara Markov, the troubled teen princess of Markovia, is rescued from kidnappers by the Titans' green-skinned adventurer, Changeling. Thus begins her quest to use her powers over earth and gravity in the cause of justice. Does this obnoxious young powerhouse have what it takes to join the team? This is the original Teen Titans team, in which Dick Grayson is still Robin.

Wonder Woman Vol. 4: Destiny Calling. DC Comics 2006 176p. Illustration
Grades: 8 9 10 11 12 Adult   741.5; Fic
1. Superhero graphic novels; 2. Wonder Woman (Fictional character); 3. Graphic novels
978-1-4012-0943-8, $19.99
It's only been a short time since Diana, dubbed Wonder Woman by the media, came to Man's World with a message of peace, only to face countless foes and stop the advancement of a third world war. Now Diana must face her greatest challenge yet: a god among men. The Olympian god Hermes has decided to grace mankind with his presence, but along with him comes a world of new troubles for the Amazon. This volume reprints stories originally published in the 1980s, when Perez re-launched Wonder Woman.

Wolfram, Amy
Teen Titans year one. Written by Amy Wolfram ; Art by Karl Kerschl & Serge LaPointe. DC Comics 2008 144p. Illustration
Grades: 7 8 9 10 11 12   741.5; Fic
1. Aquaman (Fictitious character); 2. Batman (Fictional character); 3. Flash (Fictional character); 4. Green Arrow (Fictional character); 5. Justice League (Fictional characters); 6. Robin (Fictional character); 7. Superhero graphic novels; 8. Teen Titans (Fictional characters); 9. Wonder Woman (Fictional character); 10. Graphic novels
978-1-4012-1927-7, $14.99
Suddenly, the members of the Justice League of America are acting crazy, becoming bullies, breaking the law—what has happened to Batman, Aquaman, the Flash, Green Arrow, and Wonder Woman" Their young partners, Robin, Aqualad, Kid Flash, Speedy, and Wonder Girl, decide to team up together and put things right. They're teens, they're superheroes, they're the Teen Titans. And being teens, they still do teenage things, like overindulge in pizza and soda, go out on dates and mess things up with each other, and deal with celebrity. That last is not typical of teens, but they have to learn to deal with it. This book, written by Wolfram, who wrote for the Teen Titans animated series on television, reimagines the early days of the team. The book includes some violence.

Womanthology: Heroic
Gail Simone, Camilla D'Errico, Robin Furth, Trina Robbins, Colleen Doran, Fiona Staples, Ming Doyle, Renae De Liz and others. IDW 2012 321 p.
Grades: 8 9 10 11 12   Fic
1. Comic books, strips, etc — Authorship; 2. Women artists
1613771479; 9781613771471, $50
This book is an anthology of comics content from "more than 150 women creators." The book shows "how many diverse styles and subjects can make for great comics. The different portraits and definitions of heroism encompass everything from caped fliers to historical allusions to quiet bravery." (Publishers Weekly)

Wong, Tony
The **Four** Constables Vol. 1. Director, Tony Wong ; illustrator, Andy Seto ; original story, Rui-An Wen ; translator, Yun Zhao. ComicsOne/DrMaster Publications 2004 Un Illustration
Grades: 8 9 10 11 12 Adult   741.5; Fic
1. Adventure graphic novels; 2. Martial arts; 3. Mystery graphic novels; 4. Graphic novels
1-58899-383-3, $13.95
Four of China's supremely skilled assassin/detectives serve only their Master Zhuge Zhen-Wo - The Little Flower, who in turn is head bodyguard and advisor for China's all powerful Emperor. . Yayu Sheng, "Emotionless," is a master

of weapons and devices. Yuxia Tie, "Iron Hands," possesses incredible chi and can stop the sharpest blades bare-handed. Lieshan Cui, "Life Snatcher," is highly skilled in light-foot, granting him undaunted legwork and kicks. Lingqi Len, "Cold Blooded," was raised by wolves and since learned to transfer his pain when fighting to strength, enabling him to defeat opponents much stronger than himself. Each of them is entrusted by the Emperor with the power to arrest and execute any corrupt officials or lawless criminals with the Chinese Empire. These Imperial Constables act as protectors. With their venerable skill they root out potential usurpers and discern the cause of many strange occurrences happening during the Sung Dynasty. This is a Chinese manhua series, published in full color and filled with martial arts action.

Volume 1 of 5

Wood, Brian

The **New** York Four. Written by Brian Wood ; illustrated by Kelly Ryan ; lettering by Jared K. Fletcher. DC Comics/Minx 2008 176p. Illustration
Grades: 8 9 10 11 12   **741.5; Fic**
1. Friendship; 2. Graphic novels
978-1-4012-1154-7, $9.99

Riley is a college freshman who has grown up so sheltered, protected, and disciplined by her parents that she finds it difficult to make friends. She starts seeing her older sister Angie on the sly; Angie was kicked out of the house years ago for an offense no one will tell Riley. Other than that, Riley almost lives her life through her smart phone, constantly texting to people she's never met in person. Then, just as she opens up to make friends with three fellow freshmen and helps them find work with the same research group for which she works, she "meets" someone she knows only by his user name, "sneakerfreak." Balancing classes, friends, her over-protective parents, her sister, and now this secret online romance is becoming more difficult than Riley ever thought it could be. Each of her friends also has a secret that could have consequences.

Wood, Don

Into the volcano: a graphic novel. Blue Sky Press 2008 174p. Illustration; Map
Grades: 2 3 4 5 6 7 8   **741.5; Fic**
1. Adventure graphic novels; 2. Brothers; 3. Graphic novels
978-0-439-72671-9, $18.99; 0-439-72671-9
LC 2007-51084

While their parents are away doing research, brothers Duffy and Sumo Pugg go with their cousin, Mister Come-and-Go, to Kokalaha Island, where they meet Aunt Lulu and become trapped in an erupting volcano.

"The visual format combined with nonstop action will keep reluctant readers and adventure fans turning pages to the very end." Voice Youth Advocates

Wooderson, Philip

Arf and the Three Dogs. Stone Arch Books 2006 72p. Illustration
Grades: 2 3 4 5 6 7   **741.5; Fic**
1. Humorous graphic novels; 2. Mystery graphic novels; 3. Graphic novels

978-1-59889-021-1, $21.26 lib. bdg.

When Arf is knocked down by three dogs held on a leash by the man known as Crazy Barney, he decides to get photos as proof of the wild behavior. Major Nimby blames the dog shelter, but Arf's sisters say the Major is playing tricks to close the shelter; will Arf's photos save the day" An easy text, simple panel layout, and fast-paced story make this suitable for beginning and struggling readers.

Guard Dog. Stone Arch Books 2007 80p. Illustration
Grades: 3 4 5 6 7 8 9   **741.5; Fic**
1. Mystery graphic novels; 2. Graphic novels
978-1-59889-829-3, $22.60
LC 2007-6244

Ryan would rather play his favorite video game, Guard Dog, than help his dad sell his artwork at the flea market. When the artwork is stolen, however, Ryan and his friend Steve take on the case. Soon, they're hot on the trail of the thieves, but are the clues leading them in the wrong direction" The two boys learn that a detective's work is no game. This graphic novel is written with an easy vocabulary and a simple panel layout for beginning, reluctant, and struggling readers.

Part of the Graphic Quest line.

Yakin, Boaz

★ **Marathon**. By Boaz Yakin; [illustrations by Joe Infurnari]. First Second 2012 186 p.
Grades: 6 7 8 9   **741.5/973; 741.5**
1. Adventure graphic novels; 2. Greece — History; 3. Greece — History — Persian Wars, 500-449 BC — Fiction; 4. Greece — History — Persian Wars, 500-449 BC — Juvenile fiction; 5. Marathon, Battle of, 490 BC; 6. Graphic novels
9781596436800, $16.99 ; 1596436808
LC 2011030472

This book is a graphical "account of the battle of Marathon" in which "Hippias, former king of Athens, is on his way back with a huge army of Persians to reclaim the throne and crush Athenian democracy. . . . Eucles, Athens' best runner, is charged to race the 153 miles to Sparta in hopes of finding an ally, . . . [returning] with the dismaying news that the Spartans will not be coming in time. He joins the savage fight and then runs 26 more miles over rugged mountains to Athens . . . warning of an impending surprise attack by sea." (Kirkus Reviews)

Yamamoto, Lun Lun

Swans in space, volume 1. UDON Entertainment 2009 150p. Illustration
Grades: 2 3 4 5 6 7   **741.5; Fic**
1. Humorous graphic novels; 2. Manga; 3. Science fiction graphic novels; 4. Graphic novels
978-1-897376-93-5, $8.99

Sixth grader Corona is effectively her class's president, representing them on the Cosmos Institute student council. At home, she barely tolerates the obsessive fandom displayed by her father and younger brother for the television show, Space Patrol. Imagine her chagrin when she reaches out to an odd classmate, only to find herself recruited into ... the Space Patrol! It's a real organization that works to keep the Earth and other worlds safe, and show's episodes are edited versions of actual missions. Of course, Corona must keep her work in the Space Patrol a secret from anyone who isn't a member; and since she needs to study the old episodes to learn the history, this makes her father and brother think she has become one with them, while her classmates wonder what's wrong with her. Corona must also keep up with not only her school work, which is bad enough, because she's one of the top students, but as class president she has to take responsibility for all kinds of extra activities and work; all this makes her one tired girl. This manga for younger readers is published in full color.

Yamashita, Matt
    Ghostbusters: Ghost Busted. Stories by Nathan Johnson and Matt Yamashita ; art by Chrissy Delk et al. Tokyopop 2008 Un Illustration
Grades: 7 8 9 10 11 12 Adult   **741.5; Fic**
    1. Fantasy graphic novels; 2. Ghosts; 3. Humorous graphic novels; 4. Graphic novels
978-1-4278-1459-3, $12.99
    In the time since the Ghostbusters last saved New York City (as seen in the second film), the team finds itself pretty busy. A major producer hires Ray, Peter, and Egon to save his new lavish musical from destruction, which would ruin him. Then, the mayor's former right hand man returns, intent on getting revenge on all the Ghostbusters for ruining his reputation. Meanwhile, Peter, Ray, and Egon each disappear while out on individual calls, and now it's up to Winston to find and save them. This is a global manga and includes ghostly manifestations, ectoplasm, and ghostbusting action.

Yanagawa, Sozo
    Edu-manga: Helen Adams Keller. Artist, Rie Yagi. Digital Manga Publishing 2005 160p. Illustration
Grades: 3 4 5 6 7 8   **92; 741.5**
    1. Biographical graphic novels; 2. Keller, Helen; 3. Kodomo manga; 4. Manga; 5. Graphic novels
1-56970-976-9, $9.95
    This manga, originally written for Japanese schoolchildren, covers the life of Helen Keller and of her teacher, Anne Sullivan. It uses the Atom Boy series characters to introduce her story and to cover questions between chapters. The writer also worked with the Tokyo Helen Keller Association. Young readers can see the initial struggles between young "Teacher" Sullivan and the blind, deaf and uneducated little Helen, and how they worked together so Helen could learn to communicate, and learn to learn and get an education. As an adult, Helen traveled around the U.S. and to Europe and Japan, working to help the physically handicapped; her message was don't just pity the handicapped, but help them help themselves. The book includes a timeline of her life and short biographies of some of the important people in her life.

Yang, Gene Luen
    ★ **American** born Chinese. Color by Lark Pien. First Second 2006 233p. Illustration
Grades: 7 8 9 10 11 12   **741.5; Fic**
    1. Chinese Americans; 2. Young adult literature — Works
1-59643-152-0, $16.95; 978-1-59643-152-2
                                        LC 2005-58105
    Michael L. Printz Award, 2007

In this graphic novel by Gene Luen Yang, "Jin Wang is the only Asian American boy in his new school; Danny is a young man deeply embarrassed by his visiting Chinese cousin, portrayed deliberately by the author as an ethnic clich?; and the Monkey King, a figure from Chinese lore, is desperate to be treated like a god. This . . . story relates how three characters overcome hurdles to find satisfaction within themselves." (Library Journal)
    "True to its origin as a Web comic, this story's clear, concise lines and expert coloring are deceptively simple yet expressive. Even when Yang slips in an occasional Chinese ideogram or myth, the sentiments he's depicting need no translation. Yang accomplishes the remarkable feat of practicing what he preaches with this book: accept who you are and you'll already have reached out to others." Publ Wkly

    ★ **Boxers**. Gene Luen Yang; color by Lark Pien. First Second 2013 328 p.
Grades: 7 8 9 10 11 12 Adult   **741.5**
    1. China — History — Boxer Rebellion, 1899-1901; 2. Historical fiction
1596433590; 9781596433595, $18.99
                                        LC 2013947229
National Book Award for Young People's Literature: Finalist (2013)
Boston Globe-Horn Book Honor: Fiction (2014)
    "Life in Little Bao's peaceful rural village is disrupted when . . . a priest and his phalanx of soldiers . . . arrive." They start "smashing the village god, appropriating property, and administering vicious beatings for no reason. Little Bao and his older brothers train in kung fu and swordplay." . . . Little Bao "becomes the leader of a peasant army, eventually marching to Beijing." (School Library Journal)
    "China's Boxer Rebellion is the unlikely backdrop for this graphic treatment of young villagers on the opposite sides of history. Bao wants to drive out the white devils that poison his country with opium and Christianity. Four-Girl is an unwanted daughter who finds purpose in the missionary life. Their stories collide in a moment of grace that could only be penned by the Printz Award-winning author of 'American Born Chinese.'" LJ

    ★ **Prime** baby. [by] Gene Luen Yang, colors by Derek Kirk Kim. First Second Books 2010 56p. Illustration
Grades: 6 7 8 9 10 11 12   **741.5; Fic**
    1. Extraterrestrial beings; 2. Humorous graphic novels; 3. Science fiction graphic novels; 4. Siblings; 5. Graphic novels
978-1-59643-612-1, $6.99
    Thaddeus K. Fong always preferred to be the center of his family's attention, so the birth of his little sister Maddie has really bothered him. When she's eighteen months old, he notices something about the sounds she makes; her "gaga's" come out in prime numbers. Then his math teacher says that if aliens were ever to try to make contact with humans, it would be through prime numbers. Oh no, Maddie is an intergalactic conduit for invading aliens! Except no one believes Thaddeus. Until Maddie starts burping up strange things that turn out to be little ships for sluglike aliens. They're peaceful missionary types, but that doesn't stop Thaddeus from making them seem hostile. When their parents finally believe Thaddeus, Maddie gets locked up in a research facility. Thaddeus should be ecstatic, his dumb little

sister has been put away. So why is he feeling sad? This story was originally serialized in the New York Times magazine and has been printed to preserve the original comic strip format.

"Sf readers who value humor and humanity (not just slam-bang action), Christians, newcomers to graphic novels, and fans of Yang's simultaneously childlike and sophisticated ability to create and maintain tension should all be satisfied by his new book." Booklist

★ **Saints**. By Gene Luen Yang and Lark Pien. First Second 2013 170 p.
Grades: 7 8 9 10 11 12 Adult   **741.5**
1. China — History — Boxer Rebellion, 1899-1901; 2. Historical fiction
1596436891; 9781596436893, $15.99
                                        LC 2013947228
National Book Award for Young People's Literature: Finalist (2013)
Boston Globe-Horn Book Honor: Fiction (2014)
This graphic novel, by Gene Luen Yang and Lark Pien, "follows a lonely girl . . . . Unwanted by her family, Four-Girl isn't even given a proper name until she converts to Cathclicism and is baptized by the very same priest who bullies Little Bao's village. Four-Girl, now known as Vibiana, leaves home and finds fulfillment in service to the Church, while Little Bao roams the countryside committing acts of increasing violence as his army grows." (School Library Journal)

"Yang presents a 'diptych' of graphic novels set during China's Boxer Rebellion. Boxers follows Little Bao, who learns to harness the power of ancient gods to fight the spread of Christianity; Saints centers on Four-Girl, who sits squarely on the other side of the rebellion. Yang's characteristic infusions of magical realism, bursts of humor, and distinctively drawn characters make for a compelling read." (Horn Book)

Secret coders. Gene Yuen Lang & Mike Holmes. First Second 2015 96 p. Color; Illustration
Grades: 4 5 6 7   **741.5**
1. Computer programming; 2. School stories
9781626722767, $17.99; 9781626720756; 1626722765
In this graphic novel, by Gene Yuen Lang and Mike Holmes, "Hopper, an enthusiastic 12-year-old girl . . ., has just started school at the creepy Stately Academy. After getting in a fight . . . with Eni . . ., Hopper and Eni become friends while unraveling the secrets of the school. Robotic birds, family troubles, and sinister, child-hating school administrators lead to a story both emotionally rich and rife with learning opportunities." (School Library Journal)

The **Shadow** Hero. Gene Luen Yang. Art by Sonny Liew. First Second 2014 176 p. Color; Illustration
Grades: 6 7 8 9 10   **741.5**
1. Chinese Americans — Fiction; 2. Superheroes — Fiction
1596436972; 9781596436978, $17.99
This book, by Gene Luen Yang, is about "Green Turtle, a 1940s comic book hero. . . . The Green Turtle is cast as an unlikely 19-year-old young man, Hank, the son of Chinese immigrants who own a grocery store in 1940s America. When his mother is rescued by a superhero, the loving but overbearing woman decides that it's Hank's fate to become a

hero himself, and she does everything in her power to push her son in that direction." (School Library Journal)

"Yang and Liew have crafted an origin story for the Green Turtle, a little-known . . . World War II-era comic superhero created by cartoonist Chu Hing in 1944. Much about the series remains a mystery, as Yang shares in an author's note, but according to rumors Hing wanted his star to be Chinese, and, not surprisingly for the era, his publishers balked at the idea. Now seventy years later, Yang and Liew vindicate the cartoonist by imagining the Green Turtle as 'perhaps...the first Asian American superhero.'" Horn Book

Yeh, Phil
   Dinosaurs Across America. NBM 2007 32p. Illustration
Grades: 2 3 4 5 6   **973; 741.5**
1. United States — Geography; 2. Graphic novels
978-1-56163-509-2, $12.95
Originally done as a comic book and sold by Cartoonists Across America, a literacy group working for decades to promote the use of comic books to teach literacy to children, this is now a graphic novel. Featuring Yeh's dinosaurs and Patrick Rabbit, the book devotes a half-page to each state in the U.S., packing in basic facts and a simple map along with fun little tidbits (for example, the largest privately owned cattle ranch in the U.S. happens to be in Hawaii, on the island of Hawaii).

YKids
   Curie. Youngjin Singapore 2007 148p. Illustration
Grades: 3 4 5 6 7 8 9   **92; 741.5**
1. Biographical graphic novels; 2. Curie, Marie, 1867-1934; 3. Graphic novels
978-981-05-4946-6, $14.95
Throughout her career, Marie Curie, the renowned scientist and first woman to win the Nobel Prize, had to overcome the objections of her peers and the many obstacles facing an early female scientist. This is the story of her work in discovering radium and explaining the mysteries, benefits, and dangers of radioactivity that would ultimately lead to her own death. It also recounts the enormous time and resources she devoted to the cause of peace, having witnessed herself the horrors of war. In the fictional framing story, a boy and a robot from the future seek out Marie Curie to take one particular value from her life to help them in their time; they seek her burning passion for her work.
Part of the Great Figures in History series.

   Einstein. Youngjin Singapore 2007 146p. Illustration
Grades: 3 4 5 6 7 8 9   **92; 741.5**
1. Biographical graphic novels; 2. Einstein, Albert, 1879-1955; 3. Graphic novels
978-981-05-4944-2, $14.95
A genius of enormous accomplishment, Albert Einstein overcame numerous hardships-separation from his family, religious discrimination, and the political turmoil of his day-to become one of the greatest minds of the 20th century. As a young boy, Einstein's unending curiosity and constant questioning earned him the reputation of being unfocused and inattentive. This book uses a framing story of a young boy and a robot from the future going back in time to

examine the lives of great people and find the one value that will help their situation; from Einstein, they take his insatiable curiosity.

Part of the Great Figures in History series.

Gandhi. Youngjin Singapore 2007 148p. Illustration
Grades: 3 4 5 6 7 8 9   **92; 741.5**
1. Biographical graphic novels; 2. Gandhi, Mahatma, 1869-1948; 3. Graphic novels
978-981-05-4945-9, $14.95

A champion of the poor and lower classes, Mahatma Gandhi helped transform India into the democracy it is today. Young readers of this manga-style biography will learn about the key historical events during this time and how the peaceful efforts of one humble man affected enormous change. This book presents a time line of Gandhi's life-from his roots in a middle-class family in India, to his law-school education in England, his experiences with discrimination, and his key role as a leader in the Indian independence movement. Each volume in the Great Figures in History series focuses on a key value personified by the biographical subject; in Gandhi's case, it's courage.

Part of the Great Figures in History series.

Little Women: Manga Literary Classics. Youngjin Singapore 2007 145p. Illustration
Grades: 3 4 5 6 7   **741.5; Fic**
1. Alcott, Louisa May, 1832-1888 — Adaptations; 2. Graphic novels
978-981-05-4943-5, $14.95

The story of the March girls-beautiful Meg, tomboy Jo, kind and gentle Beth, and spunky Amy-is retold manga-style and in full color. With their country embroiled in war and their father far from home, the four sisters find themselves thrust into new and trying situations, and with little money and a hard winter ahead, they must learn to adapt. In the year that follows, the girls learn about compassion, sacrifice, love, and more about themselves and each other than they ever imagined.

Treasure Island: Manga Literary Classics. Youngjin Singapore 2007 148p. Illustration
Grades: 3 4 5 6 7   **741.5; Fic**
1. Stevenson, Robert Louis, 1850-1894 — Adaptations; 2. Graphic novels
978-981-05-4942-8, $14.95

Young cabin boy Jim Hawkins throws in his lot with pirates Black Dog, Blind Pew, and the unforgettable Long John Silver in this manga-style retelling of Robert Louis Stevenson's classic adventure story. Jim, overly romantic about life on the high seas, is unprepared for the frightening events ahead, including mutiny and an armed battle that poses a grim dilemma: should his loyalty lie with Captain Smollett or Long John Silver?

Yomtov, Nel
Theseus and the Minotaur. Retold by Nel Yomtov ; illustrated by Tod Smith. Stone Arch Books 2009 72p.
Grades: 4 5 6 7 8 9   **292; 741.5**
1. Greek mythology; 2. Graphic novels
978-1-4342-1171-2, $23.93
                                                         LC 2008-32066

King Aegeus of Athens wants a son and ends up with Medea the sorceress; however, he had spent the night with Aethra of Troezen, and she bears a son she names Theseus. He grows up strong, and when he defeats a huge bully, Aethra tells him about his father and sends him to Athens. Along the way, Theseus defeats several evil men, and arrives in Athens. He's just in time to become part of the group of young people sent as sacrifices to appease Minos, King of Crete, who bears a grudge against Aegeus. Minos has a monstrous son, the half-bull half-human Minotaur, and the Athenian youths become the Minotaur's food. Theseus decides to fight the creature and gets help from Ariadne. The book includes information about the Oracle at Delphi, discussion questions, and a glossary.

Part of the Graphic Revolve series

Yoon, Paul
Everyday Science Vol. 2: At the Amusement Park. Art by Laurence Na. Youngjin Singapore 2005 180p. Illustration
Grades: 3 4 5 6 7 8   **500; 741.5**
1. Science; 2. Graphic novels
981-05-2243-6, $12.95

In this volume, every kid is talking about a science tournament in Dreamland, the biggest amusement park in town. Four friends, Daniel, Lucy, Christine, and Sam, hope to win first prize. They soon discover that the tournament questions are linked to the park's roller coasters. Young readers can learn along with Daniel, Lucy, Christine, and Sam as they investigate Newton's Laws of Motion, acceleration, action and reaction, zero gravity, and much more. Colorful illustrations, simple text, and a storyline help to make science understandable.

Yoshida, Akira
X-Men: Kitty Pryde - Shadow & Flame. Written by Akira Yoshida ; art by Paul Smith. Marvel Entertainment 2006 Un Illustration
Grades: 8 9 10 11 12 Adult   **741.5; Fic**
1. Adventure graphic novels; 2. Superhero graphic novels; 3. X-Men (Fictional characters); 4. Graphic novels
0-7851-1816-0, $14.99

A deadly mystery draws Kitty Pryde and her fire-breathing friend Lockheed to the shores of Japan. Ninjas and dragons will be the least of their worries, however, as a long-forgotten villain from Kitty's past is about to finally make his move. There's lots of ninja fighting action.

Yoshida, Tatsuo
Speed Racer: Mach go go go vol. 1 & 2, 2v. Digital Manga Publishing 2008 Illustration
Grades: 7 8 9 10 11 12 Adult   **741.5; Fic**
1. Adventure graphic novels; 2. Automobile racing; 3. Manga; 4. Graphic novels
978-1-56970-731-9, set $39.95

This two-volume set reprints the original Speed Racer manga in its entirety, released for the 40th anniversary of Speed Racer. All the characters are here: Speed, Pops, Sparky, Mom, Trixie, Spritle, Chim Chim, and the mysterious Racer X. Readers will learn how Pops had to set out on his own, how Speed became a professional racecar driver in order to help finance Pops design the special, 12 cylinder Mach 5 engine. In addition to racing, Speed has to deal with people who try to steal Pops' engine plans, rival racers who'll try any cheating tactic to win, and try to figure out who Racer X is. While the animated television series was fine for children to watch, this manga includes violent action that makes it more suitable for teen readers. A note about the title: in Japanese, "go" means "5."

Yoshizumi, Wataru

Ultra Maniac Vol. 1. Viz Media/Shojo Beat 2005 184p. Illustration
Grades: 5 6 7 8 9 10   **741.5; Fic**
   1. Humorous graphic novels; 2. Manga; 3. Romance graphic novels; 4. Shojo manga; 5. Graphic novels
   1-59116-917-8, $8.99

Shy Ayu Tateishi has just made a new friend at school. But this new friend, much to her surprise, is no ordinary classmate. Nina Sakura may look like a normal middle school girl, but she's got a big secret. She's a witch. Or, rather, she's studying to be a witch. And, apparently, she's not doing her homework. Her spells are devastating in their ineffectiveness and often result in the most embarrassing situations for poor Ayu. But things wouldn't be so bad if Nina's sorcery didn't make Ayu look silly in front of the one boy she secretly adores. All she wants is a simple love potion. What she gets, however, is a new best friend who almost flunked out of witch school. This is a five-volume manga series.

Yun, Mi-Kyung

Bride of the water god, vol. 1. Dark Horse Comics 2007 186p. Illustration
Grades: 8 9 10 11 12 Adult   **741.5**
   1. Fantasy graphic novels; 2. Romance graphic novels; 3. Graphic novels
   978-1-59307-849-2, $9.95

Soah's impoverished, drought-stricken village sacrifices her to the Water God Habaek in hopes of getting rain. Instead of dying, Soah finds herself in the land of the gods, and she meets Habaek, who is a young boy. What she doesn't know (but the reader does) is that he takes the form of an adult man at night. She's supposed to be Habaek's bride, but so far she's just an outsider who doesn't belong anywhere. This is sunjeong manwha the Korean equivalent of shojo manga.

Yune, Tommy

Speed Racer & Racer X: the origins collection. Art by Jo Chen. IDW Publishing 2008 Un Illustration
Grades: 8 9 10 11 12 Adult   **741.5; Fic**
   1. Adventure graphic novels; 2. Automobile racing; 3. Racer, Speed (Fictional character); 4. Graphic novels
   978-1-60010-211-0, $19.99

In 1999, Wildstorm Productions relaunched Speed Racer with a three-part origins story; it was successful enough to launch another three-part story telling the origins of Speed's brother, Racer X (come on, it's not a spoiler, everyone but the Racer family knows this). IDW Publishing has collected the stories into this volume. Here is the story of how Speed becomes the driver of the Mach 5, designed by Pops Racer, and here is the story of why Rex Racer left the family, how he "died," and Racer X was born from the

wreckage. There is a lot of racing action, some violence, and some mild fan service.

Zahler, Thomas F.

★ **Love** and capes, vol. 1: do you want to know a secret?. Story and art by Thomas F. Zahler. IDW Publishing 2008 160p. Illustration
Grades: 8 9 10 11 12 Adult   **741.5; Fic**
   1. Humorous graphic novels; 2. Romance graphic novels; 3. Superhero graphic novels; 4. Graphic novels
   978-1-60010-275-2, $19.99

Independent bookseller Abby falls in love with her accountant, Mark; then he confesses to her that he's the superpowered crime-fighter, the Crusader. How does one have a romantic relationship with a superhero? Even without meaning to do it, Abby gives away Mark's secret to her sister Charlotte. Oops. So begins a "heroically super situation comedy" in which Abby feels she's competing against the beautiful Amazonia (Mark's superpowered ex-girlfriend), not to mention Mark's over-protective mother, and Mark has to deal with Abby's obnoxious brother Quincy, who thinks Mark is a wimp.

Volume 1 of 4

★ **Love** and capes, vol. 2: going to the chapel. IDW Publishing 2010 192p. Illustration
Grades: 8 9 10 11 12 Adult   **741.5; Fic**
   1. Humorous graphic novels; 2. Romance graphic novels; 3. Superhero graphic novels; 4. Graphic novels
   978-1-60010-680-4, $19.99

Independent bookstore owner Abby and accountant Mark Spencer, who is also the superhero called the Crusader, have fallen deeply and completely in love. Which is wonderful, except Mark can't quite seem to figure out how to propose to Abby and almost blows it. When he gets over that hurdle, more problems crop up. For one thing, Abby wants the PERFECT wedding dress. Then, a super villain impersonates Mark and almost destroys their relationship. Abby has to find a new bookstore employee when her sister Charlotte gets the chance to go back to college in Paris, France. Abby decides she needs to understand what Mark goes through as a superhero, and she gets superpowers, and a new identity, only to learn that it's far more difficult, and tragic, than she ever imagined. And then, on the eve of the wedding, another super villain strikes, this time changing history, and only Abby has the power to put things right again, which she'll have to do if she wants to marry Mark. This story has superhero action, romance, comedy, drama, romance ... the only content that might bother some people happens when Abby and Amazonia, Mark's superhero ex-girlfriend, get drunk and bond together.

Zidrou

Ducoboo: in the corner!. Godi + Zidrou ; colour work, Véronique Grobert. Cinebook 2008 48p. Illustration
Grades: 3 4 5 6 7 8   **741.5; Fic**
   1. Humorous graphic novels; 2. School stories; 3. Graphic novels
   978-1-905460-26-7, $9.99

Ducoboo doesn't do well in school; he hardly ever gets the right answers, and he spends a lot of time in the corner with Skelly, the classroom skeleton. Desk mate Leonie, naturally, gets very high grades and Ducoboo keeps trying out new plans to copy her work. Mr. Latouche, the teacher, has to deal with a student who seems absolutely incapable of learning. This book is translated from the French, who seem to have very similar classroom situations as those here in the U.S.

Part of the Ducoboo series, originally published in France as L'eleve Ducobu Au coin!

Zirkel, Scott

A **bit** haywire. Created & illustrated by Courtney Huddleston ; written by Scott Zirkel ; inked by Jeff Dabu and Courtney Huddleston ; colored by Mike Garcia ; lettered by Greg Gatlin. Viper 2006

Grades: 5 6 7 8 9   **741.5; Fic**

1. Humorous graphic novels; 2. Superhero graphic novels; 3. Graphic novels

978-0-9777-8835-4; 0-9777883-5-0, $11.95

Owen Brice wants more than anything to be a superhero; he lives in a city protected by the Noble Seven, a superhero team led by Captain Melee and Lady Barrage. On one memorable day, Owen discovers he does have powers, but they're . . . a bit haywire. He can run super fast—but only as long as he can hold his breath. He can fly—as long as he keps his eyes closed. He teleports when camera flashes go off (the first time, he accidentally teleports his clothes off); he burns when he sneezes; he can shoot lase beams from hiseyes when he's cold. Then he discovers his parents are Captain Melee and Lady Barrage. How does one train to be a superhero when all his powers are so weird? Owen decides to give it a try.

Aaron, Jason

The **Other** Side. DC Comics/Vertigo 2007 144p. Illustration

Grades: 12 Adult   **741.5; Fic**
1. Vietnam War, 1961-1975; 2. Graphic novels
978-1-4012-1350-3, $12.99

Billy Everette from Alabama gets drafted into the Marines in 1967; in North Vietnam, Vo Binh Dai volunteers to serve in the People's Army of Vietnam. The book follows these two young men through their training and their journey towards an inevitable confrontation. Billy starts seeing horrifying ghost images of dead soldiers in various stages of decay, and he hears his rifle telling him to kill. Vo maintains a strong sense of patriotism despite the hardships of the march south to find the war. They both end up at Khe Sanh just after the Tet Offensive in February 1968.

Anyone who has seen such movies as "Full Metal Jacket" or "We Were Soldiers Once" will know what to expect in this book; the language is full of expletives and the battle scenes are brutal. Aaron and Stewart bring the harsh reality of war to readers 40 years after the fact.

Originally published as The Other Side issues #1-5.

Scalped: Indian Country. DC Comics/Vertigo 2007 128p. Illustration

Grades: 12 Adult   **741.5; Fic**
1. Mystery graphic novels; 2. Graphic novels
978-1-4012-1317-6, $9.99

Fifteen years ago, Dashiell "Dash" Bad Horse ran away from a life of abject poverty and utter hopelessness on the Prairie Rose Indian Reservation in hopes of finding something better. Now he's come back home armed with nothing but a set of nunchucks, a hell-for-leather attitude and one dark secret, to find nothing much has changed on "The Rez"—short of a glimmering new casino, and a once-proud people overcome by drugs and organized crime. Is he here to set things right or just get a piece of the action? This book has lots of graphic violence, harsh language, nudity, and sexual situations.

Thor; Volume 1: the goddess of thunder. Writer, Jason Aaron; artists, Russell Dauterman (#1-4) & Jorge Molina (#5); color artists, Matthew Wilson (#1-4) & Jorge Molina (#5); letterer, VC's Joe Sabino; cover art, Russell Dauterman & Frank Martin. Marvel Enterprises 2015 136 p. Color; Illustration

Grades: 9 10 11 12 Adult   **741.5**
1. Thor (Fictional character); 2. Women superheroes
0785192387; 9780785192381, $24.99

In this book, by Jason Aaron, illustrated by Russell Dauterman, "Mjolnir lies on the moon, unable to be lifted! Something dark has befallen the God of Thunder, leaving him unworthy for the first time ever! But when Frost Giants invade Earth, the hammer will be lifted - and a mysterious woman . . . the mighty Thor! Who is this new Goddess of Thunder? Not even Odin knows . . . but she may be Earth's only hope against the Frost Giants!" (Publisher's note)

"When the classic Thor is no longer righteous enough to wield his hero-making mallet, the only person worthy enough to take up the mantle is . . . well, you don't find out in

this volume. But the point is that it's a lady, and she's every bit up to the task, as she proves by taking on bloodthirsty Frost Giants, the Minotaur CEO of megacorporation Roxxon, and the Dark Elf Malekith." Booklist

Contains material originally published in magazine form as Thor #1-5.

Volume 1 of an ongoing series

Abadzis, Nick

★ **Laika**. First Second Books 2007 205p. Illustration

Grades: 5 6 7 8 9 10 11 12 Adult   **741.5; Fic**
1. Soviet Union — History — 1953-1991; 2. Space flight; 3. Graphic novels
1-59643-101-6; 978-1-59643-101-0

LC 2006-51907

Laika was the abandoned puppy destined to become Earth's first space traveler. This is her journey. Along with Laika, there is Korolev, once a political prisoner and now a driven engineer at the top of the Soviet space program, and Yelena, the lab technician responsible for Laika's health and life. The book depicts the dedication and struggles of the scientists and technicians who worked in the Soviet space program, based on research Abadzis did before writing this book. The book includes a bibliography of books and websites.

"Abadzis's tear-inducing and solidly researched graphic novel treatment of Laika's surpassingly tragic story is a standout." Publ Wkly

Abbott, Wes

Dogby Walks Alone. Tokyopop 2006 Un Illustration

Grades: 9 10 11 12 Adult   **741.5; Fic**
1. Amusement parks; 2. Mystery graphic novels; 3. Graphic novels
1-59816-582-8, $9.99

Dogby is the park mascot for Happyplace, the world's happiest theme park. When other, armed mascots invade Happyplace and the beautiful Princess is murdered, Dogby and his best friend Snack Girl try to find out what's happening. In this rather wacky mystery, all the characters are identified by their function (for example, P.U.M.G. - Park-Upper-Management-Guy) or their costume. Dogby never says a word, and with the masked costume, his expression never changes, yet Abbott manages to convey his emotions to the reader. This is the first volume of a global manga series.

Dogby walks alone vol. 2: Dogby walks tall. Tokyopop 2008 Un Illustration

Grades: 9 10 11 12 Adult   **741.5; Fic**
1. Humorous graphic novels; 2. Graphic novels
978-1-59816-583-8, $9.99

Dogby, the former costumed animal mascot of the Happyland amusement park, has wandered into the Alaskan wilderness, where he rescues a young boy. He finds the town where the boy lives gripped by fear and ruled by criminals. The boy's single mother struggles to make an honest living, but the criminals, led by a strangely costumed leader named Shelikof, tighten their grip even as they deal with internal struggles led by the hooded Leader. Then there's the Kodiak bear that seems to be hunting Dogby ...

Abel, Jessica

Mastering comics: drawing words & writing pictures continued. By Jessica Abel and Matt Madden. First Second 2012 Xvii, 318 p. Illustration; Color
Grades: 9 10 11 12 Adult   **741.5/1; 741.5**
    1. Cartooning — Technique; 2. Cartoonists; 3. Comic books, strips, etc — Technique; 4. Drawing
    1596436174; 9781596436176, $34.99
                                   LC 2011037023
    Jessica Abel's book "Mastering Comics," written with her husband Matt Madden, is a "course of study for the budding cartoonist. Covering advanced topics such as story composition, coloring, and file formatting, [the book] is a vital companion to the introductory content of the first volume" entitled "Drawing Words & Writing Pictures." (Publisher's note)

Abirached, Zeina

A **game** for swallows: to die, to leave, to return. Written by Zeina Abirached; art by Zeina Abirached; translation by Edward Gauvin. Graphic Universe 2012 188 p.
Grades: 7 8 9 10 11 12   **741.5**
    1. Abirached, Zeina, 1981-; 2. Beirut (Lebanon); 3. Family; 4. Lebanon — History — Civil War, 1975-1990
    0761385681; 9780761385684, $29.27
                                   LC 2011038914
    Mildred L. Batchelder Honor Book (2013)
    This graphic novel looks at "the civil war in Lebanon in the 1980s, as seen through the eyes of a child" separated from her parents. "Young Zeina [Abirached] and her brother have been sequestered within the small foyer in their apartment," which "becomes a place for neighbors in the building to congregate and seek asylum. Though war is raging and death always seems to loom near with shells falling and snipers possibly crouching behind every wall, Zeina and her neighbors try to live the best they can." (Kirkus Reviews)
    Translation of Le jeau des hirondelles.

I remember Beirut. Zeina Abirached. Graphic Universe 2014 96 p. Illustration; Map
Grades: 8 9 10 11 12 Adult   **92; 741.5**
    1. Abirached, Zeina, 1981-; 2. Beirut (Lebanon) — Biography — Juvenile literature; 3. Children and war; 4. Lebanon — History — 20th century — Juvenile literature
    1467738220; 9781467738224, $29.27
                                   LC 2013047112
    In this graphic memoir, Zeina Abirached "reveals numerous details from her childhood in Beirut during the war from 1975 to 1990 war. 'I remember' is a recurring phrase and provides a personal frame of reference for the effect of war on kids. Some are simple childhood memories. . . Inclusion of . . . maps and diagrams orient the reader and provide additional perspective." (Kirkus Reviews)
    "The blocky, naive-style pictures quietly evoke wartime fears in ways the words simply cannot—bullet holes in the sides of cars, rubble in the streets, her father's eyebrows indicating increasing sadness at the heartbreaking state of a formerly vital market." Booklist

Abnett, Dan

Gamble for Victory: Battle of Gettysburg. Osprey Publishing 2007 48p. Illustration
Grades: 3 4 5 6 7 8 9   **741.5; 973.7**
    1. Gettysburg (Pa), Battle of, 1863; 2. United States — History — 1861-1865, Civil War; 3. War; 4. Graphic novels
    978-1-84603-051-2, $9.95
    In July 1863, after having observed a forward column of Union General George G. Meade's cavalry, General Robert E. Lee sent his 75,000 men of the Army of Northern Virginia to meet the 97,000 strong Union Army of the Potomac. Of more than 2,000 land engagements of the American Civil War, Gettysburg ranks as one of the most horrific and devastating battles; more men actually fought and died on this battlefield than in any other encounter on North American soil and the battle itself marked the beginning of the end for the Confederacy. This full-color comic book includes further reading, essential information on the background, aftermath and key players of the conflict.
    Part of Osprey's Graphic History series. This book is also available in a library binding edition from the Rosen Publishing Group under the title The Battle of Gettysburg: Spilled Blood on Sacred Ground.

Abouet, Marguerite

★ **Aya:** life in Yop City. By Marguerite Abouet and Clément Oubrerie; translated by Helge Dascher. Drawn & Quarterly 2012 96 p. Color; Illustration
Grades: 10 11 12 Adult   **741.5/944; 741.5**
    1. Africa — Fiction; 2. Friendship — Fiction
    1770460829; 9781770460829, $24.95
    This book, by Marguerite Abouet and Clément Oubrerie, "is the story of the studious and clear-sighted nineteen-year-old Aya, her easygoing friends Adjoua and Bintou, and their meddling relatives and neighbors. It's . . . [an] account of the simple pleasures and private troubles of everyday life in Yop City." (Publisher's note)
    Followed by Aya: Love in Yop City

★ **Aya:** love in Yop City. By Marguerite Abouet and Clement Oubrerie; translatied by Helge Dascher. Drawn & Quarterly 2013 328 p. Color illustration
Grades: 10 11 12 Adult   **741.5; Fic**
    1. Côte d'Ivoire; 2. Graphic novels — Côte d'Ivoire; 3. Nineteen seventies; 4. Teenage girls — Côte d'Ivoire
    1770460926; 9781770460928, $24.95
                                   LC 2012545664
    This graphic novel, written by Marguerite Abouet and Clément Oubrerie, comprises the final three chapters of the 'Aya' story, . . . a lighthearted story about life in the Ivory Coast during the 1970s, a particularly thriving and wealthy time in the country's history. When a professor tries to take advantage of Aya, her plans to become a doctor are . . . shaken, and she vows to take revenge on [him]." The book includes "recipes, guides to understanding Ivorian slang, street sketches, and concluding remarks from Abouet explaining . . . social milieu." (Publisher's note)

★ **Above the Dreamless Dead: World War I in Poetry and Comics.**
Edited by Chris Duffy. First Second 2014 144 p. Illustration
Grades: 9 10 11 12 Adult   741.5
1. World War, 1914-1918; 2. World War, 1914-1918 — Poetry
1626720657; 9781626720657, $24.99
In this book edited by Chris Duffy, "various artists adapt the works of some of the most famous WWI poets, including Wilfred Owen, Siegfried Sassoon, and Isaac Rosenberg. The ... cartoonists, including Hunt Emerson, Sarah Glidden, and Stuart Immomen, use different approaches to illuminate poems known for its bitter irony and brutal honesty." (Publishers Weekly)
"The work of 'Trench Poets' from WWI is brought vividly to life by accomplished cartoonists. This stunningly effective presentation does much to inform readers of the emotional and physical horrors of war. The volume's small format renders some of the detail difficult to decipher, but anything larger might be overwhelming. There's very mature content, especially in lyrics of soldiers' songs. Reading list." Horn Book
Includes bibliographical references and index

Adamson, Heather
Charles Darwin and the Theory of Evolution. Capstone Press 2007 32p. Illustration
Grades: 3 4 5 6 7 8 9   576.8; 741.5; 92
1. Darwin, Charles, 1809-1882; 2. Evolution; 3. Naturalists; 4. Graphic novels
978-1-4296-0145-0, $25.26
LC 2007005659
This book uses the graphic novel format to tell the story of how Charles Darwin developed his controversial theory of evolution based on the research he conducted during his voyage on the HMS Beagle. The book includes additional facts and a list books for further reading.
Part of the Graphic Library Invention and Discovery series.

Adamson, Thomas K.
Lessons in Science Safety with Max Axiom, Super Scientist. Capstone/Graphic Library 2006 32p. Illustration
Grades: 5 6 7 8 9   508.2; 741.5
1. Science — Experiments; 2. Graphic novels
978-0-7368-6834-1, $18.95
Using the graphic novel format and the engaging fictional scientist character Max Axiom, a tall, muscular African American, this volume shows students conducting science experiments and demonstrates how and why to wear safety goggles, call for help when accidents occur, and safety procedures for dealing with unknown substances. This is part of the Graphic Science series.
"This will be a good choice for science classes during the opening weeks of the school year." (Booklist)

The Adventures of the Fly Volume 1
Archie Comics 2004 96p. Illustration
Grades: 3 4 5 6 7 8 9 10 11 12 Adult   741.5; Fic
1. Adventure graphic novels; 2. Superhero graphic novels
1-879794-18-7, $12.95

This book highlights one of the pioneering super-hero titles of the Silver Age: The Fly. Tommy Troy is a young boy whose world is turned upside down when he meets an emissary of the Fly World and is given a special ring that magically transforms him into the superhuman Fly. Considered an early prototype of Spider-Man, the Fly's earliest adventures were charted by some of the most legendary creative talent in comics: Jack Kirby, Joe Simon, Jack Davis, and Al Williamson. All of these artists and more are featured in this special edition that collects titanic tales from 1959 and 1960.

Aguirre-Sacasa, Roberto
★ **Afterlife** with Archie: Escape from Riverdale. Story by Roberto Aguirre-Sacasa; artwork by Francesco Francavilla; lettering by Jack Morelli. Archie Comic Publications 2014 160 p. Color; Illustration (Afterlife with Archie)
Grades: 11 12 Adult   741.5
1. Andrews, Archie (Fictional character); 2. Dogs — Fiction; 3. Witches — Fiction; 4. Zombies — Fiction
1619889080; 9781619889088, $17.99
LC 2014430277
In this book, by Roberto Aguirre-Sacasa, "[w]hen Jughead's beloved pet Hot Dog is killed in a hit and run, Jughead turns to the only person he knows who can help bring back his furry best friend—Sabrina the Teenage Witch. Using dark, forbidden magic, Sabrina is successful and Hot Dog returns to the land of the living. But he's not the same... and soon, the darkness he brings back with him from beyond the grave begins to spread." (Publisher's note)
"Not parody but serious drama, this graphic novel casts off the typical Archie comic lightheartedness and goes deep into the gut. . . . Paired with Francavilla's dead-on illustrations, the excellent writing from Aguirre-Sacasa . . . brings constant surprises while confronting the dilemma of remaining humane through crisis." LJ

Civil War: Peter Parker, Spider-Man. Writer, Roberto Aguirre-Sacasa; artist, Clayton Crain; pencilers, Angel Medina & Sean Chen; inker, Scott Hanna; colorist, Avalon's Dan Kemp. Marvel Entertainment 2007 Un Illustration
Grades: 9 10 11 12 Adult   741.5; Fic
1. Spider-Man (Fictional character); 2. Superhero graphic novels; 3. Graphic novels
0-7851-2189-7, $17.99
The Civil War has begun, sides have been chosen. Spider-Man chose to unmask himself to the whole world, and now everyone knows he's Peter Parker. Every action has consequences, but for Peter, will he pay, or will his loved ones pay?

The Sensational Spider-Man: Feral. Artist, Angel Medina, Clayton Crain. Marvel Entertainment 2007 Un Illustration
Grades: 7 8 9 10 11 12 Adult   741.5; Fic
1. Spider-Man (Fictional character); 2. Superhero graphic novels; 3. Graphic novels
978-0-7851-2126-8, $19.99
Strange changes are coming over Spidey's animalistic foes - including Dr. Curt Connors, John Jameson and Felicia Hardy - awakening the beast that dwells within them all. Spidey's beaten the Lizard, Man-Wolf and the Black Cat

before, but they've never been more vicious than they are now.

Aihara, Miki

Tokyo Boys & Girls Volume 1. Story by Satoru Akahori; art by Yukimaru Katsura. Viz Media/Shojo Beat 2005 200p. Illustration
Grades: 10 11 12 Adult   **741.5; Fic**
1. Manga; 2. Romance graphic novels; 3. Shojo manga; 4. Graphic novels
1-4215-0020-5, $8.99

Mimori Kosaka's dream comes true when she's accepted to the Meidai Attached High School and gets to wear their super-fashionable uniform. The school year starts off well when Mimori befriends the beautiful Nana, but things quickly turn sour for her when she is chosen to be the class representative. Through a series of unfortunate events, she finds herself the focus of attention by three boys and her teachers, for all the wrong reasons. Mimori is reunited with Atsushi, a boy she knew in elementary school—and it turns out he despises her for allegedly bullying him in their grade school days. In fact, he plans to exact a little revenge. The series includes sexual innuendo, brief sexual situations, and some strong language.

Akahori, Satoru

Kashimashi: Girl Meets Girl Vol. 1. Seven Seas Entertainment 2006 Un Illustration
Grades: 10 11 12 Adult   **741.5; Fic**
1. Fantasy graphic novels; 2. Manga; 3. Romance graphic novels; 4. Yuri manga; 5. Graphic novels
978-1-933164-34-2, $10.99

Being a girl is harder than it looks. For Hazumu, this couldn't be truer, because just the other day, she... was a he. Shunned by the girl of his dreams, Hazumu loses himself in the mountains and is promptly squashed by an oncoming space ship. The alien inside, feeling guilty, rebuilds Hazumu's body... but as the wrong gender! Now Hazumu must learn how to be the girl his parents always wanted while dealing with the trials and tribulations of being caught in a love triangle between two girls - his childhood friend, Tomari, and Yasuna, the girl who rejected him but is now strangely attracted to him/her. This yuri (girl-girl romance) manga was published in a shonen magazine in Japan. The book includes partial nudity and sexual situations.

Akamatsu, Ken

Love Hina: Omnibus 1. By Ken Akamatsu; translated by Satsuki Yamashita; lettered by Hope Donovan. Kodansha Comics 2011 542 p. Illustration
Grades: 11 12 Adult   **741.5**
1. Grandmothers — Fiction; 2. Japan — Fiction; 3. Manga; 4. Young men — Fiction
1935429477; 9781935429470, $19.99
LC 2011517873

In this book, by Ken Akamatsu, "Keitaro Urashima fails his entrance exams to get into Tokyo University for the second time. . . . To make things worse, his parents have kicked him out of his house. Fortunately, his grandmother owns the fabulous Hinata Lodge and has agreed to take Keitaro in as caretaker. What he doesn't know is that the lodge is actually a girl's dorm and he's the only guy around!" (Publisher's note)

Originally published in the U.S. by Tokyopop in 14 volumes

First published in 1999 by Kodansha Ltd., Tokyo as: Love Hina vol. 1-3—Vol. 1, t.p. verso.

Volume 1 of 5

Mao-Chan vol. 1. Del Rey Manga 2008 394p. Illustration
Grades: 8 9 10 11 12   **741.5; Fic**
1. Humorous graphic novels; 2. Manga; 3. Graphic novels
978-0-345-50181-3, $14.95

When incredibly cute aliens invade Japan and steal its signature landmarks, Japan unleashes the Grade School Defense Corps, made up of second-grade students, such as Mao, Misora, and Sylvie. As their grandfathers, who command Ground, Air, and Marine Defense respectively, plot to make their own granddaughters the big heroes, the girls prefer to work together to defeat the aliens. Readers must love incredible cuteness along with some fan service featuring the older teenage girls. There is very little in this volume other than the mild fan service to indicate reasons for an older teen rating the publisher rates it for ages 16 and up.

Akimoto, Nami

Ultra Cute Volume 1. Tokyopop 2006 192p. Illustration
Grades: 7 8 9 10 11 12   **741.5; Fic**
1. Humorous graphic novels; 2. Manga; 3. Romance graphic novels; 4. Shojo manga; 5. Graphic novels
1-59532-956-0, $9.99

For all 15 years of their lives, Ami and Noa have competed against each other for love with the same results: both fall for the same guy, inevitably scaring him away and leaving them boyfriend-less. But the vicious cycle is broken when the girls go to a party and each fall for two different guys! With potential love on the horizon, the sky couldn't be bluer...until Ami discovers that these two dudes are actually duds with ulterior motives. Determined to get revenge on these players, Ami vows to make her guy fall for her while she tries to protect an unsuspecting Noa.

Akimoto, Yasushi

One Missed Call 1+2. Original story by Yasushi Akimoto; manga by Mayumi Shihou. Dark Horse Comics 2007 262p. Illustration
Grades: 10 11 12 Adult   **741.5; Fic**
1. Horror graphic novels; 2. Manga; 3. Graphic novels
978-1-59307-747-1, $14.95

It's an epidemic of accidental death. Multiple college students receive odd voice-mails from themselves, messages from the future, and all they contain are the screams of their own deaths. A few days later, at the date and time of the message's posting, they die in mysterious accidents, and oddly enough, each has a candy in their mouths. The book includes some partial nudity and some violence, but the horror is mostly psychological.

Akino, Matsuri

Kamen Tantei Vol. 1. Tokyopop 2006 196p. Illustration
Grades: 8 9 10 11 12   **741.5; Fic**

1. Humorous graphic novels; 2. Mystery graphic novels; 3. Supernatural graphic novels; 4. Graphic novels
1-59816-499-6, $9.99

A pair of young aspiring mystery writers, Masato and Hakura, tries to crack the most bizarre, baffling, and hilarious cases around them. But when clues lead to a dead end, fortunately for this duo, the Masked Detective always seems to show up in the nick of time to help. There is some violence, mostly in the murder scenes.

Tokyo pet shop of horrors volume 1. Tokyopop 2008 Un Illustration
Grades: 10 11 12 Adult   **741.5; Fic**
1. Horror graphic novels; 2. Manga; 3. Graphic novels
978-1-4278-0607-9, $9.99

Several years after the mysterious Count D left Los Angeles' Chinatown, a new exotic pet shop has opened in the Shinjuku Chinatown of Tokyo. D is still selling strange pets to customers. One hardworking single mother comes seeking a pet/bodyguard for her young son, because she's plagued by horrible nightmares of her ex-husband coming to kill them. The "pet" looks like a young boy, but he's able to quiet her nightmares. A young woman comes seeking an "unlovable" pet, to find that she has a beautiful young teen boy in her house; it turns out she's an aspiring writer and he helps her find success. Each of these customers, however, find that getting what they want may exact a higher price than they expected. The book includes nonsexual partial nudity and some violence.

Alan Moore: Portrait of an Extraordinary Gentleman.
Edited by Smoky Man and Gary Spencer Millidge; with assistance from Omar Martini; introduction by Terry Gilliam. Abiogenesis Press/Top Shelf Productions 2003 352p. Illustration
Grades: 11 12 Adult   741.5
1. Graphic novels
0-946790-06-X, $14.95

This book contains comic strips, illustrations, essays, articles, anecdotes and other pieces contributed by American, English, and international comics creators paying tribute to the master of comic book writing, Alan Moore (creator of Watchmen and From Hell), as he celebrates his 50th year. 145 contributors include Neil Gaiman, Will Eisner, Bill Sienkiewicz, Dave Gibbons, Denis Kitchen, David Lloyd, Jim Valentino, Sergio Toppi, Bryan Talbot, Steve Parkhouse, Mark Millar, Howard Cruse, James Kochalka, Jose Villarrubia, Sam Kieth, Dave Sim, Oscar Zarate, DJ Paul Gambaccini, and novelist Darren Shan, to name just a few. The book includes some content not suitable for younger readers, some strong language, some nudity, and some violence. Alexovich, Aaron

Kimmie66. Written & illustrated by Aaron Alexovich; lettering by Jared K. Fletcher. DC Comics/Minx 2007 176p. Illustration
Grades: 7 8 9 10 11 12 Adult   **741.5; Fic**
1. Science fiction graphic novels; 2. Graphic novels
978-1-4012-0373-3, $9.99

In the 23rd century, people spend lots of time in online VR lairs. Telly Kade is a fairly typical teen of her time, and she tends to hang out in an online vampire lair. Right now, however, she is a little creeped out, because she has received a suicide note from her best friend, Kimmie66. And now other people seem to see Kimmie66 all over the 'net, and Telly wants to know what is really going on.
A Minx graphic novel

Serenity Rose Vol. 1: Working Through the Negativity. SLG Publishing 2005 Un Illustration
Grades: 9 10 11 12 Adult   **741.5; Fic**
1. Humorous graphic novels; 2. Witches; 3. Graphic novels
1-593620-11-X, $12.95

When you can float through the air, smash things with your brain, and conjure up monsters out of ectoplasm, you're bound to attract attention. Serenity Rose, local witch, amateur painter, and noted recluse, wants to be left alone, but she spends the day dodging goblins, goths, greasy politicians, big media parasites, and gawking tourists in the "spookiest lil' town in America." The art is cute-Goth, but there's some harsh language.

Alice, A. (Alex)
Siegfried 1; 1. Written and illustrated by Alex Alice. Archaia Entertainment, LLC 2012 144 p.
Grades: 6 7 8 9 10 11 12   **741.5**
1. Dragons; 2. Gods and goddesses; 3. Orphans
193639345X; 9781936393459, $24.95

This graphic novel by Alex Alice presents "a three-part story inspired by [Richard] Wagner's classic opera 'The Ring of the Nibelung!' Siegfried, born of the love between a mortal man and a Valkyrie, is a young orphan being raised by Mime, one of the last of the dwarf-goblin Nibelungs. Siegfried yearns to discover who his real parents were . . ., not knowing that Odin, father of the Norse gods, has a destiny planned for him: to fight the dragon Fafnir, guardian of the Rheingold!" (Publisher's note)

All Star Comics Archives Volume 11
DC Comics 2005 273p. Illustration
Grades: 7 8 9 10 11 12 Adult   **741.5; Fic**
1. Flash (Fictional character); 2. Green Lantern (Fictional character); 3. Justice Society of America (Fictional characters); 4. Superhero graphic novels; 5. Wonder Woman (Fictional character)
1-4012-0403-1, $49.95

The adventures of the world's first super-team continue in this extra-sized final volume of the series. In Volume 11, collecting All Star Comics #50-57, the JSA face the Diamond Men, Mr. Alpha, and more. The Justice Society of America included the Golden Age Flash, Green Lantern, Dr. Mid-Nite, Hawkman, Wonder Woman, Black Canary, and Atom.

Allan, Von
Li'l kids: road to God knows . . . adventures!. Von Allan Studio 2008 86p. Illustration
Grades: 7 8 9 10 11 12 Adult   **741.5; Fic**
1. Friendship; 2. Mother-daughter relationship; 3. Graphic novels
978-0-9781237-1-0, $13.95

In three interlocked short stories, readers meet Marie, a lonely eight-year-old girl, as she meets neighbor girl Kelly. Marie has been sent outside with a little ball, told by her mother to play. Kelly has to return three late videotapes to the rental store; they're all cutesy-kiddie movies she refuses to watch, after all she is eight years old. Then Marie falls asleep at the kitchen table while drawing her own superhero comic strip and dreams that her character is real. In the last story, readers meet Betty, Marie's mother. Something about her is definitely wrong, but Marie is just confused by her mother's wonky sense of time. Allan includes concept art and the outline and completed script for each story, providing readers with a look at how he puts a comic together. While Marie and Kelly are eight years old, younger readers might not see the subtle hints at trouble that Marie will face in her teen years.

Stargazer, volume one. Von Allan Studio 2010 115p. Illustration
Grades: 4 5 6 7 8 9   **741.5; Fic**
1. Adventure graphic novels; 2. Friendship; 3. Science fiction graphic novels; 4. Graphic novels

Courtesy of Von Allan Studio

978-0-9781237-2-7, $14.95
Marni's grandmother has just died, and she left a strange device that the two of them played with whenever Marni had visited. No one knows how Marni's grandmother got it, and it has never done anything. Her best friends, Elora and Sophie, come over for a last backyard campout before the weather turns cold, and when they each put a hand on the device, an extremely bright light nearly blinds them. After things seem to go back to normal, the girls go outside to find Marni's house gone, the device vanished, and none of the stars look familiar. In the morning, they pack up the little food they had brought for their campout, Elora's telescope, and Sophie's pennywhistle, and hike towards a tower Elora had spotted. They know they're in a totally strange place when they come upon a statue of nonhuman, alien creatures. As they continue, they come upon a strange house, where they find food, and then a mute, boy-sized robot. Even though the three friends bicker with each other, they work together to find a way home. Allan includes extensive notes on his writing process, and an excerpt from his script. The cover art shows one interesting looking character who doesn't appear in this volume. While their age isn't specified, the girls look to be tweens, with the slightly awkward, coltish bodies and movements of pre-adolescents. The strongest language used is one instance of the word "damn."
Volume 1 of 2

Allen, Brooke A.
★ A **home** for Mr. Easter. NBM Publishing, Inc. 2010 197p. Illustration
Grades: 8 9 10 11 12 Adult   **741.5; Fic**
1. Humorous graphic novels; 2. Rabbits; 3. Graphic novels
978-1-56163-580-1, $13.99; 1-56163-580-4

High school student Tesana is large, not too bright, strong, and has always gotten into trouble. A lonely misfit, she tries to fit in better by joining a pep rally planning committee. Once she finds the white rabbits that will be used in the pep rally, she discovers one that is very different: it lays colorful eggs that grant wishes. Tesana believes this is the real Easter Bunny, and she calls him Mr. Easter—and he talks to her. When the football team tries to take Mr. Easter away, Tesana takes them all down and then runs away. Soon they're pursued by cops, an unscrupulous and greedy pet shop owner, laboratory scientists, animal rights protesters, television news crews, a magician/con man, and her mom. Allen was a student at the Savannah School of Art and Design when she wrote this book.
"This is for mature readers who understand the humor, and would be a welcome addition for your multicultural section—female, robust, ethnic." Libr Media Connect

Allie, Scott
The **Fog**. Written by Scott Allie; art by Todd Herman. Dark Horse Comics 2005 Un Illustration
Grades: 9 10 11 12 Adult   **741.5; Fic**
1. Horror graphic novels; 2. Graphic novels
1-59307-423-9, $6.95
A group of Shanghai traders have come to America hoping to escape a string of weird deaths at the teeth and claws of unseen monsters. The arrival of a strange yet familiar fog reveals that the curse has found them, but even they don't know what that has to do with a pyromaniac refugee from the Civil War, the disappearance of one of their sons, or the terrible change coming over the Americans in this small seaside town. This story is a prequel to the motion picture "The Fog." The story has some foul language and some violence, but mostly atmospheric horror.

Allison, John
Bad Machinery 4: The Case of the Lonely One. By John Allison. Oni Press 2015 136 p. Color; Illustration
Grades: 7 8 9 10 11 12 Adult   **741.5**
1. Mystery fiction; 2. School stories
1620102129; 9781620102121, $19.99
                                        LC 2012953355
In this book, by John Allison, "a new school year brings a new classmate to Griswald's Grammar School! But he's a bit strange, and he really, really likes onions. When the whole school suddenly becomes best friends with him, Shauna seems to be the only one left out. It's up to her to peel back the mystery, one onion layer at a time." (Publishers note)

Bad machinery; 1: the case of the team spirit. John Allison; [edited by] James Lucas Jones. Oni Press 2013 112 p. Color; Illustration
Grades: 7 8 9 10 11 12 Adult   **741.5**
1. Mystery graphic novels; 2. School stories
1620100843; 9781620100844, $19.99
                                        LC 2012953355
This graphic novel, the first in John Allison's Bad Machinery series, is "set in a grammar school in a British working-class community" and follows "three earnest boys vying against three sharp-tongued girls to solve mysteries. The framing story concerns a Russian owner of a U.K.

foot-ball (soccer) team trying to bully an elderly homeowner to sell her house." (Publishers Weekly)

Bad Machinery; 2: The Case of the Good Boy. By John Allison; edited by James Lucas Jones and Jill Beaton. Oni Press 2014 136 p. Color; Illustration (Bad Machinery)

Grades: 7 8 9 10 11 12 Adult   741.5
1. Detectives — Fiction; 2. Dogs — Fiction; 3. England — Fiction; 4. Mystery fiction
1620101149; 9781620101148, $19.99

In this book, by John Allison, "everyone's favorite pre-teen British detectives are back for another case! With toddlers disappearing and rumors of a large, beast-like creature roaming the woods, Tackleford is in serious danger. And then there's Mildred's new dog Archibald . . . if you can even call it a dog. . . . Everything comes to a head once the boys get a picture of the beast and Archibald goes missing. Is there a connection?" (Publisher's note)

"The story veers between realism and fantasy, with just a touch of absurdism to keep things fun. . . . The bright, colorful art and snarky dialogue are icing on a delightful cake." Booklist

Bad Machinery; 3: The Case of the Simple Soul. By John Allison. Oni Press 2014 136 p. Color illustration; Color; Map

Grades: 7 8 9 10 11 12 Adult   741.5
1. Monsters; 2. Mystery graphic novels; 3. School stories
1620101939; 9781620101933, $19.99

In this graphic novel, by John Allison, "the Tackleford gang is back with a new case that demands solving! When Tackleford's derelict barns begin going up in flames, Linton and Sonny are on the case with a moderately mysterious new friend. Paths cross, however, when Lottie and Mildred meet a terrifying yet misunderstood creature living beneath a bridge!" (Publisher's note)

"[W]hat stands out in this work is the authentic dialogue, characters' constant questioning, and the protagonists' experiences as 'new' teenagers. Allison addresses how they are coping with physical and emotional changes, balancing friendships, and romantic relationships in a humorous way." SLJ

Originally published online as a webcomic

Giant Days 1. By John Allison and Whitney Cogar; illustrated by Lissa Treiman. Simon & Schuster 2015 128 p. Color; Illustration

Grades: 10 11 12
1. College students — Fiction; 2. Women — Fiction
1608867897; 9781608867899, $9.99

In this book, by John Allison and Whitney Cogar, illustrated by Lissa Treiman, "Susan, Esther, and Daisy started at university three weeks ago and became fast friends. Now, away from home for the first time, all three want to reinvent themselves. But in the face of hand-wringing boys, 'personal experimentation,' influenza, mystery-mold, nu-chauvinism, and the willful, unwanted intrusion of 'academia,' they may be lucky just to make it to spring alive." (Publisher's note)

Volume 1 of an ongoing series

Allred, Michael

Madman atomic comics, vol. 1. Created, written and illustrated by Michael Allred; colors by Laura Allred. Image Comics 2008 Un

Grades: 10 11 12 Adult   741.5; Fic
1. Madman (Fictional character); 2. Science fiction graphic novels; 3. Graphic novels
978-1-58240-916-0, $19.99

Frank Einstein, Madman, undergoes a bizarre, phantasmagorical, existential journey that turns out to be something going on in his subconscious self while he's in a coma. His friends Dr. Flem, Joe (Josephine), and the Atomics hook up Astroman, Frank's robotic "clone," as a technological rescue beacon to lead him through his myriad of fictional personae to his true self, but when they think both Frank and Astroman are dead, they send them up into space in a rocket. Astroman tries to go for help, but his batteries run out, then Frank is rescued by Haley FouFou, who proclaims that he is "one of the Four" who must save the universe. He sends for the Atomics to help him defeat the Crimson King, who has been infected with a cosmic virus and will turn the universe inside out if not stopped. The book is not for casual comics readers, although familiarity with previous Madman comics aren't really necessary to understand this new series. Allred challenges readers with existential discussions and elliptical plotting, and he has fun drawing in the style of many different cartoonists and artists. There's some violence and a little partial nudity, but little in the way of harsh language ("monkey spit" is the strongest epithet Frank utters).

Michael Allred's madman volume 3. Created, written and illustrated by Michael Allred; colors by Laura Allred. Image Comics 2008 Un Illustration

Grades: 9 10 11 12 Adult   741.5; Fic
1. Adventure graphic novels; 2. Science fiction graphic novels; 3. Graphic novels
978-1-58240-893-4, $17.99

This volume completes Image Comics' project of collecting and reprinting the regular Madman Comics series previously published elsewhere. This collection includes The Exit of Dr. Boiffard and G-Men From Hell, along with the Madman King-Size Super Groovy Special. Madman is Frank Einstein, a man with no memory of who or what he had been before. He has wild, surrealistic science fictional adventures with giant brains, sea monsters, frog men, demons, mutating beatniks, secret agents, and lots more. The book includes some violence.

★ **Red** rocket 7. Image Comics 2008 Un Illustration

Grades: 9 10 11 12 Adult   741.5; Fic
1. Rock music; 2. Science fiction graphic novels; 3. Graphic novels
978-1-58240-998-6, $16.99

In a wild science fiction adventure that spans the history of American rock and roll, the humanoid alien known as Red Rocket is left for dead by the villainous Enfinites, but a robotic guardian creates seven clones, each with their own ability. Seven goes on a world-spanning tour of pop music, working with such artists as Little Richard, Elvis Presley, the Beatles, and David Bowie. On his last tour, rock music journalist Lynn Hayes gets mixed up with Seven, his brother clones, and the evil Enfinites who seek to destroy all the clones and Earth, while they're at it. This book was originally published in 1998 by Dark Horse Comics in an 11x11 album size. This new edition is in the vinyl single size and includes bonus material, including an essay from Allred's editor Jamie S. Rich, an introduction by Robert Rodriguez, and an outro by Gerard Way of Chemical Romance. Allred's book predates all the rock 'n' roll graphic novels that have come out in recent years. The book includes some violence and mild language.

Amano, Akira
    Reborn, Vol. 1. Viz Media/Shonen Jump Advanced 2006 192p. Illustration
Grades: 9 10 11 12 Adult   **741.5; Fic**
    1. Humorous graphic novels; 2. Manga; 3. Shonen manga; 4. Graphic novels
    978-1-4215-0671-5, $7.99
    Hapless middle school student Tsuna doesn't do well in school, sports, or socializing. Things get weird when the pint-size assassin named Reborn arrives, announces that Tsuna is the tenth generation Mafia boss of the Vongola family, and that he will tutor the boy. Among his many weapons, Reborn has the Deathperation Shot, which he uses to get Tsuna to succeed in training; basically, if the person shot with this bullet has regrets, he or she will be reborn instantly with the temporary power to do what needs to be done. Reborn has to shoot Tsuna a lot. Violence is cartoony, the humor is wacky slapstick, but the weapons look real and assassins spring out of nowhere.

Amano, Jeff
    The **Cobbler's** Monster: A Tale of Gepetto's Frankenstein. Illustrated by Craig Rousseau. Image Comics 2006 Un Illustration
Grades: 11 12 Adult   **741.5; Fic**
    1. Horror graphic novels; 2. Graphic novels
    1-58240-629-4, $14.99
    Grieving over the death of his only son, Gepetto mixes the new science of DNA with the age-old magic of the golem to resurrect his son. But in truth, he was never very close to Victor. And the anger that burns within the heart of the monster he birthed and created, destroys everything and everyone around him. Now, Gepetto must hunt his own son. This is the story of a man and a monster who, through unspeakable horror, find their way to becoming father and son for the very first time. There's some strong language in the story, and also violence in this tale that combines Pinocchio and Frankenstein and the Jewish legend of the Golem.

    Fade from Grace. Image Comics 2005 Un Illustration
Grades: 10 11 12 Adult   **741.5; Fic**
    1. Superhero graphic novels; 2. Graphic novels
    1-58240-527-1, $14.99
    Power wanes ... fame is fleeting ... but love never fades. Grace tells the story of how John gained the power to fade through walls and doors in order to save her life, then used his powers to help people. Then, when the powers started draining more out of him, they tried to leave, put the superhero deeds behind them, but they encounter a disaster and John knows he has to help to save lives, even if his ends ...

    Red Warrior: Assassin for the Thieves World. Illustrated by Andy MacDonald. Image Comics 2006 Un Illustration
Grades: 10 11 12 Adult   **741.5; Fic**
    1. Adventure graphic novels; 2. Mystery graphic novels; 3. Graphic novels
    978-1-58240-660-2, $12.99
    Agent Tolik Kalinichenko convinces Elena - a Russian Mafia leader's daughter - to seduce an old flame who may be connected to a secret combat system called "Bespredel" (Russian for "without limits"). Elena risks her life for her country, Mother Russia, the world, but most of all, for Tolik. In a race against the clock, Tolik must destroy Bespredel's Red Warriors in time to save Elena, who has been discovered as an informant. But when war has no limits, where can love hide" The book has some strong language and violence, including martial arts fighting. Kat Amano provides an afterword describing Mixed Martial Arts, and the creators provide a bibliography on Russian organized crime and on martial arts.

    Ronin Hood of the Samurai. Illustrated by Andy MacDonald. Image Comics 2005 Un Illustration
Grades: 9 10 11 12 Adult   **741.5; Fic**
    1. Adventure graphic novels; 2. Chushingura — Adaptations; 3. Samurai; 4. Graphic novels
    1-58240-555-7, $9.99
    Masterless after his Lord falls prey to treachery, samurai Oishi of the 47 Ronin leads his faithful few to vengeance. The time has come to defend their honor and raise their swords one final time. This retelling postulates that Oishi and his men lived and fought as Robin Hood-like ronin to help poor villagers victimized by a vicious daimyo (Lord) before they wreaked vengeance for their Lord's death. The tale of the 47 ronin, also called Chushingura, is one of the most famous stories in Japan, called by some the Dd|national tale." The inevitable bloodshed is quite subdued.

America's 1st Patriotic Comic Book Hero: The Shield Volume 1

    Archie Comics 2002 96p. Illustration
Grades: 3 4 5 6 7 8 9 10 11 12 Adult   **741.5; Fic**
    1. Adventure graphic novels; 2. Superhero graphic novels
    1-879794-08-X, $12.95
    A hero with great power, strength and courage who donned the colors of the American flag. A hero who lived for democracy and protected the world from the foes of freedom! No, it's not who you think... it's THE SHIELD, who predated his well known counterpart by over a year. This historic full color trade paperback reprints his first 8 stories from PEP and SHIELD/WIZARD Comics. It includes his first appearance and origin, along with the covers of the comics they originally appeared in, dating from 1940.

Amano, Kat
    The **Wonderful** Wizard of Oz. Image Comics 2006 101p. Illustration
Grades: 3 4 5 6 7 8 9   **741.5; Fic**
    1. Adventure graphic novels; 2. Baum, L Frank; 3. Baum, L Frank — Adaptations; 4. Fantasy graphic novels; 5. Graphic novels

978-1-58240-715-9, $9.99

Baum's classic story gets a European treatment in this colorful adaptation of Dorothy's adventures in the land of Oz.

Originally published as Le Magicien D'Oz Volumes 1-3 by Guy Delcourt Productions, France.

Amano, Kozue
 Aria, vol. 3. Tokyopop 2008 Un Illustration
Grades: 8 9 10 11 12 **741.5; Fic**
 1. Manga; 2. Science fiction; 3. Shojo manga; 4. Graphic novels
 978-1-4278-0512-6, $9.99
 With the coming of Spring, Akari has now been on Neo-Venezia for one year (two Earth years). She meets a new trainee undine named Alice, who's only fourteen years old but has natural talent as a gondolier. Akari and Alicia go on a hunt for Spring and find a marvelous cherry tree near an abandoned railway track. Then Akari, Akai, and Alice go on a treasure hunt when Akari finds a small chest in the old gondola she has borrowed. When Akai runs away from Himeya, Akari finally learns who Akai really is, besides being a single undine (a journeyman). And, on the Festa del Bocolo, Akatsuki wants Akari's help in rounding up as many red roses as he can to give to Alicia. While Tokyopop has rated this series for older teens, there hasn't been any content in the first three volumes to prevent younger teens from reading these books.

 Aria, vol.4. Tokyopop 2008 182p.
Grades: 8 9 10 11 12 **741.5; Fic**
 1. Manga; 2. Science fiction graphic novels; 3. Shojo manga; 4. Graphic novels
 978-1-4278-0513-3, $9.99
 It's now summer on Neo Venezia (formerly known as Mars), and journeyman undine (gondolier) Akari and her friends receive invitations to a place called the Neverlands. It turns out to be a secluded beach, and Akari swims in the ocean for the first time in her life. She also helps a sylph an airbike-riding deliveryman make his deliveries when he crashes and loses his map. When Akari tries to find a street fair where she can buy a wind chime, she gets lost and follows President Aria (a Neo Venezian cat) to a special bar that caters only to cats. Akari, Alice, and Aika meet the legendary major fairy who founded Aria Company, a lady they call Grandma; they want to learn how to become the best undines, while she tries to help them enjoy life. Tokyopop keeps rating this series for older teens, citing fan service, nonsexual nudity, and alcohol use, but in four volumes there has been very little of any of these elements in the stories.

 Aria, volume 1. Tokyopop 2008 Un Illustration
Grades: 8 9 10 11 12 **741.5**
 1. Manga; 2. Science fiction graphic novels; 3. Shojo manga; 4. Graphic novels
 978-1-4278-0510-2, $9.99
 Aria is the sequel series to Aqua, a two-volume manga. Mars had been terraformed and is now almost completely covered in water. Various islands have become extensions of different nations on Manhome, and young Akari Mizunashi lives and works in Neo-Venezia, an exact replica of old Venice. The gondoliers of Neo-Venezia are called undines,

and Akari is a journeyman undine who loves her work. She helps an elderly tourist find his daughter, teaches her friend from the floating cities which maintain the climate about Venetian history, visits an island where the Japanese have settled and encounters a fox god, and participates in a gondola race. The publisher rates this series for older teens, but there's no content in this first volume to keep it from younger teens.

Amano, Shiro
 Kingdom Hearts II Vol. 1. Tokyopop 2007 204p. Illustration
Grades: 4 5 6 7 8 9 10 11 12 **741.5; Fic**
 1. Fantasy graphic novels; 2. Manga; 3. Shonen manga; 4. Graphic novels
 978-1-4278-0058-9, $9.99
 In the quiet little hamlet of Twilight Town, there lives a boy named Roxas. He and his friends Hayner, Pence and Olette are trying to enjoy their final days of summer vacation, when strange things begin to happen. First the group is falsely accused of stealing photos from all over town. Then they are attacked by bizarre, white creatures. But the oddest occurrences are the recurring dreams Roxas has of a boy named Sora, and the presence of a girl named Namine, who has a mysterious secret to share with Roxas. What began in Kingdom Hearts and Kingdom Hearts: Chain of Memories continues in Kingdom Hearts II.

 Kingdom Hearts, Chain of Memories, Vol. 1. Tokyopop 2006 198p. Illustration
Grades: 4 5 6 7 8 9 **741.5; Fic**
 1. Adventure graphic novels; 2. Fantasy graphic novels; 3. Graphic novels
 1-59816-637-9, $9.99
 The door to Kingdom Hearts was sealed, dealing a blow to the Heartless and restoring the worlds to normal, but Riku and King Mickey were tapped inside. Now Sora, Donald, and Goofy's search for their friends leads them to the mysterious Castle Oblivion, where a hooded figure tells them, "Ahead lies something you need, but to claim it, you must lose something dear." What could be more dear than one's own memories" This is the first of two volumes, and is published in the original Japanese right-to-left page order.

 Kingdom Hearts, Vol. 1. Tokyopop 2005 136p. Illustration
Grades: 4 5 6 7 8 9 **741.5; Fic**
 1. Adventure graphic novels; 2. Fantasy graphic novels; 3. Manga; 4. Graphic novels
 1-59816-217-9, $5.99
 When a strange storm hits his island home, 14-year-old Sora is separated from his friends and swept into a mysterious new land. There he meets Court Wizard Donald and Captain Goofy, who are on a mission to find their king, Mickey, and return him to his throne at Disney Castle. When the three learn of the Heartless, ominous creatures who feed off the darkness in the hearts of others, they join forces to recover Sora's friends, return the king to his rightful position and save the universe from the Heartless. This story is based on the popular video game and is a four volume manga series.

The Amazing Adventures of the Escapist Vol. 3
Dark Horse Comics 2006 168p. Illustration
Grades: 8 9 10 11 12 Adult   741.5; Fic
 1. Adventure graphic novels; 2. Superhero graphic novels;
3. Graphic novels
 978-1-59307-492-0, $14.95
 This volume of The Escapist features the late Will
Eisner's return to the Spirit, in a crossover tale with the
Escapist. This story became Eisner's last comics work,
completed just two weeks before the death of the comics
godfather. Also in this volume is the comics writing debut of
award-winning author and Guggenheim fellow Chris Offutt,
illustrated by Thomas Yeates. Dan Best and Eddie Campbell
contribute a fully painted story from the 1939 World's Fair in
Empire City, and 2004 Russ Manning Award winner Eric
Wight brings a polemic story from writer Jason Hall to life.
Among the other notable contributors are Howard Chaykin,
Paul Grist, Shawn Martinbrough, David Hahn, Roy Thomas,
Matt Wagner and indie stalwarts Jeffrey Brown and Jason.
The book includes some violence.

Ambaum, Gene
 Book Club: An Unshelved Collection. By Gene
Ambaum and Bill Barnes; art by Bill Barnes. Overdue
Media 2006 120p. Illustration
Grades: 7 8 9 10 11 12 Adult   741.5
 1. Humorous graphic novels; 2. Libraries; 3. Graphic
novels
 0-9740353-3-5, $17.95
 What happens in the library stays in the library. But oh,
what happens in the library! Dewey has a book club, and you
do not talk about Book Club. Colleen has a blog, but she
doesn't know everyone can read it. Someone gave vegan
Tamara a membership to the ham-of-the-month-club. And
Merv reserved every copy of the new Harry Potter for
purposes nefarious. This collection also features dozens of
full-page full-color comic-format book talks, plus a very
special storytime zombie nursery rhyme. This is the fourth
print collection of the daily web comic chronicling the
shenanigans at the Mallville Public Library.

 Frequently asked questions: an Unshelved collection.
By Gene Ambaum and Bill Barnes; art by Bill Barnes.
Overdue Media 2008 135p. Illustration
Grades: 7 8 9 10 11 12 Adult   741.5
 1. Humorous graphic novels; 2. Libraries; 3. Graphic
novels
 978-0-9740353-5-2, $17.95
 This sixth collection of the Unshelved webcomics
includes all daily and Sunday Book Club comic strips from
February 19, 2007 through February 16, 2008. It includes
"The Great Plastic Coffee Cup Lid Comic Strip Challenge,"
a week-long competition between Unshelved and Dave
Kellett's Sheldon, another webcomic. It also includes all the
special comic strips done for ALA's Cognotes, the
conference newsletter published every day of the Midwinter
Meeting and Annual Conference. The Sunday Book Club
strips are in color, each one is a full page, and constitutes a
mini-booktalk cum reader's advisory for each title, which
range from YA fiction to graphic novels to classic science
fiction and more.

 ★ **Large** print: an unshelved collection. By Gene
Ambaum and Bill Barnes; art by Bill Barnes. Overdue
Media   2010   128p.

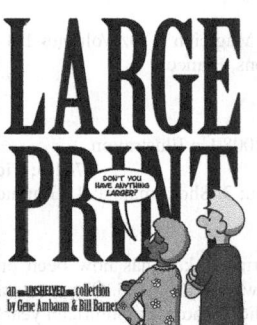

Illustration
Grades: 7 8 9 10 11 12
Adult   741.5
 1.   Humorous   graphic
novels; 2. Libraries; 3.
Graphic novels
 978-0-9740353-7-6, $11.95
 This volume collects
the daily webcomic strips of
Unshelved   from February
16, 2009 to April 26, 2010
plus the strips that originally
appeared in ALA Cognotes
in June 2009 and January
2010. It introduces a change
in format and a lower price
point, in that the Sunday

Courtesy of Overdue Media

booktalk strips are not included. The strips collected for this
volume reflect the recession, as the Mallville Public Library
deals with a public that now comes to the library to use the
computers to apply for unemployment benefits, fill out job
applications, and more. Despite the gloomy times, the strips
still find humor in the everyday happenings in the public
library. Librarians and people who like to use libraries will
find that Mallville is not so different from their local
libraries.

 Read Responsibly: An Unshelved Collection. By Gene
Ambaum and Bill Barnes; art by Bill Barnes. Overdue
Media 2007 135p. Illustration
Grades: 8 9 10 11 12 Adult   741.5
 1. Humorous graphic novels; 2. Libraries; 3. Graphic
novels
 978-0-9740353-4-5, $17.95
 The fifth year of strips about the Mallville Public
Library, its eccentric staff and even more eccentric patrons,
includes the Pimp My Bookcart sequence (that sparked a
nationwide contest) and a year's worth of full-color
full-page Unshelved Book Clubs featuring the greatest
books ever written. Probably. Plus never-before published
strips, mostly those done for American Library Association
conferences, and more.

Ambrosio, Stefan
 Wizards of Mickey, vol. 1: mouse magic. Boom!
Studios 2010 Un Illustration
Grades: 3 4 5 6 7 8 9   741.5; Fic
 1. Adventure graphic novels; 2. Fantasy graphic novels; 3.
Humorous graphic novels; 4. Mickey Mouse (Fictional
character); 5. Graphic novels
 978-1-60886-541-3, $9.99
 Wizard's apprentice Mickey loses a magic talisman
called the Diamagic when he and the village fall afoul of a
con man who steals it from them. Mickey pursues the con
man, but he learns he'll have to compete in the Great
Wizard's Tournament to win it back if he can father a team to
work with him. He ends up with Donald and Goofy, both
misfit bunglers, but somehow they'll have to compete
against Peg-Leg Pete and the Phantom Blot. This book,

originally written and published in Italy, is full of fantasy adventure and fun with recognizable Disney characters.

Amir
★ **Zahra's** paradise. Amir Khalil. First Second 2011 255 p. Illustration
Grades: 10 11 12 Adult   **741.5**
1. Iran — History — 1979-; 2. Iran — Politics and government; 3. Missing persons — Fiction; 4. Graphic novels
9781596436428 (pa); 1596436425
LC 2011017564
This book, a "Publishers Weekly" Best Comics title for 2011, is "[s]et in the aftermath of Iran's fraudulent elections of 2009 . . . [and] is the fictional story of the search for Mehdi, a young protestor who has vanished into an extrajudicial twilight zone. What's keeping his memory from being obliterated is not the law. It is the grit and guts of his mother, who refuses to surrender her son to fate, and the tenacity of his brother, a blogger, who fuses tradition and technology to explore and explode the void in which Mehdi has vanished." (Publisher's note)

Andelman, Bob
Will Eisner: A Spirited Life. M Press 2005 375p. Illustration
Grades: 9 10 11 12 Adult   **92; 741.5**
1. Artists — Biography; 2. Arts — Biography; 3. Authors — Biography; 4. Cartoonists — United States — Biography; 5. Eisner, Will, 1917-2005; 6. Literature — Biography; 7. Graphic novels
1-59582-011-6, $14.95
LC 2005026326
Internationally recognized for his genre-busting 1940s art and storytelling style on The Spirit, Will Eisner's greatest legacy may be the graphic novels he championed and created. He was an American master whose work in comics permanently altered the face of global pop culture. This biography explores Eisner's life, detailing a career that spanned 70 years and saw him educate several generations of Army soldiers in the innovative PS Magazine and create the first widely known graphic novel, A Contract with God. Eisner also introduced some of the world's greatest comics art talent: Bob Kane (Batman), Jack Kirby (Fantastic Four), Jules Feiffer, Dave Berg (MAD) and Joe Kubert (Tarzan). And he inspired generations of modern artists and writers, including Frank Miller (Sin City), Robert Crumb, Harlan Ellison, Neil Gaiman (Sandman, American Gods), Brad Bird (The Incredibles), Patrick McDonnell (Mutts) and Art Spiegelman (Maus). A Spirited Life also includes interviews with many of Eisner's contemporaries, such as Alan Moore, Dave Gibbons, Neil Gaiman, Denis Kitchen, Jim Warren, Dave Sim, Denny O'Neil and Stan Lee.
"Michael Chabon contributes a heartfelt introduction to Andelman's first-ever biography of Will Eisner (1917-2005) . . . Eisner revolutionized the field . . . from his 1940s stories featuring masked crime fighter the Spirit to his later, pioneering graphic novels but also as businessman and entrepreneur, teacher, mentor, and the inspiration of countless young artists [like Art Spiegelman]. . . . Besides verifying Eisner's impact on nearly every artist who drew comics in his wake, Andelman shows that Eisner's influence

extends to such film directors as Spielberg and Tarantino." Booklist

Anderson, Christine
The **long** tail: why the future of business is selling less of more. Art by Shane Clester. Smarter Comics 2011 80p. Illustration
Grades: 10 11 12 Adult   **658.8; 741.5**
1. Business; 2. Marketing; 3. Graphic novels
978-1-61066-006-8, $12.95
LC 2010-942329
Anderson's bestselling book about niche markets the "long tail" of the title is now a graphic novel. Adapted by comics writer Bunn, this book describes how business is changing with the rise of e-commerce that allows the success of specialty appeal items, whether various forms of media or such things as t-shirts. Wired editor-in-chief Anderson discusses the rise and fall of the music industry, the video rental industry, and the many changes in brick-and-mortar retail due to ever-changing and advancing technology. The comic book format may attract more readers among older teens and college students, who are the consumers changing things.

Anderson, Eric A.
PX! Book one: a girl and her panda. Written by Eric A. Anderson and Manny Trembley; illustrated by Manny Trembley. Image Comics 2007 Un Illustration
Grades: 6 7 8 9 10 11 12 Adult   **741.5; Fic**
1. Adventure graphic novels; 2. Humorous graphic novels; 3. Science fiction graphic novels; 4. Graphic novels
978-1-58240-820-0, $16.99; 1-58240-820-3
A young girl named Dahlia and her trusty (robot) panda sidekick set off on a journey around the world to save her missing scientist father, who has been kidnapped by Pollo, an evil goat mastermind who wants to take over the world (and yes, people keep telling him his name means chicken" in Spanish). Along the way, Dahlia meets Weatherby Ian Poppington III, a Victorian English secret agent also known as Double Aught Seven," and Wikkity Jones, a rollerskating swordsman who talks like a hillbilly and stands ready to fight ninja any time. The absurd humor is punctuated by moments of intense violent action, especially in the side story about fighting zombies. This book collects the webcomic.
Followed by: PX! v.2: in the service of the Queen (2009)

PX! book two: in the service of the Queen. Image Comics 2008 Un Illustration
Grades: 4 5 6 7 8 9 10 11 12   **741.5; Fic**
1. Adventure graphic novels; 2. Humorous graphic novels; 3. Science fiction graphic novels; 4. Graphic novels
978-1-60706-018-5, $16.99
In this second volume, Weatherby takes center stage. Dahlia's father is called to London to permanently shut down a super-computer, but villainous goat Pollo has already had two of his lackeys hack into the system and take over. When Weatherby, Wikkity, and Panda show up to help Dahlia and her dad, Double Aught Seven Weatherby discovers he has not been, nor ever was, a Double Aught

agent in the service of the Queen. However, he soon discovers that he is the only one who can get into the system, because IT had recruited him. The book, co-written by Trembley as well as illustrated by him, includes several short stories, including one created during the 24-Hour Comic Book Day. The main story doesn't have any bad language or overt violence, but a couple of the short stories include occasional use of the word "crap," and one story involves zombies.

Sam Noir Volume One. Art by Manny Trembley. Image Comics/Shadowline 2007 Un Illustration
Grades: 10 11 12 Adult 741.5; Fic
1. Adventure graphic novels; 2. Mystery graphic novels; 3. Graphic novels
978-1-58240-758-6, $15.99
Sam Noir is a samurai, and a private detective. When the woman he loves gets killed, he sets out for revenge, armed with his two swords. This violent story mixes samurai action with crime noir mystery with some pirate action.

Anderson, Ho Che
King: a comics biography. Fantagraphics 2010 312p. Illustration
Grades: 10 11 12 Adult 92; 741.5
1. African Americans — Biography; 2. African Americans — Civil rights; 3. Biographical graphic novels; 4. Civil rights activists; 5. Clergy; 6. King, Martin Luther, Jr, 1929-1968; 7. Nonfiction writers; 8. Graphic novels
978-1-60699-310-1, $34.99

"Much of the book (packaged nicely with previously unprinted material, sketches, and a somewhat beside-the-point modern-day "prelude" titled Black Dogs) tracks King from his college days in the 1950s to his death, jamming each page with noirishly drawn frames and tightly packed political debates. Though all the great moments of his civil rights battle are here (from the March on Washington to his

Courtesy of Fantagraphics

less-successful housing campaign in Chicago), Anderson doesn't resort to the cheap cinematic trick of success and fadeout. There is more disappointment here than celebration, suffused with the sorrowful sense of a long, long battle just barely begun. A crowning achievement, like the man it portrays." Publ Wkly
First published 2005

Anderson, Jameson
The **Z-boys** and Skateboarding. Capstone Press 2007 32p. Illustration
Grades: 3 4 5 6 7 8 9 741.5; 796.22
1. Skateboarding; 2. Graphic novels
978-1-4296-0150-4, $25.26
LC 2007004915

This book uses the graphic novel format to describe the birth of the Z-boys skateboarding team in Dogtown, an area of Santa Monica, in 1973, and how they influenced modern skateboarding. The book includes additional facts and a list of books for further reading.
Part of the Graphic Library Invention and Discovery series.

Anderson, Kevin J.
Grumpy old monsters. IDW Publishing 2004 96p. Illustration
Grades: 4 5 6 7 8 9 741.5; Fic
1. Humorous graphic novels; 2. Monsters; 3. Graphic novels
1-932382-35-6, $13.99
The old monsters Frankenstein's Monster, Dracula, the Mummy, and the Werewolf, have all retired and moved to the old monsters' home, where Nurse Wrentch terrorizes them and only little Tiffany Frankenstein, granddaughter of old Dr. F., comes to visit. But this time she comes with terrible news the Van Helsing Corporation is about to take possession of Castle Frankenstein, tear it down, and build luxury condominiums. The monsters decide they must come out of retirement and help Tiffany stop the horror if they can escape Nurse Wrentch!

Ando, Natsumi
The **Best** of draw! volume 3. Twomorrows Publishing 2008 256p. Illustration
Grades: 11 12 Adult 741.5
1. Comic books, strips, etc — Authorship; 2. Drawing — Technique
978-1-893905-91-7, $29.95
This volume collects articles from Draw! issues 5, 6, and 7, including interviews with the late Mike Weiringo, Bill Wray, and Dan Brereton, and tutorials on various aspects of drawing, including light and shadow, penciling hands, digital illustration, and figure drawing. The black and white illustrations include some nudity, particularly in the figure drawing tutorials.

Kitchen Princess, Vol. 2. Natsumi Ando ; story by Miyuki Kobayashi. Ballantine Books/ Del Rey Manga 2007 Un Illustration
Grades: 7 8 9 10 11 12 741.5; Fic
1. Cooking; 2. Manga; 3. Shojo manga; 4. Graphic novels
978-0-345-49659-1, $10.95
Orphaned Najika has left Hokkaido and come to the Seika Academy in Tokyo in search of the "prince" who saved her when she was a little girl. Brothers Sora and Daichi, whose parents founded the academy, discover that Najika has the gift of an absolute sense of taste; when she eats a food, she can identify all the ingredients, and she never forgets the taste. She can use this to duplicate any recipe, and she does so to win a cooking competition so she can stay at the Academy. Then she learns that Akane, who hates Najika, wants so badly to become a supermodel like her mother that she's following an extreme diet that could lead to an eating disorder. Can Najika overcome Akane's hostility to help her? Each volume includes recipes.

This is a 10 volume series
Also available in omnibus editions

Kitchen princess, vol. 9. Natsumi Ando ; story by Miyuki Kobayashi. Del Rey Manga 2009 Un Illustration
Grades: 7 8 9 10 11 12   **741.5; Fic**
1. Cooking; 2. Manga; 3. Romance graphic novels; 4. Shojo manga; 5. Graphic novels
978-0-345-51026-6, $10.99
Najika finally discovers the true identity of her Flan Prince, but she discovers that it doesn't change how she feels about Daichi, even with Seiya trying to win her over. And Daichi starts to remember things from the past, things he had forgotten and was allowed to forget. He starts to remember the family's trip to Hokkaido when his and Sora's mother was still alive, a trip that ended tragically for the family. Now that he remembers what happened, he holes up in his room and won't let anyone see him; but Najika won't stop trying to prepare food for him and to try to cheer him up, even if Daichi's father doesn't like her. The book includes recipes for dishes mentioned throughout the story.

Andrews, Mark
Tales of Colossus. Image Comics 2006 Un Illustration
Grades: 10 11 12 Adult   **741.5; Fic**
1. Adventure graphic novels; 2. Fantasy graphic novels; 3. Graphic novels
1-58240-591-3, $17.99
A knight, whose soul is trapped inside a metal monster called Colossus, lives out an immortal existence slaying evil creatures. Until one day a twisted, evil paladin wielding enchanted weapons arrives in the Kingdom with his own agenda. Their paths cross in a steel pounding, armor glinting no holds barred battle that will change a Kingdom forever. Set during the times of the Crusades, this book is filled with battles and bloodshed, with some nudity and sexual situations.

Andreyko, Marc
Manhunter: Street Justice. Marc Andreyko, writer; Jesus Saiz, penciller; Jimmy Palmiotti, inker; Steve Buccellato, colorist; Phil Balsman, Jared K. Fletcher, Pat Brosseau, letterers. DC Comics 2005 Un Illustration
Grades: 10 11 12 Adult   **741.5; Fic**
1. Superhero graphic novels; 2. Graphic novels
1-4012-0728-6, $12.99
When top federal prosecutor Kate Spencer loses a case against a super-villain, setting him free to kill again, she breaks the laws she has long upheld to become Los Angeles' newest crime fighting vigilante. Prosecuting super-villains has been her life's work But these criminals never stay locked up for good. Now, using confiscated met human weaponry she raided from an evidence locker, Kate tracks the perps who have eluded justice in the courts and delivers a long-overdue eye for an eye. She's found her true calling. She is the Manhunter. And she likes it. Plenty of violence, an anti-heroine who smokes and is willing to kill the criminals she hunts, make this superhero title one for older readers.

Manhunter: Trial by Fire. Art by Javier Pina, Jesus Saiz, Brad Walker, et al. DC Comics 2007 224p. Illustration
Grades: 10 11 12 Adult   **741.5; Fic**
1. Manhunter (Fictional character); 2. Superhero graphic novels; 3. Graphic novels
978-1-4012-1198-1, $17.99

When super criminals use the legal system to escape justice, prosecutor Kate Spencer assumed the role of vigilante, becoming the Manhunter and meting out her own brand of street justice. In this second collection, Spencer is poised to take on the trial of the year, as the eyes of the nation are on her latest case: finding the Shadow Thief guilty of murdering the hero Firestorm. As Manhunter she has to protect the Shadow Thief against other villains out to kill him. Then she learns that she's only the latest in a long line of Manhunters, and someone is killing them all. This book includes violence, foul language, and sexual situations.

Nightwing: the lost year. Marv Wolfman, Marc Andreyko, writers; Jamal Igle, Jon Bosco, Joe Bennett, pencillers; Keith Champagne, Alex Silva, Jack Jadson, inkers; Jason Wright, Edgar Delgado, colorists. DC Comics 2008 Un Illustration
Grades: 10 11 12 Adult   **741.5; Fic**
1. Adventure graphic novels; 2. Nightwing (Fictional character); 3. Superhero graphic novels; 4. Graphic novels
978-1-4012-1671-9, $14.99
Nightwing interrupts a kidnapping attempt only to realize the victim is someone from his past, Liu, his first lover. She says she works for Eddie Hwang, who used to be Metal Eddie, a criminal mastermind who tried to use a teenage Dick Grayson. Liu says Eddie has gone straight. However, the Vigilante, a ruthless killer, is hunting Eddie. Nightwing needs to find out what Eddie really wants, while trying to prevent Vigilante from killing anyone. The book includes some sexual scenes without nudity, and lots of fighting violence.

Angel: Spotlight
IDW Publishing 2006 120p. Illustration
Grades: 10 11 12 Adult   **741.5; Fic**
1. Fantasy graphic novels; 2. Horror graphic novels
978-1-600100-023-6, $19.99
This collection compiles five one-shots focusing on different members of Angel's supporting cast, each from a different creative team. Peter David and Nicola Scott focus on Illyria. Dan Jolly and Mark Pennington handle Gunn, Scott Tipton and Mike Norton feature Wesley. Jeff Mariotte and David Messina present Doyle. And Jay Faerber and Bob Gill offer up a tale of Conner. Monster fighting, demons, and internal organs are on display in the stories.

Anzai, Noboyuki
Flame of Recca Volume 1. Story and art by Nobuyuki AnzaiViz. Media 2003 184p. Illustration
Grades: 10 11 12 Adult   **741.5; Fic**
1. Fantasy graphic novels; 2. Manga; 3. Martial arts; 4. Ninja; 5. Shonen manga; 6. Graphic novels
1-59116-066-9, $9.95
Teenager Recca Hanabishi is always up for a good-natured tussle with his friends. That's because he's famous at school and around town for being a super ninja geek. Armed with the power to control flame, Recca suddenly finds himself in an awkward situation. On the day he pledges his undying ninja allegiance to a pretty classmate named Yanagi Sakoshita, a mysterious older woman pops into his life. Is she good" Is she evil" What exactly does she want" And what's the deal with tomboy, Fuko Kirisawa"

She's got the power of wind at her command. Does she want to smash Recca to smithereens, or does she simply want to kiss him" The series includes strong language, nudity, sexual innuendo, and graphic violence.
Volume 1 of 33

Aoyama, Gosho
★ **Case** Closed Volume 1. Viz Media 2004 192p. Illustration
Grades: 9 10 11 12 Adult   **741.5; Fic**
1. Manga; 2. Mystery graphic novels; 3. Shonen manga; 4. Graphic novels
1-59116-327-7, $9.95

Precocious high school student Jimmy Kudo used his keen powers of observation and astute intuition to solve mysteries that have left law enforcement officials baffled. Hot on the trail of a suspect, Jimmy is accosted from behind and fed a strange chemical which physically transforms him into a first-grader. Taking on the pseudonym Conan Edogawa (from favorite mystery writers Arthur Conan Doyle and Edgar Allan Poe), he attempts to track down the people who did this to him. But until he finds a cure for his bizarre condition, Jimmy continues to help the police solve their toughest cases, and he lives with his best friend Rachel, who thinks he's Jimmy's cousin, and her private detective father (who gets credit for cracking all the cases). The murder cases are violent and there's a little sexual innuendo; despite Jimmy's little-kid appearance, the stories are not for younger readers.

Appignanesi, Richard
Hamlet. [Richard Appignanesi, text adaptor]; illustrated by Emma Vieceli. Harry N. Abrams/Amulet Books 2007 195p. (Manga Shakespeare)
Grades: 8 9 10 11 12 Adult   **822.3; 741.5**
1. Shakespeare, William, 1564-1616 — Adaptations
978-0-8109-9324-2, $9.95; 0-8109-9324-4

Shakespeare's classic play of murder and revenge is here adapted into a manga-style graphic novel. It's now set in 2107, after global climate change has devastated the Earth. Appignanesi uses the text of the play and abridges it to fit the pages, while Vieceli's art vigorously carries the story along. The book includes a summary of the plot and a brief biography of Shakespeare.
First published in the United Kingdom

Introducing Postmodernism, Third Ed. Art by Chris Garratt. Totem Books 2005 176p. Illustration
Grades: 10 11 12 Adult   **190; 741.5**
1. Postmodernism; 2. Graphic novels
1-84046-575-1, $12.95

Postmodernism seemed to promise an end to the grim Cold War era of nuclear confrontation and oppressive ideologies. This volume uses cartoons and a spare text to trace the pedigrees of postmodernism in art, theory, science, and history, along with the ideas of Derrida, Baudrillard, Foucault, and other icons of postmodern thinking. A new edition will be published in September 2007.

A **midsummer** night's dream. Illustrated by Kate Brown. Abrams 2008 207p. (Manga Shakespeare)
Grades: 7 8 9 10   **822.3; 741.5**
1. Shakespeare, William, 1564-1616 — Adaptations

978-0-8109-9475-1, $9.95; 0-8109-9475-5
Shakespeare's comedy of romance, Faerie, and shenanigans in the forest is adapted into a manga-style graphic novel. Hermia is in love with Lysander, while Demetrius is in love with Hermia, and Helen loves Demetrius. When mischievous fairy Puck decides to have some fun with the powerful love potion he has fetched for Fairy King Oberon, chaos reigns. While the human foursome needs to sort itself out, Oberon seeks revenge against his wife, Queen Titania, by having Puck use the love potion on her so she falls in love with the first creature she sees—who happens to be a yokel to whom Puck gave a donkey's head. The text takes dialog from the original play. The book includes a plot summary and a brief biography of Shakespeare.

Romeo and Juliet. By William Shakespeare; adapted by Richard Appignanesi; illustrated by Sonia Leong. Amulet Books 2007 195p. (Manga Shakespeare)
Grades: 8 9 10 11 12   **822.3; 741.5**
1. Shakespeare, William, 1564-1616 — Adaptations
978-0-8109-9325-9, $9.95; 0-8109-9325-2
                                   LC 2006-100362
Shakespeare's classic play of star-crossed young lovers gets the manga treatment. The book is set in modern Tokyo with rival yakuza gangs and uses somewhat abridged text from the play for the dialogue.
"Although the richness of the language may be lost, the script keeps the spirit of the story intact, hitting all the major speeches." Booklist
First published in the United Kingdom

The **tempest**. Illustrated by Paul Duffield; [adaptor, Richard Appignanesi]. Abrams 2008 207p. Illustration (Manga Shakespeare)
Grades: 7 8 9 10   **822.3; 741.5**
1. Shakespeare, William, 1564-1616 — Adaptations
978-0-8109-9476-8, $9.95
Prospero and his daughter Miranda have lived on an isolated island for twelve years, after he had been deposed from his rule as Duke of Naples and cast out to sea to die. A powerful magician, Prospero has caused the survivors of a shipwreck to land on his island, in order to get his revenge, for these survivors are his enemies. Problems arise when Miranda falls in love with Ferdinand, the monster Caliban tries to use the survivors to kill Prospero, and Ariel the sprite is trying to set things right while still obeying Prospero. The book includes a plot summary and a brief biography of Shakespeare
"This adaptation would be useful both as an introduction to the play and as a companion piece for classroom study of it, using images to illuminate the Bard's eloquent poetry." SLJ

Appollo
★ **Bourbon** Island 1730. By Appollo & Lewis Trondheim; art by Lewis Trondheim; translated by Alexis Siegel. First Second Books 2008 278p. Illustration
Grades: 9 10 11 12 Adult   **741.5; Fic**
1. Adventure graphic novels; 2. Pirates; 3. Slavery; 4. Graphic novels
978-1-59643-258-1, $17.95; 1-59643-258-6
                                   LC 2007-46138

On Bourbon Island off the coast of Madagascar, a French ornithologist and his assistant are caught up in an adventure involving slavery, colonialism, and the last days of the great pirates.

"This eccentric but illuminating historical drama . . . [is] a compelling, engrossing story of people considering whether their cause is worth more to them than their lives." Publ Wkly

Aragones, Sergio

Sergio Aragones' Groo: Mightier than the Sword. Sergio Aragonés ; Mark Evanier. Dark Horse Comics 2002 Un Illustration

Grades: 7 8 9 10 11 12 Adult   **741.5; Fic**
1. Adventure graphic novels; 2. Fantasy graphic novels; 3. Humorous graphic novels; 4. Graphic novels
1-56971-612-9, $13.95

In a savage land of another era, a goodly segment of the world has long been under the heavy thumb of the evil, power-mad despot known as Pipil Khan. The tyrant wants nothing more than to name an heir and shuck his mortal coil, but one thing stands in his way: Groo. It seems Khan just can't rest easy until Groo is out of the way. He'll give his kingdom to the one of his sons who can accomplish this. One of them has a foolproof plan how to do it. Unfortunately for him, it may be that no plan is foolproof enough to thwart Groo. The book includes some comedic violence.

Sergio Aragones' Groo: The Groo Nursery. Writer/artist, Sergio Aragonés ; wordsmith, Mark Evanier ; letterer, Stan Sakai ; colorist, Tom Luth. Dark Horse Comics 2002 Un Illustration

Grades: 7 8 9 10 11 12 Adult   **741.5; Fic**
1. Adventure graphic novels; 2. Fantasy graphic novels; 3. Humorous graphic novels; 4. Graphic novels
1-56971-794-X, $11.95

In this collection, Groo visits the happy island of Felicidad and manages to stir up lots of trouble among the people. Then a minstrel sings of Groo's deeds in a country resembling Japan, only to keep finding himself in trouble. And a town that knows of Groo's dangerous reputation try to keep him out, but he's illiterate. Oy! The stories include some comic violence.

Arai, Kiyoko

Beauty Pop, Vol. 1. Story and art by Kiyoko Arai. Viz Media/Shojo Beat 2006 194p. Illustration

Grades: 7 8 9 10 11 12   **741.5; Fic**
1. Hair; 2. Shojo manga; 3. Graphic novels
978-1-4215-0575-6, $8.99

At Kiri Koshiba's high school, three popular upper classmen do occasional "Scissors Projects," working makeovers on specially selected girls. Narumi Shogo, who cuts hair, wants to become the best beautician in Japan and has won every youth competition - except one, years ago, that a younger girl won. When girls who aren't already pretty ask Narumi for a makeover, he tells them they're too ugly. Kiri helps two of the girls, working a stylist's magic that makes the girls glow; she's not interested in competition, even though her family owns a salon. Narumi wants to know who dares to be the upstart and challenge him, and he sets up

the school's cultural festival to be a haircutting duel. Will Kiri even bother to compete—
Other titles in this series are: Beauty pop, Vol. 2 (2006) (978-1-4215-0576-6); Beauty pop. Vol. 3 (2007) (978-1-4215-1009-5); Beauty pop. Vol. 4 (2007) (978-1-4215-1010-1); Beauty pop. Vol. 5 (2007) (978-1-4215-1011-8); Beauty pop. Vol. 6 (2007) (978-1-4215-1323-2); Beauty pop. Vol. 7 (2008) (978-1-4215-1784-1); Beauty pop. Vol. 8 (2008) (978-1-4215-2310-1); Beauty pop. Vol. 9 (2008) (978-1-4215-2310-1); Beauty pop. Vol. 10 (2009) (978-1-4215-2594-5)

Beauty pop, vol. 10. Viz Media/Shojo Beat 2009 200p. Illustration

Grades: 7 8 9 10 11 12   **741.5; Fic**
1. Cosmetics; 2. Hair; 3. Shojo manga; 4. Romance graphic novels; 5. Graphic novels
978-1-4215-2594-5, $8.99

The Scissors Project has been competing in the All-Japan Beauty Tournament, but for the final match, things aren't going so well. Kiri is running a high fever, Narumi has hurt his scissor hand, and his special pair of scissors has disappeared. On top of that, Narumi and Ochiai have been fighting over Kiri, so the team's harmony has gone. And Narumi's father has thrown his support behind Billy and his team. This is the final volume of the series.

Arakawa, Hiromu

★ **Fullmetal** alchemist. By Hiromu Arakawa. Viz 2005 192 p. Illustration

Grades: 8 9 10 11 12   **741.5**
1. Alchemy — Fiction; 2. Brothers — Fiction; 3. Shonen manga
1591169208; 9781591169208, $9.99

"Alchemy: the mystical power to alter the natural world. . . . When two brothers, Edward and Alphonse Elric, dabbled in this power to grant their dearest wish, one of them lost an arm and a leg...and the other became nothing but a soul locked into a body of living steel. Now Edward is an agent of the government, a slave of the military-alchemical complex, using his unique powers to obey orders." (Publisher's note)
Volume 1 of 27
Also available in VIZBIG omnibus editions

Araki, Hirohiko

JoJo's Bizarre Adventure Volume 1. Viz Media/Shonen Jump Advanced 2005 224p. Illustration

Grades: 10 11 12 Adult   **741.5; Fic**
1. Adventure graphic novels; 2. Horror graphic novels; 3. Manga; 4. Supernatural graphic novels; 5. Graphic novels
1-59116-754-X, $7.99

In a Japanese jail sits 17-year-old Jotaro Kujo: punk, fighter, delinquent...and possessed by a force beyond his control. Around the world, evil spirits are awakening: "Stands," monstrous invisible creatures which give their bearers incredible powers. To save his mother's life, Jotaro must tame his dark forces and travel around the world to Cairo, Egypt, where a hundred-year-old vampire thirsts for the blood of his family. But the road is long, and an army of evil Stand Users waits to kill JoJo and his friends... JoJo is a descendant of Jonathan Joestar, who had once defeated the evil vampire Dio. There's lots of monster/demon fighting violence, some crude humor, and strong language.

Archie Americana Series: Best of the Eighties
Archie Comics 2001 96p. Illustration
Grades: 3 4 5 6 7 8 9 10 11 12 Adult   **741.5; Fic**
1. Andrews, Archie (Fictional character); 2. Humorous graphic novels; 3. Graphic novels
1-879794-06-3, $10.95
During the 1980s pop culture ruled America; even the President was a former actor. In this volume, Archie and friends experience the punk movement, the "Urban Cowboy" craze, see the rise of MTV, get into the preppie, new wave and "Flashdance" fashions, play Trivial Pursuit, and boogie at the roller disco.
Volume 1 of 2

Archie Americana Series: Best of the Fifties
Archie Comics 1992 96p. Illustration
Grades: 3 4 5 6 7 8 9 10 11 12 Adult   **741.5; Fic**
1. Andrews, Archie (Fictional character); 2. Humorous graphic novels; 3. Graphic novels
1-879794-01-2, $10.95
Readers can journey back to the days of drive-ins and hula hoops, plaid skirts and bobby sox, Elvis and beatniks, rollerskates and sock hops in this book that reprints stories from the 1950s.

Archie Americana Series: Best of the Fifties Book 2
Archie Comics 2003 96p. Illustration
Grades: 3 4 5 6 7 8 9 10 11 12 Adult   **741.5; Fic**
1. Andrews, Archie (Fictional character); 2. Humorous graphic novels; 3. Graphic novels
1-879794-15-2, $10.95
The '50s are a fondly remembered time for many - both those who lived during the decade as well as those who discovered it through movies like Grease and TV shows like Happy Days. They were also the perfect decade for Archie to have his misadventures - whether getting tangled up in the eternal love triangle or incurring the wrath of Mr. Weatherbee, Mr. Lodge and even his father, Archie and his friends scaled new heights of hilarity. Series editor Castiglia says in the Introduction that the 1950s was the first time the U.S. had been prosperous since the 1920s; teens could do fun things, not just work to help the family, and the Archie comics reflected the rise of popular culture.

Archie Americana Series: Best of the Forties Volume 1.
Archie Comics 1991 128p. Illustration
Grades: 3 4 5 6 7 8 9 10 11 12 Adult   **741.5; Fic**
1. Andrews, Archie (Fictional character); 2. Humorous graphic novels; 3. Graphic novels
1-879794-00-4, $11.95
In 1941, Pep Comics introduced Archie Andrews, "America's newest boyfriend." Since then, Archie and his perennial teenage friends have entertained readers with their misadventures. This book includes the very first Archie story, with the first appearance of Betty and Veronica, Reggie, Jughead, Mr. Weatherbee, Miss Grundy, and the rest of the Archie characters as they originally appeared.

Archie Americana Series: Best of the Forties Book 2
Archie Comics 2002 96p. Illustration
Grades: 3 4 5 6 7 8 9 10 11 12 Adult   **741.5; Fic**
1. Andrews, Archie (Fictional character); 2. Humorous graphic novels; 3. Graphic novels
1-879794-09-8, $10.95
In 1941, Pep Comics introduced Archie Andrews, "America's newest boyfriend." Since then, Archie and his perennial teenage friends have entertained readers with their misadventures. This book includes stories from 1946 through 1949, with more slapstick and screwball comedy from Archie and the gang.

Archie Americana Series: Best of the Seventies
Archie Comics 1998 96p. Illustration
Grades: 3 4 5 6 7 8 9 10 11 12 Adult   **Fic; 741.5**
1. Andrews, Archie (Fictional character); 2. Humorous graphic novels; 3. Graphic novels
1-879794-05-5, $9.95
The decade of the 1970s was a time of transition in America, and the Archie Comics gang was right there. In this volume, Riverdale experiences the women's movement, joins in the Bicentennial celebration, sees the rise of bubble-pop, and joins the crazes for patches, pet rocks, and CB radio. Archie and the gang play "Pong" (one of the earliest video games), watch popular movies and TV shows, and go to the disco.
Volume 1 of 2

Archie Americana Series: Best of the Sixties
Archie Comics 1995 96p. Illustration
Grades: 3 4 5 6 7 8 9 10 11 12 Adult   **741.5; Fic**
1. Andrews, Archie (Fictional character); 2. Humorous graphic novels; 3. Graphic novels
1-879794-02-0, $9.95
The 1960s was a time of dreams, hopes, revolution, and social change, and the nation's youth were at the forefront. Archie and his friends came along for the ride, exploring both the fun and the mores of the times with humor. In this book readers can see the girls in slim jims, experience Beatlemania as it hits Riverdale, watch the teens become flower children, see them hit the surf, drag race, and wear mod fashions.
Volume 1 of 2

Archie Classics: The Adventures of Little Archie Volume 1
Archie Comics 2004 96p. Illustration
Grades: 3 4 5 6 7 8 9 10 11 12 Adult   **741.5; Fic**
1. Adventure graphic novels; 2. Humorous graphic novels
1-879794-17-9, $10.95
Little Archie deals with Martian invaders, secret spies, pirates, freewheeling uncles, gorillas on the loose and more! Who knew a little boy could have so many adventures? This book collects vintage Little Archie stories originally published from 1961 through 1965.

Archie's Classic Christmas Stories Volume 1
Archie Comics 2002 96p. Illustration
Grades: 3 4 5 6 7 8 9 10 11 12 Adult   **741.5; Fic**

1. Andrews, Archie (Fictional character); 2. Humorous graphic novels; 3. Graphic novels
1-879794-10-1, $10.95

Deck the halls with smiles and laughter, fa la la la la, la la la la! Since their inception, Archie and his friends have delighted readers with scores of Yuletide tales. These stories proved so popular that in 1954 an entire series devoted to stories of Holiday Cheer and Good Will to all premiered: ARCHIE'S CHRISTMAS STOCKING. Archie and his friends show their holiday spirit in this collection of classic tales from the first decade of Santa Claus himself. This book features painstaking restorations of original stories published from 1957 through 1963.

Arikawa, Hiro
★ **Library** wars, vol. 1: love & war. Story and art by Kiiro Yumi; original concept by Hiro Arikawa; [English translation & adaptation, Kinami Watabe]. Viz Media/Shojo Beat 2010 166p. Illustration
Grades: 9 10 11 12 Adult
741.5; Fic
1. Censorship; 2. Librarians; 3. Manga; 4. Shojo manga; 5. Graphic novels
978-1-4215-3488-6, $9.99

In Japan of the near future, the federal government passes the Media Betterment Act, and the Media Betterment Committee goes on book hunts to destroy any "unsuitable" book. The libraries strike back with the

Courtesy of Viz Media/Shojo Beat

Library Defense Force, a paramilitary organization dedicated to protecting the freedom to read. Iku Kasahara started to work for libraries and wants more than anything to join the Library Defense Force; she's physically very capable, but drill instructor Sergeant Dojo doesn't seem to like her very much and pushes her very hard. Iku must improve her library skills as well as her physical skills if she's to work effectively as a soldier librarian.

This book "delivers an appealing, determined female lead in the midst of an intriguing war on censorship being waged in bookstores and libraries." SLJ
First published 2008 in Japan
Volume 1 of a 14-volume series

Arima, Keitaro
Tsukuyomi: Moon Phase Vol. 1. Tokyopop 2005 162p. Illustration
Grades: 10 11 12 Adult
741.5; Fic
1. Manga; 2. Seinen manga; 3. Vampires; 4. Graphic novels
1-59532-948-X, $9.99

Cameraman Morioka Kouhei is researching Schwarz Quelle Castle in Germany. When he steps inside the castle's great walls, he discovers a mysterious little girl, Hazuki, who's been trapped there for years. Utilizing her controlling charm, Hazuki tries to get Kouhei set her free. But this sweet little girl isn't everything she appears to be... In fact, she's a vampire; and when Kouhei frees her and she follows him back to Japan, her fellow German vampires track her down to take her back home. The book includes some strong language, violence, infrequent nudity, sexual situations, and later volumes will have some torture scenes.

Arlem, Renato
Marvel Nemesis: The Imperfects. Marvel Entertainment 2005 Un Illustration
Grades: 8 9 10 11 12
741.5; Fic
1. Spider-Man (Fictional character); 2. Superhero graphic novels; 3. Wolverine (Fictional character); 4. Graphic novels
978-0-7851-1778-0, $7.99

An evil scientist sets his cross-hairs on planet Earth, in search of test subjects for his experiments, transforming even the most timid creatures into vicious fighting machines. Thousands of years later, the Thing, Wolverine, Spider-Man, and Elektra all find themselves unwilling participants in the scientist's millennia-old trials . . . or perhaps not all of them are that unwilling. This book includes some violence and strong language.

Armstrong, Jason
Ferro City, Vol. 1: The Medusa Key. Image Comics 2007 Un Illustration
Grades: 10 11 12 Adult
741.5; Fic
1. Mystery graphic novels; 2. Robots; 3. Science fiction graphic novels; 4. Graphic novels
978-1-58240-738-8, $15.99

In the world of Ferro City, ten million sentient robots live and work for their human "masters." The Robo Sapiens Act is about to come up for a vote, and if it succeeds, could crash the entire economy. An illegally created piece of technology called the Medusa Key could change everything. Private detective Cyrus Smithe gets involved when his partner Harry Weston gets the Medusa Key on behalf of a client only he knows, only to die very messily. With police and gangsters after him, Smithe needs to find the Medusa Key and find out who the mysterious client is. Armstrong calls this "robot science fiction pulp noir," which pretty much describes the feel of the book. The robots sport glass-tube heads, aircars that look like 1950s-era automobiles fly through the air, and the city is full of retro futuristic architecture, as though everything were imagined by someone in 1939.
Originally published as Ferro City issues #1-4.

Asami, Yuu
A. I revolution volume 1. Go! Comi 2007 216p. Illustration
Grades: 10 11 12 Adult
741.5; Fic
1. Manga; 2. Robots; 3. Science fiction graphic novels; 4. Graphic novels
978-1-933617-64-0, $10.99

In the middle of the twenty-first century, household robots are everywhere. Teenage Sui's father runs MG

Company, and he develops a very human-looking robot and wants Sui to "educate" it to act human. Naturally, Sui names the robot Vermillion. He has a special ability to communicate with computers without needing a physical connection, and it is this ability that makes Vermillion a target for the unscrupulous Dr. Sasaki. When Sui and Vermillion foil him, there's still trouble to come. Soon, another human-looking robot comes from another company; but this robot, whom Sui names Kira, has a secret mission and Vermillion is the target. The series includes some boy love elements, sexual innuendo, and mild violence.

Asamiya, Kia
    Junk: Record of the Last Hero Vol. 1. DrMaster Publications 2006 200p. Illustration
Grades: 10 11 12 Adult   **741.5; Fic**
    1. Manga; 2. Science fiction graphic novels; 3. Shonen manga; 4. Graphic novels
    978-1-59796-107-8, $9.95
    High school student Hiro hasn't gone back to school ever since a traumatic run-in with local bullies. Then he applies online for a new gadget, and when it arrives and he activates it, he finds himself encased within a powered armor JUNK suit. He starts going after the bullies in nightly rampages, but then he meets someone else with a JUNK suit who doesn't like the way Hiro is abusing his power. When he accidentally destroys his own home and kills his parents, he must learn to fend for himself and to choose to use his power for good or for evil. The legendary manga-ka (manga creator) Kia Asamiya has written this manga, which includes considerable violence.

Asaoka, Misuzu
    Glass Wings. Tokyopop 2006 Un Illustration
Grades: 9 10 11 12 Adult   **741.5; Fic**
    1. Fantasy graphic novels; 2. Manga; 3. Romance graphic novels; 4. Shojo manga; 5. Graphic novels
    1-59816-158-X, $9.99
    In this collection, a boy struggles with a dreaded affliction that comes between him and his true love; an orphan has the power to take on the sickness of others; a disfigured boy confronts the inner conflict between his need to survive and his desire to love. In a blend of magic and realism, Glass Wings reveals love's capacity to overcome all obstacles and replenish the human spirit in the direst of times. This book includes some violence and strong language. This is a standalone manga title.

Ashby, Ruth
    The **great** american documents: Volume 1, 1620-1830. Ruth Ashby; illustrated by Ernie Colón; editorial consultant Russell Motter. Hill and Wang 2014 160 p. Color illustration
Grades: 9 10 11 12 Adult   **741.5; 973**
    1. United States — History — Sources; 2. United States — Politics and government — Sources
    0809094606; 9780809094608, $40
                          LC 2013956401
    Written by Ruth Ashby and illustrated by Ernie Colón, "'The Great American Documents: Volume 1' introduces as series narrator none other than Uncle Sam, who walks us through twenty essential documents. Each document gets a chapter, in which Uncle Sam explains its key passages, its

origins, how it came to be written, and its impact. This graphic primer is an indispensable resource for students and anyone else who wants the facts of American history close at hand." (Publisher's note)
    "Colon uses well-designed, full-color panel layouts to eloquently blend charts and other informative graphics with straightforward images of events, clothing, and customs as well as clear, concise metaphors, all with an eye toward promoting a solid understanding of the basic facts and their impact." Booklist
    Includes bibliographical references

Ashihara, Hinako
    Sand chronicles vol. 1. Story & art by Hinako Ashihara; [translation, Kinami Watabe; English adaptation, John Werry]. Viz Media/Shojo Beat 2008 Un Illustration
Grades: 9 10 11 12   **741.5; Fic**
    1. Shojo manga; 2. Graphic novels
    978-1-4215-1477-2, $8.99
    After her parents divorce, twelve-year-old Ann Uekusa and her mother move from Tokyo to rural Shimane, to stay with Ann's grandparents. Ann finds it difficult to adjust to a small town where everybody knows everybody, and she especially has a hard time with local boy Daigo, whom she finds to be obnoxious. But when Ann's mother deliberately gets lost in the mountains around New Year's Day and dies of exposure, Ann needs the comfort of the people in Shimane, and she finally bonds with her grandmother. The publisher rates this series for older teens, citing "mature themes."
    Volume 1 of a 10-volume series

Askwith, Mark
    Silencers. Art by R.G. Taylor. Image Comics 2007 Un Illustration
Grades: 11 12 Adult   **741.5; Fic**
    1. Spies; 2. Graphic novels
    978-1-58240-728-9, $14.99
    Silencers is a compelling look at spies coming to terms with the changing face of espionage in the new world order. When the newest recruit to the Silencers is murdered, his death triggers a mission of betrayal and revenge. Violence and strong language figure in this story that invokes the themes of John LeCarre's books.

Aso, Yusuke
    The **king** of debris, volume 1. DC Comics/CMX 2009 160p. Illustration
Grades: 8 9 10 11 12   **741.5; Fic**
    1. Adventure graphic novels; 2. Manga; 3. Science fiction graphic novels; 4. Graphic novels
    978-1-4012-1879-9, $9.99
    Young android boy Citro lives happily with his human "grandfather," an old mechanic, and the mechanic's granddaughter Corona. Then Tera zooms into their life on her flying, robotic broomstick, pursued by soldiers determined to kill her and take the device she's carrying. During the fight, Grampa is killed, and Tera drops the device which activates and bonds with Citro. The device is "The God of Destruction's Heart," and it turns little Citro into a deadly and powerful killing machine. He drives off the enemy soldiers, but now he must go with Tera and Corona,

who has no other family but Citro to Altasia, where the "Heart" can be safely removed from Citro and used to defend Altasia against the enemies pursuing them. Meanwhile, word of what they have goes ahead of them, and they will have to fight to get to Altasia. This manga is full of action and fighting, but there's not too much graphic violence.

Atangan, Patrick

Songs of Our Ancestors Volume II: The Silk Tapestry and Other Chinese Folktales. NBM 2004 Un Illustration
Grades: 6 7 8 9 10   **741.5; Fic**
   1. Folklore — China; 2. Graphic novels
   1-56163-403-4, $12.95
   In three Chinese folk tales, an old woman, a young boy and a wild spirit are all bound by a passion to create, changing the world around them forever. In "The Silk Tapestry," an impoverished elderly woman's only hope against a life of hardship lies in the completion of a magical tapestry. It is said to be the key to a paradise. Already living in squalor, how much more of herself is she willing sacrifice to see her dream come to fruition" In "Sausage-Boy and his Magic Brush," a young boy's remarkable talent for paintings that come to life attracts a greedy woman. In "The Story of Pan Gu, The First Man," a lonely but wild spirit sculpts the Earth from a cosmic egg in hopes it brings others like him to keep him company.

Songs of Our Ancestors Volume III: Tree of Love. NBM 2005 Un Illustration
Grades: 6 7 8 9 10   **741.5; Fic**
   1. Folklore — India; 2. Romance graphic novels; 3. Graphic novels
   1-56163-438-7, $12.95
   This volume of Atangan's Asian folktale collection, Tree of Love, celebrates India's tradition of elevating romance to a work of art. Atangan adapts Rajput polyptych paintings of northern India and transforms them into a poetic comics experience. The story follows a prince's courtship of a flower peddler. The young prince is surprised by the difficulty in proving the worthiness of what everyone sees as a common woman. But she has a secret, a special gift bound in the beauty and power of nature. Each page ornaments Tree of Love's universal story about the intricacies of love. Atangan combined two Indian folktales to make this story: "The Flowering Tree" and "The Tree of Sorrow."

Songs of our ancestors: The yellow jar: two tales from Japanese tradition. NBM 2003 48p. Illustration (Songs of our ancestors)
Grades: 5 6 7 8 9 10 11 12   **741.5**
   1. Folklore — Japan; 2. Graphic novels
   1-56163-331-3, $12.92
                                               LC 2002-32132
   "To render two magical Japanese legends, one about a fisherman who discovers a fair maiden in a big pot, the other about a monk whose fastidiously kept garden is invaded by two chrysanthemums, Atangan charmingly adopts the sharp outlines, boldly juxtaposed color fields, and striking compositions of eighteenth-century Japanese woodblock prints." Booklist
   Other titles in this series are: Silk tapestry and other Chinese folktales (2004); Tree of love (2005)

Augustyn, Brian

Gotham by Gaslight: A Tale of the Batman. Brian Augustyn, Mike Mignola, P. Craig Russell, Eduardo Barreto. DC Comics 2006 112p. Illustration
Grades: 8 9 10 11 12 Adult   **741.5; Fic**
   1. Batman (Fictional character); 2. Science fiction graphic novels; 3. Superhero graphic novels; 4. Graphic novels
   978-1-4012-1153-0, $12.99
   In an age of mystery and superstition, how would the people of Gotham react to a weird creature of the night, a bat-garbed vigilante feared by the guilty and the innocent alike" Some would live in terror. Others would rest easier. Only one man would take no notice at all ... a man with other matters to attend to. His name" No one knows for sure. Most people know him only as Jack. Jack the Ripper. This book collects two Elseworlds adventures of Batman, Gotham by Gaslight and its sequel Master of the Future.

Auster, Paul

Hulk: is he man or monster or . . . is he both?. ABDO/Spotlight 2008 Un Illustration
Grades: 3 4 5 6 7 8 9   **741.5; Fic**
   1. Hulk (Fictional character); 2. Superhero graphic novels; 3. Graphic novels
   978-1-59961-547-9, $21.35
                                               LC 2007-52759
   Dr. Bruce Banner is ready to test his new gamma ray weapon using a monkey, when his intern Rick Jones suddenly goes to Ground Zero to save the monkey. When the test won't abort, Banner races out to save Rick, only to be caught by the gamma ray blast himself. It turns him into a giant, green monster of a man, and General Ross makes him angry. The General sends troops and weapons out to capture the Hulk, but Rick and the monkey try to help him. This is the first volume of a set of comics that provide kid-friendly, action-packed Hulk stories with little in the way of graphic violence and no bad language.
   This is a library bound edition of a Marvel Age: The Incredible Hulk comic book issue, with all advertising pages removed.

Hulk: Mayhem!. ABDO/Spotlight 2008 Un Illustration
Grades: 3 4 5 6 7 8 9   **741.5; Fic**
   1. Hulk (Fictional character); 2. Superhero graphic novels; 3. Hulk (Fictional character); 4. Graphic novels
   978-1-59961-548-6, $21.35
                                               LC 2008-101
   Bruce Banner, Rick Jones, and Monkey have been hanging out in a cabin near a ski resort in the Rocky Mountains, where Banner has been trying to build a nano-nuclear cellular reconfiguration matrix—or, as Rick calls it, a de-Hulkifier. However, they've been tracked by General "Thunderbolt" Ross, who has brought troops, Jamie Madrox (tricked out in an anti-Hulk armor), and Radioactive Man (former nuclear physicist Chen Lu) to capture the Hulk. Their efforts end up causing an avalanche, which only the Hulk seems interested in stopping before attacking his attackers. As with the other volumes, this book includes lots of action with no actual violence and no bad language.
   This is a library bound edition of a Marvel Age: The Incredible Hulk comic book issue, with all advertising pages removed.

Hulk: Radioactive. ABDO/Spotlight 2008 Un Illustration

Grades: 3 4 5 6 7 8 9   **741.5; Fic**
1. Hulk (Fictional character); 2. Superhero graphic novels; 3. Graphic novels
978-1-59961-549-3, $21.35

LC 2008-103

When General Ross and his army of Hulkbusters (soldiers in exoskeleton armor) capture Bruce Banner, Rick Jones and Monkey break into the military compound to save their friend. Then the Hulk accidentally busts out Radioactive Man while messing up the compound. In his radioactive damper, Radioactive Man is Dr. Chen Lu, and he behaves as though he's Banner's friend, although Rick and Monkey notice Lu keeps doing things that cause Bruce to start Hulking up. This volume provides lots of action in kid-friendly mode, with little real violence and no bad language.

This is a library bound edition of a Marvel Age: The Incredible Hulk comic book issue, with all advertising pages removed.

Paul Auster's City of Glass. Script adaptation, Paul Karasik and David Mazzucchelli; art, David Mazzucchelli. Avon Bks. 1994 129p. Illustration

Grades: 9 10 11 12 Adult   **741; 741.5**
0-380-77108-X; 9780380771080, $12

LC 93-91005

"Auster's acclaimed novel City of Glass, a dreamlike meditation on language and fiction in the form of a detective novel, has been translated into comics form to stunning effect. . . . This combination story, lecture and literary deconstruction begins when New York City detective novelist Daniel Quinn answers a wrong number. Donning the personas of both the detective he created and his own creator, Auster himself, Quinn attempts to protect a young man, who as a child was kept without light or language for nine years as his lunatic academic father tried to discover 'God's Language.'" (Publishers Weekly)

Avery, Ben

The **hedge** knight. [by] George R. R. Martin; Ben Avery, adapter; Mike S. Miller, artist. Marvel Enterprises 2006 160p. Illustration

Grades: 9 10 11 12 Adult   **741.5; Fic**
1. Fantasy graphic novels; 2. Knights and knighthood; 3. Graphic novels
978-0-7851-2577-8, $19.95; 978-0-7851-2578-5, $19.95

"Hulking young Dunk is the squire of an elderly warrior. When Dunk's master dies, he rides on to the next tournament in hopes of winning recognition for his knightly prowess. He acquires a squire of his own, a bald infant boy who calls himself Egg, and gives himself the more elegant title of Duncan the Tall. . . . This heroic fantasy tale reinvigorates the tired category of sword and sorcery fiction by emphasizing the human angle." Publ Wkly

Kingdoms Volume 1: The Coming Storm. Zondervan/Zonderkidz 2007 160p. Illustration

Grades: 5 6 7 8 9 10   **741.5; Fic**
1. Adventure graphic novels; 2. Graphic novels
978-0-310-71353-1, $9.99

LC 2007-3148

When Pharaoh Neco and his army marched across Judah, King Josiah recklessly led the attack and died. Now his faithful adviser Iddo remains loyal to his king's memory and labors to keep the nation faithful to the Lord even as he struggles to protect his own family. This story is set against the backdrop of the events in the Old Testament books, 1 & 2 Kings and 1 & 2 Chronicles.

Volume 1 of 8

Avery, Fiona

Arana Vol. 1: The Heart of the Spider. Art by Roger Cruz and Mark Brooks. Marvel Entertainment 2005 Un Illustration

Grades: 8 9 10 11 12 Adult   **741.5; Fic**
1. Adventure graphic novels; 2. Superhero graphic novels
0-7851-1506-4, $7.99

She's fierce, she's sassy, she sticks to walls. Anya Corazon, a.k.a. Arana, is a next-generation girl warrior. A scrappy teen from Brooklyn by day, Anya becomes the Hunter of the ancient and mystical Spider Society by night. But first, she must survive her initiation and prove herself on her first mission, all while going to high school and hiding everything from her single-parent dad. Together with her partner, the mysterious mage Miguel, Anya must fight to protect the peace of the world from the sworn enemies of the Spider Society, the evil Sisterhood of the Wasp. There's lots of super hero action here.

Arana Vol. 2: In the Beginning. Art by Roger Cruz. Marvel Entertainment 2005 Un Illustration

Grades: 8 9 10 11 12 Adult   **741.5; Fic**
1. Adventure graphic novels; 2. Superhero graphic novels
0-7851-1719-9, $7.99

Anya Corazon continues her work as Arana. What seems like a routine collar turns out to be anything but when the corrupt judge Anya captured reveals a deadly new threat to the Spider Society. While her partner Miguel tangles with an old enemy, a new one appears to challenge Anya, and he's willing to kill everyone around her.

Arana Vol. 3: Night of the Hunter. Art by Roger Cruz, Jonboy Meyers, and Francis Portella. Marvel Entertainment 2006 Un Illustration

Grades: 7 8 9 10 11 12   **741.5; Fic**
1. Adventure graphic novels; 2. Superhero graphic novels
0-7851-1853-5, $7.99

Exactly what happened to Arana's mother before she disappeared all those years ago" Startling new information on her family's past spurs Anya to launch her own personal investigation. Will history be too painful to bear" Meanwhile, the evil Sisterhood of the Wasp hosts a summit of fiends, rogues and villains so big that Arana just might have to crash the party. Hopefully, she can get a few roundhouse kicks in before someone calls the cops.

Axe, David

War Fix. Steve Olexa, David Axe. NBM 2006 96p. Illustration

Grades: 11 12 Adult   **741.5; 956.7; Fic**
1. Iraq War, 2003-; 2. Graphic novels
978-1-56163-463-7, $15.95
2006 ForeWord Graphic Novel Gold Award.

As a kid, David watched the first Iraq war on CNN. As an adult in March 2003, David is now a journalist, but he becomes obsessed with the new war in Iraq and decides he's going to go there. He tells his editor he's going to cover the elections. He buys body armor, travels to Baghdad, and joins a unit of army truckers who drive in supply convoys. He witnesses violence, death, most of it pointless. Even after he returns home, his friends and his lover can see what David hasn't realized yet - he's hooked on the violence. Brutal, honest depictions of violence and some nudity make this appropriate for older readers.

Azuma, Kiyohiko
★ **Azumanga** Daioh omnibus. Translation, Stephen Paul. Yen Press 2009 675p. Illustration
Grades: 8 9 10 11 12   **741.5; Fic**
1. High school students; 2. Humorous graphic novels; 3. Manga; 4. School stories; 5. Graphic novels
978-0-316-07738-5, $24.99
An omnibus edition of a humorous four-volume manga series featuring a Japanese suburban high school class with a ditzy teacher. The adult teachers go drinking occasionally, and there's one male teacher who ogles the girls in their P.E. uniforms.
First published 2001 in Japan

Azuma, Mayumi
Elemental Gelade Volume 1. Tokyopop 2006 192p. Illustration
Grades: 8 9 10 11 12   **741.5; Fic**
1. Adventure graphic novels; 2. Fantasy graphic novels; 3. Manga; 4. Shonen manga; 5. Graphic novels
1-59816-598-4, $9.99
During a routine raid, sky-pirate Coud Van Giruet discovers a most unusual bounty: Ren, an "Edel Raid," is a living weapon that interacts with a human to become the ultimate fighting machine. But Van Giruet soon realizes that Ren is even more prized than he first thought. When she is captured by an evil man who sells Edel Raids on the black market, Coud and the agents of Arc Aile join forces to rescue Ren. This fantasy adventure includes some violence and some mildly harsh language.

Azzarello, Brian
Batman: Broken City. Writer, Brian Azzarello; artist, Eduardo Risso; letterer, Clem Robins; colorist, Patricia Mulvihill; original series covers, Dave Johnson. DC Comics 2004 Un Illustration
Grades: 10 11 12 Adult   **741.5; Fic**
1. Batman (Fictional character); 2. Joker (Fictional character); 3. Mystery graphic novels; 4. Superhero graphic novels; 5. Graphic novels
1-4012-0214-4, $14.99
While hunting the murderer of a small boy's parents, Batman embarks on a journey of self-discovery that forces him to reflect on his life and the choices he has made. But when the Dark Knight becomes caught up in his own investigation and ruminations, he suddenly falls prey to a deadly new pair of killers that has been stalking him. A gritty, introspective tale, this noir-flavored book features appearances by the Joker, the Penguin, Killer Croc and Scarface. This story includes more violence than in most Batman stories.

Doctor 13: architecture & mortality. Brian Azzarello, writer; Cliff Chiang, artist; Patricia Mulvihill, colorist; Jared K. Fletcher, letterer. DC Comics 2007 Un Illustration
Grades: 9 10 11 12 Adult   **741.5**
1. Humorous graphic novels; 2. Superhero graphic novels; 3. Graphic novels
978-1-4012-1552-1, $14.99
Doctor 13, the world's greatest skeptic, sets out with his daughter Tracy to investigate strange doings in the French Alps. The two encounter in short order a vampire, a pirate with a flying ship, a caveman who had been frozen in ice, a mysterious boy who can answer any question for the price of a dime, a talking Nazi gorilla, a cosmic heroine with a constant runny nose, and the ghost of a Confederate general taking time off from haunting a US Army tank. Doctor 13 doesn't believe in any of them, but he works with them when they have to go up against the Architects, the shapers of the universe. The Architects have decided that Doctor 13 and his team of misfits don't belong in the world, and they beg to differ. The book includes some violence.

Lex Luthor: Man of Steel. Art by Lee Bermejo. DC Comics 2005 Illustration
Grades: 10 11 12 Adult   **741.5; Fic**
1. Lex Luthor (Fictional character); 2. Superhero graphic novels; 3. Superman (Fictional character); 4. Graphic novels
1-4012-0454-6, $12.99
Superman has been called many things since becoming a superhero, from the defender of Truth, Justice and the American Way to the Big Blue Boy Scout. Lex Luthor calls him a dangerous threat to all humanity. This book is narrated by Luthor, so the reader sees Superman from his point of view; and to Luthor, Superman is an alien being who can't be trusted. Therefore, Luthor tries to create a superhero of his own, in the form of a beautiful young woman, named Hope. The book includes some violence and sexual situations.

Loveless Vol. 1: A Kin of Homecoming. Art by Marcello Frusin. DC Comics/Vertigo 2006 128p. Illustration
Grades: 12 Adult   **741.5; Fic**
1. Western graphic novel; 2. Graphic novels
978-1-4012-1061-8, $9.99
Wes Cutter is a wanted man running from a violent past - the horrors of the Civil War, a brutal stint in a Union prison camp, and the savage fallout of Reconstruction. Now he's on a quest for the one thing in short supply: peace. Joining Wes is his beautiful wife Ruth, a woman who has been to hell and back herself - and hides dark secrets of her own. The road they travel will be a bloody one, leaving a trail of bodies stretching from Missouri to the Pacific Ocean. The book contains graphic violence, copious use of foul language, nudity, and sexual situations.

Loveless Vol. 2: Thicker Than Blackwater. Brian Azzarello, writer; Danijel Zezelj, Marcelo Frusin, Werther Dell'edera, art; Patricia Mulvihill and Martin Breccia, colorists; Clem Robins, letterer. DC Comics/Vertigo 2007 168p. Illustration
Grades: 11 12 Adult   **741.5; Fic**

1. Mystery graphic novels; 2. Western graphic novels; 3. Graphic novels
978-1-4012-1250-6, $14.99

No one in the town of Blackwater escaped the Civil War unscathed. Not former slave-turned-bounty hunter Atticus Mann. Not Ruth Cutter, who thought her husband Wes was dead, and took to the woods to fight for a lost cause. And certainly not Wes Cutter. He's suffered the worst fate of all, a Yankee made him sheriff of Blackwater and the most hated man in town. But hate him or not, the citizens of Blackwater desperately need Wes to protect them from a vicious killer who's butchering them in ever more ghastly ways. A killer who may have deep ties to Blackwater ... and to Wes' own dark past. The story includes considerable violence, profanity, and nudity.

Superman: For Tomorrow Volume One. Brian Azzarello, writer; Jim Lee, penciller; Scott Williams, inker; Alex Sinclair, colorist; Rob Leigh, Nick J. Napolitano, letterers. DC Comics 2005 Un Illustration
Grades: 10 11 12 Adult   **741.5; Fic**
1. Superhero graphic novels; 2. Superman (Fictional character); 3. Graphic novels
1-4012-0352-3, $14.99

A cataclysmic event has struck the Earth. Millions of people have vanished without a trace. No one is left unaffected - not even Superman. A year has passed, and Superman is left with many questions and very few answers. For a hero who tries to have all the answers, it's torture. And, just as the action heats up and the stakes are raised, one huge question emerges: just how far is Superman willing to go "For Tomorrow"?

Superman: For Tomorrow Volume Two. Brian Azzarello, writer; Jim Lee, penciller; Scott Williams, inker; Alex Sinclair, colorist; Rob Leigh, Nick J. Napolitano, letterers. DC Comics 2006 Illustration
Grades: 10 11 12 Adult   **741.5; Fic**
1. Superhero graphic novels; 2. Superman (Fictional character); 3. Wonder Woman (Fictional character); 4. Graphic novels
978-1-4012-0448-8, $14.99

In Volume One, a million people had seemingly vanished without a trace, including Lois Lane. In this volume, Superman is closer to discovering the mystery of the Vanishing, and comes face-to-face with the evil entity behind it all. But what desperate measures will Superman take to make things right again" And does Wonder Woman have the power to stop him" The book includes fighting violence.

Wonder Woman; Volume 1: Blood. Brian Azzarello, Cliff Chiang, Tony Akins. DC Comics 2012 160 p.
Grades: 11 12 Adult   **741.5**
1. Greek mythology — Fiction; 2. Superhero comic books, strips, etc; 3. Wonder Woman (Fictional character)
1401235638; 9781401235635, $22.99
                    LC 2011051798

In this comic book, author Brian Azzarello "gives Diana (Wonder Woman) a new origin, not as a baby her mother, Hippolyta, molded out of clay but as the illegitimate daughter of Zeus. As such, she's a target for the jealous rage of Hera, Zeus' wife, but she finds a new role as protector of a waifish young woman who's currently carrying Zeus' baby.

The king of the gods, meanwhile, has vanished." (Publishers Weekly)
Originally published in single magazine form in WONDER WOMAN 1-6—t.p. verso.
Other Wonder Woman volumes by Azzarello and Chiang are: 2: Guts; 3: Iron; 4: War

B., David
★ **Epileptic**. Pantheon Books 2005 361p. Illustration
Grades: 11 12 Adult   **741.5; 616.8**
1. Autobiographical graphic novels; 2. Epilepsy; 3. Graphic novels
0-375-42318-4, $25; 0-375-71468-5 (pa), $18.95; 9780375423185
                    LC 2004-53419

"Growing up in the 1960s and 1970s in France's Loire Valley, Jean-Christophe developed grand mal epilepsy around the age of 11. Pierre-Francois, nine, observes his brother's battle with the physical and social implications of the disease; their parents' efforts to find management of it through medical, macrobiotic, and even psychic interventions; and the author's own development in this milieu as a boy obsessed with history and warfare and as a dedicated artist." SLJ

The author's "artwork is magnificent—gorgeously bold, impressionistic representations of the world not as it is but as he's taught himself to perceive it. . . . B.'s illustrations constantly underscore his writing's wrenching psychological depth; readers can literally see how the chaos of his childhood shaped his vision and mind." Publ Wkly
Original French edition, 2002

Backder, Derf
Trashed: a graphic novel. By Derf Backderf. Abrams ComicArts 2015 256 p. Illustration
Grades: 10 11 12 Adult   **741.5**
1. Refuse and refuse disposal — Fiction; 2. Sanitation workers — Fiction
9781419714535, $24.95; 9781419714542
                    LC 2015011115

This graphic novel, by Derf Backderf, "is an ode to the crap job of all crap jobs—garbage collector. . . . [It] follows the raucous escapades of three 20-something friends as they clean the streets of pile after pile of stinking garbage, while battling annoying small-town bureaucrats, bizarre townfolk, sweltering summer heat, and frigid winter storms." (Publisher's note)

"The blocky grotesquerie of Backderf's art is well-suited to the material, and the episodic, slackerish narrative is spiked here and there by brief lessons on the history of the garbage truck, the ecology of the landfill, and an answer to the question of whether rich or poor neighborhoods generate the most trash (hint: it's not the poor). A downbeat but entertaining ode to the odiferous realities of getting by." Pub Wkly
Includes bibliographical references

Badeaux, Brandon
Star Wars: Rebellion Volume 1: My Brother, My Enemy. Dark Horse Comics 2007 Un Illustration
Grades: 8 9 10 11 12 Adult   **741.5; Fic**

1. Adventure graphic novels; 2. Science fiction graphic novels; 3. Graphic novels
9781593077112, $14.95; 1593077114

Having rescued Rebel strategist Jorin Sol from the Empire, Luke Skywalker now leads X-Wing attack runs on Imperial convoys to rustle up much needed supplies for the Rebel fleet. Little does he know that within Sol lies a secret that will put the entire Alliance in danger. What's worse, when Luke receives a coded message from Lt. Sunber, who wants to defect to the Rebel Alliance, he must decide whether to trust his old friend or obey the orders of Princess Leia who believes Tank may be part of an Imperial plot to capture the Rebellion's greatest hero.

Bagge, Peter
Apocalypse nerd. Dark Horse Comics 2008 120p. Illustration
Grades: 11 12 Adult   **741.5; Fic**
1. Adventure graphic novels; 2. End of the world; 3. Graphic novels
978-1-59307-902.4, $13.95

Software engineer Perry and his friend Gordo are just two average suburban guys (okay, maybe not Gordo, since he deals drugs) who have gone on a camping trip in the North Cascade Mountains near Seattle; but on their way up, North Korea nukes Seattle, and the two friends must find a way to survive in the mountain. They become looters, deal with others out to survive any way possible, and do things they never dreamed they would do—including killing others. The book includes lots of harsh language (including s-bombs and f-bombs), partial nudity, and violence.

Bailey, Tracey
Wonderdog, Inc.. Arcana Studio Inc. 2010 Un Illustration
Grades: 5 6 7 8 9 10   **741.5; Fic**
1. Adventure graphic novels; 2. Humorous graphic novels; 3. Graphic novels
978-1-897548-87-5, $14.95

Sixteen-year-old Ryan Robertson is a typical, nerdy type of guy, except he's got a very hot-looking girlfriend, whom his best buddy Alex just doesn't trust. The two guys are looking forward to the summer break, until Ryan's history teacher parents tell him they're going to Europe on a trip and he'll have to stay with his grandfather on a pig farm. Rachel, the hot girlfriend, wants to know where he's going, so she can visit him. When he gets there, he finds a wise-cracking grandfather, lots of chores, no Internet, no television ... and then Rachel shows up to steal a little statue of a dog from his grandfather. That's when Ryan learns that his grandfather, his parents, and a lot of other people are part of a secret organization to protect the world from the likes of Rachel, err ... Dr. Sweeney, and her nefarious colleagues who are out to rule the world and get very rich with the Fountain of Youth that the little dog statue unlocks. Now he's off to Bolivia with Pappy and siblings Seth and Amie (she's cute!), to try to stop Dr. Sweeney. Think of Indiana Jones as a grandfather who still swashbuckles, and the kind of story told in the Indiana Jones movies. Some readers may note the fairly numerous grammatical errors (using an apostrophe inappropriately), but it shouldn't distract too much from the fun story. There's a lot of action but very little actual violence.

Baillie, Liz
My brain hurts volume one. Microcosm Publishing 2008 Un Illustration
Grades: 11 12 Adult   **741.5; Fic**
1. Friendship; 2. Homosexuality; 3. Graphic novels
978-1-934620-03-8, $6

Best friends Kate and Joey are gay and trying to find some happiness with their relationships. They're also thirteen years old, love punk music, dress punk, and get into all kinds of trouble. Joey's father is in denial, Kate doesn't know how to tell her mother. Then one night, a gang of skinheads beat Joey around the head with a chain; he collapses during an interview at a Catholic school and goes into a coma. Meanwhile, one of the skinheads keeps trying to get Kate to go with him; and Kate joins a gay student club at school. The book shows kissing but no other sexual activity, there's no nudity, but there's a lot of strong language, especially the f-bomb.

Baker, Kyle
★ **How** to draw stupid and other essentials of cartooning. Watson-Guptill 2008 110p. Illustration
Grades: 8 9 10 11 12 Adult   **741.5**
1. Cartooning — Technique; 2. Graphic novels — Drawing
978-0-8230-0143-9, $16.95
                         LC 2008-922161
"Baker, an award-winning cartoonist and graphic-novel illustrator, gives aspiring cartoonists irreverent advice about how to succeed in their chosen field. He offers instruction in basic drawing techniques such as choosing the right tools and discusses the importance of learning to draw shapes, exaggerating, and using references. But the author's most inspiring advice focuses on how to succeed as a cartoonist." SLJ

King David. DC Comics/Vertigo 2002 104p. Illustration
Grades: 9 10 11 12 Adult   **221; 741.5**
1. Bible OT — Adaptations; 2. Graphic novels
978-1-56389-866-2, $19.95
Baker retells the Old Testament story of David, the shepherd boy who slew the giant Goliath and later became the King of Israel, after years of dodging King Saul's attempts to kill him. Using a hip, freewheeling style full of irreverent humor, Baker also renders the battles as the bloody messes they were.

Kyle Baker: Cartoonist. Kyle Baker Publishing 2004 126p. Illustration
Grades: 10 11 12 Adult   **741.5**
1. Humorous graphic novels; 2. Graphic novels
0-9747214-0-9, $14.95
Kyle Baker's cartoons have appeared in major magazines and newspapers, and his animation has appeared on MTV and BET. He collects new material in this book, including his recurring The Bakers," a behind-the-scenes look at his family and home life. Some cartoons include drug references and violence.

Nat Turner. Abrams 2008 207p. Illustration
Grades: 10 11 12 Adult   **92; 741.5**
1. Biographical graphic novels; 2. Revolutionaries; 3. Slavery; 4. Slaves; 5. Graphic novels
978-0-8109-9535-2; 0-8109-9535-2, $14.95
                                  LC 2008-6911
This book "follows the dark legacy of the Virginia slave rebellion and subsequent murders of at least 55 white slave owners and their families in 1831. . . . Turner is presented as a fiercely intelligent, angry, yet steadfast individual whose potential was dashed in an era of hate and inhumanity. Those characteristics are mirrored in the actions of the slaves' rebellion, in illustrations that are not for the faint of heart or the weak of stomach. The ideas brought forth here are sure to ignite debate and discussion." SLJ
Includes bibliographical references
Originally published 2006 in four volumes

Nat Turner Vol. 2: revolution. Image Comics 2006 96p. Illustration
Grades: 10 11 12 Adult   **92**
1. Biographical graphic novels; 2. Revolutionaries; 3. Slavery; 4. Slaves; 5. Turner, Nat, 1800?-1831; 6. Graphic novels
978-1-58240-792-0, $10
In this concluding volume, excerpts from The Confessions of Nat Turner alternate with wordless panels to depict the series of murders carried out by Turner and his followers as they tried to start a slave revolution based on Turner's vision. He is eventually captured and hanged. Baker doesn't editorialize with narration, instead he allows readers to draw their own conclusions about Turner and the society against which he rebelled. Some of the images will be disturbing because of the brutal acts they depict.
Originally published as Nat Turner issues #3 and 4 by Kyle Baker Publishing
Sequel to Nat Turner Encore Edition Vol. 1 (2006)

Plastic Man: On the Lam!. DC Comics 2004 Un Illustration
Grades: 6 7 8 9 10 11 12 Adult   **741.5; Fic**
1. Humorous graphic novels; 2. Plastic Man (Fictional character); 3. Superhero graphic novels; 4. Graphic novels
1-4012-0343-4, $14.95
2005 Eisner Award for Best Publication for a Younger Audience, also 2005 Eisner Award for Best Writer/Artists-Humor for Kyle Baker
Plastic Man has worked as a superhero, but he used to be the criminal Eel O'Brian, a fact he has hidden from the FBI. Now there's been a murder, and Eel O'Brian is the main (and only) suspect. When the FBI learns of his old identity, Plastic Man goes on the lam to clear himself.
Originally published as Plastic Man issues #1-6; this volume is bound in plastic

Through the looking-glass. By Lewis Carroll; adapted by Kyle Baker. Papercutz 2008 Un Illustration (Classics illustrated)
Grades: 3 4 5 6 7 8 9   **741.5; Fic**
1. Carroll, Lewis, 1832-1898 — Adaptations; 2. Fantasy graphic novels; 3. Graphic novels
978-1-59707-115-4, $9.95; 1-59707-115-3
This is Carroll's sequel to Alice's Adventures in Wonderland. This time, Alice climbs through the

looking-glass in her house and finds herself in a land with talking flowers and insects, Tweedledee and Tweedledum (who recite "The Walrus and the Carpenter—), the White Queen who needs help pinning her shawl straight, Humpty Dumpty, the Red Queen, and more. The Eisner Award-winning Baker uses a different style from his usual cartoony look here, more reminiscent of Tenniel's classic illustrations of Carroll's books.

Courtesy of Papercutz

Balak
    Last man 1: The stranger. Bastien Vive?s, Michae?l Sanlaville, Balak; English translation by Alexis Siegel. First Second 2015 207 p. Illustration
Grades: 9 10 11 12   **741.5; Fic**
1. Magic — Fiction; 2. Martial arts
1626720460; 9781626720466, $9.99
                                  LC 2014045696
In this book, "Adrian has been preparing for the annual Games for years, and he's crushed when his assigned partner manages to get sick right before the event. Richard Aldana arrives late at the Games, and he's . . . clearly from another world. . . . Aldana is also seeking a partner in order to compete, and thus magically trained boy Adrian and brutish man Aldana team up and eventually become friends." (Bulletin of the Center for Children's Books)
Originally published: Tournai, Belgium : Casterman, 2013.
Volume 1 of an ongoing series.

Balce, Nicc
    Random Encounter Volume 1. Viper Comics 2006 Un Illustration
Grades: 9 10 11 12 Adult   **741.5; Fic**
1. Adventure graphic novels; 2. Science fiction graphic novels; 3. Graphic novels
0-9754193-8-2, $9.95
Strange things are afoot at the ... Kwik Mart. With their eerie tromp through the latest Silent Kill game interrupted by a strange sound, Migo, Mica, and Mona begin a journey into the perplexing and uncharted. The discovery of a dead girl in a pool of blood on the roof of Migo's parents' Kwik Mart sends the kids' lives into a maelstrom of confusion, freakish aliens, precipitous resurrection, and enigmatic secrets. It's a wild ride into the unimaginable and astonishing, a ... random encounter. There are lots of fighting scenes and some monsters.

Baldwin, Stephen
    Spirit Warriors Book 1. B & H Publishing Group 2006 Un Illustration
Grades: 7 8 9 10 11 12   **741.5; Fic**

1. Christian life; 2. Fantasy graphic novels; 3. Graphic novels
978-0-8054-4357-8, $9.99

Six radical young teens enter the spiritual war zone every day for classic battles of good against evil in the crumbling New City. Mia, Nano, Faith, Jon, Davy, and Hailey were all mysteriously orphaned at a young age; they each have uncommon strengths. When the Elder Seiko takes over a local church and fills it with evil, the young Spirit Warriors fight back.

Baltazar, Art
 Patrick the Wolf Boy Volume 1. Devil's Due Publishing 2004 Un Illustration
Grades: 2 3 4 5 6 7 8 9 10 11 12 Adult **741.5; Fic**
 1. Humorous graphic novels; 2. Graphic novels
1-932796-27-4, $10.95

Patrick looks at first glance like the other kids in school, but he's a werewolf. A cute werewolf. He resembles Eddie Munster (from the 1960s television comedy series "The Munsters—), and he doesn't speak, although he growls a lot and sometimes howls. He gives his teacher an apple - but with a skull biting the apple. When he goes fishing with his dad, he prefers to scare the bear into giving him his catch. He loves to play tag with the neighborhood squirrel. And when Valentine's Day comes, he makes sure that his babysitter likes him better. His utterly normal parents adore him and understand his growls; so does Neve, his classmate at school.

 Patrick the Wolf Boy Volume 2. Devil's Due Publishing 2005 Un Illustration
Grades: 2 3 4 5 6 7 8 9 10 11 12 Adult **741.5; Fic**
 1. Humorous graphic novels; 2. Graphic novels
1-932796-29-0, $10.95

This volume collects previously published issues of the comic: the Super Hero Special, the Science Fiction Special, the Wedding Special, and the After School Special. In the many short stories, Patrick the Wolf Boy attends a comic book convention with his dad, plays "Star Wars" with the neighborhood kids, meets and befriends an alien kid, Zyggie, who then crashes the wedding reception of a relative, and deals with the school bully.

 Patrick the Wolf Boy Volume 3. Devil's Due Publishing 2007 Un Illustration
Grades: 2 3 4 5 6 7 8 9 10 11 12 Adult **741.5; Fic**
 1. Fantasy graphic novels; 2. Humorous graphic novels; 3. Graphic novels
978-1-932796-30-8, $12.99

The third volume of Patrick the Wolf Boy collects the Rock-n-Roll Special, the Post Father's Day Special, and the Happy Birthday Special, plus some stories written and illustrated by guest creators. Patrick meets Squatch, the baby Big Foot, accidentally bites Neve, who thinks she's turning into a werewolf, encounters various rock stars, and other adventures. In one panel, the screaming pajama lady says "crap."

 Patrick the Wolf Boy Volume 4. Devil's Due Publishing 2007 Un Illustration
Grades: 3 4 5 6 7 8 9 10 11 12 Adult **741.5; Fic**

1. Halloween; 2. Humorous graphic novels; 3. Graphic novels
978-1-932796-83-4, $12.99

This fourth collection of comics featuring Patrick the Wolf Boy focus mostly on Halloween, a natural holiday for the young wolfman ... er ... wolfboy. He plays with jack o'lanterns (he likes to wear them on his head), goes trick-or-treating with the neighbor kids, keeps trying to melt the grouchy neighbor lady after watching The Wizard of Oz, and plays with new neighbor, the Grim Reaper. The book includes a couple instances of mild language (fricken"), and one scene in which the Grim Reaper does his thing.

Barasui
 Strawberry Marshmallow Volume 1. Tokyopop 2006 184p. Illustration
Grades: 8 9 10 11 12 **741.5; Fic**
 1. Humorous graphic novels; 2. Manga; 3. Shonen manga; 4. Graphic novels
1-59816-494-5, $9.99

This series follows the lives of Nobue Ito, her younger sister Chika, and her friends Miu and Matsuri—these girls try to solve problems and help each other out, whether it's helping someone to quit smoking or organizing a sleepover at a friend's house. The girls all look very young, but Nobue and her friends are teenagers. The comedy is very Seinfeld-esque, with a little partial nudity and some cigarette smoking.

Barberi, Carlo
 Justice League Unlimited Vol. 1: United They Stand. DC Comics 2005 104p. Illustration
Grades: 4 5 6 7 8 9 **741.5; Fic**
 1. Justice League (Fictional characters); 2. Superhero graphic novels; 3. Graphic novels
1401205127; 9781401205126, $6.99

Leaping straight out of their Cartoon Network show, the Worlds Greatest Heroes have their own comics series. This inaugural collection features these tales: Divide Conquer, Poker Face, Small Time, Local Hero and Monitor Duty.

 Justice League Unlimited Vol. 2: World's Greatest Heroes. DC Comics 2006 104p. Illustration
Grades: 4 5 6 7 8 9 **741.5; Fic**
 1. Green Lantern (Fictional character); 2. Justice League (Fictional characters); 3. Superhero graphic novels; 4. Graphic novels
1-4012-1014-7, $6.99

The JLA encounter the oldest Green Lantern as they battle the terrible Triptych, journey to deep space to thwart the malicious Darkseid and travel back in time to Camelot to battle the evil Morgaine Le Fey. Plus, the crazy Creeper helps in a battle against the Madmen, while the enigmatic Question hunts down a traitor within the League itself.

 Justice League Unlimited Vol. 3: Champions of Justice. DC Comics 2006 104p. Illustration
Grades: 4 5 6 7 8 9 **741.5; Fic**
 1. Flash (Fictional character); 2. Justice League (Fictional characters); 3. Superhero graphic novels; 4. Graphic novels
978-1-4012-1015-1, $6.99

The World's Greatest Heroes travel to Atlantis to confront the gigantic menace called Umbra! Plus, the two Flashes team up to battle Mirror Master, as the entire League must take on an out-of-control Red Tornado! This volume also includes a journey to Limbo and an encounter with the deadly Mr. Atom.

Barker, Clive

The **complete** the great and secret show. Adapted by Chris Ryall; art by Gabriel Rodriguez. IDW Publishing 2007 304p. Illustration

Grades: 11 12 Adult   741.5; Fic
1. Fantasy graphic novels; 2. Graphic novels
978-1-60010-121-2; 978-1-60010-121-2 (pa), $35

Clive Barker's horror novel has been adapted to comic book form and is presented complete in this volume. In the little town of Palomo Grove, the ultimate battle between good and evil begins when unassuming postal clerk Randall Jaffe finds clues to an alternate reality in the dead letter office. The book includes nudity, some sexual situations, violence, and harsh language.

The **Thief** of Always. IDW Publishing 2005 144p. Illustration

Grades: 4 5 6 7 8 9 10   741.5; Fic
1. Fantasy graphic novels; 2. Horror graphic novels; 3. Graphic novels
1-933239-17-4, $35.00; 1-933239-38-7 (pa), $19.99

Clive Barker's fable for younger readers is adapted here into graphic novel format. Mr. Hood's Holiday House has stood for a thousand years, welcoming countless children to enjoy a blissful round of treats and holidays ... for a price. Then bored young Harvey Swick comes, and he notices disquieting little details that make him realize the place is more of a trap. Things are spooky but not terrifying, with little violence.

Originally published as The Thief of Always issues #1-3.

Barr, Mike W.

The **Maze** Agency, Volume 1. Art by Adam Hughes. IDW Publishing 2005 156p. Illustration

Grades: 9 10 11 12 Adult   741.5; Fic
1. Mystery graphic novels; 2. Graphic novels
1-933239-06-9, $24.99

Presented for the first time since their original publication in 1989 by Innovation, The Maze Agency, Vol. 1 collects writer Mike W. Barr's first adventures of private eye Jennifer Mays and her boyfriend, true-crime writer and amateur sleuth Gabriel Webb. Their expanding relationship plays a backdrop to the cases they investigate, all of them whodunits that the reader can solve along with Jen and Gabe. While most of their cases are murder mysteries, there's very little gore on the pages.

Barry, Lynda

One hundred demons. Sasquatch Bks. 2002 216p. Illustration

Grades: 10 11 12 Adult   741.5
1. Autobiographical graphic novels
1-57061-337-0; 1-57061-459-8 (pa), $17.95
LC 2002-21657

"Whether she's talking about head lice, old boyfriends, or hippies who "forgot" to pay her wages, Barry playfully explores, in "autobifictionalographical" text and art, those demons common to teens—and to us all." Booklist

★ **Picture** this: the near-sighted monkey book. With guest watercolorist Kevin Kawula. Drawn and Quarterly 2010 224 p. Color illustration

Grades: 9 10 11 12 Adult
741.5; 741.5/973
1. American wit and humor, Pictorial; 2. Animals; 3. Animals/Graphic novels; 4. Humorous graphic novels; 5. Graphic novels
1897299648;
9781897299647, $29.95
LC 2010399443

Courtesy of Drawn and Quarterly

In author Lynda Barry's book, she "asks 'Why do we stop drawing?' and 'Why do we start?' It features the return of" the character "Marlys, and introduces a new one, the Nearsighted Monkey." The book is a "graphic-memoir-how-to" and a "take home extension of Barry's traveling" writing workshop which focuses on literature illustration. (Publisher's note)

★ **What** it is. Drawn & Quarterly 2008 209p. Illustration

Grades: 7 8 9 10 11 12 Adult   818; 741.5
1. Authorship; 2. Creative writing
978-1-897299-35-7, $24.95; 1-897299-35-4
LC C2007-9047319

Independent cartoonist Lynda Barry presents an unconventional book that encourages its readers to write by using her colorful art and asking questions such as "How are monsters different?" "And how are they the same?" "Can/Do images exist without thinking?" "What is the difference between lying and pretending?" Each question appears with illustrated writing prompts and Barry's own ruminations on the topics. It's a workbook of sorts, but it also exists as a book to be read for itself.

"Every so often a book comes along that surpasses expectations, taking readers on an inspirational voyage that they don't want to leave. This is one such book." SLJ

Batman Adventures Vol. 2: Shadows & Masks

DC Comics 2004 112p. Illustration
Grades: 4 5 6 7 8 9   741.5; Fic
1. Batman (Fictional character); 2. Superhero graphic novels; 3. Graphic novels
978-1-4012-0330-2, $6.95

A deadly new gang is threatening Gotham City, and it's up to the Dark Knight Detective to take it down, from the inside. He goes on an undercover mission in this volume.

Batman Black and White Volume 3

DC Comics 2007 288p. Illustration
Grades: 10 11 12 Adult   741.5; Fic

1. Batman (Fictional character); 2. Superhero graphic novels; 3. Graphic novels
978-1-4012-1531-6, $24.99

This third volume in the series collects thirty-three stories written and illustrated by creators from the mainstream and the independent comics world, including Brian Azzarello, John Bolton, Ed Brubaker, Mike Carey, Darwyn Cooke, Todd Dezago, Paul Grist, Michael Golden, Dick Giordano, Geoff Johns, Jim Mahfood, Dwayne McDuffie, Mike Mignola, Scott Morese, Ann Nocenti, Whilce Portacio, Mark Schultz, Julius Schwartz, Judd Winick, Bill Wray, and many more. Some of the stories have overt violence.

Batman unauthorized: vigilantes, jokers, and heroes in Gotham City
Edited by Dennis O'Neil. Benbella Books, Inc. 2008 219p. Illustration (Smart pop series)
Grades: 10 11 12 Adult   **741.5**
1. Batman (Fictional character); 2. Comic books, strips, etc — History and criticism; 3. Joker (Fictional character); 4. Robin (Fictional character); 5. Graphic novels
978-1-93377130-4, $17.95; 1-933771-30-5
LC 2007-46504

Former Batman comics editor and comic book writer O'Neil edits this collection of essays about Batman and his world, written by comics writers, magazine editors, and others. Topics include the cost of being Batman, calculated to the last dollar; why Batman is the most American of superheroes; whether Bruce Wayne might be mentally ill; why Batman needs Robin more than Robin needs Batman; why Arkham Asylum is doing more harm than good for Gotham City; why Batman works better when his world remains closer to reality; and more.

Includes bibliographical references

Beagle, Peter
The last unicorn. Original story by Peter S. Beagle; adaptation by Peter B. Gillis; art by Renae De Liz. IDW 2011 167p. Illustration
Grades: 6 7 8 9 10   **741.5; Fic**
9780451450524 (rpt), $16.00; 978-1-60010-851-8, $24.99; 1-60010-851-2

"A beloved story is now a graphic novel in this excellent adaptation. . . . Much of the original novel's lyrical language has been included, and readers will be eager to find out if the unicorn will give up her quest for love, or if any of Schmendrick's spells will ever turn out right. . . . The illustrations are graceful and detailed, and inked in warm, glowing colors. This is a worthy successor to the classic novel and film." SLJ

Beatty, Scott
Nightwing: Year One. Scott Beatty & Chuck Dixon, writers ; Scott McDaniel, penciller ; Andy Owens, inker ; Gregory Wright, colorist ; Phil Balsman, letterer, DC Comics 2005 Un Illustration
Grades: 7 8 9 10 11 12 Adult   **741.5; Fic**
1. Batman (Fictional character); 2. Nightwing (Fictional character); 3. Robin (Fictional character); 4. Superhero graphic novels; 5. Teen Titans (Fictional characters); 6. Graphic novels

1-4012-0435-X, $14.99

Dick Grayson was the first Robin, the teen sidekick to the Dark Knight, Batman. Then he became Nightwing and stepped out of Batman's shadow. The story behind that transformation and how it affected Batman, the Teen Titans and Dick himself is explored in this graphic novel. When Batman fires Robin, an angry Dick Grayson is unsure of where to go. On his journey, he receives advice from Superman and aid from Deadman, and makes the decisions that lead him to become a brand new crimefighter.

Best of Josie and the Pussycats Volume 1
Archie Comics 2001 96p. Illustration
Grades: 3 4 5 6 7 8 9 10 11 12 Adult   **741.5; Fic**
1. Adventure graphic novels; 2. Humorous graphic novels; 3. Rock music; 4. Graphic novels
1-879794-07-1, $10.95

This book reprints a selection of stories about rock group Josie and the Pussycats, from their origin in 1963 to 1988. Josie, Melody, and Valerie are the Pussycats, along with their roadie Alan M., their shifty manager Alex, and his conniving sister, Alexandra. They make music, but along the way they also solve mysteries.

The Beats: a graphic history
Edited by Paul Buhle. Hill & Wang 2009 199p. Illustration Grades: 10 11 12 Adult   **810.9; 920; 741.5; 810**
1. Beat generation; 2. Biographical graphic novels; 3. Graphic novels
978-0-8090-9496-7, $22; 0-8090-9496-7
LC 2008-43350

Main writer Harvey Pekar is joined by Nancy J. Peters, Penelope Rosemont, Joyce Brabner, Trina Robbins, and Tuli Kupferberg and by artists Ed Piskor, Jay Kinney, Nick Thorkelson, Summer McClinton, Peter Kuper, Mary Fleener, Jerome Neukirch, Anne Timmons, Gary Dumm, Lance Tooks, and Jeffrey Lewis to provide a brief history of the Beat movement and the most famous writers. The stories give readers a frank glimpse into the lives of such people as Jack Kerouac, Allen Ginsburg, William Burroughs, Lawrence Ferlinghetti, most of whom started to change what was called literature in the 1940s and 1950s. Their sexual and drug habits, which both contributed to their work and hampered their lives, receive frank treatment in this book. In addition to the famous Beats, the book includes short pieces about a number of the lesser known figures in the Beat movement, including LeRoi Jones/Amiri Baraka, Gregory Corso, Diane di Prima, artist Jay DeFeo, and the famed City Lights bookstore in San Francisco. The black and white art portrays sexual activity, consumption of alcohol and drugs, smoking, and the book includes some harsh language.

Beaulieu, Jean Francios
★ The **Wonderful** Wizard of Oz. Marvel Entertainment 2009 192p. Illustration
Grades: 3 4 5 6 7 8 9 10 11 12 Adult   **741.5; Fic**
1. Adventure graphic novels; 2. Authors; 3. Baum, L Frank, 1856-1919
978-0-7851-2921-9, $29.99

A twister picks up the house Dorothy and her dog Toto are in and carries them from Kansas to the land of Oz; the house lands on top of the Wicked Witch of the East, and the Munchkins, who were her slaves, hail Dorothy as a great sorceress. All the girl wants is to get back home to Kansas, but all anyone can say is that she must go to the Emerald City and ask the Great Wizard Oz to send her home. As she travels along the Yellow Brick Road, she meets a scarecrow who wants brains so people won't think he's a dummy, a tin man who wants a heart so he can love, and a great cowardly lion who wants courage so he'll truly be king of the beasts. However, once they reach the Emerald City and each see the Wizard Oz, they learn they must do what no one, including the Wizard himself, could ever do kill the Wicked Witch of the West. Shanower's adaptation of L. Frank Baum's novel keeps all the charm of the original, while Skottie Young's art banishes any lingering images of the old Technicolor movie; Beaulieu's muted color palette works with Young's art, while Eckleberry's lettering adds to an overall effect of magic and wonder. This book will appeal to all ages

Other Oz adapations by Shanower and Young are: The Marvelous Land of Oz; Ozma of Oz; Dorothy and the Wizard in Oz; The Road to Oz; The Emerald City of Oz

Bechdel, Alison

★ **Fun** home: a family tragicomic. Houghton Mifflin 2006 232p. Illustration

Grades: 11 12 Adult   **92; 741.5**

1. Artists; 2. Authors; 3. Autobiographical graphic novels; 4. Bechdel, Alison, 1960-; 5. Biography, Individual; 6. Cartoonists; 7. Comic book writers; 8. Essayists; 9. Novelists; 10. Graphic novels

0-618-47794-2, $19.95; 978-0-618-47794-4

LC 2005-30304

Time Magazine Book of the Year for 2006

This is a memoir in graphic novel format about the author's "childhood, her father's death and their shared homosexuality. . . . The death was deemed an accident—a truck hit [Mr. Bechdel] as he crossed a road with an armful of garden brush—but Ms. Bechdel suspects suicide." (N Y Times (Late N Y Ed))

Courtesy of Houghton Mifflin

This "is one of the very best graphic novels ever." Booklist

Bedard, Tony

Turok: son of stone. Dark Horse Comics 2008 Un Illustration

Grades: 9 10 11 12 Adult   **741.5; Fic**

1. Adventure graphic novels; 2. Fantasy graphic novels; 3. Graphic novels

978-1-59582-201-7, $14.95

Turok discovers a killing beast within himself when he, his brother, and Catori, the girl they both love, encounter a group of deadly hunters from another tribe; Turok kills all of the enemies, but in his killing mode, he also cuts down his brother. The tribe exiles him. Years later, the son of the man

Turok killed comes with his tribe to slaughter Turok's people; only Catori and her son Andar survive the guns used by Chichak and his men. When Turok pursues them into a deep cave, they all find themselves in a strange underworld where dinosaurs and other prehistoric creatures live, as well as humans and a beastly tribe. This book adapts the animated feature, Turok: Son of Stone, and features art from the animation. The book includes violence and bloodshed.

Beechen, Adam

Hench. Art by Manny Bello. AiT/Planet Lar 2004 Un Illustration

Grades: 10 11 12 Adult   **741.5; Fic**

1. Superhero graphic novels; 2. Graphic novels

1-932051-17-1, $12.95

The fine line between hero and villain is just another of longtime super-villain henchman Mike Fulton's many scars. Now, faced with a terrible choice that could mean life and death for heroes, villains, his family, and himself, Mike ponders just how his normal life went so crazy. There's a little violence but mostly fighting action, and a little bit of strong language.

Justice League Unlimited: the ties that bind. Written by Adam Beechen and Paul Storrie; illustrated by Carlo Barberi, Rick Burchett and others. DC Comics 2008 Un Illustration (Justice league unlimited)

Grades: 3 4 5 6 7 8 9   **741.5; Fic**

1. Batman (Fictional character); 2. Flash (Fictional character); 3. Green Arrow (Fictional character); 4. Green Lantern (Fictional character); 5. Justice League (Fictional characters); 6. Superhero graphic novels; 7. Superman (Fictional character); 8. Wonder Woman (Fictional character); 9. Graphic novels

978-1-4012-1691-7, $12.99; 1-4012-1691-9

This version of the Justice League was created for the Cartoon Network animated series and features such superheroes as Superman, Batman, Wonder Woman, Green Lantern, the Flash, Hawkgirl, J'onn Jonnz the Martian Manhunter, Power Girl, Green Arrow, and others. The stories collected in this volume include a clash of misunderstanding with Uncle Sam and the Freedom Fighters, a jaunt backwards in time, getting involved in a lovers' spat between super villains whose fight could destroy a city, and more. The book includes superhero vs supervillain fighting action with no bloodshed.

Another title in this series is: Justice league unlimited. Heroes (2009)

Robin: Wanted. Adam Beechen, writer; Freddie Williams II , artist; Karl Kerschl with Wayne Faucher & Prentis Rollins, artists, pages 6-27. DC Comics 2007 144p. Illustration

Grades: 9 10 11 12 Adult   **741.5; Fic**

1. Batgirl (Fictional character); 2. Mystery graphic novels; 3. Robin (Fictional character); 4. Superhero graphic novels; 5. Graphic novels

978-1-4012-1225-4, $12.99

Batgirl - Cassandra Cain - is dead ... and the evidence shows that Robin is the killer. Every cop in Gotham City is looking for him now, so he has to find the real killer and clear his name. Someone keeps sending Robin clues that only he can find, and they seem to be leading to a shadowy player who is making a grab for power in the deadly League of Assassins. Solving this mystery will lead Robin to a confrontation with the new leader of the League of Assassins ... and the killer's identity will change Robin's world forever. This book has lots of fighting action.

Beimler, Hans

The **Middleman**: the Doomsday Armageddon Apocalypse. Javier Grillo-Marxuach and Hans Beimler ; art by Armando Zanker. Viper Comics 2009 68p. Illustration
Grades: 8 9 10 11 12 Adult   **741.5; Fic**
   1. Humorous graphic novels; 2. Science fiction graphic novels; 3. Graphic novels
   978-0-9802385-8-7, $7.95

This graphic novel picks up right where the ABC Family television series left off, tying up the loose ends left by the series cancellation. The television series is based on the graphic novels, but the art in this book bases the character designs on the television series and is in color. Wendy Watson works with the Middleman to maintain justice and goodness in the world, but right now things have become very complicated. Her boyfriend Tyler now works for Manservant Neville, whose corporation has developed a ... Umaster ... a solar powered cube that's supposed to help people, how is unclear. The Middleman discovers that Neville plans to use the Umaster to take over the world and destroy it so he can remake it the way he wants. And somehow, Neville has managed to counter everything the Middleman and Wendy do to stop him. There is only one possible way to defeat Manservant Neville, but it involves Chac-Mol, a Mayan talisman of great power that demands the ultimate sacrifice of the user. A brief introduction provides enough information for any reader who hasn't seen any of the television series; and the book includes annotations to explain the many pop culture references. It provides closure for fans of the television series, and provides a nice little diversion for fans of the comics series, and there's enough information for readers meeting Wendy Watson and the Middle Man for the first time.

Beland, Tom

★ **True** story swear to God archives, vol. 1. Image Comics 2008 528p. Illustration
Grades: 10 11 12 Adult   **92; 741.5**
   1. Autobiographical graphic novels; 2. Beland, Tom, 1962-; 3. Cartoonists; 4. Romance graphic novels; 5. Graphic novels
   978-1-58240-881-1, $19.99

They met at a bus stop at Disneyworld, by chance: he was a cartoonist from Napa, California, and she was a radio personality from Puerto Rico. Their chance meeting blossomed into a romance that survived a long-distance separation, a Category 5 hurricane, his leaving home to move to a new world. Tom Beland writes candidly about the ups and downs of his relationship with Lily, with his family, and all the slings and arrows of life one has to deal with daily. He originally self-published these comics, and they were collected in several trade paperbacks from AiT/PlanetLar. The book includes occasional harsh language (including s-bombs and f-bombs), sexual situations, and frank talk about sex.

True Story Swear to God Volume 1. Image Comics 2007 Un Illustration
Grades: 10 11 12 Adult   **741.5**
   1. Autobiographical graphic novels; 2. Humorous graphic novels; 3. Romance graphic novels; 4. Graphic novels
   978-1-58240-761-6, $14.99

Tom Beland is a California cartoonist who is now living on the island of Puerto Rico with the woman of his dreams he met at a bus stop a year ago in Disney World. It hasn't been easy, since his freelance clients haven't paid him in months, while demanding more work from him. But all that is going to change as Beland demands restitution... or else. And Beland starts to worry about his lack of sexual performance. There's nothing portrayed on the page, but he talks about his problem in a frank manner. There's also some strong language, including the f-word.

This book from Image Comics continues the story of True Story Swear to God that was first published by AiT/Planet Lar.

★ **True** Story Swear to God: Chances Are .... AiT/Planet Lar 2003 Un Illustration
Grades: 10 11 12 Adult   **741.5**
   1. Autobiographical graphic novels; 2. Romance graphic novels; 3. Graphic novels
   1-932051-09-0, $14.95

What are the chances of going to a theme park, on the East Coast... and meeting a person who will change your life as you know it" What are the chances of this person living on the island of San Juan, Puerto Rico, some 3,600 miles from your home in Napa Valley, California" What are the chances of a long-distance relationship such as this lasting very long" If you're California cartoonist Tom Beland and Puerto Rico journalist Lily Garcia, those chances are pretty good. This book deals with the joys of meeting someone by chance and the heartache that comes with distance. It covers the humor, anxiety, annoyances and paranoia found in every relationship. And it's all true, swear to God. Beland uses some harsh language, and some sexual situations which aren't graphic.

★ **True** Story Swear to God: This One Goes to 11. AiT/Planet Lar 2005 Un Illustration
Grades: 10 11 12 Adult   **741.5**
   1. Autobiographical graphic novels; 2. Romance graphic novels; 3. Graphic novels
   1-932051-34-1, $12.95

A relationship is tough enough when there's 3,600 miles separating two lovebirds. Toss in a category 5 hurricane named Georges, which struck Puerto Rico in 1998, and you've got some real problems. How do you pack up your life, say goodbye to everything you hold dear, and take a leap of faith based on what your heart tells you" Beland tells how. This book has some harsh language and some sexual situations.

Bell, Blake

★ **Strange** & stranger: the world of Steve Ditko. Fantagraphics Books 2008 220p. Illustration
Grades: 10 11 12 Adult   **92; 741.5**
   1. Comic books, strips, etc — History and criticism; 2. Ditko, Steve; 3. Graphic designers; 4. Spider-Man (Fictional character); 5. Graphic novels

Courtesy of Fantagraphics

978-1-56097-921-0, $39.99

Steve Ditko may be best known as the cocreator and first artist for Marvel's Spider-Man comics, but he has done much more. Bell tells Ditko's life story and covers his career which has spanned more than 50 years. He also gives Ditko's side of the story in explaining his split with Stan Lee and why he walked away from Spider-Man back in 1966. Ditko's work has been strongly influenced by author/philosopher Ayn Rand, and her Objectivist philosophy has informed his work. The book includes lots of Ditko's art, including many unpublished pieces. Bell doesn't romanticize Ditko, but provides ample reason for the artist's place in comic book history.

Bell, Gabrielle

Lucky. Drawn & Quarterly 2006 Un Illustration

Grades: 11 12 Adult   741.5
   1. Autobiographical graphic novels; 2. Graphic novels
1-897299-01-X, $16.95

Bell documents the mundane details of her below-minimum-wage, twenty-something existence in Brooklyn, New York, with a subtle humor. Her simple, unadorned drawing style and heavy narrationchronicle transient roommates who communicate only through Post-it notes; aspiring artists who sublet tiny rooms in leaky, greasy broken-down border-house loft apartments crawling with bugs, cats, and bad art. Bell tackles a string of forgettable, unrelated jobs-including nude modeling, artist's assistant, art teacher, and jewelry maker-that only serve to bolster her despair, boredom, and discomfort in her own skin. Bell's self-scrutiny leads her to dream sequences that allow her to rise above her banal actuality and hyperawareness. She uses some strong language and nudity in some of the sequences.

Bellstorf, Arne

Baby's in black: Astrid Kirchherr, Stuart Sutcliffe, and the Beatles. Arne Bellstorf. First Second 2012 196 p. Illustration

Grades: 10 11 12 Adult   **782.421; 782.42166092/2**
   1. Beatles; 2. Kirchherr, Astrid; 3. Love stories; 4. Rock musicians — England; 5. Sutcliffe, Stuart, 1940-1962
1596437715; 9781596437715, $24.99

LC 2011049680

This graphic novel tells the love story of "Stuart Sutcliffe, one of the original Beatles," and "German photographer Astrid Kirchherr." The "story offers insight into the time the Beatles spent performing together in Germany before they made it big." Despite the couple's "different languages and worlds, the pair fall into a happy, and seemingly easy, romance. But their happiness is short-lived: the Beatles are being forced to leave the country, and Stuart's health is failing." (Publishers Weekly)

Translated from the German by Michael Waaler.

Bendis, Brian Michael

Civil War: Iron Man. Marvel Entertainment 2007 Un Illustration

Grades: 9 10 11 12 Adult   741.5; Fic
   1. Captain America (Fictional character); 2. Iron Man (Fictional character); 3. Superhero graphic novels; 4. Graphic novels
0-7851-2314-8, $11.99

This book will give readers insight into why Iron Man believes that super human registration is necessary, and why he has taken it upon himself to lead the charge for its implementation. He and Captain America meet secretly to see if there's any hope of working things out before further tragedy occurs. How could these two men, once the closest of friends and staunchest of allies, end up leading opposing armies in this conflict? And when two of the Marvel heroes most affected by the conclusion of the war get together one last time, and what is said between them will set the course of the Marvel Universe for the future.

Fortune and Glory: A True Hollywood Comic Book Story. Oni Press 2000 152p. Illustration

Grades: 11 12 Adult   741.5
   1. Autobiographical graphic novels; 2. Graphic novels
978-1-929998-06-7, $14.95

Bendis has collected his miniseries into one volume. He uses the comic book format to show the stupidity of Hollywood producers, the vanity of stars like Uma Thurman and Clint Eastwood, and the mood swings and ego nosedives of a little indie comic-book creator caught up in the maelstrom of the motion picture industry as he tries to sell his comics crime caper story Goldfish in Hollywood. Bendis has since become a major writer for Marvel Comics. This collection features brand-new pages left on the cutting room floor and not included in the original comics. There's some strong language.

Civil War: Marvel Universe. Marvel Entertainment 2007 Un Illustration

Grades: 9 10 11 12 Adult   741.5; Fic
   1. Daredevil (Fictional character); 2. Superhero graphic novels; 3. Graphic novels
978-0-7851-2470-2, $11.99

Civil War is encompassing the entire Marvel Universe, and the effects of the war are being felt by every hero, villain and civilian. In Civil War: Choosing Sides, five stories shine a spotlight on the wildcards and impact players whose part in the Civil War has yet to be told - including Daredevil/Iron Fist, U.S.Agent, the Irredeemable Ant-Man, Venom and even... Howard the Duck? On Earth, the Sentry confronts his inner demons as the shadows of past and future battles tear him apart. Within The Negative Zone, the walls of 42 are pulled back to reveal the return of one of the Marvel's greatest heroes. And in She-Hulk, Civil War threatens the rights of every American super hero. So whose side will Marvel's top superhuman lawyer fight for? And how can she possibly choose, when she feels one way as She-Hulk, and another as Jen Walters?

Jinx: The Definitive Collection. By Brian Michael Bendis for David Engel. Image Comics 2001 480p. Illustration

Grades: 11 12 Adult   741.5; Fic
   1. Mystery graphic novels; 2. Graphic novels

978-1-58240-179-9, $24.95

This is a graphic crime noir novel about a bounty hunter, two grifters, and a treasure hunt that propels the character driven story. This extra large edition carries with it the entire epic story, behind the scenes/making of, script excerpts, and an art gallery. The story includes harsh language, nudity, sexual situations, and violence.

Miles Morales; Volume 1: the ultimate Spider-Man : revival. Writer, Brian Michael Bendis; artists, Dave Marquez, Mark Bagley & Andrew Hennessey. Marvel Enterprises 2014 144 p. Color; Illustration
Grades: 9 10 11 12   **741.5**
1. Spider-Man (Fictional character); 2. Superhero graphic novels
0785154175; 9780785154174, $17.99
This Spider-Man comic book was written by Brian Michael Bendis and illustrated by David Marquez. "Here we find Miles back in the red and black and still fighting in the long shadow of the late Peter Parker. Little does Miles know that lurking in that shadow is Norman Osborn and . . . Peter Parker" On the anniversary of Peter's death, is he really alive and well—" (Booklist)
Contains material originally published in single magazine form as Ultimate Spider-Man #200 and Miles Morales: ultimate Spider-Man #1-5

Powers Vol. 2: Roleplay. By Brian Michael Bendis and Michael Avon Oeming. Image Comics 2002 Un Illustration
Grades: 11 12 Adult   **741.5; Fic**
1. Mystery graphic novels; 2. Superhero graphic novels; 3. Graphic novels
1-58240-232-9, $13.95
2001 Eisner Award, Best New Series.
Detectives Christian Walker and Deena Pilgrim work out of the special homicide office in charge of cases that involve Powers, those that have talents and abilities far beyond those of normal men. This graphic novel details one of the most disturbing cases of their careers. A group of college kids who role play their favorite super-heroes are being murdered one-by-one, and unless Walker and Pilgrim can stop the killer, more kids will die. The book includes violence and copious use of harsh language, especially the f-bomb.

Powers Vol. 8: Legends. Created and produced by Brian Michael Bendis and Mike Avon Oeming; color art, Peter Pentazis. Marvel Entertainment/Icon 2004 Un Illustration
Grades: 11 12 Adult   **741.5; Fic**
1. Mystery graphic novels; 2. Superhero graphic novels; 3. Graphic novels
0-7851-1742-3, $17.95
Homicide detectives Christian Walker and Deena Pilgrim investigate murders specific to superhero cases. With all superheroes declared illegal, a bloody powers crime wave has hit the city and hit hard. A hero has returned, but is it enough to keep the city safe from the crossfire as the city's most powerful villains gun for each other in a massive turf war" And how far will Detective Deena Pilgrim go to prove she still has what it takes" The book contains lots of graphic violence, very harsh language with copious use of the f-bomb and s-bomb, and nudity.

★ **Powers:** The Definitive Hardcover Collection Vol. 1. Created and produced by Brian Michael Bendis and Mike Avon Oeming; colored by Pat Garrahy with Brian Michael Bendis. Marvel Comics 2006 456p. Illustration
Grades: 11 12 Adult   **741.5; Fic**
1. Mystery graphic novels; 2. Superhero graphic novels; 3. Graphic novels
978-0-7851-1805-3, $29.99
Volume 1 of 6
Homicide detectives Christian Walker and Deena Pilgrim investigate homicides in a city where super-powered heroes and villains live, fight, and die. Sometimes the heroes are just as flawed as the villains. And Walker has a secret of his own that gives him special insight in his investigations. The first three storylines have been remastered, reformatted, and collected in this edition which is replete with violence, harsh language, nudity, and sexual situations.
Also available in 16 paperback volumes

The **Pulse** Vol. 1: Thin Air. Illustrated by Mark Bagley. Marvel Entertainment 2004 Un Illustration
Grades: 10 11 12 Adult   **741.5; Fic**
1. Superhero graphic novels; 2. Graphic novels
0-7851-1332-0, $13.99
Former super hero and current private investigator Jessica Jones has just been offered a new job: a position with the Bugle's new super-hero section, The Pulse. Jessica's first assignment: to uncover the true identity of a former Bugle reporter's super-powered murderer. How is millionaire industrialist Norman Osborn involved in the case" And how will Jessica's discovery affect the entire Marvel Universe" The book includes some violence and strong language.

The **Road** to Civil War. Marvel Entertainment 2007 Un Illustration
Grades: 9 10 11 12 Adult   741.5; Fic
1. Fantastic Four (Fictional characters); 2. Iron Man (Fictional character); 3. Spider-Man (Fictional character); 4. Superhero graphic novels; 5. Graphic novels
978-0-7851-1974-6, $14.99
This book covers the hidden story of Marvel's secret past, the secret history of Marvel's most secret team - how they came together and how they are ripped apart. Plus: Spidey's got a new lease on life, new powers and a new costume, courtesy of his new best friend Tony Stark. So what could possibly go wrong? With clouds quickly building on the horizon, the bonds that Spider-Man now forges may very well determine his capacity to withstand a coming storm. And a mysterious object has fallen from space to crash in the Midwest, and Reed Richards of the Fantastic Four investigates.

Sam & Twitch: The Brian Michael Bendis Collection Vol. 1. Image Comics 2006 Un Illustration
Grades: 12 Adult   **741.5; Fic**
1. Mystery graphic novels; 2. Graphic novels
1-58240-583-2, $24.95
This neonoir crime series centers on the lives of New York City detectives Sam Burke and Twitch Williams and their adventures in the back alleys, deep nooks and dark crannies of the Big Apple. The hard-boiled stories are full of graphic violence and harsh language.

Sam and Twitch: The Brian Michael Bendis Collection Vol. 2. Image Comics 2007 Un Illustration
Grades: 11 12 Adult   **741.5; Fic**
   1. Mystery graphic novels; 2. Graphic novels
   978-1-58240-845-6, $24.95
   This volume collects issues 10-19 of Bendis' run on the Sam & Twitch comics series. This is a crime noir series set in New York City and focused on the lives of detectives Sam Burke and Twitch Williams. The book features the Witchcraft story arc, an Ashley Wood cover gallery, and more extras. The book contains graphic violence and very harsh language.

Ultimate Fantastic Four Vol. 1: The Fantastic. Writers, Brian Michael Bendis & Mark Millar ; pencils, Adam Kubert ; inks, Danny Miki and John Dell ; colors, Dave Stewart ; letters, Chris Eliopoulos/ Marvel Entertainment 2005 Un Illustration
Grades: 8 9 10 11 12 Adult   **741.5; Fic**
   1. Fantastic Four (Fictional characters); 2. Superhero graphic novels; 3. Graphic novels
   978-0-7851-1393-5, $12.99
   The Ultimate treatment takes the Fantastic Four back to the beginning. High school genius (and bully magnet) Reed Richards suffers at school and also at home with a father who doesn't like his "troublemaking" experiments. When Reed enrolls at a secret government-sponsored school for the most gifted minds in the world, he unwittingly embarks on the journey of a lifetime. This is a story about science, adventure, and above all else, family.

Ultimate Spider-Man: Power & Responsibility. By Brian Michael Bendis (Author), Mark Bagley (Illustrator). Marvel 2009 200 p. Color illustration
Grades: 7 8 9 10 11 12 Adult   **741.5**
   1. Spider-Man (Fictional character)
   0785139400; 9780785139409, $19.99
   In this comic book, by Brian Michael Bendis, illustrated by Mark Bagley, "Peter Parker gains super-powers after being bitten by a spider, loses his likable Uncle Ben to violent crime, and learns once again that 'with great power comes great responsibility.'" (Publisher's note)
   Collected edition originally published 2001
   Volume 1 of 21

Benjamin, Paul
   Hulk: the Hulks take Manhattan; Paul Benjamin, writer ; Juan Santacruz, penciler ; Raul Fernandez, inker ; Wilfredo Quintana, colorist ; Dave Sharpe, letterer. ABDO/Spotlight 2008 Un Illustration
Grades: 3 4 5 6 7 8 9   **741.5; Fic**
   1. Hulk (Fictional character); 2. Superhero graphic novels; 3. Hulk (Fictional character); 4. Graphic novels
   9781599615462, $21.35
                                                     LC 2008-102
   In his quest to remove the Hulk from himself, Bruce Banner hires Jamie Madrox, the Multiplying Man, to help him locate the secret laboratory of a former colleague; he hopes to use the radiation equipment there to make himself normal again. However, one of Madrox's more paranoid selves comes at just the wrong moment, and suddenly there are multiplying Hulks. As Hulk Prime tries to smash all the new Hulks, he makes more of them, and they start to take

Manhattan apart. While there's a lot of smashing action and property damage, the book maintains kid-friendly dialogue and avoids graphic violence.
   This is a library bound edition of a Marvel Age: The Incredible Hulk comic book issue, with all advertising pages removed.

   Hulk: misunderstood monster, v1. Writer, Paul Benjamin; illustrated by David Nakayama and Juan Santacruz. Marvel 2007 Illustration
Grades: 5 6 7 8 9   **741.5; Fic**
   978-0-7851-2642-3, $6.99; 0-7851-2642-2
   "See how brilliant scientist Bruce Banner was cursed to transform into the rampaging Hulk! Learn why Banner's girlfriend Betty Ross left him, why her father, General 'Thunderbolt' Ross hunts him and why Rick Jones blames himself for creating the monster." (Publisher's note)

Pantheon High, Vol. 1: Demigods & Debutantes. Art by Steven & Megumi Cummings. Tokyopop 2007 188p. Illustration
Grades: 10 11 12   **741.5; Fic**
   1. Fantasy graphic novels; 2. Mythology; 3. Graphic novels
   978-1-59816-734-4, $9.99
   Nestled in Los Angeles, Pantheon High is a high school for demigods, teens who have one divine parent from Greek, Norse, Japanese, or Egyptian mythology. Four sophomores: Grace, daughter of Norse god Tyr; Yukio, son of Japanese goddess Benten; Griffin, son of Hades; and Aziza el Ra, daughter of the Egyptian sun god - find that they are the only ones awake enough to stop another group of students who drugged the rest of the students and faculty into sleep and plan to cast a spell to take all their divine powers to become immortal, full gods.
   Full of mythological references, the book has a useful appendix that explains them. The art includes a lot of fan service (titillating angles and shots), especially panty shots, and a little nudity at the end of this volume. This is the first volume in a new global manga series.

Bennett, Anina
   Heartbreakers Meet Boilerplate. Anina Bennett and Paul Guinan. IDW Publishing 2005 100p. Illustration
Grades: 8 9 10 11 12 Adult   **741.5; Fic**
   1. Adventure graphic novels; 2. Science fiction graphic novels; 3. Graphic novels
   1-932382-86-0, $9.99
   The pioneering female action heroes, Heartbreakers, team up with the long-lost 19th-century robot, Boilerplate (already a worldwide legend), for a science fiction adventure featuring kung fu clones and robot romance. In this world, clones have won partial human rights, and rogue researchers now race to develop androids that can serve as the new slave workers.

Benson, Gabriel
   The **Ballad** of Sleeping Beauty. Mike Hawthorne, Artist. Image Comics 2006 Un Illustration
Grades: 9 10 11 12 Adult   **741.5; Fic**
   1. Fairy tales; 2. Westerns; 3. Graphic novels
   0-97668-600-7, $21.95

Hounded gunfighter Cole Jarrett chases the tale of a woman cursed to spend the rest of her days imprisoned in sleep for sins she did not commit while running from a guilt-riddled past. In this adventure, the classic fairy tale is just the beginning. The story has violence and some strong language, as the fairy tale is set in the Old West.

Bertozzi, Nick

Shackleton: Antarctic odyssey. Nick Bertozzi. First Second 2014 128 p. Illustration; Map
Grades: 5 6 7 8 9 10　　　　　　　　**741.5; 919.89**
　　1. Antarctica — Discovery and exploration — British; 2. Antarctica — Exploration; 3. Explorers — Great Britain — Biography; 4. Shackleton, Ernest Henry, Sir, 1874-1922; 5. Graphic novels
　　1596434511; 9781596434516, $16.99
　　This book by Nick Bertozzi describes how "Ernest Shackleton was one of the last great Antarctic explorers, and he led one of the most ambitious Antarctic expeditions ever undertaken. This is his story, and the story of the dozens of men who threw in their lot with him—many of whom nearly died in the unimaginably harsh conditions of the journey." (Publisher's note)
　　"Bertozzi eschews all narrative explanation, relying solely on dialogue among the crew and the detailed black-and-white panels to tell the story. The snow- and ice-bound journey is the perfect match for Bertozzi's minimal style—vast stretches of white become gasp-worthy, desolate vistas." Booklist

Best, Dan

The **amazing** remarkable MonsieurLeotard: a novel with typographical acrobatics andillustrational feats in an ideal production ofentirely new tricks, statuesque acts, andperformances. Art by Eddie Campbell. First Second Books 2008 128p. Illustration
Grades: 10 11 12 Adult　　　　　　　　**741.5; Fic**
　　1. Adventure graphic novels; 2. Circus; 3. Graphic novels
　　978-1-59643-301-4, $17.95
　　　　　　　　　　　　　　　LC 2008-23283
　　When Jules Leotard, the man who inspired the song "The Man on the Flying Trapeze," dies, his nephew Etienne takes his place as trapeze artist and head of a circus troupe. Things don't go as planned, and eventually the members of the troupe go their separate ways. They come back together many years later when Zany, the clown, gets sent to Devil's Island; on their mission to save him, they end up on the Titanic and even more adventures. The book includes some (literal) potty humor, some violence, and mild sexual situations.

★ **The Best of the Spirit**

DC Comics 2005 187p. Illustration
Grades: 7 8 9 10 11 12 Adult　　　　　　**741.5; Fic**
　　1. Spirit (Fictional character); 2. Superhero graphic novels; 3. Graphic novels
　　1-4012-0755-3, $14.99; 9781401207557
　　Legendary comics creator Will Eisner created The Spirit in 1940, and over the twelve years of its initial publication, he used it to revolutionize the cartooning medium, creating new methods of storytelling, developing new depths of characterization, and inventing such artistic

innovations as the splash page. This volume reprints 22 stories from the original run, including the origin story from 1940; the bulk of the stories were initially published in the mid- to late-1940s. These stories allow people to get acquainted with The Spirit, who was a young criminologist named Denny Colt; believed to have been murdered, he was buried in a state of suspended animation and awoke one day in the Wildwood Cemetery. He has since dedicated himself to fighting crime, wearing a suit, fedora, and mask. DC Comics started publishing a new incarnation of The Spirit in 2007, and a motion picture is in the works.

The Best of write now!

Twomorrows Publishing 2008 160p. Illustration
Grades: 11 12 Adult　　　　　　　　　　**741.5**
　　1. Comic books, strips, etc — Authorship; 2. Drawing — Technique; 3. Graphic novels — Authorship
　　978-1-893905-924, $19.95
　　This collection of articles from Write Now! Magazine features interviews with comics writers such as Brian Michael Bendis, Jeff Loeb, Todd McFarlane, and Paul Levitz, focusing on the art, craft, and business of writing comics. Other articles look at the comics writing and drawing processes, with such professionals as Mark Millar, Bendis, and J. Michael Straczynski; and other articles cover such topics as breaking into comics publishing, dealing with writer's block, and surviving in the comics industry. Comics titans Stan Lee and Will Eisner are also profiled.

Betten, Court

Harukaze bitter pop, volume 1. Tokyopop 2008 182p. Illustration
Grades: 9 10 11 12　　　　　　　　　　**741.5**
　　1. Humorous graphic novels; 2. Manga; 3. Mystery graphic novels; 4. Shonen manga; 5. Graphic novels
　　978-1-4278-0328-3, $9.99
　　Chiyoharu used to be the leader of troublemakers, until a prank got out of hand and caused a major fire; his friends were caught and took the blame, but Chiyoharu has been ostracized at school. But now it's a new term, but his plans to just get by are dashed when he meets a musclebound amnesiac who seems strangely familiar and a self-proclaimed detective who develops an instant crush on Souza (the amnesiac). The action in the story is full of comedy and riffs on established manga such as Kinnikuman, but the occasional violence can be quite shocking.

Bevard, Robby

Ninja High School Hawaii Vol. 1. Antarctic Press 2002 Un Illustration
Grades: 10 11 12 Adult　　　　　　　　**741.5; Fic**
　　1. Humorous graphic novels; 2. Martial arts; 3. Graphic novels
　　0-9768043-1-X, $12.95
　　Most people travel to Hawaii to escape from the craziness of their lives, but from the moment ninja-in-training Yumei Katana arrived at the airport, she knew this was no vacation. Klutzy assassins, philanthropist bullies, and even the landscape itself seem out to get her. Now she has to go to a school full of people who are trying to date her, kill her - or both - while still attempting to pass her

next test! What's your typical ninja girl to do" This story is full of titillating fan service and martial arts action.

Biggs, Gina
Red String, Vol. 1. Dark Horse Comics 2006 192p. Illustration
Grades: 7 8 9 10 11 12   **741.5; Fic**
1. High school life; 2. Romance graphic novels; 3. Graphic novels
978-1-59307-624-5, $9.95
First year high school student Miharu Ogawa can't believe it when her parents tell her they've arranged for her to marry the son of their friends, someone she has never met. They won't marry until they finish school, but the whole idea is repugnant. Then Miharu meets a cute guy and knows she has to fight her parents; but the cute guy she likes is Kazuo Fujiwara, the arranged fiance. Now Miharu just has to deal with gossip at school that hurts her friend Reika, and with her manipulative cousin Karen, who wants Kazuo for herself, and other problems and romantic obstacles. Biggs uses the manga format and manga-influenced art to tell her story of high school romance. Other than one panel of tastefully rendered partial nudity, there's no content to keep this from most middle school age readers.

Bilson, Danny
The **Flash:** Lightning in a Bottle. DC Comics 2007 144p. Illustration
Grades: 9 10 11 12 Adult   **741.5; Fic**
1. Superhero graphic novels; 2. Flash (Fictional character); 3. Graphic novels
978-1-4012-1229-2, $12.99
Bart Allen returned from fighting Superboy Prime inside the Speed Force at the end of the Infinite Crisis with no speed and aged four years into an adult, and also no memory of how he spent the time. One year later, he's a factory worker in Keystone City, when an accident at the factory reconnects him to the Speed Force. That same accident causes Bart's best friend Griffin Gray to gain powers, too, but they drain his life force and cause him to rapidly age. His solution - he siphons off the energy from the slowly aging original Flash, Jay Garrick; but it might kill Garrick. And Griffin's brand of justice is too harsh.

Biskup, Agnieszka
Understanding Global Warming with Max Axiom, Super Scientist. Capstone Press 2007 32p. Illustration
Grades: 3 4 5 6 7 8 9   **363.7; 741.5**
1. Greenhouse effect; 2. Graphic novels
978-1-4296-0139-9, $25.26
                         LC 2007002269
This book uses the graphic novel format to follow the adventures of super scientist Max Axiom as he explains the science behind the issue of global warming. The book includes additional facts and a list of books for further reading.
Part of the Graphic Science series.

Bizarro World
DC Comics 2005 Un Illustration
Grades: 9 10 11 12 Adult   **741.5; Fic**

1. Aquaman (Fictitious character); 2. Batman (Fictional character); 3. Flash (Fictional character); 4. Humorous graphic novels; 5. Justice League (Fictional characters); 6. Superhero graphic novels; 7. Superman (Fictional character); 8. Wonder Woman (Fictional character); 9. Graphic novels
1-4012-0657-3, $19.99
In this collection, independent comics creators take DC's super hero characters - Superman, Batman, Wonder Woman, the Flash, Aquaman, the Justice League of America, and more - and put their own vision and spin on them, mostly with lots of humor. Some of the creators included here are: Peter Bagge, Kyle Baker, Ellen Forney, Paul Hornschemeier, Tony Millionaire, Scott Morse, Johnny Ryan, Mo Willems, Raina Telgemeier, Craig Thompson, Dean Haspiel, and Evan Dorkin.

The Black Diamond Detective Agency.
Inspired by the screenplay of C. Gaby Mitchell. First Second Books 2007 138p. Illustration
Grades: 10 11 12 Adult   **741.5; Fic**
1. Mystery graphic novels; 2. Graphic novels
978-1-59643-142-3, $16.95; 1-59643-142-3
John Hardin is a desperate man. He is the sole suspect of the renowned Black Diamond Detective Agency, a private operation determined to solve the mystery of a deadly train bombing and bring its perpetrator to justice at any cost. Once a quiet Missouri corn farmer, Hardin now finds himself on the run in turn-of-the-century Chicago. Violence, harsh language, brief nudity, and an implied sexual encounter make this better for older teen and adult readers.

Black, Holly
The **Good** Neighbors; book one: Kin. Art by Ted Naifeh. Graphix 2008 117p. (The Good Neighbors)
Grades: 7 8 9 10 11 12   **741.5; Fic**
1. Fairies; 2. Fantasy graphic novels; 3. Graphic novels
978-0-439-85562-4, $16.99; 0-439-85562-4
                         LC 2007-49008
Sixteen-year-old Rue has grown up in a world much like ours, except that the human world and the world of faerie have co-existed, as good neighbors, for a long time. When Rue's mother disappears and her professor father becomes the main suspect in the murder of a young woman, Rue's life turns strange. As she digs for information to figure out what is happening in her life, Rue discovers that her mother is a faerie and has returned to that realm because of a broken promise.
"This sophisticated tale is well served by Naifeh's stylish, angular illustrations." SLJ
Other titles in this series are: Kith (2009); Kind (2010)

Blackman, Haden
Star Wars Omnibus: X-Wing Rogue Squadron Volume 1. Haden Blackman and Michael A. Stackpole. Dark Horse Comics 2006 Un Illustration
Grades: 7 8 9 10 11 12 Adult   **741.5; Fic**
1. Adventure graphic novels; 2. Science fiction graphic novels; 3. Star Wars; 4. Graphic novels
978-1-59307-572-9, $24.95
The greatest star fighters of the Rebel Alliance become the defenders of a New Republic in this massive collection

of stories featuring Wedge Antilles, hero of the Battle of Endor, and his team of ace pilots known throughout the galaxy as Rogue Squadron. Meet the Rogues for the first time and learn the fate of the galaxy immediately after the events of Return of the Jedi as the Rebellion's best pilots battle remnants of the Empire wherever its ugly agenda of fear and domination appears. Along with X-Wing Rogue Squadron: The Phantom Affair, this jam-packed volume contains never before collected material, including Star Wars X-Wing Rogue Leader #1-3, Star Wars X-Wing Rogue Squadron: The Rebel Opposition #1-4, Star Wars X-Wing Rogue Squadron: The Phantom Affair #1-4, and Star Wars Handbook: X-Wing Rogue Squadron.

Star Wars: Clone Wars Adventures Volume 2. Written by Haden Blackman, Welles Hartley ; art by the Fillbach Brothers. Dark Horse Comics 2004 Un Illustration
Grades: 6 7 8 9 10 11 12   **741.5; Fic**
   1. Adventure graphic novels; 2. Science fiction graphic novels; 3. Star Wars; 4. Graphic novels
   1-59307-271-6, $6.95
In the rolling asteroid rings above a remote planet, General Obi-Wan Kenobi and Anakin Skywalker play a deadly game of cat and mouse against Separatist droid fighters - and a squadron of highly skilled human pilots who have pledged their guns to Count Dooku. Also in this volume, Jedi Master Luminara Unuli and her Padawan Barriss Offee race against time to evacuate farmers and their families before the droid forces of General Grievous overrun their village. When Barriss and her squad of clone troopers are caught in the path of the enemy army, only fast thinking and steel resolve can save the day. And Jedi Master Mace Windu goes solo to foil a sinister Separatist plot. These stories take place approximately five months after the Battle of Geonosis.

Blain, Christophe
  Gus and his gang. First Second Books 2008 164p. Illustration
Grades: 10 11 12 Adult   **741.5; Fic**
   1. Humorous graphic novels; 2. Western stories; 3. Graphic novels
   978-1-59643-170-6, $16.95; 1-59643-170-9
                            LC 2008-23541
Gus, Gratt, and Clem are three outlaws in this French version of the Old West. Gus much prefers to rob trains, banks are too still for him. What all three of them prefer is to be with women; Gus and Gratt go girl-hunting together in towns such as El Dorado, but Clem doesn't go with them. He has a family, with Ava and their daughter Jamie; but he does have a passionate affair with a free-spirited, red-haired photographer. Everything the three men do is financed by robbing banks, trains . . . when Gus tries to case a bank, he falls for a woman who works there and ends up pretending to be a writer in order to woo her. The book doesn't follow a straightforward narrative, and the French idea of how the Old West "worked" is more than a bit eccentric. The book also includes lots of sexual content and partial nudity.

  Isaac the Pirate 1. To Exotic Lands. NBM 2003 Un Illustration
Grades: 10 11 12 Adult   **741.5; Fic**
   1. Adventure graphic novels; 2. Pirates; 3. Graphic novels

1-56163-366-6, $14.95
                             LC 2003-59288
Isaac is a talented artist with no money but with a wonderful lover back in Paris of the 18th century. He runs into a rich Captain who is taken by his abilities and hires him with a handsome stipend to come along in his voyages. It turns out he's a pirate. Isaac went to make some quick money and come back and marry the love of his life, but he has embarked upon a series of adventures on the high seas from the Caribbean to the icy North, with apparently no end in sight. Meanwhile, his girlfriend is getting attention from another ... The book includes some harsh language and violence.

  Isaac the Pirate Volume 2: The Capital. NBM 2005 Un Illustration
Grades: 10 11 12 Adult   **741.5; Fic**
   1. Adventure graphic novels; 2. Pirates; 3. Graphic novels
   1-56163-418-2, $14.95
                            LC 2004-116613
As things get bad on the pirate ship, Isaac must rescue himself from many dangers and, with the help of one of his former shipmates, a fleet-footed thief, makes his way back to Paris to seek his love, Alice, from whom he has been separated far too long. However, the bad pirating influences prove themselves hard to shake; he becomes a nimble pickpocket. Alice, however, remains elusive ... The book includes violence, strong language, nudity, and sexual situations.

Blaylock, Josh
  How to Self-Publish Comics ... Not Just Create Them. Devil's Due Publishing 2006 135p. Illustration
Grades: 9 10 11 12   **741.5**
   1. Graphic novels — Publishing; 2. Graphic novels
   978-1-932796-67-4, $14.95
This is Josh Blaylock's information packed Self Publishing guide. If there's anything that Blaylock's past ten years of publishing has taught him, there's more to making a comic book than just finding people to write and draw it. Blaylock has been writing comics since he was six years old, and has run Devil's Due Publishing for years. He includes sample contracts, information on marketing, figuring out how many copies to print, and how to exhibit at conventions. A helpful appendix shows how to read important business documents such as purchase orders, how to read a printer quote, and others.

  Misplaced: Somewhere Under the Rainbow. Devil's Due Publishing 2005 Un Illustration
Grades: 7 8 9 10 11 12   **741.5; Fic**
   1. Adventure graphic novels; 2. Science fiction graphic novels; 3. Graphic novels
   1-932796-04-5, $10.95
Alyssa is from Realm 77, a hi-tech utopia where those who question authority aren't treated kindly. Even stranger, the only person who does is Alyssa. Ostracized from her peers since childhood, and subjected to numerous medical tests by the mysterious Elders, Alyssa grows more and more intolerant of the Realm. When it's discovered she's developing incredible powers, Alyssa escapes to Earth to live a normal life in a small college town, but the Elders won't allow it. It's only when she's forced to return to the

realm that her powers truly manifest. All she wanted to do was hang out, go to some clubs, and be normal." But that's not Alyssa's destiny.

Penguin Bros.. Devil's Due Publishing 2004 Un Illustration
Grades: 7 8 9 10 11 12   741.5; Fic
1. Humorous graphic novels; 2. Penguins; 3. Superhero graphic novels; 4. Graphic novels
1-932796-20-7, $10.95

Three teenage penguins living in Chill City, Antarctica are the ones chosen to become their city's heroes, and granted Super Powers. There's only one problem - they'd rather go to concerts, hang with girlfriends, and play video games. It's sleigh cars, super powers and homework in the Penguin Bros. As Blaylock explains at the end of the book, he created the Penguin Bros. when he was six years old - and he has the drawings to prove it.

Bogaert, Harmen Meyndertsz van den
Journey into Mohawk Country. As written by H.M. van den Bogaert, with artwork by George O'Connor and color by Hilary Sycamore. First Second 2006 144p. Illustration
Grades: 8 9 10 11 12   973.2
1. New York (State) — History — 1600-1775, Colonial period; 2. United States — History — 1600-1775, Colonial period; 3. Graphic novels
1-59643-106-7, $17.95

In 1634, young Dutch trader Harmen Meyndertsz van den Bogaert, several companions, and some native guides traveled deep into what is now New York State, trading tools and weapons and trying to establish new tribal friendships to bolster Dutch trade. van den Bogaert kept a journal throughout his journeys. O'Connor has kept the original text and conducted extensive research in order to make his illustrations as authentic as possible.

Boldman, Craig
Archie Day by Day Volume 1. Archie Comics 2003 96p. Illustration
Grades: 3 4 5 6 7 8 9 10 11 12 Adult   741.5; Fic
1. Andrews, Archie (Fictional character); 2. Humorous graphic novels; 3. Graphic novels
1-879794-16-0, $10.95
Archie and his pals have been comics' most celebrated teenage humor characters for over 60 years, since 1941. Now for the first time, selections from Archie's worldwide syndicated newspaper strip are collected in this volume. This black and white edition includes a selection of daily strips from the mid-1990s, chronicling life in Riverdale, USA.

Bourne, Malcolm
Tales of Ordinary Madness. Illustrated by Mike Allred. Oni Press 2004 Un Illustration
Grades: 11 12 Adult   741.5; Fic
1. Mental illness; 2. Graphic novels
1-929998-78-3, $11.95
Everyone has problems. Every day, people's lives are peppered with a little bit of madness, things that push them over the edge and away from their sanity. Take Robert. He knows those eyes are watching him. What eyes? The ones that are everywhere, lurking in every corner, outside every

window. Then there's David, who one day had the irresistible urge to walk out into the middle of traffic. Or Mrs. Yogeswarren, who is so scared of dogs, she has to plan a route ahead of time whenever she wants to go anywhere, just so she can avoid canines of any kind. These are the sorts of people who have to go to the psychiatrist to learn to cope. But what happens when the good doctor begins to identify a little too closely with his patients" The book includes violence, strong language, nudity, and sexual situations.

Bowen, Carl
20,000 leagues under the sea. Retold by Carl Bowen ; illustrated José Alfonso Ocampo Ruiz. Stone Arch Books 2008 72p. Illustration
Grades: 4 5 6 7 8 9   741.5; Fic
1. Adventure graphic novels; 2. Science fiction graphic novels; 3. Submarines
978-1-4342-0447-9, $23.93; 978-1-4342-0497-4 (pa), $9.95

Scientist Pierre Aronnax and his servant set sail to help hunt a sea monster threatening ships, but they and master harpooner Ned Land discover that the monster is actually a submarine, the Nautilus. The submarine's leader, Captain Nemo, takes the three men captive and they journey under the sea, where they see many wonders; but they must each decide whether they should trust Nemo, who bears a bitter secret, or try to escape. This graphic novel adaptation of Verne's classic adventure novel uses simple language to help reluctant and struggling readers understand the story.

Part of the Graphic Revolve series

The **strange** case of Dr. Jekyll and Mr. Hyde. By Robert L. Stevenson; retold by Carl Bowen; illustrated by Daniel Perez. Stone Arch Books 2009 72p. Illustration
Grades: 4 5 6 7 8 9 10   741.5; Fic
1. Horror graphic novels; 2. Science fiction graphic novels; 3. Graphic novels
978-1-4342-0754-8, $23.93

LC 2008-6248

"Scientist Dr. Henry Jekyll believes every human has two minds: one good and one evil. He develops a potion to separate them from each other. Soon, his evil mind takes over, and Dr. Jekyll becomes a hideous fiend known as Mr. Hyde." (Publisher's note)

Part of the Graphic Revolve series

Brandon, Ivan
Ruule: Ganglords of Chinatown. Mike Hawthorne, Illustrator. Image Comics 2005 Un Illustration
Grades: 10 11 12 Adult   741.5; Fic
1. Adventure graphic novels; 2. Bible fiction; 3. Graphic novels
1-58240-566-2, $19.99

Chinatown has been overwhelmed by vicious biker gangs. One man is chosen to lead his people to freedom, but the price of victory is more costly than blood and darker than war. This is a bloody, violent, yet very faithful retelling of the Biblical story of Gideon's battle against the followers of the false god Baal. In this story, Baal leads a vicious group of motorcycle gangs, and one man, Gid, dares to face him and starts to build a small army of believers who want to take Chinatown back.

Braun, Eric

Booker T. Washington: Great American Educator. Capstone Press 2005 32p. Illustration
Grades: 3 4 5 6 7 8 9   **92; 741.5**
1. African Americans — Biography; 2. Biographical graphic novels; 3. Educators; 4. Washington, Booker T, 1856-1915; 5. 6. Graphic novels
0-7368-4630-1, $25.26
LC 2005001727
In graphic novel format, this book tells the life story of Booker T. Washington and his accomplishments toward promoting the education of African Americans. The book includes additional facts about Washington, a bibliography, and a list of books for further reading.
Part of the Graphic Biographies series.

Cesar Chavez: Fighting for Farmworkers. Capstone Press 2006 32p. Illustration
Grades: 3 4 5 6 7 8 9   **741.5; 331.8; 92**
1. Biographical graphic novels; 2. Chavez, Cesar, 1927-1993; 3. United Farm Workers of America; 4. Graphic novels
0-7368-4631-X, $25.26
LC 2005006460
This book uses the comic book format to recount the highlights of the life of labor leader Cesar Chavez and the boycotts he led to gain fair working conditions for farm workers. It includes additional information, a glossary, a list of books for further reading, and more.
Part of the Graphic Library, Graphic Biographies series.

The **Story** of Jamestown. Capstone Press 2006 32p. Illustration
Grades: 3 4 5 6 7 8 9   **741.5; 975.5**
1. Jamestown (Va) — History; 2. Graphic novels
0-7368-4967-X, $25.26
LC 2005013592
This book uses the comic book format to tell the story of Jamestown, the first permanent English settlement in North America. It includes additional information, a glossary, a list of books for further reading, and more.
Part of the Graphic Library, Graphic History series.

Bravo, Emile

★ **Beauty** and the Squat Bears. Illustrations by the author. Yen Press 2011 Un Illustration
Grades: 3 4 5 6 7 8 9   **741.5; Fic**
1. Bears; 2. Fairy tales; 3. Graphic novels
978-0-316-08362-1, $14.99
LC 2010-941434
When the queen's magic mirror declares that Snow White is the fairest in the land, the young princess flees the kingdom, and she finds herself at the cabin belonging to the seven squat bears. They don't want a princess, especially when she refuses to earn her keep by cleaning the cabin. What to do? Well, they need to find a prince, so they send one of the squat bears out to find a suitable prince. He meets a blue bird who claims to be an enchanted prince, they cause trouble at the ball where Cinderella is supposed to captivate Prince Charming, run into the Beast, and they all run afoul of the Fairy Godmother, who is not amused. Bravo mashes up a bunch of fairy tales in a way that will amuse anyone who has a good sense of humor and sometimes loses patience with all

those young girls waiting for a handsome prince to save them. While this is written for younger readers, adults will also have fun reading this book.
Originally published in France under the title, La Belle aux ours nains.

Courtesy of Yen Press

★ **My** mommy is in America and she met Buffalo Bill. Fanfare/Ponent Mon 2009 120p. Illustration
Grades: 6 7 8 9 10 11 12 Adult   **741.5; Fic**
1. Family life; 2. Mother; 3. School life; 4. Graphic novels
978-84-96427-85-3, $25
Essentials Award winner at the 35th Festival of Angouleme,n France, 2008; Tam Tam Literary Award 2009 from Salon du Livres et de la Presse Jeunesse, for Comic Album, age group eight to thirteen years old.
Narrator Jean has just started first grade and has a younger brother, Paul, in kindergarten. They live with their factory boss father and nanny Yvette; Jean says his mother is on a trip. As he talks about his first day at school, meeting a new friend, Alain, and fighting with Paul, he mentions his mother has been away so long he can't quite remember her. Next door neighbor Michelle claims to be receiving postcards from Jean's mother and reads them to him; they come from places such as Switzerland and the United States. As the reader sees Jean and Paul spend a day with their mother's parents and interact with their grandparents' friends, the reader understands what Jean does not: his mother is dead. This book, translated from its original French, won an award for best comic album for ages eight to thirteen; however, with the essential fact never stated and Jean deciding that he's getting too old to believe in his mother, just as he's too old to believe in Father Christmas, makes this more suitable for the upper age range, teens, and adults.

Brennan, Michael

Electric Girl. AiT/PlanetLar 2000 168p. Illustration
Grades: 5 6 7 8 9 10   **741.5; Fic**
1. Humorous graphic novels; 2. Graphic novels
0-9703555-0-5, $9.95
Virginia is an average suburban girl except for her electric powers, which cause her to zap things all the time, and except for her invisible gremlin "friend" Oogleeoog, who has been with her since she was born. The stories go back and forth in time from her early childhood to her teen years and back again as the reader learns about Virginia's powers and how they affect her life.

"Facial expressions and body postures are fluid and evocative, while the verbal text is easy to read." SLJ

Other titles is this series are: Electric Girl vol. 2 (2002); Electric Girl vol. 3 (2005)

Briggs, Raymond

★ **Ethel** & Ernest: A True Story. Pantheon 2001 104p. Illustration

Grades: 4 5 6 7 8 9 10 11 12 Adult   **741.5**

1. Biographical graphic novels; 2. Graphic novels

978-0-375-71447-4, $15.00

This is Raymond Briggs's loving depiction of his parents' lives from their chance first encounter in the 1920s until their deaths in the 1970s. Ethel and Ernest were solid members of the English working class, part of the generation that lived through the most tumultuous years of the twentieth century. They met during the Depression—she working as a maid, he as a milkman—and the reader follows them as they court and marry, make a home, raise their son, and cope with the dark days of World War II. Briggs portrays how his parents succeeded, or failed, in coming to terms with the events of their rapidly shifting world—the advent of radio, television, and telephones; the development of the atomic bomb; the moon landing; the social and political turmoil of the sixties.

Britt, Fanny

Jane, the fox & me. [written by] Fanny Britt; [illustrated by] Isabelle Arsenault; translated by Christine Morelli and Susan Ouriou. Pgw 2013 101 p.

Grades: 5 6 7 8 9   **Fic**

1. Alienation (Social psychology) — Fiction; 2. Teenage girls — Fiction

1554983606; 9781554983605, $19.95

Written by Fanny Britt, illustrated by Isabelle Arsentault, and translated by Christine Morelli and Susan Ouriou, this "graphic novel reveals the casual brutality of which children are capable, but also assures readers that redemption can be found through connecting with another, whether the other is a friend, a fictional character or even, amazingly, a fox." (Publisher's note) It "centers on Hélène, ostracized by her former friends and now a loner at school." (Horn Book Magazine)

"Britt's well-constructed narrative is achieved sensitively through Arsenault's impressionistic artwork. . . . An elegant and accessible approach to an important topic." Booklist

Britt, Mark Haven

Full-Color. Image Comics 2007 175p. Illustration

Grades: 11 12 Adult   **741.5; Fic**

1. Revenge; 2. Graphic novels

978-1-58240-840-8, $15.99

A lifetime marked with Napoleonic bosses has generated a rage in Boom that she can't contain anymore - only aim. Her target" Her boss. She's given herself one day to make it all right now that she's quit her job. That same day, Boom comes home to find an old friend standing on her fire escape. David's double-crossed a drug dealer and he's looking for help. She'll help him if he'll help her; but things don't go according to plan. The book has lots of violence, harsh language, and some partial nudity.

Broome, John

All Star Comics Archives Volume 11. DC Comics 2005 273p. Illustration

Grades: 7 8 9 10 11 12 Adult   **741.5; Fic**

1. Flash (Fictional character); 2. Green Lantern (Fictional character); 3. Justice Society of America (Fictional characters); 4. Superhero graphic novels; 5. Wonder Woman (Fictional character)

1-4012-0403-1, $49.95

The adventures of the world's first super-team continue in this extra-sized final volume of the series. In Volume 11, collecting All Star Comics #50-57, the JSA face the Diamond Men, Mr. Alpha, and more. The Justice Society of America included the Golden Age Flash, Green Lantern, Dr. Mid-Nite, Hawkman, Wonder Woman, Black Canary, and Atom.

Crisis on Multiple Earths Volume 1: The Team-Ups. DC Comics 2005 224p. Illustration

Grades: 8 9 10 11 12 Adult   **741.5; Fic**

1. Flash (Fictional character); 2. Green Lantern (Fictional character); 3. Superhero graphic novels; 4. Graphic novels

1-4012-0470-8, $14.99

This collection of stories from the 1960s features team-ups of the Silver Age DC heroes with their Golden Age counterparts, with the conceit that DC Comics dreamed up, that the Golden Age heroes are from a parallel world. And along with the heroes, of course come the super-villains. The Flash, Green Lantern, and Hourman from both worlds work with each other to defeat their villains, including Solomon Grundy, the Thinker, the Trickster, and others.

Showcase Presents: The Elongated Man Volume 1. Written by John Broome and Gardner Fox ; Art by Carmine Infantino, Neal Adams, Murphy Anderson and Gil Kane. DC Comics 2006 560p. Illustration

Grades: 6 7 8 9 10 11 12 Adult   **741.5; Fic**

1. Batman (Fictional character); 2. Elongated Man (Fictional characters); 3. Flash (Fictional character); 4. Green Lantern (Fictional character); 5. Robin (Fictional character); 6. Superhero graphic novels; 7. Graphic novels

978-1-4012-1042-7, $16.99

Ralph Dibny is the Elongated Man, a self-taught superhero who has harnessed the power of the exotic gingo fruit and attained the ability to stretch himself to fantastic lengths. As the only costumed hero whose identity has been revealed to the world, Elongated Man travels the globe with his adoring wife Sue, solving mysteries and gaining renown for his singular elastic talent. In these stories, originally published from 1960 to 1968 and reprinted here in black and white, Dibny sometimes teams up with the Flash, Batman and Robin, Green Lantern, and Zatanna. Ralph and Sue Dibny were at the heart of the Identity Crisis, so readers might want to see their early adventures.

Brosgol, Vera

★ **Anya's** ghost. First Second 2011 221p. Illustration

Grades: 9 10 11 12 Adult   **741.5; Fic**

1. Friendship; 2. Ghosts; 3. Horror graphic novels; 4. School life; 5. Graphic novels

978-1-59643-552-0, $15.99; 1-59643-713-8; 978-1-59643-552-0 (pa); 1-59643-552-6 (pa)

LC 2010-36251

"A deliciously creepy page-turning gem from first-time writer and illustrator Brosgol. . . . A moodily atmospheric spectrum of grays washes over the clean, tidy panels, setting a distinct stage before the first words appear. . . . In addition to the supernatural elements, Brosgol interweaves some savvy insights about the illusion of perfection and outward appearance. . . . A book sure to haunt its reader long after the last page is turned—exquisitely eerie." Kirkus

Brown, Box
Andre the Giant: Life and Legend. By Box Brown. First Second 2014 240 p. Illustration
Grades: 9 10 11 12 Adult   **92; 741.5**
   1. Andre, the Giant, 1946-1993; 2. Wrestling
1596438517; 9781596438514, $17.99
LC 2014466607
This book, by Box Brown, is a graphic novel biography of Andre Roussimoff. "At his peak, he weighed 500 pounds and stood nearly seven and a half feet tall. But the huge stature that made his fame also signed his death warrant. . . . [Brown draws] from historical records about Andre's life as well as a wealth of anecdotes from his colleagues in the wrestling world." (Publisher's note)
Brown "uses professional wrestling's complex narrative devices in this biography, which pulls back the curtain on Andre the Giant (Andre Rousimoff), one of the industry's most well-known figures. . . . Brown's simple, blocky art keeps the story front and center, and the down-to-earth tone allows him to avoid demonizing or lionizing his subject." Pub Wkly"
Includes bibliographical references

Brown, Don
★ Drowned City: Hurricane Katrina and New Orleans. By Don Brown. Houghton Mifflin Harcourt 2015 96 p. Color; Illustration
Grades: 7 8 9 10   **741.5; 363.34**
   1. Hurricane Katrina, 2005; 2. New Orleans (La) — History; 3. New Orleans (La) — History — 21st century
054415777X, $18.99; 9780544157774, $18.99
LC 2015458266
Robert F. Sibert Honor Book (2016)

   In this work of graphic nonfiction by Don Brown, "when the calamitous category five Katrina's gusty winds hurl into the city of New Orleans, most people have evacuated the city. The rest of the scared, stubborn, and simply stranded must face the dangers of what is to come—broken levees quickly swelling the city with water. Many families seek safety on their roofs or via floatation devices as a way to row to safety. However, some are not as fortunate." (Children's Literature)

Courtesy of Houghton Mifflin Harcourt

   "Brown's narrative is clear and precise, relying exclusively on data and statistics interspersed with quotes from residents, rescue crews, journalists, and news reports. Alone, the text might lack impact, but combined with the haunting imagery, it hits readers like a punch in the gut." Booklist
Includes bibliographical references

★ The **great** American dust bowl. By Don Brown. Houghton Mifflin Harcourt 2013 80 p.
Grades: 5 6 7 8 9   **978**
   1. Droughts — United States — History; 2. Dust Bowl Era, 1931-1939 — Juvenile literature; 3. Dust storms; 4. Dust storms — History
0547815506; 9780547815503, $18.99
Author Don Brown presents a "graphic novel of one of America's most catastrophic natural events: the Dust Bowl. On a clear, warm Sunday, April 14, 1935, a wild wind whipped up millions upon millions of these specks of dust to form a duster, a savage storm on America's high southern plains." (Publisher's note)
"In this bleak yet compelling graphic-novel-style glimpse at the Dirty Thirties, Brown crisply paces the narrative with fascinating glimpses of the sociological and geological causes of the Dust Bowl. The color brown is a recurring theme here, as Brown relies, aptly, almost entirely on shades of brown throughout. Primary source material is used liberally, as characters speak directly to the reader, documentary-style." (Horn Book)

Brown, Elman
Richard Matheson's I Am Legend. IDW Publishing 2007 244p. Illustration
Grades: 10 11 12 Adult   **741.5; Fic**
   1. Horror graphic novels; 2. Matheson, Richard; 3. Matheson, Richard — Adaptations; 4. Science fiction graphic novels; 5. Vampires; 6. Graphic novels
978-1-933239-21-7, $19.99
Robert Neville is the last human survivor of a virus that has turned the rest of the population into vampires. He spends his days hunting and killing them, and fortifying his house against them. But as the last human, he has to wonder who is normal, he or the vampires" This graphic novel adapts Matheson's science fiction/horror masterpiece. In 2007, a third movie adaptation will be released, starring Will Smith; there were two films produced previously: 1964's "The Last Man on Earth" starring Vincent Price, and 1971's "The Omega Man" starring Charlton Heston. Some scenes in the book are graphically violent.

Brown, Jeffrey
Every Girl is the End of the World for Me. Top Shelf Productions 2005 Un Illustration
Grades: 10 11 12 Adult   **741.5; Fic**
   1. Autobiographical graphic novels; 2. Humorous graphic novels; 3. Romance graphic novels; 4. Graphic novels
1-891830-77-5, $8
Autobiographical cartoonist Jeffrey Brown provides an epilogue to his Girlfriend Trilogy, detailing the day-by-day events of a three week run-in with five different girls. An ex comes back into the picture, he develops a growing but poorly chosen crush, muses on the way friends come and go in life, and comes to a realization that the end is never really the end.

Incredible Change-Bots. Top Shelf Productions 2007 Un Illustration
Grades: 8 9 10 11 12 Adult   **741.5; Fic**
  1. Humorous graphic novels; 2. Robots; 3. Science fiction graphic novels; 4. Graphic novels
978-1-891830-91-4, $15
  Far away in outer space, the Incredible Change-Bots live on the planet Electronocybercircuitron. The Awesomebots and the Fantasticons have lived in relative harmony, until Shootertron, the leader of the Fantasticons, decides to rig the election to rule the planet. The Awesomebots declare war, and over the years the Change-Bots destroy their planet. They then come to Earth, where they continue their fighting, each group gaining their own human allies. Brown has done a fun send-up of the Transformers with this story, and while there is some violence, there is very little in the way of bad language.

  Miniature Sulk. Top Shelf Productions 2005 Un Illustration
Grades: 11 12 Adult   **741.5; Fic**
  1. Autobiographical graphic novels; 2. Humorous graphic novels; 3. Graphic novels
1-891830-66-X, $8
  Brown presents a humorous short story collection featuring fiction, gags, and autobiography. The book includes My Brother Knows Kung Fu and Action Television Show. The book includes harsh language and some sexual suggestiveness.

Brown, Lars
  North world. Oni Press 2008 Un Illustration
Grades: 9 10 11 12 Adult   **741.5; Fic**
  1. Adventure graphic novels; 2. Fantasy graphic novels; 3. Graphic novels
978-1-932664-91-1, $11.95
  Conrad is a working hero who wields a sword to vanquish giant animals; he wants to work up to legend status, so when the guild wants to send him to his old home town to find a demon summoner and stop him, Conrad agrees. He has also received a wedding invitation from his ex-girlfriend. When he gets to town, he faces a group of young punks who want to challenge him, his family, and lots of old friends and foes. He starts to wonder if he really has it in him to stop a demon summoner, and it gets kind of weird when he sees a restaurant back in business that burned down just before he left home seven years before.

Brown, Tom
  Hopeless, Maine: Personal Demons. Tom and Nimue Brown. Archaia Entertainment 2012 128 p.
Grades: 10 11 12 Adult   **Fic; 741**
  1. Maine; 2. Paranormal fiction; 3. Graphic novels
1936393573; 9781936393572, $19.95
  In this gothic graphic novel, by Nimue and Tom Brown, "The small island of Hopeless, off the coast of Maine, is a breeding ground for demons, freaks, vampires, and other creatures of the night. . . . Salamandra, a young girl with one foot in our world and one foot in the otherworld, . . . navigates a life on the edge of reality." (Publisher's note)

Brubaker, Ed
  The **Authority:** Revolution Book One. Penciler, Dustin Nguyen; Inker, Richard Friend. DC Comics/Wildstorm 2005 Un Illustration
Grades: 10 11 12 Adult   **741.5; Fic**
  1. Science fiction graphic novels; 2. Superhero graphic novels; 3. Graphic novels
1-4012-0623-9, $14.99
  The Authority has settled into its role as governing body of the U.S. But with many unhappy Americans and a powerful foe working behind-the-scenes, can a second American Revolution be far behind" Can the Authority survive its internal struggles long enough to stop Paul Revere and the Sons of Liberty" The book includes lots of harsh language and violence.

  The **Authority:** Revolution Book Two. Penciler, Dustin Nguyen; Inker, Richard Friend. DC Comics/Wildstorm 2006 Un Illustration
Grades: 10 11 12 Adult   **741.5; Fic**
  1. Science fiction graphic novels; 2. Superhero graphic novels; 3. Graphic novels
978-1-4012-0947-6, $14.99
  Former StormWatch Weatherman Henry Bendix has returned from the dead and is busy remolding the Earth to his unique vision. After the debacle in the nation's capital that led to the total destruction of Washington, DC, the Authority relinquished control of the United States and all but vanished. How long can tyranny stand, before heroes will rise up? Can a teenage Jenny Quantum reunite the fractured team and make them heroes again, or has Bendix finally won the battle? The book includes lots of harsh language and violence.

  Batman: Turning Points. By Greg Rucka, Ed Brubaker, and Chuck Dixon. DC Comics 2007 124p. Illustration
Grades: 8 9 10 11 12 Adult   **741.5; Fic**
  1. Batgirl (Fictional character); 2. Batman (Fictional character); 3. Joker (Fictional character); 4. Robin (Fictional character); 5. Superhero graphic novels; 6. Graphic novels
978-1-4012-1360-2, $14.99
  Throughout the long comic book career of Batman, Gotham policeman James Gordon has been an almost constant presence. The two men's alliance and friendship formed an important element in Batman's work. This book traces the relationship from Batman's early years, to the first time Gordon meets Robin, to the time shortly after Gordon's daughter Barbara, the Batgirl, was shot by the Joker, to the Batman who took over after Bane broke Batman's back, to come back full circle when a man Gordon and Bats stopped from killing hostages in the first story returns to Gotham City.
  Originally published as Batman Turning Points issues #1-5.

  Catwoman: Wild Ride. Cameron Stewart, artist; Guy Davis, Nick Cerington, additional layouts. DC Comics 2005 Un Illustration
Grades: 9 10 11 12 Adult   **741.5; Fic**
  1. Catwoman (Fictional character); 2. Superhero graphic novels; 3. Graphic novels
1-4012-0436-8, $14.99

Selina and Holly need to get out of Gotham City, so they drive off on a road trip. But the two women are in for way more than they bargained for as they face some mysterious - and dangerous - Egyptian thieves who seem to keep crossing their paths. This volume includes guest appearances by Batman, Wildcat, Hawkman and Hawkgirl, and Captain Cold. The book has some mildly bad language and some violence.

Civil War: Captain America. Illustrators, Lee Weeks and Mike Perkins. Marvel Entertainment 2007 Un Illustration

Grades: 9 10 11 12 Adult   **741.5; Fic**
   1. Captain America (Fictional character); 2. Superhero graphic novels; 3. Graphic novels
   0-7851-2798-4, $11.99

Captain America has clashed with the government and his friends and become a renegade because of his opposition to the Super Human Registration Act. The life of his girlfriend, Agent 13, is torn apart as her superiors use her divided loyalties against her. Elsewhere, the Red Skull returns, and the Winter Soldier once again comes face-to-face with Cap; but which side will he choose" Winter Soldier, who was once Bucky Barnes, Captain America's partner, faces his first Christmas in the 21st century, and the truth of the terrible things he was forced to do as the Winter Soldier.

Criminal, Vol. 1: Coward. By Ed Brubaker and Sean Phillips. Marvel Entertainment/Icon 2007 Un Illustration

Grades: 12 Adult   **741.5; Fic**
   1. Criminals; 2. Mystery graphic novels; 3. Graphic novels
   0-7851-2439-X, $14.99

Leo plans heists; he's been a criminal since he was a young kid picking pockets. He lives by rules that keep him alive, rules that make others call him a coward. When old friend Seymour comes to him, along with crooked cop Jeff, and asks him to plan a heist of evidence (blood diamonds) from an evidence transport van, Leo doesn't want it. But when Greta, widow of a dead partner, tells him she needs the money to take care of her sick daughter, Leo takes the job. He plans everything, plans for every possible problem, except one. The target of the heist isn't diamonds, it's pure heroin. And crooked cop Jeff is ready to betray everyone. This is dark crime noir, with lots of harsh language, violence, and a little sex.

Originally published as Criminal issues #1-5.

Other volumes in this series are:Vol. 2: Lawless (2007); Vol. 3: The Dead and the dying (2008); Vol. 4: Bad night (2009); Vol. 5: The sinners (2010); Vol. 6: The last of the innocent (2011)

★ **Gotham** Central; Book One. Ed Brubaker, Greg Rucka; With Michael Lark. DC Comics 2013 235 p. Color illustration

Grades: 11 12 Adult   **741.5**
   1. Batman (Fictional character); 2. Good and evil; 3. Police; 4. Superheroes
   1401220371; 9781401220372, $19.99
                LC 2012046720

This graphic novel, by Ed Brubaker and Greg Rucka, takes place in "Gotham City: a town teeming with corrupt cops, ruthless crime lords, petty thieves à and just a small handful that would oppose them. Grizzled veteran Harvey

Bullock, Captain Maggie Sawyer, detective Renee Montoya and the GCPD are the law force that stands between order and complete anarchy." (Publisher's note)

   Series originally collected in five volumes
   Originally published in single magazine form in Gotham Central #1-10.
   In the Line of Duty
   Other Gotham Central collections are: Book two: Jokers and madmen; Book three: On the freak beat; Book four: Corrigan

The **Sandman** presents: the dead boy detectives. Illustrators Steve Leialoha and Bryan Talbot. DC Comics/Vertigo 2008 104p. Illustration

Grades: 10 11 12 Adult   **741.5; Fic**
   1. Fantasy graphic novels; 2. Ghosts; 3. Mystery graphic novels; 4. Supernatural graphic novels; 5. Graphic novels
   978-1-4012-1855-3, $12.99

Charles Rowland and Edwin Paine spend all their time reading detective stories, watching thrillers at the movie theaters, or just hanging out in their treehouse, and no one cares. Charles and Edwin are ghosts from different times in the past, who have become friends in their new existence. Now, inspired by the stories and movies, they decide to become private detectives, and they take a case from a runaway girl. Someone is killing the runaway children who live in the Underground of London, and that someone is capable of hurting even ghosts like Charles and Edwin. They encounter a man who says his family has hunted the killer for centuries and enlists their help, but is he telling the truth, or are Charles and Edwin in very deep trouble" The book includes some violence.

Sleeper: Out in the Cold. Artist, Sean Phillips. DC Comics/Wildstorm 2005 Un Illustration

Grades: 11 12 Adult   **741.5; Fic**
   1. Mystery graphic novels; 2. Spies; 3. Graphic novels
   1-4012-0115-6, $17.95

Holden Carver is part of a world-spanning secret organization headed by Tao, super-manipulator and ruthless criminal mastermind. Carver is also a sleeper agent, forced into a world of evil and treachery by master spy John Lynch, who now lies in an irreversible coma, the only living soul able to bear witness that Carver is actually one of the good guys. Now, ensnared in an ongoing game of cat and mouse, every day is a challenge for Holden to evade detection by those who think he is an ally, avoid capture by those who believe he is a traitor, and somehow survive with his soul intact. What's a spy to do when no one knows he's been left out in the cold" The book includes graphic violence, harsh language replete with f-bombs and s-bombs, nudity, and sexual situations.

Brunetti, Ivan

★ An **Anthology** of graphic fiction, cartoons, and true stories. Edited by Ivan Brunetti. Yale University Press 2006 400p. Illustration

Grades: 11 12 Adult   **741.5**
   978-0-300-11170-5; 0-300-11170-3, $28
                LC 2006-14095

"Comic art is a vital, highly personal art form in which change—rapid and unpredictable—is the norm. In this exciting new anthology, comic artist Ivan Brunetti focuses on very recent works by contemporary artists engaged in this world of change. . . . The book presents contemporary art comics produced by 75 artists, along with some classic comic strips and other related fine art and historical materials. Brunetti arranges the book to reflect the creative process itself, connecting stories and art to each other in surprising ways: nonlinear, elliptical, sometimes whimsical, even poetic. He emphasizes continuity from piece to piece, weaving themes and motifs throughout the volume." (Publisher's note)

Brunswick, Glen

The **Gray** Area Vol. 1: All of This Can be Yours. Artists Klaus Janson and John Romita Jr. Image Comics 2005 Un Illustration

Grades: 11 12 Adult   **741.5; Fic**

1. Superhero graphic novels; 2. Supernatural graphic novels; 3. Graphic novels

1-58240-485-2, $14.95

After his execution for double-crossing a drug cartel, Rudy Chance - a brutal, corrupt cop and womanizer - expects he'll wind up in Hell. Instead, he finds himself in the Gray Area, where he is forced to combat evil for an afterlife police force in order to gain a shot at redemption. Given extraordinary powers, Chance hunts down the wicked to condemn and the worthy to heal. But can he control his own dark side, or will it lead to eternal damnation" The book has foul language and considerable violence.

★ **Jersey** Gods, vol.1: I'd live and I'd die for you. Art by Dan McDaid; colors by Rachelle Rosenberg; lettering by Rus Wooton. Image Comics 2009 Un Illustration

Grades: 10 11 12 Adult   **741.5; Fic**

1. Humorous graphic novels; 2. Romance graphic novels; 3. Superhero graphic novels; 4. Graphic novels

978-1-60706-063-5, $14.99

Jersey Girl Zoe works as an assistant to the fashion editor of her local newspaper in Cherry Hill, New Jersey. She has bad luck with boyfriends who always dump her. Then she meets Barock, a god from another planet (Cumulus), when one of his fights leads him to Earth. She has to deal with her boss stealing her idea of an article series on fashion, while Barock has to deal with betrayals and infighting among the gods of his world. But they're in love; what is a Jersey mall princess to do with a planetary god" And what happens when they both get entangled with a scheme to flood the New Jersey malls with fake designer fashions" The art takes classic Jack Kirby style (big, muscular, square-jawed, clean-cut heroes) and gives it just enough of a twist to be humorous without being satirical. The book includes a lot of action and some violence; there's no nudity, but Zoe is shown in her underwear in one panel.

Brusha, Joe

Discovery channel top 10 dangerous sharks. Silver Dragon Books 2010 120p. Illustration

Grades: 3 4 5 6 7 8 9   **741.5**

1. Sharks; 2. Graphic novels

978-0-9827507-2-8, $9.99

This book presents true stories about human encounters with ten of the deadliest sharks: lemon shark, blue shark, hammerhead shark, sand tiger shark, grey reef shark, mako

shark, oceanic whitetip, tiger shark, great white shark, and bull shark. Anyone who watches Discovery Channel's Shark Week programs probably knows the stories related in this book, but most middle grade students who like to read about sharks will want to read these stories anyway. Each section starts out with a two-page spread giving facts about the particular shark, including an "attack file" listing the number of

Courtesy of Discovery Channel

recorded attacks and the number of unprovoked fatalities. Artists Anthony Spay, Shawn McCauley, Marcio Abreu, Agustin Alessio, German Nobile, HG Young, Gabriel Rearte, and Shawn Van Briesen illustrated the stories, with colors by Andrew Elder and John Hunt, and letters by Jim Campbell.

Bryant, Marc

Shangri-La. Illustrated by Hendrix Shepherd. Image Comics 2004 Un Illustration

Grades: 11 12 Adult   **741.5; Fic**

1. Mystery graphic novels; 2. Rock music; 3. Graphic novels

1-58240-352-X, $7.95

When burned out assassin Jetta Helm backs out of a hit on has been rocker Correy Stinson, the two are set on a wild chase across America. Running from the vicious hillbilly hitman Lonesome Roscoe, they're forced to do their best not to kill each other before they can turn the tables on the record label that wants them both dead. The book includes considerable violence and harsh language.

Bugs Bunny: What's Up, Doc?

DC Comics 2005 112p. Illustration

Grades: 3 4 5 6 7 8 9   **741.5; Fic**

1. Bugs Bunny (Fictional character); 2. Humorous graphic novels; 3. Graphic novels

1-4012-0516-X, $6.99

This volume collects stories about the wisecracking rabbit from the archives of Looney Tunes, sure to tickle the funny bones of both children and the childlike as Bugs goes up against Daffy Duck, Marvin the Martian, Elmer Fudd, and other unfortunates.

Bullock, Mike

Lions, tigers and bears volume 2: betrayal. Image Comics 2008 Un Illustration

Grades: 3 4 5 6 7 8 9   **741.5; Fic**

1. Adventure graphic novels; 2. Fantasy graphic novels; 3. Graphic novels

978-1-58240-930-6, $14.99

Joey and Courtney's winter wonderland is shattered when the Big Cats of the Night Pride arrive with terrible news from the Stuffed Animal Kingdom. Now all that stands between the horrible Beasties and children everywhere are Joey, Courtney, and their imaginations. For the evil

Valthraax and his minions have taken over the Crystal Castle, imprisoned King Bear, and plot to capture all children who aren't being protected by the Stuffed Animal Militia. There is some fighting violence between the Night Pride and their allies against the Beasties.

Bunn, Cullen
The **damned** volume one: Three days dead. Brian Hurtt, artist. Oni Press 2008 Un Illustration
Grades: 11 12 Adult   741.5; Fic
1. Humorous graphic novels; 2. Mafia; 3. Mystery graphic novels; 4. Supernatural graphic novels; 5. Graphic novels
978-1-932664-63-8, $14.95
In an alternate world prohibition era, gangsters still grow rich on catering to people's vices, but a more sinister power controls the crime cartels and uses human greed, gluttony, lust, and other mortal sins to fuel a much more lucrative trade: mortal souls. When a feud between two Families is supposed to end with a brokered deal, the bookkeeper brokering the deal is kidnapped. Big Al pulls gumshoe Eddie's corpse out of a ditch and puts him on the case to find the missing bookkeeper. Poor Eddie, he's already dead, but people keep killing him over and over again. The book includes considerable violence, some bad language, and occasional nudity.

Burgan, Michael
The **Boston** Massacre. Capstone Press 2006 32p. Illustration
Grades: 3 4 5 6 7 8 9   741.5; 973.3
1. Boston Massacre, 1770; 2. Graphic novels
0-7368-4368-X, $25.26
                LC 2005006462
This book uses the comic book format to tell the story of the Boston Massacre and its aftermath. It includes additional information, a glossary, a list of books for further reading, and more.
Part of the Graphic Library, Graphic History series.

The **Curse** of King Tut's Tomb. Capstone Press 2005 32p. Illustration
Grades: 3 4 5 6 7 8 9   741.5; 932
1. Tutankhamen, King of Egypt; 2. Tutankhamen, King of Egypt — Tomb; 3. Graphic novels
0-7368-3833-3, $22.60
                LC 2004020452
This volume follows the discovery and excavation of King Tutankhamen's tomb and the myth of the curse that afflicted those involved in the tomb's exploration. The book includes additional information, a glossary, a list of books for further reading, and more.
Part of the Graphic Library, Graphic History series.

The **Great** San Francisco Earthquake and Fire. Capstone Press 2007 32p. Illustration
Grades: 3 4 5 6 7 8 9   741.5; 979.4
1. Earthquakes — California; 2. San Francisco Earthquake and Fire, Calif., 1906; 3. Graphic novels
978-1-4296-0155-9, $26.25
                LC 2007014929
This book uses the graphic novel format to tell of the San Francisco earthquake of 1906 and the subsequent fires

that nearly destroyed the city. The book includes additional facts and a list of books for further reading.
Part of the Graphic Library Disasters in History series

Muhammad Ali: American Champion. Capstone Press 2007 32p. Illustration
Grades: 3 4 5 6 7 8 9   741.5; 796.8; 92
1. Ali, Muhammad; 2. Boxing; 3. Graphic novels
978-1-4296-0153-5, $26.25
                LC 2006103432
This book uses the graphic novel format to tell the life story of dynamic heavyweight boxing champion Muhammad Ali, who gained fame for his boxing skills, political views, and humanitarian efforts. The book stops short of showing Ali being rendered almost speechless by advanced Parkinson's Disease in the last couple of years. The book includes additional facts and a list of books for further reading.
Part of the Graphic Biographies series.

Burns, Charles
★ **Black** hole. Charles Burns.. Pantheon Books 2005 1 v. Illustration
Grades: 10 11 12 Adult   741.5/973; 741.5
1. Communicable diseases — Fiction; 2. High school students — Fiction; 3. Homicide — Fiction; 4. Teenagers — Fiction
9780375714726; 9780375423802; 037542380X, $29.95
                LC 2005046431
Eisner Awards: Best Graphic Album - Reprint (2006); Harvey Awards: Best Graphic Album - Previously Published (2006); Ignatz Awards: Outstanding Anthology or Collection (2006)
This book takes place in "Suburban Seattle, [in] the mid-1970s. We learn from the out-set that a strange plague has descended upon the area's teenagers, transmitted by sexual contact. The disease is manifested in any number of ways - from the hideously grotesque to the subtle (and concealable) - but once you've got it, that's it. There's no turning back. As we inhabit the heads of several key characters ù some kids who have it, some who don't, some who are about to get it ù what unfolds isn't the expected battle to fight the plague, or bring heightened awareness to it, or even to treat it. What we become witness to instead is a fascinating and eerie portrait of the nature of high school alienation itself - the savagery, the cruelty, the relentless anxiety and ennui, the longing for escape. And then the murders start." (Publisher's note)

Burns, Jason M.
A **Dummy's** Guide to Danger. Ron Chan, artist. Viper Comics 2007 Un Illustration
Grades: 11 12 Adult   741.5; Fic
1. Mystery graphic novels; 2. Graphic novels
978-0-9793680-0-4, $11.95
Private investigator Alan Sirois and his partner Mr. Bloomberg, a paraplegic ventriloquist dummy that Alan believes was shot in the back by an assailant and became crippled when the bullet lodged in his spine, track down a gruesome killer known only as the Flesh Collector. The book includes violence and harsh language.

The **Expendable** One. Brian Baugh, artist. Viper Comics 2006 Un Illustration
Grades: 10 11 12 Adult **741.5; Fic**
1. Horror graphic novels; 2. Mystery graphic novels; 3. Graphic novels
0-9754193-9-0, $11.95

Twigs Dupree was just an average, everyday forgotten townie, but then he accidentally injected himself with an experimental concoction that gave him the gift of immortality, whether he's shot in the head or strangled with a wire ... Now, along with his childhood friend Jerry, Twigs wages a war in the suburbs, playing part-time superhero with the help of a police scanner. Things take an unexpected turn when FBI agent Armstrong recruits Twigs to take down a serial killer known as the Animal. Some believe he is a werewolf, but he's the head of a killer cult. The book includes graphic violence, harsh language, and some sexual situations.

The **rabid**. Guy Lemay, artist. Viper Comics 2008 Un Illustration
Grades: 10 11 12 Adult **741.5; Fic**
1. Horror graphic novels; 2. Graphic novels
978-0-980-2385-0-1, $11.95

A dog infected with a mutated rabies virus escapes from a lab, and the disease spreads rapidly from dogs to humans. Sheriff Kevin Chase had gone home early for his son Jesse's birthday, only to find that his own dog is infected and has bitten their neighbor, who quickly becomes a ravening maniac who tries to kill them. He soon learns his entire town is infected, and he, his family, and a deputy barely make back to their office. This graphic novel reads like one of those horror movies where everyone dies, one at a time, until only a handful of people are left alive. It's full of violence and bloodshed, and there's one panel of a woman naked from the waist up (of course, she's already infected, green, and horrible looking).

The **Underworld** Railroad. Paul Tucker, artist. Viper Comics 2007 112p. Illustration
Grades: 10 11 12 Adult **741.5**
1. Fantasy graphic novels; 2. Graphic novels
978-0-9793680-3-5, $11.95

This book postulates that when a person dies while still wrongly accused, that person's spirit doesn't immediately go to Heaven or to Hell, but must wait to be cleared. In the meantime, the spirit is vulnerable and can be taken by the devil. For these spirits, a system of safe houses offers refuge. In one such safe house, Bruce welcomes the spirit of a man who was falsely accused of murdering his wife. The devil takes the form of a sexy woman who doesn't want to take no for an answer, and she tries to take the spirit by force. The book includes violence, some harsh language, and supernatural action.

Busiek, Kurt
★ **Astro** city: life in the big city. By Kurt Busiek, Brent Anderson, and Alex Ross. DC Comics 2011 192 p. Color illustration
Grades: 11 12 Adult **741.5; Fic**
1. Superhero graphic novels
1401232612; 1401232620; 9781401232610; 9781401232627, $17.99

LC 2012376788
This graphic novel, by Kurt Busiek, Brent Anderson, and Alex Ross, is set in "Astro City, a shining city on a hill where super heroes patrol the skies. . . . The city's leading super hero tries to be everywhere at once, and berates himself for every wasted second as he longs for just a moment of his own. A smalltime hood learns a hero's secret identity, and tries to figure out how to profit from the knowledge. A beat reporter gets some advice from his editor on his first day on the job." (Publisher's note)

"These heroes are intentionally written to resemble classic superheroes like Superman, Wonder Woman, and the Fantastic Four. The Astro City heroes, however, aren't derivative; the authors introduce well-developed, original characters and use them to delve into the unexplored possibilities and unanswered questions of classic superheroes as well as their relationships with the world around them." LJ

Collected volume originally published 1997
Originally published as Kurt Busiek's Astro city v. 1 #1-6.
Other Astro City volumes are: Confession (1997); Family album (1998); The tarnished angel (2000); Local heroes (2005); The dark age 1: Brothers & other strangers (2008); The dark age 2: Brother in arms (2010); Shining stars (2011); Through open doors (2014); Victory (2014)

Astro City: the dark age 1: brothers & other strangers. DC Comics/Wildstorm 2009 256p. Illustration
Grades: 10 11 12 Adult **741.5; Fic**
1. Crime; 2. Gangs; 3. Superhero graphic novels; 4. Graphic novels
978-1-4012-2077-8, $19.99

In Astro City of the 1970s, estranged brothers Charles and Royal Williams are still trying to cope with the tragedy that ripped their family apart back in 1959. Charles is an honest cop stuck with a crooked partner who keeps trying to get him to accept graft payments, while Royal has been living the life of a smalltime crook. Their lives keep intersecting with those of the superpowered, heroes and criminals alike. Throughout the book, the readers piece together the bits of flashbacks to that pivotal tragedy in 1959; when the only black superhero treats the young brothers with respect, but a battle between superhero Silver Agent and super criminals erupts into the Williams family's apartment and kills the parents. When Silver Agent walked through the apartment in pursuit of the villains and ignored the dead and surviving civilians, it crushed the boys' spirits, leaving one distrustful of all super powered beings and the other without hope of any good in life. Now, with Silver Agent convicted of murder, an impending war between super powered gangs, and the vengeful Black Velvet and Blue Knight slaughtering criminals even smalltime grifters such as Royal, it's truly a Dark Age in Astro City. The book includes some violence and some harsh language.

Conan Volume 1: The Frost-Giant's Daughter and Other Stories. Cary Nord and Thomas Yeates, illustrators. Dark Horse Comics 2005 Un Illustration
Grades: 10 11 12 Adult **741.5; Fic**
1. Adventure graphic novels; 2. Conan the Barbarian (Fictional character); 3. Fantasy graphic novels; 4. Graphic novels

1-59307-301-1, $15.95

Conan the Barbarian wars with the murderous Vanir, meets the Frost Giant's Daughter, and is taken as a slave by the ancient sorcerers of Hyperborea in this volume of new Conan adventures. Busiek and Nord adapt some of Robert E. Howard's original Conan stories and create some original stories, just as Roy Thomas and Barry Windsor-Smith had done in the 1970s. Conan prefers action to thought, and the stories are full of fighting, some nudity and sexual situations.

JLA: Syndicate Rules. Ron Garney, penciler; Dan Green, inker. DC Comics 2005 Un Illustration
Grades: 10 11 12 Adult   **741.5; Fic**
1. Adventure graphic novels; 2. Justice League of America (Fictional characters); 3. Superhero graphic novels; 4. Graphic novels
1-4012-0477-5, $17.99

Cosmic upheavals destroyed and rebuilt the antimatter universe, with their super-powered conquerors blaming the JLA. Seeking revenge against their positive matter universe counterparts, the JLA, the Crime Syndicate of Amerika breaches the barrier between universes and brings chaos to Earth. The antimatter universe's Weaponers of Qward tip the balance of power as they employ a new super-weapon that can wipe out both super-teams, and Earth's inhabitants, in a heartbeat.

★ **Marvels**. By Kurt Busiek; illustrated by Alex Ross. Marvel 2010 248 p.
Grades: 10 11 12 Adult   **741.5; 741.5/973**
1. Marvel Comics Group; 2. Superhero comic books, strips, etc
078514286X; 9780785142867, $24.99

In this comic book, by Kurt Busiek, illustrated by Alex Ross, "Welcome to New York. Here, burning figures roam the streets, men in brightly colored costumes scale the glass and concrete walls, and creatures from space threaten to devour our world. This is the Marvel Universe, where the ordinary and fantastic interact daily." (Publisher's note)

Followed by Marvels: Eye of the camera

Shockrockets: we have ignition. [by] Kurt Busiek, Stuart Immonen, and Wade Von Grawbadger. Dark Horse Comics 2004 160p. Illustration
Grades: 8 9 10 11 12   **741.5; Fic**
1. Adventure graphic novels; 2. Science fiction graphic novels; 3. Graphic novels
1-59307-129-9, $14.95

"In this graphic novel vision of 2087, Alejandro Cruz lives in a postwar world. An alien invasion has been averted but at a high cost, and people are rebuilding. Alejandro loves his family, but he doesn't want to get caught in the same dead-end jobs that his family members have had to take to survive. Then he accidentally becomes the newest pilot for the Shockrockets, the cream-of-the-crop, high-tech air squadron, and his entire life changes." Booklist

"Busiek brings the same touch of character he used in the "Astro City" series (DC Comics), making this title as much about Cruz's choices and challenges as about lasers and extreme fighter pilot moves." SLJ

Superman: Camelot Falls. Carlos Pacheco, pencils; Jesús Merino, inks . DC Comics 2007 128p. Illustration
Grades: 10 11 12 Adult   **741.5; Fic**

1. Superhero graphic novels; 2. Superman (Fictional character); 3. Graphic novels
978-1-4012-1204-9, $19.99

Everything is going well. Superman is married to Lois Lane. As Clark Kent, he's enjoying his job as reporter and doing it well. He's managed to put Intergang on the run from Metropolis. But when he goes to Kazakhstan to confront the mysterious and deadly Subjekt 17, a new enemy, Superman receives a grave warning from an ancient sorcerer: in the future, Camelot (Metropolis) will fall, and it will be his fault. The book includes a few panels with partial nudity.

★ **Superman:** secret identity. Kurt Busiek, writer; Stuart Immonen, artist, colorist, original covers; Todd Klein, letterer; Superman created by Jerry Seigel and Joe Schuster. DC Comics 2004 206p. Illustration
Grades: 10 11 12 Adult   **Fic; 741; 741.5**
1. Superhero graphic novels; 2. Superman (Comic strip); 3. Superman (Fictional character); 4. Graphic novels
1-4012-0451-1, $19.95

LC 2005-299025

"The teenage Clark Kent of this book is a Kansas farm boy, but in his world, Superman is just a comic book character, and Clark gets teased for having his name. But one day, Clark discovers that he actually has all of Superman's powers. As he starts to use them, he draws government attention—but this book isn't as much about superheroics and men in black as it is about Clark the man. . . . Strongly recommended for teen and adult superhero fans and for anyone who feels that the genre lacks "human interest." Libr J

First published in single magazine form in Superman: secret identity 1-4

The **wizard's** tale. [by] Kurt Busiek and David Wenzel. DC Comics 1998 141p. Illustration
Grades: 6 7 8 9   **741.5; Fic**
1. Graphic novels
1-56389-589-7, $19.95

Bafflerog Rumplewhisker is the most pitiful excuse for an evil wizard that ever lived, for all his evil spells end up doing good. When Lord Grimthorne, head of the Darksome Council, orders him to find the Book of Worse, the reluctant Bafflerog heads out with the toad, Gumpwort, to find it. Author Busiek and artist Wenzel have crafted a tale that honors the marks of high fantasy even while having fun with it.

Butzer, C. M.
★ **Gettysburg:** the graphic novel. Bowen Books/HarperCollins 2009 80p. Illustration
Grades: 3 4 5 6 7 8 9 10 11 12   **741.5; 973.7**
1. American speeches; 2. Gettysburg (Pa), Battle of, 1863; 3. Gettysburg address: Lincoln, Abraham; 4. Lincoln, Abraham; 5. Lincoln, Abraham — Juvenile literature; 6. Lincoln, Abraham — Work — Gettysburg address; 7. Lincoln, Abraham, 1809-1865; 8. Graphic novels
978-0-06-156176-4, $16.99; 978-0-06-156175-7 (pa), $8.99

LC 2008-10657

In the summer of 1863, everyone knew that the Battle of Gettysburg would be an important battle that could determine the course of the War Between the States, the Civil

War. What they didn't know was who would prevail. Butzer uses primary sources to play out the battle that lasted three days and caused tremendous casualties, the aftermath that nearly overwhelmed the town of Gettysburg, and the effort to build the monument to commemorate the fallen. He uses a somber blue and gray wash in his illustrations. Lincoln's famous Gettysburg Address was only 271 words long and appear in their entirety, against images of the nation's past. Some panels depicting the violence of the battles, and particularly the dead on the battlefield, could be disturbing for sensitive younger readers; but this battle was ugly and overwhelming in its violence. Butzer includes extensive end notes to explain what he depicted, and to note the sources of the dialog and narration.

Byrne, Eugene
★ **Darwin:** a graphic biography. By Eugene Byrne; illustrated by Simon Gurr. Smithsonian Books 2013 96 p. Illustration
Grades: 5 6 7 8 9 10 11 12 Adult   **B; 576.8; 576.8/2092**
1. Darwin, Charles, 1809-1882; 2. Evolution; 3. Evolution (Biology); 4. Natural selection; 5. Graphic novels
1588343529; 9781588343529, $9.95
                                        LC 2012951786
This work of graphic nonfiction by Eugene Byrne and Simon Gurr presents a "summary of [Charles] Darwin's life and achievement. . . . Darwin was an indifferent student . . .until he received an invitation to take a voyage that 'would change the course of history.' . . .The animals he encountered seemed so different . . . that he theorized that if it weren't a matter of different conditions that resulted in such 'transmutation,' they might well have had a different creator." (Kirkus Reviews)
Includes bibliographical references.

Byrne, John
Alpha Flight Classics Vol. 1. Writer & artist, John Byrne ; colorist, Andy Yanchus ; letterers, Joe Rosen [and others].. Marvel Entertainment 2007 224p. Illustration
Grades: 7 8 9 10 11 12 Adult   **741.5; Fic**
1. Superhero graphic novels; 2. Graphic novels
978-0-7851-2746-8, $24.99
Guardian, Shaman, Snowbird, Aurora, Northstar, Puck, Marrina, and Sasquatch are Canada's premiere super human strike force, Alpha Flight. The team was brought together by Department H for the greater good of humankind. They battle injustice and evil forces across the globe - including the Master of the World, Tundra, Kolomaq, Deadly Ernest and Delphine Courtney. The book features cameos by the Sub-Mariner, Invisible Woman, Wolverine and Nightcrawler.

Superman: The Man of Steel Vol. 1. Written by John Byrne and Marv Wolfman. DC Comics 1991 132p. Illustration Grades: 8 9 10 11 12 Adult   **741.5; Fic**
1. Superhero graphic novels; 2. Superman (Fictional character); 3. Graphic novels
978-0-930289-28-5, $14.99
This reprint of a 1986 book retells and reinvents the origin and early adventures of the Man of Steel. Superman begins his ascension to iconic hero as he leaves Smallville and becomes Metropolis's revered protector and guardian.

Featuring the Man of Steel's legendary first encounters with Lex Luthor, Lois Lane, and Batman, this book also includes a deadly battle with Bizarro, a fateful encounter with Lana Lang, and Superman's astonishing discovery of his Kryptonian heritage.

Cabarga, Leslie
Harvey Comics Classics Volume Two: Richie Rich, the Poor Little Rich Boy. Dark Horse Comics 2007 480p. Illustration
Grades: 3 4 5 6 7 8 9 10 11 12 Adult   **741.5**
1. Humorous graphic novels; 2. Richie Rich (Fictional character); 3. Graphic novels
978-1-59307-848-5, $19.95
This volume reprints 125 Richie Rich stories, taken from the comic's beginnings in 1953 through the 1960s. While most of the stories appear here in black and white, the book includes a 64-page section of color reprints. Richie Rich and his friends Gloria, Freckles, and Peewee enjoy not-so-everyday adventures, including playing "tycoon" in the new offices of Rich's father. Some stories feature rich cousin and antagonist Reggie.

Harvey comics classics voulme three: hot stuff: the little devil. Dark Horse Comics 2008 480p. Illustration
Grades: 3 4 5 6 7 8 9 10 11 12 Adult   **741.5; Fic**
1. Devil; 2. Humorous graphic novels; 3. Graphic novels
978-1-59307-914-7, $19.95
Hot Stuff: the Little Devil was created for Harvey Comics in 1957, and right away became the starring character in his own comic book series. This volume collects 110 stories from the Hot Stuff comics originally published from 1957 through 1966; the comic book actually remained in print until the 1980s. Back in 1957, having a little red hot devil as a main character caused some controversy, but most young children who read the comics had no problem with him. These stories involve Hot Stuff and his friends in comical misadventures just like any kid could get into, such as having to babysit a younger cousin, trying to outdo a visiting ghost, going to see a doctor (of course, Hot Stuff has to see a witch doctor).
Part of the Harvey Comics Classics series

Cabot, Meg
Avalon High: Coronation Vol. 1: the Merlin prophecy. Created and written by Meg Cabot; illustrated by Jinky Coronado. Tokyopop/HarperTeen 2007 126p. Illustration
Grades: 7 8 9 10 11 12   **741.5; Fic**
1. Arthur, King; 2. Fantasy graphic novels; 3. High school students; 4. School stories; 5. Graphic novels
978-0-06-117707-1, $9.99
Being a new student at Avalon High has been exciting for Ellie, to say the least—she's an honor student, a star on the track team, and dating the super-hot class president, Will. Who also happens to be the alleged reincarnation of King Arthur. Ellie couldn't be happier to have Will in her life, but she's also worried that his estrangement from his parents is tearing him apart. To make matters worse, Will's doubt that he really is King Arthur could prevent the Merlin Prophecy—an age of enlightenment—from occurring. Can Ellie convince Will to believe in something that even she isn't sure about? And more importantly, can she get him to

give his parents another chance? This global manga title continues Cabot's Avalon High story.

Avalon High: Coronation volume 2: Homecoming. Illustrated by Jinky Coronado. Tokyopop/HarperTeen 2008 Un Illustration
Grades: 7 8 9 10 11 12   **741.5; Fic**
1. Arthurian romances; 2. Fantasy graphic novels; 3. Romance graphic novels; 4. Graphic novels
978-0-06-117709-5, $9.99
At Avalon High School, football star Will is the reincarnated King Arthur, but he won't believe it. His brother Marco did, and he nearly killed Will and Ellie (who is the Lady of the Lake). Now kicked out of his house, Will has been staying with Ellie and her family, but things aren't going so great. Mr. Morton is convinced that if Will won't accept his destiny, the world will end. Marco has been released from the hospital, and he obliquely threatens Ellie to leave Will alone about the whole reincarnation thing. But she's having nightmares, and she doesn't know what to do. Except to try to reconcile Will with his parents.

Caldwell, Ben
Star Wars: Clone Wars Adventures Vol. 1. Dark Horse Comics 2004 Un Illustration
Grades: 5 6 7 8 9 10   **741.5; Fic**
1. Adventure graphic novels; 2. Science fiction graphic novels; 3. Star Wars; 4. Graphic novels
1-59307-243-0, $6.95
On the night-world of Nivek, Obi-Wan Kenobi and Anakin Skywalker must first overcome the limitations of fighting in the dark before they can take on the dreaded Shadowmen! Meanwhile, Jedi Masters Mace Windu and Saesee Tiin discover that push can come to shove when using the Force to fight battledroids. And, fresh from leading an underwater assault against Separatist forces on the water planet of Mon Calamari, Jedi Master Kit Fisto and his remaining clone troops reach the surface to find a new threat awaiting them. These original stories use the animated style of the Cartoon Network's "Clone Wars" cartoons and are set during the time between Star Wars Episodes 2 and 3, approximately five months after the Battle of Geonosis.
Volume 1 of 10

Calen, Tokyo
Dark Metro volume 2. Yoshkin, artist. Tokyopop 2008 168p. Illustration
Grades: 10 11 12 Adult   **741.5; Fic**
1. Horror graphic novels; 2. Manga; 3. Graphic novels
978-1-4278-0741-0, $9.99
This volume includes four stories. In Akihabara, a waitress at a maid cafe sparks jealousy and one of her customers, Morio, becomes trapped in a game by the man who wants Yuuyuu all to himself. Then a park employee finds herself in a haunted park filled with dead children, including the young boy she had befriended when he was lost at her park. An American tourist buys an old samurai sword (actually, he takes it and leaves some money) from a shop owner who warns him it is possessed; when the man draws the sword, he awakens the bloodthirsty ghost who used to own it. In all these stories, a young man helps the people out of the nightmarish situations, and in the last story,

readers see Seiya's tragic past. The book includes violence and some gore.

Callen, Kerry
Halo and Sprocket vol. 2: Natural creatures. SLG Publishing/Amaze Ink 2008 Un Illustration
Grades: 8 9 10 11 12 Adult   **741.5; Fic**
1. Angels; 2. Humorous graphic novels; 3. Robots; 4. Graphic novels
978-1-59362-131-5, $8.95
Halo the angel and Sprocket the robot live with a young woman named Katie. Their mission: to try to figure out the human race. They are puzzled by Katie's desire for privacy when she's taking a bath; they don't understand why she'll accept being clawed and bitten by a cute little kitten but won't hold a skink; and playing a trivia game causes Halo to show anger. When Halo transforms Sprocket into a human so he can experience what eating food is all about, the temporarily human Sprocket drives Katie crazy with questions about bodily functions such as burping, sneezing, and more.

Halo and Sprocket: Welcome to Humanity. SLG Publishing/Amaze Ink 2003 Un Illustration
Grades: 7 8 9 10 11 12   **741.5; Fic**
1. Humorous graphic novels; 2. Graphic novels
0-943151-81-3, $12.95
What do an extremely powerful angel, a socially inexperienced robot, and a young, single woman have in common? Apparently, aside from the house they share, not very much! Logic, metaphysics, and human nature collide as Katie tries to educate both angel and robot about humans, philosophy, and such things as the Tooth Fairy. The book includes some slightly raunchy humor.

Campbell, Bruce
Man with the Screaming Brain. Story by Bruce Campbell and David Goodman. Dark Horse Comics 2005 Un Illustration
Grades: 9 10 11 12 Adult   **741.5; Fic**
1. Horror graphic novels; 2. Graphic novels
1-59307-397-6, $13.95
B-movie megastar Bruce Campbell comes to comics with this adaptation of his feature film. Campbell put the version of the script he wanted to shoot into the hands of artists Rick Remender and Hilary Barta. Man with the Screaming Brain tells the story of a wealthy American businessman determined to exploit the crippled economy of a former Soviet state torn between communist roots and capitalist greed. But when Campbell's character hits on the wrong gypsy girl, he soon finds himself in the grip of a mad scientist with a twisted brain-transplant scheme worthy of Dr. Frankenstein. It's filled with cartoony horror movie action and some gore, with some mildly harsh language.

Campbell, Eddie
The **Fate** of the Artist. First Second Books 2006 96p. Illustration
Grades: 11 12 Adult   **741.5; Fic**
1. Art; 2. Autobiographical graphic novels; 3. Graphic novels
1-59643-133-4, $15.95

Campbell uses prose text, newspaper-style comic strips, fumetti-style strips (combining photographs with captions) and standard comic book panels to investigate the disappearance of . . . Eddie Campbell. He explores the history of art and music, portrays aspects of his own like, and uses his perpetually cursing daughter in the fumetti and other comic strips.

"In this work of art about art, assemble the pieces of the puzzle to see the beleaguered and beautiful life of the artist." (VOYA)

Campbell, Ross
The **Abandoned**. Tokyopop 2006 217p. Illustration
Grades: 10 11 12 Adult   **741.5; Fic**
  1. Horror graphic novels; 2. Graphic novels
  1-59816-434-1, $9.99
Big-hearted volunteer worker by day, unruly rocker by night, Rylie is one of the most-liked residents in the small, swampy, Southern island-town of Buffalora. When she sets her sights on Naomi, the new girl in town, love is definitely in the air. Unfortunately for Rylie, so is a storm, the kind in which nothing good ever happens... Suddenly everyone aged 23 and older dies and quickly rises from the dead. These flesh-craving zombies seek out the last remnants of youth and hope for society. With death in the air and love on their minds, Rylie and Naomi must make their way through the vast swamplands to salvation ... This global manga is full of zombie horror and gore, and nudity.

Wet Moon Book 1: Feeble Wanderings. Oni Press 2004 172p. Illustration
Grades: 11 12 Adult   **741.5; Fic**
  1. Graphic novels
  1-932664-07-6, $14.95
This story is set in the gothic, swampy southern town of Wet Moon. As Cleo Lovedrop heads off for college at the local art school, she's haunted by her melancholic past: a lost love, a lost child. An unseen social assailant spreads slander about Cleo, she is forced to deal with her two brusque roommates, and discovers unsolved mysteries about the girl who lived in her room previously. Elsewhere, Trilby deals with unsettled emotional and sexual issues, and keeping her secret habits hidden from everyone. And Audrey comes to the realization that, despite all her efforts, she always causes her friends distress, while Fern, a peculiar, deformed girl who lives in an isolated mansion in the bayous, begins to notice Cleo and her friends. As the moon grows full, lunacy and moon-calves run free. Goths, friendship, romance, sex, betrayal, gossip, cats, murder, guilt, a squirrel monkey, and all the terrible and wonderful things people do to each other. The book includes lots of harsh language, nudity, and sexual situations.

Caniff, Milton
The **Complete** Terry and the Pirates, 1934-1936. IDW Publications 2007 368p. Illustration
Grades: 6 7 8 9 10 11 12 Adult   **741.5**
  1. Adventure graphic novels; 2. Graphic novels
  978-1-60010-100-7, $49.99
This first volume in a projected series to collect the entire Milton Caniff run of the comic strip Terry and the Pirates covers the years 1934 through 1936. This volume

includes the Sunday color comics as well as the black and white dailies. In this volume, the Sunday strips told a different story from the daily strips, so the Sunday strips come first. The Sundays and dailies were merged into one storyline sometime in 1936. Young Terry Lee, his adult pal Pat Ryan, their sidekick Connie, and such villains as Captain Judas and Captain Blade, along with the Dragon Lady, provide readers with lots of high adventure. Some racial stereotypes, common for the 1930s, occur.

Cannon, Kevin
  Crater XV. By Kevin Cannon. Top Shelf Productions 2013 496 p.
Grades: 10 11 12 Adult   **741; Fic**
  1. Adventure graphic novels; 2. Science fiction graphic novels
  1603091009; 9781603091008, $19.95
This graphic novel, by Kevin Cannon, "weaves together . . . swashbuckling adventure, abandoned moon bases, bloodthirsty walruses, rogue astronauts, two-faced femme fatales, sailboat chases, Siberian pirates, international Arctic politics, and a gaggle of horny orphans. Mixed up in all of this are Army Shanks, our salty sea dog still reeling from a devastating loss, and Wendy Byrd, a plucky teenager who wants nothing more than a one-way ticket off the face of the Earth." (Publisher's note)

Far Arden. Kevin Cannon. Top Shelf Productions 2009 400p. Illustration
Grades: 10 11 12 Adult
Fic; 741.5/973
  1. Adventure graphic novels; 2. Arctic regions
  9781603090360, $19.95; 1603090363
In this graphic novel, by Kevin Cannon, "Army Shanks—crusty old sea dog and legendary brawler of the high Arctic seas . . . [has] one mission: to find the mythical island paradise known as Far Arden, which lies hidden . . . in the wintry oceans of the far North. But . . . he'll have to contend with circus performers, adorable orphans, heinous villains, bitter ex-lovers, well-meaning undergraduates, and the full might of the Royal Canadian Arctic Navy!" (Publisher's note)

Courtesy of Top Shelf Productions

Card, Orson Scott
  Red Prophet: The Tales of Alvin Maker Vol. 1. Orson Scott Card; adapted by Roland Bernard Brown; art by Renato Arlem and Miguel Montenegro. Marvel Entertainment/Dabel Brothers 2007 Un Illustration
Grades: 9 10 11 12 Adult   **741.5; Fic**
  1. Adventure graphic novels; 2. Fantasy graphic novels; 3. Graphic novels
  978-0-7851-2721-5, $19.99
In an alternate history where folk magic really works, war is brewing on the frontier. But in the midst of the conflict, two men will begin down the path towards

changing the world forever. One of them is Alvin Miller, a young boy who is the seventh son of a seventh son - and thus powerful enough to shape the world around him. The other is Tenskwa-Tawa, the Red Prophet, who will help Alvin fulfill his destiny. This book is adapted from Card's novel.

Ultimate Iron Man Vol. 1. Writer: Orson Scott Card; pencils: Andy Kubert and Mark Bagley. Marvel Entertainment 2006 Un Illustration
Grades: 10 11 12 Adult   741.5; Fic
1. Iron Man (Fictional character); 2. Superhero graphic novels; 3. Graphic novels
978-0-7851-1499-8, $14.99
Iron Man has been part of the Ultimates, but this volume gives his Ultimate origin. Due to an accident that happened before Tony Stark was born, he has grown up to be a super genius, but always in great physical pain. It's the main reason he becomes an alcoholic as an adult.

Carey, Mike
Crossing Midnight: Cut Here. Mike Carey, writer; Jim Fern, penciller; Rob Hunter, Mark Pennington, inkers; Jose Villarrubia, colorist; Todd Klein, letterer. DC Comics/Vertigo 2007 124p. Illustration
Grades: 11 12 Adult   741.5; Fic
1. Fantasy graphic novels; 2. Horror graphic novels; 3. Mystery graphic novels; 4. Graphic novels
978-1-4012-1341-1, $9.99
In present-day Nagasaki, Japan, a set of twins are born — one just before midnight and the other just after. They discover the huge impact this small difference has on their destinies when the after-midnight twin is inducted into a world of supernatural beings and events that intersects with our own world. Together, they will desperately try to stay one step ahead of their terrifying fates while they learn how far the curse afflicting them really stretches. As their father gets mixed up with Yakuza, the story builds with violence, partial nudity, and harsh language.

God Save the Queen. Written by Mike Carey; painted by John Bolton; lettering by Todd Klein. DC Comics/Vertigo 2007 Un Illustration
Grades: 11 12 Adult   741.5; Fic
1. Fairies; 2. Fantasy graphic novels; 3. Graphic novels
978-1-4012-0303-0, $19.99
Rebellious North London teenager Linda falls in with a group of slacker faeries, who use her blood to make Red Horse - heroin mixed with special human blood. Only once she's hooked and lost her best friend, Jeff, to the drug, does she learn about the faeries and about the civil war raging between two Faerie Queens: Titania and her mad predecessor, Mab. And now Linda is caught in the war, for in her drug-induced state, she can find Mab's hidden heart, which Titania needs to win the war.

Fans of Neil Gaiman's Sandman series will find familiar characters in the story, and they are the audience most ready for this work. The drug use, some nudity, brief sex scenes, and considerable harsh language, make this most appropriate for older teens and adults.

John Constantine: Hellblazer: All His Engines. Writer, Mike Carey; artist, Leonardo Manco; colorist & separator, Lee Loughridge & Zylonol Studio; letterer, Jared K. Fletcher. DC Comics/Vertigo 2006 Un Illustration
Grades: 10 11 12 Adult   741.5; Fic
1. Horror graphic novels; 2. Constantine, John (Fictional character); 3. Graphic novels
1-4012-0317-5, $14.99
When a mysterious worldwide plague starts putting millions of people into deadly comas, Earth's foremost expert on the bizarre, John Constantine, steps in with the "cure." After traveling from the dreary alleys of London to the glittering boulevards of L.A., Constantine realizes that a cadre of wicked demons and hellish monsters is behind the outbreak, and he'll have to sacrifice more than himself to put an end to the nightmare. The book includes lots of very harsh language, bloody violence, and demonic horror.

John Constantine: Hellblazer: Black Flowers. Written by Mike Carey; art by Marcelo Frusin, Tim Bradstreet, Lee Bermejo. DC Comics/Vertigo 2005 142p. Illustration
Grades: 11 12 Adult   741.5; Fic
1. Fantasy graphic novels; 2. Horror graphic novels; 3. Constantine, John (Fictional character); 4. Graphic novels
1-4012-0499-6, $14.99
For months he has felt a growing sense of foreboding, of dark forces massing just out of view. Now the signs are changing from subtle to lethally obvious, and as they manifest themselves, John Constantine's immediate priority changes to staying alive. But he will never rest until he knows just who his real enemy is. There's a whiff of apocalypse in the air, and the world's shrewdest magus is determined to find its source. The book includes lots of harsh language (complete with f-bombs), nudity, and graphic violence.

John Constantine: Hellblazer: Stations of the Cross. Written by Mike Carey; art by Leonardo Manco, Marcelo Frusin, Steve Dillon, Chris Brunner, Tim Bradstreet. DC Comics/Vertigo 2006 192p. Illustration
Grades: 11 12 Adult   741.5; Fic
1. Fantasy graphic novels; 2. Constantine, John (Fictional character); 3. Mystery graphic novels; 4. Supernatural graphic novels; 5. Graphic novels
978-1-4012-1002-1, $14.99
John Constantine is an unconcerned, somewhat amoral occultist with a British working-class background. He's a hero of sorts, who manages to come out on top through a combination of luck, trickery and genuine magical skill. This latest volume finds the hard-drinking master of bad-luck magic suffering alone in the aftermath of the near-apocalypse he unwittingly caused, with no memory of his identity or history and no powers. However, he still has his usual luck, and soon enough he's being hunted by man and demon alike - and about to make the worst mistake of his long, blood-soaked life. The book has lots of harsh language, some nudity, and considerable violence.

Neil Gaiman's Neverwhere. Mike Carey, writer; Glenn Fabry, artist; Tanya & Richard Horie, colorists; Todd Klein, letterer. DC Comics/Vertigo 2007 Un Illustration
Grades: 11 12 Adult   741.5; Fic
1. Fantasy graphic novels; 2. Gaiman, Neil, 1960- ; 3. Adaptations; 4. Graphic novels
978-1-4012-1007-6, $19.99
Ordinary Richard Mayhew lives an ordinary life in London, in an ordinary corporate job, with a domineering fiancee. Then one day he does one extraordinary thing: he

defies his fiancee to help an injured young woman, and his life changes. That young woman, Door, comes from London Below, a fantastical world made up of the bits and pieces of forgotten city and life from above. Her family has been slaughtered, she's being hunted by a pair of extremely nasty, sadistic, violent assassins, and after Richard helps her he has no choice but to go to London Below, for his entire existence in ordinary London has been wiped out, as though he has never . . . been.

Neverwhere was first a script for a BBC miniseries written by Neil Gaiman; he then adapted his script into a novel, which is now adapted into graphic novel format.

Originally published as Neverwhere issues #1-9.

★ **Re-Gifters**. Written by Mike Carey; art by Sonny Liew and Marc Hempel. DC Comics/Minx 2007 148p. Illustration

Grades: 7 8 9 10 11 12   **741.5; Fic**
  1. High school students; 2. Martial arts; 3. Romance graphic novels; 4. School stories; 5. Graphic novels
  978-1-4012-0371-9 (pa), $9.99; 1-4109-0371-X (pa)

"Jen Dik Seong, or Dixie, is having trouble getting her ki focused. Normally an outstanding hapkido student, she finds that her crush on classmate Adam is affecting her ability to fight. This is not good, as the national competition is fast approaching, and her parents expect her to do well. . . . Dixie makes a series of poor choices. She decides to spend the entry fee . . . on an elaborate birthday present for Adam. . . . This is a terrific read that features complex characters dealing with internal and external conflicts that make them believable and endearing. Lively black-and-white illustrations bring action and emotion to the story." SLJ

Spellbinders: Signs & Wonders. Writer, Mike Carey ; pencils, Mike Perkins ; inks, Drew Hennessy. Marvel Entertainment 2005 Un Illustration

Grades: 7 8 9 10 11 12 Adult   **741.5; Fic**
  1. Magic; 2. Mystery graphic novels; 3. Supernatural graphic novels; 4. Graphic novels
  0-7851-1756-3, $7.99

Getting through high school is hard enough without having to watch your back the whole time, but magic can give you a real edge over the competition. When 15-year-old Kim Vesco moves from Chicago to Salem, MA, she finds that the local student body is divided into rival factions of witches and non-witches, with both sides bidding for her allegiance. And if that weren't enough, an unknown force seems to want her... dead. Between the tribal loyalties of the schoolyard and the brutal, fight-or-die logic of the mage-war, Kim has to steer a course that will keep her alive until she can take the fight back to her enemy and reveal the true identity of someone she thought she already knew: herself.

★ The **Unwritten**: Tommy Taylor and the ship that sank twice. Mike Carey, illustrated by Peter Gross. Vertigo 2013 160 p. Color; Illustration

Grades: 11 12 Adult   **741.5; Fic**
  1. Characters and characteristics in literature; 2. Father-son relationship — Fiction; 3. Fiction; 4. Identity (Philosophical concept); 5. Wizards — Fiction
  140122976X; 9781401229764, $22.99
                                        LC 2013020333

In this graphic novel by Mike Carey, "Tom Taylor has lived his life being mistaken for Tommy Taylor, the boy wizard from the world-famous series of novels penned by Tom's long-lost father Wilson. However, after a series of strange events start to parallel the lives of both Taylors—fictional and real—Tom realizes that he might be the character on page made flesh." (Publisher's note)

"This title can serve as an entry point to the author's 'Unwritten' series, or as a standalone prequel. . . . The fictional Tommy receives his magical powers in this volume, and in a parallel narrative, Wilson crafts his first book, and orchestrates a twisted publicity stunt to make his son and his book character the same person in the eyes of the public. . . . Both story lines are equally compelling and balance each other out wonderfully." SLJ

Voodoo child volume 1. Created by Nicolas Cage and Weston Cage; written by Mike Carey; art by Dean Ruben Hyrapiet. Virgin Comics 2008 Un Illustration

Grades: 11 12 Adult   **741.5; Fic**
  1. Fantasy graphic novels; 2. Horror graphic novels; 3. Voodooism; 4. Graphic novels
  978-1-934413-13-5, $14.99

In the time just before the Civil War, when states were starting to secede from the Union, plantation owner and Union sympathizer Mason Moore is murdered and his plantation burned. His illegitimate son, Gabriel, is fatally wounded, but a voodoo bokor casts a spell on him. Gabriel isn't entirely dead, but his spirit has gone into limbo. More than a century later, Katrina has wreaked havoc upon New Orleans, and evil walks its devastated streets. And Gabriel, now a voodoo child, has woken up to take care of unfinished business. The book is full of bloody violence, harsh language, and some nudity. And yes, one of the co-authors is Nicolas Cage the actor, together with one of his sons.

Carey, Percy
  Sentences: the life of M F Grimm. Writer, Percy Carey; artist, Ronald Wimberly; gray tones, Lee Loughridge; letterer, Jared K. Fletcher. DC Comics/Vertigo 2007 128p. Illustration

Grades: 11 12 Adult   **92; 741.5**
  1. Autobiographical graphic novels; 2. Carey, Percy; 3. Gangs; 4. Rap music; 5. Graphic novels
  978-1-4012-1046-5, $19.99

Percy Carey, known in the Hip Hop world as M.F. Grimm, tells his story, from his escape from poverty on the streets to his rise in the world of Hip Hop music. Life in this world involves cutthroat competition and sometimes violence; Carey lost the use of his legs in gang violence, he has spent time in prison, and he re-invented himself. This is his story, complete with the extremely foul language of the streets, and the violence of the life he led.

Carre, Lilli
  The **fir-tree**. It Books/HarperCollins 2009 Un Illustration

Grades: 3 4 5 6 7 8 9 10 11 12 Adult   **741.5; Fic**
  1. Andersen, Hans Christian, 1805-1875 — Adaptations; 2. Christmas; 3. Christmas trees; Graphic novels
  978-0-06-178236-7, $14.99

A young fir-tree only wants to grow tall; it's never satisfied and doesn't notice the sunlight and clean air. It never rejoices in anything, but grumbles and complains. When it sees some trees being cut down and taken away, it wonders what it's missing. The birds tell of seeing the trees inside homes, beautifully decorated, and it becomes jealous. When it does grow tall and beautiful, a woodsman comes along and cuts it down, hauling it to town to become a Christmas tree in a house. It enjoys the family playing around the tree at Christmas, but after the holiday, the family throws it into a storeroom. Will the tree ever see its forest again" Lilli Carre uses delicate coloring and illustrations to adapt Andersen's sad Christmas story. Although this is suitable for young readers, adults may better appreciate the tragedy and Carre's idiosyncratic illustrations her people have long, loopy arms.

Carroll, Emily
★ **Through** the woods. Emily Carroll. Margaret K. McElderry Books 2014 208 p. Color; Illustration
Grades: 8 9 10 11 12 Adult   **741.5**
   1. Horror fiction; 2. Short stories; 3. Graphic novels
   9781442465961, $14.99; 9781442465954, $21.99
                                    LC 2013030969
Eisner Award: Best Graphic Album—Reprint (2015)
Ignatz Award: Outstanding Artist (2015)
   In this book, Emily Carroll "crafts five unsettling tales in graphic-novel format inspired by common folkloric themes—from wolves in the woods to peculiar visitors to dark possessions. In 'Our Neighbor's House,' three sisters who find themselves alone in a cabin are taken, one by one, in the middle of the night by a smiling stranger. . . . 'The Nesting Place' focus on malevolent spirit possession." (Horn Book Magazine)
   "All the tales in Carroll's debut graphic novel are fairly standard ghost stories, but it is her eerie illustrations—popping with bold color on black, glossy pages—that masterfully build terrifying tension and a keep-the-lights-on atmosphere." Booklist

Carroll, Lewis
   New Alice in Wonderland, masterpiece edition. Antarctic Press 2007 Un Illustration
Grades: 4 5 6 7 8 9   **741.5**
   1. Adventure graphic novels; 2. Fantasy graphic novels; 3. Humorous graphic novels; 4. Graphic novels
   978-0-9787725-8-1, $14.95
   Espinosa (The Courageous Princess) adapts Lewis Carroll's classic tale into a graphic novel full of pop culture references (check out the Mad Hatter, for instance). It's still the original story, which starts when the daydreaming Alice sees a rabbit checking his pocket watch and runs after him, only to find herself in a strange world with bizarre creatures.

Casey, Joe
   Godland Volume 1: Hello, Cosmic!. Art by Tom Scioli. Image Comics 2006 Un Illustration
Grades: 8 9 10 11 12 Adult   **741.5; Fic**
   1. Adventure graphic novels; 2. Science fiction graphic novels; 3. Superhero graphic novels; 4. Graphic novels
   1-58240-712-6, $14.99

The cosmic superhero epic is back and this collection is chock-full of all the "cosmic" one could ask for. Experience the glory of Commander Adam Archer, the enigmatic alien Maxim, the wacky Basil Cronus, the evil Discordia, the confusing Freidrich Nickelhead and that's just scratching the surface. The storytelling and art bring back the kind of story that Stan Lee and Jack Kirby did, with fun superhero action and very little grim, gritty content.

   Godland Volume Three: Proto-Plastic Party. Image Comics 2007 Un Illustration
Grades: 9 10 11 12 Adult   **741.5; Fic**
   1. Science fiction graphic novels; 2. Graphic novels
   978-1-58240-736-4, $14.99
   From the burning heart of a pocket dimension to the farthest reaches of our own reality, the saga of Godland continues in this third trade paperback collection. As cosmic forces of evil conspire against the Earth and all who inhabit it, its lone emissary to the stars, Commander Adam Archer, finds himself the target of humanity's mistrust and deceit. All this, and Basil still wears the body of a woman. The book includes some strong language.

   Krash bastards volume 1. Art by Axel #13. Image Comics 2008 Un Illustration
Grades: 10 11 12 Adult   **741.5; Fic**
   1. Martial arts; 2. Science fiction graphic novels; 3. Graphic novels
   978-1-58240-905-4, $9.99
   On a future world where fighters are like rock stars, monsters are an everyday occurrence, and media broadcast battles, the Krash Bastards travel in their airship the Melody Maker and battle monsters and baddies wherever they touch down. Ren, the younger brother of Krash Bastard leader Tran, runs into trouble with a gang called the Death Lords of Kwan, and when the Bastards come to the rescue, they learn that the gang's true leader is the dreaded Kau Death. He seeks a worthy mortal enemy, and thinks he might have found one in Tran. The book includes lots of sword fighting and lopping off of limbs and heads. As a bonus for anyone interested in the process of creating comics, the book includes Casey's script along with Axel 13's concept sketches.

   Rock Bottom. Art by Charlie Adlard. AiT/Planet Lar 2006 Un Illustration
Grades: 11 12 Adult   **741.5; Fic**
   1. Graphic novels
   978-1-932051-45-2, $12.95
   Thomas Dare was just an ordinary guy, who liked to play rock music with the band to blow off the steam of a week of work, who was going through a bad divorce. Then something started happening to him; first his hand was stiff, then the heavy feeling started. No doctor can stop it, he's slowly turning to stone, it's hereditary. What can one do" How does one live the last few months of life" Thomas Dare is going to find out. The story includes lots of harsh language and some non-sexual nudity.

Castellucci, Cecil
   Janes in love. By Cecil Castellucci and Jim Rugg; with lettering by Rob Clark Jr. and gray tones by Jasen Lex. DC Comics/Minx 2008 176p. Illustration (Plain Janes)

Grades: 7 8 9 10 11 12   **741.5; Fic**
1. Art; 2. Friendship; 3. High school students; 4. Romance graphic novels; 5. School stories; 6. Graphic novels
978-1-4012-1387-9 (pa), $9.99; 1-4012-1387-1 (pa)

"The second book of the PLAIN Janes series returns to the four Janes of suburban town Kent Waters and their public art "attacks" as People Loving Art in Neighborhoods (PLAIN). This time the story line is sprinkled with bits of romance as the various Janes struggle to approach their love interests for dates to the school dance and the main Jane applies for an art grant." Publ Wkly

"Castellucci deftly deals with a number of serious issues, including anxiety and depression, mortality, body image, gay relationships, and community activism. Fortunately, they never weigh down the narrative: this is a sweet, quirky story with some uplifting (though never pedantic) messages. Rugg's clean, crisp illustrations are the perfect accompaniment." SLJ

The **Plain** Janes. [illustrated by] Jim Rugg. DC Comics/Minx 2007 Un Illustration
Grades: 7 8 9 10 11 12   **741.5; Fic**
1. Art; 2. Friendship; 3. High school students; 4. School stories; 5. Graphic novels
978-1-4012-1115-8, $9.99

After a bomb attack in Metro City, Jane's parents move to suburban Kent Waters, where Jane feels lost. Then she meets three other Janes at the "reject" table in the high school lunch room, and she convinces them to help her form their own secret club: P.L.A.I.N. "People Loving Art in Neighborhoods." However, their "art attacks" cause the authorities to think that P.L.A.I.N. is a terrorist group.

"The art, inspired by Dan Clowes' work, is absolutely engaging. Packaged like manga this is a fresh, exciting use of the graphic-novel format." Booklist
Another title about the Janes is: Janes in love (2008)

Castrée, Geneviève
Susceptible. Geneviève Castrée. Drawn & Quarterly 2012 75 p.
Grades: 9 10 11 12   **741.5; 741.5/971**
1. Family; 2. Identity (Psychology); 3. Young women — Fiction; 4. Graphic novels
1770460888; 9781770460881, $19.95
LC 2013375302

In this graphic novel by Geneviève Castrée "Goglu is a daydreamer with a young working mother, a disengaged stepfather, and a father who lives five thousand miles away. Drawing, punk rock, and the promise of true independence guide Goglu to adulthood while her home—s daily chaos inevitably shapes her identity. It's a testament to the heartbreaking loss of innocence when a child is forced to be the adult amongst grownups." (Publisher's note)

Cauvin, Raoul
The **bluecoats** no. 1: Robertsonville Prison. Cinebook Ltd. 2008 48p. Illustration
Grades: 5 6 7 8 9 10   **741.5; Fic**
1. Adventure graphic novels; 2. Humorous graphic novels; 3. United States — History — 1861-1865, Civil War — Prisoners and prisons; 4. Graphic novels
978-1-90546-071-7, $11.95

Sergeant Chesterfield and Corporal Blutch are Union soldiers during the Civil War; Blutch tends to be lazy, and Chesterfield always seems to be getting him out of trouble; but after one battle, they're both in trouble when they're captured by Confederate troops and are force-marched to Robertsonville Prison. They constantly get into trouble with a soldier and camp guard named Cockroach, and Chesterfield leads multiple attempts to escape the prison. Then when they succeed, they're wearing stolen Confederate uniforms and ultimately end up in a Union prison camp. Prison camps aren't normally subjects of humor, but the humor in this book is reminiscent of the old television series Hogan's Heroes, which was set in a German prisoner of war camp.

Cavallaro, Mike
★   **Parade**   (with   fireworks).   Image Comics/Shadowlands Books 2008 70p. Illustration
Grades: 10 11 12 Adult   **741.5; Fic**
1. Italy — History — 1914-1945; 2. Graphic novels
978-1-58240-995-5, $12.99

In 1923, Italy was recovering from the Great War; the fascists were already starting to come into power and battling the socialists. In Maropati, one family gets caught up in the political infighting. Paolo, whose father owns a large olive farm, has come back from living in Chicago, where he learned all about fighting feuds and settling disagreements with guns. On the evening of the Feast of the Epiphany, things in Maropati come to a head, local fascists attack and kill Paolo's brother and cousin, and he chooses to fight back. Despite the fact that the fascists had attacked first, he's the one who is hunted, tried, and convicted, and this shatters his family. Cavallaro has based this story on what really happened to his family in Italy. This story first appeared as a webcomic, part of ACT-I-VATE, and was nominated for an Eisner Award, for Best Limited Series, in 2008. The book includes violence.

Cebulski, C. B.
X-Men: Fairy Tales. Writer, C.B. Cebulski; artist, Sana Takeda. Marvel Entertainment 2006 96p. Illustration
Grades: 9 10 11 12 Adult   **741.5; Fic**
1. Fantasy graphic novels; 2. Superhero graphic novels; 3. X-Men (Fictional characters); 4. Graphic novels
978-0-7851-2207-4, $10.99

Cebulski creates new legends, re-imagining the greatest X-Men stories through folktales, myths and fables from across the globe: Japan, Africa, Lousiana's cajun country, and Central Europe. The book includes some violence.

Chabon, Michael
The **amazing** adventures of the Escapist. Dark Horse Comics 2004 Un Color; Illustration
Grades: 9 10 11 12 Adult   **741.5**
1-59307-171-X; 9781593071714, $17.95

"Fans of Chabon's Amazing Adventures of Kavalier and Clay (2000) who long to read the actual comic-book adventures of the Escapist, the superhero created by the novel's young protagonists, have recently had the chance, thanks to the comic book of which this is the first collection. It purports to repackage the 'original' Escapist stories, dating from the 1940s. Scripting the Escapist's origin story himself,

Chabon has enlisted contributions from leading comics artists and writers, including Howard Chaykin, Kyle Baker, and Chris Ware." (Booklist)
Volume 1 of 3

Chabot, Jacob
The **Mighty** Skullboy Army. Dark Horse Comics 2007
Un Illustration
Grades: 6 7 8 9 10 11 12   **741.5; Fic**
  1. Humorous graphic novels; 2. Graphic novels
  978-1-59307-629-0, $9.95
Skullboy may be an elementary school student, but he's already the CEO of an evil corporation (so he tells everyone), and he has the Mighty Skullboy Army. Actually, he has a robot, Unit 1, and a super-intelligent monkey, Unit 2 (who is easily distracted). He keeps trying to get out of attending school, but his efforts result in silly mayhem and sometimes backfire on him.

Chadwick, Paul
  Concrete Vol. 1: Depths. Dark Horse Comics 2005
208p. Illustration
Grades: 10 11 12 Adult   **741.5; Fic**
  1. Adventure graphic novels; 2. Concrete (Fictional character); 3. Graphic novels
  1-59307-343-7, $12.95
Part man, part...rock" Over seven feet tall and weighing over a thousand pounds, he is known as Concrete but is in reality the mind of one Ronald Lithgow, trapped inside a shell of stone, a body that allows him to walk unaided on the ocean's floor or survive the crush of a thousand tons of rubble in a collapsed mineshaft...but prevents him from feeling the touch of a human hand. Depths, the first in a series of new collections reprinting the classic early Concrete stories along with never-before-collected short stories, includes the Eisner-nominated "Orange Glow" and "Vagabond," Paul Chadwick's autobiographical account of a cross-country hitchiking trip. Further volumes in the series show that Concrete collects nude paintings.

  Concrete Vol. 2: Heights. Paul Chadwick. Dark Horse Comics 2005 208 p. Illustration
Grades: 10 11 12 Adult   **741.5; Fic**
  1. Adventure graphic novels; 2. Science fiction graphic novels
  1593074204; 9781593074203, $12.95
                    LC 2006274266
"Unlike conventional superheroes, who battle costumed criminals or intergalactic foes, Concrete, aided by Larry Munro and biologist Maureen Vonnegut, uses his powers to save the world one small step at a time. Here he helps save a family farm and travels to Nepal to build a much-needed footbridge. He also takes advantage of his exceptional capabilities to enjoy unique experiences. After building the bridge, he climbs Everest solo." (Booklist)

  Concrete Vol. 3: Fragile Creature. Dark Horse Comics 2006 208p. Illustration
Grades: 10 11 12 Adult   **741.5; Fic**
  1. Concrete (Fictional character); 2. Science fiction graphic novels; 3. Graphic novels
  1-59307-464-6, $12.95

The four issue mini-series of Fragile Creature won the1992 Eisner Award for Best Finite Series/Limited Series.
When you're seven-feet plus of walking, talking stone, you're bound to draw the media spotlight, especially when you live in Tinseltown. Concrete's celebrity status is sometimes a pain in the buttress... but it does bring the occasional paycheck gig. When the producer of a low-budget science-fiction film approaches Concrete to use his prodigious strength to help save money on the film's FX budget, the siren call of Hollywood draws Concrete like a moth to a flame... a seven thousand dollar a week flame, that is. The volume includes several short stories that have not been previously collected. Some of the stories include some nudity.

  Concrete Vol. 4: Killer Smile. Dark Horse Comics 2006 206p. Illustration
Grades: 10 11 12 Adult   **741.5; Fic**
  1. Concrete (Fictional character); 2. Mystery graphic novels; 3. Graphic novels
  978-1-59307-469-2, $12.95
Standing in the shadow of celebrity has its ups and downs, as Concrete's personal assistant, Larry Munro, knows all too well. But there are darker places than any shadow, as Larry learns the hard way when he is taken hostage by a psychotic gunman who forces Larry to be his chauffeur on a road trip destined to end in disaster... unless Larry can muster the courage to act. This volume includes strong language and some violence.

  Concrete Vol. 5: Think Like a Mountain. Dark Horse Comics 2006 206p. Illustration
Grades: 10 11 12 Adult   **741.5; Fic**
  1. Adventure graphic novels; 2. Concrete (Fictional character); 3. Graphic novels
  978-1-59307-559-0, $12.95
Celebrity has its benefits... and its costs. Due to his status as the world's most unusual travel writer - being a thousand pounds of walking, talking rock will do that - Concrete is approached by a group of radical eco-warriors to see firsthand and write about their efforts to save old-growth forest. What begins as a lark soon turns into a harrowing struggle, and Concrete must decide whether to dispassionately observe or to join these people who would risk anything, even life itself, to save the planet. This volume includes some previously uncollected short stories that tie into the ecology theme. There's some strong language and a little violence.

  Concrete Vol. 6: Strange Armor. Dark Horse Comics 2006 208p. Illustration
Grades: 10 11 12 Adult   **741.5; Fic**
  1. Concrete (Fictional character); 2. Science fiction graphic novels; 3. Graphic novels
  978-1-59307-560-6, $12.95
A troubled man seeking spiritual renewal in the wilderness experiences a wholly unexpected rebirth - as a walking monolith, half a ton of animate stone able to perform astonishing feats of strength and endurance but forever denied many of life's fundamental pleasures. As Concrete, Ronald Lithgow becomes an overnight celebrity and the focus of dark government operatives desperate to keep the secret of his metamorphosis from the public.

Concrete must struggle with the loss of his humanity while discovering, perhaps for the first time, what it truly means to be human. This volume that retells Concrete's origin also includes some short stories. The book has some strong language, but the only nudity is displayed in the artwork that Concrete chooses to purchase.

Concrete Vol. 7: The Human Dilemma. Dark Horse Comics 2006 160p. Illustration
Grades: 11 12 Adult   741.5; Fic
1. Science fiction graphic novels; 2. Graphic novels
978-1-59307-462-3, $12.95

Trapped in an alien's rock-hard body, Lithgow is an accidental celebrity whose high profile is being courted by a front-page CEO. Though Concrete believes overpopulation to be an important issue, does he want to become the spokesperson for a controversial population control program" While Concrete mulls this generous proposition over with his biologist, Maureen, his longtime aide Larry Munro mulls over an entirely different sort of proposal. Life and violent death take center stage in this volume. The book includes nudity, sexual situations, and violence.

★ **Star** Wars: Empire Volume Two: Darklighter. Doug Wheatley, artist; Tomas Giorello, artist. Dark Horse Comics 2004 Un Illustration
Grades: 7 8 9 10 11 12 Adult   741.5; Fic
1. Adventure graphic novels; 2. Science fiction graphic novels; 3. Star Wars; 4. Graphic novels
1-56971-975-6, $17.95

Before Luke Skywalker, the Rebel Alliance had another hero: Biggs Darklighter. For the first time, the full story of Luke's boyhood friend is revealed; from his departure from Tatooine to attend the Imperial Academy, to his decision to lead a mutiny against the Empire and join the Rebellion, to the fateful attack on the Death Star.

The **World** Below. Dark Horse Comics 2007 190p. Illustration
Grades: 9 10 11 12 Adult   741.5; Fic
1. Adventure graphic novels; 2. Science fiction graphic novels; 3. Graphic novels
978-1-59307-360-2, $12.95

Wealthy Charles Hoy assembles a team of explorers to descend into a hole in the ground that is a passageway to an underground world. Years before, he pulled a strange machine out of the hole and used its alien technology to make his fortune. Now he wants more strange technology to make more money. The Team of Six, led by Barclay Hassler, includes tech genius George, physician Susan, Hoy's youngest son Gilbert, and street tough Layla and Regina. They have vehicles, equipment, weapons, but they encounter bizarre, dangerous creatures, weird geography, and hazards beyond anything they could have imagined. Chadwick harks back to old pulp science fiction stories for the pacing and the style of his stories here. Some violence and nongraphic sexual situations occur in the course of the stories.

Originally published as The World Below issues #1-4 and The World Below: Deeper and Stranger issues #1-4.

Chan, Queenie
The **Dreaming** Volume 1. Tokyopop 2005 194p. Illustration

Grades: 9 10 11 12 Adult   741.5; Fic
1. Mystery graphic novels; 2. Supernatural graphic novels; 3. Graphic novels
1-59816-382-5, $9.99

When twin sisters Amber and Jeanie are accepted into an exclusive Australian boarding school, their future looks bright. But the school's halls harbor a terrible secret: students have been known to wander into the surrounding bushlands and vanish ...without a trace. No one knows where they went—or why. But as Amber and Jeanie are about to learn, the key to the school's dark past may lie in the world of their dreams ... This global manga story has lots of atmospheric spookiness and some scary images.

In odd we trust. Created by Dean Koontz; written by Queenie Chan and Dean Koontz; illustrated by Queenie Chan. Del Rey 2008 224p. Illustration
Grades: 9 10 11 12 Adult   741.5; Fic
1. Ghosts; 2. Horror graphic novels; 3. Mystery graphic novels; 4. Graphic novels
978-0-345-49966-0, $10.95

Nineteen-year-old Odd Thomas works as a fry cook in small town Pico Mundo, California; people come to the diner for his pancakes (among other foods), he's easygoing and friendly. Odd also sees ghosts; the ghosts never talk, but they tend to come to him when they need something done. The latest one is a little boy. Odd's girlfriend Stormy tells him that the dead boy's babysitter, her friend, is worried about her other charge, a young girl. So psychic Odd and pistol-packing Stormy try to find the murderer before he can strike again. This original graphic novel, co-written by illustrator Queenie Chan and illustrated and formatted like manga, is a prequel to Koontz's bestselling prose novels about Odd Thomas. While it is a murder mystery, there's little in the way of actual violence portrayed in the book.

"This book is a light, diverting read that has the advantage of being a manga that isn't a part of a multivolume series." Booklist

Chantler, Scott
★ The **annotated** Northwest Passage. Oni 2007 268p. Illustration
Grades: 8 9 10 11 12 Adult   741.5; Fic
1. Adventure graphic novels; 2. Canada — History — 0-1763 (New France); 3. Graphic novels
978-1-932664-61-4, $19.95

It is the year 1755. Charles Lord, an acclaimed explorer and adventurer from England, has taken a desk job governing Fort Newcastle, a remote frontier trading post in Canada. On the eve of his retirement, Charles longs for a return to past glories and a second chance at his great unfulfilled quest, to find the fabled Northwest Passage. When Fort Newcastle is captured by the brutal French privateer Guerin Montglave and his men, Charles and a few survivors flee into the Canadian wilderness. This edition includes the first three installments of Northwest Passage, along with annotations by the creator. It includes violence and some mild harsh language.

Chao, Fred
★ **Johnny** Hiro: {half Asian, all hero}. Fred Chao; greytones by Dylan Babb; letters by Jesse Post. Tom Doherty Associates 2012 175 p.
Grades: 10 11 12 Adult   **Fic**
1. Busboys; 2. Chinese restaurants; 3. Monsters; 4. New York (NY); 5. Graphic novels
0765329379; 9780765329370, $16.99
LC 2011277796
This graphic novel focuses on the life of Johnny Hiro. "Things just happen to [him], like when a Godzilla-type monster snatches Johnny's girlfriend Mayumi . . . . Or when his boss at the sushi restaurant orders Johnny to steal a special lobster from a rival chef. Or when New York's Mayor Bloomberg intercedes with Judge Judy in a lawsuit about the damage the monster did to Johnny's apartment building. (Library Journal)
Previously collected with new material as Johnny Hiro by AdHouse Books (2009)

Chayamachi, Suguro
Devil May Cry 3 Code 1: Dante. Tokyopop 2005 186p. Illustration
Grades: 10 11 12 Adult   **741.5; Fic**
1. Fantasy graphic novels; 2. Horror graphic novels; 3. Manga; 4. Graphic novels
1-59816-031-1, $9.99
Dante is a demon slayer and bounty hunter with a demon heritage of his own that haunts his past. He's currently unemployed—and bored to death. Opportunity knocks in the form of a missing-child case, which his friend and manager, Enzo, offers him. But a four-million-dollar reward, an unexpected demon attack and a little girl named Alice all conspire to send Dante through the looking glass on a nightmarish adventure beyond his wildest imagination. Based on the violent video game, the book contains graphic violence and some strong language.

Chaykin, Howard
Barnum: In Secret Service to the USA. Written by Howard Chaykin; art by Niko Henrichon. DC Comics/Vertigo 2005 128p. Illustration
Grades: 9 10 11 12 Adult   **741.5; Fic**
1. Adventure graphic novels; 2. Fantasy graphic novels; 3. Mystery graphic novels; 4. Graphic novels
1-4012-0073-7, $19.95; 9781401200732
When brilliant inventor Nikola Tesla and a cadre of the world's richest men plot to destroy America, secret agent P.T. Barnum must assemble a team of the wildest circus freaks on the planet to save the world. Span, a teenaged human fly; Col. Dyna-Mite, a midget strongman; Plastino, a sword-swallowing rubber man; Primeva, a Brazilian animal empath; and the legendary Siamese twins Chang and Eng join Barnum on his quest to stop Tesla. The book includes some violence and some strong language.

Challengers of the Unknown: Stolen Moments, Borrowed Time. DC Comics 2006 144p. Illustration
Grades: 10 11 12 Adult   **741.5; Fic**
1. Superhero graphic novels; 2. Graphic novels
978-1-4012-0941-4, $16.99

Five extraordinary people with seemingly nothing in common share the bond of surviving a cataclysmic event. In a world devoid of superheroes, they come together and discover that all they know has been a lie, that the world we live in is not the one we believe it to be. To survive they must unite and face the true masters of our universe. It's a world where literally anything can happen, and probably will - as if living on borrowed time wasn't enough. There's a fair amount of foul language and considerable violence.

Fritz Leiber's Fafhrd and the Gray Mouser. Adaptation and script, Howard Chaykin; pencils, Mike Mignola; inks, Al Williamson; colors, Sherlyn van Valkenburgh; letters, Michael Heisler. Dark Horse Comics 2007 Un Illustration
Grades: 11 12 Adult   **741.5; Fic**
1. Adventure graphic novels; 2. Fantasy graphic novels; 3. Leiber, Fritz; 4. Leiber, Fritz — Adaptations; 5. Graphic novels
978-1-59307-713-6, $19.95
This volume, which was first published as a four-issue miniseries by Marvel Comics in 2001, adapts several of Leiber's stories about the huge northern barbarian Fafhrd and the conniving Gray Mouser. "Ill Met in Lankhmar" describes how the two meet; in "The Circle Curse" the two leave Lankhmar only to return because they're bored when away from the city; "The Bazaar of the Bizarre" offers trinkets and treasures which are really enchanted trash. In "Lean Times of Lankhmar," the two friends fall out and the Mouser works for a major thug while Fafhrd becomes a devotee of the god Issek of the Jug.
Leiber poked fun at the "sword and sorcery" type of fantasy adventure, but ended up crafting classic stories in the subgenre. Readers will find humor, swordfights, thievery, sex, and more.

Chen, Marcia
Wraithborn. DC Comics/Wildstorm 2007 Un Illustration
Grades: 10 11 12 Adult   **741.5**
1. Horror graphic novels; 2. Mystery graphic novels; 3. Graphic novels
978-1-4012-0995-7
Melanie Moore is a typical teenager, with all the usual hopes and dreams and angst that fill the teen years. All that suddenly changes when she is unexpectedly granted fantastic powers by a mysterious stranger as he lies dying. Now Melanie races to discover the secrets of her newfound abilities before those stalking her can claim the Wraithborn as their own, along with her life. This story includes nudity, strong language, and graphic violence.

Cherniss, Matt
Powerless. Matt Chernis and Peter Johnson; art by Michael Gaydos. Marvel Entertainment 2005 Un Illustration
Grades: 9 10 11 12 Adult   **741.5; Fic**
1. Daredevil (Fictional character); 2. Spider-Man (Fictional character); 3. Superhero graphic novels; 4. Wolverine (Fictional character); 5. Graphic novels
07851-1511-0, $14.99
What makes a hero? Is it his actions, or is it the results of those actions? Powerless explores what it means to be a hero in very human terms. By re-imagining Marvel's most

popular characters without superhuman powers, this story strips down to the core heroes readers have all come to know and love. These characters - including Peter Parker, Matt Murdock and Logan - were fated to be heroes. Just because Peter Parker wasn't bitten by a radioactive spider doesn't mean he didn't do battle with a madman named Norman Osborn. Matt Murdock" Blinded, yes - but with no heightened senses. However, he did become a legal champion of the poor in Hell's Kitchen, and he did cross paths with Wilson Fisk, the Kingpin. And Logan is, of course, the enigmatic - and amnesiac - drifter on the run from his past. Psychiatrist Dr. Watts suffers strange dreams and visions even as he tries to help his three patients. The book includes some violence.

Cherrywell, Steph
★ **Pepper** Penwell and the land creature of Monster Lake. [written and drawn by Steph Cherrywell].. SLG Publishing 2011 Un Illustration
Grades: 7 8 9 10 11 12 Adult   **741.5; Fic**
1. Horror graphic novels; 2. Humorous graphic novels; 3. Monsters; 4. Mystery graphic novels; 5. Graphic novels
978-1-59362-205-3, $14.95
British teenager Pepper Penwell prefers solving mysteries over school work and wants to be a detective like her father. When the latest school boots her out, Pepper takes on the case of a missing drum majorette named Lucy. Accompanied by her brother Alex, who inexplicably (it was some kind of accident) has the body of a bird, Pepper travels to Monster Lake, a town trying to establish itself as a tourist attraction based on its local monster, which is a land creature. In the town, Pepper meets strange people, any of whom could be guilty of kidnapping the wealthy and annoying Lucy. However, after Pepper does find Lucy, there's still the matter of the land monster, which is all too real. British slang (arse, bum) provides the mildly harsh language.

Cheung, Man Wai
Topspeed Underground Vol. 1. Comics One/DrMaster Publishing 2004 206p. Illustration
Grades: 10 11 12 Adult   **741.5; Fic**
1. Adventure graphic novels; 2. Automobile racing; 3. Graphic novels
1-58899-403-1, $14.95
Most of the Hong Kong street racing champions, the Four Kings, have fallen from grace, and now the streets are ruled by the 13 Ghosts. When a legendary racing god comes out of retirement to recruit some new talent, the wheel is set in motion for some major competition with the 13 to rule the streets of Asia. The children of racing icons Tien Ren and Ichiro Sakazaki step forward to prove their worth, but previous kings Fuma and Seer intervene. Lots of street racing action and some strong language spice the story.
Volume 1 of 3.

Chiba, Tomohiro
Mobile Suit Gundam: Lost War Chronicles Volume 1. Art by Masato Natsumoto. Tokyopop 2006 Un Illustration
Grades: 8 9 10 11 12 Adult   **741.5; Fic**
1. Adventure graphic novels; 2. Manga; 3. Mecha manga; 4. Graphic novels

159816-213-6, $9.99
The One Year War between the Earth Federation and the Principality of Zeon has begun—and the newest Mobile Suits are tested for battle. Captain Matt Healy leads his team into dangerous territory as the leader of a Special Forces Experimental Ken Bederstadt is a Foreign Legion Lieutenant working in alliance with Zeon. These two heroes are trying to keep everyone alive...for tomorrow.

Chilman-Blair, Kim
What's up with Bill?: Medikidz explain epilepsy. Rosen Publishing Group, Inc. 2010 40p. Illustration (Superheroes on a medical mission)
Grades: 3 4 5 6 7 8 9   **616.85; 741.5**
1. Epilepsy; 2. Graphic novels
978-1-4358-3533-7, $29.25; 1-4358-3533-6
LC 2009-29785
After teenage Bill suffers a seizure, he and his unnamed sister meet the Medikidz, a team of superheroes who help

Courtesy of Rosen Publishing

people with health problems. They take the two teens into the brain to explain how it works and what happens when a person has epilepsy. The book uses a lot of humor, especially with Gastro, who loves to eat and does things like pass gas. Chilman-Blair is a physician, and the book was reviewed by an expert for medical accuracy. The book includes a glossary of the medical terms used, a list of books for further reading, and contact information for some agencies that deal with epilepsy.
Includes glossary and bibliographical references
Part of the Superheroes on a Medical Mission series.

Chmakova, Svetlana
Dramacon, Vol. 1. Tokyopop 2005 182p. Illustration
Grades: 10 11 12 Adult   **741.5; Fic**
1. Humorous graphic novels; 2. Romance graphic novels; 3. Graphic novels
1-59816-129-6, $9.99
Amateur writer Christie (a high school junior) attends her first anime convention with her boyfriend Derek, who ogles and flirts with all the pretty cosplayers (people who dress as their favorite anime characters). She meets a handsome cosplayer who never takes off his sunglasses and other new friends who help her realize that Derek is a jerk, and when things get bad and Derek attacks her, she turns to Matt the cosplayer and her new friends for help. Chmakova employs many manga art techniques, especially the exaggeratedly small and funny chibi figures in this behind-the-scenes look at an anime convention. Nothing sexually graphic is depicted, but Christie and Derek are obviously sexually active.

★ **Nightschool:** the weirn books, volume one. [by] Svetlana Chmakova; toning artist, Dee DuPuy; lettering, JuYoun Lee. Yen Press 2009 190p. Illustration

Grades: 7 8 9 10 11 12   **741.5; Fic**
1. Mystery graphic novels; 2. Supernatural graphic novels; 3. Witches; 4. Graphic novels
978-0-7595-2859-8, $12.99

PS 13W is a regular public high school during the day, but after dark it is the Nightschool attended by werewolves, vampires, and weirns (a particular breed of witch). Sarah has just started her job as the new Night Keeper when she disappears from the school; when her younger sister Alex, a young weirn who's been homeschooled, discovers that

Courtesy of Yen Press

Sarah's existence has been wiped out from everyone's memory but hers, she sets out to investigate. Dark forces have caused Sarah's disappearance, and they seem to be watching Alex, too. Meanwhile, Daemon, the teacher of the hunters, must try to figure out what young seer Marina has seen in her visions of a broken seal and what this has to do with his students who were severely injured while they were out on a class trip to the cemetery. This urban fantasy was first published in Yen Press's manga magazine, Yen Plus.

"Manga fans and teens looking for vampire stories will devour this one and will want to find out more about these characters." SLJ
Volume 1 of 4

★ **Nightschool: the weirn books, volume two.** Svetlana Chmakova ; toning artist, Dee DuPuy ; lettering, JuYoun Lee. Yen Press 2009 196p. Illustration
Grades: 7 8 9 10 11 12   **741.5; Fic**
1. Mystery graphic novels; 2. Supernatural graphic novels; 3. Witches; 4. Graphic novels
978-0-7595-2859-8, $10.99

Alex tries to investigate Sarah's disappearance from the Nightschool, but in order to get the Nightpass that will allow her unfettered access to the school grounds, she must enroll as a student. She soon proves to be far advanced in her astral class astrals are supernatural beings bonded to witches that help them do magic. Mr. Roi teaches an advanced astral class, but he is focused on helping Daemon investigate the broken seal and to help his student hunters who remain unconscious but are also transforming. And a mysterious girl with black wings keeps tabs on Alex.

Chopra, Gotham
The **Sadhu.** Virgin Comics 2007 Un Illustration
Grades: 10 11 12 Adult   **741.5; Fic**
1. Fantasy graphic novels; 2. Superhero graphic novels; 3. Graphic novels
978-1-934413-03-6, $14.99

Sadhus do not know love or hate, desire or fear. They are detached from all emotional ties, devoting themselves to a spiritual journey said to unleash unimaginable powers. It is this ancient tradition that James Jenson is fated to tread. He's a down-on-his-luck Englishman, recruited into her majesty

Queen Victoria's army and posted with his family in Colonial India. A tragic twist of fate sends James on a journey that will force him to choose between spiritual awakening and human instinct, guiding him from a simple soldier to a spiritual warrior. The book includes some violence.

Chrono, Nanae
Momo Tama, vol. 1. Story and art by Nanae Chrono ; [translation, Beni Axia Conrad ; English adaptation, Lorelei Laird]. Tokyopop 2009 Un
Grades: 8 9 10 11 12   **741.5; Fic**
1. Fantasy graphic novels; 2. Humorous graphic novels; 3. Manga; 4. Shonen manga; 5. Graphic novels
978-1-4278-1109-7, $9.99

Kokonose Mutsu is the 9th successor to the leadership of the Mutsu family, who lead the ogres who lost their island back when Momotaro defeated them. According to the legends, Momotaro returned home from the ogres' island with treasures, but really, he was given the island. Now the latest descendant of Momotaro runs a "school" on the island that actually trains people to be senkishi, ogre hunters. Kokonose joins the school's group of new students in order to set his plan to regain the island into motion. There are a couple of problems, one of which is that he is very small; he also doesn't have much in the way of supernatural powers (although he does possess a huge ego), and everyone knows who he is. His 20-year-old roommate smokes cigarettes, the book includes some harsh language, including several uses of the s-bomb, and there is some moderate violence.

Peacemaker Volume 1. Tokyopop 2007 Un Illustration
Grades: 10 11 12 Adult   **741.5; Fic**
1. Adventure graphic novels; 2. Manga; 3. Shonen manga; 4. Graphic novels
978-1-4278-0075-6, $9.99

Tetsunosuke and Tatsunosuke are the sons of a diplomat who sought to bring peace and prosperity to Japan during the early Meiji Restoration. But when their parents are murdered before their very eyes, Tetsu seeks to join the Shinsengumi, the unofficial police who are capable of the same brutality as his parents' murderers. Wading through a sea of espionage, deception and bloodshed, the young boy must choose: should he take a step on the path to becoming a demon...or give up his rage and transform into the ultimate Peacemaker? This first volume includes violence.
Volume 1 of 5.

Church, Kevin
Cover girl. Andrew Cosby & Kevin Church, writers; Mateus Santolouco, pencils. Boom! Studios 2008 Un Illustration
Grades: 9 10 11 12 Adult   **741.5; Fic**
1. Adventure graphic novels; 2. Mystery graphic novels; 3. Graphic novels
978-1-934506-27-1, $14.99

Young struggling actor Alex Martin saves a woman whose car crashes off the road, and the videotape of his rescue helps his fortunes rise, and he snags the lead role in a high-budget action film. However, mysterious black SUVs seem to be following him, and then someone (or several someones) attempt several times to kill him. The studio hires a bodyguard, but Rachel Dodd isn't the usual type. She has to play the part of Alex's girlfriend in order to be by his side. When she and her partner Dwight manage to foil several more attempts to kill Alex, they decide they need to find out who's trying to kill Alex, and why. They soon discover it all comes back to Alex's roadside rescue of the woman, who has since disappeared from public view. This story is full of action and includes some violence and mildly bad language. Anyone who enjoys fast-paced action films with witty dialog will enjoy this. Teen girls and women may delight in the fact that the action hero is a no-nonsense woman who can shoot and fight as well as any male action movie hero.

CLAMP (Mangaka group)

★ **Cardcaptor** Sakura: Book 1. Story and art by CLAMP. Dark Horse Manga 2010 576 p. Illustration; Color
Grades: 6 7 8 9 10 **741.5**
1. Books and reading — Juvenile fiction; 2. Fantasy fiction — Juvenile fiction; 3. Magic — Juvenile fiction; 4. Wizards — Fiction
1595825223; 9781595825223, $19.99
In this book, by CLAMP, "[f]ourth-grader Sakura Kinomoto found a strange book in her father's library—a book made by the wizard Clow to store dangerous spirits sealed within a set of magical cards. But when Sakura opened it up, there was nothing left inside but Kero-chan, the book's cute little guardian beast, who informs Sakura that since the Clow cards seem to have escaped while he was asleep, it's now her job to capture them!" (Publisher's note)
"CLAMP's classic manga series (originally published in the U.S. in a 12-volume, two-series run) is being rereleased in remastered and newly translated omnibus editions that collect three books each." Booklist
Volume 1 of 4

R. G. Veda Vol. 1. English adaptation by Christine Schilling. Tokyopop 2005 198p. Illustration
Grades: 8 9 10 11 12 Adult **741.5; Fic**
1. Fantasy graphic novels; 2. Manga; 3. Shojo manga; 4. Graphic novels
1-59532-484-4, $9.99
At the dawn of creation, the world was a beautiful and tranquil place. Gods and humans lived peacefully together under the Heavenly Emperor's rule. But Taishakuten, a powerful warlord, rebelled against the King, and a violent, chaotic age began ... Three hundred years later, Kuyou, the strongest warrior in the land, hears the prophetic words of a revered stargazer: Six Stars will one day assemble and overthrow this bloody reign. Now, the quest begins to find the Six Stars and fulfill the prophecy before the heavens are torn apart. The book includes some battle violence.

Tsubasa: Reservoir Chronicle Vol. 1. Translated and adapted by Anthony Gerard ; lettered by Dana Hayward. Random House/Del Rey Manga 2004 198p. Illustration
Grades: 8 9 10 11 12 **741.5; Fic**
1. Fantasy graphic novels; 2. Manga; 3. Shonen manga; 4. Supernatural graphic novels; 5. Graphic novels
0-345-47057-5, $10.95
LC 2004-101711
Sakura is the princess of Clow-and possessor of a mysterious, misunderstood power that promises to change the world. Syaoran is her childhood friend and leader of the

archaeological dig that took his father's life. They reside in an alternate reality . . . where whatever you least expect can happen-and does. When Sakura ventures to the dig site to declare her love for Syaoran, a puzzling symbol is uncovered-which triggers a remarkable quest. Now Syaoran embarks upon a desperate journey through other worlds-all in the name of saving Sakura. This series crosses over with xxxHolic, and both of them use characters from past CLAMP manga. The book includes some violence.

XXXHolic Vol. 1. Translated and adapted by Anthony Gerard ; lettered by Dana Hayward. Random House/Del Rey Manga 2004 Un Illustration
Grades: 8 9 10 11 12 **741.5; Fic**
1. Fantasy graphic novels; 2. Manga; 3. Seinen manga; 4. Supernatural graphic novels; 5. Graphic novels
0-345-47058-3, $10.95
Watanuki Kimihiro is haunted by visions of ghosts and spirits. Seemingly by chance, he encounters a mysterious witch named Yuuko, who claims she can help. In desperation, he accepts, but realizes that he's just been tricked into working for Yuuko in order to pay off the cost of her services. Soon he's employed in her little shop-a job which turns out to be nothing like his previous work experience. Most of Yuuko's customers live in Japan, but Yuuko and Watanuki are about to have some unusual visitors named Sakura and Syaoran from a land called Clow. . . The book includes some strong language and graphic violence.

Clare, Cassandra
Clockwork angel. By Cassandra Clare, illustrated by HyeKung Baek. Yen Press 2012 222 p. (The infernal devices)
Grades: 9 10 11 12 **Fic**
1. Demonology — Fiction; 2. Fantasy fiction; 3. Fantasy graphic novels; 4. London (England) — Fiction; 5. Orphans — Fiction; 6. Secret societies — Fiction; 7. Steampunk fiction; 8. Supernatural — Fiction
0316200980; 9780316200981, $12.99
LC 2012359456
This graphic novel adaptation, by Cassandra Clare, illustrated by HyeKung Baek, is "a prequel to Cassandra Clare's 'Mortal Instruments' series. . . . [it] is the story of Tessa Gray, a sixteen-year-old American girl traveling alone to Victorian London who runs afoul of the city's sordid supernatural underworld. Rescued by the Shadowhunters of the London Institute, Tessa quickly finds herself caught up in an intrigue that may very well destroy her new friends." (Publisher's note)

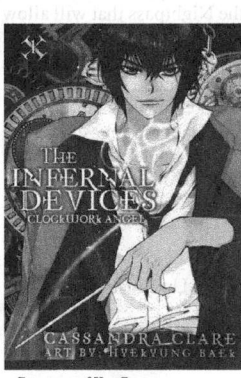
Courtesy of Yen Press

Claremont, Chris

★ **Wolverine**. Art by Frank Miller. Marvel Entertainment 2007 Un Illustration
Grades: 9 10 11 12 Adult   **741.5; Fic**
1. Superhero graphic novels; 2. Wolverine (Fictional character); 3. Graphic novels
978-0-7851-2329-3, $19.99

Originally published in the early 1980s, this was the first miniseries to delve into the character of the berserker mutant, Wolverine, and shape him into something more than a snarling fighting beast. Wolverine loves Mariko, but she is a yakuza boss's daughter; and when he follows her back to Japan, the Hand hires the ninja Yukio to kill Logan. Instead, she falls in love with him. Wolverine fights gangsters and ninja in his bid to win Mariko's heart.

★ **X-Men:** The Dark Phoenix Saga, 2nd ed.. Penciler and co-plotter, John Byrne. Marvel Entertainment 2006 200p. Illustration
Grades: 7 8 9 10 11 12 Adult   **741.5; Fic**
1. Superhero graphic novels; 2. X-Men (Fictional characters); 3. Graphic novels
978-0-7851-2213-5, $24.99

Gathered together by Professor Charles Xavier to protect a world that fears and hates them, the X-Men had fought many battles, been on adventures that spanned galaxies, grappled enemies of limitless might, but none of this could prepare them for the most shocking struggle they would ever face. One of their own members, Jean Grey, has gained power beyond all comprehension, and that power has corrupted her absolutely. Now they must decide if the life of the woman they cherish is worth the existence of the entire universe.

X-Men: The End Book One: Dreamers & Demons. Writer, Chris Claremont ; pencils, Sean Chen ; inks, Sandu Florea ; colors, Avalaon's Ian Hannin ; letters, Dave Sharpe. Marvel Entertainment 2005 Un Illustration
Grades: 7 8 9 10 11 12 Adult   **741.5; Fic**
1. Superhero graphic novels; 2. X-Men (Fictional characters); 3. Graphic novels
978-0-7851-1690-5, $14.99

It's the epic finale to the story of the Children of the Atom as X-Men scribe Chris Claremont joins with artist Sean Chen for a trilogy in the style of the Lord of the Rings movies, one that spans the length and breadth of the X-Men canon and brings the saga of Marvel's mutants to a climax. In this volume, the unthinkable happens - attackers succeed in breaching all security at the Xavier School for the Gifted and threaten the lives of all the young mutants living there.

X-Men: The End Book Three: Men & X-Men. Sean Chen, illustrator. Marvel Entertainment 2006 Un Illustration
Grades: 7 8 9 10 11 12 Adult   **741.5; Fic**
1. Superhero graphic novels; 2. X-Men (Fictional characters); 3. Graphic novels
978-0-7851-1692-9, $14.99

The endgame of the last tale of Marvel's most popular mutants begins. They've suffered through sneak attacks, betrayals, and fatalities - now, Professor X and Magneto are taking the fight back to the enemy, amidst the stars.

X-Men: The End Book Two: Heroes & Martyrs. Sean Chen, illustrator. Marvel Entertainment 2005 Un Illustration

Grades: 7 8 9 10 11 12 Adult   **741.5; Fic**
1. Superhero graphic novels; 2. X-Men (Fictional characters); 3. Graphic novels
978-0-7851-1691-2, $14.99

The Xavier Academy has been reduced to a smoldering crater in a brutal sneak attack, and the casualties number in the hundreds. Now, Cyclops must mobilize the survivors to get to the bottom of who is behind these coordinated strikes on mutants in general and the X-Men in particular.

★ **X-Men:** days of future past. Chris Claremont, art by John Byrne. Marvel Worldwide 2011 176 p.
Grades: 9 10 11 12 Adult   **741.5**
1. X-Men (Fictional characters)
0785164537; 9780785164531, $19.99
LC Bl2011037630

"Relive the legendary first journey into the dystopian future of 2013 - where Sentinels stalk the Earth, and the X-Men are humanity's only hope...until they die! Also featuring the first appearance of Alpha Flight, the return of the Wendigo, the history of the X-Men from Cyclops himself...and a demon for Christmas!" (Publisher's note)

Clevinger, Brian

Atomic Robo; Volume one: Atomic Robo and the Fightin' Scientists of Tesladyne. Words, Brian Clevinger; art and cover, Scott Wegener; colors, Ronda Pattison; letters, Jeff Powell. Red 5 Comics 2008 180 p. Color illustration (Atomic Robo)
Grades: 9 10 11 12 Adult   **741.5**
1. Robots; 2. Science fiction graphic novels; 3. Superhero comic books, strips, etc
0980930200; 9780980930207, $18.95

This graphic novel, by Brian Clevinger, illustrated by Scott Wegener and Ronda Pattison, collects the first six issues of the action comic series "Atomic Robo." "Atomic Robo and the so-called Action Scientists of Tesladyne become the go-to defense force against the unexplained! See ROBO take on Nazis, giant ants, clockwork mummies, walking pyramids, Mars, cyborgs, and his nemesis, Baron von Helsingard." (Publisher's note)

"[This] series about a scientific adventure robot created by Nikola Tesla has been . . . funny and yet surprisingly touching at times, a book that features car chases, gun fights and robots punching other robots but never uses them as an excuse to give up on being smart." ComicsAlliance
Volume 1 of an ongoing series

Cliff, Tony

★ **Delilah** Dirk and the king's shilling. Tony Cliff. First Second 2016 272 p.
Grades: 7 8 9 10 11 12   **741.5/973; 741.5**
1. Adventure and adventurers — Fiction; 2. Adventure graphic novels; 3. Espionage — Fiction; 4. Fantasy graphic novels; 5. Graphic novels
1626721556; 9781626721555, $17.99
LC 2015020653

In this graphic novel, by Tony Cliff, "globetrotting troublemaker Delilah Dirk and her loyal friend Selim are just minding their own business, peacefully raiding castles and and traipsing across enemy lines, when they attract the unwanted attention of the English Army. Before they know it, Delilah and Selim have gotten themselves accused of espionage against the British crown!" (Publisher's note)

★ **Delilah** Dirk and the Turkish Lieutenant. By Tony Cliff. First Second 2013 176 p. Illustration

Grades: 9 10 11 12   **741.5; Fic**
1. Adventure fiction; 2. Historical fiction; 3. Istanbul (Turkey) — Fiction; 4. Women adventurers — Fiction
1596438134; 9781596438132, $15.99

LC 2013947230

In this book, "Delilah Dirk has abandoned conventional court life and become a globe-trotting soldier of fortune. She is captured and held prisoner in 1800s Constantinople. Eventually she escapes, taking along the astonished Turkish Lieutenant Erdemogul Selim, whose quiet life centers around a proper cup of tea. This unlikely pair embarks on a wild journey that includes flying a ship, outwitting the Evil Pirate Captain Zakul, and escaping burning buildings." (School Library Journal)

"Plenty of fight scenes will attract male readers, in addition to females looking for strong heroines. All in all, this is a carefree romp across the Ottoman Empire with an upbeat tone that is refreshing." Lib Med Con

Clowes, Daniel

Art School Confidential: A Screenplay. Fantagraphics Books 2006 200p. Illustration

Grades: 11 12 Adult   **741.5; 808.2**
1. Artists
1-56097-678-0, $14.95

The story follows Jerome, an art student who dreams of becoming the greatest artist in the world. The film expands on a short comic story by Dan Clowes that was originally published, in black-and-white, in his hit comic book series Eightball; for this new book, the strip has been published in full-color for the first time. This scrapaook/screenplay also features the shooting script for the film, including several scenes edited out from the final cut. It also has two full-color sections with stills from the film, character designs from Clowes' sketchbook, and artwork created as set dressing by Clowes and his friends. The original story features full nudity and strong language.

★ **Ghost** world. Daniel Clowes. Fantagraphics Bks. 1997 80p. Illustration

Grades: 11 12 Adult   **741.5**
1. Female friendship; 2. Teenage girls — Fiction
1-56097-280-7 (pa), $19.95; 9781560974277
Ignatz Award: Outstanding Story (1998)
Ignatz Award: Outstanding Graphic Novel or Collection (1998)

Clugston-Major, Chynna

Blue Monday Vol. 1: The Kids are Alright. Oni Press 2003 136p. Illustration

Grades: 10 11 12 Adult   **741.5; Fic**
1. Humorous graphic novels; 2. Teenagers; 3. Graphic novels
1-929998-62-7, $11.95

Being a teenager can be a difficult job, something the adult world can never understand. While to her parents and teachers getting Adam Ant tickets is no big deal, to Bleu L. Finnegan it means everything. This could be the defining moment of her life, and there is no guarantee that she will ever achieve it. On the way, Bleu must deal with the travails of adolescence - from prank-playing, porn-addicted boys to sexist-pig radio disc jockeys to trying to figure out how to show that dreamy substitute teacher that she's his perfect mate. It all culminates on that fateful night when Bleu and her best friend, Clover, go to the club and try to get in at any cost. Nothing will bar Bleu from the pop idol of her dreams. This book includes sexual innuendo and strong language, particularly from Clover, who curses with an Irish accent. Collects the debut mini-series as well as the various short stories that preceded it in independent comic book anthologies.

Other titles in this series are: Volume 2: Absolute beginners; Volume 3: Inbetween days; Volume 4: Painted moon

Scooter Girl. Oni Press 2004 Un Illustration

Grades: 10 11 12 Adult   **741.5; Fic**
1. Humorous graphic novels; 2. Romance graphic novels; 3. Graphic novels
1-929998-88-0, $14.95

Ashton Archer has it all. He's the biggest man on his campus, he's got a family fortune waiting for him to transfer into his own account, and his closet and garage are full of the coolest accoutrements available, from flash suits to swank shoes to a zippy Vespa scooter. It appears that nothing can go wrong for this hard-hearted hottie - that is until the sexy and fashionable Margaret Sheldon motors by on her Lambretta. At that moment, Ashton's life takes a turn for the worse. Everyone at school hates him, his father declares bankruptcy, and his scooter gets run over by a truck. Even high-tailing it out of town does him no good, because wherever he goes, Margaret follows. How can he get out of the black curse this woman has placed on his life" By getting her to fall in love with him, of course. The book has some raunchy humor, plenty of strong language, some partial nudity, and sexual innuendo.

Cobley, Jason

Frankenstein: the graphic novel. [by] Mary Shelley; script adaptation Jason Cobley; American English adaptation: Joe Sutliff Sanders; linework: Declan Shalvey; coloring: Jason Cardy & Kat Nicholson; lettering: Terry Wiley. Classical Comics 2008 141p. Illustration

Grades: 6 7 8 9 10 11 12 Adult   **741.5; Fic**
1. Frankenstein (Fictional character); 2. Horror graphic novels; 3. Shelley, Mary Wollstonecraft, 1797-1851 — Adaptations; 4. Graphic novels
978-1-906332-49-5, $16.95

Young scientist Victor Frankenstein becomes obsessed with the idea that technology can create life, and works to prove his theories. However, his success doesn't bring him glory, but a living nightmare for himself and everyone around him. This graphic adaptation brings the entire book to the reader, using Shelley's original text for the dialog and narrative. Back matter includes a brief biography of Shelley, her family tree, a description of how she came to write the novel, and information on some of the various adaptations of the story to the stage and to film.

"More than a straightforward retelling, this edition invites readers to explore important social issues such as alienation, the consequences and ethics of scientific studies, as well as the nature of creation and destruction." SLJ

Also available quick text version $16.95 (ISBN: 978-1-906332-50-1)

Original text version

Coda, Gakuto

Missing: Kamikakushi no Monogatari Volume 1. Art by Rei Mutsuki. Tokyopop 2007 174p. Illustration

Grades: 9 10 11 12 Adult **741.5; Fic**
1. Fantasy graphic novels; 2. Manga; 3. Supernatural graphic novels; 4. Graphic novels
978-1-4278-0066-4, $9.99

Kyoichi Utsume, a.k.a. "His Majesty, Lord of Darkness," is a dark and compelling mystery, so much so that his fellow Literature Club members would rather discuss him than books. When "His Majesty" vanishes in front of their very eyes, his friends are left with several unanswered questions: what is the source of Kyoichi's long-standing obsession with the "other side?" And just who is Ayame, the eerily ghostlike girl Kyoichi brought to school as his girlfriend the day before he disappeared?

Cogan, Adam

The **Black** Coat: A Call to Arms. by Ben Lichius and Adam Cogan. Illustrated by Francesco Francavilla. APE Entertainment 2006 Un Illustration

Grades: 8 9 10 11 12 Adult **741.5; Fic**
1. Adventure graphic novels; 2. Supernatural graphic novels; 3. Graphic novels
978-0-9741398-8-3, $12.95

In pre-Revolutionary War New York City, the masked Black Coat and his Knights of Liberty battle the British occupation forces, and the occult. Lieutenant-General Henry Savidge has accepted the help of Lord Morrow and his shadowy organization to stop the Black Coat. Morrow and his League have brought the Krauss brothers to the Colonies; Wilhelm Krauss murders people, taking their arms, as he works to perfect a serum that will make the takers immortal. The Black Coat and his people work to prevent it, even as the Krauss' butchery is blamed on the Black Coat.

This story, combining historical fiction with the occult, is the first volume; a new miniseries of comics began publication in 2007.

Originally published as The Black Coat issues #1-4.

Cole, Allison

Never Ending Summer. Alternative Comics 2004 128p. Illustration

Grades: 10 11 12 Adult **741.5; Fic**
1. Graphic novels
1-891867-66-0, $11.95

This story is an autobiographical account that follows a group of friends through a summer filled with uncertainty and confusion. Relationships break down between boyfriends, friends, and family, throughout which the author must discover how to maintain a sense of balance. Parties, excessive drinking, and financial instability add to the commotion. The book reflects upon the immediacy of the present and the potential of events to come. There's very little in the way of strong language or sexual situations.

Colfer, Eoin

Artemis Fowl: the graphic novel. Adapted by Eoin Colfer and Andrew Donkin; art by Giovanni Rigano; color by Paolo Lammana. Hyperion Books for Children 2007 Un Illustration

Grades: 4 5 6 7 8 9 **741; 741.5; Fic**
1. Adventure graphic novels; 2. Fantasy graphic novels
978-0-7868-4881-2, $18.99; 0-7868-4881-2;
978-0-7868-4882-9 (pa), $9.99; 0-7868-4882-0 (pa)

Twelve-year-old genius and criminal mastermind Artemis Fowl runs his missing father's crime empire and gets his hands on a book that will give him access to the underground fairy world. This graphic novel adaptation gives the book a European lookd color palette

"Excellent use of color and shading gives the panels a tremendous sense of light with enchanting effect. Characters are expressively brought to life with fun, exaggerated style." SLJ

Other Artemis Fowl graphic novels are: Artemis Fowl: the Arctic incident (2009); Artemis Fowl: the eternity code (2013); Artemis Fowl: the opal deception (2014)

The **supernaturalist:** the graphic novel. Eoin Colfer; Andrew Donkin; illustrated by Giovanni Rigano and Paolo Lamanna. Miramax Books/Hyperion Books for Children 2004 267 p.

Grades: 6 7 8 9 **Fic; 741.5/9415**
1. Abandoned children; 2. Friendship — Fiction; 3. Orphans — Fiction; 4. Science fiction
0786848790; 0786851481; 9780786848799, $19.99

LC 2004044180

In this graphic novel by Eoin Colfer and Andrew Donkin, illustrated by Giovanni Rigano and Paolo Lamanna, "unwanted by his parents, Cosmo Hill is put to work by the state, testing highly dangerous products. Cosmo . . . escapes with the help of the Supernaturalists, a group of kids who have the same special abilities as Cosmo—they can see supernatural Parasites, creatures that feed on the life force of humans. The Supernaturalists patrol the city at night." (Publisher's note)

Collins, Max Allan

CSI: Crime Scene Investigation: Bad Rap. Art by Gabriel Rodriguez and Ashley Wood. IDW Publishing 2004 132p. Illustration

Grades: 10 11 12 Adult **741.5; Fic**
1. Mystery graphic novels; 2. Graphic novels
1-932382-20-8, $19.99

The duel between retro-punk rappers from the music scene in Las Vegas ends with one of them murdered. The problem for Gil Grissom and his team of crime scene investigators isn't a lack of suspects, it's too many, each with his or her own reason to want Busta Kapp dead. But when the suspects start becoming murder victims themselves, Grissom knows he's got to solve this case in a hurry, before the victim list goes off the charts. The violence is at the level shown on broadcast television in this original story based on the CSI characters.

CSI: Crime Scene Investigation: Demon House. Art by Gabriel Rodriguez and Ashley Wood. IDW Publishing 2004 120p. Illustration

Grades: 9 10 11 12 Adult **741.5; Fic**

1. Mystery graphic novels; 2. Graphic novels
1-932382-34-8, $19.99

When a real body turns up in a charity haunted house, the members of Las Vegas's CSI team - already busy on a series of armed robberies - find themselves pulling double duty. It's all tricks and no treats for Grissom and crew. Rodriguez does the art for what is happening during the course of the story, Wood does the art for the flashbacks and replays. The story includes some violence and some strong language.

Dick Tracy: The Collins Casefiles Volume 1. Chester Gould, artist, Rick Fletcher, artist. Checker Book Publishing Group 2003 164p. Illustration
Grades: 8 9 10 11 12 Adult   741.5; Fic
1. Dick Tracy (Fictional character); 2. Mystery graphic novels; 3. Graphic novels
0-9741664-2-1, $19.95
                                        LC 2003-23068
This is the first of several volumes collecting Collins' 11-year run on the Dick Tracy comic strips. He took over scripting duties from Chester Gould in 1978, although Gould maintained his byline and consulted with Collins on plot directions. Fletcher, a longtime Gould assistant, took over the drawing and worked with Collins. This volume includes the stories "Angel Top's Last Stand," "Return of Haf-and Haf," and "Big Boy's Revenge."

Johnny Dynamite: Underworld. Art by Terry Beatty. AiT/Planet Lar 2003 Un Illustration
Grades: 10 11 12 Adult   741.5; Fic
1. Horror graphic novels; 2. Mystery graphic novels; 3. Graphic novels
1-932051-10-4, $12.95
1950s tough-guy private detective Johnny Dynamite goes up against zombies in Las Vegas as well as the mob, and the zombies also have crime on their undead minds. Mob-style violence, with beatings and hits, combines with zombie killings and horror action.

Colon, Ernie
★ **After** 9/11: America's war on terror (2001-). Hill and Wang 2008 149p. Illustration; Map
Grades: 9 10 11 12 Adult   973.931; 741.5
1. Iraq War, 2003-; 2. Terrorism; 3. United States — Foreign relations; 4. United States — Politics and government; 5. Graphic novels
978-0-8090-2370-7, $16.95
                                        LC 2008-13298
In 2006, longtime comic book veterans Jacobson and Colon adapted the 9/11 Commission's report into a graphic format that made it a readable, comprehensible work for teens and adults. Now they have used the comic book treatment to cover America's War on Terror since 2001, including the wars in Iraq and in Afghanistan, summarizing events and showing the major players throughout the years. Some images can be disturbing, such as the depiction of prisoner mistreatment at Abu Ghraib and other facilities, as well as depictions of the victims of sectarian violence.

Anne Frank: the Anne Frank House authorized graphic biography. [by] Sid Jacobson and Ernie Colón. Hill and Wang 2010 152p. Illustration

Grades: 9 10 11 12 Adult   92; 741.5
978-0-8090-2684-5, $30; 978-0-8090-2685-2 (pa), $16.95
                                        LC 2010-5776
This is a "graphic biography of Anne Frank . . . covering the lives of Anne's parents, Edith and Otto; Anne's first years in Frankfurt; the rise of Nazism; the Franks' immigration to Amsterdam; war and occupation; Anne's years in the Secret Annex; betrayal and arrest; her deportation and tragic death in Bergen-Belsen; the survival of Anne's father; and his recovery and publication of her astounding diary." Publisher's note
"Panel arrangements effectively show simultaneous events happening in the life of the family and in the world, while brief 'snapshots' provide enough historical information to make motives, fears, and expectations sensible to anyone unfamiliar with the Holocaust's machinery. More than simply poignant, this biography elucidates the complex emotional aspects of living a sequestered adolescence as a brilliant, budding writer." Booklist

Conley, Steve
Astounding space thrills: Argosy Smith and the codex reckoning. IDW Publishing 2008 192p. Illustration
Grades: 9 10 11 12 Adult   741.5; Fic
1. Adventure graphic novels; 2. Science fiction graphic novels
978-1-60010-320-9, $19.99
Adventurer Argosy Smith lives on an Earth that has changed drastically due to its move thanks to some aliens time flows differently, space folds weirdly, and the Earth has basically become the library of the universe. Smith races against time (he's supposed to die on his 25th birthday, which is tomorrow) to steal a lost manuscript by Leonardo Da Vinci, discover the secret of Split-Space travel, keep two alien races from all-out war, avoid certain death at the hands of little green mercenaries hired by a several-brained-corporate head, and keep the universe from breaking apart. Oh yeah, and celebrate his birthday. The action harkens back to the kind of cosmic science fiction adventure written by E. E. "Doc" Smith, with lots of action.

Conner, Daniel
The **picture** of Dorian Gray. Adapted by Daniel Conner; illustrated by Chris Allen.. Magic Wagon/Graphic Planet 2009 32p. Illustration
Grades: 6 7 8 9 10   741.5; Fic
1. Horror graphic novels; 2. Supernatural graphic novels; 3. Wilde, Oscar, 1854-1900; 10. Wilde, Oscar, 1854-1900 — Adaptations/Graphic novels; 4. Graphic novels
978-160270-680-4, $27.07
                                        LC 2009-8597
Impossibly handsome, young Dorian Gray sits for a portrait and then impulsively wishes that he could never age and that the portrait should do so in his place. However, as life goes on, he becomes evil; he falls in love with an actress and then spurns her; he murders the portrait artist; and with every act his portrait becomes more and more grotesque while he remains a youthful, handsome fellow. This easy-reading graphic novel adaptation of Oscar Wilde's horror story makes it easier for reluctant and struggling

readers to enjoy the story. Back matter includes a brief biography of Wilde, a list of some of his other works, and a short glossary. The question of morality in the story and the violence make this more suitable for somewhat older readers, despite the simplicity of language.

This is part of the Graphic Horror Series 2.

William Shakespeare's A midsummer night's dream. Adapted by Daniel Conner; illustrated by Rod Espinosa.. ABDO/Magic Wagon 2008 48p. Illustration
Grades: 5 6 7 8 9 10   **741.5; Fic**
1. Graphic novels; 2. Shakespeare, William, 1564-1616 — Adaptations; 3. Youths' writings
978-1-60270-191-5, $28.50
                                                LC 2008-10745
In Athens, the ruler Theseus prepares to marry Hippolyta. Meanwhile, Hermia and Lysander run away to the forest because Hermia doesn't want to marry Demetrius, who follows them into the forest with Helena, whom he loves. Enter Puck, mischievous fairy who serves Oberon, the King of the Fairies. When he is ordered to find a flower whose nectar acts like a love potion and use it on Queen Titania, Puck also decides to play with the two young couples. And meanwhile again, a group of guildsmen prepare a play for their ruler's wedding. Havoc ensues. This graphic novel adaptation retains some of the original language from Shakespeare's play, while paring down the story to appeal to struggling readers. The book includes a short biography of Shakespeare, a summary of the play, a glossary, and a short selection of famous lines and phrases from the play.

Part of the Graphic Shakespeare series

Cooke, Darwyn
Batman: Ego and Other Tails. DC Comics 2007 200p. Illustration
Grades: 10 11 12 Adult   **741.5; Fic**
1. Batman (Fictional character); 2. Catwoman (Fictional character); 3. Mystery graphic novels; 4. Superhero graphic novels; 5. Graphic novels
978-1-4012-1529-3, $24.99
This volume collects Cooke's work for DC that focus on Batman and Catwoman. In Ego, after suffering physical and psychological trauma, Batman confronts himself in his mind. The book also includes Catwoman: Selina's Big Score, in which the perfect heist ... isn't. The book includes some violence and strong language.

★ **DC:** The New Frontier Vol. 1. DC Comics 2004 Un Illustration
Grades: 9 10 11 12 Adult   **741.5; Fic**
1. Batman (Fictional character); 2. Superhero graphic novels; 3. Superman (Fictional character); 4. Wonder Woman (Fictional character); 5. Graphic novels
1-4012-0350-7, $19.99; 9781401203504
2005 Eisner Award for Best Limited Series.
World War II is over. The Cold War has begun. The Age of the Superhero is in decline. But where are the heroes of tomorrow" This book recounts the dawning of the DC Universe's Silver Age from the perspective of those brave individuals who made it happen. Encounter "keepers of the flame" including Superman, Wonder Woman and Batman, who survived the anti-hero sentiment of the Cold War, as

well as eager newcomers like test pilot Hal Jordan and scientist Barry Allen, poised to become the next generation of crime fighters. The book includes some strong language and violence.

★ **DC:** The New Frontier Vol. 2. DC Comics 2005 Un Illustration
Grades: 9 10 11 12 Adult   **741.5; Fic**
1. Aquaman (Fictitious character); 2. Batman (Fictional character); 3. Flash (Fictional character); 4. Superhero graphic novels; 5. Superman (Fictional character); 6. Wonder Woman (Fictional character); 7. Graphic novels
1-4012-0461-9, $19.99
2005 Eisner Award for Best Limited Series.
It's a mystery in space as Superman, the Suicide Squad, and the Challengers of the Unknown encounter a frightening extraterrestrial life form. Could this hideous creature have anything to do with the sense of impending doom all the heroes are experiencing" Meanwhile, pilot Hal Jordan is grounded, while post-war America faces a monstrous threat older than time. Will this challenge bring America and its heroes back together or tear them apart" The book features Green Lantern, the Flash, Martian Manhunter, Aquaman, Wonder Woman, Batman, and more heroes. It includes some strong language and some violence.

The **Spirit** book two. With J. Bone and Dave Stewart. DC Comics 2008 Un Illustration
Grades: 10 11 12 Adult   **741.5; Fic**
1. Mystery graphic novels; 2. Spirit (Fictional character); 3. Graphic novels
978-1-4012-1920-8, $24.99
In this second volume of Darwyn Cooke's take on Will Eisner's iconic character, The Spirit, readers meet Silk Satin, a sultry and sexy CIA agent, the villainous Octopus, and El Morte, the criminal who died with Denny Colt only to be raised as a zombie by his mother's supernatural rites. Along the way, the Spirit also works (sort of) with cable crime reporter Ginger Coffee to find out who is killing all the cable news pundits. The book includes violence and some bloodshed.

★ **Will** Eisner's The Spirit. Written by Darwyn Cooke and Jeph Loeb; drawn by Darwyn Cooke; inks and finishes by J. Bone; colors by Dave Stewart. DC Comics 2007 192p. Illustration
Grades: 8 9 10 11 12 Adult   **741.5; Fic**
1. Batman (Fictional character); 2. Humorous graphic novels; 3. Spirit (Fictional character); 4. Superhero graphic novels; 5. Graphic novels
978-1-4012-1461-6; 978-1-4012-1618-4 (pa), $19.99
Will Eisner's character The Spirit was popular for decades. Eisner is gone, but Darwyn Cooke has taken up the pen to update The Spirit while maintaining the action, adventure, and humor of the original stories. Readers will meet Commissioner Dolan and his daughter Ellen, Ebony, bad girl P'Gell, and more. This volume also includes the Eisner Award winning Batman/The Spirit special, written by Jeph Loeb and drawn by Cooke. The upcoming live action movie directed by comics veteran Frank Miller will spark more interest in the comics. The book includes lots of action and some cartoony violence.

"This is fine, entertaining stuff that will satisfy any longtime comics fan; recommended for teens and adults." Libr J

Cooper, Nate
Build your own website: a comic guide to HTML, CSS, and WordPress. Nate Cooper. No Starch Press 2014 250 p. Illustration
Grades: 7 8 9 10 11 12   **006.7**
1. Web site development — Humor; 2. Web sites — Design — Humor
1593275226; 9781593275228, $19.95
LC 2014019597
Author Nate Cooper and illustrator Kim Gee present this "illustrated introduction to the basics of creating a website. Join Kim and her little dog Tofu as she learns HTML, the language of web pages, and CSS, the language used to style web pages, from the Web Guru and Glinda, the Good Witch of CSS." (Publisher's note)
"The comic art engages the readers and gives the broad picture of what the reader will learn from Cooper's text which follows. Best suited for beginning self-learning, it is one of the few books on the topic which entertains as well as educates."
Includes index.

Cooper, Park
Half Dead. Barb Lien-Cooper and Park Cooper; art by Jimmy Bott. Marvel Publishing/Dabel Brothers Productions 2007 Un Illustration
Grades: 10 11 12 Adult   **741.5; Fic**
1. Horror graphic novels; 2. Vampires; 3. Graphic novels
0-78551-2659-7, $10.99
In London, ballerina Romany Petrovna gets caught in a gas attack in the Underground. Vampires, called Nozzies (for Nosferatu) use the gas to spread a virus that turns people into half dead creatures; the Bureau of Parahuman and Supernatural Affairs, called PASA, deals with them - by killing them. They save Romany, however, for she has retained her mental capabilities. Half dead, she must now work for PASA, hunt and kill Nozzies and other half dead, or be destroyed. There is considerable vampire action, fighting, and shooting throughout the story.

Corzine, Amy
Jane Eyre: The graphic novel original text. Charlotte Brontë ; script adaptation Amy Corzine ; American English adaptation by Joe Sutliff Sanders ; artwork by John M. Burns ; lettering by Terry Wiley. Classical Comics 2008 144p. Illustration
Grades: 6 7 8 9 10 11 12 Adult
741.5; Fic
1. Brontë, Charlotte, 1816-1855 — Adaptations; 2. Romance

©Classical Comics

graphic novels; 3. Graphic novels
978-1-906332-47-1, $16.95
Orphaned as an infant and begrudgingly raised by an aunt who despises her, Jane Eyre begins to find some happiness at Lowood School, a charity school where she spends eight years of her life, as a student and then as a teacher. When she chafes for freedom and advertises for a position, Jane finds a job as governess at Thornfield Hall, where she meets Mr. Rochester. Love blooms, but his dark secret destroys what hope she ever had of happiness and she runs away. As life seems to reach its darkest, worst moments, things begin to look up for Jane, but will she ever find love again? This graphic adaptation uses Bronte's dialog and some of her narration straight from the original novel. Back matter includes a short biography of Bronte, a timeline of her life and career, and the Bronte family tree.
Also available quick text version $16.95 (ISBN: 978-1-906332-48-8)

Cosby, Andrew
Enigma Cipher, 112. Written by Andrew Cosby and Michael A. Nelson; art by Greg Scott. 2008 Illustration
Grades: 9 10 11 12 Adult   **741.5; Fic**
1. Adventure graphic novels; 2. Ciphers; 3. Mystery graphic novels; 4. Graphic novels
978-1-934506-13-4, $15.99
During World War II, the Nazis used a machine called Enigma to encrypt their communications, and the Allies broke that code, helping them to win the war. Now, decades later, grad student Casey Williams' professor has found a long-lost Enigma-encrypted document and has given it to his class to decipher as an assignment. He has also sent a copy to the State Department, which unleashes a deadly plot. American agents kill the professor and the other three students in the class, and when Casey tries to ask her ex-boyfriend for help, they kill him and his roommate. One detective, Merrick, believes Casey, and they end up on the run, until Casey decides she needs to decode the cipher and find out what the document contains. This book reads like an action thriller movie, reminiscent of The Pelican Brief and The Bourne Identity; there is some violence but only mildly strong language. Andrew Cosby is a comics writer who has also created two television series: Haunted (on UPN) and Eureka (on the Sci Fi Channel).

Court-Kaemon, Amy
Ratatouille. Tokyopop 2007 96p. Illustration
Grades: 2 3 4 5 6 7 8 9 10 11 12 Adult   **741.5; Fic**
1. Cooking; 2. Humorous graphic novels; 3. Rats; 4. Graphic novels
978-1-4278-0087-9, $7.99
This Cine-Manga title takes stills from Pixar's popular animated film to adapt the story into a graphic novel. Remy is a rat living in Paris, who aspires to be a chef. Linguine is a hapless young man who wishes to be a chef but has no talent. When the two meet, a partnership is born.

Crain, Dale
The **DC** Comics Rarities Archives Volume 1. DC Comics 2004 348p. Illustration
Grades: 7 8 9 10 11 12 Adult   **741.5; Fic**
1. Superhero graphic novels; 2. Graphic novels

1-4012-0007-8, $75

For the first time ever, in one huge collection, three of DC Comics' most hard to find early anthology titles are reprinted in their entirety. This is a 348-page hardcover collecting New York World's Fair 1939, New York World's Fair 1940 and Big All-American Comic Book #1 (1944). The two World's Fair Comics were specially created to be distributed at the legendary New York World's Fair of 1939-40 and feature adventures revolving around the DC heroes' visits there.

The **Seven** Soldiers of Victory Archives Volume 1. DC Comics 2005 237p. Illustration
Grades: 6 7 8 9 10 11 12 Adult   **741.5; Fic**
1. Green Arrow (Fictional character); 2. Superhero graphic novels; 3. Graphic novels
1-4012-0401-5, $49.95

Collecting Leading Comics #1-4, featuring the adventures of The Seven Soldiers of Victory: The Crimson Avenger, Green Arrow, the Shining Knight, The Vigilante, the Star-Spangled Kid, and their sidekicks Speedy, Stripesy, and Wing (yes, there were eight of them). In 1941, one year after DC Comics launched the Justice Society of America in All-Star Comics, sister company All-American Comics released Leading Comics #1 featuring its very own super-team; in these early stories they take on various criminals and villains who possess super-senses.

Superman Archives Volume 7. DC Comics 2006 237p. Illustration
Grades: 8 9 10 11 12 Adult   **741.5; Fic**
1. Superhero graphic novels; 2. Superman (Fictional character); 3. Graphic novels
978-1-4012-1051-9, $49.99

This seventh volume of the Superman Archive Editions collects issues 25-29 of Superman, with tales featuring the Man of Steel fighting subversion and sabotage on the home front during World War II, meeting mythic figures like Paul Bunyan and Hercules and foiling villains including the Toyman and the Prankster. This volume also features the first episodes of "Lois Lane, Girl Reporter." These stories were originally published in 1943 and 1944.

Crane, Jordan
The **Last** Lonely Saturday. Fantagraphics Books 2007 Un Illustration
Grades: 10 11 12 Adult
741.5; Fic
1. Ghosts; 2. Romance graphic novels; 3. Graphic novels
978-1-56097-743-8, $8

Using a deep yellow and brown palette, this almost wordless little story follows the day of an older man who gathers his letters addressed to Elinore, sets off to buy flowers, and drives out to the cemetery to visit Elinore's

Courtesy of Fantagraphics

grave. As he sits and hugs the gravestone, the spirit of Elinore comes out and starts to kiss him. In a macabre twist that is portrayed in a sweet, gentle manner, Elinore's spirit finds a way for the two of them to be together.

Crilley, Mark
★ **Akiko** pocket-size, vol. 1. Sirius Entertainment 2004 192p. Illustration
Grades: 3 4 5 6 7 8 9 10   **741.5; Fic**
1. Adventure graphic novels; 2. Science fiction graphic novels
1-579890-67-9, $11.95

Fourth-grader Akiko travels to the planet Smoo, on a mission to rescue King Froptoppit's son from the evil Alia Rellapor. Teamed up with the scruffy adventurer Spuckler, bookish Mr. Beeba, Spuckler's robot Gax, and the floating alien known as Poog, Akiko faces sea monsters, Sky Pirates, Sleeslup worms, and other dangers as they travel around the planet on their quest. Crilley also has written a series of prose fiction featuring Akiko and her friends.

★ **Brody's** ghost: book 1. Story and art by Mark Crilley. Dark Horse Books 2010 88p. Illustration
Grades: 8 9 10 11 12 Adult   **741.5; Fic**
1. Adventure graphic novels; 2. Fantasy graphic novels; 3. Ghosts; 4. Mystery graphic novels; 5. Graphic novels
978-1-59582-521-6, $6.99

In what looks like a near-future city, Brody is down and out, eking out a living by playing guitar on the streets and working part-time as a stock clerk. Then, one day, while playing his guitar, he sees the ghost of a young woman; he thinks he's seeing things, but she won't let him alone until he talks with her. Talia, the ghost, needs to do a great deed before she can get into heaven, and she has decided to solve the mystery of a serial killer called the Penny Murderer, but she needs Brody, who is a ghostseer, to help her. First, though, he needs training to bring out his ghostseer powers, because he doesn't think he has any. Enter Kagemura, the ghost of a samurai, who decides, half-unwillingly, to train Brody. This book is much grittier than Crilley's earlier works, which were more suitable for younger readers; it is aimed more at teen and adult readers and includes some fighting violence but no graphically violent content.

"The setting—an unidentified future city partially in ruins—is a masterpiece of drawing, and Brody and the other characters are equally well crafted. . . . The story is more than a match for the art: humor, action, and mystery butt up against the reality of Brody's sad life, giving him the opportunity to change who he is." Booklist

Also available in an omnibus edition

The first in a six-volume limited series. Page 4 of cover

Book 1 of 6

Miki Falls Vol. 2: Summer. HarperTeen 2007 178p. Illustration
Grades: 7 8 9 10 11 12 Adult   **741.5; Fic**
1. Romance graphic novels; 2. Supernatural graphic novels; 3. Graphic novels
978-0-06-084617-6, $7.99

Has Miki fallen too hard" It's summer, and Miki Yoshida is learning all about love. Her senior year has blossomed with promise ever since she gained Hiro Sakurai's confidence. Now, she's resolved to keep his trust as he reveals more about his secret mission and warns: "Don't get involved." But Miki fears his work might do more harm than good, and she takes control-with disastrous results. How can trying to make things right turn out so dangerously wrong" Crilley is doing this series in manga style.

Miki Falls, Book One: Spring. HarperCollins/HarperTeen 2007 176p. Illustration
Grades: 7 8 9 10 11 12   **741.5; Fic**
1. Friendship; 2. High school students; 3. School stories; 4. Graphic novels
978-0-06-084616-9, $7.99
"This is Miki Yoshida's final year of high school, and she's determined to make this the best year yet. Miki is in control . . . until Hiro Sakurai shows up. The tall, handsome new student is hiding something, and Miki wants to know what." Publisher's note
"Crilley uses mystery to drive the narrative and creates characters that the reader will care about. The black-and-white, manga-style art is beautiful." Voice Youth Advocates
Other titles in this series are: Miki Falls, Book Two: Summer; Miki Falls, Book Three: Autumn; Miki Falls, Book Four: Winter

★ **Miki** Falls: Winter. HarperCollins/HarperTeen 2008 176p. Illustration
Grades: 7 8 9 10 11 12   **741.5; Fic**
1. Adventure graphic novels; 2. Fantasy graphic novels; 3. Romance graphic novels; 4. Graphic novels
978-0-06-084619-0, $7.99
                                        LC 2007-931803
Miki and Hiro have been on the run for a while now; it's now winter and they are in the far north of Japan, trying to escape from the Deliverers led by Akuzu who are determined to tear the young couple apart and punish Hiro. Miki is equally determined to stay with Hiro, whom she loves above all else. Can love conquer all? This is the final volume of the series.

Crisis on Multiple Earths Volume 1: The Team-Ups
DC Comics 2005 224p. Illustration
Grades: 8 9 10 11 12 Adult   **741.5; Fic**
1. Flash (Fictional character); 2. Green Lantern (Fictional character); 3. Superhero graphic novels; 4. Graphic novels
1-4012-0470-8, $14.99
This collection of stories from the 1960s features team-ups of the Silver Age DC heroes with their Golden Age counterparts, with the conceit that DC Comics dreamed up, that the Golden Age heroes are from a parallel world. And along with the heroes, of course come the super-villains. The Flash, Green Lantern, and Hourman from both worlds work with each other to defeat their villains, including Solomon Grundy, the Thinker, the Trickster, and others.

Crisse, Didier
Luuna, book 1. Art by Nicolas Keramidas and Bruno Garcia. Tokyopop 2009 108p. Illustration
Grades: 9 10 11 12   **741.5; Fic**
1. Adventure graphic novels; 2. Fantasy graphic novels; 3. Graphic novels
978-1-4278-1412-8, $12.99
Luuna is a young woman of the Paumanok tribe, whose people can see and communicate with animal spirits. The

night of her coming of age ritual, when Luuna will receive her animal totem, is a bad night for it belongs to Unkui, the Evil One, who wants her soul. This night she receives two totems, a white wolf that reflects the good in her, and a black wolf that reflects her darkness. Because of this, she can't return to her tribe, and she sets out on a quest to seek help from the spirits of the earth. However, Unkui's human minions are on her trail, for he wants to totally possess her. This graphic novel has been popular in Europe, and is one of Tokyopop's new full-color graphic novels. If the art style looks vaguely familiar, it's because Keramidas has worked on some animated films, including Disney's Tarzan, The Hunchback of Notre Dame, The Emperor's New Groove, and more. The book includes some violence and a few titillating shots of Luuna.

Croall, Marie P.
Marwe: into the land of the dead: an East African legend. Author, Marie P. Croall; pencils by Ray Lago and inks by Craig Hamilton.. Lerner Publishing Group 2009 48p. Illustration
Grades: 3 4 5 6 7 8 9   **741.5; Fic**
1. Fantasy graphic novels; 2. Folklore — East Africa; 3. Graphic novels
978-0-8225-7134-6, $27.93
                                        LC 2007-1828
In this story retold from the oral tradition of the Chaga people in East Africa, Marwe lives in a village where times are hard and food is scarce. When she and her brother leave the family's bean fields to cool off at the river, monkeys destroy the entire crop. When her brother goes off to ask the family's forgiveness, Marwe sees something strange in the water and dives down; she passes through a strange doorway and finds herself in another land. Soon she learns she has come to the land of the dead, where an old woman welcomes her. Too scared to go home, Marwe stays there, and despite assurances that she needn't do anything, she works in the fields. When will Marwe think it's time to return home to her anxious and mourning family?
Part of the Graphic Universe Myths and Legends series

Psyche & eros: the lady and the monster: a Greek myth. Story by Marie Croall; pencils and inks by Ron Randall. Lerner Publishing Group 2009 48p. Illustration
Grades: 3 4 5 6 7 8 9   **741.5; Fic**
1. Fantasy graphic novels; 2. Greek mythology; 3. Graphic novels
978-0-8225-7177-3, $27.93
                                        LC 2007-43353
Psyche is a beautiful young woman, so beautiful that men start to give her gifts instead of taking them to the temple. This makes Aphrodite jealous, and she sends her son, Eros, to prick Psyche with an arrow so no man will ever fall in love with her. However, Eros falls in love with Psyche. He arranges for the Oracle to tell Psyche's father that his daughter must be taken up on a mountain to marry a monster. He only comes to her at night, and they love each other; but Psyche's sisters convince her that she should see her husband. When hot wax from her candle burns Eros and wakens him, he must leave her. Now Psyche, unable to convince any other god or goddess to help her, must go to

Aphrodite, who sets impossible tasks that Psyche manages to accomplish with help from unexpected sources.

Part of the Graphic Universe Myths and Legends series

Crosby, Andrew
   Damn Nation. Art by J. Alexander. Dark Horse Comics 2005 Un Illustration
Grades: 10 11 12 Adult   **741.5; Fic**
   1. Horror graphic novels; 2. Vampires; 3. Graphic novels
1-59307-389-5, $12.95
   The United States has been shut off from the world by concrete barricades and barbed wire - not because of what might get in, but what might get out. A vampire plague has spread from sea to shining sea, and when a small holdout of scientists trapped outside of Buffalo, N.Y. discover a cure, it's up to a Special Ops team from the President's current offices in London to go in and get it. Yet, not everyone in the world wants to see America back in the saddle again ... This story includes some incidental nudity, strong language, and considerable violence.

Crumb, Aline Kominsky
   Need More Love: A Graphic Memoir. MQ Publications Ltd 2007 383p. Illustration
Grades: 11 12 Adult   **741.5; Fic**
   1. Autobiographical graphic novels; 2. Crumb, Aline Kominsky, 1948-; 3. Graphic novels
978-1-84601-133-7, $30
   Crumb was one of the pioneers of women's comics and became well-known during the Sixties and Seventies, along with her husband R. Crumb. This is her memoir of her life, taken from her comics published over the past four decades, incorporating photos and short prose text pieces along with memorabilia. She covers not only her life, but of her family, her husband, and other movers and shakers of the art and music worlds from the Sixties into the 21st century. The book includes considerable nudity, sexual situations, and harsh language.

Cryptic Magazine
   Horror book volume 1. Image Comics 2008 Un Illustration
Grades: 10 11 12 Adult   **741.5; Fic**
   1. Horror graphic novels; 2. Short stories; 3. Graphic novels
978-1-58240-956-6, $14.99
   This volume collects stories originally published in Cryptic Magazine. Each story reworks a classic horror tale. In the first, readers will find zombies in Vietnam in the year 1968, as an American patrol finds horror in the jungle. "Creature of the Depths" takes on The Creature from the Black Lagoon, as a small troop from a struggling sideshow is hired to help trap a marauding sea creature. In "Frankenstein," years after the monster was killed, the doctor is now an opium addict, but now someone is robbing graves and kidnapping people such as the blacksmith and some prostitutes; the monster isn't dead, but he wants more creatures like himself. And in "Full Moon," a nameless man agrees to help the village priest rescue a couple of kidnapped children who were taken by a vengeful vampire; it is the night of the full moon, and the young man becomes a ravening werewolf. The stories include graphic violence and gore, some partial nudity, and some rough language.

Dabb, Andrew
   G.I. Joe, Sigma 6: big time. ABDO Spotlight 2008 Un Illustration
Grades: 3 4 5 6 7 8 9   **741.5; Fic**
   1. Adventure graphic novels; 2. G I Joe (Fictional character); 3. Graphic novels
978-1-59961-369-7, $21.35
                                              LC 2006-52226
   It's quiet time at R.O.C.C., the mobile headquarters of G.I. Joe, and Heavy Duty and Long Range are the only Joes there when they get a call from General Sato in Tokyo, Japan. Cobra Commander has been spotted, and Sato needs the Joes' help. Heavy Duty and Long Range are usually just the back up guys for the more well-known Joes (Duke, Scarlett, Snake Eyes . . .), but they have to take the mission. What they do is wreck havoc at a Yakuza club in Tokyo while trying to take down Cobra Commander. The book includes lots of action but no real violence.

   This book is a revision of issue 5 (March 2006) of G. I. Joe Sigma 6, originally published by Devils Due Publishing.

Daffy Duck: You're Despicable!
   DC Comics 2005 112p. Illustration
Grades: 3 4 5 6 7 8 9   **741.5; Fic**
   1. Daffy Duck (Fictional character); 2. Humorous graphic novels; 3. Graphic novels
1-4012-0515-1, $6.99
   It's duck season again. Everyone's favorite foul-tempered fowl explodes into his own collection with this first volume of Daffy Duck stories straight from the pages of Looney Tunes comics. Packed full of hilarity and anger management issues, this volume will warm the hearts of curmudgeons young and old everywhere. Of course you know this means war.

Dahl, Roald
   The **Gremlins:** The Lost Walt Disney Production: A Royal Air Force Story. Dark Horse Books 2006 Un Illustration
Grades: 4 5 6 7 8 9 10 11 12 Adult   **741.5; Fic**
   1. Humorous graphic novels; 2. World War, 1939-1945; 3. Graphic novels
978-1-59307-496-8, $12.95
   This is an illustrated novella, the first published work of RAF Flight Lieutenant Roald Dahl in his only collaboration with Walt Disney Studios. Originally published in 1943, the story was supposed to become a film combining live action with animation; the movie was never made, although the studio produced a lot of illustrations and samples. The story tells about one young Royal Air Force pilot named Gus, who first sees the little gremlins that wreak havoc on his plane. While the gremlins first cause lots of trouble, eventually Gus convinces them to work with the RAF.

Dakin, Glenn
   Temptation: A Battle of Wits Through All Eternity. Active Images 2004 72p. Illustration

Grades: 8 9 10 11 12 Adult   741.5
   1. Humorous graphic novels; 2. Graphic novels
0-9740567-5-8, $8.95
   It's a constant battle of wits between a hermit who lives out in the wilderness and the devil who wants his soul. While that's the main theme, there are strips in which the devil needs the hermit to babysit his little baby devils so he can see a movie, the devil tries to sell the hermit a set of encyclopedias, and more fun.

Dalrymple, Farel
   The **Wrenchies**. Farel Dalrymple. First Second 2014 304 p. Color; Illustration
Grades: 10 11 12 Adult   741.5
   1. Imaginary places; 2. Science fiction
159643421X; 9781596434219, $19.99
   In this book by Farel Dalrymple, "whatever life remains on earth is oppressed by the evil shadowsmen. Only a gang of ruthless and powerful children called the Wrenchies can hope to stand against them. When Hollis, a lonely boy from our world, is magically given access to the future world of the Wrenchies, he finally finds a place he belongs. But it is not an easy world to live in, and Hollis's quest is bigger than he ever dreamed of." (Publisher's note)
   "Clearly, it doesn't pay to demand sheer narrative coherence here, but the raw emotional weight of Dalrymple's anger forcibly tows readers through the obfuscating narrative, and the intricate, gritty, and rivetingly grotesque art, in sickly greens and browns peppered with bloody red, plays no small part in that." Booklist

Daly, Joe
   Scrublands. Fantagraphics Books 2006 126p. Illustration
Grades: 12 Adult   741.5; Fic
   1. Humorous graphic novels; 2. Graphic novels
978-1-56097-744-5, $16.95
   "Prebaby," the centerpiece of this collection, delves into creation, survival, random occurrences and the micro/macrocosm. Told entirely without dialogue, it unfolds like the storyboard to a wonky existential animated cartoon. In contrast, Daly's "Kobosh and Steve" stories come across as a series of routines by a demented Abbott and Costello. Kobosh even visits a down-on-his-luck Bruce Springsteen in one story, while another strip features a pair of micro-fauna questioning their existence as they feed off the rock legend's scalp. The book contains strong language, nudity, and some sexual situations.

Daly, Paul
   Athena Voltaire: the collected webcomics. Written by Paul Daly and Steve Bryant; art by Steve Bryant and Chad Fidler. APE Entertainment 2006 Un Illustration
Grades: 9 10 11 12 Adult   741.5; Fic
   1. Adventure graphic novels; 2. Fantasy graphic novels; 3. Graphic novels
978-0-9741398-9-0, $13.95
   In "The Terror in Tibet," adventurous pilot (and widow) Athena Voltaire agrees to guide a group of British gentlemen on an expedition into the Himalayas. The time is the 1930s, and Nazis are on the rise in Germany. Athena soon finds out that the British are up to no good, nor are the Germans

pursuing them. They're all after something in a remote monastery halfway up Mount Everest, and she decides to prevent anyone from succeeding. In "The Wrath from the Tomb," Dracula's daughter seeks revenge against the men who killed her father; she makes a mistake when she sends men to attack Athena's Arizona ranch. Teens who love the Indiana Jones and Mummy movies will enjoy Athena's adventures. The violence level is about the same as those movies, although the scene in which the vampire is run through with a spear might bother more sensitive readers.
   The stories originally appeared as webcomics, and the series was nominated for the first Eisner Award for Best Digital Comic in 2005

Danko, Dan
   Leonardo da Vinci: the renaissance man. Dan Danko, illustrated by Lalit Kumar Sharma. Campfire/Kalyani Navyug Media Pvt. Ltd. 2011 68 p.
Grades: 8 9 10   709.2
   1. Artists; 2. Artists — Italy — Biography; 3. Biographical graphic novels; 4. Inventors — Italy — Biography; 5. Leonardo, da Vinci, 1452-1519; 6. Renaissance — Italy — Biography; 7. Scientists — Italy — Biography
9380741014; 9380741200; 9789380741017; 9789380741208, $9.99
       LC 2011294404
   This graphic novel is a biography of Leonardo da Vinci. It "opens with the theft of the 'Mona Lisa' from the Louvre in 1911, then backtracks to da Vinci's turbulent childhood in Italy during the Renaissance. Throughout the tale, the mind of da Vinci is shown to be always active, always questioning, always seeking ways to create something better." (Voice of Youth Advocates)

David, Peter
   Fallen Angel: Down to Earth. Art by David Lopez. DC Comics 2007 136p. Illustration
Grades: 12 Adult   741.5; Fic
   1. Superhero graphic novels; 2. Supernatural graphic novels; 3. Graphic novels
978-1-4012-1268-1, $14.99
   Bete Noir is a quiet, almost mundane city by day; but by night it becomes a haven for crime, corruption, and the supernatural. Enter the Fallen Angel, a mysterious and powerful woman who aids people in need when they find themselves at a crossroads in their lives. If she deems a person worthy, she can be a savior; if she doesn't, that person won't live to tell the tale. In this volume, the Angel's nemesis, Black Mariah, has returned to town, and this time she's hunting the Angel. The book includes nudity, sexual situations, foul language, and violence.

   Friendly Neighborhood Spider-Man Vol. 1: Derailed. Writer, Peter David ; pencils, Mike Wieringo & Roger Cruz ; inks, Karl Kesel ... [et al.] ; colors, Paul Mounts & Chris Sotomayor. Marvel Entertainment 2006 Un Illustration
Grades: 7 8 9 10 11 12 Adult   741.5; Fic
   1. Spider-Man (Fictional character); 2. Superhero graphic novels; 3. Graphic novels
978-0-7851-2216-6, $14.99

A major character from Peter Parker's past returns, and it looks like Hobgoblin is terrorizing the skies again. Also, a woman chronicles Spider-Man's career on her blog, convinced that he has stalked her for her entire life.

I am Iron Man. Sean Chen, illustrator. Marvel Worldwide, Inc. 2010 Un Illustration
Grades: 7 8 9 10 11 12 Adult   **741.5; Fic**
1. Iron Man (Fictional character); 2. Superhero graphic novels; 3. Graphic novels
978-0-7851-4558-5, $16.99
The first Iron Man movie, released in 2008, was a major hit, but just like the other superhero movies based on Marvel Comics properties, it wasn't based on any particular Iron Man comics. This book collects a two-issue miniseries based on the movie script, written by Peter David with pencils by Sean Chen, a one-shot written by Christos Gage with pencils by Hugo Petrus, and Iron Man #200, which was written by Denny O'Neil with pencils by Mark Bright and originally published in 1985. David and Chen's comic adapts the movie script, hitting all the high points of the action. Gage and Petrus's one-shot, "Security Measures," looks at the action of the movie from the viewpoint of S.H.I.E.L.D. agent Coulson. Iron Man #200 features a battle between Iron Man and Iron Monger, who is Tony Stark's erstwhile partner Obadiah Stane. The book also includes an interview with Kevin Feige, producer of the Iron Man movie, and photos taken on the movie sets. The book actually cuts down on the amount of violence that was shown in the movie.

Marvel 1602: Fantastick Four. Art by Pascal Alixe. Marvel Entertainment 2007 Un Illustration
Grades: 9 10 11 12 Adult   **741.5; Fic**
1. Fantastic Four (Fictional characters); 2. Superhero graphic novels; 3. Graphic novels
978-0-7851-2293-7, $14.99
In the year 1602, Count Otto von Doom has an insidious plan that takes him - and the Four of the Fantastick - to the ends of the Earth. What does Doom want" Why doesn't Invisible Woman want to fight him" And what does Shakespeare have to do with it" This book spins off from Marvel 1602 written by Neil Gaiman.

Sachs & Violens. Art by George Perez. DC Comics 2006 126p. Illustration
Grades: 12 Adult   **741.5; Fic**
1. Mystery graphic novels; 2. Graphic novels
978-1-4012-1050-2, $7.99
The brutal killing of a young actress during the shooting of a snuff film sets soft core model Juanita Jean Sachs and photographer Ernie Schultz on a quest to discover those responsible. Their journey takes them from the mean streets of New York City to the back alleys of New Orleans, where they confront the utter depravity and corruption that defines the dark underbelly of American society. But they discover something else as well; something unexpected. Their destiny. This book includes considerable partial nudity, strong language, and graphic violence.

The Dark House Book of the Dead
Dark Horse Books 2005 96p. Illustration
Grades: 10 11 12 Adult   **741.5; Fic**

1. Ghosts; 2. Hellboy (Fictional character); 3. Horror graphic novels; 4. Graphic novels
1-59307-281-3, $14.95
Mike Mignola presents a Hellboy yarn combining Shakespeare and graverobbing. Also returning this volume are Jill Thompson and her collaborator Evan Dorkin with another occult canine adventure. New additions for this volume include Goon creator Eric Powell, artist Guy Davis, and the artist who spent the last twenty years making superhero comics more scary, Kelley Jones. Cover artist Gary Gianni also returns, "Old Garfield's Heart" by Conan creator Robert E. Howard. Some stories have graphically violent or nude illustrations.

The Dark House Book of Hauntings.
Dark Horse Books 2003 96p. Illustration
Grades: 9 10 11 12 Adult   **741.5; Fic**
1. Ghosts; 2. Hellboy (Fictional character); 3. Horror graphic novels; 4. Graphic novels
1-56971-958-6, $14.95
This book includes Mike Mignola's only new Hellboy adventure in 2003, in which Hellboy investigates a haunted house and discovers his own unexpected connection to the spirits within. P. Craig Russell adapts Mike Richardson's story about a child who leads friends and family into an abandoned house, and Paul Chadwick and his longtime Concrete editor Randy Stradley team up for a creepy short about a haunted suit. Jill Thompson and Evan Dorkin recount the legend of a haunted doghouse in "Strays." The Victorian ghost story "Thurnley Abbey" is illustrated by Gary Gianni. The book includes an interview with real-life seance medium L.L. Dreller, plus a new Devil's Footprints story and contributions from international artists Uli Oesterle (Germany) and Lucas Maragnon (Mexico). The stories and art are spooky with very little graphic violence.

The Dark Horse Book of Witchcraft.
Dark Horse Comics 2004 96p. Illustration
Grades: 9 10 11 12 Adult   **741.5; Fic**
1. Hellboy (Fictional character); 2. Horror graphic novels; 3. Witchcraft; 4. Graphic novels
1-59307-108-6, $14.95
This anthology conjures up eight tales of horror and magic. Mignola presents a Hellboy story; Thompson and Dorkin return to the dog characters they created in "Stray" from a previous anthology volumes. Morse presents an evocative and carefully researched tale of old Salem, digging into the madness of the accusations leveled there, which ended more than thirty lives in a few short months. The book reprints a classic Clark Ashton Smith story, "Mother of Toads," illustrated by Gary Gianni, and more. There's some strong language and some graphic images of horror and violence.

Davis, Rob
The **Motherless** Oven. By Rob Davis. SelfMadeHero 2014 160 p. Illustration
Grades: 9 10 11 12 Adult   **741.5; Fic**
1. Death — Fiction; 2. Fantasy fiction; 3. Parent-child relationship — Fiction; 4. Graphic novels
190683881X; 9781906838812, $19.95
LC 2015296214

In this graphic novel, by Rob Davis, "parents don't make children—children make parents. Scarper's father is his pride and joy, a wind-powered brass construction with a billowing sail. His mother is a Bakelite hairdryer. In this world it rains knives, and household appliances have souls. There are also no birthdays—only deathdays. Scarper's deathday is just three weeks away, and he clings to the mundane repetition of his life at home and high school for comfort." (Publisher's note)

"Davis's dark and shadow-filled art appropriately mindbends and illuminates the text. The variation in panels quickens and pulls back the pace in this enigmatic tale, with the right amount of imagery left open for interpretation." SLJ

Davison, Al
The **Spiral** Cage: An Autobiography. DC Comics 2003 141p. Illustration
Grades: 11 12 Adult   741.5
1. Autobiographical graphic novels; 2. Davison, Al, 1960-; 3. Spina bifida; 4. Graphic novels
0-9740567-1-5, $12.95

Born with severe spina bifida, doctors considered Al Davison a hopeless case, condemned to the 'spiral cage' of his own DNA. In Al's own words and pictures, this book portrays his struggle to overcome 'disability' and the prejudice that surrounds it. The book includes lots of full frontal nudity, but it's not sexual, as Davison shows how he has to struggle physically every single day. The book also includes some strong language.

Dawson, Mike
Troop 142. Mike Dawson.. Secret Acres 2011 1 v. (unpaged) Illustration
Grades: 9 10 11 12   741.5
1. Boy Scouts; 2. Camping; 3. Men — Attitudes; 4. Scouts and scouting
9780979960994, $20
         LC 2011924536

This graphic novel, originally published online where it won the 2010 Ignatz Award for Outstanding Online Comic, "follows a group of campers and counselors at a week-long scout retreat in the woods of New Jersey. It is a story as much about adults as it is adolescents, the blurred line between childhood and manhood, and the consequences of authoritative posturing. Dispensing with idyllic notions, [author Mike] Dawson describes . . . truths about boys and men, the hypocrisy of institutional morality and the resilience of Spam and the human spirit." (Publisher's note)

The DC Comics Rarities Archives Volume 1
Edited by Dale Crain. DC Comics 2004 348p. Illustration
Grades: 7 8 9 10 11 12 Adult   741.5; Fic
1. Superhero graphic novels; 2. Graphic novels
1-4012-0007-8, $75

For the first time ever, in one huge collection, three of DC Comics' most hard to find early anthology titles are reprinted in their entirety. This is a 348-page hardcover collecting New York World's Fair 1939, New York World's Fair 1940 and Big All-American Comic Book #1 (1944). The two World's Fair Comics were specially created to be distributed at the legendary New York World's Fair of 1939-40 and feature adventures revolving around the DC heroes' visits there.

The DC Encyclopedia: The Definitive Guide to the Characters of the DC Universe
Dorling Kindersley. Edited by Alastair Dougall. 2006 351p. Illustration
Grades: 6 7 8 9 10 11 12 Adult   741.5
1. Batman (Fictional character); 2. Comic books, strips, etc — United States — History and criticism — Encyclopedias; 3. DC Comics — Encyclopedias; 4. Joker (Fictional character); 5. Superman (Fictional character); 6. Wonder Woman (Fictional character); 7. Graphic novels
978-0-7566-0592-6, $40.00
         LC 2004-3379

This one-volume encyclopedia of more than 1,000 characters created by DC Comics, features some of DC's most creative artists and heroes and villains from the world famous - such as Superman, Batman, Wonder Woman, Lex Luthor, and Joker, to lesser known characters. This guide has comic book history exploding off every page.

DC's Greatest Imaginary Stories
Otto Binder [and others], writers ; C.C. Beck [and others], pencillers and inkers. DC Comics 2005 192p. Illustration
Grades: 6 7 8 9 10 11 12 Adult   741.5; Fic
1. Batman (Fictional character); 2. Flash (Fictional character); 3. Superhero graphic novels; 4. Superman (Fictional character); 5. Graphic novels
1-4012-0534-8, $19.99

This volume collects eleven stories that are totally imaginary about many of DC's heroes: Superman marries Lois Lane; in another story, he marries Lana Lang; and in yet another story, he marries Lori Lemaris the mermaid. Batman abandons his millions to drive a taxi. The Flash races into action maskless. Superman and Batman are brothers. In the wedding of the century, it's Super girl and ... Jimmy Olsen" And Shazam witnesses atomic bomb and attacks and finds that even he, the World's Mightiest Mortal, can't stop the bombs.

De Campi, Alex
Kat & Mouse. Story by Alex de Campi; art by Federica Manfredi; story by Alex de Campi; art by Federica Manfredi.. Tokyopop 2009 Un Illustration
Grades: 5 6 7 8 9   741.5; Fic
1. Mystery graphic novels; 2. Schools; 3. Graphic novels
978-1-4278-1175-2, $5.99

Kat and Mouse have pursued the thief called Artful Dodger, who has managed to elude them and the police. On the night of the Dover Academy Snow Ball, their school enemy Chloe comes to the girls for help: her diamond necklace has been stolen. They spend the evening checking clues, but an oncoming blizzard and a surprise revelation about their art teacher complicate matters. This concluding volume of the series has been long-delayed; readers might want to refresh their memory of what happened before by rereading the first three volumes before reading this one. There is no synopsis of previous events, and some characters aren't identified by name.

Kat & Mouse: Teacher torture. [by] Alex de Campi; art by Frederica Manfredi. Tokyopop 2006 96p. Illustration
Grades: 4 5 6 7 8 9   **741.5; Fic**
  1. Mystery fiction; 2. Mystery graphic novels; 3. Graphic novels
  1-59816-548-8, $5.99
  Middle schooler Kat starts at a posh school where her father has been hired as the new science teacher, but all is not well. Accidents happen in the science lab, and an anonymous student threatens worse unless Kat's dad passes all the rich, popular students. Kat decides to investigate, aided by her one new friend, Mouse, the rebellious computer nerd and would-be CSI investigator.
  Other titles in this series are: Tripped (2007); The ice storm (2007); The knave of diamonds (2009)

Kat & Mouse Vol. 2: Tripped. Tokyopop 2007 96p. Illustration
Grades: 4 5 6 7 8 9   **741.5; Fic**
  1. Mystery graphic novels; 2. Graphic novels
  978-1-59816-549-4, $5.99
  Since her arrival at Dover Academy, the one person Kat has been able to depend on is her best friend Mee-Seen, better known as Mouse. But when Mouse gets a crush on the new art teacher, a misunderstanding comes between the two friends - and a class trip to the art museum only makes it worse. When a famous painting is stolen right under their noses, will Kat and Mouse be able to smooth things out in time to catch the thief?

De Crecy, Nicolas
  Glacial Period: A Graphic Novel. NBM/ComicsLit 2006 80p. Illustration
Grades: 10 11 12   **741.5; Fic**
  1. Art; 2. Museums — France; 3. Science fiction graphic novels; 4. Graphic novels
  1-56163-483-2, $14.95; 9781561634835
  Thousands of years in the future, the world is in the midst of a glacial period, an Ice Age. All human history has been forgotten, and mankind coexists with genetically-engineered dogs who are intelligent and can speak. A small group of archeologists literally fall upon the Louvre, the great French museum, buried in snow. Their wild misinterpretations of the art works they find have a sharp, satirical bite. One of the dogs, named Hulk, encounters sculptures and statues who want to escape.
  This book is a co-edition with the Musee du Louvre and is part of a series of graphic novels that impart the artists' visions of the museum. Crecy reproduces some famous works that are all listed in the back of the book. Many of the paintings and statures are nudes.
  Originally published in France in 2005 by Musee du Louvre Editions.

De Groot, Bob
  Clifton Jade. Cinebook 2008 48p.
Grades: 5 6 7 8 9   **741.5; Fic**
  1. Adventure graphic novels; 2. Humorous graphic novels; 3. Spies; 4. Graphic novels
  978-1-905460-52-6, $11.95

  Sir Harold Wilberforce Clifton, ex-Secret Service and retired Colonel, works as a private detective, as well as leading a troop of young scouts. With the help of his housekeeper, Mrs. Partridge, who's also a dab hand at auto mechanics, he still helps the government. This time, however, he's being tailed by someone and then summoned to a retirement home where he finds his old World War II nemesis, Otto Kartoffeln, who tells him a group of neo-Nazis are searching for a long-lost Nazi treasure in order to bring about the 4th Reich. The mysterious shadow is Jade, a young agent who was trying to complete her training; now she and Clifton must stop the neo-Nazis from finding the treasure.
  Part of the Clifton series, originally published in France as Clifton Jade.

De Heer, Margreet
  Philosophy- a discovery in comics: A discovery in comics. Margreet de Heer. NBM Pub. 2012 120 p.
Grades: 11 12 Adult   **100.022; 741.5**
  1. Philosophy; 2. Philosophy — History
  1561636983; 9781561636983, $16.99
                       LC 2012938931
  This book, by Margreet de Heer, offers an "illustrated primer on philosophy. . . . Margreet de Heer visualizes the history of Western philosophy and makes it approachable for those with little knowledge of the subject. The book explains the thoughts of philosophers such as Socrates, Plato, Aristotle, Descartes, Spinoza, and Nietzsche, and ponders questions such as 'What is thinking?' 'What is reality?' 'Is there free will?' and 'Why are these ideas still important?'" (Publisher's note)

De Radiguès, Max
  Moose. Max de Radiguès. Conundrum International 2015 160 p. Illustration
Grades: 10 11 12 Adult   **741.5; Fic**
  1. Bullies; 2. Children of gay parents — Fiction
  1894994930; 9781894994934, $17
  In this graphic novel, by Max De Radigues, "Meet Joe, an average, quiet high school student who is being bullied relentlessly by classmate Jason. No longer able to ride the bus, Joe walks to school every day through the woods finding comfort in Mother Nature. On his way to school, Joe sees a moose, a poignant encounter that helps distract him from the daily indignities. The story continues through many days of continual abuse, slowly revealing more about Joe's life." (Library Journal)

DeAngelis, Jason
  No Man's Land Vol. 1. Art by Jennyson Rosero. Seven Seas Entertainment 2006 192p. Illustration
Grades: 10 11 12 Adult   **741.5; Fic**
  1. Horror graphic novels; 2. Western graphic novels; 3. Graphic novels
  1-933164-07-7, $10.99
  John Parker had it all. A decorated sharpshooter in the Civil War, he had a promising career ahead of him, a beautiful wife, and a newborn son. But after becoming embroiled in a dark and demonic conspiracy engineered by the Bakerton Detective Agency, he lost everything. Fleeing to the West, a broken man, Parker reinvents himself as No Man," a heartless gun-for-hire whose only solace comes

from hunting and killing the demons who he helped set loose. With Buntline Special in hand, a deadly revolver with a sixteen inch barrel, he blasts his way through a different kind of Old West, where strange and evil beings lurk. The book includes lots of violence and some strong language. This is a global manga title.

DeConnick, Kelly Sue

Captain Marvel; 1: in pursuit of flight. By Kelly Sue Deconnick; illustrated by Dexter Soy and Emma Rios. Marvel Worldwide 2013 136 p. Color; Illustration

Grades: 10 11 12 Adult   741.5
1. Female superhero graphic novels; 2. Superheroes — Fiction
0785165495; 9780785165491, $14.99

In this graphic novel by Kelly Sue Deconnick, illustrated by Dexter Soy and Emma Rios, "Carol Danvers has a new name, a new mission—and all the power she needs to make her own life a living hell. As the new Captain Marvel, Carol is forging from a challenge from her past! It's a firefight in the sky as the Banshee Squadron debut - but who are the Prowlers, and where has Carol seen them before" And how does secret NASA training program Mercury 13 fit in—" (Publisher's note)

Captain Marvel; Volume 2: Down. By Kelly Sue Deconnick and Christopher Sebela; illustrated by Dexter Soy and Filipe Andrade. Marvel Worldwide 2013 136 p. Color; Illustration

Grades: 10 11 12 Adult   741.5
1. Captain Marvel (Fictional character); 2. Superhero graphic novels
0785165509; 9780785165507, $14.99

In this graphic novel, by Kelly Sue Deconnick and Christopher Sebela, illustrated by Dexter Soy and Filipe Andrade, "Captain Marvel goes head to head with . . . Captain Marvel" Former Captain Monica Rambeau returns, but what's her problem with Earth's new Mightiest Hero? What threat is lurking below the ocean's surface? And can both Captain Marvels stop it before they get ship wrecked?" (Publisher's note)

Contains material originally published in magazine form as Captain Marvel #7-12—t.p. verso.

Pretty deadly; Vol. 1: The shrike. Kelly Sue Deconnick; illustrated by Emma Rios, Jordie Bellaire, Clayton Cowles. Image Comics 2014 120 p. Color; Illustration

Grades: 9 10 11 12 Adult   741.5
1. Death; 2. Women — Fiction
1607069628; 9781607069621, $9.99

In this graphic novel by Kelly Sue Deconnick, "Death's daughter rides the wind on a horse made of smoke and her face bears the skull marks of her father. Her origin story is a tale of retribution as beautifully lush as it is unflinchingly savage." (Publisher's note)

Volume 1 of an ongoing series

DeFalco, Tom

The **Amazing** Spider-Girl: Whatever Happened to the Daughter of Spider-Man?. Illustrated by Ron Frenz. Marvel Entertainment 2007 Un Illustration

Grades: 7 8 9 10 11 12 Adult   741.5; Fic

1. Spider-Girl (Fictional character); 2. Spider-Man (Fictional character); 3. Superhero graphic novels; 4. Graphic novels
978-0-7851-2341-5, $14.99

After discovering she had inherited her father's incredible powers, May "Mayday" Parker donned a costume and became the amazing Spider-Girl. Recent events have forced her to hang up her webs and lead a normal life ... but how long can May keep from web-slinging when there are villains like Hobgoblin on the loose" This volume begins collecting the second run of Spider-Girl comics; the first 100 issues were published as Spider-Girl and are being collected in digest-sized trade paperbacks. This new series, The Amazing Spider-Girl, features new numbering (from #1 and on) and is being collected in regular comic book-sized trade paperbacks.

Avengers Next: Rebirth. Written by Tom DeFalco ; pencilled by Ron Lim. Marvel Entertainment 2007 Un Illustration

Grades: 7 8 9 10 11 12   741.5; Fic
1. Avengers (Fictional characters); 2. Superhero graphic novels
978-0-7851-2518-1, $13.99

The time has come for the next generation of Avengers to choose a new lineup, but first they must battle zombie versions of themselves. Then, as Katie Power (from Power Pack) joins the team, American Dream and her friends mount a search for the missing Thunderstrike. The man called Nova guest stars when strange visitors from outer space land on Earth. And more.

Spider-Girl Presents A-Next: Second Coming. Illustrator Ron Frenz. Marvel Entertainment 2006 Un Illustration

Grades: 6 7 8 9 10 11 12   741.5; Fic
1. Captain America (Fictional character); 2. Doctor Strange (Fictional character); 3. Superhero graphic novels; 4. Graphic novels
0-7851-2131-5, $7.99

On another day unlike any other, a new collection of the World's Mightiest Heroes rocked their own remarkable reality. New heroes, such as J2 (son of Juggernaut), Thunderstrike (Kevin Masterson), Stinger (Cassie Lang), and the mysterious Mainframe, become the new Avengers. Enemies alien and Earthbound vie to end the new era of Avengerdom. This book features the heir of Captain America and the son of the Black Panther, and guest-stars Doctor Strange and the Defenders.

Spider-Girl Presents Juggernaut, Jr.: Secrets and Lies. Written by Tom DeFalco ; art by Ron Lim. Marvel Entertainment 2006 Un Illustration

Grades: 6 7 8 9 10 11 12   741.5; Fic
1. Superhero graphic novels; 2. Graphic novels
0-7851-2047-5, $7.99

Lots of people have big shoes to fill, but how many have to fill the helmet of the Juggernaut? Teenager Zane Marko grows up fast and hits the big time head first when he inherits his father's unstoppability and joins the latest generation of Avengers. J2 squares off against villains and heroes alike, including a certain green goliath who thinks he's still the strongest one there is. This volume includes the first appearances of the X-People and Wild Thing, daughter of Wolverine and Elektra.

Spider-Girl Vol. 2: Like Father, Like Daughter. Illustrated by Pat Olliffe. Marvel Entertainment 2004 Un Illustration
Grades: 7 8 9 10 11 12   **741.5; Fic**
  1. Spider-Girl (Fictional character); 2. Superhero graphic novels; 3. Graphic novels
0-7851-1657-5, $7.99
Her name is May "Mayday" Parker, and she recently learned her father was the original Spider-Man. The good news is that she's having the time of her life as she hones the amazing spider-like abilities she inherited from him. The bad news is that some of her roughest, toughest battles lie ahead - against the likes of Ladyhawk, the Kingpin of Crime, Mr. Nobody, Crazy Eight...and her own parents. She also learns that it's not easy hiding such a big part of your life from all your friends in school.

Spider-Girl Vol. 3: Avenging Allies. Written by Tom DeFalco ; illustrated by Pat Olliffe. Marvel Entertainment 2005 Un. Illustration
Grades: 7 8 9 10 11 12   **741.5; Fic**
  1. Avengers (Fictional characters); 2. Spider-Girl (Fictional character); 3. Superhero graphic novels; 4. Graphic novels
0-7851-1658-3, $7.99
The adventures of Spider-Man's daughter continue as Mayday Parker faces defeat and disgrace at the hands of Darkdevil and Kaine, then she has to prove her fighting mettle by taking on the Avengers one at a time. Plus: Beset by problems in her civilian guise, Spider-Girl teams up with Speedball to take on Mr. Abnormal, the most flexible felon of all.

Spider-Girl Vol. 4: Turning Point. Artist Pat Olliffe. Marvel Entertainment 2005 Un Illustration
Grades: 7 8 9 10 11 12   **741.5; Fic**
  1. Spider-Girl (Fictional character); 2. Spider-Man (Fictional character); 3. Superhero graphic novels; 4. Graphic novels
0-7851-1871-3, $7.99
The adventures of Spider-Man's daughter continue as Mayday once again faces Kaine, Spider-Man swings again, and Darkdevil is . . . actually nice" Plus: Meet new heroes and villains, take a peek into the fantasies of Mayday's friends, and witness the return of the Green Goblin. In May's life, she's caught between JJ (grandson of J. Jonah Jameson) and Brad; how is a girl to choose?

Spider-Girl Vol. 5: Endgame. Illustrated by Pat Olliffe. Marvel Entertainment 2006 Un Illustration
Grades: 7 8 9 10 11 12   **741.5; Fic**
  1. Spider-Girl (Fictional character); 2. Superhero graphic novels; 3. Graphic novels
0-7851-2034-3, $7.99
Spider-Girl faces trouble when her deadliest enemies join forces as the Savage Six (or is it Seven?)! But even with the help of rival/critic heroes like Darkdevil and the Buzz, can she deal with the sudden loss of her super-powers? And, naturally, that's when Normie Osborn escapes from the mental institution, convinced that he, as Green Goblin, must kill Spider-Girl.

Spider-girl Vol. 1: Legacy. Illustrated by Pat Olliffe. Marvel Comics 2004 144p. Illustration
Grades: 7 8 9 10 11 12   **741.5; Fic**
  1. Spider-Girl (Fictional character); 2. Spider-Man (Fictional character); 3. Superhero graphic novels; 4. Graphic novels
0-7851-1441-6, $7.99
In an alternate future in the Marvel Universe, Peter Parker has retired from being Spider-Man after a crippling injury; but he and Mary Jane have a daughter, May. She has just turned sixteen, and suddenly discovers she has superpowers! Soon she finds out who her father used to be, and she decides to be a superhero—but Peter knows the dangers all too well and tries to stop her. Once Mayday decides to be Spider-Girl, though, no one can stop her. This is the first of an ongoing series.

Spider-Girl Vol. 6: Too Many Spiders!. Artist Pat Olliffe. Marvel Entertainment 2006 Un Illustration
Grades: 7 8 9 10 11 12   **741.5; Fic**
  1. Spider-Girl (Fictional character); 2. Spider-Man (Fictional character); 3. Superhero graphic novels; 4. X-Men (Fictional characters); 5. Graphic novels
0-7851-2156-0, $7.99
Sworn to follow in her father's web tracks, "May Mayday" Parker's got a lot on her plate - but an upstart imitator wants to help himself to her heritage. Who is the new Spider-Man and what role will he play in Spider-Girl's reality? This volume guest-stars the Avengers of A-Next - with looks into the legacies of the FF, the X-Men and the New Warriors.

Spider-Girl Vol. 7: Betrayed. Illustrator Pat Olliffe. Marvel Entertainment 2006 Un Illustration
Grades: 7 8 9 10 11 12   **741.5; Fic**
  1. Spider-Girl (Fictional character); 2. Spider-Man (Fictional character); 3. Superhero graphic novels; 4. Graphic novels
0-7851-2157-9, $7.99
Who will lead the New York underworld? Will the Green Goblin go good or give grief? What secret is Mary Jane keeping? And who is the next true Spider-Man? This volume guest-stars the Fantastic Five.

Spider-Girl Vol. 8: Duty Calls. Illustrator Pat Olliffe. Marvel Entertainment 2007 Un Illustration
Grades: 7 8 9 10 11 12   **741.5; Fic**
  1. Adventure graphic novels; 2. Spider-Girl (Fictional character); 3. Spider-Man (Fictional character); 4. Superhero graphic novels; 5. Graphic novels
07851-2495-0, $7.99
Wall-crawling gets crowded when a new Spider-Man and Scarlet Spider swing into action, and the one true web-slinger joins Spider-Girl to clear up the costumed clonery. Plus: One of Spider-Girl's longtime foes meets his doom, prompting his family into vengeful action. And this volume introduces the MC-2 incarnation of the New Warriors.

Spider-Girl: Choices. Tom DeFalco, writer; Pat Olliffe, penciler; Al Williamson, inker; Janice Chiang, letterer; Christie Scheele, colorist; Bob Harras, chief. ABDO Spotlight 2006 Un Illustration

Grades: 5 6 7 8 9 10 11 12   **741.5; Fic**
1. Spider-Girl (Fictional character); 2. Spider-Man (Fictional character); 3. Superhero graphic novels; 4. Graphic novels
1-59961-028-0, $21.35

May, teenage daughter of Peter and Mary Jane Parker, has inherited her father's Spidey powers, but the former Spider-Man has forbidden her to use them; he doesn't want May to get crippled like him, or worse. However, May can't help but use her powers for good, so even though Peter has destroyed all the old Spider-Man equipment, May rescued some web shooters and web-cartridges. Dressed in an old gym suit and a skiing mask, she sets out to discover who has been following her father, who is working on a case involving organized crime. The book includes lots of action but little violence.

★ **Spider-Girl:** legacy . . . in black and white. ABDO Publishing Group/Spotlight 2006 Un Illustration
Grades: 5 6 7 8 9 10 11 12   **741.5; Fic**
1. Adventure graphic novels; 2. Spider-Girl (Fictional character); 3. Spider-Man (Fictional character); 4. Superhero graphic novels; 5. Graphic novels
1-59961-029-9; 978-1-59961-029-0, $21.35
                     LC 2006-44301

In an alternate Marvel Universe, Peter and Mary Jane Parker stayed married and had a daughter, May (nicknamed Mayday). Peter's superhero career as Spider-Man ended when the Green Goblin shattered his leg, and he and Mary Jane have kept all of this secret from May. Now she's fifteen years old, popular, a star basketball player " and during a game, the powers she inherited from her father kick in. As if that isn't shock enough, a new Hobgoblin comes after Peter Parker " it's another Osborne, Norman, grandson of the original Green Goblin and May's former playmate. Does she have enough Spidey powers to take him down before he hurts her parents" This is a library-bound edition of Spider-Girl #0, which was first Marvel What If #105, and which launched the Spider-Girl comics series.
Volume 1 of 12

DeFilippis, Nunzio
Destiny's Hand Volume 1. Written by Nunzio DeFilippis and Christina Weir ; illustrated by Melvin Calingo. Seven Seas Entertainment 2006 Un Illustration
Grades: 8 9 10 11 12   **741.5; Fic**
1. Adventure graphic novels; 2. Pirates; 3. Graphic novels
1-933164-11-5, $10.99

Destiny's Hand is a pirate ship that cannot be sunk, led by a dying Captain who will not give up. His final wish before he dies is to find the legendary Devil's Eye. And who does he appoint to lead his fearless crew in search of the lost treasure, but Olivia Soldana, a brash 16-year-old girl who can outdo any man. This is a global manga title published in the Japanese right-to-left format. There is hand-to-hand combat but no gore, and little strong language.

Once in a blue moon. Written by Nunzio DeFilippis & Christina Weir ; artwork by Jennifer Quick ; lettering by Jennie Jones ; design by Keith Wood ; edited by James Lucas Jones. Oni Press 2004 154p. Illustration
Grades: 6 7 8 9 10 11 12   **741.5; Fic**
1. Fantasy graphic novels; 2. Graphic novels

1-929998-83-X, $11.95

Aeslin had a magical childhood, with loving parents who read wonderful fables from the book, The Avalon Chronicles, about a fantastic world where a brave Dragon Knight and her Prince battled an Evil Wizard. Then, her parents left on a business trip from which only her mother returned. Her mother tried to erase any aspect of fantasy from Aeslin's life from that time. Now, she happens upon a new book, Once in a Blue Moon, and when she wishes she could go to Avalon to help the people, she finds herself magically transported there and learns she is the new Dragon Knight who must save the land.

Play ball. Written by Nunzio DeFilippis and Christina Weir ; illustrated by Jackie Lewis. Oni Press, Inc. 2012 144 p.
Grades: 6 7 8 9   **741.5/973; Fic**
1. Baseball; 2. School stories; 3. Women athletes
1934964794; 9781934964798, $19.99
                     LC 2011933142

This comic "traces a high school girl's struggle to join a boys' baseball team. Freckle-faced Dashiell Brody was good at softball in her private girls' school; now that she's moved to another city with her mother and older sister and they must enroll in public school, she wants to play the real game, despite stereotypical resistance from school administrators and some jocks." (Publishers Weekly)

Del Rio, Tania
Sabrina the Teenage Witch: The Magic Revisited. Archie Comics 2006 Un Illustration
Grades: 4 5 6 7 8 9   **741.5; Fic**
1. Fantasy graphic novels; 2. Humorous graphic novels; 3. Witches; 4. Graphic novels
1-879794-19-5, $7.49

The first four issues of Sabrina the Teenage Witch's "manga makeover" are collected in this special edition trade paperback. Writer-artist Tania del Rio presents these tales of magical flights of fancy and romantic intrigue... sprinkled with a dash of humor. Sabrina's awakening powers and the various love triangle combinations that have formed since keep her busy at school, on dates, and ... everywhere.

Delano, Jamie
Outlaw Nation. Art by Goran Sudzuka and Goran Parlov. Image Comics 2006 458p. Illustration
Grades: 12 Adult   **741.5; Fic**
1. Adventure graphic novels; 2. Revenge; 3. Graphic novels
978-1-58240-707-4, $15.99

Story Johnson, a hundred-year-old semi-deranged amnesiac pulp fiction-writer returns home from 25 years MIA in Vietnam. All Story wants is to recover his missing time and catch up with some legendary, larger-than-life Johnson Family members. Trouble is, a lot of cousins have "disappeared," and those that are left have put the blame on him. This story is full of graphic violence, very strong language, nudity, and sexual situations.

Delisle, Guy

★ **Pyongyang:** a journey in North Korea. Translated by Helge Dascher. Drawn & Quarterly 2005 176p. Illustration; Map

Grades: 11 12 Adult   **951.93; 741; 741.5**
   1. Korea (North); 2. Graphic novels
   1-896597-89-0; 1-897299-21-4 (pa), $14.95

This book "documents the two months French animator Delisle spent overseeing cartoon production in North Korea. . . . He records everything from the omnipresent statues and portraits of dictators Kim Il-Sung and Kim Jong-Il to the brainwashed obedience of the citizens." Booklist

"Pyongyang will appeal to multiple audiences: current events buffs, Persepolis fans and those who just love a good yarn." Publ Wkly

Shenzhen: A Travelogue from China. Drawn & Quarterly 2006 148p. Illustration

Grades: 10 11 12 Adult   **741.5**
   1. Autobiographical graphic novels; 2. Graphic novels
   1-896597-79-1, $19.95

Shenzhen details Guy Delisle's observations of life in a cold urban city in southern China in 1997 that is sealed off from the rest of the country by electric fences and armed guards. With a dry wit and a clean line, Delisle makes the most of his time spent in Asia overseeing outsourced production for a French animation company. By translating his fish-out-of-water experiences into graphic novels, Delisle is quick to find the humor and point out the differences between Western and Eastern cultures. Yet he never forgets his compassion for the simple freedoms that escape his colleagues by virtue of living in a Communist state. Delisle uses the occasional "s-word."

DeMatteis, J. M.

Abadazad: The Dream Thief by J.M. DeMatteis ; drawings by Mike Ploog ; colors by Nick Bell. Hyperion Books for Children 2006 Un Illustration

Grades: 5 6 7 8 9   **741.5; Fic**
   1. Adventure graphic novels; 2. Fantasy graphic novels; 3. Graphic novels
   1-4231-00646, $9.99

In the magical land of Abadazad, Kate needs all the help she can get when she encounters the Lanky Man. He's mean and heartless, and he wants to steal children's dreams. Everyone seems to be against her, which only makes her more determined to find her brother. And Matt is getting closer, isn't he? This story is a hybrid, combining prose text with pages of sequential art from the original comic books.

Abadazad: The Road to Inconceivable. Hyperion Books for Children 2006 Un Illustration

Grades: 5 6 7 8 9   **741.5; Fic**
   1. Adventure graphic novels; 2. Fantasy graphic novels; 3. Graphic novels
   1-4231-0062-X, $9.99

Kate's little brother Matt disappeared five years ago, and Kate thinks she will never see him again. But then she finds out that Matt is trapped in the world of Abadazad. Will Kate have the courage to look for her brother? And if she leaves home, will she ever return? This story began as comic books, but the publisher went out of business before the story was completed. Now it's published as a hybrid,

combining prose sections with pages of sequential art and spot illustrations.

★ The **stardust** kid. Boom! created by J. M. DeMatteis, writer & Mike Ploog, illustrator ; Nick Bell & Sumi Pak, color ; Dave Lanphear, lettering. Studios 2008 Un Illustration

Grades: 3 4 5 6 7 8 9 10 11 12 Adult   **741.5; Fic**
   1. Adventure graphic novels; 2. Fantasy graphic novels; 3. Graphic novels
   978-1-934506-04-2, $14.99

Twelve-year-old Cody's best friend is Paul Brightfield; they share a deep bond that goes far beyond mere friendship. What no one else knows is that Paul isn't human, he's one of the last Old Ones, ancient elemental beings who lived before man existed. One night, Paul disappears, and a hate-filled creature who has existed long buried beneath Wilde Park bursts out with a desire to destroy everything in the world. Only Cody, his little sister K.M., and his friend Alana and her little brother Nathaniel, remain, and somehow they must find The Stardust Kid and discover a way to stop the hate and restore their world. Some creatures might be frightening to younger readers, but anyone who likes the Harry Potter books shouldn't have a problem with this book.

Denson, Abby

Tough Love: High School Confidential. Manic D Press 2006 144p. Illustration

Grades: 8 9 10 11 12 Adult   **741.5; Fic**
   1. Homosexuality; 2. Romance graphic novels; 3. Graphic novels
   978-1-933149-08-0, $12.95

In this sweet teen romance graphic novel, shy Brian discovers he loves martial artist Chris, but also develops a supportive friendship with Julie, the first person he's ever told that he's gay. Denson was inspired by shonen-ai (boy love) manga to do an American comic depicting a positive, healthy relationship between two teen boys who accept what they are. The story was originally serialized in XY magazine. The boys are shown hugging and kissing, but that is all.

Desberg, Stephen

The **Scorpion:** the devil's mark. Art by Enrico Merini. Cinebook Ltd. 2008 96p. Illustration

Grades: 10 11 12 Adult   **741.5; Fic**
   1. Adventure graphic novels; 2. Rome — History; 3. Graphic novels
   978-1-905460-62-5, $19.95

In Rome of the Renaissance, a young thief called the Scorpion makes a living by unearthing relics in the depths of the Roman Catacombs, which he then sells at high prices to princes, nobles, and bishops. Then Cardinal Trebaldi declares the Scorpion must die. Trebaldi is part of a group called the Nine Families, who made a pact to rule the world back in the time of the Caesars; he has now organized an army of warrior monks to carry out his will, and he has gained the approval of the Nine Families to assassinate the Pope so he can take over and rule Rome. Somehow, the Scorpion threatens that plan. Trebaldi sets a beautiful Egyptian poisoner on the Scorpion's trail, but they will both face betrayal and confront amazing truths. The book includes lots of blade fighting and sexual innuendo without any overt nudity or sexual content.

Dezago, Todd
Spider-man and Thor: out of time. Todd Dezago, script ; Ron Lim, pencils ; Scott Koblish, inks ; Dave Sharpe, letters ; Digital Rainbow, colors. ABDO Publishing Company/Spotlight 2006 Un Illustration
Grades: 4 5 6 7 8 9   **741.5; Fic**
1. Spider-Man (Fictional character); 2. Superhero graphic novels; 3. Thor (Fictional character); 4. Graphic novels
1-59961-004-3, $21.35
It takes both Spider-Man and the Mighty Thor to deal with things when an Asgardian enemy, Kryllk, regains control of the Frostgaard Crystal; it allows him to freeze time so he and his troll hordes can conquer Midgard, er, Earth, and the gods' realm of Asgard as well. But now Kryllk faces two heroes at the same time. This is a revised, hardbound edition of the Marvel Age comic book.
Part of the Spider-Man Team Up series

Di Filippo, Paul
Top 10: Beyond the Farthest Precinct. Art by Jerry Ordway. DC Comics/America's Best Comics 2006 Un Illustration
Grades: 10 11 12 Adult   **741.5; Fic**
1. Mystery graphic novels; 2. Superhero graphic novels; 3. Graphic novels
978-1-4012-0991-9, $14.99
In Neopolis, a modern city populated exclusively by super beings, it takes a unique and powerful police force to protect and serve. The officers of Precinct 10, also known as Top Ten, encounter all manner of the super powered and the supernatural on a routine basis. It doesn't help matters when Captain Traynor (Jetman) is unceremoniously replaced. Now the officers must band together, overcome their personal squabbles, and get their city back on track, before it all comes tumbling down on their heads. The book includes some sexual situations.

Dickens, Charles, 1812-1870
Classics Illustrated Deluxe #8: Oliver Twist. By Loic Dauvillier; illustrated by Olivier Deloye. Papercutz 2012 238 p.
Grades: 6 7 8 9 10 11 12   **741.5**
1. London (England) — Fiction; 2. Orphans — Fiction; 3. Graphic novels
9781597073073; 1597073075
This graphic novel, by Charles Dickens, adapted by Loic Dauvillier, and illustrated by Olivier Deloye, is part of the "Classic Illustrated Deluxe" series. "The story is about an orphan, Oliver Twist, who endures a miserable existence in a workhouse and then is placed with an undertaker. He escapes and travels to London where he meets . . . a gang of juvenile pickpockets. Naively unaware of their unlawful activities, Oliver is led to the lair of their elderly criminal trainer Fagin." (Wikipedia)

Diggle, Andy
John Constantine, Hellblazer: Lady Constantine. Goran Sudzuka, artist; Patricia Mulvihill, colorist; Robert Solanovic, letterer. DC Comics/Vertigo 2006 96p. Illustration
Grades: 11 12 Adult   **741.5; Fic**
1. Adventure graphic novels; 2. Horror graphic novels; 3. Graphic novels
978-1-4012-0942-1, $9.99
It's 1785 England, and Johanna Constantine is a young woman with a knack for the impossible, a taste for the good life - and a knowledge of the dark arts. She accepts a dangerous assignment for king and country to retrieve a mysterious ancient chest, but hidden forces move against her, seeking the box for their own deadly purposes. The book includes nudity, sexual situations, strong language, considerable violence and horror.

The **Losers** Vol. 4: Close Quarters. Andy Diggle, writer; Jock, Ben Oliver, artists; Lee Loughridge, colorist; Clem Robins, letterer. DC Comics/Vertigo 2005 144p. Illustration
Grades: 10 11 12 Adult   **741.5; Fic**
1. Adventure graphic novels; 2. Graphic novels
1-4012-0719-7, $14.99
The Losers' pursuit of rogue C.I.A. mastermind Max has led them to London, where a potential trove of information on their quarry's financial dealings awaits them at the money-laundering offices of Cayman Credit Internationale ... provided they can get past the Company-sponsored welcoming committee. Following the money will only take them so far, though. To find out what all that cash is for, the Losers will need to head out to sea, and what they discover both above and below the waves will raise the stakes of this deadly game to a whole new level. The book includes harsh language, lots of action and some graphic violence.

The **Losers**: Ante Up. Andy Diggle, writer; Jock, artist & original series covers; Lee Loughridge, colorist; Clem Robins, letterer. DC Comics/Vertigo 2004 160p. Illustration
Grades: 10 11 12 Adult   **741.5; Fic**
1. Adventure graphic novels; 2. Graphic novels
1-4012-0198-9, $9.95
An elite U.S. Special Forces unit is targeted for assassination when they unintentionally uncover the illegal and immoral practices of the C.I.A. Believed dead and with nothing to lose, the team of wet works operatives regroup and begin a mission of revenge against the organization that betrayed them. Only as the team goes after a corrupt oil conglomerate with ties to the C.I.A., do they truly begin to realize the depths of the conspiracy they have discovered and the impossible odds of survival that they face. The book includes lots of foul language and some fairly graphic violence.
Other volumes in this series are: Double down (2004); Trifecta (2005); Close quarters (2006); Endgame (2006)

The **Losers**: Endgame. Andy Diggle, writer; Jock, Colin Wilson, artists; Lee Loughridge, colorist; Clem Robins, letterer. DC Comics/Vertigo 2006 168p. Illustration
Grades: 11 12 Adult   **741.5; Fic**
1. Adventure graphic novels; 2. Spies; 3. Graphic novels
978-1-4012-1004-5, $14.99
The seemingly unstoppable C.I.A. mastermind Max is about to play his final hand, and he's sitting on a whole pile of aces. With a brand-new country under his feet and a nuclear arsenal within his reach, Max is going all in - and the

stakes are nothing less than the global balance of power itself. As all the other players are folding, though, the Losers are still holding their cards, and they've got one last chance to raise the bet. But calling Max will cost them dearly, especially considering the joker they're about to be dealt. This book has lots of violence and copious use of foul language.

Silent Dragon. Writer, Andy Diggle; penciler, Leinil Yu; inkers, Gerry Alanguilan and Richard Friend; colors, Dave Stewart; letters, Jared K. Fletcher. DC Comics/Wildstorm 2006 Un Illustration
Grades: 10 11 12 Adult   741.5; Fic
   1. Adventure graphic novels; 2. Science fiction graphic novels; 3. Graphic novels
   978-1-4012-1104-2, $19.99
   Tokyo, A.D. 2063: the Yakuza warlord Hideaki has seized total control of Honshu's underworld while ruthlessly crushing all opposition. But his true dream is the overthrow of the government itself. Japan's hard-line military junta will do anything to stop him and they have found the ultimate pawn to set their plan in motion: Renjiro, the chief advisor to the notorious gangster. Caught between a lifetime of honor and loyalty to his Yakuza clan and the iron-fisted might of the military elite, Renjiro will find that the only way to stop a civil war and avoid total annihilation is to play both sides against the middle. The book includes partial nudity, strong language, and lots of bloody violence.

Dini, Paul
   The **World's** Greatest Super-Heroes. Stories by Alex Ross and Paul Dini ; text by Paul Dini ; art by Alex Ross ; lettering on JLA: liberty and justice by Todd Klein. DC Comics 2005 Un Illustration
Grades: 6 7 8 9 10 11 12 Adult   741.5; Fic
   1. Batman (Fictional character); 2. Justice League (Fictional characters); 3. Superhero graphic novels; 4. Superman (Fictional character); 5. Wonder Woman (Fictional character); 6. Graphic novels
   1-4012-0254-3, $49.95
                           LC 2006-159064
   This oversize hardcover volume collects the stories that DC originally published separately. Superman tries to singlehandedly end world hunger, only to face suspicion and corruption; Batman tries to stop all criminal activity; and Wonder Woman tries to free oppressed women. They each realize that, despite their super powers, they can't eradicate the problems of the world on their own. The rest of the book portrays the Justice League and highlights each member's super hero origins.

Dirge, Roman
   It ate Billy on Christmas; art by Steven Daily. Dark Horse Books 2007 Un Illustration
Grades: 4 5 6 7 8 9 10 11 12 Adult   741.5; Fic
   1. Horror graphic novels; 2. Humorous graphic novels; 3. Graphic novels
   978-1-59307-853-9, $12.95
   Lumi has been bullied by her brother Billy all her life, and this Christmas would have been more of the same, but for the weird, ugly little monster that crawled up from the abandoned well and came into their house. Mistaking it for

the stuffed puppy she had requested from her parents, Lumi watches in amazement as it devours the bullying Billy when he shoots it with darts from his new dart gun. She makes a cardboard Billy, which fools her unsuspecting and clueless parents. A few weeks later, back at school, Lumi has to face the bullies who have made her school life miserable, but she has her "puppy" in her backpack and it's hungry. . . . Dirge wrote the story and drew the black and white illustrations, while Daily provided the color paintings. The story shows the monster eating Billy in one gulp, but there's little actual violence on the pages. The dark humor and twisted story line will appeal to those who enjoy Coraline and The Wolves in the Walls by Neil Gaiman, and the weird humor of Edward Gorey cartoons.

   Lenore: Noogies. Slave Labor Graphics 1999 Un Illustration
Grades: 9 10 11 12 Adult   741.5; Fic
   1. Horror graphic novels; 2. Humorous graphic novels; 3. Graphic novels
   0-943151-03-1, $11.95
   This book collects the first four issues of the Lenore comic book series. It ventures into the dark, surreal world of a little dead girl and features stories about limbless cannibals, clock monsters, cursed vampire dolls, taxidermied friends, an obsessed would be lover, and more fuzzy animal mutilations than should be legal. The book includes some disturbing images and macabre humor.
   Other Lenore books are: Wedgies (2000); Cooties (2005); Swirlies (2012); Purple Nurples (2013)

   Something at the Window is Scratching: Children's Tales for Disturbed Children. SLG Publishing 1998 120p. Illustration
Grades: 9 10 11 12 Adult   741.5; Fic
   1. Horror graphic novels; 2. Humorous graphic novels; 3. Graphic novels
   0-943151-09-0, $9.95
   Chilling, disturbing, sickly amusing poems accompanied by equally chilling, disturbing, and sickly amusing illustrations bring to mind a very morbid Shel Silverstein with more of a horror twist. In the title tale, what's scratching at the boy's window that night is the son of the Sandman, who died after sending the boy to sleep; in order to give the creature a home, the boy tapes a tail to the creature and presents his parents with their new cat. Despite the moody, dark tone, there is no violence or bad language.

Dixon, Chuck
   The **Iron** Ghost. Art by Flint Henry and Sergio Cariello. Image Comics 2007 Un Illustration
Grades: 10 11 12 Adult   741.5; Fic
   1. Mystery graphic novels; 2. World War, 1939-1945; 3. Graphic novels
   978-1-58240-727-2, $15.99
   Berlin, Germany, 1945: The tide of the war has turned in favor of the Allies. The fall of the Nazi empire is inevitable, but there is still something even more dangerous than the ever approaching Allies to the Third Reich: The Iron Ghost, who is murdering officials in the Nazi regime. It's up to two non-Nazi German police officers to capture the Ghost. But once they discover the truth will they want to - or even be

able to - stop him? The story includes harsh language and considerable violence.

Nightwing: On the Razor's Edge. Pencilled by Greg Land et al; inked by Drew Geraci et al. DC Comics 2005 192p. Illustration
Grades: 9 10 11 12 Adult   **741.5; Fic**
1. Mystery graphic novels; 2. Nightwing (Fictional character); 3. Superhero graphic novels; 4. Graphic novels
1-4012-0437-6, $14.99

Bludhaven has seen its share of battles between its costumed protector, Nightwing, and various criminals. But when an army of ninjas arrives, it's only a harbinger of the deadliest threat yet. Shrike, long thought dead, is back, and he wants revenge on his childhood pal, Nightwing. Shrike's current master, Blockbuster, would be only too happy to see the vigilante destroyed, but Shrike wants to see to Nightwing's destruction personally.

Robin, year one. Chuck Dixon, Scott Beatty, writers; Javier Pulido, Marcos Martin, pencillers; Robert Campanella, inker; Lee Loughridge, colorist; Sean Konot, letterer. DC Comics 2008 200p. Illustration
Grades: 9 10 11 12 Adult   **741.5; Fic**
1. Batman (Fictional character); 2. Robin (Fictional character); 3. Superhero graphic novels; 4. Graphic novels
978-1-563-89805-1, $14.99

This book takes readers back to Dick Grayson's first year working as Robin, sidekick of the Batman. After his family of aerialists was murdered, Bruce Wayne took in young Dick Grayson, who helped Wayne as Batman solve the murders. Adopted by Wayne, Dick starts training to become his partner in solving crimes on the streets of Gotham City; but not everyone likes it. Captain James Gordon of the Gotham City Police thinks Dick is much too young, and he puts Batman on notice that if anything happens to hurt or kill Robin, Batman will pay. At first, Dick/Robin can easily handle the bad guys. Then he ends up working solo on a case of girls who disappear when one of his friends from school goes missing, and he goes up against the Mad Hatter. Unknown to Robin, or Batman, Two-Face is watching the young crime-fighter's progress, and he decides to test the boy—brutally. When Two-Face beats Robin badly enough to put him into a hospital, Batman "retires" Robin; but when Dick is strong enough, he runs away to live on the streets. There, he encounters Shrike, a contract killer who trains teen boys in ninja-style fighting, and joins his "school," an organization that Dick realizes Batman doesn't know exists. The book includes strong violence.

Transformers: Evolutions: Hearts of Steel; art by Guido Guidi IDW Publishing 2006 120p. Illustration
Grades: 4 5 6 7 8 9   **741.5; Fic**
1. Science fiction graphic novels; 2. Transformers (Fictional characters); 3. Graphic novels
978-1-60010-055-4, $19.99

In this new Transformers story, writer Chuck Dixon and artist Guido Guidi transplant the 'bots to the Industrial Revolution, where a charismatic hammer-man named John Henry discovers that a steam drill is really an alien robot named Bumblebee. Before he can process this information, the pair is attacked by Decepticons disguised as tanks, trains and walking engines. Is this all part of a larger scheme by Starscream" And if so, will the other Autobots arrive in time

to stop his nefarious plans? Mark Twain is among the humans who work with the Autobots.

The **Vanishers**. Illustrated by Andres Klacik. IDW Publishing 2002 80p. Illustration
Grades: 6 7 8 9 10 11 12 Adult   **741.5; Fic**
1. Adventure graphic novels; 2. Science fiction graphic novels; 3. Graphic novels
0-9712282-6-4, $12.99

From the turn of the 20th century, to medieval England, and into the far-flung future, Andy and Arvis must escape their pursuers, rescue their friends, and return to their own time. Andy's friends begin to disappear and only he remembers that they ever existed. When Andy discovers another student, Arvis Voltoz, has noticed that disappearances, he follows Arvis home and begins an adventure that takes him and Arvis through time.

Doctorow, Cory
★ **Cory** Doctorow's futuristic tales of the here and now. IDW Publishing 2008 152p. Illustration
Grades: 10 11 12 Adult   **741.5; Fic**
1. Science fiction graphic novels; 2. Short stories; 3. Graphic novels
978-1-60010-172-4, $24.99

Six short stories by noted young science fiction writer and BoingBoing.net coeditor Doctorow are adapted into the graphic format by various comics creators, including Dara Naraghi, Dan Taylor, J. C. Vaughn, James Anthony Kuhoric, Esteve Polls, Daniel Warner, Paul McCaffrey, Dustin Evans, Erich Owen, Robbie Robbins, Chris Mowry, and more. The stories include "Anda's Game," in which a twelve-year-old girl gets involved in a multi-player game in which she kills enemies and someone starts paying cash for her kills; "Craphound," in which a professional yard sale picker makes friends with one of the aliens who had come to Earth and wants to learn how to be a picker at yard sales; "After the Siege," in which Valentine and her family struggle to survive the disease turning the city's people into zombies as they try to get by during a siege; and "When Sysadmins Ruled the Earth," in which a global catastrophe destroys almost everything, except the computer techs holed up in various company buildings around the world. The stories include violence and some strong language.

In Real Life. Cory Doctorow; illustrated by Jen Wang. First Second Books 2014 192 p. Color; Illustration
Grades: 8 9 10 11 12   **741.5**
1. Computer games — Economic aspects; 2. Ethics; 3. Video games
1596436581; 9781596436589, $17.99

In this graphic novel, "online gaming and real life collide when a teen discovers the hidden economies and injustices that hide among seemingly innocent pixels. . . . Anda joins . . . a group of girls playing the game as girl avatars. . . . Another guild member named Lucy . . . asks her if she'd be interested in earning 'real cash.' . . . She's pulled into a world of real-money economies where workers 'play' the game, garnering items they can then sell for actual money to other players." (Kirkus Reviews)

"Characters come to life through Wang's . . . fluid forms and emotive faces, and her adroit shift in colors as the story moves between the physical and gaming worlds is subtle and effective." Pub Wkly

Doeden, Matt

George Washington: Leading a New Nation; by Matt Doeden ; illustrated by Cynthia Martin. Capstone Press 2006 32p. Illustration

Grades: 3 4 5 6 7 8 9   **741.5; 973.4; 92**
  1. Washington, George, 1732-1799; 2. Graphic novels
0-7368-4963-7, $25.26

                     LC 2005006530

This book uses the comic book format to recount highlights in the life of George Washington, the leader of the Continental Army during the Revolutionary War and the first President of the United States. It includes additional information, a glossary, a list of books for further reading, and more.

Part of the Graphic Library, Graphic Biographies series.

John Sutter and the California Gold Rush; by Matt Doeden ; illustrated by Ron Frenz and Charles Barnett III. Capstone Press 2006 32p. Illustration

Grades: 3 4 5 6 7 8 9   **741.5; 979.4**
  1. California — Gold discoveries; 2. Sutter, John Augustus, 1803-1880; 3. Graphic novels
0-7368-4370-1, $25.26

                     LC 2005007890

This book tells the story in comic book format of the discovery of gold at John Sutter's mill and how it changed California. It includes additional information, a glossary, a list of books for further reading, and more.

Part of the Graphic Library, Graphic History series.

Winter at Valley Forge by Matt Doeden ; illustrated by Ron Frenz and Charles Barnett III ; [colorist, Bill Anderson]. Capstone Press 2006 32p. Illustration

Grades: 3 4 5 6 7 8 9   **741.5; 973.3**
  1. Pennsylvania — History; 2. United States — History — 1775-1783, Revolution; 3. Valley Forge (Pa) — History; 4. Graphic novels
0-7368-4975-0, $25.26

                     LC 2005010145

This book uses the comic book format to tell the story of the American patriot troops during the Revolutionary War while wintering at Valley Forge, Pennsylvania. It includes additional information, a glossary, a list of books for further reading, and more.

Part of the Graphic Library, Graphic History series.

Dominguez, Richard

Frank Zamboni and the Ice-Resurfacing Machine. Capstone Press 2007 32p. Illustration

Grades: 3 4 5 6 7 8 9   **688.7; 741.5; 92**
  1. Ice skating; 2. Inventors; 3. Zamboni, Frank; 4. Graphic novels
1429601477; 9781429601474, $29.99

                     LC 2007000254

This book uses the graphic novel format to tell how Frank Zamboni created the ice-resurfacing machine, and how it affected the world of ice-based sports. The book includes additional facts and a list of books for further reading.

Part of the Graphic Library Inventions and Discovery series.

Donner, Rebecca

Burnout. Written by Rebecca Donner; illustrated by Inaki Miranda. DC Comics/Minx 2008 176p. Illustration

Grades: 7 8 9 10 11 12   **741.5; Fic**
  1. Environmental protection; 2. Romance graphic novels; 3. Graphic novels
978-1-4012-1537-8, $9.99

Danni and her mother have made another in a long series of moves, this time moving in with her mother's boyfriend, lodge owner Hank. Danni can see that Hank is an alcoholic, and he tends to take his anger out on people, including his son Haskell (with whom Danni is forced to share a room for the time being). They live in the Pacific Northwest, in a logging town, and Haskell is a hardcore environmentalist. Danni falls for him despite herself, and she begins to go with him at night to spike trees, which is an act of ecoterrorism. As home life continues to stay rough, Haskell starts to escalate his acts against logging, and Danni has to decide what to do. The book includes scenes of heavy petting.

"Miranda's superb illustrations complement the story well, whether they're showing landscapes of the Pacific Northwest, action sequences, or the eyes of a troubled girl." Publ Wkly

Doran, Colleen

A **Distant** Soil Vol. 1: The Gathering. Image Comics 1997 Un Illustration

Grades: 10 11 12 Adult   **741.5; Fic**
  1. Adventure graphic novels; 2. Fantasy graphic novels; 3. Graphic novels
1-887279-51-2, $19.95

This is the story of a young girl who is born the heir to an alien religious dynasty, one of comics' most lavish and romantic sagas. Liana and her brother Jason are orphaned and live in a research institution; they get caught up in interplanetary politics and magic. The book includes fantasy, epic scope, psychics, Arthurian legend, smart-mouthed punks, adorable gay couples, bizarre clothing, aliens, death, love, and heavy doses of humor.

A **Distant** Soil Vol. 2: The Ascendant. Image Comics 2000 Un Illustration

Grades: 10 11 12 Adult   **741.5; Fic**
  1. Adventure graphic novels; 2. Fantasy graphic novels; 3. Graphic novels
1-58240-018-0, $18.95

Liana was born the heir to an alien religious dynasty, then hidden on Earth until Rieken found her and brought her back. But the galaxy's most powerful psionic, the Avatar, already sits on the throne. Revolutionary forces on the planet have taken Jason, however, and intend to turn him into one of their weapons against the throne. Things continue to become more complicated when Jason learns his father started the Resistance movement on Ovanan, and Liana learns that Rieken is actually Seren, the Avatar, and she's a danger to him. Dangerous politics swirl around everyone. The book includes sexual suggestiveness and violence.

A **Distant** Soil Vol. 3: Aria. Image Comics 2001 Un Illustration
Grades: 11 12 Adult   **741.5; Fic**
  1. Adventure graphic novels; 2. Fantasy graphic novels; 3. Graphic novels
  1-58240-201-9, $16.95

    Rieken/Seren is the target of assassins, a pawn in a dangerous game of powerful psionics, and he makes a desperate play for freedom. But his ploy threatens to capture him in his own web of deceit, as his darkest secrets are revealed to allies and enemies alike, leading to a showdown with deadly consequences. And Liana, with powers of the Avatar, and Jason, are caught in the middle. The book includes lots of sexual situations, including same-sex relations, harsh language (including f-bombs), and violence.

A **Distant** Soil Vol. 4: Coda. Image Comics 2005 Un Illustration
Grades: 11 12 Adult   **741.5; Fic**
  1. Adventure graphic novels; 2. Fantasy graphic novels; 3. Graphic novels
  1-58240-478-X, $17.99

    Liana is born the heir to an alien religious dynasty. Possessing the power to destroy worlds with her mind, Liana is under an assassination order from the government of her father's home world. A foiled coup attempt results in a power vacuum that leaves the alien world without its treasure weapon. The aliens have no choice but to take Liana as their reluctant new Avatar. Only an angry slave and a small group of resistance fighters can free her - and the universe - from the dangers of her power. The book includes some strong language, nudity, and violence.

Dorkin, Evan
  ★ **Beasts** of Burden: animal rites. Written by Evan Dorkin; art by Jill Thompson; lettering by Jason Arthur and Jill Thompson. Dark Horse Comics 2010 184p. Illustration
Grades: 8 9 10 11 12 Adult   **741.5; Fic**
  1. Cats; 2. Dogs; 3. Mystery graphic novels; 4. Supernatural graphic novels; 5. Graphic novels
  978-1-59582-513-1, $19.99

  2010 Eisner Award for Best Publication for Teens; 2010 Eisner Award to Jill Thompson for Best Painter/Multimedia Artist for Beasts of Burden and Magic Trixie; 2005 Eisner Award for Best Short Story for 'Unfamiliar;' 2004 Eisner Award to Jill Thompson for Best Painter/Multimedia Artist (interior art) for 'Stray.'

    Burden Hill is just a nice, quiet suburban town full of houses with yards and white picket fences, demonic frogs, zombie roadkill, ghosts, etc. The humans who live in Burden Hill seem to be totally oblivious to the dangers, but the dogs, and one cat, work together to keep their town safe. Jack the beagle, Pugsley (go figure), Ace the husky, Rex the Doberman, Whitey the terrier, and Orphan the cat deal with a haunted dog house, witches, undead dogs, a werewolf, and other monsters. The book includes some mild bad language (—crap" usually from Pugs) and a fair amount of violence. This book includes the four-issue miniseries plus all of the short stories that originally appeared in The Dark Horse

Book of Hauntings, The Dark Horse Book of Witchcraft, The Dark Horse Book of the Dead, and The Dark Horse Book of Monsters. Sarah Dyer co-wrote "A Dog and His Boy" with Evan Dorkin.

    "Gorgeous artwork and a smart, witty script elevate this tale of household pets who unite to fight occult menaces in idyllic Burden Hill." Publ Wkly

Bill & Ted's Most Excellent Adventures Volume Two. Amaze Ink/SLG Publishing 2005 Un Illustration
Grades: 9 10 11 12 Adult   **741.5; Fic**
  1. Humorous graphic novels; 2. Graphic novels
  1-59362-002-0, $13.95

    The silly and fun movies "Bill and Ted's Excellent Adventure" and its sequel, "Bill and Ted's Bogus Journey" inspired a Marvel Comics series in the early 1990s. Written by Evan Dorkin, it was nominated for an Eisner Award. This second volume finds the two time-hopping headbangers on the run from a gang from Hell, on trial for tampering with time, and stuck on a planet of superheroes. There's also an invasion of inter-dimensional Bills and Teds, a pink-slipped Death, and a bogus attempt to prevent Lincoln's assassination.

Doucet, Julie
  365 days: a diary by Julie Doucet. Drawn & Quarterly 2008 360p. Illustration
Grades: 12 Adult   **741.5**
  1. Art; 2. Autobiographical graphic novels; 3. Graphic novels
  978-1-89729-915-9; 1-89729-915-X

    Doucet renounced her comics-centric lifestyle five years ago and focused on art, but the journal she started in late 2002 combines comics with art with text. Her personal narrative combines with collage, doodles, and comics panels to chronicle her life as she became part of a broader arts community. The book includes some harsh language, and one panel towards the end depicts an image combining nudity with a disturbing sexual situation.

Doxiadis, Apostolos
  ★ **Logicomix**. [written by] Apostolos Doxiadis, Christos H. Papadimitriou; art, Alecos Papadatos; color, Annie Di Donna. Bloomsbury 2009 347p. Illustration
Grades: 11 12 Adult
741.5; Fic
  1. Biographical graphic novels; 2. Essayists; 3. Logicians; 4. Mathematicians; 5. Nobel laureates for literature; 6. Nonfiction writers; 7. Philosophers; 8. Philosophy; 9. Russell, Bertrand, 1872-1970 — Fiction; 10. Graphic novels
  0-7475-9720-0, $22.95; 978-0-7475-9720-9

Courtesy of Bloomsbury

This is a "graphic novel based on the life of the philosopher and mathematician Bertrand Russell." (Publisher's note)

Doyle, Arthur Conan
The **hound** of the Baskervilles: a Sherlock Holmes mystery. By Sir Arthur Conan Doyle; retold by Martin Powell; illustrated by Daniel Perez. Stone Arch Books 2009 63p. Illustration
Grades: 4 5 6 7 8 9 10   **741.5; Fic**
   1. Holmes, Sherlock (Fictional character); 2. Mystery graphic novels; 3. Graphic novels
978-1-4342-0755-5, $23.93

LC 2008-6247

Late one night, Sir Charles Baskerville is attacked and killed outside his home in Dartmoor, England. Some say that the legendary monster, the Hound of the Baskervilles, has come back. Now Sherlock Holmes and Dr. Watson investigate the mystery, in order to protect the Baskerville heir, who has just come from America. This graphic novel adapts Doyle's one full-length mystery novel featuring his famous character.

Part of the Graphic Revolve series

Drake, Arnold
It Rhymes with Lust. Illustrations by Matt Baker and Ray Osrin. Dark Horse Books 2007 136p. Illustration
Grades: 10 11 12 Adult   **741.5; Fic**
   1. Mystery graphic novels; 2. Graphic novels
978-1-59307-728-0, $14.95

In 1950, writers Arnold Drake and Leslie Waller, both attending college on the G.I. Bill, envisioned a sophisticated, novel-length comic tailored to their peers. Collaborating with comic art master Matt Baker, known for singularly defining the genre of "good girl art" on titles such as Phantom Lady, they crafted a film-noir inspired masterwork of romance, intrigue, and moral relativity. When cynical newspaperman Hal Weber reunites with old flame Rust Masson, he finds the beguiling widow of a mining magnate willing to do anything to undermine the local political machine - her only opponent for total control of Copper City. This is a "replica edition" of the "picture novel" (as Drake called it); it will appeal most to adults, but there's little in the way of harsh language or any sexual content, and the violence is not graphically portrayed.

Drooker, Eric
Blood song: a silent ballad. Introduction by Joe Sacco. Dark Horse 2009 Un Illustration
Grades: 11 12 Adult   **741.5**
   1. Stories without words; 2. Graphic novels
978-1-59582-389-2, $19.95

"Driven by war from their rural home in Southeast Asia, a young woman and her dog ride the ocean currents to a city in the West. A deeply moving graphic novel, masterfully done." SLJ

First published 2002 by Harcourt

Dryer, Matt
Dwight T. Albatross's The Goon Noir. Dark Horse Comics 2007 Illustration

Grades: 11 12 Adult   **741.5; Fic**
   1. Horror graphic novels; 2. Humorous graphic novels; 3. Graphic novels
978-1-59307-785-3, $12.95

The horror comedy series has been described as "EC by way of Looney Tunes," so it seems fitting that comedians and horror creators put their own spin on the Goon characters. Among the distinguished creators featured in this, the very first Goon anthology, are comedians Patton Oswalt and Brian Posehn (both of Comedy Central's Comedians of Comedy and Mr. Show), Reno: 911 co-creator Thomas Lennon, B.P.R.D. scribe John Arcudi, comics great Kevin Nowlan (Tomorrow Stories, Sandman, Superman), fan-favorite Humberto Ramos (Revelations, Spider-Man), Steve Niles, Ryan Sook, Mike Ploog, Bill Morrison, Arvid Nelson, Tony Moore, Hilary Barta, Roger Langridge, Scott Allie and Todd Herman. Powell himself and frequent co-conspirators Tom Sniegoski and Mark Farmer also present the three-part "Peg Leg Full of Heaven," featuring the Little Unholy Bastards, and erstwhile publisher Dwight T. Albatross contributes a little somethin' for the ladies. Readers can expect to find zombies, monster-smashing, some gore, a little harsh language, quite a bit of sexual suggestiveness, and lots of slightly sick humor.

Duffield, Paul
Freakangels 1; Volume 1. Story Warren Ellis; artwork Paul Duffield. Avatar Press 2008 144 p.
Grades: 10 11 12 Adult
   1. Apocalyptic fiction; 2. Dystopian fiction; 3. Psychic ability; 4. Science fiction graphic novels; 5. Youth — England — London
1592910564;
9781592910564, $19.99

Courtesy of Avatar Press

"Twenty-three years ago, twelve strange children were born in England at exactly the same moment. Six years ago, the world ended. Today, eleven strange 23-year-olds live in and defend Whitechapel, maybe the last real settlement in flooded London. When a dazed, gun-toting girl appears on the outskirts with a deadly grudge against the self-proclaimed Freakangels, the kids realize that an old enemy is still alive beyond the safety of their borders... a twelfth psychic child, evil and exiled, who can program human minds to hate, and send his private, pirate armies into Whitechapel for revenge." (Publisher's note)
Volume 1 of 6

Duggan, Gerry
The **Last** Christmas. Gerry Duggan and Brian Posehn; art by Rick Remender. Image Comics 2006 Un Illustration
Grades: 11 12 Adult   **741.5; Fic**
   1. Adventure graphic novels; 2. Horror graphic novels; 3. Humorous graphic novels; 4. Santa Claus; 5. Graphic novels
978-1-58240-676-3, $14.99

After the apocalypse, no one is safe; not even at the North Pole. After marauders kill Mrs. Claus, Santa withdraws from life and turns his back on Christmas. When he finally emerges from seclusion, the old world is gone forever, and as Santa struggles to find his way in a post-apocalyptic world, can he find a way to save Christmas too? This Christmas story is for all those who love horror movies (especially with killer zombies) and action movies with lots of shooting and killing of bad guys while yelling curses.

Dumas, Alexandre

The **Count** of Monte Cristo. Wordsmith, R. Jay Nudds ; illustrator, Sankha Banerjee. Campfire 2012 111 p.
Grades: 8 9 10 11 12 Adult   **741.5**
    1. Literature — Adaptations; 2. Graphic novels
    9380028679; 9789380028675, $12.99
    This "graphic novel tells the . . . tale of revenge written by Alexandre Dumas in 1844. Set between 1815 and 1838," the book "depicts a tumultuous time in France's history when multiple powers were vying for control of the country. . . . When Edmond Dantes is unjustly arrested and placed in a prison, his anger and desire for revenge builds inside him. After his escape, he finds the means to carefully plot against his conspirators and steal away their livelihoods and happiness." (Voice of Youth Advocates)

The **three** musketeers; adapted by Bruce Buchanan ; illustrated by Amit Tayal. Campfire 2010 104p. Illustration
Grades: 3 4 5 6 7 8 9   **741.5; Fic**
    1. Adventure graphic novels; 2. Graphic novels
    978-93-80028-57-6, $12.99
    Young D'Artagnan comes to Paris, determined to become a king's musketeer, but runs into trouble with three musketeers in one day. When they band together to tight Cardinal Richelieu's forces, they become friends. The friends soon find themselves involved in averting a plot to discredit Queen Anne, and their efforts to help her cause them to run afoul of Richelieu. D'Artagnan, Athos, Porthos, and Aramis also must deal with Milady de Winter, a beautiful and deadly woman with her own agenda. This graphic novel adaptation features art that emphasizes the humor in the historical adventure. It also puts most of the violence off-panel, so the story is suitable for younger readers.

Dunn, Joeming W.

The **tell-tale** heart. Adapted by Joeming Dunn; illustrated by Rod Espinosa.. Magic Wagon/Graphic Planet 2009 32p. Illustration
Grades: 6 7 8 9 10   **741.5; Fic**
    1. Guilt; 2. Homicide; 3. Horror graphic novels; 4. Poe, Edgar Allan, 1809-1849 — Adaptations; 5. Graphic novels
    978-1-60270681-1, $27.07
                                    LC 2009-8589
    The young narrator takes care of an old man; he tells the reader he has had no reason to do harm, he never felt any greed for the old man's wealth. However, he hates what he calls the old man's vulture eye, and his hatred of that eye makes him determined to kill the old man so he would never have to look on it again. When he finally murders the old

man, however, it's not the eye, but the imagined sound of the old man's beating heart that drives the young killer insane. This easy-reading graphic novel adaptation of Edgar Allan Poe's short story provides a good introduction to Poe's work for reluctant and struggling readers; the emotional intensity of the work makes it more suitable for older readers despite the simplicity of language. Back matter includes a brief biography of Poe, a list of some of his other works, and a short glossary.
    This is part of the Graphic Horror Series 2.

Duo Brand

Cross break, vol. 1. Go! Comi 2008 Un Illustration
Grades: 10 11 12 Adult   **741.5; Fic**
    1. Adventure graphic novels; 2. Fantasy graphic novels; 3. Manga; 4. Graphic novels
    978-1-933617-74-9, $10.99
    Brothers Shinkai and Akito live in a Tokyo different from our world; in theirs, Japan now has a democracy and their father is the President. Ninth grader Akito resents Shinkai's behavior and tries to study hard, his one friend is Yaya, a strange young girl who lives next door. Then Shinkai says Akito shall study abroad and sends him to a strange world. Akito and Yaya, who had come over for help with her homework and got sent away with Akito, must deal with a world ruled by warlocks who murder with impunity. Neon befriends them, but Akito thinks he knows too much about them; but when a poisonous bug bites Yaya, Akiko needs Neon to help him find medicine to heal her. He'll figure out the world he's in as he goes. The book includes violence.

Dyer, Jamaica

★ **Weird** fishes. SLG Publishing 2009 112p. Illustration
Grades: 10 11 12 Adult   **741.5; Fic**
    1. Friendship; 2. Graphic novels
    978-1-59362-177-3, $9.95
    Dee sees giant talking ducks and her main confidant is Bones, a talking goldfish. Bunny Boy always wears a bunny suit. The two misfits have been friends for years, but now things are starting to change. Bunny Boy falls for a goth girl and actually wears a mod suit. Dee, however, has problems when her visions begin to darken, ducks become monsters, and bad things hang out in storm clouds. She needs Bunny Boy, but he seems to want more normalcy in his personal relationships. The two teens smoke cigarettes, cut school, and Bunny Boy goes to a party where people are drinking alcohol.

Dysart, Joshua

★ **Captain** Gravity and the Power of the Vril. Pencils by Sal Velluto ; inks by Bob Almond, Joe Rubenstein & Sal Velluto ; colors by Mike Garcia. Penny-Farthing Press 2006 193p. Illustration
Grades: 8 9 10 11 12   **741.5; Fic**
    1. Adventure graphic novels; 2. Superhero graphic novels; 3. Graphic novels
    0-9719012-8-7, $19.95
    Some years before, a young African American named Joshua Jones stumbled upon a mysterious stone at an archeological dig and became infused with an element from the stone that gave him power over gravity, including flight.

He hid his identity with a helmet and became Captain Gravity. Now it's the 1930s, and Joshua Jones works in Hollywood with the two friends who know his secret. They've been making Captain Gravity movies, and no one else has figured out that the hero is Black. Now, Nazis are searching for the original source of what they call Vril, Joshua's power, and they plan to use it to conquer the Earth. Only Captain Gravity can stop them, and he has to chase them all over the world and to the lost city of Atlantis.

A young, evil Adolf Hitler, an unusual hero for the time, and a story that harks back to the Golden Age of comics storytelling all add up to a great story for this time.

Swamp Thing Vol. 2: Love in Vain. Art by Enrique Breccia and Timothy Green II. DC Comics/Vertigo 2005 144p. Illustration
Grades: 11 12 Adult   741.5; Fic
1. Horror graphic novels; 2. Science fiction graphic novels; 3. Graphic novels
1-4012-0493-7, $14.99

Though he once wielded the combined power of all the Earth's elemental forces, the creature known as Swamp Thing has renounced his omnipotence and returned to his original status as the avatar of the Green, the web of energy connecting all of the world's plant life. But he is now vulnerable, and Arcane is about to break out of his eternal damnation into the world of the living. His designs for revenge threaten to sink not only the Swamp Thing and his family, but everything else under the sun into a never-ending nightmare of corruption and despair. The book includes lots of harsh language, graphic violence, nudity, and sexual situations.

Swamp Thing: Healing the Breach. Art by Enrique Breccia, Ronald Wimberly, Richard Corben. DC Comics/Vertigo 2006 144p. Illustration
Grades: 10 11 12 Adult   741.5; Fic
1. Fantasy graphic novels; 2. Superhero graphic novels; 3. Swamp Thing (Fictional character); 4. Graphic novels
1-4012-0934-3, $17.99

With the consciousness of Alec Holland still separated from its former host and scattered throughout the world, the Swamp Thing must face a new threat which is manifesting itself inside a growing dead zone in the Gulf of Mexico and contend with the gradual reassembly of the Holland mind and the pain of reintegration that its completion promises. In the meantime, a hurricane threatens the Gulf Coast area where Swamp Thing, and crippled Jordin are staying. The book includes strong language, some nudity and sexual situations, and some violence.

★ **Unknown** soldier: haunted house. DC Comics/Vertigo 2009 144p. Illustration
Grades: 11 12 Adult   741.5; Fic
1. Terrorism; 2. Uganda; 3. Graphic novels
978-1-4012-2311-3, $9.99

In 2002, Northern Uganda is a beautiful country racked by horrible brutality and war, as an insane extremist Christian rebel and his army of children terrorize their own people. Dr. Lwanga Moses had fled Uganda with his family when he was a child and Idi Amin was in power; now, he has returned to Uganda with his Ugandan wife, full of pacifist ideals and plans to bring hope and healing to his home country. Then he falls prey to the child soldiers and something deep within him erupts, and Dr. Moses becomes an unstoppable killing machine. His face disfigured, he covers it in bandages and becomes an unknown soldier, determined to do whatever it takes, however much violence and killing he must do, to stop the war. Meanwhile, his wife keeps up their medical mission, always wondering what happened to make her husband disappear. This book is full of horrific, gory violence, but with this update of the classic Unknown Soldier character, Dysart also carefully researched into Ugandan politics and conflicts to make his story as authentic as possible.

E. C. Segar
Popeye Vol. 1: I Yam What I Yam!. Fantagraphics Books 2006 182p. Illustration
Grades: 10 11 12 Adult   741.5
1. Humorous graphic novels; 2. Popeye (Fictional character); 3. Graphic novels
978-1-56097-779-7, $29.95

This is the first volume in a series that will publish all of Segar's original comic strips featuring Popeye, Olive Oyl, Wimpy, and all the other characters people have known from cartoons and a motion picture. This volume covers the years 1928 through 1930 and feature Popeye's courtship of Olive Oyl, meeting the Sea Hag, and Castor Oyl's attempts to turn Popeye into a boxing champion. With all the fighting going on, this book really isn't meant for children.

Eaglesham, Dale
Green Lantern: New Journey, Old Path. DC Comics 2001 192p. Illustration
Grades: 9 10 11 12 Adult   741.5; Fic
1. Green Lantern (Fictional character); 2. Justice League (Fictional characters); 3. Superhero graphic novels; 4. Graphic novels
1-56389-729-6, $12.95

Nero, an escaped mental patient, is bequeathed a Yellow Lantern Ring by the Qwardians. Possessing the mind of a demon and the skill of an artist, he wreaks havoc in New York City and could possibly decimate the planet. With the Justice League pushed to the limit trying to contain Nero's hordes, Green Lantern Kyle Rayner stands alone against a maniac whose power could surpass his own.

Earle-Bridges, Michele
Picture This! Shakespeare: Hamlet. Barron's Educational Series, Inc. 2006 69p. Illustration
Grades: 7 8 9 10 11 12   741.5; 822.3
1. Drama; 2. Shakespeare, William, 1564-1616 — Adaptations; 3. Graphic novels
978-0-7641-3524-8, $7.99

This adaptation combines pages done in graphic novel format with extensive excerpts from Shakespeare's Hamlet to provide an introductory reading experience for younger and struggling students. Each scene presented in the book is preceded by a brief summary, words that modern teens would find unfamiliar are briefly defined on the page, literary terms are explained.

Picture This! Shakespeare: Hamlet Teacher's Resource Book. Barron's Educational Series, Inc. 2006 58p. Illustration

Grades: 7 8 9 10 11 12   **741.5; 371.33**
1. Drama; 2. Teaching — Aids and devices; 3. Graphic novels
978-0-7641-3523-1, $9.99

Hamlet, the Shakespearean drama that is in the curriculum of many high schools in the country, is an offering in Barron's "Picture This! Shakespeare" series. This manual supplements Barron's "Picture This: Hamlet," a book presented in graphic novel style for students' use. The manual offers teachers suggestions for classroom discussions, quizzes, and activities related to the play, including reproducible activity sheets.

Picture This! Shakespeare: Julius Caesar. Barron's Educational Series, Inc. 2006 54p. Illustration
Grades: 7 8 9 10 11 12   **741.5; 822.3**
1. Shakespeare, William, 1564-1616 — Adaptations
978-0-7641-3279-7, $7.99

This adaptation combines pages done in graphic novel format with extensive excerpts from Shakespeare's Julius Caesar to provide an introductory reading experience for younger and struggling students. Each scene presented in the book is preceded by a brief summary, words that modern teens would find unfamiliar are briefly defined on the page, literary terms are explained.

Picture This! Shakespeare: Julius Caesar Teacher's Resource Book. Barron's Educational Series, Inc. 2006 58p. Illustration
Grades: 7 8 9 10 11 12   **741.5; 371.33**
1. Drama; 2. Teaching — Aids and devices; 3. Graphic novels
978-0-7641-3280-3, $9.99

Julius Caesar, the Shakespearean drama that is in the curriculum of virtually every high school in the country, is an offering in Barron's "Picture This! Shakespeare" series. This manual supplements Barron's "Picture This: Julius Caesar," a book presented in graphic novel style for students' use. The manual offers teachers suggestions for classroom discussions, quizzes, and activities related to the play, including reproducible activity sheets.

Edginton, Ian
    Hellgate London. Dark Horse Comics 2007 Un Illustration
Grades: 10 11 12 Adult   **741.5; Fic**
1. Adventure graphic novels; 2. Fantasy graphic novels; 3. Graphic novels
978-1-59307-681-8, $12.95

In 2020, MI5 agent Lyra Darius discovers a human channel house in the heart of London while tailing Lord Sumerisle, the recently resigned Home Office Minister for Internal Affairs. She's soon entangled in a bloody intrigue with Knights Templar, and everything is building up to All Hallows Eve as demons establish Hellgates to invade Earth. Years later, humans must discover the true nature of an arcane symbol known as the Sigil, if they hope to survive much longer against the demons. The book includes violence and strong language; it's based on a video game of the same name.

    Kingdom of the Wicked. Illustrated by D'Israeli. Dark Horse Comics 2004 120p. Illustration

Grades: 8 9 10 11 12 Adult   **741.5; Fic**
1. Adventure graphic novels; 2. Fantasy graphic novels; 3. Graphic novels
1-59307-187-6, $15.95

Christopher Grahame is the premier children's author of the twenty-first century, a publishing phenomenon. With his work translated into everything from Aborigine to Zulu, he is the cornerstone of a multi-million dollar, franchise spewing empire. Is it any surprise then that under all this pressure something has to give? Unfortunately, it's Chris's mind. Stricken by mysterious headaches and blackouts that plagued his childhood, Chris once again finds himself walking the avenues and boulevards of Castrovalva - the fantasy realm he dreamt up as a boy, to while away his recuperation. But like Chris, Castrovalva has also changed. Deluged in mud, blood, and barbed wire, war has come to wonderland. Chris tries to tell himself it's all a bad dream. . .so why can't he wake up? The book includes violence, strong language, and brief nudity.

    Scarlet Traces. Dark Horse Comics 2003 88p. Illustration
Grades: 9 10 11 12 Adult   **741.5; Fic**
1. Mystery graphic novels; 2. Science fiction graphic novels; 3. Graphic novels
1-56971-940-3, $14.95

A decade after the Martians' abortive assault on the Earth and their attempt to establish an invasion bridgehead on the British Isles, the industrious Victorians have assimilated the Martian technologies into their everyday lives. Hansom cabs now scuttle along the Capital's streets on multi-limbed crab legs and the terrible monopoly of the Martian heat-ray has assured the dominance of the British Empire over two thirds of the Earth's surface. However, there is something rotten at the heart of empire. When the bodies of several young women are found washed up on the Thames, drained of blood, enter Captain Robert Autumn (retired soldier turned gentleman-adventurer) and his former Sergeant Major, now manservant, Archie Currie. Together they are drawn into the mystery which leads them from the gin palaces of the East End, and the grinding poverty of the North, to Whitehall's corridors of power and the very Hall of the Martian King. The book includes violence and some strong language.

Edmondson, Nathan
    Black Widow; Volume 1: the finely woven thread. Nathan Edmondson; illustrated by Phil Noto. Marvel Enterprises 2014 144 p. Color; Illustration
Grades: 11 12 Adult   **741.5**
1. Black Widow (Fictional character); 2. Superheroes — Fiction; 3. Undercover operations — Fiction
0785188193; 9780785188193, $17.99

"The Black Widow goes undercover in Russia, but from its cold streets, the Hand of God reaches out to crush her . . . and it is as merciless as its name implies. Outmatched by the brute force of a powerful new villain, Natasha faces her deadliest test, and discovers a deadly plot unfolding that spans the entire globe." (Publisher's note)

"Edmondson's fast-paced and action-packed espionage story does an excellent job playing to the character's strengths, using her cunning to assess each situation and her agility and reflexes when it all goes to hell. Noto's luminous

watercolorlike panels—a welcome departure from more traditional superhero comics artwork—create a soft atmosphere." Booklist
Contains material originally published in magazine form as Black Widow #1-6 and All new Marvel now! point one #1—Tp verso.
Volume 1 of an ongoing series

Olympus. Written by Nathan Edmondson; art by Christian Ward. Image Comics 2009 Un Illustration
Grades: 10 11 12 Adult   **741.5; Fic**
1. Fantasy graphic novels; 2. Greek mythology; 3. Graphic novels
978-1-60706-178-6, $14.99
In Ancient Greece, Zeus granted immortality to two brothers, Castor and Pollux (most people might know them as the Gemini twins), then bound them to his service. Three thousand years later, they still serve him on Earth by hunting fugitives from Olympus and maintaining order between the human realm and the divine. This means they have to catch Hermes and cast him off Earth; when they do that, they accidentally leave an opening between the realms for Pelops, son of Tantalus, who has no love for the gods. Ward saturates his sketchy, scratchy lines with wild colors. The book includes violence and some harsh language.

Eisenberg, Adam
The **Creation** of Iron Man. Rosen Publishing Group 2006 48p. Illustration
Grades: 4 5 6 7 8 9 10   **741.5**
1. Iron Man (Fictional character); 2. Superhero graphic novels; 3. Graphic novels
978-1-4042-0767-7, $29.25
LC 2006000167
This volume discusses the unique character of Tony Stark, developed by Stan Lee and Jack Kirby, who was unable to live a normal life and invented a special iron suit that gave him superpowers. The book includes information about the times in which Lee and Kirby worked at Marvel Comics.
Part of the Action Heroes series.

Eisner, Will
★ **Comics** and sequential art: principles and practices from the legendary cartoonist. W.W. Norton 2008 175p. Illustration (The Will Eisner library)
Grades: 9 10 11 12 Adult   **741.5**
1. Comic books, strips, etc — Authorship; 2. Drawing — Technique; 3. Graphic novels — Authorship
978-0-393-33126-4; 0-393-33126-1, $22.95
LC 2008-20042
This book offers the author's ideas, theories, and advice about graphic storytelling and the uses to which the comic book art form can be applied.
First published 1985 by Poorhouse Press
A Will Eisner instructional book.

Fagin the Jew. By Will Eisner; foreword by Michael Bendis. Dark Horse 2013 136 p. Illustration
Grades: 11 12 Adult   **741.5**
1. Jews — Great Britain — Fiction
1616551267; 9781616551261, $19.99

This book is author and illustrator Will Eisner's reimagination of author Charles Dickens' character Fagin from the book "Oliver Twist." "Imagining Fagin's impoverished childhood in the slums of London and his initiation into the criminal underworld, Eisner's story counters the anti-Semitism of Victorian literature as his . . . brushwork creates . . . [a] portrait of the era." (Publisher's note)
"[T]his compelling counternarrative is framed as Fagin's apologia to Dickens and folds in plenty of historical background about Jews in Europe and England during the late 19th century." LJ
Includes bibliographical references
First published 2003

The **Last** Knight: An Introduction to Don Quixote. NBM Publishing 2000 32p. Illustration
Grades: 3 4 5 6 7 8 9 10   **741.5; Fic**
1. Adventure graphic novels; 2. Authors; 3. Cervantes Saavedra, Miguel de, 1547-1616 — Adaptations
1-56163-251-1; 978-1-56163-251-0, $15.95
LC 2001-265049
This is Eisner's graphic novel remake of Don Quixote. Here are the adventures of a Spanish country gentleman and his companion who set out, like knights of old, to search for adventure. As the subtitle says, this book hits the highlights and serves to introduce the classic tale to younger readers.

Moby Dick. NBM Publishing 2001 32p. Illustration
Grades: 3 4 5 6 7 8 9 10   **741.5; Fic**
1. Adventure graphic novels; 2. Whaling; 3. Graphic novels
1-56163-293-7, $15.95; 1-56163-294-5 (pa)
LC 2001-032989
Ishmael, a sailor, recounts the ill-fated voyage of a whaling ship led by the fanatical Captain Ahab in search of the white whale that had crippled him. Eisner's adaptation hits the highlights of the novel.

The **plot**: the secret story of the Protocols of the Elders of Zion. By Will Eisner, with an introduction by Umberto Eco. Norton 2005 Vii, 148 p. Illustration (Will Eisner library.)
Grades: 9 10 11 12 Adult   **741.5; 305.892**
1. Antisemitism; 2. Protocols of the wise men of Zion
0393060454; 0393328600; 9780393060454, $19.95
LC 2005040527
This book, by Will Eisner, "examines the astonishing conspiracy and the fabrication of The Protocols of the Elders of Zion. . . . Purported to be the actual blueprints by Jewish leaders to take over the world, the Protocols, first published in 1902, have become gospel truth to international millions. Presenting a pageant of historical figures, . . . Eisner unravels and dispels one of the most devastating hoaxes of the twentieth century." (Publisher's note)

The **Princess** and the Frog. NBM Publishing 1999 32p. Illustration
Grades: 3 4 5 6 7 8 9 10   **741.5; Fic**
1. Fairy tales; 2. Fantasy graphic novels; 3. Graphic novels
1-56163-244-9, $15.95; 1-56163-346-1 (pa)
A good prince, turned into a frog by a spiteful wizard, exacts from a princess a promise which she is reluctant to fulfill, despite his kindness and her desire not to hurt him.

Comics master Will Eisner adapted the familiar tale by the Brothers Grimm.

The **Spirit** Archives Volume 14. DC Comics 2004 192p. Illustration
Grades: 9 10 11 12 Adult   **741.5; Fic**
1. Spirit (Fictional character); 2. Superhero graphic novels; 3. Spirit (Fictional character); 4. Graphic novels
1-4012-0158-X, $49.95
LC 2001-274103
The adventures of Will Eisner's most famous creation continue in this volume reprinting the Spirit newspaper sections from 1/5/47 to 6/29/47. It features appearances by Ebony, Dolan and Ellen, the seductive P'Gell, Hoagy the Yogi, Silken Floss, Saree and more. Today's readers should understand that Eisner's depiction of Ebony, who is the Spirit's sidekick, was not considered out of place in 1947, even though many might take offense now. Eisner started developing new methods of telling a story and revolutionizing comics along the way.

The **Spirit** Archives Volume 15. DC Comics 2004 192p. Illustration
Grades: 9 10 11 12 Adult   **741.5; Fic**
1. Spirit (Fictional character); 2. Superhero graphic novels; 3. Spirit (Fictional character); 4. Graphic novels
1-4012-0162-8, $49.95
LC 2001-274103
Volume 15 reprints The Spirit newspaper sections published from July 6, 1947 to December 28, 1947, featuring the seductive P'Gell, The Octopus, a send up of Li'l Abner, and more. The stories range from broad comedy to crime noir, with plenty of comic violence.

The **spirit** book five. DC Comics 2009 Un Illustration
Grades: 9 10 11 12 Adult   741.5; Fic
1. Humorous graphic novels; 2. Mystery graphic novels; 3. Spirit (Fictional character); 4. Superhero graphic novels; 5. Spirit (Fictional character); 6. Graphic novels
978-1-4012-2642-8, $19.99
In this collection of new comics featuring the characters created by Will Eisner, The Spirit goes up against his faceless archnemesis The Octopus (in the comics readers never see his face, unlike in the 2008 motion picture) and such deadly ladies as Silken Floss and Plaster of Paris. He also takes on a Yakuza/Triad gang war, a tattooed killer, and gets caught up in a battle between leprechauns, Marines, and the undead. Creators in this volume include writers Michael Uslan and F.J. DeSanto (who also worked on the movie), Dean Motter, Michael Avon Oeming, and Mike Ploog; artists Justinio and Walden Wong, Tom Derenick, Paul Rivoche, Mike Ploog, Dan Green, and Michael Avon Oeming; colorists Trish Mulvihill, Lee Loughridge, and Paul Rivoche; and letterer Rob Leigh.
This volume collects The Spirit issues #2632.

★ The **Spirit**: Femmes fatales. DC Comics 2008 192p. Illustration
Grades: 9 10 11 12   **741.5; Fic**
1. Adventure graphic novels; 2. Mystery graphic novels; 3. Spirit (Fictional character); 4. Superhero graphic novels; 5. Spirit (Fictional character); 6. Graphic novels
978-1-4012-1973-4, $19.99

Will Eisner's The Spirit is a classic comic book hero Denny Colt, a young policeman who was killed on the job and has come back from the dead to become a masked, suited crime fighter. And while he fought crime, he also dealt with women, lots of women, some good, some bad, some plain evil, and all beautiful. This book collects 23 stories from the original twelve-year run of The Spirit that feature some of the gorgeous but deadly villainesses who made the Spirit's life . . . interesting. Readers will meet Silk Satin, P'Gell, Silken Floss, Madam Minx, and true-blue, courageous Ellen Dolan. The stories include some violence and the same kind of sexual tension found in such classic movies as The Maltese Falcon.

El Rassi, Toufic
Arab in America. Last Gasp 2008 118p. Illustration
Grades: 10 11 12 Adult   **92; 741.5**
1. Biographical graphic novels; 2. Muslims — United States
978-0-86719-673-3, $14.95
Toufic El Rassi combines a memoir of his life in America with commentary on how Muslims and Arabs have been treated in the U.S. Born in Beirut but living in the U.S. since he was a young boy, El Rassi faced ignorant prejudice and discrimination ever since his family immigrated to this country. In this book he shows how hard it is to maintain an Arab identity in a country saturated with anti-Arab propaganda, examining the roles of media and pop culture in a world with 9/11, two Gulf Wars, and other U.S. involvement in the Middle East. Readers will confront uncomfortable ideas about just what unthinking patriotism and ignorance about the real culture of the Middle East countries do to harm many who are innocent. The book includes some strong language and a few isolated panels with partial nudity.

Elder, Joshua
Mail Order Ninja, Vol. 1 written by Joshua Elder ; illustrated by Erich Owen. Tokyopop 2006 Un Illustration
Grades: 4 5 6 7 8 9   **741.5; Fic**
1. Humorous graphic novels; 2. Ninja; 3. Graphic novels
1-59816-728-6, $5.99
Timmy is a normal boy attending L. Frank Baum Elementary School in Cherry Creek, Indiana - dealing with bullies, a nasty little sister, and an even nastier super-rich girl who acts as though she owns the school. When things get really bad, Timmy decides to enter a drawing in a mail order catalog to win a ninja. Yes, a real live ninja of his very own. When Jiro arrives, Timmy soon overpowers the bullies and beats rich Felicity in the Student Body President election. But as long as Felicity's father has money, she'll find a way to get even, and she has a copy of that mail order catalog. . . . This is the first volume in a global manga series.

Eldred, Tim
★ **Grease** monkey. Written and drawn by Tim Eldred; [edited by Teresa Nielsen Hayden]. Tor 2006 352p. Illustration
Grades: 9 10 11 12 Adult   **741.5; Fic**
1. Science fiction graphic novels; 2. Graphic novels
0-7653-1325-1; 0-7653-1326-X (pa), $19.95

When hostile aliens attacked Earth and left it after killing most of the humans, another group of aliens came and offered to "uplift" one of the animal species to human intelligence so that Earth could rebuild. The dolphins turned them down, but the gorillas went for it. Some generations later, new mechanic Robin Plotnik comes to the space station called Fist of Earth, where he's assigned to work with Chief Mac Gimbensky. Mac is a no-nonsense gorilla who works on the ships of the all-woman Barbarian Squadron. He and Robin work together well, but they each have their romantic problems. This is science fiction from a viewpoint not always seen in most stories.

Eliopoulos, Chris
   Fantastic Four Presents Franklin Richards, Son of a Genius: Lab Brat. Marvel Publishing, Inc. 2007 Un Illustration
Grades: 3 4 5 6 7 8 9   **741.5; Fic**
   1. Fantastic Four (Fictional characters); 2. Humorous graphic novels; 3. Superhero graphic novels; 4. Graphic novels
   0-7851-2322-9, $7.99
   This book collects stories depicting the adventures of Franklin Richards, young son of Reed and Susan Richards of the Marvel superhero family, the Fantastic Four. Franklin and his robot companion H.E.R.B.I.E. keep sneaking into Reed's lab and playing with the devices they find; or, actually, Franklin does as H.E.R.B.I.E. tries to keep the boy out of trouble. In one story, Franklin accidentally turns his teacher and classmates into vegetables; in another he converts dishes of Jell-O into clones to go trick-or-treating for him; he tries to use a time machine to gather Christmas gifts for his family; he uses a device to make his comic book come to life; and he travels to another dimension where turkeys have evolved and become the dominant life form.
   Originally published as Franklin Richards: Son of a Genius, Everybody Loves Franklin, Super Summer Spectacular, and Happy Franksgiving.

Ellerton, Sarah
   Inverloch, Volume 1. Seven Seas 2006 Un Illustration
Grades: 4 5 6 7 8 9 10 11 12   **741.5; Fic**
   1. Adventure graphic novels; 2. Fantasy graphic novels; 3. Graphic novels
   1-933164-13-1, $14.99
   In a world where humans, elves, and other beings coexist, albeit not altogether peacefully, Acheron is a young da'kor, a horned wolf-like race that lives in the forests. He encounters a beautiful elf and takes her quest for his own - to find another elf who went missing twelve years before. Teased by his brothers as a lousy hunter, feared by humans who think da'kor are dangerous beasts, innocent Acheron finds that the world beyond the forest is full of danger, intrigue, and betrayal.
   This story began online as a webcomic.

Ellis, Grace
   ★ **Lumberjanes** 1: Beware the kitten holy. Written by Noelle Stevenson & Grace Ellis ; illustrated by Brooke Allen ; colors by Maarta Laiho. Simon & Schuster 2015 128 p. Illustration; Color (Lumberjanes)
Grades: 6 7 8 9 10 11 12 Adult   **741.5**

   1. Adventure fiction; 2. Camps — Fiction; 3. Female friendship; 4. Monsters — Fiction; 5. Summer — Fiction
1608866874; 9781608866878, $14.99
Eisner Award: Best New Series (2015)
Eisner Award: Best Publication for Teens (2015)
Harvey Award: Best New Series (2015); Harvey Award: Best Original Graphic Publication For Young Readers (2015)
   "[This] graphic novel begins mid-adventure as five campers are out after hours investigating a strange event that they all witnessed: a woman turning into a giant bear. This is just the first of many odd occurrences that Jo, April, Molly, Mal, and Ripley encounter at the summer camp for 'Hardcore Lady Types.' The Lumberjanes, as the scouts are called, band together to solve puzzles, defeat three-eyed creatures, and escape the ire of their watchful counselor Jen." (School Library Journal)
   "Humorously riffing on everything from scout badges to the X-Men to feminist heroes . . ., it's a sharp, smart, and most of all fun celebration of sisterhood." Pub Wkly
   Volume 1 of an ongoing series

Ellis, Warren
   Crecy. Story, Warren Ellis; artwork, Raulo Caceres. Avatar Press 2007 Un Illustration
Grades: 10 11 12 Adult
741.5; Fic
   1. Crecy (France), Battle of, 1346; 2. Hundred Years' War, 1339-1453; 3. War; 4. Graphic novels
   978-1-59291-040-3, $6.99
   A highly trained but under equipped army invades another country due to that country's perceived threat to home security. The

Courtesy of Avatar Press

army conducts shock-and-awe raids designed to terrify the populace. This army is soon driven to ground, and vastly outnumbered. The English army has to stand and fight, under the command of King Edward III, in Crecy, France. On 26 August 1346, modern warfare changed forever. This is the story of England's greatest battle, narrated by a fictional English longbowman. The book is full of battlefield violence and lots of very harsh language, including the f-bomb.

   Desolation Jones. Warren Ellis, writer; J.H. Williams III, artist. DC Comics/Wildstorm 2006 142p. Illustration
Grades: 12 Adult   **741.5; Fic**
   1. Mystery graphic novels; 2. Graphic novels
   978-1-4012-1150-9, $14.99
   Michael Jones used to be an MI6 field agent, and he is the first surviving victim of the Desolation Test, a radically dangerous procedure cooked up by the British government. He was kept alive intravenously while being force-fed a steady diet of horrific data and images non-stop as stimulants were continuously pumped into him, for an entire year. Now he lives in Los Angeles, where all the ex-spooks like him have been sent and kept; he works as a private

investigator to their secret underground community. Colonel Nigh, who lives for his pornography collection, needs Jones' help to recover a special piece of film - pornography starring Adolf Hitler; Nigh's troublesome daughters all play into the equation. Mature readers who enjoy such titles as Preacher and aren't troubled by nudity, violence, and considerable use of harsh language, will want to read this.

Fell Volume 1: Feral City. Written by Warren Ellis; illustrated by Ben Templesmith; lettering by Chris Eliopoulos. Image Comics 2007 Un Illustration
Grades: 11 12 Adult   **741.5; Fic**
   1. Mystery graphic novels; 2. Graphic novels
   978-1-58240-693-0, $14.99
   Detective Richard Fell is transferred over the bridge from the big city to Snowtown, a feral district whose police investigations department numbers three and a half people (one detective has no legs). Dumped in this collapsing urban trashzone, Richard Fell is starting all over again. In a place where nothing seems to make any sense, Fell clings to the one thing he knows to be true: everybody's hiding something. Considerable violence and strong language mix with a strong noir-ish mystery.

Nextwave: Agents of H.A.T.E. Vol. 1: This is What They Want. Writer, Warren Ellis; artist, Stuart Immonen. Marvel Entertainment 2006 Un Illustration
Grades: 10 11 12 Adult   **741.5; Fic**
   1. Adventure graphic novels; 2. Satire; 3. Superhero graphic novels; 4. Graphic novels
   0-7851-2278-8, $19.99
   H.A.T.E. (The Highest Anti-Terrorism Effort) put together a team of superheroes they call Nextwave: Monica Rambeau (formerly Captain Marvel and Photon), Aaron Stack (the robotic Machine Man), Tabitha Smith (X-Force's Meltdown), monster-hunter Elsa Bloodstone, and The Captain. The team was told they were supposed to fight Bizarre Weapons of Mass Destruction; however, Tabitha lifted some papers that reveal the truth: H.A.T.E. is part of the Beyond Corporation, which is the new version of the terrorist organization formerly known as Silent. The Corporation plans to test its weapons on unsuspecting American towns, so Nextwave goes rogue to stop the weapons and be the good guys. They face an awakened Fin Fang Foom (giant monster lizard), a bad cop turned robotic monster, and their former boss, Dirk Anger. There's lots of action, bad words show as a series of death's heads, and the whole thing is written as a biting satire of superheroes.

Nextwave: Agents of H.A.T.E. Vol. 2: I Kick Your Face. Writer, Warren Ellis; penciler, Stuart Immonen; inker, Wade von Grawbadger; colorist, Dave McCaig. Marvel Entertainment 2007 Un Illustration
Grades: 10 11 12 Adult   **741.5; Fic**
   1. Humorous graphic novels; 2. Superhero graphic novels; 3. Graphic novels
   0-7851-2855-7, $19.99
   In this second and final volume of the series, former Captain Marvel Monica Rambeau and the Nextwave team continue their quest to shut down H.A.T.E.'s network of Unusual Weapons of Mass Destruction. They destroy the Mindless Ones, the bizarre Broccoli Men who have been created to look like various superhero teams, and then decide to finish off S.I.L.E.N.T. itself, the uber-terrorist network

that has been funding H.A.T.E. It's a full-on superhero satire with lots of comic book action, and all the bad words appear as skulls.

Orbiter. Writer, Warren Ellis; artist, Colleen Doran. DC Comics/Vertigo 2004 104p. Illustration
Grades: 10 11 12 Adult   **741.5; Fic**
   1. Mystery graphic novels; 2. Science fiction graphic novels; 3. Graphic novels
   1-4012-0056-7, $17.95
   In the early 21st century, the space shuttle Venture has suddenly returned to Earth after disappearing ten years ago; its crew is missing, except for the catatonic pilot, and the ship is outfitted with new instrumentation, new engines, and is covered in something very much like skin, while its landing gear has Martian sand. Now a team of three specialists must discover where the Venture went, what's been done to it, and what happened to the crew. Unfortunately, most of the answers are locked up in the seemingly twisted mind of the pilot. Does he really know the truth or is he simply a demented casualty of a space mission gone wrong? The book includes some foul language.

★ **Planetary:** 2, Vol. 2. Warren Ellis, writer; John Cassaday, artist; Laura DePuy and David Baron, colorists; Ryan Cline, Bill O'Neil and Mike Heisler, letterers. DC Comics 2013 144 p. Color; Illustration
Grades: 11 12 Adult   **741.5**
   1. Adventure graphic novels; 2. Parapsychology — Fiction; 3. Superhero comic books, strips, etc
   1563897644; 9781563897641, $14.99
                                                  LC 2012046722
   This graphic novel, written by Warren Ellis and illustrated by John Cassady, the second in the "Planetary" series, "focuses on the team's mysterious benefactor, the 'Fourth Man.' After paying their final respects to a British occultist with ties to their group, Elijah Snow, Jakita Wagner, and The Drummer continue their super-human archeological studies as they visit a hidden government compound full of radioactive human guinea pigs." (Publisher's note)
   Originally published by WildStorm in single magazine form as Planetary #7-#12.

★ **Planetary:** 3: leaving the 20th century, 3. Warren Ellis & John Cassaday, writer, co-creators, artist; Laura Martin, colorist. DC Comics 2005 144 p. Color; Illustration
Grades: 11 12 Adult   **741.5**
   1. Adventure graphic novels; 2. Mystery graphic novels; 3. Science fiction graphic novels; 4. Superhero comic books, strips, etc
   1401202942; 9781401202941, $14.99
   In this graphic novel, written by Warren Ellis and illustrated by John Cassaday, the third in the "Planetary" series, "Elijah takes a look at his past, making startling revelations and recounting his participation in the first moon shot . . . in 1851!" (Publisher's note)
   Originally published in single magazine form as Planetary #13-18

★ **Planetary:** 4: spacetime archaeology. Writer, Warren Ellis; artist, John Cassaday; colorist, Laura Martin; letterer, Comicraft. WildStorm Productions 2010 224 p. Color; Illustration
Grades: 11 12 Adult   **741.5**

1. Adventure fiction; 2. Fantasy fiction; 3. Superhero comic books, strips, etc; 4. Graphic novels
1401223451; 9781401223458, $17.99

LC 2010294189

This book, by Warren Ellis, is the "fourth and final graphic novel collecting the adventures of Elijah Snow, a powerful, hundred year old man, Jakita Wagner, an extremely powerful but bored woman, and The Drummer, a man with the ability to communicate with machines. Infatuated with tracking down evidence of super-human activity, these mystery archaeologists of the late 20th Century uncover unknown paranormal secrets and histories." (Publisher's note)

"Engaging as the story itself may be, Planetary's brilliance lies more in the rich history of comics and comic lore that Ellis draws from and cleverly weaves into the narrative from beginning to end." SLJ

Originally published in single magazine form as Planetary #19-27.

★ **Planetary;** vol 1: all over the world and other stories. Warren Ellis, John Cassaday, Laura DePuy. Wildstorm 2012 160 p. Color; Illustration
Grades: 11 12 Adult   **741.5**
1. Adventure graphic novels; 2. Archaeologists — Fiction; 3. Mystery graphic novels; 4. Parapsychology — Fiction; 5. Science fiction comic books, strips, etc
1563896486; 9781563896484, $14.99

LC 2012024915

Written by Warren Ellis with art by John Cassaday, "this graphic novel features the adventures of Elijah Snow, a hundred year old man, Jakita Wagner, an extremely powerful and bored woman, and The Drummer, a man with the ability to communicate with machines. Infatuated with tracking down evidence of super-human activity, these mystery archaeologists of the late 20th Century uncover unknown paranormal secrets and histories." (Publisher's note)

Also available in an omnibus edition

Originally published by WildStorm Productions in single magazine form as Planetary #1-6 And Planetary Preview. Other volumes in this series are: Vol. 2: The fourth man; Vol. 3: Leaving the 20th century; Vol. 4: Spacetime archaeology

Ellison, Halan
Harlan Ellison's Dream Corridor, Vol. 2. Dark Horse Comics 2007 168p. Illustration
Grades: 11 12 Adult   **741.5; Fic**
1. Fantasy graphic novels; 2. Graphic novels
978-1-59307-494-4, $19.95

The words of world-renowned science-fiction author Harlan Ellison are translated onto the page by top comics creators, including Paul Chadwick, Neal Adams, Steve Rude, Gene Colan, Steve Niles, Gerard Jones, Richard Corben and the legendary Oz illustrator Eric Shanower. Most of these stories have never before seen print. Ellison uses strong language and violence a lot in his stories, which include "Opposites Attract," "One Life, Furnished in Early Poverty," "The Discarded," "Moonlighting," and more.

Endo, Hiroki
Tanpenshu Vol. 1. Dark Horse Comics 2007 230p. Illustration

Grades: 11 12 Adult   **741.5; Fic**
1. Manga; 2. Seinen manga; 3. Graphic novels
978-1-59307-637-5, $12.95

The three stories in this first volume are mature explorations of humanity's constant, fumbling attempts to find hope and meaning in a confusing, violent world. A disfigured misfit befriends a doomed yakuza outcast, a group a school kids fail to see the anger that's about to boil over from one of their own and members of an experimental theatre troupe embark on a project that will test both their friendships and the group's grasp on reality. The stories include strong language, nudity and graphic violence, and the cover may disturb some readers.

Englehart, Steve
Batman: Dark Detective. Steve Englehart, writer; Marshall Rogers, penciller; Terry Austin, inker; John Workman, letterer; Chris Chuckry, colorist. DC Comics 2005 144p. Illustration
Grades: 9 10 11 12 Adult   **741.5; Fic**
1. Batman (Fictional character); 2. Joker (Fictional character); 3. Superhero graphic novels; 4. Graphic novels
1-4012-0898-3, $14.99

When the maniacal Joker enters a gubernatorial election, the Dark Knight takes action. But Batman discovers he's in way over his head when the unexpected return of former girlfriend Silver St. Cloud leaves him torn between love and duty. With adversaries like the Joker, Two-Face, Scarecrow, and others to contend with, Batman must make a choice between his quest for justice and his affections for Silver. And his indecision could cost him everything. The story evokes the style and content of 1970s comics.

Ennis, Garth
Britton, Battler. Garth Ennis, writer; Colin Wilson, artist; colored by Jeromy Cox; lettered by Rob Leigh. DC Comics/Wildstorm 2007 Un Illustration
Grades: 10 11 12 Adult   **741.5; Fic**
1. Adventure graphic novels; 2. World War, 1939-1945; 3. Graphic novels
978-1-4012-1378-7, $19.99

In October, 1942, Allied forces are on the run from the unrelenting forces of the Nazis in North Africa. Wing Commander Robert "Battler" Britton of the Royal Air Force and his squadron are dispatched to an American airstrip to spearhead a joint action against Hitler's war machine. Now they must survive taunts, threats, and assaults ... and that's just from the Yanks. There's plenty of war action in the air and on the ground.

John Woo's Seven Brothers: Sons of Heaven, Son of Hell. Art by Jeevan Kang. Virgin Comics 2007 144p. Illustration
Grades: 10 11 12 Adult   **741.5; Fic**
1. Fantasy graphic novels; 2. Mystery graphic novels; 3. Graphic novels
978-1-934413029, $14.99

Six hundred years ago long, before history's great explorers stole the credit for their feats, mighty Chinese treasure fleets set sail to reach every continent. These voyages of discovery left behind an evil legacy and a plot by a powerful Chinese sorcerer to dominate the world. The story begins in modern day Los Angeles where an ancient Chinese prophecy must be fulfilled. Seven men with strange abilities and nothing in common but their destinies must face the Son of Hell to save the world. Action movie director John Woo created the story. The book includes lots of harsh language full of f-bombs and violence.

War Stories Vol. 2. Art by David Lloyd, Cam Kennedy, Carlos Ezquerra, Gary Erskine. DC Comics/Vertigo 2006 240p. Illustration

Grades: 10 11 12 Adult   **741.5; Fic**
  1. Spain — History — 1936-1939, Civil War; 2. World War, 1939-1945; 3. Graphic novels
978-1-4012-1039-7, $19.99

The brutality and bravery of those who served in history's greatest conflict is brought to life in this book. From the saturation bombing of the Ruhr Valley to the birth of the SAS in the deserts of North Africa, from the blasted wreckage of Guernica to the tracer-filled skies over the North Atlantic, these tales will land the reader in some of the worst combat zones the world has ever seen. Author Ennis includes historical notes at the end of the book. Readers will find strong language and wartime violence in the stories.

Espinosa, Frank

Rocketo: Journey to the Hidden Sea, Volume 1. Frank Espinosa; co-writer, Marie Taylor. Image Comics 2006 Un Illustration

Grades: 9 10 11 12 Adult   **741.5; Fic**
  1. Adventure graphic novels; 2. Science fiction graphic novels; 3. Graphic novels
1-58240-585-9, $19.99

2,000 years after the Earth shattered, the magnetic core destroyed and continents split apart, new races of men came to be. Rocketo Garrison is a Mapper; he possesses an inner compass which lights when he is ready to use it. When his parents die in a violent storm, another Mapper takes him in. When he grows up, war comes to the planet; he hides his identity as a Mapper since he had never joined the guild, and fights. Lucerne captures him and takes his Mapper senses and powers away and uses them to design killing machines that win the war. Broken and lost, Rocketo joins the shady Spiro and his motley crew on a quest to explore the Hidden Sea.

Espinosa uses a very fluid, loose, almost sketchy style that shows a lot of energy while setting up his new world of wonders and dangers.

Rocketo: Journey to the Hidden Sea, Volume 2. Frank Espinosa; co-writer, Marie Taylor. Image Comics 2007 Un Illustration

Grades: 9 10 11 12 Adult   **741.5**
  1. Adventure graphic novels; 2. Science fiction graphic novels; 3. Graphic novels
978-1-58240-735-7, $19.99

Rocketo, Spiro, and their crew had made it into the Hidden Sea, and they discover a place of beauty and peace. However, the gangster Scarletto, working for Lucerne, has been pursuing them and has taken control of the weapon created from Rocketo's Mapper powers. Scarletto is bringing war to the Hidden Sea, determined to destroy everything good. Rocketo and everyone who lives in the

Hidden Sea fight back, but the only way they can win is if Rocketo can once again light his inner compass and reawaken his Mapper powers. Libraries will want get both Volume 1 and this volume to get the complete story.

Espinosa, Rod

Around the world in 80 days. Adapted and illustrated by Rod Espinosa.. ABDO/Red Wagon 2008 32p. Illustration

Grades: 3 4 5 6 7 8 9   **741.5; Fic**
  1. Adventure graphic novels; 2. Graphic novels; 3. Verne, Jules, 1828-1905 — Adaptations
978-1-60270-050-5, $27.07

                     LC 2007-6444

In 1872, English gentleman Phileas Fogg makes a wager that he can travel around the world in just 80 days. Unfortunately, at the time of his wager, a daring robber has made off with a fortune, and Scotland Yard detective Fix is convinced Fogg is the villain. The chase is on, around the world. This comic book adaptation has been written for younger, reluctant, and struggling readers and provides highlights of the adventures in the original novel by Verne. The book includes a brief biography of Verne, a short list of some of his other works, and a brief glossary.

★ The **courageous** princess. Dark Horse Comics 2007 240p. Illustration

Grades: 3 4 5 6 7 8 9   **741.5; Fic**
  1. Fantasy graphic novels; 2. Princesses
978-1-59307-719-8, $9.95

Plain Princess Mabelrose doesn't get along with the other, prettier princesses, but her intelligence helps her when a dragon kidnaps her. Instead of waiting for rescue, Mabelrose escapes, taking a friendly hedgehog and a few useful-looking items (a pouch, a length of rope) that she doesn't know are magic.

This new edition from Dark Horse is in black and white; the previous Antarctic Press editions were in color.

Lewis and Clark. ABDO/Magic Wagon 2008 32p. Illustration (Bio-graphics)

Grades: 3 4 5 6 7 8 9   **917.8; 92; 741.5; 917**
  1. Biographical graphic novels; 2. Clark, William, 1770-1838; 3. Explorers; 4. Lewis and Clark Expedition (1804-1806); 5. Lewis, Meriwether, 1774-1809; 6. Territorial governors; 7. West (US) — Exploration; 8. Graphic novels
978-1-60270-069-7, $27.07

                     LC 2007-5578

This graphic format book tells the story of the Lewis and Clark Expedition, which explored the land of the Louisiana Purchase, as authorized in 1803 by President Thomas Jefferson. The book includes a timeline of the Expedition, a map of the route, and a list of books for further reading.

Neotopia Color Manga, Vol. 1: The Enlightened Age. Antarctic Press 2004 161p. Illustration

Grades: 7 8 9 10 11 12   **741.5; Fic**
  1. Science fiction graphic novels; 2. Graphic novels
978-1-932453-57-7, $9.99

"A young Grand Duchess who is not what she appears to be plays a role in a war to save her world . . . . The world of

Neotopia with all its different races is as much of a character as the people." (VOYA)

The battle scenes are depicted with drama but aren't traumatic. This series is an example of what has been called "Amerimanga" and "Global manga."

The **prince** of heroes, chapter I. Antarctic Press 2008 Un Illustration
Grades: 8 9 10 11 12   **741.5; Fic**
1. Adventure graphic novels; 2. Science fiction graphic novels; 3. Graphic novels
978-0-9801255-0-4, $14.95

Ronen and his mother Aiymie have lived on the planet Irdne for years; now she tells him they must leave and travel to the edge of the universe to meet his father. She refuses to tell Ronen who he is, or to what Darem clan they belong, and this has made them outcasts in Darem society. Then they learn that the Nationalist Armada, a fleet of thousands of ships, is on its way to take over Irdne, and all Darem colonials must leave. Ronen must leave his friends, and his martial arts teacher, behind. During a fight with Baron Ermont Mesozora and Baroness Mazza Mesozora, Ronen strips Mazza's clothing from her; nothing really shows, but it's clear she has lost her pants.

Estes, Max
Coffee and Donuts: A Junkyard Cats Comic. Top Shelf Productions 2006 112p. Illustration
Grades: 6 7 8 9 10 11 12 Adult   **741.5; Fic**
1. Cats; 2. Humorous graphic novels; 3. Graphic novels
1-891830-80-5, $10

Dwight and Jules live in an unused dumpster and scavenge their food; every morning a mystery person leaves coffee and donuts for them. When, desperate for money, they try (and fail) to rob an armored truck, real crooks Myles and Moose try to force them into real crime.

Hello, Again. Top Shelf Productions 2005 156p. Illustration
Grades: 11 12 Adult   **741.5; Fic**
1. Graphic novels
1-891830-63-5, $10.00

William is finding out that his past may not be buried as deep as he once thought. In fact, a colorful character from his past has just crawled out of the ground and is refusing to leave until William changes his ways. This is the tale of a drunken fisherman, an unfaithful fiancee, and a guilt ridden apartment manager, whose lives intersect with unsuspecting and dangerous consequences. The book includes some strong language and sexual situations (without any nudity).

Eto, Miyuki
Hell girl. Del Rey Manja 2008 Un Illustration
Grades: 10 11 12 Adult   **741.5; Fic**
1. Horror graphic novels; 2. Manga; 3. Graphic novels
978-0-345-50669-6, $10.99

In this volume, Ai Enma, Hell Girl, offers help to a beautiful teen idol who's being stalked by a long-ago costar of a failed children's television show; to a teenage girl who has become the victim of an obsessively possessive boyfriend who threatens the life of her childhood buddy, and to a girl with a sickly younger brother whose parents were killed by a hit-and-run driver and whose aunt and uncle take care of them only because of the money. A young girl discovers her grandmother isn't dead, but when she goes to visit her, she learns that her grandmother had used help from Hell Girl to protect her newborn daughter from a predatory landlord, and the village hates her for it. The horror is mostly psychological, but there is some violence.

Hell girl vol. 2. Del Rey Manga 2008 202p. Illustration
Grades: 10 11 12 Adult   **741.5; Fic**
1. Horror graphic novels; 2. Manga; 3. Shojo manga; 4. Graphic novels
978-0-345-50416-6, $10.95

Hell Girl is the ultimate avenger for those who have no one else to whom they can turn for help. If one goes to her website at midnight and enters the name of one's tormentor, Hell Girl will destroy that person. However, everyone who completes the contract with Hell Girl must also look forward to eternal torment in hell after death. In this volume, a spiteful figure skater tries to turn the two girls who beat her in competition against each other; a teenager only wants to save her younger sister from an abusive nanny; a boy in fragile health discovers who is stalking his best friend; the student class president can find no other way to save her friend from a vengeful new teacher. While there is no really graphic violence or bad language, the intensity of the stories make this series more appropriate for older teens.

Hell girl, vol. 4. Del Rey Manga 2008 184p. Illustration
Grades: 10 11 12 Adult   **741.5; Fic**
1. Horror graphic novels; 2. Manga; 3. Graphic novels
978-0-345-50418-0, $10.95

In this fourth volume, someone has set up a fake Hell Correspondence webpage, and students at a middle school are entering a harsh teacher's name, but the real Hell Girl, Ai Enma, does come for the real culprit. The price for her services, however, is eternal damnation of the requesters' souls. One young girl learns that her stepfather saddled his debts onto her father and then killed him. A group of neighbors take a stray dog they adopted to a woman who advertises that she will care for animals, only to discover she's abusing all of them—and the police won't listen to a bunch of kids. The book includes some violence.

Eury, Michael
The **Krypton** Companion. Twomorrows Publishing 2006 240p. Illustration
Grades: 9 10 11 12 Adult   **741.5**
1. Superhero graphic novels; 2. Superman (Fictional character); 3. Graphic novels
1-893905-61-6, $24.95

This book examines the "Superman mythology" that grew out of Superman comic books published by DC Comics from 1958 through 1986, under the direction of editors Mort Weisinger and Julius Schwartz. It includes interviews with a number of writers and artists who worked on Superman, including Neal Adams, Murphy Anderson, Steve Gerber, Jerry Siegel, Curt Swan, and many others, along with lots of art, photos, and behind-the-scenes stories.

Faerber, Jay
Noble causes archives volume one. Image Comics 2008 598p. Illustration
Grades: 10 11 12 Adult   **741.5; Fic**

1. Family life; 2. Science fiction graphic novels; 3. Superhero graphic novels; 4. Graphic novels
978-1-58240-896-5, $19.99

Normal young woman Liz Donnelly marries superhero Race Noble and gets a firsthand look at the inner workings of the celebrity superhero Noble family. Race is murdered while they're on their honeymoon, but the Nobles keep Liz with them. She finds that she has landed among some of the most dysfunctional people living a soap opera life. She has one brother-in-law who is now housed in a robotic body, another who is sort of immaterial, a sister-in-law who is pregnant and the father is one of the Noble family's greatest enemies, and the media keeps wanting to dig up as much dirt as they can, because gossip makes for high ratings. This volume reprints the early miniseries and the first twelve issues of the ongoing comics series in an economical black and white edition. The book includes violence, partial nudity, and sexual situations.

Volume 1 of 2

Fandel, Jennifer
  Jim Thorpe: Greatest Athlete in the World. By Jennifer Fandel ; illustrated by Rod Whigham. Capstone Press 2007 32p. Illustration
Grades: 3 4 5 6 7 8 9   **741.5; 796; 92**
  1. Athletes; 2. Thorpe, Jim; 3. Graphic novels
9781429601528, $29.99; 1429601523
                                   LC 2007000286
  This book uses the graphic novel format to tell the life story of Native American Jim Thorpe, star of the 1912 Olympic Games and member of the Pro Football Hall of Fame. The book includes additional facts and a list of books for further reading.
  Part of the Graphic Biographies series.

Fawkes, Ray
  One Soul. Ray Fawkes; [edited by] James Lucas Jones.. Oni Press 2011 176 p. Illustration
Grades: 11 12 Adult   **741.5**
  1. Identity (Philosophical concept); 2. Identity (Psychology); 3. Reincarnation; 4. Graphic novels
9781934964668, $24.99
                                   LC 2011922803
  Harvey Nominee: Best Graphic Novel (2012)
  Eisner Nominee: Best Graphic Album - New (2012)
  This graphic novel "follows a single soul as it's reincarnated through human history. . . . Each two-page spread is divided evenly into two three-by-three grids. Each of its 18 individual stories takes place in a single panel in that grid through the book's 88 spreads, so that to follow, say, the life of a silk heiress in Imperial China, the reader fastens the eye to a single spot in the book and then turns the pages quickly. . . . [Author Ray] Fawkes creates black-and-white tableaux of action, grief, sex and death spanning centuries. Individual spreads allow 18 characters to speak in unison, as when we see every subject's eyes widen simultaneously. When a character dies, his panel goes black for the rest of the book, and we meet the soul itself in cryptic narration." (Publishers Weekly)

Feiffer, Jules
  Explainers. Fantagraphics Books 2008 546p. Illustration
Grades: 9 10 11 12 Adult   **741.5**
  1. Humorous graphic novels; 2. Graphic novels
978-1-56097-835-0, $28.99; 1-56097-835-X
  This book collects the comic strips done by Jules Feiffer for the Village Voice, from 1956 through 1966. The alternative weekly newspaper, the only one of its kind back then, provided the then-unknown Feiffer with a forum to tackle all kinds of issues, ranging from relationships, sexuality, love, family, neuroses, politicians and politics, media, race, class, labor, religion, foreign policy, and war, among others. This is the first of four volumes planned to collect Feiffer's entire run of more than 2,000 strips. Older teen readers may be surprised to see just how timely and relevant these strips are, forty and fifty years after their original publication.

  ★ **Kill** My Mother: a graphic novel. Jules Feiffer. Liveright Publishing Corporation 2014 160 p. Illustration
Grades: 11 12 Adult   **741.5**
  1. Noir fiction; 2. Violence — Fiction; 3. Graphic novels
0871403145; 9780871403148, $27.95
                                   LC 2014005844
  "Along with three femme fatales, an obsessed daughter, and a loner heroine, 'Kill My Mother' features a fighter turned tap dancer, a small-time thug who dreams of being a hit man, a name-dropping cab driver, a communist liquor store owner, and a hunky movie star with a mind-boggling secret. Culminating in a U.S.O. tour on a war-torn Pacific island, this disparate band of old enemies congregate to settle scores." (Publisher's note)
  "The entire work feels pulled from an earlier time yet explosively modern, a madcap relic animated by an outrageous mind. An unusual, unforgettable, incomparable pulpy punch." Kirkus

  Passionella and Other Stories. Fantagraphics Books 2006 Un Illustration
Grades: 10 11 12 Adult   **741.5; Fic**
  1. Graphic novels
978-1-56097-097-2, $19.95
  This book collects Feiffer's extended graphic narratives of the late '50s and early '60s. "Excalibur and Rose" is the fable of a village comedian who embarks on a crusade in search of his serious side, which he finds in spades when he encounters his true love, the pathologically depressed Rose. "Passionella" retells Cinderella, seting it in modern Hollywood with a chimney sweep whose fairy godmother transforms her into the "mysterious exotic bewitching temptress"-and movie star-Passionella. "The Lonely Machine" is an account of one man's attempt to find the perfect relationship through robot love, and "Harold Swerg" recounts the predicament of the world's greatest athlete who'd rather stay at his

Courtesy of Fantagraphics

mundane job than compete against others, despite his country's desperate pleas to enter the Olympics. Three more graphic tales and several one-act plays round out this edition. There are some sexual situations.

Fein, Eric
The **Creation** of the Fantastic Four. Rosen Publishing Group 2006 48p. Illustration
Grades: 4 5 6 7 8 9 10   **741.5**
1. Fantastic Four (Fictional characters); 2. Superhero graphic novels; 3. Graphic novels
978-1-4042-0765-3, $29.25
LC 2005031170
Describes the history and development of the action heroes called the Fantastic Four and how they got their superpowers. Created in 1961 by the Marvel power team of Jack Kirby and Stan Lee, the Fantastic Four was the first superhero team the men created.
Part of the Action Heroes series.

The **Creation** of the Incredible Hulk. Rosen Publishing Group 2006 48p. Illustration
Grades: 4 5 6 7 8 9 10   **741.5**
1. Hulk (Fictional character); 2. Superhero graphic novels; 3. Graphic novels
978-1-4042-0764-6, $29.25
LC 2005035267
Discusses the unique character developed in 1962 by Stan Lee and Jack Kirby who was unable to live a normal life after he was affected by a gamma bomb's blast and Dr. Bruce Banner became the huge, inarticulate, super-strong Hulk. The book also includes information on the cultural climate in the U.S. at the time, and on the way the two men worked together at Marvel Comics.
Part of the Action Heroes series.

Felix, Rebecca
Exploring caves. By Rebecca Felix. Essential Library 2014 144 p. Color; Illustration (Story of exploration)
Grades: 5 6 7 8 9 10   **796.525**
1. Caves; 2. Caves — Juvenile literature; 3. Exploration
1624032494; 9781624032493, $35.64
LC 2013946594
A children's book by Rebecca Felix, part of The Story of Exploration series, "This title examines the exploration of caves. Easy-to-read, engaging text takes readers into the world's deepest caves, examines the explorers who journeyed to these dark, dangerous chambers, and traces the development of the technology and techniques that made this exploration possible." (OverDrive)
"The photographs will engage a wide audience. With some displaying, librarians may be able to offer it to people not even looking for information on the topic. This would serve nicely to round out a collection." VOYA
Includes bibliographical references and index

Ferraiolo, Jack D.
★ **Sidekicks**. Amulet 2011 309p.
Grades: 6 7 8 9   **741.5; Fic**
978-0-8109-9803-2, $16.95; 0-8109-9803-3
"By all outward appearances, Bright Boy is an average middle-school student, but at night, he becomes the sidekick

to superhero Rogue Warrior. . . . Ferraiolo is delightfully unafraid to inject irreverence into the superhero formula, adding plenty of humor to the high-adventure high jinks." Booklist

Fessenden, Larry
The **last** winter. Larry Fessenden and Robert Leaver; art by Brahm Revel. Image Comics 2008 128p. Illustration
Grades: 10 11 12 Adult   **741.5; Fic**
1. Arctic regions; 2. Horror graphic novels; 3. Science fiction graphic novels; 4. Graphic novels
978-1-58240-936-8, $12.99
Oil company troubleshooter Pollack arrives at the base of the company's advance team in the Arctic National Wildlife Refuge to find out what's holding up the team's reports. Hoffman, who is working on the environmental impact statements, says there's something wrong, the permafrost is melting, and the whole area is unsafe for building any ice roads. Then one of the team dies, and the others begin to succumb to mysterious fears. When Hoffman is recalled to corporate headquarters, the plane crashes, and there's no way out except to find help from other remote stations; there's only one skidoo left, and Pollack and Hoffman head out. Will they find help before everyone dies" The book includes some violence, partial nudity, and some harsh language. This book adapts the script for the 2006 motion picture starring Ron Perlman, which is being released on DVD in September 2008.

Fetter-Vorm, Jonathan
Trinity: a graphic history of the first atomic bomb. Jonathan Fetter-Vorm. Hill and Wang 2012 154 p. Illustration
Grades: 9 10 11 12   **623.4; 741.5; 623.4/5119**
1. Atomic bomb — History; 2. Atomic bomb — United States — History; 3 — Manhattan Projects (U.S.)
9780809094684, $22; 0809094681
LC 2011036622
This graphic novel, by Jonathan Fetter-Vorm, presents "the dramatic history of the race to build and the decision to drop the first atomic bomb. This sweeping historical narrative traces the spark of invention from the laboratories of nineteenth-century Europe to the massive industrial and scientific efforts of the Manhattan Project." (Publisher's note)
"Powerfully understated in both text and art, this matter-of-fact account of the atom bomb's development renders scientific complexity intelligible. There is no preaching here, so readers must ponder the illustrations of apocalyptic devastation in order to process the full implications of nuclear warfare." Kirkus

Fies, Brian
Mom's cancer. Abrams ComicArts 2008 115p. Illustration
Grades: 9 10 11 12 Adult   **616.99; 741.5**
1. Biographical graphic novels; 2. Cancer; 3. Graphic novels
978-0-8109-7107-3, $14.95
When writer/cartoonist Fies learned his mother had cancer and that it had already spread from her lungs, he used webcomics to depict what was happening to his mother and

the rest of the family as Mom fought the cancer. All the pain, the heartache, the little battles won, the effects on Fies' relationships with his sisters, the ultimate hope are all on the page. In the end, Mom beat the cancer. In an afterword, Fies tells the reader that some of the medications just wore down his mother's body, and she died shortly before the book was published.

First published 2006

Fiffe, Michel
    All-new ultimates: power for power. Writer: Michel Fiffe; artist: Amilcar Pinna; color artist, Nolan Woodard; letterer, VC's Clayton Cowles; cover artist, David Nakayama; assistant editor, Emily Shaw; editor, Mark Paniccia. Marvel Enterprises 2014 136 p. Color; Illustration
Grades: 9 10 11 12   **741.5**
    1. Crime — Fiction; 2. Spider-Man (Fictional character); 3. Superheroes — Fiction; 4. Youth — Fiction
    0785154272; 9780785154273, $17.99
    In this graphic novel by Michael Fiffe, illustrated by Amilcar Pinna, "Spider-Man, Black Widow, Kitty Pryde, Bombshell, Cloak and Dagger unite to tackle the vicious, rampant crime wave overtaking Hell's Kitchen! But the young Ultimates are put to the test as they try to survive their first mission: going head to head with the city's most ruthless gang, the Serpent Skulls, led by Diamondback." (Publisher's note)
    "Led by Jessica Drew, aka Spider-Woman (later Black Widow), the Ultimates include Spider-Man (Miles Morales, not Peter Parker), the romantic duo Cloak and Dagger, the volatile Bombshell, and the famous Kitty Pryde. . . . What they lack in experience, they make up for in enthusiasm and loyalty." SLJ
    Contains material originally published in magazine form as All-new Ultimates #1-6—Title page verso.

Filiu, Jean-Pierre
    Best of Enemies: A History of US and Middle East Relations: 1783-1953. Jean-Pierre Filiu, David B.. Harry N Abrams Inc. 2012 114 p. Illustration
Grades: 10 11 12 Adult   327.73056022/2; 327.730
    1. Christianity and other religions; 2. United States — Foreign relations — Middle East; 3. Graphic novels
    1906838453; 9781906838454, $24.95
    This graphic novel looks at "the history of U.S. and Middle East relations." It starts with "the murderous aggression of Gilgamesh-as-avatar . . . . [The] focus then moves to 1780s skirmishes with Muslim city-states over maritime piracy, shifting priorities of Christian and Muslim nations over oil and anti-Semitism, and the subsequent ousting by the Americans and the British of Iran's Mohammad Mossadegh." (Library Journal)

Fillbach, Matt
    Star Wars: Clone Wars Adventures Volume 8. Dark Horse Comics 2007 Un Illustration
Grades: 5 6 7 8 9 10   **741.5; Fic**
    1. Adventure graphic novels; 2. Science fiction graphic novels; 3. Star Wars; 4. Graphic novels
    978-1-59307-680-1, $6.95
    The stories in this volume take place during the Clone Wars. Luminara Unduli battles in the Arena of Doom, Aurra

Sing hunts a bounty on the Smuggler's Moon, Obi-Wan Kenobi disrupts an assassin's mission, and a battle droid makes a career change.

Fillbach, Shawn
    Maxwell Strangewell. By the Fillbach Brothers. Dark Horse Comics 2007 383p. Illustration
Grades: 9 10 11 12 Adult   **741.5; Fic**
    1. Adventure graphic novels; 2. Science fiction graphic novels; 3. Graphic novels
    978-1-59307-794-5, $19.95
    Photographer Anna Gilmour discovers a ten-foot-tall being immediately after his fall to Earth. He can't speak, but communicates through telepathic empathy, and Anna introduces him to her father as "Max." Their home is soon beset by a sea of beatific Tibetan monks, alien assassins in disguise, and heavy weapons fire. Max might not know who he is, but a lot of others sure as heck seem to. A galactic free-for-all is about to go down and Earth is ground zero. Before the final act, Anna and Max encounter a prophecy, the man in the moon, an entire race of alien accountants, and the Revolver - an innocuous-looking jogger responsible for keeping the world spinning. The book has some strong language and some violence.

Fisher, Bud
    Forever Nuts: Classic Screwball Strips: The Early Years of Mutt & Jeff. NBM 2007 192. Illustration
Grades: 10 11 12 Adult   **741.5**
    1. Mutt & Jeff (Fictional characters); 2. Graphic novels
    978-1-56163-502-3, $24.95
    One of the most long lasting and popular humor strips in history, Mutt and Jeff had many memorable moments of serious goofiness and irreverence. Here's a rediscovery of a true oddball classic maybe only outdone by the antic high living of its own creator. 2007 is the one hundredth anniversary of its start. In these early strips, alcohol consumption, smoking, gambling, and various other pursuits considered to be vices are portrayed.

Fisher, Jane Smith
    WJHC: Hold Tight!. Wilson Place Comics, Inc. 2005 96p. Illustration
Grades: 4 5 6 7 8 9 10   **741.5; Fic**
    1. Humorous graphic novels; 2. Graphic novels
    0-9744235-1-3, $11.95
    After the success of WJHC: On the Air, the crew of Jackson Hill High's wacky radio station is back. This time they struggle to save WJHC from a wicked faculty advisor who takes over the station, face the fears of reality TV when they participate on a survival-type television show, and race to claim passes to a backstage bash at the hottest concert of the year.

Fitzgerald, F. Scott
    The **curious** case of Benjamin Button: a graphic novel. Adapted by Nunzio Defilippis & Christina Weir; illustrated by Kevin Cornell. Quirk Books 2008 128p. Illustration
Grades: 9 10 11 12 Adult   **741.5; Fic**
    1. Authors; 2. Fitzgerald, F Scott (Francis Scott), 1896-1940; 3. Fitzgerald, F Scott (Francis Scott),

1896-1940 —
Adaptations; 4.
Humorous graphic
novels; 5. Novelists; 6.
Screenwriters; 7. Graphic
novels
978-1-59474-281-1,
$15.95

Courtesy of Quirk Books

LC 2008-923680
Benjamin Button
comes into the world in the
year 1860, but as a newborn
infant, he is the size of, and
looks like, a
seventy-year-old man. His
flabbergasted parents cope,
with difficulty, and
Benjamin finds he has to live his life in reverse, looking old
but with the mind and emotions of a child. When he's a
young man (but looks to be in late middle age), he marries a
young woman who likes older men, and he continues his
father's successful business. As he matures but continues to
grow younger, he becomes a military officer, and when he
looks like a teenager but is in late middle age, he attends
Harvard. Finally, in his old age, he resembles a newborn
baby and must have a nurse to take care of him. This story by
Fitzgerald was originally published in 1922; Cornell
illustrates it in sepia tones.

Fleisher, Michael
The **Original** Encyclopedia of Comic Book Heroes
Volume One, Featuring Batman. DC Comics 2007 391p.
Illustration
Grades: 9 10 11 12 Adult   **741.5**
1. Batman (Fictional character); 2. Graphic novels
978-1-4012-1355-8, $19.99
This book was originally published in 1976, and
chronicled the first twenty-six years of Batman comics.
Fleisher used the encyclopedia format to cover Batman and
all the major characters who appeared in the comics, places,
and adventures. Entries range in length from a few lines to
many pages. Illustrated in black and white with lots of
interior art from the early comics, this book is a treat for
anyone who wants to know about Batman's early career.

The **Original** Encyclopedia of Comic Book Heroes
Volume Two Featuring Wonder Woman. By Michael L.
Fleisher; assisted by Janet E. Lincoln. DC Comics 2007
253p. Illustration
Grades: 9 10 11 12 Adult   741.5
1. Wonder Woman (Fictional character); 2. Graphic novels
978-1-4012-1365-7, $19.99
Everything one ever wanted to know about DC's
Amazing Amazon " and so much more " can be found in this
in-depth volume, brought back into print for the first time in
30 years. Originally published in 1976, this comprehensive
volume includes every piece of information one could want
to know about Wonder Woman, her allies and enemies,
weapons in her quest for peace, and her adventures across
the decades. The book covers the first three decades of
Wonder Woman comics.

Fleming, Ann Marie
The **Magical** Life of Long Tack Sam: An Illustrated
Memoir. Ann Marie Fleming.. Riverhead Books 2007 170 p.
Illustration; Color
Grades: 11 12 Adult   **741.5; 793.8; 92**
1. Biographical graphic novels; 2. Long Tack Sam; 3.
Magicians; 4. Graphic novels
1594482640; 9781594482649, $20
LC 2007060352
This graphic memoir, by Ann Marie Fleming, was
"inspired by the award-winning documentary-and the life
and mystery of China's greatest magician. Who was Long
Tack Sam" He was born in 1885. He ran away from
Shangdung Province to join the circus. He was an acrobat. A
magician. A comic. An impresario. A restaurateur. A theater
owner. A world traveler. An East-West ambassador. A
mentor to Orson Welles. He was considered the greatest act
in the history of vaudeville." (Publisher's note)
Includes bibliographical references (p. 168-169)

Fletcher, Brenden
Gotham Academy; Volume 1: Welcome to Gotham
Academy. Becky Cloonan, Brenden Fletcher; illustrated by
Karl Kerschl. DC Comics 2015 160 p. Color; Illustration
Grades: 7 8 9 10 11 12   **741.5**
1. Amnesia — Fiction; 2. School stories
9781401254728, $14.99
LC 2015007185
"Gotham Academy [is] the most prestigious school in
Gotham City. Only the best and brightest students may enter
its halls, study in its classrooms, explore its secret passages,
summon its terrifying spiritsà Okay, so Gotham Academy
isn't like other schools. But Olive Silverlock isn't like other
students. After a mysterious incident over summer break,
she's back at school with a bad case of amnesia."
(Publisher's note)
"Filled with spunky and quirky characters and
unexpected plot turns, this work adds an intriguing and fresh
layer to the Batman mythos. . . . Kerschl's campy art is by
turns luminous and gloomy, enhancing Cloonan and
Fletcher's energetic and sometimes contemplative text." SLJ
Originally published in single magazine form as Gotham
Academy 1-6
Volume 1 of an ongoing series

★ **Flight, volume six**
Edited by Kazu Kibuishi. Villard Books 2009 284p.
Illustration
Grades: 8 9 10 11 12 Adult   **741.5; Fic**
1. Fantasy graphic novels; 2. Short stories; 3. Graphic
novels
978-0-345-50590-3, $25
This sixth volume of the graphic anthology series
includes stories by fifteen creators: J.P. Ahonen, Graham
Annable, Bannister, Phil Craven, Mike Dutton, Michel
Gagne, Cory Godbey, Rodolphe Guenoden, Steve Hamaker,
Kazu Kibuishi, Andrea Offermann, Richard Pose, Justin
Ridge, Rad Sechrist, and Kean Soo. Returning favorite
characters includ Jellaby by Soo, Hamaker's Fish N Chips,
Kibuishi's Daisy Kutter, and the wordless little fox Rex by
Gagne. Bannister's "Cooking Duel" stands out as a lot of
fun, as a couple makes a bet about which of them can make

the better tasting mushroom quiche; and Justin Ridge's "Dead Bunny" shows that there is a soul mate for just about anyone, including a zombie bunny.

Foglio, Kaja

Girl Genius Book Six: Agatha Heterodyne and the Golden Trilobite. Story by Kaja & Phil Foglio; drawings by Phil Foglio. Airship Entertainment 2007 Un Illustration
Grades: 9 10 11 12 Adult   **741.5; Fic**
1. Adventure graphic novels; 2. Fantasy graphic novels; 3. Humorous graphic novels; 4. Graphic novels
978-1-890856-42-7, $21.95

The Wulfenbachs discover that Agatha is still alive and come to get her. Things are complicated by the fact that Agatha is currently possessed by the evil mastermind responsible for the Long War - her mother, Lucrezia. Agatha keeps fighting back, and things get very chaotic when she keeps flipping back and forth between herself and the evil Lucrezia. This book has some violence.

Girl Genius Omnibus Edition #1. Story by Kaja & Phil Foglio; drawings by Phil Foglio. Airship Entertainment 2006 312p. Illustration
Grades: 9 10 11 12 Adult   **741.5; Fic**
1. Adventure graphic novels; 2. Science fiction graphic novels; 3. Graphic novels
978-1-890856-40-3, $14.95

In a time when the Industrial Revolution has become an all-out war, Mad Science rules the world. Agatha Clay is a student at Transylvania Polygnostic University, a complete klutz with rotten luck. But when the University is overthrown and a mechanical monster stalks the streets, it begins to look as though Agatha may carry a spark of Mad Science after all. She ends up aboard the giant airship Castle Wulfenbach, and finds an ally in Krosp the Cat (a genetic experiment with a smattering of Napoleon's brain cells); she also becomes friends with Gilgamesh, Baron Wulfenbach's son. When the Monster Engine is activated, Agatha and Gil battle it, then Agatha and Krosp make their escape. This black and white edition contains the first three volumes of the Girl Genius collection: Agatha Heterodyne & the Beetleburg Clank, Agatha Heterodyne & the Airship City, and Agatha Heterodyne & the Monster Engine. Agatha tends to do a lot of her best tech work while wearing pajamas.

Girl Genius Vol. 4: Agatha Heterodyne and the Circus of Dreams. Story by Kaja & Phil Foglio; drawings by Phil Foglio. Airship Entertainment 2005 127p. Illustration
Grades: 9 10 11 12 Adult   **741.5; Fic**
1. Adventure graphic novels; 2. Science fiction graphic novels; 3. Graphic novels
978-1-890856-36-6, $20.95

The Adventure, Romance & Mad Science continues as Agatha Heterodyne's damaged aircraft comes roughly to rest in the Wastelands. She encounters a traveling circus and proves her mettle by destroying a massive spider-clank as it attacks. Back at the airship city, a frustrated Baron Wulfenbach dispatches his son Gilgamesh and deposed pirate queen Bangaldesh DuPree to capture Agatha, whose very existence threatens the peace - but the cunning circus folk succeed in hiding Agatha, who quickly discovers she is only one of their many secrets. She begins warrior training with the circus's expert swordswoman Zeetha, meets a

strange new breed of Jagermonster, and attracts unexpected attention in saving them from the grimmest of fates. This volume is in full color. The book has some monster fighting.

Girl Genius Vol. 5: Agatha Heterodyne and the Clockwork Princess. Story by Kaja & Phil Foglio; drawings by Phil Foglio. Airship Entertainment 2006 109p. Illustration
Grades: 9 10 11 12 Adult   **741.5; Fic**
1. Adventure graphic novels; 2. Science fiction graphic novels; 3. Graphic novels
978-1-890856-39-7, $19.95

Agatha continues to travel with the circus, but they have to pass through a town where the prince confiscated one of their clanks, Tinka, who is actually one of the Muses of the Storm King. When they are ordered to play a command performance and Agatha plays Lucrezia, the prince recognizes her as a real Heterodyne. Now she's really in trouble. Meanwhile, Baron Wulfenbach discovers that he's been duped and Agatha is still alive.

Foglio, Phil

Girl Genius book seven: Agatha Heterodyne and the voice of the castle. Story by Kaja and Phil Foglio; drawings by Phil Foglio. Airship Entertainment 2008 128p. Illustration
Grades: 9 10 11 12 Adult   **741.5; Fic**
1. Adventure graphic novels; 2. Humorous graphic novels; 3. Science fiction graphic novels; 4. Graphic novels
978-1-890856-45-8, $21.95

After the battle at Sturmhalten, everyone converges on Mechanicsburg. The severely injured Baron is in the hospital, and Gilgamesh must fend off all the would-be assassins trying to strike while the Baron is weak. A fake Heterodyne heir enters Mechanicsburg and gets into the Heterodyne castle. And Agatha and her friends arrive and she manages to convince the old castle Seneschal that she just might be the real Heterodyne heir. Only the real heir will be able to control the sentient castle, but the fake one in there now plans to kill the castle. There is fighting action but no graphic violence, or harsh language, or any really objectionable content.

Foley, Ryan

Don Bluth presents Dragon's Lair, volume 1. Ryan Foley and Andy Mangels ; art by Fabio Laguna. Arcana Comics, Inc. 2008 Un Illustration
Grades: 7 8 9 10 11 12   **741.5; Fic**
1. Adventure graphic novels; 2. Fantasy graphic novels; 3. Humorous graphic novels; 4. Graphic novels
978-0-9763095-5-0, $19.95

Dirk the Daring has fought against many a villain and slain many dragons, and he has won the heart of the beautiful Princess Daphne. But all is not quite well in the land, and while they travel homeward on a trip, a huge dragon attacks and takes Daphne. The dragon is Singe, father of all the dragons slain by Dirk, and he wants revenge. Now Dirk must go on a rescue mission, while Singe wants to turn Daphne into yet another fawning, scantily-clad princess slave to join the many he already has. Based on the Dragon's Lair video game, this book is full of action as Dirk faces many obstacles on his quest.

Fontes, Justine

The **Trojan** Horse: The Fall of Troy; story by Justine & Ron Fontes ; pencils by Gordon Purcell ; inks by Barbara Schulz. Lerner Publishing Group/Graphic Universe 2007 48p. Illustration
Grades: 3 4 5 6 7 8 9   **398.2; 741.5**
    1. Greek mythology; 2. Troy (Extinct city); 3. Graphic novels
    978-0-8225-3085-5, $26.60 lib. Bdg.

This story is adapted from Virgil's Aeneid and from Smyrnacus Quintus' Posthomerica. The Trojan War has raged for ten years; then suddenly the Greek forces pull back. When the Trojans venture outside their city walls, they discover a giant wooden horse and a messenger. Should they accept this peace offering" Or is the gift horse too good to be true" This book includes a glossary and a list of books and websites for further reading.

Fontes, Ron

Atalanta: The Race Against Destiny; story by Justine & Ron Fontes ; pencils and inks by Thomas Yeates ; [coloring by Hi-Fi Design ; lettering by Bill Hauser]. Lerner Publishing Group/Graphic Universe 2007 48p. Illustration
Grades: 3 4 5 6 7 8 9
292.1; 741.5
    1. Atlanta (Greek mythology); 2. Greek mythology
    978-0-8225-5965-8, $26.60 lib bdg

Courtesy of Lerner Publishing Group/Graphic Universe

Atalanta is the best hunter and swiftest runner in the land. The Oracle at Delphi has warned her to never marry, but her father, a powerful king, insists that she choose a husband. Atalanta declares she will only marry the man who can beat her in a footrace. Can she escape her fate?

Captured by pirates. Justine & Ron Fontes ; illustrations by David Witt. Lerner Publishing Group/Graphic Universe 2007 112p. Illustration (Twisted Journeys)
Grades: 3 4 5 6 7 8 9   **741.5; Fic**
    1. Adventure graphic novels; 2. Pirates; 3. Graphic novels
    978-0-8225-6201-6, $27.93; 978-0-8225-6202-3 (pa), $7.95
                                        LC 2006-101599
In the series called Twisted Journeys, readers choose how the story will progress. Pages of text alternate with comic book-style pages. In this volume, "you" are a young boy on a voyage with your father on his ship, when pirates capture the ship. Will you fight them, or will you join them? Readers will find many scenarios played out, depending on their choices; some end well, others not so well.

Demeter & Persephone: Spring Held Hostage; story by Justine & Ron Fontes ; pencils by Steve Kurth ; inks by Barbara Schultz. Lerner Publishing Group/Graphic Universe 2007 48p. Illustration
Grades: 3 4 5 6 7 8 9   **292.1; 741.5**
    1. Demeter (Greek deity); 2. Greek mythology; 3. Persephone (Greek deity); 4. Graphic novels
    978-0-8225-5966-5, $26.60 lib. Bdg.

The goddess Demeter spreads warmth and bounty throughout the world, but when her daughter Persephone disappears and Demeter learns she has been kidnapped by Hades, the god of the underworld, her sorrow causes a permanent winter to fall upon the land. Can Demeter rescue Persephone from the underworld, and can the other gods and goddesses of Mount Olympus convince Demeter to bring back spring and summer?

Forbes, Jake

Jim Henson's Return to Labyrinth. Illustrated by Chris Lie. Tokyopop 2006 Un Illustration
Grades: 7 8 9 10 11 12 Adult   **741.5; Fic**
    1. Adventure graphic novels; 2. Fantasy graphic novels; 3. Graphic novels
    1-59816-725-1, $9.99

The Goblin King has kept a watchful eye on Toby, his minions secretly guiding and protecting the child. Legions of goblins work behind the scenes to ensure that Toby has whatever his heart desires, preparing him for the day when he will return to the Labyrinth and take his rightful place beside Jareth as the heir to the Goblin Kingdom. That day has come ... but no one has told Toby. This is an original story set in the world of the motion picture and is focused on Toby, who was a baby in the movie. This book is a global manga title.

Ford, Michael

The **Hunchback** of Notre Dame; illustrated by Penke Gelev ; retold by Michael Ford. Barron's Educational Series, Inc. 2007 48p. Illustration
Grades: 3 4 5 6 7 8 9   **741.5**
    1. Hugo, Victor; 2. Hugo, Victor, 1802-1885 — Adaptations; 3. Graphic novels
    978-0-7641-3493-7 (pa); 978-0-7641-5979-4

Abandoned as a baby and raised in the cathedral of Notre Dame, the hunchback Quasimodo lives as an outcast. The arrival of the beautiful gypsy girl Esmeralda begins a tragic series of events marked by jealousy, betrayal, and murder. This volume includes a brief biography of Hugo and of Notre Dame, and information on the importance of the novel and its adaptations.

Forget, Thomas

The **Creation** of Captain America. Rosen Publishing Group 2006 48p. Illustration
Grades: 4 5 6 7 8 9 10   **741.5**
    1. Captain America (Fictional character); 2. Superhero graphic novels; 3. Graphic novels
    978-1-4042-0766-0, $29.25
                                        LC 2005032024
Captain America has been a hero since 1940 and saved comic books and Marvel Comic Group. This volume discusses the times during which Cap was created and how

the character has changed over the years. In light of the character's death in the aftermath of the Marvel Civil War storyline that played out in comics during 2006 and 2007, this book may have wide appeal.

Part of the Action Heroes series.

Fox, Gardner

The **Atom** Archives Volume 2. Pencils by Gil Kane; inks by Murphy Anderson. DC Comics 2003 215p. Illustration

Grades: 7 8 9 10 11 12 Adult   741.5; Fic
1. Atom (Fictional character); 2. Superhero graphic novels; 3. Graphic novels
1-4012-0014-1, $49.95

This volume, reprinting The Atom issues #6-13, originally published in 1963 through 1964, features Mighty Mite's early team-ups with Hawkman and Hawkgirl, the classic villainy of Dr. Light, the return of Chronos, and much more. This Archive Edition reprints the comics in full color in a hardcover edition.

The **Green** Lantern Archives Volume 5. DC Comics 2004 239p. Illustration

Grades: 6 7 8 9 10 11 12 Adult   741.5; Fic
1. Green Lantern (Fictional character); 2. Superhero graphic novels; 3. Graphic novels
1-4012-0404-X, $49.95

LC 93-131923

This volume presents the further adventures of Green Lantern Hal Jordan "the Silver Age's science fiction-influenced hero. This time, the Emerald Gladiator squares off against foes such as Dr. Light, Hector Hammond, Evil Star, the Aerialist, and many more. This full-color Archive reprints nine tales from Green Lantern #30-38, originally published in 1964 and 1965."

Showcase Presents: Adam Strange Volume One. DC Comics 2007 510p. Illustration

Grades: 6 7 8 9 10 11 12 Adult   741.5; Fic
1. Superhero graphic novels; 2. Graphic novels
978-1-4012-1313-8, $16.99

After being mysteriously teleported to a distant world by an alien scientist, Adam Strange went from being an Earth archaeologist to a cosmic adventurer. He soon becomes the hero of the planet Rann, shuttling between his old and new worlds via the Zeta Beam. With the love of his life, Alanna, daughter of Rann's leading scientist, they embark on a series of adventures against all types of space menaces. This black and white volume reprints stories from 1958 through 1963.

Showcase Presents: Green Lantern Volume 1. DC Comics 2005 528p. Illustration

Grades: 6 7 8 9 10 11 12 Adult   741.5; Fic
1. Green Lantern (Fictional character); 2. Superhero graphic novels; 3. Graphic novels
1-4012-0759-6, $9.99

A dying alien summoned test pilot Hal Jordan and gave him the most powerful weapon in the universe: a power ring. Jordan was inducted into the universe-spanning Green Lantern Corps and assigned to protect a sector of space including Earth. His sheer willpower directs the ring to create fantastic energy constructs and with it, protect the

good from evil. In these earliest stories, readers meet the Guardians of the Universe, many of Jordan's intergalactic comrades, and some of his deadliest opponents, including Hector Hammond, Sonar, and Sinestro. The black and white reprints date from 1959 through 1962.

Showcase Presents: Hawkman Volume 1. DC Comics 2007 560p. Illustration

Grades: 7 8 9 10 11 12 Adult   741.5; Fic
1. Hawkman (Fictional character); 2. Superhero graphic novels; 3. Graphic novels
978-1-4012-1280-3, $16.99

Katar Hol and his wife Shayera, winged law officers from the planet Thanagar, visit Earth to learn about terrestrial police methods. To fit into human society, they adopt the civilian identities of Carter Hall, the curator of the Midway City Museum, and Shiera, his assistant. Dressed in their avian Thanagarian garb, Carter and Shiera patrol the skies of Midway City as Hawkman and Hawkgirl. They plunge headlong into the battle for justice against such villains as the Shadow Thief and Matter Master. With their array of alien weaponry and their scientific skill, this crime-fighting duo continue to defend Earth against nefarious threats. This book collects black and white reprints of thirty-three stories written by Fox, dating from 1961 through 1966 and featuring the work of artists such as Joe Kubert, Murphy Anderson, and Carmine Infantino.

Showcase Presents: Justice League of America Volume 1. DC Comics 2005 544p. Illustration

Grades: 6 7 8 9 10 11 12 Adult   741.5; Fic
1. Justice League of America (Fictional characters); 2. Superhero graphic novels
1-4012-0761-8, $16.99

Some of the greatest super heroes in the DC Universe united to form the Justice League of America: Superman, Batman, Wonder Woman, the Flash, Green Lantern, Martian Manhunter, and Aquaman. Together, they face such foes as Dr. Light, Dr. Destiny, Starro, Felix Faust, Amos Fortune, and the Weapons Master. This volume includes the stories in which the JLS inducts new members to the team: Green Arrow and the Atom. In light of the events in Infinite Crisis, readers might be interested to see how far back the roots of the story went - all the way back to 1960. This black and white reprint volume includes stories published from 1960 through 1962.

Fraction, Matt

Casanova; Volume 1: Luxuria. By Matt Fraction & Gabriel Bá; lettering by Sean Konot. Image Comics 2007 Un Illustration

Grades: 11 12 Adult   741.5; Fic
1. Adventure graphic novels; 2. Science fiction graphic novels; 3. Spies; 4. Graphic novels
9781582408972; 978-1-58240-689-3, $24.99

Meet Casanova Quinn: prodigal son of a law-and-order family hell-bent on keeping the world safe and sound through its organization, E.M.P.I.R.E.,; now blackmailed into betraying his father and E.M.P.I.R.E. Luxuria collects the first volume of Casanova as its titular star transforms from devil-may-care thrill-seeker into the most dangerous man in the world. What happens when the ultimate player gets played" Find out in this genre-bending story that combines spy action with science fiction. Frequent use of harsh language combines with sexual situations and violence to make this more appropriate for older teens and adults.

Also available in a deluxe hardcover edition
Other Casanova volumes are: 2: Gula; 3: Avaritia; 4: Acedia

The **Five** Fists of Science. Written by Matt Fraction; illustrated by Steven Sanders. Image Comics 2006 Un Illustration
Grades: 9 10 11 12 Adult   741.5; Fic
  1. Adventure graphic novels; 2. Science fiction graphic novels; 3. Graphic novels
  1-58240-605-7, $12.99
At the beginning of the twentieth century, Mark Twain and Nicola Tesla work to save the world from the menace of war. J.P. Morgan, Andrew Carnegie, Thomas Edison, and Guillermo Marconi are having the Innsmouth Tower built; what the world doesn't know is that they intend to summon some monstrous old gods (anyone familiar with H.P. Lovecraft and his Cthulhu Mythos will catch on immediately). Meanwhile, Twain and Tesla have been trying to interest world leaders in technology that will end all war, only to find that no one is interested. When Marconi realizes what Morgan is really planning, he tells Tesla and Twain, in hopes that their robotic machine can stop Morgan. Some harsh language and violence pepper the story.

Hawkeye: Little Hits. By Matt Fraction (Author), David Aja (Illustrator), Javier Pulido (Illustrator), Steve Lieber (Illustrator), Francesco Francavilla (Illustrator), Jesse Hamm (Illustrator). Marvel Worldwide 2013 136 p.
Grades: 11 12 Adult   741.5; Fic
  1. Avengers (Fictional characters); 2. Superheroes — Fiction; 3. Graphic novels
  0785165630; 9780785165637, $16.99
In this graphic novel, by Matt Fraction, "ace archer Clint Barton faces the digital doomsday of DVR-Mageddon! Then: Cherry's got a gun. And she looks good in it. And Hawkeye gets very, very distracted. Plus: Valentine's Day with the heartthrob of the Marvel Universe" This will be...confusing." (Publisher's note)
"Fraction's writing is superb, but it's Eisner-winning Aja's wildly creative page layouts that have matured into something truly unique and demanding of critical attention." Booklist

Hawkeye: my life as a weapon. By Matt Fraction (Author), David Aja (Illustrator), Javier Pulido (Illustrator). Marvel Worldwide 2013 136 p.
Grades: 11 12 Adult   741.5; Fic
  1. Avengers (Fictional characters); 2. Superheroes — Fiction; 3. Graphic novels
  0785165622; 9780785165620, $16.99
In this book, by Matt Fraction, "Clint Bartonûaka the self-made hero Hawkeye fights for justice! With ex-Young Avenger Kate Bishop by his side, he's out to prove himself as one of Earth's Mightiest Heroes! SHIELD recruits Clint to intercept a packet of incriminating evidenceûbefore he becomes the most wanted man in the world." (Publisher's note)

Hawkeye: Rio Bravo. By Matt Fraction; illustrated by Francesco Francavilla, David Aja and Annie Wu. Marvel Enterprises 2015 160 p. Color; Illustration
Grades: 10 11 12 Adult   741.5973; 741.5
  1. Superhero comic books, strips, etc
  0785185313; 9780785185314, $17.99
In this comic book, by Matt Fraction, "Reeling from recent events, even Hawkeye wants to know what his new status quo is. Who's with him" Who's against him" Who's trying to kill him and why" So many dang questions! And just when Clint's rock bottom couldn't arrive fast enough...his brother shows up. After a lifetime of decisions both good and bad, Clint and Barney Barton have to realize that they are brothers and ultimately, they're the only ones who can save one another." (Publisher's note)

Hawkeye; Volume 3: L.A. Woman. By Matt Fraction; illustrated by Annie Wu and Javier Pulido. Marvel Worldwide 2014 144 p. Color; Illustration
Grades: 11 12 Adult   741.5
  1. Assassins — Fiction; 2. Criminals — Fiction; 3. Los Angeles (Calif) — Fiction; 4. Musicians — Fiction
  0785183906; 9780785183907, $15.99
In this book, by Matt Fraction, illustrated by Annie Wu and Javier Pulido, "Kate Bishop heads to Los Angeles to get away from New York, life, and Clint Barton—but not away from trouble! Because Madame Masque is hanging out at poolside with the rich and famous as well! As Kate helps a reclusive and Sixties-damaged pop music genius find his lost masterpiece, Madame Masque finds Kate. By which we mean starts trying to kill her again." (Publisher's note)
"Fraction's unique brand of storytelling is both light with humor and deep with meaning, and he keeps it fresh by constantly bringing in new characters." Booklist
Contains material originally published in magazine form as Hawkeye #14, #16, #18, #20 and Annual #1—Title page verso.

★ **Fractured fables**
Edited by Jim Valentino and Kristen K. Simon; book design by Jim Valentino; cover illustration by Michael and Laura Allred from a sketch by Jim Valentino; cover design and graphics by Tim Daniel. Image Comics 2010 159p. Illustration
Grades: 6 7 8 9   741.5
  978-1-60706-269-1, $29.99; 1-60706-269-0
                           LC 2010014838
Presents, in comic book format, thirty familiar fairy tales, songs, fables, and stories as retold by such acclaimed authors and illustrators as Ben Templesmith, Jim Di Bartolo, Scott Morse, and May Ann Licudine.
"This is a great adaptation highly worth reading or just browsing the artwork and illustrations." Voice Youth Advocates

Frakes, Colleen
  Prison island: a graphic memoir. By Colleen Frakes. Houghton Mifflin Harcourt 2015 187 p. Illustration
Grades: 9 10 11 12 Adult   741.5; 741.56973
  1. Prisons — United States; 2. Washington (State)
  1942186029; 9781942186021, $16.99

In this graphic memoir, by Colleen Frake, "McNeil Island in Washington state was the home of the last prison island in the United States, accessible only by air or sea. It was also home to about fifty families, including . . . Frake's. Her parents—like nearly everyone else on the island—both worked in the prison, where her father was the prison's captain and her mother worked in security." (Publisher's note)

Frampton, Otis
   Oddly Normal. Image 2015 128 p. Illustration
Grades: 4 5 6 7 8 9   **741.5; Fic**
   1. Fantasy graphic novels; 2. Humorous graphic novels; 3. Graphic novels
   978-1-63215-226-8, $9.99
   Written and illustrated by Otis Frampton, this graphic novel describes how "Oddly must travel to Fignation to uncover the mystery of her parents' disappearance. Join Oddly as she navigates a strange new school, teenage angst, monstrous bullies, and Evil itself on an unforgettable fantasy adventure through the vibrant world of Fignation in Oddly Normal." (Publisher's note)
   Volume 1 of 3

   Oddly Normal: Family Reunion. Viper Comics 2007
Un Illustration
Grades: 4 5 6 7 8 9 10   **741.5; Fic**
   1. Fantasy graphic novels; 2. Humorous graphic novels; 3. Graphic novels
   978-0-9777883-9-2, $11.95
   In this second volume, Oddly meets Tommy Tsunami, who is a comic book hero in the real world, and her friends Reggie and Ragnar seem a bit jealous. Then Ragnar's dad returns and claims that Oopie, the creature Ragnar created and that has bonded with Oddly, holds the secret needed to continue his experiments. And the new teacher in school is actually Mr. Gooseberry in female form, with Oddly's mother's face - and he is determined to force her to ask him to help, for a price.

Freeman, Adam
   Monster Attack Network. Marc Bernardin and Adam Freeman; art by Nima Sorat. AiT/PlanetLar 2007 96p. Illustration
Grades: 10 11 12 Adult   **741.5**
   1. Adventure graphic novels; 2. Monsters; 3. Graphic novels
   978-1-932051-50-6, $12.95
   The island of Lapuatu is a paradise, except for the various giant monsters that occasionally attack. The Monster Attack Network fights the beasties and rebuilds from the destruction. When Lana Barnes starts to work for M.A.N., though, things get really crazy and monsters attack two and three at a time giant slugs, bats, and other destructive critters. Nate Klinger, one of the top first responders at M.A.N., knows something's a bit off about Lana; for one thing, she's a native Lapuatan despite her name. And the monsters have never attacked more than one at a time before she started to work. The book includes lots of foul language and monster fighting action.

Fujima, Takuya
   Free Collars Kingdom Vol. 1. Random House/Del Rey Manga 2007 240p. Illustration
Grades: 10 11 12 Adult   **741.5; Fic**
   1. Cats; 2. Fantasy graphic novels; 3. Manga; 4. Graphic novels
   978-0-345-49265-4, $10.95
   Cyan is a teenage cat (in cat years), and when his beloved young master falls ill, the parents abandon Cyan in the basement of a luxurious apartment building. Now Cyan finds himself smack-dab in the middle of the biggest feline territorial battle in Japan. While waiting for his owner to return and reclaim him, Cyan has to brave the attacks of vampy Siam and the beautiful killer Kline. He also must try to fit in with the group of oddball strays who reside in the basement, a cat gang named the Free Collars. The conceit here is that the cats are drawn as cute cat-eared humans. There's some partial nudity and sexually suggestive situations.

Fujisaki, Ryu
   Hoshin Engi Volume 1. Viz Media/Shonen Jump 2007
192p. Illustration
Grades: 8 9 10 11 12 Adult   **741.5; Fic**
   1. Adventure graphic novels; 2. Fantasy graphic novels; 3. Shonen manga; 4. Graphic novels
   978-1-4215-1362-1, $7.99
   When his clan is wiped out by a beautiful demon, young Taikobo finds himself in charge of the mysterious Hoshin Project. Its mission: find all immortals living in the human world and seal them away forever. But who do you trust—and whose side are you really on—when you've been trained to hunt demons by a demon. There is demon-fighting action.

Fujishima, Kosuke
   Oh My Goddess! Volume 1. Dark Horse Comics 2005
192p. Illustration
Grades: 8 9 10 11 12   **741.5; Fic**
   1. Fantasy graphic novels; 2. Humorous graphic novels; 3. Shonen manga; 4. Graphic novels
   1-59307-387-9, $10.95
   Alone in his dorm on a Saturday night, Nekomi Tech student Keiichi Morisato dials a wrong number that will change his life forever - reaching the Goddess Technical Help Line. Granted one wish by the charming young goddess Belldandy - a wish for anything in the world - Keiichi wishes she would stay with him always. Complications are bound to ensue from this; the immediate first being the new couple getting tossed out of the dorm - it's males only. As the hapless student and his mysterious "foreign beauty" ride around looking for a new place to stay - risking the different dangers of seeking shelter with an otaku convinced Belldandy is an imaginary woman, and a Zen priest convinced she's a sinister witch - Keiichi's still got his classes on Monday morning. How is his new "exchange student" companion going to be received on the N.I.T. campus" A little too well for normal life to ever return... This is the beginning of the series in a new edition that restores the original right-to-left page orientation and includes a notes section. This classic "harem" manga has very mild sexual innuendo and focuses more on the comedy.

Fujiyama, Kairi
    Dragon Eye, Volume 1. Ballantine Books/Del Rey Manga 2007 192p. Illustration
Grades: 8 9 10 11 12   **741.5; Fic**
    1. Adventure graphic novels; 2. Science fiction graphic novels; 3. Shonen manga; 4. Graphic novels
978-0-345-49665-2, $10.95
    Ten years before, a deadly virus devastated the world, turning its victims into bloodthirsty Dracules; human soon learned that the only cure is death. The people who rose up to fight the Dracules are called VIUS. Now, in the VIUS city Mikuni, a new recruit named Leila Mikami joins VIUS; she's determined to find a Dragon Eye, a powerful magic weapon she plans to use to get revenge for her family's death. To her surprise, bumbling recruit Issa Kazuma is actually a VIUS captain, and when top-level Dracules invade the candidates' final exam, he reveals his Dragon Eye. Leila joins Kazuma's Squad Zero as they work to protect Mikuni from Dracules. This first volume offers lots of action and monster killing.

Fukuchi, Tsubasa
    The **Law** of Ueki Vol. 1. Viz Media 2006 192p. Illustration
Grades: 7 8 9 10 11 12   **741.5; Fic**
    1. Humorous graphic novels; 2. Shonen manga; 3. Graphic novels
978-1-4215-0716-3, $9.99
    In a world of powerful celestial beings, an epic contest is being conducted to select the next king. Each Celestial selects a kid in junior high to be his champion and grants him a special power. The kids battle it out, losers are eliminated, and the winners are granted new talents. Seemingly ordinary Kosuke Ueki has been chosen to be a contender in the tournament. Granted the power to change trash into trees, Ueki has two disadvantages to overcome: one, he doesn't know he's a participant in the tournament, and two, how the heck can anyone win a battle with the power to turn trash into trees? Especially when his first opponent has power over fire?

Fukushima, Haruka
    Cherry Juice Volume 1. Tokyopop 2007 Un Illustration
Grades: 9 10 11 12   **741.5; Fic**
    1. Manga; 2. Romance graphic novels; 3. Shojo manga; 4. Graphic novels
978-1-4278-0286-6, $9.99
    After five awkward years, step-siblings Minami and Otome are finally getting along as true siblings might, even to the point of offering each other romantic advice. But when Amane, Minami's best friend, confesses his love for Otome, suddenly the siblings' peaceful relationship takes an unpredictable turn that leaves them wondering: who are they really in love with? The book has nudity, some fan service (panty shots of Otome and shirtless shots of Minami), and some sexual suggestiveness.

Fuller, Nicolle Rager
    Charles Darwin's On the Origin of Species: a graphic adaptation. [by] Michael Keller; art by Nicolle Rager Fuller. Rodale 2009 192p. Illustration
Grades: 9 10 11 12 Adult   **576.8; 741.5**

978-1-60529-697-5; 1-60529-697-X, $19.99;
978-1-60529-948-8 (pa); 1-60529-948-0 (pa), $14.99
                    LC 2009-11387
    "The graphic novel follows Origin's original chapters, combining snippets of Darwin's text with quotes from letters, illustrative examples from his time and from the present, and occasional invented dialog. Fuller's images of people seem clumsy, but her full-color plants, animals, charts, maps, and scientific accoutrements are attractive and effective.... [This] version well conveys both the science and the wonder of Origin." Libr J

Furman, Simon
    Transformers: Beast Wars: The Gathering; art by Don Figueroa. IDW Publishing 2007 Un Illustration
Grades: 4 5 6 7 8 9   **741.5; Fic**
    1. Science fiction graphic novels; 2. Transformers (Fictional characters); 3. Graphic novels
978-1-60010-025-3, $9.99
    In this story, Predacon General Magmatron is on a mission to capture the renegade Megatron, but his true intentions are fare more terrifying; he ultimately aims to bring Cybertron itself to its knees. All he need is an army, and he knows exactly where to find one. The heroic Maximals now have to battle the evil Predacons to protect their planet.

Furse, Sophie
    Moby Dick; illustrated by Penko Gelev ; retold by Sophie Furse. Barron's Educational Series, Inc. 2007 48p. Illustration
Grades: 3 4 5 6 7 8 9   **741.5**
    1. Melville, Herman — Adaptations; 2. Graphic novels
978-0-7641-5977-0; 978-0-7641-3492-0 (pa)
    Ishmael's dream of adventure on a whaling ship becomes a nightmare as the voyage turns into a struggle for survival. Captain Ahab, maimed by a monster whale, is obsessed with revenge. As the crew discovers, he is willing to risk everything to destroy that whale. This volume includes a brief biography and timeline of Melville, and information on the legacy of his novel.

Gabrych, Andersen
    Batgirl: Destruction's Daughter. Andersen Gabrych, writer; Pop Mhan et al, pencillers; Jesse Delperdang et al, inkers. DC Comics 2006 Un Illustration
Grades: 10 11 12 Adult   **741.5; Fic**
    1. Adventure graphic novels; 2. Batgirl (Fictional character); 3. Superhero graphic novels; 4. Graphic novels
978-1-4012-0896-7, $19.99
    Cassandra Cain was quickly accepted as the new Batgirl after helping Batman during Gotham's darkest hours. Trained in deadly martial arts from early childhood by a notorious assassin, Batgirl developed the uncanny ability to anticipate her opponents' movements to make her unbeatable in combat. Now, the Dark Knight's young protege is determined to discover who her true mother is, and her quest, brings her face-to-face with the League of Assassins and into mortal combat with the deadliest woman alive, Lady Shiva. It all ends in a life or death battle at the

edge of Lazarus Pit, and only one person will survive. There's a fair amount of blood shed in the many fights.

Batgirl: Kicking Assassins. Andersen Gabrych, writer; Alé Garza, Pop Mhan, pencillers; Jesse Delperdang, Andrew Pepoy, Jack Purcell, inkers. DC Comics 2005 Un Illustration

Grades: 9 10 11 12 Adult   741.5; Fic
   1. Batgirl (Fictional character); 2. Superhero graphic novels; 3. Graphic novels
   1-4012-0439-2, $14.99
   It's a fresh start for Batgirl as Cassandra Cain is building a new life for herself in Bludhaven. But with the Penguin also moving to town and setting up a criminal empire, can Batgirl keep the streets safe, or will she face something more sinister and vile than before" With the Brotherhood of Evil, Deathstroke, and the Ravager coming at her one after the other, Batgirl barely has the chance to settle into her new neighborhood before the fists start to fly. The book includes lots of fighting.

Gaiman, Neil
   The **Books** of Magic. Writer, Neil Gaiman; illustrators, John Bolton [and others]. DC Comics/Vertigo 1993 Un Illustration
Grades: 10 11 12 Adult   741.5; Fic
   1. Fantasy graphic novels; 2. Magic; 3. Supernatural graphic novels; 4. Graphic novels
   1-56389-082-8, $19.99
   A quartet of fallen mystics dubbed the "Trench Coat Brigade "is introduced in this first collection of the adventures of Timothy Hunter. John Constantine, the Phantom Stranger, Dr. Occult, and Mister E take Hunter on a tour of the magical realms. Along the way he's introduced to Vertigo's greatest practitioners of magic and must choose whether or not to join their ranks. And they must decide if he should live ... or die . While the publisher rates it for mature readers, there's little in the way of strong language or overt violence, and no nudity.

   Creatures of the Night. Neil Gaiman, writer; Michael Zulli, artist; Todd Klein, lettering. Dark Horse Comics 2004 46p. Illustration
Grades: 10 11 12 Adult   741.5; Fic
   1. Fantasy graphic novels; 2. Supernatural graphic novels; 3. Graphic novels
   1-56971-936-5, $12.95
   Artist Zulli has adapted two of Gaiman's prose short stories into comic book form. In "The Price," a mysterious black cat comes to a family living in the English countryside. Soon after he arrives, the father notices that in the mornings, the cat is scratched and bleeding. Each morning after that, the cat suffers more injuries; maybe the family isn't quite so safe in the countryside after all. "The Daughter of Owls" is a baby girl abandoned on the steps of the Dymton Church in the late 1800s. Sequestered in the convent, the girl lives in solitary silence for fourteen years, cared for after a fashion by a nun, and then by a woman in Dymton. When the woman gossips about the silent girl's beauty, the men of Dymton hatch a dastardly plot which ends in tragedy.

   ★ **Death:** The High Cost of Living. Art by Chris Bachalo, Mark Buckingham, Dave McKean. DC Comics/Vertigo 1994 104p. Illustration

Grades: 10 11 12 Adult   741.5; Fic
   1. Adventure graphic novels; 2. Fantasy graphic novels; 3. Graphic novels
   1-56389-133-6, $12.95
   A member of the Endless, a family of beings who have existed longer than the gods, Death enjoys manifesting herself in the persona of a Goth girl. She is taking her one-day-a-century holiday in New York City, where she meets suicidal teen Sexton, and they end up searching the city for the witch Mad Hettie's heart, which she has hidden away ... somewhere. Then the Eremite hunts her, to steal Death's ankh and therefore her power. The book includes some violence and some strong language.

   Death: The Time of Your Life. Art by Chris Bachalo, Mark Buckingham, Mark Pennington. DC Comics/Vertigo 1997 96p. Illustration
Grades: 10 11 12 Adult   741.5; Fic
   1. Adventure graphic novels; 2. Fantasy graphic novels; 3. Horror graphic novels; 4. Graphic novels
   1-56389-333-9, $12.99
   This is the story of Foxglove, a rising star of the music world who must wrestle with revealing her true sexual orientation as her companion, Hazel, is lured into the realm of Death. As one of the Endless, Death met the two young women on her latest once a century holiday, so it's only natural that she would appear now. The book includes some strong language, sexual situations, and some violence.

   ★ The **graveyard** book graphic novel Volume 2. Based on the novel by Neil Gaiman; adapted by P. Craig Russell; illustrated by David LaFuente, Scott Hampton, P. Craig Russell, Kevin Nowlan, Galen Showman; colorist, Lovern Kindzierski; letterer, Rick Parker. HarperCollins 2014 188 p. Color; Illustration
Grades: 5 6 7 8 9 10   741.5; Fic
   1. Cemeteries — Fiction; 2. Dead — Fiction; 3. Orphans — Fiction; 4. Supernatural — Fiction; 5. Supernatural graphic novels; 6. Graphic novels
   0062194836; 9780062194831, $19.99
                           LC 2013497350
   "Russell concludes the two-part adaptation of Gaiman's Newbery Medal winner, encompassing the final three chapters of the novel. Bod, raised by the ghostly denizens of a graveyard, is a young adult now, yearning for knowledge of the world of the living. After a showdown with a pair of school bullies . . . Bod finally confronts the ancient order who murdered his family and overcomes them with his supernatural know-how and his innate courage and cleverness." (Booklist)
   "Russell and his team of illustrators continue to do this amazing story justice with images that lead readers down a path into Bod's dark and magical graveyard world. Gaiman has the ability to weave beauty and intrigue into a story that has a strong potential to frighten." VOYA

   Marvel 1602. [Neil Gaiman, writer; Andy Kubert, illustrator; Richard Isanove, digital painting; Todd Klein, lettering]. Marvel Comics 2005 Un Illustration
Grades: 10 11 12 Adult   741.5; 741; Fic
   1. Daredevil (Fictional character); 2. Doctor Doom (Fictional character); 3. Superhero graphic novels; 4. X-Men (Fictional characters); 5. Graphic novels
   0-7851-1073-9, $24.99; 0-7851-1073-9 (pa), $19.99

This book "takes the Marvel superheroes and villains of the 1960s—the original X-Men, Daredevil, Dr. Doom, and many others—and places them in the early 17th century." Libr J

"The improbable combination works remarkably well, as the superheroes' strange abilities adapt to Elizabethan culture. This glorious adventure is peppered with Scott McKowen's gorgeous, moody cover-art woodcuts." Publ Wkly

First published in magazine form as Marvel 1602 #1-8

★ **Neil** Gaiman and Charles Vess' Stardust: being a romance within the realms of Faerie. DC Comics/Vertigo 2007 213p. Illustration
Grades: 10 11 12 Adult   **741.5; Fic**
    1. Fantasy graphic novels; 2. Graphic novels
    978-1-4012-1190-5, $39.95
In the sleepy English countryside at the dawn of the Victorian Era, young Tristran Thorn has lost his heart to beautiful Victoria Forester. But Victoria is cold and distant—as distant, in fact, as the star she and Tristran see fall from the sky on a crisp October evening. For the coveted prize of Victoria's hand, Tristran vows to retrieve the fallen star and deliver it to his beloved. It is an oath that sends the lovelorn swain into a world that is strange beyond imagining, a world populated by evil old witches, deadly clutching trees, and goblin press-gangs—a world redeemed only by true love. The story includes some sexual situations and partial nudity. This deluxe hardcover edition includes bonus material such as Gaiman's initial proposal and a number of preliminary sketches and new artwork from Vess. This illustrated novel is published by a comic book publisher and can go in either fiction or in the graphic novel section.

Neil Gaiman's Midnight Days. DC Comics/Vertigo 2000 Un Illustration
Grades: 10 11 12 Adult   **741.5; Fic**
    1. Fantasy graphic novels; 2. Horror graphic novels; 3. Graphic novels
    1-56389-517-X, $17.99
This book collects some of Gaiman's earliest work for Vertigo. Included in these never-before-reprinted and original publications are tales featuring the Golden Age Sandman, Morpheus, the Swamp Thing, and John Constantine. Some of the stories include strong language, violence, and nudity.

★ The **Sandman**, Vol. 1: Preludes and Nocturnes. Neil Gaiman, author; Sam Kieth, Mike Dringenberg, Malcolm Jones III, artists; Todd Klein, letterer; Robbie Busch, colorist. DC Comics/Vertigo 1991 236p. Illustration
Grades: 10 11 12   **741.5; Fic**
    1. Fantasy; 2. Mythology; 3. Graphic novels
    978-1-56389-011-6, $19.95
"Gaiman's stories of Morpheus, the Lord of Dream, his Endless siblings (Death, Destruction, Delirium, Desire, Destiny, and Despair), his enemies, and many figures who spring from various mythologies and folklore have changed many readers' ideas about comics and graphic novels." (VOYA)

Various artists worked with Gaiman to illustrate his stories, which include some strong depictions of violence and occasional nudity.

Other Sandman volumes are: 2: A Doll's House; 3: Dream Country; 4: Season of Mists; 5: A Game of You; 6: Fables and Reflections; 7: Brief Lives; 8: World's End; 9: The Kindly Ones; 10: The Wake

Sandman Volume 2: The Doll's House. Written by Neil Gaiman; illustrated by Mike Dringenberg et al. DC Comics/Vertigo 1991 255p. Illustration
Grades: 10 11 12 Adult   **741.5; Fic**
    1. Fantasy graphic novels; 2. Horror graphic novels; 3. Sandman (Fictional character); 4. Graphic novels
    0-930289-59-5, $19.99
                                                            LC 92-159876
In this second volume, Rose Walker is the dream vortex who must be killed to save the Dreaming. In the meantime, she wanders the world hunting for her younger brother, and along the way she attends a "Cereal" convention, which is actually a serial killers' convention. Morpheus must track down four of his major arcana dreams that were lost during his long imprisonment. And Morpheus meets once a century with Hob, a man who had wished to never die. The book includes graphic violence, some partial nudity, and strong language.

★ **Sandman** Volume 3: Dream Country. Art by Kelley Jones, Charles Vess, Colleen Doran, Malcom Jones III. DC Comics/Vertigo 1991 Un Illustration
Grades: 10 11 12 Adult   **741.5; Fic**
    1. Fantasy graphic novels; 2. Horror graphic novels; 3. Sandman (Fictional character); 4. Graphic novels
    1-56389-016-X, $14.99
                                                            LC 92-159876
This third volume collects four stories; the two standouts are "A Dream of a Thousand Cats," in which a purebred Siamese remembers her first litter of mixed-breed cats that her owners killed and ventures into the cat version of the dreaming in which Morpheus is a huge black cat and discovers her mission in life - cat owners may never look at their sleeping cats the same way again; and "A Midsummer Night's Dream" recounts the adventures of William Shakespeare and his company of players as they are summoned to perform their play to a highly select audience - King Oberon and Queen Titania of Faerie. This story won the World Fantasy Award for Best Short Story when it was first published. The book includes nudity, sexual situations, and some violence.

Sandman Volume 4: The Season of Mists. Writer Neil Gaiman; artists, Kelley Jones, Mike Dringenberg, Malcolm Jones III, Matt Wagner, Dick Giordano, George Pratt, P. Craig Russell. DC Comics/Vertigo 1994 Un Illustration
Grades: 10 11 12 Adult   **741.5; Fic**
    1. Fantasy graphic novels; 2. Horror graphic novels; 3. Sandman (Fictional character); 4. Graphic novels
    1-56389-041-0, $19.99
                                                            LC 92-159876
Lucifer has grown tired of being the lord of Hell. He kicks out the demons and the damned alike, closes up shop, and gives the key to Hell to Morpheus. Beings from all the world's mythologies converge on the lord of Dream to seize this instrument of power. All Morpheus wants is to search

for the soul of his first love, Nada, whom he had consigned to Hell long ago. The book includes violence, strong language, and nudity.

Sandman Volume 5: A Game of You. Written by Neil Gaiman; illustrated by Shawn McManus, Colleen Doran, Bryan Talbot, George Pratt, Stan Woch, and Dick Giordano. DC Comics/Vertigo 1993 Un Illustration
Grades: 10 11 12 Adult   **741.5; Fic**
1. Fantasy graphic novels; 2. Horror graphic novels; 3. Sandman (Fictional character); 4. Graphic novels
1-56389-089-5, $19.99
Take an apartment house, mix in a trans woman, a lesbian couple, some talking animals, a talking severed head, a confused heroine, and the deadly Cuckoo. Stir vigorously with a hurricane and Morpheus himself and you get this fifth installment of the Sandman series. This story stars Barbie, who first makes an appearance in The Doll's House, who here finds herself a princess in a vivid dreamworld. The book includes violence, partial nudity, and strong language.

Sandman Volume 6: Fables & Reflections. Art by Ken Williams, P. Craig Russell, Jill Thompson, John Watkiss, Shawn McManus. DC Comics/Vertigo 1994 Un Illustration
Grades: 10 11 12 Adult   **741.5; Fic**
1. Fantasy graphic novels; 2. Horror graphic novels; 3. Sandman (Fictional character); 4. Graphic novels
9781563891052, $19.99; 1563891050
Morpheus, the King of Dreams, observes and interacts with an odd assortment of historical and fictional characters throughout time. Featuring tales of kings, explorers, spies, and werewolves, this book of myth and imagination delves into the dark dreams of Augustus Caesar, Haroun Al Raschid, Marco Polo, Cain and Abel, Emperor Joshua Norton I, and Orpheus to illustrate the effects that these subconscious musings have had on the course of history and mankind. The book includes some violence, nudity, and strong language.

Sandman Volume 7: Brief Lives. Neil Gaiman, writer; Jill Thompson, penciller; Vince Locke, inker; Dick Giordano, inker. DC Comics/Vertigo 1995 Un Illustration
Grades: 10 11 12 Adult   **741.5; Fic**
1. Fantasy graphic novels; 2. Horror graphic novels; 3. Sandman (Fictional character); 4. Graphic novels
1-56389-138-7, $19.99
                        LC 92-159876
Delirium, youngest sister of the Endless, prevails upon her brother, Dream, to help her find their missing sibling, Destruction, who disappeared several centuries ago. Their travels take them through the world of the waking until a final confrontation with the missing member of the Endless and the resolution of Dream's relationship with his son change the endless forever. The book includes violence, nudity, sexual situations, and strong language.

★ The **Sandman** Volume 8: World's End. Art by Bryan Talbot, Michael Zulli, Michael Allred, John Watkiss. DC Comics/Vertigo 1995 Un Illustration
Grades: 10 11 12 Adult   **741.5; Fic**
1. Adventure graphic novels; 2. Fantasy graphic novels; 3. Sandman (Fictional character); 4. Graphic novels
1-56389-171-9, $19.99

A "reality storm" draws an unusual cast of characters together. They take shelter in a tavern, where they amuse each other with their life stories. Although Morpheus is never a focus in these stories, each has something to say about the nature of stories and dreams. The book includes some violence, some strong language, and brief partial nudity and sexual situations.

★ The **Sandman** Volume 9: The Kindly Ones. Writer, Neil Gaiman; artists, Marc Hempel et al.; colorist, Daniel Vozzo. DC Comics/Vertigo 1996 Un Illustration
Grades: 10 11 12 Adult   **741.5; Fic**
1. Adventure graphic novels; 2. Fantasy graphic novels; 3. Sandman (Fictional character); 4. Graphic novels
1-56389-205-7, $19.99
Distraught by the kidnapping and presumed death of her son Daniel, and believing Morpheus to be responsible, Lyta Hall calls the ancient wrath of the Furies down upon him. A former super heroine blames Morpheus for the death of her child and summons an ancient curse of vengeance against the Lord of Dream. The kindly ones" enter his realm and force a sacrifice that will change the Dreaming forever. The book includes violence, strong language, and partial nudity.

★ The **Sandman** Volume 10: The Wake. Art by Michael Zulli, Jon J. Muth, Charles Vess. DC Comics/Vertigo 1997 Un Illustration
Grades: 10 11 12 Adult   **741.5; Fic**
1. Adventure graphic novels; 2. Fantasy graphic novels; 3. Sandman (Fictional character); 4. Graphic novels
1-56389-279-0, $19.99
In the last chapter of the Sandman saga, the Endless and all the dreamers come to celebrate the life and mourn the passing of the King of Dreams. Meanwhile, the new Dream, who was once the boy Daniel Hall, waits for the others to come and meet him. The King is dead, long live the King. The book includes some nudity and violence.

The **Sandman**: Endless Nights. DC Comics/Vertigo 2004 Un Illustration
Grades: 11 12 Adult   **741.5; Fic**
1. Fantasy graphic novels; 2. Sandman (Fictional character); 3. Graphic novels
1-4012-0113-X, $19.99
This volume reveals the legend of the Endless, a family of magical and mythical beings who exist and interact in the real world. Born at the beginning of time, Destiny, Death, Dream, Desire, Despair, Delirium and Destruction are seven brothers and sisters who each lord over their respective realms. These seven peculiar and powerful siblings each reveal more about their true-being as they star in their own tales of curiosity and wonder. A different artist interprets each story by Gaiman. The book includes considerable nudity and sexual situations, and some violence.

★ The **Sandman**: the dream hunters. Original words by Neil Gaiman; graphicplay and art by P. Craig Russell; coloring by Lovern Kindzierski; lettering by Todd Klein. D.C. Comics/Vertigo 2009 144p. Illustration
Grades: 10 11 12 Adult   **741.5; Fic**
1. Dreams; 2. Love; 3. Supernatural graphic novels; 4. Graphic novels
978-1-4012-2424-0, $24.99

In old Japan, creatures of myth and legend live among the people. Two such creatures, a badger and a fox, make a wager to force a humble monk to leave the temple he tends alone up in the mountains. Because the young monk can see through their disguises to their true nature, both badger and fox lose the wager, and the fox falls in love with the handsome young man and remains nearby. Meanwhile, a wealthy man who has mastered demons yet cannot find peace in his soul decides to steal the young monk's inner strength for his own. The fox tries to protect the monk, and even makes a bargain with the great black fox in her dreams, to sacrifice her life for the man she loves. Then, when she suffers the consequences of the evil dreams sent by the wealthy man through his demons, the monk ventures into the Dreaming in a quest to save the fox, whom he finally realizes he loves. When he makes the decision to take back the dream that will kill him, the fox decides to take revenge on the wealthy man, the onmyoji, and comes to him as a beautiful young woman to destroy him. Russell has adapted the novella written by Gaiman and illustrated by Yoshitaka Amano. It includes some nudity.

Gallagher, John
   Buzzboy: Trouble in paradise. Sky Dog Press 2002 144p. Illustration
Grades: 5 6 7 8 9 10 11 12   **741.5; Fic**
   1. Humorous graphic novels; 2. Superhero graphic novels; 3. Graphic novels
   0-8721831-0-8, $11.95
   Imagine a superhero who jokes constantly, watches way too many old television shows, and loves junk food, and you have Buzzboy. Years before, he was sidekick to Captain Ultra, but the evil Dr. Schism destroyed all superheroes and their sidekicks, except for Captain Ultra. Now, Ultra has declared martial law in the city of New Paradise, and his police stomp out all rebellions. Then a mysterious superhero stops the Hoppers (police) it's Buzzboy, older and back from the dead! Aided by sarcastic teen sorceress Becca and reformed mad scientist Doc Cyber, Buzzboy is here to save the day.
   Another title in this series is: Buzzboy: Monsters, dreams, & milkshakes (2003)

Gallagher, Monica
   Gods & undergrads, Book 1. Lipstick Press 2007 Un Illustration
Grades: 10 11 12 Adult   **741.5; Fic**
   1. College students; 2. Greek mythology; 3. School stories; 4. Graphic novels
   978-0-9794589-0-3, $10
   College sophomore Lelaina Pentheus has decided to move on campus at Troy University, and by some chance meetings and good luck joins several juniors in an apartment. Her new friends quickly learn that Lelaina has some strange quirks, like fainting a lot, and hands that can suddenly turn hot and blister. She doesn't know why, nor why she has strange markings on her face; she was adopted as an infant. Then she gets strange messages that "they're coming——from a talking frog, from her roommate's brother, and then from a stranger who claims he's Hermes, the Greek messenger god. This book collects the first three chapters of Gallagher's story, which first appeared as webcomics at www.eatyourlipstick.com.
   Also available online as webcomic

Gallaher, David
   High moon. Art by Scott O. Brown and Steve Ellis. DC Comics 2009 Un Illustration
Grades: 10 11 12 Adult   **741.5; Fic**
   1. Horror graphic novels; 2. Werewolves; 3. Western stories; 4. Graphic novels
   978-1-4012-2462-2, $14.99
   2009 Harvey Award for Best OnLine Comics Work.
   It starts in a small town in Texas, with mysterious happenings and then the disappearance of a girl. Ex-Pinkerton detective McGregor comes to town hunting a criminal named Conroy and gets involved in the town's problems. Mr. Hunter, father of the missing girl, doesn't know the half of it; the town is filled with werewolves resentful of human progress. Conroy is a werewolf, and so is McGregor. When McGregor dies fighting the werewolves from the mines, Conroy takes his identity and continues his travels. In Ragged Rock, he finds more trouble stemming from an old hate, and the real McGregor's brother, Tristan, has come to find his brother's killer. Conroy soon learns that he can be killed, but he won't stay dead. The book includes considerable violence.
   Originally published online at www.zudacomics.com.

Gamache, Line
   Hello, Me Pretty. Conundrum Press 2007 63p. Illustration
Grades: 9 10 11 12 Adult
92; 741.5
   1. Autobiographical graphic novels; 2. Mentally handicapped children; 3. Sisters; 4. Graphic novels
   978-1-894994-23-1, $15
   The author writes of growing up with her mentally disabled sister in a small community just outside Montreal, Canada, with Expo '67 and the FLQ crisis

Courtesy of Conundrum Press

happening in the background (in October 1970, members of the Front de liberation du Quebec kidnapped two government officials; they murdered one and released the other). It is a story of people's intolerance and lack of understanding, but mostly about being different. It gives a glimpse into one family's personal trials and tribulations, woven into the tapestry of Quebec's rich culture and history. The only moment of nudity is when the author's mother gives birth to Josee.

Ganeri, Anita
   Harriet Tubman: The Life of an African-American Abolitionist. Rosen Publishing Group 2005 48p. Illustration
Grades: 3 4 5 6 7 8 9   **92; 741.5**

1. African American women; 2. Biographical graphic novels; 3. ss; 4. Tubman, Harriet, 1819 or 1820-1913; 5. Underground Railroad; 6. Graphic novels
1-4042-0245-5, $29.25

Born a slave in the United States, Harriet Tubman escaped from bondage to risk her life and newfound liberty in becoming a leading abolitionist in the years before the American Civil War. Tubman surreptitiously led hundreds of escaped Southern slaves to freedom in the North along the Underground Railroad, earning her the nickname as "the Moses of her people." This graphic novel format book tells her story. It includes additional information about the Underground Railroad and her legacy in the civil rights movement, and a list of books for further reading.

Part of the Graphic Nonfiction series.

Ganter, Amy Kim

Goosebumps: Terror Trips. Scholastic/Graphix 2007 137p. Illustration
Grades: 4 5 6 7 8 9   **741.5; Fic**
1. Horror graphic novels; 2. Stine, R L — Adaptations; 3. Graphic novels
978-0-439-85780-2, $8.99

Stine's Goosebumps series was very popular years ago, and is enjoying a resurgence of popularity with new editions of the prose books. The graphic novel adaptations, all done by well-known independent comics creators, bring the stories to a new audience. Goosebumps: Creepy Creatures is also available.

This volume adapts three of Stine's Goosebumps novels into graphic novel format. Noted independent comic creator Thompson adapts One Day at Horrorland, about one family's ordeal in a very strange, all-too-realistic amusement park. Canadian artist Tolagson adapts A Shocker on Shock Street, which depicts the horrific adventures of two kids on a movie studio lot where the horror is more than just special effects. Global manga creator Ganter adapts Deep Trouble, in which a brother and sister find a real mermaid.

Sorcerers & Secretaries, Vol. 1. Tokyopop 2006 Un Illustration
Grades: 8 9 10 11 12   **741.5; Fic**
1. Romance graphic novels; 2. Graphic novels
1-59816-409-0, $9.99

Nicole attends university and works part-time as a receptionist, but she prefers to daydream of the fantasy characters she has created and writes about in her journal. Josh, Nicole's former neighbor, works in a bookstore; he has always liked her, but could never get her to go out with him. They reconnect, but when Nicole realizes that being with Josh prevents her from writing her fantasy stories, she has to decide what's more important to her. This is a global manga story.

Geary, Rick

The **Beast** of Chicago: An Account of the Life and Crimes of Herman W. Mudgett, Known to the World as H. H. Holmes. NBM 2003 Un Illustration
Grades: 9 10 11 12 Adult   **364.152; 741.5**
1. Homicide; 2. Mystery graphic novels; 3. Graphic novels
1-56163-362-3, $8.95

Courtesy of NBM Publishing

He was the world's first serial killer and he existed in the late 19th century, operating around the Chicago World's Fair, building a literal house of horrors, replete with chutes for dead bodies, gas chambers, surgical rooms. He methodically murdered up to 200 people, mostly young women. Geary steers away from gore to focus on such things as Holmes' "lab" in his castle. The book is still not for the squeamish, but the art is restrained.

Part of the A Treasury of Victorian Murder series.

The **Borden** Tragedy: A Memoir of the Infamous Double Murder at Fall River, Mass., 1892. NBM 1997 80p. Illustration
Grades: 9 10 11 12 Adult   **364.152; 741.5**
1. Homicide; 2. Mystery graphic novels; 3. Graphic novels
1-56163-189-2, $8.95; 9781561631896

Including such details as maps of Fall River, Massachusetts as it was in 1892, Geary presents the facts and documented speculations about the case of Lizzie Borden, a thirty-year-old spinster accused and tried for murdering her parents. The popular rhyme "Lizzie Borden took an axe, gave her mother forty whacks, when she saw what she had done, she gave her father forty-one" was apparently sung to the tune of "Tararaboom deeay." Geary leaves it to the reader to decide if Lizzie was guilty or not.

Part of the A Treasury of Victorian Murder series.

Courtesy of NBM Publishing

Famous players: the mysterious death of William Desmond Taylor. NBM/ComicsLit 2009 Un Illustration
Grades: 9 10 11 12 Adult   **364.152; 741.5**
1. Homicide; 2. Motion picture directors; 3. Motion picture producers and directors; 4. Murder victims; 5. Mystery graphic novels; 6. Taylor, William Desmond, 1877-1922; 7. Graphic novels
978-1-56163-555-9, $15.95; 978-1-56163-559-7 (pa), $9.95

Hollywood in 1922 was just coming into its own as a mecca for filmmakers as the silent films became more and more popular. One of the new studios was Famous Players

Studio, and William Desmond Taylor was one of its successful directors, along with Cecil B. DeMille. Then, on the morning of February 2, 1922, Taylor's cook/valet/general house servant Henry Peavey arrived at 7:30 and found Taylor's body on the floor of the living room. He'd been shot, but by whom? As the investigation progresses, several prominent actresses come under suspicion, along with a former cook and house servant; and his own mysterious past starts to come to light. However, the police are never able to solve the case. Geary provides a list of his sources for anyone who would like to know more about this Twentieth-Century Murder mystery. He depicts the crime with little gore or violence.

This is part of the Treasury of XXth Century Murder series.

J. Edgar Hoover: a graphic biography. Hill and Wang 2008 102p. Illustration
Grades: 9 10 11 12 Adult   **363.2; 92; 741.5**
1. Biographical graphic novels; 2. FBI officials; 3. Hoover, J Edgar (John Edgar), 1895-1972; 4. United States — Federal Bureau of Investigation; 5. Graphic novels
978-0-8090-9503-2; 0-8090-9503-3, $16.95
LC 2007-25193

Rick Geary has written a biography of J. Edgar Hoover, who served in the federal government for 55 years and under eight presidents, most notably as director of the Federal Bureau of Investigation. He was appointed to that position on May 10, 1924. Geary covers Hoover's sometimes controversial career, including his refusal to involve the FBI directly into investigations of crimes against civil rights workers and the 1963 bombing in Birmingham, Alabama, and the bureau's investigation of Martin Luther King, Jr. He tastefully discusses Hoover's undercover sexual life.

"As solid, thrilling and informative a guide to the life of the America's most powerful authoritarian as one could ask for." Kirkus

★ The **Lindbergh** child: America's hero and the crime of the century. Written and illustrated by Rick Geary. NBM/ComicsLit 2008 Un Illustration; Map (Treasury of XXth century murder)
Grades: 8 9 10 11 12 Adult   **364.1; 741.5**
1. Air force officers; 2. Air pilots; 3. Generals; 4. Homicide; 5. Kidnapping; 6. Lindbergh, Charles, 1902-1974; 7. Memoirists; 8. Mystery graphic novels; 9. Graphic novels
978-1-56163-529-0, $15.95

Charles Lindbergh was an American hero following his solo crossing of the Atlantic in an airplane. He married into a wealthy family, he and his wife had a baby, they were building their dream home. Then, one night, the

Courtesy of NBM Publishing

baby was abducted from the house. Geary's account retraces all the highly publicized events, ransom notes (false and otherwise), as well as the string of colorful characters who all claimed they could help but instead snookered the Lindberghs. While Bruno Hauptmann was arrested, tried, convicted, and executed, there remain many questions about what really happened. Geary brings them up for readers to consider.

"A good example of the origins of modern forensics, crime-scene investigation, and celebrity hysteria, this work is an excellent choice for most collections." SLJ

The **lives** of Sacco and Vanzetti. Rick Geary.. NBM Comics Lit 2011 80 p. Illustration
Grades: 9 10 11 12 Adult   **345; 741.5; 345.73**
1. Anarchism and anarchists; 2. Sacco, Nicola, 1891-1927 — Trials, litigation, etc; 3. Sacco-Vanzetti case; 4. Sacco-Vanzetti Trial, Dedham, Mass, 1921; 5. United States — History — 1919-1933; 6. Vanzetti, Bartolomeo, 1888-1927 — Trials, litigation, etc
1561636053; 9781561636051, $15.99
LC 2011927818

"Geary lays out what is known and not known about the case, in which two Italian anarchist immigrants were put to death after being found guilty of robbery and murder. The . . . narrative not only details the events of the crime, manhunt, and trial but also includes information about the lives of Sacco and Vanzetti and their families." (Publishers Weekly) Includes bibliographical references.

Courtesy of NBM Publishing

Madison Square tragedy: the murder of Stanford White : 25 June, 1906. Written and illustrated by Rick Geary. NBM Pub. 2013 80 p. Illustration (Treasury of xxth century murder)
Grades: 9 10 11 12 Adult   **741.5; 364.152**
1. Murder; 2. Mystery graphic novels
1561637629; 9781561637621, $15.99
LC 2013947335

In this graphic novel, by Rick Geary, as architect Stanford White "became popular and in demand, he also became quite self-indulgent: he had a taste for budding young showgirls on Broadway, even setting up a private apartment to entertain them in. . . . When he met Evelyn Nesbit . . . he knew he was on to something special. However, Evelyn eventually married a young Pittsburgh decadent heir with a dark side who developed a deep hatred for White and what he may or may not have done to her." (Publisher's note)

"In this entry in his series recounting historical murder cases, Geary tackles an infamous crime that scandalized New York City in 1901. . . . Geary's old-fashioned black-and-white line drawings, vividly evoking the turn-of-the-century milieu, and his reliance on text-heavy captions as a sort of voice-over impart a documentary air to his thoroughly researched account." Booklist

Includes bibliographical references

The **murder** of Abraham Lincoln: a chronicle of 62 days in the life of the American Republic, March 4-May 4, 1865. Written and illustrated by Rick Geary. NBM ComicsLit 2005 Un Illustration; Map (A treasury of Victorian murder)

Grades: 7 8 9 10 11 12   **973.7**
  1. Booth, John Wilkes, 1838-1865; 2. Lawyers; 3. Lincoln, Abraham, 1809-1865 — Assassination; 4. Murderers; 5. Presidents; 6. Graphic novels
  978-1-56163-425-5; 1-56163-425-5, $15.95;
  978-1-56163-426-2 (pa); 1-56163-426-3 (pa), $8.95
                          LC 2005-41468

This graphic novel "covers Lincoln's assassination, the events that led up to it, and the aftermath. Geary also makes a point of bringing up still-unanswered questions, like the whereabouts of the missing pages of John Wilkes Booth's journal. . . . Even teens who know nothing about the tragedy will find their heads chock-full of information when they're finished reading this book." SLJ

Includes bibliographical references

Courtesy of NBM Publishing

The **Mystery** of Mary Rogers: A Chronicle of the Disappearanceand Murder of The Beautiful Segar Girl in July,1841 - A Crime Which was Never Solved - And WhichInspired the Sensational Tale by Edgar A. Poe. NBM 2001 Un Illustration

Grades: 9 10 11 12 Adult   **364.152; 741.5**
  1. Homicide; 2. Mystery graphic novels; 3. Graphic novels
  1-56163-274-0, $15.95

Mary Rogers was a compellingly beautiful lass employed in a cigar store in New York City in the mid-nineteenth century. She had a few suitors. Then, she suddenly disappeared, her body recovered in the Hudson off the Jersey side. The press had a field day with all the possible shocking possibilities. Rape... her "fooling around" between lovers...even gang rape. Never was this case solved. The hypotheses remain many. Even Edgar Allen Poe thought to have solved the case and presented that in his tale "The Mystery of Mary Roget."

Part of the A Treasury of Victorian Murder series.

The **saga** of the bloody Benders: the infamous homicidal family of Labette County, Kansas. NBM/ComicsLit 2007 Un Illustration

Grades: 9 10 11 12 Adult   **364.152; 741.5**
  1. Homicide; 2. Mystery graphic novels; 3. Graphic novels
  978-1-56163-498-9, $15.95

In Kansas, around the year 1870, the Bender family ran the Bender Inn and grocery store in Labette County, Kansas. Soon after they open their inn to travelers, people start to disappear, usually people with a fair amount of money with them. When the authorities investigate, the family disappears, and the people of Labette County make grisly discoveries in the Bender Inn's cellar. Geary includes just enough gory details for readers to comprehend the Benders' crimes. Earlier volumes in this series focused on famous nineteenth century murders and criminals, but the crimes of this more obscure family are just as dastardly for true crime aficionados.

Part of the series, A Treasury of Victorian Murders

Courtesy of NBM Publishing

★ The **terrible** Axe-Man of New Orleans. Music and lyrics by Rick Geary. NBM Publishing/ComicsLit 2010 Un Illustration; Map (Treasury of XXth century murder)

Grades: 9 10 11 12 Adult   **364.152; 741.5**
  1. Homicide; 2. Mystery graphic novels; 3. New Orleans (La) — History; 4. Graphic novels
  978-1-56163-581-8, $15.99

                          LC 2010-926782

Geary tells the story of the Terrible Axe-Man, who murdered grocers in New Orleans right after World War I. In each case, the murderer removed a piece of the door to the house, borrowed an axe found at the property, then aimed straight for the head of his victim. From May 23, 1918 to October 27, 1919, the Axe-Man killed six people and badly wounded six more, then disappeared. Geary lays out the

Courtesy of NBM Publishing

known facts, then shows some of the speculation. The black and white art helps to mitigate the violence and gore, so the book is suitable for teens who enjoy true-life mysteries.

"Geary's exacting, historically accurate approach makes this . . . a natural for true-crime fans as well as comics lovers." Booklist

Includes bibliographical references

Nights of terror! A city awash in blood!

★ **Trotsky**: a graphic biography. Hill and Wang 2009 103p. Illustration; Map
Grades: 9 10 11 12 Adult   **92; 741.5**
1. Biographical graphic novels; 2. Communism — Soviet Union; 3. Communist leaders; 4. Nonfiction writers; 5. Political leaders; 6. Revolutionaries; 7. Russia — Politics and government — 1894-1917; 8. Soviet Union — Politics and government; 9. Trotsky, Leon, 1879-1940; 10. Graphic novels
978-0-8090-9508-7, $16.95; 0-8090-9508-4
LC 2008-50235

Geary provides a graphic biography of Leon Trotsky, the "brain" behind the Russian Revolution of 1917. The book, with its black and white panel art, chronicles Trotsky's tumultuous relationships with Lenin and Stalin, the contentious debates within the revolutionary movement, Trotsky's many exiles, and his murder in Mexico in 1940.

"Geary's familiar cartoonlike drawing style and factual presentation make this title an accessible and concise introduction to Trotsky's life." SLJ

Includes bibliographical references

A novel graphic from Hill and Wang

Gelatt, Philip
Indiana Jones adventures vol. 1; script, Philip Gelatt ; art, Ethen Beavers. Dark Horse Comics 2008 Un Illustration
Grades: 4 5 6 7 8 9   **741.5; Fic**
1. Adventure graphic novels; 2. Archeology; 3. Indiana Jones (Fictional character); 4. Indiana Jones (Fictional character); 5. Graphic novels
978-1-59307-905-5, $6.95

It's winter of 1930 in Sweden, and Dr. Henry Jones Jr. (Indiana Jones) finds an ancient pre-Christian temple of a religion devoted to war; he gets a scroll while Dr. Lawrence, the pretty British archeologist with him, runs with a valuable gold ring. When Indy decides to steal the ring back from the British Museum, the unscrupulous French archeologist Belloq, who works for the Nazis, steals the scroll from Marcus Brody, Indy's friend. From London, Indy and Dr. Lawrence pursue Belloq to Egypt to recover the scroll before he can sell it to the Nazis. This original graphic novel story provides adventure suitable for younger readers.

Gelev, Penko
Dr. Jekyll and Mr. Hyde; illustrated by Penko Geleve ; retold by Fiona Macdonald. Barron's Educational Series 2008 48p. Illustration
Grades: 4 5 6 7 8 9 10   **741.5; Fic**
1. Authors; 2. Essayists; 3. Novelists; 4. Poets; 5. Science fiction graphic novels; 6. Stevenson, Robert Louis, 1850-1894 — Adaptations; 7. Graphic novels
978-0-7641-6058-5, $15.99; 978-0-7641-3782-2 (pa), $8.99

LC 2008-923897

In Victorian London, the sinister, monstrous Mr. Hyde prowls and commits murder, and he's protected by Dr. Henry Jekyll, who is a respected member of society. Why is this? Stevenson's story of good and evil is retold in the graphic format. Words from his original text are defined on the pages, and back matter includes a brief biography of Stevenson, background information about the story, and information on the various adaptations done for film and television over the years.

Part of the Graphic Classics series.

Dracula; illustrated by Penko Gelev ; retold by Fiona MacDonald. Barron's 2007 48p.
Grades: 4 5 6 7 8 9   **741.5; Fic**
1. Authors; 2. Dracula, Count (Fictional character); 3. Horror graphic novels; 4. Stoker, Bram, 1847-1912 — Adaptations; 5. Vampires; 6. Graphic novels
978-0-7641-6054-7, $15.99; 978-0-7641-3778-5 (pa), $8.99

LC 2007-925724

Englishman Jonathan Harker travels to Transylvania to meet his firm's new client, Count Dracula, only to discover the horrible truth that Dracula is a vampire and seeking new hunting grounds in England. Back home, Harker's fiancee, Mina Murray, and her friend Lucy Westenra, face danger from Dracula. This graphic novel adaptation of Stoker's novel includes a biography of Stoker, information about vampires, a list of eighteenth and nineteenth century tales of mystery and horror, a list of some of the film adaptations, and more.

Part of Barron's Graphic Classics series

Frankenstein; illustrated by Penko Gelev ; retold by Fiona MacDonald. Barron's 2008 48p. Illustration
Grades: 4 5 6 7 8 9   **741.5; Fic**
1. Authors; 2. Horror graphic novels; 3. Novelists; 4. Science fiction graphic novels; 5. Shelley, Mary Wollstonecraft, 1797-1851 — Adaptations; 6. Graphic novels
978-0-7641-6057-8, $15.99; 978-0-7641-3781-5 (pa), $8.99

LC 2006-937854

Victor Frankenstein is a brilliant medical student who has discovered the secret of bringing dead matter to life. Determined to create a living being, he gathers materials from graveyards and slaughterhouses, and creates a giant of superhuman strength, but his creature is also hideous. Horrified by what he has done, Frankenstein flees, and the creature he left behind plans his revenge. This graphic novel adaptation includes a brief biography of Shelley, a timeline of scientific and medical discoveries made during Shelley's lifetime, information on various film adaptations of her story, and more.

Part of Barron's Graphic Classics series

Gerber, Steve
Guardians of the Galaxy; 1: Tomorrow's Avengers 1. By Steve Gerber, Chris Claremont, Gerry Conway, Len Wein, Arnold Drake and Roger Stern and illustrated by Gene Colan, Sal Buscema, Don Heck, and Al Milgrom. Marvel Enterprises 2013 368 p.
Grades: 7 8 9 10 11 12   **741.5**

1. Captain America (Fictional character); 2. Doctor Strange (Fictional character); 3. Hulk (Fictional character); 4. Outer space — Fiction; 5. Space warfare — Fiction; 6. Superheroes — Fiction
0785166874; 9780785166870, $39.99

In this graphic novel, written by Steve Gerber, Chris Claremont, Gerry Conway, Len Wien, Arnold Drake and Roger Stern, "Captain America, Doctor Strange, the Thing, the Hulk and other[s] . . . join the star-spanning heroes in the greatest war the future ever saw! As the Guardians help a planet . . . rebuild, threats rise from two other worlds: one of them living, the other gone mad!" (Publisher's note)

Gianopoulos, Andrea

The **Attractive** Story of Magnetism with Max Axiom, Super Scientist by Andrea Gianopoulos ; illustrated by Cynthia Martin and Barbara Schulz. Capstone Press 2007 32p. Illustration
Grades: 3 4 5 6 7 8 9   **538; 741.5**
1. Magnetism; 2. Magnets; 3. Graphic novels
978-1-4296-0141-2, $25.26
                                                          LC 2007002262
This book uses the graphic novel format to follow the adventures of super scientist Max Axiom as he explains the science behind magnetism. The book includes additional facts and a list of books for further reading.

Part of the Graphic Science series.

Gibbons, Dave

Green Lantern Corps: Recharge. Geoff Johns, Dave Gibbons, writers; Patrick Gleason, penciller; Prentis Rollins, Christian Alamy, inkers; Phil Balsman, Pat Brosseau, Travis Lanham, letterers; Moose Baumann, colorist. DC Comics 2006 Un Illustration
Grades: 9 10 11 12 Adult   **741.5; Fic**
1. Green Lantern (Fictional character); 2. Superhero graphic novels; 3. Graphic novels
978-1-4012-0962-9, $12.99

After the return of Hal Jordan, the Guardians of the Universe have re-formed the Green Lantern Corps. The best and the brightest from across the universe find themselves chosen as members of the new Corps and summoned to the planet Oa, given power rings that turn strength of will into reality, and for training. While veteran ring-bearers gladly return to duty, some new recruits resent being drafted into the Corps against their will. Kyle Rayner, Guy Gardner, and Kilowog set out to train the new Green Lanterns, but something is making its way to Oa, something that threatens the very existence of the planet and the Guardians; can the new Corps stop it?

★ The **Originals**. DC Comics/Vertigo 2004 Un Illustration
Grades: 10 11 12 Adult   **741.5; Fic**
1. Gangs; 2. Science fiction graphic novels; 3. Graphic novels
1-4012-0355-8, $24.95
2005 Eisner Award for Best Graphic Album - New.

In a retro-futuristic city of industrial gray where hover scooters, music, and drugs rule the street, the Originals are the toughest, most stylish gang around. For two childhood friends, Lel and Bok, nothing is more important than being one of them. But being part of the crowd will bring its own deadly consequences. Gibbons draws upon the world of the Mods in 1960s England and sets it in an alternate world. Violence, harsh language, and sexual situations are part of this world.

Giffen, Keith

52 aftermath: The Four Horsemen. Keith Giffen, writer; Pat Olliffe, pencils; John Stanisci, inks. DC Comics 2008 144p. Illustration
Grades: 10 11 12 Adult   **741.5; Fic**
1. Batman (Fictional character); 2. Superhero graphic novels; 3. Superman (Fictional character); 4. Wonder Woman (Fictional character)
978-1-4012-1781-5, $19.99

During the event of 52 weeks, a cadre of scientists created the Four Horsemen of Apokolips, creatures of destructive power that killed Black Adam's family and pretty much destroyed his nation, Bialya. Black Adam destroyed the Horsemen; but, he only destroyed their physical forms. Now, War, Famine, Pestilence, and Death have returned, taking over new human hosts. Superman, Batman, and Wonder Woman are on the scene, but they might not be enough to destroy the Horsemen. Their best hope may be Dr. Cale, who helped create the Horsemen in the first place. Can she be trusted" The book includes violence.

Blue Beetle vol. 2: road trip. John Rogers & Keith Giffen, writers; Cully Hamner . . . [et al.], artists; Guy Major, colorist; Phil Balsman, Pat Brosseau, Jared K. Fletcher, letterers. DC Comics 2007 144p. Illustration
Grades: 8 9 10 11 12 Adult   **741.5; Fic**
1. Adventure graphic novels; 2. Blue Beetle (Fictional character); 3. Superhero graphic novels; 4. Graphic novels
978-1-4012-1361-9, $12.99

High school teen Jaime Reyes became the latest Blue Beetle by accident, and now he needs to know more about the scarab that has bonded with his body (something it had never done with either previous Blue Beetle). He undertakes a journey with his friend Brenda and the tattooed soldier called Peacemaker to find out what is happening to him, and his journey takes him across the country and into the furthest reaches of space.

"The use of an ethnicity not often seen in comic heroes, plus engaging characters and a fast-paced, rip-snorting second half make for a divertingly lighthearted take on a young man's quest to solve the secrets of himself." Booklist
Followed by Blue Beetle vol. 3: reach for the stars (2008)
Sequel to Blue Beetle: shellshocked (2006)

Hero Squared, Volume 1. Written by Keith Giffen and J. M. DeMatteis; art by Joe Abraham. Boom! Studios 2006 Un Illustration
Grades: 9 10 11 12 Adult   **741.5; Fic**
1. Humorous graphic novels; 2. Superhero graphic novels; 3. Graphic novels
1-4243-0422-9, $14.99

When a superhero's world is destroyed, he ends up in a parallel world (ours) in which he's a slacker; and the supervillain who destroyed her world is the slacker's girlfriend in this one. Really bad words appear as nonsense syllables, and there is considerable superhero fighting action and lots of confusion about identities.

Giffen, Keith and Alan Grant

Lobo/The Authority: Holiday Hell. Art by Simon Bisley. DC Comics/Wildstorm 2006 Un Illustration
Grades: 12 Adult   **741.5; Fic**
1. Science fiction graphic novels; 2. Superhero graphic novels; 3. Graphic novels
978-1-4012-0992-6, $17.99

In "The Lobo Paramilitary Christmas Special," Lobos tries to take out Kris Kringle himself - in a hit organized by The Easter Bunny. Next, in "The Authority/Lobo: Jingle Hell," Lobo comes to the Wildstorm Universe as a young Jenny Quantum wants him to answer for his horrible crime against Old Saint Nick. And finally, in "The Authority/Lobo: Spring Break Massacre," this series of holiday fun comes full circle as The Authority realize Lobo is still free in their universe and that he must be stopped before he collects his long-awaited bounty from the Easter Bunny. The book has crude humor, strong language, lots of graphic violence, nudity, and sexual situations between various types of consenting adults.

Gill, Joel

Strange fruit; Volume 1: Uncelebrated narratives from Black history. Words and pictures by Joel Christian Gill; foreword by Henry Louis Gates, Jr. Fulcrum Publishing 2014 176 p. Color; Illustration
Grades: 9 10 11 12 Adult   **973.04960730092/2; 741.5; 92**
1. African Americans; 2. African Americans — Biography; 3. African Americans — History — Anecdotes — Juvenile literature; 4. Heroes — United States — Biography — Juvenile literature
1938486293; 9781938486296, $23.95
LC 2014010803

This book, illustrated by Joel Christian Gill, "is a collection of stories from African American history that exemplifies success in the face of great adversity. This unique graphic anthology offers historical and cultural commentary on nine uncelebrated heroes [such as escaped slave] Henry 'Box' Brown, . . . Alexander Crummel and the Noyes Academy [and] Marshall 'Major' Taylor . . . the first black champion in any sport." (Publisher's note)

"The short narratives are conversational in tone and the accompanying detailed images convey tragic beauty. Gil doesn't shy away from portraying brutal scenes, but does so without sensationalism. The panels vary in size and orientation, pushing the momentum of each vignette forward with great success." SLJ

Gillen, Kieron

★ **Young** Avengers: mic-drop at the edge of time and space. By Kieron Gillen; illustrated by Jamie McKelvie. Marvel Enterprises 2014 112 p. Color illustration
Grades: 10 11 12 Adult   **741.5; Fic**
1. Captain America (Fictional character); 2. Heroes — Fiction; 3. Loki (Norse Deity); 4. Science fiction comic books, strips, etc; 5. Superheroes — Fiction; 6. Young adult fiction; 7. Graphic novels
9780785185307, $15.99; 0785185305

"They say you can never go home. For the Young Avengers, that's not true. They can go home - it's just that if they do, the universe may end. Better not go home then, eh" (Wait, what are you doing, Young Avengers? You've decided to go home!) The team takes on the gig to save reality, but is Kate Bishop an enemy in waiting" Is this the last we see of the loveable/strangle-able Kid Loki?" (Publisher's note)

"Gillen is an intelligent, savvy writer who gives more space to the battle's buildup and after-party than to the battle itself and even in the midst of the fight relies more on intimate character conflict than epic fisticuffs. . . . The overt focus on fluid sexuality . . . and smart teen dialogue that rings familiar and true give this series high appeal for new adults in particular." Booklist

★ **Young** avengers: style > substance. Kieron Gillen, writer; Jamie McKelvie, Mike Norton, artist; Matthew Wilson, color artist; VC's Clayton Cowles, letterer. Marvel Enterprises 2013 128 p. Illustration
Grades: 10 11 12 Adult   **741.5; Fic**
1. Superhero graphic novels; 2. Teenagers — Fiction
9780785167082, $15.99; 0785167080

In this superhero graphic novel, author Kieron Gillen and illustrator Jamie McKelvie tell the story of "Wiccan, Hulkling and Kate 'Hawkeye' Bishop with Kid Loki, Marvel Boy and Ms. America. . . . As a figure from Loki's past emerges, Wiccan makes a horrible mistake that comes back to bite everyone on their communal posteriors. Fight scenes! Fake IDs! And plentiful feels! (aka 'meaningful emotional character beats' . . .)" (Publisher's note)

"The story . . . flies by, thanks to clever banter and lightning pacing. . . . McKelvie turns in clean, polished pages with eye-popping character work and shows some real and very welcome imagination with action sequences." Booklist

Contains material originally published in magazine form Young Avengers #1-5 and Marvel now! point one #1—Tp verso

★ **Young** Avengers; Volume 2: alternative cultures. Kieron Gillen, illustrated by Kate Brown and Jamie McKelvie. Marvel Enterprises 2014 112 p. Color illustration (Young Avengers)
Grades: 9 10 11 12 Adult   **741.5**
1. Fantasy fiction; 2. Heroes; 3. Science fiction comic books, strips, etc; 4. Superhero comic books, strips, etc; 5. Young adult fiction; 6. Graphic novels
0785167099; 9780785167099, $15.99

In this comic book collection by Kieron Gillen, illustrated by Kate Brown and Jamie McKelvie, "existential horror turns cosmic horror as something emerges from the shadows of the past . . . and it seems that the Young Avengers have one more thing to worry about. The team races desperately across the multi-verse in pursuit of their missing friend, but their road trip goes crazy as it reaches its destination." (Publisher's note)

"As with the previous one, this slim volume is a quick read with snappy dialogue and fast, cleanly depicted action that pops with cinematic digital coloring effects." Booklist

Contains material originally published as Young Avengers (2013) #6-10

Gillis, Peter

Shatter. Art by Mike Saenz. AiT/Planet Lar 2006 Un Illustration

Grades: 10 11 12 Adult   **741.5; Fic**

1. Mystery graphic novels; 2. Science fiction graphic novels; 3. Graphic novels

978-1-932051-44-5, $14.95

In a near-future Chicagoland (as envisioned in the 1980s), private cop Shatter takes a contract to track down a woman who traffics in recombinant RNA. This violent and sexy mystery was originally published in the mid-1980s, and the art was done on a first-generation Macintosh with 128K of memory and a dot-matrix printer.

Gilroy, Henry

Star Wars: The Clone wars: Shipyards of doom. Ronda Pattison, illustrator; The Fillbach Brothers, illustrators. Dark Horse Comics 2008 96p. Illustration

Grades: 6 7 8 9 10   **741.5; Fic**

1. Adventure graphic novels; 2. Science fiction graphic novels; 3. Star Wars; 4. Graphic novels

978-1-59582-207-9, $7.95

In this original story based on the Star Wars: Clone Wars animated movie and television series, Anakin Skywalker, Obi-Wan Kenobi, and Anakin's Padawan Ahsoka Tano form the nucleus of a small team whose objective is to infiltrate the Banking Clan Shipyards in order to call in a bombing strike. For now, the Separatist forces have superior numbers of ships, and destroying the shipyard could help the Republic. However, once they arrive, they learn that the shipyard is using live workers instead of being fully automated, and Anakin and Obi-Wan must find a way to save the workers while still destroying the shipyards. The workers' beaten-down attitudes and refusal to be freed hampers the Jedi Knights. This graphic novel includes the same level of action and violence as the live action Star Wars movies.

Gilson, Che

Avigon: Gods & Demons. Writer Che' Gilson; artist, Jimmie Robinson. Image Comics 2005 Un Illustration

Grades: 10 11 12 Adult   **741.5; Fic**

1. Fantasy graphic novels

1-58240-503-4, $19.95

Avigon, a clockwork creation, has to escape, her mechanical world is killing her very soul. The sky is black with acrid smoke, the rivers run slick with oil, and bizarre clockwork creatures roam the streets. Above it all, eccentric and power-hungry politicians and egomaniacal clockwork masters govern with stone cold hearts. But how can Avigon escape a surreal world of machines where she herself is one" Her desperate search will lead her to the darkest regions of humanity and to the arms of her destiny. The book includes some violence.

Dark Moon Diary Volume 1. Brett Uher, illustrator/ Tokyopop 2007 Un Illustration

Grades: 8 9 10 11 12   **741.5; Fic**

1. Fantasy graphic novels; 2. Supernatural graphic novels; 3. Graphic novels

978-1-59532-844-1, $9.99

When fifteen-year-old Priscilla's parents pass away, she has nowhere to go but to her last living" relatives in the European town of Nachtwald. Once there, she learns that not only is Nachtwald populated by ghosts, werewolves, witches, and other preternatural beings, but that her relatives are vampires. Amidst the pandemonium, she turns to her diary, and slowly learns what it takes to survive a new family, new friendships, and the anxiety of high school, all while living in an unfamiliar world.

Gin, Toriko

Song of the hanging sky, vol. 2. Go! Comi 2008 Un

Grades: 10 11 12 Adult   **741.5; Fic**

1. Manga; 2. Science fiction graphic novels; 3. Graphic novels

978-1-60510-024-1, $10.99

The tribe's shaman, Across the River, is still missing, so Wolf, Another Bear, and Hello go out to search for her. This leaves the human, Jack, among the other members of the tribe, some of whom hate and fear all humans. Fair Cave shelters Jack in his tent and tells him what happened on the first Day of Destruction that left only some of the tribe's children alive. Meanwhile, Across the River is living with Rod, a blind ex-soldier, and they take in the injured boy soldier, Cherry. The humans' war is getting closer to the tribe. The book includes some mildly harsh language and some violence.

Song of the hanging sky, vol.1. Go! Comi 2008 Un Illustration

Grades: 10 11 12 Adult   **741.5; Fic**

1. Fantasy graphic novels; 2. Manga; 3. Graphic novels

978-0-933617-87-9, $10.99

Jack is a field medic in an army at war in what looks much like a World War I era world. He has left the army and lives in an isolated mountainous area with only a dog to keep him company. Then he finds a wounded boy, with wings. He nurses the boy back to health, realizing that he must be one of the legendary "birdfolk." However, when he tries to return the boy to his tribe, the others would much prefer to kill the human and keep their presence a secret. Jack needs to find a way to make them realize he's on their side and wants to help them, and that he's sick of war, fighting, and death. The book includes brief moments of partial nudity.

Gipi

Garage Band. First Second Books 2007 132p. Illustration

Grades: 8 9 10 11 12 Adult   **741.5**

1. Friendship; 2. Rock music; 3. Graphic novels

978-1-59643-206-2

LC 2006018345

Four boys - Giuliano, Stefano, Alberto, and Alex - with turbulent home lives find refuge in the music they play together and in their friendship. When their only amp blows a fuse and the deadline to make their demo tape is pressing, they decide to steal in order to replace it. Events rapidly spiral out of control: will this be the end of everything the band has worked for?

Notes for a war story. Translated by Spectrum. First Second Books 2007 126p. Illustration

Grades: 10 11 12 Adult   **741.5; Fic**
1. Crime; 2. War; 3. Graphic novels
978-1-59643-261-1, $16.95

LC 2006-49716

Giuliano, a loner among outsiders, is one of three young drifters caught up in the whirlwind of a war in the Balkans. The three boys are like passing shadows; they live in abandoned houses, dodge the occasional bomb, and steal car parts for money. Meeting Felix—a powerful, fast-talking mercenary—changes everything for them. Felix is an expert manipulator; he speaks to their ambition and to their desires for power, wealth, and purpose. They're instantly hooked, especially the trio's unofficial leader, Stefano, and they soon escalate from petty crime to working on behalf of a mafia-style militia, bullying and extorting money in Felix's name. But as Giuliano comes to realize, they don't know what they're fighting for—if they're even fighting for anything. There's some naturally occurring violence and harsh language.
Original Italian edition, 2004

Glaser, Jason

The **Buffalo** Soldiers and the American West. Capstone Press 2005 32p. Illustration
Grades: 3 4 5 6 7 8 9   **741.5; 978**
1. African American soldiers; 2. West (US); 3. Graphic novels
0-7368-4966-1, $25.26

LC 2005006527

In graphic novel format, this book tells the story of the African American soldiers known as Buffalo Soldiers, who fought against Native Americans and protected the Western Frontier of the United States. The book includes additional information about the Buffalo Soldiers, a bibliography, and a list of books for further reading.
Part of the Graphic History series.

Jackie Robinson: Baseball's Great Pioneer. Capstone Press 2005 32p. Illustration
Grades: 3 4 5 6 7 8 9   **741.5; 796.357'092; 796.357**
1. African American athletes; 2. Baseball — Biography; 3. Biographical graphic novels; 4. Robinson, Jackie, 1919-1972; 5. Graphic novels
0-7368-4633-6, $25.26

LC 2005003345

In graphic novel format, this book tells the life story of Jackie Robinson and his professional baseball career that broke the "color barrier." The book includes additional information about Robinson, including the back of a baseball card that shows his playing statistics for the 1947-1956 seasons, a bibliography, and a list of books for further reading.
Part of the Graphic Biographies series.

John Brown's raid on Harper's Ferry. Capstone Press 2005 32p. Illustration
Grades: 3 4 5 6 7 8 9   **741.5; 973.7**
1. Harpers Ferry (W Va) — History — John Brown's Raid, 1859; 2. Graphic novels
0-7368-4369-8, $25.26

LC 2004029083

This book recounts the story of John Brown's failed rebellion in Harpers Ferry in 1859, intended to start a massive slave uprising in the South and the establishment of a state in the Allegheny Mountains for freed slaves. It includes additional information, a glossary, a list of books for further reading, and more.
Part of the Graphic Library, Graphic History series.

Patrick Henry: Liberty or Death. Capstone Press 2006 32p. Illustration
Grades: 3 4 5 6 7 8 9   **741.5; 973.3; 92**
1. Biographical graphic novels; 2. Henry, Patrick, 1736-1799; 3. Graphic novels
0-7368-4970-X, $25.26

LC 2005004011

This book uses the comic book format to recount highlights of the life story of Patrick Henry, who is known as the "Voice of the American Revolution." It includes additional information, a glossary, a list of books for further reading, and more.
Part of the Graphic Library, Graphic Biographies series.

Glass, Bryan J. L.

The **mice** templar, volume one: the prophecy. Created by Bryan J.L. Glass & Michael Avon Oeming. Michael Avon Oeming, illustrator. Image Comics 2008 256p. Illustration
Grades: 6 7 8 9 10 11 12 Adult   **741.5; Fic**
1. Adventure graphic novels; 2. Fantasy graphic novels; 3. Mice; 4. Graphic novels
978-1-58240-871-2, $29.99; 1-58240-871-8

In a land populated by animals, the Mice Templar used to protect the people of the mouse kingdom, but a civil war destroyed them; the king now employs rat soldiers, and they prey upon the mouse villages. Young Karic still idolizes the Mice Templar, but everything he knows and believes is shattered when his village is raided by rats, burned, and his family captured as slaves. He survives, saved by a mysterious mouse named Pilot, who says he was once a Templar and offers to train Karic. The salmon in the river say that Karic is the one prophesied to restore the Templar, but can he truly be the one? The book includes considerable battle violence.
"Equal parts Norse myth, Arthurian legend, and Mrs. Frisby and the Rats of N.I.M.H., The Mice Templar series re-imagines the warrior animal tale with just enough of its own spin to make it well worth adding to the collection." Voice Youth Advocates
The volume is a collection of the first six issues of The mice templar
Other titles in this series are:Destiny Part One (2010)Destiny Part Two (2010)Legend (2013)A Midwinter Night's Dream (2012)

Glidden, Sarah

How to understand Israel in 60 days or less. Writer & artist, Sarah Glidden; letterer Clem Robins. Vertigo/DC Comics 2010 206p. Illustration; Map
Grades: 11 12 Adult   **915.694; 741.5**
978-1-4012-2233-8, $24.99; 9781401222345, $19.99

This book "is Sarah [Glidden]'s memoir not only of her Israeli governmentsponsored trip through Tel Aviv, Jerusalem, the Golan Heights, Masada and other famous locations, but of the emotional journey she never expected to take while she was there. Her experience clashes with her preconceived notions again and again, particularly when she tries to take a non-chaperoned trip into the West Bank. Sarah is forced to question first her political beliefs and, ultimately, her own sense of identity." (Publisher's note)

Goddard, Drew

Buffy the Vampire Slayer season eight, volume 3: Wolves at the gate. Artist, Georges Jeanty, Jo Chen. Dark Horse Comics 2008 Un Illustration

Grades: 8 9 10 11 12 Adult   **741.5; Fic**
1. Buffy the Vampire Slayer (Fictional character); 2. Fantasy graphic novels; 3. Horror graphic novels; 4. Vampires; 5. Graphic novels
978-1-59582-165-2, $15.95

A band of Japanese vampires who can transform into wolves, panthers, swarms of bees, and fog, attack the Slayer compound in Scotland, stealing Buffy's mystical scythe that she used to transform thousands of young women into Slayers. Now the only one who can help her fight these vampires is Dracula himself, and they have to travel to Japan to recover the scythe and stop the Japanese from accomplishing their plans. Meanwhile, Buffy and Satsu have one night together that seems to throw everyone else for a loop. The last panel on the last page shows Buffy and Satsu together in bed, kissing and wrapped around each other.

Goetzinger, Annie

Girl in Dior. Annie Goetzinger; translation by Joe Johnson; lettering by Ortho. NBM Pub. 2015 128 p. Color; Illustration

Grades: 9 10 11 12 Adult   **741.5**
1. Dior, Christian, 1905-1957; 2. Fashion design; 3. Fashion designers
1561639141; 9781561639144, $27.99
                                            LC 2014956278

This book, by Annie Goetzinger, "covers the 1947 groundbreaking first fashion show put on by designer Christian Dior. . . . We watch the magic happen through the eyes of Clara Nohant, a young 'fashion chronicler,' a fictional character injected into the story amid real-life modistes, drapers, pattern makers, muses, magazine editors, and movie stars who surrounded the designer." (School Library Journal)

"Goetzinger's detailed, expressive faces and figures seem to be illuminated from within, and the garments themselves are a great tribute to the author's background in fashion illustration." Booklist

Initially published in French as Jeune fille en Dior

Goldstein, Nancy

★ **Jackie** Ormes: the first African American woman cartoonist. University of Michigan Press 2008 225p. Illustration

Grades: 10 11 12 Adult   **92; 741.5**
1. African American women — Biography; 2. Cartoonists; 3. Ormes, Jackie, 1911-1985
978-0-472-11624-9, $35; 0-472-11624-X
                                            LC 2007-35395

This book covers the life and career of Jackie Ormes, who was the first African American woman cartoonist. She wrote and drew comic strips that ran in Black newspapers

such as the Pittsburgh Courier and the Chicago Defender. She was part of the Black elite in Chicago and knew other luminaries such as singer Eartha Kitt and musician/composer/conductor Duke Ellington. She was also investigated by the FBI because of her Leftist political ideas and activities. While she did such things as create Torchy paper dolls, based on her beautiful and sexy cartoon character, and cute Patty-Jo dolls, Ormes also used her comic strips to put forth her political views. This book reproduces some of her cartoons and comic strips, in both black and white and in color.

Includes bibliographical references

Gonick, Larry

★ The **cartoon** history of the modern world: Part 1: from Columbus to the U.S. Constitution. Collins 2007 259p. Illustration

Grades: 9 10 11 12 Adult   **741.5; 909.08**
1. Modern history; 2. Graphic novels
978-0-06-076004-5; 0-06-076004-4, $17.95
                                            LC 2006-49146

The book begins with a "15-page distillation of pre-Columbian America; and while Europe and North America receive most of the attention, Gonick does include at least some highlights from other parts of the world. Covering such topics as the Protestant Reformation, the British defeat of the Spanish Armada, the Copernican model of the universe, and the American Revolution, he writes and draws with considerable wit and authority, and is obviously well versed in his subject." SLJ

Followed by:The Cartoon History of the Modern World Part 2: From the Bastille to Baghdad (2009)

★ The **Cartoon** History of the Universe III: From the Rise of Arabia to the Renaissance. W. W. Norton 2002 300p. Illustration

Grades: 9 10 11 12 Adult   **741.5; 909.07**
1. World history; 2. Graphic novels
0-393-32403-6, $21.95
                                            LC 02-288002

This volume begins in the year 395, covers the birth of Islam, the Crusades, the Asian and African nations, the Mongol conquests, the Ottoman Empire, the Black Death, the Italian Renaissance, the rise of Spain, and culminates in the year 1492. The facts in the text are accompanied again by his irreverently humorous illustrations.

★ The **Cartoon** History of the Universe Volumes 1-7: From the Big Bang to Alexander the Great. Main Street Books/Doubleday & Co. 1990 368p. Illustration

Grades: 9 10 11 12 Adult   **741.5**
1. World history; 2. Graphic novels
0-385-26520-4, $22.95; 9780385265201
                                            LC 02-288002

Gonick presents a quick tour of world history, starting from the Big Bang through the life of Alexander the Great. He presents facts in the text, while his illustrations provide an irreverently humorous counterpoint. There's partial nudity with some of the ancient people.

★ The **Cartoon** History of the Universe Volumes 8-13: From the Springtime of China to the Fall of Rome. Main Street Books/Doubleday & Co. 1994 305p. Illustration

Grades: 9 10 11 12 Adult   **741.5; 902**
   1. World history; 2. Graphic novels
0-385-42093-5, $22.95

                        LC 02-288002
   Gonick presents a quick tour of world history, continuing with Alexander the Great's march to India (and his about-face), focusing on India and China, then going back to Rome and covering the Western World through the end of Justinian's reign, around 564 A.D. He also tells the story of Jeshua ben Joseph (Jesus). He presents facts in the text, while his illustrations provide an irreverently humorous counterpoint. There's partial nudity and some violence with the depictions of wars and battles.

Goodwin, Michael
   Economix: how and why our economy works (and doesn't work) in words and pictures. Michael Goodwin. Harry N. Abrams Inc. 2012 304 p. Illustration
Grades: 11 12 Adult   **330**
   1. Cost and standard of living; 2. Economic development; 3. Economics; 4. Economics
9780810988392, $19.95

                   LC 2011052119
   Author Michael Goodwin discusses the economy, "human nature and our attempts to make the most of what we've got . . . and sometimes what our neighbors have got . . . [The book explains concepts from] the beginning of Western economic thought, to markets free and otherwise, to economic failures, successes, limitations, and future possibilities." (Publisher's note)
   "This dense yet readable exegesis makes economics entertaining despite current financial shenanigans worldwide. Goodwin takes a chronological approach, starting with the history of banking in the 17th century. As he marches through four centuries of economic theories and theorists, he attempts to show what happened, what succeeded, and what went wrong in terms of both public and private good, with a focus on the reasons particular theories didn't pan out in real life." LJ
   Includes bibliographical references and index

Goodwin, Vincent
   Sir Arthur Conan Doyle's The adventure of the Red-Headed League. ABDO/Magic Wagon 2010 48p. Illustration
Grades: 4 5 6 7 8 9   **741.5; Fic**
   1. Doyle, Arthur Conan Sir, 1859-1930 — Adaptations; 2. Holmes, Sherlock (Fictional character); 3. Mystery graphic novels; 4. Novelists; 5. Graphic novels
978-1-60270-726-9, $28.50; 1-60270-726-X

           LC 2009-32460
   Consulting detective Sherlock Holmes and his friend Dr. John Watson take the case of Jabez Wilson, an ordinary tradesman with an

Courtesy of ABDO/Magic Wagon

extraordinary tale. His pawn shop assistant had found an advertisement in the newspaper asking for eligible men to apply for membership in The RedHeaded League, and he helped Mr. Wilson fight through a crowd of redheaded men and to be accepted into the League. Wilson was paid four pounds a week for a few hours' work copying out of an encyclopedia; then suddenly, all trace of the League disappeared. He wants Holmes to find out what has happened. This graphic novel adaptation has been done by Goodwin and Dunn, who are experienced creators with Antarctic Press (Dunn started the publishing house). The book includes a brief glossary, a short biography of Doyle, a listing of his published works, and a short sketching lesson by Dunn.
   Part of The Graphic Novel Adventures of Sherlock Holmes

Courtesy of ABDO/Magic Wagon

   Sir Arthur Conan Doyle's The adventure of the speckled band. Adapted by, Vincent Goodwin; illustrated by, Ben Dunn. ABDO/Magic Wagon 2010 48p. Illustration
Grades: 4 5 6 7 8 9   **741.5; Fic**
   1. Doyle, Arthur Conan Sir, 1859-1930 — Adaptations; 2. Holmes, Sherlock (Fictional character); 3. Mystery graphic novels; 4. Mystery writers
978-1-60270-727-6, $28.50; 1-60270-727-8

           LC 2009-32461
   Consulting detective Sherlock Holmes and his partner Dr. John Watson come to the aid of Miss Helen Stoner. After moving back to England from India with their stepfather, Helen's twin sister died under mysterious circumstances. Now, two years later, Helen knows something is terribly wrong in her stepfather's house. Both men suspect the gypsies that Dr. Roylott, the stepfather, has allowed to live on his property, but Holmes soon suspects something else. This graphic novel adaptation has been done by Goodwin and Dunn, who are experienced creators with Antarctic Press (Dunn started the publishing house). The book includes a brief glossary, a short biography of Doyle, a listing of his published works, and a short sketching lesson by Dunn.
   Part of The Graphic Novel Adventures of Sherlock Holmes

   Sir Arthur Conan Doyle's, The adventure of the Abbey Grange. ABDO/Magic Wagon 2010 48p. Illustration
Grades: 4 5 6 7 8 9
741.5; Fic
   1. Doyle, Arthur Conan Sir, 1859-1930 — Adaptations; 2. Holmes,

Courtesy of ABDO/Magic Wagon

Sherlock (Fictional character); 3. Mystery graphic novels; 4. Mystery writers

978-1-60270-722-1, $28.50; 1-60270-722-7

A robbery and murder have occurred, and Sir Eustace Brackenstall is dead. His wife and maid say that a gang of robbers invaded their home, tied up Lady Brackenstall and killed Sir Eustace, but Holmes doesn't believe their story. As he investigates, he learns that Sir Eustace was a cruel man, and even though Lady Brackenstall has lied, Holmes sympathizes with her. This book adapts Doyle's short story; it includes a short glossary, a brief biography of Doyle, a short drawing lesson, and a list of Doyle's other writings. Dunn's art depicts Holmes and Dr. Watson as younger men, but continues the stereotypical portrayal of Holmes with the deerstalker cap and shoulder caped coat which Doyle never had him wear in the original stories.

Part of The Graphic Novel Adventures of Sherlock Holmes series.

Sir Arthur Conan Doyle's, The adventure of the dancing men. ABDO/Magic Wagon 2010 48p. Illustration

Grades: 4 5 6 7 8 9

1. Doyle, Arthur Conan Sir, 1859-1930 — Adaptations; 2. Holmes, Sherlock (Fictional character); 3. Mystery graphic novels; 4. Mystery writers

978-1-60270-723-8, $28.50; 1-60270-723-5

Courstesy of ABDO/Magic Wagon

When strange writing that looks like dancing men starts appearing around the estate of Mr. Cubitt, he comes to Sherlock Holmes for help. He thinks it's the work of pranksters, but his American wife seems frightened. As he brings more of the writing samples to Holmes, the detective works on the case, but he may not be able to solve it before tragedy strikes the Cubitts. This book adapts Doyle's short story; it includes a short glossary, a brief biography of Doyle, a short drawing lesson, and a list of Doyle's other writings. Dunn's art depicts Holmes and Dr. Watson as younger men, but continues the stereotypical portrayal of Holmes with the deerstalker cap and shoulder caped coat which Doyle never had him wear in the original stories.

Part of The Graphic Novel Adventures of Sherlock Holmes series

Sir Arthur Conan Doyle's, The adventure of the empty house. ABDO/Magic Wagon 2010 48p. Illustration

Grades: 4 5 6 7 8 9 **741.5; Fic**

1. Doyle, Arthur Conan Sir, 1859-1930 — Adaptations; 2. Holmes, Sherlock (Fictional character); 3. Mystery graphic novels; 4. Mystery writers

978-1-60270-724-5, $28.50; 1-60270-724-3

Three years before, Dr. Watson witnessed the death of his friend Sherlock Holmes, who plummeted to his death along with archvillain Dr. Moriarty. Now, Inspector Lestrade asks Watson's help in a puzzling murder case, but it stumps Watson as well. Then, to his utter surprise, Holmes comes to him, explaining that he pretended to die. Together again, the

two men work on the case, hoping to catch one of Moriarty's dangerous henchmen. This graphic novel adapts Doyle's original story which was the "comeback" after killing Holmes in "The Final Problem." The art depicts Watson as a fairly young man, but persists in putting Holmes into the deerstalker cap and caped overcoat which Doyle's Holmes never wore. The book includes a brief drawing lesson, a short glossary, brief biography of Doyle, and a listing of his other writings.

Courtsesy of ABDO/Magic Wagon

Part of The Graphic Novel Adventures of Sherlock Holmes

Sir Arthur Conan Doyle's, the adventure of the Norwood Builder. ABDO/Magic Wagon 2010 48p. Illustration

Grades: 4 5 6 7 8 9 **741.5; Fic**

1. Holmes, Sherlock (Fictional character); 2. Mystery graphic novels; 3. Graphic novels

978-1-60270-725-2, $28.50; 1-60270-725-1

LC 2009-32459

Young solicitor Mr. McFarlane begs Holmes to clear his name when he's accused of the murder of Jonas Oldacre, the Norwood Builder. Inspector Lestrade thinks he has a solid case, and the evidence seems to implicate McFarlane, especially since Mr. Oldacre's new will made McFarlane his sole heir. Holmes points to the lack of a body, and digs up more clues in his quest to save McFarlane. This graphic novel adaptation of Doyle's short story retains the suspense of the original, but perpetuates the stereotypical portrayals of Holmes in the deerstalker and caped coat which he never wore in the original stories. The book includes a brief drawing lesson, a short glossary, a brief biography of Doyle, and a listing of his other writings.

Courtesy of ABDO/Magic Wagon

Part of The Graphic Novel Adventures of Sherlock Holmes

Goosebumps: Terror Trips

Adapted by Jill Thompson, Jamie Tolagson, and Amy Kim Ganter. Scholastic/Graphix 2007 137p. Illustration

Grades: 4 5 6 7 8 9 **741.5; Fic**

1. Horror graphic novels; 2. Stine, R L — Adaptations; 3. Graphic novels

978-0-439-85780-2, $8.99

Stine's Goosebumps series was very popular years ago, and is enjoying a resurgence of popularity with new editions of the prose books. The graphic novel adaptations, all done by well-known independent comics creators, bring the stories to a new audience. Goosebumps: Creepy Creatures is also available.

This volume adapts three of Stine's Goosebumps novels into graphic novel format. Noted independent comic creator Thompson adapts One Day at Horrorland, about one family's ordeal in a very strange, all-too-realistic amusement park. Canadian artist Tolagson adapts A Shocker on Shock Street, which depicts the horrific adventures of two kids on a movie studio lot where the horror is more than just special effects. Global manga creator Ganter adapts Deep Trouble, in which a brother and sister find a real mermaid.

Goscinny, Rene

Asterix and Caesar's Gift. Orion/Sterling Publishing 2004 48p. Illustration
Grades: 4 5 6 7 8 9 10 11 12 Adult   **741.5; Fic**
   1. Asterix (Fictional character); 2. Humorous graphic novels
   0-75286-645-1, $12.95; 0-75286-646-X (pa)
   When Legionary Tremensdelirius gets the title deeds to the little Gaulish village as a bonus, he swaps them with tavern landlord Orthopaedix for a drink. Funnily enough, Asterix and his friends aren't keen to hand over their village to anyone else. After a chieftaincy election campaign and a showdown with the Romans, both events fiercely contested, can all still end well?

Asterix and Cleopatra. Orion/Sterling Publishing 2004 48p. Illustration
Grades: 4 5 6 7 8 9 10 11 12 Adult   **741.5; Fic**
   1. Asterix (Fictional character); 2. Humorous graphic novels
   0-75286-606-0, $12.95; 0-75286-607-9 (pb)
   How can lovely Queen Cleopatra show Julius Caesar that ancient Egypt is still a great nation" Her architect Edifis recruits his Gaulish friends to help him build a magnificent palace within three months. There are villainous saboteurs to be outwitted, but Asterix, Obelix, and Getafix still find time to go sight-seeing, and leave their mark on the Pyramids and the Sphinx's nose.

Asterix and the Banquet. Orion/Sterling Publishing 2004 48p. Illustration
Grades: 4 5 6 7 8 9 10 11 12 Adult   **741.5; Fic**
   1. Asterix (Fictional character); 2. Humorous graphic novels
   0-75286-608-0, $12.95; 0-75286-609-5 (pa)
   When the Romans try to contain the threat from the Gaulish village by building a stockade around it, Asterix and Obelix lay a bet with them. They will break out and claim their right to travel freely all over Gaul, collecting the local delicacies and bringing them back to prove their point. Ham from Lutetia, fizzy wine from Durocortorum, fish stew from Massilia in the south ... soon their shopping bag is full. Outwitting Romans, a couple of treacherous Gauls, and the thieves Villanus and Unscrupulus, they set off for home ... but who's that little dog who has been following them all the way from Lutetia?

Asterix and the Cauldron. Orion/Sterling Publishing 2004 48p. Illustration
Grades: 4 5 6 7 8 9 10 11 12 Adult   **741.5; Fic**
   1. Asterix (Fictional character); 2. Humorous graphic novels
   0-75286-629-X, $9.95
   There's financial skulduggery in ancient Gaul. When local Chief Whosemoralsarelastix wants a cauldron full of money kept out of Roman hands, the cash disappears while Asterix is guarding it. He and Obelix must earn enough to repay it through fairground gladiatorial contests, trendy theatrical performances, even bank robbery - they'll try anything. But whose morals are really elastic? And how do the pirates, just for once, get an unexpected bonus?

Asterix and the Class Act. Orion/Sterling Publishing 2004 56p. Illustration
Grades: 4 5 6 7 8 9 10 11 12 Adult   **741.5; Fic**
   1. Asterix (Fictional character); 2. Humorous graphic novels
   0-75286-068-2, $12.95; 0-75286-640-0 (pa)
   This volume collects 14 stories, including the day Asterix and Obelix were born (in the middle of a fish fight); how Obelix goes back to school; fashion in ancient Gaul; how Dogmatix helps the village cockerel win a duel, and how he's adopted as a Roman mascot; Obelix's adventures under the mistletoe; the bid for the very first Gaulish Olympics, and more.

Asterix and the Laurel Wreath. Orion/Sterling Publishing 2004 48p. Illustration
Grades: 4 5 6 7 8 9 10 11 12 Adult   **741.5; Fic**
   1. Asterix (Fictional character); 2. Humorous graphic novels
   0-75286-636-2, $12.95; 0-75286-637-0 (pa)
   Chief Vitalstatistix rashly invites his brother-in-law to dine on a stew seasoned with Caesar's laurel wreath, so Asterix and Obelix must to go Rome to fetch those laurels. Hoping to get access to Caesar, they sell themselves as slaves, but can they do a deal with the corrupt Goldendelicius to swap the laurels for parsley?

Asterix in Britain. Orion/Sterling Publishing 2004 48p. Illustration
Grades: 4 5 6 7 8 9 10 11 12 Adult   **741.5; Fic**
   1. Asterix (Fictional character); 2. Humorous graphic novels
   0-85286-618-4, $12.95; 0-75286-619-2 (pa)
   The Romans have invaded Britain, but one village still holds out. Asterix and Obelix come to help, with a barrel of magic potion in hand. But to deliver the precious brew, the Gaulish heroes must face fog, rain, bad food, warm beer, and the Romans too.

★ **Asterix** the Gaul. [by] René Goscinny and Albert Uderzo. Orion Media 2004 48p. Illustration; Map
Grades: 4 5 6 7 8 9 10 11 12   **741.5; Fic**
   1. France — History; 2. Humorous graphic novels
   0-7528-6604-4, $12.95; 0-7528-6605-2 (pa), $9.95
   Meet Asterix, a diminutive but extremely strong Gaul living in ancient France during the time of the Roman Republic. Together with his friend Obelix, Asterix continually outwits the Roman Legionnaires sent to conquer Gaul for Julius Caesar. Full of puns and outrageous humor, the books also manage to teach a lot of history. This is the

first in a long-running series of graphic novels translated from the original French.

Translated from the French

Other titles in this series are: Asterix and Caesar's Gift; Asterix and Cleopatra; Asterix and the actress; Asterix and the banquet; Asterix and the big fight; Asterix and the cauldron; Asterix and the Goths; Asterix and the Great Crossing; Asterix and the laurel wreath; Asterix the legionary; Asterix and the Normans; Asterix and the Roman Agent; Asterix and the soothsayer; Asterix at the Olympic Games; Asterix in Belgium; Asterix in Britain; Asterix in Corsica; Asterix in Spain; Asterix in Switzerland; Asterix Obelix and Co.; Asterix the gladiator; Asterix The Mansions of the Gods

Asterix the Legionary. Orion/Sterling Publishing 2004 48p. Illustration
Grades: 4 5 6 7 8 9 10 11 12 Adult   **741.5; Fic**
1. Asterix (Fictional character); 2. Humorous graphic novels
0-75286-620-6, $12.95; 0-75286-621-4 (pa)

It's off to the wars for Asterix and Obelix: they've enlisted as legionnaires in order to rescue Tragicomix, whom the Romans forcibly conscripted. The two find Tragicomix and succeed in causing the biggest commotion ever on a battlefield.

Gossett, Christian
King Kong: The 8th Wonder of the World. Dark Horse Books 2006 Un Illustration
Grades: 7 8 9 10 11 12 Adult   **741.5; Fic**
1. King Kong (Fictional character); 2. Science fiction graphic novels; 3. Graphic novels
978-1-59307-472-2, $12.95

Director Carl Denham has one chance to make the film of his dreams - hire an unknown actress, kidnap his writer and board a tramp freighter for the mysterious Island of the Skull. But when hostile natives capture actress Ann Darrow, Denham and his crew will face horrors from giant spiders to bloodthirsty dinosaurs to get her back. Yet, nothing can prepare them for the revelation of the mighty wonder in whose clutches Ann truly remains - King Kong. This story adapts the screenplay for the motion picture directed by Peter Jackson, which is based on the original story by Merian C. Cooper and Edgar Wallace.

Graham, Brandon
King City Vol. 1: Cat Master. Tokyopop 2007 192p. Illustration
Grades: 11 12 Adult   **741.5; Fic**
1. Science fiction graphic novels; 2. Graphic novels
978-1-59816-982-9, $9.99

King City is a semi-futuristic city full of spy gangs, aliens, and lots of weirdness. Joe has returned to King City armed with a special cat. This cat can swallow and duplicate a key, become a weapon, a tool, almost anything Joe needs, all with a simple injection of a mysterious substance Joe keeps handy. He took on a job to duplicate a key, but now finds himself mixed up between rival gangs (he thinks). Meanwhile, his friend Pete takes a job to guard what turns out to be an aquatic alien girl, and he decides to save her. A mysterious, sexy woman helps Joe. Meanwhile, Joe's

ex-girlfriend has a new lover, but the ex-soldier is addicted to a drug called chalk, which will eventually turn his body into chalk. Some sexual situations and foul language make this story more appropriate for older teens. Graham is a noted independent comics creator trying his hand at the global manga format.

Gran, Meredith
Octopus Pie 1. By Meredith Gran. Image Comics 2016 200 p.
Grades: 11 12 Adult   **741.5**
1. Brooklyn (New York, NY) — Fiction; 2. College graduates — Fiction; 3. Roommates — Fiction
1632156326; 9781632156327, $14.99

In this book, by Meredith Gran, "we follow grumpy twenty-something Eve and her stoner roommate Hanna as they navigate post-college life. They'll take on crazed childhood rivals, troubling art scenes, the discomfort of exes, and maybe even... friendship" All this and more in the fictional, totally made-up city of Brooklyn." (Publisher's note)

(Volume 1 of an ongoing series)

Grant, Alan
Robert Louis Stevenson's Kidnapped. Adaptation by Alan Grant; illustrator, Cam Kennedy. Tundra Books 2007 Un Illustration
Grades: 6 7 8 9 10   **741.5; Fic**
1. Adventure graphic novels; 2. Stevenson, Robert Louis, 1850-1894 — Adaptations; 3. Graphic novels
978-0-88776-843-9 (pa), $11.95; 0-88776-843-1 (pa)
LC 2007921350

Kidnapped is set in 1751, during the time of the Jacobite rebellion "a tumultuous and tragic period in Scottish history. When David Balfour sets out to find his uncle, he never dreamed that he would be kidnapped " but saved from a life of slavery " and thrown from one escapade to another in the company of the fugitive, masterful swordsman Alan Breck Stewart.

"This is an engaging adaptation, aided by Kennedy's vibrant illustrations in a palette dominated by blues, greens, and sepia tones. The action scenes are exciting." SLJ

Robert Louis Stevenson's Strange case of Dr. Jekyll and Mr. Hyde. Adapted by Alan Grant; illustrated by Cam Kennedy; colored and lettered by Jamie Grant. Tundra Books 2008 40p. Illustration
Grades: 6 7 8 9 10   **741.5; Fic**
978-0-88776-882-8 (pa), $11.95; 0-88776-882-2 (pa)

The graphic canon of children's literature: the world's great kids' lit as comics and visuals
Edited by Russ Kick. Seven Stories Press 2014 480 p. Color; Illustration
Grades: 6 7 8 9 10 11 12 Adult   **741.5**
1. Children's literature; 2. Graphic novels in education; 3. Literature — Adaptations
1609805305; 9781609805302, $38.95
LC 2014010178

Edited by Russ Kick, "the original three-volume anthology 'The Graphic Canon' presented the world's classic literature—from ancient times to the late twentieth century—as eye-popping comics, illustrations, and other visual forms. In this follow-up volume, young people's literature through the ages is given new life by the best comics artists and illustrators." (Publisher's note)

"These dazzlingly varied renderings run the gamut from haunting to comical while offering visceral reminders that children's stories are often densely layered, infinitely transposable, and peddle in imagery both macabre and whimsical. It is the unfettered imagination of these stories that make them not only wildly entertaining, but also vessels of forgotten truths." Pub Wkly

The graphic canon, volume 2: from Kubla Khan to the Bronte sisters to The picture of Dorian Gray.
Edited by Russ Kick. Seven Stories Press 2012 499 p.
Grades: 11 12 Adult   741.5
1. Comic books, strips, etc — History and criticism; 2. Graphic novels in education; 3. Literature — Adaptations; 4. Literature — Collections; 5. Graphic novels
1609803787; 9781609803780, $34.95
LC 2012013176
This book, edited by Russ Kick, collects "original graphic versions of [19th-century] classic literature, from [Samuel Taylor] Coleridge's 'Kubla Khan' to Wilde's 'The Picture of Dorian Gray'. . . . Contributors include Maxon Crumb, John Porcellino, and Megan Kelso. Each selection is prefaced with a short introduction to provide context, and a rationale is included for the marriage of a particular writer with a particular artist." (Publishers Weekly)
Includes index.

Graphic Classics volume eight: Mark Twain
Edited by Tom Pomplun. Eureka Productions 2007 144p. Illustration
Grades: 9 10 11 12 Adult   741.5; 818
1. Adventure graphic novels; 2. Humorous graphic novels; 3. Short stories; 4. Twain, Mark, 1835-1910 — Adaptations; 5. Graphic novels
978-0-9787919-2-6, $11.95
This book includes an adaptation of "Tom Sawyer Abroad" by Tom Pomplun and George Sellas, "The Mysterious Stranger" by Rick Geary, "A Dog's Tale" by Lance Tooks, "The Celebrated Jumping Frog of Calaveras County" by Kevin Atkinson, and "The Carnival of Crime in Connecticut" by Antonella Caputo and Nick Miller. Also in this volume are "Is He Living or Is He Dead?," "A Curious Pleasure Excursion," and eight women artists interpret Mark Twain's "Advice to Little Girls."

"With a terrific lineup of artists and unbeatable material, Pomplun has assembled a collection of Mark Twain's work that should delight graphic novel fans and anyone seeking to boost their general cultural knowledge." Publ Wkly [review of 2004 edition]
First published 2004

Graphic Classics volume eleven: O. Henry
Edited by Tom Pomplun. Eureka Productions 2005 144p. Illustration
Grades: 7 8 9 10 11 12 Adult   741.5; Fic
1. Henry, O, 1862-1910 — Adaptations; 2. Short stories; 3. Graphic novels
978-0-9746648-2-0, $11.95

This volume of Graphics Classics adapts some of the short stories by O. Henry, the master of the surprise ending. Stories include "The Ransom of Red Chief," illustrated by Johnny Ryan, "The Gift of the Magi," illustrated by Lisa Weber, "The Caballero's Way" (the original story of the Cisco Kid), illustrated by Mark A. Nelson, and more.

Graphic Classics volume fifteen: Fantasy classics
Edited by Tom Pomplun. Eureka Productions 2008 144p. Illustration
Grades: 8 9 10 11 12 Adult   741.5; Fic
1. Fantasy graphic novels; 2. Horror graphic novels; 3. Short stories; 4. Graphic novels
978-0-9787919-3-3, $11.95
This volume provides graphic novel adaptations of Mary Shelley's Frankenstein, "Rappaccini's Daughter" by Nathaniel Hawthorne, "The Glass Dog" by L. Frank Baum, "The Dream Quest of Unknown Kadath" by H. P. Lovecraft, and poems "After the Fire" by Lord Dunsany and "The Dream-Bridge" by Clark Ashton Smith. There are a few instances of mild violence and mild language in some of the stories. Illustrators include Skot Olsen, Lance Tooks, Brad Teare, and Leong Wan Kok; adapters include Rod Lott, Lance Tooks, Antonella Caputo, and Ben Avery.

Graphic Classics volume four: H. P. Lovecraft
Edited by Tom Pomplun. Eureka Productions 2007 144p. Illustration
Grades: 7 8 9 10 11 12 Adult   741.5; Fic
1. Horror graphic novels; 2. Lovecraft, H P (Howard Phillips), 1890-1937 — Adaptations; 3. Mystery writers; 4. Short stories
978-0-9746648-9-7, $11.95
Here are comic book adaptations of stories by Lovecraft, master of the macabre and creator of the Cthulhu Mythos. It includes adaptations of "The Shadow Over Innsmouth," illustrated by Simon Gane and "Dreams in the Witch House," by Pedro Lopez. Plus: "Sweet Ermengarde," a rare comedy by Lovecraft. Returning from the previous edition are "Reanimator," "The Shadow Out of Time," "The Terrible Old Man" and "The Cats of Ulthar." Illustrations of headless corpses and monstrous beings might disturb more tender sensibilities.
First published 2002

★ **Graphic Classics volume fourteen: Gothic classics**
Edited by Tom Pomplun. Eureka Productions 2007 144p. Illustration
Grades: 7 8 9 10 11 12 Adult   741.5; Fic
1. Horror graphic novels; 2. Short stories; 3. Graphic novels
978-0-9787919-0-2, $11.95
This volume includes graphic adaptations of classic novels Carmilla by Joseph Sheridan Le Fanu, The Mysteries of Udolpho by Ann Radcliffe, and Northanger Abbey by Jane Austen, along with shorter works "The Oval Portrait" by Edgar Allan Poe, "At the Gate" by Myla Jo Closser, and "I've a Pain in My Head" by Jane Austen. Radcliffe's novel is one mentioned by Austen in Northanger Abbey and is a famous gothic novel from the late eighteenth century, considered to be the world's first best-seller. Le Fanu's vampire novel was published twenty-five years before

Stoker's Dracula. Austen wrote Northanger Abbey as a satire of the popular gothic genre.

Graphic Classics volume seven: Bram Stoker
Edited by Tom Pomplun. Eureka Productions 2007 144p. Illustration
Grades: 7 8 9 10 11 12 Adult   **741.5; Fic**
1. Fantasy graphic novels; 2. Horror graphic novels; 3. Short stories; 4. Stoker, Bram, 1847-1912 — Adaptations; 5. Graphic novels
978-0-9787919-1-9, $11.95

This collection includes a comics adaptation of Dracula by Rich Rainey and Joe Ollmann, "The Judge's House" by Gerry Alanguilan, "Torture Tower" by Onsmith Jeremi, and "The Lair of the White Worm" by South African artist Rico Schacherl. Also "The Bridal of Death," an excerpt from "The Jewel of Seven Stars" by J.B. Bonivert and "The Wondrous Child" illustrated by Evert Geradts. The book includes some violence, and one panel of partial nudity.

"A must-read for fans of horror comics, this collection also works as a good introduction to Stoker's contributions to the traditions of Gothic horror." SLJ
First published 2003

Graphic Classics Volume Twelve: Adventure Classics
Eureka Productions 2005 144p. Illustration
Grades: 8 9 10 11 12   **741.5; 808.3**
1. Adventure graphic novels; 2. Short stories; 3. Graphic novels
978-0-9746648-4-7, $11.95

This volume of the Graphic Classics series includes a selection of poems and short stories that more or less fit the adventure genre. Rudyard Kipling's poem "Gunga Din" is here, as is Robert Service's "The Shooting of Dan McGrew." Short stories include "In the Valley of the Sorceress" by Sax Rohmer, "Tigre" by Zane Grey, "Blood Money" (a Captain Blood story) by Rafael Sabatini, "The Crime of the Brigadier" (a Brigadier Gerard adventure) by Sir Arthur Conan Doyle, "The Roads We Take" by O. Henry, and more. "The Mystery of the Semi-Detached" by Edith Nesbit may surprise readers who only know her as a children's fantasy author.

Gray, Harold
★ **Harold** Gray's Little Orphan Annie volume one: Will tomorrow evercome: the complete daily comics, 1924-27: Will tomorrow ever come? IDW Publishing 2008 385p. Illustration
Grades: 2 3 4 5 6 7 8 9 10 11 12 Adult   **741.5; Fic**
1. Adventure graphic novels; 2. Little Orphan Annie (Fictional character); 3. Orphans; 4. Graphic novels
978-1-60010-140-3, $39.99

Little Orphan Annie started as a daily newspaper comic strip in one newspaper, the New York Daily News, on August 5, 1924. It became a popular strip, syndicated to newspapers all over the world. It eventually became a Broadway musical, a hit movie, and Annie became an iconic character. This book is the first comprehensive collection of Gray's comic strip and is the first volume of a series planned to collect all of Gray's Little Orphan Annie strips. She is an orphan girl living in an orphanage, with an unscrupulous director who hires Annie out for work. When wealthy Mrs.

Warbucks, trying to prove that she cares for the poor, takes Annie on a "trial" adoption, Annie eventually meets Oliver Warbucks, whom she calls "Daddy." As the strips go on, Annie undergoes many hardships and perils, facing everything with spunk and a positive attitude. She's no wilting girl, though " she can fight (she has a mean right hook) and will take on any bully. She rescues the dog she calls Sandy, who rewards her with a loyal friendship. This volume includes more than 1,000 comic strips, many of which haven't seen publication since their original newspaper appearance. During the first years of the strip's publication, the color Sunday comics had no connection to the weekday storylines, but a few Sunday pages are included in this book. This book may appeal most to adults who remember reading Little Orphan Annie in the "funnies" pages, but the stories will appeal to all ages. Contributing Editor Jeet Heer provides a biography of Harold Gray.

Gray, Justin
Daughters of the Dragon: Samurai Bullets. Written by Justin Gray and Jimmy Palmiotti; art by Luke Ross. Marvel Entertainment 2006 Un Illustration
Grades: 10 11 12 Adult   **741.5; Fic**
1. Adventure graphic novels; 2. Superhero graphic novels; 3. Graphic novels
0-7851-1944-2, $15.99

Bounty hunters Misty Knight and Colleen Wing star in this sexy action thriller, the latest project from writers Justin Gray and Jimmy Palmiotti - a mix of gritty action and biting comedy. When four less-than "super" villains - Whirlwind, 8-Ball, Humbug and Freezer Burn - skip bail and team up to rob the penthouse apartment of a wealthy publisher, they get more than they bargained for. Misty Knight and Colleen Wing are on the case. Unfortunately, so are a host of villains and assassins looking to recover what was stolen.

The **Hills** Have Eyes: The Beginning. Written by Justin Gray and Jimmy Palmiotti; art by John Higgins. HarperCollins/Fox Atomic Comics 2007 Un Illustration
Grades: 11 12 Adult   **741.5; Fic**
1. Horror graphic novels; 2. Graphic novels
978-0-06-124354-7, $17.99

Deep within the remote hills of the New Mexico desert, a group of townspeople thought wiped out by the United States government when it began above-ground atomic testing has returned to the now-irradiated land they still claim as their home. Within the eye of this nuclear storm good people will go bad, battle lines will be drawn, and a new family of mutated monstrosities must protect their own at all costs in a mind-boggling orgy of blood and vengeance. This is a book prequel to the horror movies of the same title. The book includes f-bombs galore, other strong language, and lots of graphic violence.

Jonah Hex: Face Full of Violence. Written by Justin Gray and Jimmy Palmiotti; art by Luke Ross. DC Comics/Vertigo 2006 144p. Illustration
Grades: 10 11 12 Adult   **741.5; Fic**
1. Jonah Hex (Fictional characters); 2. Western graphic novels; 3. Graphic novels
978-1-4012-1095-3, $12.99

This book collects the new stories of Jonah Hex, the former Confederate soldier turned bounty hunter, the man with the scarred face. He doles out his brand of justice with his guns, taking vengeance upon murderers, thieves, and others who victimize the weak. The book has foul language and lots of violence.

Jonah Hex: Guns of Vengeance. Written by Justin Gray and Jimmy Palmiotti; art by Luke Ross. DC Comics 2007 144p. Illustration
Grades: 11 12 Adult   **741.5; Fic**
  1. Adventure graphic novels; 2. Supernatural graphic novels; 3. Western graphic novels; 4. Graphic novels
  978-1-4012-1249-0, $12.99
Jonah Hex, a mysterious bounty hunter and thinking man's killer, was a hero to some and a villain to others—and his name was spoken in whispers. He had no friends, but he did have two companions: one was death and the other... the smell of gun smoke. Haunted by the ghosts of his past, present, and future, the bullets fly as Jonah Hex battles bounty hunters, vengeful spirits, alligators, and sideshow freaks. This Western is full of graphic violence, harsh language, and some sexual situations and nudity.

★ **Power** girl: a new beginning. Art by Amanda Conner. DC Comics 2010 Un Illustration
Grades: 9 10 11 12 Adult   **741.5; Fic**
  1. Superhero graphic novels; 2. Graphic novels
  978-1-4012-2618-3, $17.99
Kara Zor-L came from Krypton, just like her very famous cousin Kal-L, who became Superman, but she had lived in a parallel universe, known as Earth 2. Since then, she has come to this world's New York City and started all over again as Karen Starr and reopening her business, a progressive technology company called Starrware Labs. She's also Power Girl, since she has many of Superman's superpowers. Before she can get Starrware Labs fully up and running with all essential positions filled, she has to deal with a horde of fear-inducing robots sent by the Ultra-Humanite to destroy Manhattan. Then, a trio of party-crashing aliens and their pursuer start wrecking the rest of Manhattan as they fight in the streets. The book has lots of action but no really graphic violence, and some "fan service" as it's called in manga there are some panty shots, and Karen/Power Girl deals with men staring at her bust. Her costume has a cutout design on the chest, which the writers and artist treat with some great humor. Co-writer Palmiotti and artist Conner are a couple themselves, and their close work shows in sheer fun of this book.

Grayson, Devin
  Am I blue. Udon with Long Vo, Charles Park, and Saka, art and colors ; Randy Gentile, letterer. ABDO Publishing Company/Spotlight 2006 Illustration
Grades: 4 5 6 7 8 9   **741.5; Fic**
  1. Superhero graphic novels; 2. X-Men (Fictional characters); 3. Graphic novels
  978-1-59961-052-8, $21.35
                                                      LC 2006-43970
The young members of the X-Men, including Kurt (Nightcrawler), Rogue, and Kitty (Shadowcat), must attend school in town as well as train at the Xavier Academy. They must conceal their identities as super powered mutants, which is difficult for Kurt since he is normally blue-skinned; he wears an image inducer that makes him appear like a normal human. When they are assigned an essay for English composition class: "What I am at home that I can't be at school," it bothers Kurt that he can't tell the truth. This book is a revised, hardbound edition of a Marvel Age comic book issue.
Part of the X-Men: Evolution series

Nightwing: Mobbed Up. Devin Grayson, writer; Phil Hester, Cliff Chiang, pencillers; Ande Parks, inker; Phil Balsman, Nick J. Napolitano, letterers; Gretory Wright, colorist. DC Comics 2006 128p. Illustration
Grades: 10 11 12 Adult   **741.5; Fic**
  1. Nightwing (Fictional character); 2. Superhero graphic novels; 3. Graphic novels
  978-1-4012-0907-0, $12.99
Injured and dejected, cut off from all allegiances, Dick Grayson decides to turn his misery into an advantage and a new purpose. He arranges to be adopted into one of New York City's crime families. In doing so he begins a new odyssey, one that sweeps him into the depths of the criminal underworld. Try as he may, however, he can't put his crime-fighting alter ego behind him forever, so Nightwing returns. But which side is he on? There's some violence, but despite the mob, little in the way of harsh language.

Nightwing: Renegade. Devin Grayson, writer; Phil Hester et. al, pencillers; Ande Parks, Rodney Ramos, Edde Wagner, inkers. DC Comics 2006 144p. Illustration
Grades: 9 10 11 12 Adult   **741.5; Fic**
  1. Nightwing (Fictional character); 2. Robin (Fictional character); 3. Superhero graphic novels; 4. Graphic novels
  978-1-4012-0908-7, $14.99
Once he was Robin, but Dick Grayson stepped out from the shadow of the Bat to become his own hero, Nightwing. Now the events of the past year have taken a heavy toll on Dick, and he's seemingly embraced the darkness within himself. He's got a new costume, a new name - Renegade - and he serves a new master. But could Nightwing really be working for Deathstroke, the deadly assassin and his longtime nemesis" As Renegade takes Deathstroke's daughter Ravager under his wing, the two old enemies will play a dangerous game of cat and mouse. But who's manipulating whom, and what do these two brilliant minds really want from each other? Just when Nightwing thinks he has it all figured out, Deathstroke makes a move so shocking, Nightwing's world will never be the same. There's plenty of action, but little overt violence or harsh language.

Grecian, Alexander
  Proof book 2: the company of men. Art by Riley Rossmo. Image Comics 2008 Un
Grades: 9 10 11 12 Adult   **741.5; Fic**
  1. Adventure graphic novels; 2. Fantasy graphic novels; 3. Sasquatch; 4. Graphic novels
  978-1-60706-017-8, $12.99
Proof the Bigfoot has worked as part of a team investigating monsters they call cryptoids, but now a big-game hunter who specializes in killing endangered animals and cryptoids in order to eat them (along with an organization of special gourmets who like to eat monstrous creatures) wants to catch, kill, and eat Proof. In order to get him, he has killed a mother dinosaur in a remote African jungle and left the baby alive to lure Proof and his human

teammates (including one traitor). The book includes some violence. Extras in this volume include paper dolls of some of the characters and the script for one of the stories, "A Perfect Gentleman."

Seven Sons. Riley Rossmo, artist. AiT/Planet Lar 2006 120p. Illustration
Grades: 7 8 9 10 11 12 Adult   **741.5; Fic**
1. China — Folklore; 2. Graphic novels
978-1-932051-46-9, $12.95
Seven identical Chinese brothers come to America during the Gold Rush of the 1850s. When two children fall through an iced-over river, Brother Number One tries to save them by breathing the entire river into his mouth. But he can't hold it long enough for them to get to safety and lets the water go, accidentally drowning the children. When a mob of angry townspeople tries to retaliate, each of Number One's brothers takes his place, using their remarkable abilities each time to save his life. This retelling doesn't have the happy ending usually found in the children's picture books, and by moving the story to the U.S., Grecian infuses a message about intolerance and prejudice in the story.

Green Arrow/Black Canary: for better or for worse.
DC Comics 2007 200p. Illustration
Grades: 10 11 12 Adult   741.5
1. Black Canary (Fictional character); 2. Green Arrow (Fictional character); 3. Romance graphic novels; 4. Superhero graphic novels; 5. Graphic novels
978-1-4012-1446-3, $14.99
Green Arrow and Black Canary have been crime fighting partners, business partners, lovers. Somewhere along the way, they broke up. Then Green Arrow died. Or so everyone thought. Then he came back. This volume collects the stories from the past several decades, from the Silver Age to the present day, that tell the saga of the great love affair in the DC Universe. The book includes some mild sexual situations and partial nudity.

Green, Jen
Great expectations: the graphic novel: original text version. Joe Sutliff Sanders ; character designs & original artwork, John Stokes ; coloring. Classical Comics 2009 160p. Illustration
Grades: 7 8 9 10 11 12   **741.5; Fic**
1. Dickens, Charles, 1812-1870 — Adaptations; 2. Great Britain — History — 19th century; 3. Social classes; 4. Graphic novels
978-1-4205-0372-2, $32.45
                                        LC 2010-924002
In 1812, young orphaned Pip encounters an escaped convict in the graveyard near his home; that encounter changes his life. He had helped the man by stealing food and a file from his older sister's home. When the convict is recaptured, he keeps Pip's secret and claims he was the thief. As time goes by, Pip becomes his brother-inlaw's apprentice as a blacksmith, but then the eccentric Miss Havisham wants Pip to attend to her. Miss Havisham's adopted niece, Estella, calls Pip coarse and rough, which makes him determined to improve himself and become a gentleman. His wish comes true when a mysterious benefactor has Miss Havisham's solicitor, Mr. Jaggers, set Pip up in London, with expenses paid. Pip has only to keep using his nickname, to learn how

to be a gentleman, and have "great expectations." Getting his wish doesn't make him happy, however, for he wants Estella, whom he adores, to love him; Miss Havisham has raised Estella to break men's hearts as her heart was once broken by a man. Pip must also learn what is most important to him improving his social standing or standing loyal to family and friends. This graphic novel adaptation includes every chapter in Dickens' original novel; this library bound edition uses a more colloquial American adaptation, which was done by arrangement with Classical Comics, the original publisher. This adaptation is meant for reluctant and struggling readers. The artist, John Stokes, is not credited anywhere in this edition. The back matter includes a biography of Dickens, a glossary, illustrated character summaries, notes on the historical context of the novel, and a brief discussion of the different ending Dickens originally wrote.

Great expectations: the graphic novel: original text version. Classical Comics 2009 160p. Illustration
Grades: 7 8 9 10 11 12
741.5; Fic
1. Dickens, Charles, 1812-1870 — Adaptations; 2. Great Britain — History — 19th century; 3. Social classes; 4. Graphic novels
978-1-906332-59-4, $16.95

©Classical Comics

In 1812, young orphaned Pip encounters an escaped convict in the graveyard near his home; that encounter changes his life. He had helped the man by stealing food and a file from his older sister's home. When the convict is recaptured, he keeps Pip's secret and claims he was the thief. As time goes by, Pip becomes his brother-in-law's apprentice as a blacksmith, but then the eccentric Miss Havisham wants Pip to attend to her. Miss Havisham's adopted niece, Estella, calls Pip coarse and rough, which makes him determined to improve himself and become a gentleman. His wish comes true when a mysterious benefactor has Miss Havisham's solicitor, Mr. Jaggers, set Pip up in London, with expenses paid. Pip has only to keep using his nickname, to learn how to be a gentleman, and have "great expectations." Getting his wish doesn't make him happy, however, for he wants Estella, whom he adores, to love him; Miss Havisham has raised Estella to break men's hearts as her heart was once broken by a man. Pip must also learn what is most important to him improving his social standing or standing loyal to family and friends. This graphic novel adaptation includes every chapter in Dickens' original novel; the Original Text Version uses excerpts from Dickens' dialog and narration. The book includes biographical information about Dickens and information about the English justice system and Newgate prison.
Also available Quick Text edition pa $16.95 (ISBN: 978-1-906332-60-0)

Greenberg, Isabel
The **encyclopedia** of early earth: a novel. Isabel Greenberg. Little, Brown and Co. 2013 176 p.
Grades: 10 11 12 Adult   **741.5; Fic**
1. Earth — Fiction; 2. Fables; 3. Travel — Fiction
0316225819; 9780316225816, $23
LC 2013939419
Author Isabel Greenberg presents a "series of illustrated and linked tales [which] chronicles the explorations of a young man as he paddles from his home in the North Pole to the South Pole. There, he meets his true love, but their romance is ill-fated. Early Earth's unusual and finicky polarity means the lovers can never touch." (Publisher's note)

"Greenberg deeply immerses readers in the themes and lessons of world mythology, but she remarkably never merely apes classic myths the way each of Early Earth's cultures tweaks the same ideas and characters for their own myths is a veritable lesson in comparative theology." Booklist

Greenberger, Robert, ed.
Batman: War Crimes. DC Comics 2006 Un Illustration
Grades: 9 10 11 12 Adult   **741.5; Fic**
1. Batman (Fictional character); 2. Joker (Fictional character); 3. Mystery graphic novels; 4. Superhero graphic novels; 5. Graphic novels
1-4012-0903-3, $12.99
The Spoiler died during the gang war, or so Batman thought. When the media begin reporting on the Spoiler's private life and making accusations aimed at the Dark Knight, he begins an investigation that leads to a new confrontation with Gotham City's undisputed underworld boss, Black Mask. Complicating matters even further is the return of his deadliest opponent, the Joker, and the reappearance of an old foe long believed dead. The book includes violence.

Batman: War Games Act One: Outbreak. DC Comics 2005 Un Illustration
Grades: 10 11 12 Adult   **741.5; Fic**
1. Batgirl (Fictional character); 2. Batman (Fictional character); 3. Mystery graphic novels; 4. Nightwing (Fictional character); 5. Robin (Fictional character); 6. Superhero graphic novels; 7. Graphic novels
1-4012-0429-5, $14.95
Gotham City's underworld families respond to a mysterious summons for a summit. Fear, suspicion, and paranoia get the better of them and bullets fly fast and furiously. As familiar warlords fall, a new wave of chaos engulfs the city. Batman must use every available asset - Oracle, Batgirl, Nightwing, Orpheus, Onyx, and Tarantula - to preserve life and contain the trouble, while determining who is the mastermind behind the conflagration. If he doesn't figure it out soon, no one will be safe. And when someone starts targeting family members of the gang leaders, the danger spills out to parks and schools - including former Robin Tim Drake's high school.

Batman: War Games Act Three: Endgame. DC Comics 2005 Un Illustration
Grades: 10 11 12 Adult   **741.5; Fic**
1. Batman (Fictional character); 2. Mystery graphic novels; 3. Superhero graphic novels; 4. Graphic novels
1-4012-0431-7, $14.99
Black Mask has made Batman's training scenario a chilling reality. The various crime families are leaderless, and the soldiers run for their lives while trying to grab a piece of the underworld pie for themselves. Batman and his allies have failed to contain the chaos threatening the lives of Gotham City's people. The media have exploited the situation so people think Batman is acting against their best interests. Worse, he has lost the trust and support of Commissioner Akins, just when he needs it the most. Before the day is over, a friend and ally will be dead, familial ties will be broken, and the balance of power in the city will be forever altered.

Batman: War Games Act Two: Tides. DC Comics 2005 Un Illustration
Grades: 10 11 12 Adult   **741.5; Fic**
1. Batman (Fictional character); 2. Mystery graphic novels; 3. Robin (Fictional character); 4. Superhero graphic novels; 5. Graphic novels
1-4012-0430-9, $14.99
In this second volume the truth behind the criminal activity is revealed, one of Batman's agents is beaten, another killed and a new player emerges on the scene, one assumed gone for good but now ready to seize control over Gotham's underworld. Tim Drake returns to the Robin uniform to help, although he knows there will be consequences for his actions. The Dark Knight may be powerless to stop the streets from running red with blood, and the police are losing their trust in him and his colleagues.

The **essential** Batman encyclopedia. Ballantine Books 2008 388p. Illustration
Grades: 9 10 11 12 Adult   **741.5**
1. Batman (Fictional character); 2. Comic books, strips, etc — History and criticism; 3. Graphic novels
978-0-345-50106-6, $29.95
LC 2008-3016
Former DC Comics editor Greenberger has compiled a guide book that includes hundreds of entries in AZ format, covering characters, places, and organizations that have appeared in Batman comics over the decades. Entries range from a few lines to several pages and include every villain, partner, sidekick, friend and enemy that has ever appeared in the Batman universe.

Includes bibliographical references.

Showcase Presents: Jonah Hex Volume 1. DC Comics 2005 528p. Illustration
Grades: 10 11 12 Adult   **741.5; Fic**
1. Jonah Hex (Fictional character); 2. Western graphic novels; 3. Graphic novels
1-4012-0760-X, $16.99
He was a hero to some, a villain to others; and wherever he rode, people spoke his name in whispers. He had no friends, this Jonah Hex, but he did have two companions: one was death itself, the other - the acrid smell of gun smoke. These are the earliest adventures of the gunslinger, which were first published in the early 1970s, at a time when the spaghetti westerns of Sergio Leone and others had introduced tough, violent antiheroes to the American fiction staple. The stories include a considerable amount of

violence, but it's not too graphic, and very little strong language.

Will Eisner. Rosen Publishing Group 2005 112p. Illustration
Grades: 8 9 10 11 12 Adult **92; 741.5**
1. Cartoonists — Biography; 2. Graphic novels
1-4042-0286-2, $31.95

LC 2004016656

Veteran comics insider Greenberger has written this biography of Eisner, covering his long career in comics, from the 1930s through the early 2000s. Eisner created the groundbreaking comic series The Spirit, and in the 1970s started writing original graphic novels set in New York City. The Eisner Awards for comics are named after him, due to his strong influence on the industry over the decades. This volume includes a list of books for further reading and a bibliography.

Part of the Library of Graphic Novelists

Grell, Mike

The **Complete** Jon Sable, Freelance Volume 1. IDW Publishing 2005 180p. Illustration
Grades: 10 11 12 Adult **741.5; Fic**
1. Adventure graphic novels; 2. Graphic novels
1-932382-77-1, $24.99

The initial 54-page story guest-stars Ronald Reagan, and the second is Sable's famous 108-page origin saga. Sable is a mercenary willing to act as a private eye or bodyguard if the money is right and the job promises excitement. The origin story depicts how he became that way after his family was massacred. There's lots of fighting action and bloodshed in this story, originally published by First Comics in the early 1980s.

Grillo-Marxuach, Javier

★ The **Middleman:** the collected series indispensability. Viper Comics 2008 336p. Illustration
Grades: 9 10 11 12 Adult **741.5; Fic**
1. Adventure graphic novels; 2. Humorous graphic novels; 3. Science fiction graphic novels; 4. Graphic novels
978-0-9802385-4-9, $19.95

This book collects all three volumes of The Middleman comics series. Art student Wendy Watson works as a temp agency hire, when one day she's working at a scientific laboratory where things go totally wrong and a mysterious guy who calls himself The Middleman takes care of the monsters. Unfortunately for Wendy, the cover story that a gas main explosion caused all the mess also indicates that her lucky Zippo lighter, the only thing she has from her long-missing father, ignited the gas leak. Unemployed Wendy soon finds herself recruited by the Jolly Fats Wehawkin Temp Agency, which is actually the cover for The Middleman and his henchperson, robotic Ida. Wendy soon finds herself battling intelligent apes out to rule the criminal underworld, crazy Lucha Libre wrestlers, and more "exotic problems," at the side of the enigmatic, super-good guy, The Middleman. The book includes some violence, some nudity, and some sexual innuendo. The series was adapted into a television series on ABC Family which ran for one season; the DVD boxed set is scheduled for a summer 2009 release.

Grine, Chris

Chickenhare: The House of Klaus. Dark Horse Comics 2006 160p. Illustration
Grades: 7 8 9 10 11 12 **741.5**
1. Adventure graphic novels; 2. Fantasy graphic novels; 3. Graphic novels
978-1-59307-574-3, $9.95

Friends Chickenhare (who is exactly that, a cross between a chicken and a hare) and bearded turtle Abe are captives being taken to the mad taxidermist Klaus, who looks like an evil Santa. Chickenhare and Abe escape, along with obnoxious monkey Banjo and horned girl Meg; Chickenhare finds the dead goat Mr. Buttons, and the others encounter the warlike, cave-dwelling Shromph, who have a bone to pick with Klaus. A few harsh words, some violence, and implied cannibalism may be disturbing for younger readers.

Chickenhare: fire in the hole. Dark Horse Comics 2008 200p. Illustration
Grades: 7 8 9 10 11 12 Adult **741.5; Fic**
1. Adventure graphic novels; 2. Fantasy graphic novels; 3. Graphic novels
978-1-59307-907-9, $10.95

Chickenhare, his friend Abe, and their new friends Scabby, Meg and Banjo managed to escape the evil Taxidermist Klaus, but they have gone from one dangerous situation into . . . something worse. While at sea in a small boat about to be swamped by rain and waves, Banjo's brother and some warriors from the Underworld pop up, they zap the soul out of Abe and take Banjo and Meg. Chickenhare is left with Scabby and Abe's body. He must venture into the Underworld to recover Abe's soul. Meanwhile, Banjo and Meg face punishment for deserting the Underworld. And just why do the Sea Folk call Chickenhare "Your Majesty"?

Chickenhare. Chris Grine. Graphix / Scholastic 2013 160 p.
Grades: 4 5 6 7 8 9 **741.5**
1. Animals; 2. Escapes — Juvenile fiction; 3. Taxidermy — Fiction
0545485088; 9780545485081, $10.99

LC 2012936214

Author Chris Grine presents a children's comic book. "What's a chickenhare" A cross between a chicken and a rabbit, of course. And that makes Chickenhare the rarest animal around! So when he and his turtle friend Abe are captured and sold to the evil taxidermist Klaus, they've got to find a way to escape before Klaus turns them into stuffed animals. With the help of two other strange creatures, Banjo and Meg, they might even get away. But with Klaus and his thugs hot on their trail, the adventure is only just beginning for this unlikely quartet of friends." (Publisher's note)

Grist, Paul

Kane Vol. 1: Greetings from New Eden. Image Comics 2004 127p. Illustration
Grades: 10 11 12 Adult **741.5; Fic**
1. Mystery graphic novels; 2. Graphic novels
1-58240-340-6, $11.95

Detective Kane returns to active duty with the New Eden Police Dept. following a six month suspension after he shot and killed his partner Dennis Harvey. His fellow police officers give Kane a welcome back gift - a couple of bullets with his name engraved on them. Partnered with a new detective. Kate Felix, Kane soon finds out nothing has changed in the city of New Eden. In his first two days back, Kane has to deal with a siege, a kidnapping and a bomb attack. And then there's the Crime Boss of New Eden, Oscar Darke... The book includes some harsh language and violence.

Kane Vol. 2: Rabbit Hunt. Image Comics 2004 Un Illustration
Grades: 10 11 12 Adult   **741.5; Fic**
  1. Mystery graphic novels; 2. Graphic novels
  1-58240-355-4, $12.95
  It's a bad day for Mister Floppsie Whoppsie, New Eden's self-styled Rabbit for Hire. The freelance rabbit business isn't going as well as it should. He's hung over. The rent's due. There's a knock at the door and a gun-wielding homicidal maniac barges into the room. That's when things start to go downhill. And Detective Kane still can't trust anyone in the New Eden Police Department. The book includes some strong language and violence.

Kane Vol. 4: Thirty-Ninth. Image Comics 2005 Un Illustration
Grades: 10 11 12 Adult   **741.5; Fic**
  1. Mystery graphic novels; 2. Graphic novels
  1-58240-468-2, $16.95
  When Detective Kane returned to active duty with the New Eden Police Dept. following a six-month suspension in the wake of shooting and killing his partner, his fellow police officers gave him a welcome back gift: a couple of bullets with his name on them. Now, a sniper is taking pot shots at the police. An ex-cop is looking to take revenge on the cop who turned him in. There's rioting in the streets and the Mayor's been kidnapped again. It's another typical week for the police in New Eden's Precinct 39. The book has some strong language and violence.

Gross, Allan
  Cryptozoo Crew Volume 2: Call of the Thunderbird!. Jerry Carr, illustrator; NBM 2006 Un Illustration
Grades: 5 6 7 8 9 10 11 12 Adult   **741.5; Fic**
  1. Humorous graphic novels; 2. Mythical animals; 3. Graphic novels
  978-1-56163-466-8, $12.95
  In this second volume, cryptozoologist Tork Darwyn suffers nightmares about a childhood encounter with the legendary thunderbird; it's been twenty years since that day, and he must return or be cursed. In the meantime, his teacher wife Tara has learned that her school will be shut down for lack of funding. Naturally, they travel together to Alaska to find out what is driving Tork to go there.

  Cryptozoo Crew, Vol. 1. art and lettering by Jerry Carr. NBM 2005 Un Illustration
Grades: 6 7 8 9 10 11 12   **741.5; Fic**
  1. Adventure graphic novels; 2. Humorous graphic novels; 3. Monsters; 4. Graphic novels
  1-56163-437-9, $9.99
  "Preteens will enjoy the humor and adventure, while older teens will appreciate the banter between Tork and Tara

along with everything else. The black-and-white art makes the cryptids look more funny than scary, so even the squeamish can read this one without getting grossed out." (VOYA)
  Intrepid cryptozoologist Tork Darwyn hunts for cryptids, those legendary creatures such as the Loch Ness Monster, the Yeti, and others. His beautiful wife Tara works as a science teacher but often accompanies Tork on his expeditions; it's a good thing, too, because she's much smarter and gets him out of trouble a lot. There is a second volume, published in 2006.

Gross, Milt
  He Done Her Wrong: The Great American Novel. Fantagraphics Books 2005 Un Illustration
Grades: 9 10 11 12 Adult   **741.5; Fic**
  1. Adventure graphic novels; 2. Humorous graphic novels; 3. Graphic novels
  1-56097-694-2, $16.95
  The story follows the convoluted misadventures of a na?ve frontiersman with superhuman strength exploited by a larcenous robber baron who eventually double crosses our hero and steals his girl. The pursuit leads to New York City where a sordid cast of cantankerous salesmen, officious government bureaucrats, bumbling hospital attendants, a lusty widow with a defensive Chihuahua and one angry barber wreak more havoc in our characters' lives than a hundred Little Rascals in a Marx Brothers film.
  This wordless comic novel shares much with the silent comedy films of Harold Lloyd, Buster Keaton, and Charlie Chaplin. It's full of slapstick humor, with one politically incorrect gag that was the norm in 1930, this book's original year of publication.

Groth, Gary
  ★ The **Complete** Peanuts: 1950-1952. Fantagraphics Books 2004 330p. Illustration
Grades: 2 3 4 5 6 7 8 9 10 11 12 Adult   **741.5; Fic**
  1. Humorous graphic novels; 2. Peanuts (Comic strip); 3. Graphic novels
  1-56097-589-X, $28.95
  This is the first volume of a project to collect all of Schulz's Peanuts comic strips from 1950 to 2000. This volume includes the strips published from October 2, 1950 through all of 1952. These early strips featured characters younger readers may not recognize: Patty (not Peppermint Patty), Violet, Shermy, and a Snoopy who behaves like a normal dog. Schroeder is a baby who's already a whiz at the toy piano; Lucy is a toddler who already causes trouble for Charlie Brown; Linus shows up as a baby in September 1952. Lucy pulls the football trick on Charlie Brown for the first time in November 1952. This volume also includes a biography of Schulz and a long interview with him.
  Volume 1 of 26

Guggenheim, Marc
  Blade: Undead Again. Written by Marc Guggenheim; art by Howard Chaykin. Marvel Entertainment 2007 Un Illustration
Grades: 10 11 12 Adult   **741.5; Fic**
  1. Blade (Fictional character); 2. Dracula, Count (Fictional character); 3. Spider-Man (Fictional character);

4. Superhero graphic novels; 5. Wolverine (Fictional character); 6. Graphic novels
978-0-7851-2364-4, $14.99

Here are new adventures starring the popular character who's starred in three movies and a TV series. Blade encounters Spider-Man, Dracula, Dr. Doom, Wolverine... and Santa Claus" Plus, the book takes a look into Blade's mysterious past. This book includes some bloody violence, mostly vampiric and fighting vampires.

Civil War: Wolverine. Marc Guggenheim; artist, Humberto Ramos. Marvel Entertainment 2007 Un Illustration
Grades: 10 11 12 Adult   **741.5; Fic**
1. Superhero graphic novels; 2. Wolverine (Fictional character); 3. Graphic novels
978-0-7851-1980-7, $17.99

In the aftermath of the Stamford tragedy, Logan makes it his personal mission to take down the man responsible. No sooner does he begin his hunt, however, than he discovers someone else is stalking the same prey: a mysterious trio whose identity, and disturbing mission, unsettles him. This book includes some bloody violence and some strong language.

Guibert, Emmanuel
★ **Alan's** war. First Second 2008 304p. Illustration
Grades: 10 11 12 Adult   **92; 940.54; 741.5**
1. Biographical graphic novels; 2. Cope, Alan Ingram, 1925-1999; 3. Soldiers; 4. Soldiers; 5. Veterans; 6. World War, 1939-1945; 7. Graphic novels
978-1-59643-096-9; 1-59643-096-6, $24
LC 2007-46190

French cartoonist Guibert met and became friends with Alan Cope and interviewed him at length to create this book. It recreates Cope's memories of being an eighteen-year-old G.I. during World War II. Unlike the war movies that focus on battles, this book focuses on more everyday, mundane memories of the day-to-day life of a soldier. Cope frankly describes a bout with crabs (genital lice), matter-of-factly tells of casual man-to-man sexual encounters among the soldiers, and gives the reader a feel for what happened back then. He also talks about postwar relationships and travels.

This is a "poignant and frank graphic memoir of young soldier who was told to serve his country in WWII and how it changed him forever. . . . Cope and Guibert forge a story that resonates with humanity." Publ Wkly

★ The **photographer**. [by] Emmanuel Guibert, Didier Lefèvre and Frédéric Lemercier; translated by Alexis Siegel. First Second 2009 267p. Illustration; Map
Grades: 11 12 Adult   **92; 741.5; 958.1**
978-1-59643-375-5; 1-59643-375-2, $29.95

"Originally published as three volumes in France from 2003 to 2006, this graphic novel follows photojournalist Didier Lefèvre during his three months in Pakistan and Afghanistan in 1986 as he documented the medical missions of Doctors without Borders. . . . The graphic novel combines traditional comic art with some of the four thousand photographs Lefevre shot while in Afghanistan. . . . Many images will stay with readers as both horrifying and glorious. The Afghan children being treated for burns, bullet wounds, and shrapnel are page by page next to the beauty of

the Afghan mountainous landscapes. . . . [This book] has a powerful message and images of a part of the world that should be discussed more often." Voice Youth Advocates

Gulledge, Laura Lee
★ **Page** by Paige. Amulet Books 2011 Un Illustration
Grades: 7 8 9 10 11 12   **741.5; Fic**
1. Artists; 2. Friendship; 3. Humorous graphic novels; 4. New York (NY); 5. Graphic novels
0-8109-9721-5; 0-8109-9722-3 (pa);
978-0-8109-9721-9, $18.95; 978-0-8109-9722-6 (pa), $9.95

Teenage Paige Turner (blame her writer parents) moves to New York City from Virginia, and she finds the big city rather overwhelming. She decides to buy a sketchbook and sort out her thoughts and feelings in drawings. Soon she does make some friends, and she explores more of the city, but as she begins to feel happier, she clashes with her parents. All of this goes into her sketchbook journal, which she starts to show to her new friends "Jules, Longo, and Gabe. The book is organized by Paige's "rules," which she uses to try to change herself, such as "Rule #2: Draw what you know. If you feel it or see it . . . DRAW IT!"

"Gulledge's b&w illustrations are simple but well-suited to their subject matter; the work as a whole is a good-natured, optimistic portrait of a young woman evolving toward adulthood." Publ Wkly

Gunter, Miles
Zombee. Writer, Miles Gunter; artist, Victor Santos. Image Comics 2006 Un Illustration
Grades: 10 11 12 Adult   **741.5; Fic**
1. Horror graphic novels; 2. Humorous graphic novels; 3. Graphic novels
978-1-58240-662-6, $12.99

A dutiful Samurai, a madcap Ninja and a bizarro Zen Monk team up to battle the undead in Feudal Japan. Can these unlikely allies stay friends long enough to stop the zombees from taking over their homeland? Gory and violent zombie-destroying action combines with comedy and foul language (most of it very anachronistic); the cover image, with the zombie head flying amongst sprays of blood while a samurai holds his sword, lets the reader know exactly what to expect.

Gurewich, Nicholas
The **Trial** of Colonel Sweeto and other stories: a collection of the comic strips. Dark Horse Comics 2007 96p. Illustration
Grades: 11 12 Adult   **741.5**
1. Humorous graphic novels; 2. Graphic novels
978-1-59307-844-7, $14.95

Gurewich's Perry Bible Fellowship is a popular webcomic; now they're collected into this hardcover volume. The full-color strips betray a twisted sense of humor with a strong bias for the bizarre, and some strips use nudity and violence.

Hadley, Amy Reeder
Fool's gold vol. 1. Tokyopop 2006 192p. Illustration
Grades: 7 8 9 10 11 12   **741.5; Fic**

1. Humorous graphic novels; 2. Romance graphic novels; 3. Graphic novels
978-1-59816-585-2, $9.99

Penny observes that, with rare exceptions, most of the girls in her high school are fatally drawn to jerks. She starts out trying to save her best friend Katie from just such a relationship, when she decides to form her own underground club (using the geology club as a decoy) to help girls identify the jerks and avoid them. She calls such jerks Pyrites (fool's gold). She's also a dress designer and works in her young aunt's shop, even though her father objects and wants her to do better in school. She really wants to just design cool, fun and funky clothes, but her crusade against jerks takes a lot of her time. And what's going to happen when she finds a nice, cool, creative, nonjerk boy she can like" This is a global manga series.

Hage, Anika
Gothic sports vol. 3. Tokyopop 2008 196p. Illustration
Grades: 8 9 10 11 12   741.5; Fic
1. Friendship; 2. Soccer; 3. Graphic novels
978-1-59816-994-2, $9.99

Anya's quest to start the Gothic-Lolita soccer team at her school has been officially approved by the school principal. The team is excited, but when summer vacation starts, everyone has different plans that don't include soccer practice. Delia comes up with a solution: she invites the whole team to come to a cabin in the Bavarian mountains for a training camp to work on their skills. The book includes one scene with incidental and nonsexual partial nudity. This is a global manga series, translated from German.

Gothic sports, Vol. 1. Tokyopop 2007 176p. Illustration
Grades: 8 9 10 11 12   741.5; Fic
1. High school students; 2. Manga; 3. School stories; 4. Soccer
978-1-59816-992-8, $9.99

When Anya starts at Lucrece High, she wants to join one of the sports teams for which the school is famed. Since she's never played on a school's team before, she gets rejected. But this time, she's determined to succeed, so she joins with some of the other school misfits and they form their own soccer team. And with the help of a Goth-Lolita classmate, they have fantastically fashionable Goth-Lolita uniforms (even for the boys!). This is the first volume of a series translated from German, making it a global manga title.

Hakase, Mizuki
Demon Flowers: Kuruizaki no Hana Volume 1. Tokyopop 2007 Un Illustration
Grades: 10 11 12 Adult   741.5; Fic
1. Fantasy graphic novels; 2. Horror graphic novels; 3. Manga; 4. Graphic novels
978-1-4278-0298-9, $9.99

Long ago, when Japanese gods descended upon humans, their mixed offspring inherited supernatural powers, and the name Kuruizaki no hana." Now, the demon world is rising up to kill them all to take their powers; Ushitora is their assassin. Then he falls for a little boy, Masato, who is a kuruizaki no hana," and they go on the run. Along the way, Ushitora takes in orphaned girl Nao, they

form an odd but loyal family. This book includes some violence and partial nudity.

Hale, Dean
★ **Calamity** Jack [by] Shannon and Dean Hale; illustrated by Nathan Hale. Bloomsbury 2010 144p. Illustration

Courtesy of Bloomsbury

Grades: 4 5 6 7 8 9   **741.5; Fic**
1. Adventure graphic novels; 2. Fantasy graphic novels; 3. Folklore; 4. Graphic novels
9781599903736, $14.99;
9781599900766, $19.99
LC 2008-41332

In this sequel to Rapunzel's Revenge, the reader meets Jack as a child growing up in the city of Shyport; Jack has been a schemer practically since birth, but he hasn't had a whole lot of luck. His schemes usually end in unforeseen consequences. When he goes up against the giant Blunderboar, the magic beanstalk he uses to reach the giant's floating fortress destroys his neighborhood and his mother's bakery, and he just manages to leave town with a certain gold-egg-laying goose under his arm. After the events of the first book, Jack and Rapunzel come to Shyport, where Jack hopes to help his mother rebuild her bakery with the golden eggs he now has. However, they come to a city transformed Blunderboar has taken over, his security company claims to be keeping giant ants at bay, and Jack's mother is being held prisoner. Jack is still wanted for what he had done, and only Prudence, Jack's hat-loving pixie partner-in-crime, is willing to help. Then Jack and Rapunzel meet Freddie Sparksmith, newspaperman and gadget inventor, and they team up for a rescue mission. The book includes a lot of action and some non-gory violence.

Companion to: Rapunzel's Revenge

Hale, Tricia Riley
Grand Theft Galaxy, Vol. 1. Illustrated by Jim Jimenez. Tokyopop 2007 Un Illustration
Grades: 8 9 10 11 12   **741.5; Fic**
1. Humorous graphic novels; 2. Science fiction graphic novels; 3. Graphic novels
978-1-59816-713-9, $9.99

College freshman Samantha Beagley has her life all figured out. She's a pre-law student, and she lives by her charts and planners. On her eighteenth birthday, Sam loses control of her life. She receives a very strange present from her parents, and learns to her horror that they are alien thieves. Some years ago they stole a certain object, the Evo Cube, and they hid it away so well they can't remember where it is. And now the Galactic Order Directorate has found Sam's parents, and they will destroy the Earth in three days if the Evo Cube isn't returned. When her parents grab her and go off-planet to save themselves, Sam decides to find the Evo Cube herself; and that leads her to find the master thief Jackal. He turns out to be her former pet cat, Mr. Fluffy. This is the first of a global manga series.

Hall, Jason
Hellboy: the companion. Stephen Weiner, Jason Hall, Victoria Blake with additional material by Mike Mignola. Dark Horse Comics 2008 240p. Illustration
Grades: 10 11 12 Adult   **741.5**
1. Hellboy (Fictional character); 2. Horror graphic novels; 3. Graphic novels
978-1-59307-655-9, $14.95
Mike Mignola's Hellboy debuted in 1994 and has built up a growing audience for its world of Victorian occult societies, prehistoric gods, arcane Nazi experiments, and a big red demon for a good guy. Now librarian and comics historian Weiner, comics writer Hall, and journalist Blake put together a guide to Mignola's created world, illustrated with new art by Mignola as well as art from fourteen years of Hellboy from Mignola and the other artists who have worked with him over the years, including Guy Davis, Duncan Fegredo, Paul Azaceta, and others. The book includes character profiles, a timeline, and the literary heritage of Hellboy.

Hall, Jeremy
Piers Anthony Presents Revved. Art by David Nakayama. Image Comics/Top Cow Productions 2007 Un Illustration
Grades: 10 11 12 Adult   **741.5; Fic**
1. Adventure graphic novels; 2. Fantasy graphic novels; 3. Graphic novels
1-58240-779-7, $9.99
Four people are recruited by a man named Bob Gruber to form a team. Ex-racer Jack James steals the first car, a white Mazda RX-8; he becomes the White Rider. In quick succession, he helps steal three more vehicles: a red Shelby Cobra for the violent Stick, a black motorcycle for speed demon Andre, and a special jeep for Maddie. Each vehicle has a bit of the mystical "First Metal," and the riders become the new avatars of the Four Horsemen of the Apocalypse. Bob sends them on missions they believe will preserve world peace, but each time even more chaos and violence happens. Are they a force for peace or instruments to cause the end of humanity

Hall, M. C.
King Arthur and the Knights of the Round Table. Stone Arch Books 2006 63p. Illustration
Grades: 3 4 5 6 7 8 9   **741.5; Fic**
1. King Arthur — Adaptations; 2. Graphic novels
978-1-59889-048-8, $23.93
In a world of wizards, giants, and dragons, King Arthur and the Knights of the Round Table are the kingdom of Camelot's only defense against the threatening forces of evil. Fighting battles and saving those in need, the Knights of the Round Table can defeat every enemy but one - themselves. This adaptation focuses on how Arthur became King, on Lancelot and how Sir Galahad came to be born, the quest for the Holy Grail, and how Mordred brought about the end.
Part of the Graphic Revolve series.

Halliday, Ayun
Peanut. Ayun Halliday; illustrated by Paul Hoppe. Schwartz & Wade Books 2012 216 p. Color illustration
Grades: 6 7 8 9 10   **741.5**
1. Food allergy — Fiction; 2. High schools — Fiction; 3. Mothers and daughters — Fiction; 4. Moving, Household — Fiction; 5. Peanut allergy; 6. Popularity — Fiction; 7. School stories; 8. Graphic novels
037586590X, $15.99; 0375965904, $18.99; 9780375865909, $15.99; 9780375965906, $18.99
LC 2009047168
In this graphic novel by Ayun Halliday, illustrated by Paul Hoppe, "Sadie has the perfect plan to snag some friends when she transfers to Plainfield High—pretend to have a peanut allergy. But what happens when you have to hand in that student health form your unsuspecting mom was supposed to fill out? And what if your new friends want to come over and your mom serves them snacks? (Peanut butter sandwich, anyone?)" (Publisher's note)

Hama, Larry
The **Battle** of First Bull Run: The Civil War Begins. The Rosen Publishing Group 2007 48p. Illustration
Grades: 3 4 5 6 7 8 9   **741.5; 973.7**
1. Bull Run 1st Battle of, 1861; 2. United States — History — 1861-1865, Civil War; 3. War; 4. Graphic novels
978-1-4042-0776-9, $29.25
Three months after the shelling of Fort Sumter, Union and Confederate forces met for the first time in earnest combat. However, neither side was prepared at this early stage of the war, and confusion reigned on the battlefield. Finally, Confederate reinforcements forced the Union army into a

Courtesy of Rosen Publishing

panicked retreat. The intensity—and ill preparedness—of both armies convinced the nation that the conflict between the states would be a long, bloody ordeal. The book includes background information, a glossary, and a list of books for further reading.
Part of the Graphic Battles of the Civil War series. The book is also available in paperback from Osprey Publishing under the title The War is On!: Battle of First Bull Run.

The **Battle** of Guadalcanal: Land and Sea Warfare in the South Pacific. The Rosen Publishing Group 2007 48p. Illustration
Grades: 3 4 5 6 7 8 9   **741.5; 940.54**
1. Guadalcanal Island (Solomon Islands), Battle of, 1942-1943; 2. World War, 1939-1945; 3. Graphic novels
978-1-4042-0784-4, $29.25
The battle of Guadalcanal shattered the myth of Japanese invincibility. August 7, 1942, marked the first American amphibious assault of World War II, and the first attempt to secure the Japanese-controlled island of

Guadalcanal. From the ranks of the units that contested this campaign a seasoned fighting force of US veterans was created that, island by island, would sweep the Japanese back across the Pacific. This full-color comic book includes further reading, essential information on the background, aftermath and key players of the conflict.

Part of the Graphic Battles of World War II series. This book is also available in a paperback edition from Osprey Publishing, under the title Fight to the Death: Battle of Guadalcanal.

The **battle** of Iwo Jima: guerilla warfare in the Pacific. By Larry Hama; illustrated by Anthony Williams. Rosen Pub. 2007 48p. Illustration; Map (Graphic battles of World War II)

Grades: 5 6 7 8 9   **940.54**
1. Iwo Jima, Battle of, 1945; 2. World War, 1939-1945; 3. Graphic novels
978-1-4042-0781-3 (lib bdg), $29.25; 1-4042-0781-3 (lib bdg)

                       LC 2006007645

"Using a graphic novel to introduce the battle for Iwo Jima makes it very accessible. Before the graphic-novel section of the book begins, Hama provides a short, informative background piece describing the run-up to World War II, the significance of the Japanese war machine, and the importance of the tiny island of Iwo Jima. Then the graphic novel, illustrated by Williams in camouflage colors, does a terrific job of examining the ups and downs of the battle as well as the horror of so many losses—on both sides." Booklist

Includes bibliographical references

The **Battle** of the Wilderness: Deadly Inferno. The Rosen Publishing Group 2007 48p. Illustration

Grades: 3 4 5 6 7 8 9   **741.5; 973.7**
1. United States — History — 1861-1865, Civil War; 2. War; 3. Wilderness, Battle of the, 1864; 4. Graphic novels
978-1-4042-0780-6, $29.25 lib. bdg.

'The Wilderness' encompassed a 70-square-mile expanse of virtually impenetrable woodland in central Virginia, so dense it made conventional warfare impossible. The first battle of Lieutenant General Ulysses S. Grant's 1864 Overland Campaign against the Army of Northern Virginia, the Wilderness witnessed some of the fiercest fighting of the Civil War. Though outnumbered, General Lee's forces posed stiff resistance to Grant's offensive. At the end of the three day battle, the outcome was uncertain, and the fight ended in a draw. Illustrating one of the American Civil War's most tactically challenging battles, this comic strip narrative brings to life a completely new type of warfare; the likes of which had never been fought before on American soil. The book includes

Courtesy of Rosen Publishing

additional information, including a map, a glossary, and a list of books for further reading.

Part of the Graphic Battles of the Civil War series; a trade paperback edition is also available from Osprey Publishing under the title Deadly Inferno: Battle of the Wilderness.

Spider-girl presents Wild Thing: crash course. Illustrated by Ron Lim. Marvel Entertainment 2007 Un Illustration

Grades: 5 6 7 8 9 10   **741.5**
1. Adventure graphic novels; 2. Superhero graphic novels; 3. Graphic novels
978-0-7851-2606-5, $7.99

A few years in the future, in the alternate Marvel Universe where Peter Parker and Mary Jane had a daughter who has become Spider-Girl, Wolverine and Elektra got together and they had a daughter, too Rina Logan, also known as Wild Thing. She has psychic claws that work pretty much like Wolverine's claws, and she has his fast healing power. She still has to deal with high school even as she fights against bad guys, demons, evil droids, and more.

Hambly, Barbara

    Anne Steelyard: the garden of emptiness, act I: an honorary man. Written by Barbara Hambly; pencils by Alex Kosakowski and Ron Randall; colors by Mike Garcia. Penny Farthing Press 2008 Un Illustration

Grades: 9 10 11 12 Adult   **741.5; Fic**
1. Adventure graphic novels; 2. Archeology; 3. Middle East; 4. Graphic novels
978-0-9719012-9-2, $14.95

In 1908, the Middle East is a region in turmoil; while Germany and Great Britain posture at each other in a prelude to the First World War, men called the Young Turks challenge the Turkish Sultans for control of the Ottoman Empire. Archeologists excavate relics and treasures from the desert sands, their work beginning to demystify human history and managing to bring wealth and fame (or infamy) to those archeologists. Anne Steelyard is a British archeologist who wants to make that one huge discovery which will make her reputation, free her from her father and force the male-dominated field to recognize her as an equal. However, even as she tries to set up an expedition, the politics of the place and time provide obstacles from the Turkish government, from the British, and from society itself. The book includes some violence.

Other titles in this series are: The gate of dreams and starlight (2009); A thousand waters (2011)

Hamilton, Laurell K.

    Anita Blake, Vampire Hunter: Guilty Pleasures Volume 1. Laurell K. Hamilton; adapted by Stacie Ritchie (issues 1-5) & Jess Ruffner-Booth (issue 6); artwork, Brett Booth. Marvel Entertainment 2007 168p. Illustration

Grades: 10 11 12 Adult   **741.5; Fic**
1. Fantasy graphic novels; 2. Horror graphic novels
978-0-7851-2723-9, $19.99

Anita Blake lives in a world where vampires, zombies and werewolves have been declared legal citizens of the United States. Anita Blake is an "animator" - a profession that involves raising the dead for mourning relatives. But she is also known as a fearsome hunter of criminal vampires, and she's often employed to investigate cases that are far too much for conventional police. But as Anita gains the attention of the vampire masters of her hometown of St. Louis, she also risks revealing an intriguing secret about herself - the source of her unusual strength and power. The book includes vampiric violence, strong language, partial nudity, and sexual suggestiveness.

Hamilton, Tim
 Robert Louis Stevenson's Treasure Island. Penguin Young Readers Group/Puffin Books 2005 176p. Illustration
Grades: 4 5 6 7 8 9 10   **741.5; Fic**
 1. Adventure graphic novels; 2. Buried treasure; 3. Pirates; 4. Stevenson, Robert Louis, 1850-1894 — Adaptations; 5. Graphic novels
0-14-240470-5, $9.99
 Innkeeper's son Jim Hawkins befriends an old seaman who stays at the inn; when he dies, Jim finds a treasure map in the old man's seachest. When he takes it to the local magistrate, Jim finds himself caught up in a treasure hunt adventure with a ship's crew of pirates led by Long John Silver. This graphic novel adaptation keeps all the main action of the original novel. The book includes a gallery of the character models Hamilton used as well as sketched pages so readers can see some of the process.

Hanmura, Ryo
 Samurai Commando: Mission 1549 Volume 1. Original idea by Ryo Hanmura; story by Harutoshi Fukui; art by Ark Performance. DC Comics/CMX 2007 176p. Illustration
Grades: 10 11 12 Adult   **741.5; Fic**
 1. Adventure graphic novels; 2. Manga; 3. Science fiction graphic novels; 4. Seinen manga; 5. Graphic novels
978-1-4012-1438-8, $9.99
 A military test accidentally sends a unit from Japan's Self-Defense Forces (JDF) back in time to the Sengoku Jidai period in the late 16th century, the time of warfare before Ieyasu Tokugawa seized power. When the unit's actions begin to alter the present, the JDF sends a second unit to retrieve them. But Colonel Matoba, commander of the lost battalion, is determined to use his advanced technology to conquer Japan and change his country's destiny. It's up to Kashima, Matoba's former prot?g?, to stop him. But he only has a narrow window of time, and it is rapidly closing. This is the first of two volumes. The book includes battle violence and some strong language.

 TrainMan: Densha Otoko, Vol. 1. Viz Media 2006 208p. Illustration
Grades: 9 10 11 12   **741.5; Fic**
 1. Romance graphic novels; 2. Seinen manga; 3. Graphic novels
978-1-4215-0848-1, $9.99
 This is another manga version of the Train Man story from Japan, which tells the story of how a young anime fanatic uses advice from an online forum (2channel) to date and then pursue a romantic relationship with a young woman he saved from a harasser. This version utilizes most of the Japanese emoticons used by the forum members. It's written for a slightly older audience than Densha Otoko; on one page, TrainMan imagines Hermess (the young woman) in the shower.

Harbo, Christopher L.
 The **Explosive** World of Volcanoes with Max Axiom, Super Scientist. Art by Tod Smith. Capstone Press 2007 32p. Illustration
Grades: 3 4 5 6 7 8 9   **551.21; 741.5**
 1. Volcanoes; 2. Graphic novels
978-1-4296-0144-3, $25.26
                                                  LC 2006102361
 This book uses the graphic novel format to follow the adventures of super scientist Max Axiom as he explains the science behind volcanoes, describing the different types of volcanoes found all over the world. The book includes additional facts and a list of books for further reading.
 Part of the Graphic Science series.

Harmon, Paul
 Mora Vol. 1: All Beasts Will Show Their Teeth. Image Comics 2006 Un Illustration
Grades: 10 11 12 Adult   **741.5; Fic**
 1. Fantasy graphic novels; 2. Horror graphic novels; 3. Graphic novels
1-58240-588-3, $12.99
 This is the dark tale of the most powerful witch that lived, and the city that raised her. Strange creatures and ruthless beasts abound as the story follows young Mora through the treacherous City of Witches. There is violence as monsters attack and people fight back.

Harper, Charise Mericle
 Fashion Kitty. Hyperion Books for Children 2005 90p. Illustration
Grades: 3 4 5 6 7 8 9   **741.5; Fic**
 1. Cats; 2. Humorous graphic novels; 3. Graphic novels
0-7868-5134-1, $8.99
 Kiki Kittie is a very unusual cat. For one thing, she has a mouse for a pet—and that's kind of like a human having a chocolate cake for a pet. Kiki also has a natural flair for fashion, but up until a recent birthday, she was just an ordinary fashionable kitty. Then, on that day, she discovered that she had special powers: she can turn into Fashion Kitty, able to mix and match hundreds of outfits in a single second. Regular cat by day, Fashion Kitty by night, Kiki is always ready to answer a call of despair and save other cats from making fashion faux pas
 Other titles about Fashion Kitty are: Fashion Kitty versus the Fashion Queen (2007); Fashion Kitty and the unlikely hero (2008)

 Fashion Kitty Versus the Fashion Queen. Hyperion Paperbacks for Children 2007 90p. Illustration
Grades: 3 4 5 6 7 8 9   **741.5; Fic**
 1. Cats; 2. Humorous graphic novels; 3. Graphic novels
978-0-7868-3726-7, $8.99
 After her last adventure, Fashion Kitty is truly becoming a hero. At school, she is more popular than ever. She's even been mentioned in several articles in the local newspaper, (which she clips out and saves in a scrapbook, of course). But not everyone is excited about Fashion Kitty's newfound popularity. A spoiled new kitty named Cassandra

doesn't like sharing the spotlight. And when Fashion Kitty starts inspiring the other kitties at school to be more independent about their style choices, Cassandra really doesn't like it. So she hatches a plan (evil, of course) that involves lying, conniving, and outlawing bright colors and patterns. Fashion Kitty knows she must put an end to Cassandra's reign of terror. She will use her fashion sense, quick smarts, and the power of friendship to overcome fashion evil.

Harris, James S.

Shades of blue, Volume 1. Art by Rachel Nacion. D3 Digest/Devil's Due Publishing 2005 144p. Illustration
Grades: 7 8 9 10 11 12   **741.5; Fic**
   1. Superhero graphic novels; 2. Graphic novels
   1-932796-26-6, $10.95

Heidi Page's "life takes an odd turn after she awakens with blue hair and the power to control electricity. Although she tries to keep her powers from getting in the way of her normal life, weird situations pop up, and her best friend, K. T., and Marcus (who calls himself her sidekick) insist that she's the superhero for the job. This sarcastic, funny send-up of superhero comics hinges on great characterizations and an immensely likable, believable cast." Booklist

The series changed artists after the second issue. This is the first volume of a series.

Harris, Micah

Heaven's War. Micah Harris and Michael Gaydos. Image Comics 2003 118p. Illustration
Grades: 9 10 11 12 Adult   **741.5**
   1. Adventure graphic novels; 2. Fantasy graphic novels; 3. Graphic novels
   1-58240-330-9, $12.95

In this graphic novel, "J.R.R. Tolkien and C.S. Lewis are called upon by eccentric fellow fantasist Charles Williams to join him against occultist Aleister Crowley. Crowley seeks an entrance into the Heavenly realms with the intent of manipulating the angelic battles that shape human history and thus mold the world according to his will. Their conflict with Crowley will take this trio of authors . . . to the very edge of Heaven." (Publisher's note)

Hart, Christopher

The **reformed**. Del Rey Manga 2008 170p. Illustration
Grades: 10 11 12 Adult   **741.5; Fic**
   1. Fantasy graphic novels; 2. Horror graphic novels; 3. Mystery graphic novels; 4. Vampires; 5. Graphic novels
   978-0-345-49663-8, $10.95

Handsome, wealthy Giancarlo is a vampire who has lived for hundreds of years and is lonely. Then he meets Jenny, a beautiful young woman who stirs feelings he hasn't known for centuries; he's willing to become mortal again to be with her. However, brutal, ghoulish murders plaguing the city have made him the target of a relentless homicide cop. And the real killer, a dangerous vampire, also wants to destroy Giancarlo. The book includes graphic, bloody violence.

Hartley, Welles

Star Wars: Empire Volume Seven: The Wrong Side of the War. Writers, Welles Hartley, John Jackson Miller ; pencillers, Davidé Fabbri ; colorists, Davidé Fabbri, Neziti Domenico, Michael Atiyeh ; letterer, Michael David Thomas. Dark Horse Comics 2007 Un Illustration
Grades: 7 8 9 10 11 12 Adult   **741.5; Fic**
   1. Adventure graphic novels; 2. Science fiction graphic novels; 3. Star Wars; 4. Graphic novels
   978-1-59307-709-9, $17.95

Fresh from the killing fields of Jabiim, where the Empire has virtually wiped out the populace of that world, Imperial Lieutenant Janek Sunber is sent to the quiet prison base on Kalist VI. But, unbeknownst to the Empire, the Rebels have designs on Kalist Base both for its desirable fuel supplies and for the presence of a very important prisoner - one of their own who has already attracted the interest of Darth Vader. Sunber doesn't know it, but he's on a collision course with an old friend who is with the Rebels, and he finds himself wondering which of them is on the wrong side of the war. The book includes battle violence.

Wes Hartman's sky sharks. Wes Hartman and Fred Perry. Antarctic Press 2008 Un Illustration
Grades: 9 10 11 12   **741.5; Fic**
   1. Adventure graphic novels; 2. Graphic novels
   978-0-9797719-5-8, $14.95

In what looks to be an alternate world, the Sky Sharks are an independent air force for hire. They try to hire out only for jobs that will help people fight against pirates, mercenaries, and hostile forces; but their latest job in the Middle East turns out to be helpful only to Prince Ahmed. When hotshot new pilot Jason is caught messing around with Prince Ahmed's daughter, the Sky Sharks need to get out in a hurry, and the only place they can refuel their planes is War Island, run by Admiral Calloway. The Sky Sharks also learn that they're fighting against the Iron Swans, led by Monica Swan, a former Sky Shark. When Prince Ahmed teams up with a scientist who has developed a terrible weapon of mass destruction and takes over War Island, the Sky Sharks have no choice but to try and stop them. The book includes some partial nudity and lots of aerial battle action.

Hartzell, Andy

★ **Fox** bunny funny. Top Shelf Productions 2007 102p. Illustration
Grades: 9 10 11 12 Adult
741.5; Fic
   1. Animals; 2. Fantasy graphic novels; 3. Stories without words; 4. Graphic novels
   978-1-891830-97-6, $10

The rules are simple: you're either a fox or a bunny. Foxes oppress and devour, bunnies suffer and die. Everyone knows their place. Everyone's satisfied. So what happens when a secret desire puts you at odds with your society? Starting from a simple premise—and without

Courtesy of Top Shelf Productions

using a single word—this book leads the reader on a zigzag chase in and out of rabbit holes, and through increasingly strange landscapes where funny animals have serious identity problems. The tale swerves from slapstick to horror and back again before landing at the inevitable climax, in which all the old rules are shattered. Some moments of violence and dismemberment might be disturbing for some readers.

"Deftly presented in crisp black-and-white, block-print-like panels, this is a must for libraries supporting LGBT collections." Booklist

Hasegawa, K-Ske
Ballad of a shinigami, vol. 1. By Asuka Izumi; original story by K-Ske Hasegawa; translated by Sheldon Drzka. DC Comics/CMX 2009 Un Illustration
Grades: 9 10 11 12 **741.5; Fic**
1. Death; 2. Manga; 3. Shojo manga; 4. Supernatural graphic novels
978-1-4012-2058-7, $9.99
Momo is a shinigami, an angel of death; however, unlike other depictions of shinigami, she appears as a beautiful young woman in white bearing a large scythe. In this collection of stories, Momo helps people cross over from life to death, even sometimes preventing people from dying if it isn't yet their time. Makoto can see Momo and her talking cat companion, Daniel; he survived an attack that killed his mother. He has started dreaming of the attack again, but his friend Hiura helps him feel better; Momo helps him see that Hiura needs protecting or she will die at the hands of her abusive father. Then Momo and Daniel help Mitsuki see that he was not meant to die when his older sister died saving him. And an old woman on her deathbed tells Momo about her first love, even as her grandson is about to meet his. There's some violence, mostly in the nightmares experienced by Makoto.

Hashiguchi, Takashi
Yakitate!! Japan, Vol. 1. Viz Media 2006 196p. Illustration
Grades: 10 11 12 Adult **741.5; Fic**
1. Baking; 2. Bread; 3. Manga; 4. Shonen manga; 5. Graphic novels
978-1-4215-0719-4, $9.99
When still a little boy, Kazuma Azuma became fascinated with bread after meeting a baker who taught him how to bake it. He begins to experiment with baking different types of bread to find the one he can call "Ja-pan," the national bread of Japan ("pan" is Japanese for bread). At sixteen, Kazuma is almost totally self-taught, but he gets accepted as a candidate for employment at Pantasia, a bakery chain. Only one person can become the new baker at Pantasia, and Kazuma intends to win, . . . but he is totally ignorant of European bread names (such as croissants). This series is an example of a genre unique to manga, a story focused on food. Most of the action takes place in kitchens, but there's some crude humor.
Volume 1 of 26.

Hashimoto, Kyoko
Love master A, vol.1. Go! Comi 2008 Un Illustration
Grades: 7 8 9 10 11 12 **741.5; Fic**
1. Humorous graphic novels; 2. Romance graphic novels; 3. Shojo manga; 4. Graphic novels
978-1933617-60-2, $10.99
Aria starts at a new high school, hoping to have a normal school experience. Since elementary school, when she confessed her love to a classmate and was summarily rejected, she has suffered rejection all through school and earned the ironic nickname "Love Master." Now, she has renounced love. However, on her first day at school, she discovers the school's strange way of selecting Student Council members, and not only is she as a first year student a Student Council member, she is the President! And her reputation has been twisted so everyone thinks she's a real "Love Master" and wants her advice. Tonohashi High School is in for a very interesting year.

Hata, Kenjiro
Hayate the Combat Butler Volume 1. Viz Media 2006 182p. Illustration
Grades: 10 11 12 Adult **741.5; Fic**
1. Humorous graphic novels; 2. Romance graphic novels; 3. Shonen manga; 4. Graphic novels
978-1-4215-0851-1, $9.99
Hardworking teenager Hayate has a plan to pay back the yakuza—who are now the legal owners of his vital organs (thanks to his deadbeat parents): he'll kidnap someone and ransom them for a mountain of money. But things get tricky when his would-be kidnappee—who as luck would have it is the daughter of a mind-bogglingly wealthy family—mistakes Hayate's actions for a confession of love, and hires him to be her personal servant. At least his employment future is secure, or so he thinks... The book includes some strong language and mild sexual situations.

Hatori, Bisco
Millennium Snow Vol. 1. Viz Media/Shojo Beat 2007 200p. Illustration
Grades: 8 9 10 11 12 **741.5; Fic**
1. Romance graphic novels; 2. Shojo manga; 3. Vampires; 4. Graphic novels
978-1-4215-1202-0, $8.99
17-year-old Chiyuki Matsuoka was born with heart problems, and her doctors say she won't live to see the next snow. Toya is an 18-year-old vampire who hates blood and refuses to make the traditional partnership with a human, whose life-giving blood would keep them both alive for a thousand years. Can Chiyuki teach Toya to feel a passion for life, even as her own is ending? The book has some mildly strong language, and romance without graphic depictions of vampiric action.
Volume 1 of 4.

Ouran High School Host Club Volume 1. Viz Media/Shojo Beat 2005 184p. Illustration
Grades: 9 10 11 12 Adult **741.5; Fic**
1. Humorous graphic novels; 2. Manga; 3. Shojo manga; 4. Graphic novels
1-59116-915-1, $8.99
Haruhi is a scholarship student at an exclusive private school: Ouran High School, where it turns out the bespectacled, short-haired Haruhi is the only student from a lower-middle class family in attendance. Then, to make

matters worse, one day she breaks an $80,000 vase that belongs to one of the campus clubs, a mysterious outfit called the "Host Club," consisting of six superrich (and gorgeous) guys. Haruhi can't afford to pay back the cost of the vase, of course, so she's forced to work for the Host Club. And it's there that she discovers just how rich all the boys are and how different the rich are from "regular" folks ... And meanwhile, the eccentric but good-hearted rich boys are shocked to find out how life is on the other side...

Volume 1 of an 18 volume series

Hayakawa, Tomoko
The **Wallflower** 1: Yamatonadeshiko Shichihenge. Random House/Del Rey Manga 2004 224p. Illustration
Grades: 10 11 12 Adult   741.5; Fic
1. Humorous graphic novels; 2. Shojo manga; 3. Graphic novels
0-345-47912-2, $10.95

It's a gorgeous, spacious mansion, and four handsome, fifteen-year-old friends are allowed to live in it for free. There's only one condition - that within three years the guys must transform the owner's wallflower niece into a lady befitting the palace in which they all live. How hard can it be" Enter Sunako Nakahara, the agoraphobic, horror-movie-loving, pockmark-faced, frizzy-haired, fashion-illiterate recluse who tends to break into explosive nosebleeds whenever she sees anyone attractive. This project is going to take more than the four heroes ever expected: it needs a miracle. The series includes some mildly harsh language, some mild sexual situations, and mild violence.

Hayashi, Fumino
★ **Neon** Genesis Evangelion Vol. 1 2nd ed.. Viz Media 2004 184p. Illustration
Grades: 10 11 12 Adult   741.5; Fic
1. Mecha manga; 2. Science fiction graphic novels; 3. Shonen manga; 4. Graphic novels
978-1-4139-0344-7, $9.95

A handful of teenagers must pilot huge biomechanical robots — the Evangelion combat units — against monstrous "Angels" bent on destroying humanity. Among them is Shin, a very reluctant recruit whose scientist father is commander of the secret organization NERV and who has ignored his son all his life. The book includes violence, strong language, nudity, and sexual situations.

Neon Genesis Evangelion: Angelic Days Vol. 1. ADV Manga 2006 184p. Illustration
Grades: 10 11 12 Adult   741.5; Fic
1. Manga; 2. Romance graphic novels; 3. Science fiction graphic novels; 4. Shojo manga; 5. Graphic novels
978-1-4139-0344-7, $9.99

This manga series is set in the world of Neon Genesis Evangelion, but in this series, life isn't quite so angst-ridden. Choosing the right girl is more important than saving the world. The book includes some mild sexual situations.

Hayashi, Mikase
March on earth, volume one. DC Comics/CMX 2009 Un Illustration
Grades: 7 8 9 10 11 12   741.5; Fic

1. Family life; 2. Romance graphic novels; 3. Shojo manga; 4. Graphic novels
978-1-4012-1594-1, $9.99

When Yuzu was a young girl, her older sister Tsubaki raised her after their parents died. Then a few years ago, Tsubaki got pregnant and decided to have the baby and raise him as a single parent; she would never tell Yuzu who the father was. Just a few months ago, Tsubaki died in a car accident, and Yuzu, now a 10th grader in high school, has decided she will raise her nephew Shou herself. She and Shou live in an apartment in the building owned by Mrs. Kusano, who lives there with her two sons, Seita and Keita. They help her take care of Shou, but even with their help it's difficult to focus on her studies. She reads her sister's picture books to Shou, especially the last one Tsubaki wrote, called March on Earth. Yuzu wants to become a lawyer to help people, but will there be enough money from what her parents left to pay for college, after paying for rent and all the other expenses? Other teens worry about boyfriends, and whether they should go sing karaoke, but Yuzu has to take care of a two-year-old boy and worry about having enough money to buy him one Christmas present. She doesn't seem to see that Seita has fallen for her, and she seems to be oblivious to his efforts to appear before her half naked (wearing only an apron to cook curry, claiming to have just come out of the bath with only a towel around his waist, ...).

Haynes, Stephen
Macbeth. Barron's 2008 Illustration
Grades: 4 5 6 7 8 9   822.3; 741.5
1. Authors; 2. Dramatists; 3. Poets; 4. Shakespeare, William, 1564-1616 — Adaptations; 5. Graphic novels
978-0-7641-6140-7, $15.99; 978-0-7641-4009-9 (pa), $8.99
LC 2007-938484

Macbeth is a loyal retainer of King Duncan of Scotland, until three witches prophesy that he will be king. Now, nothing will stop his ambition, and Macbeth and his wife kill the king. But now that he has the throne, Macbeth is haunted by guilt and paranoia, and the murders pile up. This graphic novel adaptation of Shakespeare's play includes a brief biography of Shakespeare, background information on the real Macbeth, Scotland, and James I's campaign against witches; it also covers the superstitions about the play, and film adaptations.

Part of Barron's Graphic Classics series

Heer, Margreet de
Science, a discovery in comics. Margreet de Heer. NBM Publishing 2013 192 p. (A discovery in comics)
Grades: 9 10 11 12 Adult   500
1. Science; 2. Scientists — History
1561637505; 9781561637508, $19.99
LC 2013939851

"This history of scientific discovery, [by Margreet de Heer] is presented as a series of conversations about understanding the laws that govern the universe. . . . Beginning with the ideals of scientific observation and inquiry, the book moves to detailed chronologies of the evolutions of biology, physics, geology, etc. Much of the information is organized in time-line form, which is used to depict the gradual accumulation and transformation of concepts." (School Library Journal)

"Although the information on any one topic is very basic, a great many topics are treated, thanks to the economy of de Heer's visual presentation, and they are all handled very well, thanks to the energy of her drawing style and the vividness of Kohl's coloring." Booklist

Heinberg, Allan

Avengers: the children's crusade. Allan Heinberg, writer; Jim Cheung, penciler; Mark Morales, et al., inkers; Justin Ponsor, Paul Mounts, colorists; VC's Cory Petit, letterer. Marvel Worldwide 2012 248 p.

Grades: 9 10 11 12   **741.5/973; Fic**
1. Superhero comic books, strips, etc; 2. Voyages and travels
0785135499; 9780785135494, $29.99

In this comic book, "the Young Avengers are the heroes of tomorrow. But two of their membersùtwin brothers Wiccan and Speedùare boys without a past. When Wiccan's powers begin spiraling out of control, the team sets out to find the one person who might be able to help: the Scarlet Witch, who may be the twins' mother, and whose own uncontrollable powers once almost destroyed the Avengers and nearly wiped out the mutant race." (Publisher's note)

Young Avengers Vol. 1: Sidekicks. writer, Allan Heinberg; pencils, Jim Cheung; inks, John Dell, Mark Morales & Drew Geraci; colors, Justin Ponsor; letters, Virtual Calligraphy's Cory Petit. Marvel Entertainment 2006 Un Illustration

Grades: 9 10 11 12 Adult   **741.5; Fic**
1. Superhero graphic novels; 2. Graphic novels
978-0-7851-2018-6, $14.99

A mysterious new group of teen super heroes appears, with powers and names resembling classic Avengers Captain America, Iron Man, Thor, and the Hulk. But who are they? Where did they come from? And what right to they have to call themselves the Young Avengers? When their public activities draw the attention of Captain America and Iron Man, the old Avengers set out to learn the truth about their teenaged namesakes. Caught between a maniacal super-villain and their heroic idols, will the Young Avengers' first fight be their last stand?

Helfand, Lewis

Conquering Everest: the lives of Edmund Hillary and Tenzing Norgay. Lewis Helfand; illustrated by Amit Tayal. Campfire 2011 96p. Illustration

Grades: 3 4 5 6 7 8 9 10   **741.5; 796.522**
1. Hillary, Edmund Sir; 2. Mount Everest; 3. Mountaineering; 4. Mountaineers; 5. Nonfiction writers; 6. Tenzing Norgay, 1914-1986
978-93-80741-24-6, $12.99

Tenzing Norgay immigrated to Nepal with his Tibetan family when he was a boy, and he worked hard over the years to become one of the best Sherpas who helped the European, American, and other climbers who journeyed to Nepal to climb Mount Everest. Edmund Hillary was the son of a beekeeper from New Zealand, who became fascinated with mountain climbing during World War II. He came to Nepal in 1953 as part of a British expedition to reach Everest's

peak, and Norgay came to be the sirdar, the head Sherpa and organizer of the expedition's support system. These two men became the first to reach Everest's summit at 11:30 a.m. on May 29, 1953. This graphic novel tells the story of the two men from such different backgrounds, and their friendship. The book notes that on May 22, 2010, Californian thirteen-year-old Jordan Romero became the youngest climber to reach Everest's peak. Tayal's panels show some of the massive scale of the mountain.

Mother Teresa: Angel of the Slums. By Lewis Helfand and illustrated by Sachin Nagar. Random House Inc 2013 88 p.

Grades: 6 7 8 9   **271.9**
1. Teresa, Mother, 1910-1997
9380028709; 9789380028705, $11.99

This illustrated biography written by Lewis Helfand and illustrated by Sachin Nagar "presents the facts about Mother Teresa, born Agnes Gonxha Bojaxhiu in Macedonia in 1910. The book describes her decision to become a nun, her early work in Europe, and her path to teaching at a convent in India. From there it covers, in greater detail, her life among the poor and sick in Calcutta, and the foundation of Mother Teresa's worldwide charitable order." (Publisher's Weekly)

Nelson Mandela: the unconquerable soul. Lewis Helfand. Kalyani Navyug Media Pvt LTD 2011 115 p.

Grades: 8 9 10
1. Biographical graphic novels; 2. Mandela, Nelson, 1918-2013; 3. South Africa — History
9380741162; 9789380741161, $12.99
                                              LC 2012374765

This book is a graphic novel biography of Nelson Mandela. It "includes a brief history of 20th-century South Africa along with a full account of Mandela's full life. . . . [B]lack, white, and gray illustrations are" included. "Endnotes include a glossary and additional facts about South Africa." (School Library Journal)

Helfer, Andrew

Malcolm X: a graphic biography. Written by Andrew Helfer; art by Randy DuBurke. Hill and Wang 2006 102p. Illustration

Grades: 10 11 12 Adult   **92; 741.5**
1. African Americans — Biography; 2. Biographical graphic novels; 3. Black Muslims; 4. Malcolm X, 1925-1965; 5. Malcolm X, 1925-1965; 6. Graphic novels
978-0-8090-9504-9; 0-8090-9504-1, $15.95
                                              LC 2006-13743

The authors "tell the story of Malcolm X's short life—his meeting with Dr. Martin Luther King Jr., the two leaders describing the opposite ideological ends of the fight for civil rights; and his eventual assassination by other members of the Nation of Islam (NOI)—in narration and detailed b&white drawings, sharp as photographs in a newspaper. . . . Helfer and DuBurke have created an evocative and studied look at not only Malcolm X but the racial conflict that defined and shaped him." Publ Wkly

Ronald Reagan: a graphic biography. Written by Andrew Helfer; art by Steve Buccellato and Joe Staton. Hill and Wang 2007 102p. Illustration

Grades: 9 10 11 12 Adult   **92; 741.5**

1. Actors; 2. Biographical graphic novels; 3. Governors; 4. Presidents; 5. Reagan, Ronald, 1911-2004; 6. Graphic novels
978-0-8090-9507-0, $16.95

LC 2006-16437

This graphic novel biography covers the life of Ronald Reagan, who began as an actor and ended his career as the fortieth president of the U.S. The book discusses Reagan's work as a union president (Screen Actor's Guild), a General Motors pitchman on television, Governor of California, and his terms as President. It also covers some of the scandals that occurred during his gubernatorial and presidential terms, including the Iran/Contra arms-for-hostages deal, and the assassination attempt by John Hinkley.
Includes bibliographical references
A novel graphic from Hill and Wang

Hellboy: Weird Tales Volume One.
Dark Horse Comics 2003 Un Illustration
Grades: 10 11 12 Adult   **741.5; Fic**
1. Fantasy graphic novels; 2. Hellboy (Fictional character); 3. Horror graphic novels; 4. Mystery graphic novels; 5. Graphic novels
1-56971-622-6, $17.95
Some writers and artists - John Arcudi, Joe Casey, Bob Fingerman, Roger Langridge, Alex Maleev, Eric Powell, Steve Lieber, Sara Ryan and Andi Watson to name a few - team up to present stories of giant bats, demon children, jet-packs, haunted circuses, and rusted-out spaceships. These stories are old-fashioned pulp fun featuring Hellboy. Some stories include violence, strong language, and nudity.

Hellboy: Weird Tales Volume Two.
Dark Horse Comics 2004 Un Illustration
Grades: 9 10 11 12 Adult   **741.5; Fic**
1. Fantasy graphic novels; 2. Hellboy (Fictional character); 3. Horror graphic novels; 4. Mystery graphic novels; 5. Graphic novels
1-56971-953-5, $17.95
Writers and artists including John Cassaday, P. Craig Russell, Scott Morse, Evan Dorkin, Jill Thompson, Kia Asamiya, Craig Thompson, and others team up to present stories of satanic theaters, a vacation in hell, and romance in the back of a Cadillac - old-fashioned pulp fiction style stories featuring Hellboy. The book includes violence and some strong language."

Henderson, Sam
Magic Whistle #10. Alternative Comics 2006 Un Illustration
Grades: 11 12 Adult   **741.5; Fic**
1. Humorous graphic novels; 2. Graphic novels
1-891867-94-6, $11.95
This tenth book in the second volume collects more of Henderson's humor pieces. He has written for SpongeBob Square Pants (and been nominated for an Emmy Award), and previous volumes of Magic Whistly have been nominated for the Harvey Award for humor. He uses very low-brow humor that almost parodies low-brow humor, with intentionally crude art. There's lots of raunchy humor and some sexual situations.

Hennessey, Jonathan
★ The **Gettysburg** Address: A Graphic Adaptation. By Jonathan Hennessey and illustrated by Aaron McConnell. HarperCollins 2013 224 p.
Grades: 9 10 11 12 Adult   **973.7**
1. Gettysburg (Pa), Battle of, 1863; 2. Lincoln, Abraham, 1809-1865; 3. Speeches
0061969761; 9780061969768, $15.99
This graphic novel by Jonathan Hennessey and illustrated by Aaron McConnell "is a full-color illustrated look at Abraham Lincoln's most famous speech, the bloody battle of the Civil War that prompted it, and how they led to a defining point in the history of America. Using Lincoln—s words as a keystone, and drawing from first-person accounts, 'The Gettysburg Address' shows us the events through the eyes of those who lived through the events of the War, from soldiers to slaves." (Publisher's note)

★ The **United** States Constitution: a graphic adaptation. Written by Jonathan Hennessey; art by Aaron McConnell. Hill and Wang 2008 149p. Illustration
Grades: 9 10 11 12 Adult   **342; 741.5**
1. Constitutional history — United States; 2. United States — Constitution; 3. Graphic novels
978-0-8090-9487-5; 0-8090-9487-8, $35; 978-0-8090-9470-7 (pa); 0-8090-9470-3 (pa), $16.95

LC 2008-17927

The author and illustrator go "through the entire U. S. Constitution, article by article, amendment by amendment, explaining their meaning and implications—in comics format. Avoiding the didactic, the book succeeds in being both consistently entertaining and illuminating." Publ Wkly
Includes bibliographical references

Henson, Jim
Jim Henson's tale of sand. Written by Jim Henson and Jerry Juhl; as realized by Ramón K. Pérez; colors by Ian Herring with Ramón K. Pérez; lettering and font design by Deron Bennett based on the handwriting of Jim Henson; edited by Stephen Christy.. Archaia Entertainment 2012 152 p.
Grades: 10 11 12 Adult   **741.5**
1. Adventure graphic novels; 2. Deserts; 3. Fantasy graphic novels; 4. Southwestern States
1936393093; 9781936393091
This graphic novel "follows its hapless protagonist as he is cast out into the desert by the cheerful Sheriff Tate.... The scruffy hero is a pawn in a game whose rules are concealed from him, pursued across a surrealistic southwest U.S. by an implacable hunter and hindered by the eccentric, bizarre inhabitants of the great desolation. The prize waiting for him at the end of the chase, should he survive to reach the end, is one he will never guess at." (Publishers Weekly)

Herge
★ The **adventures** of Tintin, vol. 1: Tintin in America, Cigars of the Pharaoh, The Blue Lotus. Little, Brown 1994 192p. Illustration
Grades: 4 5 6 7 8 9   **741.5; Fic**
1. Adventure graphic novels; 2. Tintin (Fictional character); 3. Graphic novels
0-316-35940-8, $18.99

Tintin, the heroic boy reporter from France, travels to America where he outwits gangsters in Chicago of the 1930s and adventures in the Wild West; sails the Mediterranean Sea with faithful dog Snowy and finds himself in a mystery involving a movie tycoon, drugs, and cigars in an ancient Egyptian tomb; then he travels to India to finally solve the mystery. This Little, Brown edition reprints some of the early Tintin adventures published in the 1930s in a 3-in-1 volume. This is the first in a series that reprints most of the Tintin stories by Herge. Librarians and teachers should note that the books retain some stereotypical depictions of people of other cultures and remember that these were acceptable and expected at the time of original publication.

Tintin and the Picaros. Little, Brown 1978 62p. Illustration
Grades: 4 5 6 7 8 9   **741.5; Fic**
1. Adventure graphic novels; 2. Humorous graphic novels; 3. Tintin (Fictional character); 4. Graphic novels
0-316-35849-5, $10.99
                    LC 77-090973
Tintin and his friends rescue prima donna Bianca Castafiore while trying to help restore their friend Alcazar to power in San Theodoros - but they'll have to defeat General Tapioca and his troops to do it.

Tintin in Tibet. Little, Brown 1978 62p. Illustration
Grades: 4 5 6 7 8 9   **741.5; Fic**
1. Adventure graphic novels; 2. Humorous graphic novels; 3. Tintin (Fictional character); 4. Graphic novels
0-316-35839-8, $10.99
                    LC 80-191368
Tintin, Snowy, and Captain Haddock trek through the snow-covered Himalayas to rescue their friend Chang from the hands of an abominable snowman.

Tintin: The Broken Ear. Little, Brown 1978 62p. Illustration
Grades: 4 5 6 7 8 9   **741.5; Fic**
1. Adventure graphic novels; 2. Humorous graphic novels; 3. Tintin (Fictional character); 4. Graphic novels
0-316-35850-9, $10.99
                    LC 77-090970
A fetish which originally belonged to the Arumbayas tribe in San Theodoros is stolen from a museum, then returned; soon Tintin discovers that the returned fetish is a forgery. When he follows the trail of the stolen fetish, it leads him and Snowy to South America and to San Theodoros, where he gets caught in the middle of a civil war. Tintin gets into all kinds of trouble even as he tries to find out why so many people want the fetish.

★ **Tintin:** The Calculus Affair. Little, Brown 1976 62p. Illustration
Grades: 4 5 6 7 8 9   **741.5; Fic**
1. Adventure graphic novels; 2. Humorous graphic novels; 3. Tintin (Fictional character); 4. Graphic novels
0-316-35847-9, $10.99
                    LC 76-13280
Unscrupulous Bordurians have kidnapped Professor Calculus, and Tintin, Snowy, and Captain Haddock are soon on the trail again, to rescue their friend. It's no easy task to rescue the Professor and save his fantastic invention; spies

are everywhere, and Calculus lies deep in the fortress of Bakhine. But the Bordurians now have to deal with Tintin ...

Tintin: Cigars of the Pharaoh. Little, Brown 1975 62p. Illustration
Grades: 4 5 6 7 8 9   **741.5; Fic**
1. Adventure graphic novels; 2. Humorous graphic novels; 3. Tintin (Fictional character); 4. Graphic novels
0-316-35836-3, $10.99
                    LC 74-021620
Tintin and Snowy are on a cruise to Egypt when they happen to meet Professor Sophocles Sarcophagus (the first of Tintin's absent-minded professors) and join his expedition. But they become embroiled in a complicated scheme involving a fakir, cigars marked with an unusual brand, and Rajijah, the poison of madness. Tintin meets the detectives Thompson and Thomson as well as the movie mogul Rastapopolous. Herge wrote this book in 1932 then revised it in 1955.

Tintin: Destination Moon. Little, Brown 1976 62p. Illustration
Grades: 4 5 6 7 8 9   **741.5; Fic**
1. Adventure graphic novels; 2. Humorous graphic novels; 3. Tintin (Fictional character); 4. Graphic novels
0-316-35845-2, $10.99
                    LC 76-013279
Professor Calculus has designed a rocket for an expedition to the Moon. He summons Tintin and Captain Haddock (along with Snowy) to the country of Syldavia, where he's been working. Despite spies being everywhere and mysterious explosions and other problems, the rocket is soon ready to launch, and Professor Calculus wants Tintin and Captain Haddock to go with him - to the Moon.

Tintin: Explorers On the Moon. Little, Brown 1976 62p. Illustration
Grades: 4 5 6 7 8 9   **741.5; Fic**
1. Adventure graphic novels; 2. Humorous graphic novels; 3. Tintin (Fictional character); 4. Graphic novels
0-316-35846-0, $10.99
                    LC 76-013297
Tintin, Captain Haddock, and Prof. Calculus are headed for the Moon when they discover Thompson and Thomson, who had inadvertently stowed away on the rocket. But there's more trouble when they land on the Moon and go exploring, for Colonel Jorgen is there, another stowaway, and he wants revenge on Tintin.

Tintin: Flight 714. Little, Brown 1975 62p. Illustration
Grades: 4 5 6 7 8 9   **741.5; Fic**
1. Adventure graphic novels; 2. Humorous graphic novels; 3. Tintin (Fictional character); 4. Graphic novels
0-316-35837-1, $10.99
                    LC 74-021623
Tintin, Snowy, Captain Haddock, and Professor Calculus land in Djakarta and meet millionaire Mr. Carreidas, who invites them to fly to Sydney with him in his prototype jet. They find themselves in the middle of a plot to steal their new friend's fortune, and they decide to stop it.

Tintin: Land of Black Gold. Little, Brown 1975 62p. Illustration
Grades: 4 5 6 7 8 9   **741.5; Fic**

1. Adventure graphic novels; 2. Humorous graphic novels; 3. Tintin (Fictional character); 4. Graphic novels
0-316-35844-4, $10.99

LC 75-007896

The world is on the brink of a crisis when car engines begin to explode without explanation or warning; someone has been tampering with the oil supply. Tintin travels to the Middle East to investigate, and he helps Sheik Ben Kalish Ezab, whose son is kidnapped by one of Tintin's old enemies.

Tintin: Prisoners of the Sun. Little, Brown 1975 62p. Illustration
Grades: 4 5 6 7 8 9　　　　　　　**741.5; Fic**
1. Adventure graphic novels; 2. Humorous graphic novels; 3. Tintin (Fictional character); 4. Graphic novels
0-316-35843-6, $10.99

LC 75-007897

Tintin, Snowy, and Captain Haddock travel to Peru to rescue Professor Calculus. They meet Indian boy Zorrino, and they must travel into the jungle to the Andes to find their old friend.

Tintin: Red Rackham's Treasure. Little, Brown 1974 62p. Illustration
Grades: 4 5 6 7 8 9　　　　　　　**741.5; Fic**
1. Adventure graphic novels; 2. Humorous graphic novels; 3. Tintin (Fictional character); 4. Graphic novels
0-316-35834-7, $10.99

LC 73-021253

Tintin and his friends search for the pirate booty left by Captain Haddock's pirate ancestor. They're aided in their quest by the hard-of-hearing inventor, Professor Calculus.

Tintin: The Castafiore Emerald. Little, Brown 1975 62p. Illustration
Grades: 4 5 6 7 8 9　　　　　　　**741.5; Fic**
1. Adventure graphic novels; 2. Humorous graphic novels; 3. Tintin (Fictional character); 4. Graphic novels
0-316-35842-8, $10.99

Tintin and Snowy investigate when prima donna Bianca Castafiore's jewels are stolen, in particular, her emerald.

Tintin: The Seven Crystal Balls. Little, Brown 1975 62p. Illustration
Grades: 4 5 6 7 8 9　　　　　　　**741.5; Fic**
1. Adventure graphic novels; 2. Humorous graphic novels; 3. Tintin (Fictional character); 4. Graphic novels
0-316-35840-1, $10.99

LC 75-007921

Tragedy strikes the members of an expedition which returned after violating Incan burial chambers; the seven men fall into comas, one by one, and fragments of crystal are found by their bodies. Tintin, Professor Calculus, Captain Haddock, and Thompson and Thomson investigate, but then Calculus disappears - he's been kidnapped.

Hernandez, Gilbert
Chance in hell. Fantagraphics Books 2007 120p. Illustration
Grades: 11 12 Adult　　　　　　　**741.5**
1. Graphic novels
978-1-56097-833-6, $16.95

This book tells the story about a little orphan girl who lives in the slum of slums. Nobody knows who she is or where she's from, but her fellow shantytown inhabitants collectively look over her. The three-act story follows the heroine as she is adopted by a decent man who raises her well, and she eventually marries a kind, well-to-do man, only to discover that she can't relate to the good life and the comforts it provides. The book includes sexual situations and lots of foul language, but little nudity.

★ **Heartbreak** Soup: A Love and Rockets Book. Fantagraphics Books 2007 288p. Illustration
Grades: 12 Adult　　　　　　　**741.5; Fic**
1. Graphic novels
978-1-56097-783-4, $14.95

This volume collects the first half of Gilbert Hernandez's acclaimed magical-realist tales of "Palomar," the small Central American town, beginning with the groundbreaking "Sopa de Gran Pena" (which introduces most of his main cast of characters as children, plus the imposing newcomer Luba), and continuing on through such modern-day classics as "Ecce Homo," "Act of Contrition," "Duck Feet," and the great love story "For the Love of Carmen." His stories include lots of sexual situations, full nudity, and strong language.

★ **Heartbreak** Soup: A Love and Rockets Book. Fantagraphics Books 2007 256p. Illustration
Grades: 12 Adult　　　　　　　**741.5; Fic**
1. Graphic novels
978-1-56097-948-0, $14.95

This volume collects the second half of Gilbert Hernandez's acclaimed magical-realist tales of "Palomar,"

Courtesy of Fantagraphics

the small Central American town, beginning with the landmark "Human Diastrophism," the only full graphic novel length "Palomar" story ever created by Gilbert. In it, a serial killer stalks Palomar-but his depredations, hideous as they are, only serve to exacerbate the cracks in the idyllic Central American town as the modern world begins to intrude. "Diastrophism" concludes with the death (suicide) of one of Palomar's most beloved characters, and a postscript that provides one of the most hauntingly magical moments of the entire series as a rain of ashes drifts down upon Palomar. Also included are all the post-"Diastrophism" stories, in which Luba's past comes back to haunt her, and the seeds are sown for the "Palomar diaspora" that ends this book. Hernandez uses a lot of nudity, sexual situations, strong language, and violence in these stories.

Marble Season. By Gilbert Hernandez. Drawn & Quarterly 2013 128 p. Illustration
Grades: 11 12 Adult　　　　　　　**741.5**
1. Autobiographies; 2. Graphic novels
1770460861; 9781770460867, $21.95

LC 2013375524

Written by Gilbert Hernandez, this autobiographical novel "portrays the reality of life in a large family in suburban 1960s California. Pop-culture references—TV shows, comic books, and music—saturate this evocative story of a young family navigating cultural and neighborhood norms set against the golden age of the American dream and the silver age of comics." (Publisher's note)

"Neither overly rosy and romantic nor dark and dramatic, the book focuses on the real bulk of a child's daily life: the long summer months in which nothing eventful happens, the neighborhood kids who come and go, the tomboys and bullies, the temptation of small-time crime, and the confusion and innocence of early sexuality." LJ

Sloth. DC Comics/Vertigo 2006 Un Illustration
Grades: 11 12 Adult   **741.5; Fic**
  1. Teenagers; 2. Graphic novels
  978-1-4012-0366-5, $19.99
Teenager Miguel Serra had suddenly fallen into a coma; a year later he wakes up, back to normal except he moves at a very slow pace; some people call him Sloth Boy. He reconnects with his girlfriend Lita and best friend Romeo and they try to find evidence of an urban legend in the lemon orchards that surround their sleepy town. One encounter causes a change, as suddenly it was Lita who'd been in the year-long coma. She tries to catch the attention of the handsome, popular Romeo and tries to score tickets to the Romeo X concert. Soon she's having intimate relations with both Miguel and Romeo, and when they fight over her, she falls and slips into another coma. Romeo throws himself off a bridge, and Lita wakes up . . .

This is the first original graphic novel by Hernandez, who co-created Love and Rockets with his brother. Adult language and sexual situations make this more appropriate for older teens.

Hernandez, Jaime
  ★ The **Girl** from H.O.P.P.E.R.S.: A Love and Rockets Book. Fantagraphics Books 2007 288p. Illustration
Grades: 12 Adult   **741.5; Fic**
  1. Graphic novels
  978-1-56097-851-0, $14.95
In this second volume, having abandoned the sci-fi trappings of the earliest Love & Rockets stories, Hernandez refined his approach, settling on the more naturalistic environment of the fictional Los Angeles barrio, Hoppers, and the lives of the young Mexican-Americans and punk rockers who live there. A central story is "The Death of Speedy." In this volume, Maggie also begins her on-again and off-again romance with Ray D., leading to friction and an eventual separation from Hopey. Hernandez uses nudity, sexual situations, and strong language in these stories.

  ★ **Maggie** the mechanic: a love and rockets book. Fantagraphics Books 2007 276p. Illustration
Grades: 12 Adult   **741.5; Fic**
  1. Graphic novels
  978-1-56097-784-1, $14.95
This is the first of three volumes by Jaime Hernandez, collecting the adventures of the spunky Maggie, her annoying best friend and sometime lover Hopey, and their circle of friends, including their bombshell friend Penny Century, Maggie's weirdo mentor Izzy-as well as the wrestler Rena Titanon and Maggie's handsome love interest, Rand Race. Maggie the Mechanic collects the earliest, punkiest, most heavily sci-fi stories of Maggie and her circle of friends. Hernandez uses some nudity, sexual situations, and some harsh language in these stories.

Hernandez, Lea
  Rumble Girls: Silky Warrior Tansie. NBM 2003 Un Illustration
Grades: 10 11 12 Adult   **741.5; Fic**
  1. Martial arts; 2. Science fiction graphic novels; 3. Graphic novels
  1-56163-370-4, $9.95
In a future world where media is run by suits (literally, they have no bodies) and everyone watches battles between warriors in battlesuits called hardskins, orphaned Raven Tansania Ransom trains to be a hardskin pilot at the girls' school academie Juliet. When a relationship gone sour causes Raven to sign with super media corporation Enteco to become a Rumble Girl, school rival Carmen signs on, too, for she wants to destroy Raven by any means possible. The book includes lots of fighting action and some sexual activity.

Hernandez worked with the Japanese anime/manga group known as Gainax and developed her manga-esque style from her experience there. Rumble Girls originally appeared in comics issues published by Image Comics and then online as webcomics.

Herriman, George
  ★ **Krazy** & Ignatz, 1937-1938: Shifting Sands Dusts its Cheeks in Powdered Beauty. Fantagraphics Books 2006 176p. Illustration
Grades: 7 8 9 10 11 12 Adult   **741.5; Fic**
  1. Humor graphic novels; 2. Krazy Kat (Fictional character); 3. Graphic novels
  978-1-56097-734-6, $19.95
Krazy Kat is a love story, focusing on the relationships of its three main characters. Krazy Kat adored Ignatz Mouse. Ignatz Mouse simply tolerated Krazy Kat, except for recurrent onsets of targeted tumescence, which found expression in the fast delivery of bricks to Krazy's cranium. Offisa Pup loved Krazy and sought to protect "her" (Herriman always maintained that Krazy was genderless) by throwing Ignatz in jail. Each of the characters was ignorant of the others' true motivations, and this simple structure allowed Herriman to build entire worlds of meaning into the actions, building thematic depth and sweeping his readers up by the looping verbal rhythms of Krazy & Co.'s unique dialogue. Most of these strips in this volume have not seen print since originally running in Hearst newspapers over 70 years ago. This seventh volume collecting all of the comic strips, is the second one to be published in color; Herriman started doing the strip in color in 1935. Other than the brick-throwing, this book has no violence, foul language, or any other usual objectionable content. Krazy Kat cartoons were made for children in the mid-1930s, and there was a Krazy Kat animated series which aired on television in the mid-1960s.

Heuvel, Eric

A **family** secret. [English translation, Lorraine T. Miller]. Farrar, Straus and Giroux 2009 62p. Illustration
Grades: 7 8 9 10 11 12   741.5; Fic
1. Grandmothers; 2. Holocaust, 1933-1945; 3. Jews; 4. Graphic novels
0-374-32271-6; 978-0-374-42265-3 (pa), $9.99; 0-374-42265-6 (pa); 978-0-374-32271-7, $18.99
LC 2009-13943

While searching his Dutch grandmother's attic for yard sale items, Jeroen finds a scrapbook which leads Gran to tell of her experiences as a girl living in Amsterdam during the Holocaust, when her father was a Nazi sympathizer and Esther, her Jewish best friend, disappeared

This is a "moving graphic novel. . . . The art is in ink and watercolor, with very clear, highly detailed panels. . . . [A] gripping story." Booklist

Original Dutch edition, 2003

Anne Frank House

Hickman, Jonathan

★ **East** of West; Volume 1: The Promise. Jonathan Hickman, writer; Nick Dragotta, artist; Frank Martin, colors; Rus Wooton, letters. Image Comics 2013 96 p. Color illustration (East of West)
Grades: 11 12 Adult   741.5
1. Death — Fiction; 2. Four Horsemen of the Apocalypse — Fiction; 3. Revenge
1607067706; 9781607067702, $9.99

This graphic novel by Jonathan Hickman is "set in a futuristic Old West and starring none other than the Four Horsemen of the Apocalypse. But there's trouble in the ranks, it seems, between Death and his cohort. What exactly that trouble is, and a swarming host of other tantalizing questions—like what happened between the Civil War and 2066, for instance—are teased out as Death tracks down those who have wronged him." (Booklist)

First published in single magazine format as East of West #1-5.

Volume 1 of an ongoing series

The **nightly** news. Image Comics 2007 184p.
Grades: 11 12 Adult   741.5
1. Crime; 2. Mass media; 3. Graphic novels
978-1-58240-766-1, $16.99

As an act of violence spirals out of control to encompass the entirety of the news media, a cult has emerged from the errors and retractions that have ruined careers, marriages and even lives. Under direction from his cult master The Voice, The Hand leads an army of followers committed to revolution, willing to die for their cause. Targeting journalists of all kinds, they launch a campaign of terror and violence that plays out in the media. The story includes considerable violence and foul language with page design that is very different from the usual comics panels.

Hickman, Troy

Common Grounds: Baker's dozen. Image Comics/Top Cow Productions 2004 144p. Illustration
Grades: 9 10 11 12 Adult   741.5; Fic
1. Superhero graphic novels; 2. Graphic novels
978-1-58240-841-5, $14.99

Superheroes and supervillains need a place where they can relax, unwind, and not worry about the next battle. Common Grounds is just such a place—a chain of coffee shops with bakery counters, totally neutral ground. Here, hero and villain can relax and take a break in the restroom ("Head Games"), a teenage superhero who doubts herself and an older superpowered religious Jew can encourage each other ("'Sanctuary"), a group of overweight heroes can meet ("Fat Chance"), or formerly evil monsters can get custom takeout and shoot the breeze ("Where Monsters Dine"). The book includes a baker's dozen (thirteen) stories.

Hicks, Faith Erin

Friends with boys. Faith Erin Hicks. First Second 2012 Un Illustration
Grades: 6 7 8 9 10   741.5
1. Ghost stories; 2. Teenagers — Fiction; 3. Graphic novels
9781596435568, $16.99
LC 2011030470

In this graphic novel, "[the] youngest of four siblings and the only girl, Maggie is both excited and worried about starting high school after being home-schooled her whole life. . . . As Maggie makes friends with a perky indie girl named Lucy and her mysterious brother, Alistair, she broods over the loss of her mother, who recently left the family without much of an explanation, and tries to figure out what the ghost wants from her." (Bulletin of the Center for Children's Books)

★ The **Nameless** City. Faith Erin Hicks; color by Jordie Bellaire. First Second 2016 240 p. Color; Illustration
Grades: 5 6 7 8 9 10   741.5; Fic
1. Cities and towns — Fiction; 2. Fantasy graphic novels; 3. Friendship — Fiction; 4. Survival — Fiction; 5. Survival skills — Fiction
1626721564; 9781626721562, $14.99; 9781626721579
LC 2015020651

"Every nation that invades the City gives it a new name. . . . The natives don't let themselves get caught up in the unending wars. To them, their home is the Nameless City. . . . Kaidu is . . . a Dao born and bred—a member of the latest occupying nation. Rat is a native of the Nameless City. At first, she hates Kai for everything he stands for, but his love of his new home may be the one thing that can bring these two unlikely friends together." (Publisher's note)

"With comprehensive world building, well-rounded characters, and entertaining action, this expertly executed story will find a home with a wide variety of readers, all of whom will be eagerly awaiting the next installment." Booklist

★ The **war** at Ellsmere. Slave Labor Graphics 2008 156p. Illustration
Grades: 6 7 8 9 10 11   741.5; Fic
1. Friendship; 2. Humorous graphic novels; 3. School stories; 4. Graphic novels
1-59362-140-X; 978-1-59362-140-7, $12.95

Juniper is the newest scholarship student at the prestigious Ellsmere Academy; she wanted to attend there in order to increase her chances of getting into a good medical school. She's on scholarship because her mom has had to raise her alone since her father died when she was young.

Jun makes one friend at Ellsmere, Cassie, who calls herself the cliche of the poor little rich girl. Wealthy Emily calls Cassie "Orphan" because her parents ignore her, and chooses to call Jun "Project," as in Headmistress Ms. Bishop's latest project. Emily is also determined to get rid of Jun, especially when Jun encourages Cassie to work harder and even win the extra credit essay contest. Now it's war, or as Jun puts it, "It's like Upstairs Downstairs meets Lord of the Flies. In plaid skirts. And sweater vests." There's one incident when Jun punches Emily in the face.

"Hicks gives readers enough tension and quirky turns to satisfy and pleasantly surprise." Booklist

Zombies calling. SLG Publishing 2007 104p. Illustration
Grades: 8 9 10 11 12 Adult   **741.5; Fic**
1. Horror graphic novels; 2. Humorous graphic novels; 3. Zombies; 4. Graphic novels
978-1-59362-079-0, $9.95

Anglophile/zombie movie fan/college student Joss is going crazy in the middle of exams week, but when her college campus is overrun with actual zombies, she knows what to do. With her roommate Sonnet and their buddy Robyn, Joss uses the Rules gleaned from years of watching zombie movies to fight the undead hordes. When the first rule is that the ordinary person suddenly becomes a total ass-kicking cool fighter able to beat off zombies with no fighting lessons, yeah, it's cool. Except the zombies just keep coming and coming. . . . The book has some harsh language and lots of black and white zombie fighting action without gore.

Hidaka, Banri
I Hate You More than Anyone! Volume 1. DC Comics/CMX 2007 192p. Illustration
Grades: 7 8 9 10 11 12   **741.5; Fic**
1. Humorous graphic novels; 2. Romance graphic novels; 3. Shojo manga; 4. Graphic novels
978-1-4012-1310-7, $9.99

Kazuha Akiyoshi is the eldest of six children. She's very responsible and also irresistibly cute, but she is something of a tomboy who has never allowed her romantic side to show throught. Then she meets Mizushima, the first guy to treat her like a girl. He's Kazuha's first crush, but does Mizushima feel the same way about her" And then there's Sugimoto, an older guy who's determined to make himself an important part of her life, only he's the one she hates more than anyone.

Higashimura, Akiko
Princess Jellyfish 1. By Akiko Higashimura. Random House Inc 2016 400 p.
Grades: 10 11 12 Adult   **741.5**
1. Manga; 2. Tokyo (Japan) — Fiction; 3. Young women — Fiction
1632362287; 9781632362285, $19.99

In this book, by Akiko Higashimura, "Tsukimi Kurashita has a strange fascination with jellyfish. She's loved them from a young age and has carried that love with her to her new life in the big city of Tokyo. There, she resides in Amamizukan. . . . However, a chance meeting at a pet shop has Tsukimi crossing paths with one of the things that the residents of Amamizukan have been desperately trying to

avoidùa beautiful and fashionable woman!" (Publisher's note)
Volume 1 of an ongoing series

Higashiyama, Kazuko
Tactics Vol. 1. Tokyopop 2007 Un Illustration
Grades: 7 8 9 10 11 12   **741.5; Fic**
1. Fantasy graphic novels; 2. Manga; 3. Supernatural graphic novels; 4. Graphic novels
978-1-59816-960-7, $9.99

Ever since Kantarou was a child, he has been able to see and talk to various spirits. But now that Kantarou's all grown up and a folklore scholar living in the Taisho period (1912-1926), he moonlights as an exorcist solving the problems of ghosts and demons...all with the help of Haruka, the legendary demon-eating tengu. Throw in some supernatural elements, a bit of Japanese mythology, and plenty of pretty boys... There's some harsh language, but very little violence. This first volume includes language and culture notes.

The first two volumes of this series were originally published by ADV Manga in 2004-2005.

Higgins, Dustin
★ **Pinocchio**, vampire slayer. Written by Van Jensen; created and drawn by Dusty Higgins. SLG Publishing 2009 Un Illustration
Grades: 9 10 11 12 Adult   **741.5; Fic**
1. Horror graphic novels; 2. Pinocchio (Fictional character); 3. Vampires; 4. Graphic novels
978-1-59362-176-6, $10.99; 1-59362-176-0
LC 2010-278899

After a brief recap of Collodi's novel, this graphic novel takes place a few years later. Pinocchio, still a wooden puppet, now finds he has a use for lying and growing his nose—he breaks off the growth and uses it as a wooden stake to destroy vampires. The blood suckers have come to the town of Nasolungo, they killed his creator/father Geppetto, and now Pinocchio roams the streets at night, seeking vengeance upon the vampires. The book includes violence but only mild language (Pinocchio says "crap" a few times). Along with the violence, the book includes a lot of sardonic humor.

"Heavy shadows and thick lines dominate the panels and provide a midnight-black atmosphere for all the gory mayhem, but it's the humor that makes this so memorable... . There's also surprising heart at the story's center that plays with the core theme of fatherhood. There won't be many teen (or adult) graphic-novel readers who won't want this book for its concept alone, and the execution doesn't disappoint." Booklist

Other titles in this series are:Pinocchio, vampire slayer and the great puppet theater (2010); Pinocchio, vampire slayer: of wood and blood, part one (2012); Pinocchio, vampire slayer: of wood and blood, part two (2012)

Higuri, You
Cantarella, Vol. 1. Go! Comi 2005 200p. Illustration
Grades: 10 11 12   **741.5; Fic**
1. Borgia, Cesare, 1476?-1507; 2. Heads of state; 3. Manga; 4. Statesmen; 5. Graphic novels
978-0-9768957-0-1, $10.99

This is a fictional account of the life of Cesare Borgia, full of supernatural elements and hints of shonen-ai (Boys' Love) romance. In Higuri's story, Cesare's father, Cardinal Rodrigo, made a deal with Hell at Cesare's birth, and the boy has grown up with darkness within him. It is a brutal time, and there is considerable violence—both fighting and sexual.

"Cantarella offers a convoluted plot, a doomed young hero, the deep love of true friendship, family rivalries, and a struggle for the very soul of late fifteenth-century Italy." Voice Youth Advocates

Crown, vol. 2. You Higuri and Shinji Wada. Go! Media Entertainment, Inc. 2009 Un Illustration
Grades: 10 11 12 Adult   **741.5; Fic**
1. Adventure graphic novels; 2. Manga; 3. Mystery graphic novels; 4. Graphic novels
978-1-60510-006-7, $10.99

Mahiro was just an ordinary Japanese high school girl, until she learned she is a princess and heir to the throne of Regalia. Her brother Ren and his best friend Jake have become her bodyguards, for the woman who now rules Regalia will stop at nothing to keep her throne. In this volume, they first encounter the assassin named Condor, who they end up welcoming as a partner in guarding Mahiro as she tries to continue as usual in school. Then they must deal with the master assassin named Lady Angela, whom they find out is actually a man. He's been sent to kill Ren and Jake, but he decides to find out just why Mahiro needs such protection. This volume includes some violence (assassinations and murder), and some provocative art, as Angela dresses to seduce and then takes Mahiro shopping for lingerie. There are also a few hints of boy love, just hints, nothing shown.

Gorgeous Carat Vol.1. Tokyopop/BLU 2006 196p. Illustration
Grades: 10 11 12 Adult   **741.5; Fic**
1. Adventure graphic novels; 2. Romance graphic novels; 3. Shonen-ai manga; 4. Graphic novels
1-59816-102-4, $9.99

In turn-of-the- 20th-century Paris, ball gowns swirl, champagne corks pop, and precious jewels sparkle all around the city—and in the amethyst eyes of one particular young man... Florian is the only son of an impoverished noble family. When his family's 120-carat Flame of Mughal goes missing, Florian teams up with the stunning, mysterious Ray Balzac Courland to track down the dazzling gem. The trail of clues leads the duo to an abandoned castle—and a deadly secret. This boys' love action-romance follows the swashbuckling adventures of Ray and Florian as they battle crime lords, backstabbing family members, and a possible attraction to each other. The book includes some strong language, some sexual suggestiveness, and some violence.

Hiiragi, Aoi
Baron: The Cat Returns. Viz/Studio Ghibli Library 2005 222p. Illustration
Grades: 3 4 5 6 7 8 9   **741.5; Fic**
1. Cats; 2. Fantasy graphic novels; 3. Kodomo manga; 4. Manga; 5. Graphic novels
1-59116-956-9, $9.99

Awkward teen Haru saves a cat from being run over one afternoon, but she never expected the trouble it would cause. He is a cat prince, and his father wants to bring Haru into the kingdom of the cats to be his son's bride. A mysterious voice sends Haru to the Cat Office, where she meets Baron, a toy cat come to life, the fat cat Muta, and a magical crow. When the cats come and bear Haru to the kingdom of the cats, the three friends follow to help bring Haru back home.

This one-volume manga was the basis for the feature-length manga (Japanese animated film) called "The Cat Returns," which was produced by Studio Ghibli, the animation studio run by famed anime director Hayao Miyazaki and some partners.

Hill, Joe
★ **Locke** & key: welcome to Lovecraft. Written by Joe Hill; art by Gabriel Rodriguez. IDW Publishing 2008 158p. Illustration
Grades: 10 11 12 Adult   **741.5; Fic**
1. Horror graphic novels; 2. Mystery graphic novels; 3. Graphic novels
978-1-60010-237-0, $24.99; 978-1-60010-384-1 (pa), $19.99

After Rendell Locke is murdered by a former student, Sam Lesser, who then tried to find and kill the rest of the family, Nina Locke takes her children, Tyler, Kinsey, and Bode to Lovecraft, Massachusetts, to live with Rendell's brother Duncan in Keyhouse. Tyler needs to deal with the guilt he feels because of a conversation with Sam Lesser, in which he said Sam should kill his dad. Kinsey had taken Bode and hidden from Sam, keeping them both safe, but she feels as though she'll never be safe again. Bode finds a door at Keyhouse, and when he goes through it, he dies and his ghost wanders around. There's definitely something weird at Keyhouse, and something is living at the bottom of the well in the well house—something that uses both Bode and Sam Lesser—and wants revenge. The book includes bloody violence. Joe Hill is the son of Stephen King.

"This first of . . . several volumes delivers on all counts, boasting a solid story bolstered by exceptional work from Chilean artist Rodriguez . . . that resembles a fusion of Rick Geary and Cully Hamner with just a dash of Frank Quitely." Publ Wkly

Other titles in this series are: Vol 2: Head Games (2009); Vol 3: Crown of Shadows (2010); Vol 4: Keys to the Kingdom (2011); Vol 5: Clockworks (2012); Vol 6: Alpha & Omega (2014)

Himekawa, Akira
The **legend** of Zelda: the Ocarina of time, part 2. Viz Media/Viz Kids 2008 192p. Illustration
Grades: 4 5 6 7 8 9   **741.5; Fic**
1. Adventure graphic novels; 2. Fantasy graphic novels; 3. Manga; 4. Graphic novels
978-1-4215-2328-6, $7.99

After completing his training, Link begins his journey to find the remaining Sages. Meanwhile, Ganondorf continues to search for Princess Zelda and to plot the capture of Link with the aid of the witches. Twinrova. The mysterious Sheik urges Link to enter the Haunted Wasteland to find Zelda, but even as he must fight the Gerudo warriors and Twinrova, Link learns Sheik's secret "he" is actually

Zelda in disguise. But almost as soon as Link and Zelda reunite, Ganondorf captures Zelda, and Link must save her. Then, the book goes back in time to when Link was a young boy, and his friend Saria wanders into the woods; now he must find her before she becomes a "skull kid." The book includes fighting scenes and action. This manga is based on the Nintendo 64 game, The Legend of Zelda: The Ocarina of Time.

Himuro, Isao
Edu-Manga: Albert Einstein. Art by Kotaro Iwasaki. Digital Manga Publishing 2006 144p. Illustration
Grades: 3 4 5 6 7 8 9   **92; 741.5**
  1. Biographical graphic novels; 2. Einstein, Albert, 1879-1955; 3. Manga; 4. Graphic novels
1-56970-975-0, $9.95
At the age of 26, Einstein published his groundbreaking Theory of Relativity, revolutionizing the world of physics forever. Today, he is considered a true genius. From his boyhood quest for answers to some of science's most challenging questions, to his search to uncover the mysteries of the universe, Einstein's work led to both the formulation of his theories and his place as one of the most important scientists in history. Astro Boy and his friends introduce Einstein's story and present the Q&A that provides more information. The book also includes a timeline of Einstein's life.

Hina
Di Gi Charat Theater: Leave It to Piyoko!. Broccoli International USA, Inc. 2004 206p. Illustration
Grades: 3 4 5 6 7 8 9   **741.5; Fic**
  1. Humorous graphic novels; 2. Manga; 3. Graphic novels
1-932480-17-X, $9.99
Piyoko has grand evil plans to kidnap the princess of Di Gi Charat, Dejiko, and hold her for ransom. The people of her poor Planet Analogue are all counting on her and the Black Gema Gema Gang. She and her loyal henchmen "Rik, Ky, and Coo" are scheming and plotting, but for some reason her grand plans seem to keep falling apart. Take a look into the daily lives of the Black Gema Gema Gang as they figure out their plans to kidnap Dejiko while trying to survive on the little money they have left.

Hinds, Gareth
  ★ **Beowulf**. Adapted and illustrated by Gareth Hinds. Candlewick Press 2007 Un Illustration
Grades: 8 9 10 11 12 Adult   **741.5; Fic**
  1. Adventure graphic novels; 2. Beowulf; 3. Monsters; 4. Graphic novels
978-0-7636-3022-5, $21.99; 0-7636-3022-5;
978-0-7636-3023-2 (pa); 0-7636-3023-3 (pa), $9.99
                     LC 2006-49023
Graphic novel adaptation of the Old English epic poem, Beowulf
"For fantasy fans both young and old, this makes an ideal introduction to a story without which the entire fantasy genre would look very different; many scenes may be too intense for very young readers." Publ Wkly

King Lear. A play by William Shakespeare; adapted and illustrated by Gareth Hinds. Candlewick Press 2009 123p. Illustration
Grades: 7 8 9 10 11 12   **741.5; 822.3**
  978-0-7636-4343-0, $22.99; 0-7636-4343-2;
  978-0-7636-4344-7 (pa), $11.99; 0-7636-4344-0 (pa)
"Employing a range of artistic styles that convey dramatic mood, the artist begins the play almost as a fairy tale, featuring bright, softly washed drawings. Once Cordelia is cast out and things sour, the images become darker and more compact. As the king descends into madness, the art becomes downright menacing, with Lear appearing as a jagged, ghostly figure drawn with white pencil on a dark background." (Kirkus)

Macbeth. Adapted and illustrated by Gareth Hinds. Candlewick Press 2015 152 p. Color illustration; Color; Map
Grades: 8 9 10 11 12   **741.5**
  1. Kings and rulers — Fiction; 2. Murder — Fiction; 3. Scotland — Fiction; 4. Graphic novels; 5. Shakespeare, William, 1564-1616 — Adaptations
0763678023; 9780763669430; 9780763678029, $12.99
                   LC 2014939338
"Set against the moody backdrop of eleventh-century Scotland, [illustrator] Gareth Hinds's . . . interpretation takes readers into the claustrophobic mind of a man driven mad by ambition. An evil seed takes root in the mind of Macbeth, a general in the king's army, when three witches tell him he will one day be king." (Publisher's note)
"Though many lines of the original are intact, Hinds does undertake some changes to make this version more accessible to contemporary readers, and a closing note addresses those alterations. Students struggling to find an entry point into the Scottish play should look no further than this entertaining and elucidating volume." Booklist

The **merchant** of Venice: a play. By William Shakespeare; adapted and illustrated by Gareth Hinds. Candlewick Press 2008 68p. Illustration
Grades: 8 9 10 11 12 Adult   **822.3; 741.5**
  1. Shakespeare, William, 1564-1616 — Adaptations
  978-0-7636-3024-9, $21.99; 978-0-7636-3025-6 (pa), $11.99
                   LC 2007-938349
Hinds uses a sketchy art style and blue and gray tones to illustrate his graphic adaptation of Shakespeare's controversial play. He sets the play in modern Venice and uses more modern language, including prose, at the beginning of the play and then gradually returns to Shakespeare's original language for the courtroom scenes. The play tells the story of a debt owed to a Jewish merchant of Venice, of a strong-willed young woman who is determined to choose her own husband, and of the quest to save a young man from the fate of having a pound of flesh cut from him.
"Fans of the play will find this an intriguing adaptation." Publ Wkly

The **most** excellent and lamentable tragedy of Romeo & Juliet: a play by William Shakespeare. By William Shakespeare, adapted and illustrated by Gareth Hinds. Candlewick Press 2013 128 p.
Grades: 7 8 9 10   **741.5**

1. Shakespeare, William, 1564-1616 — Adaptations; 2. Shakespeare, William, 1564-1616 — Tragedies; 3. Graphic novels
0763659487; 0763668079; 9780763659486, $21.99; 9780763668075, $12.99

LC 2012950561

This book by Gareth Hinds presents a graphic novel adaptation of William Shakespeare's play "Romeo and Juliet." "The most notable change between this story and Shakespeare's original is the creative license that Hinds takes with ethnicity—he makes the characters of African, Indian, and Caucasian descent in order to promote the universality of the story. The Shakespearean language is abridged but not adapted into contemporary English." (School Library Journal)

"Cleaving to Shakespeare's words and dramatic arc, Hinds (The Merchant of Venice) creates another splendid graphic novel, tracing each scene in taut, coherent dialogue. The characters, in period dress modified by a few more contemporary touches, are poignantly specific yet universal. Hinds delivers the play's essence and beauty, its glorious language, furious conflict, yearning love, and wrenching tragedy." (Horn Book)

The **Odyssey:** a graphic novel. By Gareth Hinds. Candlewick Press 2010 248 p. Color illustration
Grades: 7 8 9 10 11 12 Adult **741.5**
1. Greek mythology; 2. Homer; 3. Mythology, Greek — Juvenile literature; 4. Odyssey; 5. Graphic novels
0763642665; 0763642681; 9780763642662, $24.99; 9780763642686

LC 2010007512

"Retells, in graphic novel format, Homer's epic tale of Odysseus, the ancient Greek hero who encounters witches and other obstacles on his journey home after fighting in the Trojan War." (Publisher's note)

Hino, Matsuri
Captive hearts, vol. 1. Viz Media/Shojo Beat 2008 200p. Illustration
Grades: 7 8 9 10 11 12 **741.5; Fic**
1. Manga; 2. Romance graphic novels; 3. Shojo manga; 4. Graphic novels
978-1-4215-1932-6, $8.99

Carefree college student Megumi Kuroishi finds his life turned upside down when the last surviving member of the Kogami family, teenage Suzuka, is found in China. That's when Megumi learns of the curse against his family, that they will serve the Kogami family for 100 generations. Whenever he looks into Suzuka's eyes, the curse overwhelms him and he becomes far too subservient; complicating matters is the fact that he does indeed find Suzuka captivating. She likes him, too, but can't trust his feelings because of the curse. The book includes two short romance stories. In "Real Storm," shy high school student Io Ayase has a huge crush on Kuji-sensei, who only wants to help her learn to deal with a pervy stalker. In "Let Time Freeze," Ayu and Yuji are childhood friends now in their senior year of high school, and she doesn't want the year to end; when it does, Yuji will go to university in Tokyo while Ayu must remain behind. Now that she loves him, the impending separation already hurts.

MeruPuri: Marchen Prince Vol. 1. Viz Media/Shojo Beat 2005 Un Illustration
Grades: 8 9 10 11 12 **741.5; Fic**
1. Fantasy graphic novels; 2. Manga; 3. Romance graphic novels; 4. Shojo manga; 5. Graphic novels
1-4215-0120-1, $8.99

All high-school freshman Airi Hoshina ever wanted was to someday live in a cozy home with a loving husband, and find joy in the little things in life. As a result, she makes it her daily mission to get to school on time because school legend has it that the longer one's non-tardy streak is, the better boyfriend one will find. But, on the way to school one morning, Airi drops her mirror, one that had been passed down to her through generations, and suddenly finds herself in a bizarre situation. Never in her wildest dreams did she expect to meet Aram, a little boy from a magical kingdom, to have emerged from the mirror in the short time it took her to track it down. The series includes some mild sexual situations.

Vampire Knight, Vol. 1. Viz Media/Shojo Beat 2007 Un Illustration
Grades: 10 11 12 **741.5; Fic**
1. Fantasy graphic novels; 2. Shojo manga; 3. Vampires; 4. Graphic novels
978-1-4215-0822-1, $8.99

Ten years ago, little Yuki was saved from a vampire attack that killed her family, and the headmaster of Cross Academy adopted her. Cross Academy has two groups of students: the normal human Day Class and the vampires of the Night Class. Yuki and Zero, a fellow Day Class student, work as guardians to keep the Academy's secret and ensure that there is only limited contact between the Classes. Vampires may not be evil, but their very appearance is extremely seductive, and Yuki and Zero have their hands full trying to maintain order. Trouble starts when some of the Night Class try to push the rules, and Zero's attitude towards them becomes even more hostile.

Hiramoto, Akira
Me and the devil blues: the unreal life of Robert Johnson vol. 1. Del Rey Manga 2008 540p. Illustration
Grades: 11 12 Adult **741.5; Fic**
1. Adventure graphic novels; 2. Blues music; 3. Blues musicians; 4. Guitarists; 5. Johnson, Robert, 1911-1938; 6. Manga; 7. Graphic novels
978-0-345-49926-4, $19.95

Robert Johnson was a legendary blues player who died very young. This manga takes his story and runs with it. In the Mississippi Delta in 1929, a young farmer named RJ desperately wants to be a bluesman, even though he can't play the guitar. One night he takes a midnight stroll and ends up at a crossroads where he meets up with someone who just might be the devil. After that night, RJ can play the blues, but he loses his former life and still has to suffer under Jim Crow laws. Then one day he meets young Clyde Barrow, who will become a different kind of legend (remember Bonnie and Clyde?) and they travel together. The American Deep South, the blues, and legendary criminals as reimagined through Japanese sensibilities and mores makes for a unique read. The book includes considerable foul language, violence, nudity, and sexual situations.

Hirano, Kohta
   Hellsing Volume 1. Dark Horse Comics 2003 208p. Illustration
Grades: 11 12 Adult   **741.5; Fic**
   1. Horror graphic novels; 2.Seinen manga; 3. Graphic novels
   1-59307-056-X, $13.95
   There's a secret organization somewhere in England created to defend the Queen and country from monsters of all sorts. Enter Hellsing, an agency, long in tooth, with the experience, know-how, and... special equipment to handle the problems that arise when vampires, ghouls, and the like take on these dark forces. The special "equipment" is another vampire, and a big pistol loaded with special silver bullets. This series focuses on the violence of destroying vampires who love to slaughter people. Some might be offended by the portrayal of the Roman Catholic Church as insanely fundamentalist and using inquisitors and brainwashed killer nuns. The series includes lots of graphic violence and harsh language.

Hitch, Bryan
   Bryan Hitch's Ultimate Comics Studio. Impact 2010 128p. Illustration
Grades: 7 8 9 10   **741.5; 741**
   1. Captain America (Fictional character); 2. Fantastic Four (Fictional characters)
   978-1-6006-1327-2, $24.99; 1-6006-1327-6

Hiwatari, Saki
   Tower of the Future, Vol. 1. DC Comics/CMX 2005 192p. Illustration
Grades: 8 9 10 11 12   **741.5; Fic**
   1. Fantasy graphic novels; 2. Romance graphic novels; 3. Shojo manga; 4. Graphic novels
   978-1-4012-0814-1, $9.99
   Takeru's mother has died, and then he finds out that his half-English father has a daughter in England; on her deathbed, Takeru's mother asked that Hyoju be allowed to move to Japan and live with them. Shocked and upset, Takeru's first reaction is anger and disgust. He then meets Ichigo, a girl his age upon whom he immediately has a crush, and a strange little boy named Zen who knows way too much about Takeru. As the series progresses, Takeru learns a little more about Zen and why he knows so much. Also, a fantasy element comes in as Takeru learns about a parasitic being called Noize, and Ichigo's adult older brother has an unhealthy fixation on her.

Hodgson, William Hope
   The **House** on the Borderland. Adapted by Simon Revelstroke and Richard Corben; art by Richard Corben. BiblioBazaar 2006 88p. Illustration
Grades: 10 11 12 Adult   **741.5; Fic**
   1. Horror graphic novels; 2. Graphic novels
   978-1-4264-3828-8, $11.99
   This book adapts Hodgson's horror novel. It sits astride two worlds, the bleak world of colorless normality, and the realms of cosmic horror where reason my yet have a last chance to conquer fear. To this ancient dwelling a challenger comes, to exorcise its shadowed curse, to plumb its pits of ultimate perversity and, perhaps, to prevent evil's emergence

into the present. This book includes strong language, violence, and brief nudity.

Hoena, B. A.
   Matthew Henson: Arctic Adventurer. Capstone Press 2005 32p. Illustration
Grades: 3 4 5 6 7 8 9   **741.5; 910; 92**
   1. African American explorers — Biography; 2. Biographical graphic novels; 3. Henson, Matthew Alexander, 1866-1955; 4. North Pole — Discover and exploration; 5. Graphic novels
   0-7368-4634-4, $25.26
                                        LC 2005005774
   In graphic novel format, this book tells the life story of African American explorer Matthew Henson and his expedition to the North Pole with Robert Peary. The book includes additional facts about Henson, a bibliography, and a list of books for further reading.
   Part of the Graphic Biographies series.

   Perseus and Medusa. By Blake A. Hoena; illustrated by Daniel Perez. Stone Arch Books 2009 72p. Illustration (Graphic revolve)
Grades: 4 5 6 7 8 9   **741.5; Fic**
   1. Greek mythology; 2. Monsters; 3. Graphic novels
   978-1-4342-1170-5 (lib bdg), $23.93; 1-4342-1170-3 (lib bdg); 978-1-4342-1394-5 (pa), $6.95; 1-4342-1386-2 (pa)
                                        LC 2008-32065
   Perseus is the son of Danae, daughter of the King of Argos, and of Zeus; due to a prophecy that Perseus would cause his death, the King puts his daughter and grandson into a wooden chest and has it cast out to sea. A fisherman rescues them, and Perseus grows up unaware of his royal lineage. King Polydectes wants Danae for himself and sends Perseus on what should be an impossible task that will kill him he wants Perseus to bring him the head of Medusa, whose gaze turns anyone into stone. Perseus enjoys the guidance and advice of gods and goddesses to accomplish his task
   This title has a "solid awareness of how to balance visual depiction and expository captions, evident right from the striking prologue. While the artwork is cartoony and the dialogue deliberately casual and modern, the style doesn't prevent the artist from providing heroic vistas, or the author from slipping in a couple of humorous moments, and the action is sufficiently thrilling." SLJ

Hogan, James P.
   The **Two** Faces of Tomorrow. Story by James P. Hogan; art and adaptation by Yukinobu Hoshino; translation, Frederik L. Schodt and Toren Smith; lettering and retouch, Tomoko Saito. Dark Horse Comics 2006 576p. Illustration
Grades: 9 10 11 12 Adult   **741.5**
   1. Computers; 2. Manga; 3. Science fiction graphic novels; 4. Graphic novels
   978-1-59307-563-7
   Midway through the 21st century, an integrated global computer network manages much of the world's affairs. A proposed major software upgrade - an artificial intelligence - will give the system an unprecedented degree of independent decision-making, but serious questions are

raised in regard to how much control can safely be given to a non-human intelligence. In order to more fully assess the system, a new space-station habitat - a world in miniature - is developed for deployment of the fully operational system, named Spartacus. This mini-world can then be "attacked" in a series of escalating tests to assess the system's responses and capabilities. If Spartacus gets out of hand, the system can be shut down and the station destroyed... unless Spartacus decides to take matters into its own hands and take the fight to Earth. This manga adaptation of Hogan's novel includes some harsh language and brief incidental nudity.

Hon, Creative
Last Fantasy Vol. 1. Story by Creative Hon; art by Yong-Wan Kwon. Tokyopop 2006 204p. Illustration
Grades: 9 10 11 12 Adult   741.5; Fic
1. Adventure graphic novels; 2. Fantasy graphic novels; 3. Humorous graphic novels; 4. Manwha; 5. Graphic novels
1-59532-526-3, $9.99
Tian and Drei von Richenstein, two unlikely heroes, embark on an adventure filled with excitement, intrigue, and a bit of comic relief. They have quite the talent for making allies into new enemies. Their (mis)adventure pits them against ferocious ogres, vengeful red dragons, an army of soldiers, and even an age-old rival. But leave it to Tian and Drei to make sure that this adventure isn't their final fantasy. In this parody of all things RPG (no, not "Really Powerful Guys"), no gaming franchise is safe in this comedy that's never dull—unlike our heroes' swords. The book contains strong language and fantasy monster-killing violence.

Hope, Jane
Introducing Buddha, New Ed.. Art by Borin Van Loon. Totem Books 2005 176p. Illustration
Grades: 10 11 12 Adult   294.3; 741.5
1. Buddhism; 2. Graphic novels
978-1-84046-633-1, $12.95
                                    LC 95-060973
This book uses cartoons and a spare text to describe the life and teachings of the Buddha. Author Jane Hope shows that enlightenment is a matter of experiencing the truth individually and by inspiration which is passed from teacher to student. The book explains the practices of meditation, Taoism and Zen. It goes on to describe the role of Buddhism in modern Asia and its growing influence on Western thought. The book includes a list of books for further reading.

Hopkins, David
Emily Edison. David Hopkins, illustrated by Brock Rizy. Viper Comics 2006 144p. Illustration
Grades: 7 8 9 10 11 12 Adult   741.5; Fic
1. Humorous graphic novels; 2. Science fiction graphic novels; 3. Graphic novels
0-9777883-2-6, $12.95
High schooler Emily has more than her share of problems; along with trying to keep up in school and survive such things as parties and boys, she has to deal with her parents' very mixed marriage. Her father is human, but her mother came from another dimension. Since their divorce, Emily has had to split her time between Earth and elsewhere; and now her grandfather wants her to live permanently in his

dimension, and he's prepared to destroy Earth to force her hand. What's a girl to do?

Hornschemeier, Paul
Let Us Be Perfectly Clear. Fantagraphics Books 2006 136p. Illustration
Grades: 11 12 Adult
741.5; Fic
1. Short stories; 2. Graphic novels
978-1-56097-752-0, $19.95

Courtesy of Fantagraphics

This is a collection of Paul Hornschemeier's full-color short stories from a variety of sources, none of which has been available to the book trade. The book is designed as a "flip book" in the tradition of the old Ace paperbacks, with one side featuring comedic work (or as comedic as Hornschemeier's mind allows), and the other decidedly more morose. On the "funny" menu, we are treated to Dr. Rodentia (an unfortunate-looking fellow with only apathy as his weapon), a detailed artist's catalogue exploring such modern masterpieces as "Accidental Late-Night Sex With a Radiator," musings on the cancerous nature of civilization as observed by a deceased cat and a cotton-based airbus, the scatological "Feelings Check," the ever pathetic Vanderbilt Millions and his fantasies of self-worth, and the multi-narrative story that started the Forlorn Funnies comics series: "The Men and Women of the Television." On the "forlorn" plate is the cold examination of the dyslexic narcoleptic and his bungled plans of murder, a sea creature's balancing of morality and sustenance, the Western romance "Wanted," a metal man's self-destructive search for meaning, and the story of two men meeting; it may disgust readers, without a single visually objectionable panel. The other stories do include strong language and some violence.

Mother, come home. With an introduction by Thomas Tennant. Fantagraphics 2004 128p. Illustration
Grades: 11 12 Adult   741.5; Fic
1. Mental illness; 2. Graphic novels
978-1-56097-973-9 (pa)
In this "story, a young child struggles with the death of his mother and his father's collapse. Clean-lined artwork leaves plenty of room for strong emotional content linked to themes of euthanasia, suicide, and depression." Booklist

Hoshino, Katsura
D.Gray-Man Volume 1. Viz Media/Shonen Jump Advanced 2006 192p. Illustration
Grades: 10 11 12 Adult   741.5; Fic
1. Adventure graphic novels; 2. Fantasy graphic novels; 3. Manga; 4. Supernatural graphic novels; 5. Graphic novels
978-1-4215-0623-4, $7.99
Set in a fictional end of the 19th century England, the story revolves around a teenage boy named Allen Walker who is cursed with a cross mark on his hand that turns his arm into an enormous weapon, which he uses to hunt down

and kill akumas. An akuma, generated by The Millenium Earl, a 1,000-year-old phantom, is implanted into a human's soul during a moment of devastation and despair. The phantom uses the demons to then carry out his goal: destroy all humankind. Allen, a 15-year-old boy, roams the Earth in search of Innocence. Washed away to unknown parts of the world after The Great Flood, Innocence is the mysterious substance used to create weapons that obliterate the akumas. The action is over-the-top in style, with lots of demon-fighting action.

Hoshino, Ryo
The **third** vol. 2. Story by Ryo Hoshino; art by Ariko Ito. Tokyopop 2008 Un Illustration
Grades: 10 11 12 Adult   **741.5; Fic**
1. Adventure graphic novels; 2. Manga; 3. Science fiction graphic novels; 4. Graphic novels
978-1-4278-0713-7, $9.99
On a world covered with sand, Honoka is a Dune Runner trainee. She has a third eye, but hers is blue, compared to the red third eye that marks the power holders on her world. As she takes on more assignments, she encounters dangers such as a deadly soldier virus, as well as Lidell, the Senior Dune Runner she has viewed as a role model. Honoka suffers doubts because she makes mistakes, but she's determined to continue on her path to becoming a strong Dune Runner, and her AI partner, Bogie, will help her. The book includes some violence.

Hosler, Jay
Clan Apis. Active Synapse 2000 158p. Illustration
Grades: 4 5 6 7 8 9 10 11 12   **741.5; Fic**
1. Bees; 2. Science; 3. Graphic novels
0-9677255-0-X, $15
"Opening with a creation myth . . . and working through the biological, sociological, and ecological changes affecting the life of Nyuki the bee, the text is a combination of authoritative science; appealing, detailed black-and-white drawings; and dialogue replete with humor, pubescent angst, political sloganeering, and more. Nyuki's colony undertakes migration to a new hive, is beset by a woodpecker, and hibernates through a winter that yields to a revitalizing spring." Booklist

★ **Evolution:** the story of life on Earth. Written by Jay Hosler; art by Zander Cannon and Kevin Cannon. Hill and Wang 2011 150p. Illustration
Grades: 9 10 11 12 Adult   **741.5; 576.8**
1. Evolution; 2. Evolution (Biology); 3. Graphic novels
0809094762; 9780809094769
LC 2010-05777
Alien scientist Bloort-183 takes King Floorsh-727 and Prince Floorsh-418 on a tour of Earth's history, explaining the theory of evolution. These are the same aliens who explored human genetics in The Stuff of Life. The illustrations by Kevin Cannon and Zander Cannon (no relation to each other) help human readers see how the theory of evolution explains the beginnings of life on Earth, the four conditions needed for natural selection, the Cambrian explosion, the Permian extinction, sexual selection, the evolution of modern humans, and the Earth scientists who studied the life forms and made the scientific

discoveries. The book includes an illustrated glossary, a list of further reading, and endpapers filled with all kinds of dinosaurs.
"This delightful book seems ideal for nonscientists who want to entertainingly brush up their knowledge of evolution as well as for students from middle school on up." Booklist

★ The **last** of the sandwalkers. Written and illustrated by Jay Hosler. First Second 2015 312 p. Illustration
Grades: 5 6 7 8 9 10   **741.5; Fic**
1. Adventure fiction; 2. Beetles — Fiction; 3. Science fiction; 4. Scientific expeditions — Fiction; 5. Graphic novels
162672024X; 9781626720244, $16.99
LC 2014045542
This book, by Jay Hosler, is about a "civilization of beetles. In this bug's paradise, beetles write books, run restaurants, and even do scientific research. But not too much scientific research is allowed by the powerful elders, who guard a terrible secret about the world outside. . . . Lucy is not one to quietly cooperate, however. This tiny field scientist defies the law of her safe but authoritarian home and leads a team of researchers out into the desert." (Publisher's note)
"Hosler's cartooning is no less meticulous than his writing and similarly retains a sense of animated energy and humor, engaging readers with characters that are far from human, but filled with humanity." Booklist
Includes bibliographical references

The **Sandwalk** Adventures: An Adventure in Evolution Told in Five Chapters. Active Synapse 2003 160p. Illustration
Grades: 4 5 6 7 8 9 10 11 12 Adult   **576.8; 741.5**
1. Darwin, Charles; 2. Evolution; 3. Science; 4. Graphic novels
0-9677255-1-8, $20
Scientist Hosler explains Darwin's theory of evolution in a whimsical fashion. Follicle mites Mara and Willy live in Darwin's left eyebrow, and by accident they discover that Darwin, whom they call the god Flycatcher, can hear Mara. He thinks he's going crazy, but as he takes his daily walks on the Sandwalk at his home in England, Darwin does his best to convince Mara and Willy that he isn't a god and tells them about evolution. Hosler uses humor and whimsy, but also did a lot of research; the book includes explanatory notes and a long bibliography of sources.

Hosoda, Mamoru
Wolf children Ame & Yuki. Original story: Mamoru Hosoda; art: Yu; character design: Yoshiyuki Sadamoto; translation: Jocelyne Allen; lettering: Tania Biswas, Lys Blakeslee. Yen Press 2014 538 p. Color; Illustration
Grades: 10 11 12 Adult   **741.5**
1. Werewolves — Fiction; 2. Widows — Fiction
031640165X; 9780316401654, $26
"When Hana falls in love with a young interloper she encounters in her college class, the last thing she expects to learn is that he is part wolf. Instead of rejecting her lover upon learning his secret, she accepts him with open arms. . . . But after what seems like a mere moment of bliss to Hana, the father of her children is tragically taken from her." (Publisher's note)

"This emotion-laden work focuses on family and community issues. . . . The soft color palette of these watercolors complements the tender emotion of the plot." Lib Med Con

Hotta, Yumi

★ **Hikaru** No Go, Volume 1. [by] Yumi Hotta and Takeshi Obata. Viz Media, LLC 2004 192p. Illustration
Grades: 5 6 7 8 9 10 11 12   741.5; Fic
1. Board games; 2. Manga; 3. Shonen manga; 4. Graphic novels
1-59116-222-X, $7.95
Sixth-grader Hikaru Shindo is not interested in intellectual pursuits, but by a twist of fate, the spirit of Fujiwara no Sai, the ghost of an ancient Go master, manages to bond with Hikaru. Now, suddenly, Hikaru can play Go, a complex board game of strategy, better than almost anyone under 18 and most adults, too. Akira, who has been raised by his Go master father, needs to know more about the upstart Hikaru, who beats him and yet seems so casual about the game. This is the first volume of an ongoing series.
Volume 1 of a 23 volume series

Howard, Josh

Dead @17: compendium edition. Viper Comics 2008 336p. Illustration
Grades: 10 11 12 Adult   741.5; Fic
1. Adventure graphic novels; 2. Horror graphic novels; 3. Graphic novels
978-0-9793680-3, $24.95
Seventeen-year-old Nara Kilday's murder is the start of a new battle between good and evil. Her best friend Hazy investigates Nara's death and uncovers a dark side that he hadn't known. Meanwhile, an evil has raised an army of the undead, intending to reshape the world in its image. Among the undead is Nara, however, and she may just be the only thing standing in the way of Armageddon. Well, Nara, Hazy and Noel, that is. This book collects the original trilogy; Howard has revised and expanded it, and this book also includes cover and pinup galleries as well as a section of fan-produced arts and photographs. The book includes nudity and bloody violence.

Dead@17: The Complete First Series, Special Edition. Viper Comics 2006 Un Illustration
Grades: 10 11 12   741.5; Fic
1. Horror graphic novels; 2. Mystery graphic novels; 3. Graphic novels
0-9754193-6-6, $14.95
Seventeen-year-old Nara has a pretty good life, but it ends suddenly when she's stabbed to death. An investigator gives best friend Hazy Nara's diary, and she finds it filled with weird, arcane symbols and writing. Then zombies rise up all over town and some attack Hazy; she's saved by - Nara. It turns out Nara is one of the Resurrected," and the person who has raised the zombies wants Nara for his own evil purposes. The book includes bloody violence and some strong language.

Dead@17: Revolution. Viper Comics 2005 Un Illustration
Grades: 10 11 12 Adult   741.5; Fic

1. Horror graphic novels; 2. Mystery graphic novels; 3. Graphic novels
0-9754193-3-1, $14.95
A political assassination plot by a mysterious group called Heaven's Militia unravels a government conspiracy with ties to Nara's past and future. She's forced to make a choice that could expose her secret to the world and puts her at odds with Noel Raddemer, her one ally. But somehow she has to stop the demon Bolabogg from achieving his goal, or the world will not survive. The book includes violence, strong language, and nudity.

Josh Howard Presents Sasquatch. Viper Comics 2007 254p. Illustration
Grades: 10 11 12 Adult   741.5; Fic
1. Fantasy graphic novels; 2. Sasquatch; 3. Graphic novels
978-0-9777883-8-5, $24.95
This anthology includes twenty stories that feature the creature variously known as Big Foot, Yeti, and Sasquatch. The stories range from gruesomely bloody ("Sawmill Horror") to silly ("Smallfoot") to ironically sweet ("Heart Mountain, WY: 1942") to fun ("The Sitter") to suitable-for-Saturday-morning-cartoons ("Sasquatch and Timmy"). Creators for the stories include Courtney Huddleston, David Hartman, Bryan Baugh, Otis Frampton, Tone Rodriguez, and Scott Zirkel.

Hudlin, Reginald

Black Panther: Civil War. Pencilers: Scot Eaton & Manuel Garcia, Koi Turnbull & Marcus To. Marvel Entertainment 2007 Un Illustration
Grades: 9 10 11 12 Adult   741.5; Fic
1. Black Panther (Fictional character); 2. Superhero graphic novels; 3. Graphic novels
978-0-7851-2235-7, $17.99
King T'Challa and Queen Ororo, Black Panther and Storm, embark on a diplomatic tour that will have them spanning the globe and beyond. Stops include Latveria (Dr. Doom), the Moon (Black Bolt and the Inhumans), Atlantis (Namor the Sub-Mariner) and the Civil War-ravaged United States, for a meeting with none other than the point man for the U.S. government's implementation of the Superhuman Registration Act: Tony Stark, T'Challa's former Avengers teammate. Will the Black Panther and Storm decide to step off the sidelines of the Civil War and get involved?

Black Panther: The Bride. Art by Scott Eaton. Marvel Entertainment 2006 Un Illustration
Grades: 9 10 11 12 Adult   741.5; Fic
1. Black Panther (Fictional character); 2. Superhero graphic novels; 3. Graphic novels
978-0-7851-2107-7, $14.99
Every king needs a queen, and the Black Panther, who is also the King of Wakanda, sets out on an epic quest to find a wife. His heart is Storm's if she'll accept his hand in marriage. The question is, does she want it? With a super hero civil war ready to explode in the U.S., and snakes in the Wakanda court preparing to make their moves, the road to the altar could not be more complicated.

Hughes, Susan

No girls allowed: tales of daring women dressed as men for love, freedom and adventure. Written by Susan Hughes;

llustrated by Willow Dawson. Kids Can Press 2008 80p. Illustration
Grades: 3 4 5 6 7 8 9   **306.7; 741.5**
1. Biographical graphic novels; 2. Transvestites; 3. Graphic novels
978-1-55453-177-6, $16.95; 978-1-55453-178-3 (pa), $9.95

LC 2007-9060846

This book collects short biographies in graphic format of young women who dressed as and pretended to be men in order to do and be what they wanted. The real Mu Lan did pretend to be her father's son in order to serve in the Chinese Emperor's army to protect her father. Hatshepsut was an Egyptian princess who was determined to be pharaoh, although that role could only go to men. Margaret Buckley was a young Englishwoman who became Dr. James Barry in the early nineteenth century. Seven women's stories are told here, and the book includes a short list of books for further reading.

Hugo, Victor
The **Hunchback** of Notre Dame by Victor Hugo ; retold by L.L. Owens ; illustrated by Greg Rebis Stone Arch Books 2006 63p. Illustration
Grades: 3 4 5 6 7 8 9   **741.5; Fic**
1. Adventure graphic novels; 2. Hugo, Victor, 1802-1885 — Adaptations; 3. Graphic novels
978-1-59889-047-1, $23.93

Hidden away in the bell tower of the Cathedral of Notre Dame, Quasimodo is treated like a beast. Although he is gentle and kind, he has the reputation of a frightening monster because of his physical deformities. He develops affection for Esmeralda, a gypsy girl who shows him kindness in return. When the girl is sentenced to an unfair death by hanging, Quasimodo is determined to save her. But those closest to Quasimodo have other plans for the gypsy. This adaptation is written for reluctant and struggling readers, and the tragic story is handled with sensitivity.
Part of the Graphic Revolve series.

Huizenga, Kevin
★ **Curses**. Drawn & Quarterly 2006 145p. Illustration
Grades: 11 12 Adult   **741.5; Fic**
1. Graphic novels
978-1-894937-86-3, $21.95

Huizenga's central character in his comics is Glenn Ganges, a seemingly middle-class man living in the suburbs whose blank-eyed wonderment at everyday experiences brings together such diverse aspects of the world as golf, theology, late-night diners, parenthood, politics, Sudanese refugees, and hallucinatory vision, into a complete experience as multifaceted as our own lives. There is some use of strong language.

Hunter, Erin
Warriors: Tigerstar & Sasha #1: into the woods. Created by Erin Hunter; written by Dan Jolley; art by Don Hudson. HarperCollins/Tokyopop 2008 108p. Illustration
Grades: 3 4 5 6 7 8 9   **741.5; Fic**
1. Adventure graphic novels; 2. Cats; 3. Graphic novels
978-0-06-154792-8, $6.99; 0-06-154792-1

Sasha was a loved, pampered kittypet, but when one of the housefolk dies and the other moves away, they leave her behind. She had always explored the woods at night, but now she has to survive on her own. Then she meets Tigerstar, leader of ShadowClan, and they spend a lot of time together as he teaches her how to improve her hunting. He even offers her membership in the clan, but he has secrets, and when Sasha discovers one of them, she has to decide if she can trust him. There are scenes of cats hunting prey such as mice and squirrels, and fighting with foxes.
Other titles in this series are:Escape from the forest (2008); Return to the clans (2009)

Hurd, Damon
Pictures of you. Art by Tatiana Gill. Alternative Comics 2007 96p.
Grades: 10 11 12 Adult   **741.5**
1. Friendship; 2. Graphic novels
978-1-934460-00-9, $11.95

One year before their chance encounter (recounted in A Strange Day), Miles and Anna live parallel lives only a few miles apart. Miles is both jealous and overprotective when Sarah, his best friend since junior high, starts spending more time with her new musician boyfriend Kyle. Anna's family is ending in divorce, and her only solace is with the boy next door, Ethan. He's a college bound musician who is growing apart from his younger sidekick, not returning Anna's romantic feelings for him. Lyrics from songs by The Cure accompany the story as Miles becomes the kind of friend Sarah needs and Anna tries to find her own path. The creators say this is the second volume of a trilogy, but it can be read on its own. There's a brief instance of partial nudity and some foul language.

Hutchison, David
Biowulf Volume 1. Antarctic Press 2007 Un Illustration
Grades: 10 11 12 Adult   **741.5; Fic**
1. Adventure graphic novels; 2. Beowulf — Adaptations; 3. Horror graphic novels; 4. Science fiction graphic novels; 5. Graphic novels
978-0-9787725-2-9, $14.95

In the staggering wreckage of Earth's future, the great King Hrothgar and his armies have known only victory after bloody victory. Now, on the brink of uniting the battling lands and bringing the long wars to an end, Hrothgar's rule is threatened. His actions have awakened the ancient evil of the Grendel, and his men are powerless to defend themselves against the demon's wrath. Only with the aid of the young hero Beowulf and a cunning trap can they hope to kill Grendel and finally know peace. In this cyberpunk adaptation, Beowulf is an Advance, a genetically engineered, cybernetically enhanced human warrior; and Grendel is a monster, but he's not the real villain. The book includes a lot of graphic, bloody violence.

Oz: The Manga. Antarctic Press 2006 Un Illustration
Grades: 4 5 6 7 8 9   **741.5; Fic**
1. Baum, L Frank — Adaptations; 2. Fantasy graphic novels; 4. Graphic novels
978-1-932453-69-0, $14.95

This is Baum's classic novel, The Wizard of Oz, adapted into manga format by Hutchison. All the characters are here:

Dorothy, Toto, the Cowardly Lion, the Tin Woodsman, the Scarecrow, the Wizard. And all the main plot elements are here, from the cyclone that blows Dorothy and Toto to Oz to the Flying Monkeys to dealing with the Wicked Witch. The art makes this adaptation shine, especially the Tin Woodsman, who is a steampunk wonder.

Hyde, Laurence
Southern Cross. Drawn & Quarterly 2007 256p. Illustration
Grades: 10 11 12 Adult　　　　　　　　　**741.5**
1. Atomic bomb — Testing; 2. Stories without words; 3. Graphic novels
978-1-897299-10-4, $24.95

This is a wordless novel, told in 118 wood engravings, about the atomic bomb testing performed by the United States in the South Pacific following World War II. This new hardcover edition is a facsimile of the original edition, published in 1951. Laurence Hyde was infuriated with the United States' continued testing in the Bikini Atoll, following the mass destruction and unthinkable horrors resulting from the atomic bombs dropped on Hiroshima and Nagasaki in August 1945. The story depicts the evacuation of the Polynesian islanders from their homes; during the evacuation, a fisherman kills a sailor who attempts to rape his wife. The couple flees with their child into the jungle to avoid capture. After the other islanders have evacuated, the Americans detonate an atom bomb on the ocean floor, and the fisherman and his family suffer horribly from the effects. The book includes nudity and depiction of the attempted rape.

Hyun, Kang-Suk
Heaven Above Heaven Volume 1. Art by Jeon Joong-Won. Tokyopop 2005 168p. Illustration
Grades: 10 11 12 Adult　　　　　　　　**741.5; Fic**
1. Adventure graphic novels; 2. Fantasy graphic novels; 3. Manhwa; 4. Graphic novels
1-59532-288-4, $9.99

Ancient prophecy foretold of a baby that would be the catalyst for the Apocalypse. At the anointed time, nine Grand Masters of Martial Arts raced to a remote mountaintop to prevent the terrible prophecy from being fulfilled. Seventeen years later, a young boy with a knack for trouble, a lust for ladies, and a wicked fighting technique has crossed paths with the child of the Apocalypse—and he's in for more kung fu action than he can handle. The book includes nudity, harsh language, and martial arts fighting violence.

I-Huan
Real/Fake Princess, Vol. 1. DrMaster Publications 2006 176p. Illustration
Grades: 6 7 8 9 10 11 12　　　　　　　　**741.5; Fic**
1. Adventure graphic novels; 2. Manhua; 3. Romance graphic novels; 4. Graphic novels
978-1-59796-079-3, $9.95

In Tang Dynasty China, the country is in great chaos due to the infamous Jin Kang Rebellion. Fearing the possible destruction that might eventually result, Concubine Liu tearfully entrusts the care of her baby daughter, Princess Yi Fu, to a common citizen named Tang Hui. Tang Hui immediately escapes with the princess to the South. A decade passes, and Emperor Gao Zon of Tang has decided he wants to find all of his long-lost relatives and has appointed Zhong Lu to the task. From there an adventure begins as Zhong Lu discovers and takes a special interest in Princess Yi Fu (renamed Zi Li), who is happily living in a quiet fishing village with her childhood crush and savior - Tang Hui. Returning with Zhong Lu to a life of royalty means leaving behind the humble life she has come to know with the commoners.

Igarashi, Daisuke
★ **Children** of the sea, vol. 1. Viz Media/Viz Signature 2009 320p. Illustration
Grades: 7 8 9 10 11 12　　　　　　**741; Fic; 741.5**
1. Adventure graphic novels; 2. Fantasy graphic novels; 3. Manga; 4. Mystery graphic novels; 5. Ocean; 6. Graphic novels
978-1-4215-2914-1, $14.99; 1-4215-2914-9

"As a young girl, Ruka sees a fish turn into light and disappear at the aquarium where her father works, but no one believes her. Years later, the mystery of the ghost of the sea unfolds before Ruka and a pair of mysterious young boys, Umi and Sora." Publ Wkly

"Igarashi's storytelling is quiet, thoughtful, and thought provoking, but it is his drawings that make this manga so amazing. Extremely detailed settings turn panels into mini-masterpieces." Booklist

Courtesy of VIZ Media LLC

Volume 1 of a 5-volume series

Ihara, Shigekatsu
Pokemon diamond and pearl adventure!, vol. 2. Viz Media/Viz Kids 2008 192p. Illustration
Grades: 3 4 5 6 7 8 9　　　　　　　　**741.5; Fic**
1. Adventure graphic novels; 2. Fantasy graphic novels; 3. Manga; 4. Graphic novels
978-1-4215-2287-6, $7.99

Hareta, Mitsumi, and their Pokemon friends continue on their quest to find Dialga, the Pokemon that rules time. They journey through the land of Sinnoh as Hareta and his partner Piglup grow stronger; they also keep ruining Team Galactic's nasty schemes. In Celestic Town, they find that Team Galactic's boss, Cyrus, has beat them to finding the first major clue to Dialga's whereabouts. And Hareta decides he needs help to become a better Trainer, but he and Piglup will have to pass Gym Leader Byron's test before he will accept them as students. There's lots of Pokemon fighting action.

Ikeda, Miyoko
Fairy navigator Runa, vol.1. Del Rey Manga 2010 186p. Illustration
Grades: 7 8 9 10 11 12　　　　　　　　**741.5; Fic**

1. Adventure graphic novels; 2. Fairies; 3. Fantasy graphic novels; 4. Magic; 5. Manga; 6. Shojo manga; 7. Graphic novels

978-0-345-52226-9, $10.99

Fourth grader Runa Rindo has lived in the Children of the Stars School ever since she was very young, it's the only home she has ever really known. All she has from her parents is a ring pendant and a small wooden box. Then two young strangers ask Runa "Are you the Legendary Girl?" And with that, her life changes. Suneri and Mokke are Fairies who can change shape to a cat (Suneri) and an owl (Mokke), and they tell Runa that she is a princess from the Fairy world. When another fairy, Kamachi, kidnaps Runa's best friend, Chae ("my name is Sae!"), Runa finds she must accept her destiny as the one who can control passage between the human and fairy worlds to save Chae.

Inada, Shiho

Ghost hunt, Vol. 1. Manga by Shiho Inada; story by Fuyumi Ono; translated by Akira Tsubasa; adapted by David Walsh; lettered by Foltz Design. Del Rey Manga 2005 216p. Illustration

Grades: 8 9 10 11 12 Adult   741.5; Fic
1. Horror graphic novels; 2. Manga; 3. Shojo manga; 4. Graphic novels

0-345-48624-2, $10.95

A decrepit old building stands on the campus of Mai's high school; every time the school tries to demolish it, unexplained accidents occur. Finally, the school hires a psychic researcher, and when Mai accidentally injures his assistant and damages an expensive camera, Shibuya (the researcher) insists she work off her debt by helping him. A miko (Shinto priestess), a Buddhist monk, and a Roman Catholic exorcist also come—but none of their methods work to stop the strange occurrences. Despite herself, Mai gets drawn into the investigation. This is the first of an ongoing manga series that provides some ghostly thrills without graphic violence, bad language, or sexual innuendo.

Inagaki, Riichiro

Eyeshield 21 Volume 1. Art by Yusuke Murata. Viz Media/Shonen Jump Advanced 2005 208p. Illustration

Grades: 10 11 12 Adult   741.5; Fic
1. Football; 2. Humorous graphic novels; 3. Manga; 4. Shonen manga; 5. Graphic novels

1-59116-752-3, $7.99

What does a wimpy kid who's been bullied all his life have to depend on but his own two feet? Sena Kobayakawa is about to start his first year in high school and he's vowed not to get picked on anymore. Unfortunately, the sadistic captain of the football team already has his eye on Sena and his lightning-fast speed. As the Devil Bats' "secret weapon," Sena uses a superhero-like secret identity, Eyeshield 21, to protect himself from other teams. This is a football story for people who don't know or like American football. The series includes crude humor, strong language, and some playing field violence.

Indiana Jones Omnibus, Volume 1

Dark Horse Comics 2008 352p.
Grades: 7 8 9 10 11 12 Adult   741.5; Fic

1. Adventure graphic novels; 2. Archeology; 3. Indiana Jones (Fictional character); 4. Graphic novels

978-1-59307-887-4, $24.95

This volume collects original comics stories starring movie hero Indiana Jones that were originally published by Dark Horse Comics in the early 1990s. Stories include Indiana Jones and the Fate of Atlantis, Indiana Jones: Thunder in the Orient, and Indiana Jones and the Arms of Gold. All of the stories predate the movies, as Indy races against the Nazis to recover and secure ancient treasures that could give great power to the owners. The book includes some violence.

Indiana Jones Omnibus: the further adventures, volume 1

Edited by Katie Moody. Dark Horse COmics 2009 366p. Illustration

Grades: 7 8 9 10 11 12   741.5; Fic
1. Adventure graphic novels; 2. Archeology; 3. Indiana Jones (Fictional character); 4. Graphic novels

978-1-59582-246-8, $24.95

This volume collects the Marvel Comics adaptation of "Raiders of the Lost Ark" and the first twelve issues of Marvel Comics' "The Further Adventures of Indiana Jones," which were originally published in the 1980s. Artists on the comics include John Byrne, Ron Frenz, Terry Austin, John Buscema, Howard Chaykin, Kerry Gammill, and a lot more. Marion Ravenwood appears in many of the further adventures, sometimes working with Indy and sometimes needing rescue by him. When she tries to open a nightclub, a gangster tries to force her into partnership with him so he can use the club as a front. In other stories, Indy travels to Africa and finds (as he has done so in the movies) that sometimes the damsel is the villain. The book includes the same level of action and violence that can be found in the movies.

Infantino, Carmine

Showcase Presents: The Elongated Man Volume 1. DC Comics 2006 560p. Illustration

Grades: 6 7 8 9 10 11 12 Adult   741.5; Fic
1. Batman (Fictional character); 2. Elongated Man (Fictional characters); 3. Flash (Fictional character); 4. Green Lantern (Fictional character); 5. Robin (Fictional character); 6. Superhero graphic novels; 7. Graphic novels

978-1-4012-1042-7, $16.99

Ralph Dibny is the Elongated Man, a self-taught superhero who has harnessed the power of the exotic gingo fruit and attained the ability to stretch himself to fantastic lengths. As the only costumed hero whose identity has been revealed to the world, Elongated Man travels the globe with his adoring wife Sue, solving mysteries and gaining renown for his singular elastic talent. In these stories, originally published from 1960 to 1968 and reprinted here in black and white, Dibny sometimes teams up with the Flash, Batman and Robin, Green Lantern, and Zatanna. Ralph and Sue Dibny were at the heart of the Identity Crisis, so readers might want to see their early adventures.

Inoue, Kazurou

Midori Days Volume 1. Viz Media 2005 190p. Illustration

Grades: 10 11 12 Adult   741.5; Fic

1. Fantasy graphic novels; 2. Romance graphic novels; 3. Shonen manga; 4. Graphic novels
1-59116-905-4, $9.99

Seiji Sawamura is the toughest seventeen-year-old in town, feared by all for his fighting prowess and his deadly "devil's right hand." But at heart, Seiji is a softy, and all he wants is an end to his seventeen-year history of being a lonely single guy. Unfortunately his tough-guy reputation only serves to decrease his popularity with the ladies. Then one day, Seiji wakes up to discover his devil's right hand" has turned into a miniature gal named Midori. Strangely enough, Midori is a real girl who is just as surprised as Seiji to find out she has now become—literally "Seiji's right hand." It turns out Midori has always had a crush on Seiji, and her desperate wish to be connected to him has somehow come true. While she is now part of his right arm, her real body is in a coma. The book includes some nudity and sexual situations.

Inoue, Takehiko
★ **Real,** volume 1. Story & art by Takehiko Inoue. Viz Media 2008 222p. Illustration
Grades: 10 11 12 Adult   **741; Fic; 741.5**
1. Basketball; 2. Manga; 3. Sports; 4. Wheelchair basketball; 5. Graphic novels
978-1-4215-1989-0, $12.99

Nomiya was the controlling rider on a motorcycle when he got into an accident that paralyzed the young woman riding with him; now he has dropped out of high school in his senior year and feels guilty. Togawa is stuck in a wheelchair but still plays basketball, which was the only thing Nomiya was good at in school. Togawa has quit the wheelchair basketball team, but he still plays. Nomiya starts playing while in a wheelchair, and they soon start a bit of a scam against regular players. They each have their own goals, but can they work together and find a better life for themselves? The book includes some harsh language, partial nudity, and Nomiya commits a bodily act against his school when he leaves.

"A compelling story of tragedy and struggle, Real is sure to appeal to teens—especially to male readers." SLJ
Original Japanese edition, 2001
Volume 1 of an ongoing series

★ **Slam** dunk, volume 1: Sakuragi. Story and art by Takehiko Inoue; English adaptation Kelly Sue DeConnick. Viz Media/Shonen Jump 2008 197p. Illustration
Grades: 8 9 10 11 12   **741.5; Fic**
1. Basketball; 2. Shonen manga; 3. Graphic novels
978-1-4215-0679-1, $7.99

Hanamichi Sakuragi is a first year student at Shohoku Prefecture High School; he's got a reputation as a bruising fighter and has suffered 50 rejections from girls who were scared of his fighting. He's looked down on sports all his life, but on this first day of high school, he meets Haruko Akagi; she's not scared of him, and she loves basketball. He falls for her completely, enough to try to play basketball. But, he has competition"Kaeda Rukawa is another first year student; he's a star basketball player, and Haruko has a huge crush on him. Then Sakuragi gets on the bad side of the basketball team captain, who happens to be Haruko's older brother. Sakuragi does everything he can to convince Takenori Akagi to let him join the team. However, he has a

long way to go before he can build the fundamental skills to play basketball effectively; will he stick it out" There's some fighting, one male student's buttocks get exposed accidentally, but there's no bad language.
Original Japanese edition, 1991
Volume 1 of a 31-volume series

★ **Vagabond,** Vol. 1. Viz 2002 Un Illustration
Grades: 11 12 Adult   **741.5; Fic**
1. Manga; 2. Musashi, Miyamoto, c 1584-1645; 3. Samurai; 4. Seinen manga; 5. Graphic novels
1-59116-034-0, $12.95

Based on the novel Musashi by Eiji Yoshikawa, this is the story of Shinmen Takezo, a young foot soldier who survived the Battle of Sekigahara, which marked the beginning of the Tokugawa Era in Japan. Destined to become the legendary sword saint Miyamoto Musashi, Takezo is a wild young brute, a cold-hearted killer who wants to make a name for himself. This first volume in the ongoing series includes sword fights, some nudity, and sexual situations.
Also available as 12 VIZBIG volumes
Volume 1 of 37

Inui, Sekihiko
Murder Princess Vol. 1. Broccoli Books 2007 208p. Illustration
Grades: 10 11 12 Adult   **Fic; 741.5**
1. Fantasy graphic novels; 2. Manga; 3. Shonen manga; 4. Graphic novels
978-1-5974-1060-1, $9.99

The world of politics is treacherous enough, but in Forland, it's deadly confusing. When her royal father is murdered by a greedy drug manufacturer, Princess Alita must step forward to take over the kingdom. Unfortunately, a freak magical mishap has trapped her in the body of Falis, the bounty hunter. Now Alita must stay disguised as a servant while the battle-savvy Falis sits on the throne in her body. Threatened by a coup and attacks from the outside, the fate of the kingdom is in the hands of Alita and Falis. Switched souls or not, there's another royal heir and Alita has to hold everything together for a little longer. As though this weren't enough to juggle, evil Professor Akamashi and his twin android assassins are out to cause some trouble of their own. Along with violence, there's a little fan service.
Volume 1 of 2

Inuki, Kanako
School Zone Vol. 1. Dark Horse Manga 2006 190p. Illustration
Grades: 10 11 12 Adult   **741.5; Fic**
1. Horror graphic novels; 2. Manga; 3. Graphic novels
978-1-59307-433-3, $12.95

Kanako Inuki presents School Zone, a series about ordinary children who encounter the strange and terrifying at their very own elementary school, and discover that many ghost stories, urban legends and superstitions are truly and horribly real. The children, ranging from first through sixth graders, encounter monsters in mirrors, horribly live dolls, murderous ghosts, and more. The book includes graphic horror violence and some strong language.

Inzana, Ryan

Ichiro. Written & illustrated by Ryan Inzana. Houghton Mifflin/Houghton Mifflin Harcourt 2012 288 p. Illustration; Color

Grades: 7 8 9 10   **741.5/973; 741.5**

1. Fantasy graphic novels; 2. Folklore — Japan; 3. Gods and goddesses — Fiction; 4. Grandfathers — Fiction; 5. Japan — Fiction; 6. Japan — History; 7. Japanese Americans; 8. Monsters — Fiction; 9. Supernatural — Fiction; 10. Supernatural graphic novels; 11. Graphic novels

0547252692; 9780547252698

LC 2011277558

This graphic novel depicts the story of Ichiro, "a young American teen, son of a Japanese immigrant and an American soldier killed in combat, [who] goes to Japan with his mother for an extended visit and begins to grapple with sophisticated cultural complexities. . . . After his mother and Japanese grandfather tell him stories of Japanese history and folklore, Ichiro has a fantastical adventure involving the Japanese myth of the shape-shifting tanuki spirit." (Kirkus Reviews)

Irving, Washington

The **legend** of Sleepy Hollow. Washington Irving (retold by Blake A. Hoena); illustrated by Tod Smith.. Stone Arch Books 2008 72p. Illustration

Grades: 4 5 6 7 8 9   **741.5; Fic**

1. Ghosts; 2. Horror graphic novels; 3. Humorous graphic novels; 4. Graphic novels

978-1-4342-0446-2, $23.93; 978-1-4342-0496-7 (pa), $9.95

LC 2007-30807

Tarrytown's new schoolmaster, Ichabod Crane, thinks little of the legend his students tell him about a headless horseman who haunts Sleepy Hollow. Crane must cross the Hollow in order to visit the Van Tassel home, for he fancies himself to be in love with Katrina Van Tassel. However, local strongarm man Brom wants Katrina for himself, and he plays mischief with Crane and the school. Eventually, the legendary ghost may play a role in this love triangle. This graphic novel adaptation of Irving's classic provides lots of humor and a few chills with a simple vocabulary, background notes on how Irving wrote his story, and discussion questions.

Part of the Graphic Revolve series

Irwin, Jane

Vogelein: clockwork faerie. [by] Jane Irwin with Jeff Berndt; foreword by Jennifer M. Contino. Fiery Studios 2003 167p. Illustration

Grades: 6 7 8 9 10 11 12

741.5; Fic

1. Fairies; 2. Fantasy graphic novels; 3. Graphic novels

0-9743110-06, $12.95

This is a "graphic novel about Vogelein, a beautiful

Courtesy of Fiery Studios

mechanical fairy created in the seventeenth century. Although she is immortal, she must be wound every 36 hours. After her old friend and caretaker dies, she must find someone new to take care of her. . . . This modern fable is a rare treasure that weaves fanciful imagination into themes of individuality, diversity, and independence. The art is beautifully shaded black and white, and it carries the narrative impeccably." Booklist

Most of the material contained within was originally printed in issues 15 of the magazine

Vogelein: Old Ghosts. Fiery Studios 2007 168p. Illustration

Grades: 7 8 9 10 11 12 Adult   **741.5; Fic**

1. Fantasy graphic novels; 2. Graphic novels

0-9743110-1-4, $12.95

Though three hundred years have passed since Alexi's death, Vogelein finds herself still haunted by the unkept promise she made to her first Guardian. Now the clockwork faerie must confront her past with the help of Mason, an itinerant musician whose spirit bears a striking resemblance to the one she desperately wants to lay to rest. As she struggles to find peace for both herself and Alexi, Vogelein discovers that centuries-old questions rarely have easy answers, intended paths reveal themselves in mysterious ways, and present-day threats strike just as suddenly as those from long ago.

Isayama, Hajime

★ **Attack** on Titan 1. Hajime Isayama. Kodansha 2012 186 p. Illustration (Attack on Titan)

Grades: 8 9 10 11 12   **741.5**

1. Giants; 2. Good and evil; 3. Horror graphic novels; 4. Shonen manga

1612620248; 9781612620244, $10.99

"Humanity has been devastated by the bizarre, giant humanoids known as the Titans. Little is known about . . . why they are bent on consuming mankind. . . . People believe their 100-meter-high walls will protect them from the Titans, but the sudden appearance of an immense Titan is about to change everything." (Publisher's note)

"Along with the setting and intricate, twisting plot, Attack on Titan derives its appeal from its willingness to bend the conventions of shounen manga. Here, friendship and burning spirit do not conquer all, and your favorite character stands a good chance of getting eaten without the opportunity to give a cool speech first." LJ

Volume 1 of an ongoing series

Ishida, Sui

Tokyo Ghoul 1. By Sui Ishida; translation, Joe Yamazaki. Viz 2015 224 p. Illustration

Grades: 10 11 12 Adult   **741.5**

1. College students — Fiction; 2. Horror fiction; 3. Manga; 4. Seinen

1421580365; 9781421580364, $12.99

"Ghouls live among us, the same as normal people in every wayùexcept their craving for human flesh. Ken Kaneki is an ordinary college student until a violent encounter turns him into the first half-human half-ghoul hybrid. Trapped between two worlds, he must survive Ghoul

turf wars, learn more about Ghoul society and master his new powers." (Publisher's note)
Volume 1 of an ongoing series

Ishihara, Yoko
★ The **manga** cookbook. Presented by the Manga University Culinary Institute; illustrations by Chihiro Hattori; [with recipes by Yoko Ishihara]. Japanime Co. Ltd. 2007 158p. Illustration
Grades: 4 5 6 7 8 9 10 11 12   **641.5; 741.5**
   1. Japanese cooking; 2. Manga; 3. Graphic novels
   978-4-921205-07-2, $14.95

Food appears frequently in manga and in anime, but just what are the characters eating" This book is an illustrated step-by-step guide to preparing some Japanese dishes, from onigiri (rice balls) to yakitori (skewered grilled chicken), oshinko (pickled vegetables), udon (Japanese noodles), to traditional sweets and desserts. Definitions of terms and ingredients used, basic cooking guidelines, and instructions on how to properly use chopsticks are all included. The recipes are authentic but have been simplified somewhat so older children and teens with some basic kitchen skills can prepare the foods. Adult supervision is recommended for younger children and for children who aren't very experienced with using knives, measuring spoons, and cooking on the stove.

Ito, Junji
Museum of Terror Volume 3: The Long Hair in the Attic. Dark Horse Manga 2006 388p. Illustration
Grades: 11 12 Adult   **741.5; Fic**
   1. Horror graphic novels; 2. Manga; 3. Graphic novels
   978-1-59307-639-9, $13.95

Junji Ito, creator and curator of this horrible museum, collects various horror stories for this volume. A beautiful young woman with long, flowing hair comes home with a broken heart, a mouse becomes entangled in her hair, and it won't let her cut it. Lovely violinists will escort you to dinner in a vampire den. Next, in a classroom full of grotesquely masked students, which one is a demon in disguise" A musician's possessed arm attacks a schoolgirl by way of his mouth, and another young man listens to the tape recording left behind by a suicide victim. Why did she kill herself, and is he safe from its influence" Swordplay, monk-ridden ruins, halls of upright corpses, and infectious radio broadcasts all come into play.

Museum of Terror: Tomie 1. Dark Horse Manga 2006 376p. Illustration
Grades: 11 12 Adult   **741.5; Fic**
   1. Horror graphic novels; 2. Manga; 3. Graphic novels
   978-1-59307-542-2, $13.95

"Tomie" is the story of an eternally youthful and beautiful high school girl, whose admirers become obsessed to the point of murdering her. Most of them tend to dismember her body; but to their horror, she is reincarnated over and over, and each body part becomes a whole Tomie. The book includes graphic violence, strong language, and nudity.

Iwaaki, Hitoshi
Parasyte vol. 3. Del Rey Manga 2008 284p. Illustration
Grades: 10 11 12 Adult   **741.5; Fic**
   1. Horror graphic novels; 2. Manga; 3. Science fiction graphic novels; 4. Seinen manga; 5. Graphic novels
   978-0-345-49825-0, $12.95

Alien parasites have invaded Earth and taken over the minds and bodies of ordinary people, in order to be able to feed on humans. Shin has been invaded by a parasite, but he stopped the invasion of his body and limited it to one arm. He can communicate with the parasite, whom he has named Migi (Japanese for right), and he can sense who is actually a parasite masquerading as a human. Now he's been approached by two mysterious victims of the invasion: Tamiya, a beautiful school teacher, and Shimada, another student. What do they really want? The book includes gory violence.

Parasyte vol.4. Del Rey Manga 2008 296p. Illustration
Grades: 10 11 12 Adult   **741.5; Fic**
   1. Horror graphic novels; 2. Manga; 3. Seinen manga; 4. Graphic novels
   978-0-345-49826-7, $14.95

Shinichi and Migi, the Parasyte that merged with him, continue their search for the Parasytes who kill humans, even as Shinichi tries to be a "normal" high school student. Then he meets Kana, a classmate who seems to have a knack for sensing the killer aliens. The fact that the aliens are getting into politics in order to gain positions of power disturbs Shinichi, but he also suspects that Migi may be infiltrating his brain, too. The book includes violence and bloodshed, and brief partial nudity.

Parasyte, Vol. 1. Ballantine Books/Del Rey Manga 2007 282p. Illustration
Grades: 11 12 Adult   **741.5; Fic**
   1. Horror graphic novels; 2. Manga; 3. Science fiction graphic novels; 4. Seinen manga; 5. Graphic novels
   978-0-345-49624-9, $12.95

Aliens come to Earth in a silent invasion, taking over human bodies; their plan is to kill and eat humans. One ordinary high school student, Shin, fights off an alien and it only manages to get into his right hand. Once the parasitic alien has matured while still stuck in Shin's right hand, it can't get to his brain. They settle into an uneasy relationship, as Migi (Japanese for "right") tries to learn everything and Shin just tries to keep up a normal appearance. Soon, though, they find other aliens, and Shin can't let the parasites take over without trying to fight back.

Iwaaki alleviates the horror with plenty of dark humor; he also uses harsh language, including f-bombs and s-bombs, and some sexual innuendo.
Originally published in a flipped (American style) manga series by Tokyopop from 1997 to 2002; this edition retains the right-to-left orientation, Japanese sound effects, and other original elements.

Iwahara, Yuji
King of Thorn Vol. 1. Tokyopop 2007 188p. Illustration
Grades: 10 11 12 Adult   **741.5; Fic**
   1. Horror graphic novels; 2. Manga; 3. Science fiction graphic novels; 4. Graphic novels
   978-1-59816-235-6, $9.99

Twin sisters . . . Separated by fate. . . Drawn together by a horrific illness. . . Kasumi and her sister, Shizuku, were infected with the Medusa virus, which slowly turns the victim to stone—and there is no cure. Hope for salvation rests in Kasumi and a select few who are put into a cryogenically frozen state until a cure is found. But Shizuku is left behind, and in the not-too-distant future, Kasumi awakens along with others who also have the virus, to find herself in an unfamiliar world with terrifying beings roaming the terrain. Despite their mistrust among themselves, they need to discover what has happened while they were in their cryogenic sleep, and protect themselves from deadly dangers. The book includes strong language and some violence.

Iwanaga, Ryoutaro

Pumpkin scissors vol. 1. Translated by Ikoi Hiroe. Del Rey Manga 2007 218p. Illustration
Grades: 10 11 12 Adult   741.5; Fic
   1. Adventure graphic novels; 2. Manga; 3. Graphic novels
   978-0-345-50119-6, $10.95

The bitter war between the Empire and the Republic of Frost has ended, but three years after the cease-fire, the Empire is still ravaged by starvation and disease, and bandits terrorize the people. Can the Imperial Army State Section III, aka Pumpkin Scissors, stop a renegade force bent on destruction? And who is the mysterious stranger helping Pumpkin Scissors? The book includes some violence and mildly harsh language.

Iwaoka, Hisae

★ **Saturn** apartments, volume 1. [translation, Matt Thorn].. Viz Signature 2010 184p. Illustration
Grades: 7 8 9 10   741; 741.5; Fic
   1. Manga; 2. Science fiction graphic novels; 3. Graphic novels
   978-1-4215-3364-3, $12.99; 1-4215-3364-2

Far in the future, humankind has left Earth to live in a gigantic ringlike structure that circles the planet. In this structure, humans have developed a class structure based on where one lives: the higher the floor on which you live, the greater your status. Mitsu has just graduated from junior high and is now expected to work as a window washer, just like his father before him. The thing is, his father disappeared while washing windows and is presumed dead. Window washing means one must get into a space suit and go out of the structure into outer space, 35 kilometers above the Earth's surface; space winds and other hazards make the work dangerous and expensive. Even as he wonders still, five years after his father's disappearance, what happened to him, Mitsu finds his job gives him a unique perspective on the lives of those who live in the Saturn Apartments. This is science fiction from the

Courtesy of VIZ Media LLC

viewpoint of the mundane service work rather than heroics of space action.

"This story of a young teen struggling to live alone will appeal to YAs, and the introspective nature of the narrative will have plenty of crossover appeal for adult readers as well." Booklist
   Reads from right to left
   Volume 1 of a 7-volume series

Jabcuda, Joshua

The **Mummy:** The rise and fall of Xango's Ax. Story by Joshua Jabcuga; artist, Stephen Mooney; colors by Lisa Jackson; letters by Robbie Robbins. IDW Publishing 2008 104p. Illustration
Grades: 9 10 11 12 Adult   741.5; Fic
   1. Adventure graphic novels; 2. Mummies; 3. Graphic novels
   978-1-60010-252-3, $17.99

Set before the events of the third Mummy movie (The Mummy: Tomb of the Dragon Emperor), adventurer Rick O'Connell tracks his son Alex to Burma, where corrupt treasure hunters have unearthed the Third Eye of Shangri-La. They've also managed to disturb the spirit of Xango, the mythical god of thunder, who wants the jewel back. Lord Hoxford, whom Alex had idolized, had led the theft; now, the O'Connells, Hoxford, and a ragtag group of poker players have to face down Xango and his revenant warriors to save the world. The book includes fighting violence, severed limbs, and beheadings.

Jablonski, Carla

Defiance. Written by Carla Jablonski; art by Leland Purvis; color by Hilary Sycamore. First Second 2011 126p. Illustration
Grades: 7 8 9 10 11 12   741.5; Fic
   978-1-59643-292-5, $16.99; 1-59643-292-6
                                                    LC 2010036253

"World War II has taken its toll on the French countryside. German soldiers patrol the towns, searching for any challenge to their rule. The Tessier siblings, Paul, Marie, and Sophie, keep their noses clean and their faces blank as the French military police tighten their grip on their small country town. But all three are secretly doing their part for the Resistance: the men and women working hard to undermine the Germans and win back France's freedom . . . even if it ends up costing them their lives." (Publisher's note)

★ **Resistance,** book 1. Art by Leland Purvis; color by Hilary Sycamore. First Second Books 2010 121p. Illustration (Resistance)
Grades: 6 7 8 9 10 11 12   741.5; Fic
   1. Adventure graphic novels; 2. France — History — 1940-1945, German occupation; 3. World War, 1939-1945 — Jews — Rescue; 4. World War, 1939-1945 — Underground movements; 5. Graphic novels
   978-1-59643-291-8, $16.99; 1-59643-291-8

Paul and his younger sister Marie live in a small village in Vichy France during World War II. Thus far, the war hasn't really touched them, but now Nazi soldiers come, and Paul's friend, Henri, and his parents are Jews and therefore in danger. When Paul and Marie try to protect Henri, their secret leaks out to members of the Resistance. Although they are young, they soon become recruits in the Resistance. Paul's incessant sketching in his book turns out to be a valuable talent, but he and Marie, and then their older sister, Sylvie, don't quite realize just how dangerous things can get. The cover is very striking, with Paul aiming a slingshot at a Nazi soldier. The Author's Note at the end of the book talks about history, the Resistance, and why the events in France during World War II should not be depicted as black and white, heroic Resistance versus villainous Vichy.

Followed by: Defiance (2011)

Jablonski, Carla.
★ **Victory**. Written by Carla Jablonski; art by Leland Purvis; color by Hilary Sycamore.. First Second 2012 123 p. Color illustration
Grades: 6 7 8 9 10 11 12   **741.5/973; 741.5**
  1. France — History; 2. France — History — German occupation, 1940-1945 — Fiction; 3. France — History — German occupation, 1940-1945 — Juvenile fiction; 4. Resistance to government — Fiction; 5. World War, 1939-1945 — France — Fiction; 6. World War, 1939-1945 — France — Juvenile fiction; 7. World War, 1939-1945 — Underground movements — France — Fiction; 8. Graphic novels
  1596432934; 9781596432932
                                              LC 2011030504
  "In this third volume in the graphic novel trilogy about the Tessier family," set during the French Resistance, "Sylvie relays information she gathers from her unwitting German boyfriend, Marie hides a man she discovers after a plane crash in the woods, and Paul is the ears of the Resistance in town. . . . At the end of the book, Paul travels to Paris to pass along information. He's on the scene for the city—s liberation." (Horn Book Magazine)
  "The storyline is brisk and edgy, complementing the worn nerves of people who have lived through war... Fans of graphic art and WWII will appreciate this book, as well as reluctant readers who are interested in historical fiction." VOYA

Jackson, B. Albers
  Rama: The legend. Art by Ashok Bhadana. Arcana Studio 2008 Un Illustration
Grades: 6 7 8 9 10 11 12   **398.2; 741.5**
  1. Adventure graphic novels; 2. Fantasy graphic novels; 3. Hindu mythology; 4. Ramayana; 5. Graphic novels
  978-0-9809204-0-6, $14.95
  The Hindu legend, The Ramayana, is retold in comic book form, adapted for Western readers. Jackson created two original characters, Rarecrow (a crow, of course) and Raj the mongoose; they tend to speak in contemporary slang. Rama is the oldest son of King Dasaratha, one of several brothers born after Vishnu blesses Dasaratha and his wives. The heavens have been wracked by war between the gods, and the evil god Ravana leads the thus-far victorious forces; Brahman had granted him a boon that he could not be defeated by anyone from the heavens or the underworld, but the gods had dismissed the humans as insignificant. As Rama and his brothers grow up, they become mighty warriors and begin to defeat the evil Ragasthas warriors, and as adults they must face Ravana himself when he kidnaps Rama's beautiful and faithful wife Sita. This graphic novel

adaptation makes the famous Hindu legend approachable for younger teen readers.

Jackson, Sherard
  Assembly. Antarctic Press 2003
Grades: 9 10 11 12   **741.5; Fic**
  1. Science fiction graphic novels; 2. Graphic novels
  1-932453-51-2; 978-1-932453-51-5, $9.99
  In a future world in which war is a constant, a young woman enters the military as a doctor, only to find she must pilot a battle suit. In one pitched battle full of violence and casualties, she makes a devastating discovery about her pacifist older sister.
  "In our time of violence all over the world, this slim book examines one teenage girl's motivation for becoming a soldier in a world consumed by war." Voice Youth Advocates

Jacobs, Edgar P.
  The **mystery** of the Great Pyramid part 1. Cinebook Ltd 2007 56p. Illustration
Grades: 7 8 9 10 11 12 Adult   **741.5; Fic**
  1. Adventure graphic novels; 2. Egypt — Antiquities; 3. Graphic novels
  978-1-905460-37-3, $13.95
  Professor Mortimer has come to Egypt on vacation with his servant, Nasir; his old friend, Professor Ahmed Rassim Bey has offered him an opportunity to satsify his passion for Egyptology by inviting him to take part in deciphering his latest discoveries. Mortimer and Bey soon realize that one of the fragments of papyrus deals with the "Chamber of Horus," a fabled crypt that could hold priceless treasures. However, Bey's assistant has been in league with villainous adventurers with their own plans to grab the treasures. . . . Jacobs was a close relative of Herge, creator of Tintin, and his adventures of Blake and Mortimer follow a similar pattern and style.
  This is a part of The Adventures of Blake and Mortimer.

Jacobson, Ryan
  Eleanor Roosevelt: First Lady of the World by Ryan Jacobson ; illustrated by Gordon Purcell and Barbara Schulz Capstone Press 2006 32p. Illustration
Grades: 3 4 5 6 7 8 9   **741.5; 973.917; 92**
  1. Biographical graphic novels; 2. Roosevelt, Eleanor, 1884-1962; 3. Graphic novels
  0-7368-4969-6, $25.26
                                              LC 2004028556
  This book uses the comic book format to describe highlights in the life and work of U.S. First Lady Eleanor Roosevelt. It includes additional information, a glossary, a list of books for further reading, and more.
  Part of the Graphic Library, Graphic Biographies series.

Jacobson, Sidney
  The **9/11** report: a graphic adaptation. By Sid Jacobson and Ernie Colón; [with a foreword by Thomas H. Kean and Lee H. Hamilton]. Hill and Wang 2006 133p. Illustration
Grades: 9 10 11 12 Adult   **973.931; 741.5**
  1. September 11 terrorist attacks, 2001; 2. Graphic novels

0-8090-5738-7; 978-0-8090-5738-2, $30;
0-8090-5739-5 (pa); 978-0-8090-5739-9 (pa), $16.95

"The book aims to make . . . [The 9/11 Commission Report] more accessible to all readers and draw in young adults. . . . This graphic adaptation is an important and necessary part of any collection." Libr J

On cover: Based on the final report of the National Commission on Terrorist Attacks upon the United States

Jacques, Brian

Redwall: the graphic novel. By Brian Jacques; illustrated by Bret Blevins; adapted by Stuart Moore; lettering by Richard Starkings. Philomel Books 2007 143p. Illustration

Grades: 4 5 6 7 8 9   **741.5; Fic**
1. Adventure graphic novels; 2. Fantasy graphic novels; 3. Mice; 4. Graphic novels

978-0-399-24481-0, $12.99; 0-399-24481-6

When Cluny the rat's army attacks Redwall Abbey, young Matthias the mouse follows in the footsteps of the long-ago hero Martin the Warrior to defend his home

"The story is a page-turner, and the detailed black-and-white drawings capture both the passion and the pathos." SLJ

Jaffe, Michele

Bad kitty volume 1: catnipped. Art by Lince. HarperCollins/Tokyopop 2008 176p. Illustration

Grades: 7 8 9 10 11 12   **741.5; Fic**
1. Humorous graphic novels; 2. Mystery graphic novels; 3. Graphic novels

978-0-06-135162-4, $9.99; 0-06-135162-8

Teenage aspiring detective Jasmine Callihan just wants to hang out with her boyfriend, rock star Jack, but while they're at the mall, trouble strikes. First, Jas finds a schoolmate's purse, then there's a jewelry store heist and the cops arrest the store owner whom she believes is innocent, then she says exactly the wrong thing to Jack, and her cousin Alyson with her Evil Hench Twin Veronique decided to join the investigation along with Jas and her best friends Roxy, Polly, and Tom. This global manga is an original story using the same characters as Jaffe's prose teen novels Bad Kitty and Kitty Kitty.

"Catnipped will be especially appreciated by fans of Jaffe's novels, but it is not necessary to have read them to enjoy this rollicking, fast-paced, and funny mystery." SLJ

James, Dan

Mosquito: An Omnilingual Nosferatu Pictomunication Novel. Top Shelf Productions/Ghostshrimp Press 2005 Un Illustration

Grades: 11 12 Adult   **741.5; Fic**
1. Horror graphic novels; 2. Stories without words; 3. Graphic novels

1-891830-686, $12.95

This is a wordless vampire story, done completely in red ink. It follows the adventure of a man who receives a curious letter containing polaroids of vampire victims and a map to the small town where it lives. The book includes some violence.

Jansson, Tove

Moomin Book One. Drawn & Quarterly 2006 96p. Illustration

Grades: 8 9 10 11 12 Adult   **741.5; Fic**
1. Humorous graphic novels; 2. Moomins (Fictional characters); 3. Graphic novels

1-894937-80-5, $19.95

Jansson is best known in the U.S. for her children's books featuring the Moomins, hippo-shaped creatures. Her comic strips have a more mature outlook. Moomin needs help getting rid of unwanted guests, but the only solution that works costs him his house. Then his scheming friend Sniff involves him in all sorts of shady get-rich-quick schemes. And when Moomin finds his long-lost parents, his father's craving for adventure causes more trouble. Snorkmaiden, Moomin's girlfriend, is just as bad as Moominpapa, and they spark a boat trip south to a resort, where the naive Moomins think they're houseguests and everyone else, including the hotel staff, assumes they're wealthy eccentrics. The childlike look of the strips belie the goings-on; this book is not really for young readers, although teens and adults will enjoy the whimsy overlaying sharp satire.

Moomin's winter follies. Trove Jansson. Enfant 2012 45 p.

Grades: 8 9 10 11 12 Adult   **741.5**
1. Moomins (Fictional characters)

1770460985; 9781770460980, $9.95

Author Tove Jansson presents a graphic novel. "Moomin wakes up one morning to find the pond frozen over, and rather than hibernate, the family decides to brave the winter weather. At first, their wintry adventure seems to be going swimmingly, until Mr. Brisk of the Great Outdoors Club takes over and forces everyone to embrace the winter sports, whether they want to or not." (Comic Vine)

Japan as viewed by 17 creators.

Fanfare/Ponent Mon 2005 254p. Illustration

Grades: 11 12 Adult   **741.5**
1. Japan; 2. Graphic novels

978-84-96427-16-7, $25

Eight stories from nine European creators about different geographic locations around Japan are combined with eight stories from eight creators from the country about their birthplace or place of residence. The result is a collection of anecdotes and tales, both ancient and modern, woven together from differing views that provide tantalizing glimpses of this land of the Rising Sun. Creators include Frederic Boilet, Nicolas de Crecy, Emmanuel Guibert, Joann Sfar, Moyoko Anno, Taiyo Matsumoto, and Jiro Taniguchi. Some of the stories include nudity, sexual situations, and foul language.

Jason

The **Iron** Wagon. Fantagraphics Books 2003 Un Illustration

Grades: 10 11 12 Adult   **741.5; Fic**
1. Mystery graphic novels; 2. Graphic novels

1-56097-541-5, $12.95

The Iron Wagon is an evocative murder mystery written in 1908 by Riverton (a pseudonym) and set in the Norwegian countryside; it, like all good murder mysteries, is a stew of passion, buried past crimes, revelations, and sharply defined characters who remain ambiguous to the very end. This novel has never been translated into English. Norwegian cartoonist Jason has adapted it into a graphic novel using his animal characters.

The **Left** Bank Gang. Fantagraphics Books 2006 46p. Illustration Grades: 10 11 12 Adult **741.5; Fic**
1. Mystery graphic novels; 2. Graphic novels 978-1-56097-742-1, $12.95

Double-crosses, violence, and harsh language pepper this little noir story that depicts Ernest Hemingway, F. Scott Fitzgerald, Ezra Pound, and James Joyce as struggling cartoonists in 1920s Paris.

Courtesy of Fantagraphics

Zelda Fitzgerald and Gertrude Stein are there, as well. Everyone is portrayed as dog-headed people, in Jason's signature art style.

Meow, Baby!. Fantagraphics Books 2005 Un Illustration
Grades: 10 11 12 Adult **741.5; Fic**
1. Humorous graphic novels; 2. Graphic novels 1-56097-695-0, $16.95

Jason unleashes his inner Scandinavian goofball with this big collection of hilarious shorter pieces. God, the Devil, mummies, vampires, zombies, werewolves, reanimated skeletons, space invaders, Death, cavemen, Godzilla and Elvis populate these most often wordless blackout gags, side by side with Jason's usual Little-Orphan-Annie-eyed, rabbit-and-bird-head protagonists - a "lighter side" of one of the best cartoonists of the new millennium. Some nudity and sexual situations, and a little violence, plus seeing what zombies eat are subtly present.

Courtesy of Fantagraphics

Jeffrey, Gary
Bob Marley: The Life of a Musical Legend. Art by Terry Riley. The Rosen Publishing Group 2007 48p. Illustration
Grades: 3 4 5 6 7 8 9 **741.5**
1. Biographical graphic novels; 2. Marley, Bob, 1945-1981; 3. Graphic novels
978-1-4042-0854-4, $29.25

This comic book format biography presents the life and musical career of legendary reggae master Marley, from his early years in Jamaica to international stardom. Additional material gives background information about Jamaica, its land and people, its music, and the Rastafarian religion. The book includes a glossary and a list of books for further reading.
Part of the Graphic Biographies

Courtesy of Rosen Publishing

Hurricane hunters and tornado chasers. Illustrated by Gianluca Garofalo. Rosen Publishing Group 2008 48p.
Grades: 3 4 5 6 7 8 9 **551.55; 741.5**
1. Meteorology; 2. Storms; 3. Vocational guidance; 4. Graphic novels
978-1-4042-1458-3, $29.25
LC 2007-42133

Courtesy of Rosen Publishing

After brief descriptions of what hurricane hunters and tornado chasers do (and why they do it), the book profiles hurricane hunter Jeffrey Masters and tornado chasers Roger Edwards and Tim Samaras, describing a memorable incident in each of their careers.
Part of the Graphic Careers series

Martin Luther King Jr.: The Life of a Civil Rights Leader. Art by Chris Forsey. Rosen Publishing Group 2006 48p. Illustration
Grades: 3 4 5 6 7 8 9
741.5; 323.1; 92
1. African Americans — Civil rights; 2. Biographical graphic novels; 3. King, Martin Luther, Jr, 1929-1968; 4. Graphic novels
978-1-4042-0858-2, $29.25
LC 2005035525

This book uses the graphic novel format to tell of the life and career of civil rights leader King. It gives additional information about segregation in the U.S. and the civil rights movement after King's death, and a list of books for further reading.
Part of the Rosen Graphic Biographies series.

Courtesy of Rosen Publishing

Oprah Winfrey: The Life of a Media Superstar. Rosen Publishing Group 2006 48p. Illustration

Grades: 3 4 5 6 7 8 9   **741.5; 791.4; 92**
1. Biographical graphic novels; 2. Television personalities; 3. Winfrey, Oprah, 1954-; 4. Graphic novels
978-1-4042-0862-9, $29.25

LC 2006001559

This book uses the graphic novel format to tell of the life and career (so far) of television personality Oprah Winfrey, who has been called the queen of daytime talk shows and was the first African American billionaire. The book includes background information on the civil rights movement and on daytime television, information on Winfrey's charitable work, and a list of books for further reading.

Part of the Rosen Graphic Biographies series.

Secret agents. Art by Terry Riley. Rosen Publishing Group 2008 48p. Illustration
Grades: 3 4 5 6 7 8 9   **327.12; 741.5**
1. Espionage; 2. Spies; 3. Graphic novels
978-14042-1464-4, $29.25

LC 2007-43334

After brief descriptions of espionage and some organizations and gadgets, the book profiles three spies. During World War II, Wulf Schmidt was airdropped into Great Britain to spy for Nazi Germany, but the British had broken the communication code and knew he was coming; he became a double agent and worked for British Intelligence for the rest of the war. Oleg Penkovsky was a Soviet Intelligence officer who started working for the British in 1961; he and his British contact were caught and tried. Penkovsky was executed for treason. Robert Baer was a career CIA case officer; this book recalls one case from 1979, in India.

Part of the Graphic Careers series

Jenkins, Paul
    Civil War: Front Line Book 1. Art by various. Marvel Entertainment 2007 Un Illustration
Grades: 9 10 11 12 Adult   **741.5; Fic**
1. Superhero graphic novels; 2. Graphic novels
978-0-7851-2312-5, $14.99

In "Embedded," reporters Sally Floyd and Ben Urich seek the truth at the heart of the war. In "The Accused," the lone survivor of the team that caused the Stamford tragedy has been found, and this vilified hero is placed under arrest for the deaths of an entire town. And his trouble is just beginning. This volume includes other stories, including the mystery of the Atlanteans.

    Civil War: Front Line Book 2. Art by various. Marvel Entertainment 2007 Un Illustration
Grades: 9 10 11 12 Adult   **741.5; Fic**
1. Superhero graphic novels; 2. Graphic novels
978-0-7851-2469-6, $14.99

In "Embedded," hot on the trail of a revelation that could explode the rift between the pro-registration and anti-registration heroes and forever change the nature of the Registration Act, the Daily Bugle's Ben Urich and Sally Floyd have the story. Can they bring the power to the people? In "The Accused," his powers are gone, he's been held culpable for the worst super-human disaster in history, and every super-villain in prison is looking to take a piece of Speedball. Will he make it out alive, and with hundreds of

deaths on his conscience, does he want to? In the meantime, Norman Osborn shoots an Atlantean ambassador, bringing the U.S. to the brink of war; and there's a traitor in Stark's group. This volume includes some violence.

Revelations. Created by Paul Jenkins and Humberto Ramos; story by Paul Jenkins; art by Humberto Ramos; colors by Leonardo Olea and Edgar Delgado; letters by Richard Starkings and Comicraft. Dark Horse Comics 2006 Un Illustration
Grades: 11 12 Adult   **741.5; Fic**
1. Catholic church; 2. Mystery graphic novels; 3. Graphic novels
978-1-59307-239-1, $17.95

When a Cardinal in line to succeed the dying Pope falls from a high window in the Vatican, a priest calls on his friend, tough London cop Charlie Northern, to investigate. Once in Rome, Northern confronts coverups and secrets as he tries to find out what happened. What he learns will shake him to his atheistic core. This violent murder mystery will appeal to fans of The Da Vinci Code and other works depicting religious conspiracies.

Originally published as Revelations issues #1-6.

Sidekick. Image Comics 2007 Un Illustration
Grades: 12 Adult   **741.5; Fic**
1. Satire; 2. Superhero graphic novels; 3. Graphic novels
978-1-58240-743-2, $16.99

This is the story of the not-so-glamorous life of Eddie Edison - also known as Superior Boy. Eddie works two jobs: delivering pizza to pay the bills and being a sidekick to the most powerful superhero on earth - to pay the bills. What's a guy to do" Discover the answer to this burning question, and get a healthy dose of evil villains, busty women, sex-fiends and more F-bombs than one can shake a stick at. The book indeed includes lots of harsh language, sexual situations, and violence.

Jensen, Van
    Pinocchio vampire slayer and the great puppet theater: a story. By [artist] Dusty Higgins and [text] Van Jensen. SLG 2010 165 p. Illustration
Grades: 9 10 11 12 Adult   **741.5; Fic**
9781593622039, $14.95

ôThe second volume of Pinocchio, Vampire Slayer follows a cast of puppets, a ghost cricket, and a human girl, Carlotta, to battle to destroy the head vampire and his associates. With an enraged disposition, Pinocchio, the main character, plots to avenge his father Geppetto's death. His former ally, Master Cherry, now a vampire, is killed by Pinocchio's hand when Cherry cannot dominate his thirst for blood. In a fit of sorrow and fury over Cherry's death, the Blue Fairy casts a spell transforming Pinocchio into a human boyùrendering him virtually defenseless against the vampires. . . . With a blend of horror and fantasy, the graphic novel unfolds layers of a unique story in comic book form. The vibrant characters breathe to life a tale that connects with readers of multiple ages.ö Voice Youth Advocates

Pinocchio, Vampire Slayer: Volume 3: Of Wood and Blood Part 1. SLG Publishing 2012 130 p.
Grades: 9 10 11 12 Adult   **741**
1. Fractured fairy tales

1593622392; 9781593622398, $10.95

This book is the final part of Van Jensen's Pinocchio series. "Pinocchio's wish to become a real boy was granted at a most disadvantageous time: he ended up marooned in the middle of the Mediterranean with the remnants of the Great Puppet Theater, while Carlotta was dragged away by the vampires. He washes ashore on an island" and must find a way to rescue Carlotta. (Voice of Youth Advocates)

Jerwa, Brandon

G. I. Joe Vol. 6: Players & Pawns. Illustrated by Tim Seeley. Devil's Due Publishing 2004 Un Illustration
Grades: 7 8 9 10 11 12 Adult **741.5; Fic**
1. Adventure graphic novels; 2. G I Joe (Fictional character); 3. Graphic novels
1-932796-18-5, $12.95

Cobra has re-established its island base, but the organization is crumbling; Destro and Zartan have both resigned, and the Baroness is caught between love and duty. While the Joes infiltrate Cobra Island, Cobra Commander makes a violent attempt on General Hawk's life and the South American nation of Sierra Gordo is invaded by a mysterious new high-tech commando unit. As the players enact their strategies, the pawns move into place. The book includes fighting action.

Jimenez, Phil

Other World Book One. Phil Jimenez, writer/penciller; Andy Lanning, inker; Jeromy Cox, colorist; Nick J. Napolitano, letterer. DC Comics/Vertigo 2006 176p. Illustration
Grades: 10 11 12 Adult **741.5**
1. Adventure graphic novels; 2. Fantasy graphic novels; 3. Graphic novels
978-1-4012-1011-3

Otherworld is an idyllic, pastoral land populated by mythological beings that battle endlessly with a nation-state made of pure technology. A group of young people - some friends, some strangers - have been plucked violently from Earth, imbued with superpowers, and brought to Otherworld. Siobhan Moynihan, a college student and an aspiring singer, is told she's the savior who will end the war and save Otherworld ... or destroy it forever. This book includes some nudity, strong language, and violence.

Teen Titans/Outsiders: The Death and Return of Donna Troy. Written by Phil Jimenez and Judd Winick; Art by Alé Garza et al. DC Comics 2006 176p. Illustration
Grades: 9 10 11 12 Adult **741.5; Fic**
1. Outsiders (Fictional characters); 2. Superhero graphic novels; 3. Teen Titans (Fictional characters); 4. Graphic novels
1-4012-0931-9, $14.99

A mysterious android from the future sparks a chain of events that leads to the death of Donna Troy, Titan member and sister to Wonder Woman. The new incarnation of the Teen Titans and the Outsiders later discover that Donna is still alive, but she doesn't seem to remember who she is and is hell-bent on destroying her friends. Will her former teammates be able to restore Donna's true self before her ultimate destiny is revealed?

JLA: The Greatest Stories Ever Told
DC Comics 2006 192p. Illustration
Grades: 9 10 11 12 Adult Fic; 741.5
1. Aquaman (Fictional character); 2. Batman (Fictional character); 3. Flash (Fictional character); 4. Green Arrow (Fictional character); 5. Green Lantern (Fictional character); 6. Justice League of America (Fictional characters); 7. Superhero graphic novels; 8. Superman (Fictional character); 9. Wonder Woman (Fictional character)
978-1-4012-0932-2, $19.99

Superman. Batman. Wonder Woman. Green Lantern. The Flash. Aquaman. Martian Manhunter. Green Arrow. Black Canary. They are the World's Greatest Super-Heroes, and they compose the Justice League of America. For over 45 years, this all-star team of DC's greatest characters has entertained generations of comics fans. And now, this new collection reprints eight of their greatest tales in one volume, covering nearly every era and incarnation of the League, from classic adventures of the Silver Age, to stories that formed the basis of the best-selling Identity Crisis, to newer tales featuring a humorous League and the return of the classic lineup.

Johns, Geoff

52, Volume One. DC Comics 2007 304p. Illustration
Grades: 10 11 12 Adult **741.5; Fic**
1. Adventure graphic novels; 2. Mystery graphic novels; 3. Science fiction graphic novels; 4. Superhero graphic novels; 5. Superman (Fictional character)
978-1-4012-1353-4, $19.99

The events of Infinite Crisis have left Superman, Batman and Wonder Woman missing, many other superheroes dead or injured. Black Adam, the long-time nemesis of Shazam, seeks to gain allies to form a group to go up against the U.S. Ralph Dibny investigates a cult built around the idea of resurrecting Superboy. The Blue Beetle tries to use information from the 25th century to gain wealth and become the next big superhero. John Steel tries to go up against ex-President Lex Luthor, who has developed a drug that can "create" superheroes. DC Comics gathered four writers, a breakdown artist (Giffen), and a host of pencillers and inkers to create a year-long weekly comic book that plays out the action in real time. Johns, Morrison, Rucka, and Waid also worked together on every issue.

Originally published as 52 issues #1-13.

Volume 1 of 4

52 Volume Two. Written by Geoff Johns, Grant Morrison, Greg Rucka, Mark Waid; Art by various. DC Comics 2007 304p. Illustration
Grades: 10 11 12 Adult **741.5; Fic**
1. Adventure graphic novels; 2. Superhero graphic novels
978-1-4012-1364-0, $19.99

Lex Luthor's created meta humans become Infinity, Inc. even as John Steel finds out that Luthor can control the power within them - including removing them. Ralph Dibny takes up the helmet of Dr. Fate. The Question and Renee Montoya travel to Kahndaq, on the trail of Intergang's weapons. Black Adam and Isis get married. Booster Gold's dubious heroism ends badly. Supernova bothers Luthor. Adam Strange, Animal Man, and Starfire escape from the planet where they had been trapped, with help from ... Lobo"

The year without Superman, Batman, and Wonder Woman continues. The book includes some sexually suggestive scenes, violence, and some strong language.

The **Flash:** The Secret of Barry Allen. Geoff Johns, writer; Howard Porter & Livesay, artists; James Sinclair, colorist; Nick J. Napolitano, Rob Leigh, Pat Brosseau, letterers. DC Comics 2005 Un Illustration
Grades: 9 10 11 12 Adult   **741.5; Fic**
1. Flash (Fictional character); 2. Superhero graphic novels; 3. Graphic novels
1-4012-0723-5, $19.99
This volume details the events in Wally West's life as he regains his memory of being the Flash. He carefully chooses which friends and allies to whom he will again reveal his identity. Then, he and his pal Nightwing are confronted with the return of Gorilla Grodd, more savage than ever. But the biggest shock in the Fastest Man Alive's life comes when he reads a letter from his mentor and predecessor, Barry Allen, revealing a dark decision that haunted him to the day he died. And after reading it, Wally needs to reassess what it means to be a hero in a world growing ever darker.

The **Flash:** crossfire. [by] Geoff Johns, writer; Scott Kolins, Rich Burchett, Justiniano, pencillers; Doug Hazlewood, Dan Panosian, Walden Wong, inkers; James Sinclair, colorist; Gaspar Saladino, Bill Oakley, letterers; Brian Bolland, Scott Kolins, original cover. DC Comics 2004 212p. Illustration
Grades: 10 11 12 Adult   **741.5; Fic**
1. Flash (Fictional character); 2. Superhero graphic novels; 3. Graphic novels
1-4012-0195-4, $17.95
LC 2004-555611
"Eight . . . rogues have joined forces to take over Flash's town of Keystone City. As if that weren't enough, the Thinker, an artificial intelligence with a personality—a walking computer virus of sorts—is attempting to absorb the minds of the city's inhabitants, including Flash's. Writer Johns demonstrates his ability to reinvigorate the series' classic elements. . . . Teens will appreciate it as mainstream superhero fare, executed with complexity and flair." Booklist

The **Flash:** Wonderland. Geoff Johns, writer; Angel Unzueta, penciller; Doug Hazlewood, inker; Tom McCraw, colorist; Gaspar, letterer. DC Comics 2007 144p. Illustration

Grades: 9 10 11 12 Adult   **741.5; Fic**
1. Flash (Fictional character); 2. Superhero graphic novels; 3. Graphic novels
978-1-4012-1489-0, $12.99
The Flash, Wally West, finds himself on a parallel Earth in which there's no Speed Force, and without that energy source, he has no power. The cops think he's a murderer, and the only one who can help him is one of his enemies, Captain Cold, who's also in the same world. They join forces to try to get back to their Earth, but they've got to find out who brought them here.

Green Lantern: No Fear. Geoff Johns, writer; Darwyn Cook [and others], pencillers. DC Comics 2006 Un Illustration
Grades: 10 11 12 Adult   **741.5; Fic**

1. Green Lantern (Fictional character); 2. Superhero graphic novels; 3. Graphic novels
978-14012-0466-2, $24.99
Hal Jordan has been resurrected and redeemed. Now it's tie to get on with his life as Green Lantern, protector of space sector 2814. But even as he returns to the skies as an Air Force pilot, Jordan faces new threats from his old foes. The deadly Manhunter androids and the mutated Shark return with shocking violence ... yet they are just precursors to even greater dangers. A maddened Black Hand embarks on a murderous rampage just as the Lantern finds himself the object of an alien race's insidious plan to harvest humans as living weapons of war. Johns works with artists Carlos Pacheco, Ethan Van Sciver, Darwyn Cooke, and Simone Bianchi in the stories collected here. There is some strong language, and violence, some graphic.

Green Lantern: Rebirth. Geoff Johns, writer; Ethan van Sciver, penciller; Prentis Rollins [and others], inkers; Rob Leigh, letterer; Moose Baumann, colorist. DC Comics 2005 Un Illustration
Grades: 9 10 11 12 Adult   **741.5; Fic**
1. Green Lantern (Fictional character); 2. Superhero graphic novels; 3. Graphic novels
978-1-4012-0465-5, $14.99
He was the greatest Green Lantern of them all. Then Hal Jordan went mad and ultimately died in an attempt to redeem himself. But fate was not done with him. Kyle Rayner, the sole Green Lantern, crashes back to Earth with a coffin bearing Hal Jordan's body, saying feverishly, "Parallax is coming." And Hal Jordan has returned. And so has Parallax, and the Spectre. Will one of them win and possess Jordan forever? Or can he become the Green Lantern once again?

Green Lantern Vol. 2: Revenge of the Green Lanterns. Written by Geoff Johns; pencilled by Carlos Pacheco, Ethan Van Sciver, Ivan Reis. DC Comics 2006 Un Illustration
Grades: 9 10 11 12 Adult   **741.5; Fic**
1. Green Lantern (Fictional character); 2. Superhero graphic novels; 3. Graphic novels
1401209602; 9781401209605, $14.99
The Green Lantern Corps kept peace and order throughout the universe for millenia, until their greatest warrior, Hal Jordan of Earth, destroyed them. The Corps had been resurrected, and Jordan, freed of the alien entity that drove him to madness, had been fully reinstated as a Green Lantern of Earth. But now, after the events of the Infinite Crisis, Jordan is in trouble again, and a Green Lantern whom he thought he had killed years ago has returned with vengeance on his mind. Jordan and fellow Green Lantern Guy Gardner travel to the home world of the Corps' greatest enemies, the android Manhunters, to save the Lanterns.

Infinite Crisis. Geoff Johns, writer; Phil Jimenez [and others], pencillers. DC Comics 2006 262p. Illustration
Grades: 9 10 11 12 Adult   **741.5; Fic**
1. Superhero graphic novels; 2. Graphic novels
978-1-4012-0959-9, $24.99
Four heroes, trapped in limbo since the original Crisis on Infinite Earths, are about to reveal themselves: one is dying, one wants to save her and restore an entire world that vanished and the other two seek unrivaled power. The plan they concoct is literally earth-shattering, and the world's

greatest superheroes may not be enough to stop their attempt to alter the very nature of reality.

JSA Presents Stars and S.T.R.I.P.E.. writer, Geoff Johns ; penciller, Lee Moder ; inker, Dan Davis ; colorist, Tom MccCraw ; letterer, Bill Oakely. DC Comics 2007 192p. Illustration
Grades: 8 9 10 11 12 Adult   **741.5; Fic**
1. Superhero graphic novels; 2. Graphic novels
978-1-4012-1390-9, $17.99

Courtney Whitmore is just your typical teenage girl trying to make it through high school, but she's about to stumble upon a secret that will make her life a lot more complicated. Her new stepfather, Pat Dugan, was once Stripesy, sidekick of the Golden Age hero The Star-Spangled Kid. Finding the Kid's old costume, Courtney modifies it for herself and becomes the new Star-Spangled Kid, aiming to fight crime and annoy the heck out of her stepfather. But Dugan isn't about to let his new daughter get into any danger. Putting his mechanical skills to work, he creates a robotic suit called S.T.R.I.P.E., and joins Courtney's battle for justice. They fight side-by-side - and sometimes with each other - taking on aliens, cults, new villains, and more. These stories are the first that Johns wrote in comics, back in 1999.

JSA: Black Vengeance. Geoff Johns, writer; Don Kramer, penciller; Keith Champagne, inker. DC Comics 2006 208p. Illustration
Grades: 10 11 12 Adult   **741.5; Fic**
1. Justice Society of America (Fictional characters); 2. Superhero graphic novels; 3. Graphic novels
978-1-4012-0966-7, $19.99

The JSA's former comrade, the Spectre, is now without a human host and running rampant, dealing out a brutal form of justice, encouraged by the new Eclipso. Atom-Smasher, also a former JSA member, seeks forgiveness for his actions in Kahndaq. Before the JSA decides whether or not to readmit him, Khandaq's ruler, Black Adam, summons the atomic hero back to the Middle East. When the JSA follow, all are forced to re-examine what it means to be a hero.

JSA: Lost. Geoff Johns, writer; Dave Gibbons [and others], pencillers. DC Comics 2005 208p. Illustration
Grades: 9 10 11 12 Adult   **741.5; Fic**
1. Science fiction graphic novels; 2. Superhero graphic novels; 3. Graphic novels
1-4012-0722-7, $19.99

The first Hourman sits alone at the end of time, having given his life to protect humanity. Sand, former chairman of the JSA, became one with the planet Earth to keep it whole. Hal Jordan sacrificed himself to become the new Spectre and keep the world safe. Now the JSA find themselves visiting old friends and new, rectifying injustices, aware that as they fix one problem, an even larger one is brewing in the time stream. The end of this volume contains spoilers about the killer's identity in the Identity Crisis. The book includes lots of superhero action and some violence.

JSA: Mixed Signals. Geoff Johns and Keith Champagne. DC Comics 2006 144p. Illustration
Grades: 10 11 12 Adult   **741.5; Fic**
1. Superhero graphic novels; 2. Graphic novels
978-1-4012-0967-4, $14.99

The JSA gets word from their ally, Airwave, that an intergalactic war has begun. Meanwhile, recent events have left all of the magic-based heroes vulnerable, and the ancient, evil magician Mordru plans to take full advantage of the situation. And when Golden Age legend Liberty Belle's powers go out of control, Stargirl is the only one who can figure out what to do.

Power Girl. Geoff Johns, Paul Levitz, Paul Kupperberg, writers; Amanda Conner et al., pencillers. DC Comics 2006 176p. Illustration
Grades: 9 10 11 12 Adult   **741.5; Fic**
1. Adventure graphic novels; 2. Superhero graphic novels; 3. Graphic novels
978-1-4012-0968-1, $14.99

Who is Power Girl? Is she Superman's cousin from a parallel world? Is she the granddaughter of an ancient Atlantean sorcerer? Is she a pawn in a game of cosmic chess that threatens the known universe" Whoever she is, she's playing a major role in recent DC Universe titles. In these stories, some dating back to 1975, her reality keeps changing. The more recent stories include a little bit of suggestiveness.

Superman: That Healing Touch. Writers, Greg Rucka, Geoff Johns & Jeremy Johns; pencillers, Matthew Clark [and others]. DC Comics 2005 168p. Illustration
Grades: 9 10 11 12 Adult   **741.5; Fic**
1. Superhero graphic novels; 2. Superman (Fictional character); 3. Graphic novels
1-4012-0453-8, $14.99

Ruin is out to kill Superman and those closest to him. He has unleashed Replikon and his son to soften up the Man of Steel, but now he unleashes his deadliest attack yet, twin Parasites who can sap the life from even a Kryptonian. Lois Lane, still recovering from a gunshot wound, Lana Lang, and Jimmy Olsen are all threatened. And each time, Superman insists that no one will die on his watch.

Superman: Up, Up and Away!. Geoff Johns and Kurt Busiek ; art by Pete Woods and Renato Guedes. DC Comics 2006 192p. Illustration
Grades: 8 9 10 11 12 Adult   **741.5; Fic**
1. Green Lantern (Fictional character); 2. Superhero graphic novels; 3. Superman (Fictional character); 4. Graphic novels
978-1-4012-0954-4, $14.99

In the wake of Infinite Crisis, Superman had lost his powers. For the past year, as Clark Kent he has worked with the help of his super-powered allies, Green Lantern, Supergirl, and Hawkgirl, to keep Metropolis safe. Now, Lex Luthor has been acquitted of his past crimes, and he has managed to get his hands on a powerful and ancient Kryptonian artifact and plans to use it to destroy Superman once and for all. What can a powerless Superman do—

Superman; Volume 6: the men of tomorrow. Geoff Johns, writer; John Romita Jr, Klaus Janson, artists. DC Comics 2015 256 p. Color; Illustration
Grades: 10 11 12 Adult   **741.5; Fic**
1. Superhero graphic novels; 2. Superman (Fictional character)
1401252397; 9781401252397, $24.99
LC 2015008050

"Enter Ulysses, the Man of Tomorrow, into the Man of Steel's life. This strange visitor shares many of Kal-El's experiences, including having been rocketed from a world with no future. New and exciting mysteries and adventures await. Plus, Perry White offers Clark a chance to return to The Daily Planet!" (Publisher's note)

Collects Superman #32-39 (New 52 relaunch)

Teen Titans Vol. 1: A Kid's Game. Geoff Johns, writer; Mike McKone & Tom Grummett, pencillers; Marlo Alquiza & Nelson, inkers; Jeremy Cox, colorist; Comicraft, letterer. DC Comics 2004 Un Illustration

Grades: 9 10 11 12 Adult   **741.5; Fic**
1. Batman (Fictional character); 2. Flash (Fictional character); 3. Robin (Fictional character); 4. Superhero graphic novels; 5. Superman (Fictional character); 6. Teen Titans (Fictional characters); 7. Graphic novels
1-4012-0308-6, $9.95

As the adolescent sidekicks of the world's most powerful heroes, Robin, Superboy, Wonder Girl, and Impulse have fought alongside their mentors in many battles. But when Cyborg, a former teen hero, realizes that this new generation of super-heroes needs to be guided and trained, he recruits the young adventurers into the new Teen Titans. Now as Earth's future champions begin working together as a unified team, they quickly learn the true consequences of the path they have chosen. Featuring Batman, Superman, Wonder Woman and the Flash, this action-packed volume includes the Teen Titans' inaugural adventures as they face off against the deadly mercenary Deathstroke, contend with the fanatical villainy of Brother Blood and take on the heroes of the Justice League. The level of action and some violence puts this beyond most young fans of the Cartoon Network series, "Teen Titans Go."

Teen Titans Vol. 4: The Future is Now. writers, Geoff Johns and Mark Waid ; pencillers, Mike McKone ... [et al.]. DC Comics 2005 Un Illustration

Grades: 8 9 10 11 12 Adult   **741.5; Fic**
1. Science fiction graphic novels; 2. Superhero graphic novels; 3. Teen Titans (Fictional characters); 4. Graphic novels
1-4012-0475-9, $9.99

The Titans' weekends are usually a chance to get away from it all, but this time they've gone to the 31st century, where they must help the Legion of Super-Heroes stop a threat known as the Fatal Five Hundred. Their return trip drops them off ten years into their future, and they don't like what they see. And when they finally get back home, they meet Speedy, who has arrived just in time to help them fight Dr. Light.

Teen Titans Vol. 6: Titans Around the World. Geoff Johns, writer; Mike McKone & Tom Grummett, pencillers; Marlo Alquiza & Nelson, inkers; Jeromy Cox, colorist ; Comicraft, letterer. DC Comics 2007 192p. Illustration

Grades: 9 10 11 12 Adult   **741.5; Fic**
1. Robin (Fictional character); 2. Superhero graphic novels; 3. Teen Titans (Fictional characters); 4. Graphic novels
978-1-4012-1217-9, $14.99

The tragic events of Infinite Crisis tore apart the Teen Titans. It's one year later, and the core members of the Titans return to re-form the team. Robin, Wonder Girl, and Cyborg

go with interim members Kid Devil and Ravager on a journey to find their former colleagues, but they discover there had been a traitor in their ranks. With the identity and intent of the saboteur unknown, the team must be ready at all times for an assault. They meet with the Doom Patrol and fight the Brotherhood of Evil.

Johns, W. E.

Biggles Spitfire parade. Cinebook Ltd. 2008 48p. Illustration

Grades: 5 6 7 8 9 10   **741.5; Fic**
1. Adventure graphic novels; 2. World War, 1939-1945 — Aerial operations; 3. Graphic novels
978-1-905460-54-0, $11.95

James Bigglesworth, known as Biggles, takes command of 666 Fighter Squadron of the RAF during World War II. He has two flights of eccentric pilots who patrol the skies and protect England from enemy aircraft that attack from Germany. Sometimes they have to protect their own airfield from Stukas and JU88s (German bombers), and from Messerschmitts (German fighters) with their Spitfires. Biggles also has a friendly rivalry with an acquaintance who commands a squadron of Hurricanes. The book is full of air combat action, and while there is little graphic violence, people do die. This graphic novel is adapted by a French comics creator from the novels by W. E. Johns, who was a pilot himself during WWI.

Johnson, Crockett

Barnaby: 1942-1943, 1. By Crockett Johnson. Fantagraphics 2012 318 p. Illustration; Color

Grades: 10 11 12 Adult   **741.5; 741.5/6973**
1. Boys; 2. Children; 3. Fairies
9781606995228, $35; 1606995227

LC 2013363489

This volume, by Crockett Johnson, presents the collected comic strips of "Barnaby" from 1942-1943, which "revolved around a precocious five-year-old named Barnaby Baxter and his fairly godfather Jackeen J. O'Malley. Yet O'Malley, a cigar-chomping, bumbling con-artist and fast-talker, was not your typical protector." (Publisher's note)

Johnson, Dan

Sinbad: The legacy. Wordsmith, Dan Johnson; illustrator, Naresh Kumar; colorist, Ajo Kurian; letterer, Laxmi Chand Gupta. Campfire 2011 86 p. Color illustration

Grades: 7 8 9 10   **813.6; Fic**
1. Historical fiction; 2. Sea stories; 3. Sinbad the Sailor (Legendary character); 4. Graphic novels
8190751557; 9788190751551, $12.99

LC 2011287737

In this graphic novel, "[w]hen King Haakim sends his teenage son Habib on a voyage to teach him" maturity, "the spoiled brat makes enemies of Sinbad's crew and is responsible for the ship being blown off course and forced to anchor near islands full of dangerous giant animals, beautiful cannibal women, and [a] . . . death-obsessed kingdom. Despite this, Sinbad rescues the prince from his blunders, while relating the tale of his own . . . adventures that helped him grow up." (Publishers Weekly)

Johnson, Dan Curtis
    Batman: Snow. J.H. Williams III, Dan Curtis Johnson, story; Dan Curtis Johnson, script & dialogue; Seth Fisher, art; Dave Stewart, colors; Phil Balsman, letterer. DC Comics 2007 128p. Illustration
Grades: 9 10 11 12 Adult   **741.5; Fic**
    1. Adventure graphic novels; 2. Batman (Fictional character); 3. Superhero graphic novels; 4. Graphic novels
    978-1-4012-1265-0, $14.99
    At the dawn of his career, Batman recruits allies for his war on crime in order to really protect Gotham City. Everything changes when a brilliant scientist's desperate attempt to save the life of his terminally ill wife goes tragically wrong, and a new type of threat is born. As Batman faces his first super-powered villain, Mr. Freeze, he begins to realize that malfeasance comes in many deadly forms, and some offenders are more powerful than he. How will the crime fighter overcome this new menace while protecting not only his associates, but also the innocent citizens of Gotham? This book has lots of action and some mildly harsh language.

Johnson, Mat
    ★ **Incognegro.** Art by Warren Pleece. DC Comics/Vertigo 2008 136p. Illustration
Grades: 10 11 12 Adult   **741.5; Fic**
    1. African Americans — Southern states; 2. Mystery graphic novels; 3. Graphic novels
    9781401210977, $19.99
    In the early 20th century, light-skinned African American reporters risked their lives to cover the lynching murders of African Americans in the South; this process of "passing" was called "going incognegro." Zane Pinchback is a reporter from Harlem who has just narrowly escaped from one such reporting assignment when his editor sends him back down to Mississippi; this time, the man charged with murdering a white woman is Pinchback's own twin brother. He decides to investigate and find the real murderer in order to free his brother, but a Ku Klux Klansman has also come to town hunting the "Incognegro" reporter. This book portrays hangings and mutilations and uses the "n" word as it was used during the time period.

Johnson, Peter
    Supernatural: Origins. Writer, Peter Johnson; artist, Matthew Dow Smith; colorist, J.D. Mettler; letterer, Greg Thompson. DC Comics/Wildstorm 2008 144p. Illustration
Grades: 10 11 12 Adult   **741.5; Fic**
    1. Horror graphic novels; 2. Graphic novels
    978-1-4012-1701-3, $14.99
    This book is a prequel to the television series, "Supernatural." After witnessing the murder of his wife at the hands of . . . something evil . . . John Winchester finds no answers in town until a psychic shows him it was supernatural. As he goes on the road with his two young sons, Dean and Sam, Winchester finds himself on a path that will lead him towards much more than mere vengeance for his wife's death. The book includes gory violence.

Johnson, R. Kikuo
    Night Fisher. Fantagraphics Books 2005 144. Illustration

Grades: 11 12 Adult   **741.5; Fic**
    1. Bildungsromans; 2. Graphic novels
    1-56097-719-1, $12.95
    Loren Foster was handed an island paradise when he moved to the island of Maui in Hawaii with his dentist father six years ago. But, with the end of high school just around the corner, his best friend Shane has grown distant. Their friendship is put to the test when they get mixed up in a frivolous crime that leads to an arrest. Some drug use, strong language, and a sexual situation occur.

Johnston, Antony
    Julius. Written by Antony Johnston; illustrated & lettered by Brett Weldele. Oni Press 2004 138p. Illustration
Grades: 10 11 12 Adult   **741.5; Fic**
    1. Gangs; 2. Shakespeare, William, 1564-1616 — Adaptations; 3. Graphic novels
    1-929998-80-5, $14.95
    After years of infighting and turf wars, organized crime in the neighborhood is finally united under one leader. Julius is the gangster king of London's East End and his public persona is as beloved as it would be were he true royalty. But in private, his generals conspire and contemplate ways to remove Julius for their own selfish gain. This reworking of Shakespeare's classic tale of betrayal, corruption, manipulation, narcissism, and the violence spawned by each, gives the play a new power and relevance for a modern audience. Gangland killings and harsh language occur throughout the story.

    The **Long** Haul. Writer, Antony Johnston; artist, Eduardo Barreto; letterer, Marshall Dillon. Oni Press 2005 176p. Illustration
Grades: 9 10 11 12 Adult   **741.5; Fic**
    1. Adventure graphic novels; 2. Western graphic novels; 3. Graphic novels
    1-932664-05-X, $14.95
    The year is 1871 and a government grant of $100,000 in bonds (the last payment for the building of the Central Pacific Railroad from San Francisco to Promontory) is about to be sent from Chicago to the Western Pacific offices in San Francisco, over 2000 miles of railroad away. A Pinkerton agent has been brought in to oversee security, and the details for this operation are top secret. But professional thief Cody Plummer has discovered the plans... and the prize is too sweet to resist. With so much money at stake, this is no ordinary train: it can't be stopped, it can't be blown open, the safe weighs 2,000 pounds, and there are fourteen armed guards between Cody, the crew of ex-outlaws and old partners he's assembled, and the money. Sounds like pretty good odds to Cody. The book includes minimal violence, brief partial nudity, and no harsh language.

Jolley, Dan
    Alien Incident on Planet J. By Dan Jolley; illustrated by Matt Wendt; [coloring by Hi-Fi Design; lettering by Marshall Dillon].. Lerner Publishing Group/Graphic Universe 2008 112p. Illustration
Grades: 3 4 5 6 7 8 9   **741.5; Fic**
    1. Adventure graphic novels; 2. Plot-your-own stories; 3. Science fiction graphic novels

978-0-8225-6998-5, $27.93; 978-0-8225-8876-4 (pa), $7.93

LC 2007-44116

In this new take on the "Choose Your Own Adventure" type of book that combines pages of prose text with pages of comic book sequences, you are a young human stuck on Planet J; your spaceship needs a new part, and you'll never get off this planet if you don't make peace with the Makanuk, the Zirifubi, and the Frongo. Some choices will end badly, others will be better, and the choices are all up to the reader.

This is Volume 8 of the Twisted Journeys series.

Escape from Pyramid X. Art by Matt Wendt. Lerner Publishing Group/Graphic Universe 2007 112p. Illustration (Twisted Journeys)

Grades: 3 4 5 6 7 8 9   **741.5; Fic**
1. Adventure graphic novels; 2. Mummies; 3. Graphic novels
978-0-8225-6777-6, $27.93; 978-0-8225-6779-0 (pa), $7.95

LC 2006-101598

In the series called Twisted Journeys, readers choose how the story will progress. Pages of text alternate with comic book-style pages. In this volume, you the reader are a student who won an essay contest to be part of an archeological dig led by Professor Emil Snackport, at the site of a newly discovered pyramid. In some story lines, you encounter smugglers, in others, a malevolent mummy. Readers will find many scenarios played out, depending on their choices; some end well, others not so well.

The **girl** who owned a city. By O.T. Nelson; adapted by Dan Jolley; illustrated by Joe?lle Jones; coloring by Jenn Manley Lee. Graphic Universe 2012 125 p.

Grades: 6 7 8 9 10   **741.5**
1. Adventure graphic novels; 2. Apocalyptic fiction; 3. Children; 4. Dystopian juvenile fiction; 5. Science fiction; 6. Survival — Fiction; 7. Graphic novels
9780761349037; 9780761356349; 0761356347

LC 2009033270

This graphic novel, by Dan Jolley, O.T. Nelson, and illustrated by Joelle Jones, describes a post-apocalyptic world. "A deadly virus killed every adult on Earth, leaving only us kids behind. . . . I have to make sure we stay alive. . . . I figured out how to give the kids on Grand Avenue food, homes, and protection against the gangs. But Tom Logan and his army are determined to take away what we've built and rule the streets themselves." (Publisher's note)

The **hero** twins: against the lords of death: a Mayan myth. Story by Dan Jolley ; pencils and inks by David Witt. Lerner Publishing Group/Graphic Universe 2008 48p. Illustration

Grades: 3 4 5 6 7 8 9   **398.2; 741.5**
1. Adventure graphic novels; 2. Mayas — Folklore; 3. Graphic novels
978-0-8225-7495-8, $26.60

LC 2007-25897

The Hero Twins, Hunahpu and Xbalanque, were blessed by the Mayan gods with special powers. However, their incredible skill at playing Pok-ta-Pok, the Mayan ball game, angers the Lords of Xibalba, rulers of the Land of the Dead. When the Lords challenge them to a Pok-ta-Pok game in Xibalba, the twins know they must use all of their powers and cunning to defeat the Lords' many challenges. Comics veteran Jolley consulted several translations of the Popol Vuh, artist Witt studied books on Mayan culture, architecture and art, and Mesoamerican folklore expert John Bierhorst reviewed the story to ensure accuracy and respect for Mayan culture.

Part of the Graphic Myths & Legends series

Pigling: a Cinderella story: a Korean tale. Art by Anne Timmons. Graphic Universe 2008 48p. Illustration (Graphic myths and legends)

Grades: 3 4 5 6 7 8 9   **741.5; Fic**
1. Fairy tales; 2. Korea — Folklore; 3. Graphic novels
978-0-8225-7174-2, $27.93; 0-8225-7174-9

LC 2007-40891

In old Korea, in a time when magic still exists, Pear Blossom lives happily with her parents. But when her mother dies, her father quickly remarries a spiteful woman and her mean daughter, and they turn Pear Blossom's life into misery. They treat her like a servant and call her Pigling. Omoni (mother in Korean) makes impossible demands of Pear Blossom, and each time magical creatures help her achieve the tasks. Then on the day of a festival, a handsome magistrate sees Pear Blossom on the road, and she runs away, frightened, leaving a sandal behind.

The **Smoking** Mountain: The Story of Popocatepetl and Iztaccihuatl: An Aztec Legend. Art by David Witt. Lerner Publishing Group 2009 48p. Illustration

Grades: 3 4 5 6 7 8 9   **741.5; Fic**
1. Aztecs — Folklore; 2. Fantasy graphic novels; 3. Graphic novels
978-0-8225-7178-0, $27.93

LC 2007-20028

Back when the Aztec Empire was at its peak, the Emperor has a favorite daughter, Iztaccihuatl (called Izta); he is troubled by an enemy nation, the Tlaxcalans, and the soldier Popocatepetl (called Popo) is the Emperor's great military leader. Popo and Izta fall in love at first sight when the Emperor honors Popo for his accomplishments, and they meet in secret. However, Cuetlachtli is a jealous soldier who wants to destroy Popo, and he finds his chance when the Emperor catches the two lovers together and tells Popo he can only marry Izta if he brings back the head of the Tlaxcalan king. Searching for the enemy takes a long, hard time, and Cuetlachtli sends a messenger back to Tenochtitlan with word that Popo has died, which sends Izta into a decline. When victorious Popo returns, he finds his lover dead, and takes her to the top of a mountain where he stands over her until his death. Now there are two mountains in Mexico, named for the two lovers. Jolley sets the story as one told by a Mexican tour guide, using contemporary language; artist Witt conducted research to make the art look as authentic as possible. The book includes a list of books, websites, and DVDs for more information and entertainment.

Part of the Graphic Universe Myths and Legends series

The **time** travel trap. Illustrated by Matt Wendt. Graphic Universe 2008 111p. Illustration (Twisted journeys)

Grades: 3 4 5 6 7 8 9   **741.5; Fic**
1. Adventure graphic novels; 2. Plot-your-own stories; 3. Science fiction graphic novels; 4. Graphic novels

978-0-7613-9472-3 (lib bdg), $27.93; 0-7613-9472-9 (lib bdg); 978-0-8225-8874-0 (pa), $7.95; 0-8225-8874-9 (pa)

LC 2007-6101

In this new take on the "Choose Your Own Adventure" type of book that combines pages of prose text with pages of comic book sequences, you are caught in a time machine a fellow student built for the school's science fair. Depending on the choices, you could end up at a medieval joust, facing woolly mammoths and "cavemen," or future aliens. Some choices will end badly, others will be better, and the choices are all up to the reader.

This is Volume 7 of the Twisted Journeys series.

Vampire hunt. Illustrated by Gregory Titus; [coloring by Hi-Fi Design; lettering by Marshall Dillon]. Lerner Publishing Group/Graphic Universe 2008 112p. Illustration
Grades: 3 4 5 6 7 8 9   **741.5; Fic**
1. Adventure graphic novels; 2. Plot-your-own stories; 3. Science fiction graphic novels; 4. Vampires; 5. Graphic novels
978-0-8225-8877-1, $27.93; 978-0-8225-8879-5 (pa), $7.95

LC 2007-043732

In this new take on the "Choose Your Own Adventure" type of book that combines pages of prose text with pages of comic book sequences, you are a vampire, and you must defend yourself and your castle from vampire hunters. Some choices will end badly, others will be better, and the choices are all up to the reader.

This is Volume 7 of the Twisted Journeys series

Warriors: Ravenpaw's path: vol. 1, shattered peace. Created by Erin Hunter ; written by Dan Jolley ; art by James L. Barry. Tokyopop/HarperCollins 2009 Un Illustration
Grades: 3 4 5 6 7 8 9   **741.5; Fic**
1. Adventure graphic novels; 2. Cats; 3. Graphic novels
978-0-06-158865-2 (pa), $6.99

LC 2009-920733

Ravenpaw used to be part of Thunderclan, but he left the clan and has lived on the twolegs' farm with his friend Barley, mostly to stay away from Tigerstar. Life is quiet, peaceful, with plenty of mice to hunt in the cozy barn. Then other cats come seeking shelter, because Minty, the female, is about to give birth to her kits. Barley knows there's something bad about the cats, as he comes upon the males teaching the kits how to fight and kill other cats. Ravenpaw and Barley had always left the chickens alone and only hunted mice; after a fire damages the barn, they find the other cats have returned and plan to make the farm their territory. When the other cats kill some chicks, the farmer sees only Ravenpaw and Barley, who had tried to stop the killing, and the twoleg blames them. Now they must leave the farm, but Ravenpaw doesn't think he can return to the clan. This manga-style graphic novel is an original story featuring characters from Erin Hunter's fiction series.

Warriors: the rise of Scourge. Created by Erin Hunter ; written by Dan Jolley ; art by Bettina M. Kurkoski. Tokyopop/HarperCollins 2008 106p. Illustration
Grades: 3 4 5 6 7 8 9   **741.5; Fic**
1. Adventure graphic novels; 2. Cats; 3. Graphic novels
978-0-06-147867-3, $6.99

LC 2007-935239

Scourge, leader of the Bloodclan, is a violent, fierce cat and enemy of the Thunderclan cats. This story tells of his life before he became the leader, before he became Scourge. He started life as the kittypet named Tiny, the runt of his litter, despised by his bigger litter mates. Fascinated by the woods outside the fence where he lives, he ventures out to explore, and one day runs into forest cats from Thunderclan who injure him. Convinced the twoleg family will drown him as an unwanted kitten, Tiny lives among the strays in the alleys. A series of happenstances establish a reputation for toughness and he changes his name to Scourge. What he really wants, though, is to settle things with the Thunderclan cat who almost killed him. The fights between cats might be upsetting for younger readers.

Wrapped up in you. By Dan Jolley; illustrated by Natalie Nourigat. Graphic Universe 2012 127 p.
Grades: 6 7 8 9 10 11 12   **741.5; Fic**
1. Horror graphic novels; 2. Horror stories; 3. Love stories; 4. Mummies; 5. Mummies — Fiction; 6. North Carolina — Fiction; 7. Supernatural graphic novels; 8. Witches — Fiction; 9. Graphic novels
0761368566; 9780761368564, $29.27

LC 2011044655

This graphic novel, by Dan Jolley, illustrated by Natalie Nourigat, is book 6 in the "My Boyfriend Is a Monster" series. "Prince Pachacutec—or 'Chuck'—is a man with a past. He died tragically five hundred years ago, but that's all ancient history as far as Staci is concerned. He is everything she could want. . . . But the witches aren't willing to live and let live. Will Staci fight for Chuck? Or do the witches have a point when they say reanimated corpses make bad boyfriends?" (Publisher's note)

Jones, Bruce
Deadman: Deadman Walking. Bruce Jones, writer; John Watkiss, artist. DC Comics 2007 128p. Illustration
Grades: 11 12 Adult   **741.5; Fic**
1. Mystery graphic novels; 2. Superhero graphic novels; 3. Supernatural graphic novels; 4. Graphic novels
978-1-4012-1236-0, $12.99

Brandon Cayce is about to find out the answers to the question of what happens after we die; unfortunately, he's going to find out by becoming a dead man himself. Now come new questions. Why did his brother crash an airliner, killing everyone aboard - including Brandon? Why does Brandon find himself drawn to Sarah, his sister-in-law and onetime love? Who are those men trying to kill him ... and can you even kill a Deadman? The book includes a lot of violence, some nudity and sexual situations.

Nightwing: Brothers in Blood. Bruce Jones, writer; Joe Dodd, Paco Diaz, Robert Teranishi, pencillers; Bit, Nathan Massengill, Wes Craig, inkers; Javier Rodriguez Studio, Guy Major, colorists. DC Comics 2007 168p. Illustration
Grades: 10 11 12 Adult   **741.5; Fic**
1. Nightwing (Fictional character); 2. Robin (Fictional character); 3. Superhero graphic novels; 4. Graphic novels
978-1-4012-1224-7, $14.99

After Bludhaven was destroyed in the Infinite Crisis, Dick Grayson relocated to New York City. It's a year later, and he has new friends, a new flame, and new criminal masterminds to fight. But, there's also another Nightwing, one who kills criminals without mercy - it's Jason Todd, the former Robin who succeeded Dick but was then killed by the Joker. He's been resurrected, but his idea of justice is twisted. And New York City has meta-human criminal kingpins, the Pierce brothers, who want both Nightwings dead. The book includes some sexual situations along with superhero violence.

Jones, Gerard
Dragon Ball Z (vizbig edition vol. 1). Viz Media/Shonen Jump 2008 528p. Illustration
Grades: 7 8 9 10 11 12   **741.5; Fic**
1. Adventure graphic novels; 2. Manga; 3. Martial arts; 4. Shonen manga; 5. Graphic novels
978-1-4215-2064-3, $17.99
The first three volumes of DragonBall Z are now collected in a larger size volume. The Saiyans are an alien race of deadly warriors who wipe out entire planets for their own profit and gain. When the Saiyans set their sights on Earth, it's up to Son Goku to fight off the invaders with his superhuman strength. This series is an almost nonstop series of martial arts action scenes, so there's lots of fighting and yelling, but no harsh language.
Also available in 26 individual volumes
Volume 1 of 9

Jones, Sabrina
★ **Isadora** Duncan: a graphic biography. Hill & Wang 2008 129p. Illustration
Grades: 9 10 11 12 Adult   **92; 792.8; 741.5**
1. Biographical graphic novels; 2. Dancers; 3. Duncan, Isadora, 1878-1927; 4. Graphic novels
978-0-8090-9497-4, $18.95
                                                    LC 2008-17928
Dancer Isadora Duncan thrilled and appalled her audiences at the turn of the twentieth century and beyond; she chose to wear freeflowing costumes with no corsets or other confining undergarments, and she danced barefoot. She used choreographic elements from the ancient Greeks, with flowing movements as free as her garments. Jones sifts through the various books about Duncan, from the autobiography and others, with all their contradictory information, to depict a unique and contradictory woman who deeply influenced modern dance well beyond her death. The black and white art shows Duncan always in Greek-styled gowns. There are two panels which show nudity in the context of Duncan's dance performances.
Includes bibliographical references.

    Race to incarcerate: a graphic retelling. Sabrina Jones and Marc Mauer. The New Press 2013 128 p. Illustration
Grades: 9 10 11 12 Adult   **364.6; 364.6\0973**
1. Administration of criminal justice — United States; 2. Crime prevention — United States; 3. Criminal justice, Administration of — United States; 4. Discrimination in criminal justice administration — United States; 5. Imprisonment — United States; 6. Prison sentences — United States; 7. Prisons — United States; 8. Graphic novels
1595585419; 9781595585417, $17.95
                                                    LC 2012049688

"Jones channels the tradition of liberal-Left political cartooning to give this graphic documentary a dynamic, woodcut-like look that galvanizes its adaptation of Mauer's tract of the same name. Its subject is imprisonment in the U.S., especially, since the war on drugs was launched in the 1980s, the push to jail as many as possible (as it sometimes seems). Since the opening of the first 'penitentiary' in 1829 and preceded by 'getting tough on crime' policies, the war on drugs has reversed the emphasis on rehabilitation in U.S. prisons." (Booklist)
Includes bibliographical references and index
Based on Race to Incarcerate by Marc Mauer.

Jones, Steve
Introducing Genetics, New ed.. Steve Jones and Borin Van Loon. Totem Books 2005 176p. Illustration
Grades: 10 11 12 Adult   **576.5; 741.5**
1. Genetics; 2. Graphic novels
978-1-84046-636-2, $12.95
This book uses cartoons and a spare text to provide an introductory guide to the study of genetics, form Mendel to the human gene map and the treatment of inborn disease. It shows how DNA was discovered, and explains how some genes may act in their own interests as much as in the interests of those who carry them. Jones is a professor of genetics. The book includes a list of books for further reading.

Joy, Bob, ed.
Batman: The Greatest Stories Ever Told Volume Two. DC Comics 2007 208p. Illustration
Grades: 7 8 9 10 11 12 Adult   **741.5; Fic**
1. Batgirl (Fictional character); 2. Batman (Fictional character); 3. Joker (Fictional character); 4. Superhero graphic novels; 5. Graphic novels
978-1-4012-1214.8, $19.99
This volume includes stories from different periods in the nearly seventy-year career of Batman, from 1940 to 2003. He goes up against classic villains - the Joker, Killer Croc, the Penguin; he meets Batgirl (Barbara Gordon); deals with crooked businessmen and other criminals.

    Flash: The Greatest Stories Ever Told. DC Comics 2007 208p. Illustration
Grades: 6 7 8 9 10 11 12 Adult   **741.5; Fic**
1. Flash (Fictional character); 2. Superhero graphic novels; 3. Graphic novels
978-1-4012-1372-5, $19.99
Jay Garrick, Barry Allen, and Wally West are all men who have donned the symbol of the yellow lightning bolt to combat evil as the Flash. Each hero with his own unique style of commanding a mastery over momentum, they have fought separately and together over the years. This volume collects stories that see them pitted against such villains as Gorilla Grodd, the Reverse Flash, the Fiddler, and many others. This volume also includes the story of Barry and Iris' wedding.

    The **Helmet** of fate. DC Comics 2007 128p. Illustration
Grades: 8 9 10 11 12 Adult   **741.5**
1. Superhero graphic novels; 2. Supernatural graphic novels; 3. Graphic novels
978-1-4012-1470-8, $14.99

The tenth age of magic is about to begin, but it needs a new champion, a new Dr. Fate. The Helmet of Fate seeks a new master and encounters some of the most powerful beings of the supernatural world on its quest. Candidates include Zauriel from JLA, Black Alice from Birds of Prey, Shadowpact's Detective Chimp (what!?), as well as Sargon the Sorcerer and Ibis the Invincible. Who will become the successor to Dr. Fate? The book includes some violence and some mild harsh language.

Showcase Presents: Batgirl Volume 1. DC Comics 2007 552p. Illustration
Grades: 6 7 8 9 10 11 12 Adult   **741.5; Fic**
   1. Batgirl (Fictional character); 2. Superhero graphic novels; 3. Graphic novels
   978-1-4012-1367-1, $16.99
   In the late 1960s, DC Comics added a new character to the world of Batman and Robin: Batgirl. Daughter of Commissioner Jim Gordon, Barbara Gordon is a librarian who relocates to Gotham City and soon dons her costume as the crime fighting Batgirl. This volume of black and white reprints includes her early adventures, from 1967 through 1975. The cover art notwithstanding, Batgirl is a woman of action.

Showcase Presents: Batman Vol. 1. DC Comics 2006 552p. Illustration
Grades: 6 7 8 9 10 11 12 Adult   **741.5; Fic**
   1. Batman (Fictional character); 2. Superhero graphic novels; 3. Graphic novels
   1-4012-1086-4, $16.99
   The spotlight's on Batman in this volume featuring Detective Comics #327-342 and Batman #164-174. The Dynamic Duo take on some of their most enduring Rogues Gallery members, including Penguin, the Riddler, and the Outsider in these classic Silver Age stories from the era of famed editor Julius Schwartz. This Showcase edition reprints the comics in black and white.

Showcase Presents: Batman Vol. 2. DC Comics 2007 510p. Illustration
Grades: 6 7 8 9 10 11 12 Adult   **741.5; Fic**
   1. Batgirl (Fictional character); 2. Batman (Fictional character); 3. Joker (Fictional character); 4. Riddler (Fictitious character); 5. Robin (Fictional character); 6. Superhero graphic novels; 7. Graphic novels
   978-1-4012-1362-6, $16.99
   Over 500 pages of classic adventures are included in this volume collecting Silver Age tales of Batman and Robin as they face their most enduring enemies, including the Joker, Poison Ivy, the Riddler, Blockbuster, and many others. These are the stories that inspired the Dynamic Duo's 1960s TV series, which featured Batman's astonishing detective skills and impressive array of Bat-gadgets. The stories, reprinted in black and white, date from 1965 and 1966.

Superman/Doomsday: The Collected Edition. DC Comics 2006 412p. Illustration
Grades: 10 11 12 Adult   **741.5; Fic**
   1. Superhero graphic novels; 2. Superman (Fictional character); 3. Graphic novels
   978-1-4012-1107-3, $19.99

Doomsday killed Superman. Now the Man of Steel wants payback. Superman travesl to the nightmare world of Apokolips for a confrontation with Doomsday, the creature who cost the Man of Steel his life. With the help of the mysterious, time-traveling Waverider, superman at last discovers the shocking truth of his greatest enemy's origin. And just when he thinks the terror is finally over, the murderous juggernaut returns to Earth more powerful than ever.

Superman: The Amazing Transformations of Jimmy Olsen. DC Comics 2007 192p. Illustration
Grades: 6 7 8 9 10 11 12 Adult   **741.5; Fic**
   1. Humorous graphic novels; 2. Superhero graphic novels; 3. Superman (Fictional character); 4. Graphic novels
   978-1-4012-1369-5, $14.99
   Cub reporter Jimmy Olsen stars in this light-hearted volume collecting some of his most memorable adventures from the late 1950s and 1960s, all of which guest-star Superman. While investigating crime for The Daily Planet, Jimmy undergoes one startling transformation after another, gaining temporary super-powers as Elastic Lad and becoming a Giant Turtle Man, The Wolf-Man of Metropolis, The Human Porcupine and much more. At times like these, Superman finds that he must not only protect Metropolis from Jimmy, but Jimmy from himself.

Judal
   Vampire Game Vol.1. Tokyopop 2003 193p. Illustration
Grades: 8 9 10 11 12   **741.5; Fic**
   1. Fantasy graphic novels; 2. Humorous graphic novels; 3. Shojo manga; 4. Graphic novels
   1-59182-369-2, $9.99
   In an epic battle, valiant King Phelios defeats the evil vampire King Duzell, but both monarchs are mortally wounded. As the two lay dying, Duzell prophesies that they will meet again, in another place and another time, and vows that he will be triumphant. Hundreds of years later, Duzell comes back as a menacing baby wildcat who is rescued from the wild and adopted by Ishtar, the great-granddaughter of his nemesis, King Phelios. Ishtar is a playful girl with an iron will and a penchant for pranks, a trait that distresses her caretaker, Sir Keld, and a dashing imperial guard, Captain Dales. Ishtar is not, however, the reincarnation of Phelios, leaving the now-feline Duzell to continue his quest for revenge - without letting his new owner know that he is hell-bent on destroying her family ... but would Ishtar even care about that if she knew" The book includes some strong language, some violence, and some brief sexual situations.

DC Showcase presents Booster Gold volume 1. DC Comics 2008 624p. Illustration
Grades: 8 9 10 11 12 Adult   **741.5; Fic**
   1. Booster Gold (Fictional character); 2. Superhero graphic novels; 3. Graphic novels
   978-1-4012-1655-9, $16.99
   This volume collects the entire run of the Booster Gold comics series written and drawn by Dan Jurgens and published from 1986 through 1988. Michael Jon Carter lives in the 25th century, and he wants thrills, wealth, and fame. He "borrows" items from the Space Museum and travels back in time to the twentieth century, where he uses his

knowledge of things to come to build an empire and become the super hero, Booster Gold. His constant self-promotion annoys and offends the heroic community, and eventually he will have to learn that fame and fortune come at a price. DC brought Booster Gold back for its 2007 crossover event, 52, but here readers can find the original "anti-superhero."

Justice League Adventures Vol. 1: The Magnificent Seven
DC Comics 2004 112p. Illustration
Grades: 4 5 6 7 8 9   **741.5; Fic**
1. Batman (Fictional character); 2. Flash (Fictional character); 3. Green Lantern (Fictional character); 4. Justice League (Fictional characters); 5. Superhero graphic novels; 6. Superman (Fictional character); 7. Wonder Woman (Fictional character); 8. Graphic novels
1-4012-0179-2, $6.95
The World's Greatest Heroes: Martian Manhunter, Green Lantern, Hawkgirl, the Flash, Wonder Woman, Batman, and Superman battle against villainy from all corners of the globe, and beyond. Among other villains, they fight Chronos the Time Thief and Screamthief.

Justice League Adventures Vol. 2: Friends and Foes
DC Comics 2004 112p. Illustration
Grades: 4 5 6 7 8 9   **741.5; Fic**
1. Batman (Fictional character); 2. Flash (Fictional character); 3. Green Lantern (Fictional character); 4. Justice League (Fictional characters); 5. Superhero graphic novels; 6. Superman (Fictional character); 7. Wonder Woman (Fictional character); 8. Graphic novels
1-4012-0180-6, $6.95
The World's Greatest Heroes: Martian Manhunter, Green Lantern, Hawkgirl, the Flash, Wonder Woman, Batman, and Superman - return to thwart another round of wrongdoers, and the threats come from all sides. Brainiac and Poison Ivy are just a couple of the super villains they face.

Ka, Olivier
★ **Why** I killed Peter. Story, Olivier Ka; adaptation & art, Alfred; color, Henri Meunier. NBM 2008 112p. Illustration
Grades: 10 11 12 Adult   **741.5**
1. Biographical graphic novels; 2. Catholic church — Clergy; 3. Child sexual abuse; 4. Graphic novels
978-1-56163-543-6, $18.95
Olivier Ka writes of his life and of the lifelong effect of one particular act. He grows up in France, the child of what he describes as hippie parents. Their lifestyle is very open, and young Olivier sees adults naked a lot, and his parents sleep with other partners quite often. Into this comes young priest Peter, a liberal type of cleric who wears shirts and jeans rather than cassocks and other vestments, who plays the guitar during services. Olivier likes him a lot, because Peter really talks with him and listens, more like a fun uncle than a priest. Over the years, Peter remains a part of the family, and Olivier goes to his summer camps. Then the summer Olivier is twelve, Peter asks him to do something that makes Olivier uncomfortable. They will sleep side by side in their own sleeping bags, but completely naked "to be equal," and they will massage each other's belly. It starts out like that, but ends . . . well. Olivier continues to go to the summer camps until he's fifteen, but he and Peter never do anything like that again. Years later, as an adult, Olivier suffers emotional problems, and attending services in a Catholic church makes him physically ill. Eventually, when his own daughter is twelve years old, Olivier writes this story, makes a friend who is an artist, and they create the graphic novel. And Olivier confronts Peter after so many years. The act Peter committed with Olivier is not depicted on the page, but there is nudity and some sexual situations, along with strong language.

Kafka, Franz
Kafka: Give It Up! And Other Short Stories. NBM/ComicsLit 1995 63p. Illustration
Grades: 10 11 12 Adult   **741.5; Fic**
1. Graphic novels
978-1-56163-449-1, $8.95
Peter Kuper adapts and illustrates nine stories by Kafka: "A Little Fable," "The Bridge," "Give It Up!," "A Hunger Artist," "dA Fratricide," "The Helmsman," "The Trees," "The Top," and "The Vulture."

Kagami, Takaya
Seraph of the end; Vol 1: vampire reign. By Takaya Kagami, Daisuke Furuya, illustrated by Yamato Yamamoto. Viz 2014 197 p. Illustration
Grades: 9 10 11 12   **741.5**
1. Manga; 2. Vampires
1421571501; 9781421571508, $9.99
"After a catastrophic epidemic kills every adult on earth, vampires arise from the shadows to enslave the remaining human population. Yuichiro escapes from captivity and joins the Japanese Imperial Demon Army. But before he's allowed to fight . . ., he has to . . . make new friends with his fellow aspiring monster slayers!" (Publisher's note)
"Yamamoto's black-and-white illustrations are eye-catching and powerful, capturing architectural details of crumbling cities, extreme close-ups of conflicted characters, explosions, and fight scenes with equal skill." SLJ
Volume 1 of an ongoing series

Kaishaku
Key Princess Story: Eternal Alice Rondo Vol. 1. DrMaster Publications 2007 188p. Illustration
Grades: 10 11 12 Adult   **741.5; Fic**
1. Adventure graphic novels; 2. Fantasy graphic novels; 3. Shonen manga; 4. Graphic novels
978-1-59796-113-2, $9.95
When Aruto Kirihara, an aspiring writer moved by the classic tale Alice in Wonderland, meets a group of magically gifted young girls, the literary fuel for a new and truly fantastic "Alice" story is revealed. This is an adventure of a hopeful scribe and a group of girls with special powers, the Alice Police, in pursuit of the missing third book of Alice called "Eternal Alice." This series includes some fan service shots and partial nudity.

Kakalios, James

The **Physics** of Superheroes. James Kakalios.. Gotham Books 2009 424 p.

Grades: 11 12 Adult   530

1. Batman (Fictional character); 2. Heroes and heroines; 3. Physics — Study and teaching; 4. Spider-Man (Fictional character); 5. Superman (Fictional character)

1592405088; 9781592405084, $18

LC 2009028814

"With The Physics of Superheroes, named one of the best science books of 2005 by Discover, he introduced his colorful approach to an even wider audience. Now Kakalios presents a totally updated, expanded edition that features even more superheroes and findings from the cutting edge of science. With three new chapters and completely revised throughout with a splashy, redesigned package, the book that explains why Spider-Man's webbing failed his girlfriend, the probable cause of Krypton's explosion, and the Newtonian physics at work in Gotham City is electrifying from cover to cover." (Publisher's Note)

"By combining his love for physics with his love of comic books, . . . Kakalios has written a book for the general reader [that covers] all of the basic points in a first-level college physics course and is difficult to put down. . . . That all of this is accomplished with enough humor to make you laugh aloud is an added bonus." Pub Wkly

Includes bibliographical references and index

Kamio, Yoko

Boys Over Flowers (Hana Yori Dango) Volume 1. Viz Media/Shojo 2003 208p. Illustration

Grades: 9 10 11 12 Adult   741.5; Fic

1. Romance graphic novels; 2. Shojo manga; 3. Graphic novels

1-56931-996-0, $9.99

When her only friend, Makiko, accidentally offends F4 leader Tsukasa, Tsukushi boldly defends her. Enraged, Tsukasa puts the dreaded red tag in Tsukushi's locker - a sign that she is now a target for the abuse of the F4 gang and the entire school. But when Tsukushi fights the gang with their own weapon, Tsukasa finds himself falling for her. Tsukushi comes from a poor family but attends a prestigious school ruled by the rich students; she manages to hold her own against any bullying. There's some violence in the bullying, and some sexual situations.

Kanari, Youzaburou

Gimmick! volume 1. Story by Youzaburou Kanari; art by Kuroko Yabuguchi. Viz Media 2008 226p. Illustration

Grades: 10 11 12 Adult   741.5; Fic

1. Adventure graphic novels; 2. Manga; 3. Mystery graphic novels; 4. Graphic novels

978-1-4215-1778-0, $9.99

Kohei Nagase is a prodigy in creating makeup and special effects, and he runs Studio Gimmick with his stuntman friend and sidekick, Kannazuki. While Kohei depends on Ms Shiho to help him find paying work for movie and television studios, his passion for creating makeup effects leads him to helping people. For instance, a young starlet wants to escape her sleazy manager and reunite with her boyfriend. Then there's the actress who had been in a horrible accident and wants to hide the hideous scar on her

body when the studio wants to film a nude scene. Then a horror theme park hires Kohei to redo the zombie dummies, but he runs afoul of the original makeup artist, who is determined to destroy the park in vengeance for being fired. Kohei is a bit sukebe and ecchi (kind of perverted) and visibly lusts after the beautiful young actresses, but his passion for makeup rules everything for him. The stories include some frontal nudity and some violence.

Kindaichi Case Files Vol. 14: The Gentleman Thief. Story by Yozaburo Kanari; art by Fumiya Sato. Tokyopop 2006 Un Illustration

Grades: 9 10 11 12 Adult   741.5; Fic

1. Manga; 2. Mystery graphic novels; 3. Shonen manga; 4. Graphic novels

1-59532-698-7, $9.99

11th grader Hajime Kindaichi is considered a slacker, but he's actually a genius detective and the grandson of famous detective Kousuke Kindaichi. In this volume, Hajime and his best friend Miyuki travel to Aomori with Detective Kenmochi to try to prevent a thief from stealing a painting from artist Gozo Gamou, who has assembled a party to unveil his painting. The Gentleman Thief issues a challenge to Kindaichi, then raises the stakes by committing murder. Each volume in the series is a standalone murder mystery involving locked rooms and serial murders; in each volume, at least one body is found partially nude.

The **Kindaichi** case files vol. 17: the undying butterflies. Tokyopop 2008 Un Illustration

Grades: 8 9 10 11 12 Adult   741.5; Fic

1. Manga; 2. Mystery graphic novels; 3. Graphic novels

978-1-59532-701-7, $9.99

The article about the discoverer of a rediscovered species of butterfly is not the sort of thing that teenage detective Hajime Kindaichi would care about, but the photograph included with the article catches his eye; the assistant to Madarame, the butterfly expert, looks identical to Eiji Touno, a killer Kindaichi had uncovered and whom he thought had died in a massive fire. Kindaichi, best friend Miyuki, and their detective buddy Itsuki, travel to Madarame's impressive estate to uncover the mystery about Touno. However, while they are there, murders begin to occur, starting tragically with Madarame's youngest daughter Ruri, who is only twelve years old. Can Kindaichi match wits with the murderer and stop him? There is little bloodshed or overt violence in this murder mystery, and one instance of nonsexual partial nudity.

Kindaichi Case Files Volume 1: The Opera House Murders. Tokyopop 2003 186p. Illustration

Grades: 8 9 10 11 12 Adult   741.5; Fic

1. Manga; 2. Mystery graphic novels; 3. Shonen manga; 4. Graphic novels

1-59182-354-4, $9.99

Teenager Hajime Kindaichi is a slacker, but a genius at solving mysteries, which is needed when the Fudo High drama club travels to a hotel on an isolated island to rehearse the play, 'Phantom of the Opera.' People start turning up dead, murdered in ways appearing in the play, and with no way off the island, Hajime better find the killer before everyone dies. The book includesgraphic violence, some strong language, and some nudity (usually the dead bodies).

Kanata, Konami

★ **Chi's** sweet home, volume 1. Vertical, Inc. 2010 166p. Illustration

Grades: 5 6 7 8 9 10 11 12 Adult   **741.5; Fic**

1. Cats; 2. Humorous graphic novels; 3. Manga; 4. Graphic novels

9781-934287-81-1

Young kitten Chi gets separated from her family while out on a stroll, then she meets little boy Yohei and his parents. They take her home, even though their apartment building has a strict no pets policy. While they try to find someone to take her in, they feed her, give her a cozy bed, set up a box with shredded newspaper for a litter box, and do their best to help her. Even though readers can read what she's thinking, Chi behaves just like a cat, with cat problems such as thinking the litter box is a wonderful play area instead of the place to do her business, and taking fright at Yohei's "vrooming" as he plays with his toy cars. The book is great for younger readers as well as anyone who likes cats. There is one panel where Yohei is sitting on the toilet while Chi is in her litter box in the bathroom, and a scene at the veterinarian's office where the doctor sticks a thermometer in to take Chi's temperature. And, of course, Chi tends to urinate in inappropriate places.

Also available in 3-in-1 omnibus editions
Volume 1 of 12

Kanda, Takayuki

Edu-Manga: Ludwig van Beethoven. Art by Naoko Takase. Digital Manga Publishing 2006 144p. Illustration

Grades: 3 4 5 6 7 8 9   **92; 741.5**

1. Beethoven, Ludwig van; 2. Biographical graphic novels; 3. Manga; 4. Graphic novels

1-56970-973-4, $9.95

Beethoven stands as one of the greatest musical minds the world has ever seen, with such famous works as his Symphony No. 9 ("Ode to Joy") and the classic piano piece "Fur Elise." The onset of deafness was only one of many hardships he had to face, but his strength and desire to do battle with his turbulent life led him to create the many musical pieces the world cherishes today. This manga format biography uses Astro Boy and his friends to introduce the story, present more information in a Q&A format, and provides a timeline to Beethoven's life.

Kane, Bob

Batman Archives Volume 1. Bob Kane and Bill Finger. DC Comics 1990 304p. Illustration

Grades: 7 8 9 10 11 12 Adult   **741.5; Fic**

1. Batman (Fictional character); 2. Robin (Fictional character); 3. Superhero graphic novels; 4. Graphic novels

978-0-930289-60-7, $39.95

When a young Bruce Wayne watched in horror as his parents were murdered, the legend of the Batman was born. Collected here are the first stories of the masked vigilante as they were originally printed in 1939. These stories include the classic first appearance of the Batman and the introduction of his teenage ally, Robin. These early adventures show how a dark and grim character and his humorous and light sidekick were masterfully combined to create one of the most enduring partnerships of all time.

The **Batman** Chronicles Volume Two. Bob Kane and Bill Finger. DC Comics 2006 224p. Illustration

Grades: 7 8 9 10 11 12 Adult   **741.5; Fic**

1. Batman (Fictional character); 2. Catwoman (Fictional character); 3. Joker (Fictional character); 4. Robin (Fictional character); 5. Superhero graphic novels; 6. Graphic novels

978-1-4012-0790-8, $14.99

This series reprints the Batman comics in chronological order; this second volume includes stories originally published in 1940. Batman is becoming more of a father figure to Robin; the villains become more colorful, the scientists get madder; the Dynamic Duo take on the Joker, Catwoman, Clayface, and more classic Bat-villains.

Batman in the eighties. Batman created by Bob Kane; [introduction by John Wells]. DC Comics 2004 191p. Illustration

Grades: 9 10 11 12 Adult   **741; 741.5; Fic**

1. Batgirl (Fictional character); 2. Batman (Comic strip); 3. Batman (Fictional character); 4. Robin (Fictional character); 5. Superhero graphic novels; 6. Graphic novels

1-4012-0241-1, $19.95

The events featured in this collection "include Dick Grayson's transformation into Nightwing, Barbara Gordon's final days as Batgirl and the introduction of not one, but two new versions of Robin. The stories in this volume may not include the greatest highlights of the decade, but do serve to round out many of the events that affected the Batman mythos during the 1980's." Libr Media Connect

Batman in the forties. Batman created by Bob Kane; [introduction by Bill Schelly]. DC Comics 2004 192p. Illustration

Grades: 9 10 11 12 Adult   **741; 741.5; Fic**

1. Batman (Fictional character); 2. Catwoman (Fictional character); 3. Joker (Fictional character); 4. Robin (Fictional character); 5. Superhero graphic novels; 6. Graphic novels

1-4012-0206-3, $19.95

"The 17 selections include such milestones as Batman's first appearance in May 1939, the two-page story of his origins from November 1939, and the 1940 introduction of his young partner, Robin. . . . Other stories feature early appearances by some of Batman's most renowned arch-enemies: the Joker, Catwoman, and Two-Face. . . . Most compelling are the earliest stories; crude as they are, their naive verve and raw directness remain effective." Booklist

Originally published (1939-1949) in single magazine form as Batman 7, 15, 20, 31, 37, 47, 48, 49, Detective Comics 27, 33, 38, 49, 80, Real Fact Comics 5, Star-Spangled Comics 70, World's Finest Comics 30

Kang, E-Jin

Good Luck Volume 1. Tokyopop 2007 Un Illustration

Grades: 8 9 10 11 12   **741.5; Fic**

1. Manhwa; 2. Romance graphic novels; 3. Graphic novels

978-1-59816-761-0, $9.99

Shi-Hyun is pure bad luck. That's what everyone says ... and in some ways, she believes it. So for their protection asnd her own, she's developed a hard shell that keeps people at bay. But when Shi-Hyun transfers to a new school, an array of new characters comes into her life. The Queen Bee has a cool personality and the fighting skills to match. The Cold Prince has the looks and demeanor to make all the girls swoon. And what about the nice girl, Hee-Soo, the only one who'll come near Shi-Hyun? Well, she has an agenda of her own ...

Kanigher, Robert
Showcase Presents: The Haunted Tank Volume 1. Art by Joe Kubert and Russ Heath. DC Comics 2006 560p. Illustration
Grades: 7 8 9 10 11 12 Adult   741.5; Fic
1. Ghosts; 2. World War, 1939-1945; 3. Graphic novels
1-4012-0789-8, $16.99
What happens when the ghost of General J. E. B. Stuart, a long-deceased Confederate general, returns to act as a protector to his namesake, Sgt. Jeb Stuart, commander of a tank in North Africa during World War II" These stories combine the fast-paced action of war with a supernatural bent. This black and white volume reprints the first thirty-three tales of the Haunted Tank, dating from 1961 to 1966. Writer Kanigher was just voted into the Eisner Awards Hall of Fame as a Judges' Choice in 2007.

Showcase Presents: Wonder Woman Vol. 1. DC Comics 2007 528p. Illustration
Grades: 6 7 8 9 10 11 12 Adult   741.5; Fic
1. Superhero graphic novels; 2. Wonder Woman (Fictional character); 3. Graphic novels
978-1-4012-1373-2, $16.99
Wonder Woman faces some of her deadliest challenges as she battles a variety of aliens and robots, and confronts the evil menaces of the Time Master, the Gadget Maker, Dike of Deception, and one of her most incessant foes, the Angle Man. This volume also includes the re-done origin of Wonder Woman, and some of her teenage adventures as Wonder Girl. Created by William Moulton Marston as a strong, liberated warrior in 1941, these adventures published in the late 1950s and early 1960s cast Wonder Woman in a more "traditional" female superhero role.

Kanno, Aya
Blank slate volume 1. Viz Media/Shojo Beat 2008 Un Illustration
Grades: 10 11 12 Adult   741.5; Fic
1. Adventure graphic novels; 2. Mystery graphic novels; 3. Shojo manga; 4. Graphic novels
978-1-4215-1924-1, $8.99
Zen is a beautiful young man with no memory of who or what he was, all he knows is that he gets urges to kill and he does so. The nation of Amata had been taken over by the Galayans twenty years ago, and Zen inadvertently gets involved with the resistance when he kidnaps the Galay general's daughter Rian. He ends up with Hakka, an unlicensed doctor who helps the Amatans. But what does Hakka know about Zen? This book includes considerable violence.

Otomen; Volume 1. Story & art by Aya Kanno. Viz Media 2010 208 p. Illustration
Grades: 8 9 10 11 12   741.5; Fic
1. Dating (Social customs) — Fiction; 2. Shojo manga; 3. Teenagers — Fiction

1421521865; 9781421521862, $9.99
"Asuka Masamune is a guy who loves girly things—sewing, knitting, making cute stuffed animals and reading shojo comics. But in a world where boys are expected to act manly, Asuka must hide his beloved hobbies and play the part of a masculine jock instead. Ryo Miyakozuka, on the other hand, is a girl who can't sew or bake a cake to save her life. Asuka finds himself drawn to Ryo, but she likes only the manliest of men! Can Asuka ever show his true self to anyone, much less to the girl that he's falling for?" (Publisher's note)
"Although the art is as sugary and cute as Asuka himself, with lots of sparkling and glitter in the periphery, hidden among all the prettiness are important themes of individuality and being true to yourself, making this an empowering read for teenage girls." Booklist
Volume 1 of 18

Soul Rescue Volume 1. Tokyopop 2006 Un Illustration
Grades: 8 9 10 11 12   741.5; Fic
1. Adventure graphic novels; 2. Fantasy graphic novels; 3. Shonen manga; 4. Graphic novels
1-59816-672-7, $9.99
When Angels are supposed to epitomize all that is perfect in love and mercy, where does a rogue angel fit into it all? Renji is one of heaven's most powerful but overly violent angels. As punishment for going too far in the last great battle against the demons, Renji is banished to Earth. His mission? Saving 10,000 souls. But for an angel who's never known anything outside of fighting, there may be nothing in Heaven or Hell that can help him. Where bad boy angels must learn to love humanity, it's all in the Soul Rescue. The series includes some fighting action.

Kaplan, Arie
Speed Racer: chronicles of the racer. Art by Robby Musso and German Torres. IDW Publishing 2008 Un Illustration
Grades: 5 6 7 8 9 10 11 12 Adult   741.5; Fic
1. Adventure graphic novels; 2. Automobile racing; 3. Racer, Speed (Fictional character); 4. Graphic novels
978-1-60010-213-4, $17.99
After a race in which something happens to Speed's Mach 5 and he's saved by Racer X, Pop Racer gives Speed a book, The Chronicles of the Racer. For thousands of years, there has been one Racer in their family, one who is destined to win. And for those thousands of years, the Racer has dealt with a villain who is associated with Mercury. From ancient Rome to medieval England to eighteenth century pirates and onward, Speed finds himself reliving his ancestors' experiences after he sneaks into Mercury Studios, and he finds himself face-to-face with the same man who has battled his ancestors through the centuries. This book collects the four-issue miniseries of original stories based on the Speed Racer characters.

Kardy, Glenn
Manga University Presents . . . Kana de Manga Special Edition: Japanese Sound FX!. Writer, Glenn Kardy; artist, Chihiro Hattori. Japanime Co. Ltd./Manga University 2007 110p. Illustration
Grades: 6 7 8 9 10 11 12 Adult   495.6; 741.5

1. Japanese language; 2. Manga; 3. Graphic novels
978-4-921205-12-6, $9.99

What does a cat's meow sound like in Japanese? How about the grumble of an empty stomach, the wail of a police car's siren or the crash of an ocean wave? Japanese manga artists rely heavily upon onomatopoeia—sound-effect words—and this entry in the Kana de Manga / Kanji de Manga language-learning series includes illustrated examples of those sounds in action. It features more than 100 Japanese onomatopoeia and their English equivalents in categories such as "Humans," "Animals," "Machines" and "Nature." The text is written in both English and Japanese hiragana.

Manga University Presents ... Kana de Manga: A Fun, Easy Way to Learn the ABCs of Japanese!. Text by Glenn Kardy ; art by Chihiro Hattori. Japanime Co. Ltd 2004 113p. Illustration
Grades: 5 6 7 8 9 10 11 12 Adult   **495.6; 741.5**
1. Japanese language — Teaching — Aids and devices; 2. Manga; 3. Graphic novels
4-921205-01-9, $9.99

This book uses original manga artwork to teach students how to read, write and pronounce the Japanese hiragana and katakana alphabets, also known as "kana." Author Glenn Kardy and artist Chihiro Hattori have teamed up to create this book for manga enthusiasts who are interested in more than just pretty pictures. In addition to presenting the kana, the book illustrates stroke order in writing the characters, and each hiragana character is shown with a word, its definition, an illustration, and opportunities for practice in writing the character.

Manga University Presents ... Kanji de Manga: The Comic Book That Teaches You How to Read and Write Japanese! Created by Glenn Kardy ; art by Chihiro Hattori. Volume 1. Japanime Co. Ltd 2004 113p. Illustration
Grades: 5 6 7 8 9 10 11 12 Adult   **495.6; 741.5**
1. Japanese language — Teaching — Aids and devices; 2. Manga; 3. Graphic novels
4-921205-02-7, $9.99

This book uses original comic artwork to teach readers how to identify and write the most common Japanese kanji ideographs. It introduces 80 basic kanji that all Japanese schoolchildren are required to learn before entering the third grade, or for those who wish to pass Level 4 of the Japanese Language Proficiency Test for non-native speakers of Japanese. Each page features its own comic strip, kanji pronunciation guide, stroke order, and English explanations.

Manga University Presents ... Kanji deManga: The Comic Book That Teaches You How to Read and Write Japanese! Volume 2. Japanime Co. Ltd 2005 113p. Illustration
Grades: 7 8 9 10 11 12 Adult   **495.6; 741.5**
1. Japanese language — Teaching — Aids and devices; 2. Manga; 3. Graphic novels
4-921205-03-5, $9.99

The second volume in this series - using original comic artwork to teach readers how to identify and write the most common Japanese kanji ideographs - introduces 80 more kanji that all Japanese school children are required to learn by the time they graduate from sixth grade, or for those who wish to pass Level 3 of the Japanese Language Proficiency Test for non-native speakers of Japanese. Each page features its own comic strip, kanji pronunciation guide, stroke order, and English explanations.

Manga University Presents ... Kanji deManga: The Comic Book That Teaches You How to Read and Write Japanese! Volume 3. Japanime Co. Ltd 2005 113p. Illustration
Grades: 7 8 9 10 11 12 Adult   **495.6; 741.5**
1. Japanese language — Teaching — Aids and devices; 2. Manga; 3. Graphic novels
4-921205-04-3, $9.99

The third volume in this series - using original comic artwork to teach readers how to identify and write the most common Japanese kanji ideographs - introduces 80 more kanji that all Japanese school children are required to learn by the time they graduate from sixth grade, or for those who wish to pass Level 3 of the Japanese Language Proficiency Test for non-native speakers of Japanese. Each page features its own comic strip, kanji pronunciation guide, stroke order, and English explanations.

Manga University Presents ... Kanji deManga: The Comic Book That Teaches You How to Read and Write Japanese! Volume 4. Japanime Co. Ltd 2006 144p. Illustration
Grades: 7 8 9 10 11 12 Adult   **495.6; 741.5**
1. Japanese language — Teaching — Aids and devices; 2. Manga; 3. Graphic novels
4-921205-09-4, $9.99

The fourth volume in this series - using original comic artwork to teach readers how to identify and write the most common Japanese kanji ideographs - introduces 80 more kanji that all Japanese school children are required to learn by the time they graduate from sixth grade, or for those who wish to pass Level 3 of the Japanese Language Proficiency Test for non-native speakers of Japanese. Each page features its own comic strip, kanji pronunciation guide, stroke order, and English explanations.

Kari, Erika
Vampire Doll: Guilt-na-Zan Vol. 1. Tokyopop 2006 196p. Illustration
Grades: 8 9 10 11 12 Adult   **741.5; Fic**
1. Horror graphic novels; 2. Humorous graphic novels; 3. Manga; 4. Graphic novels
1-59816-519-4, $9.99

Guilt-na-Zan is a vampire aristocrat who has been sealed into a cross for more than 100 years. When he is released by Kyoji, a powerful exorcist from the family that first banished the vampire, Guilt-na-Zan is resurrected as a female doll and can only transform into his real form when he sucks blood from Kyoji's sister Tonae. Kyoji uses Guilt-na-Zan and his old servant Vincent as Tonae's bodyguards at school. They also have to deal with black sheep brother Kyoichi, who constantly tries to steal old family artifacts, trying to gain occult power. The series includes some mild sexual encounters.

Kariya, Tetsu
Oishinbo a la carte: the joy of rice. Story by Tetsu Kariya ; art by Akira Hanasaki. Viz Signature Edition 2009 268p. Illustration

Grades: 8 9 10 11 12 Adult   741.5; Fic
1. Cooking; 2. Manga; 3. Rice; 4. Graphic novels
978-1-4215-2144-2, $12.99

This volume collects the Oishinbo stories centering on rice, the supreme staple of the Japanese diet. As Yamaoka continues, with the help of other Tozai News staffers, to work on the newspaper's Ultimate Menu to celebrate its 100th anniversary, they examine rice. Among other stories, Yamaoka rails against the importing of rice from other countries; he shows that organic rice farming could be unhealthy depending on the farm's location; and he helps the company cafeteria chef attract more business by focusing on homestyle rice dishes. The big competition between the Ultimate Menu and the Supreme Menu is rice balls (omusubi). The stories here may help American readers understand a little more about how important rice is to Japanese culture, and they may want to try some of the dishes. The book includes a recipe for scallop rice, which is published in color with photos. As with the other volumes, this book includes stories that originally appeared throughout the original manga series, so the characters' lives and relationships change abruptly from story to story.

Oishinbo a la carte: vegetables. Story by Tetsu Kariya ; art by Akira Hanasaki. Viz Media/Viz Signature 2009 268p. Illustration
Grades: 8 9 10 11 12 Adult   741.5; Fic
1. Cooking — Vegetables; 2. Manga; 3. Graphic novels
978-1-4215-2143-5,
$12.99

Tozai News reporter Yamaoka Shiro and his colleagues continue their quest for the Ultimate Menu. In this volume, he competes against his father Kaibara, who represents rival newspaper Teito Times and their Supreme Menu, in a competition involving the vegetables cabbage and turnip. In other stories, Yamaoka and his friends use asparagus as a way to reunite a culinary specialist and a pottery artist who broke up years ago; and they

Courtesy of VIZ Media LLC

help Tomii's son get over his hatred of eggplant. A number of the stories discuss the debate between organic cultivation and the use of pesticides and imported vegetable types. Since the stories are selected from the Oishinbo series to fit into themes, they skip around in time and lack a real narrative flow. The book is suitable for teens, but the main appeal may be to adults, especially to those who want to read about food. The artist's focus on presenting all the vegetables so realistically and in great detail may just make the reader hungry.

Katakura, Masanori-Ookamigumi
Kurohime Vol. 1. Viz Media/Shonen Jump Advanced 2007 182p. Illustration
Grades: 10 11 12 Adult   741.5; Fic

1. Adventure graphic novels; 2. Fantasy graphic novels; 3. Manga; 4. Shonen manga; 5. Graphic novels
978-1-4215-1366-9, $7.99

Kurohime is a big busty witch with the command of magical guns. She was once foolish enough to challenge the Gods and in doing so was punished. A curse was put on her that turned her into a little girl. The only way she can break this curse and turn back in to her big bad buxom self is to fall in love. Master gunman Zero searches the land for the legendary Kurohime, because she saved him as a child and impressed upon him the importance of justice and helping others. He meets a young girl named Himeko; little does he know that she is actually Kurohime. This book includes lots of sexual suggestiveness and some violence.

Katin, Miriam
We are on our own: a memoir. Drawn & Quarterly 2006 122p. Illustration
Grades: 9 10 11 12 Adult   92; 741; 741.5
1. Animators; 2. Artists; 3. Autobiographical graphic novels; 4. Cartoonists; 5. Holocaust, 1933-1945; 6. Illustrators; 7. Katin, Miriam; 8. World War, 1939-1945
1-896597-20-3, $19.95

LC 2005-9063602

In this WWII memoir, the author recounts "how she and her mother faked their deaths and fled Budapest after the Nazis occupied the city. With forged papers obtained from a black marketer, they escaped to the countryside in the guise of a servant girl and her illegitimate child. Katin relates their harrowing lives there and her mother's desperate search for her missing husband after the war. . . . This impressive book belongs in all serious graphic novel collections and is also a natural for Jewish studies." Booklist

Kawahara, Kazune
High school debut vol. 1. VizMedia/Shojo Beat 2008 184p. Illustration
Grades: 7 8 9 10 11 12   741.5; Fic
1. Manga; 2. Romance graphic novels; 3. Shojo manga; 4. Graphic novels
978-1-4215-1481-9, $8.99

Haruna used to be interested only in softball and manga, but now that she's starting in high school, she wants to change her focus, to find a boyfriend and have a fun romance. The problem is, no boy will hit on her. She's done her research in magazines, but nothing is working. Then a friend's comment causes her to decide to find a coach who will help her attract boys. Upperclassman Yoh Komiyama agrees to help her, but only if Haruna promises to not fall in love with him. It's a struggle, though, for Yoh's sister and his friends decide to tag along for fun. There's one scary moment when a guy tries to abduct Haruna.

★ **My** Love Story!!; Volume 1. Story, Kazune Kawahara; art, Aruko; English adaptations, Ysabet Reinhardt MacFarlane; translation, JN Productions. Viz 2014 184 p. Illustration
Grades: 8 9 10 11 12   741.5
1. Man-woman relationship — Fiction; 2. Shojo manga
1421571447; 9781421571447, $9.99

In this graphic novel, by Kazune Kawahara, "Takeo is big and manly in a macho kind of way. His best friend,

Sunakawa, is handsome in a pretty/pointy-haired way, which means that girls always find him attractive. One day Takeo rescues a girl named Yamato from a groper on the train, and she starts falling in love with him. Unfortunately for Takeo, he is too dense to realize this and spends most of the story convinced that Yamato is really in love with Sunakawa." (School Library Journal)

Volume 1 of an ongoing series

Showcase Presents: Teen Titans Volume 1. DC Comics 2006 528p. Illustration
Grades: 6 7 8 9 10 11 12 Adult   741.5; Fic
1. Flash (Fictional character); 2. Robin (Fictional character); 3. Superhero graphic novels; 4. Teen Titans (Fictional characters); 5. Graphic novels
978-1-4012-0788-5, $16.99

The Teen Titans were all sidekicks to such heroes as Batman, Wonder Woman, Aquaman, and the Flash. When teen heroes Robin, Aqualad, and Kid Flash joined together, they became a forced to be reckoned with. Wonder Girl quickly joined them, and occasionally Speedy would come, and they all proved they were just as capable of defeating the bad guys and saving the world as their mentors, while still being teens and having fun. The black and white reprinted stories originally appeared from 1964 through 1968. Today's teens will get a kick out of what the writers thought was cool "teen speak" back then.

Superman: The Greatest Stories Ever Told Volume Two. DC Comics 2006 192p. Illustration
Grades: 7 8 9 10 11 12 Adult   741.5; Fic
1. Superhero graphic novels; 2. Superman (Fictional character); 3. Graphic novels
978-1-4012-0956-8, $19.99

This volume includes nine stories from different times in Superman's career. Readers can experience Superman's first meeting with the other dimensional imp Mr. Mxyztplk, his return to Krypton, a deadly battle against the team of Lex Luthor and Brainiac, an after-life adventure with Pa Kent, his greatest secret revealed, and more.

Kawase, Natsuna
The **Lapis** Lazuli crown, vol. 1. DC Comics/CMX 2009 Un Illustration
Grades: 6 7 8 9 10 11 12   741.5; Fic
1. Magic; 2. Manga; 3. Romance graphic novels; 4. Shojo manga; 5. Graphic novels
978-1-4012-2120-1, $9.99

Teenage Miel is a member of the Violette family, which once was influential due to having so many important magicians who protected the kingdom of Savarin. Now, her older sister Sara is a strong magician, but Miel won't use her talent. The problem is Miel has talent but no control, which tends to get her into trouble. Then she meets a handsome young man on the street, and after he eggs her into using her magic, she learns he is really the reclusive Prince Radian. Will her desire to be his friend and work in the palace be enough to motivate her to practice using her magical powers" Can she be the one who will protect the kingdom again" The book includes a short backup story, "Daisy Romance," in which Hinagiku tries to protect her house from the thief who calls himself New Moon, only to get help from

the thief to catch an impostor using his name. All the romance in both stories is very innocent and sweet.

Kawashima, Tadashi
Alive Vol. 1. Story by Tadashi Kawashima; art by Adachitoka. Random House/Del Rey Manga 2007 200p. Illustration
Grades: 10 11 12 Adult   741.5; Fic
1. Shonen manga; 2. Graphic novels
978-0-345-49746-8, $10.95

A strange virus is making its way around the globe, causing its victims to commit suicide, and becoming a lethal pandemic in less than a week. Then Taisuke finds his shy, withdrawn friend Hiro, who has always been the target of bullies, on the roof of their high school, with the bloody, dead bodies of the four bullies. And when Hiro turns on him, Taisuke discovers he has powers, too. What's going on? This first volume raises lots of questions. The book includes some harsh language and graphic violence.

Kazumi, Yuana
Million Tears Vol. 1. Tokyopop 2007 Un Illustration
Grades: 8 9 10 11 12   741.5; Fic
1. Family life; 2. Mystery graphic novels; 3. Shojo manga; 4. Graphic novels
978-1-4278-0056-5, $9.99

When friends and loved ones begin to disappear and no one else remembers them, Hiromu's sense of reality begins to crumble—until the day he runs into a mysterious figure who can erase a person's very existence, and tells Hiromu he's another "destiny thief." This is the first of two volumes.

Keatinge, Joe
Shutter; Volume 1: Wanderlost. Joe Keatinge; illustrated by Leila Del Duca, Owen Gieni, Ed Brisson. Image Comics 2014 136 p. Color illustration
Grades: 11 12 Adult   741.5; Fic
1. Explorers; 2. Family secrets — Fiction
1632151456; 9781632151452, $9.99

In this graphic novel by Joe Keatinge, illustrated by Leila Del Duca, Owen Gieni, and Ed Brisson, "Kate Kristopher, once the most famous explorer of an Earth far more fantastic than the one we know, is forced to return to the adventurous life she left behind when a family secret threatens to destroy everything she spent her life protecting." (Publisher's note)

"Keatinge and Del Duca have created a contemporary world that teems with casual miracles and feels all the more real and lived in for it. Crammed with the elements of children's storybooks, the art offers soft lines and a panoply of almost-recognizable storybook figures that honor those hallowed childhood recollections." Booklist

Originally published in single magazine form as Shutter #1-6

Volume 1 of an ongoing series

Keith, Sam
Batman: Secrets. Sam Kieth, writer, artist; Alex Sinclair, colorist; Rob Leigh, Phil Balsman, Travis Lanham, letterers. DC Comics 2007 128p. Illustration
Grades: 9 10 11 12 Adult   741.5; Fic

1. Batman (Fictional character); 2. Joker (Fictional character); 3. Superhero graphic novels; 4. Graphic novels
978-1-4012-1212-4, $12.99

This is a story that pits the Dark Knight against the Joker—all under the unforgiving eye of the media. Their confrontation is caught on film, and Gotham City's protector appears to pummel his archenemy without mercy. The Joker uses this to frame Batman in the court of public opinion while the media hover like vultures, ready to convict before all the facts are in. But it gets worse when the Joker threatens someone from Bruce Wayne's past, and this brings back tormented memories that Batman has kept hidden for years. Keith's eccentric art style might not be to everyone's taste.

Kelly, Joe

★ **Captain** Stoneheart and the Truth Fairy. Image Comics 2008 Un Illustration
Grades: 5 6 7 8 9 10 11 12 Adult   **741.5; Fic**
1. Adventure graphic novels; 2. Fairies; 3. Fantasy graphic novels; 4. Pirates; 5. Graphic novels
978-1-58240-865-1, $19.99

The story, in rhyming text with lushly drawn and colored art, tells the tale of the pirate named Captain Stoneheart, a fierce and angry pirate who won't let people tell him what to do. After attacking a peaceful ship and killing everyone on it, his crew discovers a caged fairy in the hold, and Stoneheart knows he can wreak havoc and scourge the world with her powers. Somehow they connect even through his anger, and when she finds a way to save Stoneheart and his crew even when she is free to leave the pirates and save herself, Stoneheart starts to change. Alas, the good times can't last, and he commits one final act that destroys everything and everyone around him because he won't let anyone tell him what to do, even if he loves that one person. There is some fighting violence, and there are some monsters, so this is not a story for very young readers. Older elementary school age children who love the old fairy tales with the tragic endings will be able to handle this story.

★ **I kill giants.** Image Comics 2009 Un Illustration
Grades: 8 9 10 11 12   **741.5; Fic**
1. Family life; 2. Fantasy graphic novels; 3. Giants; 4. Graphic novels
978-1-60706-092-5, $15.99

Fifth-grader Barbara Thorson appears to be a smart-aleck troublemaker, and she does get into trouble at school, with great regularity. She has no friends, she has to deal with teachers and a principal who don't understand her, with the bully Taylor, with Sophie, the new girl who wants to be her friend, and now with a school psychologist. She has no time for this nonsense, she is a giant killer, with her mighty weapon she calls Coveleski (after Stanley Coveleski, a baseball player in the early twentieth century). What writer Kelly reveals slowly to the reader is Barbara's real family situation: her mother is dying, her older sister is trying to keep the family together, and Barbara is convinced that if she can slay the Titan, a huge giant, she can keep her mother alive. While Barbara is young, the story has an emotional intensity better suited for older teens.

Justice League Elite Volume One. Doug Mahnke, collaborator; John Byrne, collaborator; Tom Nguyen, collaborator. DC Comics 2005 Un Illustration

Grades: 9 10 11 12 Adult   **741.5; Fic**
1. Justice League (Fictional characters); 2. Superhero graphic novels; 3. Graphic novels
1-4012-0481-3, $19.99

Conflicting goals causes a schism among the Justice League of America. As a result, several members of the JLA choose to do undercover work with Vera Black and her super-powered team, the Elite. Their first assignment: infiltrate a small brotherhood of assassins gathering to hit a major political target. Heroes find themselves suddenly allied with deadly foes. Can this group function effectively enough to do their job" And if they can't, what happens to the world" The book includes some strong language, although most of it is masked in nonsense symbols, and violence.

Space Ghost. Joe Kelly, writer ; Ariel Olivetti, illustrator ; Richard Starkings, letterer. DC Comics 2005 Un Illustration
Grades: 8 9 10 11 12 Adult   **741.5; Fic**
1. Superhero graphic novels; 2. Graphic novels
1-4012-0721-9, $14.99

The masked avenger of the cartoon spaceways has been a popular character since his introduction to television in 1966. Since then, people have wondered who he is, how he got those power bands and why he protects the galaxy from evil. Now his story is told for the first time ever, and readers will learn the tragic circumstances that led to his donning a cowl and his first battle with arch nemesis Zorak. This is not the funny character from Cartoon Network.

Kelly, Walt

Walt Kelly's Our Gang Vol. 1. Fantagraphics Books 2006 104p. Illustration
Grades: 4 5 6 7 8 9 10 11 12 Adult   **741.5; Fic**
1. Friendship; 2. Humorous graphic novels; 3. Graphic novels
978-1-56097-753-7, $12.95

Kelly's longest-running continuing comics series based on the "real-life" characters of MGM's durable short-film series, "Our Gang" (a.k.a. "The Little Rascals"). Kelly's Our Gang harks back to the days before television, when kids spent most of their time playing outdoors, limited only by each other's imagination and ingenuity. This is the first in a series of books reprinting Walt Kelly's Our Gang stories. Suitable for both adults and children, they have been restored from their comic book appearance. These stories were originally published in 1942 and 1943.

Volume 1 of 4

Kelso, Megan

The **Squirrel** Mother: Stories. Fantagraphics Books 2006 147p. Illustration
Grades: 10 11 12 Adult   **741.5; Fic**
1. Graphic novels
978-1-56097-746-9, $16.95

Kelso's work is characterized by subject matter that fits roughly into two disparate camps: personal and semi-autobiographical stories that draw heavily on the details of her childhood and adolescence, and stories about the idea of America and American history, such as a trilogy of short pieces about Alexander Hamilton. This book

features 15 stories, including two stories, "Meow Face" and "Aide de Camp," done especially for this volume. The personal stories are each self-contained but in a sense take place in the same world where similar characters inhabit different stories. The "America" stories are broader in subject matter, taking on events of political and historical significance and wrestling with ideas having to do with the American experience.

Kennedy, Mike

Aliens vs. Predator: civilized beasts. Mike Kennedy; illustrated by Roger Robinson. Dark Horse Comics 2008 Un Illustration

Grades: 9 10 11 12 Adult   **741.5; Fic**
1. Horror graphic novels; 2. Science fiction graphic novels; 3. Graphic novels
978-1-59307-342-8, $6.95

It was supposed to have been a short business tour, but the group has been stranded on the remote planet for eight months. The humans have been aided by a Predator they've named Smiley, and occasionally they have to hunt an alien out to kill them. When a rescue ship arrives, however, it is crewed by illegal synthetic humans, then everyone gets mixed into the Predators' new hunt of Aliens. Whoever wins, the humans will lose. The book includes considerable violence, including the tearing off of limbs.

Alien vs. Predator: Thrill of the Hunt. Story, Mike Kennedy; pencils, Roger Robinson with Dustin Weaver. Dark Horse Comics 2004 Un Illustration

Grades: 10 11 12 Adult   **741.5; Fic**
1. Horror graphic novels; 2. Science fiction graphic novels; 3. Graphic novels
1-59307-257-0, $6.95

In the future, after a technological catastrophe that started a second dark age, all memory of vicious bug-like aliens and brutal predatory aliens that hunted humans has been forgotten. Now, mankind has reached out to space again, and humans are once again caught in the middle of a deadly struggle between the two most lethal species ever encountered. And once again, whoever wins ... humans lose. The book includes some bloody violence.

Superman: Infinite City. Art by Carlos Meglia. DC Comics 2005 96p. Illustration

Grades: 8 9 10 11 12 Adult   **741.5; Fic**
1. Superhero graphic novels; 2. Superman (Fictional character); 3. Graphic novels
978-1-4012-0066-4, $17.99

When a villain uses a very powerful weapon in Metropolis, Clark and Lois trace him back to an old town called Infinite City. They find the town abandoned, except for a doorway that leads to another amazing world.... the true Infinite City, where magic and science happily coexist.

Superman and Lois step through the magic portal and become embroiled in a war for power on the other side. One faction wants to stay in its dimension, and another wants to branch out to our world. Superman will meet a doppelganger called the Warden, who shares the Kryptonian's might but not his intellect. He will also come across the architect of this world, a robot leader who claims to be what remains of his father Jor-El.

Kesel, Barbara

Legends of the Dark Crystal, vol. 1: The Garthim Wars. Written by Barbara Randall Kesel ; illustrated by Heidi Arnhold and Max Kim. Tokyopop 2007 192p. Illustration

Grades: 8 9 10 11 12 Adult   **741.5**
1. Adventure graphic novels; 2. Fantasy graphic novels; 3. Graphic novels
978-1-59816-701-6, $9.99

Lahr and Neffi are gentle and fun-loving Gelflings who enjoy the simple pleasures of life. Their world is turned upside down when the violent Garthim attack their villages, and after a narrow escape, the two Gelflings must join forces and learn how to become leaders to help another Gelfling village defend themselves against the Garthim. This story is a prequel to the Jim Henson film, The Dark Crystal. It includes some violence.

Kashyap, Keshni

Tina's mouth. Keshni Kashyap; illustrated by Mari Araki.. Houghton Mifflin Harcourt 2011 242 p. Illustration

Grades: 9 10 11 12   **741.5/973; 741.5**
1. California, Southern — Fiction; 2. East Indian Americans — Fiction; 3. Girls; 4. High schools — Fiction; 5. Individuality — Fiction; 6. Schools — Fiction; 7. Teenagers; 8. Graphic novels
9780618945191

LC 2011030439

This book tells the story of "Tina, an Indian-American living in San Francisco, [who] writes an illustrated diary to Jean-Paul Sartre as part of a semester-long existentialism class in this . . . coming-of-age story. . . . Tina's best friend ditches her for a boy and Tina has a crush on someone but has trouble making it work. . . . A story about Krishna lends the book its title. Tina is not religious herself, but she and her peers are exploring different religions as they grapple with racial identity." (Publishers Weekly) Ketcham, Hank

★ **Hank Ketcham's Complete Dennis the Menace (Volume 1): 1951-1952.**

Fantagraphics Books 2005 590p. Illustration
Grades: 2 3 4 5 6 7 8 9 10 11 12 Adult   **741.5; Fic**
1. Dennis the Menace (Fictional character); 2. Humorous graphic novels; 3. Graphic novels
1-56097-680-2, $24.95

This volume is the first of a series that will reprint every Dennis the Menace cartoon. The first cartoon was published in sixteen newspapers on March 12, 1951, and the cartoon was soon picked up by many more newspapers. This volume collects the daily single-panel cartoons from March 1951 through December 1952. In these cartoons, readers meet five-and-a-half-year-old Dennis Mitchell, his parents, retired neighbors George and Martha Wilson, Dennis' dog Ruff, and neighborhood pals Joey and Margaret. Every cartoon hearkens back to the positive aspects of growing up in suburban Middle America and the joys (mostly) of being a child. While older adults will catch all the references to past popular culture (i.e. Hopalong Cassidy), younger readers will enjoy the humor arising from everyday situations.

Kibuishi, Kazu, ed.

Flight v2. [editor/art director, Kazu Kibuishi]. Villard 2007 432p. Illustration
Grades: 10 11 12 Adult   **741.5**
  1. Fantasy graphic novels; 2. Short stories
  978-0-345-49637-9, $24.95
In this themed story collection, "more than 30 accomplished young artists take off on the theme, sometimes loosely construed, of flight. . . . At more than 400 pages, there is something in this elegantly produced collection for everyone, including readers who usually snub comics." Booklist
Stories are by various authors; previously published by Image Comics; v1 published 2004 by Image Comics; Villard edition published 2007

★ **Flight** v3. [editor/art director, Kazu Kibuishi]... Ballantine Books 2006 351p. Illustration
Grades: 9 10 11 12 Adult   **741.5**
  1. Fantasy graphic novels; 2. Short stories; 3. Graphic novels
  978-0-345-49039-1; 0-345-49039-8, $24.95
                        LC 2006-45883
This third volume of Flight includes 26 short stories by mostly young writers, many of whom have webcomics. Some, such as Michael Gagne and Becky Cloonan, have published a number of books. The stories range from whimsical interludes to ironic fables to mini-epics of derring-do; ironically, most of the stories have only a tangential connection to the theme of flight.
Sequel to Flight v2 (2005)

Flight volume five. Villard Books 2008 364p. Illustration
Grades: 9 10 11 12 Adult   **741.5; Fic**
  1. Short stories; 2. Graphic novels
  978-0-345-50589-7, $25
This latest volume contains twenty-one stories from creators such as Svetlana Chmakova, Dave Roman, Phil Craven, Kean Soo, Scott Campbell, Graham Annable, editor Kibuishi, and others. The stories include another episode in the adventures of Jellaby, the true meaning of baseball and what it is to be a true professional player ("Beisbol 2—), another episode in Michael Gagne's "The Saga of Rex," and a tale of what happens when a trio of high-tech "Worry Dolls" goes to work to help an unemployed actor. In this volume, the stories are somewhat longer than in previous volumes and most have actual plots to go with the artwork. Stories range from realistic to the fantastic, from whimsical to dramatic to tragic.

★ **Flight,** volume six. Villard Books 2009 284p. Illustration
Grades: 8 9 10 11 12 Adult   **741.5; Fic**
  1. Fantasy graphic novels; 2. Short stories; 3. Graphic novels
  978-0-345-50590-3, $25

This sixth volume of the graphic anthology series includes stories by fifteen creators: J.P. Ahonen, Graham Annable, Bannister, Phil Craven, Mike Dutton, Michel Gagne, Cory Godbey, Rodolphe Guenoden, Steve Hamaker, Kazu Kibuishi, Andrea Offermann, Richard Pose, Justin Ridge, Rad Sechrist, and Kean Soo. Returning favorite characters includ Jellaby by Soo, Hamaker's Fish N Chips, Kibuishi's Daisy Kutter, and the wordless little fox Rex by Gagne. Bannister's "Cooking Duel" stands out as a lot of fun, as a couple makes a bet about which of them can make the better tasting mushroom quiche; and Justin Ridge's "Dead Bunny" shows that there is a soul mate for just about anyone, including a zombie bunny.

Flight: Volume Four. Random House/Villard 2007 344p. Illustration
Grades: 9 10 11 12 Adult   **741.5; Fic**
  1. Fantasy graphic novels; 2. Short stories; 3. Graphic novels
  978-0-345-49040-7, $24.95
This fourth volume of the graphic novel anthology series includes 25 stories by creators ranging from veterans such as Michel Gagne and Graham Annable to newer creators such as Clio Chiang and Neil Babra. Most of the artists have webcomics; a number of them work in animation (Gagne most recently worked on the motion picture Ratatouille); some have worked on major graphic novel projects - Lark Pien colored Gene Yang's American Born Chinese, and Raina Telgemeier works on the graphic novel adaptations of The Baby-Sitters Club. While there is little harsh language and no nudity, some of the stories have more mature themes.

★ **Flight:** Volume One. Edited by Kazu Kibuishi. Villard 2007 207 p.
Grades: 9 10 11 12 Adult   **741.5; 741.5/973**
  0345496361; 9780345496362, $27
This comic book, edited by Kazu Kibuishi, includes work from "Bengal, Bill Mudron, Catia Chien, Chris Appelhans, Clio Chiang, Derek Kirk Kim, Dylan Meconis, Enrico Casarosa, Erika Moen, Hope Larson, Jacob Magraw-Mickelson, Jake Parker, Jen Wang, Joel Carroll, Kazu Kibuishi, Khang Le, Neil Babra, Philip Craven, Rad Sechrist, and Vera Brosgol." (Publisher's note)
Volume 1 of 8

Kidd, Chip

Mythology: the DC Comics art of Alex Ross. Text by Chip Kidd; introduction by M. Night Shymalan; photography by Geoff Spear. Pantheon Bks. 2003 Un Illustration; Color
Grades: 9 10 11 12 Adult   **741.5\092; 741; 741.5**
  0-375-42240-4, $35
                        LC 2003-46740
"Ross's gouache painted art glows on the pages. Interspersed with quotations by the artist and those who know him, Kidd's sparse text takes readers on a brief tour of Ross's childhood to his early days in advertising and comic books, finally ending with the limited series "Kingdom Come" (Warner, 1998), which combined hyper-realistic artwork with unusually complex storytelling. The book not only displays samples of finished works but also includes

sketches, photographs of live models, and comic art dating back to the 1930s." SLJ

Kieth, Sam
　The **Maxx** Volume 1. DC Comics/Wildstorm 2003 Unp. Illustration
Grades: 10 11 12 Adult　　　　　　　**741.5; Fic**
　1. Adventure graphic novels; 2. Fantasy graphic novels; 3. Graphic novels
　1-4012-0124-5, $17.95
　Thinking himself a typical superhero, Maxx is a homeless bum living in a cardboard box, aided by freelance social worker Julie Winters. Maxx travels to another world, "The Outback," where he's a hero and saves Julie from strange imaginary creatures and from his ultimate enemy, Mr. Gone. The reader also meets Sarah, who wants to be a writer, is mad at her mom, and is too chicken to kill herself. People who like their superhero comics very postmodern, existential, and very strange will like this. The book has some violence.

　Star Wars: Clone Wars Adventures Volume 2. Dark Horse Comics 2004 Un Illustration
Grades: 6 7 8 9 10 11 12　　　　　　　**741.5; Fic**
　1. Adventure graphic novels; 2. Science fiction graphic novels; 3. Star Wars; 4. Graphic novels
　1-59307-271-6, $6.95
　In the rolling asteroid rings above a remote planet, General Obi-Wan Kenobi and Anakin Skywalker play a deadly game of cat and mouse against Separatist droid fighters - and a squadron of highly skilled human pilots who have pledged their guns to Count Dooku. Also in this volume, Jedi Master Luminara Unuli and her Padawan Barriss Offee race against time to evacuate farmers and their families before the droid forces of General Grievous overrun their village. When Barriss and her squad of clone troopers are caught in the path of the enemy army, only fast thinking and steel resolve can save the day. And Jedi Master Mace Windu goes solo to foil a sinister Separatist plot. These stories take place approximately five months after the Battle of Geonosis.

　Zero Girl. Story and art, Sam Kieth; additional inks, Jim Sinclair; colors, Nick Bell, Alex Sinclair; letters, Naghmeh Zand. DC Comics/Wildstorm 2001 114p. Illustration
Grades: 9 10 11 12 Adult　　　　　　　**741.5; Fic**
　1. Fantasy graphic novels; 2. Graphic novels
　1-56389-851-9, $14.95
　Amy Smootster is a high school social outcast who lives her life content in her own world. But it seems that Amy's world is full of strange happenings such as the spontaneous appearances of puddles of water around her and two-sided conversations with insects. And there's something weird with her and circles and the fact that squares are inimical to her. With the help of her guidance counselor (upon whom she has a crush), Amy eventually accepts and embraces her abnormal abilities and discovers her place in the world.

　Zero Girl: Full Circle. Writer/artist, Sam Kieth; colorist, Alex Sinclair; letterer, John Layman. DC Comics/Wildstorm 2003 110p. Illustration
Grades: 9 10 11 12 Adult　　　　　　　**741.5; Fic**
　1. Fantasy graphic novels; 2. Graphic novels

　1-4012-0170-9, $17.95
　Amy Smootster's now an adult, working as a guidance counselor. Her former crush, Tim Foster, is now a single parent with a troubled daughter. Tim enlists Amy's aid in helping her adjust, but the young girl, Nikki, has plans - and abilities - of her own. The book includes some strong language.

Kikuta, Michiyo
　Mamotte! Lollipop Vol. 1. Random House/Del Rey Manga 2007 224p. Illustration
Grades: 8 9 10 11 12 Adult　　　　　　　**741.5; Fic**
　1. Fantasy graphic novels; 2. Shojo manga; 3. Graphic novels
　978-0-345-49623-2, $10.95
　Junior high schooler Nina is ready to fall in love. She's looking for a boy who's cute and sweet-and strong enough to support her when the chips are down. But what happens when Nina's dream comes true . . . twice? One day, two cute boys literally fall from the sky: they're both wizards and they've come to the Human World to take the Magic Exam. The boys' success on this test depends on protecting Nina from evil, so now Nina has a pair of cute magical boys chasing her everywhere she goes. But, because Nina accidentally swallowed a magic "crystal pearl" that is part of the Magic Exam, Zero and Ichi aren't the only wizards around her, and some are willing to do just about anything to get their hands on the magic pearl.

Kim, Derek Kirk
　★ **Good** as Lily. Written by Derek Kirk Kim; illustrated by Jesse Hamm; lettering by Jared K. Fletcher. DC Comics/Minx 2007 Un Illustration
Grades: 7 8 9 10 11 12　　　　　　　**741.5; Fic**
　1. Fantasy graphic novels; 2. Humorous graphic novels; 3. Graphic novels
　978-1-4012-1381-7, $9.99
　"On her eighteenth birthday, Korean American Grace suddenly finds herself surrounded by three very corporeal essences of herself: as a small child, as a 30-year-old woman, and as "a cranky old fart." Each of these incarnations is at an emotional precipice, which teenage Grace helps resolve, allowing the other self to quietly disappear. . . . Kim's pacing and plotting are excellent, and Hamm's black, white, and gray artwork is lively, witty, and full of appropriate comedy and melodrama." Booklist

　Same difference. Derek Kirk Kim.. First Second 2011 90p. Illustration
Grades: 9 10 11 12 Adult　　　　　　　**741.5**
　1. Family — Fiction; 2. Love — Fiction; 3. Short stories; 4. Youth — Fiction; 5. Graphic novels
　9781596436572; 1596436573
　　　　　　　　　　　　　　LC 2010052663
　This graphic-novel-style collection of short stories is concerned with young people, and gives particular focus to romantic and familial relationships. "The title story focuses on 20-somethings Nancy and Simon, who are racked with guilt. Why" Simon has turned down a date with a friend because she is blind, and Nancy has read love letters meant for someone else-and answered them, giving the jilted ex-boyfriend false hope. Through a series of credible

coincidences, both eventually make amends. . . . [The] collection also includes stories about high school track, weed wacking, familial relationships, celebrity interviews, and autobiographical tales." (School Libr J)

Kim, Dong Wook

Angel Cup Volume 1. Written by Dong Wook Kim; illustrated by Jae Ho Youn. Tokyopop 2006 208p. Illustration

Grades: 9 10 11 12   741.5; Fic
   1. Manwha; 2. Sports; 3. Graphic novels
   1-59532-303-1, $9.99

Even though So-jin thinks of Shin-bee as her rival at soccer, Shin-bee seems more interested in managing the boys' team at So-jin's school rather than leading the girls' team to victory. When the boys on the soccer team make disparaging remarks about girls, So-jin wants to put together a collection of female athletes to meet the challenge from the boys. Now the game is approaching, and so far So-jin is a few members short of a full squad. The book contains some titillating angle shots of the girls.

Kim, Ho Sik

My sassy girl. Illustrated by Dae Hong Min. Comics One 2003 130p. Illustration

Grades: 9 10 11 12   741; Fic; 741.5
   1. Graphic novels
   1-58899-342-6, $13.95

"College-age Geon-woo meets a strange and exceedingly sassy young woman who yearns for him one moment and treats him with hostility the next. Geon-woo's psychic tribulations and peaks of infatuation are depicted in hilarious detail as he morphs from suave guy to blithering toddler in response to the girl's demands and egregiously mean tricks. . . . The narrative flows seamlessly among the captioned thoughts, and the artwork, replete with manga-derived angles and vantage points, is beautifully colored to show off anger-reddened faces, European hair colors, gaudy modern streets, and crowded subways. Readers will sympathize with Geon-woo as they wait to see what shenanigans his sassy girl will pull next." Booklist
   Vol. 1
   Volume 1 of 6

Kim, Jae-Hwan

War Angels Vol. 1. Tokyopop 2007 172p. Illustration
Grades: 10 11 12   741.5; Fic
   1. Adventure graphic novels; 2. Fantasy graphic novels; 3. Manwha; 4. Graphic novels
   978-1-4278-0188-3, $9.99

Salvation can be Hell... It's the year 2504. In the aftermath of an apocalyptic war, the surviving humans are ruled by the Beasterians, animal-human hybrids created to be the ultimate soldiers, but who instead became merciless tyrants. Doomed to extinction, humanity's future rests with the savior whose birth is foretold by the Post-Testament Bible. This manwha has harsh language and graphic violence.

Kim, June

12 Days. Tokyopop 2006 Un Illustration
Grades: 10 11 12 Adult   741.5; Fic
   1. Romance graphic novels; 2. Graphic novels
   1-59816-691-3, $9.99

When Jackie's ex-lover Noah (another woman) dies, she decides the best and quickest way to get over the love of her life is to hold a personal ritual with Noah's ashes. Jackie consumes the ashes in the form of smoothies for 12 days—hoping the pain will subside with her profound reaction to Noah's death. The book includes some same-sex sexual situations, depicted tastefully.

Kindt, Matt

2 Sisters: A Super-Spy Graphic Novel. Top Shelf Productions 2004 334p. Illustration
Grades: 9 10 11 12 Adult   741.5; Fic
   1. Adventure graphic novels; 2. Spies
   1-891830-58-9, $19.95

This World War II era spy thriller spans not only the globe, but time as well - from England to Spain and from ancient Roman times through the era of Pirates and Buccaneers. This spy story is the backdrop for the unique tale of two sisters, their relationship and the secrets they share. Readers will find a world of shady gypsies, mysterious rockets, buried treasure, pen-guns, cyanide teeth, and romance. The book includes violence.

Pistolwhip. Top Shelf Productions 2001 120p. Illustration
Grades: 10 11 12 Adult   741.5; Fic
   1. Adventure graphic novels; 2. Mystery graphic novels; 3. Graphic novels
   1-891830-23-6, $14.95

                                        LC 2002-280685
Readers will find a naive bellhop's struggle towards a life's ambition, an expatriate musician on the run, a young woman's battle with her paranoia and her past, and the mysterious figure who wants to control their lives. Set in an exotic atmosphere of a by-gone era, this is a tale crafted with a crime noir feel. The book includes violence and some strong language.

Super Spy. Top Shelf Productions 2007 336p. Illustration
Grades: 9 10 11 12 Adult   741.5; S C
   1. Adventure graphic novels; 2. Spies; 3. World War, 1939-1945; 4. Graphic novels
   978-1-891830-96-9, $19.95

Set during World War II, the book follows the everyday life of several spies as they go about their work. A writer hides secret messages in the text of the children's picture book he's writing; the wife of a German officer desperately needs to escape with her child; a female German master assassin encounters several of the Allied spies, with mostly fatal results. As the stories go on, the reader starts to see the interweaving connections between them. Some violence is depicted on the pages, but there's no nudity and little in the way of harsh language.

King, Stacy

Pride and prejudice. Adapted by Stacy King; illustrated by Po Tse. Udon Entertainment 2014 369 p. Illustration

Grades: 9 10 11 12 Adult   **741.5**
1. Manga
1927925177; 9781927925171, $24.99

In this manga adaption by Stacy King, "Pride & Prejudice is delightfully transformed. . . . All of the joy, heartache, and romance of Jane Austen's original [is] perfectly illuminated by the sumptuous art of manga-ka Po Tse." (Publisher's note)

Kinney, Sarah

Nancy Drew, girl detective #14: Sleight of Dan. Stefan Petrucha & Sarah Kinney, writers ; Sho Murase, artist ; with 3D CG elements and color by Carlos Jose Guzman. Papercutz 2008 Un Illustration
Grades: 3 4 5 6 7 8 9   **741.5; Fic**
1. Adventure graphic novels; 2. Drew, Nancy (Fictional character); 3. Mystery graphic novels; 4. Graphic novels
978-1-59707-108-6, $12.95; 978-1-59707-107-9 (pa), $7.95

The assistant for magician Dan Deville has disappeared, and Nancy tries to find Tina. It all started when Nancy attended one of Dan's magic shows with buddies George and Bess, and George challenged Nancy to figure out the magician's tricks. Now, though Nancy runs into a large anaconda while trying to find Tina, and large snakes are definitely not fun.

Volume 14 of the Nancy Drew, Girl Detective series

Kipling, Rudyard

Jungle book adapted by Jean-Blaise Mitildji ; illustrated by TieKo. IDW Publishing 2009 62p. Illustration
Grades: 5 6 7 8 9   **741.5; Fic**
1. Adventure graphic novels; 2. Children's authors; 3. India; 4. Kipling, Rudyard, 1865-1936 — Adaptations; 5. Wolves; 6. Graphic novels
978-1-60010-352-0, $14.99

This graphic novel adapts Kipling's tale of Mowgli, the boy who was raised by wolves, educated by Baloo the bear and Bagheera the panther, the enemy of Shere Khan the tiger. When the wolf pack overthrows the wise Akela and order Mowgli to leave, he returns to the human village, but he never feels completely comfortable among them. When Shere Khan comes to hunt him, Mowgli fights with Akela at his side, but this causes the people to reject him. This adaptation, originally published in France, stays true to Kipling's original story; at the beginning of the tale, Mowgli is naked, although the one panel showing him from the front is a longer-distance shot. The book includes biographical information about Kipling, historical background on the British Empire and on India in the nineteenth century, and an analysis of the story.

Kirby, Jack

Jack Kirby's Fourth World Omnibus Volume Two. Image Comics 2007 396p. Illustration
Grades: 7 8 9 10 11 12 Adult   **741.5; Fic**
1. Superhero graphic novels; 2. Graphic novels
978-1-4012-1357-2, $49.99

DC collects four series by Kirby — The New Gods, The Forever People, Mister Miracle, and Superman's Pal Jimmy Olsen — in chronological order as they originally appeared. These comics spanned galaxies, from the streets of Metropolis to the far-flung worlds of New Genesis and Apokolips, as cosmic-powered heroes and villains struggled for supremacy.In this second volume, the evil Darkseid's schemes continue to unfold while the New Gods, the Forever People, Mr. Miracle and other heroes battle his many minions.

Jack Kirby's Fourth World Omnibus, Volume One. DC Comics 2007 396p. Illustration
Grades: 8 9 10 11 12 Adult   **741.5; Fic**
1. Science fiction graphic novels; 2. Superhero graphic novels; 3. Graphic novels
978-1-4012-1344-2, $49.99

In the 1970s, legendary comics creator Kirby left Marvel Comics to work for DC Comics, writing and drawing several new series and also taking over Superman's Pal Jimmy Olsen. This volume collects the first three issues of his new series, plus the start of his run on Jimmy Olsen, from issue #133. With the Fourth World storylines in Kirby's New Gods, Forever People, and Mister Miracle, he created new mythologies and epic storylines. This hardcover edition uses a flat paper that shows off the inks and colors brilliantly.

Jack Kirby's Omac: one man army corps. Jack Kirby, writer/penciller ; D. Bruce Berry, Mike Royer, inkers and letterers. DC Comics 2008 176p. Illustration
Grades: 7 8 9 10 11 12 Adult   **741.5; Fic**
1. Superhero graphic novels; 2. Graphic novels
978-1-4012-1790-7, $24.99

In the 1970s, comics master creator Jack Kirby shocked the comics industry when he left Marvel Comics to work for the opposition DC Comics. He created new characters and new worlds. Among them was an unusual science fiction concept: OMAC, One Man Army Corps. Corporate nobody Buddy Blank is changed by the artificial intelligence "Brother Eye" into a superpowered agent of the Global Peace Agency, fighting bizarre menaces in a disturbing, near-future world. This book collects the complete 8-issue saga as published by DC; readers will note it ends in a cliffhanger that was never resolved.

Silver Star. Image Comics 2007 152p. Illustration
Grades: 8 9 10 11 12 Adult   **741.5; Fic**
1. Superhero graphic novels; 2. Graphic novels
978-1-58240-764-7, $34.99

Chronicling the rise of Homo-Geneticus, the New Breed of humanity that spawns both Silver Star (Morgan Miller) and the nefarious Darius Brumm. Silver Star was Kirby's final creation and one of only two creator-owned projects published by Pacific Comics in the early '80s. This volume also includes the original screenplay, written by Kirby and Steve Sherman, upon which Kirby based the comic.

Silver Star: Graphite Edition. Twomorrows Publishing 2006 Un Illustration
Grades: 8 9 10 11 12 Adult   **741.5; Fic**
1. Adventure graphic novels; 2. Science fiction graphic novels; 3. Graphic novels
1-893905-55-1, $19.95

Jack Kirby first conceptualized Silver Star in the mid-1970s as a movie screenplay, complete with illustrations to sell the idea to Hollywood. Too far ahead of its time for Tinseltown, Jack instead adapted his Visual

Novel" as a six-issue mini-series for Pacific Comics in the early 1980s, making it the last original creation of his career. Now, in Silver Star: Graphite Edition, King" Kirby's final series is collected at last, this time reproduced from his un-inked pencil art. This is the complete story of Homo-Geneticus, the New Breed of humanity that spawns both hero (Silver Star) and villain (the nefarious Darius Drumm). The book includes Kirby's screenplay, including illustrations and never-published character sketches. Plus there are pin-ups and other rare Kirby art, and an historical overview to put it all in perspective.

Kirishima, Takeru
   Kanna Volume 1. Go! Comi 2007 180p. Illustration
Grades: 10 11 12 Adult   **741.5; Fic**
   1. Adventure graphic novels; 2. Fantasy graphic novels; 3. Manga; 4. Graphic novels
   978-1-933617-55-8, $10.99
   Kagura was perfectly happy living a normal, leisurely life... until an adorable little girl shows up in his house one day and starts calling him "Daddy—! As his once-normal life turns upside down around him, he sets off to unravel the child's mystery, embarking on a journey which will change everything... The book includes some bloody violence, as minions of the Black God are after the little girl, Kanna. There's also a slightly pervy character who's into moe - cute little girls - in anime, and he likes to give Kanna anime costumes to wear.

Kirkman, Robert
   Capes, volume one: punching the clock. Writer, Robert Kirkman; artist, Mark Englert. Image Comics 2007 144p. Illustration
Grades: 10 11 12 Adult   **741.5**
   1. Adventure graphic novels; 2. Superhero graphic novels; 3. Graphic novels
   978-1-58240-756-2, $17.99
   Imagine living in a world where superhero is just another job title. Capes Incorporated is a business that employs superpowered individuals to protect the city of New York, and occasionally the world. Superheroes such as the Meteor Twins, The American Champion, strong man Bolt, and the new guy, Kid Thor, are all on the payroll; they're superheroes who punch a time clock, take lunch breaks, and get overtime. Along with fighting violence, there's some harsh language and a few sexual situations and some partial nudity.

   Invincible Vol. 8: My Favorite Martian. Writer, Robert Kirkman; penciler, inker, Ryan Ottley; colorist, Bill Crabtree; letterer, Rus Wooten. Image Comics 2007 Un Illustration
Grades: 9 10 11 12 Adult   **741.5; Fic**
   1. Invincible (Fictional character); 2. Superhero graphic novels; 3. Graphic novels
   978-1-58240-683-1, $14.99
   Invincible battles the Reanimen on the campus of Upstate University to save his roommate William. Meanwhile, unbeknownst to him trouble is brewing - trouble of Martian origin. Invincible must assemble a team of Earth's mightiest defenders to go out into space and prevent

what could well be the end of mankind. On top of that, as Mark, he's got girlfriend trouble.

   Invincible: Ultimate Collection Volume 2. Robert Kirkman, writer; Ryan Ottley, Penciler; Inker, Bill Crabtree; Rus Wooton, Letterer. Image Comics 2006 Un Illustration
Grades: 9 10 11 12 Adult   **741.5; Fic**
   1. Invincible (Fictional character); 2. Superhero graphic novels; 3. Graphic novels
   1-58240-594-8, $34.99
   In the aftermath of Mark's revelation concerning his father, he's forced to pick up the pieces of his life and carry on. Everything is different now - his family, his friends, his colleagues. The world has become a strange and unfamiliar place. He faces insurmountable odds, countless super-villains, otherworldly threats ... and graduating from high school, starting college ... Nobody told him being a superhero would be easy, but nobody told him it'd be this hard, either. When Invincible fights, he gets hurt and it shows, so there's some blood.

   Invincible: ultimate collection, Vol. 1. Ryan Ottley, penciler, inker; Bill Crabtree, colorist. Image Comics 2005 400p. Illustration
Grades: 9 10 11 12   **741.5; Fic**
   1. Superhero graphic novels; 2. Graphic novels
   1-58240-500-X, $34.95
   High school senior Mark Grayson develops super powers, but it's only logical because his father is superhero Omni-Man. Soon enough Mark gets a costume, a mask, and a name: Invincible. He also joins a team of teenage superheroes as they track down the person who is turning fellow students into walking bombs. Then Mark learns that evil sometimes wears the face of someone familiar, someone respected, and loved. And he'll need all the power he can muster to save himself—and Earth. This edition includes extra features, including a sketchbook section.
   "The story is compelling, presenting teenage melodrama without a trace of condescension, and even the inevitable superhero-crush-on-a-girl-he-can-never-have subplot receives a fresh spin." Voice Youth Advocates
   Originally published as Invincible, issues #1-13

   The **Irredeemable** Ant-Man: Low-Life. Writer, Robert Kirkman; penciler, Phil Hester; inker, Ande Parks. Marvel Entertainment 2007 Un Illustration
Grades: 9 10 11 12 Adult   **741.5; Fic**
   1. Superhero graphic novels; 2. Graphic novels
   978-0-7851-1962-3, $9.99
   When a low-level S.H.I.E.L.D. agent gets a hold of Hank Pym's new Ant-Man suit, the Marvel Universe is in trouble. He's not concerned with saving the world or helping others. He's concerned with getting through the day and getting a leg up on life. He's not going to use his powers responsibly, he's going to use them for the betterment of himself. He's Ant-Man, a new "hero" for the modern world.

   Tales of the Realm. Concept by Val Staples and Matt Tyree; written by Robert Kirkman; art by Matt Tyree. Image Comics 2004 Un Illustration
Grades: 9 10 11 12 Adult   **741.5; Fic**
   1. Adventure graphic novels; 2. Fantasy graphic novels; 3. Humorous graphic novels; 4. Graphic novels
   1-58240-394-5, $14.95

What if we rode dragons to work every day? What if myth and fantasy were real? The Realm is full of the hustle and bustle of life on Earth as it is today, with a little twist... Dragons and ogres, sword and sorcery are the norms in The Realm, seamlessly blended with our familiar human counterparts. This adventure follows the lives of three television show actors as they fight to make it big in Hollywood while interacting with a world very much like our own, but oh-so different. The book has some magical violence and some strong language.

Tech jacket, Vol. 1: Lost & found. [by] Robert Kirkman and E. J. Su. Image Comics 2003 144p. Illustration
Grades: 6 7 8 9 10 11 12   **741.5; Fic**
1. Adventure graphic novels; 2. Science fiction graphic novels; 3. Graphic novels
1-58240-314-7, $12.95
Teenage Zach Thompson stumbles upon a crashed space ship with a dying alien; Geldarian gives his Tech Jacket to Zach. The Tech Jackets gave the physically weak Geldarians the ability to do their work; on the physically fit Zach, it gives him great power. But, even as his father deals with gangsters trying to take his hardware store, Zach learns that possessing the Tech Jacket gives him great responsibility, and the Geldarians need him.

The **Walking** Dead. Written by Robert Kirkman; Pencilled/inked by Tony Moore and Charlie Adlard. Image Comics 2006 Un Illustration
Grades: 10 11 12 Adult   **741.5; Fic**
1. Horror graphic novels; 2. Graphic novels
978-1-58240-619-0, $29.99
This hardcover features the first 12 issues of the hit series along with the covers for the issues in one oversized hardcover volume. An epidemic of apocalyptic proportions has swept the globe, causing the dead to rise and feed on the living. In a matter of months, society has crumbled. Rick Grimes finds himself one of the few survivors in this terrifying future. A couple months ago he was a small town cop who had never fired a shot and only ever saw one dead body. Separated from his family, he must now sort through all the death and confusion to try and find his wife and son. And when he finds them, along with a few other survivors, they must try to find a place of safety, for the walking dead are everywhere. The book includes lots of zombie violence, strong language, and some sexual situations.
Also available in trade paperback, omnibus, and compendium editions
Previously published as The Walking Dead issues #1-12.
Book 1 of an ongoing series

Kishi, Daimuro
Time Guardian, Vol. 1. DC Comics/CMX 2007 198p. Illustration
Grades: 5 6 7 8 9 10 11 12   **741.5; Fic**
1. Fantasy graphic novels; 2. Manga; 3. Shojo manga; 4. Graphic novels
1-4012-1161-5, $9.99
High school student Miu stumbles upon a mysterious pawnshop that trades time for people's memories. Shop owner Tokiya hires Miu to be his Time Go-Between to work

with his customers, but she must never speak of the shop to anyone.

Kishimoto, Masashi
★ **Naruto.** vol. 1, The tests of the Ninja. Story and art by Masashi Kishimoto; [English adaptation by Jo Duffy]. Viz 2003 186p. Illustration
Grades: 7 8 9 10 11 12   **741.5; Fic**
1. Manga; 2. Martial arts; 3. Shonen manga; 4. Graphic novels
1-56931-900-6; 978-1-56931-900-0, $7.95
"Teen orphan Naruto wants to become the greatest ninja of all, despite the fact that most people in his village have despised him from birth because a terrible demon has been imprisoned in his body. . . . Teens love this series." Voice Youth Advocates
First published 1999 in Japan
Volume one of an ongoing series; ?This graphic novel contains material that was originally published in English in Shonen jump #6-10? Verso of title page
Volume 1 of 72

Kishimoto, Seishi
O-Parts Hunter Vol. 1. Viz Media 2006 185p. Illustration
Grades: 10 11 12 Adult   **741.5; Fic**
1. Adventure graphic novels; 2. Fantasy graphic novels; 3. Manga; 4. Shonen manga; 5. Graphic novels
978-1-4215-0855-9, $9.99
In the not too distant future, mankind fights over relics from an ancient civilization called O-Parts, each of which contain incredible powers. Some people with special abilities to use the O-Parts to their full potential are known as O.P.T.s (or O-Parts Tacticians). Jio is a young boy with a tragic past who only trusts one thing in the world: money. He is actually a very powerful O.P.T., and inside him sleeps a demon of incredible ferocity. He meets up with a girl named Ruby who, like her famous father before her, wants to become a treasure hunter. Though Jio doesn't believe in friendship, he agrees to be Ruby's bodyguard, and together they go on a dangerous quest to discover as many O-Parts as they can. The story uses some harsh language and violence, occasionally graphic. Mangaka Kishimoto is twin brother to Masashi Kishimoto, mangaka of Naruto.

Kishiro, Yukito
Battle Angel Alita Vol. 1: Rusty Angel. Viz Media 2003 Un Illustration
Grades: 10 11 12 Adult   **741.5; Fic**
1. Manga; 2. Science fiction graphic novels; 3. Seinen manga; 4. Graphic novels
1-56931-945-6, $9.95
When Doc Ido, a talented cyberphysician, finds cyborg Alita's head in a junk heap, she has lost all memory of her past life. But when he reconstructs her, she discovers her body still instinctively remembers the Panzer Kunst, the most powerful cyborg fighting technique ever known. In the post-apocalyptic world of the Scrapyard, as the secrets of Alita's past unfold, each day is a struggle for survival. The book includes graphic violence and strong language.
Volume 1 of 9

Kita, Naoe

The **Empty** Empire Volume 1. DC Comics/CMX 2006 192p. Illustration
Grades: 7 8 9 10 11 12   **741.5; Fic**
1. Science fiction graphic novels; 2. Shojo manga; 3. Graphic novels
1-4012-1121-6, $9.99

Long ago, the Emperor possessed great mystical powers. Now, a young boy wonders if he will have them as well. With no memories and only a rose-shaped scar on his forehead as a clue, he ponders his legacy while on the run with the girl who rescued him from a group of armed warriors. She takes him to a scientist who identifies Rose as the Emperor's clone and believes that this young boy must assume the mantle of leadership. But opposing forces with their own agenda have created another clone from the Emperor's DNA...and now the struggle for power begins. The book includes some mildly strong language and some violence.

Kitchen, Alexa

Drawing Comics is Easy! (Except When It's Hard). Denis Kitchen Publishing Company 2006 Un Illustration
Grades: 2 3 4 5 6 7 8 9 10 11 12 Adult   **741.5**
1. Drawing; 2. Graphic novels
0-9710080-6-X, $19.95

Drawing Comics is Easy! (Except When It's Hard!) is entirely the work of a seven-year-old (at the time) prodigy cartoonist, who in 2007 was ten years old. Though seemingly aimed at a peer audience of other children, this idiosyncratic How-To book will appeal to readers of any age, especially those interested in cartooning and the creative process. Kitchen is the daughter of Denis Kitchen, who's been in the comics industry as a publisher and agent for many years.

Klavan, Laurence

★ **Brain** camp. By Susan Kim and Laurence Klavan; illustrated by Faith Erin Hicks. First Second 2010 151p. Illustration
Grades: 7 8 9 10   **741.5; Fic**
1. Camps; 2. Horror graphic novels; 3. Mystery graphic novels; 4. Science fiction graphic novels; 5. Graphic novels
978-1-59643-366-3, $16.99; 1-59643-366-3

Jenna and Lucas are both under-achieving young teens who suddenly receive invitations to join the Fielding Camp for the summer. Pressed by their respective parents to attend, Jenna and Lucas both notice some strange things at the camp, and neither feels like eating the nasty slop served at every meal. The other campers are either intellectually challenged bullies, misfits, or supersmart zombies. At first Dwayne, a self-described spaz, befriends them, but when his cabin "wins" ice cream treats at dinner, Lucas sees the camp counselors sneaking in that night to "inoculate" all his cabin mates. Lucas and Jenna work against time to escape the camp and develop an antidote.

The authors present a "well-rounded adventure here, as the far-out (and kind of gross) climax mixes with genuine insight into dealing with parents, fitting into a new crowd, and handling the pressures of performance. Hicks' line work

is cool enough to assuage older readers who might be suspicious of the summer-camp setting." Booklist

Kleid, Neil

Brownsville. Written by Neil Kleid; illustrated by Jake Allen. NBM 2006 208p. Illustration
Grades: 10 11 12 Adult   **741.5; 973.9**
1. Gangs; 2. United States — History — 20th century; 3. Graphic novels
1-56163-458-1, $18.95

Brownsville, in Brooklyn, New York, was an impoverished part of the city in the early twentieth century. Filled with tenements and poor Jews, it became the breeding ground for criminals. This book follows the lives of Allie Tanennbaum, Abe Reles, and other young hoods organized by Louis Lepke Buchalter into the deadly "Murder, Inc." in the 1930s.

"The history of Jewish gangsters is often overshadowed by images of The Godfather and stories of the Italian mafia, but the events and players come to life in the stark images of this historical overview." (VOYA)

Jack London's Call of the Wild. Art by Alex Nino. Puffin Graphics 2006 176p. Illustration
Grades: 5 6 7 8 9 10   **741.5; Fic**
1. Adventure graphic novels; 2. Dogs; 3. London, Jack; 4. London, Jack — Adaptations; 5. Graphic novels
0-14-240571-X, $10.99

Buck was a pampered dog on Judge Miller's estate in Santa Clara, California of 1897; then one of Judge Miller's men sold Buck to a broker selling sled dogs to the men flocking to the Yukon in the Gold Rush of that time. A strong dog, Buck manages to survive and even thrive under masters good and bad. This volume includes the artist's sketch gallery and sample script pages.

Klein, Grady

The **cartoon** introduction to statistics. By Grady Klein and Alan Dabney, Ph.D. Hill and Wang, a Division of Farrar, Straus and Giroux 2013 240 p.
Grades: 7 8 9 10 11 12   **519.5**
1. Mathematical statistics; 2. Statistics; 3. Graphic novels
0809033593; 9780809033591, $17.95
LC 2012030027

This book, by Grady Klien and Alan Dabney, explores statistics in humorous cartoon illustrations. "Separating the book into two main parts (hunting statistics and gathering parameters) for readers both in and outside the classroom, they explore the key foundational concepts of statistics and the perils of improper methods. They round out the book with the 'Math Cave,' which provides easy access to the formulas every student will want to have close at hand." (Publisher's note)

The **Lost** Colony Book 2: The red menace. First Second Books 2007 120p. Illustration
Grades: 10 11 12 Adult   **741.5; Fic**
1. Adventure graphic novels; 2. Humorous graphic novels; 3. Graphic novels
978-1-59643-098-3, $16.95

In the second installment of The Lost Colony series, the beloved and not-so-beloved islanders confront war profiteering, the Native American Wars, and other unwelcome visitors to their hidden realm. Along with magic potions, stage tricks, and farting contests, the book includes tragedy, controversy, and even shameful secrets. Some characters use racial slurs, and some are drawn as seeming stereotypes, but patient and discerning readers will see Klein's intent.

The lost colony, book 3: Last rights. First Second Books 2008 152p. Illustration

Grades: 9 10 11 12 Adult   **741.5; Fic**
  1. Graphic novels
  978-1-59643-099-0, $18.95

The arrival of Buck Swagger, a smarmy preacher, on the island bodes no good for Birdy or for Louis. It's bad enough Birdy has to deal with the death of her grandfather at the hands of her old nanny, and that her father has become obsessed with getting revenge, now it seems her mother has had an affair with Swagger—and is continuing with it, now that he's there. Louis has had his own run-ins with Swagger, who used Louis as a slave until Birdy bought him and brought him to the island. Old Patricia tries to warn Birdy that trouble has come, but no one will listen to Birdy, except maybe Louis. And the rock bugs fit in somehow. Patricia says they killed Birdy's grandfather because he was evil and they were protecting the island, but no one will believe that when Birdy repeats it. Klein continues his exploration of race relations and American history in this third volume of Lost Colony. The book includes some violence, partial nudity, and strong language.

Kleist, Richard
  Johnny Cash: I see a darkness: a graphic novel. [translated from the German edition by Michael Waaler]. Abrams ComicArts 2009 221p. Illustration

Grades: 11 12 Adult   **92; 741.5**
  978-0-8109-8463-9, $17.95
                    LC 2010-279149

The author "presents a biography (with seemingly invented dialog that stays true to the facts) focusing on Cash's turning points: from his poor family's 1935 relocation to a New Deal-created cotton farming community, through his troubled first marriage, endless touring, the amphetamine abuse of his early musical career, and climaxing with a famous, highly charged 1968 concert at California's Folsom Prison. Kleist also dramatizes several of Cash's songs and relates the tragic story of Glen Sherley, a Folsom inmate who sent Cash a song he had written hoping Cash would play it in the show. The ruggedness of Kleist's black-and-white illustrations suits their subject, as the stark portrayal of Cash's withdrawal from drugs is inventive and harrowing. . . . This thoughtful and compelling portrait of a towering talent with a tortured soul is recommended for all teen and adult music fans." Libr J

Klimowski, Andrzej
  Dr. Jekyll and Mr. Hyde: a graphic novel. Illustrated and adapted by Andrzej Klimowski and Danusia Schejbal. Sterling 2009 122p. Illustration

Grades: 6 7 8 9   **741; 741.5**
  1. Graphic novels; 2. Horror graphic novels; 3. Stevenson, Robert Louis, 1850-1894 — Adaptations
  978-1-4114-1595-9 (pa), $14.95; 1-4114-1595-7 (pa)

This graphic novel adaptation of Robert Louis Stevenson's story "is the story of a respectable London doctor who ends up leading a dreadful double life—as a doctor, and as a cold-blooded murderer." Publisher's note

"Klimowski captures a . . . formal air with a literal but still quick-moving adaptation, and Schejbal's grainy art displays a Richard Sala-like sense of both grit and unease. . . . Overall, this will have the most appeal for readers with an eye for the moody and strange." Booklist

Kneece, Mark
  The **Bristol** Board Jungle. Bob Pendarvis, Mark Kneece. NBM 2004 144p. Illustration

Grades: 9 10 11 12 Adult   **741.5**
  1. Graphic novels — Technique
  1-56163-379-8, $11.95
                    LC 2003-70631

Here is a full college class on creating comics... in a graphic novel. Readers can learn the secrets of the trade while attending an actual class and getting to know the students. This book is written and drawn by two professors of the Savannah College of Art & Design with a class of their best seniors, who each illustrate one chapter.

The **Twilight** Zone: the after hours. Adaptation by Mark Kneece; illustrated by Rebekah Isaacs. Walker & Company 2008 Un Illustration

Grades: 5 6 7 8 9 10   **741.5; Fic**
  1. Supernatural graphic novels; 2. Twilight zone (Television program); 3. Graphic novels
  978-0-8027-9716-2, $16.99; 978-0-8027-9717-9 (pa), $9.99
                    LC 2008-4310

Marsha White visits a department store to buy an advertised gold thimble, is taken by elevator to a floor with empty display cases except for one, which has the thimble, and she deals with an odd saleswoman who knows her name. When Marsha is in the elevator, she discovers the thimble is defective and tries to complain, but the manager insists there is no eighteenth floor, the store has no elevator, and the store has never carried gold thimbles. As she begins to leave, Marsha faints at the sight of a mannequin that looks exactly like the strange saleswoman, and she's put into a back room to recover. When she wakes up, the store has been closed and she's locked in. This is an actual episode of the old Twilight Zone television show.

"Kneece's adaptation is quick and enjoyable and introduces a classic TV series to a new generation of readers. Isaacs's illustrations are clean, distinct and cinematic in scope, employing an interesting variety of angles." Kirkus

The **Twilight** Zone: walking distance. Adaptation from Rod Serling's original script by Mark Kneece; illustrated by Dove McHargue. Walker & Company 2008 Un Illustration

Grades: 5 6 7 8 9 10   **741.5; Fic**
  1. Supernatural graphic novels; 2. Twilight zone (Television program); 3. Graphic novels
  978-0-8027-9714-8, $16.99; 978-0-8027-9715-5 (pa), $9.99
                    LC 2008-4273

Thirty-nine-year-old businessman Martin Sloan's car blows a tire as he's driving, and he realizes he is within walking distance of his hometown. Leaving his car to be repaired, he decides to walk there. However, when he reaches town, he has also gone back in time. Can he find his boyhood self and give his younger self advice? Or will everyone think he's just crazy? This is an actual episode of the old Twilight Zone television show.

The story is "exceptionally well told and . . . [is] brilliantly adapted to a new medium." SLJ

Knisley, Lucy

An **Age of License.** Lucy Knisley. Fantagraphics 2014 208 p. Illustration; Color; Map

Grades: 11 12 Adult   **92; 741.5**

1. Autobiographical graphic novels; 2. Europe — Description and travel

1606997688; 9781606997680, $19.99

"'An Age of License' is [author Lucy] Knisley's comics travel memoir recounting her charming (and romantic!) adventures. It's punctuated by whimsical visual devices (such as a 'new experiences' funnel); peppered with the cute cats she meets along the way; and, of course, features her hallmark—drawings and descriptions of food that will make your mouth water." (Publisher's note)

"Knisley makes memoir comics seem both sophisticated and approachableùand beyond these, useful in helping an individual delve into and communicate personal issues." LJ

★ **Relish:** My Life in the Kitchen. By Lucy Knisley. First Second 2013 192 p.

Grades: 9 10 11 12 Adult   **92; 741.5**

1. Cooking; 2. Food

1596436239; 9781596436237, $17.99

Alex Award Winner (2014)

This book is a memoir from food-lover Lucy Knisley. "Having grown up surrounded by delicious food, thanks to her gourmand father and earthy superchef mother, Knisley looks back on her childhood and adolescence through her roving palette and voracious appetite for new tastes and experiences. With each memory Knisley shares, she shows that life, like a good meal, should be savored and that all food—even junk food—is more than 'just fuel.'" (Publishers Weekly)

"Knisley tempers any navel-gazing impulses with humor, humility, and honesty. . . . Just about everything in this rambling memoir is handled with good cheer." Booklist

Ko, Ya-Seong

Redrum Three Twenty Seven Volume 1. Tokyopop 2006 Un Illustration

Grades: 10 11 12 Adult   **741.5; Fic**

1. Horror graphic novels; 2. Manwha; 3. Mystery graphic novels; 4. Graphic novels

1-59816-506-2, $9.99

When a group of seven young college students go off to enjoy a weekend getaway at a remote mountain villa, secrets that haunt the friends are unveiled—which lead to bizarre love triangles, tragic relationships, and deadly betrayal. And when hallucinations and strange disappearances begin, their dream vacation turns into a nightmare... The book includes strong language and violence.

Kobayashi, Jin

School Rumble, Vol. 1. Ballantine Books/Del Rey Manga 2006 182p. Illustration

Grades: 10 11 12 Adult   **741.5; Fic**

1. Humorous graphic novels; 2. Romance graphic novels; 3. Shonen manga; 4. Graphic novels

0-345-49147-5, $10.95

Second-year high school student Tsukamoto Tenma (this series uses Japanese name order, so Tenma is her first name) starts the new school year determined to declare her love for Karasuma Oji. Notorious juvenile delinquent Harima Kenji has a crush on Tenma and has returned to school in hopes of declaring his love for her. Karasuma seems totally oblivious to all that's going on around him. Tenma's younger sister Yakumo is the one who cooks and takes care of Tenma; she also possesses the ability to read the minds of people who have feelings for her. Tenma and Kenji each engage in hilariously over-the-top efforts to declare their love for the objects of their affection, but they never succeed. Meanwhile, boys are starting to notice Yakumo.

Kobayashi, Miyuki

Kitchen princess vol. 6. Del Rey Manga 2008 Un Illustration

Grades: 8 9 10 11 12   **741.5; Fic**

1. Cooking; 2. Shojo manga; 3. Graphic novels

978-0-345-50194-3, $10.95

On the eve of the dessert contest finals, Sora is hit by a truck. In the hospital, he tells Najika that he isn't her Flan Prince, then dies. Stunned by his death, and by his confession, Najika loses her sense of taste. She loses the competition, and the Director, Sora's father, orders her to leave the academy minutes before the memorial service. However, Daichi offers to take Sora's place at the academy and give up on his own dreams, if Najika can stay. She loses her scholarship, is forced into the regular classes, and almost everyone at the academy shuns her, blaming her for Sora's death.

Kochalka, James

The **Cute** Manifesto. Alternative Comics 2005 Un Illustration

Grades: 11 12 Adult   **741.5**

1. Autobiographical graphic novels; 2. Humorous graphic novels; 3. Graphic novels

1-891867-73-3, $19.95

In a dangerously uncertain world, Kochalka plots a theoretical path to happiness. Collecting some of his thoughtful work, this book struggles with all the big issues: comics and art, birth and death, technology and joy, and everything in between. It collects "The Horrible Truth about Comics," "Reinventing Everything" parts 1 and 2, "Sunburn," "The Cute Manifesto," and even "Kochalka's Craft is the Enemy" essays. The book includes harsh language and brief nudity.

Monkey vs. Robot. Top Shelf Productions 2000 144p. Illustration

Grades: 5 6 7 8 9 10 11 12   **741.5; Fic**

1. Graphic novels

1-891830-15-5, $14.95

The book is almost wordless, allowing the reader to imagine one's own narrative. While there is violence, it's not graphic, and this little fable provides much food for thought. "A very simply illustrated black and white pictorial narrative about a battle between a monkey community and a self-run robot factory encroaching on the monkeys' unspoiled forest domain." Publ Wkly

Another title in this series is: Monkey vs. Robot and the crystal of power (2003)

Peanutbutter & Jeremy's best book ever. Alternative Comics 2003 280p. Illustration
Grades: 4 5 6 7 8 9 10 11 12   741.5; Fic
1. Friendship; 2. Humorous graphic novels; 3. Graphic novels
1-891867-46-6, $14.95

Peanutbutter is a sweet cat who acts like a hardworking office cat but usually naps on top of the paperwork, and Jeremy is a troublemaking crow; and they are friends. Jeremy may seem spiteful and sometimes does very mean things to Peanutbutter, such as pretending to threaten the cat with a pistol, but most of the stories are silly and fun.

Pinky & Stinky. Top Shelf Productions 2002 208p. Illustration
Grades: 4 5 6 7 8 9 10 11 12 Adult   741.5; Fic
1. Adventure graphic novels; 2. Friendship; 3. Humorous graphic novels; 4. Graphic novels
1-891830-29-7, $17.95

Pinky & Stinky are fat little piglets, but just because they're cuties doesn't mean that they're not brave astronauts! When they embark on a daring mission to be the first pigs on Pluto, things go horribly wrong and they crash land on the moon. There they meet some not-so-friendly moon men, and end up in the middle of a conflict between the American space program and a race of alien ice creatures.

Koike, Kazuo
Lone wolf and cub omnibus. 1. By Kazuo Koike; illustrated by Goseki Kojima. Dark Horse Manga 2013 706 p. Illustration
Grades: 9 10 11 12 Adult   741.5; 741.5952
1. Samurai
1616551348; 9781616551346, $19.99

This graphic novel, by Kazuo Koike, illustrated by Goseki Kojima, is a "samurai epic. . . . [It] begins its second life at Dark Horse Manga with new, larger editions of over 700 pages." (Publisher's note)

Also available in 28 single volumes
Volume 1 of 12

Path of the Assassin Vol. 1: Serving in the Dark. By Kazuo Koike & Goseki Kojima. Dark Horse Manga 2006 314p. Illustration
Grades: 11 12 Adult   741.5; Fic
1. Adventure graphic novels; 2. Manga; 3. Samurai; 4. Seinen manga; 5. Graphic novels
978-1-59307-502-6, $9.95

This is the story of Hattori Hanzo, the fabled master ninja whose duty was to protect Tokugawa Ieyasu. Ieyasu was the shogun who would unite Japan into one great nation. But before he could do that, he had to grow up and learn how to love the ladies. As the secret caretaker of such an influential future leader, not only does Hanzo use vast and varied ninja talents, but in living closely with Ieyasu, he forms a close friendship with the young shogun. The two men get into bawdy escapades, the book includes nudity, strong language, and graphic violence.

Komura, Ayumi
Mixed vegetables, vol. 1. Viz Media/Shojo Beat 2008 Un Illustration
Grades: 7 8 9 10 11 12   741.5; Fic
1. Cooking; 2. Romance graphic novels; 3. Shojo manga; 4. Graphic novels
978-1-4215-1967-8, $8.99

Hanayu Ashitaba is the daughter of the Patisserie Ashitaba, a famous pastry shop, but ever since she was a little girl she has wanted to become a sushi chef. Hayato Hyuga is the son of the famed Sushi Hyuga, but all he's ever wanted to be is a pastry chef, even though he's got mad skills with the knives. Both of them are students at the Oikawa High School Cooking Department, where Hanayu has decided she needs to make Hayato fall for her and marry her. However, Hayato wants Hanayu to teach him more about pastry making.

Volume 1 of 8

Konomi, Takeshi
The **Prince** of Tennis, Vol. 1. Viz Media, LLC 2004 192p. Illustration
Grades: 6 7 8 9 10   741.5; Fic
1. Shonen manga; 2. Tennis; 3. Graphic novels
1-59116-435-4, $7.95

"Ryoma is a former U.S. junior tennis champion who attends a Japanese academy, where his skill and natural talent make him nearly unbeatable. The younger students are inspired by him, but he's ruffling the feathers of the older tennis team members. Then the journalists appear, trying to discover the next champion, adding to the pressure. There's lots of tennis action, dramatically illustrated, and the characters, already pretty boys, are made even more attractive with their intensity." Publ Wkly

Volume 1 of 42

Kouga, Yun
Earthian Vol.1. Tokyopop/BLU 2005 400p. Illustration
Grades: 10 11 12 Adult   741.5; Fic
1. Manga; 2. Romance graphic novels; 3. Science fiction graphic novels; 4. Shonen-ai manga; 5. Graphic novels
1-59816-006-0, $14.99

Angels are among us. They are scattered across the globe, living in our neighborhoods, observing humanity—the Earthian—in crisis...Chihaya and Kagetsuya have known each other since their days at school. They are friends...and possibly more. These two angels roam the world, compiling lists of the positive and negative traits of humanity. In the process they become involved in the lives of various humans, full of despair: An astronaut about to venture on a dangerous mission, a sorceress running from the mafia, and a mysterious artificially created human are just a few of those beings who Chihaya puts himself at risk to help, much to Kagetsuya's dismay. But after a meeting of angels, it is discovered that a dreaded disease is plaguing a growing legion of angels. Salvation possibly lies in the fallen angel Lord Seraphim—and as Chihaya and Kagetsuya search to find him, he turns up in the most unlikely of places... This is a Boy Love/shonen-ai manga title. It includes some violence and strong language; nudity occurs in the fourth (and final) volume.

Loveless Volume 1. Tokyopop 2006 202p. Illustration
Grades: 10 11 12 Adult   **741.5; Fic**
1. Fantasy graphic novels; 2. Manga; 3. Mystery graphic novels; 4. Romance graphic novels; 5. Shonen-ai manga; 6. Graphic novels
1-59816-221-7, $9.99
The mystery behind the death of his older brother was just the beginning...When 12-year-old Ritsuka discovers a posthumous message from his brother indicating he was murdered, he becomes involved in a shadowy world of spell battles and secret names. Together with the mysterious Soubi, the search to find Seimei's killer and uncover the truth begins. But in a world where everyone has cat ears and mere words have unbelievable power, how can you find true friendship and happiness when your very name is Loveless" The romance is boy/boy, and the book includes fighting violence.

Kouno, Fumiyo
Town of evening calm, Country of cherry blossoms. Last Gasp 2006 104p. Illustration
Grades: 9 10 11 12 Adult   **741.5; Fic**
1. Atomic bomb victims; 2. Japan — History — 1952-; 3. Manga; 4. Graphic novels
978-0-86719-665-8, $9.99
In 1955, Hiroshima has been recovering from the devastation of the Atom Bomb in August 1945. Minami is one of the survivors of the bomb, and she tries not to remember the events of that day when most of her family died. She even pushes away Uchikoshi, a co-worker who likes her, feeling guilty that she survived when so many didn't; but when she finally comes to terms with her past and allows Uchikoshi in, radiation sickness manifests. Fifty years later, old school friends Nanami and Toko run into each other as Nanami follows her father who has been behaving oddly; he goes to Hiroshima, for he is Minami's younger brother. This quiet, one-volume manga uses gentle, sweet art to bring home to readers the lingering after-effects of the bombing of Hiroshima.

Kovalic, John
★ **Here** Be Snapdragons. Art by Liz Rathke. Dork Storm Press 2006 120p. Illustration
Grades: 3 4 5 6 7 8 9 10 11 12 Adult   **741.5; Fic**
1. Children; 2. Humorous graphic novels; 3. Graphic novels
1-930964-52-8, $12.99
'Everybody Loves Gilly,' 2003 Origins Award for Graphic Fiction (Origins International Game Expo).
The Snapdragons are fraternal twins Jake and Jody, Cooper, Benjamin, and the years-younger Mitze, along with Jake and Jody's cat Huey. They are neighbors and friends, they love role-playing games and video games. Cooper's dad is a gamer, Jake and Jody's mother is clueless (she buys

years-old Halloween costumes at a discount, unaware that the characters aren't popular any more), and they all often get babysat by Goth-cute teen Gilly, who can be a very cool Dungeon Master. One of the stories has Jake and Jody sent to their room without supper and they start quoting Wild Things by Maurice Sendak as their room begins to transform . . .

Krahulik, Mike
Penny Arcade Vol. 2: Epic Legends of the Magic Sword Kings. Jerry Holkins and Mike Krahulik. Dark Horse Comics 2006 160p. Illustration
Grades: 10 11 12 Adult   **741.5**
1. Humorous graphic novels; 2. Video games; 3. Graphic novels
978-1-59307-541-5, $12.95
This volume collects the web comic strips posted online throughout 2001. Gamers Gabe and Tycho contend with games that were new back then (e.g. Onimusha) and systems such as Playstation (the first one) and Gamecube. Foul language abounds, along with sexual innuendo and generally raunchy humor. The creators' comments appear on every page.

Kreie, Chris
Lost: A Tale of Survival. Art by Marcus Smith. Stone Arch Books 2007 88p. Illustration
Grades: 3 4 5 6 7 8 9   **741.5; Fic**
1. Adventure graphic novels; 2. Graphic novels
978-1-59889-828-6, $22.60
                                                       LC 2007-6245
Every summer, Eric and his dad head to the Boundary Waters Canoe Area in northern Minnesota. This year, Eric has brought his friend Cris, and the boys want to explore the wilderness on their own. When they set out in their canoe, Cris and Eric promise to return before dark. But, shortly into the trip, the river becomes a violent rapids the boys can't avoid, and Cris is injured. Now Eric must race against time to find the camp and save his friend. This graphic novel is written with an easier vocabulary for struggling and reluctant readers.
Part of the Graphic Quest line of books.

Krensky, Stephen
Comic book century: the history of American comic books. Twenty-First Century Books 2007 112p. Illustration
Grades: 5 6 7 8 9 10   **741.5; 741**
978-0-8225-6654-0, $30.60; 0-8225-6654-0
                                                       LC 2006-20795
"Part of a series that focuses on American History, this book highlights America's love and hate relationship with comic books. Starting with the 1930s, each chapter focuses on an era of the comics. Highlighted areas include the rise of Superman and Batman in the late 1930s, comics during World War II, the creation of the Comics Code Authority, Stan Lee's Marvel superhero creations, underground comix, and more." (VOYA)

Kris
A **bag** of marbles. Based on the memoir by Joseph Joffo; adapted by Kris; illustrated by Vincent Bailly; translated by

Edward Gauvin. Graphic Universe 2013 126 p. Color;
Illustration
Grades: 6 7 8 9 10   **940.53; 741.5; B**
1. Children and war — Fiction; 2. France — History —
German occupation, 1940-1945 — Fiction; 3. Holocaust,
1939-1945; 4. Holocaust, Jewish (1939-1945) — France
— Fiction; 5. Jews — France — Fiction; 7. Joffo, Joseph
— Fiction; 8. Joffo, Maurice — Fiction; 10. World War,
1939-1945 — France; 12. Graphic novels
1467715166; 9781467707008; 9781467715164, $9.95;
9781467716512

LC 2013002284

In this book by Joseph Joffo, set "in 1941 in occupied
Paris, brothers Maurice and Joseph play a last game of
marbles before running home to their father's barbershop.
With the German occupation threatening their family's
safety, the boys' parents decide Maurice and Joseph must
disguise themselves and flee to their older brothers in the
free zone. Surviving the long journey will take every scrap
of ingenuity and courage they can muster. And if they hope
to elude the Nazis, they must never, under any
circumstances, admit to being Jewish."

"This graphic-novel adaptation of Joffo's 1973 memoir
of the same name succeeds in melding sensitive and accurate
imagery with the original narrative flow of a young secular
Jewish boy's experiences in occupied France." Booklist

Krohn, Katherine
The **1918** Flu Pandemic by Katherine Krohn ; illustrated
by Bob Hall, Keith Williams, and Charles Barnett, III.
Capstone Press 2007 32p. Illustration
Grades: 3 4 5 6 7 8 9   **614.5; 741.5**
1. Influenza; 2. Graphic novels
978-1-4296-0158-0, $26.25

LC 2007000004

This book uses the graphic novel format to tell of the
1918 outbreak of a mysterious influenza virus that killed
millions of people worldwide, making it the deadliest
pandemic in history. The book includes additional facts and
a list of books for further reading.
Part of the Graphic Library Disasters in History series.

The **earth-shaking** facts about earthquakes with Max
Axiom, super scientist. Illustrated by Tod Smith and Al
Milgrom. Capstone Press 2008 32p. Illustration
Grades: 3 4 5 6 7 8 9   **551.2; 741.5**
1. Earthquakes; 2. Graphic novels
978-1-4296-1328-6, $26.26

LC 2007-25091

Young readers learn about earthquakes, how they
happen, why they happen, the damage they cause, and
what's being done to study them and help people be better
prepared to deal with them. Back matter includes more
information about earthquakes, a glossary, and a short list of
books for further reading.
Part of the Graphic Science series.

Krueger, Jim
Justice Volume One. Jim Krueger and Alex Ross, story
; Doug Braithwaite and Alex Ross, art. DC Comics 2006
160p. Illustration
Grades: 8 9 10 11 12 Adult   **741.5; Fic**

1. Justice League of America (Fictional characters); 2.
Superhero graphic novels; 3. Graphic novels
978-1-4012-0969-8, $19.99

The Justice League of America are the World's Greatest
Super-Heroes, but now villains - the Riddler, Lex Luthor,
Poison Ivy, Captain Cold, and others are banding together
and making sweeping, worldwide changes that appear to be
noble acts. But, one by one the members of the JLA are being
taken down; will anyone be left to truly protect the people of
Earth?

Kubert, Joe
Sgt. Rock: The Prophecy. By Joe Kubert ; colors by Joe
Kubert with Pete Carlsson. DC Comics 2007 144p.
Illustration
Grades: 10 11 12 Adult   **741.5; Fic**
1. Sgt Rock (Fictional character); 2. War stories; 3. World
War, 1939-1945; 4. Graphic novels
978-1-4012-1248-3, $17.99

It's late 1943, and Sgt. Rock and Easy Company go on a
covert mission far from the Allied front lines. They land in
Vilnius, Lithuania, a no-man's-land caught between Nazi
forces and Russia's Red Army. Rock has orders to contact
the civilian partisans and get a valuable religious object from
them and take it to safety. However, the object turns out to be
a young rabbi named David, whom the people believe is
their Messiah. Now Easy Company has to take him across
hostile, war-torn territory to Riga, in Latvia, facing cold
weather, Nazis, collaborators, minefields, and more.

Kubert made Sgt. Rock the iconic figure he is today, and
this story marks his return to the character. The book is full
of fighting action, hard-bitten dialog, and everything that
marks a classic World War II combat story. People who like
the motion picture "Saving Private Ryan" will like Sgt. Rock
(and this story has none of the profanity).

Yossel: April 19, 1943: a story of the Warsaw Ghetto
Uprising. Ibooks; Simon & Schuster 2003 121p. Illustration
Grades: 9 10 11 12 Adult   **940.53; Fic**
1. Holocaust, 1933-1945; 2. Warsaw (Poland) — History
— Uprising of 1943; 3. Graphic novels
0-7434-7516-X, $24.95

"Imagining his life as it might have been had his parents
not left for America in 1926, Kubert portrays himself as a
ghetto youngster whose drawing ability ingratiates him with
the Nazis, allowing him to overhear their plans and aid the
underground resistance. Besides depicting life in the ghetto
with shocking vividness, Kubert shows the barbarism of the
concentration camps through the eyes of an escapee. In a
striking departure from standard comics presentation, the
artwork is printed in rough, penciled form rather than as
finished ink drawings. The visual looseness this gives to
work that is stylized by mainstream-comics standards
conjures a potent intimacy that adds to the story's impact."
Booklist

Kubo, Tite
★ **Bleach**, Vol. 1. [story and art by Tite Kubo; English
adaptation, Lance Caselman; translation, Joe Yamazaki]. Viz
Shonen Jump 2004 190p. Illustration
Grades: 9 10 11 12   **741.5; Fic**

1. Adventure graphic novels; 2. Shonen manga; 3. Supernatural graphic novels; 4. Graphic novels
1-59116-441-9, $7.95

Teenage Ichigo Kurasaki has always been able to see ghosts, but that never really affected his life, until the night a Hollow, an evil spirit that preys on humans, attacks him. Soul Reaper Rukia Kuchiki tries to help Ichigo save himself and his family, but somehow he manages to absorb all her powers. Now he's a Soul Reaper, and he must work to protect the innocent from the Hollows. This is the first volume of an ongoing manga series that is full of fighting action and irreverent humor.

Volume 1 of an ongoing series

Kuper, Peter
The **jungle**. [based on the story by] Upton Sinclair; adapted by Peter Kuper. Papercutz 2010 Un Illustration (Classics Illustrated)
Grades: 9 10 11 12 Adult   741.5; Fic
1. Chicago (Ill); 2. Immigrants; 3. Meat industry; 4. Sinclair, Upton, 1878-1968 — Adaptations; 5. Socialist leaders; 6. Graphic novels
978-1-59707-192-5, $9.99

"Jurgis and his family have immigrated to America from Lithuania, settled in Chicago, and found jobs in the meatpacking plant. The family seems to be living the American dream: having their own home, and a means of support, even if the work is hard and disgusting. Peter Kuper's dark, colored, cartoon-style illustrations, framed in black, bring to life Sinclair's original work and highlight the atrocities perpetuated upon the Rudkus family." Libr Media Connect
First published 1991 by First Publishing

The **metamorphosis**. [based on the story by] Franz Kafka; adapted by Peter Kuper. Crown 2003 77p. Illustration
Grades: 8 9 10 11 12   741.5; Fic
1. Kafka, Franz, 1883-1924 — Adaptations
1-4000-4795-1; 1-4000-5299-8 (pa), $10.95; 9781400052998
LC 2003-273589

"Gregor Samsa wakes up and discovers he has been changed into a giant cockroach. Thus begins "The Metamorphosis," and Kuper translates this story masterfully with his scratchboard illustrations. The text is more spare, but the visuals are so strongly rendered that little of the original is changed or omitted." SLJ

Sticks and stones: an epic in pictures. Three Rivers Press 2004 Un Illustration
Grades: 10 11 12 Adult   741.5; Fic
1. Stories without words; 2. Graphic novels
1-4000-5257-2, $13.95
LC 2004-45969

"A stone giant is born from a volcano and demands the fealty of the people around him. He makes them build him a stone castle; then he discovers a nearby peaceful village made entirely of wood and sets about conquering it and plundering its resources. Meanwhile, a small resistance front develops, led by a woman from the stone tribe and a boy from the wood tribe, and eventually the stone empire and its despot meet a grim fate. Kuper's narrative is beautifully

constructed, from its grand sweep to its minute details." Publ Wkly

Kupperberg, Paul
Archie: the married life. Written by Paul Kupperberg; pencils by Fernando Ruiz, Pat & Tim Kennedy; inking by Al Milgrom and Bob Smith; letters by Janice Chiang and Jack Moretti; coloring by Glenn Whitmore. Archie Comic Publications 2013 320 p. Color illustration
Grades: 9 10 11 12 Adult   741.5/973; Fic
1. Andrews, Archie (Fictional character); 2. Marriage — Fiction
1936975351; 9781936975358, $19.99
LC 2013409812

This graphic novel by Paul Kupperberg "explores Archie Andrews' life down two paths—if he had married girl-next-door Betty Cooper or wealthy socialite Veronica Lodge. In this volume, things really start getting interesting, as the mysterious Dilton Doiley subplots that have been bubbling just below the surface since the series' beginning start to affect... well, everything!" (Publisher's note)

"Eye-opening for longtime fanatics and an invigorating soap opera for newcomers." Booklist

Kurata, Hideyuki
R. O. D. (Read or Dream) Volume 1. Story by Hideyuki Kurata; art by Ran Ayanaga. Viz Media 2007 Un Illustration
Grades: 10 11 12 Adult   741.5; Fic
1. Fantasy graphic novels; 2. Manga; 3. Seinen manga; 4. Graphic novels
978-1-4215-0510-7, $9.99

Michelle is a romantic daydreamer and hardcore book collector. Maggie is a soft-spoken bookworm who always gets mistaken for a boy. Anita is a tomboy who doesn't have time for reading. Together, they're the Paper Sisters, three very different siblings united by a strange power. Michelle, Maggie and Anita all have the ability to control paper in any way they desire. And from their Hong Kong detective agency, they solve any and all cases involving books. In this volume, the sisters check out books from a secret library, use the power of literature to save the planet from an alien attack, and finally organize their massive book collection. There's never a dull moment at Paper Sisters Detective Company. The book includes some nudity and fan service (titillating pictures designed to appeal to male readers).

Train + Train, Vol. 1. Original story by Hideyuki Kurata ; art by Tomomasa Takuma. Go! Comi 2007 196p. Illustration
Grades: 8 9 10 11 12 Adult   741.5; Fic
1. Adventure graphic novels; 2. High school students; 3. Manga; 4. Graphic novels
978-1-933617-18-3, $10.99

Reiichi and Liae have come to the planet Deloca to board the high school train. On Deloca, different schools run on special trains, with stops where students complete certain assignments; they live in dorms on the trains. Reiichi and Liae are registered to board the "General" school train. Arena Pendleton, on the other hand, has determined to board the Special Train, and she won't let anyone stop her, not even the men her wealthy grandfather has hired to capture her and bring her home. In Ideo City, where the students must board their respective trains, Reiichi accidentally gets involved in a run-in between Arena and Kong Seeval, who intends to take Arena home. Reiichi and Arena become handcuffed together, and he has no choice but to board the Special Train. There's lots of action but little in the way of violence or bad language in this first of a manga series.

Kure, Yuki
La Corda D'Oro, Volume 1. Viz Media/Shojo Beat 2006 Un Illustration
Grades: 7 8 9 10 11 12   **741.5; Fic**
1. Music; 2. Shojo manga; 3. Violinists; 4. Graphic novels
978-1-4215-0583-1, $8.99
Kahoko is a second-year (junior) general education student at Seison Academy, which also has a famous music school. Every few years, the Academy holds a music competition in which only the best students are selected to participate. However, this year the director selects Kahoko. She has just encountered a "fata," a music fairy, whom very few can see. The fairy gives her a magical violin and tells Kahoko she must participate in the competition. While some of the music students consider Kahoko to be an interloper, several of the boys find her intriguing and help her. Even with a magical violin, Kahoko still needs to learn to find the right connection with the music in order to play well.

Kurkoski, Bettina
My Cat Loki Vol. 1. Tokyopop 2006 Un Illustration
Grades: 8 9 10 11 12   **741.5; Fic**
1. Cats; 2. Fantasy graphic novels; 3. Graphic novels
978-1-59816-731-3, $9.99
As a child, Ameya had always considered his cat more a sibling than a pet. As the years went by, their bond grew ever tighter. But the day his feline "brother" died was the day Ameya withdrew from the world. Several years later, Ameya encounters a drenched stray cat in the park. Little does he know what fate has in store for him... Most of the time, the cats in this global manga look like cats, but sometimes they're drawn as catboys and catgirls.

My Cat Loki Vol. 2. Tokyopop 2007 Un Illustration
Grades: 8 9 10 11 12   **741.5; Fic**
1. Cats; 2. Fantasy graphic novels; 3. Graphic novels
978-1-59816-732-0, $9.99
It's a warm and sunny day when Ameya makes his way to his favorite cafe and fate rears its strange and beautiful head. When a young woman named Luci literally stumbles into Ameya's life, will the encounter lead to something more? She is just like him—a struggling artist who has a strong relationship with her pet, and she's more than a little clumsy, in a totally adorable way. But neither Loki nor Miss Chacha find Ameya's growing interest in the newcomer to be even the least bit cute; Loki doesn't care for Luci's cat Calli at all. What's a lonely cat and a heartsick agent to do?

Kurosawa, Edo
50 Things We Love About Japan written by Edo Kurosawa ; illustrated by Atsuhisa Okura. Japanime Co. Ltd. 2007 112p. Illustration
Grades: 5 6 7 8 9 10 11 12 Adult   **741.5; 952**
1. Japan; 2. Graphic novels
978-4-921205-08-9, $9.99

From anime to karaoke to kaiten-zushi, this little book features manga illustrations and prose to offer the rest of the world a glimpse at what the Japanese love most about the country they call home. Manga readers and anime fans will find explanations for the some of the cultural elements found in the books and films.

Kurtz, Scott
How to make Webcomics. Brad Guigar, Dave Kellett, Scott Kurtz, Kris Straub. Image Comics 2008 195p. Illustration
Grades: 10 11 12 Adult   **741.5**
1. Graphic novels — Study and teaching; 2. Web sites — Design
978-1-58240-870-5, $12.99
Four webcomics creators have banded together to help readers make webcomics on their own. As they say in the introduction, this isn't a basic how to cartoon book. They address readers who already draw their cartoons and want to find a way to publish their work. Publishing on the web means the cartoonist is working for himself or herself and is not beholden to a publisher or syndicate. The book includes information on putting together a business plan, for self-publishing cartoonists must deal with the nitty-gritty of business decisions as well as the creative work of making the cartoons. The book also covers the basics of web design, whether to set up a subscription system, publishing one's comics in book form, even how to set up a booth at a comics convention.

Truth, Justin, and the American Way. Written by Aaron Williams and Scott Kurtz ; illustrated by Giuseppe Ferrario. Image Comics 2007 Un Illustration
Grades: 8 9 10 11 12 Adult   **741.5; Fic**
1. Humorous graphic novels; 2. Superhero graphic novels; 3. Graphic novels
978-1-58240-705-0, $14.99
1980s-era slacker Justin is supposed to get married this weekend, but due to a colossal mix-up, the silly t-shirt his friends got him for his bachelor party has been switched with an alien suit. When clueless Justin puts it on, the suit molds to his body, and when an FBI agent after the suit crashes the party, Justin learns what the suit can do. Before the weekend is over, Justin will have to fight not only FBI, but also aliens who want their property back. Filled with references to television shows and movies from the 1980s, the wacky story will appeal to younger teens even if they don't catch all the references.

Kusakawa, Nari
Recipe for Gertrude. DC Comics/CMX 2006 200p. Illustration
Grades: 6 7 8 9 10 11 12   **741.5; Fic**
1. Humorous graphic novels; 2. Manga; 3. Shojo manga; 4. Supernatural graphic novels; 5. Graphic novels
978-1-4012-1110-3, $9.99
Sahara is a normal high school girl whose life gets turned upside down when she meets "Gertrude," a 100-year-old demon who looks like a teen-age boy. Gertrude is a man-made demon, constructed from the parts of various other demons and brought to life through a "recipe" from an ancient spell book. Gertrude searches for the recipe, in order

to learn more about his origin and destroy the formula so that it can never be repeated. Sahara becomes his resourceful ally in Gertrude's quest and they are aided by some very comical and non-threatening demons. There's a little bit of violence as Gertrude and Sahara fight with various demons and other creepy enemies. This is a five-volume manga series that was completed in 2007.

Kwitney, Alisa

Token. Illustrated by Joelle Jones. DC Comics/Minx 2008 176p. Illustration
Grades: 7 8 9 10 11 12   **741.5; Fic**
1. Shoplifting; 2. Graphic novels
978-1-4012-1538-5, $9.99

Almost-sixteen Shira lives in Miami's South Beach in the mid-1980s, in a hotel with her attorney father, her grandmother, and elderly friend Minerva. She's sort of a spaz at sports, the popular girls at her Jewish high school think she's weird, and her father has started dating his new secretary. Life isn't good. She impulsively starts shoplifting just to feel something, and then she meets Rafael, a streetwise boy who decides to teach her the finer points of stealing. And more.

Kye, Seung-Hui

Recast Volume 1. Tokyopop 2006 192p. Illustration
Grades: 8 9 10 11 12   **741.5; Fic**
1. Adventure graphic novels; 2. Fantasy graphic novels; 3. Manwha; 4. Graphic novels
1-59816-664-6, $9.99

JD has grown up in a country village with his magician grandfather; they live in a world divided into different realms, and suddenly a "puppet" from the fourth realm attacks JD. He defeats it, but now his grandfather knows that time is running out; he used much of his power and sacrificed his immortality to recast his magic into JD, but bounty hunters from the fourth realm and the church's warriors from the fifth realm are now coming to find JD before the recast spell is complete. JD is destined for greatness, but only if he can survive. This manwha, Korean comics, series, is full of fighting action, with martial arts and monsters.

Kyle, Craig

New X-Men: Childhood's End Vol. 1. Mark Brooks, Illustrator. Marvel Entertainment 2006 Un Illustration
Grades: 9 10 11 12 Adult   **741.5; Fic**
1. Superhero graphic novels; 2. X-Men (Fictional characters); 3. Graphic novels
978-0-7851-1831-2, $10.99

The New X-men deal with the changed world after the events of the House of M (in which many mutants lost their powers). Will X-23 join the team, can anyone trust her" Will friendships persevere" Will the kids survive" No one is safe, and not everyone will live through the changes, not when the rules have changed and the safety is off.

Lagos, Alexander

The **sons** of liberty. Created and written by Alexander Lagos and Joseph Lagos; art by Steve Walker; color by Oren Kramek; letters by Chris Dickey. Random House 2010 Un Illustration
Grades: 6 7 8 9 10 11 12   **741.5; Fic**
1. Adventure graphic novels; 2. African Americans; 3. Superhero graphic novels; 4. United States — History — 1600-1775, Colonial period; 5. Graphic novels
978-0-375-85670-9, $18.99; 0-375-85670-6; 978-0-375-95667-6 (lib bdg), $21.99; 0-375-95667-6 (lib bdg); 978-0-375-85667-9 (pa), $12.99; 0-375-85667-9 (pa)

In the mid-eighteenth century American colonies, Graham and Brody work as slaves on a tobacco plantation not far from Philadelphia. When they run away after injuring the plantation owner's son for threatening another slave, they seek Benjamin Lay, an eccentric abolitionist who might give them shelter. Instead, William Franklin, son of Benjamin Franklin, finds them and conducts unknown experiments on them.

"History offers few villains as vile as slaveholders, but this graphic novel is far from being a simple revenge thriller. The use of historical figures and well-researched (but embellished) history, and a willingness to flesh out characters and set up situations to pay off in future installments, makes for an uncommonly complex, literate, and satisfying adventure." Booklist

The **sons** of liberty 2: death and taxes. Created and written by Alexander Lagos and Joseph Lagos; art by Steve Walker; color by Oren Kramek; letters by Chris Dickey. Random House Children's Books 2011 Un Illustration
Grades: 6 7 8 9 10 11 12   **741.5; Fic**
1. Adventure graphic novels; 2. African Americans; 3. Superhero graphic novels; 4. United States — History — 1600-1775, Colonial period
978-0-375-85671-9, $18.99; 978-0-375-85668-6 (pa), $12.99

"Graham and Brody, escaped slaves gifted with superpowers, remain at the center of this continuing pre-Revolutionary War saga of political intrigue and reimagined history. As Benjamin Franklin seeks to stop the stamp tax from falling on the colonies and enemies attack his good name, Graham attempts to arrange an escape back to Africa along with his love, the slave girl Isabel. . . . The embellishments, literate dialogue, and several historical truths—effectively counterpointed with glossy contemporary art—keep things fun and suspenseful." Booklist

Lane, Miles

Star Wars: Clone Wars Volume 7: When They Were Brothers. Written by Haden Blackman and Miles Lane ; art by Brian Ching and Nicola Scott. Dark Horse Comics 2005 Un. Illustration
Grades: 7 8 9 10 11 12 Adult   **741.5; Fic**
1. Adventure graphic novels; 2. Science fiction graphic novels; 3. Star Wars; 4. Graphic novels
1-59307-396-8, $17.95

Consumed by the belief that the Dark Jedi Asajj Ventress still lives, Obi-Wan Kenobi has temporarily forsaken his duties and recruited Anakin Skywalker in his desperate hunt for Ventress. But Anakin believes that Obi-Wan is chasing a ghost-because he himself killed Ventress. And Anakin's doubts about his former Master's quest are not assuaged when, following the trail of the rumors of Ventress' existence, they walk into a trap set by their old enemies, the bounty hunter Durge and Count Dooku. The book includes battle violence.

Langridge, Roger

The **Muppet** Show comic book: on the road. Writer, Roger Langridge ; art, Shelli Paroline & Roger Langridge ; colors, Digikore Studios, Mickey Clausen & Eric Cobain ; letters, Shelli Paroline & Deron Bennett. Boom! Kids 2010 Un Illustration

Grades: 3 4 5 6 7 8 9 10 11 12 Adult   **741.5; Fic**
   1. Humorous graphic novels; 2. Muppets (Fictional characters); 3. Travel; 4. Graphic novels
978-1-60886-516-1, $9.99

The Muppets' theater must undergo massive repairs, so the crew takes their show on the road. Standup comedian Fozzie tries to go on his own as a solo act, while Kermit and the rest of the motley group hires a caravan of buses and trailers to find small towns where they can perform. One place, Little Statwald, seems to be populated almost completely by relatives of old curmudgeons Stadler and Waldorf, who all delight in heckling the hapless performers. Langridge draws the main Muppets story, while Shelli Paroline draws the Pigs in Space episodes. The stories have been written to appeal to younger readers, while adults who remember the old Muppets television series will also enjoy the comics.

★ **Thor,** the mighty avenger, v.1.. Illustrated by Chris Samnee. Marvel 2011 Un Illustration

Grades: 8 9 10 11 12   **741.5; 741**
   1. Thor (Fictional character)
978-0-7851-4121-1, $14.99; 0-7851-4121-9

"Readers meet the mysterious blond-haired God of Thunder with no memory when historian Jane Foster watches him get tossed out of a Norse exhibition one day. After the gallant fellow helps her out and she takes him in, an utterly charming romance ensues. . . . Langridge deserves top marks for taking a character whose story possibilities might seem limited and imbuing him with a fresh and highly entertaining life. . . . Samnee's art grounds the vigorous superhero action with expressive faces, subtle lighting tones, and an individual style that makes the drama sing." Booklist

Lapham, David

Batman: City of Gotham. David Lapham, writer; Ramon Bachs, penciler; Nathan Massengill, inker; Jason Wright, colorist; Jared K. Fletcher, letterer. DC Comics 2006 288p. Illustration

Grades: 10 11 12 Adult   **741.5; Fic**
   1. Batman (Fictional character); 2. Mystery graphic novels; 3. Superhero graphic novels; 4. Graphic novels
978-1-4012-0897-4, $19.99

Dave Lapham, the creator of the ultra-gritty noir series Stray Bullets, weaves a story of the Dark Knight facing an unspeakable crime. Batman first investigates the deaths of six teenage girls, then he learns of even worse crimes. As he tries to shut down a drug ring that's turned deadly, Bruce Wayne must contend with a wayward 14-year-old who's getting dangerously close to Gotham's underworld. In Gotham City, not every villain wears a mask; not every hero wears a cape; not every victim is innocent; and some secrets should remain buried. This volume includes violence.

Silverfish. DC Comics/Vertigo 2007 Un Illustration
Grades: 11 12 Adult   **741.5; Fic**
   1. Mystery graphic novels; 2. Graphic novels
978-1-4012-1048-9, $24.99

What starts as a childish bid for her father's affections turns into nail-biting suspense when teenaged Mia searches her new stepmother's purse, only to find a secret stash of money, a bloody knife and a mysterious address book. In the meantime, Daniel is on the trail of the woman who betrayed him; and the silverfish he keeps seeing in his mind's eye are telling him to kill again.

The **Spectre:** Infinite Crisis Aftermath. Written by David Lapham and Will Pfeifer; pencilled by Eric Battle and Cliff Chiang. DC Comics 2007 144p. Illustration
Grades: 10 11 12 Adult   **741.5; Fic**
   1. Spectre (Fictional character); 2. Superhero graphic novels; 3. Supernatural graphic novels; 4. Graphic novels
978-1-4012-1380-0, $12.99

After losing his human host, The Spectre ran rampant across the DC Universe, destroying all sources of magic. Now, the spirit of vengeance has been joined with a new host: the spirit of murdered Detective Crispus Allen from the Gotham City Police Department. But Allen wants nothing to do with the Spectre or his holy mission—even if it means jeopardizing his chance for redemption. The Spectre's vengeance tends to be quite bloody.

Larsen, Erik

Savage Dragon Archives Volume 1. Image Comics 2006 616p. Illustration
Grades: 10 11 12 Adult   **741.5; Fic**
   1. Hellboy (Fictional character); 2. Mystery graphic novels; 3. Superhero graphic novels; 4. Graphic novels
978-1-58240-723-4, $19.99

The earliest adventures are collected for the first time in one volume as Savage Dragon defends Chicago from Overlord and the Vicious Circle. Savage Dragon, a big, green, fin-headed alien with no memory of his early life before being found in an empty field in Chicago, is a superhero who actually works as a police officer with the Chicago Police Department. This is the complete Overlord epic from start to finish, culminating in a battle that can only end one way. Guest-starring the WildC.A.T.S and the Teenage Mutant Ninja Turtles. This black and white reprint volume includes a lot of fighting violence, some strong language, and some skimpy women's costumes.

Savage Dragon Archives Volume 2. Image Comics 2006 616p. Illustration
Grades: 10 11 12 Adult   **741.5; Fic**
   1. Mystery graphic novels; 2. Superhero graphic novels; 3. Graphic novels
9781582407371, $19.99; 1582407371

This volume kicks off with an all-out gang war in the streets of Chicago and builds to the destruction of the planet Earth itself. Dragon goes from cop to corpse and to hell and back. This book features the birth of Dragon's son, the death and rebirth of Darklords and Dragon's ascension to the head of Special Operations Strikeforce. Guest-starring Spawn,

Hellboy, the Maxx, the Teenage Mutant Ninja Turtles, and God. The book has lots of fighting violence, harsh language, some nudity and sexual situations.

Larson, Hope

★ **Chiggers**. [by] Hope Larson; lettered by Jason Azzopardi. Atheneum Books for Young Readers 2008 170p. Illustration

Grades: 5 6 7 8 9   **741.5; Fic**
1. Camps — Fiction; 2. Friendship; 3. Graphic novels
978-1-4169-3584-1, $17.99; 978-1-4169-3587-2 (pa), $9.99

LC 2008-09557

When Abby returns to the same summer camp she always goes to, she is dismayed to find that her old friends have changed, and the only person who wants to be her friend is the strange new girl, Shasta.

"Chiggers provides a ticket to summer fun. Larson delicately handles both the usual middle-school angst and the additional pressures that come with being somewhat different. . . . The content is perfect for upper elementary and middle school students." SLJ

Gray horses. Oni Press 2006 Un Illustration

Grades: 9 10 11 12 Adult   **741.5; Fic**
1. Dreams; 2. Graphic novels
1-932664-36-X, 14.95

LC 2006-280748

French exchange student Noemie has traveled to Onion City on her own, where she makes friends with free-spirited Anna, a neighbor and baker's daughter who sculpts in bread. As she walks around the city, she finds herself the target of a mysterious young photographer. However, it's in her dreams that things are weird. Every night she dreams of a girl named Marcy who finds help from a talking horse to get away from her mother; she must find a place to hide a photograph before her mother burns everything "contaminated" from illness. As the dreams progress every night, Noemie is more able to live in the moment. Much of the text is bilingual.

Who is AC?. Hope Larson; illustrated by Tintin Pantoja. Atheneum Books for Young Readers 2013 176 p.

Grades: 7 8 9 10 11 12   **741.5/973; Fic**
1. Female superhero graphic novels; 2. Superheroes — Fiction; 3. Graphic novels
1442426500; 9781442426504, $14.99; 9781442465404, $21.99

LC 2011052616

In this book, "Lin, a zine-writing 15-year-old who's just moved to a small town, becomes an unwitting Sailor Moon-style superhero, activated by mysterious cellphone messages and visited by a 'dispatcher' who nags her until she suits up. Her nemesis is a shadowy villain who possesses a glamorous rich girl in order to snare a boy named Trace." (Publishers Weekly)

Lash, Batton

Archie: the high school chronicles, book one: freshman year. Script, Batton Lash ; pencils, Bill Galvan ; inks, Bob Smith, Al Milgrom ; letters, Jack Morelli ; colors, Glenn Whitmore. Archie Comic Publications, Inc. 2009 120p. Illustration

Grades: 4 5 6 7 8 9 10   **741.5; Fic**

1. Andrews, Archie (Fictional character); 2. High school; 3. Humorous graphic novels; 4. Graphic novels
978-1-879794-40-5, $10.95

Lash, creator of Supernatural Law, writes the story never before written about Archie Andrews and all his friends in all the decades of Archie comics (since the 1940s) what was it like for the gang to start high school" This story starts at the end of summer vacation, and everyone is looking forward to a new start at a new school especially Archie, who constantly got into trouble with his old school principal. The one bad thing is that Jughead has to leave town, because his father has got a new job. On the very first day of school, Archie already gets into trouble with the Principal and yikes! it's Mr. Weatherbee, his old nemesis. Weatherbee has more problems than just dealing with Archie, however; the superintendent doesn't like him and wants to find a way to get him fired. Top that off with Archie facing off against upper classmen bullies, and freshman year is shaping up to be interesting, in a painful way. Galvan's art shows Archie, Jughead, Betty, Veronica, and Reggie as very recognizably themselves but looking young enough to be fourteen years old. This book could be a great entry point for anyone who has never read any Archie comics before.

Mister Negativity and Other Tales of Supernatural Law. Exhibit A Press 2004 170p. Illustration

Grades: 8 9 10 11 12 Adult   **741.5; Fic**
1. Humorous graphic novels; 2. Supernatural graphic novels; 3. Graphic novels
0-9633954-8-3, $15.95

LC 2003113227

Attorneys Wolff & Byrd represent clients that include Nagy D'Viti, a fellow with such a negative attitude that he physically repels people, Huberis the Dybbuk, a born again demon seeking church membership, Nicky Gorillo, a gangster who has literally become a gorilla mob boss, Steven Gink, a horror novelist in a coma who summons them through their dreams, Susann, the Muse of Potboilers, who sues the author she has "inspired," and Perry Otter, a boy magician with an unusual affliction.

Sonovawitch! And Other tales of Supernatural Law. Exhibit A Press 2000 166p. Illustration

Grades: 9 10 11 12 Adult   **741.5; Fic**
1. Horror graphic novels; 2. Humorous graphic novels; 3. Law; 4. Graphic novels
0-9633954-6-7, $14.95

Alanna Wolff and Jeff Byrd are attorneys who represent the supernatural and the supernaturally afflicted. In this volume, their clients include "Dr. Life," a physician dedicated to reviving the dead; "Bugsy" Renfield, a vampire member of the Nosferatu crime cartel; Ygor, a hunchback charged with teaching Satanism to preschool children; Martin Woodhull, accused of "hexual harassment" when his mother, a witch, puts a

Courtesy of Exhibit A Press

love spell on one of his co-workers; Dekoo Kei, a Japanese holy man who guards a jewel that can unleash the power of the giant reptilian monster, the Gormagon; and Barry Hopper, a nice guy whose soul has accidentally possessed the body of the demon Wasistlos, who is not too happy to deal with its "inner human." And their secretary, Mavis, has an adventure all her own.

Tales of supernatural law. Exhibit A Press 2005 184p. Illustration

Grades: 9 10 11 12 Adult   **741.5; Fic**
   1. Humorous graphic novels; 2. Lawyers; 3. Supernatural graphic novels; 4. Graphic novels

0-9633954-9-1, $16.95

This volume reprints the first eight issues of the ongoing comics series that used to be called Wolff & Byrd, Counselors of the Macabre and is now called Supernatural Law. Alanna Wolff and Jeff Byrd provide legal services for monsters, vampires, zombies, ghosts, and other things that go bump in the night. In these stories, they help a couple who foolishly used a monkey's paw

Courtesy of Exhibit A Press

to make wishes, another couple whose house becomes haunted every full moon, a supermodel seeking redress for a curse, a horror television host accused of exposing children to violence, a swamp monster who would like his fifteen minutes of fame, and the interdimensional being Th'Lulu.

Lasko-Gross, Miss
   Escape from Special. Fantagraphics Books 2006 Un Illustration

Grades: 10 11 12 Adult   **741.5; Fic**
   1. Autobiographical graphic novels; 2. Girls; 3. Graphic novels

978-1-56097-804-6, $16.95

   This semi-autobiographical graphic novel uses short episodes to depict the childhood and teen years of Melissa. Sometimes willful, she gets into trouble at school, is branded "special" (as in special education), has very few friends, and has to see a therapist. With biting honesty, Melissa endures the casual cruelty of so-called friends, mis-uses bad words to comic effect, and questions why she should do things like attend Jewish school when her parents don't go to Temple. Occasional nudity and harsh language occur throughout the book.

Courtesy of Fantagraphics

Lassieur, Allison
   Clara Barton: Angel of the Battlefield. Illustrated by Brian Bascle. Capstone Press 2006 32p. Illustration

Grades: 3 4 5 6 7 8 9   **741.5; 361.7; 92**
   1. Barton, Clara, 1821-1912; 2. Biographical graphic novels; 3. Graphic novels

0-7368-4632-8, $25.26

                LC 2005008122

   This book uses the comic book format to describe highlights in the life and work of Clara Barton, who served as a Civil War nurse and started the American Red Cross. It includes additional information, a glossary, a list of books for further reading, and more.

   Part of the Graphic Library, Graphic Biographies series.

   Lords of the Sea: The Vikings Explore the North Atlantic. Illustrated by Ron Frenz and Charles Barnett III. Capstone Press 2006 32p. Illustration

Grades: 3 4 5 6 7 8 9   **741.5; 948**
   1. Vikings; 2. Graphic novels

0-7368-4974-2, $25.26

                LC 2005007891

   This book uses the comic book format to tell the story of the Vikings' exploration of the North Atlantic and their discovery of North America. It includes additional information, a glossary, a list of books for further reading, and more.

   Part of the Graphic Library, Graphic History series.

Lat
   Kampung boy. First Second 2006 141p. Illustration

Grades: 7 8 9 10 11 12 Adult   **741.5; Fic**
   1. Family life; 2. Malaysia; 3. Muslims; 4. Graphic novels

1-59643-121-0, $16.95

                LC 2005-34135

   "Malaysian cartoonist Lat uses the graphic novel format to share the story of his childhood in a small village, or kampung. From his birth and adventures as a toddler to the enlargement of his world as he attends classes in the village, makes friends, and, finally, departs for a prestigious city boarding school, this autobiography is warm, authentic, and wholly engaging." Booklist

   First published 1979 in Malaysia with title: Lat, the kampung boy

   ★ **Town** boy. First Second Books 2007 191p. Illustration

Grades: 7 8 9 10 11 12 Adult   **741.5; Fic**
   1. Bildungsromans; 2. Humorous graphic novels; 3. Malaysia; 4. Graphic novels

978-1-59643-331-1, $16.95; 1-59643-331-0

                LC 2006-102857

   In this sequel to Kampung Boy, it's the late 1960s and Mat is now a teenager attending a boarding school in the town of Ipoh, far from his kampung. He discovers bustling streets, hip music, heady literature, budding romance, and through it all his growing passion for art.

Latour, Jason
   Spider-Gwen; Volume 0: Most Wanted?. Written by Jason Latour, art by Robbi Rodriguez. Marvel Enterprises 2015 112 p.

Grades: 9 10 11 12 Adult   **741.5**

1. Female superhero comic books, strips, etc; 2. Spider-Woman (Fictional character); 3. Superhero comic books, strips, etc
0785197737; 9780785197737, $16.99
"Gwen Stacy is Spider-Woman, but you knew that already. What you DON'T know is what friends and foes are waiting for her in the aftermath of Spider-Verse! From the fan-favorite creative team that brought you Spider-Gwen's origin story in EDGE OF SPIDER-VERSE, Jason Latour and Robbie Rodriguez!" (Publisher's note)
Originally published in single issue form as Spider-Gwen #1-5
First volume of an ongoing series

Layman, John
★ **Chew,** volume one: taster's choice. Written & lettered by John Layman; drawn & coloured by Rob Guillory. Image Comics 2009 Un Illustration
Grades: 10 11 12 Adult   **741.5; Fic**
1. Cannibalism; 2. Mystery graphic novels; 3. Science fiction graphic novels; 4. Graphic novels
978-1-60706-159-5, $9.99
Police detective Tony Chu is a good detective with a weird secret: he's Cibopathic he gets psychic impressions from whatever he eats. It means he is a vegetarian, but it also means he can learn important facts about a case by nibbling on the corpse of a murder victim. Aside from the ôewwwwö factor, he tends to have a high success rate in solving his cases. In his world, the FDA (yes, Food and Drug Administration) has become the most powerful law enforcement agency on the planet, and chicken is a forbidden food because of the avian flu. The FDA's Special Crimes Division makes Tony one of their agents and gives him their strangest, sickest, most bizarre unsolved cases, hoping to use his Cibopathic abilities to close them. This story includes cannibalism, violence, some gore, and some bad language. It has also been cited by many comics reviewers as one of the top comics series of 2009.
Volume 1 of an ongoing series

Lee, Stan
Essential Fantastic Four Vol. 1, 2nd ed.. Art by Jack Kirby. Marvel Entertainment 2005 Un Illustration
Grades: 7 8 9 10 11 12 Adult   **741.5; Fic**
1. Fantastic Four (Fictional characters); 2. Hulk (Fictional character); 3. Superhero graphic novels; 4. Graphic novels
978-0-7851-1828-2, $16.99
This massive trade paperback collects the first 20 issues of The Fantastic Four plus the Annual #1. Reprinted in black and white, this volume lets readers get the origin and early stories as originally written by Lee and drawn by Kirby. The Fantastic Four fights against Skrulls, Sub-Mariner, The Impossible Man, The Hulk, the Red Ghost, The Thinker, Doctor Doom (who first appeared in issue #5), the Puppet Master, and many more super villains.

★ **Stan** Lee's How todraw comics: from the legendary co-creator ofSpider-Man, the Incredible Hulk, Fantastic Four,X-Men, and Iron Man. Watson-Guptill Publication 2010 224p. Illustration
Grades: 9 10 11 12 Adult   **741.5**

1. Comic books, strips, etc — Authorship; 2. Drawing — Technique; 3. Fantastic Four (Fictional characters); 4. Hulk (Fictional character); 5. Iron Man (Fictional character); 6. Spider-Man (Fictional character); 7. X-Men (Fictional characters); 8. Graphic novels
978-0-8230-0083-8, $24.99
     LC 2010-5781
The author "includes chapters on creating comics with computer programs and online resources and how to get work in the 21st century. The book begins with a brief history of comics, then focuses on action-adventure style, romance, humor, horror, and Japanese manga. This is the one book anyone interested in drawing comics should own." Libr J
Includes bibliographical references

Stan's soapbox: The collection. Marvel Entertainment 2008 144p. Illustration
Grades: 9 10 11 12 Adult   **741.5; 814**
1. Fantastic Four (Fictional characters); 2. Spider-Man (Fictional character); 3. X-Men (Fictional characters); 4. Graphic novels
978-0-9797602-9-7, $14.99
Stan Lee is probably one of the best-known faces of American comics, he helped to create many of the iconic superhero characters published by Marvel Comics, including the Fantastic Four, Spider-Man, and the X-Men. As an editor for Marvel, he wrote editorials that ran in every Marvel comic published from 1967-1980; these were called "Stan's Soapbox." This book, published as a co-venture with the Hero Initiative as a fundraiser to help comic creators in financial need, collects all of the Stan's Soapbox editorials from those Marvel comics. Readers can go back in time as they read what Lee wrote; the book also includes the major events happening in the U.S. and the world during those years

Lee, Tony
★ **Outlaw:** the legend of Robin Hood: a graphic novel. Written by Tony Lee; illustrated by Sam Hart; colored by Artur Fujita. Candlewick Press 2009 Un Illustration
Grades: 7 8 9 10 11 12   **741.5; Fic**
1. Adventure graphic novels; 2. Great Britain — History — 1154-1399, Plantagenets; 3. Robin Hood (Legendary character); 4. Graphic novels
978-0-7636-4399-7, $21.99; 0-7636-4399-8; 978-0-7636-4400-0 (pa), $11.99; 0-7636-4400-5 (pa)
     LC 2008-943331
In this retelling of the Robin Hood legend, it's the year 1192, and Robin of Loxley has returned home from the Crusades after receiving news of his father's death. The Sheriff of Nottingham and Sir Guy of Gisburn govern Nottingham at the pleasure of Prince John. When Gisburn treacherously stabs Robin in a murder attempt, Robin escapes to Sherwood Forest, where the outlaws befriend him. With the help of such men as Little John and Friar Tuck, he organizes the outlaws and they start hurting Prince John where it matters—in his moneybags.
"Lee's excellent rendition of the famed selfless hero goes hand-in-hand with Hart's expressive illustrations, featuring lots of closeups and dramatic lighting and a

beautiful jewel-toned palette. Teens will get caught up in this exciting page-turner." SLJ

Starship TroopersVol. 1: Blaze of Glory. Story Tony Lee; art Sam Hart and Rod Reis. Markosia 2006 Un Illustration
Grades: 10 11 12 Adult   **741.5; Fic**
1. Adventure graphic novels; 2. Science fiction graphic novels; 3. Graphic novels
1-905692-05-6, $14.95
Based on the science fiction novel by Robert Heinlein, this book tells the story of the Starship Troopers, human soldiers who fight a war against aliens they call "bugs." Rookie Will Tanner joins Tamari's Tigers, one of the fiercest units in the mobile infantry in time for their next mission, to rescue the survivors of Alamar "Alamo" Bay from a planet of bugs. The book is full of combat action and harsh language.

Lee, Young-You
Priceless Volume 1. Tokyopop 2006 192p. Illustration
Grades: 9 10 11 12 Adult   **741.5; Fic**
1. Humorous graphic novels; 2. Manwha; 3. Romance graphic novels; 4. Graphic novels
1-59816-309-4, $9.99
After her mother goes on the lam because of a business scam, Lang-bee is alone to fend for herself. She repays the people ripped-off by her mom with the money she makes working for her fellow students, taking on their school cleaning duties. When Lang-bee pursues her love interest Dan Won, the rich heir to a corporate empire, she competes against archrival Yuka Lee. Then Jimmy, a teenager just a little older than Lang-bee, shows up and claims her mother plans to marry him, and he tries to be her "father." This is a rags-to-riches story filled with love triangles, double-crosses, and mysterious pasts.

LeGrow, M. Alice
Bizenghast Vol. 1. Tokyopop 2005 Un Illustration
Grades: 9 10 11 12 Adult   **741.5; Fic**
1. Fantasy graphic novels; 2. Horror graphic novels; 3. Graphic novels
1-59532-743-6, $9.99
Time passes in every town...except one. When Dinah moves to the forgotten town of Bizenghast after her parents die, she uncovers a terrifying collection of lost souls that leads her to the brink of insanity. One thing becomes painfully clear: the residents of Bizenghast are just dying to come home. This is a global manga title.

Lehmann, Matthias
Hwy 115. Fantagraphics Books 2006 Un Illustration
Grades: 12 Adult   **741.5; Fic**
1. Mystery graphic novels; 2. Graphic novels
978-1-56097-733-9, $19.95
Two detectives, Ren? and Agatha, are on the tracks of Robert Illot, a serial killer whose modus operandi is to suffocate his victim with various objects (including chickens and lightbulbs) along the highways and byways of France. As they get closer and closer to catching up with him, seeking out and interrogating men and women from his past life at the insane asylum, he always stays one step ahead and

the row of corpses grows longer and longer... In this lengthy original graphic novel by Matthias Lehmann, dreams and flashbacks converge with the ongoing narrative, with graphically depicted sex and lots of murders.

Lemire, Jeff
★ **Descender:** Tin Stars Book one. By Jeff Lemire; illustrated by Dustin Nguyen. Image Comics 2015 160 p.
Grades: 9 10 11 12 Adult   **741.5; 741.5/973**
1. Androids — Fiction; 2. Robots — Fiction; 3. Science fiction comic books, strips, etc
1632154269; 9781632154262, $9.99
                     LC Bl2015040509
In this science fiction comic book, by Jeff Lemire, illustrated by Dustin Nguyen, "Young Robot boy TIM-21 and his companions struggle to stay alive in a universe where all androids have been outlawed and bounty hunters lurk on every planet." (Publisher's note)
Volume 1 of an ongoing series

★ **Essex** County, Vol. 1: Tales from the Farm. Top Shelf Productions 2007 Un Illustration
Grades: 10 11 12 Adult
741.5; Fic
1. Farm life; 2. Friendship; 3. Orphans; 4. Graphic novels
978-1-891830-88-4, $9.95

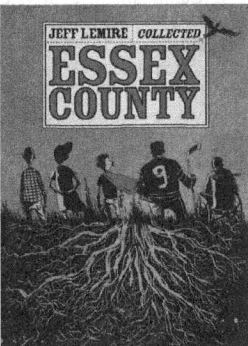
Courtesy of Top Shelf Productions

Orphaned ten-year-old Lester lives with his bachelor uncle Ken on a southwestern Ontario farm. He constantly wears a mask and cape, imagining that he's protecting the place from invading space aliens. Uncle Ken doesn't know how to deal with Lester, and their relationship becomes strained. Only one grown-up, Jimmy, who runs the gas station and convenience store, can connect with Lester on his level.
"Lemire enriches this rather familiar scenario with telling, particularizing detail, ensuring that this time the old heartwarming routine is unforgettably special." Booklist

Essex County, vol. 2: Ghost stories. Top Shelf Productions 2007 224p. Illustration
Grades: 10 11 12 Adult   **741.5; Fic**
1. Brothers; 2. Hockey; 3. Graphic novels
978-1-891830-94-5, $14.95
Ghost Story follows the lives and relationship of brothers Lou and Vince Lebeuf over the course of nearly seven decades. Elder brother Lou, now a deaf and lonely man, lives out his final days on his farm full of guilt and regret for the decisions he made that tore his family apart. From their childhood on the farm, to Toronto in the 1950s (where they both played professional hockey), Lou is left to revisit his life, his decisions and his regrets. This is the second volume of Lemire's stories of Essex County.

★ **Essex** County, vol. 3: The country nurse. Top Shelf Productions 2008 127p. Illustration

Grades: 10 11 12 Adult   **741.5; Fic**
1. Family life; 2. Graphic novels
978-1-891830-95-2, $9.95

In this third and final volume in the Essex County trilogy, the story follows country nurse Anne Morgan through one day as she drives around the county to visit patients. In between her meetings with Jimmy at the gas station, Ken and his nephew Lester at the farm, and learning that elderly Mr. LeBeuf, Jimmy's father, had died the previous night, readers see the story of an orphanage that existed almost a century ago. When it burned down one night and the caretaker died getting all the children out, the nun in charge led them on a cold winter hike to find shelter and help in Essex County. Anne is a descendant of the nun, while Jimmy, Ken, and Lester are all descendants of one orphan. And all their stories come together as Anne makes her rounds of the day.

"Well written and beautifully drawn, this wonderful close to a powerful trilogy is ideal for fans of realistic stories in comics." SLJ

Green Arrow; Volume 4: The kill machine. Jeff Lemire, writer; Andrea Sorrentino, artist. DC Comics 2014 Un Color; Illustration
Grades: 9 10 11 12 Adult   **741.5; Fic**
1. Green Arrow (Fictional character); 2. Superhero comic books, strips, etc
9781401246907, $16.99; 1401246907
                       LC 2013045547

"A mysterious villian called Komodo knows Oliver's secrets and uses them to rob Oliver of all his wealth and his company. Now on the run from this seemingly unstoppable force, Oliver finds himself in a mystery involving the island where he first became Green Arrow and his father! Everything will change for the Emerald Archer in this new beginning for the character." (Publisher's note)

Other Green Arrow volumes by Lemire and Sorrentino are: 5: The outsiders war; 6: Broken

Hawkeye: all-new Hawkeye. By Jeff Lemire; illustrated by Ramon Perez. Marvel Enterprises 2015 112 p. Color; Illustration
Grades: 11 12 Adult   **741.5; 741.5**
1. Superhero comic books, strips, etc
0785194037; 9780785194033, $15.99

In this comic book, by Jeff Lemire, illustrated by Ramon Perez, "Hawkeye returns. . . . With Kate Bishop, his trusted ward and protege (not titles she would use) back at his side, Team Hawkeye is thrown into an all new adventure spanning two generations of avenging archers. Past and present lives collide as Kate and Clint face a threat that will challenge everything they know about what it means to be Hawkeye." (Publisher's note)

Teen Titans; Volume 1: Earth One. Written by Jeff Lemire; pencils by Terry Dodson. DC Comics 2014 144 p. Color; Illustration
Grades: 10 11 12 Adult   **741.5**
1. Superhero comic books, strips, etc; 2. Teen Titans (Fictional characters); 3. Teenagers
1401245560; 9781401245566, $22.99
                       LC 2014032609

This book, by Jeff Lemire and Terry Dodson, is a "new original graphic novel in DC's popular 'Earth One' series. . . . The Teen Titans never felt like normal kids... but they had no idea how right they were. Their seemingly idyllic Oregon upbringing hides a secret — one that will bring killers, shamans, and extraterrestrials down on their heads, and force them into an alliance that could shake the planet to its foundations!" (Publisher's note)

"Rather than more minor tinkering with the teenaged super-hero team, this graphic novel is a full-scale reboot: what if, in an alternative world, circumstances brought together young people who echo the regular Teen Titans but are totally different people" . . . Lemire's (Essex County) script exploits teen angst efficiently and with some fresh imagination, while the Dodsons (Wonder Woman) produce lovely art, especially in panels showing Navajo seer Raven." Pub Wkly

Trillium. Jeff Lemire, writer & artist; Jeff Lemire, Jose Villarrubia, colorists; Carlos M. Mangual, letterer. DC Comics/Vertigo 2014 192 p. Color; Illustration
Grades: 11 12 Adult   **741.5**
1. Love stories; 2. Science fiction graphic novels; 3. Time travel
1401249000; 9781401249007, $16.99
                       LC 2014011939

Eisner Nominee: Best Limited Series (2014)

This graphic novel, by Jeff Lemire, with color by Jose Villarrubia and lettering by Carlos M. Mangual, "spins the tale of two star-crossed loved through space in time. . . . [In] the year 3797, . . . botanist Nika Temsmith is researching a strange species on a remote science station near the outermost rim of colonized space. . . . [In] 1921, . . . English explorer William Pike leads an expedition into the dense jungles of Peru in search of the fabled 'Lost Temple of the Incas.'" (Publisher's note)

"Lemire's art excels, combining his trademark sketchiness with gorgeous watercolors. But it's the layouts that take the book to new heights of creativity. Lemire tells two stories at once by turning the panels upside down, disorienting the reader as much as his heroes." Pub Wkly

Lemke, Donald B.
The **Brave** Escape of Ellen and William Craft. Capstone Press 2006 32p. Illustration
Grades: 3 4 5 6 7 8 9   **741.5; 306.3; 92**
1. Craft, Ellen, 1826-1891; 2. Craft, William, 1824-1900; 3. Fugitive slaves — United States — Biography; 4. Slavery — United States; 5. Graphic novels
0-7368-4973-4, $25.26
                       LC 2005008084

This book uses the comic book format to tell the story of Ellen and William Craft's escape from slavery in Georgia to freedom in Pennsylvania. It includes additional information, a glossary, a list of books for further reading, and more.

Part of the Graphic Library, Graphic History series.

Investigating the scientific method with Max Axiom, super scientist. Illustrated by Tod Smith and Al Milgrom. Capstone Press 2008 32p. Illustration
Grades: 3 4 5 6 7 8 9   **507; 741.5**
1. Science — Methodology; 2. Graphic novels
978-1-42961329-3, $26.26
                       LC 2007-22792

Super scientist Max Axiom, who has powers gained from a freak accident, takes young readers on a journey to learn about the scientific method and how scientists use it to begin their investigations into problems that need solving; readers also learn how to use it themselves in their class work. Back matter includes more historical tidbits of information, a short glossary, and a list of books for further reading.

Part of the Graphic Science series

The **Schoolchildren's** Blizzard. Capstone Press 2007 32p. Illustration
Grades: 3 4 5 6 7 8 9   **741.5; 977**
1. Blizzards; 2. Middle West; 3. Graphic novels
978-1-4296-0157-3, $26.25
                                        LC 2007000259
This book uses the graphic novel format to tell of the devastating 1888 blizzard that suddenly exploded across the Great Plains and killed hundreds of children as they walked home from school. The book includes additional facts and a list of booksfor further reading.

Part of the Graphic Library Disasters in History series.

Lenkov, Peter M.
Fort: Prophet of the Unexplained. Script, Peter M. Lenkov; art, Frazer Irving; letters, Digital Chameleon. Dark Horse Comics 2003 Un Illustration
Grades: 9 10 11 12 Adult   **741.5; Fic**
1. Adventure graphic novels; 2. Fantasy graphic novels; 3. Horror graphic novels; 4. Mystery graphic novels; 5. Graphic novels
1-56971-781-8, $9.95
It's the end of the 19th century and the city of New York has been plagued by fish falling from the sky, strange lights in the night, bizarre collections of microbial goo, and vanishing citizens. It's up to one man to expose the truth behind these events... Charles Fort. A mild mannered librarian by day, Fort seeks out the truth and exposes the bizarre to the light of day, with the aid of young newspaper boy H.P. Lovecraft. The book includes some violence.

Lent, Michael
P.R.E.Y.: Origin of the Species. Written by Michael Lent ; adapted by Mike Raicht ; art by Bong Dazo and Alex Sanchez, Marvel Entertainment/Dabel Brothers 2007 Un Illustration
Grades: 7 8 9 10 11 12 Adult   **741.5; Fic**
1. Horror graphic novels; 2. Science fiction graphic novels; 3. Graphic novels
978-0-7851-2658-4, $10.99
The Prometheus Corporation has unearthed something ancient and dangerous in its underwater excavations, and now it's come to the surface to make humanity its prey. Their solution" To lure the thing back in the sea and kill everything within a five mile radius, effectively covering the corporation's tracks. And so a disgraced marine biologist must race against the clock and find a way to keep the ocean from being destroyed by the corporation before something even more dangerous is unleashed on mankind. The book includes some strong language and some violence.

Lerner, Emily Ryan
Showcase Presents: Superman Volume 2. DC Comics 2006 576p. Illustration
Grades: 7 8 9 10 11 12 Adult   **741.5; Fic**
1. Superhero graphic novels; 2. Superman (Fictional character); 3. Graphic novels
978-1-4012-1041-0, $16.99
The beginning of the 1960s ushered in a new era for Superman. These Silver Age exploits see Superman confront a wide array of villains, explore the planet Krypton, and overcome Kryptonite exposure, become a Bizarro, and more. The stories, reprinted here in black and white, date from December 1959 through May 1961.

Levine, David
American presidents. Fantagraphics Books 2008 128p. Illustration
Grades: 9 10 11 12 Adult   **352.23; 741.5**
1. Cartoons and caricatures; 2. Presidents — United States
978-1-60699-130-5, $19.99
Cartoonist and caricaturist Levine has drawn the most powerful men of the free world for more than 50 years. This book collects his portraits of the American presidents, from Washington through George W. Bush (and some of their important colleagues); it includes caricatures of Bush Cabinet members and appointees, and the various candidates who ran for President in 2008, including Senator Hillary Clinton, Rudy Giulani, Senator John McCain, and President-Elect Barack Obama. Levine used his art to point out what he considered to be shortcomings, phoniness, duplicity, and venality in the various administrations throughout American history.

Levitz, Paul
The **Huntress:** Darknight Daughter. DC Comics 2006 224p. Illustration
Grades: 8 9 10 11 12 Adult   **741.5; Fic**
1. Batman (Fictional character); 2. Catwoman (Fictional character); 3. Superhero graphic novels; 4. Graphic novels
978-1-4012-09131, $19.99
She is unique in comics, the daughter of a hero and a villain: the Earth-Two Batman and Catwoman. Helena Wayne was trained by her parents to become a superb athlete, and she studied law with the hope of bringing criminals to justice. But after Catwoman is blackmailed to resume her life of crime, leading to her death, Helena dons a costume and crossbow to become the Huntress to avenge her mother. This volume collects the stories originally published in the 1970s and 1980s.

JSA: Ghost Stories. Paul Levitz, writer; George Pérez [and others], pencillers. DC Comics 2006 144p. Illustration
Grades: 10 11 12 Adult   **741.5; Fic**
1. Batman (Fictional character); 2. Justice Society of America (Fictional characters); 3. Superhero graphic novels; 4. Graphic novels
978-1-4012-1196-7, $12.99
Near the end of Infinite Crisis, Power Girl learns of a Golden Age adventure in which Batman and Superman battled the Gentleman Ghost. One year later, the members of the JSA are haunted by ghosts of their departed loved ones. As it becomes clear the two incidents are connected, the JSA

becomes the target of the Gentleman Ghost and his undead army. How will the JSA end this supernatural slaughter, when the only being who knows how to stop it is the ghost of Batman?

Justice Society Volume One. Paul Levitz and Gerry Conway. DC Comics 2006 224p. Illustration
Grades: 7 8 9 10 11 12 Adult   **741.5; Fic**
1. Flash (Fictional character); 2. Green Lantern (Fictional character); 3. Justice Society of America (Fictional characters); 4. Robin (Fictional character); 5. Superhero graphic novels; 6. Graphic novels
978-1-4012-0970-4, $14.99

The volume collects stories originally published in the 1970s, when DC revived the very first superhero team that was originally created in 1940: the Justice Society of America. This incarnation of the Justice Society includes the Golden Age Flash and Green Lantern, Hawkman, Dr. Fate, Wildcat, Dr. Mid-Nite, Robin, Power Girl, and the Star-Spangled Kid. Artists on this run include Wally Wood, Joe Staton, Keith Giffen, and Ric Estrada.

Justice Society Vol. 2. Written by Paul Levitz ; art by Joe Staton, Bob Layton, Joe Giella, Dave Hunt. DC Comics 2007 224p. Illustration
Grades: 8 9 10 11 12 Adult   **741.5; Fic**
1. Batman (Fictional character); 2. Flash (Fictional character); 3. Green Lantern (Fictional character); 4. Justice Society of America (Fictional characters); 5. Robin (Fictional character); 6. Superhero graphic novels; 7. Superman (Fictional character); 8. Graphic novels
978-1-4012-1194-3, $14.99

The Justice Society of America was the first comic book super-team, created in All Star Comics in the 1940s. They faded into obscurity until they were revived in the 1970s. This volume includes stories from the 1970s, featuring Superman, the Flash, Green Lantern, Hawkman, Dr. Fate, Wildcat, Robin, Power Girl, Star-Spangled Kid, and the Huntress. Among other stories in this volume, Batman dies, and Huntress is his daughter.

Lewis, A. David
The **lone** and level sands. Artists, Marvin Perry Mann and Jennifer Rodgers. Archaia Studio 2006 147p. Illustration
Grades: 9 10 11 12 Adult   **741.5; Fic**
1. Bible — OT — Exodus; 2. Egypt — History; 3. Graphic novels
1-932386-12-2, $17.95

Told mostly from the viewpoint of the Pharaoh, this book recounts the well-known story of the Exodus. Moses is portrayed as an old desert rascal, and Ramses II finds himself buffeted on all sides as he contends with a God who speaks through his family and friends and manipulates him to bring about the freedom of the Hebrews.

"The plot moves with inexorable tragedy toward its conclusion, but the book never reads like a catalogue of vignettes about the miseries the Egyptians and Hebrews inflicted on each other. Instead, it is a powerful, moving reconsideration of an otherwise familiar tale. It is guaranteed to provoke." Voice Youth Advocates

First published 2005 in black and white by Caption Box

Lewis, Corey Sutherland
Sharknife Volume 1. Oni Press 2006 Un Illustration
Grades: 8 9 10 11 12 Adult   **741.5; Fic**
1. Humorous graphic novels; 2. Martial arts; 3. Graphic novels
1-932664-17-3, $9.95

The Guandong Factory isn't like other restaurants. It's five stories tall, produces more peach dumplings per day than most eateries do in a decade, and it's the home of Sharknife - a mystical protector charged with protecting the establishment from those who would do it harm. But who is this mysterious yet colorful being? Once just a simple busboy, now Caesar Ives is something more - a crazy red rocket hero destined for greatness. But can Caesar juggle both lives - nabbing the girl (the super-sexy Chieko Momuza), and stopping the wide assortment of bizarre baddies that would love to do his precious eatery harm? There's lots of martial arts action.

Lewis, Edith Patton
The **claws** come out: astounding tales of broads and monsters. IDW Publishing 2007 152p. Illustration
Grades: 10 11 12 Adult   **741.5**
1. Fantasy graphic novels; 2. Horror graphic novels; 3. Humorous graphic novels; 4. Graphic novels
978-160010-120-5, $19.99

The subtitle may sound rude (come on, calling women broads?), but all the women in the stories are strong, capable, willing to fight off monsters, vampires, and zombies. A young woman goes on a date for the first time in years, not knowing her ideal guy is a vampire. A teenage girl walking home after a date has a close encounter of the strange kind, but the aliens end up in trouble. An apathetic scientist/aspiring rock star works late at the lab defrosting the Abominable Snowman and finds trouble when a power outage allows the creature to get free. A fortune teller accidentally starts a zombie epidemic with a very powerful love potion. Lewis plays horror for laughs, with some violence and sexual innuendo.

Lewis, John
★ **March:** Book One. John Lewis; [co-written by] Andrew Aydin; [art by] Nate Powell. Top Shelf Productions 2013 121 p. Illustration
Grades: 8 9 10 11 12 Adult   **92; 741.5**
1. African Americans — Civil rights; 2. Civil rights movements — United States; 3. Lewis, John, 1940 February 21-
9781603093002, $14.95

                    LC 2013218903
Coretta Scott King (Author) Honor Book (2014)

This graphic novel, by U.S. congressman John Lewis, "in collaboration with co-writer Andrew Aydin and New York Times best-selling artist Nate Powell . . . spans John Lewis' youth in rural Alabama, his life-changing meeting with Martin Luther King, Jr., the birth of the Nashville Student Movement, and their battle to tear down segregation through nonviolent lunch counter sit-ins, building to a . . . climax on the steps of City Hall." (Publisher's note)

"This is superb visual storytelling that establishes a convincing, definitive record of a key eyewitness to significant social change." SLJ

★ **March:** Book Two. By John Lewis and Andrew Aydin; illustrated by Nate Powell. Top Shelf Productions 2015 192 p. Illustration

Grades: 8 9 10 11 12 Adult   **92; 741.5**
1. African American civil rights workers; 2. African American legislators; 3. African Americans — Civil rights; 4. Civil rights movements; 5. Civil rights workers — United States; 6. Legislators — United States
9781603094009, $19.95; 1603094008

                   LC Bl2015004150

This graphic novel, by John Lewis and Andrew Aydin, illustrated by Nate Powell, "takes us behind the scenes of some of the most pivotal moments of the Civil Rights Movement. . . . After the success of the Nashville sit-in campaign, John Lewis is more committed than ever to changing the world through nonviolence — but as he and his fellow Freedom Riders board a bus into the vicious heart of the deep south, they will be tested like never before." (Publisher's note)

"Heroism and steadiness of purpose continue to light up Lewis' frank, harrowing account of the civil rights movement's climactic days. . . . The contrast between the dignified marchers and the vicious, hate-filled actions and expressions of their tormentors will leave a deep impression on readers." Kirkus

Lie, Bjorn Rune
    The **wolf's** whistle. By B.R. Lie and S.J. Donaldson.. Nobrow 2012 88 p. Illustration; Color

Grades: 4 5 6 7 8 9 10   **741.5; Fic**
1. Fractured fairy tales; 2. Revenge — Fiction
1907704035; 9781907704031, $18.00

    This children's book by Bjorn Rune Lie "digs into the troubled upbringing of one of storydom's most maligned figures: the house-blowing-down wolf. As a wolf cub, little Robert loved superhero comics . . . which led to much torment at the hands of three piggish brothers. Robert grows up to be not much . . . when the building owned by the Honeyroasts burns down with three of Robert's best friends trapped inside, the spark of vengeance and justice is kindled in the wolf." (Booklist)

Lieberman, A. J.
    Martian Manhunter: The Others Among Us. DC Comics 2007 208p. Illustration

Grades: 10 11 12 Adult   **741.5; Fic**
1. Justice League (Fictional characters); 2. Martian Manhunter (Fictional character); 3. Superhero graphic novels; 4. Graphic novels
978-1-4012-1335-0, $19.99

    J'onn J'onzz, the Martian Manhunter, came to Earth years ago to warn all of humanity of an impending invasion. He believed himself to be the sole surviving member of his race and thus decided to use his incredible super-powers to help safeguard the people of his adopted world as a member of the Justice League of America. His discovery of a Martian artifact on Earth sets him on a quest to discover the origin of the relic which leads to a stunning discovery, the

ramifications of which will forever change the way he sees himself, humanity and his destiny. He discovers that a shadowy branch of the U.S. government has imprisoned and experimented upon a group of Green Martians. Why were they being held captive, and what mysterious predator still stalks the survivors of Mars? His quest for truth will bring J'onn into conflict with humans, with every friend he has made on this planet. This book includes violence.

Ligotti, Thomas
    The **Nightmare** factory: based on the stories of Thomas Ligotti. HarperCollins/Fox Atomic Comics 2007 Illustration

Grades: 10 11 12 Adult   **741.5**
1. Horror graphic novels; 2. Graphic novels
978-0-06-124353-0, $17.99

    In the universe of horror master Thomas Ligotti, clowns take part in a sinister winter festival, a scheming girlfriend makes reality itself come unraveled, a crumbling asylum's destruction unleashes a greater horror, and a mysterious Teatro comes and goes, leaving only shattered dreams in its wake. Ligotti's tales of terror take the reader to places few would suspect exist, where madness is only a thought away. This book adapts four of Ligotti's chilling tales by writers and artists Stuart Moore, Joe Harris, Colleen Doran (The Sandman), Ben Templesmith (30 Days of Night), Ted McKeever (Batman), and Michael Gaydos (Alias). Ligotti provides introductions to each story. Violence, some harsh language, and some nudity appear in some of the stories.

Lim, Ron
    Spider-Girl Presents Juggernaut, Jr.: Secrets and Lies. Marvel Entertainment 2006 Un Illustration

Grades: 6 7 8 9 10 11 12   **741.5; Fic**
1. Superhero graphic novels; 2. Graphic novels
0-7851-2047-5, $7.99

    Lots of people have big shoes to fill, but how many have to fill the helmet of the Juggernaut" Teenager Zane Marko grows up fast and hits the big time head first when he inherits his father's unstoppability and joins the latest generation of Avengers. J2 squares off against villains and heroes alike, including a certain green goliath who thinks he's still the strongest one there is. This volume includes the first appearances of the X-People and Wild Thing, daughter of Wolverine and Elektra.

Limke, Jeff
    Isis and Osiris: To the Ends of the Earth. Story by Jeff Limke ; pencils and inks by David Witt. Lerner Publishing Group/Graphic Universe 2007 48p. Illustration

Grades: 3 4 5 6 7 8 9   **398.2; 741.5**
1. Egyptian mythology; 2. Isis (Egyptian deity); 3. Osiris (Egyptian deity); 4. Graphic novels
978-0-8225-3086-2, $26.60 lib. Bdg.

    Osiris is the greatest king and god of the land of the Nile. He is a generous ruler, and the people love and worship him, along with his wife and queen, the goddess Isis. But Osiris's jealous brother Set has a terrible plan to get rid of Osiris forever and take his place on the Egyptian throne. Isis uses her magic and her love to save Osiris and conquer Set.

The book includes a glossary and a list of books for further reading.

Jason: Quest for the Golden Fleece. Story by Jeff Limke ; pencils by Tim Seely ; inks by Barbara Schulz. Lerner Publishing Group/Graphic Universe 2007 48p. Illustration
Grades: 3 4 5 6 7 8 9   292.1; 741.5
 1. Greek mythology; 2. Jason (Greek mythology); 3. Graphic novels
978-0-8225-5967-2, $26.60 lib bdg

Jason's uncle Pelias had stole the throne when Jason was a child; now a young man, Jason must prove himself by retrieving the priceless Golden Fleece from the far-off land of Colchis. He gathers a ship of heroes, the Argonauts, to aid him in his quest; but when they arrive in Colchis, the king insists that Jason prove himself in dangerous trials, and the king's daughter, Medea, has plans for Jason. This retelling is based on the heroic poem by Apollonius of Rhodes. The book includes a glossary and a list of books and websites for further reading.

King Arthur: Excalibur Unsheathed. Story by Jeff Limke ; pencils and inks by Thomas Yeates. Lerner Publishing Group/Graphic Universe 2007 48p. Illustration
Grades: 3 4 5 6 7 8 9   398.2; 741.5
 1. Arthurian romances; 2. Malory, Sir Thomas, 15th c — Adaptations; 3. Graphic novels
978-0-8225-3083-1, $26.60 lib. Bdg.

This story is adapted from Sir Thomas Malory's Le Morte D'Arthur. Young squire Arthur's life, and that of England, changes the day he pulls out the mysterious Sword in the Stone. Guided by Merlin the magician, Arthur takes his place as King of England. Can he win peace and freedom for his country" The book includes a glossary and a list of books for further reading.

The **treasure** of Mount Fate. Jeff Limke ; illustrated by Clint Hilinski. Lerner Publishing Group/Graphic Universe 2007 112p. Illustration (Twisted Journeys)
Grades: 3 4 5 6 7 8 9   741.5; Fic
 1. Adventure graphic novels; 2. Graphic novels
978-0-8225-6205-4, $27.93; 978-0-8225-6206-1 (pa), $7.95
                                        LC 2006-101596
In the series called Twisted Journeys, readers choose how the story will progress. Pages of text alternate with comic book-style pages. In this volume, you are a young knight who comes to Mount Fate in search of a treasure. In some storylines, you encounter a trapped wizard, in others a monstrous borkadrac, in yet others such hazards as fireballs, and a talking dragon. Readers will find many scenarios played out, depending on their choices; some end well, others not so well.

Lin, Yali
 Hawthorne's the Scarlet letter: the Manga edition. Adapted by Adam Sexton ; illustrated by Yali Lin. Wiley Publishing 2009 186p. Illustration
Grades: 5 6 7 8 9 10 11 12   741.5; Fic
 1. Hawthorne, Nathaniel, 1804-1864 — Adaptations; 2. Graphic novels
978-0-470-14889-1, $9.99

Hester Prynne, a young married woman in puritanical Massachusetts, stands in public shame when she bears a child long after her husband had disappeared. She refuses to identify the father of her child and instead wears the scarlet letter A always. The young minister Arthur Dimmesdale lives with his guilt in secret, but the physician, Roger Chillingworth, is actually Hester's husband, returned for vengeance. He vows to find the man who fathered Pearl, Hester's daughter, and destroy him. Meanwhile, Pearl grows up in a society that shuns her mother, and she comes to see the A as her mother's badge of honor. This book is a manga style adaptation of Hawthorne's novel.

Little, Jason
 Shutterbug follies. Doubleday Graphic Novels 2002 153p. Illustration
Grades: 10 11 12 Adult   741.5
 1. Mystery graphic novels; 2. Graphic novels
0-385-50346-6, $24.95
                                        LC 2002-727189
This novel was "originally serialized as both a weekly newspaper comic strip and a web comics serial. . . . Scrappy 18-year-old Bee is working in a New York photo lab when a picture of a naked female corpse that's not quite what it appears to be piques her interest. Her amateur investigation of its photographer leads her to an ever-deepening mystery, a friendly cab driver, a cute but nervous photo assistant, some scary doings with the Russian mob and finally, into deadly danger." Publ Wkly

"With nearly implausible coincidences, a dash of slapstick humor, and a few red herrings, this is a detective romp, and the ending panel leaves readers breathlessly awaiting a sequel." SLJ

Livingston, Todd
 America Jr.. Written by Nick Capetanakis & Todd Livingston; illustrated by Brendon Fraim & Brian Fraim. Image Comics 2007 96p. Illustration
Grades: 9 10 11 12 Adult   741.5; Fic
 1. Humorous graphic novels; 2. Politics; 3. Graphic novels
978-1-58240-829-3, $9.99

Millerstown is a typical small, quiet middle America kind of town, but then the town's clerk discovers a bombshell in the town's charter: it was only a temporary part of the U.S., and the time ran out the day before. Suddenly, it's an independent nation right in the middle of the USA. "Led" by Mayor Thornton and advised by young retired Hollywood lawyer Darren, the people of Millerstown have to take care of all the day-today business of being an independent nation, such as naming their country (America Jr.), creating a national anthem, getting ready for elections. . . . The book collects the first 150 strips of the webcomic, and it includes some visual sexual innuendo.

Lobdell, Scott
 Hardy Boys, undercover brothers #14: Haley Danelle's top eight. Paulo Henrique Marcondes, artist. Papercutz 2008 Un Illustration
Grades: 3 4 5 6 7 8 9   741.5; Fic
 1. Adventure graphic novels; 2. Hardy Boys (Fictional characters); 3. Mystery graphic novels; 4. Graphic novels

978-1-59707-114-7, $12.95; 978-1-59707-113-0 (pa), $7.95

Cute little computer nerd and horse expert Haley Danelle needs the help of the Hardy Boys; she has been an ATAC operative and knows who they are. Her top friends on her MyFacePlace social network page are disappearing, one by one, and she wants Joe and Frank to help her stop it and find her friends. But things soon turn deadly, and Joe and Frank find themselves in trouble.

Volume 14 of the Hardy Boys, Undercover Brothers series

The **Hardy** boys, undercover brothers #15: Live free, die hardy!. Paulo Henrique Marcondes, artist. Papercutz 2008 Un Illustration
Grades: 3 4 5 6 7 8 9   **741.5; Fic**
1. Adventure graphic novels; 2. Hardy Boys (Fictional characters); 3. Mystery graphic novels; 4. Graphic novels
978-1-59707-124-6, $12.95; 978-1-59707-123-9 (pa), $7.95

When the guys at A.T.A.C. decide to throw Fenton Hardy a surprise party, some uninvited guests show up. The Noir Sisters, Nicolina and Shira, an evil counterpart to Frank and Joe Hardy, show up with their henchmen and get in because the security system was temporarily shut down to allow the invited guests to come in. It's going to be up to Frank and Joe to find a way to take down the bad guys without letting anyone get hurt.

Part of The Hardy Boys, Undercover Brothers series.

The **Hardy** Boys, Undercover Brothers #7: The Opposite Numbers. Daniel Rendon, Paulo Henrique, Sidney Lima, artist. NBM/Papercutz 2006 112p. Illustration
Grades: 4 5 6 7 8 9   **741.5; Fic**
1. Adventure graphic novels; 2. Mystery graphic novels; 3. Graphic novels
1-59707-035-1, $12.95; 1-59707-034-3, $7.95

Traveling across the country on the maiden voyage of a bullet train, the Hardy Boys find themselves framed for murder. But they can't depend on A.T.A.C. (American Teens Against Crime) to help them, because every indication is that it's the super secret spy organization, founded by their own father, that framed them.

The **Hardy** Boys: Undercover Brothers #1: The Ocean of Osyria. Lea Hernandez, artist. NBM/Papercutz 2005 Un Illustration
Grades: 3 4 5 6 7 8 9   **741.5; Fic**
1. Hardy Boys (Fictional characters); 2. Mystery graphic novels; 3. Graphic novels
1-59707-005-X, $12.95; 1-59707-001-7 (pa)

After rescuing Jackpot, a kidnapped prize-winning racehorse, Frank and Joe are stunned to return to Bayport and discover that the Department of International Security has arrested their best friend, Chet Morton, for stealing a priceless art treasure. The Hardy Boys decide the only way to clear their friend is to journey to the Middle East and find the Ocean of Osyria themselves.

The **Hardy** Boys: Undercover Brothers #2: Identity Theft. Daniel Rendon, artist. NBM/Papercutz 2005 Un Illustration
Grades: 3 4 5 6 7 8 9   **741.5; Fic**

1. Hardy Boys (Fictional characters); 2. Mystery graphic novels; 3. Graphic novels
978-1-59707-007-2, $12.95; 978-1-59707-003-4 (pa)

Joe and Frank Hardy first crack a case involving sky-diving diamond smugglers, then take on a case of stolen identity. Joy Gallagher claims another girl is now living her life, with her parents, and in her body. Is this girl insane, or can her fantastic story actually be true?

The **Hardy** Boys: Undercover Brothers #3: Mad House. Daniel Rendon, artist. NBM/Papercutz 2005 Un Illustration
Grades: 3 4 5 6 7 8 9   **741.5; Fic**
1. Hardy Boys (Fictional characters); 2. Mystery graphic novels; 3. Graphic novels
978-1-59707-011-9, $12.95; 978-1-59707-010-2 (pa)

No sooner do Frank and Joe Hardy rescue a member of Her Majesty's Secret Service (who says he's shaken, not stirred), than they're off on a new top-secret ATAC (American Teens Against Crime) mission. Frank and Joe must go undercover on a new reality TV show called 'Mad House,' to discover how far the producers are willing to go risking the contestants' lives for the sake of huge ratings. The plot thickens when the producer of Mad House turns up murdered.

The **Hardy** Boys: Undercover Brothers #4: Malled. Daniel Rendon, artist. NBM/Papercutz 2005 Un Illustration
Grades: 3 4 5 6 7 8 9   **741.5; Fic**
1. Hardy Boys (Fictional characters); 2. Mystery graphic novels; 3. Graphic novels
978-1-59707-015-7, $12.95; 978-1-59707-014-0 (pb)

Frank and Joe Hardy finish up a case helping a fellow ATAC (American Teens Against Crime) agent, who sharp-eyed fans may recognize despite her Alias. Things seem to quiet down when ATAC sends Frank and Joe undercover to investigate a new Mall opening in Bayport, due to several suspicious accidents there. But things get exciting when the night before the big opening, Joe, Frank, and seven others are mysteriously locked in the mall with a murderer on the loose. If that wasn't enough, everything that could go horribly wrong in a mall, does: a flood caused by water beds; an electrocution at an electronics shop; a bow and arrow used to kill in the Sporting Goods store; a runaway elevator; a damsel in distress in the dress shop; fire in the food court; and much, much more.

The **Hardy** Boys: Undercover Brothers #5: Sea You, Sea Sea You, Sea Me. Daniel Rendon, artist. NBM/Papercutz 2006 112p. Illustration
Grades: 3 4 5 6 7 8 9   **741.5; Fic**
1. Hardy Boys (Fictional characters); 2. Mystery graphic novels; 3. Graphic novels
978-1-59707-023-2, $12.95; 978-1-59707-022-5 (pb)

When a series of suspicious mishaps befall several deep sea fishing boats, the Hardy Boys are called into action by ATAC (American Teens Against Crime) before any more teen green horns can be hurt. But while in the past Frank and Joe have battled terrorists, master criminals, and multinational corporations, the undercover brothers have no experience fighting the fury of the ocean.

The **Hardy** Boys: Undercover Brothers #6: Hyde & Shriek. Art by Daniel Rendon. NBM/Papercutz 2006 112p. Illustration

1. Hardy Boys (Fictional characters); 2. Mystery graphic novels; 3. Graphic novels
978-1-59707-029-4, $12.95; 978-1-59707-028-7 (pb)

When a visiting dignitary's daughter is scheduled to attend a party at a horror-themed restaurant in New York City, ATAC agents Joe and Frank Hardy are enlisted as undercover protection. But in a building where anything can happen, where the walls literally have ears, can the Hardy Boys find and stop the assassin who has targeted Sangita before it is too late?

The **Hardy** Boys: Undercover Brothers #7: The Opposite Numbers. Daniel Rendon, Paulo Henrique, Sidney Lima, artist. NBM/Papercutz 2006 112p. Illustration
Grades: 3 4 5 6 7 8 9   **741.5; Fic**
1. Hardy Boys (Fictional characters); 2. Mystery graphic novels; 3. Graphic novels
978-1-59707-035-5, $12.95; 978-1-59707-034-3 (pb)

Traveling across the country on the maiden voyage of a bullet train, the Hardy Boys find themselves framed for murder, even after their heroic efforts to save others. But they can't depend on A.T.A.C. (American Teens Against Crime) to help them, because every indication is that it's the super secret spy organization, founded by their father, that framed them.

The **Hardy** Boys: Undercover Brothers #8: Board to Death. Paulo Henrique, artist. NBM/Papercutz 2007 112p. Illustration
Grades: 3 4 5 6 7 8 9   **741.5; Fic**
1. Hardy Boys (Fictional characters); 2. Mystery graphic novels; 3. Graphic novels
978-1-59707-054-6, $12.95; 978-1-59707-053-9 (pb)

Frank and Joe Hardy go undercover at a major skateboarding contest in Venice, California to find out which competitor is trying to kill off the competition, literally. The list of suspects includes Dex Thom, a skilled skateboarder whose parents wanted him to be a musical prodigy, the Pink Shadow, a girl of mystery, and her equally secretive trainer, Mr. Moto, and the Wraith, a dark and brooding young man. Will Frank and Joe solve the mystery before the killer discovers their real mission, and eliminates them?

The **Hardy** Boys: Undercover Brothers #9: To Die or Not to Die?. Paulo Henrique, artist. NBM/Papercutz 2007 112p. Illustration
Grades: 3 4 5 6 7 8 9   **741.5; Fic**
1. Hardy Boys (Fictional characters); 2. Mystery graphic novels; 3. Graphic novels
978-1-59707-063-8, $12.95; 978-1-59707-062-1 (pb)

At a nationwide drama competition, Frank and Joe Hardy must go undercover to discover which contestant has been knocking off the competition by any means possible - including deadly force. While Joe keeps an eye on all of the backstage drama, Frank, posing as a competing drama student, may be distracted from his mission by the romantic attentions of a beautiful acting student named Joelle. Things get further complicated when Joelle becomes the only eyewitness to the red-haired woman who is their number one suspect! Will Frank's stage debut be the Hardy Boys final bow?

High Roads. Writer: Scott Lobdell; pencils: Leinil Francis Yu. DC Comics/Wildstorm 2003 Un Illustration

Grades: 10 11 12 Adult   **741.5; Fic**
1. Adventure graphic novels; 2. Humorous graphic novels; 3. Graphic novels
1-4012-0033-8, $14.95

This volume tells the story of a mismatched group of ne'er-do-wells and misfits who find themselves involved in a treasure hunt of most improbable proportions. Nic Highroad and his friends - a washed-up British actor, a failed Kamikaze pilot, and Hitler's former mistress - set out to steal Hitler's most prized possession, and end up trying to save the world. Along the way, they have to fight off a Nazi-ninja corps, jump from a moving train, and outsmart the Master Race; but in the end, Hitler's FINAL final solution comes to something of an unexpected conclusion. The book includes violence, harsh language, nudity, and sexual situations.

Loeb, Jeph
Batman: Dark Victory. Written by Jeph Loeb; art by Tim Sale. DC Comics 2014 400 p.
Grades: 9 10 11 12 Adult   **741.5; Fic**
1. Batman (Fictional character); 2. Crime; 3. Serial killers
1401244017; 9781401244019, $24.99
     LC 2013041357

This collection "continues the story of 'The Long Halloween.' It is early in Batman's crimefighting career, when James Gordon, Harvey Dent, and the vigilante himself were all just beginning their roles as Gotham's protectors. Once a town controlled by organized crime, Gotham City suddenly finds itself being run by lawless freaks, such as Poison Ivy, Mr. Freeze, and the Joker. Witnessing his city's dark evolution, the Dark Knight completes his transformation into the city's greatest defender." (Publisher's note)
Collected edition originally published 2001
Dark victory

Batman: Hush. Jeph Loeb, writer; Jim Lee, penciller; Scott Williams, inker; Richard Starkings, letterer; Alex Sinclair, colorist; Jim Lee & Scott Williams, original series covers; Batman created by Bob Kane. DC Comics 2009 320 p. Illustration; Color
Grades: 9 10 11 12 Adult   **741.5/973; 741.5**
1. Batman (Fictional character); 2. Batman (Fictional character)
1401223176; 9781401223175, $24.99
     LC 2009502034

This comic book, by Jeph Loeb, "is a thrilling mystery of action, intrigue, and deception, . . . in which Batman sets out to discover the identity of a mysterious mastermind using the Joker, Riddler, Ra's al Ghul and the Dark Knight's other enemies - and allies - as pawns in a plan to wreak havoc." (Publisher's note)
Originally published in single magazine form in Batman 608-619, Wizard 0—t.p. verso.

★ **Batman**: The Long Halloween. Jeph Loeb, writer; Tim Sale, artist; Gregory Wright, colors; Richard Starkings & Comicraft, letters. DC Comics 1999 375p. Illustration
Grades: 9 10 11 12 Adult   **741.5; Fic**
1. Batman (Fictional character); 2. Mystery graphic novels; 3. Superhero graphic novels; 4. Graphic novels
1563894270; 9781563894275, $19.99
     LC 99-218572

Taking place during Batman's early days of crime fighting, this collection tells the story of a mysterious killer who murders his prey only on holidays. Working with District Attorney Harvey Dent and Lieutenant James Gordon, Batman races against the calendar as he tries to discover who Holiday is before he claims his next victim each month. This story also ties into the events that transform Harvey Dent into Batman's deadly enemy, Two-Face. The book includes some violence

Catwoman: When in Rome. Jeph Loeb, writer; Tim Sale, artist; Dave Stewart, colorist; Richard Starkings, lettering. DC Comics 2005 Un Illustration
Grades: 10 11 12 Adult   741.5; Fic
  1. Catwoman (Fictional character); 2. Joker (Fictional character); 3. Mystery graphic novels; 4. Superhero graphic novels; 5. Graphic novels
  1-4012-0432-5, $19.99; 1-4012-0717-0 (pa), $12.99
Catwoman travels to Rome with some unfinished business with the Falcone crime family. Accompanied by the Riddler, she dreams almost nightly about Batman, which annoys her to no end; she has gone to see Don Verinni, but even as she's talking to him, he dies from the Joker's poison. With help from local Sicilian hitman Christopher Castillo, Catwoman and Riddler get away, but when more mobsters come after her with Mr. Freeze's ice gun, Catwoman knows something is definitely wrong in Rome.
  With frequent flashes of partial nudity and considerable violence, this title is more appropriate for older teens and adults.
  Originally published as Catwoman: When in Rome issues #1-6 and Batman: Dark Victory issue #13.

Superman/Batman: Supergirl. Jeph Loeb, writer; Michael Turner, artist. DC Comics 2005 Un Illustration
Grades: 10 11 12 Adult   741.5; Fic
  1. Batman (Fictional character); 2. Superhero graphic novels; 3. Superman (Fictional character); 4. Wonder Woman (Fictional character); 5. Graphic novels
  1-4012-0250-0, $12.99
Batman has discovered something strange on the bottom of Gotham Bay which leads him to a mysterious and powerful teenaged girl who's bent on destroying Gotham City. What's her connection to Superman? Why does Wonder Woman want to hide her from the outside world? Will Darkseid succeed in recruiting her into doing his bidding? Who is she?

Superman/Batman Vol. 3: Absolute Power. Jeph Loeb, writer; Carlos Pacheco, penciller; Jesús Merino, inker; Ivan Reis, additional pencils; Laura Martin, colorist; Richard Starkings, letterer. DC Comics 2005 Un Illustration
Grades: 10 11 12 Adult   741.5; Fic
  1. Batman (Fictional character); 2. Science fiction graphic novels; 3. Superhero graphic novels; 4. Superman (Fictional character); 5. Graphic novels
  1-4012-0714-6, $12.99
The Earth wakes up one day to a brand-new world order, on in which Superman and Batman rule with an iron fist. Humankind has a choice: obey or die. How did things get this way? And is anyone left who can stop them? Before long, Superman and Batman are sent careening through a series of bizarre alternate dimensions, facing an assortment

of DC characters, including Kamandi, Sgt. Rock, Haunted Tank, Jonah Hex, and many more.

Superman/Batman Volume 4: Vengeance. Jeph Loeb, writer; Ed McGuinness, penciller; Dexter Vines, inker. DC Comics 2006 Un Illustration
Grades: 9 10 11 12 Adult   741.5; Fic
  1. Batman (Fictional character); 2. Superhero graphic novels; 3. Superman (Fictional character); 4. Graphic novels
  978-1-4012-1043-4, $19.99
Superman and Batman travel to an alternate Earth to kill the man responsible for the death of Lois Lane. And now the Maximums, the mightiest heroes from a world of super-soldiers, hulking monsters, and Norse gods have crossed dimensional barriers seeking to avenge their fallen comrade. It's a tale of nonstop action with guest stars from infinite earths, but who's really behind all of this?

Superman: Our Worlds at War. Writers, Jeph Loeb et al.; artists, Phil Jimenez et al. DC Comics 2006 512p. Illustration
Grades: 9 10 11 12 Adult   741.5; Fic
  1. Green Lantern (Fictional character); 2. Superhero graphic novels; 3. Superman (Fictional character); 4. Wonder Woman (Fictional character); 5. Graphic novels
  978-1-4012-1129-5, $24.99
Imperiex has been unleashed. As planets are destroyed in its mighty wake and with Earth in its path as it seeks to remake the universe in its twisted image, Superman is forced to form alliances with President Lex Luthor and Darkseid, even as he also joins with such heroes as Wonder Woman, Green Lantern, and many others. For once, this looks like a job that not even Superman can handle.

Lolos, Vasilis
  The **last** call volume 1. Oni Press 2007 Un Illustration
Grades: 10 11 12 Adult   741.5; Fic
  1. Mystery graphic novels; 2. Supernatural graphic novels; 3. Graphic novels
  978-1-932664-69-0, $11.95
Teenagers Sam and Alec have gone joyriding in Alec's mother's car, jamming to heavy metal rock, when the car dies, and something hits them. They awaken to find themselves on a strange train with very odd people. The conductor throws Alec off the train, and Sam meets some of the other passengers on the train. When he goes back to the compartment where he and Alec woke up on the train, he witnesses the murder of the ticketed passenger who had the compartment. Now Sam works with Mr. S, the shadow person who existed in dead Benny's body, to try to find out who murdered him. The book includes some harsh language, including occasional use of the f-bomb, and some violence.

Lott, Renee
  Festering romance. Oni Press 2009 184p.
Grades: 9 10 11 12 Adult   741.5; Fic
  1. Ghosts; 2. Romance graphic novels; 3. Graphic novels
  978-1-934964-18-7, $11.95
College student Janet prefers to spend her time in her apartment, playing video games with her roommate and best friend Paul who happens to be a ghost. However, her friends keep setting her up on blind dates, and then one of them,

Derek, turns out to be a nice guy. Subsequent dates don't go so well, though, because Derek also has a ghostly roommate Carol, who in life was his girlfriend. Janet and Derek blame each other for not telling the truth about their ghostly companions, but they each need to face the truth of why Paul and Carol are still with them. The book includes only some mildly bad language (crap, pissed off).

Loux, Matthew
★ **Salt** water taffy: the seaside adventures of Jack and Benny, vol. 4: Caldera's revenge, part 1. Oni Press 2011 Un Illustration
Grades: 3 4 5 6 7 8 9   **741.5; Fic**
  1. Adventure graphic novels; 2. Brothers; 3. Humorous graphic novels; 4. Whales; 5. Graphic novels
  978-1-934964-62-0, $5.99
  As Jack and Benny's summer vacation in Chowder Bay continues, Captain Hollister gives the boys a book called The Hidden History of Chowder Bay. The boys find it difficult to read, so they jump at the chance to investigate when a spooky whaling ship appears in the bay. The local fishermen talk about something attacking their boats in the bay, and the brothers soon discover that the culprit is the legendary whale called Caldera. But just what is that spooky whaling ship doing in the bay" This volume ends in a cliffhanger. Readers who enjoy rollicking adventure and a little whimsy (talking giant squid who like grilled hot dogs) will enjoy this book.

    Sidescrollers. Oni Press 2006 Un Illustration
Grades: 10 11 12 Adult   **741.5; Fic**
  1. Friendship; 2. Humorous graphic novels; 3. Graphic novels
  1-932664-50-5, $11.95
  Brian, Brad, and Matt are the kind of young man who works just enough to get by and be able to play video games, eat junk food, and hang around. Things change when their neighbor Amber, who works with them at the local McGreggor's, is going to the big local rock show where Brian's brother's band will be playing. Unfortunately for the guys, she's going with Dick (he'd rather be called Richard), the bully football player. Since Matt is sweet on Amber, the guys decide they have to save her from Dick, and their quest gets them out of the house, on the road, and in a whole lot of trouble. The book includes strong language, including the s-bomb and f-bomb, some sexual innuendo, and some fistfight violence.

Love, Jeremy
★ **Bayou,** volume one. Created by Jeremy Love; colors by Patrick Morgan. Zuda Comics/DC Comics 2009 Un Illustration
Grades: 9 10 11 12 Adult   **741.5; Fic**
  1. African Americans; 2. Fantasy graphic novels; 3. Monsters; 4. Graphic novels
  978-1-4012-2382-3, $14.99
  2009 Glyph Comics Awards: Story of the Year, Best Writer, Best Artist, Best Female Character (Lee), Best Comic Strip
  In a little southern town called Charon in 1933, Lee Wagstaff lives the kind of precarious life that African Americans under Jim Crow laws had to have. She's friends

with white Lily Westmoreland, but that friendship doesn't protect her when Lily's mother accuses Lee of theft. Then Lily disappears, victim of a swamp monster, and the town's white men haul her father off to jail, most likely to face a lynching. Lee has to find Lily to save her father, but when she goes to the swamp where Lily disappeared, she falls into a strange land of monsters. There she meets Bayou, a blues-singing swamp monster who helps her, and Lee faces the evil in the strange land to find and save her friend. This book collects the first four chapters of the webcomic by Love, which was one of the first webcomics from Zuda, run by DC Comics. The book includes disturbing images of hanged people, and a white man hits Lee so hard she flies through the air and lands on her back with her face torn up. The "n" word is represented by "n*****" while other harsh language is plainly written. The book contains enough violence to bother squeamish and sensitive readers.
  "Extremely beautiful, scary and wonderful, this . . . comic takes readers to a pair of almost familiar, frequently threatening worlds." Publ Wkly
  Volume 1 of 2

Lovecraft, H. P. (Howard Phillips)
  The **Lovecraft** Anthology 2: A Graphic Collection of H.P. Lovecrafts Short Stories. H. P. Lovecraft; edited by Dan Lockwood; illustrated by Alice Duke.. Harry N Abrams Inc 2012 128 p.
Grades: 11 12 Adult   **741.5/942; 741.5; S C**
  1. Horror fiction; 2. Short stories
  1906838437; 9781906838430, $19.95
  This book presents "a graphic anthology of tales" by horror fiction author H. P. Lovecraft. "From the insidious mutations of 'The Shadow over Innsmouth' to the mindbending threat of 'The Call of Cthulhu,' this collection explores themes of insanity, inherited guilt, and arcane ritual." (Publisher's note)

Luedke, Robert James
  Eye Witness: A Fictional Tale of Absolute Truth. Head Press Publishing 2004 96p. Illustration
Grades: 9 10 11 12 Adult   **741.5; Fic**
  1. Adventure graphic novels; 2. Graphic novels
  978-0-9758924-0-4, $13.99
  Amid the violence and chaos of the present day Middle East, remarkably preserved first century documents are discovered by seismic researchers beneath the foundations of present day Jerusalem. None of the experts called in by the Israeli government can decipher this mysterious text, so as a last resort they call in American archeologist, Dr. Terry Harper, known around the world as, "The Bone Man." What Dr. Harper finds through his translation, is a previously undiscovered, eyewitness account of Jesus' final week in Jerusalem. Will it confirm or discount the Gospel accounts of this event that have guided people for thousands of years" Only Dr. Harper has the key to unlocking this mystery & and sharing it may cost him his life.

Lung, Khoo Fuk
  Ultraman Tiga, Vol. 1: Return of the warrior. [by] Tony Wong and Khoo Fuk Lung. Dark Horse Comics 2004 128p. Illustration
Grades: 7 8 9 10   **741.5; Fic**

1. Monsters; 2. Science fiction graphic novels; 3. Superhero graphic novels; 4. Ultraman (Fictional character); 5. Graphic novels
1-59307-119-1, $15.95

A cultural icon in Hong Kong and Japan, Ultraman has punched, kicked and karate-chopped in TV shows and movies for nearly four decades. Now this incarnation of Ultraman, called Tiga, finds the 100-foot-tall hero revived in the year 2049 and finding a world ill-equipped to handle the onslaught of gigantic beasts that are attacking all over the world. There is a second volume: Past Sins, Future Dangers.

"Wong's script moves briskly from one fight scene to the next, and Lung's art effectively uses line work and color. The duo is capable of winking knowingly at readers while still taking the story seriously enough to be compelling." Publ Wkly

Lutes, Jason
★ **Houdini:** the handcuff king. Art by Nick Bertozzi. Hyperion Books for Children/Jump at the Sun 2007 90p. Illustration (Center for Cartoon Studies presents)
Grades: 4 5 6 7 8 9 10 **92; 741.5**
1. Biographical graphic novels; 2. Houdini, Harry, 1874-1926; 3. Magicians; 4. Magicians; 5. Graphic novels
978-0-7868-3902-5, $16.99; 978-0-7868-3903-2 (pa), $9.99

On May 1, 1908, magician Harry Houdini performed one of his famous handcuff escapes, this time in handcuffs and leg irons, while jumping off the Cambridge Bridge in Massachusetts into the frigid Boston River. This graphic novel takes the reader through Houdini's day, from 5:00 a.m. as he makes his preparations, makes a practice jump, coaches his wife Bess on how she's to help him, and then makes the jump.

This is a "fascinating graphic novel.... The format will instantly draw a lot of attention from readers and then hold on to it. Lutes and Bertozzi use grayscale comic panels to share their story about the life of Harry Houdini in a unique way.... The book resembles a hybrid between fiction and nonfiction, and the ingenious choice of format will appeal to a broad age range of readers." Voice Youth Advocates

Jar of Fools. Drawn & Quarterly 2003 152p. Illustration
Grades: 10 11 12 Adult **741.5; Fic**
1. Graphic novels
1-896597-72-6, $16.95

Haunted by the death of his escape-artist brother and a failed romance, the remaining hope of washed-up stage magician Ernie Weiss lies in his aging mentor, Al Flosso. But Al is slipping further into senility with each passing day. Meanwhile, Esther O'Dea, Ernie's ex-love, struggles to find peace in her own life, and a con man named Nathan Lender sets some mysterious plans for Ernie's future in motion in his efforts to make things right for his twelve-year-old daughter Claire.

Luthi, Morgan
Snow, Vol. 1. Tokyopop 2006 Un Illustration
Grades: 9 10 11 12 Adult **741.5; Fic**
1. Adventure graphic novels; 2. Science fiction graphic novels; 3. Graphic novels

1-59816-743-X, $9.99
The gigantic Warmongers created the Ghost of Destruction, a human-shaped weapon that can destroy entire planets. Hub is a planet full of misfits and gangs, and one day a young man with a scarred face wanders into Refuse City and inadvertently helps a rebel gang called the Crows, led by Kat. Snow, the young man, and Kat each have secrets in their past, but Snow's secrets could destroy Hub.

Lyga, Barry
★ **Wolverine:** worst day ever. By Barry Lyga; artist, Todd Nauck. Marvel Publishing 2009 184p. Illustration
Grades: 5 6 7 8 9 **741.5; Fic**
1. Humorous graphic novels; 2. Superhero graphic novels; 3. Wolverine (Fictional character); 4. Graphic novels
978-0-7851-3757-3, $14.99; 0-7851-3757-2

Teenager Eric Mattias has just recently discovered he has mutant powers. Very sucky mutant powers: suddenly no one notices him even when he's in the same room. He's not invisible, but he might as well be, and people don't even notice him when he speaks. Eric decides to follow Wolverine around and see if he can't pick up a few pointers about living a loner-type life, as the adamantium-clawed mutant tends to do. Only when they end up in a remote forested area does Eric realize he may not have made the smartest move, because someone else has come, someone who is as strong as Wolverine, and maybe meaner: Sabretooth.

"It's a coming-of-age tale with bursts of action that's sure to appeal to its large, built-in audience." Booklist

Lynch, Brian
Spike: shadow puppets. Brian Lynch; illustrated by Franco Urru. IDW Publishing 2007 112p. Illustration
Grades: 10 11 12 Adult **741.5; Fic**
1. Fantasy graphic novels; 2. Spike (Fictional character); 3. Vampires; 4. Graphic novels
978-1-60010-112-0, $17.99

The vampire named Spike teams up with green-skinned Lorne to take on the demonic puppets of "Smile Time," who have moved to Japan and taken their evil there. The children who watch the show lose their souls, and Spike decides to save them. Even when he and Lorne attack the puppets and find themselves turned into puppets. The book includes mild harsh language and some puppet killing violence.

Ma, Wing Shing
Chinese Hero, Tales of the Blood Sword, Vol. 1. DrMaster Publications, Inc. 2007 270p. Illustration
Grades: 8 9 10 11 12 Adult **741.5; Fic**
1. Adventure graphic novels; 2. Martial arts; 3. Graphic novels
978-1-59796-041-1, $19.95

When he was a child, Hero's family was attacked and killed by a practitioner of Northern Mantis kung fu. This assassin was tasked, by the affluent head of a local triad, to retrieve Hero's family heirloom - the legendary Blood Sword. Barely escaping with his life, Hero has now reached adulthood, having mastered several forms of kung fu to aid him in his lifelong endeavor to safeguard the family treasure. But now his enemies turn their gaze to his newborn son. This series is full of full-color kung fu action. This is a Chinese manhua.

MacHale, D. J.

★ **Pendragon** book one: the merchant of death graphic novel. Adapted and illustrated by Carla Speed McNeil. Aladdin Paperbacks 2008 172p. Illustration
Grades: 5 6 7 8 9 10
741.5; Fic
1. Adventure graphic novels; 2. Fantasy graphic novels; 3. Graphic novels
978-1-4169-5080-6, $9.99; 1-4169-5080-X
LC 2007-937920

Courtesy of Aladdin Paperbacks

Fourteen-year-old Bobby Pendragon has had a good life with a loving family, friends, and sports, but it all changes the night his Uncle Press takes him into New York City, to a deserted subway station that contains a gate that leads them to another world. On Denduron, a peaceful tribe called the Milago face annihilation from the Bedowan, and Uncle Press expects Bobby to help him stop it. Press is what he calls a Traveler, and he says Bobby is one, too, and they have a job to do. Bobby is able to write journals and send them home to his best friends Mark and Courtney. Meanwhile, he needs to learn so much, can he do it in time to help—and stay alive?

"This graphic-format adaptation streamlines the already fast-moving experience, providing satisfying interpretations of favorite characters and situations." Booklist

Mack, Stan

★ **Taxes,** the tea party, and those revolting rebels: a comics history of the American revolution. Stan Mack. NBM Pub. 2012 166 p.
Grades: 9 10 11 12 Adult **741.5**
1. United States — History — 1600-1775, Colonial period; 2. United States — History — 1775-1783, Revolution; 3. United States — Politics and government — 1775-1783, Revolution; 4. Wit and humor
1561636975; 9781561636976, $14.99
LC 2012938930

This historical comic book, by Stan Mack, is a humorous narrative overview of the U.S. Revolutionary War. "This graphic account of the birth of the United States stars a chubby, insecure King George III, rebellious and misunderstood colonists, and loudmouthed and insensitive aristocrats, providing information about the Boston Tea Party and the revolt against the status quo." (Publisher's note)

Macklin, Ken

The **weasel** patrol. Illustrated by Lela Dowling. About Comics/About Infinity 2009 104p. Illustration
Grades: 7 8 9 10 11 12 Adult **741.5; Fic**
1. Humorous graphic novels; 2. Science fiction graphic novels; 3. Weasels; 4. Graphic novels
978-0-9790750-8-7, $9.99

When criminals strike, the intergalactic troopers called the Weasel Patrol will ferret out the bad guys every time. Despite their utter lack of planning, attentiveness, cohesion, or competence, they always succeed, even if their favorite tactic when faced with danger is to run away. This book includes twelve comedic adventures, in which the weasels face mythical monsters (Big Foot), aliens, kidnapped cattle in disguise, and the ever-ready bad guy Reefer Rick. Willy, Leroy, Biff, Roscoe, and Bob are the genetically uplifted Weasel Patrol. The book includes mild, cartoony violence and no bad language and no nudity. Villainous Reefer Rick smokes. Artist Dowling includes fun little details, such as the Acme name on some of the gadgets.

MacPherson, Dwight L.

Kid Houdini and the silver dollar misfits. Art by Worth Gowell and Kevin Conley. Viper Comics 2008 Un Illustration
Grades: 3 4 5 6 7 8 9 **741.5; Fic**
1. Houdini, Harry, 1874-1926; 2. Magicians; 3. Mystery graphic novels; 4. Nonfiction writers; 5. Supernatural graphic novels; 6. Graphic novels
978-0—9802385-2-5, $9.95

In 1886, ten-year-old Harry Houdini runs away from home, only to find himself a prisoner in Professor Murat's circus. Harry joins the "freak" children: Lydia the snake girl (and her snake Terra), Hans the legless boy, and Jacques and Joe the Siamese twins and they form a detective agency that will solve mysteries for the fee of a silver dollar. Near Kansas City, a girl named Bea hires them to find her missing father whom she fears was kidnapped. However, when the gang gets to her house, they discover that her mother has now been kidnapped, too. It all has to do with a treasure map that leads to a lost gold mine, and the gang needs to solve that mystery in order to find Bea's parents. A young Harry Houdini and his friends make a fun team and they face some supernatural elements in their cases, much like the old Scooby-Doo cartoons "and with a similar scary-fun factor."

Mad About the Fifties

Grant Geissman, editor. E.C. Publications/MAD Books 2005 Un. Illustration
Grades: 8 9 10 11 12 Adult **741.5**
1. Humorous graphic novels; 2. Satire; 3. Graphic novels
1-4012-0753-7, $12.99

MAD Magazine was founded in 1952 as a ten-cent comic book that parodied other comic books; three years later it became a twenty-five cent (cheap!) magazine. This volume collects some of the regular features and parodies of television programs and movies of the decade. Some of the advertising parodies feature tobacco and alcohol products, and some parodies portray the imbibing of alcohol products.

Mad About the Sixties: The Best of the Decade

Grant Geissman, editor. Mad Books/E.C. Publications 1997 Un Illustration
Grades: 7 8 9 10 11 12 Adult **741.5; Fic**
1. Humorous graphic novels; 2. Satire; 3. Graphic novels
1-4012-0754-5, $9.99

Alfred E. Newman as a flower child? Ecch! Here is a look back at the Sixties from the satire magazine, full of send-ups, takeoffs, and put-ons from the decade that gave the world Timothy Leary and Tiny Tim. Along with Spy vs. Spy, Sergio Aragones' "Mad Marginals," Don Martin's lunacies, and Snappy Answers to Stupid Questions, this volume includes TV satires such as Star Blecch, Bats-Man, and The Phewgitive, and movie takeoffs 201 Min. of a Space Idiocy, East Side Story, and Flawrence of Arabia. Back in the 1960s, preteens read the magazine and most of them turned out okay ...

Madara, Sai

Mamoru the shadow protector volume 1. DrMaster Publications 2008 168p. Illustration

Grades: 7 8 9 10 11 12   **741.5; Fic**

1. Humorous graphic novels; 2. Manga; 3. Ninja; 4. Graphic novels

978-1-59796-183-7, $9.95

LC 2008-249015

Mamoru Kagemori seems to be just an ordinary, boring high school boy, but he's really the eldest son of a ninja clan that has been charged with guarding their neighbors, the Konnyakus, for four hundred years. Mamoru must secretly guard Yuna Konnyaku, his classmate; she's a total klutz and rather ditzy, and gets into all kinds of trouble. Take, for example, the fact that she witnessed a drug deal without even realizing what went on; now, the criminals want her dead, and Mamoru has to stop them all. The book includes some minor fan service and some mild violence.

Madden, Matt

★ **Drawing** words & writing pictures: making comics: from manga, graphic novels, and beyond. [by] Jessica Abel & Matt Madden. First Second Books 2008 Xxi, 282 p. Illustration

Grades: 9 10 11 12 Adult   **741.5**

1. Cartooning — Technique; 2. Comic books, strips, etc — Authorship; 3. Drawing — Technique; 4. Graphic novels — Authorship

1596431318; 9781596431317, $34.99

LC 2007044125

Authors Jessica Abel and Matt Madden present "a course on comic creation — for college classes or for independent study — that centers on storytelling and concludes with making a finished comic. With chapters on lettering, story structure, and panel layout, the fifteen lessons offered — each complete with homework, extra credit activities and supplementary reading suggestions — provide a solid introduction for people interested in making their own comics." (Publisher's note)

"This book offers step-by-step entry into a complicated series of skills in a nonscary and approachable way." Libr J

Includes bibliographical references (p. 261-265) and index

Maeda, Jun

Hibiki's magic, vol. 1. Art by Rei Izumi. Tokyopop 2007 234p. Illustration

Grades: 7 8 9 10 11 12   **741.5; Fic**

1. Fantasy graphic novels; 2. Magic; 3. Manga; 4. Graphic novels

978-1-59816-766-5, $9.99

Hibiki works as a sorcerer's assistant, but she's lousy at magic; her best talent is making tea. When criminal ruffians interrupt an experiment, her master's soul becomes trapped in a squirrellike gusk and his body is destroyed when the

house's magical defenses are triggered by the intrusion. Bereft of her master, Hibiki comes to the big city, Kamigusk, where she is taken to Kamisaid Academy and welcomed as an expert magic user, but what can she do" The story includes some mild bad language, minor fan service, and mild violence.

Maeda, Mahiro

Gankutsuou: the Count of Monte Cristo, vol.. Del Rey Manga 2008 220p. Illustration

Grades: 10 11 12 Adult   **741.5; Fic**

1. Authors; 2. Biographers; 3. Dramatists; 4. Dumas, Alexandre, 1802-1870; 5. Dumas, Alexandre, 1802-1870 — Adaptations; 6. Magazine editors; 7. Manga; 8. Novelists; 9. Science fiction graphic novels; 10. Graphic novels

978-0-345-50520-0, $10.95

In the future, young Parisian nobleman Albert and his friend Franz travel to Luna, the moon, for a vacation, where they meet the Count of Monte Cristo, a wealthy aristocrat from the far reaches of the galaxy. Albert becomes fascinated by the man, who seems to be free in every sense of the word. What he doesn't know is that his father, General Morcerf, wealthy banker Baron Danglars, and Attorney General de Villefort, conspired together to destroy Edmond Dantes a quarter-century ago; and that Edmond Dantes is now the Count of Monte Cristo. He has returned to Paris for his own dark purposes of revenge upon all Albert loves. This science fictional version of Alexandre Dumas' novel is based on the anime series. The book includes some sexual situations, some nudity, and bloody violence.

Maeda, Tomo

Black Sun Silver Moon, Vol. 1. Go! Comi 2007 192p. Illustration

Grades: 10 11 12 Adult   **741.5; Fic**

1. Fantasy graphic novels; 2. Manga; 3. Supernatural graphic novels; 4. Graphic novels

978-1-933617-20-6, $10.99

Eighteen-year-old Taki had taken a job cleaning the church of Shikimi-sensei in order to work off his late father's debt; then he discovered that his main job is to hunt and kill demons and zombies. After working for a while - cleaning the church by day and slaying monsters by night - he notices that the townspeople shun Shikimi-sensei. Then Shikimi-sensei tells Taki that someday Taki will have to kill him, for his silver hair and eyes are signs that Shikimi-sensei will eventually become a zombie. This volume also includes a back-up story, "Magic Words," about a king who still looks like a little boy and his search for a worthy queen.

Mahler, Nicolas

Lone Racer. Top Shelf Productions 2007 92p. Illustration

Grades: 11 12 Adult   **741.5; Fic**

1. Humorous graphic novels; 2. Racing; 3. Graphic novels

978-1-891830-69-3, $12.95

Years before, Lone Racer was a champion; now, he keeps plugging away despite taunts from the younger racers. He does it for his hospitalized wife. When he's not at the track or the hospital, he's at Bar Juanjo with old racing pal Rubber. When mechanic-turned-cop Irksome talks Lone

Racer into a bank robbery and then chickens out, things get dire, and Racer decides he has to win a race to regain his self-respect. His "middling love-affair," which he breaks off because he can't stop thinking about his wife, adds more adult content to the book, along with the bar scenes. Mahler's art style is different - bodies curve oddly and heads are nothing but hats and noses; he also uses black, white and dull brick red for color.

" . . . this corny-old-movie scenario is, thanks largely to its looks, delightfully ludicrous." (Booklist)

Mairowitz, David Zane
Kafka. [by] David Zane Mairowitz and Robert Crumb; edited by Richard Appignanesi. Fantagraphics Books 2007 176p. Illustration
Grades: 10 11 12 Adult   **92; 741.5**
1. Biographical graphic novels; 2. Kafka, Franz, 1883-1924; 3. Graphic novels
978-1-56097-806-0, $14.95
This book combines a biography of Kafka with illustrated plot descriptions of many of his works, including The Metamorphosis. Crumb renders the stories in comic book form, while the biographical information is presented mostly in text.

Majiko!
St. Lunatic High School Volume 1. Tokyopop 2007 Un Illustration
Grades: 8 9 10 11 12   **741.5; Fic**
1. Horror graphic novels; 2. Humorous graphic novels; 3. Manga; 4. Graphic novels
978-1-59816-944-7, $9.99
Forced to attend the prestigious St. Lunatic School when her brother gets a needed teaching job there, Niko Kanzaki discovers a haunting secret in her demon-filled night-classes. She applies higher learning to find out the differences between humans and demons, but the handsome and mysterious Ren shows her that the races also share some things in common... High school—filled with cute boys, delicious secrets, and debonair demons...oh, my.

Maki, Yoko
Aishiteruze Baby Vol. 1. Viz Media/Shojo Beat 2006 Un Illustration
Grades: 8 9 10 11 12 Adult   **741.5; Fic**
1. Shojo manga; 2. Graphic novels
978-1-4215-0711-8, $19.95
Kippei Katakura is a 17-year-old playboy who spends his time chasing girls, careless of their feelings. But when his 5-year-old cousin Yuzuyu comes to live with his family after her mother's sudden disappearance, Kippei is put in charge of taking care of her. As Kippei gets to know Yuzuyu and starts to understand how she feels, he also begins to realize that all girls were like Yuzuyu once... Kippei has a lot to figure out, like what to make for Yuzuyu's lunch and how to drop her off at kindergarten while still getting to high school on time. Kippei is enjoying his time with Yuzuyu, but not everyone is happy about it. The girls at school miss their quality time with Kippei, and one decides to play dirty to get him back.

Malam, John
Oliver Twist. Illustrated by Penko Gelev; retold by John Malam.. Barron's 2006 48p. Illustration
Grades: 3 4 5 6 7 8 9   **741.5; Fic**
1. Dickens, Charles, 1812-1870 — Adaptations; 2. Great Britain — History — 19th century; 3. Graphic novels
978-0-7641-5975-6, $15.99; 978-0-7641-3490-6 (pa), $8.99
LC 2005-936253
Born in a workhouse and immediately orphaned, Oliver Twist seems destined for a life of misery. He survives childhood years filled with neglect, hunger, and violence, but on his eighth birthday, he must start to work in the workhouse, and his troubles begin. Soon after he gets into trouble for daring to ask for more food, he's sent out to work and falls in with the evil Bill Sikes and Fagin, who run a group of raggedy young thieves. The book includes a brief biography of Dickens, a time line of world events during his life, a brief essay on the poor in London, and descriptions of some of the theatrical and motion picture adaptations of the story.
Part of the Graphic Classics series.

Manabe, Shohei
Dead End Vol. 1. Tokyopop 2005 214p. Illustration
Grades: 11 12 Adult   **741.5; Fic**
1. Horror graphic novels; 2. Manga; 3. Science fiction graphic novels; 4. Seinen manga; 5. Graphic novels
1-59532-161-6, $9.99
Shirou is just an ordinary poor construction worker who happens to stumble into a life-changing event that has him screaming, There's no place like home." In the midst of his confusion and panic, a mysterious companion tells him that all of his questions will be answered and his memory restored if he recovers five friends in three days. Meanwhile, he's being pursued by killers. The book includes lots of graphic violence, harsh language, and some nudity.

Mangels, Andy
Iron man: beneath the armor. Del Rey Books 2008 216p. Illustration
Grades: 8 9 10 11 12 Adult   **741.5**
1. Iron Man (Fictional character); 2. Graphic novels
978-0-345-50615-3, $19.95
This book gives readers lots of information about Marvel Comics' hero, Iron Man. Millionaire industrialist and genius Tony Stark creates the armor and together, human and machine become Iron Man. Readers will find the history of Iron Man, from his debut in the 1960s to the movie which opened on May 2, 2008. They will see an overview of the armor's design evolution through the decades, and also find profiles of the characters who have appeared in Iron Man comics, from Tony Stark himself to Virginia "Pepper" Potts, James Rhodes, villains such as Mandarin, Crimson Dynamo, Fin Fang Foom, and many more.

Manglobe
Samurai Champloo Vol. 1. Iillustrated by Masaru Gotsubo. Tokyopop 2005 177p. Illustration
Grades: 8 9 10 11 12 Adult   **741.5; Fic**

1. Adventure graphic novels; 2. Humorous graphic novels; 3. Manga; 4. Samurai; 5. Shonen manga; 6. Graphic novels
1-59182-282-3, $9.99

In a world full of evil, a hardworking waitress, an arrogant mercenary and a mysterious samurai meet. Through a series of misunderstandings, Fuu, Mugen and Jin find themselves running from officials and wanted by the law. Together they form an uneasy alliance to search for the enigmatic Sunflower Samurai. Along the way they come across misleading characters, ninjas, assassins and a prince in disguise. Their journey proves to be nothing less than a roller coaster ride of battles, danger, desperation and companionship. The book includes some strong language and some fighting violence.

Manning, Matthew K.
Wolverine: inside the world of the living weapon. Written by Matthew K. Manning. DK 2009 199p. Illustration
Grades: 6 7 8 9   741.5
1. X-Men (Fictional characters)
978-0-7566-4547-2, $24.95; 0-7566-4547-6
LC 2009284799
"Super-fans can learn about Wolverine's comic book debut (a cameo in a Hulk comic in 1974), and the development of his character, his story, the X-Men, and more." (Publisher's note)

Mansfield, Andy
The **All-New** All-Different X-Men Pop-Up. Candlewick Press 2007 Un Illustration
Grades: K 1 2 3 4 5 6 7 8 9 10 11 12 Adult   741.5; Fic
1. Pop-up books; 2. Superhero graphic novels; 3. X-Men (Fictional characters); 4. Graphic novels
978-0-7636-3462-9, $24.99

This pop-up book uses excerpts from classic X-Men comics, paper engineering, and pull-out fact files to profile the X-Men, including Cyclops, Storm, Nightcrawler, Wolverine, Colossus, and Banshee, along with nemesis Magneto and mini-profiles of the original X-Men.

Marchetto, Marisa Acocella
Cancer Vixen: A True Story. By Marisa Acocella Marchetto. Pantheon Books 2009 211 p. Color; Illustration
Grades: 11 12 Adult   92; 741.5
1. Autobiographical graphic novels; 2. Breast — Cancer; 3. Marchetto, Marisa Acocella; 4. Graphic novels
037571474X; 9780375714740, $16.95
LC 200640967
"In this graphic memoir, Marisa Acocella Marchetto tells the story of her eleven-month, ultimately triumphant bout with breast cancer—from diagnosis to cure, and every challenging step in between." Publisher's note
"The fashion details are great fun, drawn in a spare loose style, but it's the heart of her story, the support and love she gets from her family and friends, that make Cancer Vixen a universal story that's hard to put down." Publ Wkly

Marcus, Ken
Super human resources season one. Justin Bleep, illustration; Ken Marcus, story. Ape Entertainment 2009 Un Illustration
Grades: 9 10 11 12 Adult   741.5; Fic
1. Humorous graphic novels; 2. Superhero graphic novels; 3. Graphic novels
978-1-934944-68-4, $12.95

Super Crises International hires out super heroes people with capes, claws, radioactive half-lives, ... And, like any business, it has a human resources office that keeps up with expense reports, payroll, cleaning up the conference rooms after crossovers gone wrong ... Tim from Temps-RUs comes to SCI to work in accounts receivable, and he soon learns that running a super hero business is definitely not fun. Something is not right with the bills, and Gordon from the corporate office threatens to shut down the office. On top of that, the office copier has attained sentience and decides to destroy all organic life, and his boss in Accounts plans to destroy SCI. Just another day at the office ... The book includes some superhero fighting violence with no bloodshed.

Marshall, Gary
Studio space: the world's greatest comic illustrators at work. Interviews & edited by Joel Meadows & Gary Marshall. Image Comics 2008 318p. Illustration
Grades: 10 11 12 Adult   741.5
1. Cartoonists; 2. Graphic novels
978-1-58240-909-2, $49.99; 978-1-58240-908-5 (pa), $29.99

Twenty modern comics artists talk about their careers, their work, and their working methods. Each of them is photographed in his studio, and samples of their artwork are included. The artists are: Brian Bolland, Tim Bradstreet, Howard Chaykin, Steve Dillon, Tommy Lee Edwards, Duncan Fegredo, Dave Gibbons, Adam Hughes, Joe Kubert, Jim Lee, Mike Mignola, Frank Miller, Sean Phillips, George Pratt, Alex Ross, Tim Sale, Walt Simonson, Bryan Talbot, Dave Taylor, and Sergio Toppi.

Martin, George R. R.
The **Hedge** Knight II: sworn sword. George R.R. Martin and Ben Avery ; artist, Mike Miller. Marvel Entertainment 2008 Un Illustration
Grades: 8 9 10 11 12 Adult   741.5; Fic
1. Adventure graphic novels; 2. Fantasy graphic novels; 3. Knights and knighthood; 4. Graphic novels
978-0-7851-2650-8, $19.99

Dunk, who is now Ser Duncan the Tall, has roamed Westeros as a hedge knight, accompanied by his squire, Egg. Now they're employed by Ser Eustace of Standfast, whose land suffers a severe drought because of his dispute with Lady Rohanna, whom many call the "Red Widow." Dunk tries to find a peaceful settlement to the feud, even as he deals with his strong attraction to Lady Rohanna. The book includes some fighting violence and mild sexual innuendo, and one scene of partial nudity.

Martinson, Lars
Tonoharu: part one. Pliant Press/Top Shelf Productions 2008 128p. Illustration

Grades: 11 12 Adult   **741.5; Fic**
1. Japan; 2. Teachers; 3. Graphic novels
978-1-9801023-2-1, $19.95

                    LC 2007-940522

Daniel Wells looks back at his first year working as an assistant junior high school teacher in rural Japan as he must make a decision whether to renew his contract or leave Japan. In Tonoharu, he leads an isolated, almost monastic life, hampered by his lack of Japanese language skills and ignorance of Japanese culture. He wonders why his predecessor lasted only one year, and whether he will last beyond that as well. Meanwhile, he tries to work with the teachers at school and tries to pursue a relationship with another American teacher who lives a few towns away by train. This volume includes some harsh language, including the s-bomb, and some partial nudity.

Marunas, Nathaniel
  Manga Claus, Honor, Loyalty, Tinsel: The Blade of Kringle. Penguin Group/Razorbill 2006 80p. Illustration
Grades: 4 5 6 7 8 9   **741.5; Fic**
1. Fantasy graphic novels; 2. Ninja; 3. Santa Claus; 4. Graphic novels
1-59514-134-0, $12.99

It's the night before Christmas Eve, and disgruntled elf Fritz, determined to show he belongs in Production and not Laundry, uses a dark magic spell on a ninja nutcracker. It's only supposed to cause a little damage and then he, Fritz, can use a spell to stop it. However, things go terribly wrong when elf Wallace fights back, the evil nutcracker lands in the furnace, and evil spell embers land on a pile of teddy bears. Yes, now an army of evil ninja teddy bears wreaks havoc at the North Pole, and Santa must stop them, with the help of a special pair of Japanese samurai swords.

Marvel Adventures: Spider-Man Volume One
  Marvel Entertainment 2006 Un Illustration
Grades: 4 5 6 7 8 9   **741.5; Fic**
1. Spider-Man (Fictional character); 2. Superhero graphic novels; 3. Graphic novels
978-0-7851-2432-0, $19.99

This hardcover collects the first two volumes of Marvel Adventures Spider-Man. What separates the super-villains from just plain old villains" When they escape from prison, regular villains might lay low for a while and enjoy the sweetness of freedom. But not a super-villain like Doctor Octopus - the minute he's free, he's gathering up the most dangerous crew ever assembled: the Vulture, Electro, Kraven the Hunter, Sandman and Mysterio. And they've all got one thing on their minds: bringing down Spider-Man once and for all. Also, catch the story that started it all: the origin of Spider-Man. Stories also include the return of the Human Torch, the villainy of the Scorpion, and more.

Marvel Comics Group (Firm)
  Wolverine: inside the world of the living weapon. Written by Matthew K. Manning. DK 2009 199p. Illustration
Grades: 6 7 8 9   **741.5**
1. X-Men (Fictional characters)
978-0-7566-4547-2, $24.95; 0-7566-4547-6
                    LC 2009284799

Marvel Romance Redux: Another Kind of Love
  Marvel Entertainment 2007 Un Illustration
Grades: 9 10 11 12 Adult   **741.5; Fic**
1. Humorous graphic novels; 2. Romance graphic novels; 3. Graphic novels
978-0-7851-2090-2, $13.99

Current Marvel writers take some of the old Marvel romance comics (written and illustrated by such past Marvel luminaries as Jack Kirby - and not a single female writer) and put in new dialogue that play the stories for laughs. The new dialogues some sexual suggestiveness.

Marz, Ron
  Ion, Guardian of the Universe Vol. 1: The Torchbearer. Art by Tom Grindberg and Greg Tocchini. DC Comics 2007 208p. Illustration
Grades: 9 10 11 12 Adult   **741.5; Fic**
1. Green Lantern (Fictional character); 2. Superhero graphic novels; 3. Graphic novels
978-1-4012-1197-6, $14.99

Kyle Raynor was the last of the Green Lanterns, but he had helped to bring back the Green Lantern Corps. Now, as Ion, he has more power than he had ever imagined, but is it a boon or a curse? He has been acting out of character and left a wake of senseless destruction and unanswered questions. Can rogue Green Lantern Hal Jordan help him figure out what's going on?

  Samurai: Heaven and Earth. Art by Luke Ross. Dark Horse Comics 2006 Un Illustration
Grades: 11 12 Adult   **741.5; Fic**
1. Adventure graphic novels; 2. Samurai; 3. Graphic novels
1-59307-388-7, $14.95

How far will a man travel for love? What battles will he fight? Will he cross heaven and earth to be by the side of the woman he loves? Beginning in feudal Japan of 1704, Samurai: Heaven & Earth follows Shiro, a lone samurai warrior sworn to be reunited with the love of his life who has been spirited away by his enemies. His pursuit of Yoshiko will carry him farther than he could have imagined - from his native Japan to the sprawling empire of China, across Europe, and finally to Paris itself. There, in the fabled halls of King Louis XIV's Versailles, he must cross blades with the greatest swordsmen ever known if he is to reclaim his love. Readers will find nudity, sexual situations, and violence (including beheadings).

Masamune, Shirow
  Black magic. Dark Horse Manga 2008 200p. Illustration
Grades: 10 11 12 Adult   **741.5; Fic**
1. Manga; 2. Science fiction graphic novels; 3. Graphic novels
978-1-59307-696-2, $14.95

Millions of years ago, the planet Venus teemed with life and an advanced civilization. In this past, the Nemesis supercomputer controls government functions, with bioroid "executors" created to carry out the system's utopian edicts. But trouble brews, even in good times, as different executors vie for control of Nemesis; these struggles force the governing system to secretly create Duna Typhon, a super-bioroid "sleeper." Raised among humans, she possesses awesome magical powers to be used to protect Nemesis. That time has now come. This was Masamune's first published manga series. The book includes some violence and harsh language.

Mashiba, Shin
    Yumekui Kenbun: Nightmare Inspector volume 1. Viz Media 2008 184p. Illustration
Grades: 9 10 11 12 Adult   **741.5; Fic**
  1. Dreams; 2. Fantasy graphic novels; 3. Manga; 4. Graphic novels
  978-1-4215-1758-2, $9.99
    In Japan, during the Taisho Era (1920s), there is a special place where people who suffer nightmares can go for help. At the Silver Star Tea House, Hiruko is a special kind of private investigator who can rid people of their darkest visions, for the price of eating their nightmares. In this first volume, Hiruko helps a young gatekeeper who suffers nightmares about his beautiful master, but when Hiruko enters the nightmare, he learns the gatekeeper's secret and true nature. He also helps a young woman who suffers nightmares of losing pieces of herself (her eyes, her hand, etc.), a young fan who dreams that his favorite movie star commits suicide, an unforgiving son whose father haunts his dreams, a young man who can never see the face of the ideal woman in his dreams. Some stories end in O. Henry-type twists; some stories include some violence.

Mashima, Hiro
    Fairy tale vol. 1. Translated and adapted by William Flanagan; lettered by North Market Street Graphics. Del Rey Manga 2008 202p. Illustration
Grades: 8 9 10 11 12   **741.5; Fic**
  1. Fantasy graphic novels; 2. Humorous graphic novels; 3. Manga; 4. Graphic novels
  978-0-345-50133-2, $10.95
    Cute girl wizard Lucy wants to join the Fairy Tail, a club for the most powerful wizards (and the most troublesome " they tend to do stuff such as blow up harbors while fighting the bad guys). However, her ambitions land her in the clutches of a gang of unsavory pirates led by a devious magician, who plan to sell her into slavery. Her only hope is Natsu, a strange boy she has met on her travels. Natsu is not the typical hero: he gets motion sickness, eats like a pig, and his best friend is a talking cat. He is a member of the Fairy Tail, however. The book includes some mild fan service (usually cleavage shots), consumption of alcohol, and lots of magical fighting.
  Volume 1 of an ongoing series

Massey, Jim
    Maintenance, volume 3: Fighting occupants of interstellar craft. Robbi Rodriguez, illustrator. Oni Press 2008 104p. Illustration
Grades: 10 11 12 Adult   **741.5; Fic**
  1. Adventure graphic novels; 2. Humorous graphic novels; 3. Science fiction graphic novels; 4. Graphic novels
  978-1-934964-05-7, $9.95
    When smooth talking aliens kidnap Mendy from the receptionist desk, Terromax janitors Doug and Manny form

a team to rescue her. It's not exactly a dream team: K'Arl (an amnesiac alien with a flying saucer), Manshark (pretty much exactly what his name describes), Dr. Woodfern (who has a "thing" about monkeys) and his new invention, the Invisolux, the very hairy Dr. Papritz and his handy new Zappy Stick, and a zombie cat and the two janitors, of course. The book has some violence and the ick factor can get pretty high (such as when the zombie cat jumps into an alien's mouth and starts eating him from the inside out).

    Maintenance volume 1: it's a dirty job . . .. Robbi Rodriguez, artist. Oni Press 2007 88p. Illustration
Grades: 10 11 12 Adult   **741.5; Fic**
  1. Humorous graphic novels; 2. Science fiction graphic novels; 3. Graphic novels
  $9.95
    Doug and Manny work as custodians at TerroMax Inc., the world's biggest and best evil science think tank. The messes they have to clean up include toxic spill monsters and a talking manshark who wants to go out on the town. They also have to worry about the mad scientists, would-be dictators, and the cute young woman who works at reception. The book includes some harsh language, including the s-bomb, and some violence.

    Maintenance volume 2: fantastic sewage & other stories. Robbi Rodriguez, illustrator. Oni Press 2008 82p.
Grades: 10 11 12 Adult   **741.5; Fic**
  1. Humorous graphic novels; 2. Science fiction graphic novels; 3. Graphic novels
  978-1-932664-76-8, $9.95
    Doug and Manny work as custodians at TerroMax Inc., the world's biggest and best evil science think tank. In this volume, Dr. Dorothy blackmails Doug and Manny into letting him shrink them so they can go into his toilet and destroy some microcreatures he flushed down the toilet. Now the two custodians have to deal with several kinds of poo monsters. The book includes harsh language, lots of poo, and some violence.

Matheny, Bill
    The **Batman** Strikes! Vol. 1: Crime Time; illustrated by Terry Beatty, Christopher Jones et al. DC Comics 2005 Un Illustration
Grades: 4 5 6 7 8 9   **741.5; Fic**
  1. Batman (Fictional character); 2. Joker (Fictional character); 3. Superhero graphic novels; 4. Graphic novels
  1-4012-0509-7, $6.99
    This book boasts five action-packed adventures of the Dark Knight Detective: Penguin Rising, City of Bats, Outlaw and Disorder, Without a Chance and Deadly Partner. Batman goes up against the Penguin, the Joker, Manbat, and other villains.

    The **Batman** Strikes! Vol. 2: In Darkest Knight. DC Comics 2005 Un Illustration
Grades: 4 5 6 7 8 9   **741.5; Fic**
  1. Batman (Fictional character); 2. Catwoman (Fictional character); 3. Joker (Fictional character); 4. Superhero graphic novels; 5. Graphic novels
  1-4012-0510-0, $6.99
    Evil can't hide, and neither can the rogues' gallery of villains who take on Gotham City's Dark Knight Detective.

Catwoman, Mr. Freeze, Firefly, the Joker, and Man-Bat try their luck in this volume.

The **Batman** Strikes!: duty calls. Bill Matheny, J. Torres ; illustrated by Christopher Jones, Terry Beatty ; Colored by Heroic Age ; Lettered by Phil Balsman, Travis Lanham. DC Comics 2007 144p. Illustration
Grades: 3 4 5 6 7 8 9   **741.5; Fic**
1. Adventure graphic novels; 2. Batgirl (Fictional character); 3. Batman (Fictional character); 4. Catwoman (Fictional character); 5. Superhero graphic novels; 6. Graphic novels
978-1-4012-1548-4, $12.99
This volume of Bat-stories is based on the new WB Kids cartoon series. Batman takes on Clayface, the Penguin, the Riddler, Catwoman, and Poison Ivy; Batgirl steps in because Pamela Isley used to be Barbara Gordon's friend. The stories have lots of action, fast quips, and no foul language or actual violence.

Matoh, Sanami
Ra-I. Tokyopop 2006 196p. Illustration
Grades: 7 8 9 10 11 12   **741.5; Fic**
1. Manga; 2. Mystery graphic novels; 3. Romance graphic novels; 4. Shojo manga; 5. Graphic novels
1-59816-663-8, $9.99
Al Foster is a private detective whose workaday life suddenly shakes up with the arrival of thirteen-year-old Rai Spencer, youngest son of the billionaire Spencer family, genius child prodigy, and unrepentant smart aleck. Rai also has telekinetic powers that can knock out anyone who stands in his path. His older sister Rei sports a mean left hook. What Rai desperately needs is someone to figure out who has been trying to kill him for the past month. This is a standalone manga.

Matsui, Yusei
Assassination classroom 1: Time for assassination. Yusei Matsui. Viz 2014 192 p. Illustration
Grades: 9 10 11 12   **741.5**
1. Assassination — Fiction; 2. Manga; 3. School stories; 4. Shonen manga
1421576074; 9781421576077, $9.99
In this graphic novel, by Yusei Matsui, "the students in Class 3-E of Kunugigaoka Junior High have a new teacher: an alien octopus with bizarre powers and unlimited strength, who's just destroyed the moon and is threatening to destroy the earth—unless they can kill him first! . . . Will the deed be accomplished through pity, brute force or poison . . . " And what chance does their teacher have of repairing his students' tattered self-esteem—" (Publisher's note)
"This book begins as a simple adventure story, but the further teens get into the story, the more they will see the subtext of 'bad' students becoming empowered to find their real talents. Matsui's artwork is filled with action and humor, capturing the realistic aspects of the human characters and the smiley face and tentacles of the alien." SLJ
Volume 1 of an ongoing series

Matsumoto, Natsumi
St. [heart] dragon girl, vol. 1. Viz Media/Shojo Beat 2008 Un Illustration

Grades: 7 8 9 10 11 12   **741.5; Fic**
1. Fantasy graphic novels; 2. Manga; 3. Romance graphic novels; 4. Shojo manga; 5. Graphic novels
978-1-4215-2010-0, $8.99
High schooler Momoka Sendou, nicknamed Dragon Girl, is a martial artist; her childhood friend Ryuga Kou is a Chinese sorcerer who banishes demons. They have helped each other over the years, but now the Serpent King has threatened to take Ryuga's cousin Shunran as his bride. Ryuga knows he needs more strength, so he tries to summon the clan's dragon spirit to possess him, but Momoka sees only a threat to her friend and pushes him out of the way; the dragon enters her instead. Ryuga does possess the power to seal or unseal the dragon within Momoka, so now they really have to work together to fight the demons, especially the Serpent King. Complicating matters is the little fact that Momoka loves Ryuga but won't tell him, even though everyone around them knows it.

St. Dragon Girl, vol. 2. Viz Media/Shojo Beat 2009 Un Illustration
Grades: 7 8 9 10 11 12   **741.5; Fic**
1. Magic; 2. Manga; 3. Martial arts; 4. Romance graphic novels; 5. Shojo manga; 6. Graphic novels
978-1-4215-2011-7, $8.99
Childhood friends, Momoka is a martial artist and Ryuga is a Chinese magic master; Momoka is possessed by a dragon spirit that only Ryuga can unseal whenever its strength is needed. When the Kenpo class goes on a training camp in the old school building, Momoka finds "her" peach tree; but now she learns that a demon that had been trapped beneath the tree is trying to get free, and it possesses her classmates then Ryuga. Somehow she's going to have to defeat it. One would think she wouldn't need the dragon during the school's festival. Momoka stars in the Kenpo class's play, but when she takes a break to enjoy the festival with Ryuga, thieves steal the sword she was using it belongs to Ryuga's family, and she must get it back. Then a new transfer student comes to school, and it's Ryuga's cousin, Raika. She says they're promised to each other and wants Momoka's help to make sure Ryuga will fall in love with her; the problem is Momoka loves Ryuga herself. The book includes martial arts action and a few chaste kisses.

Matsumoto, Nina
Yokaiden, volume 1. Del Rey Manga 2008 Un Illustration Grades: 6 7 8 9 10 11 12   **741.5; Fic**
1. Fantasy graphic novels; 2. Folklore — Japan; 3. Monsters; 4. Graphic novels
978-0-345-50327-5, $10.95
In what looks like 18th or 19th-century Japan, young Hamachi Uramaki lives with his crotchety old grandmother (his parents died years before); he's obsessed with yokai, Japan's legendary monsters and other supernatural creatures, and he desperately wants to meet one. He does encounter a kappa who fell into a trap, and Hamachi saves the creature he names Madkap. When Hamachi returns home after selling bamboo in town, he finds his grandmother dead and thinks Madkap did it (grandmother had set the kappa trap). He decides to enter the yokai realm to find Madkap and get revenge; but once Hamachi enters, the trick is to survive, for the yokai realm is not meant for humans. This is a global manga story that uses Western page order (left to

right). Matsumoto features lesser-known yokai, such as the chochin obake, the paper lantern ghost, and the namahage, an ogre who disciplines naughty children by crippling them for a while. The book includes some violence and mild bad language.

"Matsumoto's manga is silly fun, anchored by a clueless but plucky hero and a dry sense of humor. Taking place in a fantasy setting close to historical Japan, Hamachi's adventures read like lighthearted folktales centered on the wide variety of yokai and the various means of dealing with them." Booklist

Matsumoto, Tomo
 Beauty is the Beast Volume 1. Viz Media/Shojo Beat 2005 184p. Illustration
 Grades: 7 8 9 10 11 12   **741.5; Fic**
 1. Humorous graphic novels; 2. Romance graphic novels; 3. Shojo manga; 4. Graphic novels
 1-4215-0289-5, $8.99
 When bubbly eleventh-grader Eimi Yamashita finds out that her parents are relocating for work, she decides to strike out on her own and move into a dormitory for girls. Little does Eimi suspect the exciting romantic adventures that await her there. Eimi's fellow residents are a little bit crazy, but a whole lot of fun. They've got a secret mission planned for Eimi's new resident initiation...and it has something to do with sneaking into the boys dormitory across the street and returning with a special keepsake! Can Eimi pull it off without getting caught by one of the handsomest (and cruelest) boys in the dorm?

Matsushita, Yoko
 Descendants of Darkness Vol. 1. Viz Media/Shojo 2004 200p. Illustration
 Grades: 10 11 12 Adult   **741.5; Fic**
 1. Fantasy graphic novels; 2. Humorous graphic novels; 3. Manga; 4. Shojo manga; 5. Graphic novels
 1-59116-507-5, $9.99
 As a Shinigami, a Guardian of Death, Asato Tsuzuki has a lot to think about. First of all, there are all those dead people. Someone's got to escort them safely to the afterlife. Then there's all that bureaucracy. The affairs of death come with a lot of paperwork, budgetary concerns and endless arcana. Combining supernatural action with heavy dollops of romance, sex and humor, this book proves one thing: Death is big business...and business is good. The book includes graphic violence, some strong language, and some sexual situations.

Matsuzuki, Kou
 Happy Cafe, vol. 1. Tokyopop 2010 194p. Illustration
 Grades: 7 8 9 10 11 12   **741.5; Fic**
 1. Humorous graphic novels; 2. Manga; 3. Restaurants; 4. Romance graphic novels; 5. Shojo manga; 6. Graphic novels
 978-1-4278-1730-3, $10.99
 Sixteen-year-old Uru lives by herself because her mother has married a younger man (stepfather is 29) and she wants to give them privacy. She decides she has to help pay her bills, so she gets a part time job as a waitress at the Cafe Bonheur (which means Happy Cafe), where she meets Shindo and Ichiro, two very handsome but rather grumpy

young men. Uru is a major klutz, which is a liability for a waitress, but Shindo and Ichiro manage to save her most of the time. Shindo is especially cranky, and Ichiro seems to be eating all the time" he tends to fall asleep when he's hungry. Despite all that, Uru enjoys working at the cafe, but she's under pressure to get good scores on her school exams, or her mother has threatened to make her move back home. When Uru helps another teenager live her dream of being a model, Mitsuka texts her a question that puts Uru in a fluster? "Is that dark haired crank your crush or something?" The romance is light, with very little suggestiveness. Instead of the usual chibi characters to express deep emotions, Matsuzuki uses very simple round-headed figures.

Matthews, Brett
 The **Lone** Ranger. Brett Matthews, writer ; Sergio Cariello, artist ; Dean White, colorist ; Simon Bowland, lettering ; John Cassaday, cover artist & art direction.   Dynamite Entertainment 2007 160p. Illustration
 Grades: 8 9 10 11 12 Adult
 741.5; Fic
 1. Adventure graphic novels; 2. Lone Ranger (Fictional character); 3. Western stories; 4. Graphic novels

Courtesy of Dynamite Entertainment

 978-1-933305-39-4, $24.99; 978-1-933305-40-0 (pa), $19.99
 "A fiery horse with the speed of light, a cloud of dust, and a hearty "Hi Yo Silver!" The Lone Ranger ..." A popular radio show starting in the 1930s that became a popular television show that ran from 1949 through 1957, a few film serials (extremely hard to find), some paperback novels, and a movie in 1981, The Lone Ranger became an iconic figure. In March 2008, Disney Studios announced it's planning to make a new Lone Ranger movie. In the meantime, Dynamite Entertainment started publishing Lone Ranger comics in 2006. This Lone Ranger is different from the old radio and television shows, and so is Tonto. These aren't the squeaky clean heroes one might expect, although they are heroic. This volume shows the origin of the Lone Ranger, from a young Texas Ranger who has just joined his father and brother. They are ambushed and all killed, except for John. Tonto, a Native American of unknown tribal nation, takes care of John; he has killed all of the killers. When John recovers from his wounds, they set off to find out who ordered the killing, while the reader knows that another killer is murdering all the dead Rangers' families. This book includes some graphic violence.

Texas Ranger John Reid seeks revenge for the murders of his family and friends, only to find justice . . . and that he's something greater than he ever thought he could be. Together with Tonto, he rides against rich criminals like Cavendish and the politicians Cavendish backs. This new version of the Lone Ranger includes more violence than some might remember from the old television show and books.

The **Lone** Ranger, volume II: lines not crossed. John Cassaday, artist; Paul Pope, artist; Sergio Cariello, artist. Dynamite Entertainment 2008 Un
Grades: 9 10 11 12 Adult   **741.5; Fic**
1. Lone Ranger (Fictional character); 2. Mystery graphic novels; 3. Western stories; 4. Graphic novels
978-1-933305-70-7, $14.99
The Lone Ranger continues his quest to take down Butch Cavendish's various illegal businesses, hitting the crime boss in his pocketbook, even as Cavendish tries to use big-city politics to his advantage. Then, the Ranger and Tonto need to find the truth about a shootout when they stop a lynching. The ranchers say the Mexican they caught is a cold-blooded killer, he says it was all due to a misunderstanding; but what should they do when they discover there is fault on both sides" This is not the Lone Ranger of the old radio serial and television show, but a tougher story with two conflicted heroes. The book includes some violence.

Serenity: Those Left Behind. Story by Joss Whedon & Brett Matthews ; script by Brett Matthews ; art by Will Conrad ; colors by Laura Martin ; letters by Michael Heisler ; front cover art by Adam Hughes ; back cover art by Sean Phillips. Dark Horse Comics 2006 Un Illustration
Grades: 8 9 10 11 12 Adult   **741.5; Fic**
1. Adventure graphic novels; 2. Science fiction graphic novels; 3. Graphic novels
1-59307-449-2, $9.95
Penned by Firefly creator Whedon and Brett Matthews, who wrote several episodes of the show, this book follows a ship full of mercenaries, fugitives and one law-abiding prostitute in their pursuit for fast cash and a little peace along the fringes of space. The ragtag crew of Serenity take on a scavenger mission with the hopes of earning enough dough to disappear for a while. Only too late do they realize the whole gig is orchestrated by an old enemy eager remake their acquaintance with the help of some covert-operatives known only as the Blue Gloves. The book includes some violence; most of the strong language is written in Chinese characters so most readers won't know what is being said.

Serenity: Better days. Script by Joss Whedon and Brett Matthews ; art by Will Conrad ; colors by Michelle Madsen ; letters by Michael Heisler. Dark Horse Books 2008 Un Illustration
Grades: 8 9 10 11 12 Adult   **741.5; Fic**
1. Adventure graphic novels; 2. Science fiction graphic novels; 3. Graphic novels
978-1-59582-162-1, $9.95
Mal Reynolds and his ragtag crew take their ship Serenity to the far frontiers of space, as far from the Alliance as they can get. They have actually succeeded in pulling off a heist, and got a much larger than expected payoff from the guy who hired them. However, while the crew members fantasize about what each will do with the newfound wealth, the Alliance is hunting for whoever stole their high-tech weapon and will do whatever it takes to get it back. The book includes some mild sexual innuendo and some violence. This is an original story based on the "Firefly" television series and characters that Joss Whedon created.

Max
Bardin the Superrealist. Fantagraphics Books 2006 82p. Illustration
Grades: 10 11 12 Adult   **741.5; Fic**
1. Humorous graphic novels; 2. Graphic novels
978-1-56097-759-9, $19.95
Everyman Bardin finds himself suddenly transported (well, at least his upper half) to another dimension, where an "Andalusian Dog" (a reference to Buñuel's Un Chien Andalou) serves as his ill-tempered guide. In a series of vignettes, gags, illustrations, text pieces, and dream stories, ping-ponging back between the surrealist world and the "real" world, Bard?n examines, questions, and defends his own beliefs, convictions and philosophies while tangling with the Dog and the Holy Trinity in a variety of guises (including a familiar-looking mouse with red shorts and white gloves). In other stories, he imagines himself in a painting by Brueghel the Elder, tries to deal with his onanism in a productive way, is enlightened, dodges his real "creator" Max in the street, has several nightmares and hallucinations, and, in the book's climactic episode, "The Sound and the Fury," battles a bona fide dragon. There are some sexual situations and some other adult situations regarding the male's gender-defining organs.

Maxwell, Matt
Strangeways: murder moon. Highway 62 Press 2008 144p. Illustration
Grades: 10 11 12 Adult   **741.5; Fic**
1. Fantasy graphic novels; 2. Horror graphic novels; 3. Werewolves; 4. Western stories; 5. Graphic novels
978-0-9796957-0-4, $13.95
In the year 1868, ex-Army officer Seth Collins works as a stagecoach guard and tries to forget the horrors of the Civil War. However, he now faces a different kind of horror: something hunts the people of Silver Branch, including Collins' estranged sister; a strange, seemingly unkillable wolf prowls the wilderness, stalking and killing people from the town. The people have their own secrets, and soon Collins finds himself trapped between the obligations of family and friendship, between the secretive townspeople and the killing beast. The book includes violence and some strong language.

Mazzotta, Antony
Bombaby: The Screen Goddess. SLG Publishing/AmazeInk Comics 2004 Un Illustration
Grades: 10 11 12 Adult   **741.5; Fic**
1. Fantasy graphic novels; 2. Graphic novels
1-59362-003-9, $13.95
Sangeeta Mukherjee is the daughter of well-to-do, traditional parents, dealing with a bratty little sister and an arranged marriage when an out-of-body experience reveals that she is not an ordinary young woman. Sangeeta is, in fact, the reincarnation of India's ancient protector, the Goddess of Mumbai. But how will Sangeeta use this new-found power" Can she make a difference in a male-dominated society" Sangeeta must defy traditional expectations to choose what kind of life she wants and discover her true self. There is some violence in the story.

McCarthy, Tom

Tintin and the secret of literature. Granta Books 2007 211p. Illustration

Grades: 10 11 12 Adult   741.5

1. Graphic novels — History and criticism; 2. Tintin (Fictional character)

978-1-86207-831-9, $29.95

McCarthy examines Herge's Tintin books and asks the question: are they literature? From there he takes the reader on a journey through the books and notes connections between plot elements and characters to Herge's personal life. Whether or not the reader agrees with McCarthy's assertions and conclusions, anyone who has read and enjoyed the Tintin books will enjoy the speculations about Herge's family connections and the way he took on established religion.

McCay, Winsor

Winsor McCay: Early Works Volume 1. Checker Book Publishing Group 2003 201p. Illustration

Grades: 10 11 12 Adult   741.5; Fic

1. Humorous graphic novels; 2. Graphic novels

0-9741664-0-5, $19.95

LC 2003-12920

This volume is a collection of turn-of-the-century rarities from cartooning and animation pioneer, Winsor McCay: Tales of the Jungle Imps," Little Sammy Sneeze," Dreams of a Rarebit Fiend," and Pilgrim's Progress." Best known for Little Nemo in Slumberland, and the seminal animated feature Gertie the Dinosaur, McCay puts his artistic talent and whimsical humor on full display here. Readers should note that when these stories were first published in the early 1900s (Tales of the Jungle Imps" was published in 1903), McCay's artistic vision of the jungle imps" wasn't considered racist."

McCloud, Scott

Reinventing comics: how imagination and technology are revolutionizing an art form. Paradox Press 2000 237p. Illustration

Grades: 11 12 Adult   741; 741.5

0-06-095350-0, $22.95

LC 00-710457

The author maps out "'12 revolutions', which, he believes, need to take place for comics to survive and finally be recognized as a legitimate art form. The topics progress from the oldest of comic-related arguments (seeking respect) to the use of computer technology to renew and expand its audience. These brilliantly presented discussions concern comics as literature, comics as art, creators' rights, industry innovation, and public perception, among other topics." Libr J

★ **Understanding** comics: the invisible art. HarperPerennial 1994 215p. Illustration

Grades: 9 10 11 12 Adult   741.5

0-06-097625-X, $22.95; 9780060976255

McCloud "conducts a genial, well-researched and funny tour of virtually every historical and perceptual aspect of comics, which he calls 'sequential art,' that is, art that consists of sequences of words and pictures. Beginning in the 11th century with the Bayeux tapestry, he examines

pre-Columbian picture languages and the printing press, presenting a quick survey of the historical development of early sequential pictures into the specialized visual language of comics. . . . He dissects the vocabulary of the medium, cheerfully analyzing the psychological power of comics and their central role in our ultra-visual culture." (Publishers Weekly)

Includes bibliographical references

First published 1993 by Kitchen Sink Press

McCreery, Conor

★ **Kill** Shakespeare, vol. 1: a sea of troubles. Created and written by Conor McCreery and Anthony Del Col; art by Andy Belanger; colors by Ian Herring; lettering by Chris Mowry, Robbie Robbins, and Neil Uyetake. IDW Publishing 2010 Un Illustration

Grades: 10 11 12 Adult   741.5; Fic

1. Adventure graphic novels; 2. Authors; 3. Dramatists; 4. Fantasy graphic novels; 5. Poets; 6. Shakespeare, William, 1564-1616 — Adaptations; 7. Graphic novels

978-1-60010-781-8, $19.99

A shipwrecked Hamlet finds himself in England with Richard III, who wants his help to find and kill the wizard, Will Shakespeare, so that Richard can rule with impunity. Haunted by his father's ghost, who tells Hamlet that killing Shakespeare will let him live again, Hamlet agrees to help the English king. Then he discovers that the Lady Juliet Capulet leads an army of rebellion, aided by Othello and Falstaff. They fight against the corrupt Richard, who consults the witch Hecate (who has her own agenda). Falstaff says that Hamlet is the prophesied Shadow King, who will aid the rebellion, while Richard and his allies only want to use Hamlet to destroy Shakespeare, but all agree that only Hamlet can lead them to the wizard. The book includes bloody action and sexual situations, making this more suited to older teens.

"McCreery and Del Col spin an engrossing action-adventure tale of satisfying complexity, full of mystery, deceit, and gory violence, starring a hero who once again must marshal his determination and decide his path." Libr J

Other titles in this series are: Volume two: the blast of war (2011); Volume three: the tide of blood (2013)

★ **Kill** Shakespeare 3: The Tide of Blood. Conor McCreery and Anthony Del Col, illustrated by Andy Belanger. IDW Publishing 2013 140 p. Color; Illustration

Grades: 10 11 12 Adult   741.5

1. Shakespeare, William, 1564-1616 — Adaptations; 2. Graphic novels

1613777329; 9781613777329, $19.99

"With Richard III and Lady Macbeth defeated, Hamlet, Juliet, Othello, and Romeo face an even greater danger—Prospero, a rogue wizard who plans to destroy all of creation! Hamlet must embark on a perilous journey to a remote island whose inhabitants have gone mad and want the Dane's blood . . . if they aren't beaten to the chase by one of Hamlet's allies." (Publisher's note)

"There's more action, wizardry, and gore than the Bard himself was apt to include, but clever echoes of dialogue, intense emotional turnabouts, and imaginatively theatrical art recall the plays in satisfying ways." - Booklist

Kill Shakespeare; Volume 2: the blast of war. Created and written by Conor McCreery and Anthony Del Col; art by Andy Belanger; colors by Ian Herring; lettering by Chris Mowry, Neil Uyetake, and Shawn Lee; original series edits by Tom Waltz.. IDW 2011 148 p.

Grades: 10 11 12 Adult   **741.5**
 1. Shakespeare, William, 1564-1616 — Characters; 2. Shakespeare, William, 1564-1616 — Fiction
 1613770251; 9781613770252, $19.99

This book, the second volume of the comic book series, presents a "sweeping fantasy of magic, war, betrayal, and love [which] is set in a world where Shakespeare's characters dwell and Shakespeare himself is an absent god struggling with a heavy conscience. The second volume builds to the climactic finale of Hamlet's quest to find the creator god Shakespeare and return peace to a land torn apart by an evil army led by Richard III and Lady Macbeth. Joined by love interest Juliet, the warrior Othello, the wise fool Falstaff, and the spy Iago, Hamlet has built an army of rebels, the prodigals, who hold off their enemies while he searches for their creator. But even victory comes at a cost as friends and foes die in a great final battle." (Publishers Wkly)

"[A]n appropriate air of grandeur and theatricality is much on display, brought forth all the more in Belanger's spectacular and inventive page compositions." Booklist

McCulloch, Derek
 ★ **Stagger** Lee. Drawn by Shepherd Hendrix. Image Comics 2006 232p. Illustration

Grades: 10 11 12 Adult   **741.5; Fic**
 1. Folk songs — United States; 2. Graphic novels
 1-58240-607-3, $17.99

What is known: On Christmas of 1895, in Bill Curtis' saloon in St. Louis, "Stag" Lee Shelton shot Billy Lyons. There have been many songs written about this incident, using some version or another of his name: Stacker Lee, Stack-A-Lee, Stack O'Lee, and more. This graphic novel, part historical fiction, part historical essay, examines the legend that grew in the many songs written and sung about the incident. The book contains some sexual situations and some strong language along with some violence.

McDaniel, Scott
 Nightwing: Year One. DC Comics 2005 Un Illustration

Grades: 7 8 9 10 11 12 Adult   **741.5; Fic**
 1. Batman (Fictional character); 2. Nightwing (Fictional character); 3. Robin (Fictional character); 4. Superhero graphic novels; 5. Teen Titans (Fictional characters); 6. Graphic novels
 1-4012-0435-X, $14.99

Dick Grayson was the first Robin, the teen sidekick to the Dark Knight, Batman. Then he became Nightwing and stepped out of Batman's shadow. The story behind that transformation and how it affected Batman, the Teen Titans and Dick himself is explored in this graphic novel. When Batman fires Robin, an angry Dick Grayson is unsure of where to go. On his journey, he receives advice from Superman and aid from Deadman, and makes the decisions that lead him to become a brand new crimefighter.

McDonald, John
 Henry V: the graphic novel: original text version. [by] William Shakespeare; script adaptation, John McDonald; pencils, Neill Cameron ...; editor in chief, Clive Bryant. Classical Comics 2008 143p. Illustration

Grades: 8 9 10 11 12 Adult   **822.3; 741.5**
 1. Shakespeare, William, 1564-1616 — Adaptations
 978-1-906332-41-9, $16.95

This graphic novel adaptation of Shakespeare's play uses a full and unabridged text combined with full color comic book style illustrations. Young King Henry V goes to war against France when he learns he has a legitimate claim to the French

Also available plain text version (ISBN: 978-1-906332-42-6) and quick text version (ISBN: 978-1-906332-43-3) ea $16.95

First published 2007 in the United Kingdom

McDuffie, Dwayne
 Static shock: rebirth of the cool. J. H. Williams, illustrator; Don Kramer, illustrator; Joe Benitez, illustrator). DC Comics 2009 192p. Illustration

Grades: 9 10 11 12 Adult   **741.5; Fic**
 1. African Americans; 2. Science fiction graphic novels; 3. Superhero graphic novels; 4. Graphic novels
 978-1-4012-2262-8, $19.99

In 1993, Milestone Comics published superhero comics written for African American readers, featuring African American superheroes. One of those heroes was Static, an inner city teenager imbued with the power of lightning and electricity. DC Comics has brought back Static by reprinting the two Milestone Comics miniseries. High school teen Virgil Hawkins is just trying to survive high school, getting by without joining gangs, and trying to get a date with the girl he really likes. He's also Static, with electromagnetic powers he gained on a night the city calls "The Big Bang." The problem is, he's not the only one who gained super powers of one kind or another that night, and most of those who did are using their powers to help them commit more crimes. Static wants to be a hero, but he faces incredible odds, including his own family's situation. The book includes some harsh language, at least one usage of the one-fingered salute, and violence.

McElroy, Alan
 The **Best** of Curse of the Spawn. Danny Miki, artist; Dwayne Turner, artist. Image Comics 2006 Un Illustration

Grades: 11 12 Adult   **741.5; Fic**
 1. Horror graphic novels; 2. Superhero graphic novels; 3. Supernatural graphic novels; 4. Graphic novels
 1-58240-616-2, $16.99

Meet new Spawns and delve deeply into the cast and characters of the regular series Spawn mythos as well. This book features 23 handpicked issues of this series written by the author of the Spawn movie, Allen McElroy. The character was created by Todd McFarlane, one of the founding members of Image Comics, and his series was one of those that influenced comics in the 1990s. This black and white volume is formatted similarly to the DC Showcase and Marvel Essential reprint series. Readers should expect to find violence, strong language, and some incidental nudity.

McFarlane, Todd

Spawn Collection Volume 1. Story and art, Todd McFarlane; coloring, Steve Oliff, Reuben Rude and Olyoptics. Image Comics 2005 Un Illustration

Grades: 11 12 Adult — **741.5; Fic**

1. Fantasy graphic novels; 2. Horror graphic novels; 3. Mystery graphic novels; 4. Graphic novels

1-58240-563-8, $19.95

Al Simmons, formerly a soldier, was resurrected from the ashes of his own grave. Reborn as a creature from the depths of Hell, disfigured, homeless, and alone, this new warrior known as Spawn now wanders the shadowy alleys of New York City in search of his past life. Robbed of his memories and identity, this freshly created man whose body is nothing more than scars and torn flesh becomes a protector of the weak, the poor, the downtrodden, and other victims of circumstance. While Spawn tries to piece together his confusing existence, an unwelcome mentor reveals the purpose of his abrupt return to earth. But since this guide comes from the dark side, can he be trusted to tell the truth? And just what is the truth? In this twisted world of shadow players, nothing is as it appears. The book includes graphic violence and harsh language.

McGraw, Royal

Batman: Detective. J. H. Williams, illustrator; Don Kramer, illustrator; Joe Benitez, illustrator). DC Comics 2007 144p. Illustration

Grades: 9 10 11 12 Adult — **741.5; Fic**

1. Batman (Fictional character); 2. Joker (Fictional character); 3. Superhero graphic novels; 4. Graphic novels

978-1-4012-1239-1, $14.99

He is in peak physical condition, with a high-tech arsenal at his disposal, but it is perhaps his unequaled detective skills that make Batman the most formidable opponent of the countless deadly villains of Gotham City. In this volume, the Dark Knight faces the Joker, the Riddler, the Penguin, and Poison Ivy, as well as some brand-new villains, while pushing himself to the limit to solve crimes. But can even the most powerful mind outthink unpredictable and crazy foes?

McGruder, Aaron

Birth of a nation: a comic novel. Aaron McGruder and Reginald Hudlin; illustrated by Kyle Baker. Three Rivers Press 2005 144p. Illustration

Grades: 10 11 12 Adult — **741.5; Fic**

1. Humorous graphic novels; 2. Political satire; 3. Graphic novels

978-1-4000-8316-9, $14.95

LC 2004047838

East St. Louis, Illinois ("the inner city without an outer city"), is an impoverished town, but Fred Fredericks, its idealistic mayor, rallies his fellow citizens to the polls for the presidential election, only to find hundreds of them turned away for trumped-up reasons. As a result of the mass disenfranchisement of East St. Louis, a radical right-wing junta led by a dim-witted Texas governor seizes the Oval Office. Prodded by shady black billionaire and old friend John Roberts, Fredericks devises a radical plan of protest: East St. Louis will secede from the Union. Roberts' financial dealings result in East St. Louis becoming flush with money.

Problems set in almost immediately: controversies rage over the name and national anthem of the new country (they decide on the Republic of Blackland with an anthem sung to the tune of the theme from Good Times), and local thug Roscoe becomes a warlord and turns his gang into a paramilitary force. When the U.S. military begins to move in, Fredericks is forced to decide whether his protest is worth taking all the way. The book includes some strong language, partial nudity, and sexual situations.

McKay, Sharon E.

War brothers: the graphic novel. Sharon E. McKay, Daniel Lafrance ; art by Daniel Lafrance. Annick Press 2013 176 p. Illustration

Grades: 8 9 10 11 12 — **741.5/971; Fic**

1. Kidnapping; 2. Lord's Resistance Army

1554514894; 9781554514892, $27.95

In this graphic novel, "14-year-old Jacob and his friends are just starting school at George Jones Seminary for Boys. The story tells of their subsequent kidnapping and near induction into the Lord's Resistance Army (LRA). Complete innocents at first, the boys endure near starvation, grueling conditions, and physical violence as they travel out of northern Uganda and into Sudan." (School Library Journal)

McKeever, Sean

The **loyalty** thing. Art by Takeshi Miyazawa. Spotlight 2006 Un Illustration

Grades: 4 5 6 7 8 9 — **741.5; Fic**

1. Romance graphic novels; 2. Spider-Man (Fictional character); 3. Superhero graphic novels; 4. Watson, Mary Jane (Fictional character); 5. Graphic novels

9781599610375, $21.35

LC 2006-75006

Mary Jane suffers the attention of a couple of pranksters who have targeted her for their practical jokes. Flash almost gets into trouble when he tries to "question" them with his fists, then he nearly gets into trouble with Liz when he forgets (on purpose) to register for Homecoming King. Meanwhile, Mary Jane is ready to break up with Harry, but she finally feels the magic when he kisses her. But what's going to happen when she finds Flash's notebook in her backpack?

Part of the Marvel Age: Mary Jane series. This is an edited version of an issue originally published by Marvel in 2005, with all advertisements removed.

Mary Jane Vol. 1: Circle of Friends. Art by Takeshi Miyazawa. Marvel Entertainment Group 2004 96p. Illustration

Grades: 5 6 7 8 9 10 11 12 — **741.5; Fic**

1. Romance graphic novels; 2. Spider-Man (Fictional character); 3. Superhero graphic novels; 4. Graphic novels; 4. Watson, Mary Jane (Fictional character)

0-7851-1467-X, $6.99

High school student Mary Jane Watson hangs out with her friends (including nerdy Peter Parker) and starts dating old friend Harry Osborn even as she fantasizes about the new costumed superhero in town: Spider-Man. In this series, high school romance and friendships take center stage while the superhero action happens off the page and in the sidelines. This is the first of two volumes, then a new ongoing comics series called Spider-Man Loves Mary Jane continues the story.

The **money** thing. Art by Takeshi Miyazawa. ABDO/Spotlight 2006 Un Illustration
Grades: 4 5 6 7 8 9   **741.5; Fic**
1. Romance graphic novels; 2. Spider-Man (Fictional character); 3. Superhero graphic novels; 4. Watson, Mary Jane (Fictional character); 5. Graphic novels
978-1-59961-038-2, $21.35
                    LC 2006-55059
Harry Osborn is rich and loves to spend money on his dates with Mary Jane, but she's starting to feel that she should do something to get money to pay for some things on her own, such as that really beautiful prom dress she's been looking at. She tries job after job after job, and fails at each one for one reason or another, and the long hours have taken a toll on her school work and on her social life. What's going to give?
Part of the Marvel Age: Mary Jane series. This is an edited version of an issue originally published by Marvel in 2005, with all advertisements removed.

The **real** thing. Art by Takeshi Miyazawa. ABDO/Spotlight 2006 Un Illustration
Grades: 4 5 6 7 8 9   **741.5; Fic**
1. Mary Jane Watson (Fictional character); 2. Romance graphic novels; 3. Spider-Man (Fictional character); 4. Superhero graphic novels; 5. Watson, Mary Jane (Fictional character)
978-1-59961-039-9, $21.35
                    LC 2006-75007
Pressured by best friend Liz to start dating Harry Osborn so she and Harry can double date with Liz and Flash, Mary Jane has her doubts. When she sees him treat nerdy Peter Parker with affection, she decides to try a date. However, as she rides the train on the way home, a fight between Spider-Man and Electro upends the train car and she nearly falls out. Spider-Man saves her and takes her home. Uh-oh, now she's crushing on Spider-Man, how could Harry compete?
Part of the Marvel Age: Mary Jane series. This is an edited version of an issue originally published by Marvel in 2005, with all advertisements removed.

Sentinel #1: Salvage. Art by UDON. ABDO/Spotlight 2004 Un Illustration
Grades: 4 5 6 7 8 9   **741.5; Fic**
1. Robots; 2. Science fiction graphic novels; 3. Graphic novels
978-1-59961-316-1, $21.35
                    LC 2006-50623
Juston Seyfert is a teenage loner type, living with his father and younger brother at the Seyfert Salvage yard. Juston and his friends are the school misfits and face beatings and ridicule from the jocks and popular students. One day, while fooling around in the yard, he finds a strange control chip and ends up putting it into his homemade battle 'bot, but when he turns on the remote, the toy takes off and breaks through the salvage yard fence. What Juston and his friends don't know is that there is a broken-to-pieces Sentinel out there in the woods, and the control chip belongs to it.
This book was originally published as Sentinel #1 by Marvel Comics' Marvel Age line; this book reprints the story without all the advertisements in the original comic.

Sentinel #2: Discovery. Art by UDON. ABDO/Spotlight 2004 Un Illustration
Grades: 4 5 6 7 8 9   **741.5; Fic**
1. Robots; 2. Science fiction graphic novels; 3. Graphic novels
978-1-59961-317-8, $21.35
                    LC 2006-50623
When his dad and younger brother go on an overnight trip to haul junkers to Chicago, Juston has to stay home alone, but it gives him a chance to talk with cute senior Jessie, who doesn't mind hanging out with a younger guy. Then that night, Juston finds something weird in the salvage yard's building—a half-destroyed Sentinel. Juston doesn't realize that the Sentinels were created to destroy mutants; he just knows that the one he's got is a way cool robot with artificial intelligence so he can talk with it.
This book was originally published as Sentinel #2 by Marvel Comics' Marvel Age line; this book reprints the story without all the advertisements in the original comic.

Sentinel #3: Pet project. Art by UDON. ABDO/Spotlight 2004 Un Illustration
Grades: 4 5 6 7 8 9   **741.5; Fic**
1. Robots; 2. Science fiction graphic novels; 3. Graphic novels
978-1-59961-318-5, $21.35
                    LC 2006-50623
Juston has decided to keep the giant robot he's rebuilding a secret from everyone, which causes a rift in his relationship with his younger brother, Christopher, and with his father—actually, with all his friends, too. When he does some research on the Internet, Juston discovers he's got a Sentinel. Now what's he going to do?
This book was originally published as Sentinel #3 by Marvel Comics' Marvel Age line; this book reprints the story without all the advertisements in the original comic.

Sentinel #4: Rebuilding. Art by UDON. ABDO/Spotlight 2004 Un Illustration
Grades: 4 5 6 7 8 9   **741.5; Fic**
1. Robots; 2. Science fiction graphic novels; 3. Graphic novels
978-1-59961-319-2, $21.35
                    LC 2006-50623
As Juston continues to rebuild the Sentinel, he becomes so consumed with what he's doing that he's practically abandoned all his friends. The jocks, however, haven't forgotten him. Once Juston gets the Sentinel rebuilt enough, he constructs a platform for himself to ride piggyback on the robot and they go out to the woods to test the Sentinel's weapons.
This book was originally published as Sentinel #4 by Marvel Comics' Marvel Age line; this book reprints the

story without all the advertisements in the original comic.

Sentinel #6: Primary targets. Art by UDON. ABDO/Spotlight 2004 Un Illustration
Grades: 4 5 6 7 8 9   **741.5; Fic**
1. Robots; 2. Science fiction graphic novels; 3. Graphic novels
978-1-59961-321-5, $21.35
                 LC 2006-50623
Juston has given his Sentinel a mission, and Greg and Josh are the primary targets. The robot attacks the school in broad daylight, identifying itself as an alien machine; then Juston races in and stops the robot. He's declared a hero, even by the jocks who only the day before beat him up. However, Juston isn't sure he's done the right thing. And he doesn't know it yet, but the Sentinel has now recovered enough of its memory to get back to its primary mission—to annihilate mutants.
This book was originally published as Sentinel #6 by Marvel Comics' Marvel Age line; this book reprints the story without all the advertisements in the original comic.

Sentinel Vol. 3: Past Imperfect. Art by Scott Hepburn and Joe Vriens. Marvel Entertainment 2006 Un Illustration
Grades: 8 9 10 11 12   **741.5; Fic**
1. Adventure graphic novels; 2. Robots; 3. Graphic novels
0-7851-1914-0, $7.99
After using his refurbished government weapon of mutant destruction to make himself popular, one would think Juston Seyfert would be on top of the world. Instead, he's run away from home, torn up inside by the guilt brought on by his selfish acts. Now in search of his mother, who left his family at an early age, Juston must figure out what to do with his life. And if he doesn't figure it out soon, there are a couple government types who would be more than happy to figure it out for him.

Sentinel, part 5: test mission. Art by UDON. ABDO/Spotlight 2004 Un Illustration
Grades: 4 5 6 7 8 9   **741.5; Fic**
1. Robots; 2. Science fiction graphic novels; 3. Graphic novels
978-1-59961-320-8, $21.35
                 LC 2006-50623
Jocks Josh and Greg have beat up Juston's friend Alex, and their girlfriends have spread a false rumor about Juston guaranteed to anger Jessie. Then they beat up Juston and humiliate him in front of most of the school. Juston decides it's time to get revenge, and he's going to use the Sentinel to do it.
This book was originally published as Sentinel #5 by Marvel Comics' Marvel Age line; this book reprints the story without all the advertisements in the original comic.

Spider-Man Loves Mary Jane, Vol. 2: The New Girl. Art by Takeshi Miyazawa and Valentine de Landro. Marvel Entertainment 2006 Un Illustration
Grades: 6 7 8 9 10   **741.5; Fic**
1. Romance graphic novels; 2. Spider-Man (Fictional character); 3. Superhero graphic novels; 4. Graphic novels
0-7851-2265-6, $7.99

This is the second trade paperback collection of the continuing comic book series that focuses on Mary Jane Watson and everyone in the high school rather than on Spider-Man. Mary Jane gets dumped by football player Ned Leeds and spirals into despair, almost missing the fact that her friend Peter Parker has just lost his Uncle Ben. As Liz, Flash, and Harry try to cheer her up, Mary Jane also has afterschool conversations with Spider-Man, who has his own problems trying to catch a villain named The Looter. Mary Jane discovers she really likes Peter, but new girl Gwen Stacy has latched onto him. Meanwhile, Spider-Man/Peter thinks Mary Jane likes Harry. . . .
Originally published as Spider-man Loves Mary Jane issues #6-10.

The **trust** thing. Art by Takeshi Miyazawa. ABDO/Spotlight 2006 Un Illustration
Grades: 4 5 6 7 8 9   **741.5; Fic**
1. Romance graphic novels; 2. Spider-Man (Fictional character); 3. Superhero graphic novels; 4. Watson, Mary Jane (Fictional character); 5. Graphic novels
978-1-59961-040-5, $21.35
                 LC 2006-55061
While Mary Jane is still daydreaming about Spider-Man, her best friend Liz is having major trust issues with boyfriend Flash. Certain that he's seeing someone else, she enlists Mary Jane, even Peter Parker, to find out what's going on. Meanwhile, MJ has to figure out if she wants to keep dating rich Harry Osborn.
Part of the Marvel Age: Mary Jane series. This is an edited version of an issue originally published by Marvel in 2005, with all advertisements removed.

McNamara, Jason
    Continuity. Illustrated by Tony Talbert. AiT/Planet Lar 2006 Un Illustration
Grades: 11 12 Adult   **741.5; Fic**
1. Dreams; 2. Graphic novels
978-1-932051-43-8, $12.95
Alicia's life as a typical suburban misfit takes a horrific turn as her dreams begin to alter reality. She quickly finds herself orphaned, pregnant, and on the run from a pharmaceutical police state. Now she's fighting to stay awake and restore the world she once knew. But when a lonely doctor offers Alicia redemption, will she accept? Or will her dreams tear reality apart" Harsh language and some violence make this more appropriate for older teens and adult readers.

First Moon. Illustrated by Tony Talbert. Ait/Planet Lar 2006 Un Illustration
Grades: 9 10 11 12 Adult   **741.5; Fic**
1. Horror graphic novels; 2. Monsters; 3. United States — History; 4. Graphic novels
978-1-932051-47-6, $12.95
In 1587, 110 settlers established an English colony on the island of Roanoke Virginia; shortly after, they disappeared, and their fate has remained a mystery. In present-day Berkeley, California, eleven-year-old Ben makes an appalling discovery about his parents and runs into the woods. In 1587, the colonists mistakenly attacked Indian allies, then compounded their error by attacking other Indians. In the present, Ben becomes lost in the woods,

comes upon a strange house, catches a mysterious train, then sees his parents pursuing him, in monstrous animal forms. In 1587, the obsessive desire to find and control copper mines leads some colony leaders to torture an Indian woman; their violent hostility causes her people to attack and kill most of the colonists. The survivors remain isolated in eternal night. Ben jumps from the train to find himself among the colonists who have lived there since 1587. They are shapechangers, as are his parents, and now Ben, too. But his parents chose to live in the world, and they must leave while it is still the full moon in Berkeley, or be forced to remain. McNamara includes historical information on what is known about Roanoke and provides a bibliography; his story is fiction, but most of what is portrayed about the past is based on his research.

The **Martian** confederacy, volume 1. Paige Braddock, illustrator. Girl Twirl Comics 2008 143p. Illustration
Grades: 10 11 12 Adult   **741.5; Fic**
  1. Humorous graphic novels; 2. Mars (Planet); 3. Mystery graphic novels; 4. Science fiction graphic novels; 5. Graphic novels
  978-0-9794207-1-9, $15
Mars in the year 3535 is pretty much a dump, with toxic air and stripped of its natural resources by the corporations that run the planet. Boone, Spinner (a bear) and Lou (a female android) are smalltime outlaws who take on the crooked Alcalde when he steals a professor's cure for the toxic air. As illustrator Braddock says, the story is basically The Dukes of Hazzard on Mars, with redneck good ol' boy outlaws doing the right thing against the corrupt government. However, Lou is no Daisy Duke, but a tough fighter. There is some violence, mostly fist fights, and some brief sexual situations and partial nudity.

McNeil, Carla Speed
  The **Finder** library; Volume 2. By Carla Speed McNeil. Dark Horse Books 2012 636 p. Illustration
Grades: 11 12 Adult   **741.5; 973**
  1. Science fiction graphic novels
  159582653X; 9781595826534, $24.99
"Since 1996, Finder has set the bar for science-fiction storytelling, with a lush, intricate world and compelling characters. Now, Dark Horse is proud to present four more story arcs of Carla Speed McNeil's groundbreaking series in a single, affordably priced volume!" (Publisher's note)

  The **Finder** Library; Volume one. Illustrated by the author. Dark Horse 2011 630 p. Illustration
Grades: 11 12 Adult   **741.5; 973**
  1. Science fiction graphic novels
  1595826521; 9781595826527, $24.99
This science fiction graphic novel anthology, by Carla Speed McNeil, collects and reprints several of the author's Eisner Award-winning graphic novels within the "Finder" series. This volume includes the novels "Sin-Eater," "Talisman," and "King of the Cats," along with commentary and footnotes from the author. (Publisher's note)

McNiven, Steve
  Civil War. Writer, Mark Millar; penciler, Steve McNiven. Marvel Entertainment 2007 Un Illustration
Grades: 9 10 11 12 Adult   **741.5; Fic**

  1. Captain America (Fictional character); 2. Iron Man (Fictional character); 3. Superhero graphic novels; 4. Graphic novels
  0-7851-2179-X, $24.99
The landscape of the Marvel Universe is changing, and it's time to choose: Whose side are you on? A conflict has been brewing for more than a year, and a single misstep by a costumed superhero costs thousands of lives and ignites the fuse of a superhero civil war. Teams, friendships, and families begin to fall apart as they must choose. What is the choice? The government wants to register all super powered individuals. Iron Man agrees and takes the government's side. Captain America sees registration as a step down the slippery slope towards the abolishment of civil rights for superheroes.

Meathaus Vol. 8: Headgames.
  Alternative Comics 2006 Un Illustration
Grades: 11 12 Adult   **741.5; Fic**
  1. Short stories; 2. Graphic novels
  1-891867-92-X, $14.95
This eighth volume of the Meathaus anthology series features works by a variety of Meathaus favorites, including James Jean, Becky Cloonan, Tomer Hanuka, Brandon Graham, Jim Campaell, Tom Herpich, Dash Shaw, Scott Morse, Jim Mahfood, Jim Rugg, Farel Dalrymple, and more. Each story is just a few pages long, many include harsh language and nudity, some have violence.

Mechner, Jordan
  Solomon's thieves. Artwork by LeUyen Pham & Alex Puvilland. First Second 2010 139p. Illustration
Grades: 6 7 8 9 10   **741.5; Fic**
  1. France — History — 0-1328; 2. Knights and knighthood; 3. Middle Ages; 4. Graphic novels
  978-1-59643-391-5, $12.99; 1-59643-391-4
                    LC 2010-282641
Life as a Templar Knight returning from the Crusades is dull" bread, beans, and lots and lots of walking. But after Martin stumbles upon his lost love (now married—to someone else), things begin to get more interesting very quickly. There's a vast conspiracy afoot to destroy the Templar Order and steal their treasure. Soon, Martin finds himself one of the only Templars out of prison—and out for revenge!
"Pham and Puvilland . . . are again in top form, balancing grainy, hatched textures and clean spaces to lend a weighty historical feel as a vibrant sense of kineticism brings the action sequences to life." Booklist
Includes bibliographical references

Medley, Linda
  ★ **Castle** waiting. Fantagraphics 2006 456p. Illustration
Grades: 5 6 7 8 9 10 11 12   **741.5; Fic**
  1. Fairy tales; 2. Fantasy graphic novels; 3. Graphic novels
  1-56097-747-7, $29.95
All of Medley's previously self-published comics are collected here in one volume for the first time. The titular castle was the home of Sleeping Beauty, whose story is retold from the viewpoint of the flibbertigibbet ladies in waiting. After the flighty princess awakens with the kiss of a

handsome but not too bright prince, the castle becomes a sanctuary for various misfits. Readers will find references to many fairy tales, folk tales, and nursery rhymes in Medley's book, and her clean, clear black-and-white art reflects the works of classic illustrators such as Arthur Rackham.

Courtesy of Fantagraphics

Castle waiting; Volume II. By Linda Medley; [graphic design by Adam Grano; edited by Kim Thompson]. Fantagraphics Books 2013 464 p. Color; Illustration

Grades: 5 6 7 8 9 10 11 12 **741.5/973; 741.5**
1. Fairy tales
1606996339; 9781606996331, $29.99
LC 2014381744

In this graphic novel, by Linda Medley, "Lady Jain settles into her new life. . . . Unexpected visitors result in the discovery and exploration of a secret passageway, not to mention an epic bowling tournament. A quest for ladies' underpants, the identity of her baby son Pindar's father, the education of Simon, Rackham and Chess arguing about the "manly arts," and an escape-prone goat are just a few of the elements in this . . . new volume." (Publisher's note)

Meister, Todd
Little Scrowlie Volume One: The Call of Cuthbert. Jennifer Feinberg, illustrator. SLG Publishing 2004 Un Illustration

Grades: 9 10 11 12 Adult **741.5; Fic**
1. Fantasy graphic novels; 2. Horror graphic novels; 3. Graphic novels
1-59362-000-4, $10.95

A particularly scrowlie cat and her friends - human, feline, and ghostly - get tangled in the tentacles of an aging fashionista's nefarious clothing conspiracy. Can over privileged goth chick Elizabeth, would-be wizard James, and a couple of jumpy housecats foil this foul plan? Or will the Lovecraftian beastie known only as "Cuthbert" overcome all of them? The book includes some violence and horror scenes, but no bad language.

Melbourne, Drew
ArchEnemies, Volume 1: Sinners & Saints. Pencils, Yvel Guichet; inks, Joe Rubenstein. Dark Horse Comics 2007 Un Illustration

Grades: 10 11 12 Adult **741.5; Fic**
1. Humorous graphic novels; 2. Superhero graphic novels; 3. Graphic novels
978-1-59307-699-3, $12.95

Vince and Ethan are practically strangers, but they've ended up as roommates in order to share an affordable apartment. Ethan is a total slob, while the intense Vince needs neatness; they're the proverbial odd couple and they really, really hate each other. What neither of them realizes is

that they're also super powered archenemies: Vince is the Underlord (a villain) while Ethan is Star Fighter (a hero). Vince comes from a family of super villains, and his brother Anton has just murdered their father. When the roommates actually reconcile a bit and Ethan travels with Vince to the funeral, Anton and his hugely menacing minion try to kill all the people at the funeral, and Ethan becomes Star Fighter to stop the slaughter. Maybe the two don't hate each other quite as much as they thought. . . .

Originally published as ArchEnemies issues #1-4.

Melchior-Durand, Stéphane
The **golden** compass; volume 1: the graphic novel.. Adapted and illustrated by Stéphane Melchior-Durand and Clément Oubrerie; coloring by Clément Oubrerie with Philippe Bruno. Alfred A. Knopf 2015 80 p. Color; Illustration

Grades: 6 7 8 9 10 **741.5; 741.5/973**
1. Fantasy; 2. Fantasy graphic novels; 3. Pullman, Philip, 1946- Golden compass — Adaptations; 4. Graphic novels
9780553523713, $18.99; 9780553523720; 9780553523867
LC 2015005828

In this graphic novel adaptation of the young adult fantasy by Philip Pullman, adapted and illustrated by St?phane Melchior-Durand and Cl?ment Oubrerie, "Lyra Belacqua is content to run wild among the scholars of Jordan College, with her daemon familiar always by her side. But the arrival of her fearsome uncle, Lord Asriel, draws her to the heart of a terrible struggleùa struggle born of Gobblers and stolen children, and a mysterious substance known as Dust." (Publisher's note)

Originally published by Gallimard Jeunesse, Paris, France, in 2014—Copyright page.

Meltzer, Brad
Green Arrow: The Archer's Quest. DC Comics 2003 176p. Illustration

Grades: 9 10 11 12 Adult **741.5; Fic**
1. Adventure graphic novels; 2. Green Arrow (Fictional character); 3. Superhero graphic novels; 4. Graphic novels
1-4012-0044-3, $14.95

Oliver Queen, the Green Arrow, has come back from the dead; certain items were supposed to have been destroyed once he was dead, but it never happened. Now, he and his former sidekick now known as Arsenal travel around, seeking those legendary artifacts in order to protect those people Oliver loves. The book includes some violence.

★ **Identity** Crisis. Rags Morales, penciller; Michael Bair, inker. DC Comics 2005 Un Illustration

Grades: 9 10 11 12 Adult **741.5; Fic**
1. Green Arrow (Fictional character)
978-1-4012-0688-8, $24.99; 978-1-4012-0458-7 (pa)

It's been said that super-heroes keep secret identities to protect their loved ones. Elongated Man (Ralph Dibny) is one of the few without a confidential alter ego. So when his wife, Sue, is murdered in her own home, the tragedy hits the crime fighting community like a sledgehammer. As the fraternity of champions begins scouring the country for clues and suspects, Green Arrow, Hawkman, Black Canary, the Atom, and Zatanna stay behind, with a powerful secret to protect. Things get worse when other superheroes' family members receive threatening notes. And when the secret is discovered, the ramifications will forever change the world of super-powered heroes and villains.

Justice League of America: The Tornado's Path. DC Comics 2007 228p. Illustration
Grades: 9 10 11 12 Adult   **741.5; Fic**
    1. Batman (Fictional character); 2. Justice League of America (Fictional characters); 3. Superhero graphic novels; 4. Superman (Fictional character); 5. Wonder Woman (Fictional character); 6. Graphic novels
978-1-4012-1349-7, $24.99

After traumatic events shattered the Justice League, trust was in short supply, but after it's all over, Superman, Batman, and Wonder Woman meet to choose who will become members of the new Justice League; but while they meet in secret, dark forces move against their friends and allies. A mysterious organization has helped the android Justice Leaguer known as Red Tornado to transfer his consciousness into the human body he's always wanted. But their motives may not have Red Tornado's best interests in mind. Instead, this is only the first step in a sinister conspiracy of super villains. The Justice League will have to rise again to save Red Tornado, and the world. But who will answer the call? The violence and fighting result in bloodshed.

Meyer, Scott
    Help is on the way: a collection of basic instructions. Dark Horse Books 2008 120p. Illustration
Grades: 10 11 12 Adult   **741.5; Fic**
    1. Humorous graphic novels; 2. Graphic novels
978-1-59307-995-6, $9.95

This book collects Meyer's web comic called Basic Instructions. Using a four-panel format, he covers a variety of situations with wry humor, from How to Win an Argument to How to Pick a Password to How to Disguise a Yawn, and many more. The black and white art is fairly static, with a cast of characters Meyer uses and reuses. The humor is in the text, with a lot of fast-looking dialog. Many of the situations deal with marriage and with the workplace, while a number of them will resonate with those in the "nerd culture;" language is only mildly harsh (calling someone an "ass").

Michelinie, David
    Superman Adventures Vol. 3: Last Son of Krypton. Written by Mark Millar, David Michelinie ; illustrated by Aluir Amancio, Ron Boyd, Terry Austin, Mike Manley, Neil Vokes. DC Comics 2006 112p. Illustration
Grades: 4 5 6 7 8 9   **741.5; Fic**
    1. Superhero graphic novels; 2. Superman (Fictional character); 3. Graphic novels
978-1-4012-1037-3, $6.99

Superman confronts his own past as he encounters survivors from Krypton, including his parents, Jor-El and Lara. Plus, someone wants to expose Clark's secret to Lex Luthor and the world. Will an encounter with Dr. Fate mean the end of Superman—"

Midorikawa, Shin
    Aventura vol. 1. Del Rey Manga 2007 188p. Illustration
Grades: 8 9 10 11 12   **741.5; Fic**
    1. Adventure graphic novels; 2. Fantasy graphic novels; 3. Magic; 4. Manga; 5. Graphic novels
978-0-345-49744-4, $10.95

Since ancient days, the Gaius School of Witchcraft and Wizardry has trained the fiercest swordsmen and the most powerful wizards. Now one boy could become the greatest of them all. If he studies hard. If he is true to his friends. If he believes. And if he survives. The book includes some mild violence.

The Mighty Crusaders: Origin of a Super-Team
    Archie Comics 2003 96p. Illustration
Grades: 3 4 5 6 7 8 9 10 11 12 Adult   **741.5; Fic**
    1. Humorous graphic novels; 2. Superhero graphic novels; 3. Graphic novels
1-879794-14-4, $12.95

It's a pop-art explosion as some of the wildest heroes in the history of comic books unite to form one of the most beloved super-teams of the Sixties: The Shield, The Black Hood, The Comet, The Fly, and Fly Girl. Relive the excitement as this intrepid team of heroes meet, fight super-villains as well as each other, come up with a name for their team and even recruit new members. It's all here in this colorful collection reprinting classic stories originally appearing in Fly-Man #31, #32 and #33 as well as Mighty Crusaders #1. It features restoration of all stories, and faithful recoloring.

Mignola, Mike
    B.P.R.D. Volume 1: Hollow Earth & Other Stories, Rev. ed.. Dark Horse Comics 2004 Un Illustration
Grades: 10 11 12 Adult   **741.5; Fic**
    1. Fantasy graphic novels; 2. Hellboy (Fictional character); 3. Horror graphic novels; 4. Mystery graphic novels
1-59307-280-5, $17.95

This volume collects stories recounting the adventures of the Bureau for Paranormal Research and Defense, featuring Hellboy supporting characters Abe Sapien, Liz Sherman, and others. Beneath the treacherous South Seas and under a ravaged monastery, Abe Sapien and the other weird agents of the BPRD uncover homesick bones, mad science, and the junkyard at the center of the earth. The book includes violence and some strong language.

    B.P.R.D. Volume 4: The Dead. Story by Mike Mignola and John Arcudi; art by Guy Davis; colors by Dave Stewart. Dark Horse Comics 2005 Un Illustration
Grades: 10 11 12 Adult   **741.5; Fic**
    1. Adventure graphic novels; 2. Fantasy graphic novels; 3. Horror graphic novels; 4. Graphic novels
1-59307-380-1, $17.95

The Bureau for Paranormal Research and Defense and their new team leader Captain Benjamin Daimio, a former corpse himself, moves into their new headquarters only to unearth a gigantic long-buried secret involving United States government covert experiments and Nazi scientists. Abe Sapien, still reeling from the revelation of his former life as a Victorian scientist, meets his long-dead wife in their crumbling home by the sea. This tale of the walking dead, madness, the Spear of Destiny, and a monstrous gateway to heaven includes some strong language and some violence.

B.P.R.D.: The Black Flame. Story by Mike Mignola and John Arcudi; art by Guy Davis; colors by Dave Stewart; letters by Clem Robins. Dark Horse Comics 2006 Un Illustration
Grades: 10 11 12 Adult   **741.5; Fic**
  1. Fantasy graphic novels; 2. Horror graphic novels
  978-1-59307-550-7, $17.95
  The Bureau for Paranormal Research and Defense faces its worst tragedy ever as the war against the plague of frogs reaches a devastating new level. Heralded by a bizarre villain from the B.P.R.D.'s past, an ancient monster-god marches across the American heartland portending an end to the reign of men, and leaving a permanent mark on the Bureau. The book includes some horror violence.

B.P.R.D.: killing ground. Story by Mike Mignola and John Arcudi; art by Guy Davis. Dark Horse Comics 2008 Un Illustration
Grades: 10 11 12 Adult   **741.5; Fic**
  1. Horror graphic novels; 2. Mystery graphic novels; 3. Supernatural graphic novels; 4. Graphic novels
  978-1-59307-956-7, $17.95
  The secret of Captain Daimio's resurrection in Bolivia comes back to haunt the B.P.R.D. as Liz struggles to free herself from her nightmares and Johann abandons his responsibilities in favor of pleasures of the flesh in his new, superhuman body. The book includes violence and incidental partial nudity. A wendigo-type monster has escaped, Kate Corrigan is in charge of chasing it down, and Daimio has a deep connection.

B.P.R.D.: Plague of Frogs. Mike Mignola, Guy Davis, et al. Dark Horse Comics 2005 Un Illustration
Grades: 10 11 12 Adult   **741.5; Fic**
  1. Hellboy (Fictional character); 2. Horror graphic novels; 3. Supernatural graphic novels; 4. Graphic novels
  1-59307-288-0, $17.95
  Introduced in the first Hellboy book, Abe Sapien has remained one of the most intriguing mysteries of Mignola's work. The story of Abe's origins unfolds as the Bureau for Paranormal Research and Defense try to stop the monstrous frog men from the first Hellboy graphic novel, Seed of Destruction. The plague begins its spread across America, and the BPRD has its work cut out for it. There's some violence and some strong language in the book.

B.P.R.D.: The Universal Machine. Written by Mike Mignola and John Acudi; Art by Guy Davis et al; Color by Dave Stewart. Dark Horse Comics 2007 Un Illustration
Grades: 10 11 12 Adult   **741.5; Fic**
  1. Fantasy graphic novels; 2. Hellboy (Fictional character); 3. Horror graphic novels
  978-1-59307-710-5, $17.95
  After the catastrophic encounter with the monster-god Katha-Hem, Dr. Kate Corrigan travels to rural France in search of an ancient text that might undo the death of Roger. Back at the Bureau for Paranormal Research and Defense, Captain Daimio tells the story of his own death, Johann Kraus confesses a bizarre love triangle arising from one of

his s?ances, Abe recalls a mission with Hellboy during his early days at the B.P.R.D., and Liz reveals a weird tale of the family members she killed while discovering her firestarter powers. There's no nudity, but lots of monsters and monster fighting.

Hellboy Volume 1: Seed of Destruction 2nd ed.. By Mike Mignola; script by John Byrne; miniseries colors by Mark Chiarello. Dark Horse Comics 2003 Un Illustration
Grades: 9 10 11 12 Adult   **741.5; Fic**
  1. Fantasy graphic novels; 2. Hellboy (Fictional character); 3. Horror graphic novels; 4. Mystery graphic novels; 5. Graphic novels
  9781593070946; 1-59307-094-2, $17.95
  When strangeness threatens to engulf the world, a strange man will come to save it. Sent to investigate a mystery with supernatural overtones, the good-guy big red demon, Hellboy, discovers the secrets of his own origins, and his link to the Nazi occultists who promised Hitler a final solution in the form of a demonic avatar. The book includes some violence and horror.
  Other Hellboy volumes are: 2: Wake the Devil; 3: The Chained Coffin and Others; 4: The Right Hand of Doom; 5: Conqueror Worm; 6: Strange Places; 7: The Troll Witch and Others; 8: Darkness Calls; 9: The Wild Hunt; 10: The Crooked Man and Others; 11: The Bride of Hell and Others; 12: The Storm and the Fury; 13: Hellboy in Mexico

Hellboy Volume 2: Wake the Devil, 2nd ed.. By Mike Mignola; colored by James Sinclair; lettered by Pat Brosseau. Dark Horse Comics 2003 Un Illustration
Grades: 9 10 11 12 Adult   **741.5; Fic**
  1. Fantasy graphic novels; 2. Hellboy (Fictional character); 3. Horror graphic novels; 4. Mystery graphic novels; 5. Graphic novels
  1-59307-095-0, $17.95
  A murder in a New York wax museum and a missing corpse lead Hellboy into ancient Romanian castles on the trail of a sleeping legend: the original nobleman vampire. Nazi scientists prepare for the return of their occult master and the end of the world, and Hellboy confronts his purpose on earth. The book includes some violence, strong language and some nonsexual partial nudity.

Hellboy Volume 3: The Chained Coffin and Others 2nd ed.. By Mike Mignola; colored by James Sinclair, Matthew Hollingsworth, & Dave Stewart. Dark Horse Comics 2004 Un Illustration
Grades: 9 10 11 12 Adult   **741.5; Fic**
  1. Fantasy graphic novels; 2. Hellboy (Fictional character); 3. Horror graphic novels; 4. Mystery graphic novels; 5. Graphic novels
  1-59307-091-8, $17.95
  This volume collects short stories Mignola wrote for various other publications; it includes The Corpse," which some critics think is the best Hellboy story he has written. Mignola provides notes before each story. The book includes some violence, strong language, and nonsexual partial nudity.

Hellboy Volume 4: The Right Hand of Doom 2nd ed.. By Mike Mignola; colored by Dave Stewart; lettered by Pat

Brosseau; edited by Scott Allie. Dark Horse Comics 2004
Un Illustration
Grades: 9 10 11 12 Adult   741.5; Fic
    1. Fantasy graphic novels; 2. Hellboy (Fictional
character); 3. Horror graphic novels; 4. Mystery graphic
novels; 5. Graphic novels
1-59307-093-4, $17.95
    This volume collects more Hellboy short stories
Mignola wrote for various other publications; it includes
Pancakes," a cute two-page story set when he was a young
demon. The Right Hand of Doom" is a long story that takes
up most of the volume. The book includes some violence and
strong language.

    Hellboy Volume 5: Conqueror Worm 2nd ed.. By Mike
Mignola; colored by Dave Stewart; lettered by Pat Brosseau;
introduction by Guillermo del Toro; edited by Scott Allie.
Dark Horse Comics 2004 Un Illustration
Grades: 9 10 11 12 Adult   741.5; Fic
    1. Fantasy graphic novels; 2. Hellboy (Fictional
character); 3. Horror graphic novels; 4. Mystery graphic
novels; 5. Graphic novels
1-59307-092-6, $17.95
2002 Eisner Award for Best Limited Series.
    At the end of World War II, American
costumed-adventurer Lobster Johnson led an Allied attack
on Hitler's space program, but not before the Nazis were
able to launch the first man into space. Now, after sixty
years, Hellboy is partnered with an artifical man - a
Frankenstein's monster implanted by Bureau scientists with
a bomb - to travel to the ruined castle in Norway to intercept
the returning capsule, and its single passenger. . .the
conqueror worm. The book includes violence, strong
language, and partial nudity.

    Hellboy Volume 6: Strange Places. Colored by Dave
Stewart; lettered by Clem Robins. Dark Horse Comics 2006
Un Illustration
Grades: 9 10 11 12 Adult   741.5; Fic
    1. Fantasy graphic novels; 2. Hellboy (Fictional
character); 3. Horror graphic novels; 4. Mystery graphic
novels; 5. Graphic novels
978-1-59307-475-3, $17.95
    After leaving the Bureau for Paranormal Research and
Defense, Hellboy's travels take him briefly to Africa, then
for a two-year stint at the bottom of the ocean. An ancient
witch doctor, a giant fish woman and keeper of the secret
history of the universe force Hellboy to either accept his role
in the coming apocalypse, or have that role stolen from him.
Weird undersea creatures and talking lions populate this
turning-point adventure, which reveals secrets buried since
Hellboy's very creation. The book includes some violence
and strong language.

    Hellboy volume 8: Darkness calls. Story by Mike
Mignola; art by Duncan Fegredo; colored by Dave Stewart.
Dark Horse Comics 2008 Un Illustration
Grades: 10 11 12 Adult   741.5; Fic
    1. Fantasy graphic novels; 2. Hellboy (Fictional
character); 3. Horror graphic novels; 4. Graphic novels
978-1-59307-896-6, $19.95
    Hellboy has finally returned from his adventures at sea,
but no sooner has he settled on land than a conclave of
witches drags him from his respite and into the heart of

Russian folklore, where he becomes the quarry of the
powerful and bloodthirsty witch Baba Yaga. Bent on
revenge for the eye she had lost to Hellboy, Baba Yaga has
enlisted the aid of Koshchei, a deathless warrior who will
stop at nothing to destroy Hellboy. Meanwhile, in England,
the Gruagach and his minions seek to regain the powers they
once had over the world. The book includes brief partial
nudity and a lot of bloodshed.

    Jenny Finn: doom messiah. Created and written by
Mike Mignola and Troy Nixey. Boom! Studios 2008 Un
Illustration
Grades: 11 12 Adult   741.5; Fic
    1. Fantasy graphic novels; 2. Horror graphic novels; 3.
Graphic novels
978-1-934506-14-1, $14.99
    In Victorian London, wherever the mysterious Jenny
Finn goes, death and destruction follow in her wake as a
plague sweeps through the city, affecting men. Meanwhile,
someone is murdering and eviscerating whores.
Goodhearted butcher Joe thinks Jenny Finn is an innocent
girl who doesn't belong in the bad part of the city, and in his
efforts to help her, he becomes embroiled in a battle between
good and evil, with secret societies, an invasion of
monstrous sea creatures, and a murderous artist. The book
includes nudity, scenes in a whorehouse, harsh language,
and violence.

    Zombie World: Champion of the Worms. Pat McEown,
illustrator. Dark Horse Comics 2005 80p. Illustration
Grades: 9 10 11 12 Adult   741.5; Fic
    1. Horror graphic novels; 2. Graphic novels
1-59307-407-7, $8.95
    A small-town museum is plagued by odd disturbances
and missing persons - all part of the arcane work of their
newest arrival, Azzul Gotha, a 42,000-year-old Hyperborean
mummy bent upon sacrificing mankind to his ancient worm
gods. There's some brief nudity of ghosts and monsters, and
horror violence.

Mihara, Mitsukazu
    Beautiful People. Tokyopop 2006 190p. Illustration
Grades: 10 11 12 Adult   741.5; Fic
    1. Josei manga; 2. Manga; 3. Graphic novels
1-59816-243-8, $9.99
    In this anthology, a young boy tries to grant the ultimate
wish to a magical snow princess; two strangers struggle to
survive an apocalyptic world—and each other; the lonely
victim of a bully takes solace in the world of the Internet; and
a woman who has had extensive cosmetic surgery learns the
frightening truth about what real beauty is; a vampire takes
in an abandoned child with plans to consume her, but
decades slip by as he enjoys her innocent affection. The
book includes some strong language, violence, nudity, and
sexual situations.

    Haunted House. Tokyopop 2006 198p. Illustration
Grades: 10 11 12   741.5; Fic
    1. Horror graphic novels; 2. Humorous graphic novels; 3.
Manga; 4. Graphic novels
1-59816-321-3, $9.99
    Meet Sabato Obiga, a hapless young teen trying to find
himself in the world, which is made all but impossible by his

frighteningly flamboyant family (sometimes they look very much like the Addams Family). Scaring away every girl he brings home, Sabato's family seems to revel in his misery—but could there be more to their torment than meets the eye? The book includes some strong language.

Mikimoto, Haruhiko
   Mobile Suit Gundam Ecole du Ciel Vol. 1. Tokyopop 2005 Un Illustration
Grades: 8 9 10 11 12 Adult   741.5; Fic
   1. Mecha manga; 2. Science fiction graphic novels; 3. Graphic novels
   1-59532-851-3, $9.99
   Ecole du Ciel is where aspiring pilots train to become Top Gundam. The year is 0085 of the Universal Century. Daughter of a brilliant professor, Asuna is a below-average student at Ecole du Ciel. But with the world spiraling toward war, Asuna is headed for a crash course in danger, battle, and most of all, love. This story is set in the original Gundam universe, and is full of mecha (giant battle robot) battles.

Milky, D. J.
   Princess Ai Volume 1. Created by Courtney Love & D.J. Milky ; illustrated by Misaho Kujiradou ; written by Misaho Kujiradou and D.J. Milky. Tokyopop 2004 192p. Illustration
Grades: 7 8 9 10 11 12   741.5; Fic
   1. Fantasy graphic novels; 2. Manga; 3. Romance graphic novels; 4. Shojo manga; 5. Graphic novels
   1-59182-669-1, $9.99
   Ai finds herself lost, alone and penniless on the cold, hard streets of Tokyo. With flickers of memory, she must piece together clues about who she is, how she ended up on Earth and the secret of the ornate heart-shaped box she carries with her. Sparks fly when Kent, a complicated young college student, offers his help...and possibly more. But time is running out, as the clashing forces of love and chaos close in around her... This is the first of a three-volume series created by rocker Courtney Love and co-written and illustrated by Misaho Kujiradou.

Millar, Mark
   Chosen. Art, Peter Gross; colors, Jeanne McGee. Dark Horse Comics 2005 Un Illustration
Grades: 10 11 12 Adult   741.5; Fic
   1. Supernatural graphic novels; 2. Graphic novels
   1-59307-213-9, $17.95
   Imagine you're twelve years old and suddenly discover that you are the returned Jesus Christ. You can turn water into wine, make the crippled walk and perhaps even raise the dead. What do you and your family do, and how does it affect you knowing that you're destined to grow up and take part in a conflict that people have been waiting almost two thousand years for" The book contains strong language, including the f-bomb.

   Superman Adventures Vol. 4: The Man of Steel. Written by Mark Millar, Evan Dorkin and Sarah Dyer ; illustrated by Aluir Amancio, Terry Austin, Bret Blevins. DC Comics 2006 112p. Illustration
Grades: 4 5 6 7 8 9   741.5; Fic

   1. Superhero graphic novels; 2. Superman (Fictional character); 3. Graphic novels
   978-1-4012-1038-0, $6.99
   The battle never ends for the Man of Steel - especially when his greatest enemies will stop at nothing in order to destroy him. Superman confronts Toyman, Multi-Face, Parasite, the mischievous Mr. Mxyzptlk, and Brainiac.

   Superman: Red Son. Mark Millar, Dave Johnson, Kilian Plunkett, Andrew Robinson, Walden Wong. DC Comics 2014 168 p. Color; Illustration
Grades: 11 12 Adult   741.5; 741.5/973
   1. Superman (Fictional character)
   1401247113; 9781401247119, $17.99
                                 LC 2013049659
   Eisner Nominee: Best Limited Series (2004)
   This comic book, by Mark Millar, illustrated by Dave Johnson, Kilian Plunkett, Andrew Robinson, and Walden Wong, "is a vivid tale of Cold War paranoia, that reveals how the ship carrying the infant who would later be known as Superman lands in the midst of the 1950s Soviet Union. Raised on a collective, the infant grows up and becomes a symbol to the Soviet people, and the world changes drastically from what we know." (Publisher's note)
   Red Son

   Wanted. Pencils and inks by J.G. Jones. Top Cow 2008 208p. Illustration
Grades: 11 12 Adult   741.5; Fic
   1. Mystery graphic novels; 2. Superhero graphic novels; 3. Graphic novels
   978-1-58240-497-4, $19.99
   Wesley Gibson is a typical office worker, a nobody with a boring life . . . until he discovers that he is the son of "The Killer," a member of an underground fraternity of supervillains who've been running the world since 1986. After his father is killed, Wesley becomes the new Killer and he joins the villains while trying to unravel the mystery of his father's murder. This book is the basis for the motion picture starring Jamie MacElvoy and Angelina Jolie that was released during the summer of 2008. The book includes lots of graphic violence, very harsh language (with lots of f-bombs), and nudity.

Miller, Connie Colwell
   Elizabeth Cady Stanton: Women's Rights Pioneer. Illustrated by Cynthia Martin. Capstone Press 2006 32p. Illustration
Grades: 3 4 5 6 7 8 9   741.5; 305.42; 92
   1. Stanton, Elizabeth Cady, 1815-1902; 2. Women — Suffrage — United States — History; 3. Graphic novels
   0-7368-4971-8, $25.26
                                 LC 2005009211
   This book uses the comic book format to describe the life and career of women's suffragist Elizabeth Cady Stanton. It includes additional information, a glossary, a list of books for further reading, and more.
   Part of the Graphic Library, Graphic Biographies series.

Miller, Frank
   300. Dark Horse Comics 1999 88p. Illustration
Grades: 10 11 12 Adult   741.5; Fic
   1. Thermopylae, Battle of, 480 BC; 2. Graphic novels

978-1-56971-402-7, $30

Miller paints a highly fictionalized, stylized account of the Battle of Thermopylae, where the Spartan King Leonidas and a relatively small band of Spartans held off the massive army of Emperor Xerxes of Persia long enough for Athens to gather its troops for the final showdown. The Spartans all died, but their sacrifice saved Greece in the end. Watercolor paintings by artist Varley use an earthy palette to depict the stark landscape and violent battles. This book is the basis for the hit motion picture released in March 2007.

★ **Batman,** the Dark Knight returns. Frank Miller; with Klaus Janson and Lynn Varley. DC Comics 2013 198 p.
Grades: 11 12 Adult   **741.5; 741.5/973**
    1. Batman (Fictional character); 2. Robin (Fictional character); 3. Superheroes
1563893428; 9781563893421, $19.99
                                    LC 2013008716
This graphic novel, by Frank Miller, "completely reinvents the legend of Batman. . . . The Dark Knight returns in a blaze of fury, taking on a whole new generation of criminals and matching their level of violence. He is soon joined by a new Robin—a girl named Carrie Kelley, who proves to be just as invaluable as her predecessors. But can Batman and Robin deal with the threat posed by their deadliest enemies, after years of incarceration have made them into perfect psychopaths? (Publisher's note)
Originally published in single magazine form as Batman, the Dark Knight returns 1-4.

Batman: the Dark Knight strikes again. [by] Frank Miller, Lynn Varley, Todd Klein, Batman created by Bob Kane. DC Comics 2002 247p. Illustration
Grades: 10 11 12 Adult   741.5; Fic
    1. Batman (Comic strip); 2. Batman (Fictional character); 3. Superhero graphic novels; 4. Graphic novels
1-56389-844-6; 1-56389-929-9 (pa), $19.99
                                    LC 2003-544916
"Batman leads the opposition in a dystopian near-future when security concerns have spurred a repressive crackdown. Other costumed heroes side with either the government or Batman. . . . The book's authoritarian society resonates with the post-9/11 environment, though Miller's cheekiness dispels notions that this is serious commentary." Booklist
Originally published in single magazine form as Batman: the Dark Knight strikes again 1-3
    Based on Batman comic strip
    Sequel to Batman: the Dark Knight returns (1986)

Batman: Year One. DC Comics 2005 168p. Illustration
Grades: 8 9 10 11 12 Adult   **741.5; Fic**
    1. Batman (Fictional character); 2. Catwoman (Fictional character); 3. Superhero graphic novels; 4. Graphic novels
978-1-4012-0752-6, $14.99
In the late-1980s, after publishing Miller's Batman: The Dark Knight Returns, DC realized they should remain faithful to the original roots of Batman. Miller then wrote this book, which reinvents the very early years of Batman as a superhero. In this book, Jim Gordon arrives in Gotham City to work in the police department and discovers the high level of corruption there; Batman encounters Selina, who becomes Catwoman, for the first time; and he develops some

of the weapons he uses to fight crime. This new edition includes preliminary sketches and other extras.

★ **Sin** City Vol. 1: The Hard Goodbye. Dark Horse Comics 2005 208p. Illustration
Grades: 11 12 Adult   **741.5; Fic**
    1. Mystery graphic novels; 2. Graphic novels
1-59307-293-7, $17
Sin City is the place - tough as leather and dry as tinder. Love is the fuel, and Marv has the match ... not to mention a condition." He's gunning after Goldie's killer, so it's time to watch this town burn. Frank Miller is one of modern comic's first talents to publish a comic book that he created, crafted, and owned. That book is Sin City, which grew from the wellspring of Miller's passionate desire to create a comic book with two distinct qualities - it wouldn't be a superhero comic, and it had to be a crime comic. Enter Marv and Goldie. And a psychotic killer. And a crime-drenched town. And a corrupted diocese. The stark black and white art includes nudity and graphic violence, along with lots of harsh language.

Sin City Vol. 2: A Dame to Kill For. Dark Horse Comics 2005 208p. Illustration
Grades: 11 12 Adult   **741.5; Fic**
    1. Mystery graphic novels; 2. Graphic novels
1-59307-294-5, $17
It's one of those hot nights, dry and windless. The kind that makes people do sweaty, secret things. Dwight's thinking of all the ways he's screwed up and what he'd give for one clear chance to wipe the slate clean, to dig his way out of the numb gray hell that is his life. And he'd give anything. Just to cut loose. Just to feel the fire. One more time. And then Ava calls. Dwight thinks it's love, but Ava just needs him to kill her rich husband and she betrays him. No one does that to Dwight and gets away with it. This book includes lots of harsh language, graphic violence, nudity, and sexual situations.

Miller, John Jackson
Star Wars: Knights of the Old Republic Volume One: Commencement. Script, John Jackson Miller ; art, Brian Ching and Travel Foreman, ; colors, Michael Atiyeh ; lettering, Michael Heisler ; cover art, Travis Charest. Dark Horse Comics 2006 Un Illustration
Grades: 8 9 10 11 12 Adult   **741.5; Fic**
    1. Adventure graphic novels; 2. Science fiction graphic novels; 3. Graphic novels
978-1-59307-640-5, $18.95
Thousands of years before Luke Skywalker would destroy the Death Star in that fateful battle above Yavin 4, one lone Padawan would become a fugitive hunted by his own Masters, charged with murdering every one of his fellow Jedi-in-training. From criminals hiding out in the treacherous under-city of the planet Taris, to a burly, mysterious droid recovered from the desolate landscape of a cratered moon, Padawan Zayne Carrick will find unexpected allies in his desperate race to clear his name before the unmerciful authorities enact swift retribution upon him.

Miller, Mike S.

Lullaby: Wisdom seeker. [by] Ben Avery, Mike S. Miller, and Hector Sevilla. Alias Enterprises 2005 96p. Illustration

Grades: 4 5 6 7 8 9   741.5; Fic

1. Fantasy graphic novels; 2. Graphic novels

1-933428-62-7, $9.99

In this book, Alice never left Wonderland, she grew up to become the Queen's warrior. When dark magic threatens the world, Alice, haunted by vague memories of another life, sets out to discover the cause, and on the way she encounters the Pied Piper, Little Red Riding Hood (who is a werewolf), Jim Hawkins (from Treasure Island), and Pinocchio, as they all travel to Oz.

Milligan, Peter

Infinity Inc.: Luthor's monsters. Illustrated by Max Fiumara, Pete Woods ... [et al.]. DC Comics 2008 128p. Illustration

Grades: 10 11 12 Adult   741.5; Fic

1. Mystery graphic novels; 2. Superhero graphic novels; 3. Graphic novels

978-1-4012-1816-4, $14.99

Infinity Inc. was a new superhero team, made up of young people who gained their super-powers thanks to Lex Luthor's metagene-manipulating Everyman Project. When they'd served their purpose, Luthor cut off their powers and abandoned them. More than a year later, the young ex-heroes have undergone just about every kind of therapy, but something is starting to happen to them. Natasha, John Henry Steel's niece, was a member of Infinity Inc., and suddenly she turns to a gaseous form and disappears. He tries to track her down, but someone else, who also was part of Infinity Inc, is tracking down his former teammates with an entirely different agenda in mind. The book includes violence.

Millionaire, Tony

Billy Hazelnuts. Fantagraphics Books 2005 111. Illustration

Grades: 9 10 11 12 Adult   741.5; Fic

1. Adventure graphic novels; 2. Humorous graphic novels; 3. Graphic novels

1-56097-701-9, $19.95

This book transmutes nursery rhymes and the golem myth into a storybook about Becky, girl scientist, her friend Billy Hazelnuts (who was created from cooking ingredients by tailless mice), and their journey to find the missing moon while battling an evil steam-driven alligator with a seeing-eye skunk. Millionaire fuses the darker spirit of older fairy tales with an adventure story, throws gender politics into the mix, and uses his highly detailed, old-fashioned looking art to pull it all together.

Sock Monkey: The Inches Incident. Dark Horse Comics 2007 88p. Illustration

Grades: 7 8 9 10 11 12 Adult   741.5; Fic

1. Fantasy graphic novels; 2. Toys; 3. Graphic novels

978-1-59307-842-3, $12.95

Inches the doll was the cutest in the whole house. Loved by everyone, the world was Inches' oyster. Then one day something happened... The Sock Monkey and Mr. Crow became concerned for their diminutive friend, but by then it was too late. The truth sent the terrified Sock Monkey and Crow fleeing for their lives, for Inches had been invaded by a colony of evil ants. The sight of ants swarming over Inches and other things might be too creepy-crawly for some readers; the violence is aimed at toys rather than people, however, this is not a book for younger readers.

Sock Monkey: Uncle Gabby. Dark Horse Comics 2004 Un Illustration

Grades: 8 9 10 11 12 Adult   741.5; Fic

1. Adventure graphic novels; 2. Humorous graphic novels; 3. Graphic novels

1-59307-026-8, $14.95

Uncle Gabby, the Sock Monkey, and Drinky the crow set off on a journey to solve the mystery of unremembered memories. This looks like a children's book, but the underlying bitter sweetness of a lost past and longing is more suited to teens and adults.

Mina, Denise

John Constantine: Hellblazer: Empathy is the Enemy. Leonardo Manco, artist; Jared K. Fletcher, letterer. DC Comics/Vertigo 2006 168p. Illustration

Grades: 11 12 Adult   741.5; Fic

1. Horror graphic novels; 2. John Constantine (Fictional character); 3. Mystery graphic novels; 4. Graphic novels

978-1-4012-1066-3, $14.99

Beginning with a chance meeting in a London pub, occultist Constantine finds himself swept along on the road to Glasgow, Scotland, where the murder rate is soaring and the most popular diet consists of cigarettes, whiskey and sugar, in other words, a city where Constantine feels right at home. But things are different this time. Constantine has been cursed with the worst thing he can feel: empathy for his fellow human beings. He'll need to get over that before he confronts what awaits him in Glasgow: an angry ghost, an ancient cult, a magus as powerful as Constantine himself, and a horror beyond his imagination, and he's already seen the worst hell has to offer. The story has copious use of strong language, nudity, and considerable violence.

John Constantine: Hellblazer: The Red Right Hand. DC Comics/Vertigo 2007 144p. Illustration

Grades: 11 12 Adult   741.5; Fic

1. Horror graphic novels; 2. John Constantine (Fictional character); 3. Graphic novels

978-1-4012-1342-8, $14.99

When his friends and relatives are in trouble, the last person they'd dare turn to is John Constantine. But this time, there is no other option. As Praexis demons father around Glasgow, feasting on the bloody roil of emotions there, a larger threat looms. Soldiers and guns can't contain the deadly infection of empathy that has turned the Scottish city into a ghost town. Time is running out, and unless Constantine can pull a trick out of his trench coat sleeve, the whole world is going to succumb to the empathy plague. And the first to go will be Constantine's last few remaining intimates - who are already suffering from exposure to his horrific memories. The book includes lots of harsh language, violence, and horrific images.

Minekura, Kazuya

Bus Gamer: 1999-2001 The Pilot Edition. Tokyopop 2006 240p. Illustration

Grades: 10 11 12 Adult   **741.5; Fic**
1. Adventure graphic novels; 2. Games; 3. Manga; 4. Graphic novels
1-59816-327-2, $9.99

When Toki, Nobuto, and Kazuo are hired to play the "Biz" Game, company secrets and insane amounts of money collide in a frenzied competition that starts out as an innovative way to win some cash. But as the game goes on, the players are ushered into a world filled with mystery, deceit, and murder. Suddenly, they realize what is truly at stake: their very lives. The book contains harsh language and violence.

Wild Adapter Vol. 1. Tokyopop 2007 Un Illustration
Grades: 12 Adult   **741.5; Fic**
1. Manga; 2. Mystery graphic novels; 3. Graphic novels
978-1-59816-978-2, $9.99

Makoto Kubota wandered through life, not taking things too seriously or looking too deep within himself. His job as the head of the Izumo Group's youth gang kept him pleasantly occupied with yakuza wars, mahjong and assassinations... Until the day he stumbled upon a strange drug called Wild Adapter that produces bizarre side-effects—including beast-like violent behavior and death. Forever changed, Kubota becomes entangled with a drifter named Minoru Tokito, and the two form an unlikely companionship that draws them deeper into the mystery of Wild Adapter... The book includes harsh language and graphic violence, later volumes will include some nudity as well.

Misako Rocks!

Biker girl. Story and art by Misako Rocks. Hyperion Paperbacks 2006 Un Illustration
Grades: 3 4 5 6 7 8 9   **741.5; Fic**
1. Adventure graphic novels; 2. Bicycles; 3. Graphic novels
0-7868-3676-8, $7.99

LC 2005-57428

"In this manga-style adventure, a young girl becomes a reluctant superhero after she inherits a bike with magical powers. . . . This fast-paced and well-executed story is . . . bound to be popular." Booklist

Rock and Roll Love. Hyperion Paperbacks 2007 Un Illustration
Grades: 5 6 7 8 9 10   **741.5; Fic**
1. Romance graphic novels; 2. Student exchange programs; 3. Graphic novels
978-0-7868-3685-7, $7.99

Sixteen-year-old high school student Misako comes to the U.S. as an exchange student for a year. Missouri is very different from Tokyo, but her host family and their teenage daughter, Natalie, make her welcome. Misako soon makes friends at high school, and feels comfortable enough to join a summer puppet camp in Wisconsin. There, she meets Zac, a rock and roll musician, and her dream boy. Given to strong enthusiasms, Misako falls hard for Zac, but he says he only wants to be friends. Will she ever get him to change his mind about her?

Misako Rocks! (real surname Takashima) moved to the U.S. from Japan as a teenager; this book is based on her own experiences.

Mitsuki, Lay

Yggdrasil vol. 1. Go! Comi 2008 Un Illustration
Grades: 9 10 11 12 Adult   **741.5; Fic**
1. Fantasy graphic novels; 2. Manga; 3. Video games; 4. Graphic novels
978-1-933617-91-6, $10.99

It's the near-future, and online gaming is all the rage. Teenage gamer Ko has more of an edge than others, since his father works for the company that produces the biggest online game out there . . . at least, he had an edge, until someone hacks his account and starts playing his Phantom character that no one is supposed to know about. Ko is determined to find out who's been logging into his game, but he and his friends may have found more than they bargained for as they delve deeper into the fabulous world of Yggdrasil . . .

Miyabe, Miyuki

Brave Story Volume 1. Art by Yoichiro Ono. Tokyopop 2007 198p. Illustration
Grades: 10 11 12 Adult   **741.5; Fic**
1. Adventure graphic novels; 2. Fantasy graphic novels; 3. Manga; 4. Shonen manga; 5. Graphic novels
978-1-4278-0489-1, $9.99

Life couldn't be more average for junior high school student Wataru, whose only real skill is playing video games. His parents' divorce is bad, but life is normal. That all changes in the blink of an eye when a mysterious transfer student comes to his school and drags him into a land of magic and monsters. Now, Wataru must face challenges he could not imagine in even his wildest dreams. There's some strong language and lots of monster fighting in this book, based on a novel which became a popular anime in Japan.
978-1-4215-2018-6, $8.99

Miyamoto, Yuki

Cafe Kichijouji De Vol. 1. Digital Manga Publishing 2005 156p. Illustration
Grades: 9 10 11 12 Adult   **741.5; Fic**
1. Humorous graphic novels; 2. Manga; 3. Shojo manga; 4. Graphic novels
1-56970-949-1, $12.95

The staff at Cafe Kichijouji are a wacky bunch. When five guys of wildly different personalities get together, every day is a day full of raucous mayhem. They're the source of continual headaches for the poor cafe master who oversees them all. From disastrous shopping excursions to dealing with demonic scone batter, the wackiness at the cafe never ends. Even the most menial activities are fraught with disaster and weirdness when these five are around. This is a three-volume series.

Miyazaki, Hayao

★ **Nausicaa** of the Valley of the Wind, Vol. 1. Viz Media 2004 136p. Illustration
Grades: 7 8 9 10 11 12   **741.5; Fic**

1. Manga; 2. Science fiction graphic novels; 3. Graphic novels

978-1-59116-408-1, $9.95

In a world devastated by ecological disaster and war, pockets of humanity exist in the vast wastelands. When some begin another war that could totally destroy the world, hope rests upon one young girl, Nausicaa, who can communicate with the strange creatures of the wasteland.

"Miyazaki is best known for his anime features . . . This tale contains all the classic elements of Miyazaki's films . . ." (VOYA)

This is a seven-volume series.

Miyuki, Takahashi

Musashi #9, Vol. 1. [translation and adaptation by Tony Ogasawara]. CMX Manga 2005 206p. Illustration

Grades: 9 10 11 12 Adult   **741.5; Fic**

1. Adventure graphic novels; 2. Manga; 3. Spies; 4. Graphic novels

1-4012-0540-2, $9.95

Musashi #9 is the code name for one of the top operatives of ultimate Blue, a secret organization operating independently of any government, whose goal is to maintain world peace. A teenager who displays incredible martial arts skills, wields weapons with aplomb, moves with stealth, and uses disguises, Musashi #9 protects tough teen girl Yayoi when assassins come after her, helps an ex-FBI agent save his kidnapped sister, protects a Russian scientist and his son from spies, and helps two teen boys who stumble upon terrorists targeting the Russian president. The reader discovers, along with Yayoi, that Musashi #9 is actually a girl who usually disguises herself as a boy. This is the first volume of an ongoing manga series. There's lots of action, but minimal graphic depictions of violence and little in the way of harsh language or adult content.

Mizukami, Wataru

Four-eyed prince, v1. Del Rey Manga 2009 184p. Illustration

Grades: 8 9 10 11 12   **741.5; Fic**

1. Manga; 2. Romance graphic novels; 3. Shojo manga; 4. Graphic novels

978-0-345-51624-4, $10.99

High school student Sachiko has a huge crush on upper classman Akihiko, but he claims to have absolutely no interest in her. He's quiet, studious, wears glasses, but something about him attracts Sachiko. Then, to her horror, when her long-gone mother summons Sachiko to live with her and her new family, Sachiko discovers Akihiko is her mother's stepson. She will have to live in the same home with the boy who rejected her and who objected to her moving in. When he leaves the house at night, Sachiko follows him, gets caught in a downpour in a strange neighborhood, and a handsome young bartender named Akira helps her. Except he's not Akira, he's Akihiko a warm, friendly, confident guy that all the girls want. Akihiko wants Sachiko to keep his secret, but she's torn between his two personalities. This volume includes another short story. There are a few "beefcake" shots of Akihiko/Akira shirtless, and one panel in the short story showing Sakamoto (the girl) lying down naked and face down while being massaged.

Mizuki, Shigeru

NonNonBa. Shigeru Mizuki; translation by Jocelyne Allen. Drawn & Quarterly 2012 408 p. Illustration; Color

Grades: 7 8 9 10 11 12 Adult   **741.5/952; 741.5**

1. Autobiographical graphic novels; 2. Cartoonists — Japan — Biography; 3. Folklore — Japan; 4. Grandmothers; 5. Grandparent- grandchild relationship; 6. Mizuki, Shigeru, 1922-2015 — Childhood and youth; 7. Yokai (Japanese folklore)

1770460721; 9781770460720, $26.95

LC 2012427667

This graphic novel, by Shigeru Mizuki, translated by Jocelyne Allen, is "a poetic memoir detailing his interest in yokai (spirit monsters). Mizuki's childhood experiences with yokai influenced the course of his life and oeuvre; he is now known as the forefather of yokai manga. . . . Mizuki explores the legacy left him by his childhood explorations of the spirit world, explorations encouraged by his grandmother, a grumpy old woman named NonNonBa." (Publisher's note)

Includes bibliographical references

Manga format; reads from back to front, right to left.

Mizuki, Shioko

Crossroad, Vol. 1. Go! Comi 2005 200p. Illustration

Grades: 10 11 12 Adult   **741.5; Fic**

1. Family life; 2. Manga; 3. Romance graphic novels; 4. Shojo manga; 5. Graphic novels

0-9768957-2-2, $10.99

Kajitsu has lived with her grandmother while her irresponsible mother, Rumiko, has flitted from one relationship to another. But now, her grandmother has died, and at fifteen Kajitsu is alone. Then her mother shows up, as well as Taro and Natsu, two of Kajitsu's stepbrothers. Before they know it Rumiko has run off again, but this time she has left behind a little girl, Satsuki. They have to make the best of the situation and live together as a sort of family, even though they have no blood connection to each other. Moments of broad comedy alternate with drama as the step-siblings try to settle into something resembling normal life.

Cy-believers. Go! Comi 2008 Un Illustration

Grades: 10 11 12 Adult   **741.5; Fic**

1. Humorous graphic novels; 2. Manga; 3. School stories; 4. Graphic novels

978-1-933617-76-3, $10.99

Rui has just transferred to a new high school in hope of finding some independence from a controlling family. Unfortunately, her fiance has been using his power as Public Safety Commissioner of the school to shut down many of the school's clubs. And Nijo seems to think he can control Rui's life at the school, which she doesn't like at all. With the help of a couple of cute computer nerds, Rui sets up a new club, the Cy-Believers. This volume includes some sexual situations.

Three in love, vol. 1. Go! Comi 2008 Un Illustration

Grades: 10 11 12 Adult   **741.5; Fic**

1. Humorous graphic novels; 2. Manga; 3. Romance graphic novels; 4. Graphic novels

978-1-60510-015-9, $10.99

Machiru has always been first-place in everything she has done, and she can't stand it when anyone else seems to do better than she can, so when Hanakago transfers into school and immediately makes a play for Machiru's childhood friend Suruga, Machiru can't let Hanakago have him as a boyfriend. They become a threesome, with the two girls constantly trying to outmaneuver each other. Complicating matters Ichiro has always tried to protect Hanakago and has a crush on her, and Hiroo has been Machiru's friend for years. The book so far only shows some kissing, but there's a fair amount of talk about romance and sex.

Mizushiro, Setona
After School Nightmare Volume 1. Go! Comi 2006 200p. Illustration
Grades: 10 11 12 Adult   **741.5; Fic**
1. Horror graphic novels; 2. Manga; 3. Shojo manga; 4. Supernatural graphic novels; 5. Graphic novels
978-1-933617-16-9, $10.99
You have just awakened to find your darkest, ugliest secret revealed to classmates who would do anything to destroy you. This is what's happened to Ichijou Mashiro, whose elite school education turns into the most horrifying experience of his life when he's enlisted by a mysterious school nurse to take an after-hours class. Only those who pass the class will graduate, and the only way for Mashiro to pass is to enter into a nightmare world... where his body and soul will be at the mercy of his worst enemies. Can Mashiro keep his life-long secret - that he is not truly a he nor entirely a she? Or will he finally be "outted" in the most humiliating way possible? The book includes graphic violence, strong language, and sexual situations.

Mizuto, Aqua
Yume Kira Dream Shoppe. Viz Media/Shojo Beat 2007 186p. Illustration
Grades: 7 8 9 10 11 12   **741.5; Fic**
1. Fantasy graphic novels; 2. Romance graphic novels; 3. Shojo manga; 4. Graphic novels
978-1-4215-1173-3, $8.99
They say that any dream can be made true in exchange for something dear to you. The Yume Kira Dream Shoppe flies through the dusk sky as Rin the shopkeeper listens for wishes that travel on the wind. With the help of his assistant Alpha (a stuffed rabbit), Rin uses the magical wares of the Dream Shoppe to make desires a reality ... But it costs the wisher something dear to the person. In the first story, a tree that has never bloomed falls in love with the music played by a young man, then the tree falls in love with the young man; she wishes for a human form so she can tell him how much his music means to her. Then she finds out he suffers from a disease that will take away the use of his hands, and she wants to change her wish ... In the second story, Alpha is the one who makes the wish, and at the end of the story, he leaps off a bridge so the young girl who owned him won't be dependent on him; it's so much like a suicide that it might disturb younger readers who might otherwise enjoy this book.

Mochizuki, Jun
Pandora hearts; Volume 1. Jun Mochizuki; [translation, Tomo Kimura; lettering, Tania Biswas]. Yen Press 2013 187 p. Illustration
Grades: 8 9 10 11 12   **741.5; Fic**
1. False imprisonment; 2. Nobility — Fiction
0316076074; 9780316076074, $13
"The air of celebration surrounding fifteen-year-old Oz Vessalius's coming-of-age ceremony quickly turns to horror when he is condemned for a sin about which he knows nothing. He is thrown into an eternal, inescapable prison known as the Abyss from which there is no escape. There, he meets a young girl named Alice, who is not what she seems. Now that the relentless cogs of fate have begun to turn, do they lead only to crushing despair for Oz, or is there some shred of hope for him to grasp on to—" (Publisher's note)
Volume 1 of 24

Mochizuki, Minetaro
Dragon Head Vol. 1. Tokyopop 2006 223p. Illustration
Grades: 11 12 Adult   **741.5; Fic**
1. Apocalyptic fiction; 2. Manga; 3. Science fiction graphic novels; 4. Seinen manga; 5. Graphic novels
1-59532-914-5, $9.99
The end of everyone was just the beginning...Returning home by train after a class trip, Teru Aoki takes a most frightening ride inside a mountain tunnel. When the train derails, nearly everyone aboard is killed. Amidst the bloody carnage, Teru discovers two survivors—but salvation is far from their grasp. As they try to dig out from the wreck in order to come up with a plan to stay alive, the lack of light and food, combined with the stench of death and decay, will lead one member of the group down a dark and demented path. And with sudden, violent earthquakes shaking the tunnel, escaping to the outside world may lead them to an even greater danger... Violence, strong language, partial nudity, and sexual situations occur in the series.

Modan, Rutu
Exit Wounds. Drawn & Quarterly 2007 160p. Illustration
Grades: 12 Adult   **741.5; Fic**
1. Israelis; 2. Mystery graphic novels; 3. Graphic novels
1-897299-06-0, $19.95
Israeli taxi driver Koby Franco lives and works in Tel Aviv; he lives with his Aunt Ruby and Uncle Aryeh, and he hasn't seen his father in a long time. One evening he gets a fare; Numi is a soldier, and she tells Koby she thinks his father may have been killed in a terrorist bombing in Hadera. He reluctantly helps her, against the advice of his family, and he and Numi try to trace his father's last few months and see whether he died or not. As they do this, Koby must deal with his feelings about a father who never really connected with his own family. Angry with Numi because she'd had an affair with his father, Koby eventually becomes her friend, and then her lover. The book includes one fairly graphic sex scene without any nudity.

Moeller, Christopher
Iron Empires: Faith Conquers. Lettering by James Greer and Steve Haynie. Dark Horse Comics 2004 Un Illustration

Grades: 9 10 11 12 Adult   **741.5; Fic**
1. Science fiction graphic novels; 2. Graphic novels
1-59307-015-2, $17.95
In the far future, eight weary nations are scattered among three million light years of the Milky Way Galaxy, all that is left of a once vast human civilization. The Vaylen Terror has ravaged humanity through the years, seizing a thousand worlds in a bloody rush, then pausing for decades of consolidation During these intervals of calm, the empires rebuild, rearm, then wage war on their neighbors. In this volume, readers will meet tough, uncompromising warrior-priest Trevor Faith, battling for his life and conscience on a border world. The book includes some strong language and lots of fighting violence.

Iron Empires: Sheva's War. Dark Horse Comics 2004 Un Illustration
Grades: 9 10 11 12 Adult   **741.5; Fic**
1. Science fiction graphic novels; 2. Graphic novels
1-59307-110-8, $17.95
In the far future, eight weary nations are scattered among three million light years of the Milky Way Galaxy, all that is left of a once vast human civilization. The Vaylen Terror has ravaged humanity through the years, seizing a thousand worlds in a bloody rush, then pausing for decades of consolidation During these intervals of calm, the empires rebuild, rearm, then wage war on their neighbors. In this volume, readers will meet the beautiful Karsan noblewoman, Ahmi Sheva. As the planet she despises but is duty-bound to defend is caught up in an empire-wide catastrophe, Sheva finds herself fighting, not just for survival, but for her humanity. The book includes strong language and violence.

Molebash, Wes
You'll Have That Vol. 1. Viper Comics 2006 64p. Illustration
Grades: 9 10 11 12 Adult   **741.5; Fic**
1. Humorous graphic novels; 2. Married people; 3. Graphic novels
0-9777883-1-8, $4.95
LC 2002-280685
This book follows the lives of Andy and Katie, a newlywed couple in their twenties, as they try to figure out life together. In the first published volume of the webcomic strip You'll Have That, newlyweds Andy and Katie battle noisy neighbors, have an unpleasant restaurant visit, and cope with the everyday struggles of married life. The book includes some mildly strong language.

Momochi, Reiko
Confidential Confessions: Deai Volume 1. Tokyopop 2006 216p. Illustration
Grades: 10 11 12 Adult   **741.5; Fic**
1. Manga; 2. Mystery graphic novels; 3. Shojo manga; 4. Graphic novels
1-59816-3868, $9.99
Welcome to the seedy underbelly of the enormous deai-kei industry, where men pay exorbitant fees to send emails to various girls whom they hope one day to meet in person. Rika is a young teen in need of a job. When the opportunity to join a deai-kei site presents itself, she decides

to go for it—the money is good and the interaction seems innocent enough. But the longer Rika works, the more her inhibitions and boundaries are pushed to the limit—and she begins heading down a path from which there is no return. While this story is fictional, it's based on fact, and the situation of high school girls dating older men for money has been touched on in several other manga titles. This is the first of two volumes. The book includes strong language, partial nudity, sexual situations, and violence.

Moon, Fabio
De: Tales: Stories from Urban Brazil. Fábio Moon and Gabriel Bá. Dark Horse Comics 2006 112p. Illustration
Grades: 10 11 12 Adult   **741.5; Fic**
1. Graphic novels
978-1-19307-485-2, $14.95
This collection of short stories features Moon and Ba, who are twins, working together, in tandem, or separately - trading off on the roles of writing and illustrating, sharing those roles or flying solo. Brimming with all the details of human life, their tales move from the urban reality of their home in Sao Paulo to the magical realism of their Latin American background. Some stories feature brief partial nudity and sexual situations and some mild harsh language.

MOONSHOT: The Indigenous Comics Collection
Edited by Hope Nicholson. Alternate History Comics Inc 2015 176 p. Illustration
Grades: 6 7 8 9 10 11 12 Adult   **741.5**
1. American literature — Native American authors; 2. Graphic novels
0987715259;
9780987715258, $17.99

This comic anthology, edited by Hope Nicholson, "from traditional stories to exciting new visions of the future, . . . presents some of the finest comic book and graphic novel work in North America. The traditional stories presented in the book are with the permission from the elders in their respective communities, making this a truly genuine, never-before-seen publication." (Publisher's note)

Courtesy of Alternate History

"This collection of folklore from a powerhouse team of Native authors, including Buffy Sainte-Marie and Richard Van Camp, will wow readers with traditional and futuristic tales based on tribal-specific cultural teachings. . . . The full-page illustrations in some selections and the bright colors in others add depth and understanding to the narratives. The artwork is as diverse as the stories collected." SLJ

Moorcock, Michael
Michael Moorcock's Elric: The Making of a Sorcerer. Writer, Michael Moorcock; artist, Walter Simonson;

colorist, Steve Oliff; letterer, John Workman. DC Comics 2007 Un Illustration
Grades: 9 10 11 12 Adult   **741.5; Fic**
  1. Adventure graphic novels; 2. Fantasy graphic novels; 3. Graphic novels
  978-1-4012-1334-3, $19.99

This graphic novel reveals an untold chapter from the novels starring the classic sword and sorcery character Elric. Young Elric must first learn to protect his beloved homeland from raiders. Then, he must learn the perils of making pacts with the magical world in return for protection and power in order to become a prince and ascend to the throne of Melnibone. He'll have to learn to temper his youthful enthusiasm with wisdom if he is going to rule the Bright Empire. There is some incidental nudity, along with battles.

Moore, Alan
  Alan Moore's Complete WildC.A.T.S.. Art by various. DC Comics/Wildstorm 2007 400p. Illustration
Grades: 10 11 12 Adult   **741.5; Fic**
  1. Superhero graphic novels; 2. Graphic novels
  978-1-4012-1545-3, $29.99

Moore's defining run on the super-hero team known as WildC.A.T.s is collected into a single volume, one in which he is assisted by Travis Charest and other artists. He envisioned a saga of honor, adventure, and betrayal that is presented here in complete form. The book includes violence and strong language.

  ★ **Batman:** the killing joke: the deluxe edition. Brian Bolland, art and colors. DC Comics 2008 Un Illustration
Grades: 10 11 12 Adult   **741.5; Fic**
  1. Batgirl (Fictional character); 2. Batman (Fictional character); 3. Joker (Fictional character); 4. Superhero graphic novels; 5. Graphic novels
  978-1-4012-1667-2, $17.99

This story was originally published in 1988, and it set Barbara Gordon on the path to become Oracle. The Joker says one bad day is all that separates the sane from the psychotic, and he sets out to prove it by driving Commissioner Jim Gordon insane by hurting his daughter Barbara. She has been Batgirl, but all her training and skills can't stop the Joker from shooting her in the spine. Then he takes Commissioner Gordon. Batman has to find the Joker and stop him. This story also reveals the origin of the Joker. This book includes violence and nonsexual partial nudity.

  ★ **From** Hell. Top Shelf Productions 2000 Un Illustration
Grades: 11 12 Adult   **741.5; Fic**
  1. Jack the Ripper murders, London (England), 1888; 2. Mystery graphic novels; 3. Graphic novels
  0-9585783-4-6, $35

Legendary comics writer Alan Moore and artist Eddie Campbell have created a hallucinatory piece of crime fiction about Jack the Ripper. Detailing the events that led up to the Whitechapel murders and the cover-up that followed, Moore posits the theory that a Masonic conspiracy covered up the involvement of Queen Victoria's grandson. He tells the story from the viewpoint of the victims, of the police investigating the case, and of the killer. The book includes graphic violence and depiction of the murder victims, harsh language, and nudity.

The **League** of Extraordinary Gentlemen: Black Dossier. Art by Kevin O'Neill. DC Comics/America's Best Comics 2007 208p. Illustration
Grades: 12 Adult   **741.5**
  1. Adventure graphic novels; 2. Spies; 3. Graphic novels
  978-1-4012-0306-1, $29.99

Britain in 1958 is not the world we knew; the country is still at war with Germany (led by Hynkel). The League of Extraordinary Gentlemen had been disbanded after the last world war, and the members of the "Murray Group" were labelled impersons. But now, the ever-youthful Mina Murray and a rejuvenated Allan Quatermain return to London and retrieve the Black Dossier, a legendary volume that details all the known facts about the league, going back centuries. Government spies pursue them, including one rather smarmy young agent called Jimmie (who likes his martinis stirred not shaken), Bulldog Drummond, and others. The book includes lots of full-frontal nudity, sexual situations, foul language, and violence.

Promethea Book Five. Alan Moore, writer; J.H. Williams III, penciller & painter; Mick Gray, inker; Jose Villarrubia, Jeromy Cox, coloring. DC Comics/America's Best Comics 2005 160p. Illustration
Grades: 10 11 12 Adult   **741.5; Fic**
  1. Adventure graphic novels; 2. Fantasy graphic novels; 3. Graphic novels
  1-4012-0620-4, $14.99

Sophie, the new personification of the goddess Promethea, went into hiding after government agents destroyed her world. As the years have passed, Sophie has suppressed the goddess within her, but now, with the help of Tom Strong, the government is closing in on her again, and she has no choice but to release the mystic power of Promethea, thereby unleashing an apocalypse upon the world and everyone in it, both foe and friend. This is the final volume of the series. The book includes nudity, sexual situations, harsh language, and violence.

Promethea Book One. Alan Moore, J.H. Williams III, Mick Gray. DC Comics/America's Best Comics 2001 160p. Illustration
Grades: 10 11 12 Adult   **741.5; Fic**
  1. Adventure graphic novels; 2. Fantasy graphic novels; 3. Graphic novels
  1-56389-667-2, $14.99

Sophie Bangs was a just an ordinary college student in a futuristic New York when a simple assignment changed her life forever. While researching Promethea, a mythical warrior woman, Sophie receives a cryptic warning to cease her investigations. Ignoring the cautionary notice, she continues her studies and is almost killed by a shadowy creature when she learns the secret of Promethea. Surviving the encounter, Sophie soon finds herself transformed into Promethea, the living embodiment of the imagination. Her trials have only begun as she must master the secrets of her predecessors before she is destroyed by Promethea's ancient enemy. The book includes some strong language, partial nudity, and violence.
Volume 1 of 5

  Smax Collected Edition. Alan Moore, writer; Zander Cannon, artist; Andrew Currie, Richard Friend, inkers; Ben Dimagmaliw, Wildstorm FX, coloring; Todd Klein, lettering, logo and design. DC Comics/America's Best Comics 2004 Un Illustration

Grades: 10 11 12 Adult   **741.5; Fic**
1. Adventure graphic novels; 2. Humorous graphic novels; 3. Science fiction graphic novels; 4. Graphic novels

1-4012-0290-X, $12.99

Jeff Smax, a major character in Alan Moore's Top 10 series, must return to his home world after many years on Earth. Accompanied by his fellow Neopolis Precinct Ten police officer Robin Toybox Slinger, he must face a myriad of challenges ranging from cutting through mountainous red tape to go on a quest, doing battle with the most monstrous of all dragons, and adapting to a world where the laws of physics are not only unheard of, they just plain don't work. And then there's Jeff's sister ... While there's little in the way of bad language and the violence is mostly against fantasy monsters, the book does include some sexual suggestiveness. And in Jeff's world, sex with one's sister is normal.

Terra Obscura Vol. Two. Alan Moore and Peter Hogan, co-plotters ; Peter Hogan, scripts ; Yanick Paquette, pencils ; Karl Story, inks ; Jeremy Cox, colors. DC Comics/Wildstorm 2005 Un Illustration

Grades: 8 9 10 11 12 Adult   **741.5; Fic**
1. Science fiction graphic novels; 2. Superhero graphic novels; 3. Graphic novels

1-4012-0622-0, $14.99

Just as things have returned to normal for everyone on Terra Obscura, including the members of S.M.A.S.H., a mysterious object appears on the edge of their galaxy, and it's on a collision course with the planet. Even more distressing is that the object appears to be the spacecraft of long-lost hero Captain Future. As the ship nears, time anomalies crop up over the entire planet, wreaking terrible havoc the closer the ship gets. Can Tom Strange and the other heroes unravel this mystery before it spells doom for the entire planet?

Tom Strong's Terrific Tales Book One. DC Comics/Wildstorm 2005 Un Illustration

Grades: 10 11 12 Adult   **741.5; Fic**
1. Adventure graphic novels; 2. Humorous graphic novels; 3. Science fiction graphic novels; 4. Graphic novels

1-4012-0029-X, $17.99

        LC Bd 05-068084

This anthology of stories features the science-fantasy exploits of heroine Jonni Future, the escapades of young Tom Strong in his early days on the exotic island of Attabar Teru, stories starring Tom's daughter Tesla and the intelligent ape King Solomon, and more. Moore works with noted independent comics artists such as Peter Bagge, Peter Kuper, Jaime Hernandez, and Sergio Aragones, among many others. The book includes some nudity.

Top 10 Book Two. Alan Moore, writer; Gene Ha, finishing artist; Zander Cannon, layout artist; Alex Sinclair, Wildstorm FX, coloring; Todd Klein, lettering, logos and design. DC Comics/Wildstorm 2002 Un Illustration

Grades: 10 11 12 Adult   **741.5; Fic**
1. Fantasy graphic novels; 2. Superhero graphic novels; 3. Graphic novels

1-56389-966-3, $14.95

Imagine a city where every citizen, from poorest slum-dweller to corporate honcho, has unusual powers and abilities - not to mention an alter ego and costume. How would you police such a city" Neopolis is the city of super powered citizens, and the police officers of Precinct Ten are also super powered. In this volume, they investigate the murder of an ex-sidekick rock star, deal with a murderous police commissioner who kills one of their own, and just try to get by each day. The book includes violence, nudity, and sexual situations.

Top 10: Book One. Alan Moore, writer; Gene Ha, finishing artist; Zander Cannon, layout artist; Wildstorm FX, coloring; Todd Klein, lettering, logos and design. DC Comics/America's Best Comics 2000 Un Illustration

Grades: 9 10 11 12 Adult   **741.5; Fic**
1. Mystery graphic novels; 2. Superhero graphic novels; 3. Graphic novels

1-56389-668-0, $17.95

Imagine a city where every citizen, from poorest slum-dweller to corporate honcho, has unusual powers and abilities, not to mention an alter ego and a costume. How does one police such a city? Rookie cop Robyn Singer is about to find out in her first day as part of Precinct 10 in Neopolis.

Top 10: The Forty-Niners. Alan Moore, writer; Gene Ha, artist; Art Lyon, colorist; Todd Klein, lettering, logos and design. DC Comics/America's Best Comics 2005 Un Illustration

Grades: 10 11 12 Adult   **741.5; Fic**
1. Superhero graphic novels; 2. Graphic novels

1-4012-0573-9, $17.99

This is the tale of Neopolis, a modern metropolis with a citizenry made up exclusively of super beings. In this city where everyone is blessed with powers, it takes a unique and powerful police force to protect and serve. The officers of Precinct 10 encounter all manner of the super powered and the supernatural on a routine basis. The TOP 10 team of writer Alan Moore and artist Gene Ha reunites for a graphic novel that delves into the past, revealing the origins of Neopolis and the first officers of Top Ten, from 1949. Discover the original Top 10 officers who blazed the trail and made Neopolis the city it is today. Some sexual situations and superhero violence occur in the book.

★ **V** for vendetta. Written by Alan Moore; art by David Lloyd; coloring by David Lloyd, Steve Whitaker, Siobhan Dodds; lettering by Jenny O'Connor, Steve Craddock, Elitta Fell. DC Comics 2008 288p. Illustration

Grades: 10 11 12 Adult   **741.5; Fic**
1. Science fiction graphic novels; 2. Graphic novels

978-1-4012-0841-7; 1-4012-0841-X, $19.99

The book is set in an alternate world in which England has embraced fascism after a devastating war has destroyed a lot of the world; it's 1997, and a young woman named Eve tries prostitution, only to be caught by the police on her first night. A man wearing a Guy Fawkes mask saves her, and thus begins his campaign to restore human spirit by rebelling against the oppressive government. Known only as V, he uses terror tactics and murder to dismantle the government. Occasional nudity, some violence, and harsh language along with a complex plot make this a book for mature-minded readers.

Originally published in single magazine form in the United States as V for Vendetta 1-10—Title page

★ **Watchmen**. Alan Moore, writer; Dave Gibbons, illustrator/letterer; John Higgins, colorist. DC Comics 2005 Illustration
Grades: 11 12 Adult   741.5; Fic
1. Superhero graphic novels; 2. Graphic novels
1-4012-0713-8; 978-0-930289-23-2 (pa)
1988 Eisner Award for Best Finite Series, Best Graphic Album, Best Writer, Best Writer/Artist; 1988 Hugo Award for Other Forms; 2005 listed in Time Magazine's 100 Greatest English Language Novels; 2006 Eisner Award to Watchmen Absolute Edition for Best Archival Collection, Comic Books

This graphic novel "begins with the paranoid delusions of a half-insane hero called Rorschach. But is Rorschach really insane or has he in fact uncovered a plot to murder super-heroes and, even worse, millions of innocent civilians" On the run from the law, Rorschach reunites with his former teammates in a desperate attempt to save the world and their lives." Publisher's note

"Nearly 20 years after the original publication, "Watchmen" shows an eerie prescience: the symmetry between current events and the conclusion of its story, concerning a villain who believes he can stave off real war by distracting the populace with a trumped-up one, and an act of mass murder perpetrated in the heart of New York City, is almost too fearful to bear." N Y Times Book Rev

Originally published in single magazine form as Watchmen 1-12; trade paperback edition still available Issued in slipcase. Awards: 1988 Eisner Award for Best Finite Series, Best Graphic Album, Best Writer, Best Writer/Artist; 1988 Hugo Award for Other Forms; 2005 listed in Time Magazine's 100 Greatest English Language Novels; 2006 Eisner Award to Watchmen Absolute Edition for Best Archival Collection, Comic Books

Wild Worlds. DC Comics/Wildstorm 2007 320p. Illustration
Grades: 12 Adult   741.5; Fic
1. Adventure graphic novels; 2. Horror graphic novels; 3. Superhero graphic novels; 4. Graphic novels
978-1-4012-1379-4, $24.99
Celebrated comics writer Alan Moore presents his take on some of Wildstorm's characters: WildC.A.T.s, Deathblow, Voodoo, and Majestic, and special guest star Spawn (from Image Comics), all of whom live in exotic, sometimes even outlandish, worlds: a stripper turned superhero turned private detective; a world populated by the clones of a secret agent; a time-twisted tale of a man who travels years into the future merely to find that even there, his past remains out of reach; and the last story of an immortal at the end of time. The book includes lots of violence, harsh language, and nudity.

Moore, B. Clay

Battle Hymn: Farewell to the First Golden Age. Drawn by Jeremy Haun. Image Comics 2006 Un Illustration
Grades: 10 11 12 Adult   741.5; Fic
1. Superhero graphic novels; 2. Graphic novels
1-58240-565-4, $14.99
It's 1944, and the first gathering of super-powered heroes may well be the last. In the waning days of World War II, at the dawn of the nuclear age, super-powered beings are emerging from the shadows of conflict, beginning with the arrival of the Artificial Man. Now the United States government has assembled this collection of genetic misfits, patriotic zealots, and half-human creatures to help with the war effort. At least, that's the official version of the story. Who lives? Who dies? And what exactly does the government have planned for the "heroes?" The book includes harsh language, violence, and brief sexual situations.

Casey Blue, beyond tomorrow. Writer, B. Clay Moore; pencils, Carlo Barberi; inks, Jacob Eguren. DC Comics/Wildstorm 2009 144p. Illustration
Grades: 10 11 12 Adult   741.5; Fic
1. Adventure graphic novels; 2. Science fiction graphic novels; 3. Graphic novels
978-1-4012-2208-6, $19.99
Casey Blue is an ordinary teenager, going to high school and playing on the volleyball team, living a nice, normal, suburban life. Then, one night it all goes weird. Leaving her brother Craig's downtown apartment after a visit, Casey feels a strange buzzing in her head, walks to another apartment building, goes up to one of the apartments, rings the doorbell, and when a man answers and opens the door, she brutally beats him to death. When she gets into her car afterwards, she can't remember how she got all that blood all over her. She also has nightmares about a future in which aliens have enslaved all humans. The news blares out the story of the murder of an industrialist who lived near Craig, and Casey starts to investigate on the Internet; this connects her to a young man in Brazil. An FBI agent comes after Casey and tries to kill her, then Craig's new neighbor Angela grabs Casey and tells her she is one of the few who will defend the world against aliens who are "Seeding" humans with a mind-controlling virus. Casey's nightmares are showing her the future. That strange buzzing in her head lets her know when a Seeded human is near, and her duty is to kill that person, no matter what. However, there are Seeded humans everywhere, hunting Casey and the other defenders being trained to fight. The story includes considerable bloody violence, and Casey seems to have a much curvier, busty body than most sixteen-year-olds.

Hawaiian Dick Volume 1: Byrd of Paradise. Written by B. Clay Moore; drawn by Steven Griffin, Nick Derington. Image Comics 2003 136p. Illustration
Grades: 10 11 12 Adult   741.5; Fic
1. Mystery graphic novels; 2. Supernatural graphic novels; 3. Graphic novels
978-1-58240-317-5, $14.95
In 1953 Hawaii, the supernatural manifestations of the islands' myths and legends lie just around every corner. Exiled stateside detective Byrd finds himself immersed in a dark paradise of exotic bar girls, murdered beauties, and high speed chases along the scenic Hawaiian coast, and the mysterious Night Marchers of the Pali Highway. The psychic Madame Chan, the eccentric but deadly Bishop Masaki and a restless corpse complete the mix in this slice of tropical noir. Violence and some strong language feature in

the story in which Honolulu and its Chinatown of the time feature prominently (and accurately).

Hawaiian Dick Volume 2: The Last Resort. Written by B. Clay Moore; drawn by Steven Griffin, Nick Derington. Image Comics 2006 Un Illustration
Grades: 10 11 12 Adult   **741.5; Fic**
  1. Mystery graphic novels; 2. Supernatural graphic novels; 3. Graphic novels
978-1-58240-664-0, $14.99
  In Hawaii of the early 1950s, it's gangsters, guns and ghosts as Byrd is caught between warring gangs in a beautiful Hawaiian bay turned red with blood. Also, his Honolulu police detective friend Mo and Byrd's secretary Kahami decide to visit the Seaside Sands resort and get mixed up in trouble as well. The locals on the island know something bad is going to happen to all the haoles (white men), the gangs just don't know that yet. There's a lot of shooting and killing in this book.

The **Leading** Man. Written by B. Clay Moore; illustrated by Jeremy Haun; colored by Dave Bryant; lettered by Tom Bolton. Oni Press 2007 144p. Illustration
Grades: 10 11 12 Adult   **741.5; Fic**
  1. Adventure graphic novels; 2. Mystery graphic novels; 3. Spies; 4. Graphic novels
978-1-932664-57-7, $14.95
  There's more to the world's hottest actor than sexy starlets, tabloid gossip and primo parts, because Nick Walker isn't just a Hollywood hunk, he's also the world's greatest super spy. When a routine investigation off the coast of France turns up a terrorist training facility, Nick Walker must juggle espionage and screen time in this explosive and astonishing adventure. The book includes harsh language, violence, and sexual situations.

Moore, J. Stuart
  Stuart Moore's Para. Penny-Farthing Press 2006 177p. Illustration
Grades: 9 10 11 12 Adult   **741.5; Fic**
  1. Science — Experiments; 2. Science fiction graphic novels; 3. Graphic novels
0-9719012-4-4, $19.95
  When Sara Eric was ten years old, her scientist father built a huge supercollider, but there was an accident that killed everyone. Nineteen years later, the supercollider has finally cooled off enough from the radiation for scientists to go in and investigate. Dr. Andersen, Dr. Eric's best friend, is leading the scientists, and Sara insists on going. However, the FBI has sent a Special Agent as well, and the team finds only more mysteries when they can't find any bodies. They do find the word "Para" scrawled all over the walls of the lab, and soon they discover a mysterious gateway that leads . . . elsewhere. It will be up to Sara, the non-scientist, to figure out what happened nineteen years before.

Moore, Richard
  Boneyard Volume 1. NBM 2005 96p. Illustration
Grades: 9 10 11 12 Adult   **741.5; Fic**
  1. Humorous graphic novels; 2. Supernatural graphic novels; 3. Graphic novels
978-1-56163-427-9, $10.95

Michael Paris has inherited a plot in the remote town of Raven Hollow. As he arrives, he gets to find out what a doozie that is: he's inherited a cemetery that the villagers want razed. Why" It's haunted with apparently frightening creatures putting a curse on the whole town. But when Paris actually gets to meet some of the denizens of his inherited headache, it turns out they aren't all that bad (Abbey the vampire, in fact, is quite cute) and maybe the evil is not where it may seem... This book was originally published in black and white; this edition is in full color.

  Boneyard Volume 2. NBM 2006 96p. Illustration
Grades: 9 10 11 12 Adult   **741.5; Fic**
  1. Humorous graphic novels; 2. Supernatural graphic novels; 3. Graphic novels
978-1-56163-487-3, $11.95
  Now that Beelzebub has been dealt a blow, it's the turn of the IRS to make Paris' life hell. But then, a certain beauteous Roxanna miraculously appears looking to solve all monetary problems. Paris resists as best he can, even putting on a monsters boxing contest to raise money, but the lures and the pressures... how strong can he stay? And as if that's not enough, Nessie the sexy gill girl (think of a female Creature from the Black Lagoon) and Abbey the vampire contend for Paris' affections. This book was originally published in black and white; this edition is in full color. The book includes some sexual innuendo.

  Boneyard Volume 3. NBM 2008 96p. Illustration
Grades: 10 11 12 Adult   **741.5; Fic**
  1. Humorous graphic novels; 2. Supernatural graphic novels; 3. Graphic novels
978-1-56163-515-3, $12.95
  Glump devises a wondrous scheme to do a Monsters on the Beach special swimsuit issue to help the cash-strapped Michael Paris. Never mind that Glump is hiding a much worse scheme within the scheme. On a darker note, Roxanne shows her true powerful demonic self, resulting in a potentially deadly showdown with Abbey. With this volume, Moore kicks the sensual sexiness of the female characters up a notch. This is the color edition; the black and white edition, published in 2004, seems to be unavailable.

  Boneyard Volume 4. NBM 2005 Un Illustration
Grades: 10 11 12 Adult   **741.5; Fic**
  1. Humorous graphic novels; 2. Supernatural graphic novels; 3. Graphic novels
978-1-56163-424-8, $9.95
  As Abbey recovers from her showdown with the much more powerful Lilith (who had disguised herself as Roxanne), swamp girl Nessie starts taking the upper hand in her pursuit of Michael (never mind she's married to Frankenstein monster-like Brutus). Meanwhile, Glump continues his schemes to rule the world, this time launching the "Doomsday Frog.DD However, everyone comes together to face a new threat: zombies sprouting up from the cemetery. And Michael discovers that not all monsters are ... nice. The book includes some partial nudity and sexual situations, and violence. This is the original black and white edition.

  Boneyard Volume 5. NBM 2006 Un Illustration
Grades: 10 11 12 Adult   **741.5; Fic**

1. Humorous graphic novels; 2. Supernatural graphic novels; 3. Graphic novels
978-1-56163-479-8, $9.95

After dealing with the zombie mess from the previous volume, Abbey, Michael and the Boneyard gang have to confront a two-pronged threat: a huge, masked,chainsaw-wielding serial killer in a girl's summer camp and the Pumpkinhead, whose very presence puts all in the 'yard into fevered sleep. Abbey barely survives the confrontation with the chainsaw brute, now it's up to Michael to face the worst threat, with Nodoze and a baseball bat. This book includes violence and some sexual innuendo.

Moore, Stuart
   Lone. Dark Horse Comics 2004 Un Illustration
Grades: 9 10 11 12 Adult   **741.5; Fic**
   1. Adventure graphic novels; 2. Science fiction graphic novels; 3. Western graphic novels; 4. Graphic novels
1-59307-265-1, $14.95

LC Bd 05-187024
Ravenous zombies have overrun the post-apocalyptic town of Desolation. Sharpshooter Luke and her older brother, Mark, are desperate. Their only hope is to track down and enlist the help of a gunman legendary in the western wasteland, a man known only as Lone. But if they find him, can they trust him" Cletus, a geezer who claims to know Lone, seems to know more than he's saying - especially after Luke mentions how the zombies are being controlled by a strange figure that bleeds yellow. And what are Gunfathers," anyway" After fighting off radiation-twisted mutants for two weeks, Luke and Mark are ready for answers. This is an example of the genre called weird Westerns." The book includes violence and some strong language.

   Wolverine: Blood & Sorrow. Writers, Stuart Moore, Rob Williams, David Lapham; artists, C.P. Smith, Laurence Campbell, David Aja. Marvel Entertainment 2007 Un Illustration
Grades: 10 11 12 Adult   741.5; Fic
   1. Superhero graphic novels; 2. Wolverine (Fictional character); 3. Graphic novels
978-0-7851-2607-2, $13.99

In "The Package," Logan must escape from an army of killers deep in the heart of war-torn Africa - with a baby strapped to his chest. In "Better to Give ...," a suicide cult dressed as elves has taken a Manhattan department store hostage on Christmas Eve. And Logan is one of the shoppers. In "The House of Blood and Sorrow," Wolverine lies at the edge of death in a Nebraska cornfield after crashing to Earth from the edge of the atmosphere where he'd been battling a giant robot. And then, things get bad. In "The Healing," Logan lies gutted in a Northwest forest, surrounded by wolves, as his body tries to heal. The book includes violence.

Moore, Terry
   ★ **Strangers** in Paradise Pocket Book 1. Abstract Studio 2003 360p. Illustration
Grades: 11 12 Adult   **741.5; Fic**
   1. Mystery graphic novels; 2. Graphic novels
1-892597-26-8, $17.95

Katchoo is a beautiful young woman living a quiet life with everything going for her. She's smart, independent and very much in love with her best friend, Francine. Then Katchoo meets David, a gentle but persistent young man who is determined to win Katchoo's heart. The resulting love triangle is a touching comedy of romantic errors until Katchoo's former employer comes looking for her and $850,000 in missing mob money. As her idyllic life begins to fall apart, Katchoo discovers no one can be trusted and that the past she thought she left behind now threatens to destroy her and everything she loves, including Francine. This thick pocket book edition collects several of the original trade paperback volumes. The story includes strong language, sexual situations, nudity, and some violence.

   ★ **Strangers** in Paradise Pocket Book 2. Abstract Studio 2004 344p. Illustration
Grades: 10 11 12 Adult   **741.5; Fic**
   1. Friendship; 2. Graphic novels
1-892597-29-8, $17.95

The second Strangers In Paradise pocket book finds Katchoo following David to California where she comes face to face with Darcy Parker. When Darcy makes Katchoo an offer she can't refuse, Katchoo transforms from prey to predator and begins to spin a web of her own. This book features 5 pages of Jim Lee art to open the story, hero-style. Also included is the most popular Strangers in Paradise short story ever—the Xena parody, "Warrior Princess." This volume collects several of the original trade paperback collections, including Vol. 6, High School. This volume includes violence, strong language, nudity, and sexual situations.

   ★ **Strangers** in Paradise Pocket Book 3. Abstract Studio 2004 372p. Illustration
Grades: 10 11 12 Adult   **741.5; Fic**
1-892597-30-4, $17.95

In this third pocket book volume, Francine is stuck in a bad marriage and Katchoo is a successful artist but keeps everyone at a distance. David's mysterious past links him even closer to Katchoo, who still can't escape the Mafia life she had led with Darcy Parker. There are more friendships, breakups, makeups, and action. Readers should expect to find strong language, nudity, and sexual situations along with a little violence.

   ★ **Strangers** in Paradise Pocket Book 4. Abstract Studio 2005 360p. Illustration
Grades: 10 11 12 Adult   **741.5; Fic**
   1. Friendship; 2. Graphic novels
1-892597-31-1, $17.95

Katchoo still loves Francine, but her wild past and dangerous enemies, such as Mafia types, prove to be more than Francine can handle. Meanwhile, David wants more than friendship with Katchoo. And then Francine, on the verge of another marriage, calls it off and decides to return to Houston and see what will happen with Katchoo. This fourth pocket book volume collects three of the original trade paperback collections.

   ★ **Strangers** in Paradise Pocket Book 5. Abstract Studio 2005 376p. Illustration
Grades: 10 11 12 Adult   **741.5; Fic**
   1. Friendship; 2. Graphic novels

1-892597-38-1, $17.95

While David finds solace with Katchoo, Francine can think of nothing but her past relationship with her former best friend and brings home a tattoo to prove it. It seems that Katchoo is destined to move on without Francine into the world of glitz, glamour, and art showings with her stunning display of 100 nudes. As Katchoo becomes the toast of the town, Francine finds herself looking for peace in the Caribbean. Our unlikely friends seem to be drifting apart until they are set on a collision course back to Houston. This pocket book volume also includes the Molly & Poo stories, which are illustrated prose stories set in Victorian England. Strong language, nudity, sexual situations, and violence punctuate the stories.

★ **Strangers** in Paradise Pocket Book 6. Abstract Studio 2007 272p. Illustration

Grades: 10 11 12 Adult   **741.5; Fic**
1. Friendship; 2. Graphic novels
1-892597-39-X, $17.95

Brad and Francine prepare to move to Houston, while free spirit Casey gets involved in the lives of her new roommates in Las Vegas and discovers a stalker. Back in Houston, Casey and David get Katchoo and Francine together again. Then David has to tell Casey and Katchoo his secret, a medical condition that may kill him. And in the final story, Francine leaves the cheating Brad and tries to reconnect with Katchoo, but she learns she's going to have to fight for her. This series lasted 90 issues and has ended the way Moore wanted it to. The stories include strong language, nudity, sexual situations, and violence.

Morgan, Melanie J.
Betty & Veronica: Bad Boy Trouble. Art by Steven Butler. Archie Comics 2007 112p. Illustration

Grades: 4 5 6 7 8 9 10   **741.5; Fic**
1. Humorous graphic novels; 2. Romance graphic novels; 3. Graphic novels
978-1-879794-25-2, $7.49

When Nick St. Clair rides into Riverdale on his motorcycle, Veronica is smitten. She likes Nick's air of assurance and his knack for getting noticed. The only problem is Nick gets noticed for all the wrong things. Nick quickly alienates all of Ronnie's friends, especially Betty, as he keeps trying to hit on her even as he dates Ronnie. Is this handsome rebel the boy of Veronica's dreams, or just plain trouble" This particular story has caused some stir among longtime Archie fans, because of the drastic artistic makeover of the Riverdale teens.

Mori, Kaoru
A **bride's** story, v1. Kaoru Mori. Yen Press 2011 192 p. Illustration

Grades: 11 12 Adult   **741.5**
1. Arranged marriage — Fiction; 2. Asia, Central — History — 19th century; 3. Man-woman relationships; 4. Silk Road; 5. Women — China
0316180998; 9780316180993, $17

LC 2012450076

In this graphic novel, author "Kaoru Mori brings the nineteenth-century Silk Road to lavish life, chronicling the story of Amir Halgal, a young woman from a nomadic tribe

Courtesy of Yen Press

betrothed to a twelve-year-old boy eight years her junior. Coping with cultural differences, blossoming feelings for her new husband, and expectations from both her adoptive and birth families, Amir strives to find her role as she settles into a new life and a new home in a society quick to define that role for her." (Publisher's note)

"By the end of this first volume, the plot is only beginning to bloom, but there is ample enjoyment in watching the small, everyday activities that make up the family's life—laundry, hunting, raising children. Amir's cheerfulness is infectious, both to her new family and to readers." Booklist

Volume 1 of an ongoing series

Emma 1. Kaori Mori; translation, Sheldon Drzka; lettering, Abigail Blackman. Yen Press 2015 386 p. Illustration

Grades: 10 11 12 Adult   **741.5**
1. Great Britain — History — Victoria, 1837-1901 — Fiction; 2. Household employees; 3. Shojo manga
0316302236; 9780316302234, $35

In this manga by Kaoru Mori, translated by Sheldon Drzka, "calling upon his former governess, William Jones, gentleman, is startled when his knock is answered by an uncommonly beautiful servant, the soft-spoken Emma. Throughout his visit, William's eyes drift to the maid whenever she enters the room, and he contrives to meet Emma socially as she goes about her errands. But London society is a web of strict codes and divisions." (Publisher's note)

Originally published in Japan; Previously published in the U.S. by CMX

Volume 1 of 4

Shirley volume 1. Del Rey Manga 2008 200p. Illustration

Grades: 8 9 10 11 12 Adult   **741.5; Fic**
1. Household employees; 2. Manga; 3. Graphic novels
978-1-4012-1777-8, $9.99

In Edwardian England, the independent Miss Bennett runs a cafe, but finds she has no time to take care of her house, so she advertises for a house maid. Young Shirley Madison answers the advertisement, and despite her very young age—she's only 13—she proves to be a competent maid and a good companion. In other stories, two maids take care of their young master, a five-year-old boy, but they don't know how to relieve his loneliness; and an experienced maid must deal with her bored master's pranks that have driven away most of the household help.

Morinaga, Ai
My Heavenly Hockey Club Vol. 1. Ballantine Books/Del Rey Manga 2007 212p. Illustration

Grades: 8 9 10 11 12 Adult   **741.5; Fic**

1. Hockey; 2. Humorous graphic novels; 3. Shojo manga;
4. Graphic novels
978-0-345-49904-2, $10.95

Hana Suzuki loves only two things in life: eating and sleeping. So when handsome classmate Izumi Oda asks Hana, his major crush, to join the school hockey club, persuading her proves to be a difficult task. True, the Grand Hockey Club is full of boys, and all the boys are super-cute, but given a choice, Hana prefers a sizzling steak to a hot date. Then Izumi mentions the field trips to fancy resorts. Now Hana can't wait for the first away game, with its promise of delicious food and luxurious linens. Of course there's also the getting up early, working hard, and playing well with others. How will Hana survive?

Morris, Steve
Blessed Thistle. Dark Horse Comics 2007 86p. Illustration
Grades: 11 12 Adult   **741.5; Fic**
1. Horror graphic novels; 2. Mystery graphic novels; 3. Graphic novels
978-1-59307-630-6, $9.95

Morris won Dark Horse's 2005 New Recruits Contest, resulting in publication of his first graphic novel.

Several stories come together: a desperate young man breaks into a house and finds the owner awake inside; a school teacher returns from a tropical vacation carrying a disturbing secret; a girl's playground bullying triggers a horrifying event. Some harsh language, violence, and ironic plot twists.

Morrison, Grant
All-Star Superman, Volume One. Written by Grant Morrison; pencilled by Frank Quitely. DC Comics 2007 160p. Illustration
Grades: 8 9 10 11 12 Adult   **741.5; Fic**
1. Superhero graphic novels; 2. Superman (Fictional character); 3. Graphic novels
978-1-4012-0914-8; 978-1-4012-1102-8 (pa), $12.99
Eisner Award: Best New Series (2006)

Writer Morrison and artist Quitely present several episodes in the life of the iconic superhero, Superman. When he saves a group of scientists from burning up in the sun, what no one realizes is that uber-villain Lex Luthor set up everything in order to kill Superman, who absorbed so much solar radiation that it is now slowly killing him. Once Superman learns that he is dying, he sets out to give Lois Lane a birthday she will never forget, by giving her his powers for one day. Then, when Jimmy Olsen takes charge of the science think tank P.R.O.J.E.C.T. for one day, they discover black kryptonite, which makes Superman turn evil. And, in his guise as Clark Kent, he interviews Lex Luthor in prison, but super-villain Parasite is taken from his shielded cell and begins to absorb Superman's powers, causing chaos.

Also available as a single volume collecting all 12 issues
Originally published as All-Star Superman issues #1-6
Volume 1 of 2

Batman and son. Grant Morrison, writer; Andy Kubert, penciller; Jesse Delperdang, inker; Guy Major, Dave Stewart, colorists; Jared K. Fletcher, Rob Leigh, Nick J. Napolitano, letterers. DC Comics 2007 200p. Illustration
Grades: 9 10 11 12 Adult   Fic; 741.5

1. Batman (Fictional character); 2. Joker (Fictional character); 3. Superhero graphic novels; 4. Graphic novels
978-1-4012-1240-7, $24.99

Talia, daughter of archvillain Ra's al Ghul and Batman's onetime love, returns with a teenage boy she claims is Batman's son. She leaves Damian with Batman, but while the boy has Batman's skills, he was raised among the League of Assassins and doesn't share his father's morals. Soon, both Tim Drake, Bruce Wayne's newly adopted heir, and the faithful Alfred, become Damian's targets. The book also includes an interlude about the Joker, and a story set in the future, when Damian becomes Batman. The book includes some gory violence.]

Batman: Arkham Asylum: A Serious House on Serious Earth. Written by Grant Morrison; illustrated by Dave McKean; lettered by Gaspar Saladino. DC Comics 2004 Un Illustration
Grades: 11 12 Adult   **741.5; Fic**
1. Batman (Fictional character); 2. Horror graphic novels; 3. Joker (Fictional character); 4. Superhero graphic novels; 5. Graphic novels
1-4012-0425-2, $17.99
                                        LC 2006-276659

In this painted graphic novel, the inmates of Arkham Asylum have taken over Gotham's detention center for the criminally insane on April Fools Day, demanding Batman in exchange for their hostages. Accepting their challenge, Batman is forced to live and endure the personal hells of the Joker, Scarecrow, Poison Ivy, Two-Face and many other sworn enemies in order to save the innocents and retake the prison. During his run through this gauntlet, the Dark Knight's own sanity is placed in jeopardy. This edition also reproduces the original script with annotations by Morrison and editor Karen Berger. The book includes violence and some disturbing images.

Doom Patrol; Volume 1: Crawling from the Wreckage. Written by Grant Morrison; pencillers, Richard Case, Doug Braithwaite; inkers, Scott Hanna, Carlos Garzon, John Nyberg; colorists, Daniel Vozza and Michele Wolfman; letterer, John Workman. DC Comics 2004 190 p. Color; Illustration
Grades: 10 11 12 Adult   **741.5; Fic**
1. Superhero comic books, strips, etc
9781563890345, $19.99; 1563890348

"The new Doom Patrol puts itself back together after nearly being destroyed, and things start to get a lot weirder for everybody. The Chief leads Robotman, the recently formed Rebis and new member Crazy Jane against the Scissormen, part of a dangerous philosophical location that has escaped into our world and is threatening to engulf reality itself." (Publisher's note)

Other Doom Patrol volumes by Morrison are: The Painting That Ate Paris; Down Paradise Way; Musclebound; Magic Bus; Planet Love

Doom Patrol Book 5: Magic Bus. Writer, Grant Morrison; pencillers, Richard Case, Ken Stacey. DC Comics 2007 208p. Illustration
Grades: 11 12 Adult   **741.5; Fic**
1. Doom Patrol (Fictional character); 2. Superhero graphic novels; 3. Graphic novels
978-1-4012-1202-5, $19.99

This book reprints stories originally published in 1992; Morrison took a 1960s team and radically remade it, creating a weird team who fight utter weirdness. In this volume, Mr. Nobody and his new slate of Dadaists hit the presidential candidate trail. But when the team's members start going their own ways, they don't seem to see the danger growing in their midst, that threatens not only the Doom Patrol, but the world as well. The book includes some nudity, foul language, and violence, some of which might be disturbing.

Doom Patrol Volume 4: Musclebound. Written by Grant Morrison; artists, Richard Case and others. DC Comics 2006 256p. Illustration
Grades: 10 11 12 Adult   **741.5**
1. Doom Patrol (Fictional character); 2. Science fiction graphic novels; 3. Superhero graphic novels; 4. Graphic novels
978-1-4012-0999-5
Reality has always been flexible around the Doom Patrol, a bit too flexible if one is looking for some peace and quiet. But for the World's Strangest Heroes, staving off the annihilation of free will or the reformatting of the universe into an artistic statement is all in a day's work, not to mention the everyday assassination attempts and visits from Satan. From the sinister workings of the Ant Farm deep beneath the Pentagon to the inevitable return of the New New New Brotherhood of Dada, threats to the very structure of existence continue to bubble up. In these showdowns, only the weirdest will survive - fortunately, nobody out-weirds the Doom Patrol. Morrison has worked with a veritable host of artists on the stories collected in this volume. The stories include some strong language, partial nudity, sexual innuendo and situations, and some violence.

★ **Joe** the Barbarian. By Grant Morrison and illustrated by Sean Murphy. Vertigo 2013 224 p.
Grades: 10 11 12 Adult   **741.5/9411; 741.5**
1. Diabetes — Fiction; 2. Hallucinations and illusions — Fiction; 3. Graphic novels
1401237479; 9781401237479, $19.99
                      LC 2012047802
In this graphic novel by Grant Morrison "Joe is an imaginative young kid of 11 who happens to suffer from type 1 diabetes. Without supervision and insulin, he can easily slip into a delirious, disassociative state that presages coma and death. One fateful day, his condition causes him to believe he has entered a vivid fantasy world in which he is the lost savior — a fantastic land based on the layout and contents of his home." (Publisher's note)
Originally published in a single magazine form in Joe the Barbarian 1-8.

Kid Eternity. Grant Morrison, writer; Duncan Fegredo, artist; Gaspar Saladino, letterer. DC Comics/Vertigo 2006 Un Illustration
Grades: 10 11 12 Adult   **741.5; Fic**
1. Fantasy graphic novels; 2. Horror graphic novels; 3. Graphic novels
1-4012-0933-5, $14.99
Comics visionary Grant Morrison re-imagines the character of Kid Eternity, a young man who died before his true time and returns to Earth as a ghostly spirit, along with his guardian Mister Keeper. This book follows the terrifying

night of aspiring stand-up comedian Jerry Sullivan as he joins Kid Eternity, who just escaped from Hell, on a quest back there to free Mister Keeper. Then the Kid learns he's been used as a pawn in the struggle between Order and Chaos. The book includes considerable violence and harsh language (f-bombs and s-bombs included).

The **Multiversity** deluxe edition. Grant Morrison, Frank Quitely, Ivan Reis. DC Comics 2015 448 p. Color; Illustration
Grades: 9 10 11 12 Adult   **741.5/973; 741.5**
1. Superhero comic books, strips, etc
1401256821; 9781401256821, $49.99
                      LC 2015014166
This comic book, by Grant Morrison, presents "a cast of unforgettable heroes from 52 alternative Earths of the DC Multiverse! Prepare to meet the Vampire League of Earth-43, the Justice Riders of Earth-18, Superdemon, Doc Fate, the super-sons of Superman and Batman, the rampaging Retaliators of Earth-8, the Atomic Knights of Justice, Dino-Cop, Sister Miracle, Lady Quark and the latest, greatest Super Hero of Earth-Prime: YOU!" (Publisher's note)

Supergods: what masked vigilantes,miraculous mutants, and a sun god from Smallvillecan teach us about being human. Spiegel & Grau 2011 444p. Illustration
Grades: 11 12 Adult   **741.5**
1. Comic books, strips, etc — United States; 2. Heroes; 3. Superheroes; 4. Superman (Fictional character); 5. Wolverine (Fictional character)
1-4000-6912-2; 978-1-4000-6912-5
                      LC 2010053712
A graphic novelist presents a history of the superhero in American comic books and movies. Index.
Includes bibliographical references

Superman - Action Comics; Volume 1. Grant Morrison, Rags Morales, Andy Kubert. DC Comics 2012 256 p.
Grades: 7 8 9 10 11 12 Adult   **Fic; 741.5/9411**
1. Adventure fiction; 2. Superhero comic books, strips, etc; 3. Superman (Fictional character)
1401235468; 9781401235468, $24.99
                      LC 2012010313
This comic book anthology, by Grant Morrison, illustrated by Rags Morales, presents volume one of "The New 52" re-launch of the DC Comics Superman series. This collection includes the first eight issues of the series, depicting "humanity's first encounters with Superman, before he became one of the world's greatest super heroes." (Publisher's note)
Originally published in single magazine form in ACTION COMICS 1-8—t.p. verso.

Vimanarama. Grant Morrison, writer; Philip Bond, artist; Brian Miller, colorist; Todd Klein, letterer. DC Comics/Vertigo 2005 104p. Illustration
Grades: 9 10 11 12 Adult   **741.5; Fic**
1. Fantasy graphic novels; 2. Graphic novels
1-4012-0496-1, $12.99
Beneath the town of Bradford, England, a buried city of wonders holds an ancient evil; Ali and Sofia, two teenagers nervously anticipating their arranged marriage, accidentally

awaken the evil. They must call upon the equally ancient Prince Ben Rama and his Ultrahadeen to drive the darkness back.

WE 3. DC Comics/Vertigo 2005 Un Illustration
Grades: 10 11 12 Adult   **741.5; Fic**
1. Animal experimentation; 2. Science fiction graphic novels; 3. Graphic novels
1-4012-0495-3, $12.99
2005 Eisner Award for Best Artist for Frank Quitely; this series was cited.

A top-secret research facility has taken a dog, a cat, and a rabbit and used cybernetics to transform the pets into armored smart weapons. The WE 3 are very successful; their enhanced intelligence allows them to communicate verbally with each other and adapt to any situation to carry out their mission. However, they're only prototypes, and when the project scientists advance to the next stage, the WE 3 are to be terminated. What the scientists and military brass haven't counted on is that their smart weapons possess enough reasoning to escape. Now Bandit the dog, Tinker the cat, and Pirate the rabbit are loose, and they want to find "Home." And they're ready to kill to find it.
Originally published as WE 3 issues #1-3.

Morrison, Robbie
White Death. Rob Morrison, Charlie Adlard. AiT/Planet Lar 2002 Un Illustration
Grades: 11 12 Adult   **741.5; Fic**
1. World War, 1914-1918; 2. Graphic novels
0-9709360-6-0, $12.95
It's 1916, and World War I, the Great War, is lurching across Europe. The Italian Front stretches across the Trentino mountain range, and Pietro Aquasanta has returned home only to find it a mass of trenches and death. If the enemy soldiers and their guns don't get you, the avalanches, the White Death, will. The men take comfort with the whores whenever they can to help them deal with the boredom and terror of the front. Harsh language, sexual situations, and the bloody violence of war permeate the story.

Wildcats: Nemesis. Pencilled by Talent Caldwell. DC Comics/Wildstorm 2006 208p. Illustration
Grades: 11 12 Adult   **741.5; Fic**
1. Mystery graphic novels; 2. Science fiction graphic novels; 3. Superhero graphic novels; 4. Graphic novels
978-1-4012-1105-90, $19.99; 978-1-4012-1105-9, $19.99
Zealot and her Coda sisters are the elite warrior-class on their homeworld of Khera, feared throughout the galaxy. A single name, however, strikes fear and hatred into their hearts: Nemesis. Frames for the betrayal and slaughter of Kheran military forces on Earth at the dawn of mankind, rogue warrior Charis Adrastea embarks on an epic quest. Hunted by former friends and foes alike, she is determined to clear her name and bring those responsible to justice. She'll soon discover a conspiracy that threatens the entire universe, but can one woman fight an entire war alone" The book includes lots of graphic violence, some nudity and sexual situations, and strong language.

Morrow, John
Kirby five-oh!: celebrating 50 years of the king of comics. [edited by John Morrow]. Twomorrows Publishing 2008 165p. Illustration
Grades: 7 8 9 10 11 12 Adult   **741.5**
1. Cartoonists; 2. Comic books, strips, etc — History and criticism; 3. Kirby, Jack, 1917-1994
978-1-893905-89-4, $19.95

LC 2008-299709

In celebration of Jack Kirby's 50-year career in comics, this book features lists of such things as the best Kirby story published each year from 1938 through 1987, the best covers from each decade, Kirby's best 50 character designs, and more. The book includes a color section of photographs and art from his career.

Morse, Scott
Noble Boy. Adhouse Books/Red Window, Inc. 2006 Un Illustration
Grades: 9 10 11 12 Adult   **92; 741.5**
1. Animation; 2. Biographical graphic novels; 3. Noble, Maurice; 4. Noble, Maurice; 5. Graphic novels
0-9774715-0-0, $12.95
Using a board book design and a Dr. Seuss-style rhyming text, Morse creates a tribute to Maurice Noble, an animation designer whose works people know, even if they don't know his name. Noble worked for Walt Disney on such films as Fantasia, Snow White, Bambi, and other famous animated films. During World War II he met Theodore Geisel (better known as Dr. Seuss). After the war, Noble worked for Chuck Jones, and with Jones he worked on the cartoon version of How the Grinch Stole Christmas. In the later years with Jones, Morse came to work at the studio and Noble befriended and trained him. Morse uses full-color, full-page paintings that aren't so much representative as symbolic of the philosophy of desing Nobel taught him. One page, showing Noble gleefully and playfully peeing into a toilet across the room is the only image that could raise objections.

★ **Tiger!** Tiger! Tiger!. Adhouse Books/Red Window, Inc. 2008 48p. Illustration
Grades: 10 11 12 Adult   **741.5**
1. Courage; 2. Imagination; 3. Graphic novels
978-0-9774715-3-9, $14.95
Drawing himself and his family members as tigers, Morse ruminates on personal courage, keeping one's imagination strong, living in the same moment as his young son, and getting by day-today. He includes his day in downtown Oakland when he had to report for jury duty, and fills the pages with sketches of the people encountered in the jury pool and around the town. This is not a standard graphic novel with a regular story, but readers will be able to ask the same questions of themselves and perhaps come to their own conclusions about how to face life with courage from within and how to find joy in the little moments of life. While there is nothing here that should be objectionable, Morse's thoughts are best understood by older teens and adults.

Morvan, Jean David
★ **Classics** illustrated deluxe #6: the three Musketeers. [by] Alexandre Dumas; adapted by Jean David Morvan,

Michel Dufranne, Rubèn, and Marie Galopin. Papercutz 2011 Un Illustration
Grades: 5 6 7 8 9 10 11 12 Adult   741.5; Fic
1. Adventure graphic novels; 2. Dumas, Alexandre, 1802-1870 — Adaptations; 3. France — History — 1589-1789, Bourbons; 4. Graphic novels
978-1-59707-253-3, $21.99; 978-1-59707-252-6 (pa), $16.99

In seventeenth-century France, young D'Artagnan initially quarrels with, then befriends, three musketeers and joins them in trying to outwit the enemies of the king and queen. This adaptation is suitable for many readers from age ten and up, but parents, teachers, and librarians might want to consider the visual depictions of sexual tensions and situations that might go over most young readers' heads in prose (there are some heaving bosoms, perspiring men, and a couple of scenes in bed), and the violence (most of it occurs off-panel). The book's endpapers include Dumas' introduction to his novel, an Epilogue, a brief biography of Dumas, and an illustrated character guide.

This book is a 70th Anniversary Edition of Classics Illustrated

Motter, Dean
    ★ **Electropolis:** the infernal machine. Dark Horse Books 2009 152p.
Grades: 10 11 12 Adult   741.5; Fic
1. Mystery graphic novels; 2. Robots; 3. Science fiction graphic novels; 4. Graphic novels
978-1-59582-363-2, $14.95

Menlo Park used to be a janitor robot in Electra City, but a private detective reprogrammed him to be his partner. Then, Jacob Ladder committed suicide by jumping off the Diogenes Tower, the tallest structure in the world. Sixteen years later, Menlo Park is still a private detective, complete with trench coat, fedora, and cigar and his new partner, Anesta. Femme fatale Tess LaCoyle comes to tell Park and Anesta that Jake didn't commit suicide, but was murdered. They reopen the investigation, which leads to a complicated situation full of twists and betrayals, and a mysterious object called the Astrolabe. Motter creates a future city that harkens back to the look of such films as the silent "Metropolis," and a noir mystery plot that could have come from the mind of Dashiell Hammett. The book includes some violence.

Mucci, Tim
    Tom Sawyer. Adapted by Tim Mucci; illustrated by Rad Sechrist.. Sterling 2008 Un Illustration
Grades: 3 4 5 6 7 8 9   741.5; Fic
1. Adventure graphic novels; 2. Twain, Mark, 1835-1910 — Adaptations
978-1-4027-3399-4, $6.95
                                        LC 2007-41162
Tom Sawyer lives in a small town along the Mississippi River, where he does his best to avoid Aunt Polly's list of chores and skips school so he can go fishing. When he and his friend Huckleberry Finn witness a murder, their first thought is to run away. This graphic novel adaptation includes a brief biography of Mark Twain.

Part of the All-Action Classics series.

Mukai, Natsumi
    +Anima, Vol. 1. Tokyopop 2006 194p. Illustration
Grades: 7 8 9 10 11 12   741.5; Fic
1. Adventure graphic novels; 2. Fantasy graphic novels; 3. Shonen manga; 4. Graphic novels
1-59816-347-7, $9.99

In an alternate world, +Anima are people who possess animal-like powers. Cooro, who has the black wings of a crow, befriends a boy named Husky who can live and breathe underwater. The two boys escape the circus and meet Senri, who has the powers of a bear. They just want to find a place where they can live in peace, but normal humans fear and shun them, or try to use them as the circus did. In the city called Octopus they encounter Nana, a bat-winged +Anima who has been stealing to live.

Volume 1 of 10

Mulligan, Brennan Lee
    Strong   Female Protagonist; Book one. Brennan Lee Mulligan and Molly Ostertag. Top Shelf Productions 2014 220 p. Illustration
Grades: 11 12 Adult
741.5
1. College students — Fiction; 2. Superheroes — Fiction
0692246185;
9780692246184, $19.95
"Alison Green, aka Mega Girl, lives in a dark world fraught with difficult relationships. She is a

Courtesy of Top Shelf Productions

biodynamic, who, along with other young people who possess special capabilities, rejects her role as a superhero and attempts to revert to the life of a 'normal' college freshman. However, . . . she encounters situations that test her resolve to no longer use her powers." (School Library Journal)

Originally appeared as a webcomic

Munroe, Kevin
    El Zombo Fantasma. Dave Wilkins, Kevin Munroe, writers; Sean Galloway, Tony Washington, illustrators. Dark Horse Comics 2004 Un Illustration
Grades: 9 10 11 12 Adult   741.5; Fic
1. Mystery graphic novels; 2. Superhero graphic novels; 3. Graphic novels
1-59307-284-8, $9.95

El Zombo Fantasma was the most famous and notorious Mexican wrestler on the planet, up until he was murdered ... apparently for throwing a match. Now the luchador has fallen into a strange land of purgatory, and the only way to avoid an eternity of fiery damnation is to return to Los Angeles and guard the well-being of a struggling young spitfire, ten-year-old Belisa Montoya. However, this role as an undead guardian angel gives El Zombo the opportunity to hunt down his killer ... and unearth far more than he bargained for. The violence is very much like television's pro wrestling shows; the book does have some strong language.

Olympus Heights. IDW Publishing 2005 152p. Illustration
Grades: 9 10 11 12 Adult   **741.5; Fic**
1. Adventure graphic novels; 2. Fantasy graphic novels; 3. Graphic novels
1-932382-55-0, $19.99
Oliver Dobbs likes working for the local museum in Olympus Heights, Indiana. His run-ins with deity have been limited - so far - to statuary that turns up, without warning or explanation, at the museum's loading dock. Now, that's about to change. When he discovers that Zeus is his next door neighbor, and that he's suddenly become involved in an ancient feud, Oliver embarks on the adventure of his life. The book includes fantasy violence.

Mutou, Hiromu
Never Give Up Volume 1. Tokyopop 2006 Un Illustration
Grades: 8 9 10 11 12 Adult   **741.5; Fic**
1. Humorous graphic novels; 2. Manga; 3. Romance graphic novels; 4. Shojo manga; 5. Graphic novels
1-59816-165-2, $9.99
Kiri's fashion-model dad passed on his stunningly attractive masculine looks to his only child...unfortunately, Kiri is a girl. Tohya is the love of Kiri's life—in order to protect him as he enters the world of male modeling, Kiri becomes a male model herself. But things get a bit complicated on the catwalk when others start to fall for Kiri's male alter ego. The book includes some partial nudity and some strong language.

Murashe, Sho
Me2 Volume 1. Written by Sho Murase and Matt Anderson; illustrated by Sho Murase. Tokyopop 2007 Un Illustration
Grades: 10 11 12   **741.5; Fic**
1. Fantasy graphic novels; 2. Mystery graphic novels; 3. Graphic novels
978-1-4278-0063-3, $9.99
Aki is a shy, introverted teen trying to cope with the death of her older brother. This, coupled with the daily pressures being the most bullied kid in school, lead to her having mysterious blackouts. Entire days begin to be unaccounted for as Aki finds strange items in her closet. Adding to her bewilderment is that the cutest boy in school suddenly takes an interest in her. As Aki wonders if her grip on reality is slowly slipping away, something even more shocking might be behind everything ... Fans of the television series "Heroes" will catch on quickly to Aki's situation in this global manga tale of psychological suspense.

Myers, Walter Dean, 1937-2014
Monster: a graphic novel. By Walter Dean Myers; adapted for graphic novel by Guy A. Sims; illustrated by Dawud Anyabwile. HarperTeen, an imprint of HarperCollinsPublishers 2015 160 p. Illustration
Grades: 8 9 10 11 12   **741.5; Fic**

1. African Americans — Fiction; 2. Bildungsromans; 3. Myers, Walter Dean, 1937-2014 Monster — Adaptations; 4. Prisons — Fiction; 5. Self-perception — Fiction; 6. Teenagers; 7. Trials (Murder) — Fiction; 8. Graphic novels
0062275003; 9780062274991; 9780062275004, $17.99
LC 2013043138
This graphic novel by Guy Sims, illustrated by Dawud Anyabwile, and adapted from the novel by Walter Dean Myers, is a "coming-of-age story about Steve Harmon, a teenager awaiting trial for a murder and robbery. As Steve acclimates to juvenile detention and goes to trial, he envisions the ordeal as a movie." (Publisher's note)
"Using panels like a filmstrip, Sims and Anyabwile achieve several remarkably cinematic effects: alternating grids and splash pages captures the tension between close-up and long shots; the use of jittery lettering and uneven word balloons injects deeper anxiety into the sound design; having a jury view the events recounted in testimony as a movie audience creates incisive visual metaphors." Booklist

Nagatomo, Haruno
Draw your own Manga: beyond the basics. Translated by Francoise White. Kodansha International 2005 111p. Illustration
Grades: 7 8 9 10 11 12   **741.5; 741**
1. Graphic novels — Drawing; 2. Manga — Drawing
4-7700-2304-9, $19.95; 978-4-7700-2304-9
"This advanced manual looks at how to enhance manga with a range of special effects as well as how to use various types of color ink, markers, and airbrushes to reach more creative levels. Supplemented by an interview with the immensely popular Japanese sports manga artist Shinji Mizushima, this book is recommended for any cartoon or animation library." Libr J
Also available: Draw your own Manga; all the basics (2003)

Naifeh, Ted
Courtney Crumrin & the Coven of Mystics. Oni Press 2003 Un Illustration
Grades: 7 8 9 10 11 12   **741.5; Fic**
1. Fantasy graphic novels; 2. Magic; 3. Supernatural graphic novels; 4. Graphic novels
1-929998-59-3, $11.95
When the night things of Courtney's community start causing trouble, it's up to the girl to find out why. The Coven of Mystics blames the hobgoblin initially but quickly turns its ire to Skarrow, a night thing in service to the town's most reclusive witch. Uncle Aloysius doesn't believe the disturbances are that easy to explain. His dismissal of the Coven's alleged culprit starts Courtney down a twisted path that leads to the true mastermind behind all the horror. But does Courtney stand a chance against a being that powerful and manipulative? This is a darker book than the first volume.

Courtney Crumrin and the fire thief's tale. Oni Press 2007 62p. Illustration
Grades: 7 8 9 10 11 12 Adult   **741.5; Fic**
1. Fantasy graphic novels; 2. Horror graphic novels; 3. Werewolves; 4. Graphic novels

978-1-932664-85-0, $5.95

Courtney travels with Uncle Aloysius to Romania, where they stay with Alexi Markovic, an old friend of Uncle Aloysius. Things aren't quite right there, though; the townspeople hunt wolves at night unnatural wolves, werewolves. Markovic's daughter has fallen in love with a Romany man even though her father has arranged her betrothal to an influential man in town. Courtney gets involved against Uncle Aloysius' wishes, and learns more than she wanted about werewolf origins and thwarted love.

Courtney Crumrin and the night things. Oni Press 2005 128p. Illustration
Grades: 5 6 7 8 9 10 11 12   741.5; Fic
1. Fantasy graphic novels; 2. Supernatural graphic novels; 3. Graphic novels
1-929998-60-0, $11.95

Courtney's social-climber parents take her out of her comfortable city neighborhood and move into an upscale suburb to live with her creepy Great-Uncle Aloysius in her spooky old house. She has to face uppity classmates and things that go bump in the night; but she ends up making friends with the spooks! Courtney deals with magic and the supernatural, but she's no altruistic Harry Potter; in this series, magic sometimes bites hard.

Other titles in this series are: Courtney Crumrin and the coven of Mystics (2003); Courtney Crumrin in the twilight kingdom (2004); Courtney Crumrin's monstrous holiday (2009); Courtney Crumrin: the witch next door (2014); Courtney Crumrin: the final spell (2014)

Courtney Crumrin in the Twilight Kingdom. Oni Press 2004 Un Illustration
Grades: 7 8 9 10 11 12   741.5; Fic
1. Fantasy graphic novels; 2. Magic; 3. Supernatural graphic novels; 4. Graphic novels
1-932664-01-7, $11.95

Courtney has changed schools yet again, but this time she's in the Coven's special class for magical studies. But when a student spell goes wrong and leaves one of her classmates cursed, can Courtney lead the kids into Goblin Town and find a cure, or will misfortune follow the group straight to the Twilight Kingdom" And the law keeper, Templeton, intends to stop Courtney from what he considers her most terrible crime yet.

Courtney Crumrin's monstrous holiday. Oni Press, Inc. 2009 192p. Illustration
Grades: 7 8 9 10 11 12   741.5; Fic
1. Fantasy graphic novels; 2. Horror graphic novels; 3. Graphic novels
978-1-934964-11-8, $11.95

Courtney accompanies Uncle Aloysius on his trip through Europe, and their first stop is in Romania. He has come to visit with an old friend, Professor Alexi Markovic, but they soon find they have stumbled into a family turmoil. Morkovic's daughter Magda loves a young Gypsy, but the local bully and noble (even if he has denounced his title), Petru has claimed Magda as his betrothed. Courtney learns that some of the wolves in the woods surrounding Markovic's house are werewolves, and Petru and his men hunt them, convinced that they are members of the Gypsy group in town. Courtney thinks she's helping a romantic young couple only to be disillusioned by Magda's attitude.

Then, in Krumrhein, Germany, she meets a handsome young man named Wolfgang and maybe falls a little in love with him. Which turns out to be a bad thing, for Wolfgang is a vampire. Aloysius had come there for he has learned he has cancer and doesn't want to die; but when he discovers that something is draining the life blood from Courtney, he knows he needs to save her.

Nakahara, Aya
Love*Com Vol. 1. Story and art by Aya Nakahara; [translation & English adaptation, Pookie Rolf]. Viz Media/Shojo Beat 2007 Un Illustration
Grades: 8 9 10 11 12   741.5; Fic
1. Humorous graphic novels; 2. Manga; 3. Romance graphic novels; 4. Shojo manga; 5. Graphic novels
978-1-4215-1343-0, $8.99

Risa Koizumi is the tallest girl in class, and the last thing she wants is the humiliation of standing next to Atsushi Otoni, the shortest guy. Fate and the whole school have other ideas, and the two find themselves cast as the unwilling stars of a bizarre romantic comedy duo. Rather than bow to the inevitable, Risa and Atsushi join forces to pursue their true objects of affection. But in the quest for love, will their budding friendship become something more complex?

First published 2001 in Japan
Volume 1 of a 17-volume series

Nakajo, Hisaya
Hana-Kimi: For You in Full Bloom Volume 1. Viz Media/Shojo 2004 184p. Illustration
Grades: 10 11 12 Adult   741.5; Fic
1. Humorous graphic novels; 2. Romance graphic novels; 3. Shojo manga; 4. Graphic novels
1-59116-329-3, $9.95

Japanese-American track-and-field star Mizuki has transferred to a high school in Japan...but not just any school. To be close to her idol, high jumper Izumi Sano, she's going to an all-guys' high school...and disguising herself as a boy. But as fate would have it, they're more than classmates...they're roommates. Now, Mizuki must keep her secret in the classroom, the locker room, and her own bedroom. And her classmates—and the school nurse—must cope with a new transfer student who may make them question their own orientation... The book includes some strong language, brief nudity, and sexual situations.

Sugar Princess volume 1: skating to win. Story & art by Hisaya Nakajo. Viz Media/Shojo Beat 2008 184p. Illustration
Grades: 7 8 9 10 11 12   741.5; Fic
1. Ice skating; 2. Manga; 3. Romance graphic novels; 4. Shojo manga; 5. Graphic novels
978-1-4215-1930-2, $8.99; 1-4215-1930-5

Maya Kurinoko takes her little brother to the local ice-skating rink with free tickets, but he won't skate unless she does a jump just like they saw on television the night before. So, she attempts a double axel, and lands it. Skating coach Eishi Todo sees her make the jump and scouts her as an ice skater. He wants famous skater Shun Kano (who attends Maya's high school she's in junior high) to coach and then partner with her, but Shun doesn't want it. However,

Maya loves ice skating and realizes it may be the one thing she can be good at doing, and she's willing to persevere.
Followed by: Sugar pincess. Vol. 2 : skating to win (2008)
Orginal Japanese editon, 2005

Nakamura, Yoshiki
Skip Beat! Vol. 1. Viz Media/Shojo Beat 2006 Un Illustration
Grades: 8 9 10 11 12   **741.5; Fic**
1. Entertainers; 2. Humorous graphic novels; 3. Shojo manga; 4. Graphic novels
978-1-4215-0585-5, $8.99
Kyoko Mogami has followed her true love, Sho, to Tokyo, where he wants to become an idol, a pop star. Idols can be pop singers or actors, and young hopefuls audition at talent agencies hoping to become the next big star. Sho succeeds, then he tosses Kyoko aside, saying that she's boring. Now Kyoko wants revenge, and thinks the best way to get it is to become an idol and eclipse Sho; but the talent agency rejects her audition. Is revenge an appropriate motivation? Kyoko doesn't care.
Nakamura uses different visual techniques to show characters' feelings, and with Kyoko's emotions in particular, especially her anger.
Volume 1 of 36

Nakano, Hitori
Densha Otoko: The Story of the Train Man Who Fell in Love with a Girl, Vol. 1. Written by Hitori Nakano ; illustrated by Wataru Watanabe. DC Comics/CMX 2006 182p. Illustration
Grades: 8 9 10 11 12   **741.5; Fic**
1. Romance graphic novels; 2. Shonen manga; 3. Graphic novels
978-1-4012-1141-7, $9.99
In Tokyo, a hapless otaku (nerdy anime fanatic) saves a pretty young woman from a harasser on the train. She sends him an expensive thank you gift, and members of the 2channel online forum encourage him and advise him as he first wants to ask her on a date, and then realizes he really likes her and wants a relationship. This off-beat romance is supposedly based on actual events; this series is one of several versions of manga adapted from Nakano's original novel.

Nakazawa, Keiji
Barefoot Gen: Hadashi no Gen : a cartoon story of Hiroshima. By Keiji Nakazawa; translated by Project Gen. New Society Publishers 1987 284 p. Illustration
Grades: 10 11 12 Adult   **741.5; 741.5/952**
1. Hiroshima (Japan) — Bombardment, 1945
0865710945; 0865710953; 0867196025; 9780867196023, $14.95
                                    LC 88187202
This book, by Keiji Nakazawa, is "an all-new translation of the author's first-person experiences of Hiroshima and its aftermath. [It] is a reminder of the suffering war brings to innocent people. . . . Volume one of this ten-part series details the events leading up to and

immediately following the atomic bombing of Hiroshima." (Publisher's note)
Volume 1 of 10

Nanatsuki, Kyoichi
Project Arms Volume 1. Created by Ryoji Minagawa and Kyoichi Nantsuki. Viz Media 2003 216p. Illustration
Grades: 10 11 12 Adult   **741.5; Fic**
1. Science fiction graphic novels; 2. Shonen manga; 3. Graphic novels
1-56931-889-1, $9.95
The future is a world of nano-machines, cybernetic assassins, powerful telekinetic opponents, and a secret organization dedicated to bringing forth the next evolution of humankind. Ryo Takatsuki thinks he's just a normal kid in high school, but strange things start happening—the new guy in school is trying to kill him; secret agents with high-powered weapons and modified limbs show up and start hunting him down; then his own body begins to transform into something grotesque and out of control. In order to find out what is going on, Ryo must come face to face with the underground world of secret organizations, fierce mercenary agents, and the secrets of his own mysterious past... The book includes graphic violence and harsh language.

Naraghi, Dara
Lifelike. IDW Publishing 2007 112p. Illustration
Grades: 10 11 12 Adult   **741.5; Fic**
1. Short stories; 2. Graphic novels
978-1-60010-122-9, $19.99
Iranian-born writer Naraghi works with artists such as Marvin Mann, Tom Williams, and Adrian Barbu to illustrate this collection of slice-of-life stories. The stories range from crime noir to love stories to war memoirs to humorous conversation pieces, all populated by a multicultural, multiethnic cast of characters. Some stories include harsh language, violence, and partial nudity.

Naruse, Kaori
Pretear, Volume 1. ADV Manga 2004 188p. Illustration
Grades: 6 7 8 9 10 11 12   **741.5; Fic**
1. Fantasy graphic novels; 2. Manga; 3. Shojo manga; 4. Graphic novels
1-4139-0144-1, $9.99
Naruse combines elements of fairy tales such as Cinderella and Snow White with fantasy adventure in this four-volume series.
"Himeno's alcoholic novelist father marries a rich businesswoman with two snobby daughters. They treat [Himeno] terribly, of course, but she . . . is goodhearted, virtuous, and patient. Himeno. . . [meets] seven knights who use leafe, a substance emitted by everything in the natural world. The Princess of Disaster wants to destroy all the leafe so the world will die. The knights need Himeno to become the Pretear so they can combine with her and combat the princess." SLJ

Narushima, Yuri
The **Young** Magician Volume 1. DC Comics/CMX 2005 240p. Illustration

Grades: 11 12 Adult **741.5; Fic**
1. Fantasy graphic novels; 2. Shojo manga; 3. Graphic novels
1-4012-0737-5, $9.99

A battle has broken out among rival sorcerers. The most nefarious group, the Necromancers, is killing young girls in Hong Kong to read the future in their entrails. Carno, a human youth raised by Aeromancers in a different dimension, is summoned back to his homeworld to join in the battle. Does Carno have what it takes to survive in a world of political alliances and emotional entanglements" The series includes graphic violence, harsh language, and nudity.

Nathanson, Jeff
Indiana Jones and the Kingdom of the Crystal Skull. Dark Horse Comics 2008 Un Illustration
Grades: 7 8 9 10 11 12 Adult **741.5; Fic**
1. Adventure graphic novels; 2. Indiana Jones (Fictional character); 3. Indiana Jones (Fictional character); 4. Graphic novels
978-1-59307-952-9, $12.95

It's now the 1950s, and Dr. Henry Jones Jr."Indiana Jones—is still getting into trouble. After escaping from Russians in Area 51, he's approached by a rebellious, motorcycle-riding young man who needs his help finding his mother in South America. That trip leads Indy into an adventure with an amazing discovery and unexpected companions—and the Russians, who want the treasure for themselves. This book adapts the story and screenplay from the fourth Indiana Jones motion picture that opened in May 2008. The book includes violence and icky scenes involving soldier ants.

Natsume, Yoshinori
Batman: death mask. DC Comics 2008 Un Illustration
Grades: 10 11 12 Adult **741.5; Fic**
1. Batman (Fictional character); 2. Manga; 3. Superhero graphic novels; 4. Graphic novels
978-1-4012-1924-6, $9.99

In this original manga story published in the manga format (with right-to-left orientation), Batman confronts a new killer whose arrival coincides with the arrival of a Japanese businessman with a new scheme for Gotham's rich. The killer slices off the faces of his victims; and in Bruce Wayne's nightmares, he confronts a shadowy figure who resembles Batman but with a different kind of mask. Bruce will have to delve into his past, to the time he trained in martial arts in Japan as a young man, to find the answer and identity of the killer. The book includes violence. Natsume's art is dynamic, his Batman is a muscular, athletic fighter, but his Bruce Wayne looks quite different from the regular DC comic art.

Togari Vol. 1. Viz Media 2007 192p. Illustration
Grades: 10 11 12 Adult **741.5; Fic**
1. Fantasy graphic novels; 2. Horror graphic novels; 3. Shonen manga; 4. Graphic novels
978-1-4215-1355-3, $9.99

Tobe is a ruthless killer from medieval Japan who's been suffering in Hell for 300 years. After what seems like an eternity, he's finally given a chance for redemption—armed with the magical wooden sword Togari, he's sent to modern-day Tokyo to destroy 108 malevolent demons in 108 days. However, these demons must be vanquished without causing harm to their possessed human hosts. Will the baffling ways of the modern world and his own criminal tendencies make Tobe's quest against evil an unwinnable war? Fast-paced action seasoned with a touch of moral philosophizing combines with considerable violence, and in this first volume, nudity.

Natsumi Mukai
+Anima, Vol. 1. Tokyopop 2006 194p. Illustration
Grades: 7 8 9 10 11 12 **741.5; Fic**
1. Adventure graphic novels; 2. Fantasy graphic novels; 3. Shonen manga; 4. Graphic novels
1-59816-347-7, $9.99

In an alternate world, +Anima are people who possess animal-like powers. Cooro, who has the black wings of a crow, befriends a boy named Husky who can live and breathe underwater. The two boys escape the circus and meet Senri, who has the powers of a bear. They just want to find a place where they can live in peace, but normal humans fear and shun them, or try to use them as the circus did. In the city called Octopus they encounter Nana, a bat-winged +Anima who has been stealing to live.

The underlying themes of tolerance (or the lack thereof) and prejudice are very much like the themes of the X-Men comics. There's some violence, but in the early volumes it's been fairly mild.

Nauck, Todd
Wildguard Vol. 1: Casting Call. Image Comics 2005 Un Illustration
Grades: 9 10 11 12 Adult **741.5; Fic**
1. Adventure graphic novels; 2. Superhero graphic novels; 3. Graphic novels
1-58240-470-4, $17.95

The cameras are rolling for the auditions of a new made-for-TV superteam: WildGuard. Hundreds of superheroes will try out, but only five will have what it takes to make the team... if they survive. Join a host of heroes through the agony of competition and unforeseen dangers, as they hope to be selected by a panel of judges, including the mysterious Producer X.

With Stan Lee's reality television series, "Who Wants to Be a Superhero?" airing its second season on the Sci-Fi Channel during the summer of 2007, this title is no longer so off the wall.

Nelson, Arvid
Hellgate London, vol. 1. Arvid Nelson, Lee Tae-Hang. Tokyopop 2008 Un Illustration
Grades: 10 11 12 Adult **741.5; Fic**
1. Horror graphic novels; 2. Graphic novels
978-1-4278-0700-7, $10.99

Rugby scholarship college student John Fowler gets mixed up in his team members' prank which results in the awakening of an ancient evil to which he is related. They've uncovered the skeleton of a body which was buried in a fashion used for those who were witches or worshipped devils. John and his sister Lindsey fight a lot, but they find they must work together when they learn that their long-dead father was a Knight Templar, and that the body John accidentally dug up is that of their many times great-grandfather Isaac, who sided with evil, and that they now possess Isaac's pendant, which is a key to something they must prevent the awakened Isaac from possessing. This is a prequel to the video game of the same title, and includes considerable gory violence and British harsh language. The book is also in a global manga format.

Rex Mundi Book One: The Guardian of the Temple. Writer, Arvid Nelson; artist, Eric J. Dark Horse Comics 2006 Un Illustration
Grades: 10 11 12 Adult   **741.5; Fic**
  1. Fantasy graphic novels; 2. Horror graphic novels; 3. Graphic novels
  978-1-59307-652-8, $16.95
  When a medieval scroll disappears from a Paris church, Doctor Julien Sauniere investigates, uncovering a series of horrific ritual murders and an ancient secret society. Julien cannot let these shadowy figures retreat into the darkness, lest they take up their killing once again. His investigation turns into a one-man quest into the bizarre secrets of the Catholic Church. The story is set in a world where the American Civil War ended in a stalemate, the Catholic Church controls Europe, and sorcery determines political power. Violent murders occur along with some incidental nudity. Older teen fans of The Da Vinci Code might like this story.

Nicholls, Stan
  Orcs: forged for war. Stan Nicholls; illustrated and adapted by Joe Flood. First Second 2011 204 p. Illustration
Grades: 10 11 12   **741.5**
  1. Adventure graphic novels; 2. Fantasy graphic novels; 3. Monsters
  1596434554; 9781596434554, $17.99
                    LC 2011009786
  This graphic novel, by Stan Nicholls, illustrated and adapted by Joe Flood, "follows a ruthless and deadly cohort of warrior orcs as they fight their way free of the dominion of an evil human enchantress. . . . With high fantasy on one side and the . . . gruesome battlefields of graphic novel[s] . . . on the other, [the novel] presents the world of its ogre-like protagonists with technicolor violence and moments of unexpected sympathy." (Publisher's note)

Nicieza, Fabian
  Civil War: Thunderbolts. Writer, Fabian Nicieza; pencilers, Tom Grummett, Dave Ross. Marvel Entertainment 2007 Un Illustration
Grades: 9 10 11 12 Adult   **741.5; Fic**
  1. Superhero graphic novels; 2. Graphic novels
  0-7851-1947-7, $13.99
  The Super Human Registration Act has been signed into law, sides are being chosen, but what side do the former villains called the Thunderbolts fall on" Well, their identities are already public knowledge, and they sure can get good publicity by hunting down renegade heroes, so ... it's time for the Thunderbolts to, err, kick some spandex butt. Except, they also wear spandex, so ...

Civil War: X-Men Universe. Peter David, Fabian Nicieza; artists, Dennis Carlo, Barry Windsor-Smith. Marvel Entertainment 2007 Un Illustration
Grades: 9 10 11 12 Adult   **741.5; Fic**
  1. Deadpool (Fictional character); 2. Superhero graphic novels; 3. X-Men (Fictional characters); 4. Graphic novels
  978-0-7851-2243-2, $13.99
  The divisiveness of Civil War has spread to X-Factor: half of them want to cooperate with the government; the other half wants to take a stand against it. Quicksilver's return to the team may well decide whether X-Factor stays together or cracks apart. Plus: Cable and Deadpool find themselves on opposite sides of the fence, and both refuse to budge. It's going to lead to a fight, but this one may change both their lives.

Nickel, Scott
  The **Day** of the Field Trip Zombies. Illustrated by Cedric Hohnstadt. Stone Arch Books 2007 40p. Illustration
Grades: 3 4 5 6 7 8 9   **741.5; Fic**
  1. Horror graphic novels; 2. Humorous graphic novels; 3. Zombies; 4. Graphic novels
  978-1-59889-834-7, $21.26
                    LC 2007-3175
  Trevor is a fifth-grade expert on zombies. In fact, he's a zombie-buster. When his class takes a field trip to an aquarium, the evil scientist Dr. Brainium turns the students into radio-controlled zombies. Only Trevor can rescue them, but first he has to escape an army of psycho penguins. The book is written with an easy vocabulary for reluctant and struggling readers.
  Part of the Graphic Sparks series.

  Jimmy Sniffles: Up the President's Nose. Illustrated by Steve Harpster. Stone Arch Books 2007 40p. Illustration
Grades: 3 4 5 6 7 8 9   **741.5; Fic**
  1. Humorous graphic novels; 2. Science fiction graphic novels; 3. Graphic novels
  978-1-59889-837-8, $21.26
                    LC 2007-3179
  The President is suffering a strange allergic reaction, and his life could be in danger. Jimmy Sniffles, the kid with the super-powered nose, is shrunk down to microscopic size to enter the President's nose and sniff out the problem. He finds evil lurking there, but there's still more trouble in the lab, too. The book is written with an easy vocabulary for struggling and reluctant readers.
  Part of the Graphic Sparks line of books.

  The **Monster** of Lake Lobo. Illustrated by Enrique Corts. Stone Arch Books 2007 40p. Illustration
Grades: 3 4 5 6 7 8 9   **741.5; Fic**
  1. Fantasy graphic novels; 2. Mystery graphic novels; 3. Graphic novels
  978-1-59889-836-1, $21.26
                    LC 2007-3178
  When Kevin and his dad visit Lake Lobo, their summer vacation suddenly turns creepy. Who made the claw marks outside their cabin window? What is howling in the night? Local legends say a strange creature prowls the woods. Could Kevin's new dog hold the secret to the Monster of

Lake Lobo? This graphic novel is written with an easy vocabulary for reluctant and struggling readers.
Part of the Graphic Sparks line of books.

Nightow, Yasuhiro
  Trigun Maximum Volume 1: The Hero Returns. Dark Horse Comics 2004 192p. Illustration
Grades: 10 11 12 Adult   741.5; Fic
  1. Adventure graphic novels; 2. Science fiction graphic novels; 3. Seinen manga; 4. Graphic novels
  1-59307-196-5, $9.95
  Vash the Stampede disappeared for two years after blasting a crater onto the moon orbiting the desert planet he saved from annihilation. But, with good and bad people alike trying to track him down he won't stay lost for long. He teams up again with Wolfwood, and learns of a new villain named Knives. As with the original manga series, humor combines with lots of fighting action; this time there's more violence, and some nudity and harsh language.

  Trigun Volume 1. Dark Horse Comics 2003 360p. Illustration
Grades: 9 10 11 12 Adult   741.5; Fic
  1. Adventure graphic novels; 2. Manga; 3. Science fiction graphic novels; 4. Shonen manga; 5. Graphic novels
  1-59307-052-7, $14.95
  Somehow, the past has placed a sixty billion double dollar bounty on Vash's head and the gunslinging pacifist can't seem to get away from money grubbing, itchy-trigger-finger citizenry. Find out why Vash is worth so much money dead. Feel the clumsy worry of the unfortunate citizens of the pulverous planet. Follow the follies of an unlikely hero in a forbidding world. Join Vash the Stampede " with his troubled past and uncanny ability to dodge a gazillion bullets " and a cavalcade of unlucky characters on a dusty, desert planet in the distant future. This series combines Old West action with high-tech weaponry and some crazy humor as bounty hunters and a couple of insurance investigators hunt for Vash. The series includes some harsh language, violence, partial nudity, and brief mild sexual innuendo.

Nihei, Tsutomu
  Blame! Volume 1. Tokyopop 2005 250p. Illustration
Grades: 10 11 12 Adult   741.5; Fic
  1. Science fiction graphic novels; 2. Seinen manga; 3. Graphic novels
  1-59532-834-3, $9.99
  In a future world rife with decay and destruction, Killy is a man of few words who packs one very powerful gun. He wanders an endless labyrinth of cyberdungeons filled with concrete and steel, fighting off cyborgs and other bizarre silicate creatures. Everyone is searching for the Net Terminal Genes, but no one is quite certain what kind of power they contain. The answer may lie hidden among the scattered human settlements of this vast and desolate future world. The book includes graphic violence, some strong language, and some suggestive images.

Niles, Steve
  ★ **30** Days of Night. Steve Niles, story; Ben Templesmith, art; Robbie Robbins, letters & design. IDW Publishing 2003 104p. Illustration
Grades: 10 11 12 Adult   741.5; Fic
  1. Horror graphic novels; 2. Vampires; 3. Graphic novels
  0-9719775-5-0, $17.99
  The long night of winter is coming to Barrow, Alaska; it's normal, and the people living in this isolated town don't mind. However, this particular winter, a band of vampires has decided to come up to Barrow for the month-long night and play. Sheriff Eben Olemaun and his deputy, wife Stella, and the people of Barrow have no idea of the terror and death they face when vampires can roam freely all night, all thirty days of it.
  This is pure, raw horror with monstrous vampires; these are not the romantic, sexy vampires of so many supernatural romances, but nasty, ugly, blood-sucking monsters. Templesmith's art and the technique of setting his panels on black pages adds a claustrophobic element that adds to the horror.

  30 Days of Night: Dark Days. Steve Niles and Ben Templesmith. IDW Publishing 2004 144p. Illustration
Grades: 10 11 12 Adult   741.5; Fic
  1. Horror graphic novels; 2. Vampires; 3. Graphic novels
  1-932382-16-X, $19.99
  In this sequel, the action shifts from Barrow, Alaska to Los Angeles, as Stella Olemaun, her life forever altered by the vampires' assault and her husband's death, rededicates herself to wiping out vampires and alerting the world to their shadowed existence. Along the way, she meets new allies and new foes - lots and lots of enemies. The book includes lots of graphic violence and harsh language.

  30 Days of Night: Return to Barrow. Written by Steve Niles; illustrated by Ben Templesmith. IDW Publishing 2004 144p. Illustration
Grades: 11 12 Adult   741.5; Fic
  1. Horror graphic novels; 2. Vampires; 3. Graphic novels
  1-932382-36-4, $19.99
  Three years before, vampires came to Barrow, Alaska at the beginning of the long winter night and slaughtered most of the town's inhabitants. Sheriff Olemaun died saving the town and his deputy wife died fighting vampires elsewhere. Now a new sheriff has come to town four days before the winter night, and the vampires are returning to destroy Barrow for good. Monstrous, evil creatures who slaughter viciously with lots of bloodshed combine with Templesmith's art that promotes a claustrophobic feeling of terror in this sequel to 30 Days of Night.
  Originally published as 30 Days of Night: Return to Barrow issues #1-6.

  30 Days of Night: Eben & Stella. Written by Steve Niles, Kelly Sue DeConnick; art by Justin Randall. IDW Publications 2007 104p. Illustration
Grades: 11 12 Adult   741.5
  1. Horror graphic novels; 2. Vampires; 3. Graphic novels
  978-1-60010-107-6, $17.99
  Stella Olemaun managed to bring back her vampire husband Eben back from beyond, but he came back hungry. Now, she's got a vampire baby the new would-be queen wants; the vampires have Eben; and vampire hunter Alice

and her husband want to destroy them all. The book includes lots of graphic bloody violence and foul language.

Batman: Gotham County Line. Steve Niles, writer; Scott Hampton, artist. DC Comics 2006 160p. Illustration
Grades: 10 11 12 Adult   **741.5; Fic**
1. Batman (Fictional character); 2. Horror graphic novels; 3. Superhero graphic novels; 4. Graphic novels
978-1-4012-0905-6, $17.99

Batman investigates a series of murders in the suburbs, and faces an enemy he doesn't believe in. He faces the undead, and he must defeat them, or lose his sanity. The horror element and graphic violence in fighting the undead makes this for more mature readers than for most Batman titles.

Checkmate: Big Book of Horror. IDW Publishing 2006 Un Illustration
Grades: 6 7 8 9 10 11 12 Adult   **741.5; Fic**
1. Horror graphic novels; 2. Shelley, Mary Wollstonecraft, 1797-1851 — Adaptations; 3. Stoker, Bram, 1847-1912 — Adaptations; 4. Wells, H G — Adaptations; 5. Graphic novels
978-1-600100-14-7, $19.99

Modern horror master Niles (30 Days of Night) retells three classic tales: Frankenstein, War of the Worlds, and Dracula. This book is not so much an adaptation of the stories as it is a telling inspired by the original novels. Scott Morse illustrates Frankenstein, Ted McKeever paints War of the Worlds, and Richard Sala does the honors for Dracula. Each artist paints full-page and double-page spreads in full color, with Niles' prose appearing on each page. Niles focuses on the main plot of each story; for example, in Dracula, the entire section dealing with Lucy Westenra and her suitors is omitted, so the reader only meets Jonathan Harker, Mina Murray, and Dr. Van Helsing. This book serves best as a brief introduction or as an accompaniment to the original novels.

Originally published as three separate volumes under the series title Little Book of Horror.

The **Creeper:** welcome to Creepsville. Steve Niles, writer; Justiniano, Steve Scott, pencillers; Walden Wong, Dan Green, inkers; Chris Chuckry, colorist; Pat Brosseau, letterer. DC Comics 2007 160p. Illustration
Grades: 10 11 12 Adult   **741.5**
1. Batman (Fictional character); 2. Superhero graphic novels; 3. Graphic novels
978-1-4012-1554-5, $19.99

The newest face in Gotham City is both a freak and a hero. When TV pundit Jack Ryder gets mixed up in a mob hit on a mad scientist, he finds himself transformed into the superstrong, super-agile, and quite possibly insane Creeper ... Or does the Creeper find himself transformed into Jack Ryder" The Creeper/Ryder try to find out what Dr. Yatz was really up to, with the help of Batman. While there is little in the way of foul language, the book includes fighting violence.

The **Cryptics**. IDW Publishing 2008 48p. Illustration
Grades: 4 5 6 7 8 9   **741.5; Fic**
978-1-60010-254-7, $17.99

The classic movie monsters: the Wolf Man, Dracula, Dr.Jekyll/Mr. Hyde, and the Creature from the Black

Lagoon, have moved to the suburbs, and they have kids. Jackie Jekyll (who turns into Hyde), Wolfy (whose mother is The Bride of Frankenstein go figure), Drac, and Sea-Boy do the usual suburban going-to-school, playing in the back yard, sorts of things, except when Wolfy suddenly disappears and the rest have to go find him in the afterlife. The book collects lots of short episodes in the lives of suburban kid monsters. The stories are all humorous, but the fact that the main characters are all monsters may be too much for very sensitive young readers. On the other hand, young readers who like a touch of the scary and macabre will have fun. Roman is the coauthor as well as main artist; one story, "Front Line," is illustrated by Billy Martin, and "Identity Crisis" features art by Robert Iza, Dylan McCrae, Kris Anka, Vidar Cornelius, Shane Long, Fabian "Monk" Schlaga, and David Igo. The book also includes pinup art by various artists.

This was originally published by Image Comics as The Cryptics Issues #13.

Freaks of the Heartland. Story by Steve Niles; art and lettering by Greg Ruth. Dark Horse Comics 2005 Un Illustration
Grades: 10 11 12 Adult   **741.5; Fic**
1. Fantasy graphic novels; 2. Horror graphic novels; 3. Graphic novels
1-59307-029-2, $17.95

Some folks would call Trevor's brother a monster. But to Trevor, Will is just another kid trapped in a dark reality he can't comprehend. When the situation moves from bad to worse, and their father threatens to do away with Will, Trevor learns that they're not alone - that "freak" children were born to other families in Gristlewood Valley. And just as they were all born at the same time, it seems their sad, frustrated, and emotionally spent parents seem to be hatching a plan to see that they disappear at the same time. Against all odds, and with nothing but love for his brother in his heart, Trevor is going to do whatever he can to get Will, and the other freak children, out of harm's way, if it's not already too late. The book includes fairly graphic violence and harsh language.

Fused Vol. 1: Canned Heat. Sstory. Steve Niles; art, Paul Lee, Brad Rader, and Ben Templesmith. Dark Horse Comics 2004 Un Illustration
Grades: 10 11 12 Adult   **741.5; Fic**
1. Science fiction graphic novels; 2. Graphic novels
1-59307-192-2, $12.95

Mark Haggerty was a promising young robotics engineer until his body became fused with an experimental robot suit during a routine testing session. Trapped inside a body that's not his own, and suddenly the unwilling pawn in a deadly struggle between obsessive egos and misguided military forces, Mark's life is forever changed. With his human body consumed more each day by the Cy-bot suit, his marriage suffering the consequences of his transformation, and the most dangerous elements in the world closing in around him, Mark's only recourse is to keep fighting - until he gets his life back. The book includes strong language and violence.

Fused Vol. 2: Think Like a Machine. Story, Steve Niles; art, Josh Medors & Peter Repovski. Dark Horse Comics 2004 Un Illustration

Grades: 10 11 12 Adult   **741.5; Fic**
1. Adventure graphic novels; 2. Fantasy graphic novels; 3. Horror graphic novels; 4. Graphic novels
1-59307-263-5, $12.95

In a world of subtle horrors, Elizabeth Mason is about to meet one monster she never counted on - herself. On the day of her 18th birthday Liz undergoes a strange metamorphosis which, for reasons unknown, causes her to transform into the monster called Crush whenever she bleeds. As if growing up isn't hard enough without that, Liz soon has to deal with a deadly, ruthless agent tailing her... with teenage werewolves. At least she has her best friend, Jen Tanaka, to count on. And what at first seems to be a curse may be the very thing that leads her to understand who she truly is. The book has some strong language and violence.

Last Train to Deadsville: A Cal McDonald Mystery. Art by Kelley Jones. Dark Horse Comics 2005 Un Illustration
Grades: 10 11 12 Adult   **741.5; Fic**
1. Horror graphic novels; 2. Humorous graphic novels; 3. Mystery graphic novels; 4. Graphic novels
1-59307-107-8, $14.95

Detective of the weird Cal McDonald knows that the teen redneck on his porch isn't anything to worry about, but the sex-crazed succubus the kid summoned in a love spell gone wrong is a big problem. She's turned the entire male population of the kid's hometown into a throng of murderous monsters. But what's worse - dealing with the demon-possessed town, or with a girlfriend who's hinting at commitment? The book includes harsh language, violence, and sexual suggestiveness.

The **Nail**. Rob Zombie and Steve Niles; art by Nat Jones. Dark Horse Comics 2005 Un Illustration
Grades: 11 12 Adult   **741.5; Fic**
1. Horror graphic novels; 2. Graphic novels
1-59307-173-6, $14.95

Hunted in one of the most desolate regions of America, preyed upon by an evil that does not sleep, Rex Hauser is The Nail - and it's time he took a stand. A semi-pro wrestler, Hauser has been touring the country performing at small-time arenas until the fateful night he and his family run afoul of a bloodthirsty gang of Satanic bikers stalking the North Dakota Badlands. Now he's a lone man fighting for the survival of his loved ones in a no-holds-barred standoff against the forces of Hell itself. The book includes nudity, sexual situations, and lots of very harsh language and graphic violence. This book is co-written by rock star and horror film maker Rob Zombie.

Nilsen, Anders
Dogs & Water. Drawn & Quarterly 2007 96p. Illustration
Grades: 10 11 12 Adult   **741.5**
1. Graphic novels
978-1-897299-08-1

A young man wandering a nameless path has only a stuffed bear as a companion, which inertly endures his desperation, anger, and musings along the way. The landscape is cold and bleak with few landmarks, and offers only precarious encounters with animals and armed men. These interactions are rife with instinct, the drive for survival, and human ethics concerning the killed and injured. He finds acceptance with a pack of dogs, though their nature is wild and their potential threat is as unsettling as the sudden presence of a massive pipeline on the horizon. The road disappears and only blind circumstance remains. All is uncertain and all can be lost, but he continues on regardless. This is for the thoughtful reader who doesn't mind a little bit of harsh language and some violence.

Monologues for the Coming Plague. Fantagraphics Books 2006 260p. Illustration
Grades: 11 12 Adult   **741.5; Fic**
1. Humorous graphic novels; 2. Graphic novels
978-1-56097-718-6, $18.95

This book ranges from riffs on the gag cartoon to paranoid soliloquies of a surrealistic apocalypse, with references to contemporary politics, pop culture, religion, plays on language, and sequential abstractions. The "characters" (all unnamed) are abstract humans (one man's head is drawn as a big scribble), a bird, a dog, and a dinosaur. Nilsen uses a form of Automatic Writing, an aesthetic mode championed by Andre Breton at the beginning of the twentieth century that became the foundation of the Surrealist Movement. Some nudity, strong language, and violence occur, but the utter simplicity of Nilsen's art belies deep thought and sly humor.

Ninomiya, Tomoko
Nodame Cantabile, Vol. 1. Ballantine Books/Del Rey Manga 2005 188p. Illustration
Grades: 10 11 12 Adult   **741.5; Fic**
1. Music; 2. Romance graphic novels; 3. Shojo manga; 4. Graphic novels
0-345-48172-0, $10.95
2004 Kodansha Manga Award for Shojo Manga.

Music student Shinichi Chiaki dreams of becoming a conductor, but his fear of flying and arrogant attitude hold him back. Then he meets Megumi Noda, who has a natural talent for piano, but she can't read a music score, she's a slovenly mess, and her apartment is a disaster area. Shinichi starts working with her, and Megumi falls for him. Romantic complications, new friendships, and music ensue. There are some mild sex scenes.

Nishimori, Hiroyuki
Cheeky Angel Vol. 1. Viz Media 2004 200p. Illustration
Grades: 10 11 12 Adult   **741.5; Fic**
1. Humorous graphic novels; 2. Manga; 3. Romance graphic novels; 4. Shonen manga; 5. Graphic novels
1-59116-397-8, $9.95

Megumi, a nine-year-old martial arts enthusiast and all around rapscallion always wanted to be, the manliest man on Earth." After saving a sorcerer from a group of local toughs, Megumi is presented with a magic genie which can grant any wish. Unfortunately, this genie misconstrues Megumi's desire as wanting to become the, womanliest woman on Earth," and in a flash, Megumi's Y chromosome is swapped for an X. Six years later...Megumi is the hottest girl in school, but has stayed true to his/her tough talkin', punk stompin' ways. If that's not enough, Genzo, the baddest dude in town, is smitten by Megumi's womanly wiles" ... The series includes some strong language and some violence, very little partial nudity.

Nishino, Jyutaroh

Steel fist Riku vol. 1. DC Comics/CMX 2008 162p. Illustration

Grades: 9 10 11 12 Adult   **741.5; Fic**

1. Humorous graphic novels; 2. Manga; 3. Martial arts; 4. Graphic novels

978-1-4012-1752-5, $9.99

Teenage Riku lives with Rocky, her gruff, adopted dad ("Call me Sensei!" he roars when she calls him Pops), who trained her in martial arts. In their world, semi-humans are common, such as a Pig Man, or the fact that Riku has a fist of steel. Rocky now runs a shop selling celebrity photos, but he used to be a professional martial artist. When the daughter of his old master ventures into the shop, Rocky kidnaps her in order to demand a rematch, 20 years after the fact, with his old rival Utsugizaki. This doesn't sit well with Riku, and she decides to take matters into her own hands. The book includes some raunchy humor and fan service (Riku's powers become even stronger when her breasts are unbound); Rocky is obsessed with women's breasts and suffers many nosebleeds (manga symbol for sexual arousal) while watching his DVDs, and characters declare that they're pissed off or that someone is a pain in the butt.

Niz, Xavier

Paul Revere's Ride. Illustrated by Brian Bascle. Capstone Press 2006 32p. Illustration

Grades: 3 4 5 6 7 8 9   **741.5; 973.3**

1. Concord (Mass), Battle of, 1775; 2. Lexington (Mass), Battle of, 1775; 3. Massachusetts — History; 4. United States — History — 1775-1783, Revolution; 5. Graphic novels

0-7368-4965-3, $25.26

LC 200500652

This book uses the comic book format to tell the story of Paul Revere's ride to Lexington in April 1775 to warn colonists of approaching British troops. It includes additional information, a glossary, a list of books for further reading, and more.

Part of the Graphic Library, Graphic History series.

No, Yee-Jung

The **Visitor** Vol. 1. Tokyopop 2006 178p. Illustration

Grades: 9 10 11 12 Adult   **741.5; Fic**

1. Horror graphic novels; 2. Manwha; 3. Mystery graphic novels; 4. Graphic novels

1-59816-342-2, $9.99

Beautiful Hyo-Bin Na is the new girl in high school that everyone is dying to meet, but she is not a normal student. Hyo-Bin is cursed with supernatural abilities that she can't quite understand...or control. Every night she's haunted by disturbing dreams, while during the day she lives in fear—not of those around her, but of herself. Then she discovers another classmate, Mi-Soo, has the same dreams; what can this mean" The book includes some strong language and violence.

Nobleman, Marc Tyler

★ **Boys** of steel: the creators of Superman. Illustrated by Ross MacDonald. Alfred A. Knopf 2008 Un Illustration

Grades: 3 4 5 6 7 8 9   **741.5**

1. Artists; 2. Biographical graphic novels; 3. Cartoonists; 4. Cartoonists; 5. Comic book writers; 6. Illustrators; 7. Shuster, Joe, 1914-1992; 8. Siegel, Jerry, 1914-1996; 9. Superman (Fictional character); 10. Graphic novels

978-0-375-83802-6, $16.99; 978-0-375-93802-3 (lib. bdg.), $19.99

LC 2007-41606

This picture book tells the story of Jerry Siegel and Joe Shuster, two teenagers living in Depression-era Cleveland, Ohio, who became friends and started writing stories together. One night they created the character who would become Superman. A text section at the back of the book tells of the struggle Siegel and Shuster had after they sold rights to Superman to the company that is now DC Comics. After Superman became wildly successful and made lots of money for DC Comics, Siegel and Shuster saw none of it. They started a legal fight that did end up with DC providing a financial settlement; Siegel's family was finally awarded half of the U.S. copyright to the material in Action Comics #1 in March 2008. Shuster's family is now asserting its right to the other half of the copyright, and negotiations are ongoing.

Noh, Mi Young

Threads of Time Volume 1. Tokyopop 2004 178p. Illustration

Grades: 9 10 11 12 Adult   **741.5; Fic**

1. Adventure graphic novels; 2. Fantasy graphic novels; 3. Manwha; 4. Graphic novels

1-59812-780-9, $9.99

The most frightening thing about Moon Bin Kim's nightmare is that he doesn't appear to be dreaming, this modern high school student lives a parallel life in the 13th century as the son of a prominent warrior family. When friends and family in his present-day existence assume roles in his historical life, Moon Bin struggles to learn exactly who he is and why his life spans hundreds of years across space, time, and consciousness. The book includes some nudity, strong language, and teen smoking.

Nolen-Weathington, Eric

Modern masters volume sixteen: Mike Allred. Twomorrows Publishing 2008 120p. Illustration

Grades: 11 12 Adult   **741.5**

1. Allred, Mike; 2. Comic books, strips, etc — History and criticism; 3. Graphic novels — History and criticism

978-1-893905-86-3, $14.95

Mike Allred grew up in the 1960s and 1970s, then published his first comic in 1989. In 1991, he sprung his hip, Pop-inspired creation Madman upon the world. His first series of Madman comics won the Harvey Award for Best New Series. Allred is also an actor, filmmaker, and rock musician. This book features a long interview with Allred and includes lots of black and white reproductions of his art.

★ **Modern** Masters volume twenty-five: Jeff Smith. TwoMorrows Publishing 2011 117p. Illustration

Grades: 6 7 8 9 10 11 12 Adult   **741.5**

Courtesy of TwoMorrows Publishing

1. Artists; 2. Authors; 3. Cartoonists; 4. Comic books, strips, etc — History and criticism; 5. Graphic novels — History and criticism; 6. Smith, Jeff
978-1-60549-024-3, $15.95
This volume in the Modern Masters series focuses on Jeff Smith, creator of Bone. In an interview that covers his childhood, college career, and early work before becoming a cartoonist, Smith talks about how he created Fone Bone when he was just five years old. The artwork in the book includes young Smith's hand-created comics from his childhood. Only a couple of "craps" slip out. The book includes mostly black and white art and photographs, with a few color illustrations from the Bone comics.

Nonaka, Eiji
Cromartie High School, Vol. 1. [translated by Brendan Frayne]. ADV Manga 2005 158p. Illustration
Grades: 10 11 12 Adult   **741.5; Fic**
1. High school students; 2. Humorous graphic novels; 3. Manga; 4. School stories; 5. Graphic novels
1-4139-0257-X, $10.95
Takashi Kamiyama enrolled at Cromartie High School, the worst high school in Tokyo, to help a friend, who then flunked the entrance exam. Now he's stuck in a school filled with juvenile delinquents, street toughs, and some very strange characters. They include a shirtless guy who looks like Freddy Mercury and never says anything, a gorilla who is smarter than everyone else, and Mechazawa, who looks like a canister-shaped robot. American readers may not be aware that, in Japan, students must pass entrance exams to get into the high school of their choice. It doesn't matter how rich your family is if you can't pass an entrance exam with a high enough score to get into a top school. This is the first volume of an ongoing manga full of wacky and sometimes deadpan humor.

North, Ryan
Adventure Time. Ryan North; illustrated by Braden Lamb and Shelli Paroline. Simon & Schuster 2012 128 p. Color; Illustration
Grades: 3 4 5 6 7 8 9 10   **741.5**
1. Adventure fiction; 2. Imaginary places
1608862801; 9781608862801, $14.99
"The totally algebraic adventures of Finn and Jake have come to the comic book page! The Lich, a super-lame, SUPER-SCARY skeleton dude, has returned to the the Land of Ooo, and he's bent on total destruction! Luckily, Finn and Jake are on the case . . . but can they succeed against their most destructive foe yet?" (Publisher's note)
"The comic series has been every bit as good as the show, with epic magic battles with an evil Lich, a multi-part

time travel story, and a host of backup strips by some of the best indie cartoonists out there." Comics Alliance
Volume 1 of an ongoing series

★ The **unbeatable** Squirrel Girl; Volume 1: Squirrel power!. Ryan North; illustrated by Erica Henderson. Marvel Enterprises 2015 136 p. Color; Illustration
Grades: 7 8 9 10 11 12 Adult   **741.5**
1. Female superhero graphic novels; 2. Squirrel Girl (Fictional character); 3. Squirrels — Fiction; 4. Superheroes — Fiction
0785197028; 9780785197027, $15.99
In this comic by Ryan North, illustrated by Erica Henderson, "supervillains and criminals meet their match . . . Squirrel Girl, aka Doreen Green, a college freshman with the appearance, speed, and agility of a squirrel. When Galactus threatens Earth, the heroine must rely on more than strength to defeat the Devourer of Worlds. She may have extraordinary strength . . . but it is her ability to form connections with people that proves to be her most powerful asset." (School Library Journal)
Contains material originally published in magazine form as The Unbeatable Squirrel Girl #1-4 and Marvel Super-Heroes #8
Volume 1 of an ongoing series

Novgorodoff, Danica
Slow storm. First Second 2008 172p. Illustration
Grades: 9 10 11 12   **741.5; Fic**
978-1-5964-3250-5, $17.95; 1-5964-3250-0
LC 2007-46202

Nowak, Naomi
Unholy kinship. NBM 2006 Un Illustration
Grades: 10 11 12 Adult   **741.5; Fic**
1. Dreams; 2. Mental illness; 3. Sisters; 4. Graphic novels
1-56163-482-4, $9.95
Young college student Luca has taken care of her mentally unstable older sister Gae ever since their single mother became a permanent resident of St. Mark's Asylum for the Demented. As the fall term starts, Luca starts having strange dreams as Gae begins to deteriorate emotionally. The doctors and nurses from St. Mark's Asylum claim they want to help Gae, but their drugs make things worse. And the dreams become stranger, until Luca can't be sure what is real. The cool tones of the artwork underscore the building sense of doom as the story progresses.

O'Connor, George
Aphrodite: Goddess of love. George O'Connor. First Second 2014 76 p. Color; Illustration (Olympians)
Grades: 6 7 8 9   **741.5**
1. Aphrodite (Greek deity); 2. Gods and goddesses — Fiction; 3. Graphic novels
1596437391; 1596439475; 9781596437395, $9.99; 9781596439474, $16.99
This graphic novel, volume six of the Olympians series on Greek mythology, by George O'Connor, "turns the spotlight on Aphrodite, the goddess of love. . . . O'Connor tackles the story of the Aphrodite from her dramatic birth (emerging from sea-foam) to her role in the Trojan War." (Publisher's note)

"Like the prior volumes, this book injects the mythology with an accessible modern sensibility through its colorful, action-packed graphic storytelling." Horn Book

Includes bibliographical references

Other titles in this series are:Zeus (2010); Athena (2010); Hera (2011); Hades (2012); Poseidon (2013); Ares (2015)

Ares: bringer of war. George O'Connor. First Second Books 2015 80 p. Color; Illustration (Olympians)
Grades: 4 5 6 7 8 9   **741.5**
1. Ares (Greek deity); 2. Greek mythology; 3. Trojan War
1626720134; 1626720142; 9781626720138; 9781626720145, $16.99

LC 2014041225

This graphic novel by George O'Connor "continues in the tenth year of the fabled Trojan War where two infamous gods of war go to battle. The spotlight is thrown on Ares, god of war, and primarily focuses on his battle with the clever and powerful Athena. As the battle culminates and the gods try to one-up each other to win, the human death toll mounts." (Publisher's note)

"In this nuanced, multilayered view of the usually vilified bringer of war, O'Connor continues his exceptional graphic novel series about the Greek gods. . . . The author's extensive notes amusingly explain connections to The Odyssey, The Aeneid, and the series' previous works." SLJ

A Neal Porter Book.

Other titles in this series are: Athena: Grey-eyed Goddess (2010); Zeus: King of the Gods (2010); Hera: The Goddess and her Glory (2011); Hades: Lord of the Dead (2012); Poseidon: Earth Shaker (2013); Aphrodite: Goddess of Love (2014)

★ **Olympians:** Athena, grey-eyed goddess. First Second Books 2010 78p. Illustration
Grades: 4 5 6 7 8 9   **741.5; Fic**
1. Athena (Greek deity); 2. Fantasy graphic novels; 3. Gods and goddesses; 4. Greek mythology; 5. Graphic novels
978-1-59643-432-5, $9.99

The Fates retell five tales of the goddess Athena, daughter of Zeus, a warrior and also the goddess of wisdom. The first story tells of her birth, which is unlike any other, god or human; the second and third stories tell a couple of versions of how she took the name Pallas. The fourth story recounts Athena's dealings with Medusa, and how young demigod Perseus finally killed her. The events in these stories also provide Athena with her Aegis, one of her great weapons, which incorporates the impenetrable skin of the giant Pallas and the snakes from Medusa's head with the cape Zeus made from the skin of the goat Amalthea, who had nurtured him as a child. The Fates then tell of the weaving contest between Athena and the skilled but arrogant human woman, Arachne. O'Connor includes notes that provide more information about some of the historical background, discussion questions, a bibliography, and suggestions for further reading. His full-color art utilizes some of the style of super hero comics. This is the second of twelve planned volumes.

O'Donnell, Liam
Media meltdown: a graphic guide adventure. Written by Liam O'Donnell; illustrated by Mike Deas. Orca Book Publishers 2009 Un Illustration
Grades: 6 7 8 9 10
741.5; Fic
1. Media literacy; 2. Mystery graphic novels; 3. Graphic novels
978-1-55469-065-7 (pa), $9.95; 1-55469-065-X (pa)

Courtesy of Orca Publishers

LC 2009-927573

Pema and Bounce find a new housing development going up in the middle of what used to be their favorite biking trail, and then they learn that the developer is trying to force Jagroop's farmer father to sell his land. Pema's older sister Nima has been working as an intern at the local TV station, and she tries to help the teens put together a news story about what's happening. Then they learn that the developer buys a lot of advertising on the station, and he gets the station owner to pressure the producer to kill their story. They need to get their story out, but since traditional media won't help them, they turn to alternate media on the internet and a little guerilla newscasting by Nima to stop the developer and preserve their land.

This "is an excellent choice for developing media literacy. . . . The design and layout are colorful and fast paced. The text is well written and paired with useful imagery." SLJ

★ **Power** play. Illustrated by Mike Deas. Orca Book Publishers 2011 64p. Illustration (Graphic guide adventure)
Grades: 3 4 5 6 7 8 9   **741; 741.5; Fic**
1. Mystery graphic novels; 2. Graphic novels
978-1-55469-069-5, $9.95; 1-55469-069-2

Siblings Devin and Nadia team up with their friend Marcus, Marcus' stepbrother Bounce, and Bounce's best friend Pema when they all attend the World Leaders Summit, where Marcus' father, Dr. Ashmore is scheduled to speak. The friends find themselves mixed up in a fight between some of the most powerful people in the world and those who want more equitable rights to clean water and other environmental concerns. They investigate when one

Courtesy of Orca Publishers

of Dr. Ashmore's assistants is murdered at the summit, and Dr. Ashmore receives threats.

"An enjoyable story with educational value, this strong mystery is presented along with information about world politics, power, and the benefits of political protest for social good." Booklist

Ramp rats: a graphic guide adventure. Written by Liam O'Donnell; illustrated by Mike Deas. Orca Book Publishers 2008 Un Illustration
Grades: 3 4 5 6 7 8 9   **741.5; Fic**
1. Bullies; 2. Friendship; 3. Skateboarding; 4. Graphic novels
978-1-55143-880-1 (pa), $9.95; 1-55143-880-1 (pa)
LC 2008-928577
"Benny (nicknamed Bounce) just wants to use the cool new skate park with his friend Pema, but older bullying Crunch and his friends have taken over the park. . . . Aside from the action-packed story, great characters, and colorful artwork, this graphic-novel adventure includes an array of practical skateboarding tips for beginners. The story also delivers a deft message about standing up to bullies." Booklist

System Shock. Stone Arch Books 2007 88p. Illustration
Grades: 4 5 6 7 8 9   **741.5; Fic**
1. Science fiction graphic novels; 2. Video games; 3. Graphic novels
978-1-59889-083-9 li, $22.60; 978-1-59889-214-7 (pa)
LC 2006007185
In a futuristic society, Daniel, Jack, and Jemma find themselves lost in a virtual reality game. To make matters worse, every video-game villain seems to be pursuing them. Even if they defeat the evil Cyborgs, the controllers in Realworld are working on wiping the corrupt system clean. If the friends don't find a way out soon, they are in danger of being erased forever. This graphic novel is written at an easy level for reluctant and struggling readers.
Part of the Graphic Quest series.

O'Malley, Bryan Lee
Scott Pilgrim's Precious Little Life, Vol. 1. Oni Press 2004 Un Illustration
Grades: 10 11 12 Adult   **741.5; Fic**
1. Humorous graphic novels; 2. Martial arts; 3. Romance graphic novels; 4. Graphic novels
1-932664-08-4, $11.95
Twenty-three-year-old musician Scott Pilgrim is going steady with a Chinese high school girl (it's totally platonic), when he starts seeing a rollerblading girl in his dreams, at the library, at a party. . . She's Ramona Flowers, and Scott totally falls for her, just as Knives (his high school girl friend) wants to start heating up their relationship. Then, Scott discovers that he will have to fight Ramona's seven evil ex-boyfriends before he and Ramona can get together. It's wacky romance and martial arts action.
Also available in full-color hardcover editions
Other titles in this series are: Scott Pilgrim vs. the World (2005); Scott Pilgrim & the Infinite Sadness (2006); Scott Pilgrim Gets It Together (2007); Scott Pilgrim vs. the Universe (2009); Scott Pilgrim's Finest Hour (2010)

★ **Seconds**. Bryan Lee O'Malley. Ballantine Books 2014 336 p. Color; Illustration
Grades: 11 12 Adult   **741.5**
1. Restaurants — Fiction; 2. Graphic novels
0345529375; 9780345529374, $25

LC 2013456979
In this graphic novel by Bryan Lee O'Malley, "Katie's got it pretty good. She's a talented young chef, she runs a successful restaurant, and she has big plans to open an even better one. Then, all at once, progress on the new location bogs down, her charming ex-boyfriend pops up, her fling with another chef goes sour, and her best waitress gets badly hurt. And just like that, Katie's life goes from pretty good to not so much." (Publisher's note)
"O'Malley's engaging narrative voice hasn't diminished—ïeven the self-absorbed Katie is likeable enough to root for, although it's obvious that she's making things worse for herself. O'Malley's sweet, nimble art, now in color, has acquired more confidence: the plot unfolds cinematically, and his character designs are more appealing than ever." Pub Wkly

O'Neil, Dennis
★ **Green** Lantern, Green Arrow. Dennis O'Neil, Elliot Maggin, writers; Neal Adams, penciller; Neal Adams, Dick Giordano, Frank Giacoia, Dan Adkins, Berni Wrightson, inkers; Cory Adams, Jack Adler, colorists; John Costanza, Joe Letterese, letterers. DC Comics 2012 361 p. Color illustration
Grades: 10 11 12 Adult   **741.5**
1. Green Arrow (Fictional character); 2. Green Lantern (Fictional character); 3. Superheroes
1401235174; 9781401235178, $29.99
LC 2013363523
In this comic book collection, "Green Lantern Hal Jordan continued his usual cosmic-spanning adventures, as he used his amazing Power Ring to police Sector 2814 against universe-threatening menaces. Meanwhile, on Earth, Oliver Queen, the archer known as Green Arrow, was confronting menaces of a different kind: racism, poverty, drugs, and other social ills!" (Publisher's note)
Originally published in single magazine form in Green Lantern 76-87, 89; Flash 217-219, 226. Green Lantern/Green Arrow 1-7.

The **Question:** Zen and violence. Dennis O'Neil, writer; Denys Cowan, penciller. DC Comics 2007 174p. Illustration
Grades: 11 12 Adult   **741.5; Fic**
1. Crime; 2. Superhero graphic novels; 3. Graphic novels
978-1-4012-1579-8, $19.99
Investigative reporter Vic Sage, who is also the faceless, morally conflicted avenger known as The Question, works to bring down the politically corrupted mayor of Hub City and his advisers, but they have hired the mercenary Lady Shiva, who defeats him in combat and the henchmen of the crooked Rev. Hatch throw him into the river. But, Sage is not dead, he's rescued and healed, and told to find Richard Dragon. He stays with Dragon for a year, training in martial arts and disciplining himself. When he returns to Hub City, he now has the focus to go after the criminals and politicians mucking up the city. The book includes lots of violence and some harsh language.

O, Se-Yong
Buja's diary. NBM 2005 280p. Illustration
Grades: 11 12 Adult   **741.5; Fic**

1. Korea (South); 2. Graphic novels
1-56163-448-4; 978-1-56163-448-4, $19.95

LC 2005-50519

The thirteen "stories by this Korean "manwha" (comic book) author relate poignant tales of distressed humanity struggling with family, history, and culture. . . . Although O's eye is not unsympathetic, the world he depicts is unforgiving, sometimes graphically so. . . . Originally published in 1995, this book is a thoughtful examination of the human condition in the Korea of the recent past as well as universally." Voice Youth Advocates

Oakley, Mark
  Thieves & kings. [by Mark Oakley]. I Box Pub 1998 154p. Illustration
  Grades: 4 5 6 7 8 9 10 11 12   **741.5; Fic**
    1. Adventure graphic novels; 2. Fantasy graphic novels; 3. Graphic novels
  0-9681025-0-6, $18.95

LC 2003-446777

In a story that mixes pages of text with pages of comic book art, the reader meets the young thief Rubel, who has returned home from a long voyage to find things no longer as they were. He has to deal with soldiers and pirates, princes and princesses, a strange young wizard, and a mysterious Shadow Lady.
  Originally published as individual issues of the Thieves & kings comic series, beginning in 1994
  Volume 1 of 5

  Thieves & Kings Presents The Walking Mage. I Box Publishing 2006 Un Illustration
  Grades: 5 6 7 8 9 10 11 12   **741.5; Fic**
    1. Fantasy graphic novels; 2. Humorous graphic novels; 3. Graphic novels
  0-9681025-5-7, $9.95

In the world of Thieves & Kings, the royal wizard, Quinton Zempfester, has lost his job. Again. This time, though, his name has also been added to the top of the kingdom's list of most wanted criminals. Unfairly accused by the dark witch who has seized the throne, Quinton decides that perhaps a little treason might not be such a bad idea after all ... This book chronicles a side adventure in the series, and is done completely in comic book panels rather than the mix of prose and panels used in the main series.

Obara, Shinji
  Samurai Champloo Film Manga Vol. 1. Bandai Entertainment 2006 194p. Illustration
  Grades: 8 9 10 11 12 Adult   **741.5; Fic**
    1. Adventure graphic novels; 2. Humorous graphic novels; 3. Manga; 4. Samurai; 5. Graphic novels
  978-1-59409-523-8, $10.99

After causing a great riot at a teahouse, Mugen and Jin are arrested by the magistrate and set to be executed. In exchange for helping them, teahouse maid Fuu makes them promise to travel with her to find a samurai who smells like a sunflower." When they leave her behind, Mugen and Jin each end up getting hired as a bodyguard by the two rival groups that rule a town. However, they both promised Fuu they wouldn't kill each other until they finish helping her. The anime series combines samurai drama with hip-hop

sensibilities; this manga uses frames from the anime. Foul language is replaced by nonsense symbols, but there is still considerable fighting violence. The anime was directed by Shinichiro Watanabe.
  "It is a fascinating exploration of two brilliant young men and their intricate relationship even as the story explores the idea of 'the ends justify the means.'" (VOYA)
  Also available in 2-in-1 editions
  Volume 1 of a 12 volume series

Obata, Yuki
  ★ **We** were there, vol. 1. Story & art by Yuki Obata. Viz Media/Shojo Beat 2008 Un Illustration
  Grades: 10 11 12   **741.5; Fic**
    1. Manga; 2. Romance graphic novels; 3. Shojo manga; 4. Graphic novels

Fifteen-year-old Nanami Takahashi has just started high school, with high hopes for making friends and doing well, but things don't go as smoothly as she had hoped. She struggles with math, then she gets sort of railroaded into being the class president. She also falls for Motoharu Yano, an irresponsible boy who somehow is the most popular person in the class. His carefree attitude covers his grief for the death of his girlfriend, an older girl whose younger sister is their classmate, Yuri Yamamoto. Nanami struggles with classwork, with the responsibilities of being class president, and with her conflicting feelings about Motoharu. Some of the black and white art looks airbrushed; these pages occur at the beginning of each chapter. Viz has rated this series for older teens due to sexual themes, but they don't occur in this first volume.
  Original Japanese edition, 2002
  Volume 1 of 18

Ocampo, Ruiz, Jose Alfonso
  20,000 leagues under the sea. Stone Arch Books 2008 72p. Illustration
  Grades: 4 5 6 7 8 9   **741.5; Fic**
    1. Adventure graphic novels; 2. Science fiction graphic novels; 3. Submarines
  978-1-4342-0447-9, $23.93; 978-1-4342-0497-4 (pa), $9.95

Scientist Pierre Aronnax and his servant set sail to help hunt a sea monster threatening ships, but they and master harpooner Ned Land discover that the monster is actually a submarine, the Nautilus. The submarine's leader, Captain Nemo, takes the three men captive and they journey under the sea, where they see many wonders; but they must each decide whether they should trust Nemo, who bears a bitter secret, or try to escape. This graphic novel adaptation of Verne's classic adventure novel uses simple language to help reluctant and struggling readers understand the story.
  Part of the Graphic Revolve series

Ocha, Machiko
  Train Man: A Shojo Manga. Manga by Machiko Ocha; original story by Hitori Nakano. Del Rey Manga 2006 192p. Illustration
  Grades: 9 10 11 12   **741.5; Fic**
    1. Romance graphic novels; 2. Shojo manga; 3. Graphic novels
  978-0-345-49619-5, $10.95

This is another version of the story also told in Densha Otoko and in Train Man: Densha Otoko. In this version, the story of a young anime fan who saves a pretty young woman and then pursues a romantic relationship with the help of an online forum is told in one volume. The art style is the softer, more romantic look from shojo manga (manga for girls and teen girls), although there is one panel depicting a page from an adult-oriented manga that Train Man reads. The book also includes an essay that gives background information about the supposedly true story that inspired the novel, the several manga series, a movie, and a television series.

Ochi, Yoshihiko
Atelier Marie and Elie, Zarlburg Alchemist. Tokyopop 2008 159p. Illustration
Grades: 8 9 10 11 12   **741.5; Fic**
1. Adventure graphic novels; 2. Fantasy graphic novels; 3. Humorous graphic novels; 4. Manga; 5. Graphic novels
978-1-59816-528-9, $9.99
Millie accidentally puts a tadpole into a magical barrel in her workshop, and now Ingrid, Marie, and Elie need to find a watery home for the creature before it does too much damage to the town. Then, along with demon Strafe, they go on a journey to deliver medicines and such, only to encounter troublesome magical beasts. The book includes some minor fan service with a few skimpy women's tops.

Atelier Marie and Elie, Zarlburg Alchemist Vol. 2. Tokyopop 2007 Un Illustration
Grades: 8 9 10 11 12   **741.5; Fic**
1. Adventure graphic novels; 2. Fantasy graphic novels; 3. Manga; 4. Graphic novels
978-1-59816-526-5, $9.99
Alchemists Marie and Elie run their shop, teach two young elves, build a better flying broom, take down some thieves, and help a half-demon half-human warrior friend. Now if they can just manage to do all that without blowing up Zarlburg around them ... The book includes some mild violence.

Atelier Marie and Elie: Zarlburg Alchemist Volume 1. Tokyopop 2007 162p. Illustration
Grades: 7 8 9 10 11 12 Adult   **741.5; Fic**
1. Fantasy graphic novels; 2. Manga
978-1-59816-525-8, $9.99
Welcome to the Zarlburg Royal Magic Academy" producers of the best alchemists in the world. When Marie, Zalburg's prodigal daughter and premier alchemist, returns to her alma mater after thrilling journeys in many foreign lands, she suddenly realizes things are not too exciting at home. But all that changes after running into fellow alchemist Elie, who has plans to open an alchemy workshop and become famous. Now, adventure comes to them in all shapes and sizes—curious elves, flying broomsticks, giant monsters, and explosive bombs. It's all inside Yoshihiko Ochi's new manga series based on the popular video game franchise. There's lots of monster fighting action.

Oda, Eiichiro
★ **One** Piece Volume 1. Viz Media/Shonen Jump 2003 216p. Illustration
Grades: 8 9 10 11 12 Adult   **741.5; Fic**

1. Adventure graphic novels; 2. Fantasy graphic novels; 3. Manga; 4. Shonen manga; 5. Graphic novels
1-56931-901-4, $7.95
Monkey D. Luffy's main ambition is to become a pirate, inspired by listening to the tales of the buccaneer "Red-Haired" Shanks. When he accidentally eats the Gum-Gum Fruit, it gives him strange powers to stretch like rubber, but doing so also invokes the fruit's curse: anybody who consumes it can never learn to swim. Nevertheless, Monkey and his crewmate Roronoa Zoro, master of the three-sword fighting style, sail the Seven Seas of swashbuckling adventure in search of the elusive treasure "One Piece." As the series goes on, Luffy gains more crew and they encounter sea monsters, far away kingdoms, cloud island, and super powered pirates of every shape, size, and description - which means lots of epic and comical fight scenes.
Volume 1 of an ongoing series

Oeming, Michael Avon
Bastard Samurai Vol. 1, 2nd printing. Conceived, co-written and inked by Mike Avon Oeming; written and co-created by Miles Gunter; penciled, colored and co-created by Kelsey Shannon. Image Comics 2007 Un Illustration
Grades: 11 12 Adult   **741.5; Fic**
1. Adventure graphic novels; 2. Samurai
978-1-58240-746-3, $12.99
Jiro is a student of the KoZu Sword School, an underground training camp in midtown Manhattan that takes in orphans and twists and transforms them into Bushido warriors. The Yakuza use these kids in death matches staged across the city rooftops where Japanese businessmen gamble heavily on the always-fatal outcome. This killing life is all Jiro has ever known. But a rendezvous with fate is about to change all of that when he learns his latest kill is his own long-lost older brother. In one moment Jiro realizes that everything he has lived for is a lie. The Samurai live by the Bushido code, one of which is rectitude: the righting of wrongs. Now he sets out on a campaign of vengeance, determined to topple the entire organization. The story is full of foul language, some sexual situations, and lots of fighting action and violence, with plenty of beheadings.

Blood River. Written by Michael Avon Oeming and Daniel Berman; artwork by Brian Quinn; lettering by Adam Levine. Image Comics 2005 Un Illustration
Grades: 10 11 12 Adult   **741.5; Fic**
1. Graphic novels
1-58240-509-3, $7.99
Sex, Drugs and Zeppelin! In the 1970s, four life-long friends plan their escape from a small town in New Jersey. They like to have drug parties out in the woods, but one night they find that fate, nature or some monstrous power has other plans for them... Based on a true story. Readers will find a recount of a true incident from the summer of 1916. Besides the use of drugs, readers will encounter considerable harsh language.

The **Cross** Bronx. Writers, Michael Avon Oeming and Ivan Brandon; artist, Michael Avon Oeming. Image Comics 2007 Un Illustration
Grades: 12 Adult   **741.5; Fic**

1. Mystery graphic novels; 2. Supernatural graphic novels; 3. Graphic novels
978-1-58240-690-9, $14.99

In New York City, veteran detective Rafael Aponte catches a homicide case that's not exactly a gang hit, but is definitely bloody and awful. Aponte finds a gun at the scene, and he learns it belonged to a beat cop who was killed on the job years before. When he visits the widow, he finds out their daughter is in the hospital, in a coma; she'd been repeatedly raped, beaten, then thrown out of a car. Soon Aponte realizes that the widow may be using dark arts to have her daughter's spirit take vengeance on those who hurt her, such as the men killed in the first homicide case.

This powerful story includes a lot of violence, harsh language, and some nudity.

Originally published as The Cross Bronx issues #1-4

Ogishima, Chiaki
Heat Guy J. Original story by Kazuki Akane and Satelight; character design by Nobuteru Yuki; art and story by Chiaki Ogishima. Tokyopop 2005 224p. Illustration
Grades: 10 11 12 Adult   **741.5; Fic**
1. Manga; 2. Mystery graphic novels; 3. Science fiction graphic novels; 4. Shonen manga; 5. Graphic novels
1-59182-777-9, $9.99

Daisuke Aurora works with the special division of peacekeepers in the city of Jewde, one of the largest cities on the planet. He and his android partner, Heat Guy J, team up to make sure that anything illegal stays off the streets and out of circulation. However, their presence doesn't sit too well with the local mob leader—a ruthless, unbalanced, well-armed son of the late Don, who is out to prove that he is not too young to take over the family business. In the city that never sleeps, will Daisuke and Heat Guy J sleep with the fishes? The book includes violence, strong language, partial nudity, and sexual situations.

Ogiwara, Noriko
The **Good** Witch of the West, Vol. 1. Tokyopop 2006 Un Illustration
Grades: 7 8 9 10 11 12 Adult   **741.5; Fic**
1. Fantasy graphic novels; 2. Shojo manga; 3. Graphic novels
1-59816-620-4, $9.99

Fifteen-year-old Firiel has grown up with her reclusive astronomer father, his devoted servants, and his apprentice, Rune. Life is basically good, until the night Firiel attends the Count's ball. She wears a necklace from her dead mother, and it turns out the necklace identifies her as one of the heirs to the throne of Graal. Her father, Professor Dee, has been branded a heretic, and now that people know Firiel is the daughter of Princess Edilene, events have been set into motion, bringing danger and death to the people she loves. This is the first volume of a manga series.

Oh! Great
Air Gear Vol. 1. Random House/Del Rey Manga 2006 Un Illustration
Grades: 10 11 12 Adult   **741.5; Fic**
1. Adventure graphic novels; 2. Shonen manga
978-0-345-49278-4, $10.95

LC Bd 06-250081

Itsuki Minami is the toughest kid at Higashi Junior High School, plus he lives with the mysterious and sexy Noyamano sisters. Life is never dull, but it becomes dangerous when Itsuki leads his school to victory over some vindictive Westside punks with gangster connections. Now he stands to lose his school, his friends, and everything he cares about. But in his darkest hour, the Noyamano girls come to Itsuki's aid. They can teach him a powerful skill that will save their school from the gangsters' siege-and introduce Itsuki to a thrilling and terrifying new world. The series includes crude humor, violence, partial nudity, sexual situations (including hints at sexual violence), and harsh language.

Ohba, Tsugumi
Death Note, Vol. 1. Story by Tsugumi Ohba; art by Takeshi Obata. Viz Shonen Jump Advanced 2005 196p. Illustration
Grades: 10 11 12   **741.5; Fic**
1. Manga; 2. Suspense graphic novels; 3. Graphic novels
1-4215-0168-6, $7.99

When brilliant, bored high school student Light Kagami finds a Death Note, a notebook that belongs to a shinigami (Japanese death god), he decides to improve the world by ridding it of criminals. The police frown upon the murders and investigate, and the brilliant and eccentric young detective known only as L joins the police in Japan to hunt the killer. Light has Ryuk, the shinigami whose Death Note he's using, so the game is on.

Oima, Yoshitoki
A **silent** voice; Volume 1. Yoshitoki Oima; translation, lettering, Steven LeCroy. Kodansha 2015 186 p. Illustration
Grades: 7 8 9 10   **741.5; Fic**
1. Bullies; 2. Deaf children; 3. School stories
163236056X; 9781632360564, $10.99

"Shoya is a bully. When Shoko, a girl who can't hear, enters his elementary school class, she becomes their favorite target. . . . But the children's cruelty goes too far. Shoko is forced to leave the school, and Shoya ends up shouldering all the blame. Six years later, the two meet again. Can Shoya make up for his past mistakes, or is it too late?" (Publisher's note)

Volume 1 of 7

Okabayashi, Kensuke
Manga for dummies. Wiley Publishing, Inc. 2007 416p. Illustration (—For dummies)
Grades: 9 10 11 12 Adult   **741.5**
1. Graphic novels — Drawing; 2. Manga
978-0-470-08025-2, $19.99

LC 2006-939589

This guide, written and illustrated by Okabayashi, who teaches art at the Educational Alliance Art School in New York City and who has interned with manga creators in Japan, shows aspiring manga artists how to create characters, how to draw weapons, cars, animals, and more, how to create plotlines and storyboards, how to convey motion and emotion, and more.

Okamoto, Kazuhiro
  Translucent Volume One. Dark Horse Comics 2007
192p. Illustration
Grades: 7 8 9 10 11 12   **741.5; Fic**
  1. Humorous graphic novels; 2. Manga; 3. Romance
graphic novels; 4. Graphic novels
  978-1-59307-647-4, $9.95
  Eighth grader Shizuka is an introverted girl, dealing
with schoolwork, boys, and a medical condition - the
Translucent Syndrome - that begins to turn her invisible. She
finds support with Mamoru, a hyperactive boy who is falling
for Shizuka despite her condition, and with Keiko, another
girl who suffers from this illness and has finally turned
completely invisible. The mysterious disease that these teens
struggle with becomes a metaphor in the ordinary lives of the
students in their classes, as they try to work their way
through their friendships and romances. There are brief
moments of partial nudity.

Okuda, Hitoshi
  No Need for Tenchi! Vol. 1 (2nd edition). Viz Media
2004 184p. Illustration
Grades: 8 9 10 11 12 Adult   **741.5; Fic**
  1. Adventure graphic novels; 2. Humorous graphic
novels; 3. Shonen manga; 4. Graphic novels
  1-59116-610-1, $9.99
  The trouble and fun began when ordinary teenager
Tenchi Masaki inadvertently released the legendary demon
Ryoko from his grandfather's shrine. Turned out Ryoko was
actually a marooned space pirate; since then, she's become
Tenchi's unwanted houseguest, attracting a host of other
troublemaking alien women: Ayeka, a haughty alien pricess;
Sasami, her mischievous little sister; and Washu, Ryoko's
mad-scientist "mother." Add Ryo-oh-Ki, an adorable little
carrot-eating spaceship, and you've got one full Shinto
shrine. Now Tenchi's troubles double—in the form of
Minagi, a dead-ringer for Ryoko who attacks our hapless
friends and then conveniently develops amnesia. But Minagi
is just a pawn of the alien warrior Yakage, who plans to steal
Tenchi's miraculous sword and abduct Ayeka. And the only
hero who has what it takes to rescue the kidnapped princess
is...Ryoko. The series includes some sexual innuendo,
raunchy humor, comic violence, and a little strong language.

Oliver, Simon
  The **Exterminators** Vol. 1: The Bug Brothers. Simon
Oliver, writer; Tony Moore, artist; Brian Buccellato,
colorist; Pat Brosseau, letter; Philip Bond, cover artist. DC
Comics/Vertigo 2006 128p. Illustration
Grades: 11 12 Adult   **741.5; Fic**
  1. Horror graphic novels; 2. Graphic novels
  978-1-4012-1064-9, $9.99
  This book focuses on a dysfunctional group of bug
killers prowling the barrios and bungalows of Los Angeles.
Henry James, the newest exterminator, sees the job as a way
to cleanse the sins of his dark past; he has a hard time getting
his view across to his careerist girlfriend, sociopathic partner
and the general bunch of freaks he calls co-workers.
Meanwhile, what Henry and the "bug brothers" of
Bug-Bee-Gone Co. don't understand is that human beings
may be the true pests - and bugs could be the real
exterminator. This book has graphic violence, some nudity

and sexual situations, and lots and lots of nasty bugs, rats,
and other pests.

Olliffe, Pat
  Spider-Girl Vol. 3: Avenging Allies. Marvel
Entertainment 2005 Un. Illustration
Grades: 7 8 9 10 11 12   **741.5; Fic**
  1. Avengers (Fictional characters); 2. Spider-Girl
(Fictional character); 3. Superhero graphic novels; 4.
Graphic novels
  0-7851-1658-3, $7.99
  The adventures of Spider-Man's daughter continue as
Mayday Parker faces defeat and disgrace at the hands of
Darkdevil and Kaine, then she has to prove her fighting
mettle by taking on the Avengers one at a time. Plus: Beset
by problems in her civilian guise, Spider-Girl teams up with
Speedball to take on Mr. Abnormal, the most flexible felon
of all.

Olson, Kay Melchisedech
  Benjamin Franklin: An American Genius. Illustrated
by Barabara Schulz and Gordon Purcell. Capstone Press
2006 32p. Illustration
Grades: 3 4 5 6 7 8 9   **741.5; 973.3; 92**
  1. Franklin, Benjamin, 1706-1790; 2. Graphic novels
  0-7368-4269-8, $25.26
                                             LC 2005003964
  This book uses the comic book format to recount
highlights in the life of American statesman and inventor
Benjamin Franklin. It includes additional information, a
glossary, a list of books for further reading, and more.
  Part of the Graphic Library, Graphic Biographies series.

  Betsy Ross and the American Flag. Illustrated by Anna
Maria Cool, Sam Delarosa, and Charles Barnett III.
Capstone Press 2006 32p. Illustration
Grades: 3 4 5 6 7 8 9   **741.5; 973.3; 92**
  1. Flags; 2. Ross, Betsy, 1752-1836; 3. United States —
History — 1775-1783, Revolution; 4. Graphic novels
  0-7368-4962-9, $25.26
                                             LC 2005006461
  This book uses the comic book format to tell the story of
the life of Betsy Ross and the legend of her sewing the first
American flag. It includes additional information, a
glossary, a list of books for further reading, and more.
  Part of the Graphic Library, Graphic History series.

  Frank Zamboni and the Ice-Resurfacing Machine by
Kay Melchisedech Olson ; illustrated by Richard
Dominguez and Charles Barnett, III. Capstone Press 2007
32p. Illustration
Grades: 3 4 5 6 7 8 9   **688.7; 741.5; 92**
  1. Ice skating; 2. Inventors; 3. Zamboni, Frank; 4. Graphic
novels
  1429601477; 9781429601474, $29.99
                                             LC 2007000254
  This book uses the graphic novel format to tell how
Frank Zamboni created the ice-resurfacing machine, and
how it affected the world of ice-based sports. The book
includes additional facts and a list of books for further
reading.
  Part of the Graphic Library Inventions and Discovery
series.

Olson, Nathan

Nathan Hale: Revolutionary Spy. Illustrated by Cynthia Martin and Brent Schoonover. Capstone Press 2006 32p. Illustration

Grades: 3 4 5 6 7 8 9   **741.5; 973.3; 92**
1. Biographical graphic novels; 2. Hale, Nathan, 1755-1776; 3. Graphic novels
0-7368-4968-8, $25.26

                     LC 2005007894

This book uses the comic book format to recount highlights of the life story of Revolutionary War hero and spy Nathan Hale. It includes additional information, a glossary, a list of books for further reading, and more.

Part of the Graphic Library, Graphic Biographies series.

One (Manga author)

★ One-punch man; Volume 1. Story by One; art by Yusuke Murata. Viz 2015 189 p. Illustration

Grades: 8 9 10 11 12 Adult   **741.5; Fic**
1. Manga; 2. Superheroes; 3. Graphic novels
1421585642; 9781421585642, $9.99

Eisner Nominee: Best U.S. Edition of International Material—Asia (2015)

"Saitama passes the eyeball test when it comes to superheroes, from his lifeless expression to his bald head to his unimpressive physique. However, this average-looking guy has a not-so-average problem—he just can't seem to find an opponent strong enough to take on! Every time a promising villain appears, he beats the snot out of 'em with one punch!" (Publisher's note)

"The story is fast-paced, humorous, and entertaining in a way that looks and feels like an action movie." SLJ

Volume 1 of an ongoing series

Ono, Fuyumi

Ghost hunt, Vol. 1. Manga by Shiho Inada; story by Fuyumi Ono; translated by Akira Tsubasa; adapted by David Walsh; lettered by Foltz Design. Del Rey Manga 2005 216p. Illustration

Grades: 8 9 10 11 12 Adult   **741.5; Fic**
1. Horror graphic novels; 2. Manga; 3. Shojo manga; 4. Graphic novels
0-345-48624-2, $10.95

A decrepit old building stands on the campus of Mai's high school; every time the school tries to demolish it, unexplained accidents occur. Finally, the school hires a psychic researcher, and when Mai accidentally injures his assistant and damages an expensive camera, Shibuya (the researcher) insists she work off her debt by helping him. A miko (Shinto priestess), a Buddhist monk, and a Roman Catholic exorcist also come—but none of their methods work to stop the strange occurrences. Despite herself, Mai gets drawn into the investigation. This is the first of an ongoing manga series that provides some ghostly thrills without graphic violence, bad language, or sexual innuendo.

Ono, Natsume

★ Gente: the people of Ristorante Paradiso, volume 1. Story and art by Natsume Ono; translation Joe Yamazaki. Viz Signature 2010 Un Illustration

Grades: 10 11 12 Adult   **741.5; Fic**

1. Family; 2. Josei manga; 3. Manga; 4. Restaurants; 5. Graphic novels
978-1-4215-3251-6, $12.99

In this companion and prequel to Ono's Ristorante Paradiso, readers meet the various handsome, mature, bespectacled men who staff Casetta dell'Orso, a popular restaurant in Rome. The stories in this volume include how Lorenzo, the owner, decides to choose the type of men that his wife Olga finds attractive; how cranky Luciano tries to hide his kind heart even as he babysits his young grandson; how playboy Vito meets a lonely college student at a health club; and more. Ono's somewhat sketchy art style is vastly different from the typical manga, more European than Japanese. While this is rated for Older Teens by the publisher, there is no content to raise any concerns, but its gentle, quiet stories focused on adults may appeal more to older teens and adults.

First volume of an ongoing series

Onote, Sora

Metamo Kiss, Volume 1. Tokyopop 2007 168p. Illustration

Grades: 9 10 11 12 Adult   **741.5; Fic**
1. Humorous graphic novels; 2. Romance graphic novels; 3. Shojo manga; 4. Graphic novels
978-1-59816-827-3, $9.99

Kohamaru has moved from the countryside to meet his family for the first time, when he literally runs into a girl at the train station, and they switch bodies. Nanao, the girl he ran into, wants to date Konatsu, who is Kohamaru's fraternal twin brother. The switched bodies, well, that's a family trait, and one generally can only switch with one's soul mate. Konatsu can't switch bodies, but somehow his kiss can cause Kohamaru and Nano to get back into their own bodies. Nanao will do what it takes to get close to Konatsu, who doesn't care about her; meanwhile, hapless Kohamaru is caught in the middle.

Oprisko, Kris

The Complete Metal Gear Solid. Written by Kris Oprisko; art by Ashley Wood. IDW Publishing 2006 Un Illustration

Grades: 10 11 12 Adult   **741.5; Fic**
1. Adventure graphic novels; 2. Science fiction graphic novels; 3. Graphic novels
978-1-60010031-7, $55.00; 978-1-600100-17-1 (pa), $35.00

This graphic novel adapts the storyline from the popular console game. Infiltration expert Solid Snake attempts to save the world from a band of genetically enhanced terrorists who have overrun a secret weapons facility in Alaska. Metal Gear Solid is a shooting game, and this book is full of shooting and fighting sequences.

Orff, Joel

Thunderhead Underground Falls. Alternative Comics 2007 Un Illustration

Grades: 10 11 12 Adult   **741.5**
1. Friendship; 2. Graphic novels
1-891867-88-1

Jack, a young army reservist, has one weekend left before shipping out for combat in the Middle East. He and a friend find themselves behind the wheel of his parent's car, driving farther and farther west into a snowy landscape. The book is an impressionistic exploration of Jack's flight from his future, as well as an exploration of this place that he's pledged his life to fight for. Jack and his friends want to experience the simple freedom of taking a drive, of seeing familiar things before his outlook is changed forever by the violence that he knows he will soon face. As the hours go by, Jack begins to consider desertion, but he knows that if he stays to hold onto the life that he knows, it will still be changed forever.

Orr, Tamra
Manga artists. [by] Tamra Orr. Rosen Publishing Group 2009 64p. Illustration (Extreme careers)
Grades: 4 5 6 7 8 9   **741.5**
1. Graphic novels — Authorship; 2. Manga — Authorship; 3. Vocational guidance
978-1-4042-1854-3, $29.25

LC 2007-50666

This book provides an introduction to manga as a format of Japanese comics, including a brief history and mentions some famous mangaka (manga creators). It also provides information on what it's like to be a mangaka in Japan, and how to become a manga-style artist in the U.S.
Includes glossary and bibliographical references
Part of the Extreme Careers series

Osada, Yuko
Toto! the wonderful adventure vol.1. Del Rey Manga 2008 204p. Illustration
Grades: 7 8 9 10 11 12   **741.5; Fic**
1. Adventure graphic novels; 2. Dogs; 3. Humorous graphic novels; 4. Shonen manga; 5. Graphic novels
978-0-345-50147-9, $10.95

Orphaned Kakashi is a small-town boy with a big dream, to travel around the world like his long-lost explorer father. He's so determined to leave his little island home that he stows away on board a zeppelin. What he doesn't know is that the Man Chicken crime family has hijacked the zeppelin. What they don't know is that the zeppelin carries a cargo that the military wants back at any cost. Could it possibly be the cute little puppy Kakashi befriends in the cargo hold? When the military attacks the zeppelin, the Boss of the Man Chicken family straps the last parachute onto Kakashi and kicks him out of the burning aircraft. On the ground, Kakashi meets Dorothy, a girl about his age who names the puppy Toto. Neither of them knows why the military wants the dog so badly. Just what is Toto? The book includes some violence and Kakashi shouts a lot.

Toto! the wonderful adventure vol.2. Del Rey Manga 2008 202p. Illustration
Grades: 7 8 9 10 11 12 Adult   **741.5; Fic**
1. Adventure graphic novels; 2. Manga; 3. Science fiction graphic novels; 4. Graphic novels
978-0-345-50555-2, $10.95

In this second volume, Dorothy and Kakashi have been trapped in a burning building by the Nassau Imperial Army, who are there to recover Toto, their "test subject." The cute little dog had turned into a gigantic monster, but Toto saves Dorothy and Kakashi. When the Army then tries to destroy

Toto and Kakashi gets to him first, they merge, and the dog bracelet that had been around Toto's neck is now on Kakashi's right wrist. When danger threatens, Toto the monstrous weapon emerges from Kakashi's hand. The two kids flee to Dego City, hoping to catch a train to Emerald, but the Nassau Army has occupied the city and destroyed all the trains to use the metal for weapons. Kakashi and Dorothy meet Millica, an older girl who saves them, and the soldier Noil, who would much rather become a standup comedian. The book includes some violence and mild fan service.

Osborne, Rob
1000 Steps to World Domination. AiT/Planet Lar 2004 Un Illustration
Grades: 9 10 11 12 Adult   **741.5; Fic**
1. Humorous graphic novels; 2. Graphic novels
1-932051-26-0, $12.95
2003 Isotope Award for Excellence in Mini-Comics; 2004 Broken Frontier Paper Screen Gem Award for Humor.

Can one achieve world domination by writing comics? With a supportive spouse, one can do a lot. But what about talking chiimpanzees in plaid suits - or clown suits" The dog is not impressed.

Sunset City, For Active Senior Living. AiT/Planet Lar 2005 Un Illustration
Grades: 12 Adult   **741.5; Fic**
1. Retirement communities; 2. Graphic novels
1-932051-41-4, $9.95

Sunset City is a typical retirement community. Its residents enjoy golf and gossip and they all seem content to fritter away their golden years. Except Frank McDonald. A retired widower, he wrestles with the question: why am I here? Reading the newspaper, Frank keeps up on the minutia of the day; it provides a buzz to an otherwise humdrum life. One morning, Frank is overcome by a startling story, and he does something extraordinary: he takes life by the balls. The story includes some harsh language and violence, and the climactic scene may bother some readers.

Osborne, Wayne
FX. Art by John Byrne. IDW Publishing 2008 160p. Illustration
Grades: 7 8 9 10 11 12 Adult   **741.5; Fic**
1. Adventure graphic novels; 2. Humorous graphic novels; 3. Superhero graphic novels; 4. Graphic novels
978-1-60010-274-5, $19.99

Teenager Tom Talbot was playing with his best friend when Jack accidentally hit Tom so hard he went into a coma. When Tom recovers, he discovers that he's got the power to make what he imagines be real; he discovers this when they're playing around in an alley and Tom imagines he's got a bazooka and really destroys a dumpster. He cobbles together a masked costume, and finds himself fighting superpowered giant talking apes, nasty weapons-bearing lizards, and more. But someone notices him and decides he wants Tom's powers Lord Everos, the Father of Death. And it's not just Tom, either; Vicki, the class weirdo, does really talk with the dead, and Lord Everos wants her, too. And that's not the worst of it, for apparently Tom was never supposed to get the power of the thunderbolt, and a whole pantheon of heroes has just arrived to stop him. Oops again.

Ostrander, John
The **Legend** of Grimjack, Volume 1. Script, John Ostrander; art, Timothy Truman. IDW Publishing 2005 125p. Illustration
Grades: 10 11 12 Adult   **741.5; Fic**
1. Adventure graphic novels; 2. Fantasy graphic novels; 3. Graphic novels
1-932382-51-8, $19.99
Gathering all of the earliest GrimJack stories from the comic book series of the 1980s in one tome for the first time, The Legend of GrimJack, Volume One introduces the major characters and origin stories and also includes the GrimJack/Starslayer crossover saga. This volume also includes a brand new story and art as well as critical background information heretofore unrevealed. The book is full of grim, gritty action with considerable violence; the comics were originally published by First Comics in 1983 and 1984.

Star Wars: Clone Wars Volume 1: The Defense of Kamino. John Ostrander and Haden Blackman. Dark Horse Comics 2003 Un Illustration
Grades: 7 8 9 10 11 12 Adult   **741.5; Fic**
1. Adventure graphic novels; 2. Science fiction graphic novels; 3. Star Wars; 4. Graphic novels
1-56971-962-4, $14.95
Two undercover Jedi discover a Separatist plan to destroy the cloning facility on the watery world of Kamino, thus crippling the Republic's ability to maintain their clone army. Obi-Wan Kenobi and Anakin Skywalker are part of a Jedi fighter squadron sent to protect the installation. Meanwhile, Mace Windu, the leader of the Jedi Council, must deal with a rift in the Jedi ranks—a matter that reveals a Jedi traitor and a new Dark Jedi working in league with Dooku. Mace is considered one of the best swordsmen in the galaxy, but can he stand up to the sword master who taught him everything he knows—including the mysterious technique known as Vaapad. The book includes battle violence.
Volume 1 of 9

Star Wars: Clone Wars Volume 2: Victories and Sacrifices. Written by Haden Blackman and John Ostrander; Pencillers Tomás Giorello, Brian Ching, and Jan Duursema; Inkers Dan Parsons, Joe Weems, Curtis Arnold. Dark Horse Comics 2003 Un Illustration
Grades: 7 8 9 10 11 12 Adult   **741.5; Fic**
1. Adventure graphic novels; 2. Science fiction graphic novels; 3. Star Wars; 4. Graphic novels
1-56971-969-1, $14.95
From one of the swamp moons of Naboo, to the war-torn cityscapes of Brentaal IV, the battles of the Clone Wars have thrown the galaxy into turmoil. New Separatist threats, ranging from deadly biological weapons, to dark Jedi, to unkillable alien bounty hunters, have the loyalist Jedi and their clone troops pushed to their limits. This graphic novel collection contains three separate, yet linked stories of heroism and sacrifice. The book includes battle violence.

Star Wars: Clone Wars Volume 3: Last Stand on Jabiim. Written by Haden Blackman and John Ostrander; Pencillers

Brian Ching and Jan Duursema; Inkers Dan Parsons and Victor Llamas. Dark Horse Comics 2004 Un Illustration
Grades: 7 8 9 10 11 12 Adult   **741.5; Fic**
1. Adventure graphic novels; 2. Science fiction graphic novels; 3. Star Wars; 4. Graphic novels
1-59307-006-3, $14.95
General Obi-Wan Kenobi and his Padawan Anakin Skywalker find themselves in command of a regiment of Clone Troopers on the muddy battlefields of the rain world of Jabiim. With their supply lines stretched thin and reinforcements unable to land due to the perpetual storms, the Jedi and their army have become easy targets for the rebel Alto Stratus and his elite Nimbus warriors. The situation goes from bad to worse when General Kenobi is listed missing in action, and Anakin is teamed with a group of other masterless young Jedi on a doomed mission to hold the last line in the Republic's defense.

Star Wars: Clone Wars Volume 6: On the Fields of Battle. Written by John Ostrander; pencilled by Jan Duursema; inked by Dan Parsons; colored by Brad Anderson. Dark Horse Comics 2005 Un Illustration
Grades: 7 8 9 10 11 12 Adult   **741.5; Fic**
1. Adventure graphic novels; 2. Science fiction graphic novels; 3. Star Wars; 4. Graphic novels
1-59307-352-6, $17.95
Mace Windu leads an elite Jedi strike force against an army of trained killers in a demonstration of Jedi power and resolve... Aayla Secura must confront her former Master in an effort to retrieve the plans for a weapon that has already destroyed a world... Obi-Wan Kenobi and Anakin Skywalker must joins forces with a renegade Jedi to prevent a fleet of warships from falling into the hands of the enemy...

Star Wars: Clone Wars Volume 8: The Last Siege, the Final Truth. Written by John Ostrander; pencilled by Jan Duursema; inked by Dan Parsons; colored by Brad Anderson. Dark Horse Comics 2006 Un Illustration
Grades: 7 8 9 10 11 12 Adult   **741.5; Fic**
1. Adventure graphic novels; 2. Science fiction graphic novels; 3. Star Wars; 4. Graphic novels
1-59307-482-4, $17.95
Beneath the surface of this Outer Rim planet, the Dark Jedi Sora Bulq has begun cloning an army of Morgukai assassins. Unwilling to leave this grave new threat unchecked, the Jedi and their armies soon find themselves entrenched in a five-month siege. Now, time and resources have run out, and it's up to a crack team of Jedi, led by Quinlan Vos and Aayla Secura, to infiltrate the Separatist base. The book includes battle violence.

Star Wars: Clone Wars Volume 9: Endgame. Written by John Ostrander and Welles Hartley; art by Jan Duursema and Douglas Wheatley. Dark Horse Comics 2006 Un Illustration
Grades: 7 8 9 10 11 12 Adult   **741.5; Fic**
1. Adventure graphic novels; 2. Science fiction graphic novels; 3. Star Wars; 4. Graphic novels
978-1-59307-553-8, $17.95
Suddenly, clone troopers are turning on the Jedi and killing them; it's Order 66. In the jungles of the Wookiee homeworld Kashyyyk, Quinlan Vos wages a battle of impossible odds against his own troops to protect his loved ones. On the icy Outer Rim world of Toola, Jedi Master Kai

Huddora takes a terrified Padawan into his charge after her own master falls to Order 66. Amidst the forests of New Plymto, Dass Jennir finds himself in league with a band of rebels he'd led attacks against only days before. And Darth Vader hunts for Obi Wan Kenobi.

Star Wars: Empire Volume One: Betrayal. Scott Allie and Ryan Benjamin. Dark Horse Comics 2003 Un Illustration
Grades: 7 8 9 10 11 12 Adult   **741.5; Fic**
1. Adventure graphic novels; 2. Science fiction graphic novels; 3. Star Wars; 4. Graphic novels
1-56971-964-0, $12.95
In the weeks before the events in Star Wars: A New Hope, as the Death Star is readied for its fateful first mission, a power-hungry cabal of Grand Moffs and Imperial Officers embark on a dangerous plan to kill Emperor Palpatine and Darth Vader and seize control of the Empire. When word that a Jedi has made an appearance on a backwater world lures Vader away from his master, the cabal makes its move. But even the galaxy isn't enough of a prize to sate the ambitions of some of the conspirators, and before long the would-be assassins are turning on one another. Their plans are further complicated by the actions of bounty hunter Boba Fett. And, of course, they may have fatally underestimated the cunning of their primary target: Emperor Palpatine.

Star Wars: Empire Volume Six: In the Shadows of Their Fathers. writers, Thomas Andrews, Scott Allie ; artists, Adriana Melo, Joe Corroney, Michel LaCombe. Dark Horse Comics 2006 Un Illustration
Grades: 7 8 9 10 11 12 Adult   **741.5; Fic**
1. Adventure graphic novels; 2. Science fiction graphic novels; 3. Star Wars; 4. Graphic novels
978-1-59307-627-6, $17.95
Luke Skywalker confronts the legacy of the Jedi father he never knew in an epic story involving Princess Leia, Darth Vader and the fate of an entire planet! When Luke and Leia travel to Jabiim recruiting allies for the fledgling Rebellion, they unwittingly set into motion events that will ignite one man's betrayal of his people, pit rebel hero against rebel hero and attract the attention of the Empire's deadliest enforcer - Darth Vader. The book includes battle violence.

Star Wars: Legacy, Volume One: Broken. Story, John Ostrander and Jan Duuresma ; script, John Ostrander ; pencils, Jan Duuresma ; inks, Dan Parsons ; colors, Brad Anderson ; lettering, Michael David Thomas ; cover art, Adam Hughes. Dark Horse Comics 2007 Un Illustration
Grades: 7 8 9 10 11 12   **741.5; Fic**
1. Adventure graphic novels; 2. Science fiction graphic novels; 3. Star Wars; 4. Graphic novels
978-1-59307-716-7, $17.95
125 years have passed since the events in Return of the JedI and the days of the New JedI Order. There is a new evil gripping the galaxy, shattering a resurgent Empire and seeking to destroy the last of the JedI. Even as their power is failing, the JedI hold onto one final hope, the last remaining heir to the Skywalker legacy: Cade, who has rejected the way of the JedI. The book's fighting action is at the same level as the motion picture series.

Suicide Squad: from the ashes. John Ostrander, writer; Javier Pina, Robin Riggs, Jesus Saiz, pencillers; Robin Riggs, inker; Jason Wright, colorist. DC Comics 2008 192p. Illustration
Grades: 11 12 Adult   **741.5; Fic**
1. Adventure graphic novels; 2. Science fiction graphic novels; 3. Superhero graphic novels; 4. Graphic novels
978-1-4012-1866-9, $19.99
Rick Flag commanded the Suicide Squad, a team of villains used to conduct covert operations missions in return for their freedom. He died in a nuclear blast while battling terrorism in Qurac " or did he" Years later, he has returned, and finds himself caught between two commanders: Amanda Waller, former coleader of Checkmate, and General Wade Eiling, who started the Suicide Squad. The new Suicide Squad, which includes old members Deadshot, Bronze Tiger, and Nightshade, goes on a mission to assassinate the Board members that run a huge conglomerate that has developed a deadly bioweapon; but Eiling has found a way to compromise the mission and take out his old enemies, especially Mrs. Waller. This book includes lots of graphic violence.

Otsuka, Eiji
The **Kurosagi** Corpse Delivery Service Vol. 1. Story by Eiji Ohtsuka; art by Housui Yamazaki. Dark Horse Comics 2006 202p. Illustration
Grades: 12 Adult   **741.5; Fic**
1. Horror graphic novels; 2. Mystery graphic novels; 3. Shonen manga; 4. Graphic novels
978-1-59307-555-2, $10.95
Five young students at a Buddhist university, three guys and two girls, find little call for their job skills in today's Tokyo... among the living, that is. But all that stuff in college they were told would never pay off - channeling, dowsing, ESP - gives them a direct line to the dead... the dead who are still trapped in their corpses and can't move on to the next reincarnation. The five form the Kurosagi ("Black Heron" - their ominous bird logo) Corpse Delivery Service: whether suicide, murder, accident, or illness, they'll carry your body wherever it needs to go to free your soul! The kids from Kurosagi can smell a customer a mile away - it's a good thing one of the girls majored in embalming. Lots of violent murders, dismemberments, nudity, and strong language are present.

MPD-Psycho No. 1. Original story and script, Eiji Otsuka; art, Sho-u Tajima. Dark Horse Comics 2007 186p. Illustration
Grades: 12 Adult   **741.5; Fic**
1. Horror graphic novels; 2. Manga; 3. Mystery graphic novels; 4. Graphic novels
978-1-59307-770-9, $10.95
Tokyo police detective Kobayashi Yousuke's life is changed forever after a serial killer notices something "special" about him. That same killer mutilates Kobayashi's girlfriend and kick-starts a "multiple personality battle" within Kobayashi that pushes him into a complex tempest of interconnected deviants and evil forces. After prison he works for a private detective organization, and the cases are all bloody and weird. The book shows lots of graphic violence and nudity, along with strong language. This series is very popular in Japan.

Ottaviani, Jim
Bone sharps, cowboys, and thunder lizards: a tale of Edwin Drinker Cope, Othniel Charles Marsh, and the gilded age of paleontology. By Jim Ottaviani & Big Time Attic. G.T. Labs 2005 165p. Illustration
Grades: 9 10 11 12 Adult   **560**
1. Biographical graphic novels; 2. Cope, E D (Edward Drinker), 1840-1897; 3. Fossils; 4. Marsh, Othniel Charles, 1831-1899; 5. Paleontologists; 6. Zoologists; 7. Graphic novels
0-9660106-6-3; 978-0-9660106-6-4, $22.95
LC 2005-920326
"Ottaviani portrays the heyday of American dinosaur hunting with a ripsnorting Western feel. Rival scientist/dinosaur hunters Marsh and Cope play out their real-life drama in a mostly accurate historical telling. Copious notes at the back of the book point out where Ottaviani departs from the facts; science and history become fun in his hands." Voice Youth Advocates
Includes bibliographical references
Title from cover

Dignifying science: stories about women scientists. Written by Jim Ottaviani and illustrated by Donna Barr . . . [et al.]. G.T. Labs 2009 142p. Illustration
Grades: 6 7 8 9 10 11 12
920
1. Biographical graphic novels; 2. Women scientists; 3. Graphic novels
978-0-9788037-3-5, $16.95; 0-9788037-3-5

Courtesy Jim Ottaviani and G.T. Labs; art by Ramona Fradon and Linda Medley

Ottaviani provides biographical sketches of women scientists such as Lise Meitner, Rosalind Franklin, Barbara McClintock, and Hedy Lamarr (yes, the actress was also an inventor); all the stories are illustrated by women comics artists, including Lea Hernandez, Linda Medley, Anne Timmons, and others.
First published 1999

Fallout. Jim Ottaviani et al. G.T. Labs 2001 239 p. Illustration
Grades: 11 12 Adult
1. Atomic bomb; 2. Nuclear energy; 3. Nuclear weapons
0966010639; 9780966010633, $24.95
LC 2001091068
In this nonfiction graphic novel about atomic bombs, by Jim Ottaviani, "the focus . . . is on the scientists themselves — in particular J. Robert Oppenheimer and Leo Szilard, whose lives offer a cautionary tale about the uneasy alliance between the military, the government, and the beginnings of 'big science.'" (Publisher's note)

★ **Feynman**. Written by Jim Ottaviani; art by Leland Myrick; coloring by Hilary Sycamore. First Second 2011 262 p. Illustration; Color
Grades: 9 10 11 12 Adult   **B; 92; 530.092**

1. Atomic bomb; 2. Biography, Individual; 3. Feynman, Richard Phillips, 1918-1988; 4. Musicians — Biography; 5. Nobel Prizes; 6. Physicists
1596432594; 9781596432598, $29.99; 9781596438279, $19.99; 9781451722406, $33.99
LC 2010036260
Author Jim Ottaviani presents a "graphic novel biography . . . [of] Nobel-winning quantum physicist, adventurer, musician, world-class raconteur, and one of the greatest minds of the twentieth century: Richard Feynman . . . [The book] tells the story of the great man's life from his childhood in Long Island to his work on the Manhattan Project and the Challenger disaster." (Publisher's note)
"This is a fascinating look at the life of an eccentric genius, a man who worked on the Manhattan Project, won a Nobel Prize, was the first great physicist to teach freshmen classes, and was the investigator into the cause of the Challenger explosion who discovered the problem was the 0-rings. This work was so entertaining it was difficult to put down." Voice Youth Advocates

The **Imitation** Game: Alan Turing Decoded. Jim Ottaviani; illustrated by Leland Purvis. Harry N Abrams Inc 2016 240 p. Illustration
Grades: 9 10 11 12 Adult   **92; 741.5**
1. Mathematicians — Biography; 2. Turing, Alan Mathison, 1912-1954
1419718932; 9781419718939, $24.95
This graphic novel, by Jim Ottaviani and illustrated by Leland Purvis, "present[s] a historically accurate graphic novel biography of English mathematician and scientist Alan Turing. [It covers] Turing's life and groundbreaking research—as an unconventional genius who was arrested, tried, convicted, and punished for being openly gay, and whose innovative work still fuels the computing and communication systems that define our modern world." (Publisher's note)

Levitation: physics and psychology in the service of deception. [by] Jim Ottaviani and Janine Johnston; lettering by Tom Orzechowski. G. T. Labs 2007 71p. Illustration
Grades: 6 7 8 9 10 11 12 Adult   **793.8; 741.5**
1. Magic tricks; 2. Graphic novels
978-0-9788037-0-4, $12.95
This book tells the story of how John Neville Maskelyne developed the stage magic trick of levitation, of the American Harry Kellar, who acquired the trick through devious means, of the old school engineer Guy Jarrett, who perfected the magicians' tricks, and of stage performer Howard Thurston, who inherited the levitation trick from Kellar and ruined it. Or did he? The book includes notes and reprints of old posters and other information on the magicians.
Includes bibliographical references
A General Tektronics Labs book

Primates: The Fearless Science of Jane Goodall, Dian Fossey, and Biruté Galdikas. Jim Ottaviani; illustrated by Maris Wicks. First Second 2013 133 p. Color; Illustration
Grades: 5 6 7 8 9 10 11 12 Adult   **741.5; 599.8**
1. Fossey, Dian, 1932-1985; 2. Galdikas, Birute, 1946-; 3. Goodall, Jane, 1934-; 4. Primates
1596438657; 9781596438651, $19.99
LC 2013427678

This nonfiction graphic novel, by Jim Ottaviani, illustrated by Maris Wicks, presents an "account of the three greatestáprimatologists of the last century: Jane Goodall, Dian Fossey, and Birut? Galdikas. These three ground-breaking researchers were all students of the great Louis Leakey, and each made profound contributions to primatology—and to our own understanding of ourselves." (Publisher's note)

"More story than study, the book provides an accessible introduction to Goodall's, Fossey's and Galdikas' lives and work." Kirkus

Includes bibliographical references, page 138

Suspended in language: Niels Bohr's life, discoveries, and the century he shaped. Written by Jim Ottaviani; illustrated and lettered by Leland Purvis. G.T. Labs 2009 318p. Illustration

Grades: 10 11 12 Adult **92**
1. Biographical graphic novels; 2. Bohr, Niels Henrik David, 1885-1962; 3. Nobel laureates for physics; 4. Physicists; 5. Quantum theory; 6. Graphic novels
978-0-9788037-2-8, $24.95

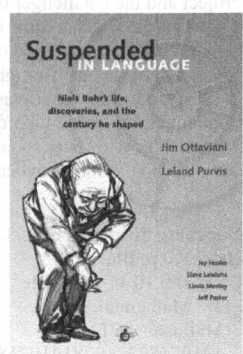

Courtesy of G.T. Labs

"Quantum physics gets an accessible yet substantive introduction through art that mixes fantasy and realism. Great for teens who like science." Booklist

Includes bibliographical references

First published 2004

Additional art by Jay Hosler, Roger Langridge, Steve Leialoha, Linda Medley, and Jeff Parker.

★ **T-Minus:** the race to the moon. [illustrated by] Zander Cannon, Kevin Cannon. Aladdin 2009 124p. Illustration

Grades: 4 5 6 7 8 9 10 11 12 Adult **629.45; 741.5**

Courtesy of Aladdin Paperbacks

1. Apollo project; 2. Gemini project; 3. Space flight to the moon; 4. Graphic novels
978-1-4169-8682-9, $21.99; 1-4169-8682-0;
978-1-4169-4960-2 (pa), $12.99; 1-4169-4960-7 (pa)
LC 2009-920999

Ottaviani, Zander Cannon, and Kevin Cannon show what happened when the U.S. and the U.S.S.R. started the space race in the 1950s, and how it progressed to the NASA Apollo 11 mission which landed two men on the moon in July of 1969.

"Organized as a countdown, making the outcome seem inevitable, the frequent, prominent sidebars list a type of rocket, the duration of its flight, and whether the mission was a success or a failure. There are more than 30 attempts chronicled, and the shift between Soviet and U.S. successes creates an interesting balance in the narrative. . . . Ottaviani is particular with facts and eager to inspire readers with regard to the scientific process." SLJ

★ **Wire** mothers: Harry Harlow and the science of love. [by] Jim Ottaviani [and] Dylan Meconis. G.T. Labs 2007 84p. Illustration

Grades: 9 10 11 12 Adult **152.4; 741.5**
1. Harlow, Harry F, 1905-1981; 2. Love; 3. Psychologists; 4. Graphic novels
978-0-9788037-1-1, $12.95; 0-9788037-1-X
LC 2007-900136

Courtesy of G.T. Labs

In the 1950s, psychologists warned parents about the dangers of too much love; in fact, they denied love was anything more than a base instinct based on the need for food. When scientist Harry Harlow began his experiments on mother love, was more than just an outsider trying to make his name. He was also an unhappy man who knew in his gut the truth about what love, and its absence, meant, and he set about to prove it. His experiments on monkeys and their stark results shocked the world. The emotional intensity of his experiments might be overwhelming for younger readers.

"This nonfiction graphic novel retelling psychologist Harry Harlow's famous experiments is as disturbing as it is excellent." Publ Wkly

Includes bibliographical references

A General Tektronics Labs book

Out of picture: art from the outside looking in volume 2

Villard Books 2008 238p. Illustration

Grades: 10 11 12 Adult **741.5; Fic**
1. Short stories; 2. Graphic novels
978-0-345-49873-1, $30

Animation production artists who have worked together at Blue Sky Studios have put together another volume of short stories in comics form. In one story, a giant of a man wants only to become a farmer, but the military has hunted him down because he was a biological weapon used by them to win a war; now, he can't be allowed to live. In another story, a young boy takes his first airplane ride and sees a strange being riding on the wing, fly-fishing in the sky. In another story, three friends "a cat, a pigeon, and a grumpy gargoyle " need to find a new home when their antique shop home is destroyed. None of the stories uses graphic violence or much in the way of harsh language, but the moods and intensity of emotion make the book more suitable for older teens and adults.

Page, Philip

Picture This! Shakespeare: A Midsummer Night's Dream. Barron's Educational Series, Inc. 2002 58p. Illustration

Grades: 7 8 9 10 11 12   **741.5; 822.3**
1. Drama; 2. Shakespeare, William, 1564-1616 — Adaptations; 3. Graphic novels
0-7641-3142-7, $7.95
This adaptation combines pages done in graphic novel format with extensive excerpts from Shakespeare's A Midsummer Night's Dream to provide an introductory reading experience for younger and struggling students. Each scene presented in the book is preceded by a brief summary, words that modern teens would find unfamiliar are briefly defined on the page, literary terms are explained.

Picture This! Shakespeare: Macbeth. Barron's Educational Series, Inc. 2002 56p. Illustration
Grades: 7 8 9 10 11 12   **741.5; 822.3**
1. Drama; 2. Shakespeare, William, 1564-1616 — Adaptations; 3. Graphic novels
978-0-7641-3140-0, $7.99
This adaptation combines pages done in graphic novel format with extensive excerpts from Shakespeare's Macbeth to provide an introductory reading experience for younger and struggling students. Each scene presented in the book is preceded by a brief summary, words that modern teens would find unfamiliar are briefly defined on the page, literary terms are explained.

Picture This! Shakespeare: Romeo and Juliet. Barron's Educational Series, Inc. 2005 58p. Illustration
Grades: 7 8 9 10 11 12   **741.5; 822.3**
1. Drama; 2. Shakespeare, William, 1564-1616 — Adaptations; 3. Graphic novels
978-0-7641-3144-8, $7.99
This adaptation combines pages done in graphic novel format with extensive excerpts from Shakespeare's Romeo and Juliet to provide an introductory reading experience. Each scene presented in the book is preceded by a brief summary, words that modern teens would find unfamiliar are briefly defined on the page, literary terms are explained.

Picture This! Shakespeare: Twelfth Night or, What You Will. Barron's Educational Series, Inc. 2005 58p. Illustration
Grades: 7 8 9 10 11 12   **822.3; 741.5**
1. Shakespeare, William, 1564-1616 — Adaptations
978-0-7641-3147-9, $7.95
This adaptation combines pages done in graphic novel format with extensive excerpts from Shakespeare's Twelfth Night to provide an introductory reading experience for younger and struggling students. Each scene presented in the book is preceded by a brief summary, words that modern teens would find unfamiliar are briefly defined on the page, literary terms are explained.

Picture This! Shakespeare: Twelfth Night Teacher's Resource Book. Barron's Educational Series, Inc. 2005 59p. Illustration
Grades: 7 8 9 10 11 12   **741.5; 371.33**
1. Drama; 2. Teaching — Aids and devices; 3. Graphic novels
0-7641-3148-6, $9.95
Twelfth Night, the Shakespearean drama that is in the curriculum of many high schools in the country, is an offering in Barron's "Picture This! Shakespeare" series. This manual supplements Barron's "Picture This: Twelfth Night," a book presented in graphic novel style for students'

use. The manual offers teachers suggestions for classroom discussions, quizzes, and activities related to the play, including reproducible activity sheets.

Pak, Greg
    X-Men: Phoenix: Endsong. Writer, Greg Pak; penciler, Greg Land. Marvel Entertainment 2005 Un Illustration
Grades: 9 10 11 12 Adult   **741.5; Fic**
1. Superhero graphic novels; 2. X-Men (Fictional characters); 3. Graphic novels
978-0-7851-1924-1, $14.99
The mysterious and powerful Phoenix Force is life incarnate, and yet it consumes whole worlds in a moment. Its long history with the X-Men is fraught with tragedy... especially concerning one of the most beloved of their number, Jean Grey. What will happen when the Phoenix returns to Earth in search of the one mortal who could ever contain its power... only to find her dead?

Palmiotti, Jimmy
    21 Down: The Conduit. Jimmy Palmiotti, Justin Gray and Jesus Saiz. DC Comics/Wildstorm 2003 Un Illustration
Grades: 10 11 12 Adult   **741.5; Fic**
1. Mystery graphic novels; 2. Graphic novels
1-4012-0120-2, $19.95
Preston Kills is a 20-year-old tattoo artist from Coney Island who has the power to see the final moments before and after a person's death; no one with similar powers has lived past their 21st birthday, and his homicide cop brother Robert has exploited Preston's powers to advance his career. Enter FBI agent Mickey Rinaldi, who is investigating the situation of super-powered teens who die early. She and Preston meet at his tattoo shop, follow the trail of a serial killer, and try to come to terms with love, loss, and the hope of surviving 21 Down. The book includes violence, strong language, and partial nudity.

    Hawkman: Rise of the Golden Eagle. Written by Justin Gray and Jimmy Palmiotti; pencilled by Christopher Moeller et al. DC Comics 2006 208p. Illustration
Grades: 10 11 12 Adult   **741.5; Fic**
1. Hawkman (Fictional character); 2. Superhero graphic novels; 3. Graphic novels
978-1-4012-1092-2, $17.99
In Ancient Egypt, he was known as Prince Khufu. Today he is called Carter Hall. Archaeologist. Winged Warrior. Hawkman. He's lived thousands of lives - his soul reincarnated again and again, destined forever to be reunited with his true love until now. Prince Khufu's "soul mate" has been reincarnated into the body of Kendra Saunders - also known as Hawkgirl, but with no memories of her past lives, Kendra has made it quite clear she wants nothing to do with Hawkman. Now the two heroes must figure out a way to work together as they unravel the mysteries within the enigmatic southern epicenter called St. Roch, travel to exotic lands, and battle an alliance of adversaries from the past. The book has some violence beyond superhero fighting.

    Uncle Sam and the Freedom Fighters. Written by Justin Gray and Jimmy Palmiotti; art by Daniel Acuna. DC Comics 2007 208p. Illustration
Grades: 10 11 12 Adult   **741.5; Fic**
1. Superhero graphic novels; 2. Graphic novels

978-1-4012-1336-7, $14.99

Meet the all-new Phantom Lady, Doll Man, Human Bomb and the Ray - members of the government task force known as SHADE, the country's first line of defense against super-powered threats and terrorists in the wake of the Infinite Crisis. When the resurrected Uncle Sam makes them realize that Father Time has used them to further his own interests that will harm the United States, they work with Uncle Sam as the new Freedom Fighters. There is considerable violence in this superhero title.

Papadatos, Alekos

Democracy. Concept, Alecos Papadatos; story, Alecos Papadatos & Abraham Kawa; script, Abraham Kawa; art direction & drawings, Alecos Papadatos; colouring, Annie Di Donna. Bloomsbury 2015 236 p. Color; Illustration

Grades: 11 12 Adult   **741.5**
    1. Athens (Greece) — Fiction; 2. Democracy; 3. War stories
    1608197190; 9781608197194, $27

This book by Alecos Papadatos, Abraham Kawa, and Annie Di Donna "opens in 490 B.C., with Athens at war. The hero of the story, Leander, is trying to rouse his comrades for the morrow's battle against a far mightier enemy, and begins to recount his own life, having borne direct witness to the evils of the old tyrannical regimes and to the emergence of a new political system. The tale that emerges is one of daring, danger, and big ideas, of the death of the gods and the tortuous birth of democracy." (Publisher's note)

"Papadatos's lively and energetic art illuminates battles, alliances, political machinations, and vivid personalities, and Di Donna's intense coloring is gloriously rich without a touch of gaudiness. For those interested in further background, the extensive back matter features useful commentary on both legendary and historical figures and concepts." Pub Wkly

Parent, Dan

Archie Comics Presents: The Love Showdown. Archie Comics 1994 Un Illustration

Grades: 3 4 5 6 7 8 9 10 11 12 Adult   **741.5; Fic**
    1. Andrews, Archie (Fictional character); 2. Archie (Fictional character); 3. Humorous graphic novels; 4. Graphic novels
    1-879794-03-9, $4.95

In the mid-1990s, Archie Comics announced that Archie might finally choose between Betty and Veronica, after the love triangle had lasted since 1941; the story was published as a crossover among the four Archie comics series. This volume reprints the stories.

Park, Eun Ah

Bird Kiss Vol. 1. Tokyopop 2006 Un Illustration

Grades: 8 9 10 11 12 Adult   **741.5; Fic**
    1. Humorous graphic novels; 2. Manwha; 3. Romance graphic novels; 4. Graphic novels
    1-59816-491-0, $9.99

Miyoul is a feisty, boy-crazed girl who is in love with Guelin, a talk, dark, and handsome high school boy. But Heerack—short, scrawny, and too dorky to be given the time of day—has the hots for Miyoul, and worships her every move. Of course, Miyoul is awfully embarrassed by him and

tries to avoid him like the plague. And of course, it doesn't work. This Korean manwha is filled with the trials and tribulations of high school—and some wacky, slapstick moments.

Park, Hee Jung

Hotel Africa volume one. Tokyopop 2008 Un Illustration

Grades: 10 11 12 Adult   **741.5; Fic**
    1. Graphic novels
    978-1-4278-0575-1, $12.99

The narrator, a young man named Elvis, tells stories about the Hotel Africa, a small hotel run by his mother and grandmother, located in the middle of the Utah desert. To this place come a strange young Native American named Geo and a couple of young vagabonds. The book includes some harsh language. This is Korean manwha.

Park, Joong-Ki

Shaman Warrior, Volume One. Dark Horse Comics 2006 214p. Illustration

Grades: 11 12 Adult   **741.5; Fic**
    1. Adventure graphic novels; 2. Fantasy graphic novels; 3. Manwha; 4. Graphic novels
    978-1-59307-638-2, $12.95

Warrior Wizard Yarong and his faithful servant Batu travel to the desert wastelands of Kugai on a mission for their king. However, they find only an overwhelming force of fighters led by a warrior who seeks to kill Yarong. The two warriors face on attack after the other, until Yarong realizes he is going to die; he sends Batu away, to find Yarong's baby daughter Yaki. They have been betrayed by their General for political expediency. This was a top-selling manwha in Korea; the kinetic, violent story will appeal to older readers who enjoy Lone Wolf & Cub, Blade of the Immortal, and other warrior epics.

Park, Min-Seo

Blazin' Barrels Volume 1. Tokyopop 2005 186p. Illustration

Grades: 8 9 10 11 12 Adult   **741.5; Fic**
    1. Adventure graphic novels; 2. Science fiction graphic novels; 3. Western graphic novels; 4. Graphic novels
    1-59532-559-X, $9.99

Sting may look harmless and naive, but he's really an excellent fighter and a wannabe bounty hunter in the futuristic Wild West. When he comes across a notice that advertises a reward for the criminal outfit named Gold Romany, he decides that capturing the all-girl gang of bad guys is his ticket to fame and fortune. The book includes some strong language and sexual suggestiveness, along with some violence.

Park, Sang-Sun

The **Tarot** Cafe Volume 1. Tokyopop 2005 176p. Illustration

Grades: 9 10 11 12 Adult   **741.5; Fic**
    1. Fantasy graphic novels; 2. Manwha; 3. Supernatural graphic novels; 4. Graphic novels
    1-59532-555-7, $9.99

Pamela is a tarot card reader who helps supernatural beings living in the human world. She'll help anyone, whether they're a love-stricken cat, a vampire spending eternal life running from his one true love, an unattractive waitress looking for the man of her dreams, or even a magician who creates a humanoid doll to serve the woman he loves. Although Pamela is good-natured, she has a deep dark secret that she must deal with before she can move on to the next life. The book includes some violence and one bondage scene.

Parker, Jeff
The **Avengers**: finding Zemo. Art by Manuel Garcia and Scott Koblish. ABDO Publishing Company/Spotlight 2008 Un Illustration
Grades: 4 5 6 7 8 9   **741.5; Fic**
1. Avengers (Fictional characters); 2. Captain America (Fictional character); 3. Hulk (Fictional character); 4. Iron Man (Fictional character); 5. Spider-Man (Fictional character); 6. Storm (Fictional character); 7. Superhero graphic novels; 8. Wolverine (Fictional character); 9. Graphic novels
978-1-59961-383-3, $21.35
                                        LC 2007-20254
A ceremony to honor Captain America is attacked by his old enemy, Baron Zemo, in a new giant attack robot. While the Avengers battle the robot, Zemo kidnaps Captain America. Now, the rest of the team must find Zemo and Cap. This Avengers team includes Storm, Spider-Man, Iron Man, Wolverine, the Hulk, and Giant-Girl. This is a revised, hardbound edition of the Marvel Adventures comic book.
Part of the Avengers series

The **avengers**: heroes assembled, v1. Artist, Manuel Garcia. Marvel 2006 Illustration
Grades: 5 6 7 8 9   **741.5; Fic**
1. Avengers (Fictional characters); 2. Captain America (Fictional character); 3. Spider-Man (Fictional character); 4. Storm (Fictional character); 5. Wolverine (Fictional character)
978-0-7851-2306-4, $6.99; 0-7851-2306-7

Fantastic four: law of the jungle. Manuel Garcia, pencils ; Scott Koblish, inks ; A. Crossley, colors. ABDO Publishing Company/Spotlight 2008 Un Illustration
Grades: 4 5 6 7 8 9   **741.5; Fic**
1. Black Panther (Fictional character); 2. Fantastic Four (Fictional characters); 3. Superhero graphic novels; 4. Graphic novels
978-1-59961-390-1, $21.35
                                        LC 2007-20255
The Fantastic Four find themselves fighting the Black Panther and discover that the rare metal they had purchased was stolen from Wakandia, the Black Panther's home country in Africa. When they investigate, they discover the thieves plan to steal again, and the team heads to Wakandia to help the Black Panther stop the criminals. If only he'll stop and listen to them before destroying them. This is a revised, hardbound edition of the Marvel Adventures comic book issue.
Part of the Fantastic Four series

Meteor men. Written by Jeff Parker; illustrated by Sandy Jarrell; colored by Kevin Volo; lettered by Crank!. Oni Press 2014 133 p. Color; Illustration
Grades: 8 9 10 11   **741.5; Fic**
1. Extraterrestrial beings; 2. Human-alien encounters — Fiction; 3. Science fiction graphic novels
1620101513; 9781620101513, $19.99
Eisner Nominee: Best Publication for Teens (2015)
"On a summer night, Alden Baylor sits in a field watching the largest meteor shower in human history. What begins as teenage adventure becomes something more—the celestial event brings travelers who will change the world completely, and Alden discovers a connection to one of them. How does a young man who had to grow up fast handle the invasion of his planet? Can Alden keep humanity from oblivion?" (Publisher's note)
"Parker combines the familiar concept with gentle domesticity and deliberate humanism, thus circumventing clich? and providing an accessible perspective to the logical and realistic extensions of such an event." SLJ

Parks, Ande
Capote in Kansas. Written by Ande Parks; illustrated by Chris Samnee; lettered by Ande Parks. Oni Press 2005 121p. Illustration
Grades: 10 11 12   **741.5; 92; Fic**
1. Biographical graphic novels; 2. Capote, Truman; 3. Graphic novels
1-932664-29-7, $11.95
This book is Parks' fictional account of what Truman Capote might have done during his time in Kansas as he researched the story that became his bestselling book, In Cold Blood. As Capote begins to connect with Perry Smith, one of the killers, and with investigators and others, he also meets the ghost of teenage Nancy Mae Clutter, one of the victims. This book predated the movie Capote, starring Philip Seymour Hoffman, but it might appeal to the movie's fans. A few harsh words and Capote's open homosexuality should not deter most libraries from getting this book.

Union Station. Written by Ande Parks; illustrated by Eduardo Barreto. Oni Press 2003 116p. Illustration
Grades: 11 12 Adult   **364.1; 741.5**
1. Crimes — United States; 2. FBI; 3. Graphic novels
1-929998-69-4, $11.95
Kansas City, 1933. Frank Nash is a petty criminal who has been pinched by the Feds and is being brought back into town by train. When FBI agent Reed Vetterli heads down to Union Station to meet Nash and his uniformed escort, he has no reason to suspect that there will be any action. Neither does Charles Thompson, a reporter sent down to the station just to see what the fuss is for. Little do they know that Frank's buddy, Vern Miller, is going to bust him out. Nash may not be a big time player, but he's still earned some loyalty. The resulting clash ends in a massacre, with no one knowing who pulled the trigger first - or even who pulled it at all. Rumor has it that Pretty Boy Floyd was on the scene, but no one knows for sure, and J. Edgar Hoover doesn't particularly care. He just wants Floyd's butt in an electric chair, and when Vetterli, Miller, and Thompson find themselves in the way of Hoover's justice, they can't duck for cover fast enough. This graphic novel is based on a true incident. The book includes violence and strong language.

Pascoe, Jim

Hellboy Animated Vol. 2: The Judgment Bell. Written by Jim Pascoe, art by Ricky Lacy. Dark Horse Comics 2007 Un Illustration

Grades: 7 8 9 10 11 12 **741.5; Fic**
1. Fantasy graphic novels; 2. Hellboy (Fictional character); 3. Horror graphic novels; 4. Graphic novels
978-1-59307-799-0, $6.25

In "The Judgment Bell," written by Jim Pascoe and drawn by Rick Lacy a figure from Dr. Broom's past wreaks havoc on the children of a small Polish village. And in a backup story written and drawn by Hellboy Animated creator Tad Stones, a young Hellboy is once again stirred to heroism by the radio adventures of Lobster Johnson, only to cause chaos.

Undertown Volume 1. Art by Jake Myler. Tokyopop 2007 Un Illustration

Grades: 7 8 9 10 11 12 **741.5; Fic**
1. Adventure graphic novels; 2. Fantasy graphic novels; 3. Graphic novels
978-1-4278-0103-6, $9.99

Sama is so sad that tears have literally stained his cheeks. His father has congestive heart failure, and doctors only give him a month to live. With nowhere to turn, Sama grabs his teddy bear and crawls under his bed...magically entering a portal to a fantastic realm called Undertown, where his teddy bear comes to life. Sama looks for the Sugar Stone: a "secret something" that might be able to heal his dad. But The Cloud—the wicked leader of the Insect Insurgents—hunts for the Stone, as well ... This global manga has some violence and darker moments that could disturb younger readers.

Patterson, James

Daniel X: alien hunter: a graphic novel. James Patterson & Leopoldo Gout ; art by Klaus Lyngeled, Jon Girin & Joseph McLamb. Little, Brown and Company 2008 128p. Illustration

Grades: 6 7 8 9 10 11 12 **741.5; Fic**
1. Extraterrestrial beings; 2. Science fiction graphic novels; 3. Graphic novels
978-0-316004-25-1, $9.99; 0-31600-425-1

When his parents were murdered, young Daniel inherited the List of Alien Outlaws and took over his father's job as Alien Hunter; his family were also aliens, and Daniel possesses the ability to shape-shift and to conjure up anybody and anything out of thin air. He's been hunting aliens on the list for years, and now he's in Tokyo, going after Number 7. That alien has been running a "game" in which he releases an alien creature for alien bounty hunters to hunt, and the more destruction they cause in the process, the better. This time is different, however, when Daniel learns that Number 7 has a teenage son, and that son is somewhat alienated from his father. This graphic novel is a companion to the novel The Dangerous Days of Daniel X, which is the first of a series of novels.

Patton, Michael F.

The **cartoon** introduction to philosophy. Michael F. Patton and Kevin Cannon; Illustrated by Kevin Cannon. Hill & Wang 2015 176 p. Illustration

Grades: 11 12 Adult **100; 741.5**
1. Cartoons and caricatures; 2. Philosophy; 3. Philosophy — Introductions; 4. Graphic novels
0809033623; 9780809033621, $17.95
LC 2014029343

In this book, authors "Michael F. Patton and Kevin Cannon introduce us to the grand tradition of examined living. With the wisecracking Heraclitus as our guide, we travel down the winding river of philosophy, meeting influential thinkers from nearly three millennia of Western thought and witnessing great debates over everything from ethics to the concept of the self to the nature of reality." (Publisher's note)

"The dynamic, cartoony illustrations might lead some to assume that this title is a little more accessible than it actually is, but anyone with an interest in learning about the philosophers and philosophical concepts that have shaped 21st-century life without having to plow their way through a dry textbook will find this title a stimulating delight." LJ

Includes bibliographical references

Pedrosa, Cyril

Three shadows. Translated by Edward Gauvin. First Second Books 2008 270p. Illustration

Grades: 10 11 12 Adult **741.5; Fic**
1. Family life; 2. Graphic novels
978-1-59643-239-0, $15.95; 1-59643-239-X
LC 2007-38499

Life is good for the family, mother, father, and son Joachim. Then one night they find three shadows, figures on horseback, watching them, and Joachim is frightened. The parents dismiss his fears at first, but their presence every day, every night, begins to wear on them. Finally, the father decides to leave and take Joachim far away, from the shadows. But wherever the two go, the shadows follow. The book includes some nudity and violence.

Pekar, Harvey

Macedonia: what does it take to stop a war?. [by] Harvey Pekar and Heather Robinson; illustrated by Ed Piskor. Villard Books 2007 163p. Illustration

Grades: 10 11 12 Adult **979.7; 741.5**
1. Eastern Europe; 2. Graphic novels
978-0-345-49899-1, $17.95
LC 2006-42106

For years Heather Roberson, a passionate peace activist, has argued that war can always be avoided. But she has repeatedly faced counterarguments that fighting is an inescapable consequence of world conflicts. Indeed, Heather finds proving her point to be a little tricky without examples to bolster her case. So she does something a little crazy: She sets out for far-off Macedonia, a landlocked country north of Greece and west of Bulgaria, to explore a region that has edged-repeatedly-close to the brink of violence, only to refrain. In the process, Heather is tangled in red tape, ripped off by cabdrivers and hotel clerks, hit on by creepy guys, secretly photographed, and mistaken for a spy. She also creates unlikely friendships, learns that getting lost means seeing something new, and makes some startling discoveries. War is hell and peace is difficult but conflict is always necessary. As written by Pekar and illustrated by

Piskor, the book includes some harsh language and a few images of violence, but has no nudity or sexual situations.

Quitter. Harvey Pekar, writer; Dean Haspiel, artist; Lee Loughridge, gray tones; Pat Brosseau, letters. DC Comics/Vertigo 2005 Un Illustration
Grades: 10 11 12 Adult   **92; 741.5**
1. Autobiographical graphic novels; 2. Monsters; 3. Pekar, Harvey; 4. Pekar, Harvey; 5. Graphic novels
1-4012-0399-X, $19.95

Harvey Pekar is now a famed independent comics creator, whose series American Splendor was adapted into a hit motion picture. In this book, he recounts his childhood, teen years, and early adulthood and examines the experiences that shaped his life. He gives an unflinchingly honest portrait of a boy who used fighting to get a tough reputation, who needed to excel in sports and academics and would quit if he felt he couldn't achieve what he wanted. He allows the reader to see into his soul.

Students for a Democratic Society: a graphic history. Written by Harvey Pekar; art by Gary Dumm; edited by Paul Buhle. Hill & Wang 2008 214p. Illustration
Grades: 10 11 12 Adult   **378.1; 741.5**
1. College students — Political activity; 2. Students for a Democratic Society — History; 3. Graphic novels
978-0-8090-9539-1, $22; 978-0-8090-8939-0 (pa), $16
LC 2007-40641

Students for a Democratic Society formed as an organization in 1960, but had its roots as a New Left group in the League for Industrial Democracy, founded in 1905 with members such as Jack London and Upton Sinclair. The members in 1960 included Al Haber and Tom Hayden, and one of their most famous documents is the Port Huron Statement of 1962. By the late 1960s, with opposition to the Vietnam War in full swing, a radical subgroup called the Weathermen became more violent. Graphic novelist Pekar is joined by members of the SDS in telling the story of the organization, which dissolved soon after its 1969 convention. The book includes some harsh language and violence.

"The book acts like a sophisticated handbook on an often misunderstood organization. It's good comics and excellent history." Publ Wkly

Pendergast, Sara
★ **U-X-L** graphic novelists, 3v. [by] Tom Pendergast and Sara Pendergast; Sarah Hermsen, project editor. U-X-L/Thomson Gale 2007 Lxii, 634 Illustration
Grades: 9 10 11 12 Adult   **920.003**
1. Cartoonists — Dictionaries; 2. Graphic novels — Dictionaries; 3. Reference books
1-4144-0440-9; 978-1-4144-0440-0, set $181
LC 2006-13711

The three volumes include 75 alphabetically-arranged articles that profile authors, illustrators, and author-illustrators, and include European, American, and Japanese creators. The introduction provides some history of graphic novels, and there is a separate essay on manga.

"This accessible and readable survey of a timely topic should generate considerable attention in school library media center and public library collections. Well researched and documented, with subject and language appropriate for

its intended audience, this set is highly recommended." Booklist
Includes bibliographical references

Perez, Daniel
The **strange** case of Dr. Jekyll and Mr. Hyde. By Robert L. Stevenson; retold by Carl Bowen; illustrated by Daniel Perez.. Stone Arch Books 2009 72p. Illustration
Grades: 4 5 6 7 8 9 10   **741.5; Fic**
1. Horror graphic novels; 2. Science fiction graphic novels; 3. Graphic novels
978-1-4342-0754-8, $23.93
LC 2008-6248

"Scientist Dr. Henry Jekyll believes every human has two minds: one good and one evil. He develops a potion to separate them from each other. Soon, his evil mind takes over, and Dr. Jekyll becomes a hideous fiend known as Mr. Hyde." (Publisher's note)
Part of the Graphic Revolve series

Perez, George
The **New** Teen Titans: Terra Incognito. DC Comics 2006 224p. Illustration
Grades: 7 8 9 10 11 12 Adult   **741.5; Fic**
1. Robin (Fictional character); 2. Superhero graphic novels; 3. Teen Titans (Fictional characters); 4. Graphic novels
978-1-4012-0972-8, $19.99

Tara Markov, the troubled teen princess of Markovia, is rescued from kidnappers by the Titans' green-skinned adventurer, Changeling. Thus begins her quest to use her powers over earth and gravity in the cause of justice. Does this obnoxious young powerhouse have what it takes to join the team" This is the original Teen Titans team, in which Dick Grayson is still Robin.

Wonder Woman Vol. 4: Destiny Calling. DC Comics 2006 176p. Illustration
Grades: 8 9 10 11 12 Adult   **741.5; Fic**
1. Superhero graphic novels; 2. Wonder Woman (Fictional character); 3. Graphic novels
978-1-4012-0943-8, $19.99

It's only been a short time since Diana, dubbed Wonder Woman by the media, came to Man's World with a message of peace, only to face countless foes and stop the advancement of a third world war. Now Diana must face her greatest challenge yet: a god among men. The Olympian god Hermes has decided to grace mankind with his presence, but along with him comes a world of new troubles for the Amazon. This volume reprints stories originally published in the 1980s, when Perez re-launched Wonder Woman.

Perry, Fred
Gold Digger Pocket Manga Vol. 1. Antarctic Press 1991 158p. Illustration
Grades: 10 11 12 Adult   **741.5; Fic**
1. Adventure graphic novels; 2. Fantasy graphic novels; 3. Humorous graphic novels; 4. Graphic novels
1-932453-00-8, $9.99

Gina "Gold Digger" Diggers—archaeologist, adventurer, and super-scientist—travels the world with her adopted were-cheetah sister, Britanny (called Cheetah), in search of knowledge, excitement, and treasure . . . as well as a cute guy, here and there. In this collection of the very first Gold Digger stories, Gina and Brit have to foil the dragon Dreadwing's attempt to control Merlin's Time Raft. Then, the pair are off on a wild journey to mythic places around the globe (and off it), including Shangri-La, Atlantis, and the Garden of Eden - all to stop the evil Atlantean wizard Gyphon from using his people's ancient artifacts to rule the world. The two sexy young women face a lot of action and get into a lot of martial arts fights. This series is one of the early American manga, now more commonly called global manga.

Perry, James II

Oranges crows, vol. 1. By James Perry II; art by Ryo Kayakami. Tokyopop 2009 Un
Grades: 9 10 11 12   **741.5; Fic**
1. Adventure graphic novels; 2. Fantasy graphic novels; 3. Magic; 4. Graphic novels
978-1-4278-1228-5, $10.99

Cierra, a young witch, broke the one unforgivable law of her society when she tried to create her own magic; her experiment burned down a major research lab and injured her friend Natalie, who is also the Mayor's daughter. For her crime, Cierra was exiled to the Wilderness for five years; it's a barren wasteland populated by witch-devouring Fairies and violent and bloodthirsty Forsaken. She has managed to survive on her own for her entire sentence, and now the authorities drag her back to civilization, where she still faces suspicion, and her former best friend is cold and bitter. Adjustment to her new situation in a world she no longer knows becomes much harder when Cierra realizes she has a freakish new ability that links her to the terrifying Fairies, and that she's expected to guide an expedition into the Wilderness.

Pet avengers classic

Marvel Entertainment 2009 208p. Illustration
Grades: 7 8 9 10 11 12 Adult   **741.5; Fic**
1. Adventure graphic novels; 2. Pets; 3. Superhero graphic novels; 4. Graphic novels
9780785139669, $24.99

This volume collects the various Marvel Pets stories, from 1960 to 2007, with each story featuring a different pet, from Lockjaw the teleporting dog to Kitty Pryde's dragon Lockheed to Brightwind the winged horse, and many more. Lockjaw, Lockheed, Redwing the falcon, the cat named Niels, and Zabu the saber tooth tiger all starred in th 2009 mini series titled Pet Avengers. Some of the stories in this collection include violence.

Peterson, Scott

Batman Adventures Vol. 1: Rogues' Gallery. DC Comics 2004 112p. Illustration
Grades: 4 5 6 7 8 9   **741.5; Fic**
1. Batman (Fictional character); 2. Catwoman (Fictional character); 3. Joker (Fictional character); 4. Superhero graphic novels; 5. Graphic novels
9781401203290, $6.95

Gotham City's greatest villains, including the Joker, Harley Quinn, Catwoman, the Penguin, Poison Ivy, and Ra's

al Ghul, all take their turn against the World's Greatest Detective. Crime never sleeps, and neither does Batman.

Petrou, Das

Ring of Roses. Written by Das Petrou; penciled and inked by John Watkiss. Image Comics 2005 142p. Illustration
Grades: 10 11 12 Adult   **741.5; Fic**
1. Mystery graphic novels; 2. Science fiction graphic novels; 3. Graphic novels
1-58240-425-9, $12.95

Ring of Roses is set in London in an alternate 21st century in which the Church rules England with an iron hand but has begun to lose its grip. Then six high-powered priests are brutally murdered on the Thames. Samuel Waterhouse, the flamboyant barrister hired to investigate, soon realizes he is out of his depth, so he hires a hardened criminal, William Barnett, to assist him. Barnett rams through a delicate web of conspiracy like an express train through a scout troop's tent. Meanwhile, the bubonic plague breaks out and thousands are dying. Throughout all this chaos, Waterhouse and Barnett are treading on the toes of the immensely powerful figures behind the scenes. This story was originally published years before The Da Vinci Code; readers will find some similarities. The book includes violence, strong language, and sexual situations.

Petrucci, Michele

Due. SLG Publishing 2005 Un Illustration
Grades: 11 12 Adult   **741.5; Fic**
1. Mystery graphic novels; 2. Graphic novels
1-59362-016-0, $12.95

Keires, in ancient Greek, means "hands" - the essence of creation. As a killer murders and mutilates his victims without any apparent logic, a misogynist detective, a university teacher searching for perfection, a sculptor trying to forget his awful past, and a group of students get involved in a tale of blood and suspicion. Everything revolves around a mysterious death that will lead the characters to a bitter end, where innocence and guilt mix together and truth proves herself to be just the last work created by the hands of man. With Silver Salts, it all begins when Bob Keller, photographer of the Los Angeles Herald, gets a call to cover a simple murder story. But Bob is used to looking at details through the lens of his camera, and knows the truth is not as it seems. Things hidden inside his own mind will slowly be revealed like a latent image developed with the help of the silver salts. The book includes some strong language, violence, and nudity. Translated from Italian; the title means "two."

Petrucha, Stefan

Nancy Drew, girl detective #15: Tiger counter. Stefan Petrucha & Sarah Kinney, writers ; Sho Murase, artist. Papercutz 2008 Un Illustration
Grades: 3 4 5 6 7 8 9   **741.5; Fic**
1. Drew, Nancy (Fictional character); 2. Mystery graphic novels; 3. Tigers; 4. Graphic novels
978-1-59707-119-2, $12.95; 978-1-59707-118-5 (pa), $7.95

Due to a lack of mysteries to keep them occupied, Nancy, Bess, and George have been volunteering at the

River Heights Animal Protection Center, where Jack Kingsley has been rescuing wild animals. They get a rescue call, only to find that old Mrs. Eartha has a house full of cats. Then, while driving back to town, they come upon a wrecked truck, and the driver says he was transporting a tiger that escaped. Jack hunts it with a tranquilizer gun, but Nancy soon finds more tiger tracks. Just how many tigers were in that truck, and why were they being transported to River Heights?

Nancy Drew, Girl Detective #1: The Demon of River Heights. Stefan Petrucha, writer ; Sho Murase, artist. NBM/Papercutz 2005 Un Illustration
Grades: 4 5 6 7 8 9   **741.5; Fic**
  1. Adventure graphic novels; 2. Mystery graphic novels; 3. Graphic novels
  1-59707-004-1, $12.95; 1-59707-000-9, $7.95
Everyone's favorite girl detective makes her graphic novel debut. Nancy also makes her debut in a horror film concerning a monstrous River Heights urban legend - but is it really an urban legend, or does the River Heights Demon truly exist? And will Nancy, Bess, and George live long enough to find out? This graphic novel series updates Nancy and her friends to the twenty-first century, but she's still a klutz.

Nancy Drew: Girl Detective #2: Writ in Stone. Stefan Petrucha, writer ; Sho Murase, artist. NBM/Papercutz 2005 112p. Illustration
Grades: 3 4 5 6 7 8 9   **741.5; Fic**
  1. Drew, Nancy (Fictional character); 2. Mystery graphic novels; 3. Graphic novels
  978-1-59707-006-5, $12.95; 978-1-59707-002-7 (pb)
It's double trouble for America's favorite girl detective when Owen Zucker, a sweet young boy Nancy has often babysat, is missing and a shore stone marker found on the coast of California, which may prove the Chinese discovered America in 1421, before Columbus, is stolen. Will Nancy, with the help of her best friends, Bess and George, be able to solve two baffling mysteries at the same time, while all of River Heights is watching?

Nancy Drew: Girl Detective #3: The Haunted Dollhouse. Sho Murase, artist. NBM/Papercutz 2005 112p. Illustration
Grades: 3 4 5 6 7 8 9   **741.5; Fic**
  1. Drew, Nancy (Fictional character); 2. Mystery graphic novels; 3. Graphic novels
  978-1-59707-009-6, $12.95; 978-1-59707-008-9 (pb)
River Heights is celebrating 'Nostalgia Week' and everyone in town is dressing up and acting like it was 1930 - including Nancy, Bess, and George. Nancy even drives a roadster (just as the original Nancy Drew did in the novels 75 years before). But when scenes of crimes displayed in Emma Blavatsky's antique dollhouse start coming true, Nancy has a full-blown mystery on her hands. Nancy's shocked when she stakes out the dollhouse, and witnesses a doll version of herself murdered. Will that scene become reality too?

Nancy Drew: Girl Detective #4: The Girl Who Wasn't There. Sho Murase, artist. NBM/Papercutz 2005 112p. Illustration
Grades: 3 4 5 6 7 8 9   **741.5; Fic**

  1. Drew, Nancy (Fictional character); 2. Mystery graphic novels; 3. Graphic novels
  978-1-59707-013-3, $12.95; 978-1-59707-012-2 (pb)
Nancy gets a call for help late one night from a girl she befriended over the phone when getting technical support to help fix her computer. When the line goes dead, Nancy is determined to get to the bottom of things. Soon, Nancy, her Dad, and friends George and Bess are on their way to India to find Kalpana, the girl who wasn't there. Then Nancy is captured by Sahadev the crime lord, who wants to sacrifice her to Kali.

Nancy Drew: Girl Detective #5: The Fake Heir. Stefan Petrucha, writer ; Daniel Vaughn Ross, artist. NBM/Papercutz 2006 112p. Illustration
Grades: 3 4 5 6 7 8 9   **741.5; Fic**
  1. Drew, Nancy (Fictional character); 2. Mystery graphic novels; 3. Graphic novels
  978-1-59707-025-6, $12.95; 978-1-59707-024-9 (pb)
Nancy, Bess and George find the wreck of an old yacht with a safe inside full of jewelry worth a small fortune. Jack and Amelia Druthers, who were clients of Nancy's dad Carson Drew, owned the yacht. Their will leaves everything to Anton Druthers, specifically excluding his wife Tanya (whom the cousins hated), but no one's seen him for ten years and the rumor is that Mrs. Druthers murdered him. Things take a surprising turn when suddenly Mr. Druthers reappears. But then Mrs. Druthers disappears. Can Nancy Drew solve the mystery of the fake heir? And what does that spider bite have to do with anything?

Nancy Drew: Girl Detective #6: Mr. Cheeters is Missing. Stefan Petrucha, writer ; Sho Murase, artist. NBM/Papercutz 2006 112p. Illustration
Grades: 3 4 5 6 7 8 9   **741.5; Fic**
  1. Drew, Nancy (Fictional character); 2. Mystery graphic novels; 3. Graphic novels
  978-1-59707-031-7, $12.95; 978-1-59707-030-0 (pb)
When the eccentric Blanche Porter reports that her beloved Mr. Cheeters has vanished, it isn't a standard missing persons case. As Nancy Drew soon discovers, Mr. Cheeters is a pet chimp. Or is he? Based on a preliminary investigation and information obtained from Blanche's brother, Lawrence, the River Heights police dismiss the case as bogus, doubting that there ever was a Mr. Cheeters to begin with. But when Nancy Drew discovers there's a missing diamond necklace as well, she's on the case. Can Nancy, along with Bess and George, recover the great ape and the necklace, or has Blanche Porter made a monkey out of Nancy Drew?

Nancy Drew: Girl Detective #7: The Charmed Bracelet. Daniel Vaughn Ross, artist. NBM/Papercutz 2006 112p. Illustration
Grades: 3 4 5 6 7 8 9   **741.5; Fic**
  1. Drew, Nancy (Fictional character); 2. Mystery graphic novels; 3. Graphic novels
  978-1-59707-037-9, $12.95; 978-1-59707-036-2 (pb)
Ned Nickerson has been arrested for shoplifting, and Nancy Drew is threatened with a lawsuit. A rare computer chip has been stolen from Rackham Industries. It all gets even more exciting when Nancy receives a mysterious charm bracelet in the mail - and soon a crime is committed

for each charm. Will Nancy, even with the help of Bess and George, be able to find the real culprit and save Ned?

Nancy Drew: Girl Detective #8: Global Warning. Stefan Petrucha, writer ; Sho Murase, artist. NBM/Papercutz 2006 112p. Illustration
Grades: 3 4 5 6 7 8 9   **741.5; Fic**
1. Drew, Nancy (Fictional character); 2. Mystery graphic novels; 3. Graphic novels
978-1-59707-052-2, $12.95; 978-1-59707-051-5 (pb)
At a new Bio-Dome facility in River Heights, Nancy, Bess, and George get swept up in a mystery involving five different world environments encased within giant domes, animals and all. It's founded and funded by famed environmentalist billionaire, Cheri Goale. But before the Bio-Dome officially opens, a gross green substance destroys one of the domes and Sasquatch appears within the Arctic dome, creating havoc and endangering the future of the facility. Nancy Drew investigates, but is soon trapped within the dome with the legendary Bigfoot.

Nancy Drew: Girl Detective #9: Ghost in the Machinery. Sho Murase, artist. NBM/Papercutz 2007 112p. Illustration
Grades: 3 4 5 6 7 8 9   **741.5; Fic**
1. Drew, Nancy (Fictional character); 2. Mystery graphic novels; 3. Graphic novels
978-1-59707-061-4, $12.95; 978-1-59707-058-4 (pb), $7.95
On a mission sponsored by young, rich, and handsome Ralph Credo, Nancy teams up with eccentric scientist Roy Hinkley to find an amazing high efficiency engine able to operate at an amazing 200 miles per gallon. The experimental engine, mounted on a tank, was part of an experiment during the final days of World War II. There's just one problem, the engine and the tank are haunted. "Ghost In The Machinery" is the first in a series of three Nancy Drew adventures entitled "The High Miles Mystery."

Nancy Drew: Girl Detective Vol. 10: The Disoriented Express. Stefan Petrucha & Sarah Kinney, writers ; Sho Murase, artist. NBM/Papercutz 2007 Un Illustration
Grades: 4 5 6 7 8 9   **741.5; Fic**
1. Drew, Nancy (Fictional character); 2. Mystery graphic novels; 3. Graphic novels
978-1-59707-066-9, $7.95
On its journey to Professor Hinkley's research facility, Nancy Drew must protect an amazing creation that could possibly end the world's energy crisis. Unstable and dangerous, the super fuel-efficient engine must be transported by a private train. But dark forces are at work, attempting to shanghai the miracle machine - literally at every turn by using computers to jam the switches. But while Nancy, and her friend George, attempt to determine which sinister suspect is behind these despicable acts, they soon realize that if their adversaries can't succeed at stealing this miraculous machine, they'll destroy the train, along with everything, and everyone on it. "The Disoriented Express" is the second in a series of three Nancy Drew adventures entitled "The High Miles Mystery."

Petty, J. T. (John T.)
The **Fall** of the House of West. By Paul Pope and J. T. Petty; illustrated by David Rubín. First Second 2015 160 p. Illustration (Battling Boy)
Grades: 7 8 9 10 11 12   **741.5; Fic**
1. Father-daughter relationship — Fiction; 2. Gods; 3. Monsters; 4. Mothers — Fiction; 5. Secrets — Fiction; 6. Graphic novels
162672010X; 9781626720107, $9.99
In this graphic novel, by Paul Pope and J. T. Petty, illustrated by David Rubín, "Aurora West is on the verge of solving the mystery of her mother's death, but it's hard keeping her efforts a secret from her grieving father, the legendary monster-hunter Haggard West. Between her school work and her hours training and hunting with her dad, Aurora is hard-pressed to find time to be a secret sleuth. But she's nothing if not persistent." (Publisher's note)
"Rubín's frenetic black-and-white illustrations stylistically complement Pope and Petty's breakneck-paced plotting. True to the genre, the story explores notions of good and evil but provides no easy answers." Kirkus

The **Rise** of Aurora West. By Paul Pope, J. T. Petty, illustrated by David Rubín. First Second Books 2014 160 p. Illustration (Battling Boy)
Grades: 7 8 9 10 11 12   **741.5**
1. Adventure graphic novels; 2. Female superhero graphic novels
1626722684; 9781626722682, $17.99
In this graphic novel, by Paul Pope and J. T. Petty, illustrated by David Rub?n, the "world introduced in . . . 'Battling Boy' is rife with monsters and short on heroes. . . . But in this action-driven extension of the Battling Boy universe, we see it through a new pair of eyes: Aurora West, daughter of Arcopolis's last great hero, Haggard West." (Publisher's note)
"Since Aurora and her father were only briefly mentioned in the previous installment, this volume does a wonderful job of fleshing out their characters further; readers see an Aurora that's not as confident in her abilities, and a slightly jaded and darker side to her heroic father. Pope's gritty, experimental art from the original Battling Boy has been replaced by Rubin's more traditional style, giving a '60s 'Silver Age' appearance to the work." SLJ

Peyer, Tom
Go boy 7, Vol. 1: Ready set go!. [by] Tom Peyer and Jon Sommariva. Rocket Comics/Dark Horse Comics 2004 96p. Illustration
Grades: 6 7 8 9 10 11 12   **741.5; Fic**
1. Science fiction graphic novels; 2. Graphic novels
1-56971-937-3, $12.95
When Jonny Zero's family jet is shot down, he survives only because his uncle uses his experimental nanotech plasm to save his life. Now Jonny is more than human, which is a good thing, because Uncle Noah and his Go Base are under attack by the forces of The Cultist, an evil madman out to destroy all thinking life. The problem is, he's still just a young teen and a wee bit impulsive when taking action. The action and violence level is similar to what preteens might see in a PG rated movie.
Another title in this series is: Go boy 7 Vol 2: The human factor, written by Brian Augustyn (2004)

Peyo

The **Smurfs** anthology; Vol. 1. Peyo. Papercutz 2013 190 p. Color illustration (The Smurfs graphic novels)
Grades: 4 5 6 7 8 9 10 11 12 Adult   **741.5**
1597074179; 9781597074179, $19.99
1. Smurfs (Fictional characters)

"Newly remastered and presented in original publication order, along with a Smurfy collection of historical notes and photographs, the stories in this volume," by Belgian comics artist Peyo, "introduce us to Papa Smurf, Gargamel, Smurfette, and the rest of the village." (Publisher's note)

The **Smurfs** anthology; Vol. 2. Peyo. Papercutz 2013 192 p. Color illustration
Grades: 4 5 6 7 8 9 10 11 12 Adult   **741.5**
1597074454; 9781597074452, $19.99
1. Smurfs (Fictional characters)

"Newly remastered and presented in original publication order, along with a Smurfy collection of historical notes and photographs, this volume," by Belgian comics artist Peyo, "introduces us to Smurfette and features a 'Johan and Peewit' story never before seen in the U.S." (Publisher's note)

"[A] delightful and instructive mix of Peyo's colorful tales. A series of essays interspersed throughout the collection provides social and historical context for the cartoons." Booklist

Translated from the French

Pfeifer, Will

Captain Atom: Armageddon. Written by Will Pfeifer; penciled by Giuseppe Camuncoli; inked by Sandra Hope. DC Comics/Wildstorm 2007 224p. Illustration
Grades: 10 11 12 Adult   **741.5; Fic**
1. Superhero graphic novels; 2. Graphic novels
978-1-4012-1106-6, $19.99

In the DC Universe, Captain Atom was saving the world by piloting a spaceship into a kryptonite asteroid that was headed for Earth. But at the point of impact, something happens and throws him into another world, a darker world, where superhumans are feared, even the "heroes." Atom first encounters Majestic, who immediately fights him. Then they discover that Atom's appearance in the Wildstorm Universe will end up destroying everything, unless he can find a way home. That's the problem, so far they can't find a way to get him back to where he belongs. This story has more violence than most superhero stories.

Catwoman: It's Only a Movie. Will Pfeifer, writer; David Lopez, penciller; Alvaro Lopez, inker; Jeromy Cox, colorists; Jared K. Fletcher, letterer. DC Comics 2007 168p. Illustration
Grades: 10 11 12 Adult   **741.5; Fic**
1. Catwoman (Fictional character); 2. Mystery graphic novels; 3. Superhero graphic novels; 4. Graphic novels
978-1-4012-1337-4, $19.99

Selina Kyle has prowled the skyline of Gotham City as Catwoman, the protector of the East End, for years. But one year ago, following the events of Infinite Crisis, she became pregnant and decided to leave the costumed world behind. In this volume, the father of Catwoman's baby is revealed. Learn the fallout from Catwoman's killing of Black Mask,

including the horrible price she paid for vengeance and why she chose to bring a baby into the world. Plus, Selina pays a visit to Superman's home, Metropolis. There is some graphic violence.

Catwoman: The Replacements. Will Pfeifer, writer; David Lopez, penciller; Alvaro Lopez, inker; Jeromy Cox, Brad Anderson, colorists; Jared K. Fletcher, letterer. DC Comics 2006 144p. Illustration
Grades: 10 11 12 Adult   **741.5; Fic**
1. Catwoman (Fictional character); 2. Superhero graphic novels; 3. Graphic novels
978-1-4012-1213-1, $14.99

Selina Kyle has prowled the skyline of Gotham City as Catwoman, the protector of the East End, for years. But one year ago, she became pregnant and decided to leave the costumed world behind. Now, a new inexperienced Catwoman continues Selina's trade cloaked in the shadows and tries to restore order in the streets, while the original feline fatale has her hands full with the baby who's become the most important person in her life. Will it be too late for Selina to return when she questions her decision to step away from her crimefighting life? The book includes more violence than in most superhero comics.

Phelan, Matt

★ The **storm** in the barn. Candlewick Press 2009 201p. Illustration
Grades: 4 5 6 7 8 9   **741.5; Fic**
1. Adventure graphic novels; 2. Dust storms; 3. Kansas; 4. Monsters; 5. United States — History — 1933-1945; 6. Graphic novels
978-0-7636-3618-0, $24.99; 0-7636-3618-5;
978-0-7636-5290-6 (pa), $14.99; 0-7636-5290-3 (pa)

In Kansas of 1937, the land has been in the grip of the Dust Bowl for four years, and eleven-year-old Jack Carter has seen his family worn down by it. But the day Jack outruns a dust storm all the way home from town, he glimpses something odd in the abandoned Talbot barn, and he tries to find the courage to go into the barn and confront what is there.

"Children can read this as a work of historical fiction, a piece of folklore, a scary story, a graphic novel, or all four. Written with simple, direct language, it—s an almost wordless book: the illustrations" shadowy grays and blurry lines eloquently depict the haze of the dust. A complex but accessible and fascinating book." SLJ

Phillipson, Phil

God the Dyslexic DoG. Written and created by Brian & Philip Phillipson; art by Alex Nino. Bliss on Tap Publishing 2006 Un Illustration
Grades: 10 11 12 Adult   **741.5; Fic**
1. Fantasy graphic novels; 2. Gods and goddesses; 3. Graphic novels
978-0-9763768-6-6, $19.95

An old poet writes words of wisdom and hides them in a box, christens his loyal dog God, and gives them both to Pandora with the warning that the box should never be opened. All the gods exist, the Greek gods, the Mayan gods, the Egyptians, and all others, but one of them, Dionysus, also known as Bacchus, wants to die. The only way he can is to get Pandora to open the box, which he does trick her into doing. He traps her in the box and carries it with him for a thousand years, during which doG lives but can't remember who and what he is. Eventually doG becomes one of Pavlov's experimental animals, and when his fellow dogs howl at the full moon, they release the Mayan gods from their limbo and set events into motion again. For what" They want the world to end in 2011. Bacchus wants the world to end period. And when doG does finally drool at Pavlov's signal, a new god is created: Darwin. And Darwin wants to destroy all humans; he decides to make all the gods deities of different animals, to turn on humans. The only one who can stop him is doG, and his new human master, Nez, the dyslexic son of a psychic who talks to animals. The book includes some violence and alcohol consumption.

Pien, Lark
   ★ **American** born Chinese. Color by Lark Pien. First Second 2006 233p. Illustration
Grades: 7 8 9 10 11 12   **741.5; Fic**
   1. Chinese Americans; 2. Young adult literature — Works
   1-59643-152-0, $16.95; 978-1-59643-152-2
                                        LC 2005-58105
Michael L. Printz Award, 2007
   In this graphic novel by Gene Luen Yang, "Jin Wang is the only Asian American boy in his new school; Danny is a young man deeply embarrassed by his visiting Chinese cousin, portrayed deliberately by the author as an ethnic clich?; and the Monkey King, a figure from Chinese lore, is desperate to be treated like a god. This . . . story relates how three characters overcome hurdles to find satisfaction within themselves." (Library Journal)
   "True to its origin as a Web comic, this story's clear, concise lines and expert coloring are deceptively simple yet expressive. Even when Yang slips in an occasional Chinese ideogram or myth, the sentiments he's depicting need no translation. Yang accomplishes the remarkable feat of practicing what he preaches with this book: accept who you are and you'll already have reached out to others." Publ Wkly

Pini, Wendy
   ★ **Elfquest** Archives Vol. 1. By Wendy and Richard Pini. DC Comics 2003 216p. Illustration
Grades: 9 10 11 12 Adult   **741.5; Fic**
   1. Adventure graphic novels; 2. Elves; 3. Fantasy graphic novels; 4. Graphic novels
   1-4012-0128-8, $49.99
   Existing on a prehistoric world, the World of Two Moons, in which humans and elves are bitter enemies, the Wolfriders live a dangerous life of fatal battles, deadly hunts, and tribal traditions. Proud of their history but unaware of their origin, the Wolfriders are on an eternal quest to learn the mysteries of their past. This hardcover edition includes the Wolfriders' fateful battle with a band of humans, their surprising discovery of another clan of elves, and Cutter's first meeting with the enchanting healer, Leetah. The Pinis started publishing the Elfquest stories as black and white comics in the mid-1970s; this is a full-color deluxe hardcover edition of the first five issues. The book includes partial nudity, brief sexual situations, and violence.

   ★ **Elfquest** Archives Vol. 2. By Wendy and Richard Pini. DC Comics 2005 226p. Illustration
Grades: 9 10 11 12 Adult   **741.5; Fic**
   1. Adventure graphic novels; 2. Elves; 3. Fantasy graphic novels; 4. Graphic novels
   1-4012-0129-6, $49.99
   The Wolfriders have found sanctuary, and Cutter and Leetah become lifemates. But their peace is threatened once more by men, and the trolls, and by the twin mysteries of the Forbidden Grove and Blue Mountain. The book includes some violence and brief partial nudity.

   ★ **Elfquest** Archives Vol. 3. By Wendy and Richard Pini. DC Comics 2005 224p. Illustration
Grades: 9 10 11 12 Adult   **741.5; Fic**
   1. Adventure graphic novels; 2. Elves; 3. Fantasy graphic novels; 4. Graphic novels
   1-4012-0412-0, $49.99
   This third volume collects Elfquest #11-15. When Leetah and some of the others try to catch up to Cutter to warn him of danger, they are taken as slaves into the towering and mysterious Blue Mountain, stronghold of the ancient elves called the Gliders. There Cutter and the Wolfriders must face the evil Winnowill, who wields strong magic, to save family and friends. The book includes violence, partial nudity, and sexual situations.

Elfquest: The Searcher and the Sword. By Wendy and Richard Pini. DC Comics 2005 96p. Illustration
Grades: 9 10 11 12 Adult   **741.5; Fic**
   1. Adventure graphic novels; 2. Elves; 3. Fantasy graphic novels; 4. Graphic novels
   1-4012-0184-9, $14.99
                                        LC 2004-304577
   In this tale, the elves must adapt to a world without the Troll smiths, who forged their weapons and tools. They must seek the secret of ancient troll metallurgy. Painfully aware of her human heritage, Shuna leaves her adoptive family of Wolfriders and embarks on a quest to unite elves and humans in peace. The book includes some violence.

Elfquest: The Discovery. Written by Wendy & Richard Pini ; script, art, letters, and colors by Wendy Pini. DC Comics 2006 128p. Illustration
Grades: 8 9 10 11 12 Adult   **741.5; Fic**
   1. Adventure graphic novels; 2. Fantasy graphic novels; 3. Graphic novels
   1-4012-0958-0, $14.99
   Wonder and danger mount as the Wolfrider chief's son Sunstream finds romance in the form of the lovely sea elf Brill and fierce hostility whe he exposes her long-hidden tribe, the Wave Dancers. Rule by fear of the "Landers" who hunt and slay his folk, the mighty mer-chief Surge will do anything, even destroy Sunstream and Brill's happiness, to keep his tribe secret and safe. This full-color story is the first new Elfquest story in years.

Pins, Arthur de
   Zombillenium: Gretchen. By Arthur de Pins. NBM Publishing 2013 48 p. (Zombillenium)
Grades: 10 11 12 Adult   **741.5; Fic**
   1. Amusement parks; 2. Vampires
   1561637343; 9781561637348, $14.99

LC 2013936651

In this graphic novel, by Arthur de Pins, "Francis von Bloodt, a vampire and good family man, operates the one-of-a-kind theme park Zombiellenium. But this unique amusement park doesn't just hire anyone: mere mortals need not apply—only genuine werewolves, vampires, zombies, and other citizens from the undead community are employed." (Publisher's note)

Piskor, Ed

Wizzywig. Ed Piskor. Top Shelf Productions 2012 288 p. Illustration
Grades: 11 12 Adult
741.5
1. Computer hackers — Fiction; 2. Telephones — Fiction
1603090975;
9781603090971, $19.95

This graphic novel, "inspired by tales of real-life hackers . . . follows the story of Kevin 'Boingthump' Phenicle, who gets his start tapping into telephone lines as a teenager and works his way up to infiltrating the phone company and its database. At his side is his best (and indeed only) friend, Winston, who goes from helping Kevin with his hacking to defending him on the radio when Kevin is eventually caught and incarcerated." (Publishers Weekly)

Courtesy of Top Shelf Productions

"With heavy technology content and social-issue relevance, plus hacker and comics industry in-jokes, this is a techie's dream read, enhanced by Piskor's thorough research and judiciously unpretty black-and-white art." LJ

Plaka, Christine

Yonen Buzz Volume 1. Tokyopop 2006 188p. Illustration
Grades: 9 10 11 12 Adult   **741.5; Fic**
1. Rock music; 2. Graphic novels
1-59816-403-1, $9.99

Four young musicians stand at a new threshold of their musical career. With Plastic Chew, the band they created in high school, set on a path to rock 'n' roll stardom, will the demands of jobs, schoolwork, and relationships get in the way? Can they be true to their artistic vision without becoming sellouts? No matter what happens, this band keeps on rockin' ... determined to not let anything derail their rock odyssey. This is a global manga, originally published in German. The book includes some mildly harsh language.

PLUS

Hanami: International love story vol. 2. Art by Sung Jae Park. Dark Horse Comics 2007 204p. Illustration
Grades: 8 9 10 11 12 Adult   **741.5**
1. Humorous graphic novels; 2. Romance graphic novels; 3. Graphic novels
978-1-59307-738-9, $9.95

Joonho's first kiss came from Hanami, not Sae-un oops. Hanami still believes that Sae-un is just a friend, not a girlfriend, and things are going to get even more tangled if Joonho doesn't get over his guilt and act soon. But first he has to buy a cell phone, because Sae-un is fed up with his poor calling habits, and she makes him promise never to give the number to any other girl. In order to afford the thing, though, he has to get a job... at a fast-food restaurant... with David Bacon. At least his female coworkers are cute ... There's a brief instance of partial nudity and some fighting. This is a manwha (Korean comic) series.

Poe, Marshall

Turning Points: Little Rock nine. Illustrated by Ellen Lindner. Simon & Schuster/Aladdin Paperbacks 2008 122p. Illustration
Grades: 3 4 5 6 7 8 9   **741.5; Fic**
1. African Americans — Civil rights; 2. African Americans — Education; 3. United States — History — 1953-1961; 4. Graphic novels
978-1-4169-5066-0, $7.99

LC 2007-937918

Sixteen-year-old William McNally and fifteen-year-old Thomas Johnson both live in Little Rock, Arkansas, in the summer of 1957. They both love baseball and teasing their little sisters. There's just one big difference: William is white, and Thomas, the son of the McNally family's maid, is black. After the U.S. Supreme Court rules in favor of desegregating public schools, Little Rock Central High School prepares to enroll its first nine African-American students, and William and Thomas are caught in the middle of a storm. William's family has divided over the issue, and Thomas' parents don't want him to get hurt and forbid him to try to enter the school. The book portrays the issues of the time and the personal beliefs of both sides to let readers see what it was like back then. William, Thomas, and their families are fictional, but what happened at Little Rock Central High School is an important part of American history.

Pope, Paul

Batman: Year 100. By Paul Pope; colorist, Jose Villarrubia; letters, Jared K. Fletcher & John Workman. DC Comics 2007 232p. Illustration
Grades: 10 11 12 Adult   **741.5; Fic**
1. Batman (Fictional character); 2. Science fiction graphic novels; 3. Superhero graphic novels; 4. Graphic novels
978-1-4012-1192-9, $19.99

This is a futuristic mystery of epic proportions set in a dark, dystopian world devoid of privacy and filled with government conspiracies, psychic police, holographic caller ID and absolutely no room for "secret identities." In Gotham City, 2039, a federal agent is murdered and a contingent of Washington's top agents is hot on the suspect's trail. The Batman, a forgotten icon from the past, is wanted for the murder. Amid the chaos Gotham City Police Detective Gordon, grandson of the former commissioner, discovers that the man they are chasing shouldn't exist at all. The book has some bloody violence and some strong language.

★ **Battling** Boy. Paul Pope; colors by Hilary Sycamore. First Second 2013 208 p. Illustration
Grades: 7 8 9 10 11 12   **741.5; Fic**
1. Fantasy graphic novels; 2. Superhero graphic novels

1596438053; 9781596431454, $15.99; 9781596438057, $24.99

LC 2013030815

Eisner Award: Best Publication for Teens (2014)

In this book, "the hero Haggard West helps battle the evil forces of Sadisto and his hooded ghouls. However, in a shocking turn of events, evil triumphs over good, and the metropolis is left without protection. In a world far, far away, a 13-year-old son of a god has been chosen to help Earth fight the onslaught of monsters as a rite of passage. Sent with only a few possessions, including an array of magical T-shirts, Battling Boy helps the cityùbut he finds he cannot do it alone." (Kirkus Reviews)

"This is a sophisticated tale for younger readers, but Pope manages to both grant full-scale wish fulfillment and acknowledge the limitations of young boys with equal aplomb. His art, meanwhile, looks like nothing else in comics, with ropy, sinewy figures, dynamic action, and gritty urban design all captured in panels that have the rough, subversive tone of classic punk album covers." Booklist

Popgun, volume one: a graphic mixtape.
Image Comics 2007 448p. Illustration
Grades: 11 12 Adult   **741.5**
1. Short stories; 2. Graphic novels
978-1-58240-824-8, $29.99

This anthology of graphic short stories rams through the various genres with stories from comics veterans and newcomers, including Eric Larsen, Mike Allred, Dan Hipp, Rick Remender, Phil Yeh, Richard Starkings, Jamie S. Rich, Jim Mahfood, Leah Moore, and many more. Many of the stories include nudity, sexual situations, harsh language, and violence.

Porcellino, John
    King-Cat Classix. Drawn & Quarterly 2007 384p. Illustration
Grades: 10 11 12 Adult   **741.5**
1. Autobiographical graphic novels; 2. Graphic novels
978-1-894937-91-7, $29.95

This large collection focuses on the first fifty issues of Porcellino's autobiographical comics, with extensive endnotes and an index, along with selections of all the extra ephemera that makes an individual issue of King-Cat a unique experience-essays, articles, stories, and letters from friends. Included are more than two hundred and fifty pages of comics, ranging from Porcellino's earliest scrawls to his later, minimalist delineations. The comics range through all of his concerns-family, family pets, the natural world, work, music, romance. He uses some strong language and some sexual situations.

    Perfect Example. Drawn & Quarterly 2005 Un Illustration
Grades: 10 11 12 Adult   **741.5; Fic**
1. Autobiographical graphic novels; 2. Graphic novels
1-896597-75-0, $16.95

A melancholic memoir of saying goodbye to the familiar road trips, drunken concerts, and late-night make-out sessions all swirl together in this coming-of-age graphic novel by King Cat cartoonist John Porcellino. Tackling the pain and uncertainty of the pivotal summer before college, Porcellino's story is drawn in his minimalist

style. Perfect Example is a collection of Porcellino's self-published King Cat comics. Porcellino uses strong language throughout.

    Thoreau at Walden. By John Porcellino, from the writings of Henry David Thoreau; introduction by D.B. Johnson. Hyperion 2008 Viii, 99 p. Illustration; Map (Center for Cartoon Studies presents)
Grades: 8 9 10 11 12 Adult   **818/.303; 741.5**
1. American authors; 2. Thoreau, Henry David, 1817-1862; 3. Walden Woods (Mass) — Social life and customs; 4. Graphic novels
1423100387; 1423100395; 9781423100386, $16.99; 9781423100393

LC 2007061358

This graphic novel, by John Porcellino, "introduces . . . Henry David Thoreau. . . . Thoreau's writings, excerpted out of chronological order, are recast into a narrative that moves from the philosopher's self-ostracism from society and his time at Walden and into the feeling of calm reverie he took from his experiences." (Booklist)

"Presents in graphic novel format an account of the two years that Thoreau spent at Walden Pond, excerpted from Thoreau's writings." Publisher's note

Includes bibliographical references (p. 99)

Postcards: True Stories That Never Happened.
Random House/Villard 2007 152p. Illustration
Grades: 10 11 12 Adult   **741.5**
1. Short stories; 2. Graphic novels
978-0-345-49850-2

Sixteen short stories inspired by antique postcards are in this anthology. Writers and artists include Tom Beland, Harvey Pekar, Stuart Moore, Neil Kleid, A. David Lewis, Ande Parks, and others. Stories range from the elegeiac (Beland's "Time") to ironic ("Best Side Out" by Antony Johnston) to dark horror ("Send Louis His Underwear" by Matt Dembicki) to heroic (Robert Tinnell's "The Midnight Caller's Holiday in Hades").

Powell, Eric
    Billy the Kid's Old Timey Oddities. Writer, Eric Powell; artist, Kyle Hotz; colorist, Eric Powell; letterer, Michael Heisler. Dark Horse Comics 2006 Un Illustration
Grades: 10 11 12 Adult   **741.5; Fic**
1. Horror graphic novels; 2. Monsters; 3. Graphic novels
1-59307-448-4, $13.95

Notorious outlaw and gunslinger William Henry McCarty - known as Billy the Kid - faked his death and is alive and well when Fineas Sproule, the four-armed owner of a sideshow called Sproule's Biological Curiosities, identifies him and then makes an offer the Kid can't refuse. They seek a mystical gem called the Golem's Heart, and they must travel from the U.S. to Europe, to an isolated castle that is home to Victor Frankenstein. They need Billy's prowess with guns to protect them on their journey. When they arrive in the village near the castle, however, everyone is captured by the mad scientist, who plans to conduct horrible and nasty experiments on everyone. Billy has thought of his companions as freaks, but they're nothing like the pitiable monsters created by Frankenstein. This will appeal to horror movie fans who love monsters.

Originally published as Billy the Kid's Old Timey Oddities issues #1-4.

The **Goon** Vol. 1: Nothin' But Misery. By Eric Powell; colors by Eric and Robin Powell. Dark Horse Comics 2003 Un Illustration

Grades: 9 10 11 12 Adult   **741.5; Fic**

    1. Horror graphic novels; 2. Humorous graphic novels; 3. Graphic novels; 4. Goon (fictional character)

1-56971-998-5, $15.95

Bones will be broken and heads will roll! An insane priest is building himself an army of the undead and filling the town with zombies, and there's only one man who can put them in their place: the man they call Goon. This volume collects The Goon series and The Goon Color Special, originally published by Albatross Exploding Funny Books, presented here for the first time in full color. Readers meet Goon, his pal Frankie, and lots of weird monsters in a story that mixes crime noir, horror, and slapstick comedy. The monsters and zombies look like they just came out of an old EC horror comic; they look icky but funny at the same time.

The **Goon**: Heaps of Ruination. By Eric Powell; color assists by Robin Powell [and others]; Hellboy sequence and dialogue by Mike Mignola; colors by Dave Stewart; letters by Clem Robins. Dark Horse Comics 2005 Un Illustration

Grades: 10 11 12 Adult   **741.5; Fic**

    1. Fantasy graphic novels; 2. Hellboy (Fictional character); 3. Horror graphic novels; 4. Humorous graphic novels; 5. Graphic novels; 6. Goon (fictional character)

1-59307-292-9, $12.95

All undead minions and other variegated doers of badness who rouse up trouble with the honest folks of Lonely Street answer to the Goon. Robot or alien, werewolf or vampire, zombie or gorilla (or zombie-gorilla), it makes no difference to the Goon - he'll serve them up a mouthful of broken teeth right quick, as evidenced by the tales collected in this third volume chronicling the triumphs and tragedies of the lone man brave enough to stand against the Zombie Priest and his ghoulish army. This volume also includes a very special guest appearance by Hellboy co-written and drawn by Hellboy creator, Mike Mignola. The book includes some strong language and comic horror violence.

The **Goon**: My Murderous Childhood (and Other Grievous Yarns). Dark Horse Comics 2004 Un Illustration

Grades: 10 11 12 Adult   **741.5; Fic**

    1. Fantasy graphic novels; 2. Horror graphic novels; 3. Humorous graphic novels; 4. Graphic novels; 5. Goon (Fictional character)

1-59307-109-4, $13.95

The Goon and Franky have been best friends ever since they were tykes. Find out how the two little ankle-biters became best pals and how they muscled their way into the rackets of big-time crime-boss, Labrazio - who, incidentally, nobody's seen in a while. Franky and the Goon are going to have to take on a horde of zombies, an army of hoboes, a couple of grave robbing freaks, a guy with a gold head and his killer robot, a pie-crazed skunk ape, one homely, man-crazy sea hag, and a whole lot of other things that smell just as bad, if not worse. The book includes some strong language and lots of comic horror violence.

The **Goon**: Rough Stuff. By Eric Powell; colors by Dave Stewart. Dark Horse Comics 2004 Un Illustration

Grades: 10 11 12 Adult   **741.5; Fic**

    1. Fantasy graphic novels; 2. Horror graphic novels; 3. Humorous graphic novels; 4. Graphic novels; 5. Goon (Fictional character)

1-59307-086-1, $12.95

This volume presents the origin of Eric Powell's The Goon, the earliest stories published for the first time. The Zombie Priest has just set up shop on Lonely Street and intends to build an undead army, and the Goon's the only man who can stop him. His early battles with the undead are mixed with stories of the Goon's youth, as the reader meets his circus-freak family and learns how he came to be the head of a notorious crime family. Also included in this volume is a look at the creation of the Goon and his world with a special "Evolution of The Goon" sketchbook section. The book includes some strong language and violence.

The **Goon**: Virtue and the Grim Consequences Thereof. Dark Horse Comics 2006 Un Illustration

Grades: 10 11 12 Adult   **741.5; Fic**

    1. Fantasy graphic novels; 2. Horror graphic novels; 3. Humorous graphic novels; 4. Graphic novels; 5. Goon (Fictional character)

1-59307-456-5, $16.95

2005 Eisner Awards for Best Continuing Series and for Best Humor Publication.

Giant man-eating eyeballs from another dimension, mad scientists, rampaging killer robots and the Ghost of Christmas Past - no, there's nothing out of the ordinary in the world of The Goon. This volume collects five tales following the exploits of the man known only as The Goon as he fights his through a horde of killer robots and even creatures from another dimension to help save his sometimes friend and ally Dr. Hieronymous Alloy from a mysterious disease. But there are plenty of bumps along the way, ultimately landing the Goon in Cade's Island Penitentiary, proving once more that no good deed goes unpunished. The book includes comic horror violence and strong language.

The **Goon**: Wicked Inclinations. Dark Horse Comics 2006 Un Illustration

Grades: 10 11 12 Adult   **741.5; Fic**

    1. Fantasy graphic novels; 2. Horror graphic novels; 3. Humorous graphic novels; 4. The Goon (Fictional character); 5. Graphic novels

978-1-59307-646-7, $14.95

The tide has turned in Goon's war against the undead hordes of the Zombie Priest - or has it? With Buzzard now preventing the harvest of any fresh corpses from the cemetery, the Priest grows desperate. So desperate, that he unleashes incantations of previously unseen power to create a whole new breed of minion - one that may be beyond even the strength of the Goon to contain. But one pays a price for conjuring such evil into the world, and the Zombie Priest quickly discovers that the cost of such power may be far more than he bargained for. The book includes strong language and comic horror violence, lots of it.

Powell, Martin

Sherlock Holmes Mysteries Volume Two. Art by Seppo Makinen. Moonstone 2004 Un Illustration

Grades: 9 10 11 12 Adult　　　　　　**741.5; Fic**
1. Mystery graphic novels; 2. Holmes, Sherlock (Fictional character); 3. Graphic novels
0-9748501-4-4, $14.95

In Return of the Devil," the many drug addicts of London have fallen victim to a poisonous supply of cocaine, trapping Sherlock Holmes himself within its deadly grip. The Great Detective is submerged in a world of nightmares where the evil Professor Moriarty still lives, and Holmes' dream of love with Irene Adler, The Woman, seems to have become a reality. Holmes must do battle against his very soul, at last facing his most terrible enemy: himself. In The Loch Ness Horror," Holmes is lured out of retirement when the Vatican calls upon him to investigate the bizarre murder of a priest. He swiftly deduces that this is no ordinary crime, and that an immensely powerful holy relic has been stolen from the secret vaults. Aleister Crowley, the self proclaimed Most Wicked Man in the World," casts his evil designs against all humanity in a mad scheme to arouse Doomsday. Meanwhile, Dr. Watson returns to Baskerville Hall, where something demonic is once again haunting the fog-shrouded moors. The book includes some violence and some strong language.

The **Swiss** family Robinson. By Johann D. Wyss; retold by Martin Powell; illustrated by Gerardo Sandoval.. Stone Arch Books 2009 74p. Illustration

Grades: 4 5 6 7 8 9 10　　　　　　**741.5; Fic**
1. Adventure graphic novels; 2. Shipwrecks; 3. Survival after airplane accidents, shipwrecks, etc; 4. Wyss, Johann David, 1743-1818 — Adaptations
978-1-4342-0756-2, $23.93

　　　　　　　　　　　　　　LC 2008-6249

In the early nineteenth century, a Swiss family survives a shipwreck and land on a deserted island. They build a life for themselves there, salvaging materials from the wrecked ship and using the plants and other things they find on the island. However, some of the creatures living on the island could be deadly. This graphic novel adaptation of Wyss's classic adventure novel includes information about real-life castaways and uninhabited islands. An interesting note, the novel has never been out of print for almost 200 years and has gone through almost 200 editions.

Part of the Graphic Revolve series

Powell, Nate

★ **Swallow** me whole. Top Shelf Productions 2008 Un Illustration

Grades: 10 11 12 Adult　　　　　　**741.5; Fic**
1. Mental illness; 2. Graphic novels
978-1-60309-033-9, $20.95

Stepsiblings Ruth and Perry share their secrets with each other; Ruth hears insects talking to her, and Perry has to deal with a tiny wizard who forces him to draw all the time. In high school, Ruth is diagnosed as an obsessive compulsive with schizophrenic tendencies, while Perry manages to hide his wizard. Ruth sees cicadas and other insects always surrounding her, to the point that she thinks she's completely covered with them and she can fly. Her Memaw (grandmother) warns her that what she sees can

swallow her whole. This book includes considerable use of foul language, especially the f-bomb, and the story takes a very thoughtful, mature reader to comprehend what is happening.

Pratchett, Terry

The **Discworld** graphic novels: The colour of magic & The light fantasic. Adapted by Scott Rockwell; illustrated by Steven Ross. HarperCollins 2008 Un Illustration

Grades: 9 10 11 12 Adult　　　　　　**741.5; Fic**
1. Fantasy graphic novels; 2. Humorous graphic novels; 3. Graphic novels
978-0-06-168596-5, $24.95

Discworld is a flat world, sitting on the backs of four elephants who hurtle through space balanced on a giant turtle. Terry Pratchett has been publishing his comic fantasy series for about 25 years; this volume collects the graphic novel adaptations of the first two novels in the series. Originally published in the U. K. in 1993, they are published for the first time in the U. S. The stories feature the spectacularly inept wizard Rincewind, who acts as a tour guide for the naive tourist named Twoflower—and for his sentient Luggage. The book includes some violence and sexual innuendo.

Priddy, Joel

The **gift** of the Magi. It Books/HarperCollins 2009 Un Illustration

Grades: 5 6 7 8 9 10 11 12 Adult　　　　**741.5; Fic**
1. Christmas; 2. Gifts; 3. Henry, O, 1862-1910 — Adaptations; 4. Graphic novels
978-0-06-178239-8, $14.99

Della and Jim are a young married couple, struggling to make ends meet when Jim's pay has been cut. It's Christmas time, but despite squeezing every penny, Della has managed to save only a little bit of money, and it's not enough to buy Jim a good present. He owns a gold pocket watch, and Della wants to buy him a chain for it. She has only one thing of value that she can sell her beautiful, long, long hair. Out of her love for Jim, Della sacrifices her hair. And, of course, Jim has sacrificed his gold pocket watch in order to buy beautiful hair combs for Della's gorgeous hair. As O. Henry says, they "most unwisely sacrificed for each other the greatest treasures of their house," but also that "of all who give gifts these two were the wisest." Joel Priddy's adaptation of this classic story uses black and white illustrations except when Della lets down her hair to consider her one treasure. He preserves much of O. Henry's original prose, which means that younger readers will have to look up a lot of words to understand the story. This book is suitable for younger readers but will also appeal to teens and adults.

Prince, Liz

★ **Tomboy:** A Graphic Memoir. By Liz Prince. Zest Books 2014 256 p. Illustration

Grades: 7 8 9 10 11 12 Adult　　　**741.5; 305.309; 92**
1. Cartoonists — Caricatures and cartoons; 2. Cartoonists — United States — Biography; 3. Gender identity; 4. Gender role; 5. Prince, Liz; 6. Sex differences (Psychology); 7. Sex role; 8. Stereotype (Social psychology); 9. Graphic novels

1936976552;
9781936976553, $15.99
LC 2014034070
This memoir, by Liz Prince, "is a graphic novel about refusing gender boundaries, yet unwittingly embracing gender stereotypes at the same time, and realizing later in life that you can be just as much of a girl in jeans and a T-shirt as you can in a pink tutu." (Publisher's note)

Courtesy of Zest Books

"Prince's honest voice and self-deprecating humor help make young Liz a sympathetic and relatable character. The simply rendered black-and-white panel drawings have an unpretentious quality, in keeping with the narrative tone." Horn Book

The psychology of superheroes: an unauthorized exploration
Edited by Robin S. Rosenberg with Jennifer Canzoneri. BenBella Books, Inc. 2008 259p. Bibliographic footnotes; Illustration (BenBella Books psychology of popular culture series)
Grades: 10 11 12 Adult   741.5
1. Conduct of life; 2. Hulk (Fictional character); 3. Justice League (Fictional characters); 4. Spider-Man (Fictional character); 5. Superheroes (Fictional characters) — Psychology; 6. Superman (Fictional character); 7. Wonder Woman (Fictional character); 8. X-Men (Fictional characters)
1-933771-31-3; 978-1-933771-31-1, $17.95
LC 2007-41418
This book collects essays about superheroes from several psychological viewpoints, ranging from the positive moral aspects of superheroes to gender stereotypes, prejudice, anti-heroes, the place of Arkham Asylum (the notorious place where DC super villains get locked up), the role of rage in The Incredible Hulk, and more. Editor Rosenberg is a clinical psychologist, and many of the contributors hold degrees in psychology and have faculty positions at various universities.
Includes bibliographical references

Pruett, Joe
Kilroy Is Here. Image Comics 2006 Un Illustration
Grades: 11 12 Adult   741.5; Fic
1. Horror graphic novels; 2. Mystery graphic novels; 3. Graphic novels
1-58240-587-5, $24.99
A being of unknown origin and power who is drawn to scenes of human suffering, Kilroy is an avenger of the innocent and protector of the weak. In the stories collected here, he appears at such places as Tiananmen Square in 1989, Sarajevo, Mogadishu, anywhere people suffer unjustly and are unjustly killed, he's there to take vengeance. The book includes some strong language, sexual situations, and graphic violence.

The **Nameless:** The Director's Cut. Writer, Joe Pruett; artists, Phil Hester, Bruce McCorkindale. ImageComics 2006 Un Illustration
Grades: 10 11 12 Adult   741.5; Fic
1. Fantasy graphic novels; 2. Horror graphic novels; 3. Graphic novels
1-58240-499-2, $15.99
He is a man without a past, without a future, and without a name. An evil hides in the shadows of modern day Mexico City, feeding on the thousands of abandoned and unwanted street children that plague the night. This "nameless" man finds himself drawn into the midst of a very real modern horror with its origins found in the mythical bloodthirsty rites of the extinct Aztec Empire. The violent rituals and gods of the sun worshipping tribe somehow hold a key to his past. The nameless man knows that if he survives and learns the ancient secrets, he will have to live with the answers. The book includes violence.

Untouchables. Writer, Joe Pruett; artist, John Kissee. Image Comics 2006 Un Illustration
Grades: 10 11 12 Adult   741.5; Fic
1. Mystery graphic novels; 2. Graphic novels
978-1-58240-359-6, $16.99
Twenty years after the fall of Capone and the rise to fame of Ness comes a new group of Treasury agents code-named Untouchables. Prohibition never ended, and it now includes not only liquor, but tobacco and firearms. Joseph Tarpley comes to lead the new Untouchables in Chicago. Gun fights, car chases, gangsters, nightclubs and sexy dames galore can be found throughout this hard-boiled, alternate take on the days of the mob and the officers who hunted them.

Puckett, Kelly
Kinetic. Kelley Puckett, writer; Warren Pleece, artist. DC Comics 2005 Un Illustration
Grades: 9 10 11 12 Adult   741.5; Fic
1. Teenagers; 2. Graphic novels
1-4012-0472-4, $9.99
Tom Morrell is a sickly and disabled ultra-loser facing the daily hell of high school. Worse yet, his sole means of emotional support is his loving but smothering mother who fears he'll drop dead at any moment. And the worst part is, she's right. Tom's only escape is the super-heroic exploits of Kinetic, his favorite comic-book hero. But unbeknownst to Tom, he's got some powers of his own, and they're going to change his life - assuming they manifest themselves before Tom reaches the end of his rope and decides that life isn't worth living. Foul language is represented by nonsense syllables.

Pyle, Kevin C.
Blindspot. Henry Holt & Company 2007 Un Illustration
Grades: 5 6 7 8 9 10 11 12 Adult   741.5; Fic
1. Friendship; 2. Graphic novels
978-0-8050-7998-2 (pa), $13.95; 0-8050-7998-X (pa)
LC 2006041155
Dean and his friends have created an entire world in the woods behind their suburban housing development. In their army fantasy, they're at war, and Dean is the daring captain

leading his troops through episodes of intrigue and danger. But no fantasy can last forever. A run-in with a homeless man in the woods snaps the boys back to reality, and little by little the real world pervades their imagined universe and drives them apart.

★ **Katman**. Henry Holt and Co. 2009 Un Illustration
Grades: 7 8 9 10 11 12   **741.5; Fic**
   1. Cats; 2. Friendship; 3. Graphic novels
978-0-8050-8285-2, $12.99; 0-8050-8285-9
                                      LC 2008-937398
Kit is a bored sixteen-year-old with nothing to do one summer when he starts feeding stray cats. He loves it when cool, artistic Jess helps him out, even though he has to endure constant taunting by her disaffected metalhead friends. They make fun of him for being like the local cat lady, but Kit doesn't care—especially after Jess draws him an anime-style avatar named Katman.

"Beautifully simple and straightforward." Voice Youth Advocates

Quesada, Joe
   NYX: Wannabe. Writer, Joe Quesada; artists, Josh Middleton, Robert Teranishi. Marvel Entertainment 2006 Un Illustration
Grades: 10 11 12 Adult   **741.5; Fic**
   1. Adventure graphic novels; 2. Superhero graphic novels; 3. X-Men (Fictional characters); 4. Graphic novels
0-7851-1243-X, $19.99
The X-Men's dream has always been one of creating hope from despair - in a young mutant's darkest hour Charles Xavier will always be just around the corner, ready with open arms and a helping hand. But Xavier can't be everywhere at once. What becomes of a group of young mutants that have to rely on themselves for everything from food to shelter to love? Wayward angels with dirty faces who, instead of preparing for Magneto's next big assault, must learn to survive in the cold, harsh world of the city that never sleeps. The world of the X-Men is brought to the streets, and the struggle for survival has never been more uncertain...

Quick, Jennifer
   Once in a blue moon. [by] Nunzio DeFilippis, Chistina Weir, and Jennifer Quick. Oni Press 2004 154p. Illustration
Grades: 6 7 8 9 10 11 12   **741.5; Fic**
   1. Fantasy graphic novels; 2. Graphic novels
1-929998-83-X, $11.95
Aeslin had a magical childhood, with loving parents who read wonderful fables from the book, The Avalon Chronicles, about a fantastic world where a brave Dragon Knight and her Prince battled an Evil Wizard. Then, her parents left on a business trip from which only her mother returned. Her mother tried to erase any aspect of fantasy from Aeslin's life from that time. Now, she happens upon a new book, Once in a Blue Moon, and when she wishes she could go to Avalon to help the people, she finds herself magically transported there and learns she is the new Dragon Knight who must save the land.

Quinn, Jason
   Gandhi: My Life is My Message. By Jason Quinn; illustrated by Naresh Kumar. Random House Inc 2014 212 p. Color; Illustration
Grades: 8 9 10 11 12 Adult   **92; 741.5**
   1. Gandhi, Mahatma, 1869-1948
9380741227; 9789380741222, $16.99
This book by Jason Quinn, illustrated by Naresh Kumar, focuses on the life of "Mohandas Karamchand Gandhi, better known as the Mahatma or Great Soul. . . . We discover the man behind the legend, following him from his birth in the Indian coastal town of Porbandar in 1869, to the moment of his tragic death at the hands of an assassin in January 1948, just months after the Independence of India." (Publisher's note)

"Just as the writing eloquently intertwines explication with reenactments of dramatic, poignant events, the panels are meticulously arranged to move the reader's attention from broad and busy scenes to intimate close-ups." Booklist

   Steve Jobs: genius by design. By Jason Quinn; illustrated by Amit Tayal. Random House Inc 2012 104 p. Illustration; Color
Grades: 7 8 9 10 11 12 Adult   **92; 741.5**
   1. Apple Inc — Officials & employees; 2. Biographical graphic novels; 3. Computer industry; 4. Jobs, Steve, 1955-2011
9380028768; 9789380028767, $12.99
This graphic novel, by Jason Quinn, illustrated by Amit Tayal, presents a biography of the 20th-century technology entrepreneur and Apple Inc. founder Steve Jobs. "Steve Jobs and his inventions changed the world we live in." The book ranges "from his birth and his adoption, through the advent of the computer age and on into the digital age. Forced out of the company he created, his indomitable vision allowed him to change the world of computers, movies, music and telecommunications." (Publisher's note)

"This cleverly designed volume provides a concise but well-balanced view of Steve Jobs the wunderkind, including his difficult personality and complex genius." Booklist

Quitely, Frank
   All-Star Superman, Volume One. Written by Grant Morrison; pencilled by Frank Quitely. DC Comics 2007 160p. Illustration
Grades: 8 9 10 11 12 Adult   **741.5; Fic**
   1. Superhero graphic novels; 2. Superman (Fictional character); 3. Graphic novels
978-1-4012-0914-8; 978-1-4012-1102-8 (pa), $12.99
Eisner Award: Best New Series (2006)
Writer Morrison and artist Quitely present several episodes in the life of the iconic superhero, Superman. When he saves a group of scientists from burning up in the sun, what no one realizes is that uber-villain Lex Luthor set up everything in order to kill Superman, who absorbed so much solar radiation that it is now slowly killing him. Once Superman learns that he is dying, he sets out to give Lois Lane a birthday she will never forget, by giving her his powers for one day. Then, when Jimmy Olsen takes charge of the science think tank P.R.O.J.E.C.T. for one day, they discover black kryptonite, which makes Superman turn evil. And, in his guise as Clark Kent, he interviews Lex Luthor in prison, but super-villain Parasite is taken from his shielded

cell and begins to absorb Superman's powers, causing chaos.

Also available as a single volume collecting all 12 issues
Originally published as All-Star Superman issues #1-6
Volume 1 of 2

Rabagliati, Michel

Paul Has a Summer Job. Drawn & Quarterly 2003 Un Illustration
Grades: 10 11 12 Adult   **741.5; Fic**
  1. Graphic novels
  1-896597-54-8, $16.95

Paul is outraged that he is forced to stop his high school art training, but he's been asked to put art aside because his other grades are so terribly low. Defiant, he quits school and anticipates a summer of leisure. But instead Paul follows the path of so many Quebecois teenagers: he lands a job as a counselor at one of the many summer camps in the mountains outside the city. There he finds himself guiding a motley band of kids, misfits and troublemakers, much like himself. The book includes some nudity, sexual situations, and strong language.

Paul Moves Out. Drawn & Quarterly 2005 Un Illustration
Grades: 10 11 12 Adult   **741.5; Fic**
  1. Graphic novels
  1-896597-87-4, $19.95

Nineteen-year-old Paul takes another step into adulthood by moving out of his parents' house and into his first apartment with his girlfriend, enjoying life's pleasures as well as confronting its challenges. He attends art school in Montreal and must deal with the fact that a charismatic professor is gay. The book includes strong language and some sexual situations.

Ragawa, Marimo

Baby & Me, Vol. 1. Viz Media/Shojo Beat 2006 200p. Illustration
Grades: 6 7 8 9 10 11 12 Adult   **741.5; Fic**
  1. Family; 2. Humorous graphic novels; 3. Shojo manga
  1-4215-0234-8, $8.99

Young Takuya has it tough. After his mother passed away it has been his job to take care of his baby brother, Minoru while their father, Harumi, works the long hours of a Japanese "salaryman." Takuya must sacrifice the playtime usually associated with childhood for the responsibilities of an adult. Cooking, cleaning, sewing and scolding are all now an integral part of the sixth-grader's life. "All work and no play" has Takuya incredibly frustrated and resentful of his little brother. Will Takuya find it in his heart to love the brother who is causing him so much grief" This isn't so much a soap opera drama as it is a comedy with dramatic moments.

Raicht, Mike

Hulk: big green men. Mike Raicht, writer ; Alex Sanchez, pencils ; J. Rauch, colors ; Dave Sharpe, letters ; Shane Davis & J. Rauch, cover. ABDO Publishing Company/Spotlight 2006 Un Illustration
Grades: 4 5 6 7 8 9   **741.5; Fic**

  1. Hulk (Fictional character); 2. Superhero graphic novels; 3. Graphic novels
  1-59961-042-6, $21.35

                LC 2005-57558

When Bruce Banner finds himself in Roswell, he finds all the inhabitants wear strange collars and act spaced out—except for a teenage girl. What they don't know is that she's really a Skrull, as are her parents, and their people have finally come to rescue them. But now her family doesn't want to leave, and when the Skrulls hurt Bruce, he becomes The Hulk and rampages against the "little green men." This is a revised, hardbound edition of the Marvel Age comic book.

Part of the Hulk series

Hulk: The abomination. Mike Raicht, writer; Ryan Odagawa, pencils; J. Rauch, colors; Dave Sharpe, letters; Shane Davis & J. Rauch, cover.. ABDO Spotlight 2006 Un Illustration
Grades: 3 4 5 6 7 8 9   **741.5; Fic**
  1. Hulk (Fictional character); 2. Superhero graphic novels; 3. Graphic novels
  1-59961-045-0, $21.35

                LC 2005-57557

Dr. Bruce Banner was conducting research on gamma rays when he was exposed and became the Hulk. However, he can return to his human form when he's not stressed or upset or angry. Emil Blonsky worked on the project, too, and after Banner left he tried to carry on the work and experimented on himself. However, he became a monster some call the Abomination, and in his anger over not being able to change back, he takes it out on towns, and people. He rampages in Texas, and Banner travels there in hopes of stopping him; but Blonsky only succeeds in causing Banner to turn into the Hulk. Young readers who have seen the new Incredible Hulk movie that premiered in June 2008 will know the Abomination from the movie.

This is a revision of a Dec. 2004 issue of Incredible Hulk from the Marvel Age line.

Spider-man: Spidey strikes back Vol. 1 digest. Mike Raicht and Todd Dezago. Marvel Comics 2005 96p. Illustration
Grades: 4 5 6 7 8 9   **741.5; Fic**
  1. Spider-Man (Fictional character); 2. Superhero graphic novels; 3. Graphic novels
  0-7851-1632-X, $5.99

Tired of saving the day and getting no respect, Spider-Man considers taking a break from his superhero duties, which leaves the city wide open for the likes of the Sandman and the Enforcers. Will Spidey let it all go to pot, or will he step up to the plate and take one for the team? This volume collects Marvel Age Spider-Man issues 17-20. Previous volumes were published under the series title Marvel Age Spider-Man. The Marvel Age titles are being collected and published in the digest size, similar to manga, and at an affordable price. The Marvel Age series are aimed at younger audiences than the other superhero titles from Marvel.

★ The **Stuff** of Legend; Omnibus one. By Mike Raicht and Brian Smith; illustrated by Charles Paul Wilson III. Th3rd World Studios 2014 284 p. Color illustration (The Stuff of Legend)

Grades: 8 9 10 11 12 Adult **741.5**
1. Kidnapping; 2. Rescues; 3. Toys; 4. Graphic novels
9780983216193; 0989574482; 9780989574488, $29.99
"This hardcover collection brings together the first two volumes. . . . As Allied forces fight the enemy on Europe's war-torn beaches, another battle begins in a child's bedroom in Brooklyn when the nightmarish Boogeyman snatches a boy and takes him to the realm of the Dark. The child's playthings, led by the toy soldier known as the Colonel, band together to stage a daring rescue. On their perilous mission they will confront the boy's bitter and forgotten toys, as well as betrayal in their own ranks." (Publisher's note)
"Wilson renders the harrowing closet netherworld with full-fleshed detailing and sepia tones that nail both the 1940s time frame and the classicism of children's stories. But don't mistake this for a kids' comic⸺the violence is often explicit, and the Boogeyman creepy enough to slither his way right back onto grownups' most-terrifying lists." Booklist

★ The **stuff** of legend; Omnibus two. By Mike Raicht and Brian Smith; illustrated by Charles Paul Wilson III. Th3rd World Studios 2014 270 p. Color illustration (The Stuff of Legend)
Grades: 8 9 10 11 12 Adult **741.5**
1. Horror comic books, strips, etc; 2. Kidnapping; 3. Toys; 4. Graphic novels
0989574490; 9780989574495, $34.99
The second omnibus edition "finds our toys at a crossroads. Unable to find their boy, our loyal toys' bonds have been tested and broken. Now scattered across The Dark, the toys must decide whether to continue their search or admit defeat and return home." (Publisher's note)

Raiku, Makoto
Zatch Bell! Volume 1. Viz Media 2005 192p. Illustration
Grades: 9 10 11 12 Adult **741.5; Fic**
1. Fantasy graphic novels; 2. Humorous graphic novels; 3. Manga; 4. Shonen manga; 5. Graphic novels
1-59116-586-5, $9.99
Kiyo is a brilliant junior high student whose inflated ego (and tendency to blow the grading curve) has made him a major target for teasing at school. So his father sends him a bizarre birthday present - a strange boy named Zatch Bell - to help him make friends and reform his bad attitude. Zatch brings with him a mysterious red Volume of spells, and Kiyo discovers that Zatch has magic powers that are unleashed by reading from the book. But there are more surprises - Zatch is a Mamodo who must fight against the 99 other Mamodo who were sent to Earth in order to become the Mamodo King, and Kiyo is now along for the ride. There are lots of fight scenes.

Raiti, Ashly
Mark of the Succubus Volume 1. Story by Ashly Raiti; art by Irene Flores. Tokyopop 2005 Un Illustration
Grades: 9 10 11 12 **741.5; Fic**
1. Fantasy graphic novels; 2. Supernatural graphic novels; 3. Graphic novels
1-59816-266-7, $9.99
Maeve, a succubus-in-training, is sent to the human world to learn how to hone her skills of seduction. But things

get a bit complicated when she sets her sights on Aiden, a smart but unmotivated student at her new high school. Meanwhile, the head succubus of the Demon World has sent a spy to make sure Maeve doesn't step out of line. But between Aiden's witchy girlfriend, his nutty best friend, biology class, and Demon World conspiracies, Maeve is going to be lucky to make it out of high school alive. There's surprisingly little in the way of seduction going on in this global manga story, no nudity, and only mildly strong language.

Scary Book Volume 3: Faces. Dark Horse Manga 2006 232p. Illustration
Grades: 8 9 10 11 12 **741.5; Fic**
1. Horror graphic novels; 2. Manga; 3. Shojo manga; 4. Graphic novels
978-1-59307-487-6, $13.95
This is the third volume of the anthology series. In "Fear," Aiko is always ignored and neglected when compared to her beautiful older sister, Momoko. But when Momoko is horribly disfigured in an accident and goes mad, it's up to Aiko to bring home young girls her sister can use... to make a new face. And in "The Coincidental Letter," a young girl named Yoko, in a fit of mischief, sends an insulting letter to a made-up girl at a made-up address warning her of a horrible fate. However, by incredible coincidence, both the girl and the address are real, and everything in the letter starts coming true. Both stories rely on psychological suspense rather than violent horror, although there is some mildly strong language and a little violence in the first story.

Rall, Ted
2024. NBM/ComicsLit 2001 96p. Illustration
Grades: 10 11 12 Adult **741.5; Fic**
1. Satire; 2. Science fiction graphic novels; 3. Graphic novels
1-56163-279-1, $16.95
Move forward two decades. The giant media moguls and software companies have become the new big brothers. They want the best for everyone. They know what's best for everyone. And society has chosen to be consumer heaven with no questions asked. A terrifying future where the past doesn't matter and no one cares. The motto to live by: "yes, no, whatever." Ted Rall updates and spoofs 1984 in a look at where the U.S. could be headed. Rall uses harsh language and some sexual situations.

Silk road to ruin: is Central Asia the new Middle East?. NBM 2006 303p. Illustration; Map
Grades: 11 12 Adult **958**
1. Central Asia; 2. Graphic novels
1-56163-454-9; 978-1-56163-454-5, $22.95
LC 2006-42041
"Moving between narrative and graphic novella interludes, . . . [the author] recounts several trips that he has made in the past decade to the five "Stans," those Central Asian nations that were so recently part of the USSR. . . . Rall takes readers on scary bus trips where armed guards threaten Westerners. . . . Diarrhea is a constant and bloody companion. Sports include a deadly horseback event in which opponents whip one another in the eyes." Voice Youth Advocates

Rall's "awestruck descriptions of the region's natural beauty, crowded bazaars, and chaotic sporting tournaments will make adventurous readers want to see it all firsthand." SLJ

Includes bibliographical references

Thor and Loki: In the Land of Giants. Lerner Publishing Group/Graphic Universe 2007 48p. Illustration
Grades: 3 4 5 6 7 8 9   **741.5; 398.2**
  1. Loki (Norse deity); 2. Norse mythology; 3. Thor (Norse deity); 4. Graphic novels
978-0-8225-3087-9, $26.60 lib. Bdg.

Thor the powerful god of thunder, and his brother Loki, the trickster, are eager to solve an argument: does strength always win, or do brains always beat brawn" To find an answer, they travel to the strange and forbidding land of giants. There they face a series of challenges that will prove once and for all which god is right. Or will it" The book includes a glossary and a list of books for further reading.

Randolph, Grace
  Marvel her-oes. Art by Craig Rousseau. Marvel Worldwide, Inc. 2010 Un Illustration
Grades: 7 8 9 10 11 12   **741.5; Fic**
  1. High schools; 2. Superhero graphic novels; 3. Teenagers; 4. Graphic novels
978-0-7851-4842-5, $14.99

Janet Van Dyne has to deal with the perils of high school while keeping a major secret: she can shrink to the size of a wasp, and she can shoot energy blasts from her hands. Then she discovers that snooty Namora also has superpowers, and then she discovers that her best friend Jenny Walters also has powers. The school definitely has secrets, so do Janet's parents, and now she, Namora, and Jenny have to figure out what's going on. This book collects the four-issue miniseries that re-imagines the origins of some of Marvel's female superheroes in a manner that doesn't require the reader to know much about the Marvel Universe. The book also includes the first issue of Savage She-Hulk #1 from 1980.

Rauch, Mac
  Buckaroo Banzai: Return of the Screw. Story, Earl Mac Rauch; adaptation/new material, Joe Gentile; pencils, Steven Thompson; inks, Keith Williams; colors, Ken Wolak with Dave Alusik and Wally Lowe; letters, Erik Enervold. Moonstone 2007 120p. Illustration
Grades: 9 10 11 12 Adult   **741.5; Fic**
  1. Adventure graphic novels; 2. Mystery graphic novels; 3. Science fiction graphic novels; 4. Graphic novels
978-1-933076-26-3, $16.95

Everyone's favorite adventurer/surgeon/rock star is back again just in time to save the world. Along with his Hong Kong Cavaliers, Banzai must battle more than one surprise arch enemy, each with their own motives, but all acting in concert to bring Banzai (and the universe as we know it) to his knees. All this sandwiched between a couple of great rock and roll guitar solos, a few surgical procedures, a crazy gun battle on land and air, Buck's one chance for the ultimate revenge, his soul in turmoil, all the chicks digging him, engineering synchronicity, pretty toilets, a human pickle and a giant sombrero. The book includes some mildly strong language and some violence.

Rawson, David
  Chiaroscuro: The Private Lives of Leonardo da Vinci. DC Comics/Vertigo 2005 264p. Illustration
Grades: 11 12 Adult   **741.5; 92; Fic**
  1. Art; 2. Leonardo, da Vinci; 1452-1519; 3. Graphic novels
1-4012-0498-8, $24.99

He was the ultimate Renaissance man, but what was Leonardo da Vinci really like? This historical drama follows the life of Leonardo as witnessed by his "Little Devil," Salai, a low-born youth whose beauty entranced da Vinci enough for the artist to adopt him, and whose quest for acceptance from the maestro led him to both love and betray the man. The creators conducted a lot of research, and this graphic novel has a full-page bibliography. The book contains harsh language, nudity, and sexual situations.

Realbuzz Studios
  Goofyfoot Gurl vol. 1: Let There be Lighten Up!. Written by Pat McGreal and David Rawson; pencilled by Chaz Truog; inked by Rafael Kayanan; colored by Carla Feeny and Lovern Kindzierski; lettered by Clem Robins and John Costanza. Thomas Nelson 2007 96p. Illustration
Grades: 5 6 7 8 9   **741.5**
  1. Friendship; 2. Religion; 3. Surfing; 4. Graphic novels
978-1-59554-389-9, $10.99

Surfer girl Suki, called Goofyfoot for her right-foot-forward stance on her surfboard, and her friends hang out at the beach in Orange County, California. But everyone's got their own problems: a serious lack of funds, a new young stepmother, parents who are never around, and even the possibility of an arranged marriage. But Suki finds a way to bring some happiness and good times to her friends.

  Serenity #2: Stepping Out. Thomas Nelson 2007 96p. Illustration
Grades: 5 6 7 8 9 10   **741.5; Fic**
  1. Christian life; 2. Friendship; 3. Graphic novels
978-1-59554-384-4, $9.99

The Prayer Club kids are nice, but that doesn't mean they can't be tough. Serenity is starting to warm up to the Christian teens who made her their project" by showing her an unconditional love she's never experienced before. But when she tries ducking responsibility for wrecking Kimberly's car, that unconditional love turns tough. Can Serenity understand it's for her own good?

  Serenity #3: Basket Case. Thomas Nelson 2007 96p. Illustration
Grades: 5 6 7 8 9 10   **741.5; Fic**
  1. Christian life; 2. Friendship; 3. Graphic novels
978-1-59554-385-1, $9.99

Serenity laughs at responsibility, but there's nothing funny about this job ... She disses a health class assignment that has teens caring for chicken eggs 24/7 to simulate the round-the-clock nurturing a baby requires. But when an overwhelming responsibility falls in Serenity's lap, where can she get help - from the friends she has mocked, or the God she doesn't quite believe in?

  Serenity #4: Rave-n-Rant. Thomas Nelson 2007 96p. Illustration
Grades: 5 6 7 8 9 10   **741.5; Fic**

1. Christian life; 2. Friendship; 3. Graphic novels
978-1-59554-386-8, $9.99

Serenity begins to share her soul with her Prayer Club friends, and is angered to find that, while they say they love Serenity, they don't always like her. The teen with the blue hair and attitude takes her frustrations to God, but soon decides He isn't listening ... until a surprise ending makes Serenity realize there may be something to prayer after all.

Serenity #5: Snow Biz. Thomas Nelson 2007 96p. Illustration
Grades: 5 6 7 8 9 10   **741.5; Fic**
1. Christian life; 2. Friendship; 3. Graphic novels
978-1-59554-387-5, $9.99

Serenity views a Prayer Club ski trip as one more opportunity to drive a wedge between Derek and Kimberly. But while hotdogging on the slopes, Serenity takes a major tumble, breaking her leg and seriously bruising her ego. Who's going to care for her wounds - both physical and spiritual?

Serenity #6: You Shall Love. Thomas Nelson 2007 96p. Illustration
Grades: 5 6 7 8 9 10   **741.5; Fic**
1. Christian life; 2. Friendship; 3. Graphic novels
978-1-59554-388-2, $9.99

A broken bone—and heart—finds Serenity at a major crossroad. Her leg's in a cast, the power's out, and Serenity's bored stiff. Searching for answers and willing to risk everything, Serenity picks up the Bible she received when she first visited the Prayer Club. Before long, she's pestering her friends with spiritual questions and getting serious about some major life changes. There's healing for the broken—and unexpected new challenges—in this story.

Serenity Vol. 1: Bad Girl in Town. Thomas Nelson 2007 96p. Illustration
Grades: 4 5 6 7 8 9   **741.5; Fic**
1. Friendship; 2. Graphic novels
978-1-59554-383-7, $9.99

Everyone needs a little Serenity—or do they? She's only five feet tall and 98 pounds - but she's one tense bundle of attitude and anger. Serenity's life is a mess on every front. Now she's got one last shot at a fresh start . . . but her new school seems to just be adding new problems. Being the "New Kid" isn't making life any easier. But her friends might have just what she's been searching for - if they don't drive her crazy first, with their Christian beliefs. Can she be like them?

Reaves, Michael
The **Irregulars** ... In the Service of Sherlock Holmes. Written by Steven-Elliot Altman & Michael Reaves; illustrated by Bong Dazo; lettered by Simon Bowland; cover by Ben Templesmith. Dark Horse Comics 2005 Un Illustration
Grades: 9 10 11 12 Adult   **741.5; Fic**
1. Horror graphic novels; 2. Mystery graphic novels; 3. Graphic novels
1-59307-303-8, $12.95

A madman stalks the streets of London's Whitechapel slum, leaving a trail of grisly murders in his wake. The police have only one suspect: a prominent and respected physician named John Watson. The master detective Sherlock Holmes, in order to solve the most fantastic mystery of his career and save his greatest friend from the gallows, employs a band of young street urchins to infiltrate the alleys of Whitechapel. They can go everywhere, see everything, overhear everyone. They are the Baker Street Irregulars, and this is the most fantastic and terrifying adventure of their lives, as they uncover an evil unlike anything Sherlock Holmes has ever faced, and end up in a nightmare future. Grisly murders and horrific sights along with some strong language occur.

Reed, Gary
Bram Stoker's Dracula: The Graphic Novel. Illustrated by Becky Cloonan. Puffin Graphics 2006 176p. Illustration
Grades: 6 7 8 9 10 11 12   **741.5; Fic**
1. Dracula, Count (Fictional character); 2. Horror graphic novels; 3. Stoker, Bram, 1847-1912 — Adaptations; 4. Vampires; 5. Graphic novels
0-14-240572-8, $10.99

When Jonathan Harker travels to Transylvania to meet his firm's client, Count Dracula, he discovers his host's terrifying secret: Dracula is a vampire. The monster moves to England and targets young Lucy Westenra, and then Harker's fiancee, Mina Murray. Harker joins with Dr. Van Helsing and several other men who have pledged to destroy the vampire. This volume includes notes by Reed and Cloonan, some of Cloonan's sketches, and pages that show her early art for the book.

Mary Shelley's Frankenstein: the graphic novel. Art by Frazer Irving. Puffin Graphics 2005 176p. Illustration
Grades: 5 6 7 8 9 10 11 12   **741.5; Fic**
1. Horror graphic novels; 2. Novelists; 3. Shelley, Mary Wollstonecraft, 1797-1851 — Adaptations; 4. Graphic novels
0-14-240407-1, $9.99

Scientist Victor Frankenstein decided to create a man, only to create something he deemed a monster.

"Reed concentrates on the emotional anguish of the story, ably capturing the rage, the hurt, and the guilt of both monster and creator. Irving . . . creates a hazy, suitably murky black-and-white backdrop, never exploiting the violence inherent in the monster's quest for vengeance." Booklist

The **Red** Diaries. Gary Reed; artists, Laurence Campbell, Chris Jones and Larry Shuput. Image Comics 2006 168p. Illustration
Grades: 10 11 12 Adult   **741.5; Fic**
1. Mystery graphic novels; 2. Graphic novels
978-1-58240-622-0, $16.95

Marilyn Monroe, John F. Kennedy, the Mob, Fidel Castro, J. Edgar Hoover, the CIA... It was a conspiracy of secrets, a conspiracy of murder. All was revealed in Marilyn's diaries, her Red Diaries, and it is about to blow everything out into the open more than thirty years later. Raven, Inc., a group used to investigating the paranormal, does a favor for someone and starts hunting for Marilyn Monroe's lost Red Diaries. There's some strong language and nudity, mostly from the notorious Playboy photographs of Marilyn Monroe.

Renfield: A Tale of Madness. Written and created by Gary Reed; illustrated and lettered by Galen Showman. Image Comics 2006 192p. Illustration

Grades: 9 10 11 12 Adult   **741.5; Fic**
1. Horror graphic novels; 2. Vampires; 3. Graphic novels
978-1-58240-674-9, $19.99
This book delves into the story of the bug-eating asylum
inmate Renfield, from Bram Stoker's Dracula. Renfield
foretold the coming of the vampire to England. Possessed by
almost demonic forces and impassioned with the zeal of a
religious fanatic, Renfield must struggle to grasp the
overwhelming need to serve the darkness against his own
humanity. There is some violence in this story that retells
part of the story of Dracula, and particularly of Mina Harker,
from Renfield's viewpoint.

Saint Germaine: Shadows Fall. Writer Gary Reed; artist
Vince Locke. Image Comics 2005 Un Illustration
Grades: 10 11 12 Adult   **741.5; Fic**
1. Horror graphic novels; 2. Graphic novels
1-58240-562-X, $14.99
An immortal being who has died 1,000 deaths, Saint
Germaine has traversed the paths of mankind for untold
years with his companion, Lilith. But Lilith's disappearance
and the perils of the modern world direct him to undertake a
new quest - to surrender his immortality. The book has some
strong images of violence.

Regnaud, Jean
★ **My** mommy is in America and she met Buffalo Bill.
Jean Regnaud & Émile Bravo (artist). Fanfare/Ponent Mon
2009 120p. Illustration
Grades: 6 7 8 9 10 11 12 Adult   **741.5; Fic**
1. Family life; 2. Mother; 3. School life; 4. Graphic novels
978-84-96427-85-3, $25
Essentials Award winner at the 35th Festival of
Angouleme,n France, 2008; Tam Tam Literary Award
2009 from Salon du Livres et de la Presse Jeunesse, for
Comic Album, age group eight to thirteen years old.
Narrator Jean has just started first grade and has a
younger brother, Paul, in kindergarten. They live with their
factory boss father and nanny Yvette; Jean says his mother is
on a trip. As he talks about his first day at school, meeting a
new friend, Alain, and fighting with Paul, he mentions his
mother has been away so long he can't quite remember her.
Next door neighbor Michelle claims to be receiving
postcards from Jean's mother and reads them to him; they
come from places such as Switzerland and the United States.
As the reader sees Jean and Paul spend a day with their
mother's parents and interact with their grandparents'
friends, the reader understands what Jean does not: his
mother is dead. This book, translated from its original
French, won an award for best comic album for ages eight to
thirteen; however, with the essential fact never stated and
Jean deciding that he's getting to old to believe in his mother,
just as he's too old to believe in Father Christmas, makes this
more suitable for the upper age range, teens, and adults.

Reilly, Chris
The **weirdly** world of strange eggs. Chris Reilly, Steve
Ahlquist, and Jeremy Mann. Amaze Ink/SLG Publishing
2007 80p. Illustration
Grades: 5 6 7 8 9 10   **741.5**
1. Adventure graphic novels; 2. Fantasy graphic novels; 3.
Humorous graphic novels; 4. Graphic novels

978-1-59362-085-1, $7.95
Kip and Kelly have a pretty quiet life on the farm with
their father (who generally stays behind the newspaper);
Kelly performs all kinds of scientific experiments while Kip
always wants adventure. Then they encounter Roger Rogers,
who gives them a strange egg" that hatches into a creature
they name Hooper. When Roger comes with another egg,
Hooper tricks him and takes it, and this time the egg hatches
a creature that looks like a party hat and excretes vampire
bats. As Kip and Kelly fight off the party hat, bats, and even
a monster tree, they learn to protect thos they love and trust
those who want to help them (such as the ex B-movie actress
veterinarian).

Reilly, Christopher P.
Punch and Judy: Twice Told Tales. Written by
Christopher P. Reilly; art by Darron Laessig & Jorge
Santillan; additional paintings by Jon Foster. SLG
Publishing 2005 Un Illustration
Grades: 10 11 12 Adult   **741.5; Fic**
1. Fantasy graphic novels; 2. Humorous graphic novels; 3.
Graphic novels
1-59362-015-2, $7.95
In The Comical Tragedy of Punch and Judy, Mr. Punch
brandishes his infamous stick against all foes who threaten
his precious and impressive nose, including his squalling
baby, his quarrelsome wife Judy, Mr. Scaramouche and his
dog Toby, the hangman and, finally, the Devil himself. In
Punch and Judy: A Grand Guignol, Mr. Punch, not content
with killing the Devil, taking over Hell and outlawing
Goodness, sets his sight on the pinnacle of achievements:
Getting on Santa's Nice List. Or if that doesn't work, ruining
Christmas for the last two good children on Earth. The first
story is a retelling of the traditional English puppet show
(actually, there are versions all over Europe) that dates back
at least to the mid-seventeenth century, with roots in the
commedia dell'arte. The stories are full of shocking violence
that seems much more sinister than in the puppet shows.

Remender, Rick
Fear Agent Volume One: Re-Ignition. Pencils, Tony
Moore. Dark Horse Comics 2007 Un Illustration
Grades: 9 10 11 12 Adult   **741.5; Fic**
1. Adventure graphic novels; 2. Science fiction graphic
novels; 3. Graphic novels
978-1-59307-764-8, $13.95
Heath Huston, an alien exterminator, stumbles upon a
plot by a race called the Dressites to send feeders to Earth.
The feeders are a life-form that consumes all organic matter
until a planet is destroyed. When Huston and the human
scientist, Mara, try to go in Huston's AI ship to Earth, they
discover that the ship has taken on a type of hyper-fuel it
can't handle, and they crashland on a planet in its distant
past, whose dominant race invaded Earth. Huston is the last
of the Fear Agents, elite soldiers of Earth, and he thinks he
can prevent the invasion by changing the past.
Originally published by Image Comics as Fear Agent
issues #1-4.

Fear Agent Volume Two: My Way. Dark art by Jerome
Opeña. Horse Comics 2007 Un Illustration
Grades: 11 12 Adult   **741.5; Fic**

719

1. Adventure graphic novels; 2. Science fiction graphic novels; 3. Graphic novels
978-1-59307-766-2, $14.95

Lost, beaten and trapped in the past, Heath Huston must face the demons of his inevitable future when he finds himself face to face with the automaton regime responsible for robbing him of all he loves. With the knowledge that the Feeders are progressing ever closer to Earth, will Heath be able to get payback from the automaton empire in time to save his home planet from the scourge of an alien infestation? This volume has nudity, sexual situations, harsh language, and violence.

Strange Girl Vol. 1: Girl Afraid. Artists, Eric Nguyen, Joelle Comtois. Image Comics 2005 Un Illustration
Grades: 11 12 Adult   **741.5; Fic**
1. Horror graphic novels; 2. Supernatural graphic novels; 3. Graphic novels
978-1-58240-543-8, $12.99

Ten years after the Rapture, beautiful occultist Bethany Black and her pet runt demon Bloato embark on a road trip to the last open gateway to heaven, in hopes of befriending God and escaping hell on earth. The book includes considerable graphic violence, harsh language, and some nudity.

Strange Girl Vol. 2: Heaven Knows I'm Miserable Now. Artists, Eric Nguyen, Harper Jaten and Jerome Opena. Image Comics 2006 Un Illustration
Grades: 11 12 Adult   **741.5; Fic**
1. Horror graphic novels; 2. Supernatural graphic novels; 3. Graphic novels
978-1-58240-642-8, $14.99

There's a point in every journey where there seems to be no light - no hope. After returning to the human stronghold, Dead Western, Bethany Black learns there is little hope she'll ever find respite from hell on Earth. The book includes considerable graphic violence, harsh language, and some nudity.

Tales of the fear agent. Dark Horse Comics 2008 Un Illustration
Grades: 11 12 Adult   **741.5; Fic**
1. Horror graphic novels; 2. Humorous graphic novels; 3. Science fiction graphic novels; 4. Graphic novels
978-1-59307-959-8, $14.95

Heath Huston, the Fear Agent, lost his family and most of his life when invading aliens pretty much destroyed the Earth. This volume collects stories of his first ten years working as an alien exterminator. Huston spends much of his time as drunk as possible, and many of the stories include violence, harsh language, and partial nudity. The stories possess the style of 1950's science fiction and horror stories, with a lot of humor and action. Writers include Rick Remender, who created the Fear Agent, Kieron Dwyer, Steve Niles, Hilary Barta, Eric Nguyen, C. B. Cebulski, and more.

Uncanny Avengers: the red shadow. Rick Remender, illustrated by John Cassaday. Marvel Worldwide 2013 136 p.
Grades: 10 11 12 Adult   **741.5; Fic**
1. Avengers (Fictional characters); 2. Captain America (Fictional character); 3. Thor (Fictional character); 4. Wolverine (Fictional character); 5. X-Men (Fictional characters)

0785168443; 9780785168447, $24.99

In this graphic novel by Rick Remender, "Captain America creates a sanctioned Avengers unit comprised of Avengers and X-Men, humans and mutants working together...so why is Professor Xavier's dream more at risk than ever" The Red Skull has returned - straight out of the 1940s and full of hatred - and his rebirth will alter the Marvel Universe forever!" (Publisher's note)

"[D]ense, intelligent writing that asks significant questions; a battle not only of arms but of ideologies; and a cast of characters that gives movie stars like Captain America, Thor, and Wolverine their due without ignoring the rich personalities of lesser-known players. . . . Cassaday's art, the most purely gorgeous in contemporary superhero comics [is] so clean and clear the pages practically glow with life." Booklist

Renier, Aaron
   Spiral-bound. Top Shelf Productions 2005 144p. Illustration
Grades: 4 5 6 7 8 9
741.5; Fic
1. Mystery graphic novels; 2. Graphic novels
1-891830-50-3, $14.95

"Turnip the elephant is using the summer to find his artistic voice through sculpture, his friend Stucky the dog is building a submarine, and Ana the rabbit is working on the town's underground

Courtesy of Top Shelf Productions

newspaper. Their stories all wind around the town's deep, dark secret about the monster that lives in the pond. . . . The characters seem like real children, wholesome without being too sweet, and Renier's art is light and fun, a sort of Babar meets underground comix." Booklist

Revel, Brahm
   Guerillas Volume 2: Volume 2. Brahm Revel; [edited by] Charlie Chu. Oni Press, Inc 2012 120 p.
Grades: 11 12 Adult   **741; Fic**
1. Military personnel — United States; 2. Monkeys; 3. Vietnam War, 1961-1975
1934964999; 9781934964996, $17.99
                    LC 2012930679

In this book by Brahm revel "Private John Francis Clayton's strange tour of duty in Vietnam gets stranger as he struggles with the unbelievable facts he is faced with. The elite platoon of simian soldiers he's encountered don't make any more sense to him than the war he's been sent to fight, but is this squad of chain-smoking chimps the most dangerous force in the jungle, or are they merely a distraction from the larger evil growing in the wild?" (Publisher's note)

Reyes, Luis
   Star Trek the Manga Volume 1: Shinsei Shinsei. Tokyopop 2006 Un Illustration
Grades: 7 8 9 10 11 12 Adult   **741.5; Fic**

1. Adventure graphic novels; 2. Science fiction graphic novels; 3. Star Trek; 4. Graphic novels
1-59816-744-8, $9.99

Ten writers and artists deliver tales of triumph aboard the original NCC-1701, the starship Enterprise, featuring the characters from the original television series. These new stories venture into the terrain of social politics, personal reflection ... and bare-knuckled brawls between Captain Kirk and various alien creatures, Spock's unflappable logic, Dr. McCoy's flare for drama, Scotty's perpetual struggle to keep the engines running smoothly, and more. The stories are written and illustrated as global manga.

Star Trek the Manga: Uchu. Tokyopop 2008 Un Illustration
Grades: 7 8 9 10 11 12 Adult   **741.5; Fic**
1. Science fiction graphic novels; 2. Star trek (Television program); 3. Graphic novels
978-1-4278-0787-8, $10.99

This third collection of manga-style stories set in the original Star Trek universe includes "Art of War" by Star Trek: The Next Generation actor Wil Wheaton and artist E. J. Su, "Bandi" by The Trouble with Tribbles writer David Gerrold and artist Don Hudson, "Inalienable Rights" by Nathaniel Bowden and artist Heidi Arnhold, and "The Humanitarian" by Luis Reyes and artist Nate Watson. Kirk has an encounter with a Klingon that makes both men rethink their hatred; the Bandi is yet another alien creature that has invaded the Enterprise, this one is highly empathic and can influence peoples' emotions; Kirk and his command team visit a planet and find a society in which bureaucracy runs wild; and Spock has command of the Enterprise during a very difficult situation, when a huge explosion causes major casualties of the Enterprise crew. People who like Star Trek's original series and characters will find stories in keeping with the philosophy of that series.

Rhoades, Shirrel

★ **Comic** books: how the industry works. Afterword by Stan Lee. Peter Lang Publishing, Inc. 2008 406p. Illustration
Grades: 11 12 Adult   **741.5**
1. Comic books, strips, etc — History and criticism; 2. Graphic novels — History and criticism; 3. Publishers and publishing
978-0-8204-8892-9, $32.95
                                        LC 2007-32719

Rhoades, who was publisher of Marvel Comics after Stan Lee and has worked in publishing for more than forty years, gives an insider's look at how the comic book industry works. He discusses how superhero characters are created, how comic books are put together, how they're sold, how comics' intellectual property is licensed to other industries, adapting comics to television and movies, what manga is all about, and the move of graphic novels into bookstores. The chapters are broken down into subsections, and there are frequent sidebars with labels such as "speak up," "flashback," "comics trivia!" and others that provide even more tidbits of information in a highly readable format.

★ A **complete** history of American comic books. Afterword by Steve Geppi. Peter Lang Publishing Inc. 2008 353p. Illustration
Grades: 9 10 11 12 Adult   **741.5**

1. Comic books, strips, etc — History and criticism; 2. Graphic novels — History and criticism
978-1-4331-0110-6; 1-4331-0110-6, $119.95; 978-1-4331-0107-6 (pa); 1-4331-0107-6 (pa), $39.95
                                        LC 2007-43460

Rhoades, former publisher of Marvel Comics (after Stan Lee stepped down to move to Hollywood and focus on Marvel Comics in the movies), dates the beginning of the American comic book to the 1930s, when the format was first used. He covers the history of comics from that time to the present, covering all the big names (Will Eisner, Jack Kirby, Stan Lee, etc.). The book is peppered with fun sidebars with such labels as "flashback," "comics trivia," "looking back," "true facts," and so one. These help to make the book fun to read. Rhoades doesn't employ a straight narrative, but includes interviews, the side bars, comics milestones, a list of fanboys who have and had careers in comics, and a comic book quiz.
Includes bibliographical references

Richardson, Mike

47 Ronin. Writer, Mike Richardson; artist, Stan Sakai. Dark Horse 2014 151 p. Color; Illustration
Grades: 11 12 Adult   **741.5**
1. Samurai
1595829547; 9781595829542, $19.99

Written by Mike Richardson and illustrated by Stan Sakai, "this collection of the acclaimed [comic book] mini-series recounts this sweeping saga of honor and violence in all its grandeur. Opening with the tragic incident that sealed the fate of Lord Asano, 47 Ronin follows a dedicated group of Asano's vassals on their years-long path of vengeance!" (Publisher's note)

"Richardson, founder of Dark Horse Comics, and Sakai, creator of the long-running and award-laden Usagi Yojimbo samurai series, combine talents to produce this terrific graphic interpretation of one of Japan's most important sagas. . . . The level of talent, the research, and the attention to both narrative and artistic detail shine through in this volume." LJ

Living with the dead. Artist, Ben Stenbeck. Dark Horse Comics 2008 Un Illustration
Grades: 11 12 Adult   **741.5; Fic**
1. Horror graphic novels; 2. Humorous graphic novels; 3. Zombies; 4. Graphic novels
978-1-59307-906-2, $9.95

A virus has doomed most of humanity to become zombies, but hard rockers Straw and Whip have managed to survive, going out disguised as zombies, pilfering what they need from deserted stores and malls. Then they meet Betty, saving her when there are too many zombies attacking for her to whack with a golf club. Her presence messes up the tight friendship and partnership the two guys have had, as they each get jealous about her. And their jealousy (and her need to kill zombies) makes them careless. The book includes lots of graphic violence.

The **secret**. Story by Mike Richardson; art and covers by Jason Shawn Alexander; letters by Clem Robbins. Dark Horse Comics 2007 112p. Illustration
Grades: 10 11 12 Adult   **741.5**

1. Horror graphic novels; 2. Mystery graphic novels; 3. Graphic novels
978-1-59307-821-8, $12.95

When outsider Tommy Morris gets invited to Pam's party, he finds she and her friends making prank phone calls to randomly punched numbers. When someone answers, they say "I know your secret." Then one of the calls gets weird when the person on the other end responds. When they go out to the park late at night, someone does show up, and his behavior scares them. And the next day, someone calls Pam on her cell phone and says How do you know my secret?" She disappears that afternoon, and her friends and the police think Tommy is involved. Now he can't stop until he finds Pam, to clear himself.

Ricketts, Mark
Night Trippers. Written by Mark Ricketts; illustrated by Micah Farritor. Image Comics 2006 184p. Illustration
Grades: 10 11 12 Adult   **741.5; Fic**
1. Horror graphic novels; 2. Vampires; 3. Graphic novels
978-1-58240-606-0, $16.99

Once upon a time in swinging London, around 1966, there was a serial killer who loved Elvis, a fab foursome that worshipped Satan, trendy vampires looking for kicks, an ancient and hungry evil, young and hungry love... and there was revolution in the air. Get your trip together, baby. Tune in, turn on and fang out. The book includes some strong language and violence (especially vampire killing).

Ridley, John
The **American** Way. Written by John Ridley; penciled by Georges Jeanty. DC Comics/Wildstorm 2007 192p. Illustration
Grades: 10 11 12 Adult   **741.5; Fic**
1. Science fiction graphic novels; 2. Superhero graphic novels; 3. Graphic novels
978-1-4012-1256-8, $19.99

The 1960s were a decade of incredible change for America. It was a time of innocence. It was a time of optimism. It was a time of heroes. In the early '40s, the United States government hatched a plan to create the Civil Defense Corps: a group of "super-heroes" who could fight alien invasions, evil super-powered beings and communism, all in front of an adoring public, courtesy of television. But that dream was far from reality by the 60s, as new C.D.C. Marketing Director Wesley Catham is about to discover. How far will America go to protect its dream of a better tomorrow? White racists use the n-word, plus there's violence, and other foul language.

The **Authority:** Human on the Inside. Written by John Ridley; art by Ben Oliver. DC Comics/Wildstorm 2004 Un Illustration
Grades: 9 10 11 12 Adult   **741.5; Fic**
1. Superhero graphic novels; 2. Graphic novels
1-4012-0069-9, $17.99

The Authority, Earth's last defense, have performed godlike acts in defense of the planet, whether defeating ancient gods or fending off interdimensional invasion forces. But these brave acts haven't always endeared them to many in power.... particularly in the United States. The President, tired of being embarrassed by what he views as a

bunch of costumed freaks, sets a plan in motion that could very well destroy the Authority from the inside, a plan so cunning it'll shake the Authority to their very core. With an unexpected threat from the future on Earth's doorstep, it could very well mean global extinction. The book has some violence and strong language.

Rieber, John Ney
The **Books** of Magic Book 4: Transformations. John Ney Rieber, writer; Peter Gross, artist; Sherilyn van Valkenburgh, Nathan Eyring, colorists; Richard Starkings & Comicraft, letterer. DC Comics/Vertigo 1998 128p. Illustration
Grades: 10 11 12 Adult   **741.5; Fic**
1. Fantasy graphic novels; 2. Magic; 3. Timothy Hunter (Fictional character); 4. Graphic novels
1-56389-417-3; 978-1-56389-417-6, $12.95
                                          LC 99-229773

The son of a manipulative sorceress and a mystical falconer, Tim Hunter is destined to become the most powerful mage in the world. But as the young Londoner comes to terms with his abilities and future, he must deal with demons and wizards looking to claim his power. In the fourth volume of this enrapturing series, Tim's magical adventures continue as he has a remarkable encounter with Death, transforms himself into a cat, faces off against an ancient enchantress and "celebrates" his fourteenth birthday. The book includes some strong language and partial nudity.

The **Books** of Magic Book 5: Girl in the Box. John Ney Rieber, writer; Peter Gross, Peter Snejbjerg, artists. DC Comics/Vertigo 1999 192p. Illustration
Grades: 10 11 12 Adult   **741.5; Fic**
1. Fantasy graphic novels; 2. Magic; 3. Timothy Hunter (Fictional character); 4. Graphic novels
1-56389-539-0, $14.95
                                          LC 2001-265347

Possessing infinite magical powers, Tim Hunter will become the Earth's greatest sorcerer. But as the fourteen-year-old boy begins his ascension to powerful mage, he must navigate the everyday travails of adolescence. Looking to escape his personal troubles, Tim runs away to America only to find his problems multiplying. Allying himself with a shape-shifting succubus in the form of a female model, the young wizard learns lessons of treachery and friendship as he contends with a seductive mermaid who is lost in the desert and Cupid and Psyche, two disillusioned gods looking to adapt to modern ways. The book includes strong language, partial nudity, and violence.

The **Books** of Magic Book 6: The Burning Girl. John Ney Rieber, Peter Gross, writers; Peter Snejbjerg, Peter Gross, artists; Nathan Eyring, Sherilyn Van Valkenburgh, colorists; Richard Starkings & Comicraft/LA, letter. DC Comics/Vertigo 2000 224p. Illustration
Grades: 10 11 12 Adult   **741.5; Fic**
1. Fantasy graphic novels; 2. Magic; 3. Timothy Hunter (Fictional character); 4. Graphic novels
1-56389-619-2, $17.95
                                          LC 00-708603

An adolescent boy with unimaginable power, Tim Hunter is destined to become the greatest magic wielder of all time. But after a mystical adventure traps the young wizard in the mythical land of Faerie, he finds himself caught up in the alternate realm's war with Hell. Now in order to save himself and the inhabitants of Faerie from an impending holocaust, the reactionary sorcerer must free his girlfriend from his jealous mother's curse while simultaneously warding off the legions of the underworld. The book includes some strong language and violence.

The **Books** of Magic Book 7: Death After Death. John Ney Rieber, writer; Peter Gross, Jill Thompson, Temujin, Richard Case, artists. DC Comics/Vertigo 2001 224p. Illustration
Grades: 10 11 12 Adult   **741.5; Fic**
  1. Fantasy graphic novels; 2. Magic; 3. Timothy Hunter (Fictional character); 4. Graphic novels
1-56389-740-7, $19.95
Since learning that he would become a wizard of infinite power, young Tim Hunter has been cursed with a life of loss and death. Tired of the misery that has become his adolescence, the fourteen year-old mage releases all of his magic unto the universe. But as a war between Heaven and Hell erupts over the newly released power, Tim learns that his impulsive action may lead to the end of all Creation. Now the completely powerless sorcerer must find a way to outmaneuver and manipulate an assortment of angels, demons, and deities in order to regain his magic or watch as all of existence ceases to be. The book includes violence, some strong language, and nudity.

G. I. Joe Reloaded Vol. 1: In the Name of Patriotism. Devil's Due Publishing 2004 Un Illustration
Grades: 7 8 9 10 11 12 Adult   **741.5; Fic**
  1. Adventure graphic novels; 2. G I Joe (Fictional character); 3. Graphic novels
1-932796-23-1, $12.95
The Threat: Unknown. The Mission: Critical. The Team: G.I. Joe. United by the twisted strategic genius of a madman, a deadly cabal of conspirators unleashes a savage assault on the very heart of America. The nation is defenseless against these faceless paramilitary hordes whose dread insignia is a striking cobra... Until a rogue Lieutenant Colonel forges a handful of hard-hitting soldiers into the ultimate elite fighting force: G.I. Joe. The book includes fighting action.

Riordan, Rick
  Percy Jackson & the Olympians, book one: the lightning thief: the graphic novel. Adapted by Robert Venditti; art by Attila Futaki; color by José Villarrubia; layouts by Orpheus Collar; lettering by Chris Dickey. Hyperion Books for Children 2010 Un Illustration
Grades: 5 6 7 8 9 10   **741.5; Fic**
  1. Adventure graphic novels; 2. Fantasy graphic novels; 3. Greek mythology; 4. Graphic novels
978-1-4231-1696-7, $19.99; 978-1-4321-1710-0 (pa), $9.99
Twelve-year-old Percy Jackson has had a hard time in school, but when a teacher transforms into a Fury and tries to kill him during a field trip to the museum, his life becomes even more complicated. He learns that he is the son of one of the Greek gods and a human woman, and then he learns that he should never have been born, and that the gods think he has stolen Zeus's master lightning bolt. Percy, his best friend

Grover (a satyr), and Annabeth, daughter of Athena, have ten days to recover the lightning bolt and prevent all-out war among the Olympians. This graphic novel adapts Riordan's novel, NOT the movie. Futaki makes the water action look great in an adaptation that should make the book fans happy.

The **red** pyramid: the graphic novel. Rick Riordan; adapted by Orpheus Collar; lettered by Jared Fletcher. Disney/Hyperion Books 2012 Un Color; Illustration (The Kane chronicles)
Grades: 4 5 6 7 8 9   **741.5**
  1. Brothers and sisters — Fiction; 2. Egyptian mythology — Fiction; 3. Magic — Fiction
1423150694; 1423150686; 9781423150695, $12.99; 9781423150688, $21.99
LC 2012007905
"Since their mother's death, Sadie and Carter have become near-strangers. While Sadie has lived with her grandparents in London, Carter has traveled the world with their father, the famed Egyptologist Dr. Julius Kane. One night, Dr. Kane brings the siblings to the British Museum, where he hopes to set things right for his family. Instead, he unleashes the Egyptian god Set, who banishes him to oblivion and forces the children to flee for their lives." (Publisher's note)
"Out of necessity, much of the dialogue is dedicated to explaining actions and events, but a constant stream of humor prevents the reader from getting bogged down by logistics. The colorful artwork has an almost painting-like quality, . . . and some clever visual jokes and thoughtful use of panels make good use of the format." VOYA

Rivkah
  Steady Beat, Vol. 1. Tokyopop 2005 Un Illustration
Grades: 8 9 10 11 12   **741.5; Fic**
  1. Homosexuality; 2. Lesbians; 3. Romance graphic novels; 4. Graphic novels
1-59816-135-0, $9.99
Sixteen-year-old Leah finds a love letter in her older sister's things; it's signed "Jessica." That wouldn't really be a problem, except that their single mother is a conservative Republican politician and they live in a conservative Texas town. And someone wants to blackmail Sarai through Leah. While she's trying to keep Sarai's secret, Leah meets Elijah, who has a gay father. This is a global manga series.

Robbins, Trina
  Go Girl!: Robots Gone Wild!. Dark Horse Comics 2007 183p. Illustration
Grades: 4 5 6 7 8 9 10   **741.5**
  1. Go Girl! (Fictional character); 2. Superhero graphic novels; 3. Graphic novels
978-1-59307-409-8
Video games can get too realistic, as the flying teenager, Go Girl! discovers in "Prisoners of the Machine," when she and her friends find themselves trapped inside a computer, menaced by giant anime-robots. And in "Double Trouble," Go Girl!'s arch-enemies create a robot that looks just like her, except that it has the mind of a master criminal. How can our heroine convince the cops that she didn't rob that bank, when everyone saw her do it? Plus, Go Girl!'s sidekick,

Haseena, tired of always being rescued by the flying teen, takes up sleuthing herself in "Haseena Ross, Girl Detective."

Hedy Lamarr and a Secret Communication System. Illustrated by Cynthia Martin and Anne Timmons. Capstone Press 2007 32p. Illustration
Grades: 3 4 5 6 7 8 9   **621.384; 741.5; 92; 621.384092**
1. Biographical graphic novels; 2. Inventions; 3. Lamarr, Hedy, 1914-2000; 4. Graphic novels
978-0-7368-6479-4, $25.26
LC 2006004104
This volume tells the story of how gorgeous Hollywood star Hedy Lamarr came up with the idea for a secret communication system back in the early days of World War II, which would much later become the basis for wireless technology. The book provides additional information, a glossary, a list of books for further reading, and more.
Part of the Graphic Library, Inventions and Discovery series.

Robinson, Alex
★ A **kidnapped** Santa Claus. It Books/HarperCollins 2009 Un Illustration
Grades: 4 5 6 7 8 9   **741.5; Fic**
1. Adventure graphic novels; 2. Baum, L Frank, 1856-1919 — Adaptations; 3. Christmas; 4. Santa Claus; 4. Graphic novels
978-0-06-178240-4, $14.99
Santa Claus lives in the Laughing Valley, with the fairies on one side of the valley in the Forest of Burzee. On the other side of the valley stands a mountain that contains the caves of the daemons, Selfishness, Envy, Hatred, and Repentance. On this Christmas Eve, the daemons hatch a diabolical plot to destroy Christmas. When they can't convince Santa to be selfish, envious, or to hate people, they kidnap him. Santa's helpers, led by the young fairy named Wisk, decide they need to save Christmas when the big man doesn't show up, so they set out to deliver the presents all around the world. There's one big problem Wisk can't find Santa's list; they have to improvise. Baum's story provides a different type of Christmas adventure; his Santa doesn't live at the North Pole, and his helpers aren't elves. Robinson, who's known for his adult graphic novels, makes Wisk a girl fairy with big cats-eye glasses. During the battle to rescue Santa from the daemons, one of Santa's helpers named Nuter loses his head, which might disturb some younger readers (he doesn't die).

Too cool to be forgotten. Top Shelf Productions 2008 128p. Illustration
Grades: 11 12 Adult
741.5; Fic
1. Humorous graphic novels; 2. School stories; 3. Time travel; 4. Graphic novels
978-1-891830-98-3, $14.95
Andy Wicks is in his forties and a longtime smoker who has tried just

Courtesy of Top Shelf Productions

about everything to quit smoking. Now he's going to try hypnosis, what's the worst thing that could happen? Well, when he wakes up, he finds himself back in high school, in 1985, as his high school sophomore self. Is he doomed to relive all his mistakes, or can he use his return as a second chance to get things right? Things like asking out that girl from math class. . . . Then he finds himself reliving time with his father, who died of Lou Gehrig's disease in 1985 after a sudden decline. Is this, after all, what he really needs to do? The book includes quite a bit of harsh language and lots of drinking and smoking at a party."

Tricked. Top Shelf Productions 2005 350p. Illustration
Grades: 11 12 Adult   **741.5; Fic**
1. Mystery graphic novels; 2. Rock music; 3. Graphic novels
1-891830-73-2, $19.95
Ignatz Award: Outstanding Graphic Novel (2006)
The story follows the lives of six people: a reclusive rock legend, a heartbroken waitress, a counterfeiter, an obsessive crank, a lost daughter, and a backstabbing lover, whose lives are unconnected until an act of violence brings them spiraling in on each other. The story includes nudity and strong language.

Robinson, Dave
Introducing Ethics. Dave Robinson, Chris Garratt. Totem Books 2005 176p. Illustration
Grades: 10 11 12 Adult   **170; 741.5**
1. Ethics; 2. Graphic novels
1-84046-580-8, $12.95
What are the acceptable limits of scientific investigation and genetic engineering, the rights and wrongs of animal rights, euthanasia and civil disobedience? This book confronts these dilemmas, tracing arguments of moral thinkers, including Socrates, Plato, Aristotle, and brings us up to date with postmodern critics. Using cartoons and a spare text, this book provides an introductory look at ethics; it includes a list of books for further reading.

Introducing Kierkegaard, Rev. ed. Dave Robinson and Oscar Zarate. Totem Books 2007 176p. Illustration
Grades: 10 11 12 Adult   **142; 741.5**
1. Existentialism; 2. Kierkegaard, Soren, 1813-1855; 3. Philosophy; 4. Graphic novels
978-1-84046-758-1, $12.95
Soren Kierkegaard is regarded as the founder of Existentialism and the first modern theologian. Philosophy, in Kierkegaard's radical view, was of no use unless it permanently changed people's lives. His distrust of grand abstract schemes, particularly Hegel's, and his insistence that philosophy is essentially writing also identify him as a forerunner of postmodernism. This book uses cartoons and a spare text to introduce readers to the ideas and life of Kierkegaard; it includes a list of books for further reading.

Introducing Philosophy.   Dave Robinson, Judy Groves. Totem Books 2004 176p. Illustration
Grades: 10 11 12 Adult   **100; 741.5**
1. Philosophy; 2. Graphic novels
1-84046-576-X, $12.95
This volume uses cartoons and a spare text to provide an introductory guide to the thinking of all the significant

philosophers of the Western world, from Heraclitus to Derrida. It examines and explains their key arguments and ideas. The book includes a list of books for further reading.

Robinson, James
   Batman: Face the Face. James Robinson, writer; Leonard Kirk, Don Kramer, pencillers. DC Comics 2006 192p. Illustration
Grades: 10 11 12 Adult   741.5; Fic
   1. Batman (Fictional character); 2. Mystery graphic novels; 3. Robin (Fictional character); 4. Superhero graphic novels; 5. Graphic novels
   978-1-4012-0910-0, $14.99
   One year ago, Batman and Robin disappeared from Gotham City. Before his departure, Batman chose a guardian to protect Gotham's citizens from the city's usual predators. Now, the Dynamic Duo return to find that some of their most notorious foes are being brutally murdered, leaving Batman to wonder if the man he entrusted to carry on in his place has confused justice with vengeance. With James Gordon back as Commissioner and Harvey Bullock back on the Gotham police force, it's almost like old times. But Bruce Wayne also has a decision to make about Tim Drake. The book includes some graphic violence.

   ★ **Leave** It to Chance Vol. II: Trick or Threat & Other Stories. James Robinson & Paul Smith ; with George Freeman, inks ; Jeromy Cox, color art ; and Amie Grenier, lettering. Image Comics 2003 Un Illustration
Grades: 5 6 7 8 9 10   741.5; Fic
   1. Adventure graphic novels; 2. Fantasy graphic novels; 3. Horror graphic novels; 4. Graphic novels
   1-58240-278-7, $14.95
   In "Trick or Threat," Chance helps a boy save his pet monkey from being sacrificed by a gang of cultists. Then her father sends Chance away to a boarding school (to keep her out of trouble), but there she has to face the ghost of the evil pirate Captain Hitch. Back home in Devil's Echo, Chance goes to the mall with her new friends from school, but they have to confront "The Phantom of the Mall." The book includes cartoony horror violence.

   ★ **Leave** It to Chance Vol. III: Monster Madness & Other Stories. Image Comics 2003 Un Illustration
Grades: 5 6 7 8 9 10   741.5; Fic
   1. Adventure graphic novels; 2. Fantasy graphic novels; 3. Horror graphic novels; 4. Graphic novels
   1-58240-298-1, $14.95
   Chance Falconer is the mischievous 14-year- old daughter of Lucas Falconer, who is the mystical guardian for the city of Devil's Echo and its most prominent supernatural detective. Devil's Echo faces an all-new threat, as classic matinee monsters literally come to life and walk off a movie screen to wreak havoc in the streets. It's all-out excitement as Chance and her friends try to stop them, but the most shocking secret of all is who is really behind the mayhem. Then Chance helps a zombie hockey star hunt for the men who killed him. The book includes some cartoony horror action.

   Leave it to Chance: Shaman's rain. [by] James Robinson & Paul Smith. Image Comics 2002 Un Illustration
Grades: 5 6 7 8 9 10   741.5; Fic

   1. Fantasy graphic novels; 2. Horror graphic novels; 3. Graphic novels
   1-58240-253-1, $14.95
   "Chance Falconer is a 14-year-old only child born into a family of municipal sorcerers that has protected the city of Devil's Echo for centuries. Chance can't wait to start training in the family business, but her father decides he doesn't want a girl joining the family's dangerous profession. Predictably, it's not long before she stumbles onto a dead body and a kidnapping in progress, and soon enough she's got a full-fledged mystery on her hands. . . . This is a girl power comic written with a younger audience in mind. The smartest cops are female, the violence is G-rated and the story is fast-paced, brightly colored and as wholesome as it gets." Publ Wkly
   Other titles in this series are: Leave it to Chance, Vol. 2: Trick or treat (2003); Leave it to Chance, Vol. 3: Monster madness (2003)

Robinson, James Dale
   Earth 2; Volume 1. James Robinson, writer; Nicola Scott, Eduardo Pansica, pencillers; Trevor Scott, Sean Parsons, inkers.. DC Comics 2013 160 p.
Grades: 9 10 11 12   **741.5/973; Fic**
   1. Flash (Fictional character); 2. Green Lantern (Fictional character); 3. Justice League (Fictional characters); 4. Superheroes — Fiction
   1401237746; 9781401237745, $22.99
                                                    LC 2012046491
   This graphic novel, by James Robinson, Nicola Scott, and Trevor Scott "reimagine[s] the classic Justice Society of America. Earth's greatest heroes have defeated grave threats from Apokolips. Left in their stead is a group of young, untrained heroes who pick up the pieces in the . . . aftermath. The Flash, Green Lantern, Hawkgirl and the Atom are humanity's . . . guardians, but not the ones we've all known. These are different heroes, in a strange and foreign world with dangerous new villains." (Publisher's note)
   Originally published in single magazine form in Earth 2 1-6.

Robinson, Jimmie
   Evil & malice save the world!. Image Comics/Silverline Books 2009 128p. Illustration
Grades: 5 6 7 8 9 10   **741.5; Fic**
   1. Humorous graphic novels; 2. Sisters; 3. Superhero graphic novels; 4. Graphic novels
   978-1-60706-091-8, $14.99
   Evelyn and Malinda are the twin daughters of Dooplis City's top villain, the Black Eye, but they want to go see superhero Goldie Gal at a public appearance. She has come to help unveil a new computer system, the Max2000, that will automate many city functions. However, just at the moment of the unveiling, villains Coldheart, Chef, and Drip take out Goldie Gal and try to steal the Max2000. The damage they do in town threatens Evelyn's and Malinda's only friend Cindy, so they fight the villains to save her. The local newscaster catches just enough of the action to decide that Dooplis City has two new heroes and names them Evil and Malice. The girls decide to steal a bunch of their father's gadgets, since they have no superpowers of their own, and even though Dad is a villain, they set out to be heroes. Funny

that every time they try to help, they end up destroying stuff. The villainous trio pretends to team up with the Black Eye, but plan to destroy him once they get the Max2000, so the girls know they have to save their father. There's a lot of superhero-type action, with buildings getting destroyed and things blowing up, but very little actual violence. Evie and Mal are very girly girls who still manage to handle a lot of action, and they learn that their conflict between villainous and heroic impulses comes because their mother was a superhero who married her chief villainous opponent. Bright cartoony colors and action along with lots of humor make this a much lighter-hearted story than Runaways.

Rogers, John

Blue Beetle: Shellshocked. Writers, Keith Giffen & John Rogers; Cully Hamner . . . [et al], pencillers; Phil Balsman, Pat Brosseau, letterers; David Self, Guy Major, colorists; Cully Hamner, Phil Moy, Duncan Rouleau, Jack Purcell, inkers. DC Comics 2006 144p. Illustration
Grades: 8 9 10 11 12 Adult   **741.5; Fic**
1. Adventure graphic novels; 2. Blue Beetle (Fictional character); 3. Superhero graphic novels; 4. Graphic novels
978-1-4012-0965-0, $12.99
Ted Kord, the Blue Beetle, is dead; but the Blue Beetle scarab has chosen a new guardian, El Paso teenager Jaime Reyes. Supernatural powers can be a blessing or a curse, and when it comes to the powers of the Scarab, you don't get one without the other. The new hero will now have to deal with increasingly strange and dangerous days ahead, as he learns to handle his new skills while intergalactic trouble comes looking for him.

Rol, Ruud van der

The **search**. [by] Eric Heuvel, Ruud van der Rol [and] Lies Schippers; [English translation by Lorraine T. Miller]. Farrar, Straus and Giroux 2009 61p. Illustration
Grades: 5 6 7 8 9   **741.5; Fic**
1. Grandmothers — Fiction; 2. Holocaust survivors — Fiction; 3. Holocaust, 1933-1945; 4. Jews — Netherlands — Fiction; 5. Graphic novels
978-0-374-36517-2, $18.99; 978-0-374-46455-4 (pa), $9.99
                                   LC 2009-13603
After recounting her experience as a Jewish girl living in Amsterdam during the Holocaust, Esther, helped by her grandson, embarks on a search to discover what happened to her parents before they died in a concentration camp.

Esther, her grandson Daniel, and her friend Helena's grandson Jeroen visit the Dutch farm where Esther hid during the Nazi occupation of the Netherlands during World War II. She tells her story, of how she managed to escape the Nazi roundup of Jews, but how her family died in a concentration camp. Daniel helps her find an old friend from the farm, now living in Israel, and he tells her what happened to her family in Auschwitz. The book depicts some of the horrendous, horrible things that happened but does it without graphic violence or gore.

Roman, Dave

Agnes Quill: an anthology of mystery. All transcripts written by Dave Roman; illustrated by Jason Ho, Raina Telgemeier, Jeff Zornow and Dave Roman. SLG Publishing 2006 130p. Illustration
Grades: 7 8 9 10 11 12   **741.5**
1. Horror graphic novels; 2. Mystery graphic novels; 3. Graphic novels
978-1-59362-052-3, $10.95
Orphaned teen Agnes Quill lives in the city of Legerdemain and carries on a family tradition; she can see and communicate with ghosts, and she works as a detective to help them. Her cases range from recovering the mummified head of a ghost's old body in order to save the valuable necklace hidden there, to helping a little girl ghost find her doll, to helping a man find his legs, and more. Roman works with artists including Raina Telgemeier, and their styles range from childlike cartoons to gloomy, atmospheric art full of shadows.

"The variety of drawing styles and Agnes' story of being a teenage detective who can see the dead among the living combine in an interesting read that will likely keep readers' attention." Voice Youth Advocates

Jax Epoch and the Quicken Forbidden: Borrowed Magic. John Green, illustrator. AiT/PlanetLar 2003 152p. Illustration
Grades: 7 8 9 10 11 12 Adult   **741.5; Fic**
1. Science fiction graphic novels; 2. Graphic novels
1-932051-11-2, $14.95
When teenager Jax stumbles into an interdimensional portal, she "borrows" several items: an ancient book, a pair of gloves, and a pair of boots. When she returns home through the portal, things are a bit . . . off. Her little escapade has caused magic to leak into her world, and now she's deep in trouble, unstuck in time and on trial for the crime of crossing dimensions. The story continues in Volume 2: Separation Anxiety.

"Jax is a great character - quite real but with flaws that get her into deep trouble while possessing the aplomb to get herself out." (VOYA)

Followed by Volume 2: Separation Anxiety

Romance Without Tears

Edited by John Benson. Fantagraphics Books 2004 160p. Illustration
Grades: 8 9 10 11 12 Adult   **741.5; Fic**
1. Romance graphic novels; 2. Graphic novels
1-56097-558-X, $22.95
This revisionist collection of romance comics stories from the '50s challenges the cliché of the "tear-stained face" that later dominated the genre and became widely known and vilified as a tiresome icon of moral uplift. Editor Benson has picked stories that portray stron young women who learn from their mistakes and choose their guys, and get themselves out of trouble. The stories were all originally published by Archer St. John in the late-1940s to mid-1950s.

Rosa, Don

Walt Disney's Uncle $crooge and Donald Duck: the Son of the sun. [written and drawn by Don Rosa; lettered by John Clark]. Fantagraphics Books 2014 207 p. Color; Illustration
Grades: 7 8 9 10 11 12 Adult   **741.5**
1. Ducks — Fiction; 2. Fictional characters

1606997424; 9781606997420, $29.99

LC 2012287668

This collection by Don Rosa, featuring Disney's Donald Duck and Scrooge McDuck, is "filled with epic adventures, like hunting for buried treasure or recovering stolen money. . . . At the end of each volume are whole pages of reference notes, explaining each comic in depth and addressing Rosa's process and nods to previous works." (School Library Journal)

"When Rosa began creating Uncle Scrooge comics in 1987, his work instilled childish wonder in readers. Disney comics had entirely disappeared from circulation, and those that had just preceded the fall had become completely hackneyedùrife with repeating storylines and drab artwork. But under Rosa's creative flair, a zippy, glamorous franchise suddenly appeared, with riveting stories and detailed yet kinetic artwork. While remaining totally true to Scrooge McDuck's ornery persona, Rosa turned the moody miser into a plucky adventurer worthy of Tintin." Pub Wkly

Other titles in this series are: Return to plain awful (2014); Treasure under glass (2015)

Rosca, Madeleine
   Hollow Fields Omnibus collection. Seven Seas Entertainment 2009 Un Illustration
Grades: 5 6 7 8 9 10   **741.5; Fic**
   1. Adventure graphic novels; 2. Science fiction graphic novels; 3. Graphic novels
978-1-934876-72-5, $14.99
Rosca is an Australian global manga creator who won one of the inaugural International Manga Awards 'Shorei' awards given by the Japanese government in 2007.

   Lucy Snow was supposed to start school at a nice elementary school in town, but she manages to lose her way in a forest and finds herself at Miss Weaver's Academy for the Scientifically Gifted and Ethically Unfettered a school for archvillains in training. Lucy's fellow students are all learning how to be mad scientists and evil geniuses, with classes such as Live Taxidermy, Cross-Species Body-Part Transplantation, and Killer Robot Construction. Hollow Fields, as the school is also called, also has a practice guaranteed to make everyone compete to do well: the student with the lowest grades at the end of the week is sent to the windmill for detention, and thus far no student has ever returned. Miss Weaver has experimented on herself, as have all the Engineers who teach; what the reader learns is that they need new, young blood to keep their stitched-together bodies going, for they are all more than a hundred years old. Befriended by a talking box that calls itself Doctor Bleak, Lucy struggles to hold her own in her classes, despite her innate niceness. She decides she needs to discover just what goes on in the windmill, and how she can make things right. The book includes some mild violence.

Rosenkranz, Patrick
   ★ **Rebel** visions: the underground comix revolution, 1963-1975. Fantagraphics Books 2008 292p. Illustration
Grades: 11 12 Adult   **741.5**
   1. Cartoonists; 2. Comic books, strips, etc — History and criticism; 3. Graphic novels
978-1-56097-706-3, $34.99

"The most lasting artistic legacy of the 1960s hippie movement, other than its music, is its eye-poppingly transgressive underground comics—black-and-white pamphlets that spread the counterculture message of sex, drugs, and rebellion to freak and straight alike. Rosencranz thoroughly documents the phenomenon, providing a year-by-year account of the underground scene, from 1968's Zap #1, which artist R. Crumb sold from a baby carriage on the streets of Haight Ashbury, to its crash in 1973 in the wake of obscenity rulings and a crackdown on head shops. . . . Rosencranz's writing may lack flair, but with personalities this colorful (the artists themselves provide fly-on-the-wall reminiscences) and art this outrageous (reprinted on nearly every page) to write about, who needs it?" Booklist

Ross, Steve
   Marked. Seabury Books 2005 Un Illustration
Grades: 9 10 11 12 Adult   **225; 741.5**
   1. Bible NT Mark — Adaptations; 2. Graphic novels
1-59627-002-0, $20
   An occupied country. A people infested with demons. A time of revolution. A liberator rises. One of the oldest stories in human history comes alive in this telling of the Gospel of Mark. Join a carpenter as he changes the world. This is a human story of passion and murder. Of a compassionate man brutally killed and yet alive. Ross has set the story in a futuristic, urban world.

Rouleau, Duncan
   Metal Men. DC Comics 2008 Un Illustration
Grades: 9 10 11 12 Adult   **741.5; Fic**
   1. Robots; 2. Superhero graphic novels; 3. Graphic novels
978-1-40112-1845-4, $24.99
   The Metal Men series was part of the Silver Age of comics. Now, they're back with a new origin story. Doc Will Magnus created androids from elements: Gold, Platinum, Mercury, Lead, Iron, Tin, and Copper; he used devices he calls responsometers to power them. However, the responsometers are also ancient weapons that that control the very fabric of the world, and things from the past hunt the "thief" who stole their weapons. Magnus and the Metal Men must also deal with his ex-mentor, T. O. Morrow, the toxic creature called Chemo, and Magnus' own brother. The book includes fighting, most of it machine against machine.

   The **Nightmarist**. Active Images 2006 Un Illustration
Grades: 11 12 Adult   **741.5; Fic**
   1. Horror graphic novels; 2. Graphic novels
1-9766761-8-4, $14.99
   When an entity calling himself the Nightmarist appears in Beth Sorenson's dreams, claiming to protect her from forces plotting to twist her will, Beth's reality begins to crack. With horrors closing in around her, while awake and asleep, Beth must decide—has she gone crazy? Have her dreams become ground zero in a battle for the future of mankind? Can she trust The Nightmarist? Her choices may cost more than her soul. The book includes violence and some strong language.

Rubio, Kevin
   Star Wars: Tag & Bink Were Here. Pencils by Lucas Marangon. Dark Horse Comics 2006 Un Illustration

Grades: 7 8 9 10 11 12 Adult   **741.5; Fic**
1. Adventure graphic novels; 2. Humorous graphic novels; 3. Science fiction graphic novels; 4. Star Wars; 5. Graphic novels
978-1-59307-641-2, $14.95

Rebel officers Tag Greenley and Bink Otauna were minding their own business aboard a familiar, princess-harboring freighter when they suddenly found themselves under siege. Now under attack by the Empire, they will choose life over a noble death and "borrow" the armor off a pair of deceased stormtroopers. Their new disguises might get them off the freighter alive, but they'll also lead Tag and Bink on an adventure neither could have predicted. Chock-full of appearances by everyone's favorite Star Wars characters, Tag & Bink weaves the pair's misadventures into the movies themselves. No setting is safe as they traverse the galaxy from the Death Star to the Sarlacc pit to Cloud City to Endor.

Rucka, Greg
   Batwoman: elegy. Greg Rucka, writer; J.H. Williams III, artist; Dave Stewart, colorist; Todd Klein, letters.. DC Comics 2010 1 v. Color illustration
Grades: 11 12 Adult   741.5
1. Batwoman (Fictional character); 2. Mentally ill — Fiction; 3. Superheroes — Fiction; 4. Graphic novels
9781401226923, $24.99; 1401226922

LC 2010283560

In this graphic novel, "Batwoman battles a madwoman known only as Alice, inspired by Alice in Wonderland, who sees her life as a fairy tale and everyone around her as expendable! Batwoman must stop Alice from unleashing a toxic death cloud over all of Gotham City—but Alice has more up her sleeve than just poison, and Batwoman's life will never ever be the same." (Publisher's note)

"[A] nuanced, literary, and culturally charged story, but the real knockout element is Williams' art nouveau inspired compositions." Booklist

Checkmate: A King's Game. Greg Rucka, Jesus Saiz, Cliff Richards. DC Comics 2007 166p. Illustration
Grades: 10 11 12 Adult   **741.5; Fic**
1. Green Lantern (Fictional character); 2. International security; 3. Superhero graphic novels; 4. Graphic novels
978-1-4012-1220-9, $14.99

After the events of Identity Crisis, Checkmate is re-chartered by the U.N. to deal with metahuman threats. It's a joint partnership between human and metahuman leaders, and they have titles based on chess. The White King is Alan Scott, the original Green Lantern, the White Queen is Doctor Amanda Waller, who used to work for Lex Luthor; the Black Queen in Sasha Bordeaux, a former super villain, and the Black King is Israeli Col. Taleb Beni Khalid. Checkmate is not immune to politics; the organization already faces dissolution that the leaders can stop only if they can learn which nation wants to dissolve Checkmate, even as they battle against terrorists Kobra and the Kali Yuga. Filled with action, politics, internal conflicts, and sexual tensions, this is a continuing comics series.

Originally published as Checkmate issues #1-7.

The **OMAC** Project: Countdown to Infinite Crisis. Art by Jesus Saiz and Cliff Richards. DC Comics 2005 Un Illustration
Grades: 9 10 11 12 Adult   **741.5; Fic**
1. Superhero graphic novels; 2. Superman (Fictional character); 3. Wonder Woman (Fictional character); 4. Graphic novels
1-4012-0837-1, $14.99

Originally designed by Batman, the Brother I satellite has been usurped by the government's Checkmate spy division, and Checkmate in its turn has been usurped by the insane Maxwell Lord, who reprograms the satellite and other technology to serve his twisted goals. Blue Beetle stumbled on the secret first, and paid for that knowledge with his life. Earth's super-heroes have to contend with OMACs, normal humans who can be turned into armored warriors with a single command. Now, Lord has taken possession of Superman's mind, forcing Wonder Woman to take action, an action that will forever change her relationship with her colleagues.

Superman: Unconventional Warfare. Writer, Greg Rucka; pencillers, Matthew Clark, Renado Guedes, Paul Pelletier. DC Comics 2005 160p. Illustration
Grades: 9 10 11 12 Adult   **741.5; Fic**
1. Superhero graphic novels; 2. Superman (Fictional character); 3. Graphic novels
1-4012-0449-X, $14.95

Superman has been away for a time, but now he's back in Metropolis and is putting his life in order. As Clark Kent, he finds himself assigned to ride along with the Metropolis Special Crimes Unit and is glad he did. A souped-up Replikon comes calling, the harbinger of a new, deadly threat to not only the Man of Steel but also all of Metropolis. Meanwhile, Lois Lane is an embedded reporter in Umec and her experiences are no less dangerous. Away from familiar turf, distanced from the man she loves, Lois witnesses a different kind of courage. The book includes some violence.

Whiteout Volume 1: The Definitive Edition. Written by Greg Rucka; illustrated & lettered by Steve Lieber. Oni Press 2007 128p. Illustration
Grades: 11 12 Adult   **741.5; Fic**
1. Mystery graphic novels; 2. Graphic novels
978-1-932664-70-6, $13.95

One of Oni Press' earliest and most acclaimed books returns in a brand new re-mastered and re-formatted edition. U.S. Marshal Carrie Stetko has made Antarctica her home. In the vastness of The Ice, she found peace ... Or at least that's what she thought, until someone commits a murder in her jurisdiction and the lawwoman is forced to use her detective skills once more or become another victim to this mysterious killer. The book includes violence and harsh language, including copious use of the f-bomb.

Whiteout Volume 2: Melt, The Definitive Edition. Written by Greg Rucka; illustrated & lettered by Steve Lieber. Oni Press 2007 120p. Illustration
Grades: 11 12 Adult   **741.5; Fic**
1. Mystery graphic novels; 2. Graphic novels
978-1-932664-71-3, $13.95

2000 Eisner Award for Best Finite Series/Limited Series.

One of Oni Press' earliest and most acclaimed books returns in a brand new re-mastered and re-formatted edition. U.S. Marshal Carrie Stetko investigates the explosion that destroyed a Russian science station that may have been a cache for weapons. The book includes violence, copious harsh language, nudity and sexual situations.

Wonder Woman: Eyes of the Gorgon. Greg Rucka, writer; Drew Johnson, James Raiz, Sean Phillips, pencillers; Ray Snyder, Sean Phillips, inkers; Richard & Tanya Horie, colorists; Todd Klein, letterer. DC Comics 2005 Un Illustration
Grades: 9 10 11 12 Adult   **741.5; Fic**
1. Justice League (Fictional characters); 2. Superhero graphic novels; 3. Wonder Woman (Fictional character); 4. Graphic novels
1-4012-0797-9, $19.99
As Diana tries to avert war at the White House, the deadly Medousa comes calling, and Wonder Woman's world is turned completely upside-down as she must face the Gorgon in a final confrontation that has tragic consequences for Diana and her loved ones. She must also prove herself once again to her comrades in the Justice League of America, and to the world. The book has superhero fighting action.

Wonder Woman: Land of the Dead. Greg Rucka, Geoff Johns, writers; Drew Johnson et al, pencillers. DC Comics 2006 128p. Illustration
Grades: 9 10 11 12 Adult   **741.5; Fic**
1. Flash (Fictional character); 2. Superhero graphic novels; 3. Wonder Woman (Fictional character); 4. Graphic novels
1-4012-0938-6, $12.99
Just as Wonder Woman is starting to deal with her blindness (self-inflicted, in order to defeat Medusa), the Cheetah returns and teams up with another villain known for speed: The Reverse Flash. Wally West, the real Flash, joins forces with Wonder Woman to stop the villainous duo from causing untold havoc. Then, the goddess Athena sends Wonder Woman on a journey to retrieve Hermes from the Underworld. Joined by Wonder Girl and Ferdinand the Minotaur, Wonder Woman must face unimagined peril to complete her mission. But should she succeed, what will Diana ask in return from the all-seeing Goddess of Wisdom?

Wonder Woman: Mission's End. Pencilled by Cliff Richards, et al. DC Comics 2006 Un Illustration
Grades: 10 11 12 Adult   **741.5; Fic**
1. Superhero graphic novels; 2. Superman (Fictional character); 3. Wonder Woman (Fictional character); 4. Graphic novels
978-1-4012-1093-9, $19.99
Wonder Woman had only recently regained her sight, when she was forced into battling against Superman, whose mind was being controlled by Max Lord. She could only stop Lord by crossing the line and doing something no superhero had done before, and her action forever changes her relationship with Superman, and the whole world. Then Infinite Crisis hits, and a swarm of OMAC robots descends upon her island home and she must fight even more.

Rudahl, Sharon
A **dangerous** woman: the graphic biography of Emma Goldman. The New Press 2007 115p. Illustration
Grades: 10 11 12 Adult
335; 92; 741.5
1. Anarchism and anarchists; 2. Anarchists; 3. Biographical graphic novels; 4. planning advocates; 5. Goldman, Emma, 1869-1940; 6. Memoirists
978-1-59558-064-1, $17.95

Courtesy of The New Press

LC 2007-15415
Emma Goldman was a revolutionary activist, speaker, writer, and feminist and anarchist. An immigrant to the U.S., she spoke out against inhumane working conditions, taught contraception, and opposed conscription for World War I. She founded the Free Speech League (a precursor to the ACLU), and the magazine Mother Earth. When she was deported to Russia just after the Bolshevik Revolution, she became disillusioned with the authoritarianism she found there, and she ended up supporting the fight against fascism in the Spanish Civil War. Rudahl based her graphic novel on Goldman's autobiography. The book includes nudity, sexual situations, and some violence.

Rugg, Jim
The **Plain** Janes. [illustrated by] Jim Rugg. DC Comics/Minx 2007 Un Illustration
Grades: 7 8 9 10 11 12   **741.5; Fic**
1. Art; 2. Friendship; 3. High school students; 4. School stories; 5. Graphic novels
978-1-4012-1115-8, $9.99
After a bomb attack in Metro City, Jane's parents move to suburban Kent Waters, where Jane feels lost. Then she meets three other Janes at the "reject" table in the high school lunch room, and she convinces them to help her form their own secret club: P.L.A.I.N."People Loving Art in Neighborhoods. However, their "art attacks" cause the authorities to think that P.L.A.I.N. is a terrorist group.
"The art, inspired by Dan Clowes' work, is absolutely engaging. Packaged like manga this is a fresh, exciting use of the graphic-novel format." Booklist
Another title about the Janes is: Janes in love (2008)

Street Angel. Created and written by Jim Rugg and Brian Maruca; drawn by Jim Rugg. SLG Publishing 2005 208p. Illustration
Grades: 10 11 12 Adult   **741.5; Fic**
1. Adventure graphic novels; 2. Homeless persons; 3. Graphic novels
1-59362-012-8, $14.95
Homeless, orphaned, rarely in school, twelve-year-old skateboarder Jesse "Street Angel" Sanchez uses her board skills and kung fu to fight crime on the streets of Wilkesborough, the worst ghetto in Angel City. She has to fight Dr. Pangaea and his ninja forces, deal with time-warping pirates and Inca warriors, go dumpster-diving

to find food . . . Jesse does a lot of slicing and dicing with her handy sword and knows how to handle automatic weapons as well in the many graphically depicted fight scenes.

Originally published as Street Angel issues #1-5.

Runton, Andy
★ **Owly** Vol. 2: Just a Little Blue. Top Shelf Productions 2005 127p. Illustration
Grades: K 1 2 3 4 5 6 7 8 9 10 11 12 Adult   **741.5; Fic**
1. Friendship; 2. Stories without words; 3. Graphic novels
1-891830-64-3, $10

Owly is a kind, yet lonely, little owl who's always on the search for new friends and adventure. Owly learns that sometimes you have to make sacrifices and work at things that are important, especially friendship. He and Wormy try to help a stubborn bluebird by building a new home, but the bluebird rejects it and them.

★ **Owly** Vol. 3: Flying Lessons. Top Shelf Productions 2005 143p. Illustration
Grades: K 1 2 3 4 5 6 7 8 9 10 11 12 Adult   **741.5; Fic**
1. Friendship; 2. Stories without words; 3. Graphic novels
1-891830-76-7, $10

Owly figures out why he can't fly (he failed his childhood flying lessons), and helps another forest creature with his own flying problems. The flying squirrel is frightened by Owly, for he knows owls are hunters, but Owly isn't like that. How can he convince the squirrel he just wants to be friends?

★ **Owly** vol. 4: a time to be brave. Top Shelf Productions 2007 132p. Illustration
Grades: K 1 2 3 4 5 6 7 8 9 10 11 12 Adult   **741.5; Fic**
1. Fantasy graphic novels; 2. Friendship; 3. Owls; 4. Stories without words; 5. Graphic novels
978-1-891830-89-1, $10

A new visitor comes to the forest, but Wormy is scared of him because Owly had just read stories about a scary dragon, and the visitor seems to look scary. The visitor is just as scared of Owly. Things aren't just as they seem, and everyone soon finds out that a little bravery and a lot of friendship can fix just about anything. This is the latest volume in Runton's nearly wordless series about Owly and his friends.

★ **Owly** volume five: tiny tales. Top Shelf Productions 2008 175p. Illustration
Grades: K 1 2 3 4 5 6 7 8 9 10 11 12 Adult   **741.5; Fic**
1. Friendship; 2. Humorous graphic novels; 3. Graphic novels
978-1-60309-019-3, $10

This volume gathers short stories about Owly and his friends, including stories originally published for Free Comic Book Day issues from Top Shelf Productions, the first Owly mini-comics, drawings of Owly before he met Wormy, and more. Among the stories, Owly saves a friend from drowning in the cold river when the ice cracks, only to get caught in the hole himself; Owly finds a way to keep both the bees and hummingbirds happy when they get into a "turf" battle; Owly helps a friend when she falls and breaks the fancy potted plant she bought for a present; and more.

★ **Owly:** The way home and The bittersweet summer. [by] Andy Runton. Top Shelf 2004 160p. Illustration
Grades: K 1 2 3 4 5 6 7 8 9 10 11 12   **741.5; Fic**
1. Friendship; 2. Owls; 3. Graphic novels
1-891830-62-7, $10

LC 2005298860

Rotund little Owly befriends Wormy despite their differences, and together they help a couple of hummingbirds and learn that friendship doesn't end with separation.

"The whimsical black-and-white art is done with great facility for expressing emotion, and Runton's reliance on icons and pictures in lieu of the usual dialogue makes the story perfect for give-and-take between children and their parents." Booklist

Other titles in this series are: Owly: Just a little blue (2005); Owly: Flying lessons (2005); Owly: A time to be brave (2007); Owly: Tiny tales (2008)

Rushkoff, Douglas
Testament: West of Eden. Writer, Douglas Rushkoff; artist, Liam Sharp; Jim Devlin, colorist; Todd Klein, letterer. DC Comics. Vertigo 2007 128p. Illustration
Grades: 11 12 Adult   **741.5; Fic**
1. Fantasy graphic novels; 2. Graphic novels
978-1-4012-1201-8, $12.99

Rushkoff continues to retell stories from the Bible his way in this second volume. Alan Stern creates a new kind of life inside his laptop computer, but he and his wife Greta discover that playing in the realm of the gods has catastrophic consequences. Then their son Jake lives as a fugitive from the police-state. His former classmate Alec works to speed billionaire Pierre Fallow's push for a single, global currency based solely on artificial intelligence. The only way to stop them is for Jake to defy the gods and take the story to places the Bible would never have dared to go. The nudity, sexual situations, and language make this a book for mature readers. It will also offend anyone who is a devout Christian.

Russell, P. Craig
Fairy Tales of Oscar Wilde Vol. 4: The Devoted Friend & The Nightingale and the Rose. NBM Publishing 2004 Un Illustration
Grades: 5 6 7 8 9   **741.5; Fic**
1. Fantasy graphic novels; 2. Graphic novels
978-1-56163-391-3, $16.99

This volume adapts "The Devoted Friend," on what constitutes real friendship, and "The Nightingale and the Rose," a story of sacrifice to love with a cruel twist. In both stories, innocence is sacrificed to cynicism and shallowness.

★ The **graveyard** book graphic novel Volume 1. Based on the novel by Neil Gaiman; adapted by P. Craig Russell; illustrated by Kevin Nowlan, P. Craig Russell, Tony Harris, Scott Hampton, Galen Showman, Jill Thompson, Stephen B. Scott; colorist, Lovern Kindzierski; letterer, Rick Park. HarperCollins 2014 188 p. Color; Illustration
Grades: 5 6 7 8 9 10   **741.5; Fic**
1. Cemeteries — Fiction; 2. Orphans — Fiction; 3. Graphic novels; 4. Gaiman, Neil, 1960- — Adaptations
9780062194817, $19.99; 006219481X

LC 2013953799

This graphic novel is an adaptation of the "Newbery Medal-winning novel, [where] Bod is an unusual boy . . ., the only living resident of a graveyard. Raised from infancy by the ghosts, werewolves, and other cemetery denizens, Bod has learned the antiquated customs of his guardians' time as well as their ghostly teachings." (Publisher's note)

"Russell brings his decades of comics know-how to this lovely, lyrical adaptation of [Gaiman's] well-loved, Newbery Medal—winning book. Not content to rely exclusively on his own distinctive talents, Russell has enlisted some of the industry's greatest contemporary illustrators as contributors, who fill the panels with appropriately gothic tones. In order to give ample room to the novel's twists and turns, the adaptation has been divided into two parts." Booklist

Ruth, Greg
  Sudden Gravity (A Tale of the Panopticon). Dark Horse Comics 2006 168p. Illustration
  Grades: 11 12 Adult   **741.5; Fic**
  1. Horror graphic novels; 2. Mystery graphic novels; 3. Graphic novels
  978-1-59307-565-1, $10.95
  Built on a site of great and forgotten power, the mammoth Bentham International Hospital was to be the very definition of modern medical science at its best. But over the years, the spectres and dark secrets of the Hospital began to bore away at its heart, leaving its foundations cracked and vulnerable to the oldest of horrors and nightmares. When a prominent Commissioner of the City's Housing and Urban Development Department is brought to the Panopticon for evaluation after murdering her family, the haunted secrets of the hospital begin to unravel, leaving no one untouched. Julius, the prosthetic boy in room 13 is waking up. The black eggs are found. The lines between the patients and the doctors are blurring. This is where the end begins. Every cure is paid with a curse and every sin is birthed anew as the once brilliant light of modern medicine forsakes the world for the shadows it can no longer hide. The book includes strong language, some violence, and disturbing scenes.

Ryall, Chris
  Beowulf. Based on the screenplay by Neil Gaiman & Roger Avery; written by Chris Ryall; art and cover by Gabriel Rodriguez. IDW Publishing 2007 104p. Illustration
  Grades: 10 11 12 Adult   **741.5; Fic**
  1. Beowulf — Adaptations; 2. Fantasy graphic novels; 3. Graphic novels
  978-1-60010-128-1, $17.99
  This graphic novel adaptation of the motion picture screenplay written by Neil Gaiman and Roger Avary takes liberties with the original epic. In this version, the warrior Beowulf slays the monster Grendel who has slain many of King Hrothgar's warriors, but is seduced by Grendel's demon mother. This story states that Grendel is Hrothgar's son. It basically turns the epic saga upside down, showing that the heroes bring about the monsters. The book includes harsh language, nudity, and graphic violence.

Saavedra, Scott
  Dr. Radium Battles Phill, King of the Pill Bugs!. Amaze Ink/SLG Publishing 2004 112p. Illustration
  Grades: 7 8 9 10 11 12 Adult   **741.5; Fic**
  1. Humorous graphic novels; 2. Science fiction graphic novels; 3. Graphic novels
  0-943151-84-8, $9.95
  Before "Dexter's Laboratory" and before "Jimmy Neutron," there was Dr. Radium, the last scientist left standing in the "perfect" world of tomorrow. Ignored by society and feared by his assistant, Dr. Radium pursues Science with happy disregard for knowledge, progress, or safety. Stuck with Penny, a girl from the present presently trapped in the future, Dr. Radium suffers distractions from giant scientist rats, screaming dinosaurs, and Phill, one very mad King of the Pill Bugs.

Sable, Mark
  Grounded, Vol. 1: Powerless. Writer/creator, Mark Sable; artist, Paul Azaceta. Image Comics 2006 160p. Illustration
  Grades: 10 11 12 Adult   **741.5; Fic**
  1. High school students; 2. School stories; 3. Superhero graphic novels; 4. Graphic novels
  978-1-58240-641-1, $14.99
  Ever since he was a little boy, Jonathan just knew that superheroes are real, and that he would eventually come into his power. Now he's in high school, and he has just discovered that he was right all along superheroes are real. In fact, his parents are two of the most famous heroes in the world. Disillusionment sets in when he catches his father in bed with another woman. He also has to face the fact that he has no powers at all, which doesn't help when his parents put him into a school for the children of heroes; he's the only one who doesn't have any. Even as he deals with bullying and nasty pranks, he learns that there's a dark side to the powers.
  Originally published as a comics miniseries

Sacco, Joe
  The **fixer:** a story from Sarajevo. Joe Sacco. Drawn and Quarterly 2003 105p. Illustration
  Grades: 9 10 11 12 Adult
  741; 741.5
  9781896597607, $24.95
  "Joe Sacco goes behind the scene of war correspondence to reveal the anatomy of the big scoop. He begins by returning us to the dying days of Balkan conflict and introduces us to his own fixer; a man looking to squeeze the last bit of profit

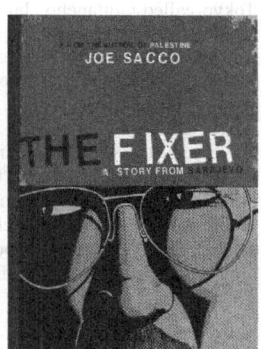

Courtesy of Drawn & Quarterly

from Bosnia before the reconstruction begins. Thanks to a complex relationship with the fixer Joe discovers the crimes of opportunistic warlords and gangsters who run the countryside in times of war. But the west is interested in a different spin on the stories coming out of Bosnia. Almost ten years later, Joe meets up with his fixer and sees how the new Bosnian government has 'dealt' with these criminals and Joe ponders who is holding the reins of power these days." (Publisher's note)

Safe area Gorazde. Fantagraphics Bks. 2000 227p. Illustration
Grades: 10 11 12 Adult   **949.7; 741.5; 949.702**
1-56097-392-7, $28.95; 1-56097-470-2 (pa), $19.95

Sacco "spent five months in Bosnia in 1996, immersing himself in the human side of life during wartime, researching stories that are rarely found in conventional news coverage. The book focuses on the Muslim-held enclave of Gorazde, which was besieged by Bosnian Serbs during the war. Sacco lived for a month in Gorazde, entering before the Muslims trapped inside had access to the outside world, electricity or running water." (Publisher's note)

Said, Fehed
The **Clarence** Principle. Writer, Fehed Said; artist, Shari Chankhamma. SLG Publishing 2007 Un Illustration
Grades: 11 12 Adult   **741.5; Fic**
1. Death; 2. Fantasy graphic novels; 3. Graphic novels
978-1-59362-064-6, $12.95

After Clarence commits suicide, he wakes up to find a message written on the bathroom mirror; he opens the door and finds himself in a bizarre afterlife where he meets whimsical and strange people. Some images may be disturbing for more sensitive readers (such as the people with vacant holes instead of eyes, complete with zippers, and some dismemberments).

Saijyo, Shinji
★ **Iron** Wok Jan! Volume 1. DRMaster Publications 2002 190p. Illustration
Grades: 9 10 11 12 Adult   **741.5; Fic**
1. Cooking; 2. Manga; 3. Shonen manga; 4. Graphic novels
1-58899-256-7, $9.95

Jan is a talented young chef at a top class restaurant in Tokyo called Gottancho. Jan is really arrogant and full of self-confidence regarding his cooking technique. He always challenges Kiriko—a talented chef of Gottancho. Both Jan and Kiriko have entered a cooking competition. Who will win? As the series progresses, Jan competes with every chef; he's actually more the villain with his maniacal approach to cooking. There's lots of cooking action, even recipes. Some female characters are drawn to emphasize certain physical attributes. There's also some violence; some of Jan's competitors use violence (such as breaking his hand or arm) to gain an advantage. The food competitions in the manga are like television's Iron Chef taken to the extreme.

Saint-Exupéry, Antoine de
★ The **little** prince by Joann Sfar. Adapted from the book by Antoine de Saint-Exupéry; translated by Sarah Ardizzone; colour by Brigitte Findakly. Houghton Mifflin Harcourt 2010 110p. Illustration
Grades: 5 6 7 8 9   **741; Fic; 741.5**
1. Extraterrestrial beings; 2. Fantasy graphic novels; 3. Saint-Exupéry, Antoine de, 1900-1944 — Adaptations; 4. Graphic novels
978-0-547-33802-6, $19.99; 0-547-33802-3

Courtesy of Houghton Mifflin Harcourt

"On the surface, this is a straight graphic-novel retelling of the narrator pilot getting stranded in the desert, where he meets a curious little boy who claims to be from a wee planet very far away. . . . The ultimately tricky task is to honor the source but not sound like an adaptation (otherwise, why not just read the original?) and Sfar nails it on both counts. . . . Everything is handled with both reverence and ingenuity." Booklist

Sakai, Stan
★ **Usagi** Yojimbo, book one: The Ronin. Fantagraphics Books 1999 144p. Illustration
Grades: 7 8 9 10 11 12 **741.5; Fic**
1. Adventure graphic novels; 2. Japan; 3. Rabbits; 4. Samurai; 5. Usagi Yojimbo (Fictional character); 6. Graphic novels
0-930193-35-0; 978-0-930193-35-5, $15.95

Courtesy of Fantagraphics

LC 93-239124
This series contains the adventures of Miyamoto Usagi, a ronin samurai rabbit in 17th-century Japan.
First published 1987
Vol. 1 of an ongoing series; Vols. 1-7 published by Fantagraphics; Vols. 8-25 published by Dark Horse Comics

★ **Usagi** Yojimbo: Yokai. Created, written, and illustrated by Stan Sakai. Dark Horse Books 2009 62p. Illustration
Grades: 6 7 8 9 10 11 12 Adult   **741.5; Fic**
1. Adventure graphic novels; 2. Japan; 3. Monsters; 4. Samurai; 5. Usagi Yojimbo (Fictional character); 6. Graphic novels
978-1-59582-362-5, $14.95

LC 2009-20024
As he walks through a spooky forest at night, samurai rabbit Usagi Yojimbo encounters a woman who begs him to find her daughter, who was kidnapped and dragged into the forest. That night, the yokai—monsters, demons, and spirits from Japanese folklore—are amassing for a once-a-century attempt to take over the living world. Armed only with his swords and his wit, Usagi can't hope to win against so many supernatural beings, but luckily Sasuke the Demon Queller has come, knowing about the yokais' plan, and together they fight the gathered monsters. The fighting is not graphic or bloody, and the monsters and demons aren't too scary looking for most younger readers.

"Sakai's art deftly demonstrates that comics can be simultaneously cartoony and scary. . . . Usagi Yojimbo is a genuine pleasure for readers of all ages." Publ Wkly

Sakuishi, Harold
 Beck: Mongolian Chop Squad, Vol. 1. Tokyopop 2005 214p. Illustration
Grades: 10 11 12 Adult   **741.5; Fic**
 1. Humorous graphic novels; 2. Rock music; 3. Shonen manga; 4. Graphic novels
1-59532-770-3, $9.99
 Fourteen-year-old Yukio Tanaka is one heck of a boring guy. He has no hobbies, a weak taste in music, and only a small vestige of a personality. His shy and somewhat neurotic personality makes him his own worst enemy. Little does he know that his life will be forever changed when he meets rocker Ryusuke Minami, an unpredictable sixteen-year-old with a cool dog named Beck. Ryusuke has just returned to Japan from America, and when he inspires Yukio to get into music, the two begin a journey through the world of rock 'n' roll dreams. The series includes some fan service, harsh language, fight scenes and some sexual situations along with lots of music and raucous comedy.

Sakura, Kenichi
 Dragon drive. Vol. 1, D-break. Story & art by Ken-ichi Sakura. Viz Media/Shonen Jump 2007 195p. Illustration
Grades: 6 7 8 9 10   **741.5; Fic**
 1. Manga; 2. Shonen manga; 3. Video games; 4. Graphic novels
978-1-4215-1187-0, $7.99; 1-4215-1187-8
 Reiji Ozora knows that he's no good at anything, people keep telling him that. Then best friend Maiko takes him to a secret center where people play a virtual reality game, Dragon Drive. Reiji signs up and finds that, despite the fact that his virtual dragon, Chibi, is small and weak, together they have more power than meets the eye. While they play the game, they're in a world called Rikyu, where everything feels all too real; can Reiji, Chibi, and their friends be in real danger?
 Other titles in the Dragon Drive series are: Dragon drive. Vol. 2 : another world (2007); Dragon drive. Vol. 3: believe (2007); Dragon drive. Vol. 4: hero (2007); Dragon drive. Vol. 5: mission (2007); Dragon drive. Vol. 6: hope (2008); Dragon drive. Vol. 7: decisive battle (2008); Dragon drive. Vol. 8: excitement (2008); Dragon drive. Vol. 9: reshuffle (2008); Dragon drive. Vol. 10: departure (2008); Dragon drive. Vol. 11: trust (2008); Dragon drive. Vol. 12: promise (2009); Dragon drive. Vol. 13: reunion (2009); Dragon drive. Vol. 14: wait (2009)

Sakuragi, Yukiya
 Inubaka: Crazy for Dogs, Vol. 1. Viz Media 2007 210p. Illustration
Grades: 10 11 12 Adult   **741.5; Fic**
 1. Dogs; 2. Manga; 3. Seinen manga; 4. Graphic novels
978-1-4215-1149-8, $9.99
 Naive Suguri wants to move to Tokyo and pursue a career now that she's finished high school. Teppei owns Woofles, a new pet store, and desperately needs someone to help take care of the dogs in his store. When Suguri's dog Lupin scores sexually with a purebred Labrador Retriever that Teppei wants to breed to get puppies to sell, Suguri ends up working at Woofles to make up for it. A fair amount of fan service (mostly panty shots), a little sexual innuendo, and lots of dog pee and poop make this title more appropriate for older teens who love dogs.

Sakurai, Ami
 Made in Heaven Vol. 1. Written by Ami Sakurai; illustrated by Yukari Yashiki. Tokyopop 2006 204p. Illustration
Grades: 10 11 12 Adult   **741.5; Fic**
 1. Josei manga; 2. Romance graphic novels; 3. Science fiction graphic novels; 4. Graphic novels
1-59816-164-4, $9.99
 After a near-fatal car accident, surgeons rebuilt Reiji with prosthetic parts and renamed him Himejima Kazemichi. It was a second chance at life, but there was no guarantee that his new body would last. As his artificial heart runs down, Kazemichi embarks on a journey to discover what his life really means, and live—and love—to the fullest. Along the way, he uncovers dark secrets about his past, including the organization that was responsible for resurrecting him... But the story is not always what it seems. The book includes some strong language, brief violence, nudity, and sexual situations.

Sakurai, Susugi
 Short sunzen! volume 1. Tokyopop 2008 Un Illustration
Grades: 10 11 12   **741.5**
 1. Humorous graphic novels; 2. Romance graphic novels; 3. Shojo manga; 4. Graphic novels
978-1-59816-937-9, $9.99
 Satsuki is a rough and tumble girl, ready to fight any time; she attends a high school with a reputation for rowdiness and violence. Her classmate, Aya Sendo, is just as tough, except with Satsuki. In the short episodes in this volume, readers can see Aya likes Satsuki a lot, but she's basically clueless and likes him as a friend. As time goes on, they spend more time together, and their friendship deepens. Will it ever go beyond that? The book includes some harsh language, fighting, and some mild sexual situations.

Sakurakoji, Kanoko
 Backstage Prince, Vol. 1. Viz Media/Shojo Beat 2007 188p. Illustration
Grades: 8 9 10 11 12 Adult   **741.5; Fic**
 1. Kabuki; 2. Romance graphic novels; 3. Shojo manga; 4. Graphic novels
978-1-4215-1172-6, $8.99
 High school freshman Akari stumbles into hottie Ryusei Horiuchi and hurts him with her school bag. That evening, she stumbles upon the kabuki theater where he, as famous kabuki actor Shonosuke Ichimura, is performing, and becomes his backstage assistant. Ryusei is very shy and aloof, and he's only opened up to his cat, Mr. Ken, and now to Akari; and she, despite herself, has fallen hard for Ryusei. Can an ordinary girl and a handsome, famous actor be together?

Sala, Richard
★ **Cat** burglar black. First Second 2009 126p. Illustration
Grades: 5 6 7 8 9 10   **741.5; Fic**
1. Mystery graphic novels; 2. Orphans; 3. Graphic novels
978-1-59643-144-7, $16.99; 1-59643-144-X

K.'s aunt, who works at the Bellsong Academy for Girls, has invited K. to attend the school. But as soon as she arrives, K. notices some strange goings-on: her aunt has suddenly taken ill; there are only three other students and no regular classes; and a statue speaks to K. when no one else is around.

"The story is structured like a lighthearted cross between a fable and a horror film, but only ever teetering on the edge of horror without depicting it. This could have resulted in a mishmash, but Sala elegantly dances through the creepy and the sweet." SLJ

Mad Night. Fantagraphics Books 2005 231p. Illustration
Grades: 9 10 11 12 Adult   **741.5; Fic**
1. Humorous graphic novels; 2. Mystery graphic novels; 3. Graphic novels
1-56097-681-0, $18.95

Judy Drood, girl detective, along with her friend and reluctant aide, Kasper Keene, investigate a series of murders at Lone Mountain College. Imagine Nancy Drew in a noir mystery, mixed in with macabre and humorous elements from Lemony Snicket books and Charles Addams cartoons.

"Reading a Sala comic is a unique experience, both jarring and fun, good for a rainy day or a stormy night." (PW)

Salvatore, R. A.
DemonWars Vol. 1: The Demon Awakens. Art by Tim Seeley. Devil's Due Publishing 2007 Un Illustration
Grades: 8 9 10 11 12 Adult   **741.5; Fic**
1. Adventure graphic novels; 2. Fantasy graphic novels; 3. Graphic novels
978-1-932796-89-6, $18.99

A fearsome evil has awakened in the land of Corona. A demon determined to spread death and misery has unleashed his goblins and giants to ravage the settlements of the frontier. Two orphans, Pony and Elbryan, have survived the attacks. Taken in by elves, Elbryan grows up to be a formidable ranger. Meanwhile, on a far-off island, a shower of gemstones falls onto the black sand shores; these heaven-sent stones carry power for both good and evil. One young monk must liberate them from the corrupt monastery that harvests them. The book includes some violence.

The **Legend** of Drizzt Book 1: Homeland. R.A. Salvatore, writer; Andrew Dabb, script; Tim Seeley, pencils. Devil's Due Publishing 2005 Un Illustration
Grades: 9 10 11 12 Adult   **741.5; Fic**
1. Adventure graphic novels; 2. Fantasy graphic novels; 3. Graphic novels
1-932796-40-1, $14.95

Travel back to strange and exotic Menzoberranzan, the vast city of the drow and homeland to Icewind Dale hero Drizzt Do'Urden. The young prince of a royal house, Drizzt grows to maturity in the vile world of his dark kin. Possessing honor beyond the scope of his unprincipled

society, young Drizzt faces an inevitable dilemma. Can he live in a world that rejects integrity" The story includes lots of fighting action.

SAM (Special Academic Manga)
Leonardo da Vinci. Y.kids/Youngjin Singapore Pte. Ltd. 2008 152p. Illustration
Grades: 3 4 5 6 7 8 9   **92; 741.5**
1. Art; 2. Artists; 3. Biographical graphic novels; 4. Leonardo, da Vinci, 1452-1519; 5. Painters; 6. Scientists; 7. Writers on science; 8. Graphic novels
978-981-057555-7, $14.95

This graphic format biography of da Vinci uses the conceit that an adventurer from the Planet Mud seeks to learn about the great people of Earth's history in an effort to save the people of Mud, who face a disease that drains their mental powers. In the course of his search in this volume, readers learn about the life and work Leonardo da Vinci, who was a painter, scientist, mathematician, engineer, inventor, anatomist, sculptor, architect, musician, and writer. The book includes a time line of da Vinci's life, and a list of books and websites for further reading.

Part of the Great Figures in History series

Samura, Hiroaki
★ **Blade** of the Immortal Book 1: Blood of a Thousand. Dark Horse Manga 1997 136p. Illustration
Grades: 11 12 Adult   **741.5; Fic**
1. Adventure graphic novels; 2. Samurai; 3. Seinen manga; 4. Graphic novels
1-56971-239-5, $14.95
1998 winner of Japan's Media Arts Award; 2000 Eisner Award for Best U.S. Edition of Foreign Material

"To end his eternal suffering, he must slay one thousand enemies!" Manji, a ronin warrior of feudal Japan, has been cursed with immortality. To rid himself of this curse and end his life of misery, he must slay one thousand evil men. His quest begins when a young girl named Rin seeks his help in taking revenge on her parents' killers . . . and his quest won't end until the blood of a thousand has spilled. The problem comes in judging who is truly evil. This series includes lots of graphic violence, much harsh language, partial nudity, sexual situations, and anachronistic situations and dialog.

Volume 1 of 30

Ohikkoshi. Dark Horse Manga 2006 252p. Illustration
Grades: 10 11 12 Adult   **741.5**
1. Humorous graphic novels; 2. Romance graphic novels; 3. Seinen manga; 4. Graphic novels
978-1-59307-622-1

"Ohikkoshi" follows the turbulent paths of several twenty-something art students as they fall in love, fall in lust, play in rock bands, ride motorbikes, eat, sleep (together) and try to avoid making life decisions while drunk. This romantic comedy is a "Japanese Art School Confidential" packed with absurd humor, obscure Death Metal references and some dramatic revelations. In "Luncheon of Tears Diary" Natsumi Funabashi, a virgin, is an aspiring manga creator on a quest for love and a fulfilling career. Along the way, she has to cope with overzealous men, gang warfare, a mahjong addiction and a lascivious manga editor. This collection is rounded off by Samura's "Kyoto Super

Barhopping Journal: Bloodbath at Midorogaike," a rare, autobiographical travel piece. Samura is best known in the US for his manga series Blade of the Immortal. The book has some mildly strong language, brief violence, brief partial nudity, and sexual situations.

San Giacomo, Michael
Tales of the Starlight drive in. By Michael San Giacomo and twenty-three talented artists. Image Comics 2008 Un Illustration
Grades: 10 11 12 Adult   **741.5; Fic**
1. Motion picture theaters; 2. Graphic novels
978-1-58240-948-1, $19.99
The thirty-one stories in this book tell the tale of the Starlight Drive In movie theater, from 1955 to 2008. It's also the story of Adam Powell, who is a little boy whose family just moved into the house across the street from the theater in 1955. As the years go by, Adam sneaks into the theater, is befriended by Neil, who works there, becomes an assistant manager, and eventually owns the drive in. The stories are connected to the movies that were hits during the particular years and trace the declining fortunes of most drive ins. Some stories include harsh language, violence, and a rape scene.

Sanbe, Kei
Testarotho Volume 1. DC Comics/CMX 2005 192p. Illustration
Grades: 11 12 Adult   **741.5; Fic**
1. Fantasy graphic novels; 2. Manga; 3. Shonen manga; 4. Graphic novels
1-4012-0742-1, $9.99
In a dark future, rival warriors of warring sects persecute nonbelievers and die for their faith. But a disillusioned young novice and a deadly gun-toting priest may be about to change all that... Young Capria has completed her studies at the Arsenal School and has begun her internship with the Elysia Unification Council under Father Garrincha. But no lessons could prepare this sheltered novice for the outside world, where rebels battle against the dreaded Testarotho." Heretics are tried and burned at the stake, warring religious factions battle for power, and the common people live a miserable life in feudal servitude. Can she bring a spark of hope to a world filled with destruction and madness? Maybe if she lives long enough. The book includes nudity, harsh language, and graphic violence.

Sandoval, Tony
Doomboy. Tony Sandoval; translated by Mike Kennedy. Magnetic Press 2014 136 p. Illustration
Grades: 10 11 12 Adult   **741.5; Fic**
1. Rock musicians — Fiction; 2. Teenagers — Fiction
0991332474; 9780991332472, $24.99
Eisner Nominee: Best Publication for Teens (2014)
"Sandoval . . . places cartoon artwork—featuring a wan color palette and oddly large heads on slender bodies—and a well-detailed social scene replete with bands, friendships, breakups and jealousies against the familiar context of adolescent loss and longing to produce a story that is intimate in scale yet epic in emotional terms." LJ

Sanjo, Riku
Beet the Vandel Buster Vol. 1. Viz Media/Shonen Jump 2004 178p. Illustration
Grades: 6 7 8 9 10 11 12   **741.5; Fic**
1. Adventure graphic novels; 2. Fantasy graphic novels; 3. Manga; 4. Shonen manga; 5. Graphic novels
1-59116-690-X, $7.99
The Vandel Busters are a roving band of certified monster destroyers. Beet's biggest ambition in life is to become a Buster, but what can you say about a monster hunter who can barely stand the pain when he receives the mystical brand of a Level 1 Vandel Buster? Still, Beet is ready for action, and when a nearby town is invaded by demons, he rushes to help—without a clue as to how to trounce even a single member of the rampaging horde. But not knowing how formidable the Vandels are might work to his advantage because he doesn't know enough to be scared. Beet is about to learn that being a hero may be more than he bargained for... The book includes monster fighting action.

Santacruz, Juan
Hulk: misunderstood monster, v1. Writer, Paul Benjamin; illustrated by David Nakayama and Juan Santacruz. Marvel 2007 Illustration
Grades: 5 6 7 8 9   **741.5; Fic**
978-0-7851-2642-3, $6.99; 0-7851-2642-2

Santiago, Wilfred
21: the story of Roberto Clemente : a graphic novel. Wilfred Santiago.. Fantagraphics 2011 148p. Illustration
Grades: 11 12 Adult   **92; 741.5**
1. Baseball; 2. Baseball players; 3. Clemente, Roberto, 1934-1972; 4. Graphic novels
978-1-56097-892-3, $22.99
This book "is an all-ages graphic biography of baseball star Roberto Clemente: No other baseball player dominated the 1960s like him and no other Latin American player achieved his numbers. '21' chronicles his early days growing up in rural Puerto Rico, the highlights of his career (including the 1960s World Series), the prejudice he faced, his private life and his humanitarian mission." (trplteens.wordpress.com)
Includes bibliographic references.

Sardar, Ziauddin
Introducing Cultural Studies, Third Ed.. Ziauddin Sardar and Borin Van Loon. Totem Books 2005 176p. Illustration
Grades: 10 11 12 Adult   **301; 741.5**
1. Sociology; 2. Graphic novels
978-1-84046-587-7, $12.95
Cultural studies is a discipline that claims not to be a discipline, a radical critical approach for understanding racial, national, social, and gender identities. This book uses cartoons and a spare text to provide an introductory look, covering its origins in Great Britain and the U.S., examining the ideas of its leading exponents and providing a flavor of its use around the world. The book includes a list of books for further reading."

Introducing Islam. Ziauddin Sardar, Zafar Abbas Malik; edited by Richard Appignanesi. Totem Books 2004 176p. Illustration
Grades: 10 11 12 Adult   **297; 741.5**
1. Islam; 2. Graphic novels
1-84046-582-4, $12.95
This introductory guide recounts the history of Islam from the birth of the Prophet Muhammad to its status as a global culture and political force today, explaining the message of the Qur'ran and the features of Islamic law. Using cartoons and a spare text, this book shows how Muslims everywhere are trying to live their faith and are struggling to shape new Islamic ideas and ideals in a globalized world. It includes a list of books for further reading, and definitions of Islamic terms are defined in the index.

Sarkar, Sam
Caliber: first canon of justice. Writer Sam Sarkar; artist Garrie Gastonny. Radical Books 2009 Un Illustration
Grades: 10 11 12 Adult   **741.5; Fic**
1. Adventure graphic novels; 2. Arthurian romances — Adaptations; 3. Western stories; 4. Graphic novels
978-1-935417-00-2, $14.95
Arthurian legend gets updated to the American West of the nineteenth century. In the town of Telacoma in the Pacific Northwest, certain men, led by Mr. Leary, run things the way they want, which includes getting the railroad to come through town and bring more business. Years before, these men caused Captain Pendergon and his men to die in a forced battle with the Native Americans on the reservation which was needed for the railroad. Now, Pendergon's son Arthur has returned to reclaim his birthright. Jean Michel Whitefeather is a shaman who once thought Arthur's father was the one to wield the gun forged from the metal of the sword Excalibur. Now he decides he must help Arthur fight against the corruption in Telacoma. They won't be alone; his old friend Gwen works in the saloon, a gunfighter named Lance comes to town, and Gwen's friend Sheng Yi helps them because she knows Arthur will help to free her father. Readers who know the stories of King Arthur and the Knights of the Round Table will find familiar story elements and characters, while those who don't know much about the old stories can enjoy a new Western adventure. The book includes violence and some partial nudity and mild sexual situations.

Sato, Yuki
Yokai doctor, vol. 1. Del Rey Manga 2009 218p. Illustration
Grades: 10 11 12   **741.5; Fic**
1. Humorous graphic novels; 2. Manga; 3. Supernatural graphic novels; 4. Graphic novels
978-0-345-51238-3, $10.99
Yokai are mysterious, troublemaking demons and spirits that have tormented Japan for centuries. High school student Kotoko's grandfather exorcised them for a living, and Kotoko has inherited the ability to see yokai, although she doesn't really have the skills to exorcise them; that doesn't stop her from trying when her fellow students beg her to do so. Then she meets transfer student Kuro, who actually tries to help the yokai! He's a yokai doctor, and

somehow she finds herself helping him. The story includes lots of innuendo, as Kuro finds the human female form to be irresistably fascinating and he manages to accidentally touch girls' breasts, see up girls' skirts, stumble into the girls' locker room, and other bits of fan service. Despite that, he's rather naive and endearing as he tries to fit into the human world and high school society.

Satrapi, Marjane
Chicken with plums. Pantheon Books 2006 84p. Illustration
Grades: 11 12 Adult   **92; 741.5**
1. Biographical graphic novels; 2. Khan, Nasser Ali, d 1958; 3. Lute players; 4. Graphic novels
0-375-42415-6; 978-0-375-42415-1, $16.95
              LC 2006-43156
In graphic novel format, the author chronicles "the life of her great-uncle Nasser Ali Khan. A revered musician, he takes to his bed and refuses sustenance after his frustrated wife breaks his tar—an Iranian lute—over her knee. It takes him eight days to die, and in that time Satrapi reveals the futures of his children and unearths his past. . . . Satrapi's deceptively simple, remarkably powerful drawings match the precise but flexible prose she employs in adapting to her multiple roles as educator, folklorist, and grand-niece." New Yorker

★ The **complete** Persepolis. Pantheon Books 2007 341p. Illustration
Grades: 11 12 Adult   **92; 741.5**
1. Autobiographical graphic novels; 2. Cartoonists; 3. Iran; 4. Satrapi, Marjane, 1969-; 5. Graphic novels
978-0-375-71483-2, $24.95
              LC 2007-60106
Ignatz Award: Outstanding Graphic Novel (2005)
Also published in two separate volumes 2003-2004
"Persepolis is the story of Satrapi's unforgettable childhood and coming of age within a large and loving family in Tehran during the Islamic Revolution; of the contradictions between private life and public life in a country plagued by political upheaval; of her high school years in Vienna facing the trials of adolescence far from her family; of her homecoming—both sweet and terrible; and, finally, of her self-imposed exile from her beloved homeland. It is the chronicle of a girlhood and adolescence at once outrageous and familiar, a young life entwined with the history of her country yet filled with the universal trials and joys of growing up." (Publisher's note)

Embroideries. Pantheon Books 2005 134p. Illustration
Grades: 11 12 Adult   **955; Fic**
1. Iran; 2. Women — Iran; 3. Graphic novels
0-375-42305-2, $16.95
              LC 2004-58660
This book "explores the lives of Iranian women young and old. The book begins with Satrapi arriving for afternoon tea at her grandmother's house. There, her mother, aunt and their group of friends tell stories about their lives as women, and, more specifically, the men they've lived with and through." Publ Wkly
"Discussions of sex are frank and explicit and laced with high humor. . . . Satrapi's simple black-and-white

cartooning style is tremendously effective, expertly portraying emotional nuances with just a few lines." Libr J

Satterlee, Chuck
Of Bitter Souls, Vol. 1: Saints & Sinners, Collected Edition. Created and written by Chuck Satterlee; art by Norm Breyfoble. Markosia Enterprises 2006 Un Illustration
Grades: 10 11 12 Adult   741.5; Fic
1. Superhero graphic novels; 2. Supernatural graphic novels; 3. Graphic novels
1-905692-07-2, $16.95
In New Orleans, a pastor named Secord chooses four very flawed individuals: a crooked cop, a prostitute, a drug addict, and an inveterate gambler, and grants them powers based on their character flaws. They use their powers against arcane enemies, such as vampires, ghosts, werewolves, demons, and other supernatural creatures, as they learn to trust each other and themselves. The book includes a pin-up gallery by other artists, and several prose stories.
Originally published as Of Bitter Souls issues #1-6.

Sava, Scott Christian
The **dreamland** chronicles book two. Blue Dream Studios 2007 176p. Illustration
Grades: 5 6 7 8 9 10 11 12   741.5; Fic
1. Adventure graphic novels; 2. Dreaming; 3. Fantasy graphic novels; 4. Graphic novels
978-0-9789168-3-1, $19.95
LC 2007-932090
Alexander Carter continues his adventures in Dreamland every night, as he and his friends escape the Dragon Lord Nicodemus' prison with the help of Felicity, a catgirl with tiger stripes, and continue their search for the King and Queen of Elves, Nastajia's parents. The problem is, Nastajia doesn't trust Felicity and thinks she could be a spy for Nicodemus. Meanwhile, the friends find themselves in the undersea cave of the Kraken, which is a much more immediate danger to them all.

The **Dreamland** Chronicles: Book One. Blue Dream Studios 2006 Un Illustration
Grades: 5 6 7 8 9 10 11 12 Adult   741.5; Fic
1. Adventure graphic novels; 2. Fantasy graphic novels; 3. Graphic novels
978-0-9789168-0-0, $19.95
College student Alexander Carter has found a key that takes him back to the land of his childhood dreams. Every night he enters Dreamland, a magical world filled with dragons, fairies, and giants. Reunited with his childhood friends Paddington, Kiwi, and Nastajia, Alexander now embarks on a quest to save Dreamland from war with the Nightmare Realm. But, will his daytime life as a college student interfere? Colorful 3-D animated art makes the story look like a computer game.

Gary the pirate. Art by Tracy Bailey. IDW Publishing 2009 112p. Illustration
Grades: 4 5 6 7 8 9   741.5; Fic
1. Adventure graphic novels; 2. Humorous graphic novels; 3. Pirates; 4. Graphic novels
978-1-60010-312-4, $12.99
Gary, a teenage Sky Pirate from the secret floating city Pirate Cove, owes Stinky a lot for ruining his watch,

dumping a chocolate ice cream sundae on his head, and messing up his ship all accidentally, because Gary is a klutz. Gary is also a lousy thief for a pirate. While searching for treasure, he sees thirteen-year-old Judy in the park with her grandmother. She complains to her grandmother about all the boys she knows how could she ever want to date any of them" They're either bullies, computer nerds, too cool for anyone, or just totally clueless. When klutzy Gary breaks into her bedroom in search of the brooch her grandmother just gave her (it's treasure, after all), she wants him to take her on his ship to see Pirate Cove. True to his klutzy nature, though, Gary manages to crash his ship into Stinky's ship, and now they're in big trouble. The pirates may brandish their swords, but there's no actual violence, only cartoony action.

The **lab:** hey . . . test this!. Astonish Factory 2004 120p. Illustration
Grades: 5 6 7 8 9   741.5; Fic
1. Humorous graphic novels; 2. Science fiction graphic novels; 3. Graphic novels
0-9721259-3-0, $14.95
"A collection of previously published comics and original stories that highlight the working relationship between Livingston, a scientist mole, and his goofball assistant, Esteban, a weasel whose ultrasensitivity to chemicals makes him an excellent test subject for new products. With bright, colorful pictures, the stories usually consist of observing Esteban's outlandish reactions to Livingston's concoctions, such as floating to the ceiling, shrinking to microscopic size, or singing uncontrollably." SLJ

Pet Robots. Art by Diego Jourdan. Blue Dream Studios 2007 Un Illustration
Grades: 3 4 5 6 7 8 9   741.5; Fic
1. Humorous graphic novels; 2. Robots; 3. Science fiction graphic novels; 4. Graphic novels
978-0-9789168-2-4, $19.95
LC 2007902577
Four students - Jake, Chris, Tammy, and Tommy - get lost while on a field trip to the Rooty Tooty Toy Company. In their quest to find they way back to the rest of the class, the stumble upon a room inhabited only by four military robots. That night they're followed home by the robots: Skye, Rock, Aqua, and Wind. As the kids get to know their new robotic friends, they must also avoid the evil owner of the Rooty Tooty Toy Company, Vandenburger Meisterburger. He wants his robots back and he's willing to do anything to get them.

Scalera, Buddy
Decoy: Storm of the Century. Buddy Scalera and Courtney Huddleston. Penny-Farthing Press 2003 151p. Illustration
Grades: 5 6 7 8 9 10 11 12 Adult   741.5; Fic
1. Adventure graphic novels; 2. Friendship; 3. Science fiction graphic novels; 4. Graphic novels
0-9719012-0-1, $17.95
He's the champion of justice and fast one-liners, a green shape-shifting alien from the planet Nacrum whose primary purpose in life is to protect the innocent and to one-up his roommate in an ongoing battle of pranks and bad jokes. All

goes well until a subterranean encounter with a long-forgotten threat changes Decoy's life and threatens the friendship with his only ally on the planet: his best friend. Faced with an identity crisis of cosmic proportions, loveable alien Decoy must team up with his buddy, rookie cop Bobby Luck, to battle meteorological and psychological disaster.

Schaffer, Dan
  The **Scribbler:** Unzip Your Head. Image Comics 2006 Un Illustration
  Grades: 11 12 Adult   **741.5; Fic**
  1. Multiple personality; 2. Mystery graphic novels; 3. Graphic novels
  978-1-58240-700-5, $7.99
  Suki has multiple personalities; she hears voices; she's nuts. But she's getting experimental treatment, the Siamese Burn Therapy, an experimental machine designed to eliminate multiple personalities. And it works. Suki is down to her last unwanted identity, but now she's losing time and the machine is changing into something that's going to turn her world inside out. And that unwanted identity... what do you do when it turns out to be you" The book includes violence, strong language, and some sexual situations.

Schigiel, Gregg
  X-babies: stars reborn. Written by Gregg Schigiel ; art by Jacob Chabot. Marvel Worldwide 2010 Un Illustration
  Grades: 4 5 6 7 8 9 10   **741.5; Fic**
  1. Adventure graphic novels; 2. Cyclops (Fictional character); 3. Humorous graphic novels; 4. Nightcrawler (Fictional character); 5. Storm (Fictional character); 6. Superhero graphic novels; 7. Wolverine (Fictional character); 8. X-Men (Fictional characters); 9. Graphic novels
  978-0-7851-4380-2, $14.99
  In Mojoworld, where everything is televised, Mojo had created the X-Babies, child-sized versions of the X-Men, and the X-Babies have been the top-rated stars, but then Mr. Veech takes over and replaces the X-Babies with cute, safe, friendly versions who don't fight, but do such things as grow and eat! vegetables. The X-Babies know something is wrong, and they set out to find out what's happening. As they break out of their imprisonment and seek answers, they encounter lots of modified cutesy versions of other kid heroes. Younger readers will enjoy the wise-cracking kiddie versions of Wolverine, Storm, Cyclops, Rogue, Colossus, Kitty Pryde, and Nightcrawler. The other kid heroes whom the X-Babies meet were stars of Marvel's mid-1980s kid-centric Star Comics line, including Top Dog, Wally the Wizard, Planet Terry, and Royal Roy. There is no bad language (Wolverine says "poot" a lot), and lots of action with little violence.
  Originally published as X-Babies issues #14

Schrag, Ariel
  Stuck in the middle: seventeen comics from an unpleasant age. Edited by Ariel Schrag. Viking 2007 210p. Illustration
  Grades: 7 8 9 10 11 12   **741.5; Fic**
  1. Middle schools; 2. Teenagers; 3. Graphic novels
  978-0-670-06221-8, $18.99
                                      LC 2006-52581

This book collects seventeen short stories about the perils of middle school, each by independent comics creators, including editor Schrag, her younger sister Tania Schrag, Aaron Renier, Daniel Clowes, Gabrielle Bell, and others. Stories include the experience of being the new kid in school, getting betrayed by your best friend, being a Jewish nonathlete at a Christian sports summer camp, finding a creative outlet despite having attention deficit disorder, and more of the everyday bad situations and joys of being twelve and thirteen years old. Some harsh language (one story is also called "Shit") reflects the reality of young teen life.

Schreiber, Ellen
  Vampire kisses: blood relatives volume 2. Art by Rem. HarperCollins/Tokyopop 2008 Un Illustration
  Grades: 7 8 9 10 11 12   **741.5; Fic**
  1. Horror graphic novels; 2. Romance graphic novels; 3. Vampires; 4. Graphic novels
  978-0-06-134082-6, $9.99
  Raven and Alexander face enough challenges about their relationship—she's human, he's a vampire—but things get really complicated when Alexander's half-vampire cousin Claude shows up with his gang. They're looking for a stash of vials filled with blood that will turn them into pure vampires. Since that would mean disastrous trouble, Raven and Alexander must come up with a plan to outwit Claude. This is the second volume of Schreiber's global manga story based on her vampire romance novels for teens.

Schultz, Brandon
  Blokhedz, Vol. 1: Genesis. Created by Mark & Mike Davis ; written by Mark & Mike Davis, Brandon Schultz. Pocket Books 2007 Un Illustration
  Grades: 8 9 10 11 12   **741.5; Fic**
  1. Fantasy graphic novels; 2. Rap music; 3. Graphic novels
  978-1-4165-4073-1, $12.95
  In the decaying Monarch projects of Empire City, teenage Blak aspires to become a big rap star, while his older brother Konzaquenz, who recently got out of prison for gang activity, wants to unite all the Monarch neighborhoods. Old friend Bloko, who runs the local recording industry, and the gangs, sees Konz as a problem. When gang members kill Konz, Blak gets drawn into Bloko's schemes. What no one realizes, yet, is that Blak's rhymes have a mystical power, fed by the Original People upon whose burial grounds Monarch was built. Soon Blak will have to choose his path. Bad words are present but not completely spelled out ("sh*t" for example), so the content is appropriate for older middle school and high school readers.
  "This is urban fiction mixed with the supernatural and depicted in a colorful, dynamic, animated style." (VOYA - upcoming, Aug 07 issue)

Schultz, Mark
  The **stuff** of life: a graphic guide to genetics and DNA. Written by Mark Schultz; art by Zander Cannon and Kevin Cannon. Hill and Wang 2009 150p. Illustration
  Grades: 9 10 11 12 Adult   **576.5; 741.5**
  1. Genetics; 2. Graphic novels
  978-0-8090-8946-8, $30; 978-0-8090-8947-5 (pa), $14.95

Eisner and Harvey Award winning writer Schultz uses the device of an alien writing a report to describe genetics and DNA in five chapters, from molecular structure of Earth organisms to sexual reproduction to genetic inheritance to genetic counseling and the genome Project and beyond. The black and white cartoons add some humor to the sound information, and the book includes a list of suggested reading ranging from magazines and books to websites, along with a glossary of terms.

Includes bibliographical references

Superman and Batman Versus Aliens and Predators. Writer, Mark Schultz; artist, Ariel Olivetti; letterer, Todd Klein. DC Comics/Dark Horse Comics 2007 Un Illustration
Grades: 9 10 11 12 Adult   **741.5; Fic**
1. Aliens (Fictional characters); 2. Batman (Fictional character); 3. Predators (Fictional characters); 4. Superhero graphic novels; 5. Superman (Fictional character); 6. Graphic novels
978-1-4012-1328-2, $12.99

DC's iconic heroes square off against two of the most popular movie aliens in a joint publishing venture. There's lots of fighting action, but not as intense as in the movies, and with little harsh language.

A lost colony of Predators has lived under a dormant volcano in the Andes mountains for centuries, but volcanic activity has begun, their home is unsafe, and they've come out, and started killing humans. Superman and Batman have fought them before and want to send them back to their home planet, but the Terrestrial Defense Initiative wants to destroy all the aliens and they're willing to kill Superman and Batman to do it.

Schutz, Diana
The **Amazing** Adventures of the Escapist Vol. 3. Dark Horse Comics 2006 168p. Illustration
Grades: 8 9 10 11 12 Adult   **741.5; Fic**
1. Adventure graphic novels; 2. Superhero graphic novels; 3. Graphic novels
978-1-59307-492-0, $14.95

This volume of The Escapist features the late Will Eisner's return to the Spirit, in a crossover tale with the Escapist. This story became Eisner's last comics work, completed just two weeks before the death of the comics godfather. Also in this volume is the comics writing debut of award-winning author and Guggenheim fellow Chris Offutt, illustrated by Thomas Yeates. Dan Best and Eddie Campbell contribute a fully painted story from the 1939 World's Fair in Empire City, and 2004 Russ Manning Award winner Eric Wight brings a polemic story from writer Jason Hall to life. Among the other notable contributors are Howard Chaykin, Paul Grist, Shawn Martinbrough, David Hahn, Roy Thomas, Matt Wagner and indie stalwarts Jeffrey Brown and Jason. The book includes some violence.

Schwark, Mike
Van Von Hunter Vol. 1. By Ron Kaulfersch and Mike Schwark. Kaplan Publishing/Tokyopop 2007 173p. Illustration (Kaplan SAT/ACT vocabulary-building manga)
Grades: 8 9 10 11 12 Adult   **741.5; Fic**

1. Adventure graphic novels; 2. Fantasy graphic novels; 3. Humorous graphic novels; 4. Vocabulary; 5. Graphic novels
978-1-4277-5494-3, $9.99

The forces of evil have returned to the Kingdom of Dikay. All hope is lost. There will be strife and clamorous discord. The people need a hero. Is there no one around who can vanquish the malevolent tyranny" Uhm. . . . Anyone. . . . Anyone" Enter the legendary Van Von Hunter, the Hunter of Evil. . . . This Kaplan edition includes more than 300 SAT/ACT vocabulary words identified and defined on the pages where they appear.

Schwartz, David B.
Meltdown: The Definitive Collection. Written by David B. Schwartz; artwork and lettering by Sean Wang. Image Comics 2007 Un Illustration
Grades: 10 11 12 Adult   **741.5; Fic**
1. Superhero graphic novels; 2. Graphic novels
978-1-58240-821-7, $14.99

Caliente, the Flare, is dying. His own super-powers are eating him alive, melting him down from within. During his final days, Cal must struggle with his volatile life and the questionable decisions he's made along the way, hoping to find redemption before time runs out. See the final moments that prove what a hero can - and should - be. The story has considerable violence.

Schwarzman, Mat
Beginner's Guide to Community-Based Arts. Keith Knight, Mat Schwarzman and many others. New Village Press 2005 171p. Illustration
Grades: 10 11 12 Adult   **741.5; 701**
1. Art and society; 2. Graphic novels
978-0-9766054-3-0
                                        LC 2005929142

Ten transformative local arts projects come alive in this illustrated training manual for youth leaders and teachers. This energetic guidebook demonstrates the enormous power of art in grass-roots social change. It presents proven models of community-based arts programs, plus techniques, discussion questions, and plentiful resources.

Schweizer, Chris
★ **Crogan's** loyalty. Chris Schweizer; [edited by] James Lucas Jones. Oni Press, Inc. 2012 150 p. Color; Illustration
Grades: 8 9 10 11 12 Adult   **741.5**
1. Adventure graphic novels; 2. United States — History — 1775-1783, Revolution
9781934964408, $14.99; 1934964409
                                        LC 2011943514

"Schweizer takes another bite out of history in this story of two brothers divided by the American Revolution. Charlie, the elder Crogan and a Loyalist ranger, is infuriated that his younger brother would turn rebel, stating 'There's a passion that makes most young men wanna tear society down because they ain't in charge of it.' Meanwhile, Will, a colonial scout, is no less incensed that his older brother would stand for a tyrant against his own country." (Booklist)

★ **Crogan's** march. Oni Press 2009 212p. Illustration
Grades: 8 9 10 11 12 Adult   **741.5; Fic**
1. Adventure graphic novels; 2. Imperialism; 3. North Africa — World history — 20th century; 4. Graphic novels
978-1-934964-24-8, $14.95

When brothers Eric and Cory squabble at the dinner table, their father tells them the story of Peter Crogan, one of their ancestors, who fought in the French Foreign Legion in 1912. Crogan's five-year term of service is one month from completion when he's asked to stay and become an officer. His unit is stationed in North Africa, where the French hold territory and depend on the French Foreign Legion to police the territory, putting down the rebellious attacks of the Tuaregs. He finds himself torn between the heroic Captain Poitelet (who tends to be the sole survivor of various battles) and the grizzled sergeant who actually cares about the people the Legion polices. When Crogan's unit escorts a caravan that endures an attack by Tuaregs, the captain's reckless actions endanger everyone, and Crogan must find help. Schweizer's story includes the kind of violence military actions cause, but very little in the way of bad language. Some may wince at the heavily French-accented English of some of the characters (—zee Daughters of France send zem out to all of zee units," etc.). This action-packed historical fiction graphic novel will appeal to teens, but adults who remember such novels as Beau Geste by Percival Christopher Wren (and the movies, of course) will also enjoy reading Schweizer's tale.

This book is part of The Crogan Adventures series
Sequel to: Crogan's vengeance (2008)

★ **Crogan's** vengeance. Book design by Keith Wood; edited by James Lucas Jones with Jill Beaton. Oni Press 2008 185p. Illustration
Grades: 8 9 10 11 12 Adult   **741.5; Fic**
1. Adventure graphic novels; 2. Pirates; 3. Graphic novels
978-1-934964-06-4, $14.95

Catfoot Crogan serves as an honest and honorable sailor on a ship commanded by an unjust captain when the ship is taken over by pirates. In order to save their lives, the sailors all take the oath to become pirates, but Crogan immediately runs afoul of D'Or, a brutal man who enjoys torturing others. Catfoot is a pirate, but he's determined to remain as honest and honorable as he can be, which continually puts him in danger. This swashbuckling tale shows a less romantic story than Rafael Sabatini's Captain Blood, with more violence, but it is more action-oriented than merely violent.

"Filled with mutiny, ferocious storms, shark-infested waters, commandeering of ships, and—of course—swashbuckling sword fights, this book has high teen appeal." SLJ
Part of the Crogan Adventures series

Scott, Jerry
★ **Chillax.** By Jerry Scott; illustrated by Jim Borgman. HarperTeen 2013 256 p. Illustration
Grades: 7 8 9 10   **Fic**
1. Concerts — Fiction; 2. Teenagers — Fiction
9780062228512, $9.99; 006222851X
LC 2013931374
"Jeremy Duncan, high school sophomore and future rock god, offers up a comedic outlook on teenage life,

including school, parents, chores, bands, and friends. Jeremy and his best friend, Hector Garcia, are planning to [go] to a rock concert without parental supervision. But the . . . concert falls on the same night their friend Tim is donating bone marrow for his mom, a cancer patient. Jeremy and Hector are determined to go to the show for Tim." (Publisher's note)

Scrambly, Crab
The **13th** of Never. SLG Publishing 2004 72p. Illustration
Grades: 9 10 11 12 Adult   **741.5; Fic**
1. Fantasy graphic novels; 2. Horror graphic novels; 3. Graphic novels
0-943151-90-2, $7.95

Cursed with bad luck and trapped in a monotonous life, an unfortunate young man named Zazil longs to escape from the drudgery of his waking life and the troubled thoughts that haunt him. A good luck charm that Zazil finds in a dusty curio shop proves to be his ticket away from the mundane, but it brings him everything but good luck. When soul-stealing creatures called Charnoks pursue Zazil through strange lands and ghost trains, he must use his wits and courage to escape them - and finally face his past. This illustrated novel has no bad language or real violence, but has a macabre feel.

Seagle, Steven T.
American Virgin: Head. Steven T. Seagle; art by Becky Cloonan. DC Comics/Vertigo 2006 112p. Illustration
Grades: 11 12 Adult   **741.5; Fic**
1. Mystery graphic novels; 2. Revenge; 3. Graphic novels
978-1-4012-1065-6, $9.99

Adam Chamberlain is a youth minister and author, head of a national virginity movement. When his fiancee, Cassie, is brutally murdered in Africa, Adam travels there with his black-sheep stepsister Cyndi, trying to discover meaning in Cassie's death. Confronted by hit men, paparazzi, pornography, and even the voice of God, Adam finds himself lost in a vortex of spiritually uncharted territory. This series has nudity, strong language, and violence.

Kafka. By Steven T. Seagle & Stefano Gaudiano; lettering by Richard Starkings. Active Images 2006 Un Illustration
Grades: 10 11 12 Adult   **741.5; Fic**
1. Adventure graphic novels; 2. Mystery graphic novels; 3. Graphic novels
0-9766761-5-X, $14.99

Dan Hutton lost everything ... his name, his past, his wife, his life. Having lived in a witness relocation program for years, Dan is told his new identity has been compromised, by two different groups who each claim to be CIA operatives. Unable to trust anyone, Dan runs back to the world that took everything he loved, hoping he can reclaim his past. The book is filled with suspense and action with very little violence.

Sandman Mystery Theatre: The Scorpion. Matt Wagner, Steven T. Seagle, writers; Guy Davis, artist; David Hornung, colorist; John Costanza, letterer. DC Comics 2006 104p. Illustration
Grades: 10 11 12 Adult   **741.5; Fic**

1. Mystery graphic novels; 2. Graphic novels
1-4012-1040-6, $12.99

This reimagination of the original Golden Age Sandman finds Wesley Dodds still driven by his dreams to fight injustice in the dark of night while trying to make sense of a world slipping into the madness of war. Taking on a twisted anti-capitalist vigilante wielding a poisoned whip who calls himself the Scorpion, Dodds finds himself closer than ever to death—and to revealing his secret life to his paramour, Dian Belmont. Readers will find some harsh language, including ethnic slurs uttered by villains, and some violence.

Secret identities: the Asian American superhero anthology
New Press 2009 194p. Illustration
Grades: 9 10 11 12 Adult   **741.5; Fic**
1. Asian Americans; 2. Superhero graphic novels; 3. Graphic novels
978-1-59558-398-7, $21.95

LC 2009-1536

Yang, Shen, Chow, and coeditor Jerry Ma have put together a collection of twenty-six stories by Asian American creators about Asian American superheroes. The book is divided into sections: War and Remembrance, Many Masks, When Worlds Collide, Girl Power, Ordinary Heroes, and From Headline to Hero. The Preface, the Prologue, all section introductions, and the Epilogue, are all done in comic book format. Creators include Gene Luen Yang, Greg Pak, Dustin Nguyen, Kazu Kibuishi, Cliff Chiang, Christine Norrie, and many more. Some stories deal with the Nisei soldiers of the 100th Battalion/442nd Regimental Combat Team during World War II, others confront the idea that the Asian character can only be the sidekick, still others explore the stereotypical attitudes of some Americans toward Asian Americans. The book includes some violence and some harsh language.

Segami, Akira
Kagetora, volume 1. Del Rey Manga 2008 202p. Illustration
Grades: 8 9 10 11 12   **741.5; Fic**
1. Humorous graphic novels; 2. Manga; 3. Martial arts; 4. Romance graphic novels; 5. Graphic novels
978-0-345-49141-6, $10.95

Young ninja Kagetora arrives at the Toudou family dojo on assignment, and he learns that he must teach martial arts to the family hime (princess), Yuki. The problem is, Yuki is a total, absolute klutz; she's also tiny and absolutely cute and charming. As he tries his best to train her, Kagetora finds himself doing the forbidden—he's falling for Yuki. How can he perform his duty? On top of that, Yuki's best friend Aki, one of the Toudou's top students, has been protecting Yuki for years and resents Kagetora's presence. The book includes a lot of fan service, which actually ties into the plot as Kagetora can't help but look at Yuki, even though he knows that his feelings are not appropriate.

Seino, Shizuru
Heaven!! Volume 1. Tokyopop 2007 Un Illustration
Grades: 9 10 11 12 Adult   **741.5; Fic**

1. Fantasy graphic novels; 2. Manga; 3. Romance graphic novels; 4. Shojo manga; 5. Graphic novels
978-1-59816-816-7, $9.99

Rinne is a girl who not only can see and exorcise ghosts with a paper fan (called a harisen). When she's saved from becoming a ghost by the school punk, he ends up in a coma. Fortunately, that doesn't stop their unique relationship from forging: Rinne and her rescuer's now-disembodied spirit must defend his prone body from being possessed by a muddled collection of local ghosts. When Rinne fails in her task, an ancient playboy god takes over the punk's body—leaving him to inhabit a pink stuffed monkey. There's some harsh language and quite a bit of mildly suggestive behavior.

Sen, Jai
★ **Garlands** of Moonlight. Written by Jai Sen; illustrated by Rizky Wasisto Edi. Shoto Press 2002 86p. Illustration
Grades: 9 10 11 12 Adult   **741.5; Fic**
1. Horror graphic novels; 2. Vampires; 3. Graphic novels
0-9717564-0-6, $4.59

LC 03-311055

Silent and merciless, a creature of darkness has come to prey on an island village. Babies vanish, mothers are murdered, and the threat of evil grows with each night. The village becomes a battleground as the onrush of the twentieth century clashes with tradition—and the restless spirits of the island's mythical past... Set in late colonial Indonesia, this book relates a Malay vampire legend in graphic novel format. Printed in a black and silver duotone, the book captures the feel of turn-of-the-century daguerreotype photographs. There is some violence.
Malay Mysteries Book 1

Seo, Eun-Jin
Fantamir Volume 1. Tokyopop 2007 Un Illustration
Grades: 8 9 10 11 12   **741.5; Fic**
1. Fantasy graphic novels; 2. Manwha; 3. Graphic novels
978-1-4278-0290-3, $9.99

When a mysterious incident causes Mir to lose her magical abilities, she decides to retire as successor to the Sorceress and become a student in a normal school. To her surprise, she enrolls in a school with a special connection to her family, and before she knows it, she's in trouble with the uber-popular Ba-ri, who has challenged her to a duel.

Peppermint Volume 1. Tokyopop 2006 Un Illustration
Grades: 8 9 10 11 12   **741.5; Fic**
1. Humorous graphic novels; 2. Manwha; 3. Romance graphic novels; 4. Graphic novels
1-59816-681-6, $9.99

What do you do when true love is just beyond your reach? Hey is a normal high school girl who has a crush on the hot teen singer EZ. But whenever she tries to work up the nerve to confess her feeling toward him, middle schooler Eo always gets in the middle of things. Pop star EZ may never think of Hey as anything more than a fan ... But dealing with people thinking Eo is her boyfriend may get Hey in big trouble.

Seth

Clyde Fans Book 1. Drawn & Quarterly 2004 156p. Illustration

Grades: 11 12 Adult   **741.5; Fic**
1. Graphic novels
1-896597-84-X, $19.95

This book focuses on the lives of two brothers and their fan manufacturing company. After one more disastrous attempt at selling, Simon returns to the office defeated and unsure of what he'll do next. Even after studying manuals on the art of selling, he still can't seem to clinch that final deal. In the eyes of his brother Abraham, he is a failure. Simon's plight is reminiscent of Arthur Miller's play, "Death of a Salesman." Here, Seth explores the complex and fascinating relationship of the two brothers behind Clyde Fans. There's one brief scene of incidental nudity.

Wimbledon Green: The Greatest Comic Book Collector in the World. Drawn & Quarterly 2005 Un Illustration

Grades: 11 12 Adult   **741.5; Fic**
1. Collectors and collecting; 2. Graphic novels
1-896597-93-9, $19.95

Meet Wimbledon Green, the self-proclaimed world's greatest comic-book collector who brokered the world's best comic-book deal in the history of collecting. Comic-book retailers, auctioneers, and conventioneers from around North America, as well as Green's collecting rivals, weigh in on the man and his vast collection of comic books. Are Green's intentions honorable? Does he truly love comics or is he driven by the need to conquer? Lastly, is he really even Wimbledon Green?

Seto, Andy

The **Four** Constables Vol. 1. ComicsOne/DrMaster Publications 2004 Un Illustration

Grades: 8 9 10 11 12 Adult   **741.5; Fic**
1. Adventure graphic novels; 2. Martial arts; 3. Mystery graphic novels; 4. Graphic novels
1-58899-383-3, $13.95

Four of China's supremely skilled assassin/detectives serve only their Master Zhuge Zhen-Wo - The Little Flower, who in turn is head bodyguard and advisor for China's all powerful Emperor. . Yayu Sheng, "Emotionless," is a master of weapons and devices. Yuxia Tie, "Iron Hands," possesses incredible chi and can stop the sharpest blades bare-handed. Lieshan Cui, "Life Snatcher," is highly skilled in light-foot, granting him undaunted legwork and kicks. Lingqi Len, "Cold Blooded," was raised by wolves and since learned to transfer his pain when fighting to strength, enabling him to defeat opponents much stronger than himself. Each of them is entrusted by the Emperor with the power to arrest and execute any corrupt officials or lawless criminals with the Chinese Empire. These Imperial Constables act as protectors. With their venerable skill they root out potential usurpers and discern the cause of many strange occurrences happening during the Sung Dynasty. This is a Chinese manhua series, published in full color and filled with martial arts action.

Volume 1 of 5

Sewell, Anna

Black Beauty. Retold by L.L. Owens ; illustrated by Jennifer Tanner. Stone Arch Books 2006 63p. Illustration

Grades: 3 4 5 6 7 8 9   **741.5; Fic**
1. Sewell, Anna, 1820-1878 — Adaptations; 2. Graphic novels
978-1-59889-046-4, $23.93

Black Beauty, a handsome colt living in Victorian England, has a happy childhood growing up in the peaceful countryside. In his later years, he encounters cruelty, human suffering, and a tragic fire. Things go from bad to worse when his new owners begin renting him out for profit. Black Beauty endures a life of mistreatment and disrespect in a world that shows little regard for the happiness of animals. This adaptation is written for reluctant and struggling readers.

Part of the Graphic Revolve series.

Sexton, Adam

Twain's the adventure of Huckleberry Finn: the Manga edition. Art by Hyeondo Park. Wiley Publishing 2009 186p.

Grades: 5 6 7 8 9 10 11 12   **741.5; Fic**
1. Adventure graphic novels; 2. Authors; 3. Essayists; 4. Humorists; 5. Humorous graphic novels; 6. Memoirists; 7. Novelists; 8. Satirists; 9. Slaves; 10. Twain, Mark, 1835-1910; 11. Graphic novels
978-0-470-15287-4, $9.99

Huckleberry Finn, son of a ne'er-do-well, has been living with Tom Sawyer and his Aunt Polly ever since they helped solve a murder. Now, his father wants Huck's share of the reward money. When Huck gets away, he decides he has to run; he encounters Jim, a slave who has run away from his owner, and they set out on a raft down the Mississippi River, where they encounter other murderers, con artists, thieves, feuding families, and more. This is a manga-style adaptation of Twain's classic adventure. While the original novel has faced challenges because of certain language, this book does not include the inflammatory words.

Sexy Chix: Anthology of Women Cartoonists.

Dark Horse Comics 2006 104p. Illustration

Grades: 10 11 12 Adult   **741.5; Fic**
1. Short stories; 2. Women; 3. Graphic novels
1-59307-238-4, $12.95

Don't let the title fool you - this isn't the average collection of comics featuring impossibly proportioned vixens in spandex. This time around the sexy chix in question are the writers and artists behind the comics, representing some of the best and brightest talent contributing to the medium of comics and graphic novels today. With stories ranging from mainstream adventures to comic shorts to autobiography, Sexy Chix is devoted to the under-recognized contingent of female cartoonists in an overwhelmingly male-oriented industry. It's about time these creators get to tell the stories they want to, and the result is a variety of artistic visions and styles. Among the sexy chicks are New York Times best-selling author Joyce Carol Oates, Eisner Award-winning illustrator Jill Thompson (Scary Godmother), A Distant Soil writer/artist Colleen Doran, Bitchy Bitch creator Roberta Gregory, DC Comics writer Gail Simone, novelist Sarah Grace McCandless (Grosse Pointe Girl) and many, many more.

Some stories include nudity, sexual situations, harsh language, and violence.

Sfar, Joann

Dungeon Vol. 1: Duck Heart. [by] Joann Sfar & Lewis Trondheim. NBM 2003 96p. Illustration
Grades: 7 8 9 10 11 12   741.5; Fic
1. Fantasy graphic novels; 2. Humorous graphic novels; 3. Graphic novels
1-56163-401-8, $14.95

"As a result of some unfortunate accidents, Herbert, usually a lowly messenger in the great Dungeon, is called upon to defend it from all manner of beasties. In his endeavors to become a warrior, he is helped by his friend Marvin the vegetarian dragon and by the Dungeon Keeper. Although there's a solid dose of cartoon-style violence and gore, teens will appreciate Herbert's pseudo-slacker attitude, which turns him into an accidental hero time and time again." Booklist

Other titles in this series are: Dungeon, the early years: the night shirt (2005); Zenith: the barbarian princess (2005)

Dungeon: Parade Vol. 1: A Dungeon Too Many. By Joann Sfar, Lewis Trondheim & Manu Larcenet. NBM 2007 Un Illustration
Grades: 6 7 8 9 10 11 12 Adult   741.5; Fic
1. Adventure graphic novels; 2. Fantasy graphic novels; 3. Humorous graphic novels; 4. Graphic novels
978-1-56163-495-8, $9.95

Marvin the Vegetarian Dragon and Herbert the Duck do battle with the new, rival dungeon next door that is actually a theme park. Then, Herbert finds a magic lamp that has one wish left, and he and Marvin set out on a quest to find a dying sage to get advice on the best wish.

Klezmer, Book One: Tales of the Wild East. First Second Books 2006 140p. Illustration
Grades: 11 12 Adult   741.5
1. Jews; 2. Musicians; 3. Graphic novels
1-59643-198-9

Klezmer tells a tale of love, friendship, survival, and the joy of making music in pre-World War II Eastern Europe. Noah is perfectly content as the leader of a traveling klezmer band, until his bandmates are brutally murdered by rival musicians. He sets out for Odessa alone, but is joined by Chava, a beautiful girl with a voice like an angel. Meanwhile, Yaacov is expelled from his yeshiva for stealing; he too makes his way to Odessa along with Vincenzo, a violinist, and Tshokola, a gypsy entertainer. When these five misfits finally come together, they must set aside their differences and learn to work together (and rock a crowd) through their music. Some nudity and a fair amount of violence make this better for older readers.

Little Vampire Does Kung Fu!. Stories and drawings by Joann Sfar ; colors by Walter. Simon & Schuster Books for Young Readers 2003 Un Illustration
Grades: 4 5 6 7 8 9   741.5; Fic
1. Fantasy graphic novels; 2. Humorous graphic novels; 3. Vampires; 4. Graphic novels
0-689-85769-1, $12.95

LC 2003-045770

Jeffrey the jerk is a bully and everyone knows it. Little Vampire isn't about to stand around and watch him pick on his best friend, Michael. There's only one thing to do: travel to the highest mountain and seek kung fu lessons from the master... There's an icky moment when Little Vampire's monster friends spit up bits of Jeffrey (whom they ate) and they try to put him together again.

The **professor's** daughter. [story by] Joann Sfar & [illustrated by] Emmanuel Guibert; translated by Alexis Siegel. First Second Books 2007 63p. Illustration
Grades: 7 8 9 10 11 12 Adult   741.5
1. Humorous graphic novels; 2. Mummies; 3. Romance graphic novels; 4. Graphic novels
978-1-59643-130-0; 1-59643-130-X, $16.95

LC 2006-22177

In Victorian London, Lillian, the daughter of a famed archeologist, has fallen in love with the mummy of Imhotep IV; he thinks that Lillian bears a strong resemblance to this long-dead wife. Their love faces many obstacles, from Lillian's father, the police, a pirate who is actually Imhotep III (yes, the father and another mummy), even Queen Victoria herself. Dainty Victorian manners mix with broad farce and black comedy in a beautifully illustrated book with muted colors and sepia tones.

The **rabbi's** cat. Pantheon Books 2005 142p. Illustration
Grades: 11 12 Adult   741.5; Fic
1. France — History — 1914-1940; 2. Jews; 3. North Africa; 4. Rabbis; 5. Graphic novels
0-375-42281-1, $21.95; 0-375-71464-2 (pa), $16.95

LC 2004-61406

"A slinky gray cat lives with a rabbi and his beautiful young daughter. One day, the feline eats their parrot, only to find that he has gained the bird's ability to talk. Witty and highly intelligent, the cat immediately decides that he wants to learn more about Judaism, from the Kabbalah to the Torah. . . . There is plenty for teens to like—humor, romance, and theological questioning combined with a folkloric quality to bring to life a multifaceted work." SLJ

Vampire loves. Color by Audré Jardel; translation by Alexis Siegel. First Second Books 2006 187p. Illustration
Grades: 9 10 11 12 Adult   741.5; Fic
1. Romance graphic novels; 2. Vampires; 3. Graphic novels
978-1-59643-093-8; 1-59643-093-1, $16.95

LC 2005-21498

When the vampire Ferdinand breaks up with Lani, his cheating girlfriend, he starts looking for love and romance. In the process he meets the vampire sisters Ritaline and Aspirine, tries his hand at detective work, goes on a cruise and meets the ghost, Sigh, and gets mixed up in a fight between mummy pirates and Professor Joseph Bell.

"Edgy and creepy but at the same time universal and normal, Vampire Loves is a unique study in contrasts that will be a pleasurable discovery for graphic novel enthusiasts." Voice Youth Advocates

First published in four volumes in France with title: Grand vampire

Shaffer, Neal

The **Awakening**. Written by Neal Shaffer; illustrated by Luca Genovese; lettering by Manfredi Toraldo. Oni Press 2004 104p. Illustration

Grades: 10 11 12 Adult   **741.5; Fic**
1. Horror graphic novels; 2. Mystery graphic novels; 3. Graphic novels

1-932664-00-9, $9.95

Francesca, the only child of an affluent family, is excited to be attending one of the most prestigious boarding schools in New England. Unfortunately, things go horribly wrong when, shortly after her arrival, she finds one of her classmates brutally murdered, sending her into a deep shock, putting her into a coma. Even worse, immediately following the tragic incident, Francesca begins to have visions of which girl will be slain next, and even though she has awakened, she's unable to tell anyone about it. Is this a new horror being visited on the longstanding institution, or is it something much more, going to the core of the school itself, to an evil that defies description? The book includes strong language, violence, and some nudity.

Shakespeare, William

William Shakespeare's King Lear. Illustrated by Ian Pollock. Black Dog & Leventhal/Workman Publishing 2006 148p. Illustration

Grades: 7 8 9 10 11 12 Adult   **741.5; 822.3**
1. Shakespeare, William, 1564-1616 — Adaptations; 2. Graphic novels

978-1-57912-617-9, $12.95

This graphic novel adaptation of King Lear, originally published in 1984, uses excerpted text from the play together with full-color illustrations to tell the story of the king whose ill-fated attempts to learn which of his daughters loves him best causes loss and madness.

Part of the Shakespeare Graphic Library.

William Shakespeare's King Lear. Adapted by Brian Farrens; illustrated by Ben Dunn.. ABDO/Magic Wagon 2008 48p. Illustration

Grades: 5 6 7 8 9 10   **822.3; 741.5**
1. Shakespeare, William, 1564-1616 — Adaptations; 2. Graphic novels

978-1-60270-189-2, $28.50

LC 2008-10739

King Lear divides his kingdom among his three daughters but disowns Cordelia, the youngest, when she refuses to flatter him with insincerity. Then his older daughters renege on their promise to care for him, and he goes mad and roams the countryside. Meanwhile, Edmund, the illegitimate son of the Earl of Gloucester, plays political games in his quest for power. This graphic novel adaptation retains some of the original language from Shakespeare's play, while paring down the story to appeal to struggling readers. The book includes a short biography, a summary of the play, a glossary, and a short selection of famous lines and phrases from the play.

Part of the Graphic Shakespeare series

William Shakespeare's Macbeth. Illustrated by Von. Black Dog & Leventhal/Workman Publishing 1982 92p. Illustration

Grades: 7 8 9 10 11 12 Adult   **741.5; 822.3**

1. Shakespeare, William, 1564-1616 — Adaptations; 2. Graphic novels

978-1-57912-621-6, $12.95

This graphic novel adaptation of Macbeth, originally published in 1982, uses excerpted text from the play together with full-color illustrations to tell the story of the Thane of Cawdor who listens to a trio of witches and slays the King of Scotland to take his throne.

Part of the Shakespeare Graphic Library

William Shakespeare's Othello. Adapted by Vincent Goodwin; illustrated by Chris Allen.. ABDO/Magic Wagon 2008 48p. Illustration

Grades: 5 6 7 8 9 10   **822.3; 741.5**
1. Shakespeare, William, 1564-1616 — Adaptations; 2. Graphic novels

978-1-60270-192-2, $28.50

LC 2008-10743

Othello the Moor is a successful general, married to the beautiful Desdemona. Life should be good, but he's incredibly jealous of anyone who looks at his wife. Iago wants Othello's position and decides that he should destroy Othello by fabricating an affair between Desdemona and Cassio. This graphic novel adaptation keeps some of the original dialog from Shakespeare's play while paring down the action to simplify it for readers who would struggle with the original. The book includes a short biography of Shakespeare, a summary of the plot, a glossary, and a sampling of famous lines and phrases.

Part of the Graphic Shakespeare series

William Shakespeare's Twelfth night. Adapted by Vincent Goodwin illustrated by Cynthia Martin. ABDO/Magic Wagon 2008 48p. Illustration

Grades: 5 6 7 8 9 10   **822.3; 741.5**
1. Shakespeare, William, 1564-1616 — Adaptations; 2. Graphic novels

978-1-60270-195-3, $28.50

LC 2008-10747

Twins Viola and Sebastian are separated in a shipwreck. Viola decides to disguise herself as a man since she's alone, and this sets the stage for mixed-up identities and a comic love triangle. This graphic novel adaptation retains some of the original language from Shakespeare's play, while paring down the story to appeal to struggling readers. The book includes a short biography, a summary of the play, a glossary, and a short selection of famous lines and phrases from the play.

Part of the Graphic Shakespeare series

Shan, Darren

Cirque du Freak, vol. 1. Art by Takahiro Arai. Yen Press 2009 Un Illustration

Grades: 6 7 8 9 10   **741.5; Fic**
1. Authors; 2. Horror graphic novels; 3. Manga; 4. Novelists; 5. Shan, Darren, 1972- — Adaptations; 6. Vampires; 7. Graphic novels

978-0-7595-3041-6, $10.99

Middle schoolers Darren and Steve hustle soccer games against older players for money; Steve obsesses over horror movies, while Darren has a huge fascination with spiders. When a mysterious stranger hands Darren a flyer advertising a Cirque du Freak, he and Steve decide they must attend. At the circus, they discover that the freaks in the show are true monsters, not the usual hokey hoaxes, and Darren loves the monstrous spider. Then Steve decides that Mr. Crepsley, the spider handler, is a vampire, and Steve wants more than anything to become a vampire. However, Mr. Crepsley rejects him after tasting his blood Steve is too bloodthirsty. Then Darren steals Madame Octa, the spider, only to lose control of her while she's out of her cage and she bites Steve.

Courtesy of Yen Press

Crepsley comes for his pet and tells Darren he'll save Steve, but only if Darren will become his assistant and become a vampire. This book is the English translation of the original Japanese manga that is based on Shan's novel.

Shanower, Eric

Age of Bronze vol. 1: A Thousand Ships. Image Comics 2001 223p. Illustration (Age of bronze)
Grades: 10 11 12   **741.5; Fic**
1. Greek mythology; 2. Trojan War; 3. Graphic novels
1-58240-212-4; 1-58240-200-0 (pa), $19.95
Shanower includes frank sex scenes and doesn't shy away from the brutal violence of war.
This is "the first part of a seven-volume graphic novel about the Trojan War. . . . The book begins with the story of Paris, the milk-white bull and the kidnapping of Helen, and goes up to the start of the war." Publ Wkly
"This series retells the story of the Trojan War, going back to the young Trojan prince Paris and the petty rivalry of several goddesses that set the events into motion. Shanower conducted extensive reasearch of the world of that time—its technology, architecture, clothing, armor, and weapons. His books are more "real" than any Hollywood movie depiction." Voice Youth Advocates
Includes bibliographical references
Other books in the Age of Bronze series include:
Betrayal (2008); Sacrifice (2004)

Age of bronze volume 3A: Betrayal part one. Image Comics 2007 176p. Illustration
Grades: 10 11 12 Adult   **741.5; Fic**
1. Adventure graphic novels; 2. Greek mythology; 3. Troy (Extinct city)
978-1-58240-755-5, $17.99
The graphic novel retelling of the story of the Trojan War continues, as High King Agamemnon's army passes the island of Tenedos on its journey to conquer Troy. When a snake bites Philoktetes on the foot, his cries of pain bother the army so much that Odysseus must find a solution. Then, the Achaeans send an embassy to Troy in hopes of preventing a war. This book includes some nudity and sexual situations as well as some violence. Shanower includes a lengthy bibliography of historical sources.
Sequel to Sacrifice (2004)

Age of Bronze: Betrayal part 2. By Eric Shanower. Image Comics 2013 176 p. Illustration
Grades: 10 11 12 Adult   **741.5**
1. Greece — Fiction; 2. Trojan War — Fiction; 3. Graphic novels
1607067579; 9781607067573
In this graphic novel, written and illustrated by Eric Shanower, "the Trojan plain fills with death as Achaean forces clash in blood with the Trojan army. In the city of Troy, Pandarus pulls the strings to put Troilus in Cressida's bed. But when Cressida is ripped away to the enemy camp, how far will Troilus fight" (Publisher's note)
"Shanower's graphic-novel retelling of the Trojan War is one of the great artistic visions of the comics medium. Where both mythology and heroic-adventure comics typically lean toward vast spectacle and archetypal characters, Shanower is uncompromising in his sharp, humanizing focus. Betrayal, Part 2, the second part of the third part of Shanower's projected seven-part series, begins with Achilles and his Myrmidons invading the beach of Troy and ends with Troilus' breakdown during a bloody skirmish with a squad of Achaeans. . . . Seldom has a work shined so brightly on every page." Booklist

Age of Bronze: Sacrifice. Image Comics 2004 223p. Illustration; Map (Age of bronze)
Grades: 10 11 12 Adult   **741; 741.5; Fic**
1. Greek mythology; 2. Trojan War; 3. Graphic novels
1-58240-360-0; 1-58240-399-6 (pa), $19.95
"Sacrifice begins by recapitulating the story thus far. Paris sails back to Troy, just as self-regarding and shortsighted as when he left. Thrilled with his own prize (Helen), he has no understanding of the political complications. Priam does, but he is swayed by the machinations of Helen and by Hecuba's generosity. Not only are the major characters (Achilles, Klytemnestra, Odysseus) complex, but even a minor player like Telephus is carefully developed." SLJ
Includes bibliographical references
Followed by Betrayal (2008)
This is the second book in the author's projected seven-volume graphic novel about the Trojan War. The first volume, A thousand ships, was published in 2001

Little Nemo: Return to Slumberland. Written by Eric Shanower; illustrated by Gabriel Rodriguez. IDW Publishing 2015 120 p. Color; Illustration
Grades: 10 11 12 Adult   **741.5**
1. Dreaming; 2. Friendship
1631400592; 9781631400599, $21.99
Eisner Award: Best Limited Series (2015)
This graphic novel, by Eric Shanower, illustrated by Gabriel Rodriguez, "sees King Morpheus' daughter, in the Royal Palace of Slumberland, selecting her next-playmate—Nemo! Only Nemo has no interest in being anyone's playmate, dream or no dream!" (Publisher's note)
Originally published as: Little Nemo: Return to Slumberland, issues #1-4

Shazam!: the greatest stories ever told
DC Comics 2008 224p. Illustration
Grades: 4 5 6 7 8 9 10 11 12 Adult   **741.5; Fic**
1. Adventure graphic novels; 2. Captain Marvel (Fictional character); 3. Superhero graphic novels; 4. Graphic novels
978-1-4012-1674-0, $24.99

This book collects comics stories about Captain Marvel dating from 1940 to 1998. Captain Marvel predated Superman as a comic book superhero; young newsboy Billy Batson could transform into the flying superhero by shouting the magic word "Shazam!" This gave him the wisdom of Solomon, the strength of Hercules, the stamina of Atlas, the power of Zeus, the courage of Achilles, and the speed of Mercury. In these fourteen stories, he battles against such foes as Dr. Sivana, Mr. Mind, and the Monster Society of Evil.

Sheikman, Alex
Robotika. Archaia Studios Press 2006 128p. Illustration
Grades: 11 12 Adult   **741.5; Fic**
1. Adventure graphic novels; 2. Science fiction graphic novels; 3. Graphic novels
978-1-932386-21-9, $19.95

In a future world full of human/machine hybrids and organic technology, a samurai named Niko serves the Queen. When a new piece of technology that can revolutionize the world and render cyborgs obsolete is stolen and its inventor killed, the Queen sends Niko to retrieve it. He must fight and kill many warriors along the way and succeeds, only to see the Queen destroy the object to create a hair ornament. He gives up the sword, but still joins yojimbo (wandering masterless samurai bodyguards) Cherokee Geisha and Uri Bronski to protect a caravan of pilgrims seeking their god's temple.

Sheikman uses color, differing visual styles, even vertical lettering (for Cherokee Geisha's speech), and combines genre elements of the Western, samurai action, and science fiction to create a story set in a well-realized world. Two short stories give background on Cherokee Geisha and Bronski.

Originally published as Robotika issues #1-4.

Shelley, Mary Wollstonecraft, 1797-1851
Frankenstein. Retold by Michael Burgan ; illustrated by Dennis Calero. Stone Arch Books 2007 72p. Illustration
Grades: 3 4 5 6 7 8 9   **741.5; Fic**
1. Horror graphic novels; 2. Science fiction graphic novels; 3. Graphic novels
978-1-59889-830-9, $23.93
LC 2007-6199

The young scientist Victor Frankenstein has created something amazing and horrible at the same time, a living being out of dead flesh and bone. His creation, however, turns out to be a monster. Frankenstein's creation quickly discovers that his hideous appearance frightens away any companions. Now, Frankenstein must stop his creation before the monster's loneliness turns to violence. The book is written with an easy vocabulary for struggling and reluctant readers, and it includes facts about the novel.

Part of the Graphic Revolve series.

Shen, Prudence
★ **Nothing** Can Possibly Go Wrong. By Prudence Shen, illustrated by Faith Erin Hicks. First Second 2013 288 p.
Grades: 7 8 9 10   **741.5/973; Fic**
1. Cheerleading — Juvenile fiction; 2. Robots — Juvenile fiction; 3. School stories
159643659X; 9781596436596, $16.99

In this juvenile graphic novel, by Prudence Shen, illustrated by Faith Erin Hicks, "you wouldn't expect Nate and Charlie to be friends. Charlie's the laid-back captain of the basketball team, and Nate is the neurotic, scheming president of the robotics club. But they are friends, however unlikely—until Nate declares war on the cheerleaders. At stake is funding that will either cover a robotics competition or new cheerleading uniforms—but not both." (Publisher's note)

"Shen's plot ably balances drama, humor, angst, and robotic geekery, giving the book an immediate YA appeal, but one that's broad enough to be enjoyable to older readers, as well. Visually, Hicks's wide-eyed, inky b&w panels infuse the characters with real emotion and personality, capturing the book's heartfelt youthfulness." Pub Wkly

Shepard, Aaron
Robin Hood. Retold by Aaron Shepard and Anne L. Watson ; illustrated by Jennifer Tanner. Stone Arch Books 2006 63p. Illustration
Grades: 3 4 5 6 7 8 9   **741.5; Fic**
1. Adventure graphic novels; 2. Robin Hood (Legendary character); 3. Graphic novels
978-1-59889-049-5, $23.93

Robin Hood and his band of outlaws are the heroes of Sherwood Forest. Taking from the rich and giving to the poor, Robin Hood and his loyal followers fight for the oppressed and against the evil Sheriff of Nottingham. Among the adventures recounted are how Robin meets Little John and Friar Tuck, helping Alan-a-Dale marry his true love, Eleanor, and Robin entering the Sheriff's archery contest even though it's a trap. This adaptation is written for reluctant and struggling readers.

Part of the Graphic Revolve series.

Sherman, M. Zachary
SOCOM: Seal Team Seven Vol. 1. Writer, M. Zachary Sherman; Roberto de la Torre, artist. Image Comics 2006 Un Illustration
Grades: 10 11 12 Adult   **741.5; Fic**
1. Adventure graphic novels; 2. Science fiction graphic novels; 3. Graphic novels
1-58240-586-7, $12.99

When a submarine is mysteriously downed in the Persian Gulf, CIA tactician Douglas Griffin is reactivated into his former SEAL team to investigate. Simultaneously, a string of mystifying attacks pits the U.S. Navy against the underwater Kingdom of Atlantis in a full-blown war against humanity's extinction. With the threat of global devastation imminent, twisting realities lead the SEALs from Atlantis' 5000 fathoms to the even deeper political waters of the U.S. government. The book includes lots of harsh language and violence.

Shiga, Jason
Bookhunter. Sparkplug Comics 2007 Un Illustration
Grades: 10 11 12 Adult   **741.5; Fic**
   1. Humorous graphic novels; 2. Librarians; 3. Mystery
graphic novels; 4. Graphic novels
978-0-9742715-6-9, $15
   When a rare Caxton Bible is stolen from the Oakland
Public Library in 1973, Agent Bay of the Library Police is on
the case. Reading very much like a police procedural
mystery, but set in the library, Bookhunter combines humor,
library technology of the early 1970s, and lots of action
movie tropes. The book includes a few harsh words and
some violence.

   Meanwhile. Abrams/Amulet 2010 Un Illustration
Grades: 4 5 6 7 8 9   **741.5**
   1. Science fiction graphic novels; 2. Graphic novels
0-8109-8423-7; 978-0-8109-8423-3, $15.95
                                              LC 2009-39844
   In this choose-your-own adventure graphic novel, a boy
stumbles on the laboratory of a mad scientist who asks him
to choose between testing a mind-reading device, a time
machine, and a doomsday machine. (Bull Cent Child Books)

Shigematsu, Takako
   King of the lamp. Go! Comi 2007 208p. Illustration
Grades: 11 12 Adult   **741.5; Fic**
   1. Manga; 2. Romance graphic novels; 3. Graphic novels
978-1-933617-46-6, $10.99
   In this one-volume manga, teenage girls in the throes of
unrequited love encounter a mysterious merchant who sells a
magic lamp. This lamp hold a genie, who is actually a king
from a far land who lived long ago; because he took one
thousand beautiful girls for his harem, he was imprisoned in
the lamp and must grant the wishes of one thousand girls
who are looking for love. What each girl learns, however, is
that he can exact a price from them for their wishes, and the
price ranges from a kiss to sex. Hinata loves Togo, but her
older sister has been dating him. When Togo gets into an
accident and is blinded, Hinata wishes that she could sound
like her unfaithful sister and comfort Togo. Enter the prince,
who grants her wish. Pretending to be her sophisticated older
sister isn't easy, but Hinata discovers the hardest part is she's
falling more deeply in love with Togo. This is just one of
several stories. Each of them ends with the characters having
sex, although it's not graphically portrayed; but there is
partial nudity.

Shigeno, Shuichi
   Initial D Volume 1. Tokyopop 2002 229p. Illustration
Grades: 8 9 10 11 12 Adult   **741.5; Fic**
   1. Automobile racing; 2. Seinen manga; 3. Graphic novels
1-931514-98-4, $9.99
   Tak Fujiwara spends a lot of time behind the wheel,
delivering tofu for his dad's shop. He races down the
treacherous roads of Mount Akina all the time, and without
even realizing it, he has mastered racing techniques that take
most drivers a lifetime to learn. None of his friends realize
this, because they're too busy watching the local street
racing team. When the Red Suns, an outside team, shows up
to challenge the Akina Speed Stars, it doesn't look good for
the local team; then a mysterious Trueno Eight Six shows up

and the driver exhibits great skill. Who is the driver" The
book includes some strong language and some sexual
situations (the girl Tak likes is dating older men for money).

Shiki, Satoshi
   Kami-Kaze Volume 1. Tokyopop 2006 268p.
Illustration
Grades: 12 Adult   **741.5; Fic**
   1. Fantasy graphic novels; 2. Horror graphic novels; 3.
Manga; 4. Seinen manga; 5. Graphic novels
1-59532-924-2, $9.99
   Everyone is after the legendary Girl of Water, whose
blood can unlock the trans-dimensional prison that holds the
fabled 88 beasts...and unleash them unto our world. The only
problem is that no one knows where the Girl of Water is, nor
do they know if the power she wields has awakened in
whatever body she has chosen to possess. Intent on tracking
her down, a host of supernatural warriors descends upon
Tokyo, all thirsting for the imminent destruction of mankind.
All, that is, except one rogue swordsman, who is
inexplicably duty-bound to protect the Girl of Water at all
costs. The book is full of explicit, graphic violence and
extremely harsh language, along with some nudity and
sexual situations.

Shimabukuro, Mitsutoshi
   Toriko, vol. 1. Viz
Media/Shonen Jump 2010
208p. Illustration
Grades: 8 9 10 11 12 Adult
741.5; Fic
   1. Adventure graphic
novels; 2. Food; 3.
Humorous graphic novels;
4. Hunting; 5. Manga; 6.
Graphic novels
978-1-4215-3509-8, $9.99
   Toriko is a Gourmet
Hunter, who earns huge
bounties for finding
ferocious, delicious foods.
We're not talking salmon
fishing or deer hunting here,
but eight-legged alligators and rare fruit guarded by
four-armed, bloodthirsty gorilla-type creatures. Toriko
himself has a huge appetite for the rare foods, and sometimes
eats most of what he's supposed to bring to the fancy
restaurants that hire him. Komatsu, the head chef at Igo, a
restaurant that caters to those wealthy enough to afford the
rare foods, tags along with Toriko, who is a muscular giant of
a man. This odd couple forms a friendship born in their
mutual love of fine foods. The book is full of crazy action,
lots of bugeyed, drop-jawed, slapstick moments, and some
potty humor.

Courtesy of VIZ Media LLC

Shimizu, Aki
   Qwan Vol. 1. Tokyopop 2005 180p. Illustration
Grades: 9 10 11 12 Adult   **741.5; Fic**
   1. Adventure graphic novels; 2. Fantasy graphic novels; 3.
Manga; 4. Graphic novels
1-59532-534-4, $9.99

In the mystical lands of Han Dynasty China (206 B.C.-A.S. 220), where magical beings are a part of everyday life, Qwan is a strange amnesiac boy who can devour demons and absorb their power. However, he's looking for more than a quick bite. Qwan's quest is to find the sutra known as the Essential Arts of Peace, an ancient verse which will ultimately reveal the ultimate purpose of his existence. The book includes violence, mildly strong language, and mild sexual situations.

Shimizu, Reiko
   Moon Child. DC Comics/CMX 2006 192p. Illustration
Grades: 10 11 12 Adult   **741.5; Fic**
   1. Manga; 2. Romance graphic novels; 3. Science fiction graphic novels; 4. Shojo manga; 5. Graphic novels
   1-4012-0825-8, $9.99
   According to prophecy, a half-mermaid, half-human girl will either bring an end to the feud between humanity and the mer-people, or bring about the destruction of all life on Earth. When the mer-man named Shona returns to Earth to find the girl, he meets a young boy suffering from amnesia. The boy, Jimmy, joins Shona in his search. Will they be able to avert the prophecy, or will finding the secret of Jimmy's identity delay them and set Earth on the path to destruction" One of the secondary characters, an old black woman, is drawn in a stereotypical fashion. This series includes some partial nudity, sexual situations, and some mild violence.

Shimizu, Takashi
   Ju-On 2. Story by Takashi Shimizu; Manga adaptation by Meimu. Dark Horse Manga 2006 Un Illustration
Grades: 10 11 12 Adult   **741.5; Fic**
   1. Horror graphic novels; 2. Manga; 3. Graphic novels
   978-1-59307-531-6, $9.95
   When horror movie queen Kyoko Harase signs on to appear in a made-for-television special investigating a haunted house, she has no idea that her life has begun to resemble the films that made her an icon. Gruesome and eerie incidents soon plague the cast and crew as an ominous presence pervades their private affairs. What sits just below the surface, burning to manifest itself and satisfy a deep-seated rage" This standalone volume contains strong language and graphic violence.

Shimoku, Kio
   Genshiken: The Society for the Study of Modern Visual Culture, Vol. 1. Ballantine Books/Del Rey Manga 2005 190p. Illustration
Grades: 10 11 12 Adult   **741.5; Fic**
   1. College students; 2. Humorous graphic novels; 3. Seinen manga; 4. Graphic novels
   0-345-48169-0, $10.95
   College freshmen Kenji Sasahara, Makoto Kousaka, and Saki Kasukabe must join a social circle (college clubs in Japan are important avenues of student social life); Sasahara and Kousaka end up joining Genshiken, which is the ultimate otaku club, combining anime, manga, games, doujinshi, and cosplay in one organization. Saki doesn't want Kousaka, whom she considers to be her boyfriend, to be with these people, but she gets sucked into the club despite herself. The doujinshi, which are manga fanzines,

are filled with pornographic images (which the reader doesn't usually see); Kousaka has lots of pornographic video games, and there is some fan service. This series gives an insider's look at the otaku lifestyle even while satirizing it.

Shinjo, Mayu
   Demon Love Spell. Story and art by Mayu Shinjo; translated and adapted by Tetsuchiro Miyaki; touch-up art & lettering by Inori Fukuda Trant. Viz 2012 155 p.
Grades: 10 11 12 Adult   **741.5/952; Fic**
   1. Spirits — Fiction; 2. Supernatural — Fiction
   142154945X; 9781421549453, $9.99
   In this book by Mayu Shinjo "Miko is a shrine maiden who has never had much success at seeing or banishing spirits. Then she meets Kagura, a . . . demon who feeds off women's feelings of passion and love. Kagura's insatiable appetite has left many girls at school brokenhearted, so Miko casts a spell to seal his powers. Surprisingly the spell works—sort of—but now Kagura is after her!" (Publisher's note)
Translated from the Japanese.
Book reads right to left in the original Japanese format.

Shinkai, Makoto
   ★ **Hoshi** No Koe: The Voices of a Distant Star. Original concept by Makaoto Shinkai; manga adaptation by Mizu Sahara. Tokyopop 2006 232p. Illustration
Grades: 8 9 10 11 12 Adult   **741.5; Fic**
   1. Manga; 2. Romance graphic novels; 3. Science fiction graphic novels; 4. Graphic novels
   1-59816-529-1, $9.99
   In the mid-twenty-first century, high school student Mikako joins a research team heading out to space on a U.N. ship, to explore recent contact with aliens called the Tarsians. Her friend Noboru stays behind on Earth. While he continues with school, he receives cell-phone text messages, his only contact with Mikako. As her ship travels farther away, the low-priority messages take longer to reach Noboru, and he grows older while Mikako remains a teenager. Even as he considers moving on with his life, Noboru learns that love will find a way. This one-volume manga adapts the anime film; however, it stands alone as a story.

Shiomi, Chika
   Canon Vol. 1. DC Comics/CMX 2007 200p. Illustration
Grades: 8 9 10 11 12 Adult   **741.5; Fic**
   1. Horror graphic novels; 2. Shojo manga; 3. Vampires; 4. Graphic novels
   978-1-4012-1163-9, $9.99
   Suspense and the supernatural collide in the tale of Canon—the only student to escape the bloody vampire attack that takes the lives of her fellow classmates. But she doesn't get very far before she is captured, bitten and turned into a vampire herself. Struggling against the terrible needs that compel the undead, Canon commits herself to using her powers for good. She'll do whatever she can to avenge the death of her friends and her own unfortunate fate. Joining forces with Fuui—a talking vampire crow—she begins her quest to find Rodd, Lord of the Vampires. There's some mildly harsh language and lots of fighting vampire attacks,

but nothing more than has been seen in most Buffy the Vampire Slayer or Angel episodes on television.

Night of the Beasts Volume 1. Go! Comi 2006 200p. Illustration
Grades: 10 11 12 Adult   **741.5; Fic**
1. Horror graphic novels; 2. Manga; 3. Shojo manga; 4. Supernatural graphic novels; 5. Graphic novels
978-1-933617-14-5, $10.99

Aria's got a reputation as the toughest girl in school because she can't resist taking on bullies - especially guys who aggressively hit on innocent girls. Which is why she's taken by surprise when her first kiss is stolen by a complete stranger. Not only does he keep making moves on her, but it seems like every time they meet, it's at the latest crime scene of a murder spree that's plaguing Aria's neighborhood. How is it that he seems to know all about the supernatural murderer of these innocent girls? And how will Aria react to his claim only she can save him from a destiny so bloody that even the violent deeds of black demon slaughtering victims all over town will pale in comparison? The book includes mildly strong language, some bloody violence, and mild sexual situations.

Yurara, Vol. 1. Viz Media/Shojo Beat 2007 192p. Illustration
Grades: 10 11 12 Adult   **741.5; Fic**
1. Fantasy graphic novels; 2. Ghosts; 3. Manga; 4. Shojo manga; 5. Graphic novels
978-1-4215-1350-8, $8.99

Translated by JN Productions. First year high school student Yurara Tsukinowa is a quiet girl; she has seen ghosts most of her life, but has kept it a secret from anyone outside her family. Since she reacts emotionally in the presence of ghosts, she has a reputation for being weird. At school, she meets Mei Tendo and Yako Hoshino, two handsome boys who have powers to ward off vengeful spirits. When she's threatened by the ghost of a girl at her classroom desk, Yurara's guardian spirit manifests herself; this dark-haired, bold girl has the power to release souls. Yurara has to fend off Mei's teasing advances and her female classmates' jealousy while trying to figure out just what she can now do. The story features some supernatural violence and sexual innuendo.

Shirodaira, Kyo
The **record** of a fallen vampire vol. 1. Story by Kyo Shirodaira; art by Yuri Kimura. Viz Media 2008 208p. Illustration
Grades: 9 10 11 12 Adult   **741.5; Fic**
1. Fantasy graphic novels; 2. Manga; 3. Vampires; 4. Graphic novels
978-1-4215-1773-5, $9.99

Long, long ago, Vampire King Akabara "Red Rose" Strauss lost both his kingdom and his queen, whose power went out of control when she tried to save her husband. Since humans were unable to kill the queen, they sealed her away then erected thousands of fake seals so that Akabara would never find her. For centuries, Akabara has hunted down seals and destroyed them one by one, always pursued by dhampires, half human/half vampire beings determined to destroy all vampires, and by the Black Swan. The Black Swan possesses a young human girl every fifty years, giving her the power to destroy the Vampire King and his queen. Now Akabara faces the 49th Black Swan; each new incarnation is stronger than the last. The series includes graphic, bloody violence and some harsh language.

Shirow, Masamune
The **ghost** in the shell. Story and art by Shirow Masamune; translation and English adaptation, Frederik L. Schodt and Toren Smith. Kodansha Comics 2009 348 p. Illustration; Color
Grades: 11 12 Adult   **741.5; 741.5/952**
1. Androids — Fiction; 2. Cyborgs
9781935429012, $26.99

LC 2010292697

In this book, by Shirow Masamune, "the line between man and machine has been inexorably blurred. . . . In this rapidly converging landscape, cyborg superagent Major Motoko Kusanagi is charged to track down the craftiest and most dangerous terrorists and cybercriminals. . . . When Major Kusanagi tracks the cybertrail of one such master hacker, the Puppeteer, her quest leads her into a world beyond information and technology." (Publisher's note)

Translated and adapted from the Japanese.

Other titles in this series are: Ghost in the Shell 2: Man-Machine Interface; Ghost in the Shell 1.5: Human-Error Processor

Shone, Rob
Muhammad Ali: The Life of a Boxing Hero. Art by Nick Spender. Rosen Publishing Group 2006 48p. Illustration
Grades: 3 4 5 6 7 8 9   **741.5; 796.8; 92**
1. African American athletes; 2. Ali, Muhammad, 1942-; 3. Biographical graphic novels; 4. Boxing — Biography; 5. Graphic novels
978-1-4042-0856-8, $29.25

LC 2005035521

This book uses the graphic novel format to tell of the life and career of boxing great Muhammad Ali. He started his career as Cassius Clay but changed his name when he converted to the Nation of Islam. He used his fame as a boxer to advocate against U.S. involvement in Vietnam, and to raise funds for charity. The book includes a list of all his boxing matches, and a list of books for further reading.

Part of the Rosen Graphic Biographies series.

Nelson Mandela: The Life of an African Statesman. Art by Neil Reed. The Rosen Publishing Group 2007 48p. Illustration
Grades: 3 4 5 6 7 8 9   **92; 741.5**
1. Biographical graphic novels; 2. Mandela, Nelson, 1918-2013; 3. Graphic novels
978-1-4042-0860-5, $29.25

After presenting information about South Africa and the apartheid system, the book presents a comic book style biography of Nelson Mandela, from his childhood through his adult life spent fighting apartheid from outside and within prison. Additional material describes the 1993 elections that brought Mandela and his political party, the ANC, to power in a new South Africa. The book includes a glossary and a list of books for further reading.

Part of the Graphic Biographies series.

Rosa Parks: The Life of a Civil Rights Heroine. Rosen Publishing Group 2006 48p. Illustration
Grades: 3 4 5 6 7 8 9   **741.5; 323.092; 323**
1. African American women — Alabama — Montgomery — Biography; 2. African Americans — Civil rights — Alabama — Montgomery — History — 20th century; 3. Biographical graphic novels; 4. Parks, Rosa, 1913-2005; 5. Graphic novels
978-1-4042-0864-3, $29.25
                               LC 2006002735
    This book uses the graphic novel format to tell of the life of Rosa Parks and her act of defiance that inspired the Montgomery Bus Boycott. Additional information explains Jim Crow laws and briefly covers the civil rights movement. The bookes a list of books for further reading.
    Part of the Rosen Graphic Biographies series.

War correspondents. Illustrated by Chris Forsey. Rosen Publishing Group 2008 48p. Illustration
Grades: 3 4 5 6 7 8 9   **070.4; 741.5**
1. Adie, Kate; 2. Journalists; 3. Newspaper editors; 4. Television reporters; 5. Graphic novels
978-1-4042-1449-1, $29.25
                               LC 2007-45936
    After brief descriptions of early war reporting and the development of broadcast news from the front, the book profiles three war correspondents. Ernie Pyle made the life and wartime plight of the common soldier come alive for the folks back home; he was the first embedded journalist, staying with troops on the front. He was killed in action on Okinawa in 1945. Sydney Schanberg went to Cambodia in 1973 and witnessed the "killing fields" there. He wrote about a bombing incident in Neak Leung, when a B52 accidentally bombed the town and killed 137 people, injuring 258 more. Dith Pran, his fellow journalist from Cambodia, died on March 30, 2008. BBC journalist Kate Adie was embedded with Coalition Forces during Desert Storm, the first Gulf war, in 1990. During this war, the embedded journalists used technology to broadcast directly from the war front.
    Part of the Graphic Careers series

Shonen, Sasaki
    Lunar Legend Tsukihime Vol. 1. DrMaster Publications 2006 208p. Illustration
Grades: 10 11 12 Adult   **741.5; Fic**
1. Horror graphic novels; 2. Shonen manga; 3. Graphic novels
978-1-59796-075-5, $9.95
    A childhood accident has left young Shiki Tohno with the ability to see the hidden lines or weak points in all things - be they organic or inanimate. By striking or cutting along these lines Shiki can slice through anything. Unfortunately the giftomes packaged with a nearly irresistable urge to kill using his new ability. The story includes graphic violence and some sexual situations.

Showcase Presents The Flash, Volume One
    DC Comics 2007 509p. Illustration
Grades: 7 8 9 10 11 12 Adult   **741.5; Fic**
1. Flash (Fictional character); 2. Superhero graphic novels; 3. Graphic novels

978-1-4012-1327-5, $16.99
    A freak accident gives Central City police scientist Barry Allen fantastic super-speed abilities. Inspired by his favorite childhood comic book hero, Allen uses the name the Flash and uses his powers to help humanity. He soon finds himself facing such villains as Captain Cold, Mirror Master, Gorilla Grodd, the Pied Piper, Weather Wizard, and more. This volume collects 39 stories from the 1950s and 1960s in black and white.

Showcase Presents Superman Family Volume One
    Otto Binder [and others], writers ; C.C. Beck [and others], pencillers and inkers. DC Comics 2006 572p. Illustration
Grades: 6 7 8 9 10 11 12 Adult   **741.5; Fic**
1. Jimmy Olsen (Fictional character); 2. Lois Lane (Fictional character); 3. Superhero graphic novels; 4. Superman (Fictional character); 5. Graphic novels
978-1-4012-0787-8, $16.99
    This volume spotlights Superman's girlfriend Lois Lane and his pal Jimmy Olsen. Learn more about these two dynamic personalities in their solo stories as each braves danger for the latest scoop. These stories from the 1950s also introduceing elements such as the Daily Planet's Flying Newsroom and Jimmy's penchant for disguises. The Showcase series reprints the older comics stories in black and white collections.

Showcase Presents The Unknown Soldier Volume 1
    DC Comics 2006 552p. Illustration
Grades: 8 9 10 11 12 Adult   **741.5; Fic**
1. Adventure graphic novels; 2. Unknown Soldier (Fictional character); 3. Graphic novels
978-1-4012-1090-8, $16.99
    His face hideously disfigured by a grenade explosion in the early days of World War II, the young man who would become the Unknown Soldier was determined to continue fighting for his country. His true identity kept top secret, he became the perfect covert operative, using a multitude of disguises to carry out his exploits against the Axis powers. The first 38 adventures of the Unknown Soldier are collected in this black and white reprint volume, with stories dating from 1970 through 1975.

Showcase Presents: Green Arrow Volume 1
    Otto Binder [and others], writers ; C.C. Beck [and others], pencillers and inkers. DC Comics 2006 528p. Illustration
Grades: 7 8 9 10 11 12 Adult   **741.5; Fic**
1. Green Arrow (Fictional character); 2. Superhero graphic novels; 3. Graphic novels
1-4012-0785-5, $16.99
    Millionaire Oliver Queen mastered the bow and arrow as a matter of survival when he was trapped on a desert island. Back home in Star City, he chose to use his newfound skills as the costumed champion Green Arrow. With his sidekick, Speedy, he tackled crooks and solved mysteries with energy, style, and the occasional boxing glove arrow. The stories collected in this black and white volume were originally published from 1958 through 1969

Showcase Presents: The House of Mystery Volume 1
DC Comics 2006 552p. Illustration
Grades: 7 8 9 10 11 12 Adult   741.5; Fic
    1. Horror graphic novels; 2. Supernatural graphic novels;
3. Graphic novels
978-1-4012-0786-1, $16.99
    Just beyond the door of the House of Mystery await
spine-chilling (and some rib-tickling) stories of the
supernatural, tales of ghosts and witches, ghouls and
gargoyles, all hosted by Cain, the caretaker of the House.
This black and white volume reprints House of Mystery
issues 174-194, dating from 1968 through 1971. Some of the
stories have a "Twilight Zone" feel, others are a little more
gruesome.

Showcase Presents: Legion of Super-Heroes Volume 1
DC Comics 2007 552p. Illustration
Grades: 7 8 9 10 11 12 Adult   741.5; Fic
    1. Legion of Super-Heroes (Fictional characters); 2.
Superhero graphic novels; 3. Graphic novels
978-1-4012-1382-4, $16.99
    The Legion of Super-Heroes, teenagers from across the
cosmos, each with a unique ability, are the sworn protectors
of the galaxy. Headquartered in their Super-Hero Club
House, Lightning Lad, Saturn Girl, and Cosmic Boy have
high standards for young hopeful champions wishing to join
their ranks. With the largest roster of any super-team of the
2960s, they patrol all sectors of the universe to ensure peace
and justice for all sentient beings. This volume collects black
and white reprints of stories originally published from 1958
through 1964.

Showcase Presents: Martian Manhunter Volume 1
DC Comics 2007 544p. Illustration
Grades: 7 8 9 10 11 12 Adult   741.5; Fic
    1. Martian Man hunter (Fictional character); 2. Superhero
graphic novels; 3. Graphic novels
978-1-4012-1368-8, $16.99
    After being accidentally teleported to Earth, Martian
J'onn J'onzz finds himself stranded in a strange new world,
with no way home. Using his powers to disguise his
appearance, J'onn J'onzz adopts the name of deceased
Denver police detective John Jones. With this new identity,
he joins the Middleton Police force, secretly using his
powers to help the inhabitants of Earth. Jack Miller and Joe
Samachson were principal writers on the series in the early
years, and artist Joe Certa did all the pencils; this black and
white volume reprints stories originally published from
1953 through 1962.

**Showcase Presents: Metamorpho, the Element Man
Volume 1**
DC Comics 2005 560p. Illustration
Grades: 7 8 9 10 11 12 Adult   741.5; Fic
    1. Science fiction graphic novels; 2. Superhero graphic
novels; 3. Graphic novels
1-4012-0762-6, $16.99
    Adventurer Rex Mason would do almost anything for
the right price, but he ended up paying with his own
humanity for stealing the legendary Orb of Ra for
millionaire industrialist Simon Stagg. The mysterious relic
transformed Rex into a freakish "element" man. with the

ability to transform his body into hundreds of different
substances. Calling himself Metamorpho, Rex considered
his life cursed and sought a way to reverse the Orb's powers.
Along the way, Stagg used Metamorpho's unique skills for
his own purposes, and the Element Man would go along,
since it meant more time with Stagg's gorgeous daughter
Sapphire. The stories in this black and white volume date
from 1964 through 1966.

Showcase Presents: Sgt. Rock
DC Comics 2007 543p. Illustration
Grades: 8 9 10 11 12 Adult   741.5
    1. Adventure graphic novels; 2. Sgt Rock (Fictional
character); 3. World War, 1939-1945; 4. Graphic novels
978-1-4012-1713-6, $16.99
    Sgt. Rock, created by Robert Kanigher, was an ordinary
soldier fighting in World War II. The stories collected in this
volume, published from 1959 through 1962, depict Rock
and his Easy Company fighting against evil during the war.
Even today, Sgt. Rock is a symbol of patriotism and of
America's fighting spirit. The stories include battle action.

Showcase Presents: Superman Volume 1
    Otto Binder [and others], writers ; C.C. Beck [and
others], pencillers and inkers. DC Comics 2005 560p.
Illustration
Grades: 6 7 8 9 10 11 12 Adult   741.5; Fic
    1. Superhero graphic novels; 2. Superman (Fictional
character); 3. Graphic novels
1-4012-0758-8, $9.99
    This first volume in the Showcase Presents Library of
Classics features stories about Superman dating from 1958
through 1959. The adventure collected here have influenced
the history of Superman and his extended family. From the
introduction of his first love, the mermaid Lori Lemaris, to
the introduction of his cousin Supergirl, Superman faces his
most dangerous opponents, including Bizarro, Metallo, and
Brainiac.

Showcase Presents: Superman Volume 2
DC Comics 2006 576p. Illustration
Grades: 7 8 9 10 11 12 Adult   741.5; Fic
    1. Superhero graphic novels; 2. Superman (Fictional
character); 3. Graphic novels
978-1-4012-1041-0, $16.99
    The beginning of the 1960s ushered in a new era for
Superman. These Silver Age exploits see Superman
confront a wide array of villains, explore the planet Krypton,
and overcome Kryptonite exposure, become a Bizarro, and
more. The stories, reprinted here in black and white, date
from December 1959 through May 1961.

Showcase Presents: Teen Titans Volume 1
DC Comics 2006 528p. Illustration
Grades: 6 7 8 9 10 11 12 Adult   741.5; Fic
    1. Flash (Fictional character); 2. Robin (Fictional
character); 3. Superhero graphic novels; 4. Teen Titans
(Fictional characters); 5. Graphic novels
978-1-4012-0788-5, $16.99
    The Teen Titans were all sidekicks to such heroes as
Batman, Wonder Woman, Aquaman, and the Flash. When

teen heroes Robin, Aqualad, and Kid Flash joined together, they became a forced to be reckoned with. Wonder Girl quickly joined them, and occasionally Speedy would come, and they all proved they were just as capable of defeating the bad guys and saving the world as their mentors, while still being teens and having fun. The black and white reprinted stories originally appeared from 1964 through 1968. Today's teens will get a kick out of what the writers thought was cool "teen speak" back then.

Siddell, Thomas
 Gunnerkrigg Court: orientation. [by] Tom Siddell. Archaia Studios Press 2009 296p. Illustration
 Grades: 6 7 8 9 10 11 12   **741; Fic; 741.5**
 978-1-932386-34-9, $26.95; 1-932386-34-3
 Other titles in this series are: Vol. 2: Research (2009); Vol. 3: Reason (2011); Vol. 4: Materia (2013); Vol. 5: Refine (2015)
 "Antimony Carver is a precocious and preternaturally self-possessed young girl starting her first year of school at gloomy Gunnerkrigg Court, a very British boarding school that has robots running around along side body-snatching demons, forest gods, and the odd mythical creature. The opening volume in the series follows Antimony through her orientation year: the people she meets, the strange things that happen, and the things she causes to happen as she and her new friend, Kat, unravel the mysteries of the Court and deal with the everyday adventures of growing up." (Publisher's note)

Siegel, Jerry
 The **Superman** Chronicles Volume Three. Superman created by Jerry Siegel & Joe Shuster ; all stories written by Jerry Siegel and illustrated by Joe Shuster. DC Comics 2007 190p. Illustration
 Grades: 6 7 8 9 10 11 12 Adult   **741.5; Fic**
 1. Superhero graphic novels; 2. Superman (Fictional character); 3. Graphic novels
 978-1-4012-1374-9, $14.99
 In this third volume of the adventures of Superman presented in chronological order, the Man of Steel faces the villain who would plague him ever since: Lex Luthor. Clark Kent and Lois Lane become European war correspondents covering the conflicts that will eventually become World War II. And Superman maintains his reputation as the champion of the oppressed by battling jewel thieves, blackmailers, and predatory monsters.

 The **Superman** Chronicles Volume Two. Superman created by Jerry Siegel & Joe Shuster ; all stories written by Jerry Siegel and illustrated by Joe Shuster. DC Comics 2007 192p. Illustration
 Grades: 7 8 9 10 11 12 Adult   **741.5; Fic**
 1. Superhero graphic novels; 2. Superman (Fictional character); 3. Graphic novels
 978-1-4012-1215-5, $14.99
 Experience the history of Superman with this series that reprints the early adventures of the Man of Tomorrow in chronological order. This volume features classic tales from 1939 and 1940 written and illustrated by Superman co-creators Jerry Siegel and Joe Shuster, in which the Man of

Tomorrow battles crooked politicians and slumlords as he brings justice to the downtrodden masses.

 Superman: The World's Finest Comics Archives Volume 1. DC Comics 2004 240p. Illustration
 Grades: 7 8 9 10 11 12 Adult   **741.5; Fic**
 1. Superhero graphic novels; 2. Superman (Fictional character); 3. Graphic novels
 1-4012-0151-2, $49.99
 This Archives volume collects Superman stories from World's Finest Comics, dating from 1939 through 1944, with stories by the original creators, Siegel and Schuster. In these early adventures, Superman battled "regular" criminals, and his super powers were but a fraction of what they are in current Superman comics. These full-color reprints are bound in a sturdy hardcover edition.

Sierra, Sergio A.
 Frankenstein by Mary Shelley: a Dark graphic novel. Adaptation Sergio A. Sierra; illustration Meritxell Ribas. Enslow Publishers 2013 95 p.
 Grades: 6 7 8 9 10 11 12 Adult   **741.5**
 1. Horror stories; 2. Monsters — Fiction; 3. Graphic novels; 4. Frankenstein (Fictional character)
 0766040844; 9780766040847, $25.26
                                    LC 2011035826
 This book is a black-and-white graphic novel adaptation of Mary Shelley's 19th-century gothic novel "Frankenstein." The plot tells the "tale of a monster, assembled by a scientist from parts of dead bodies, who develops a mind of his own as he learns to loathe himself and hate his creator." (WorldCat)
 Includes bibliographical references.

Sievert, Tim
 That salty air. Top Shelf Productions 2008 116p. Illustration
 Grades: 10 11 12 Adult   **741.5; Fic**
 1. Bereavement; 2. Fishing; 3. Ocean; 4. Graphic novels
 978-1-60309-005-6, $10
 Fisherman Hugh has treated the ocean and its inhabitants with respect and reverence, but when he receives word that his mother died by drowning at sea, he acts as though the ocean itself has betrayed him. His loyal wife MaryAnne has just learned that she's pregnant, and she tries to help her husband. But he returns to fishing with a vengeful attitude that nearly destroys him. A mystical giant squid figures in Hugh's struggles deal with his grief and with the world.

Siku
 The **manga** Bible: from Genesis to Revelation. [by] Siku ; concept and art, Siku ; script, Akinsiku. Doubleday 2008 218p. Illustration
 Grades: 8 9 10 11 12   **220.9; 741.5**
 1. Bible; 2. Graphic novels
 978-0-385-52431-5, $12.95
                                    LC 2007-42413
 This graphic novel with some manga influences hits the highlights of the Bible, all the way from Genesis to Revelation, with stops for the story of Adam and Eve's fall into sin, the story of Abraham and Sarah, Joseph's fall into

slavery and rise to power in Egypt, Moses and the Exodus of the Israelites to Canaan, on to the story of Ruth the Moabite, her descendant David who became King, to the Babylonian Captivity and the prophet Daniel, to John the Baptist, the three-year journey of Jesus who was crucified, died, and rose from the dead to show that He was the Son of God, to the work of Paul, who started as an enemy of the new Christians but became one of the great apostles, to John's writing of the Revelation. The angular, almost sketchy art combines with casual, slangy dialogue to make the stories more accessible to those who may have never read the Bible, but even with some violence and partial nudity, the stories are still faithful to the original text.

Silady, Matt
The **Homeless** Channel. AiT/Planet Lar 2007 162p. Illustration
Grades: 10 11 12 Adult   741.5
   1. Homeless persons; 2. Graphic novels
  978-1-932051-49-0
   When Darcy Shaw starts a 24-hour cable network called The Homeless Channel, she thinks she's got everything figured out. But confronted with an unexpected romance, a sibling out on the streets and corporate sponsors who think they know what's best for her network, Darcy starts to wonder which is more important: saving the world or saving herself. The book includes some sexual situations and strong language.

Silvermoon, Crystal
Les misérables. Victor Hugo; adapted by Crystal Silvermoon; illustrated by SunNeko Lee. Udon Entertainment 2014 337 p. Illustration; Color (Manga Classics)
Grades: 8 9 10 11 12   741.5; Fic
   1. France — History — 1789-1799, Revolution; 2. Manga
  1927925169; 9781927925164, $19.99
   In this graphic novel adaptation by Crystal Silvermoon, illustrated by SunNeko Lee, "Victor Hugo's classic novel of love & tragedy during the French Revolution is reborn in this fantastic new manga edition! The gorgeous art of TseMei Lee brings to life the tragic stories of Jean Valjean, Inspector Javert, and the beautiful Fantine, in this epic adaptation of Les Miserables!" (Publisher's note)
   "All major plot points and iconic scenes are included in the text and art, and both work seamlessly to tell the story.... The characters, for the most part, are instantly recognizable. It is clear that research has gone into making this adaptation." VOYA

Simmons, Josh
House. Fantagraphics Books 2007 Un Illustration
Grades: 11 12 Adult   741.5; Fic
   1. Horror graphic novels; 2. Graphic novels
  978-1-56097-855-8, $12.95
   In the thick of a dense wood, a young man comes upon a decrepit house and two teen-aged girls, who quickly decide to explore the abandoned house together. Simmons captures the aloof ennui and deep curiosity of being a teenager-that is, until events force them to confront their own mortality. One of the girls takes a horrible fall, and her clothes are torn; for the rest of the book she is partially nude because of it.

Simon, Kristen Koerner
  ★ **Fractured** fables. Edited by Jim Valentino and Kristen K. Simon; book design by Jim Valentino; cover illustration by Michael and Laura Allred from a sketch by Jim Valentino; cover design and graphics by Tim Daniel. Image Comics 2010 159p. Illustration
Grades: 6 7 8 9   741.5
  978-1-60706-269-1, $29.99; 1-60706-269-0
                    LC 2010014838

Simone, Gail
Birds of Prey Vol. 4: The Battle Within. Gail Simone, writer; Joe Bennett [and others], pencillers. DC Comics 2006 240p. Illustration
Grades: 9 10 11 12 Adult   741.5
   1. Adventure graphic novels; 2. Birds of Prey (Fictional characters); 3. Superhero graphic novels; 4. Graphic novels
  978-1-4012-1096-0
   Oracle and the others have left Gotham after their headquarters was destroyed but continue their work, stopping a young witch with a split personality, then taking on a met human vigilante who calls herself Harvest and kills unpunished killers. However, Oracle's controlling ways have caused Huntress to remove herself and go after Gotham mobsters on her own. Black Canary enlists the help of Wildcat in Singapore to go after drug dealers, while back home Oracle is overcome by the techno-virus left in her body after she had defeated Brainiac. There's lots of fighting action, but little graphic violence.

Birds of Prey Vol. 5: Perfect Pitch. Gail Simone, writer; Paulo Siqueira [and others], pencillers. DC Comics 2007 Illustration
Grades: 10 11 12 Adult   741.5; Fic
   1. Batgirl (Fictional character); 2. Birds of Prey (Fictional characters); 3. Joker (Fictional character); 4. Superhero graphic novels; 5. Graphic novels
  978-1-4012-1191-2, $17.99
   After being paralyzed by the Joker, former Batgirl Barbara Gordon became Oracle and formed a crime-fighting team with other female heroes including the martial artist with a devastating sonic scream, Black Canary, the vigilante known as the Huntress and the mysterious Lady Blackhawk. In this collection, the team is shaken up as members depart and new teammates are added to the roster. Who will be asked to join Oracle in her all-new Birds Of Prey? Who will refuse, and who will fly the coop for good? There's lots of hand-to-hand fighting in this book.

Birds of Prey: Between Dark & Dawn. Gail Simone, writer; Ed Benes et al, pencillers. DC Comics 2006 Un Illustration
Grades: 9 10 11 12 Adult   741.5; Fic
   1. Birds of Prey (Fictional characters); 2. Justice League (Fictional characters); 3. Superhero graphic novels; 4. Graphic novels
  978-1-4012-0940-7, $14.99
   Huntress goes undercover to infiltrate a religious cult with a dangerous secret and a hidden operative, while Black Canary and Oracle uncover the true nature of Sovereign Brusaw's organization. It all leads to the Huntress's battle against former Justice League member Vixen. Oracle wages

a private, internal battle against Brainiac, who has infected her with a techno-organic virus. Finally, the Birds must face the aftermath of the Gotham Gang War, leading to a decision that changes the team's fate forever.

Birds of Prey: Of Like Minds. Gail Simone, writer; Ed Benes, penciller; Alex Lei with Rob Lea, inkers; Hi-Fi, colorist; John E. Workman, Rob Leigh, Jared K. Fletcher, letterers; Ed Benes, Alex Lei with Rob Lei, original series covers. DC Comics 2004 143 p. Color; Illustration
Grades: 9 10 11 12 Adult   741.5
1. Black Canary (Fictional character); 2. Catwoman (Fictional character); 3. Female superhero graphic novels
9781401201920, $14.99; 140120192X
LC 2005295809
"The wheelchair-bound Oracle (Barbara Gordon, formerly Batgirl) now fights crime as a superhacker and cyberspy. Her field agent, Dinah Lance, is the Black Canary, a tough martial artist. When a case goes wrong, and a blackmailer called Savant captures the Canary, he threatens to kill her unless Oracle can supply him with a choice piece of information: the secret identity of Batman." (Library Journal)
Originally published in single magazine form in Birds of prey #56-61

Birds of Prey: Sensei & Student. [Gail Simone, writer; Ed Benes ... [et al.], pencillers; Alex Lei ... [et al.], inkers; Hi-Fi, colorist; Jared K. Fletcher, Rob Leigh, Nick Napolitano, letterers]. DC Comics 2005 Un Color; Illustration
Grades: 9 10 11 12 Adult   741.5
1. Black Canary (Fictional character); 2. Female superhero comic books, strips, etc; 3. Huntress (Fictional character); 4. Oracle (Fictional character)
9781401204341, $17.99; 1401204341
"Black Canary goes to China on a mission of mercy and runs into the DC Universe's most deadly combatant; Lady Shiva! Shiva is acting with a hidden agenda, making Canary an offer that could change the course of her life. Meanwhile, Oracle's life is tearing at the seams as the information she feeds out to aid her various heroes starts going strangely and dangerously awry! Not to mention Huntress stumbling upon some of her secrets!" (Publisher's note)
Originally published in single magazine form in Birds of Prey #62-68—t.p. verso.

Gen 13: Best of a Bad Lot. Talent Caldwell, penciller. DC Comics/Wildstorm 2007 Un Illustration
Grades: 10 11 12 Adult   741.5; Fic
1. Gen 13 (Fictional characters); 2. Superhero graphic novels; 3. Graphic novels
978-1-4012-1323-7, $14.99
The life of a teenager can be a strange experience, but when super-powers are added to the mix things get a whole lot more confusing. Meet Caitlin, Sarah, Roxy, Bobby, and Eddie " outcast teenagers from different parts of the country who quickly learn they all have something in common: abilities far beyond those of their classmates. Discover the secret to their wonderful and scary powers and what role the nefarious Tabula Rasa and International Operations play in their lives as they learn to work as a team. Jim Lee and J. Scott Campbell created Gen 13 in the 1990s; this is a fresh

start for the team. This book has a lot of violence in addition to the superhero action.

Killer Princesses. Written by Gail Simone; illustrated by Lea Hernandez; cover colors by Laura Martin. Oni Press 2002 96p. Illustration
Grades: 10 11 12 Adult   741.5; Fic
1. Humorous graphic novels; 2. Mystery graphic novels; 3. Graphic novels
978-1-929998-31-9, $9.95
Meet Charity, Faith, and Hope: the girls of the Tri-Omega Sorority. To some, they're the most popular girls on their campus, but to others, they're the most unstoppable, cruel, and dangerous (not to mention dumbest) assassins in the world! They might not have the highest IQ, but they sure do know how to kick the crap out of the bad guys. The girls jump, skip, and river dance their way into a military base to bust the heads of evil villains and stop a nuclear weapon from being unleashed by a terrorist's spoiled son. Then they attend a splendid gala event which is hosted by someone from their sorority Mother's past who wants to kill her. They go up against some of the cutest Russian terrorists to hit this side of the Pacific, and deal with a new sorority sister. Danger, intrigue, and hilarity ensue as the girls race against the clock to save the day and get back home in time to look good for class. The story includes some strong language, violence, and sexual suggestiveness.

The **marvelous** adventures of Guz Beezer with the X-Men: X marks the Mutant. Jason Lethcoe, art. ABDO Spotlight 2006 Un Illustration
Grades: 3 4 5 6 7 8 9   741.5; Fic
1. Adventure graphic novels; 2. Humorous graphic novels; 3. Superhero graphic novels; 4. Graphic novels
1-59961-050-7, $21.35
Gus Beezer, major comics fan and collector, is convinced he's a mutant like the X-Men, even when his comic book skit at school results in major trouble and gets him grounded. What he keeps missing is that his baby sister Tillie is the one getting him into trouble at home. Another story runs on the bottom part of the page, and looks like a homemade comic written and drawn by Gus, featuring him as Marvel Boy and his baby sister as the town-consuming villain.
This book is a revision of an issue of The Marvelous Adventures of Gus Beever, originally published by Marvel's Marvel Age line.

Secret Six: Six Degrees of Devastation. Gail Simone, writer; Brad Walker, penciller; Jimmy Palmiotti, inker. DC Comics 2007 128p. Illustration
Grades: 11 12 Adult   741.5; Fic
1. Adventure graphic novels; 2. Superhero graphic novels; 3. Graphic novels
978-1-4012-1231-5, $14.99
The mysterious team of misfits walks the line between good and evil and takes on the dirtiest, craziest tasks in the DC Universe. Their first mission, to rescue one of their own from a North Korean prison before he's executed, leads them to the realization that someone is trying to have them all killed. The book includes lots of graphic violence, considerable nudity, sexual situations, and strong language.

Superman: Strange Attractors. Written by Gail Simone; pencilled by John Byrne. DC Comics 2006 Un Illustration
Grades: 9 10 11 12 Adult   **741.5; Fic**
  1. Superhero graphic novels; 2. Superman (Fictional character); 3. Graphic novels
  1401209173; 9781401209179, $14.99
  First, Superman must contend with Dr. Polaris, but something's just not right with the good doctor ... Then, Dr. Psycho comes to Metropolis to mess with Superman's head. And with his Secret Society comrade Black Adam not far behind, a throw down between Adam and Superman is a certainty. Plus, Satanus, the Queen of Fables, and Livewire make Superman's life a living nightmare.

Welcome to Tranquility, book one. DC Comics/Wildstorm 2007 144p. Illustration
Grades: 10 11 12 Adult   **741.5; Fic**
  1. Crime; 2. Superhero graphic novels; 3. Graphic novels
  978-1-4012-1516-3, $19.99
  Tranquility is like any other small town in America, except for one thing—it's the town where superpowered beings go when they want to retire and raise families. From the Golden Age to the Modern Age, heroes and villains alike live in Tranquility, and the unique blend of personalities and conflicts causes headaches for local law enforcement. When a camera crew comes with a reporter to film a news segment about the town, things get turned upside down by a murder, and it becomes clear Tranquility isn't . . . tranquil. The book includes violence and harsh language.

Welcome to Tranquility, book two. Gail Simone, writer; Neil Googe, artist. DC Comics/Wildstorm 2008 144p. Illustration
Grades: 10 11 12 Adult   **741.5; Fic**
  1. Horror graphic novels; 2. Superhero graphic novels; 3. Zombies; 4. Graphic novels
  978-1-4012-1773-0, $19.99
  Tranquility, the town where retired superheroes and villains live side-by-side, was rocked by violence and murders, but has been recovering. Now, zombies keep coming back from the dead. It's up to Sheriff Tommy Lindo to find out what's happening, but it's going to take all the retired heroes and villains, and some thought long dead, to fight the powerful demon who wants the human infestation gone from the city. The book includes some partial nudity and lots of violence, especially zombie fighting.

Sinclair, Alex
  Tom Strong Book Five. Written by Steve Aylett, Brian K. Vaughan, Mark Schultz, Peter Hogan, Ed Brubaker; Pencilled by Peter Snejbjerg, Shawn McManus, Pasqual Ferry, Duncan Fegredo, Chris Sprouse. DC Comics 2005 Un Illustration
Grades: 10 11 12 Adult   **741.5; Fic**
  1. Adventure graphic novels; 2. Science fiction graphic novels; 3. Superhero graphic novels; 4. Tom Strong (Fictional character); 5. Graphic novels
  1-4012-0624-7, $24.99
  In this volume, other writers have taken over from Alan Moore, who created Tom Strong and his world. Tom and his associates face an ancient menace in the sky; a young woman who distorts reality; and an unusual art thief who

brings paintings to life. In a two-part story, Tom is an ordinary schlub who just dreams about being a science super hero; his psychiatrist keeps trying to make him understand that holding on to the dreams is holding him back from reality.

Sizer, Paul
  ★ **Little** White Mouse Omnibus Edition. Cafe Digital Studios 2006 447p. Illustration
Grades: 6 7 8 9 10 11 12   **741.5; Fic**
  1. Science fiction graphic novels; 2. Graphic novels
  978-0-9768565-5-9, $24.95
  "In a far future universe, teenaged Loo is the lone survivor of the mysterious destruction of a luxury space liner. She finds an abandoned space mining station, where she must evade a security system that seeks to destroy an intruder such as her, and find a way home before the automated life systems fail. With its strong and appealing young female protagonist, Sizer's story is science fiction that girls will love." (VOYA)
  Originally published in serial form, and then as a four-volume series from Blue Line Pro.

Moped army, Vol. 1. Cafe Digital Comics 2005 136p. Illustration
Grades: 10 11 12 Adult   **741.5; Fic**
  1. Science fiction graphic novels; 2. Graphic novels
  0-9768565-4-9; 978-0-9768565-4-2, $12.95
  This graphic novel is set in the same universe as Little White Mouse (2005). "Feeling unsatisfied with her circumscribed life and rich, cruel boyfriend, a privileged teenaged girl runs away to the lower city where the poor dwell, finding a home and a new "family" among the young rebels who call themselves the Moped Army. Even readers who don't like science fiction will enjoy this story that depends on strong characterization." Voice Youth Advocates

Slade, Christian
  ★ **Korgi**, Book 1: Sprouting Wings. Top Shelf Productions 2007 88p. Illustration
Grades: 2 3 4 5 6 7 8 9 10 11 12 Adult   **741.5; Fic**
  1. Dogs; 2. Fantasy graphic novels; 3. Stories without words; 4. Graphic novels
  978-1-891830-90-7, $10
  In this wordless book, a young Mollie (woodland people) named Ivy and her young Korgi companion named Sprout embark on adventures in Korgi Hollow, an enchanted place. When they wander from the Mollie village, the two fall through a hole in the ground and find nasty, monstrous creatures who want to eat them. As they deal with the danger and make their escape, Ivy and Sprout both discover new talents. Slade's extensively cross-hatched yet delicate art is highly expressive, and readers young and old will have no trouble figuring out what is going on. The Korgi are based on Welsh corgi dogs, of which Slade and his wife have two.

Korgi, book 2. Top Shelf Productions 2008 Un Illustration
Grades: 3 4 5 6 7 8 9 10 11 12 Adult   **741.5; Fic**
  1. Adventure graphic novels; 2. Fantasy graphic novels; 3. Stories without words; 4. Graphic novels
  978-1-60309-010-0, $10

In this second wordless volume, the young Mollie named Ivy and her Korgi cub Sprout, experience a harrowing adventure. Someone has been hunting the Mollies and cutting off their wings. Ivy and Sprout rescue one older Mollie named Art and his Korgi when they fall into a deep trap in the woods; then as Ivy flies, a barbed arrow cuts one of her wings off. She and Sprout see a strange creature carrying her wing and they follow him to his place, where he hangs all the Mollie wings like trophies. Ivy decides she wants her wing back, but she and Sprout will have to fight the creature and his automated and nasty bots.

Small, David
★ **Stitches:** a memoir. W.W. Norton 2009 329p. Illustration
Grades: 10 11 12 Adult   **92; 741.5**
1. Art teachers; 2. Artists; 3. Authors; 4. Autobiographical graphic novels; 5. Cancer; 6. Children's authors; 7. Family life; 8. Illustrators; 9. Small, David, 1945-; 10. Graphic novels
978-0-393-06857-3, $23.95; 0-393-06857-9
LC 2009-22526
David Small grew up in a dysfunctional family, with a radiologist father who was distant, an angry mother who expressed her anger in eloquent silences, and an older brother who played drums a lot to express his frustrations. When he was eleven, he had a lump, a growth, on the side of his neck. Nothing was done until he was fourteen. He thought he was going in for a minor surgery to remove the cyst from his neck; instead, there were two surgeries, and when he woke up, he had no voice—a vocal cord was removed. He later learned he had cancer, something his parents refused to discuss. After he finds his mother in bed with another woman and his father confesses that he exposed him to x-rays when he was very young, Small leaves home at age sixteen, with little except his dreams that his art could be his life. In one early scene, Small shows the indignities wrought upon his body by his father, including an enema. In another scene, young Small and his older brother look at their father's medical books and see a woman's breast and a man's penis; towards the end of the book, Small draws his grandmother stripping all her clothes off and dancing wildly after setting her house on fire. Other than these few images, Small's depictions of his horrible childhood and teen years are quiet and low-key.
"Emotionally raw, artistically compelling and psychologically devastating graphic memoir of childhood trauma." Kirkus

Smalley, Roger
Dolley Madison Saves History. Illustrated by Anna Maria Cool, Scott Rosema, Charles Barnett III. Capstone Press 2006 32p. Illustration
Grades: 3 4 5 6 7 8 9   **741.5; 973.5; 92**
1. Biographical graphic novels; 2. Madison, Dolley, 1768-1849; 3. War of 1812; 4. Washington (DC); 5. Graphic novels
0-7368-4972-6, $25.26
LC 2005008465
This book uses the comic book format to recount the story of First Lady Dolley Madison's actions during the War of 1812, when Washington, D.C. was invaded by British

troops. It includes additional information, a glossary, a list of books for further reading, and more.
Part of the Graphic Library, Graphic History series.

Smith, Andy J.
Jeremy Kreep: Fang Fairy. Stone Arch Books 2007 40p. Illustration
Grades: 3 4 5 6 7 8 9   **741.5; Fic**
1. Fantasy graphic novels; 2. Humorous graphic novels; 3. Graphic novels
978-1-59889-835-4, $21.26
LC 2007-3176
Jeremy Kreep has a problem. Something has snagged a baby tooth from beneath his brother's pillow and left a puddle of slime. Now Jeremy and his best friend Nessy go off to find the truth behind the tooth fairy. Is the creature just a silly superstition, or a real-life collector of fangs? This graphic novel is written with an easy vocabulary for reluctant and struggling readers.
Part of the Graphic Sparks line of books.

Smith, Dwayne Alexander
Speed Racer. Art by Dwayne Alexander Smith. Seven Seas Entertainment 2007 Un Illustration
Grades: 8 9 10 11 12 Adult   **741.5; Fic**
1. Adventure graphic novels; 2. Automobile racing; 3. Racer, Speed (Fictional character); 4. Graphic novels
978-1-933164-33-5, $9.99
The popular cartoon character Speed Racer is back in an original global manga story. Speed comes from a family with racing in its blood; his older brother Rex presumably died in an accident. Speed drives the Mach 5 and, in this book, he's participating in a grueling three-day, 900 mile race. His main opponent, Adam Matic, determines to win at any cost and tries to sabotage the Mach 5, but on the second day of the race, he's the one who dies. His father, the mad scientist Otto Matic, takes Adam's heart and builds a cyborg version of his son to carry on; but Adam 2 also retains the original man's hatred and tries to kill Speed. Several publishers are bringing Speed Racer back to the U.S. in book form, and a new live-action movie is scheduled for a May 2008 release. This one has lots of action and some violence that makes it more suitable for teen readers.

Smith, Ian
Emily & the intergalactic lemonade stand. [by] Ian Smith and Tyson Smith. Amaze Ink/Slave Labor Graphics 2004 96p. Illustration
Grades: 4 5 6 7 8 9   **741.5; Fic**
1. Humorous graphic novels; 2. Science fiction graphic novels; 3. Graphic novels
0-943151-96-1, $12.95
Eleven-year-old Emily runs a lemonade stand with the help of her pet robot, Juicer; she wants to earn enough money to buy a pony. Complicating matters is neighborhood rival Daisy, who wants to beat Emily because cute Jace Tanner hangs around Emily (he actually only likes robots). Then aliens invade, and the military wants Juicer, because they think he's the perfect weapon. And little alien warrior Pheef wants blood, can he help it he's so cute and tiny? The defense of Earth depends on Emily; can it survive?

Oddjob: The Collected Stories Volume 1. By Ian and Tyson Smith. Slave Labor Graphics 2002 Un Illustration
Grades: 9 10 11 12 Adult   **741.5; Fic**
1. Humorous graphic novels; 2. Mystery graphic novels; 3. Graphic novels
0-943151-63-5, $19.95

The odd has arrived. Moe is the Investigator of the Odd, the man called when the going gets too strange for the police, too askew for the FBI, too creepy for the CIA. His exploits with his unemployable sidekick clown Robin, and ball player Moose Mulligan span eight issues and five mad scientists, as well as living gummi men, sloths, Amish cyborgs, and exploding echidna. The collection comes complete with a newly unearthed story, commentary, and rare case files.

Smith, Jeff
★ **Bone** Book Seven: ghost circles. Scholastic/GRAPHIX 2008 152p. Illustration
Grades: 3 4 5 6 7 8 9 10 11 12 Adult   **741.5; Fic**
1. Adventure graphic novels; 2. Fantasy graphic novels; 3. Graphic novels
978-0-439-70629-2, $19.99; 978-0-439-70634-6 (pa), $9.99
                                        LC 2007-9568403
The Bone cousins, Gran'ma Ben, Thorn, and their loyal rat creature cub Bartleby venture on a journey through the mysterious ghost circles to Atheia, the old city of the royal family. Meanwhile, the Barrelhaven villagers and the Veni Yan face enemy hordes. Steve Hamaker is the colorist for this full color version of Smith's comic epic.

★ **Bone** vol. 8: treasure hunters. Scholastic/Graphix 2008 138p. Illustration
Grades: 5 6 7 8 9 10 11 12 Adult   **741.5; Fic**
1. Adventure graphic novels; 2. Fantasy graphic novels; 3. Graphic novels
978-0-439-70630-8, $18.95; 978-0-439-70633-9 (pa), $9.99
                                        LC 2008-9568403
The Bone cousins, Gran'ma Ben, and Thorn reach the city of Atheia, where they prepare to battle the Lord of the Locusts. Meanwhile, Thorn's visions are becoming more threatening and Phoney Bone is convinced Atheia is rich in gold, and he is determined to find it. But all is not well in Atheia, and Thorn is in great danger, not only from Briar and the Lord of the Locusts. This edition is in full color, done by Steve Hamaker.

★ **Bone:** out from Boneville. Scholastic Graphix 2005 144p. Illustration
Grades: 4 5 6 7 8 9 10 11 12   **741.5; Fic**
1. Adventure graphic novels; 2. Fantasy graphic novels; 3. Graphic novels
0-439-70623-8, $18.95; 0-439-70640-8 (pa), $9.99
"The story follows three cousins who have been thrown out of their town for cheating the citizens. Shortly thereafter, they are separated. Each Bone stumbles into a mysterious valley full of odd creatures that reveal strange happenings. The story is well paced with smooth transitions. It is dark,

witty, mysterious, and exciting. The full-color art reflects that of classic comic books." SLJ
Also available Bone: one volume edition $39.95 from Cartoon Books (ISBN 1-8889-6314-X)
Other titles in this series are: Bone: the great cow race (vol. 2); Bone: eyes of the storm (vol. 3); Bone: the dragonslayer (vol. 4); Bone: Rock Jaw: master of the Eastern border (vol. 5); Bone: old man's cave (vol. 6); Bone: ghost circles (vol. 7); Bone: treasure hunters (vol. 8); Bone: crown of horns (vol. 9)

Smith, Kevin
Spider-Man and the Black Cat: The Evil That Men Do. Writer, Kevin Smith; artist, Terry Dodson. Marvel Entertainment 2007 Un Illustration
Grades: 10 11 12 Adult   **741.5; Fic**
1. Spider-Man (Fictional character); 2. Superhero graphic novels; 3. Graphic novels
978-0-7851-1079-8, $14.99
The mysterious disappearance of an old friend brings Felicia Hardy, the Black Cat, to New York in search of answers, and a certain web-slinging ex-lover of hers is following the same trail. How long will it take before they do some... catching up" This book is written by filmmaker and former comic store owner Kevin Smith (of Jay and Silent Bob fame). The book includes some sexually suggestive content.

Smith, Mark Andrew
The **amazing** Joy Buzzards volume 1: here come the spiders. Written by Mark Andrew Smith; art by Dan Hipp. Image Comics 2008 Un Illustration
Grades: 9 10 11 12 Adult   741.5; Fic
1. Fantasy graphic novels; 2. Humorous graphic novels; 3. Rock music; 4. Spies; 5. Graphic novels
978-1-58240-918-4, $19.99
Rockers Gabe, Biff, and Stevo are the Amazing Joy Buzzards, a hot rock band managed by Dalton, who works for the Creative International Artists Agency. Yes, its initials read "CIA." And yes, it is the covert government agency. The boys in the band have no idea that they're a front for intelligence agency covert operations. They get into enough trouble on their own, such as when Stevo becomes a giant monster, or when Gabe stars in a movie and movie star Brick Brannigan is nearly killed, or when the boys throw a free concert and the entire audience is turned into bloodthirsty zombies, ... This book collects the first two trade paperback volumes of the adventures of the Amazing Joy Buzzards, and Image Comics has been publishing a new ongoing comic book series of more rocking, bopping, fantastical, super spy type stories. There is some violence and some brief moments of sexual innuendo.

Aqua Leung. Mark Andrew Smith; art by Paul Maybury. Image Comics 2008 Un Illustration
Grades: 9 10 11 12 Adult   **741.5; Fic**
1. Adventure graphic novels; 2. Fantasy graphic novels; 3. Ocean; 4. Graphic novels
978-1-58240-863-7, $17.99
Adam Leung has never quite fit in, especially at school. Then one day he comes home and finds his parents slaughtered and the murderer waiting for him. Atlantean warriors save him and take him under the ocean, where

Adam finds he can breathe, and he learns that he is the son of the king. Taking back his true name of Aqua, he begins the process of learning everything about his true home so he can undertake the journey to take back his father's kingdom from the evil lords who rule over it. The book includes violence, bloodshed and military battles.

The **New** Brighton Archeological Society book one: The castle of Galomar. Created by Mark Andrew Smith & Matthew Weldon. Image Comics 2009 Un Illustration
Grades: 4 5 6 7 8 9   **741.5; Fic**
1. Adventure graphic novels; 2. Fairies; 3. Fantasy graphic novels; 4. Goblins; 5. Graphic novels
978-1-58240-973-3, $17.99
When their parents die on an archeological expedition, two sets of siblings Joss and Cooper, and Brad and Becka, come to live on the estate where their parents lived as children. They first discover bottled ghosts when Becka accidentally falls through a secret door, then they find an old clubhouse connected to the estate's manor house by a tunnel. The clubhouse holds lots of books about different kinds of monsters and other creatures. And then, when they go camping, they find a society of goblins, including Mitch, who knew their parents. There, the four find themselves caught in the middle of a war between the fairies and the goblins, all for possession of powerful books. Mitch's parents tell the children about the evil Galomar, who seeks to possess all the magic books in the world. They decide to infiltrate the castle in order to try to stop Galomar. This fantasy adventure includes some action but little actual killing (the goblins use maple syrup to make the fairies' wings too sticky to fly, among other tactics).

Smith, Paul
X-Men: Kitty Pryde - Shadow & Flame. Marvel Entertainment 2006 Un Illustration
Grades: 8 9 10 11 12 Adult   **741.5; Fic**
1. Adventure graphic novels; 2. Superhero graphic novels; 3. X-Men (Fictional characters); 4. Graphic novels
0-7851-1816-0, $14.99
A deadly mystery draws Kitty Pryde and her fire-breathing friend Lockheed to the shores of Japan. Ninjas and dragons will be the least of their worries, however, as a long-forgotten villain from Kitty's past is about to finally make his move. There's lots of ninja fighting action.

Smith, Tyson
Dream Maiden Megan. Tyson Smith and Ian Smith ; Art by Ian Smith. SLG Publishing/Amaze Ink 2008 93p. Illustration
Grades: 8 9 10 11 12   **741.5; Fic**
1. Fantasy graphic novels; 2. Humorous graphic novels; 3. Graphic novels
978-1-59362-129-2, $8.95
High school student Jef is a good student who now works as a manager at a coffee bar. He has no time for sleep, which causes a problem for Dream Maiden Megan, who needs to get Jef to sleep and dream. However, once he finds out she can't leave until he sleeps, he refuses to do so because she's beautiful and he isn't lucky with girls. Megan decides to set up shop in his closet and brings in her friends, such as a monster in the closet and some other dream

maidens. And they plot to make Jef fall asleep even as he does everything in his power to stay awake. Megan finally figures out she needs to set up Jef on a date, but no one will go out with him. . . . There's some violence, especially with Maiden-in-Training Tulip, who likes to bash Jef in the head.

Sniegoski, Tom
Talent. Written by Christopher Golden & Tom Sniegoski; art by Paul Azaceta; colors by Ron Riley; letters by Marshall Dillon. Boom! Studios 2007 120p. Illustration
Grades: 10 11 12 Adult   **741.5**
1. Mystery graphic novels; 2. Graphic novels
978-1-934506-05-9, $14.99
When a plane crashes, sole survivor Nicholas Dane discovers he can channel his dead fellow passengers' talents. Chased by the killers who destroyed the plane, Dane stays one step ahead of death, while putting the pieces of the mystery together. Aided by a ... spirit ... Dane soon learns that some of the passengers on the ill-fated flight were killers working for the organization now hunting him. The book includes violence.

Snyder, Scott
Batman; Volume 1: The court of owls. Scott Snyder, writer; Greg Capullo, penciller; Jonathan Glapion, inker. DC Comics 2012 Un Color; Illustration (New 52)
Grades: 9 10 11 12 Adult   **741.5**
1. Batman (Fictional character); 2. Superhero comic books, strips, etc
1401235425; 9781401235420, $16.99
"After a series of brutal murders rocks Gotham City, Batman begins to realize that perhaps these crimes go far deeper than appearances suggest. As the Caped Crusader begins to unravel this deadly mystery, he discovers a conspiracy going back to his youth and beyond to the origins of the city he's sworn to protect. Could the Court of Owls, once thought to be nothing more than an urban legend, be behind the crime and corruption" Or is Bruce Wayne losing his grip on sanity and falling prey to the pressures of his war on crime?" (Publisher's note)

Soda, Masahito
Firefighter! Daigo of Fire Company M Volume 1. Viz Media 2003 208p. Illustration
Grades: 9 10 11 12 Adult   **741.5; Fic**
1. Adventure graphic novels; 2. Firefighters; 3. Manga; 4. Shonen manga; 5. Graphic novels
1-56931-955-3, $9.95
Fire, smoke, adrenaline, and fear—when everyone is running to escape from a fire, a few courageous people are running to jump right into the thick of it. Firefighters put their own lives on the line to protect others and Daigo Asahina has always dreamed of becoming one. He's eighteen years old, fresh out of the training academy, and has been newly assigned to Medaka-Ga-Hama fire station. Cocky and overconfident, Daigo responds to a few calls and is quickly humbled and put in his place—he's still got a lot to learn before he can call himself a true firefighter. There's some mildly bad language and mild violence in the stories that focus on Daigo and his fellow firefighters and their job.
Volume 1 of 20

Sohn, Emily
   The **Illuminating** World of Light with Max Axiom, Super Scientist. Capstone Press 2007 32p. Illustration
Grades: 3 4 5 6 7 8 9   **535; 741.5**
   1. Light; 2. Graphic novels
978-1-4296-0140-X, $25.26
                LC 2007002264
   This book uses the graphic novel format to follow the adventures of super scientist Max Axiom as he explains the science behind light, including how the human eye sees light. The book includes additional facts and a list of books for further reading.
   Part of the Graphic Science series.

Sommariva, Jon
   Go boy 7, Vol. 1: Ready set go!. [by] Tom Peyer and Jon Sommariva. Rocket Comics/Dark Horse Comics 2004 96p. Illustration
Grades: 6 7 8 9 10 11 12   **741.5; Fic**
   1. Science fiction graphic novels; 2. Graphic novels
1-56971-937-3, $12.95
   When Jonny Zero's family jet is shot down, he survives only because his uncle uses his experimental nanotech plasm to save his life. Now Jonny is more than human, which is a good thing, because Uncle Noah and his Go Base are under attack by the forces of The Cultist, an evil madman out to destroy all thinking life. The problem is, he's still just a young teen and a wee bit impulsive when taking action. The action and violence level is similar to what preteens might see in a PG rated movie.
   Another title in this series is: Go boy 7 Vol 2: The human factor, written by Brian Augustyn (2004)

Son, Hee-Joon
   IDeNTITY Volume 1. Written by Hee-Joon Son; illustrated by Youn-Kyung Kim. Tokyopop 2005 192p. Illustration
Grades: 9 10 11 12 Adult   **741.5; Fic**
   1. Adventure graphic novels; 2. Fantasy graphic novels; 3. Manwha; 4. Graphic novels
1-59532-345-7, $9.99
   In real life, Roto, Boromid and Ah-Dol are average kids with average problems, but in the virtual world of Lost Saga, they're heroes. They might even become legends...if they can stop bickering long enough to level up. Whether it's werewolves running rampant or a gorgeous pair of troublesome thieves, our boys must be ready for anything, because in Lost Saga nothing is what it seems and murder can happen with a click of a mouse. The book includes fantasy gaming violence, some strong language, and some sexual suggestiveness.

Song, Ji-Hyung
   XS Hybrid Vol. 1. Dark Horse Comics 2007 192p. Illustration
Grades: 11 12 Adult   **741.5; Fic**
   1. Manwha; 2. Science fiction graphic novels; 3. Graphic novels
978-1-59307-628-3, $10.95
   In a strange future where gifted, "hybrid" humans police the planet, Mina is a likeable tomboy with growing psychic powers. When a young boy falls into a coma after

gazing into her eyes, it's clear that there's more to Mina than her pretty looks. This young boy, Huin Chang, grows up to be quite a daredevil, and his awkward, secret love for Mina fuels his protective fire when mysterious men arrive, bringing the violence of the "hybrid" world with them. The book includes considerable graphic violence and use of foul language.

Sonic the Hedgehog: The Beginning
   Archie Comics 2003 96p. Illustration
Grades: 3 4 5 6 7 8 9 10 11 12 Adult   **741.5; Fic**
   1. Adventure graphic novels; 2. Humorous graphic novels; 3. Sonic the Hedgehog (Fictional character); 4. Graphic novels
1-879794-12-8, $10.95
   In 1993, Sonic the Hedgehog sped his way from video games to comic books, and has been going strong ever since. Now, readers can enjoy his earliest comic book adventures with this edition that reprints the first appearances of Tails, Princess Sally, Antoine, Rotor, Uncle Chuck, and Muttski. Fans can also marvel at Sonic's magic rings, the freedom emeralds, and King Acorn's magic crown; while booing and hissing at the villainous Robotnik, his evil Swat-Bots, and his myriad dastardly devices.

Soo, Kean
   ★ **Jellaby:** monster in the city. Hyperion Books 2009 172p. Illustration
Grades: 4 5 6 7 8 9   **741.5; Fic**
   1. Fantasy graphic novels; 2. Friendship; 3. Monsters; 4. Graphic novels
1-4231-0565-6 (pa); 978-1-4231-0565-7 (pa), $9.99
   Beginning right where the first book ended, Portia, Jason, and Jellaby continue on their way to Toronto, walking after Portia panicked and they got off the train. They're searching for a way home for Jellaby, and they think a door somewhere in Exhibition Place, where the Canadian National Exhibition is taking place, holds a clue. Portia feels torn between wanting to help her friend yet not wanting to say goodbye forever, and her ambivalence causes a rift between her and Jason. When she doesn't want to trust a masked magician who seems to know too much about them and Jellaby, Portia leaves Jason. They all end up in the Automotive Building, where the masked man leads Jason and Jellaby down below the building, while Portia seems to find her long lost father. But is he really her father, and just what is waiting for Jason and Jellaby under the Automotive Building? Soo again uses a mostly purple color palette.
   Another title in the author's series about Jellaby

   ★ **Jellaby;** Volume 1: the lost monster. By Kean Soo. Stone Arch Books 2014 160 p. Color; Illustration (Jellaby)
Grades: 4 5 6 7 8 9   **741.5**
   1. Extraterrestrial beings — Fiction; 2. Friendship — Fiction; 3. Human-alien encounters; 4. Monsters — Fiction
1434291952; 9781434264206, $12.95 ; 9781434291950, $19.99
                LC 2013037026
   "Portia has just moved to a new neighborhood with her mom. Adjusting to life without a father is hard enough, but school is boring and her classmates are standoffish. . . . But things start to get better when Portia mounts a midnight

excursion into the woods behind her house where she discovers a shy and sweet purple monster. Life with Jellaby is exciting, but Portia's purple friend has secrets of his own." (Publisher's note)

"Soo grounds the story in a fairly gritty contemporary reality, where kids deal with bullies and well-meaning adults try to help. Clear, clean lines and easy-to-follow panel layouts round out the package." Booklist

First published 2008

Originally published: New York : Hyperion Books for Children, 2008.A Capstone imprint.

Sorachi, Hideaki

Gin Tama Vol. 1. Viz Media/Shonen Jump Advanced 2007 216p. Illustration

Grades: 10 11 12 Adult　　　　　**741.5; Fic**
1. Humorous graphic novels; 2. Manga; 3. Shonen manga; 4. Graphic novels
978-1-4215-1358-4, $7.99

The samurai didn't stand a chance. First, the aliens invaded Japan. Next, they took all the jobs. And then they confiscated everyone's swords. So what does a hotheaded former samurai like Sakata "Gin" Gintoki do to make ends meet" Take any odd job that comes his way, even if it means losing his dignity. Sleazy alien moneylenders, monsters on the rampage, and a ticking time bomb may all be in a day's work for Gin, but a drop in his blood sugar level means trouble for everyone. Some harsh language and lots of fighting action fill this alternate history comedy.

Sorano, Kaili

Monochrome factor, volume 1. Tokyopop 2007 182p. Illustration

Grades: 8 9 10 11 12　　　　　**741.5**
1. Manga; 2. Shonen manga; 3. Supernatural graphic novels; 4. Graphic novels
978-1-4278-0069-5, $9.99

Akira Nikaido is the ultimate slacker, able to skip entire days of school with relative impunity. Then, one day a mysterious man named Shirogane confronts him and when Akira refuses to listen to him, he tells him to meet him at the school that night. Due to circumstances beyond his control, Akira finds himself at the school and a shadow monster attacks. When Akira ignores Shirogane's warning and runs past a psychic barrier, he becomes caught in the shadow world, and now the only way to live is for Akira to become a shin, a creature of the shadow world just like Shirogane, and work to restore the balance between the human and shadow worlds. The book includes some minor incidental partial nudity, some mildly harsh language and some violence.

Soria, Gabriel

★ **Life** sucks. [text by] Jessica Abel, Gabe Soria; [art by] Warren Pleece; coloring by Hilary Sycamore. First Second Books 2008 186p. Illustration

Grades: 10 11 12 Adult　　　　　**741.5; Fic**
1. Horror graphic novels; 2. Humorous graphic novels; 3. Romance graphic novels; 4. Vampires; 5. Graphic novels
978-1-59643-107-2, $19.95; 1-59643-107-5

Anyone who thinks the vampire life is all romantic and ethereal better have another think. Dave can tell them, it sucks. He's the night manager for a convenience store, and

he's a vampire, "made" by his boss (master), Radu. He's not the only one; in their neighborhood, most of the shops are owned by vampires who make their night managers vampires. Dave can't make himself drink from humans, so he drinks bottled blood. His roommate is human but tolerant. Then Dave sees the perfect girl, Rosa, one of the goth vampire groupies who hangs out in the neighborhood. However, surfer/slacker Wes, whom Dave replaced as the night manager, also has his eye on Rosa, and Wes isn't above killing to get his way. The book includes some violence (including the tearing off of one girl's head), and some harsh language.

"Warren Pleece's art marvelously captures the humor of the mundane that lends the book's crew of late-night wage-slave vamps believability and energy. A really fun read!" Booklist

Spangler, Bill

Tom Corbett: space cadet. Art by John DaCosta and Wilson Ramos Jr.. Bluewater Productions 2010 96p. Illustration

Grades: 7 8 9 10 11 12 Adult　　　　　**741.5; Fic**
1. Adventure graphic novels; 2. Science fiction graphic novels; 3. Tom Corbett, Space Cadet (Television series); 4. Graphic novels
978-1-4507-0014-6, $15.95

In the year 2251 A.D., Solar Guard Cadets Tom Corbett, Roger Manning, and Astro Deaver come to Rescue Station RSA-4 to conduct routine maintenance, but instead they find big trouble when the fully automated station doesn't respond to their computers, and the robots attack them. When the cadets manage to stop an alien robot that had taken over the station, they take it back to the Academy, where Solar Guard scientists discover that it isn't alien, but based on the old designs of Dr. Sanderson Dale of Earth. Then robot-run ships attack every planet of the Solar System except Earth, with a demand that humans leave space and return to Earth or face destruction. The Solar Alliance's only hope is to find Dr. Dale's original software, in order to reboot the robots of the One State. This space adventure is an original story set in the universe created for the Tom Corbett, Space Cadet television series that aired in the 1950s, as well as the novels and comics that were spun off the series. Spangler wrote some of the comics published in the 1990s. DaCosta's full-color art uses a retro/epic look for the outer space architecture and ships. This book was originally published as a four-issue miniseries of comic books.

Spencer, Nick

Morning Glories: Volume 1: for a better future. Nick Spencer, words; Joe Eisma, art; Rodin Esquejo, covers; Alex Sollazzo, colors; Johnny Lowe, letters. Image 2011 192 p. Illustration

Grades: 9 10 11 12 Adult　　　　　**741.5**
1. Good and evil — Fiction; 2. School stories
1607063077; 9781607063070, $9.99
Originally published in single magazine form as Morning Glories #1-6

"Morning Glory Academy is one of the most prestigious prep schools in the country . . . but something sinister and deadly lurks behind its walls. When six gifted, but troubled, students arrive, they find themselves trapped and fighting for their lives as the secrets of the academy reveal themselves." (Publisher's note)

"[C]ompelling character studies, mind games, and action-packed sequences [feature] in this gorgeously inked mystery." Booklist

Volume 1 of an ongoing series

Morning Glories: Volume. 2 All Will Be Free. Nick Spencer, illustrated by Joe Eisma and Rodin Esquejo. Image Comics 2011 168 p. Color; Illustration

Grades: 10 11 12 Adult   **741.5; Fic**
1. Good and evil — Fiction; 2. School stories; 3. Graphic novels
1607064073; 9781607064077, $12.99

"It's the Glories' first day of school, and they've already landed themselves in detention! Now, anywhere else that might just mean the start of a bad year, but they're about to find out when you're enrolled at Morning Glory Academy, corporal punishment takes on a whole new-and deadly-meaning!" (Publisher's note)

"Zoe, Hunter, Jun, Jade, Ike, and Casey . . . continue to fight for survival while trying to figure out who they can trust among the staff and their fellow students. Meanwhile, snippets of their pasts are revealed in flashbacks but only serve to bring about more questions than answers." (Booklist)

Collects issues 7-12—P. [4] of cover

Morning Glories: Volume 3: P.E.. Nick Spencer, illustrated by Joe Eisma and Rodin Esquejo. Image Comics 2012 240 p. Color; Illustration

Grades: 10 11 12 Adult   **741.5; Fic**
1. Good and evil — Fiction; 2. School stories; 3. Graphic novels
1607065584; 9781607065586, $14.99

"When the faculty cancels classes and sends the students on an outing in the nearby woods, all hell breaks loose, sending the Glories on a mysterious journey through time and space. Nothing is what it seems to be as Academy's hold on the kids collapses and new threats emerge!" (Publisher's note)

"Following an ensemble cast makes identifying with characters a challenge, but the momentum of the plot should carry readers along." LJ

Collects: Morning Glories issues 13-19

Morning Glories: Volume four: Truants. Nick Spencer, illustrated by Joe Eisma. Image Comics 2013 216 p. Color; Illustration

Grades: 10 11 12 Adult   **741.5; Fic**
1. School stories; 2. Graphic novels
1607067277; 9781607067276, $14.99

"Still reeling from the climactic events of 'P.E.,' the Glories find themselves lost in time and space, confronted by a new group of students who might be even more dangerous than the faculty themselves—the truants!" (Publisher's note)

Originally published in single magazine form as Morning glories #20-25

Morning Glories: Volume five: Tests. Nick Spencer, illustrated by Joe Eisma. Image Comics 2013 136 p. Color; Illustration

Grades: 10 11 12 Adult   **741.5**
1. School stories; 2. Graphic novels

1607067749; 9781607067740, $12.99

"The Glories are scattered, The Faculty broken, and The Truants on the attack!"(Publisher's note)

Originally published in single magazine form Morning Glories, #26-29—T.p. verso

Morning Glories: Volume six: Demerits. Nick Spencer, illustrated by Joe Eisma. Image Comics 2013 144 p. Color; Illustration

Grades: 10 11 12 Adult   **741.5**
1. School stories; 2. Graphic novels
1607068230; 9781607068235, $14.99

"After the climactic events of the Season Two premiere, the Glories and the Truants find themselves more lost than ever before, haunted by the things they've seen and done" (Publisher's note)

Originally published in single magazine form Morning Glories, #30-34

Morning Glories: Volume seven: Honors. Nick Spencer, illustrated by Joe Eisma. Image Comics 2014 124 p. Color; Illustration

Grades: 10 11 12 Adult   **741.5**
1. School stories; 2. Graphic novels
1607069431; 9781607069430, $12.99

"The Truants are back in class, and that means new mysteries abound! And whatever happened to Abraham? The answer to that question and more as Season Two races on! Collects the suspense-filled arc 'Honors.'" (Publisher's note)

Originally published in single magazine form as Morning glories, #35-38

Spider-Man: The Birth of Venom

Marvel Entertainment 2007 Un Illustration
Grades: 8 9 10 11 12 Adult   **741.5; Fic**
1. Fantastic Four (Fictional characters); 2. Spider-Man (Fictional character); 3. Superhero graphic novels; 4. Graphic novels
978-0-7851-2498-6, $29.99

The Beyonder's Battleworld might seem a strange place to get new threads, but it's Spider-Man who becomes unraveled when his new symbiotic, shape-changing costume attempts to darken his life as well as his fashion sense. But ridding himself of his black costume proves an even greater mistake when its alien enmity bonds with mortal madness to form our hero's most dedicated enemy, Venom. Other stories include the first appearances of Puma and the Rose, Mary Jane Watson's startling secret, and the debut of the battling . . . Bag-Man" The Black Cat, the Fantastic Four and other Marvel characters appear.

Spider-Man: Saga of the Sandman

Marvel Entertainment 2007 176p. Illustration
Grades: 7 8 9 10 11 12 Adult   **741.5; Fic**
1. Fantastic Four (Fictional characters); 2. Hulk (Fictional character); 3. Spider-Man (Fictional character); 4. Superhero graphic novels; 5. Graphic novels
978-0-7851-2497-9, $19.99

It was no day at the beach when criminal Flint Marko was mutated into one of Marveldom's most versatile villains. This book recounts his origins and some of the best battles between Sandman, Spider-Man, the Fantastic Four and the Hulk.

Spiegelman, Art

★ **In** the shadow of no towers. Pantheon Books 2004 Illustration

Grades: 10 11 12 Adult   **741; 973.931; 741.5**
1. September 11 terrorist attacks, 2001; 2. Graphic novels
0-375-42307-9, $19.95

                     LC 2004-43870

This is a "memoir of the attacks on the World Trade Center, which Spiegelman witnessed from close range, a rant on their effects on the world at large and within the author, and a monograph on the Sunday newspaper comic strips of the early 20th century." N Y Times Book Rev

The author "provides a hair-raising and wry account of his family's frantic efforts to locate one another on September 11 as well as a morbidly funny survey of his trademark sense of existential doom. . . . This is a powerful and quirky work of visual storytelling by a master comics artist." Publ Wkly

★ **Maus:** a survivor's tale, 2v in 1. Art Spiegelman.. Pantheon Bks. 1996 295 p. Illustration; Map; Color

Grades: 7 8 9 10 11 12 Adult   **741.5; 92; 940.53**
1. Biographical graphic novels; 2. Holocaust, 1933-1945; 3. Spiegelman, Vladek; 4. Graphic novels
0-679-40641-7, $35

                     LC 96-32796

Awards: 1992 Pulitzer Prize Special Award; Eisner Award for Best Graphic Album: Reprint for Maus II; Harvey Award for Best Graphic Album of Previously Published Work (for Maus II); 1993 Los Angeles Times Book Prize for Fiction (for Maus II)

"An undisputed classic and award-winning title (including a Pulitzer Prize in 1992) in which renowned cartoonist Spiegelman depicts his father's experiences as a World War II Nazi concentration camp survivor. The memoir is also a chronicle of Spiegelman's relationship with his father as we witness their visits and disagreements. The black-and-white drawings are straightforward, but with an interesting twist: all of the Jews are depicted as mice and the Nazis as cats." LJ

Also available: paperback boxed set edition $23.25 (ISBN 0141014083)

A combined edition of Maus I : My father bleeds history (1986) and Maus II : And here my troubles began (1991)

★ **MetaMaus.** Pantheon Books 2011 299p. Illustration

Grades: 11 12 Adult   **92; 741.5**
1. Autobiographical graphic novels; 2. Cartoonists; 3. Holocaust survivors; 4. Holocaust, 1933-1945; 5. Spiegelman, Art; 6. Graphic novels
978-0-375-42394-9, $35

                   LC 2010052045

The New York cartoonist traces the creative process that went into drawing his Pulitzer Prizewinning classic, revealing the sources of his inspiration and describing his parents' emotional struggles as Holocaust survivors after the end of World War II.

Spotnitz, Frank

The **X-files**. Writers, Frank Spotnitz, Marv Wolfman, Doug Moench; artist, Brina Denham; colors, Kelsey Shannon and Carlos Badilla; letters, Ed Dukeshire. DC Comics/Wildstorm 2009 176p. Illustration

Grades: 9 10 11 12 Adult   **741.5; Fic**
1. Supernatural graphic novels; 2. X-files (Television program); 3. Graphic novels
978-1-4012-2527-8, $19.99

FBI agents Fox Mulder and Dana Scully investigate several cases that involve possession, then a murder case that involves a company conducting secret research for the U.S. government. The Lone Gunmen help Mulder uncover the company's wrongdoing. A murder investigation in San Francisco sees Mulder and Scully go up against members of the Tong underworld. Then, the two travel to the Badlands to investigate a series of disappearances that leads them deep underground, to a Netherworld inhabited by strange creatures. Spotnitz worked as a producer and screenwriter for the television series; Wolfman and Moench are veteran DC Comics creators.

Spradlin, Michael P.

Spy goddess volume 1: the chase for the chalice. Created by Michael P. Spradlin ; script by Rachel Manija Brown ; illustrated by Rainbow Buddy. HarperCollins/Tokyopop 2008 Un Illustration

Grades: 7 8 9 10 11 12   **741.5; Fic**
1. Adventure graphic novels; 2. Spies; 3. Graphic novels
978-0-06-136299-6, $9.99

Rachel Buchanan and her fellow Blackthorn Academy spy students travel with Headmaster Mr. Kim to Japan, where Simon Blankenship and his Mithrian followers have stolen another Mithrian artifact. In between the shopping (by both guys and gals), Pilar and Rachel suspect that their local police contacts are actually Mithrians. Then Rachel gets kidnapped, for Blankenship is convinced she is the goddess Etherea, his mortal enemy, and sacrificing her will awaken the god Mithras within him. This graphic novel is a sequel to the prose Spy Goddess novels and has been put into manga format. It includes some martial arts fighting violence.

Stanley, John

Little Lulu vol. 17: The Valentine. Writer, John Stanley ; artists, John Stanley, Irving Tripp. Dark Horse Comics 2007 228p. Illustration

Grades: 3 4 5 6 7 8 9 10 11 12 Adult   **741.5**
1. Friendship; 2. Humorous graphic novels; 3. Little Lulu (Fictional character); 4. Graphic novels
978-1-59307-686-3, $10.95

In this seventeenth volume, Lulu gets into more fun mischief, tricking Tubby into taking a sponge for a walk, rescuing a pair of pants from the tough west side gang, and defeating the clubhouse boys in a snowball war. She also tells neighborhood little terror Alvin more stories of Witch Hazel, and during a day at the beach, she tries to win a doll at the ball throwing booth where Tubby is working.

★ **Little** Lulu, vol. 1: My dinner with Lulu. [by] John Stanley and Irving Tripp. Dark Horse Comics 2005 200p. Illustration

Grades: 4 5 6 7 8 9 10 11 12 Adult   **741.5; Fic**

1. Friendship; 2. Humorous graphic novels; 3. Graphic novels

1-59307-318-6, $9.95

Lulu Moppet plays with best friend Tubby, except when he hangs out with the other neighborhood boys and tries to keep girls out of their clubhouse; she deals with terrible toddler Alvin by weaving extravagant tales featuring herself; and other everyday adventures. This is the first volume of a series that will eventually reprint every Little Lulu comic for new young readers.

Volume 1 of 29

Little Lulu, volume 21: Miss Feeny's folly and other stories. John Stanley & Irving Tripp. Dark Horse Comics 2009 200p. Illustration

Grades: 1 2 3 4 5 6 7 8 9 10 11 12 Adult   741.5; Fic

1. Friendship; 2. Humorous graphic novels; 3. Little Lulu (Fictional character); 4. Graphic novels

978-1-59582-365-6, $14.95

This volume collects the Little Lulu stories from issues #100 to 105 of the Dell Comics series. Lulu and Annie carry on their battle with the boys over the boys' clubhouse, Lulu tells little Alvin more stories of the poor little girl and the wicked Witch Hazel, Tubby goes to the dentist, all the neighbor kids have to attend Miss Feeny's dance party, Tubby and then Lulu each have to clean up parts of their houses and try to trick the other into helping, and more. These stories are mostly in full color, with just a few one-page stories in black and white.

Little Lulu: the alamo and other stories. John Stanley & Irving Tripp. Dark Horse Comics 2009 200p. Illustration

Grades: 1 2 3 4 5 6 7 8 9 10 11 12 Adult   741.5; Fic

1. Humorous graphic novels; 2. Little Lulu (Fictional character); 3. Graphic novels

978-1-59582-293-2, $14.95

With this nineteenth volume of Little Lulu reprints, the comics are in full color; this volume collects issues 88 through 93, originally published by Dell Comics in 1955 through 1956. Among the stories in this volume, Tubby and the boys try to trick Lulu and Annie into digging a well, Tubby's parents pay Lulu to keep him company while they go out, and Lulu and Annie get revenge on Tubby and the boys by dousing them with water bombs while the boys are wearing their Davy Crockett coonskin caps. These stories appeal to younger readers as well as adults who remember reading the original comic books.

★ **Nancy,** volume 1: the Johnny Stanley Library. From the comic strip by Ernie Bushmiller ; script and layout by John Stanley ; finished art by Dan Gormley. Drawn & Quarterly 2009 128p. Illustration

Grades: 2 3 4 5 6 7 8 9 10 11 12 Adult   741.5; Fic

1. Humorous graphic novels; 2. Nancy Drew (Fictional character); 3. Graphic novels

978-1-897299-77-7, $24.95

LC C2009-901565-X

The comic book character Nancy was created by Ernie Bushmiller; Dell Comics published the comics scripted by John Stanley with art by Dan Gormley starting with issue 146 in 1957. In these stories, Nancy meets Oona Goosepimple, a spooky girl who lives in a haunted house, has an incredible run of bad luck because of what she thinks is a four-leaf clover, and has all kinds of everyday

adventures and misadventures with her friend Sluggo, their nemesis Spike, neighborhood rich kid Rollo, and her Aunt Fritzi. Always short of money yet needing some to buy ice cream sodas and other treats, many of Nancy's adventures with Sluggo involve various moneymaking schemes to get the dime needed (those were the days ...). The kinds of adventures the kids have are somewhat similar to Stanley's other work on

Courtesy of Drawn & Quarterly

Little Lulu, but set in an urban environment rather than the suburban neighborhood of Lulu and her friends. The book, designed by Seth, retains the soft original coloring of the old comics, with the paper even looking like old comics (but much sturdier). This book should have the same all-ages appeal as Little Lulu; the 2009 Free Comic Book Day issue featuring Nancy was a big hit with readers five years old and up to adults who remembered reading Nancy comics when they were kids.

Star Trek the Manga Volume 1: Shinsei Shinsei

Tokyopop 2006 Un Illustration

Grades: 7 8 9 10 11 12 Adult   741.5; Fic

1. Adventure graphic novels; 2. Science fiction graphic novels; 3. Star Trek; 4. Graphic novels

1-59816-744-8, $9.99

Ten writers and artists deliver tales of triumph aboard the original NCC-1701, the starship Enterprise, featuring the characters from the original television series. These new stories venture into the terrain of social politics, personal reflection ... and bare-knuckled brawls between Captain Kirk and various alien creatures, Spock's unflappable logic, Dr. McCoy's flare for drama, Scotty's perpetual struggle to keep the engines running smoothly, and more. The stories are written and illustrated as global manga.

Star Trek the Manga: Uchu

Tokyopop 2008 Un Illustration

Grades: 7 8 9 10 11 12 Adult   741.5; Fic

1. Science fiction graphic novels; 2. Star trek (Television program); 3. Graphic novels

978-1-4278-0787-8, $10.99

This third collection of manga-style stories set in the original Star Trek universe includes "Art of War" by Star Trek: The Next Generation actor Wil Wheaton and artist E. J. Su, "Bandi" by The Trouble with Tribbles writer David Gerrold and artist Don Hudson, "Inalienable Rights" by Nathaniel Bowden and artist Heidi Arnhold, and "The Humanitarian" by Luis Reyes and artist Nate Watson. Kirk has an encounter with a Klingon that makes both men rethink their hatred; the Bandi is yet another alien creature that has invaded the Enterprise, this one is highly empathic and can influence peoples' emotions; Kirk and his command team visit a planet and find a society in which bureaucracy runs wild; and Spock has command of the Enterprise during a very difficult situation, when a huge explosion causes major casualties of the Enterprise crew. People who like Star Trek's original series and characters will find stories in keeping with the philosophy of that series.

Star Wars Adventures: Han Solo and the Hollow Moon of Khorya
Dark Horse Books 2009 80p. Illustration
Grades: 5 6 7 8 9   **741.5; Fic**
   1. Adventure graphic novels; 2. Science fiction graphic novels; 3. Star Wars; 4. Graphic novels
978-1-58582-198-0, $7.95
   Approximately one year before they meet Luke Skywalker and Obi-Wan Kenobi, Han Solo and his first mate Chewbacca get into major trouble with the gangster Sollima. Han must team up with his treacherous former partner, Billal Batross, to retrieve an accounting droid currently in the hands of the Empire; meanwhile, Chewie is supposed to be held as a hostage, but Sollima orders him into the gladiatorial games. Han discovers that Billal is just as shady and treacherous as ever when his "partner" betrays him to the Imperial forces on Khorya. And Chewie, who was supposed to be killed, defeats one opponent after another and becomes the champion of the games. The book provides lots of action without showing graphic violence.

Star Wars: Clone Wars Adventures Volume 3
Dark Horse Comics 2005 Un Illustration
Grades: 6 7 8 9 10 11 12   **741.5; Fic**
   1. Adventure graphic novels; 2. Science fiction graphic novels; 3. Star Wars; 4. Graphic novels
1-59307-307-0, $6.95
   Asajj Ventress and Durge pit themselves against General Grievous; Republic commandos battle through the streets of Ord Mantell to recover a most precious cargo; and JedI Master Yoda brings law to a lawless town, whether they want it or not. These stories take place approximately six months after the Battle of Geonosis.

Star Wars: Clone Wars Adventures Volume 4
Dark Horse Comics 2005 Un Illustration
Grades: 6 7 8 9 10 11 12   **741.5; Fic**
   1. Adventure graphic novels; 2. Science fiction graphic novels; 3. Star Wars; 4. Graphic novels
1-59307-402-6, $6.95
   As the Clone Wars burn across the galaxy and the true intentions of the Sith are revealed, the true heroes of the conflict emerge. Chewbacca leads the Wookiees against the Republic invaders on the jungle world of Kashyyyk; R2-D2 and C-3PO uncover a plot to assassinate Padme; an orphaned refugee witnesses the rough life of a Clone Trooper firsthand, and Anakin Skywalker fights alongside Serra Keto, a young Jedi who will play a part in his descent into the dark side.

Star Wars: Clone Wars Adventures Volume 5
Dark Horse Comics 2006 Unp. Illustration
Grades: 5 6 7 8 9 10   **741.5; Fic**
   1. Adventure graphic novels; 2. Science fiction graphic novels; 3. Star Wars; 4. Graphic novels
1-59307-483-2, $6.95

As the fires of the Clone Wars burn across the galaxy, heroes on both sides of the conflict emerge, and no matter what the outcome, the galaxy will be forever changed. In this volume, the JedI Aayla Secura journeys into the heart of darkness to save an Ewok village; a clone commander learns firsthand of the sacrifices the Separatists will make for their cause; Bail Organa (Leia's adoptive father) infiltrates a dangerous world to rescue a friend; and the Padawan Joc Sah gets caught in the crosshairs of Order 66. These stories take place just before and during the events of Star Wars Episode III: The Revenge of the Sith.

Star Wars: Clone Wars Adventures Volume 6
Dark Horse Comics 2006 Un Illustration
Grades: 5 6 7 8 9 10   **741.5; Fic**
   1. Adventure graphic novels; 2. Science fiction graphic novels; 3. Star Wars; 4. Graphic novels
978-1-59307-567-5, $6.95
   The Clone Wars grind through the galaxy, shaking every system to its core and testing loyalties on both sides of the conflict. In this volume, Saesee Tiin steals a secret Separatist fighter, Ki-Adi-Mundi and Rivi-Anu rescue an army of clone troopers, clone commandos battle in the clouds of a gas planet, and Plo Koon and Kit Fisto get trapped in an underwater prison. These stories take place just before and during the events in Star Wars Episode III: Revenge of the Sith.

Star Wars: Clone Wars Adventures Volume 7
Dark Horse Comics 2007 Un Illustration
Grades: 5 6 7 8 9 10   **741.5; Fic**
   1. Adventure graphic novels; 2. Science fiction graphic novels; 3. Star Wars; 4. Graphic novels
978-1-59307-678-8, $6.95
   The fate of the galaxy hangs in the balance, the Republic and Confederacy taking their fight from the cold reaches of space to exotic alien worlds. In this volume, Obi-Wan Kenobi and Anakin Skywalker are attacked by giant monsters; Padme Naberrie becomes a spy; Bultar Swan storms an impenetrable fortress, and three friends rob a back guarded by an army of clones. These adventures take place some time during the Clone Wars.

Star Wars: Clone Wars Volume 5: The Best Blades
Dark Horse Comics 2004 Un Illustration
Grades: 7 8 9 10 11 12 Adult   **741.5; Fic**
   1. Adventure graphic novels; 2. Science fiction graphic novels; 3. Star Wars; 4. Graphic novels
1-59307-273-2, $17.95
   The darkest days of the Clone Wars have arrived, when even victories are cause for abiding sorrow; when the hopes for a brighter future are lost in the turmoil of a divided galaxy; and when friendships are tools of convenience and the reason for betrayals. From political intrigue within the Senate to bloody battlefields on exotic worlds, the war has left its mark on the bystanders as well as the combatants. Obi-Wan Kenobi and Anakin Skywalker battle for survival, Senator Bail Organa struggles to preserve freedom within the Republic, and Master Yoda strives to prevent an old friend from plunging a system into war in four stories from the Clone Wars. The book includes battle violence.

Star Wars: Empire Volume Five: Allies and Adversaries
Written by Jeremy Barlow and Ron Marz ; art by Brandon Badeaux, Jeff Johnson, et al. Dark Horse Comics 2006 Un Illustration
Grades: 7 8 9 10 11 12 Adult   **741.5; Fic**
1. Adventure graphic novels; 2. Science fiction graphic novels; 3. Star Wars; 4. Graphic novels
1-59307-466-2, $14.95
Luke Skywalker fights side-by-side with a shipwrecked veteran from the Clone Wars, Han Solo's flirtations with an old flame land him in the fire, and BoShek (the galaxy's second-coolest smuggler) attracts a whole lot of blaster fire from Rebels and Imperials alike in this collection featuring some of the most unexpected stories in the era of the Empire. Whether it's BoShek transporting an innocent-enough looking girl, Han making a supply run for the resource-strapped Alliance or Luke flying escort for a Rebel Intelligence team on a supposedly deserted planet, these adventures may start as routine missions, but their endings are anything but predictable. The book includes battle violence.

Star Wars: Empire Volume Four: The Heart of the Rebellion
Dark Horse Comics 2005 Un Illustration
Grades: 7 8 9 10 11 12 Adult   **741.5; Fic**
1. Adventure graphic novels; 2. Science fiction graphic novels; 3. Star Wars; 4. Graphic novels
1-59307-308-9, $17.95
She was the catalyst that helped to turn a rag-tag rebellion into the Rebel Alliance. She provided the impetus for the 'Heroes of Yavin' in their attack on the Death Star. And she was the spark that ignited the flames of passion in one of the galaxy's most notorious rogues. 'She,' of course, is Princess Leia, the leader—and heart—of the Rebellion against Palpatine's galactic Empire. The four stories in this volume follow Leia from the weeks just before the events in A New Hope, to the time just before The Empire Strikes Back—from her first transforming experience with armed rebellion, to facing the ramifications of consequences of the destruction of her home planet, to the beginnings of true love. The book includes some battle violence.

Star Wars: Empire Volume Three: The Imperial Perspective
Dark Horse Comics 2004 Un Illustration
Grades: 7 8 9 10 11 12 Adult   **741.5; Fic**
1. Adventure graphic novels; 2. Science fiction graphic novels; 3. Star Wars; 4. Graphic novels
1-59307-128-0, $17.95
A loyal Stormtrooper, thwarted by the very bureaucracy which he serves, struggles to track down a Rebel saboteur on board the Death Star in the days and hours before the fateful Rebel attack. Darth Vader, the sole survivor of the explosion of the Death Star, crash lands on a primitive world where savagery is the key to survival. A young Imperial lieutenant learns all service comes at a price when his small company of Stormtroopers is attacked by thousands of angry aliens. Assassins vow revenge on the man responsible for killing their families - the Dark Lord, Darth Vader. These four tales are all told from the point of view of the major villains of the Star Wars galaxy - the Imperials. But, as these stories show,

even the bad guys are no strangers to loyalty, honor, and sacrifice. The book includes battle violence.

Star Wars: Tales Volume 6
Dark Horse Comics 2006 232p. Illustration
Grades: 7 8 9 10 11 12 Adult   **741.5; Fic**
1. Adventure graphic novels; 2. Science fiction graphic novels; 3. Star Wars; 4. Graphic novels
1-59307-447-6, $19.95
The vastness of the Star Wars galaxy hosts an ever-unfolding mythology, filled with character-driven stories of loss and tragedy, of heroism and redemption. Collected here are ten such tales - adventures that traverse and illuminate every era in the Star Wars mythos. From the life-affirming lessons of the Force to the moral and emotional fall-out that comes with giving oneself over to the ways of the Sith, these stories will change the way readers see that galaxy far, far away.

Starkings, Richard
★ Elephantmen: Wounded Animals. Writer, Richard Starkings; artist, Moritat. Image Comics 2007 Un Illustration
Grades: 10 11 12 Adult   **741.5; Fic**
1. Mystery graphic novels; 2. Science fiction graphic novels; 3. Graphic novels
978-1-58240-691-6, $24.99
They were genetically engineered to be super-human weapons of mass destruction, but now they must walk amongst the people they were created to destroy and face hatred and fear every day. Ebony Hide is one of them, an Elephantman. Even when he is befriended by a small girl, Hide is still haunted by his past and is forced to recognize that suspicion and contempt will always be his constant companions. The book includes some violence and strong language.
Volume 1 of an ongoing series

Hip Flask: Concrete Jungle (The Big Here & the Long Now). Richard Starkings and Joe Casey; art by Ladronn. Image Comics 2007 96p. Illustration
Grades: 10 11 12 Adult   **741.5; Fic**
1. Mystery graphic novels; 2. Science fiction graphic novels; 3. Graphic novels
978-1-58240-679-4, $29.95
2162: They are the survivors of genetic engineering experiments and indoctrination by Doctor Kazushi Nikken and MAPPO, a sinister organization which sought to create superhuman weapons of mass destruction. Now, freed and rehabilitated by the United Nations Intelligence Taskforce, the ?nhumans" now live amongst men. Legitimized by the Elephantmen Act, they are nevertheless denied the right to bear arms and must survive on their wits alone... Business person Ebony's organization has been targeted by someone, while private investigator Hip Flask tries to find a mystery aircar. The book includes violence and strong language.

Tim Sale: black and white (revised and expanded). Brought to you by Richard Starkings & John 'JG' Roshell with Tim Sale. Image Comics 2008 272p. Illustration
Grades: 10 11 12 Adult   **741.5**
1. Artists; 2. Batman (Fictional character); 3. Catwoman (Fictional character); 4. Comic books, strips, etc —

History and criticism; 5. Daredevil (Fictional character); 6. Graphic novels — History and criticism; 7. Hulk (Fictional character); 8. Illustrators; 9. Sale, Tim; 10. Superman (Fictional character)
978-1-58240-880-4, $39.99

Comics artist Tim Sale is well known because of the art he did for the television series "Heroes," but he's been in the comics business for a long time before that. This book collects a lot of his work, from his earliest years in the Buscema School in the 1970s, to his work on "Heroes." In between, Sale has worked on books for Marvel (Daredevil: Yellow and Hulk: Gray among others) and DC (Superman for All Seasons, Batman: The Long Halloween, Catwoman, and more) as well as independent work such as Thieves' World and Billi 99. The book includes interviews with Sale, a sketchbook section of his art, and more. Some images include partial nudity.

Stassen, Jean-Philippe
Deogratias: a tale of Rwanda. [by] Stassen; translated by Alex Siegel. Roaring Brook 2006 79p. Illustration
Grades: 11 12 Adult   **741.5; Fic**
1. Genocide; 2. Rwanda; 3. Graphic novels
1-59643-103-2; 978-1-59643-103-4, $17.95
                                                       LC 2005-17576
In this "fictionalized account of the Rwandan genocide, readers meet Deogratias, a teenaged Hutu. His friends Benina and Apollinaria are Tutsi—a race that is being ethnically cleansed by Hutu extremists. As the conflict escalates, Deogratias witnesses murders and is forced to become involved in brutal acts of violence. He suffers a mental breakdown. The story is told through a series of flashbacks while he skates the line between rational and insane. Stassen spares his readers none of the brutality and visceral cruelties of this atrocity. Scenes of rape, harsh language, and some sexual content solidly designate this book for a mature audience. . . . A masterful work with vibrant, confident art, this book will stay with and haunt its readers." SLJ

Staton, Joe
Justice Society Vol. 2. DC Comics 2007 224p. Illustration
Grades: 8 9 10 11 12 Adult   **741.5; Fic**
1. Batman (Fictional character); 2. Flash (Fictional character); 3. Green Lantern (Fictional character); 4. Justice Society of America (Fictional characters); 5. Robin (Fictional character); 6. Superhero graphic novels; 7. Superman (Fictional character); 8. Graphic novels
978-1-4012-1194-3, $14.99
The Justice Society of America was the first comic book super-team, created in All Star Comics in the 1940s. They faded into obscurity until they were revived in the 1970s. This volume includes stories from the 1970s, featuring Superman, the Flash, Green Lantern, Hawkman, Dr. Fate, Wildcat, Robin, Power Girl, Star-Spangled Kid, and the Huntress. Among other stories in this volume, Batman dies, and Huntress is his daughter.

Steinbach, Hans Hanzo
Midnight Opera Vol. 1. Tokyopop 2005 Un Illustration
Grades: 8 9 10 11 12 Adult   **741.5; Fic**

1. Fantasy graphic novels; 2. Horror graphic novels; 3. Graphic novels
1-59816-265-9, $9.99
For nearly a millennium, undead creatures have blended into a Europe driven by religious dogma... Ein DeLaLune is an underground Goth metal sensation on the Paris music scene, tragic and beautiful. He has the edge on other Goth music powerhouses...he's undead, a fact he's kept hidden for centuries. But his newfound fame might just bring out the very phantoms of his past from whom he has been hiding for centuries, including his powerful brother, Leroux. And if the two don't reconcile, the entire undead nation could rise up from the depths of modern society to lay waste to mankind. There's fighting action between the two undead brothers.

Stern, Roger
Captain America: War & Remembrance 2nd ed.. Artist, John Byrne ; inker, Rubinstein, Joe. Marvel Entertainment 2007 207p. Illustration
Grades: 8 9 10 11 12 Adult   **741.5; Fic**
1. Avengers (Fictional characters); 2. Captain America (Fictional character); 3. Superhero graphic novels; 4. Graphic novels
978-0-7851-2693-5, $24.99
Captain America's endless war on crime and tyranny sets him against new enemies and old, from an army of robot replicas to the black deeds of Baron Blood. Plus: Cap for president? This book guest-stars the Avengers, S.H.I.E.L.D. and Union Jack, and features Cobra, Mister Hyde and Batroc the Leaper. This is the complete Stern/Byrne run, culminating with the standard-setting version of Cap's origin. Byrne co-scripted as well as pencilled the art.

Spider-Man Visionaries: Roger Stern Vol. 1. Marvel Entertainment 2007 256p. Illustration
Grades: 7 8 9 10 11 12 Adult   **741.5; Fic**
1. Spider-Man (Fictional character); 2. Superhero graphic novels; 3. Graphic novels
978-0-7851-2710-9, $24.99
Roger Stern sets his stamp on Spider-Man and his supporting cast with a collection of costumed criminals, would-be alien abductors, and gangsters both local and imported. Spidey is up against Belladonna, the Vulture, the Prowler, the Smuggler, Mysterio, a roomful of aliens, and an abundance of gas. These stories were originally published in the 1980s, and Stern worked with a number of different artists, including Steve Leialoha and Marie Severin.

Stevenson, Noelle
★ **Nimona.** By Noelle Stevenson. HarperCollins Childrens Books 2015 272 p.
Grades: 7 8 9 10 11 12   **741.5**
1. Fantasy graphic novels; 2. Good and evil — Fiction; 3. Heroes and heroines; 4. Magic; 5. Shapeshifting
0062278231; 9780062278234, $17.99
Eisner Nominee: Best Digital/Web Comic (2015)
National Book Award Finalist: Young People's Literature (2015)
In this graphic novel, by Noelle Stevenson, "Nimona is an impulsive young shapeshifter with a knack for villainy. Lord Ballister Blackheart is a villain with a vendetta. As sidekick and supervillain, Nimona and Lord Blackheart are

about to wreak some serious havoc. Their mission: prove to the kingdom that Sir Ambrosius Goldenloin and his buddies at the Institution of Law Enforcement and Heroics aren't the heroes everyone thinks they are." (Publisher's note)

"This celebrated webcomic, a mash-up of medieval culture with modern science and technology, is now available in print. . . . Action scenes dominate as Nimona shifts with Hulk-like ferocity from frightful creatures such as a fire-breathing dragon to a docile cat or a timid child. Dialogue is fresh and witty with an abundance of clever lines." SLJ

Stevenson, Robert Louis, 1850-1894

Kidnapped. Adapted by Mark Jones ; art by Naresh Kumar. Kalyani Navyug Media Pvt. Ltd/Campfire Classics 2010 80p. Illustration

Grades: 3 4 5 6 7 8 9   **741.5; Fic**
  1. Adventure graphic novels; 2. Stevenson, Robert Louis, 1850-1894 — Adaptations
  978-9-380028-52-1, $9.99

When David Balfour's father dies and he has no family left, he leaves home and goes to the house of Shaws upon the advice of his father's agent; there, he finds an uncle he had never known. However, instead of welcoming David, Ebenezer Balfour arranges for the boy to be kidnapped on a ship to be taken to the American colonies and sold into slavery. When the ship causes a smaller boat to capsize, the crew takes on the lone survivor, the adventurer Alan Breck. David befriends Breck and helps him when the crew tries to murder the man, and when the ship wrecks near the Scottish shore, David washes up alone and must find his way through the Highlands. This graphic novel adaptation was originally published in India. It includes some background information about the Jacobite Risings against the English, and some other information about the characters Stevenson created. The book does depict some sword fighting and shooting, but with little gore.

Treasure Island. Retold by Wim Coleman and Pat Perrin ; illustrated by Greg Rebis. Stone Arch Books 2007 63p. Illustration

Grades: 3 4 5 6 7 8 9   **741.5; Fic**
  1. Adventure graphic novels; 2. Stevenson, Robert Louis, 1850-1894 — Adaptations
  978-1-59889-050-1, $23.93

Young Jim Hawkins discovers an old treasure map and sets out on a harrowing voyage to a faraway island, in the company of Dr. Livesey and Mr. Trelawney. The violent sea is just the first of many obstacles, as Jim soon learns that most of the ship's crew are dangerous pirates seeking the same treasure, and they're led by Long John Silver. This adaptation is written for reluctant and struggling readers.

Part of the Graphic Revolve series.

Stewart, Cameron

The **Apocalipstix**. By Ray Fawkes & Cameron Stewart. Oni Press 2008 Un Illustration

Grades: 9 10 11 12 Adult   **741.5; Fic**
  1. Adventure graphic novels; 2. Humorous graphic novels; 3. Rock music; 4. Science fiction graphic novels; 5. Graphic novels
  978-1-932664-45-4, $11.95

Mandy, Megumi, and Dot were on track to be one of the greatest rock bands in the world until Armageddon hit and nuked most of it. The three survived and decided they would go on an "End of the World" tour with a group name like The Apocalipstix, it seemed appropriate. Riding an armored tour bus, the trio deals with road pirates who turn out to be major fans, giant ants just like in the old movies, and a rock contest with gasoline as the big prize. Megumi speaks mostly in Japanese, which is shown in the word balloons in Japanese text with English subtitles. All three can kick butt, and there's plenty of fistfights and giant ant fighting going on.

★ **Batgirl;** Volume 1: Batgirl of Burnside. Written by Cameron Stewart & Brenden Fletcher; art by Babs Tarr; breakdown art by Cameron Stewart. DC Comics 2015 176 p. Color; Illustration

Grades: 10 11 12 Adult   **741.5**
  1. Batgirl (Fictional character)
  9781401253325, $24.99
                              LC 2015006319

"Barbara Gordon's ready for a fresh start. She's packing her bags, crossing the bridge, and heading to Gotham's coolest neighborhood: Burnside. And when a freak fire burns up her costume and gear, Babs has the chance to become a whole new Batgirl! But she barely slips on her new DIY costume before Batgirl starts trending as Gotham's first viral vigilante—and attracting a new wave of enemies." (Publisher's note)

"While most attempts at updating an established character to tap into the youth culture zeitgeist feel phony and fall flat, this reinvigoration of Batgirl manages to be big fun and actually tuned in to Millennial culture. . . . The supporting cast is diverse and fully developed, and the action is intense, rendered in a bright, dynamic style that evokes animation with just a hint of Japanese influence." LJ

Stine, R. L.

Goosebumps Graphix: Scary Summer. Scholastic/Graphix 2007 137p. Illustration

Grades: 4 5 6 7 8 9   **741.5; Fic**
  1. Horror graphic novels; 2. Graphic novels
  978-0-439-85782-6, $8.99

Someone's creeping through the garden, doing nasty things! Dean Haspiel, a veteran of Batman and Justice League comics, knows just how to portray "The Revenge of the Lawn Gnomes." In his comic series like The Bakers and Plastic Man, Kyle Baker proves he's one funny artist, the perfect guy to draw a story about fun and games at camp—until "The Horror at Camp Jellyjam" is uncovered. And Courtney Crumrin creator Ted Naifeh adapts and illustrates "Ghost Beach," in which Terri and Jerry go on vacation with some of their father's cousins and meet other kids who dress in old-fashioned clothes and caution them about ghosts.

Stok, Barbara

Vincent. By Barbara Stok; translation by Laura Watkinson. SelfMadeHero 2014 144 p. Color; Illustration

Grades: 9 10 11 12 Adult   **92; 741.5**
  1. Gogh, Vincent van, 1853-1890
  1906838798; 9781906838799, $19.95
                            LC 2014431349

This biography, by Barbara Stok, "documents the brief and intense period of creativity Vincent van Gogh (1853-1890) spent in Arles, Provence, in southern France. Here van Gogh dreams of setting up an artists' studioùa haven where he and his friends can paint together. But attacks of mental illness leave the painter confused and disoriented. . . . Throughout this period of intense emotion and hardship, Vincent's brother Theo stands by him." (Publisher's note)

"Stok doesn't try to reproduce van Gogh's visuals; instead, she uses heavy lines, solid colors, and minimal background details to focus attention on characters and history. When she breaks away from this pattern—in jagged panel lines showing van Gogh's slipping sanity, or the brilliance of his paintings exploding behind him—it's emotionally charged and made all the more immediate by the iconography." Pub Wkly

Text in English, translated from the Dutch

Stoker, Bram, 1847-1912

Bram Stoker's Dracula. Adapted by Tim Mucci, writer, Ben Caldwell, penciller/colorist, Bill Halliar, inker. Sterling 2008 Un Illustration

Grades: 5 6 7 8 9 10 11 12   **741.5; Fic**
1. Authors; 2. Horror graphic novels; 3. Novelists; 4. Stoker, Bram, 1847-1912 — Adaptations; 5. Graphic novels
978-1-4027-3152-5, $6.95

LC 2007-41554

English estate agent Jonathan Harker travels to Transylvania to meet his firm's new client, Count Dracula, but the young man discovers his host's evil secret. He escapes and returns to England, but the Count has traveled there, too, determined to settle in new land where he can find more victims, for Dracula is a vampire. Harker, his fiancee Mina Murray, and their friends are not safe from evil. This graphic novel adaptation includes background information about the real person who was the model for Stoker's villain, and a brief biography of Stoker.

Part of the All-Action Classics series.

Dracula. Retold by Michael Burgan ; illustrated by José Alfonso Ocampo Ruiz ; cover color by Benny Fuentes ; interior color by Protobunker Studio. Stone Arch Books 2008 72p. Illustration

Grades: 4 5 6 7 8 9   **741.5; Fic**
1. Horror graphic novels; 2. Vampires; 3. Graphic novels; 4. Stoker, Bram, 1847-1912 — Adaptations
978-1-4342-0448-6, $23.93; 978-1-4342-0498-1 (pa), $9.95

LC 2007-30805

Jonathan Harker and his fiancee, Mina Murray, become entangled in the affairs of the man who calls himself Count Dracula when Harker is sent by his firm to Transylvania. There, Harker learns that Dracula is a vampire. Then Dracula comes to London, where Mina's friend Lucy Westenra becomes a victim. Aided by Dr. Van Helsing, Jack Steward, and Arthur Holcombe, they hunt Dracula to stop him from killing anyone else. This graphic novel adaptation uses simple language to help reluctant and struggling readers understand the story.

Part of the Graphic Revolve series.

Stokoe, James

Won ton soup: a space trucker cooking opera, vol.1. Oni Press 2007 Un Illustration

Grades: 10 11 12 Adult   **741.5**
1. Cooking; 2. Humorous graphic novels; 3. Science fiction graphic novels; 4. Graphic novels
978-1-932664-60-7, $11.95

Space trucker Johnny Boyo used to be the best student at the Plaxos Cooking School, but he gave it all up to travel in space for a year. Now, he and his partner Deacon have returned to Plaxos for needed repairs after a space ninja attack. Johnny reconnects with his girlfriend Citrus and his old cooking master Mongolius Grahm, but a visit to the school results in a cooking challenge from the twins from Nebula 5; they have a psychic connection and absorb flavors through their pores. The book includes violence, some harsh language, and verbal sexual innuendo.

Stolarz, Laurie Faria

Black is for beginnings. Adaptation by Barbara Randall Kesel; artwork by Janina Gørrissen. Llewellyn Publications/Flux 2009 160p. Illustration

Grades: 8 9 10 11 12   **741.5; Fic**
1. Dreams; 2. Romance graphic novels; 3. Supernatural graphic novels; 4. Graphic novels
978-0-7387-1438-7, $9.95; 0-7387-1438-0

When Stacey, a college student and hereditary witch, again begins to have disturbing dreams about her former boyfriend and a little girl who was murdered years earlier, she knows that the dreams are trying to tell her something important, but she does not know what

"The story's weirdo flashes of humor make the darkness bearable, as do the everyday settings of a pizza parlor and dorm room. A unique and somewhat unhinged blend of realism and fantasy." Booklist

Stone, Carl S.

Dragon Arms Vol. 2: Chaos Blade. Creator/graphic designer David Hutchison; writer, Carl S. Stone. Antarctic Press 2004 Un Illustration

Grades: 9 10 11 12   **741.5; Fic**
1. Adventure graphic novels; 2. Fantasy graphic novels; 3. Graphic novels
1-932453-66-0, $9.99

The King of Landres, Eon, once beloved hero of legend, has become corrupted by his power. His armies, allied with the monstrous Majin, swarm across the continent of Lordez, annihilating all who resist them and conquering nation after nation in a seemingly unstoppable tide of violence. However, new hope has arisen with the reemergence of the legendary wizard Anrack, who once fought side by side with Eon against the abominable Dragon Kings. Gathered about him is a small yet powerful assemblage of would-be heroes, each wielding items and abilities far beyond the norm. With a cache of powerful weaponry having been destroyed, Anrack prepares to lead his band to acquire the legendary and heavily guarded Chaos Blade. When Eon decides to take a more personal hand in things, though, Anrack's allies find they may not be able to overcome their newest task. This is a global manga title. The book includes violence.

Stones, Tad

Hellboy Animated Volume 1: The Black Wedding. Jim Pasco and Tad Stones ; Pencils by Fabio Laguna and Rick Lacy. Dark Horse Comics 2007 Un Illustration
Grades: 7 8 9 10 11 12 Adult   **741.5; Fic**
1. Fantasy graphic novels; 2. Hellboy (Fictional character); 3. Horror graphic novels; 4. Graphic novels
978-1-59307-700-6, $6.95

In the lead feature, "The Black Wedding," written by Jim Pascoe and drawn by Rick Lacy, Liz Sherman is kidnapped by an ancient cult, dragging the entire Bureau for Paranormal Research and Defense into a horrifying tale of witchcraft and possession. Tad Stones and Fabio Laguna team up in "Pyramid of Death," in which radio hero Lobster Johnson inspires a young Hellboy to inflict some imaginary justice of his own, causing havoc on the military base where he lives. The art matches the style used in the Hellboy Animated features shown on Cartoon Network, and the horror is kept to a level suitable for younger teen readers.

Storrie, Paul D.

Amaterasu: Return of the Sun. Pencils and inks by Ron Randall. Lerner Publications Company/Graphic Universe 2007 48p. Illustration
Grades: 3 4 5 6 7 8 9   **299.5; 741.5**
1. Amaterasu Omikami (Shinto deity); 2. Mythology, Japanese
978-0-8225-5968-9 li, $26.60

In this retelling of a Japanese myth, the Shinto goddess of the sun, Amaterasu, hides from her jealous brother Susano, the god of storms; the world plunges into cold and darkness without the sun. The other gods must find a way to lure Amaterasu out of hiding and keep Susano from harming her or anyone else. The book includes a glossary and a list of books and websites for further reading.

Hercules: The Twelve Labors. Story by Paul Storrie ; pencils by Steve Kurth ; inks by Barbara Schulz. Lerner Publishing Group/Graphic Universe 2007 48p. Illustration
Grades: 3 4 5 6 7 8 9   **398.2; 741.5**
1. Greek mythology; 2. Heracles (Greek mythology); 3. Graphic novels
978-0-8225-3084-8, $26.60 lib. Bdg.

Hercules was born half-god, half-man, the son of Zeus, King of the gods, and a mortal mother. Zeus's wife Hera resents her stepson, so she dupes Hercules into performing a series of twelve seemingly impossible labors that will test not only his legendary strength, but also his courage, cunning, and fighting skills. The book includes a glossary and a list of books for further reading.

Nightmare on Zombie Island. Illustrated by David Witt. Graphic Universe 2008 111p. Illustration (Twisted journeys)
Grades: 3 4 5 6 7 8 9   **741.5; Fic**
1. Adventure graphic novels; 2. Plot-your-own stories; 3. Science fiction graphic novels; 4. Graphic novels
978-0-8225-6198-9 (lib bdg), $27.93;
978-0-8225-6200-9 (pa), $7.95
LC 2007-10823

In this new take on the "Choose Your Own Adventure" type of book that combines pages of prose text with pages of comic book sequences, you have joined your best friend

Jimmy and his famous explorer aunt, Dr. Chase, on a trip to an island with an abandoned plantation. Unfortunately, you discover only after your arrival that there are zombies on the island, undead pirates cursed by the plantation's workers. Can any of you escape? Some choices will end badly, others will be better, and the choices are all up to the reader.

This is Volume 6 of the Twisted Journeys series.

Robin Hood: Outlaw of Sherwood Forest. Pencils and inks by Thomas Yeates. Lerner Publishing Group/Graphic Universe 2007 48p. Illustration
Grades: 3 4 5 6 7 8 9   **398.2; 741.5**
1. Robin Hood (Legendary character); 2. Graphic novels
978-0-8225-5964-1, $26.60 lib. Bdg.

Fooled into committing a crime by the King's foresters, young Robin Hood finds himself branded an outlaw. As he takes refuge in Sherwood Forest, he meets other hideaways who also had found themselves unjustly branded outlaws. Under Robin's leadership, they form a band of "merry men" who exact justice against the unfair laws of the land by stealing from the rich and giving their loot to the poor. Robin's exploits enrage the Sheriff of Nottingham, who vows to capture his foe at any cost.

Terror in Ghost Mansion. Illustrated by Sandy Carruthers. Lerner Publishing Group/Graphic Universe 2007 112p. Illustration (Twisted Journeys)
Grades: 3 4 5 6 7 8 9   **741.5; Fic**
1. Ghosts; 2. Horror graphic novels; 3. Graphic novels
978-0-8225-6776-9, $27.93; 978-0-8225-6778-3 (pa), $7.95
LC 2006-101597

In the series called Twisted Journeys, readers choose how the story will progress. Pages of text alternate with comic book-style pages. In this volume, you and your friends are out on a stormy Halloween night when your car ends up in a ditch while trying not to hit a kid on the road. When the cell phone won't work, you all go up to a big house, where the butler says there is no phone or electricity, but you should stay for the night. However, the house is full of ghosts, and most of them are evil. Readers will find many scenarios played out, depending on their choices; some end well, others not so well.

William Tell: one against an Empire: a Swiss legend. Story by Paul D. Storrie; pencils and inks by Thomas Yeates.. Lerner Publishing Group 2009 48p. Illustration
Grades: 3 4 5 6 7 8 9   **741.5; Fic**
1. Adventure graphic novels; 2. Tell, Wilhelm; 3. Graphic novels
978-0-8225-7175-9, $27.93
LC 2007-38657

The Swiss hunter William Tell has lived a quiet life of peace, but now the free cantons have been overrun with Austrian governors and officials who threaten and punish the citizens for no reason than that they're misusing their power against the people. Tell is forced by Gessler, the governor, to shoot an apple on top of his son's head, or they will both be killed. This is when he decides he must act against the tyranny. Storrie retold the story using sources such as the 1804 play written by Friedrich Schiller and P. G. Wodehouse's William Tell Told Again (published in 1904). The book includes a list of books for further reading and websites with music from the opera by Rossini (some readers may recognize some of the music that has often been used in cartoons and one famous radio and television series, "The Lone Ranger").

Part of the Graphic Universe Myths and Legends series

Yu the Great: Conquering the Flood. Story by Paul D. Storrie ; pencils and inks by Sandy Carruthers. Lerner/Graphic Universe 2007 48p. Illustration
Grades: 4 5 6 7 8 9 **398.2; 741.5**
1. Da Yu; 2. Folklore — China; 3. Graphic novels
978-0-8225-3088-6, $26.60

When ancient China suffers from a flood caused by angry gods, the emperor begs the hero, Yu, to save the land and the people. Accompanied by a dragon and a tortoise given by his great-grandfather the Yellow Emperor, ruler of the gods, Yu sets out to save China. This story is based on the real Chinese hero, who founded the Xia Dynasty. This is a volume in the Graphic Myths and Legends series.

"The volume maintains the tone and look of an old Chinese tale (Storrie cites his sources at the end) while imbuing it with the dynamic art and feel of a contemporary comic book." (Booklist)

Straczynski, J. Michael
Bullet Points. J Michael Straczynski and Tommy Lee Edwards. Marvel Entertainment 2007 Un Illustration
Grades: 9 10 11 12 Adult **741.5; Fic**
1. Hulk (Fictional character); 2. Iron Man (Fictional character); 3. Spider-Man (Fictional character); 4. Superhero graphic novels; 5. Graphic novels
978-0-7851-2010-0, $13.99

It's World War II, and America needs a super soldier. Only one man possesses the formula to create the perfect fighting machine from volunteer Steve Rogers. But when a deadly bullet kills Dr. Erskine along with his bodyguard, M.P. Ben Parker, Steve's destiny - and that of the Marvel Universe - is changed forever. Steve Rogers becomes Iron Man. Years after the war, a rebellious teenage Peter Parker gets lost on a testing field and accidentally irradiated with gamma rays, becoming the Hulk. Dr. Bruce Banner gets bitten by a spider exposed to gamma rays and becomes Spider-Man. All of them, and every other super powered hero, is needed when Galactus comes to devour the planet.

Civil War: Fantastic Four. Writers, J. Michael Straczynski & Dwayne McDuffie; penciller, Mike McKone; inkers, Andy Lanning, Kris Justice, & Cam Smith; colorist, Paul Mounts. Marvel Entertainment 2007 Un Illustration
Grades: 9 10 11 12 Adult **741.5; Fic**
1. Fantastic Four (Fictional characters); 2. Superhero graphic novels; 3. Graphic novels
0-7851-2227-3, $17.99

One member of the Fantastic Four lies hospitalized, a casualty of the Civil War that has fragmented the superhuman community. Another member of the team is secretly helping the opposition. Amid the tumult and tensions, the Fantastic Four is breaking up. Who will toe the line with the government, who will join the resistanace, and who will leave the battlefield altogether?

Civil War: The Amazing Spider-Man. Writer, J. Michael Straczynski; penciler, Ron Garney et al. Marvel Entertainment 2007 Un Illustration

Grades: 9 10 11 12 Adult **741.5; Fic**
1. Spider-Man (Fictional character); 2. Superhero graphic novels; 3. Graphic novels
0-7851-2237-0, $17.99

Life couldn't be more complicated - or more dangerous - for Peter Parker. After rushing to the aftermath of the Stamford Massacre to offer aid to its victims, Peter travels with Tony Stark to Washington, D.C. and the White House, where the enactment of the Super Human Registration Act appears imminent. As the world braces for the implications of legislation that will forever change the societal status of super heroes, Peter is forced to make an important personal decision, maybe the most important decision of his life. As Civil War tears apart the super hero community, will Spidey stay true to that decision?

Strait, Sonny
We Shadows Vol. 1. Tokyopop 2007 188p. Illustration
Grades: 7 8 9 10 11 12 **741.5; Fic**
1. Fantasy graphic novels; 2. Humorous graphic novels; 3. Graphic novels
978-1-4278-0104-3, $9.99

There is a song—it is a key to unlocking a gateway into a world of Shadows. A dark yet magical place where faeries, ogres and hobgoblins co-exist. One such creature is Goat, a homely being considered insane by the others. Her only friend is a talking mushroom who assures her she is a "fairy princess in training." However the truth of Goat's destiny is far more interesting ... And then there's poor Tucker, an accountant who blacks out for hours at a time, and who may just be someone, or something, other than merely human. This global manga has some nudity that doesn't show any crucial parts.

Strazewski, Len
Speed Racer volume 1. Len Strazewski and Brian Thomas ; illustrated by Gary Washington and Jill Thompson. IDW Publishing 2008 120p. Illustration
Grades: 7 8 9 10 11 12 **741.5; Fic**
1. Adventure graphic novels; 2. Automobile racing; 3. Racer, Speed (Fictional character); 4. Graphic novels
978-1-60010-174-8, $19.99

This book collects the first five issues of the Speed Racer comic originally published by Now Comics. In these stories the reader sees the origin of Speed Racer and the Mach 5, the first encounter with Racer X, and a very strange situation with a racing team called The V-Team that participates in a demolition derby as well as in Speed's next race. The book includes some minimal fan service and some violence with crashes during the races.

Strip Search
Dark Horse Comics 2004 128p. Illustration
Grades: 9 10 11 12 Adult **741.5; Fic**
1. Short stories; 2. Graphic novels
1-59307-099-3, $14.95

More than a dozen young artists and writers strut their stuff in this collection. These strips are culled from Dark Horse's on-line comics talent search/contest, Strip Search, and represent the best of the strips posted in 2002 and 2003. Some stories include harsh language and some violence.

Strokes, Johanna

Death Valley. Story by Andrew Cosby; written by Johanna Stokes; pencils and inks by Rhoald Marcellus; colored by Arif Priyanto; lettered by Marshall Dillon. Boom! Studios 2007 Un Illustration

Grades: 9 10 11 12 Adult   **741.5; Fic**
  1. Horror graphic novels; 2. Zombies; 3. Graphic novels
978-1-934506-08-0, $14.99

Sam and some of her high school senior classmates hold an "End of the World" rave in their school's old bomb shelter, when the trap door closes and sticks, shutting them in over night. When they manage to open it, they find something has happened, and everyone they meet has become a bloodthirsty zombie. As they try to stay alive and to find shelter, Sam's knowledge of guns and self-defense (thanks to her military father) comes in handy, but the overwhelming numbers of zombies in San Fernando Valley means that the odds are against them; and the students fall, one by one ... Cosby (cocreator and head writer) and Stokes also write for Eureka, a fun television science fiction show that airs during the summers on SyFy, and the art by Marcellus doesn't go overboard with gory details just enough to satisfy readers who want some horror.

Stuck in the middle: seventeen comics from an unpleasant age

Edited by Ariel Schrag. Viking 2007 210p. Illustration

Grades: 7 8 9 10 11 12   **741.5; Fic**
  1. Middle schools; 2. Teenagers; 3. Graphic novels
978-0-670-06221-8, $18.99

                                          LC 2006-52581

This book collects seventeen short stories about the perils of middle school, each by independent comics creators, including editor Schrag, her younger sister Tania Schrag, Aaron Renier, Daniel Clowes, Gabrielle Bell, and others. Stories include the experience of being the new kid in school, getting betrayed by your best friend, being a Jewish nonathlete at a Christian sports summer camp, finding a creative outlet despite having attention deficit disorder, and more of the everyday bad situations and joys of being twelve and thirteen years old. Some harsh language (one story is also called "Shit") reflects the reality of young teen life.

Sturges, Matthew

Blue Beetle: boundaries. Matthew Sturges, writer; Rafael Albuquerque, Andre Coelho, artists; Guy Major, colorist; Travis Lanham, Swands, Sal Cipriano, letterers. DC Comics 2009 Un Illustration

Grades: 9 10 11 12   **741.5; Fic**
  1. Blue Beetle (Fictional character); 2. Superhero graphic novels; 3. Graphic novels
978-1-4012-2162-1, $14.99

El Paso teenager Jaime Reyes, the latest Blue Beetle, has managed to fight off an alien invasion (with the help of family and friends), learned how to communicate with the alien scarab that has grafted itself onto him and given him super powers. But now, illegal aliens hopped up on some new kind of drug and Intergang have come to El Paso, along with a new Doctor Polaris, and again they've involved Jaime's family and friends. And that's not all the city's District Attorney has deputized Blue Beetle to help protect the border from crossings by illegal aliens, and that has

angered many of the Mexican American residents of El Paso. The book includes lots of super powered fighting action without too much actual violence.

Sturm, James

James Sturm's America: God, gold, and golems. Drawn & Quarterly 2007 192p. Illustration

Grades: 10 11 12 Adult   **741.5; Fic**
  1. Baseball; 2. Gold mines and mining; 3. Revivals; 4. United States — History; 5. Graphic novels
978-1-897299-05-0, $24.95

This book compiles three of Sturm's stories that are set in quieter periods of American history, during relatively peaceful non-war and pre-Depression times. "The Revival," set around 1801, portrays frontier life and early religious revival movements as a couple makes their way from Ohio westward and stop off at a camp where people push themselves into religious frenzies. "Hundreds of Feet Below Daylight" examines the people who continue gold mining after the euphoria has died down and life becomes tough. Some readers may be shocked by the brutality exhibited by some of the miners who so desperately hunt for money. "The Golem's Mighty Swing" features a Jewish professional baseball team traveling the country just trying to get by in the 1920s. Facing racial and religious taunts and sometimes violence, they try a gimmick—disguising their African American player as a golem—in order to generate ticket sales.

"Social issues, including racial prejudice and intolerance, poverty, and family dynamics, are broached via both plot and character. . . . This [is] an easy crossover graphic novel for readers who enjoy American history made into well-told stories." Booklist

★ **Satchel** Paige: striking out Jim Crow by James Sturm & Rich Tommaso. Hyperion Books for Children/Jump at the Sun 2007 90p. Illustration

Grades: 4 5 6 7 8 9 10   **92; 741.5**
  1. African Americans — Biography; 2. Baseball; 3. Baseball players; 4. Biographical graphic novels; 5. Paige, Satchel, 1906-1982; 6. Graphic novels
978-0-7868-3901-8, $9.99; 978-0-7868-3900-1, $16.99

Narrated by an African American who played in the Negro Leagues for a short time, this book sketches part of the career of Leroy "Satchel" Paige, a star of the Negro Leagues. Young Emmet scored a run off Paige in a game, but suffered a career-ending knee injury. Readers get a sense of the rough life African Americans faced in the south during the 1920s, 1930s, and 1940s. Then Paige and his team come to Tuckwilla, Alabama in 1944 to play an all-White team, and Emmet and his son attend the game and watch how Paige and his team take apart the home boys. There's one panel showing a man who has been lynched and hanged; most of the violence is mentioned but not depicted on the pages.

Part of The Center for Cartoon Studies Presents series

Suburbia, Liz

★ **Sacred** Heart. Liz Suburbia. Fantagraphics 2015 312 p. Illustration

Grades: 11 12 Adult   **741.5; Fic**
  1. Mystery fiction; 2. Teenagers

1606998412; 9781606998410, $24.99

LC 2015942121

Alex Award (2016)

In this graphic novel, by Liz Suburbia, "the children of . . . Alexandria are just trying to live like normal teens until their parents' promised return from a mysterious, four-year religious pilgrimage, and Ben Schiller is no exception. She's just trying to take care of her sister . . . and get through her teen years. But her relationship with her best friend is changing, her younger sister is hiding a dark secret, and a terrible tragedy is coming for them all." (Publisher's note)

Sumerak, Marc

Big trouble at the Big Top!. GuriHiru, art; ABDO/Spotlight 2007 Un

Grades: 3 4 5 6 7 8 9   **741.5; Fic**

1. Adventure graphic novels; 2. Nightcrawler (Fictional character); 3. Power Pack (Fictional characters); 4. Superhero graphic novels; 5. X-Men (Fictional characters); 6. Graphic novels

978-1-59961-219-5, $21.35

LC 2007-130032

Marvel's youngest superheroes, the Power Pack (siblings Alex, Julie, Jack, and Katie) team up with Nightcrawler of the X-Men. The Power family has gone to the circus, but Katie is deathly afraid of clowns and won't go into the Big Top. Meanwhile, Nightcrawler has gone to visit an old friend who works in the circus, only to come under the influence of the Ringmaster and his Circus of Crime. Can the Power Pack stop the criminals and save Nightcrawler?

Part of the X-Men Power Pack series. This is a revision of the February 2006 issue of Marvel Age X-Men Power Pack, with all advertisements removed.

Costumes on!. GuriHiru, art; ABDO/Spotlight 2007 Un Illustration

Grades: 3 4 5 6 7 8 9   **741.5; Fic**

1. Adventure graphic novels; 2. Power Pack (Fictional characters); 3. Superhero graphic novels; 4. Wolverine (Fictional character); 5. X-Men (Fictional characters); 6. Graphic novels

978-1-59961-220-1, $21.35

LC 2007-130030

Marvel's youngest superheroes, the Power Pack (siblings Alex, Julie, Jack, and Katie) team up with Wolverine on Halloween. The Power family attends the big Halloween party, and Jack's convinced his Wolverine costume will win the contest until he sees that half the kids at the party are wearing Wolverine costumes. When he makes little sister Katie cry, she runs out to the woods, where she encounters the real Wolverine, who has to deal with Sabretooth with a little help from Power Pack.

Part of the X-Men Power Pack series. This is a revision of the December 2005 issue of Marvel Age X-Men Power Pack, with all advertisements removed.

Fantastic Four Presents Franklin Richards, Son of a Genius: Lab Brat. Written by Marc Sumerak ; art by Chris Eliopoulis Marvel Publishing, Inc. 2007 Un Illustration

Grades: 3 4 5 6 7 8 9   **741.5; Fic**

1. Fantastic Four (Fictional characters); 2. Humorous graphic novels; 3. Superhero graphic novels; 4. Graphic novels

0-7851-2322-9, $7.99

This book collects stories depicting the adventures of Franklin Richards, young son of Reed and Susan Richards of the Marvel superhero family, the Fantastic Four. Franklin and his robot companion H.E.R.B.I.E. keep sneaking into Reed's lab and playing with the devices they find; or, actually, Franklin does as H.E.R.B.I.E. tries to keep the boy out of trouble. In one story, Franklin accidentally turns his teacher and classmates into vegetables; in another he converts dishes of Jell-O into clones to go trick-or-treating for him; he tries to use a time machine to gather Christmas gifts for his family; he uses a device to make his comic book come to life; and he travels to another dimension where turkeys have evolved and become the dominant life form.

Originally published as Franklin Richards: Son of a Genius, Everybody Loves Franklin, Super Summer Spectacular, and Happy Franksgiving.

Franklin Richards, son of a genius: not-so-secret invasion. Art by Chris Eliopoulos. Marvel Entertainment 2009 Un Illustration

Grades: 3 4 5 6 7 8 9   **741.5; Fic**

1. Fantastic Four (Fictional characters); 2. Humorous graphic novels; 3. Superhero graphic novels; 4. Graphic novels

978-0-7851-3369-8, $9.99

This latest volume includes stories featuring Franklin Richards, son of Reed and Sue Richards of the Fantastic Four. Young Franklin, aided and abetted (albeit reluctantly) by his robot companion H.E.R.B.I.E., builds a replica of the first Iron Man robotic armor, drinks one of his dad's formulas and proceeds to belch HUGELY, de-ages his dad so they can play together, and then a multiplicity of Franklin Richards in many different timelines get into similar trouble. There are more stories, lots of silly humor and superhero action, drawn by coauthor Eliopoulos.

Hulk and Power Pack: Pack Smash!. Art by Gary Martin and David Williams. Marvel Entertainment 2007 Un Illustration

Grades: 3 4 5 6 7 8 9   **741.5; Fic**

1. Hulk (Fictional character); 2. Power Pack (Fictional characters); 3. Superhero graphic novels; 4. Graphic novels

0-7851-2490-X, $6.99

Zero-G, Lightspeed, Mass Master, and Energizer are Marvel's youngest superheroes, Power Pack. And they couldn't be more excited to meet their father's new colleague, the world-famous Dr. Bruce Banner. But when the kids find out what happens every time the good doctor becomes angry, he becomes the Hulk. Will the Pack be able to stand by their new friend, even if it may mean fighting every other hero in the Marvel Universe?

Leader of the pack. Art by Gurihiru. ABDO/Spotlight 2007 Un Illustration

Grades: 3 4 5 6 7 8 9   **741.5; Fic**

1. Adventure graphic novels; 2. Cyclops (Fictional character); 3. Power Pack (Fictional characters); 4. Superhero graphic novels; 5. X-Men (Fictional characters); 6. Graphic novels

978-1-59961-221-8, $21.35

LC 2007-130029

Marvel's youngest superheroes, the Power Pack (siblings Alex, Julie, Jack, and Katie) team up with Cyclops of the X-Men. When the kids try to help the X-Men fight the Marauders, they end up causing enough of a distraction for the villains to get away. When Julie and Greg go to the lab where he interns, though, they discover that his boss, Dr. Essex, is actually Mr. Sinister, and the Marauders have captured Cyclops. This time, the Power Pack is determined to save Cyclops and do things right.

Part of the X-Men Power Pack series. This is a revision of the March 2006 issue of Marvel Age X-Men Power Pack, with all advertisements removed.

Machine Teen: History 101001. Illustrated by Mike Hawthorne. Marvel Entertainment 2005 Un Illustration
Grades: 8 9 10 11 12   **741.5; Fic**
1. Adventure graphic novels; 2. Science fiction graphic novels; 3. Graphic novels
0-7851-1799-7, $7.99
Adam Aaronson is the ideal teenager. Straight "A" student, Captain of the West Tech football team, smart, handsome, charismatic. Every boy wants to be him. Every girl wants to be with him. But after a series of debilitating seizures, Adam makes a discovery that will shake his very reality to the core - the fact that he isn't real at all, but a sophisticated android created by a rogue scientist. Adam must now begin to decrypt the truth about his origins and what it truly means to be human. It's not easy being the perfect teen ... even when you're built that way.

Mind over matter. ABDO/Spotlight 2007 Un Illustration
Grades: 3 4 5 6 7 8 9   **741.5; Fic**
1. Adventure graphic novels; 2. Beast (Fictional character); 3. Power Pack (Fictional characters); 4. Superhero graphic novels; 5. X-Men (Fictional characters); 6. Graphic novels
978-1-59961-222-5, $21.35
                                        LC 2007-130026
Marvel's youngest superheroes, the Power Pack (siblings Alex, Julie, Jack, and Katie) team up with The Beast of the X-Men. The Power family has come to the Science Expo, where their father has a booth, and Dr. Hank McCoy, otherwise known as The Beast of the X-Men, is the keynote speaker. However, there's trouble when the shape-changing villain, Mystique, uses Dr. Power's appearance to steal The Beast's genetic analyzer. In order to save their father, the Power Pack teams up with The Beast to find and stop Mystique.

Part of the X-Men Power Pack series. This is a revision of the January 2006 issue of Marvel Age X-Men Power Pack, with all advertisements removed.

Power Pack: I know what we did that summer. Art by Gurihiru. ABDO Spotlight 2006 Un Illustration
Grades: 3 4 5 6 7 8 9   **741.5; Fic**
1. Adventure graphic novels; 2. Power Pack (Fictional characters); 3. Superhero graphic novels; 4. Graphic novels
1-59961-033-7, $21.35
A new school year is about to start, and Kate Power, youngest of the Power Pack siblings, has written a report about the team for her summer report. The problem is, as all her siblings point out, that public exposure will bring great

risk to them. This does not sit well with Kate, and it's up to oldest brother Alex to calm her down. However, her use of her power is detected by their alien enemies, the Snark, and one of them comes to Earth, determined to capture the Power Pack.

Sun Tzu
The **art** of war. Sun Tzu; illustrated by Shane Clester; adapted by Cullen Bunn and Shane Clester. Roundtable Press 2011 Un Illustration
Grades: 9 10 11 12 Adult   **741.5**
1. Competition; 2. Philosophers; 3. Strategy; 4. Sun-tzu, 6th cent BC — Adaptations
978-1-61066-010-5, $12.95
Sun Tzu's classic book on strategy has now been adapted into a graphic novel. This adaptation is more a summary of the principles of strategy discussed in The Art of War, illustrated by Clester using modern situations to demonstrate the principles. For example, Sun Tzu's statement that "he who wishes to fight must first count the cost" is depicted with rival gangsters. This short book can't replace the original, but it provides a good summary of the main points and serves as an introduction for high school students and busy adults who may not have the time to read the whole original text.

Superman/Batman: The Greatest Stories Ever Told.
DC Comics 2007 192p. Illustration
Grades: 9 10 11 12 Adult   741.5; Fic
1. Batman (Fictional character); 2. Superhero graphic novels; 3. Superman (Fictional character); 4. Graphic novels
978-1-4012-1227-8, $19.99
They are two of the world's biggest icons, and they couldn't be more different. One is the most powerful being on the planet with an array of superpowers, a shining symbol of hope embodying truth, justice, and the American way. The other has no powers, but has trained his mind and body to the peak of perfection, a dark vigilante determined to strike fear into evildoers' hearts. Together, this popular and unlikely pair starred in numerous team-ups over several decades; this book collects ten of those stories, from 1952 to the 2000s.

Suzuki, Koji
The **Ring** Vol. 4: Birthday. Dark Horse Manga 2004 159p. Illustration
Grades: 10 11 12 Adult   **741.5; Fic**
1. Horror graphic novels; 2. Manga; 3. Graphic novels
1-59307-267-8, $12.95
This volume of the Ring series collects three short stories that provide background clues about the evil Sadako and what makes her otherworldly scheme work so well. "Coffin in the Sky" relates Mai Takano's last days gestating the next Sadako; Lemon Heart" tells a story of Sadako's ill-fated young love; and Sakado" takes the reader to the icy depths of the tragic young psychic girl's creeping vengeance. The book includes nudity and harsh language."

Suzuki, Yasushi

    Purgatory Kabuki. DrMaster Publications Inc. 2008
150p. Illustration
Grades: 10 11 12 Adult   **741.5; Fic**
    1. Manga; 2. Samurai; 3. Supernatural graphic novels; 4.
Graphic novels
978-1-59796-070-0, $9.95
    This is a samurai action story set in the underworld of
the afterlife. For reasons unknown, former samurai
Imanotsurugi is obsessed with leaving the afterlife. To die in
battle is a samurai's greatest honor. Yet, he must claim 1,000
swords from the fallen warriors who now share residence in
the dark underworld. By these means alone, this highly
skilled blades master will be allowed admittance back into
the living world. But to what end" Upon what purpose does
he sharpen his edge" The story borrows heavily from various
Japanese legends and myths, and the art is reminiscent of
ukiyo-e. The book includes considerable violence with its
many sword fights.

Suzumi, Atsushi

    Haridama magic cram school. Translated and adapted
by Kaya Laterman.. Del Rey Manga 2008 202p. Illustration
Grades: 7 8 9 10 11 12   **741.5; Fic**
    1. Fantasy graphic novels; 2. Magic; 3. Manga; 4. Graphic
novels
978-0-345-50136-3, $10.95
                            LC 2008-299354
    Kokuyo and Harika are sorcery students, but they're
Obsidians, wizards who must use special stones set in
swords to help them cast spells. Other sorcery students think
they're inferior because they lack both yin and yang. But
Kokuyo and Harika do have something no one else has: the
power of friendship. They'll have to figure it out, but when
they work together, they don't need their swords. This is a
one-volume manga.

Swift, Jonathan

    Gulliver's travels. Jonathan Swift (retold by Donald B.
Lemke); illustrated by Cynthia Martin.. Stone Arch Books
2008 72p. Illustration
Grades: 4 5 6 7 8 9   **741.5; Fic**
    1. Adventure graphic novels; 2. Satire; 3. Graphic novels
978-1-4342-0449-3, $23.93; 978-1-4342-0499-8 (pa),
$9.95
                            LC 2007-30806
    Sailor Lemuel Gulliver finds himself shipwrecked on
the island of Lilliput, where he is captured by tiny people no
taller than six inches. When he leaves Lilliput and tries to go
home, he ends up in the country of Blefuscu, a land of giants
where he is considered to be nothing more than an intelligent
animal and pet. This graphic novel adaptation includes only
the first two voyages of Gulliver but does summarize the
third and fourth voyages.
    Part of the Graphic Revolve series.

Tachibana, Yutaka

    Gatcha Gacha Vol. 1. Tokyopop 2006 204p. Illustration
Grades: 8 9 10 11 12   **741.5; Fic**
    1. Humorous graphic novels; 2. Romance graphic novels;
3. Shojo manga; 4. Graphic novels
978-1-59816-153-9, $9.99

    Yuri has a big crush on Yabe, but Yabe has decided the
only girl he will ever seriously date is Motoko. So what's the
problem? Yuri and Motoko are friends, and Motoko doesn't
want to have anything to do with Yabe. But is she secretly
harboring a crush on him, too? Will they ever get this mess
straightened out? Only time will tell if love will tear these
best friends apart in this love triangle—that may get another
member. Yuri has a bad reputation from having so many
skeevy boyfriends who have dumped her; Motoko is a tough
girl. The book includes some strong language and some
school fight scenes. This series is not to be confused with the
shonen manga series, Gacha Gacha by Tamakoshi.

Taira, Shino

    Bogle, vol. 2. by Shino Taira & Yuko Ichiju. Go! Comi
2008 200p. Illustration
Grades: 9 10 11 12   **741.5; Fic**
    1. Mystery graphic novels; 2. Romance graphic novels; 3.
Shojo manga; 4. Graphic novels
978-1-933617-96-1, $10.99
    Asuka Hamuro has started at a new high school because
her older brother has taken a detective position in Tokyo.
She had been a secret "cat" thief to help people in Okinawa;
now, in her new school, she becomes part of a group called
Bogle. Two upperclassmen students and a teacher are all in
the group, and they use a website to take on jobs. Everything
they do is to help people, but because they are thieves, the
police are trying to hunt them down; Asuka's brother is one
of them.

    Bogle, vol. 2. Go! Comi 2008 200p. Illustration
Grades: 7 8 9 10 11 12   **741.5; Fic**
    1. Mystery graphic novels; 2. Romance graphic novels; 3.
Shojo manga; 4. Graphic novels
978-1-933617-97-8, $10.99
    The secret organization called Bogle operates as
"chivalrous thieves," helping people recover items taken
from them. High school student Asuka Hamuro is their
newest recruit, and she's been doing well, until the night they
steal a statue and she drops it while they're escaping from the
house from which they stole it. Worse, she dropped it right in
front of a dog, and the house belongs to a schoolmate who
has shown interest in Asuko. Later, Asuko's police detective
brother arrests fellow Bogle member Masato's older brother,
a physician whose patient has died under suspicious
circumstances. Can Bogle find out what's really happening"
The book includes romantic moments but no sexual content
or actual violence.

Takabayashi, Tomo

    Kyo Kara Maoh, volume 1. Tokyopop 2008 Un
Illustration
Grades: 8 9 10 11 12   **741.5; Fic**
    1. Fantasy graphic novels; 2. Shojo manga; 3. Graphic
novels
978-1-4278-1099-1, $9.99
    Teenager Yuri Shibuya tries to stop a student mugging,
only to be beaten and dragged to a restroom where the bullies
dunk his head in the toilet; except, instead of just getting
dunked, Yuri gets sucked into and through the toilet and
comes out into a strange world. There, he learns that he is the
King of the Mazoku, who are magic working demons hated

by the humans who also inhabit the world. As King, Yuri is supposed to possess magic skills and powers, too, but he doesn't yet know how to access or use them. And since he doesn't know the customs of the land, he also finds himself engaged to a young man who hates him and must also fight a duel. With all the bishonen (beautiful young men) and the fact that same sex relationships are considered to be normal, this manga has some boy love manga aspects, although there's very little in the way of sexual content in this first volume.

Takada, Rie
Gaba Kawa. Viz Media/Shojo Beat 2008 Un Illustration
Grades: 7 8 9 10 11 12   **741.5; Fic**
    1. Fantasy graphic novels; 2. Romance graphic novels; 3. Shojo manga; 4. Supernatural graphic novels; 5. Graphic novels
    978-1-4215-2259-3, $8.99
    Young demon Rara has come to Earth to attend high school and draw human souls to darkness. She's had a crush on a master demon she has been calling Aku, and she already has a rival, the ruthless demon Bibi. Then Rara does the unthinkable—she falls for a human boy named Retsu Aku. Despite the fact that she'll lose a power when she uses it to help a human, she does so, she can't help it. And Retsu is different from other boys, he can sense ghosts and supernatural beings; he likes Rara because she's so open in her affection for him. However, as Rara continues to lose her powers, the other demons decide to punish her and offer her only one recourse—she must kill Retsu in order to regain her powers, or disappear forever. There's very little in the way of fan service or violence; Rara and Bibi often appear in chibi (super-cute miniaturized) form when they get excited or upset. This is a standalone, one volume manga story.

    Happy Hustle High Volume 1. Viz Media/Shojo 2005 190p. Illustration
Grades: 10 11 12 Adult   **741.5; Fic**
    1. Romance graphic novels; 2. Shojo manga; 3. Graphic novels
    1-59116-912-7, $9.99
    Hanabi Ozora is a rambunctious 16-year-old tomboy who comes to the rescue of her less assertive friends—sometimes in exchange for food. So what does she do when, all of a sudden, her all-girls school is integrated with an all-boys school? She meets and falls in love—naturally—with one of the three most popular boys in the Student Council, Yasuaki Garaku. Unfortunately, Yasuaki doesn't care for girls... but when the girls' Student Council clashes head-on with the boys' Student Council, Hanabi steps in to become a member—hoping she'll change Yasuaki's mind. The book includes crude humor, sexual situations (in Vol. 5, the girls decide to attack sexual perverts who expose themselves to the girls) and some strong language. This is a 5-volume manga series.

Takagi, Ryo
    The **Devil** Within Volume 1. Go! Comi 2007 Un Illustration
Grades: 10 11 12 Adult   **741.5; Fic**

    1. Fantasy graphic novels; 2. Humorous graphic novels; 3. Shojo manga; 4. Graphic novels
    978-1-933617-22-0, $10.99
    Rion's convinced that men are devils and only little boys are angels, that is, innocent. And just when she's found the boy of her dreams, she finds herself forced by her father into an engagement to a trio of suitors. While fighting off their advances and trying to win over the heart of her reluctant young love, Tenshi, she discovers the shocking secret of the handsome trio... and something sinister about herself. The book includes a lot of sexual innuendo but so far no graphic depictions and no nudity.

Takahashi, Kazuki
    Yu-Gi-Oh! Duelist Volume 1. Viz Media/Shonen Jump 2005 216p. Illustration
Grades: 7 8 9 10 11 12 Adult   **741.5; Fic**
    1. Adventure graphic novels; 2. Games; 3. Shonen manga; 4. Graphic novels
    1-59116-614-4, $7.95
    In the second saga of the Yu-Gi-Oh! epic, Duel Monsters is the world's most popular collectible card game-but to Yugi, it's the most dangerous game of all. Entering the Duel Monsters world championship, Yugi fights ruthless opponents like game designer Maximillion Pegasus and teenage multimillionaire Kaiba Seto, hoping to discover the origin of the game...and his own powers. When Yugi beat Kaiba, little did he know the consequences: a trip through Kaiba's "Death T" - a theme park of death - and a series of evil spells against Yugi's family. It doesn't help that Kaiba's little brother also has a score to settle. There's more gaming violence in the manga series compared to what has been shown on American television; this is not a book for younger children.

    Yu-Gi-Oh! Millenium World Volume 1. Viz Media/Shonen Jump 2005 200p. Illustration
Grades: 7 8 9 10 11 12 Adult   **741.5; Fic**
    1. Adventure graphic novels; 2. Games; 3. Shonen manga; 4. Graphic novels
    1-59116-878-3, $7.95
    This is the final Yu-Gi-Oh! story. After hundreds of battles, Yugi has finally gathered all the Egyptian God Cards... the key to unlocking his memories of his past life as an Egyptian pharaoh. When Ryo Bakura gives him the Millennium Eye, Yugi opens the door to the "world of memory," and his mind travels back in time to ancient Egypt, when the magic and monsters were real. Now Yugi and his friends must explore the world of Yugi's forgotten past...and fight an enemy who has been waiting for them for 3,000 years. The manga contains more action and violence in the gaming action than has been shown in the animated series that has aired on American television; this series is not for younger children.

Takahashi, Rumiko
    ★ **InuYasha:** Volume One. By Rumiko Takahashi. Viz 2009 562 p.
Grades: 7 8 9 10 11 12   **741.5; 741.5/952**
    1. Japanese mythology; 2. Manga
    1421532808; 9781421532806, $19.99
                                        LC Bl2009031710

In this book, by Rumiko Takahashi, "Kagome is a modern Japanese high school girl. Never the type to believe in myths and legends, her world view dramatically changes when, one day, she's pulled out of her own time and into another! There, in Japan's ancient past, Kagome discovers more than a few of those dusty old legends are true, and that her destiny is linked to one legendary creature in particular—the dog like half-demon called Inuyasha!" (Publisher's note)

Originally published in 56 individual volumes
Volume 1 of 18

One-pound gospel, vol. 1. Viz Media 2008 242p. Illustration
Grades: 10 11 12 Adult   **741.5; Fic**
1. Boxing; 2. Humorous graphic novels; 3. Manga; 4. Shonen manga; 5. Graphic novels
978-1-4215-2030-8, $9.99

Kosaku Hatanaka is a talented boxer, but he suffers from an insatiable appetite that makes it extremely difficult to make weight for his boxing matches (he's a featherweight who should weigh 126 pounds). He drives his poor coach crazy and tends to lose matches because he has to starve himself to lose weight, which saps his strength. Then he meets Sister Angela, a novice nun who tries to help him; she's so cute, Kosaku has a crush on her. Between his coach at Mukaida's Gym and Sister Angela's prayers, Kosaku starts to win his bouts—but usually with such bizarre circumstances and incredible luck that his opponents hate him. The boxing action is pretty well done and fairly graphic; this volume doesn't include much at all in the way of strong language, but Viz has put a warning about strong language and realistic violence on the title page. This series was originally published starting in 1989 and is now released in Viz's now standard unflipped tankobon size book.
Volume 1 of 4

Ranma 1/2. Rumiko Takahashi, translated from Japanese by Gerard Jones & Matt Thorn. Viz Media 2014 359 p. Illustration
Grades: 10 11 12 Adult   **741.5**
1. Gender role — Fiction; 2. Manga
1421565943; 9781421565941, $14.99

"One day, teenaged martial artist Ranma Saotome went on a training mission with his father and ended up taking a dive into some cursed springs at a legendary training ground in China. Now, every time he's splashed with cold water, he changes into a girl. His father, Genma, changes into a panda! What's a half-guy, half-girl to do?" (Publisher's note)

"One of the bestselling manga from the early '90s, a gender-bending rom-com mixed with copious martial arts action, returns in this rerelease. World-class martial artist Ranma Saotome has been cursed with a special fate: when doused with cold water, he turns into a girl. This oddity is little more than an irritation to him until he becomes engaged to Akane Tendo, a prodigiously strong fighter who also happens to hate men." Pub Wkly

38 volumes originally released in Japan from 1987-1996

Takahashi, Yashichiro
Shakugan no Shana Vol. 1. Viz Media 2007 Un Illustration

Grades: 10 11 12   **741.5; Fic**
1. Fantasy graphic novels; 2. Shonen manga; 3. Graphic novels
978-1-4215-1195-5, $9.99

Yuuji Sakai, a high school student who expected his very normal life to last forever, is dead. While on his way home one day the world suddenly freezes, people are engulfed by blue flames and a monster resembling a large doll seems to swallow them. Just as the monster prepares to consume Yuuji, a sword-wielding girl in black attire with flaming red eyes and hair that burns like embers saves him. The girl calls herself a "Flame Haze" who hunts the Tomogara (formally "Guze no Tomogara," or Crimson Denizens in English), creatures from another world. When Yuuji notices a blue flame in his chest, the Flame Haze tells him that the "real" Yuuji died some time ago, and that he is a "Torch—, a temporary replacement for erased humans. Torches take on the forms of those erased persons, but before long, they will vanish from the memories of the living. Unfazed by his apparent death, Yuuji befriends the strange girl and names her "Shana". Shana is surprised to find that Yuuji is not a normal Torch, but instead a special kind called a "Mistes": he has a "hougu" inside him, and an extremely powerful and valuable one at that. Shana resolves to protect Yuuji from the Tomogara, who would use the hougu to disrupt the balance of the world, and Yuuji decides to join Shana in her fight. This series has some violence and some incidental nudity.

Takahiro
Akame ga kill!; Volume 1. Story, Takahiro; art, Tetsuya Tashiro; translation, Christine Dashiell; lettering, James Dashiell. Yen Press 2015 238 p. Illustration
Grades: 9 10 11 12   **741.5; Fic**
1. Manga; 2. Shonen manga; 3. Teenagers — Japan
0316259462; 9780316259460, $13
LC 2015373812

In this shonen manga graphic novel, by Takahiro, art by Tetsuya Tashiro, translated by Christine Dashiell, "Tatsumi dreams of earning enough money for his impoverished village by working in the Capital—but . . . he's robbed by a buxom beauty upon arrival! Penniless, Tatsumi is taken in by the lovely Miss Aria, but just when his Capital dreams seem in reach yet again, Miss Aria's mansion is besieged by Night Raid—a team of ruthless assassins." (Publisher's note)
Volume 1 of an ongoing series

Takako, Shimura
Wandering son: Volume One. Shimura Takako; translated by Matt Thorn. Fantagraphics 2011 192 p. Illustration
Grades: 7 8 9 10   **Fic**
1. Bildungsromans; 2. Manga; 3. Puberty; 4. Sex role; 5. Transgender people; 6. Graphic novels
1606994166; 9781606994160, $19.99

This manga "tells the story of a friendship between Shuichi, a young boy who wishes he were a girl, and Yoshino, a young girl who wishes she were a boy. . . . Shuichi's impulses toward a female identity feel confusing and shameful to him, and it's the girls in his life-first Yoshino, and then Saori-who point out his difference and encourage it. . . . Both children are teased mercilessly by their classmates, whose sexual development, while perhaps more socially normative, is just as confusing to them." (Publishers Weekly)

Wandering son: Volume Three. Shimura Takako; translated by Matt Thorn. Fantagraphics Books 2012 200 p.
Grades: 7 8 9 10   **741.5; Fic**
1. Friendship; 2. Secrets — Fiction; 3. Transgender people
1606995332; 9781606995334, $19.99
In this graphic novel, by Shimura Takako, "Shuichi and his friend Yoshino have a secret: Shuichi is a boy who wants to be a girl, and Yoshino is a girl who wants to be a boy. But one day . . . their secret is exposed, and the two find themselves the target of sixth-grade cruelty. Their friendship is strained, . . . and their mentor, Yuki, reveals the harder reality of being transgendered. Meanwhile, Shuichi's sister, Maho, realizes her dream of becoming a model, and drags Shuichi along." (Publisher's note)

Wandering son: Volume Two. Shimura Takako; translated by Matt Thorn. Fantagraphics Books 2012 200 p.
Grades: 7 8 9 10   **741.5; Fic**
1. Bildungsromans; 2. Middle schools — Fiction; 3. Transgender people
1606994565; 9781606994566, $19.99
"In the second volume of Shimura Takako's [Wandering Son series], . . . transgendered protagonists, Shuichi and Yoshino, have entered the sixth grade. Shuichi spends a precious gift of cash from his grandmother on a special present for himself, a purchase that triggers a chain of events in which his sister Maho learns his secret, and Shuichi inadvertently steals the heart of a boy Maho in interested in." (Publisher's note)
"While the first volume served as an introduction to Shuichi and Yoshino's lives, their stories and identities really begin to evolve in this lovely, exciting, and surprising follow-up." Booklist

Wandering son; Volume four. Shimura Takako; [translation: Matt Thorn]. Fantagraphics Books 2013 219 p.
Grades: 7 8 9 10   **741.5; Fic**
1. Friendship; 2. Gender identity; 3. Gender role; 4. Middle schools — Juvenile fiction
1606996053; 9781606996058, $19.99
                                    LC 2013363244
This book, by Shimura Takako, the fourth in the series, "continues the story of Nitori Shuichi, a girl who wants to be a boy named Takatsuki Yoshino. . . . The story is filled with mixed signals, rumors, unrequited love, boys and girls fighting over one another, and love-hate relationships. . . . And as the characters get ready to enter middle school, with its gender-specific uniforms, each one is being pushed to conform to society's standards." (School Library Journal)

Takamisaki, Ryo
Megaman NT Warrior Vol. 1. Viz/Viz Kids 2004 186p. Illustration
Grades: 4 5 6 7 8 9   **741.5; Fic**
1. Science fiction graphic novels; 2. Shonen manga; 3. Graphic novels
1-59116-465-6, $7.95
The year is 200X and everyone is now connected to the Cyber Network. People carry their own PET (Personal terminal) and are paired up with an artificial intelligence program called a NetNavi (or NetNavigator). Computers have turned the world into a bright and shiny utopia, but there's always trouble in paradise. While the invention of the PET and NetNavis has brought great benefits to the world, computer hacking, virus spreading, and other high-tech crimes are becoming a major problem. A sinister organization by the name of World Three has appeared, and they've vowed to destroy this technological wonderland. Enter Lan Hikari, an intensely curious and cheerful fifth grader. Synchronized with his NetNavigator, MegaMansupercharged, he becomes a super-charged dynamo. In and out of the Net, Lan and MegaMan do their best to thwart World Three's neverending quest to take over the world. The book includes some raunchy humor and lots of action.

Pokemon: the rise of Darkrai. Viz Media/VizKids 2008 Un Illustration
Grades: 2 3 4 5 6 7 8 9   **741.5; Fic**
1. Adventure graphic novels; 2. Fantasy graphic novels; 3. Manga; 4. Graphic novels
978-1-4215-2289-0, $7.99
Ash and his friends come to Alamos Town, home of the Space-Time Towers, and while touring the town, they discover that the town's special garden has been ransacked. Some of the townspeople blame Darkrai, a sinister looking Pokemon that said to haunt the garden. However, Alamos Town faces much more peril when two powerful Pokemon that control time and space battle each other; it should be impossible for them to meet, and unless Ash and the others "and perhaps Darkrai" can stop them, Alamos Town will be destroyed. This book includes a lot of Pokemon fighting action; the panels are so filled with details that very young readers might find it difficult to follow the action.

Takanashi, Mitsuba
Crimson Hero, Vol. 1. Viz Media/Shojo Beat 2005 Un Illustration
Grades: 8 9 10 11 12   **741.5; Fic**
1. Science fiction graphic novels; 2. Shonen manga; 3. Graphic novels
978-1-4215-0140-6, $8.99
First year high school student Nobara wants more than anything to play volleyball, and she enrolled in Crimson Field High School to do so. However, her mother, who runs the high class ryotei restaurant called Seiryu, has used her wealth and position to eliminate the girls' volleyball club in order to force Nobara to be her successor in running the restaurant. Incensed at her mother's actions, Nobara runs away from home; she ends up in the dorm with the boys on volleyball scholarships and works for them as cook and clean-up maid for room and board. And she works to start a new girls' volleyball club at school.

The **Devil** Does Exist Volume 1. DC Comics/CMX 2005 192p. Illustration
Grades: 7 8 9 10 11 12   **741.5; Fic**
1. Manga; 2. Romance graphic novels; 3. Shojo manga; 4. Graphic novels
1-4012-0545-3, $9.99
High school is difficult for most kids. But for Kayano, a shy girl whose single mother seems to work all the time, it's

even worse than usual. She's so afraid of drawing attention to herself, in fact, that she can't tell the handsome Kamijo how much she loves him-until one day she finally gets up the courage to write him a letter confessing her feelings. But her plans go awry when the letter falls into the hands of the school's most notorious student, Edogawa Takeru. To Kayano, Takeru seems to be Satan himself. Not only is he devilishly handsome, he is the son of the school's principal. Even the teachers dare not stand up to him. Kayano, appalled by how badly her first attempt at a social life has gone, thinks she can struggle through, and get her letter back. But, Takeru enjoys watching her suffer. Just when she thinks she's solved the problem, her mother comes home to announce she's getting married-to principal Edogawa. Now Kayano will have to live with this devil Takeru 24/7. How will she cope with this literal living hell?" The book includes some mild strong language, mild violence, and some brief sexual situations.

Takarai, Saori

Manga Moods: 40 Faces + 80 Phrases. Japanime Co. Ltd./Manga University 2006 96p. Illustration
Grades: 6 7 8 9 10 11 12 Adult   741.5
  1. Manga; 2. Graphic novels
  978-4-921205-13-3, $12.95
  A raised eyebrow, a curled lip, a wink of the eye. All it takes is a single stroke of the pen to instantly change a manga character's mood from one extreme to the other: glad to sad, sassy to shy, angry to embarrassed. In addition, each of the facial expressions is labeled with the Japanese word for the mood being depicted, along with common Japanese conversational phrases and English translations, making this book fun for aspiring artists, language enthusiasts and manga fans. As a bonus, the 46 basic hiragana, as well as contracted hiragana and two-dash and one-circle hiragana characters are shown for those who want to start learning to write Japanese.

Takaya, Natsuki

  ★ **Fruits** Basket Collector's Edition, Vol. 1. Natsuki Takaya. Yen Press 2016 400 p. Illustration
Grades: 7 8 9 10 11 12   Fic
  1. Family — Fiction; 2. Secrets — Fiction
  0316360163; 9780316360166, $20
  "After a family tragedy turns her life upside down, plucky high schooler Tohru Honda takes matters into her own hands and moves out...into a tent! Unfortunately for her, she pitches her new home on private land belonging to the mysterious Sohma clan, and it isn't long before the owners discover her secret." (Publisher's note)
  Originally published in the U.S. by Tokyopop

  Phantom dream, vol. 1. Tokyopop 2008 Un Illustration
Grades: 10 11 12   741.5; Fic
  1. Fantasy graphic novels; 2. Manga; 3. Romance graphic novels; 4. Shojo manga; 5. Graphic novels
  978-1-4278-1089-2, $9.99
  High school student Tamaki Otoya is the latest Monshu, or head priest, at his family's temple. He's also a shugoshi, an exorcist of jaki, demons born of negative emotions. Tamaki has never wanted the responsibility, but as the only son and heir, he has no choice. Best friend (and lover) Asahi

keeps encouraging him, but Tamaki tries to avoid his fate, until a childhood friend becomes possessed by jashin (extreme negative emotions). Then a boy who committed suicide comes back to life but filled with jashin. The boy only wants to be able to raise and study butterflies, but his parents have pressured him so much . Then a member of the Gekka family returns, demanding that the temple hand over the Suigekka, the demon sword. The book includes some violence, nudity, and sexual situations.

Takei, Hiroyuki

  Shaman King Volume 1. Viz Media/Shonen Jump 2003 204p. Illustration
Grades: 8 9 10 11 12 Adult   741.5; Fic
  1. Adventure graphic novels; 2. Shonen manga; 3. Supernatural graphic novels; 4. Graphic novels
  1-56931-902-2, $7.95
  When he takes a shortcut through a cemetery, Manta Oyamada meets a strange kid with headphones - surrounded by ghosts. The kid is the teenage shaman Yoh Asakura. Tapping the supernatural swordfighting powers of samurai ghost Admidamaru, Yoh fights Bokuto no Ryu, a sword-wielding gang member. But an even more dangerous opponent is stalking Yoh and Manta - a Chinese shaman who wants to possess Amidamaru.

Takemoto, Novala

  Kamikaze Girls. Story by Novala Takemoto; art by Yukio Kanesada; English translation & adaptation, Tomo Kimura. Viz Media/Shojo Beat 2006 190p. Illustration
Grades: 10 11 12 Adult   741.5; Fic
  1. Manga; 2. Shojo manga; 3. Graphic novels
  978-1-4215-0268-7, $8.99
  Momoko is a Lolita stranded in the boondocks of rural Ibaraki prefecture, although she'd much rather be living in the Palace of Versailles. Ichigo is a member of a girls-only biker gang who firmly believes in honor, loyalty, and fist fighting. Together this unlikely duo strikes out on a journey to find a legendary embroiderer who might just be able to make their dreams come true. The book includes some strong language, some violence, and teen smoking. This is a standalone one volume manga.

Takemiya, Keiko

  ★ To **Terra** Volume One. Vertical, Inc. 2007 343p. Illustration
Grades: 9 10 11 12 Adult   741.5; Fic
  1. Manga; 2. Psychics; 3. Science fiction graphic novels; 4. Shojo manga; 5. Graphic novels
  9781932234671, $13.95; 1932234675
  The future. Having driven Terra to the brink of environmental collapse, humanity decides to reform itself by ushering in the age of Superior Domination (S.D.), a system of social control in which children are no longer the offspring of parents but progeny of a universal computer. The new social order, however, results in an unexpected byproduct: the Mu, a mutant race with extrasensory powers who are forced in exile by The System. The saga begins on educational planet Ataraxia, where Jomy Marcus Shin, a brash and unpredictable teenager, is nervously preparing to enter adult society. When his Maturity Check goes wrong, the Mu intervene in the great hope that Jomy, who possesses

Mu telepathy and human physical strength, can lead them back home, to Terra...

Volume 1 of 3

Takemura, Masaharu

The **manga** guide to biochemistry. Masaharu Takemura, Kikuyaro, Office Sawa. Oreilly & Associates Inc 2011 Xii, 253 p. Illustration

Grades: 11 12 Adult   **572**

1. Biochemistry

1593272766; 9781593272760, $24.95; 1593274211; 9781593274214, $24.95

LC 2011038517

In this work of graphic nonfiction, "Kumi explores the mysteries of her body's inner workings." Topics include "biopolymers like DNA and proteins, the metabolic processes that turn our food into energy, and the enzymes that fuel our bodies' chemical reactions." Also discussed are "the metabolism of substances like carbohydrates, lipids, proteins, and alcohol . . . mitochondria . . . DNA transcription . . . [and] enzyme kinetics." (Publisher's note)

Includes index.

Takeuchi, Mick

Her Majesty's Dog, Vol. 1. Go! Comi 2005 200p. Illustration

Grades: 10 11 12 Adult   **741.5; Fic**

1. Romance graphic novels; 2. Shojo manga; 3. Supernatural graphic novels; 4. Graphic novels

0-9768957-3-0, $10.99

New students Amane and Hyoue cause a stir in their high school because they kiss so much. Amane is a psychic, Hyoue is actually her guardian demon-dog, and he feeds on her life force by their kisses. Together, they hunt demons, but in school they need to learn how to deal with everyday hazards such as bullies, jealousy, and making friends. This series combines teen romance with supernatural horror.

Takeuchi, Naoko

★ **Sailor** Moon; Volume 1. [Naoko Takeuchi; translator/adapter, William Flanagan]. Kodansha Comics 2011 240 p. Illustration; Color

Grades: 5 6 7 8 9 10   **741.5**

1. Good and evil — Fiction; 2. Shojo manga; 3. Teenage girls — Fiction; 4. Teenage girls — Japan; 5. Women heroes

1935429744; 9781935429746, $10.99

LC 2012374271

"Usagi Tsukino is a normal girl until she meets up with Luna, a talking cat, who tells her that she is Sailor Moon. As Sailor Moon, Usagi must fight evils and enforce justice, in the name of the Moon and the mysterious Moon Princess. She meets other girls destined to be Sailor Senshi (Sailor Scouts), and together, they fight the forces of evil!" (Publisher's note)

First published in Japan in 2003 by Kodansha Ltd., Tokyo, as Bishoujosenshi Sailor Moon Shinsoban—End pages.

Volume 1 of 12

Takizaki, Mamiya

Element line vol.1. Tokyopop 2008 Un Illustration

Grades: 10 11 12 Adult   **741.5; Fic**

1. Adventure graphic novels; 2. Fantasy graphic novels; 3. Manga

978-1-4278-0527-0, $9.99

On a world devastated by monstrous Rizoms, humanity lives in the remaining cities, surrounded by huge walls called Shields and protected by soldiers of the Guild. Laolyth was a great hero among the Guild, but he disappeared fourteen years ago. Kam, an orphan boy brought to live in the city of Grisfynn, is preparing to become a Guild member, which would allow him to travel as a guard for merchant caravans going between the fortified cities. However, he also hides a dangerous secret: he is the son of Laolyth, and something is happening to his body, making him fear he will become a Rizom. Meanwhile, the heir to the Guild's grand master discovers that his mother has been a political manipulator and revealed some of the Guild's deepest secrets. The series includes considerable bloody violence.

Takizawa, Seiho

Who Fighter with Heart of Darkness. Dark Horse Manga 2006 208p. Illustration

Grades: 10 11 12 Adult   **741.5; Fic**

1. Seinen manga; 2. War; 3. Graphic novels

978-1-59307-626-9, $11.95

The first story in this anthology, "Who Fighter," is a play on the legendary "Foo Fighters," the nickname given to the mysterious, UFO-like fireballs that were sighted by World War II pilots. An ace Japanese pilot manages to shoot one of the fireballs down... or does he? As ominous signs and visions begin to follow in his steps, the bewildered pilot wonders if he's lost not only his memory of the incident-but also his very mind. "Heart of Darkness" is Takizawa's take on the Joseph Conrad novel. A Japanese war hero, Colonel Kurutsu, has gone rogue, setting up his own private kingdom deep upriver in the jungles of Burma. A young captain, sent to execute Kurutsu, finds that the true reasons for the Colonel's "desertion" are very different from what he was told. Finally, a short piece, "Tanks," closes out the collection with a surreal voyage through one hundred years of armored vehicle battles. The book includes some violence and some mildly strong language.

Talbot, Bryan

★ **Alice** in Sunderland: An Entertainment. Dark Horse Comics 2007 324p. Illustration

Grades: 10 11 12 Adult   **741.5**

1. Fantasy graphic novels

978-1-59307-673-3

Sunderland was once the greatest center of learning in Christendom and the birthplace of English consciousness. In the time of Lewis Carroll it was the greatest shipbuilding port in the world, and here are buried the roots of Carroll's surreal masterpiece, Alice in Wonderland. Talbot mixes fact and fiction in his meditation on myth, history, storytelling. The book includes some strong language, particularly Briticisms.

★ The **tale** of one bad rat. Dark Horse 2010 Un Illustration

Grades: 9 10 11 12 Adult   741.5; Fic
1. Child sexual abuse; 2. Runaway teenagers; 3. Graphic novels
978-1-59582-493-6, $19.99

This book's "heroine is teenager Helen Potter, who has run away from an abusive father and whose path to recovery takes her from a squat in London to refuge at an inn in the British countryside. Along the way, she meets characters and situations that Talbot derives from the work of Helen's namesake, Beatrix Potter, whose life he symbolically links to Helen's. Talbot's vivid, realistic full-color illustration brilliantly evokes the story's settings, yet even more effective are his compassionate characterizations." Booklist
First published 1995
This volume collects issues one through four of the Dark Horse comic-book series Verso of title page

Talbot, Mary M.
Dotter of her father's eyes. Mary M. Talbot; art by Bryan Talbot. Diamond Comic Distributors 2012 96 p. Illustration; Color
Grades: 11 12 Adult   741.5
1. Atherton, James S; 2. Bildungsromans; 3. Joyce, James, 1882-1941
1595828508; 9781595828507, $14.99
Costa Biography Award Winner 2012

Author Mary M. Talbot's book "contrasts two coming of age narratives: that of Lucia, the daughter of James Joyce, and that of author Mary Talbot, daughter of the eminent Joycean scholar James S Atherton. Social expectations and gender politics, thwarted ambitions and personal tragedy are played out against two contrasting historical backgrounds." (mary-talbot.co.uk)
Includes bibliographical references.

Tamaki, Jillian
★ **SuperMutant** Magic Academy. Jillian Tamaki. Drawn & Quarterly 2015 274 p. Illustration
Grades: 10 11 12 Adult   741.5
1. Canada; 2. Fantasy graphic novels; 3. Private schools; 4. School stories; 5. Teenagers — Fiction
1770461981; 9781770461987, $22.95
LC 2015376543

In this graphic novel, author Jillian Tamaki "paints a teenaged world filled with just as much ennui and uncertainty, but also with a sharp dose of humor and irreverence. . . . The SuperMutant Magic Academy is a prep school for mutants and witches, but their paranormal abilities take a backseat to everyday teen concerns. Science experiments go awry, bake sales are upstaged, and the new kid at school is a cat who will determine the course of human destiny." (Publisher's note)
"There are flickering moments of transcendent wisdom and kindness, but the overall tone is one of insouciant, salty resignation to the mundane realities of existence. Simultaneously heartbreaking and hilarious." Booklist

Tamaki, Mariko
★ **Emiko** superstar. Written by Mariko Tamaki; illustrated by Steve Rolston. DC Comics/Minx 2008 149p. Illustration
Grades: 7 8 9 10 11 12   741.5; Fic

1. Performance art; 2. Racially mixed people; 3. Graphic novels
978-1-4012-1536-1, $9.99

"Emiko, a half-Japanese, half-Caucasian Canadian, is a self-described geek facing a summer of babysitting and isolation. Things change when she stumbles upon an underground performing art scene inspired by Andy Warhol's Factory. She eventually takes to the stage . . . and achieves minor celebrity. Soon, though, Emiko must face the troubling complexities in the lives of her new friends and the consequences of her own questionable actions. . . . Rolston's playful, vibrant b&w illustrations bring the characters to life." Publ Wkly

★ **Skim**. Words by Mariko Tamaki; drawings by Jillian Tamaki. Groundwood Books 2008 144p. Illustration
Grades: 7 8 9 10 11 12   741; 741.5; Fic
1. Friendship; 2. Humorous graphic novels; 3. School stories; 4. Graphic novels
088899964X; 0-88899-753-1; 9780888999641, 12.95; 978-0-88899-753-1, $18.95
Ignatz Award: Outstanding Graphic Novel (2008)

Skim is Kimberly Keiko Cameron, a not-slim half-Japanese would-be Wiccan goth who attends a private school. When classmate Katie Matthews' ex-boyfriend commits suicide, concerned guidance counselors descend upon the school because so many of the student body goes into mourning overdrive. The popular clique starts a new club, Girls Celebrate Life, and make Katie their project, especially after she falls off her roof and breaks both arms. Kim and her best friend Lisa observe all this, but counselors target Kim for her goth tendencies and are convinced she'll become suicidal any moment. All she is, is in love with her English teacher, Ms. Archer, who seems to reciprocate and then leaves the school. As Lisa starts to get sucked into the GLC, Kim and Katie tentatively begin a new friendship. There is only one rather chaste kiss between Kim and Ms. Archer. Artist Jillian Tamaki draws Kim to look like a classical Heian period Japanese woman.

★ **This** One Summer. Mariko Tamaki, Jillian Tamaki. First Second 2014 320 p. Illustration
Grades: 7 8 9 10 11 12 Adult   741.5; Fic
1. Friendship — Fiction; 2. Vacations — Fiction; 3. Graphic novels
159643774X, 17.99; 1626720940, 21.99; 9781626720947, $21.99; 9781596437746, 17.99
Caldecott Honor Book (2015)
Printz Honor Book (2015)
Eisner Award: Best Graphic Album—New (2015)
Ignatz Award: Outstanding Graphic Novel (2014)
Harvey Nominee: Best Artist (2015)
Harvey Nominee: Best Graphic Album of Original Work (2015)
Harvey Nominee: Best Original Graphic Publication For Young Readers (2015)

In this young adult graphic novel written by Mariko Tamaki and illustrated by Jillian Tamaki, "Every summer, Rose goes with her mom and dad to a lake house in Awago Beach. . . . Rosie's friend Windy is always there, too, like the little sister she never had. But this summer is different. . . . It's a summer of secrets, and sorrow, and growing up, and it's a good thing Rose and Windy have each other." (Publisher's note)

"This captivating graphic novel presents a fully realized picture of a particular time in a young girl's life, an in-between summer filled with yearning and a sense of ephemerality." SLJ

Tamura, Yumi

Basara Volume 1. Viz Media/Shojo 2003 200p. Illustration

Grades: 10 11 12 Adult   **741.5; Fic**
1. Adventure graphic novels; 2. Fantasy graphic novels; 3. Romance graphic novels; 4. Shojo manga; 5. Graphic novels

1-53961-974-X, $9.99

Born under a prophecy that will liberate and unite a post-apocalyptic Japan, Sarasa has had to take her brother Tatara's place as the "Boy of Destiny." Fighting for the oppressed, Sarasa journeys across Japan to gain allies and defeat her enemies—all while keeping her identity a secret. Ironically, while she leads her people in rebellion against the Red King, she falls in love with him before realizing who he is. The series includes nudity, sexual situations, and violence.

Tan, Shaun

★ The **arrival**. Arthur A. Levine Books 2007 Un Illustration

Grades: 6 7 8 9 10   **741.5; Fic**
1. Immigrants; 2. Stories without words; 3. Graphic novels

0-439-89529-4, $19.99; 9780439895293

LC 2006-21706

Boston Globe-Horn Book Award special citation (2008)

In this wordless graphic novel, a man leaves his homeland and sets off for a new country, where he must build a new life for himself and his family.

"Young readers will be fascinated by the strange new world the artist creates. . . . They will linger over the details in the beautiful sepia pictures and will likely pick up the book to pore over it again and again." SLJ

Tanabe, Yellow

Kekkaishi, Vol. 1. Viz Action 2005 192p. Illustration
Grades: 9 10 11 12 Adult   **741.5; Fic**
1. Shonen manga; 2. Supernatural graphic novels; 3. Graphic novels

1-59116-968-2, $9.99

Junior high student Yoshimori Sumimura is a kekkaishi, a demon hunter; it's the family business. The Yukimuras next door are also kekkaishi, rivals of the Sumimuras. Their daughter Tokine is also a demon hunter. Yoshimori would much rather become a pastry chef, but he can't let Tokine always get the demons. This is the first of an ongoing manga series that has lots of demon hunting action but not too much violence, and considerable humor.

Tanaka, Masashi

Gon vol.6. DC Comics/CMX 2008 Un Illustration
Grades: 6 7 8 9 10 11 12 Adult   **741.5; Fic**
1. Gon (Fictional character); 2. Manga; 3. Stories without words; 4. Graphic novels

978-1-4012-1278-0, $5.99

In this volume, Gon acquires headgear—a bird's nest with three orphaned chicks falls onto his head when he headbutts a tree, and the three young birds are in for the ride of their life as Gon goes his way. Then he and a band of ragtag creatures make their way through a forest and a fire. And he befriends an old elephant as they make their way to a goal only the old elephant knows. The book includes animal-on-animal violence.

Gon Volume 1. DC Comics/CMX 2007 Un Illustration
Grades: 6 7 8 9 10 11 12 Adult   **741.5; Fic**
1. Humorous graphic novels; 2. Manga; 3. Stories without words; 4. Graphic novels

978-1-4012-1273-5, $5.99

Volume 1 of 7

A tiny dinosaur with a feisty attitude marches across the wilderness defending the friendly and furry from the mean and hungry. Told entirely without words, the stories highlight the detailed art and visual storytelling ability of creator Masashi Tanaka. This new edition from CMX restores the book to its original right-to-left orientation.

Gon volume 5. DC Comics/CMX 2008 Un Illustration
Grades: 7 8 9 10 11 12 Adult   **741.5; Fic**
1. Animals; 2. Gon (Fictional character); 3. Manga; 4. Graphic novels

978-1-4012-1277-3, $5.99

In this book-length episode, Gon starts out by exploring an anthill, then defending prairie dogs against a coyote. When an earthquake sends Gon, a prairie dog and the adult coyote and its pup underground, they unite against a giant spider that traps the pup. They must deal with various giant insects (ants, pillbugs, mayflies), bats, and the deadly huge spider. People who don't like to see so many creepy crawlies on the page may want to skip this book.

Gon volume 4. DC Comics/CMX 2008 Un Illustration
Grades: 7 8 9 10 11 12 Adult   **741.5; Fic**
1. Adventure graphic novels; 2. Dinosaurs; 3. Gon (Fictional character); 4. Manga; 5. Graphic novels

978-1-4012-1275-6, $5.99

Gon, the little dinosaur living in the time of mammals, is back for more wordless adventures. First, he finds a turtle shell and decides to try it on, only to find he can't get out of it. He ends up doing his best to protect the newly hatched sea turtles as they face a gauntlet of hungry predators in their journey to the sea. Then Gon finds himself in the desert with several savannah animals after a tornado dumps them there, and has to save them. The book includes predator/prey animal violence; some readers might get upset to see the baby turtles being eaten by so many other animals.

Tanemura, Arina

Full Moon Vol. 1: O Sagashite. Viz Media/Shojo Beat 2005 200p. Illustration
Grades: 7 8 9 10   **741.5; Fic**
1. Fantasy graphic novels; 2. Manga; 3. Romance graphic novels; 4. Shojo manga; 5. Graphic novels

1-59116-928-3, $8.99

Young Mitsuki loves singing and dreams of becoming a pop star. Unfortunately, a malignant tumor in her throat prevents her from pursuing her passion. However, her life turns around when two surprisingly fun-loving harbingers of death appear to grant Mitsuki a temporary reprieve from her illness and give her singing career a magical push start. They transform her into a 16-year-old, and she becomes a sensation, but when one of the spirits falls in love with Mitsuki, complications abound.

I-O-N. Viz Media/Shojo Beat 2008 208p. Illustration
Grades: 7 8 9 10 11 12   **741.5; Fic**
1. Humorous graphic novels; 2. Psychokinesis; 3. Romance graphic novels; 4. Shojo manga; 5. Graphic novels
978-1-4215-1800-8, $8.99

Ion Tsuburagi chants the letters of her first name as a charm to bring good luck when she needs it; in school, she uses it to get away from Kouki Shiraishi, the Student Council President, who has vowed to make Ion his girlfriend. Then she meets Mikado Horai, the president of the Psychic Powers Research Society at school, and she touches a mysterious substance he's been developing. Now, chanting "ION" gives her telekinetic powers. This is a one-volume manga by the creator of Kamikaze Kaito Jeanne, Full Moon, and The Gentlemen's Alliance.

Kamikaze Kaito Jeanne, Vol. 1. DC Comics/CMX 2006 176p. Illustration
Grades: 6 7 8 9 10   **741.5; Fic**
1. Fantasy graphic novels; 2. Shojo manga; 3. Supernatural graphic novels; 4. Graphic novels
978-1-4012-0555-3, $9.99

Sixteen-year-old Maron Kusakabe is a high school student, but she's also the reincarnation of Joan of Arc (called here by her French name, Jeanne d'Arc). At night, Maron takes the magical form of Kamikaze Kaito Jeanne, and with the help of angel-in-training Finn, she steals paintings that have been possessed by demons in order to save the paintings' owners from the demons' enchantments. Jeanne soon has a rival, Kaito Sinbad; coincidentally, in school Maron meets a transfer student, Chiaki. She also has to deal with the determined investigations of her friend Miyako, daughter of a police detective. This seven-volume manga series finished publication in 2007.

Short-tempered Melancholic and other stories. Viz Media/Shojo Beat 2008 192p. Illustration
Grades: 7 8 9 10 11 12   **741.5; Fic**
1. Humorous graphic novels; 2. Manga; 3. Romance graphic novels; 4. Shojo manga; 5. Graphic novels
978-1-4215-1801-5, $8.99

This manga collects some of Tanemura's early, shorter manga works, including her debut story, "The Style of the Second Love." In this story, Mana secretly like's her friend's boyfriend, but the younger Nakamura is determined to win Mana's heart. In "Short Tempered Melancholic," female ninja Kajika Yamano's job is to protect her family's legendary weapon, but when Fujisaki, an older boy she likes, tells her she should act more ladylike, Kajika tries to give up all ninja deeds. Minori falls in love with Takato, who shared his umbrella with her one rainy afternoon. Now, she thinks "Rainy Afternoons are for Romantic Heroines" and "forgets" her umbrella every time it rains. Then Yuri sends her penpal Ryo a picture of her best friend Karin instead of one of herself, because Karin is prettier. But "This Love is Nonfiction," and now Ryo wants to meet her. Now she has to

send Karin, but Yuri can't help but follow, then she meets up with a weird guy.

Time stranger Kyoko, volume 1. Viz Media/Shojo Beat 2008 Un Illustration
Grades: 10 11 12   **741.5; Fic**
1. Fantasy graphic novels; 2. Manga; 3. Shojo manga; 4. Graphic novels
978-1-4215-1797-1, $8.99

In the 30th century, all of Earth is united into one kingdom, Earth Nation, and Kyoko Suomi is the princess. She has lived among the commoners, attending school with almost no one knowing her true identity. As her sixteenth birthday approaches, Kyoko really doesn't want to end her days at school; her only option is to find a way to revive her twin sister, Ui, who has been in a magical sleep for these sixteen years. Kyoko must find 12 holy stones and 12 telepaths to move the clock that has stopped time. And Dragon Tribe brothers Sakataki and Hizuki, her bodyguards, end up on the trip as well.

Tangent Comics, volume one.
DC Comics 2007 206p. Illustration
Grades: 9 10 11 12 Adult   741.5
1. Flash (Fictional character); 2. Green Lantern (Fictional character); 3. Superhero graphic novels; 4. Graphic novels
978-1-4012-1530-9, $19.99

In 1997, DC published a series of comics featuring familiar character names, but they were all ... different. The Atom had atomic powers, the Flash (a woman) was made of light, the Metal Men weren't robots but soldiers, the Green Lantern was a woman and used an artifact to raise the dead for one final mission, and so on. Now, DC has collected some of the stories into this trade paperback collection.

Taniguchi, Jiro
The **Ice** wanderer and other stories. Fanfare/Ponent Mon 2007 244p. Illustration
Grades: 10 11 12 Adult   **741.5; Fic**
1. Adventure graphic novels; 2. Manga; 3. Graphic novels
978-84-96427-33-4, $21.99

This volume collects six short stories by Taniguchi, which deal with the relationship of man to nature. Lost in the Great North, two men are saved by an old hunter who recounts a strange legend to them. Surrounded by wolves and fighting for their survival, two explorers head for Alaska to bury their companion. A marine biologist begins a quest to find the mythical graveyard of whales. An inexperienced young city boy goes abalone hunting with a young teenage girl and they get swept out to sea by sudden rough weather. Some stories include some violence.

Tatsumi, Yoshihiro
Abandon the Old in Tokyo. Drawn & Quarterly 2006 Un Illustration
Grades: 12 Adult   **741.5; Fic**
1. City and town life — Japan; 2. Manga
1-894937-87-2, $19.95

Abandon the Old in Tokyo continues to delve into the urban underbelly of 1960s Tokyo, exposing not only the seedy dealings of the Japanese everyman but Tatsumi's maturation as a story writer. These stories were originally published in 1970, and most of them feature burned-out, defeated men in relationships with dissatisfied, shrewish women. His considerable use of strong language, sexual situations and nudity make his work most appropriate for older, mature-minded teens and adults.

★ The **Push** Man and Other Stories. Drawn & Quarterly 2005 208p. Illustration
Grades: 12 Adult   **741.5; Fic**
  1. City and town life — Japan; 2. Manga; 3. Graphic novels
  1-896597-85-8, $19.95
  Tatsumi is considered the grandfather of alternate manga for the adult reader; the stories in this collection date back to the late 1960s and explore the darker aspects of Japanese urban life. The look of his art is very different from most manga, and his stories comment on the interplay between an overwhelming, bustling, crowded, modern society and the troubled emotional and sexual life of the individual. He invented the term "gekiga" ("dramatic pictures") in 1957 to describe his manga Strong sexual overtones, violence, and strong language make Tatsumi's work more suitable for older, mature-minded teens and adults.

Taylor, G. P.
  The **Tizzle** Sisters & Erik. Illustrated by Dan Boultwood. Markosia Enterprises Ltd 2006 182p. Illustration
Grades: 5 6 7 8 9 10 11 12   **741.5; Fic**
  1. Adventure graphic novels; 2. Twins; 3. Graphic novels
  978-1-905692-22-4, $20.01
  Almost identical twins, Sadie and Saskia Tizzle have lived in St. Dunstan's School for Wayward Children ever since their actress mother left them there and never returned. When an eccentric writer decides to take Saskia to adopt her and separates the twins, she sets wild adventures into motion. Saskia finds herself in a house of intrigue with ghosts, seances, a treasure hunt, and a secret twin; while Sadie and Erik make a harrowing escape from St. Dunstan's just ahead of the police.
  Noted fantasy author Taylor (Shadowmancer, 2003) teams up with British comics veterans Lee and Boultwood to create what they call an "illustronovella," which alternates pages of prose and comic book panels to tell the story.

Taylor, R. G.
  Growing up with comics. All illustrations by R. G. Taylor. Desperado Publishing 2008 Un Illustration
Grades: 10 11 12 Adult   **741.5; 920**
  1. Biographical graphic novels; 2. Books and reading; 3. Hulk (Fictional character); 4. Spider-Man (Fictional character); 5. Spirit (Fictional character); 6. Graphic novels
  978-1-935002-12-3, $16.99
  This book collects stories about the writers' various experiences as comic book readers. Some of the writers own or work in comics shops, others are comic book creators, some just continued to be comic book readers into adulthood. Many of the stories center on a particular comic book that made an impression upon the writer. The art shows them as adults, but also depicts the comics they loved when they were kids. It gives a glimpse into childhoods of the past and how one's love for a comic book, be it a Spider-Man or Hulk or The Spirit, could transform one's life.

Taylor, Sarah Stewart
  Amelia Earhart: this broad ocean. [illustrations by] Ben Towle; with an introduction by Eileen Collins. Disney/Hyperion Books 2010 78p. Illustration
Grades: 5 6 7 8 9   **741.5; 741; 92**
  1. Earhart, Amelia, 1898-1937
  978-1-4231-1337-9 (lib bdg), $17.99; 1-4231-1337-3 (lib bdg)
                                      LC 2009-29321
  "Grace, an aspiring young journalist, is excited when Amelia Earhart arrives in her town of Trepassey, Newfoundland, on June 4, 1928. Earhart wants to become the first female passenger to cross the Atlantic Ocean by air. Grace is there to see them and to receive Earhart's telegram announcing their arrival in Ireland." (Publisher's note)
  "This approach brings the legendary aviation pioneer and her fame into a manageable context. . . . Reluctant readers, adventure fans, and those who themselves yearn for the skies will be sucked right into the immediacy here." Bull Cent Child Books

Templeton, Ty
  Howard the duck: media duckling. Writer, Ty Templeton; artist, Juan Bobillo. Marvel Entertainment 2008 Un Illustration
Grades: 9 10 11 12 Adult   **741.5; Fic**
  1. Howard the Duck (Fictional character); 2. Humorous graphic novels; 3. Graphic novels
  978-0-7851-2776-5, $11.99
  Steve Gerber's creation, Howard the Duck, is back. The trouble starts when fraternal twin physicists who were unsuccessful on their duck hunt encounter cabbie Howard and decide he'll be their hunting trophy. When he beats them up with their own rifles, he's caught on video by his friend Beverly's play director, Serge, who puts the video online. Renegade science organization A.I.M.'s media-mad creature M.O.D.O.T. (Mental Organism Designed Only for Talking) decides to use the video to turn Howard into a media sensation and help him take over the world. The story includes cartoony violence and Beverly is often clad in her stage costume of fig leaves.

TenNapel, Doug
  Bad Island. Created, written, and drawn by Doug TenNapel. Graphix 2011 218p. Illustration
Grades: 6 7 8 9 10   **741.5**
  1. Adventure graphic novels; 2. Extraterrestrial beings; 3. Family life; 4. Father-son relationship; 5. Survival after airplane accidents, shipwrecks, etc
  0545314798; 0545314801 (pa); 9780545314794, $24.99; 9780545314800 (pa)
                                      LC 2011276008
  "Dad has decided to take Reese, who is too cool for family outings, and his sister, Janine, on a fishing trip. The vacation takes an unexpected turn when their boat capsizes during a storm and they find themselves marooned on a strange island. To their horror, the family slowly realizes that the island is the submerged body of a giant creature, escaped

from another world. The story alternates between the shipwreck survivors and the faraway world that created this "island." Both stories feature conflict between an adolescent son and his father. . . . Ultimately, both rebellious adolescents grow up and find their place as young men." (School Libr J)

"Though father, mother, teenage son, and tween daughter face the various dangers like a gang of Indiana Joneses, their family stresses are believable. . . . A clever, old-fashioned adventure with some modern twists and a lighthearted tone." Booklist

Black Cherry. Image Comics 2007 Un Illustration
Grades: 11 12 Adult   **741.5; Fic**
1. Horror graphic novels; 2. Mystery graphic novels; 3. Science fiction graphic novels; 4. Graphic novels
978-1-58240-830-9, $17.99

Down-on-his-luck Mafioso Eddie Paretti is so desperate for cash he's agreed to steal a dead body from his own mob boss. Things only get worse when he discovers the body isn't human. With few options and fewer people he can trust, Eddie calls on the man who raised him, Father McHugh. The priest tells Eddie that the body was stolen from his monastery by the Mafia. Father McHugh is accompanied by Mary, a beautiful woman Eddie swears looks just like a stripper he once fell in love with named Black Cherry. The book is full of very foul language (f-bombs and s-bombs galore), nudity, sexual situations, and graphic violence. It also has a deeply-felt religious core that may confuse some readers. TenNapel has written a foreword for readers that explains it.

Creature Tech. Top Shelf Productions 2002 208p. Illustration
Grades: 8 9 10 11 12 Adult   **741.5; Fic**
1. Science fiction graphic novels; 2. Graphic novels
978-1-891830-34-1, $17.95

Resurrected by the Shroud of Turin, the zombified Dr. Jameson intends to finish what he started 150 years ago—destroying the earth with a giant space eel. Standing in his way is Dr. Ong, a would-be pastor turned scientist who now works in a government research facility infamously known as "Creature Tech." Aided by an unlikely cast of rednecks, symbiotic aliens, and a CIA-trained mantid, Dr. Ong embarks on a journey of faith, love, and self-discovery. All in a day's work at Creature Tech. There's some mild violence and language.

Earthboy Jacobus. Image Comics 2005 272p. Illustration
Grades: 7 8 9 10 11 12 Adult   **741.5; Fic**
1. Science fiction graphic novels; 2. Graphic novels
1-58240-492-5, $17.95

"The alien settings are vivid, weird, and even bordering on goofy, but this story's very human characters provide a grounding that keeps the reader involved and believing. The heavily inked black-and-white panels serve well for quiet scenes as well as those bursting with action or bathroom jokes." (VOYA)

Ex-Marine and Chief of Police "Chief" Edwards hits a whale while driving home; he rescues a boy from the inside and becomes an "instant" father. Jacobus comes from a rather nasty parallel world, and Chief has to teach the boy to defend himself against the enemies who inevitably come. When they end up in Jacobus' world, the values "Chief" had

instilled comprise the well from which Jacobus can draw strength.

Flink. Image Comics 2007 122p. Illustration
Grades: 6 7 8 9 10 11 12 Adult   **741.5; Fic**
1. Adventure graphic novels; 2. Sasquatch; 3. Graphic novels
978-1-58240-891-0, $13.99; 1-58240-891-2

Conrad is flying with his father on his first hunting trip when the plane crashes in the wilderness. When Conrad comes to after the crash, he's completely alone, with only the clothes on his back, a handheld game player, and a pocketknife his father had just given him. When he wakes up from a sleep, he finds a deerskin wrapped around him and follows a trail of berries; a Bigfoot named Flink has saved him. Now they have to deal with a rabid she-bear that injures Flink; he needs his brother's medicine to heal, but the Bigfoot community hates humans who hunt them. How can Flink convince them that Conrad is harmless? The book includes some violence and one scene where Conrad pees on a tree.

Gear. Image Comics 2007 Un Illustration
Grades: 7 8 9 10 11 12   **741.5; Fic**
1. Adventure graphic novels; 2. Animals; 3. Fantasy graphic novels; 4. War; 5. Graphic novels
978-1-58240-680-0, $14.99

In a world populated only with animals, the cats of Newton need to find a way to defend themselves against the dogs and the bugs. The dogs and cats have metal guardians that they ride and operate like walking armored robots, and other technology. What the dogs want, especially crime boss Big Tomato, is the Forbidden Mechanism that dog scientist Dr. Pilk has hidden in Newton. This graphic novel started as a black and white comic series, then a graphic novel in 1998. Nickelodeon hired TenNapel to do a cartoon series, Catscratch, based on Gear; it went on the air in 2005. Then Image Comics published Gear in color. TenNapel used Japanese bamboo brushes and sumi ink to draw the art. The book includes considerable violence; characters die, a war is raging.

Ghostopolis. Created, written, and drawn by Doug TenNapel.. Graphix 2010 266 p. Illustration
Grades: 7 8 9 10   **741.5**
1. Ghosts; 2. Graphic novels
9780545210287, $12.99; 9780545210270, $24.99; 0545210275

LC 20090942984

This graphic novel tells the story of an "agent for the Supernatural Immigration Task Force, . . . Frank Gallows[, whose] . . . job [is] to catch ghosts on Earth and send them back to the afterlife. However, during one particularly tricky deportation, he accidentally zaps a young-living-boy. Garth Hale suddenly finds himself surrounded by mummies and goblins in a crumbling, ghastly city, with a skeleton horse and his long-departed grandfather as his only friends. Gallows comes crashing into the afterlife, as well, on a daring rescue mission. As this bumbling team tries to find a way home, they end up face to face with the evil ruler of Ghostopolis, who doesn't look too kindly upon mortals in his city." (Kirkus)

Iron West. Image Comics 2006 160p. Illustration

Grades: 8 9 10 11 12 Adult   **741.5; Fic**
1. Science fiction graphic novels; 2. Western stories; 3. Graphic novels
978-1-58240-630-5, $14.99

Preston Struck has worked as a con artist and crooked gambler, but when he encounters a horde of technological killers while escaping bounty hunters, he discovers an unfortunate streak of responsibility. Awakened by greedy miners, an alien artifact has begun manufacturing humanoid form robots to kill every human, starting with the town of Twain Harte. Aided by a wizened shaman, a Sasquatch, and the not-too-trusting sheriff, Struck reluctantly sets out to stop the killer robots.

TenNapel uses well-worn cliches of American Westerns and turns them on their heads, including Native American stereotypes, the saloon gal with a heart of gold. The level of violence is similar to that seen in any classic Western movie (think John Wayne films). "This finely balanced piece of work is polished with style." Voice Youth Advocates

Tommysaurus Rex. Image Comics 2005 110p. Illustration
Grades: 5 6 7 8 9 10 11 12   **741.5; Fic**
1. Dinosaurs; 2. Graphic novels
1-58240-395-3, $11.95

When Ely loses his dog, Tommy, in a car accident, his parents send him to Grandpa Joe's farm for the summer. He discovers a live, 40-foot Tyrannosaurus Rex in a cave on the farm, and soon the boy and his pet dinosaur cause a big ruckus in town. Ely promises to train the dinosaur he names Tommysaurus, but not if the town's bully, Randy, has his way.

Tetzner, Lisa
The **Black** Brothers: A Novel in Pictures. Art by Hannes Binder. Front Street 2004 144p. Illustration
Grades: 4 5 6 7 8 9   **741.5; Fic**
1. Chimney sweeps; 2. Graphic novels
1-932425-04-7, $16.95

In rural Italy, thirteen-year-old Giorgio is sold to a man who supplies chimney sweeps for Milan. After a treacherous journey in which most of the other boys die, Giorgio goes to work for a man whose wife resents another mouth to feed and starves him. He is sent up into chimneys with no training or guidance for how to do the dangerous work. After nearly dying, he is befriended by a doctor and finds the Black Brothers, a group of chimney sweeps who swear loyalty to each other.

This illustrated novel was originally published in German in 1941, and the translation's tone is similar to other children's books, such as Emil and the Detectives.

Tezuka, Osamu
Apollo's Song. Vertical, Inc. 2007 541p. Illustration
Grades: 10 11 12 Adult   **741.5; Fic**
1. Love; 2. Manga; 3. Graphic novels
978-1-932234-66-4, $19.95

The gods, with their poetic justice, can be unrelenting. Just ask the young cynic Shogo, who sinned against love. Electroshock therapy was only meant to bring him face to face with his own violent misdeeds, but instead landed him in the court of a stern goddess. If the encounter was a hallucination, then it's a hallucination that starts to encroach on reality in this tale. Shogo is sentenced to fall in love with the same woman over and over again, through all time and many incarnations, beginning with him as a guard and the woman a young Jew being transported to a concentration camp during World War II. The book has strong language, lots of nudity and sexual situations.

Astro Boy books 1 and 2. Dark Horse Comics 2008 424p. Illustration
Grades: 3 4 5 6 7 8 9 10 11 12 Adult   **741.5; Fic**
1. Adventure graphic novels; 2. Astro Boy (Fictional character); 3. Robots; 4. Science fiction graphic novels; 5. Graphic novels
978-1-59582-153-9, $14.95

When a scientist loses his young son, he builds a robot to look exactly like the boy, but when he activates the robot, the scientist becomes repulsed and rejects him. Professor Ochanomizu (gotta love the name, it means tea water and is also a famous Tokyo neighborhood) rescues the boy robot from a circus and names him Astro Boy. He deals with aliens, with people who would use robots to commit crimes, and with adventures in outer space. This new edition collects the first two volumes of the Dark Horse manga editions.

Also available in omnibus editions
Volumes 1 and 2 of a 23 volume series

★ **Black** Jack, volume 1. Vertical, Inc. 2008 287p. Illustration
Grades: 9 10 11 12 Adult   **741.5; Fic**
1. Manga; 2. Medical practice; 3. Surgeons; 4. Graphic novels
978-1-934287-27-9, $16.95

Black Jack is the only known name for a mysterious, scarred surgeon from Japan who can perform surgical miracles but is considered to be a creepy mercenary. He will perform highly risky surgeries for an exorbitant price, and he's unlicensed. However, most people don't realize that he actually does a lot for more altruistic reasons as well. In this first volume that reprints the original stories by pioneer mangaka (manga creator) Tezuka, stories include one in which Black Jack operates on a crime boss's son using the body of an unjustly convicted man; and one where he removes a teratoid cystoma from a unidentified wealthy and famous woman, but he refuses to kill the cystoma, which contains the body parts of the woman's unborn twin. While there are some surgical scenes that might not be for the squeamish, the stories offer little in the way of graphic violence or bad language while providing action and some thought about ethics and morals.

"With genre-spanning stories—horror, sci-fi, romance—and Tezuka's signature blend of drama, bathos and extreme broad comedy jammed together on every page, Black Jack is a wild but extravagantly entertaining ride." Publ Wkly

Volume 1 of 17

★ **Buddha** Volume 1: Kapilavastu. Vertical, Inc. 2003 400p. Illustration
Grades: 10 11 12 Adult   **741.5; Fic**
1. Buddhism; 2. Manga; 3. Graphic novels
1-932234-56-X (pa); 1-932234-43-8, $24.95; 9781932234565, $14.95

In this first of eight volumes, Tezuka starts the story of Buddha before the birth of the prince Siddhartha. His fictional characters, the slave Chapra, the pariah Tatta, the monk Naradatta, and many others, populate the story and will have an effect on the prince's life. The book includes sexual situations and considerable nudity; the pariahs never wore clothes. Tezuka also throws in a lot of humorous and anachronistic comments; but underlying everything is a profoundly deep understanding of Buddhism. The book also includes some violence.

★ **Ode** to Kirihito. Vertical, Inc. 2006 822p. Illustration
Grades: 10 11 12 Adult   **741.5; Fic**
1. Seinen manga; 2. Graphic novels
978-1-93-223464-0, $24.95

It may or may not be contagious. There seems to be no cure for it. Yet, Monmow Disease, a life-threatening condition that transforms a person into a dog-like beast, is not the only villain in this shocking medical thriller. Young doctor Kirihito Osanai investigates the source of the disease, only to be infected himself. Then he discovers his betrayal by the medical community, the violent reactions of most of society because of the deformity of his facial features, and he sets out around the world to find a cure. The book includes violence, nudity, rape, and some strong language.

Also available as two separate volumes

Phoenix Vol. 10: Sun, Part One. Viz Media/Signature 2007 339p. Illustration
Grades: 10 11 12 Adult   **741.5; Fic**
1. Manga; 2. Religion; 3. Science fiction graphic novels; 4. Graphic novels
978-1-4215-0972-3, $15.99

This volume in Tezuka's Phoenix series covers two vastly different time periods; in 663 A.D., a young soldier named Harima is punished by the enemy general by putting a wolf's head on him. Rescued by an old woman, he travels with her and a Japanese general to Japan. Harima suffers nightmares in which he sees visions of a future world; Bando Suguru is a warrior in the twenty-first century, fighting on behalf of banished humans. In the seventh century, Harima battles against those who would force Buddhism upon the people; in the twenty-first century, Suguru battles against the Church of Light, which has forced "unbelievers" to hide underground. This volume has some partial nudity and such violence as beheadings.

Phoenix Vol. 5: Resurrection. Viz Media/Editor's Choics 2004 324p. Illustration
Grades: 10 11 12 Adult   **741.5; Fic**
1. Manga; 2. Science fiction graphic novels; 3. Graphic novels
1-59116-593-8, $15.95

In the year 3344, Prof. Saruta lands on the moon and meets and acquires Robita in his final form. On Earth, the Robita model robots, now sentient, rebel in the only way left open to robots programmed to obey. And Leon, miraculously brought back to life after dying in an accident, realizes he was murdered and tries to remember what he was doing that would get him killed. There's some violence and some sexual suggestiveness.

Phoenix Vol. 7: Civil War Part One. Viz Media/Signature 2006 424p. Illustration

Grades: 10 11 12 Adult   **741.5; Fic**
1. Manga; 2. Graphic novels
978-1-4215-0517-6, $15.95

At the end of the Heian Period (12th century), a hunter named Benta comes to Kyoto in search of his abducted fiance, Obuu. Obuu is forced to become the attendant of a powerful man of the time, who wishes to cheat death and extend the life of his clan by obtaining the legendary phoenix. Meanwhile, dissent is brewing among a people fed up with their corrupt government. Kyoto is on the verge of a civil war. The book includes violence, strong language, and some sexual situations.

Phoenix Volume 8: Civil War Part Two. Viz/Signature 2006 338p. Illustration
Grades: 10 11 12 Adult   **741.5; Fic**
1. Manga; 2. Graphic novels
978-1-4215-0518-3, $15.99

This volume continues the story of the turbulent events of 12th century Japan, when the Taira and Minamoto clans fought each other; one of the stories about this was is called the Heike Monogatari. The everyman Benta has become an unwilling samurai, witness to senseless killings and the replacement of one brutal regime with another even more so. The book also includes Tezuka's retelling of the Japanese fable Hagoromo-densest, called here "Robe of Feathers," which he illustrates as though it's a play being enacted on stage. The book includes some sexual content, strong language, and violence.

Thomas, Roy

The **Chronicles** of Conan Volume 1: Tower of the Elephant and Other Stories. Written by Roy Thomas; illustrated by Barry Windsor-Smith and others. Dark Horse Comics 2003 166p. Illustration
Grades: 9 10 11 12 Adult   **741.5; Fic**
1. Adventure graphic novels; 2. Conan the Barbarian (Fictional character); 3. Fantasy graphic novels; 4. Graphic novels
1-59307-016-0, $15.95

In the early 1970s, Robert E. Howard's Conan the Barbarian exploded on to the comics scene. Writer Roy Thomas teamed with a young artist named Barry Smith, and together the two mapped out Conan adventures over the course of their 24-issue run together. Thomas and Smith defined Conan for a generation of comics readers, and now those stories are collected here in a series of trade paperbacks. This series features completely remastered color and text corrections, and contains material not available for nearly thirty years. Some of the stories are original, others adapt the original Howard stories; they all include action and violence and some suggestive scenes, as Conan fights warriors and monsters and encounters beautiful, sexy women.

The **man** in the iron mask, volume 1: The three Musketeers. Writer, Roy Thomas ; penciler, Hugo Petrus ; inker, Tom Palmer ; letterer, Joe Caramagna ; colorist, June Chung ; editors, Ralph Macchio, Nicole Boose. L. ABDO/Spotlight 2009 Un
Grades: 6 7 8 9 10 11 12   **741.5; Fic**

1. Adventure graphic novels; 2. Dumas, Alexandre, 1802-1870 — Adaptations; 3. France — History — 1589-1789, Bourbons; 4. Graphic novels
978-1-59961-594-3, $21.35

LC 2008-35321

In this Marvel Comics adaptation of Alexandre Dumas' Man in the Iron Mask, the reader first receives a summary of The Three Musketeers, then this story gets rolling. Aramis, now a Bishop, is still scheming; this time, he's determined to finagle the release of a young man named Philippe from the Bastille. Philippe is the younger twin brother of Louis XIV, and the new King has made enemies of the former Musketeers. This book is part of the Marvel Illustrated line of classics adaptations.

This is a library bound edition that doesn't include any of the advertisements from the original Marvel Illustrated comic book issue.

Thompson, Bart A.
Mummy. Adapted by Bart A. Thompson ; illustrated by Brian Miroglio ; based upon the works of Bram Stoker. ABDO/Magic Wagon 2008 Un Illustration
Grades: 4 5 6 7 8 9   **741.5**
1. Horror graphic novels; 2. Mummies; 3. Graphic novels
978-1-60270-061-1, $27.07

LC 2007-16370

In ancient Egypt, Queen Tera had herself mummified and she swore she would return to life. During an expedition to Egypt in 1947, Abel Trelawney and John Corbeck uncovered her tomb. Today, all is ready for her return. This graphic novel adapts Stoker's Jewel of Seven Stars, which was the basis for the classic horror movie, The Mummy." While there is some violence, the level of horror in this adaptation has been toned down to be suitable for younger readers. Part of the Graphic Horror series

Thompson, Craig
★ **Blankets:** an illustrated novel. Top Shelf 2003 582p. Illustration
Grades: 10 11 12 Adult   **Fic; 741; 92; 741.5**
1. Artists; 2. Autobiographical graphic novels; 3. Cartoonists; 4. Family life; 5. Illustrators; 6. Thompson, Craig, 1975-; 7. Graphic novels
1-891830-43-0, $29.95; 9781891830433

LC 2004-297892

This "memoir recreates the confusion, emotional pain and isolation of the author's rigidly fundamentalist Christian upbringing, along with the trepidation of growing into maturity. Skinny, naive and spiritually vulnerable, Thompson and his younger brother manage to survive their parents' overbearing discipline (the brothers are sometimes forced to sleep in "the cubbyhole," a forbidding and claustrophobic storage chamber) through flights of childhood fancy and a mutual love of drawing . . . Thompson manages to explore adolescent social yearnings, the power of young love and the complexities of sexual attraction with a rare combination of sincerity, pictorial lyricism and taste. His exceptional b&w drawings balance representational precision with a bold and wonderfully expressive line for pages of ingenious, inventively composed and poignant imagery." Publ Wkly

Carnet de Voyage: Travel Journal Volume One. Top Shelf Productions 2004 224p. Illustration
Grades: 10 11 12 Adult   **741.5; 910**
1. Autobiographical graphic novels; 2. Travel; 3. Graphic novels
1-891830-60-0, $14.95

Craig Thompson spent three months traveling through Barcelona, the Alps, and France, as well as Morocco, researching his next graphic novel, Habibi. Spontaneous sketches and a travelogue diary document his adventures and quiet moments, creating a portrait of countries, culture and the wandering artist. Very occasional partial nudity and mild harsh language punctuate Thompson's narrative.

Goodbye, Chunky Rice. Pantheon 2006 128p. Illustration
Grades: 9 10 11 12   **741.5; Fic**
1. Graphic novels
978-0-375-71476-4, $12.95

"Little turtle Chunky Rice sets out on a voyage hoping to find something (the reader never knows what); he has left behind his best friend, the mouse deer Dandel, and finds himself on a strange little ship run by a captain with a dark past." (VOYA)

This little book is filled with poignant longing, deep regrets, reconciliation, and a sense of redemption.

This was originally published in 1999 by Top Shelf Productions.

Thompson, Jill
Death: At Death's Door. DC Comics/Vertigo 2003 204p. Illustration
Grades: 10 11 12 Adult   **741.5; Fic**
1. Adventure graphic novels; 2. Fantasy graphic novels; 3. Horror graphic novels; 4. Humorous graphic novels; 5. Graphic novels
1-56389-938-8, $9.95

A member of the Endless, a family of beings who have existed longer than the gods, Death enjoys manifesting herself in the persona of a Goth girl. Along with her siblings, she interacts and influences the lives of humans on a daily basis. In this shojo manga-style adventure, Death's little sisters, Delirium and Despair, have thrown a party at her apartment for hell's escapees. But as the festivities get out of control, it falls on Death's black-clad shoulders to regain order and save the afterlife - not to mention her carpet. Despair is always drawn as nude. The events in this book occur around the time of the Sandman volume, Season of Mists.

The **Little** Endless Storybook. DC Comics/Vertigo 2004 Un Illustration
Grades: 9 10 11 12 Adult   **741.5; Fic**
1. Adventure graphic novels; 2. Fantasy graphic novels; 3. Graphic novels
14012-0428-7, $15.95

Jill Thompson takes Neil Gaiman's the Endless and draws them as little children in this story. Puppy Barnabas has been entrusted with watching and protecting Delirium, who is always easily ... distracted. When he leaves her for just a minute or so, she gets lost. He searches the waking world but can't find her. Now, he must travel to the strange and unlikely realms of each of the Endless to see if

Delirium's siblings have seen their missing sister. While the pictures are cute and the book resembles a child's picture book, the story has enough of an edge to make it more suitable for older teens. Despair is, as always, drawn as nude.

Scary Godmother: Wild About Harry. Sirius Entertainment 2001 Un Illustration

Grades: 6 7 8 9 10 11 12   **741.5; Fic**
1. Humorous graphic novels; 2. Monsters; 3. Supernatural graphic novels; 4. Graphic novels
1-57989-046-6, $9.95

Obnoxiously lazy, selfish, boorish, gluttonous Harry the Werewolf has worn out his mother, Irene the fortune teller. Encouraged by Scary Godmother and her other Fright Side friends, Irene orders Harry out of her house to earn his own living and find his own place to stay. Of course Harry first tries freeloading off his friends, but eventually he has to get a job, working for the Fright Brothers.

This story is for older audiences than the picture book format Scary Godmother books, and is in regular comic book format with black-and-white art. Another title in this format is Scary Godmother: Ghoul's Out for Summer.

Originally published as Scary Godmother: Wild About Harry issues #1-3

Thompson, Robbie
Silk: the life and times of Cindy Moon. By Robbie Thompson; illustrated by Stacey Lee. Marvel Enterprises 2015 160 p. Color; Illustration

Grades: 10 11 12 Adult
1. Women superheroes
0785197044; 9780785197041, $19.99

In this comic book, by Robbie Thompson, illustrated by Stacey Lee, "Cindy Moon . . . learned that she had been bitten by the same radioactive spider from the first arc of AMAZING SPIDER-MAN. She then went on to save Peter Parker's life (more than once!) and traverse the Spider-Verse alongside Spider-Woman. Now, as SILK, Cindy is on her own in New York City, searching for her past, defining her own future, and webbing up wrong-doers along the way!" (Publisher's note)

Volume 1 of an ongoing series

Thrash, Maggie
★ **Honor** girl: a graphic memoir. Maggie Thrash. Candlewick Press 2015 272 p. Color; Illustration

Grades: 9 10 11 12   **92; 741.5**
1. Camps; 2. Lesbians; 3. Teenage girls; 4. Thrash, Maggie
076367382X; 9780763673826, $19.99
       LC 2014951805
LA Times Book Prize Finalist: Graphic Novel/Comics (2015)

This graphic memoir, by Maggie Thrash, relates how the author "has spent basically every summer of her fifteen-year-old life at the one-hundred-year-old Camp Bellflower for Girls, set deep in the heart of Appalachia. . . . A split-second of innocent physical contact pulls Maggie into a gut-twisting love for a . . . female counselor named Erin. But Camp Bellflower is an impossible place for a girl to fall in love with another girl." (Publisher's note)

"Thrash finds both heartwarming support from her friends and smarmy disapproval from adults in the southern camp, and although she doesn't deny her burgeoning

feelings, her revelation doesn't result in easy confidence, either. Though the understated artwork might not appeal to all readers, this honest, raw, and touching graphic memoir will resonate with teens coming to terms with identities of all stripes." Booklist

Thung, Diana
★ **Captain** Long Ears. SLG Publishing 2010 168p. Illustration

Grades: 5 6 7 8 9 10 11 12 Adult   **741.5; Fic**
1. Adventure graphic novels; 2. Amusement parks; 3. Death; 4. Graphic novels
978-1-59362-187-2, $12.95

Eight-year-old Michael, aka Captain Long Ears, goes on a mission to Headquarters (an amusement park) with Captain Jam, who is actually his purple toy stuffed gorilla. They're searching for Captain Big Nose, who is Michael's father; he's been gone "on a mission" for two years. In Headquarters, Captain Long Ears and Captain Jam encounter monsters (a preschool teacher and a park attendant), then they find a large crate in a locked enclosure. When they open the crate, they find a young elephant the boy calls "Little Big Nose." They decide they must save Little Big Nose, so they hide in the park overnight. Meanwhile, Michael's mother comes home late from work and doesn't realize her son is missing until the next day. Back in the park, Michael has several dreams of his father leaving him behind. He's so caught up in his fantasy of Captain Long Ears that he doesn't realize the dangers he faces in trying to save the young elephant from abusive handlers. Thung's art shows most of the action through Michael's imagination; readers soon realize that Michael hasn't accepted his father's death. The use of words such as "ass," "caca brain," and other childish epithets may cause more conservative schools to carefully consider their purchase. This imaginary adventure and exploration of the mourning process brings to mind such books as The Bridge to Terabithia and has a similar emotional impact. Despite Michael's young age, this book is more suited to upper elementary and middle school age readers on up.

Tiede, Dirk I.
Paradigm shift part one: equilibrium. Dirk Tiede Cartoons & Illustrations 2006 98p. Illustration

Grades: 10 11 12 Adult   **741.5; Fic**
1. Adventure graphic novels; 2. Mystery graphic novels; 3. Graphic novels
978-0-9789717-1-7, $9.95

Chicago cops and partners Kate and Mike stumble onto a major case when they shake down an informer for information that leads them to Chinatown and a pool hall brawl that leaves Kate shot. In the hospital, the emergency room staff tells her she's not seriously hurt, but she knows she lost a lot of blood, too much for it to be a minor injury. Meanwhile, she and Mike are pulled off that case and told to investigate a mauling death that might be homicide. The victim looks as though he had been attacked by a monstrous animal. Can Kate's nightmare, in which she becomes the creature, be a clue to what's going on" This global manga story was originally published in 2003 and is still available online under that original ISBN (978-1591098690). The book includes one panel with partial nudity, some violence, and the occasional use of harsh language, including s-bomb and f-bomb.

Tieri, Frank

Civil War: War Crimes. Writer, Frank Tieri; artist, Staz Johnson. Marvel Entertainment 2007 Un Illustration
Grades: 10 11 12 Adult   **741.5; Fic**
1. Captain America (Fictional character); 2. Iron Man (Fictional character); 3. Superhero graphic novels; 4. Graphic novels
0-7851-2652-X, $17.99

Wilson Fisk, the incarcerated ex-Kingpin of Crime, proposes a deal to Iron Man, to use his underworld connections to help track down Captain America and his anti-Registration underground in exchange for consideration on his sentence. But can the Kingpin be trusted, or is he playing a deeper game" In a Civil War prequel story, career criminal Jackie Dio, fresh out of prison, finds the New York underworld has changed, and he finds trouble. If he's going to have a shot at surviving, he may have to find the shadowy figure known only as "The Consultant" - that is, if he even exists. There is more graphic violence in this title, and some strong language.

Tillieux, Maurice

Murder by high tide. [by] M. Tillieux. Fantagraphics 2011 92p. Illustration
Grades: 11 12 Adult
741.5; Fic
1. Mystery graphic novels; 2. Graphic novels
978-1-60699-451-1, $18.99

Courtesy of Fantagraphics

"Dapper private detective Gil Jordan is the star of these funny adventure stories, aided by ex-burglar assistant Crackerjack, eccentric friend Inspector Crouton, and no-nonsense secretary Miss Midge. "Murder by High Tide" sets an antiques dealer's death at an irresistible location, on a tidal causeway leading to the decrepit Tower of the Merrie Knight. And in "Leap of Faith," escaped convict Joe the Syringe stays one leap ahead of the good guys as he seeks revenge on his attorney. Plausibility may not be the watchword here, but no matter: these are a ton of fun and the full-color art, beautifully produced and fairly bursting with sweat beads, stink lines, and other emanata, is an animated delight." Booklist
Translated from the French

Timony, Bobby

★ The night owls. Peter Timony and Bobby Timony. DC Comics/Zuda Comics 2010 Un Illustration
Grades: 9 10 11 12 Adult   **741.5; Fic**
1. Humorous graphic novels; 2. Mystery graphic novels; 3. Supernatural graphic novels; 4. Graphic novels
978-1-4012-2673-2, $14.99

Occult specialist Ernest Baxter, fighting flapper girl Mindy Markus, and Roscoe the Gargoyle are the Night Owls, a private detective agency specializing in supernatural cases involving such creatures as vampires, werewolves, ghosts, and other things that go bump in the night. Some of the cases in this volume include the murderous, faceless Mr. You, who steals people's faces, bootleggers with banshees, and a jealous ghost of an actor who haunts his old theater. Most of the book is illustrated in sepia tones, except for the stories set in the fairy tale kingdom that is Mindy's real home. It includes some on-page violence, including a strangulation. This book collects the Night Owls webcomic originally posted at www.zuda.com.

Tinnell, Robert

The **Black** Forest. Written by Todd Livingston & Robert Tinnell; illustrated by Neil Vokes; lettered by Anthony Schiavino & Adam Levine. Image Comics 2004 104p. Illustration
Grades: 10 11 12 Adult   **741.5; Fic**
1. Adventure graphic novels; 2. Fantasy graphic novels; 3. Horror graphic novels; 4. Graphic novels
1-58240-350-3, $9.95

During World War I, in the battle between good and evil, evil just got creative. The Germans are developing a mysterious weapon to break through the trenches. American pilot Jack Shannon and Archie Caldwell, Britain's greatest stage magician, are sent behind enemy lines, into the heart of the supernatural vortex that is the Black Forest. There, in a remote castle, they match wits with evil occultist Avery Dye, who aims to use Frankenstein's Monster as a template to create an army of unstoppable re-animated dead. In order to thwart the forces of evil, Jack and Archie will be forced to battle Nosferatu, werewolves, a sorcerer, and Frankenstein's Monster himself. The book includes violence.

The **Faceless:** A Terry Sharp Story. Image Comics 2005 64p. Illustration
Grades: 10 11 12 Adult   **741.5; Fic**
1. Fantasy graphic novels; 2. Horror graphic novels; 3. Humorous graphic novels; 4. Graphic novels
978-1-58240-516-2, $6.99

Once upon a time in England, 1962. By day, Terry Sharp is a successful director of horror films, consumer of cocktails, and chaser of skirts. By night, the horror is real as he battles tirelessly against a Satanic conspiracy that reaches the highest levels of government. Sharp's willing to go to hell... so you won't have to. The book includes mildly bad language and some violence as Sharp fights the Faceless.

Tinsley, Kevin

Stonehaven: Milk Cartons & Dog Biscuits. Kevin Tinsley, words & colors; Phil Singer, art. Stickman Graphics 2004 214p. Illustration
Grades: 10 11 12 Adult   **741.5; Fic**
1. Fantasy graphic novels; 2. Mystery graphic novels; 3. Graphic novels
0-9675423-3-2; 0-9675423-4-0 (pa)

Ranger Dan Parsons comes from the Far Reaches to the big city, Stonehaven, searching for his runaway teenage daughter. He's forced to ask half-elf private detective Victor Jardine for help, and they soon find out that Melody Parsons faces danger from her friends, including one young man who has dabbled in dark magic to transform into a werewolf. Can

Parsons and Jardine save Melody while also dealing with the police, the werewolf Wild Pack, and the Tong?

Tinsley combines hard-boiled crime noir with high fantasy and the supernatural in this story. Stonehaven bears some resemblance to New York City. Singer uses subdued, earthy tones for the art. Bloody murders that look like werewolf attacks make this more suitable for older readers.

Tipton, David

Star Trek: miror images. David and Scott Tipton ; art by Sara Pichelli and David Messina. IDW Publishing 2010 128p. Illustration

Grades: 6 7 8 9 10 11 12 Adult   **741.5; Fic**
1. Adventure graphic novels; 2. Science fiction graphic novels; 3. Star Trek; 4. Graphic novels
978-1-60010-179-3, $19.99

This volume collects a series of one-shots (standalone comics issues), each devoted to one of the alien races featured in the Star Trek series. Readers meet the Gorns, Vulcans, Andorians, Orions, the Borg, and the Romulans in stories that also give the aliens' point of view. The stories are set in the various time periods of the Star Trek universe; for example, Captain Clark Terrell and Pavel Chekov (before they were captured by Khan in "The Wrath of Khan") and their landing party encounter the Gorns on a planet designed to train Gorn warriors, while Captain Picard encounters the Borg.

Star Trek: Klingons: blood will tell. IDW Publishing 2007 168p. Illustration

Grades: 7 8 9 10 11 12 Adult   **741.5; Fic**
1. Science fiction graphic novels; 2. Star Trek; 3. Graphic novels
978-1-60010-108-3, $24.99

In this volume, readers look back at some of the most famous encounters between the United Federation of Planets and the Klingon Empire, from the Klingon perspective. Kahnrah must decide if he will side with Gorkon and ask the Federation for aid in a time of crisis for all Klingons, and he seeks enlightenment from the actions of his relatives who encountered such Federation officers as Captain James T. Kirk of the starship Enterprise. The book includes the Klingon language variant of the first comic book issue.

Star Trek: Klingons: blood will tell. David and Scott Tipton ; art by David Messina. IDW Publishing 2007 168p. Illustration

Grades: 7 8 9 10 11 12 Adult   **741.5; Fic**
1. Science fiction graphic novels; 2. Star Trek; 3. Graphic novels
978-1-60010-108-3, $24.99

In this volume, readers look back at some of the most famous encounters between the United Federation of Planets and the Klingon Empire, from the Klingon perspective. Kahnrah must decide if he will side with Gorkon and ask the Federation for aid in a time of crisis for all Klingons, and he seeks enlightenment from the actions of his relatives who encountered such Federation officers as Captain James T. Kirk of the starship Enterprise. The book includes the Klingon language variant of the first comic book issue.

Tobe, Keiko

With the Light: Raising an Autistic Child (Hikari to Tomoni). Yen Press 2007 528p. Illustration

Grades: 8 9 10 11 12 Adult
741.5; Fic
1. Autism; 2. Manga; 3. Graphic novels
978-0-7595-2356-2, $14.99

Courtesy of Yen Press

Born during the sunrise - an auspicious beginning - the Azumas' newborn son is named Hikaru, which means "light." But during one play date, his son is slightly different from the other children. In this alternately heartwarming and bittersweet tale, a young mother tries to cope with both the overwhelming discovery of her child's autism and the trials of raising him while keeping her family together. This fictional story is based on true accounts; and the book includes notes about how parents can deal with certain situations depicted in the story.

Volume 1 of 8

Tobin, Paul

Bandette: Presto!. By Paul Tobin, illustrated by Collen Coover, edited by Brendan Wright. Dark Horse Books 2013 144 p. (Bandette)

Grades: 7 8 9 10 11 12 Adult   **741.5**
1. Burglars; 2. Organized crime — Fiction; 3. Paris (France); 4. Teenage girls — Fiction; 5. Thieves
1616552794; 9781616552794, $14.99

LC 2013024226

Eisner Award: Best Digital Comic (2013)

In this graphic novel by Paul Tobin and Colleen Coover, "the world's greatest thief is a costumed teen burglar in swinging Paris by the nome d'arte of Bandette! But it's not all breaking hearts and purloining masterpieces when a rival thief discovers that an international criminal organization wants Bandette dead!" (Publisher's note)

"[O]ne of the brightest, and most fun, comics of the year." Pub Wkly

Another title about Bandette is: Stealers keepers! (2015)

Toboso, Yana

Black butler, vol. 1. [translation: Tomo Kimura; lettering: Tania Biswas].. Yen Press 2010 184p. Illustration
Grades: 10 11 12 Adult
741.5; Fic
1. Fantasy graphic novels; 2. Household employees; 3. Manga; 4. Mystery graphic novels; 5. Graphic novels
978-0-316-08084-2, $10.99

In an alternate England, the young Earl Phantomhive,

Courtesy of Yen Press

Ciel, lives just outside London; he's only twelve years old, but he runs a massive toy manufacturing company, aided by his butler Sebastian. In this world, magic coexists with science and technology, cars from the early twentieth century drive the roads and Ciel tests video games. Sebastian commands the other workers: Finnian the Gardener (who tends to kill plants), Mey-Rin the klutzy housemaid, and Baldroy the chef, who always has a cigarette dangling from the corner of his mouth. The dapper butler always finds a way to save the day, whether it's transforming a destroyed courtyard into a Japanese rock garden, teaching his young charge to dance the waltz, or saving him from gangsters. He is too good to be true; he is, as he says, "a devil of a butler." The book includes some graphic violence and occasional, mildly bad language ("bastard," "damned").

First volume in an ongoing series

Togashi, Yoshihiro
 YuYu Hakusho Vol. 1. Viz Media/Shonen Jump 2003 208p. Illustration
Grades: 8 9 10 11 12 Adult   **741.5; Fic**
 1. Fantasy graphic novels; 2. Shonen manga; 3. Supernatural graphic novels; 4. Graphic novels
 1-56931-904-9, $7.95
 Yusuke Urameshi was a tough teen delinquent until one selfless act changed his life...by ending it. When he died saving a little kid from a speeding car, the afterlife didn't know what to do with him, so it gave him a second chance at life. Now, Yusuke is a ghost with a mission, performing good deeds at the behest of Botan, the spirit guide of the dead, and Koenma, her pacifier-sucking boss from the "other side." But what strange things await him on the borderline between life and death? It's going to include a lot of battles against supernatural creatures. The series includes some strong language, lots of supernatural martial arts fighting action, and some mildly suggestive humor.

Tokeino, Hari
 Me and My Brothers Vol. 1. Tokyopop 2007 Un Illustration
Grades: 8 9 10 11 12   **741.5; Fic**
 1. Family life; 2. Humorous graphic novels; 3. Shojo manga; 4. Graphic novels
 978-1-4278-0071-8, $9.99
 When Sakura, a fourteen-year-old orphaned girl, discovers she has four half-brothers, her world is turned upside down as they're all forced to live under one roof ... Masashi, the eldest at 25, is a romance novelist; Takashi is a teacher now working as a substitute in Sakura's school; Tsuyoshi works several part-time jobs; and Takeshi is in 11th grade. Sakura has been so used to living quietly with her grandmother that adjusting to the controlled chaos of having four brothers in the house isn't so easy.

Tomasi, Peter J.
 Light Brigade. Peter J. Tomasi, story and words; Peter Snejbjerg, artist; Bjarne Hansen, colorist; Ken Lopez and Rob Leigh, letterers. DC Comics 2005 Un Illustration
Grades: 10 11 12 Adult   **741.5; Fic**
 1. Supernatural graphic novels; 2. World War, 1939-1945; 3. Graphic novels
 1-4012-0795-2, $19.99

In the middle of World War II, American soldier Chris Staros just wants to survive so he can go home and raise his son after learning that his wife has died. He and his fellow soldiers soon learn that they have to worry about a lot more than surviving attacks by a superior Nazi force. Their captain is the immortal centurion who thrust his spear into Jesus' side at the Crucifixion almost two millenia before; he's been tracking and killing grigori, the fallen angels and the nephillim, their half-angel/half-mortal children. Now, he and the small band of American soldiers under his command must find the Sword of God before the last grigori and his nephillim do and prevent them from storming Heaven's Gate.

Originally published as a four-issue miniseries.

Tomine, Adrian
 ★ Shortcomings. Drawn & Quarterly 2007 108p. Illustration
Grades: 10 11 12 Adult   **741.5; Fic**
 1. Graphic novels
 978-1-897299-16-6, $19.95; 1-897299-16-8
 Ben Tanaka, a Japanese American in his late twenties, has trouble. His girlfriend, Miko, suspects that Ben's wandering eye is doing so in the direction of white women. This accusation, and its various implications, becomes the subject of heated, spiraling debate, setting in motion a story that pits California against New York (they both live in Berkeley), devotion against desire, and truth against truth. The book includes some strong language, nudity, and sexual situations.

Tooks, Lance
 Lucifer's Garden of Verses Volume Three: The Student (Or Nude Descending a Staircase ... Head First). NBM/ComicsLit 2004 80p. Illustration
Grades: 10 11 12 Adult   **741.5; Fic**
 1. Art; 2. Horror graphic novels; 3. Graphic novels
 1-56163-446-8, $15.95
 Inspired by the German silent film classic "The Student of Prague", this is the story of Andre Baldwin, a down-on-his-luck would-be Basquiat who enters into a Faustian bargain with a powerful art critic in exchange for status, riches and the love of a woman. Acquanetta Scapinelli is the critic in question, and she recounts this bitter tale with sardonic delight... "For what shall it profit a man if he gain the whole world and lose his own soul?" This book includes harsh language, violence, and some sexual situations.

 Lucifer's Garden of Verses, Volume One: The Devil on Fever Street. NBM/ComicsLit 2005 Un Illustration
Grades: 11 12 Adult   **741.5; Fic**
 1. Devil; 2. Romance graphic novels; 3. Graphic novels
 1-56163-409-3, $15.95
 Satan awakens, after a hundred-year sleep, depressed and disillusioned. It is a mere seven days before he's expected to bring Armageddon to Earth and he is wracked with spiritual doubt and severe performance anxiety. He decides that and old-fashioned temptation will be just the thing to return him to form. His chosen temptee: Black Lily, the purest, most virtuous woman on Earth. Alas, he may

have met his match or more... Nudity and sexual situations as Satan falls in love.

Volume 1 of 4

Toriyama, Akira

Cowa!. Story and art by Akira Toriyama; translation & English adaptation Alexander O. Smith, et. al.. Viz Media/Shonen Jump 2008 208p. Illustration

Grades: 5 6 7 8 9 10 11 12   741.5; Fic
1. Humorous graphic novels; 2. Manga; 3. Monsters; 4. Graphic novels
978-1-4215-1805-3, $7.99; 1-4215-1805-8

Mischievous Paifu is half-vampire and half-werekoala, and he's usually getting into lots of trouble with his best buddy, Jose the ghost. When the Monster Flu sweeps through town, the doctor says that without medicine, everyone will die. The only person who makes the medicine is the witch who lives hundreds of miles away, and all the adults except for the doctor are ill. Paifu and Jose team up with grumpy ex-sumo wrestler Maruyama to make the journey; will they make it before they get sick? The book includes some potty humor (Jose farts a lot) and lots of fighting scenes (Toriyama created Dragon Ball Z).

Original Japanese edition, 1997

Dr. Slump Volume 1. Viz Media/Shonen Jump 2005 192p. Illustration

Grades: 9 10 11 12 Adult   741.5; Fic
1. Humorous graphic novels; 2. Manga; 3. Shonen manga; 4. Graphic novels
1-59116-950-X, $7.99

When goofy inventor Senbei Norimaki (his name means seaweed-wrapped rice cracker) creates a precocious robot named Arale, his masterpiece turns out to be more than he bargained for, for she is very strong; however, she's nearsighted. Senbei scrambles to get Arale in working order so the rest of Penguin Village won't have reason to suspect she's not really a girl. But first Senbei needs to find her a pair of glasses and some clothes... It doesn't help that Arale also talks to poop. The book includes some sexual innuendo, crude humor, and lots of silliness.

Volume 1 of 18

Jaco the galactic patrolman. Story and art, Akira Toriyama; translation, Tetsuichiro Miyaki; touch-up art and lettering, James Gaubatz. Viz 2015 245 p. Illustration

Grades: 7 8 9 10 11 12   741.5
1. Interplanetary voyages; 2. Manga; 3. Police — Fiction
1421566303; 9781421566306, $9.99

"Retired scientist Omori lives alone on a deserted island while continuing his research into time-travel. His quiet life is interrupted when galactic patrolman Jaco crash-lands and decided to move in with him. Can Jaco get along with the old man long enough to save the earth from a dangerous threat—" (Publisher's note)

"Dragon Ball creator Toriyama returns to comedic serials with the story of an eccentric alien who befriends a grumpy old man. . . . Toriyama's punchy dialogue and waggish spirit are still intact, and his art, although pared down, remains sharp in its sense of movement and pace in this back-to-basics one-off from one of the industry's giants." Pub Wkly

Torres, Alissa

★ **American** widow. Illustrated by Sungyoon Choi. Villard Books 2008 209p. Illustration

Grades: 11 12 Adult   92; 974.7; 741.5
1. Autobiographical graphic novels; 2. Educators; 3. Memoirists; 4. September 11 terrorist attacks, 2001; 5. Torres, Alissa; 6. Widows; 7. Graphic novels
978-0-345-50069-4, $22

LC 2008-08396

Alissa Torres' husband Luis had just started his new job in the World Trade Center on September 10, 2001. The next day, he died in the terrorist attacks that destroyed the twin towers. Alissa was more than seven months pregnant. In this book, she recounts the personal struggles she suffered as a pregnant "terror widow," first heaped upon with sympathy, then publicly scorned. She describes the tragedies suffered by all the families who lost loved ones on September 11, 2001 and the frustrations they experienced dealing with bureaucrats as they tried to get even the smallest physical trace of their loved ones.

The author's "tragedy of errors inspires anger on her behalf, although the story is calmly and beautifully told. Choi's simple and attractive line art is set off by turquoise wash, yielding to a full-color photo at the end when Alissa embraces her life anew." Libr J

Torres, J.

Alison Dare, Little Miss Adventures Volume 2. Oni Press 2005 Un Illustration

Grades: 4 5 6 7 8 9   741.5; Fic
1. Adventure graphic novels
1-932664-25-4, $11.95

Alison Dare is back in this new collection of stories, including her report about her experience at her mother's excavation site in Egypt (with the true story coming right after). Then Alison and her boarding school friends journey into the Heart of the Maiden." The costumed avenger The Blue Scarab encounters villains while gift shopping. And world renowned archaeologist Dr. Alice Dare teaches a thing or two about museum mayhem.

Blue Beetle: reach for the stars. John Rogers, J. Torres, Keith Giffen, writers ; Rafael Albuquerque, David Baldeon, Freddie Williams II, pencillers ; Rafael Albuquerque, Steve Bird, Dan Davis, inkers ; Guy Major, colorist ; Phil Balsman, Pat Brosseau, letterers. DC Comics 2008 168p. Illustration

Grades: 8 9 10 11 12 Adult   741.5; Fic
1. Adventure graphic novels; 2. Green Lantern (Fictional character); 3. Superhero graphic novels; 4. Teen Titans (Fictional characters); 5. Graphic novels
978-1-4012-1642-9, $14.99

In the previous volume, teenager Jaime Reyes discovered that the scarab fused to his spine that turns him into the Blue Beetle was created by aliens. Now he learns that those aliens are invading Earth, but they're doing it so insidiously that humans are welcoming the Reach and no one will believe one boy from Texas. It's up to Jaime, his friends, and some other superheroes, such as Green Lantern Guy Gardner and the Teen Titans, to try to stop them. The book includes some violence.

Days Like This. Written by J. Torres ; illustrated by Scott Chantler. Oni Press 2003 Un Illustration

Grades: 6 7 8 9 10 11 12 Adult   **741.5; Fic**
   1. Rock music; 2. Graphic novels
1-929998-48-1, $8.95

It's the early 1960s, and rock'n'roll and r&b are ushering in a new golden age of pop music. Tina & the Tiaras, three teenage girl singers, songwriter Karen Prince, and new music mogul Anna Solomon team to create a new girl group sound and move up the charts.

Degrassi the Next Generation Extra Credit Vol. 1: Turning Japanese. Art by Ed Northcott. Pocket Books 2006 Un Illustration
Grades: 8 9 10 11 12   **741.5; Fic**
   1. Graphic novels
978-1-4165-3076-3, $9.95

It's the end of Ellie's senior year, and as though final exams aren't enough to worry about, she's been placed in a compromising position by one of her bosses at a comic book company. Is quitting her only option? J.T. turns to the Internet to help cope with the recent troubles in his life. But now he spends most of his time locked in his room, and he can't seem to move on. Is his new habit just making his problems worse? This original story follows the sixth season of the popular television series.

Degrassi the Next Generation Extra Credit Vol. 2: Suddenly Last Summer. Art by Ramon Perez. Pocket Books 2007 Un Illustration
Grades: 8 9 10 11 12   **741.5; Fic**
   1. Graphic novels
978-1-4165-3077-0, $9.95

Emma gets her groove back with the help of group therapy and a family trip to New York City. But as she returns to her old self, her relationship with Peter begins to suffer. Is he helping Emma recover, or holding her back? In the meantime, while coaching at basketball camp, Jimmy finds himself dealing with the fallout of a hazing incident. Was the initiation just a prank, or did it cross the line? When the police get involved, Jimmy is faced with a tough decision. This is another original story set during the summer vacation following the sixth season of the popular television series.

Love as a Foreign Language Omnibus Ed. Vol. 1. Written by J. Torres; illustrated by Eric Kim. Oni Press 2006 200p. Illustration
Grades: 9 10 11 12   **741.5; Fic**
   1. Humorous graphic novels; 2. Romance graphic novels; 3. Graphic novels
978-1-932664-41-6, $11.95

Joel has been living and working in Seoul, South Korea for almost a year, teaching English in a hagwon, a private school that teaches various subjects to students of all ages. He hates feeling isolated (he doesn't speak Korean), the food gives him indigestion, he can't find English language comics, he's tired of fighting the giant cockroach in his apartment. But, just as he's decided to quit at the end of his one-year contract, he meets Hana, the school's new secretary, and he's smitten with love. Can he get her to like him? Should he stay in case there's a chance?

Joel and the other adults go to bars, there's a humorous moment with Koreans mispronouncing the word "clap" with

an "r" instead of the "l." This is a funny, sweet romance from the guy's point of view.

This was originally published in several square-bound volumes by Oni Press in 2005.

Ninja scroll. Writer, J. Torres; artist, Michael Chang Ting Yu. DC Comics/Wildstorm 2007 144p. Illustration
Grades: 10 11 12 Adult   **741.5; Fic**
   1. Ninja; 2. Supernatural graphic novels; 3. Graphic novels
978-1-4012-1318-3, $19.99

Jubei Kibagami was a ninja, now he's a wandering ronin who wants nothing more than a good night's sleep. One thing after another keeps him awake, though—demons, devils, bloodthirsty tengu—and he must fight over and over again. The book includes considerable violence and some partial nudity.

Teen Titans Go! Vol. 1: Truth, Justice, Pizza!. DC Comics 2004 112p. Illustration
Grades: 3 4 5 6 7 8 9   **741.5; Fic**
   1. Humorous graphic novels; 2. Robin (Fictional character); 3. Superhero graphic novels; 4. Teen Titans (Fictional characters); 5. Graphic novels
1-4012-0333-7, $6.95

They're too young to drive, but not too young to save the world. The world's hottest heroes: Robin, Beast Boy, Raven, Cyborg, and Starfire, show how it's done Titan-style, as they go up against teen super villains Gizmo, Jinx, and Mammoth. Things get icky when Raven's bad dad, Trigon, comes out from a huge zit on Raven's forehead (ewwww ...).

Teen Titans Go! Vol. 2: Heroes on Patrol!. DC Comics 2004 112p. Illustration
Grades: 3 4 5 6 7 8 9   **741.5; Fic**
   1. Humorous graphic novels; 2. Superhero graphic novels; 3. Teen Titans (Fictional characters); 4. Graphic novels
1-4012-0334-5, $6.95

In this volume, the Teen Titans encounter the battling brothers, Thunder and Lightning; Starfire has to deal with her naughty sister Blackfire; they encounter Aqualad; and more.

Teen Titans Go! Vol. 3: Bring It On!. Written by J. Torres, Adam Beechen. DC Comics 2005 104p. Illustration
Grades: 3 4 5 6 7 8 9   **741.5; Fic**
   1. Humorous graphic novels; 2. Superhero graphic novels; 3. Teen Titans (Fictional characters); 4. Graphic novels
1-4012-0511-9, $6.99

Terra rejoins the Titans to fight Slade's robots; the teen superheroes fight Mumbo; Beast Boy tries to help a man stricken with werewolfism; Speedy joins the Titans to fight Plasmus; and they go up against Kwiz Kid, who's mad at Robin because his ex-girlfriend has a crush on Robin.

Teen Titans Go! Vol. 4: Ready for Action!. DC Comics 2005 104p. Illustration
Grades: 3 4 5 6 7 8 9   **741.5; Fic**
   1. Humorous graphic novels; 2. Superhero graphic novels; 3. Teen Titans (Fictional characters); 4. Graphic novels
978-1-4012-0985-8, $6.99

In this volume, the Titans confront a rampaging Wildebeest, teach the hot-tempered Hotshot the value of patience, battle an army of zombies, find themselves trapped in a deadly video game with the Titans East and more.

Teen Titans Go! Vol. 5: On the Move!. DC Comics 2006 104p. Illustration
Grades: 3 4 5 6 7 8 9   **741.5; Fic**
1. Humorous graphic novels; 2. Robin (Fictional character); 3. Superhero graphic novels; 4. Teen Titans (Fictional characters); 5. Graphic novels
978-1-4012-0986-5, $6.99

In this collection, among other stories the Titans must stop Beast Boy, who's been turned into the terrifying vegetarian monster Garsaurus Rex; Robin is tempted to the dark side by Slade; and the Titans crash a comic book convention to discover the secret of Red X.

Teen Titans Go!: Titans Together!. DC Comics 2007 144p. Illustration
Grades: 3 4 5 6 7 8 9   **741.5**
1. Robin (Fictional character); 2. Superhero graphic novels; 3. Teen Titans (Fictional characters); 4. Graphic novels
978-1-4012-1563-7, $12.99

This volume collects eight adventures of the Teen Titans as seen in the animated series, Teen Titans Go! Robin leads the young team that includes Cyborg, Beast Boy, Raven, and Starfire. The stories have lots of action and bad puns as Beast Boy makes a movie, the Titans find themselves in an alien fighting arena, and Robin's future self, Nightwing, comes when time goes a little haywire and an evil Robin shows up.

Toume, Kei
Kuro Gane Vol. 1. By Kei Toume; translated by Akira Tsubasa; adapted by Alex Kent. Random House/Del Rey Manga 2007 224p. Illustration
Grades: 9 10 11 12   **741.5; Fic**
1. Adventure graphic novels; 2. Seinen manga; 3. Graphic novels
978-0-345-49203-6, $10.95

Avenging his father's murder is a matter of honor for the young samurai Jintetsu. But it turns out that the killer is a corrupt government official-and now the powers that be are determined to hunt Jintetsu down like an animal. There's only one problem: Jintetsu is already dead. Torn to pieces by a pack of dogs, Jintetsu's ravaged body has been found by Genkichi, outcast and master inventor. Genkichi gives the dead boy a new, indestructible steel body and a talking sword, Haganemaru, just what he'll need to face down the gang that's terrorizing his hometown and the mobster who ordered his father's hit. But what about Otsuki, the beautiful girl he left behind? Steel armor is defense against any sword, but it can't save Jintetsu from the pain in his heart. The story has some mildly harsh language and some violence. This is a five-volume series.

Towle, Ben
Midnight sun. SLG Publishing 2007 Un Illustration
Grades: 10 11 12 Adult   **741.5; Fic**
1. Arctic regions; 2. Graphic novels
978-1-59362-088-2, $14.95

In 1928, an Italian airship expedition to the North Pole disappears shortly after radioing that it has reached the North Pole. The stranded members of the airship crew prepare for a stay on the drifting icepack where they've crashed, hoping to survive until rescuers can find them. A newspaper reporter who drinks too much in speakeasies is sent to the Arctic on board a Russian rescue ship to cover the story; there, he meets the Russian reporter whose boyfriend is a member of the airship crew. There are scenes of drinking.

Toyama, Ema
Pixie Pop: Gokkun Pucho Vol. 1. Tokyopop 2007 Un Illustration
Grades: 7 8 9 10 11 12   **741.5; Fic**
1. Humorous graphic novels; 2. Manga; 3. Romance graphic novels; 4. Shojo manga; 5. Graphic novels
978-1-59816-813-6, $9.99

Mayu, the daughter of a cafe owner, is down-in-the-dumps and unlucky in love...until she meets Pucho, the magical fairy of beverages. Now, whenever Mayu drinks something, she transforms! But there's a catch—milk makes her grow (into a giant), water turns her invisible, and pork soup turns her into a cute little piglet. Only Pucho can reverse the transformations. But what will help her win the man of her dreams?

Tran, G. B.
Vietnamerica: a family's journey. Written and illustrated by GB Tran.. Villard Books 2010 279 p. Color illustration
Grades: 11 12 Adult   **741.5**
1. Artists; 2. Illustrators; 3. Vietnamese Americans — Biography; 4. Graphic novels
0345508726; 9780345508720, $30

                 LC 2011283144

In this personal memoir, drawn in the style of a graphic novel, the author tries to make sense of a shattered family history. [G. B.] Tran was born in America shortly after his family fled Vietnam during the fall of Saigon. However, he sees how deeply his parents still feel connected to their homeland, even as they can't fully admit their dismay at being cut off from it. . . . By visiting Vietnam and exploring memories, Tran learns how his grandfather, a lifelong Vietminh supporter, was horrified at the brutal results of the Communist victory and how his father became a glum autocrat after his career as an artist was destroyed. He watches how his parents interact uneasily with the swarm of relatives and friends they left behind. (Publishers Weekly)

Trondheim, Lewis
A.L.I.E.E.E.N.. First Second Books 2006 Un Illustration
Grades: 8 9 10 11 12   **741.5; Fic**
1. Humorous graphic novels; 2. Science fiction graphic novels; 3. Stories without words; 4. Graphic novels
978-1-59643-095-2, $12.95

According to the title page, the full title is Archives of Lost Issues and Earthly Editions of Extraterrestrial Novelties. The book purports to be an alien comic book, and all dialog is in an alien script, rendering it basically wordless for human readers. In several separate stories, little creatures suffer injuries, perpetrate bullying violence on others, suffer extreme pooping, and other bizarre and weird experiences.

The dark humor in this book will appeal to teens who enjoy snarky attitudes and macabre humor.
Originally published in France in 2004 by Editions Breal.

Astronauts of the future. [by] Lewis Trondheim, Manu Larcenet. NBM 2004 96p. Illustration
Grades: 7 8 9 10 11 12   **741.5; Fic**
   1. Science fiction graphic novels; 2. Graphic novels
1-561-63407-7, $14.95
                   LC 2004-49960
This story "begins as a witty, gentle tale of two precocious youngsters, Gil and Martina, whose estrangement from their classmates and parents leads them to conclude that others are either, as Martina insists, aliens, or, according to Gil, robots. Initially wryly depicting the loneliness and alienation of brainy children and their joy at discovering simpatico souls—think Calvin and Hobbes meets To Be and to Have—the story suddenly swirls into an outrageous but compelling science-fiction epic." Booklist

Dungeon: Twilight Vol. 2: Joann Sfar, Lewis Trondheim, story. Armageddon. NBM 2006 Un Illustration
Grades: 10 11 12 Adult   **741.5; Fic**
   1. Adventure graphic novels; 2. Fantasy graphic novels; 3. Graphic novels
978-1-56163-477-4, $14.95
Marvin, saved at the last minute from certain death in a duel by his young warrior admirer Marvin the Red, simply cannot be let to die like he wishes. Whatever he loses, he regains in different powers. He's even become invincible. It's to the point where he'd rather exchange body parts to get back his mortality. But then he is led to a discovery that may make continuing to live actually worth it. Unlike the first Dungeon series, this one includes more violence, some nudity, and sexual situations.

Li'l Santa. NBM Publishing 2002 Un Illustration
Grades: 3 4 5 6 7 8 9 10 11 12 Adult   **741.5; Fic**
   1. Fantasy graphic novels; 2. Humorous graphic novels; 3. Santa Claus; 4. Stories without words; 5. Graphic novels
1-56163-335-6, $14.95
                   LC 2002-32131
You have no idea what Santa must go through, all the way up there at the North Pole, until you read this fully silent graphic novel. Besides the huge yearly job that faces him, the North Pole is no friendly place, what with Impies and a Snow Dragon and the like. Santa must use all his best cunning to make all the world's kids happy.

Little nothings: the curse of the umbrella. NBM Publishing 2008 126p. Illustration
Grades: 9 10 11 12 Adult   **92; 741.5**
   1. Biographical graphic novels; 2. Humorous graphic novels; 3. Graphic novels
978-1-56163-523-8, $14.95
                   LC 2008-113013
French cartoonist Trondheim, creator of the Dungeon series, A.L.I.E.E.E.N., Mr. O, and many other comics, collects here little snippets of everyday life, covering everything from being the plant-killer of all time (nothing he tries to grow ever survives), getting kittens as pets, dealing with a wife who tells him that wearing a t-shirt under a short-sleeved shirt is ugly, realizing that his eleven-year-old son is too jaded by horror movies to be scared by "Alien," the inconvenience of having athletic shoes with hidden metal that set off airport security alarms, and more "little nothings."

Mister i. NBM 2007 32p. Illustration
Grades: 10 11 12 Adult   **741.5; Fic**
   1. Humorous graphic novels; 2. Stories without words; 3. Graphic novels
978-1-56163-486-6, $13.95
This volume has page after page of goofy gags crammed with little frames showing the mishaps of Mr. i, who, no matter what he tries, whether getting a pie out of an oven or getting an apple, always ends up killed, poor fellah. The humor is full of cartoony violence, and although it's not gory, will be disturbing for younger readers.

The **Spiffy** Adventures of McConey: Harum Scarum. Fantagraphics Books 1998 48p. Illustration
Grades: 8 9 10 11 12 Adult   **741.5; Fic**
   1. Humorous graphic novels; 2. Mystery graphic novels; 3. Science fiction graphic novels; 4. Graphic novels
1-56097-288-2, $10.95
This is a story about horrible monsters and science gone awry ... about kidnappings, murder, arson, and pitiless beatings ... about fairy dust, time machines, and the teleportation cap ... about sinister commies, double agents, and corrupt commissioners ... about the niceties of tipping and the precise location of the jugular vein. McConey the bunny and his friends blunder and wisecrack their way through a monstrous mystery.

Tiny tyrant. Lewis Trondheim; translated by Alexis Siegel; illustrated by Fabrice Parme. First Second 2007 124 p. Color illustration
Grades: 4 5 6 7 8 9 10 11 12 Adult   **741.5/944; Fic**
   1. Humorous graphic novels; 2. Kings and rulers — Fiction; 3. Graphic novels
9781596430945, $12.95; 159643094X
                   LC 2006021479
Translations into English of eight French stories originally published by Delacourt, 2001-2004.
"In this illustrated collection of eight translated French stories, King Ethelbert rules as much by whim as by moral or regal standards; this lack of perspective can be excused, though, since he's only six. . . . Grades three to eight." (Bull Cent Child Books)
"Tiny child-king Ethelbert is spoiled and difficult, expecting to have his every whim fulfilled-or else. . . . In the end, though, he becomes a hero. The dynamic cartoons are filled with details and riddled with humor; most pages have between six and eight small pictures. . . . This title will have wide appeal. It's young and accessible enough for elementary-grade kids, but teens will also be charmed by the rascally king." SLJ

Tsang, Evonne
   I love him to pieces: or my date is dead weight or he only loves me for my brains. Illustrated by Janina Gorrissen. Graphic Universe 2011 123p. Illustration (My boyfriend is a monster)
Grades: 6 7 8 9 10 11 12   **741.5; Fic**

1. Horror graphic novels; 2. Humorous graphic novels; 3. Romance graphic novels; 4. Zombies; 5. Graphic novels
978-0-7613-6004-9 (lib bdg), $29.27; 0-7613-6004-2 (lib bdg); 978-0-7613-7079-6 (pa), $9.95; 0-7613-7079-X (pa)

LC 2010-30774

Dicey Bell, star of her high school baseball team in St. Petersburg, Florida, falls for Jack Chen, the star of the science program, and she wangles her way into partnering with Jack on a school project. They work together well, like each other a lot, and things look good for a romance, when a weird infection hits the city. The infection attacks the brain and turns the infected people into human flesh-craving monsters. Dicey and Jack try to get to safety, but find themselves surrounded by zombie-like monsters. This story combines romance with zombie fighting in a story that works like a lighter version of The Walking Dead; the extra subtitles on the title page indicate the humor: "My Date is Dead Weight, or He Only Loves Me For My Brains." Gorrissen's black and white art makes the teens look like teens, and the zombies look yucky and scary without being too icky for most teen readers. This is the first volume in a series of standalone stories, each taking on a different kind of monster.

Tsutsui, Yasutaka
    Telepathic Wanderers Volume 1. Story by Yasutaka Tsutsui; art by Sayaka Yamazaki. Tokyopop 2005 192p. Illustration
Grades: 11 12 Adult   741.5; Fic
    1. Manga; 2. Mystery graphic novels; 3. Seinen manga; 4. Graphic novels
1-59532-938-2, $9.99
    When Nanase, a beautiful young telepath, return to her hometown, she stumbles across others possessing telepathic powers, and her life suddenly turns to chaos. On a train she meets Tsuneo, a man with the power to tell the future, and dire predictions for the riders of the train! Will Nanase find her way to safety in time" The book includes nudity, sexual situations, very harsh language, and violence.

Tucci, Billy
    ★ **Sgt.** Rock: the lost battalion. DC Comics 2009 Un Illustration
Grades: 10 11 12 Adult   741.5; Fic
    1. Japanese Americans; 2. Sgt Rock (Fictional character); 3. Soldiers; 4. World War, 1939-1945; 5. Graphic novels
978-1-4012-2533-9, $24.99
    After the Allied force landing at Normandy in 1944, Sgt. Frank Rock and his Easy Company are attached to the 141st Infantry and march deep into the Vosges Mountains, their assignment to open an avenue straight into the heart of Germany. However, the German forces have dug in deeply with snipers, Tiger tanks, and elite infantry troops, ready to keep the Americans trapped until reinforcements come to help them destroy the Allies. As Sgt. Rock and his men, along with the rest of the Lost Battalion, try to hang on with dwindling ammunition and rations, American commanders keep trying to send help. Everyone fails, except for the "Little Iron Men" of the 442nd Regimental Combat Team. These Japanese American soldiers, many of whom have family forced to live in internment camps, are the only hope

for the Lost Battalion; and Hitler has just ordered their execution. This story does portray the violence of war, but Tucci keeps his art fairly subdued and the language pretty clean (dang, nuts, etc.). He heavily researched this book so the facts are there, he just added the fictional Sgt. Rock and Easy Company to the real soldiers. Anyone who wants to get a feeling for what war was like for the everyday Army soldier will get it in this story, with no glorification of fighting or violence.

Tucci, William
    Shi: Ju-Nen. Story and illustrations by Billy Tucci. Dark Horse Comics 2005 Un Illustration
Grades: 10 11 12 Adult   741.5; Fic
    1. Adventure graphic novels; 2. Ninja; 3. Graphic novels
1-59307-451-4, $12.95
    Ana Ishikawa returns to her native Japan where she desperately tries to avert an all out war between the secretive sects of the Kyoto and Nara Sohei. And with the Narans on the verge of annihilation, the Kyoto Sohei are about to rub it in - with the encouragement of the Yakuza and with potentially disastrous consequences. Once again, Ana in the guise of Death Incarnate, will take up the naginata and don her grandfather's Kabuki face paint in order to save both cities, even if it means turning to her father's murderer Masahiro Arashi to do so. The book includes lots of violence and some skimpy clothing on Tomoe and Shi.

Turner, James.
    Rex Libris volume one: I, Librarian. [written and illustrated by James Turner]. Slave Labor Graphics 2007 Un Illustration
Grades: 10 11 12 Adult   741.5; Fic
    1. Fantasy graphic novels; 2. Humorous graphic novels; 3. Librarians; 4. Graphic novels
978-1-59362-062-2, $14.95
    Rex Libris is the head librarian at Middleton Public Library, the best public library ever, with a vast collection including many rare items. He also has to deal with demons, space aliens, and other odd library patrons. And when a book is overdue, he will go to whatever lengths it takes to get the book back. In this volume, Rex must travel to another planet to confront the powerful Space Warlord Vaglox, who has not returned the Principia Mathematica. Meanwhile, his fellow librarians (including Circe the witch from Homer's Odyssey) must fend off a manifestation of bloodthirsty Vandals set on burning the library. The book includes some harsh language, including the s-bomb.

Twain, Mark, 1835-1910
    The **Adventures** of Tom Sawyer. Retold by M.C. Hall ; illustrated by Daniel Strickland. Stone Arch Books 2006 63p. Illustration
Grades: 3 4 5 6 7 8 9   741.5; Fic
    1. Adventure graphic novels; 2. Twain, Mark, 1835-1910 — Adaptations; 3. Graphic novels
978-1-59889-045-7, $23.93
    Tom Sawyer is the cleverest of characters, constantly outwitting those around him. Then there is Huckleberry Finn, the envy of the town's schoolchildren because he has the rare gift of complete freedom, never attending school or answering to anyone but himself. After Tom and Huck

witness a murder, they find themselves on a series of adventures that lead them to some seriously frightening situations. This adaptation is written for reluctant and struggling readers.

Part of the Graphic Revolve series.

Classics illustrated delux #4: the adventures of Tom Sawyer. Adapted by Jean David Morvan, Frederique Voulyze and Severine LeFebvre. Papercutz 2009 Un Illustration

Grades: 4 5 6 7 8 9 10   **741.5; Fic**
   1. Adventure graphic novels; 2. Twain, Mark, 1835-1910
   — Adaptations
   978-1-59707-152-9, $17.95; 978-1-59707-153-6 (pa), $13.95

Orphan Tom Sawyer lives with his half-brother Sid at Aunt Polly's house, where he messes up in school and plays hooky as often as possible; he plays practical jokes with his buddy Huckleberry Finn, crushes on Becky Thatcher, and generally has a happy life. Then Tom and Huck witness a murder, and it changes their lives. This graphic novel adaptation was originally published in France and is translated by Joe Johnson for Papercutz; artist Lefebvre's work shows strong anime influences.

Tyler, Joe
   Grimm Fairy Tales Vol. 1. Joe Tyler and Ralph Tedesco. Zenescope Entertainment 2007 Un Illustration
Grades: 10 11 12 Adult   **741.5; Fic**
   1. Fairy tales; 2. Fantasy graphic novels; 3. Graphic novels
   978-0-9786874-0-3, $15.99

For more than two hundred years the powerful stories of the Brothers Grimm have enchanted millions of readers around the world. This book explores the original darker side of these classic stories while updating the original works. In these stories, morality is tested and the results of one's actions have consequences. Red Riding Hood faces a werewolf; Cinderella seeks vengeance for the years of torture she suffered; Hansel and Gretel run away from horrors at home only to find worse in the woods; Sleeping Beauty learns that narcissism can be a gruesome trait; an envious sister marries the Robber Bridegroom before she realizes her danger; a desperate beauty strikes a deal with Rumpelstiltskin, but he triumphs after all. The book includes violence and reprints the very sexy and suggestive covers from the original issues.

Tynion, James, IV
   The **woods;** Volume 1: The arrow. James Tynion IV; illustrated by Michael Dialynas. Boom! Studios 2014 96 p. Color; Illustration
Grades: 11 12 Adult   **741.5**
   1. High school students — Fiction; 2. Missing persons; 3. Science fiction graphic novels
   1608864545; 9781608864546, $9.99

"On October 16, 2013, 437 students, 52 teachers, and 24 additional staff from Bay Point Preparatory High School in suburban Milwaukee, WI vanished without a trace. Countless light years away, far outside the bounds of the charted universe, 513 people find themselves in the middle of an ancient, primordial wilderness. Where are they? The answers will prove stranger than anyone could possibly imagine. (Publisher's note)

"Tynion pulls no punches as he puts these kids through hell, and in the few moments they are allowed to stop to take a breath, they reveal very unique and original personalities, making them less like horror stereotypes and more like real, breathing kids." Booklist

Volume 1 of an ongoing series

Type-Moon
   Fate stay night, volume 1. Art by Nishiwaki. Tokyopop 2008 196p. Illustration
Grades: 8 9 10 11 12   **741.5; Fic**
   1. Fantasy graphic novels; 2. Grail; 3. Magic; 4. Shonen manga; 5. Graphic novels
   978-1-4278-1037-3, $9.99

When he was still a little boy, Shirou Emiya was the lone survivor of a devastating fire that destroyed his entire village; a magus saved him and raised him. Now in high school, Shirou helps the various school clubs with minor mechanical repairs, but he really wants to follow his stepfather's footsteps and become a hero of justice. Then one afternoon he stumbles upon two men fighting with swords and causing major magical havoc. That day he discovers he's a magus, and he's now in the middle of a new war between the Seven Magi to win the Holy Grail, and he has a magical servant, the Saber (who looks like a young woman). If he refuses to join in the war, many innocent lives will be lost, just like his home village. The book includes considerable fighting violence, some strong language; any moderate sexuality mentioned in the book's rating hasn't appeared in the first volume.

Ubukata, Tou
   Le Chevalier D'Eon, Volume 1. Story by Tou Ubukata; manga by Kiriko Yumeji. Ballantine Books/Del Rey Manga 2007 Un Illustration
Grades: 11 12 Adult   **741.5; Fic**
   1. France — History — 1589-1789, Bourbons; 2. Manga; 3. Supernatural graphic novels; 4. Graphic novels
   0-345-59622-1, $10.95

During the reign of King Louis XV of France, Paris experiences a series of horrific murders. Young virginal women are slowly drained of their blood, which serves as the "ink" for nefarious books of poetry written by men who want to transform themselves into superhuman monsters. Slacker police officer D'Eon de Beaumont, who is actually a secret operative working for the King, is the repository for his slain sister Lia's soul; when she possesses D'Eon's body, she wields a powerful, supernatural sword that she uses to destroy the killer poets. The black and white art helps to mitigate the bloody killings and the violence of the battles between Sphinx (Lia) and the monsters. This manga series is very loosely based on a historical character; D'Eon de Beaumont was a transvestite who served King Louis XV.

Uderzo
   ★ **Asterix** the Gaul. [by] René Goscinny and Albert Uderzo. Orion Media 2004 48p. Illustration; Map
Grades: 4 5 6 7 8 9 10 11 12   **741.5; Fic**
   1. France — History; 2. Humorous graphic novels
   0-7528-6604-4, $12.95; 0-7528-6605-2 (pa), $9.95

Meet Asterix, a diminutive but extremely strong Gaul living in ancient France during the time of the Roman Republic. Together with his friend Obelix, Asterix continually outwits the Roman Legionnaires sent to conquer Gaul for Julius Caesar. Full of puns and outrageous humor, the books also manage to teach a lot of history. This is the first in a long-running series of graphic novels translated from the original French.

Translated from the French

Other titles in this series are: Asterix and Caesar's Gift; Asterix and Cleopatra; Asterix and the actress; Asterix and the banquet; Asterix and the big fight; Asterix and the cauldron; Asterix and the Goths; Asterix and the Great Crossing; Asterix and the laurel wreath; Asterix the legionary; Asterix and the Normans; Asterix and the Roman Agent; Asterix and the soothsayer; Asterix at the Olympic Games; Asterix in Belgium; Asterix in Britain; Asterix in Corsica; Asterix in Spain; Asterix in Switzerland; Asterix Obelix and Co.; Asterix the gladiator; Asterix The Mansions of the Gods

Ueda, Miwa

Papillon, vol. 1. Del Rey Manga 2008 184p. Illustration
Grades: 8 9 10 11 12   **741.5; Fic**
1. Manga; 2. Romance graphic novels; 3. Shojo manga; 4. Graphic novels
978-0-345-50519-4, $10.05

Hana and Ageha are twins, but they were raised separately for years. Now they're in high school, and Hana is totally glamorous and popular, while Ageha is quiet, and shy and everyone thinks of her as plain. Ageha has a crush on Ryuhei, a classmate who was her childhood play buddy while she lived in the country, but Hana decides to date him. A college student who works as the school's counselor tries to get Ageha to open up and strive for what she wants, but his first scheme results in making her a laughingstock of her class. He calls her a chrysallis, but can she break out and become the butterfly?

Papillon, vol. 2. Del Rey Manga 2009 186p. Illustration
Grades: 8 9 10 11 12   **741.5; Fic**
1. Manga; 2. Romance graphic novels; 3. Shojo manga; 4. Graphic novels
978-0-345-50592-7, $10.99

Ichijiku-sensei has been trying to help Ageha get out from twin sister Hana's shadow and get her friend Ryusei see her as girlfriend material, but when Ageha sees Ryuseia and Hana kissing when he's supposed to pick her up to visit her grandmother in the hospital, Ageha goes alone. Ageha has felt for so many years that her mother didn't want her, that it comes as a shock when her mother follows her as Ichijiku-sensei seems to be leading her into a love hotel. Then, when Ageha runs into the street, her mother saves her from being run over and suffers a head injury. Ageha is able to tell her mother how she feels, and the healing process begins. Hana isn't sure she wants this. But now, Ageha no longer wants Ryusei; she's falling for Ichijiku-sensei. The book includes some mildly suggestive scenes.

Ueda, Rinko

Tail of the Moon Vol. 1. Viz Media/Shojo Beat 2006 196p. Illustration

Grades: 10 11 12 Adult   **741.5; Fic**
1. Humorous graphic novels; 2. Manga; 3. Ninja; 4. Romance graphic novels; 5. Shojo manga; 6. Graphic novels
978-1-4215-0764-4, $8.99

Sometimes it seems like Usagi is hopeless. Sure, she's good with healing herbs, but she's the granddaughter of the leader of a prestigious ninja village and she's such a klutz that she's never made it out of the kiddie class. Finally frustrated with Usagi's lack of progress, her grandfather sends her to marry Hattori Hanzo, leader of the ninja clan's main branch, and have lots of ninja babies. But Hanzo has no interest in her or her child bearing potential. After years of goofing around, Usagi is finally determined to reach her goals—she's going to become a ninja and capture Hanzo's heart. This series combines ninja action with romance with lots of bare-chested men and some sexual situations.

Ugawa, Hiroki

Shrine of the Morning Mist Volume 1. Tokyopop 2006 192p. Illustration
Grades: 9 10 11 12 Adult   **741.5; Fic**
1. Fantasy graphic novels; 2. Manga; 3. Romance graphic novels; 4. Shojo manga; 5. Graphic novels
1-59816-343-4, $9.99

Sisters Kurako, Yuzu and Tama are miko, Shinto priestesses, entrusted with keeping an eye on the often volatile spirit world. But when you're a teenager like Yuzu, you want nothing more than to lead a normal life and deal with growing up and falling in love. Enter Tadahiro, the sisters' cousin, who has a mysterious connection to Yuzu's past—and a strained relationship with his other relatives. However, family drama may have to wait. The spirit world suddenly shifts out of balance, unleashing demons into the world who have set their sights on Tadahiro... There is some violence as the monsters try to get Tadahiro.

Umezu, Kazuo

The **Drifting** Classroom Vol. 1. Viz Media/Shojo 2006 194p. Illustration
Grades: 11 12 Adult   **741.5; Fic**
1. Horror graphic novels; 2. Manga; 3. Shonen manga; 4. Graphic novels
978-1-4215-0722-4, $9.99

In the aftermath of a strange earthquake, an entire elementary school vanishes, leaving nothing but a hole in the ground. While parents mourn and authorities investigate, the students and teachers of find themselves somewhere far away...somewhere cold and dark... a lifeless, nightmarish wasteland among which their school stands like a lone fortress. As panic turns to terror, as the rules start to fall apart, a 6th-grade boy named Sho and his friends must try to survive in a hostile new world... The book includes some brutal, graphic violence.

According to Jason Thompson in Manga: The Complete Guide (he also edited this manga series), this was originally published in Japan for younger readers; given the brutal nature of the violence depicted, here in the U.S. it's rated for older teen and adult readers.

Scary Book Volume 1: Reflections. Kazuo Umezu; translation, Kumar Sivasubramanian. Dark Horse Manga 2006 231p. Illustration
Grades: 10 11 12 Adult   **741.5; Fic**
1. Horror graphic novels; 2. Manga; 3. Shojo manga; 4. Graphic novels
978-1-59307-476-0, $13.95
This book offers two tales: "Mirror," in which a narcissistic girl's reflection begins to take ruthless command of her life; and "Demon of Vengeance," where a sadistic warlord bent on seeking retribution for his selfish and reckless son's injuries finds the tables of revenge turned against him. Umezu is considered a master of horror manga; these stories were originally published in the 1960s and 1970s in Japan. This book includes some violence and some strong language.
Other titles in this series are: Volume 2: Insects; Volume 3: Faces

Scary Book Volume 3: Faces. Dark Horse Manga 2006 232p. Illustration
Grades: 8 9 10 11 12   **741.5; Fic**
1. Horror graphic novels; 2. Manga; 3. Shojo manga; 4. Graphic novels
978-1-59307-487-6, $13.95
This is the third volume of the anthology series. In "Fear," Aiko is always ignored and neglected when compared to her beautiful older sister, Momoko. But when Momoko is horribly disfigured in an accident and goes mad, it's up to Aiko to bring home young girls her sister can use... to make a new face. And in "The Coincidental Letter," a young girl named Yoko, in a fit of mischief, sends an insulting letter to a made-up girl at a made-up address warning her of a horrible fate. However, by incredible coincidence, both the girl and the address are real, and everything in the letter starts coming true. Both stories rely on psychological suspense rather than violent horror, although there is some mildly strong language and a little violence in the first story.

Umino, Chica
Honey and Clover vol. 1. Viz Media/Shojo Beat 2008 184p. Illustration
Grades: 10 11 12 Adult   **741.5; Fic**
1. Humorous graphic novels; 2. Romance graphic novels; 3. Shojo manga; 4. Graphic novels
978-1-4215-1504-5, $8.99
College sophomore art student Takemoto thinks his greatest worries in life are finding ways to eat more meat and getting to class on time, but with his friends, life is not so tame. Morita has been a senior for years, because he keeps missing a crucial freshman class; he tends to disappear for days or weeks at a time and return with lots of cash. Yamada works part time for a woman on whom he has a major crush. Then Professor Hanamoto's cousin's daughter Hagumi starts attending college; she looks younger than 18 and she's an art prodigy. And Takemoto has fallen completely for her. The story includes some mild sexual innuendo.

Unita, Yumi
★ **Bunny** drop vol. 1. [translation, Kaori Inoue; lettering, Alexis Eckerman].. Yen Press 2010 196p. Illustration
Grades: 8 9 10 11 12 Adult
741.5; Fic
1. Josei manga; 2. Unmarried fathers; 3. Graphic novels
978-0-7595-3122-2, $12.99

Courtesy of Yen Press

Thirty-year-old bachelor Daikichi is a salaryman, a junior executive, living on his own in Tokyo. When he goes home for his grandfather's funeral, he discovers that his grandfather had a younger lover who left him with a little girl, Rin (which makes her his aunt). The lover is nowhere to be found, and none of Daikichi's relatives will have anything to do with Rin, who won't talk to anyone but sticks close to Daikichi, who closely resembles his grandfather. When no one will step forward to take care of the six-year-old, Daikichi impulsively decides he will. Once he brings Rin home, the reality of his new situation finally dawns on him; Daikichi is now a single father and has to provide care for Rin. There's one scene with Rin and Daikichi together in their furo bath (a very typical Japanese family scene), and a few panels with Rin and Daikichi in their underwear. In one chapter, Daikichi has to deal with Rin's night time bedwetting, and Rin is shown changing her clothes.
"This sweet-natured manga shows the joys, frustrations, and quirks of family life; and while it is aimed at teens, it would also be more than welcome in the hands of adult readers." Booklist
First published 2006 in Japan

★ **Bunny** drop, vol. 2. Yen Press 2010 206p. Illustration
Grades: 8 9 10 11 12 Adult   **741.5; Fic**
1. Humorous graphic novels; 2. Single-parent families; 3. Graphic novels
978-0-7595-3119-2, $12.99
Thirty-year-old bachelor Daikichi Kawachi had impulsively decided to become the guardian of his dead grandfather's illegitimate child, six-year-old Rin, when all the other relatives refused to help her. The reality of the responsibilities he's taken on have hit, and he makes a risky job transfer in order to have more time for Rin. Now, he has to navigate the choices for school as he must enroll Rin in elementary school, and he continues to search for Rin's mother. Being a parent is not easy, and being a male single parent is even harder. And just how is he

Courtesy of Yen Press

supposed to help when Rin says her classmates tell her she is not cute? Picture a bachelor trying to brush a little girl's hair into pigtails.

Urasawa, Naoki

★ **Monster;** Volume 1. Story & art by Naoki Urasawa; translation & English adaptation, Camellia Nieh; lettering, Steve Dutro; editor, Mike Montesa. Viz Media 2014 418 p. Illustration; Color

Grades: 10 11 12 Adult **741.5**
1. Physicians — Fiction; 2. Serial killers — Fiction
142156906X; 9781421569062, $19.99

"Dr. Tenma is the third son in a family of doctors, who left Japan years ago to work under his idol in a hospital in Dusseldorf, Germany. . . . He's on the fast track to promotion and power, until he refuses the hospital director's order to leave the victim of a brutal crime on the table and go help the mayor instead. Suddenly he goes from the cusp of a bright future to a grunt. His fiance leaves him, his promotion is given away, and his patients are removed from his care. But when the men who took everything from Tenma wind up suddenly dead, he's set down a path that will change his life forever." (School Library Journal)
Volume 1 of 9

★ **Naoki** Urasawa's 20th century boys, vol. 1. Viz Media 2009 216p.

Grades: 10 11 12 Adult **741.5; Fic**
1. Manga; 2. Mystery graphic novels; 3. Graphic novels
978-1-59116-922-2, $12.99

In 1997, Kenji has given up his dream of being a rock musician and manages his family's convenience store. When one of his childhood friends, a science teacher, commits suicide, Kenji starts to think back to 1969, when he and his friends created a hideaway, swore to do what they could to save the world, and buried a time capsule with a symbol they designed drawn on top. In 1997, that symbol starts showing up as grafitti in Kenji's neighborhood. And a strange cult led by a man who calls himself "Friend" uses that symbol (an eye with a hand pointing upward). As Kenji reunites with his buddies, they talk about what they did in 1969, and they dig up the time capsule. Does it have anything to do with their friend Donkey's death? The book includes graphic violence and partial nudity.
Volume 1 of 22.

★ **Pluto:** Urasawa x Tezuka, vol. 1. By Naoki Urasawa. Viz Media 2009 200 p. Illustration

Grades: 9 10 11 12 Adult **741.5; Fic**
1. Astro Boy (Fictional character); 2. Manga; 3. Mystery graphic novels; 4. Robots; 5. Robots — Fiction; 6. Graphic novels
1421519186; 9781421519180, $12.99

"In a distant future where sentient humanoid robots pass for human, someone or some thing is out to destroy the seven great robots of the world. Europol's top detective Gesicht is assigned to investigate these mysterious robot serial murdersùthe only catch is that he himself is one of the seven targets." (Publisher's note)
Original Japanese edition, 2004
Volume 1 of 8

Urrea, Luis Alberto

★ **Mr.** Mendoza's paintbrush. Artwork by Christopher Cardinale; color masking and compositing, Anthony Cardinale; design, Anne M. Giangiulio. Cinco Puntos Press 2010 Un Illustration

Grades: 7 8 9 10 11 12 Adult **741.5; Fic**
1. Artists; 2. Humorous graphic novels; 3. Mexico; 4. Graphic novels
978-1-933693-23-1, $17.95

LC 2008-11636

Rosario is a small town in the Sinaloa region of Mexico, nestled into a wet, green, mango-sweet subtropical landscape. There, Mr. Mendoza wields his paintbrush to write graffiti with a purpose. When Mr. Mendoza catches the young narrator and his best friend Jaime spying on the girls who are swimming, he strips them, writes graffiti all over their bodies, and chases the naked boys down the street through town. He also appoints himself as the town's conscience and angers the authorities with his graffiti on the town's whorehouse, bridge, and other places. Then, one day, he takes his paint and paintbrush to the center square and paints steps into the sky and walks up until he disappears. Women and girls are shown in their underwear, and the naked boys are shown only from the back. The talk of sex, the way the boys sneak peeks at the girls and one of the town's women, make this book suitable for teens even though the format resembles a picture book.

"Not only does the art perfectly capture the mood of the piece—from the blocky woodcuts to the muted earth tones—but it also reinforces the lucid dreamlike quality of its magical realism, serving as an enticing invitation to further explore the genre." Horn Book Guide

Urushibara, Yuki

Mushishi 1. Random House/Del Rey Manga 2007 240p. Illustration

Grades: 10 11 12 Adult **741.5:; 741.5**
1. Fantasy graphic novels; 2. Seinen manga; 3. Graphic novels
978-0-345-49621-8

The mushi are a primitive life-form that has existed long before humans came to be. Some mushi can co-exist peacefully with mankind, but some are deadly to humans. Ginko is a mushi-shi, a master who has studied the mushi and knows how to control them, and to destroy them if need be. He travels the countryside of old Japan, ending infestations and helping people when he can. The publisher has rated this for older teens, but there's little in the way of overt violence, harsh language, or any other content issues in this first volume. As a seinen manga, this was published in Japan for adult men.
Volume 1 of 10

Valentino, Serena

Gloomcookie, Volume Five: The Final Curtain. Written by Serena Valentino; drawn by Ted Naifeh; art assistant: Tristan Crane; lettering assistants: Eric Russell & Nikki Coffman. SLG Publishing 2007 Un Illustration

Grades: 9 10 11 12 Adult **741.5; Fic**
1. Fantasy graphic novels; 2. Supernatural graphic novels; 3. Graphic novels
978-1-59362-066-0, $15.95

In this volume of the Gloomcookie series, the Carnival Wars are over. Sebastien killed the evil Marguerite in the previous volume, but he feels guilty. The curse on Lex and Damion has been broken, but now Damion is overprotective of Lex. Meanwhile, Vermilion (a bad goth poet) thinks he has found his true love; but Moon Raven does not have the dark powers she has claimed. Can Sebastien and Lex help their friends, and themselves? There's enough information for first-time readers to piece together what has gone on before. Although the atmosphere is very gothic and dark, there's no violence or nudity, just lots of dark humor and some gentle drama.

Originally published as Gloomcookie issues #24-28.

Nightmares & Fairy Tales Volume Three: 1140 Rue Royale. Written by Serena Valentino; art by Crab Scrambly. SLG Publishing 2007 Un Illustration
Grades: 10 11 12 Adult   741.5; Fic
   1. Horror graphic novels; 2. Graphic novels
   978-1-59362-065-3, $14.95
   In antebellum New Orleans, Delphine Lalaurie tortured and killed her slaves in the house at 1140 Rue Royale. Now, decades later, elderly Victoria and her niece Rebecca have come to live in the house. Everyone tells them the house is haunted, and both Victoria and Rebecca see visions of the past. One of the spirits in the house possesses Rebecca and shows her the horrible, evil acts perpetrated upon the slaves and servants, and she realizes she must help the victims find peace.

This volume stands alone as a complete story. Older teens who enjoy moody, atmospheric, Gothic horror stories will like this.

Originally published as Nightmares & Fairy Tales issues #13-18.

Van Lente, Fred

Action Philosophers Giant-Size Thing Vol. 2. By Fred Van Lente and Ryan Dunlavey. Evil Twin Comics 2007 94p. Illustration
Grades: 9 10 11 12 Adult   180; 741.5
   1. Philosophers; 2. Graphic novels
   978-0-9778329-1-0, $8.95
   Karl Marx: The People's Hero! Jacques Derrida: The Deconstructonator! St. Thomas Aquinas: The Scholastic Spastic! Isaac ben-Luria: Rabbi of the Mystic Arts! They're not just great thinkers, ... They also make great comics. This book collects issues #4-6 of the Action Philosophers series, detailing the lives and thoughts of the men above, plus Machiavelli, Sartre, Descartes, Kierkegaard, Wittgenstein. There's just a little bit of strong language in this volume.

Action philosophers!. By Fred Van Lente and Ryan Dunlavey. Evil Twin Comics 2006 92p. Illustration
Grades: 10 11 12   100
   1. Humorous graphic novels; 2. Philosophy; 3. Graphic novels
   0-9778329-0-2; 978-0-9778329-0-3, $6.95
   This book combines a summary of the basic tenets of philosophers Plato, Bodhidharma, Nietzsche, Thomas Jefferson, St. Augustine, Ayn Rand, Sigmund Freud, Carl Jung, and Joseph Campbell with irreverent artistic portrayals. Imagine Plato as a masked wrestler (shouting "Plato smash!"), or Bodhidharma as a kung fu master. The

section on Freud frankly discusses and portrays some of his more controversial psychosexual ideas.

The **comic** book history of comics. By Fred Van Lente and Ryan Dunlavey. IDW Pub. 2012 224 p. Illustration; Map
Grades: 10 11 12   741.5/9; 741.5
   1. Comic books, strips, etc — History
   1613771975; 9781613771976, $21.99
   This book by Fred Van Lente and Ryan Dunlavy "trac[es] comics from the late 19th century through the next 100 years, and cover[s] the creative, business, and social factors that shaped them.... It takes ... detours that trace the flow of underground comics, explaining the economics of the direct market and the speculative implosion of the 1990s with a clear sense of how these affect content, and delving into the histories of European, English, and Japanese scenes." (Publishers Weekly)

Destructive reentry. Fred Van Lente, writer ; James Cordeiro, penciler ; Gary Erskine, inker ; Martegod Gracia, colorist ; Dave Sharpe, letterer ; Skottie Young, cover. ABDO/Spotlight 2009 Un Illustration
Grades: 4 5 6 7 8 9   741.5; Fic
   1. Iron Man (Fictional character); 2. Superhero graphic novels; 3. Graphic novels
   978-1-59961-589-9, $21.35
                    LC 2008-33395
   Iron Man heads out to space in an attempt to prevent the Stark International lab station Delphi-1 from falling out of orbit and crashing onto Earth. When he arrives, he finds big trouble: Living Laser has taken control of the lab and is forcing the scientists to use the nanotechnology there to build him a new body. His battle with Iron Man interrupts the process, and instead of a new body for Living Laser, a new entity of ever-regenerating nanobots with LL's paranoia comes to life. Now Iron Man and Living Laser must team up to stop the entity and save Earth.

This Spotlight edition reprints the comic originally published by Marvel as part of its Marvel Age imprint, without all the advertisements. This is part of the Iron Man Set II.

Ghost of a chance. Fred Van Lente, writer ; Graham Nolan, penciler ; Victor Olazaba, inker ; Martegod Gracia, colorist ; Dave Sharpe, letterer ; Skottie Young, cover. ABDO/Spotlight 2009 Un Illustration
Grades: 4 5 6 7 8 9   741.5; Fic
   1. Iron Man (Fictional character); 2. Superhero graphic novels; 3. Graphic novels
   978-1-59961-590-5, $21.35
                    LC 2008-33396
   Dr. Doom captures Stark International executives, including Rhodey and Pepper, claiming they invaded Latverian air space while they were flying to a mountain chalet for a conference. Stark, who had stayed behind to work on a new invention, uses his untried stealth armor to infiltrate Doom's fortress and rescue his people.

This Spotlight edition reprints the comic originally published by Marvel as part of its Marvel Age imprint, without all the advertisements. This is part of the Iron Man Set II.

Marvel Adventures: Fantastic Four: Monsters & Mysteries. Art by Clay Mann. Marvel Entertainment 2007 Un Illustration
Grades: 3 4 5 6 7 8 9   **741.5; Fic**
1. Fantastic Four (Fictional characters); 2. Superhero graphic novels; 3. Graphic novels
978-0-7851-2380-4, $6.99
Mr. Fantastic, the Invisible Woman, the Human Torch, and the Thing go for a wild ride adventures and encounter the Mole Man, the Skrulls, Rama-Tut, and the Sub-Mariner.

Pirated!. Fred Van Lente, writer ; Rafa Sandoval, penciler ; Roger Bonet, inker ; Martegod Gracia, colorist ; Dave Sharpe, letterer ; Skottie Young, cover. ABDO/Spotlight 2009 Un Illustration
Grades: 4 5 6 7 8 9   **741.5; Fic**
1. Iron Man (Fictional character); 2. Superhero graphic novels; 3. Graphic novels
978-1-59961-591-2, $21.35
                                LC 2008-33397
While using his deep-sea armor to investigate shipwrecks, Stark stumbles upon the hideout of modern pirates, led by the man who calls himself Commander Kraken. They specialize in stealing technology and strip the armor from Stark; they plan to attack Hydrobase, where Kraken used to work as a scientist before he was accused of stealing his own technological secrets. Unarmed, shot out of Kraken's submarine through its torpedo tube, Stark must find a way to survive and get his armor back.
This Spotlight edition reprints the comic originally published by Marvel as part of its Marvel Age imprint, without all the advertisements. This is part of the Iron Man Set II.

The simple life. Fred Van Lente, writer ; Rafa Sandoval, penciler ; Roger Bonet, inker ; Ulises Arreola, colorist ; Dave Sharpe, letterer ; Skottie Young, cover. ABDO/Spotlight 2009 Un Illustration
Grades: 4 5 6 7 8 9   **741.5; Fic**
1. Iron Man (Fictional character); 2. Superhero graphic novels; 3. Graphic novels
978-1-59961-592-9, $21.35
                                LC 2008-33398
Flying over the Alleghenies to a meeting, Stark finds himself under attack by a superpowered assassin; she shorts out his suit's power but can't finish him off when a jetliner interrupts the fight. Iron Man crash lands near a remote settlement where the people have given up on modern technology to live in peace. However, one of the women there used to work in a Stark International factory and harbors great bitterness toward Stark for closing the factory. When the assassin returns to finish him off, how will he fight her off without armor and without harming the people who saved his life?
This Spotlight edition reprints the comic originally published by Marvel as part of its Marvel Age imprint, without all the advertisements. This is part of the Iron Man Set II.

Spider-man: fashion victims. Fred Van Lente, writer ; Michael O'Hare, pencils ; Cory Hamscher, inks ; GURU eFX, colors ; Scherberger, Paris and GURU eFX, cover ; Dave Sharpe, letterer. ABDO Publishing Company/Spotlight 2008 Un Illustration

Grades: 4 5 6 7 8 9   **741.5; Fic**
1. Spider-Man (Fictional character); 2. Superhero graphic novels; 3. Graphic novels
978-1-59961-395-6, $21.35
                                LC 2007-20239
When Spider-Man suddenly finds himself battling newbie villains in high-tech suits marked with a "T—, he knows he's got to find the source who is supplying them with the means to commit crimes. But when he finds the Tinkerer, how will he be able to stop him" This is a revised, hardbound edition of the Marvel Adventures Spider-Man comic book issue #21.
Part of the Spider-Man Set III

Van Meter, Jen
Hopeless Savages. Art by Christine Norrie and Chynna Clugston-Major. Oni Press 2002 128p. Illustration
Grades: 7 8 9 10 11 12 Adult   **741.5; Fic**
1. Family; 2. Humorous graphic novels; 3. Rock music; 4. Graphic novels
1-929998-24-4, $13.95
Family ties are the earliest ties that bind, setting the tone for the paths we will take in our future. So what if your father is Dirk Hopeless and your mother Nikki Savage, a superstar couple from the days of punk rock? When you're born a rebel, what can you possibly do to make yourself stand apart? For Rat Hopeless-Savage, the answer is to leave home and become a normal citizen with a nine-to-five job.

Hopeless Savages Vol. 2: Ground Zero. Art by Christine Norrie, Chynna Clugston-Major, Andi Watson, and Bryan Lee O'Malley. Oni Press 2004 128p. Illustration
Grades: 7 8 9 10 11 12 Adult   **741.5; Fic**
1. Family; 2. Humorous graphic novels; 3. Rock music; 4. Romance graphic novels; 5. Graphic novels
1-929998-99-6, $11.95
When you're sixteen, the world is a different place. When you're Zero Hopeless-Savage, the youngest daughter of rock stars Dirk Hopeless and Nikki Savage, the world is practically unrecognizable. Imagine you're in the midst of high school, you have your first band, and WHAMMO! Some boy comes along who doesn't think you're a total freak, and you think he's pretty swell, too. But before you can do anything about it, there's a TV crew outside your house that wants to chronicle the gossip and scandals of your parents' careers, and a massive misunderstanding has gotten you grounded. How's a self-respecting young lady supposed to handle all that?

Hopeless Savages Vol. 3: Too Much Hopeless. Art, Christine Norrie and Ross Campbell. Oni Press 2004 Un Illustration
Grades: 7 8 9 10 11 12 Adult   **741.5; Fic**
1. Family; 2. Humorous graphic novels; 3. Martial arts; 4. Romance graphic novels; 5. Graphic novels
1-929998-85-6, $11.95
This was supposed to be a leisurely vacation. Arsenal Hopeless-Savage has a rematch with an old high school rival in a kung-fu tournament in Hong Kong. She and her brother Twitch figured they could turn it into a nice jaunt with their boyfriends to meet their aging grandmother, a renowned Chinese fortune teller. Too bad Grandma Shi didn't phone ahead to tell them that it was going to be the trip from Hell. It

begins at the airport when a shady character slips something into Arsenal's bag, putting the quartet on the radar of the local bad guys, the British secret service, and the Hong Kong police. It becomes even more complicated when the rest of the Hopeless-Savage clan decides to join the middle children in Asia, getting caught up in the international intrigue themselves. Arsenal is the only person that can get them all out of the jam they're in, and for her it's all too much. Twitch's gay relationship is treated matter-of-factly.

JSA Classified: Honor Among Thieves. Jen Van Meter, Peter J. Tomasi, writers; Patrick Olliffe, Don Kramer, pencillers; Ruy Jose, Drew Geraci, Keith Champagne, inkers; Nathan Eyring, John Kalisz, colorist: Rob Leigh, letterer. DC Comics 2007 128p. Illustration
Grades: 9 10 11 12 Adult   **741.5; Fic**
1. Flash (Fictional character); 2. Justice Society of America (Fictional characters); 3. Superhero graphic novels; 4. Graphic novels
978-1-4012-1218-6, $14.99
The villainous Injustice Society re-forms with a new mission: break into the Justice Society of America's headquarters to steal the key of Prometheus. But a flurry of betrayals and the loss of a teammate might threaten any chance that the Injustice Society has. Plus, a mysterious figure has gained control of the Spear of Destiny and is using it to pit the Flash and Wildcat against each other.

Van Sciver, Noah
★ The **Hypo**: The Melancholic Young Lincoln. Noah Van Sciver. Fantagraphics 2012 192 p. Illustration
Grades: 11 12 Adult   **92; 973.7092; 741.5**
1. Biographical graphic novels; 2. Depression (Psychology); 3. Lincoln, Abraham, 1809-1865
1606996193; 9781606996195, $24.99
This graphic novel, by Noah Van Sciver, "is based on [Abraham] Lincoln's battle with depression. . . . [It] follows the twenty-something Abraham Lincoln as . . . a rising Whig in the state's legislature as he arrives in Springfield, IL to practice law. . . . But, as time passes and uncertainty creeps in, young Lincoln is forced to battle a dark cloud of depression brought on by a chain of defeats and failures culminating into a nervous breakdown that threatens his life and sanity." (Publisher's note)
"A thoroughly engaging graphic novel that seamlessly balances investigation and imagination." Pub Wkly

Vance, Steve
★ **Bad** girls. Steve Vance, writer ; Jennifer Graves, Christine Norrie, pencillers ; Jennifer Graves, J. Bone, Daniel Krall, inkers ; Kurt Hathaway, letterer. DC Comics 2009 128p. Illustration
Grades: 8 9 10 11 12   **741.5; Fic**
1. Humorous graphic novels; 2. Schools; 3. Superhero graphic novels; 4. Graphic novels
978-1-4012-2359-5, $14.99
Lauren's first day at San Narciso High becomes a disaster when she collides with the school's uber-nerd Ronald and gets on the wrong side of the school's queen bee cheerleaders led by Tiffany. Things only get worse as the days go by, then Lauren unknowingly helps to create even more trouble when Tiffany, Brittany, Ashley, and Destinee all drink from Ronald's thermos that Lauren had been holding. That thermos held Ronald's secret science project, a potion that gives the drinker super powers. Oh, and all that stuff about "with great power comes great responsibility?" Pffft! These girls decide to have their own kind of fun at the expense of everyone else. So how is Lauren supposed to stop them? Ronald decides to give her a dose of his potion, and now suddenly she can read minds. How is that supposed to help? Meanwhile, a couple of sinister government agents come to town, and the science teacher wants to find out just what Ronald has been doing ...

Vanholme, Virginie
Scared to death, bk 1: the vampire from the Marshes. Illustrated by Mauricet. Cinebook 2008 48p. Illustration
Grades: 5 6 7 8 9   **741.5; Fic**
1. Horror graphic novels; 2. Mystery graphic novels; 3. Vampires; 4. Graphic novels
978-1-905460-47-2, $11.95

Young teen friends Robin and Max sneak a look into Robin's father's files. He's a forensic scientist who gets called in to investigate mysterious deaths. They read the file on the death of a man who was found in the rushes in the local park, full of little holes all over his body. Max believes the man was killed by vampires, and the two boys go to the library to do research, camp out in Robin's yard but nothing seems to happen except that they interrupt the work of a poacher. However, there are vampires out there, and now they're watching Robin and Max. There's just enough spookiness and blood for upper elementary and middle school age readers who want some horror without being grossed out by excessive gore.
Part of the Scared to Death series, originally published in France as Mort de Trouille Le vampire des marais.

Vankin, Deborah
Poseurs. [written by Deborah Vankin; illustrated by Rick Mays; lettering by Robert Clark, Jr., Clem Robins and Drew Gill].. Image Comics 2011 149p. Illustration
Grades: 8 9 10 11 12   **741.5; Fic**
1. Friendship; 2. Kidnapping; 3. Mystery graphic novels; 4. Graphic novels
978-1-60706-358-2, $16.99
Jenna's friendship with Mac, a busboy, and Pouri, a Taiwanese partygoer, is tested when Pouri suggests that Jenna and Mac help her stage her own kidnapping in order to to avoid flunking out of school and being sent back to Taiwan. This book was originally meant to be part of DC Comics' Minx line; Mays' black and white art looks clear and spare in the larger size pages of this Image Comics publication. One page shows a nude young woman whose naughty parts are covered by sushi, and on another page, Pouri throws a drink into a man's lap; other than these, there's no overt violence, no bad language (just a lot of Mac-isms), and the one time Jenna and Mac are in bed together, they are fully clothed. The cover copy states "Gossip Girl meets Bret Easton Ellis for the comic book crowd," but the book stays teen friendly throughout.

Varon, Sara

Robot dreams. First Second 2007 205p. Illustration
Grades: 3 4 5 6 7 8 9 10 11 12 Adult   **741; 741.5; Fic**
1. Dogs; 2. Robots; 3. Graphic novels
978-1-59643-108-9 (pa), $16.95; 1-59643-108-3 (pa)
LC 2006-52640
The friendship between a dog and a robot is portrayed in this wordless graphic novel. (Bull Cent Child Books)
"Varon's drawing style is uncomplicated, and her colors are clean and refreshing. Although her story seems equally simple, it is invested with true emotion." Booklist

Sweaterweather. Alternative Comics 2006 96p. Illustration
Grades: 3 4 5 6 7 8 9   **741.5; Fic**
1. Animals; 2. Friendship; 3. Stories without words; 4. Graphic novels
1-891867-93-8, $14.95
A turtle, a rabbit, and other creatures venture out on a wordless snowy journey full of friendship and sweetness. Varon includes interactive bits to the book, such as paper dolls, postcards, and stamps.
First published 2003

Vaughan, Brian K.

Batman: false faces. Pencilled by Scott McDaniel, Rick Burchett, Scott Kolins, Marcos Martin. DC Comics 2008 160p. Illustration
Grades: 10 11 12 Adult   **741.5; Fic**
1. Batman (Fictional character); 2. Superhero graphic novels; 3. Wonder Woman (Fictional character); 4. Graphic novels
978-1-4012-1640-5, $19.99
Throughout his crimefighting career, the Dark Knight has managed to balance his double life as Batman and billionaire Bruce Wayne. But he has taken on other identities as well, including that of criminal Matches Malone. What happens when leading multiple lives becomes too much to handle? As Batman faces old enemies the Ventriloquist and the Mad Hatter, his greatest adversary may be his own secret lives. And Wonder Woman faces a crisis of her own, when Clayface steals part of the source of her power, and she must enlist the help of Donna Troy. The book includes some violence.

Buffy the Vampire Slayer season eight volume 2: No future for you. Writers, Brian K. Vaughan and Joss Whedon ; art by Georges Jeanty. Dark Horse Comics 2008 Un Illustration
Grades: 8 9 10 11 12 Adult   **741.5; Fic**
1. Buffy the Vampire Slayer (Fictional character); 2. Fantasy graphic novels; 3. Horror graphic novels; 4. Graphic novels
978-1-59307-963-5, $15.95
While Buffy is busy trying to uncover just who or what "Twilight" is, Giles recruits Faith to carry out an undercover mission. A Slayer in Great Britain has gone rogue, and she must be stopped. Since she's the daughter of a Peer, Faith has to make like Eliza Doolittle and learn how to become a "lady" in order to infiltrate into the upper crust world to carry out her mission. It's only when she's in the middle of the job that she learns this rogue Slayer is messing around with evil

magic and wants to slay Buffy. The book includes brief partial nudity and some violence.

Doctor Strange: The Oath. Writer, Brian K. Vaughan; art, Marcos Martin. Marvel Enterprises 2007 Un Illustration
Grades: 9 10 11 12 Adult   **741.5; Fic**
1. Doctor Strange (Fictional character); 2. Superhero graphic novels; 3. Graphic novels
0-7851-2211-7, $13.99
Doctor Stephen Strange embarks on the most important paranormal investigation of his career, as he sets out to solve an attempted murder - his own. And with his most trusted friend, Wong, also at death's door, Strange turns to an unexpected corner of the Marvel Universe to recruit a new ally. The Night Nurse runs a clandestine clinic for superheroes, but she insists on accompanying Doctor Strange on his quest to find help for Wong.

★ The **Escapists**. Dark Horse Books 2009 176p. Illustration
Grades: 10 11 12 Adult   **741.5; Fic**
1. Adventure graphic novels; 2. Graphic novels
978-1-59582-361-8, $14.95
Inspired by Michael Chabon's Pulitzer Prizewinning novel, The Amazing Adventures of Kavalier and Clay, this story shows what it's like to start with nothing in Cleveland, Ohio, and end up with a comic so hot a major corporation wants to steal it from you. Maxwell Roth spends his inheritance to buy the rights to The Escapist, the comic book character created by Kavalier and Clay decades ago, and he and his high school friend Case Weaver set out to make new comics of The Escapist. Artist Denny Jones joins them, and together the three create a new comic book series that makes a smash debut. Then, Omnigrip Corporation, which long ago sold the rights away, wants it back. When Roth says no, the corporation uses every dirty trick to force him to sell the rights back. The story of Roth, Weaver, and Jones is intermixed with adventures of the Escapist from the old comics. Artists Steve Rolston and Philip Bond illustrate the present-day story of the three independent comics creators, while Jason Shawn Alexander and Eduardo Barreto illustrate the classic Escapist stories. The book includes some violence and some harsh language.

★ **Ex** Machina Vol. 1: The First Hundred Days. Brian K Vaughan; art by Tony Harris. DC Comics/Wildstorm 2005 Un Illustration
Grades: 10 11 12 Adult   **741.5; Fic**
1. Politics; 2. Superhero graphic novels; 3. Graphic novels
978-1-4012-0612-3, $9.99
This book tells the story of civil engineer Mitchell Hundred, who becomes America's first living, breathing super-hero after a strange accident gives him amazing powers. Eventually Mitchell tires of risking his life merely to maintain the status quo, retires from masked crime fighting, and runs for mayor of New York City, winning by a landslide. But Mayor Hundred has to worry about more than just budget problems and an antagonistic governor, especially when a mysterious hooded figure begins assassinating plow drivers during the worst snowstorm in the city's history. Strong language and some violence figures into this political superhero story.
Volume 1 of 10

★ **Pride** of Baghdad. Written by Brian K. Vaughan; art by Niko Henrichon; lettered by Todd Klein. DC Comics/Vertigo 2006 136p. Illustration

Grades: 10 11 12   **741.5; Fic**
1. Animals; 2. Iraq; 3. War; 4. Iraq War
1-4012-0314-0, $19.99

Vaughan based his original graphic novel on an incident that occurred in 2003, when the Allied forces began bombing Baghdad. The bombs destroy the wall of the Baghdad Zoo, and a small group of lions escapes into the city, only to encounter death and destruction they can't comprehend. All they want is freedom to live and hunt their prey, but they become the most innocent victims of war. Graphic scenes of violence as bombs kill animals could provoke intense emotional reactions.

Runaways Vol. 2: Teenage Wasteland. Pencils, Adrian Alphona and Takeshi Miyazawa. Marvel Entertainment 2004 Un Illustration

Grades: 8 9 10 11 12   **741.5; Fic**
1. Adventure graphic novels; 2. Runaways (Fictional characters); 3. Superhero graphic novels; 4. Graphic novels
0-7851-1415-7, $7.99

Still on the run from their super-villain parents, the motley crew of super-powered kids finds a kindred spirit in a daring young stranger and welcomes him into their fold. But will this dashing young man help the teens defeat their villainous parents, or tear them apart. Then Marvel's original teen runaway crime fighters, Cloak and Dagger, are sent to catch the runaways.

Runaways Vol. 3: The Good Die Young. Writer, Brian K. Vaughan ; penciler, Adrian Alphona ; inks, Craig Yeung ; colors, UDON's Christina Strain. Marvel Entertainment 2005 Un Illustration

Grades: 8 9 10 11 12   **741.5; Fic**
1. Adventure graphic novels; 2. Runaways (Fictional characters); 3. Superhero graphic novels; 4. Graphic novels
0-7851-1684-2, $7.99

The world as people know it is about to end and the Runaways are the only hope to prevent it. But if the fledgling teenage heroes are going to succeed, they may have to become just as evil as their villainous parents. The Runaways have learned how their parents' criminal organization began, and now they must decide how it should end. As the Runaways' epic battle against their evil parents reaches its shocking conclusion, the team's mole stands revealed, and blood must be shed. Which kids will still be standing when the smoke finally clears?

Runaways Vol. 4: True Believers. Writer, Brian K. Vaughan ; penciler, Adrian Alphona ; inker, Craig Yeung ; colorist, UDON's Christina Strain ; letterer, Virtual Calligraphy's Randy Gentile & Dave Sharpe. Marvel Entertainment 2005 Un Illustration

Grades: 8 9 10 11 12   **741.5; Fic**
1. Adventure graphic novels; 2. Runaways (Fictional characters); 3. Superhero graphic novels; 4. Graphic novels
0-7851-1705-9, $7.99

Now that the evil Pride is gone, nearly every bad guy in the Marvel Universe is trying to fill the power vacuum in Los Angeles, and the Runaways are the only heroes who can stop them. Plus: What does a mysterious new team of young heroes want with the Runaways, and which fan-favorite Marvel characters are part of this group?

Runaways Vol. 5: Escape to New York. Writer, Brian K. Vaughan ; penciler, Adrian Alphona ; inks, Craig Yeung ; colors, UDON's Christina Strain. Marvel Entertainment 2006 Un Illustration

Grades: 8 9 10 11 12   **741.5; Fic**
1. Adventure graphic novels; 2. Runaways (Fictional characters); 3. Superhero graphic novels; 4. Graphic novels
0-7851-1901-9, $7.99

When a dangerous alien invades Los Angeles, the Runaways' own Karolina Dean may be the only hero in the Marvel Universe who can stop him ... but at what cost" Then, the Runaways embark on a coast-to-coast adventure. When Clock is accused of a crime he didn't commit, the vigilante is forced to turn to the teenage Runaways for help. They go on a road trip to New York City. Meanwhile, back in LA, someone is tracking the teens, and it can't be good.

Runaways Vol. 6: Parental Guidance. Writer, Brian K. Vaughan ; penciler, Adrian Alphona ; inker, Craig Yeung. Marvel Entertainment 2006 Un Illustration

Grades: 8 9 10 11 12   **741.5; Fic**
1. Adventure graphic novels; 2. Runaways (Fictional characters); 3. Superhero graphic novels; 4. Graphic novels
0-7851-1952-3, $7.99

The Pride is back as an all-new group, and they have it in for the Runaways. And when Molly is separated from her teammates, she must survive a night alone on the mean streets of Los Angeles. The eleven-year-old mutant girl soon hooks up with a new group of runaways, but is their mysterious leader a hero or a villain" In this volume, a member of the team dies.

Runaways Vol. 7: Live Fast. Brian K. Vaughan, writer ; Adrian Alphona, Mike Norton, pencilers. Marvel Entertainment 2007 Un Illustration

Grades: 8 9 10 11 12   **741.5; Fic**
1. Adventure graphic novels; 2. Runaways (Fictional characters); 3. Superhero graphic novels; 4. Graphic novels
978-0-7851-2267-8, $7.99

The Runaways say good-bye to the past, and make hard decisions about their future. Plus: Still reeling from the events of Young Avengers/Runaways (part of Marvel's Civil War), the teenage heroes must now confront a horrific enemy who threatens to tear the team apart.

★ **Runaways,** Vol. 1: Pride & Joy. Writer, Brian K. Vaughan ; pencils, Adrian Alphona ; inks, David Newbold and Craig Yeung ; colors, Brian Reber. Marvel Entertainment 2004 Un Illustration

Grades: 7 8 9 10 11 12   **741.5; Fic**
1. Runaways (Fictional characters); 2. Science fiction graphic novels; 3. Superhero graphic novels; 4. Graphic novels
0-7851-1379-7, $7.99

All young people believe their parents are evil ... but what if they really are" Meet Alex, Karolina, Gert, Chase,

Molly and Nico - whose lives are about to take an unexpected turn. When these six young friends discover their parents are all secretly super-powered villains, the shocked teens find strength in one another. Together, they run away from home and straight into the adventure of their lives - vowing to turn the tables on their evil legacy. This is the first volume of an ongoing series.

Originally published as Runaways issues #1-6.

Other Runaways volumes are: 2: Teenage Wasteland; 3: The Good Die Young; 4: True Believers; 5: Escape to New York; 6: Parental Guidance; 7: Live Fast; 8: Dead End Kids; 9: Dead Wrong; 10: Rock Zombies; 11: Homeschooling

Y: The Last Man Vol. 1: Unmanned. Written by Brian K. Vaughn; art by Pia Guerra. DC Comics/Vertigo 2003 128p. Illustration
Grades: 10 11 12 Adult   **741.5; Fic**
1. Science fiction graphic novels; 2. Graphic novels
978-1-56389-980-5, $12.99
Escape artist Yorick Brown and his male pet monkey are the only surviving males left on Earth after a plague instantaneously kills all the other males on the planet. As women take over ... everything ... latter-day Amazons declare all men must die, Yorick's congresswoman mother arranges protection for him, and mysterious Israeli soldiers seem highly amused. The story includes strong language, nudity, and violence.
Volume 1 of 10

Veitch, Alan
Swamp Thing: Infernal Triangles. Steve Bissette, Artist. DC Comics/Vertigo 1988 Un Illustration
Grades: 10 11 12 Adult   **741.5; Fic**
1. Superhero graphic novels; 2. Swamp Thing (Fictional character); 3. Graphic novels
978-1-4012-1008-3, $19.99
After much trial and error, the elemental entity known as the Swamp Thing has succeeded in harnessing the life-force of his successor into the one form with which he can co-exist, a new human soul, to be born of his love Abby, with help from the sardonic magus John Constantine. But even as the couple begin preparing for their impending domesticity, forces far beyond their intimate world are conspiring to drive them apart once more. There's no nudity or graphic violence, little harsh language, but the themes are mature.

Veitch, Rick
Swamp Thing Vol. 8: Spontaneous Generation. Rick Veitch, Alfredo Alcala; Tatjana Wood, colorist; John Costanza, letterer. DC Comics 2005 Un Illustration
Grades: 11 12 Adult   **741.5; Fic**
1. Superhero graphic novels; 2. Swamp Thing (Fictional character); 3. Graphic novels
1-4012-0793-6, $19.99
When the Swamp Thing returned to Earth from the endless void of space, he discovered that a replacement had been created to take his place as the avatar of Earth's plant life. He resolves to find a way to coexist with the new, as-yet unborn spirit, but each attempt he makes causes the embryonic elemental to become more corrupt. Swamp Thing can think of only one more way to try, and it needs John

Constantine, the Hellblazer, to make it work. This book includes violence, some strong language, nudity, and sexual situations.

Venditti, Robert
Blue Bloods: the graphic novel. By Melissa de la Cruz; adapted by Robert Venditti; art by Alina Urusov; illustrations by Disney Enterprises, Inc.. Hyperion 2013 112 p. Color illustration
Grades: 8 9 10 11 12   **741.5/973; Fic**
1. New York (NY) — Fiction; 2. Secrets — Fiction; 3. Supernatural graphic novels; 4. Teenagers; 5. Vampires — Fiction; 6. Wealth — Fiction; 7. Graphic novels
9781423134466, $19.99; 9781423134473, $11.99; 142313446X

LC 2011053237
In this graphic novel, written by Melissa de la Cruz, adapted by Robert Venditti, and illustrated by Alina Urusov, the focus is on a group of New York teenagers. "Schuyler Van Alen is a loner, and happy that way. But when she turns fifteen, her life dramatically changes. A mosaic of blue veins appears on her arms, and she begins to have memories of another time and place. When a classmate is found dead at a night club, the mystery deepens." (Publisher's note)

The **homeland** directive. Illustrated by Mike Huddleston. Top Shelf Productions 2011 148p. Color illustration
Grades: 11 12 Adult   **741.5**
1. Bioterrorism — Fiction; 2. Mystery fiction; 3. Political corruption — Fiction; 4. Suspense fiction
9781803090247 (pa);
9781603090247

This book tells the story of Dr. Laura Regan, head of the U.S. National Center for Infectious Diseases. "When her research partner is murdered and Laura is blamed for the crime, she finds herself at the heart of a vast and deadly conspiracy." (Publisher's note).

Courtesy of Top Shelf Productions

"A cabinet minister decides to persuade the public that more trackable behavior is in the service of antiterrorist surveillance. But since his incentive involves virally induced 'justified' death for thousands along the way, Regan throws in with the good feds to stop a developing plague and expose the minister. Not that she has much choice: the bad fed operatives are out to kill her since she created the vaccine that could stop their plot cold." (Libr J)

The **sea** of monsters: the graphic novel. By Rick Riordan; adapted by Robert Venditti; art by Attila Futaki; colors by Tamas Gaspar; lettering by Chris Dickey. Disney-Hyperion Books 2013 128 p. Color illustration
(Percy Jackson & the Olympians)
Grades: 5 6 7 8 9 10   **741.5; Fic**

1. Fathers and sons — Fiction; 2. Greek mythology; 3. Monsters — Fiction; 4. Poseidon (Greek deity) — Fiction; 5. Graphic novels
1423145291; 9781423145295, $19.99; 9781423145509
LC 2011012356

In this graphic novel, by Rick Riordan, adapted by Robert Venditti, and illustrated by Attila Futaki and Tamas Gaspar, "when an innocent game of dodgeball among Percy and his classmates turns into a death match against an ugly gang of cannibal giants, things get...well, ugly. And the unexpected arrival of his friend Annabeth brings more bad news: the magical borders that protect Camp Half-Blood have been poisoned by a mysterious enemy, and unless a cure is found, the only safe haven for demigods will be destroyed." (Publisher's note)

"This is a good summary presentation of the original novel, with active and effective art." Lib Med Con.

The **Surrogates**. Created and written by Robert Venditti; illustrated and colored by Brett Weldele. Top Shelf Productions 2006 208p. Illustration
Grades: 10 11 12 Adult   **741.5; Fic**
1. Mystery graphic novels; 2. Science fiction graphic novels; 3. Graphic novels
1-891830-87-2, $19.95

The year is 2054, and life has been reduced to a data feed. The fusing of virtual reality and cybernetics has ushered in the era of the surrogate, a new technology that lets users interact with the world without ever leaving their homes. It's a perfect world, and it's up to Detectives Harvey Greer and Pete Ford of the Metro Police Department to keep it that way. But to do so they'll need to stop a techno-terrorist bent on returning society to a time when people lived their lives instead of merely experiencing them. There's some violence in the story.

Verheiden, Mark
Aliens Omnibus Volume 1. Art by various. Dark Horse Comics 2007 384p. Illustration
Grades: 10 11 12 Adult   **741.5; Fic**
1. Adventure graphic novels; 2. Science fiction graphic novels
978-1-59307-727-3, $24.95

The first three Dark Horse Aliens stories based on the movies are collected in this volume: Outbreak, Nightmare Asylum, and Female War. Outbreak starts thirteen years after the events of the movie Aliens; Billie is in a mental institution suffering from nightmares about what happened at the colony outpost of Rim, and Wilks is in prison. They're both offered a chance to return to Rim. In Female War, Ripley must go with another team of Marines to another planet for another "bug hunt." The stories use strong language and show violence as the humans fight the Aliens.

The **American**. Dark Horse Comics 2005 368p. Illustration
Grades: 11 12 Adult   **741.5; Fic**
1. Superhero graphic novels; 2. Graphic novels
1-59307-419-0, $14.95

He's the ultimate American hero. Since the fifties, he has been a symbol of hope and courage for the entire nation, an indestructible one-man army standing tall for freedom, justice, and the American way - but what about truth" When

reporter Dennis Hough is assigned to cover a story about his boyhood hero, he begins to see the cracks in the legend. Does The American have feet of clay? Or is he himself a victim of a larger conspiracy?

Superman: Sacrifice: Countdown to Infinite Crisis. Greg Rucka, Mark Verheiden, Gail Simone, writers; Ed Benes [and others], pencillers. DC Comics 2005 Un Illustration
Grades: 10 11 12 Adult   **741.5; Fic**
1. Superhero graphic novels; 2. Superman (Fictional character); 3. Wonder Woman (Fictional character); 4. Graphic novels
1-4012-0919-X, $14.99

The pivotal story that forever alters the relationship between Superman and Wonder Woman is collected here for the first time. Max Lord has taken over Superman's mind and has him in his total thrall. With his peers and loved ones threatened, Superman is helpless. But not Wonder Woman, who must battle past the Man of Steel and decisively end the threat. Her actions, and the repercussions, are explored in this story that leads into Infinite Crisis. Some of the fighting in this book is brutal.

Superman: The Journey. Mark Verheiden, writer; Ed Benes et al., pencillers. DC Comics 2006 144p. Illustration
Grades: 9 10 11 12 Adult   **741.5; Fic**
1. Flash (Fictional character); 2. Superhero graphic novels; 3. Superman (Fictional character); 4. Graphic novels
1-4012-0918-1, $14.99

Even the Man of Steel needs to get away from it all, and when he tries to relocate his Fortress of Solitude to South America, a chain of events begins that will test his bravery more than ever. After his first contact with an OMAC, a cybernetic being set to destroy all super-heroes, Superman then must contend with the arrival in Metropolis of Bizarro, as well as Zoom, the Reverse-Flash. Then Blackrock returns with more power than ever; and Lex Luthor seeks deadly vengeance, again.

Verne, Jules, 1828-1905
Around the world in 80 days. Adapted by Chrys Millien ; illustrated by Flo Demolis. IDW Publishing 2009 60p. Illustration
Grades: 5 6 7 8 9   **741.5; Fic**
1. Adventure graphic novels; 2. Verne, Jules, 1828-1905 — Adaptations; 3. Graphic novels
978-1-60010-394-0, $14.99

This graphic novel Verne's globe-trotting adventures of Phileas Fogg, English gentleman, his newly-hired French manservant, Passepartout, and the English detective, Fix, who pursues Fogg, convinced he is a master bank robber. Fogg makes a bet with fellow members of the Reform Club in 1872

Courtesy of IDW Publishing

that he can travel around the world in eighty days, but his precipitous departure makes Scotland Yard suspect him. The three men travel through India, where Fogg saves a beautiful young Indian woman from being burned alive, to Hong Kong, then Japan and then across the United States and onward. This adaptation was originally published in France. The book includes biographical information about Verne, historical information about what the world was like in the 1870s, and an analysis of the novel.

Journey to the Center of the Earth. Retold by Davis Worth Miller and Katherine McLean Brevard ; illustrated by Greg Rebis. Stone Arch Books 2007 72p. Illustration
Grades: 3 4 5 6 7 8 9   **741.5; Fic**
1. Adventure graphic novels; 2. Science fiction graphic novels; 3. Graphic novels
978-1-59889-832-3, $23.93
                                    LC 2007-6202
Axel Lidenbrock and his uncle find a mysterious message inside the 300-year-old book. The dusty note describes a secret passageway to the center of the earth, and Axel reluctantly joins his uncle on a quest. Soon they are descending deeper and deeper into the heart of a volcano. With their guide, Hans, the men discover underground rivers, oceans, strange rock formations, and prehistoric monsters. They also run into danger, which threatens to trap them below the surface forever. The book is written with an easy vocabulary for reluctant and struggling readers, and it includes facts about the real center of the Earth.
Part of the Graphic Revolve series.

Vernon, Ursula
★ **Digger:** the complete Omnibus edition. By Ursula Vernon. Sofawolf Press, Inc. 2013 850 p.
Grades: 9 10 11 12 Adult   **741.5; Fic**
1. Adventure graphic novels; 2. Wombats
1936689324; 9781936689323, $29.44
Hugo Award: Best Graphic Story (2012)
This graphic novel, by Ursula Vernon, is "about a particularly no-nonsense wombat who finds herself stuck on the wrong end of a one-way tunnel in a strange land where nonsense seems to be the specialty. Now, with the help of a talking statue of a god, an outcast hyena, a shadow-being of indeterminate origin, and an oracular slug she seeks to find out where she is and how to go about getting back to her Warren." (Publisher's note)

Vess, Charles
The **Book** of Ballads. Tor 2004 192p. Illustration
Grades: 11 12 Adult   **741.5; 808.81**
1. Ballads; 2. Graphic novels
0-765-31214-X, $24.95
"Vess shows off his ability to use a wide variety of styles and formats. . . . The ballad from which each story is taken is written in its traditional form at the end of each tale." (VOYA)
Artist Vess works with authors such as Charles de Lint, Neil Gaiman, Jane Yolen, Jeff Smith, and others who adapt ballads from the English, Scottish, and Irish traditions. Moods range from comedic hilarity (such as in "Galtee Farmer") to the somber lover's test ("Sovay"). Many of the stories include nudity and some sexual content.

Vinton, Will
Jack Hightower. Created and written by Will Vinton and Andrew Wiese; art by Fabio Laguna; colors by Rain Beredo; letters by Nate Piekos. Dark Horse Comics 2006 Un Illustration
Grades: 10 11 12 Adult   **741.5; Fic**
1. Adventure graphic novels; 2. Humorous graphic novels; 3. Spies; 4. Graphic novels
978-1-59307-392-3, $14.95
Secret agent Jack Hightower was at the height of his career when something BIG happened. Now the world-class operative and infamous ladies man is seeing things from a whole new perspective... a very, very different perspective, to say the least. Tall, daring, and handsome, Jack had it all - a stellar career, beautiful women, and more power and influence than he could shake a supermodel at. But despite it all, Jack longed for one thing that eluded him - the capture of his long-time archnemesis, Dr. Litigious Savant. On the fateful night when Jack's dream of cornering the elusive Savant is realized, things go terribly, dreadfully wrong, and Jack gets cut down to size by one of the doctor's insidious inventions... the size of your average action figure, to be exact. Partial nudity, sexual situations, alcohol consumption and violence are all here, in a book that is a big departure from Claymation animator Vinton's usual work.

Vollmar, Rob
Bluesman. Rob Vollmar & Pablo Callejo. NBM Publishing/ComicsLit 2008 208p. Illustration
Grades: 10 11 12 Adult   **741.5; Fic**
1. African Americans — Southern states; 2. Blues music; 3. Graphic novels
978-1-56163-532-0, $24.95
All Lem Taylor ever wanted was to play the blues. In Arkansas in the late 1920s, life isn't easy for African Americans, whatever their ambitions. When he and piano player Ironwood Malcott play at Shug's speakeasy out in the woods, they catch the attention of a man who says if they get to Memphis, he'll record their songs. However, while staying the night with a young woman, a young white man comes and kills Ironwood and the young woman. Taylor is wounded, and another woman comes and chases him out before she kills the white man. Taylor is trying to get to Memphis any way he can, but the white folk in town want revenge for the white man's murder (never mind the three dead blacks). The only white man who cares about justice is the sheriff. The story was originally published in three parts. It includes graphic violence, sexual situations, and harsh language.

The **castaways.** Illustrated by Pablo G. Callejo. NBM/ComicsLit 2007 64p. Illustration
Grades: 6 7 8 9 10 11 12   **741.5; Fic**
1. United States — History — 1919-1933; 2. Graphic novels
978-1-56163-492-7, $17.95
"Afraid that he's just a burden on his family, 13-year-old Tucker Freeman lets himself be driven away from home and jumps on a freight train heading west. His inexperience makes him vulnerable to all the angry, desperate people looking for any way they can survive during America's economic collapse, but fortunately he's taken under the wing of Elijah Hopkins, an elderly colored man who introduces

him to the cooperative hobo subculture. . . . Vollmer's script, based on family reminiscences, rings true; his dialogue has the vocabulary and the rhythms of real people talking. . . . Callejo's art creates a solid setting in which Tucker's experience can reveal squalor or grace." Publ Wkly

An expanded and newly illustrated edition of the title first published 2002 by Absence of Ink Comic Press

Voloj, Julian

Ghetto Brother: Warrior to Peacemaker. Julian Voloj; illustrated by Claudia Ahlering. NBM Publishing 2015 128 p. Illustration

Grades: 11 12 Adult   **92; 741.5**

1. Gangs; 2. Melendez, Benjy; 3. Peace movements; 4. Puerto Ricans — New York (NY)

1561639486; 9781561639489, $12.99

This graphic novel by Julian Voloj, illustrated by Claudia Ahlering, "tells the true story of Benjy Melendez, a Bronx legend, son of Puerto-Rican immigrants, who founded, at the end of the 1960s, the notorious Ghetto Brothers gang. From the seemingly bombed-out ravages of his neighborhood, wracked by drugs, poverty, and violence, he managed to extract an incredibly positive energy from this riot ridden era: his multiracial gang promoted peace rather than violence." (Publisher's note)

"Using Melendez as narrator-protagonist, Voloj places the seminal events of November and December 1971 in the contexts of post-WWII Puerto Rican immigration and difficult assimilation to New York, and of Melendez's personal development as he learned of and adopted his Jewish heritage. Ahlering bases her artwork partly on news and documentary photography, although she doesn't incorporate or copy photos but draws on them for detail, composition, and tonal variety." Booklist

Von Sholly, Pete

Pete Von Sholly's Extremely Weird Stories. Dark Horse Comics 2006 96p. Illustration

Grades: 11 12 Adult   **741.5; Fic**

1. Fantasy graphic novels; 2. Horror graphic novels; 3. Graphic novels

978-1-59307-554-5, $14.95

Von Sholly uses the European fumetti style of using photographs and combines them with special effects to illustrate his horror stories that seem to come right out of the monster movies of the 1950s and 1960s. There are some pretty gruesome, graphically violent and horrifying images, and some sexual situations.

Pete Von Sholly's Morbid. Dark Horse Comics 2003 96p. Illustration

Grades: 10 11 12 Adult   **741.5; Fic**

1. Fantasy graphic novels; 2. Horror graphic novels; 3. Satire; 4. Graphic novels

1-59307-028-4, $14.95

While employing the European "fumetti" format of using photographs instead of drawn art, this book goes beyond that simple approach; custom-sculpted models, costumed actors, and mind-boggling computer-generated "special effects" come together to create a visual storytelling format. The stories themselves run the gamut from tongue-in-cheek lampoons of '50s drive-in movies to horror

in the Lovecraft tradition. The book includes strong language and some sexually suggestive scenes.

Pete Von Sholly's Morbid 2: Dead But Not Out!. Dark Horse Comics 2005 96p. Illustration

Grades: 10 11 12 Adult   **741.5; Fic**

1. Fantasy graphic novels; 2. Horror graphic novels; 3. Satire; 4. Graphic novels

1-59307-289-9, $14.95

Von Sholly takes the European "fumetti" method to its next level with custom-sculpted models, costumed actors, and computer-generated special effects. In this volume, stories include parodies of Lost World type stories with dinosaurs invading the modern world, to Lovecraftian monsters in the graveyard (and one brave young woman to fight them), to ghost stories, and more. The book includes harsh language, violence, and some sexually suggestive scenes.

Wada, Shinji

Crown, vol. 1. Story, Shinji Wada; art, You Higuri. Go! Comi 2008 Un Illustration

Grades: 10 11 12 Adult   **741.5; Fic**

1. Adventure graphic novels; 2. Manga; 3. Graphic novels

978-1-60510-005-0, $10.99

Teenage orphan Mahiro has been living with the owners of a Chinese takeout restaurant while working several jobs to earn money after relatives took over her parents' house when they died. Suddenly two very handsome young men show up at her construction site job, sweep her into their car, drive to her parents' home and evict the bad relatives, then take her to a condominium. One of the men is Mahiro's long-lost brother, Ren, the other is his best friend Jake; they have worked as mercenaries but now have come to protect Mahiro. She is the rightful heir to the throne of a small island kingdom, she possesses the jewel called the Crown, and the current queen, her stepmother, wants Mahiro dead so she can take over the country. Ren and Jake are very good at what they do, and they have to be, because the queen of Regalia decides to send a small army to Tokyo to kill Mahiro. The book includes violence and fan service (including partial nudity) to appeal to both male and female readers.

Wagahara, Satoshi

The **devil** is a part-timer!; Volume One. Satoshi Wagahara; illustrated by Akio Hiiragi. Yen Press 2015 176 p.

Grades: 7 8 9 10 11 12

1. Demonology — Fiction; 2. Devil — Fiction; 3. Fantasy; 4. Fast food restaurants — Fiction; 5. Manga

9780316383134; 0316383139 $13

LC 2015028390

"This comical tale of a demon-lord-turned-fry-slinger follows the daily travails of (former) Devil King Sadao Maou and his general Shiro Ashiya as they navigate the complexities of life in modern-day Tokyo. Having suffered utter defeat at the hands of a plucky hero, they've been banished to earth and stripped of magical power. And if that wasn't enough, that pesky hero is still hell bent on finishing the job. Artist Akio Hiiragi brings Satoshi Wagahara's story to hilarious life in this manga adaptation of the hit light novel series." (Publisher's note)

Volume 1 of an ongoing series

Wagner, John

A **History** of Violence. Written by John Wagner; art by Vince Locke; lettering by Bob Lappan. DC Comics/Vertigo 2004 286p. Illustration

Grades: 11 12 Adult   **741.5; Fic**

1. Mystery graphic novels; 2. Revenge; 3. Graphic novels
978-1-56389-367-4, $9.99

It was just another quiet day at McKenna's Diner—until a couple of wanted killers walked in looking for trouble. Instead, they got bullets, and Tom McKenna got to be an instant media celebrity. That got him a lot of attention from some people he thought he'd escaped long ago. The kind of people who never forget a face—even after twenty years... Now Tom must confront a group of cold-blooded mobsters intent on settling the score. As much as he tries to deny it, he's a man with a history of violence—and with the lives of his family hanging in the balance, he'll do anything to make sure his secret past stays buried...forever. This story has lots of graphic violence and strong language. This original graphic novel was originally published in 1997.

Wagner, Josh

Sky pirates of Neo Terra. Art by Camilla D'Errico. Image Comics 2010 Un Illustration

Grades: 7 8 9 10 11 12   **741.5; Fic**

1. Adventure graphic novels; 2. Fantasy graphic novels; 3. Science fiction graphic novels; 4. Graphic novels
978-1-60706-324-7, $17.99

The world of Neo Terra blends forgotten technology with natural magic, and glide-wing racing is its major sport. Reckless young glide-wing pilot Billy Boom Boom wants to help his friend Ricket, a young master mechanic whose father was taken by the Pirate King. Sky Pirates have been trying to take over everything, including the glide-wing races. After a race that Billy wins, a huge monstrous creature crashes in among the spectators, but he's actually got word of Ricket's father; Wurl tells the young racers that Ricket's father is on the Forgotten Isle, captive of the Pirate King and the Witch Queen. Billy and his main rival, Rena, set out on their glide-wings to rescue Ricket's father. However, the Witch Queen has her own plans; she's using the master mechanic to improve "Mother," a machine that finds a person's Dark Side and magnifies it to overcome one's better nature. And Mother has corrupted Ricket's father. This book is based on the video game co-created by D'Errico and Sean Megaw, Tyler Sigman, and Jeff Simpson. D'Errico's manga-influenced art blazes with brightly saturated colors in this story of adventure that also explores the meaning of heroism and of friendships. There is some violent action, but nothing excessive for most younger teens.

Wagner, Matt

Batman and the Monster Men: Dark Moon Rising. Matt Wagner, story and art; Dave Stewart, colors; Rob Leigh, letters; Matt Wagner, covers. DC Comics 2006 144p. Illustration

Grades: 10 11 12 Adult   **741.5; Fic**

1. Batman (Fictional character); 2. Mystery graphic novels; 3. Superhero graphic novels; 4. Graphic novels
978-1-4012-1091-5, $14.99

It has been one year since the mysterious Batman first appeared to protect the people of Gotham. In that time, he has waged war on the common criminals and members of organized crime who have plagued his city. But the brutal massacre of some of the city's most notorious gangsters reveals that a far more dangerous threat is emerging, one for which the young Bruce Wayne is woefully unprepared: genetically engineered, horribly mutated men who have developed a taste for human flesh. They are the stuff of nightmare. And as they wreak havoc on Gotham's criminal community, Batman soon discovers that even the woman he loves may be threatened. Can the Dark Knight stop the carnage, or will he become the next victim of the Monster Men" The book includes violence, some graphic.

Batman/Superman/Wonder Woman: Trinity. DC Comics 2003 208p. Illustration

Grades: 9 10 11 12 Adult   **741.5; Fic**

1. Batman (Fictional character); 2. Superhero graphic novels; 3. Superman (Fictional character); 4. Wonder Woman (Fictional character); 5. Graphic novels
1-4012-0187-3, $17.99

When Batman's greatest nemesis, Ra's al Ghul, recruits Bizarro and an Amazon warrior to aid him in his plan to create global chaos, the Dark Knight Detective suddenly finds himself working with the Man of Steel and the Amazon Princess, Wonder Woman. Looking to thwart the madman's plot to simultaneously destroy all satellite communications as well as all of the world's oil reserves, Earth's greatest heroes reluctantly band together. But if Batman, Superman and Wonder Woman are to have any hope of stopping Ra's nuclear missile assault, they will first need to overcome their own biases and reconcile their differing philosophies. The book includes some violence.

Grendel: Devil's Legacy. Creator-writer-cover artist: Matt Wagner; pencillers-inkers, Arnold & Jacob Pander; inkers Jay Geldhof, Rich Rankin; colorist: Jeromy Cox; letterer: Steve Haynie. Dark Horse Comics 2001 120p. Illustration

Grades: 10 11 12 Adult   **741.5; Fic**

1. Mystery graphic novels; 2. Science fiction graphic novels; 3. Supernatural graphic novels; 4. Graphic novels
1-56971-662-5, $29.95

The mind of a vigilante murderer is complex, wrought with anger and blood; it echoes through time in ancestral screams for revenge. And the cycle of death that comes from such a spirit is often endless and tragic. Such is the story of Christine Spar, adopted granddaughter of the terribly notorious, yet rich and graceful Hunter Rose, a.k.a. the original Grendel. It's the near future, and Spar takes her son, Anson, to see a kabuki show, not knowing what tragedy lies ahead. The mysterious leader of the troupe cuts a terrifying figure, cat-like and dangerous, with an odd fixation for Spar and her son. Soon Anson disappears, and Spar takes up the mantle of Grendel to hunt for him. So the cycle begins. The book includes violence and harsh language.

Madame Xanadu: disenchanted. Matt Wagner, writer; Amy Reeder Hadley, penciller. DC Comics/Vertigo 2009 Un Illustration

Grades: 10 11 12 Adult 741.5; Fic
1. Fantasy graphic novels; 2. Magic; 3. Graphic novels
978-1-4012-2291-8, $12.99

In the days of King Arthur and Camelot, Nimue used woodland magic. Despite her power, the warnings of a stranger with glowing eyes comes too late for her to save the land against the machinations of Merlin and her own sister, Morgana. Using her herb lore to maintain her youth, Nimue next shows up in the court of Kublai Khan, where she is known as the Western Seer. Again, the Phantom Stranger shows up, this time with the party of Marco Polo, who become targets of a plot to discredit the Westerners. Nimue helps, only to learn that it wasn't enough, and the Stranger abandons her in the middle of the Gobi Desert. Then she appears in France, known there as Madame Xanadu, a favorite of Queen Marie Antoinette. This time, Nimue reads the portents for herself and knows that the Revolution will topple the King; the Phantom Stranger appears again, but because she can't trust him, she ends up imprisoned, betrayed by the former Queen whom she believed to be a friend, and Nimue has to trick Death herself. In London of the 1880s, Madame Xanadu tries to help the prostitutes of Whitechapel, but the Phantom Stranger says the murders committed by Jack the Ripper serve a larger purpose and he thwarts her again. In New York City of the 1930s, Nimue has found another magician, John Zatara and they are lovers, but the Phantom Stranger comes again and this time Nimue decides to trap him. What consequences will her actions have upon the people around her, including a heroic policeman named James Corrigan" The book includes some gory violence, some harsh language, some sexual suggestiveness and one not-very-graphic rape scene. This series, in its pamphlet comic issue form, was nominated for four Eisner Awards in 2009: Best Writer, Best Cover Artist, Best New Series, and Best Penciler Inker Team.

Volume 1 of 4

Sandman Mystery Theater: Dr. Death and The Night of the Butcher. Matt Wagner, Steven T. Seagle, writers; Guy Davis, Vince Locke, artists; David Hornung, colorist; John Costanza, Gaspar Saladino, letterers. DC Comics/Vertigo 2007 210p. Illustration
Grades: 10 11 12 Adult 741.5; Fic
1. Mystery graphic novels; 2. Sandman (Fictional character); 3. Supernatural graphic novels; 4. Graphic novels
978-1-4012-1237-7, $19.99

Wesley Dodds is driven by his dreams to fight injustice in the dark of night. Donning a gas mask, fedora, business suit and cape, Dodds goes after evildoers as the vigilante known only as The Sandman. Dr. Death and the Night of the Butcher follows Wesley Dodds through two new cases of serial murderers, each more grisly than the last. But the real challenge for The Sandman will be holding on to his paramour, Dian Belmont, once she finally uncovers his secret career. This volume includes strong language, some sexual situations, and some violence.

Wagner, Richard
Richard Wagner's The Ring of the Nibelung Volume One. Adapted for comics by P. Craig Russell; translated by Patrick Mason; colored by Lovern Kindzierski; lettered by Galen Showman. Dark Horse Comics 2002 Un Illustration

Grades: 9 10 11 12 Adult 741.5; Fic
1. Fantasy graphic novels; 2. Norse mythology; 3. Opera; 4. Graphic novels
1-56971-666-8, $21.95
2001 Eisner Award for Best Limited Series; 2001 Eisner Award to P. Craig Russell for Best Penciller/Inker of Penciller/Inker Team.

The Rhinegold and The Valkyrie comprise the first volume of Russell's adaptation of the Ring cycle by German composer Richard Wagner. Woton has exhausted himself and his godly resources to have a mighty fortress built with the labor of the giants, Fasolt and Fafnir. But in his bargaining with them, he has promised the fair Freia, keeper of the golden apple tree whose fruit gives power and immortality to the gods. The giants come to collect their pay, and only Log?, the trickster god, can find something to offer the giants in exchange: the Rhinegold. The only problem is, Woton doesn't have the Rhinegold yet.

Richard Wagner's The Ring of the Nibelung Volume Two. Adapted for comics by P. Craig Russell; translated by Patrick Mason; colored by Lovern Kindzierski; lettered by Galen Showman. Dark Horse Comics 2002 Un Illustration
Grades: 9 10 11 12 Adult 741.5; Fic
1. Fantasy graphic novels; 2. Norse mythology; 3. Opera; 4. Graphic novels
1-56971-734-6, $21.95
2001 Eisner Award for Best Limited Series; 2001 Eisner Award to P. Craig Russell for Best Penciller/Inker of Penciller/Inker Team.

This volume adapts Wagner's Siegfried and Gotterdammerung: The Twilight of the Gods. Siegfried is separated from his love, the Valkyrie Brunhilde, and even the All-Father himself cannot make things right. In the conclusion, all of creation hangs in the balance because of gods meddling in the affairs of man - all over the gold of the Rhinemaids.

Waid, Mark
Amazing Spider-Man: family business. By Mark Waid and James Robinson; illustrated by Gabriele Dell'Otto and Werther Dell'Edera. Marvel Enterprises 2014 112 p. Color; Illustration
Grades: 9 10 11 12 Adult 741.5
1. Spider-Man (Fictional character)
0785184406; 9780785184409, $24.99

In this graphic novel, by Mark Waid and James Robinson, "someone has Spider-Man in their crosshairs and the only person in the Marvel Universe who can save him is . . . Peter Parker's sister—! As the web-slinger meets family he never knew, will she end up becoming his greatest ally . . . or the one who damns him" And what does the KINGPIN have to do with it—" (Publisher's note)

"Waid's story is perfectly blended, with all the one-liners and gags that fans have come to expect as well as a level of mystery and intrigue that's a welcome addition. And with four villains vying for the death of Spider-Man (one literally dug up from the past), this original graphic novel is certainly not short on action." Booklist

★ **Daredevil**. Writer, Mark Waid; artists, Paolo Rivera, Marcos Martin. Marvel 2013 Color illustration (Daredevil (2011))

Grades: 10 11 12 Adult   **741.5**
1. Daredevil (Fictional character); 2. Spider-Man (Fictional character); 3. Superhero comic books, strips, etc
0785168060; 9780785168065, $34.99

"Matt Murdock is back in New York and hoping to resuscitate his law practice, but not everyone is happy to see him. And Daredevil hits the streets as Klaw, master of sound, makes his deadly return! Then, a blind client holds the key to a global conspiracy perpetrated by some familiar foes. Can Daredevil protect him long enough to bring down an international criminal organization? And when a piece of cutting-edge technology goes missing, Daredevil and Punisher team up to track it down and clear the Black Cat of the crime. But is Black Cat really innocent?! And after someone exhumes Battlin' Jack Murdock's grave, DD heads underground to find the villain responsible." (Publisher's note)

Collects Daredevil (2011) 1-10, 10.1; Amazing Spider-Man (1963) 677
Volume 1 of 2 (hardcover collection)

    Legion of Super-Heroes Vol. 1: Teenage Revolution. Mark Waid, writer ; Barry Kitson, penciller. DC Comics 2005 Un Illustration
Grades: 8 9 10 11 12 Adult   **741.5; Fic**
1. Science fiction graphic novels; 2. Superhero graphic novels; 3. Graphic novels
1-4012-0482-1, $14.99

Poverty, famine, war, and disease have been eliminated in the early days of the 31st century. The Dawning Millenium is utopian: shining, optimistic, hopeful ... and deadly dull. Dull, that is, until a team of bright, defiant, super-powered teenagers from different worlds assemble. The come together as activists and fierce dreamers, crusading to make a difference in a society that has forgotten how to change. Cosmic Boy, Lightning Lad, Saturn Girl, and the rest of the Legion of Super-Heroes fight for freedom and justice while learning from, and learning to tolerate, one another.

    Legion of Super-Heroes Vol. 2: Death of a Dream. Mark Waid, writer; Barry Kitson, penciller. DC Comics 2006 Un Illustration
Grades: 9 10 11 12 Adult   **741.5; Fic**
1. Legion of Super-Heroes (Fictional characters); 2. Superhero graphic novels; 3. Graphic novels
978-1-4012-0971-1, $14.99

A bright, defiant, energized team of super-powered teenagers from different worlds joins forces to form a legion of passionate activists that crusade to leave their mark on a complacent society that has forgotten how to fight for change. A hidden mastermind plans the downfall of the United Planets, and only the Legion has the combined knowledge and power needed to stop him. But a struggle for control of the team has split the Legion into two clashing factions. Can the members put aside their personal differences in time to stop the intergalactic menace?

    Supergirl and the Legion of Super-Heroes: Strange Visitor from Another Century. Mark Waid, writer; Barry Kitson [and others], pencillers; Mick Gray [and others], inkers. DC Comics 2006 144p. Illustration
Grades: 10 11 12 Adult   **741.5; Fic**

1. Mystery graphic novels; 2. Superhero graphic novels; 3. Graphic novels
978-1-4012-0916-2, $14.99

In the 31st century, the rebel teens of the Legion of Super-Heroes has ended the greatest threat to the peace and stability of the galaxy. The United Planets was to make the Legion an officially sanctioned peace-keeping force. Then, 21st-century hero Supergirl arrives in their time, with no memory of how she got there and no idea how to get back, so she applies for full-time Legionnaire membership. The story includes superhero action, and some violence in a locked-room mystery.

    Superman: Birthright. Mark Waid, writer; Leinil Francis Yu, penciller; Gerry Alanguilan, inker; Dave McCaig, colorist; Comicraft, letterer. DC Comics 2004 304p. Illustration
Grades: 9 10 11 12 Adult   **741.5; Fic**
1. Superhero graphic novels; 2. Superman (Fictional character); 3. Graphic novels
1-4012-0252-7, $19.99

                           LC 2005-284647

The whole world knows that Superman fights for truth and justice ... but why does he? What drives a farm boy from Kansas to divide his life between posing as a mild-mannered reporter and embarking on a career as a super hero? This book retells the origin of Superman, from his infancy through his first appearance as Superman, and why Lex Luthor is so obsessed with destroying him.

Walker, Landry Q.

The **super** scary monster show, featuring Little Gloomy. Written by Landry Walker; drawn by Eric Jones; tones by Rikki Simons. Amaze Ink/SLG Publishing 2008 Un Illustration
Grades: 3 4 5 6 7 8 9   **741.5; Fic**
1. Horror graphic novels; 2. Humorous graphic novels; 3. Graphic novels
978-1-59362-103-2, $9.95; 1-59362-103-5

This book collects the three issues (so far) of The Super Scary Monster Show comics. Little Gloomy, her friends, and her enemies, live in the world called Frightsylvania. Gloomy deals with an alien who crashlands in her backyard and wants to take over the world (she has plenty of "pet" monsters in her house who take care of her problem). Carl the squid lies to his parents about taking over the world and enslaving all its creatures, then they come for a visit. . . . Gloomy buys a golden scorpion as a gift for her friend the Mummy, but it turns out to be cursed, and everyone around her suffers accidents. The witch Evey has come up with a new spell to torment Gloomy, but it hits werewolf buddy Larry instead and shrinks him. There are plenty more stories, all written with tongue-in-cheek humor and just a touch of horror for younger readers. Gloomy does not suffer fools gladly, so the invading alien gets eaten (off page), and other inimical creatures suffer similar fates, so this book shouldn't be given to younger readers who are sensitive and don't like any violence. There is little in the way of any gore or overt violence, except for poor Frank, whose body parts often come apart.

Wallace, Daniel

★ The **DC** Comics encyclopedia: the definitive guide to the characters of the DC universe. Text by Scott Beatty . . . [et al.]; updated text by Dan Wallace. DK Pub. 2008 399p. Illustration

Grades: 9 10 11 12 Adult   **741.5**

978-0-7566-4119-1; 0-7566-4119-5, $40

                     LC 2008-300609

The authors "meticulously profile 1000 DC heroes and villains created since DC's 1935 founding. The entries are organized alphabetically, by character name, while introductory insets consistently detail first appearance, hero/villain status, physical statistics, and special powers. A genuinely essential DC character reference." Libr J

Walsh, David

Shugo chara!, v1-v6. Peach-Pit; translated by June Kato; adapted by David Walsh; lettered by North Market Street Graphics. Del Rey/Ballantine Books 2007 Illustration

Grades: 5 6 7 8 9   **741.5; Fic**

978-0-345-49745-1 (v1), $10.95

                     LC 2007296632

Volume 1 of 12

"Everybody at Seiyo Elementary thinks that stylish and super cool Amu has it all: But nobody knows the real Amu, a shy girl who wishes she had the courage to truly be herself. Changing Amu's life is going to take more than wishes and dreams—it's going to take a little magic! One morning, Amu finds a surprise in her bed: three strange little eggs. Each egg contains a Guardian Character, an angel-like being who can give her the power to be someone new." (Publisher's note)

Waltz, Tom

Children of the grave. Illustrated by Casey Maloney. IDW Publishing 2007 122p. Illustration

Grades: 11 12 Adult   **741.5; Fic**

1. Atrocities; 2. War; 3. Graphic novels

978-1-60010-166-3, $19.99

Team Orphan, a three-man Special Forces team, have orders to assassinate Colonel Akbar Assan, a terrorist who is on a mission to massacre all the children of his enemies. When the squad locates a mass grave site, the men get a weird feeling when they see all the graves are empty. And as they continue on their mission, each man is haunted by the dead in his own past, while Lt. Michael Drake also sees the dead children. The book includes graphic violence, copious use of harsh language, and a rape scene.

This book was published in 2006 in black and white.

Finding peace. Tom Waltz; [artist], Nathan St. John; design and letters by Neil Uyetake. IDW Publishing 2008 Un Illustration

Grades: 10 11 12 Adult   **741.5; Fic**

1. War; 2. Graphic novels

978-1-60010-218-9, $14.99

Set in an unnamed country that could be anywhere in the Middle East or Latin America or Eastern Europe, three stories in reverse chronological order tell the tale of an unending civil war that destroys too many lives. The first story shows just how dangerous a "peacekeeping" tour of duty can be, as a young soldier recalls a violent riot and the death of a fellow peacekeeper from a sniper's bullet. In the second story, a soldier watches his female sergeant during a raid as they hunker in a bunker and realizes that her momentary vulnerability both humanizes her and makes her a stronger soldier in his eyes. A young civilian girl narrates the third story, as she watches her country torn apart by civil war and brutal violence and is forced to make a final stand herself. St. John's sketchy illustrations depict the violence in such a way that readers won't feel brutalized by blood and gore yet will feel the impact and horror of war.

Wang, Sean

Runners, Book 1: Bad Goods. Serve Man Press 2005 168p. Illustration

Grades: 8 9 10 11 12

741.5; Fic

1. Adventure graphic novels; 2. Science fiction graphic novels; 3. Graphic novels

0-9768517-0-9, $14.95

Courtesy of Serve Man Press

Reluctant smuggler Roka Nostaco and the crew of his ship, the Khoruysa Brimia, were just trying to complete a job for the mob, but they find themselves fighting space pirates, bounty hunters, and just about everyone in Oniaka City Station. And it's all over some cargo they retrieved from another ship, the Tique Amara. Or is it because of the mysterious young woman they found unconscious in the Amara's cargo hold? Wang has taken a chance by making almost all of his characters nonhumanoid aliens. This story is everything Star Wars should have been.

Warren, Adam

Livewires Vol. 1: Clockwork Thugs, Yo. Story & layouts: Adam Warren; penciler: Rick Mays. Marvel Entertainment 2005 Un Illustration

Grades: 9 10 11 12 Adult   **741.5; Fic**

1. Robots; 2. Science fiction graphic novels; 3. Graphic novels

0-7851-1519-6, $7.99

Hollowpoint Ninja. Gothic Lolita. Cornfed. Stem Cell. Social Butterfly. They're nanobuilt human form combat mecha, with "smartware" bodies specialized for covert ops and Artificially Intelligent minds programmed for suicidal loyalty. They're the superhuman products of a top-secret, quasi-governmental R&D program with a unique agenda: namely, to seek out and destroy other top-secret, quasi-governmental R&D programs. And in the ultra-tech underbelly of a Marvel Universe infested with mad super-geniuses, homebrewed WMDs, and bootlegged alien technologies, they have a lot of work to do...

Watanabe, Taeko

Kaze Hikaru, Vol. 1. Viz Shojo Beat 2005 190p. Illustration

Grades: 10 11 12 Adult   **741.5; Fic**

1. Japan — History — 0-1868; 2. Manga; 3. Shojo manga;
4. Graphic novels
1-4125-0189-9, $9.99
"The talk of catamites and homosexual sex among the young men of the Mibu-Roshi and the almost perpetually drunken state of their older members make this title more suited to older teens." (VOYA)

In the waning years of the Tokugawa Shogunate, a band of young samurai called the Mibu-Roshi, gathers in Tokyo. They are loyal to the Shogun and will eventually become the Shinsengumi. Fifteen-year-old Seizaburo Kamiya, who has lost his father and brother to murderous supporters of the Emperor, joins the Mibu-Roshi, and young master swordsman Okita Soji befriends him. Soon, though, Soji learns Seizaburo's secret - he's actually a girl. He agrees to keep her secret and Sei becomes a mainstay in the group, but that doesn't end her danger.

Watanabe, Yoshitomo
Beyond the Beyond Volume 1. Tokyopop 2006 194p.
Illustration
Grades: 6 7 8 9 10 11 12   **741.5; Fic**
1. Adventure graphic novels; 2. Fantasy graphic novels; 3. Manga; 4. Graphic novels
1-59816-371-X, $9.99

Sixth-grader Futaba feels smothered by his older siblings' overprotective actions, so when Kiara literally falls from the sky and a mysterious, sinister warrior immediately comes to threaten her, Futaba decides to take action. Kiara then transports herself and Futaba to a magical realm, where she must find her master in order to join with him and become powerful; in the meantime, almost everyone hunts her, calling her the Amaranthine. The two encounter Lady Belbel, a powerful wizard who looks like a cute bunny, and a mysterious prince named Virid, who has a twin brother also named Virid.

Most of the time, the story feels like a children's fantasy, but every so often it's punctuated by violence that would bother younger readers. It combines shojo and shonen elements.

Watase, Yuu
Absolute Boyfriends Volume 1. Viz Media/Shojo Beat 2006 208p. Illustration
Grades: 10 11 12 Adult   **741.5; Fic**
1. Humorous graphic novels; 2. Romance graphic novels; 3. Shojo manga; 4. Graphic novels
978-1-4215-0016-4, $8.99

Shy high school student Riko Izawa aches for a boyfriend but guys just won't look her way. Then one day she signs up for a three-day trial of a mysterious "lover figurine," and the next thing she knows, a cute naked guy is delivered to her doorstep—and he wants to be her boyfriend. Has Riko died and gone to heaven? The cute naked guy (she names him Night) turns out to be smart, super nice, stylish and a gourmet chef. Plus, he looks like a million bucks ... Trouble is, that's about what he's going to cost Riko because she didn't return him in time. The book includes partial nudity, sexual innuendo, and some slightly strong language.

Ceres: Celestial Legend Vol. 1: Aya. Viz Media/Shojo 2003 208p. Illustration

Grades: 10 11 12 Adult   **741.5; Fic**
1. Horror graphic novels; 2. Manga; 3. Romance graphic novels; 4. Science fiction graphic novels; 5. Shojo manga; 6. Graphic novels
1-56931-980-4, $9.95

Aya and her twin brother Aki thought they were going to a celebration of their sixteenth birthday at their grandfather's home, but the funeral-like atmosphere tips them off that something's not right. Their "birthday present" turns out to be a mummified hand—the power of which forces an awakening within Aya, and painful wounds all over Aki's body. Grandfather Mikage announces that Aki will be heir to the Mikage fortune, and Aya must die. Aya has allies in the athletic cook and martial artist Yûhi, and the attractive, mysterious Tôya. But can even two handsome and resourceful guys save Aya when it's her own power that's out of control? The series includes nudity, sexual situations, strong language, and violence.

Fushigi Yugi Genbu Kaiden Volume 1. Viz Media/Shojo Beat 2005 200p. Illustration
Grades: 10 11 12 Adult   **741.5; Fic**
1. Adventure graphic novels; 2. Fantasy graphic novels; 3. Manga; 4. Shojo manga; 5. Graphic novels
1-59116-896-1, $8.99

When schoolgirl Takiko Okuda attempts to destroy her father's translation of "The Universe of the Four Gods," she is instead literally sucked into the story, becoming the Priestess of Genbu in an epic journey to find the seven Celestial Warriors. In her first encounter, she meets the mysterious Limdo, one of the Celestial Warriors who has a tattoo of the Chinese character for "woman" on his chest. As it turns out, it's there for a good reason: Limdo can not only summon the wind as one of his special powers, but also transform into a woman! Caught up in pursuit, because Limdo is regarded an outlaw, Takiko falls in with the bowman Chamka, who is hunting Limdo. Chamka regards Takiko an outlaw as well, but they eventually become traveling companions, for it seems Chamka is a one of the seven Celestial Warriors as well ... This prequel series to Fushigi Yugi is darker, more violent, and has more nudity than the original series.

★ **Fushigi** yugi: the mysterious play. By Yuu Watase. VIZ Media LLC 2009 573 p. Illustration; Color
Grades: 9 10 11 12   **741.5**
1. Books and reading — Fiction; 2. Fantasy fiction; 3. Quests (Expeditions); 4. Teenage girls; 5. Women heroes; 6. Graphic novels
142152290X; 9781421522906, $17.99
"Miaka Yuki is an ordinary junior-high student who is suddenly whisked away into the world of a book, The Universe Of The Four Gods. There she becomes the priestess of the god Suzaku, and is charged with finding all seven of her Celestial-Warrior protectors." (Publisher's note)
Volume 1 of 6 ; VIZBIG 3-in-1 edition

Watson, Andi
Clubbing. Written by Andi Watson ; illustrated by Josh Howard. DC Comics/Minx 2007 176p. Illustration
Grades: 7 8 9 10 11 12   **741.5**

1. Mystery graphic novels; 2. Teenagers; 3. Graphic novels
978-1-4012-0370-2, $9.99

Spoiled, rebellious Charlotte "Lottie" Brook lives in London, but her parents send her to Yorkshire to work at her grandparents' country club, and Lottie has to trade her trendy platform boots for Wellies to walk around the muck outside, and she has to learn all about golf clubs. But something's not quite right out there, and Lottie discovers the body of another employee. Along with Howard, the only other young person at the club, Lottie uncovers bizarre evidence and begins to suspect her own grandfather of murder. The book includes a short glossary of English slang.

Princess at midnight. Image Comics 2008 Un Illustration
Grades: 4 5 6 7 8 9 10   **741.5; Fic**
1. Fantasy graphic novels; 2. Princesses; 3. War; 4. Graphic novels
978-1-58240-928-3, $5.99; 1-58240-928-5

Holly Crescent and her twin brother Henry lead sheltered lives as home-schooled children by day; their parents don't want any harm to come to their children after they were born prematurely and their early lives were so worrisome. At night, however, Holly becomes Princess of Castle Waxing, where life is good until the Horrible Horde takes over one of her favorite picnic spots. All too soon, her nights are spent in warfare against the Horde, and her days in reading books on war strategy. And when she wins, she's not satisfied with winning, she must pursue more warfare against the Horde, even as her dragon Chancellor warns her of overspending and the consequences of war on her people.

Watsuki, Nobuhiro
Rurouni Kenshin: Meiji swordsman romantic story [Vol. 1]. Story and art by Nobuhiro Watsuki; [English adaptation, Gerard Jones; translation, Kenichiro Yagi; touch-up art & lettering, Steve Dutro].. Viz 2008 576p. Illustration
Grades: 10 11 12   **741.5; Fic**
1. Japan — History — 1868-1945; 2. Manga; 3. Graphic novels
978-1-4215-2073-5, $17.99

"The story of a young wandering samurai—who bears a reverse blade sword and strives not to kill after seeing and committing much bloodshed in the battles to bring the Emperor back to power in 1868—becomes much more than mere historical saga. Kenshin's relationships with new and old friends and enemies makes compelling storytelling." Voice Youth Advocates

This twenty-eight volume series was completed in late 2006

Way, Daniel
Wolverine: Origins & Endings. Writer, Daniel Way; artists, Javier Saltares and Mark Texeira. Marvel Entertainment 2006 Un Illustration
Grades: 11 12 Adult   **741.5; Fic**
1. Superhero graphic novels; 2. Wolverine (Fictional character); 3. Graphic novels
978-0-7851-1979-1, $13.99

Left shaken at ground zero after the cataclysmic events of House M, Logan has no choice but to soldier on, as he's done so many times before - but has the burden now become too great" In his lifetime, Logan has been both a hero and a villain, a player and a pawn... but what is he now" This book includes some bloody violence.

Wolverine: Origins Vol. 1. Born in Blood. Writer, Daniel Way; artist, Steve Dillon. Marvel Entertainment 2007 Un Illustration
Grades: 11 12 Adult   **741.5; Fic**
1. Superhero graphic novels; 2. Wolverine (Fictional character); 3. Graphic novels
978-0-7851-2287-6, $13.99

Armed with the one thing that could kill him, as well as key clues to his very existence, Logan embarks on the first leg of a long and bloody quest for vengeance against those who once enslaved him. No longer feeling the need to play it quiet, Logan's first strike elicits a Condition Critical response from the U.S. government. With no other choice, they drop their bomb - when Logan hits D.C., someone's going to be waiting for him. This book includes considerable violence.

Wolverine: Origins Vol. 2: Savior. Writer, Daniel Way; artist, Steve Dillon. Marvel Entertainment 2007 Un Illustration
Grades: 10 11 12 Adult   **741.5; Fic**
1. Superhero graphic novels; 2. Wolverine (Fictional character); 3. Graphic novels
978-0-7851-2286-9, $19.99

Completely shattered by recent revelations, Logan must now ask himself some hard - almost impossible - questions, such as whether he can continue on his quest...or if he even should. Though he now remembers who he was, the more pressing question becomes who - and what - is he now" Answering these questions will take the help of one of Logan's closest friends, and one of his deadliest enemies: Omega Red. The book includes some violence.

Weiner, Stephen
The **Will** Eisner companion: the pioneering spirit of the father of the graphic novel. [by] N.C. Christopher Couch and Stephen Weiner; introduction by Dennis O'Neil; afterword by Denis Kitchen. DC Comics 2004 174p. Illustration
Grades: 11 12 Adult   **741.5**
1. Comic books, strips, etc.; 2. Eisner, Will, 1917-2005
1-4012-0422-8; 1-4012-0423-6 (pa), $12.99

"This book is part mini-biography and part summary of the major works of the man who invented and reinvented the art of the graphic novel." SLJ

"Wherever Eisner's books—either the Spirit collections that DC Comics is lavishly republishing, or the graphic novels—have proven popular, their fans will value this authoritative supplement to them." Booklist

Includes bibliographical references

Weing, Drew
Set to sea. Fantagraphics 2010 Un Illustration
Grades: 8 9 10 11 12   **Fic; 741; 741.5**
978-1-60699-368-2, $16.99; 1-60699-368-2

"The unnamed hero is a poet who writes overblown verse about the wonders of sea life, while trying to pay his bar bill with promises of book dedications. That attitude quickly changes when he's shanghaied aboard a clipper bound for Hong Kong." Publ Wkly

The author "has produced a beautiful gem here, with minimal dialogue, one jolting battle scene, and each small page owned by a single panel filled with art whose figures have a comfortable roundness dredged up from the cartoon landscapes of our childhood unconscious, even as the intensely crosshatched shadings suggest the darkness that sometimes traces the edges of our lives. . . . [This book] is playful, atmospheric, dark, wistful, and wise." Booklist

Weinstein, Lauren

Girl stories. By Lauren R. Weinstein. Henry Holt 2006 237p. Illustration

Grades: 7 8 9 10 11 12 Adult   **741.5; Fic**
  1. Friendship; 2. Girls; 3. Humorous graphic novels; 4. Graphic novels
  978-0-8050-7863-3, $16.95; 0-8050-7863-0
                                        LC 2005-46205
  "Smart, creative Lauren sheds her geeky rep in high school in Weinstein's collection of comic strips, which have to intimacy of a teen's diary. The color-washed sketches have an edgy quality." Booklist

Weir, Christina

Amazing Agent Luna Volume 1. Nunzio Defilippis and Christina Weir ; artist, Shiei. Seven Seas Entertainment 2005 184p. Illustration

Grades: 8 9 10 11 12 Adult   **741.5; Fic**
  1. Adventure graphic novels; 2. Science fiction graphic novels
  193316400X; 9781933164007, $10.99
  This is the story of Luna, the perfect secret agent. A girl grown in a lab from the finest genetic material, she has been trained since her birth fifteen years ago to be the U.S. government's ultimate espionage weapon. But now she is given an assignment that will test her abilities to the utmost - high school. In order to uncover an evil plot, the government sends Luna to a prominent high school to pose as a student. But the one thing Luna has not been trained to handle is her own feelings. They are powerful and out of control, like your average teen, but without parents or the usual interaction with her peers to guide her. Putting her in high school is lighting the fuse on an emotional bomb of adolescent confusion, especially when she starts making friends, creating rivals, and having her first big crush on bad boy Jonah, the son of her arch-nemesis, Count Von Brucken.
  Volume 1 of 11

Maria's Wedding. Nunzio Defilippis and Christina Weir ; art by Jose Garibaldi. Oni Press 2003 88p. Illustration

Grades: 8 9 10 11 12 Adult   **741.5; Fic**
  1. Family; 2. Weddings; 3. Graphic novels
  1-929998-57-0, $10.95
  Few events exude as much joy, happiness, and hope as a wedding, and for the Pirellis these ceremonies mean even more. Pirelli weddings are about tradition and family as much as they're about the happy couple, or at least they used to be. When Joseph Pirelli married Matthew it rocked the clan to its knees. Now a year later, the tension and downright animosity between different factions of the family have

turned Maria's special day into a powder keg. And poor Frankie, Joseph's outspoken brother, is holding the match. But while some fear the fuse being lit, others in the family are ready for and secretly looking forward to the blow-up. Frankie, on the other hand, thinks his reputation for speaking his mind is undeserved. He just wants to see his favorite cousin get married and maybe rekindle his childhood romance with Maria's maid of honor, Brenna. Can Frankie balance the Pirellis expectations of him with his own or will the scales tip and bring the whole ceremony crashing down?

The **Tomb**. Written by Nunzio DeFilippis & Christina Weir; illustrated by Christopher Mitten; design by Keith Wood; cover by Christopher Mitten & Guy Major. Oni Press 2004 144p. Illustration

Grades: 9 10 11 12 Adult   **741.5; Fic**
  1. Adventure graphic novels; 2. Horror graphic novels; 3. Graphic novels
  1-929998-95-3, $14.95
  In 1922, Lord Earl Carnarvon financed the Egyptian expedition that unearthed King Tut's tomb. While the fact that the dig gained a reputation for being "cursed" is well known, Mathias Fowler slipped away into anonymity. Fowler, an American on the team, had grown obsessed with the Ancient Egyptians and when he returned to the States it was with several stolen artifacts in tow. Fowler had become so consumed by the era that when he died, he killed all of his household staff and had them buried in his mansion with him - a modern day Pharaoh's Tomb. Almost 60 years after Fowler's death, Jessica Parrish, archeologist and would-be Indiana Jones, has been hired to assemble and lead a team into the house to take back the missing pieces and disable the booby traps that have already cost one unfortunate group their lives. Can Parrish and her comrades navigate the elaborate deathtraps with their persons intact or will the curse of Tut's tomb just add to its mounting body count" Strong language and violence pepper this horror story.

Weissman, Steven

The **Kid** Firechief. Fantagraphics Books 2004 96p. Illustration

Grades: 4 5 6 7 8 9   **741.5; Fic**
  1. Adventure graphic novels; 2. Fire fighters; 3. Graphic novels
  1-56097-596-2, $12.95
  Even though he's just a poor orphaned boy, it's a well-known fact that there's no greater firefighter than Olaf Oedwards, a.k.a. "Kid Firechief." Olaf and his assistant chief (and guardian) Smoky Joe put out fires all over the city and forests of Milltown and as far as... Ancient Rome" This adventure romp features characters including the infant rappers D.J. Diaper and M.C. Nu-Born ("This li'l piggy kept it real/while this li'l piggy was chillin'/This li'l piggy said 'Talk to the hand'/while this li'l piggy was illin'"), local school reporter "Nosy" Rosie Cheeks, Olaf's arch-nemesis Hotfoot, and Olaf's forest ranger cousin, Oella Oedwards. The book uses orange ink on light yellow paper.

White flower day. Fantagraphics 2002 112p. Illustration

Grades: 5 6 7 8 9 10 11 12 Adult   **741.5; Fic**
  1. Humorous graphic novels
  1-56097-514-8, $14.95

This book will appeal to older children who enjoy such things as "The Grim Adventures of Billy and Mandy" on Cartoon Network, with its somewhat gross and twisted humor.

"Scratch panels highlighted in ocher cast {a} jaundiced pall over three . . . twisted tales of rascaldom. They feature the Frankenstein-like Pullapart Boy, devilish L'il Bloody, and several equally weird young characters who venture forth to create mayhem, from innocent to morbid." Booklist

Another 'Yikes' book

Wells, H. G.

Classics illustrated #12: The Island of Dr. Moreau. Adapted by Steven Grant ; Illustrated by Eric Vincent. Papercutz 2011 Un Illustration

Grades: 7 8 9 10 11 12 Adult   **741.5; Fic**
  1. Authors; 2. Historians; 3. Horror graphic novels; 4. Novelists; 5. Science fiction writers; 6. Wells, H G (Herbert George), 1866-1946; 7. Wells, H G (Herbert George), 1866-1946 — Adaptations; 8. Writers on politics; 9. Writers on science; 10. Graphic novels
  978-1-59707-235-9, $9.99

Edward Prendick is the sole survivor of a shipwreck when a passing ship picks him up. It carries a strange cargo of animals, a doctor, who takes care of Prendick, and an odd man who looks more like an ape. Montgomery, the doctor, is taking the animals to a small island he won't name, and Prendick ends up with them when the drunken ship's captain casts him off. On that island, Prendick discovers half-human, half-beast creatures, all created by the arrogant Dr. Moreau. This book adapts Wells' classic story; it was originally published in 1990 as part of the Classics Illustrated line published by First Comics. This edition includes an interview with Steven Grant, who wrote the adaptation.

The **Invisible** Man. Retold by Terry Davis ; illustrated by Dennis Calero. Stone Arch Books 2007 72p. Illustration

Grades: 3 4 5 6 7 8 9   **741.5; Fic**
  1. Mystery graphic novels; 2. Science fiction graphic novels; 3. Graphic novels
  978-1-59889-831-6, $23.93

                    LC 2007-6200

Late one night, a mysterious man, covered from head to toe in bandages, wanders into a tiny English village. After a series of burglaries, the villagers grow suspicious. Who is this man" Where did he come from" When they attempt to arrest the stranger, he suddenly reveals his secret: he is invisible. How can anyone stop the Invisible Man" The book is written with an easy vocabulary for struggling and reluctant readers, and it includes facts about invisibility.

Part of the Graphic Revolve series.

The **Time** Machine. retold by Terry Davis ; illustrated by José Alfonso Ocampo Ruiz. Stone Arch Books 2007 72p. Illustration

Grades: 3 4 5 6 7 8 9   **741.5; Fic**
  1. Adventure graphic novels; 2. Science fiction graphic novels; 3. Graphic novels
  978-1-59889-833-0, $23.93

                    LC 2007-6201

A scientist invents a machine that he claims will travel through time, but his friends laugh at the idea. So the Time Traveler climbs aboard his machine and ends up thousands of years in the future. He meets a race of gentle humans called the Eloi, but he is soon swept up in a fight for his life against evil underground creatures known as Morlocks. Even worse, his Time Machine, his only chance to escape, is trapped deep inside the Morlock caverns. This book is written with an easy vocabulary for struggling and reluctant readers, and it includes some scientific speculations about the future.

Part of the Graphic Revolve series

The **war** of the worlds. By H.G. Wells; retold by Davis Miller and Katherine M. Brevard; illustrated by Jose Alfonso Ocampo Ruiz. Stone Arch Books 2009 72p. Illustration

Grades: 4 5 6 7 8 9 10   **741.5; Fic**
  1. Science fiction graphic novels; 2. Graphic novels
  978-1-4342-0757-9, $23.93

                    LC 2008-6250

In 1894, a strange meteorite crashes down near London, England. When George and other residents of Woking investigate the site, they discover a large alien cylinder. Suddenly, it's activated and begins destroying everything in its path. And George finds out there are more of the things elsewhere in the country. The people eventually learn that England has been invaded by Martians, and they are definitely not friendly. This graphic novel adaptation includes information about the Halloween 1938 radio hoax in which this story was dramatized in such a way that people in the U.S. thought they were in fact being invaded by deadly aliens.

Part of the Graphic Revolve series

Wells, Zeb

Civil War: Young Avengers & Runaways. Writer, Zeb Wells ; artist, Stefano Caseli ; color art, Daniele Rundoni ; letterer, Virtual Calligraphy's Cory Petit. Marvel Entertainment 2007 Un Illustration

Grades: 8 9 10 11 12 Adult   **741.5; Fic**
  1. Runaways (Fictional characters); 2. Superhero graphic novels; 3. Graphic novels
  0-7851-2317-2, $11.99

As the Civil War goes on between the two super hero camps, and the public turns against their heroes, and the teen Runaways get caught up in the struggle despite their best efforts to stay out of the fight. When the Young Avengers offer their assistance, how can the Runaways believe they're on the same side?

Fantastic Four/Iron Man: Big in Japan. Writer, Zeb Wells; artist, Steve Fisher. Marvel Entertainment 2006 Un Illustration

Grades: 9 10 11 12 Adult   **741.5; Fic**
  1. Fantastic Four (Fictional characters); 2. Humorous graphic novels; 3. Iron Man (Fictional character); 4. Superhero graphic novels; 5. Graphic novels
  0-7851-1776-8, $12.99

The Fantastic Four, the world's first super-hero big-monster battling squad, and playboy industrialist Tony Stark have descended on the Land of the Rising Sun to dedicate the opening of the Kaiju Museum and Celebration. It's an all-out romp with big monsters a-go-go as Droom, Giganto and Eerok, the giant ape - along with hundreds of manic '50s Marvel monsters - return to trample all over Tokyo and a Japanese worshipper of the kaiju (that means giant monster, by the way) warps reality.

Marvel Adventures Spider-Man Vol. 4: Concrete Jungle. Pencilled by Patrick Scherberger. Marvel Entertainment 2006 Un Illustration
Grades: 3 4 5 6 7 8 9   **741.5; Fic**
1. Spider-Man (Fictional character); 2. Superhero graphic novels; 3. Graphic novels
978-0-7851-2005-6, $6.99
Spider-Man stars in four stories featuring the Mad Thinker, the Chameleon, the Black Cat, and Doctor Octopus.

Shekhar Kapur's Snake Woman Vol. 1: A Snake in the Grass. Created by Shekhar Kapur; script, Zeb Wells; art, Michael Gaydos. Virgin Comics 2007 Un Illustration
Grades: 10 11 12 Adult   **741.5; Fic**
1. Fantasy graphic novels; 2. Horror graphic novels; 3. Graphic novels
978-1-934413-01-2, $14.99
Jessica Peterson is learning first-hand that the cycle of revenge cannot be broken. Without understanding why, she finds herself turning into a creature - a vicious Snakewoman. Her mission - to avenge a centuries old wrong that was conceived half a world away, deep in the jungles of India. Terrified by her true nature and hunted by a mysterious organization known only as "The 68," Jessica must confront the monster that lurks inside her before it is too late. The book includes strong language, violence, and sexual situations.

Welvaert, Scott R.
Helen Keller: Courageous Advocate. By Scott R. Welvaert ; illustrated by Cynthia Martin and Keith Tucker. Capstone Press 2006 32p. Illustration
Grades: 3 4 5 6 7 8 9   **741.5; 362.4; 92**
1. Biographical graphic novels; 2. Keller, Helen, 1880-1968; 3. Graphic novels
0-7368-4964-5, $25.26
                                           LC 2005006463
This book uses the comic book format to recount highlights of the life of Helen Keller, a blind and deaf woman who became an author and advocate for the blind and other physically handicapped people. It includes additional information, a glossary, a list of books for further reading, and more.
Part of the Graphic Library, Graphic Biographies series.

Wenzel, David
The **wizard's** tale. [by] Kurt Busiek and David Wenzel. DC Comics 1998 141p. Illustration
Grades: 6 7 8 9   **741.5; Fic**
1. Graphic novels
1-56389-589-7, $19.95
Bafflerog Rumplewhisker is the most pitiful excuse for an evil wizard that ever lived, for all his evil spells end up doing good. When Lord Grimthorne, head of the Darksome Council, orders him to find the Book of Worse, the reluctant Bafflerog heads out with the toad, Gumpwort, to find it. Author Busiek and artist Wenzel have crafted a tale that

honors the marks of high fantasy even while having fun with it.

Werry, John
Millennium Snow Vol. 1. Viz Media/Shojo Beat 2007 200p. Illustration
Grades: 8 9 10 11 12   **741.5; Fic**
1. Manga; 2. Romance graphic novels; 3. Shojo manga; 4. Vampires; 5. Graphic novels
978-1-4215-1202-0, $8.99
17-year-old Chiyuki Matsuoka was born with heart problems, and her doctors say she won't live to see the next snow. Toya is an 18-year-old vampire who hates blood and refuses to make the traditional partnership with a human, whose life-giving blood would keep them both alive for a thousand years. Can Chiyuki teach Toya to feel a passion for life, even as her own is ending" The book has some mildly strong language, and romance without graphic depictions of vampiric action.
Volume 1 of 4

West, David
Astronauts. Illustrated by Jim Robbins. Rosen Publishing Group 2008 48p. Illustration
Grades: 3 4 5 6 7 8 9   **629.45; 741.5**
1. Astronautics — Vocational guidance; 2. Astronauts; 3. Graphic novels
978-1-4042-1461-3, $29.25
                                           LC 2007-45208
After brief descriptions of living and working conditions in space and the training one undergoes to become an astronaut, the book profiles three astronauts. Yuri Alexeyevich Gagarin was the first person to go into space; he was a Russian cosmonaut. Dr. Jerry Linenger lived and worked on the Russian space station Mir in 1997, when a fire broke out in the space station. And Thomas D. Jones flew on the space shuttle Atlantis, on its 2000 mission, STS-98.
Part of the Graphic Careers series

Fighter pilots. Illustrated by James Field. Rosen Publishing Group 2008 48p. Illustration
Grades: 3 4 5 6 7 8 9   **358.4; 741.5**
1. Air pilots; 2. Military aeronautics; 3. Graphic novels
978-1-4042-1455-2, $29.25
                                           LC 2007-41458
After brief descriptions of the rise of fighters in air combat and of the evolution of jet fighters, this book profiles three pilots. Lieutenant Edwin C. Parsons flew with the Escadrille Lafayette during World War I. Pilot Office Geoffrey Wellum piloted a Royal Air Force Spitfire during the Battle of Britain in 1940. Lieutenant Randall H. Cunningham was a Navy fighter pilot who became the first fighter ace (he shot down at least five enemy aircraft) of the Vietnam War. This is the same man who, in 2005, pleaded guilty of graft for taking bribes while serving in the U.S. Congress. His later crimes do not take away from his fighter pilot accomplishments.
Part of the Graphic Careers series

Race car drivers. Illustrated by Peter Wilks and Geoff Ball. Rosen Publishing Group 2008 48p. Illustration
Grades: 3 4 5 6 7 8 9   **796.72; 741.5**
1. Automobile racing; 2. Graphic novels

978-1-4042-1452-1, $29.25

LC 2007-45174

After brief descriptions of early car racing and of the different types of car racing (NASCAR, Formula One, etc.), the book profiles three racers. Argentinian driver Juan Manuel Fangio is considered one of the best Formula One race car drivers, and he recalls the 1957 race at the Nurburgring in Germany. Dale Earnhardt, Sr. was one of the best-known NASCAR racers in the U.S. In 1996, he crashed during the Diehard 500; despite his injuries (a broken collarbone and sternum), he drove in Indianapolis, although he had to stop before finishing. The next week, he raced in Watkins Glen, New York, and finished in sixth place. He died in 2001, in a crash at the Daytona 500. The third driver profiled in this book is Formula One rookie Lewis Hamilton, who started at age seven with remote-controlled car races and spent his teen years winning Kart races in Great Britain (Karts are small racecars). He became a Formula One race driver in 2006.

Part of the Graphic Careers series

Westerfeld, Scott

Uglies: Shay's story. Created by Scott Westerfeld; written by Scott Westerfeld and Devin Grayson; illustrations by Steven Cummings. Del Rey 2012 160 p. Illustration
Grades: 7 8 9 10   **741.5**
1. Beauty, Personal — Fiction; 2. Conformity; 3. Dystopian graphic novels; 4. Friendship — Fiction; 5. Plastic surgery; 6. Science fiction
9780606264754, $22.10; 0345527224; 9780345527226, $10.99

LC 2012374898

This young adult graphic novel retells the story of author Scott Westerfeld's dystopia "Uglies" from "the point of view of recurring frenemy Shay." It is "set in a . . . future time when discord is suppressed through ruthlessly enforced conformity and obligatory plastic surgery at age 16. . . . Shay yearns for freedom. An encounter with the flawed and alluring David, a covert envoy from the Smoke, a secret community of nonconformists, may offer Shay the escape she craves." (Publishers Weekly)

Followed by:Uglies: Cutters (2012)

Whedon, Joss

★ **Astonishing** X-Men Vol. 1: Gifted. writer, Joss Whedon; artist, John Cassaday; colorist, Laura Martin; letterer, Chris Eliopoulos. Marvel Entertainment 2004 Un Illustration
Grades: 9 10 11 12 Adult   **741.5; Fic**
1. Superhero graphic novels; 2. X-Men (Fictional characters); 3. Graphic novels
978-0-7851-1531-1, $14.99
Eisner Award: Best Continuing Series (2006)
Eisner Award: Best Penciller/Inker (2005)

Cyclops and Emma Frost re-form the X-Men with the express purpose of "astonishing" the world. But when breaking news regarding the mutant gene unexpectedly hits the airwaves, will it derail their new plans before they even get started. As demand for the mutant cure reaches near-riot levels, the X-Men go head-to-head with the enigmatic Ord, with an unexpected ally - and some unexpected adversaries - tipping the scales.

Other Astonishing X-Men volumes by Whedon and Cassaday are: 2: Dangerous; 3: Torn; 4: Unstoppable

Buffy the Vampire Slayer season eight, volume 1: the long way home. Writer, Joss Whedon ; artists, Georges Jeanty, Andy Owens, Jo Chen. Dark Horse Comics 2007 136p. Illustration
Grades: 9 10 11 12 Adult   **741.5; Fic**
1. Adventure graphic novels; 2. Horror graphic novels; 3. Vampires; 4. Graphic novels
978-1-59307-784-6, $24.95

This first omnibus volume begins at the beginning - The Origin, a faithful adaptation of creator Joss Whedon's original screenplay for the film that started it all. The newly-chosen slayer's road to Sunnydale continues in Viva Las Buffy and Slayer, Interrupted. Next, high school, the Scoobies and an English librarian lead the way into Season One continuity. Plus, The Goon creator Eric Powell provides pencils to "All's Fair," featuring Spike and Drusilla at the 1933 World's Fair. This omnibus project will publish the Buffy graphic novels in chronological order. There are scenes of violence in fighting vampires and other monsters.

Buffy the Vampire Slayer season eight, volume 1: the long way home. Dark Horse Comics 2007 136p. Illustration
Grades: 8 9 10 11 12 Adult   **741.5**
1. Adventure graphic novels; 2. Buffy the Vampire Slayer (Fictional character); 3. Horror graphic novels; 4. Graphic novels
978-1-59307-822-5, $15.95

The television series of Buffy the Vampire Slayer lasted seven seasons; this volume begins the comics-only eighth season. Buffy and her friends may have destroyed the Hellmouth, but all is not fun and games, as an old enemy returns, younger sister Dawn experiences some "growing pains," and a former decoy Slayer has her own troubles. There is a considerable amount of monster fighting.

Fray. Created and written by Joss Whedon; penciller, Karl Moline; inker, Andy Owens; colorists, Dave Stewart, Michelle Madsen; letterer, Michelle Madsen. Dark Horse Comics 2003 Un Illustration
Grades: 9 10 11 12 Adult   **741.5; Fic**
1. Adventure graphic novels; 2. Monsters; 3. Graphic novels
1-56971-751-6, $19.95

Hundreds of years in the future, Manhattan has become a deadly slum, run by mutant crime-lords and disinterested cops. Stuck in the middle is a young girl who thought she had no future, but learns she has a great destiny. In a world so poisoned that it doesn't notice the monsters on its streets, how can a street kid like Fray unite a fallen city against a demonic plot to consume mankind" Creator Whedon set this story in the future of Buffy the Vampire Slayer's world, with Fray a new slayer, aided by a demonic Watcher. The story has some violence and mild harsh language.

Runaways: dead end kids. Writer, Joss Whedon ; artist, Michael Ryan. Marvel Entertainment 2008 Un Illustration
Grades: 7 8 9 10 11 12 Adult   **741.5; Fic**
1. Adventure graphic novels; 2. Runaways (Fictional characters); 3. Superhero graphic novels; 4. Graphic novels
978-0-7851-2853-3, $19.99

When the team's Los Angeles hideout is compromised, they flee to New York, where they become mixed up with Kingpin, and he pressures them to pull a "minor" heist. When the Punisher shows up, with more killers behind him, the Runaways make a desperate escape and find themselves a hundred years in the past. They find that there are other "specials" in that time, too, and more danger, even as they try to find a way back home.

Wheeler, Shannon
    Screw Heaven, When I Die I'm Going to Mars. Dark Horse Comics 2007 144p. Illustration
Grades: 9 10 11 12 Adult   **741.5; Fic**
    1. Humorous graphic novels; 2. Graphic novels
    978-1-59307-820-1, $12.95
    This new collection of Wheeler's comic strips blends the coffee-fueled cynicism of "Too Much Coffee Man" with the slightly more tender take on humor found in "How to Be Happy" and "Postage Stamp Funnies." He takes aim at lots of things that deserve to be made fun of, from the insipidity of coffee culture to the sad state of the American political system to the horrendous reality of dating. And all this without a single bad word (except what's in the title) or bit of violence.

    Too Much Coffee Man: How to Be Happy. Dark Horse Books 2005 144p. Illustration
Grades: 10 11 12 Adult   **741.5; Fic**
    1. Humorous graphic novels; 2. Graphic novels
    1-59307-353-4, $12.95
    Too Much Coffee Man has been percolating in the comics underground for years now, and like everything else that was once "alternative," he's sold out, been used by the man (as an advertising tool for Hewlitt Packard and Converse, among others), and is now middle-aged, depressed, broke, and cynical. Who better to write a book, then, called How to be Happy" Political humor, some strong language, and some violence appear in the short comic strips collected here.

White, Shane
    North Country. NBM/ComicsLit 2005 94p. Illustration
Grades: 10 11 12 Adult   **741.5; Fic**
    1. Autobiographical graphic novels; 2. Graphic novels
    978-1-56163-435-4, $13.95
    Sometimes, you have to escape your past to get to the truth. After years of being away from the northern New York town where he grew up and making a life for himself, Shane finally travels back home. On his way, his mind is flooded with the memories of his blue-collar family under tremendous pressure and pushed to the breaking point by alcoholism and abuse. For a kid growing up in this, the pain can be tremendous. As an adult, resentment battles reconciliation. There's some harsh language, but the scenes of physical abuse, while never truly graphically portrayed, could be disturbing.

White, Steve
    The **Battle** of Midway: the destruction of the Japanese fleet. Illustrated by Richard Elson.The Rosen Publishing Group 2007 48p. Illustration
Grades: 3 4 5 6 7 8 9   **741.5; 940.54**

1. Midway, Battle of, 1942; 2. War; 3. World War, 1939-1945; 4. Graphic novels
978-1-4042-0783-7, $29.25

Courtesy of Rosen Publishing

    One of the most important naval battles in history, Midway marked a crucial turning point in the war in the Pacific. With a fleet that had dominated this theater since the attack on Pearl Harbor, the Japanese anticipated certain victory against the US forces, but the attack was not a surprise. The US Navy sank four irreplaceable aircraft carriers, and cleared the way for the island-hopping US counterattack. This book also includes eight pages of authoritative information, placing the battle in its historical context, describing the key players, and its build-up and aftermath.
    Part of the Graphic Battles of World War II series. This book is also available in a paperback edition from Osprey Publishing, under the title The Empire Falls: Battle of Midway.

    Pearl Harbor: A Day of Infamy. Illustrated by Jerrold Spahm. The Rosen Publishing Group 2007 48p. Illustration
Grades: 3 4 5 6 7 8 9   **741.5; 940.54**
    1. Pearl Harbor (Oahu, Hawaii), Attack on, 1941; 2. War; 3. World War, 1939-1945; 4. Graphic novels
    978-1-4042-0785-1, $29.25
    On December 7, 1941, the Japanese Navy launched a surprise attack on American military bases in Pearl Harbor, Hawaii. Masterfully planned and executed, the attack devastated the US Pacific Fleet; in less than two hours, Japanese aircraft had sunk or damaged all eight US battleships anchored in the harbor and had destroyed 151 planes. Thrust into battle, the United States could have only one response: war. This book portrays the attack that drove the United States into World War II in full-color comic book narrative. Featuring the personal stories of front-line heroes like Ken Taylor, George Welch, and mess attendant Dorie Miller, it also provides background material - causes and consequences, key players, and a glossary of terms - as well as a list of additional resources.
    Part of the Graphic Battles of World War II series. This book is also available in a paperback edition from Osprey Publishing, under the title Day of Infamy: Attack on Pearl Harbor.

Whitta, Gary
    Death Jr. Vol. 1. Gary Whitta & Ted Naifeh. Image Comics 2005 Un Illustration
Grades: 8 9 10 11 12 Adult   **741.5; Fic**
    1. Adventure graphic novels; 2. Fantasy graphic novels; 3. Horror graphic novels; 4. Graphic novels
    1-58240-526-3, $14.99
    When a school field trip to the local museum coincides with coming-of-age angst and an overly inquisitive friend (a cute goth girl named Pandora), Junior releases an ancient evil into the world... and it's up to him to fix it. He's helped

by his friends Stigmartha, whose hands bleed when she gets nervous; Smith & Weston, two twins conjoined at the head and The Seep, a foul-mouthed, armless, legless fetus in a tube. He's your average, everyday, happy-go-lucky middle-school student... who just happens to be the son of the grim reaper.

Death Jr. Vol. 2. Gary Whitta & Ted Naifeh. Image Comics 2007 Un Illustration
Grades: 7 8 9 10 11 12   **741.5; Fic**
1. Horror graphic novels; 2. Humorous graphic novels; 3. Graphic novels
978-1-58240-682-4, $14.99
Death Jr. returns with all of his friends in a new adventure that finds him filling a summer internship with his father at Terminal Industries, while the rest of the gang heads off to summer camp. Can they manage to survive the summer unscathed? And what is DJ going to do when he causes his father, the Grim Reaper, to be fired and his mom has to get a job?

My dead girlfriend, Vol. 1. Tokyopop 2007 Un Illustration
Grades: 8 9 10 11 12 Adult   **741.5; Fic**
1. High school students; 2. Romance graphic novels; 3. School stories; 4. Supernatural graphic novels; 5. Graphic novels
978-1-59816-996-6, $9.99
As a perfectly normal boy, Finney Bleak stands out among the monsters and ghosts of his town and in school, Mephisto Prep. He's the youngest in a family known for the many weird and wacky ways everyone has died. In school, Finney must deal with bullies such as Karl the Frankenstein-type monster, teen vampire Drake, and others. He had one memorable night at the carnival with the perfect girl, Jenny, months ago, but she never made it to the meeting they had arranged for the next day. Now, as he's chased in the woods by Karl and company, somebody comes to his aid—it's Jenny, who's now a ghost. So, nobody's ever perfect, right? This is another global manga title, the first of a projected series.

The Wicked West II: Abomination & Other Tales.
Image Comics 2006 192p. Illustration
Grades: 10 11 12 Adult   **741.5; Fic**
1. Horror graphic novels; 2. Supernatural graphic novels; 3. Graphic novels
978-1-58240-661-8, $15.99
Cotton Coleridge is a cowboy who lives in an Old West out of a horror show nightmare. The "lightning rod for the supernatural" faces zombies, ghosts, resurrectionists, giant flies, carnivorous slugs, demons and lots of pure evil in this collection of 22 short stories by lots of different creators, including Todd Livingston, Robert Tinnell, Neil Vokes, Mike Baron, Chris Moreno, Michael Avon Oeming, Mark Ricketts, Filip Sablik, and many others. There's some harsh language and lots of fighting and monster killing. Wight, Eric

Wight, Joseph
Twilight X: Storm Vol. 1. Antarctic Press 2004 Un Illustration
Grades: 10 11 12   **741.5; Fic**

1. Adventure graphic novels; 2. Science fiction graphic novels; 3. War; 4. Graphic novels
1-932453-63-6, $9.99
The final battle of World War Three begins with a clash of armies that must win or die forever. Old America unleashes a Navy task force against the hordes of a brutal fascist army controlling Central America and the Caribbean. But a mysterious force known only as Elysium, commanding technology in the heavens, has chosen this moment to end the war once and for all. Caught between them all, Jed Saxon, a soldier of Old America, faces not just his own destruction but the loss of his only friends. Earth itself has released its fury in the form of a massive hurricane, capable of sweeping everyone and everything into oblivion. The book includes battlefield violence, brief sexual situations, and harsh language (including the s-bomb). This is a global manga title.

Williams, Aaron
PS 238, volume VI: senseless acts of tourism!. Do Gooder Press 2008 Un Illustration
Grades: 3 4 5 6 7 8 9 10 11 12 Adult   **741.5; Fic**
1. Humorous graphic novels; 2. Superhero graphic novels; 3. Graphic novels
978-1-933288-49-9, $15.99
After the town had been pretty much leveled by invading aliens and repair work begins, Miss Kyle takes a vacation to Las Vegas. However, Zodon has convinced Poly and Julie that Miss Kyle is leaving for good, so they hitch a ride on the plane. They don't know that others are following and trying to kidnap Zodon. Meanwhile, Flea has hitched a ride on the bad guys' jet. Once they all get to Las Vegas, they end up helping the Masquerade Casino catch the person who has been cheating and winning too much in the casino. Meanwhile, back at PS 238, Tyler is stuck in a stasis pod because he was infected with an alien virus that could destroy the world; then Tom comes and takes Tyler, or at least a part of his soul, to make a crucial decision about whether humanity should continue to gain super powers. And then Cecil, who still sees aliens everywhere, goes with mysterious millionaire Kent Allard to scout out possible aliens. There's lots of superhero action going on, all of it at kid-friendly level.

PS 238: To the Cafeteria . . . For Justice!. Henchman Publishing/Dork Storm Press 2005 Un Illustration
Grades: 4 5 6 7 8 9 10 11 12 Adult   **741.5; Fic**
1. Elementary schools; 2. Humorous graphic novels; 3. Superhero graphic novels; 4. Graphic novels
1-933288-13-2, $15.99
PS 238 is the only public school for metahuman children, where the students learn how to use their powers, socialize with normal as well as super-powered classmates, and have fun adventures. In this second volume, the students learn about the importance of primary sources for history research (time traveling Tom brings a girl to the present to give them straight information about her father). Also, Tyler, son of two superheroes who hasn't yet come into his powers, spends some time training with the vigilante hero, Revenant. And in shop class, the students make some super accessories. The first volume is not available, but readers

can pick up on things from this volume. This is a continuing series.

PS238 Vol. III: No Child Left Behind!. Dork Storm Press/Henchman Publishing 2006 Un Illustration
Grades: 5 6 7 8 9 10 11 12 Adult   **741.5; Fic**
1. Adventure graphic novels; 2. Humorous graphic novels; 3. Superhero graphic novels; 4. Graphic novels
1-933288-24-8, $15.99

In this third volume, readers meet Malphast, the child of divine and not-so-divine parents, who involves almost everyone in a cosmic game of four-square. Then Tom Davidson discovers an unusual castle floating outside of time and space. And Harold Nelson, after whom PS238's "Rainmaker Program" was named, has decided that a sizeable number of students need to be "rescued" from the school. Tyler works with the Revenant to save his friends from Nelson.

Williams, Rob
Star Wars: Rebellion Volume 1: My Brother, My Enemy. Script, Rob Williams ; "Crossroads" script, Thomas Andrews ; art, Brandon Badeaux and Michel Lacombe ; colors, Wil Glass ; lettering, Michael Heisler. Dark Horse Comics 2007 Un Illustration
Grades: 8 9 10 11 12 Adult   **741.5; Fic**
1. Adventure graphic novels; 2. Science fiction graphic novels; 3. Graphic novels
9781593077112, $14.95; 1593077114

Having rescued Rebel strategist Jorin Sol from the Empire, Luke Skywalker now leads X-Wing attack runs on Imperial convoys to rustle up much needed supplies for the Rebel fleet. Little does he know that within Sol lies a secret that will put the entire Alliance in danger. What's worse, when Luke receives a coded message from Lt. Sunber, who wants to defect to the Rebel Alliance, he must decide whether to trust his old friend or obey the orders of Princess Leia who believes Tank may be part of an Imperial plot to capture the Rebellion's greatest hero.

Willingham, Bill
Day of Vengeance: Countdown to Infinite Crisis. Written by Bill Willingham and Judd Winick; pencilled by Ian Churchill, Justiano, Ron Wagner. DC Comics 2005 Un Illustration
Grades: 9 10 11 12 Adult   **741.5; Fic**
1. Adventure graphic novels; 2. Superhero graphic novels; 3. Superman (Fictional character); 4. Graphic novels
1-4012-0840-1, $12.99

Eclipso, the original spirit of vengeance, needs a new human host. The Spectre, the current spirit of vengeance, has just lost its human host and is vulnerable. When Eclipso seeks a new body, it first tries to control Superman; it takes Captain Marvel, the World's Mightiest Marvel, to stop him. Inhabiting the body of a familiar, tortured soul, Eclipso sets its sights on seducing the Spectre and destroying Earth's practitioners of magic. Seven heroes stand in their way. All very different. All with different goals at stake. And then they find an eighth, a girl who might be the most powerful teenager in the universe. Can this group, who call themselves Shadowpact, stop the angry spirits of vengeance?

Fables Vol 8: Wolves. Art by Mark Buckingham and Shawn McManus. DC Comics/Vertigo 2006 160p. Illustration
Grades: 10 11 12 Adult   **741.5; Fic**
1. Adventure graphic novels; 2. Fantasy graphic novels; 3. Graphic novels
978-1-4012-1001-4, $17.99

Fabletown's ex-sheriff Bigby Wolf and ex-deputy mayor (and power behind King Cole's former mayoral throne) Snow White finally tie the knot in this arc from the series about the fairy-tale characters who walk among us (or, at least, New Yorkers). That can't happen before Mowgli finds missing, moping Bigby and the latter undertakes a reprisal mission against the Adversary. This eighth volume includes some violence, strong language, and nudity.

★ **Fables** Vol. 1: Legends in Exile. Art by Lan Medina. DC Comics/Vertigo 2002 128p. Illustration
Grades: 10 11 12 Adult   **741.5; Fic**
1. Fantasy graphic novels; 2. Mystery graphic novels; 3. Graphic novels
1-56389-942-6, $9.99; 9781401237554

In Fabletown, where fairy tale legends live alongside regular New Yorkers, the question on everyone's mind is who killed Rose Red" But only the Big Bad Wolf can actually solve the case (since he's the Fabletown sheriff) - and, along with Rose's sister Snow White, keep the Fabletown community from coming apart at the seams. The book includes strong language, violence, nudity, and sexual situations.
Also available in deluxe hardcover editions
Volume 1 of a 22 volume series

Fables Vol. 2: Animal Farm. Written by Bill Willingham; art by Mark Buckingham. DC Comics/Vertigo 2003 128p. Illustration
Grades: 10 11 12 Adult   **741.5; Fic**
1. Fantasy graphic novels; 2. Graphic novels
1-4012-0077-X, $12.95

In upstate New York, the non-human Fable characters have lived for centuries on a farm, miles from mankind. But all is not well on the farm - and a conspiracy to free them from the shackles of their perceived imprisonment may lead to a war that could wrest control of the Fables community away from Snow White. Goldilocks and the Three Little Pigs inflame the farm's inhabitants with fiery revolutionary rhetoric, and both Snow White and her sister Rose Red face threats to their lives. The book includes violence and some strong language.

Fables Vol. 3: Storybook Love. Written by Bill Willingham; art by Mark Buckingham. DC Comics/Vertigo 2004 190p. Illustration
Grades: 10 11 12 Adult   **741.5; Fic**
1. Fantasy graphic novels; 2. Graphic novels
1-4012-0256-X, $14.99

In the Fables' world, there isn't a lot of happily-ever-after to go around. As refugees from the lands of make-believe, the Fables have been driven from their storybook realms and forced to blend into the mundane world. But that doesn't mean they don't have any room for romance, or the pain, betrayal, and jealous rage that go along with it. In fact, love may be blooming between two of the most hard-bitten, no-nonsense Fables around - Snow White and Bigby Wolf. Meanwhile, Bigby teams up with several other Fables to stop a reporter from publishing a story that exposes the Fables and the lives they've built in New York. The book includes violence.

Fables Vol. 5: The Mean Seasons. Written by Bill Willingham; art by Mark Buckingham. DC Comics/Vertigo 2005 168p. Illustration
Grades: 11 12 Adult   741.5; Fic
   1. Adventure graphic novels; 2. Fantasy graphic novels; 3. Graphic novels
   1-4012-0486-4, $14.99
With the Battle of Fabletown won, and the surrounding city of New York none the wiser, the Fables have gained a little time for rebuilding and reflection, in between the interrogation of the Adversary's agent and the anticipation of Snow White's impending motherhood. For Bigby Wolf, the father of the soon-to-be newborns, that means a visit with an old friend, and a reminiscence of another, even deadlier war. For the new Mayor of Fabletown, Prince Charming, it means a rude awakening to the harsh realities of civic administration, and its conflicting demands. And for Snow herself, it means a long, painful labor, and a series of joyful, heart wrenching surprises. The book includes some violence, brief sexual situations, and strong language.

Fables Vol. 6: Homelands. Written by Bill Willingham; art by Mark Buckingham. DC Comics/Vertigo 2005 192p. Illustration
Grades: 10 11 12 Adult   741.5; Fic
   1. Adventure graphic novels; 2. Fantasy graphic novels; 3. Graphic novels
   1-4012-0500-3, $14.99
The Fables have beaten back the Adversary's first advance into their world, but now they must prepare themselves for the war that is sure to follow. Jack decides to skip town and heads for Hollywood, where he becomes a sleazy movie mogul. Boy Blue appropriates some weapons and heads back to the Homelands, killing enemies as he makes his way to the heart of enemy territory. The story features some nudity and sexual situations, some strong language, and considerable violence.

Fables: Arabian Nights (And Days). Written by Bill Willingham; art by Mark Buckingham. DC Comics/Vertigo 2006 Un Illustration
Grades: 10 11 12 Adult   741.5; Fic
   1. Fantasy graphic novels; 2. Graphic novels
   978-1-4012-1000-7, $14.99
Now that the Adversary's identity has been revealed, it's time to begin making preparations in earnest for the defense of the Fabletown stronghold. That means forging new alliances with whoever remains unconquered by the Adversary's legions. But the arrival in Fabletown of a delegation from the Arabian Homelands shows just how tricky this kind of coalition-building can be ... especially when one side is concealing Weapons of Magical Destruction. This volume includes some strong language and violence.

Robin: Days of Fire and Madness. Bill Willingham, writer; Scott McDaniel, penciller; Andy Owens, inkers; Guy Major, colorist; Phil Balsam, letterer. DC Comics 2006 144p. Illustration

Grades: 9 10 11 12 Adult   741.5; Fic
   1. Mystery graphic novels; 2. Robin (Fictional character); 3. Superhero graphic novels; 4. Graphic novels
   978-1-4012-0911-7, $14.99
Recruited into a covert military team by the mysterious and powerful man known only as the Veteran, Robin realizes that he has entered an entirely new world of danger when his first assignment takes him to the Middle East where he and his new teammates engage an enemy of unimaginable horror, flesh-eating demons. Back home, the battle continues as the Teen Wonder comes face to face with the inexplicable resurrection of his former girlfriend - determined to kill Robin in order to stay with Tim Drake forever - even as the city of Bludhaven suffers an attack by the supremely powerful, supremely deadly OMACs. Can the mystical superheroes of Shadowpact save Robin and his newfound allies? Or will this be his final battle? Lots of superhero fighting and demon fighting.

Robin/Batgirl: Fresh Blood. Bill Willingham, Andersen Gabrych, writers; Damion Scott, Ale' Garza & Jesse Delperdang, artists. DC Comics 2005 Un Illustration
Grades: 9 10 11 12 Adult   741.5; Fic
   1. Batgirl (Fictional character); 2. Nightwing (Fictional character); 3. Robin (Fictional character); 4. Superhero graphic novels; 5. Graphic novels
   1-4012-0433-3, $12.99
After the traumatic events of Batman: War Games, two of Gotham's youngest heroes, Robin and Batgirl, relocate to Bludhaven, where they must pick up the pieces of their lives and start anew. But before they can get fully settled in, they discover they have new threats to face, including Nightwing's enemy Shrike and their old friend the Penguin. In order to save the day, the two heroes realize there's only one thing they can do: battle each other to the death.

Robin: To Kill a Bird. Bill Willingham, writer ; Damion Scott, Giusseppe Camuncoli, Scott McDaniel, Pop Mhan, pencillers ; Sandra Hope, Damion Scott, Andy Owens, inkers ; Guy Major, colorist ; Phil Balsam, Jared K. Fletcher, Rob Leigh, letterers. DC Comics 2006 Un Illustration
Grades: 8 9 10 11 12 Adult   741.5; Fic
   1. Robin (Fictional character); 2. Superhero graphic novels; 3. Graphic novels
   978-1-4012-0909-4, $14.99
It's a brand-new start for Batman's sidekick, Robin: a new town (Bludhaven), a new school, new adventures and new problems. Before our hero can fully recover from the recent deaths of his father and girlfriend Spoiler, he must come face to face with his enemies: the Penguin, the Dark Rider, the Veteran, and a mysterious archer who seems to want the Boy Wonder dead. There's lots of superhero fighting action.

The **Sandman** Presents: Thessaly, Witch for Hire. Written by Bill Willingham; illustrated by Shawn McManus; colored by Pamela Rambo. DC Comics/Vertigo 2005 96p. Illustration
Grades: 10 11 12 Adult   741.5; Fic
   1. Supernatural graphic novels; 2. Witches; 3. Graphic novels
   1-4012-0497-X, $12.99
She's the world's oldest and most powerful witch, but nothing has prepared Thessaly for the persistence of

lovesick ghost Fetch, or the conniving, underhanded lengths he'll go to in order to win her heart. It's bad enough he attached her name to a monster-slaying business card, but now he's agreed to take on the universe's ultimate destructive force, and that's just plain stupid. Faced with this kind of courtship, it'll be a miracle if Thessaly can survive long enough to smack some sense into Fetch's intangible head ... never mind stopping the unstoppable doom he's unleashed. There's some nudity and some strong language, and lots of monster-killing violence.

Shadowpact: The Pentacle Plot. Written by Bill Willingham; art by Bill Willingham, Cory Walker, Steve Scott, Tom Derenick, Shawn McManus. DC Comics 2007 168p. Illustration
Grades: 9 10 11 12 Adult   741.5; Fic
  1. Mystery graphic novels; 2. Superhero graphic novels; 3. Supernatural graphic novels; 4. Graphic novels
  978-1-4012-1230-8, $14.99
  Nightmaster, Ragman, Nightshade, Blue Devil, Enchantress, and Detective Chimp are Shadowpact, magical heroes who explore the darkest corners of the DC Universe, fighting the mystical villains that other heroes can't, or won't. In this volume, they must content with their evil counterparts known as the Pentacle, and deal with the fact that they've lost a whole year in their lives. There's supernatural monster fighting and some incidental partial nudity.

Teen Titans Vol. 5: Life and Death. Geoff Johns, Bill Willingham, Tony S. Daniel, Scott McDaniel. DC Comics 2006 210p. Illustration
Grades: 10 11 12 Adult   741.5; Fic
  1. Robin (Fictional character); 2. Superhero graphic novels; 3. Teen Titans (Fictional characters); 4. Graphic novels
  978-1-4012-0978-0, $14.99
  The line between life and death is crossed as the Teen Titans must confront the deceased members of the team that have seemingly returned from the dead. As Donna Troy recruits the mightiest members of the team to battle in the Infinite Crisis, Robin is confronted by his predecessor, the bygone Boy Wonder, Jason Todd. The remaining Titans face the onslaught of Brother Blood and his army of followers which include the deceased Titans Aquagirl, Omen, Hawk, and Dove. As the Crisis hits, Superboy teams up with all of the reserve members of the team to battle his evil counterpart from another dimension. There is considerable violence in the personal battles.

Wilson, G. Willow
  ★ **Air,** vol. 1: letters from lost countries. G. Willow Wilson, writer; M.K. Perker, artist; Chris Chuckry, colorist; Jared K. Fletcher, letterer. DC Comics/Vertigo 2009 144p. Illustration
Grades: 11 12 Adult   741.5; Fic
  1. Adventure graphic novels; 2. Fantasy graphic novels; 3. Graphic novels
  978-1-4012-2153-9, $9.99
  Blythe works as a stewardess on Clearfleet Airlines, an odd choice of career for someone suffering from acrophobia, but that's what she does. As she works on various flights, she keeps encountering a man who changes his appearance and

name every time she sees him; she suspects he could be a terrorist, but he never actually does anything. Then one day a man approaches her on a flight to Amsterdam and tells her he's part of a group called the Etesians, and they fight terrorists. One of the Etesians asks Blythe to deliver a briefcase, but when the fellow with the ever-changing identity tells her to check inside, she finds plans to hijack one of the Clearfleet jets. This gets her into bad trouble, and things start to get very weird. Zayn finally tells her his real name when they start a sexual relationship, then one day after he's been gone on an assignment for too long, he sends Blythe a letter from a country that doesn't exist. Or does it" Along the way, Blythe starts to figure out that things aren't quite normal at the airline, and the Etesians are really bad people. The book includes some violence, including scenes of torture (that really aren't too graphic), some sexual situations, and the occasional s-bomb and f-bomb.

  ★ **Cairo.** Written by G. Willow Wilson; art by M.K. Perker; lettered by Travis Lanham. DC Comics/Vertigo 2007 160p. Illustration
Grades: 9 10 11 12 Adult   741.5; Fic
  1. Adventure graphic novels; 2. Fantasy graphic novels; 3. Graphic novels
  978-1-4012-1140-0, $24.99
  A stolen hookah, a spiritual underworld, and a genie on the run change the lives of five strangers in Cairo. A drug runner, a down-on-his-luck journalist, an American expatriate, a troubled young student, and a female Israeli soldier end up all working together to help the jinn that Lebanese American Shaheed calls Shams to recover a special box from the evil magic-wielding drug lord Nar. The book includes some violence.
  "Scripting and art complement each other well in an adventure with lots of appeal for readers willing to try a literary graphic novel and for those simply looking for the next good one." Booklist

  ★ **Ms.** Marvel 1: No Normal. Writer, G. Willow Wilson; artist, Adrian Alphona. Marvel Enterprises 2014 120 p. Color; Illustration
Grades: 9 10 11 12 Adult   741.5
  1. Female superhero comic books, strips, etc; 2. Muslim women — Fiction
  078519021X; 9780785190219, $15.99
  Hugo Award: Best Graphic Story (2015)
  In this comic, written by G. Willow Wilson and illustrated by Adrian Alphona, "Kamala Khan is an ordinary girl from Jersey City—until she is suddenly empowered with extraordinary gifts. But who truly is the all-new Ms. Marvel? Teenager? Muslim? Inhuman? Find out as . . . Kamala discovers the dangers of her newfound powers [and] she unlocks a secret behind them as well." (Publisher's note)
  "Wilson's story touches on many issues bubbling up around comics today—diversity, gender, culture, sexuality—though never with a heavy hand. The story is the focus here, and together with Alphona's playful and stylish artwork, Wilson offers a superhero comic full to bursting with heart and charm." Booklist
  Contains material originally published in magazine form as Ms. Marvel #1-5 and All-new Marvel now! point one #1—Title page

Ms. Marvel 2: Generation Why. By G. Willow Wilson; illustrated by Jacob Wyatt and Adrian Alphona. Marvel Enterprises 2015 136 p. Color; Illustration
Grades: 9 10 11 12 Adult   741.5
1. Female superhero comic books, strips, etc; 2. Muslim women — Fiction; 3. Pakistani Americans — Fiction; 4. Teenage girls — Fiction; 5. Wolverine (Fictional character); 6. Women superheroes
0785190228; 9780785190226, $15.99
"Who is the Inventor, and what does he want with the all-new Ms. Marvel and all her friends?" Maybe Wolverine can help! Kamala may be fan-girling out when her favorite (okay maybe Top Five) super hero shows up, but that won't stop her from protecting her hometown.? (Publisher's note)
"Alphona's distinctive panels make great use of exaggerated angles and distorted figures, and his line work, more intricate than most comic-book artists', packs each page with captivating, tongue-in-cheek detail." Booklist
Contains material originally published in magazine form as Ms. Marvel #6-11—Title page verso.

Ms. Marvel: Crushed. G. Willow Wilson; illustrated by Takeshi Miyazawa and Elmo Bondoc. Marvel Enterprises 2015 112 p. Color; Illustration
Grades: 9 10 11 12 Adult   741.5
1. Female superhero graphic novels; 2. Pakistani Americans; 3. Superhero; 4. Teenage girls; 5. Valentine's Day
0785192271; 9780785192275, $15.99
In this graphic novel by G. Willow Wilson, illustrated by Takeshi Miyazawa and Elmo Bondoc, "Love is in the air in Jersey City as Valentine's Day arrives! Kamala Khan may not be allowed to go to the school dance...but Ms. Marvel is! Well sort of - by crashing it attempting to capture Asgard's most annoying trickster! Yup, it's a special Valentine's Day story featuring Marvel's favorite charlatan, Loki!" (Publisher's note)
"As always, Wilson's rollicking superhero action is sprinkled with both hilarity and meaningful cultural commentary, and Kamala herself is as appealing as ever." Booklist
Contains material originally published in magazine form as Ms. Marvel #12-15 and S.H.I.E.L.D #2.

Wilson, Sean Michael
A **Christmas** Carol: The graphic novel original text by Charles Dickens. Illustrated by Mike Collins. Classical Comics 2008 144p. Illustration
Grades: 6 7 8 9 10 11 12 Adult   741.5; Fic
1. Christmas; 2. Dickens, Charles, 1812-1870 — Adaptations; 3. Ghosts; 4. Graphic novels
978-1-906332-51-8, $16.95
Miserly Ebenezer Scrooge has pronounced "Bah, humbug!" against Christmas, but on this Christmas Eve night, the ghost of his dead partner Jacob Marley visits him and proclaims his only hope to escape Marley's fate is to endure the visits of the Ghosts of Christmas Past, Present, and Future. Scrooge sees his past as a hopeful young man who slowly becomes bitter and obsessed with money as a means to avoid poverty, sees how his relatives and employees view him in the present, and how his future death is a matter of joy. This graphic adaptation uses dialog and narration taken directly from Dickens' novel. Back matter

includes a short biography of Dickens, a description of a typical Victorian period Christmas celebration, a description of the harsh poverty in London of the mid-nineteenth century, and more.
Also available quick text version $16.95 (ISBN: 978-1906332-52-5)

Winget, Larry

Courtesy of Smarter Comics

Shut up, stop whining and get a life: a kick-butt approach to a better life. Larry Winget; illustrated by Shane Clester; adapted by Cullen Bunn. Smarter Comics 2011 80p. Illustration
Grades: 10 11 12 Adult
646.7; 741.5
1. Self-help techniques; 2. Self-improvement; 3. Graphic novels
978-1-61066-002-0, $12.95
Larry Winget's bestselling self-help book is now a graphic novel. Self-described "Pitbull of Personal Development" Winget's approach takes aim at the usual advice found in most self-help books; he says that people need to take responsibility for their own lives, acknowledge their mistakes, learn from them, and change what they need to change in order to achieve their goals, whatever they may be. Even if one doesn't agree with everything he says, his approach is refreshing and full of common sense advice. Comics writer Bunn adapts Winget's prose, and comics illustrator Clester uses a lot of humor in the art to make Winget's points. Older teens and college students may discover that this book can truly help them.

Winick, Judd
Batman: Harley and Ivy. Writers, Paul Dini and Judd Winick; Art by Ronnie Del Carmen, Joe Chiodo, Bruce Timm, Shane Glines. DC Comics 2007 136p. Illustration
Grades: 10 11 12 Adult   741.5; Fic
1. Batman (Fictional character); 2. Humorous graphic novels; 3. Superhero graphic novels; 4. Graphic novels
978-1-4012-1333-6, $14.99
The sexy, madcap super-villain duo of Harley Quinn and Poison Ivy plan to take down Batman once and for all in this volume that collects the miniseries Batman: Harley and Ivy, written and drawn by Paul Dini and Bruce Timm, who created Batman: The Animated Series. The book also includes Harley and Ivy: Love on the Lam, written by Judd Winick and painted by Joe Chiodo, and "The Bet," a newly colored short story. Partial nudity and some suggestive scenes occur throughout the stories.

Batman: Under the Hood. Judd Winick, writer; Doug Mahnke, Paul Lee, pencillers; Tom Nguye, Cam Smith, inkers; Alex Sinclair, colorist. DC Comics 2005 Un Illustration
Grades: 10 11 12 Adult   741.5; Fic

1. Batman (Fictional character); 2. Superhero graphic novels; 3. Graphic novels
1-4012-0756-1, $9.99

While battling new criminal chieftains brought in by new Gotham crime boss Black Mask, Batman is confronted with a hidden face from the past. The Red Hood seems to be fighting the Black Mask for territory, but who is wearing the mask, and what will he do to Batman" Revelations from the past start to haunt the Dark Knight. This book contains quite a bit of violent fighting action.

Batman: Under the Hood Volume Two. Judd Winick, writer; Doug Mahnke, Shane Davis, Eric Battle, pencillers; Tom Nguyen [and others], inkers; Alex Sinclair, colorist; Pat Brosseau, Jarek K. Fletcher, Travis Lanham, letterers. DC Comics 2006 Un Illustration

Grades: 10 11 12 Adult   **741.5; Fic**
1. Batman (Fictional character); 2. Joker (Fictional character); 3. Robin (Fictional character); 4. Superhero graphic novels; 5. Graphic novels
978-1-4012-0901-8, $9.99

The Red Hood has been unmasked, and it's ... Jason Todd. Who was once Robin, successor to Dick Grayson, and killed by the Joker. He's changed, he wants revenge against the Joker, he wants power, he's angry at Batman. As the Red Hood, he's been taking over Black Mask's territory, and there will be a showdown. This book contains lots of violent fighting action.

★ The **big** book of Barry Ween, boy genius. Oni Press 2009 368p. Illustration

Grades: 10 11 12 Adult   **741.5; Fic**
1. Adventure graphic novels; 2. Humorous graphic novels; 3. Science fiction graphic novels; 4. Graphic novels
978-1-934964-02-6, $19.95

This volume collects all the Barry Ween comics published previously in three miniseries and then trade paperbacks, plus it includes a full-color one-shot story called "Barry Ween Ween Out Color Special." This last story, co-written with Greg Rucka, puts Barry into Antarctica U.S. Marshal Carrie Stetko's territory; Barry and best friend Jeremy blast into Antarctica instead of the movie theater, and Barry's terraforming procedure to keep them from freezing to death has gone way out of control, creating a tropical jungle environment that will keep growing unless Barry can stop it. Barry Ween is a ten-year-old super genius with an extremely foul mouth, his best friend Jeremy is a doofus who obsesses about sexual matters (a typical comment: "Will you look at the triceratops. Big lizard, tiny penis. No wonder they're extinct."). The stories include some violence, lots of f-bombs and s-bombs and other foul language, lots of sexual inferences and innuendo, and lots of hilarity. Teens who can handle the language and violence will enjoy this. The first trade paperback: The Adventures of Barry Ween, Boy Genius, was included in the 2002 YALSA Popular Paperbacks list, Graphic Novels: Superheroes and Beyond.

Green Arrow: Crawling Through the Wreckage. Judd Winick, writer; Scott McDaniel, penciller; Andy Owens, inker; Guy Major, colorist; Pat Brosseau, letterer. DC Comics 2007 144p. Illustration

Grades: 9 10 11 12 Adult   **741.5; Fic**

1. Green Arrow (Fictional character); 2. Superhero graphic novels; 3. Graphic novels
978-1-4012-1232-2, $12.99

After the Infinite Crisis has left Star City devastated and without resources, Oliver Queen - the Green Arrow - takes steps to save his home town ... by becoming the Mayor. The problem is that politics, executive powers, and his explosive arrows can't fix what's wrong with Star City. Someone is importing tainted drugs and causing the addicts to turn into mindless killers, corporate raiders want to take over the city and turn it into glitzy casinos and unaffordable housing, and on top of it all, someone has hired the world's deadliest assassin - Deathstroke - to kill Queen. The Mayor's plans include performing gay marriages, in order to attract people to come to Star City and spend money in its hotels and restaurants, and Green Arrow teams up with a former crime kingpin turned superhero to try to keep the ghettos safer until he can bring the walls down. There's some harsh language and lots of fighting.

Green Arrow: Straight Shooter. Judd Winick, writer; Phil Hester, penciller; Ande Parks, inker; Guy Major, colorist; Sean Konot, letterer. DC Comics 2004 144p. Illustration

Grades: 9 10 11 12 Adult   **741.5; Fic**
1. Green Arrow (Fictional characters); 2. Superhero graphic novels; 3. Graphic novels
1-4012-0200-4, $12.95

     LC 2004-301698

When Green Arrow discovers corporate corruption in Star City, he goes after those responsible. The last thing he expects is a fight with a 3-ton ogre. And more than one of them. As he delves into this mystery, he also falls into an unexpected romance, with tragic results. The book includes violence, some strong language, and brief sexual situations.

Green Lantern: brother's keeper. Judd Winick, writer; Dale Eaglesham {et al.}, pencillers; Rodney Ramos {et al.}, inkers; Moose Baumann, Rob Ro, Alex Bleyaert, colorists; Chris Eliopoulos, Kurt Hathaway, letterers. DC Comics 2003 124p. Illustration

Grades: 9 10 11 12   **741.5; Fic**
1. Green Lantern (Comic strip); 2. Green Lantern (Fictional character); 3. Superhero graphic novels; 4. Graphic novels
1-401-20078-8, $12.95

     LC 2004-297241

"Terry, Kyle's assistant and friend, has been beaten to the brink of death by men who "don't like faggots." As Terry lays in a coma, the Green Lantern takes a leaf from Batman's book, tracking down and punishing each offender. . . . Add this graphic novel to the collection, especially if other Green Lantern novels are well read. Remember this title, too, for the student writing the term paper on gay/lesbian issues in pop culture. The slick style with consistent color use, realistic dialogue, background information, and thoughtful afterward, make this a well-rounded, successful graphic novel." Libr Media Connect

Originally published in single magazine form in Green Lantern 151-155 and Green Lantern secret files 3.—t.p. Verso

Outsiders Volume 5: The Good Fight. Judd Winick, writer; Matthew Clark [and others], pencillers. DC Comics 2007 192p. Illustration

Grades: 9 10 11 12 Adult   **741.5; Fic**

1. Outsiders (Fictional characters); 2. Superhero graphic novels; 3. Graphic novels

978-1-4012-1195-0, \$14.99

The Outsiders have been thought dead for months. Then, deep undercover in the African country of Mali, trying to save innocent lives and stop a civil war, they are discovered. With a new team consisting of members from teams past and one former super-villain, the team finds itself at odds with an entire nation, not to mention the super-hero community. Also, the Outsiders try to thwart the Brotherhood of Evil's plot to sell metahumans to the underworld.

Outsiders: Crisis Intervention. Judd Winick, Jen Van Meter, writers; Matthew Clark, Dietrich Smith, penciller; Art Thibert, Steve Bird, inkers. DC Comics 2006 128p. Illustration

Grades: 9 10 11 12 Adult   **741.5; Fic**

1. Outsiders (Fictional characters); 2. Superhero graphic novels; 3. Graphic novels

1-4012-0973-4, \$12.99

The Outsiders are left reeling after the revelation of one of their members' ultimate betrayal. Before they can pick up the pieces, they must face a rematch with the Fearsome Five and Sabbac, who now has the power of the Seven Deadly Sins. Plus, with Infinite Crisis looming, Donna Troy recruits half the team, along with other heroes, for an important mission in space, while the rest must contend with the villainous Secret Society.

Outsiders: Wanted. Judd Winick, writer; Tom Raney, ChrisCross, Ivan Reis, pencillers; Scott Hanna, Sean Parsons, Marc Campos, inkers; Gina Going, Sno-Cone, colorists; John Workman, Comicraft, Nick Napolitano, letterers; Tom Raney & Scott Hanna, Michael Golden, original series covers. DC Comics 2005 Un Illustration

Grades: 9 10 11 12 Adult   **741.5; Fic**

1. Outsiders (Fictional characters); 2. Superhero graphic novels; 3. Graphic novels

1-4012-0460-0, \$14.99

In this third volume, the team works with John Walsh to take down a child abduction ring that had once had Grace before her powers kicked in. Then they find out just who has been funding the team, and the knowledge has Nightwing steamed. Things get worse when Roy, who thought he'd been getting intel for the Outsiders from Batman, discovers who really was doing it. Just as the team was starting to gel, the Outsiders become a team in crisis. The book includes strong language and violence, and alien sexual situations.

★ **Pedro** & me: friendship, loss, & what I learned. Henry Holt and Co. 2009 187p. Illustration

Grades: 7 8 9 10 11 12   **362.1**

1. AIDS (Disease); 2. AIDS activists; 3. AIDS patients; 4. Biographical graphic novels; 5. Friendship; 6. Real world (Television program); 7. Television personalities; 8. Graphic novels

978-0-8050-8964-6, \$16.99

2001 Robert F. Sibert Honor Book

In this "volume—part graphic novel, part memoir—professional cartoonist Winick pays tribute to his Real World housemate and friend Pedro Zamora, an AIDS activist who died of the disease in 1994." Publ Wkly

First published 2000

Superman/Shazam/First Thunder. Judd Winick, writer ; Joshua Middleton, artist ; Nick J. Napolitano, letterer. DC Comics 2006 128p. Illustration

Grades: 8 9 10 11 12 Adult   **741.5; Fic**

1. Shazam (Fictional character); 2. Superhero graphic novels; 3. Superman (Fictional character); 4. Graphic novels

978-1-4012-0923-0, \$12.99

With one word, young orphan Billy Batson transforms into a man imbued with the powers of the gods, but even one gifted with the Wisdom of Solomon can learn from a Superman. While Superman must stop members of a cult from stealing ancient artifacts from the Metropolis Natural History Museum, Billy must battle giant robots rampaging through Fawcett City. These separate events lead the heroes to cross paths, and a mighty friendship is formed as Earth's most powerful defenders team up to stop such menaces as Lex Luthor, Dr. Sivana, Eclipso, and the monstrous Lord Sabbac. There's some violence, and the climax is heartbreaking.

The **Trials** of Shazam! Volume One. Judd Winick, writer; Howard Porter, artist; Rob Leigh, letterer. DC Comics 2007 Un Illustration

Grades: 9 10 11 12 Adult   **741.5; Fic**

1. Captain Marvel (Fictional character); 2. Fantasy graphic novels; 3. Superhero graphic novels; 4. Graphic novels

978-1-4012-1331-2, \$14.99

Given powers by an ancient and mysterious wizard, boy reporter Billy Batson need only say the word "Shazam!" and he is transformed into the powerful adult hero Captain Marvel. Magical turmoil in the aftermath of INFINITE CRISIS force Captain Marvel to give up his role as Earth's Mightiest Mortal to keep the supernatural under control. Freddie Freeman, also known as Captain Marvel Jr., has been left powerless by these events, but is given the opportunity to take over the mantle of his mentor if he can pass tests administered by the gods themselves. The only catch is that he has to earn each of his super-abilities from scratch.

Wisna, Chris

Doris Danger, volume one: Giant monster adventures. SLG Publishing 2009 96p. Illustration

Grades: 8 9 10 11 12 Adult   **741.5; Fic**

1. Humorous graphic novels; 2. Monsters; 3. Graphic novels

978-1-59362-180-3, \$9.95

Intrepid ace photo-journalist Doris Danger seeks out the truth about giant alien monsters, and her quest takes her to isolated islands, jungles in Africa, rural Kansas, the Niagara Falls, and many other places where mysterious military officials cover up the existence of creatures such as Splazoo, Kockh, and Spoosh. Also, everywhere she goes in search of the giant alien monsters, the Monster Liberation Army shows up. The book reads like a collection of stories from a magazine, and Wisna's black and white art resembles the old Jack Kirby monster comics of the 1950s and 1960s.

Wolfman, Marv

Homeland: The Illustrated History of the State of Israel. Marv Wolfman, writer; Mario Ruiz, illustrator and graphic designer; William J. Rubin, executive editor. Nachschon Press 2007 124p. Illustration

Grades: 9 10 11 12 Adult   305.892; 741.5; 956.94
1. Israel — History; 2. Israelis; 3. Jews; 4. Palestine; 5. Graphic novels
978-0-9771507-0-0, $19.95

Using the conceit that a university professor is teaching a class, this book covers about 4,000 years of history in the Middle East, focused on Israel. It goes back to the Biblical narrative of Abram's journey from Mesopotamia, quickly progresses to the Middle Ages, explains the complicated circumstances surrounding the Zionist movement and efforts to establish the modern state of Israel, and covers the recent situations there. Readers may not be so familiar with the history of Israel and the Jews beyond the Old Testament narratives, the World War II Holocaust, and the current struggles. This book gives a concise explanation of the history which is valuable whether or not one supports Israel today.

The **New** Teen Titans: Terra Incognito. Marv Wolfman, writer ; George Pérez, penciller ; Romeo Tanghal, Pablo Markos, inkers ; Adrienne Roy, colorist. DC Comics 2006 224p. Illustration

Grades: 7 8 9 10 11 12 Adult   741.5; Fic
1. Robin (Fictional character); 2. Superhero graphic novels; 3. Teen Titans (Fictional characters); 4. Graphic novels
978-1-4012-0972-8, $19.99

Tara Markov, the troubled teen princess of Markovia, is rescued from kidnappers by the Titans' green-skinned adventurer, Changeling. Thus begins her quest to use her powers over earth and gravity in the cause of justice. Does this obnoxious young powerhouse have what it takes to join the team? This is the original Teen Titans team, in which Dick Grayson is still Robin.

Superman: The Man of Steel Vol. 5. Written by Marv Wolfman, Jerry Ordway, and John Byrne; pencilled by Jerry Ordway and John Byrne. DC Comics 2006 210p. Illustration

Grades: 9 10 11 12 Adult   741.5; Fic
1. Joker (Fictional character); 2. Superhero graphic novels; 3. Superman (Fictional character); 4. Graphic novels
978-1-4012-0948-3, $19.99

Superman and the staff of the Daily Planet uncover a gang war raging in the city's notorious "Suicide Slum." Journalistic integrity is put to the test when it is revealed that Perry White's son is involved. Will the Daily Planet run a story that will ruin the life of one of their own" And what is the identity of the new protector of the streets, who emerges amid the havoc" Also, love is in the air, as Superman finds himself romantically involved with Big Barda, the amazon from the planet Apokolips, and with Cat Grant. Along with his ever-present nemesis Lex Luthor, Superman faces the

evil of Sleez, the Joker, and that fiendish magical imp from the Fifth Dimension, Mr. Mxyzptlk. These stories were originally published in 1987.

Wonder Woman Vol. 4: Destiny Calling. DC Comics 2006 176p. Illustration

Grades: 8 9 10 11 12 Adult   741.5; Fic
1. Superhero graphic novels; 2. Wonder Woman (Fictional character); 3. Graphic novels
978-1-4012-0943-8, $19.99

It's only been a short time since Diana, dubbed Wonder Woman by the media, came to Man's World with a message of peace, only to face countless foes and stop the advancement of a third world war. Now Diana must face her greatest challenge yet: a god among men. The Olympian god Hermes has decided to grace mankind with his presence, but along with him comes a world of new troubles for the Amazon. This volume reprints stories originally published in the 1980s, when Perez re-launched Wonder Woman.

Wolfram, Amy

Teen Titans year one. Written by Amy Wolfram ; Art by Karl Kerschl & Serge LaPointe. DC Comics 2008 144p. Illustration

Grades: 7 8 9 10 11 12   741.5; Fic
1. Aquaman (Fictitious character); 2. Batman (Fictional character); 3. Flash (Fictional character); 4. Green Arrow (Fictional character); 5. Justice League (Fictional characters); 6. Robin (Fictional character); 7. Superhero graphic novels; 8. Teen Titans (Fictional characters); 9. Wonder Woman (Fictional character); 10. Graphic novels
978-1-4012-1927-7, $14.99

Suddenly, the members of the Justice League of America are acting crazy, becoming bullies, breaking the law—what has happened to Batman, Aquaman, the Flash, Green Arrow, and Wonder Woman" Their young partners, Robin, Aqualad, Kid Flash, Speedy, and Wonder Girl, decide to team up together and put things right. They're teens, they're superheroes, they're the Teen Titans. And being teens, they still do teenage things, like overindulge in pizza and soda, go out on dates and mess things up with each other, and deal with celebrity. That last is not typical of teens, but they have to learn to deal with it. This book, written by Wolfram, who wrote for the Teen Titans animated series on television, reimagines the early days of the team. The book includes some violence.

Womanthology: Heroic

Gail Simone, Camilla D'Errico, Robin Furth, Trina Robbins, Colleen Doran, Fiona Staples, Ming Doyle, Renae De Liz and others. IDW 2012 321 p.

Grades: 8 9 10 11 12   Fic
1. Comic books, strips, etc — Authorship; 2. Women artists
1613771479; 9781613771471, $50

This book is an anthology of comics content from "more than 150 women creators." The book shows "how many diverse styles and subjects can make for great comics. The different portraits and definitions of heroism encompass everything from caped fliers to historical allusions to quiet bravery." (Publishers Weekly)

Wong, Tony

The **Four** Constables Vol. 1. Director, Tony Wong ; illustrator, Andy Seto ; original story, Rui-An Wen ; translator, Yun Zhao. ComicsOne/DrMaster Publications 2004 Un Illustration
Grades: 8 9 10 11 12 Adult   741.5; Fic
    1. Adventure graphic novels; 2. Martial arts; 3. Mystery graphic novels; 4. Graphic novels
    1-58899-383-3, $13.95

Four of China's supremely skilled assassin/detectives serve only their Master Zhuge Zhen-Wo - The Little Flower, who in turn is head bodyguard and advisor for China's all powerful Emperor. . Yayu Sheng, "Emotionless," is a master of weapons and devices. Yuxia Tie, "Iron Hands," possesses incredible chi and can stop the sharpest blades bare-handed. Lieshan Cui, "Life Snatcher," is highly skilled in light-foot, granting him undaunted legwork and kicks. Lingqi Len, "Cold Blooded," was raised by wolves and since learned to transfer his pain when fighting to strength, enabling him to defeat opponents much stronger than himself. Each of them is entrusted by the Emperor with the power to arrest and execute any corrupt officials or lawless criminals with the Chinese Empire. These Imperial Constables act as protectors. With their venerable skill they root out potential usurpers and discern the cause of many strange occurrences happening during the Sung Dynasty. This is a Chinese manhua series, published in full color and filled with martial arts action.
Volume 1 of 5

Wood, Brian

The **Couriers**. Brian Wood and Rob G. AiT/Planet Lar 2003 Un Illustration
Grades: 11 12 Adult   741.5; Fic
    1. Adventure graphic novels; 2. Mystery graphic novels; 3. Graphic novels
    1-932051-06-6, $12.95

The story is set in New York City, featuring Moustafa and Special: mercenary couriers. They do the work the normal couriers are only barely aware of: intelligence, large cash transfers, protection, assassinations, blockade-running ... you name it. But there is one job they always knew they would refuse, known as a biologic." But when their latest package turns out to be a young deaf/mute girl from Nepal, with a gone-rogue Chinese Red Army Brigade hot on her heels, how can they NOT get involved" The book is full of action, with lots of harsh language (f-bombs and s-bombs all over the place) and graphic violence.

The **Couriers** 02: Dirtbike Manifesto. Brian Wood and Rob G. AiT/Planet Lar 2004 Un Illustration
Grades: 11 12 Adult   741.5; Fic
    1. Adventure graphic novels; 2. Graphic novels
    1-932051-18-X, $12.95

Sometimes Moustafa and Special, The Couriers, run guns. It's not the most admirable job in the world to take on, but they have rent to pay and ammo to buy, and M has acquired a rather expensive new hobby: building the ultimate motocross dirtbike from scratch. But their latest gig goes bad... all kinds of wrong... and it ticks them off. They head to upstate New York to track the guns to the source and to get a little vengeance and get P-A-I-D in the process. In those small New York towns, the slow economy has hit hard,

the streets are dead on a weekend, and half the shops are boarded up. There are lots of angry people with too much time on their hands, and half of them own guns. They don't need two young arrogant punks from The City to roll into town like they own the place ... The book includes lots of harsh language with f-bombs and s-bombs flying all over, and lots of graphic violence.

The **Couriers** 03: The Ballad of Johnny Funwrecker. Brian Wood and Rob G. AiT/Planet Lar 2005 Un Illustration
Grades: 11 12 Adult   741.5; Fic
    1. Mystery graphic novels; 2. Graphic novels
    1932051-31-7, $12.95

Book Three in the Couriers saga hits the rewind button on the lives of everybody's two favorite urban mercenary couriers and goes back, way back, to 1993. Moustafa's a dirtbag grunge kid selling weed by the cube at Astor Place, and Special's a riot grrrl with a mean streak, looking to carve a place for herself in the criminal underworld. How do these two unlikely partners meet up and become the tight-knit team they are now" Meet Johnny Funwrecker, the hilarious larger-than-life Chinatown mob boss and role model for little street rat hooligans all over. The book contains lots of violence, drug dealing, very harsh language, and some nudity.

Couscous Express. Brian Wood, Brett Weldele. AiT/Planet Lar 2001 Un Illustration
Grades: 10 11 12 Adult   741.5; Fic
    1. Mystery graphic novels; 2. Graphic novels
    1-9709360-2-8, $12.95

Scooter enthusiast and spoiled brat, Olive Yassin, delivers food for her parents' award-winning Middle Eastern restaurant, Couscous Express. She hates it. It's boring. She would much rather be hanging out with her courier-mercenary boyfriend, Moustafa. But when the local branch of the stylish and dangerous Turkish Scooter Mafia make a move against the restaurant, she knows she has to do something, anything, to protect her family. This book combines delicious food, automatic weapons fire, and scooter culture into an adrenaline-fueled story of love, family, war, and the best hummus recipe in New York City. Readers will find lots of harsh language and violence.

Demo, Second ed.. written by Brian Wood; illustrated by Becky Cloonan; lettered by Ryan Yount. AiT/Planet Lar 2003 Un Illustration
Grades: 11 12 Adult   741.5; Fic
    1. Graphic novels
    1-932051-42-2, $19.95

This book collects the twelve issues of Demo, with twelve stories about young people coming to terms with particular powers they have. These are not necessarily superhero-type powers, but anyone who watched the television series Heroes, which debuted in 2006, will find these stories to be very much in line with what the series depicted. Strong language, some sexual situations, and violence will make this more appropriate for older readers.

DMZ Vol. 1: On the Ground. Brian Wood, Riccardo Burchielli. DC Comics/Vertigo 2006 128p. Illustration
Grades: 11 12 Adult   741.5
    1. Adventure graphic novels; 2. Graphic novels
    978-1-4012-1062-5

In the near future, America's worst nightmare has come true. With military adventurism overseas bogging down the Army and National Guard, the U.S. government mistakenly neglects the very real threat of anti-establishment militias scattered across the 50 states. Like a sleeping giant, Middle America rises up and violently pushes its way to the shining seas, coming to a standstill at the line in the sand - Manhattan. Or as the world now knows it, the DMZ. Matty Roth, a nave aspiring photojournalist, lands a dream gig following a veteran war correspondent into the heart of the DMZ. Things soon go terribly wrong, and Matty finds himself lost and alone in a world he's only seen on television. This story has lots of harsh language and violence.

Volume 1 of 12

The **New** York Four. Written by Brian Wood ; illustrated by Kelly Ryan ; lettering by Jared K. Fletcher. DC Comics/Minx 2008 176p. Illustration
Grades: 8 9 10 11 12   **741.5; Fic**
1. Friendship; 2. Graphic novels
978-1-4012-1154-7, $9.99

Riley is a college freshman who has grown up so sheltered, protected, and disciplined by her parents that she finds it difficult to make friends. She starts seeing her older sister Angie on the sly; Angie was kicked out of the house years ago for an offense no one will tell Riley. Other than that, Riley almost lives her life through her smart phone, constantly texting to people she's never met in person. Then, just as she opens up to make friends with three fellow freshmen and helps them find work with the same research group for which she works, she "meets" someone she knows only by his user name, "sneakerfreak." Balancing classes, friends, her over-protective parents, her sister, and now this secret online romance is becoming more difficult than Riley ever thought it could be. Each of her friends also has a secret that could have consequences.

Supermarket. Written by Brian Wood; illustrated by Kristian. IDW Publishing 2006 102p. Illustration
Grades: 11 12 Adult   **741.5; Fic**
1. Adventure graphic novels; 2. Organized crime; 3. Graphic novels
978-1-600100-09-3, $17.99

In the future world of Supermarket, legitimate and black-market economies rule the City, overseen by the vying factions of the Yakuza and Porno Swede crime families. Convenience store clerk and sixteen-year old suburban wise-ass Pella Suzuki suddenly finds herself in the middle of it all, heir to an empire she couldn't possibly inherit, but hitmen on both sides aren't taking any chances. Pella's world is full of violence and harsh language.

Wooderson, Philip
Guard Dog. Stone Arch Books 2007 80p. Illustration
Grades: 3 4 5 6 7 8 9   **741.5; Fic**
1. Mystery graphic novels; 2. Graphic novels
978-1-59889-829-3, $22.60
LC 2007-6244

Ryan would rather play his favorite video game, Guard Dog, than help his dad sell his artwork at the flea market. When the artwork is stolen, however, Ryan and his friend Steve take on the case. Soon, they're hot on the trail of the

thieves, but are the clues leading them in the wrong direction? The two boys learn that a detective's work is no game. This graphic novel is written with an easy vocabulary and a simple panel layout for beginning, reluctant, and struggling readers.

Part of the Graphic Quest line.

Woodfin, Rupert
Introducing Aristotle, New Edition. Rupert Woodfin & Judy Groves. Totem Books 2006 176p. Illustration
Grades: 10 11 12 Adult   **100; 741.5**
1. Ancient philosophy; 2. Aristotle, 384-322 BC; 3. Graphic novels
978-1-84046-759-8, $12.95

Aristotle was named the "master of those who know" He is a foundational thinker in every field of inquiry. He established logic as a systematic discipline, conceived the earliest rules of science, developed a rational psychology, a political science and an outline of sociology, and gave us a virtue theory of ethics that is still a model today. His contributions to metaphysics continue to permeate modern philosophy. He supplied the first theory of aesthetics, which still provides the basis of debates today. Aristotle's authority extended beyond his time to influence Islamic society and medieval scholasticism. For fifteen hundred years he remained the paradigm of knowledge itself, until scientific empiricism in the 17th century is said to have discredited his methods. Is this true" How 'scientific' is Aristotle'? This volume uses cartoons and a spare text to introduce readers to Aristotle's philosophy; it includes a list of books for further reading.

Wright, Edgar
Shaun of the Dead. Adapted by Chris Ryall; penciled and inked by Zach Howard. Dark Horse Comics 2005 104p. Illustration
Grades: 10 11 12 Adult   **741.5; Fic**
1. Graphic novels
1-933239-43-3, $17.95

This "director's cut" adaptation of the romantic zombie comedy - produced with the full participation of the movie's co-writer/director and co-writer/star, Edgar Wright and Simon Pegg - features deleted scenes and other never-before-seen material. This volume also contains movie storyboards, production stills, and additional bonus material courtesy of Edgar and Simon. The book features zombie violence and some strong language.

Yabuki, Kentaro
Black Cat, Volume 1. Viz Media/Shonen Jump 2006 200p. Illustration
Grades: 10 11 12 Adult   **741.5; Fic**
1. Adventure graphic novels; 2. Shonen manga; 3. Graphic novels
978-1-4215-0605-0, $7.99

Translated by JN Productions. Train Heartnet, known as "Black Cat," worked as a top assassin for a secret organization called Chronos, but quit. Now he's a sweeper, a bounty hunter, partnered with the one-eyed Sven. Even as Train has to deal with assassins from his past, he and Sven go after wanted men for the bounties. Then beautiful thief Rinslet Walker proposes that they partner with her to take down a weapons smuggler who is developing dangerous new weapons. At first glance, Train's world is similar to ours, but science fictional elements such as nanotechnology and mystical elements of chi come into play as well. Sven seems to always have a cigarette in hand, and Train seems to always find someone he has to fight, but in the first four volumes there hasn't been any gratuitous cleavage or panty shots.

Yagami, Yu
Hikkatsu! Strike a Blow to Vivify, vol. 1. Go! Comi 2007 196p. Illustration
Grades: 10 11 12 Adult 741.5
1. Science fiction graphic novels; 2. Shonen manga; 3. Graphic novels
978-1-933617-57-2, $10.99
In the future, geomagnetic abnormalities make every day a struggle to survive. Static electricity storms are bad enough, but the human race faces its greatest threat from ordinary, everyday appliances that go on the blink. But Shota is mastering his Repair Blow technique so he can do more than just beat machines. The book includes some mild violence and harsh language.

Yagi, Norihiro
Claymore Vol. 1. Viz Media/Shonen Jump Advanced 2006 188p. Illustration
Grades: 10 11 12 Adult 741.5; Fic
1. Fantasy graphic novels; 2. Horror graphic novels; 3. Shonen manga; 4. Graphic novels
978-1-4215-0618-0, $7.99
A Claymore - a female warrior named for the sword she carries - travels from medieval village to village to destroy Yoma, monsters who disguise themselves as humans and who are almost impossible to kill. Claymores are half-humans, half-demons who willingly transformed themselves by mixing their blood with monster's blood. Clare, nicknamed silver-eyed killer, is such a powerful Claymore, she can slay a Yoma using only one hand. But she must constantly struggle to keep from becoming a monster herself. The book includes a considerable amount of monster-slaying violence.

Yakin, Boaz
★ **Marathon.** By Boaz Yakin; [illustrations by Joe Infurnari]. First Second 2012 186 p.
Grades: 6 7 8 9 741.5/973; 741.5
1. Adventure graphic novels; 2. Greece — History; 3. Greece — History — Persian Wars, 500-449 BC — Fiction; 4. Greece — History — Persian Wars, 500-449 BC — Juvenile fiction; 5. Marathon, Battle of, 490 BC; 6. Graphic novels
9781596436800, $16.99 ; 1596436808
LC 2011030472
This book is a graphical "account of the battle of Marathon" in which "Hippias, former king of Athens, is on his way back with a huge army of Persians to reclaim the throne and crush Athenian democracy. . . . Eucles, Athens' best runner, is charged to race the 153 miles to Sparta in hopes of finding an ally, . . . [returning] with the dismaying news that the Spartans will not be coming in time. He joins the savage fight and then runs 26 more miles over rugged mountains to Athens . . . warning of an impending surprise attack by sea." (Kirkus Reviews)

Yamashita, Matt
Ghostbusters: Ghost Busted. Stories by Nathan Johnson and Matt Yamashita ; art by Chrissy Delk et al. Tokyopop 2008 Un Illustration
Grades: 7 8 9 10 11 12 Adult 741.5; Fic
1. Fantasy graphic novels; 2. Ghosts; 3. Humorous graphic novels; 4. Graphic novels
978-1-4278-1459-3, $12.99
In the time since the Ghostbusters last saved New York City (as seen in the second film), the team finds itself pretty busy. A major producer hires Ray, Peter, and Egon to save his new lavish musical from destruction, which would ruin him. Then, the mayor's former right hand man returns, intent on getting revenge on all the Ghostbusters for ruining his reputation. Meanwhile, Peter, Ray, and Egon each disappear while out on individual calls, and now it's up to Winston to find and save them. This is a global manga and includes ghostly manifestations, ectoplasm, and ghostbusting action.

Yamazaki, Housui
Mail Vol. 1. Dark Horse Comics/Dark Horse Manga 2006 210p. Illustration
Grades: 10 11 12 741.5; Fic
1. Horror graphic novels; 2. Shonen manga; 3. Graphic novels
978-1-59307-566-8, $10.95
Private detective Reiji Akiba has a theory about those awkward moments and weird coincidences we all encounter in life. They are actually encounters with the dead - their way of sending us a message. But you may not want to open such strange mail from beyond - not unless you can see the ghostly attachment, like Akiba can. And not unless you carry a gun that can kill what isn't alive, like Akiba's aptly named Kagutsuchi, "the tool between God and earth" digging a divine grave to lay to rest the evil dead. This first volume opens with a model's photo shoot at what was a lovely riverside. But someone's thrown their trash away here: human bones. When the negatives in the darkroom reveal hidden horror, it's time for the magazine to hire Akiba. The answers lie in the secret basement of a shunned house... but they don't lie peacefully. This horror manga includes some nudity, violence, and some disturbing images.

Yamazaki, Toru
Octopus Girl Vol. 1. Dark Horse Manga 2006 190p. Illustration
Grades: 12 Adult 741.5; Fic
1. Horror graphic novels; 2. Humorous graphic novels; 3. Manga; 4. Graphic novels
978-1-59307-540-8, $12.95
Good school girl Takako is horribly bullied by other students in school, including having her mouth stuffed with octopus (she's allergic). The next day, she wakes up to find she has mutated into a hybrid form, with a human head upon an octopus body; she decides to exact bloody revenge upon her tormenters. The book mixes sick, crass humor with gross-out violence and horror, nudity, and harsh language.

Yang, Gene Luen

★ **American** born Chinese. Color by Lark Pien. First Second 2006 233p. Illustration

Grades: 7 8 9 10 11 12   741.5; Fic

1. Chinese Americans; 2. Young adult literature — Works

1-59643-152-0, $16.95; 978-1-59643-152-2

LC 2005-58105

Michael L. Printz Award, 2007

In this graphic novel by Gene Luen Yang, "Jin Wang is the only Asian American boy in his new school; Danny is a young man deeply embarrassed by his visiting Chinese cousin, portrayed deliberately by the author as an ethnic clich?; and the Monkey King, a figure from Chinese lore, is desperate to be treated like a god. This . . . story relates how three characters overcome hurdles to find satisfaction within themselves." (Library Journal)

"True to its origin as a Web comic, this story's clear, concise lines and expert coloring are deceptively simple yet expressive. Even when Yang slips in an occasional Chinese ideogram or myth, the sentiments he's depicting need no translation. Yang accomplishes the remarkable feat of practicing what he preaches with this book: accept who you are and you'll already have reached out to others." Publ Wkly

★ **Boxers**. Gene Luen Yang; color by Lark Pien. First Second 2013 328 p.

Grades: 7 8 9 10 11 12 Adult   741.5

1. China — History — Boxer Rebellion, 1899-1901; 2. Historical fiction

1596433590; 9781596433595, $18.99

LC 2013947229

National Book Award for Young People's Literature: Finalist (2013)

Boston Globe-Horn Book Honor: Fiction (2014)

"Life in Little Bao's peaceful rural village is disrupted when . . . a priest and his phalanx of soldiers . . . arrive." They start "smashing the village god, appropriating property, and administering vicious beatings for no reason. Little Bao and his older brothers train in kung fu and swordplay." . . . Little Bao "becomes the leader of a peasant army, eventually marching to Beijing." (School Library Journal)

"China's Boxer Rebellion is the unlikely backdrop for this graphic treatment of young villagers on the opposite sides of history. Bao wants to drive out the white devils that poison his country with opium and Christianity. Four-Girl is an unwanted daughter who finds purpose in the missionary life. Their stories collide in a moment of grace that could only be penned by the Printz Award-winning author of 'American Born Chinese.'" LJ

★ The **eternal** smile: three stories. First Second 2009 170p. Illustration

Grades: 9 10 11 12   741.5; Fic

978-1-59643-156-0, $16.95; 1-59643-156-3

★ **Level** up. First Second Books 2011 160p. Illustration

Grades: 10 11 12 Adult   741.5; Fic

1. Angels; 2. Bildungsromans; 3. Chinese Americans; 4. College students; 5. Graphic novels

978-1-59643-235-2, $15.99

LC 2010-36257

"Pham's watercolor artwork, mostly in muted pallet, is a perfect match for Yang's story. This gentle tale of loss and redemption, family responsibility, and dreams might not be to all teens' tastes (especially by the end), but the mix of fantasy and realism will please the right crowd." Voice Youth Advocates

★ **Prime** baby. [by] Gene Luen Yang, colors by Derek Kirk Kim. First Second Books 2010 56p. Illustration

Grades: 6 7 8 9 10 11 12   741.5; Fic

1. Extraterrestrial beings; 2. Humorous graphic novels; 3. Science fiction graphic novels; 4. Siblings; 5. Graphic novels

978-1-59643-612-1, $6.99

Thaddeus K. Fong always preferred to be the center of his family's attention, so the birth of his little sister Maddie has really bothered him. When she's eighteen months old, he notices something about the sounds she makes; her "gaga's" come out in prime numbers. Then his math teacher says that if aliens were ever to try to make contact with humans, it would be through prime numbers. Oh no, Maddie is an intergalactic conduit for invading aliens! Except no one believes Thaddeus. Until Maddie starts burping up strange things that turn out to be little ships for sluglike aliens. They're peaceful missionary types, but that doesn't stop Thaddeus from making them seem hostile. When their parents finally believe Thaddeus, Maddie gets locked up in a research facility. Thaddeus should be ecstatic, his dumb little sister has been put away. So why is he feeling sad" This story was originally serialized in the New York Times magazine and has been printed to preserve the original comic strip format.

"Sf readers who value humor and humanity (not just slam-bang action), Christians, newcomers to graphic novels, and fans of Yang's simultaneously childlike and sophisticated ability to create and maintain tension should all be satisfied by his new book." Booklist

★ **Saints**. By Gene Luen Yang and Lark Pien. First Second 2013 170 p.

Grades: 7 8 9 10 11 12 Adult   741.5

1. China — History — Boxer Rebellion, 1899-1901; 2. Historical fiction

1596436891; 9781596436893, $15.99

LC 2013947228

National Book Award for Young People's Literature: Finalist (2013)

Boston Globe-Horn Book Honor: Fiction (2014)

This graphic novel, by Gene Luen Yang and Lark Pien, "follows a lonely girl . . . . Unwanted by her family, Four-Girl isn't even given a proper name until she converts to Catholicism and is baptized by the very same priest who bullies Little Bao's village. Four-Girl, now known as Vibiana, leaves home and finds fulfillment in service to the Church, while Little Bao roams the countryside committing acts of increasing violence as his army grows." (School Library Journal)

"Yang presents a 'diptych' of graphic novels set during China's Boxer Rebellion. Boxers follows Little Bao, who learns to harness the power of ancient gods to fight the spread of Christianity; Saints centers on Four-Girl, who sits squarely on the other side of the rebellion. Yang's characteristic infusions of magical realism, bursts of humor, and distinctively drawn characters make for a compelling read." (Horn Book)

The **Shadow** Hero. Gene Luen Yang. Art by Sonny Liew. First Second 2014 176 p. Color; Illustration
Grades: 6 7 8 9 10   **741.5**
  1. Chinese Americans — Fiction; 2. Superheroes — Fiction
  1596436972; 9781596436978, $17.99
  This book, by Gene Luen Yang, is about "Green Turtle, a 1940s comic book hero. . . . The Green Turtle is cast as an unlikely 19-year-old young man, Hank, the son of Chinese immigrants who own a grocery store in 1940s America. When his mother is rescued by a superhero, the loving but overbearing woman decides that it's Hank's fate to become a hero himself, and she does everything in her power to push her son in that direction." (School Library Journal)
  "Yang and Liew have crafted an origin story for the Green Turtle, a little-known . . . World War II-era comic superhero created by cartoonist Chu Hing in 1944. Much about the series remains a mystery, as Yang shares in an author's note, but according to rumors Hing wanted his star to be Chinese, and, not surprisingly for the era, his publishers balked at the idea. Now seventy years later, Yang and Liew vindicate the cartoonist by imagining the Green Turtle as 'perhaps...the first Asian American superhero.'" Horn Book

Yazawa, Ai
  Nana, Volume One. Viz Media/Shojo Beat 2006 Un Illustration
Grades: 11 12 Adult   **741.5; Fic**
  1. Josei manga; 2. Manga; 3. Romance graphic novels; 4. Shojo manga; 5. Graphic novels
  978-1-4215-0108-6, $8.99
  Two young women, both named Nana, both the same age, but different in personalities, each want to move to Tokyo. Nana Komatsu is somewhat immature, and so far her life has revolved around men. Nana Osaki is a punk rock vocalist with an attitude to match; she wants to make her band a success. Nana K wants to be with her friends even if she failed all the college entrance exams; she also wants to become more self-reliant. The two Nanas meet on the train to Tokyo, then meet again when looking for an affordable apartment. The series includes considerable strong language and sexual situations.
  Volume 1 of 21

YKids
  Curie. Youngjin Singapore 2007 148p. Illustration
Grades: 3 4 5 6 7 8 9   **92; 741.5**
  1. Biographical graphic novels; 2. Curie, Marie, 1867-1934; 3. Graphic novels
  978-981-05-4946-6, $14.95
  Throughout her career, Marie Curie, the renowned scientist and first woman to win the Nobel Prize, had to overcome the objections of her peers and the many obstacles facing an early female scientist. This is the story of her work in discovering radium and explaining the mysteries, benefits, and dangers of radioactivity that would ultimately lead to her own death. It also recounts the enormous time and resources she devoted to the cause of peace, having witnessed herself the horrors of war. In the fictional framing story, a boy and a robot from the future seek out Marie Curie to take one particular value from her life to help them in their time; they seek her burning passion for her work.
  Part of the Great Figures in History series.

  Einstein. Youngjin Singapore 2007 146p. Illustration
Grades: 3 4 5 6 7 8 9   **92; 741.5**
  1. Biographical graphic novels; 2. Einstein, Albert, 1879-1955; 3. Graphic novels
  978-981-05-4944-2, $14.95
  A genius of enormous accomplishment, Albert Einstein overcame numerous hardships-separation from his family, religious discrimination, and the political turmoil of his day-to become one of the greatest minds of the 20th century. As a young boy, Einstein's unending curiosity and constant questioning earned him the reputation of being unfocused and inattentive. This book uses a framing story of a young boy and a robot from the future going back in time to examine the lives of great people and find the one value that will help their situation; from Einstein, they take his insatiable curiosity.
  Part of the Great Figures in History series.

  Gandhi. Youngjin Singapore 2007 148p. Illustration
Grades: 3 4 5 6 7 8 9   **92; 741.5**
  1. Biographical graphic novels; 2. Gandhi, Mahatma, 1869-1948; 3. Graphic novels
  978-981-05-4945-9, $14.95
  A champion of the poor and lower classes, Mahatma Gandhi helped transform India into the democracy it is today. Young readers of this manga-style biography will learn about the key historical events during this time and how the peaceful efforts of one humble man affected enormous change. This book presents a time line of Gandhi's life-from his roots in a middle-class family in India, to his law-school education in England, his experiences with discrimination, and his key role as a leader in the Indian independence movement. Each volume in the Great Figures in History series focuses on a key value personified by the biographical subject; in Gandhi's case, it's courage.
  Part of the Great Figures in History series.

Yokoyama, Akira
  Project X: Fairlady Z/240Z. Digital Manga Publishing 2006 206p. Illustration
Grades: 9 10 11 12   **629.222; 741.5**
  1. Automobiles — Design and construction; 2. Manga; 3. Nissan automobiles; 4. Graphic novels
  1-56970-957-2, $12.95
  Adapted to manga from the NHK television documentary series, Project X, this title tells the story of how visionary Nissan auto designers developed the 240Z, which became a stylish yet practical sports car.
  "This documentary manga has all the drama of any well-told story, with a breathless pace that carries the reader along. ... Anyone who likes the 240Z or cars in general will enjoy this behind-the-scenes look at how auto design is done." (VOYA)

Yomtov, Nel
  Theseus and the Minotaur. Retold by Nel Yomtov ; illustrated by Tod Smith. Stone Arch Books 2009 72p.
Grades: 4 5 6 7 8 9   **292; 741.5**
  1. Greek mythology; 2. Graphic novels

978-1-4342-1171-2, $23.93

LC 2008-32066

King Aegeus of Athens wants a son and ends up with Medea the sorceress; however, he had spent the night with Aethra of Troezen, and she bears a son she names Theseus. He grows up strong, and when he defeats a huge bully, Aethra tells him about his father and sends him to Athens. Along the way, Theseus defeats several evil men, and arrives in Athens. He's just in time to become part of the group of young people sent as sacrifices to appease Minos, King of Crete, who bears a grudge against Aegeus. Minos has a monstrous son, the half-bull half-human Minotaur, and the Athenian youths become the Minotaur's food. Theseus decides to fight the creature and gets help from Ariadne. The book includes information about the Oracle at Delphi, discussion questions, and a glossary.

Part of the Graphic Revolve series

Yoon, Jae-ho
In Dream World Vol. 1. Tokyopop 2005 198p. Illustration

Grades: 9 10 11 12 Adult   **741.5; Fic**
1. Adventure graphic novels; 2. Fantasy graphic novels; 3. Manwha; 4. Graphic novels
1-59532-516-6, $9.99

Nightmares are bad enough when you are asleep, but in this land of dreams, Nightmares are real, physical monsters. Drake, Hanee and Kyle fight these Nightmares with "In Dream Cards," magical cards that have unusual and devastating powers. Those who wield the cards are masters of their elements. But just how did our heroes become entangled in this dream world? And what will it take to get home? The book includes violence and partial nudity.

Yoshida, Akira
Conan and the Demons of Khitai. Writer, Akira Yoshida; artist, Paul Lee; letterers, Richard Starkings and Comicraft's Albert Deschesne; cover artist, Pat Lee and Dream Engine. Dark Horse Comics 2006 Un Illustration

Grades: 11 12 Adult   **741.5; Fic**
1. Adventure graphic novels; 2. Conan the Barbarian (Fictional character); 3. Fantasy graphic novels; 4. Graphic novels
978-1-59307-543-9, $12.95

Set many years in the future from the ongoing series, this book marks Conan's first appearance as King in Dark Horse's comics revival of the legendary fantasy hero. When King Conan receives an invitation from the Eastern kingdom of Khitai to open trade in precious jewels and spices, he decides that he will travel into this long-mysterious land. Yet to do so is perilous, as those who have requested his company may have far more devious intentions, and beasts unseen by Western eyes lurk amidst the shadows. The book contains graphic, bloody violence as men fight monstrous beasts.

X-Men: Kitty Pryde - Shadow & Flame. Written by Akira Yoshida ; art by Paul Smith. Marvel Entertainment 2006 Un Illustration

Grades: 8 9 10 11 12 Adult   **741.5; Fic**
1. Adventure graphic novels; 2. Superhero graphic novels; 3. X-Men (Fictional characters); 4. Graphic novels

0-7851-1816-0, $14.99

A deadly mystery draws Kitty Pryde and her fire-breathing friend Lockheed to the shores of Japan. Ninjas and dragons will be the least of their worries, however, as a long-forgotten villain from Kitty's past is about to finally make his move. There's lots of ninja fighting action.

Yoshida, Sunao
Trinity Blood Vol. 1. Story by Sunao Yoshida; illustrated by Kiyo Kyujo. Tokyopop 2006 178p. Illustration

Grades: 10 11 12 Adult   **741.5; Fic**
1. Fantasy graphic novels; 2. Horror graphic novels; 3. Manga; 4. Vampires; 5. Graphic novels
1-59816-674-3, $9.99

In a dark and distant future, Armageddon has giving rise to the fabled Second Moon—and a perpetual war between the vampires and the humans. Esther is a nun in the city of Istavan. When she crosses paths with Abel Nightroad, a priest sent from the Vatican to combat the local order of vampires, the two form a holy alliance to battle the most evil of threats: Gyula, the leader of the vampires. In this gothic-action series the very survival of the human race is at stake. The book includes some violence.

Yoshida, Tatsuo
Speed Racer: Mach go go go vol. 1 & 2, 2v. Digital Manga Publishing 2008 Illustration

Grades: 7 8 9 10 11 12 Adult   **741.5; Fic**
1. Adventure graphic novels; 2. Automobile racing; 3. Manga; 4. Graphic novels
978-1-56970-731-9, set $39.95

This two-volume set reprints the original Speed Racer manga in its entirety, released for the 40th anniversary of Speed Racer. All the characters are here: Speed, Pops, Sparky, Mom, Trixie, Spritle, Chim Chim, and the mysterious Racer X. Readers will learn how Pops had to set out on his own, how Speed became a professional racecar driver in order to help finance Pops design the special, 12 cylinder Mach 5 engine. In addition to racing, Speed has to deal with people who try to steal Pops' engine plans, rival racers who'll try any cheating tactic to win, and try to figure out who Racer X is. While the animated television series was fine for children to watch, this manga includes violent action that makes it more suitable for teen readers. A note about the title: in Japanese, "go" means "5."

Yoshinaga, Fumi
Antique Bakery Vol. 1. Digital Manga Publishing 2005 192p. Illustration

Grades: 10 11 12 Adult   **741.5; Fic**
1. Humorous graphic novels; 2. Josei manga; 3. Manga; 4. Romance graphic novels; 5. Shojo manga; 6. Graphic novels
1-56970-946-7, $12.95

Three young men run a European style bakery and cafe in a former antique shop. Tachibana, the manager, and master pastry chef Ono are thirty-two years old and former high school classmates. Twenty-one-year-old Eiji is a boxer forced to retire because of eye injuries; he lives to eat fine pastries and has apprenticed himself to Ono. Ono is shy in the kitchen, but he's gay and seems to charm even straight men, except for Tachibana and Eiji. The stories revolve around their interactions in the bakery, and around some of their customers, in comedy that never degenerates into sitcom cliches. One scene showing Ono and a young man having sex doesn't show much graphically, yet it is perfectly clear what is happening. The books include lots of pointers about French pastries. This is a four-volume series.

Yoshizaki, Seimu
★ **Kingyo** used books, vol. 1. [translation, Adrienne Weber]. Viz Media/Viz Signature 2010 191p. Illustration
Grades: 9 10 11 12 Adult
741.5; Fic
1. Books and reading; 2. Manga; 3. Graphic novels
978-1-4215-3362-9, $12.99

Courtesy of Viz Media

This manga collects several stories based in or connected to Kingyo Used Books, a used manga store in Tokyo. An art student finds inspiration in a manga series based on the life of the famous artist Hokusai; a silly gag manga helps an archer regain his focus in time for a match; a young Japanese man raised in the U.S. uses an old detective manga series from the 1950s to model his life; the manga store owner's son tries to get away from manga by living in Europe, where he discovers that comics are everywhere; a busy housewife rekindles the passion in her life when she rediscovers a shojo manga featuring a dreamy male protagonist. While there is no violence or bad language, all the main characters are adults.

Yoshizumi, Wataru
Ultra Maniac Vol. 1. Viz Media/Shojo Beat 2005 184p. Illustration
Grades: 5 6 7 8 9 10
741.5; Fic
1. Humorous graphic novels; 2. Manga; 3. Romance graphic novels; 4. Shojo manga; 5. Graphic novels
1-59116-917-8, $8.99

Shy Ayu Tateishi has just made a new friend at school. But this new friend, much to her surprise, is no ordinary classmate. Nina Sakura may look like a normal middle school girl, but she's got a big secret. She's a witch. Or, rather, she's studying to be a witch. And, apparently, she's not doing her homework. Her spells are devastating in their ineffectiveness and often result in the most embarrassing situations for poor Ayu. But things wouldn't be so bad if Nina's sorcery didn't make Ayu look silly in front of the one boy she secretly adores. All she wants is a simple love potion. What she gets, however, is a new best friend who almost flunked out of witch school. This is a five-volume manga series.

Young, Ethan
Tails : Book 1. Ethan Young. Hermes Press 2012 160 p.
Grades: 10 11 12 Adult
741; Fic
1. Artists; 2. Superhero comic books, strips, etc
161345015X; 9781613450154, $15.99

LC 2012934894
Ethan may seem like your typical struggling cartoonist. The trouble is, Ethan's just too hapless to realize it yet. As his life gets weirder in the real world, it also does on the comic page. Before he knows it, Ethan gets in over his head when fantasy and reality combine — and then things get really weird.

Young, Larry
Astronauts in Trouble: Master Flight Plan. AiT/Planet Lar 2003 Un Illustration
Grades: 9 10 11 12 Adult
741.5; Fic
1. Science fiction graphic novels; 2. Graphic novels
1-932051-16-3, $16.95

"Live from the Moon" launches fifty years after Armstrong's one small step. The world's richest man claims the moon as his own personal property... and Channel Seven is there! "Space: 1959" is a period adventure featuring an earlier generation of the Channel Seven newshounds from "Live from the Moon". They uncover the story of Col. Lloyd Macadam's top-secret moon-shot program. Macadam's plans are accelerated when a Russian spy commandeers the rocket and the Colonel must choose between his country and his life. "One Shot, One Beer" picks up ten years after the events of "Live from the Moon" where space jockeys relate tales of life on Earth's desolate sister, far from home. The stories portray lots of action.

Young-Oh, Kim
Banya: The Explosive Delivery Man Vol. 1. Dark Horse Comics 2006 Un Illustration
Grades: 10 11 12 Adult
741.5; Fic
1. Adventure graphic novels; 2. Fantasy graphic novels; 3. Manwha; 4. Graphic novels
978-1-59307-614-6, $12.95

With a worldwide war raging between humans and monsters, the young delivery men of the Gaya Desert Post Office do not pledge allegiance to any country or king. They are banded together by a pledge to deliver. "Fast. Precise. Secure." Banya, the craziest and craftiest of the bunch, will stop at nothing to get a job done. Known as the "Explosive Delivery Man" for his risk taking, bold resolve, and impeccable record, Banya agrees to complete a wounded soldier's mission to transport a parcel of great importance - not knowing what dangers lie in store for him and his friends. As their arduous journey begins, Banya promises, "There isn't a delivery I can't make. I always deliver." Kim Young-Oh's fantastical world is filled with unique monsters, vicious swordplay, and a dash of hotfooted humor.

Youngquist, Jeff
Spider-Man: Saga of the Sandman. Marvel Entertainment 2007 176p. Illustration
Grades: 7 8 9 10 11 12 Adult
741.5; Fic
1. Fantastic Four (Fictional characters); 2. Hulk (Fictional character); 3. Spider-Man (Fictional character); 4. Superhero graphic novels; 5. Graphic novels
978-0-7851-2497-9, $19.99

It was no day at the beach when criminal Flint Marko was mutated into one of Marveldom's most versatile villains. This book recounts his origins and some of the best battles between Sandman, Spider-Man, the Fantastic Four and the Hulk.

Yukimura, Makoto
 Planetes Omnibus 1. By Makoto Yukimura. Random House Inc 2015 528 p.
Grades: 10 11 12 Adult
 1. Outer space — Exploration — Fiction; 2. Science fiction graphic novels; 3. Space colonies — Fiction; 4. Space debris — Fiction
 1616559217; 9781616559212, $19.99
 In this book, by Makoto Yukimura, "It's the 2070s, and mankind has conquered space, making interplanetary travel possible and igniting the imaginations of the world. It's also vastly increased the amount of dangerous space debris, and someone has to clean it up. Hachimaki, Yuri, and Fee are a crew on that beat, each with their own goals, tendencies, and personal problems." (Publisher's note)
 Originally published in the U.S. by Tokyopop in 4 volumes
 Volume 1 of 2

Yun, Mi-Kyung
 Bride of the water god, vol. 1. Dark Horse Comics 2007 186p. Illustration
Grades: 8 9 10 11 12 Adult   **741.5**
 1. Fantasy graphic novels; 2. Romance graphic novels; 3. Graphic novels
 978-1-59307-849-2, $9.95
 Soah's impoverished, drought-stricken village sacrifices her to the Water God Habaek in hopes of getting rain. Instead of dying, Soah finds herself in the land of the gods, and she meets Habaek, who is a young boy. What she doesn't know (but the reader does) is that he takes the form of an adult man at night. She's supposed to be Habaek's bride, but so far she's just an outsider who doesn't belong anywhere. This is sunjeong manwha the Korean equivalent of shojo manga.

Yune, Tommy
 Speed Racer & Racer X: the origins collection. Art by Jo Chen. IDW Publishing 2008 Un Illustration
Grades: 8 9 10 11 12 Adult   **741.5; Fic**
 1. Adventure graphic novels; 2. Automobile racing; 3. Racer, Speed (Fictional character); 4. Graphic novels
 978-1-60010-211-0, $19.99
 In 1999, Wildstorm Productions relaunched Speed Racer with a three-part origins story; it was successful enough to launch another three-part story telling the origins of Speed's brother, Racer X (come on, it's not a spoiler, everyone but the Racer family knows this). IDW Publishing has collected the stories into this volume. Here is the story of how Speed becomes the driver of the Mach 5, designed by Pops Racer, and here is the story of why Rex Racer left the family, how he "died," and Racer X was born from the wreckage. There is a lot of racing action, some violence, and some mild fan service.

Yurkovich, David
 Less Than Heroes. Top Shelf Productions 2004 152p. Illustration

Grades: 10 11 12 Adult   **741.5; Fic**
 1. Superhero graphic novels; 2. Graphic novels
 1-891830-51-1, $14.95
 In the city of Philadelphia there is a tall building at 18th and Market Streets atop of which live four individuals. They are the official protectors of the city. Their job is to be around when traditional law enforcement fails. But are they really heroes? Meet Philadelphia's contracted super-hero team, Threshold. A quartet more interested in milk and cookies than crime and punishment. A team more concerned with battling indigestion than their arch enemies. Sure, they have super-powers. They can leap tall buildings, fly, and do all the stuff other heroes do. More than human? Probably. Less than heroes? Without a doubt. While there's little in the way of overt violence or strong language, the story itself has more appeal to mature readers.

Zahler, Thomas F.
 ★ **Love** and capes, vol. 1: do you want to know a secret?. Story and art by Thomas F. Zahler. IDW Publishing 2008 160p. Illustration
Grades: 8 9 10 11 12 Adult   **741.5; Fic**
 1. Humorous graphic novels; 2. Romance graphic novels; 3. Superhero graphic novels; 4. Graphic novels
 978-1-60010-275-2, $19.99
 Independent bookseller Abby falls in love with her accountant, Mark; then he confesses to her that he's the superpowered crime-fighter, the Crusader. How does one have a romantic relationship with a superhero? Even without meaning to do it, Abby gives away Mark's secret to her sister Charlotte. Oops. So begins a "heroically super situation comedy" in which Abby feels she's competing against the beautiful Amazonia (Mark's superpowered ex-girlfriend), not to mention Mark's over-protective mother, and Mark has to deal with Abby's obnoxious brother Quincy, who thinks Mark is a wimp.
 Volume 1 of 4

 ★ **Love** and capes, vol. 2: going to the chapel. IDW Publishing 2010 192p. Illustration
Grades: 8 9 10 11 12 Adult   **741.5; Fic**
 1. Humorous graphic novels; 2. Romance graphic novels; 3. Superhero graphic novels; 4. Graphic novels
 978-1-60010-680-4, $19.99
 Independent bookstore owner Abby and accountant Mark Spencer, who is also the superhero called the Crusader, have fallen deeply and completely in love. Which is wonderful, except Mark can't quite seem to figure out how to propose to Abby and almost blows it. When he gets over that hurdle, more problems crop up. For one thing, Abby wants the PERFECT wedding dress. Then, a super villain impersonates Mark and almost destroys their relationship. Abby has to find a new bookstore employee when her sister Charlotte gets the chance to go back to college in Paris. France. Abby decides she needs to understand what Mark goes through as a superhero, and she gets superpowers, and a new identity, only to learn that it's far more difficult, and tragic, than she ever imagined. And then, on the eve of the wedding, another super villain strikes, this time changing history, and only Abby has the power to put things right again, which she'll have to do if she wants to marry Mark. This story has superhero action, romance, comedy, drama, romance ... the only content that might bother some people

happens when Abby and Amazonia, Mark's superhero ex-girlfriend, get drunk and bond together.

Zekuu, To-ru
    Shiki Tsukai Volume 1. Random House/Del Rey Manga 2007 Un Illustration
    Grades: 9 10 11 12   **741.5; Fic**
    1. Fantasy graphic novels; 2. Manga; 3. Graphic novels
    978-0-345-49925-7, $10.95
    On the day he turns fourteen, Akira discovers his destiny: He's a shiki tsukai, a warrior with the magical power to control the seasons. He also meets the beautiful Koyomi, another warrior, who is sworn to protect him. For there are evil forces intent on destroying Akira-and the entire universe. The book includes fighting violence and some sexual suggestiveness.

Zimmerman, Dwight Jon
    The **hammer** and the anvil: Frederick Douglass, Abraham Lincoln, and the end of slavery in America. Dwight Jon Zimmerman; illustrated by Wayne Vansant; foreword by James M. McPherson; editorial consultant, Craig Symonds. Hill and Wang 2012 Ix, 150 p. Color illustration; Color; Map
    Grades: 10 11 12 Adult   **B; 973.7092/2; 973.7092**
    1. Abolitionists — Biography; 2. African American abolitionists — Biography; 3. Antislavery movements — United States — History — 19th century; 4. Douglass, Frederick, 1818-1895; 5. Lincoln, Abraham, 1809-1865; 6. Presidents — United States — Biography; 7. Presidents — United States
    0809053586; 9780809053582, $24.95; 9780809053599, $15.95; 0809053594
                                 LC 2011032361
    This book presents a "graphic biography" of "Abraham Lincoln and Frederick Douglass. For both men, the book . . . show[s] the challenges that they faced as children, their efforts to overcome difficult circumstances, and the very real impact both men had on shaping the social and political consciousness of their times. It draws parallels between the humble circumstances of their early years . . . [and] look[s] at the difficulties both men faced and what motivated them." (Publishers Weekly)
    Includes bibliographical references.
    A novel graphic from Hill and Wang.

Zinn, Howard
    A **people's** history of American empire: a graphic adaptation. By Howard Zinn, Mike Konopacki, and Paul Buhle. Henry Holt and Company/Metropolitan Books 2008 275p.
    Grades: 10 11 12 Adult   **973; 741.5**
    1. College teachers; 2. Historians; 3. Nonfiction writers; 4. Social activists; 5. United States — Foreign relations; 6. United States — History; 7. United States — History; 8. United States — Territorial expansion; 9. Zinn, Howard, 1922-2010 — Adaptations; 10. Graphic novels
    978-0-8050-7779-7, $30; 978-0-8050-8744-4 (pa), $17
                                 LC 2007-31150
    First published in 1980, A People's History of the United States triggered a revolution in the way history is told, chronicling events as they were lived, from the bottom up. Now Howard Zinn, historian Paul Buhle, and cartoonist Mike Konopacki have collaborated to retell a chapter of A People's History: the centuries-long story of America's actions in the world. Narrated by Zinn, this version opens with the events of 9/11 and then jumps back to explore the cycles of U.S. expansionism from Wounded Knee to Iraq, stopping along the way at World War I, Central America, Vietnam, and the Iranian revolution. The book also follows the story of Zinn, the son of poor Jewish immigrants, from his childhood in the Brooklyn slums to his role as one of America's leading historians. The Civil Rights Movement is also included. The book includes images of violence, both in photographs and drawn art.

Zinsmeister, Karl
    Combat Zone: True Tales of GIs in Iraq. Marvel Entertainment 2005 Un Illustration
    Grades: 9 10 11 12 Adult   **Fic; 741.5**
    1. Iraq War, 2003-; 2. Graphic novels
    0-7851-1516-1, $19.99
    Longtime embedded journalist Karl Zinsmeister (Boots on the Ground: A Month with the 82nd Airborne in the Battle for Iraq) and penciler Dan Jurgens (Thor, Superman) chronicle three months in the lives of the 82nd Airborne in the Battle for Iraq in this series. As Zinsmeister states in his introduction, the stories are all based on real-life accounts; he changed the names of the soldiers and in some cases combined some of the incidents. The book includes battlefield violence and some mildly strong language.

Zirkel, Scott
    A **bit** haywire. Created & illustrated by Courtney Huddleston ; written by Scott Zirkel ; inked by Jeff Dabu and Courtney Huddleston ; colored by Mike Garcia ; lettered by Greg Gatlin. Viper 2006
    Grades: 5 6 7 8 9   **741.5; Fic**
    1. Humorous graphic novels; 2. Superhero graphic novels; 3. Graphic novels
    978-0-9777-8835-4; 0-9777883-5-0, $11.95
    Owen Brice wants more than anything to be a superhero; he lives in a city protected by the Noble Seven, a superhero team led by Captain Melee and Lady Barrage. On one memorable day, Owen discovers he does have powers, but they're . . . a bit haywire. He can run super fast—but only as long as he can hold his breath. He can fly—as long as he keps his eyes closed. He teleports when camera flashes go off (the first time, he accidentally teleports his clothes off); he burns when he sneezes; he can shoot lase beams from hiseyes when he's cold. Then he discovers his parents are Captain Melee and Lady Barrage. How does on train to be a superhero when all his powers are so weird" Owen decides to give it a try.

Zograf, Aleksandar
    Regards from Serbia: A Cartoonist's Diary of a Crisis in Serbia. Top Shelf Productions 2007 Un Illustration
    Grades: 10 11 12 Adult   **741.5**
    1. Autobiographical graphic novels; 2. War; 3. Graphic novels
    978-1-891830-42-6, $19.95

Serbian cartoonist Zograf used diary comics and email to reach out to other cartoonists when NATO bombs started falling on his town, Pancero, in 1999. This book collects those comics and emails, along with Zograf's earlier comics from the early 1990s, to give readers a local view of what to most Americans was a distant conflict.

Courtesy of Top Shelf Productions

Zub, Jim

★ **Skullkickers:** 1000 Opas and a dead body. Writer/creator, Jim Zub; line art, Edwin Huang and Chris Stevens; colors, Misty Coates and Chris Stevens. Image Comics 2011 Un Illustration

Grades: 9 10 11 12 Adult   **Fic; 741.5**

1. Adventure graphic novels; 2. Fantasy graphic novels; 3. Humorous graphic novels; 4. Graphic novels

978-1-60706-366-7, $9.99

First published in magazine form as Skullkickers #1-5 Volume 1 of 6

Adult

Aaron, Jason

The **Other** Side. DC Comics/Vertigo 2007 144p. Illustration

Grades: 12 Adult   **741.5; Fic**

1. Vietnam War, 1961-1975; 2. Graphic novels

978-1-4012-1350-3, $12.99

Billy Everette from Alabama gets drafted into the Marines in 1967; in North Vietnam, Vo Binh Dai volunteers to serve in the People's Army of Vietnam. The book follows these two young men through their training and their journey towards an inevitable confrontation. Billy starts seeing horrifying ghost images of dead soldiers in various stages of decay, and he hears his rifle telling him to kill. Vo maintains a strong sense of patriotism despite the hardships of the march south to find the war. They both end up at Khe Sanh just after the Tet Offensive in February 1968.

Anyone who has seen such movies as "Full Metal Jacket" or "We Were Soldiers Once" will know what to expect in this book; the language is full of expletives and the battle scenes are brutal. Aaron and Stewart bring the harsh reality of war to readers 40 years after the fact.

Originally published as The Other Side issues #1-5.

Scalped: Indian Country. DC Comics/Vertigo 2007 128p. Illustration

Grades: 12 Adult   **741.5; Fic**

1. Mystery graphic novels; 2. Graphic novels

978-1-4012-1317-6, $9.99

Fifteen years ago, Dashiell "Dash" Bad Horse ran away from a life of abject poverty and utter hopelessness on the Prairie Rose Indian Reservation in hopes of finding something better. Now he's come back home armed with nothing but a set of nunchucks, a hell-bent-for-leather attitude and one dark secret, to find nothing much has changed on "The Rez"—short of a glimmering new casino, and a once-proud people overcome by drugs and organized crime. Is he here to set things right or just get a piece of the action? This book has lots of graphic violence, harsh language, nudity, and sexual situations.

Southern Bastards; Volume 1: here was a man. By Jason Aaron, illustrated by Jason LaTour. Image Comics 2014 128 p. Color; Illustration

Grades: Adult   **Fic; 741.5**

1. Alabama — Fiction; 2. Crime; 3. Vigilantes

1632150166; 9781632150165, $9.99

"What does old Earl Tubb do when he returns home to Craw County, Ala., only to find the place a veritable criminal fiefdom run by Euless Boss, the local high school football coach" Why, pick up the stick helpfully cleaved by lightning from a tree growing out of his daddy's grave and start meting out justice just like his father, the old sheriff, did." (Publishers Weekly)

Volume 1 of an ongoing series

Thor; Volume 1: the goddess of thunder. Writer, Jason Aaron; artists, Russell Dauterman (#1-4) & Jorge Molina (#5); color artists, Matthew Wilson (#1-4) & Jorge Molina (#5); letterer, VC's Joe Sabino; cover art, Russell Dauterman & Frank Martin. Marvel Enterprises 2015 136 p. Color; Illustration

Grades: 9 10 11 12 Adult   **741.5**

1. Thor (Fictional character); 2. Women superheroes

0785192387; 9780785192381, $24.99

In this book, by Jason Aaron, illustrated by Russell Dauterman, "Mjolnir lies on the moon, unable to be lifted! Something dark has befallen the God of Thunder, leaving him unworthy for the first time ever! But when Frost Giants invade Earth, the hammer will be lifted - and a mysterious woman . . . the mighty Thor! Who is this new Goddess of Thunder? Not even Odin knows . . . but she may be Earth's only hope against the Frost Giants!" (Publisher's note)

"When the classic Thor is no longer righteous enough to wield his hero-making mallet, the only person worthy enough to take up the mantle is . . . well, you don't find out in this volume. But the point is that it's a lady, and she's every bit up to the task, as she proves by taking on bloodthirsty Frost Giants, the Minotaur CEO of megacorporation Roxxon, and the Dark Elf Malekith." Booklist

Contains material originally published in magazine form as Thor #1-5.

Volume 1 of an ongoing series

Abadzis, Nick

★ **Laika.** First Second Books 2007 205p. Illustration

Grades: 5 6 7 8 9 10 11 12 Adult   **Fic; 741.5**

1. Soviet Union — History — 1953-1991; 2. Space flight; 3. Graphic novels

1-59643-101-6; 978-1-59643-101-0

LC 2006-51907

Laika was the abandoned puppy destined to become Earth's first space traveler. This is her journey. Along with Laika, there is Korolev, once a political prisoner and now a driven engineer at the top of the Soviet space program, and Yelena, the lab technician responsible for Laika's health and life. The book depicts the dedication and struggles of the scientists and technicians who worked in the Soviet space program, based on research Abadzis did before writing this book. The book includes a bibliography of books and websites.

"Abadzis's tear-inducing and solidly researched graphic novel treatment of Laika's surpassingly tragic story is a standout." Publ Wkly

Abbott, Wes

Dogby Walks Alone. Tokyopop 2006 Un Illustration

Grades: 9 10 11 12 Adult   **741.5; Fic**

1. Amusement parks; 2. Mystery graphic novels; 3. Graphic novels

1-59816-582-8, $9.99

Dogby is the park mascot for Happyplace, the world's happiest theme park. When other, armed mascots invade Happyplace and the beautiful Princess is murdered, Dogby and his best friend Snack Girl try to find out what's happening. In this rather wacky mystery, all the characters are identified by their function (for example, P.U.M.G. - Park-Upper-Management-Guy) or their costume. Dogby never says a word, and with the masked costume, his expression never changes, yet Abbott manages to convey his emotions to the reader. This is the first volume of a global manga series.

Dogby walks alone vol. 2: Dogby walks tall. Tokyopop 2008 Un Illustration
Grades: 9 10 11 12 Adult   **741.5; Fic**
1. Humorous graphic novels; 2. Graphic novels
978-1-59816-583-8, $9.99
: Dogby, the former costumed animal mascot of the Happyland amusement park, has wandered into the Alaskan wilderness, where he rescues a young boy. He finds the town where the boy lives gripped by fear and ruled by criminals. The boy's single mother struggles to make an honest living, but the criminals, led by a strangely costumed leader named Shelikof, tighten their grip even as they deal with internal struggles led by the hooded Leader. Then there's the Kodiak bear that seems to be hunting Dogby ...

Abel, Jessica
   Mastering comics: drawing words & writing pictures continued. By Jessica Abel and Matt Madden. First Second 2012 Xvii, 318 p. Illustration; Color
Grades: 9 10 11 12 Adult   **741.5/1; 741.5**
1. Cartooning — Technique; 2. Cartoonists; 3. Comic books, strips, etc — Technique; 4. Drawing
1596436174; 9781596436176, $34.99
                              LC 2011037023
Jessica Abel's book "Mastering Comics," written with her husband Matt Madden, is a "course of study for the budding cartoonist. Covering advanced topics such as story composition, coloring, and file formatting, [the book] is a vital companion to the introductory content of the first volume" entitled "Drawing Words & Writing Pictures." (Publisher's note)

Abirached, Zeina
   I remember Beirut. Zeina Abirached. Graphic Universe 2014 96 p. Illustration; Map
Grades: 8 9 10 11 12 Adult   **741.5; 92**
1. Abirached, Zeina, 1981-; 2. Beirut (Lebanon) — Biography; 3. Beirut (Lebanon) — Biography — Juvenile literature; 4. Children and war; 5. Lebanon — History — 20th century; 6. Lebanon — History — 20th century — Juvenile literature; 7. War
1467738220; 9781467738224, $29.27
                              LC 2013047112
In this graphic memoir, Zeina Abirached "reveals numerous details from her childhood in Beirut during the war from 1975 to 1990 war. 'I remember' is a recurring phrase and provides a personal frame of reference for the effect of war on kids. Some are simple childhood memories. . . . Inclusion of . . . maps and diagrams orient the reader and provide additional perspective." (Kirkus Reviews)
   "The blocky, naive-style pictures quietly evoke wartime fears in ways the words simply cannot—bullet holes in the sides of cars, rubble in the streets, her father's eyebrows indicating increasing sadness at the heartbreaking state of a formerly vital market." Booklist

Abouet, Marguerite
   ★ **Aya:** life in Yop City. By Marguerite Abouet and Clément Oubrerie; translated by Helge Dascher. Drawn & Quarterly 2012 96 p. Color; Illustration
Grades: 10 11 12 Adult   **741.5/944; 741.5**
1. Africa — Fiction; 2. Friendship — Fiction
1770460829; 9781770460829, $24.95
   This book, by Marguerite Abouet and Clément Oubrerie, "is the story of the studious and clear-sighted nineteen-year-old Aya, her easygoing friends Adjoua and Bintou, and their meddling relatives and neighbors. It's . . . [an] account of the simple pleasures and private troubles of everyday life in Yop City." (Publisher's note)
   Followed by Aya: Love in Yop City

   ★ **Aya:** love in Yop City. By Marguerite Abouet and Clément Oubrerie; translatied by Helge Dascher. Drawn & Quarterly 2013 328 p. Color illustration
Grades: 10 11 12 Adult   **741.5; Fic**
1. Côte d'Ivoire; 2. Graphic novels — Côte d'Ivoire; 3. Ivory Coast; 4. Nineteen seventies; 5. Teenage girls — Côte d'Ivoire
1770460926; 9781770460928, $24.95
                              LC 2012545664
This graphic novel, written by Marguerite Abouet and Clément Oubrerie, comprises the final three chapters of the 'Aya' story, . . . a lighthearted story about life in the Ivory Coast during the 1970s, a particularly thriving and wealthy time in the country's history. When a professor tries to take advantage of Aya, her plans to become a doctor are . . . shaken, and she vows to take revenge on [him]." The book includes "recipes, guides to understanding Ivorian slang, street sketches, and concluding remarks from Abouet explaining . . . social milieu." (Publisher's note)

★ **Above the Dreamless Dead: World War I in Poetry and Comics.**
   Edited by Chris Duffy. First Second 2014 144 p. Illustration
Grades: 9 10 11 12 Adult   **741.5**
1. World War, 1914-1918; 2. World War, 1914-1918 — Poetry
1626720657; 9781626720657, $24.99
   In this book edited by Chris Duffy, "various artists adapt the works of some of the most famous WWI poets, including Wilfred Owen, Siegfried Sassoon, and Isaac Rosenberg. The . . . cartoonists, including Hunt Emerson, Sarah Glidden, and Stuart Immomen, use different approaches to illuminate poems known for its bitter irony and brutal honesty." (Publishers Weekly)
   "The work of 'Trench Poets' from WWI is brought vividly to life by accomplished cartoonists. This stunningly effective presentation does much to inform readers of the emotional and physical horrors of war. The volume's small format renders some of the detail difficult to decipher, but anything larger might be overwhelming. There's very mature content, especially in lyrics of soldiers' songs. Reading list." Horn Book
   Includes bibliographical references and index

The Adventures of the Fly Volume 1
Archie Comics 2004 96p. Illustration
Grades: 3 4 5 6 7 8 9 10 11 12 Adult   **741.5; Fic**
1. Adventure graphic novels; 2. Superhero graphic novels
1-879794-18-7, $12.95

This book highlights one of the pioneering super-hero titles of the Silver Age: The Fly. Tommy Troy is a young boy whose world is turned upside down when he meets an emissary of the Fly World and is given a special ring that magically transforms him into the superhuman Fly. Considered an early prototype of Spider-Man, the Fly's earliest adventures were charted by some of the most legendary creative talent in comics: Jack Kirby, Joe Simon, Jack Davis, and Al Williamson. All of these artists and more are featured in this special edition that collects titanic tales from 1959 and 1960.

Aguirre-Sacasa, Roberto
★ **Afterlife** with Archie: Escape from Riverdale. Story by Roberto Aguirre-Sacasa; artwork by Francesco Francavilla; lettering by Jack Morelli. Archie Comic Publications 2014 160 p. Color; Illustration (Afterlife with Archie)
Grades: 11 12 Adult   **741.5**
1. Andrews, Archie (Fictional character); 2. Dogs — Fiction; 3. Witches — Fiction; 4. Zombies — Fiction
1619889080; 9781619889088, $17.99
                                        LC 2014430277
In this book, by Roberto Aguirre-Sacasa, "[w]hen Jughead's beloved pet Hot Dog is killed in a hit and run, Jughead turns to the only person he knows who can help bring back his furry best friend - Sabrina the Teenage Witch. Using dark, forbidden magic, Sabrina is successful and Hot Dog returns to the land of the living. But he's not the same... and soon, the darkness he brings back with him from beyond the grave begins to spread." (Publisher's note)

"Not parody but serious drama, this graphic novel casts off the typical Archie comic lightheartedness and goes deep into the gut. . . . Paired with Francavilla's dead-on illustrations, the excellent writing from Aguirre-Sacasa . . . brings constant surprises while confronting the dilemma of remaining humane through crisis." LJ

Civil War: Peter Parker, Spider-Man. Writer, Roberto Aguirre-Sacasa; artist, Clayton Crain; pencilers, Angel Medina & Sean Chen; inker, Scott Hanna; colorist, Avalon's Dan Kemp. Marvel Entertainment 2007 Un Illustration
Grades: 9 10 11 12 Adult   **741.5; Fic**
1. Spider-Man (Fictional character); 2. Superhero graphic novels; 3. Graphic novels
0-7851-2189-7, $17.99
The Civil War has begun, sides have been chosen. Spider-Man chose to unmask himself to the whole world, and now everyone knows he's Peter Parker. Every action has consequences, but for Peter, will he pay, or will his loved ones pay?

The **Sensational** Spider-Man: Feral. Artist, Angel Medina, Clayton Crain. Marvel Entertainment 2007 Un Illustration
Grades: 7 8 9 10 11 12 Adult   **741.5; Fic**
1. Spider-Man (Fictional character); 2. Superhero graphic novels; 3. Graphic novels

978-0-7851-2126-8, $19.99
Strange changes are coming over Spidey's animalistic foes - including Dr. Curt Connors, John Jameson and Felicia Hardy - awakening the beast that dwells within them all. Spidey's beaten the Lizard, Man-Wolf and the Black Cat before, but they've never been more vicious than they are now.

Ahrens, Lois
The **Real** cost of prisons comix. [edited by] Lois Ahrens. Comics by Lois Ahrens, Craig Gilmore, Ruth Wilson Gilmore, et al. PM Press 2008 72 p. Illustration
Grades: Adult   **365/.973**
1. Prisoners; 2. Prisoners — Social aspects — United States; 3. Prisoners — United States; 4. Prisons; 5. Prisons — Social aspects — United States; 6. Prisons — United States
1604860340; 9781604860344, $14.95
                                        LC 2008929092
This nonfiction graphic novel, edited by Lois Ahrens, "provides a crash course in what drives mass incarceration, the human and community costs, and how to stop the numbers from going even higher. This volume collects the three comic books published by the Real Cost of Prisons Project." (Publisher's note)
Includes bibliographical references

Aihara, Miki
Tokyo Boys & Girls Volume 1. Story by Satoru Akahori; art by Yukimaru Katsura. Viz Media/Shojo Beat 2005 200p. Illustration
Grades: 10 11 12 Adult   **741.5; Fic**
1. Manga; 2. Romance graphic novels; 3. Shojo manga; 4. Graphic novels
1-4215-0020-5, $8.99
Mimori Kosaka's dream comes true when she's accepted to the Meidai Attached High School and gets to wear their super-fashionable uniform. The school year starts off well when Mimori befriends the beautiful Nana, but things quickly turn sour for her when she is chosen to be the class representative. Through a series of unfortunate events, she finds herself the focus of attention by three boys and her teachers, for all the wrong reasons. Mimori is reunited with Atsushi, a boy she knew in elementary school—and it turns out he despises her for allegedly bullying him in their grade school days. In fact, he plans to exact a little revenge. The series includes sexual innuendo, brief sexual situations, and some strong language.

Akahori, Satoru
Kashimashi: Girl Meets Girl Vol. 1. Story by Satoru Akahori ; art by Yukimaru Katsura. Seven Seas Entertainment 2006 Un Illustration
Grades: 10 11 12 Adult   **741.5; Fic**
1. Fantasy graphic novels; 2. Manga; 3. Romance graphic novels; 4. Yuri manga; 5. Graphic novels
978-1-933164-34-2, $10.99
Being a girl is harder than it looks. For Hazumu, this couldn't be truer, because just the other day, she... was a he. Shunned by the girl of his dreams, Hazumu loses himself in the mountains and is promptly squashed by an oncoming space ship. The alien inside, feeling guilty, rebuilds

Hazumu's body... but as the wrong gender! Now Hazumu must learn how to be the girl his parents always wanted while dealing with the trials and tribulations of being caught in a love triangle between two girls - his childhood friend, Tomari, and Yasuna, the girl who rejected him but is now strangely attracted to him/her. This yuri (girl-girl romance) manga was published in a shonen magazine in Japan. The book includes partial nudity and sexual situations.

Akamatsu, Ken
    Love Hina: Omnibus 1. By Ken Akamatsu; translated by Satsuki Yamashita; lettered by Hope Donovan. Kodansha Comics 2011 542 p. Illustration
Grades: 11 12 Adult   **741.5**
    1. Grandmothers — Fiction; 2. Japan — Fiction; 3. Manga; 4. Young men — Fiction
1935429477; 9781935429470, $19.99
                      LC 2011517873
    In this book, by Ken Akamatsu, "Keitaro Urashima fails his entrance exams to get into Tokyo University for the second time. . . . To make things worse, his parents have kicked him out of his house. Fortunately, his grandmother owns the fabulous Hinata Lodge and has agreed to take Keitaro in as caretaker. What he doesn't know is that the lodge is actually a girl's dorm and he's the only guy around!" (Publisher's note)
    Originally published in the U.S. by Tokyopop in 14 volumes
    First published in 1999 by Kodansha Ltd., Tokyo as: Love Hina vol. 1-3—Vol. 1, t.p. verso.
    Volume 1 of 5

Akimoto, Yasushi
    One Missed Call 1+2. Original story by Yasushi Akimoto; manga by Mayumi Shihou. Dark Horse Comics 2007 262p. Illustration
Grades: 10 11 12 Adult   **741.5; Fic**
    1. Horror graphic novels; 2. Manga; 3. Graphic novels
978-1-59307-747-1, $14.95
    It's an epidemic of accidental death. Multiple college students receive odd voice-mails from themselves, messages from the future, and all they contain are the screams of their own deaths. A few days later, at the date and time of the message's posting, they die in mysterious accidents, and oddly enough, each has a candy in their mouths. The book includes some partial nudity and some violence, but the horror is mostly psychological.

Akino, Matsuri
    Tokyo pet shop of horrors volume 1. Tokyopop 2008 Un Illustration
Grades: 10 11 12 Adult   **741.5; Fic**
    1. Horror graphic novels; 2. Manga; 3. Graphic novels
978-1-4278-0607-9, $9.99
    Several years after the mysterious Count D left Los Angeles' Chinatown, a new exotic pet shop has opened in the Shinjuku Chinatown of Tokyo. D is still selling strange pets to customers. One hardworking single mother comes seeking a pet/bodyguard for her young son, because she's plagued by horrible nightmares of her ex-husband coming to kill them. The "pet" looks like a young boy, but he's able to quiet her nightmares. A young woman comes seeking an

"unlovable" pet, to find that she has a beautiful young teen boy in her house; it turns out she's an aspiring writer and he helps her find success. Each of these customers, however, find that getting what they want may exact a higher price than they expected. The book includes nonsexual partial nudity and some violence.

Alan Moore: Portrait of an Extraordinary Gentleman.
    Abiogenesis Press/Top Shelf Productions 2003 352p. Illustration
Grades: 11 12 Adult   **741.5**
    1. Graphic novels
0-946790-06-X, $14.95
    This book contains comic strips, illustrations, essays, articles, anecdotes and other pieces contributed by American, English, and international comics creators paying tribute to the master of comic book writing, Alan Moore (creator of Watchmen and From Hell), as he celebrates his 50th year. 145 contributors include Neil Gaiman, Will Eisner, Bill Sienkiewicz, Dave Gibbons, Denis Kitchen, David Lloyd, Jim Valentino, Sergio Toppi, Bryan Talbot, Steve Parkhouse, Mark Millar, Howard Cruse, James Kochalka, Jose Villarrubia, Sam Kieth, Dave Sim, Oscar Zarate, DJ Paul Gambaccini, and novelist Darren Shan, to name just a few. The book includes some content not suitable for younger readers, some strong language, some nudity, and some violence.

Alexovich, Aaron
    Kimmie66. Written & illustrated by Aaron Alexovich; lettering by Jared K. Fletcher. DC Comics/Minx 2007 176p. Illustration
Grades: 7 8 9 10 11 12 Adult   **741.5; Fic**
    1. Science fiction graphic novels; 2. Graphic novels
978-1-4012-0373-3, $9.99
    In the 23rd century, people spend lots of time in online VR lairs. Telly Kade is a fairly typical teen of her time, and she tends to hang out in an online vampire lair. Right now, however, she is a little creeped out, because she has received a suicide note from her best friend, Kimmie66. And now other people seem to see Kimmie66 all over the 'net, and Telly wants to know what is really going on.
    A Minx graphic novel

    Serenity Rose Vol. 1: Working Through the Negativity. SLG Publishing 2005 Un Illustration
Grades: 9 10 11 12 Adult   **741.5; Fic**
    1. Humorous graphic novels; 2. Witches; 3. Graphic novels
1-593620-11-X, $12.95
    When you can float through the air, smash things with your brain, and conjure up monsters out of ectoplasm, you're bound to attract attention. Serenity Rose, local witch, amateur painter, and noted recluse, wants to be left alone, but she spends the day dodging goblins, goths, greasy politicians, big media parasites, and gawking tourists in the "spookiest lil' town in America." The art is cute-Goth, but there's some harsh language.

All Star Comics Archives Volume 11
    DC Comics 2005 273p. Illustration
Grades: 7 8 9 10 11 12 Adult   **741.5; Fic**

1. Flash (Fictional character); 2. Green Lantern (Fictional character); 3. Justice Society of America (Fictional characters); 4. Superhero graphic novels; 5. Wonder Woman (Fictional character)
1-4012-0403-1, $49.95

The adventures of the world's first super-team continue in this extra-sized final volume of the series. In Volume 11, collecting All Star Comics #50-57, the JSA face the Diamond Men, Mr. Alpha, and more. The Justice Society of America included the Golden Age Flash, Green Lantern, Dr. Mid-Nite, Hawkman, Wonder Woman, Black Canary, and Atom.

Allan, Von
Li'l kids: road to God knows . . . adventures!. Von Allan Studio 2008 86p. Illustration
Grades: 7 8 9 10 11 12 Adult   **741.5; Fic**
1. Friendship; 2. Mother-daughter relationship; 3. Graphic novels
978-0-9781237-1-0, $13.95

In three interlocked short stories, readers meet Marie, a lonely eight-year-old girl, as she meets neighbor girl Kelly. Marie has been sent outside with a little ball, told by her mother to play. Kelly has to return three late videotapes to the rental store; they're all cutesy-kiddie movies she refuses to watch, after all she is eight years old. Then Marie falls asleep at the kitchen table while drawing her own superhero comic strip and dreams that her character is real. In the last story, readers meet Betty, Marie's mother. Something about her is definitely wrong, but Marie is just confused by her mother's wonky sense of time. Allan includes concept art and the outline and completed script for each story, providing readers with a look at how he puts a comic together. While Marie and Kelly are eight years old, younger readers might not see the subtle hints at trouble that Marie will face in her teen years.

Allen, Brooke A.
★ A **home** for Mr. Easter. NBM Publishing, Inc. 2010 197p. Illustration
Grades: 8 9 10 11 12 Adult   **741.5; Fic**
1. Humorous graphic novels; 2. Rabbits; 3. Graphic novels
978-1-56163-580-1, $13.99; 1-56163-580-4

High school student Tesana is large, not too bright, strong, and has always gotten into trouble. A lonely misfit, she tries to fit in better by joining a pep rally planning committee. Once she finds the white rabbits that will be used in the pep rally, she discovers one that is very different: it lays colorful eggs that grant wishes. Tesana believes this is the real Easter Bunny, and she calls him Mr. Easter—and he talks to her. When the football team tries to take Mr. Easter away, Tesana takes them all down and then runs away. Soon they're pursued by cops, an unscrupulous and greedy pet shop owner, laboratory scientists, animal rights protesters, television news crews, a magician/con man, and her mom. Allen was a student at the Savannah School of Art and Design when she wrote this book.

"This is for mature readers who understand the humor, and would be a welcome addition for your multicultural section—female, robust, ethnic." Libr Media Connect

Allie, Scott
The **Fog**. Written by Scott Allie; art by Todd Herman. Dark Horse Comics 2005 Un Illustration
Grades: 9 10 11 12 Adult   **741.5; Fic**
1. Horror graphic novels; 2. Graphic novels
1-59307-423-9, $6.95

A group of Shanghai traders have come to America hoping to escape a string of weird deaths at the teeth and claws of unseen monsters. The arrival of a strange yet familiar fog reveals that the curse has found them, but even they don't know what that has to do with a pyromaniac refugee from the Civil War, the disappearance of one of their sons, or the terrible change coming over the Americans in this small seaside town. This story is a prequel to the motion picture "The Fog." The story has some foul language and some violence, but mostly atmospheric horror.

Allison, John
Bad Machinery 4: The Case of the Lonely One. By John Allison. Oni Press 2015 136 p. Color; Illustration
Grades: 7 8 9 10 11 12 Adult   **741.5**
1. Mystery fiction; 2. School stories
1620102129; 9781620102121, $19.99
LC 2012953355

In this book, by John Allison, "a new school year brings a new classmate to Griswald's Grammar School! But he's a bit strange, and he really, really likes onions. When the whole school suddenly becomes best friends with him, Shauna seems to be the only one left out. It's up to her to peel back the mystery, one onion layer at a time." (Publishers note)

Bad machinery; 1: the case of the team spirit. John Allison; [edited by] James Lucas Jones. Oni Press 2013 112 p. Color; Illustration
Grades: 7 8 9 10 11 12 Adult   **741.5**
1. Mystery graphic novels; 2. School stories
1620100843; 9781620100844, $19.99
LC 2012953355

This graphic novel, the first in John Allison's Bad Machinery series, is "set in a grammar school in a British working-class community" and follows "three earnest boys vying against three sharp-tongued girls to solve mysteries. The framing story concerns a Russian owner of a U.K. foot-ball (soccer) team trying to bully an elderly homeowner to sell her house." (Publishers Weekly)

Bad Machinery; 2: The Case of the Good Boy. By John Allison; edited by James Lucas Jones and Jill Beaton. Oni Press 2014 136 p. Color; Illustration (Bad Machinery)
Grades: 7 8 9 10 11 12 Adult   **741.5**
1. Detectives — Fiction; 2. Dogs — Fiction; 3. England — Fiction; 4. Mystery fiction
1620101149; 9781620101148, $19.99

In this book, by John Allison, "everyone's favorite pre-teen British detectives are back for another case! With toddlers disappearing and rumors of a large, beast-like creature roaming the woods, Tackleford is in serious danger. And then there's Mildred's new dog Archibald . . . if you can even call it a dog. . . . Everything comes to a head once the boys get a picture of the beast and Archibald goes missing. Is there a connection—" (Publisher's note)

"The story veers between realism and fantasy, with just a touch of absurdism to keep things fun. . . . The bright, colorful art and snarky dialogue are icing on a delightful cake." Booklist

Bad Machinery; 3: The Case of the Simple Soul. By John Allison. Oni Press 2014 136 p. Color illustration; Color; Map
Grades: 7 8 9 10 11 12 Adult   **741.5**
1. Monsters; 2. Mystery graphic novels; 3. School stories
1620101939; 9781620101933, $19.99
In this graphic novel, by John Allison, "the Tackleford gang is back with a new case that demands solving! When Tackleford's derelict barns begin going up in flames, Linton and Sonny are on the case with a moderately mysterious new friend. Paths cross, however, when Lottie and Mildred meet a terrifying yet misunderstood creature living beneath a bridge!" (Publisher's note)

"[W]hat stands out in this work is the authentic dialogue, characters' constant questioning, and the protagonists' experiences as 'new' teenagers. Allison addresses how they are coping with physical and emotional changes, balancing friendships, and romantic relationships in a humorous way." SLJ
Originally published online as a webcomic

Allred, Michael
Madman atomic comics, vol. 1. Created, written and illustrated by Michael Allred; colors by Laura Allred. Image Comics 2008 Un
Grades: 10 11 12 Adult   **741.5; Fic**
1. Madman (Fictional character); 2. Science fiction graphic novels; 3. Graphic novels
978-1-58240-916-0, $19.99
Frank Einstein, Madman, undergoes a bizarre, phantasmagorical, existential journey that turns out to be something going on in his subconscious self while he's in a coma. His friends Dr. Flem, Joe (Josephine), and the Atomics hook up Astroman, Frank's robotic "clone," as a technological rescue beacon to lead him through his myriad of fictional personae to his true self, but when they think both Frank and Astroman are dead, they send them up into space in a rocket. Astroman tries to go for help, but his batteries run out, then Frank is rescued by Haley FouFou, who proclaims that he is "one of the Four" who must save the universe. He sends for the Atomics to help him defeat the Crimson King, who has been infected with a cosmic virus and will turn the universe inside out if not stopped. The book is not for casual comics readers, although familiarity with previous Madman comics aren't really necessary to understand this new series. Allred challenges readers with existential discussions and elliptical plotting, and he has fun drawing in the style of many different cartoonists and artists. There's some violence and a little partial nudity, but little in the way of harsh language ("monkey spit" is the strongest epithet Frank utters).

Michael Allred's madman volume 3. Created, written and illustrated by Michael Allred; colors by Laura Allred. Image Comics 2008 Un Illustration
Grades: 9 10 11 12 Adult   **741.5; Fic**
1. Adventure graphic novels; 2. Science fiction graphic novels; 3. Graphic novels

978-1-58240-893.4, $17.99
This volume completes Image Comics' project of collecting and reprinting the regular Madman Comics series previously published elsewhere. This collection includes The Exit of Dr. Boiffard and G-Men From Hell, along with the Madman King-Size Super Groovy Special. Madman is Frank Einstein, a man with no memory of who or what he had been before. He has wild, surrealistic science fictional adventures with giant brains, sea monsters, frog men, demons, mutating beatniks, secret agents, and lots more. The book includes some violence.

★ **Red** rocket 7. Image Comics 2008 Un Illustration
Grades: 9 10 11 12 Adult   **741.5; Fic**
1. Rock music; 2. Science fiction graphic novels; 3. Graphic novels
978-1-58240-998-6, $16.99
In a wild science fiction adventure that spans the history of American rock and roll, the humanoid alien known as Red Rocket is left for dead by the villainous Enfinites, but a robotic guardian creates seven clones, each with their own ability. Seven goes on a world-spanning tour of pop music, working with such artists as Little Richard, Elvis Presley, the Beatles, and David Bowie. On his last tour, rock music journalist Lynn Hayes gets mixed up with Seven, his brother clones, and the evil Enfinites who seek to destroy all the clones and Earth, while they're at it. This book was originally published in 1998 by Dark Horse Comics in an 11x11 album size. This new edition is in the vinyl single size and includes bonus material, including an essay from Allred's editor Jamie S. Rich, an introduction by Robert Rodriguez, and an outro by Gerard Way of Chemical Romance. Allred's book predates all the rock 'n' roll graphic novels that have come out in recent years. The book includes some violence and mild language.

Rocketeer adventures: Vol. 1. Mike Allred, Kurt Busiek and John Cassaday. IDW Pub. 2011 128 p.
Grades: Adult   **741.5/973; Fic**
1. Rocketeer (Fictional character); 2. Superhero comic books, strips, etc
1613770340; 9781613770344, $24.99
This graphic novel anthology, by Mike Allred, Kurt Busiek and John Cassaday, presents adventures of the 1930s hero, the Rocketeer. "Dave Stevens' The Rocketeer was an instant hit . . . in the early 1980s. Stevens' . . . distinctive artwork and . . . story was inspired by the adventure pulp novels of the era The Rocketeer was set in. . . . Now, . . . [this book] present[s] new interpretations of The Rocketeer by some of today's finest talents." (Publisher's note)

Alpert, Abby
Read on— graphic novels: reading lists for every taste. Abby Alpert. Libraries Unlimited 2012 Xxi, 177 p.
Grades: Adult   **016.7415**
1. Best books; 2. Graphic novels — Bibliography; 3. Libraries — Special collections; 4. Public libraries — United States — Book lists; 5. Readers' advisory services — United States
1591588251; 1610691555; 9781591588252, $40; 9781610691550
                        LC 2011039792

This book on graphic novels by Abby Alpert, part of the Read On series, offers "more than 500 original annotations organized within 70 thematic lists. The broad selection of titles is further categorized by key appeal elements, including story, character, setting, language, and mood, providing unique access points that allow discovery of interests to transcend subject headings in catalogs." (Publisher's note)

"This accessible guide is equally effective for collection building, readers' advisory, or individual perusal, and most public collections will find it perceptive and helpful. Recommended." Booklist

Includes index.

Amano, Akira

Reborn, Vol. 1. Viz Media/Shonen Jump Advanced 2006 192p. Illustration

Grades: 9 10 11 12 Adult   **741.5; Fic**

  1. Humorous graphic novels; 2. Manga; 3. Shonen manga; 4. Graphic novels

978-1-4215-0671-5, $7.99

Hapless middle school student Tsuna doesn't do well in school, sports, or socializing. Things get weird when the pint-size assassin named Reborn arrives, announces that Tsuna is the tenth generation Mafia boss of the Vongola family, and that he will tutor the boy. Among his many weapons, Reborn has the Deathperation Shot, which he uses to get Tsuna to succeed in training; basically, if the person shot with this bullet has regrets, he or she will be reborn instantly with the temporary power to do what needs to be done. Reborn has to shoot Tsuna a lot. Violence is cartoony, the humor is wacky slapstick, but the weapons look real and assassins spring out of nowhere.

Amano, Jeff

The **Cobbler's** Monster: A Tale of Gepetto's Frankenstein. Illustrated by Craig Rousseau. Image Comics 2006 Un Illustration

Grades: 11 12 Adult   **741.5; Fic**

  1. Horror graphic novels; 2. Graphic novels

1-58240-629-4, $14.99

Grieving over the death of his only son, Gepetto mixes the new science of DNA with the age-old magic of the golem to resurrect his son. But in truth, he was never very close to Victor. And the anger that burns within the heart of the monster he birthed and created, destroys everything and everyone around him. Now, Gepetto must hunt his own son. This is the story of a man and a monster who, through unspeakable horror, find their way to becoming father and son for the very first time. There's some strong language in the story, and also violence in this tale that combines Pinocchio and Frankenstein and the Jewish legend of the Golem.

Fade from Grace. Image Comics 2005 Un Illustration

Grades: 10 11 12 Adult   **741.5; Fic**

  1. Superhero graphic novels; 2. Graphic novels

1-58240-527-1, $14.99

Power wanes ... fame is fleeting ... but love never fades. Grace tells the story of how John gained the power to fade through walls and doors in order to save her life, then used his powers to help people. Then, when the powers started draining more out of him, they tried to leave, put the superhero deeds behind them, but they encounter a disaster and John knows he has to help to save lives, even if his ends ...

Red Warrior: Assassin for the Thieves World. Illustrated by Andy MacDonald. Image Comics 2006 Un Illustration

Grades: 10 11 12 Adult   **741.5; Fic**

  1. Adventure graphic novels; 2. Mystery graphic novels; 3. Graphic novels

978-1-58240-660-2, $12.99

Agent Tolik Kalinichenko convinces Elena - a Russian Mafia leader's daughter - to seduce an old flame who may be connected to a secret combat system called "Bespredel" (Russian for "without limits"). Elena risks her life for her country, Mother Russia, the world, but most of all, for Tolik. In a race against the clock, Tolik must destroy Bespredel's Red Warriors in time to save Elena, who has been discovered as an informant. But when war has no limits, where can love hide" The book has some strong language and violence, including martial arts fighting. Kat Amano provides an afterword describing Mixed Martial Arts, and the creators provide a bibliography on Russian organized crime and on martial arts.

Ronin Hood of the Samurai. Image Comics 2005 Un Illustration

Grades: 9 10 11 12 Adult   **741.5; Fic**

  1. Adventure graphic novels; 2. Chushingura — Adaptations; 3. Samurai; 4. Graphic novels

1-58240-555-7, $9.99

Masterless after his Lord falls prey to treachery, samurai Oishi of the 47 Ronin leads his faithful few to vengeance. The time has come to defend their honor and raise their swords one final time. This retelling postulates that Oishi and his men lived and fought as Robin Hood-like ronin to help poor villagers victimized by a vicious daimyo (Lord) before they wreaked vengeance for their Lord's death. The tale of the 47 ronin, also called Chushingura, is one of the most famous stories in Japan, called by some the Dd|national tale." The inevitable bloodshed is quite subdued.

The Amazing Adventures of the Escapist Vol. 3

Dark Horse Comics 2006 168p. Illustration

Grades: 8 9 10 11 12 Adult   **741.5; Fic**

  1. Adventure graphic novels; 2. Superhero graphic novels; 3. Graphic novels

978-1-59307-492-0, $14.95

This volume of The Escapist features the late Will Eisner's return to the Spirit, in a crossover tale with the Escapist. This story became Eisner's last comics work, completed just two weeks before the death of the comics godfather. Also in this volume is the comics writing debut of award-winning author and Guggenheim fellow Chris Offutt, illustrated by Thomas Yeates. Dan Best and Eddie Campbell contribute a fully painted story from the 1939 World's Fair in Empire City, and 2004 Russ Manning Award winner Eric Wight brings a polemic story from writer Jason Hall to life. Among the other notable contributors are Howard Chaykin, Paul Grist, Shawn Martinbrough, David Hahn, Roy Thomas, Matt Wagner and indie stalwarts Jeffrey Brown and Jason. The book includes some violence.

Ambaum, Gene

Book Club: An Unshelved Collection. by Gene Ambaum and Bill Barnes ; art by Bill Barnes. Overdue Media 2006 120p. Illustration

Grades: 7 8 9 10 11 12 Adult   **741.5**

1. Humorous graphic novels; 2. Libraries; 3. Graphic novels

0-9740353-3-5, $17.95

What happens in the library stays in the library. But oh, what happens in the library! Dewey has a book club, and you do not talk about Book Club. Colleen has a blog, but she doesn't know everyone can read it. Someone gave vegan Tamara a membership to the ham-of-the-month-club. And Merv reserved every copy of the new Harry Potter for purposes nefarious. This collection also features dozens of full-page full-color comic-format book talks, plus a very special storytime zombie nursery rhyme. This is the fourth print collection of the daily web comic chronicling the shenanigans at the Mallville Public Library.

Frequently asked questions: an Unshelved collection. By Gene Ambaum and Bill Barnes ; art by Bill Barnes. Overdue Media 2008 135p. Illustration

Grades: 7 8 9 10 11 12 Adult   **741.5**

1. Humorous graphic novels; 2. Libraries; 3. Graphic novels

978-0-9740353-5-2, $17.95

This sixth collection of the Unshelved webcomics includes all daily and Sunday Book Club comic strips from February 19, 2007 through February 16, 2008. It includes "The Great Plastic Coffee Cup Lid Comic Strip Challenge," a week-long competition between Unsheleved and Dave Kellett's Sheldon, another webcomic. It also includes all the special comic strips done for ALA's Cognotes, the conference newsletter published every day of the Midwinter Meeting and Annual Conference. The Sunday Book Club strips are in color, each one is a full page, and constitutes a mini-booktalk cum reader's advisory for each title, which range from YA fiction to graphic novels to classic science fiction and more.

★ **Large** print: an unshelved collection. By Gene Ambaum and Bill Barnes ; art by Bill Barnes. Overdue Media 2010 128p. Illustration

Grades: 7 8 9 10 11 12 Adult   **741.5**

1. Humorous graphic novels; 2. Libraries; 3. Graphic novels

978-0-9740353-7-6, $11.95

Courtesy of Overdue Media

This volume collects the daily webcomic strips of Unshelved from February 16, 2009 to April 26, 2010 plus the strips that originally appeared in ALA Cognotes in June 2009 and January 2010. It introduces a change in format and a lower price point, in that the Sunday booktalk strips are not included. The strips collected for this volume reflect the recession, as the Mallville Public Library deals with a public that now comes to the library to use the computers to apply for unemployment benefits, fill out job applications, and more. Despite the gloomy times, the strips still find humor in the everyday happenings in the public library. Librarians and people who like to use libraries will find that Mallville is not so different from their local libraries.

Read Responsibly: An Unshelved Collection. By Gene Ambaum and Bill Barnes ; art by Bill Barnes. Overdue Media 2007 135p. Illustration

Grades: 8 9 10 11 12 Adult   **741.5**

1. Humorous graphic novels; 2. Libraries; 3. Graphic novels

978-0-9740353-4-5, $17.95

The fifth year of strips about the Mallville Public Library, its eccentric staff and even more eccentric patrons, includes the Pimp My Bookcart sequence (that sparked a nationwide contest) and a year's worth of full-color full-page Unshelved Book Clubs featuring the greatest books ever written. Probably. Plus never-before published strips, mostly those done for American Library Association conferences, and more.

America's 1st Patriotic Comic Book Hero: The Shield Volume 1

Archie Comics 2002 96p. Illustration

Grades: 3 4 5 6 7 8 9 10 11 12 Adult   **741.5; Fic**

1. Adventure graphic novels; 2. Superhero graphic novels

1-879794-08-X, $12.95

A hero with great power, strength and courage who donned the colors of the American flag. A hero who lived for democracy and protected the world from the foes of freedom! No, it's not who you think... it's THE SHIELD, who predated his well known counterpart by over a year. This historic full color trade paperback reprints his first 8 stories from PEP and SHIELD/WIZARD Comics. It includes his first appearance and origin, along with the covers of the comics they originally appeared in, dating from 1940.

Amir

★ **Zahra's** paradise. Amir Khalil. First Second 2011 255 p. Illustration

Grades: 10 11 12 Adult   **741.5**

1. Iran — History — 1979-; 2. Iran — Politics and government; 3. Missing persons — Fiction; 4. Graphic novels

9781596436428 (pa); 1596436425

LC 2011017564

This book, a "Publishers Weekly" Best Comics title for 2011, is "[s]et in the aftermath of Iran's fraudulent elections of 2009 . . . [and] is the fictional story of the search for Mehdi, a young protestor who has vanished into an extrajudicial twilight zone. What's keeping his memory from being obliterated is not the law. It is the grit and guts of his mother, who refuses to surrender her son to fate, and the tenacity of his brother, a blogger, who fuses tradition and technology to explore and explode the void in which Mehdi has vanished." (Publisher's note)

★ **An Anthology of graphic fiction, cartoons, and true stories.**
Edited by Ivan Brunetti. Yale University Press 2006 400p. Illustration
Grades: 11 12 Adult   **741.5**
978-0-300-11170-5; 0-300-11170-3, $28
                                    LC 2006-14095
"Comic art is a vital, highly personal art form in which change—rapid and unpredictable—is the norm. In this exciting new anthology, comic artist Ivan Brunetti focuses on very recent works by contemporary artists engaged in this world of change. . . . The book presents contemporary art comics produced by 75 artists, along with some classic comic strips and other related fine art and historical materials. Brunetti arranges the book to reflect the creative process itself, connecting stories and art to each other in surprising ways: nonlinear, elliptical, sometimes whimsical, even poetic. He emphasizes continuity from piece to piece, weaving themes and motifs throughout the volume." (Publisher's note)

Andelman, Bob
Will Eisner: A Spirited Life. M Presss 2005 375p. Illustration
Grades: 9 10 11 12 Adult   **92; 741.5**
1. Artists — Biography; 2. Arts — Biography; 3. Authors — Biography; 4. Cartoonists — Biography; 5. Cartoonists — United States — Biography; 6. Eisner, Will, 1917-2005; 7. Literature — Biography; 8. Graphic novels
1-59582-011-6, $14.95
                                    LC 2005026326
Internationally recognized for his genre-busting 1940s art and storytelling style on The Spirit, Will Eisner's greatest legacy may be the graphic novels he championed and created. He was an American master whose work in comics permanently altered the face of global pop culture. This biography explores Eisner's life, detailing a career that spanned 70 years and saw him educate several generations of Army soldiers in the innovative PS Magazine and create the first widely known graphic novel, A Contract with God. Eisner also introduced some of the world's greatest comics art talent: Bob Kane (Batman), Jack Kirby (Fantastic Four), Jules Feiffer, Dave Berg (MAD) and Joe Kubert (Tarzan). And he inspired generations of modern artists and writers, including Frank Miller (Sin City), Robert Crumb, Harlan Ellison, Neil Gaiman (Sandman, American Gods), Brad Bird (The Incredibles), Patrick McDonnell (Mutts) and Art Spiegelman (Maus). A Spirited Life also includes interviews with many of Eisner's contemporaries, such as Alan Moore, Dave Gibbons, Neil Gaiman, Denis Kitchen, Jim Warren, Dave Sim, Denny O'Neil and Stan Lee.
"Michael Chabon contributes a heartfelt introduction to Andelman's first-ever biography of Will Eisner (1917-2005) . . . Eisner revolutionized the field . . . from his 1940s stories featuring masked crime fighter the Spirit to his later, pioneering graphic novels but also as businessman and entrepreneur, teacher, mentor, and the inspiration of countless young artists [like Art Spiegelman]. . . . Besides verifying Eisner's impact on nearly every artist who drew comics in his wake, Andelman shows that Eisner's influence extends to such film directors as Spielberg and Tarantino." Booklist

Anderson, Christine
The **long** tail: why the future of business is selling less of more. Art by Shane Clester. Smarter Comics 2011 80p. Illustration
Grades: 10 11 12 Adult   **658.8; 741.5**
1. Business; 2. Marketing; 3. Graphic novels
978-1-61066-006-8, $12.95
                                    LC 2010-942329
Anderson's bestselling book about niche markets the "long tail" of the title is now a graphic novel. Adapted by comics writer Bunn, this book describes how business is changing with the rise of e-commerce that allows the success of specialty appeal items, whether various forms of media or such things as t-shirts. Wired editor-in-chief Anderson discusses the rise and fall of the music industry, the video rental industry, and the many changes in brick-and-mortar retail due to ever-changing and advancing technology. The comic book format may attract more readers among older teens and college students, who are the consumers changing things.

Anderson, Eric A.
PX! Book one: a girl and her panda. Written by Eric A. Anderson and Manny Trembley; illustrated by Manny Trembley. Image Comics 2007 Un Illustration
Grades: 6 7 8 9 10 11 12 Adult   **741.5; Fic**
1. Adventure graphic novels; 2. Humorous graphic novels; 3. Science fiction graphic novels; 4. Graphic novels
978-1-58240-820-0, $16.99; 1-58240-820-3
A young girl named Dahlia and her trusty (robot) panda sidekick set off on a journey around the world to save her missing scientist father, who has been kidnapped by Pollo, an evil goat mastermind who wants to take over the world (and yes, people keep telling him his name means chicken" in Spanish). Along the way, Dahlia meets Weatherby Ian Poppington III, a Victorian English secret agent also known as Double Aught Seven," and Wikkity Jones, a rollerskating swordsman who talks like a hillbilly and stands ready to fight ninja any time. The absurd humor is punctuated by moments of intense violent action, especially in the side story about fighting zombies. This book collects the webcomic.
Followed by: PX! v.2: in the service of the Queen (2009)

Sam Noir Volume One. Art by Manny Trembley. Image Comics/Shadowline 2007 Un Illustration
Grades: 10 11 12 Adult   **741.5; Fic**
1. Adventure graphic novels; 2. Mystery graphic novels; 3. Graphic novels
978-1-58240-758-6, $15.99
Sam Noir is a samurai, and a private detective. When the woman he loves gets killed, he sets out for revenge, armed with his two swords. This violent story mixes samurai action with crime noir mystery with some pirate action.

Anderson, Ho Che
King: a comics biography. Fantagraphics 2010 312p. Illustration
Grades: 10 11 12 Adult   **741.5; 92**
1. African Americans — Biography; 2. African Americans — Civil rights; 3. Biographical graphic novels;

Courtesy of Fantagraphics

4. Civil rights activists; 5. Clergy; 6. King, Martin Luther, Jr, 1929-1968
978-1-60699-310-1, $34.99

"Much of the book (packaged nicely with previously unprinted material, sketches, and a somewhat beside-the-point modern-day "prelude" titled Black Dogs) tracks King from his college days in the 1950s to his death, jamming each page with noirishly drawn frames and tightly packed political debates. Though all the great moments of his civil rights battle are here (from the March on Washington to his less-successful housing campaign in Chicago), Anderson doesn't resort to the cheap cinematic trick of success and fadeout. There is more disappointment here than celebration, suffused with the sorrowful sense of a long, long battle just barely begun. A crowning achievement, like the man it portrays." Publ Wkly
First published 2005

Ando, Natsumi
The **Best** of draw! volume 3. Twomorrows Publishing 2008 256p. Illustration
Grades: 11 12 Adult   **741.5**
1. Comic books, strips, etc — Authorship; 2. Drawing — Technique
978-1-893905-91-7, $29.95
This volume collects articles from Draw! issues 5, 6, and 7, including interviews with the late Mike Weiringo, Bill Wray, and Dan Brereton, and tutorials on various aspects of drawing, including light and shadow, penciling hands, digital illustration, and figure drawing. The black and white illustrations include some nudity, particularly in the figure drawing tutorials.

Andrews, Mark
Tales of Colossus. Image Comics 2006 Un Illustration
Grades: 10 11 12 Adult   **741.5; Fic**
1. Adventure graphic novels; 2. Fantasy graphic novels; 3. Graphic novels
1-58240-591-3, $17.99
A knight, whose soul is trapped inside a metal monster called Colossus, lives out an immortal existence slaying evil creatures. Until one day a twisted, evil paladin wielding enchanted weapons arrives in the Kingdom with his own agenda. Their paths cross in a steel pounding, armor glinting no holds barred battle that will change a Kingdom forever. Set during the times of the Crusades, this book is filled with battles and bloodshed, with some nudity and sexual situations.

Andreyko, Marc
Manhunter: Street Justice. Marc Andreyko, writer; Jesus Saiz, penciller; Jimmy Palmiotti, inker; Steve Buccellato, colorist; Phil Balsman, Jared K. Fletcher, Pat Brosseau, letterers. DC Comics 2005 Un Illustration

Grades: 10 11 12 Adult   **741.5; Fic**
1. Superhero graphic novels; 2. Graphic novels
1-4012-0728-6, $12.99
When top federal prosecutor Kate Spencer loses a case against a super-villain, setting him free to kill again, she breaks the laws she has long upheld to become Los Angeles' newest crime fighting vigilante. Prosecuting super-villains has been her life's work But these criminals never stay locked up for good. Now, using confiscated met human weaponry she raided from an evidence locker, Kate tracks the perps who have eluded justice in the courts and delivers a long-overdue eye for an eye. She's found her true calling. She is the Manhunter. And she likes it. Plenty of violence, an anti-heroine who smokes and is willing to kill the criminals she hunts, make this superhero title one for older readers.

Manhunter: Trial by Fire. Art by Javier Pina, Jesus Saiz, Brad Walker, et al. DC Comics 2007 224p. Illustration
Grades: 10 11 12 Adult   **741.5; Fic**
1. Manhunter (Fictional character); 2. Superhero graphic novels; 3. Graphic novels
978-1-4012-1198-1, $17.99
When super criminals use the legal system to escape justice, prosecutor Kate Spencer assumed the role of vigilante, becoming the Manhunter and meting out her own brand of street justice. In this second collection, Spencer is poised to take on the trial of the year, as the eyes of the nation are on her latest case: finding the Shadow Thief guilty of murdering the hero Firestorm. As Manhunter she has to protect the Shadow Thief against other villains out to kill him. Then she learns that she's only the latest in a long line of Manhunters, and someone is killing them all. This book includes violence, foul language, and sexual situations.

Nightwing: the lost year. Marv Wolfman, Marc Andreyko, writers; Jamal Igle, Jon Bosco, Joe Bennett, pencillers; Keith Champagne, Alex Silva, Jack Jadson, inkers; Jason Wright, Edgar Delgado, colorists. DC Comics 2008 Un IllustrationDC Comics 2008 Un Illustration
Grades: 10 11 12 Adult   **741.5; Fic**
1. Adventure graphic novels; 2. Nightwing (Fictional character); 3. Superhero graphic novels; 4. Graphic novels
978-1-4012-1671-9, $14.99
Nightwing interrupts a kidnapping attempt only to realize the victim is someone from his past, Liu, his first lover. She says she works for Eddie Hwang, who used to be Metal Eddie, a criminal mastermind who tried to use a teenage Dick Grayson. Liu says Eddie has gone straight. However, the Vigilante, a ruthless killer, is hunting Eddie. Nightwing needs to find out what Eddie really wants, while trying to prevent Vigilante from killing anyone. The book includes some sexual scenes without nudity, and lots of fighting violence.

Angel: Spotlight
IDW Publishing 2006 120p. Illustration
Grades: 10 11 12 Adult   **741.5; Fic**
1. Fantasy graphic novels; 2. Horror graphic novels
978-1-600100-023-6, $19.99
This collection compiles five one-shots focusing on different members of Angel's supporting cast, each from a different creative team. Peter David and Nicola Scott focus on Illyria. Dan Jolly and Mark Pennington handle Gunn,

Scott Tipton and Mike Norton feature Wesley. Jeff Mariotte and David Messina present Doyle. And Jay Faerber and Bob Gill offer up a tale of Conner. Monster fighting, demons, and internal organs are on display in the stories.

Anno, Moyoko
In clothes called fat. Comic by Moyoco Anno; translation provided by Vertical, Inc. Vertical Inc. 2014 258 p. Illustration
Grades: Adult   **741.5; Fic**
1. Josei manga; 2. Self-esteem — Fiction; 3. Weight loss — Fiction; 4. Young women — Fiction
9781939130433, $16.95; 1939130433
LC 2014030099
In this graphic novel, by Moyoco Anno, "Noko appears to be living a great life: she's got a good job and a loving boyfriend, but beneath a thin veneer is a young woman who is struggling with her self-image and self-confidence as she fights to keep her weight down. To Noko, being 5 pounds overweight means being miles away from happiness in her love life and in her workplace." (Publisher's note)
"Anno's illustrations of binges and purges, bony bodies and sallow faces are haunting, effective, and suit the story perfectly." LJ
Complete edition originally published in Japanese as Shibou to iu na no fuku wo kite: kanzenban by Shodensha in 2002—Colophon

Aoyama, Gosho
★ **Case** Closed Volume 1. Viz Media 2004 192p. Illustration
Grades: 9 10 11 12 Adult   **741.5; Fic**
1. Manga; 2. Mystery graphic novels; 3. Shonen manga; 4. Graphic novels
1-59116-327-7, $9.95
Precocious high school student Jimmy Kudo used his keen powers of observation and astute intuition to solve mysteries that have left law enforcement officials baffled. Hot on the trail of a suspect, Jimmy is accosted from behind and fed a strange chemical which physically transforms him into a first-grader. Taking on the pseudonym Conan Edogawa (from favorite mystery writers Arthur Conan Doyle and Edgar Allan Poe), he attempts to track down the people who did this to him. But until he finds a cure for his bizarre condition, Jimmy continues to help the police solve their toughest cases, and he lives with his best friend Rachel, who thinks he's Jimmy's cousin, and her private detective father (who gets credit for cracking all the cases). The murder cases are violent and there's a little sexual innuendo; despite Jimmy's little-kid appearance, the stories are not for younger readers.

Appignanesi, Richard
Hamlet. [Richard Appignanesi, text adaptor]; illustrated by Emma Vieceli. Harry N. Abrams/Amulet Books 2007 195p. (Manga Shakespeare)
Grades: 8 9 10 11 12 Adult   **822.3; 741.5**
1. Shakespeare, William, 1564-1616 — Adaptations
978-0-8109-9324-2, $9.95; 0-8109-9324-4
Shakespeare's classic play of murder and revenge is here adapted into a manga-style graphic novel. It's now set in 2107, after global climate change has devastated the Earth.

Appignanesi uses the text of the play and abridges it to fit the pages, while Vieceli's art vigorously carries the story along. The book includes a summary of the plot and a brief biography of Shakespeare.
First published in the United Kingdom

Introducing Postmodernism, Third Ed. Art by Chris Garratt. Totem Books 2005 176p. Illustration
Grades: 10 11 12 Adult   **190; 741.5**
1. Postmodernism; 2. Graphic novels
1-84046-575-1, $12.95
Postmodernism seemed to promise an end to the grim Cold War era of nuclear confrontation and oppressive ideologies. This volume uses cartoons and a spare text to trace the pedigrees of postmodernism in art, theory, science, and history, along with the ideas of Derrida, Baudrillard, Foucault, and other icons of postmodern thinking. A new edition will be published in September 2007.

Appollo
★ **Bourbon** Island 1730. By Appollo & Lewis Trondheim; art by Lewis Trondheim; translated by Alexis Siegel. First Second Books 2008 278p. Illustration
Grades: 9 10 11 12 Adult   **741.5; Fic**
1. Adventure graphic novels; 2. Pirates; 3. Slavery; 4. Graphic novels
978-1-59643-258-1, $17.95; 1-59643-258-6
LC 2007-46138
On Bourbon Island off the coast of Madagascar, a French ornithologist and his assistant are caught up in an adventure involving slavery, colonialism, and the last days of the great pirates.
"This eccentric but illuminating historical drama . . . [is] a compelling, engrossing story of people considering whether their cause is worth more to them than their lives." Publ Wkly

Aragones, Sergio
Sergio Aragones' Groo: Mightier than the Sword. Sergio Aragonés ; Mark Evanier. Dark Horse Comics 2002 Un Illustration
Grades: 7 8 9 10 11 12 Adult   **741.5; Fic**
1. Adventure graphic novels; 2. Fantasy graphic novels; 3. Humorous graphic novels; 4. Graphic novels
1-56971-612-9, $13.95
In a savage land of another era, a goodly segment of the world has long been under the heavy thumb of the evil, power-mad despot known as Pipil Khan. The tyrant wants nothing more than to name an heir and shuck his mortal coil, but one thing stands in his way: Groo. It seems Khan just can't rest easy until Groo is out of the way. He'll give his kingdom to the one of his sons who can accomplish this. One of them has a foolproof plan how to do it. Unfortunately for him, it may be that no plan is foolproof enough to thwart Groo. The book includes some comedic violence.

Sergio Aragones' Groo: The Groo Nursery. Writer/artist, Sergio Aragonés ; wordsmith, Mark Evanier ; letterer, Stan Sakai ; colorist, Tom Luth. Dark Horse Comics 2002 Un Illustration
Grades: 7 8 9 10 11 12 Adult   **741.5; Fic**
1. Adventure graphic novels; 2. Fantasy graphic novels; 3. Humorous graphic novels; 4. Graphic novels

1-56971-794-X, $11.95

In this collection, Groo visits the happy island of Felicidad and manages to stir up lots of trouble among the people. Then a minstrel sings of Groo's deeds in a country resembling Japan, only to keep finding himself in trouble. And a town that knows of Groo's dangerous reputation try to keep him out, but he's illiterate. Oy! The stories include some comic violence.

Araki, Hirohiko

JoJo's Bizarre Adventure Volume 1. Viz Media/Shonen Jump Advanced 2005 224p. Illustration
Grades: 10 11 12 Adult   **741.5; Fic**
1. Adventure graphic novels; 2. Horror graphic novels; 3. Manga; 4. Supernatural graphic novels; 5. Graphic novels
1-59116-754-X, $7.99

In a Japanese jail sits 17-year-old Jotaro Kujo: punk, fighter, delinquent...and possessed by a force beyond his control. Around the world, evil spirits are awakening: "Stands," monstrous invisible creatures which give their bearers incredible powers. To save his mother's life, Jotaro must tame his dark forces and travel around the world to Cairo, Egypt, where a hundred-year-old vampire thirsts for the blood of his family. But the road is long, and an army of evil Stand Users waits to kill JoJo and his friends... JoJo is a descendant of Jonathan Joestar, who had once defeated the evil vampire Dio. There's lots of monster/demon fighting violence, some crude humor, and strong language.

Rohan at the Louvre. Hirohiko Araki. NBM Pub. 2012 128 p. Color illustration
Grades: Adult   **Fic; 741.5/952; 741.5**
1. Adolescence; 2. Artists; 3. Fantasy fiction; 4. Supernatural graphic novels
1561636150; 9781561636150, $19.99
               LC 2011944475

This fantasy graphic novel "tells of a young man's encounter with a mysterious divorcee who moves into his grandmother's boarding house." As a teen, Rohan's manga art "attract[s] the attention of the beautiful, apparently emotionally disturbed boarder, who tells him of the darkest, most evil painting ever crafted." She disappears after destroying his work. "Ten years later, Rohan . . . discovers the mysterious evil painting is housed in one of the [Louvre] museum's closed wings." (Publishers Weekly)

Archie Americana Series: Best of the Eighties
Archie Comics 2001 96p. Illustration
Grades: 3 4 5 6 7 8 9 10 11 12 Adult   **741.5; Fic**
1. Andrews, Archie (Fictional character); 2. Humorous graphic novels; 3. Graphic novels
1-879794-06-3, $10.95

During the 1980s pop culture ruled America; even the President was a former actor. In this volume, Archie and friends experience the punk movement, the "Urban Cowboy" craze, see the rise of MTV, get into the preppie, new wave and "Flashdance" fashions, play Trivial Pursuit, and boogie at the roller disco.

Volume 1 of 2

Archie Americana Series: Best of the Fifties
Archie Comics 1992 96p. Illustration

Grades: 3 4 5 6 7 8 9 10 11 12 Adult   **741.5; Fic**
1. Andrews, Archie (Fictional character); 2. Humorous graphic novels; 3. Graphic novels
1-879794-01-2, $10.95

Readers can journey back to the days of drive-ins and hula hoops, plaid skirts and bobby sox, Elvis and beatniks, rollerskates and sock hops in this book that reprints stories from the 1950s.

Archie Americana Series: Best of the Fifties Book 2
Archie Comics 2003 96p. Illustration
Grades: 3 4 5 6 7 8 9 10 11 12 Adult   **741.5; Fic**
1. Andrews, Archie (Fictional character); 2. Humorous graphic novels; 3. Graphic novels
1-879794-15-2, $10.95

The '50s are a fondly remembered time for many - both those who lived during the decade as well as those who discovered it through movies like Grease and TV shows like Happy Days. They were also the perfect decade for Archie to have his misadventures - whether getting tangled up in the eternal love triangle or incurring the wrath of Mr. Weatherbee, Mr. Lodge and even his father, Archie and his friends scaled new heights of hilarity. Series editor Castiglia says in the Introduction that the 1950s was the first time the U.S. had been prosperous since the 1920s; teens could do fun things, not just work to help the family, and the Archie comics reflected the rise of popular culture.

Archie Americana Series: Best of the Forties Volume 1
Archie Comics 1991 128p. Illustration
Grades: 3 4 5 6 7 8 9 10 11 12 Adult   **741.5; Fic**
1. Andrews, Archie (Fictional character); 2. Humorous graphic novels; 3. Graphic novels
1-879794-00-4, $11.95

In 1941, Pep Comics introduced Archie Andrews, "America's newest boyfriend." Since then, Archie and his perennial teenage friends have entertained readers with their misadventures. This book includes the very first Archie story, with the first appearance of Betty and Veronica, Reggie, Jughead, Mr. Weatherbee, Miss Grundy, and the rest of the Archie characters as they originally appeared.

Archie Americana Series: Best of the Forties Book 2
Archie Comics 2002 96p. Illustration
Grades: 3 4 5 6 7 8 9 10 11 12 Adult   **741.5; Fic**
1. Andrews, Archie (Fictional character); 2. Archie (Fictional character); 3. Humorous graphic novels; 4. Graphic novels
1-879794-09-8, $10.95

In 1941, Pep Comics introduced Archie Andrews, "America's newest boyfriend." Since then, Archie and his perennial teenage friends have entertained readers with their misadventures. This book includes stories from 1946 through 1949, with more slapstick and screwball comedy from Archie and the gang.

Archie Americana Series: Best of the Seventies
Archie Comics 1998 96p. Illustration
Grades: 3 4 5 6 7 8 9 10 11 12 Adult   **Fic; 741.5**
1. Andrews, Archie (Fictional character); 2. Humorous graphic novels; 3. Graphic novels

1-879794-05-5, $9.95

The decade of the 1970s was a time of transition in America, and the Archie Comics gang was right there. In this volume, Riverdale experiences the women's movement, joins in the Bicentennial celebration, sees the rise of bubble-pop, and joins the crazes for patches, pet rocks, and CB radio. Archie and the gang play "Pong" (one of the earliest video games), watch popular movies and TV shows, and go to the disco.

Volume 1 of 2

Archie Americana Series: Best of the Sixties
Archie Comics 1995 96p. Illustration
Grades: 3 4 5 6 7 8 9 10 11 12 Adult   **741.5; Fic**
1. Andrews, Archie (Fictional character); 2. Humorous graphic novels; 3. Graphic novels
1-879794-02-0, $9.95

The 1960s was a time of dreams, hopes, revolution, and social change, and the nation's youth were at the forefront. Archie and his friends came along for the ride, exploring both the fun and the mores of the times with humor. In this book readers can see the girls in slim jims, experience Beatlemania as it hits Riverdale, watch the teens become flower children, see them hit the surf, drag race, and wear mod fashions.

Volume 1 of 2

Archie Classics: The Adventures of Little Archie Volume 1
Archie Comics 2004 96p. Illustration
Grades: 3 4 5 6 7 8 9 10 11 12 Adult   **741.5; Fic**
1. Adventure graphic novels; 2. Humorous graphic novels
1-879794-17-9, $10.95

Little Archie deals with Martian invaders, secret spies, pirates, freewheeling uncles, gorillas on the loose and more! Who knew a little boy could have so many adventures" This book collects vintage Little Archie stories originally published from 1961 through 1965.

Archie's Classic Christmas Stories Volume 1
Archie Comics 2002 96p. Illustration
Grades: 3 4 5 6 7 8 9 10 11 12 Adult   **741.5; Fic**
1. Andrews, Archie (Fictional character); 2. Humorous graphic novels; 3. Graphic novels
1-879794-10-1, $10.95

Deck the halls with smiles and laughter, fa la la la la, la la la la! Since their inception, Archie and his friends have delighted readers with scores of Yuletide tales. These stories proved so popular that in 1954 an entire series devoted to stories of Holiday Cheer and Good Will to all premiered: ARCHIE'S CHRISTMAS STOCKING. Archie and his friends show their holiday spirit in this collection of classic tales from the first decade of Santa Claus himself. This book features painstaking restorations of original stories published from 1957 through 1963.

Archie Comics Presents: The Love Showdown
Archie Comics 1994 Un Illustration
Grades: 3 4 5 6 7 8 9 10 11 12 Adult   **741.5; Fic**
1. Andrews, Archie (Fictional character); 2. Humorous graphic novels; 3. Graphic novels

1-879794-03-9, $4.95

In the mid-1990s, Archie Comics announced that Archie might finally choose between Betty and Veronica, after the love triangle had lasted since 1941; the story was published as a crossover among the four Archie comics series. This volume reprints the stories.

Arikawa, Hiro
★ **Library** wars, vol. 1: love & war. Story and art by Kiiro Yumi; original concept by Hiro Arikawa; [English translation & adaptation, Kinami Watabe]. Viz Media/Shojo Beat 2010 166p. Illustration
Grades: 9 10 11 12 Adult
741.5; Fic
1. Censorship; 2. Librarians; 3. Manga; 4. Shojo manga; 5. Graphic novels
978-1-4215-3488-6, $9.99

Courtesy of VIZ Media LLC

In Japan of the near future, the federal government passes the Media Betterment Act, and the Media Betterment Committee goes on book hunts to destroy any "unsuitable" book. The libraries strike back with the Library Defense Force, a paramilitary organization dedicated to protecting the freedom to read. Iku Kasahara started to work for libraries and wants more than anything to join the Library Defense Force; she's physically very capable, but drill instructor Sergeant Dojo pushes her very hard. Iku must improve her library skills as well as her physical skills if she's to work effectively as a soldier librarian.

This book "delivers an appealing, determined female lead in the midst of an intriguing war on censorship being waged in bookstores and libraries." SLJ

First published 2008 in Japan

Volume 1 of a 14-volume series

Arima, Keitaro
Tsukuyomi: Moon Phase Vol. 1. Tokyopop 2005 162p. Illustration
Grades: 10 11 12 Adult   **741.5; Fic**
1. Manga; 2. Seinen manga; 3. Vampires; 4. Graphic novels
1-59532-948-X, $9.99

Cameraman Morioka Kouhei is researching Schwarz Quelle Castle in Germany. When he steps inside the castle's great walls, he discovers a mysterious little girl, Hazuki, who's been trapped there for years. Utilizing her controlling charm, Hazuki tries to get Kouhei set her free. But this sweet little girl isn't everything she appears to be... In fact, she's a vampire; and when Kouhei frees her and she follows him back to Japan, her fellow German vampires track her down to take her back home. The book includes some strong language, violence, infrequent nudity, sexual situations, and later volumes will have some torture scenes.

Armstrong, Jason
Ferro City, Vol. 1: The Medusa Key. Image Comics 2007 Un Illustration
Grades: 10 11 12 Adult   741.5; Fic
1. Mystery graphic novels; 2. Robots; 3. Science fiction graphic novels; 4. Graphic novels
978-1-58240-738-8, $15.99

In the world of Ferro City, ten million sentient robots live and work for their human "masters." The Robo Sapiens Act is about to come up for a vote, and if it succeeds, could crash the entire economy. An illegally created piece of technology called the Medusa Key could change everything. Private detective Cyrus Smithe gets involved when his partner Harry Weston gets the Medusa Key on behalf of a client only he knows, only to die very messily. With police and gangsters after him, Smithe needs to find the Medusa Key and find out who the mysterious client is. Armstrong calls this "robot science fiction pulp noir," which pretty much describes the feel of the book. The robots sport glass-tube heads, aircars that look like 1950s-era automobiles fly through the air, and the city is full of retro futuristic architecture, as though everything were imagined by someone in 1939.
Originally published as Ferro City issues #1-4.

Asami, Yuu
A. I revolution volume 1. Go! Comi 2007 216p. Illustration
Grades: 10 11 12 Adult   741.5; Fic
1. Manga; 2. Robots; 3. Science fiction graphic novels; 4. Graphic novels
978-1-933617-64-0, $10.99

In the middle of the twenty-first century, household robots are everywhere. Teenage Sui's father runs MG Company, and he develops a very human-looking robot and wants Sui to "educate" it to act human. Naturally, Sui names the robot Vermillion. He has a special ability to communicate with computers without needing a physical connection, and it is this ability that makes Vermillion a target for the unscrupulous Dr. Sasaki. When Sui and Vermillion foil him, there's still trouble to come. Soon, another human-looking robot comes from another company; but this robot, whom Sui names Kira, has a secret mission and Vermillion is the target. The series includes some boy love elements, sexual innuendo, and mild violence.

Asamiya, Kia
Junk: Record of the Last Hero Vol. 1. DrMaster Publications 2006 200p. Illustration
Grades: 10 11 12 Adult   741.5; Fic
1. Manga; 2. Science fiction graphic novels; 3. Shonen manga; 4. Graphic novels
978-1-59796-107-8, $9.95

High school student Hiro hasn't gone back to school ever since a traumatic run-in with local bullies. Then he applies online for a new gadget, and when it arrives and he activates it, he finds himself encased within a powered armor JUNK suit. He starts going after the bullies in nightly rampages, but then he meets someone else with a JUNK suit who doesn't like the way Hiro is abusing his power. When he accidentally destroys his own home and kills his parents, he must learn to fend for himself and to choose to use his power

for good or for evil. The legendary manga-ka (manga creator) Kia Asamiya has written this manga, which includes considerable violence.

Asano, Inio
Nijigahara Holograph. By Inio Asano; translated by Matt Thorn. Fantagraphics 2014 200 p. Illustration
Grades: Adult   741.5
1. Curses — Fiction; 2. Murder — Fiction; 3. Mystery fiction; 4. School children — Fiction
1606995839; 9781606995839, $29.99

In this magna, by Inio Asano, "as butterflies ominously proliferate in town, the rumor of a mysterious creature lurking in the tunnel behind the school spreads among the children. When the body of Ari Kimura's mother is found by this tunnel's entrance, . . . the legend seems to be confirmed. . . . In order to appease the wrath of the beast, the children decide to offer it a sacrifice: The unfortunate Ari?, whom they believe to be the cause of the curse." (Publisher's note)
"Asano . . . delivers a dark and twisted psychological horror story that links together a series of characters and tragic events in one timeline that have devastating ramifications for a second timeline. Equal parts beautiful and highly disturbing, this story of love and loss, obsession and vengeance, is sometimes too opaque to be easily understood, but it has the kind of depth and layers that encourage multiple readings." Pub Wkly

Asaoka, Misuzu
Glass Wings. Tokyopop 2006 Un Illustration
Grades: 9 10 11 12 Adult   741.5; Fic
1. Fantasy graphic novels; 2. Romance graphic novels; 3. Shojo manga; 4. Graphic novels
1-59816-158-X, $9.99

In this collection, a boy struggles with a dreaded affliction that comes between him and his true love; an orphan has the power to take on the sickness of others; a disfigured boy confronts the inner conflict between his need to survive and his desire to love. In a blend of magic and realism, Glass Wings reveals love's capacity to overcome all obstacles and replenish the human spirit in the direst of times. This book includes some violence and strong language. This is a standalone manga title.

Ashby, Ruth
The **great** american documents: Volume 1, 1620-1830. Ruth Ashby; illustrated by Ernie Colón; editorial consultant Russell Motter. Hill and Wang 2014 160 p. Color illustration
Grades: 9 10 11 12 Adult   741.5; 93
1. United States — History — Sources; 2. United States — Politics and government — Sources
0809094606; 9780809094608, $40

LC 2013956401
Written by Ruth Ashby and illustrated by Ernie Colón, "'The Great American Documents: Volume 1' introduces as series narrator none other than Uncle Sam, who walks us through twenty essential documents. Each document gets a chapter, in which Uncle Sam explains its key passages, its origins, how it came to be written, and its impact. This graphic primer is an indispensable resource for students and anyone else who wants the facts of American history close at hand." (Publisher's note)

"Colon uses well-designed, full-color panel layouts to eloquently blend charts and other informative graphics with straightforward images of events, clothing, and customs as well as clear, concise metaphors, all with an eye toward promoting a solid understanding of the basic facts and their impact." Booklist

Includes bibliographical references

Askwith, Mark

Silencers. Art by R.G. Taylor. Image Comics 2007 Un Illustration

Grades: 11 12 Adult   **741.5; Fic**

1. Spies; 2. Graphic novels

978-1-58240-728-9, $14.99

Silencers is a compelling look at spies coming to terms with the changing face of espionage in the new world order. When the newest recruit to the Silencers is murdered, his death triggers a mission of betrayal and revenge. Violence and strong language figure in this story that invokes the themes of John LeCarre's books.

Augustyn, Brian

Gotham by Gaslight: A Tale of the Batman. Brian Augustyn, Mike Mignola, P. Craig Russell, Eduardo Barreto. DC Comics 2006 112p. Illustration

Grades: 8 9 10 11 12 Adult   **741.5; Fic**

1. Batman (Fictional character); 2. Science fiction graphic novels; 3. Superhero graphic novels; 4. Graphic novels

978-1-4012-1153-0, $12.99

In an age of mystery and superstition, how would the people of Gotham react to a weird creature of the night, a bat-garbed vigilante feared by the guilty and the innocent alike? Some would live in terror. Others would rest easier. Only one man would take no notice at all ... a man with other matters to attend to. His name? No one knows for sure. Most people know him only as Jack. Jack the Ripper. This book collects two Elseworlds adventures of Batman, Gotham by Gaslight and its sequel Master of the Future.

Auster, Paul

Paul Auster's City of Glass. Script adaptation, Paul Karasik and David Mazzucchelli; art, David Mazzucchelli. Avon Bks. 1994 129p. Illustration

Grades: 9 10 11 12 Adult   **741; 741.5**

0-380-77108-X; 9780380771080, $12

                         LC 93-91005

"Auster's acclaimed novel City of Glass, a dreamlike meditation on language and fiction in the form of a detective novel, has been translated into comics form to stunning effect. . . . This combination story, lecture and literary deconstruction begins when New York City detective novelist Daniel Quinn answers a wrong number. Donning the personas of both the detective he created and his own creator, Quinn attempts to protect a young man, who as a child was kept without light or language for nine years as his lunatic academic father tried to discover 'God's Language.'" (Publishers Weekly)

Avery, Ben

The hedge knight. [by] George R. R. Martin; Ben Avery, adapter; Mike S. Miller, artist. Marvel Enterprises 2006 160p. Illustration

Grades: 9 10 11 12 Adult   **741.5; Fic**

1. Fantasy graphic novels; 2. Knights and knighthood; 3. Graphic novels

978-0-7851-2577-8, $19.95; 978-0-7851-2578-5, $19.95

"Hulking young Dunk is the squire of an elderly warrior. When Dunk's master dies, he rides on to the next tournament in hopes of winning recognition for his knightly prowess. He acquires a squire of his own, a bald little boy who calls himself Egg, and gives himself the more elegant title of Duncan the Tall. . . . This heroic fantasy tale reinvigorates the tired category of sword and sorcery fiction by emphasizing the human angle." Publ Wkly

Avery, Fiona

Arana Vol. 1: The Heart of the Spider. Art by Roger Cruz and Mark Brooks. Marvel Entertainment 2005 Un Illustration

Grades: 8 9 10 11 12 Adult   **741.5; Fic**

1. Adventure graphic novels; 2. Superhero graphic novels

0-7851-1506-4, $7.99

She's fierce, she's sassy, she sticks to walls. Anya Corazon, a.k.a. Arana, is a next-generation girl warrior. A scrappy teen from Brooklyn by day, Anya becomes the Hunter of the ancient and mystical Spider Society by night. But first, she must survive her initiation and prove herself on her first mission, all while going to high school and hiding everything from her single-parent dad. Together with her partner, the mysterious mage Miguel, Anya must fight to protect the peace of the world from the sworn enemies of the Spider Society, the evil Sisterhood of the Wasp. There's lots of super hero action here.

Arana Vol. 2: In the Beginning. Art by Roger Cruz. Marvel Entertainment 2005 Un Illustration

Grades: 8 9 10 11 12 Adult   **741.5; Fic**

1. Adventure graphic novels; 2. Superhero graphic novels

0-7851-1719-9, $7.99

Anya Corazon continues her work as Arana. What seems like a routine collar turns out to be anything but when the corrupt judge Anya captured reveals a deadly new threat to the Spider Society. While her partner Miguel tangles with an old enemy, a new one appears to challenge Anya, and he's willing to kill everyone around her.

Axe, David

War Fix. Steve Olexa, David Axe. NBM 2006 96p. Illustration

Grades: 11 12 Adult   **741.5; 956.7; Fic**

1. Iraq War, 2003-; 2. Graphic novels

978-1-56163-463-7, $15.95

2006 ForeWord Graphic Novel Gold Award.

As a kid, David watched the first Iraq war on CNN. As an adult in March 2003, David is now a journalist, but he becomes obsessed with the new war in Iraq and decides he's going to go there. He tells his editor he's going to cover the elections. He buys body armor, travels to Baghdad, and joins a unit of army truckers who drive in supply convoys. He witnesses violence, death, most of it pointless. Even after he returns home, his friends and his lover can see what David hasn't realized yet - he's hooked on the violence. Brutal, honest depictions of violence and some nudity make this appropriate for older readers.

War is boring: bored stiff, scared to death in the world's worst war zones. David Axe and Matt Bors. New American Library 2010 124p. Illustration

Grades: Adult   **92; 741.5**

978-0-451-23011-9, $12.95

"As a correspondent for The Washington Times, C-SPAN and BBC Radio, Axe flew from conflict to conflict, reveling in death, danger, and destruction abroad while, back in D.C., his apartment gathered dust, his plants died, and his relationships withered. War reporting was physically, emotionally, and financially draining-and disillusioning. Loosely based on the web comic of the same name, with extensive new material, War Is Boring takes us to Lebanon and Somalia; to arms bazaars across the United States; to Detroit, as David tries to reconnect with his family-and to Chad, as David attempts to bring attention to the Darfur genocide." (Publisher's note)

Azzarello, Brian

Batman: Broken City. Writer, Brian Azzarello; artist, Eduardo Risso; letterer, Clem Robins; colorist, Patricia Mulvihill; original series covers, Dave Johnson. DC Comics 2004 Un Illustration

Grades: 10 11 12 Adult   **741.5; Fic**

1. Batman (Fictional character); 2. Joker (Fictional character); 3. Mystery graphic novels; 4. Superhero graphic novels; 5. Graphic novels

1-4012-0214-4, $14.99

While hunting the murderer of a small boy's parents, Batman embarks on a journey of self-discovery that forces him to reflect on his life and the choices he has made. But when the Dark Knight becomes caught up in his own investigation and ruminations, he suddenly falls prey to a deadly new pair of killers that has been stalking him. A gritty, introspective tale, this noir-flavored book features appearancesby the Joker, the Penguin, Killer Croc and Scarface. This story includes more violence than in most Batman stories.

100 bullets: the deluxe edition. Brian Azzarello, writer; Eduardo Risso, artist. DC Comics 2011 456 p. Color illustration

Grades: Adult   **741.5/973; 741.5**

1. Crime

1401232019; 1401250564; 9781401232016, $49.99; 9781401250560, $24.99

LC 2011534002

This graphic novel, by Brian Azzarello, illustrated by Eduardo Risso, "features a mysterious agent named Graves who approaches ordinary citizens and gives them an opportunity to exact revenge on a person who has wronged them. Offering his clients an attache case containing proof of the deed and a gun, he guarantees his 'clients' full immunity for all of their actions, including 'murder.' This volume collects 100 Bullets #1-19." (Publisher's note)

Originally collected in 13 volumes

Originally published in single magazine form.

Volume 1 of 5

Doctor 13: architecture & mortality. Brian Azzarello, writer; Cliff Chiang, artist; Patricia Mulvihill, colorist; Jared K. Fletcher, letterer. DC Comics 2007 Un Illustration

Grades: 9 10 11 12 Adult   **741.5**

1. Humorous graphic novels; 2. Superhero graphic novels; 3. Graphic novels

978-1-4012-1552-1, $14.99

Doctor 13, the world's greatest skeptic, sets out with his daughter Tracy to investigate strange doings in the French Alps. The two encounter in short order a vampire, a pirate with a flying ship, a caveman who had been frozen in ice, a mysterious boy who can answer any question for the price of a dime, a talking Nazi gorilla, a cosmic heroine with a constant runny nose, and the ghost of a Confederate general taking time off from haunting a US Army tank. Doctor 13 doesn't believe in any of them, but he works with them when they have to go up against the Architects, the shapers of the universe. The Architects have decided that Doctor 13 and his team of misfits don't belong in the world, and they beg to differ. The book includes some violence.

Lex Luthor: Man of Steel. Art by Lee Bermejo. DC Comics 2005 Illustration

Grades: 10 11 12 Adult   **741.5; Fic**

1. Lex Luthor (Fictional character); 2. Superhero graphic novels; 3. Superman (Fictional character); 4. Graphic novels

1-4012-0454-6, $12.99

Superman has been called many things since becoming a superhero, from the defender of Truth, Justice and the American Way to the Big Blue Boy Scout. Lex Luthor calls him a dangerous threat to all humanity. This book is narrated by Luthor, so the reader sees Superman from his point of view; and to Luthor, Superman is an alien being who can't be trusted. Therefore, Luthor tries to create a superhero of his own, in the form of a beautiful young woman, named Hope. The book includes some violence and sexual situations.

Loveless Vol. 1: A Kin of Homecoming. Art by Marcello Frusin. DC Comics/Vertigo 2006 128p. Illustration

Grades: 12 Adult   **741.5; Fic**

1. Western graphic novel; 2. Graphic novels

978-1-4012-1061-8, $9.99

Wes Cutter is a wanted man running from a violent past - the horrors of the Civil War, a brutal stint in a Union prison camp, and the savage fallout of Reconstruction. Now he's on a quest for the one thing in short supply: peace. Joining Wes is his beautiful wife Ruth, a woman who has been to hell and back herself - and hides dark secrets of her own. The road they travel will be a bloody one, leaving a trail of bodies stretching from Missouri to the Pacific Ocean. The book contains graphic violence, copious use of foul language, nudity, and sexual situations.

Loveless Vol. 2: Thicker Than Blackwater. Brian Azzarello, writer; Danijel Zezelj, Marcelo Frusin, Werther Dell'edera, art; Patricia Mulvihill and Martin Breccia, colorists; Clem Robins, letterer.

Grades: 11 12 Adult   **741.5; Fic**

1. Mystery graphic novels; 2. Western graphic novels; 3. Graphic novels

978-1-4012-1250-6, $14.99

No one in the town of Blackwater escaped the Civil War unscathed. Not former slave-turned-bounty hunter Atticus

Mann. Not Ruth Cutter, who thought her husband Wes was dead, and took to the woods to fight for a lost cause. And certainly not Wes Cutter. He's suffered the worst fate of all, a Yankee made him sheriff of Blackwater and the most hated man in town. But hate him or not, the citizens of Blackwater desperately need Wes to protect them from a vicious killer who's butchering them in ever more ghastly ways. A killer who may have deep ties to Blackwater ... and to Wes' own dark past. The story includes considerable violence, profanity, and nudity.

Superman: For Tomorrow Volume One. Brian Azzarello, writer; Jim Lee, penciller; Scott Williams, inker; Alex Sinclair, colorist; Rob Leigh, Nick J. Napolitano, letterers. DC Comics 2005 Un Illustration
Grades: 10 11 12 Adult   **741.5; Fic**
   1. Superhero graphic novels; 2. Superman (Fictional character); 3. Graphic novels
   1-4012-0352-3, $14.99
A cataclysmic event has struck the Earth. Millions of people have vanished without a trace. No one is left unaffected - not even Superman. A year has passed, and Superman is left with many questions and very few answers. For a hero who tries to have all the answers, it's torture. And, just as the action heats up and the stakes are raised, one huge question emerges: just how far is Superman willing to go "For Tomorrow?"

Superman: For Tomorrow Volume Two. Brian Azzarello, writer; Jim Lee, penciller; Scott Williams, inker; Alex Sinclair, colorist; Rob Leigh, Nick J. Napolitano, letterers. DC Comics 2006 Illustration
Grades: 10 11 12 Adult   **741.5; Fic**
   1. Superhero graphic novels; 2. Superman (Fictional character); 3. Wonder Woman (Fictional character); 4. Graphic novels
   978-1-4012-0448-8, $14.99
In Volume One, a million people had seemingly vanished without a trace, including Lois Lane. In this volume, Superman is closer to discovering the mystery of the Vanishing, and comes face-to-face with the evil entity behind it all. But what desperate measures will Superman take to make things right again? And does Wonder Woman have the power to stop him? The book includes fighting violence.

Wonder Woman; Volume 1: Blood. Brian Azzarello, Cliff Chiang, Tony Akins. DC Comics 2012 160 p.
Grades: 11 12 Adult   **741.5**
   1. Greek mythology — Fiction; 2. Superhero comic books, strips, etc; 3. Wonder Woman (Fictional character)
   1401235638; 9781401235635, $22.99
                                         LC 2011051798
In this comic book, author Brian Azzarello "gives Diana (Wonder Woman) a new origin, not as a baby her mother, Hippolyta, molded out of clay but as the illegitimate daughter of Zeus. As such, she's a target for the jealous rage of Hera, Zeus' wife, but she finds a new role as protector of a waifish young woman who's currently carrying Zeus' baby. The king of the gods, meanwhile, has vanished." (Publishers Weekly)
Originally published in single magazine form in WONDER WOMAN 1-6—t.p. verso.

Other Wonder Woman volumes by Azzarello and Chiang are: 2: Guts; 3: Iron; 4: War

B., David
   Black paths. David B. SelfMadeHero 2011 128 p. Color illustration
Grades: Adult   **741.5; Fic**
   1. Fascism — Italy; 2. Historical fiction; 3. Graphic novels
   190683833X; 9781906838331, $24.95
                                         LC 2011507750
This graphic novel, by David B., takes place during the Interwar period. "When the Austro-Hungarian Empire disintegrated after World War I, ... Gabriele d'Annunzio ... stormed the city [of Fiume] with 3,000 Italian nationalists. D'Annunzio declared Fiume a free republic and himself commander.... David B. uses this real event as a backdrop .. . [for] the tragic love story of a beautiful torch singer and a young soldier haunted by the horrors of trench warfare." (Publisher's note)

★ **Epileptic.** Pantheon Books 2005 361p. Illustration
Grades: 11 12 Adult   **741.5; 616.8**
   1. Autobiographical graphic novels; 2. Epilepsy; 3. Graphic novels
   0-375-42318-4, $25; 0-375-71468-5 (pa), $18.95; 9780375423185
                                         LC 2004-53419
"Growing up in the 1960s and 1970s in France's Loire Valley, Jean-Christophe developed grand mal epilepsy around the age of 11. Pierre-Francois, nine, observes his brother's battle with the physical and social implications of the disease; their parents' efforts to find management of it through medical, macrobiotic, and even psychic interventions; and the author's own development in this milieu as a boy obsessed with history and warfare and as a dedicated artist." SLJ
The author's "artwork is magnificent—gorgeously bold, impressionistic representations of the world not as it is but as he's taught himself to perceive it. ... B.'s illustrations constantly underscore his writing's wrenching psychological depth; readers can literally see how the chaos of his childhood shaped his vision and mind." Publ Wkly
Original French edition, 2002

Backder, Derf
   My friend Dahmer. Written & illustrated by Derf Backderf. Abrams ComicArts 2012 221 p.
Grades: Adult   **741.5**
   1. Autobiographical graphic novels; 2. Dahmer, Jeffrey; 3. Friendship; 4. High school
   9781419702167
                                         LC 2011285306
Alex Award (2013)
This book is an exploration of notorious serial killer Jeffrey Dahmer by his high-school classmate. . . . In this graphic novel, [Derf] Backderf interweaves his memories of Dahmer with additional information gleaned from news reports, public interviews, and the memories of other classmates and community members. The book traces Dahmer's progression from experimenting with roadkill to . . . his first human victim just post-high school. (Bulletin of the Center for Children's Books)

Trashed: a graphic novel. By Derf Backderf. Abrams ComicArts 2015 256 p. Illustration

Grades: 10 11 12 Adult   **741.5**

1. Refuse and refuse disposal — Fiction; 2. Sanitation workers — Fiction

9781419714535, $24.95; 9781419714542

LC 2015011115

This graphic novel, by Derf Backderf, "is an ode to the crap job of all crap jobs—garbage collector. . . . [It] follows the raucous escapades of three 20-something friends as they clean the streets of pile after pile of stinking garbage, while battling annoying small-town bureaucrats, bizarre townfolk, sweltering summer heat, and frigid winter storms." (Publisher's note)

"The blocky grotesquerie of Backderf's art is well-suited to the material, and the episodic, slackerish narrative is spiked here and there by brief lessons on the history of the garbage truck, the ecology of the landfill, and an answer to the question of whether rich or poor neighborhoods generate the most trash (hint: it's not the poor). A downbeat but entertaining ode to the odiferous realities of getting by." Pub Wkly

Includes bibliographical references

Bagge, Peter

Apocalypse nerd. Dark Horse Comics 2008 120p. Illustration

Grades: 11 12 Adult   **741.5; Fic**

1. Adventure graphic novels; 2. End of the world; 3. Graphic novels

978-1-59307-902.4, $13.95

Software engineer Perry and his friend Gordo are just two average suburban guys (okay, maybe not Gordo, since he deals drugs) who have gone on a camping trip in the North Cascade Mountains near Seattle; but on their way up, North Korea nukes Seattle, and the two friends must find a way to survive in the mountain. They become looters, deal with others out to survive any way possible, and do things they never dreamed they would do—including killing others. The book includes lots of harsh language (including s-bombs and f-bombs), partial nudity, and violence.

Woman Rebel: The Margaret Sanger Story. Peter Bagge. Drawn and Quarterly 2013 104 p. Illustration

Grades: Adult   **741.5; 92**

1. Birth control; 2. Sanger, Margaret, 1879-1966; 3. Women political activists

1770461264; 9781770461260, $21.95

Author peter Bagge presents a "biography of [Margaret Sanger,] the social and political maverick, jam-packed with fact and fun. In his signature cartoony, rubbery style, Bagge presents the life of the birth-control activist, educator, nurse, mother, and protofeminist from her birth in the late nineteenth century to her death after the invention of the birth control pill." (Publisher's note)

Courtesy of Drawn & Quarterly

Baillie, Liz

My brain hurts volume one. Microcosm Publishing 2008 Un Illustration

Grades: 11 12 Adult   **741.5; Fic**

1. Friendship; 2. Homosexuality; 3. Graphic novels

978-1-934620-03-8, $6

Best friends Kate and Joey are gay and trying to find some happiness with their relationships. They're also thirteen years old, love punk music, dress punk, and get into all kinds of trouble. Joey's father is in denial, Kate doesn't know how to tell her mother. Then one night, a gang of skinheads beat Joey around the head with a chain; he collapses during an interview at a Catholic school and goes into a coma. Meanwhile, one of the skinheads keeps trying to get Kate to go with him; and Kate joins a gay student club at school. The book shows kissing but no other sexual activity, there's no nudity, but there's a lot of strong language, especially the f-bomb.

Baker, Kyle

★ **How** to draw stupid and other essentials of cartooning. Watson-Guptill 2008 110p. Illustration

Grades: 8 9 10 11 12 Adult   **741.5**

1. Cartooning — Technique; 2. Graphic novels — Drawing

978-0-8230-0143-9, $16.95

LC 2008-922161

"Baker, an award-winning cartoonist and graphic-novel illustrator, gives aspiring cartoonists irreverent advice about how to succeed in their chosen field. He offers instruction in basic drawing techniques such as choosing the right tools and discusses the importance of learning to draw shapes, exaggerating, and using references. But the author's most inspiring advice focuses on how to succeed as a cartoonist." SLJ

King David. DC Comics/Vertigo 2002 104p. Illustration

Grades: 9 10 11 12 Adult   **741.5; 221**

1. Bible OT — Adaptations; 2. Graphic novels

978-1-56389-866-2, $19.95

Baker retells the Old Testament story of David, the shepherd boy who slew the giant Goliath and later became the King of Israel, after years of dodging King Saul's attempts to kill him. Using a hip, freewheeling style full of irreverent humor, Baker also renders the battles as the bloody messes they were.

Kyle Baker: Cartoonist. Kyle Baker Publishing 2004 126p. Illustration

Grades: 10 11 12 Adult   **741.5**

1. Humorous graphic novels; 2. Graphic novels

0-9747214-0-9, $14.95

Kyle Baker's cartoons have appeared in major magazines and newspapers, and his animation has appeared on MTV and BET. He collects new material in this book, including his recurring "The Bakers," a behind-the-scenes look at his family and home life. Some cartoons include drug references and violence.

Nat Turner. Abrams 2008 207p. Illustration

Grades: 10 11 12 Adult   **741.5; 92**

1. Biographical graphic novels; 2. Revolutionaries; 3. Slavery; 4. Slaves; 5. Turner, Nat, 1800?-1831; 6. Graphic novels

978-0-8109-9535-2; 0-8109-9535-2, $14.95

LC 2008-6911

This book "follows the dark legacy of the Virginia slave rebellion and subsequent murders of at least 55 white slave owners and their families in 1831. . . . Turner is presented as a fiercely intelligent, angry, yet steadfast individual whose potential was dashed in an era of hate and inhumanity. Those characteristics are mirrored in the actions of the slaves' rebellion, in illustrations that are not for the faint of heart or the weak of stomach. The ideas brought forth here are sure to ignite debate and discussion." SLJ

Includes bibliographical references

Originally published 2006 in four volumes

Nat Turner Vol. 2: revolution. Image Comics 2006 96p. Illustration

Grades: 10 11 12 Adult **92**

1. Biographical graphic novels; 2. Revolutionaries; 3. Slavery; 4. Slaves; 5. Turner, Nat, 1800?-1831; 6. Graphic novels

978-1-58240-792-0, $10

In this concluding volume, excerpts from The Confessions of Nat Turner alternate with wordless panels to depict the series of murders carried out by Turner and his followers as they tried to start a slave revolution based on Turner's vision. He is eventually captured and hanged. Baker doesn't editorialize with narration, instead he allows readers to draw their own conclusions about Turner and the society against which he rebelled. Some of the images will be disturbing because of the brutal acts they depict.

Originally published as Nat Turner issues #3 and 4 by Kyle Baker Publishing

Sequel to Nat Turner Encore Edition Vol. 1 (2006)

Plastic Man: On the Lam!. DC Comics 2004 Un Illustration

Grades: 6 7 8 9 10 11 12 Adult **741.5; Fic**

1. Humorous graphic novels; 2. Plastic Man (Fictional character); 3. Superhero graphic novels; 4. Graphic novels

1-4012-0343-4, $14.95

2005 Eisner Award for Best Publication for a Younger Audience, also 2005 Eisner Award for Best Writer/Artists-Humor for Kyle Baker

Plastic Man has worked as a superhero, but he used to be the criminal Eel O'Brian, a fact he has hidden from the FBI. Now there's been a murder, and Eel O'Brian is the main (and only) suspect. When the FBI learns of his old identity, Plastic Man goes on the lam to clear himself.

Originally published as Plastic Man issues #1-6, this volume is bound in plastic

Balce, Nicc

Random Encounter Volume 1. Viper Comics 2006 Un Illustration

Grades: 9 10 11 12 Adult **741.5; Fic**

1. Adventure graphic novels; 2. Science fiction graphic novels; 3. Graphic novels

0-9754193-8-2, $9.95

Strange things are afoot at the ... Kwik Mart. With their eerie tromp through the latest Silent Kill game interrupted by a strange sound, Migo, Mica, and Mona begin a journey into the perplexing and uncharted. The discovery of a dead girl in a pool of blood on the roof of Migo's parents' Kwik Mart sends the kids' lives into a maelstrom of confusion, freakish aliens, precipitous resurrection, and enigmatic secrets. It's a wild ride into the unimaginable and astonishing, a ... random encounter. There are lots of fighting scenes and some monsters.

Baltazar, Art

Patrick the Wolf Boy Volume 1. Devil's Due Publishing 2004 Un Illustration

Grades: 2 3 4 5 6 7 8 9 10 11 12 Adult **741.5; Fic**

1. Humorous graphic novels; 2. Graphic novels

1-932796-27-4, $10.95

Patrick looks at first glance like the other kids in school, but he's a werewolf. A cute werewolf. He resembles Eddie Munster (from the 1960s television comedy series "The Munsters"), and he doesn't speak, although he growls a lot and sometimes howls. He gives his teacher an apple - but with a skull biting the apple. When he goes fishing with his dad, he prefers to scare the bear into giving him his catch. He loves to play tag with the neighborhood squirrel. And when Valentine's Day comes, he makes sure that his babysitter likes him better. His utterly normal parents adore him and understand his growls; so does Neve, his classmate at school.

Patrick the Wolf Boy Volume 2. Devil's Due Publishing 2005 Un Illustration

Grades: 2 3 4 5 6 7 8 9 10 11 12 Adult **741.5; Fic**

1. Humorous graphic novels; 2. Graphic novels

1-932796-29-0, $10.95

This volume collects previously published issues of the comic: the Super Hero Special, the Science Fiction Special, the Wedding Special, and the After School Special. In the many short stories, Patrick the Wolf Boy attends a comic book convention with his dad, plays "Star Wars" with the neighborhood kids, meets and befriends an alien kid, Zyggie, who then crashes the wedding reception of a relative, and deals with the school bully.

Patrick the Wolf Boy Volume 3. Devil's Due Publishing 2007 Un Illustration

Grades: 2 3 4 5 6 7 8 9 10 11 12 Adult **741.5; Fic**

1. Fantasy graphic novels; 2. Humorous graphic novels; 3. Graphic novels

978-1-932796-30-8, $12.99

The third volume of Patrick the Wolf Boy collects the Rock-n-Roll Special, the Post Father's Day Special, and the Happy Birthday Special, plus some stories written and illustrated by guest creators. Patrick meets Squatch, the baby Big Foot, accidentally bites Neve, who thinks she's turning into a werewolf, encounters various rock stars, and other adventures. In one panel, the screaming pajama lady says "crap."

Patrick the Wolf Boy Volume 4. Devil's Due Publishing 2007 Un Illustration

Grades: 3 4 5 6 7 8 9 10 11 12 Adult **741.5; Fic**

1. Halloween; 2. Humorous graphic novels; 3. Graphic novels

978-1-932796-83-4, $12.99

This fourth collection of comics featuring Patrick the Wolf Boy focus mostly on Halloween, a natural holiday for the young wolfman ... er ... wolfboy. He plays with jack o'lanterns (he likes to wear them on his head), goes trick-or-treating with the neighbor kids, keeps trying to melt the grouchy neighbor lady after watching The Wizard of Oz, and plays with new neighbor, the Grim Reaper. The book includes a couple instances of mild language (fricken"), and one scene in which the Grim Reaper does his thing.

Barker, Clive
The **complete** the great and secret show. Adapted by Chris Ryall; art by Gabriel Rodriguez. IDW Publishing 2007 304p. Illustration
Grades: 11 12 Adult   **741.5; Fic**
  1. Fantasy graphic novels; 2. Graphic novels
  978-1-60010-121-2; 978-1-60010-121-2 (pa), $35
Clive Barker's horror novel has been adapted to comic book form and is presented complete in this volume. In the little town of Palomo Grove, the ultimate battle between good and evil begins when unassuming postal clerk Randall Jaffe finds clues to an alternate reality in the dead letter office. The book includes nudity, some sexual situations, violence, and harsh language.

Barr, Mike W.
The **Maze** Agency, Volume 1. Art by Adam Hughes. IDW Publishing 2005 156p. Illustration
Grades: 9 10 11 12 Adult   **741.5; Fic**
  1. Mystery graphic novels; 2. Graphic novels
  1-933239-06-9, $24.99
Presented for the first time since their original publication in 1989 by Innovation, The Maze Agency, Vol. 1 collects writer Mike W. Barr's first adventures of private eye Jennifer Mays and her boyfriend, true-crime writer and amateur sleuth Gabriel Webb. Their expanding relationship plays a backdrop to the cases they investigate, all of them whodunits that the reader can solve along with Jen and Gabe. While most of their cases are murder mysteries, there's very little gore on the pages.

Barry, Lynda
One hundred demons. Sasquatch Bks. 2002 216p. Illustration
Grades: 10 11 12 Adult   **741.5**
  1. Autobiographical graphic novels
  1-57061-337-0; 1-57061-459-8 (pa), $17.95
                                  LC 2002-21657
"Whether she's talking about head lice, old boyfriends, or hippies who "forgot" to pay her wages, Barry playfully explores, in "autobifictionalographical" text and art, those demons common to teens—and to us all." Booklist

★ **Picture** this: the near-sighted monkey book. With guest watercolorist Kevin Kawula. Drawn and Quarterly 2010 224 p. Color illustration
Grades: 9 10 11 12 Adult   **741.5; 741.5/973**
  1. American wit and humor, Pictorial; 2. Animals; 3. Animals/Graphic novels; 4. Humorous graphic novels; 5. Graphic novels
  1897299648; 9781897299647, $29.95
                                  LC 2010399443

Courtesy of Drawn & Quarterly

In author Lynda Barry's book, she "asks 'Why do we stop drawing?' and 'Why do we start?' It features the return of" the character "Marlys, and introduces a new one, the Nearsighted Monkey." The book is a "graphic-memoir-how-to" and a "take home extension of Barry's traveling" writing workshop which focuses on literature illustration. (Publisher's note)

★ **What** it is. Drawn & Quarterly 2008 209p. Illustration
Grades: 7 8 9 10 11 12 Adult   **818; 741.5**
  1. Authorship; 2. Creative writing
  978-1-897299-35-7, $24.95; 1-897299-35-4
                                  LC C2007-9047319
Independent cartoonist Lynda Barry presents an unconventional book that encourages its readers to write by using her colorful art and asking questions such as "How are monsters different?" "And how are they the same?" "Can/Do images exist without thinking?" "What is the difference between lying and pretending?" Each question appears with illustrated writing prompts and Barry's own ruminations on the topics. It's a workbook of sorts, but it also exists as a book to be read for itself.
"Every so often a book comes along that surpasses expectations, taking readers on an inspirational voyage that they don't want to leave. This is one such book." SLJ

Beaton, Kate
Hark! A vagrant. Drawn and Quarterly 2011 168p. Illustration
Grades: Adult   **741.5**
  1770460608; 9781770460607
                                  LC 2011505458
The book offers a collection of comic strips by author Kate Beaton, "a series of short gag cartoons, primarily about history and literature, with a particularly Canadian bent. . . . Comics about long-suffering heroines like Jane Eyre, Laura Secord, and 'Every Lady Scientist in History Who Ever Did Anything Until Now' highlight the absurdities of gender disparity. . . . A number of these comics are driven simply by absurdity itself: a kingdom whose royal mascot is a fat pony; a sexy Batman; and teens who solve crimes in a real-life fashion: by hiding behind the

Courtesy of Drawn & Quarterly

school, smoking weed, and lying about it later." (Quill & Quire)

Includes index.

★ **Step** Aside, Pops: A Hark! a Vagrant Collection. Kate Beaton. Drawn & Quarterly 2015 160 p. Illustration
Grades: Adult   **741.5**
1. Cartoons and caricatures; 2. Wit and humor; 3. World history
1770462082; 9781770462083, $19.95

In this collection of comics by Kate Beaton, "Ida B. Wells, the Black Prince, and Benito Jußrez burst off the pages . . . armed with modern-sounding quips and amusingly on-point repartee. Kate Beaton's second [Drawn and Quarterly] book brings her hysterically funny gaze to bear on these and even more historical, literary, and contemporary figures." (Publisher's note)

"The widely lauded Beaton has created a tidy niche for herself in gag strips that deflate history and literature's more grandiose personalities with highbrow intellectualism and lowbrow barbs." Booklist

Includes index

The Beats: a graphic history.
Edited by Paul Buhle. Hill & Wang 2009 199p.
Illustration
Grades: 10 11 12 Adult   **810.9; 920; 741.5; 810**
1. Beat generation; 2. Biographical graphic novels; 3. Graphic novels
978-0-8090-9496-7, $22; 0-8090-9496-7
LC 2008-43350

Main writer Harvey Pekar is joined by Nancy J. Peters, Penelope Rosemont, Joyce Brabner, Trina Robbins, and Tuli Kupferberg and by artists Ed Piskor, Jay Kinney, Nick Thorkelson, Summer McClinton, Peter Kuper, Mary Fleener, Jerome Neukirch, Anne Timmons, Gary Dumm, Lance Tooks, and Jeffrey Lewis to provide a brief history of the Beat movement and the most famous writers. The stories give readers a frank glimpse into the lives of such people as Jack Kerouac, Allen Ginsburg, William Burroughs, Lawrence Ferlinghetti, most of whom started to change what was called literature in the 1940s and 1950s. Their sexual and drug habits, which both contributed to their work and hampered their lives, receive frank treatment in this book. In addition to the famous Beats, the book includes short pieces about a number of the lesser known figures in the Beat movement, including LeRoi Jones/Amiri Baraka, Gregory Corso, Diane di Prima, artist Jay DeFeo, and the famed City Lights bookstore in San Francisco. The black and white art portrays sexual activity, consumption of alcohol and drugs, smoking, and the book includes some harsh language.

Beatty, Scott
Nightwing: Year One. Scott Beatty & Chuck Dixon, writers ; Scott McDaniel, penciller ; Andy Owens, inker ; Gregory Wright, colorist ; Phil Balsman, letterer, DC Comics 2005 Un Illustration
Grades: 7 8 9 10 11 12 Adult   **Fic; 741.5**
1. Batman (Fictional character); 2. Nightwing (Fictional character); 3. Robin (Fictional character); 4. Superhero graphic novels; 5. Teen Titans (Fictional characters); 6. Graphic novels
1-4012-0435-X, $14.99

Dick Grayson was the first Robin, the teen sidekick to the Dark Knight, Batman. Then he became Nightwing and stepped out of Batman's shadow. The story behind that transformation and how it affected Batman, the Teen Titans and Dick himself is explored in this graphic novel. When Batman fires Robin, an angry Dick Grayson is unsure of where to go. On his journey, he receives advice from Superman and aid from Deadman, and makes the decisions that lead him to become a brand new crimefighter.

Beaulieu, Jean Francios
★ The **Wonderful** Wizard of Oz. Marvel Entertainment 2009 192p. Illustration
Grades: 3 4 5 6 7 8 9 10 11 12 Adult   **Fic; 741.5**
1. Adventure graphic novels; 2. Authors; 3. Baum, L Frank, 1856-1919; 4. Children's authors; 5. Dramatists; 6. Fantasy graphic novels; 7. Journalists; 8. Graphic novels
978-0-7851-2921-9, $29.99

A twister picks up the house Dorothy and her dog Toto are in and carries them from Kansas to the land of Oz; the house lands on top of the Wicked Witch of the East, and the Munchkins, who were her slaves, hail Dorothy as a great sorceress. All the girl wants is to get back home to Kansas, but all anyone can say is that she must go to the Emerald City and ask the Great Wizard Oz to send her home. As she travels along the Yellow Brick Road, she meets a scarecrow who wants brains so people won't think he's a dummy, a tin man who wants a heart so he can love, and a great cowardly lion who wants courage so he'll truly be king of the beasts. However, once they reach the Emerald City and each see the Wizard Oz, they learn they must do what no one, including the Wizard himself, could ever do kill the Wicked Witch of the West. Shanower's adaptation of L. Frank Baum's novel keeps all the charm of the original, while Skottie Young's art banishes any lingering images of the old Technicolor movie; Beaulieu's muted color palette works with Young's art, while Eckleberry's lettering adds to an overall effect of magic and wonder. This book will appeal to all ages
Other Oz adapations by Shanower and Young are: The Marvelous Land of Oz; Ozma of Oz; Dorothy and the Wizard in Oz; The Road to Oz; The Emerald City of Oz

Beazley, Mark D.
Essential Official Handbook of the Marvel Universe Vol. 1. Marvel Entertainment 2006 Un Illustration
Grades: 7 8 9 10 11 12 Adult   **741.5**
1. Marvel Comics — History and criticism; 2. Graphic novels
978-0-7851-1933-3, $16.99

This massive trade paperback collects the original fifteen issues of the Official Handbook of the Marvel Universe. Here, readers will find character profiles, descriptions of alien races, heroes, villains, and information on gadgets, weapons, vehicles, buildings, and lands that have appeared in Marvel Comics over the years.

Pet avengers classic. Marvel Entertainment 2009 208p. Illustration
Grades: 7 8 9 10 11 12 Adult   **741.5; Fic**
1. Adventure graphic novels; 2. Pets; 3. Superhero graphic novels; 4. Graphic novels
978-0-7851-1366-9, $24.99

This volume collects the various Marvel Pets stories, from 1960 to 2007, with each story featuring a different pet, from Lockjaw the teleporting dog to Kitty Pryde's dragon Lockheed to Brightwind the winged horse, and many more. Lockjaw, Lockheed, Redwing the falcon, the cat named Niels, and Zabu the saber tooth tiger all starred in th 2009 mini series titled Pet Avengers. Some of the stories in this collection include violence.

Spider-Man: The Birth of Venom. Marvel Entertainment 2007 Un Illustration
Grades: 8 9 10 11 12 Adult   **Fic; 741.5**
1. Fantastic Four (Fictional characters); 2. Spider-Man (Fictional character); 3. Superhero graphic novels; 4. Graphic novels
978-0-7851-2498-6, $29.99
The Beyonder's Battleworld might seem a strange place to get new threads, but it's Spider-Man who becomes unraveled when his new symbiotic, shape-changing costume attempts to darken his life as well as his fashion sense. But ridding himself of his black costume proves an even greater mistake when its alien enmity bonds with mortal madness to form our hero's most dedicated enemy, Venom. Other stories include the first appearances of Puma and the Rose, Mary Jane Watson's startling secret, and the debut of the battling . . . Bag-Man? The Black Cat, the Fantastic Four and other Marvel characters appear.

Bechdel, Alison
★ **Are** you my mother?: a comic drama. Alison Bechdel. Houghton Mifflin Harcourt 2012 286 p.
Grades: Adult   **741.5/973; 741.5; B**
1. Autobiographical graphic novels; 2. Bechdel, Alison, 1960-; 3. Cartoonists — Biography; 4. Cartoonists — United States; 5. Mother-daughter relationship
0618982507; 9780618982509
LC 2012010582
In this book, "[Alison] Bechdel not only searches for keys to [her relationship with her mother] but perhaps even for surrogate mothers, through therapy, girlfriends and the writing of Virginia Woolf, Adrienne Rich, Alice Miller and others. Yet the primary inspiration in this literary memoir is psychoanalyst Donald Winnicott, whose life and work Bechdel explores along with her own." (Kirkus Reviews)

★ **Fun** home: a family tragicomic. Houghton Mifflin 2006 232p. Illustration

Courtesy of Houghton Mifflin

Grades: 11 12 Adult   **92; 741.5**
1. Autobiographical graphic novels; 2. Bechdel, Alison, 1960-; 3. Biography, Individual; 4. Cartoonists; 5. Comic book writers; 6. Essayists
0-618-47794-2, $19.95; 978-0-618-47794-4
LC 2005-30304
Time Magazine Book of the Year for 2006
This is a memoir in graphic novel format about the author's "childhood, her father's death and their shared homosexuality. . . . The death was deemed an accident—a truck hit [Mr. Bechdel] as he crossed a road with an armful of garden brush—but Ms. Bechdel suspects suicide." (N Y Times (Late N Y Ed))
This "is one of the very best graphic novels ever." Booklist

Bedard, Tony
Turok: son of stone. Dark Horse Comics 2008 Un Illustration
Grades: 9 10 11 12 Adult   **741.5; Fic**
1. Adventure graphic novels; 2. Fantasy graphic novels; 3. Graphic novels
978-1-59582-201-7, $14.95
Turok discovers a killing beast within himself when he, his brother, and Catori, the girl they both love, encounter a group of deadly hunters from another tribe; Turok kills all of the enemies, but in his killing mode, he also cuts down his brother. The tribe exiles him. Years later, the son of the man Turok killed comes with his tribe to slaughter Turok's people; only Catori and her son Andar survive the guns used by Chichak and his men. When Turok pursues them into a deep cave, they all find themselves in a strange underworld where dinosaurs and other prehistoric creatures live, as well as humans and a beastly tribe. This book adapts the animated feature, Turok: Son of Stone, and features art from the animation. The book includes violence and bloodshed.

Beechen, Adam
Hench. Art by Manny Bellow. AiT/Planet Lar 2004 Un Illustration
Grades: 10 11 12 Adult   **741.5; Fic**
1. Superhero graphic novels; 2. Graphic novels
1-932051-17-1, $12.95
The fine line between hero and villain is just another of longtime super-villain henchman Mike Fulton's many scars. Now, faced with a terrible choice that could mean life and death for heroes, villains, his family, and himself, Mike ponders just how his normal life went so crazy. There's a little violence but mostly fighting action, and a little bit of strong language.

Robin: Wanted. Adam Beechen, writer; Freddie Williams II , artist; Karl Kerschl with Wayne Faucher & Prentis Rollins, artists, pages 6-27. DC Comics 2007 144p. Illustration
Grades: 9 10 11 12 Adult   **Fic; 741.5**
1. Batgirl (Fictional character); 2. Mystery graphic novels; 3. Robin (Fictional character); 4. Superhero graphic novels; 5. Graphic novels
978-1-4012-1225-4, $12.99
Batgirl - Cassandra Cain - is dead ... and the evidence shows that Robin is the killer. Every cop in Gotham City is looking for him now, so he has to find the real killer and clear his name. Someone keeps sending Robin clues that only he can find, and they seem to be leading to a shadowy player who is making a grab for power in the deadly League of Assassins. Solving this mystery will lead Robin to a confrontation with the new leader of the League of Assassins ... and the killer's identity will change Robin's world forever. This book has lots of fighting action.

Beimler, Hans

The **Middleman**: the Doomsday Armageddon Apocalypse. Javier Grillo-Marxuach and Hans Beimler ; art by Armando Zanker. Viper Comics 2009 68p. Illustration
Grades: 8 9 10 11 12 Adult   **741.5; Fic**
  1. Humorous graphic novels; 2. Science fiction graphic novels; 3. Graphic novels
978-0-9802385-8-7, $7.95

This graphic novel picks up right where the ABC Family television series left off, tying up the loose ends left by the series cancellation. The television series is based on the graphic novels, but the art in this book bases the character designs on the television series and is in color. Wendy Watson works with the Middleman to maintain justice and goodness in the world, but right now things have become very complicated. Her boyfriend Tyler now works for Manservant Neville, whose corporation has developed a ... Umaster ... a solar powered cube that's supposed to help people, how is unclear. The Middleman discovers that Neville plans to use the Umaster to take over the world and destroy it so he can remake it the way he wants. And somehow, Neville has managed to counter everything the Middleman and Wendy do to stop him. There is only one possible way to defeat Manservant Neville, but it involves Chac-Mol, a Mayan talisman of great power that demands the ultimate sacrifice of the user. A brief introduction provides enough information for any reader who hasn't seen any of the television series; and the book includes annotations to explain the many pop culture references. It provides closure for fans of the television series, and provides a nice little diversion for fans of the comics series, and there's enough information for readers meeting Wendy Watson and the Middle Man for the first time.

Beland, Tom

★ **True** story swear to God archives, vol. 1. Image Comics 2008 528p. Illustration
Grades: 10 11 12 Adult   **92; 741.5**
  1. Autobiographical graphic novels; 2. Beland, Tom, 1962-; 3. Cartoonists; 4. Romance graphic novels; 5. Graphic novels
978-1-58240-881-1, $19.99

They met at a bus stop at Disneyworld, by chance: he was a cartoonist from Napa, California, and she was a radio personality from Puerto Rico. Their chance meeting blossomed into a romance that survived a long-distance separation, a Category 5 hurricane, his leaving home to move to a new world. Tom Beland writes candidly about the ups and downs of his relationship with Lily, with his family, and all the slings and arrows of life one has to deal with daily. He originally self-published these comics, and they were collected in several trade paperbacks from AiT/PlanetLar. The book includes occasional harsh language (including s-bombs and f-bombs), sexual situations, and frank talk about sex.

True Story Swear to God Volume 1. Image Comics 2007 Un Illustration
Grades: 10 11 12 Adult   **741.5**
  1. Autobiographical graphic novels; 2. Humorous graphic novels; 3. Romance graphic novels; 4. Graphic novels
978-1-58240-761-6, $14.99

Tom Beland is a California cartoonist who is now living on the island of Puerto Rico with the woman of his dreams he met at a bus stop a year ago in Disney World. It hasn't been easy, since his freelance clients haven't paid him in months, while demanding more work from him. But all that is going to change as Beland demands restitution... or else. And Beland starts to worry about his lack of sexual performance. There's nothing portrayed on the page, but he talks about his problem in a frank manner. There's also some strong language, including the f-word.

This book from Image Comics continues the story of True Story Swear to God that was first published by AiT/Planet Lar.

★ **True** Story Swear to God: Chances Are .... AiT/Planet Lar 2003 Un Illustration
Grades: 10 11 12 Adult   **741.5**
  1. Autobiographical graphic novels; 2. Romance graphic novels; 3. Graphic novels
1-932051-09-0, $14.95

What are the chances of going to a theme park, on the East Coast... and meeting a person who will change your life as you know it" What are the chances of this person living on the island of San Juan, Puerto Rico, some 3,600 miles from your home in Napa Valley, California" What are the chances of a long-distance relationship such as this lasting very long" If you're California cartoonist Tom Beland and Puerto Rico journalist Lily Garcia, those chances are pretty good. This book deals with the joys of meeting someone by chance and the heartache that comes with distance. It covers the humor, anxiety, annoyances and paranoia found in every relationship. And it's all true, swear to God. Beland uses some harsh language, and some sexual situations which aren't graphic.

★ **True** Story Swear to God: This One Goes to 11. AiT/Planet Lar 2005 Un Illustration
Grades: 10 11 12 Adult   **741.5**
  1. Autobiographical graphic novels; 2. Romance graphic novels; 3. Graphic novels
1-932051-34-1, $12.95

A relationship is tough enough when there's 3,600 miles separating two lovebirds. Toss in a category 5 hurricane named Georges, which struck Puerto Rico in 1998, and you've got some real problems. How do you pack up your life, say goodbye to everything you hold dear, and take a leap of faith based on what your heart tells you" Beland tells how. This book has some harsh language and some sexual situations.

Bell, Blake

I Have to Live with This Guy!. Twomorrows Publishing 2002 208p. Illustration
Grades: Adult Professional   **741.5**
  1. Comic books, strips, etc — History and criticism; 2. Graphic novels
1-893905-16-0, $19.95

Will Eisner did what? Alan Moore said that Dave Sim is really like that? Take a deep look into what it's been like living with comic book creators over the past 60 years, with the people who know them best. This book explores the lives of the partners and wives of Will Eisner, Alan Moore, Stan Lee, Joe Kubert, Harvey Kurtzman, John Romita, Gene

Colan, Dan DeCarlo, Dick Ayers, Archie Goodwin, Ric Estrada, Dave Sim, Howard Cruse, Dave Cooper, and more. In addition to sharing memories and anecdotes found nowhere else, their better halves have also opened up private files to unearth personal photos, mementos, and never-before-seen art by an interesting mix of creators in comics. Some of the illustrations show partial nudity.

★ **Strange** & stranger: the world of Steve Ditko. Fantagraphics Books 2008 220p. Illustration

Grades: 10 11 12 Adult **92; 741.5**
1. Comic books, strips, etc — History and criticism; 2. Ditko, Steve; 3. Graphic designers; 4. Spider-Man (Fictional character); 5. Graphic novels
978-1-56097-921-0, $39.99

Steve Ditko may be best known as the cocreator and first artist for Marvel's Spider-Man comics, but he has done much more. Bell tells Ditko's life story and covers his career which has

Courtesy of Fantagraphics

spanned more than 50 years. He also gives Ditko's side of the story in explaining his split with Stan Lee and why he walked away from Spider-Man back in 1966. Ditko's work has been strongly influenced by author/philosopher Ayn Rand, and her Objectivist philosophy has informed his work. The book includes lots of Ditko's art, including many unpublished pieces. Bell doesn't romanticize Ditko, but provides ample reason for the artist's place in comic book history.

Bell, Gabrielle
Lucky. Drawn & Quarterly 2006 Un Illustration
Grades: 11 12 Adult **741.5**
1. Autobiographical graphic novels; 2. Graphic novels
1-897299-01-X, $16.95

Bell documents the mundane details of her below-minimum-wage, twenty-something existence in Brooklyn, New York, with a subtle humor. Her simple, unadorned drawing style and heavy narrationchronicle transient roommates who communicate only through Post-it notes; aspiring artists who sublet tiny rooms in leaky, greasy broken-down border-house loft apartments crawling with bugs, cats, and bad art. Bell tackles a string of forgettable, unrelated jobs-including nude modeling, artist's assistant, art teacher, and jewelry maker-that only serve to bolster her despair, boredom, and discomfort in her own skin. Bell's self-scrutiny leads her to dream sequences that allow her to rise above her banal actuality and hyperawareness. She uses some strong language and nudity in some of the sequences.

The **Voyeurs.** Gabrielle Bell. Consortium Book Sales & Dist 2012 160 p.
Grades: Adult **741.5**
1. Bell, Gabrielle, 1976-; 2. Cartoonists — Biography
098468140X; 9780984681402, $24.95

This book by "autobiographical cartoonist [Gabrielle] Bell" presents a "series of full-color vignettes that document

her life as part of a free-floating community of indie comics artists drifting between the neighborhood bars of Brooklyn and L.A. and an international and domestic circuit of comics conventions." It includes "drawings of her life, lovers, friends and neurotic obsessions." (Publishers Weekly)

Bell, Marc
Stroppy. By Marc Bell. Farrar Straus & Giroux 2015 64 p. Color illustration
Grades: Adult **741.5/971; 741.5**
1. Contests — Fiction; 2. Factories — Fiction; 3. Graphic novels
1770462058; 9781770462052, $21.95
LC 2014481388

In this graphic novel, by Marc Bel, Our hapless hero, Stroppy, is minding his business, working a menial job in one of Monsieur Moustache's factories, when a muscular fellah named Sean blocks up the assembly line. Sean's there to promote an All-Star Schnauzer Bandûorganized songwriting contest, which he does enthusiastically and at the expense of Stroppy's livelihood, home, and face. Hoping for a cash prize, Stroppy submits a work by his friend Clancy the Poet. (Publisher's note)

Bellstorf, Arne
Baby's in black: Astrid Kirchherr, Stuart Sutcliffe, and the Beatles. Arne Bellstorf. First Second 2012 196 p. Illustration
Grades: 10 11 12 Adult **782.421; 782.42166092/2**
1. Beatles; 2. Kirchherr, Astrid; 3. Love stories; 4. Rock musicians — England; 5. Sutcliffe, Stuart, 1940-1962
1596437715; 9781596437715, $24.99
LC 2011049680

This graphic novel tells the love story of "Stuart Sutcliffe, one of the original Beatles," and "German photographer Astrid Kirchherr." The "story offers insight into the time the Beatles spent performing together in Germany before they made it big." Despite the couple's "different languages and worlds, the pair fall into a happy, and seemingly easy, romance. But their happiness is short-lived: the Beatles are being forced to leave the country, and Stuart's health is failing." (Publishers Weekly)

Translated from the German by Michael Waaler.

Bendis, Brian Michael
Civil War: Iron Man. Marvel Entertainment 2007 Un Illustration
Grades: 9 10 11 12 Adult **741.5; Fic**
1. Captain America (Fictional character); 2. Iron Man (Fictional character); 3. Superhero graphic novels; 4. Graphic novels
0-7851-2314-8, $11.99

This book will give readers insight into why Iron Man believes that super human registration is necessary, and why he has taken it upon himself to lead the charge for its implementation. He and Captain America meet secretly to see if there's any hope of working things out before further tragedy occurs. How could these two men, once the closest of friends and staunchest of allies, end up leading opposing armies in this conflict" And when two of the Marvel heroes most affected by the conclusion of the war get together one last time, and what is said between them will set the course of the Marvel Universe for the future.

Civil War: Marvel Universe. Marvel Entertainment 2007 Un Illustration
Grades: 9 10 11 12 Adult   **Fic; 741.5**
1. Daredevil (Fictional character); 2. Superhero graphic novels; 3. Graphic novels
978-0-7851-2470-2, $11.99

Civil War is encompassing the entire Marvel Universe, and the effects of the war are being felt by every hero, villain and civilian. In Civil War: Choosing Sides, five stories shine a spotlight on the wildcards and impact players whose part in the Civil War has yet to be told - including Daredevil/Iron Fist, U.S.Agent, the Irredeemable Ant-Man, Venom and even... Howard the Duck" On Earth, the Sentry confronts his inner demons as the shadows of past and future battles tear him apart. Within The Negative Zone, the walls of 42 are pulled back to reveal the return of one of the Marvel's greatest heroes. And in She-Hulk, Civil War threatens the rights of every American super hero. So whose side will Marvel's top superhuman lawyer fight for" And how can she possibly choose, when she feels one way as She-Hulk, and another as Jen Walters?

Fortune and Glory: A True Hollywood Comic Book Story. Oni Press 2000 152p. Illustration
Grades: 11 12 Adult   741.5
1. Autobiographical graphic novels; 2. Graphic novels
978-1-929998-06-7, $14.95

Bendis has collected his miniseries into one volume. He uses the comic book format to show the stupidity of Hollywood producers, the vanity of stars like Uma Thurman and Clint Eastwood, and the mood swings and ego nosedives of a little indie comic-book creator caught up in the maelstrom of the motion picture industry as he tries to sell his comics crime caper story Goldfish in Hollywood. Bendis has since become a major writer for Marvel Comics. This collection features brand-new pages left on the cutting room floor and not included in the original comics. There's some strong language.

Jessica Jones; Volume 1: Alias. By Brian Michael Bendis. Michael Gaydos, artist ; Matt Hollingsworth, colorist. Marvel Enterprises 2015 216 p. Color; Illustration
Grades: Adult   **741.5; Fic**
1. Private investigators — Fiction; 2. Superhero comic books, strips, etc
0785198555; 9780785198550, $24.99

"Meet Jessica Jones. Once upon a time, she was a costumed super hero - but not a very good one. . . . The self-destructive would-be Avenger is now the owner and sole employee of Alias Investigations - a small, private-investigative firm specializing in superhuman cases. When she uncovers the potentially explosive secret of one hero's true identity, Jessica's life immediately becomes expendable." (Publisher's note)
Collected edition originally published 2002 as Alias
Volume 1 of 4

Jinx: The Definitive Collection. By Brian Michael Bendis for David Engel. Image Comics 2001 480p. Illustration
Grades: 11 12 Adult   **741.5; Fic**

1. Mystery graphic novels; 2. Graphic novels
978-1-58240-179-9, $24.95

This is a graphic crime noir novel about a bounty hunter, two grifters, and a treasure hunt that propels the character driven story. This extra large edition carries with it the entire epic story, behind the scenes/making of, script excerpts, and an art gallery. The story includes harsh language, nudity, sexual situations, and violence.

Powers Vol. 2: Roleplay. By Brian Michael Bendis and Michael Avon Oeming. Image Comics 2002 Un Illustration
Grades: 11 12 Adult   **741.5; Fic**
1. Mystery graphic novels; 2. Superhero graphic novels; 3. Graphic novels
1-58240-232-9, $13.95
2001 Eisner Award, Best New Series.

Detectives Christian Walker and Deena Pilgrim work out of the special homicide office in charge of cases that involve Powers, those that have talents and abilities far beyond those of normal men. This graphic novel details one of the most disturbing cases of their careers. A group of college kids who role play their favorite super-heroes are being murdered one-by-one, and unless Walker and Pilgrim can stop the killer, more kids will die. The book includes violence and copious use of harsh language, especially the f-bomb.

Powers Vol. 8: Legends. Created and produced by Brian Michael Bendis and Mike Avon Oeming; color art, Peter Pentazis. Marvel Entertainment/Icon 2004 Un Illustration
Grades: 11 12 Adult   **741.5; Fic**
1. Mystery graphic novels; 2. Superhero graphic novels; 3. Graphic novels
0-7851-1742-3, $17.95

Homicide detectives Christian Walker and Deena Pilgrim investigate murders specific to superhero cases. With all superheroes declared illegal, a bloody powers crime wave has hit the city and hit hard. A hero has returned, but is it enough to keep the city safe from the crossfire as the city's most powerful villains gun for each other in a massive turf war? And how far will Detective Deena Pilgrim go to prove she still has what it takes? The book contains lots of graphic violence, very harsh language with copious use of the f-bomb and s-bomb, and nudity.

★ **Powers:** The Definitive Hardcover Collection Vol. 1. Created and produced by Brian Michael Bendis and Mike Avon Oeming; colored by Pat Garrahy with Brian Michael Bendis. Marvel Comics 2006 456p. Illustration
Grades: 11 12 Adult   **741.5; Fic**
1. Mystery graphic novels; 2. Superhero graphic novels; 3. Graphic novels
978-0-7851-1805-3, $29.99
Volume 1 of 6

Homicide detectives Christian Walker and Deena Pilgrim investigate homicides in a city where super-powered heroes and villains live, fight, and die. Sometimes the heroes are just as flawed as the villains. And Walker has a secret of his own that gives him special insight in his investigations. The first three storylines have been remastered, reformatted, and collected in this edition which is replete with violence, harsh language, nudity, and sexual situations.

Also available in 16 paperback volumes

The **Pulse** Vol. 1: Thin Air. Illustrated by Mark Bagley. Marvel Entertainment 2004 Un Illustration
Grades: 10 11 12 Adult   **741.5; Fic**
1. Superhero graphic novels; 2. Graphic novels
0-7851-1332-0, $13.99

Former super hero and current private investigator Jessica Jones has just been offered a new job: a position with the Bugle's new super-hero section, The Pulse. Jessica's first assignment: to uncover the true identity of a former Bugle reporter's super-powered murderer. How is millionaire industrialist Norman Osborn involved in the case" And how will Jessica's discovery affect the entire Marvel Universe" The book includes some violence and strong language.

The **Road** to Civil War. Marvel Entertainment 2007 Un Illustration
Grades: 9 10 11 12 Adult   **741.5; Fic**
1. Fantastic Four (Fictional characters); 2. Iron Man (Fictional character); 3. Spider-Man (Fictional character); 4. Superhero graphic novels; 5. Graphic novels
978-0-7851-1974-6, $14.99

This book covers the hidden story of Marvel's secret past, the secret history of Marvel's most secret team - how they came together and how they are ripped apart. Plus: Spidey's got a new lease on life, new powers and a new costume, courtesy of his new best friend Tony Stark. So what could possibly go wrong" With clouds quickly building on the horizon, the bonds that Spider-Man now forges may very well determine his capacity to withstand a coming storm. And a mysterious object has fallen from space to crash in the Midwest, and Reed Richards of the Fantastic Four investigates.

Sam & Twitch: The Brian Michael Bendis Collection Vol. 1. Image Comics 2006 Un Illustration
Grades: 12 Adult   **741.5; Fic**
1. Mystery graphic novels; 2. Graphic novels
1-58240-583-2, $24.95

This neonoir crime series centers on the lives of New York City detectives Sam Burke and Twitch Williams and their adventures in the back alleys, deep nooks and dark crannies of the Big Apple. The hard-boiled stories are full of graphic violence and harsh language.

Sam and Twitch: The Brian Michael Bendis Collection Vol. 2. Image Comics 2007 Un Illustration
Grades: 11 12 Adult   **741.5; Fic**
1. Mystery graphic novels; 2. Graphic novels
978-1-58240-845-6, $24.95

This volume collects issues 10-19 of Bendis' run on the Sam & Twitch comics series. This is a crime noir series set in New York City and focused on the lives of detectives Sam Burke and Twitch Williams. The book features the Witchcraft story arc, an Ashley Wood cover gallery, and more extras. The book contains graphic violence and very harsh language.

Torso. Created and written by Brian Michael Bendis and Mark Andreyko; illustrated and lettered by Brian Michael Bendis. Marvel 2012 Un Illustration

Grades: Adult   **741.5; 364.152**
1. Mystery graphic novels; 2. Serial killers
078515356X; 9780785153566, $24.99

This graphic novel, created and written by Brian Michael Bendis and Mark Andreyko, illustrated and lettered by Brian Michael Bendis, winner of the 1999 Eisner Award for Comic Book Excellence, collects issues 1-5 of the comic book series "Torso." This volume tells "the gripping tale of Eliot Ness' chase of America's first serial killer: the mysterious torso killer!" (Publisher's note)

Collected edition originally published 2001

Ultimate comics Spider-Man; Volume 1. By Brian Michael Bendis, illustrated by Sara Pichelli. Marvel 2012 136 p.
Grades: Adult   **Fic; 741.5/973**
1. Spider-Man (Fictional character); 2. Superhero graphic novels
0785157123; 9780785157120, $24.99

In this graphic novel by Brian Michael Bendis, illustrated by Sara Pichelli, "Miles Morales IS the new Spider-Man! What's the secret behind his powers, and how will he master them? What new and familiar enemies will rise to challenge this all-new Spider-Man? And will Miles live up to Peter Parker's legacy?" (Publisher's note)

Volume 1 of 5

Ultimate Fantastic Four Vol. 1: The Fantastic. Writers, Brian Michael Bendis & Mark Millar ; pencils, Adam Kubert ; inks, Danny Miki and John Dell ; colors, Dave Stewart ; letters, Chris Eliopoulos/ Marvel Entertainment 2005 Un Illustration
Grades: 8 9 10 11 12 Adult   **741.5; Fic**
1. Fantastic Four (Fictional characters); 2. Superhero graphic novels; 3. Graphic novels
978-0-7851-1393-5, $12.99

The Ultimate treatment takes the Fantastic Four back to the beginning. High school genius (and bully magnet) Reed Richards suffers at school and also at home with a father who doesn't like his "troublemaking" experiments. When Reed enrolls at a secret government-sponsored school for the most gifted minds in the world, he unwittingly embarks on the journey of a lifetime. This is a story about science, adventure, and above all else, family.

Ultimate Spider-Man: Power & Responsibility. By Brian Michael Bendis (Author), Mark Bagley (Illustrator). Marvel 2009 200 p. Color illustration
Grades: 7 8 9 10 11 12 Adult   **741.5**
1. Spider-Man (Fictional character)
0785139400; 9780785139409, $19.99

In this comic book, by Brian Michael Bendis, illustrated by Mark Bagley, "Peter Parker gains super-powers after being bitten by a spider, loses his likable Uncle Ben to violent crime, and learns once again that 'with great power comes great responsibility.'" (Publisher's note)

Collected edition originally published 2001

Volume 1 of 21

Bennett, Anina
Heartbreakers Meet Boilerplate. Anina Bennett and Paul Guinan. IDW Publishing 2005 100p. Illustration
Grades: 8 9 10 11 12 Adult   **741.5; Fic**

1. Adventure graphic novels; 2. Science fiction graphic novels; 3. Graphic novels

1-932382-86-0, $9.99

The pioneering female action heroes, Heartbreakers, team up with the long-lost 19th-century robot, Boilerplate (already a worldwide legend), for a science fiction adventure featuring kung fu clones and robot romance. In this world, clones have won partial human rights, and rogue researchers now race to develop androids that can serve as the new slave workers.

Benson, Gabriel

The **Ballad** of Sleeping Beauty. Mike Hawthorne, Artist. Image Comics 2006 Un Illustration

Grades: 9 10 11 12 Adult   **741.5; Fic**

1. Fairy tales; 2. Westerns; 3. Graphic novels

0-97668-600-7, $21.95

Hounded gunfighter Cole Jarrett chases the tale of a woman cursed to spend the rest of her days imprisoned in sleep for sins she did not commit while running from a guilt-riddled past. In this adventure, the classic fairy tale is just the beginning. The story has violence and some strong language, as the fairy tale is set in the Old West.

The best American comics 2011

Edited and with an introduction by Alison Bechdel; Jessica Abel & Matt Madden, series editors. Houghton Mifflin Harcourt 2011 332p. Illustration (Best American series)

Grades: Adult   **741.5**

1. Graphic novels

978-0-547-33362-5, $25

Collects original comic strips from American authors and illustrators published in 2011 in graphic novels.

First published 2006

The Best American Comics 2014

Edited by Scott McCloud, Bill Kartalopoulos. Houghton Mifflin Harcourt 2014 400 p. Illustration

Grades: Adult   **741.5**

1. Anthologies; 2. Comic books, strips, etc — United States

0544106008; 9780544106000, $25

In this anthology, edited by Scott McCloud and Bill Kartalopoulos, the "editor . . . highlights the diverse number and styles of comics . . . . The 'big names'—Los Bros. Hernandez, Charles Burns, R. and Aline Crumb—are well represented in a section dubbed, tongue-in-cheek, as 'The Usual Suspects,' but a myriad of alt-comics, minicomics, and webcomics" are also included. (Publishers Weekly)

"Most of the inclusions are excerpts from larger works, and given the structural innovations of comic form, many of them are represented in a format different from the original. . . The spirit of discovery makes this a good launching point for readers interested in the genre's variety and limitless possibility." Kirkus

The best American comics 2015

Edited by Jonathan Lethem, Bill Kartalopoulos. Houghton Mifflin Harcourt 2015 379 p. Illustration; Color

Grades: Adult   **741.5**

1. Comic books, strips, etc — United States

9780544107700, $25; 0544107705

LC 2006233298

This book, edited by Jonathan Lethem and Bill Kartalopoulos, presents an anthology of U.S. based comics and graphic novels. Comic book authors featured within the volume include "Gabrielle Bell, Mat Brinkman, Roz Chast, Anya Davidson, Eleanor Davis, Jules Feiffer, Blaise Larmee, Raymond Pettibon, Ed Piskor, Joe Sacco, Esther Pearl Watson, and others." (Publisher's note)

Best of Josie and the Pussycats Volume 1

Archie Comics 2001 96p. Illustration

Grades: 3 4 5 6 7 8 9 10 11 12 Adult   **741.5; Fic**

1. Adventure graphic novels; 2. Humorous graphic novels; 3. Rock music; 4. Graphic novels

1-879794-07-1, $10.95

This book reprints a selection of stories about rock group Josie and the Pussycats, from their origin in 1963 to 1988. Josie, Melody, and Valerie are the Pussycats, along with their roadie Alan M., their shifty manager Alex, and his conniving sister, Alexandra. They make music, but along the way they also solve mysteries.

★ The Best of the Spirit

DC Comics 2005 187p. Illustration

Grades: 7 8 9 10 11 12 Adult   **741.5; Fic**

1. Spirit (Fictional character); 2. Superhero graphic novels; 3. Graphic novels

1-4012-0755-3, $14.99; 9781401207557

Legendary comics creator Will Eisner created The Spirit in 1940, and over the twelve years of its initial publication, he used it to revolutionize the cartooning medium, creating new methods of storytelling, developing new depths of characterization, and inventing such artistic innovations as the splash page. This volume reprints 22 stories from the original run, including the origin story from 1940; the bulk of the stories were initially published in the mid- to late-1940s. These stories allow people to get acquainted with The Spirit, who was a young criminologist named Denny Colt; believed to have been murdered, he was buried in a state of suspended animation and awoke one day in the Wildwood Cemetery. He has since dedicated himself to fighting crime, wearing a suit, fedora, and mask. DC Comics started publishing a new incarnation of The Spirit in 2007, and a motion picture is in the works.

Best, Dan

The **amazing** remarkable Monsieur Leotard: a novel with typographical acrobatics andillustrational feats in an ideal production of entirely new tricks, statuesque acts, and performances. Art by Eddie Campbell. First Second Books 2008 128p. Illustration

Grades: 10 11 12 Adult   **741.5; Fic**

1. Adventure graphic novels; 2. Circus; 3. Graphic novels

978-1-59643-301-4, $17.95

LC 2008-23283

When Jules Leotard, the man who inspired the song "The Man on the Flying Trapeze," dies, his nephew Etienne takes his place as trapeze artist and head of a circus troupe. Things don't go as planned, and eventually the members of the troupe go their separate ways. They come back together many years later when Zany, the clown, gets sent to Devil's Island; on their mission to save him, they end up on the Titanic and even more adventures. The book includes some (literal) potty humor, some violence, and mild sexual situations.

The Best of write now!.
Twomorrows Publishing 2008 160p. Illustration
Grades: 11 12 Adult   **741.5**
1. Comic books, strips, etc — Authorship; 2. Drawing — Technique; 3. Graphic novels — Authorship
978-1-893905-924, $19.95

This collection of articles from Write Now! Magazine features interviews with comics writers such as Brian Michael Bendis, Jeff Loeb, Todd McFarlane, and Paul Levitz, focusing on the art, craft, and business of writing comics. Other articles look at the comics writing and drawing processes, with such professionals as Mark Millar, Bendis, and J. Michael Straczynski; and other articles cover such topics as breaking into comics publishing, dealing with writer's block, and surviving in the comics industry. Comics titans Stan Lee and Will Eisner are also profiled.

Bevard, Robby
Ninja High School Hawaii Vol. 1. Antarctic Press 2002 Un Illustration
Grades: 10 11 12 Adult   **741.5; Fic**
1. Humorous graphic novels; 2. Martial arts; 3. Graphic novels
0-9768043-1-X, $12.95

Most people travel to Hawaii to escape from the craziness of their lives, but from the moment ninja-in-training Yumei Katana arrived at the airport, she knew this was no vacation. Klutzy assassins, philanthropist bullies, and even the landscape itself seem out to get her. Now she has to go to a school full of people who are trying to date her, kill her - or both - while still attempting to pass her next test! What's your typical ninja girl to do" This story is full of titillating fan service and martial arts action.

Bilson, Danny
The **Flash:** Lightning in a Bottle. DC Comics 2007 144p. Illustration
Grades: 9 10 11 12 Adult   **741.5; Fic**
1. Superhero graphic novels; 2. Flash (Fictional character); 3. Graphic novels
978-1-4012-1229-2, $12.99

Bart Allen returned from fighting Superboy Prime inside the Speed Force at the end of the Infinite Crisis with no speed and aged four years into an adult, and also no memory of how he spent the time. One year later, he's a factory worker in Keystone City, when an accident at the factory reconnects him to the Speed Force. That same accident causes Bart's best friend Griffin Gray to gain powers, too, but they drain his life force and cause him to rapidly age. His solution - he siphons off the energy from the slowly aging original Flash, Jay Garrick; but it might kill Garrick. And Griffin's brand of justice is too harsh.

Bissette, Stephen
Swamp Thing: Infernal Triangles. DC Comics/Vertigo 1988 Un Illustration
Grades: 10 11 12 Adult   **741.5; Fic**
1. Superhero graphic novels; 2. Swamp Thing (Fictional character); 3. Graphic novels
978-1-4012-1008-3, $19.99

After much trial and error, the elemental entity known as the Swamp Thing has succeeded in harnessing the life-force of his successor into the one form with which he can co-exist, a new human soul, to be born of his love Abby, with help from the sardonic magus John Constantine. But even as the couple begin preparing for their impending domesticity, forces far beyond their intimate world are conspiring to drive them apart once more. There's no nudity or graphic violence, little harsh language, but the themes are mature.

Bizarro World
DC Comics 2005 Un Illustration
Grades: 9 10 11 12 Adult   **741.5; Fic**
1. Aquaman (Fictitious character); 2. Batman (Fictional character); 3. Flash (Fictional character); 4. Humorous graphic novels; 5. Justice League (Fictional characters); 6. Superhero graphic novels; 7. Superman (Fictional character); 8. Wonder Woman (Fictional character); 9. Graphic novels
1-4012-0657-3, $19.99

In this collection, independent comics creators take DC's super hero characters - Superman, Batman, Wonder Woman, the Flash, Aquaman, the Justice League of America, and more - and put their own vision and spin on them, mostly with lots of humor. Some of the creators included here are: Peter Bagge, Kyle Baker, Ellen Forney, Paul Hornschemeier, Tony Millionaire, Scott Morse, Johnny Ryan, Mo Willems, Raina Telgemeier, Craig Thompson, Dean Haspiel, and Evan Dorkin.

Blackman, Haden
Star Wars Omnibus: X-Wing Rogue Squadron Volume 1. Haden Blackman and Michael A. Stackpole. Dark Horse Comics 2006 Un Illustration
Grades: 7 8 9 10 11 12 Adult   **741.5; Fic**
1. Adventure graphic novels; 2. Science fiction graphic novels; 3. Star Wars; 4. Graphic novels
978-1-59307-572-9, $24.95

The greatest star fighters of the Rebel Alliance become the defenders of a New Republic in this massive collection of stories featuring Wedge Antilles, hero of the Battle of Endor, and his team of ace pilots known throughout the galaxy as Rogue Squadron. Meet the Rogues for the first time and learn the fate of the galaxy immediately after the events of Return of the Jedi as the Rebellion's best pilots battle remnants of the Empire wherever its ugly agenda of fear and domination appears. Along with X-Wing Rogue Squadron: The Phantom Affair, this jam-packed volume contains never before collected material, including Star Wars X-Wing Rogue Leader #1-3, Star Wars X-Wing Rogue Squadron: The Rebel Opposition #1-4, Star Wars X-Wing Rogue Squadron: The Phantom Affair #1-4, and Star Wars Handbook: X-Wing Rogue Squadron.

Blain, Christophe
Gus and his gang. First Second Books 2008 164p.
Illustration
Grades: 10 11 12 Adult   **741.5; Fic**
1. Humorous graphic novels; 2. Western stories; 3.
Graphic novels
978-1-59643-170-6, $16.95; 1-59643-170-9
LC 2008-23541
Gus, Gratt, and Clem are three outlaws in this French
version of the Old West. Gus much prefers to rob trains,
banks are too still for him. What all three of them prefer is to
be with women; Gus and Gratt go girl-hunting together in
towns such as El Dorado, but Clem doesn't go with them. He
has a family, with Ava and their daughter Jamie; but he does
have a passionate affair with a free-spirited, red-haired
photographer. Everything the three men do is financed by
robbing banks, trains . . . when Gus tries to case a bank, he
falls for a woman who works there and ends up pretending to
be a writer in order to woo her. The book doesn't follow a
straightforward narrative, and the French idea of how the
Old West "worked" is more than a bit eccentric. The book
also includes lots of sexual content and partial nudity.

Isaac the Pirate 1. To Exotic Lands. NBM 2003 Un
Illustration
Grades: 10 11 12 Adult   **741.5; Fic**
1. Adventure graphic novels; 2. Pirates; 3. Graphic novels
1-56163-366-6, $14.95
LC 2003-59288
Isaac is a talented artist with no money but with a
wonderful lover back in Paris of the 18th century. He runs
into a rich Captain who is taken by his abilities and hires him
with a handsome stipend to come along in his voyages. It
turns out he's a pirate. Isaac went to make some quick money
and come back and marry the love of his life, but he has
embarked upon a series of adventures on the high seas from
the Caribbean to the icy North, with apparently no end in
sight. Meanwhile, his girlfriend is getting attention from
another ... The book includes some harsh language and
violence.

Isaac the Pirate Volume 2: The Capital. NBM 2005 Un
Illustration
Grades: 10 11 12 Adult   **741.5; Fic**
1. Adventure graphic novels; 2. Pirates; 3. Graphic novels
1-56163-418-2, $14.95
LC 2004-116613
As things get bad on the pirate ship, Isaac must rescue
himself from many dangers and, with the help of one of his
former shipmates, a fleet-footed thief, makes his way back to
Paris to seek his love, Alice, from whom he has been
separated far too long. However, the bad pirating influences
prove themselves hard to shake; he becomes a nimble
pickpocket. Alice, however, remains elusive ... The book
includes violence, strong language, nudity, and sexual
situations.

Bocquet, José-Louis
Kiki de Montparnasse. Catel & Bocquet; [translated
from the Belgian edition by Nora Mahony]. SelfMadeHero
2011 416 p. Illustration
Grades: Adult   **759.4; 741.5**

1. Artists' models; 2. Artists' models — France —
Biography; 3. Kiki, 1901-1953; 4. Painters; 5. Women —
France — History
9781906838256, $24.95
LC 2011431146
This book offers a graphic biography of artist model and
actress Alice Prin, better known as Kiki de Montparnasse. In
"bohemian Montparnasse [in Paris, France] of the 1920s,
Kiki escaped poverty to become one of the most charismatic
figures of the avant-garde years between the wars. Partner to
[artist] Man Ray, and one of the first emancipated women of
the 20th century, Kiki made her mark with her freedom of
style, word, and thought that could be learned from only one
school - the school of life." (Amazon.com)
Includes bibliographical references (p. 413-415)

Boldman, Craig
Archie Day by Day Volume 1. Archie Comics 2003
96p. Illustration
Grades: 3 4 5 6 7 8 9 10 11 12 Adult   **741.5; Fic**
1. Andrews, Archie (Fictional character); 2. Humorous
graphic novels; 3. Graphic novels
1-879794-16-0, $10.95
Archie and his pals have been comics' most celebrated
teenage humor characters for over 60 years, since 1941.
Now for the first time, selections from Archie's worldwide
syndicated newspaper strip are collected in this volume. This
black and white edition includes a selection of daily strips
from the mid-1990s, chronicling life in Riverdale, USA.

Bourdain, Anthony
Get Jiro!. Anthony Bourdain, Joel Rose, Langdon Foss.
DC Comics 2012 160 p.
Grades: Adult   **741.5**
1. Cooks; 2. Food — Social aspects; 3. Japanese cooking;
4. Sushi
1401228275; 9781401228279, $24.99
LC 2011052113
This graphic novel is set in "futuristic Los Angeles,"
where "food culture rules all social life, copping to corporate
honchos. People even sing about food at karaoke bars. Two
reigning culinary empires control the town like mafia, and
both want new-in-town sushi chef Jiro on their team. But
Jiro has his own plans and prevails by cleverly pitting both
sides against each other, snotty international omnivores vs.
holistic purists." (Library Journal)

Bourne, Malcolm
Tales Tales of Ordinary Madness. Illustrated by Mike
Allred. Oni Press 2004 Un Illustration Ordinary Madness.
Oni Press 2004 Un Illustration
Grades: 11 12 Adult   **741.5; Fic**
1. Mental illness; 2. Graphic novels
1-929998-78-3, $11.95
Everyone has problems. Every day, people's lives are
peppered with a little bit of madness, things that push them
over the edge and away from their sanity. Take Robert. He
knows those eyes are watching him. What eyes? The ones
that are everywhere, lurking in every corner, outside every
window. Then there's David, who one day had the
irresistible urge to walk out into the middle of traffic. Or
Mrs. Yogeswarren, who is so scared of dogs, she has to plan

a route ahead of time whenever she wants to go anywhere, just so she can avoid canines of any kind. These are the sorts of people who have to go to the psychiatrist to learn to cope. But what happens when the good doctor begins to identify a little too closely with his patients" The book includes violence, strong language, nudity, and sexual situations.

Brabner, Joyce
Our cancer year. By Joyce Brabner and Harvey Pekar; illustrations by Frank Stack. Four Walls Eight Windows 1994 252 p. Illustration
Grades: Adult   **741.5; B; 362.1/96994/0092**
1. Cancer; 2. Cancer — Personal narratives; 3. Pekar, Harvey, 1939-2010
1568580118; 9781568580111, $19.95
LC 94010523
This graphic novel, by Joyce Brabner and Harvey Pekar, with illustrations by Frank Stack, "center[s] on the year that they found out that Pekar had cancer; the year that also saw Operation Desert Shield turn into Operation Desert Storm. Drawing upon the many personal trials they faced, Pekar and Brabner create a portrait of a man beset with fears both real and imagined." (Amazon)

Brandon, Ivan
Ruule: Ganglords of Chinatown. Mike Hawthorne, Illustrator. Image Comics 2005 Un Illustration
Grades: 10 11 12 Adult   **741.5; Fic**
1. Adventure graphic novels; 2. Bible fiction; 3. Graphic novels
1-58240-566-2, $19.99
Chinatown has been overwhelmed by vicious biker gangs. One man is chosen to lead his people to freedom, but the price of victory is more costly than blood and darker than war. This is a bloody, violent, yet very faithful retelling of the Biblical story of Gideon's battle against the followers of the false god Baal. In this story, Baal leads a vicious group of motorcycle gangs, and one man, Gid, dares to face him and starts to build a small army of believers who want to take Chinatown back.

Brenner, Robin E.
★ Understanding manga and anime. Libraries Unlimited 2007 335p. Illustration
Grades: Adult Professional   **025.2; 741.5**
1. Anime; 2. Libraries — Collection development; 3. Libraries — Special collections; 4. Manga — Study and teaching
978-1-59158-332-5, $40; 1-59158-332-2
LC 2007-9773
The author "provides thorough explanations of manga and anime vocabulary, potential censorship issues because of cultural disparities, and typical Manga conventions. . . . No professional collection could possibly be complete without this all-inclusive and exceptional work." Voice Youth Advocates

Briggs, Raymond
★ Ethel & Ernest: A True Story. Pantheon 2001 104p. Illustration
Grades: 4 5 6 7 8 9 10 11 12 Adult   **741.5**

1. Biographical graphic novels; 2. Graphic novels
978-0-375-71447-4, $15.00
This is Raymond Briggs's loving depiction of his parents' lives from their chance first encounter in the 1920s until their deaths in the 1970s. Ethel and Ernest were solid members of the English working class, part of the generation that lived through the most tumultuous years of the twentieth century. They met during the Depression—she working as a maid, he as a milkman—and the reader follows them as they court and marry, make a home, raise their son, and cope with the dark days of World War II. Briggs portrays how his parents succeeded, or failed, in coming to terms with the events of their rapidly shifting world—the advent of radio, television, and telephones; the development of the atomic bomb; the moon landing; the social and political turmoil of the sixties.

Britt, Mark Haven
Full-Color. Image Comics 2007 175p. Illustration
Grades: 11 12 Adult   **741.5; Fic**
1. Revenge; 2. Graphic novels
978-1-58240-840-8, $15.99
A lifetime marked with Napoleonic bosses has generated a rage in Boom that she can't contain anymore - only aim. Her target" Her boss. She's given herself one day to make it all right now that she's quit her job. That same day, Boom comes home to find an old friend standing on her fire escape. David's double-crossed a drug dealer and he's looking for help. She'll help him if he'll help her; but things don't go according to plan. The book has lots of violence, harsh language, and some partial nudity.

Brittenham, Skip
Anomaly. Skip Brittenham and Brian Haberlin. Ingram Pub Services 2012 370 p.
Grades: Adult   **741.5**
1. Interplanetary voyages — Fiction; 2. Political corruption — Fiction; 3. Science fiction
0985334207; 9780985334208, $75.00
In this book, set in 2717, "an interplanetary first contact mission to an unexplored, sentient-inhabited planet dubbed Anomaly unwittingly finds itself set up by a corrupt government official who . . . arranges for them to be stranded without hope of returning. All previous expeditions from a conglomerate-run Earth . . . were presumed lost, and when this team's technology falls victim to the planet's polymer-devouring organisms, the survivors must contend with an unknown and hostile environment without the benefit of equipment or supplies." (Publishers Weekly)

Broome, John
Showcase Presents: The Elongated Man Volume 1. Written by John Broome and Gardner Fox ; Art by Carmine Infantino, Neal Adams, Murphy Anderson and Gil Kane. DC Comics 2006 560p. Illustration
Grades: 6 7 8 9 10 11 12 Adult   **741.5; Fic**
1. Batman (Fictional character); 2. Elongated Man (Fictional characters); 3. Flash (Fictional character); 4. Green Lantern (Fictional character); 5. Robin (Fictional character); 6. Superhero graphic novels; 7. Graphic novels
978-1-4012-1042-7, $16.99

Ralph Dibny is the Elongated Man, a self-taught superhero who has harnessed the power of the exotic gingo fruit and attained the ability to stretch himself to fantastic lengths. As the only costumed hero whose identity has been revealed to the world, Elongated Man travels the globe with his adoring wife Sue, solving mysteries and gaining renown for his singular elastic talent. In these stories, originally published from 1960 to 1968 and reprinted here in black and white, Dibny sometimes teams up with the Flash, Batman and Robin, Green Lantern, and Zatanna. Ralph and Sue Dibny were at the heart of the Identity Crisis, so readers might want to see their early adventures.

Brosgol, Vera
★ **Anya's** ghost. First Second 2011 221p. Illustration
Grades: 9 10 11 12 Adult   **741.5; Fic**
1. Friendship; 2. Ghosts; 3. Horror graphic novels; 4. School life; 5. Young adult literature — Works; 6. Graphic novels
978-1-59643-552-0, $15.99; 1-59643-713-8; 978-1-59643-552-0 (pa); 1-59643-552-6 (pa)
           LC 2010-36251
"A deliciously creepy page-turning gem from first-time writer and illustrator Brosgol. . . . A moodily atmospheric spectrum of grays washes over the clean, tidy panels, setting a distinct stage before the first words appear. . . . In addition to the supernatural elements, Brosgol interweaves some savvy insights about the illusion of perfection and outward appearance. . . . A book sure to haunt its reader long after the last page is turned—exquisitely eerie." Kirkus

Brown, Box
Andre the Giant: Life and Legend. By Box Brown. First Second 2014 240 p. Illustration
Grades: 9 10 11 12 Adult   **741.5; 92**
1. Actors; 2. Andre, the Giant, 1946-1993; 3. Wrestling
1596438517; 9781596438514, $17.99
           LC 2014466607
This book, by Box Brown, is a graphic novel biography of Andre Roussimoff. "At his peak, he weighed 500 pounds and stood nearly seven and a half feet tall. But the huge stature that made his fame also signed his death warrant. . . . [Brown draws] from historical records about Andre's life as well as a wealth of anecdotes from his colleagues in the wrestling world." (Publisher's note)
Brown "uses professional wrestling's complex narrative devices in this biography, which pulls back the curtain on Andre the Giant (Andre Rousimoff), one of the industry's most well-known figures. . . . Brown's simple, blocky art keeps the story front and center, and the down-to-earth tone allows him to avoid demonizing or lionizing his subject." Pub Wkly"
Includes bibliographical references

Brown, Chester
Louis Riel: a comic-strip biography. Chester Brown.. Drawn and Quarterly 2003 272 p. Illustration
Grades: Adult   **741.5/971; 741.5**
1. Riel, Louis, 1844-1885
1896597637; 9781896597638, $24.95
           LC 2004396047

Courtesy of Drawn & Quarterly

"Chester Brown reveals in the dusty closet of Canadian history there are some skeletons that won't stop rattling. To some Louis Riel was one of the founding fathers of a nation but to others he was a murderer who nearly tore a country apart. A man so charismatic he was elected to government twice while in exile with a prize on his head—but so impassioned his dramatic behavior cast serious doubts on his sanity. Riel took on the army, the government, the Queen, and even the Church in the name of freedom." (Publisher's note)
Includes bibliographical references (p. 269) and index

Brown, Elman
Richard Matheson's I Am Legend. IDW Publishing 2007 244p. Illustration
Grades: 10 11 12 Adult   **741.5; Fic**
1. Horror graphic novels; 2. Matheson, Richard; 3. Matheson, Richard — Adaptations; 4. Science fiction graphic novels; 5. Vampires; 6. Graphic novels
978-1-933239-21-7, $19.99
Robert Neville is the last human survivor of a virus that has turned the rest of the population into vampires. He spends his days hunting and killing them, and fortifying his house against them. But as the last human, he has to wonder who is normal, he or the vampires" This graphic novel adapts Matheson's science fiction/horror masterpiece. In 2007, a third movie adaptation will be released, starring Will Smith; there were two films produced previously: 1964's "The Last Man on Earth" starring Vincent Price, and 1971's "The Omega Man" starring Charlton Heston. Some scenes in the book are graphically violent.

Brown, Jeffrey
Every Girl is the End of the World for Me. Top Shelf Productions 2005 Un Illustration
Grades: 10 11 12 Adult   **741.5; Fic**
1. Autobiographical graphic novels; 2. Humorous graphic novels; 3. Romance graphic novels; 4. Graphic novels
1-891830-77-5, $8
Autobiographical cartoonist Jeffrey Brown provides an epilogue to his Girlfriend Trilogy, detailing the day-by-day events of a three week run-in with five different girls. An ex comes back into the picture, he develops a growing but poorly chosen crush, muses on the way friends come and go in life, and comes to a realization that the end is never really the end.

Incredible Change-Bots. Top Shelf Productions 2007 Un Illustration
Grades: 8 9 10 11 12 Adult   **741.5; Fic**
1. Humorous graphic novels; 2. Robots; 3. Science fiction graphic novels; 4. Graphic novels
978-1-891830-91-4, $15

Far away in outer space, the Incredible Change-Bots live on the planet Electronocybercircuitron. The Awesomebots and the Fantasticons have lived in relative harmony, until Shootertron, the leader of the Fantasticons, decides to rig the election to rule the planet. The Awesomebots declare war, and over the years the Change-Bots destroy their planet. They then come to Earth, where they continue their fighting, each group gaining their own human allies. Brown has done a fun send-up of the Transformers with this story, and while there is some violence, there is very little in the way of bad language.

A **Matter** of Life. Written and illustrated by Jeffrey Brown. Top Shelf Productions 2013 96 p. Illustration
Grades: Adult   **741.5/973; Fic**
1. Family; 2. Graphic novels
1603092668, $14.95; 9781603092661
In this graphic novel, author and illustrator Jeffrey Brown "draws upon memories of three generations of Brown men: himself, his minister father, and his preschooler son Oscar. Weaving through time, passing through the quiet suburbs and colorful cities of the midwest, their stories slowly assemble into [an] answer to the big questions: matters of life and death, family and faith, and the search for something beyond oneself. (Publisher's note)

Miniature Sulk. Top Shelf Productions 2005 Un Illustration
Grades: 11 12 Adult   **741.5; Fic**
1. Autobiographical graphic novels; 2. Humorous graphic novels; 3. Graphic novels
1-891830-66-X, $8
Brown presents a humorous short story collection featuring fiction, gags, and autobiography. The book includes "My Brother Knows Kung Fu" and "Action Television Show." The book includes harsh language and some sexual suggestiveness.

Brown, Lars
  North world. Oni Press 2008 Un Illustration
Grades: 9 10 11 12 Adult   **741.5; Fic**
1. Adventure graphic novels; 2. Fantasy graphic novels; 3. Graphic novels
978-1-932664-91-1, $11.95
Conrad is a working hero who wields a sword to vanquish giant animals; he wants to work up to legend status, so when the guild wants to send him to his old home town to find a demon summoner and stop him, Conrad agrees. He has also received a wedding invitation from his ex-girlfriend. When he gets to town, he faces a group of young punks who want to challenge him, his family, and lots of old friends and foes. He starts to wonder if he really has it in him to stop a demon summoner, and it gets kind of weird when he sees a restaurant back in business that burned down just before he left home seven years before.

Brown, Tom
  Hopeless, Maine: Personal Demons. Tom and Nimue Brown. Archaia Entertainment 2012 128 p.
Grades: 10 11 12 Adult   **Fic; 741**
1. Maine; 2. Paranormal fiction; 3. Graphic novels
1936393573; 9781936393572, $19.95

In this gothic graphic novel, by Nimue and Tom Brown, "The small island of Hopeless, off the coast of Maine, is a breeding ground for demons, freaks, vampires, and other creatures of the night. . . . Salamandra, a young girl with one foot in our world and one foot in the otherworld, . . . navigates a life on the edge of reality." (Publisher's note)

Brownstein, Charles
  ★ **Eisner/Miller**. Dark Horse Books 2005 352p. Illustration
Grades: Adult Professional   **741.5**
1. Graphic novels — History and criticism; 2. Miller, Frank, 1957-; 3. Graphic novels
1-56971-755-9, $19.95
Culture-curious readers and life-long fans of comics are invited to read along as two of the medium's greatest contributors - legendary innovator and godfather of sequential art Will Eisner, and the modern master of cinematic comics storytelling, Frank Miller, discuss the ins-and-outs of this compelling and often controversial art form. The conversations took place in 2002, and were recorded by Brownstein. The book features rare, behind-the-scenes photos of Eisner, Miller, and other notable creators. Some of the reproduced art includes nudity and violence.

Brubaker, Ed
  The **Authority:** Revolution Book One. Penciler, Dustin Nguyen; Inker, Richard Friend. DC Comics/Wildstorm 2005 Un Illustration
Grades: 10 11 12 Adult   **741.5; Fic**
1. Science fiction graphic novels; 2. Superhero graphic novels; 3. Graphic novels
1-4012-0623-9, $14.99
The Authority has settled into its role as governing body of the U.S. But with many unhappy Americans and a powerful foe working behind-the-scenes, can a second American Revolution be far behind" Can the Authority survive its internal struggles long enough to stop Paul Revere and the Sons of Liberty" The book includes lots of harsh language and violence.

  The **Authority:** Revolution Book Two. Penciler, Dustin Nguyen; Inker, Richard Friend. DC Comics/Wildstorm 2006 Un Illustration
Grades: 10 11 12 Adult   **741.5; Fic**
1. Science fiction graphic novels; 2. Superhero graphic novels; 3. Graphic novels
978-1-4012-0947-6, $14.99
Former StormWatch Weatherman Henry Bendix has returned from the dead and is busy remolding the Earth to his unique vision. After the debacle in the nation's capital that led to the total destruction of Washington, DC, the Authority relinquished control of the United States and all but vanished. How long can tyranny stand, before heroes will rise up? Can a teenage Jenny Quantum reunite the fractured team and make them heroes again, or has Bendix finally won the battle? The book includes lots of harsh language and violence.

  Batman: Turning Points. By Greg Rucka, Ed Brubaker, and Chuck Dixon. DC Comics 2007 124p. Illustration
Grades: 8 9 10 11 12 Adult   **741.5; Fic**

1. Batgirl (Fictional character); 2. Batman (Fictional character); 3. Joker (Fictional character); 4. Robin (Fictional character); 5. Superhero graphic novels; 6. Graphic novels
978-1-4012-1360-2, $14.99

Throughout the long comic book career of Batman, Gotham policeman James Gordon has been an almost constant presence. The two men's alliance and friendship formed an important element in Batman's work. This book traces the relationship from Batman's early years, to the first time Gordon meets Robin, to the time shortly after Gordon's daughter Barbara, the Batgirl, was shot by the Joker, to the Batman who took over after Bane broke Batman's back, to come back full circle when a man Gordon and Bats stopped from killing hostages in the first story returns to Gotham City.

Originally published as Batman Turning Points issues #1-5.

Catwoman: Wild Ride. Cameron Stewart, artist ; Guy Davis, Nick Cerington, additional layouts. DC Comics 2005 Un Illustration
Grades: 9 10 11 12 Adult   741.5; Fic
1. Catwoman (Fictional character); 2. Superhero graphic novels; 3. Graphic novels
1-4012-0436-8, $14.99

Selina and Holly need to get out of Gotham City, so they drive off on a road trip. But the two women are in for way more than they bargained for as they face some mysterious - and dangerous - Egyptian thieves who seem to keep crossing their paths. This volume includes guest appearances by Batman, Wildcat, Hawkman and Hawkgirl, and Captain Cold. The book has some mildly bad language and some violence.

Civil War: Captain America. Illustrators, Lee Weeks and Mike Perkins. Marvel Entertainment 2007 Un Illustration
Grades: 9 10 11 12 Adult   741.5; Fic
1. Captain America (Fictional character); 2. Superhero graphic novels; 3. Graphic novels
0-7851-2798-4, $11.99

Captain America has clashed with the government and his friends and become a renegade because of his opposition to the Super Human Registration Act. The life of his girlfriend, Agent 13, is torn apart as her superiors use her divided loyalties against her. Elsewhere, the Red Skull returns, and the Winter Soldier once again comes face-to-face with Cap; but which side will he choose" Winter Soldier, who was once Bucky Barnes, Captain America's partner, faces his first Christmas in the 21st century, and the truth of the terrible things he was forced to do as the Winter Soldier.

The **Fade** Out; Act one. By Ed Brubaker; illustrated by Sean Phillips; colors by Elizabeth Breitweiser. Image Comics 2015 120 p. Color; Illustration
Grades: Adult   741.5; Fic
1. Actresses — Fiction; 2. Hollywood (Calif) — Fiction; 3. Motion pictures — Fiction; 4. Noir fiction
1632151715; 9781632151711, $9.99

This book, by Ed Brubaker, "is an epic noir set in the world of noir itself, the backlots and bars of Hollywood at the end of its Golden Era. A movie stuck in endless reshoots, a writer damaged from the war and lost in the bottle, a dead movie star and the lookalike hired to replace her. Nothing is what it seems in the place where only lies are true." (Publisher's note)

"Waking up from a complete blackout, screenwriter Charlie Parish finds himself half drunk next to the dead body of Valeria Sommers, the starlet of his latest film. As Parish struggles to cover his tracks and uncover details about her death, the studio and its players attempt to distance themselves from Sommers and finish the picture without her. Similar to Brubaker's Fatale series, this is noir at its finest, filled with gritty, deeply flawed characters with twisted motivations, trying to stay one step ahead of each other." Booklist

Contains material originally published in magazine form as The Fade Out #1-4

Volume 1 of 3

Fatale: Death Chases Me. Ed Brubaker and Sean Phillips. Image Comics 2012 144 p.
Grades: Adult   741.5
1. Historical fiction; 2. Love stories; 3. Paranormal fiction
1607065630; 9781607065630, $14.99

In this book, "[o]ccult forces and gut-wrenching horror collide in 1950s San Francisco, as a corrupt cop and a smitten reporter go toe-to-toe over Jo, an ageless beauty with the looks of a Vargas girl and the heart of a rattle snake, who is desperate to escape the grasp of a satanic cult and their demonic, shape-shifting leader." (Publishers Weekly)

Contains material originally published in magazine form as Fatale #1-5.

Volume 1 of 5

Fatale: West of Hell. By Ed Brubaker and illustrated by Sean Phillips, Dave Stewart, and Bettie Breitweiser. Image comics 2013 128 p.
Grades: Adult   Fic; 741.5
1. Historical fiction; 2. Immortality
1607067439; 9781607067436, $14.99

In this graphic novel, by Ed Brubaker and illustrated by Sean Phillips, Dave Stewart, and Bettie Breitweiser, "four stories here focus on the antiheroine's search for self-knowledge as we follow her and her predecessors through Dust Bowl Texas, medieval France, the Wild West, and WWII Europe. Tantalizing hints about the forces that spawned her and the unseen, Lovecraftian world that surrounds her are planted throughout the pages." (Booklist)

★ **Gotham** Central; Book One. Ed Brubaker, Greg Rucka; With Michael Lark. DC Comics 2013 235 p. Color illustration
Grades: 11 12 Adult   741.5
1. Batman (Fictional character); 2. Good and evil; 3. Police; 4. Superheroes
1401220371; 9781401220372, $19.99

LC 2012046720

This graphic novel, by Ed Brubaker and Greg Rucka, takes place in "Gotham City: a town teeming with corrupt cops, ruthless crime lords, petty thieves à and just a small handful that would oppose them. Grizzled veteran Harvey Bullock, Captain Maggie Sawyer, detective Renee Montoya and the GCPD are the law force that stands between order and complete anarchy." (Publisher's note)

Series originally collected in five volumes

Originally published in single magazine form in Gotham Central #1-10.

In the Line of Duty

Other Gotham Central collections are: Book two: Jokers and madmen; Book three: On the freak beat; Book four: Corrigan

The **Sandman** presents: the dead boy detectives. Illustrators Steve Leialoha and Bryan Talbot. DC Comics/Vertigo 2008 104p. Illustration

Grades: 10 11 12 Adult   **741.5; Fic**

1. Fantasy graphic novels; 2. Ghosts; 3. Mystery graphic novels; 4. Supernatural graphic novels; 5. Graphic novels

978-1-4012-1855-3, $12.99

Charles Rowland and Edwin Paine spend all their time reading detective stories, watching thrillers at the movie theaters, or just hanging out in their treehouse, and no one cares. Charles and Edwin are ghosts from different times in the past, who have become friends in their new existence. Now, inspired by the stories and movies, they decide to become private detectives, and they take a case from a runaway girl. Someone is killing the runaway children who live in the Underground of London, and that someone is capable of hurting even ghosts like Charles and Edwin. They encounter a man who says his family has hunted the killer for centuries and enlists their help, but is he telling the truth, or are Charles and Edwin in very deep trouble" The book includes some violence.

★ **Scene** of the crime. By Ed Brubaker and illustrated by Michael Lark and Sean Phillips. Image Comics 2012 128 p.

Grades: Adult   **741.5**

1. Crime; 2. Mystery graphic novels; 3. Noir fiction

1607066327; 9781607066323, $24.99

This graphic novel by Ed Brubaker presents "a hard-hitting mystery story set in a modern-day "Chinatown" that garnered nominations for Best Mini-series and Best Writer in the 2000 Eisner Awards. Also included in this new collection are behind-the-scenes art and stories, a new foreword by Brubaker, and many other extras." (Publisher's note)

Sleeper: Out in the Cold. Artist, Sean Phillips. DC Comics/Wildstorm 2005 Un Illustration

Grades: 11 12 Adult   **741.5; Fic**

1. Mystery graphic novels; 2. Spies; 3. Graphic novels

1-4012-0115-6, $17.95

Holden Carver is part of a world-spanning secret organization headed by Tao, super-manipulator and ruthless criminal mastermind. Carver is also a sleeper agent, forced into a world of evil and treachery by master spy John Lynch, who now lies in an irreversible coma, the only living soul able to bear witness that Carver is actually one of the good guys. Now, ensnared in an ongoing game of cat and mouse, every day is a challenge for Holden to evade detection by those who think he is an ally, avoid capture by those who believe he is a traitor, and somehow survive with his soul intact. What's a spy to do when no one knows he's been left out in the cold" The book includes graphic violence, harsh language replete with f-bombs and s-bombs, nudity, and sexual situations.

Brunetti, Ivan

★ **Aesthetics:** a memoir. By Ivan Brunetti. Yale University Press 2013 120 p. Illustration

Grades: Adult   **759.13**

1. Artists — Biography; 2. Cartoonists — Biography

0300184409; 9780300184402, $25

LC 2012950659

This autobiography, written by cartoonist and illustrator Ivan Brunetti, traces his artistic trajectory and output, from youthful doodles to his latest cover illustrations and comic strips." It includes "previously unpublished materials, including working drawings, sketches for cartoons, book covers, personal photographs, and items from the artist's collection of toys and handmade objects. In an introductory essay and captions, Brunetti explains . . . his creative process and aesthetic sensibility." (Publisher's note)

Brunswick, Glen

The **Gray** Area Vol. 1: All of This Can be Yours. Artists Klaus Janson and John Romita Jr. Image Comics 2005 Un Illustration

Grades: 11 12 Adult   **741.5; Fic**

1. Superhero graphic novels; 2. Supernatural graphic novels; 3. Graphic novels

1-58240-485-2, $14.95

After his execution for double-crossing a drug cartel, Rudy Chance - a brutal, corrupt cop and womanizer - expects he'll wind up in Hell. Instead, he finds himself in the Gray Area, where he is forced to combat evil for an afterlife police force in order to gain a shot at redemption. Given extraordinary powers, Chance hunts down the wicked to condemn and the worthy to heal. But can he control his own dark side, or will it lead him to eternal damnation" The book has foul language and considerable violence.

★ **Jersey** Gods, vol.1: I'd live and I'd die for you. Art by Dan McDaid; colors by Rachelle Rosenberg; lettering by Rus Wooton. Image Comics 2009 Un Illustration

Grades: 10 11 12 Adult   **741.5; Fic**

1. Humorous graphic novels; 2. Romance graphic novels; 3. Superhero graphic novels; 4. Graphic novels

978-1-60706-063-5, $14.99

Jersey Girl Zoe works as an assistant to the fashion editor of her local newspaper in Cherry Hill, New Jersey. She has bad luck with boyfriends who always dump her. Then she meets Barock, a god from another planet (Cumulus), when one of his fights leads him to Earth. She has to deal with her boss stealing her idea of an article series on fashion, while Barock has to deal with betrayals and infighting among the gods of his world. But they're in love; what is a Jersey mall princess to do with a planetary god" And what happens when they both get entangled with a scheme to flood the New Jersey malls with fake designer fashions" The art takes classic Jack Kirby style (big, muscular, square-jawed, clean-cut heroes) and gives it just enough of a twist to be humorous without being satirical. The book includes a lot of action and some violence; there's no nudity, but Zoe is shown in her underwear in one panel.

Bryant, Marc

Shangri-La. Illustrated by Hendrix Shepherd. Image Comics 2004 Un Illustration

Grades: 11 12 Adult 741.5; Fic

1. Mystery graphic novels; 2. Rock music; 3. Graphic novels

1-58240-352-X, $7.95

When burned out assassin Jetta Helm backs out of a hit on has been rocker Correy Stinson, the two are set on a wild chase across America. Running from the vicious hillbilly hitman Lonesome Roscoe, they're forced to do their best not to kill each other before they can turn the tables on the record label that wants them both dead. The book includes considerable violence and harsh language.

Building literacy connections with graphic novels: page by page, panel by panel

Edited by James Bucky Carter.. National Council of Teachers of English 2007 164p. Illustration

Grades: Adult Professional 428; 741.5

1. Graphic novels — History and criticism; 2. Language arts; 3. Literacy; 4. Peter Pan (Fictional character); 5. Teaching; 6. X-Men (Fictional characters)

978-0-8141-0392-0; 0-8141-0392-8, $30.95

LC 2007-2806

Each chapter presents practical suggestions for the classroom as it pairs a graphic novel with a more traditional text or examines connections between multiple sources. Some of the pairings include The Scarlet Letter and Katherine Arnoldi's The Amazing True" Story of a Teenage Single Mom; Oliver Twist and Will Eisner's Fagin the Jew; Young adult literature and Marjane Satrapi's Persepolis; Dante's Inferno and an X-Men story; classic fantasies (Peter Pan, The Wizard of Oz, and Alice in Wonderland) and Farel Dalrymple's Pop Gun War; traditional and graphic novel versions of Beowulf. These pairings open up a double world of possibilities-in words and images-to all kinds of learners, from reluctant readers and English language learners to gifted students and those who are critically exploring relevant social issues. An appendix recommends additional graphic novels for use in middle and high school classrooms.

Includes bibliographical references (p. 157-160)

Bunn, Cullen

The damned volume one: Three days dead. Brian Hurtt, artist. Oni Press 2008 Un Illustration

Grades: 11 12 Adult 741.5; Fic

1. Humorous graphic novels; 2. Mafia; 3. Mystery graphic novels; 4. Supernatural graphic novels; 5. Graphic novels

978-1-932664-63-8, $14.95

In an alternate world prohibition era, gangsters still grow rich on catering to people's vices, but a more sinister power controls the crime cartels and uses human greed, gluttony, lust, and other mortal sins to fuel a much more lucrative trade: mortal souls. When a feud between two Families is supposed to end with a brokered deal, the bookkeeper brokering the deal is kidnapped. Big Al pulls gumshoe Eddie's corpse out of a ditch and puts him on the case to find the missing bookkeeper. Poor Eddie, he's already dead, but people keep killing him over and over again. The book includes considerable violence, some bad language, and occasional nudity.

Burns, Charles

★ **Black** hole. Charles Burns.. Pantheon Books 2005 1 v. Illustration

Grades: 10 11 12 Adult 741.5/973; 741.5

1. Communicable diseases — Fiction; 2. High school students — Fiction; 3. Homicide — Fiction; 4. Teenagers — Fiction

9780375714726; 9780375423802; 037542380X, $29.95

LC 2005046431

Eisner Awards: Best Graphic Album - Reprint (2006); Harvey Awards: Best Graphic Album - Previously Published (2006); Ignatz Awards: Outstanding Anthology or Collection (2006)

This book takes place in "Suburban Seattle, [in] the mid-1970s. We learn from the out-set that a strange plague has descended upon the area's teenagers, transmitted by sexual contact. The disease is manifested in any number of ways - from the hideously grotesque to the subtle (and concealable) - but once you've got it, that's it. There's no turning back. As we inhabit the heads of several key characters ù some kids who have it, some who don't, some who are about to get it ù what unfolds isn't the expected battle to fight the plague, or bring heightened awareness to it, or even to treat it. What we become witness to instead is a fascinating and eerie portrait of the nature of high school alienation itself ù the savagery, the cruelty, the relentless anxiety and ennui, the longing for escape. And then the murders start."(Publisher's note)

The hive. Charles Burns. Pantheon Books 2012 56 p.

Grades: Adult 741.5/973; 741.5

1. Man-woman relationship — Fiction; 2. Monsters — Fiction; 3. Graphic novels

0307907880; 9780307907882, $21.95

LC 2012002185

This graphic novel by Charles Burns is "the second volume of a trilogy begun in 'X'ed Out'. . . . We return to Doug, the protagonist, whose recounting of his relationship with a young woman shifts back and forth between the less surreal of the book's two environments and another where his apparent alter ego works in a dreary factory/ hospital providing books to its monster patients." (Publishers Week)

★ **Sugar** Skull. Charles Burns. Pantheon Books 2014 64 p. Illustration

Grades: Adult Fic; 741.5

1. Fantasy graphic novels; 2. Hallucinations and illusions

9780307907905, $23; 0307907902

LC 2014000699

This graphic novel, by Charles Burns, "the third volume in a trilogy concludes a renowned graphic artist's hallucinatory descent into comic-book hell—and it doesn't end prettily. . . . Without ever resorting to a linear narrative, he concludes the story of Doug that began in 'X'ed Out' and continued with 'The Hive.' Sober for more than a year, he suffers a massive relapse when he returns to his former punk-rock haunts and sees some people who would rather not see him. Yet his dream life and waking life aren't clearly delineated, for Doug or for the reader" (Kirkus Reviews)

"Burns demands and rewards attentive reading, letting the novel unfold in a fractured chronology and employing patterns of repeated imagery and color to draw connections between the two narratives. He brings them together into something altogether new that blends bildungsroman with visceral horror to elucidate the mental state of his protagonist." LJ

Sequel to: The Hive (2012)

★ **X'ed** out. Charles Burns. Pantheon Books 2010 56 p. Color illustration

Grades: Adult   **Fic; 741.5**

1. Dreams; 2. Graphic novels
9780307379139, $21.95; 0307379132

LC 2010005394

In this fantasy graphic novel, by Charles Burns, "Doug is having a strange night. A weird buzzing noise on the other side of the wall has woken him up, and there, across the room, next to a huge hole torn out of the bricks, sits his beloved cat, Inky. Who died years ago. But who's nonetheless slinking out through the hole, beckoning Doug to follow." (Publisher's note)

"Burns's control of the story is masterful—the recurring imagery make it unclear just which is the reality and which is the dream. His sharply delineated art captures a grotesque yet sympathetic view of kids thrust far beyond a world that they can control or even understand." Pub Wkly

Followed by: The Hive (2012)

Burns, Jason M.

A **Dummy's** Guide to Danger. Ron Chan, artist. Viper Comics 2007 Un Illustration

Grades: 11 12 Adult   **741.5; Fic**

1. Mystery graphic novels; 2. Graphic novels
978-0-9793680-0-4, $11.95

Private investigator Alan Sirois and his partner Mr. Bloomberg, a paraplegic ventriloquist dummy that Alan believes was shot in the back by an assailant and became crippled when the bullet lodged in his spine, track down a gruesome killer known only as the Flesh Collector. The book includes violence and harsh language.

The **Expendable** One. Bryan Baugh, artist. Viper Comics 2006 Un Illustration

Grades: 10 11 12 Adult   **741.5; Fic**

1. Horror graphic novels; 2. Mystery graphic novels; 3. Graphic novels
0-9754193-9-0, $11.95

Twigs Dupree was just an average, everyday forgotten townie, but then he accidentally injected himself with an experimental concoction that gave him the gift of immortality, whether he's shot in the head or strangled with a wire ... Now, along with his childhood friend Jerry, Twigs wages a war in the suburbs, playing part-time superhero with the help of a police scanner. Things take an unexpected turn when FBI agent Armstrong recruits Twigs to take down a serial killer known as the Animal. Some believe he is a werewolf, but he's the head of a killer cult. The book includes graphic violence, harsh language, and some sexual situations.

The **rabid**. Guy Lemay, artist. Viper Comics 2008 Un Illustration

Grades: 10 11 12 Adult   **741.5; Fic**

1. Horror graphic novels; 2. Graphic novels
978-0-980-2385-0-1, $11.95

A dog infected with a mutated rabies virus escapes from a lab, and the disease spreads rapidly from dogs to humans.

Sheriff Kevin Chase had gone home early for his son Jesse's birthday, only to find that his own dog is infected and has bitten their neighbor, who quickly becomes a ravening maniac who tries to kill them. He soon learns his entire town is infected, and he, his family, and a deputy barely make back to their office. This graphic novel reads like one of those horror movies where everyone dies, one at a time, until only a handful of people are left alive. It's full of violence and bloodshed, and there's one panel of a woman naked from the waist up (of course, she's already infected, green, and horrible looking).

The **Underworld** Railroad. Paul Tucker, artist. Viper Comics 2007 112p. Illustration

Grades: 10 11 12 Adult   **741.5**

1. Fantasy graphic novels; 2. Graphic novels
978-0-9793680-3-5, $11.95

This book postulates that when a person dies while still wrongly accused, that person's spirit doesn't immediately go to Heaven or to Hell, but must wait to be cleared. In the meantime, the spirit is vulnerable and can be taken by the devil. For these spirits, a system of safe houses offers refuge. In one such safe house, Bruce welcomes the spirit of a man who was falsely accused of murdering his wife. The devil takes the form of a sexy woman who doesn't want to take no for an answer, and she tries to take the spirit by force. The book includes violence, some harsh language, and supernatural action.

Busiek, Kurt

★ **Astro** city: life in the big city. By Kurt Busiek, Brent Anderson, and Alex Ross. DC Comics 2011 192 p. Color illustration

Grades: 11 12 Adult   **741.5; Fic**

1. Superhero graphic novels
1401232612; 1401232620; 9781401232610; 9781401232627, $17.99

LC 2012376788

This graphic novel, by Kurt Busiek, Brent Anderson, and Alex Ross, is set in "Astro City, a shining city on a hill where super heroes patrol the skies. . . . The city's leading super hero tries to be everywhere at once, and berates himself for every wasted second as he longs for just a moment of his own. A smalltime hood learns a hero's secret identity, and tries to figure out how to profit from the knowledge. A beat reporter gets some advice from his editor on his first day on the job." (Publisher's note)

"These heroes are intentionally written to resemble classic superheroes like Superman, Wonder Woman, and the Fantastic Four. The Astro City heroes, however, aren't derivative; the authors introduce well-developed, original characters and use them to delve into the unexplored possibilities and unanswered questions of classic superheroes as well as their relationships with the world around them." LJ

Collected volume originally published 1997

Originally published as Kurt Busiek's Astro city v. 1 #1-6.

Other Astro City volumes are: Confession (1997); Family album (1998); The tarnished angel (2000); Local heroes (2005); The dark age 1: Brothers & other strangers (2008); The dark age 2: Brother in arms

(2010); Shining stars (2011); Through open doors (2014); Victory (2014)

Astro City: the dark age 1: brothers & other strangers. DC Comics/Wildstorm 2009 256p. Illustration
Grades: 10 11 12 Adult   **741.5; Fic**
1. Crime; 2. Gangs; 3. Superhero graphic novels; 4. Graphic novels
978-1-4012-2077-8, $19.99

In Astro City of the 1970s, estranged brothers Charles and Royal Williams are still trying to cope with the tragedy that ripped their family apart back in 1959. Charles is an honest cop stuck with a crooked partner who keeps trying to get him to accept graft payments, while Royal has been living the life of a smalltime crook. Their lives keep intersecting with those of the superpowered, heroes and criminals alike. Throughout the book, the readers piece together the bits of flashbacks to that pivotal tragedy in 1959; when the only black superhero treats the young brothers with respect, but a battle between superhero Silver Agent and super criminals erupts into the Williams family's apartment and kills the parents. When Silver Agent walked through the apartment in pursuit of the villains and ignored the dead and surviving civilians, it crushed the boys' spirits, leaving one distrustful of all super powered beings and the other without hope of any good in life. Now, with Silver Agent convicted of murder, an impending war between super powered gangs, and the vengeful Black Velvet and Blue Knight slaughtering criminals even smalltime grifters such as Royal, it's truly a Dark Age in Astro City. The book includes some violence and some harsh language.

Astro City: Through Open Doors. Kurt Busiek; [illustrated by] Brent Anderson. DC Comics/Vertigo 2014 161 p. Color; Illustration (Astro City)
Grades: Adult   **741.5**
1. Imaginary places; 2. Superhero comic books, strips, etc
1401247520; 9781401247522, $24.99
LC 2013049638

Author and illustrator "Kurt Busiek and Brent Anderson launch their next epic in the world of Astro City when a mysterious door appears, heralding the arrival of the Ambassador. But when an ordinary man is caught in a cosmic conflict, it is up to favorites like Samaritan and Honor Guard, as well as new heroes, to rise to the occasion and save the world!" (Publisher's note)

"When this Eisner and Harvey Award-winning series returned after a hiatus, it relaunched with four excellent stories of the human side of superheroes, collected in Shining Stars. In this succeeding volume, preeminent comics scribe Busiek . . . reveals the reverse: the extraordinary side of more ordinary folk living among superpowered movers and shakers." LJ

Conan Volume 1: The Frost-Giant's Daughter and Other Stories. Cary Nord and Thomas Yeates, illustrators. Dark Horse Comics 2005 Un Illustration
Grades: 10 11 12 Adult   **741.5; Fic**
1. Adventure graphic novels; 2. Conan the Barbarian (Fictional character); 3. Fantasy graphic novels; 4. Graphic novels
1-59307-301-1, $15.95

Conan the Barbarian wars with the murderous Vanir, meets the Frost Giant's Daughter, and is taken as a slave by the ancient sorcerers of Hyperborea in this volume of new Conan adventures. Busiek and Nord adapt some of Robert E. Howard's original Conan stories and create some original stories, just as Roy Thomas and Barry Windsor-Smith had done in the 1970s. Conan prefers action to thought, and the stories are full of fighting, some nudity and sexual situations.

JLA: Syndicate Rules. Ron Garney, penciler; Dan Green, inker. DC Comics 2005 Un Illustration
Grades: 10 11 12 Adult   **741.5; Fic**
1. Adventure graphic novels; 2. Justice League of America (Fictional characters); 3. Superhero graphic novels; 4. Graphic novels
1-4012-0477-5, $17.99

Cosmic upheavals destroyed and rebuilt the antimatter universe, with their super-powered conquerors blaming the JLA. Seeking revenge against their positive matter universe counterparts, the JLA, the Crime Syndicate of Amerika breaches the barrier between universes and brings chaos to Earth. The antimatter universe's Weaponers of Qward tip the balance of power as they employ a new super-weapon that can wipe out both super-teams, and Earth's inhabitants, in a heartbeat.

★ **Marvels**. By Kurt Busiek; illustrated by Alex Ross. Marvel 2010 248 p.
Grades: 10 11 12 Adult   **741.5; 741.5/973**
1. Marvel Comics Group; 2. Superhero comic books, strips, etc
078514286X; 9780785142867, $24.99

In this comic book, by Kurt Busiek, illustrated by Alex Ross, "Welcome to New York. Here, burning figures roam the streets, men in brightly colored costumes scale the glass and concrete walls, and creatures from space threaten to devour our world. This is the Marvel Universe, where the ordinary and fantastic interact daily." (Publisher's note)

Followed by Marvels: Eye of the camera

Superman: Camelot Falls. Carlos Pacheco, pencils; Jesús Merino, inks. DC Comics 2007 128p. Illustration
Grades: 10 11 12 Adult   **741.5; Fic**
1. Superhero graphic novels; 2. Superman (Fictional character); 3. Graphic novels
978-1-4012-1204-9, $19.99

Everything is going well. Superman is married to Lois Lane. As Clark Kent, he's enjoying his job as reporter and doing it well. He's managed to put Intergang on the run from Metropolis. But when he goes to Kazakhstan to confront the mysterious and deadly Subjekt 17, a new enemy, Superman receives a grave warning from an ancient sorcerer: in the future, Camelot (Metropolis) will fall, and it will be his fault. The book includes a few panels with partial nudity.

★ **Superman:** secret identity. Kurt Busiek, writer; Stuart Immonen, artist, colorist, original covers; Todd Klein, letterer; Superman created by Jerry Seigel and Joe Schuster. DC Comics 2004 206p. Illustration
Grades: 10 11 12 Adult   **Fic; 741; 741.5**
1. Superhero graphic novels; 2. Superman (Comic strip); 3. Superman (Fictional character); 4. Graphic novels
1-4012-0451-1, $19.95
LC 2005-299025

"The teenage Clark Kent of this book is a Kansas farm boy, but in his world, Superman is just a comic book character, and Clark gets teased for having his name. But one day, Clark discovers that he actually has all of Superman's powers. As he starts to use them, he draws government attention—but this book isn't as much about superheroics and men in black as it is about Clark the man. . . . Strongly recommended for teen and adult superhero fans and for anyone who feels that the genre lacks "human interest." Libr J

First published in single magazine form in Superman: secret identity 1-4

Butler, Blair

Heart. Blair Butler. Image Comics 2012 120 p. Illustration
Grades: Adult   **741.5; 741**
1. Mixed martial arts
1607065789; 9781607065784, $12.99

This graphic novel tells the story of "Oren 'Rooster' Redmond, who is looking for more than what his desk job affords him. With a brother already - a mixed martial artist, "Oren trades in watching the sport for an opportunity of self-exploration to find out exactly what he's made of—and what he discovers about himself makes for a story that is, at its heart, eminently human." (Publishers Weekly)

Byrne, Eugene

★ **Darwin**: a graphic biography. By Eugene Byrne; illustrated by Simon Gurr. Smithsonian Books 2013 96 p. Illustration
Grades: 5 6 7 8 9 10 11 12 Adult
B; 576.8; 576.8/2092
1. Darwin, Charles, 1809-1882; 2. Evolution; 3. Evolution (Biology); 4. Natural selection; 5. Graphic novels
1588343529;
9781588343529, $9.95
LC 2012951786

Courtesy of Smithsonian Books

This work of graphic nonfiction by Eugene Byrne and Simon Gurr presents a "summary of [Charles] Darwin's life and achievement. . . . Darwin was an indifferent student . . .until he received an invitation to take a voyage that 'would change the course of history.' . . .The animals he encountered seemed so different . . . that he theorized that if it weren't a matter of different conditions that resulted in such 'transmutation,' they might well have had a different creator." (Kirkus Reviews)

Includes bibliographical references.

Byrne, John

Alpha Flight Classics Vol. 1. Writer & artist, John Byrne ; colorist, Andy Yanchus ; letterers, Joe Rosen [and others].. Marvel Entertainment 2007 224p. Illustration
Grades: 7 8 9 10 11 12 Adult   **741.5; Fic**
1. Superhero graphic novels; 2. Graphic novels
978-0-7851-2746-8, $24.99

Guardian, Shaman, Snowbird, Aurora, Northstar, Puck, Marrina, and Sasquatch are Canada's premiere super human strike force, Alpha Flight. The team was brought together by Department H for the greater good of humankind. They battle injustice and evil forces across the globe - including the Master of the World, Tundra, Kolomaq, Deadly Ernest and Delphine Courtney. The book features cameos by the Sub-Mariner, Invisible Woman, Wolverine and Nightcrawler.

Superman: The Man of Steel Vol. 1. Written by John Byrne and Marv Wolfman. DC Comics 1991 132p. Illustration
Grades: 8 9 10 11 12 Adult   **741.5; Fic**
1. Superhero graphic novels; 2. Superman (Fictional character); 3. Graphic novels
978-0-930289-28-5, $14.99

This reprint of a 1986 book retells and reinvents the origin and early adventures of the Man of Steel. Superman begins his ascension to iconic hero as he leaves Smallville and becomes Metropolis's revered protector and guardian. Featuring the Man of Steel's legendary first encounters with Lex Luthor, Lois Lane, and Batman, this book also includes a deadly battle with Bizarro, a fateful encounter with Lana Lang, and Superman's astonishing discovery of his Kryptonian heritage.

Superman: The Man of Steel Vol. 5. DC Comics 2006 210p. Illustration
Grades: 9 10 11 12 Adult   **Fic; 741.5**
1. Joker (Fictional character); 2. Superhero graphic novels; 3. Superman (Fictional character); 4. Graphic novels
978-1-4012-0948-3, $19.99

Superman and the staff of the Daily Planet uncover a gang war raging in the city's notorious "Suicide Slum." Journalistic integrity is put to the test when it is revealed that Perry White's son is involved. Will the Daily Planet run a story that will ruin the life of one of their own? And what is the identity of the new protector of the streets, who emerges amid the havoc? Also, love is in the air, as Superman finds himself romantically involved with Big Barda, the amazon from the planet Apokolips, and with Cat Grant. Along with his ever-present nemesis Lex Luthor, Superman faces the evil of Sleez, the Joker, and that fiendish magical imp from the Fifth Dimension, Mr. Mxyzptlk. These stories were originally published in 1987.

Cabarga, Leslie

Harvey Comics Classics Volume Two: Richie Rich, the Poor Little Rich Boy. Dark Horse Comics 2007 480p. Illustration
Grades: 3 4 5 6 7 8 9 10 11 12 Adult   **741.5**
1. Humorous graphic novels; 2. Richie Rich (Fictional character); 3. Graphic novels
978-1-59307-848-5, $19.95

This volume reprints 125 Richie Rich stories, taken from the comic's beginnings in 1953 through the 1960s. While most of the stories appear here in black and white, the book includes a 64-page section of color reprints. Richie Rich and his friends Gloria, Freckles, and Peewee enjoy not-so-everyday adventures, including playing "tycoon" in the new offices of Rich's father. Some stories feature rich cousin and antagonist Reggie.

Harvey comics classics voulme three: hot stuff: the little devil. Dark Horse Comics 2008 480p. Illustration
Grades: 3 4 5 6 7 8 9 10 11 12 Adult   **741.5; Fic**
1. Devil; 2. Humorous graphic novels; 3. Graphic novels
978-1-59307-914-7, $19.95

Hot Stuff: the Little Devil was created for Harvey Comics in 1957, and right away became the starring character in his own comic book series. This volume collects 110 stories from the Hot Stuff comics originally published from 1957 through 1966; the comic book actually remained in print until the 1980s. Back in 1957, having a little red hot devil as a main character caused some controversy, but most young children who read the comics had no problem with him. These stories involve Hot Stuff and his friends in comical misadventures just like any kid could get into, such as having to babysit a younger cousin, trying to outdo a visiting ghost, going to see a doctor (of course, Hot Stuff has to see a witch doctor).

Part of the Harvey Comics Classics series

Calen, Tokyo
Dark Metro volume 2. Yoshkin, artist. Tokyopop 2008 168p. Illustration
Grades: 10 11 12 Adult   **741.5; Fic**
1. Horror graphic novels; 2. Manga; 3. Graphic novels
978-1-4278-0741-0, $9.99

This volume includes four stories. In Akihabara, a waitress at a maid cafe sparks jealousy and one of her customers, Morio, becomes trapped in a game by the man who wants Yuuyuu all to himself. Then a park employee finds herself in a haunted park filled with dead children, including the young boy she had befriended when he was lost at her park. An American tourist buys an old samurai sword (actually, he takes it and leaves some money) from a shop owner who warns him it is possessed; when the man draws the sword, he awakens the bloodthirsty ghost who used to own it. In all these stories, a young man helps the people out of the nightmarish situations, and in the last story, readers see Seiya's tragic past. The book includes violence and some gore.

Callen, Kerry
Halo and Sprocket vol. 2: Natural creatures. SLG Publishing/Amaze Ink 2008 Un Illustration
Grades: 8 9 10 11 12 Adult   **741.5; Fic**
1. Angels; 2. Humorous graphic novels; 3. Robots; 4. Graphic novels
978-1-59362-131-5, $8.95

Halo the angel and Sprocket the robot live with a young woman named Katie. Their mission: to try to figure out the human race. They are puzzled by Katie's desire for privacy when she's taking a bath; they don't understand why she'll accept being clawed and bitten by a cute little kitten but won't hold a skink; and playing a trivia game causes Halo to show anger. When Halo transforms Sprocket into a human so he can experience what eating food is all about, the temporarily human Sprocket drives Katie crazy with questions about bodily functions such as burping, sneezing, and more.

Campbell, Bruce
Man with the Screaming Brain. Story by Bruce Campbell and David Goodman. Dark Horse Comics 2005 Un Illustration
Grades: 9 10 11 12 Adult   **741.5; Fic**
1. Horror graphic novels; 2. Graphic novels
1-59307-397-6, $13.95

B-movie megastar Bruce Campbell comes to comics with this adaptation of his feature film. Campbell put the version of the script he wanted to shoot into the hands of artists Rick Remender and Hilary Barta. Man with the Screaming Brain tells the story of a wealthy American businessman determined to exploit the crippled economy of a former Soviet state torn between communist roots and capitalist greed. But when Campbell's character hits on the wrong gypsy girl, he soon finds himself in the grip of a mad scientist with a twisted brain-transplant scheme worthy of Dr. Frankenstein. It's filled with cartoony horror movie action and some gore, with some mildly harsh language.

Campbell, Ross
The **Abandoned**. Tokyopop 2006 217p. Illustration
Grades: 10 11 12 Adult   **741.5; Fic**
1. Horror graphic novels; 2. Graphic novels
1-59816-434-1, $9.99

Big-hearted volunteer worker by day, unruly rocker by night, Rylie is one of the most-liked residents in the small, swampy, Southern island-town of Buffalora. When she sets her sights on Naomi, the new girl in town, love is definitely in the air. Unfortunately for Rylie, so is a storm, the kind in which nothing good ever happens... Suddenly everyone aged 23 and older dies and quickly rises from the dead. These flesh-craving zombies seek out the last remnants of youth and hope for society. With death in the air and love on their minds, Rylie and Naomi must make their way through the vast swamplands to salvation ... This global manga is full of zombie horror and gore, and nudity.

Campbell, Eddie
ALEC: 'the years have pants'; a life-sized Omnibus. Eddie Campbell. Top Shelf 2009 638 p. Illustration
Grades: Adult   **741.5**
1. Autobiographical graphic novels; 2. Campbell, Eddie; 3. Graphic novels
1603090479; 9781603090476, $49.95; 978i603090254

This book, by Eddie Campbell, collects the author's "autobiographical comics. . . . The ALEC stories present a version of Campbell's own life, filtered through the alter ego of 'Alec MacGarry.' Over many years, we witness Alec's (and Eddie's) progression 'from beer to wine' - wild nights at the pub, existential despair, the hunt for love, the quest for art, becoming a 'responsible breadwinner,' feeling lost at his own movie premiere, and much more!" (Publisher's note)

★ **Bacchus** 1. By Eddie Campbell. IDW 2015 560 p.
Grades: Adult   **741**
1603090266; 9781603090261, $39.99

This book, by Eddie Campbell, "collects the first half of the Bacchus saga (including Immortality Isn't Forever, The Gods of Business, Doing the Islands with Bacchus, The Eyeball Kid: One Man Show, and Earth, Water, Air & Fire) with new notes and commentary by the author." (Publisher's note)

The **Fate** of the Artist. First Second Books 2006 96p. Illustration
Grades: 11 12 Adult   **741.5; Fic**
1. Art; 2. Autobiographical graphic novels; 3. Graphic novels
1-59643-133-4, $15.95

Campbell uses prose text, newspaper-style comic strips, fumetti-style strips (combining photographs with captions) and standard comic book panels to investigate the disappearance of . . . Eddie Campbell. He explores the history of art and music, portrays aspects of his own like, and uses his perpetually cursing daughter in the fumetti and other comic strips.

"In this work of art about art, assemble the pieces of the puzzle to see the beleaguered and beautiful life of the artist." (VOYA)

The **lovely** horrible stuff. Eddie Campbell. Top Shelf Productions 2012 95 p. Illustration
Grades: Adult   **332.4/0222; 332.4; 741.5**
1. Money; 2. Personal finance
1603091521; 9781603091527, $14.95

In this work of graphic nonfiction, "Eddie Campbell . . . presents a . . . journey into the wilderness of personal finance. With his trademark blend of research, anecdote, autobiography, and fantasy, Campbell explores how money underwrites human relationships. . . . The result is a . . . graphic essay . . . ranging from the imaginary wealth of Ponzi schemes and television pilots to the all-too-tangible stone currency of the Micronesian island of Yap." (Publisher's note)

Campbell, Ross
Wet Moon Book 1: Feeble Wanderings. Oni Press 2004 172p. Illustration
Grades: 11 12 Adult   **741.5; Fic**
1. Graphic novels
1-932664-07-6, $14.95

This story is set in the gothic, swampy southern town of Wet Moon. As Cleo Lovedrop heads off for college at the local art school, she's haunted by her melancholic past: a lost love, a lost child. An unseen social assailant spreads slander about Cleo, she is forced to deal with her two brusque roommates, and discovers unsolved mysteries about the girl who lived in her room previously. Elsewhere, Trilby deals with unsettled emotional and sexual issues, and keeping her secret habits hidden from everyone. And Audrey comes to the realization that, despite all her efforts, she always causes her friends distress, while Fern, a peculiar, deformed girl who lives in an isolated mansion in the bayous, begins to notice Cleo and her friends. As the moon grows full, lunacy and moon-calves run free. Goths, friendship, romance, sex, betrayal, gossip, cats, murder, guilt, a squirrel monkey, and all the terrible and wonderful things people do to each other. The book includes lots of harsh language, nudity, and sexual situations.

Campbell, T.
A **History** of Webcomics v1.0: The Golden Age: 1993-2005. Antarctic Press 2006 Un Illustration

Grades: Adult Professional   **741.5; 004.6**
1. Comic books, strips, etc — History; 2. Internet — History; 3. Webcomics — History; 4. Graphic novels
978-0-9768043-9-0, $14.95

Comics creator Campbell reviews the first twelve or so years of webcomics, from the very earliest days of the Internet, to a look at possible futures. He looks at "classic" webcomics such as Sluggy Freelance, PvP, Penny Arcade, and Megatokyo, along with their creators. He also covers other pioneers, such as Scott McCloud, Steve Conley, and many others who helped shape webcomics; networks such as Moderntales and Keenspot; the thorny problems of advertising and merchandising; and more. Some of the webcomics discussed include sexual content and harsh language.

Caniff, Milton
The **Complete** Terry and the Pirates, 1934-1936. IDW Publications 2007 368p. Illustration
Grades: 6 7 8 9 10 11 12 Adult   **741.5**
1. Adventure graphic novels; 2. Graphic novels
978-1-60010-100-7, $49.99

This first volume in a projected series to collect the entire Milton Caniff run of the comic strip Terry and the Pirates covers the years 1934 through 1936. This volume includes the Sunday color comics as well as the black and white dailies. In this volume, the Sunday strips told a different story from the daily strips, so the Sunday strips come first. The Sundays and dailies were merged into one storyline sometime in 1936. Young Terry Lee, his adult pal Pat Ryan, their sidekick Connie, and such villains as Captain Judas and Captain Blade, along with the Dragon Lady, provide readers with lots of high adventure. Some racial stereotypes, common for the 1930s, occur.

Cannon, Kevin
Crater XV. By Kevin Cannon. Top Shelf Productions 2013 496 p.
Grades: 10 11 12 Adult   **741; Fic**
1. Adventure graphic novels; 2. Science fiction graphic novels
1603091009; 9781603091008, $19.95

This graphic novel, by Kevin Cannon, "weaves together . . . swashbuckling adventure, abandoned moon bases, bloodthirsty walruses, rogue astronauts, two-faced femme fatales, sailboat chases, Siberian pirates, international Arctic politics, and a gaggle of horny orphans. Mixed up in all of this are Army Shanks, our salty sea dog still reeling from a devastating loss, and Wendy Byrd, a plucky teenager who wants nothing more than a one-way ticket off the face of the Earth." (Publisher's note)

Far Arden. Kevin Cannon. Top Shelf Productions 2009 400p. Illustration
Grades: 10 11 12 Adult   **Fic; 741.5/973**
1. Adventure graphic novels; 2. Arctic regions
9781603090360, $19.95; 1603090363

In this graphic novel, by Kevin Cannon, "Army Shanks—crusty old sea dog and legendary brawler of the high Arctic seas . . . [has] one mission: to find the mythical island paradise known as Far Arden, which lies hidden . . . in the wintry oceans of the far North. But . . . he'll have to contend with circus performers, adorable orphans, heinous villains, bitter ex-lovers, well-meaning undergraduates, and the full might of the Royal Canadian Arctic Navy!" (Publisher's note)

Courtesy of Top Shelf Productions

Card, Orson Scott
Red Prophet: The Tales of Alvin Maker Vol. 1. Orson Scott Card; adapted by Roland Bernard Brown; art by Renato Arlem and Miguel Montenegro. Marvel Entertainment/Dabel Brothers 2007 Un Illustration
Grades: 9 10 11 12 Adult　　　　　**741.5; Fic**
　1. Adventure graphic novels; 2. Fantasy graphic novels; 3. Graphic novels
　978-0-7851-2721-5, $19.99
　In an alternate history where folk magic really works, war is brewing on the frontier. But in the midst of the conflict, two men will begin down the path towards changing the world forever. One of them is Alvin Miller, a young boy who is the seventh son of a seventh son - and thus powerful enough to shape the world around him. The other is Tenskwa-Tawa, the Red Prophet, who will help Alvin fulfill his destiny. This book is adapted from Card's novel.

Ultimate Iron Man Vol. 1. Writer: Orson Scott Card; pencils: Andy Kubert and Mark Bagley. Marvel Entertainment 2006 Un Illustration
Grades: 10 11 12 Adult　　　　　**741.5; Fic**
　1. Iron Man (Fictional character); 2. Superhero graphic novels; 3. Graphic novels
　978-0-7851-1499-8, $14.99
　Iron Man has been part of the Ultimates, but this volume gives his Ultimate origin. Due to an accident that happened before Tony Stark was born, he has grown up to be a super genius, but always in great physical pain. It's the main reason he becomes an alcoholic as an adult.

Carey, Mike
Crossing Midnight: Cut Here. Mike Carey, writer; Jim Fern, penciller; Rob Hunter, Mark Pennington, inkers; Jose Villarrubia, colorist; Todd Klein, letterer. DC Comics/Vertigo 2007 124p. Illustration
Grades: 11 12 Adult　　　　　**741.5; Fic**
　1. Fantasy graphic novels; 2. Horror graphic novels; 3. Mystery graphic novels; 4. Graphic novels
　978-1-4012-1341-1, $9.99
　In present-day Nagasaki, Japan, a set of twins are born — one just before midnight and the other just after. They discover the huge impact this small difference has on their destinies when the after-midnight twin is inducted into a world of supernatural beings and events that intersects with our own world. Together, they will desperately try to stay one step ahead of their terrifying fates while they learn how far the curse afflicting them really stretches. As their father

gets mixed up with Yakuza, the story builds with violence, partial nudity, and harsh language.

God Save the Queen. Written by Mike Carey; painted by John Bolton; lettering by Todd Klein. DC Comics/Vertigo 2007 Un Illustration
Grades: 11 12 Adult　　　　　**741.5; Fic**
　1. Fairies; 2. Fantasy graphic novels; 3. Graphic novels
　978-1-4012-0303-0, $19.99
　Rebellious North London teenager Linda falls in with a group of slacker faeries, who use her blood to make Red Horse - heroin mixed with special human blood. Only once she's hooked and lost her best friend, Jeff, to the drug, does she learn about the faeries and about the civil war raging between two Faerie Queens: Titania and her mad predecessor, Mab. And now Linda is caught in the war, for in her drug-induced state, she can find Mab's hidden heart, which Titania needs to win the war.
　Fans of Neil Gaiman's Sandman series will find familiar characters in the story, and they are the audience most ready for this work. The drug use, some nudity, brief sex scenes, and considerable harsh language, make this most appropriate for older teens and adults.

John Constantine: Hellblazer: All His Engines. Writer, Mike Carey; artist, Leonardo Manco; colorist & separator, Lee Loughridge & Zylonol Studio; letterer, Jared K. Fletcher. DC Comics/Vertigo 2006 Un Illustration
Grades: 10 11 12 Adult　　　　　**741.5; Fic**
　1. Horror graphic novels; 2. John Constantine (Fictional character); 3. Graphic novels
　1-4012-0317-5, $14.99
　When a mysterious worldwide plague starts putting millions of people into deadly comas, Earth's foremost expert on the bizarre, John Constantine, steps in with the "cure." After traveling from the dreary alleys of London to the glittering boulevards of L.A., Constantine realizes that a cadre of wicked demons and hellish monsters is behind the outbreak, and he'll have to sacrifice more than himself to put an end to the nightmare. The book includes lots of very harsh language, bloody violence, and demonic horror.

John Constantine: Hellblazer: Black Flowers. Written by Mike Carey; art by Marcelo Frusin, Tim Bradstreet, Lee Bermejo. DC Comics/Vertigo 2005 142p. Illustration
Grades: 11 12 Adult　　　　　**741.5; Fic**
　1. Fantasy graphic novels; 2. Horror graphic novels; 3. John Constantine (Fictional character); 4. Graphic novels
　1-4012-0499-6, $14.99
　For months he has felt a growing sense of foreboding, of dark forces massing just out of view. Now the signs are changing from subtle to lethally obvious, and as they manifest themselves, John Constantine's immediate priority changes to staying alive. But he will never rest until he knows just who his real enemy is. There's a whiff of apocalypse in the air, and the world's shrewdest magus is determined to find its source. The book includes lots of harsh language (complete with f-bombs), nudity, and graphic violence.

John Constantine: Hellblazer: Stations of the Cross. Written by Mike Carey; art by Leonardo Manco, Marcelo Frusin, Steve Dillon, Chris Brunner, Tim Bradstreet. DC Comics/Vertigo 2006 192p. Illustration

Grades: 11 12 Adult   **741.5; Fic**
1. Fantasy graphic novels; 2. John Constantine (Fictional character); 3. Mystery graphic novels; 4. Supernatural graphic novels; 5. Graphic novels
978-1-4012-1002-1, $14.99

John Constantine is an unconcerned, somewhat amoral occultist with a British working-class background. He's a hero of sorts, who manages to come out on top through a combination of luck, trickery and genuine magical skill. This latest volume finds the hard-drinking master of bad-luck magic suffering alone in the aftermath of the near-apocalypse he unwittingly caused, with no memory of his identity or history and no powers. However, he still has his usual luck, and soon enough he's being hunted by man and demon alike - and about to make the worst mistake of his long, blood-soaked life. The book has lots of harsh language, some nudity, and considerable violence.

★ **Lucifer;** Book 1. Mike Carey, writer; Scott Hampton ... [et al.], artists; Daniel Vozzo, colorist; Todd Klein, Ellie de Ville, letterers; Neil Gaiman, consultant. Vertigo 2013 381 p. Color; Illustration
Grades: Adult   **Fic; 741.5**
1. Angels; 2. Devil; 3. Fantasy fiction
9781401240264, $29.99; 1401240267

"Cast out of Heaven, thrown down to rule in Hell, Lucifer Morningstar has resigned his post and abandoned his kingdom for the mortal city of Los Angeles. Emerging from the pages of writer Neil Gaiman's award-winning seriesThe Sandman, the former Lord of Hell is now enjoying a quiet retirement as the propretor of Lux, L.A.'s most elite piano bar. But now an assignment from the Creator Himself is going to change all that." (Publisher's note)
Also available as 11 volumes
Book 1 of 5

Neil Gaiman's Neverwhere. Mike Carey, writer; Glenn Fabry, artist; Tanya & Richard Horie, colorists; Todd Klein, letterer. DC Comics/Vertigo 2007 Un Illustration
Grades: 11 12 Adult   **741.5; Fic**
1. Fantasy graphic novels; 2. Gaiman, Neil — Adaptations; 3. Graphic novels
978-1-4012-1007-6, $19.99

Ordinary Richard Mayhew lives an ordinary life in London, in an ordinary corporate job, with a domineering fiancee. Then one day he does one extraordinary thing: he defies his fiancee to help an injured young woman, and his life changes. That young woman, Door, comes from London Below, a fantastical world made up of the bits and pieces of forgotten city and life from above. Her family has been slaughtered, she's being hunted by a pair of extremely nasty, sadistic, violent assassins, and after Richard helps her he has no choice but to go to London Below, for his entire existence in ordinary London has been wiped out, as though he has never . . . been.

Neverwhere was first a script for a BBC miniseries written by Neil Gaiman; he then adapted his script into a novel, which is now adapted into graphic novel format.
Originally published as Neverwhere issues #1-9.

Spellbinders: Signs & Wonders. Writer, Mike Carey ; pencils, Mike Perkins ; inks, Drew Hennessy. Marvel Entertainment 2005 Un Illustration
Grades: 7 8 9 10 11 12 Adult   **741.5; Fic**

1. Magic; 2. Mystery graphic novels; 3. Supernatural graphic novels; 4. Graphic novels
0-7851-1756-3, $7.99

Getting through high school is hard enough without having to watch your back the whole time, but magic can give you a real edge over the competition. When 15-year-old Kim Vesco moves from Chicago to Salem, MA, she finds that the local student body is divided into rival factions of witches and non-witches, with both sides bidding for her allegiance. And if that weren't enough, an unknown force seems to want her... dead. Between the tribal loyalties of the schoolyard and the brutal, fight-or-die logic of the mage-war, Kim has to steer a course that will keep her alive until she can take the fight back to her enemy and reveal the true identity of someone she thought she already knew: herself.

The **unwritten:** dead man's knock. Mike Carey & Peter Gross, script, story, art; Ryan Kelly, finishes; Chris Chuckry, Jeanne McGee, colorists; Todd Klein, letterer. DC Comics/Vertigo 2011 160 p.
Grades: Adult   **741.5; 741.5/973**
1. Fantasy graphic novels; 2. Identity (Philosophical concept); 3. Magicians; 4. Secret societies
1401230466; 9781401230463, $14.99
                    LC 2012376086

This is the third graphic novel in Mike Carey's Unwritten series. Here, a "malevolent, ancient secret society that twists stories to its will becomes the clarified antagonist of Tommy [Taylor] and pals, but its ultimate intentions remain foggy.... Our heroes are left on the verge of chasing down a certain great white whale." (Booklist)
Originally published in single magazine form as The unwritten 13-18—t.p. verso.

The **unwritten:** leviathan. Mike Carey & Peter Gross, script, story, art; Vince Locke, Al Davison, finishes; Chris Chuckry, colorist; Todd Klein, letterer; Yuko Shimizu, cover artist. Vertigo/DC Comics 2011 144 p.
Grades: Adult   **741.5; 741.5/973**
1. Fantasy graphic novels; 2. Identity (Philosophical concept); 3. Magicians
1401232922; 9781401232924, $14.99
                    LC 2011275327

This is the fourth graphic novel in Mike Carey's Unwritten series featuring Tom Taylor. Here, Tom "gets sucked into the narrative of 'Moby-Dick.' But the walls between stories are porous, and Tom soon rubs elbows with Sinbad, Baron Munchhausen, Pinocchio, and Frankenstein's monster, who knows way more about what's going on than any stitched-together lug ought to." (Booklist)
Originally published in single magazine form as The unwritten 19-24—t.p. verso.

The **unwritten:** on to genesis. Mike Carey & Peter Gross, script, story, art; Vince Locke, finishes, 1930 sequences; Christ Chuckry, colorist; Todd Klein, letter; Yuko Shimizu, covers. DC Comics 2012 144 p.
Grades: Adult   **741.5; 741.5/973**
1. Fantasy graphic novels; 2. Father-son relationship; 3. Identity (Philosophical concept); 4. Magicians
1401233597; 9781401233594, $14.99
                    LC 2012372869

This is the fifth graphic novel in Mike Carey's Unwritten series featuring Tom Taylor. Here, Tom "gradually chips away at his origin by learning about his father's history. The gang discovers that Tom's father once worked for the very cartel that killed him and was instrumental in creating another living fictional character, the Tinker, predating Tom by decades." (Booklist)

Originally published in single magazine form as The unwritten 25-30.

The **unwritten**: Tommy Taylor and the bogus identity. By Mike Carey and illustrated by Peter Gross. Vertigo 2010 144 p.

Grades: Adult   **741.5/973; 741.5**
1. Characters and characteristics in literature; 2. Characters and characteristics in literature; 3. Conspiracies — Fiction; 4. Identity (Philosophical concept); 5. Magicians; 6. Magicians
1401225659; 9781401225650, $14.99

LC 2010292145

In this graphic novel by Mike Carey a "scandal reveals that Tom might really be a boy-wizard. Tom comes into contact with a very mysterious, very deadly group that's secretly kept tabs on him. To protect his own life and discover the truth behind his origins, Tom will travel the world, eventually finding himself at locations all featured on a very special map — one kept by the deadly group that charts places throughout world history where fictions have impacted . . . reality." (Publisher's note)

Originally published in single magazine form as The unwritten 1-5—t.p. verso.

Volume 1 of 11

★ The **Unwritten**: Tommy Taylor and the ship that sank twice. Mike Carey, illustrated by Peter Gross. Vertigo 2013 160 p. Color; Illustration

Grades: 11 12 Adult   **741.5; Fic**
1. Characters and characteristics in literature; 2. Father-son relationship — Fiction; 3. Fiction; 4. Identity (Philosophical concept); 5. Wizards — Fiction
140122976X; 9781401229764, $22.99

LC 2013020333

In this graphic novel by Mike Carey, "Tom Taylor has lived his life being mistaken for Tommy Taylor, the boy wizard from the world-famous series of novels penned by Tom's long-lost father Wilson. However, after a series of strange events start to parallel the lives of both Taylors—fictional and real—Tom realizes that he might be the character on page made flesh." (Publisher's note)

"This title can serve as an entry point to the author's 'Unwritten' series, or as a standalone prequel. . . . The fictional Tommy receives his magical powers in this volume, and in a parallel narrative, Wilson crafts his first book, and orchestrates a twisted publicity stunt to make his son and his book character the same person in the eyes of the public. . . . Both story lines are equally compelling and balance each other out wonderfully." SLJ

The **unwritten**: Tommy Taylor and the war of words. Mike Carey & Peter Gross, script, story, art; M.K. Perker, Dean Ormston, Vince Locke, finishes. DC Comics 2012 240 p.

Grades: Adult   **741.5/973; 741.5**

1. Characters and characteristics in literature; 2. Fame — Psychological aspects; 3. Fantasy graphic novels; 4. Fiction; 5. Identity (Philosophical concept)
1401235603; 9781401235604, $16.99

LC 2012022581

This comic book is the sixth volume in Mike Carey's "Unwritten" series. "Before his mysterious disappearance and untimely death, the world-famous fantasy author Wilson Taylor helped bring two enduring creations into the world: Tommy Taylor, the fictional boy wizard who starred in his best selling book . . . and Tom Taylor, his real-life son. Armed with his father's journals, Tom Taylor begins a journey to uncover the truth behind how he came into this world." (Publisher's note)

Originally published in single magazine form in The Unwritten 31-35, 31.5-35.5.

The **unwritten**; 2: inside man. By Mike Carey and illustrated by Peter Gross. Vertigo 2010 168 p.

Grades: Adult   **741.5/973; 741.5**
1. Escapes — Fiction; 2. Identity (Philosophical concept); 3. Magic; 4. Magicians; 5. Time travel; 6. Graphic novels
1401228739; 9781401228736, $12.99

LC 2010526112

In this graphic novel by Mike Carey "when an enormous scandal reveals that Tom might really be a boy-wizard made flesh, Tom comes into contact with a very mysterious, very deadly group that's secretly kept tabs on him. In this volume, Tom arrives at Donostia prison in Southern France and falls into the orbit of another story: The Song of Roland. His escape from Donostia jail takes him to Stuttgart in 1940, a ghost city inhabited by . . . Josef Goebbels, and a tortured soul who's crying out for rescue." (Publisher's note)

2—Spine.

Originally published in single magazine form as The unwritten 6-12—t.p. verso.

The **Unwritten**; Volume 10. Mike Carey, writer; Peter Gross, Al Davison, artists. DC Comics/Vertigo 2014 128 p. Color; Illustration

Grades: Adult   **741.5**
1. Characters and characteristics in literature; 2. Conspiracies — Fiction; 3. Fantasy fiction; 4. Magicians
1401250556; 9781401250553, $14.99

LC 2014014691

In this book, by Mike Carey and Peter Gross, "Tom Taylor is stranded at the beginning of all creation! Lost in the unwritten scenes of all the world's stories, Tom Taylor is headed back to reality — and all the gods and beasts and monsters ever imagined can't stop him. But there's a toll on the road that may be too high for him or anyone to pay." (Publisher's note)

Originally published in single magazine form in The Unwritten: Apocalypse #1-5.

The **unwritten**; Volume 11: apocalypse. Mike Carey; illustrated by Peter Gross. DC Comics/Vertigo 2015 176 p. Color; Illustration

Grades: Adult   **Fic; 741.5**
1. Adventure fiction; 2. Fantasy comic books, strips, etc; 3. Storytelling — Fiction
1401253482; 9781401253486, $16.99

"Tom Taylor—the real-life counterpart of his father's famous fictional boy-wizard creation, a living bridge between our reality and the realities of every tale ever told—knows the power of stories only too well. Now he's the star of his most important story yet. It's a quest straight out of King Arthur, filled with black knights, ensorcelled swords, and maidens who are fair to a fault." (Publisher's note)

Originally published in single magazine form in THE UNWRITTEN: APOCALYPSE #6-12

The **Unwritten;** volume 7, Vol. 7. Mike Carey, Peter Gross. DC Comics/Vertigo 2013 144 p. Color; Illustration
Grades: Adult   **741.5**
1. Characters and characteristics in literature; 2. Identity — Fiction
1401238068; 9781401238063, $14.99
LC 2012047806
"Tom Taylor made big strides in his battle against the cabal in the last volume, but after that victory, his world is starting to unravel. His friends are questioning him and people are beginning to notice the slow apocalypse of disappearing stories. Tom can only do so much to stave it off, but luckily there are a few new characters in the mix, including a unicorn who provides rhyming, enigmatic prophesies at inopportune moments." Booklist

Originally published in single magazine form in The Unwritten 36-41

The **Unwritten;** volume 8, Vol. 8. Mike Carey; [illustrated by] Peter Gross. DC Comics/Vertigo 2014 176 p. Color; Illustration
Grades: Adult   **Fic; 741.5**
1. Dead — Fiction; 2. Fantasy fiction
1401243010; 9781401243012, $16.99
LC 2013040735
"Tommy ventures into the land of the dead to find and rescue Lizzie. But the journey through Hades pits Tommy against all kinds of enemies of undead. But none of these encounters prepare him for his meeting with the king—or for the responsibilities he has to take on for some very familiar damned souls." (Publisher's note)

Voodoo child volume 1. Created by Nicolas Cage and Weston Cage; written by Mike Carey; art by Dean Ruben Hyrapiet. Virgin Comics 2008 Un Illustration
Grades: 11 12 Adult   **741.5; Fic**
1. Fantasy graphic novels; 2. Horror graphic novels; 3. Voodooism; 4. Graphic novels
978-1-934413-13-5, $14.99
In the time just before the Civil War, when states were starting to secede from the Union, plantation owner and Union sympathizer Mason Moore is murdered and his plantation burned. His illegitimate son, Gabriel, is fatally wounded, but a voodoo bokor casts a spell on him. Gabriel isn't entirely dead, but his spirit has gone into limbo. More than a century later, Katrina has wreaked havoc upon New Orleans, and evil walks its devastated streets. And Gabriel, now a voodoo child, has woken up to take care of unfinished business. The book is full of bloody violence, harsh language, and some nudity. And yes, one of the co-authors is Nicolas Cage the actor, together with one of his sons.

Carey, Percy
Sentences: the life of M F Grimm. writer, Percy Carey; artist, Ronald Wimberly; gray tones, Lee Loughridge; letterer, Jared K. Fletcher. DC Comics/Vertigo 2007 128p. Illustration
Grades: 11 12 Adult   **741.5; 92**
1. Autobiographical graphic novels; 2. Carey, Percy; 3. Gangs; 4. Rap music; 5. Graphic novels
978-1-4012-1046-5, $19.99
Percy Carey, known in the Hip Hop world as M.F. Grimm, tells his story, from his escape from poverty on the streets to his rise in the world of Hip Hop music. Life in this world involves cutthroat competition and sometimes violence; Carey lost the use of his legs in gang violence, he has spent time in prison, and he re-invented himself. This is his story, complete with the extremely foul language of the streets, and the violence of the life he led.

Carre, Lilli
The **fir-tree.** It Books/HarperCollins 2009 Un Illustration
Grades: 3 4 5 6 7 8 9 10 11 12 Adult   **741.5; Fic**
1. Andersen, Hans Christian, 1805-1875 — Adaptations; 2. Christmas; 3. Christmas trees; Graphic novels
978-0-06-178236-7, $14.99
A young fir-tree only wants to grow tall; it's never satisfied and doesn't notice the sunlight and clean air. It never rejoices in anything, but grumbles and complains. When it sees some trees being cut down and taken away, it wonders what it's missing. The birds tell of seeing the trees inside homes, beautifully decorated, and it becomes jealous. When it does grow tall and beautiful, a woodsman comes along and cuts it down, hauling it to town to become a Christmas tree in a house. It enjoys the family playing around the tree at Christmas, but after the holiday, the family throws it into a storeroom. Will the tree ever see its forest again" Lilli Carre uses delicate coloring and illustrations to adapt Andersen's sad Christmas story. Although this is suitable for young readers, adults may better appreciate the tragedy and Carre's idiosyncratic illustrations her people have long, loopy arms.

Carroll, Emily
★ **Through** the woods. Emily Carroll. Margaret K. McElderry Books 2014 208 p. Color; Illustration
Grades: 8 9 10 11 12 Adult   **741.5**
1. Horror fiction; 2. Short stories; 3. Graphic novels
9781442465961, $14.99; 9781442465954, $21.99
LC 2013030969
Eisner Award: Best Graphic Album—Reprint (2015)
Ignatz Award: Outstanding Artist (2015)
In this book, Emily Carroll "crafts five unsettling tales in graphic-novel format inspired by common folkloric themes—from wolves in the woods to peculiar visitors to dark possessions. In 'Our Neighbor's House,' three sisters who find themselves alone in a cabin are taken, one by one, in the middle of the night by a smiling stranger. . . . 'The Nesting Place' focus on malevolent spirit possession." (Horn Book Magazine)

"All the tales in Carroll's debut graphic novel are fairly standard ghost stories, but it is her eerie illustrations—popping with bold color on black, glossy pages—that masterfully build terrifying tension and a keep-the-lights-on atmosphere." Booklist

Casey, Joe

Godland Volume 1: Hello, Cosmic!. Art by Tom Scioli. Image Comics 2006 Un Illustration

Grades: 8 9 10 11 12 Adult   **741.5; Fic**

1. Adventure graphic novels; 2. Science fiction graphic novels; 3. Superhero graphic novels; 4. Graphic novels

1-58240-712-6, $14.99

The cosmic superhero epic is back and this collection is chock-full of all the "cosmic" one could ask for. Experience the glory of Commander Adam Archer, the enigmatic alien Maxim, the wacky Basil Cronus, the evil Discordia, the confusing Freidrich Nickelhead and that's just scratching the surface. The storytelling and art bring back the kind of story that Stan Lee and Jack Kirby did, with fun superhero action and very little grim, gritty content.

Godland Volume Three: Proto-Plastic Party. Image Comics 2007 Un Illustration

Grades: 9 10 11 12 Adult   **741.5; Fic**

1. Science fiction graphic novels; 2. Graphic novels

978-1-58240-736-4, $14.99

From the burning heart of a pocket dimension to the farthest reaches of our own reality, the saga of Godland continues in this third trade paperback collection. As cosmic forces of evil conspire against the Earth and all who inhabit it, its lone emissary to the stars, Commander Adam Archer, finds himself the target of humanity's mistrust and deceit. All this, and Basil still wears the body of a woman. The book includes some strong language.

Krash bastards volume 1. Image Comics 2008 Un Illustration

Grades: 10 11 12 Adult   **741.5; Fic**

1. Martial arts; 2. Science fiction graphic novels; 3. Graphic novels

978-1-58240-905-4, $9.99

On a future world where fighters are like rock stars, monsters are an everyday occurrence, and media broadcast battles, the Krash Bastards travel in their airship the Melody Maker and battle monsters and baddies wherever they touch down. Ren, the younger brother of Krash Bastard leader Tran, runs into trouble with a gang called the Death Lords of Kwan, and when the Bastards come to the rescue, they learn that the gang's true leader is the dreaded Kau Death. He seeks a worthy mortal enemy, and thinks he might have found one in Tran. The book includes lots of sword fighting and lopping off of limbs and heads. As a bonus for anyone interested in the process of creating comics, the book includes Casey's script along with Axel 13's concept sketches.

Rock Bottom. Art by Charlie Adlard. AiT/Planet Lar 2006 Un Illustration

Grades: 11 12 Adult   **741.5; Fic**

1. Graphic novels

978-1-932051-45-2, $12.95

Thomas Dare was just an ordinary guy, who liked to play rock music with the band to blow off the steam of a week of work, who was going through a bad divorce. Then something started happening to him; first his hand was stiff,

then the heavy feeling started. No doctor can stop it, he's slowly turning to stone, it's hereditary. What can one do" How does one live the last few months of life" Thomas Dare is going to find out. The story includes lots of harsh language and some non-sexual nudity.

Cavallaro, Mike

★   **Parade**   (with   fireworks).   Image Comics/Shadowlands Books 2008 70p. Illustration

Grades: 10 11 12 Adult   **741.5; Fic**

1. Italy — History — 1914-1945; 2. Graphic novels

978-1-58240-995-5, $12.99

In 1923, Italy was recovering from the Great War; the fascists were already starting to come into power and battling the socialists. In Maropati, one family gets caught up in the political infighting. Paolo, whose father owns a large olive farm, has come back from living in Chicago, where he learned all about fighting feuds and settling disagreements with guns. On the evening of the Feast of the Epiphany, things in Maropati come to a head, local fascists attack and kill Paolo's brother and cousin, and he chooses to fight back. Despite the fact that the fascists had attacked first, he's the one who is hunted, tried, and convicted, and this shatters his family. Cavallaro has based this story on what really happened to his family in Italy. This story first appeared as a webcomic, part of ACT-I-VATE, and was nominated for an Eisner Award, for Best Limited Series, in 2008. The book includes violence.

Cebulski, C. B.

X-Men: Fairy Tales. Writer, C.B. Cebulski; artist, Sana Takeda. Marvel Entertainment 2006 96p. Illustration

Grades: 9 10 11 12 Adult   **741.5; Fic**

1. Fantasy graphic novels; 2. Superhero graphic novels; 3. X-Men (Fictional characters); 4. Graphic novels

978-0-7851-2207-4, $10.99

Cebulski creates new legends, re-imagining the greatest X-Men stories through folktales, myths and fables from across the globe: Japan, Africa, Lousiana's cajun country, and Central Europe. The book includes some violence.

Chabon, Michael

The **amazing** adventures of the Escapist. Dark Horse Comics 2004 Un Color; Illustration

Grades: 9 10 11 12 Adult   **741.5**

1-59307-171-X; 9781593071714, $17.95

"Fans of Chabon's Amazing Adventures of Kavalier and Clay (2000) who long to read the actual comic-book adventures of the Escapist, the superhero created by the novel's young protagonists, have recently had the chance, thanks to the comic book of which this is the first collection. It purports to repackage the 'original' Escapist stories, dating from the 1940s. Scripting the Escapist's origin story himself, Chabon has enlisted contributions from leading comics artists and writers, including Howard Chaykin, Kyle Baker, and Chris Ware." (Booklist)

Volume 1 of 3

Chadwick, Paul

Concrete Vol. 1: Depths. Dark Horse Comics 2005 208p. Illustration

Grades: 10 11 12 Adult   **741.5; Fic**
  1. Adventure graphic novels; 2. Concrete (Fictional character); 3. Graphic novels
  1-59307-343-7, $12.95

Part man, part...rock" Over seven feet tall and weighing over a thousand pounds, he is known as Concrete but is in reality the mind of one Ronald Lithgow, trapped inside a shell of stone, a body that allows him to walk unaided on the ocean's floor or survive the crush of a thousand tons of rubble in a collapsed mineshaft...but prevents him from feeling the touch of a human hand. Depths, the first in a series of new collections reprinting the classic early Concrete stories along with never-before-collected short stories, includes the Eisner-nominated "Orange Glow" and "Vagabond," Paul Chadwick's autobiographical account of a cross-country hitchiking trip. Further volumes in the series show that Concrete collects nude paintings.

Concrete Vol. 2: Heights. Paul Chadwick. Dark Horse Comics 2005 208 p. Illustration
Grades: 10 11 12 Adult   **Fic; 741.5**
  1. Adventure graphic novels; 2. Science fiction graphic novels
  1593074204; 9781593074203, $12.95
                         LC 2006274266
"Unlike conventional superheroes, who battle costumed criminals or intergalactic foes, Concrete, aided by Larry Munro and biologist Maureen Vonnegut, uses his powers to save the world one small step at a time. Here he helps save a family farm and travels to Nepal to build a much-needed footbridge. He also takes advantage of his exceptional capabilities to enjoy unique experiences. After building the bridge, he climbs Everest solo." (Booklist)

Concrete Vol. 3: Fragile Creature. Dark Horse Comics 2006 208p. Illustration
Grades: 10 11 12 Adult   **741.5; Fic**
  1. Concrete (Fictional character); 2. Science fiction graphic novels; 3. Graphic novels
  1-59307-464-6, $12.95
The four issue mini-series of Fragile Creature won the1992 Eisner Award for Best Finite Series/Limited Series.

When you're seven-feet plus of walking, talking stone, you're bound to draw the media spotlight, especially when you live in Tinseltown. Concrete's celebrity status is sometimes a pain in the buttress... but it does bring the occasional paycheck gig. When the producer of a low-budget science-fiction film approaches Concrete to use his prodigious strength to help save money on the film's FX budget, the siren call of Hollywood draws Concrete like a moth to a flame... a seven thousand dollar a week flame, that is. The volume includes several short stories that have not been previously collected. Some of the stories include some nudity.

Concrete Vol. 4: Killer Smile. Dark Horse Comics 2006 206p. Illustration
Grades: 10 11 12 Adult   **741.5; Fic**
  1. Concrete (Fictional character); 2. Mystery graphic novels; 3. Graphic novels
  978-1-59307-469-2, $12.95
Standing in the shadow of celebrity has its ups and downs, as Concrete's personal assistant, Larry Munro,

knows all too well. But there are darker places than any shadow, as Larry learns the hard way when he is taken hostage by a psychotic gunman who forces Larry to be his chauffeur on a road trip destined to end in disaster... unless Larry can muster the courage to act. This volume includes strong language and some violence.

Concrete Vol. 5: Think Like a Mountain. Dark Horse Comics 2006 206p. Illustration
Grades: 10 11 12 Adult   **741.5; Fic**
  1. Adventure graphic novels; 2. Concrete (Fictional character); 3. Graphic novels
  978-1-59307-559-0, $12.95
Celebrity has its benefits... and its costs. Due to his status as the world's most unusual travel writer - being a thousand pounds of walking, talking rock will do that - Concrete is approached by a group of radical eco-warriors to see firsthand and write about their efforts to save old-growth forest. What begins as a lark soon turns into a harrowing struggle, and Concrete must decide whether to dispassionately observe or to join these people who would risk anything, even life itself, to save the planet. This volume includes some previously uncollected short stories that tie into the ecology theme. There's some strong language and a little violence.

Concrete Vol. 6: Strange Armor. Dark Horse Comics 2006 208p. Illustration
Grades: 10 11 12 Adult   **741.5; Fic**
  1. Concrete (Fictional character); 2. Science fiction graphic novels; 3. Graphic novels
  978-1-59307-560-6, $12.95
A troubled man seeking spiritual renewal in the wilderness experiences a wholly unexpected rebirth - as a walking monolith, half a ton of animate stone able to perform astonishing feats of strength and endurance but forever denied many of life's fundamental pleasures. As Concrete, Ronald Lithgow becomes an overnight celebrity and the focus of dark government operatives desperate to keep the secret of his metamorphosis from the public. Concrete must struggle with the loss of his humanity while discovering, perhaps for the first time, what it truly means to be human. This volume that retells Concrete's origin also includes some short stories. The book has some strong language, but the only nudity is displayed in the artwork that Concrete chooses to purchase.

Concrete Vol. 7: The Human Dilemma. Dark Horse Comics 2006 160p. Illustration
Grades: 11 12 Adult   **741.5; Fic**
  1. Science fiction graphic novels; 2. Graphic novels
  978-1-59307-462-3, $12.95
Trapped in an alien's rock-hard body, Lithgow is an accidental celebrity whose high profile is being courted by a front-page CEO. Though Concrete believes overpopulation to be an important issue, does he want to become the spokesperson for a controversial population control program" While Concrete mulls this generous proposition over with his biologist, Maureen, his longtime aide Larry Munro mulls over an entirely different sort of proposal. Life and violent death take center stage in this volume. The book includes nudity, sexual situations, and violence.

★ **Star** Wars: Empire Volume Two: Darklighter. Doug Wheatley, artist; Tomas Giorello, artist. Dark Horse Comics 2004 Un Illustration

Grades: 7 8 9 10 11 12 Adult   741.5; Fic
  1. Adventure graphic novels; 2. Science fiction graphic novels; 3. Star Wars; 4. Graphic novels
  1-56971-975-6, $17.95

Before Luke Skywalker, the Rebel Alliance had another hero: Biggs Darklighter. For the first time, the full story of Luke's boyhood friend is revealed; from his departure from Tatooine to attend the Imperial Academy, to his decision to lead a mutiny against the Empire and join the Rebellion, to the fateful attack on the Death Star.

The **World** Below. Dark Horse Comics 2007 190p. Illustration

Grades: 9 10 11 12 Adult   741.5; Fic
  1. Adventure graphic novels; 2. Science fiction graphic novels; 3. Graphic novels
  978-1-59307-360-2, $12.95

Wealthy Charles Hoy assembles a team of explorers to descend into a hole in the ground that is a passageway to an underground world. Years before, he pulled a strange machine out of the hole and used its alien technology to make his fortune. Now he wants more strange technology to make more money. The Team of Six, led by Barclay Hassler, includes tech genius George, physician Susan, Hoy's youngest son Gilbert, and street tough Layla and Regina. They have vehicles, equipment, weapons, but they encounter bizarre, dangerous creatures, weird geography, and hazards beyond anything they could have imagined. Chadwick harks back to old pulp science fiction stories for the pacing and the style of his stories here. Some violence and nongraphic sexual situations occur in the course of the stories.

Originally published as The World Below issues #1-4 and The World Below: Deeper and Stranger issues #1-4.

Chaffee, Graham
  Good Dog. W W Norton & Co Inc 2013 80 p.
Grades: Adult   741.5
  1. Dogs
  1606996363; 9781606996362, $16.99

This graphic novel tells "the story of stray dog Ivan and his struggles with troubling nightmares, his unsure nomadic existence, and his desire to find a group he can fit in with." Ivan "weigh[s] the states of living as a tethered house pet like his bulldog pal Kirby against the wild freedom of living as a member of a roving pack of strays led by Sasha, a charismatic Malamute with questionable visions of tribal leadership and warrior's glory." (Publishers Weekly)

Chan, Queenie
  The **Dreaming** Volume 1. Tokyopop 2005 194p. Illustration
Grades: 9 10 11 12 Adult   741.5; Fic
  1. Mystery graphic novels; 2. Supernatural graphic novels; 3. Graphic novels
  1-59816-382-5, $9.99

When twin sisters Amber and Jeanie are accepted into an exclusive Australian boarding school, their future looks bright. But the school's halls harbor a terrible secret: students have been known to wander into the surrounding bushlands and vanish ...without a trace. No one knows where they went—or why. But as Amber and Jeanie are about to learn, the key to the school's dark past may lie in the world of their dreams ... This global manga story has lots of atmospheric spookiness and some scary images.

In odd we trust. Created by Dean Koontz; written by Queenie Chan and Dean Koontz; illustrated by Queenie Chan. Del Rey 2008 224p. Illustration

Grades: 9 10 11 12 Adult   741.5; Fic
  1. Ghosts; 2. Horror graphic novels; 3. Mystery graphic novels; 4. Graphic novels
  978-0-345-49966-0, $10.95

Nineteen-year-old Odd Thomas works as a fry cook in small town Pico Mundo, California; people come to the diner for his pancakes (among other foods), he's easygoing and friendly. Odd also sees ghosts; the ghosts never talk, but they tend to come to him when they need something done. The latest one is a little boy. Odd's girlfriend Stormy tells him that the dead boy's babysitter, her friend, is worried about her other charge, a young girl. So psychic Odd and pistol-packing Stormy try to find the murderer before he can strike again. This original graphic novel, co-written by illustrator Queenie Chan and illustrated and formatted like manga, is a prequel to Koontz's bestselling prose novels about Odd Thomas. While it is a murder mystery, there's little in the way of actual violence portrayed in the book.

"This book is a light, diverting read that has the advantage of being a manga that isn't a part of a multivolume series." Booklist

Chantler, Scott
  ★ The **annotated** Northwest Passage. Oni 2007 268p. Illustration
Grades: 8 9 10 11 12 Adult   741.5; Fic
  1. Adventure graphic novels; 2. Canada — History — 0-1763 (New France); 3. Graphic novels
  978-1-932664-61-4, $19.95

It is the year 1755. Charles Lord, an acclaimed explorer and adventurer from England, has taken a desk job governing Fort Newcastle, a remote frontier trading post in Canada. On the eve of his retirement, Charles longs for a return to past glories and a second chance at his great unfulfilled quest, to find the fabled Northwest Passage. When Fort Newcastle is captured by the brutal French privateer Guerin Montglave and his men, Charles and a few survivors flee into the Canadian wilderness. This edition includes the first three installments of Northwest Passage, along with annotations by the creator. It includes violence and some mild harsh language.

Chao, Fred
  ★ **Johnny** Hiro: {half Asian, all hero}. Fred Chao; greytones by Dylan Babb; letters by Jesse Post. Tom Doherty Associates 2012 175 p.
Grades: 10 11 12 Adult   Fic
  1. Busboys; 2. Chinese restaurants; 3. Monsters; 4. New York (NY); 5. New York (NY); 6. Graphic novels
  0765329379; 9780765329370, $16.99

  LC 2011277796

This graphic novel focuses on the life of Johnny Hiro. "Things just happen to [him], like when a Godzilla-type monster snatches Johnny's girlfriend Mayumi . . . . Or when his boss at the sushi restaurant orders Johnny to steal a special lobster from a rival chef. Or when New York's Mayor Bloomberg intercedes with Judge Judy in a lawsuit about the damage the monster did to Johnny's apartment building. (Library Journal)

Previously collected with new material as Johnny Hiro by AdHouse Books (2009)

Charlesworth, Kate

The **cartoon** history of time. Kate Charlesworth and John Gribbin. Dover Publications 2013 64 p.
Grades: Adult   530.11; 741.5
1. Space and time — Juvenile literature; 2. Time — History — Caricatures and cartoons
0486490971; 9780486490977, $19.95
                              LC 2012049026
This graphic novel, by Kate Charlesworth and John Gribbin, focuses on the history of time. "What is time? How did it begin, and where will it end" Is time travel possible? How does the universe expand, and where do black holes come from? Junior Chicken and Alexis, the Quantum Cat, examine these and other extraordinary concepts, explaining the substance of Stephen Hawking's A Brief History of Time." (Publisher's note)

Reprint of: Cartoon history of time / Kate Charlesworth, John Gribbin. — London : McDonald & Co., Ltd, 1990.

Chast, Roz

★ **Can't** We Talk About Something More Pleasant?: A Memoir. Roz Chast. St. Martin's Press 2014 240 p. Color; Illustration
Grades: Adult   741.5; 818.6
1. Aging parents
9781608198061, $28; 1608198065
National Book Critics Circle Award: Autobiography (2014)

In this memoir, author Roz Chast "brings her signature wit to the topic of aging parents. Spanning the last several years of their lives and told through four-color cartoons, family photos, and documents, and a narrative as rife with laughs as it is with tears, Chast's memoir is both comfort and comic relief for anyone experiencing the life-altering loss of elderly parents." (Publisher's note)

Courtesy of St. Martin's

Chast "brings her parents and herself to life in the form of her characteristic scratchy-lined, emotionally expressive characters, making the story both more personal and universal." Pub Wkly

Chayamachi, Suguro

Devil May Cry 3 Code 1: Dante. Tokyopop 2005 186p. Illustration
Grades: 10 11 12 Adult   741.5; Fic
1. Fantasy graphic novels; 2. Horror graphic novels; 3. Manga; 4. Graphic novels
1-59816-031-1, $9.99
Dante is a demon slayer and bounty hunter with a demon heritage of his own that haunts his past. He's currently unemployed—and bored to death. Opportunity knocks in the form of a missing-child case, which his friend and manager, Enzo, offers him. But a four-million-dollar reward, an unexpected demon attack and a little girl named Alice all conspire to send Dante through the looking glass on a nightmarish adventure beyond his wildest imagination. Based on the violent video game, the book contains graphic violence and some strong language.

Chaykin, Howard

Barnum: In Secret Service to the USA. Written by Howard Chaykin; art by Niko Henrichon. DC Comics/Vertigo 2005 128p. Illustration
Grades: 9 10 11 12 Adult   741.5; Fic
1. Adventure graphic novels; 2. Fantasy graphic novels; 3. Mystery graphic novels; 4. Graphic novels
1-4012-0073-7, $19.95; 9781401200732
When brilliant inventor Nikola Tesla and a cadre of the world's richest men plot to destroy America, secret agent P.T. Barnum must assemble a team of the wildest circus freaks on the planet to save the world. Span, a teenaged human fly; Col. Dyna-Mite, a midget strongman; Plastino, a sword-swallowing rubber man; Primeva, a Brazilian animal empath; and the legendary Siamese twins Chang and Eng join Barnum on his quest to stop Tesla. The book includes some violence and some strong language.

Challengers of the Unknown: Stolen Moments, Borrowed Time. DC Comics 2006 144p. Illustration
Grades: 10 11 12 Adult   741.5; Fic
1. Superhero graphic novels; 2. Graphic novels
978-1-4012-0941-4, $16.99
Five extraordinary people with seemingly nothing in common share the bond of surviving a cataclysmic event. In a world devoid of superheroes, they come together and discover that all they know has been a lie, that the world we live in is not the one we believe it to be. To survive they must unite and face the true masters of our universe. It's a world where literally anything can happen, and probably will - as if living on borrowed time wasn't enough. There's a fair amount of foul language and considerable violence.

Fritz Leiber's Fafhrd and the Gray Mouser. Adaptation and script, Howard Chaykin; pencils, Mike Mignola; inks, Al Williamson; colors, Sherlyn van Valkenburgh; letters, Michael HeislerDark Horse Comics 2007 Un Illustration
Grades: 11 12 Adult   741.5; Fic
1. Adventure graphic novels; 2. Fantasy graphic novels; 3. Leiber, Fritz; 4. Leiber, Fritz — Adaptations; 5. Graphic novels
978-1-59307-713-6, $19.95
This volume, which was first published as a four-issue miniseries by Marvel Comics in 2001, adapts several of Leiber's stories about the huge northern barbarian Fafhrd

and the conniving Gray Mouser. "Ill Met in Lankhmar" describes how the two meet; in "The Circle Curse" the two leave Lankhmar only to return because they're bored when away from the city; "The Bazaar of the Bizarre" offers trinkets and treasures which are really enchanted trash. In "Lean Times of Lankhmar," the two friends fall out and the Mouser works for a major thug while Fafhrd becomes a devotee of the god Issek of the Jug.

Leiber poked fun at the "sword and sorcery" type of fantasy adventure, but ended up crafting classic stories in the subgenre. Readers will find humor, swordfights, thievery, sex, and more.

Chen, Marcia

Wraithborn. DC Comics/Wildstorm 2007 Un Illustration
Grades: 10 11 12 Adult   **741.5**
1. Horror graphic novels; 2. Mystery graphic novels; 3. Graphic novels
978-1-4012-0995-7

Melanie Moore is a typical teenager, with all the usual hopes and dreams and angst that fill the teen years. All that suddenly changes when she is unexpectedly granted fantastic powers by a mysterious stranger as he lies dying. Now Melanie races to discover the secrets of her newfound abilities before those stalking her can claim the Wraithborn as their own, along with her life. This story includes nudity, strong language, and graphic violence.

Cherniss, Matt

Powerless. Matt Chernis and Peter Johnson; art by Michael Gaydos. Marvel Entertainment 2005 Un Illustration
Grades: 9 10 11 12 Adult   **741.5; Fic**
1. Daredevil (Fictional character); 2. Spider-Man (Fictional character); 3. Superhero graphic novels; 4. Wolverine (Fictional character); 5. Graphic novels
07851-1511-0, $14.99

What makes a hero? Is it his actions, or is it the results of those actions? Powerless explores what it means to be a hero in very human terms. By re-imagining Marvel's most popular characters without superhuman powers, this story strips down to the core heroes readers have all come to know and love. These characters - including Peter Parker, Matt Murdock and Logan - were fated to be heroes. Just because Peter Parker wasn't bitten by a radioactive spider doesn't mean he didn't do battle with a madman named Norman Osborn. Matt Murdock" Blinded, yes - but with no heightened senses. However, he did become a legal champion of the poor in Hell's Kitchen, and he did cross paths with Wilson Fisk, the Kingpin. And Logan is, of course, the enigmatic - and amnesiac - drifter on the run from his past. Psychiatrist Dr. Watts suffers strange dreams and visions even as he tries to help his three patients. The book includes some violence.

Cherrywell, Steph

★ **Pepper** Penwell and the land creature of Monster Lake. [written and drawn by Steph Cherrywell].. SLG Publishing 2011 Un Illustration
Grades: 7 8 9 10 11 12 Adult   **741.5; Fic**
1. Horror graphic novels; 2. Humorous graphic novels; 3. Monsters; 4. Mystery graphic novels; 5. Graphic novels

978-1-59362-205-3, $14.95

British teenager Pepper Penwell prefers solving mysteries over school work and wants to be a detective like her father. When the latest school boots her out, Pepper takes on the case of a missing drum majorette named Lucy. Accompanied by her brother Alex, who inexplicably (it was some kind of accident) has the body of a bird, Pepper travels to Monster Lake, a town trying to establish itself as a tourist attraction based on its local monster, which is a land creature. In the town, Pepper meets strange people, any of whom could be guilty of kidnapping the wealthy and annoying Lucy. However, after Pepper does find Lucy, there's still the matter of the land monster, which is all too real. British slang (arse, bum) provides the mildly harsh language.

Cheung, Man Wai

Topspeed Underground Vol. 1. Comics One/DrMaster Publishing 2004 206p. Illustration
Grades: 10 11 12 Adult   **741.5; Fic**
1. Adventure graphic novels; 2. Automobile racing; 3. Graphic novels
1-58899-403-1, $14.95

Most of the Hong Kong street racing champions, the Four Kings, have fallen from grace, and now the streets are ruled by the 13 Ghosts. When a legendary racing god comes out of retirement to recruit some new talent, the wheel is set in motion for some major competition with the 13 to rule the streets of Asia. The children of racing icons Tien Ren and Ichiro Sakazaki step forward to prove their worth, but previous kings Fuma and Seer intervene. Lots of street racing action and some strong language spice the story.

Volume 1 of 3

Chiba, Tomohiro

Mobile Suit Gundam: Lost War Chronicles Volume 1. Art by Masato Natsumoto. Tokyopop 2006 Un Illustration
Grades: 8 9 10 11 12 Adult   **741.5; Fic**
1. Adventure graphic novels; 2. Manga; 3. Mecha manga; 4. Graphic novels
159816-213-6, $9.99

The One Year War between the Earth Federation and the Principality of Zeon has begun—and the newest Mobile Suits are tested for battle. Captain Matt Healy leads his team into dangerous territory as the leader of a Special Forces Experimental Ken Bederstadt is a Foreign Legion Lieutenant working in alliance with Zeon. These two heroes are trying to keep everyone alive...for tomorrow.

Chmakova, Svetlana

Dramacon, Vol. 1. Tokyopop 2005 182p. Illustration
Grades: 10 11 12 Adult   **741.5; Fic**
1. Humorous graphic novels; 2. Romance graphic novels; 3. Graphic novels
1-59816-129-6, $9.99

Amateur writer Christie (a high school junior) attends her first anime convention with her boyfriend Derek, who ogles and flirts with all the pretty cosplayers (people who dress as their favorite anime characters). She meets a handsome cosplayer who never takes off his sunglasses and other new friends who help her realize that Derek is a jerk, and when things get bad and Derek attacks her, she turns to

Matt the cosplayer and her new friends for help. Chmakova employs many manga art techniques, especially the exaggeratedly small and funny chibi figures in this behind-the-scenes look at an anime convention. Nothing sexually graphic is depicted, but Christie and Derek are obviously sexually active.

Chopra, Gotham

The **Sadhu**. Virgin Comics 2007 Un Illustration

Grades: 10 11 12 Adult   **741.5; Fic**
1. Fantasy graphic novels; 2. Superhero graphic novels; 3. Graphic novels
978-1-934413-03-6, $14.99

Sadhus do not know love or hate, desire or fear. They are detached from all emotional ties, devoting themselves to a spiritual journey said to unleash unimaginable powers. It is this ancient tradition that James Jenson is fated to tread. He's a down-on-his-luck Englishman, recruited into her majesty Queen Victoria's army and posted with his family in Colonial India. A tragic twist of fate sends James on a journey that will force him to choose between spiritual awakening and human instinct, guiding him from a simple soldier to a spiritual warrior. The book includes some violence.

Chrono, Nanae

Peacemaker Volume 1. Tokyopop 2007 Un Illustration

Grades: 10 11 12 Adult   **741.5; Fic**
1. Adventure graphic novels; 2. Manga; 3. Shonen manga; 4. Graphic novels
978-1-4278-0075-6, $9.99

Tetsunosuke and Tatsunosuke are the sons of a diplomat who sought to bring peace and prosperity to Japan during the early Meiji Restoration. But when their parents are murdered before their very eyes, Tetsu seeks to join the Shinsengumi, the unofficial police who are capable of the same brutality as his parents' murderers. Wading through a sea of espionage, deception and bloodshed, the young boy must choose: should he take a step on the path to becoming a demon...or give up his rage and transform into the ultimate Peacemaker? This first volume includes violence.

Volume 1 of 5

Church, Kevin

Cover girl. Andrew Cosby & Kevin Church, writers; Mateus Santolouco, pencils. Boom! Studios 2008 Un Illustration

Grades: 9 10 11 12 Adult   **741.5; Fic**
1. Adventure graphic novels; 2. Mystery graphic novels; 3. Graphic novels
978-1-934506-27-1, $14.99

Young struggling actor Alex Martin saves a woman whose car crashes off the road, and the videotape of his rescue helps his fortunes rise, and he snags the lead role in a high-budget action film. However, mysterious black SUVs seem to be following him, and then someone (or several someones) attempt several times to kill him. The studio hires a bodyguard, but Rachel Dodd isn't the usual type. She has to play the part of Alex's girlfriend in order to be by his side. When she and her partner Dwight manage to foil several more attempts to kill Alex, they decide they need to find out who's trying to kill Alex, and why. They soon discover it all

comes back to Alex's roadside rescue of the woman, who has since disappeared from public view. This story is full of action and includes some violence and mildly bad language. Anyone who enjoys fast-paced action films with witty dialog will enjoy this. Teen girls and women may delight in the fact that the action hero is a no-nonsense woman who can shoot and fight as well as any male action movie hero.

Chwast, Seymour

Dante's Divine comedy: a graphic adaptation. Adapted by Seymour Chwast. Bloomsbury 2010 127 p. Illustration

Grades: Adult

741.5
1. Dante Alighieri, 1265-1321; 2. Future life
1608190846;
9781608190843, $20
LC 2009044551

Courtesy of Bloomsbury

In this version of "Dante's Divine Comedy", by Seymour, "Dante and his guide Virgil don fedoras and wander through noirish realms of Hell, Purgatory, and Paradise in this classic satire of human foibles." (Publisher's note)

Chwast "meets his match in one of the cornerstones of Western literature. Distilling Dante's three volumes into little more than 100 pages of large panels (many of them page-sized), he adheres to the tri-partite structure of the original without overburdening the spirit with reverence." Kirkus

★ The **odyssey**. [Homer]; adapted by Seymour Chwast.. Bloomsbury 2012 128 p. Illustration (All-action classics)

Grades: Adult   **741.5/973; 741.5; Fic**
1. Adventure graphic novels; 2. Epic literature; 3. Homer; 4. Homer — Adaptations; 5. Odysseus (Greek mythology); 6. Graphic novels
9781608194865, $20.00

LC 2012010047

In this graphic retelling of Homer's "The Odyssey," "Odysseus faces storm and shipwreck, a terrifying man-eating Cyclops, the alluring but deadly Sirens, and the fury of the sea-god Poseidon as he makes his ten-year journey home from the Trojan War. While Odysseus struggles to make it home, his wife, Penelope, fights a different kind of battle as her palace is invaded by forceful, greedy men who tell her that Odysseus is dead and she must choose a new husband." (Publisher's note)

This graphic novel adaptation of Homer's classic epic is "a crackling adventure that also penetrates the recessess of the human heart. . . . Caldwell's art has the force and vibrant life of a Samurai Jack cartoon." Booklist

CLAMP

R. G. Veda Vol. 1. English adaptation by Christine Schilling. Tokyopop 2005 198p. Illustration

Grades: 8 9 10 11 12 Adult 741.5; Fic
1. Fantasy graphic novels; 2. Manga; 3. Shojo manga; 4. Graphic novels
1-59532-484-4, $9.99

At the dawn of creation, the world was a beautiful and tranquil place. Gods and humans lived peacefully together under the Heavenly Emperor's rule. But Taishakuten, a powerful warlord, rebelled against the King, and a violent, chaotic age began ... Three hundred years later, Kuyou, the strongest warrior in the land, hears the prophetic words of a revered stargazer: Six Stars will one day assemble and overthrow this bloody reign. Now, the quest begins to find the Six Stars and fulfill the prophecy before the heavens are torn apart. The book includes some battle violence.

Claremont, Chris
★ **Wolverine**. Art by Frank Miller. Marvel Entertainment 2007 Un Illustration
Grades: 9 10 11 12 Adult 741.5; Fic
1. Superhero graphic novels; 2. Wolverine (Fictional character); 3. Graphic novels
978-0-7851-2329-3, $19.99

Originally published in the early 1980s, this was the first miniseries to delve into the character of the berserker mutant, Wolverine, and shape him into something more than a snarling fighting beast. Wolverine loves Mariko, but she is a yakuza boss's daughter; and when he follows her back to Japan, the Hand hires the ninja Yukio to kill Logan. Instead, she falls in love with him. Wolverine fights gangsters and ninja in his bid to win Mariko's heart.

★ **X-Men**: The Dark Phoenix Saga, 2nd ed.. Penciler and co-plotter, John Byrne. Marvel Entertainment 2006 200p. Illustration
Grades: 7 8 9 10 11 12 Adult 741.5; Fic
1. Superhero graphic novels; 2. X-Men (Fictional characters); 3. Graphic novels
978-0-7851-2213-5, $24.99

Gathered together by Professor Charles Xavier to protect a world that fears and hates them, the X-Men had fought many battles, been on adventures that spanned galaxies, grappled enemies of limitless might, but none of this could prepare them for the most shocking struggle they would ever face. One of their own members, Jean Grey, has gained power beyond all comprehension, and that power has corrupted her absolutely. Now they must decide if the life of the woman they cherish is worth the existence of the entire universe.

X-Men: The End Book One: Dreamers & Demons. Writer, Chris Claremont ; pencils, Sean Chen ; inks, Sandu Florea ; colors, Avalaon's Ian Hannin ; letters, Dave Sharpe. Marvel Entertainment 2005 Un Illustration
Grades: 7 8 9 10 11 12 Adult 741.5; Fic
1. Superhero graphic novels; 2. X-Men (Fictional characters); 3. Graphic novels
978-0-7851-1690-5, $14.99

It's the epic finale to the story of the Children of the Atom as X-Men scribe Chris Claremont joins with artist Sean Chen for a trilogy in the style of the Lord of the Rings movies, one that spans the length and breadth of the X-Men canon and brings the saga of Marvel's mutants to a climax. In this volume, the unthinkable happens - attackers succeed in breaching all security at the Xavier School for the Gifted and threaten the lives of all the young mutants living there.

X-Men: The End Book Three: Men & X-Men. Sean Chen, illustrator. Marvel Entertainment 2006 Un Illustration
Grades: 7 8 9 10 11 12 Adult 741.5; Fic
1. Superhero graphic novels; 2. X-Men (Fictional characters); 3. Graphic novels
978-0-7851-1692-9, $14.99

The endgame of the last tale of Marvel's most popular mutants begins. They've suffered through sneak attacks, betrayals, and fatalities - now, Professor X and Magneto are taking the fight back to the enemy, amidst the stars.

X-Men: The End Book Two: Heroes & Martyrs. Sean Chen, illustrator. Marvel Entertainment 2005 Un Illustration
Grades: 7 8 9 10 11 12 Adult 741.5; Fic
1. Superhero graphic novels; 2. X-Men (Fictional characters); 3. Graphic novels
978-0-7851-1691-2, $14.99

The Xavier Academy has been reduced to a smoldering crater in a brutal sneak attack, and the casualties number in the hundreds. Now, Cyclops must mobilize the survivors to get to the bottom of who is behind these coordinated strikes on mutants in general and the X-Men in particular.

★ **X-Men**: days of future past. Chris Claremont, art by John Byrne. Marvel Worldwide 2011 176 p.
Grades: 9 10 11 12 Adult 741.5
1. X-Men (Fictional characters)
0785164537; 9780785164531, $19.99
LC Bl2011037630

"Relive the legendary first journey into the dystopian future of 2013 - where Sentinels stalk the Earth, and the X-Men are humanity's only hope...until they die! Also featuring the first appearance of Alpha Flight, the return of the Wendigo, the history of the X-Men from Cyclops himself...and a demon for Christmas!—" (Publisher's note)

Clevinger, Brian
Atomic Robo; Volume one: Atomic Robo and the Fightin' Scientists of Tesladyne. Words, Brian Clevinger; art and cover, Scott Wegener; colors, Ronda Pattison; letters, Jeff Powell. Red 5 Comics 2008 180 p. Color illustration (Atomic Robo)
Grades: 9 10 11 12 Adult 741.5
1. Robots; 2. Science fiction graphic novels; 3. Superhero comic books, strips, etc
0980930200; 9780980930207, $18.95

This graphic novel, by Brian Clevinger, illustrated by Scott Wegener and Ronda Pattison, collects the first six issues of the action comic series "Atomic Robo." "Atomic Robo and the so-called Action Scientists of Tesladyne become the go-to defense force against the unexplained! See ROBO take on Nazis, giant ants, clockwork mummies, walking pyramids, Mars, cyborgs, and his nemesis, Baron von Helsingard." (Publisher's note)

"[This] series about a scientific adventure robot created by Nikola Tesla has been . . . funny and yet surprisingly touching at times, a book that features car chases, gun fights and robots punching other robots but never uses them as an excuse to give up on being smart." ComicsAlliance
Volume 1 of an ongoing series

Clowes, Daniel

Art School Confidential: A Screenplay. Fantagraphics Books 2006 200p. Illustration
Grades: 11 12 Adult   **741.5; 808.2**
1. Artists
1-56097-678-0, $14.95
The story follows Jerome, an art student who dreams of becoming the greatest artist in the world. The film expands on a short comic story by Dan Clowes that was originally published, in black-and-white, in his hit comic book series Eightball; for this new book, the strip has been published in full-color for the first time. This scrapaook/screenplay also features the shooting script for the film, including several scenes edited out from the final cut. It also has two full-color sections with stills from the film, character designs from Clowes' sketchbook, and artwork created as set dressing by Clowes and his friends. The original story features full nudity and strong language.

The **complete** eightball. By Daniel Clowes; [edited by] Eric Reynolds. Fantagraphics Books, Inc. 2015 454 p. Color; Illustration
Grades: Adult   **741.5**
1. Anthologies; 2. Underground comic books, strips, etc
9781606997574, $119.99; 1606997572
LC 2014951638
"This is a two-volume, slipcased facsimile edition of the Daniel Clowes comics anthology; it contains the original installments of Ghost World, the short that the film Art School Confidential was based on, and much more." (Publisher's note)
Originally published as Eightball issues #1-18

★ **Ghost** world. Daniel Clowes. Fantagraphics Bks. 1997 80p. Illustration
Grades: 11 12 Adult   **741.5**
1. Female friendship; 2. Teenage girls — Fiction
1-56097-280-7 (pa), $19.95; 9781560974277
Ignatz Award: Outstanding Story (1998)
Ignatz Award: Outstanding Graphic Novel or Collection (1998)

Clugston-Major, Chynna

Blue Monday Vol. 1: The Kids are Alright. Oni Press 2003 136p. Illustration
Grades: 10 11 12 Adult   **Fic; 741.5**
1. Humorous graphic novels; 2. Teenagers; 3. Graphic novels
1-929998-62-7, $11.95
Being a teenager can be a difficult job, something the adult world can never understand. While to her parents and teachers getting Adam Ant tickets is no big deal, to Bleu L. Finnegan it means everything. This could be the defining moment of her life, and there is no guarantee that she will ever achieve it. On the way, Bleu must deal with the travails of adolescence - from prank-playing, porn-addicted boys to sexist-pig radio disc jockeys to trying to figure out how to show that dreamy substitute teacher that she's his perfect mate. It all culminates on that fateful night when Bleu and her best friend, Clover, go to the club and try to get in at any cost. Nothing will bar Bleu from the pop idol of her dreams. This book includes sexual innuendo and strong language, particularly from Clover, who curses with an Irish accent.

Collects the debut mini-series as well as the various short stories that preceded it in independent comic book anthologies.
Other titles in this series are: Volume 2: Absolute beginners; Volume 3: Inbetween days; Volume 4: Painted moon

Scooter Girl. Oni Press 2004 Un Illustration
Grades: 10 11 12 Adult   **741.5; Fic**
1. Humorous graphic novels; 2. Romance graphic novels; 3. Graphic novels
1-929998-88-0, $14.95
Ashton Archer has it all. He's the biggest man on his campus, he's got a family fortune waiting for him to transfer into his own account, and his closet and garage are full of the coolest accoutrements available, from flash suits to swank shoes to a zippy Vespa scooter. It appears that nothing can go wrong for this hard-hearted hottie - that is until the sexy and fashionable Margaret Sheldon motors by on her Lambretta. At that moment, Ashton's life takes a turn for the worse. Everyone at school hates him, his father declares bankruptcy, and his scooter gets run over by a truck. Even high-tailing it out of town does him no good, because wherever he goes, Margaret follows. How can he get out of the black curse this woman has placed on his life" By getting her to fall in love with him, of course. The book has some raunchy humor, plenty of strong language, some partial nudity, and sexual innuendo.

Cobley, Jason

Frankenstein: the graphic novel. [by] Mary Shelley; script adaptation Jason Cobley; American English adaptation: Joe Sutliff Sanders; linework: Declan Shalvey; coloring: Jason Cardy & Kat Nicholson; lettering: Terry Wiley. Classical Comics 2008 141p. Illustration
Grades: 6 7 8 9 10 11 12 Adult   **741.5; Fic**
1. Frankenstein (Fictional character); 2. Horror graphic novels; 3. Shelley, Mary Wollstonecraft, 1797-1851 — Adaptations; 4. Graphic novels
978-1-906332-49-5, $16.95
Young scientist Victor Frankenstein becomes obsessed with the idea that technology can create life, and works to prove his theories. However, his success doesn't bring him glory, but a living nightmare for himself and everyone around him. This graphic adaptation brings the entire book to the reader, using Shelley's original text for the dialog and narrative. Back matter includes a brief biography of Shelley, her family tree, a description of how she came to write the novel, and information on some of the various adaptations of the story to the stage and to film.
"More than a straightforward retelling, this edition invites readers to explore important social issues such as alienation, the consequences and ethics of scientific studies, as well as the nature of creation and destruction." SLJ
Also available quick text version $16.95 (ISBN: 978-1-906332-50-1)
Original text version

Coda, Gakuto

Missing: Kamikakushi no Monogatari Volume 1. Art by Rei Mutsuki. Tokyopop 2007 174p. Illustration
Grades: 9 10 11 12 Adult   **741.5; Fic**

1. Fantasy graphic novels; 2. Manga; 3. Supernatural graphic novels; 4. Graphic novels
978-1-4278-0066-4, $9.99

Kyoichi Utsume, a.k.a. "His Majesty, Lord of Darkness," is a dark and compelling mystery, so much so that his fellow Literature Club members would rather discuss him than books. When "His Majesty" vanishes in front of their very eyes, his friends are left with several unanswered questions: what is the source of Kyoichi's long-standing obsession with the "other side?" And just who is Ayame, the eerily ghostlike girl Kyoichi brought to school as his girlfriend the day before he disappeared?

Cogan, Adam
The **Black** Coat: A Call to Arms. by Ben Lichius and Adam Cogan. Illustrated by Francesco Francavilla. APE Entertainment 2006 Un Illustration
Grades: 8 9 10 11 12 Adult   **741.5; Fic**
1. Adventure graphic novels; 2. Supernatural graphic novels; 3. Graphic novels
978-0-9741398-8-3, $12.95

In pre-Revolutionary War New York City, the masked Black Coat and his Knights of Liberty battle the British occupation forces, and the occult. Lieutenant-General Henry Savidge has accepted the help of Lord Morrow and his shadowy organization to stop the Black Coat. Morrow and his League have brought the Krauss brothers to the Colonies; Wilhelm Krauss murders people, taking their arms, as he works to perfect a serum that will make the takers immortal. The Black Coat and his people work to prevent it, even as the Krauss' butchery is blamed on the Black Coat.

This story, combining historical fiction with the occult, is the first volume; a new miniseries of comics began publication in 2007.

Originally published as The Black Coat issues #1-4.

Cole, Allison
Never Ending Summer. Alternative Comics 2004 128p. Illustration
Grades: 10 11 12 Adult   **741.5; Fic**
1. Graphic novels
1-891867-66-0, $11.95

This story is an autobiographical account that follows a group of friends through a summer filled with uncertainty and confusion. Relationships break down between boyfriends, friends, and family, throughout which the author must discover how to maintain a sense of balance. Parties, excessive drinking, and financial instability add to the commotion. The book reflects upon the immediacy of the present and the potential of events to come. There's very little in the way of strong language or sexual situations.

Collins, Max Allan
CSI: Crime Scene Investigation: Bad Rap. Art by Gabriel Rodriguez and Ashley Wood. IDW Publishing 2004 132p. Illustration
Grades: 10 11 12 Adult   **741.5; Fic**
1. Mystery graphic novels; 2. Graphic novels
1-932382-20-8, $19.99

The duel between retro-punk rappers from the music scene in Las Vegas ends with one of them murdered. The problem for Gil Grissom and his team of crime scene investigators isn't a lack of suspects, it's too many, each with his or her own reason to want Busta Kapp dead. But when the suspects start becoming murder victims themselves, Grissom knows he's got to solve this case in a hurry, before the victim list goes off the charts. The violence is at the level shown on broadcast television in this original story based on the CSI characters.

CSI: Crime Scene Investigation: Demon House. Art by Gabriel Rodriguez and Ashley Wood. IDW Publishing 2004 120p. Illustration
Grades: 9 10 11 12 Adult   **741.5; Fic**
1. Mystery graphic novels; 2. Graphic novels
1-932382-34-8, $19.99

When a real body turns up in a charity haunted house, the members of Las Vegas's CSI team - already busy on a series of armed robberies - find themselves pulling double duty. It's all tricks and no treats for Grissom and crew. Rodriguez does the art for what is happening during the course of the story, Wood does the art for the flashbacks and replays. The story includes some violence and some strong language.

Dick Tracy: The Collins Casefiles Volume 1. Chester Gould, artist, Rick Fletcher, artist. Checker Book Publishing Group 2003 164p. Illustration
Grades: 8 9 10 11 12 Adult   **741.5; Fic**
1. Dick Tracy (Fictional character); 2. Mystery graphic novels; 3. Graphic novels
0-9741664-2-1, $19.95
LC 2003-23068

This is the first of several volumes collecting Collins' 11-year run on the Dick Tracy comic strips. He took over scripting duties from Chester Gould in 1978, although Gould maintained his byline and consulted with Collins on plot directions. Fletcher, a longtime Gould assistant, took over the drawing and worked with Collins. This volume includes the stories "Angel Top's Last Stand," "Return of Haf-and Haf," and "Big Boy's Revenge."

Johnny Dynamite: Underworld. Art by Terry Beatty. AiT/Planet Lar 2003 Un Illustration
Grades: 10 11 12 Adult   **741.5; Fic**
1. Horror graphic novels; 2. Mystery graphic novels; 3. Graphic novels
1-932051-10-4, $12.95

1950s tough-guy private detective Johnny Dynamite goes up against zombies in Las Vegas as well as the mob, and the zombies also have crime on their undead minds. Mob-style violence, with beatings and hits, combines with zombie killings and horror action.

★ **Road** to Perdition. Written by Max Allan Collins; art by Richard Piers Rayner; lettering by Bob Lappan. Pocket Books 2002 302 p.
Grades: Adult   **741.5; 741.5/973**
1. Father-son relationship; 2. Mafia; 3. Revenge
0743442245; 9780743442244, $14
LC 2002510761

In this book, by Max Allan Collins, illustrated by Richard Piers Rayner, "Michael O'Sullivan is a deeply religious family man who works as the chief enforcer for an Irish mob family. But after O'Sullivan's eldest son witnesses one of his father's hits, the godfather orders the death of his entire family. Barely surviving an encounter that takes his wife and youngest son, O'Sullivan and his only remaining child embark on a dark and violent mission of retribution against his former boss." (Publisher's note)

Collins, Stephen
The **Gigantic** Beard That Was Evil. By Stephen Collins. St. Martin's Press 2014 240 p. Illustration
Grades: Adult   **741.5; Fic**
  1. Beards — Fiction; 2. Fables
  1250050391; 9781250050397, $20
    In this fable tale, by Stephen Collins, "on the island of Here, livin's easy. Conduct is orderly. Lawns are neat. Citizens are clean shaven—and Dave is the most fastidious of them all. Dave is bald, but for a single hair. He loves drawing, his desk job, and the Bangles. But on one fateful day, his life is upended . . . by an unstoppable (yet pretty impressive) beard." (Publisher's note)
    "Collins' illustrations are lush, rounded affairs with voluptuous shading across oblong planes. . . . With its archetypical conflict and deliberate dissection of language, the story seems aimed at delivering a moral, but the tale ultimately throws its aesthetics into abstraction rather than didacticism." Kirkus

Colon, Ernie
 ★ **After** 9/11: America's war on terror (2001-). Hill and Wang 2008 149p. Illustration; Map
Grades: 9 10 11 12 Adult   **973.931; 741.5**
  1. Iraq War, 2003-; 2. Terrorism; 3. United States — Foreign relations; 4. United States — Politics and government; 5. Graphic novels
  978-0-8090-2370-7, $16.95
                          LC 2008-13298
    In 2006, longtime comic book veterans Jacobson and Colon adapted the 9/11 Commission's report into a graphic format that made it a readable, comprehensible work for teens and adults. Now they have used the comic book treatment to cover America's War on Terror since 2001, including the wars in Iraq and in Afghanistan, summarizing events and showing the major players throughout the years. Some images can be disturbing, such as the depiction of prisoner mistreatment at Abu Ghraib and other facilities, as well as depictions of the victims of sectarian violence.

  Anne Frank: the Anne Frank House authorized graphic biography. [by] Sid Jacobson and Ernie Colón. Hill and Wang 2010 152p. Illustration
Grades: 9 10 11 12 Adult   **92; 741.5**
  978-0-8090-2684-5, $30; 978-0-8090-2685-2 (pa), $16.95
                          LC 2010-5776
    This is a "graphic biography of Anne Frank . . . covering the lives of Anne's parents, Edith and Otto; Anne's first years in Frankfurt; the rise of Nazism; the Franks' immigration to Amsterdam; war and occupation; Anne's years in the Secret Annex; betrayal and arrest; her deportation and tragic death in Bergen-Belsen; the survival of Anne's father; and his recovery and publication of her astounding diary." Publisher's note
    "Panel arrangements effectively show simultaneous events happening in the life of the family and in the world,

while brief 'snapshots' provide enough historical information to make motives, fears, and expectations sensible to anyone unfamiliar with the Holocaust's machinery. More than simply poignant, this biography elucidates the complex emotional aspects of living a sequestered adolescence as a brilliant, budding writer." Booklist

Conley, Steve
 Astounding space thrills: Argosy Smith and the codex reckoning. IDW Publishing 2008 192p. Illustration
Grades: 9 10 11 12 Adult   **741.5; Fic**
  1. Adventure graphic novels; 2. Science fiction graphic novels
  978-1-60010-320-9, $19.99
    Adventurer Argosy Smith lives on an Earth that has changed drastically due to its move thanks to some aliens time flows differently, space folds weirdly, and the Earth has basically become the library of the universe. Smith races against time (he's supposed to die on his 25th birthday, which is tomorrow) to steal a lost manuscript by Leonardo Da Vinci, discover the secret of Split-Space travel, keep two alien races from all-out war, avoid certain death at the hands of little green mercenaries hired by a several-brained-corporate head, and keep the universe from breaking apart. Oh yeah, and celebrate his birthday. The action harkens back to the kind of cosmic science fiction adventure written by E. E. "Doc" Smith, with lots of action.

Cooke, Darwyn
 Batman: Ego and Other Tails. DC Comics 2007 200p. Illustration
Grades: 10 11 12 Adult   **741.5; Fic**
  1. Batman (Fictional character); 2. Catwoman (Fictional character); 3. Mystery graphic novels; 4. Superhero graphic novels; 5. Graphic novels
  978-1-4012-1529-3, $24.99
    This volume collects Cooke's work for DC that focus on Batman and Catwoman. In Ego, after suffering physical and psychological trauma, Batman confronts himself in his mind. The book also includes Catwoman: Selina's Big Score, in which the perfect heist ... isn't. The book includes some violence and strong language.

 ★ **DC:** The New Frontier Vol. 1. DC Comics 2004 Un Illustration
Grades: 9 10 11 12 Adult   **741.5; Fic**
  1. Batman (Fictional character); 2. Superhero graphic novels; 3. Superman (Fictional character); 4. Wonder Woman (Fictional character); 5. Graphic novels
  1-4012-0350-7, $19.99; 9781401203504
  2005 Eisner Award for Best Limited Series.
    World War II is over. The Cold War has begun. The Age of the Superhero is in decline. But where are the heroes of tomorrow" This book recounts the dawning of the DC Universe's Silver Age from the perspective of those brave individuals who made it happen. Encounter "keepers of the flame" including Superman, Wonder Woman and Batman, who survived the anti-hero sentiment of the Cold War, as well as eager newcomers like test pilot Hal Jordan and scientist Barry Allen, poised to become the next generation

of crime fighters. The book includes some strong language and violence.

★ **DC:** The New Frontier Vol. 2. DC Comics 2005 Un Illustration
Grades: 9 10 11 12 Adult   **Fic; 741.5**
   1. Aquaman (Fictitious character); 2. Batman (Fictional character); 3. Flash (Fictional character); 4. Superhero graphic novels; 5. Superman (Fictional character); 6. Wonder Woman (Fictional character); 7. Graphic novels
1-4012-0461-9, $19.99
2005 Eisner Award for Best Limited Series.
   It's a mystery in space as Superman, the Suicide Squad, and the Challengers of the Unknown encounter a frightening extraterrestrial life form. Could this hideous creature have anything to do with the sense of impending doom all the heroes are experiencing" Meanwhile, pilot Hal Jordan is grounded, while post-war America faces a monstrous threat older than time. Will this challenge bring America and its heroes back together or tear them apart" The book features Green Lantern, the Flash, Martian Manhunter, Aquaman, Wonder Woman, Batman, and more heroes. It includes some strong language and some violence.

   Parker: The hunter. Darwyn Cooke. IDW Pub. 2009 140 p.
Grades: Adult   **741.5/973; Fic**
   1. Adventure graphic novels; 2. Crime; 3. Criminals; 4. Revenge
1600104932; 9781600104930, $24.99
   This graphic novel, illustrated by Darwyn Cooke, is an adaptation of the 1962 crime novel "The Hunter," by Richard Stark. "Betrayed by the woman he loved and double-crossed by his partner in crime, Parker makes his way cross-country with only one thought burning in his mind—to coldly exact his revenge and reclaim what was taken from him!" (Publisher's note)

   Parker: the score. Darwyn Cooke. IDW Pub. 2012 144 p.
Grades: Adult   **Fic; 741.5/971**
   1. Adventure graphic novels; 2. Crime; 3. Mystery fiction; 4. Theft — Fiction
1613772084; 9781613772089, $24.99
Harvey Award: Best Graphic Album of Original Work (2013)
   This graphic novel, illustrated by Darwyn Cooke, is an adaptation of the 1964 crime novel "The Score," by Richard Stark. "Parker becomes embroiled in a plot with a dozen partners in crime to pull off what might be the ultimate heist—robbing an entire town. Everything was going fine for a while, and then things got bad." (Publisher's note)

   Richard Stark's Parker: The outfit. Illustrated by the author. IDW 2010 160 p. Illustration
Grades: Adult   **741.5/973; Fic**
   1. Criminals; 2. Stark, Richard — Adaptations; 3. Suspense fiction
1600107621; 9781600107627, $24.99
   In this graphic novel, by Darwyn Cooke, "after he evens the score with those who betrayed him and recovers the money he was cheated out of from the syndicate, Parker is riding high, living in swank hotels and enjoying the finer things in life again. Until, that is, he's fingered by a squealer who rats him out to The Outfit for the price they put on his head." (Publisher's note)

   The **Spirit** book two. With J. Bone and Dave Stewart. DC Comics 2008 Un Illustration
Grades: 10 11 12 Adult   **741.5; Fic**
   1. Mystery graphic novels; 2. Spirit (Fictional character); 3. Spirit (Fictional character); 4. Graphic novels
978-1-4012-1920-8, $24.99
   In this second volume of Darwyn Cooke's take on Will Eisner's iconic character, The Spirit, readers meet Silk Satin, a sultry and sexy CIA agent, the villainous Octopus, and El Morte, the criminal who died with Denny Colt only to be raised as a zombie by his mother's supernatural rites. Along the way, the Spirit also works (sort of) with cable crime reporter Ginger Coffee to find out who is killing all the cable news pundits. The book includes violence and some bloodshed.

   ★ **Will** Eisner's The Spirit. Written by Darwyn Cooke and Jeph Loeb; drawn by Darwyn Cooke; inks and finishes by J. Bone; colors by Dave Stewart. DC Comics 2007 192p. Illustration
Grades: 8 9 10 11 12 Adult   **741.5; Fic**
   1. Batman (Fictional character); 2. Humorous graphic novels; 3. Spirit (Fictional character); 4. Superhero graphic novels; 5. Graphic novels
978-1-4012-1461-6; 978-1-4012-1618-4 (pa), $19.99
   Will Eisner's character The Spirit was popular for decades. Eisner is gone, but Darwyn Cooke has taken up the pen to update The Spirit while maintaining the action, adventure, and humor of the original stories. Readers will meet Commissioner Dolan and his daughter Ellen, Ebony, bad girl P'Gell, and more. This volume also includes the Eisner Award winning Batman/The Spirit special, written by Jeph Loeb and drawn by Cooke. The upcoming live action movie directed by comics veteran Frank Miller will spark more interest in the comics. The book includes lots of action and some cartoony violence.
   "This is fine, entertaining stuff that will satisfy any longtime comics fan; recommended for teens and adults." Libr J

Cooper, Park
   Half Dead. Barb Lien-Cooper and Park Cooper; art by Jimmy Bott. Marvel Publishing/Dabel Brothers Productions 2007 Un Illustration
Grades: 10 11 12 Adult   **741.5; Fic**
   1. Horror graphic novels; 2. Vampires; 3. Graphic novels
0-78551-2659-7, $10.99
   In London, ballerina Romany Petrovna gets caught in a gas attack in the Underground. Vampires, called Nozzies (for Nosferatu) use the gas to spread a virus that turns people into half dead creatures; the Bureau of Parahuman and Supernatural Affairs, called PASA, deals with them - by killing them. They save Romany, however, for she has retained her mental capabilities. Half dead, she must now work for PASA, hunt and kill Nozzies and other half dead, or be destroyed. There is considerable vampire action, fighting, and shooting throughout the story.

Corman, Leela

Unterzakhn. Leela Corman. Schocken Books 2012 203 p. Illustration

Grades: Adult   **741.5/973; 741.5**

1. Immigrants — New York (State) — New York; 2. Lower East Side (New York, NY); 3. Twin sisters

9780805242591, $24.95; 0805242597

                       LC 2011043769

"For six-year-old Esther and Fanya, the teeming streets of New York's Lower East Side circa 1910 are both a fascinating playground and a place where life's lessons are learned quickly and often cruelly. In drawings that capture both the tumult and the telling details of that street life, Unterzakhn (Yiddish for 'Underthings') tells the story of these sisters." (Publisher's note)

Corzine, Amy

Jane Eyre: The graphic novel original text. Charlotte Brontë ; script adaptation Amy Corzine ; American English adaptation by Joe Sutliff Sanders ; artwork by John M. Burns ; lettering by Terry Wiley. Classical Comics 2008 144p. Illustration

Grades: 6 7 8 9 10 11 12 Adult   **741.5; Fic**

1. Brontë, Charlotte, 1816-1855 — Adaptations; 2. Romance graphic novels; 3. Graphic novels

978-1-906332-47-1, $16.95

Orphaned as an infant and begrudgingly raised by an aunt who despises her, Jane Eyre begins to find some happiness at Lowood School, a charity school where she spends eight years of her life, as a student and then as a teacher. When she chafes for freedom and advertises for a position, Jane finds a job as governess at Thornfield

©*Classical Comics*

Hall, where she meets Mr. Rochester. Love blooms, but his dark secret destroys what hope she ever had of happiness and she runs away. As life seems to reach its darkest, worst moments, things begin to look up for Jane, but will she ever find love again? This graphic adaptation uses Bronte's dialog and some of her narration straight from the original novel. Back matter includes a short biography of Bronte, a timeline of her life and career, and the Bronte family tree.

Also available quick text version $16.95 (ISBN: 978-1-906332-48-8)

Cosby, Andrew

Enigma Cipher, 112. Written by Andrew Cosby and Michael A. Nelson; art by Greg Scott. 2008 Illustration

Grades: 9 10 11 12 Adult   **741.5; Fic**

1. Adventure graphic novels; 2. Ciphers; 3. Mystery graphic novels; 4. Graphic novels

978-1-934506-13-4, $15.99

During World War II, the Nazis used a machine called Enigma to encrypt their communications, and the Allies broke that code, helping them to win the war. Now, decades

later, grad student Casey Williams' professor has found a long-lost Enigma-encrypted document and has given it to his class to decipher as an assignment. He has also sent a copy to the State Department, which unleashes a deadly plot. American agents kill the professor and the other three students in the class, and when Casey tries to ask her ex-boyfriend for help, they kill him and his roommate. One detective, Merrick, believes Casey, and they end up on the run, until Casey decides she needs to decode the cipher and find out what the document contains. This book reads like an action thriller movie, reminiscent of The Pelican Brief and The Bourne Identity; there is some violence but only mildly strong language. Andrew Cosby is a comics writer who has also created two television series: Haunted (on UPN) and Eureka (on the Sci Fi Channel).

Court-Kaemon, Amy

Ratatouille. Tokyopop 2007 96p. Illustration

Grades: 2 3 4 5 6 7 8 9 10 11 12 Adult   **741.5; Fic**

1. Cooking; 2. Humorous graphic novels; 3. Rats; 4. Graphic novels

978-1-4278-0087-9, $7.99

This Cine-Manga title takes stills from Pixar's popular animated film to adapt the story into a graphic novel. Remy is a rat living in Paris, who aspires to be a chef. Linguine is a hapless young man who wishes to be a chef but has no talent. When the two meet, a partnership is born.

Crane, Jordan

The **Last** Lonely Saturday. Fantagraphics Books 2007 Un Illustration

Grades: 10 11 12 Adult   **741.5; Fic**

1. Ghosts; 2. Romance graphic novels; 3. Graphic novels

978-1-56097-743-8, $8

Using a deep yellow and brown palette, this almost wordless little story follows the day of an older man who gathers his letters addressed to Elinore, sets off to buy flowers, and drives out to the cemetery to visit Elinore's grave. As he sits and hugs the gravestone, the spirit of Elinore comes out and starts to kiss him. In a macabre twist that is portrayed in a sweet, gentle manner, Elinore's spirit finds a way for the two of them to be together.

Courtesy of Fantagraphics

Crilley, Mark

★ **Brody's** ghost: book 1. Story and art by Mark Crilley. Dark Horse Books 2010 88p. Illustration

Grades: 8 9 10 11 12 Adult   **741.5; Fic**

1. Adventure graphic novels; 2. Fantasy graphic novels; 3. Ghosts; 4. Mystery graphic novels; 5. Graphic novels

978-1-59582-521-6, $6.99

In what looks like a near-future city, Brody is down and out, eking out a living by playing guitar on the streets and working part-time as a stock clerk. Then, one day, while playing his guitar, he sees the ghost of a young woman; he thinks he's seeing things, but she won't let him alone until he talks with her. Talia, the ghost, needs to do a great deed before she can get into heaven, and she has decided to solve the mystery of a serial killer called the Penny Murderer, but she needs Brody, who is a ghostseer, to help her. First, though, he needs training to bring out his ghostseer powers, because he doesn't think he has any. Enter Kagemura, the ghost of a samurai, who decides, half-unwillingly, to train Brody. This book is much grittier than Crilley's earlier works, which were more suitable for younger readers; it is aimed more at teen and adult readers and includes some fighting violence but no graphically violent content.

"The setting—an unidentified future city partially in ruins—is a masterpiece of drawing, and Brody and the other characters are equally well crafted. . . . The story is more than a match for the art: humor, action, and mystery butt up against the reality of Brody's sad life, giving him the opportunity to change who he is." Booklist

Also available in an omnibus edition

The first in a six-volume limited series. Page 4 of cover

Book 1 of 6

Miki Falls Vol. 2: Summer. HarperTeen 2007 178p. Illustration

Grades: 7 8 9 10 11 12 Adult   **741.5; Fic**
 1. Romance graphic novels; 2. Supernatural graphic novels; 3. Graphic novels
 978-0-06-084617-6, $7.99

Has Miki fallen too hard" It's summer, and Miki Yoshida is learning all about love. Her senior year has blossomed with promise ever since she gained Hiro Sakurai's confidence. Now, she's resolved to keep his trust as he reveals more about his secret mission and warns: "Don't get involved." But Miki fears his work might do more harm than good, and she takes control-with disastrous results. How can trying to make things right turn out so dangerously wrong? Crilley is doing this series in manga style.

Crisis on Multiple Earths Volume 1: The Team-Ups
 DC Comics 2005 224p. Illustration

Grades: 8 9 10 11 12 Adult   **741.5; Fic**
 1. Flash (Fictional character); 2. Green Lantern (Fictional character); 3. Superhero graphic novels; 4. Graphic novels
 1-4012-0470-8, $14.99

This collection of stories from the 1960s features team-ups of the Silver Age DC heroes with their Golden Age counterparts, with the conceit that DC Comics dreamed up, that the Golden Age heroes are from a parallel world. And along with the heroes, of course come the super-villains. The Flash, Green Lantern, and Hourman from both worlds work with each other to defeat their villains, including Solomon Grundy, the Thinker, the Trickster, and others.

Crosby, Andrew
 Damn Nation. Art by J. Alexander. Dark Horse Comics 2005 Un Illustration

Grades: 10 11 12 Adult   **741.5; Fic**
 1. Horror graphic novels; 2. Vampires; 3. Graphic novels
 1-59307-389-5, $12.95

The United States has been shut off from the world by concrete barricades and barbed wire - not because of what

might get in, but what might get out. A vampire plague has spread from sea to shining sea, and when a small holdout of scientists trapped outside of Buffalo, N.Y. discover a cure, it's up to a Special Ops team from the President's current offices in London to go in and get it. Yet, not everyone in the world wants to see America back in the saddle again ... This story includes some incidental nudity, strong language, and considerable violence.

Crumb, Aline Kominsky
 Need More Love: A Graphic Memoir. MQ Publications Ltd 2007 383p. Illustration

Grades: 11 12 Adult   **741.5; Fic**
 1. Autobiographical graphic novels; 2. Crumb, Aline Kominsky, 1948-; 3. Graphic novels
 978-1-84601-133-7, $30

Crumb was one of the pioneers of women's comics and became well-known during the Sixties and Seventies, along with her husband R. Crumb. This is her memoir of her life, taken from her comics published over the past four decades, incorporating photos and short prose text pieces along with memorabilia. She covers not only her life, but of her family, her husband, and other movers and shakers of the art and music worlds from the Sixties into the 21st century. The book includes considerable nudity, sexual situations, and harsh language.

Crumb, R.
 The **book** of Genesis. Illustrated by R. Crumb. W.W. Norton 2009 Un Illustration; Map

Grades: Adult   **741.5; 222**
 978-0-393-06102-4; 0-393-06102-7, $24.95
          LC 2009-14303

An illustrated adaptation of the entire book of Genesis, providing the biblical accounts of the Creation, Adam and Eve, Cain and Abel, Noah and the ark, the Tower of Babel, and other people and events.

"This is the Bible that distressed 19th-century English philanthropist and man of letters Thomas Bowdler: not stories for sweet-faced kiddies, but sex and blood. . . . We could not expect less from the patriarch of underground comix—themselves notorious for sex and violence and deals gone sour. Indeed, Crumb's muscular, detailed black-and-white seems ideally suited to Old Testament scuffles and seaminess." Libr J

The **Life** and death of Fritz the cat. By R. Crumb. Fantagraphics Books 2012 92 p. Illustration

Grades: Adult   **741.5; 741.5/973**
 1. American wit and humor, Pictorial; 2. Caricatures and cartoons — United States; 3. Cats — Fiction; 4. Underground comic books, strips, etc; 5. Graphic novels
 1606994808; 9781606994801, $19.99
          LC 2012289388

This comic book, by R. Crumb, "contains all the Fritz [the Cat] stories from the earliest sketchbook-drawn tales . . . to the wild adventure stories . . . all the way to the despairing 'Fritz the Cat, Superstar' with its infamous ice-pick ending. Plus an introduction by Crumb, sketchbook pages, and more." (Publisher's note)

First paperback edition, May 1993.

The **R.** Crumb handbook. [by] R. Crumb and Peter Poplaski. MQ Publications 2005 437p. Illustration
Grades: Adult   **741.5; 741**
  1-84072-716-0, $25
  "The eight chapters, which read as if straight from the horse's mouth, are reflective and philosophical more than strictly autobiographical. As in the comics in which he portrays himself, Crumb tries to explain his life and art, and if he often trails off to "I dunno," his pessimistic skepticism sounds out loud and clear. The sixties sex-and-drugs revolution may have "liberated" him to portray his most embarrassing sex fantasies, but he doesn't think that sea change in mores was really all that good. His most perverse stories, some of which reappear here, contain the heat as well as the hilarity of satire. Besides those, a staggering wealth of his other art, dating from childhood to last year, and many photos, personal and public, occupy perhaps two-thirds of the pages." (Booklist)

Crumb, Sophie
  Sophie Crumb: evolution of a crazy artist. Edited by S., A., & R. Crumb.. W.W. Norton & Co. 2011 271 p. Illustration; Color
Grades: Adult   **741.092; 741.5**
  1. Crumb, Sophie — Themes, motives
  0393079961; 9780393079968, $27.95
                    LC 2010020364
  This book, by Sophie Crumb, edited by Aline Kominsky-Crumb and R. Crumb, "charts a young artist's life through her own drawings-from toddlerhood to motherhood. . . . Revealing how an original artistic sensibility is both innate and nurtured, the book features six separate developmental stages, including Sophie's earliest drawings, the elaborate fantasy world of her childhood, her late adolescent rebellion, and her coming of age." (Publisher's note)
  Evolution of a crazy artist

Cruse, Howard
  The **complete** Wendel. By Howard Cruse. Universe Pub. 2011 288 p. Illustration
Grades: Adult   **FIC**
  1. Gay men; 2. Gay youth — Fiction
  0789322161; 9780789322166
                    LC 2010934608
  This book is a compilation of Howard Cruse's comic strip "Wendel," which was published in the newspaper "The Advocate" in the 1980s. "Cruse's feature was an episodic chronicle of life as experienced by young Wendel Trupstock, his lover Ollie and their friends, who collectively represented a particular slice of the American LGBT demographic during a particularly stressful period in recent history, when the afterglow of gay liberation collided with the AIDS epidemic and the ascendancy of Moral Majority-fueled homophobia. Simultaneously a mirror of the days' new events and a comedic portrayal of everyday queer life, drawing Wendel required . . . what the cartoonist calls an "elasticity of tone," balancing lightheartedness with pain, erotic mischief with mundane follies." (Kirkus)

Cryptic Magazine
  Horror book volume 1. Image Comics 2008 Un Illustration
Grades: 10 11 12 Adult   **741.5; Fic**
  1. Horror graphic novels; 2. Short stories; 3. Graphic novels
  978-1-58240-956-6, $14.99
  This volume collects stories originally published in Cryptic Magazine. Each story reworks a classic horror tale. In the first, readers will find zombies in Vietnam in the year 1968, as an American patrol finds horror in the jungle. "Creature of the Depths" takes on The Creature from the Black Lagoon, as a small troop from a struggling sideshow is hired to help trap a marauding sea creature. In "Frankenstein," years after the monster was killed, the doctor is now an opium addict, but now someone is robbing graves and kidnapping people such as the blacksmith and some prostitutes; the monster isn't dead, but he wants more creatures like himself. And in "Full Moon," a nameless man agrees to help the village priest rescue a couple of kidnapped children who were taken by a vengeful vampire; it is the night of the full moon, and the young man becomes a ravening werewolf. The stories include graphic violence and gore, some partial nudity, and some rough language.

Cunningham, Darryl
  How to fake a moon landing: exposing the myths of science denial. Darryl Cunningham. Abrams ComicArts 2013 176 p.
Grades: Adult   **001.9**
  1. Debates and debating; 2. Pseudoscience; 3. Science
  1419706896; 9781419706899, $16.95
                    LC 2012042210
  In this book author-illustrator Darryl Cunningham looks at . . . hot-button science topics and presents a fact-based, visual assessment of current thinking and research on eight different issues. [He] incorporates comics, photographs, and diagrams to create substantive but easily accessible reportage. Cunningham's distinctive illustrative style shows how information is manipulated by all sides; his easy-to-follow narratives allow readers to draw their own fact-based conclusions." (Publisher's note)
  Includes bibliographical references

  Psychiatric tales: 11 graphic stories about mental illness. Darryl Cunningham. Bloomsbury 2010 139 p. Illustration
Grades: Adult

  1. Cunningham, Darryl; 2. Graphic medicine; 3. Mental health services — Fiction; 4. Mental illness; 5. Psychiatric hospital care; 6. Psychiatric Tales: 11 Graphic Stories About Mental Illness (Book)
  1608192784; 9781608192786, $17; 9781906653088

Courtesy of Bloomsbury

This graphic novel, by Darryl Cunningham, presents the author's depiction of mental illness and its care. "Having worked for years as a health care assistant in a hospital's psychiatric ward, he states his intent to counter the stigma surrounding mental illness and to represent the patients who suffer from 'this most mysterious group of illnesses.'" (Publishers Weekly)

R. Crumb Draws the Blues. By Robert Crumb. Last Gasp 1993 100 p. Illustration
Grades: Adult
1. Short stories — Collections
0867194014; 9780867194012, $16.95
This book, by Robert Crumb, includes comic strips and stories. "Brought together for the first time from all stages of his career these strips range from the silly to the serious. Real people and real problems are the substance of stories like Jelly Roll Morton's Voodoo Curse and Patton while Crumb's celebrated light-hearted zaniness can be seen in Cubist Be-Bop Comics, The Old Songs are The Best Songs and Sunny side up." (Publisher's note)

Dahl, Roald
The **Gremlins:** The Lost Walt Disney Production: A Royal Air Force Story. Dark Horse Books 2006 Un Illustration
Grades: 4 5 6 7 8 9 10 11 12 Adult   741.5; Fic
1. Humorous graphic novels; 2. World War, 1939-1945; 3. Graphic novels
978-1-59307-496-8, $12.95
This is an illustrated novella, the first published work of RAF Flight Lieutenant Roald Dahl in his only collaboration with Walt Disney Studios. Originally published in 1943, the story was supposed to become a film combining live action with animation; the movie was never made, although the studio produced a lot of illustrations and samples. The story tells about one young Royal Air Force pilot named Gus, who first sees the little gremlins that wreak havoc on his plane. While the gremlins first cause lots of trouble, eventually Gus convinces them to work with the RAF.

Dakin, Glenn
Temptation: A Battle of Wits Through All Eternity. Active Images 2004 72p. Illustration
Grades: 8 9 10 11 12 Adult   741.5
1. Humorous graphic novels; 2. Graphic novels
0-9740567-5-8, $8.95
It's a constant battle of wits between a hermit who lives out in the wilderness and the devil who wants his soul. While that's the main theme, there are strips in which the devil needs the hermit to babysit his little baby devils so he can see a movie, the devil tries to sell the hermit a set of encyclopedias, and more fun.

Dalrymple, Farel
Meathaus Vol. 8: Headgames. Alternative Comics 2006 Un Illustration
Grades: 11 12 Adult   741.5; Fic
1. Short stories; 2. Graphic novels
1-891867-92-X, $14.95
This eighth volume of the Meathaus anthology series features works by a variety of Meathaus favorites, including James Jean, Becky Cloonan, Tomer Hanuka, Brandon Graham, Jim Campaell, Tom Herpich, Dash Shaw, Scott Morse, Jim Mahfood, Jim Rugg, Farel Dalrymple, and more. Each story is just a few pages long, many include harsh language and nudity, some have violence.

The **Wrenchies**. Farel Dalrymple. First Second 2014 304 p. Color; Illustration
Grades: 10 11 12 Adult   741.5
1. Imaginary places; 2. Science fiction
159643421X; 9781596434219, $19.99
In this book by Farel Dalrymple, "whatever life remains on earth is oppressed by the evil shadowsmen. Only a gang of ruthless and powerful children called the Wrenchies can hope to stand against them. When Hollis, a lonely boy from our world, is magically given access to the future world of the Wrenchies, he finally finds a place he belongs. But it is not an easy world to live in, and Hollis's quest is bigger than he ever dreamed of." (Publisher's note)
"Clearly, it doesn't pay to demand sheer narrative coherence here, but the raw emotional weight of Dalrymple's anger forcibly tows readers through the obfuscating narrative, and the intricate, gritty, and rivetingly grotesque art, in sickly greens and browns peppered with bloody red, plays no small part in that." Booklist

Daly, Joe
Scrublands. Fantagraphics Books 2006 126p. Illustration
Grades: 12 Adult   741.5; Fic
1. Humorous graphic novels; 2. Graphic novels
978-1-56097-744-5, $16.95
"Prebaby," the centerpiece of this collection, delves into creation, survival, random occurrences and the micro/macrocosm. Told entirely without dialogue, it unfolds like the storyboard to a wonky existential animated cartoon. In contrast, Daly's "Kobosh and Steve" stories come across as a series of routines by a demented Abbott and Costello. Kobosh even visits a down-on-his-luck Bruce Springsteen in one story, while another strip features a pair of micro-fauna questioning their existence as they feed off the rock legend's scalp. The book contains strong language, nudity, and some sexual situations.

Daly, Paul
Athena Voltaire: the collected webcomics. APE Entertainment 2006 Un Illustration
Grades: 9 10 11 12 Adult   741.5; Fic
1. Adventure graphic novels; 2. Fantasy graphic novels; 3. Graphic novels
978-0-9741398-9-0, $13.95
In "The Terror in Tibet," adventurous pilot (and widow) Athena Voltaire agrees to guide a group of British gentlemen on an expedition into the Himalayas. The time is the 1930s, and Nazis are on the rise in Germany. Athena soon finds out that the British are up to no good, nor are the Germans pursuing them. They're all after something in a remote monastery halfway up Mount Everest, and she decides to prevent anyone from succeeding. In "The Wrath from the Tomb," Dracula's daughter seeks revenge against the men who killed her father; she makes a mistake when she sends men to attack Athena's Arizona ranch. Teens who love the

Indiana Jones and Mummy movies will enjoy Athena's adventures. The violence level is about the same as those movies, although the scene in which the vampire is run through with a spear might bother more sensitive readers.

The stories originally appeared as webcomics, and the series was nominated for the first Eisner Award for Best Digital Comic in 2005

The Dark Horse Book of Witchcraft
Dark Horse Comics 2004 96p. Illustration
Grades: 9 10 11 12 Adult   **Fic; 741.5**
1. Hellboy (Fictional character); 2. Horror graphic novels; 3. Witchcraft; 4. Graphic novels
1-59307-108-6, $14.95
This anthology conjures up eight tales of horror and magic. Mignola presents a Hellboy story; Thompson and Dorkin return to the dog characters they created in "Stray" from a previous anthology volumes. Morse presents an evocative and carefully researched tale of old Salem, digging into the madness of the accusations leveled there, which ended more than thirty lives in a few short months. The book reprints a classic Clark Ashton Smith story, "Mother of Toads," illustrated by Gary Gianni, and more. There's some strong language and some graphic images of horror and violence.

The Dark House Book of the Dead
Dark Horse Books 2005 96p. Illustration
Grades: 10 11 12 Adult   **741.5; Fic**
1. Ghosts; 2. Hellboy (Fictional character); 3. Horror graphic novels; 4. Graphic novels
1-59307-281-3, $14.95
Mike Mignola presents a Hellboy yarn combining Shakespeare and graverobbing. Also returning this volume are Jill Thompson and her collaborator Evan Dorkin with another occult canine adventure. New additions for this volume include Goon creator Eric Powell, artist Guy Davis, and the artist who spent the last twenty years making superhero comics more scary, Kelley Jones. Cover artist Gary Gianni also returns, "Old Garfield's Heart" by Conan creator Robert E. Howard. Some stories have graphically violent or nude illustrations.

The Dark House Book of Hauntings
Dark Horse Books 2003 96p. Illustration
Grades: 9 10 11 12 Adult   **741.5; Fic**
1. Ghosts; 2. Hellboy (Fictional character); 3. Horror graphic novels; 4. Graphic novels
1-56971-958-6, $14.95
This book includes Mike Mignola's only new Hellboy adventure in 2003, in which Hellboy investigates a haunted house and discovers his own unexpected connection to the spirits within. P. Craig Russell adapts Mike Richardson's story about a child who leads friends and family into an abandoned house, and Paul Chadwick and his longtime Concrete editor Randy Stradley team up for a creepy short about a haunted suit. Jill Thompson and Evan Dorkin recount the legend of a haunted doghouse in "Strays." The Victorian ghost story "Thurnley Abbey" is illustrated by Gary Gianni. The book includes an interview with real-life seance medium L.L. Dreller, plus a new Devil's Footprints story and contributions from international artists Uli

Oesterle (Germany) and Lucas Maragnon (Mexico). The stories and art are spooky with very little graphic violence.

David, Peter
Fallen Angel: Down to Earth. Art by David Lopez. DC Comics 2007 136p. Illustration
Grades: 12 Adult   **741.5; Fic**
1. Superhero graphic novels; 2. Supernatural graphic novels; 3. Graphic novels
978-1-4012-1268-1, $14.99
Bete Noir is a quiet, almost mundane city by day; but by night it becomes a haven for crime, corruption, and the supernatural. Enter the Fallen Angel, a mysterious and powerful woman who aids people in need when they find themselves at a crossroads in their lives. If she deems a person worthy, she can be a savior; if she doesn't, that person won't live to tell the tale. In this volume, the Angel's nemesis, Black Mariah, has returned to town, and this time she's hunting the Angel. The book includes nudity, sexual situations, foul language, and violence.

Friendly Neighborhood Spider-Man Vol. 1: Derailed. Writer, Peter David ; pencils, Mike Wieringo & Roger Cruz ; inks, Karl Kesel ... [et al.] ; colors, Paul Mounts & Chris Sotomayor. Marvel Entertainment 2006 Un Illustration
Grades: 7 8 9 10 11 12 Adult   **741.5; Fic**
1. Spider-Man (Fictional character); 2. Superhero graphic novels; 3. Graphic novels
978-0-7851-2216-6, $14.99
A major character from Peter Parker's past returns, and it looks like Hobgoblin is terrorizing the skies again. Also, a woman chronicles Spider-Man's career on her blog, convinced that he has stalked her for her entire life.

I am Iron Man. Sean Chen, illustrator. Marvel Worldwide, Inc. 2010 Un Illustration
Grades: 7 8 9 10 11 12 Adult   **741.5; Fic**
1. Iron Man (Fictional character); 2. Superhero graphic novels; 3. Graphic novels
978-0-7851-4558-5, $16.99
The first Iron Man movie, released in 2008, was a major hit, but just like the other superhero movies based on Marvel Comics properties, it wasn't based on any particular Iron Man comics. This book collects a two-issue miniseries based on the movie script, written by Peter David with pencils by Sean Chen, a one-shot written by Christos Gage with pencils by Hugo Petrus, and Iron Man #200, which was written by Denny O'Neil with pencils by Mark Bright and originally published in 1985. David and Chen's comic adapts the movie script, hitting all the high points of the action. Gage and Petrus's one-shot, "Security Measures," looks at the action of the movie from the viewpoint of S.H.I.E.L.D. agent Coulson. Iron Man #200 features a battle between Iron Man and Iron Monger, who is Tony Stark's erstwhile partner Obadiah Stane. The book also includes an interview with Kevin Feige, producer of the Iron Man movie, and photos taken on the movie sets. The book actually cuts down on the amount of violence that was shown in the movie.

Marvel 1602: Fantastick Four. Art by Pascal Alixe. Marvel Entertainment 2007 Un Illustration
Grades: 9 10 11 12 Adult   **741.5; Fic**

1. Fantastic Four (Fictional characters); 2. Superhero graphic novels; 3. Graphic novels
978-0-7851-2293-7, $14.99

In the year 1602, Count Otto von Doom has an insidious plan that takes him - and the Four of the Fantastick - to the ends of the Earth. What does Doom want? Why doesn't Invisible Woman want to fight him? And what does Shakespeare have to do with it? This book spins off from Marvel 1602 written by Neil Gaiman.

Sachs & Violens. Art by George Perez. DC Comics 2006 126p. Illustration
Grades: 12 Adult · · · · · · · · · · · · · · · · · **741.5; Fic**
1. Mystery graphic novels; 2. Graphic novels
978-1-4012-1050-2, $7.99

The brutal killing of a young actress during the shooting of a snuff film sets soft core model Juanita Jean Sachs and photographer Ernie Schultz on a quest to discover those responsible. Their journey takes them from the mean streets of New York City to the back alleys of New Orleans, where they confront the utter depravity and corruption that defines the dark underbelly of American society. But they discover something else as well; something unexpected. Their destiny. This book includes considerable partial nudity, strong language, and graphic violence.

Davis, Eleanor
How to be happy. Eleanor Davis. Fantagraphics Books 2014 145 p. Illustration; Color
Grades: Adult · **741.5**
1. Comic books, strips, etc — United States; 2. Emotions; 3. Happiness
1606997408; 9781606997406, $24.99
LC 2013497415
Ignatz Award: Outstanding Anthology or Collection (2015)

This book by Eleanor Davis "is the artist's first collection of graphic/literary short stories. [H]er narratives . . . are at once compelling and elusive, pregnant with mystery and a deeply satisfying emotional resonance." (Publisher's note)

"What's most noticeable when the stories are laid up against one another is her varied visual approach, adapting her style to best fit the material. . . . The stories' subjects are equally diverse: a back-to-the-land cult falls apart under a despotic leader; a future dystopia lies on the verge of ecological collapse; a pair of youngsters explores an abandoned house; participants in an 'emotional boot camp' learn how to express grief." Booklist

Davis, Rob
The **Motherless** Oven. By Rob Davis. SelfMadeHero 2014 160 p. Illustration
Grades: 9 10 11 12 Adult · · · · · · · · · · · · · · **Fic; 741.5**
1. Death — Fiction; 2. Fantasy fiction; 3. Parent-child relationship — Fiction; 4. Graphic novels
190683881X; 9781906838812, $19.95
LC 2015296214

In this graphic novel, by Rob Davis, "parents don't make children—children make parents. Scarper's father is his pride and joy, a wind-powered brass construction with a billowing sail. His mother is a Bakelite hairdryer. In this world it rains knives, and household appliances have souls. There are also no birthdays—only deathdays. Scarper's deathday is just three weeks away, and he clings to the mundane repetition of his life at home and high school for comfort." (Publisher's note)

"Davis's dark and shadow-filled art appropriately mindbends and illuminates the text. The variation in panels quickens and pulls back the pace in this enigmatic tale, with the right amount of imagery left open for interpretation." SLJ

Davison, Al
The **Spiral** Cage: An Autobiography. DC Comics 2003 141p. Illustration
Grades: 11 12 Adult · · · · · · · · · · · · · · · · · · · **741.5**
1. Autobiographical graphic novels; 2. Davison, Al, 1960-; 3. Spina bifida; 4. Graphic novels
0-9740567-1-5, $12.95

Born with severe spina bifida, doctors considered Al Davison a hopeless case, condemned to the 'spiral cage' of his own DNA. In Al's own words and pictures, this book portrays his struggle to overcome 'disability' and the prejudice that surrounds it. The book includes lots of full frontal nudity, but it's not sexual, as Davison shows how he has to struggle physically every single day. The book also includes some strong language.

Davodeau, Etienne
★ The **initiates:** a comic artist and a wine artisan exchange jobs. Etienne Davodeau. NBM Pub. 2013 272 p.
Grades: Adult · · · · · · · · · · · · · · · · · **741.5/944; 741.5**
1. Wine and wine making; 2. Work
1561637033; 9781561637034, $29.99
LC 2012953818

This graphic novel, by Etienne Davodeau, "offers a look at the daily devotion to craft in two dissimilar professions. Etienne Davodeau is a comic artist . . ., Richard Leroy is a winemaker. . . . But filled with good will and curiosity, the two men exchange professions, and Étienne goes to work in Richard's vineyards and cellar, while Richard, in return, leaps into the world of comics . . ., ultimately revealing that their endeavors and aspirations are not much different." (Publisher's note)

"The excellent writing, characterizations, and tranquil-yet-stimulating vibe make this a treat to savor

Courtesy of NBM Publishing

slowly, like wine. Davodeau's smoky realism, though black-and-white, manages to suggest the full range of wine-growing climate shifts. ... Unfortunately, Davodeau is not as forthcoming about how he personally creates comics as Leroy is about the vintner's craft." LJ

Lulu anew. Étienne Davodeau; translation by Joe Johnson; lettering by Ortho. NBM Pub. 2015 160 p. Illustration
Grades: Adult   **741.5; Fic**
1. Life change events — Fiction; 2. Unemployment — Fiction
1561639729; 9781561639724, $27.99
LC 2014956688

In this novel by Etienne Davodeau "at the end of yet another unproductive job interview, Lulu, on a whim, takes off for the shore just to get away from it all. She's got a husband and kids left bewildered but it's nothing against them. This is just her time, getting away from the grind and with no other plan than savoring it. Surprised at her own temerity, she meets other people on the edge of the world. " (Publisher's note)

"Using a cinematic panel structure, Davodeau tightens or spreads out the width of each tier's panels to accommodate pauses, reflection, conflict, and action. A raucous party's kinetic action rat-a-tat-tats through smaller panels; wider panels are used to show wandering through the night, and the occasional full-page single panel drops the tempo to slow reflection and contemplation." Pub Wkly

The DC Comics Rarities Archives Volume 1
Edited by Dale Crain. DC Comics 2004 348p. Illustration
Grades: 7 8 9 10 11 12 Adult   **741.5; Fic**
1. Superhero graphic novels; 2. Graphic novels
1-4012-0007-8, $75

For the first time ever, in one huge collection, three of DC Comics' most hard to find early anthology titles are reprinted in their entirety. This is a 348-page hardcover collecting New York World's Fair 1939, New York World's Fair 1940 and Big All-American Comic Book #1 (1944). The two World's Fair Comics were specially created to be distributed at the legendary New York World's Fair of 1939-40 and feature adventures revolving around the DC heroes' visits there.

The DC Encyclopedia: The Definitive Guide to the Characters of the DC Universe
Dorling Kindersley. Edited by Alastair Dougall. 2006 351p. Illustration
Grades: 6 7 8 9 10 11 12 Adult   **741.5**
1. Batman (Fictional character); 2. Comic books, strips, etc — United States — History and criticism — Encyclopedias; 3. DC Comics — Encyclopedias; 4. Joker (Fictional character); 5. Superman (Fictional character); 6. Wonder Woman (Fictional character); 7. Graphic novels
978-0-7566-0592-6, $40.00
LC 2004-3379

This one-volume encyclopedia of more than 1,000 characters created by DC Comics, features some of DC's most creative artists and heroes and villains from the world famous - such as Superman, Batman, Wonder Woman, Lex Luthor, and Joker, to lesser known characters. This guide has comic book history exploding off every page.

DC's Greatest Imaginary Stories
Otto Binder [and others], writers ; C.C. Beck [and others], pencillers and inkers. DC Comics 2005 192p. Illustration
Grades: 6 7 8 9 10 11 12 Adult   **Fic; 741.5**
1. Batman (Fictional character); 2. Flash (Fictional character); 3. Superhero graphic novels; 4. Superman (Fictional character); 5. Graphic novels
1-4012-0534-8, $19.99

This volume collects eleven stories that are totally imaginary about many of DC's heroes: Superman marries Lois Lane; in another story, he marries Lana Lang; and in yet another story, he marries Lori Lemaris the mermaid. Batman abandons his millions to drive a taxi. The Flash races into action maskless. Superman and Batman are brothers. In the wedding of the century, it's Super girl and ... Jimmy Olsen" And Shazam witnesses atomic bomb and attacks and finds that even he, the World's Mightiest Mortal, can't stop the bombs.

De Heer, Margreet
Philosophy- a discovery in comics: A discovery in comics. Margreet de Heer. NBM Pub. 2012 120 p.
Grades: 11 12 Adult   **100.022/2; 100.022; 741.5**
1. Philosophy; 2. Philosophy — History
1561636983; 9781561636983, $16.99
LC 2012938931

This book, by Margreet de Heer, offers an "illustrated primer on philosophy. . . . Margreet de Heer visualizes the history of Western philosophy and makes it approachable for those with little knowledge of the subject. The book explains the thoughts of philosophers such as Socrates, Plato, Aristotle, Descartes, Spinoza, and Nietzsche, and ponders questions such as 'What is thinking?' 'What is reality?' 'Is there free will?' and 'Why are these ideas still important?'" (Publisher's note)

De Radiguès, Max
Moose. Max de Radiguès. Conundrum International 2015 160 p. Illustration
Grades: 10 11 12 Adult   **Fic; 741.5**
1. Bullies; 2. Children of gay parents — Fiction
1894994930;
9781894994934, $17

In this graphic novel, by Max De Radigues, "Meet Joe, an average, quiet high school student who is being bullied relentlessly by classmate Jason. No longer able to ride the bus, Joe walks to school every day through the woods finding comfort in Mother Nature. On his way to school, Joe sees a moose, a poignant encounter that helps distract him from the daily indignities. The story

Courtesy of Conundrum International

continues through many days of continual abuse, slowly revealing more about Joe's life." (Library Journal)

DeAngelis, Jason

No Man's Land Vol. 1. Art by Jennyson Rosero. Seven Seas Entertainment 2006 192p. Illustration

Grades: 10 11 12 Adult   **741.5; Fic**

1. Horror graphic novels; 2. Western graphic novels; 3. Graphic novels

1-933164-07-7, $10.99

John Parker had it all. A decorated sharpshooter in the Civil War, he had a promising career ahead of him, a beautiful wife, and a newborn son. But after becoming embroiled in a dark and demonic conspiracy engineered by the Bakerton Detective Agency, he lost everything. Fleeing to the West, a broken man, Parker reinvents himself as No Man," a heartless gun-for-hire whose only solace comes from hunting and killing the demons who he helped set loose. With Buntline Special in hand, a deadly revolver with a sixteen inch barrel, he blasts his way through a different kind of Old West, where strange and evil beings lurk. The book includes lots of violence and some strong language. This is a global manga title.

DeConnick, Kelly Sue

Bitch Planet; Volume 1: Extraordinary Machine. By Kelly Sue DeConnick and Valentine De Landro. Image Comics 2015 136 p. Color; Illustration

Grades: Adult   **Fic; 741.5**

1. Prisoners — Fiction; 2. Science fiction graphic novels; 3. Women — Fiction

1632153661; 9781632153661, $9.99; 9780606378147; 0606378146

This graphic novel, by Kelly Sue DeConnick and Valentine De Landro, is a "riff on women-in-prison sci-fi exploitation. In a future just a few years down the road in the wrong direction, a woman's failure to comply with her patriarchal overlords will result in exile to the meanest penal planet in the galaxy. When the newest crop of fresh femmes arrive, can they work together to stay alive or will hidden agendas, crooked guards, and the deadliest sport on (or off!) Earth take them to their maker?" (Publisher's note)

"Though this sounds like it could get exploitative, DeConnick and De Landro never miss an opportunity to shine a light on sexism, revealing tender backstories for the characters and showcasing the ugly language of the men in power. De Landro expertly uses color to heighten the mood—noxious greens and yellows subtly highlight moments of sexist rhetoric, while the prisoners are rendered in warmer, more realistic tones." Booklist

Book 1 originally published in magazine form as Bitch Planet #1-5.

Captain Marvel; 1: in pursuit of flight. By Kelly Sue Deconnick; illustrated by Dexter Soy and Emma Rios. Marvel Worldwide 2013 136 p. Color; Illustration

Grades: 10 11 12 Adult   **741.5**

1. Female superhero graphic novels; 2. Superheroes — Fiction

0785165495; 9780785165491, $14.99

In this graphic novel by Kelly Sue Deconnick, illustrated by Dexter Soy and Emma Rios, "Carol Danvers has a new name, a new mission—and all the power she needs to make her own life a living hell. As the new Captain Marvel, Carol is forging from a challenge from her past! It's a firefight in the sky as the Banshee Squadron debut - but who are the Prowlers, and where has Carol seen them before? And how does secret NASA training program Mercury 13 fit in?" (Publisher's note)

Captain Marvel; Volume 2: Down. By Kelly Sue Deconnick and Christopher Sebela; illustrated by Dexter Soy and Filipe Andrade. Marvel Worldwide 2013 136 p. Color; Illustration

Grades: 10 11 12 Adult   **741.5**

1. Captain Marvel (Fictional character); 2. Superhero graphic novels

0785165509; 9780785165507, $14.99

In this graphic novel, by Kelly Sue Deconnick and Christopher Sebela, illustrated by Dexter Soy and Filipe Andrade, "Captain Marvel goes head to head with . . . Captain Marvel" Former Captain Monica Rambeau returns, but what's her problem with Earth's new Mightiest Hero" What threat is lurking below the ocean's surface" And can both Captain Marvels stop it before they get ship wrecked?" (Publisher's note)

Contains material originally published in magazine form as Captain Marvel #7-12—t.p. verso.

Pretty deadly; Vol. 1: The shrike. Kelly Sue Deconnick; illustrated by Emma Rios, Jordie Bellaire, Clayton Cowles. Image Comics 2014 120 p. Color; Illustration

Grades: 9 10 11 12 Adult   **741.5**

1. Death; 2. Women — Fiction

1607069628; 9781607069621, $9.99

In this graphic novel by Kelly Sue Deconnick, "Death's daughter rides the wind on a horse made of smoke and her face bears the skull marks of her father. Her origin story is a tale of retribution as beautifully lush as it is unflinchingly savage." (Publisher's note)

Volume 1 of an ongoing series

DeFalco, Tom

The **Amazing** Spider-Girl: Whatever Happened to the Daughter of Spider-Man?. Illustrated by Ron Frenz. Marvel Entertainment 2007 Un Illustration

Grades: 7 8 9 10 11 12 Adult   **741.5; Fic**

1. Spider-Girl (Fictional character); 2. Spider-Man (Fictional character); 3. Superhero graphic novels; 4. Graphic novels

978-0-7851-2341-5, $14.99

After discovering she had inherited her father's incredible powers, May "Mayday" Parker donned a costume and became the amazing Spider-Girl. Recent events have forced her to hang up her webs and lead a normal life ... but how long can May keep from web-slinging when there are villains like Hobgoblin on the loose? This volume begins collecting the second run of Spider-Girl comics; the first 100 issues were published as Spider-Girl and are being collected in digest-sized trade paperbacks. This new series, The Amazing Spider-Girl, features new numbering (from #1 and on) and is being collected in regular comic book-sized trade paperbacks.

DeForge, Michael
   Very Casual. Michael DeForge. Koyama Press 2013 152 p. Illustration; Color
Grades: Adult
741.5
   1. Comic books, strips, etc — Canada; 2. Fantasy graphic novels
0987963074; 9780987963079, $15
   LC 2013464167
Ignatz Award: Outstanding Anthology or Collection (2013)

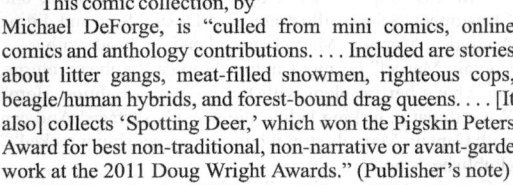

Courtesy of Koyama Press

   This comic collection, by Michael DeForge, is "culled from mini comics, online comics and anthology contributions. . . . Included are stories about litter gangs, meat-filled snowmen, righteous cops, beagle/human hybrids, and forest-bound drag queens. . . . [It also] collects 'Spotting Deer,' which won the Pigskin Peters Award for best non-traditional, non-narrative or avant-garde work at the 2011 Doug Wright Awards." (Publisher's note)
   "While often willfully unsettling, DeForge's work resonates on many levels." Pub Wkly

Delano, Jamie
   John Constantine, Hellblazer: original sins. Jamie Delano, John Ridgway, Alfredo Alcala, Rick Veitch, Tom Mandrake. DC Comics 2012 287 p. Color illustration
Grades: Adult   **741.5/973; 741.5**
   1. Superhero comic books, strips, etc
1401230067; 9781401230067, $19.99
   LC 2012021662
   This comic book, by Jamie Delano, John Ridgway, Alfredo Alcala, Rick Veitch, and Tom Mandrake, "is the first of a series of new HELLBLAZER editions starring Vertigo's longest running antihero, John Constantine, England's chain-smoking, low-rent magus. This first collection is a loosely connected series of tales of John's early years where Constantine was at his best and at his worst, all at the same time." (Publisher's note)
   Originally published in single magazine form as John Constantine, Hellblazer 1-9 and Swamp Thing 76-77.
   Volume 1 of an ongoing series

   Outlaw Nation. Art by Goran Sudzuka and Goran Parlov. Image Comics 2006 458p. Illustration
Grades: 12 Adult   **741.5; Fic**
   1. Adventure graphic novels; 2. Revenge; 3. Graphic novels
978-1-58240-707-4, $15.99
   Story Johnson, a hundred-year-old semi-deranged amnesiac pulp fiction-writer returns home from 25 years MIA in Vietnam. All Story wants is to recover his missing time and catch up with some legendary, larger-than-life Johnson Family members. Trouble is, a lot of cousins have "disappeared," and those that are left have put the blame on him. This story is full of graphic violence, very strong language, nudity, and sexual situations.

Delisle, Guy
   Burma chronicles. Drawn & Quarterly 2008 262p. Illustration
Grades: Adult   **741.5; 959.1**
   1. Myanmar — Politics and government; 2. Myanmar — Social conditions
978-1-897299-50-0, $19.95
   "Delisle follows accounts of sojourns in North Korea (Pyongyang, 2005) and China (Shenzhen, 2006) by chronicling a stint in yet another authoritarian society, Burma, to which he accompanied his wife, a Doctors without Borders administrator, to care for their infant son. He again uses wryly simple cartooning to amusingly recount his culture shock, much of which again stemmed from the host society's repressiveness, replete with censorship, Internet surveillance, and travel restrictions." (Booklist)

   Jerusalem: chronicles from the Holy City. Guy Delisle; coloured by Lucie Firoud and Guy Delisle; translated from the French by Helge Dascher. Drawn & Quarterly 2012 336 p. Illustration; Color
Grades: Adult   **915.694**
   1. Israel — Social conditions; 2. Israel-Arab conflicts; 3. Jerusalem — Description; 4. Muslims — Israel; 5. Graphic novels
1770460713; 9781770460713, $24.95
   In this graphic novel, "Guy Delisle . . . lays . . . a cultural road map of contemporary Jerusalem, utilizing the . . . stranger in a strange land point of view. . . . He . . . examines the impact of the conflict on the lives of people on both sides of the wall while . . . recounting the quotidian: checkpoints, traffic jams, and holidays, . . . observing the Christian, Jewish, and Muslim populations that call Jerusalem home." (Publisher's note)

   ★ **Pyongyang:** a journey in North Korea. Translated by Helge Dascher. Drawn & Quarterly 2005 176p. Illustration; Map
Grades: 11 12 Adult   **951.93; 741; 741.5**
   1. Korea (North); 2. Graphic novels
1-896597-89-0; 1-897299-21-4 (pa), $14.95
   This book "documents the two months French animator Delisle spent overseeing cartoon production in North Korea. . . . He records everything from the omnipresent statues and portraits of dictators Kim Il-Sung and Kim Jong-Il to the brainwashed obedience of the citizens." Booklist
   "Pyongyang will appeal to multiple audiences: current events buffs, Persepolis fans and those who just love a good yarn." Publ Wkly

   Shenzhen: A Travelogue from China. Drawn & Quarterly 2006 148p. Illustration
Grades: 10 11 12 Adult   **741.5**
   1. Autobiographical graphic novels; 2. Graphic novels
1-896597-79-1, $19.95
   Shenzhen details Guy Delisle's observations of life in a cold urban city in southern China in 1997 that is sealed off from the rest of the country by electric fences and armed guards. With a dry wit and a clean line, Delisle makes the most of his time spent in Asia overseeing outsourced production for a French animation company. By translating his fish-out-of-water experiences into graphic novels, Delisle is quick to find the humor and point out the differences between Western and Eastern cultures. Yet he

never forgets to relay his compassion for the simple freedoms that escape his colleagues by virtue of living in a Communist state. Delisle uses the occasional "s-word."

User's guide to neglectful parenting. Guy Delisle; translation by Helge Dascher. Drawn & Quarterly 2013 190 p. Illustration

Grades: Adult **306.874/2; 306.874**
1. Fatherhood; 2. Parenting; 3. Parenting; 4. Graphic novels
1770461175; 9781770461178, $12.95

LC 2013414780

In this book, by Guy Delisle, translated by Helge Dascher, "Quick, light vignettes play on the worries and cares any young parent might have, and offer wry solutions to the petty frustrations of being a dad who works from home." (Publisher's note)

Other titles in this series are: Even more bad parenting advice (2014); The owner's manual to terrible parenting (2015)

DeMatteis, J. M.
★ The **stardust** kid. Boom! created by J. M. DeMatteis, writer & Mike Ploog, illustrator ; Nick Bell & Sumi Pak, color ; Dave Lanphear, lettering. Studios 2008 Un Illustration

Grades: 3 4 5 6 7 8 9 10 11 12 Adult **741.5; Fic**
1. Adventure graphic novels; 2. Fantasy graphic novels; 3. Graphic novels
978-1-934506-04-2, $14.99

Twelve-year-old Cody's best friend is Paul Brightfield; they share a deep bond that goes far beyond mere friendship. What no one else knows is that Paul isn't human, he's one of the last Old Ones, ancient elemental beings who lived before man existed. One night, Paul disappears, and a hate-filled creature who has existed long buried beneath Wilde Park bursts out with a desire to destroy everything in the world. Only Cody, his little sister K.M., and his friend Alana and her little brother Nathaniel, remain, and somehow they must find The Stardust Kid and discover a way to stop the hate and restore their world. Some creatures might be frightening to younger readers, but anyone who likes the Harry Potter books shouldn't have a problem with this book.

Denson, Abby
Tough Love: High School Confidential. Manic D Press 2006 144p. Illustration

Grades: 8 9 10 11 12 Adult **741.5; Fic**
1. Homosexuality; 2. Romance graphic novels; 3. Graphic novels
978-1-933149-08-0, $12.95

In this sweet teen romance graphic novel, shy Brian discovers he loves martial artist Chris, but also develops a supportive friendship with Julie, the first person he's ever told that he's gay. Denson was inspired by shonen-ai (boy love) manga to do an American comic depicting a positive, healthy relationship between two teen boys who accept what they are. The story was originally serialized in XY magazine. The boys are shown hugging and kissing, but that is all.

Desberg, Stephen
The **Scorpion:** the devil's mark. Art by Enrico Merini. Cinebook Ltd. 2008 96p. Illustration

Grades: 10 11 12 Adult **741.5; Fic**
1. Adventure graphic novels; 2. Rome — History; 3. Graphic novels
978-1-905460-62-5, $19.95

In Rome of the Renaissance, a young thief called the Scorpion makes a living by unearthing relics in the depths of the Roman Catacombs, which he then sells at high prices to princes, nobles, and bishops. Then Cardinal Trebaldi declares the Scorpion must die. Trebaldi is part of a group called the Nine Families, who made a pact to rule the world back in the time of the Caesars; he has now organized an army of warrior monks to carry out his will, and he has gained the approval of the Nine Families to assassinate the Pope so he can take over and rule Rome. Somehow, the Scorpion threatens that plan. Trebaldi sets a beautiful Egyptian poisoner on the Scorpion's trail, but they will both face betrayal and confront amazing truths. The book includes lots of blade fighting and sexual innuendo without any overt nudity or sexual content.

Di Filippo, Paul
Top 10: Beyond the Farthest Precinct. Art by Jerry Ordway. DC Comics/America's Best Comics 2006 Un Illustration

Grades: 10 11 12 Adult **741.5; Fic**
1. Mystery graphic novels; 2. Superhero graphic novels; 3. Graphic novels
978-1-4012-0991-9, $14.99

In Neopolis, a modern city populated exclusively by super beings, it takes a unique and powerful police force to protect and serve. The officers of Precinct 10, also known as Top Ten, encounter all manner of the super powered and the supernatural on a routine basis. It doesn't help matters when Captain Traynor (Jetman) is unceremoniously replaced. Now the officers must band together, overcome their personal squabbles, and get their city back on track, before it all comes tumbling down on their heads. The book includes some sexual situations.

Diaz Canales, Juan
Blacksad: Amarillo. Written by Juan Di?az Canales; illustrated by Juanjo Guarnido; translation by Katie LaBarbera and Neal Adams; lettering by Tom Orzechowski and Lois Buhalis. Dark Horse Books 2014 63 p. Color; Illustration

Grades: Adult **741.5**
1. Detectives — Fiction; 2. Murder — Fiction; 3. Nineteen fifties; 4. Nineteen fifties — Fiction
1616555254; 9781616555252, $17.99

LC 2015295612

In this book, written by Juan D?az Canales and illustrated by Juanjo Guarnido, "[detective John] Blacksad lands a side job driving a rich Texan's prized yellow Cadillac Eldorado across 1950s America, hitting the back roads from New Orleans to Tulsa. But before long, the car is stolen and Blacksad finds himself mixed up in another murder, with roughneck bikers, a shifty lawyer, one down-and-out Beat generation writer, and some sinister circus folk!" (Publisher's note)

"[W]hile the script is a solid Chandler-esque thriller, it's Guarnido's animation-influenced artwork that's the true draw here, with each panel rife with detail, color, and unforgettable character designs." Pub Wkly

★ **Blacksad**. Text [by] Juan Canales Díaz; illustrated [by] Juanjo Guarnido. Dark Horse 2010 184p. Color; Illustration
Grades: Adult   741.5
1. Mystery graphic novels; 2. Noir fiction; 3. Private investigators — Fiction
9781595823939, $29.99
Harvey Award: Best American Edition of Foreign Material (2011)
"This noir thriller set in 1950s America stars a cast of anthropomorphic animals, with the dirty-handed hero an impeccably trenchcoated black cat. John Blacksad is a sort of private investigator, and these three stories visit territory both familiar and unusual. Our hero's lost love is inexplicably murdered, a misinterpreted killing rocks a white supremacist movement, and a coterie of radical intelligentsia crosses agendas with a version of Commie-hunter Joe McCarthy." (Library Journal)
"All of this material is riveting, and Guarnido's artwork is atmospheric and full of indelibly captured characters—he's a true master of the form. Blacksad is a comics classic, and American readers are fortunate to have these first three in one volume." Pub Wkly

Blacksad: A Silent Hell. Writer, Juan Diaz Canales; artist, Juanjo Guarnido. Dark Horse 2012 108 p. Color illustration
Grades: Adult   Fic; 741.5
1. Mystery graphic novels; 2. Noir fiction; 3. Private investigators — Fiction
1595829318; 9781595829313, $19.99
"Detective John Blacksad returns, with a new case that takes him to a 1950s New Orleans filled with hot jazz and cold-blooded murder! Hired to discover the fate of a celebrated pianist, Blacksad finds his most dangerous mystery yet in the midst of drugs, voodoo, the rollicking atmosphere of Mardi Gras, and the dark underbelly that it hides!" (Publisher's note)
"If Walt Disney ever made an adult-themed, anthropomorphic Philip Marlowe movie, it might resemble this popular series. . . . Canales's plot is populated by a colorful mixture of Americana: burlesque houses, snake-oil merchants, Mardi Gras, and the haunted soul of the blues are all key elements in this vibrant, atmospheric noir mystery. The authentic local details of Guarnido's art are balanced by whimsical character design and humor." Pub Wkly

Diggle, Andy
John Constantine, Hellblazer: Lady Constantine. Goran Sudzuka, artist; Patricia Mulvihill, colorist; Robert Solanovic, letterer. DC Comics/Vertigo 2006 96p. Illustration
Grades: 11 12 Adult   741.5; Fic
1. Adventure graphic novels; 2. Horror graphic novels; 3. Graphic novels
978-1-4012-0942-1, $9.99
It's 1785 England, and Johanna Constantine is a young woman with a knack for the impossible, a taste for the good

life - and a knowledge of the dark arts. She accepts a dangerous assignment for king and country to retrieve a mysterious ancient chest, but hidden forces move against her, seeking the box for their own deadly purposes. The book includes nudity, sexual situations, strong language, considerable violence and horror.

The **Losers** Vol. 4: Close Quarters. Andy Diggle, writer; Jock, Ben Oliver, artists; Lee Loughridge, colorist; Clem Robins, letterer. DC Comics/Vertigo 2005 144p. Illustration
Grades: 10 11 12 Adult   741.5; Fic
1. Adventure graphic novels; 2. Graphic novels
1-4012-0719-7, $14.99
The Losers' pursuit of rogue C.I.A. mastermind Max has led them to London, where a potential trove of information on their quarry's financial dealings awaits them at the money-laundering offices of Cayman Credit Internationale ... provided they can get past the Company-sponsored welcoming committee. Following the money will only take them so far, though. To find out what all that cash is for, the Losers will need to head out to sea, and what they discover both above and below the waves will raise the stakes of this deadly game to a whole new level. The book includes harsh language, lots of action and some graphic violence.

The **Losers**: Ante Up. Andy Diggle, writer; Jock, artist & original series covers; Lee Loughridge, colorist; Clem Robins, letterer. DC Comics/Vertigo 2004 160p. Illustration
Grades: 10 11 12 Adult   Fic; 741.5
1. Adventure graphic novels; 2. Graphic novels
1-4012-0198-9, $9.95
An elite U.S. Special Forces unit is targeted for assassination when they unintentionally uncover the illegal and immoral practices of the C.I.A. Believed dead and with nothing to lose, the team of wet works operatives regroup and begin a mission of revenge against the organization that betrayed them. Only as the team goes after a corrupt oil conglomerate with ties to the C.I.A., do they truly begin to realize the depths of the conspiracy they have discovered and the impossible odds of survival that they face. The book includes lots of foul language and some fairly graphic violence.
Other volumes in this series are: Double down (2004); Trifecta (2005); Close quarters (2006); Endgame (2006)

The **Losers**: Endgame. Andy Diggle, writer; Jock, Colin Wilson, artists; Lee Loughridge, colorist; Clem Robins, letterer. DC Comics/Vertigo 2006 168p. Illustration
Grades: 11 12 Adult   741.5; Fic
1. Adventure graphic novels; 2. Spies; 3. Graphic novels
978-1-4012-1004-5, $14.99
The seemingly unstoppable C.I.A. mastermind Max is about to play his final hand, and he's sitting on a whole pile of aces. With a brand-new country under his feet and a nuclear arsenal within his reach, Max is going all in - and the stakes are nothing less than the global balance of power itself. As all the other players are folding, though, the Losers are still holding their cards, and they've got one last chance to raise the bet. But calling Max will cost them dearly, especially considering the joker they're about to be dealt. This book has lots of violence and copious use of foul language.

Silent Dragon. Writer, Andy Diggle; penciler, Leinil Yu; inkers, Gerry Alanguilan and Richard Friend; colors, Dave Stewart; letters, Jared K. Fletcher. DC Comics/Wildstorm 2006 Un Illustration
Grades: 10 11 12 Adult **741.5; Fic**
1. Adventure graphic novels; 2. Science fiction graphic novels; 3. Graphic novels
978-1-4012-1104-2, $19.99
Tokyo, A.D. 2063: the Yakuza warlord Hideaki has seized total control of Honshu's underworld while ruthlessly crushing all opposition. But his true dream is the overthrow of the government itself. Japan's hard-line military junta will do anything to stop him and they have found the ultimate pawn to set their plan in motion: Renjiro, the chief advisor to the notorious gangster. Caught between a lifetime of honor and loyalty to his Yakuza clan and the iron-fisted might of the military elite, Renjiro will find that the only way to stop a civil war and avoid total annihilation is to play both sides against the middle. The book includes partial nudity, strong language, and lots of bloody violence.

Dillon, Glyn
The **Nao** of Brown. Glyn Dillon. Self Made Hero 2012 206 p.
Grades: Adult **741.5**
1. Art — Fiction; 2. Japanese Americans — Fiction; 3. Meditation — Fiction; 4. Obsessive-compulsive disorder — Fiction
1906838429; 9781906838423, $24.95
In this novel by Glyn Dillon "Nao Brown, who's 'hafu' (half Japanese, half English), is . . . suffering from obsessive-compulsive disorder (OCD) and fighting violent urges to harm other people. . . . [But] she wants to get her design and illustration career off the ground; and she wants to find love, perfect love. . . . She also meets Gregory, an interesting washing-machine repairman, and Ray, an art teacher at the Buddhist Center. She begins to draw and meditate to ease her mind and open her heart." (Publisher's note)

Dini, Paul
The **World's** Greatest Super-Heroes. Stories by Alex Ross and Paul Dini ; text by Paul Dini ; art by Alex Ross ; lettering on JLA: liberty and justice by Todd Klein. DC Comics 2005 Un Illustration
Grades: 6 7 8 9 10 11 12 Adult **Fic; 741.5**
1. Batman (Fictional character); 2. Justice League (Fictional characters); 3. Superhero graphic novels; 4. Superman (Fictional character); 5. Wonder Woman (Fictional character); 6. Graphic novels
1-4012-0254-3, $49.95
LC 2006-159064
This oversize hardcover volume collects the stories that DC originally published separately. Superman tries to singlehandedly end world hunger, only to face suspicion and corruption; Batman tries to stop all criminal activity; and Wonder Woman tries to free oppressed women. They each realize that, despite their super powers, they can't eradicate the problems of the world on their own. The rest of the book portrays the Justice League and highlights each member's super hero origins.

Dirge, Roman
It ate Billy on Christmas; art by Steven Daily. Dark Horse Books 2007 Un Illustration
Grades: 4 5 6 7 8 9 10 11 12 Adult **741.5; Fic**
1. Horror graphic novels; 2. Humorous graphic novels; 3. Graphic novels
978-1-59307-853-9, $12.95
Lumi has been bullied by her brother Billy all her life, and this Christmas would have been more of the same, but for the weird, ugly little monster that crawled up from the abandoned well and came into their house. Mistaking it for the stuffed puppy she had requested from her parents, Lumi watches in amazement as it devours the bullying Billy when he shoots it with darts from his new dart gun. She makes a cardboard Billy, which fools her unsuspecting and clueless parents. A few weeks later, back at school, Lumi has to face the bullies who have made her school life miserable, but she has her "puppy" in her backpack and it's hungry. . . . Dirge wrote the story and drew the black and white illustrations, while Daily provided the color paintings. The story shows the monster eating Billy in one gulp, but there's little actual violence on the pages. The dark humor and twisted story line will appeal to those who enjoy Coraline and The Wolves in the Walls by Neil Gaiman, and the weird humor of Edward Gorey cartoons.

Lenore: Noogies. Slave Labor Graphics 1999 Un Illustration
Grades: 9 10 11 12 Adult **Fic; 741.5**
1. Horror graphic novels; 2. Humorous graphic novels; 3. Graphic novels
0-943151-03-1, $11.95
This book collects the first four issues of the Lenore comic book series. It ventures into the dark, surreal world of a little dead girl and features stories about limbless cannibals, clock monsters, cursed vampire dolls, taxidermied friends, an obsessed would be lover, and more fuzzy animal mutilations than should be legal. The book includes some disturbing images and macabre humor.
Other Lenore books are: Wedgies (2000); Cooties (2005); Swirlies (2012); Purple Nurples (2013)

Something at the Window is Scratching: Children's Tales for Disturbed Children. SLG Publishing 1998 120p. Illustration
Grades: 9 10 11 12 Adult **741.5; Fic**
1. Horror graphic novels; 2. Humorous graphic novels; 3. Graphic novels
0-943151-09-0, $9.95
Chilling, disturbing, sickly amusing poems accompanied by equally chilling, disturbing, and sickly amusing illustrations bring to mind a very morbid Shel Silverstein with more of a horror twist. In the title tale, what's scratching at the boy's window that night is the son of the Sandman, who died after sending the boy to sleep; in order to give the creature a home, the boy tapes a tail to the creature and presents his parents with their new cat. Despite the moody, dark tone, there is no violence or bad language.

Dixon, Chuck
The **Iron** Ghost. Art by Flint Henry and Sergio Cariello. Image Comics 2007 Un Illustration
Grades: 10 11 12 Adult **741.5; Fic**

1. Mystery graphic novels; 2. World War, 1939-1945; 3. Graphic novels
978-1-58240-727-2, $15.99

Berlin, Germany, 1945: The tide of the war has turned in favor of the Allies. The fall of the Nazi empire is inevitable, but there is still something even more dangerous than the ever approaching Allies to the Third Reich: The Iron Ghost, who is murdering officials in the Nazi regime. It's up to two non-Nazi German police officers to capture the Ghost. But once they discover the truth will they want to - or even be able to - stop him? The story includes harsh language and considerable violence.

Nightwing: On the Razor's Edge. Pencilled by Greg Land et al; inked by Drew Geraci et al. DC Comics 2005 192p. Illustration
Grades: 9 10 11 12 Adult   **741.5; Fic**
1. Mystery graphic novels; 2. Nightwing (Fictional character); 3. Superhero graphic novels; 4. Graphic novels
1-4012-0437-6, $14.99

Bludhaven has seen its share of battles between its costumed protector, Nightwing, and various criminals. But when an army of ninjas arrives, it's only a harbinger of the deadliest threat yet. Shrike, long thought dead, is back, and he wants revenge on his childhood pal, Nightwing. Shrike's current master, Blockbuster, would be only too happy to see the vigilante destroyed, but Shrike wants to see to Nightwing's destruction personally.

Robin, year one. DC Comics 2008 200p. Illustration
Grades: 9 10 11 12 Adult   **741.5; Fic**
1. Batman (Fictional character); 2. Robin (Fictional character); 3. Superhero graphic novels; 4. Graphic novels
978-1-563-89805-1, $14.99

This book takes readers back to Dick Grayson's first year working as Robin, sidekick of the Batman. After his family of aerialists was murdered, Bruce Wayne took in young Dick Grayson, who helped Wayne as Batman solve the murders. Adopted by Wayne, Dick starts training to become his partner in solving crimes on the streets of Gotham City; but not everyone likes it. Captain James Gordon of the Gotham City Police thinks Dick is much too young, and he puts Batman on notice that if anything happens to hurt or kill Robin, Batman will pay. At first, Dick/Robin can easily handle the bad guys. Then he ends up working solo on a case of girls who disappear when one of his friends from school goes missing, and he goes up against the Mad Hatter. Unknown to Robin, or Batman, Two-Face is watching the young crime-fighter's progress, and he decides to test the boy—brutally. When Two-Face beats Robin badly enough to put him into a hospital, Batman "retires" Robin; but when Dick is strong enough, he runs away to live on the streets. There, he encounters Shrike, a contract killer who trains teen boys in ninja-style fighting, and joins his "school," an organization that Dick realizes Batman doesn't know exists. The book includes strong violence.

The **Vanishers.** Illustrated by Andres Klacik. IDW Publishing 2002 80p. Illustration
Grades: 6 7 8 9 10 11 12 Adult   **741.5; Fic**
1. Adventure graphic novels; 2. Science fiction graphic novels; 3. Graphic novels
0-9712282-6-4, $12.99

From the turn of the 20th century, to medieval England, and into the far-flung future, Andy and Arvis must escape their pursuers, rescue their friends, and return to their own time. Andy's friends begin to disappear and only he remembers that they ever existed. When Andy discovers another student, Arvis Voltoz, has noticed that disappearances, he follows Arvis home and begins an adventure that takes him and Arvis through time.

Doctorow, Cory
★ **Cory** Doctorow's futuristic tales of the here and now. IDW Publishing 2008 152p. Illustration
Grades: 10 11 12 Adult   **741.5; Fic**
1. Science fiction graphic novels; 2. Short stories; 3. Graphic novels
978-1-60010-172-4, $24.99

Six short stories by noted young science fiction writer and BoingBoing.net coeditor Doctorow are adapted into the graphic format by various comics creators, including Dara Naraghi, Dan Taylor, J. C. Vaughn, James Anthony Kuhoric, Esteve Polls, Daniel Warner, Paul McCaffrey, Dustin Evans, Erich Owen, Robbie Robbins, Chris Mowry, and more. The stories include "Anda's Game," in which a twelve-year-old girl gets involved in a multi-player game in which she kills enemies and someone starts paying cash for her kills; "Craphound," in which a professional yard sale picker makes friends with one of the aliens who had come to Earth and wants to learn how to be a picker at yard sales; "After the Siege," in which Valentine and her family struggle to survive the disease turning the city's people into zombies as they try to get by during a siege; and "When Sysadmins Ruled the Earth," in which a global catastrophe destroys almost everything, except the computer techs holed up in various company buildings around the world. The stories include violence and some strong language.

Doran, Colleen
A **Distant** Soil Vol. 1: The Gathering. Image Comics 1997 Un Illustration
Grades: 10 11 12 Adult   **741.5; Fic**
1. Adventure graphic novels; 2. Fantasy graphic novels; 3. Graphic novels
1-887279-51-2, $19.95

This is the story of a young girl who is born the heir to an alien religious dynasty, one of comics' most lavish and romantic sagas. Liana and her brother Jason are orphaned and live in a research institution; they get caught up in interplanetary politics and magic. The book includes fantasy, epic scope, psychics, Arthurian legend, smart-mouthed punks, adorable gay couples, bizarre clothing, aliens, death, love, and heavy doses of humor.

A **Distant** Soil Vol. 2: The Ascendant. Image Comics 2000 Un Illustration
Grades: 10 11 12 Adult   **741.5; Fic**
1. Adventure graphic novels; 2. Fantasy graphic novels; 3. Graphic novels
1-58240-018-0, $18.95

Liana was born the heir to an alien religious dynasty, then hidden on Earth until Rieken found her and brought her back. But the galaxy's most powerful psionic, the Avatar, already sits on the throne. Revolutionary forces on the planet have taken Jason, however, and intend to turn him into one of their weapons against the throne. Things continue to become more complicated when Jason learns his father started the Resistance movement on Ovanan, and Liana learns that Rieken is actually Seren, the Avatar, and she's a danger to him. Dangerous politics swirl around everyone. The book includes sexual suggestiveness and violence.

A **Distant** Soil Vol. 3: Aria. Image Comics 2001 Un Illustration
Grades: 11 12 Adult   **741.5; Fic**
1. Adventure graphic novels; 2. Fantasy graphic novels; 3. Graphic novels
1-58240-201-9, $16.95
Rieken/Seren is the target of assassins, a pawn in a dangerous game of powerful psionics, and he makes a desperate play for freedom. But his ploy threatens to capture him in his own web of deceit, as his darkest secrets are revealed to allies and enemies alike, leading to a showdown with deadly consequences. And Liana, with powers of the Avatar, and Jason, are caught in the middle. The book includes lots of sexual situations, including same-sex relations, harsh language (including f-bombs), and violence.

A **Distant** Soil Vol. 4: Coda. Image Comics 2005 Un Illustration
Grades: 11 12 Adult   **741.5; Fic**
1. Adventure graphic novels; 2. Fantasy graphic novels; 3. Graphic novels
1-58240-478-X, $17.99
Liana is born the heir to an alien religious dynasty. Possessing the power to destroy worlds with her mind, Liana is under an assassination order from the government of her father's home world. A foiled coup attempt results in a power vacuum that leaves the alien world without its treasure weapon. The aliens have no choice but to take Liana as their reluctant new Avatar. Only an angry slave and a small group of resistance fighters can free her - and the universe - from the dangers of her power. The book includes some strong language, nudity, and violence.

Dorff, Matt
The **Book** of revelation. Matt Dorff; illustrated by Chris Koelle. Zondervan 2013 187 p. Illustration
Grades: Adult   **228.0022**
1. Bible stories; 2. Good and evil; 3. Revelation
0310421403; 9780310421405, $19.99
        LC 2012941745
This book is a graphic novel adaptation of the Bible's book of Revelation translated by Mark B. Arey and Philemon D. Sevastiades, adapted by Matt Dorff, and illustrated by Chirs Koelle. "Stand in the Apostle John's sandals and watch the New Testament's climactic war between good and evil unfold. . . . See the Lamb, the Seven-Headed Dragon, and the Beast . . . Discover anew the story of the ultimate fulfillment of John's faith as the final battle is fought between God and Satan." (Publisher's note)
Translated from the Greek by Fr. Mark Abey and Fr. Philemon Sevastiades.

Dorkin, Evan
★ **Beasts** of Burden: animal rites. Written by Evan Dorkin; art by Jill Thompson; lettering by Jason Arthur and Jill Thompson. Dark Horse Comics 2010 184p. Illustration
Grades: 8 9 10 11 12 Adult   **741.5; Fic**
1. Cats; 2. Dogs; 3. Mystery graphic novels; 4. Supernatural graphic novels; 5. Graphic novels
978-1-59582-513-1, $19.99
2010 Eisner Award for Best Publication for Teens; 2010 Eisner Award to Jill Thompson for Best Painter/Multimedia Artist for Beasts of Burden and Magic Trixie; 2005 Eisner Award for Best Short Story for 'Unfamiliar;' 2004 Eisner Award to Jill Thompson for Best Painter/Multimedia Artist (interior art) for 'Stray.'
Burden Hill is just a nice, quiet suburban town full of houses with yards and white picket fences, demonic frogs, zombie roadkill, ghosts, etc. The humans who live in Burden Hill seem to be totally oblivious to the dangers, but the dogs, and one cat, work together to keep their town safe. Jack the beagle, Pugsley (go figure), Ace the husky, Rex the Doberman, Whitey the terrier, and Orphan the cat deal with a haunted dog house, witches, undead dogs, a werewolf, and other monsters. The book includes some mild bad language (—crap" usually from Pugs) and a fair amount of violence. This book includes the four-issue miniseries plus all of the short stories that originally appeared in The Dark Horse Book of Hauntings, The Dark Horse Book of Witchcraft, The Dark Horse Book of the Dead, and The Dark Horse Book of Monsters. Sarah Dyer co-wrote "A Dog and His Boy" with Evan Dorkin.
"Gorgeous artwork and a smart, witty script elevate this tale of household pets who unite to fight occult menaces in idyllic Burden Hill." Publ Wkly

Bill & Ted's Most Excellent Adventures Volume Two. Amaze Ink/SLG Publishing 2005 Un Illustration
Grades: 9 10 11 12 Adult   **741.5; Fic**
1. Humorous graphic novels; 2. Graphic novels
1-59362-002-0, $13.95
The silly and fun movies "Bill and Ted's Excellent Adventure" and its sequel, "Bill and Ted's Bogus Journey" inspired a Marvel Comics series in the early 1990s. Written by Evan Dorkin, it was nominated for an Eisner Award. This second volume finds the two time-hopping headbangers on the run from a gang from Hell, on trial for tampering with time, and stuck on a planet of superheroes. There's also an invasion of inter-dimensional Bills and Teds, a pink-slipped Death, and a bogus attempt to prevent Lincoln's assassination.

Doucet, Julie
365 days: a diary by Julie Doucet. Drawn & Quarterly 2008 360p. Illustration
Grades: 12 Adult   **741.5**
1. Art; 2. Autobiographical graphic novels; 3. Graphic novels
978-1-89729-915-9; 1-89729-915-X
Doucet renounced her comics-centric lifestyle five years ago and focused on art, but the journal she started in late 2002 combines comics with art with text. Her personal narrative combines with collage, doodles, and comics panels to chronicle her life as she became part of a broader arts

community. The book includes some harsh language, and one panel towards the end depicts an image combining nudity with a disturbing sexual situation.

Doxiadis, Apostolos
★   Logicomix.
[written by] Apostolos
Doxiadis, Christos H.
Papadimitriou; art, Alecos
Papadatos; color, Annie Di
Donna. Bloomsbury 2009
347p. Illustration
Grades: 11 12 Adult
741.5; Fic
1. Biographical graphic
novels; 2. Essayists; 3.
Logicians;   4.
Mathematicians;   5.
Mathematics; 6. Nobel
laureates for literature;
7. Nonfiction writers; 8.
Philosophers; 9. Philosophy; 10. Russell, Bertrand, 1872-1970 — Fiction; 12. Graphic novels
0-7475-9720-0, $22.95; 978-0-7475-9720-9

Courtesy of Bloomsbury

This is a "graphic novel based on the life of the philosopher and mathematician Bertrand Russell." (Publisher's note)

Drake, Arnold
It Rhymes with Lust. Illustrations by Matt Baker and Ray Osrin. Dark Horse Books 2007 136p. Illustration
Grades: 10 11 12 Adult   **741.5; Fic**
1. Mystery graphic novels; 2. Graphic novels
978-1-59307-728-0, $14.95

In 1950, writers Arnold Drake and Leslie Waller, both attending college on the G.I. Bill, envisioned a sophisticated, novel-length comic tailored to their peers. Collaborating with comic art master Matt Baker, known for singularly defining the genre of "good girl art" on titles such as Phantom Lady, they crafted a film-noir inspired masterwork of romance, intrigue, and moral relativity. When cynical newspaperman Hal Weber reunites with old flame Rust Masson, he finds the beguiling widow of a mining magnate willing to do anything to undermine the local political machine - her only opponent for total control of Copper City. This is a "replica edition" of the "picture novel" (as Drake called it); it will appeal most to adults, but there's little in the way of harsh language or any sexual content, and the violence is not graphically portrayed.

Drooker, Eric
Blood song: a silent ballad. Introduction by Joe Sacco. Dark Horse 2009 Un Illustration
Grades: 11 12 Adult   **741.5**
1. Stories without words; 2. Graphic novels
978-1-59582-389-2, $19.95

"Driven by war from their rural home in Southeast Asia, a young woman and her dog ride the ocean currents to a city in the West. A deeply moving graphic novel, masterfully done." SLJ
First published 2002 by Harcourt

Dryer, Matt
Dwight T. Albatross's The Goon Noir. Dark Horse Comics 2007 Illustration
Grades: 11 12 Adult   **741.5; Fic**
1. Horror graphic novels; 2. Humorous graphic novels; 3. Graphic novels
978-1-59307-785-3, $12.95

The horror comedy series has been described as "EC by way of Looney Tunes," so it seems fitting that comedians and horror creators put their own spin on the Goon characters. Among the distinguished creators featured in this, the very first Goon anthology, are comedians Patton Oswalt and Brian Posehn (both of Comedy Central's Comedians of Comedy and Mr. Show), Reno: 911 co-creator Thomas Lennon, B.P.R.D. scribe John Arcudi, comics great Kevin Nowlan (Tomorrow Stories, Sandman, Superman), fan-favorite Humberto Ramos (Revelations, Spider-Man), Steve Niles, Ryan Sook, Mike Ploog, Bill Morrison, Arvid Nelson, Tony Moore, Hilary Barta, Roger Langridge, Scott Allie and Todd Herman. Powell himself and frequent co-conspirators Tom Sniegoski and Mark Farmer also present the three-part "Peg Leg Full of Heaven," featuring the Little Unholy Bastards, and erstwhile publisher Dwight T. Albatross contributes a little somethin' for the ladies. Readers can expect to find zombies, monster-smashing, some gore, a little harsh language, quite a bit of sexual suggestiveness, and lots of slightly sick humor.

Duffield, Paul
Freakangels 1; Volume
1. Story Warren Ellis;
artwork Paul Duffield.
Avatar Press 2008 144 p.
Grades: 10 11 12 Adult

1. Apocalyptic fiction; 2.
Dystopian fiction; 3.
Psychic ability; 4. Science
fiction graphic novels; 5.
Youth — England —
London
1592910564;
9781592910564, $19.99
"Twenty-three years
ago, twelve strange children
were born in England at

Courtesy of Avatar Press

exactly the same moment. Six years ago, the world ended. Today, eleven strange 23-year-olds live in and defend Whitechapel, maybe the last real settlement in flooded London. When a dazed, gun-toting girl appears on the outskirts with a deadly grudge against the self-proclaimed Freakangels, the kids realize that an old enemy is still alive beyond the safety of their borders... a twelfth psychic child, evil and exiled, who can program human minds to hate, and send his private, pirate armies into Whitechapel for revenge." (Publisher's note)
Volume 1 of 6

Duggan, Gerry
The **infinite** horizon. Written by Gerry Duggan; art by Phil Noto; lettering by Ed Dukeshire. Image Comics 2012 175 p. Color illustration

Grades: Adult   **Fic; 741.5/973; 741.5**
1. Adventure graphic novels; 2. Apocalyptic fiction; 3. Science fiction graphic novels
1582409722; 9781582409726, $17.99

This graphic novel, by Gerry Duggan, is a post-apocalyptic science fiction story. "The Eisner-nominated series inspired by The Odyssey is finally completed and collected. The Soldier With No Name survived years of war only to be stranded halfway across the globe when the conflict ended. Getting home means going through the hell: escaping shipwrecks, beating a vicious opponent wearing a cycloptic combat armor, and resisting the siren's call of a predatory society." (Publisher's note)

The **Last** Christmas. Gerry Duggan and Brian Posehn; art by Rick Remender. Image Comics 2006 Un Illustration
Grades: 11 12 Adult   **741.5; Fic**
1. Adventure graphic novels; 2. Horror graphic novels; 3. Humorous graphic novels; 4. Santa Claus; 5. Graphic novels
978-1-58240-676-3, $14.99

After the apocalypse, no one is safe; not even at the North Pole. After marauders kill Mrs. Claus, Santa withdraws from life and turns his back on Christmas. When he finally emerges from seclusion, the old world is gone forever, and as Santa struggles to find his way in a post-apocalyptic world, can he find a way to save Christmas too" This Christmas story is for all those who love horror movies (especially with killer zombies) and action movies with lots of shooting and killing of bad guys while yelling curses.

Dumas, Alexandre
The **Count** of Monte Cristo. Wordsmith, R. Jay Nudds ; illustrator, Sankha Banerjee. Campfire 2012 111 p.
Grades: 8 9 10 11 12 Adult   **741.5**
1. Literature — Adaptations; 2. Graphic novels
9380028679; 9789380028675, $12.99

This "graphic novel tells the . . . tale of revenge written by Alexandre Dumas in 1844. Set between 1815 and 1838," the book "depicts a tumultuous time in France's history when multiple powers were vying for control of the country. . . . When Edmond Dantes is unjustly arrested and placed in a prison, his anger and desire for revenge builds inside him. After his escape, he finds the means to carefully plot against his conspirators and steal away their livelihoods and happiness." (Voice of Youth Advocates)

Duo Brand
Cross break, vol. 1. Go! Comi 2008 Un Illustration
Grades: 10 11 12 Adult   **741.5; Fic**
1. Adventure graphic novels; 2. Fantasy graphic novels; 3. Manga; 4. Graphic novels
978-1-933617-74-9, $10.99

Brothers Shinkai and Akito live in a Tokyo different from our world; in theirs, Japan now has a democracy and their father is the President. Ninth grader Akito resents Shinkai's behavior and tries to study hard, his one friend is Yaya, a strange young girl who lives next door. Then Shinkai says Akito shall study abroad and sends him to a strange world. Akito and Yaya, who had come over for help with her homework and got sent away with Akito, must deal with a world ruled by warlocks who murder with impunity. Neon befriends them, but Akito thinks he knows too much about them; but when a poisonous bug bites Yaya, Akiko needs Neon to help him find medicine to heal her. He'll figure out the world he's in as he goes. The book includes violence.

Durieux, Christian
An **enchantment**. Christian Durieux. NBM Pub. 2013 72 p.
Grades: Adult   **741.5/9493; 741.5**
1. Fantasy graphic novels; 2. Louvre (Paris, France)
9781561637058, $19.99
        LC 2012950214

This graphic novel is part of the ComicsLit Louvre series, a series of graphic novels commissioned by the Louvre art museum. In this entry, Belgian artist Christian Durieux "imagines the director of the museum as a faded grey bureaucrat on the verge of retirement, who is swept away into the building's nighttime vastness by a mysterious and pixieish muse. As they playfully romp beneath the ancient works of art, . . . the aged and cynical director muses on literature and politics." (Publishers Weekly)

Dyer, Jamaica
★ **Weird** fishes. SLG Publishing 2009 112p. Illustration
Grades: 10 11 12 Adult   **741.5; Fic**
1. Friendship; 2. Graphic novels
978-1-59362-177-3, $9.95

Dee sees giant talking ducks and her main confidant is Bones, a talking goldfish. Bunny Boy always wears a bunny suit. The two misfits have been friends for years, but now things are starting to change. Bunny Boy falls for a goth girl and actually wears a mod suit. Dee, however, has problems when her visions begin to darken, ducks become monsters, and bad things hang out in storm clouds. She needs Bunny Boy, but he seems to want more normalcy in his personal relationships. The two teens smoke cigarettes, cut school, and Bunny Boy goes to a party where people are drinking alcohol.

Dysart, Joshua
Swamp Thing Vol. 2: Love in Vain. Art by Enrique Breccia and Timothy Green II. DC Comics/Vertigo 2005 144p. Illustration
Grades: 11 12 Adult   **741.5; Fic**
1. Horror graphic novels; 2. Science fiction graphic novels; 3. Graphic novels
1-4012-0493-7, $14.99

Though he once wielded the combined power of all the Earth's elemental forces, the creature known as Swamp Thing has renounced his omnipotence and returned to his original status as the avatar of the Green, the web of energy connecting all of the world's plant life. But he is now vulnerable, and Arcane is about to break out of his eternal damnation into the world of the living. His designs for revenge threaten to sink not only the Swamp Thing and his family, but everything else under the sun into a never-ending nightmare of corruption and despair. The book includes lots of harsh language, graphic violence, nudity, and sexual situations.

Swamp Thing: Healing the Breach. Art by Enrique Breccia, Ronald Wimberly, Richard Corben. DC Comics/Vertigo 2006 144p. Illustration

Grades: 10 11 12 Adult   741.5; Fic
1. Fantasy graphic novels; 2. Superhero graphic novels; 3. Swamp Thing (Fictional character); 4. Graphic novels
1-4012-0934-3, $17.99

With the consciousness of Alec Holland still separated from its former host and scattered throughout the world, the Swamp Thing must face a new threat which is manifesting itself inside a growing dead zone in the Gulf of Mexico and contend with the gradual reassembly of the Holland mind and the pain of reintegration that its completion promises. In the meantime, a hurricane threatens the Gulf Coast area where Swamp Thing, and crippled Jordin are staying. The book includes strong language, some nudity and sexual situations, and some violence.

★ **Unknown** soldier: haunted house. DC Comics/Vertigo 2009 144p. Illustration

Grades: 11 12 Adult   741.5; Fic
1. Terrorism; 2. Uganda; 3. Graphic novels
978-1-4012-2311-3, $9.99

In 2002, Northern Uganda is a beautiful country racked by horrible brutality and war, as an insane extremist Christian rebel and his army of children terrorize their own people. Dr. Lwanga Moses had fled Uganda with his family when he was a child and Idi Amin was in power; now, he has returned to Uganda with his Ugandan wife, full of pacifist ideals and plans to bring hope and healing to his home country. Then he falls prey to the child soldiers and something deep within him erupts, and Dr. Moses becomes an unstoppable killing machine. His face disfigured, he covers it in bandages and becomes an unknown soldier, determined to do whatever it takes, however much violence and killing he must do, to stop the war. Meanwhile, his wife keeps up their medical mission, always wondering what happened to make her husband disappear. This book is full of horrific, gory violence, but with this update of the classic Unknown Soldier character, Dysart also carefully researched into Ugandan politics and conflicts to make his story as authentic as possible.

E. C. Segar
   Popeye Vol. 1: I Yam What I Yam!. Fantagraphics Books 2006 182p. Illustration

Grades: 10 11 12 Adult   741.5
1. Humorous graphic novels; 2. Popeye (Fictional character); 3. Graphic novels
978-1-56097-779-7, $29.95

This is the first volume in a series that will publish all of Segar's original comic strips featuring Popeye, Olive Oyl, Wimpy, and all the other characters people have known from cartoons and a motion picture. This volume covers the years 1928 through 1930 and feature Popeye's courtship of Olive Oyl, meeting the Sea Hag, and Castor Oyl's attempts to turn Popeye into a boxing champion. With all the fighting going on, this book really isn't meant for children.

Eaglesham, Dale
   Green Lantern: New Journey, Old Path. DC Comics 2001 192p. Illustration

Grades: 9 10 11 12 Adult   Fic; 741.5
1. Green Lantern (Fictional character); 2. Justice League (Fictional characters); 3. Superhero graphic novels; 4. Graphic novels
1-56389-729-6, $12.95

Nero, an escaped mental patient, is bequeathed a Yellow Lantern Ring by the Qwardians. Possessing the mind of a demon and the skill of an artist, he wreaks havoc in New York City and could possibly decimate the planet. With the Justice League pushed to the limit trying to contain Nero's hordes, Green Lantern Kyle Rayner stands alone against a maniac whose power could surpass his own.

Edginton, Ian
   Hellgate London. Dark Horse Comics 2007 Un Illustration

Grades: 10 11 12 Adult   741.5; Fic
1. Adventure graphic novels; 2. Fantasy graphic novels; 3. Graphic novels
978-1-59307-681-8, $12.95

In 2020, MI5 agent Lyra Darius discovers a human charnel house in the heart of London while tailing Lord Sumerisle, the recently resigned Home Office Minister for Internal Affairs. She's soon entangled in a bloody intrigue with Knights Templar, and everything is building up to All Hallows Eve as demons establish Hellgates to invade Earth. Years later, humans must discover the true nature of an arcane symbol known as the Sigil, if they hope to survive much longer against the demons. The book includes violence and strong language; it's based on a video game of the same name.

   Kingdom of the Wicked. Illustrated by D'Israeli. Dark Horse Comics 2004 120p. Illustration

Grades: 8 9 10 11 12 Adult   741.5; Fic
1. Adventure graphic novels; 2. Fantasy graphic novels; 3. Graphic novels
1-59307-187-6, $15.95

Christopher Grahame is the premier children's author of the twenty-first century, a publishing phenomenon. With his work translated into everything from Aborigine to Zulu, he is the cornerstone of a multi-million dollar, franchise spewing empire. Is it any surprise then that under all this pressure something has to give? Unfortunately, it's Chris's mind. Stricken by mysterious headaches and blackouts that plagued his childhood, Chris once again finds himself walking the avenues and boulevards of Castrovalva - the fantasy realm he dreamt up as a boy, to while away his recuperation. But like Chris, Castrovalva has also changed. Deluged in mud, blood, and barbed wire, war has come to wonderland. Chris tries to tell himself it's all a bad dream. . .so why can't he wake up? The book includes violence, strong language, and brief nudity.

   Scarlet Traces. Dark Horse Comics 2003 88p. Illustration

Grades: 9 10 11 12 Adult   741.5; Fic
1. Mystery graphic novels; 2. Science fiction graphic novels; 3. Graphic novels
1-56971-940-3, $14.95

A decade after the Martians' abortive assault on the Earth and their attempt to establish an invasion bridgehead on the British Isles, the industrious Victorians have assimilated the Martian technologies into their everyday lives. Hansom cabs now scuttle along the Capital's streets on multi-limbed crab legs and the terrible monopoly of the Martian heat-ray has assured the dominance of the British Empire over two thirds of the Earth's surface. However, there is something rotten at the heart of empire. When the bodies of several young women are found washed up on the Thames, drained of blood, enter Captain Robert Autumn (retired soldier turned gentleman-adventurer) and his former Sergeant Major, now manservant, Archie Currie. Together they are drawn into the mystery which leads them from the gin palaces of the East End, and the grinding poverty of the North, to Whitehall's corridors of power and the very Hall of the Martian King. The book includes violence and some strong language.

Edmondson, Nathan

Black Widow; Volume 1: the finely woven thread. Nathan Edmondson; illustrated by Phil Noto. Marvel Enterprises 2014 144 p. Color; Illustration
Grades: 11 12 Adult   741.5
1. Black Widow (Fictional character); 2. Superheroes — Fiction; 3. Undercover operations — Fiction
0785188193; 9780785188193, $17.99
"The Black Widow goes undercover in Russia, but from its cold streets, the Hand of God reaches out to crush her . . . and it is as merciless as its name implies. Outmatched by the brute force of a powerful new villain, Natasha faces her deadliest test, and discovers a deadly plot unfolding that spans the entire globe." (Publisher's note)
"Edmondson's fast-paced and action-packed espionage story does an excellent job playing to the character's strengths, using her cunning to assess each situation and her agility and reflexes when it all goes to hell. Noto's luminous watercolorlike panels—a welcome departure from more traditional superhero comics artwork—create a soft atmosphere." Booklist
Contains material originally published in magazine form as Black Widow #1-6 and All new Marvel now! point one #1—Tp verso.
Volume 1 of an ongoing series

Olympus. Art by Chris Ward. Image Comics 2009 Un Illustration
Grades: 10 11 12 Adult   741.5; Fic
1. Fantasy graphic novels; 2. Greek mythology; 3. Graphic novels
978-1-60706-178-6, $14.99
In Ancient Greece, Zeus granted immortality to two brothers, Castor and Pollux (most people might know them as the Gemini twins), then bound them to his service. Three thousand years later, they still serve him on Earth by hunting fugitives from Olympus and maintaining order between the human realm and the divine. This means they have to catch Hermes and cast him off Earth; when they do that, they accidentally leave an opening between the realms for Pelops, son of Tantalus, who has no love for the gods. Ward saturates his sketchy, scratchy lines with wild colors. The book includes violence and some harsh language.

Eisner, Will

★ **Comics** and sequential art: principles and practices from the legendary cartoonist. W.W. Norton 2008 175p. Illustration (The Will Eisner library)
Grades: 9 10 11 12 Adult   741.5
1. Comic books, strips, etc — Authorship; 2. Drawing — Technique; 3. Graphic novels — Authorship
978-0-393-33126-4; 0-393-33126-1, $22.95
LC 2008-20042
This book offers the author's ideas, theories, and advice about graphic storytelling and the uses to which the comic book art form can be applied.
First published 1985 by Poorhouse Press
A Will Eisner instructional book Cover

★ **The contract** with God trilogy: life on Dropsie Avenue. Will Eisner. W.W. Norton 2005 498 p. Illustration
Grades: Adult   741.5; Fic
1. Bronx (New York, NY)
0393061051; 9780393061055, $35
LC 2005053944
"Comics veteran [Will] Eisner launched a second career with 'A Contract with God' (1978), one that . . . led the way for the contemporary graphic novel. Two further Depression-era books set on the same fictitious street in the Bronx followed. In the wake of Eisner's . . . death [in 2005], the three are here gathered into a single volume." (Booklist)
Life on Dropsie Avenue

Fagin the Jew. By Will Eisner; foreword by Michael Bendis. Dark Horse 2013 136 p. Illustration
Grades: 11 12 Adult   741.5
1. Jews — Great Britain — Fiction
1616551267; 9781616551261, $19.99
This book is author and illustrator Will Eisner's reimagination of author Charles Dickens' character Fagin from the book "Oliver Twist." "Imagining Fagin's impoverished childhood in the slums of London and his initiation into the criminal underworld, Eisner's story counters the anti-Semitism of Victorian literature as his . . . brushwork creates . . . [a] portrait of the era." (Publisher's note)
"[T]his compelling counternarrative is framed as Fagin's apologia to Dickens and folds in plenty of historical background about Jews in Europe and England during the late 19th century." LJ
Includes bibliographical references
First published 2003

★ **Graphic** Storytelling and Visual Narrative. Poorhouse Press 1996 164p. Illustration
Grades: Adult Professional   741.5
1. Graphic novels — Teaching — Aids and devices; 2. Graphic novels
0-9614728-2-0, $22.99
A companion to Comics & Sequential Art, this book takes the principles examined in that title and applies them to the process of graphic storytelling. Eisner shows comic artists, filmmakers and graphic designers how to craft stories in a visual medium. Readers will learn everything from the fine points of graphic storytelling to the big picture of the comics medium, including how to: Use art that enhances your story, rather than obscuring it; wield images like narrative tools; write and illustrate effective dialogue; and

develop ideas that can be turned into dynamic stories. These lessons and more are illustrated with storytelling samples from Eisner himself along with other comic book favorites, including Pulitzer Prize-winner Art Spiegelman, Robert Crumb, Milton Caniff and Al Capp.

★ **Last** day in Vietnam: a memory. Written and illustrated by Will Eisner and edited by Diana Schutz. Dark Horse Comics 2000 79 p.
Grades: Adult **741.5; 741.5/973**
1. Soldiers; 2. Vietnam War, 1961-1975
1569715009; 1616551208; 9781616551209, $17.99
LC 00710474
This graphic novel by Will Eisner "recounts the artist's own experiences with soldiers engaged not only in the daily hostilities of war but also in larger, more personal combat. Some of the stories in this novel are comical, some heartrending, some frightening, yet all display the incredible insight into humanity characteristic of Eisner's entire oeuvre."
Cover title.

Life, in pictures: autobiographical stories. Will Eisner.. W.W. Norton & Co. 2007 493 p. (Will Eisner library.)
Grades: Adult **741.5; 92**
1. Cartoonists — United States — Biography; 2. Eisner, Will
0393061078; 9780393061079, $29.95
LC 2007032339
This graphic novel, by Will Eisner, offers "an intimate self-portrait of the American icon Will Eisner, and a chronicle of the career that launched a new art form. . . . 'The Dreamer' and 'To the Heart of the Storm' describe Eisner's gritty early life and career, while 'The Name of the Game' chronicles a personal history of his wife's family. Finally, two shorter pieces illuminate the bookends of a legendary career." (Publisher's note)

The **plot:** the secret story of the Protocols of the Elders of Zion. By Will Eisner, with an introduction by Umberto Eco. Norton 2005 Vii, 148 p. Illustration (Will Eisner library.)
Grades: 9 10 11 12 Adult **741.5; 305.892**
1. Antisemitism; 2. Protocols of the wise men of Zion
0393060454; 0393328600; 9780393060454, $19.95
LC 2005040527
This book, by Will Eisner, "examines the astonishing conspiracy and the fabrication of The Protocols of the Elders of Zion. . . . Purported to be the actual blueprints by Jewish leaders to take over the world, the Protocols, first published in 1902, have become gospel truth to international millions. Presenting a pageant of historical figures, . . . Eisner unravels and dispels one of the most devastating hoaxes of the twentieth century." (Publisher's note)

PS magazine: the best of the Preventive maintenance monthly. [by] Will Eisner; introduction by Peter J. Schoomaker; preface by Ann Eisner; selected and with commentary by Eddie Campbell. Abrams ComicArts 2011 272p. Illustration
Grades: Adult **741.5**
1. Repairing; 2. United States — Army; 3. Graphic novels
978-0-8109-9748-6, $21.95
LC 2011012342

"From 1951 to 1971, between The Spirit and A Contract with God, Eisner produced PS Magazine for the army in order to teach the common soldier how best to use, maintain, repair, and requisition their equipment. From explaining how to load a truck correctly to why it won't start, Eisner used a combination of humor, sound technical writing, and graphic storytelling to educate the soldiers. . . . With Eisner's wonderful artwork and clarity of style making sometimes difficult concepts easy to understand, it's no wonder PS Magazine was so popular with military personnel. A fascinating document for both fans of Eisner and military history buffs." Publ Wkly

The **Spirit** Archives Volume 14. DC Comics 2004 192p. Illustration
Grades: 9 10 11 12 Adult **741.5; Fic**
1. Spirit (Fictional character); 2. Superhero graphic novels; 3. Spirit (Fictional character); 4. Graphic novels
1-4012-0158-X, $49.95
LC 2001-274103
The adventures of Will Eisner's most famous creation continue in this volume reprinting the Spirit newspaper sections from 1/5/47 to 6/29/47. It features appearances by Ebony, Dolan and Ellen, the seductive P'Gell, Hoagy the Yogi, Silken Floss, Saree and more. Today's readers should understand that Eisner's depiction of Ebony, who is the Spirit's sidekick, was not considered out of place in 1947, even though many might take offense now. Eisner started developing new methods of telling a story and revolutionizing comics along the way.

The **Spirit** Archives Volume 15. DC Comics 2004 192p. Illustration
Grades: 9 10 11 12 Adult **741.5; Fic**
1. Spirit (Fictional character); 2. Superhero graphic novels; 3. Spirit (Fictional character); 4. Graphic novels
1-4012-0162-8, $49.95
LC 2001-274103
Volume 15 reprints The Spirit newspaper sections published from July 6, 1947 to December 28, 1947, featuring the seductive P'Gell, The Octopus, a send up of Li'l Abner, and more. The stories range from broad comedy to crime noir, with plenty of comic violence.

El Rassi, Toufic
Arab in America. Last Gasp 2008 118p. Illustration
Grades: 10 11 12 Adult **92; 741.5**
1. Biographical graphic novels; 2. Muslims — United States
978-0-86719-673-3, $14.95
Toufic El Rassi combines a memoir of his life in America with commentary on how Muslims and Arabs have been treated in the U.S. Born in Beirut but living in the U.S. since he was a young boy, El Rassi faced ignorant prejudice and discrimination ever since his family immigrated to this country. In this book he shows how hard it is to maintain an Arab identity in a country saturated with anti-Arab propaganda, examining the roles of media and pop culture in a world with 9/11, two Gulf Wars, and other U.S. involvement in the Middle East. Readers will confront uncomfortable ideas about just what unthinking patriotism and ignorance about the real culture of the Middle East countries do to harm many who are innocent. The book

includes some strong language and a few isolated panels with partial nudity.

Eldred, Tim

★ **Grease** monkey. Written and drawn by Tim Eldred; [edited by Teresa Nielsen Hayden]. Tor 2006 352p. Illustration
Grades: 9 10 11 12 Adult   **741.5; Fic**
1. Science fiction graphic novels; 2. Graphic novels
0-7653-1325-1; 0-7653-1326-X (pa), $19.95

When hostile aliens attacked Earth and left it after killing most of the humans, another group of aliens came and offered to "uplift" one of the animal species to human intelligence so that Earth could rebuild. The dolphins turned them down, but the gorillas went for it. Some generations later, new mechanic Robin Plotnik comes to the space station called Fist of Earth, where he's assigned to work with Chief Mac Gimbensky. Mac is a no-nonsense gorilla who works on the ships of the all-woman Barbarian Squadron. He and Robin work together well, but they each have their romantic problems. This is science fiction from a viewpoint not always seen in most stories.

Ellis, Grace

★ **Lumberjanes** 1: Beware the kitten holy. Written by Noelle Stevenson & Grace Ellis ; illustrated by Brooke Allen ; colors by Maarta Laiho. Simon & Schuster 2015 128 p. Illustration; Color (Lumberjanes)
Grades: 6 7 8 9 10 11 12 Adult   **741.5**
1. Adventure fiction; 2. Camps — Fiction; 3. Female friendship; 4. Monsters — Fiction; 5. Summer — Fiction
1608866874; 9781608866878, $14.99
Eisner Award: Best New Series (2015)
Eisner Award: Best Publication for Teens (2015)
Harvey Award: Best New Series (2015); Harvey Award: Best Original Graphic Publication For Young Readers (2015)

"[This] graphic novel begins mid-adventure as five campers are out after hours investigating a strange event that they all witnessed: a woman turning into a giant bear. This is just the first of many odd occurrences that Jo, April, Molly, Mal, and Ripley encounter at the summer camp for 'Hardcore Lady Types.' The Lumberjanes, as the scouts are called, band together to solve puzzles, defeat three-eyed creatures, and escape the ire of their watchful counselor Jen." (School Library Journal)

"Humorously riffing on everything from scout badges to the X-Men to feminist heroes . . ., it's a sharp, smart, and most of all fun celebration of sisterhood." Pub Wkly

Volume 1 of an ongoing series

Ellis, Warren

The **Authority:** relentless. By Warren Ellis. WildStorm/DC Comics 2000 192 p. Color illustration
Grades: Adult
1. Superhero comic books, strips, etc
1563896613; 9781563896613, $17.99

This comic book, by Warren Ellis, focuses on "superheroes with believable personalities and community spirit. Two story arcs, each encompassing terror and evil on a global scale, pit the group of seven against armies of superhumans dispatched in scenes reminiscent of the best action movies." (Publisher's note)

Volume 1 of 4

Crecy. Story, Warren Ellis; artwork, Raulo Caceres. Avatar Press 2007 Un Illustration
Grades: 10 11 12 Adult
741.5; Fic
1. Crecy (France), Battle of, 1346; 2. Hundred Years' War, 1339-1453; 3. War; 4. Graphic novels
978-1-59291-040-3, $6.99

Courtesy of Avatar Press

A highly trained but under equipped army invades another country due to that country's perceived threat to home security. The army conducts shock-and-awe raids designed to terrify the populace. This army is soon driven to ground, and vastly outnumbered. The English army has to stand and fight, under the command of King Edward III, in Crecy, France. On 26 August 1346, modern warfare changed forever. This is the story of England's greatest battle, narrated by a fictional English longbowman. The book is full of battlefield violence and lots of very harsh language, including the f-bomb.

Desolation Jones. Warren Ellis, writer; J. H. Williams III, artist. DC Comics/Wildstorm 2006 142p. Illustration
Grades: 12 Adult   **741.5; Fic**
1. Mystery graphic novels; 2. Graphic novels
978-1-4012-1150-9, $14.99

Michael Jones used to be an MI6 field agent, and he is the first surviving victim of the Desolation Test, a radically dangerous procedure cooked up by the British government. He was kept alive intravenously while being force-fed a steady diet of horrific data and images non-stop as stimulants were continuously pumped into him, for an entire year. Now he lives in Los Angeles, where all the ex-spooks like him have been sent and kept; he works as a private investigator to their secret underground community. Colonel Nigh, who lives for his pornography collection, needs Jones' help to recover a special piece of film - pornography starring Adolf Hitler; Nigh's troublesome daughters all play into the equation. Mature readers who enjoy such titles as Preacher and aren't troubled by nudity, violence, and considerable use of harsh language, will want to read this.

Fell Volume 1: Feral City. Written by Warren Ellis; illustrated by Ben Templesmith; lettering by Chris Eliopoulos. Image Comics 2007 Un Illustration
Grades: 11 12 Adult   **741.5; Fic**
1. Mystery graphic novels; 2. Graphic novels
978-1-58240-693-0, $14.99

Detective Richard Fell is transferred over the bridge from the big city to Snowtown, a feral district whose police investigations department numbers three and a half people (one detective has no legs). Dumped in this collapsing urban trashzone, Richard Fell is starting all over again. In a place where nothing seems to make any sense, Fell clings to the one thing he knows to be true: everybody's hiding something. Considerable violence and strong language mix with a strong noir-ish mystery.

Global frequency. Written by Warren Ellis; illustrated by Garry Leach ... [et al.]; David Baron, Art Lyon, colorists; Michael Heisler, letterer.. DC Comics 2013 288 p. Color illustration

Grades: Adult   **Fic; 741.5/973**
1. Rescue work — Fiction; 2. Graphic novels
1401237975; 9781401237974, $19.99

         LC 2012040864

This graphic novel, written by Warren Ellis, "collects the entire 12 issue Global Frequency storyline in one trade paperback. Global Frequency is a worldwide rescue organization. Manned by 1001 operatives, the Frequency is made up of experts in fields as diverse as bio-weapon engineering and Le Parkour Running. Each agent-equipped with a special mobile vid-phone-is specifically chosen by Miranda Zero, enigmatic leader of the Global Frequency, based on proximity [and] expertise." (Publisher's note)

Originally published in single magazine form in Global Frequency 1-12.

Nextwave: Agents of H.A.T.E. Vol. 1: This is What They Want. Writer, Warren Ellis; artist, Stuart Immonen. Marvel Entertainment 2006 Un Illustration

Grades: 10 11 12 Adult   **741.5; Fic**
1. Adventure graphic novels; 2. Satire; 3. Superhero graphic novels; 4. Graphic novels
0-7851-2278-8, $19.99

H.A.T.E. (The Highest Anti-Terrorism Effort) put together a team of superheroes they call Nextwave: Monica Rambeau (formerly Captain Marvel and Photon), Aaron Stack (the robotic Machine Man), Tabitha Smith (X-Force's Meltdown), monster-hunter Elsa Bloodstone, and The Captain. The team was told they were supposed to fight Bizarre Weapons of Mass Destruction; however, Tabitha lifted some papers that reveal the truth: H.A.T.E. is part of the Beyond Corporation, which is the new version of the terrorist organization formerly known as Silent. The Corporation plans to test its weapons on unsuspecting American towns, so Nextwave goes rogue to stop the weapons and be the good guys. They face an awakened Fin Fang Foom (giant monster lizard), a bad cop turned robotic monster, and their former boss, Dirk Anger. There's lots of action, bad words show as a series of death's heads, and the whole thing is written as a biting satire of superheroes.

Nextwave: Agents of H.A.T.E. Vol. 2: I Kick Your Face. Writer, Warren Ellis; penciler, Stuart Immonen; inker Wade von Grawbadger; colorist, Dave McCaig. Marvel Entertainment 2007 Un Illustration

Grades: 10 11 12 Adult   **741.5; Fic**
1. Humorous graphic novels; 2. Superhero graphic novels; 3. Graphic novels
0-7851-2855-7, $19.99

In this second and final volume of the series, former Captain Marvel Monica Rambeau and the Nextwave team continue their quest to shut down H.A.T.E.'s network of Unusual Weapons of Mass Destruction. They destroy the Mindless Ones, the bizarre Broccoli Men who have been created to look like various superhero teams, and then decide to finish off S.I.L.E.N.T. itself, the uber-terrorist network

that has been funding H.A.T.E. It's a full-on superhero satire with lots of comic book action, and all the bad words appear as skulls.

Orbiter. Writer, Warren Ellis; artist, Colleen Doran. DC Comics/Vertigo 2004 104p. Illustration

Grades: 10 11 12 Adult   **741.5; Fic**
1. Mystery graphic novels; 2. Science fiction graphic novels; 3. Graphic novels
1-4012-0056-7, $17.95

In the early 21st century, the space shuttle Venture had suddenly returned to Earth after disappearing ten years ago; its crew is missing, except for the catatonic pilot, and the ship is outfitted with new instrumentation, new engines, and is covered in something very much like skin, while its landing gear has Martian sand. Now a team of three specialists must discover where the Venture went, what's been done to it, and what happened to the crew. Unfortunately, most of the answers are locked up in the seemingly twisted mind of the pilot. Does he really know the truth or is he simply a demented casualty of a space mission gone wrong? The book includes some foul language.

★ **Planetary:** 2, Vol. 2. Warren Ellis, writer; John Cassaday, artist; Laura DePuy and David Baron, colorists; Ryan Cline, Bill O'Neil and Mike Heisler, letterers. DC Comics 2013 144 p. Color; Illustration

Grades: 11 12 Adult   **741.5**
1. Adventure graphic novels; 2. Parapsychology — Fiction; 3. Superhero comic books, strips, etc
1563897644; 9781563897641, $14.99

         LC 2012046722

This graphic novel, written by Warren Ellis and illustrated by John Cassady, the second in the "Planetary" series, "focuses on the team's mysterious benefactor, the 'Fourth Man.' After paying their final respects to a British occultist with ties to their group, Elijah Snow, Jakita Wagner, and The Drummer continue their super-human archeological studies as they visit a hidden government compound full of radioactive human guinea pigs." (Publisher's note)

Originally published by WildStorm in single magazine form as Planetary #7-#12.

★ **Planetary:** 3: leaving the 20th century, 3. Warren Ellis & John Cassaday, writer, co-creators, artist; Laura Martin, colorist. DC Comics 2005 144 p. Color; Illustration

Grades: 11 12 Adult   **741.5**
1. Adventure graphic novels; 2. Mystery graphic novels; 3. Science fiction graphic novels; 4. Superhero comic books, strips, etc
1401202942; 9781401202941, $14.99

In this graphic novel, written by Warren Ellis and illustrated by John Cassaday, the third in the "Planetary" series, "Elijah takes a look at his past, making startling revelations and recounting his participation in the first moon shot . . . in 1851!" (Publisher's note)

Originally published in single magazine form as Planetary #13-18

★ **Planetary:** 4: spacetime archaeology. Writer, Warren Ellis; artist, John Cassaday; colorist, Laura Martin; letterer, Comicraft. WildStorm Productions 2010 224 p. Color; Illustration

Grades: 11 12 Adult   **741.5**

1. Adventure fiction; 2. Fantasy fiction; 3. Superhero comic books, strips, etc; 4. Graphic novels
1401223451; 9781401223458, $17.99

LC 2010294189

This book, by Warren Ellis, is the "fourth and final graphic novel collecting the adventures of Elijah Snow, a powerful, hundred year old man, Jakita Wagner, an extremely powerful but bored woman, and The Drummer, a man with the ability to communicate with machines. Infatuated with tracking down evidence of super-human activity, these mystery archaeologists of the late 20th Century uncover unknown paranormal secrets and histories." (Publisher's note)

"Engaging as the story itself may be, Planetary's brilliance lies more in the rich history of comics and comic lore that Ellis draws from and cleverly weaves into the narrative from beginning to end." SLJ

Originally published in single magazine form as Planetary #19-27.

★ **Planetary:** vol 1: all over the world and other stories. Warren Ellis, John Cassaday, Laura DePuy. Wildstorm 2012 160 p. Color; Illustration
Grades: 11 12 Adult   741.5
1. Adventure graphic novels; 2. Archaeologists — Fiction; 3. Mystery graphic novels; 4. Parapsychology — Fiction; 5. Science fiction comic books, strips, etc
1563896486; 9781563896484, $14.99

LC 2012024915

Written by Warren Ellis with art by John Cassaday, "this graphic novel features the adventures of Elijah Snow, a hundred year old man, Jakita Wagner, an extremely powerful and bored woman, and The Drummer, a man with the ability to communicate with machines. Infatuated with tracking down evidence of super-human activity, these mystery archaeologists of the late 20th Century uncover unknown paranormal secrets and histories." (Publisher's note)

Also available in an omnibus edition

Originally published by WildStorm Productions in single magazine form as Planetary #1-6 And Planetary Preview. Other volumes in this series are: Vol. 2: The fourth man; Vol. 3: Leaving the 20th century; Vol. 4: Spacetime archaeology

StormWatch; Volume one. Warren Ellis, story; Tom Raney ... [et al.], pencils; Randy Elliott, Richard Bennett, inks; Gina Going, colors. DC Comics 2012 296 p. Color illustration
Grades: Adult   741.5/973; 741.5; Fic
1. Adventure fiction; 2. Superhero comic books, strips, etc; 3. Superhero graphic novels
1401234208; 9781401234201, $29.99

LC 2012374614

This comic book anthology, written by Warren Ellis and illustrated by Tom Raney, collects in hardcover graphic novel format volume 1 of the DC Comics series following the adventures of the United Nations-sponsored superhero team Stormwatch, originally created by Jim Lee as part of the Wildstorm Universe. (Wikipedia)

StormWatch created by Jim Lee and Brandon Choi.
Originally published by WildStorm in single magazine form in Stormwatch 37-47.—t.p. verso.

★ **Transmetropolitan:** back on the street. Warren Ellis, writer; Darick Robertson, penciller. DC Comics 2012 142 p.
Grades: Adult   741.5/973; 741.5
1. Journalists; 2. Journalists
1401220843; 9781401220846, $14.99

LC 2012017896

In this comic book, by Warren Ellis, illustrated by Darick Robertson, "After years of selfimposed exile from a civilization rife with degradation and indecency, cynical journalist Spider Jerusalem is forced to return to a job he hates and a city he loathes. Working as an investigative reporter for the newspaper The Word, Spider attacks the injustices of his surreal 23rd century surroundings." (Publisher's note)

Originally published in single magazine form as TRANSMETROPOLITAN 1-6.

Volume 1 of 10

Ellison, Halan

Harlan Ellison's Dream Corridor, Vol. 2. Dark Horse Comics 2007 168p. Illustration
Grades: 11 12 Adult   741.5; Fic
1. Fantasy graphic novels; 2. Graphic novels
978-1-59307-494-4, $19.95

The words of world-renowned science-fiction author Harlan Ellison are translated onto the page by top comics creators, including Paul Chadwick, Neal Adams, Steve Rude, Gene Colan, Steve Niles, Gerard Jones, Richard Corben and the legendary Oz illustrator Eric Shanower. Most of these stories have never before seen print. Ellison uses strong language and violence a lot in his stories, which include "Opposites Attract," "One Life, Furnished in Early Poverty," "The Discarded," "Moonlighting," and more.

Endo, Hiroki

Tanpenshu Vol. 1. Dark Horse Comics 2007 230p. Illustration
Grades: 11 12 Adult   741.5; Fic
1. Manga; 2. Seinen manga; 3. Graphic novels
978-1-59307-637-5, $12.95

The three stories in this first volume are mature explorations of humanity's constant, fumbling attempts to find hope and meaning in a confusing, violent world. A disfigured misfit befriends a doomed yakuza outcast, a group a school kids fail to see the anger that's about to boil over from one of their own and members of an experimental theatre troupe embark on a project that will test both their friendships and the group's grasp on reality. The stories include strong language, nudity and graphic violence, and the cover may disturb some readers.

Englehart, Steve

Batman: Dark Detective. DC Comics 2005 144p. Illustration
Grades: 9 10 11 12 Adult   Fic; 741.5
1. Batman (Fictional character); 2. Joker (Fictional character); 3. Superhero graphic novels; 4. Graphic novels
1-4012-0898-3, $14.99

When the maniacal Joker enters a gubernatorial election, the Dark Knight takes action. But Batman discovers he's in way over his head when the unexpected return of former girlfriend Silver St. Cloud leaves him torn between love and duty. With adversaries like the Joker, Two-Face, Scarecrow, and others to contend with, Batman must make a choice between his quest for justice and his affections for Silver. And his indecision could cost him everything. The story evokes the style and content of 1970s comics.

Ennis, Garth
   Britton, Battler. Garth Ennis, writer; Colin Wilson, artist; colored by Jeremy Cox; lettered by Rob Leigh. DC Comics/Wildstorm 2007 Un Illustration
Grades: 10 11 12 Adult   741.5; Fic
   1. Adventure graphic novels; 2. War; 3. World War, 1939-1945; 4. Graphic novels
978-1-4012-1378-7, $19.99
   In October, 1942, Allied forces are on the run from the unrelenting forces of the Nazis in North Africa. Wing Commander Robert "Battler" Britton of the Royal Air Force and his squadron are dispatched to an American airstrip to spearhead a joint action against Hitler's war machine. Now they must survive taunts, threats, and assaults ... and that's just from the Yanks. There's plenty of war action in the air and on the ground.

   John Woo's Seven Brothers: Sons of Heaven, Son of Hell. Art by Jeevan Kang. Virgin Comics 2007 144p. Illustration
Grades: 10 11 12 Adult   741.5; Fic
   1. Fantasy graphic novels; 2. Mystery graphic novels; 3. Graphic novels
978-1-934413029, $14.99
   Six hundred years ago long, before history's great explorers stole the credit for their feats, mighty Chinese treasure fleets set sail to reach every continent. These voyages of discovery left behind an evil legacy and a plot by a powerful Chinese sorcerer to dominate the world. The story begins in modern day Los Angeles where an ancient Chinese prophecy must be fulfilled. Seven men with strange abilities and nothing in common but their destinies must face the Son of Hell to save the world. Action movie director John Woo created the story. The book includes lots of harsh language full of f-bombs and violence.

   ★ **Preacher;** Book One: Gone to Texas. Garth Ennis, writer; Steve Dillon, artist; Matt Hollingsworth and Pamela Rambo, colorists; Clem Robins, letterer. Vertigo 2009 352 p. Illustration
Grades: Adult   741.5
   1. Horror graphic novels; 2. Supernatural graphic novels; 3. Western stories
140122279X; 1401240453, $19.99; 9781401222796, $39.99; 9781401240455
   "Merging with a bizarre spiritual force called Genesis, Texan Preacher Jesse Custer becomes completely disillusioned with the beliefs that he had dedicated his entire life to. Now possessing the power of 'the word,' an ability to make people do whatever he utters, Custer begins a violent and riotous journey across the country. Joined by his gun-toting girlfriend Tulip and the hard drinking Irish vampire Cassidy, the Preacher loses faith in both man and God as he witnesses dark atrocities and improbable

calamities during his exploration of America." (Publisher's note)
   Originally collected in 9 volumes
   Book 1 of 6

   War Stories Vol. 2. Art by David Lloyd, Cam Kennedy, Carlos Ezquerra, Gary Erskine. DC Comics/Vertigo 2006 240p. Illustration
Grades: 10 11 12 Adult   741.5; Fic
   1. Spain — History — 1936-1939, Civil War; 2. World War, 1939-1945; 3. Graphic novels
978-1-4012-1039-7, $19.99
   The brutality and bravery of those who served in history's greatest conflict is brought to life in this book. From the saturation bombing of the Ruhr Valley to the birth of the SAS in the deserts of North Africa, from the blasted wreckage of Guernica to the tracer-filled skies over the North Atlantic, these tales will land the reader in some of the worst combat zones the world has ever seen. Author Ennis includes historical notes at the end of the book. Readers will find strong language and wartime violence in the stories.

Espinosa, Frank
   Rocketo: Journey to the Hidden Sea, Volume 1. Frank Espinosa; co-writer, Marie Taylor. Image Comics 2006 Un Illustration
Grades: 9 10 11 12 Adult   741.5; Fic
   1. Adventure graphic novels; 2. Science fiction graphic novels; 3. Graphic novels
1-58240-585-9, $19.99
   2,000 years after the Earth shattered, the magnetic core destroyed and continents split apart, new races of men came to be. Rocketo Garrison is a Mapper; he possesses an inner compass which lights when he is ready to use it. When his parents die in a violent storm, another Mapper takes him in. When he grows up, war comes to the planet; he hides his identity as a Mapper since he had never joined the guild, and fights. Lucerne captures him and takes his Mapper senses and powers away and uses them to design killing machines that win the war. Broken and lost, Rocketo joins the shady Spiro and his motley crew on a quest to explore the Hidden Sea.
   Espinosa uses a very fluid, loose, almost sketchy style that shows a lot of energy while setting up his new world of wonders and dangers.

   Rocketo: Journey to the Hidden Sea, Volume 2. Frank Espinosa; co-writer, Marie Taylor. Image Comics 2007 Un Illustration
Grades: 9 10 11 12 Adult   741.5
   1. Adventure graphic novels; 2. Science fiction graphic novels; 3. Graphic novels
978-1-58240-735-7, $19.99
   Rocketo, Spiro, and their crew had made it into the Hidden Sea, and they discover a place of beauty and peace. However, the gangster Scarletto, working for Lucerne, has been pursuing them and has taken control of the weapon created from Rocketo's Mapper powers. Scarletto is bringing war to the Hidden Sea, determined to destroy everything good. Rocketo and everyone who lives in the Hidden Sea fight back, but the only way they can win is if Rocketo can once again light his inner compass and

reawaken his Mapper powers. Libraries will want get both Volume 1 and this volume to get the complete story.

Estes, Max

Coffee and Donuts: A Junkyard Cats Comic. Top Shelf Productions 2006 112p. Illustration
Grades: 6 7 8 9 10 11 12 Adult   **741.5; Fic**
   1. Cats; 2. Humorous graphic novels; 3. Graphic novels
   1-891830-80-5, $10

Dwight and Jules live in an unused dumpster and scavenge their food; every morning a mystery person leaves coffee and donuts for them. When, desperate for money, they try (and fail) to rob an armored truck, real crooks Myles and Moose try to force them into real crime.

Hello, Again. Top Shelf Productions 2005 156p. Illustration
Grades: 11 12 Adult   **741.5; Fic**
   1. Graphic novels
   1-891830-63-5, $10.00

William is finding out that his past may not be buried as deep as he once thought. In fact, a colorful character from his past has just crawled out of the ground and is refusing to leave until William changes his ways. This is the tale of a drunken fisherman, an unfaithful fiancee, and a guilt ridden apartment manager, whose lives intersect with unsuspecting and dangerous consequences. The book includes some strong language and sexual situations (without any nudity).

Eto, Miyuki

Hell girl. Del Rey Manja 2008 Un Illustration
Grades: 10 11 12 Adult   **741.5; Fic**
   1. Horror graphic novels; 2. Manga; 3. Graphic novels
   978-0-345-50669-6, $10.99

In this volume, Ai Enma, Hell Girl, offers help to a beautiful teen idol who's being stalked by a long-ago costar of a failed children's television show; to a teenage girl who has become the victim of an obsessively possessive boyfriend who threatens the life of her childhood buddy, and to a girl with a sickly younger brother whose parents were killed by a hit-and-run driver and whose aunt and uncle take care of them only because of the money. A young girl discovers her grandmother isn't dead, but when she goes to visit her, she learns that her grandmother had used help from Hell Girl to protect her newborn daughter from a predatory landlord, and the village hates her for it. The horror is mostly psychological, but there is some violence.

Hell girl vol. 2. Del Rey Manga 2008 202p. Illustration
Grades: 10 11 12 Adult   **741.5; Fic**
   1. Horror graphic novels; 2. Manga; 3. Shojo manga; 4. Graphic novels
   978-0-345-50416-6, $10.95

Hell Girl is the ultimate avenger for those who have no one else to whom they can turn for help. If one goes to her website at midnight and enters the name of one's tormentor, Hell Girl will destroy that person. However, everyone who completes the contract with Hell Girl must also look forward to eternal torment in hell after death. In this volume, a spiteful figure skater tries to turn the two girls who beat her in competition against each other; a teenager only wants to save her younger sister from an abusive nanny; a boy in fragile health discovers who is stalking his best friend; the

student class president can find no other way to save her friend from a vengeful new teacher. While there is no really graphic violence or bad language, the intensity of the stories make this series more appropriate for older teens.

Hell girl, vol. 4. Del Rey Manga 2008 184p. Illustration
Grades: 10 11 12 Adult   **741.5; Fic**
   1. Horror graphic novels; 2. Manga; 3. Graphic novels
   978-0-345-50418-0, $10.95

In this fourth volume, someone has set up a fake Hell Correspondence webpage, and students at a middle school are entering a harsh teacher's name, but the real Hell Girl, Ai Enma, does come for the real culprit. The price for her services, however, is eternal damnation of the requesters' souls. One young girl learns that her stepfather saddled his debts onto her father and then killed him. A group of neighbors take a stray dog they adopted to a woman who advertises that she will care for animals, only to discover she's abusing all of them—and the police won't listen to a bunch of kids. The book includes some violence.

Eury, Michael

Comics Gone Ape!: The Missing Link to Primates in Comics. Twomorrows Publishing 2007 144p. Illustration
Grades: Adult Professional   **741.5**
   1. Comic books, strips, etc — History; 2. Gorillas; 3. Monkeys; 4. Orangutans; 5. Primates; 6. Graphic novels
   978-1-893905-62-7, $16.95

This is a fairly lighthearted look at a fun topic in comics, apes. From King Kong to Banana Sunday, this book looks at the use of apes as characters in comics, ranging from the mainstream comics (Marvel and DC) to independent titles. Chapters discuss the various portrayals of King Kong in films and comics, and also Planet of the Apes. The book also includes interviews with comics creators who have done major works featuring apes, including Arthur Adams, Tim Eldred, Joe Kubert, Tony Millionaire, and Anne Timmons. Lots of comics covers, some interior art, and previously unseen sketches are reproduced in black and white.

The **Krypton** Companion. Twomorrows Publishing 2006 240p. Illustration
Grades: 9 10 11 12 Adult   **741.5**
   1. Superhero graphic novels; 2. Superman (Fictional character); 3. Graphic novels
   1-893905-61-6, $24.95

This book examines the "Superman mythology" that grew out of Superman comic books published by DC Comics from 1958 through 1986, under the direction of editors Mort Weisinger and Julius Schwartz. It includes interviews with a number of writers and artists who worked on Superman, including Neal Adams, Murphy Anderson, Steve Gerber, Jerry Siegel, Curt Swan, and many others, along with lots of art, photos, and behind-the-scenes stories.

Evanier, Mark

Kirby: king of comics. Mark Evanier; introduction by Neil Gaiman. Abrams 2008 224p. Illustration
Grades: Adult   **92; 741.5**
   9780810994478, $45; 0-8109-9447-X

   LC 2007016321

Faerber, Jay

Noble causes archives volume one. Image Comics 2008 598p. Illustration

Grades: 10 11 12 Adult **741.5; Fic**
1. Family life; 2. Science fiction graphic novels; 3. Superhero graphic novels; 4. Graphic novels
978-1-58240-896-5, $19.99

Normal young woman Liz Donnelly marries superhero Race Noble and gets a firsthand look at the inner workings of the celebrity superhero Noble family. Race is murdered while they're on their honeymoon, but the Nobles keep Liz with them. She finds that she has landed among some of the most dysfunctional people living a soap opera life. She has one brother-in-law who is now housed in a robotic body, another who is sort of immaterial, a sister-in-law who is pregnant and the father is one of the Noble family's greatest enemies, and the media keeps wanting to dig up as much dirt as they can, because gossip makes for high ratings. This volume reprints the early miniseries and the first twelve issues of the ongoing comics series in an economical black and white edition. The book includes violence, partial nudity, and sexual situations.

Volume 1 of 2

Fagan, Jody Condit

Comic book collections for libraries. [by] Bryan D. Fagan and Jody Condit Fagan; foreword by Stan Sakai; cover art by Derek Steed. Libraries Unlimited 2011 162p.

Grades: Adult Professional **025.2; 025**
978-1-59884-511-2 (pa), $45; 1-59884-511-X (pa); 978-1-59884-512-9 (e-book), $45

LC 2010052532

"This thorough guide focuses on creating a core collection for adults, though much of it will also be useful for youth librarians. It begins with a brief history of comics, then moves on to a detailed explanation of their structure, including the arcs, crossovers, and continuity essential to understanding the Marvel and DC universes. An annotated list of major publishers, writers, artists, and terms follows, along with a breakdown of genres in the medium, covering not just superheroes and manga but also Westerns, crime, romance, and more. The authors give detailed information about creating, maintaining, cataloging, and promoting a collection; circulation policies; and sample Marc records and circulation reports." (School Library Journal)

Farmer, Joyce

Special Exits: a graphic memoir. Illustrated by the author. Fantagraphics 2010 208p. Illustration

Grades: Adult **741.5; 92**
1. Aging parents; 2. Autobiographical graphic novels
9781606993811, $26.99; 160699381X; 1606997602; 9781606997604, $22.99

"Joyce Farmer's memoir chronicles the decline of the author's parents' health, their relationship with one another and with their their daughter, and how they cope with the day-to-day emotional fragility of the most taxing time of their lives." (Publisher's note)

Fawkes, Ray

One Soul. Ray Fawkes; [edited by] James Lucas Jones.. Oni Press 2011 176 p. Illustration

Grades: 11 12 Adult **741.5**
1. Identity (Philosophical concept); 2. Identity (Psychology); 3. Reincarnation; 4. Graphic novels
9781934964668, $24.99

LC 2011922803

Harvey Nominee: Best Graphic Novel (2012)
Eisner Nominee: Best Graphic Album - New (2012)

This graphic novel "follows a single soul as it's reincarnated through human history. . . . Each two-page spread is divided evenly into two three-by-three grids. Each of its 18 individual stories takes place in a single panel in that grid through the book's 88 spreads, so that to follow, say, the life of a silk heiress in Imperial China, the reader fastens the eye to a single spot in the book and then turns the pages quickly. . . . [Author Ray] Fawkes creates black-and-white tableaux of action, grief, sex and death spanning centuries. Individual spreads allow 18 characters to speak in unison, as when we see every subject's eyes widen simultaneously. When a character dies, his panel goes black for the rest of the book, and we meet the soul itself in cryptic narration." (Publishers Weekly)

Feiffer, Jules

Explainers. Fantagraphics Books 2008 546p. Illustration

Grades: 9 10 11 12 Adult **741.5**
1. Humorous graphic novels; 2. Graphic novels
978-1-56097-835-0, $28.99; 1-56097-835-X

This book collects the comic strips done by Jules Feiffer for the Village Voice, from 1956 through 1966. The alternative weekly newspaper, the only one of its kind back then, provided the then-unknown Feiffer with a forum to tackle all kinds of issues, ranging from relationships, sexuality, love, family, neuroses, politicians and politics, media, race, class, labor, religion, foreign policy, and war, among others. This is the first of four volumes planned to collect Feiffer's entire run of more than 2,000 strips. Older teen readers may be surprised to see just how timely and relevant these strips are, forty and fifty years after their original publication.

★ **Kill** My Mother: a graphic novel. Jules Feiffer. Liveright Publishing Corporation 2014 160 p. Illustration

Grades: 11 12 Adult **741.5**
1. Noir fiction; 2. Violence — Fiction; 3. Graphic novels
0871403145; 9780871403148, $27.95

LC 2014005844

"Along with three femme fatales, an obsessed daughter, and a loner heroine, 'Kill My Mother' features a fighter turned tap dancer, a small-time thug who dreams of being a hit man, a name-dropping cab driver, a communist liquor store owner, and a hunky movie star with a mind-boggling secret. Culminating in a U.S.O. tour on a war-torn Pacific island, this disparate band of old enemies congregate to settle scores." (Publisher's note)

"The entire work feels pulled from an earlier time yet explosively modern, a madcap relic animated by an outrageous mind. An unusual, unforgettable, incomparable pulpy punch." Kirkus

Passionella and Other Stories. Fantagraphics Books 2006 Un Illustration

Grades: 10 11 12 Adult **741.5; Fic**

1. Graphic novels
978-1-56097-097-2,
$19.95

This book collects Feiffer's extended graphic narratives of the late '50s and early '60s. "Excalibur and Rose" is the fable of a village comedian who embarks on a crusade in search of his serious side, which he finds in spades when he encounters his true love, the pathologically depressed Rose. "Passionella" retells Cinderella, seting it in modern Hollywood with a chimney sweep whose fairy godmother transforms her into the "mysterious exotic bewitching temptress" -and movie star-Passionella."The Lonely Machine" is an account of one man's attempt to find the perfect relationship through robot love, and "Harold Swerg" recounts the predicament of the world's greatest athlete who'd rather stay at his mundane job than compete against others, despite his country's desperate pleas to enter the Olympics. Three more graphic tales and several one-act plays round out this edition. There are some sexual situations.

Fessenden, Larry
The **last** winter. Larry Fessenden and Robert Leaver; art by Brahm Revel. Image Comics 2008 128p. Illustration
Grades: 10 11 12 Adult   **741.5; Fic**
1. Arctic regions; 2. Horror graphic novels; 3. Science fiction graphic novels; 4. Graphic novels
978-1-58240-936-8, $12.99

Oil company troubleshooter Pollack arrives at the base of the company's advance team in the Arctic National Wildlife Refuge to find out what's holding up the team's reports. Hoffman, who is working on the environmental impact statements, says there's something wrong, the permafrost is melting, and the whole area is unsafe for building any ice roads. Then one of the team dies, and the others begin to succumb to mysterious fears. When Hoffman is recalled to corporate headquarters, the plane crashes, and there's no way out except to find help from other remote stations; there's only one skidoo left, and Pollack and Hoffman head out. Will they find help before everyone dies" The book includes some violence, partial nudity, and some harsh language. This book adapts the script for the 2006 motion picture starring Ron Perlman, which is being released on DVD in September 2008.

Fies, Brian
Mom's cancer. Abrams ComicArts 2008 115p. Illustration
Grades: 9 10 11 12 Adult   **616.99; 741.5**
1. Biographical graphic novels; 2. Cancer; 3. Graphic novels
978-0-8109-7107-3, $14.95

When writer/cartoonist Fies learned his mother had cancer and that it had already spread from her lungs, he used webcomics to depict what was happening to his mother and the rest of the family as Mom fought the cancer. All the pain, the heartache, the little battles won, the effects on Fies' relationships with his sisters, the ultimate hope are all on the page. In the end, Mom beat the cancer. In an afterword, Fies tells the reader that some of the medications just wore down his mother's body, and she died shortly before the book was published.
First published 2006

Filiu, Jean-Pierre
Best of Enemies: A History of US and Middle East Relations: 1783-1953. Jean-Pierre Filiu, David B.. Harry N Abrams Inc. 2012 114 p. Illustration
Grades: 10 11 12 Adult   **327.73056022/2; 327.730**
1. Christianity and other religions; 2. United States — Foreign relations — Middle East; 3. Graphic novels
1906838453; 9781906838454, $24.95

This graphic novel looks at "the history of U.S. and Middle East relations." It starts with "the murderous aggression of Gilgamesh-as-avatar . . . . [The] focus then moves to 1780s skirmishes with Muslim city-states over maritime piracy, shifting priorities of Christian and Muslim nations over oil and anti-Semitism, and the subsequent ousting by the Americans and the British of Iran's Mohammad Mossadegh." (Library Journal)

Fillbach, Shawn
Maxwell Strangewell. By the Fillbach Brothers. Dark Horse Comics 2007 383p. Illustration
Grades: 9 10 11 12 Adult   **741.5; Fic**
1. Adventure graphic novels; 2. Science fiction graphic novels; 3. Graphic novels
978-1-59307-794-5, $19.95

Photographer Anna Gilmour discovers a ten-foot-tall being immediately after his fall to Earth. He can't speak, but communicates through telepathic empathy, and Anna introduces him to her father as "Max." Their home is soon beset by a sea of beatific Tibetan monks, alien assassins in disguise, and heavy weapons fire. Max might not know who he is, but a lot of others sure as heck seem to. A galactic free-for-all is about to go down and Earth is ground zero. Before the final act, Anna and Max encounter a prophecy, the man in the moon, an entire race of alien accountants, and the Revolver - an innocuous-looking jogger responsible for keeping the world spinning. The book has some strong language and some violence.

Fingerman, Bob
Maximum Minimum Wage. By Bob Fingerman. Image Comics 2013 360 p.
Grades: Adult   **741.5**
1. Cartoonists; 2. Cities and towns — Fiction
1607066742; 9781607066743, $34.99

This collection of comic strips by Bob Fingerman "is the workaday saga of cartoonist Rob Hoffman and his . . . girlfriend, Sylvia. With their colorful crew of friends, they forge ahead against the brutal indifference of their hometown. This definitive edition includes the original 72-page "pilot" episode (Minimum Wage Book One) and the revised "director's cut" of the main storyline. Plus, a bonus color section featuring original cover paintings and guest pin-ups." (Publisher's note)

Fisher, Bud
 Forever Nuts: Classic Screwball Strips: The Early Years of Mutt & Jeff. NBM 2007 192. Illustration
Grades: 10 11 12 Adult   **741.5**
 1. Mutt & Jeff (Fictional characters); 2. Graphic novels
978-1-56163-502-3, $24.95
 One of the most long lasting and popular humor strips in history, Mutt and Jeff had many memorable moments of serious goofiness and irreverence. Here's a rediscovery of a true oddball classic maybe only outdone by the antic high living of its own creator. 2007 is the one hundredth anniversary of its start. In these early strips, alcohol consumption, smoking, gambling, and various other pursuits considered to be vices are portrayed.

Fitzgerald, F. Scott
 The **curious** case of Benjamin Button: a graphic novel. Adapted by Nunzio Defilippis & Christina Weir; illustrated by Kevin Cornell. Quirk Books 2008 128p. Illustration
Grades: 9 10 11 12 Adult   **741.5; Fic**
 1. Authors; 2. Fitzgerald, F Scott (Francis Scott), 1896-1940 — Adaptations; 3. Humorous graphic novels; 4. Novelists; 5. Screenwriters; 6. Graphic novels
978-1-59474-281-1,
$15.95
    LC 2008-923680
 Benjamin Button comes into the world in the year 1860, but as a newborn infant, he is the size of, and looks like a seventy-year-old man. His flabbergasted parents cope, with difficulty, and Benjamin finds he has to live his life in reverse, looking old but with the mind and emotions of a child. When he's a young man (but looks to be in late middle age), he marries a young woman who likes older men, and he

Courtesy of Quirk Books

continues his father's successful business. As he matures but continues to grow younger, he becomes a military officer, and when he looks like a teenager but is in late middle age, he attends Harvard. Finally, in his old age, he resembles a newborn baby and must have a nurse to take care of him. This story by Fitzgerald was originally published in 1922; Cornell illustrates it in sepia tones.

Fleisher, Michael
 The **Original** Encyclopedia of Comic Book Heroes Volume Two Featuring Wonder Woman. DC Comics 2007 253p. Illustration
Grades: 9 10 11 12 Adult   **741.5**
 1. Wonder Woman (Fictional character); 2. Graphic novels
978-1-4012-1365-7, $19.99
 Everything one ever wanted to know about DC's Amazing Amazon " and so much more " can be found in this

in-depth volume, brought back into print for the first time in 30 years. Originally published in 1976, this comprehensive volume includes every piece of information one could want to know about Wonder Woman, her allies and enemies, weapons in her quest for peace, and her adventures across the decades. The book covers the first three decades of Wonder Woman comics.

Fleming, Ann Marie
 The **Magical** Life of Long Tack Sam: An Illustrated Memoir. Ann Marie Fleming.. Riverhead Books 2007 170 p. Illustration; Color
Grades: 11 12 Adult   **741.5; 793.8; 92**
 1. Biographical graphic novels; 2. Long Tack Sam; 3. Magicians; 4. Graphic novels
1594482640; 9781594482649, $20
    LC 2007060352
 This graphic memoir, by Ann Marie Fleming, was "inspired by the award-winning documentary-and the life and mystery of China's greatest magician. Who was Long Tack Sam" He was born in 1885. He ran away from Shangdung Province to join the circus. He was an acrobat. A magician. A comic. An impresario. A restaurateur. A theater owner. A world traveler. An East-West ambassador. A mentor to Orson Welles. He was considered the greatest act in the history of vaudeville. (Publisher's note)
 Includes bibliographical references (p. 168-169)

★ **Flight, volume six**
 Edited by Kazu Kibuishi. Villard Books 2009 284p. Illustration
Grades: 8 9 10 11 12 Adult   **741.5; Fic**
 1. Fantasy graphic novels; 2. Short stories; 3. Graphic novels
978-0-345-50590-3, $25
 This sixth volume of the graphic anthology series includes stories by fifteen creators: J.P. Ahonen, Graham Annable, Bannister, Phil Craven, Mike Dutton, Michel Gagne, Cory Godbey, Rodolphe Guenoden, Steve Hamaker, Kazu Kibuishi, Andrea Offermann, Richard Pose, Justin Ridge, Rad Sechrist, and Kean Soo. Returning favorite characters includ Jellaby by Soo, Hamaker's Fish N Chips, Kibuishi's Daisy Kutter, and the wordless little fox Rex by Gagne. Bannister's "Cooking Duel" stands out as a lot of fun, as a couple makes a bet about which of them can make the better tasting mushroom quiche; and Justin Ridge's "Dead Bunny" shows that there is a soul mate for just about anyone, including a zombie bunny.

Foglio, Kaja
 Girl Genius Book Six: Agatha Heterodyne and the Golden Trilobite. Story by Kaja & Phil Foglio; drawings by Phil Foglio. Airship Entertainment 2007 Un Illustration
Grades: 9 10 11 12 Adult   **741.5; Fic**
 1. Adventure graphic novels; 2. Fantasy graphic novels; 3. Humorous graphic novels; 4. Graphic novels
978-1-890856-42-7, $21.95
 The Wulfenbachs discover that Agatha is still alive and come to get her. Things are complicated by the fact that Agatha is currently possessed by the evil mastermind responsible for the Long War - her mother, Lucrezia. Agatha keeps fighting back, and things get very chaotic when she

keeps flipping back and forth between herself and the evil Lucrezia. This book has some violence.

Girl Genius Omnibus Edition #1. Story by Kaja & Phil Foglio; drawings by Phil Foglio. Airship Entertainment 2006 312p. Illustration
Grades: 9 10 11 12 Adult   **741.5; Fic**
   1. Adventure graphic novels; 2. Science fiction graphic novels; 3. Graphic novels
978-1-890856-40-3, $14.95

In a time when the Industrial Revolution has become an all-out war, Mad Science rules the world. Agatha Clay is a student at Transylvania Polygnostic University, a complete klutz with rotten luck. But when the University is overthrown and a mechanical monster stalks the streets, it begins to look as though Agatha may carry a spark of Mad Science after all. She ends up aboard the giant airship Castle Wulfenbach, and finds an ally in Krosp the Cat (a genetic experiment with a smattering of Napoleon's brain cells); she also becomes friends with Gilgamesh, Baron Wulfenbach's son. When the Monster Engine is activated, Agatha and Gil battle it, then Agatha and Krosp make their escape. This black and white edition contains the first three volumes of the Girl Genius collection: Agatha Heterodyne & the Beetleburg Clank, Agatha Heterodyne & the Airship City, and Agatha Heterodyne & the Monster Engine. Agatha tends to do a lot of her best tech work while wearing pajamas.

Girl Genius Vol. 4: Agatha Heterodyne and the Circus of Dreams. Story by Kaja & Phil Foglio; drawings by Phil Foglio. Airship Entertainment 2005 127p. Illustration
Grades: 9 10 11 12 Adult   **741.5; Fic**
   1. Adventure graphic novels; 2. Science fiction graphic novels; 3. Graphic novels
978-1-890856-36-6, $20.95

The Adventure, Romance & Mad Science continues as Agatha Heterodyne's damaged aircraft comes roughly to rest in the Wastelands. She encounters a traveling circus and proves her mettle by destroying a massive spider-clank as it attacks. Back at the airship city, a frustrated Baron Wulfenbach dispatches his son Gilgamesh and deposed pirate queen Bangaldesh DuPree to capture Agatha, whose very existence threatens the peace - but the cunning circus folk succeed in hiding Agatha, who quickly discovers she is only one of their many secrets. She begins warrior training with the circus's expert swordswoman Zeetha, meets a strange new breed of Jagermonster, and attracts unexpected attention in saving them from the grimmest of fates. This volume is in full color. The book has some monster fighting.

Girl Genius Vol. 5: Agatha Heterodyne and the Clockwork Princess. Story by Kaja & Phil Foglio; drawings by Phil Foglio. Airship Entertainment 2006 109p. Illustration
Grades: 9 10 11 12 Adult   **741.5; Fic**
   1. Adventure graphic novels; 2. Science fiction graphic novels; 3. Graphic novels
978-1-890856-39-7, $19.95

Agatha continues to travel with the circus, but they have to pass through a town where the prince confiscated one of their clanks, Tinka, who is actually one of the Muses of the Storm King. When they are ordered to play a command performance and Agatha plays Lucrezia, the prince recognizes her as a real Heterodyne. Now she's really in

trouble. Meanwhile, Baron Wulfenbach discovers that he's been duped and Agatha is still alive.

Foglio, Phil
   Girl genius book seven: Agatha Heterodyne and the voice of the castle. Airship Entertainment 2008 128p. Illustration
Grades: 9 10 11 12 Adult   **741.5; Fic**
   1. Adventure graphic novels; 2. Humorous graphic novels; 3. Science fiction graphic novels; 4. Graphic novels
978-1-890856-45-8, $21.95

After the battle at Sturmhalten, everyone converges on Mechanicsburg. The severely injured Baron is in the hospital, and Gilgamesh must fend off all the would-be assassins trying to strike while the Baron is weak. A fake Heterodyne heir enters Mechanicsburg and gets into the Heterodyne castle. And Agatha and her friends arrive and she manages to convince the old castle Seneschal that she just might be the real Heterodyne heir. Only the real heir will be able to control the sentient castle, but the fake one in there now plans to kill the castle. There is fighting action but no graphic violence, or harsh language, or any really objectionable content.

Forbes, Jake
   Jim Henson's Return to Labyrinth. Illustrated by Chris Lie. Tokyopop 2006 Un Illustration
Grades: 7 8 9 10 11 12 Adult   **741.5; Fic**
   1. Adventure graphic novels; 2. Fantasy graphic novels; 3. Graphic novels
1-59816-725-1, $9.99

The Goblin King has kept a watchful eye on Toby, his minions secretly guiding and protecting the child. Legions of goblins work behind the scenes to ensure that Toby has whatever his heart desires, preparing him for the day when he will return to the Labyrinth and take his rightful place beside Jareth as the heir to the Goblin Kingdom. That day has come ... but no one has told Toby. This is an original story set in the world of the motion picture and is focused on Toby, who was a baby in the movie. This book is a global manga title.

Forney, Ellen
   ★ **Marbles:** mania, depression, Michelangelo, and me : a graphic memoir. By Ellen Forney. Gotham Books 2012 248 p.
Grades: Adult   **741.5/973; 741.5; B**
   1. Cartoonists; 2. Forney, Ellen; 3. Manic-depressive illness; 4. Graphic novels
1592407323; 9781592407323, $20
                  LC 2012014588

"Eisner nominee [Ellen] Forney confesses her struggles with being diagnosed as bipolar in this . . . memoir. Beginning with the manic episode that led to her diagnosis, Forney chronicles her journey toward reconciling the dual natures of bipolar disorder: a dangerous disease, but also a source of inspiration for many artists." She uses cartoons, realistic illustrations, and photographs "to chronicle her outer life while revealing her inner state of mind." (Publishers Weekly)

Fox, Gardner

The **Atom** Archives Volume 2. Pencils by Gil Kane; inks by Murphy Anderson. DC Comics 2003 215p. Illustration

Grades: 7 8 9 10 11 12 Adult   **741.5; Fic**
1. Atom (Fictional character); 2. Superhero graphic novels; 3. Graphic novels
1-4012-0014-1, $49.95

This volume, reprinting The Atom issues #6-13, originally published in 1963 through 1964, features Mighty Mite's early team-ups with Hawkman and Hawkgirl, the classic villainy of Dr. Light, the return of Chronos, and much more. This Archive Edition reprints the comics in full color in a hardcover edition.

The **Green** Lantern Archives Volume 5. DC Comics 2004 239p. Illustration

Grades: 6 7 8 9 10 11 12 Adult   **741.5; Fic**
1. Green Lantern (Fictional character); 2. Superhero graphic novels; 3. Graphic novels
1-4012-0404-X, $49.95

                                  LC 93-131923

This volume presents the further adventures of Green Lantern Hal Jordan " the Silver Age's science fiction-influenced hero. This time, the Emerald Gladiator squares off against foes such as Dr. Light, Hector Hammond, Evil Star, the Aerialist, and many more. This full-color Archive reprints nine tales from Green Lantern #30-38, originally published in 1964 and 1965.

Showcase Presents: Adam Strange Volume One. DC Comics 2007 510p. Illustration

Grades: 6 7 8 9 10 11 12 Adult   **741.5; Fic**
1. Superhero graphic novels; 2. Graphic novels
978-1-4012-1313-8, $16.99

After being mysteriously teleported to a distant world by an alien scientist, Adam Strange went from being an Earth archaeologist to a cosmic adventurer. He soon becomes the hero of the planet Rann, shuttling between his old and new worlds via the Zeta Beam. With the love of his life, Alanna, daughter of Rann's leading scientist, they embark on a series of adventures against all types of space menaces. This black and white volume reprints stories from 1958 through 1963.

Showcase Presents: Green Lantern Volume 1. DC Comics 2005 528p. Illustration

Grades: 6 7 8 9 10 11 12 Adult   **741.5; Fic**
1. Green Lantern (Fictional character); 2. Superhero graphic novels; 3. Graphic novels
1-4012-0759-6, $9.99

A dying alien summoned test pilot Hal Jordan and gave him the most powerful weapon in the universe: a power ring. Jordan was inducted into the universe-spanning Green Lantern Corps and assigned to protect a sector of space including Earth. His sheer willpower directs the ring to create fantastic energy constructs and with it, protect the good from evil. In these earliest stories, readers meet the Guardians of the Universe, many of Jordan's intergalactic comrades, and some of his deadliest opponents, including Hector Hammond, Sonar, and Sinestro. The black and white reprints date from 1959 through 1962.

Showcase Presents: Hawkman Volume 1. DC Comics 2007 560p. Illustration

Grades: 7 8 9 10 11 12 Adult   **741.5; Fic**
1. Hawkman (Fictional character); 2. Superhero graphic novels; 3. Graphic novels
978-1-4012-1280-3, $16.99

Katar Hol and his wife Shayera, winged law officers from the planet Thanagar, visit Earth to learn about terrestrial police methods. To fit into human society, they adopt the civilian identities of Carter Hall, the curator of the Midway City Museum, and Shiera, his assistant. Dressed in their avian Thanagarian garb, Carter and Shiera patrol the skies of Midway City as Hawkman and Hawkgirl. They plunge headlong into the battle for justice against such villains as the Shadow Thief and Matter Master. With their array of alien weaponry and their scientific skill, this crime-fighting duo continue to defend Earth against nefarious threats. This book collects black and white reprints of thirty-three stories written by Fox, dating from 1961 through 1966 and featuring the work of artists such as Joe Kubert, Murphy Anderson, and Carmine Infantino.

Showcase Presents: Justice League of America Volume 1. DC Comics 2005 544p. Illustration

Grades: 6 7 8 9 10 11 12 Adult   **Fic; 741.5**
1. Justice League of America (Fictional characters); 2. Superhero graphic novels
1-4012-0761-8, $16.99

Some of the greatest super heroes in the DC Universe united to form the Justice League of America: Superman, Batman, Wonder Woman, the Flash, Green Lantern, Martian Manhunter, and Aquaman. Together, they face such foes as Dr. Light, Dr. Destiny, Starro, Felix Faust, Amos Fortune, and the Weapons Master. This volume includes the stories in which the JLS inducts new members to the team: Green Arrow and the Atom. In light of the events in Infinite Crisis, readers might be interested to see how far back the roots of the story went - all the way back to 1960. This black and white reprint volume includes stories published from 1960 through 1962.

Fraction, Matt

The **Five** Fists of Science. Written by Matt Fraction; illustrated by Steven Sanders. Image Comics 2006 Un Illustration

Grades: 9 10 11 12 Adult   **741.5; Fic**
1. Adventure graphic novels; 2. Science fiction graphic novels; 3. Graphic novels
1-58240-605-7, $12.99

At the beginning of the twentieth century, Mark Twain and Nicola Tesla work to save the world from the menace of war. J.P. Morgan, Andrew Carnegie, Thomas Edison, and Guillermo Marconi are having the Innsmouth Tower built; what the world doesn't know is that they intend to summon some monstrous old gods (anyone familiar with H.P. Lovecraft and his Cthulhu Mythos will catch on immediately). Meanwhile, Twain and Tesla have been trying to interest world leaders in technology that will end all war, only to find that no one is interested. When Marconi realizes what Morgan is really planning, he tells Tesla and Twain, in hopes that their robotic machine can stop Morgan. Some harsh language and violence pepper the story.

Hawkeye: Little Hits. By Matt Fraction (Author), David Aja (Illustrator), Javier Pulido (Illustrator), Steve Lieber (Illustrator), Francesco Francavilla (Illustrator), Jesse Hamm (Illustrator). Marvel Worldwide 2013 136 p.
Grades: 11 12 Adult   Fic; 741.5
1. Avengers (Fictional characters); 2. Superheroes — Fiction; 3. Graphic novels
0785165630; 9780785165637, $16.99
In this graphic novel, by Matt Fraction, "ace archer Clint Barton faces the digital doomsday ofûDVR-Mageddon! Then: Cherry's got a gun. And she looks good in it. And Hawkeye gets very, very distracted. Plus: Valentine's Day with the heartthrob of the Marvel Universe" This will be...confusing." (Publisher's note)
"Fraction's writing is superb, but it's Eisner-winning Aja's wildly creative page layouts that have matured into something truly unique and demanding of critical attention." Booklist

Hawkeye: my life as a weapon. By Matt Fraction (Author), David Aja (Illustrator), Javier Pulido (Illustrator). Marvel Worldwide 2013 136 p.
Grades: 11 12 Adult   Fic; 741.5
1. Avengers (Fictional characters); 2. Superheroes — Fiction; 3. Graphic novels
0785165622; 9780785165620, $16.99
In this book, by Matt Fraction, "Clint Bartonûaka the self-made hero Hawkeye fights for justice! With ex-Young Avenger Kate Bishop by his side, he's out to prove himself as one of Earth's Mightiest Heroes! SHIELD recruits Clint to intercept a packet of incriminating evidenceûbefore he becomes the most wanted man in the world." (Publisher's note)

Hawkeye: Rio Bravo. By Matt Fraction; illustrated by Francesco Francavilla, David Aja and Annie Wu. Marvel Enterprises 2015 160 p. Color; Illustration
Grades: 10 11 12 Adult   741.5973; 741.5
1. Superhero comic books, strips, etc
0785185313; 9780785185314, $17.99
In this comic book, by Matt Fraction, "Reeling from recent events, even Hawkeye wants to know what his new status quo is. Who's with him" Who's against him" Who's trying to kill him and why" So many dang questions! And just when Clint's rock bottom couldn't arrive fast enough...his brother shows up. After a lifetime of decisions both good and bad, Clint and Barney Barton have to realize that they are brothers and ultimately, they're the only ones who can save one another." (Publisher's note)

Hawkeye; Volume 3: L.A. Woman. By Matt Fraction; illustrated by Annie Wu and Javier Pulido. Marvel Worldwide 2014 144 p. Color; Illustration
Grades: 11 12 Adult   741.5
1. Assassins — Fiction; 2. Criminals — Fiction; 3. Los Angeles (Calif) — Fiction; 4. Musicians — Fiction
0785183906; 9780785183907, $15.99
In this book, by Matt Fraction, illustrated by Annie Wu and Javier Pulido, "Kate Bishop heads to Los Angeles to get away from New York, life, and Clint Barton—but not away from trouble! Because Madame Masque is hanging out at poolside with the rich and famous as well! As Kate helps a reclusive and Sixties-damaged pop music genius find his

lost masterpiece, Madame Masque finds Kate. By which we mean starts trying to kill her again." (Publisher's note)
"Fraction's unique brand of storytelling is both light with humor and deep with meaning, and he keeps it fresh by constantly bringing in new characters." Booklist
Contains material originally published in magazine form as Hawkeye #14, #16, #18, #20 and Annual #1—Title page verso.

ODY-C; Volume 1: Off to far Ithicaa. Matt Fraction, Christian Ward. Image Comics 2015 136 p. Illustration
Grades: Adult   Fic; 741.5
1. Epic literature; 2. Science fiction
1632153769; 9781632153760, $9.99
This book, by Matt Fraction, illustrated by Christian Ward, is a "mind-bending, gender-shattering epic science fiction retelling of Homer's Odyssey starting with the end of a great war in the stars and the beginning of a very long journey home for Odyssia and her crew of warriors." (Publisher's note)
This hallucinatory sf recasting of Homer's Odyssey doesn't simply swap the gender of its protagonist—it takes place in a universe where men have suffered genocide at the hands of a paranoid Zeus.... Ward fills the pages to bursting with incredible varicolored psychedelic imagery, bringing extraordinary vividness to scenes of space travel, grotesqueries such as the multibreasted Cyclops, and depictions of nudity, sex, and copious gore." LJ
Volume 1 of an ongoing series

Sex Criminals; 1: one weird trick. Matt Fraction, illustrated by Chip Zdarsky. Image Comics 2014 128 p. Color; Illustration
Grades: Adult   741.5
1. Bank robberies — Fiction; 2. Graphic novels
1607069466; 9781607069461, $9.99
Eisner Award: Best New Series (2014)
Harvey Award: Best New Series (2014)
In this comic book series by Matt Fraction, illustrated by Chip Zdarsky, "Suzie's just a regular gal with an irregular gift: when she has sex, she stops time. One day she meets Jon and it turns out he has the same ability. And sooner or later they get around to using their gifts to do what we'd ALL do: rob a couple banks." (Publisher's note)
A "funny, engaging, and inventive new comic book about sex, love, and fighting the man, with a clever sci-fi twist." Comics Alliance
Volume 1 of an ongoing series

Sex Criminals; 2: Two Worlds, One Cop. By Matt Fraction; illustrated by Chip Zdarsky. Image Comics 2015 128 p. Color; Illustration
Grades: Adult   741.5
1. Love stories; 2. Man-woman relationship — Fiction; 3. Sex — Fiction
1632151936; 9781632151933, $14.99
This graphic novel, by Matt Fraction and illustrated by Chip Zdarsky, "finds the honeymoon to be over for Jon and Suzie. Once the thrill of new lust fades, where do you go" Come along and laff and love with Matt and Chip as they brimp back ceaselessly against the past." (Publisher's note)
"At times, Jon and Suzie break the fourth wall, revealing their hookups and complicated feelings they have for themselves and for each other. Even with all the sex in

this book—and there's a lot of frank, candid sex—it's at these moments that we truly see them naked, and it's their emotional chemistry that's at the heart of this intimate narrative." Booklist

Frakes, Colleen

Prison island: a graphic memoir. By Colleen Frakes. Houghton Mifflin Harcourt 2015 187 p. Illustration

Grades: 9 10 11 12 Adult   **741.5; 741.56973**

1. Prisons — United States; 2. Washington (State)

1942186029; 9781942186021, $16.99

In this graphic memoir, by Colleen Frake, "McNeil Island in Washington state was the home of the last prison island in the United States, accessible only by air or sea. It was also home to about fifty families, including . . . Frake's. Her parents —like nearly everyone else on the island —both worked in the prison, where her father was the prison's captain and her mother worked in security." (Publisher's note)

Francavilla, Francesco

The **Black** Beetle 1: No Way Out. By Francesco Francavilla and edited by Jim Gibbons. Dark Horse 2013 152 p. Illustration

Grades: Adult   **741.5**

1. Organized crime; 2. Superheroes — Fiction

1616552026; 9781616552022, $19.99

In this comic by Francesco Francavilla, "the Black Beetle . . .witnesses an explosion that decimates the city's organized crime community, killing dozens. No one gets away with mass murder when the Black Beetle's on the case. When Colt City cries out for justice, there's one man who will answer!" (Publisher's note)

Volume 1 of an ongoing series

Freeman, Adam

Monster Attack Network. Marc Bernardin and Adam Freeman; art by Nima Sorat. AiT/PlanetLar 2007 96p. Illustration

Grades: 10 11 12 Adult   **741.5**

1. Adventure graphic novels; 2. Monsters; 3. Graphic novels

978-1-932051-50-6, $12.95

The island of Lapuatu is a paradise, except for the various giant monsters that occasionally attack. The Monster Attack Network fights the beasties and rebuilds from the destruction. When Lana Barnes starts to work for M.A.N., though, things get really crazy and monsters attack two and three at a time giant slugs, bats, and other destructive critters. Nate Klinger, one of the top first responders at M.A.N., knows something's a bit off about Lana; for one thing, she's a native Lapuatan despite her name. And the monsters have never attacked more than one at a time before she started to work. The book includes lots of foul language and monster fighting action.

Fujima, Takuya

Free Collars Kingdom Vol. 1. Random House/Del Rey Manga 2007 240p. Illustration

Grades: 10 11 12 Adult   **741.5; Fic**

1. Cats; 2. Fantasy graphic novels; 3. Manga; 4. Graphic novels

978-0-345-49265-4, $10.95

Cyan is a teenage cat (in cat years), and when his beloved young master falls ill, the parents abandon Cyan in the basement of a luxurious apartment building. Now Cyan finds himself smack-dab in the middle of the biggest feline territorial battle in Japan. While waiting for his owner to return and reclaim him, Cyan has to brave the attacks of vampy Siam and the beautiful killer Kline. He also must try to fit in with the group of oddball strays who reside in the basement, a cat gang named the Free Collars. The conceit here is that the cats are drawn as cute cat-eared humans. There's some partial nudity and sexually suggestive situations.

Fujisaki, Ryu

Hoshin Engi Volume 1. Viz Media/Shonen Jump 2007 192p. Illustration

Grades: 8 9 10 11 12 Adult   **741.5; Fic**

1. Adventure graphic novels; 2. Fantasy graphic novels; 3. Shonen manga; 4. Graphic novels

978-1-4215-1362-1, $7.99

When his clan is wiped out by a beautiful demon, young Taikobo finds himself in charge of the mysterious Hoshin Project. Its mission: find all immortals living in the human world and seal them away forever. But who do you trust—and whose side are you really on—when you've been trained to hunt demons by a demon. There is demon-fighting action.

Fuller, Nicolle Rager

Charles Darwin's On the Origin of Species: a graphic adaptation. [by] Michael Keller; art by Nicolle Rager Fuller. Rodale 2009 192p. Illustration

Grades: 9 10 11 12 Adult   **576.8; 741.5**

978-1-60529-697-5; 1-60529-697-X, $19.99;

978-1-60529-948-8 (pa); 1-60529-948-0 (pa), $14.99

LC 2009-11387

"The graphic novel follows Origin's original chapters, combining snippets of Darwin's text with quotes from letters, illustrative examples from his time and from the present, and occasional invented dialog. Fuller's images of people seem clumsy, but her full-color plants, animals, charts, maps, and scientific accoutrements are attractive and effective.... [This] version well conveys both the science and the wonder of Origin." Libr J

Gabrych, Andersen

Batgirl: Destruction's Daughter. Andersen Gabrych, writer; Pop Mhan et al, pencillers; Jesse Delperdang et al, inkers. DC Comics 2006 Un Illustration

Grades: 10 11 12 Adult   **741.5; Fic**

1. Adventure graphic novels; 2. Batgirl (Fictional character); 3. Superhero graphic novels; 4. Graphic novels

978-1-4012-0896-7, $19.99

Cassandra Cain was quickly accepted as the new Batgirl after helping Batman during Gotham's darkest hours. Trained in deadly martial arts from early childhood by a notorious assassin, Batgirl developed the uncanny ability to anticipate her opponents' movements to make her unbeatable in combat. Now, the Dark Knight's young protege is determined to discover who her true mother is, and her quest, brings her face-to-face with the League of Assassins and into mortal combat with the deadliest woman alive, Lady Shiva. It all ends in a life or death battle at the edge of Lazarus Pit, and only one person will survive. There's a fair amount of blood shed in the many fights.

Batgirl: Kicking Assassins. Andersen Gabrych, writer; Ale Garza, Pop Mhan, pencillers; Jesse Delperdang, Andrew Pepoy, Jack Purcell, inkers. DC Comics 2005 Un Illustration
Grades: 9 10 11 12 Adult   **741.5; Fic**
1. Batgirl (Fictional character); 2. Superhero graphic novels; 3. Graphic novels
1-4012-0439-2, $14.99

It's a fresh start for Batgirl as Cassandra Cain is building a new life for herself in Bludhaven. But with the Penguin also moving to town and setting up a criminal empire, can Batgirl keep the streets safe, or will she face something more sinister and vile than before" With the Brotherhood of Evil, Deathstroke, and the Ravager coming at her one after the other, Batgirl barely has the chance to settle into her new neighborhood before the fists start to fly. The book includes lots of fighting.

Gaiman, Neil
The **Books** of Magic. Writer, Neil Gaiman; illustrators, John Bolton [and others]. DC Comics/Vertigo 1993 Un Illustration
Grades: 10 11 12 Adult   **741.5; Fic**
1. Fantasy graphic novels; 2. Magic; 3. Supernatural graphic novels; 4. Graphic novels
1-56389-082-8, $19.99

A quartet of fallen mystics dubbed the "Trench Coat Brigade "is introduced in this first collection of the adventures of Timothy Hunter. John Constantine, the Phantom Stranger, Dr. Occult, and Mister E take Hunter on a tour of the magical realms. Along the way he's introduced to Vertigo's greatest practitioners of magic and must choose whether or not to join their ranks. And they must decide if he should live ... or die. While the publisher rates it for mature readers, there's little in the way of strong language or overt violence, and no nudity.

Creatures of the Night. Neil Gaiman, writer; Michael Zulli, artist; Todd Klein, lettering. Dark Horse Comics 2004 46p. Illustration
Grades: 10 11 12 Adult   **741.5; Fic**
1. Fantasy graphic novels; 2. Supernatural graphic novels; 3. Graphic novels
1-56971-936-5, $12.95

Artist Zulli has adapted two of Gaiman's prose short stories into comic book form. In "The Price," a mysterious black cat comes to a family living in the English countryside. Soon after he arrives, the father notices that in the mornings, the cat is scratched and bleeding. Each morning after that, the cat suffers more injuries; maybe the family isn't quite so safe in the countryside after all. "The Daughter of Owls" is a baby girl abandoned on the steps of the Dymton Church in the late 1800s. Sequestered in the convent, the girl lives in solitary silence for fourteen years, cared for after a fashion by a nun, and then by a woman in Dymton. When the woman gossips about the silent girl's beauty, the men of Dymton hatch a dastardly plot which ends in tragedy.

★ **Death:** The High Cost of Living. Art by Chris Bachalo, Mark Buckingham, Dave McKean. DC Comics/Vertigo 1994 104p. Illustration
Grades: 10 11 12 Adult   **741.5; Fic**
1. Adventure graphic novels; 2. Fantasy graphic novels; 3. Graphic novels
1-56389-133-6, $12.95

A member of the Endless, a family of beings who have existed longer than the gods, Death enjoys manifesting herself in the persona of a Goth girl. She is taking her one-day-a-century holiday in New York City, where she meets suicidal teen Sexton, and they end up searching the city for the witch Mad Hettie's heart, which she has hidden away ... somewhere. Then the Eremite hunts her, to steal Death's ankh and therefore her power. The book includes some violence and some strong language.

Death: The Time of Your Life. Art by Chris Bachalo, Mark Buckingham, Mark Pennington. DC Comics/Vertigo 1997 96p. Illustration
Grades: 10 11 12 Adult   **741.5; Fic**
1. Adventure graphic novels; 2. Fantasy graphic novels; 3. Horror graphic novels; 4. Graphic novels
1-56389-333-9, $12.99

This is the story of Foxglove, a rising star of the music world who must wrestle with revealing her true sexual orientation as her companion, Hazel, is lured into the realm of Death. As one of the Endless, Death met the two young women on her latest once a century holiday, so it's only natural that she would appear now. The book includes some strong language, sexual situations, and some violence.

Marvel 1602. [Neil Gaiman, writer; Andy Kubert, illustrator; Richard Isanove, digital painting; Todd Klein, lettering]. Marvel Comics 2005 Un Illustration
Grades: 10 11 12 Adult   **741.5; 741; Fic**
1. Daredevil (Fictional character); 2. Doctor Doom (Fictional character); 3. Superhero graphic novels; 4. X-Men (Fictional characters); 5. Graphic novels
0-7851-1073-9, $24.99; 0-7851-1073-9 (pa), $19.99

This book "takes the Marvel superheroes and villains of the 1960s—the original X-Men, Daredevil, Dr. Doom, and many others—and places them in the early 17th century." Libr J

"The improbable combination works remarkably well, as the superheroes' strange abilities adapt to Elizabethan culture. This glorious adventure is peppered with Scott McKowen's gorgeous, moody cover-art woodcuts." Publ Wkly

First published in magazine form as Marvel 1602 #1-8

★ **Neil** Gaiman and Charles Vess' Stardust: being a romance within the realms of Faerie. DC Comics/Vertigo 2007 213p. Illustration
Grades: 10 11 12 Adult   **741.5; Fic**
1. Fantasy graphic novels; 2. Graphic novels
978-1-4012-1190-5, $39.95

In the sleepy English countryside at the dawn of the Victorian Era, young Tristran Thorn has lost his heart to beautiful Victoria Forester. But Victoria is cold and distant—as distant, in fact, as the star she and Tristran see fall from the sky on a crisp October evening. For the coveted prize of Victoria's hand, Tristran vows to retrieve the fallen star and deliver it to his beloved. It is an oath that sends the lovelorn swain into a world that is strange beyond imagining, a world populated by evil old witches, deadly clutching trees, and goblin press-gangs—a world redeemed only by true love. The story includes some sexual situations and partial nudity. This deluxe hardcover edition includes bonus material such as Gaiman's initial proposal and a number of preliminary sketches and new artwork from Vess. This illustrated novel is published by a comic book publisher and can go in either fiction or in the graphic novel section.

Neil Gaiman's Midnight Days. DC Comics/Vertigo 2000 Un Illustration
Grades: 10 11 12 Adult   **741.5; Fic**
1. Fantasy graphic novels; 2. Horror graphic novels; 3. Graphic novels
1-56389-517-X, $17.99
This book collects some of Gaiman's earliest work for Vertigo. Included in these never-before-reprinted and original publications are tales featuring the Golden Age Sandman, Morpheus, the Swamp Thing, and John Constantine. Some of the stories include strong language, violence, and nudity.

★ The **Sandman** Volume 10: The Wake. Art by Michael Zulli, Jon J. Muth, Charles Vess. DC Comics/Vertigo 1997 Un Illustration
Grades: 10 11 12 Adult   **741.5; Fic**
1. Adventure graphic novels; 2. Fantasy graphic novels; 3. Sandman (Fictional character); 4. Graphic novels
1-56389-279-0, $19.99
In the last chapter of the Sandman saga, the Endless and all the dreamers come to celebrate the life and mourn the passing of the King of Dreams. Meanwhile, the new Dream, who was once the boy Daniel Hall, waits for the others to come and meet him. The King is dead, long live the King. The book includes some nudity and violence.

Sandman Volume 2: The Doll's House. Written by Neil Gailman; illustrated by Mike Dringenberg et al. DC Comics/Vertigo 1991 255p. Illustration
Grades: 10 11 12 Adult   **741.5; Fic**
1. Fantasy graphic novels; 2. Horror graphic novels; 3. Sandman (Fictional character); 4. Graphic novels
0-930289-59-5, $19.99
                                        LC 92-159876
In this second volume, Rose Walker is the dream vortex who must be killed to save the Dreaming. In the meantime, she wanders the world hunting for her younger brother, and along the way she attends a "Cereal" convention, which is actually a serial killers' convention. Morpheus must track down four of his major arcana dreams that were lost during his long imprisonment. And Morpheus meets once a century with Hob, a man who had wished to never die. The book includes graphic violence, some partial nudity, and strong language.

★ **Sandman** Volume 3: Dream Country. Art by Kelley Jones, Charles Vess, Colleen Doran, Malcolm Jones III. DC Comics/Vertigo 1991 Un Illustration
Grades: 10 11 12 Adult   **741.5; Fic**
1. Fantasy graphic novels; 2. Horror graphic novels; 3. Sandman (Fictional character); 4. Graphic novels
1-56389-016-X, $14.99
                                        LC 92-159876

This third volume collects four stories; the two standouts are "A Dream of a Thousand Cats," in which a purebred Siamese remembers her first litter of mixed-breed cats that her owners killed and ventures into the cat version of the dreaming in which Morpheus is a huge black cat and discovers her mission in life - cat owners may never look at their sleeping cats the same way again; and "A Midsummer Night's Dream" recounts the adventures of William Shakespeare and his company of players as they are summoned to perform their play to a highly select audience - King Oberon and Queen Titania of Faerie. This story won the World Fantasy Award for Best Short Story when it was first published. The book includes nudity, sexual situations, and some violence.

Sandman Volume 4: The Season of Mists. DC Comics/Vertigo 1994 Un Illustration
Grades: 10 11 12 Adult   **741.5; Fic**
1. Fantasy graphic novels; 2. Horror graphic novels; 3. Sandman (Fictional character); 4. Graphic novels
1-56389-041-0, $19.99
                                        LC 92-159876
Lucifer has grown tired of being the lord of Hell. He kicks out the demons and the damned alike, closes up shop, and gives the key to Hell to Morpheus. Beings from all the world's mythologies converge on the lord of Dream to seize this instrument of power. All Morpheus wants is to search for the soul of his first love, Nada, whom he had consigned to Hell long ago. The book includes violence, strong language, and nudity.

Sandman Volume 5: A Game of You. Written by Neil Gailman; illustrated by Shawn McManus, Colleen Doran, Bryan Talbot, George Pratt, Stan Woch, and Dick Giordano. DC Comics/Vertigo 1993 Un Illustration
Grades: 10 11 12 Adult   **741.5; Fic**
1. Fantasy graphic novels; 2. Horror graphic novels; 3. Sandman (Fictional character); 4. Graphic novels
1-56389-089-5, $19.99
Take an apartment house, mix in a trans woman, a lesbian couple, some talking animals, a talking severed head, a confused heroine, and the deadly Cuckoo. Stir vigorously with a hurricane and Morpheus himself and you get this fifth installment of the Sandman series. This story stars Barbie, who first makes an appearance in The Doll's House, who here finds herself a princess in a vivid dreamworld. The book includes violence, partial nudity, and strong language.

Sandman Volume 6: Fables & Reflections. Art by Kent Williams, P Craig Russell, Jill Thompson, John Watkiss, Shawn McManus. DC Comics/Vertigo 1994 Un Illustration
Grades: 10 11 12 Adult   **Fic; 741.5**
1. Fantasy graphic novels; 2. Horror graphic novels; 3. Sandman (Fictional character); 4. Graphic novels
9781563891052, $19.99; 1563891050
Morpheus, the King of Dreams, observes and interacts with an odd assortment of historical and fictional characters throughout time. Featuring tales of kings, explorers, spies, and werewolves, this book of myth and imagination delves into the dark dreams of Augustus Caesar, Haroun Al Raschid, Marco Polo, Cain and Abel, Emperor Joshua Norton I, and Orpheus to illustrate the effects that these subconscious musings have had on the course of history and

mankind. The book includes some violence, nudity, and strong language.

Sandman Volume 7: Brief Lives. Neil Gaiman, writer; Jill Thompson, penciller; Vince Locke, inker; Dick Giordano, inker. DC Comics/Vertigo 1995 Un Illustration
Grades: 10 11 12 Adult   **741.5; Fic**
  1. Fantasy graphic novels; 2. Horror graphic novels; 3. Sandman (Fictional character); 4. Graphic novels
1-56389-138-7, $19.99
                              LC 92-159876
Delirium, youngest sister of the Endless, prevails upon her brother, Dream, to help her find their missing sibling, Destruction, who disappeared several centuries ago. Their travels take them through the world of the waking until a final confrontation with the missing member of the Endless and the resolution of Dream's relationship with his son change the endless forever. The book includes violence, nudity, sexual situations, and strong language.

★ The **Sandman** Volume 8: World's End. Art by Bryan Talbot, Michael Zulli, Michael Allred, John Watkiss. DC Comics/Vertigo 1995 Un Illustration
Grades: 10 11 12 Adult   **741.5; Fic**
  1. Adventure graphic novels; 2. Fantasy graphic novels; 3. Sandman (Fictional character); 4. Graphic novels
1-56389-171-9, $19.99
A "reality storm" draws an unusual cast of characters together. They take shelter in a tavern, where they amuse each other with their life stories. Although Morpheus is never a focus in these stories, each has something to say about the nature of stories and dreams. The book includes some violence, some strong language, and brief partial nudity and sexual situations.

★ The **Sandman** Volume 9: The Kindly Ones. Writer, Neil Gaiman; artists, Marc Hempel et al.; colorist, Daniel Vozzo. DC Comics/Vertigo 1996 Un Illustration
Grades: 10 11 12 Adult   **741.5; Fic**
  1. Adventure graphic novels; 2. Fantasy graphic novels; 3. Sandman (Fictional character); 4. Graphic novels
1-56389-205-7, $19.99
Distraught by the kidnapping and presumed death of her son Daniel, and believing Morpheus to be responsible, Lyta Hall calls the ancient wrath of the Furies down upon him. A former super heroine blames Morpheus for the death of her child and summons an ancient curse of vengeance against the Lord of Dream. The "kindly ones" enter his realm and force a sacrifice that will change the Dreaming forever. The book includes violence, strong language, and partial nudity.

The **Sandman**: Endless Nights. DC Comics/Vertigo 2004 Un Illustration
Grades: 11 12 Adult   **741.5; Fic**
  1. Fantasy graphic novels; 2. Sandman (Fictional character); 3. Graphic novels
1-4012-0113-X, $19.99
This volume reveals the legend of the Endless, a family of magical and mythical beings who exist and interact in the real world. Born at the beginning of time, Destiny, Death, Dream, Desire, Despair, Delirium and Destruction are seven brothers and sisters who each lord over their respective realms. These seven peculiar and powerful siblings each reveal more about their true-being as they star in their own

tales of curiosity and wonder. A different artist interprets each story by Gaiman. The book includes considerable nudity and sexual situations, and some violence.

★ The **Sandman**: Overture. Written by Neil Gaiman; art by J.H. Williams III; colors by Dave Stewart; letters by Todd Klein. DC Comics/Vertigo 2015 224 p. Color; Illustration
Grades: Adult   **Fic; 741.5**
  1. Death; 2. Fantasy graphic novels; 3. Metaphysics — Fiction
1401248969; 9781401248963, $24.99
                       LC 2015028077
This graphic novel is author "Neil Gaiman's return to the art form that made him famous, ably abetted by artistic luminary JH Williams III whose . . . images provide an epic scope to The Sandman's origin story. From the birth of a galaxy to the moment that Morpheus is captured, THE SANDMAN: OVERTURE will feature cameo appearances by fan-favorite characters such as The Corinthian, Merv Pumpkinhead and, of course, the Dream King's siblings: Death, Desire, Despair, Delirium, Destruction and Destiny." (Publisher's note)
"Infinitely adaptable, Williams's dazzling art recalls everyone from Alphonse Mucha to Jack Kirby. Gaiman is in fine form as well—it is a true pleasure to watch him plumb the depths of weirdness that made Sandman a classic." Pub Wkly
Originally published in single magazine form in THE SANDMAN: OVERTURE 1-6

★ The **Sandman**: the dream hunters. Original words by Neil Gaiman; graphic play and art by P. Craig Russell; coloring by Lovern Kindzierski; lettering by Todd Klein. D.C. Comics/Vertigo 2009 144p. Illustration
Grades: 10 11 12 Adult   **741.5; Fic**
  1. Dreams; 2. Love; 3. Supernatural graphic novels; 4. Graphic novels
978-1-4012-2424-0, $24.99
In old Japan, creatures of myth and legend live among the people. Two such creatures, a badger and a fox, make a wager to force a humble monk to leave the temple he tends alone up in the mountains. Because the young monk can see through their disguises to their true nature, both badger and fox lose the wager, and the fox falls in love with the handsome young man and remains nearby. Meanwhile, a wealthy man who has mastered demons yet cannot find peace in his soul decides to steal the young monk's inner strength for his own. The fox tries to protect the monk, and even makes a bargain with the great black fox in her dreams, to sacrifice her life for the man she loves. Then, when she suffers the consequences of the evil dreams sent by the wealthy man through his demons, the monk ventures into the Dreaming in a quest to save the fox, whom he finally realizes he loves. When he makes the decision to take back the dream that will kill him, the fox decides to take revenge on the wealthy man, the onmyoji, and comes to him as a beautiful young woman to destroy him. Russell has adapted the novella written by Gaiman and illustrated by Yoshitaka Amano. It includes some nudity.

Violent cases: words & pictures. Neil Gaiman, Dave McKean. Kitchen Sink Press 1997 64 p. Color illustration
Grades: Adult   **741.5/973; 741.5**

1. Imagination — Fiction; 2. Memory — Fiction
0878165371; 0878165576; 1616552107;
9781616552107, $19.99

LC 99183676

This novel, by Neil Gaiman and Dave McKean, "presents the often murky nexus between memory and imagination, revealed through the narrator's cloudy childhood remembrance of a visit to Al Capone's osteopath and the impact of his seedy stories on an impressionable youth." (Publisher's note)
Words & pictures; Words and pictures

Gallagher, Monica
   Gods & undergrads, Book 1. Lipstick Press 2007 Un Illustration
Grades: 10 11 12 Adult   **741.5; Fic**
   1. College students; 2. Greek mythology; 3. School stories; 4. Graphic novels
978-0-9794589-0-3, $10

College sophomore Lelaina Pentheus has decided to move on campus at Troy University, and by some chance meetings and good luck joins several juniors in an apartment. Her new friends quickly learn that Lelaina has some strange quirks, like fainting a lot, and hands that can suddenly turn hot and blister. She doesn't know why, nor why she has strange markings on her face; she was adopted as an infant. Then she gets strange messages that "they're coming"—from a talking frog, from her roommate's brother, and then from a stranger who claims he's Hermes, the Greek messenger god. This book collects the first three chapters of Gallagher's story, which first appeared as webcomics at www.eatyourlipstick.com.
Also available online as webcomic

Gallaher, David
   High moon. Art by Scott O. Brown and Steve Ellis. DC Comics 2009 Un Illustration
Grades: 10 11 12 Adult   **741.5; Fic**
   1. Horror graphic novels; 2. Werewolves; 3. Western stories; 4. Graphic novels
978-1-4012-2462-2, $14.99
2009 Harvey Award for Best OnLine Comics Work.

It starts in a small town in Texas, with mysterious happenings and then the disappearance of a girl. Ex-Pinkerton detective McGregor comes to town hunting a criminal named Conroy and gets involved in the town's problems. Mr. Hunter, father of the missing girl, doesn't know the half of it; the town is filled with werewolves resentful of human progress. Conroy is a werewolf, and so is McGregor. When McGregor dies fighting the werewolves from the mines, Conroy takes his identity and continues his travels. In Ragged Rock, he finds more trouble stemming from an old hate, and the real McGregor's brother, Tristan, has come to find his brother's killer. Conroy soon learns that he can be killed, but he won't stay dead. The book includes considerable violence.
Originally published online at www.zudacomics.com.

Gamache, Line
   Hello, Me Pretty. Conundrum Press 2007 63p. Illustration
Grades: 9 10 11 12 Adult   **741.5; 92**

Hello, Me Pretty
Line Gamache

Courtesy of Conundrum Press

1. Autobiographical graphic novels; 2. Mentally handicapped children; 3. Sisters; 4. Graphic novels
978-1-894994-23-1, $15

The author writes of growing up with her mentally disabled sister in a small community just outside Montreal, Canada, with Expo '67 and the FLQ crisis happening in the background (in October 1970, members of the Front de liberation du Quebec kidnapped two government officials; they murdered one and released the other). It is a story of people's intolerance and lack of understanding, but mostly about being different. It gives a glimpse into one family's personal trials and tribulations, woven into the tapestry of Quebec's rich culture and history. The only moment of nudity is when the author's mother gives birth to Josee.

Garrett, Greg
   Holy Superheroes!: Exploring Faith & Spirituality in Comic Books. NavPress/Pinon Press 2005 191p. Illustration
Grades: Adult Professional   **741.5**
   1. Fantastic Four (Fictional characters); 2. Graphic novels — Ethical aspects; 3. Graphic novels — Religious aspects; 4. Superman (Fictional character); 5. X-Men (Fictional characters); 6. Graphic novels
1-57683-576-6, $12.99

Comic books have become a twenty-first-century mythology. Garrett explores this mythology and extracts truths belied by glossy art, superhuman characters, and fast-paced action. Comic books can inspire and influence people's understanding of good versus evil, personal sacrifice, and duty and faith, and Garrett uses characters such as the X-Men, Superman, and the Fantastic Four (among many others) as examples.

Gauld, Tom
   Goliath. Tom Gauld. Drawn & Quarterly 2012 96 p. Illustration
Grades: Adult   **741.5/9411; 741.5**
   1. Battles — Fiction; 2. Goliath (Biblical giant); 3. Goliath (Biblical giant)
1770460659; 9781770460652, $19.95

LC 2012397951

This graphic novel by Tom Gauld is a retelling of the Biblical story of David and Goliath. "Gauld turns the brute into a hapless lug doomed by his own meekness. . . . With the armies of the the Philistines and the Israelites at an impasse, a Philistine captain concocts a crazy scheme to flaunt Goliath's intimidating size and wage psychological warfare on the enemy. He ignores Goliath's objections . . . reasoning that no one would be nutty enough to take on such a mountain of a man." (Booklist)

   You're All Just Jealous of My Jetpack: Cartoons. By Tom Gauld. Farrar Straus & Giroux 2013 160 p.

Grades: Adult   **741.5**
1. Cartoons and caricatures
1770461043; 9781770461048, $19.95
           LC 2013375548
This book by Tom Gauld is "a collection of cartoons made for [newspaper] 'The Guardian.' [It] distills perfectly Gauld's dark humor, impeccable timing, and distinctive style. Arrests by the fiction police and imaginary towns designed by Tom Waits intermingle hilariously with piercing observations about human behavior and whimsical imaginings of the future. Gauld [creates] work infused with a deep understanding of both literary and cartoon history." (Publisher's note)

Geary, Rick

The **Beast** of Chicago: An Account of the Lifeand Crimes of Herman W. Mudgett, Known to theWorld as H. H. Holmes. NBM 2003 Un Illustration
Grades: 9 10 11 12 Adult   **364.152; 741.5**
1. Homicide; 2. Mystery graphic novels; 3. Graphic novels
1-56163-362-3, $8.95
He was the world's first serial killer and he existed in the late 19th century, operating around the Chicago World's Fair, building a literal house of horrors, replete with chutes for dead bodies, gas chambers, surgical

Courtesy of NBM Publishing

rooms. He methodically murdered up to 200 people, mostly young women. Geary steers away from gore to focus on such things as Holmes' "lab" in his castle. The book is still not for the squeamish, but the art is restrained.
Part of the A Treasury of Victorian Murder series.

The **Borden** Tragedy: A Memoir of the Infamous Double Murder at Fall River, Mass., 1892. NBM 1997 80p. Illustration
Grades: 9 10 11 12 Adult   **364.152; 741.5**
1. Homicide; 2. Mystery graphic novels; 3. Graphic novels
1-56163-189-2, $8.95; 9781561631896
Including such details as maps of Fall River, Massachusetts as it was in 1892, Geary presents the facts and documented speculations about the case of Lizzie Borden, a thirty-year-old spinster accused and tried for murdering her parents. The popular rhyme "Lizzie Borden took an axe, gave

Courtesy of NBM Publishing

her mother forty whacks, when she saw what she had done, she gave her father forty-one" was apparently sung to the tune of "Tararaboomdeeay." Geary leaves it to the reader to decide if Lizzie was guilty or not.
Part of the A Treasury of Victorian Murder series.

Famous players: the mysterious death of William Desmond Taylor. NBM/ComicsLit 2009 Un Illustration
Grades: 9 10 11 12 Adult   **364.152; 741.5**
1. Homicide; 2. Motion picture directors; 3. Motion picture producers and directors; 4. Murder victims; 5. Mystery graphic novels; 6. Taylor, William Desmond, 1877-1922; 7. Graphic novels
978-1-56163-555-9, $15.95; 978-1-56163-559-7 (pa), $9.95
Hollywood in 1922 was just coming into its own as a mecca for filmmakers as the silent films became more and more popular. One of the new studios was Famous Players Studio, and William Desmond Taylor was one of its successful directors, along with Cecil B. DeMille. Then, on the morning of February 2, 1922, Taylor's cook/valet/general house servant Henry Peavey arrived at 7:30 and found Taylor's body on the floor of the living room. He'd been shot, but by whom? As the investigation progresses, several prominent actresses come under suspicion, along with a former cook and house servant; and his own mysterious past starts to come to light. However, the police are never able to solve the case. Geary provides a list of his sources for anyone who would like to know more about this Twentieth-Century Murder mystery. He depicts the crime with little gore or violence.
This is part of the Treasury of XXth Century Murder series.

J. Edgar Hoover: a graphic biography. Hill and Wang 2008 102p. Illustration
Grades: 9 10 11 12 Adult   **363.2; 92; 741.5**
1. Biographical graphic novels; 2. FBI officials; 3. Hoover, J Edgar (John Edgar), 1895-1972; 4. United States — Federal Bureau of Investigation; 5. Graphic novels
978-0-8090-9503-2; 0-8090-9503-3, $16.95
           LC 2007-25193
Rick Geary has written a biography of J. Edgar Hoover, who served in the federal government for 55 years and under eight presidents, most notably as director of the Federal Bureau of Investigation. He was appointed to that position on May 10, 1924. Geary covers Hoover's sometimes controversial career, including his refusal to involve the FBI directly into investigations of crimes against civil rights workers and the 1963 bombing in Birmingham, Alabama, and the bureau's investigation of Martin Luther King, Jr. He tastefully discusses Hoover's undercover sexual life.
"As solid, thrilling and informative a guide to the life of the America's most powerful authoritarian as one could ask for." Kirkus

★ The **Lindbergh** child: America's hero and the crime of the century. Written and illustrated by Rick Geary. NBM/ComicsLit 2008 Un Illustration; Map (Treasury of XXth century murder)
Grades: 8 9 10 11 12 Adult   **364.1; 741.5**
1. Air force officers; 2. Air pilots; 3. Generals; 4. Homicide; 5. Kidnapping; 6. Lindbergh, Charles,

1902-1974; 7. Memoirists; 8. Mystery graphic novels; 9. Graphic novels
978-1-56163-529-0, $15.95

Charles Lindbergh was an American hero following his solo crossing of the Atlantic in an airplane. He married into a wealthy family, he and his wife had a baby, they were building their dream home. Then, one night, the baby was abducted from the house. Geary's account retraces all the highly publicized events, ransom notes (false and

Courtesy of NBM Publishing

otherwise), as well as the string of colorful characters who all claimed they could help but instead snookered the Lindberghs. While Bruno Hauptmann was arrested, tried, convicted, and executed, there remain many questions about what really happened. Geary brings them up for readers to consider.

"A good example of the origins of modern forensics, crime-scene investigation, and celebrity hysteria, this work is an excellent choice for most collections." SLJ

The **lives** of Sacco and Vanzetti. Rick Geary.. NBM Comics Lit 2011 80 p. Illustration
Grades: 9 10 11 12 Adult   **345; 741.5; 345.73**
1. Anarchism and anarchists; 2. Sacco, Nicola, 1891-1927 — Trials, litigation, etc; 3. Sacco-Vanzetti case; 4. Sacco-Vanzetti Trial, Dedham, Mass, 1921; 5. Trials (Murder) — Massachusetts — Dedham; 6. United States — History — 1919-1933; 7. Vanzetti, Bartolomeo, 1888-1927 — Trials, litigation, etc
1561636053; 9781561636051, $15.99

LC 2011927818
"Geary lays out what is known and not known about the case, in which two Italian anarchist immigrants were put to death after being found guilty of robbery and murder. The . . . narrative not only details the events of the crime, manhunt, and trial but also includes information about the lives of Sacco and Vanzetti and their families." (Publishers Weekly)
Includes bibliographical references.

Madison Square tragedy: the murder of Stanford White : 25 June, 1906. Written and illustrated by Rick Geary. NBM Pub. 2013 80 p. Illustration (Treasury of xxth century murder)
Grades: 9 10 11 12 Adult   **741.5; 364.152**
1. Murder; 2. Mystery graphic novels
1561637629; 9781561637621, $15.99

LC 2013947335
In this graphic novel, by Rick Geary, as architect Stanford White "became popular and in demand, he also became quite self-indulgent: he had a taste for budding young showgirls on Broadway, even setting up a private apartment to entertain them in. . . . When he met Evelyn

Nesbit . . . he knew he was on to something special. However, Evelyn eventually married a young Pittsburgh decadent heir with a dark side who developed a deep hatred for White and what he may or may not have done to her." (Publisher's note)

"In this entry in his series recounting historical murder cases, Geary tackles an infamous crime that scandalized New York City in 1901. . . . Geary's old-fashioned black-and-white line drawings, vividly evoking the turn-of-the-century milieu, and his reliance on text-heavy captions as a sort of voice-over impart a documentary air to his thoroughly researched account." Booklist
Includes bibliographical references

The **Mystery** of Mary Rogers: A Chronicle of the Disappearanceand Murder of The Beautiful Segar Girl in July,1841 - A Crime Which was Never Solved - And WhichInspired the Sensational Tale by Edgar A. Poe. NBM 2001 Un Illustration
Grades: 9 10 11 12 Adult   **364.152; 741.5**
1. Homicide; 2. Mystery graphic novels; 3. Graphic novels
1-56163-274-0, $15.95
Mary Rogers was a compellingly beautiful lass employed in a cigar store in New York City in the mid-nineteenth century. She had a few suitors. Then, she suddenly disappeared, her body recovered in the Hudson off the Jersey side. The press had a field day with all the possible shocking possibilities. Rape... her "fooling around" between lovers...even gang rape. Never was this case solved. The hypotheses remain many. Even Edgar Allen Poe thought to have solved the case and presented that in his tale "The Mystery of Mary Roget."
Part of the A Treasury of Victorian Murder series.

The **saga** of the bloody Benders: the infamous homicidal family of Labette County, Kansas. NBM/ComicsLit 2007 Un Illustration
Grades: 9 10 11 12 Adult   **364.152; 741.5**
1. Homicide; 2. Mystery graphic novels; 3. Graphic novels
978-1-56163-498-9, $15.95
In Kansas, around the year 1870, the Bender family ran the Bender Inn and grocery store in Labette County, Kansas. Soon after they open their inn to travelers, people start to disappear, usually people with a fair amount of money with them. When the authorities investigate, the family disappears, and the people of Labette County make grisly discoveries in the Bender Inn's cellar. Geary includes just enough gory details for readers to comprehend the Benders' crimes. Earlier volumes in this series focused on famous nineteenth century murders and criminals, but the crimes of this more obscure family are just as dastardly for true crime aficionados.
Part of the series, A Treasury of Victorian Murders

★ The **terrible** Axe-Man of New Orleans. Music and lyrics by Rick Geary. NBM Publishing/ComicsLit 2010 Un Illustration; Map (Treasury of XXth century murder)
Grades: 9 10 11 12 Adult   **364.152; 741.5**
1. Homicide; 2. Mystery graphic novels; 3. New Orleans (La) — History; 4. Graphic novels
978-1-56163-581-8, $15.99

LC 2010-926782
Geary tells the story of the Terrible Axe-Man, who murdered grocers in New Orleans right after World War I. In

each case, the murderer removed a piece of the door to the house, borrowed an axe found at the property, then aimed straight for the head of his victim. From May 23, 1918 to October 27, 1919, the Axe-Man killed six people and badly wounded six more, then disappeared. Geary lays out the known facts, then shows some of the speculation. The black and white art helps to mitigate the violence and gore, so the book is suitable for teens who enjoy true-life mysteries.

"Geary's exacting, historically accurate approach makes this . . . a natural for true-crime fans as well as comics lovers." Booklist

Includes bibliographical references

Nights of terror! A city awash in blood!

Courtesy of NBM Publishing

★ **Trotsky**: a graphic biography. Hill and Wang 2009 103p. Illustration; Map

Grades: 9 10 11 12 Adult   **92; 741.5**

1. Biographical graphic novels; 2. Communism — Soviet Union; 3. Communist leaders; 4. Nonfiction writers; 5. Political leaders; 6. Revolutionaries; 7. Russia — Politics and government — 1894-1917; 8. Soviet Union — Politics and government; 9. Trotsky, Leon, 1879-1940; 10. Graphic novels

978-0-8090-9508-7, $16.95; 0-8090-9508-4

LC 2008-50235

Geary provides a graphic biography of Leon Trotsky, the "brain" behind the Russian Revolution of 1917. The book, with its black and white panel art, chronicles Trotsky's tumultuous relationships with Lenin and Stalin, the contentious debates within the revolutionary movement, Trotsky's many exiles, and his murder in Mexico in 1940.

"Geary's familiar cartoonlike drawing style and factual presentation make this title an accessible and concise introduction to Trotsky's life." SLJ

Includes bibliographical references

A novel graphic from Hill and Wang

Georges, Nicole J.

Calling Dr. Laura: a graphic memoir. Nicole J. Georges. Houghton Mifflin Harcourt 2013 260 p. Illustration

Grades: Adult   **B; 741.5; 92**

1. Autobiographical graphic novels; 2. Family secrets; 3. Georges, Nicole J; 4. Identity (Psychology); 5. Lesbians' writings

0547615590; 9780547615592, $16.95

LC 2012022389

Lambda Award: Graphic Novel (2014)

This graphic novel by Nicole J. Georges tells how when she "was two years old, her family told her that her father

was dead. When she was twenty-three, a psychic told her he was alive. Her sister, saddled with guilt, admits that the psychic is right and that the whole family has conspired to keep him a secret. Sent into a tailspin about her identity, Nicole turns to radio talk-show host Dr. Laura Schlessinger for advice." (Publisher's note)

"Georges' quirky, big-faced, and evocative drawings, tempered by a variety of panel sizes, show the bespectacled author as she comes to terms with her mother's lies to her as a child about her father being dead. . . . An excellent graphic memoir offering engaging insights for those who share—or don't share—any of Georges' worries and traits." Booklist

Getz, Trevor R.,

Abina and the important men: a graphic history. Trevor R. Getz, Liz Clarke. Oxford University Press 2012 Xix, 179 p. Color; Illustration

Grades: Adult   **306.3; 741.5**

1. Mansah, Abina — Trials, litigation, etc; 2. Slavery — Law and legislation — Ghana — History — 19th century; 3. Women slaves — Ghana — History — 19th century

0199844399; 9780199844395, $15.95

LC 2011031033

"The story of Abina Mansah—a woman 'without history' who was wrongfully enslaved, escaped to British-controlled territory, and then took her former master to court—takes place in the complex world of the Gold Coast at the onset of late nineteenth-century colonialism. Slavery becomes a contested ground, as cultural practices collide with an emerging wage economy and British officials turn a blind eye to the presence of underpaid domestic workers in the households of African merchants. The main scenes of the story take place in the courtroom, where Abina strives to convince a series of 'important men'—a British judge, two Euro-African attorneys, a wealthy African country 'gentleman,' and a jury of local leaders—that her rights matter." (Publisher's note)

"Oxford heavily promotes this book as a near-revolution in the pedagogy of African history. While it is not quite that innovative, it is an excellent teaching tool on Africa, slavery, women's and legal history, and historical methodology." Choice

Includes bibliographical references

Gibbons, Dave

Green Lantern Corps: Geoff Johns, Dave Gibbons, writers; Patrick Gleason, penciller; Prentis Rollins, Christian Alamy, inkers; Phil Balsman, Pat Brosseau, Travis Lanham, letterers; Moose Baumann, colorist. Recharge. DC Comics 2006 Un Illustration

Grades: 9 10 11 12 Adult   **Fic; 741.5**

1. Green Lantern (Fictional character); 2. Superhero graphic novels; 3. Graphic novels

978-1-4012-0962-9, $12.99

After the return of Hal Jordan, the Guardians of the Universe have re-formed the Green Lantern Corps. The best and the brightest from across the universe find themselves chosen as members of the new Corps and summoned to the planet Oa, given power rings that turn strength of will into reality, and for training. While veteran ring-bearers gladly return to duty, some new recruits resent being drafted into the Corps against their will. Kyle Rayner, Guy Gardner, and

Kilowog set out to train the new Green Lanterns, but something is making its way to Oa, something that threatens the very existence of the planet and the Guardians; can the new Corps stop it?

★ The **Originals**. DC Comics/Vertigo 2004 Un Illustration
Grades: 10 11 12 Adult   **741.5; Fic**
1. Gangs; 2. Science fiction graphic novels; 3. Graphic novels
1-4012-0355-8, $24.95
2005 Eisner Award for Best Graphic Album - New.

In a retro-futuristic city of industrial gray where hover scooters, music, and drugs rule the street, the Originals are the toughest, most stylish gang around. For two childhood friends, Lel and Bok, nothing is more important than being one of them. But being part of the crowd will bring its own deadly consequences. Gibbons draws upon the world of the Mods in 1960s England and sets it in an alternate world. Violence, harsh language, and sexual situations are part of this world.

Gilson, Che
Avigon: Gods & Demons. Writer Che Gilson; artist, Jimmie Robinson. Image Comics 2005 Un Illustration
Grades: 10 11 12 Adult   **741.5; Fic**
1. Fantasy graphic novels
1-58240-503-4, $19.95

Avigon, a clockwork creation, has to escape, her mechanical world is killing her very soul. The sky is black with acrid smoke, the rivers run slick with oil, and bizarre clockwork creatures roam the streets. Above it all, eccentric and power-hungry politicians and egomaniacal clockwork masters govern with stone cold hearts. But how can Avigon escape a surreal world of machines where she herself is one" Her desperate search will lead her to the darkest regions of humanity and to the arms of her destiny. The book includes some violence.

Giffen, Keith
52 aftermath: The Four Horsemen. Keith Giffen, writer; Pat Olliffe, p encils; John Stanisci, ins. DC Comics 2008 144p. Illustration
Grades: 10 11 12 Adult   **741.5; Fic**
1. Batman (Fictional character); 2. Superhero graphic novels; 3. Superman (Fictional character); 4. Wonder Woman (Fictional character)
978-1-4012-1781-5, $19.99

During the event of 52 weeks, a cadre of scientists created the Four Horsemen of Apokolips, creatures of destructive power that killed Black Adam's family and pretty much destroyed his nation, Bialya. Black Adam destroyed the Horsemen; but, he only destroyed their physical forms. Now, War, Famine, Pestilence, and Death have returned, taking over new human hosts. Superman, Batman, and Wonder Woman are on the scene, but they might not be enough to destroy the Horsemen. Their best hope may be Dr. Cale, who helped create the Horsemen in the first place. Can she be trusted" The book includes violence.

Blue Beetle vol. 2: road trip. John Rogers & Keith Giffen, writers; Cully Hamner . . . [et al.], artists; Guy Major,

colorist; Phil Balsman, Pat Brosseau, Jared K. Fletcher, letterers. DC Comics 2007 144p. Illustration
Grades: 8 9 10 11 12 Adult   **741.5; Fic**
1. Adventure graphic novels; 2. Blue Beetle (Fictional character); 3. Superhero graphic novels; 4. Graphic novels
978-1-4012-1361-9, $12.99

High school teen Jaime Reyes became the latest Blue Beetle by accident, and now he needs to know more about the scarab that has bonded with his body (something it had never done with either previous Blue Beetle). He undertakes a journey with his friend Brenda and the tattooed soldier called Peacemaker to find out what is happening to him, and his journey takes him across the country and into the furthest reaches of space.

"The use of an ethnicity not often seen in comic heroes, plus engaging characters and a fast-paced, rip-snorting second half make for a divertingly lighthearted take on a young man's quest to solve the secrets of himself." Booklist
Followed by Blue Beetle vol. 3: reach for the stars (2008)
Sequel to Blue Beetle: shellshocked (2006)

Hero Squared, Volume 1. Written by Keith Giffen and J. M. DeMatteis; art by Joe Abraham. Boom! Studios 2006 Un Illustration
Grades: 9 10 11 12 Adult   **741.5; Fic**
1. Humorous graphic novels; 2. Superhero graphic novels; 3. Graphic novels
1-4243-0422-9, $14.99

When a superhero's world is destroyed, he ends up in a parallel world (ours) in which he's a slacker; and the supervillain who destroyed her world is the slacker's girlfriend in this one. Really bad words appear as nonsense syllables, and there is considerable superhero fighting action and lots of confusion about identities.

Gill, Joel
Strange fruit; Volume 1: Uncelebrated narratives from Black history. Words and pictures by Joel Christian Gill; foreword by Henry Louis Gates, Jr. Fulcrum Publishing 2014 176 p. Color; Illustration
Grades: 9 10 11 12 Adult   **973.04960730092/2; 741.5; B**
1. African Americans; 2. African Americans — Biography; 3. African Americans — Biography — Juvenile literature; 4. African Americans — History — Anecdotes; 5. African Americans — History — Anecdotes — Juvenile literature; 6. Heroes — United States — Biography; 7. Heroes — United States — Biography — Juvenile literature; 8. Success; 9. Graphic novels
1938486293; 9781938486296, $23.95
                                        LC 2014010803
This book, illustrated by Joel Christian Gill, "is a collection of stories from African American history that exemplifies success in the face of great adversity. This unique graphic anthology offers historical and cultural commentary on nine uncelebrated heroes [such as escaped slave] Henry 'Box' Brown, . . . Alexander Crummel and the Noyes Academy [and] Marshall 'Major' Taylor . . . the first black champion in any sport." (Publisher's note)

"The short narratives are conversational in tone and the accompanying detailed images convey tragic beauty. Gil doesn't shy away from portraying brutal scenes, but does so without sensationalism. The panels vary in size and orientation, pushing the momentum of each vignette forward with great success." SLJ

Gillen, Kieron

The **wicked** + the divine; Volume 1: The Faust act. By Kieron Gillen; illustrated by Jamie McKelvie. Image Comics 2014 144 p. Color; Illustration

Grades: Adult   **741.5**
1. Gods and goddesses — Fiction; 2. Immortality — Fiction
1632150190; 9781632150196, $9.99

LC 2014501185

Eisner Nominee: Best New Series (2015)

"Every ninety years, twelve gods incarnate as humans. They are loved. They are hated. In two years, they are dead. . . . [G]ods are the ultimate pop stars and pop stars are the ultimate gods. But remember: just because you're immortal, doesn't mean you're going to live forever." (Publisher's note)

"A series of horrifying events backstage after the goddess Amaterasu's latest concert thrusts a mortal woman named Laura into a quest to help clear the reincarnated-as-female Lucifer of a murder she did not commit. . . . Little is revealed at this stage of the narrative, but the solid storytelling and clean, gorgeous artwork will keep readers engrossed and eager for more." Pub Wkly

Originally published in single magazine form as The wicked + the divine #1-5

Volume 1 of an ongoing series

The **Wicked** + the Divine; Volume 2: Fandemonium. Kieron Gillen; illustrated by Jamie McKelvie and Matt Wilson. Image Comics 2015 168 p. Color illustration

Grades: Adult   **741.5; Fic**
1. Conspiracies — Fiction; 2. Gods and goddesses
1632153270; 9781632153272, $14.99

Eisner Nominee: Best New Series (2015)

This is the second volume of an "urban fantasy series where gods are the ultimate pop stars and pop stars are the ultimate gods. Following the tragic and unjust death of Lucifer, it takes a revelation from Inanna to draw Laura back into the worlds of Gods and Superstardom to try and discover the truth behind a conspiracy to subvert divinity." (Publisher's note)

"As Laura does, we delve more deeply into the Pantheon's origins and the book's motivating theme—namely how a search for identity can lead us to define ourselves through celebrity and pop culture. This all makes for a script that satisfyingly favors exploration over sheer thrills, with art providing masterful support. While the keen linework and psychedelic colors counterpoint this complexity, looking deeper reveals delightful and subtle playfulness with form." Booklist

★ **Young** Avengers: mic-drop at the edge of time and space. By Kieron Gillen; illustrated by Jamie McKelvie. Marvel Enterprises 2014 112 p. Color illustration

Grades: 10 11 12 Adult   **Fic; 741.5**
1. Captain America (Fictional character); 2. Heroes — Fiction; 3. Loki (Norse Deity); 4. Science fiction comic books, strips, etc; 5. Superheroes — Fiction; 6. Young adult fiction; 7. Graphic novels

9780785185307, $15.99; 0785185305

"They say you can never go home. For the Young Avengers, that's not true. They can go home - it's just that if they do, the universe may end. Better not go home then, eh (Wait, what are you doing, Young Avengers? You've decided to go home!) The team takes on the gig to save reality, but is Kate Bishop an enemy in waiting" Is this the last we see of the loveable/strangle-able Kid Loki?" (Publisher's note)

"Gillen is an intelligent, savvy writer who gives more space to the battle's buildup and after-party than to the battle itself and even in the midst of the fight relies more on intimate character conflict than epic fisticuffs. . . . The overt focus on fluid sexuality . . . and smart teen dialogue that rings familiar and true give this series high appeal for new adults in particular." Booklist

★ **Young** avengers: style > substance. Kieron Gillen, writer; Jamie McKelvie, Mike Norton, artist; Matthew Wilson, color artist; VC's Clayton Cowles, letterer. Marvel Enterprises 2013 128 p. Illustration

Grades: 10 11 12 Adult   **Fic; 741.5**
1. Superhero graphic novels; 2. Teenagers — Fiction
9780785167082, $15.99; 0785167080

In this superhero graphic novel, author Kieron Gillen and illustrator Jamie McKelvie tell the story of "Wiccan, Hulkling and Kate 'Hawkeye' Bishop with Kid Loki, Marvel Boy and Ms. America. . . . As a figure from Loki's past emerges, Wiccan makes a horrible mistake that comes back to bite everyone on their communal posteriors. Fight scenes! Fake IDs! And plentiful feels! (aka 'meaningful emotional character beats' . . .)" (Publisher's note)

"The story . . . flies by, thanks to clever banter and lightning pacing. . . . McKelvie turns in clean, polished pages with eye-popping character work and shows some real and very welcome imagination with action sequences." Booklist

Contains material originally published in magazine form Young Avengers #1-5 and Marvel now! point one #1—Tp verso

★ **Young** Avengers; Volume 2: alternative cultures. Kieron Gillen, illustrated by Kate Brown and Jamie McKelvie. Marvel Enterprises 2014 112 p. Color illustration (Young Avengers)

Grades: 9 10 11 12 Adult   **741.5**
1. Fantasy fiction; 2. Heroes; 3. Science fiction comic books, strips, etc; 4. Superhero comic books, strips, etc; 5. Young adult fiction; 6. Graphic novels
0785167099; 9780785167099, $15.99

In this comic book collection by Kieron Gillen, illustrated by Kate Brown and Jamie McKelvie, "existential horror turns cosmic horror as something emerges from the shadows of the past . . . and it seems that the Young Avengers have one more thing to worry about. The team races desperately across the multi-verse in pursuit of their missing friend, but their road trip goes crazy as it reaches its destination." (Publisher's note)

"As with the previous one, this slim volume is a quick read with snappy dialogue and fast, cleanly depicted action that pops with cinematic digital coloring effects." Booklist

Contains material originally published as Young Avengers (2013) #6-10

Gillis, Peter
  Shatter. Art by Mike Saenz. AiT/Planet Lar 2006 Un
Illustration
Grades: 10 11 12 Adult   **741.5; Fic**
  1. Mystery graphic novels; 2. Science fiction graphic
novels; 3. Graphic novels
  978-1-932051-44-5, $14.95
  In a near-future Chicagoland (as envisioned in the
1980s), private cop Shatter takes a contract to track down a
woman who traffics in recombinant RNA. This violent and
sexy mystery was originally published in the mid-1980s, and
the art was done on a first-generation Macintosh with 128K
of memory and a dot-matrix printer.

Gin, Toriko
  Song of the hanging sky, vol. 2. Go! Comi 2008 Un
Grades: 10 11 12 Adult   **741.5; Fic**
  1. Manga; 2. Science fiction graphic novels; 3. Graphic
novels
  978-1-60510-024-1, $10.99
  The tribe's shaman, Across the River, is still missing, so
Wolf, Another Bear, and Hello go out to search for her. This
leaves the human, Jack, among the other members of the
tribe, some of whom hate and fear all humans. Fair Cave
shelters Jack in his tent and tells him what happened on the
first Day of Destruction that left only some of the tribe's
children alive. Meanwhile, Across the River is living with
Rod, a blind ex-soldier, and they take in the injured boy
soldier, Cherry. The humans' war is getting closer to the
tribe. The book includes some mildly harsh language and
some violence.

  Song of the hanging sky, vol.1. Go! Comi 2008 Un
Illustration
Grades: 10 11 12 Adult   **741.5; Fic**
  1. Fantasy graphic novels; 2. Manga; 3. Graphic novels
  978-0-933617-87-9, $10.99
  Jack is a field medic in an army at war in what looks
much like a World War I era world. He has left the army and
lives in an isolated mountainous area with only a dog to keep
him company. Then he finds a wounded boy, with wings. He
nurses the boy back to health, realizing that he must be one
of the legendary "birdfolk." However, when he tries to
return the boy to his tribe, the others would much prefer to
kill the human and keep their presence a secret. Jack needs to
find a way to make them realize he's on their side and wants
to help them, and that he's sick of war, fighting, and death.
The book includes brief moments of partial nudity.

Gipi
  Garage Band. First Second Books 2007 132p.
Illustration
Grades: 8 9 10 11 12 Adult   **741.5**
  1. Friendship; 2. Rock music; 3. Graphic novels
  978-1-59643-206-2
                                       LC 2006018345
  Four boys - Giuliano, Stefano, Alberto, and Alex - with
turbulent home lives find refuge in the music they play
together and in their friendship. When their only amp blows
a fuse and the deadline to make their demo tape is pressing,
they decide to steal in order to replace it. Events rapidly

spiral out of control: will this be the end of everything the
band has worked for?

  Notes for a war story. Translated by Spectrum. First
Second Books 2007 126p. Illustration
Grades: 10 11 12 Adult   **741.5; Fic**
  1. Crime; 2. War; 3. Graphic novels
  978-1-59643-261-1, $16.95
                                       LC 2006-49716
  Giuliano, a loner among outsiders, is one of three young
drifters caught up in the whirlwind of a war in the Balkans.
The three boys are like passing shadows; they live in
abandoned houses, dodge the occasional bomb, and steal car
parts for money. Meeting Felix—a powerful, fast-talking
mercenary—changes everything for them. Felix is an expert
manipulator; he speaks to their ambition and to their desires
for power, wealth, and purpose. They're instantly hooked,
especially the trio's unofficial leader, Stefano, and they soon
escalate from petty crime to working on behalf of a
mafia-style militia, bullying and extorting money in Felix's
name. But as Giuliano comes to realize, they don't know
what they're fighting for—if they're even fighting for
anything. There's some naturally occurring violence and
harsh language.
  Original Italian edition, 2004

Gladstone, Brooke
  ★ The **influencing** machine: Brooke Gladstone on the
media. Illustrated by Josh Neufeld; with additional penciling
by Randy Jones and Susann Ferris-Jones.. W. W. Norton
2011 Xxii, 170p Illustration; Color
Grades: Adult   **302.23**
  1. Broadcast journalism; 2. Gladstone, Brooke; 3.
Journalism; 4. Mass media
  0393077799, $23.95; 9780393077797, $16.95
                                       LC 2011009820
  This work of graphic nonfiction explores the ôhistory of
media's influence. . . . [F]rom the 'Acta Diurna' posted in
ancient Rome to the outcries over President Adams's Alien
and Sedition Acts and McCarthy's Red Scare, [Brooke]
Gladstone traces not only the birth of the press, but also its
various muzzles. The press will not always stay silent, as she
illustrates with Daniel Ellsberg and the Pentagon Papers. . . .
Yet government opacity still abounds, and Gladstone
pointedly wonders if secrecy really makes us safer. . . .
Gladstone points to seven key biases that cognizant media
consumers should worry about: commercial, bad news,
status quo, access, visual, narrative, and fairness. These
dovetail . . . into a . . . discussion of war journalism.ö
(Publishers Weekly)
  Includes bibliographical references (p. 163-170).

Glass, Bryan J. L.
  The **mice** templar, volume one: the prophecy. Created
by Bryan J.L. Glass & Michael Avon Oeming. Michael Avon
Oeming, illustrator. Image Comics 2008 256p. Illustration
Grades: 6 7 8 9 10 11 12 Adult   **Fic; 741.5**
  1. Adventure graphic novels; 2. Fantasy graphic novels; 3.
Mice; 4. Graphic novels
  978-1-58240-871-2, $29.99; 1-58240-871-8
  In a land populated by animals, the Mice Templar used
to protect the people of the mouse kingdom, but a civil war

destroyed them; the king now employs rat soldiers, and they prey upon the mouse villages. Young Karic still idolizes the Mice Templar, but everything he knows and believes is shattered when his village is raided by rats, burned, and his family captured as slaves. He survives, saved by a mysterious mouse named Pilot, who says he was once a Templar and offers to train Karic. The salmon in the river say that Karic is the one prophesied to restore the Templar, but can he truly be the one? The book includes considerable battle violence.

"Equal parts Norse myth, Arthurian legend, and Mrs. Frisby and the Rats of N.I.M.H., The Mice Templar series re-imagines the warrior animal tale with just enough of its own spin to make it well worth adding to the collection." Voice Youth Advocates

The volume is a collection of the first six issues of The mice templar

Other titles in this series are: Destiny Part One (2010) Destiny Part Two (2010) Legend (2013) A Midwinter Night's Dream (2012)

Glidden, Sarah
How to understand Israel in 60 days or less. Writer & artist, Sarah Glidden; letterer Clem Robins. Vertigo/DC Comics 2010 206p. Illustration; Map
Grades: 11 12 Adult   **915.694; 741.5**
978-1-4012-2233-8, $24.99; 9781401222345, $19.99

This book "is Sarah [Glidden]'s memoir not only of her Israeli governmentsponsored trip through Tel Aviv, Jerusalem, the Golan Heights, Masada and other famous locations, but of the emotional journey she never expected to take while she was there. Her experience clashes with her preconceived notions again and again, particularly when she tries to take a non-chaperoned trip into the West Bank. Sarah is forced to question first her political beliefs and, ultimately, her own sense of identity." (Publisher's note)

Goddard, Drew
Buffy the Vampire Slayer season eight, volume 3: Wolves at the gate. Artist, Georges Jeanty, Jo Chen. Dark Horse Comics 2008 Un Illustration
Grades: 8 9 10 11 12 Adult   **741.5; Fic**
1. Buffy the Vampire Slayer (Fictional character); 2. Fantasy graphic novels; 3. Horror graphic novels; 4. Vampires; 5. Graphic novels
978-1-59582-165-2, $15.95

A band of Japanese vampires who can transform into wolves, panthers, swarms of bees, and fog, attack the Slayer compound in Scotland, stealing Buffy's mystical scythe that she used to transform thousands of young women into Slayers. Now the only one who can help her fight these vampires is Dracula himself, and they have to travel to Japan to recover the scythe and stop the Japanese from accomplishing their plans. Meanwhile, Buffy and Satsu have one night together that seems to throw everyone else for a loop. The last panel on the last page shows Buffy and Satsu together in bed, kissing and wrapped around each other.

Goetzinger, Annie
Girl in Dior. Annie Goetzinger; translation by Joe Johnson; lettering by Ortho. NBM Pub. 2015 128 p. Color; Illustration
Grades: 9 10 11 12 Adult   **741.5**
1. Dior, Christian, 1905-1957; 2. Fashion design; 3. Fashion designers
1561639141; 9781561639144, $27.99
                                        LC 2014956278

This book, by Annie Goetzinger, "covers the 1947 groundbreaking first fashion show put on by designer Christian Dior. . . . We watch the magic happen through the eyes of Clara Nohant, a young 'fashion chronicler,' a fictional character injected into the story amid real-life modistes, drapers, pattern makers, muses, magazine editors, and movie stars who surrounded the designer." (School Library Journal)

"Goetzinger's detailed, expressive faces and figures seem to be illuminated from within, and the garments themselves are a great tribute to the author's background in fashion illustration." Booklist

Initially published in French as Jeune fille en Dior

Goldsmith, Francisca
Graphic novels now: building, managing, and marketing a dynamic collection. American Library Association 2005 113p. Illustration
Grades: Adult Professional   **025.2**
1. Libraries — Special collections
0-8389-0904-3, $35
                                        LC 2005-12653

This book begins with a "theoretical discussion of graphic novels: an illustrative definition . . .; a brief but informative history of the format; and a number of well-reasoned arguments for bringing the genre into library collections. The latter half of the book provides many concrete suggestions for creating, maintaining, promoting, and defending a graphic-novel collection." SLJ

Includes bibliographical references

The **readers'** advisory guide to graphic novels. American Library Association 2010 124p.
Grades: Adult Professional   **025.2; 025**
978-0-8389-1008-5, $45; 0-8389-1008-4
                                        LC 2009-25239

Goldstein, Nancy
★ **Jackie** Ormes: the first African American woman cartoonist. University of Michigan Press 2008 225p. Illustration
Grades: 10 11 12 Adult   **92; 741.5**
1. African American women — Biography; 2. Cartoonists; 3. Ormes, Jackie, 1911-1985
978-0-472-11624-9, $35; 0-472-11624-X
                                        LC 2007-35395

This book covers the life and career of Jackie Ormes, who was the first African American woman cartoonist. She wrote and drew comic strips that ran in Black newspapers such as the Pittsburgh Courier and the Chicago Defender. She was part of the Black elite in Chicago and knew other luminaries such as singer Eartha Kitt and musician/composer/conductor Duke Ellington. She was also investigated by the FBI because of her Leftist political ideas and activities. While she did such things as create Torchy paper dolls, based on her beautiful and sexy cartoon character, and cute Patty-Jo dolls, Ormes also used her comic strips to put forth her political views. This book reproduces some of her cartoons and comic strips, in both black and white and in color.

Includes bibliographical references

Goldstein, Sophie
The **oven**. By Sophie Goldstein. Adhouse Books 2015 80 p. Color; Illustration
Grades: Adult
741.5
1. Dystopian fiction; 2. Dystopias
1935233335;
9781935233336, $12.95
LC 2015270630
Ignatz Award: Outstanding Graphic Novel (2015)
In this book, by Sophie Goldstein, "Ozone depletion and dwindling resources have driven the human race into domed cities where population controls are strictly enforced. When a young couple goes looking for an anti-government paradise in the desert they may have found more than they bargained for." (Publisher's note)

Courtesy of Adhouse Books

Gonick, Larry
The **cartoon** guide to calculus. Larry Gonick. William Morrow 2011 Illustration
Grades: Adult
515.0207; 745.5
0061689092; 9780061689093
LC 2011279176
In this nonfiction graphic novel, Larry Gonick "master cartoonist, former Harvard instructor, and creator of the New York Times bestselling, Harvey Award-winning Cartoon Guide series now does for calculus what he previously did for science and history: making a complex subject comprehensible, fascinating, and fun through witty text and light-hearted graphics." (Publisher's note)

The **cartoon** guide to statistics. {by} Larry Gonick & Woollcott Smith; {il. by Larry Gonick}. HarperPerennial 1993 230 p. Illustration
Grades: Adult
741.5; 519.5
1. Statistics; 2. Statistics — Caricatures and cartoons
0062731025; 9780062731029, $17.99
LC 92054683
This book, by Larry Gonick and Woollcott Smith, "covers all the central ideas of modern statistics: the summary and display of data, probability in gambling and medicine, random variables, Bernoulli Trials, the Central Limit Theorem, hypothesis testing, confidence interval estimation, and much more—all explained in simple, clear, and yes, funny illustrations." (Publisher's note)
Includes bibliographical references (p. 221-223) and index

★ The **cartoon** history of the modern world. Part II: From the Bastille to Baghdad. Larry Gonick. Harper 2009 260 p.
Grades: Adult
909.080; 909.0802/07
1. History, Modern; 2. Modern history
0060760087; 9780060760083, $23.99
LC 2006049146
This graphic novel, by Larry Gonick, part of the "Cartoon History" series, "opens with the Enlightenment and rolls across Napoleon, the fall of the Ottoman Empire, World War I and II, and all the way to our recent imbroglios in Iraq and Afghanistan." (Publisher's note)
Includes bibliographical references and indexes

★ The **cartoon** history of the modern world: Part 1: from Columbus to the U.S. Constitution. Collins 2007 259p. Illustration
Grades: 9 10 11 12 Adult
741.5; 909.08
1. Modern history; 2. Graphic novels
978-0-06-076004-5; 0-06-076004-4, $17.95
LC 2006-49146
The book begins with a "15-page distillation of pre-Columbian America; and while Europe and North America receive most of the attention, Gonick does include at least some highlights from other parts of the world. Covering such topics as the Protestant Reformation, the British defeat of the Spanish Armada, the Copernican model of the universe, and the American Revolution, he writes and draws with considerable wit and authority, and is obviously well versed in his subject." SLJ
Followed by:The Cartoon History of the Modern World Part 2: From the Bastille to Baghdad (2009)

★ The **cartoon** history of the United States. Larry Gonick. HarperPerennial 1991 392 p.
Grades: Adult
973.020
1. United States — History; 2. United States — History
0062730983 ($9.95); 9780062730985, $17.99
LC 91055037
This graphic novel about the history of the United States, by Larry Gonick, is part of the "Cartoon Guide" series. "From the first English colonies to the Gulf War and the S&L debacle, Larry Gonick spells it all out from his unique cartoon perspective." (Publisher's note)
Includes index.

★ The **Cartoon** History of the Universe III: From the Rise of Arabia to the Renaissance. W. W. Norton 2002 300p. Illustration
Grades: 9 10 11 12 Adult
741.5; 909.07
1. World history; 2. Graphic novels
0-393-32403-6, $21.95
LC 02-288002
This volume begins in the year 395, covers the birth of Islam, the Crusades, the Asian and African nations, the Mongol conquests, the Ottoman Empire, the Black Death, the Italian Renaissance, the rise of Spain, and culminates in the year 1492. The facts in the text are accompanied again by his irreverently humorous illustrations.

★ The **Cartoon** History of the Universe Volumes 1-7: From the Big Bang to Alexander the Great. Main Street Books/Doubleday & Co. 1990 368p. Illustration
Grades: 9 10 11 12 Adult
741.5; 902.07

1. World history; 2. Graphic novels
0-385-26520-4, $22.95; 9780385265201

LC 02-288002

Gonick presents a quick tour of world history, starting from the Big Bang through the life of Alexander the Great. He presents facts in the text, while his illustrations provide an irreverently humorous counterpoint. There's partial nudity with some of the ancient people.

★ The **Cartoon** History of the Universe Volumes 8-13: From the Springtime of China to the Fall of Rome. Main Street Books/Doubleday & Co. 1994 305p. Illustration
Grades: 9 10 11 12 Adult   **741.5; 902.07; 902**
1. World history; 2. Graphic novels
0-385-42093-5, $22.95

LC 02-288002

Gonick presents a quick tour of world history, continuing with Alexander the Great's march to India (and his about-face), focusing on India and China, then going back to Rome and covering the Western World through the end of Justinian's reign, around 564 A.D. He also tells the story of Jeshua ben Joseph (Jesus). He presents facts in the text, while his illustrations provide an irreverently humorous counterpoint. There's partial nudity and some violence with the depictions of wars and battles.

Goodwin, Michael

Economix: how and why our economy works (and doesn't work) in words and pictures. Michael Goodwin. Harry N. Abrams Inc. 2012 304 p. Illustration
Grades: 11 12 Adult   **330**
1. Cost and standard of living; 2. Economic development; 3. Economics; 4. Economics
9780810988392, $19.95

LC 2011052119

Author Michael Goodwin discusses the economy, "human nature and our attempts to make the most of what we've got . . . and sometimes what our neighbors have got . . . [The book explains concepts from] the beginning of Western economic thought, to markets free and otherwise, to economic failures, successes, limitations, and future possibilities." (Publisher's note)

"This dense yet readable exegesis makes economics entertaining despite current financial shenanigans worldwide. Goodwin takes a chronological approach, starting with the history of banking in the 17th century. As he marches through four centuries of economic theories and theorists, he attempts to show what happened, what succeeded, and what went wrong in terms of both public and private good, with a focus on the reasons particular theories didn't pan out in real life." LJ
Includes bibliographical references and index

Gorman, Michele

Getting graphic!: comics for kids. With a foreword by Jeff Smith; and original comic art by Jimmy Gownley. Linworth Books 2007 84p. Illustration
Grades: Adult Professional   **741.5**
1. Graphic novels — Bibliography; 2. Graphic novels — History and criticism
978-1-58683-327-5, $24.95

LC 2007-35033

Gorman presents annotated bibliographies of recommended graphic novels for children ages 6-12 to help librarians develop a quality, age-appropriate graphic novel collection that includes fiction, nonfiction, and manga. Amelia Rules! creator Jimmy Gownley created a comic story featuring his characters, just for this book. The book entries include the title, author, year of publication, publisher, ISBNs (both 10-digit and 13-digit), an annotation, and an age range recommendation. Gorman provides series annotations for series published by Capstone, Stone Arch, Rosen, Lerner, and other educational publishers.
Includes glossary and bibliographical references

Goscinny, Rene

Asterix and Caesar's Gift. Orion/Sterling Publishing 2004 48p. Illustration
Grades: 4 5 6 7 8 9 10 11 12 Adult   **741.5; Fic**
1. Asterix (Fictional character); 2. Humorous graphic novels
0-75286-645-1, $12.95; 0-75286-646-X (pa)

When Legionary Tremensdelirius gets the title deeds to the little Gaulish village as a bonus, he swaps them with tavern landlord Orthopaedix for a drink. Funnily enough, Asterix and his friends aren't keen to hand over their village to anyone else. After a chieftaincy election campaign and a showdown with the Romans, both events fiercely contested, can all still end well?

Asterix and Cleopatra. Orion/Sterling Publishing 2004 48p. Illustration
Grades: 4 5 6 7 8 9 10 11 12 Adult   **741.5; Fic**
1. Asterix (Fictional character); 2. Humorous graphic novels
0-75286-606-0, $12.95; 0-75286-607-9 (pb)

How can lovely Queen Cleopatra show Julius Caesar that ancient Egypt is still a great nation" Her architect Edifis recruits his Gaulish friends to help him build a magnificent palace within three months. There are villainous saboteurs to be outwitted, but Asterix, Obelix, and Getafix still find time to go sight-seeing, and leave their mark on the Pyramids and the Sphinx's nose.

Asterix and the Banquet. Orion/Sterling Publishing 2004 48p. Illustration
Grades: 4 5 6 7 8 9 10 11 12 Adult   **741.5; Fic**
1. Asterix (Fictional character); 2. Humorous graphic novels
0-75286-608-0, $12.95; 0-75286-609-5 (pa)

When the Romans try to contain the threat from the Gaulish village by building a stockade around it, Asterix and Obelix lay a bet with them. They will break out and claim their right to travel freely all over Gaul, collecting the local delicacies and bringing them back to prove their point. Ham from Lutetia, fizzy wine from Durocortorum, fish stew from Massilia in the south ... soon their shopping bag is full. Outwitting Romans, a couple of treacherous Gauls, and the thieves Villanus and Unscrupulus, they set off for home ... but who's that little dog who has been following them all the way from Lutetia?

Asterix and the Cauldron. Orion/Sterling Publishing 2004 48p. Illustration
Grades: 4 5 6 7 8 9 10 11 12 Adult   **741.5; Fic**

1. Asterix (Fictional character); 2. Humorous graphic
novels
0-75286-629-X, $9.95

There's financial skulduggery in ancient Gaul. When
local Chief Whosemoralsarelastix wants a cauldron full of
money kept out of Roman hands, the cash disappears while
Asterix is guarding it. He and Obelix must earn enough to
repay it through fairground gladiatorial contests, trendy
theatrical performances, even bank robbery - they'll try
anything. But whose morals are really elastic? And how to
the pirates, just for once, get an unexpected bonus?

Asterix and the Class Act. Orion/Sterling Publishing
2004 56p. Illustration
Grades: 4 5 6 7 8 9 10 11 12 Adult   **741.5; Fic**
1. Asterix (Fictional character); 2. Humorous graphic
novels
0-75286-068-2, $12.95; 0-75286-640-0 (pa)

This volume collects 14 stories, including the day
Asterix and Obelix were born (in the middle of a fish fight);
how Obelix goes back to school; fashion in ancient Gaul;
how Dogmatix helps the village cockerel win a duel, and
how he's adopted as a Roman mascot; Obelix's adventures
under the mistletoe; the bid for the very first Gaulish
Olympics, and more.

Asterix and the Laurel Wreath. Orion/Sterling
Publishing 2004 48p. Illustration
Grades: 4 5 6 7 8 9 10 11 12 Adult   **741.5; Fic**
1. Asterix (Fictional character); 2. Humorous graphic
novels
0-75286-636-2, $12.95; 0-75286-637-0 (pa)

Chief Vitalstatistix rashly invites his brother-in-law to
dine on a stew seasoned with Caesar's laurel wreath, so
Asterix and Obelix must go Rome to fetch those laurels.
Hoping to get access to Caesar, they sell themselves as
slaves, but can they do a deal with the corrupt
Goldendelicius to swap the laurels for parsley?

Asterix in Britain. Orion/Sterling Publishing 2004 48p.
Illustration
Grades: 4 5 6 7 8 9 10 11 12 Adult   **741.5; Fic**
1. Asterix (Fictional character); 2. Humorous graphic
novels
0-85286-618-4, $12.95; 0-75286-619-2 (pa)

The Romans have invaded Britain, but one village still
holds out. Asterix and Obelix come to help, with a barrel of
magic potion in hand. But to deliver the precious brew, the
Gaulish heroes must face fog, rain, bad food, warm beer, and
the Romans too.

Asterix the Legionary. Orion/Sterling Publishing 2004
48p. Illustration
Grades: 4 5 6 7 8 9 10 11 12 Adult   **741.5; Fic**
1. Asterix (Fictional character); 2. Humorous graphic
novels
0-75286-620-6, $12.95; 0-75286-621-4 (pa)

It's off to the wars for Asterix and Obelix: they've
enlisted as legionnaires in order to rescue Tragicomix, whom
the Romans forcibly conscripted. The two find Tragicomix
and succeed in causing the biggest commotion ever on a
battlefield.

Gossett, Christian
King Kong: The 8th Wonder of the World. Dark Horse
Books 2006 Un Illustration
Grades: 7 8 9 10 11 12 Adult   **741.5; Fic**
1. King Kong (Fictional character); 2. Science fiction
graphic novels; 3. Graphic novels
978-1-59307-472-2, $12.95

Director Carl Denham has one chance to make the film
of his dreams - hire an unknown actress, kidnap his writer
and board a tramp freighter for the mysterious Island of the
Skull. But when hostile natives capture actress Ann Darrow,
Denham and his crew will face horrors from giant spiders to
bloodthirsty dinosaurs to get her back. Yet, nothing can
prepare them for the revelation of the mighty wonder in
whose clutches Ann truly remains - King Kong. This story
adapts the screenplay for the motion picture directed by
Peter Jackson, which is based on the original story by
Merian C. Cooper and Edgar Wallace.

Grace, Sina
Not My Bag. Written and illustrated by Sina Grace;
design, S. Steven Struble. Image Comics 2012 96 p.
Illustration
Grades: Adult   **741.5**
1. Fashion — Fiction; 2. Gay men — Fiction; 3. Identity
(Psychology) — Fiction; 4. Retail trade — Fiction
1607065975; 9781607065975, $12.99

"[Sina] Grace draws upon his experience in retail to
craft a graphic novel that gives us a window into the life of
an artist who is forced to take a job he doesn't really want in
order to pay the bills." It presents both a "celebration of
fashion . . . and the introspection of the artist as he looks back
on the relationships that have served to define him. . . . The
protagonist's reliance on his partner's understanding and
support gets him through the retail ordeal." (Publishers
Weekly)

Graham, Brandon
King City Vol. 1: Cat Master. Tokyopop 2007 192p.
Illustration
Grades: 11 12 Adult   **741.5; Fic**
1. Science fiction graphic novels; 2. Graphic novels
978-1-59816-982-9, $9.99

King City is a semi-futuristic city full of spy gangs,
aliens, and lots of weirdness. Joe has returned to King City
armed with a special cat. This cat can swallow and duplicate
a key, become a weapon, a tool, almost anything Joe needs,
all with a simple injection of a mysterious substance Joe
keeps handy. He took on a job to duplicate a key, but now
finds himself mixed up between rival gangs (he thinks).
Meanwhile, his friend Pete takes a job to guard what turns
out to be an aquatic alien girl, and he decides to save her. A
mysterious, sexy woman helps Joe. Meanwhile, Joe's
ex-girlfriend has a new lover, but the ex-soldier is addicted
to a drug called chalk, which will eventually turn his body
into chalk. Some sexual situations and foul language make
this story more appropriate for older teens. Graham is a
noted independent comics creator trying his hand at the
global manga format.

Prophet 3: Empire. By Brandon Graham; illustrated by
Simon Roy; Giannis Milonogiannis (Contributor), Malachi

Ward (Contributor), Matt Sheean (Contributor). Image Comics 2014 128 p. Color; Illustration

Grades: Adult **741.5**

1. Science fiction; 2. Science fiction comic books, strips, etc

1607068583; 9781607068587, $14.99

"The Earth Empire is now rebuilt and gaining a stronger grasp on Earthspace. Facing an even more menacing new threat, Old Man Prophet and his team look for the help of an old ally." (Publisher's note)

"Prophet was originally created by Rob Liefeld in 1992 for Image's 'Youngblood' series, and far-future versions of other Image characters from that time appear here—but no knowledge of them is necessary to appreciate the worldbuilding present. Each artist on the series follows a different set of characters, illustrating only scenes featuring them, and each one renders amazing scientific visions—living starships, grotesque genetically engineered posthumans, truly alien aliens, and all manner of organic technology—with exceptional vividness." LJ

Collects PROPHET #32 & 34-38

Prophet; 2: Brothers. Story by Brandon Graham and Simon Roy; art by Simon Roy, Farel Dalrymple, Giannis Milonogiannis, and Brandom Graham. Image Comics 2013 172 p. Color; Illustration

Grades: Adult **741.5**

1. Prophecies — Fiction; 2. War stories; 3. Graphic novels

1607067498; 9781607067498, $14.99

"The distant future war continues! Old man Prophet is awake now and searching across the universe for old allies that have survived the centuries since the last war." (Publisher's note)

Collects PROPHET #27-31 and 33

Gran, Meredith

Octopus Pie 1. By Meredith Gran. Image Comics 2016 200 p.

Grades: 11 12 Adult **741.5**

1. Brooklyn (New York, NY) — Fiction; 2. College graduates — Fiction; 3. Roommates — Fiction

1632156326; 9781632156327, $14.99

In this book, by Meredith Gran, "we follow grumpy twenty-something Eve and her stoner roommate Hanna as they navigate post-college life. They'll take on crazed childhood rivals, troubling art scenes, the discomfort of exes, and maybe even... friendship" All this and more in the fictional, totally made-up city of Brooklyn." (Publisher's note)

The graphic canon of children's literature: the world's great kids' lit as comics and visuals

Edited by Russ Kick. Seven Stories Press 2014 480 p. Color; Illustration

Grades: 6 7 8 9 10 11 12 Adult **741.5**

1. Children's literature; 2. Graphic novels in education; 3. Literature — Adaptations

1609805305; 9781609805302, $38.95

LC 2014010178

Edited by Russ Kick, "the original three-volume anthology 'The Graphic Canon' presented the world's classic literature—from ancient times to the late twentieth century—as eye-popping comics, illustrations, and other visual forms. In this follow-up volume, young people's literature through the ages is given new life by the best comics artists and illustrators." (Publisher's note)

"These dazzlingly varied renderings run the gamut from haunting to comical while offering visceral reminders that children's stories are often densely layered, infinitely transposable, and peddle in imagery both macabre and whimsical. It is the unfettered imagination of these stories that make them not only wildly entertaining, but also vessels of forgotten truths." Pub Wkly

Graphic Classics volume eight: Mark Twain

Edited by Tom Pomplun. Eureka Productions 2007 144p. Illustration

Grades: 9 10 11 12 Adult **741.5; 818**

1. Adventure graphic novels; 2. Humorous graphic novels; 3. Short stories; 4. Twain, Mark, 1835-1910 — Adaptations; 5. Graphic novels

978-0-9787919-2-6, $11.95

This book includes an adaptation of "Tom Sawyer Abroad" by Tom Pomplun and George Sellas, "The Mysterious Stranger" by Rick Geary, "A Dog's Tale" by Lance Tooks, "The Celebrated Jumping Frog of Calaveras County" by Kevin Atkinson, and "The Carnival of Crime in Connecticut" by Antonella Caputo and Nick Miller. Also in this volume are "Is He Living or Is He Dead?," "A Curious Pleasure Excursion," and eight women artists interpret Mark Twain's "Advice to Little Girls."

"With a terrific lineup of artists and unbeatable material, Pomplun has assembled a collection of Mark Twain's work that should delight graphic novel fans and anyone seeking to boost their general cultural knowledge." Publ Wkly [review of 2004 edition]

First published 2004

Graphic Classics volume eleven: O. Henry

Edited by Tom Pomplun. Eureka Productions 2005 144p. Illustration

Grades: 7 8 9 10 11 12 Adult **741.5; Fic**

1. Henry, O, 1862-1910 — Adaptations; 2. Short stories; 3. Graphic novels

978-0-9746648-2-0, $11.95

This volume of Graphics Classics adapts some of the short stories by O. Henry, the master of the surprise ending. Stories include "The Ransom of Red Chief," illustrated by Johnny Ryan, "The Gift of the Magi," illustrated by Lisa Weber, "The Caballero's Way" (the original story of the Cisco Kid), illustrated by Mark A. Nelson, and more.

Graphic Classics volume fifteen: Fantasy classics

Edited by Tom Pomplun. Eureka Productions 2008 144p. Illustration

Grades: 8 9 10 11 12 Adult **741.5; Fic**

1. Fantasy graphic novels; 2. Horror graphic novels; 3. Short stories; 4. Graphic novels

978-0-9787919-3-3, $11.95

This volume provides graphic novel adaptations of Mary Shelley's Frankenstein, "Rappaccini's Daughter" by Nathaniel Hawthorne, "The Glass Dog" by L. Frank Baum, "The Dream Quest of Unknown Kadath" by H. P. Lovecraft, and poems "After the Fire" by Lord Dunsany and "The

Dream-Bridge" by Clark Ashton Smith. There are a few instances of mild violence and mild language in some of the stories. Illustrators include Skot Olsen, Lance Tooks, Brad Teare, and Leong Wan Kok; adapters include Rod Lott, Lance Tooks, Antonella Caputo, and Ben Avery.

Graphic Classics volume four: H. P. Lovecraft
Edited by Tom Pomplun. Eureka Productions 2007 144p. Illustration
Grades: 7 8 9 10 11 12 Adult   741.5; Fic
1. Horror graphic novels; 2. Lovecraft, H P (Howard Phillips), 1890-1937 — Adaptations; 3. Mystery writers; 4. Short stories
978-0-9746648-9-7, $11.95
Here are comic book adaptations of stories by Lovecraft, master of the macabre and creator of the Cthulhu Mythos. It includes adaptations of "The Shadow Over Innsmouth," illustrated by Simon Gane and "Dreams in the Witch House," by Pedro Lopez. Plus: "Sweet Ermengarde," a rare comedy by Lovecraft. Returning from the previous edition are "Reanimator," "The Shadow Out of Time," "The Terrible Old Man" and "The Cats of Ulthar." Illustrations of headless corpses and monstrous beings might disturb more tender sensibilities.
First published 2002

★ **Graphic Classics volume fourteen: Gothic classics**
Edited by Tom Pomplun. Eureka Productions 2007 144p. Illustration
Grades: 7 8 9 10 11 12 Adult   741.5; Fic
1. Horror graphic novels; 2. Short stories; 3. Graphic novels
978-0-9787919-0-2, $11.95
This volume includes graphic adaptations of classic novels Carmilla by Joseph Sheridan Le Fanu, The Mysteries of Udolpho by Ann Radcliffe, and Northanger Abbey by Jane Austen, along with shorter works "The Oval Portrait" by Edgar Allan Poe, "At the Gate" by Myla Jo Closser, and "I've a Pain in My Head" by Jane Austen. Radcliffe's novel is one mentioned by Austen in Northanger Abbey and is a famous gothic novel from the late eighteenth century, considered to be the world's first best-seller. Le Fanu's vampire novel was published twenty-five years before Stoker's Dracula. Austen wrote Northanger Abbey as a satire of the popular gothic genre.

Graphic Classics volume seven: Bram Stoker
Edited by Tom Pomplun. Eureka Productions 2007 144p. Illustration
Grades: 7 8 9 10 11 12 Adult   741.5; Fic
1. Fantasy graphic novels; 2. Horror graphic novels; 3. Short stories; 4. Stoker, Bram, 1847-1912 — Adaptations; 5. Graphic novels
978-0-9787919-1-9, $11.95
This collection includes a comics adaptation of Dracula by Rich Rainey and Joe Ollmann, "The Judge's House" by Gerry Alanguilan, "Torture Tower" by Onsmith Jeremi, and "The Lair of the White Worm" by South African artist Rico Schacherl. Also "The Bridal of Death," an excerpt from "The Jewel of Seven Stars" by J.B. Bonivert and "The Wondrous Child" illustrated by Evert Geradts. The book includes some violence, and one panel of partial nudity.

"A must-read for fans of horror comics, this collection also works as a good introduction to Stoker's contributions to the traditions of Gothic horror." SLJ
First published 2003

Gravett, Paul
Graphic novels: everything you need to know. Collins Design 2005 192p. Illustration
Grades: Adult Professional   741.5
1. Graphic novels — History and criticism
0-06-082425-5; 978-0-06-082425-9, $24.95
"Selecting 30 highly recommended works from many countries . . . [the author] groups them in separate chapters by theme (childhood, fantasy, crime, sex, superheroes) and devotes a two-page spread to each work, presenting sample pages and discussing them in annotations. . . . This is a genuinely substantial contribution to the growing literature on graphic novels." Libr J
Includes bibliographical references

Manga: Sixty Years of Japanese Comics. Harper Design International/HarperCollins 2004 176p. Illustration
Grades: Adult Professional   741.5
1. Manga; 2. Graphic novels
1-85669-391-0, $24.95
This book presents an accessible and highly-illustrated introduction to the development and diversity of Japanese comics from 1945 to the present. Featuring graphics and extracts from a wide range of manga, the book covers such themes as the specific attributes of manga in contrast to American and European comics; the life and career of Osamu Tezuka, creator of Astro Boy and originator of story manga; boys' comics from the 1960s to the present; the genres and genders of girls' and women's comics; the darker, more realistic themes of gekiga " violent samurai, disturbing horror and apocalyptic science fiction; issues of censorship and protest; and manga's role as a major Japanese export and global influence. Some illustrations from the more adult manga show nudity and sexual situations, as well as violence.

Gray, Harold
★ Harold Gray'sLittle Orphan Annie volume one: Will tomorrow evercome: the complete daily comics, 1924-27: Willtomorrow ever come? The complete daily comics,1924-27. IDW Publishing 2008 385p. Illustration
Grades: 2 3 4 5 6 7 8 9 10 11 12 Adult   Fic; 741.5
1. Adventure graphic novels; 2. Little Orphan Annie (Fictional character); 3. Orphans; 4. Graphic novels
978-1-60010-140-3, $39.99
Little Orphan Annie started as a daily newspaper comic strip in one newspaper, the New York Daily News, on August 5, 1924. It became a popular strip, syndicated to newspapers all over the world. It eventually became a Broadway musical, a hit movie, and Annie became an iconic character. This book is the first comprehensive collection of Gray's comic strip and is the first volume of a series planned to collect all of Gray's Little Orphan Annie strips. She is an orphan girl living in an orphanage, with an unscrupulous director who hires Annie out for work. When wealthy Mrs. Warbucks, trying to prove that she cares for the poor, takes Annie on a "trial" adoption, Annie eventually meets Oliver

Warbucks, whom she calls "Daddy." As the strips go on, Annie undergoes many hardships and perils, facing everything with spunk and a positive attitude. She's no wilting girl, though " she can fight (she has a mean right hook) and will take on any bully. She rescues the dog she calls Sandy, who rewards her with a loyal friendship. This volume includes more than 1,000 comic strips, many of which haven't seen publication since their original newspaper appearance. During the first years of the strip's publication, the color Sunday comics had no connection to the weekday storylines, but a few Sunday pages are included in this book. This book may appeal most to adults who remember reading Little Orphan Annie in the "funnies" pages, but the stories will appeal to all ages. Contributing Editor Jeet Heer provides a biography of Harold Gray.

Gray, Justin
  Daughters of the Dragon: Samurai Bullets. Written by Justin Gray and Jimmy Palmiotti; art by Khari Evans. Marvel Entertainment 2006 Un Illustration
Grades: 10 11 12 Adult   **741.5; Fic**
  1. Adventure graphic novels; 2. Superhero graphic novels; 3. Graphic novels
  0-7851-1944-2, $15.99
  Bounty hunters Misty Knight and Colleen Wing star in this sexy action thriller, the latest project from writers Justin Gray and Jimmy Palmiotti - a mix of gritty action and biting comedy. When four less-than "super" villains - Whirlwind, 8-Ball, Humbug and Freezer Burn - skip bail and team up to rob the penthouse apartment of a wealthy publisher, they get more than they bargained for. Misty Knight and Colleen Wing are on the case. Unfortunately, so are a host of villains and assassins looking to recover what was stolen.

  The **Hills** Have Eyes: The Beginning. Written by Justin Gray and Jimmy Palmiotti; art by John Higgins. HarperCollins/Fox Atomic Comics 2007 Un Illustration
Grades: 11 12 Adult   **741.5; Fic**
  1. Horror graphic novels; 2. Graphic novels
  978-0-06-124354-7, $17.99
  Deep within the remote hills of the New Mexico desert, a group of townspeople thought wiped out by the United States government when it began above-ground atomic testing has returned to the now-irradiated land they still claim as their home. Within the eye of this nuclear storm good people will go bad, battle lines will be drawn, and a new family of mutated monstrosities must protect their own at all costs in a mind-boggling orgy of blood and vengeance. This is a book prequel to the horror movies of the same title. The book includes f-bombs galore, other strong language, and lots of graphic violence.

  Jonah Hex: Face Full of Violence. Written by Justin Gray and Jimmy Palmiotti; art by Luke Ross. DC Comics/Vertigo 2006 144p. Illustration
Grades: 10 11 12 Adult   **741.5; Fic**
  1. Jonah Hex (Fictional characters); 2. Western graphic novels; 3. Graphic novels
  978-1-4012-1095-3, $12.99
  This book collects the new stories of Jonah Hex, the former Confederate soldier turned bounty hunter, the man with the scarred face. He doles out his brand of justice with his guns, taking vengeance upon murderers, thieves, and

others who victimize the weak. The book has foul language and lots of violence.

  Jonah Hex: Guns of Vengeance. Written by Justin Gray and Jimmy Palmiotti; art by Luke Ross. DC Comics 2007 144p. Illustration
Grades: 11 12 Adult   **741.5; Fic**
  1. Adventure graphic novels; 2. Supernatural graphic novels; 3. Western graphic novels; 4. Graphic novels
  978-1-4012-1249-0, $12.99
  Jonah Hex, a mysterious bounty hunter and thinking man's killer, was a hero to some and a villain to others—and his name was spoken in whispers. He had no friends, but he did have two companions: one was death and the other... the smell of gun smoke. Haunted by the ghosts of his past, present, and future, the bullets fly as Jonah Hex battles bounty hunters, vengeful spirits, alligators, and sideshow freaks. This Western is full of graphic violence, harsh language, and some sexual situations and nudity.

  ★ **Power** girl: a new beginning. Art by Amanda Conner. DC Comics 2010 Un Illustration
Grades: 9 10 11 12 Adult   **741.5; Fic**
  1. Superhero graphic novels; 2. Graphic novels
  978-1-4012-2618-3, $17.99
  Kara Zor-L came from Krypton, just like her very famous cousin Kal-L, who became Superman, but she had lived in a parallel universe, known as Earth 2. Since then, she has come to this world's New York City and started all over again as Karen Starr and reopening her business, a progressive technology company called Starrware Labs. She's also Power Girl, since she has many of Superman's superpowers. Before she can get Starrware Labs fully up and running with all essential positions filled, she has to deal with a horde of fear-inducing robots sent by the Ultra-Humanite to destroy Manhattan. Then, a trio of party-crashing aliens and their pursuer start wrecking the rest of Manhattan as they fight in the streets. The book has lots of action but no really graphic violence, and some "fan service" as it's called in manga there are some panty shots, and Karen/Power Girl deals with men staring at her bust. Her costume has a cutout design on the chest, which the writers and artist treat with some great humor. Co-writer Palmiotti and artist Conner are a couple themselves, and their close work shows in sheer fun of this book.

Grayson, Devin
  Nightwing: Mobbed Up. Devin Grayson, writer; Phil Hester, Cliff Chiang, pencillers; Ande Parks, inker; Phil Balsman, Nick J. Napolitano, letterers; Gretory Wright, colorist. DC Comics 2006 128p. Illustration
Grades: 10 11 12 Adult   **741.5; Fic**
  1. Nightwing (Fictional character); 2. Superhero graphic novels; 3. Graphic novels
  978-1-4012-0907-0, $12.99
  Injured and dejected, cut off from all allegiances, Dick Grayson decides to turn his misery into an advantage and a new purpose. He arranges to be adopted into one of New York City's crime families. In doing so he begins a new odyssey, one that sweeps him into the depths of the criminal underworld. Try as he may, however, he can't put his crime-fighting alter ego behind him forever, so Nightwing

returns. But which side is he on" There's some violence, but despite the mob, little in the way of harsh language.

Nightwing: Renegade. Devin Grayson, writer; Phil Hester et. al, pencillers; Ande Parks, Rodney Ramos, Edde Wagner, inkers. DC Comics 2006 144p. Illustration
Grades: 9 10 11 12 Adult   **Fic; 741.5**
1. Nightwing (Fictional character); 2. Robin (Fictional character); 3. Superhero graphic novels; 4. Graphic novels
978-1-4012-0908-7, $14.99

Once he was Robin, but Dick Grayson stepped out from the shadow of the Bat to become his own hero, Nightwing. Now the events of the past year have taken a heavy toll on Dick, and he's seemingly embraced the darkness within himself. He's got a new costume, a new name - Renegade - and he serves a new master. But could Nightwing really be working for Deathstroke, the deadly assassin and his longtime nemesis" As Renegade takes Deathstroke's daughter Ravager under his wing, the two old enemies will play a dangerous game of cat and mouse. But who's manipulating whom, and what do these two brilliant minds really want from each other" Just when Nightwing thinks he has it all figured out, Deathstroke makes a move so shocking, Nightwing's world will never be the same. There's plenty of action, but little overt violence or harsh language.

Grecian, Alexander
Proof book 2: the company of men. Art by Riley Rossmo. Image Comics 2008 Un
Grades: 9 10 11 12 Adult   **741.5; Fic**
1. Adventure graphic novels; 2. Fantasy graphic novels; 3. Sasquatch; 4. Graphic novels
978-1-60706-017-8, $12.99

Proof the Bigfoot has worked as part of a team investigating monsters they call cryptoids, but now a big-game hunter who specializes in killing endangered animals and cryptoids in order to eat them (along with an organization of special gourmets who like to eat monstrous creatures) wants to catch, kill, and eat Proof. In order to get him, he has killed a mother dinosaur in a remote African jungle and left the baby alive to lure Proof and his human teammates (including one traitor). The book includes some violence. Extras in this volume include paper dolls of some of the characters and the script for one of the stories, "A Perfect Gentleman."

Seven Sons. Riley Rossmo, artist. AiT/Planet Lar 2006 120p. Illustration
Grades: 7 8 9 10 11 12 Adult   **741.5; Fic**
1. China — Folklore; 2. Graphic novels
978-1-932051-46-9, $12.95

Seven identical Chinese brothers come to America during the Gold Rush of the 1850s. When two children fall through an iced-over river, Brother Number One tries to save them by breathing the entire river into his mouth. But he can't hold it long enough for them to get to safety and lets the water go, accidentally drowning the children. When a mob of angry townspeople tries to retaliate, each of Number One's brothers takes his place, using their remarkable abilities each time to save his life. This retelling doesn't have the happy ending usually found in the children's picture books, and by moving the story to the U.S., Grecian infuses a message about intolerance and prejudice in the story.

Green Arrow/Black Canary: for better or for worse.
DC Comics 2007 200p. Illustration
Grades: 10 11 12 Adult   **741.5**
1. Black Canary (Fictional character); 2. Green Arrow (Fictional character); 3. Romance graphic novels; 4. Superhero graphic novels; 5. Graphic novels
978-1-4012-1446-3, $14.99

Green Arrow and Black Canary have been crime fighting partners, business partners, lovers. Somewhere along the way, they broke up. Then Green Arrow died. Or so everyone thought. Then he came back. This volume collects the stories from the past several decades, from the Silver Age to the present day, that tell the saga of the great love affair in the DC Universe. The book includes some mild sexual situations and partial nudity.

Green, Justin
Binky Brown meets the holy Virgin Mary. Justin Green. McSweeney's Books 2009 63 p. Illustration
Grades: Adult   **741.5**
1. Catholic Church; 2. Underground comic books, strips, etc
9781934781555, $29; 193478155X

LC 2014427888
"A lost classic of underground cartooning, Binky Brown Meets the Holy VirginMary is Justin Green's autobiographical portrayal of his struggle withreligion and his own neuroses. Binky Brown is a young Catholic battling allthe usual problems of adolescencepuberty, parents, and the fear that thestrange ray of energy emanating from his private parts will strike a pictureof the Virgin Mary." (Publisher's note)

"This Rosetta Stone of autobiographical comics—or perhaps more appropriately, in this case, 'confessional' comics—receives the deluxe treatment it so richly deserves with this beautiful over-sized edition featuring art reproduced directly from the original pages." Pub Wkly

Greenberg, Isabel
The **encyclopedia** of early earth: a novel. Isabel Greenberg. Little, Brown and Co. 2013 176 p.
Grades: 10 11 12 Adult   **741.5; Fic**
1. Earth — Fiction; 2. Fables; 3. Travel — Fiction
0316225819; 9780316225816, $23

LC 2013939419
Author Isabel Greenberg presents a "series of illustrated and linked tales [which] chronicles the explorations of a young man as he paddles from his home in the North Pole to the South Pole. There, he meets his true love, but their romance is ill-fated. Early Earth's unusual and finicky polarity means the lovers can never touch." (Publisher's note)

"Greenberg deeply immerses readers in the themes and lessons of world mythology, but she remarkably never merely apes classic mythsùthe way each of Early Earth's cultures tweaks the same ideas and characters for their own myths is a veritable lesson in comparative theology." Booklist

Greenberger, Robert, ed.
Batman: War Crimes. DC Comics 2006 Un Illustration
Grades: 9 10 11 12 Adult   **Fic; 741.5**

1. Batman (Fictional character); 2. Joker (Fictional character); 3. Mystery graphic novels; 4. Superhero graphic novels; 5. Graphic novels
1-4012-0903-3, $12.99

The Spoiler died during the gang war, or so Batman thought. When the media begin reporting on the Spoiler's private life and making accusations aimed at the Dark Knight, he begins an investigation that leads to a new confrontation with Gotham City's undisputed underworld boss, Black Mask. Complicating matters even further is the return of his deadliest opponent, the Joker, and the reappearance of an old foe long believed dead. The book includes violence.

Batman: War Games Act One: Outbreak. DC Comics 2005 Un Illustration
Grades: 10 11 12 Adult   **Fic; 741.5**
1. Batgirl (Fictional character); 2. Batman (Fictional character); 3. Mystery graphic novels; 4. Nightwing (Fictional character); 5. Robin (Fictional character); 6. Superhero graphic novels; 7. Graphic novels
1-4012-0429-5, $14.95

Gotham City's underworld families respond to a mysterious summons for a summit. Fear, suspicion, and paranoia get the better of them and bullets fly fast and furiously. As familiar warlords fall, a new wave of chaos engulfs the city. Batman must use every available asset - Oracle, Batgirl, Nightwing, Orpheus, Onyx, and Tarantula - to preserve life and contain the trouble, while determining who is the mastermind behind the conflagration. If he doesn't figure it out soon, no one will be safe. And when someone starts targeting family members of the gang leaders, the danger spills out to parks and schools - including former Robin Tim Drake's high school.

Batman: War Games Act Three: Endgame. DC Comics 2005 Un Illustration
Grades: 10 11 12 Adult   **741.5; Fic**
1. Batman (Fictional character); 2. Mystery graphic novels; 3. Superhero graphic novels; 4. Graphic novels
1-4012-0431-7, $14.99

Black Mask has made Batman's training scenario a chilling reality. The various crime families are leaderless, and the soldiers run for their lives while trying to grab a piece of the underworld pie for themselves. Batman and his allies have failed to contain the chaos threatening the lives of Gotham City's people. The media have exploited the situation so people think Batman is acting against their best interests. Worse, he has lost the trust and support of Commissioner Akins, just when he needs it the most. Before the day is over, a friend and ally will be dead, familial ties will be broken, and the balance of power in the city will be forever altered.

Batman: War Games Act Two: Tides. DC Comics 2005 Un Illustration
Grades: 10 11 12 Adult   **741.5; Fic**
1. Batman (Fictional character); 2. Mystery graphic novels; 3. Robin (Fictional character); 4. Superhero graphic novels; 5. Graphic novels
1-4012-0430-9, $14.99

In this second volume the truth behind the criminal activity is revealed, one of Batman's agents is beaten, another killed and a new player emerges on the scene, one

assumed gone for good but now ready to seize control over Gotham's underworld. Tim Drake returns to the Robin uniform to help, although he knows there will be consequences for his actions. The Dark Knight may be powerless to stop the streets from running red with blood, and the police are losing their trust in him and his colleagues.

The **essential** Batman encyclopedia. Ballantine Books 2008 388p. Illustration
Grades: 9 10 11 12 Adult   **741.5**
1. Batman (Fictional character); 2. Comic books, strips, etc — History and criticism; 3. Graphic novels
978-0-345-50106-6, $29.95

LC 2008-3016

Former DC Comics editor Greenberger has compiled a guide book that includes hundreds of entries in AZ format, covering characters, places, and organizations that have appeared in Batman comics over the decades. Entries range from a few lines to several pages and include every villain, partner, sidekick, friend and enemy that has ever appeared in the Batman universe.

Includes bibliographical references.

Will Eisner. Rosen Publishing Group 2005 112p. Illustration
Grades: 8 9 10 11 12 Adult   **741.5; 92**
1. Cartoonists — Biography; 2. Graphic novels
1-4042-0286-2, $31.95

LC 2004016656

Veteran comics insider Greenberger has written this biography of Eisner, covering his long career in comics, from the 1930s through the early 2000s. Eisner created the groundbreaking comic series The Spirit, and in the 1970s started writing original graphic novels set in New York City. The Eisner Awards for comics are named after him, due to his strong influence on the industry over the decades. This volume includes a list of books for further reading and a bibliography.

Part of the Library of Graphic Novelists

Grell, Mike
The **Complete** Jon Sable, Freelance Volume 1. IDW Publishing 2005 180p. Illustration
Grades: 10 11 12 Adult   **741.5; Fic**
1. Adventure graphic novels; 2. Graphic novels
1-932382-77-1, $24.99

The initial 54-page story guest-stars Ronald Reagan, and the second is Sable's famous 108-page origin saga. Sable is a mercenary willing to act as a private eye or bodyguard if the money is right and the job promises excitement. The origin story depicts how he became that way after his family was massacred. There's lots of fighting action and bloodshed in this story, originally published by First Comics in the early 1980s.

Griffith, Bill
Invisible Ink: My Mother's Love Affair With a Famous Cartoonist. By Bill Griffith. W W Norton & Co Inc 2015 208 p. Illustration
Grades: Adult   **741.5973; 741.5**

1. Cartoonists; 2. Mother-son relationship; 3. Parent-child relationship
1606998951; 9781606998953, $29.99

LC 2015937719

This book, a memoir by Bill Griffith, "uncovers his mother's secret life which included an affair with a cartoonist and crime novelist in the 1950s and '60s. . . . Alternating between past and present, . . . Griffith recreates the quotidian habits of suburban Levittown and the professional and cultural life of mid-century Manhattan in the 1950s and '60s as seen through his mother's and his own teenage eyes." (Publisher's note)

Grillo-Marxuach, Javier
★ The **Middleman:** the collected series indispensability. Viper Comics 2008 336p. Illustration
Grades: 9 10 11 12 Adult   **741.5; Fic**
1. Adventure graphic novels; 2. Humorous graphic novels; 3. Science fiction graphic novels; 4. Graphic novels
978-0-9802385-4-9, $19.95

This book collects all three volumes of The Middleman comics series. Art student Wendy Watson works as a temp agency hire, when one day she's working at a scientific laboratory where things go totally wrong and a mysterious guy who calls himself The Middleman takes care of the monsters. Unfortunately for Wendy, the cover story that a gas main explosion caused all the mess also indicates that her lucky Zippo lighter, the only thing she has from her long-missing father, ignited the gas leak. Unemployed Wendy soon finds herself recruited by the Jolly Fats Wehawkin Temp Agency, which is actually the cover for The Middleman and his henchperson, robotic Ida. Wendy soon finds herself battling intelligent apes out to rule the criminal underworld, crazy Lucha Libre wrestlers, and more "exotic problems," at the side of the enigmatic, super-good guy, The Middleman. The book includes some violence, some nudity, and some sexual innuendo. The series was adapted into a television series on ABC Family which ran for one season; the DVD boxed set is scheduled for a summer 2009 release.

Grine, Chris
    Chickenhare: fire in the hole. Dark Horse Comics 2008 200p. Illustration
Grades: 7 8 9 10 11 12 Adult   **741.5; Fic**
1. Adventure graphic novels; 2. Fantasy graphic novels; 3. Graphic novels
978-1-59307-907-9, $10.95

Chickenhare, his friend Abe, and their new friends Scabby, Meg and Banjo managed to escape the evil Taxidermist Klaus, but they have gone from one dangerous situation into . . . something worse. While at sea in a small boat about to be swamped by rain and waves, Banjo's brother and some warriors from the Underworld pop up, they zap the soul out of Abe and take Banjo and Meg. Chickenhare is left with Scabby and Abe's body. He must venture into the Underworld to recover Abe's soul. Meanwhile, Banjo and Meg face punishment for deserting the Underworld. And just why do the Sea Folk call Chickenhare "Your Majesty?"

Grist, Paul
    Kane Vol. 1: Greetings from New Eden. Image Comics 2004 127p. Illustration
Grades: 10 11 12 Adult   **741.5; Fic**
1. Mystery graphic novels; 2. Graphic novels
1-58240-340-6, $11.95

Detective Kane returns to active duty with the New Eden Police Dept. following a six month suspension after he shot and killed his partner Dennis Harvey. His fellow police officers give Kane a welcome back gift - a couple of bullets with his name engraved on them. Partnered with a new detective, Kate Felix, Kane soon finds out nothing has changed in the city of New Eden. In his first two days back, Kane has to deal with a siege, a kidnapping and a bomb attack. And then there's the Crime Boss of New Eden, Oscar Darke... The book includes some harsh language and violence.

    Kane Vol. 2: Rabbit Hunt. Image Comics 2004 Un Illustration
Grades: 10 11 12 Adult   **741.5; Fic**
1. Mystery graphic novels; 2. Graphic novels
1-58240-355-4, $12.95

It's a bad day for Mister Floppsie Whoppsie, New Eden's self-styled Rabbit for Hire. The freelance rabbit business isn't going as well as it should. He's hung over. The rent's due. There's a knock at the door and a gun-wielding homicidal maniac barges into the room. That's when things start to go downhill. And Detective Kane still can't trust anyone in the New Eden Police Department. The book includes some strong language and violence.

    Kane Vol. 4: Thirty-Ninth. Image Comics 2005 Un Illustration
Grades: 10 11 12 Adult   **741.5; Fic**
1. Mystery graphic novels; 2. Graphic novels
1-58240-468-2, $16.95

When Detective Kane returned to active duty with the New Eden Police Dept. following a six-month suspension in the wake of shooting and killing his partner, his fellow police officers gave him a welcome back gift: a couple of bullets with his name on them. Now, a sniper is taking pot shots at the police. An ex-cop is looking to take revenge on the cop who turned him in. There's rioting in the streets and the Mayor's been kidnapped again. It's another typical week for the police in New Eden's Precinct 39. The book has some strong language and violence.

Gross, Allan
    Cryptozoo Crew Volume 2: Call of the Thunderbird!. Jerry Carr, illustrator; NBM 2006 Un Illustration
Grades: 5 6 7 8 9 10 11 12 Adult   **741.5; Fic**
1. Humorous graphic novels; 2. Mythical animals; 3. Graphic novels
978-1-56163-466-8, $12.95

In this second volume, cryptozoologist Tork Darwyn suffers nightmares about a childhood encounter with the legendary thunderbird; it's been twenty years since that day, and he must return or be cursed. In the meantime, his teacher wife Tara has learned that her school will be shut down for lack of funding. Naturally, they travel together to Alaska to find out what is driving Tork to go there.

Gross, Milt

He Done Her Wrong: The Great American Novel. Fantagraphics Books 2005 Un Illustration

Grades: 9 10 11 12 Adult   **741.5; Fic**

1. Adventure graphic novels; 2. Humorous graphic novels; 3. Graphic novels

1-56097-694-2, $16.95

The story follows the convoluted misadventures of a na?ve frontiersman with superhuman strength exploited by a larcenous robber baron who eventually double crosses our hero and steals his girl. The pursuit leads to New York City where a sordid cast of cantankerous salesmen, officious government bureaucrats, bumbling hospital attendants, a lusty widow with a defensive Chihuahua and one angry barber wreak more havoc in our characters' lives than a hundred Little Rascals in a Marx Brothers film.

This wordless comic novel shares much with the silent comedy films of Harold Lloyd, Buster Keaton, and Charlie Chaplin. It's full of slapstick humor, with one politically incorrect gag that was the norm in 1930, this book's original year of publication.

Gruber, Jonathan

Health care reform: what it is, why it's necessary, how it works. Jonathan Gruber, with HP Newquist; illustrated by Nathan Schreiber. Hill and Wang 2011 151 p.

Grades: Adult   **362.1**

1. Access to health care; 2. Health care reform — United States; 3. Medical care; 4. Medical care — Costs; 5. Medical care — United States; 6. Medical policy — United States

0809053977; 0809094622; 9780809053971; 9780809094622

LC 2011020495

This book is "[a] cartoon-driven examination of what's wrong with the American way of health care—and why the legislative reform of 2010 was necessary." (Kirkus) "It delivers information . . . through an earnest but informal lecture by a cartoon version of an expert—in this case [Jonathan] Gruber, an MIT economics professor who helped craft Massachusetts's successful health care reform plan as well as the Affordable Care Act, which has been the subject of so much confusion and deliberate misinformation. He begins the presentation by confronting a small group of people with the enormous medical bills they could receive after medical treatment, then moves from the individual to the national level to show that our present system is unfair and unsustainable." (Publishers Wkly)

A graphic explanation of the PPACA act.

Grunwald, Jennifer

I am Iron Man. Edited by Jennifer Grunwald. Marvel Worldwide, Inc. 2010 Un Illustration

Grades: 7 8 9 10 11 12 Adult   **741.5; Fic**

1. Iron Man (Fictional character); 2. Superhero graphic novels; 3. Graphic novels

978-0-7851-4558-5, $16.99

The first Iron Man movie, released in 2008, was a major hit, but just like the other superhero movies based on Marvel Comics properties, it wasn't based on any particular Iron Man comics. This book collects a two-issue miniseries based on the movie script, written by Peter David with pencils by Sean Chen, a one-shot written by Christos Gage with pencils by Hugo Petrus, and Iron Man #200, which was written by Denny O'Neil with pencils by Mark Bright and originally published in 1985. David and Chen's comic adapts the movie script, hitting all the high points of the action. Gage and Petrus's one-shot, "Security Measures," looks at the action of the movie from the viewpoint of S.H.I.E.L.D. agent Coulson. Iron Man #200 features a battle between Iron Man and Iron Monger, who is Tony Stark's erstwhile partner Obadiah Stane. The book also includes an interview with Kevin Feige, producer of the Iron Man movie, and photos taken on the movie sets. The book actually cuts down on the amount of violence that was shown in the movie.

Guggenheim, Marc

Blade: Undead Again. Written by Marc Guggenheim; art by Howard Chaykin. Marvel Entertainment 2007 Un Illustration

Grades: 10 11 12 Adult   **741.5; Fic**

1. Blade (Fictional character); 2. Dracula, Count (Fictional character); 3. Spider-Man (Fictional character); 4. Superhero graphic novels; 5. Wolverine (Fictional character); 6. Graphic novels

978-0-7851-2364-4, $14.99

Here are new adventures starring the popular character who's starred in three movies and a TV series. Blade encounters Spider-Man, Dracula, Dr. Doom, Wolverine... and Santa Claus" Plus, the book takes a look into Blade's mysterious past. This book includes some bloody violence, mostly vampiric and fighting vampires.

Civil War: Wolverine. Marc Guggenheim; artist, Humberto Ramos. Marvel Entertainment 2007 Un Illustration

Grades: 10 11 12 Adult   **741.5; Fic**

1. Superhero graphic novels; 2. Wolverine (Fictional character); 3. Graphic novels

978-0-7851-1980-7, $17.99

In the aftermath of the Stamford tragedy, Logan makes it his personal mission to take down the man responsible. No sooner does he begin his hunt, however, than he discovers someone else is stalking the same prey: a mysterious trio whose identity, and disturbing mission, unsettles him. This book includes some bloody violence and some strong language.

Rocketeer adventures: Vol. 2. Peter David, Marc Guggenheim, Stan Sakai, illustrated by Bill Sienkiewicz, Sandy Plunkett. IDW Pub. 2012 136 p. Illustration

Grades: Adult   **Fic; 741.5/973**

1. Rocketeer (Fictional character); 2. Superhero comic books, strips, etc

161377401X; 9781613774014, $24.99

This graphic novel anthology, featuring authors Marc Guggenheim, Sandy Plunkett, Peter David, and others, presents a second volume of adventures of the 1930s hero, the Rocketeer. "Dave Stevens' . . . distinctive artwork and . . . story was inspired by the adventure pulp novels of the era The Rocketeer was set in. . . . Now, . . . [this book] present[s] new interpretations of The Rocketeer by some of today's finest talents." (Publisher's note)

Guibert, Emmanuel

★ **Alan's** war. First Second 2008 304p. Illustration
Grades: 10 11 12 Adult   **92; 940.54; 741.5**
1. Biographical graphic novels; 2. Cope, Alan Ingram,
1925-1999; 3. Soldiers; 4. Soldiers; 5. Veterans; 6. World
War, 1939-1945; 7. Graphic novels
978-1-59643-096-9; 1-59643-096-6, $24

LC 2007-46190

French cartoonist Guibert met and became friends with
Alan Cope and interviewed him at length to create this book.
It recreates Cope's memories of being an eighteen-year-old
G.I. during World War II. Unlike the war movies that focus
on battles, this book focuses on more everyday, mundane
memories of the day-to-day life of a soldier. Cope frankly
describes a bout with crabs (genital lice), matter-of-factly
tells of casual man-to-man sexual encounters among the
soldiers, and gives the reader a feel for what happened back
then. He also talks about postwar relationships and travels.

This is a "poignant and frank graphic memoir of young
soldier who was told to serve his country in WWII and how
it changed him forever. . . . Cope and Guibert forge a story
that resonates with humanity." Publ Wkly

How the World Was: A California Childhood.
Emmanuel Guibert; translated by Kathryn M. Pulver. First
Second 2014 160 p.
Grades: Adult   **741.5**
1. Cope, Alan; 2. Friendship; 3. Veterans — United States
1596436646; 9781596436640, $19.99

This book "is Emmanuel Guibert's moving return to
documenting the life of his friend [American veteran named
Alan Cope]. Cope grew up in California during the great
depression, and this remarkable graphic novel details the
little moments that make a young man's life...while
capturing the scope of America during the great depression."
(Publisher's note)

★ The **photographer**. [by] Emmanuel Guibert, Didier
Lefèvre and Frédéric Lemercier; translated by Alexis Siegel.
First Second 2009 267p. Illustration; Map
Grades: 11 12 Adult   **92; 741.5; 958.1**
978-1-59643-375-5; 1-59643-375-2, $29.95

"Originally published as three volumes in France from
2003 to 2006, this graphic novel follows photojournalist
Didier Lefèvre during his three months in Pakistan and
Afghanistan in 1986 as he documented the medical missions
of Doctors without Borders. . . . The graphic novel combines
traditional comic art with some of the four thousand
photographs Lefevre shot while in Afghanistan. . . . Many
images will stay with readers as both horrifying and
glorious. The Afghan children being treated for burns, bullet
wounds, and shrapnel are page by page next to the beauty of
the Afghan mountainous landscapes. . . . [This book] has a
powerful message and images of a part of the world that
should be discussed more often." Voice Youth Advocates

Gunter, Miles

Zombee. Writer, Miles Gunter; artist, Victor Santos.
Image Comics 2006 Un Illustration
Grades: 10 11 12 Adult   **741.5; Fic**
1. Horror graphic novels; 2. Humorous graphic novels; 3.
Graphic novels
978-1-58240-662-6, $12.99

A dutiful Samurai, a madcap Ninja and a bizarro Zen
Monk team up to battle the undead in Feudal Japan. Can
these unlikely allies stay friends long enough to stop the
zombees from taking over their homeland? Gory and violent
zombie-destroying action combines with comedy and foul
language (most of it very anachronistic); the cover image,
with the zombie head flying amongst sprays of blood while a
samurai holds his sword, lets the reader know exactly what
to expect.

Gurewich, Nicholas

The **Trial** of Colonel Sweeto and other stories: a
collection of the comic strips. Dark Horse Comics 2007 96p.
Illustration
Grades: 11 12 Adult   **741.5**
1. Humorous graphic novels; 2. Graphic novels
978-1-59307-844-7, $14.95

Gurewich's Perry Bible Fellowship is a popular
webcomic; now they're collected into this hardcover
volume. The full-color strips betray a twisted sense of humor
with a strong bias for the bizarre, and some strips use nudity
and violence.

Hagio, Moto

The **heart** of Thomas. By Moto Hagio, translated by
Matt Thorn. Fantagraphics Books 2013 515 p.
Grades: Adult   **Fic; 741.5/952**
1. School stories; 2. Shojo manga
1606995510; 9781606995518, $39.99

This shojo manga graphic novel, by Moto Hagio,
translated by Matt Thorn, follows the emotional struggles of
a high school boy, set in a "boarding school in Germany,
sometime in the latter 20th Century. Fourteen year-old
Thomas Werner falls from a lonely pedestrian overpass to
his death immediately after sending a single, brief letter to a
schoolmate." (Publisher's note)

Hakase, Mizuki

Demon Flowers: Kuruizaki no Hana Volume 1.
Tokyopop 2007 Un Illustration
Grades: 10 11 12 Adult   **741.5; Fic**
1. Fantasy graphic novels; 2. Horror graphic novels; 3.
Manga; 4. Graphic novels
978-1-4278-0298-9, $9.99

Long ago, when Japanese gods descended upon
humans, their mixed offspring inherited supernatural
powers, and the name Kuruizaki no hana." Now, the demon
world is rising up to kill them all to take their powers;
Ushitora is their assassin. Then he falls for a little boy,
Masato, who is a kuruizaki no hana," and they go on the run.
Along the way, Ushitora takes in orphaned girl Nao, they
form an odd but loyal family. This book includes some
violence and partial nudity.

Hall, Jason

Hellboy: the companion. Stephen Weiner, Jason Hall,
Victoria Blake with additional material by Mike Mignola.
Dark Horse Comics 2008 240p. Illustration
Grades: 10 11 12 Adult   **741.5**
1. Hellboy (Fictional character); 2. Horror graphic novels;
3. Graphic novels

978-1-59307-655-9, $14.95

Mike Mignola's Hellboy debuted in 1994 and has built up a growing audience for its world of Victorian occult societies, prehistoric gods, arcane Nazi experiments, and a big red demon for a good guy. Now librarian and comics historian Weiner, comics writer Hall, and journalist Blake put together a guide to Mignola's created world, illustrated with new art by Mignola as well as art from fourteen years of Hellboy from Mignola and the other artists who have worked with him over the years, including Guy Davis, Duncan Fegredo, Paul Azaceta, and others. The book includes character profiles, a timeline, and the literary heritage of Hellboy.

Hall, Jeremy

Piers Anthony Presents Revved. Art by David Nakayama. Image Comics/Top Cow Productions 2007 Un Illustration

Grades: 10 11 12 Adult   **741.5; Fic**
  1. Adventure graphic novels; 2. Fantasy graphic novels; 3. Graphic novels
  1-58240-779-7, $9.99

Four people are recruited by a man named Bob Gruber to form a team. Ex-racer Jack James steals the first car, a white Mazda RX-8; he becomes the White Rider. In quick succession, he helps steal three more vehicles: a red Shelby Cobra for the violent Stick, a black motorcycle for speed demon Andre, and a special jeep for Maddie. Each vehicle has a bit of the mystical "First Metal," and the riders become the new avatars of the Four Horsemen of the Apocalypse. Bob sends them on missions they believe will preserve world peace, but each time even more chaos and violence happens. Are they a force for peace or instruments to cause the end of humanity?

Hall, Justin

No straight lines: four decades of queer comics. Justin Hall. Fantagraphics Books 2012 308 p.

Grades: Adult   **741.5**
  1. Comic books, strips, etc — History and criticism; 2. Homosexuality; 3. LGBT comic books, strips, etc
  1606995065; 9781606995068, $35

This book, edited by Justin Hall, presents an exploration into lesbian, gay, bisexual and transgendered comic books and artists. "The insular nature of the world of queer cartooning . . . created a fascinating artistic scene. LGBT comics have been an uncensored, internal conversation within the queer community, and thus provide a unique window into the hopes, fears, and fantasies of queer people for the last four decades." (Publisher's note)

Includes bibliographical references.

Hambly, Barbara

Anne Steelyard: the garden of emptiness, act I: an honorary man. Written by Barbara Hambly; pencils by Alex Kosakowski and Ron Randall; colors by Mike Garcia. Penny Farthing Press 2008 Un Illustration

Grades: 9 10 11 12 Adult   **Fic; 741.5**
  1. Adventure graphic novels; 2. Archeology; 3. Middle East; 4. Graphic novels
  978-0-9719012-9-2, $14.95

In 1908, the Middle East is a region in turmoil; while Germany and Great Britain posture at each other in a prelude to the First World War, men called the Young Turks challenge the Turkish Sultans for control of the Ottoman Empire. Archeologists excavate relics and treasures from the desert sands, their work beginning to demystify human history and managing to bring wealth and fame (or infamy) to those archeologists. Anne Steelyard is a British archeologist who wants to make that one huge discovery which will make her reputation, free her from her father and force the male-dominated field to recognize her as an equal. However, even as she tries to set up an expedition, the politics of the place and time provide obstacles from the Turkish government, from the British, and from society itself. The book includes some violence.

Other titles in this series are: The gate of dreams and starlight (2009); A thousand waters (2011)

Hamilton, Laurell K.

Anita Blake, Vampire Hunter: Guilty Pleasures Volume 1. Laurell K. Hamilton; adapted by Stacie Ritchie (issues 1-5) & Jess Ruffner-Booth (issue 6); artwork, Brett Booth. Marvel Entertainment 2007 168p. Illustration

Grades: 10 11 12 Adult   **741.5; Fic**
  1. Fantasy graphic novels; 2. Horror graphic novels
  978-0-7851-2723-9, $19.99

Anita Blake lives in a world where vampires, zombies and werewolves have been declared legal citizens of the United States. Anita Blake is an "Animator" - a profession that involves raising the dead for mourning relatives. But she is also known as a fearsome hunter of criminal vampires, and she's often employed to investigate cases that are far too much for conventional police. But as Anita gains the attention of the vampire masters of her hometown of St. Louis, she also risks revealing an intriguing secret about herself - the source of her unusual strength and power. The book includes vampiric violence, strong language, partial nudity, and sexual suggestiveness.

Hanmura, Ryo

Samurai Commando: Mission 1549 Volume 1. Original idea by Ryo Hanmura; story by Harutoshi Fukui; art by Ark Performance. DC Comics/CMX 2007 176p. Illustration

Grades: 10 11 12 Adult   **741.5; Fic**
  1. Adventure graphic novels; 2. Manga; 3. Science fiction graphic novels; 4. Seinen manga; 5. Graphic novels
  978-1-4012-1438-8, $9.99

A military test accidentally sends a unit from Japan's Self-Defense Forces (JDF) back in time to the Sengoku Jidai period in the late 16th century, the time of warfare before Ieyasu Tokugawa seized power. When the unit's actions begin to alter the present, the JDF sends a second unit to retrieve them. But Colonel Matoba, commander of the lost battalion, is determined to use his advanced technology to conquer Japan and change his country's destiny. It's up to Kashima, Matoba's former protege, to stop him. But he only has a narrow window of time, and it is rapidly closing. This is the first of two volumes. The book includes battle violence and some strong language.

Harkham, Sammy
Everything together: collected stories. Sammy Harkham. Distributed Art Pub Inc 2012
Grades: Adult   **741.5**
1. Short stories; 2. Graphic novels
0985159502; 9780985159504

Author Sammy Harkham presents a book of short-story comics, which condense vast amounts of emotion and information into nuanced cartoon narratives . . . At the center of the book are two vastly different tales: 'Poor Sailor,' a sea-faring myth of a man gone to find wealth for his love; and 'Somersaulting,' a kind of fever dream of teenagers in love, wiling away the summer. (Publisher's note)

These stories originally appeared in different forms in Vice, Mome, Drawn and Quarterly Showcase, Kramers Ergot, Crickets, etc.

Harmon, Paul
Mora Vol. 1: All Beasts Will Show Their Teeth. Image Comics 2006 Un Illustration
Grades: 10 11 12 Adult   **741.5; Fic**
1. Fantasy graphic novels; 2. Horror graphic novels; 3. Graphic novels
1-58240-588-3, $12.99

This is the dark tale of the most powerful witch that lived, and the city that raised her. Strange creatures and ruthless beasts abound as the story follows young Mora through the treacherous City of Witches. There is violence as monsters attack and people fight back.

Harras, Bob, ed.
Superman: Emperor Joker. Various artists and writers.. DC Comics 2007 256p. Illustration
Grades: 10 11 12 Adult   **Fic; 741.5**
1. Joker (Fictional character); 2. Superhero graphic novels; 3. Superman (Fictional character); 4. Graphic novels
978-1-4012-1193-6, $14.99

In this topsy-turvy tale of a world gone wrong, the Man of Steel is a hunted villain, while his imperfect duplicate, Bizarro, is hailed as a champion. With the heroes of the JLA altered almost beyond recognition, it's up to Superman to help his allies rediscover their true selves in an incredible struggle against the Joker, Emperor of the Universe.

Harris, Micah
Heaven's War. Micah Harris and Michael Gaydos. Image Comics 2003 118p. Illustration
Grades: 9 10 11 12 Adult   **741.5**
1. Adventure graphic novels; 2. Fantasy graphic novels; 3. Graphic novels
1-58240-330-9, $12.95

In this graphic novel, "J.R.R. Tolkien and C.S. Lewis are called upon by eccentric fellow fantasist Charles Williams to join him against occultist Aleister Crowley. Crowley seeks an entrance into the Heavenly realms with the intent of manipulating the angelic battles that shape human history and thus mold the world according to his will. Their conflict with Crowley will take this trio of authors . . . to the very edge of Heaven." (Publisher's note)

Hart, Christopher
The **reformed**. Del Rey Manga 2008 170p. Illustration
Grades: 10 11 12 Adult   **741.5; Fic**
1. Fantasy graphic novels; 2. Horror graphic novels; 3. Mystery graphic novels; 4. Vampires; 5. Graphic novels
978-0-345-49663-8, $10.95

Handsome, wealthy Giancarlo is a vampire who has lived for hundreds of years and is lonely. Then he meets Jenny, a beautiful young woman who stirs feelings he hasn't known for centuries; he's willing to become mortal again to be with her. However, brutal, ghoulish murders plaguing the city have made him the target of a relentless homicide cop. And the real killer, a dangerous vampire, also wants to destroy Giancarlo. The book includes graphic, bloody violence.

Hart, Tom
Rosalie Lightning: a graphic memoir. By Tom Hart and Rosalie Lightning AND Leela Corman and the residents of New York City, Gainesville, Florida, New Mexico, AND Hawaii, as well as various singer-songwriters, film directors, actors, animators, comic artists, donors, lovers and. St. Martin's Press 2016 272 p. Illustration
Grades: Adult   **741.5/973; 741.5**
1. Cartoonists; 2. Cartoonists — United States — Biography; 3. Children and death; 4. Father-daughter relationship; 5. Grief; 6. Hart, Tom, 1969- — Family; 7. Parent-child relationship
9781250049940, $19.99

LC 2015039334

This book, a memoir by Tom Hart, is ôabout the untimely death of his young daughter, Rosalie. His heart-breaking and emotional illustrations strike readers to the core, and take them along his family's journey through loss. Hart uses the graphic form to articulate his and his wife's on-going search for meaning in the aftermath of Rosalie's death, exploring themes of grief, hopelessness, rebirth, and eventually finding hope again.ö (Publisher's note)

Hartley, Welles
Star Wars: Empire Volume Seven: The Wrong Side of the War. Writers, Welles Hartley, John Jackson Miller ; pencillers, Davidé Fabbri ; colorists, Davidé Fabbri, Neziti Domenico, Michael Atiyeh ; letterer, Michael David Thomas. Dark Horse Comics 2007 Un Illustration
Grades: 7 8 9 10 11 12 Adult   **741.5; Fic**
1. Adventure graphic novels; 2. Science fiction graphic novels; 3. Star Wars; 4. Graphic novels
978-1-59307-709-9, $17.95

Fresh from the killing fields of Jabiim, where the Empire has virtually wiped out the populace of that world, Imperial Lieutenant Janek Sunber is sent to the quiet prison base on Kalist VI. But, unbeknownst to the Empire, the Rebels have designs on Kalist Base both for its desirable fuel supplies and for the presence of a very important prisoner - one of their own who has already attracted the interest of Darth Vader. Sunber doesn't know it, but he's on a collision course with an old friend who is with the Rebels, and he finds himself wondering which of them is on the wrong side of the war. The book includes battle violence.

Hartzell, Andy

★ **Fox** bunny funny. Top Shelf Productions 2007 102p. Illustration
Grades: 9 10 11 12 Adult
741.5; Fic
1. Animals; 2. Fantasy graphic novels; 3. Stories without words; 4. Graphic novels
978-1-891830-97-6, $10

Courtesy of Top Shelf Productions

The rules are simple: you're either a fox or a bunny. Foxes oppress and devour, bunnies suffer and die. Everyone knows their place. Everyone's satisfied. So what happens when a secret desire puts you at odds with your society? Starting from a simple premise—and without using a single word—this book leads the reader on a zigzag chase in and out of rabbit holes, and through increasingly strange landscapes where funny animals have serious identity problems. The tale swerves from slapstick to horror and back again before landing at the inevitable climax, in which all the old rules are shattered. Some moments of violence and dismemberment might be disturbing for some readers.

"Deftly presented in crisp black-and-white, block-print-like panels, this is a must for libraries supporting LGBT collections." Booklist

Harvey, Robert C.

The **Art** of the Comic Book: An Aesthetic History. University Press of Mississippi 1996 288p. Illustration
Grades: Adult Professional
741.5
1. Comic books, strips, etc — History and criticism; 2. Graphic novels
0-87805-758-7, $19.95
LC 95-377

Harvey traces the evolution of the comic book as a dynamic narrative art, taking it from its beginnings in the 1930s through the mid-1990s. Enhanced by many illustrations, this examination includes work from both the mainstream and alternative comics creators.

Part of the Studies in Popular Culture series.

Hashiguchi, Takashi

Yakitate!! Japan, Vol. 1. Viz Media 2006 196p. Illustration
Grades: 10 11 12 Adult
741.5; Fic
1. Baking; 2. Bread; 3. Manga; 4. Shonen manga; 5. Graphic novels
978-1-4215-0719-4, $9.99

When still a little boy, Kazuma Azuma became fascinated with bread after meeting a baker who taught him how to bake it. He begins to experiment with baking different types of bread to find the one he can call "Ja-pan," the national bread of Japan (—pan" is Japanese for bread). At sixteen, Kazuma is almost totally self-taught, but he gets accepted as a candidate for employment at Pantasia, a bakery chain. Only one person can become the new baker at Pantasia, and Kazuma intends to win, . . . but he is totally ignorant of European bread names (such as croissants). This series is an example of a genre unique to manga, a story focused on food. Most of the action takes place in kitchens, but there's some crude humor.

Volume 1 of 26

Hata, Kenjiro

Hayate the Combat Butler Volume 1. Viz Media 2006 182p. Illustration
Grades: 10 11 12 Adult
741.5; Fic
1. Humorous graphic novels; 2. Manga; 3. Romance graphic novels; 4. Shonen manga; 5. Graphic novels
978-1-4215-0851-1, $9.99

Hardworking teenager Hayate has a plan to pay back the yakuza—who are now the legal owners of his vital organs (thanks to his deadbeat parents): he'll kidnap someone and ransom them for a mountain of money. But things get tricky when his would-be kidnappee—who as luck would have it is the daughter of a mind-bogglingly wealthy family—mistakes Hayate's actions for a confession of love, and hires him to be her personal servant. At least his employment future is secure, or so he thinks... The book includes some strong language and mild sexual situations.

Hatori, Bisco

Ouran High School Host Club Volume 1. Viz Media/Shojo Beat 2005 184p. Illustration
Grades: 9 10 11 12 Adult
741.5; Fic
1. Humorous graphic novels; 2. Manga; 3. Shojo manga; 4. Graphic novels
1-59116-915-1, $8.99

Haruhi is a scholarship student at an exclusive private school: Ouran High School, where it turns out the bespectacled, short-haired Haruhi is the only student from a lower-middle class family in attendance. Then, to make matters worse, one day she breaks an $80,000 vase that belongs to one of the campus clubs, a mysterious outfit called the "Host Club," consisting of six superrich (and gorgeous) guys. Haruhi can't afford to pay back the cost of the vase, of course, so she's forced to work for the Host Club. And it's there that she discovers just how rich all the boys are and how different the rich are from "regular" folks ... And meanwhile, the eccentric but good-hearted rich boys are shocked to find out how life is on the other side...

Volume 1 of an 18 volume series

Hayakawa, Tomoko

The **Wallflower** 1: Yamatonadeshiko Shichihenge. Random House/Del Rey Manga 2004 224p. Illustration
Grades: 10 11 12 Adult
741.5; Fic
1. Humorous graphic novels; 2. Manga; 3. Shojo manga; 4. Graphic novels
0-345-47912-2, $10.95

It's a gorgeous, spacious mansion, and four handsome, fifteen-year-old friends are allowed to live in it for free. There's only one condition - that within three years the guys must transform the owner's wallflower niece into a lady befitting the palace in which they all live. How hard can it be? Enter Sunako Nakahara, the agoraphobic, horror-movie-loving, pockmark-faced, frizzy-haired, fashion-illiterate recluse who tends to break into explosive nosebleeds whenever she sees anyone attractive. This project is going to take more than the four heroes ever expected: it needs a miracle. The series includes some mildly harsh language, some mild sexual situations, and mild violence.

Hayashi, Fumino

★ **Neon** Genesis Evangelion Vol. 1 2nd ed.. Viz Media 2004 184p. Illustration

Grades: 10 11 12 Adult **741.5; Fic**

1. Manga; 2. Mecha manga; 3. Science fiction graphic novels; 4. Shonen manga; 5. Graphic novels

978-1-4139-0344-7, $9.95

A handful of teenagers must pilot huge biomechanical robots — the Evangelion combat units — against monstrous ?ngels" bent on destroying humanity. Among them is Shin, a very reluctant recruit whose scientist father is commander of the secret organization NERV and who has ignored his son all his life. The book includes violence, strong language, nudity, and sexual situations.

Neon Genesis Evangelion: Angelic Days Vol. 1. ADV Manga 2006 184p. Illustration

Grades: 10 11 12 Adult **741.5; Fic**

1. Manga; 2. Romance graphic novels; 3. Science fiction graphic novels; 4. Shojo manga; 5. Graphic novels

978-1-4139-0344-7, $9.99

This manga series is set in the world of Neon Genesis Evangelion, but in this series, life isn't quite so angst-ridden. Choosing the right girl is more important than saving the world. The book includes some mild sexual situations.

Hayden, Jennifer

★ The **Story** of My Tits. By Jennifer Hayden. Top Shelf Productions 2015 352 p. Illustration

Grades: Adult **362.196994490090; 741.5**

1. Breast cancer

1603090541; 9781603090544, $29.99

This book is a "graphic memoir and a cancer narrative. . . . When Jennifer Hayden was diagnosed with breast cancer at the age of 43, she realized that her tits told a story. Across a lifetime, they'd held so many meanings: hope and fear, pride and embarrassment, life and death. And then they were gone. Now, their story has become a way of understanding her story." (Publisher's note)

Hayes, Nick

The **rime** of the modern mariner. By Nick Hayes. Penguin Group USA 2011 336 p. Color illustration

Grades: Adult **Fic; 741.5**

1. Marine pollution — Fiction; 2. Refuse and refuse disposal — Fiction; 3. Refuse and refuse disposal — Fiction; 4. Sailors — Fiction; 5. Sea stories

0670025801; 9780670025800, $32.00

LC 2011459032

This graphic novel by Nick Hayes is an adaptation of Samuel Taylor Coleridge's "The Rime of the Ancient Mariner." "Hayes turns Coleridge's 1797 apocalyptic epic into an ecological warning, wherein a careless litterbug of a businessman is accosted by a sailor with burning eyes and a tale of woe. Part of the story mirrors Coleridge's (a carelessly murdered bird brings damnation upon the crusty mariner's vessel), but the atmospherics are more charged with the dangers of modernity." (Publishers Weekly)

Heer, Margreet de

Science, a discovery in comics. Margreet de Heer. NBM Publishing 2013 192 p. (A discovery in comics)

Grades: 9 10 11 12 Adult **500**

1. Science; 2. Scientists — History

1561637505; 9781561637508, $19.99

LC 2013939851

"This history of scientific discovery, [by Margreet de Heer] is presented as a series of conversations about understanding the laws that govern the universe. . . . Beginning with the ideals of scientific observation and inquiry, the book moves to detailed chronologies of the evolutions of biology, physics, geology, etc. Much of the information is organized in time-line form, which is used to depict the gradual accumulation and transformation of concepts." (School Library Journal)

"Although the information on any one topic is very basic, a great many topics are treated, thanks to the economy of de Heer's visual presentation, and they are all handled very well, thanks to the energy of her drawing style and the vividness of Kohl's coloring." Booklist

Heinberg, Allan

Young Avengers Vol. 1: Sidekicks. Writer, Allan Heinberg; pencils, Jim Cheung; inks, John Dell, Mark Morales & Drew Geraci; colors, Justin Ponsor; letters, Virtual Calligraphy's Cory Petit. Marvel Entertainment 2006 Un Illustration

Grades: 9 10 11 12 Adult **Fic; 741.5**

1. Superhero graphic novels; 2. Graphic novels

978-0-7851-2018-6, $14.99

A mysterious new group of teen super heroes appears, with powers and names resembling classic Avengers Captain America, Iron Man, Thor, and the Hulk. But who are they" Where did they come from" And what right to they have to call themselves the Young Avengers" When their public activities draw the attention of Captain America and Iron Man, the old Avengers set out to learn the truth about their teenaged namesakes. Caught between a maniacal super-villain and their heroic idols, will the Young Avengers' first fight be their last stand?

Helfer, Andrew

Malcolm X: a graphic biography. Written by Andrew Helfer; art by Randy DuBurke. Hill and Wang 2006 102p. Illustration

Grades: 10 11 12 Adult **92; 741.5**

1. African Americans — Biography; 2. Biographical graphic novels; 3. Black Muslim leaders; 4. Black Muslims; 5. Civil rights activists; 6. Malcolm X, 1925-1965; 7. Malcolm X, 1925-1965; 8. Graphic novels

978-0-8090-9504-9; 0-8090-9504-1, $15.95

LC 2006-13743

The authors "tell the story of Malcolm X's short life—his meeting with Dr. Martin Luther King Jr., the two leaders describing the opposite ideological ends of the fight for civil rights; and his eventual assassination by other members of the Nation of Islam (NOI)—in narration and detailed b&white drawings, sharp as photographs in a newspaper. . . . Helfer and DuBurke have created an evocative and studied look at not only Malcolm X but the racial conflict that defined and shaped him." Publ Wkly

Ronald Reagan: a graphic biography. Written by Andrew Helfer; art by Steve Buccellato and Joe Staton. Hill and Wang 2007 102p. Illustration
Grades: 9 10 11 12 Adult   **92; 741.5**
 1. Actors; 2. Biographical graphic novels; 3. Governors; 4. Presidents; 5. Presidents — United States; 6. Reagan, Ronald, 1911-2004; 7. Reagan, Ronald, 1911-2004; 8. Graphic novels
978-0-8090-9507-0, $16.95
          LC 2006-16437
 This graphic novel biography covers the life of Ronald Reagan, who began as an actor and ended his career as the fortieth president of the U.S. The book discusses Reagan's work as a union president (Screen Actor's Guild), a General Motors pitchman on television, Governor of California, and his terms as President. It also covers some of the scandals that occurred during his gubernatorial and presidential terms, including the Iran/Contra arms-for-hostages deal, and the assassination attempt by John Hinkley.
 Includes bibliographical references
 A novel graphic from Hill and Wang

Henderson, Sam
 Magic Whistle #10. Alternative Comics 2006 Un Illustration
Grades: 11 12 Adult   **741.5; Fic**
 1. Humorous graphic novels; 2. Graphic novels
1-891867-94-6, $11.95
 This tenth book in the second volume collects more of Henderson's humor pieces. He has written for SpongeBob Square Pants (and been nominated for an Emmy Award), and previous volumes of Magic Whistly have been nominated for the Harvey Award for humor. He uses very low-brow humor that almost parodies low-brow humor, with intentionally crude art. There's lots of raunchy humor and some sexual situations.

Hellboy: Weird Tales Volume One.
 Dark Horse Comics 2003 Un Illustration
Grades: 10 11 12 Adult   **741.5; Fic**
 1. Fantasy graphic novels; 2. Hellboy (Fictional character); 3. Horror graphic novels; 4. Mystery graphic novels; 5. Graphic novels
1-56971-622-6, $17.95
 Some writers and artists - John Arcudi, Joe Casey, Bob Fingerman, Roger Langridge, Alex Maleev, Eric Powell, Steve Lieber, Sara Ryan and Andi Watson to name a few - team up to present stories of giant bats, demon children, jet-packs, haunted circuses, and rusted-out spaceships. These stories are old-fashioned pulp fun featuring Hellboy. Some stories include violence, strong language, and nudity.

Hellboy: Weird Tales Volume Two.
 Dark Horse Comics 2004 Un Illustration
Grades: 9 10 11 12 Adult   **741.5; Fic**
 1. Fantasy graphic novels; 2. Hellboy (Fictional character); 3. Horror graphic novels; 4. Mystery graphic novels; 5. Graphic novels
1-56971-953-5, $17.95

Writers and artists including John Cassaday, P. Craig Russell, Scott Morse, Evan Dorkin, Jill Thompson, Kia Asamiya, Craig Thompson, and others team up to present stories of satanic theaters, a vacation in hell, and romance in the back of a Cadillac - old-fashioned pulp fiction style stories featuring Hellboy. The book includes violence and some strong language."

Hennessey, Jonathan
 The **comic** book story of beer. By Jonathan Hennessey and Mike Smith; artwork by Aaron McConnell. Ten Speed Press 2015 180 p. Color; Illustration
Grades: Adult   **663; 663/.42; 741.5**
 1. Beer — History; 2. Brewing — History
9781607746355, $18.99
          LC 2014044184
 This nonfiction graphic novel, by Jonathan Hennessey and Mike Smith, illustrated by Aaron McConnell, "recounts the many-layered past and present of beer through dynamic pairings of pictures and meticulously researched insight into the history of the world's favorite brew." (Publisher's note)
 Includes bibliographical references

 ★ The **Gettysburg** Address: A Graphic Adaptation. By Jonathan Hennessey and illustrated by Aaron McConnell. HarperCollins 2013 224 p.
Grades: 9 10 11 12 Adult   **973.7**
 1. Gettysburg (Pa), Battle of, 1863; 2. Lincoln, Abraham, 1809-1865; 3. Speeches
0061969761; 9780061969768, $15.99
 This graphic novel by Jonathan Hennessey and illustrated by Aaron McConnell "is a full-color illustrated look at Abraham Lincoln's most famous speech, the bloody battle of the Civil War that prompted it, and how they led to a defining point in the history of America. Using Lincoln—s words as a keystone, and drawing from first-person accounts, 'The Gettysburg Address' shows us the events through the eyes of those who lived through the events of the War, from soldiers to slaves." (Publisher's note)

 ★ The **United** States Constitution: a graphic adaptation. Written by Jonathan Hennessey; art by Aaron McConnell. Hill and Wang 2008 149p. Illustration
Grades: 9 10 11 12 Adult   **342; 741.5**
 1. Constitutional history — United States; 2. United States — Constitution; 3. Graphic novels
978-0-8090-9487-5; 0-8090-9487-8, $35;
978-0-8090-9470-7 (pa); 0-8090-9470-3 (pa), $16.95
          LC 2008-17927
 The author and illustrator go "through the entire U. S. Constitution, article by article, amendment by amendment, explaining their meaning and implications—in comics format. Avoiding the didactic, the book succeeds in being both consistently entertaining and illuminating." Publ Wkly
 Includes bibliographical references

Henson, Jim
 Jim Henson's tale of sand. Written by Jim Henson and Jerry Juhl; as realized by Ramón K. Pérez; colors by Ian Herring with Ramón K. Pérez; lettering and font design by Deron Bennett based on the handwriting of Jim Henson; edited by Stephen Christy.. Archaia Entertainment 2012 152 p.

Grades: 10 11 12 Adult   741.5
1. Adventure graphic novels; 2. Deserts; 3. Fantasy graphic novels; 4. Southwestern States
1936393093; 9781936393091

This graphic novel "follows its hapless protagonist as he is cast out into the desert by the cheerful Sheriff Tate. . . . The scruffy hero is a pawn in a game whose rules are concealed from him, pursued across a surrealistic southwest U.S. by an implacable hunter and hindered by the eccentric, bizarre inhabitants of the great desolation. The prize waiting for him at the end of the chase, should he survive to reach the end, is one he will never guess at." (Publishers Weekly)

Herald, Nathan
   Graphic novels for young readers: a genre guide for ages 4-14. Libraries Unlimited 2011 188p. (Genreflecting advisory series)
Grades: Adult Professional   025.2
1. Children's literature; 2. Graphic novels — Bibliography; 3. Graphic novels
1-59884-395-8; 978-1-59884-395-8, $40
                                                LC 2010044947
Includes bibliographical references
   "The annotated entries are laid out in eight chapters organized by major genre, and from action and adventure to educational. Within chapters, the titles, 600 in all, are arranged alphabetically into popular subgenres such as superheroes, mythology, sports, and many more." (School Library Journal)

Hernandez, Gilbert
   Chance in hell. Fantagraphics Books 2007 120p. Illustration
Grades: 11 12 Adult   741.5
1. Graphic novels
978-1-56097-833-6, $16.95

This book tells the story about a little orphan girl who lives in the slum of slums. Nobody knows who she is or where she's from, but her fellow shantytown inhabitants collectively look over her. The three-act story follows the heroine as she is adopted by a decent man who raises her well, and she eventually marries a kind, well-to-do man, only to discover that she can't relate to the good life and the comforts it provides. The book includes sexual situations and lots of foul language, but little nudity.

★ **Heartbreak** Soup: A Love and Rockets Book. Fantagraphics Books 2007 288p. Illustration
Grades: 12 Adult
741.5; Fic
1. Graphic novels
978-1-56097-783-4, $14.95

Courtesy of Fantagraphics

This volume collects the first half of Gilbert Hernandez's acclaimed magical-realist tales of "Palomar," the small Central American town, beginning with the groundbreaking "Sopa de Gran Pena" (which introduces most of his main cast of characters as children, plus the imposing newcomer Luba), and continuing on through such modern-day classics as "Ecce Homo," "Act of Contrition," "Duck Feet," and the great love story "For the Love of Carmen." His stories include lots of sexual situations, full nudity, and strong language.

★ **Heartbreak** Soup: A Love and Rockets Book. Fantagraphics Books 2007 256p. Illustration
Grades: 12 Adult   741.5; Fic
1. Graphic novels
978-1-56097-948-0, $14.95

This volume collects the second half of Gilbert Hernandez's acclaimed magical-realist tales of "Palomar," the small Central American town, beginning with the landmark "Human Diastrophism," the only full graphic novel length "Palomar" story ever created by Gilbert. In it, a serial killer stalks Palomar-but his depredations, hideous as they are, only serve to exacerbate the cracks in the idyllic Central American town as the modern world begins to intrude. "Diastrophism" concludes with the death (suicide) of one of Palomar's most beloved characters, and a postscript that provides one of the most hauntingly magical moments of the entire series as a rain of ashes drifts down upon Palomar. Also included are all the post-"Diastrophism" stories, in which Luba's past comes back to haunt her, and the seeds are sown for the "Palomar diaspora" that ends this book. Hernandez uses a lot of nudity, sexual situations, strong language, and violence in these stories.

   Julio's Day. Gilbert Hernandez. W W Norton & Co Inc 2013 112 p.
Grades: Adult   Fic; 741.5/973
1. Life cycle, Human; 2. Graphic novels
1606996061; 9781606996065, $19.99

This book, by Gilbert Hernandez, "traces the life of a 100-year-old man from cradle to grave in this fictional graphic novel. It begins in the year 1900, with the scream of a newborn. It ends, 100 pages later, in the year 2000, with the death rattle of a 100-year-old man. The infant and the old man are both Julio, and Gilbert Hernandez's . . . graphic novel, . . . traces one life—indeed, one century in a human life—through a series of carefully crafted . . . vignettes." (Publisher's note)

   Marble Season. By Gilbert Hernandez. Drawn & Quarterly 2013 128 p. Illustration
Grades: 11 12 Adult   741.5
1. Autobiographies; 2. Graphic novels
1770460861; 9781770460867, $21.95
                                                LC 2013375524
Written by Gilbert Hernandez, this autobiographical novel "portrays the reality of life in a large family in suburban 1960s California. Pop-culture references—TV shows, comic books, and music—saturate this evocative story of a young family navigating cultural and neighborhood norms set against the golden age of the American dream and the silver age of comics." (Publisher's note)

   "Neither overly rosy and romantic nor dark and dramatic, the book focuses on the real bulk of a child's daily life: the long summer months in which nothing eventful happens, the neighborhood kids who come and go, the tomboys and bullies, the temptation of small-time crime, and the confusion and innocence of early sexuality." LJ

Ofelia: a Love and Rockets book. Gilbert Hernandez. Fantagraphics Books 2015 249 p.
Grades: Adult   **741.5**
   1. California; 2. Families; 3. Latin Americans; 4. Graphic novels
   1606998064; 9781606998069, $19.99
                   LC 2014501184
  "In Ofelia, the sisters, the kids, and the cousins are all settled comfortably in California after leaving Palomar in Luba and Her Family. Luba and her cousin Ofelia's relationship has always been fraught, but when Ofelia threatens to write a book about Luba, past memories, secrets, resentments, and pain resurface. Meanwhile, Luba's childrenùgenius Socorro, recently out-and-proud Doralis, and prickly Maricelaùshow that a talent for trouble may be hereditary. . . ." (Publisher's note)
  "The latest Complete Love and Rockets Library volume presents content previously collected in Luba: The Book of Ofelia (2006) and Luba (2009) in the sequence of its publication in the serial Love and Rockets. It's the engrossing, sexually explicit, violent, and satirical soap opera (no other term fits) of the incredibly pneumatic Martinez sisters, originally of Palomar, somewhere in Central America, but now long settled and successful in greater L.A." Booklist
  These stories originally appeared in Luba #3-9, Luba's comics and stories #2-5, and Measles #3— Title page verso.||Fifth volume collecting Gilbert Hernandez's complete Love and rockets—Page 4 of cover.

★ **Palomar:** the heartbreak soup stories. Gilbert Hernandez. Fantagraphics; Turnaround 2003 522 p. Illustration
Grades: Adult   **741.5; 741.59/73**
   1. City and town life — United States; 2. Latin Americans — Fiction
   1560975393; 9781560975397, $39.95
                   LC 2006355302
  This book, by Gilbert Hernandez, "collects every 'Heartbreak Soup' story from 1993 to 2002 in one 500-page deluxe hardcover edition, presenting the epic for the first time as the single novel it was always intended to be. Palomar is the mythical Central American town where the "Heartbreak Soup" stories take place. The stories weave in and out of the town's entire population, crafting an intricate tapestry of Latin American experience." (Publisher's note)

Sloth. DC Comics/Vertigo 2006 Un Illustration
Grades: 11 12 Adult   **741.5; Fic**
   1. Teenagers; 2. Graphic novels
   978-1-4012-0366-5, $19.99
  Teenager Miguel Serra had suddenly fallen into a coma; a year later he wakes up, back to normal except he moves at a very slow pace; some people call him Sloth Boy. He reconnects with his girlfriend Lita and best friend Romeo and they try to find evidence of an urban legend in the lemon orchards that surround their sleepy town. One encounter causes a change, as suddenly it was Lita who'd been in the year-long coma. She tries to catch the attention of the handsome, popular Miguel and tries to score tickets to the Romeo X concert. Soon she's having intimate relations with

both Miguel and Romeo, and when they fight over her, she falls and slips into another coma. Romeo throws himself off a bridge, and Lita wakes up . . .
  This is the first original graphic novel by Hernandez, who co-created Love and Rockets with his brother. Adult language and sexual situations make this more appropriate for older teens.

Hernandez, Jaime
  ★ The **Girl** from H.O.P.P.E.R.S.: A Love and Rockets Book. Fantagraphics Books 2007 288p. Illustration
Grades: 12 Adult   **741.5; Fic**
   1. Graphic novels
   978-1-56097-851-0, $14.95
  In this second volume, having abandoned the sci-fi trappings of the earliest Love & Rockets stories, Hernandez refined his approach, settling on the more naturalistic environment of the fictional Los Angeles barrio, Hoppers, and the lives of the young Mexican-Americans and punk rockers who live there. A central story is "The Death of Speedy." In this volume, Maggie also begins her on-again and off-again romance with Ray D., leading to friction and an eventual separation from Hopey. Hernandez uses nudity, sexual situations, and strong language in these stories.

Love and rockets; No. 7: new stories. By Gilbert Hernandez, Jaime Hernandez. Fantagraphics 2015 100 p. Illustration
Grades: Adult   **741.5; Fic**
   1. Mexican Americans; 2. Women — Fiction; 3. Graphic novels
   160699770X; 9781606997703, $14.99
  In this comic, by Gilbert Hernandez and Jaime Hernandez, "Maggie and Hopey take a much-needed break from their humdrum domestic lives and go on a road trip to visit a 'sick friend.' And, when the cat's away, Ray visits some old, sick friends of his own. Plus Tonta's nutty family!" (Publisher's note)
  "The latest volume in the current incarnation of Love and Rockets series as an annual trade paperback (it began as a comic book series in 1981) conveys an overall air of regrouping, as Jaime reunites lifelong pals Maggie and Hopey for a road trip, and Gilbert returns briefly to the fictional Latin American village of Palomar and casts his sometimes-actress character Fritz in a goofy costume epic featuring Aladdin and a spaceship." Booklist

The **Love** Bunglers. By Jaime Hernandez. Fantagraphics 2014 104 p. Illustration (Love and Rockets)
Grades: Adult   **741.5**
   1. Interpersonal relations
   1606997297;
   9781606997291, $19.99
  This book, by Jaime Hernandez, "[c]ontains the critically acclaimed and award-winning short comic 'Browntown,' as well as other stories chronicling the life and loves of . . . Hernandez's longtime . . . heroine Maggie. . . . After a lifetime of losses, Maggie

Courtesy of Fantagraphics

finds, in the second half, her longtime off and on lover, Ray Dominguez." (Publisher's note)

"Hernandez (Love and Rockets), one of graphic storytelling's modern masters, returns readers to the mundane world of his most lasting creation, Maggie Chascarillo. . . . This rich tapestry of superb, deceptively minimalist artwork and characterization is rounded out with extended flashbacks to Maggie's adolescence that shed light on how her early experiences affect her actions well into adulthood." Pub Wkly

★ **Maggie** the mechanic: a love and rockets book. Fantagraphics Books 2007 276p. Illustration
Grades: 12 Adult   **741.5; Fic**
1. Graphic novels
978-1-56097-784-1, $14.95

This is the first of three volumes by Jaime Hernandez, collecting the adventures of the spunky Maggie, her annoying best friend and sometime lover Hopey, and their circle of friends, including their bombshell friend Penny Century, Maggie's weirdo mentor Izzy-as well as the wrestler Rena Titanon and Maggie's handsome love interest, Rand Race. Maggie the Mechanic collects the earliest, punkiest, most heavily sci-fi stories of Maggie and her circle of friends. Hernandez uses some nudity, sexual situations, and some harsh language in these stories.

Hernandez, Lea
Rumble Girls: Silky Warrior Tansie. NBM 2003 Un Illustration
Grades: 10 11 12 Adult   **741.5; Fic**
1. Martial arts; 2. Science fiction graphic novels; 3. Graphic novels
1-56163-370-4, $9.95

In a future world where media is run by suits (literally, they have no bodies) and everyone watches battles between warriors in battlesuits called hardskins, orphaned Raven Tansania Ransom trains to be a hardskin pilot at the girls' school academie Juliet. When a relationship gone sour causes Raven to sign with super media corporation Enteco to become a Rumble Girl, school rival Carmen signs on, too, for she wants to destroy Raven by any means possible. The book includes lots of fighting action and some sexual activity.

Hernandez worked with the Japanese anime/manga group known as Gainax and developed her manga-esque style from her experience there. Rumble Girls originally appeared in comics issues published by Image Comics and then online as webcomics.

Herriman, George
★ **Krazy** & Ignatz, 1937-1938: Shifting Sands Dusts its Cheeks in Powdered Beauty. Fantagraphics Books 2006 176p. Illustration
Grades: 7 8 9 10 11 12 Adult   **741.5; Fic**
1. Humor graphic novels; 2. Krazy Kat (Fictional character); 3. Graphic novels
978-1-56097-734-6, $19.95

Krazy Kat is a love story, focusing on the relationships of its three main characters. Krazy Kat adored Ignatz Mouse. Ignatz Mouse simply tolerated Krazy Kat, except for recurrent onsets of targeted tumescence, which found

expression in the fast delivery of bricks to Krazy's cranium. Offisa Pup loved Krazy and sought to protect "her" (Herriman always maintained that Krazy was genderless) by throwing Ignatz in jail. Each of the characters was ignorant of the others' true motivations, and this simple structure allowed Herriman to build entire worlds of meaning into the actions, building thematic depth and sweeping his readers up by the looping verbal rhythms of Krazy & Co.'s unique dialogue. Most of these strips in this volume have not seen print since originally running in Hearst newspapers over 70 years ago. This seventh volume collecting all of the comic strips, is the second one to be published in color; Herriman started doing the strip in color in 1935. Other than the brick-throwing, this book has no violence, foul language, or any other usual objectionable content. Krazy Kat cartoons were made for children in the mid-1930s, and there was a Krazy Kat animated series which aired on television in the mid-1960s.

Heuet, Stéphane
In Search of Lost Time: Swann's way. Marcel Proust; adaptation and drawings by Ste?phane Heuet; translated by Arthur Goldhammer. Liveright Publishing Corporation 2015 224 p. Color illustration; Map
Grades: Adult   **741.5**
1. France — History — 1815-1914 — Fiction; 2. France — Social life and customs — 19th century; 3. Memory — Fiction; 4. Graphic novels
1631490354; 9781631490354, $26.95
                                    LC 2014048982

This graphic novel, by Marcel Proust, adapted and illustrated by Stephane Heuet, and translated by Arthur Goldhammer, "re-presents Proust in graphic form for anyone who has always dreamed of reading him but was put off by the sheer magnitude of the undertaking. This graphic adaptation reveals the fundamental architecture of Proust's work while displaying a remarkable fidelity to his language as well as the novel's themes of time, art, and the elusiveness of memory." (Publisher's note)

Hicklenton, John
100 months: the end of all things. By Johnny Hicklenton; art & words, John Hicklenton; layout, Adam Lavis; foreword, Pat Mills. Cutting Edge Press 2010 170 p. Color illustration
Grades: Adult   **741.5**
1. Capitalism — Fiction; 2. Environmental degradation; 3. Graphic novels
0956544525; 9780956544520, $29.95
                                    LC 2010467752

This graphic novel is a parable of environmental devastation, depicting the quest of Mara, Warrior and Earth Goddess, as she seeks revenge against the Longpig: a Satanic personification of capitalism, red in tooth and claw, whose followers, a legion of the damned, look quite a lot like us. The world of the Longpig is rich in killing fields and scenes of mass crucifixion that recall Goya, Blake, and Bacon, and represents a true crossover of the graphic novel form with fine art. . . . This book was drawn and written in foreknowledge of [Hicklenton—s] imminent death, and its insight into universal themes of life, death, salvation, and damnation seems to come from a place between worlds." (Publisher's note)

Hickman, Jonathan
★ **East** of West; Volume 1: The Promise. Jonathan Hickman, writer; Nick Dragotta, artist; Frank Martin, colors; Rus Wooton, letters. Image Comics 2013 96 p. Color illustration (East of West)
Grades: 11 12 Adult   **741.5**
1. Death — Fiction; 2. Four Horsemen of the Apocalypse — Fiction; 3. Revenge
1607067706; 9781607067702, $9.99
  This graphic novel by Jonathan Hickman is "set in a futuristic Old West and starring none other than the Four Horsemen of the Apocalypse. But there's trouble in the ranks, it seems, between Death and his cohort. What exactly that trouble is, and a swarming host of other tantalizing questions—like what happened between the Civil War and 2066, for instance—are teased out as Death tracks down those who have wronged him." (Booklist)
First published in single magazine format as East of West #1-5.
Volume 1 of an ongoing series

★ **East** of West: Volume three: There is no us. By Jonathan Hickman; illustrated by Nick Dragotta. Image Comics 2014 144 p. Color; Illustration
Grades: Adult   **741.5; Fic**
1. Apocalyptic fiction; 2. Graphic novels
9781632151148, $14.99; 1632151146
  The series' third volume, written by Jonathan Hickman and illustrated by Nick Dragotta, "sees the breaking apart of the future-scape of America as the world races forward towards the apocalypse." (Publisher's note)
  "[T]he already uneasy alliance between the Horsemen's Chosen is destroyed, as a series of betrayals between the different factions marches everyone closer to war and Armageddon. Hickman focuses less on action and more on setup, as many of the characters achieve new positions of power, ready to flex their newfound muscles once the guns are drawn." Booklist

★ **East** of West; Volume 2: We Are All One. By Jonathan Hickman; illustrated by Nick Dragotta. Image Comics 2014 144 p. Color; Illustration (East of West)
Grades: Adult   **741.5**
1. Death — Fiction; 2. Four Horsemen of the Apocalypse — Fiction
1607068559; 9781607068556, $14.99
  "In the second volume of this weird western series, the three Horsemen of the Apocalypse continue to manipulate the Chosen, the American leaders sworn to the message, as they plot to bring about the end of the world. Death, the betrayed Horseman, rides out on a quest to locate his kidnapped son, but a new character, the Ranger, attempts to derail both groups' plans. . . . Hickman focuses on atmosphere and environment, with slow pacing and sudden quick-on-the-draw action, adding a touch of Lovecraftian horror and epic sci-fi for good measure." Booklist
Contains material originally published as East of West #6-10.

Manhattan Projects Volume 1. By Jonathan Hickman, illustrated by Nick Pitarra, Jordie Bellaire. Image Comics 2012 Color illustration
Grades: Adult   **741.5/973; 741.5**
1. Science fiction graphic novels; 2. Scientists
1607066084; 9781607066088, $14.99
  This graphic novel, by Jonathan Hickman, illustrated by Nick Pitarra and Jordie Bellaire, images "that the Manhattan Project was really just a front for Oppenheimer, Einstein, Feynman, et al., to get into the really out-there stuff in Los Alamos . . . while Japanese teleportation machines . . ., concurrent universes accessed by an enigmatic portal-stone, and shady bargains with warring alien races . . . [challenge] humanity's fate." (Booklist)
Volume 1 of an ongoing series

The **nightly** news. Image Comics 2007 184p.
Grades: 11 12 Adult   **741.5**
1. Crime; 2. Mass media; 3. Graphic novels
978-1-58240-766-1, $16.99
  As an act of violence spirals out of control to encompass the entirety of the news media, a cult has emerged from the errors and retractions that have ruined careers, marriages and even lives. Under direction from his cult master The Voice, The Hand leads an army of followers committed to revolution, willing to die for their cause. Targeting journalists of all kinds, they launch a campaign of terror and violence that plays out in the media. The story includes considerable violence and foul language with page design that is very different from the usual comics panels.

Hickman, Troy
Common Grounds: Baker's dozen. Image Comics/Top Cow Productions 2004 144p. Illustration
Grades: 9 10 11 12 Adult   **741.5; Fic**
1. Superhero graphic novels; 2. Graphic novels
978-1-58240-841-5, $14.99
  Superheroes and supervillains need a place where they can relax, unwind, and not worry about the next battle. Common Grounds is just such a place—a chain of coffee shops with bakery counters, totally neutral ground. Here, hero and villain can relax and take a break in the restroom ("Head Games"), a teenage superhero who doubts herself and an older superpowered religious Jew can encourage each other ("Sanctuary"), a group of overweight heroes can meet ("Fat Chance"), or formerly evil monsters can get custom takeout and shoot the breeze ("Where Monsters Dine"). The book includes a baker's dozen (thirteen) stories.

Hicks, Faith Erin
Zombies calling. SLG Publishing 2007 104p. Illustration
Grades: 8 9 10 11 12 Adult   **741.5; Fic**
1. Horror graphic novels; 2. Humorous graphic novels; 3. Zombies; 4. Graphic novels
978-1-59362-079-0, $9.95
  Anglophile/zombie movie fan/college student Joss is going crazy in the middle of exams week, but when her college campus is overrun with actual zombies, she knows what to do. With her roommate Sonnet and their buddy Robyn, Joss uses the Rules gleaned from years of watching zombie movies to fight the undead hordes. When the first

rule is that the ordinary person suddenly becomes a total ass-kicking cool fighter able to beat off zombies with no fighting lessons, yeah, it's cool. Except the zombies just keep coming and coming. . . . The book has some harsh language and lots of black and white zombie fighting action without gore.

Higashimura, Akiko

Princess Jellyfish 1. By Akiko Higashimura. Random House Inc 2016 400 p.

Grades: 10 11 12 Adult   **741.5**

1. Manga; 2. Tokyo (Japan) — Fiction; 3. Young women — Fiction

1632362287; 9781632362285, $19.99

In this book, by Akiko Higashimura, "Tsukimi Kurashita has a strange fascination with jellyfish. She's loved them from a young age and has carried that love with her to her new life in the big city of Tokyo. There, she resides in Amamizukan. . . . However, a chance meeting at a pet shop has Tsukimi crossing paths with one of the things that the residents of Amamizukan have been desperately trying to avoid̀ua beautiful and fashionable woman!" (Publisher's note)

Volume 1 of an ongoing series

Higgins, Dustin

★ **Pinocchio,** vampire slayer. Written by Van Jensen; created and drawn by Dusty Higgins. SLG Publishing 2009 Un Illustration

Grades: 9 10 11 12 Adult   **Fic; 741.5**

1. Horror graphic novels; 2. Pinocchio (Fictional character); 3. Vampires; 4. Graphic novels

978-1-59362-176-6, $10.99; 1-59362-176-0

LC 2010-278899

After a brief recap of Collodi's novel, this graphic novel takes place a few years later. Pinocchio, still a wooden puppet, now finds he has a use for lying and growing his nose—he breaks off the growth and uses it as a wooden stake to destroy vampires. The blood suckers have come to the town of Nasolungo, they killed his creator/father Geppetto, and now Pinocchio roams the streets at night, seeking vengeance upon the vampires. The book includes violence but only mild language (Pinocchio says "crap" a few times). Along with the violence, the book includes a lot of sardonic humor.

"Heavy shadows and thick lines dominate the panels and provide a midnight-black atmosphere for all the gory mayhem, but it's the humor that makes this so memorable. . . . There's also surprising heart at the story's center that plays with the core theme of fatherhood. There won't be many teen (or adult) graphic-novel readers who won't want this book for its concept alone, and the execution doesn't disappoint." Booklist

Other titles in this series are:Pinocchio, vampire slayer and the great puppet theater (2010); Pinocchio, vampire slayer: of wood and blood, part one (2012); Pinocchio, vampire slayer: of wood and blood, part two (2012)

Higgins, Kyle

C.O.W.L. 1: Principles of Power. By Kyle Higgins and Alec Siegel; illustrated by Rod Reis. Image Comics 2014 128 p. Color; Illustration; Map

Grades: Adult   **741.5**

1. Chicago (Ill) — Fiction; 2. Good and evil; 3. Superhero graphic novels

1632151111; 9781632151117, $9.99

In this graphic novel, by Kyle Higgins and Alec Siegel, illustrated by Rod Reis, "the 'Chicago Organized Workers League' [is] the world's first Super-Hero Labor Union! While C.O.W.L. once stood as a beacon of hope against an epidemic of organized crime and . . . Super-Villains, the union now faces its fiercest foe yet-a disillusioned public. In targeting the last of the great villains, C.O.W.L. attempts to prove its value to the world and to each other." (Publisher's note)

"In the spirit of books like Watchmen (1987), C.O.W.L. offers an interesting commentary on the moral issues superheroes face and how society might actually react to them." Booklist

Originally published in single magazine form as C.O.W.L. #1-5.

Volume 1 of an ongoing series

Higuri, You

Crown, vol. 2. You Higuri and Shinji Wada. Go! Media Entertainment, Inc. 2009 Un Illustration

Grades: 10 11 12 Adult   **741.5; Fic**

1. Adventure graphic novels; 2. Manga; 3. Mystery graphic novels; 4. Graphic novels

978-1-60510-006-7, $10.99

Mahiro was just an ordinary Japanese high school girl, until she learned she is a princess and heir to the throne of Regalia. Her brother Ren and his best friend Jake have become her bodyguards, for the woman who now rules Regalia will stop at nothing to keep her throne. In this volume, they first encounter the assassin named Condor, who they end up welcoming as a partner in guarding Mahiro as she tries to continue as usual in school. Then they must deal with the master assassin named Lady Angela, whom they find out is actually a man. He's been sent to kill Ren and Jake, but he decides to find out just why Mahiro needs such protection. This volume includes some violence (assassinations and murder), and some provocative art, as Angela dresses to seduce and then takes Mahiro shopping for lingerie. There are also a few hints of boy love, just hints, nothing shown.

Gorgeous Carat Vol.1. Tokyopop/BLU 2006 196p. Illustration

Grades: 10 11 12 Adult   **741.5; Fic**

1. Adventure graphic novels; 2. Manga; 3. Romance graphic novels; 4. Shonen-ai manga; 5. Graphic novels

1-59816-102-4, $9.99

In turn-of-the- 20th-century Paris, ball gowns swirl, champagne corks pop, and precious jewels sparkle all around the city—and in the amethyst eyes of one particular young man... Florian is the only son of an impoverished noble family. When his family's 120-carat Flame of Mughal goes missing, Florian teams up with the stunning, mysterious Ray Balzac Courland to track down the dazzling gem. The trail of clues leads the duo to an abandoned castle—and a deadly secret. This boys' love action-romance follows the swashbuckling adventures of Ray and Florian as they battle crime lords, backstabbing family members, and a possible attraction to each other. The book includes some strong language, some sexual suggestiveness, and some violence.

Hill, Joe
★ **Locke** & key: welcome to Lovecraft. Written by Joe Hill; art by Gabriel Rodriguez. IDW Publishing 2008 158p. Illustration
Grades: 10 11 12 Adult **Fic; 741.5**
1. Horror graphic novels; 2. Mystery graphic novels; 3. Graphic novels
978-1-60010-237-0, $24.99; 978-1-60010-384-1 (pa), $19.99

After Rendell Locke is murdered by a former student, Sam Lesser, who then tried to find and kill the rest of the family, Nina Locke takes her children, Tyler, Kinsey, and Bode to Lovecraft, Massachusetts, to live with Rendell's brother Duncan in Keyhouse. Tyler needs to deal with the guilt he feels because of a conversation with Sam Lesser, in which he said Sam should kill his dad. Kinsey had taken Bode and hidden from Sam, keeping them both safe, but she feels as though she'll never be safe again. Bode finds a door at Keyhouse, and when he goes through it, he dies and his ghost wanders around. There's definitely something weird at Keyhouse, and something is living at the bottom of the well in the well house—something that uses both Bode and Sam Lesser—and wants revenge. The book includes bloody violence. Joe Hill is the son of Stephen King.

"This first of . . . several volumes delivers on all counts, boasting a solid story bolstered by exceptional work from Chilean artist Rodriguez . . . that resembles a fusion of Rick Geary and Cully Hamner with just a dash of Frank Quitely." Publ Wkly

Other titles in this series are: Vol 2: Head Games (2009); Vol 3: Crown of Shadows (2010); Vol 4: Keys to the Kingdom (2011); Vol 5: Clockworks (2012); Vol 6: Alpha & Omega (2014)

Hinds, Gareth
★ **Beowulf**. Adapted and illustrated by Gareth Hinds. Candlewick Press 2007 Un Illustration
Grades: 8 9 10 11 12 Adult **741.5; Fic**
1. Adventure graphic novels; 2. Beowulf; 3. Monsters; 4. Graphic novels
978-0-7636-3022-5, $21.99; 0-7636-3022-5; 978-0-7636-3023-2 (pa); 0-7636-3023-3 (pa), $9.99
LC 2006-49023
Graphic novel adaptation of the Old English epic poem, Beowulf

"For fantasy fans both young and old, this makes an ideal introduction to a story without which the entire fantasy genre would look very different; many scenes may be too intense for very young readers." Publ Wkly

The **merchant** of Venice: a play. By William Shakespeare; adapted and illustrated by Gareth Hinds. Candlewick Press 2008 68p. Illustration
Grades: 8 9 10 11 12 Adult **822.3; 741.5**
1. Shakespeare, William, 1564-1616 — Adaptations
978-0-7636-3024-9, $21.99; 978-0-7636-3025-6 (pa), $11.99
LC 2007-938349

Hinds uses a sketchy art style and blue and gray tones to illustrate his graphic adaptation of Shakespeare's controversial play. He sets the play in modern Venice and uses more modern language, including prose, at the beginning of the play and then gradually returns to Shakespeare's original language for the courtroom scenes. The play tells the story of a debt owed to a Jewish merchant of Venice, of a strong-willed young woman who is determined to choose her own husband, and of the quest to save a young man from the fate of having a pound of flesh cut from him.

"Fans of the play will find this an intriguing adaptation." Publ Wkly

The **Odyssey**: a graphic novel. By Gareth Hinds. Candlewick Press 2010 248 p. Color illustration
Grades: 7 8 9 10 11 12 Adult **741.5**
1. Greek mythology; 2. Homer; 3. Mythology, Greek — Juvenile literature; 4. Odyssey; 5. Graphic novels
0763642665; 0763642681; 9780763642662, $24.99; 9780763642686
LC 2010007512

"Retells, in graphic novel format, Homer's epic tale of Odysseus, the ancient Greek hero who encounters witches and other obstacles on his journey home after fighting in the Trojan War." (Publisher's note)

Hiramoto, Akira
Me and the devil blues: the unreal life of Robert Johnson vol. 1. Del Rey Manga 2008 540p. Illustration
Grades: 11 12 Adult **741.5; Fic**
1. Adventure graphic novels; 2. Blues music; 3. Blues musicians; 4. Guitarists; 5. Johnson, Robert, 1911-1938; 6. Manga; 7. Singers; 8. Songwriters; 9. Graphic novels
978-0-345-49926-4, $19.95

Robert Johnson was a legendary blues player who died very young. This manga takes his story and runs with it. In the Mississippi Delta in 1929, a young farmer named RJ desperately wants to be a bluesman, even though he can't play the guitar. One night he takes a midnight stroll and ends up at a crossroads where he meets up with someone who just might be the devil. After that night, RJ can play the blues, but he loses his former life and still has to suffer under Jim Crow laws. Then one day he meets young Clyde Barrow, who will become a different kind of legend (remember Bonnie and Clyde?) and they travel together. The American Deep South, the blues, and legendary criminals are reimagined through Japanese sensibilities and mores makes for a unique read. The book includes considerable foul language, violence, nudity, and sexual situations.

Hirano, Kohta
Hellsing Volume 1. Dark Horse Comics 2003 208p. Illustration
Grades: 11 12 Adult **741.5; Fic**
1. Horror graphic novels; 2. Manga; 3. Seinen manga; 4. Graphic novels
1-59307-056-X, $13.95

There's a secret organization somewhere in England created to defend the Queen and country from monsters of all sorts. Enter Hellsing, an agency, long in tooth, with the experience, know-how, and... special equipment to handle the problems that arise when vampires, ghouls, and the like take on these dark forces. The special "equipment" is another vampire, and a big pistol loaded with special silver bullets. This series focuses on the violence of destroying vampires who love to slaughter people. Some might be offended by the portrayal of the Roman Catholic Church as insanely fundamentalist and using inquisitors and brainwashed killer nuns. The series includes lots of graphic violence and harsh language.

Hodgson, William Hope
The **House** on the Borderland. Adapted by Simon Revelstroke and Richard Corben; art by Richard Corben. BiblioBazaar 2006 88p. Illustration
Grades: 10 11 12 Adult   **741.5; Fic**
   1. Horror graphic novels; 2. Graphic novels
   978-1-4264-3828-8, $11.99
   This book adapts Hodgson's horror novel. It sits astride two worlds, the bleak world of colorless normality, and the realms of cosmic horror where reason my yet have a last chance to conquer fear. To this ancient dwelling a challenger comes, to exorcise its shadowed curse, to plumb its pits of ultimate perversity and, perhaps, to prevent evil's emergence into the present. This book includes strong language, violence, and brief nudity.

Hogan, James P.
The **Two** Faces of Tomorrow. Story by James P. Hogan; art and adaptation by Yukinobu Hoshino; translation, Frederik L. Schodt and Toren Smith; lettering and retouch, Tomoko Saito. Dark Horse Comics 2006 576p. Illustration
Grades: 9 10 11 12 Adult   **741.5**
   1. Computers; 2. Manga; 3. Science fiction graphic novels; 4. Graphic novels
   978-1-59307-563-7
   Midway through the 21st century, an integrated global computer network manages much of the world's affairs. A proposed major software upgrade - an artificial intelligence - will give the system an unprecedented degree of independent decision-making, but serious questions are raised in regard to how much control can safely be given to a non-human intelligence. In order to more fully assess the system, a new space-station habitat - a world in miniature - is developed for deployment of the fully operational system, named Spartacus. This mini-world can then be "attacked" in a series of escalating tests to assess the system's responses and capabilities. If Spartacus gets out of hand, the system can be shut down and the station destroyed... unless Spartacus decides to take matters into its own hands and take the fight to Earth. This manga adaptation of Hogan's novel includes some harsh language and brief incidental nudity.

Hogan, Peter
Resident Alien 1: Welcome to Earth!. writer, Peter Hogan ; artwork, colors, and letters, Steve Parkhouse. Dark Horse 2013 96 p. Illustration
Grades: Adult   **741; Fic**
   1. Mystery graphic novels; 2. Science fiction graphic novels
   1616550171; 9781616550172, $14.99
   In this graphic novel, "Harry is a space alien who lives as a recluse on Earth. His isolation comes to an end when the town doctor in the rural area he chooses to live in is murdered and the police need another doctor to fill out the death certificate. Harry not only fulfills that request, but ends up subbing for the deceased doctor, navigating human society, and trying to solve the murder." (Publishers Weekly)

Hon, Creative
Last Fantasy Vol. 1. Story by Creative Hon; art by Yong-Wan Kwon. Tokyopop 2006 204p. Illustration
Grades: 9 10 11 12 Adult   **741.5; Fic**
   1. Adventure graphic novels; 2. Fantasy graphic novels; 3. Humorous graphic novels; 4. Manwha; 5. Graphic novels
   1-59532-526-3, $9.99
   Tian and Drei von Richenstein, two unlikely heroes, embark on an adventure filled with excitement, intrigue, and a bit of comic relief. They have quite the talent for making allies into new enemies. Their (mis)adventure pits them against ferocious ogres, vengeful red dragons, an army of soldiers, and even an age-old rival. But leave it to Tian and Drei to make sure that this adventure isn't their final fantasy. In this parody of all things RPG (no, not "Really Powerful Guys"), no gaming franchise is safe in this comedy that's never dull—unlike our heroes' swords. The book contains strong language and fantasy monster-killing violence.

Hope, Jane
Introducing Buddha, New Ed.. Art by Borin Van Loon. Totem Books 2005 176p. Illustration
Grades: 10 11 12 Adult   **294.3; 741.5**
   1. Buddhism; 2. Graphic novels
   978-1-84046-633-1, $12.95

LC 95-060973
   This book uses cartoons and a spare text to describe the life and teachings of the Buddha. Author Jane Hope shows that enlightenment is a matter of experiencing the truth individually and by inspiration which is passed from teacher to student. The book explains the practices of meditation, Taoism and Zen. It goes on to describe the role of Buddhism in modern Asia and its growing influence on Western thought. The book includes a list of books for further reading.

Hopkins, David
Emily Edison. David Hopkins, illustrated by Brock Rizy. Viper Comics 2006 144p. Illustration
Grades: 7 8 9 10 11 12 Adult   **741.5; Fic**
   1. Humorous graphic novels; 2. Science fiction graphic novels; 3. Graphic novels
   0-9777883-2-6, $12.95
   High schooler Emily has more than her share of problems; along with trying to keep up in school and survive such things as parties and boys, she has to deal with her parents' very mixed marriage. Her father is human, but her mother came from another dimension. Since their divorce, Emily has had to split her time between Earth and elsewhere; and now her grandfather wants her to live permanently in his dimension, and he's prepared to destroy Earth to force her hand. What's a girl to do?

Hornschemeier, Paul

Let Us Be Perfectly Clear. Fantagraphics Books 2006 136p. Illustration

Grades: 11 12 Adult

741.5; Fic

1. Short stories; 2. Graphic novels

978-1-56097-752-0, $19.95

Courtesy of Fantagraphics

This is a collection of Paul Hornschemeier's full-color short stories from a variety of sources, none of which has been available to the book trade. The book is designed as a "flip book" in the tradition of the old Ace paperbacks, with one side featuring comedic work (or as comedic as Hornschemeier's mind allows), and the other decidedly more morose. On the "funny" menu, we are treated to Dr. Rodentia (an unfortunate-looking fellow with only apathy as his weapon), a detailed artist's catalogue exploring such modern masterpieces as "Accidental Late-Night Sex With a Radiator," musings on the cancerous nature of civilization as observed by a deceased cat and a cotton-based airbus, the scatological "Feelings Check," the ever pathetic Vanderbilt Millions and his fantasies of self-worth, and the multi-narrative story that started the Forlorn Funnies comics series: "The Men and Women of the Television." On the "forlorn" plate is the cold examination of the dyslexic narcoleptic and his bungled plans of murder, a sea creature's balancing of morality and sustenance, the Western romance "Wanted," a metal man's self-destructive search for meaning, and the story of two men meeting; it may disgust readers, without a single visually objectionable panel. The other stories do include strong language and some violence.

Mother, come home. With an introduction by Thomas Tennant. Fantagraphics 2004 128p. Illustration

Grades: 11 12 Adult

741.5; Fic

1. Mental illness; 2. Graphic novels

978-1-56097-973-9 (pa)

In this "story, a young child struggles with the death of his mother and his father's collapse. Clean-lined artwork leaves plenty of room for strong emotional content linked to themes of euthanasia, suicide, and depression." Booklist

Hoshino, Katsura

D.Gray-ManVolume 1. Viz Media/Shonen Jump Advanced 2006 192p. Illustration

Grades: 10 11 12 Adult

741.5; Fic

1. Adventure graphic novels; 2. Fantasy graphic novels; 3. Manga; 4. Supernatural graphic novels; 5. Graphic novels

978-1-4215-0623-4, $7.99

Set in a fictional end of the 19th century England, the story revolves around a teenage boy named Allen Walker who is cursed with a cross mark on his hand that turns his arm into an enormous weapon, which he uses to hunt down and kill akumas. An akuma, generated by The Millenium Earl, a 1,000-year-old phantom, is implanted into a human's soul during a moment of devastation and despair. The phantom uses the demons to then carry out his goal: destroy all humankind. Allen, a 15-year-old boy, roams the Earth in search of Innocence. Washed away to unknown parts of the world after The Great Flood, Innocence is the mysterious substance used to create weapons that obliterate the akumas. The action is over-the-top in style, with lots of demon-fighting action.

Hoshino, Ryo

The third vol. 2. Story by Ryo Hoshino; art by Ariko Ito. Tokyopop 2008 Un Illustration

Grades: 10 11 12 Adult

741.5; Fic

1. Adventure graphic novels; 2. Manga; 3. Science fiction graphic novels; 4. Graphic novels

978-1-4278-0713-7, $9.99

On a world covered with sand, Honoka is a Dune Runner trainee. She has a third eye, but hers is blue, compared to the red third eye that marks the power holders on her world. As she takes on more assignments, she encounters dangers such as a deadly soldier virus, as well as Lidell, the Senior Dune Runner she has viewed as a role model. Honoka suffers doubts because she makes mistakes, but she's determined to continue on her path to becoming a strong Dune Runner, and her AI partner, Bogie, will help her. The book includes some violence.

Hosler, Jay

★ Evolution: the story of life on Earth. Written by Jay Hosler; art by Zander Cannon and Kevin Cannon. Hill and Wang 2011 150p. Illustration

Grades: 9 10 11 12 Adult

741.5; 576.8

1. Evolution; 2. Evolution (Biology); 3. Graphic novels

0809094762; 9780809094769

LC 2010-05777

Alien scientist Bloort-183 takes King Floorsh-727 and Prince Floorsh-418 on a tour of Earth's history, explaining the theory of evolution. These are the same aliens who explored human genetics in The Stuff of Life. The illustrations by Kevin Cannon and Zander Cannon (no relation to each other) help human readers see how the theory of evolution explains the beginnings of life on Earth, the four conditions needed for natural selection, the Cambrian explosion, the Permian extinction, sexual selection, the evolution of modern humans, and the Earth scientists who studied the life forms and made the scientific discoveries. The book includes an illustrated glossary, a list of further reading, and endpapers filled with all kinds of dinosaurs.

"This delightful book seems ideal for nonscientists who want to entertainingly brush up their knowledge of evolution as well as for students from middle school on up." Booklist

The Sandwalk Adventures: An Adventure in Evolution Told in Five Chapters. Active Synapse 2003 160p. Illustration

Grades: 4 5 6 7 8 9 10 11 12 Adult

576.8; 741.5

1. Darwin, Charles; 2. Evolution; 3. Science; 4. Graphic novels

0-9677255-1-8, $20

Scientist Hosler explains Darwin's theory of evolution in a whimsical fashion. Follicle mites Mara and Willy live in Darwin's left eyebrow, and by accident they discover that Darwin, whom they call the god Flycatcher, can hear Mara. He thinks he's going crazy, but as he takes his daily walks on the Sandwalk at his home in England, Darwin does his best to convince Mara and Willy that he isn't a god and tells them about evolution. Hosler uses humor and whimsy, but also did a lot of research; the book includes explanatory notes and a long bibliography of sources.

Hosoda, Mamoru
   Wolf children Ame & Yuki. Original story: Mamoru Hosoda; art: Yu; character design: Yoshiyuki Sadamoto; translation: Jocelyne Allen; lettering: Tania Biswas, Lys Blakeslee. Yen Press 2014 538 p. Color; Illustration
Grades: 10 11 12 Adult   **741.5**
   1. Werewolves — Fiction; 2. Widows — Fiction
031640165X; 9780316401654, $26
   "When Hana falls in love with a young interloper she encounters in her college class, the last thing she expects to learn is that he is part wolf. Instead of rejecting her lover upon learning his secret, she accepts him with open arms.... But after what seems like a mere moment of bliss to Hana, the father of her children is tragically taken from her." (Publisher's note)
   "This emotion-laden work focuses on family and community issues. . . . The soft color palette of these watercolors complements the tender emotion of the plot." Lib Med Con

Howard, Josh
   Dead @17: compendium edition. Viper Comics 2008 336p. Illustration
Grades: 10 11 12 Adult   **741.5; Fic**
   1. Adventure graphic novels; 2. Horror graphic novels; 3. Graphic novels
978-0-9793680-3, $24.95
   Seventeen-year-old Nara Kilday's murder is the start of a new battle between good and evil. Her best friend Hazy investigates Nara's death and uncovers a dark side that he hadn't known. Meanwhile, an evil has raised an army of the undead, intending to reshape the world in its image. Among the undead is Nara, however, and she may just be the only thing standing in the way of Armageddon. Well, Nara, Hazy and Noel, that is. This book collects the original trilogy; Howard has revised and expanded it, and this book also includes cover and pinup galleries as well as a section of fan-produced arts and photographs. The book includes nudity and bloody violence.

   Dead@17: Revolution. Viper Comics 2005 Un Illustration
Grades: 10 11 12 Adult   **741.5; Fic**
   1. Horror graphic novels; 2. Mystery graphic novels; 3. Graphic novels
0-9754193-3-1, $14.95
   A political assassination plot by a mysterious group called Heaven's Militia unravels a government conspiracy with ties to Nara's past and future. She's forced to make a choice that could expose her secret to the world and puts her at odds with Noel Raddemer, her one ally. But somehow she has to stop the demon Bolabogg from achieving his goal, or the world will not survive. The book includes violence, strong language, and nudity.

   Josh Howard Presents Sasquatch. Viper Comics 2007 254p. Illustration
Grades: 10 11 12 Adult   **741.5; Fic**

   1. Fantasy graphic novels; 2. Sasquatch; 3. Graphic novels
978-0-9777883-8-5, $24.95
   This anthology includes twenty stories that feature the creature variously known as Big Foot, Yeti, and Sasquatch. The stories range from gruesomely bloody ("Sawmill Horror") to silly ("Smallfoot") to ironically sweet ("Heart Mountain, WY: 1942") to fun ("The Sitter") to suitable-for-Saturday-morning-cartoons ("Sasquatch and Timmy"). Creators for the stories include Courtney Huddleston, David Hartman, Bryan Baugh, Otis Frampton, Tone Rodriguez, and Scott Zirkel.

Howe, Sean
   Marvel Comics: the untold story. By Sean Howe. Harper 2012 485 p.
Grades: Adult   **741.5/973; 741.5**
   1. Comic books, strips, etc — History; 2. Comic books, strips, etc — United States — History and criticism; 3. Marvel Comics Group; 4. Superhero comic books, strips, etc; 5. United States — History — 20th century
0061992100; 9780061992100, $26.99
                                            LC 2012015058
   Author Sean Howe presents a book on the history of Marvel Comics. Howe "reveals the outsized personalities behind the scenes, including Martin Goodman, the self-made publisher who forayed into comics after a get-rich-quick tip in 1939 . . . and Jack Kirby, the World War II veteran who'd co-created Captain America in 1940 and, twenty years later, developed with Lee the bulk of the company's marquee characters in a three-year frenzy of creativity that would be the grounds for future legal battles and endless debates." (Publisher's note)
   Includes bibliographical references and index

Hudlin, Reginald
   Black Panther: Civil War. Pencilers: Scot Eaton & Manuel Garcia, Koi Turnbull & Marcus To. Marvel Entertainment 2007 Un Illustration
Grades: 9 10 11 12 Adult   **741.5; Fic**
   1. Black Panther (Fictional character); 2. Superhero graphic novels; 3. Graphic novels
978-0-7851-2235-7, $17.99
   King T'Challa and Queen Ororo, Black Panther and Storm, embark on a diplomatic tour that will have them spanning the globe and beyond. Stops include Latveria (Dr. Doom), the Moon (Black Bolt and the Inhumans), Atlantis (Namor the Sub-Mariner) and the Civil War-ravaged United States, for a meeting with none other than the point man for the U.S. government's implementation of the Superhuman Registration Act: Tony Stark, T'Challa's former Avengers teammate. Will the Black Panther and Storm decide to step off the sidelines of the Civil War and get involved?

   Black Panther: The Bride. Art by Scot Eaton. Marvel Entertainment 2006 Un Illustration
Grades: 9 10 11 12 Adult   **741.5; Fic**
   1. Black Panther (Fictional character); 2. Superhero graphic novels; 3. Graphic novels
978-0-7851-2107-7, $14.99
   Every king needs a queen, and the Black Panther, who is also the King of Wakanda, sets out on an epic quest to find a wife. His heart is Storm's if she'll accept his hand in

marriage. The question is, does she want it? With a super hero civil war ready to explode in the U.S., and snakes in the Wakanda court preparing to make their moves, the road to the altar could not be more complicated.

Huizenga, Kevin
★ **Curses.** Drawn & Quarterly 2006 145p. Illustration
Grades: 11 12 Adult **Fic; 741.5**
1. Graphic novels
978-1-894937-86-3, $21.95

Huizenga's central character in his comics is Glenn Ganges, a seemingly middle-class man living in the suburbs whose blank-eyed wonderment at everyday experiences brings together such diverse aspects of the world as golf, theology, late-night diners, parenthood, politics, Sudanese refugees, and hallucinatory vision, into a complete experience as multifaceted as our own lives. There is some use of strong language.

Gloriana: Glenn Ganges comics. By Kevin H. Huizenga. Drawn & Quarterly. Distributed in the USA by Farrar, Straus and Giroux 2012 117 p.
Grades: Adult **741.5**
1. Everyday life; 2. Social interaction
1770460616; 9781770460614, $19.95
LC 2012452358

In this comic book, "Kevin Huizenga exposes the mechanics that underpin everyday life. His protagonist, Glenn Ganges, has conversations about dish soap and library visits that are both faithful depictions of the mundane interactions we all have and so much more: existential dissections of the units that construct our lives." (Publisher's note)

Humphries, Sam
Sacrifice. By Sam Humphries, illustrated by Dalton Rose, edited by Daniel Chabon. Dark Horse 2013 168 p.
Grades: Adult **741.5; Fic**
1. Aztecs — Fiction; 2. Time travel
1595829857; 9781595829856, $19.99

This graphic novel, by Sam Humphries, asks "what happens when a troubled youth is plucked from modern society and thrust though time and space on a psychedelic journey into the heart of the Aztec civilization. [Readers] join Hector on a one-way trip through the past, the present, and the psychedelic into the glory of the Aztec Empire." (Publisher's note)

"Fascinating history combines with fantasy and science fiction . . . [a]s Hector slides through time." Pub Wkly

Hurd, Damon
Pictures of you. Art by Tatiana Gill. Alternative Comics 2007 96p.
Grades: 10 11 12 Adult **741.5**
1. Friendship; 2. Graphic novels
978-1-934460-00-9, $11.95

One year before their chance encounter (recounted in A Strange Day), Miles and Anna live parallel lives only a few miles apart. Miles is both jealous and overprotective when Sarah, his best friend since junior high, starts spending more time with her new musician boyfriend Kyle. Anna's family is ending in divorce, and her only solace is with the boy next door, Ethan. He's a college bound musician who is growing apart from his younger sidekick, not returning Anna's romantic feelings for him. Lyrics from songs by The Cure accompany the story as Miles becomes the kind of friend Sarah needs and Anna tries to find her own path. The creators say this is the second volume of a trilogy, but it can be read on its own. There's a brief instance of partial nudity and some foul language.

Hutchison, David
Biowulf Volume 1. Antarctic Press 2007 Un Illustration
Grades: 10 11 12 Adult **741.5; Fic**
1. Adventure graphic novels; 2. Beowulf — Adaptations; 3. Horror graphic novels; 4. Science fiction graphic novels; 5. Graphic novels
978-0-9787725-2-9, $14.95

In the staggering wreckage of Earth's future, the great King Hrothgar and his armies have known only victory after bloody victory. Now, on the brink of uniting the battling lands and bringing the long wars to an end, Hrothgar's rule is threatened. His actions have awakened the ancient evil of the Grendel, and his men are powerless to defend themselves against the demon's wrath. Only with the aid of the young hero Beowulf and a cunning trap can they hope to kill Grendel and finally know peace. In this cyberpunk adaptation, Beowulf is an Advance, a genetically engineered, cybernetically enhanced human warrior; and Grendel is a monster, but he's not the real villain. The book includes a lot of graphic, bloody violence.

Hyde, Laurence
Southern Cross. Drawn & Quarterly 2007 256p. Illustration
Grades: 10 11 12 Adult **741.5**
1. Atomic bomb — Testing; 2. Stories without words; 3. Graphic novels
978-1-897299-10-4, $24.95

This is a wordless novel, told in 118 wood engravings, about the atomic bomb testing performed by the United States in the South Pacific following World War II. This new hardcover edition is a facsimile of the original edition, published in 1951. Laurence Hyde was infuriated with the United States' continued testing in the Bikini Atoll, following the mass destruction and unthinkable horrors resulting from the atomic bombs dropped on Hiroshima and Nagasaki in August 1945. The story depicts the evacuation of the Polynesian islanders from their homes; during the evacuation, a fisherman kills a sailor who attempts to rape his wife. The couple flees with their child into the jungle to avoid capture. After the other islanders have evacuated, the Americans detonate an atom bomb on the ocean floor, and the fisherman and his family suffer horribly from the effects. The book includes nudity and depiction of the attempted rape.

Hyun, Kang-Suk
Heaven Above Heaven Volume 1. Art by Jeon Joong-Won. Tokyopop 2005 168p. Illustration
Grades: 10 11 12 Adult **741.5; Fic**
1. Adventure graphic novels; 2. Fantasy graphic novels; 3. Manwha; 4. Graphic novels
1-59532-288-4, $9.99

Ancient prophecy foretold of a baby that would be the catalyst for the Apocalypse. At the anointed time, nine Grand Masters of Martial Arts raced to a remote mountaintop to prevent the terrible prophecy from being fulfilled. Seventeen years later, a young boy with a knack for trouble, a lust for ladies, and a wicked fighting technique has crossed paths with the child of the Apocalypse—and he's in for more kung fu action than he can handle. The book includes nudity, harsh language, and martial arts fighting violence.

Ilya

The **Mammoth** book of cult comics. Edited by Ilya. Running Press Book Publishers 2013 448 p. Illustration

Grades: Adult   **741.5**

1. Underground comic books, strips, etc

0762454687; 9780762454686, $17.95

LC 2014940740

This book "culls material from rare and lesser-known self-published and small-press comics, some recent but most going back to the 1990s, and many originally published as photocopied minicomics." Included is "'Hummingbird,' Gregory Benton's first issue of an unrealized series about a dysfunctional family reunion." (Publishers Weekly)

"Ilya's selection of comics spanning from 1983 to 2006—cult comics if in the UK, alternative comics in the U.S.—is altogether outstanding. The variety of style and subject is gratifyingly broad yet exclusive." Booklist

Immonen, Kathryn

Russian Olive to Red King. Kathryn Immonen and Stuart Immonen. AdHouse Books 2015 176 p. Color; Illustration

Grades: Adult   **741.5; Fic**

1. Depression (Psychology); 2. Grief — Fiction

1935233343; 9781935233343, $24.95

"When your lover may be dead, how long can you hold on to what remains? To whatever is left of you? A plane crash, a package, her dog, her voice. A notebook, his writer's block, and heat-distorted summer memories of a search for Jumbo the Elephant and an absent father." (Publisher's note)

Inada, Shiho

Ghost hunt, Vol. 1. Manga by Shiho Inada; story by Fuyumi Ono; translated by Akira Tsubasa; adapted by David Walsh; lettered by Foltz Design. Del Rey Manga 2005 216p. Illustration

Grades: 8 9 10 11 12 Adult   **741.5; Fic**

1. Horror graphic novels; 2. Manga; 3. Shojo manga; 4. Graphic novels

0-345-48624-2, $10.95

A decrepit old building stands on the campus of Mai's high school; every time the school tries to demolish it, unexplained accidents occur. Finally, the school hires a psychic researcher, and when Mai accidentally injures his assistant and damages an expensive camera, Shibuya (the researcher) insists she work off her debt by helping him. A miko (Shinto priestess), a Buddhist monk, and a Roman Catholic exorcist also come—but none of their methods work to stop the strange occurrences. Despite herself, Mai gets drawn into the investigation. This is the first of an ongoing manga series that provides some ghostly thrills without graphic violence, bad language, or sexual innuendo.

Inagaki, Riichiro

Eyeshield 21 Volume 1. Art by Yusuke Murata. Viz Media/Shonen Jump Advanced 2005 208p. Illustration

Grades: 10 11 12 Adult   **741.5; Fic**

1. Football; 2. Humorous graphic novels; 3. Manga; 4. Shonen manga; 5. Graphic novels

1-59116-752-3, $7.99

What does a wimpy kid who's been bullied all his life have to depend on but his own two feet? Sena Kobayakawa is about to start his first year in high school and he's vowed not to get picked on anymore. Unfortunately, the sadistic captain of the football team already has his eye on Sena and his lightning-fast speed. As the Devil Bats' "secret weapon," Sena uses a superhero-like secret identity, Eyeshield 21, to protect himself from other teams. This is a football story for people who don't know or like American football. The series includes crude humor, strong language, and some playing field violence.

Indiana Jones Omnibus, Volume 1

Dark Horse Comics 2008 352p.

Grades: 7 8 9 10 11 12 Adult   **741.5; Fic**

1. Adventure graphic novels; 2. Archeology; 3. Indiana Jones (Fictional character); 4. Graphic novels

978-1-59307-887-4, $24.95

This volume collects original comics stories starring movie hero Indiana Jones that were originally published by Dark Horse Comics in the early 1990s. Stories include Indiana Jones and the Fate of Atlantis, Indiana Jones: Thunder in the Orient, and Indiana Jones and the Arms of Gold. All of the stories predate the movies, as Indy races against the Nazis to recover and secure ancient treasures that could give great power to the owners. The book includes some violence.

Inoue, Kazurou

Midori Days Volume 1. Viz Media 2005 190p. Illustration

Grades: 10 11 12 Adult   **741.5; Fic**

1. Fantasy graphic novels; 2. Romance graphic novels; 3. Shonen manga; 4. Graphic novels

1-59116-905-4, $9.99

Seiji Sawamura is the toughest seventeen-year-old in town, feared by all for his fighting prowess and his deadly "devil's right hand." But at heart, Seiji is a softy, and all he wants is an end to his seventeen-year history of being a lonely single guy. Unfortunately his tough-guy reputation only serves to decrease his popularity with the ladies. Then one day, Seiji wakes up to discover his devil's right hand" has turned into a miniature gal named Midori. Strangely enough, Midori is a real girl who is just as surprised as Seiji to find out she has now become—literally "Seiji's right hand." It turns out Midori has always had a crush on Seiji, and her desperate wish to be connected to him has somehow come true. While she is now part of his right arm, her real body is in a coma. The book includes some nudity and sexual situations.

Inoue, Takehiko

★ **Real,** volume 1. Story & art by Takehiko Inoue. Viz Media 2008 222p. Illustration

Grades: 10 11 12 Adult **741; Fic; 741.5**
1. Basketball; 2. Manga; 3. Sports; 4. Wheelchair basketball; 5. Graphic novels
978-1-4215-1989-0, $12.99

Nomiya was the controlling rider on a motorcycle when he got into an accident that paralyzed the young woman riding with him; now he has dropped out of high school in his senior year and feels guilty. Togawa is stuck in a wheelchair but still plays basketball, which was the only thing Nomiya was good at in school. Togawa has quit the wheelchair basketball team, but he still plays. Nomiya starts playing while in a wheelchair, and they soon start a bit of a scam against regular players. They each have their own goals, but can they work together and find a better life for themselves? The book includes some harsh language, partial nudity, and Nomiya commits a bodily act against his school when he leaves.

"A compelling story of tragedy and struggle, Real is sure to appeal to teens—especially to male readers." SLJ

Original Japanese edition, 2001

Volume 1 of an ongoing series

★ **Vagabond,** Vol. 1. Viz 2002 Un Illustration

Grades: 11 12 Adult **Fic; 741.5**
1. Manga; 2. Musashi, Miyamoto, c 1584-1645; 3. Samurai; 4. Seinen manga; 5. Graphic novels
1-59116-034-0, $12.95

Based on the novel Musashi by Eiji Yoshikawa, this is the story of Shinmen Takezo, a young foot soldier who survived the Battle of Sekigahara, which marked the beginning of the Tokugawa Era in Japan. Destined to become the legendary sword saint Miyamoto Musashi, Takezo is a wild young brute, a cold-hearted killer who wants to make a name for himself. This first volume in the ongoing series includes sword fights, some nudity, and sexual situations.

Also available as 12 VIZBIG volumes

Volume 1 of 37

Inui, Sekihiko

Murder Princess Vol. 1. Broccoli Books 2007 208p. Illustration

Grades: 10 11 12 Adult **Fic; 741.5**
1. Fantasy graphic novels; 2. Manga; 3. Shonen manga; 4. Graphic novels
978-1-5974-1060-1, $9.99

The world of politics is treacherous enough, but in Forland, it's deadly confusing. When her royal father is murdered by a greedy drug manufacturer, Princess Alita must step forward to take over the kingdom. Unfortunately, a freak magical mishap has trapped her in the body of Falis, the bounty hunter. Now Alita must stay disguised as a servant while the battle-savvy Falis sits on the throne in her body. Threatened by a coup and attacks from the outside, the fate of the kingdom is in the hands of Alita and Falis. Switched souls or not, there's another royal heir and Alita has to hold everything together for a little longer. As though this weren't enough to juggle, evil Professor Akamashi and

his twin android assassins are out to cause some trouble of their own. Along with violence, there's a little fan service.

Volume 1 of 2

Inuki, Kanako

School Zone Vol. 1. Dark Horse Manga 2006 190p. Illustration

Grades: 10 11 12 Adult **741.5; Fic**
1. Horror graphic novels; 2. Manga; 3. Graphic novels
978-1-59307-433-3, $12.95

Kanako Inuki presents School Zone, a series about ordinary children who encounter the strange and terrifying at their very own elementary school, and discover that many ghost stories, urban legends and superstitions are truly and horribly real. The children, ranging from first through sixth graders, encounter monsters in mirrors, horribly live dolls, murderous ghosts, and more. The book includes graphic horror violence and some strong language.

Irving, Christopher

Comics Introspective Volume One: Peter Bagge. Twomorrows Publishing 2007 122p. Illustration

Grades: Adult Professional **741.5**
1. Bagge, Peter; 2. Graphic novels
978-1-893905-83-2, $16.95

Peter Bagge's work runs the gamut from political (his strips for reason.com), to absurdist and satirical (the Batboy strip for Weekly World News), and dramatic (Apocalypse Nerd). From his Seattle studio, Bagge lets journalist Christopher Irving in on everything from just what was on his mind with his long-running Gen X comic Hate!, to what's going on in his head as a political satirist. This volume features an assortment of artwork picked by Bagge himself. The book includes some strong language, and some of the art includes sexual situations.

Irwin, Jane

Vogelein: Old Ghosts. Fiery Studios 2007 168p. Illustration

Grades: 7 8 9 10 11 12 Adult **741.5; Fic**
1. Fantasy graphic novels; 2. Graphic novels
0-9743110-1-4, $12.95

Though three hundred years have passed since Alexi's death, Vogelein finds herself still haunted by the unkept promise she made to her first Guardian. Now the clockwork faerie must confront her past with the help of Mason, an itinerant musician whose spirit bears a striking resemblance to the one she desperately wants to lay to rest. As she struggles to find peace for both herself and Alexi, Vogelein discovers that centuries-old questions rarely have easy answers, intended paths reveal themselves in mysterious ways, and present-day threats strike just as suddenly as those from long ago.

Ishida, Sui

Tokyo Ghoul 1. By Sui Ishida; translation, Joe Yamazaki. Viz 2015 224 p. Illustration

Grades: 10 11 12 Adult **741.5**
1. College students — Fiction; 2. Horror fiction; 3. Manga; 4. Seinen
1421580365; 9781421580364, $12.99

"Ghouls live among us, the same as normal people in every wayùexcept their craving for human flesh. Ken Kaneki is an ordinary college student until a violent encounter turns him into the first half-human half-ghoul hybrid. Trapped between two worlds, he must survive Ghoul turf wars, learn more about Ghoul society and master his new powers." (Publisher's note)

Volume 1 of an ongoing series

Ito, Junti

GYO 1-2: The Death Stench Creeps. Junji Ito. Viz 2015 400 p. Illustration

Grades: Adult   741.5
1. Horror fiction; 2. Manga
1421579154; 9781421579153, $22.99

In this work graphic novel work of manga by Junji ito "something is rotten in Okinawa... The floating smell of death hangs over the island. What is it" A strange, legged fish appears on the scene. So begins Tadashi and Kaori's spiral into the horror and stench of the sea." (Publisher's note)

Museum of Terror Volume 3: The Long Hair in the Attic. Dark Horse Manga 2006 388p. Illustration

Grades: 11 12 Adult   741.5; Fic
1. Horror graphic novels; 2. Manga; 3. Graphic novels
978-1-59307-639-9, $13.95

Junji Ito, creator and curator of this horrible museum, collects various horror stories for this volume. A beautiful young woman with long, flowing hair comes home with a broken heart, a mouse becomes entangled in her hair, and it won't let her cut it. Lovely violinists will escort you to dinner in a vampire den. Next, in a classroom full of grotesquely masked students, which one is a demon in disguise? A musician's possessed arm attacks a schoolgirl by way of his mouth, and another young man listens to the tape recording left behind by a suicide victim. Why did she kill herself, and is he safe from its influence" Swordplay, monk-ridden ruins, halls of upright corpses, and infectious radio broadcasts all come into play.

Museum of Terror: Tomie 1. Dark Horse Manga 2006 376p. Illustration

Grades: 11 12 Adult   741.5; Fic
1. Horror graphic novels; 2. Manga; 3. Graphic novels
978-1-59307-542-2, $13.95

"Tomie" is the story of an eternally youthful and beautiful high school girl, whose admirers become obsessed to the point of murdering her. Most of them tend to dismember her body; but to their horror, she is reincarnated over and over, and each body part becomes a whole Tomie. The book includes graphic violence, strong language, and nudity.

Uzumaki: spiral into horror. By Junji Ito. Viz 2013 634 p. Illustration; Color

Grades: Adult   741.5
1. Horror graphic novels; 2. Manga
1421561328; 9781421561325, $27.99

In this book, by Junji Ito, "Kur?zu-cho, a small fogbound town on the coast of Japan, is cursed. According to Shuichi Saito . . . their town is haunted not by a person or being but by a pattern: uzumaki, the spiral, the hypnotic

secret shape of the world. It manifests itself in small ways: seashells, ferns, whirlpools in water, whirlwinds in air. And in large ways: the spiral marks on people's bodies, the insane obsessions of Shuichi's father, the voice from the cochlea in your inner ear." (Publisher's note)

Iwaaki, Hitoshi

Parasyte vol. 3. Del Rey Manga 2008 284p. Illustration
Grades: 10 11 12 Adult   741.5; Fic
1. Horror graphic novels; 2. Manga; 3. Science fiction graphic novels; 4. Seinen manga; 5. Graphic novels
978-0-345-49825-0, $12.95

Alien parasites have invaded Earth and taken over the minds and bodies of ordinary people, in order to be able to feed on humans. Shin has been invaded by a parasite, but he stopped the invasion of his body and limited it to one arm. He can communicate with the parasite, whom he has named Migi (Japanese for right), and he can sense who is actually a parasite masquerading as a human. Now he's been approached by two mysterious victims of the invasion: Tamiya, a beautiful school teacher, and Shimada, another student. What do they really want? The book includes gory violence.

Parasyte vol.4. Del Rey Manga 2008 296p. Illustration
Grades: 10 11 12 Adult   741.5; Fic
1. Horror graphic novels; 2. Manga; 3. Seinen manga; 4. Graphic novels
978-0-345-49826-7, $14.95

Shinichi and Migi, the Parasyte that merged with him, continue their search for the Parasytes who kill humans, even as Shinichi tries to be a "normal" high school student. Then he meets Kana, a classmate who seems to have a knack for sensing the killer aliens. The fact that the aliens are getting into politics in order to gain positions of power disturbs Shinichi, but he also suspects that Migi may be infiltrating his brain, too. The book includes violence and bloodshed, and brief partial nudity.

Parasyte, Vol. 1. Ballantine Books/Del Rey Manga 2007 282p. Illustration
Grades: 11 12 Adult   741.5; Fic
1. Horror graphic novels; 2. Manga; 3. Science fiction graphic novels; 4. Seinen manga; 5. Graphic novels
978-0-345-49624-9, $12.95

Aliens come to Earth in a silent invasion, taking over human bodies; their plan is to kill and eat humans. One ordinary high school student, Shin, fights off an alien and it only manages to get into his right hand. Once the parasitic alien has matured while still stuck in Shin's right hand, it can't get to his brain. They settle into an uneasy relationship, as Migi (Japanese for "right") tries to learn everything and Shin just tries to keep up a normal appearance. Soon, though, they find other aliens, and Shin can't let the parasites take over without trying to fight back.

Iwaaki alleviates the horror with plenty of dark humor; he also uses harsh language, including f-bombs and s-bombs, and some sexual innuendo.

Originally published in a flipped (American style) manga series by Tokyopop from 1997 to 2002; this edition retains the right-to-left orientation, Japanese sound effects, and other original elements.

Iwahara, Yuji

King of Thorn Vol. 1. Tokyopop 2007 188p. Illustration
Grades: 10 11 12 Adult   **741.5; Fic**
1. Horror graphic novels; 2. Manga; 3. Science fiction graphic novels; 4. Graphic novels
978-1-59816-235-6, $9.99

Twin sisters . . . Separated by fate. . . Drawn together by a horrific illness. . . Kasumi and her sister, Shizuku, were infected with the Medusa virus, which slowly turns the victim to stone—and there is no cure. Hope for salvation rests in Kasumi and a select few who are put into a cryogenically frozen state until a cure is found. But Shizuku is left behind, and in the not-too-distant future, Kasumi awakens along with others who also have the virus, to find herself in an unfamiliar world with terrifying beings roaming the terrain. Despite their mistrust among themselves, they need to discover what has happened while they were in their cryogenic sleep, and protect themselves from deadly dangers. The book includes strong language and some violence.

Iwanaga, Ryoutaro

Pumpkin scissors vol. 1. Translated by Ikoi Hiroe. Del Rey Manga 2007 218p. Illustration
Grades: 10 11 12 Adult   **741.5; Fic**
1. Adventure graphic novels; 2. Manga; 3. Graphic novels
978-0-345-50119-6, $10.95

The bitter war between the Empire and the Republic of Frost has ended, but three years after the cease-fire, the Empire is still ravaged by starvation and disease, and bandits terrorize the people. Can the Imperial Army State Section III, aka Pumpkin Scissors, stop a renegade force bent on destruction" And who is the mysterious stranger helping Pumpkin Scissors" The book includes some violence and mildly harsh language.

Jabcuda, Joshua

The **Mummy:** The rise and fall of Xango's Ax. Story by Joshua Jabcuga; artist, Stephen Mooney; colors by Lisa Jackson; letters by Robbie Robbins. IDW Publishing 2008 104p. Illustration
Grades: 9 10 11 12 Adult   **741.5; Fic**
1. Adventure graphic novels; 2. Mummies; 3. Graphic novels
978-1-60010-252-3, $17.99

Set before the events of the third Mummy movie (The Mummy: Tomb of the Dragon Emperor), adventurer Rick O'Connell tracks his son Alex to Burma, where corrupt treasure hunters have unearthed the Third Eye of Shangri-La. They've also managed to disturb the spirit of Xango, the mythical god of thunder, who wants the jewel back. Lord Hoxford, whom Alex had idolized, had led the theft; now, the O'Connells, Hoxford, and a ragtag group of poker players have to face down Xango and his revenant warriors to save the world. The book includes fighting violence, severed limbs, and beheadings.

Jackson, Jack

Jack Jackson's American History: Los Tejanos & Lost Cause. W W Norton & Co Inc 2013 320 p.
Grades: Adult   **976.4**
1. United States — History; 2. Graphic novels

1606995049; 9781606995044, $35

This book is a collection of two historical graphic novels by late artist Jack Jackson. "'Lost Cause' . . . is a . . . history of mob violence . . . that uses the Taylor-Sutton feud in post-Civil War southern Texas" to view "many white Texans' reactions to Reconstruction." The second story is 'Los Tejanos,' which follows the tragic history of Juan Seguin, a heroic tejano who fought brilliantly for Texas's independence." (Publishers Weekly)

Jacobs, Edgar P.

The **mystery** of the Great Pyramid part 1. Cinebook Ltd 2007 56p. Illustration
Grades: 7 8 9 10 11 12 Adult   **741.5; Fic**
1. Adventure graphic novels; 2. Egypt — Antiquities; 3. Graphic novels
978-1-905460-37-3, $13.95

Professor Mortimer has come to Egypt on vacation with his servant, Nasir; his old friend, Professor Ahmed Rassim Bey has offered him an opportunity to satsify his passion for Egyptology by inviting him to take part in deciphering his latest discoveries. Mortimer and Bey soon realize that one of the fragments of papyrus deals with the "Chamber of Horus," a fabled crypt that could hold priceless treasures. However, Bey's assistant has been in league with villainous adventurers with their own plans to grab the treasures. . . . Jacobs was a close relative of Herge, creator of Tintin, and his adventures of Blake and Mortimer follow a similar pattern and style.

This is a part of The Adventures of Blake and Mortimer.

Jacobson, Sidney

The **9/11** report: a graphic adaptation. By Sid Jacobson and Ernie Colón; [with a foreword by Thomas H. Kean and Lee H. Hamilton]. Hill and Wang 2006 133p. Illustration
Grades: 9 10 11 12 Adult   **973.931; 741.5**
1. September 11 terrorist attacks, 2001; 2. Graphic novels
0-8090-5738-7; 978-0-8090-5738-2, $30;
0-8090-5739-5 (pa); 978-0-8090-5739-9 (pa), $16.95

"The book aims to make . . . [The 9/11 Commission Report] more accessible to all readers and draw in young adults. . . . This graphic adaptation is an important and necessary part of any collection." Libr J

On cover: Based on the final report of the National Commission on Terrorist Attacks upon the United States

James, Dan

Mosquito: An Omnilingual Nosferatu Pictomunication Novel. Top Shelf Productions/Ghostshrimp Press 2005 Un Illustration
Grades: 11 12 Adult   **741.5; Fic**
1. Horror graphic novels; 2. Stories without words; 3. Graphic novels
1-891830-686, $12.95

This is a wordless vampire story, done completely in red ink. It follows the adventure of a man who receives a curious letter containing polaroids of vampire victims and a map to the small town where it lives. The book includes some violence.

Jansson, Tove
    Moomin Book One. Drawn & Quarterly 2006 96p.
Illustration
Grades: 8 9 10 11 12 Adult   **741.5; Fic**
    1. Humorous graphic novels; 2. Moomins (Fictional
    characters); 3. Graphic novels
    1-894937-80-5, $19.95
    Jansson is best known in the U.S. for her children's
books featuring the Moomins, hippo-shaped creatures. Her
comic strips have a more mature outlook. Moomin needs
help getting rid of unwanted guests, but the only solution
that works costs him his house. Then his scheming friend
Sniff involves him in all sorts of shady get-rich-quick
schemes. And when Moomin finds his long-lost parents, his
father's craving for adventure causes more trouble.
Snorkmaiden, Moomin's girlfriend, is just as bad as
Moominpapa, and they spark a boat trip south to a resort,
where the naive Moomins think they're houseguests and
everyone else, including the hotel staff, assumes they're
wealthy eccentrics. The childlike look of the strips belie the
goings-on; this book is not really for young readers,
although teens and adults will enjoy the whimsy overlaying
sharp satire.

    Moomin's winter follies. Trove Jansson. Enfant 2012
45 p.
Grades: 8 9 10 11 12 Adult   **741.5**
    1. Moomins (Fictional characters)
    1770460985; 9781770460980, $9.95
    Author Tove Jansson presents a graphic novel.
"Moomin wakes up one morning to find the pond frozen
over, and rather than hibernate, the family decides to brave
the winter weather. At first, their wintry adventure seems to
be going swimmingly, until Mr. Brisk of the Great Outdoors
Club takes over and forces everyone to embrace the winter
sports, whether they want to or not." (Comic Vine)

Japan as viewed by 17 creators.
    Fanfare/Ponent Mon 2005 254p. Illustration
Grades: 11 12 Adult   **741.5**
    1. Japan; 2. Graphic novels
    978-84-96427-16-7, $25
    Eight stories from nine European creators about
different geographic locations around Japan are combined
with eight stories from eight creators from the country about
their birthplace or place of residence. The result is a
collection of anecdotes and tales, both ancient and modern,
woven together from differing views that provide tantalizing
glimpses of this land of the Rising Sun. Creators include
Frederic Boilet, Nicolas de Crecy, Emmanuel Guibert, Joann
Sfar, Moyoko Anno, Taiyo Matsumoto, and Jiro Taniguchi.
Some of the stories include nudity, sexual situations, and
foul language.

Jason
    Hey, wait.... By Jason; [edited and translated from the
Norwegian by Kim Thompson]. Fantagraphics 2001 64 p.
Illustration
Grades: Adult   **741.5**
    1. Comic books, strips, etc — Norway
    9781560974635, $12.95; 156097463X
    Harvey Award: Best New Talent (2002)

"This superbly evocative graphic novella by the
award-winning Norwegian cartoonist Jason (his first
appearance in the English language) starts off as a
melancholy childhood memoir and then, with a shocking
twist midway through, becomes the summary of lives lived,
wasted, and lost." (Publisher's note)

    The **Iron** Wagon. Fantagraphics Books 2003 Un
Illustration
Grades: 10 11 12 Adult   **741.5; Fic**
    1. Mystery graphic novels; 2. Graphic novels
    1-56097-541-5, $12.95
    The Iron Wagon is an evocative murder mystery written
in 1908 by Riverton (a pseudonym) and set in the Norwegian
countryside; it, like all good murder mysteries, is a stew of
passion, buried past crimes, revelations, and sharply defined
characters who remain ambiguous to the very end. This
novel has never been translated into English. Norwegian
cartoonist Jason has adapted it into a graphic novel using his
animal characters.

Courtesy of Fantagraphics

    The **Left** Bank Gang.
Fantagraphics Books 2006
46p. Illustration
Grades: 10 11 12 Adult
                    741.5; Fic
    1. Mystery graphic novels;
    2. Graphic novels
    978-1-56097-742-1, $12.95
    Double-crosses,
violence, and harsh
language pepper this little
noir story that depicts Ernest
Hemingway, F. Scott
Fitzgerald, Ezra Pound, and
James Joyce as struggling
cartoonists in 1920s Paris.
Zelda Fitzgerald and
Gertrude Stein are there, as
well. Everyone is portrayed as dog-headed people, in Jason's
signature art style.

    Meow, Baby!. Fantagraphics
Books 2005 Un Illustration
Grades: 10 11 12 Adult
741.5; Fic
    1. Humorous graphic novels; 2.
    Graphic novels
    1-56097-695-0, $16.95
    Jason unleashes his inner
Scandinavian goofball with this
big collection of hilarious shorter
pieces. God, the Devil, mummies,
vampires, zombies, werewolves,
reanimated skeletons, space
invaders, Death, cavemen,
Godzilla and Elvis populate these most often wordless
blackout gags, side by side with Jason's usual
Little-Orphan-Annie-eyed, rabbit- and-bird-head
protagonists - a "lighter side" of one of the best cartoonists
of the new millennium. Some nudity and sexual situations,
and a little violence, plus seeing what zombies eat are subtly
present.

Courtesy of Fantagraphics

Jenkins, Paul

Civil War: Front Line Book 1. Art by various. Marvel Entertainment 2007 Un Illustration

Grades: 9 10 11 12 Adult   **741.5; Fic**
  1. Superhero graphic novels; 2. Graphic novels
978-0-7851-2312-5, $14.99

In "Embedded," reporters Sally Floyd and Ben Urich seek the truth at the heart of the war. In "The Accused," the lone survivor of the team that caused the Stamford tragedy has been found, and this vilified hero is placed under arrest for the deaths of an entire town. And his trouble is just beginning. This volume includes other stories, including the mystery of the Atlanteans.

Civil War: Front Line Book 2. Art by various. Marvel Entertainment 2007 Un Illustration

Grades: 9 10 11 12 Adult   **741.5; Fic**
  1. Superhero graphic novels; 2. Graphic novels
978-0-7851-2469-6, $14.99

In "Embedded," hot on the trail of a revelation that could explode the rift between the pro-registration and anti-registration heroes and forever change the nature of the Registration Act, the Daily Bugle's Ben Urich and Sally Floyd have the story. Can they bring the power to the people? In "The Accused," his powers are gone, he's been held culpable for the worst super-human disaster in history, and every super-villain in prison is looking to take a piece of Speedball. Will he make it out alive, and with hundreds of deaths on his conscience, does he want to? In the meantime, Norman Osborn shoots an Atlantean ambassador, bringing the U.S. to the brink of war; and there's a traitor in Stark's group. This volume includes some violence.

Revelations. Created by Paul Jenkins and Humberto Ramos; story by Paul Jenkins; art by Humberto Ramos; colors by Leonardo Olea and Edgar Delgado; letters by Richard Starkings and Comicraft. Dark Horse Comics 2006 Un Illustration

Grades: 11 12 Adult   **741.5; Fic**
  1. Catholic church; 2. Mystery graphic novels; 3. Graphic novels
978-1-59307-239-1, $17.95

When a Cardinal in line to succeed the dying Pope falls from a high window in the Vatican, a priest calls on his friend, tough London cop Charlie Northern, to investigate. Once in Rome, Northern confronts coverups and secrets as he tries to find out what happened. What he learns will shake him to his atheistic core. This violent murder mystery will appeal to fans of The Da Vinci Code and other works depicting religious conspiracies.

Originally published as Revelations issues #1-6.

Sidekick. Image Comics 2007 Un Illustration

Grades: 12 Adult   **741.5; Fic**
  1. Satire; 2. Superhero graphic novels; 3. Graphic novels
978-1-58240-743-2, $16.99

This is the story of the not-so-glamorous life of Eddie Edison - also known as Superior Boy. Eddie works two jobs: delivering pizza to pay the bills and being a sidekick to the most powerful superhero on earth - to pay the bills. What's a guy to do" Discover the answer to this burning question, and get a healthy dose of evil villains, busty women, sex-fiends and more F-bombs than one can shake a stick at. The book indeed includes lots of harsh language, sexual situations, and violence.

Jensen, Van

Pinocchio vampire slayer and the great puppet theater: a story. By [artist] Dusty Higgins and [text] Van Jensen. SLG 2010 165 p. Illustration

Grades: 9 10 11 12 Adult   **Fic; 741.5**
9781593622039, $14.95

The second volume of Pinocchio, Vampire Slayer follows a cast of puppets, a ghost cricket, and a human girl, Carlotta, to battle to destroy the head vampire and his associates. With an enraged disposition, Pinocchio, the main character, plots to avenge his father Geppetto's death. His former ally, Master Cherry, now a vampire, is killed by Pinocchio's hand when Cherry cannot dominate his thirst for blood. In a fit of sorrow and fury over Cherry's death, the Blue Fairy casts a spell transforming Pinocchio into a human boỳrendering him virtually defenseless against the vampires.... With a blend of horror and fantasy, the graphic novel unfolds layers of a unique story in comic book form. The vibrant characters breathe to life a tale that connects with readers of multiple ages. Voice Youth Advocates

Pinocchio, Vampire Slayer: Volume 3: Of Wood and Blood Part 1. SLG Publishing 2012 130 p.

Grades: 9 10 11 12 Adult   **741**
  1. Fractured fairy tales
1593622392; 9781593622398, $10.95

This book is the final part of Van Jensen's Pinocchio series. "Pinocchio's wish to become a real boy was granted at a most disadvantageous time: he ended up marooned in the middle of the Mediterranean with the remnants of the Great Puppet Theater, while Carlotta was dragged away by the vampires. He washes ashore on an island" and must find a way to rescue Carlotta. (Voice of Youth Advocates)

Jerwa, Brandon

G. I. Joe Vol. 6: Players & Pawns. Illustrated by Tim Seeley. Devil's Due Publishing 2004 Un Illustration

Grades: 7 8 9 10 11 12 Adult   **741.5; Fic**
  1. Adventure graphic novels; 2. G I Joe (Fictional character); 3. Graphic novels
1-932796-18-5, $12.95

Cobra has re-established its island base, but the organization is crumbling; Destro and Zartan have both resigned, and the Baroness is caught between love and duty. While the Joes infiltrate Cobra Island, Cobra Commander makes a violent attempt on General Hawk's life and the South American nation of Sierra Gordo is invaded by a mysterious new high-tech commando unit. As the players enact their strategies, the pawns move into place. The book includes fighting action.

Jimenez, Phil

Other World Book One. Phil Jimenez, writer/penciller; Andy Lanning, inker; Jeromy Cox, colorist; Nick J. Napolitano, letterer. DC Comics/Vertigo 2006 176p. Illustration

Grades: 10 11 12 Adult   **741.5**
  1. Adventure graphic novels; 2. Fantasy graphic novels; 3. Graphic novels

978-1-4012-1011-3

Otherworld is an idyllic, pastoral land populated by mythological beings that battle endlessly with a nation-state made of pure technology. A group of young people - some friends, some strangers - have been plucked violently from Earth, imbued with superpowers, and brought to Otherworld. Siobhan Moynihan, a college student and an aspiring singer, is told she's the savior who will end the war and save Otherworld ... or destroy it forever. This book includes some nudity, strong language, and violence.

Teen Titans/Outsiders: The Death and Return of Donna Troy. Written by Phil Jimenez and Judd Winick; Art by Alé Garza et al. DC Comics 2006 176p. Illustration
Grades: 9 10 11 12 Adult   **741.5; Fic**
1. Outsiders (Fictional characters); 2. Superhero graphic novels; 3. Teen Titans (Fictional characters); 4. Graphic novels
1-4012-0931-9, $14.99
A mysterious android from the future sparks a chain of events that leads to the death of Donna Troy, Titan member and sister to Wonder Woman. The new incarnation of the Teen Titans and the Outsiders later discover that Donna is still alive, but she doesn't seem to remember who she is and is hell-bent on destroying her friends. Will her former teammates be able to restore Donna's true self before her ultimate destiny is revealed?

Johns, Geoff
52, Volume One. DC Comics 2007 304p. Illustration
Grades: 10 11 12 Adult   **Fic; 741.5**
1. Adventure graphic novels; 2. Mystery graphic novels; 3. Science fiction graphic novels; 4. Superhero graphic novels; 5. Superman (Fictional character)
978-1-4012-1353-4, $19.99
The events of Infinite Crisis have left Superman, Batman and Wonder Woman missing, many other superheroes dead or injured. Black Adam, the long-time nemesis of Shazam, seeks to gain allies to form a group to go up against the U.S. Ralph Dibny investigates a cult built around the idea of resurrecting Superboy. The Blue Beetle tries to use information from the 25th century to gain wealth and become the next big superhero. John Steel tries to go up against ex-President Lex Luthor, who has developed a drug that can "create" superheroes. DC Comics gathered four writers, a breakdown artist (Giffen), and a host of pencillers and inkers to create a year-long weekly comic book that plays out the action in real time. Johns, Morrison, Rucka, and Waid also worked together on every issue.
Originally published as 52 issues #1-13.
Volume 1 of 4

52 Volume Two. Written by Geoff Johns, Grant Morrison, Greg Rucka, Mark Waid; Art by various. DC Comics 2007 304p. Illustration
Grades: 10 11 12 Adult   **741.5; Fic**
1. Adventure graphic novels; 2. Superhero graphic novels
978-1-4012-1364-0, $19.99
Lex Luthor's created meta humans become Infinity, Inc. even as John Steel finds out that Luthor can control the power within them - including removing them. Ralph Dibny takes up the helmet of Dr. Fate. The Question and Renee Montoya travel to Kahndaq, on the trail of Intergang's

weapons. Black Adam and Isis get married. Booster Gold's dubious heroism ends badly. Supernova bothers Luthor. Adam Strange, Animal Man, and Starfire escape from the planet where they had been trapped, with help from ... Lobo" The year without Superman, Batman, and Wonder Woman continues. The book includes some sexually suggestive scenes, violence, and some strong language.

The **Flash:** The Secret of Barry Allen. DC Comics 2005 Un Illustration
Grades: 9 10 11 12 Adult   **741.5; Fic**
1. Flash (Fictional character); 2. Superhero graphic novels; 3. Graphic novels
1-4012-0723-5, $19.99
This volume details the events in Wally West's life as he regains his memory of being the Flash. He carefully chooses which friends and allies to whom he will again reveal his identity. Then, he and his pal Nightwing are confronted with the return of Gorilla Grodd, more savage than ever. But the biggest shock in the Fastest Man Alive's life comes when he reads a letter from his mentor and predecessor, Barry Allen, revealing a dark decision that haunted him to the day he died. And after reading it, Wally needs to reassess what it means to be a hero in a world growing ever darker.

The **Flash:** crossfire. [by] Geoff Johns, writer; Scott Kolins, Rich Burchett, Justiniano, pencillers; Doug Hazlewood, Dan Panosian, Walden Wong, inkers; James Sinclair, colorist; Gaspar Saladino, Bill Oakley, letterers; Brian Bolland, Scott Kolins, original cover. DC Comics 2004 212p. Illustration
Grades: 10 11 12 Adult   **741.5; Fic**
1. Flash (Fictional character); 2. Superhero graphic novels; 3. Graphic novels
1-4012-0195-4, $17.95
                                    LC 2004-555611
"Eight ... rogues have joined forces to take over Flash's town of Keystone City. As if that weren't enough, the Thinker, an artificial intelligence with a personality—a walking computer virus of sorts—is attempting to absorb the minds of the city's inhabitants, including Flash's. Writer Johns demonstrates his ability to reinvigorate the series' classic elements. . . . Teens will appreciate it as mainstream superhero fare, executed with complexity and flair." Booklist

The **Flash:** Wonderland. Geoff Johns, writer; Angel Unzueta, penciller; Doug Hazlewood, inker; Tom McCraw, colorist; Gaspar, letterer. DC Comics 2007 144p. Illustration
Grades: 9 10 11 12 Adult   **741.5; Fic**
1. Flash (Fictional character); 2. Superhero graphic novels; 3. Flash (Fictional character); 4. Graphic novels
978-1-4012-1489-0, $12.99
The Flash, Wally West, finds himself on a parallel Earth in which there's no Speed Force, and without that energy source, he has no power. The cops think he's a murderer, and the only one who can help him is one of his enemies, Captain Cold, who's also in the same world. They join forces to try to get back to their Earth, but they've got to find out who brought them here.

Green Lantern: No Fear. Geoff Johns, writer; Darwyn Cook [and others], pencillers. DC Comics 2006 Un Illustration

Grades: 10 11 12 Adult   **741.5; Fic**
1. Green Lantern (Fictional character); 2. Superhero graphic novels; 3. Graphic novels
978-14012-0466-2, $24.99

Hal Jordan has been resurrected and redeemed. Now it's tie to get on with his life as Green Lantern, protector of space sector 2814. But even as he returns to the skies as an Air Force pilot, Jordan faces new threats from his old foes. The deadly Manhunter androids and the mutated Shark return with shocking violence ... yet they are just precursors to even greater dangers. A maddened Black Hand embarks on a murderous rampage just as the Lantern finds himself the object of an alien race's insidious plan to harvest humans as living weapons of war. Johns works with artists Carlos Pacheco, Ethan Van Sciver, Darwyn Cooke, and Simone Bianchi in the stories collected here. There is some strong language, and violence, some graphic.

Green Lantern: Rebirth. Geoff Johns, writer; Ethan van Sciver, penciller; Prentis Rollins [and others], inkers; Rob Leigh, letterer; Moose Baumann, colorist. DC Comics 2005 Un Illustration
Grades: 9 10 11 12 Adult   **741.5; Fic**
1. Green Lantern (Fictional character); 2. Superhero graphic novels; 3. Graphic novels
978-1-4012-0465-5, $14.99

He was the greatest Green Lantern of them all. Then Hal Jordan went mad and ultimately died in an attempt to redeem himself. But fate was not done with him. Kyle Rayner, the sole Green Lantern, crashes back to Earth with a coffin bearing Hal Jordan's body, saying feverishly, "Parallax is coming." And Hal Jordan has returned. And so has Parallax, and the Spectre. Will one of them win and possess Jordan forever? Or can he become the Green Lantern once again?

Green Lantern Vol. 2: Revenge of the Green Lanterns. DC Comics 2006 Un Illustration
Grades: 9 10 11 12 Adult   **741.5; Fic**
1. Green Lantern (Fictional character); 2. Superhero graphic novels; 3. Graphic novels
1401209602; 9781401209605, $14.99

The Green Lantern Corps kept peace and order throughout the universe for millenia, until their greatest warrior, Hal Jordan of Earth, destroyed them. The Corps had been resurrected, and Jordan, freed of the alien entity that drove him to madness, had been fully reinstated as a Green Lantern of Earth. But now, after the events of the Infinite Crisis, Jordan is in trouble again, and a Green Lantern whom he thought he had killed years ago has returned with vengeance on his mind. Jordan and fellow Green Lantern Guy Gardner travel to the home world of the Corps' greatest enemies, the android Manhunters, to save the Lanterns.

Infinite Crisis. Geoff Johns, writer; Phil Jimenez [and others], pencillers. DC Comics 2006 262p. Illustration
Grades: 9 10 11 12 Adult   **741.5; Fic**
1. Superhero graphic novels; 2. Graphic novels
978-1-4012-0959-9, $24.99

Four heroes, trapped in limbo since the original Crisis on Infinite Earths, are about to reveal themselves: one is dying, one wants to save her and restore an entire world that vanished and the other two seek unrivaled power. The plan they concoct is literally earth-shattering, and the world's greatest superheroes may not be enough to stop their attempt to alter the very nature of reality.

JSA: Mixed Signals. Geoff Johns and Keith Champagne. DC Comics 2006 144p. Illustration
Grades: 10 11 12 Adult   **741.5; Fic**
1. Superhero graphic novels; 2. Graphic novels
978-1-4012-0967-4, $14.99

The JSA gets word from their ally, Airwave, that an intergalactic war has begun. Meanwhile, recent events have left all of the magic-based heroes vulnerable, and the ancient, evil magician Mordru plans to take full advantage of the situation. And when Golden Age legend Liberty Belle's powers go out of control, Stargirl is the only one who can figure out what to do.

JSA Presents Stars and S.T.R.I.P.E.. writer, Geoff Johns ; penciller, Lee Moder ; inker, Dan Davis ; colorist, Tom MccCraw ; letterer, Bill Oakely. DC Comics 2007 192p. Illustration
Grades: 8 9 10 11 12 Adult   **741.5; Fic**
1. Superhero graphic novels; 2. Graphic novels
978-1-4012-1390-9, $17.99

Courtney Whitmore is just your typical teenage girl trying to make it through high school, but she's about to stumble upon a secret that will make her life a lot more complicated. Her new stepfather, Pat Dugan, was once Stripesy, sidekick of the Golden Age hero The Star-Spangled Kid. Finding the Kid's old costume, Courtney modifies it for herself and becomes the new Star-Spangled Kid, aiming to fight crime and annoy the heck out of her stepfather. But Dugan isn't about to let his new daughter get into any danger. Putting his mechanical skills to work, he creates a robotic suit called S.T.R.I.P.E., and joins Courtney's battle for justice. They fight side-by-side - and sometimes with each other - taking on aliens, cults, new villains, and more. These stories are the first that Johns wrote in comics, back in 1999.

JSA: Black Vengeance. Geoff Johns, writer; Don Kramer, penciller; Keith Champagne, inker. DC Comics 2006 208p. Illustration
Grades: 10 11 12 Adult   **741.5; Fic**
1. Justice Society of America (Fictional characters); 2. Superhero graphic novels; 3. Graphic novels
978-1-4012-0966-7, $19.99

The JSA's former comrade, the Spectre, is now without a human host and running rampant, dealing out a brutal form of justice, encouraged by the new Eclipso. Atom-Smasher, also a former JSA member, seeks forgiveness for his actions in Kahndaq. Before the JSA decides whether or not to readmit him, Khandaq's ruler, Black Adam, summons the atomic hero back to the Middle East. When the JSA follow, all are forced to re-examine what it means to be a hero.

JSA: Lost. Geoff Johns, writer; Dave Gibbons [and others], pencillers. DC Comics 2005 208p. Illustration
Grades: 9 10 11 12 Adult   **741.5; Fic**
1. Science fiction graphic novels; 2. Superhero graphic novels; 3. Graphic novels
1-4012-0722-7, $19.99

The first Hourman sits alone at the end of time, having given his life to protect humanity. Sand, former chairman of the JSA, became one with the planet Earth to keep it whole.

Hal Jordan sacrificed himself to become the new Spectre and keep the world safe. Now the JSA find themselves visiting old friends and new, rectifying injustices, aware that as they fix one problem, an even larger one is brewing in the time stream. The end of this volume contains spoilers about the killer's identity in the Identity Crisis. The book includes lots of superhero action and some violence.

Justice League; Volume 1. By Geoff Johns and illustrated by Jim Lee and Scott Williams. DC Comics 2013 192 p.

Grades: Adult   **741.5/973; 741.5**
1. Justice League (Fictional characters); 2. Superhero graphic novels
1401237886; 9781401234614; 9781401237882, $16.99
LC 2011051844

This graphic novel by Geoff Johns presents "an all-new origin story for the Justice League! Batman has stumbled upon a dark evil that threatens to destroy the earth. The Dark Knight must trust an alien, a scarlet speedster, an accidental teenage hero, a space cop, an Amazon Princess and an undersea monarch. Will this combination of Superman, The Flash, Cyborg, Green Lantern, Wonder Woman and Aquaman be able to put aside their differences and come together to save the world" (Publisher's note)
Originally published in single magazine form in JUSTICE LEAGUE 1-6—t.p. verso.

Justice League; Volume 2. Geoff Johns, writer; Jim Lee ... [et .al], pencilers; Alex Sinclair ... [et .al], colorists; Sal Cipriano, Patrick Brossesau, Nick Napolitano, letters. DC Comics 2012 160 p.

Grades: Adult   **741.5; 741.5/973**
1. Justice League (Fictional characters); 2. Superheroes — Fiction
1401237649; 9781401237646, $24.99; 9781401237653
LC 2012040572

This graphic novel, written by Geoff Johns and illustrated by Jim Lee and Scott Williams features the Justice League. "Their never-ending battle against evil results in casualties beyond its super-powered . . . combatants. Unbeknownst to Earth—s greatest champions, their greatest triumph may contain the seeds of their greatest defeat. For heroes are not the only people who face tragedy and are reborn as something greater than they were before. Villains can take this journey, too." (Publisher's note)
Originally published in single magazine form in Justice League 7-12.

Power Girl. Geoff Johns, Paul Levitz, Paul Kupperberg, writers; Amanda Conner et al., pencillers. DC Comics 2006 176p. Illustration

Grades: 9 10 11 12 Adult   **741.5; Fic**
1. Adventure graphic novels; 2. Superhero graphic novels; 3. Graphic novels
978-1-4012-0968-1, $14.99

Who is Power Girl" Is she Superman's cousin from a parallel world" Is she the granddaughter of an ancient Atlantean sorcerer" Is she a pawn in a game of cosmic chess that threatens the known universe" Whoever she is, she's playing a major role in recent DC Universe titles. In these stories, some dating back to 1975, her reality keeps

changing. The more recent stories include a little bit of suggestiveness.

Superman: That Healing Touch. Writers, Greg Rucka, Geoff Johns & Jeremy Johns; pencillers, Matthew Clark [and others]. DC Comics 2005 168p. Illustration

Grades: 9 10 11 12 Adult   **741.5; Fic**
1. Superhero graphic novels; 2. Superman (Fictional character); 3. Graphic novels
1-4012-0453-8, $14.99

Ruin is out to kill Superman and those closest to him. He has unleashed Replikon and his son to soften up the Man of Steel, but now he unleashes his deadliest attack yet, twin Parasites who can sap the life from even a Kryptonian. Lois Lane, still recovering from a gunshot wound, Lana Lang, and Jimmy Olsen are all threatened. And each time, Superman insists that no one will die on his watch.

Superman: Up, Up and Away!. Geoff Johns and Kurt Busiek ; art by Pete Woods and Renato Guedes. DC Comics 2006 192p. Illustration

Grades: 8 9 10 11 12 Adult   **741.5; Fic**
1. Green Lantern (Fictional character); 2. Superhero graphic novels; 3. Superman (Fictional character); 4. Graphic novels
978-1-4012-0954-4, $14.99

In the wake of Infinite Crisis, Superman had lost his powers. For the past year, as Clark Kent he has worked with the help of his super-powered allies, Green Lantern, Supergirl, and Hawkgirl, to keep Metropolis safe. Now, Lex Luthor has been acquitted of his past crimes, and he has managed to get his hands on a powerful and ancient Kryptonian artifact and plans to use it to destroy Superman once and for all. What can a powerless Superman do?

Superman; Volume 6: the men of tomorrow. Geoff Johns, writer; John Romita Jr, Klaus Janson, artists. DC Comics 2015 256 p. Color; Illustration

Grades: 10 11 12 Adult   **741.5; Fic**
1. Superhero graphic novels; 2. Superman (Fictional character)
1401252397; 9781401252397, $24.99
LC 2015008050

"Enter Ulysses, the Man of Tomorrow, into the Man of Steel's life. This strange visitor shares many of Kal-El's experiences, including having been rocketed from a world with no future. New and exciting mysteries and adventures await. Plus, Perry White offers Clark a chance to return to The Daily Planet!" (Publisher's note)
Collects Superman #32-39 (New 52 relaunch)

Teen Titans Vol. 1: A Kid's Game. Geoff Johns, writer; Mike McKone & Tom Grummett, pencillers; Marlo Alquiza & Nelson, inkers; Jeremy Cox, colorist; Comicraft, letterer. DC Comics 2004 Un Illustration

Grades: 9 10 11 12 Adult   **741.5; Fic**
1. Batman (Fictional character); 2. Flash (Fictional character); 3. Robin (Fictional character); 4. Superhero graphic novels; 5. Superman (Fictional character); 6. Teen Titans (Fictional characters); 7. Graphic novels
1-4012-0308-6, $9.95

As the adolescent sidekicks of the world's most powerful heroes, Robin, Superboy, Wonder Girl, and Impulse have fought alongside their mentors in many battles. But when Cyborg, a former teen hero, realizes that this new generation of super-heroes needs to be guided and trained, he recruits the young adventurers into the new Teen Titans. Now as Earth's future champions begin working together as a unified team, they quickly learn the true consequences of the path they have chosen. Featuring Batman, Superman, Wonder Woman and the Flash, this action-packed volume includes the Teen Titans' inaugural adventures as they face off against the deadly mercenary Deathstroke, contend with the fanatical villainy of Brother Blood and take on the heroes of the Justice League. The level of action and some violence puts this beyond most young fans of the Cartoon Network series, "Teen Titans Go."

Teen Titans Vol. 4: The Future is Now. writers, Geoff Johns and Mark Waid ; pencillers, Mike McKone ... [et al.]. DC Comics 2005 Un Illustration
Grades: 8 9 10 11 12 Adult **741.5; Fic**
1. Science fiction graphic novels; 2. Superhero graphic novels; 3. Teen Titans (Fictional characters); 4. Graphic novels
1-4012-0475-9, $9.99
The Titans' weekends are usually a chance to get away from it all, but this time they've gone to the 31st century, where they must help the Legion of Super-Heroes stop a threat known as the Fatal Five Hundred. Their return trip drops them off ten years into their future, and they don't like what they see. And when they finally get back home, they meet Speedy, who has arrived just in time to help them fight Dr. Light.

Teen Titans Vol. 6: Titans Around the World. Geoff Johns, writer; Mike McKone & Tom Grummett, pencillers; Marlo Alquiza & Nelson, inkers; Jeromy Cox, colorist; Comicraft, letterer. DC Comics 2007 192p. Illustration
Grades: 9 10 11 12 Adult **Fic; 741.5**
1. Robin (Fictional character); 2. Superhero graphic novels; 3. Teen Titans (Fictional characters); 4. Graphic novels
978-1-4012-1217-9, $14.99
The tragic events of Infinite Crisis tore apart the Teen Titans. It's one year later, and the core members of the Titans return to re-form the team. Robin, Wonder Girl, and Cyborg go with interim members Kid Devil and Ravager on a journey to find their former colleagues, but they discover there had been a traitor in their ranks. With the identity and intent of the saboteur unknown, the team must be ready at all times for an assault. They meet with the Doom Patrol and fight the Brotherhood of Evil.

Johnson, Crockett
Barnaby: 1942-1943, 1. By Crockett Johnson. Fantagraphics 2012 318 p. Illustration; Color
Grades: 10 11 12 Adult **741.5; 741.5/6973**
1. Boys; 2. Children; 3. Fairies
9781606995228, $35; 1606995227
LC 2013363489
This volume, by Crockett Johnson, presents the collected comic strips of "Barnaby" from 1942-1943, which "revolved around a precocious five-year-old named Barnaby Baxter and his fairly godfather Jackeen J. O'Malley. Yet O'Malley, a cigar-chomping, bumbling con-artist and

fast-talker, was not your typical protector." (Publisher's note)

Johnson, Dan Curtis
Batman: Snow. J.H. Williams III, Dan Curtis Johnson, story; Dan Curtis Johnson, script & dialogue; Seth Fisher, art; Dave Stewart, colors; Phil Balsman, letterer. DC Comics 2007 128p. Illustration
Grades: 9 10 11 12 Adult **741.5; Fic**
1. Adventure graphic novels; 2. Batman (Fictional character); 3. Superhero graphic novels; 4. Graphic novels
978-1-4012-1265-0, $14.99
At the dawn of his career, Batman recruits allies for his war on crime in order to really protect Gotham City. Everything changes when a brilliant scientist's desperate attempt to save the life of his terminally ill wife goes tragically wrong, and a new type of threat is born. As Batman faces his first super-powered villain, Mr. Freeze, he begins to realize that malfeasance comes in many deadly forms, and some offenders are more powerful than he. How will the crime fighter overcome this new menace while protecting not only his associates, but also the innocent citizens of Gotham? This book has lots of action and some mildly harsh language.

Johnson, Mat
★ **Incognegro**. Art by Warren Pleece. DC Comics/Vertigo 2008 136p. Illustration
Grades: 10 11 12 Adult **741.5; Fic**
1. African Americans — Southern states; 2. Mystery graphic novels; 3. Graphic novels
9781401210977, $19.99
In the early 20th century, light-skinned African American reporters risked their lives to cover the lynching murders of African Americans in the South; this process of "passing" was called "going incognegro." Zane Pinchback is a reporter from Harlem who has just narrowly escaped from one such reporting assignment when his editor sends him back down to Mississippi; this time, the man charged with murdering a white woman is Pinchback's own twin brother. He decides to investigate and find the real murderer in order to free his brother, but a Ku Klux Klansman has also come to town hunting the "Incognegro" reporter. This book portrays hangings and mutilations and uses the "n" word as it was used during the time period.

Right state. Written by Mat Johnson; art by Andrea Mutti; letters by Pat Brosseau. DC Comics 2012 144 p.
Grades: Adult **741.5**
1. Adventure graphic novels; 2. Militia movements; 3. Militia movements — Fiction; 4. Presidents — Assassination attempts; 5. Presidents — United States — Assassination — Fiction
1401229433; 9781401229436, $24.99
LC 2012019780
This graphic novel, by Mat Johnson, illustrated by Andrea Mutti, "follows . . . a militia group that's plotting to assassinate the . . . President of the U.S. . . . [While] ex-Special Forces war hero turned conservative media pundit . . . Ted Akers' . . . politics make him a hero to the right-wing fringe and no friend to the current Administration, he takes the assignment . . . to stop a

President from dying and a country from being ripped apart." (Publisher's note)

Johnson, Peter
   Supernatural: Origins. Writer, Peter Johnson; artist, Matthew Dow Smith; colorist, J.D. Mettler; letterer, Greg Thompson. DC Comics/Wildstorm 2008 144p. Illustration
Grades: 10 11 12 Adult   **741.5; Fic**
   1. Horror graphic novels; 2. Graphic novels
   978-1-4012-1701-3, $14.99
   This book is a prequel to the television series, "Supernatural." After witnessing the murder of his wife at the hands of . . . something evil . . . John Winchester finds no answers in town until a psychic shows him it was supernatural. As he goes on the road with his two young sons, Dean and Sam, Winchester finds himself on a path that will lead him towards much more than mere vengeance for his wife's death. The book includes gory violence.

Johnson, R. Kikuo
   Night Fisher. Fantagraphics Books 2005 144. Illustration
Grades: 11 12 Adult   **741.5; Fic**
   1. Bildungsromans; 2. Graphic novels
   1-56097-719-1, $12.95
   Loren Foster was handed an island paradise when he moved to the island of Maui in Hawaii with his dentist father six years ago. But, with the end of high school just around the corner, his best friend Shane has grown distant. Their friendship is put to the test when they get mixed up in a frivolous crime that leads to an arrest. Some drug use, strong language, and a sexual situation occur.

Johnston, Antony
   Julius. Written by Antony Johnston; illustrated & lettered by Brett Weldele. Oni Press 2004 138p. Illustration
Grades: 10 11 12 Adult   **741.5; Fic**
   1. Gangs; 2. Shakespeare, William, 1564-1616 — Adaptations; 3. Shakespeare, William, 1564-1616 — Adaptations; 4. Graphic novels
   1-929998-80-5, $14.95
   After years of infighting and turf wars, organized crime in the neighborhood is finally united under one leader. Julius is the gangster king of London's East End and his public persona is as beloved as it would be were he true royalty. But in private, his generals conspire and contemplate ways to remove Julius for their own selfish gain. This reworking of Shakespeare's classic tale of betrayal, corruption, manipulation, narcissism, and the violence spawned by each, gives the play a new power and relevance for a modern audience. Gangland killings and harsh language occur throughout the story.

   The **Long** Haul. Writer, Antony Johnston; artist, Eduardo Barreto; letterer, Marshall Dillon. Oni Press 2005 176p. Illustration
Grades: 9 10 11 12 Adult   **741.5; Fic**
   1. Adventure graphic novels; 2. Western graphic novels; 3. Graphic novels
   1-932664-05-X, $14.95
   The year is 1871 and a government grant of $100,000 in bonds (the last payment for the building of the Central Pacific Railroad from San Francisco to Promontory) is about to be sent from Chicago to the Western Pacific offices in San Francisco, over 2000 miles of railroad away. A Pinkerton agent has been brought in to oversee security, and the details for this operation are top secret. But professional thief Cody Plummer has discovered the plans... and the prize is too sweet to resist. With so much money at stake, this is no ordinary train: it can't be stopped, it can't be blown open, the safe weighs 2,000 pounds, and there are fourteen armed guards between Cody, the crew of ex-outlaws and old partners he's assembled, and the money. Sounds like pretty good odds to Cody. The book includes minimal violence, brief partial nudity, and no harsh language.

Jones, Bruce
   Deadman: Deadman Walking. Bruce Jones, writer; John Watkiss, artist. DC Comics 2007 128p. Illustration
Grades: 11 12 Adult   **741.5; Fic**
   1. Mystery graphic novels; 2. Superhero graphic novels; 3. Supernatural graphic novels; 4. Graphic novels
   978-1-4012-1236-0, $12.99
   Brandon Cayce is about to find out the answers to the question of what happens after we die; unfortunately, he's going to find out by becoming a dead man himself. Now come new questions. Why did his brother crash an airliner, killing everyone aboard - including Brandon? Why does Brandon find himself drawn to Sarah, his sister-in-law and onetime love? Who are those men trying to kill him ... and can you even kill a Deadman? The book includes a lot of violence, some nudity and sexual situations.

   Nightwing: Brothers in Blood. Bruce Jones, writer; Joe Dodd, Paco Diaz, Robert Teranishi, pencillers; Bit, Nathan Massengill, Wes Craig, inkers; Javier Rodriguez Studio, Guy Major, colorists. DC Comics 2007 168p. Illustration
Grades: 10 11 12 Adult   **Fic; 741.5**
   1. Nightwing (Fictional character); 2. Robin (Fictional character); 3. Superhero graphic novels; 4. Graphic novels
   978-1-4012-1224-7, $14.99
   After Bludhaven was destroyed in the Infinite Crisis, Dick Grayson relocated to New York City. It's a year later, and he has new friends, a new flame, and new criminal masterminds to fight. But, there's also another Nightwing, one who kills criminals without mercy - it's Jason Todd, the former Robin who succeeded Dick but was then killed by the Joker. He's been resurrected, but his idea of justice is twisted. And New York City has meta-human criminal kingpins, the Pierce brothers, who want both Nightwings dead. The book includes some sexual situations along with superhero violence.

Jones, Gerard
   ★ **Men** of Tomorrow: Geeks, Gangsters and the Birth of the Comic Book. Basic Books 2005 384p. Illustration
Grades: Adult Professional   **741.5**
   1. Comic books, strips, etc — History and criticism; 2. Popular culture — United States; 3. Graphic novels
   0-465-03657-0, $15
                                        LC 2004009031
   Jones chronicles the early history of the comic book, focusing on Jerry Siegel and Joe Schuster, who created Superman, and on Harry Donenfeld, a pornographer and

bootlegger looking for a way to beat the censors, and on his partner Jack Liebowitz, who forsook radical socialism for hardcore capitalism. Many of the early leaders in the comics industry were Jewish, and Jewish and Yiddish culture informed many of the comics superheroes.

Jones, Sabrina
★ **Isadora** Duncan: a graphic biography. Hill & Wang 2008 129p. Illustration
Grades: 9 10 11 12 Adult   **92; 792.8; 741.5**
1. Biographical graphic novels; 2. Dancers; 3. Duncan, Isadora, 1878-1927; 4. Graphic novels
978-0-8090-9497-4, $18.95
LC 2008-17928
Dancer Isadora Duncan thrilled and appalled her audiences at the turn of the twentieth century and beyond; she chose to wear freeflowing costumes with no corsets or other confining undergarments, and she danced barefoot. She used choreographic elements from the ancient Greeks, with flowing movements as free as her garments. Jones sifts through the various books about Duncan, from the autobiography and others, with all their contradictory information, to depict a unique and contradictory woman who deeply influenced modern dance well beyond her death. The black and white art shows Duncan always in Greek-styled gowns. There are two panels which show nudity in the context of Duncan's dance performances.
Includes bibliographical references.

Race to incarcerate: a graphic retelling. Sabrina Jones and Marc Mauer. The New Press 2013 128 p. Illustration
Grades: 9 10 11 12 Adult   **364.6; 364.6\0973**
1. Administration of criminal justice — United States; 2. Crime prevention; 3. Crime prevention — United States; 4. Criminal justice, Administration of — United States; 5. Discrimination in criminal justice administration — United States; 6. Imprisonment — United States; 7. Prison sentences — United States — Comic books, strrips, etc; 8. Prisons — United States; 9. Graphic novels
1595585419; 9781595585417, $17.95
LC 2012049688
"Jones channels the tradition of liberal-Left political cartooning to give this graphic documentary a dynamic, woodcut-like look that galvanizes its adaptation of Mauer's tract of the same name. Its subject is imprisonment in the U.S., especially, since the war on drugs was launched in the 1980s, the push to jail as many as possible (as it sometimes seems). Since the opening of the first 'penitentiary' in 1829 and preceded by 'getting tough on crime' policies, the war on drugs has reversed the emphasis on rehabilitation in U.S. prisons." (Booklist)
Includes bibliographical references and index
Based on Race to Incarcerate by Marc Mauer.

Jones, Steve
Introducing Genetics, New ed.. Steve Jones and Borin Van Loon. Totem Books 2005 176p. Illustration
Grades: 10 11 12 Adult   **576.5; 741.5**
1. Genetics; 2. Graphic novels
978-1-84046-636-2, $12.95
This book uses cartoons and a spare text to provide an introductory guide to the study of genetics, form Mendel to the human gene map and the treatment of inborn disease. It shows how DNA was discovered, and explains how some genes may act in their own interests as much as in the interests of those who carry them. Jones is a professor of genetics. The book includes a list of books for further reading.

Joy, Bob
Batman: The Greatest Stories Ever Told Volume Two. DC Comics 2007 208p. Illustration
Grades: 7 8 9 10 11 12 Adult   **741.5; Fic**
1. Batgirl (Fictional character); 2. Batman (Fictional character); 3. Joker (Fictional character); 4. Superhero graphic novels; 5. Graphic novels
978-1-4012-1214.8, $19.99
This volume includes stories from different periods in the nearly seventy-year career of Batman, from 1940 to 2003. He goes up against classic villains - the Joker, Killer Croc, the Penguin; he meets Batgirl (Barbara Gordon); deals with crooked businessmen and other criminals.

Flash: The Greatest Stories Ever Told. DC Comics 2007 208p. Illustration
Grades: 6 7 8 9 10 11 12 Adult   **Fic; 741.5**
1. Flash (Fictional character); 2. Superhero graphic novels; 3. Graphic novels
978-1-4012-1372-5, $19.99
Jay Garrick, Barry Allen, and Wally West are all men who have donned the symbol of the yellow lightning bolt to combat evil as the Flash. Each hero with his own unique style of commanding a mastery over momentum, they have fought separately and together over the years. This volume collects stories that see them pitted against such villains as Gorilla Grodd, the Reverse Flash, the Fiddler, and many others. This volume also includes the story of Barry and Iris' wedding.

The **Helmet** of fate. DC Comics 2007 128p. Illustration
Grades: 8 9 10 11 12 Adult   **741.5**
1. Superhero graphic novels; 2. Supernatural graphic novels; 3. Graphic novels
978-1-4012-1470-8, $14.99
The tenth age of magic is about to begin, but it needs a new champion, a new Dr. Fate. The Helmet of Fate seeks a new master and encounters some of the most powerful beings of the supernatural world on its quest. Candidates include Zauriel from JLA, Black Alice from Birds of Prey, Shadowpact's Detective Chimp (what!—), as well as Sargon the Sorcerer and Ibis the Invincible. Who will become the successor to Dr. Fate" The book includes some violence and some mild harsh language.

Showcase Presents: Batgirl Volume 1. DC Comics 2007 552p. Illustration
Grades: 6 7 8 9 10 11 12 Adult   **741.5; Fic**
1. Batgirl (Fictional character); 2. Superhero graphic novels; 3. Graphic novels
978-1-4012-1367-1, $16.99
In the late 1960s, DC Comics added a new character to the world of Batman and Robin: Batgirl. Daughter of Commissioner Jim Gordon, Barbara Gordon is a librarian who relocates to Gotham City and soon dons her costume as the crime fighting Batgirl. This volume of black and white

reprints includes her early adventures, from 1967 through 1975. The cover art notwithstanding, Batgirl is a woman of action.

Showcase Presents: Batman Vol. 1. DC Comics 2006 552p. Illustration
Grades: 6 7 8 9 10 11 12 Adult   **741.5; Fic**
  1. Batman (Fictional character); 2. Superhero graphic novels; 3. Graphic novels
  1-4012-1086-4, $16.99
The spotlight's on Batman in this volume featuring Detective Comics #327-342 and Batman #164-174. The Dynamic Duo take on some of their most enduring Rogues Gallery members, including Penguin, the Riddler, and the Outsider in these classic Silver Age stories from the era of famed editor Julius Schwartz. This Showcase edition reprints the comics in black and white.

Showcase Presents: Batman Vol. 2. DC Comics 2007 510p. Illustration
Grades: 6 7 8 9 10 11 12 Adult   **Fic; 741.5**
  1. Batgirl (Fictional character); 2. Batman (Fictional character); 3. Joker (Fictional character); 4. Riddler (Fictitious character); 5. Robin (Fictional character); 6. Superhero graphic novels; 7. Graphic novels
  978-1-4012-1362-6, $16.99
Over 500 pages of classic adventures are included in this volume collecting Silver Age tales of Batman and Robin as they face their most enduring enemies, including the Joker, Poison Ivy, the Riddler, Blockbuster, and many others. These are the stories that inspired the Dynamic Duo's 1960s TV series, which featured Batman's astonishing detective skills and impressive array of Bat-gadgets. The stories, reprinted in black and white, date from 1965 and 1966.

Superman/Doomsday: The Collected Edition. DC Comics 2006 412p. Illustration
Grades: 10 11 12 Adult   **741.5; Fic**
  1. Superhero graphic novels; 2. Superman (Fictional character); 3. Graphic novels
  978-1-4012-1107-3, $19.99
Doomsday killed Superman. Now the Man of Steel wants payback. Superman travesl to the nightmare world of Apokolips for a confrontation with Doomsday, the creature who cost the Man of Steel his life. With the help of the mysterious, time-traveling Waverider, superman at last discovers the shocking truth of his greatest enemy's origin. And just when he thinks the terror is finally over, the murderous juggernaut returns to Earth more powerful than ever.

Superman: The Amazing Transformations of Jimmy Olsen. DC Comics 2007 192p. Illustration
Grades: 6 7 8 9 10 11 12 Adult   **741.5; Fic**
  1. Humorous graphic novels; 2. Superhero graphic novels; 3. Superman (Fictional character); 4. Graphic novels
  978-1-4012-1369-5, $14.99
Cub reporter Jimmy Olsen stars in this light-hearted volume collecting some of his most memorable adventures from the late 1950s and 1960s, all of which guest-star Superman. While investigating crime for The Daily Planet, Jimmy undergoes one startling transformation after another, gaining temporary super-powers as Elastic Lad and

becoming a Giant Turtle Man, The Wolf-Man of Metropolis, The Human Porcupine and much more. At times like these, Superman finds that he must not only protect Metropolis from Jimmy, but Jimmy from himself.

Jurgens, Dan
  Combat Zone: True Tales of GIs in Iraq. Marvel Entertainment 2005 Un Illustration
Grades: 9 10 11 12 Adult   **Fic; 741.5**
  1. Iraq War, 2003-; 2. Graphic novels
  0-7851-1516-1, $19.99
Longtime embedded journalist Karl Zinsmeister (Boots on the Ground: A Month with the 82nd Airborne in the Battle for Iraq) and penciler Dan Jurgens (Thor, Superman) chronicle three months in the lives of the 82nd Airborne in the Battle for Iraq in this series. As Zinsmeister states in his introduction, the stories are all based on real-life accounts; he changed the names of the soldiers and in some cases combined some of the incidents. The book includes battlefield violence and some mildly strong language.

  DC Showcase presents Booster Gold volume 1. DC Comics 2008 624p. Illustration
Grades: 8 9 10 11 12 Adult   **741.5; Fic**
  1. Booster Gold (Fictional character); 2. Superhero graphic novels; 3. Graphic novels
  978-1-4012-1655-9, $16.99
This volume collects the entire run of the Booster Gold comics series written and drawn by Dan Jurgens and published from 1986 through 1988. Michael Jon Carter lives in the 25th century, and he wants thrills, wealth, and fame. He "borrows" items from the Space Museum and travels back in time to the twentieth century, where he uses his knowledge of things to come to build an empire and become the super hero, Booster Gold. His constant self-promotion annoys and offends the heroic community, and eventually he will have to learn that fame and fortune come at a price. DC brought Booster Gold back for its 2007 crossover event, 52, but here readers can find the original "anti-superhero."

Ka, Olivier
  ★ **Why** I killed Peter. Story, Olivier Ka; adaptation & art, Alfred; color, Henri Meunier. NBM 2008 112p. Illustration
Grades: 10 11 12 Adult   **741.5**
  1. Biographical graphic novels; 2. Catholic church — Clergy; 3. Child sexual abuse; 4. Graphic novels
  978-1-56163-543-6, $18.95
Olivier Ka writes of his life and of the lifelong effect of one particular act. He grows up in France, the child of what he describes as hippie parents. Their lifestyle is very open, and young Olivier sees adults naked a lot, and his parents sleep with other partners quite often. Into this comes young priest Peter, a liberal type of cleric who wears shirts and jeans rather than cassocks and other vestments, who plays the guitar during services. Olivier likes him a lot, because Peter really talks with him and listens, more like a fun uncle than a priest. Over the years, Peter remains a part of the family, and Olivier goes to his summer camps. Then the summer Olivier is twelve, Peter asks him to do something that makes Olivier uncomfortable. They will sleep side by side in their own sleeping bags, but completely naked "to be

equal," and they will massage each other's belly. It starts out like that, but ends . . . well. Olivier continues to go to the summer camps until he's fifteen, but he and Peter never do anything like that again. Years later, as an adult, Olivier suffers emotional problems, and attending services in a Catholic church makes him physically ill. Eventually, when his own daughter is twelve years old, Olivier writes this story, makes a friend who is an artist, and they create the graphic novel. And Olivier confronts Peter after so many years. The act Peter committed with Olivier is not depicted on the page, but there is nudity and some sexual situations, along with strong language.

Kafka, Franz
Kafka: Give It Up! And Other Short Stories. NBM/ComicsLit 1995 63p. Illustration
Grades: 10 11 12 Adult 741.5; Fic
1. Graphic novels
978-1-56163-449-1, $8.95
Peter Kuper adapts and illustrates nine stories by Kafka: "A Little Fable," "The Bridge," "Give It Up!," "A Hunger Artist," "dA Fratricide," "The Helmsman," "The Trees," "The Top," and "The Vulture."

Kaishaku
Key Princess Story: Eternal Alice Rondo Vol. 1. DrMaster Publications 2007 188p. Illustration
Grades: 10 11 12 Adult 741.5; Fic
1. Adventure graphic novels; 2. Fantasy graphic novels; 3. Manga; 4. Shonen manga; 5. Graphic novels
978-1-59796-113-2, $9.95
When Aruto Kirihara, an aspiring writer moved by the classic tale Alice in Wonderland, meets a group of magically gifted young girls, the literary fuel for a new and truly fantastic "Alice" story is revealed. This is an adventure of a hopeful scribe and a group of girls with special powers, the Alice Police, in pursuit of the missing third book of Alice called "Eternal Alice." This series includes some fan service shots and partial nudity.

Kakalios, James
The **Physics** of Superheroes. James Kakalios.. Gotham Books 2009 424 p.
Grades: 11 12 Adult 530
1. Batman (Fictional character); 2. Heroes and heroines; 3. Physics — Study and teaching; 4. Spider-Man (Fictional character); 5. Superman (Fictional character)
1592405088; 9781592405084, $18
LC 2009028814
"With The Physics of Superheroes, named one of the best science books of 2005 by Discover, he introduced his colorful approach to an even wider audience. Now Kakalios presents a totally updated, expanded edition that features even more superheroes and findings from the cutting edge of science. With three new chapters and completely revised throughout with a splashy, redesigned package, the book that explains why Spider-Man's webbing failed his girlfriend, the probable cause of Krypton's explosion, and the Newtonian physics at work in Gotham City is electrifying from cover to cover." (Publisher's Note)
"By combining his love for physics with his love of comic books, . . . Kakalios has written a book for the general

reader [that covers] all of the basic points in a first-level college physics course and is difficult to put down. . . . That all of this is accomplished with enough humor to make you laugh aloud is an added bonus." Pub Wkly
Includes bibliographical references and index

Kamio, Yoko
Boys Over Flowers (Hana Yori Dango) Volume 1. Viz Media/Shojo 2003 208p. Illustration
Grades: 9 10 11 12 Adult 741.5; Fic
1. Manga; 2. Romance graphic novels; 3. Shojo manga; 4. Graphic novels
1-56931-996-0, $9.99
When her only friend, Makiko, accidentally offends F4 leader Tsukasa, Tsukushi boldly defends her. Enraged, Tsukasa puts the dreaded red tag in Tsukushi's locker - a sign that she is now a target for the abuse of the F4 gang and the entire school. But when Tsukushi fights the gang with their own weapon, Tsukasa finds himself falling for her. Tsukushi comes from a poor family but attends a prestigious school ruled by the rich students; she manages to hold her own against any bullying. There's some violence in the bullying, and some sexual situations.

Kanari, Youzaburou
Gimmick! volume 1. Viz Media 2008 226p. Illustration
Grades: 10 11 12 Adult 741.5; Fic
1. Adventure graphic novels; 2. Manga; 3. Mystery graphic novels; 4. Graphic novels
978-1-4215-1778-0, $9.99
Kohei Nagase is a prodigy in creating makeup and special effects, and he runs Studio Gimmick with his stuntman friend and sidekick, Kannazuki. While Kohei depends on Ms Shiho to help him find paying work for movie and television studios, his passion for creating makeup effects leads him to helping people. For instance, a young starlet wants to escape her sleazy manager and reunite with her boyfriend. Then there's the actress who had been in a horrible accident and wants to hide the hideous scar on her body when the studio wants to film a nude scene. Then a horror theme park hires Kohei to redo the zombie dummies, but he runs afoul of the original makeup artist, who is determined to destroy the park in vengeance for being fired. Kohei is a bit sukebe and ecchi (kind of perverted) and visibly lusts after the beautiful young actresses, but his passion for makeup rules everything for him. The stories include some frontal nudity and some violence.

Kindaichi Case Files Vol. 14: The Gentleman Thief. Story by Yozaburo Kanari; art by Fumiya Sato. Tokyopop 2006 Un Illustration
Grades: 9 10 11 12 Adult 741.5; Fic
1. Manga; 2. Mystery graphic novels; 3. Shonen manga; 4. Graphic novels
1-59532-698-7, $9.99
11th grader Hajime Kindaichi is considered a slacker, but he's actually a genius detective and the grandson of famous detective Kousuke Kindaichi. In this volume, Hajime and his best friend Miyuki travel to Aomori with Detective Kenmochi to try to prevent a thief from stealing a painting from artist Gozo Gamou, who has assembled a party to unveil his painting. The Gentleman Thief issues a

challenge to Kindaichi, then raises the stakes by committing murder. Each volume in the series is a standalone murder mystery involving locked rooms and serial murders; in each volume, at least one body is found partially nude.

The **Kindaichi** case files vol. 17: the undying butterflies. Tokyopop 2008 Un Illustration
Grades: 8 9 10 11 12 Adult   **741.5; Fic**
1. Manga; 2. Mystery graphic novels; 3. Graphic novels
978-1-59532-701-7, $9.99
The article about the discoverer of a rediscovered species of butterfly is not the sort of thing that teenage detective Hajime Kindaichi would care about, but the photograph included with the article catches his eye; the assistant to Madarame, the butterfly expert, looks identical to Eiji Touno, a killer Kindaichi had uncovered and whom he thought had died in a massive fire. Kindaichi, best friend Miyuki, and their detective buddy Itsuki, travel to Madarame's impressive estate to uncover the mystery about Touno. However, while they are there, murders begin to occur, starting tragically with Madarame's youngest daughter Ruri, who is only twelve years old. Can Kindaichi match wits with the murderer and stop him? There is little bloodshed or overt violence in this murder mystery, and one instance of nonsexual partial nudity.

Kindaichi Case Files Volume 1: The Opera House Murders. Tokyopop 2003 186p. Illustration
Grades: 8 9 10 11 12 Adult   **741.5; Fic**
1. Manga; 2. Mystery graphic novels; 3. Shonen manga; 4. Graphic novels
1-59182-354-4, $9.99
Teenager Hajime Kindaichi is a slacker, but a genius at solving mysteries, which is needed when the Fudo High drama club travels to a hotel on an isolated island to rehearse the play, 'Phantom of the Opera.' People start turning up dead, murdered in ways appearing in the play, and with no way off the island, Hajime better find the killer before everyone dies. The book includesgraphic violence, some strong language, and some nudity (usually the dead bodies).

Kanata, Konami
★ **Chi's** sweet home, volume 1. Vertical, Inc. 2010 166p. Illustration
Grades: 5 6 7 8 9 10 11 12 Adult   **741.5; Fic**
1. Cats; 2. Humorous graphic novels; 3. Manga; 4. Graphic novels
9781-934287-81-1
Young kitten Chi gets separated from her family while out on a stroll, then she meets little boy Yohei and his parents. They take her home, even though their apartment building has a strict no pets policy. While they try to find someone to take her in, they feed her, give her a cozy bed, set up a box with shredded newspaper for a litter box, and do their best to help her. Even though readers can read what she's thinking, Chi behaves just like a cat, with cat problems such as thinking the litter box is a wonderful play area instead of the place to do her business, and taking fright at Yohei's "vrooming" as he plays with his toy cars. The book is great for younger readers as well as anyone who likes cats. There is one panel where Yohei is sitting on the toilet while Chi is in her litter box in the bathroom, and a scene at the veterinarian's office where the doctor sticks a thermometer

in to take Chi's temperature. And, of course, Chi tends to urinate in inappropriate places.
Also available in 3-in-1 omnibus editions
Volume 1 of 12

Kane, Bob
Batman Archives Volume 1. Bob Kane and Bill Finger. DC Comics 1990 304p. Illustration
Grades: 7 8 9 10 11 12 Adult   **Fic; 741.5**
1. Batman (Fictional character); 2. Robin (Fictional character); 3. Superhero graphic novels; 4. Graphic novels
978-0-930289-60-7, $39.95
When a young Bruce Wayne watched in horror as his parents were murdered, the legend of the Batman was born. Collected here are the first stories of the masked vigilante as they were originally printed in 1939. These stories include the classic first appearance of the Batman and the introduction of his teenage ally, Robin. These early adventures show how a dark and grim character and his humorous and light sidekick were masterfully combined to create one of the most enduring partnerships of all time.

The **Batman** Chronicles Volume Two. Bob Kane and Bill Finger. DC Comics 2006 224p. Illustration
Grades: 7 8 9 10 11 12 Adult   **Fic; 741.5**
1. Batman (Fictional character); 2. Catwoman (Fictional character); 3. Joker (Fictional character); 4. Robin (Fictional character); 5. Superhero graphic novels; 6. Graphic novels
978-1-4012-0790-8, $14.99
This series reprints the Batman comics in chronological order; this second volume includes stories originally published in 1940. Batman is becoming more of a father figure to Robin; the villains become more colorful, the scientists get madder; the Dynamic Duo take on the Joker, Catwoman, Clayface, and more classic Bat-villains.

Batman in the eighties. Batman created by Bob Kane; [introduction by John Wells]. DC Comics 2004 191p. Illustration
Grades: 9 10 11 12 Adult   **741; 741.5; Fic**
1. Batgirl (Fictional character); 2. Batman (Comic strip); 3. Batman (Fictional character); 4. Robin (Fictional character); 5. Superhero graphic novels; 6. Graphic novels
1-4012-0241-1, $19.95
The events featured in this collection "include Dick Grayson's transformation into Nightwing, Barbara Gordon's final days as Batgirl and the introduction of not one, but two new versions of Robin. The stories in this volume may not include the greatest highlights of the decade, but do serve to round out many of the events that affected the Batman mythos during the 1980's." Libr Media Connect

Batman in the forties. Batman created by Bob Kane; [introduction by Bill Schelly]. DC Comics 2004 192p. Illustration
Grades: 9 10 11 12 Adult   **741; 741.5; Fic**
1. Batman (Fictional character); 2. Catwoman (Fictional character); 3. Joker (Fictional character); 4. Robin (Fictional character); 5. Superhero graphic novels; 6. Graphic novels
1-4012-0206-3, $19.95

"The 17 selections include such milestones as Batman's first appearance in May 1939, the two-page story of his origins from November 1939, and the 1940 introduction of his young partner, Robin. . . . Other stories feature early appearances by some of Batman's most renowned arch-enemies: the Joker, Catwoman, and Two-Face. . . . Most compelling are the earliest stories; crude as they are, their naive verve and raw directness remain effective." Booklist

Originally published (1939-1949) in single magazine form as Batman 7, 15, 20, 31, 37, 47, 48, 49, Detective Comics 27, 33, 38, 49, 80, Real Fact Comics 5, Star-Spangled Comics 70, World's Finest Comics 30

Kanigher, Robert
Showcase Presents: The Haunted Tank Volume 1. Art by Joe Kubert and Russ Heath. DC Comics 2006 560p. Illustration
Grades: 7 8 9 10 11 12 Adult   **741.5; Fic**
1. Ghosts; 2. World War, 1939-1945; 3. Graphic novels
1-4012-0789-8, $16.99
What happens when the ghost of General J. E. B. Stuart, a long-deceased Confederate general, returns to act as a protector to his namesake, Sgt. Jeb Stuart, commander of a tank in North Africa during World War II" These stories combine the fast-paced action of war with a supernatural bent. This black and white volume reprints the first thirty-three tales of the Haunted Tank, dating from 1961 to 1966. Writer Kanigher was just voted into the Eisner Awards Hall of Fame as a Judges' Choice in 2007.

Showcase Presents: Wonder Woman Vol. 1. DC Comics 2007 528p. Illustration
Grades: 6 7 8 9 10 11 12 Adult   **741.5; Fic**
1. Superhero graphic novels; 2. Wonder Woman (Fictional character); 3. Graphic novels
978-1-4012-1373-2, $16.99
Wonder Woman faces some of her deadliest challenges as she battles a variety of aliens and robots, and confronts the evil menaces of the Time Master, the Gadget Maker, Dike of Deception, and one of her most incessant foes, the Angle Man. This volume also includes the re-done origin of Wonder Woman, and some of her teenage adventures as Wonder Girl. Created by William Moulton Marston as a strong, liberated warrior in 1941, these adventures published in the late 1950s and early 1960s cast Wonder Woman in a more "traditional" female superhero role.

Kannenberg, Gene
500 essential graphic novels: the ultimate guide. Collins Design 2008 528p. Illustration
Grades: Adult Professional   **741.5**
1. Graphic novels — Bibliography
978-0-06-147451-4, $24.95
Divided into ten chapters (Adventure, NonFiction, Crime and Mystery, Fantasy, General Fiction, Horror, Humor, Science Fiction, Superheroes, War), the book lists the Top 10 books in each category and then "the best of the rest." Each entry has a color photo of the cover, a star rating for quality, short plot synopsis, a short critical review (one paragraph long), plus a suggested age rating. Kannenberg includes books that are no longer in print, which may limit this book's usefulness for collection development.

Kanno, Aya
Blank slate volume 1. Viz Media/Shojo Beat 2008 Un Illustration
Grades: 10 11 12 Adult   **741.5; Fic**
1. Adventure graphic novels; 2. Manga; 3. Mystery graphic novels; 4. Shojo manga; 5. Graphic novels
978-1-4215-1924-1, $8.99
Zen is a beautiful young man with no memory of who or what he was, all he knows is that he gets urges to kill and he does so. The nation of Amata had been taken over by the Galayans twenty years ago, and Zen inadvertently gets involved with the resistance when he kidnaps the Galay general's daughter Rian. He ends up with Hakka, an unlicensed doctor who helps the Amatans. But what does Hakka know about Zen? This book includes considerable violence.

Kaplan, Arie
Speed Racer: chronicles of the racer. Art by Robby Musso and German Torres. IDW Publishing 2008 Un Illustration
Grades: 5 6 7 8 9 10 11 12 Adult   **741.5; Fic**
1. Adventure graphic novels; 2. Automobile racing; 3. Racer, Speed (Fictional character); 4. Graphic novels
978-1-60010-213-4, $17.99
After a race in which something happens to Speed's Mach 5 and he's saved by Racer X, Pop Racer gives Speed a book, The Chronicles of the Racer. For thousands of years, there has been one Racer in their family, one who is destined to win. And for those thousands of years, the Racer has dealt with a villain who is associated with Mercury. From ancient Rome to medieval England to eighteenth century pirates and onward, Speed finds himself reliving his ancestors' experiences after he sneaks into Mercury Studios, and he finds himself face-to-face with the same man who has battled his ancestors through the centuries. This book collects the four-issue miniseries of original stories based on the Speed Racer characters.

Kardy, Glenn
Manga University Presents . . . Kana de Manga Special Edition: Japanese Sound FX!. Writer, Glenn Kardy; artist, Chihiro Hattori. Japanime Co. Ltd./Manga University 2007 110p. Illustration
Grades: 6 7 8 9 10 11 12 Adult   **495.6; 741.5**
1. Japanese language; 2. Manga; 3. Graphic novels
978-4-921205-12-6, $9.99
What does a cat's meow sound like in Japanese? How about the grumble of an empty stomach, the wail of a police car's siren or the crash of an ocean wave? Japanese manga artists rely heavily upon onomatopoeia—sound-effect words—and this entry in the Kana de Manga / Kanji de Manga language-learning series includes illustrated examples of those sounds in action. It features more than 100 Japanese onomatopoeia and their English equivalents in categories such as "Humans," "Animals," "Machines" and "Nature." The text is written in both English and Japanese hiragana.

Manga University Presents ... Kana de Manga: A Fun, Easy Way to Learn the ABCs of Japanese!. Text by Glenn

Kardy ; art by Chihiro Hattori Japanime Co. Ltd 2004 113p. Illustration

Grades: 5 6 7 8 9 10 11 12 Adult   **495.6; 741.5**
  1. Japanese language — Teaching — Aids and devices; 2. Manga; 3. Graphic novels
  4-921205-01-9, $9.99

This book uses original manga artwork to teach students how to read, write and pronounce the Japanese hiragana and katakana alphabets, also known as "kana." Author Glenn Kardy and artist Chihiro Hattori have teamed up to create this book for manga enthusiasts who are interested in more than just pretty pictures. In addition to presenting the kana, the book illustrates stroke order in writing the characters, and each hiragana character is shown with a word, its definition, an illustration, and opportunities for practice in writing the character.

Manga University Presents ... Kanji deManga: The Comic Book That Teaches You How to Read and Write Japanese! Volume 1. Created by Glenn Kardy ; art by Chihiro Hattori. Japanime Co. Ltd 2004 113p. Illustration

Grades: 5 6 7 8 9 10 11 12 Adult   **495.6; 741.5**
  1. Japanese language — Teaching — Aids and devices; 2. Manga; 3. Graphic novels
  4-921205-02-7, $9.99

This book uses original comic artwork to teach readers how to identify and write the most common Japanese kanji ideographs. It introduces 80 basic kanji that all Japanese schoolchildren are required to learn before entering the third grade, or for those who wish to pass Level 4 of the Japanese Language Proficiency Test for non-native speakers of Japanese. Each page features its own comic strip, kanji pronunciation guide, stroke order, and English explanations.

Manga University Presents ... Kanji deManga: The Comic Book That Teaches You How to Read and Write Japanese! Volume 2. Japanime Co. Ltd 2005 113p. Illustration

Grades: 7 8 9 10 11 12 Adult   **495.6; 741.5**
  1. Japanese language — Teaching — Aids and devices; 2. Manga; 3. Graphic novels
  4-921205-03-5, $9.99

The second volume in this series - using original comic artwork to teach readers how to identify and write the most common Japanese kanji ideographs - introduces 80 kanji that all Japanese school children are required to learn by the time they graduate from sixth grade, or for those who wish to pass Level 3 of the Japanese Language Proficiency Test for non-native speakers of Japanese. Each page features its own comic strip, kanji pronunciation guide, stroke order, and English explanations.

Manga University Presents ... Kanji deManga: The Comic Book That Teaches You How to Read and Write Japanese! Volume 3. Japanime Co. Ltd 2005 113p. Illustration

Grades: 7 8 9 10 11 12 Adult   **495.6; 741.5**
  1. Japanese language — Teaching — Aids and devices; 2. Manga; 3. Graphic novels
  4-921205-04-3, $9.99

The third volume in this series - using original comic artwork to teach readers how to identify and write the most common Japanese kanji ideographs - introduces 80 more

kanji that all Japanese school children are required to learn by the time they graduate from sixth grade, or for those who wish to pass Level 3 of the Japanese Language Proficiency Test for non-native speakers of Japanese. Each page features its own comic strip, kanji pronunciation guide, stroke order, and English explanations.

Manga University Presents ... Kanji deManga: The Comic Book That Teaches You How to Read and Write Japanese! Volume 4. Japanime Co. Ltd 2006 144p. Illustration

Grades: 7 8 9 10 11 12 Adult   **495.6; 741.5**
  1. Japanese language — Teaching — Aids and devices; 2. Manga; 3. Graphic novels
  4-921205-09-4, $9.99

The fourth volume in this series - using original comic artwork to teach readers how to identify and write the most common Japanese kanji ideographs - introduces 80 more kanji that all Japanese school children are required to learn by the time they graduate from sixth grade, or for those who wish to pass Level 3 of the Japanese Language Proficiency Test for non-native speakers of Japanese. Each page features its own comic strip, kanji pronunciation guide, stroke order, and English explanations.

Kari, Erika
  Vampire Doll: Guilt-na-Zan Vol. 1. Tokyopop 2006 196p. Illustration

Grades: 8 9 10 11 12 Adult   **741.5; Fic**
  1. Horror graphic novels; 2. Humorous graphic novels; 3. Manga; 4. Graphic novels
  1-59816-519-4, $9.99

Guilt-na-Zan is a vampire aristocrat who has been sealed into a cross for more than 100 years. When he is released by Kyoji, a powerful exorcist from the family that first banished the vampire, Guilt-na-Zan is resurrected as a female doll and can only transform into his real form when he sucks blood from Kyoji's sister Tonae. Kyoji uses Guilt-na-Zan and his old servant Vincent as Tonae's bodyguards at school. They also have to deal with black sheep brother Kyoichi, who constantly tries to steal old family artifacts, trying to gain occult power. The series includes some mild sexual encounters.

Kariya, Tetsu
  Oishinbo a la carte: the joy of rice. Story by Tetsu Kariya ; art by Akira Hanasaki. Viz Signature Edition 2009 268p. Illustration

Grades: 8 9 10 11 12 Adult   **741.5; Fic**
  1. Cooking; 2. Manga; 3. Rice; 4. Graphic novels
  978-1-4215-2144-2, $12.99

This volume collects the Oishinbo stories centering on rice, the supreme staple of the Japanese diet. As Yamaoka continues, with the help of other Tozai News staffers, to work on the newspaper's Ultimate Menu to celebrate its 100th anniversary, they examine rice. Among other stories, Yamaoka rails against the importing of rice from other countries; he shows that organic rice farming could be unhealthy depending on the farm's location; and he helps the company cafeteria chef attract more business by focusing on homestyle rice dishes. The big competition between the Ultimate Menu and the Supreme Menu is rice balls (omusubi). The stories here may help American readers understand a little more about how important rice is to Japanese culture, and they may want to try some of the dishes. The book includes a recipe for scallop rice, which is published in color with photos. As with the other volumes, this book includes stories that originally appeared throughout the original manga series, so the characters' lives and relationships change abruptly from story to story.

Courtesy of Viz Media

Oishinbo a la carte: vegetables. Story by Tetsu Kariya ; art by Akira Hanasaki. Viz Media/Viz Signature 2009 268p. Illustration
Grades: 8 9 10 11 12 Adult
741.5; Fic
1. Cooking — Vegetables; 2. Manga; 3. Graphic novels
978-1-4215-2143-5, $12.99
Tozai News reporter Yamaoka Shiro and his colleagues continue their quest for the Ultimate Menu. In this volume, he competes against his father Kaibara, who represents rival newspaper Teito Times and their Supreme Menu, in a competition involving the vegetables cabbage and turnip. In other stories, Yamaoka and his friends use asparagus as a way to reunite a culinary specialist and a pottery artist who broke up years ago; and they help Tomii's son get over his hatred of eggplant. A number of the stories discuss the debate between organic cultivation and the use of pesticides and imported vegetable types. Since the stories are selected from the Oishinbo series to fit into themes, they skip around in time and lack a real narrative flow. The book is suitable for teens, but the main appeal may be to adults, especially to those who want to read about food. The artist's focus on presenting all the vegetables so realistically and in great detail may just make the reader hungry.

Katakura, Masanori-Ookamigumi
Kurohime Vol. 1. Viz Media/Shonen Jump Advanced 2007 182p. Illustration
Grades: 10 11 12 Adult
741.5; Fic
1. Adventure graphic novels; 2. Fantasy graphic novels; 3. Manga; 4. Shonen manga; 5. Graphic novels
978-1-4215-1366-9, $7.99
Kurohime is a big busty witch with the command of magical guns. She was once foolish enough to challenge the Gods and in doing so was punished. A curse was put on her that turned her into a little girl. The only way she can break this curse and turn back in to her big bad buxom self is to fall in love. Master gunman Zero searches the land for the legendary Kurohime, because she saved him as a child and impressed upon him the importance of justice and helping others. He meets a young girl named Himeko; little does he know that she is actually Kurohime. This book includes lots of sexual suggestiveness and some violence.

Katchor, Ben
Hand drying in America. Ben Katchor. Pantheon Books 2013 160 p.

Grades: Adult
741.5/973; Fic
1. Cartoons and caricatures; 2. Urbanization; 3. Graphic novels
0307906906; 9780307906908, $29.95
LC 2012018003
This is a collection of four years' worth of cartoonist Ben Katchor's "cartoons about urban living. . . . Some of the . . . stories involve buildings with peculiar characteristics—the shoe-fitting bench in 'The Symbolic Building,' or 'The Souvenir Museum,' where a single souvenir is offered for sale in the gift shop." (Kirkus)

Katin, Miriam
Letting It Go. Miriam Katin. Farrar Straus & Giroux 2013 160 p. Illustration
Grades: Adult
940.53
1. Berlin (Germany) — Description; 2. Holocaust survivors; 3. Katin, Miriam
1770461035; 9781770461031, $24.95
In this memoir graphic novel, by Miriam Katin, "a Holocaust survivor and mother, Katin's world is turned upside down by the news that her adult son is moving to Berlin, a city she's villainized for the past forty years. As she struggles to accept her son's decision, she visits the city twice, first to see her son and then to attend a museum gala featuring her own artwork. What she witnesses firsthand is a city coming to terms with its traumatic past, much as Katin is herself." (Publisher's note)

We are on our own: a memoir. Drawn & Quarterly 2006 122p. Illustration
Grades: 9 10 11 12 Adult
92; 741; 741.5
1. Animators; 2. Artists; 3. Autobiographical graphic novels; 4. Cartoonists; 5. Holocaust, 1933-1945; 6. Illustrators; 7. Katin, Miriam; 8. Katin, Miriam; 9. World War, 1939-1945
1-896597-20-3, $19.95
LC 2005-9063602
In this WWII memoir, the author recounts "how she and her mother faked their deaths and fled Budapest after the Nazis occupied the city. With forged papers obtained from a black marketer, they escaped to the countryside in the guise of a servant girl and her illegitimate child. Katin relates their harrowing lives there and her mother's desperate search for her missing husband after the war. . . . This impressive book belongs in all serious graphic novel collections and is also a natural for Jewish studies." Booklist

Kawasaki, Anton
Batman Black and White Volume 3. DC Comics 2007 288p. Illustration
Grades: 10 11 12 Adult
741.5; Fic
1. Batman (Fictional character); 2. Superhero graphic novels; 3. Graphic novels
978-1-4012-1531-6, $24.99
This third volume in the series collects thirty-three stories written and illustrated by creators from the mainstream and the independent comics world, including Brian Azzarello, John Bolton, Ed Brubaker, Mike Carey, Darwyn Cooke, Todd Dezago, Paul Grist, Michael Golden, Dick Giordano, Geoff Johns, Jim Mahfood, Dwayne McDuffie, Mike Mignola, Scott Morese, Ann Nocenti,

Whilce Portacio, Mark Schultz, Julius Schwartz, Judd Winick, Bill Wray, and many more. Some of the stories have overt violence.

JLA: The Greatest Stories Ever Told. DC Comics 2006 192p. Illustration

Grades: 9 10 11 12 Adult   Fic; 741.5

1. Aquaman (Fictitious character); 2. Batman (Fictional character); 3. Flash (Fictional character); 4. Green Arrow (Fictional character); 5. Green Lantern (Fictional character); 6. Justice League of America (Fictional characters); 7. Superhero graphic novels; 8. Superman (Fictional character); 9. Wonder Woman (Fictional character)

978-1-4012-0932-2, $19.99

Superman. Batman. Wonder Woman. Green Lantern. The Flash. Aquaman. Martian Manhunter. Green Arrow. Black Canary. They are the World's Greatest Super-Heroes, and they compose the Justice League of America. For over 45 years, this all-star team of DC's greatest characters has entertained generations of comics fans. And now, this new collection reprints eight of their greatest tales in one volume, covering nearly every era and incarnation of the League, from classic adventures of the Silver Age, to stories that formed the basis of the best-selling Identity Crisis, to newer tales featuring a humorous League and the return of the classic lineup.

Superman/Batman: The Greatest Stories Ever Told. DC Comics 2007 192p. Illustration

Grades: 9 10 11 12 Adult   741.5; Fic

1. Batman (Fictional character); 2. Superhero graphic novels; 3. Superman (Fictional character); 4. Graphic novels

978-1-4012-1227-8, $19.99

They are two of the world's biggest icons, and they couldn't be more different. One is the most powerful being on the planet with an array of superpowers, a shining symbol of hope embodying truth, justice, and the American way. The other has no powers, but has trained his mind and body to the peak of perfection, a dark vigilante determined to strike fear into evildoers' hearts. Together, this popular and unlikely pair starred in numerous team-ups over several decades; this book collects ten of those stories, from 1952 to the 2000s.

Kawashima, Tadashi

Alive Vol. 1. Story by Tadashi Kawashima; art by Adachitoka. Random House/Del Rey Manga 2007 200p. Illustration

Grades: 10 11 12 Adult   741.5; Fic

1. Manga; 2. Shonen manga; 3. Graphic novels

978-0-345-49746-8, $10.95

A strange virus is making its way around the globe, causing its victims to commit suicide, and becoming a lethal pandemic in less than a week. Then Taisuke finds his shy, withdrawn friend Hiro, who has always been the target of bullies, on the roof of their high school, with the bloody, dead bodies of the four bullies. And when Hiro turns on him, Taisuke discovers he has powers, too. What's going on? This first volume raises lots of questions. The book includes some harsh language and graphic violence.

Keatinge, Joe

Glory 1: The Once and Future Destroyer. Written by Joe Keatinge; illustrated by Ross Campbell. Image Comics 2012 144 p. Color illustration

Grades: Adult   741.5

1. Science fiction comic books, strips, etc; 2. Graphic novels

1607066041; 9781607066040, $9.99

Authors Joe Keatinge and Ross Campbell present a collection of comic stories featuring the fictional character Glory. "After missing for almost a decade, GLORY's whereabouts are uncovered by a lone reporter, but the globe-spanning conspiracy keeping her hidden from humanity could make her return more dangerous than anyone ever anticipated! This first collection . . . reintroduces GLORY to a new century by revealing secrets from her past, journeying to the far-flung future and beginning a war unlike any we've seen before." (Publisher's note)

Shutter; Volume 1: Wanderlost. Joe Keatinge; illustrated by Leila Del Duca, Owen Gieni, Ed Brisson. Image Comics 2014 136 p. Color illustration

Grades: 11 12 Adult   Fic; 741.5

1. Explorers; 2. Family secrets — Fiction

1632151456; 9781632151452, $9.99

In this graphic novel by Joe Keatinge, illustrated by Leila Del Duca, Owen Gieni, and Ed Brisson, "Kate Kristopher, once the most famous explorer of an Earth far more fantastic than the one we know, is forced to return to the adventurous life she left behind when a family secret threatens to destroy everything she spent her life protecting." (Publisher's note)

"Keatinge and Del Duca have created a contemporary world that teems with casual miracles and feels all the more real and lived in for it. Crammed with the elements of children's storybooks, the art offers soft lines and a panoply of almost-recognizable storybook figures that honor those hallowed childhood recollections." Booklist

Originally published in single magazine form as Shutter #1-6

Volume 1 of an ongoing series

Keith, Sam

Batman: Secrets. Sam Kieth, writer, artist; Alex Sinclair, colorist; Rob Leigh, Phil Balsman, Travis Lanham, letterers. DC Comics 2007 128p. Illustration

Grades: 9 10 11 12 Adult   741.5; Fic

1. Batman (Fictional character); 2. Joker (Fictional character); 3. Superhero graphic novels; 4. Graphic novels

978-1-4012-1212-4, $12.99

This is a story that pits the Dark Knight against the Joker—all under the unforgiving eye of the media. Their confrontation is caught on film, and Gotham City's protector appears to pummel his archenemy without mercy. The Joker uses this to frame Batman in the court of public opinion while the media hover like vultures, ready to convict before all the facts are in. But it gets worse when the Joker threatens someone from Bruce Wayne's past, and this brings back tormented memories that Batman has kept hidden for years. Keith's eccentric art style might not be to everyone's taste.

Kelly, Joe

★ **Captain** Stoneheart and the Truth Fairy. Image Comics 2008 Un Illustration
Grades: 5 6 7 8 9 10 11 12 Adult   **741.5; Fic**
1. Adventure graphic novels; 2. Fairies; 3. Fantasy graphic novels; 4. Pirates; 5. Graphic novels
978-1-58240-865-1, $19.99

The story, in rhyming text with lushly drawn and colored art, tells the tale of the pirate named Captain Stoneheart, a fierce and angry pirate who won't let people tell him what to do. After attacking a peaceful ship and killing everyone on it, his crew discovers a caged fairy in the hold, and Stoneheart knows he can wreak havoc and scourge the world with her powers. Somehow they connect even through his anger, and when she finds a way to save Stoneheart and his crew even when she is free to leave the pirates and save herself, Stoneheart starts to change. Alas, the good times can't last, and he commits one final act that destroys everything and everyone around him because he won't let anyone tell him what to do, even if he loves that one person. There is some fighting violence, and there are some monsters, so this is not a story for very young readers. Older elementary school age children who love the old fairy tales with the tragic endings will be able to handle this story.

★ **Deadpool** Classic 1. Marvel 2008 256 p. Color; Illustration
Grades: Adult   **741.5**
1. Deadpool (Fictional character); 2. Superhero comic books, strips, etc
9780785131243, $29.99; 0785131248

"Deadpool, with sidekick Weasel in tow, sets out on a quest for romance, money, and mayhem - not necessarily in that order - only to learn he's being hunted by an enemy he killed years before! As if that isn't enough, the Juggernaut crashes into the action, and it's the unstoppable vs. the un-shut-up-able!" (Publisher's note)

Justice League Elite Volume One. Doug Mahnke, collaborator; John Byrne, collaborator; Tom Nguyen, collaborator. DC Comics 2005 Un Illustration
Grades: 9 10 11 12 Adult   **741.5; Fic**
1. Justice League (Fictional characters); 2. Superhero graphic novels; 3. Graphic novels
1-4012-0481-3, $19.99

Conflicting goals causes a schism among the Justice League of America. As a result, several members of the JLA choose to do undercover work with Vera Black and her super-powered team, the Elite. Their first assignment: infiltrate a small brotherhood of assassins gathering to hit a major political target. Heroes find themselves suddenly allied with deadly foes. Can this group function effectively enough to do their job" And if they can't, what happens to the world" The book includes some strong language, although most of it is masked in nonsense symbols, and violence.

Space Ghost. Joe Kelly, writer ; Ariel Olivetti, illustrator ; Richard Starkings, letterer. DC Comics 2005 Un Illustration
Grades: 8 9 10 11 12 Adult   **741.5; Fic**
1. Superhero graphic novels; 2. Graphic novels
1-4012-0721-9, $14.99

The masked avenger of the cartoon spaceways has been a popular character since his introduction to television in 1966. Since then, people have wondered who he is, how he got those power bands and why he protects the galaxy from evil. Now his story is told for the first time ever, and readers will learn the tragic circumstances that led to his donning a cowl and his first battle with arch nemesis Zorak. This is not the funny character from Cartoon Network.

Kelly, Walt

Walt Kelly's Our Gang Vol. 1. Fantagraphics Books 2006 104p. Illustration
Grades: 4 5 6 7 8 9 10 11 12 Adult   **741.5; Fic**
1. Friendship; 2. Humorous graphic novels; 3. Graphic novels
978-1-56097-753-7, $12.95

Kelly's longest-running continuing comics series was based on the "real-life" characters of MGM's durable short-film series, "Our Gang" (a.k.a. "The Little Rascals"). Kelly's Our Gang harks back to the days before television, when kids spent most of their time playing outdoors, limited only by each other's imagination and ingenuity. This is the first in a series of books reprinting Walt Kelly's Our Gang stories. Suitable for both adults and children, they have been restored from their comic book appearance. These stories were originally published in 1942 and 1943.

Volume 1 of 4

Kelso, Megan

The **Squirrel** Mother: Stories. Fantagraphics Books 2006 147p. Illustration
Grades: 10 11 12 Adult   *Courtesy of Fantagraphics*
741.5; Fic
1. Graphic novels
978-1-56097-746-9, $16.95

Kelso's work is characterized by subject matter that fits roughly into two disparate camps: personal and semi-autobiographical stories that draw heavily on the details of her childhood and adolescence, and stories about the idea of America and American history, such as a trilogy of short pieces about Alexander Hamilton. This book features 15 stories, including two stories, "Meow Face" and "Aide de Camp," done especially for this volume. The personal stories are each self-contained but in a sense take place in the same world where similar characters inhabit different stories. The "America" stories are broader in subject matter, taking on events of political and historical significance and wrestling with ideas having to do with the American experience.

Kennedy, Mike

Alien vs. Predator: Thrill of the Hunt. Story, Mike Kennedy; pencils, Roger Robinson with Dustin Weaver. Dark Horse Comics 2004 Un Illustration
Grades: 10 11 12 Adult   **741.5; Fic**

1. Horror graphic novels; 2. Science fiction graphic novels; 3. Graphic novels
1-59307-257-0, $6.95

In the future, after a technological catastrophe that started a second dark age, all memory of vicious bug-like aliens and brutal predatory aliens that hunted humans has been forgotten. Now, mankind has reached out to space again, and humans are once again caught in the middle of a deadly struggle between the two most lethal species ever encountered. And once again, whoever wins ... humans lose. The book includes some bloody violence.

Aliens vs. Predator: civilized beasts. Mike Kennedy; illustrated by Roger Robinson. Dark Horse Comics 2008 Un Illustration
Grades: 9 10 11 12 Adult   **741.5; Fic**
1. Horror graphic novels; 2. Science fiction graphic novels; 3. Graphic novels
978-1-59307-342-8, $6.95

It was supposed to have been a short business tour, but the group has been stranded on the remote planet for eight months. The humans have been aided by a Predator they've named Smiley, and occasionally they have to hunt an alien out to kill them. When a rescue ship arrives, however, it is crewed by illegal synthetic humans, then everyone gets mixed into the Predators' new hunt of Aliens. Whoever wins, the humans will lose. The book includes considerable violence, including the tearing off of limbs.

Superman: Infinite City. Art by Carlos Meglia. DC Comics 2005 96p. Illustration
Grades: 8 9 10 11 12 Adult   **741.5; Fic**
1. Superhero graphic novels; 2. Superman (Fictional character); 3. Graphic novels
978-1-4012-0066-4, $17.99

When a villain uses a very powerful weapon in Metropolis, Clark and Lois trace him back to an old town called Infinite City. They find the town abandoned, except for a doorway that leads to another amazing world.... the true Infinite City, where magic and science happily coexist. Superman and Lois step through the magic portal and become embroiled in a war for power on the other side. One faction wants to stay in its dimension, and another wants to branch out to our world. Superman will meet a doppelganger called the Warden, who shares the Kryptonian's might but not his intellect. He will also come across the architect of this world, a robot leader who claims to be what remains of his father Jor-El.

Kesel, Barbara
Legends of the Dark Crystal, vol. 1: The Garthim Wars. Written by Barbara Randall Kesel ; illustrated by Heidi Arnhold and Max Kim. Tokyopop 2007 192p. Illustration
Grades: 8 9 10 11 12 Adult   **741.5**
1. Adventure graphic novels; 2. Fantasy graphic novels; 3. Graphic novels
978-1-59816-701-6, $9.99

Lahr and Neffi are gentle and fun-loving Gelflings who enjoy the simple pleasures of life. Their world is turned upside down when the violent Garthim attack their villages, and after a narrow escape, the two Gelflings must join forces and learn how to become leaders to help another Gelfling village defend themselves against the Garthim. This story is a prequel to the Jim Henson film, The Dark Crystal. It includes some violence.

Ketcham, Hank
★ **Hank** Ketcham's Complete Dennis the Menace (Volume 1): 1951-1952. Fantagraphics Books 2005 590p. Illustration
Grades: 2 3 4 5 6 7 8 9 10 11 12 Adult   **741.5; Fic**
1. Dennis the Menace (Fictional character); 2. Humorous graphic novels; 3. Graphic novels
1-56097-680-2, $24.95

This volume is the first of a series that will reprint every Dennis the Menace cartoon. The first cartoon was published in sixteen newspapers on March 12, 1951, and the cartoon was soon picked up by many more newspapers. This volume collects the daily single-panel cartoons from March 1951 through December 1952. In these cartoons, readers meet five-and-a-half-year-old Dennis Mitchell, his parents, retired neighbors George and Martha Wilson, Dennis' dog Ruff, and neighborhood pals Joey and Margaret. Every cartoon hearkens back to the positive aspects of growing up in suburban Middle America and the joys (mostly) of being a child. While older adults will catch all the references to past popular culture (i.e. Hopalong Cassidy), younger readers will enjoy the humor arising from everyday situations.

Khoury, George
Modern Masters Volume Ten: Kevin Maguire. Twomorrows Publishing 2007 128p. Illustration
Grades: Adult Professional   **741.5**
1. Captain America (Fictional character); 2. Justice League (Fictional characters); 3. X-Men (Fictional characters); 4. Graphic novels
978-1-893905-66-5, $14.95

In 1987, a year after Watchmen and Dark Knight Returns turned comics grim and gritty, artist Kevin Maguire proved that comics could still be fun, with the release of the "all-new" Justice League. His style was the perfect match for the humorous dialogue and character-driven stories, and the unlikely series quickly developed a large following. But the glue that held the series together was Maguire's ability to convey emotion on the page. The Justice League, Captain America, the X-Men, the Defenders... they are all actors on Maguire's stage, and he directs them with the ability of a true Modern Master. This new volume in the Modern Masters series features a career-spanning interview and tons of artwork, including a large gallery section featuring many rare and unpublished sketches and finished pieces.

Kibuishi, Kazu, ed.
Flight v2. [editor/art director, Kazu Kibuishi]. Villard 2007 432p. Illustration
Grades: 10 11 12 Adult   **741.5**
1. Fantasy graphic novels; 2. Short stories
978-0-345-49637-9, $24.95

In this themed story collection, "more than 30 accomplished young artists take off on the theme, sometimes loosely construed, of flight. . . . At more than 400 pages, there is something in this elegantly produced collection for

everyone, including readers who usually snub comics."
Booklist
Stories are by various authors; previously published by
Image Comics; v1 published 2004 by Image Comics;
Villard edition published 2007

★ **Flight** v3. [editor/art director, Kazu Kibuishi]..
Ballantine Books 2006 351p. Illustration
Grades: 9 10 11 12 Adult   **741.5**
1. Fantasy graphic novels; 2. Short stories; 3. Graphic
novels
978-0-345-49039-1; 0-345-49039-8, $24.95
LC 2006-45883
This third volume of Flight includes 26 short stories by
mostly young writers, many of whom have webcomics.
Some, such as Michael Gagne and Becky Cloonan, have
published a number of books. The stories range from
whimsical interludes to ironic fables to mini-epics of
derring-do; ironically, most of the stories have only a
tangential connection to the theme of flight.
Sequel to Flight v2 (2005)

Flight volume five. Villard Books 2008 364p.
Illustration
Grades: 9 10 11 12 Adult   **741.5; Fic**
1. Short stories; 2. Graphic novels
978-0-345-50589-7, $25
This latest volume contains twenty-one stories from
creators such as Svetlana Chmakova, Dave Roman, Phil
Craven, Kean Soo, Scott Campbell, Graham Annable, editor
Kibuishi, and others. The stories include another episode in
the adventures of Jellaby, the true meaning of baseball and
what it is to be a true professional player ("Beisbol 2—),
another episode in Michael Gagne's "The Saga of Rex," and
a tale of what happens when a trio of high-tech "Worry
Dolls" goes to work to help an unemployed actor. In this
volume, the stories are somewhat longer than in previous
volumes and most have actual plots to go with the artwork.
Stories range from realistic to the fantastic, from whimsical
to dramatic to tragic.

Flight: Volume Four. Random House/Villard 2007
344p. Illustration
Grades: 9 10 11 12 Adult   **741.5; Fic**
1. Fantasy graphic novels; 2. Short stories; 3. Graphic
novels
978-0-345-49040-7, $24.95
This fourth volume of the graphic novel anthology
series includes 25 stories by creators ranging from veterans
such as Michel Gagne and Graham Annable to newer
creators such as Clio Chiang and Neil Babra. Most of the
artists have webcomics; a number of them work in animation
(Gagne most recently worked on the motion picture
Ratatouille); some have worked on major graphic novel
projects - Lark Pien colored Gene Yang's American Born
Chinese, and Raina Telgemeier works on the graphic novel
adaptations of The Baby-Sitters Club. While there is little
harsh language and no nudity, some of the stories have more
mature themes.

★ **Flight:** Volume One. Edited by Kazu Kibuishi.
Villard 2007 207 p.
Grades: 9 10 11 12 Adult   **741.5; 741.5/973**
0345496361; 9780345496362, $27

This comic book, edited by Kazu Kibuishi, includes
work from "Bengal, Bill Mudron, Catia Chien, Chris
Appelhans, Clio Chiang, Derek Kirk Kim, Dylan Meconis,
Enrico Casarosa, Erika Moen, Hope Larson, Jacob
Magraw-Mickelson, Jake Parker, Jen Wang, Joel Carroll,
Kazu Kibuishi, Khang Le, Neil Babra, Philip Craven, Rad
Sechrist, and Vera Brosgol." (Publisher's note)
Volume 1 of 8

Kidd, Chip
Mythology: the DC Comics art of Alex Ross. Text by
Chip Kidd; introduction by M. Night Shymalan;
photography by Geoff Spear. Pantheon Bks. 2003 Un
Illustration; Color
Grades: 9 10 11 12 Adult   **741.5\092; 741; 741.5**
0-375-42240-4, $35
LC 2003-46740
"Ross's gouache painted art glows on the pages.
Interspersed with quotations by the artist and those who
know him, Kidd's sparse text takes readers on a brief tour of
Ross's childhood to his early days in advertising and comic
books, finally ending with the limited series "Kingdom
Come" (Warner, 1998), which combined hyper-realistic
artwork with unusually complex storytelling. The book not
only displays samples of finished works but also includes
sketches, photographs of live models, and comic art dating
back to the 1930s." SLJ

Kieth, Sam
The **Maxx** Volume 1. DC Comics/Wildstorm 2003 Unp.
Illustration
Grades: 10 11 12 Adult   **741.5; Fic**
1. Adventure graphic novels; 2. Fantasy graphic novels; 3.
Graphic novels
1-4012-0124-5, $17.95
Thinking himself a typical superhero, Maxx is a
homeless bum living in a cardboard box, aided by freelance
social worker Julie Winters. Maxx travels to another world,
"The Outback," where he's a hero and saves Julie from
strange imaginary creatures and from his ultimate enemy,
Mr. Gone. The reader also meets Sarah, who wants to be a
writer, is mad at her mom, and is too chicken to kill herself.
People who like their superhero comics very postmodern,
existential, and very strange will like this. The book has
some violence.

Zero Girl. Story and art, Sam Kieth; additional inks, Jim
Sinclair; colors, Nick Bell, Alex Sinclair; letters, Naghmeh
Zand. DC Comics/Wildstorm 2001 114p. Illustration
Grades: 9 10 11 12 Adult   **741.5; Fic**
1. Fantasy graphic novels; 2. Graphic novels
1-56389-851-9, $14.95
Amy Smootster is a high school social outcast who lives
her life content in her own world. But it seems that Amy's
world is full of strange happenings such as the spontaneous
appearances of puddles of water around her and two-sided
conversations with insects. And there's something weird
with her and circles and the fact that squares are inimical to
her. With the help of her guidance counselor (upon whom
she has a crush), Amy eventually accepts and embraces her
abnormal abilities and discovers her place in the world.

Zero Girl: Full Circle. Writer/artist, Sam Kieth; colorist, Alex Sinclair; letterer, John Layman. DC Comics/Wildstorm 2003 110p. Illustration
Grades: 9 10 11 12 Adult   **741.5; Fic**
 1. Fantasy graphic novels; 2. Graphic novels
 1-4012-0170-9, $17.95

Amy Smootster's now an adult, working as a guidance counselor. Her former crush, Tim Foster, is now a single parent with a troubled daughter. Tim enlists Amy's aid in helping her adjust, but the young girl, Nikki, has plans - and abilities - of her own. The book includes some strong language.

Kikuta, Michiyo
 Mamotte! Lollipop Vol. 1. Random House/Del Rey Manga 2007 224p. Illustration
Grades: 8 9 10 11 12 Adult   **741.5; Fic**
 1. Fantasy graphic novels; 2. Shojo manga; 3. Graphic novels
 978-0-345-49623-2, $10.95

Junior high schooler Nina is ready to fall in love. She's looking for a boy who's cute and sweet-and strong enough to support her when the chips are down. But what happens when Nina's dream comes true . . . twice? One day, two cute boys literally fall from the sky: they're both wizards and they've come to the Human World to take the Magic Exam. The boys' success on this test depends on protecting Nina from evil, so now Nina has a pair of cute magical boys chasing her everywhere she goes. But, because Nina accidentally swallowed a magic "crystal pearl" that is part of the Magic Exam, Zero and Ichi aren't the only wizards around her, and some are willing to do just about anything to get their hands on the magic pearl.

Kim, Derek Kirk
 Same difference. Derek Kirk Kim.. First Second 2011 90p. Illustration
Grades: 9 10 11 12 Adult   **741.5**
 1. Family — Fiction; 2. Love — Fiction; 3. Short stories; 4. Youth — Fiction; 5. Graphic novels
 9781596436572; 1596436573

                    LC 2010052663
This graphic-novel-style collection of short stories is concerned with young people, and gives particular focus to romantic and familial relationships. "The title story focuses on 20-somethings Nancy and Simon, who are racked with guilt. Why? Simon has turned down a date with a friend because she is blind, and Nancy has read love letters meant for someone else-and answered them, giving the jilted ex-boyfriend false hope. Through a series of credible coincidences, both eventually make amends. . . . [The] collection also includes stories about high school track, weed wacking, familial relationships, celebrity interviews, and autobiographical tales." (School Libr J)

Kim, June
 12 Days. Tokyopop 2006 Un Illustration
Grades: 10 11 12 Adult   **741.5; Fic**
 1. Romance graphic novels; 2. Graphic novels
 1-59816-691-3, $9.99

When Jackie's ex-lover Noah (another woman) dies, she decides the best and quickest way to get over the love of her life is to hold a personal ritual with Noah's ashes. Jackie consumes the ashes in the form of smoothies for 12 days—hoping the pain will subside with her profound reaction to Noah's death. The book includes some same-sex sexual situations, depicted tastefully.

Kindt, Matt
 2 Sisters: A Super-Spy Graphic Novel. Top Shelf Productions 2004 334p. Illustration
Grades: 9 10 11 12 Adult   **741.5; Fic**
 1. Adventure graphic novels; 2. Spies
 1-891830-58-9, $19.95

This World War II era spy thriller spans not only the globe, but time as well - from England to Spain and from ancient Roman times through the era of Pirates and Buccaneers. This spy story is the backdrop for the unique tale of two sisters, their relationship and the secrets they share. Readers will find a world of shady gypsies, mysterious rockets, buried treasure, pen-guns, cyanide teeth, and romance. The book includes violence.

 Mind MGMT; Volume one. Created, written, and illustrated by Matt Kindt; foreword by Damon Lindelof. Dark Horse 2013 152 p.
Grades: Adult   **741.5/973; 741.5**
 1. Brainwashing — Fiction; 2. Journalists; 3. Women journalists
 1595827978; 9781595827975, $19.99

                    LC 2012041667
In this graphic novel by Matt Kindt and edited by Brendan Wright, a young journalist "reporting on a commercial flight where everyone aboard lost their memories . . . stumbles onto a much bigger story - the top-secret Mind Management program. Her ensuing journey involves weaponized psychics, hypnotic advertising, talking dolphins, and seemingly immortal pursuers, as she attempts to find the flight's missing passenger, the man who was MIND MGMT's greatest success - and its most devastating failure." (Publisher's note)

 Pistolwhip. Top Shelf Productions 2001 120p. Illustration
Grades: 10 11 12 Adult   **741.5; Fic**
 1. Adventure graphic novels; 2. Mystery graphic novels; 3. Graphic novels
 1-891830-23-6, $14.95

                    LC 2002-280685
Readers will find a naive bellhop's struggle towards a life's ambition, an expatriate musician on the run, a young woman's battle with her paranoia and her past, and the mysterious figure who wants to control their lives. Set in an exotic atmosphere of a by-gone era, this is a tale crafted with a crime noir feel. The book includes violence and some strong language.

 Red Handed: The Fine Art of Strange Crimes. Matt Kindt. First Second 2013 272 p.
Grades: Adult   **741.5/973; Fic**
 1. Humorous graphic novels; 2. Mystery graphic novels
 159643662X; 9781596436626, $26.99

This graphic novel, by Matt Kindt, is set in "the city of Red Wheelbarrow, where . . . there has been a rash of crimes so eccentric and random that even Detective Gould is stumped. Will he discover the connection between the compulsive chair thief, the novelist who uses purloined street signs to write her magnum opus, and the photographer whoásecretlyádocuments peoples' most anguished personal moments?" (Publisher's note)

Super Spy. Top Shelf Productions 2007 336p. Illustration

Grades: 9 10 11 12 Adult   **741.5; S C**
  1. Adventure graphic novels; 2. Spies; 3. World War, 1939-1945; 4. Graphic novels
  978-1-891830-96-9, $19.95

Set during World War II, the book follows the everyday life of several spies as they go about their work. A writer hides secret messages in the text of the children's picture book he's writing; the wife of a German officer desperately needs to escape with her child; a female German master assassin encounters several of the Allied spies, with mostly fatal results. As the stories go on, the reader starts to see the interweaving connections between them. Some violence is depicted on the pages, but there's no nudity and little in the way of harsh language.

King, Frank
  ★ **Walt** & Skeezix: 1921 & 1922; Book 1. By Frank O. King; edited by Chris Ware. Drawn & Quarterly 2005 400 p. Illustration; Color

Grades: Adult   **741.5**
  1. Adoption; 2. Families; 3. Family life; 4. Fathers and sons; 5. Father-son relationship
  9781896597645, $29.95; 1896597645
  Eisner Nominee: Best Archival Collection (2007)
  Harvey Nominee: Best Domestic Reprint Project (2006)

This comic strip anthology, by Frank O. King, edited by Chris Ware, "is the first-ever collection of the classic twentieth-century newspaper strip 'Gasoline Alley.' . . . Not only does this volume reprint the first two years of the strip in which King's friendly and nostalgic imagination took shape but each book in the series features an eighty-page color introduction by Jeet Heer of Canada's 'National Post.'" (Publisher's note)

"Drawn & Quarterly has inaugurated an ambitious series that will eventually reprint the entire Gasoline Alley strip, as written and drawn by the late Frank King. . . . Gasoline Alley is pure Americana, set in a neighborhood where all the men are infatuated with their automobiles, tinkering with and talking about them endlessly. Disrupting the calm murmur of shoptalk is Skeezix, an orphan left on the doorstep of the chubby and friendly Walt, one of the Alley's only unattached men." Kirkus

Other collections in this series are: Walt & Skeezix: 1923-1924 (2006); Walt & Skeezix: 1925-1926 (2007); Walt & Skeezix: 1927-1928 (2010); Walt & Skeezix: 1929-1930 (2011); Walt Before Skeezix (2014); Walt & Skeezix: 1931-1932 (2015)

King, Stacy
  Pride and prejudice. Adapted by Stacy King; illustrated by Po Tse. Udon Entertainment 2014 369 p. Illustration

Grades: 9 10 11 12 Adult   **741.5**
  1. Manga
  1927925177; 9781927925171, $24.99

In this manga adaption by Stacy King, "Pride & Prejudice is delightfully transformed. . . . All of the joy, heartache, and romance of Jane Austen's original [is] perfectly illuminated by the sumptuous art of manga-ka Po Tse." (Publisher's note)

King, Stephen
  The **dark** man: an illustrated poem. By Stephen King and illustrated by Glenn Chadbourne. Cemetery Dance Publications 2013 88 p.

Grades: Adult   **811**
  1. American poetry — 20th century; 2. Fictional characters
  1587674211; 9781587674211, $25

In this book, illustrator Glenn Chadbourne presents an illustrated version of a poem by Stephen King. "Stephen King first wrote about the Dark Man in college after he envisioned a faceless man in cowboy boots and jeans and a denim jacket forever walking the roads. Later this dark man would come to be known around the world as one of King's greatest villains, Randall Flagg." (Publisher's note)

Kinney, Jay
  Anarchy Comics: The Complete Collection. Edited by Jay Kinney. Independent Pub Group 2012 224 p.

Grades: Adult   **741**
  1. Anarchism
  1604865318; 9781604865318, $20

This comic anthology, edited by Jay Kinney, "brings together the legendary four issues of 'Anarchy Comics,' the underground comic that melded anarchist politics with a punk sensibility, producing a . . . mix of satire, revolt, and artistic experimentation. The anthology [also] features previously unpublished work by Jay Kinney and Sharon Rudahl, along with a detailed introduction by Kinney that traces the history of the comic he founded." (Publisher's note)

Kirby, Jack
  Jack Kirby's Fourth World Omnibus Volume Two. Image Comics 2007 396p. Illustration

Grades: 7 8 9 10 11 12 Adult   **741.5; Fic**
  1. Superhero graphic novels; 2. Graphic novels
  978-1-4012-1357-2, $49.99

DC collects four series by Kirby — The New Gods, The Forever People, Mister Miracle, and Superman's Pal Jimmy Olsen — in chronological order as they originally appeared. These comics spanned galaxies, from the streets of Metropolis to the far-flung worlds of New Genesis and Apokolips, as cosmic-powered heroes and villains struggled for supremacy.In this second volume, the evil Darkseid's schemes continue to unfold while the New Gods, the Forever People, Mr. Miracle and other heroes battle his many minions.

Jack Kirby's Fourth World Omnibus, Volume One. DC Comics 2007 396p. Illustration

Grades: 8 9 10 11 12 Adult   **741.5; Fic**
  1. Science fiction graphic novels; 2. Superhero graphic novels; 3. Graphic novels
  978-1-4012-1344-2, $49.99

In the 1970s, legendary comics creator Kirby left Marvel Comics to work for DC Comics, writing and drawing several new series and also taking over Superman's Pal Jimmy Olsen. This volume collects the first three issues of his new series, plus the start of his run on Jimmy Olsen, from issue #133. With the Fourth World storylines in Kirby's New Gods, Forever People, and Mister Miracle, he created new mythologies and epic storylines. This hardcover edition uses a flat paper that shows off the inks and colors brilliantly.

Jack Kirby's Omac: one man army corps. Jack Kirby, writer/penciller ; D. Bruce Berry, Mike Royer, inkers and letterers. DC Comics 2008 176p. Illustration
Grades: 7 8 9 10 11 12 Adult   **741.5; Fic**
1. Superhero graphic novels; 2. Graphic novels
978-1-4012-1790-7, $24.99
In the 1970s, comics master creator Jack Kirby shocked the comics industry when he left Marvel Comics to work for the opposition DC Comics. He created new characters and new worlds. Among them was an unusual science fiction concept: OMAC, One Man Army Corps. Corporate nobody Buddy Blank is changed by the artificial intelligence "Brother Eye" into a superpowered agent of the Global Peace Agency, fighting bizarre menaces in a disturbing, near-future world. This book collects the complete 8-issue saga as published by DC; readers will note it ends in a cliffhanger that was never resolved.

Silver Star. Image Comics 2007 152p. Illustration
Grades: 8 9 10 11 12 Adult   **741.5; Fic**
1. Superhero graphic novels; 2. Graphic novels
978-1-58240-764-7, $34.99
Chronicling the rise of Homo-Geneticus, the New Breed of humanity that spawns both Silver Star (Morgan Miller) and the nefarious Darius Brumm. Silver Star was Kirby's final creation and one of only two creator-owned projects published by Pacific Comics in the early '80s. This volume also includes the original screenplay, written by Kirby and Steve Sherman, upon which Kirby based the comic.

Silver Star: Graphite Edition. Twomorrows Publishing 2006 Un Illustration
Grades: 8 9 10 11 12 Adult   **741.5; Fic**
1. Adventure graphic novels; 2. Science fiction graphic novels; 3. Graphic novels
1-893905-55-1, $19.95
Jack Kirby first conceptualized Silver Star in the mid-1970s as a movie screenplay, complete with illustrations to sell the idea to Hollywood. Too far ahead of its time for Tinseltown, Jack instead adapted his Visual Novel" as a six-issue mini-series for Pacific Comics in the early 1980s, making it the last original creation of his career. Now, in Silver Star: Graphite Edition, King" Kirby's final series is collected at last, this time reproduced from his un-inked pencil art. This is the complete story of Homo-Geneticus, the New Breed of humanity that spawns both hero (Silver Star) and villain (the nefarious Darius Drumm). The book includes Kirby's screenplay, including illustrations and never-published character sketches. Plus there are pin-ups and other rare Kirby art, and an historical overview to put it all in perspective.

Kirishima, Takeru
Kanna Volume 1. Go! Comi 2007 180p. Illustration
Grades: 10 11 12 Adult   **741.5; Fic**
1. Adventure graphic novels; 2. Fantasy graphic novels; 3. Manga; 4. Graphic novels
978-1-933617-55-8, $10.99
Kagura was perfectly happy living a normal, leisurely life... until an adorable little girl shows up in his house one day and starts calling him "Daddy—! As his once-normal life turns upside down around him, he sets off to unravel the child's mystery, embarking on a journey which will change everything... The book includes some bloody violence, as minions of the Black God are after the little girl, Kanna. There's also a slightly pervy character who's into moe - cute little girls - in anime, and he likes to give Kanna anime costumes to wear.

Kirkman, Robert
Capes, volume one: punching the clock. Writer, Robert Kirkman; artist, Mark Englert. Image Comics 2007 144p. Illustration
Grades: 10 11 12 Adult   **741.5**
1. Adventure graphic novels; 2. Superhero graphic novels; 3. Graphic novels
978-1-58240-756-2, $17.99
Imagine living in a world where superhero is just another job title. Capes Incorporated is a business that employs superpowered individuals to protect the city of New York, and occasionally the world. Superheroes such as the Meteor Twins, The American Champion, strong man Bolt, and the new guy, Kid Thor, are all on the payroll; they're superheroes who punch a time clock, take lunch breaks, and get overtime. Along with fighting violence, there's some harsh language and a few sexual situations and some partial nudity.

Invincible Vol. 8: My Favorite Martian. Writer, Robert Kirkman; penciler, inker, Ryan Ottley, colorist, Bill Crabtree, letterer, Rus Wooten. Image Comics 2007 Un Illustration
Grades: 9 10 11 12 Adult   **741.5; Fic**
1. Invincible (Fictional character); 2. Superhero graphic novels; 3. Graphic novels
978-1-58240-683-1, $14.99
Invincible battles the Reanimen on the campus of Upstate University to save his roommate William. Meanwhile, unbeknownst to him trouble is brewing - trouble of Martian origin. Invincible must assemble a team of Earth's mightiest defenders to go out into space and prevent what could well be the end of mankind. On top of that, as Mark, he's got girlfriend trouble.

Invincible: Ultimate Collection Volume 2. Robert Kirkman, writer; Ryan Ottley, Penciler Inker, Bill Crabtree; Rus Wooton, Letterer. Image Comics 2006 Un Illustration
Grades: 9 10 11 12 Adult   **741.5; Fic**
1. Invincible (Fictional character); 2. Superhero graphic novels; 3. Graphic novels
1-58240-594-8, $34.99
In the aftermath of Mark's revelation concerning his father, he's forced to pick up the pieces of his life and carry on. Everything is different now - his family, his friends, his colleagues. The world has become a strange and unfamiliar

place. He faces insurmountable odds, countless super-villains, otherworldly threats ... and graduating from high school, starting college ... Nobody told him being a superhero would be easy, but nobody told him it'd be this hard, either. When Invincible fights, he gets hurt and it shows, so there's some blood.

The **Irredeemable** Ant-Man: Low-Life. Writer, Robert Kirkman; penciler, Phil Hester; inker, Ande Parks. Marvel Entertainment 2007 Un Illustration
Grades: 9 10 11 12 Adult   **741.5; Fic**
1. Superhero graphic novels; 2. Graphic novels
978-0-7851-1962-3, $9.99
When a low-level S.H.I.E.L.D. agent gets a hold of Hank Pym's new Ant-Man suit, the Marvel Universe is in trouble. He's not concerned with saving the world or helping others. He's concerned with getting through the day and getting a leg up on life. He's not going to use his powers responsibly, he's going to use them for the betterment of himself. He's Ant-Man, a new "hero" for the modern world.

Tales of the Realm. Concept by Val Staples and Matt Tyree; written by Robert Kirkman; art by Matt Tyree. Image Comics 2004 Un Illustration
Grades: 9 10 11 12 Adult   **741.5; Fic**
1. Adventure graphic novels; 2. Fantasy graphic novels; 3. Humorous graphic novels; 4. Graphic novels
1-58240-394-5, $14.95
What if we rode dragons to work every day? What if myth and fantasy were real? The Realm is full of the hustle and bustle of life on Earth as it is today, with a little twist... Dragons and ogres, sword and sorcery are the norms in The Realm, seamlessly blended with our familiar human counterparts. This adventure follows the lives of three television show actors as they fight to make it big in Hollywood while interacting with a world very much like our own, but oh-so different. The book has some magical violence and some strong language.

Tech jacket, Vol. 1: Lost & found. [by] Robert Kirkman and E. J. Su. Image Comics 2003 144p. Illustration
Grades: 6 7 8 9 10 11 12   **741.5; Fic**
1. Adventure graphic novels; 2. Science fiction graphic novels; 3. Graphic novels
1-58240-314-7, $12.95
Teenage Zach Thompson stumbles upon a crashed space ship with a dying alien; Geldarian gives his Tech Jacket to Zach. The Tech Jackets gave the physically weak Geldarians the ability to do their work; on the physically fit Zach, it gives him great power. But, even as his father deals with gangsters trying to take his hardware store, Zach learns that possessing the Tech Jacket gives him great responsibility, and the Geldarians need him.

Kishimoto, Seishi
O-Parts Hunter Vol. 1. Viz Media 2006 185p. Illustration
Grades: 10 11 12 Adult   **741.5; Fic**
1. Adventure graphic novels; 2. Fantasy graphic novels; 3. Manga; 4. Shonen manga; 5. Graphic novels
978-1-4215-0855-9, $9.99
In the not too distant future, mankind fights over relics from an ancient civilization called O-Parts, each of which

contain incredible powers. Some people with special abilities to use the O-Parts to their full potential are known as O.P.T.s (or O-Parts Tacticians). Jio is a young boy with a tragic past who only trusts one thing in the world: money. He is actually a very powerful O.P.T., and inside him sleeps a demon of incredible ferocity. He meets up with a girl named Ruby who, like her famous father before her, wants to become a treasure hunter. Though Jio doesn't believe in friendship, he agrees to be Ruby's bodyguard, and together they go on a dangerous quest to discover as many O-Parts as they can. The story uses some harsh language and violence, occasionally graphic. Mangaka Kishimoto is twin brother to Masashi Kishimoto, mangaka of Naruto.

Kishiro, Yukito
Battle Angel Alita Vol. 1: Rusty Angel. Viz Media 2003 Un Illustration
Grades: 10 11 12 Adult   **741.5; Fic**
1. Manga; 2. Science fiction graphic novels; 3. Seinen manga; 4. Graphic novels
1-56931-945-6, $9.95
When Doc Ido, a talented cyberphysician, finds cyborg Alita's head in a junk heap, she has lost all memory of her past life. But when he reconstructs her, she discovers her body still instinctively remembers the Panzer Kunst, the most powerful cyborg fighting technique ever known. In the post-apocalyptic world of the Scrapyard, as the secrets of Alita's past unfold, each day is a struggle for survival. The book includes graphic violence and strong language.
Volume 1 of 9

Kitchen, Alexa
Drawing Comics is Easy! (Except When It's Hard). Denis Kitchen Publishing Company 2006 Un Illustration
Grades: 2 3 4 5 6 7 8 9 10 11 12 Adult   **741.5**
1. Drawing; 2. Graphic novels
0-9710080-6-X, $19.95
Drawing Comics is Easy! (Except When It's Hard!) is entirely the work of a seven-year-old (at the time) prodigy cartoonist, who in 2007 was ten years old. Though seemingly aimed at a peer audience of other children, this idiosyncratic How-To book will appeal to readers of any age, especially those interested in cartooning and the creative process. Kitchen is the daughter of Denis Kitchen, who's been in the comics industry as a publisher and agent for many years.

Kitchen, Denis
The **art** of Harvey Kurtzman: the mad genius of comics. By Denis Kitchen and Paul Buhle; introduction by Art Spiegelman; designed by Kitchen, Lind & Associates. Abrams Comicarts 2009 241p. Illustration
Grades: Adult   **741.5**
978-0-8109-7296-4; 0-8109-7296-4, $40
LC 2008-04809
"Retrace the strands that led to a lot of current American satire — including The Simpsons, Saturday Night Live and The Daily Show — and sooner or later you end up at Harvey Kurtzman. A comic mastermind who created Mad Magazine and Playboy's 'Little Annie Fanny,' Kurtzman also happened to discover Robert Crumb and gave Gloria Steinem her first job. . . . [This volume] explores the life and

art of the famous satirist, weaving together the story of Kurtzman's career with a collection of the artist's images and illustrations." NPR

Kleid, Neil
Brownsville. Written by Neil Kleid; illustrated by Jake Allen. NBM 2006 208p. Illustration
Grades: 10 11 12 Adult   741.5; 973.9
1. Gangs; 2. United States — History — 20th century; 3. Graphic novels
1-56163-458-1, $18.95
Brownsville, in Brooklyn, New York, was an impoverished part of the city in the early twentieth century. Filled with tenements and poor Jews, it became the breeding ground for criminals. This book follows the lives of Allie Tanennbaum, Abe Reles, and other young hoods organized by Louis Lepke Buchalter into the deadly "Murder, Inc." in the 1930s.
"The history of Jewish gangsters is often overshadowed by images of The Godfather and stories of the Italian mafia, but the events and players come to life in the stark images of this historical overview." (VOYA)

Klein, Grady
The Lost Colony Book 2: The red menace. First Second Books 2007 120p. Illustration
Grades: 10 11 12 Adult   741.5; Fic
1. Adventure graphic novels; 2. Humorous graphic novels; 3. Graphic novels
978-1-59643-098-3, $16.95
In the second installment of The Lost Colony series, the beloved and not-so-beloved islanders confront war profiteering, the Native American Wars, and other unwelcome visitors to their hidden realm. Along with magic potions, stage tricks, and farting contests, the book includes tragedy, controversy, and even shameful secrets. Some characters use racial slurs, and some are drawn as seeming stereotypes, but patient and discerning readers will see Klein's intent.

The lost colony, book 3: Last rights. First Second Books 2008 152p. Illustration
Grades: 9 10 11 12 Adult   741.5; Fic
1. Graphic novels
978-1-59643-099-0, $18.95
The arrival of Buck Swagger, a smarmy preacher, on the island bodes no good for Birdy or for Louis. It's bad enough Birdy has to deal with the death of her grandfather at the hands of her old nanny, and that her father has become obsessed with getting revenge, now it seems her mother has had an affair with Swagger—and is continuing with it, now that he's there. Louis has had his own run-ins with Swagger, who used Louis as a slave until Birdy bought him and brought him to the island. Old Patricia tries to warn Birdy that trouble has come, but no one will listen to Birdy, except maybe Louis. And the rock bugs fit in somehow. Patricia says they killed Birdy's grandfather because he was evil and they were protecting the island, but no one will believe that when Birdy repeats it. Klein continues his exploration of race relations and American history in this third volume of Lost Colony. The book includes some violence, partial nudity, and strong language.

Kleist, Reinhard
The **Boxer:** The True Story of Holocaust Survivor Harry Haft. Reinhard Kleist. Harry N Abrams Inc 2014 200 p. Illustration
Grades: Adult   92; 741.5
1. Boxers (Sports); 2. Haft, Harry, 1925-2007; 3. Holocaust survivors; 4. Graphic novels
1906838771; 9781906838775, $22.95
                    LC 2014464671
"Shrimpy but scrappy, teenager Hertzko Haft helps his struggling Jewish family survive Nazi occupation of Poland. But just before he is to marry his love, Leah, Hertzko is sent to a work camp and then to Auschwitz. Over four years, he keeps alive by canny friendships, smuggling, and learning to box in tournaments held to entertain Nazi camp officers. Finally, Hertzko escapes and turns professional boxer, seeking the missing Leah." (Library Journal)
"Drawn in stark black and white panels, characterized by a visceral sharpness of lines and angles, Kleist's narrative is set in a perfect visual landscape." Pub Wkly

Johnny Cash: I see a darkness: a graphic novel. [translated from the German edition by Michael Waaler]. Abrams ComicArts 2009 221p. Illustration
Grades: 11 12 Adult   741.5; 92
978-0-8109-8463-9, $17.95
                    LC 2010-279149
The author "presents a biography (with seemingly invented dialog that stays true to the facts) focusing on Cash's turning points: from his poor family's 1935 relocation to a New Deal-created cotton farming community, through his troubled first marriage, endless touring, the amphetamine abuse of his early musical career, and climaxing with a famous, highly charged 1968 concert at California's Folsom Prison. Kleist also dramatizes several of Cash's songs and relates the tragic story of Glen Sherley, a Folsom inmate who sent Cash a song he had written hoping Cash would play it in the show. The ruggedness of Kleist's black-and-white illustrations suits their subject, as the stark portrayal of Cash's withdrawal from drugs is inventive and harrowing. . . . This thoughtful and compelling portrait of a towering talent with a tortured soul is recommended for all teen and adult music fans." Libr J

Knaak, Richard
Warcraft: The Sunwell Trilogy Vol. 1: Dragon Hunt. Written by Richard A. Knaak; illustrated by Jae-Hwan Kim. Kaplan Publishing/Tokyopop 2007 160p. Illustration (Kaplan SAT/ACT vocabulary-building manga)
Grades: 8 9 10 11 12 Adult   741.5; Fic
1. Adventure graphic novels; 2. Fantasy graphic novels; 3. Vocabulary; 4. Graphic novels
978-1-4277-5495-0, $9.99
The story follows the adventures of Kalec, a blue dragon who has taken human form to escape the forces that seek to destroy his race, and Anveena, a maiden with secrets of her own. What starts as a flight for survival turns into a quest to save the entire High Elven Kingdom from the forces of the Undead Scourge. This Kaplan edition adds more than 300 SAT/ACT vocabulary words with their definitions on the same pages where they appear. The entire Tokyopop

edition appears in full size with additional borders added to accommodate the words and definitions.

Kneece, Mark
The **Bristol** Board Jungle. Bob Pendarvis, Mark Kneece. NBM 2004 144p. Illustration
Grades: 9 10 11 12 Adult   **741.5**
1. Graphic novels — Technique; 2. Graphic novels
1-56163-379-8, $11.95
                                      LC 2003-70631
Here is a full college class on creating comics... in a graphic novel. Readers can learn the secrets of the trade while attending an actual class and getting to know the students. This book is written and drawn by two professors of the Savannah College of Art & Design with a class of their best seniors, who each illustrate one chapter.

Knisley, Lucy
An **Age** of License. Lucy Knisley. Fantagraphics 2014 208 p. Illustration; Color; Map Grades: 11 12 Adult
                                      741.5; 92
1. Autobiographical graphic novels; 2. Europe — Description and travel
1606997688; 9781606997680, $19.99
"'An Age of License' is [author Lucy] Knisley's comics travel memoir recounting her charming (and romantic!) adventures. It's punctuated by whimsical visual devices (such as a 'new experiences' funnel); peppered with the cute cats she meets along the way; and, of course, features her hallmark—drawings and descriptions of food that will make your mouth water." (Publisher's note)
"Knisley makes memoir comics seem both sophisticated and approachableùand beyond these, useful in helping an individual delve into and communicate personal issues." LJ

★ **Relish:** My Life in the Kitchen. By Lucy Knisley. First Second 2013 192 p.
Grades: 9 10 11 12 Adult   **741.5; 92**
1. Cooking; 2. Food
1596436239; 9781596436237, $17.99
Alex Award Winner (2014)
This book is a memoir from food-lover Lucy Knisley. "Having grown up surrounded by delicious food, thanks to her gourmand father and earthy superchef mother, Knisley looks back on her childhood and adolescence through her roving palette and voracious appetite for new tastes and experiences. With each memory Knisley shares, she shows that life, like a good meal, should be savored and that all food—even junk food—is more than 'just fuel.'" (Publishers Weekly)
"Knisley tempers any navel-gazing impulses with humor, humility, and honesty. . . . Just about everything in this rambling memoir is handled with good cheer." Booklist

Ko, Ya-Seong
Redrum Three Twenty Seven Volume 1. Tokyopop 2006 Un Illustration
Grades: 10 11 12 Adult   **741.5; Fic**
1. Horror graphic novels; 2. Manwha; 3. Mystery graphic novels; 4. Graphic novels
1-59816-506-2, $9.99

When a group of seven young college students go off to enjoy a weekend getaway at a remote mountain villa, secrets that haunt the friends are unveiled—which lead to bizarre love triangles, tragic relationships, and deadly betrayal. And when hallucinations and strange disappearances begin, their dream vacation turns into a nightmare... The book includes strong language and violence.

Kobayashi, Jin
School Rumble, Vol. 1. Ballantine Books/Del Rey Manga 2006 182p. Illustration
Grades: 10 11 12 Adult   **741.5; Fic**
1. Humorous graphic novels; 2. Manga; 3. Romance graphic novels; 4. Shonen manga; 5. Graphic novels
0-345-49147-5, $10.95
Second-year high school student Tsukamoto Tenma (this series uses Japanese name order, so Tenma is her first name) starts the new school year determined to declare her love for Karasuma Oji. Notorious juvenile delinquent Harima Kenji has a crush on his has and returned to school in hopes of declaring his love for her. Karasuma seems totally oblivious to all that's going on around him. Tenma's younger sister Yakumo is the one who cooks and takes care of Tenma; she also possesses the ability to read the minds of people who have feelings for her. Tenma and Kenji each engage in hilariously over-the-top efforts to declare their love for the objects of their affection, but they never succeed. Meanwhile, boys are starting to notice Yakumo.

Kochalka, James
American elf; book 1: the collected sketchbook diaries of James Kochalka, October 26, 1998 to December 31, 2003. James Kochalka; [with an introduction by Moby]. Top Shelf Productions 2004 Un Illustration
Grades: Adult   **741.5; 92**
1. Cartoonists — United States — Diaries
1-891830-49-X; 9781891830495, $29.95
                                      LC 2015506393
"Since October 26, 1998, independent comics creator Kochalka has kept a journal in comics. Each day's square of one, two, three, or the conventional four panels illustrates a nice or funny or pointed exchange between him and Amy, his wife; an encounter with their cat, Spandy; an interchange with a friend; recording or performing with his rock band; bike riding or driving; partying or traveling; attending a comics convention; appreciating, or not, the pleasures of the day; struggling with that day's entry." (Booklist)
"As a cartoonist, Kochalka is a great reducer, conveying more in one or two panels than many cartoonists do in one or two pages. On top of that, he makes readers consider the simple pleasures of voyeurism—why do we want to read about his life" Why does he want to discuss it—" Pub Wkly
Volume 1 of 4

The **Cute** Manifesto. Alternative Comics 2005 Un Illustration
Grades: 11 12 Adult   **741.5**
1. Autobiographical graphic novels; 2. Humorous graphic novels; 3. Graphic novels
1-891867-73-3, $19.95
In a dangerously uncertain world, Kochalka plots a theoretical path to happiness. Collecting some of his

thoughtful work, this book struggles with all the big issues: comics and art, birth and death, technology and joy, and everything in between. It collects "The Horrible Truth about Comics," "Reinventing Everything" parts 1 and 2, "Sunburn," "The Cute Manifesto," and even Kochalka's Craft is the Enemy" essays. The book includes harsh language and brief nudity.

Pinky & Stinky. Top Shelf Productions 2002 208p. Illustration
Grades: 4 5 6 7 8 9 10 11 12 Adult   **741.5; Fic**
1. Adventure graphic novels; 2. Friendship; 3. Humorous graphic novels; 4. Graphic novels
1-891830-29-7, $17.95

Pinky & Stinky are fat little piglets, but just because they're cuties doesn't mean that they're not brave astronauts! When they embark on a daring mission to be the first pigs on Pluto, things go horribly wrong and they crash land on the moon. There they meet some not-so-friendly moon men, and end up in the middle of a conflict between the American space program and a race of alien ice creatures.

Koike, Kazuo
Lone wolf and cub omnibus. 1. By Kazuo Koike; illustrated by Goseki Kojima. Dark Horse Manga 2013 706 p. Illustration
Grades: 9 10 11 12 Adult   **741.5; 741.5952**
1. Samurai
1616551348; 9781616551346, $19.99

This graphic novel, by Kazuo Koike, illustrated by Goseki Kojima, is a "samurai epic. . . . [It] begins its second life at Dark Horse Manga with new, larger editions of over 700 pages." (Publisher's note)
Also available in 28 single volumes
Volume 1 of 12

Path of the Assassin Vol. 1: Serving in the Dark. Dark Horse Manga 2006 314p. Illustration
Grades: 11 12 Adult   **741.5; Fic**
1. Adventure graphic novels; 2. Manga; 3. Samurai; 4. Seinen manga; 5. Graphic novels
978-1-59307-502-6, $9.95

This is the story of Hattori Hanzo, the fabled master ninja whose duty was to protect Tokugawa Ieyasu. Ieyasu was the shogun who would unite Japan into one great nation. But before he could do that, he had to grow up and learn how to love the ladies. As the secret caretaker of such an influential future leader, not only does Hanzo use vast and varied ninja talents, but in living closely with Ieyasu, he forms a close friendship with the young shogun. The two men get into bawdy escapades, the book includes nudity, strong language, and graphic violence.

Kominsky-Crumb, Aline
Drawn together: the collected works of R. and A. Crumb. Aline & R. Crumb. Liveright 2012 272 p. Illustration; Color
Grades: Adult   **B; 741.5/973; 741.5**
1. Cartoonists — United States — Biography; 2. Cartoons and caricatures; 3. Crumb, R; 4. Kominsky-Crumb, Aline, 1948; 5. Married people
087140429X; 9780871404299, $29.95

LC 2012013566
In this book by R. and Aline Crumb, a "[s]emi-autobiographical [account], the stories reveal sordid details about the romantic relationship of the Crumbs, from their active (and somewhat violent) sex life in their youth to their still deviant sexual life in their sixties. Plagued by self-hatred, the creators spend most of each panel in dialogue with each other about how awful the world is, how self-deprecating they are, or how much they want to have sex." (Publishers Weekly)

Kouga, Yun
Earthian Vol.1. Tokyopop/BLU 2005 400p. Illustration
Grades: 10 11 12 Adult   **741.5; Fic**
1. Manga; 2. Romance graphic novels; 3. Science fiction graphic novels; 4. Shonen-ai manga; 5. Graphic novels
1-59816-006-0, $14.99

Angels are among us. They are scattered across the globe, living in our neighborhoods, observing humanity—the Earthian—in crisis...Chihaya and Kagetsuya have known each other since their days at school. They are friends...and possibly more. These two angels roam the world, compiling lists of the positive and negative traits of humanity. In the process they become involved in the lives of various humans, full of despair: An astronaut about to venture on a dangerous mission, a sorceress running from the mafia, and a mysterious artificially created human are just a few of those beings who Chihaya puts himself at risk to help, much to Kagetsuya's dismay. But after a meeting of angels, it is discovered that a dreaded disease is plaguing a growing legion of angels. Salvation possibly lies in the fallen angel Lord Seraphim—and as Chihaya and Kagetsuya search to find him, he turns up in the most unlikely of places... This is a Boy Love/shonen-ai manga title. It includes some violence and strong language; nudity occurs in the fourth (and final) volume.

Loveless Volume 1. Tokyopop 2006 202p. Illustration
Grades: 10 11 12 Adult   **741.5; Fic**
1. Fantasy graphic novels; 2. Manga; 3. Mystery graphic novels; 4. Romance graphic novels; 5. Shonen-ai manga; 6. Graphic novels
1-59816-221-7, $9.99

The mystery behind the death of his older brother was just the beginning...When 12-year-old Ritsuka discovers a posthumous message from his brother indicating he was murdered, he becomes involved in a shadowy world of spell battles and secret names. Together with the mysterious Soubi, the search to find Seimei's killer and uncover the truth begins. But in a world where everyone has cat ears and mere words have unbelievable power, how can you find true friendship and happiness when your very name is Loveless" The romance is boy/boy, and the book includes fighting violence.

Kouno, Fumiyo
Town of evening calm, Country of cherry blossoms. Last Gasp 2006 104p. Illustration
Grades: 9 10 11 12 Adult   **741.5; Fic**
1. Atomic bomb victims; 2. Japan — History — 1952-; 3. Manga; 4. Graphic novels

978-0-86719-665-8, $9.99

In 1955, Hiroshima has been recovering from the devastation of the Atom Bomb in August 1945. Minami is one of the survivors of the bomb, and she tries not to remember the events of that day when most of her family died. She even pushes away Uchikoshi, a co-worker who likes her, feeling guilty that she survived when so many didn't; but when she finally comes to terms with her past and allows Uchikoshi in, radiation sickness manifests. Fifty years later, old school friends Nanami and Toko run into each other as Nanami follows her father who has been behaving oddly; he goes to Hiroshima, for he is Minami's younger brother. This quiet, one-volume manga uses gentle, sweet art to bring home to readers the lingering after-effects of the bombing of Hiroshima.

Kovalic, John
★ **Here** Be Snapdragons. Art by Liz Rathke. Dork Storm Press 2006 120p. Illustration
Grades: 3 4 5 6 7 8 9 10 11 12 Adult   741.5; Fic
1. Children; 2. Humorous graphic novels; 3. Graphic novels
1-930964-52-8, $12.99
'Everybody Loves Gilly,' 2003 Origins Award for Graphic Fiction (Origins International Game Expo).
The Snapdragons are fraternal twins Jake and Jody, Cooper, Benjamin, and the years-younger Mitze, along with Jake and Jody's cat Huey. They are neighbors and friends, they love role-playing games and video games. Cooper's dad is a gamer, Jake and Jody's mother is clueless (she buys years-old Halloween costumes at a discount, unaware that the characters aren't popular any more), and they all often get babysat by Goth-cute teen Gilly, who can be a very cool Dungeon Master. One of the stories has Jake and Jody sent to their room without supper and they start quoting Wild Things by Maurice Sendak as their room begins to transform . . .

Krahulik, Mike
Penny Arcade Vol. 2: Epic Legends of the Magic Sword Kings. Jerry Holkins and Mike Krahulik. Dark Horse Comics 2006 160p. Illustration
Grades: 10 11 12 Adult   741.5
1. Humorous graphic novels; 2. Video games; 3. Graphic novels
978-1-59307-541-5, $12.95
This volume collects the web comic strips posted online throughout 2001. Gamers Gabe and Tycho contend with games that were new back then (e.g. Onimusha) and systems such as Playstation (the first one) and Gamecube. Foul language abounds, along with sexual innuendo and generally raunchy humor. The creators' comments appear on every page.

Krigstein, B. (Bernard)
Messages in a Bottle: Comic Book Stories by B. Krigstein. By B. Krigstein; edited and produced by Greg Sadowski. W W Norton & Co Inc 2013 272 p. Illustration; Color
Grades: Adult   Fic; 741.5/973
1606995804; 9781606995808, $35
LC 2012462153

This anthology, by Marie Severin, edited by Greg Sadowski, features comics by Bernard Krigstein. "Krigstein began his career . . . during the 1940s and finished it as a respected fine artist and illustrator—but comics historians know him for his explosively creative 1950s. . . . Greg Sadowski . . . has assembled the very best of Krigstein's comics work, . . . running through every genre popular at the time." (Publisher's note)

Kristiansen, Teddy H.
The **Red** Diary: The Re(a)d Diary Flipbook. Steven T. Seagle, Teddy H. Kristiansen. Image Comics 2012 65 p. Color; Illustration
Grades: Adult   741.5; Fic
1. Diaries; 2. Identity — Fiction; 3. War
1607065606; 9781607065609, $29.99
This book presents a "dual-story graphic novel" by Teddy Kristiansen and Steven T. Seagle. "Published in French, Kristiansen's original story chronicles the search of a biographer for the truth behind the life of an unknown artist who died during WWI. Seagle uses the same images to tell a different tale of war, art, and identity, as an old man searches to connect to the diaries of his youth. Seagle . . . had not read the original before creating his own story." (Publishers Weekly)

Krueger, Jim
Justice Volume One. Jim Krueger and Alex Ross, story ; Doug Braithwaite and Alex Ross, art. DC Comics 2006 160p. Illustration
Grades: 8 9 10 11 12 Adult   741.5; Fic
1. Justice League of America (Fictional characters); 2. Superhero graphic novels; 3. Graphic novels
978-1-4012-0969-8, $19.99
The Justice League of America are the World's Greatest Super-Heroes, but now villains - the Riddler, Lex Luthor, Poison Ivy, Captain Cold, and others are banding together and making sweeping, worldwide changes that appear to be noble acts. But, one by one the members of the JLA are being taken down; will anyone be left to truly protect the people of Earth?

Kubert, Joe
Joe Kubert Presents. By Joe Kubert; colors by Joe Kubert with Pete Carlsson. Joe Kubert, Sam Glanzman. DC Comics 2013 304 p. Color; Illustration
Grades: Adult   741.5
1. Military personnel; 2. War; 3. Graphic novels
1401243304; 9781401243302, $19.99
LC 2013026713
This book, by Joe Kubert with illustrations from Brian Buniak and Sam Glanzman, is an "anthology-style graphic novel with original stories with far ranging characters and settings. Included in this new collection are tales featuring heroes from his most famous works, Sgt. Rock and Hawkman, as well as the gritty war epics he is best known for." (Publisher's note)
"The project is a testament not only to Kubert's talent but to the sort of solid, straightforward storytelling largely missing from contemporary mainstream comics; as such, its

greatest appeal will be to older readers who prefer his old-school approach." Booklist

Originally published in single magazine form as JOE KUBERT PRESENTS 1-6.

Sgt. Rock: The Prophecy. DC Comics 2007 144p. Illustration
Grades: 10 11 12 Adult   **741.5; Fic**
1. Sgt Rock (Fictional character); 2. War stories; 3. World War, 1939-1945; 4. Graphic novels
978-1-4012-1248-3, $17.99

It's late 1943, and Sgt. Rock and Easy Company go on a covert mission far from the Allied front lines. They land in Vilnius, Lithuania, a no-man's-land caught between Nazi forces and Russia's Red Army. Rock has orders to contact the civilian partisans and get a valuable religious object from them and take it to safety. However, the object turns out to be a young rabbi named David, whom the people believe is their Messiah. Now Easy Company has to take him across hostile, war-torn territory to Riga, in Latvia, facing cold weather, Nazis, collaborators, minefields, and more.

Kubert made Sgt. Rock the iconic figure he is today, and this story marks his return to the character. The book is full of fighting action, hard-bitten dialog, and everything that marks a classic World War II combat story. People who like the motion picture "Saving Private Ryan" will like Sgt. Rock (and this story has none of the profanity).

Yossel: April 19, 1943: a story of the Warsaw Ghetto Uprising. Ibooks; Simon & Schuster 2003 121p. Illustration
Grades: 9 10 11 12 Adult   **940.53; Fic**
1. Holocaust, 1933-1945; 2. Warsaw (Poland) — History — Uprising of 1943; 3. Graphic novels
0-7434-7516-X, $24.95

"Imagining his life as it might have been had his parents not left for America in 1926, Kubert portrays himself as a ghetto youngster whose drawing ability ingratiates him with the Nazis, allowing him to overhear their plans and aid the underground resistance. Besides depicting life in the ghetto with shocking vividness, Kubert shows the barbarism of the concentration camps through the eyes of an escapee. In a striking departure from standard comics presentation, the artwork is printed in rough, penciled form rather than as finished ink drawings. The visual looseness this gives to work that is stylized by mainstream-comics standards conjures a potent intimacy that adds to the story's impact." Booklist

Kuper, Peter
The **jungle**. [based on the story by] Upton Sinclair; adapted by Peter Kuper. Papercutz 2010 Un Illustration (Classics Illustrated)
Grades: 9 10 11 12 Adult   **741.5; Fic**
1. Authors; 2. Biographers; 3. Chicago (Ill); 4. Immigrants; 5. Meat industry; 6. Novelists; 7. Sinclair, Upton, 1878-1968 — Adaptations; 8. Socialist leaders; 9. Graphic novels
978-1-59707-192-5, $9.99

"Jurgis and his family have immigrated to America from Lithuania, settled in Chicago, and found jobs in the meatpacking plant. The family seems to be living the American dream: having their own home, and a means of support, even if the work is hard and disgusting. Peter

Kuper's dark, colored, cartoon-style illustrations, framed in black, bring to life Sinclair's original work and highlight the atrocities perpetuated upon the Rudkus family." Libr Media Connect

First published 1991 by First Publishing

Ruins. By Peter Kuper. Harry N Abrams Inc 2015 328 p. Color; Illustration
Grades: Adult   **741.5973; 741.5**
1. Married people — Fiction; 2. Mexican Americans — Fiction; 3. Monarch butterflies; 4. Graphic novels
1906838984; 9781906838980, $29.95

In this book, by author Peter Kuper, Samantha and George are a couple heading towards a sabbatical year in the quaint Mexican town of Oaxaca. . . . For both of them, it will be a collision course with political and personal events that will alter their paths and the town of Oaxaca forever. In tandem, the remarkable and arduous journey that a Monarch butterfly endures on its annual migration from Canada to Mexico is woven into Ruins. (Publisher's note)

Sticks and stones: an epic in pictures. Three Rivers Press 2004 Un Illustration
Grades: 10 11 12 Adult   **741.5; Fic**
1. Stories without words; 2. Graphic novels
1-4000-5257-2, $13.95
     LC 2004-45969

"A stone giant is born from a volcano and demands the fealty of the people around him. He makes them build him a stone castle; then he discovers a nearby peaceful village made entirely of wood and sets about conquering it and plundering its resources. Meanwhile, a small resistance front develops, led by a woman from the stone tribe and a boy from the wood tribe, and eventually the stone empire and its despot meet a grim fate. Kuper's narrative is beautifully constructed, from its grand sweep to its minute details." Publ Wkly

Kupperberg, Paul
Archie: the married life. 3. Written by Paul Kupperberg; pencils by Fernando Ruiz, Pat & Tim Kennedy; inking by Al Milgrom and Bob Smith; letters by Janice Chiang and Jack Moretti; coloring by Glenn Whitmore. Archie Comic Publications 2013 320 p. Color illustration
Grades: 9 10 11 12 Adult   **741.5/973; Fic**
1. Andrews, Archie (Fictional character); 2. Marriage — Fiction
1936975351; 9781936975358, $19.99
     LC 2013409812

This graphic novel by Paul Kupperberg "explores Archie Andrews' life down two paths—if he had married girl-next-door Betty Cooper or wealthy socialite Veronica Lodge. In this volume, things really start getting interesting, as the mysterious Dilton Doiley subplots that have been bubbling just below the surface since the series' beginning start to affect... well, everything!" (Publisher's note)

"Eye-opening for longtime fanatics and an invigorating soap opera for newcomers." Booklist

Kurata, Hideyuki
R. O. D. (Read or Dream) Volume 1. Story by Hideyuki Kurata; art by Ran Ayanaga. Viz Media 2007 Un Illustration
Grades: 10 11 12 Adult   **741.5; Fic**

1. Fantasy graphic novels; 2. Manga; 3. Seinen manga; 4. Graphic novels
978-1-4215-0510-7, $9.99

Michelle is a romantic daydreamer and hardcore book collector. Maggie is a soft-spoken bookworm who always gets mistaken for a boy. Anita is a tomboy who doesn't have time for reading. Together, they're the Paper Sisters, three very different siblings united by a strange power. Michelle, Maggie and Anita all have the ability to control paper in any way they desire. And from their Hong Kong detective agency, they solve any and all cases involving books. In this volume, the sisters check out books from a secret library, use the power of literature to save the planet from an alien attack, and finally organize their massive book collection. There's never a dull moment at Paper Sisters Detective Company. The book includes some nudity and fan service (titillating pictures designed to appeal to male readers).

Train + Train, Vol. 1. Original story by Hideyuki Kurata ; art by Tomomasa Takuma. Go! Comi 2007 196p. Illustration
Grades: 8 9 10 11 12 Adult   **741.5; Fic**
1. Adventure graphic novels; 2. High school students; 3. Manga; 4. Graphic novels
978-1-933617-18-3, $10.99

Reiichi and Liae have come to the planet Deloca to board the high school train. On Deloca, different schools run on special trains, with stops where students complete certain assignments; they live in dorms on the trains. Reiichi and Liae are registered to board the "General" school train. Arena Pendleton, on the other hand, has determined to board the Special Train, and she won't let anyone stop her, not even the men her wealthy grandfather has hired to capture her and bring her home. In Ideo City, where the students must board their respective trains, Reiichi accidentally gets involved in a run-in between Arena and Kong Seeval, who intends to take Arena home. Reiichi and Arena become handcuffed together, and he has no choice but to board the Special Train. There's lots of action but little in the way of violence or bad language in this first of a manga series.

Kurosawa, Edo

50 Things We Love About Japan written by Edo Kurosawa ; illustrated by Atsuhisa Okura. Japanime Co. Ltd. 2007 112p. Illustration
Grades: 5 6 7 8 9 10 11 12 Adult   **741.5; 952**
1. Japan; 2. Graphic novels
978-4-921205-08-9, $9.99

From anime to karaoke to kaiten-zushi, this little book features manga illustrations and prose to offer the rest of the world a glimpse at what the Japanese love most about the country they call home. Manga readers and anime fans will find explanations for the some of the cultural elements found in the books and films.

Kurotaki, Jan

Everybody Cosplay!. ADV Manga 2007 Un Illustration
Grades: 8 9 10 11 12 Adult   **741.5; 792**
1. Costume; 2. Graphic novels
978-1-4139-0365-2, $19.99

Kurotaki is a cosplayer and columnist for the magazine Newtype USA. In this book, she has collected some of her columns over the years that show off some of her anime and gaming costumes. Cosplay, which is dressing up as a favorite character and assuming that character's personality, has become a popular activity among American anime fans who attend conventions. Readers can see the details of Kurotaki's costumes in the color photographs, while her comments describe some of the unique features and explains a little bit about her process of making the costumes. While not strictly manga-related, this book will appeal to manga and anime fans.

Kurtz, Scott

How to make Webcomics. Brad Guigar, Dave Kellett, Scott Kurtz, Kris Straub. Image Comics 2008 195p. Illustration
Grades: 10 11 12 Adult   **741.5**
1. Graphic novels — Study and teaching; 2. Web sites — Design
978-1-58240-870-5, $12.99

Four webcomics creators have banded together to help readers make webcomics on their own. As they say in the introduction, this isn't a basic how to cartoon book. They address readers who already draw their cartoons and want to find a way to publish their work. Publishing on the web means the cartoonist is working for himself or herself and is not beholden to a publisher or syndicate. The book includes information on putting together a business plan, for self-publishing cartoonists must deal with the nitty-gritty of business decisions as well as the creative work of making the cartoons. The book also covers the basics of web design, whether to set up a subscription system, publishing one's comics in book form, even how to set up a booth at a comics convention.

Truth, Justin, and the American Way. Written by Aaron Williams and Scott Kurtz ; illustrated by Giuseppe Ferrario. Image Comics 2007 Un Illustration
Grades: 8 9 10 11 12 Adult   **741.5; Fic**
1. Humorous graphic novels; 2. Superhero graphic novels; 3. Graphic novels
978-1-58240-705-0, $14.99

1980s-era slacker Justin is supposed to get married this weekend, but due to a colossal mix-up, the silly t-shirt his friends got him for his bachelor party has been switched with an alien suit. When clueless Justin puts it on, the suit molds to his body, and when an FBI agent after the suit crashes the party, Justin learns what the suit can do. Before the weekend is over, Justin will have to fight not only FBI, but also aliens who want their property back. Filled with references to television shows and movies from the 1980s, the wacky story will appeal to younger teens even if they don't catch all the references.

Kurtzman, Harvey

Corpse on the Imjin!: and other stories. Harvey Kurtzman. Fantagraphics Books 2012 227 p.
Grades: Adult   **741.5**
1. Short stories; 2. War
1606995456; 9781606995457, $28.99

Author Harvey Kurtzman presents a book of short comic stories related to warfare. The book contains stories from cartoonists "including such giants as designer extraordinaire Alex Toth, Marvel comics stalwart Gene Colan, and a pre-Sgt. Rock Joe Kubert... and such unexpected guests as . . . artist Dave Berg and DC comics veteran Ric Estrada." (Publisher's note)

Kyle, Craig
New X-Men: Childhood's End Vol. 1. Mark Brooks, Illustrator. Marvel Entertainment 2006 Un Illustration
Grades: 9 10 11 12 Adult   741.5; Fic
1. Superhero graphic novels; 2. X-Men (Fictional characters); 3. Graphic novels
978-0-7851-1831-2, $10.99
The New X-men deal with the changed world after the events of the House of M (in which many mutants lost their powers). Will X-23 join the team, can anyone trust her" Will friendships persevere" Will the kids survive" No one is safe, and not everyone will live through the changes, not when the rules have changed and the safety is off.

Lane, Miles
Star Wars: Clone Wars Volume 7: When They Were Brothers. Written by Haden Blackman and Miles Lane ; art by Brian Ching and Nicola Scott. Dark Horse Comics 2005 Un. Illustration
Grades: 7 8 9 10 11 12 Adult   741.5; Fic
1. Adventure graphic novels; 2. Science fiction graphic novels; 3. Star Wars; 4. Graphic novels
1-59307-396-8, $17.95
Consumed by the belief that the Dark Jedi Asajj Ventress still lives, Obi-Wan Kenobi has temporarily forsaken his duties and recruited Anakin Skywalker in his desperate hunt for Ventress. But Anakin believes that Obi-Wan is chasing a ghost-because he himself killed Ventress. And Anakin's doubts about his former Master's quest are not assuaged when, following the trail of the rumors of Ventress' existence, they walk into a trap set by their old enemies, the bounty hunter Durge and Count Dooku. The book includes battle violence.

Langridge, Roger
The Muppet Show comic book: on the road. Writer, Roger Langridge ; art, Shelli Paroline & Roger Langridge ; colors, Digikore Studios, Mickey Clausen & Eric Cobain ; letters, Shelli Paroline & Deron Bennett. Boom! Kids 2010 Un Illustration
Grades: 3 4 5 6 7 8 9 10 11 12 Adult   741.5; Fic
1. Humorous graphic novels; 2. Muppets (Fictional characters); 3. Travel; 4. Graphic novels
978-1-60886-516-1, $9.99
The Muppets' theater must undergo massive repairs, so the crew takes their show on the road. Standup comedian Fozzie tries to go on his own as a solo act, while Kermit and the rest of the motley group hires a caravan of buses and trailers to find small towns where they can perform. One place, Little Statwald, seems to be populated almost completely by relatives of old curmudgeons Stadler and Waldorf, who all delight in heckling the hapless performers. Langridge draws the main Muppets story, while Shelli Paroline draws the Pigs in Space episodes. The stories have

been written to appeal to younger readers, while adults who remember the old Muppets television series will also enjoy the comics.

Lanzac, Abel
Weapons of Mass Diplomacy. By Abel Lanzac, illustrated by Christophe Blain, translated by Edward Gauvin. Harry N Abrams Inc 2014 200 p. Color; Illustration
Grades: Adult   741.5
1. United States — Foreign opinion — France; 2. War on Terrorism, 2001-2009 — Influence; 3. Graphic novels
190683878X; 9781906838782, $24.95
LC 2014501285
"In 2003, France opposed the U.S. military juggernaut's initiative to chastise Iraq for presumed 'weapons of mass destruction.' With a nail-biting tale conjuring both Dilbert and Franz Kafka's satires, Lanzac (pseudonym of former diplomatic staffer Antonin Baudry) fictionalizes the personalities and power plays leading up to this real and courageous decision. . . . The hapless Arthur Vlaminck (Baudry's nom-de-toon) signs on as speechwriter for French foreign minister Alexandre Taillard de Vorms. Buffeted by clouds of doublespeak and doublethink as the crisis builds, Arthur gradually realizes that his infuriating boss is actually a gutsy visionary." (Library Journal)
"Besides the Quai d'Orsay, other settings include far-flung embassies and the UN; besides the Minister and Arthur, several other characters are also drolly realized by ace French adventure-comedy cartoonist Blain—all in his characteristic mixture of caricatural figures and highly realistic settings." Booklist

Lapham, David
Batman: City of Gotham. David Lapham, writer; Ramon Bachs, penciler; Nathan Massengill, inker; Jason Wright, colorist; Jared K. Fletcher, letterer. DC Comics 2006 288p. Illustration
Grades: 10 11 12 Adult   741.5; Fic
1. Batman (Fictional character); 2. Mystery graphic novels; 3. Superhero graphic novels; 4. Graphic novels
978-1-4012-0897-4, $19.99
Dave Lapham, the creator of the ultra-gritty noir series Stray Bullets, weaves a story of the Dark Knight facing an unspeakable crime. Batman first investigates the deaths of six teenage girls, then he learns of even worse crimes. As he tries to shut down a drug ring that's turned deadly, Bruce Wayne must contend with a wayward 14-year-old who's getting dangerously close to Gotham's underworld. In Gotham City, not every villain wears a mask; not every hero wears a cape; not every victim is innocent; and some secrets should remain buried. This volume includes violence.

Silverfish. DC Comics/Vertigo 2007 Un Illustration
Grades: 11 12 Adult   741.5; Fic
1. Mystery graphic novels; 2. Graphic novels
978-1-4012-1048-9, $24.99
What starts as a childish bid for her father's affections turns into nail-biting suspense when teenaged Mia searches her new stepmother's purse, only to find a secret stash of money, a bloody knife and a mysterious address book. In the meantime, Daniel is on the trail of the woman who betrayed

him; and the silverfish he keeps seeing in his mind's eye are telling him to kill again.

The **Spectre:** Infinite Crisis Aftermath. Written by David Lapham and Will Pfeifer; pencilled by Eric Battle and Cliff Chiang. DC Comics 2007 144p. Illustration
Grades: 10 11 12 Adult   **741.5; Fic**
  1. Spectre (Fictional character); 2. Superhero graphic novels; 3. Supernatural graphic novels; 4. Graphic novels
  978-1-4012-1380-0, $12.99
    After losing his human host, The Spectre ran rampant across the DC Universe, destroying all sources of magic. Now, the spirit of vengeance has been joined with a new host: the spirit of murdered Detective Crispus Allen from the Gotham City Police Department. But Allen wants nothing to do with the Spectre or his holy mission—even if it means jeopardizing his chance for redemption. The Spectre's vengeance tends to be quite bloody.

Larsen, Erik
  Savage Dragon Archives Volume 1. Image Comics 2006 616p. Illustration
Grades: 10 11 12 Adult   **Fic; 741.5**
  1. Hellboy (Fictional character); 2. Mystery graphic novels; 3. Superhero graphic novels; 4. Graphic novels
  978-1-58240-723-4, $19.99
    The earliest adventures are collected for the first time in one volume as Savage Dragon defends Chicago from Overlord and the Vicious Circle. Savage Dragon, a big, green, fin-headed alien with no memory of his early life before being found in an empty field in Chicago, is a superhero who actually works as a police officer with the Chicago Police Department. This is the complete Overlord epic from start to finish, culminating in a battle that can only end one way. Guest-starring the WildC.A.T.S and the Teenage Mutant Ninja Turtles. This black and white reprint volume includes a lot of fighting violence, some strong language, and some skimpy women's costumes.

  Savage Dragon Archives Volume 2. Image Comics 2006 616p. Illustration
Grades: 10 11 12 Adult   **741.5; Fic**
  1. Mystery graphic novels; 2. Superhero graphic novels; 3. Graphic novels
  9781582407371, $19.99; 1582407371
    This volume kicks off with an all-out gang war in the streets of Chicago and builds to the destruction of the planet Earth itself. Dragon goes from cop to corpse and to hell and back. This book features the birth of Dragon's son, the death and rebirth of Darklords and Dragon's ascension to the head of Special Operations Strikeforce. Guest-starring Spawn, Hellboy, the Maxx, the Teenage Mutant Ninja Turtles, and God. The book has lots of fighting violence, harsh language, some nudity and sexual situations.

Larson, Hope
  Gray horses. Oni Press 2006 Un Illustration
Grades: 9 10 11 12 Adult   **741.5; Fic**
  1. Dreams; 2. Graphic novels
  1-932664-36-X, 14.95

                      LC 2006-280748
    French exchange student Noemie has traveled to Onion City on her own, where she makes friends with free-spirited Anna, a neighbor and baker's daughter who sculpts in bread. As she walks around the city, she finds herself the target of a mysterious young photographer. However, it's in her dreams that things are weird. Every night she dreams of a girl named Marcy who finds help from a talking horse to get away from her mother; she must find a place to hide a photograph before her mother burns everything "contaminated" from illness. As the dreams progress every night, Noemie is more able to live in the moment. Much of the text is bilingual.

Lash, Batton
  Mister Negativity and Other Tales of Supernatural Law. Exhibit A Press 2004 170p. Illustration
Grades: 8 9 10 11 12 Adult   **741.5; Fic**
  1. Humorous graphic novels; 2. Supernatural graphic novels; 3. Graphic novels
  0-9633954-8-3, $15.95
                      LC 2003113227
    Attorneys Wolff & Byrd represent clients that include Nagy D'Viti, a fellow with such a negative attitude that he physically repels people, Huberis the Dybbuk, a born again demon seeking church membership, Nicky Gorillo, a gangster who has literally become a gorilla mob boss, Steven Gink, a horror novelist in a coma who summons them through their dreams, Susann, the Muse of Potboilers, who sues the author she has "inspired," and Perry Otter, a boy magician with an unusual affliction.

  Sonovawitch! And Other tales of Supernatural Law. Exhibit A Press 2000 166p. Illustration
Grades: 9 10 11 12 Adult   **741.5; Fic**
  1. Horror graphic novels; 2. Humorous graphic novels; 3. Law; 4. Graphic novels
  0-9633954-6-7, $14.95
    Alanna Wolff and Jeff Byrd are attorneys who represent the supernatural and the supernaturally afflicted. In this volume, their clients include "Dr. Life," a physician dedicated to reviving the dead; "Bugsy" Renfield, a vampire member of the Nosferatu crime cartel; Ygor, a hunchback charged with teaching Satanism to preschool children; Martin Woodhull, accused of "hexual harassment" when his mother, a witch, puts a love spell on one of his co-workers; Dekoo Kei, a Japanese holy man who guards a jewel that can unleash the power of the giant reptilian monster, the Gormagon; and Barry Hopper, a nice guy whose soul has accidentally possessed the body of the demon Wasistlos, who is not too happy to deal with its "inner human." And their secretary, Mavis, has an adventure all her own.

  Tales of supernatural law. Exhibit A Press 2005 184p. Illustration
Grades: 9 10 11 12 Adult
741.5; Fic
  1. Humorous graphic novels; 2. Lawyers; 3. Supernatural graphic novels; 4. Graphic novels
  0-9633954-9-1, $16.95
    This volume reprints the first eight issues of the ongoing comics series that used to be called Wolff & Byrd, Counselors

Courtesy of Exhibit A Press

of the Macabre and is now called Supernatural Law. Alanna Wolff and Jeff Byrd provide legal services for monsters, vampires, zombies, ghosts, and other things that go bump in the night. In these stories, they help a couple who foolishly used a monkey's paw to make wishes, another couple whose house becomes haunted every full moon, a supermodel seeking redress for a curse, a horror television host accused of exposing children to violence, a swamp monster who would like his fifteen minutes of fame, and the interdimensional being Th'Lulu.

Lasiuta, Tim

Brush Strokes with Greatness: The Life & Art of Joe Sinnott. Twomorrows Publishing 2007 136p. Illustration
Grades: Adult Professional **741.5**
1. Biographical graphic novels; 2. Sinnott, Joe, 1929-; 3. Graphic novels
978-1-893905-72-6, $17.95

Joe Sinnott is a true living legend. During his 56-plus-year career in comic books, he has worked in every genre, and for almost every publisher. This book celebrates the career of the versatile artist, as he demonstrates his passion for his craft. In it, Joe shares his experiences working on Marvel's leading titles, memories of working with Lee and Kirby, and rare and unpublished artwork from his personal files. This book features dozens of colleagues and co-workers paying tribute to Joe and his body of work, plus an extended art gallery and a checklist of Joe's career.

Lasko-Gross, Miss

Escape from Special. Fantagraphics Books 2006 Un Illustration
Grades: 10 11 12 Adult
741.5; Fic
1. Autobiographical graphic novels; 2. Girls; 3. Graphic novels
978-1-56097-804-6, $16.95

This semi-autobiographical graphic novel uses short episodes to depict the childhood and teen years of Melissa. Sometimes willful, she gets into trouble at school, is branded "special" (as in special education), has very few friends, and has to see a therapist.

Courtesy of Fantagraphics

With biting honesty, Melissa endures the casual cruelty of so-called friends, mis-uses bad words to comic effect, and questions why she should do things like attend Jewish school when her parents don't go to Temple. Occasional nudity and harsh language occur throughout the book.

Lat

Kampung boy. First Second 2006 141p. Illustration
Grades: 7 8 9 10 11 12 Adult **741.5; Fic**
1. Family life; 2. Malaysia; 3. Muslims; 4. Graphic novels
1-59643-121-0, $16.95

LC 2005-34135

"Malaysian cartoonist Lat uses the graphic novel format to share the story of his childhood in a small village, or kampung. From his birth and adventures as a toddler to the enlargement of his world as he attends classes in the village, makes friends, and, finally, departs for a prestigious city boarding school, this autobiography is warm, authentic, and wholly engaging." Booklist
First published 1979 in Malaysia with title: Lat, the kampung boy

★ **Town** boy. First Second Books 2007 191p. Illustration
Grades: 7 8 9 10 11 12 Adult **741.5; Fic**
1. Bildungsromans; 2. Humorous graphic novels; 3. Malaysia; 4. Graphic novels
978-1-59643-331-1, $16.95; 1-59643-331-0

LC 2006-102857

In this sequel to Kampung Boy, it's the late 1960s and Mat is now a teenager attending a boarding school in the town of Ipoh, far from his kampung. He discovers bustling streets, hip music, heady literature, budding romance, and through it all his growing passion for art.

Latour, Jason

Spider-Gwen; Volume 0: Most Wanted?. Written by Jason Latour, art by Robbi Rodriguez. Marvel Enterprises 2015 112 p.
Grades: 9 10 11 12 Adult **741.5**
1. Female superhero comic books, strips, etc; 2. Spider-Woman (Fictional character); 3. Superhero comic books, strips, etc
0785197737; 9780785197737, $16.99

"Gwen Stacy is Spider-Woman, but you knew that already. What you DON'T know is what friends and foes are waiting for her in the aftermath of Spider-Verse! From the fan-favorite creative team that brought you Spider-Gwen's origin story in EDGE OF SPIDER-VERSE, Jason Latour and Robbie Rodriguez!" (Publisher's note)
Originally published in single issue form as Spider-Gwen #1-5
First volume of an ongoing series

Lavie, Boaz

The **Divine**. Written by Boaz Lavie; illustrated by Asaf Hanuka, Tomer Hanuka. First Second 2015 160 p. Color; Illustration
Grades: Adult **741.5; Fic**
1. Fantasy comic books, strips, etc; 2. Magic; 3. War stories
9781596436749, $19.99; 1596436743

LC 2014047292

In this graphic novel, written by Boaz Lavie, illustrated by Asaf Hanuka and Tomer Hanuka, "Mark's out of the military . . . with his boring, safe civilian job doing explosives consulting. But you never really get away from war. So it feels inevitable when his old army buddy Jason comes calling, with a lucrative military contract for a mining job in an obscure South-East Asian country called Quanlom. They'll have to operate under the radar—Quanlom is being torn apart by civil war." (Publisher's note)

"Once in Quanlom the mood pivots from merely ominous to outright wartime nightmare, as Mark is taken prisoner by some particularly vicious preadolescent rebels. The story gets more and more violent and fantasy-like from there. The Hanukas' layered illustrations coat everything with a hyperreal glaze, accentuating the story's dreamlike aspects." Pub Wkly

Layman, John

★ **Chew,** volume one: taster's choice. Written & lettered by John Layman; drawn & coloured by Rob Guillory. Image Comics 2009 Un Illustration
Grades: 10 11 12 Adult   **741.5; Fic**
1. Cannibalism; 2. Mystery graphic novels; 3. Science fiction graphic novels; 4. Graphic novels
978-1-60706-159-5, $9.99
Police detective Tony Chu is a good detective with a weird secret: he's Cibopathic he gets psychic impressions from whatever he eats. It means he is a vegetarian, but it also means he can learn important facts about a case by nibbling on the corpse of a murder victim. Aside from the ôewwwwö factor, he tends to have a high success rate in solving his cases. In his world, the FDA (yes, Food and Drug Administration) has become the most powerful law enforcement agency on the planet, and chicken is a forbidden food because of the avian flu. The FDA's Special Crimes Division makes Tony one of their agents and gives him their strangest, sickest, most bizarre unsolved cases, hoping to use his Cibopathic abilities to close them. This story includes cannibalism, violence, some gore, and some bad language. It has also been cited by many comics reviewers as one of the top comics series of 2009.
Volume 1 of an ongoing series

Leavitt, Sarah

★ **Tangles:** A Story About Alzheimer's, My Mother, and Me. Sarah Leavitt. Skyhorse Pub. 2012 127 p. Illustration; Portrait
Grades: Adult   **362.1**
1. Alzheimer's disease; 2. Autobiographies; 3. Family life
1616086394; 9781616086398, $14.95
"In this . . . graphic memoir, Sarah Leavitt reveals how Alzheimer's disease transformed her mother Midge — and her family — forever.... Sarah shares her family's journey .. . managing to find moments of happiness. Midge, a Harvard-educated intellectual, struggles to comprehend the simplest words; Sarah's father Rob slowly adapts to his new role as full-time caretaker . . . Sarah and her sister Hannah argue, laugh, and grieve together." (Publisher's note)

Lee, Elaine

Starstruck. Elaine Lee, [writer]; M.W. Kaluta, [artist]; Lee Moyer, [painter]; [Todd Klein, letterer; Charles Vess, Galactic Girl Guides inker; John Workman, G.G.G. letterer; Scott Dunbier, editor]. IDW Publishing 2012 360 p. Illustration; Color
Grades: Adult   **741.5**
1. Astrology — Fiction; 2. Love — Fiction; 3. New Jersey — Fiction; 4. Overweight persons — Fiction; 5. Science fiction comic books, strips, etc; 6. Supernatural — Fiction
1613774397; 9781613774397($7.95 Can.), $34.99
LC 2010021636
The book presents a collection of "all 13 issues of the completely remastered Starstruck series by Elaine Lee and Michael Wm. Kaluta." The collection presents "360 pages of Starstruck and Galactic Girl Guides adventures, covers, pin-ups, glossary, [and] postcards." The book also

introduces new artwork and presents a look into the world of Starstruck. (Comic Vine)

Lee, Stan

Amazing Fantastic Incredible: A Marvelous Memoir. By Stan Lee, Peter David, and Colleen Doran. Simon & Schuster 2015 192 p. Color; Illustration
Grades: Adult   **92; 741.5**
1. Comic books, strips, etc — Authorship; 2. Lee, Stan, 1922-
1501107720; 9781501107726, $30
In this graphic novel memoir, "Stan Lee- comic book legend and cocreator of Spider-Man, the X-Men, the Avengers, the Incredible Hulk, and a legion of other Marvel superhero - shares his iconic legacy and the story of how modern comics came to be." (Publisher's note)

Essential Fantastic Four Vol. 1, 2nd ed.. Art by Jack Kirby. Marvel Entertainment 2005 Un Illustration
Grades: 7 8 9 10 11 12 Adult   **Fic; 741.5**
1. Fantastic Four (Fictional characters); 2. Hulk (Fictional character); 3. Superhero graphic novels; 4. Graphic novels
978-0-7851-1828-2, $16.99
This massive trade paperback collects the first 20 issues of The Fantastic Four plus the Annual #1. Reprinted in black and white, this volume lets readers get the origin and early stories as originally written by Lee and drawn by Kirby. The Fantastic Four fights against Skrulls, Sub-Mariner, The Impossible Man, The Hulk, the Red Ghost, The Thinker, Doctor Doom (who first appeared in issue #5), the Puppet Master, and many more super villains.

★ **Stan** Lee's How todraw comics: from the legendary co-creator ofSpider-Man, the Incredible Hulk, Fantastic Four, X-Men, and Iron Man. Watson-Guptill Publication 2010 224p. Illustration
Grades: 9 10 11 12 Adult   **741.5**
1. Comic books, strips, etc — Authorship; 2. Drawing — Technique; 3. Fantastic Four (Fictional characters); 4. Hulk (Fictional character); 5. Iron Man (Fictional character); 6. Spider-Man (Fictional character); 7. X-Men (Fictional characters); 8. Graphic novels
978-0-8230-0083-8, $24.99
LC 2010-5781
Includes bibliographical references
The author "includes chapters on creating comics with computer programs and online resources and how to get work in the 21st century. The book begins with a brief history of comics, then focuses on action-adventure style, romance, humor, horror, and Japanese manga. This is the one book anyone interested in drawing comics should own." Libr J

Stan's soapbox: The collection. Marvel Entertainment 2008 144p. Illustration
Grades: 9 10 11 12 Adult   **741.5; 814**
1. Fantastic Four (Fictional characters); 2. Spider-Man (Fictional character); 3. X-Men (Fictional characters); 4. Graphic novels
978-0-9797602-9-7, $14.99
Stan Lee is probably one of the best-known faces of American comics, he helped to create many of the iconic superhero characters published by Marvel Comics,

including the Fantastic Four, Spider-Man, and the X-Men. As an editor for Marvel, he wrote editorials that ran in every Marvel comic published from 1967-1980; these were called "Stan's Soapbox." This book, published as a co-venture with the Hero Initiative as a fundraiser to help comic creators in financial need, collects all of the Stan's Soapbox editorials from those Marvel comics. Readers can go back in time as they read what Lee wrote; the book also includes the major events happening in the U.S. and the world during those years

Lee, Tony
   Starship TroopersVol. 1: Blaze of Glory. Story Tony Lee; art Sam Hart and Rod Reis. Markosia 2006 Un Illustration
Grades: 10 11 12 Adult   **741.5; Fic**
   1. Adventure graphic novels; 2. Science fiction graphic novels; 3. War; 4. Graphic novels
   1-905692-05-6, $14.95
   Based on the science fiction novel by Robert Heinlein, this book tells the story of the Starship Troopers, human soldiers who fight a war against aliens they call "bugs." Rookie Will Tanner joins Tamari's Tigers, one of the fiercest units in the mobile infantry in time for their next mission, to rescue the survivors of Alamar "Alamo" Bay from a planet of bugs. The book is full of combat action and harsh language.

Lee, Young-You
   Priceless Volume 1. Tokyopop 2006 192p. Illustration
Grades: 9 10 11 12 Adult   **741.5; Fic**
   1. Humorous graphic novels; 2. Manwha; 3. Romance graphic novels; 4. Graphic novels
   1-59816-309-4, $9.99
   After her mother goes on the lam because of a business scam, Lang-bee is alone to fend for herself. She repays the people ripped-off by her mom with the money she makes working for her fellow students, taking on their school cleaning duties. When Lang-bee pursues her love interest Dan Won, the rich heir to a corporate empire, she competes against archrival Yuka Lee. Then Jimmy, a teenager just a little older than Lang-bee, shows up and claims her mother plans to marry him, and he tries to be her "father." This is a rags-to-riches story filled with love triangles, double-crosses, and mysterious pasts.

LeGrow, M. Alice
   Bizenghast Vol. 1. Tokyopop 2005 Un Illustration
Grades: 9 10 11 12 Adult   **741.5; Fic**
   1. Fantasy graphic novels; 2. Horror graphic novels; 3. Graphic novels
   1-59532-743-6, $9.99
   Time passes in every town...except one. When Dinah moves to the forgotten town of Bizenghast after her parents die, she uncovers a terrifying collection of lost souls that leads her to the brink of insanity. One thing becomes painfully clear: the residents of Bizenghast are just dying to come home. This is a global manga title.

Lehman, Timothy
   Manga: masters of the art. HarperCollins/Collins Design 2005 255p. Illustration
Grades: Adult Professional   **741.5**
   1. Graphic novels — Authorship; 2. Manga — Authorship
   978-0-06-083331-2, $24.95
                        LC 2005-930652
   This is a practical reference book, a look at how this artwork makes it from concept to reality, and a commentary on the format. The artists featured are: Kia Asamiya (Silent M÷bius, Batman: Child of Dreams), CLAMP (Chobits, Tsubasa), Takehiko Inoue (Vagabond, Slam Dunk), Erica Sakurazawa (Between the Sheets, The Aromatic Bitters), Jiro Taniguchi (Icaro, The Walking Man), Yuko Tsuno (Swing Shell), Tatsuya Egawa (Golden Boy, Tokyo University Story), Suehiro Maruo (Mr. Arashi's Amazing Freak Show), Reiko Okano (Onmyoji, Fancy Dance), Mafuyu Hiroki (Apples), Miou Takaya (Crazy Heaven, Map of Sacred Pain), and Usamaru Furuya (Short Cuts, Palepoli). They discuss how they became interested in manga, their first published work, where they get their ideas, the creative process, tips and techniques, artistic influences, the genre itself, and much more. Illustrations and photographs of each artist's most seminal works are accompanied by extensive, explanatory captions. Some of the art depicts nudity, sexual situations, and violence.
   Fans "will be fascinated by the behind-the-scenes details and the generous samples from stories that prompt seeking out more." Booklist

Lehmann, Matthias
   Hwy 115. Fantagraphics Books 2006 Un Illustration
Grades: 12 Adult   **741.5; Fic**
   1. Mystery graphic novels; 2. Graphic novels
   978-1-56097-733-9, $19.95
   Two detectives, Ren? and Agatha, are on the tracks of Robert Illot, a serial killer whose modus operandi is to suffocate his victim with various objects (including chickens and lightbulbs) along the highways and byways of France. As they get closer and closer to catching up with him, seeking out and interrogating men and women from his past life at the insane asylum, he always stays one step ahead and the row of corpses grows longer and longer... In this lengthy original graphic novel by Matthias Lehmann, dreams and flashbacks converge with the ongoing narrative, with graphically depicted sex and lots of murders.

Lemelman, Gusta
   Mendel's daughter: a memoir. Gusta Lemelman, Martin Lemelman. Free Press 2006 217p. Illustration
Grades: Adult   **92; 741.5**
   074329162X; 9780743291620, $24.99
                        LC 2006045180
   "In 1989 Martin Lemelman videotaped his mother, Gusta, as she opened up about her childhood in 1930s Poland and her eventual escape from Nazi persecution. Mendel's Daughter . . . is Lemelman's loving transcription of his mother's harrowing testimony, bringing her narrative to life with his own powerful black-and-white drawings, interspersed with reproductions of actual photographs, documents and other relics from that era." (Publisher's note)

Lemire, Jeff

Animal Man; Volume 1: The hunt. Jeff Lemire, writer; Travel Foreman, artist. DC Comics 2012 144 p. Color illustration

Grades: Adult   **741.5/973; 741.5**

1. Family life — Fiction; 2. Superhero comic books, strips, etc; 3. Superheroes — Fiction

1401235077; 9781401235079, $14.99

LC 2011051856

This comic book by Jeff Lemire, illustrated by Travel Foreman, includes issues 1-6 of "Animal Man." "As a part of the . . . DC Comics-The New 52 event of September 2011, . . . Buddy Baker has gone from 'super' man to family man—but is he strong enough . . . when . . . his young daughter . . . manifest[s] her own dangerous powers" . . . [T]hings take a turn for the worse as Buddy begins a startling transformation of his own that will lead him on a journey into the heart of The Red." (Publisher's note)

"Lemire scripts likable characters and relatable family dynamics, even as he ratchets up the creepiness, ably abetted by Foreman's stark-lined and sinewy art, which basks in the varied ways the human form can be twisted into hideous shapes" Booklist

Originally published in single magazine form in ANIMAL MAN 1-6—t.p. verso.

Other Animal Man volumes written by Jeff Lemire are: 2: Animal vs. Man (2012); 3: Rotworld: The Red Kingdom (2013); 4: Splinter Species (2014); 5: Evolve or Die! (2014)

Animal Man; Volume 2. Jeff Lemire, writer; Steve Pugh, Travel Foreman, Timothy Green II, Alberto Ponticelli, pencillers. DC Comics 2012 176 p. Illustration; Color

Grades: Adult   **741.5/973; Fic**

1. Justice League (Fictional characters); 2. Superhero comic books, strips, etc

1401238009; 9781401238001, $16.99

LC 2012032137

This graphic novel, by Jeff Lemire, illustrated by Steve Pugh and Timothy Green, is volume two of the DC Comics "Animal Man" series. "Ever since he discovered his daughter's connection to the Red—the strange source of his powers and the mystical connective tissue between all life on the planet—Buddy Baker and his family have been on the run. But when Buddy goes missing, his family receives assistance from John Constantine and the Justice League Dark." (Publisher's note)

Originally published in single magazine form in Animal Man 0, 7-11, Animal Man Annual 1.

★ **Descender:** Tin Stars Book one. By Jeff Lemire; illustrated by Dustin Nguyen. Image Comics 2015 160 p.

Grades: 9 10 11 12 Adult   **741.5; 741.5/973**

1. Androids — Fiction; 2. Robots — Fiction; 3. Science fiction comic books, strips, etc

1632154269; 9781632154262, $9.99

LC Bl2015040509

In this science fiction comic book, by Jeff Lemire, illustrated by Dustin Nguyen, "Young Robot boy TIM-21 and his companions struggle to stay alive in a universe where all androids have been outlawed and bounty hunters lurk on every planet." (Publisher's note)

Volume 1 of an ongoing series

★ **Essex** County, Vol. 1: Tales from the Farm. Top Shelf Productions 2007 Un Illustration

Grades: 10 11 12 Adult   **741.5; Fic**

1. Farm life; 2. Friendship; 3. Orphans; 4. Graphic novels

978-1-891830-88-4, $9.95

Orphaned ten-year-old Lester lives with his bachelor uncle Ken on a southwestern Ontario farm. He constantly wears a mask and cape, imagining that he's protecting the place from invading space aliens. Uncle Ken doesn't know how to deal with Lester, and their relationship becomes strained. Only one grown-up, Jimmy, who runs the gas station and convenience store, can connect with Lester on his level.

"Lemire enriches this rather familiar scenario with telling, particularizing detail, ensuring that this time the old heartwarming routine is unforgettably special." Booklist

Essex County, vol. 2: Ghost stories. Top Shelf Productions 2007 224p. Illustration

Grades: 10 11 12 Adult   **741.5; Fic**

1. Brothers; 2. Hockey; 3. Graphic novels

978-1-891830-94-5, $14.95

Ghost Story follows the lives and relationship of brothers Lou and Vince Lebeuf over the course of nearly seven decades. Elder brother Lou, now a deaf and lonely man, lives out his final days on his farm full of guilt and regret for the decisions he made that tore his family apart. From their childhood on the farm, to Toronto in the 1950s (where they both played professional hockey), Lou is left to revisit his life, his decisions and his regrets. This is the second volume of Lemire's stories of Essex County.

★ **Essex** County, vol. 3: The country nurse. Top Shelf Productions 2008 127p. Illustration

Grades: 10 11 12 Adult

741.5; Fic

1. Family life; 2. Graphic novels

978-1-891830-95-2, $9.95

In this third and final volume in the Essex County trilogy, the story follows country nurse Anne Morgan through one day as

Courtesy of Top Shelf Productions

she drives around the county to visit patients. In between her meetings with Jimmy at the gas station, Ken and his nephew Lester at the farm, and learning that elderly Mr. LeBeuf, Jimmy's father, had died the previous night, readers see the story of an orphanage that existed almost a century ago. When it burned down one night and the caretaker died getting all the children out, the nun in charge led them on a cold winter hike to find shelter and help in Essex County. Anne is a descendant of the nun, while Jimmy, Ken, and Lester are all descendants of one orphan. And all their stories come together as Anne makes her rounds of the day.

"Well written and beautifully drawn, this wonderful close to a powerful trilogy is ideal for fans of realistic stories in comics." SLJ

Green Arrow; Volume 4: The kill machine. Jeff Lemire, writer; Andrea Sorrentino, artist. DC Comics 2014 Un Color; Illustration
Grades: 9 10 11 12 Adult   **741.5; Fic**
1. Green Arrow (Fictional character); 2. Superhero comic books, strips, etc
9781401246907, $16.99; 1401246907
                                        LC 2013045547
"A mysterious villain called Komodo knows Oliver's secrets and uses them to rob Oliver of all his wealth and his company. Now on the run from this seemingly unstoppable force, Oliver finds himself in a mystery involving the island where he first became Green Arrow and his father! Everything will change for the Emerald Archer in this new beginning for the character." (Publisher's note)
Other Green Arrow volumes by Lemire and Sorrentino are: 5: The outsiders war; 6: Broken

Hawkeye: all-new Hawkeye. By Jeff Lemire; illustrated by Ramon Perez. Marvel Enterprises 2015 112 p. Color; Illustration
Grades: 11 12 Adult   **741.5; 741.5/973**
1. Superhero comic books, strips, etc
0785194037; 9780785194033, $15.99
In this comic book, by Jeff Lemire, illustrated by Ramon Perez, "Hawkeye returns. . . . With Kate Bishop, his trusted ward and protege (not titles she would use) back at his side, Team Hawkeye is thrown into an all new adventure spanning two generations of avenging archers. Past and present lives collide as Kate and Clint face a threat that will challenge everything they know about what it means to be Hawkeye." (Publisher's note)

Sweet tooth; 1: out of the deep woods. Jeff Lemire, story & art; Jose Villarrubia, colors; Pat Brosseau, letters. DC Comics 2012 128 p. Color; Illustration (Sweet Tooth)
Grades: Adult   **Fic; 741.5**
1. Animal mutation; 2. Apocalyptic fiction; 3. End of the world; 4. Science fiction graphic novels
1401226965; 9781401226961, $12.99
                                        LC 2012017902
This graphic novel, by Jeff Lemire, "tells the story of Gus, a rare new breed of human/animal hybrid children, [who] has been raised in isolation following an inexplicable pandemic that struck a decade earlier. Now, with the death of his father he's left to fend for himself . . . until he meets a hulking drifter named Jepperd who promises to help him. Jepperd and Gus set out on a post-apocalyptic journey into the devastated American landscape to find 'The Preserve' a refuge for hybrids." (Publisher's note)
"Sweet Tooth is often visually stunning and even cinematic. It primarily uses a muted palette that reflects the darkness of this postapocalyptic world, but bright colors burst from the page during moments of violence, and there are quite a few of those in this book." SLJ
Originally published in single magazine form as Sweet Tooth #1-5
Volume 1 of a six-volume series

Sweet tooth; 3: animal armies. Jeff Lemire, story & art; Jose Villarrubia, colors; Pat Brosseau, letters. Vertigo/DC Comics 2011 142 p. Color; Illustration
Grades: Adult   **741.5**

1. Apocalyptic fiction; 2. Plague — Fiction; 3. Science fiction graphic novels; 4. Survival skills — Fiction
1401231705; 9781401231705, $14.99
                                        LC 2011534366
"Gus is now at the mercy of a ruthless militia who believe his past is the key to their future. And when they leave their fortified compound to hunt down Gus's history, an unlikely alliance may be his only chance to get out." (Publisher's note)
"Though there are game-changing plot twists and bloodshed to spare in this third arc of Lemire's postpandemic comic, the most interesting development is the thickening stew of biblical allusions. . . . Lemire's artwork, notable for its rough-edged style and formal playfulness, remains in full lockstep with his commanding storytelling." Booklist

Sweet tooth; 4: Endangered Species. Jeff Lemire, story & art; Jose Villarrubia, Jeff Lemire, colors; Pat Brosseau, letters; additional art by Nate Powell. Vertigo 2012 176 p. Color; Illustration (Sweet Tooth)
Grades: Adult   **741.5**
1. Animal mutation; 2. Missing persons; 3. Survival
1401233619; 9781401233617, $16.99
                                        LC 2012048547
"Gus reluctantly joins Jepperd on missing persons hunt, but the tension between the two continues to grow. Meanwhile, Singh and Johnny come face to face with a deadly new threat, and Lucy and the girls meet Walter Fish, an enigmatic survivor who may have more to offer than meets the eye. Will this lead to a new sanctuary for them, or something far more dangerous—" (Publisher's note)
"As with any story centered on stringing out the revelation of critical information, the trick is to make the journey worth it. Lemire's artwork, with a roughly hewn style that gets more brutally elegant with each issue and a constant stream of formal playfulness, is perfectly suited for the task." Booklist

Sweet tooth; 5: unnatural habitats. Jeff Lemire. Vertigo 2012 155 p. Illustration (Sweet Tooth)
Grades: Adult   **741.5**
1. Scientific expeditions — Fiction; 2. Secrets — Fiction
1401237231; 9781401237233, $14.99
                                        LC 2012023758
"As the mysterious Captain James Thacker and his crew man a deadly expedition, they will uncover secrets centuries old, but what does any of this have to do with Gus and Jepperd" Plus, while Jeppard, Singh and Gus make plans to head to Alaska, things start to deteriorate for the rest of the group back at the sanctuary!" (Publisher's note)

Sweet Tooth; 6: Wild Game. Jeff Lemire. Vertigo 2013 197 p. Color; Illustration (Sweet Tooth)
Grades: Adult   **741.5**
1. Epidemics — Fiction; 2. War
1401240291; 9781401240295, $16.99
                                        LC 2013003528
"Dr. Singh arrives in Alaska and uncovers the origins of Gus and the hybrid children and the cause of the plague that decimated the world. And as Gus and Jepperd finally arrive in Alaska and come face to face with the truth, the militia continues to bear down on them." (Publisher's note)

"Lemire comes as a package deal, both writing and drawing the story, and in that synergy, his words and art live harmoniously on the page, from expression to action, allowing his deceptively simplistic drawing style to shine." Booklist

Teen Titans; Volume 1: Earth One. Written by Jeff Lemire; pencils by Terry Dodson. DC Comics 2014 144 p. Color; Illustration

Grades: 10 11 12 Adult　　　　　　　　**741.5**
1. Superhero comic books, strips, etc; 2. Teen Titans (Fictional characters); 3. Teenagers
1401245560; 9781401245566, $22.99
　　　　　　　　　　　　　　　LC 2014032609
This book, by Jeff Lemire and Terry Dodson, is a "new original graphic novel in DC's popular 'Earth One' series. . . . The Teen Titans never felt like normal kids... but they had no idea how right they were. Their seemingly idyllic Oregon upbringing hides a secret — one that will bring killers, shamans, and extraterrestrials down on their heads, and force them into an alliance that could shake the planet to its foundations!" (Publisher's note)
"Rather than more minor tinkering with the teenaged super-hero team, this graphic novel is a full-scale reboot: what if, in an alternative world, circumstances brought together young people who echo the regular Teen Titans but are totally different people" . . . Lemire's (Essex County) script exploits teen angst efficiently and with some fresh imagination, while the Dodsons (Wonder Woman) produce lovely art, especially in panels showing Navajo seer Raven." Pub Wkly

Trillium. Jeff Lemire, writer & artist; Jeff Lemire, Jose Villarrubia, colorists; Carlos M. Mangual, letterer. DC Comics/Vertigo 2014 192 p. Color; Illustration

Grades: 11 12 Adult　　　　　　　　**741.5**
1. Love stories; 2. Science fiction graphic novels; 3. Time travel
1401249000; 9781401249007, $16.99
　　　　　　　　　　　　　　　LC 2014011939
Eisner Nominee: Best Limited Series (2014)
This graphic novel, by Jeff Lemire, with color by Jose Villarrubia and lettering by Carlos M. Mangual, "spins the tale of two star-crossed loved through space in time. . . . [In] the year 3797, . . . botanist Nika Temsmith is researching a strange species on a remote science station near the outermost rim of colonized space. . . . [In] 1921, . . . English explorer William Pike leads an expedition into the dense jungles of Peru in search of the fabled 'Lost Temple of the Incas.'" (Publisher's note)
"Lemire's art excels, combining his trademark sketchiness with gorgeous watercolors. But it's the layouts that take the book to new heights of creativity. Lemire tells two stories at once by turning the panels upside down, disorienting the reader as much as his heroes." Pub Wkly

The **underwater** welder. By Jeff Lemire. Top Shelf Productions 2012 220 p.
Grades: Adult　　　　　　　　**Fic**
1. Fatherhood; 2. Welders (Persons); 3. Graphic novels
1603090746; 9781603090742, $19.95
This graphic novel by Jeff Lemire follows Jack Joseph, "an underwater welder on an oilrig off the coast of Nova Scotia . . . [dealing with] the pressures of impending

fatherhood. As Jack dives deeper and deeper, he seems to pull further and further away from his young wife and their unborn son. But then, something happens deep on the ocean floor. Jack has a strange and mind-bending encounter that will change the course of his life forever!" (Publisher's note)

Lenkov, Peter M.
　　Fort: Prophet of the Unexplained. Script, Peter M. Lenkov; art, Frazer Irving; letters, Digital Chameleon. Dark Horse Comics 2003 Un Illustration
Grades: 9 10 11 12 Adult　　　　　**741.5; Fic**
1. Adventure graphic novels; 2. Fantasy graphic novels; 3. Horror graphic novels; 4. Mystery graphic novels; 5. Graphic novels
1-56971-781-8, $9.95
It's the end of the 19th century and the city of New York has been plagued by fish falling from the sky, strange lights in the night, bizarre collections of microbial goo, and vanishing citizens. It's up to one man to expose the truth behind these events... Charles Fort. A mild mannered librarian by day, Fort seeks out the truth and exposes the bizarre to the light of day, with the aid of young newspaper boy H.P. Lovecraft. The book includes some violence.

Lent, Michael
　　P.R.E.Y.: Origin of the Species. Written by Michael Lent ; adapted by Mike Raicht ; art by Bong Dazo and Alex Sanchez, Marvel Entertainment/Dabel Brothers 2007 Un Illustration
Grades: 7 8 9 10 11 12 Adult　　　　**741.5; Fic**
1. Horror graphic novels; 2. Science fiction graphic novels; 3. Graphic novels
978-0-7851-2658-4, $10.99
The Prometheus Corporation has unearthed something ancient and dangerous in its underwater excavations, and now it's come to the surface to make humanity its prey. Their solution" To lure the thing back in the sea and kill everything within a five mile radius, effectively covering the corporation's tracks. And so a disgraced marine biologist must race against the clock and find a way to keep the ocean from being destroyed by the corporation before something even more dangerous is unleashed on mankind. The book includes some strong language and some violence.

Leong, Sonia
　　101 top tips from professional manga artists. Sonia Leong, Hayden Scott Baron. Barrons Educational Series, Inc. 2013 176 p.
Grades: Adult　　　　　　　　**741.5**
1. Drawing — Technique; 2. Japanese art; 3. Manga — Study and teaching
1438002068; 9781438002064, $22.99
　　　　　　　　　　　　　　　LC 2012948428
This book, by Sonia Leong and Hayden Scott Baron, focuses on the Japanese drawing known as manga. "With additional insights from a select group of fellow professionals, this illustration-packed book covers all aspects of manga art, presenting advice and instruction on . . . everything an illustrator needs to know in order to create successful manga art for a variety of media." (Publisher's note)

"Freelance comic artist and illustrator Leong and several contributing artists provide over 100 tips grouped and organized around basic topics, highlighting key aspects of manga such as character design, backgrounds, props, software and media, and even practices of successful professionals." LJ

Levine, David
   American presidents. Fantagraphics Books 2008 128p. Illustration
Grades: 9 10 11 12 Adult   352.23; 741.5
   1. Cartoons and caricatures; 2. Presidents — United States
   978-1-60699-130-5, $19.99
   Cartoonist and caricaturist Levine has drawn the most powerful men of the free world for more than 50 years. This book collects his portraits of the American presidents, from Washington through George W. Bush (and some of their important colleagues); it includes caricatures of Bush Cabinet members and appointees, and the various candidates who ran for President in 2008, including Senator Hillary Clinton, Rudy Giulani, Senator John McCain, and President-Elect Barack Obama. Levine used his art to point out what he considered to be shortcomings, phoniness, duplicity, and venality in the various administrations throughout American history.

Levitz, Paul
   The **Huntress:** Darknight Daughter. Paul Levitz and Joe Staton. DC Comics 2006 224p. Illustration
Grades: 8 9 10 11 12 Adult   741.5; Fic
   1. Batman (Fictional character); 2. Catwoman (Fictional character); 3. Superhero graphic novels; 4. Graphic novels
   978-1-4012-09131, $19.99
   She is unique in comics, the daughter of a hero and a villain: the Earth-Two Batman and Catwoman. Helena Wayne was trained by her parents to become a superb athlete, and she studied law with the hope of bringing criminals to justice. But after Catwoman is blackmailed to resume her life of crime, leading to her death, Helena dons a costume and crossbow to become the Huntress to avenge her mother. This volume collects the stories originally published in the 1970s and 1980s.

   JSA: Ghost Stories. Paul Levitz, writer; George Pérez [and others], pencillers. DC Comics 2006 144p. Illustration
Grades: 10 11 12 Adult   Fic; 741.5
   1. Batman (Fictional character); 2. Justice Society of America (Fictional characters); 3. Superhero graphic novels; 4. Graphic novels
   978-1-4012-1196-7, $12.99
   Near the end of Infinite Crisis, Power Girl learns of a Golden Age adventure in which Batman and Superman battled the Gentleman Ghost. One year later, the members of the JSA are haunted by ghosts of their departed loved ones. As it becomes clear the two incidents are connected, the JSA becomes the target of the Gentleman Ghost and his undead army. How will the JSA end this supernatural slaughter, when the only being who knows how to stop it is the ghost of Batman?

   Justice Society Volume One. Paul Levitz and Gerry Conway. DC Comics 2006 224p. Illustration
Grades: 7 8 9 10 11 12 Adult   741.5; Fic

1. Flash (Fictional character); 2. Green Lantern (Fictional character); 3. Justice Society of America (Fictional characters); 4. Robin (Fictional character); 5. Superhero graphic novels; 6. Graphic novels
   978-1-4012-0970-4, $14.99
   The volume collects stories originally published in the 1970s, when DC revived the very first superhero team that was originally created in 1940: the Justice Society of America. This incarnation of the Justice Society includes the Golden Age Flash and Green Lantern, Hawkman, Dr. Fate, Wildcat, Dr. Mid-Nite, Robin, Power Girl, and the Star-Spangled Kid. Artists on this run include Wally Wood, Joe Staton, Keith Giffen, and Ric Estrada.

   Justice Society Vol. 2. Written by Paul Levitz ; art by Joe Staton, Bob Layton, Joe Giella, Dave Hunt. DC Comics 2007 224p. Illustration
Grades: 8 9 10 11 12 Adult   741.5; Fic
   1. Batman (Fictional character); 2. Flash (Fictional character); 3. Green Lantern (Fictional character); 4. Justice Society of America (Fictional characters); 5. Robin (Fictional character); 6. Superhero graphic novels; 7. Superman (Fictional character); 8. Graphic novels
   978-1-4012-1194-3, $14.99
   The Justice Society of America was the first comic book super-team, created in All Star Comics in the 1940s. They faded into obscurity until they were revived in the 1970s. This volume includes stories from the 1970s, featuring Superman, the Flash, Green Lantern, Hawkman, Dr. Fate, Wildcat, Robin, Power Girl, Star-Spangled Kid, and the Huntress. Among other stories in this volume, Batman dies, and Huntress is his daughter.

Lewis, A. David
   The **lone** and level sands. Artists, Marvin Perry Mann and Jennifer Rodgers. Archaia Studio 2006 147p. Illustration
Grades: 9 10 11 12 Adult   741.5; Fic
   1. Bible — OT — Exodus; 2. Egypt — History; 3. Graphic novels
   1-932386-12-2, $17.95
   Told mostly from the viewpoint of the Pharaoh, this book recounts the well-known story of the Exodus. Moses is portrayed as an old desert rascal, and Ramses II finds himself buffeted on all sides as he contends with a God who speaks through his family and friends and manipulates him to bring about the freedom of the Hebrews.
   "The plot moves with inexorable tragedy toward its conclusion, but the book never reads like a catalogue of vignettes about the miseries the Egyptians and Hebrews inflicted on each other. Instead, it is a powerful, moving reconsideration of an otherwise familiar tale. It is guaranteed to provoke." Voice Youth Advocates
   First published 2005 in black and white by Caption Box

Lewis, Corey Sutherland
   Sharknife Volume 1. Oni Press 2006 Un Illustration
Grades: 8 9 10 11 12 Adult   741.5; Fic
   1. Humorous graphic novels; 2. Martial arts; 3. Graphic novels
   1-932664-17-3, $9.95

The Guandong Factory isn't like other restaurants. It's five stories tall, produces more peach dumplings per day than most eateries do in a decade, and it's the home of Sharknife - a mystical protector charged with protecting the establishment from those who would do it harm. But who is this mysterious yet colorful being? Once just a simple busboy, now Caesar Ives is something more - a crazy red rocket hero destined for greatness. But can Caesar juggle both lives - nabbing the girl (the super-sexy Chieko Momuza), and stopping the wide assortment of bizarre baddies that would love to do his precious eatery harm? There's lots of martial arts action.

Lewis, Edith Patton
The **claws** come out: astounding tales of broads and monsters. IDW Publishing 2007 152p. Illustration
Grades: 10 11 12 Adult   741.5
1. Fantasy graphic novels; 2. Horror graphic novels; 3. Humorous graphic novels; 4. Graphic novels
978-160010-120-5, $19.99
The subtitle may sound rude (come on, calling women broads?), but all the women in the stories are strong, capable, willing to fight off monsters, vampires, and zombies. A young woman goes on a date for the first time in years, not knowing her ideal guy is a vampire. A teenage girl walking home after a date has a close encounter of the strange kind, but the aliens end up in trouble. An apathetic scientist/aspiring rock star works late at the lab defrosting the Abominable Snowman and finds trouble when a power outage allows the creature to get free. A fortune teller accidentally starts a zombie epidemic with a very powerful love potion. Lewis plays horror for laughs, with some violence and sexual innuendo.

Lewis, John
★ **March:** Book One. John Lewis; [co-written by] Andrew Aydin; [art by] Nate Powell. Top Shelf Productions 2013 121 p. Illustration
Grades: 8 9 10 11 12 Adult   741.5; 92
1. African Americans — Civil rights; 2. Civil rights movements — United States; 3. Lewis, John, 1940 February 21-
9781603093002, $14.95
LC 2013218903
Coretta Scott King (Author) Honor Book (2014)
This graphic novel, by U.S. congressman John Lewis, "in collaboration with co-writer Andrew Aydin and New York Times best-selling artist Nate Powell . . . spans John Lewis' youth in rural Alabama, his life-changing meeting with Martin Luther King, Jr., the birth of the Nashville Student Movement, and their battle to tear down segregation through nonviolent lunch counter sit-ins, building to a . . . climax on the steps of City Hall." (Publisher's note)
"This is superb visual storytelling that establishes a convincing, definitive record of a key eyewitness to significant social change." SLJ

★ **March:** Book Two. By John Lewis and Andrew Aydin; illustrated by Nate Powell. Top Shelf Productions 2015 192 p. Illustration
Grades: 8 9 10 11 12 Adult   741.5; 92

1. African American civil rights workers; 2. African American legislators; 3. African Americans — Civil rights; 4. Civil rights movements; 5. Civil rights workers — United States; 6. Legislators — United States
9781603094009, $19.95; 1603094008
LC Bl2015004150
This graphic novel, by John Lewis and Andrew Aydin, illustrated by Nate Powell, "takes us behind the scenes of some of the most pivotal moments of the Civil Rights Movement. . . . After the success of the Nashville sit-in campaign, John Lewis is more committed than ever to changing the world through nonviolence—but as he and his fellow Freedom Riders board a bus into the vicious heart of the deep south, they will be tested like never before." (Publisher's note)
"Heroism and steadiness of purpose continue to light up Lewis' frank, harrowing account of the civil rights movement's climactic days. . . . The contrast between the dignified marchers and the vicious, hate-filled actions and expressions of their tormentors will leave a deep impression on readers." Kirkus

Lewis, Jon
True Swamp: choose your poison. Jon Lewis. Uncivilized Books 2012 160 p.
Grades: Adult   741; Fic
1. Frogs
0984681426; 9780984681426, $19.95
This graphic novel, part of the True Swamp series, focuses on "Lenny the Frog . ., an amphibian with a constant inner dialogue of self-doubt, brought on by his interaction with other swamp life. Lenny second-guesses himself at every turn, whether he's facing the swamp fairies, battling for his life against a human, or visiting the creepy resident of a wayward human skull—it's all a catalyst for self-examination, as well as investigation of the big picture." (Publishers weekly)

Ligotti, Thomas
The **Nightmare** factory: based on the stories of Thomas Ligotti. HarperCollins/Fox Atomic Comics 2007 Illustration
Grades: 10 11 12 Adult   741.5
1. Horror graphic novels; 2. Graphic novels
978-0-06-124353-0, $17.99
In the universe of horror master Thomas Ligotti, clowns take part in a sinister winter festival, a scheming girlfriend makes reality itself come unraveled, a crumbling asylum's destruction unleashes a greater horror, and a mysterious Teatro comes and goes, leaving only shattered dreams in its wake. Ligotti's tales of terror take the reader to places few would suspect exist, where madness is only a thought away. This book adapts four of Ligotti's chilling tales by writers and artists Stuart Moore, Joe Harris, Colleen Doran (The Sandman), Ben Templesmith (30 Days of Night), Ted McKeever (Batman), and Michael Gaydos (Alias). Ligotti provides introductions to each story. Violence, some harsh language, and some nudity appear in some of the stories.

Li Kunwu
A **Chinese** Life. Written by Philippe Ôtie and Li Kunwu ; illustrated by Li Kunwu ; translated by Edward Gauvin. Harry N Abrams Inc 2012 691p. Illustration; Color

Grades: Adult 951.05092; 741.5
1. China — History; 2. Li Kunwu; 3. Graphic novels
1906838550; 9781906838553, $27.50
LC 2012464492
Kunwu's book focuses on the "creation of the People's Republic of China in 1949." It "chronicles the rise and reign of Chairman Mao Zedong, and his sweeping, often cataclysmic vision for the most populated country on the planet." The book reflects "the real life of the book's artist" and presents an autobiography of Li Kunwu. (Publisher's note)
Translated from the French edition.

Lieberman, A. J.
Martian Manhunter: The Others Among Us. A.J. Lieberman and Al Barrionuevo. DC Comics 2007 208p. Illustration
Grades: 10 11 12 Adult 741.5; Fic
1. Justice League (Fictional characters); 2. Martian Manhunter (Fictional character); 3. Superhero graphic novels; 4. Graphic novels
978-1-4012-1335-0, $19.99
J'onn J'onzz, the Martian Manhunter, came to Earth years ago to warn all of humanity of an impending invasion. He believed himself to be the sole surviving member of his race and thus decided to use his incredible super-powers to help safeguard the people of his adopted world as a member of the Justice League of America. His discovery of a Martian artifact on Earth sets him on a quest to discover the origin of the relic which leads to a stunning discovery, the ramifications of which will forever change the way he sees himself, humanity and his destiny. He discovers that a shadowy branch of the U.S. government has imprisoned and experimented upon a group of Green Martians. Why were they being held captive, and what mysterious predator still stalks the survivors of Mars" His quest for truth will bring J'onn into conflict with humans, with every friend he has made on this planet. This book includes violence.

Little, Jason
Shutterbug follies. Doubleday Graphic Novels 2002 153p. Illustration
Grades: 10 11 12 Adult 741.5
1. Mystery graphic novels; 2. Graphic novels
0-385-50346-6, $24.95
LC 2002-727189
This novel was "originally serialized as both a weekly newspaper comic strip and a web comics serial. . . . Scrappy 18-year-old Bee is working in a New York photo lab when a picture of a naked female corpse that's not quite what it appears to be piques her interest. Her amateur investigation of its photographer leads her to an ever-deepening mystery, a friendly cab driver, a cute but nervous photo assistant, some scary doings with the Russian mob and finally, into deadly danger." Publ Wkly
"With nearly implausible coincidences, a dash of slapstick humor, and a few red herrings, this is a detective romp, and the ending panel leaves readers breathlessly awaiting a sequel." SLJ

Livingston, Todd
America Jr.. Written by Nick Capetanakis & Todd Livingston; illustrated by Brendon Fraim & Brian Fraim. Image Comics 2007 96p. Illustration
Grades: 9 10 11 12 Adult 741.5; Fic
1. Humorous graphic novels; 2. Politics; 3. Graphic novels
978-1-58240-829-3, $9.99
Millerstown is a typical small, quiet middle America kind of town, but then the town's clerk discovers a bombshell in the town's charter: it was only a temporary part of the U.S., and the time ran out the day before. Suddenly, it's an independent nation right in the middle of the USA. "Led" by Mayor Thornton and advised by young retired Hollywood lawyer Darren, the people of Millerstown have to take care of all the day-today business of being an independent nation, such as naming their country (America Jr.), creating a national anthem, getting ready for elections. . . . The book collects the first 150 strips of the webcomic, and it includes some visual sexual innuendo.

Lobdell, Scott
High Roads. Writer: Scott Lobdell; pencils: Leinil Francis Yu. DC Comics/Wildstorm 2003 Un Illustration
Grades: 10 11 12 Adult 741.5; Fic
1. Adventure graphic novels; 2. Humorous graphic novels; 3. Graphic novels
1-4012-0033-8, $14.95
This volume tells the story of a mismatched group of ne'er-do-wells and misfits who find themselves involved in a treasure hunt of most improbable proportions. Nic Highroad and his friends - a washed-up British actor, a failed Kamikaze pilot, and Hitler's former mistress - set out to steal Hitler's most prized possession, and end up trying to save the world. Along the way, they have to fight off a Nazi-ninja corps, jump from a moving train, and outsmart the Master Race; but in the end, Hitler's FINAL final solution comes to something of an unexpected conclusion. The book includes violence, harsh language, nudity, and sexual situations.

Loeb, Jeph
Batman: Dark Victory. Written by Jeph Loeb; art by Tim Sale. DC Comics 2014 400 p.
Grades: 9 10 11 12 Adult Fic; 741.5
1. Batman (Fictional character); 2. Crime; 3. Serial killers
1401244017; 9781401244019, $24.99
LC 2013041357
This collection "continues the story of 'The Long Halloween.' It is early in Batman's crimefighting career, when James Gordon, Harvey Dent, and the vigilante himself were all just beginning their roles as Gotham's protectors. Once a town controlled by organized crime, Gotham City suddenly finds itself being run by lawless freaks, such as Poison Ivy, Mr. Freeze, and the Joker. Witnessing his city's dark evolution, the Dark Knight completes his transformation into the city's greatest defender." (Publisher's note)
Collected edition originally published 2001
Dark victory

Batman: Hush. Jeph Loeb, writer; Jim Lee, penciller; Scott Williams, inker; Richard Starkings, letterer; Alex Sinclair, colorist; Jim Lee & Scott Williams, original series

covers; Batman created by Bob Kane. DC Comics 2009 320 p. Illustration; Color
Grades: 9 10 11 12 Adult   **741.5/973; 741.5**
1. Batman (Fictional character); 2. Batman (Fictional character)
1401223176; 9781401223175, $24.99
LC 2009502034

This comic book, by Jeph Loeb, "is a thrilling mystery of action, intrigue, and deception, . . . in which Batman sets out to discover the identity of a mysterious mastermind using the Joker, Riddler, Ra's al Ghul and the Dark Knight's other enemies - and allies - as pawns in a plan to wreak havoc." (Publisher's note)

Originally published in single magazine form in Batman 608-619, Wizard 0—t.p. verso.

★ **Batman:** The Long Halloween. DC Comics 1999 375p. Illustration
Grades: 9 10 11 12 Adult   **Fic; 741.5**
1. Batman (Fictional character); 2. Mystery graphic novels; 3. Superhero graphic novels; 4. Graphic novels
1563894270; 9781563894275, $19.99
LC 99-218572

Taking place during Batman's early days of crime fighting, this collection tells the story of a mysterious killer who murders his prey only on holidays. Working with District Attorney Harvey Dent and Lieutenant James Gordon, Batman races against the calendar as he tries to discover who Holiday is before he claims his next victim each month. This story also ties into the events that transform Harvey Dent into Batman's deadly enemy, Two-Face. The book includes some violence

Catwoman: When in Rome. DC Comics 2005 Un Illustration
Grades: 10 11 12 Adult   **Fic; 741.5**
1. Catwoman (Fictional character); 2. Joker (Fictional character); 3. Mystery graphic novels; 4. Superhero graphic novels; 5. Graphic novels
1-4012-0432-5, $19.99; 1-4012-0717-0 (pa), $12.99

Catwoman travels to Rome with some unfinished business with the Falcone crime family. Accompanied by the Riddler, she dreams almost nightly about Batman, which annoys her to no end; she has gone to see Don Verinni, but even as she's talking to him, he dies from the Joker's poison. With help from local Sicilian hitman Christopher Castillo, Catwoman and Riddler get away, but when more mobsters come after her with Mr. Freeze's ice gun, Catwoman knows something is definitely wrong in Rome.

With frequent flashes of partial nudity and considerable violence, this title is more appropriate for older teens and adults.

Originally published as Catwoman: When in Rome issues #1-6 and Batman: Dark Victory issue #13.

Superman/Batman: Supergirl. Jeph Loeb, writer; Michael Turner, artist. DC Comics 2005 Un Illustration
Grades: 10 11 12 Adult   **Fic; 741.5**
1. Batman (Fictional character); 2. Superhero graphic novels; 3. Superman (Fictional character); 4. Wonder Woman (Fictional character); 5. Graphic novels
1-4012-0250-0, $12.99

Batman has discovered something strange on the bottom of Gotham Bay which leads him to a mysterious and powerful teenaged girl who's bent on destroying Gotham City. What's her connection to Superman? Why does Wonder Woman want to hide her from the outside world? Will Darkside succeed in recruiting her into doing his bidding? Who is she?

Superman/Batman Vol. 3: Absolute Power. Jeph Loeb, writer; Carlos Pacheco, penciller; Jesuus Merino, inker; Ivan Reis, additional pencils; Laura Martin, colorist; Richard Starkings, letterer. DC Comics 2005 Un Illustration
Grades: 10 11 12 Adult   **741.5; Fic**
1. Batman (Fictional character); 2. Science fiction graphic novels; 3. Superhero graphic novels; 4. Superman (Fictional character); 5. Graphic novels
1-4012-0714-6, $12.99

The Earth wakes up one day to a brand-new world order, on in which Superman and Batman rule with an iron fist. Humankind has a choice: obey or die. How did things get this way" And is anyone left who can stop them? Before long, Superman and Batman are sent careening through a series of bizarre alternate dimensions, facing an assortment of DC characters, including Kamandi, Sgt. Rock, Haunted Tank, Jonah Hex, and many more.

Superman/Batman Volume 4: Vengeance. DC Comics 2006 Un Illustration
Grades: 9 10 11 12 Adult   **741.5; Fic**
1. Batman (Fictional character); 2. Superhero graphic novels; 3. Superman (Fictional character); 4. Graphic novels
978-1-4012-1043-4, $19.99

Superman and Batman travel to an alternate Earth to kill the man responsible for the death of Lois Lane. And now the Maximums, the mightiest heroes from a world of super-soldiers, hulking monsters, and Norse gods have crossed dimensional barriers seeking to avenge their fallen comrade. It's a tale of nonstop action with guest stars from infinite earths, but who's really behind all of this?

Superman: Our Worlds at War. DC Comics 2006 512p. Illustration
Grades: 9 10 11 12 Adult   **741.5; Fic**
1. Green Lantern (Fictional character); 2. Superhero graphic novels; 3. Superman (Fictional character); 4. Wonder Woman (Fictional character); 5. Graphic novels
978-1-4012-1129-5, $24.99

Imperiex has been unleashed. As planets are destroyed in its mighty wake and with Earth in its path as it seeks to remake the universe in its twisted image, Superman is forced to form alliances with President Lex Luthor and Darkseid, even as he also joins with such heroes as Wonder Woman, Green Lantern, and many others. For once, this looks like a job that not even Superman can handle.

Lolos, Vasilis
The **last** call volume 1. Oni Press 2007 Un Illustration
Grades: 10 11 12 Adult   **741.5; Fic**
1. Mystery graphic novels; 2. Supernatural graphic novels; 3. Graphic novels
978-1-932664-69-0, $11.95

Teenagers Sam and Alec have gone joyriding in Alec's mother's car, jamming to heavy metal rock, when the car dies, and something hits them. They awaken to find themselves on a strange train with very odd people. The conductor throws Alec off the train, and Sam meets some of the other passengers on the train. When he goes back to the compartment where he and Alec woke up on the train, he witnesses the murder of the ticketed passenger who had the compartment. Now Sam works with Mr. S, the shadow person who existed in dead Benny's body, to try to find out who murdered him. The book includes some harsh language, including occasional use of the f-bomb, and some violence.

Lott, Renee
 Festering romance. Oni Press 2009 184p.
Grades: 9 10 11 12 Adult   **741.5; Fic**
 1. Ghosts; 2. Romance graphic novels; 3. Graphic novels
978-1-934964-18-7, $11.95
 College student Janet prefers to spend her time in her apartment, playing video games with her roommate and best friend Paul who happens to be a ghost. However, her friends keep setting her up on blind dates, and then one of them, Derek, turns out to be a nice guy. Subsequent dates don't go so well, though, because Derek also has a ghostly roommate Carol, who in life was his girlfriend. Janet and Derek blame each other for not telling the truth about their ghostly companions, but they each need to face the truth of why Paul and Carol are still with them. The book includes only some mildly bad language (crap, pissed off).

Loux, Matthew
 Sidescrollers. Oni Press 2006 Un Illustration
Grades: 10 11 12 Adult   **741.5; Fic**
 1. Friendship; 2. Humorous graphic novels; 3. Graphic novels
1-932664-50-5, $11.95
 Brian, Brad, and Matt are the kind of young man who works just enough to get by and be able to play video games, eat junk food, and hang around. Things change when their neighbor Amber, who works with them at the local McGreggor's, is going to the big local rock show where Brian's brother's band will be playing. Unfortunately for the guys, she's going with Dick (he'd rather be called Richard), the bully football player. Since Matt is sweet on Amber, the guys decide they have to save her from Dick, and their quest gets them out of the house, on the road, and in a whole lot of trouble. The book includes strong language, including the s-bomb and f-bomb, some sexual innuendo, and some fistfight violence.

Love, Jeremy
 ★ **Bayou,** volume one. Created by Jeremy Love; colors by Patrick Morgan. Zuda Comics/DC Comics 2009 Un Illustration
Grades: 9 10 11 12 Adult   **Fic; 741.5**
 1. African Americans; 2. Fantasy graphic novels; 3. Monsters; 4. Graphic novels
978-1-4012-2382-3, $14.99
2009 Glyph Comics Awards: Story of the Year, Best Writer, Best Artist, Best Female Character (Lee), Best Comic Strip
 In a little southern town called Charon in 1933, Lee Wagstaff lives the kind of precarious life that African Americans under Jim Crow laws had to live. She's friends with white Lily Westmoreland, but that friendship doesn't

protect her when Lily's mother accuses Lee of theft. Then Lily disappears, victim of a swamp monster, and the town's white men haul her father off to jail, most likely to face a lynching. Lee has to find Lily to save her father, but when she goes to the swamp where Lily disappeared, she falls into a strange land of monsters. There she meets Bayou, a blues-singing swamp monster who helps her, and Lee faces the evil in the strange land to find and save her friend. This book collects the first four chapters of the webcomic by Love, which was one of the first webcomics from Zuda, run by DC Comics. The book includes disturbing images of hanged people, and a white man hits Lee so hard she flies through the air and lands on her back with her face torn up. The "n" word is represented by "n*****" while other harsh language is plainly written. The book contains enough violence to bother squeamish and sensitive readers.
 "Extremely beautiful, scary and wonderful, this . . . comic takes readers to a pair of almost familiar, frequently threatening worlds." Publ Wkly
 Volume 1 of 2

Lovecraft, H. P. (Howard Phillips)
 The **Lovecraft** Anthology 2: A Graphic Collection of H.P. Lovecrafts Short Stories. H. P. Lovecraft; edited by Dan Lockwood; illustrated by Alice Duke.. Harry N Abrams Inc 2012 128 p.
Grades: 11 12 Adult   **741.5/942; 741.5; S C**
 1. Horror fiction; 2. Short stories
1906838437; 9781906838430, $19.95
 This book presents "a graphic anthology of tales" by horror fiction author H. P. Lovecraft. "From the insidious mutations of 'The Shadow over Innsmouth' to the mindbending threat of 'The Call of Cthulhu,' this collection explores themes of insanity, inherited guilt, and arcane ritual." (Publisher's note)

Lowe, John
 Working Methods: Comic Creators Detail Their Storytelling and Artistic Processes. Twomorrows Publishing 2007 176p. Illustration
Grades: Adult Professional   **741.5**
 1. Comic books, strips, etc — Technique; 2. Graphic novels
978-1-893905-73-3, $21.95
 Professional comic artists interpret scripts every day as they successfully transform the written word into the visual form. This book puts the minds of comic artists under the microscope, highlighting the intricacies of the creative process step by step. For this book, three short scripts are each interpreted in different ways by professional comic artists to illustrate the varied ways in which they "see" and "solve" the problem of making a script succeed in comic form. The book documents the creative and technical choices Mark Schultz, Tim Levins, Jim Mahfood, Scott Hampton, Kelsey Shannon, Chris Brunner, Sean Murphy and Pat Quinn make as they tell a story,. Hundreds of illustrated examples document the artists' processes, and interviews clarify their individual approaches regarding storytelling and layout choices.

Luedke, Robert James

Eye Witness: A Fictional Tale of Absolute Truth. Head Press Publishing 2004 96p. Illustration

Grades: 9 10 11 12 Adult $\qquad$ **741.5; Fic**
1. Adventure graphic novels; 2. Graphic novels

978-0-9758924-0-4, $13.99

Amid the violence and chaos of the present day Middle East, remarkably preserved first century documents are discovered by seismic researchers beneath the foundations of present day Jerusalem. None of the experts called in by the Israeli government can decipher this mysterious text, so as a last resort they call in American archeologist, Dr. Terry Harper, known around the world as, "The Bone Man—. What Dr. Harper finds through his translation, is a previously undiscovered, eyewitness account of Jesus' final week in Jerusalem. Will it confirm or discount the Gospel accounts of this event that have guided people for thousands of years" Only Dr. Harper has the key to unlocking this mystery & and sharing it may cost him his life.

Lust, Ulli

★ **Today** Is the Last Day of the Rest of Your Life. By Ulli Lust and translated by Kim Thompson. W W Norton & Co Inc 2012 460 p.

Grades: Adult $\qquad$ **741.5; 741.5/943 B**
1. Italy — Description and travel; 2. Summer; 3. Teenage girls — Travel

160699557X; 9781606995570, $35

Ignatz Award: Outstanding Graphic Novel (2013)

This graphic memoir by Ulli Lust, winner of the 2011 Angouleme "Revelation" prize, " recalls when "in 1984, a rebellious,17-year-old, punked-out Ulli Lust set out for a wild hitchhiking trip across Italy, from Naples through Verona and Rome and ending up in Sicily. Lust meticulously shows the who, where, when, and how (specifically, how an often penniless young girl can survive for months on the road) of a sometimes dangerous and sometimes exhilarating journey." (Publisher's note)

Lutes, Jason

★ **Berlin,** city of stones: a work of fiction. By Jason Lutes. Drawn & Quarterly 2000 209 p.

Grades: Adult $\qquad$ **741.5; 741.5/973**
1. Berlin (Germany) — Fiction; 2. College students — Fiction; 3. Journalists — Fiction

1896597297; 9781896597294, $22.95

LC Bl2007002819

This book "presents the first part of Jason Lutes' . . . trilogy, set in the twilight years of Germany's Weimar Republic. Kurt Severing, a journalist, and Marthe Muller, an art student, are the central figures in a broad cast of characters intertwined with the historical events unfolding around them. City of Stones covers eight months in Berlin, from September 1928 to May Day, 1929, . . . documenting the hopes and struggles of its inhabitants." (Publisher's note)

Jar of Fools. Drawn & Quarterly 2003 152p. Illustration

Grades: 10 11 12 Adult $\qquad$ **741.5; Fic**
1. Graphic novels

1-896597-72-6, $16.95

Haunted by the death of his escape-artist brother and a failed romance, the remaining hope of washed-up stage magician Ernie Weiss lies in his aging mentor, Al Flosso. But Al is slipping further into senility with each passing day. Meanwhile, Esther O'Dea, Ernie's ex-love, struggles to find peace in her own life, and a con man named Nathan Lender sets some mysterious plans for Ernie's future in motion in his efforts to make things right for his twelve-year-old daughter Claire.

Luthi, Morgan

Snow, Vol. 1. Tokyopop 2006 Un Illustration

Grades: 9 10 11 12 Adult $\qquad$ **741.5; Fic**
1. Adventure graphic novels; 2. Science fiction graphic novels; 3. Graphic novels

1-59816-743-X, $9.99

The gigantic Warmongers created the Ghost of Destruction, a human-shaped weapon that can destroy entire planets. Hub is a planet full of misfits and gangs, and one day a young man with a scarred face wanders into Refuse City and inadvertently helps a rebel gang called the Crows, led by Kat. Snow, the young man, and Kat each have secrets in their past, but Snow's secrets could destroy Hub.

Lynch, Brian

Spike: shadow puppets. Brian Lynch; illustrated by Franco Urru. IDW Publishing 2007 112p. Illustration

Grades: 10 11 12 Adult $\qquad$ **741.5; Fic**
1. Fantasy graphic novels; 2. Spike (Fictional character); 3. Vampires; 4. Graphic novels

978-1-60010-112-0, $17.99

The vampire named Spike teams up with green-skinned Lorne to take on the demonic puppets of "Smile Time," who have moved to Japan and taken their evil there. The children who watch the show lose their souls, and Spike decides to save them. Even when he and Lorne attack the puppets and find themselves turned into puppets. The book includes mild harsh language and some puppet killing violence.

Ma, Wing Shing

Chinese Hero, Tales of the Blood Sword, Vol. 1. DrMaster Publications, Inc. 2007 270p. Illustration

Grades: 8 9 10 11 12 Adult $\qquad$ **741.5; Fic**
1. Adventure graphic novels; 2. Martial arts; 3. Graphic novels

978-1-59796-041-1, $19.95

When he was a child, Hero's family was attacked and killed by a practitioner of Northern Mantis kung fu. This assassin was tasked, by the affluent head of a local triad, to retrieve Hero's family heirloom - the legendary Blood Sword. Barely escaping with his life, Hero has now reached adulthood, having mastered several forms of kung fu to aid him in his lifelong endeavor to safeguard the family treasure. But now his enemies turn their gaze to his newborn son. This series is full of full-color kung fu action. This is a Chinese manhua.

Mack, Stan

★ **Taxes,** the tea party, and those revolting rebels: a comics history of the American revolution. Stan Mack. NBM Pub. 2012 166 p.

Grades: 9 10 11 12 Adult   **741.5**
1. United States — History — 1600-1775, Colonial period; 2. United States — History — 1775-1783, Revolution; 3. United States — Politics and government — 1775-1783, Revolution; 4. Wit and humor
1561636975; 9781561636976, $14.99
LC 2012938930
This historical comic book, by Stan Mack, is a humorous narrative overview of the U.S. Revolutionary War. "This graphic account of the birth of the United States stars a chubby, insecure King George III, rebellious and misunderstood colonists, and loudmouthed and insensitive aristocrats, providing information about the Boston Tea Party and the revolt against the status quo." (Publisher's note)

Macklin, Ken
The **weasel** patrol. Illustrated by Lela Dowling. About Comics/About Infinity 2009 104p. Illustration
Grades: 7 8 9 10 11 12 Adult   **741.5; Fic**
1. Humorous graphic novels; 2. Science fiction graphic novels; 3. Weasels; 4. Graphic novels
978-0-9790750-8-7, $9.99
When criminals strike, the intergalactic troopers called the Weasel Patrol will ferret out the bad guys every time. Despite their utter lack of planning, attentiveness, cohesion, or competence, they always succeed, even if their favorite tactic when faced with danger is to run away. This book includes twelve comedic adventures, in which the weasels face mythical monsters (Big Foot), aliens, kidnapped cattle in disguise, and the ever-ready bad guy Reefer Rick. Willy, Leroy, Biff, Roscoe, and Bob are the genetically uplifted Weasel Patrol. The book includes mild, cartoony violence and no bad language and no nudity. Villainous Reefer Rick smokes. Artist Dowling includes fun little details, such as the Acme name on some of the gadgets.

Mad About the Fifties
Grant Geissman, editor. E.C. Publications/MAD Books 2005 Un. Illustration
Grades: 8 9 10 11 12 Adult   **741.5**
1. Humorous graphic novels; 2. Satire; 3. Graphic novels
1-4012-0753-7, $12.99
MAD Magazine was founded in 1952 as a ten-cent comic book that parodied other comic books; three years later it became a twenty-five cent (cheap!) magazine. This volume collects some of the regular features and parodies of television programs and movies of the decade. Some of the advertising parodies feature tobacco and alcohol products, and some parodies portray the imbibing of alcohol products.

Mad About the Sixties: The Best of the Decade
Grant Geissman, editor. Mad Books/E.C. Publications 1997 Un Illustration
Grades: 7 8 9 10 11 12 Adult   **741.5; Fic**
1. Humorous graphic novels; 2. Satire; 3. Graphic novels
1-4012-0754-5, $9.99
Alfred E. Newman as a flower child" Ecch! Here is a look back at the Sixties from the satire magazine, full of send-ups, takeoffs, and put-ons from the decade that gave the world Timothy Leary and Tiny Tim. Along with Spy vs. Spy, Sergio Aragones' "Mad Marginals," Don Martin's

lunacies, and Snappy Answers to Stupid Questions, this volume includes TV satires such as Star Blecch, Bats-Man, and The Phewgitive, and movie takeoffs 201 Min. of a Space Idiocy, East Side Story, and Flawrence of Arabia. Back in the 1960s, preteens read the magazine and most of them turned out okay ...

Madden, Matt
★ **Drawing** words & writing pictures: making comics: from manga, graphic novels, and beyond. [by] Jessica Abel & Matt Madden. First Second Books 2008 Xxi, 282 p. Illustration
Grades: 9 10 11 12 Adult   **741.5**
1. Cartooning — Technique; 2. Comic books, strips, etc — Authorship; 3. Drawing — Technique; 4. Graphic novels — Authorship
1596431318; 9781596431317, $34.99
LC 2007044125
Authors Jessica Abel and Matt Madden present "a course on comic creation — for college classes or for independent study — that centers on storytelling and concludes with making a finished comic. With chapters on lettering, story structure, and panel layout, the fifteen lessons offered — each complete with homework, extra credit activities and supplementary reading suggestions — provide a solid introduction for people interested in making their own comics." (Publisher's note)
This book offers step-by-step entry into a complicated series of skills in a nonscary and approachable way. Libr J
Includes bibliographical references (p. 261-265) and index

Maeda, Mahiro
Gankutsuou: the Count of Monte Cristo, vol.. Del Rey Manga 2008 220p. Illustration
Grades: 10 11 12 Adult   **741.5; Fic**
1. Authors; 2. Biographers; 3. Dramatists; 4. Dumas, Alexandre, 1802-1870; 5. Dumas, Alexandre, 1802-1870 — Adaptations; 6. Magazine editors; 7. Manga; 8. Novelists; 9. Science fiction graphic novels; 10. Graphic novels
978-0-345-50520-0, $10.95
In the future, young Parisian nobleman Albert and his friend Franz travel to Luna, the moon, for a vacation, where they meet the Count of Monte Cristo, a wealthy aristocrat from the far reaches of the galaxy. Albert becomes fascinated by the man, who seems to be free in every sense of the word. What he doesn't know is that his father, General Morcerf, wealthy banker Baron Danglars, and Attorney General de Villefort, conspired together to destroy Edmond Dantes a quarter-century ago; and that Edmond Dantes is now the Count of Monte Cristo. He has returned to Paris for his own dark purposes of revenge upon all Albert loves. This science fictional version of Alexandre Dumas' novel is based on the anime series. The book includes some sexual situations, some nudity, and bloody violence.

Maeda, Tomo
Black Sun Silver Moon, Vol. 1. Go! Comi 2007 192p. Illustration
Grades: 10 11 12 Adult   **741.5; Fic**

1. Fantasy graphic novels; 2. Manga; 3. Supernatural graphic novels; 4. Graphic novels
978-1-933617-20-6, $10.99

Eighteen-year-old Taki had taken a job cleaning the church of Shikimi-sensei in order to work off his late father's debt; then he discovered that his main job is to hunt and kill demons and zombies. After working for a while - cleaning the church by day and slaying monsters by night - he notices that the townspeople shun Shikimi-sensei. Then Shikimi-sensei tells Taki that someday Taki will have to kill him, for his silver hair and eyes are signs that Shikimi-sensei will eventually become a zombie. This volume also includes a back-up story, "Magic Words," about a king who still looks like a little boy and his search for a worthy queen.

Mahler, Nicolas
Lone Racer. Top Shelf Productions 2007 92p. Illustration
Grades: 11 12 Adult   **741.5; Fic**
1. Humorous graphic novels; 2. Racing; 3. Graphic novels
978-1-891830-69-3, $12.95

Years before, Lone Racer was a champion; now, he keeps plugging away despite taunts from the younger racers. He does it for his hospitalized wife. When he's not at the track or the hospital, he's at Bar Juanjo with old racing pal Rubber. When mechanic-turned-cop Irksome talks Lone Racer into a bank robbery and then chickens out, things get dire, and Racer decides he has to win a race to regain his self-respect. His "middling love-affair," which he breaks off because he can't stop thinking about his wife, adds more adult content to the book, along with the bar scenes. Mahler's art style is different - bodies curve oddly and heads are nothing but hats and noses; he also uses black, white and dull brick red for color.

" . . . this corny-old-movie scenario is, thanks largely to its looks, delightfully ludicrous." (Booklist)

Mairowitz, David Zane
Kafka. [by] David Zane Mairowitz and Robert Crumb; edited by Richard Appignanesi. Fantagraphics Books 2007 176p. Illustration
Grades: 10 11 12 Adult   **92; 741.5**
1. Authors; 2. Biographical graphic novels; 3. Kafka, Franz, 1883-1924; 4. Kafka, Franz, 1883-1924; 5. Novelists; 6. Poets; 7. Graphic novels
978-1-56097-806-0, $14.95

This book combines a biography of Kafka with illustrated plot descriptions of many of his works, including The Metamorphosis. Crumb renders the stories in comic book form, while the biographical information is presented mostly in text.

Authors names reversed on cover

Maki, Yoko
Aishiteruze Baby Vol. 1. Viz Media/Shojo Beat 2006 Un Illustration
Grades: 8 9 10 11 12 Adult   **741.5; Fic**
1. Shojo manga; 2. Graphic novels
978-1-4215-0711-8, $19.95

Kippei Katakura is a 17-year-old playboy who spends his time chasing girls, careless of their feelings. But when his 5-year-old cousin Yuzuyu comes to live with his family after her mother's sudden disappearance, Kippei is put in charge of taking care of her. As Kippei gets to know Yuzuyu and starts to understand how she feels, he also begins to realize that all girls were like Yuzuyu once... Kippei has a lot to figure out, like what to make for Yuzuyu's lunch and how to drop her off at kindergarten while still getting to high school on time. Kippei is enjoying his time with Yuzuyu, but not everyone is happy about it. The girls at school miss their quality time with Kippei, and one decides to play dirty to get him back.

Manabe, Shohei
Dead End Vol. 1. Tokyopop 2005 214p. Illustration
Grades: 11 12 Adult   **741.5; Fic**
1. Horror graphic novels; 2. Manga; 3. Science fiction graphic novels; 4. Seinen manga; 5. Graphic novels
1-59532-161-6, $9.99

Shirou is just an ordinary poor construction worker who happens to stumble into a life-changing event that has him screaming, There's no place like home." In the midst of his confusion and panic, a mysterious companion tells him that all of his questions will be answered and his memory restored if he recovers five friends in three days. Meanwhile, he's being pursued by killers. The book includes lots of graphic violence, harsh language, and some nudity.

Mangels, Andy
Iron man: beneath the armor. Del Rey Books 2008 216p. Illustration
Grades: 8 9 10 11 12 Adult   **741.5**
1. Iron Man (Fictional character); 2. Graphic novels
978-0-345-50615-3, $19.95

This book gives readers lots of information about Marvel Comics' hero, Iron Man. Millionaire industrialist and genius Tony Stark creates the armor and together, human and machine become Iron Man. Readers will find the history of Iron Man, from his debut in the 1960s to the movie which opened on May 2, 2008. They will see an overview of the armor's design evolution through the decades, and also find profiles of the characters who have appeared in Iron Man comics, from Tony Stark himself to Virginia "Pepper" Potts, James Rhodes, villains such as Mandarin, Crimson Dynamo, Fin Fang Foom, and many more.

Manglobe
Samurai Champloo Vol. 1. Iillustrated by Masaru Gotsubo. Tokyopop 2005 177p. Illustration
Grades: 8 9 10 11 12 Adult   **741.5; Fic**
1. Adventure graphic novels; 2. Humorous graphic novels; 3. Manga; 4. Samurai; 5. Shonen manga; 6. Graphic novels
1-59182-282-3, $9.99

In a world full of evil, a hardworking waitress, an arrogant mercenary and a mysterious samurai meet. Through a series of misunderstandings, Fuu, Mugen and Jin find themselves running from officials and wanted by the law. Together they form an uneasy alliance to search for the enigmatic Sunflower Samurai. Along the way they come across misleading characters, ninjas, assassins and a prince in disguise. Their journey proves to be nothing less than a roller coaster ride of battles, danger, desperation and companionship. The book includes some strong language and some fighting violence.

Samurai Champloo Vol. 2. Tokyopop 2006 177p. Illustration

Grades: 8 9 10 11 12 Adult   **741.5; Fic**
1. Adventure graphic novels; 2. Humorous graphic novels; 3. Manga; 4. Samurai; 5. Shonen manga; 6. Graphic novels
1-59816-215-2, $9.99

When rumors of a mysterious figure with a vendetta against samurai start to spread, Mugen and Jin volunteer to take care of the killer before the body count rises any further. But after a grueling, explosive battle, they discover that the samurai killer is on a mission of his own—to collect the swords of a thousand defeated warriors. Could this vicious swordsman be the link to the elusive the Sunflower Samurai" The book includes some strong language and fighting violence. This is the second and last volume in the series.

Mansfield, Andy
The **All-New** All-Different X-Men Pop-Up. Candlewick Press 2007 Un Illustration

Grades: K 1 2 3 4 5 6 7 8 9 10 11 12 Adult   **741.5; Fic**
1. Pop-up books; 2. Superhero graphic novels; 3. X-Men (Fictional characters); 4. Graphic novels
978-0-7636-3462-9, $24.99

This pop-up book uses excerpts from classic X-Men comics, paper engineering, and pull-out fact files to profile the X-Men, including Cyclops, Storm, Nightcrawler, Wolverine, Colossus, and Banshee, along with nemesis Magneto and mini-profiles of the original X-Men.

Marchetto, Marisa Acocella
Cancer Vixen: A True Story. By Marisa Acocella Marchetto. Pantheon Books 2009 211 p. Color; Illustration

Grades: 11 12 Adult   **741.5; 92**
1. Autobiographical graphic novels; 2. Breast — Cancer; 3. Breast cancer; 4. Breast cancer; 5. Marchetto, Marisa Acocella; 6. Graphic novels
037571474X; 9780375714740, $16.95
LC 200640967

The author "tells the story of her eleven-month, ultimately triumphant bout with breast cancer—from diagnosis to cure, and every challenging step in between." Publisher's note

"The fashion details are great fun, drawn in a spare loose style, but it's the heart of her story, the support and love she gets from her family and friends, that make Cancer Vixen a universal story that's hard to put down." Publ Wkly

Marcus, Ken
Super human resources season one. Justin Bleep, illustration; Ken Marcus, story. Ape Entertainment 2009 Un Illustration

Grades: 9 10 11 12 Adult   **741.5; Fic**
1. Humorous graphic novels; 2. Superhero graphic novels; 3. Graphic novels
978-1-934944-68-4, $12.95

Super Crises International hires out super heroes people with capes, claws, radioactive half-lives, ... And, like any business, it has a human resources office that keeps up with

expense reports, payroll, cleaning up the conference rooms after crossovers gone wrong ... Tim from Temps-RUs comes to SCI to work in accounts receivable, and he soon learns that running a super hero business is definitely not fun. Something is not right with the bills, and Gordon from the corporate office threatens to shut down the office. On top of that, the office copier has attained sentience and decides to destroy all organic life, and his boss in Accounts plans to destroy SCI. Just another day at the office ... The book includes some superhero fighting violence with no bloodshed.

Maroh, Julie
★ **Blue** Is the Warmest Color. By Julie Maroh. Arsenal Pulp Press 2013 160 p.

Grades: Adult   **741.5; Fic**
1. Dating (Social customs); 2. Lesbians; 3. Lesbians — Fiction; 4. Lesbians — Identity; 5. Love stories
1551525143; 9781551525143, $19.95
LC 2013432454

In this graphic novel by Julie Maroh, "a young woman named Clementine discovers herself and the elusive magic of love when she meets a confident blue-haired girl named Emma: a lesbian love story . . . that bristles with the energy of youth and rebellion and the eternal light of desire." (Publisher's note)

"Though a bit of a period piece, a lovely and wholehearted coming-out story." Kirkus

Marshall, Gary
Studio space: the world's greatest comic illustrators at work. Interviews & edited by Joel Meadows & Gary Marshall. Image Comics 2008 318p. Illustration

Grades: 10 11 12 Adult   **741.5**
1. Cartoonists; 2. Graphic novels
978-1-58240-909-2, $49.99; 978-1-58240-908-5 (pa), $29.99

Twenty modern comics artists talk about their careers, their work, and their working methods. Each of them is photographed in his studio, and samples of their artwork are included. The artists are: Brian Bolland, Tim Bradstreet, Howard Chaykin, Steve Dillon, Tommy Lee Edwards, Duncan Fegredo, Dave Gibbons, Adam Hughes, Joe Kubert, Jim Lee, Mike Mignola, Frank Miller, Sean Phillips, George Pratt, Alex Ross, Tim Sale, Walt Simonson, Bryan Talbot, Dave Taylor, and Sergio Toppi.

Martin, George R. R.
The **Hedge** Knight II: sworn sword. George R.R. Martin and Ben Avery ; artist, Mike Miller. Marvel Entertainment 2008 Un Illustration

Grades: 8 9 10 11 12 Adult   **741.5; Fic**
1. Adventure graphic novels; 2. Fantasy graphic novels; 3. Knights and knighthood; 4. Graphic novels
978-0-7851-2650-8, $19.99

Dunk, who is now Ser Duncan the Tall, has roamed Westeros as a hedge knight, accompanied by his squire, Egg. Now they're employed by Ser Eustace of Standfast, whose land suffers a severe drought because of his dispute with Lady Rohanna, whom many call the "Red Widow." Dunk tries to find a peaceful settlement to the feud, even as he deals with his strong attraction to Lady Rohanna. The book includes some fighting violence and mild sexual innuendo, and one scene of partial nudity.

Martinson, Lars
   Tonoharu: part one. Pliant Press/Top Shelp Productions 2008 128p. Illustration
Grades: 11 12 Adult   **741.5; Fic**
   1. Japan; 2. Teachers; 3. Graphic novels
978-1-9801023-2-1, $19.95
                                              LC 2007-940522
   Daniel Wells looks back at his first year working as an assistant junior high school teacher in rural Japan as he must make a decision whether to renew his contract or leave Japan. In Tonoharu, he leads an isolated, almost monastic life, hampered by his lack of Japanese language skills and ignorance of Japanese culture. He wonders why his predecessor lasted only one year, and whether he will last beyond that as well. Meanwhile, he tries to work with the teachers at school and tries to pursue a relationship with another American teacher who lives a few towns away by train. This volume includes some harsh language, including the s-bomb, and some partial nudity.

Marz, Ron
   Ion, Guardian of the Universe Vol. 1: The Torchbearer. Art by Tom Grindberg and Greg Tocchini. DC Comics 2007 208p. Illustration
Grades: 9 10 11 12 Adult   **741.5; Fic**
   1. Green Lantern (Fictional character); 2. Superhero graphic novels; 3. Graphic novels
978-1-4012-1197-6, $14.99
   Kyle Raynor was the last of the Green Lanterns, but he had helped to bring back the Green Lantern Corps. Now, as Ion, he has more power than he had ever imagined, but is it a boon or a curse? He has been acting out of character and left a wake of senseless destruction and unanswered questions. Can rogue Green Lantern Hal Jordan help him figure out what's going on?

   Samurai: Heaven and Earth. Art by Luke Ross. Dark Horse Comics 2006 Un Illustration
Grades: 11 12 Adult   **741.5; Fic**
   1. Adventure graphic novels; 2. Samurai; 3. Graphic novels
1-59307-388-7, $14.95
   How far will a man travel for love? What battles will he fight? Will he cross heaven and earth to be by the side of the woman he loves? Beginning in feudal Japan of 1704, Samurai: Heaven & Earth follows Shiro, a lone samurai warrior sworn to be reunited with the love of his life who has been spirited away by his enemies. His pursuit of Yoshiko will carry him farther than he could have imagined - from his native Japan to the sprawling empire of China, across Europe, and finally to Paris itself. There, in the fabled halls of King Louis XIV's Versailles, he must cross blades with the greatest swordsmen ever known if he is to reclaim his love. Readers will find nudity, sexual situations, and violence (including beheadings).

Masamune, Shirow
   Black magic. Dark Horse Manga 2008 200p. Illustration
Grades: 10 11 12 Adult   **741.5; Fic**
   1. Manga; 2. Science fiction graphic novels; 3. Graphic novels
978-1-59307-696-2, $14.95
   Millions of years ago, the planet Venus teemed with life and an advanced civilization. In this past, the Nemesis supercomputer controls government functions, with bioroid "executors" created to carry out the system's utopian edicts. But trouble brews, even in good times, as different executors vie for control of Nemesis; these struggles force the governing system to secretly create Duna Typhon, a super-bioroid "sleeper." Raised among humans, she possesses awesome magical powers to be used to protect Nemesis. That time has now come. This was Masamune's first published manga series. The book includes some violence and harsh language.

Mashiba, Shin
   Yumekui Kenbun: Nightmare Inspector volume 1. Viz Media 2008 184p. Illustration
Grades: 9 10 11 12 Adult   **741.5; Fic**
   1. Dreams; 2. Fantasy graphic novels; 3. Manga; 4. Graphic novels
978-1-4215-1758-2, $9.99
   In Japan, during the Taisho Era (1920s), there is a special place where people who suffer nightmares can go for help. At the Silver Star Tea House, Hiruko is a special kind of private investigator who can rid people of their darkest visions, for the price of eating their nightmares. In this first volume, Hiruko helps a young gatekeeper who suffers nightmares about his beautiful master, but when Hiruko enters the nightmare, he learns the gatekeeper's secret and true nature. He also helps a young woman who suffers nightmares of losing pieces of herself (her eyes, her hand, etc.), a young fan who dreams that his favorite movie star commits suicide, an unforgiving son whose father haunts his dreams, a young man who can never see the face of the ideal woman in his dreams. Some stories end in O. Henry-type twists; some stories include some violence.

Massey, Jim
   Maintenance, volume 3: Fighting occupants of interstellar craft. Robbi Rodriguez, illustrator. Oni Press 2008 104p. Illustration
Grades: 10 11 12 Adult   **741.5; Fic**
   1. Adventure graphic novels; 2. Humorous graphic novels; 3. Science fiction graphic novels; 4. Graphic novels
978-1-934964-05-7, $9.95
   When smooth talking aliens kidnap Mendy from the receptionist desk, Terromax janitors Doug and Manny form a team to rescue her. It's not exactly a dream team: K'Arl (an amnesiac alien with a flying saucer), Manshark (pretty much exactly what his name describes), Dr. Woodfern (who has a "thing" about monkeys) and his new invention, the Invisolux, the very hairy Dr. Papritz and his handy new Zappy Stick, and a zombie cat and the two janitors, of course. The book has some violence and the ick factor can

get pretty high (such as when the zombie cat jumps into an alien's mouth and starts eating him from the inside out).

Maintenance volume 1: it's a dirty job . . .. Oni Press 2007 88p. Illustration
Grades: 10 11 12 Adult   **741.5; Fic**
1. Humorous graphic novels; 2. Science fiction graphic novels; 3. Graphic novels
978-1-932664-62-1, $9.95

Doug and Manny work as custodians at TerroMax Inc., the world's biggest and best evil science think tank. The messes they have to clean up include toxic spill monsters and a talking manshark who wants to go out on the town. They also have to worry about the mad scientists, would-be dictators, and the cute young woman who works at reception. The book includes some harsh language, including the s-bomb, and some violence.

Maintenance volume 2: fantastic sewage & other stories. Robbie Rodriguez, illustrator. Oni Press 2008 82p.
Grades: 10 11 12 Adult   **741.5; Fic**
1. Humorous graphic novels; 2. Science fiction graphic novels; 3. Graphic novels
978-1-932664-76-8, $9.95

Doug and Manny work as custodians at TerroMax Inc., the world's biggest and best evil science think tank. In this volume, Dr. Dorothy blackmails Doug and Manny into letting him shrink them so they can go into his toilet and destroy some microcreatures he flushed down the toilet. Now the two custodians have to deal with several kinds of poo monsters. The book includes harsh language, lots of poo, and some violence.

Matsumoto, Taiyo
Sunny Volume 1; 1. By Taiyo Matsumoto. Viz 2013 224 p.
Grades: Adult   **741.5**
1. Automobiles — Fiction; 2. Orphans
1421555255; 9781421555256, $22.99

In this graphic novel by Taiyo Matsumoto, a "Nissan Sunny 1200 may look like a broken-down old car in front of a Japanese home for orphans. To the children and teens of the orphanage, though, the Sunny is a clubhouse, a spaceship, a getaway vehicle, and one of the few places that is truly theirs after they are abandoned by their parents. Readers catch glimpses of each of the orphans' lives, both the imaginary adventures they devise while in the Sunny and the sometimes heartbreaking ones outside of it." (Publisher's note)

Matsushita, Yoko
Descendants of Darkness Vol. 1. Viz Media/Shojo 2004 200p. Illustration
Grades: 10 11 12 Adult   **741.5; Fic**
1. Fantasy graphic novels; 2. Humorous graphic novels; 3. Manga; 4. Shojo manga; 5. Graphic novels
1-59116-507-5, $9.99

As a Shinigami, a Guardian of Death, Asato Tsuzuki has a lot to think about. First of all, there are all those dead people. Someone's got to escort them safely to the afterlife. Then there's all that bureaucracy. The affairs of death come with a lot of paperwork, budgetary concerns and endless arcana. Combining supernatural action with heavy dollops

of romance, sex and humor, this book proves one thing: Death is big business...and business is good. The book includes graphic violence, some strong language, and some sexual situations.

Matthews, Brett
The **Lone** Ranger. Brett Matthews, writer ; Sergio Cariello, artist ; Dean White, colorist ; Simon Bowland, lettering ; John Cassaday, cover artist & art direction. Dynamite Entertainment 2007 160p. Illustration
Grades: 8 9 10 11 12 Adult
741.5; Fic
1. Adventure graphic novels; 2. Lone Ranger (Fictional character); 3. Western stories; 4. Graphic novels
978-1-933305-39-4, $24.99; 978-1-933305-40-0 (pa), $19.99

Courtesy of Dynamite Entertainment

"A fiery horse with the speed of light, a cloud of dust, and a hearty "Hi Yo Silver!" The Lone Ranger ..." A popular radio show starting in the 1930s that became a popular television show that ran from 1949 through 1957, a few film serials (extremely hard to find), some paperback novels, and a movie in 1981, The Lone Ranger became an iconic figure. In March 2008, Disney Studios announced it's planning to make a new Lone Ranger movie. In the meantime, Dynamite Entertainment started publishing Lone Ranger comics in 2006. This Lone Ranger is different from the old radio and television shows, and so is Tonto. These aren't the squeaky clean heroes one might expect, although they are heroic. This volume shows the origin of the Lone Ranger, from a young Texas Ranger who has just joined his father and brother. They are ambushed and all killed, except for John. Tonto, a Native American of unknown tribal nation, takes care of John; he has killed all of the killers. When John recovers from his wounds, they set off to find out who ordered the killing, while the reader knows that another killer is murdering all the dead Rangers' families. This book includes some graphic violence.

Texas Ranger John Reid seeks revenge for the murders of his family and friends, only to find justice . . . and that he's something greater than he ever thought he could be. Together with Tonto, he rides against rich criminals like Cavendish and the politicians Cavendish backs. This new version of the Lone Ranger includes more violence than some might remember from the old television show and books.

The **Lone** Ranger, volume II: lines not crossed. John Cassaday, artist; Paul Pope, artist; Sergio Cariello, artist. Dynamite Entertainment 2008 Un
Grades: 9 10 11 12 Adult   **741.5; Fic**
1. Lone Ranger (Fictional character); 2. Mystery graphic novels; 3. Western stories; 4. Graphic novels
978-1-933305-70-7, $14.99

The Lone Ranger continues his quest to take down Butch Cavendish's various illegal businesses, hitting the crime boss in his pocketbook, even as Cavendish tries to use big-city politics to his advantage. Then, the Ranger and Tonto need to find the truth about a shootout when they stop a lynching. The ranchers say the Mexican they caught is a cold-blooded killer, he says it was all due to a misunderstanding; but what should they do when they discover there is fault on both sides" This is not the Lone Ranger of the old radio serial and television show, but a tougher story with two conflicted heroes. The book includes some violence.

Serenity: Those Left Behind. Story by Joss Whedon & Brett Matthews ; script by Brett Matthews ; art by Will Conrad ; colors by Laura Martin ; letters by Michael Heisler ; front cover art by Adam Hughes ; back cover art by Sean Phillips. Dark Horse Comics 2006 Un Illustration
Grades: 8 9 10 11 12 Adult   **741.5; Fic**
    1. Adventure graphic novels; 2. Science fiction graphic novels; 3. Graphic novels
    1-59307-449-2, $9.95
    Penned by Firefly creator Whedon and Brett Matthews, who wrote several episodes of the show, this book follows a ship full of mercenaries, fugitives and one law-abiding prostitute in their pursuit for fast cash and a little peace along the fringes of space. The ragtag crew of Serenity take on a scavenger mission with the hopes of earning enough dough to disappear for a while. Only too late do they realize the whole gig is orchestrated by an old enemy eager remake their acquaintance with the help of some covert-operatives known only as the Blue Gloves. The book includes some violence; most of the strong language is written in Chinese characters so most readers won't know what is being said.

Serenity: Better days. Script by Joss Whedon and Brett Matthews ; art by Will Conrad ; colors by Michelle Madsen ; letters by Michael Heisler. Dark Horse Books 2008 Un Illustration
Grades: 8 9 10 11 12 Adult   **741.5; Fic**
    1. Adventure graphic novels; 2. Science fiction graphic novels; 3. Graphic novels
    978-1-59582-162-1, $9.95
    Mal Reynolds and his ragtag crew take their ship Serenity to the far frontiers of space, as far from the Alliance as they can get. They have actually succeeded in pulling off a heist, and got a much larger than expected payoff from the guy who hired them. However, while the crew members fantasize about what each will do with the newfound wealth, the Alliance is hunting for whoever stole their high-tech weapon and will do whatever it takes to get it back. The book includes some mild sexual innuendo and some violence. This is an original story based on the "Firefly" television series and characters that Joss Whedon created.

Matz

Cyclops. Volume one. [by] Jacomon & Matz; written by Matz; illustrated by Luc Jacamon; translated by Matz and Edward Gauvin. Archaia Entertainment 2011 116p. Illustration
Grades: Adult   **741.5; Fic**
    1. Mass media; 2. Science fiction graphic novels; 3. Soldiers; 4. War
    978-1-936393-11-4, $19.95

"In the year 2054, the United Nations has outsourced its peacekeeping missions to Multicorp Security. Multicorp pads its bottom line by broadcasting battles live (the camera eye in their helmets leads the troops to be nicknamed Cyclops) and by building story lines around heroes such as Doug Pistoia, a brainy ex-athlete who has a knack for soldiering. But as Pistoia's heroics on the Iran-Turkey border and in Argentina make him a huge star, he begins to question how much of his reality show is actually real. Collecting the first two parts of a four-part series, Cyclops, v.1, asks big questions and sets the stage for further conflict." Booklist
    "Sharp art, relevant political commentary, and sexy, action-packed story make this . . . [a] winner." Publ Wkly
    Translated from the French. ?MR, GV. N, SSC: this book contains adult content, graphic violence, nudity and strong sexual content; it is intended for mature readers Jacket

Max

Bardin the Superrealist. Fantagraphics Books 2006 82p. Illustration
Grades: 10 11 12 Adult   **741.5; Fic**
    1. Humorous graphic novels; 2. Graphic novels
    978-1-56097-759-9, $19.95
    Everyman Bardin finds himself suddenly transported (well, at least his upper half) to another dimension, where an "Andalusian Dog" (a reference to Buñuel's Un Chien Andalou) serves as his ill-tempered guide. In a series of vignettes, gags, illustrations, text pieces, and dream stories, ping-ponging back between the surrealist world and the "real" world, Bardin examines, questions, and defends his own beliefs, convictions and philosophies while tangling with the Dog and the Holy Trinity in a variety of guises (including a familiar-looking mouse with red shorts and white gloves). In other stories, he imagines himself in a painting by Brueghel the Elder, tries to deal with his onanism in a productive way, is enlightened, dodges his real "creator" Max in the street, has several nightmares and hallucinations, and, in the book's climactic episode, "The Sound and the Fury," battles a bona fide dragon. There are some sexual situations and some other adult situations regarding the male's gender-defining organs.

Maxwell, Matt

Strangeways: murder moon. Highway 62 Press 2008 144p. Illustration
Grades: 10 11 12 Adult   **741.5; Fic**
    1. Fantasy graphic novels; 2. Horror graphic novels; 3. Werewolves; 4. Western stories; 5. Graphic novels
    978-0-9796957-0-4, $13.95
    In the year 1868, ex-Army officer Seth Collins works as a stagecoach guard and tries to forget the horrors of the Civil War. However, he now faces a different kind of horror: something hunts the people of Silver Branch, including Collins' estranged sister; a strange, seemingly unkillable wolf prowls the wilderness, stalking and killing people from the town. The people have their own secrets, and soon Collins finds himself trapped between the obligations of family and friendship, between the secretive townspeople and the killing beast. The book includes violence and some strong language.

Mazur, Dan

Comics: the modern history of a global art form. Dan Mazur, Alexander Danner. Thames & Hudson Inc. 2013 319 p. Illustration; Color

Grades: Adult   741.5

1. Graphic novels — History and criticism

9780500290965, $39.95

LC 2012954355

"This is the history of comics around the world from the late 1960s to the dawn of the 21st century.Comics is a richly illustrated narrative of extraordinary scope. Examples from all over the world include everything from Crumb and Kirby to RAW; from Metal Hurlant to Marjane Satrapi to nouvelle manga; from both the American mainstream and underground to the evolving and influential British scene." (Publisher's note)

"The topical approach of individual chapters sometimes confuses the overall chronology, but this richly dense treatise will be best read cover-to-cover anyway, as the authors' contextualizing of works and trends builds firmly throughout the text." Choice

Mazzotta, Antony

Bombaby: The Screen Goddess. SLG Publishing/AmazeInk Comics 2004 Un Illustration

Grades: 10 11 12 Adult   741.5; Fic

1. Fantasy graphic novels; 2. Graphic novels

1-59362-003-9, $13.95

Sangeeta Mukherjee is the daughter of well-to-do, traditional parents, dealing with a bratty little sister and an arranged marriage when an out-of-body experience reveals that she is not an ordinary young woman. Sangeeta is, in fact, the reincarnation of India's ancient protector, the Goddess of Mumbai. But how will Sangeeta use this new-found power" Can she make a difference in a male-dominated society" Sangeeta must defy traditional expectations to choose what kind of life she wants and discover her true self. There is some violence in the story.

Mazzucchelli, David

★ **Asterios** polyp. Written and illustrated by David Mazzucchelli. Pantheon 2009 320 p. Illustration

Grades: Adult   741.5; 741.5973

1. Middle aged men — Fiction

0307377326; 9780307377326, $35

LC 2008027859

Eisner Award: Best Graphic Album: New (2010); Eisner Award: Best Writer/Artist (2010)

The protagonist of this graphic novel is Asterios Polyp, a ômiddle-aged, meagerly successful architect and teacher, aesthete and womanizer, whose life is wholly upended when his New York City apartment goes up in flames. (Publisher's note)

McCabe, Joseph

Hanging Out with the Dream King: Conversations with Neil Gaiman and His Collaborators. Fantagraphics Books 2004 297p. Illustration

Grades: Adult Professional   741.5; 92

1. Graphic novels

1-56097-617-9, $17.95

This book presents a thorough look at Gaiman's work not only through his eyes, but through the eyes of his many collaborators. Artists, writers, editors, musicians-over two-dozen creators share their thoughts on working with Gaiman and present a mosaic portrait of the writer whose name has become synonymous with modern fantasy. Although the book's scope is not limited to Gaiman's best-selling comic book creation The Sandman, it features comprehensive interviews with all of the major Sandman artists, including Charles Vess, P. Craig Russell, Bryan Talbot, and Jill Thompson, as well as well as rare and exclusive interviews with Sandman co-creators Sam Kieth and Mike Dringenberg. And, much as Gaiman has done throughout his career, this book breaks down the walls of media and genre, presenting those who may have discovered the writer's work through one storytelling medium with doors through which they may find his other creations. Thus, admirers of Gaiman's children's books with Dave McKean will discover his adult work with Gene Wolfe and Terry Pratchett; fans of his novels will discover his comics; and everyone will have the chance to meet Gaiman's folk-rock bands-the Flash Girls and Folk Underground. Musicians Alice Cooper and Tori Amos are also interviewed.

McCarthy, Tom

Tintin and the secret of literature. Granta Books 2007 211p. Illustration

Grades: 10 11 12 Adult   741.5

1. Graphic novels — History and criticism; 2. Tintin (Fictional character)

978-1-86207-831-9, $29.95

McCarthy examines Herge's Tintin books and asks the question: are they literature? From there he takes the reader on a journey through the books and notes connections between plot elements and characters to Herge's personal life. Whether or not the reader agrees with McCarthy's assertions and conclusions, anyone who has read and enjoyed the Tintin books will enjoy the speculations about Herge's family connections and the way he took on established religion.

McCay, Winsor

★ **Little** Nemo in Slumberland: So Many Splendid Sundays!. By Winsor McCay. Last Gasp of San Francisco 2006 156 p.

Grades: Adult   741

0983550409; 9780983550402, $125

This book, by Winsor McCay, is the winner of the "Will Eisner" award and two "Harvey Kurtzman" awards. It is a "reproduction of the . . . comic strip, . . . 'Little Nemo in Slumberland.' This is the third printing of . . . a best-of collection from 1905-1910, with 8 pages more than the first two printings and enhanced restoration throughout. Every page is printed in the original size and colors." (Publisher's note)

Winsor McCay: Early Works Volume 1. Checker Book Publishing Group 2003 201p. Illustration

Grades: 10 11 12 Adult   741.5; Fic

1. Humorous graphic novels; 2. Graphic novels

0-9741664-0-5, $19.95

LC 2003-12920

This volume is a collection of turn-of-the-century rarities from cartooning and animation pioneer, Winsor McCay: Tales of the Jungle Imps," Little Sammy Sneeze," Dreams of a Rarebit Fiend," and Pilgrim's Progress." Best known for Little Nemo in Slumberland, and the seminal animated feature Gertie the Dinosaur, McCay puts his artistic talent and whimsical humor on full display here. Readers should note that when these stories were first published in the early 1900s (Tales of the Jungle Imps" was published in 1903), McCay's artistic vision of the jungle imps" wasn't considered racist."

McCloud, Scott

★ **Making** Comics: Storytelling Secrets of Comics, Manga and Graphic Novels. HarperCollins 2006 265p. Illustration

Grades: Adult Professional   **741.5**
  1. Graphic novels
978-0-06-078094-4, $22.95

In Making Comics, McCloud focuses his analysis on the art form itself, exploring the creation of comics, from the broadest principles to the sharpest details (like how to accentuate a character's facial muscles in order to form the emotion of disgust rather than the emotion of surprise.) And he does all of it through his cartoon stand-in narrator, mixing dry humor and legitimate instruction. McCloud shows his reader how to master the human condition through word and image in a minimalistic way, using the form itself to show how to do it.

Reinventing comics: how imagination and technology are revolutionizing an art form. Paradox Press 2000 237p. Illustration

Grades: 11 12 Adult   **741; 741.5**
0-06-095350-0, $22.95
              LC 00-710457

The author maps out "'12 revolutions', which, he believes, need to take place for comics to survive and finally be recognized as a legitimate art form. The topics progress from the oldest of comic-related arguments (seeking respect) to the use of computer technology to renew and expand its audience. These brilliantly presented discussions concern comics as literature, comics as art, creators' rights, industry innovation, and public perception, among other topics." Libr J

★ The **Sculptor**. By Scott McCloud. First Second 2015 496 p. Illustration

Grades: Adult   **741.5; Fic**
  1. Death — Fiction; 2. Love stories; 3. Sculptors — Fiction; 4. Graphic novels
9781596435735, $29.99; 1596435739
              LC 2014043831

In this graphic novel, by Scott McCloud, "David Smith is giving his life for his art—literally. Thanks to a deal with Death, the young sculptor gets his childhood wish: to sculpt anything he can imagine with his bare hands. But now that he only has 200 days to live, deciding what to create is harder than he thought, and discovering the love of his life at the 11th hour isn't making it any easier!" (Publisher's note)

McCloud "offers exquisite silent passages and modulated panel sizes that guide the reader's emotional journey through powerful shifts and deepen David's compelling character, all while employing a straightforward art style masquerading as simple cartooning shorthand. His brilliant pacing and unobtrusive manipulation of the space between panels creates intimate, intense moments." Booklist

★ **Understanding** comics: the invisible art. HarperPerennial 1994 215p. Illustration

Grades: 9 10 11 12 Adult   **741.5**
  0-06-097625-X, $22.95; 9780060976255

McCloud "conducts a genial, well-researched and funny tour of virtually every historical and perceptual aspect of comics, which he calls 'sequential art,' that is, art that consists of sequences of words and pictures. Beginning in the 11th century with the Bayeux tapestry, he examines pre-Columbian picture languages and the printing press, presenting a quick survey of the historical development of early sequential pictures into the specialized visual language of comics. . . . He dissects the vocabulary of the medium, cheerfully analyzing the psychological power of comics and their central role in our ultra-visual culture." (Publishers Weekly)

Includes bibliographical references
First published 1993 by Kitchen Sink Press

McCreery, Conor

★ **Kill** Shakespeare, vol. 1: a sea of troubles. Created and written by Conor McCreery and Anthony Del Col; art by Andy Belanger; colors by Ian Herring; lettering by Chris Mowry, Robbie Robbins, and Neil Uyetake. IDW Publishing 2010 Un Illustration

Grades: 10 11 12 Adult   **Fic; 741.5**
  1. Adventure graphic novels; 2. Authors; 3. Dramatists; 4. Fantasy graphic novels; 5. Poets; 6. Shakespeare, William, 1564-1616 — Adaptations; 7. Shakespeare, William, 1564-1616 — Adaptations; 8. Graphic novels
978-1-60010-781-8, $19.99

A shipwrecked Hamlet finds himself in England with Richard III, who wants his help to find and kill the wizard, Will Shakespeare, so that Richard can rule with impunity. Haunted by his father's ghost, who tells Hamlet that killing Shakespeare will let him live again, Hamlet agrees to help the English king. Then he discovers that the Lady Juliet Capulet leads an army of rebellion, aided by Othello and Falstaff. They fight against the corrupt Richard, who consults the witch Hecate (who has her own agenda). Falstaff says that Hamlet is the prophesied Shadow King, who will aid the rebellion, while Richard and his allies only want to use Hamlet to destroy Shakespeare, but all agree that only Hamlet can lead them to the wizard. The book includes bloody action and sexual situations, making this more suited to older teens.

"McCreery and Del Col spin an engrossing action-adventure tale of satisfying complexity, full of mystery, deceit, and gory violence, starring a hero who once again must marshal his determination and decide his path." Libr J

Other titles in this series are: Volume two: the blast of war (2011); Volume three: the tide of blood (2013)

Kill Shakespeare 3: The Tide of Blood. Conor McCreery and Anthony Del Col, illustrated by Andy Belanger. IDW Publishing 2013 140 p. Color; Illustration

Grades: 10 11 12 Adult **741.5**
1. Shakespeare, William, 1564-1616 — Adaptations; 2. Graphic novels
1613777329; 9781613777329, $19.99

"With Richard III and Lady Macbeth defeated, Hamlet, Juliet, Othello, and Romeo face an even greater danger—Prospero, a rogue wizard who plans to destroy all of creation! Hamlet must embark on a perilous journey to a remote island whose inhabitants have gone mad and want the Dane's blood . . . if they aren't beaten to the chase by one of Hamlet's allies." (Publisher's note)

"There's more action, wizardry, and gore than the Bard himself was apt to include, but clever echoes of dialogue, intense emotional turnabouts, and imaginatively theatrical art recall the plays in satisfying ways." - Booklist

Kill Shakespeare; Volume 2: the blast of war. Created and written by Conor McCreery and Anthony Del Col; art by Andy Belanger; colors by Ian Herring; lettering by Chris Mowry, Neil Uyetake, and Shawn Lee; original series edits by Tom Waltz.. IDW 2011 148 p.
Grades: 10 11 12 Adult **741.5**
1. Shakespeare, William, 1564-1616 — Characters; 2. Shakespeare, William, 1564-1616 — Fiction
1613770251; 9781613770252, $19.99

This book, the second volume of the comic book series, presents a "sweeping fantasy of magic, war, betrayal, and love [which] is set in a world where Shakespeare's characters dwell and Shakespeare himself is an absent god struggling with a heavy conscience. The second volume builds to the climactic finale of Hamlet's quest to find the creatorgod Shakespeare and return peace to a land torn apart by an evil army led by Richard III and Lady Macbeth. Joined by love interest Juliet, the warrior Othello, the wise fool Falstaff, and the spy Iago, Hamlet has built an army of rebels, the prodigals, who hold off their enemies while he searches for their creator. But even victory comes at a cost as friends and foes die in a great final battle." (Publishers Wkly)

"[A]n appropriate air of grandeur and theatricality is much on display, brought forth all the more in Belanger's spectacular and inventive page compositions." Booklist

McCulloch, Derek

Gone to Amerikay. Written by Derek McCulloch; art by Colleen Doran; colors by José Villarrubia; letters by Jared K. Fletcher. DC Comics 2012 144 p.
Grades: Adult **741.5**
1. Immigrants; 2. Immigrants — New York (State) — New York; 3. Ireland — Emigration and immigration; 4. Irish Americans; 5. Irish Americans — New York (State) — New York; 6. Missing persons; 7. New York (NY) — Social conditions; 8. United States — Emigration and immigration
1401223516; 9781401223519, $24.99
LC 2011278790

This graphic novel tells three intertwined stories. "Irish hopeful Ciara O'Dwyer relocates to New York's notorious slums to await a husband who never arrives; decades later the mystery of what happened to Fintan O"Dwyer remains unsolved until a specter from the past points the way to a resolution. We also meet 1960s Johnnie McCormack, a roughshod would-be actor who comes to terms with his sexual orientation; and 2010s euro millionaire Lewis Healy." (Publishers Weekly)

★ **Stagger** Lee. Drawn by Shepherd Hendrix. Image Comics 2006 232p. Illustration
Grades: 10 11 12 Adult **741.5; Fic**
1. Folk songs — United States; 2. Graphic novels
1-58240-607-3, $17.99

What is known: On Christmas of 1895, in Bill Curtis' saloon in St. Louis, "Stag" Lee Shelton shot Billy Lyons. There have been many songs written about this incident, using some version or another of his name: Stacker Lee, Stack-A-Lee, Stack O'Lee, and more. This graphic novel, part historical fiction, part historical essay, examines the legend that grew in the many songs written and sung about the incident. The book contains some sexual situations and some strong language along with some violence.

McDonald, John

Henry V: the graphic novel: original text version. [by] William Shakespeare; script adaptation, John McDonald; pencils, Neill Cameron ...; editor in chief, Clive Bryant. Classical Comics 2008 143p. Illustration
Grades: 8 9 10 11 12 Adult **822.3; 741.5**
1. Shakespeare, William, 1564-1616 — Adaptations
978-1-906332-41-9, $16.95

This graphic novel adaptation of Shakespeare's play uses a full and unabridged text combined with full color comic book style illustrations. Young King Henry V goes to war against France when he learns he has a legitimate claim to the French

Also available plain text version (ISBN: 978-1-906332-42-6) and quick text version (ISBN: 978-1-906332-43-3) ea $16.95
First published 2007 in the United Kingdom

McDuffie, Dwayne

Static shock: rebirth of the cool. Writers, Dwayne McDuffie, Robert L. Washington III; artist, John Paul Leon. DC Comics 2009 192p. Illustration
Grades: 9 10 11 12 Adult **741.5; Fic**
1. African Americans; 2. Science fiction graphic novels; 3. Superhero graphic novels; 4. Graphic novels
978-1-4012-2262-8, $19.99

In 1993, Milestone Comics published superhero comics written for African American readers, featuring African American superheroes. One of those heroes was Static, an inner city teenager imbued with the power of lightning and electricity. DC Comics has brought back Static by reprinting the two Milestone Comics miniseries. High school teen Virgil Hawkins is just trying to survive high school, getting by without joining gangs, and trying to get a date with the girl he really likes. He's also Static, with electromagnetic powers he gained on a night the city calls "The Big Bang." The problem is, he's not the only one who gained super powers of one kind or another that night, and most of those who did are using their powers to help them commit more crimes. Static wants to be a hero, but he faces incredible odds, including his own family's situation. The book includes some harsh language, at least one usage of the one-fingered salute, and violence.

McElroy, Alan

The **Best** of Curse of the Spawn. Danny Miki, artist; Dwayne Turner, artist. Image Comics 2006 Un Illustration

Grades: 11 12 Adult **741.5; Fic**

1. Horror graphic novels; 2. Superhero graphic novels; 3. Supernatural graphic novels; 4. Graphic novels

1-58240-616-2, $16.99

Meet new Spawns and delve deeply into the cast and characters of the regular series Spawn mythos as well. This book features 23 handpicked issues of this series written by the author of the Spawn movie, Allen McElroy. The character was created by Todd McFarlane, one of the founding members of Image Comics, and his series was one of those that influenced comics in the 1990s. This black and white volume is formatted similarly to the DC Showcase and Marvel Essential reprint series. Readers should expect to find violence, strong language, and some incidental nudity.

McFarlane, Todd

Spawn Collection Volume 1. Story and art, Todd McFarlane; coloring, Steve Oliff, Reuben Rude and Olyoptics. Image Comics 2005 Un Illustration

Grades: 11 12 Adult **741.5; Fic**

1. Fantasy graphic novels; 2. Horror graphic novels; 3. Mystery graphic novels; 4. Graphic novels

1-58240-563-8, $19.95

Al Simmons, formerly a soldier, was resurrected from the ashes of his own grave. Reborn as a creature from the depths of Hell, disfigured, homeless, and alone, this new warrior known as Spawn now wanders the shadowy alleys of New York City in search of his past life. Robbed of his memories and identity, this freshly created man whose body is nothing more than scars and torn flesh becomes a protector of the weak, the poor, the downtrodden, and other victims of circumstance. While Spawn tries to piece together his confusing existence, an unwelcome mentor reveals the purpose of his abrupt return to earth. But since this guide comes from the dark side, can he be trusted to tell the truth? And just what is the truth? In this twisted world of shadow players, nothing is as it appears. The book includes graphic violence and harsh language.

McGraw, Royal

Batman: Detective. J. H. Williams, illustrator; Don Kramer, illustrator; Joe Benitez, illustrator). DC Comics 2007 144p. Illustration

Grades: 9 10 11 12 Adult **Fic; 741.5**

1. Batman (Fictional character); 2. Joker (Fictional character); 3. Superhero graphic novels; 4. Graphic novels

978-1-4012-1239-1, $14.99

He is in peak physical condition, with a high-tech arsenal at his disposal, but it is perhaps his exceptional detective skills that make Batman the most formidable opponent of the countless deadly villains of Gotham City. In this volume, the Dark Knight faces the Joker, the Riddler, the Penguin, and Poison Ivy, as well as some brand-new villains, while pushing himself to the limit to solve crimes. But can even the most powerful mind outthink unpredictable and crazy foes?

McGruder, Aaron

Birth of a nation: a comic novel. Aaron McGruder and Reginald Hudlin; illustrated by Kyle Baker. Three Rivers Press 2005 144p. Illustration

Grades: 10 11 12 Adult **741.5; Fic**

1. Humorous graphic novels; 2. Political satire; 3. Graphic novels

978-1-4000-8316-9, $14.95

LC 2004047838

East St. Louis, Illinois (—the inner city without an outer city—), is an impoverished town, but Fred Fredericks, its idealistic mayor, rallies his fellow citizens to the polls for the presidential election, only to find hundreds of them turned away for trumped-up reasons. As a result of the mass disenfranchisement of East St. Louis, a radical right-wing junta led by a dim-witted Texas governor seizes the Oval Office. Prodded by shady black billionaire and old friend John Roberts, Fredericks devises a radical plan of protest: East St. Louis will secede from the Union. Roberts' financial dealings result in East St. Louis becoming flush with money. Problems set in almost immediately: controversies rage over the name and national anthem of the new country (they decide on the Republic of Blackland with an anthem sung to the tune of the theme from Good Times), and local thug Roscoe becomes a warlord and turns his gang into a paramilitary force. When the U.S. military begins to move in, Fredericks is forced to decide whether his protest is worth taking all the way. The book includes some strong language, partial nudity, and sexual situations.

McGuire, Richard

★ **Here**. Richard McGuire. Pantheon Books 2014 304 p. Illustration

Grades: Adult **741.5; Fic**

1. Buildings; 2. Rooms

0375406506; 9780375406508, $35

LC 2014003489

In this book, author Richard McGuire presents "the long-awaited fulfillment of a pioneering comic vision. 'Here' is the story of a corner of a room and of the events that have occurred in that space over the course of hundreds of thousands of years." (Publisher's note)

"McGuire's quiet artwork in a subdued full-color palette reveals nuanced gestures beautifully, sometimes with precise lines, others in sketchy sepia tones, all of which emphasize the passage of time. The concept is stunningly simple, and in laying bare the universality of existenceùits beauty, ugliness, and mundanityùit is utterly moving." Booklist

McLeod, Kagan

Infinite kung fu. Top Shelf Productions 2011 464p. Illustration

Grades: Adult

741.5; Fic

1. Kung fu; 2. Martial arts; 3. Superhero graphic novels; 4. Graphic novels

978-1-891830-83-9, $24.95

"Originally self-published in 2000 and collected here for the

Courtesy of Top Shelf Productions

first time—and including enough previously unseen pages to nearly double its size"McLeod's genre-blending opus is not merely a kung-fu epic. It's a dystopian, zombie, kung fu epic. Lei Kung is a humble soldier until the eight immortals reveal that his destiny is to defeat their former students so that he may heal a world in which reincarnation has gone horribly wrong, and corpses rise to battle the living. Seldom has a creator's love of a genre been as evident as in McLeod's meticulous homage to the heyday of martial-arts cinema. . . . Add heaping helpings of zombie gore, a well-imagined future world, and some gritty, street-style line work that suggests the 1970s, and the result is something irresistibly infectious—for those with special tastes." Booklist

McNamara, Jason
    Continuity. Illustrated by Tony Talbert. AiT/Planet Lar 2006 Un Illustration
Grades: 11 12 Adult   **741.5; Fic**
    1. Dreams; 2. Graphic novels
    978-1-932051-43-8, $12.95
    Alicia's life as a typical suburban misfit takes a horrific turn as her dreams begin to alter reality. She quickly finds herself orphaned, pregnant, and on the run from a pharmaceutical police state. Now she's fighting to stay awake and restore the world she once knew. But when a lonely doctor offers Alicia redemption, will she accept? Or will her dreams tear reality apart" Harsh language and some violence make this more appropriate for older teens and adult readers.

    First Moon. Illustrated by Tony Talbert. Ait/Planet Lar 2006 Un Illustration
Grades: 9 10 11 12 Adult   **741.5; Fic**
    1. Horror graphic novels; 2. Monsters; 3. United States — History; 4. Graphic novels
    978-1-932051-47-6, $12.95
    In 1587, 110 settlers established an English colony on the island of Roanoke Virginia; shortly after, they disappeared, and their fate has remained a mystery. In present-day Berkeley, California, eleven-year-old Ben makes an appalling discovery about his parents and runs into the woods. In 1587, the colonists mistakenly attacked Indian allies, then compounded their error by attacking other Indians. In the present, Ben becomes lost in the woods, comes upon a strange house, catches a mysterious train, then sees his parents pursuing him, in monstrous animal forms. In 1587, the obsessive desire to find and control copper mines leads some colony leaders to torture an Indian woman; their violent hostility causes her people to attack and kill most of the colonists. The survivors remain isolated in eternal night. Ben jumps from the train to find himself among the colonists who have lived there since 1587. They are shapechangers, as are his parents, and now Ben, too. But his parents chose to live in the world, and they must leave while it is still the full moon in Berkeley, or be forced to remain. McNamara includes historical information on what is known about Roanoke and provides a bibliography; his story is fiction, but most of what is portrayed about the past is based on his research.

    The **Martian** confederacy, volume 1. Girl Twirl Comics 2008 143p. Illustration

Grades: 10 11 12 Adult   **741.5; Fic**
    1. Humorous graphic novels; 2. Mars (Planet); 3. Mystery graphic novels; 4. Science fiction graphic novels; 5. Graphic novels
    978-0-9794207-1-9, $15
    Mars in the year 3535 is pretty much a dump, with toxic air and stripped of its natural resources by the corporations that run the planet. Boone, Spinner (a bear) and Lou (a female android) are smalltime outlaws who take on the crooked Alcalde when he steals a professor's cure for the toxic air. As illustrator Braddock says, the story is basically The Dukes of Hazzard on Mars, with redneck good ol' boy outlaws doing the right thing against the corrupt government. However, Lou is no Daisy Duke, but a tough fighter. There is some violence, mostly fist fights, and some brief sexual situations and partial nudity.

McNeil, Carla Speed
    The **Finder** library; Volume 2. By Carla Speed McNeil. Dark Horse Books 2012 636 p. Illustration
Grades: 11 12 Adult   **741.5; 741.5/973**
    1. Science fiction graphic novels
    159582653X; 9781595826534, $24.99
    "Since 1996, Finder has set the bar for science-fiction storytelling, with a lush, intricate world and compelling characters. Now, Dark Horse is proud to present four more story arcs of Carla Speed McNeil's groundbreaking series in a single, affordably priced volume!" (Publisher's note)

    The **Finder** Library; Volume one. Illustrated by the author. Dark Horse 2011 630 p. Illustration
Grades: 11 12 Adult   **741.5/973; 741.5**
    1. Science fiction graphic novels
    1595826521; 9781595826527, $24.99
    This science fiction graphic novel anthology, by Carla Speed McNeil, collects and reprints several of the author's Eisner Award-winning graphic novels within the "Finder" series. This volume includes the novels "Sin-Eater," "Talisman," and "King of the Cats," along with commentary and footnotes from the author. (Publisher's note)

    Finder: Third World. Story, art, and cover by Carla Speed McNeil; colors by Jenn Manley Lee and Bill Mudron. Random House Inc 2014 169 p. Illustration
Grades: Adult   **741.5**
    1. Science fiction graphic novels; 2. Thieves
    1616554673; 9781616554675, $19.99
    This graphic novel by Carla Speed McNeil presents a "turning point in the life of Jaeger, a major character in this mysterious, complex, sci-fi flavored world and the intriguing, wily heart of Finder itself! There's never been a metropolis, slum, or building that Jaeger couldn't infiltrate, escape, and/or loot—until now!" (Publisher's note)
    "McNeil's naturalistic dialogue and her lithe, expressively drawn characters highlight her impressive art chops, and the short tales have a kinetic immediacy, while the longer ones have a slow, dreamlike pace." Pub Wkly

McNiven, Steve
    Civil War. Writer, Mark Millar; penciler, Steve McNiven. Marvel Entertainment 2007 Un Illustration
Grades: 9 10 11 12 Adult   **741.5; Fic**

1. Captain America (Fictional character); 2. Iron Man (Fictional character); 3. Superhero graphic novels; 4. Graphic novels
0-7851-2179-X, $24.99

The landscape of the Marvel Universe is changing, and it's time to choose: Whose side are you on? A conflict has been brewing for more than a year, and a single misstep by a costumed superhero costs thousands of lives and ignites the fuse of a superhero civil war. Teams, friendships, and families begin to fall apart as they must choose. What is the choice? The government wants to register all super powered individuals. Iron Man agrees and takes the government's side. Captain America sees registration as a step down the slippery slope towards the abolishment of civil rights for superheroes.

Means, Greg

The **Cute** Girl Network. By Greg Means, and MK Reed, illustrated by Joe Flood. First Second 2013 179 p.
Grades: Adult   **741.5**
1. Dating (Social customs); 2. Dating (Social customs) — Fiction; 3. Love stories; 4. Single women — Social networks
1596437510; 9781596437517, $17.99
    LC 2013031420

In this graphic novel by MK Reed, Greg Means, and Joe Flood, "Jane's new in town. When she wipes out on her skateboard right in front of Jack's food cart, she finds herself agreeing to go on a date with him. Jane's psyched that her love life is taking a turn for the friskier, but it turns out that Jack has a spotty romantic history. Cue the Cute Girl Network—a phone tree information-pooling group of local single women. Poor Jane is about to learn every detail of Jack's past misadventures." (Publisher's note)

"The snappy dialog is very well matched by Flood's blocky, black-and-white art." LJ

Meathaus Vol. 8: Headgames.

Alternative Comics 2006 Un Illustration
Grades: 11 12 Adult   **741.5; Fic**
1. Short stories; 2. Graphic novels
1-891867-92-X, $14.95

This eighth volume of the Meathaus anthology series features works by a variety of Meathaus favorites, including James Jean, Becky Cloonan, Tomer Hanuka, Brandon Graham, Jim Campaell, Tom Herpich, Dash Shaw, Scott Morse, Jim Mahfood, Jim Rugg, Farel Dalrymple, and more. Each story is just a few pages long, many include harsh language and nudity, some have violence.

Mechner, Jordan

★ **Templar**. By Jordan Mechner and illustrated by LeUyen Pham and Alex Puvilland. First Second 2013 480 p.
Grades: Adult   **741.5**
1. Crusades — Fiction; 2. Knights and knighthood; 3. Popes
1596433930; 9781596433939, $39.99

In this graphic novel by Jordan Mechner "Martin is one of a handful of Templar Knights to escape when the king of France and the pope conspire to destroy the noble order. The king aims to frame the Templars for heresy, execute all of them, and make off with their legendary treasure. That's the

plan, anyway, but Martin and several other surviving knights mount a counter-campaign to regain the lost treasure of the Knights Templar." (Publisher's note)

Meister, Todd

Little Scrowlie Volume One: The Call of Cuthbert. Jennifer Feinberg, illustrator. SLG Publishing 2004 Un Illustration
Grades: 9 10 11 12 Adult   **741.5; Fic**
1. Fantasy graphic novels; 2. Horror graphic novels; 3. Graphic novels
1-59362-000-4, $10.95

A particularly scrowlie cat and her friends - human, feline, and ghostly - get tangled in the tentacles of an aging fashionista's nefarious clothing conspiracy. Can over privileged goth chick Elizabeth, would-be wizard James, and a couple of jumpy housecats foil this foul plan" Or will the Lovecraftian beastie known only as "Cuthbert" overcome all of them" The book includes some violence and horror scenes, but no bad language.

Melbourne, Drew

ArchEnemies, Volume 1: Sinners & Saints. Pencils, Yvel Guichet; inks, Joe Rubenstein. Dark Horse Comics 2007 Un Illustration
Grades: 10 11 12 Adult   **741.5; Fic**
1. Humorous graphic novels; 2. Superhero graphic novels; 3. Graphic novels
978-1-59307-699-3, $12.95

Vince and Ethan are practically strangers, but they've ended up as roommates in order to share an affordable apartment. Ethan is a total slob, while the intense Vince needs neatness; they're the proverbial odd couple and they really, really hate each other. What neither of them realizes is that they're also super powered archenemies: Vince is the Underlord (a villain) while Ethan is Star Fighter (a hero). Vince comes from a family of super villains, and his brother Anton has just murdered their father. When the roommates actually reconcile a bit and Ethan travels with Vince to the funeral, Anton and his hugely menacing minion try to kill all the people at the funeral, and Ethan becomes Star Fighter to stop the slaughter. Maybe the two don't hate each other quite as much as they thought. . . .

Originally published as ArchEnemies issues #1-4.

Meltzer, Brad

Green Arrow: The Archer's Quest. DC Comics 2003 176p. Illustration
Grades: 9 10 11 12 Adult   **741.5; Fic**
1. Adventure graphic novels; 2. Green Arrow (Fictional character); 3. Superhero graphic novels; 4. Graphic novels
1-4012-0044-3, $14.95

Oliver Queen, the Green Arrow, has come back from the dead; certain items were supposed to have been destroyed once he was dead, but it never happened. Now, he and his former sidekick now known as Arsenal travel around, seeking those legendary artifacts in order to protect those people Oliver loves. The book includes some violence.

★ **Identity** Crisis. Rags Morales, penciller; Michael Bair, inker. DC Comics 2005 Un Illustration
Grades: 9 10 11 12 Adult   **741.5; Fic**

1. Green Arrow (Fictional character)
978-1-4012-0688-8, $24.99; 978-1-4012-0458-7 (pa)

It's been said that super-heroes keep secret identities to protect their loved ones. Elongated Man (Ralph Dibny) is one of the few without a confidential alter ego. So when his wife, Sue, is murdered in her own home, the tragedy hits the crime fighting community like a sledgehammer. As the fraternity of champions begins scouring the country for clues and suspects, Green Arrow, Hawkman, Black Canary, the Atom, and Zatanna stay behind, with a powerful secret to protect. Things get worse when other superheroes' family members receive threatening notes. And when the secret is discovered, the ramifications will forever change the world of super-powered heroes and villains.

Justice League of America: The Tornado's Path. DC Comics 2007 228p. Illustration
Grades: 9 10 11 12 Adult   **Fic; 741.5**
1. Batman (Fictional character); 2. Justice League of America (Fictional characters); 3. Superhero graphic novels; 4. Superman (Fictional character); 5. Wonder Woman (Fictional character); 6. Graphic novels
978-1-4012-1349-7, $24.99

After traumatic events shattered the Justice League, trust was in short supply, but after it's all over, Superman, Batman, and Wonder Woman meet to choose who will become members of the new Justice League; but while they meet in secret, dark forces move against their friends and allies. A mysterious organization has helped the android Justice Leaguer known as Red Tornado to transfer his consciousness into the human body he's always wanted. But their motives may not have Red Tornado's best interests in mind. Instead, this is only the first step in a sinister conspiracy of super villains. The Justice League will have to rise again to save Red Tornado, and the world. But who will answer the call" The violence and fighting result in bloodshed.

Merey, Ilike
A + e 4ever: a graphic novel. Lethe Press 2011 214 p.
Grades: Adult   **FIC**
1. Androgyny — Fiction; 2. Friendship; 3. Lesbians — Fiction; 4. Love; 5. Teenagers
1590213904; 9781590213902

This book tells the story of "Asher Machnik [who] is a teenage boy cursed with a beautiful androgynous face. Guys punch him, girls slag him and by high school he's developed an intense fear of being touched. Art remains his only escape from an otherwise emotionally empty life. Eulalie Mason is the lonely, tough-talking . . . [lesbian] from school who befriends Ash. The only one to see and accept all of his sides as a loner, a fellow artist and a best friend, she's starting to wonder if ash is ever going to see all of her. . . . [The book] is a graphic novel set in that ambiguous crossroads where love and friendship, boy and girl, straight and gay meet." (Publisher's note)

Meyer, Scott
Help is on the way: a collection of basic instructions. Dark Horse Books 2008 120p. Illustration
Grades: 10 11 12 Adult   **741.5; Fic**
1. Humorous graphic novels; 2. Graphic novels

978-1-59307-995-6, $9.95

This book collects Meyer's web comic called Basic Instructions. Using a four-panel format, he covers a variety of situations with wry humor, from How to Win an Argument to How to Pick a Password to How to Disguise a Yawn, and many more. The black and white art is fairly static, with a cast of characters Meyer uses and reuses. The humor is in the text, with a lot of fast-looking dialog. Many of the situations deal with marriage and with the workplace, while a number of them will resonate with those in the "nerd culture;" language is only mildly harsh (calling someone an "ass").

The Mighty Crusaders: Origin of a Super-Team
Archie Comics 2003 96p. Illustration
Grades: 3 4 5 6 7 8 9 10 11 12 Adult   **741.5; Fic**
1. Humorous graphic novels; 2. Superhero graphic novels; 3. Graphic novels
1-879794-14-4, $12.95

It's a pop-art explosion as some of the wildest heroes in the history of comic books unite to form one of the most beloved super-teams of the Sixties: The Shield, The Black Hood, The Comet, The Fly, and Fly Girl. Relive the excitement as this intrepid team of heroes meet, fight super-villains as well as each other, come up with a name for their team and even recruit new members. It's all here in this colorful collection reprinting classic stories originally appearing in Fly-Man #31, #32 and #33 as well as Mighty Crusaders #1. It features restoration of all stories, and faithful recoloring.

Mignola, Mike
B.P.R.D. Volume 1: Hollow Earth & Other Stories, Rev. ed.. Dark Horse Comics 2004 Un Illustration
Grades: 10 11 12 Adult   **741.5; Fic**
1. Fantasy graphic novels; 2. Hellboy (Fictional character); 3. Horror graphic novels; 4. Mystery graphic novels
1-59307-280-5, $17.95

This volume collects stories recounting the adventures of the Bureau for Paranormal Research and Defense, featuring Hellboy supporting characters Abe Sapien, Liz Sherman, and others. Beneath the treacherous South Seas and under a ravaged monastery, Abe Sapien and the other weird agents of the BPRD uncover homesick bones, mad science, and the junkyard at the center of the earth. The book includes violence and some strong language.

B.P.R.D. Volume 4: The Dead. Story by Mike Mignola and John Arcudi; art by Guy Davis; colors by Dave Stewart. Dark Horse Comics 2005 Un Illustration
Grades: 10 11 12 Adult   **741.5; Fic**
1. Adventure graphic novels; 2. Fantasy graphic novels; 3. Horror graphic novels; 4. Graphic novels
1-59307-380-1, $17.95

The Bureau for Paranormal Research and Defense and their new team leader Captain Benjamin Daimio, a former corpse himself, moves into their new headquarters only to unearth a gigantic long-buried secret involving United States government covert experiments and Nazi scientists. Abe Sapien, still reeling from the revelation of his former life as a Victorian scientist, meets his long-dead wife in their crumbling home by the sea. This tale of the walking dead, madness, the Spear of Destiny, and a monstrous gateway to heaven includes some strong language and some violence.

B.P.R.D.: The Black Flame. Story by Mike Mignola and John Arcudi; art by Guy Davis; colors by Dave Stewart ; letters by Clem Robins. Dark Horse Comics 2006 Un Illustration
Grades: 10 11 12 Adult   **741.5; Fic**
  1. Fantasy graphic novels; 2. Horror graphic novels
  978-1-59307-550-7, $17.95
    The Bureau for Paranormal Research and Defense faces its worst tragedy ever as the war against the plague of frogs reaches a devastating new level. Heralded by a bizarre villain from the B.P.R.D.'s past, an ancient monster-god marches across the American heartland portending an end to the reign of men, and leaving a permanent mark on the Bureau. The book includes some horror violence.

B.P.R.D.: killing ground. Story by Mike Mignola and John Arcudi; art by Guy Davis. Dark Horse Comics 2008 Un Illustration
Grades: 10 11 12 Adult   **741.5; Fic**
  1. Horror graphic novels; 2. Mystery graphic novels; 3. Supernatural graphic novels; 4. Graphic novels
  978-1-59307-956-7, $17.95
    The secret of Captain Daimio's resurrection in Bolivia comes back to haunt the B.P.R.D. as Liz struggles to free herself from her nightmares and Johann abandons his responsibilities in favor of pleasures of the flesh in his new, superhuman body. The book includes violence and incidental partial nudity. A wendigo-type monster has escaped, Kate Corrigan is in charge of chasing it down, and Daimio has a deep connection.

B.P.R.D.: Plague of Frogs. Mike Mignola, Guy Davis, et al. Dark Horse Comics 2005 Un Illustration
Grades: 10 11 12 Adult   **Fic; 741.5**
  1. Hellboy (Fictional character); 2. Horror graphic novels; 3. Supernatural graphic novels; 4. Graphic novels
  1-59307-288-0, $17.95
    Introduced in the first Hellboy book, Abe Sapien has remained one of the most intriguing mysteries of Mignola's work. The story of Abe's origins unfolds as the Bureau for Paranormal Research and Defense try to stop the monstrous frog men from the first Hellboy graphic novel, Seed of Destruction. The plague begins its spread across America, and the BPRD has its work cut out for it. There's some violence and some strong language in the book.

B.P.R.D.: The Universal Machine. Written by Mike Mignola and John Acudi; Art by Guy Davis et al; Color by Dave Stewart. Dark Horse Comics 2007 Un Illustration
Grades: 10 11 12 Adult   **741.5; Fic**
  1. Fantasy graphic novels; 2. Hellboy (Fictional character); 3. Horror graphic novels
  978-1-59307-710-5, $17.95
    After the catastrophic encounter with the monster-god Katha-Hem, Dr. Kate Corrigan travels to rural France in search of an ancient text that might undo the death of Roger. Back at the Bureau for Paranormal Research and Defense, Captain Daimio tells the story of his own death, Johann Kraus confesses a bizarre love triangle arising from one of

his s?ances, Abe recalls a mission with Hellboy during his early days at the B.P.R.D., and Liz reveals a weird tale of the family members she killed while discovering her firestarter powers. There's no nudity, but lots of monsters and monster fighting.

Hellboy in Hell: the descent. Story and art by Mike Mignola; colored by Dave Stewart; lettered by Clem Robins. Dark Horse 2014 144 p. Illustration; Color
Grades: Adult   **741.5**
  1. Hell — Fiction; 2. Hellboy (Fictional character)
  1616554444; 9781616554446, $17.99
                LC 2012278136
    "Hellboy creator . . . Mike Mignola returns to draw Hellboy's ongoing story for the first time since 'Hellboy: The Conqueror Worm.' It's a story only Mignola could tell, as more of Hellboy's secrets are at last revealed, in the most bizarre depiction of Hell you've ever seen!" (Publisher's note)
    "Creator Mignola . . . celebrates Hellboy's 20th anniversary by killing him off and sending him back from whence he came: Hell. . . . Despite the grotesquery of his characters, they look believable in their horrific settings, and Mignola's simple but elegant panel design should be studied by everyone who is or who wants to be a cartoonist. The script is a delight, too, as Hellboy's down-to-earth anger and everyman astonishment remains funny and refreshing." Pub Wkly
  Volume 1 of an ongoing series

Hellboy Volume 1: Seed of Destruction 2nd ed.. By Mike Mignola; script by John Byrne; miniseries colors by Mark Chiarello. Dark Horse Comics 2003 Un Illustration
Grades: 9 10 11 12 Adult   **741.5; Fic**
  1. Fantasy graphic novels; 2. Hellboy (Fictional character); 3. Horror graphic novels; 4. Mystery graphic novels; 5. Graphic novels
  9781593070946; 1-59307-094-2, $17.95
    When strangeness threatens to engulf the world, a strange man will come to save it. Sent to investigate a mystery with supernatural overtones, the good-guy big red demon, Hellboy, discovers the secrets of his own origins, and his link to the Nazi occultists who promised Hitler a final solution in the form of a demonic avatar. The book includes some violence and horror.
  Other Hellboy volumes are: 2: Wake the Devil; 3: The Chained Coffin and Others; 4: The Right Hand of Doom; 5: Conqueror Worm; 6: Strange Places; 7: The Troll Witch and Others; 8: Darkness Calls; 9: The Wild Hunt; 10: The Crooked Man and Others; 11: The Bride of Hell and Others; 12: The Storm and the Fury; 13: Hellboy in Mexico

Hellboy Volume 2: Wake the Devil, 2nd ed.. By Mike Mignola; colored by James Sinclair; lettered by Pat Brosseau. Dark Horse Comics 2003 Un Illustration
Grades: 9 10 11 12 Adult   **741.5; Fic**
  1. Fantasy graphic novels; 2. Hellboy (Fictional character); 3. Horror graphic novels; 4. Mystery graphic novels; 5. Graphic novels
  1-59307-095-0, $17.95
    A murder in a New York wax museum and a missing corpse lead Hellboy into ancient Romanian castles on the

trail of a sleeping legend: the original nobleman vampire. Nazi scientists prepare for the return of their occult master and the end of the world, and Hellboy confronts his purpose on earth. The book includes some violence, strong language and some nonsexual partial nudity.

Hellboy Volume 3: The Chained Coffin and Others 2nd ed.. By Mike Mignola; colored by James Sinclair, Matthew Hollingsworth, & Dave Stewart. Dark Horse Comics 2004 Un Illustration

Grades: 9 10 11 12 Adult   **741.5; Fic**
1. Fantasy graphic novels; 2. Hellboy (Fictional character); 3. Horror graphic novels; 4. Mystery graphic novels; 5. Graphic novels
1-59307-091-8, $17.95

This volume collects short stories Mignola wrote for various other publications; it includes The Corpse," which some critics think is the best Hellboy story he has written. Mignola provides notes before each story. The book includes some violence, strong language, and nonsexual partial nudity.

Hellboy Volume 4: The Right Hand of Doom 2nd ed.. by Mike Mignola; colored by Dave Stewart; lettered by Pat Brosseau; edited by Scott Allie. Dark Horse Comics 2004 Un Illustration

Grades: 9 10 11 12 Adult   **741.5; Fic**
1. Fantasy graphic novels; 2. Hellboy (Fictional character); 3. Horror graphic novels; 4. Mystery graphic novels; 5. Graphic novels
1-59307-093-4, $17.95

This volume collects more Hellboy short stories Mignola wrote for various other publications; it includes Pancakes," a cute two-page story set when he was a young demon. The Right Hand of Doom" is a long story that takes up most of the volume. The book includes some violence and strong language.

Hellboy Volume 5: Conqueror Worm 2nd ed.. By Mike Mignola; colored by Dave Stewart; lettered by Pat Brosseau; introduction by Guillermo del Toro; edited by Scott Allie. Dark Horse Comics 2004 Un Illustration

Grades: 9 10 11 12 Adult   **741.5; Fic**
1. Fantasy graphic novels; 2. Hellboy (Fictional character); 3. Horror graphic novels; 4. Mystery graphic novels; 5. Graphic novels
1-59307-092-6, $17.95

2002 Eisner Award for Best Limited Series.

At the end of World War II, American costumed-adventurer Lobster Johnson led an Allied attack on Hitler's space program, but not before the Nazis were able to launch the first man into space. Now, after sixty years, Hellboy is partnered with an artifical man - a Frankenstein's monster implanted by Bureau scientists with a bomb - to travel to the ruined castle in Norway to intercept the returning capsule, and its single passenger. . .the conqueror worm. The book includes violence, strong language, and partial nudity.

Hellboy Volume 6: Strange Places. Colored by Dave Stewart; lettered by Clem Robins. Dark Horse Comics 2006 Un Illustration

Grades: 9 10 11 12 Adult   **741.5; Fic**

1. Fantasy graphic novels; 2. Hellboy (Fictional character); 3. Horror graphic novels; 4. Mystery graphic novels; 5. Graphic novels
978-1-59307-475-3, $17.95

After leaving the Bureau for Paranormal Research and Defense, Hellboy's travels take him briefly to Africa, then for a two-year stint at the bottom of the ocean. An ancient witch doctor, a giant fish woman and keeper of the secret history of the universe force Hellboy to either accept his role in the coming apocalypse, or have that role stolen from him. Weird undersea creatures and talking lions populate this turning-point adventure, which reveals secrets buried since Hellboy's very creation. The book includes some violence and strong language.

Hellboy volume 8: Darkness calls. Story by Mike Mignola; art by Duncan Fegredo; colored by Dave Stewart. Dark Horse Comics 2008 Un Illustration

Grades: 10 11 12 Adult   **741.5; Fic**
1. Fantasy graphic novels; 2. Hellboy (Fictional character); 3. Horror graphic novels; 4. Graphic novels
978-1-59307-896-6, $19.95

Hellboy has finally returned from his adventures at sea, but no sooner has he settled on land than a conclave of witches drags him from his respite and into the heart of Russian folklore, where he becomes the quarry of the powerful and bloodthirsty witch Baba Yaga. Bent on revenge for the eye she had lost to Hellboy, Baba Yaga has enlisted the aid of Koshchei, a deathless warrior who will stop at nothing to destroy Hellboy. Meanwhile, in England, the Gruagach and his minions seek to regain the powers they once had over the world. The book includes brief partial nudity and a lot of bloodshed.

Jenny Finn: doom messiah. Boom! Studios 2008 Un Illustration

Grades: 11 12 Adult   **741.5; Fic**
1. Fantasy graphic novels; 2. Horror graphic novels; 3. Graphic novels
978-1-934506-14-1, $14.99

In Victorian London, wherever the mysterious Jenny Finn goes, death and destruction follow in her wake as a plague sweeps through the city, affecting men. Meanwhile, someone is murdering and eviscerating whores. Goodhearted butcher Joe thinks Jenny Finn is an innocent girl who doesn't belong in the bad part of the city, and in his efforts to help her, he becomes embroiled in a battle between good and evil, with secret societies, an invasion of monstrous sea creatures, and a murderous artist. The book includes nudity, scenes in a whorehouse, harsh language, and violence.

Zombie World: Champion of the Worms. Pat McEown, illustrator. Dark Horse Comics 2005 80p. Illustration

Grades: 9 10 11 12 Adult   **741.5; Fic**
1. Horror graphic novels; 2. Graphic novels
1-59307-407-7, $8.95

A small-town museum is plagued by odd disturbances and missing persons - all part of the arcane work of their newest arrival, Azzul Gotha, a 42,000-year-old Hyperborean mummy bent upon sacrificing mankind to his ancient worm gods. There's some brief nudity of ghosts and monsters, and horror violence.

Mihara, Mitsukazu

Beautiful People. Tokyopop 2006 190p. Illustration
Grades: 10 11 12 Adult **741.5; Fic**
1. Josei manga; 2. Manga; 3. Graphic novels
1-59816-243-8, $9.99

In this anthology, a young boy tries to grant the ultimate wish to a magical snow princess; two strangers struggle to survive an apocalyptic world—and each other; the lonely victim of a bully takes solace in the world of the Internet; and a woman who has had extensive cosmetic surgery learns the frightening truth about what real beauty is; a vampire takes in an abandoned child with plans to consume her, but decades slip by as he enjoys her innocent affection. The book includes some strong language, violence, nudity, and sexual situations.

Mikimoto, Haruhiko

Mobile Suit Gundam Ecole du Ciel Vol. 1. Tokyopop 2005 Un Illustration
Grades: 8 9 10 11 12 Adult **741.5; Fic**
1. Mecha manga; 2. Science fiction graphic novels; 3. Graphic novels
1-59532-851-3, $9.99

Ecole du Ciel is where aspiring pilots train to become Top Gundam. The year is 0085 of the Universal Century. Daughter of a brilliant professor, Asuna is a below-average student at Ecole du Ciel. But with the world spiraling toward war, Asuna is headed for a crash course in danger, battle, and most of all, love. This story is set in the original Gundam universe, and is full of mecha (giant battle robot) battles.

Millar, Mark

Chosen. Dark Horse Comics 2005 Un Illustration
Grades: 10 11 12 Adult **741.5; Fic**
1. Supernatural graphic novels; 2. Graphic novels
1-59307-213-9, $17.95

Imagine you're twelve years old and suddenly discover that you are the returned Jesus Christ. You can turn water into wine, make the crippled walk and perhaps even raise the dead. What do you and your family do, and how does it affect you knowing that you're destined to grow up and take part in a conflict that people have been waiting almost two thousand years for" The book contains strong language, including the f-bomb.

Superior. Writer, Mark Millar; penciler, Leinil Yu; Gerry Alanguilan with Jason Paz & Jeff Huet, inkers; Sunny Gho, Javier Tartaglia & Dave McCaig, colorists; Clayton Cowles, letterer. Marvel 2012 200 p. Color illustration
Grades: Adult **Fic; 741.5973**
1. Children with physical disabilities; 2. Superhero comic books, strips, etc; 3. Superhero graphic novels
0785136185; 9780785136187, $24.99; 9780785153177, $19.99

This comic book anthology, by Mark Millar and illustrated by Leinil Francis Yu, collects the first seven issues of the "Superior" series in graphic novel format. "Simon Pooni had it all going for him . . . [b]ut that was when he could still move his legs. Now, he's living with multiple sclerosis, missing all the little things he used to take for granted, and escaping into the world of movies and comics

with his best friend. Then . . . SUPERIOR entered his life." (Publisher's note)
Collects Superior # 1-7.

Superman: Red Son. Mark Millar, Dave Johnson, Kilian Plunkett, Andrew Robinson, Walden Wong. DC Comics 2014 168 p. Color; Illustration
Grades: 11 12 Adult **741.5; 741.5/973**
1. Superman (Fictional character)
1401247113; 9781401247119, $17.99

LC 2013049659
Eisner Nominee: Best Limited Series (2004)

This comic book, by Mark Millar, illustrated by Dave Johnson, Kilian Plunkett, Andrew Robinson, and Walden Wong, "is a vivid tale of Cold War paranoia, that reveals how the ship carrying the infant who would later be known as Superman lands in the midst of the 1950s Soviet Union. Raised on a collective, the infant grows up and becomes a symbol to the Soviet people, and the world changes drastically from what we know." (Publisher's note)

Wanted. Pencils and inks by J.G. Jones. Top Cow 2008 208p. Illustration
Grades: 11 12 Adult **741.5; Fic**
1. Mystery graphic novels; 2. Superhero graphic novels; 3. Graphic novels
978-1-58240-497-4, $19.99

Wesley Gibson is a typical office worker, a nobody with a boring life . . . until he discovers that he is the son of "The Killer," a member of an underground fraternity of supervillains who've been running the world since 1986. After his father is killed, Wesley becomes the new Killer and he joins the villains while trying to unravel the mystery of his father's murder. This book is the basis for the motion picture starring Jamie MacElvoy and Angelina Jolie that was released during the summer of 2008. The book includes lots of graphic violence, very harsh language (with lots of f-bombs), and nudity.

Miller, Frank

300. Dark Horse Comics 1999 88p. Illustration
Grades: 10 11 12 Adult **741.5; Fic**
1. Thermopylae, Battle of, 480 BC; 2. Graphic novels
978-1-56971-402-7, $30

Miller paints a highly fictionalized, stylized account of the Battle of Thermopylae, where the Spartan King Leonidas and a relatively small band of Spartans held off the massive army of Emperor Xerxes of Persia long enough for Athens to gather its troops for the final showdown. The Spartans all died, but their sacrifice saved Greece in the end. Watercolor paintings by artist Varley use an earthy palette to depict the stark landscape and violent battles. This book is the basis for the hit motion picture released in March 2007.

★ **Batman,** the Dark Knight returns. Frank Miller; with Klaus Janson and Lynn Varley. DC Comics 2013 198 p.
Grades: 11 12 Adult **741.5; 741.5/973**
1. Batman (Fictional character); 2. Robin (Fictional character); 3. Superheroes
1563893428; 9781563893421, $19.99

LC 2013008716
This graphic novel, by Frank Miller, "completely reinvents the legend of Batman. . . . The Dark Knight returns

in a blaze of fury, taking on a whole new generation of criminals and matching their level of violence. He is soon joined by a new Robin—a girl named Carrie Kelley, who proves to be just as invaluable as her predecessors. But can Batman and Robin deal with the threat posed by their deadliest enemies, after years of incarceration have made them into perfect psychopaths?" (Publisher's note)

Originally published in single magazine form as Batman, the Dark Knight returns 1-4.

Batman: the Dark Knight strikes again. [by] Frank Miller, Lynn Varley, Todd Klein, Batman created by Bob Kane. DC Comics 2002 247p. Illustration
Grades: 10 11 12 Adult   **741.5; Fic**
1. Batman (Comic strip); 2. Batman (Fictional character); 3. Superhero graphic novels; 4. Graphic novels
1-56389-844-6; 1-56389-929-9 (pa), $19.99
LC 2003-544916

"Batman leads the opposition in a dystopian near-future when security concerns have spurred a repressive crackdown. Other costumed heroes side with either the government or Batman. . . . The book's authoritarian society resonates with the post-9/11 environment, though Miller's cheekiness dispels notions that this is serious commentary." Booklist

Originally published in single magazine form as Batman: the Dark Knight strikes again 1-3
Based on Batman comic strip
Sequel to Batman: the Dark Knight returns (1986)

Batman: Year One. DC Comics 2005 168p. Illustration
Grades: 8 9 10 11 12 Adult   **741.5; Fic**
1. Batman (Fictional character); 2. Catwoman (Fictional character); 3. Superhero graphic novels; 4. Graphic novels
978-1-4012-0752-6, $14.99

In the late-1980s, after publishing Miller's Batman: The Dark Knight Returns, DC realized they should remain faithful to the original roots of Batman. Miller then wrote this book, which reinvents the very early years of Batman as a superhero. In this book, Jim Gordon arrives in Gotham City to work in the police department and discovers the high level of corruption there; Batman encounters Selina, who becomes Catwoman, for the first time; and he develops some of the weapons he uses to fight crime. This new edition includes preliminary sketches and other extras.

★ **Daredevil** by Frank Miller & Klaus Janson Omnibus. By Frank Miller, Marv Wolfman, Roger McKenzie, David Michelinie; illustrated by Klaus Janson. Marvel Enterprises 2013 840 p.
Grades: Adult   **741.5**
1. Daredevil (Fictional character); 2. Science fiction comic books, strips, etc; 3. Superheroes
0785185682; 9780785185680, $99.99

This graphic novel, by Frank Miller, Marv Wolfman, Roger McKenzie, and David Michelinie, illustrated by Klaus Janson, "herald one of Daredevil's greatest eras, just in time for the Kingpin and Bullseye's efforts to rob the Man Without Fear of everything he holds dear! Featuring the first appearances of Elektra, Stick and the Hand!" (Publisher's note)

★ **Daredevil:** born again. By Frank Miller; illustrated by David Mazzucchelli. Marvel Worldwide 2010 203 p. Color illustration (Daredevil)
Grades: Adult   **741.5**
1. Daredevil (Fictional character); 2. Science fiction comic books, strips, etc; 3. Superheroes
0785134816; 9780785134817, $19.99

This graphic novel, by Frank Miller, illustrated by David Mazzucchelli, is the "definitive Daredevil tale! Karen Page, Matt Murdock's former lover, has traded away the Man Without Fear's secret identity for a drug fix. Now, Daredevil must find strength as the Kingpin of Crime wastes no time taking him down as low as a human can get." (Publisher's note)

Contains material originally published in magazine form as Daredevil #226-233.

Hard boiled. By Frank Miller; illustrated by Geof Darrow. Dark Horse Books 2000 124 p. Color illustration
Grades: Adult   **741.5**
1. Science fiction graphic novels
1878574582; 9781878574589, $16.95

In this graphic novel, by Frank Miller, illustrated by Geof Darrow, "Carl Seltz is a suburban insurance investigator, a loving husband, and devoted father. Nixon is a berserk, homicidal tax collector racking up mind-boggling body counts in a diseased urban slaughterhouse. Unit Four is the ultimate robot killing machine - and the last hope of the future's enslaved mechanical servants. And they're all the same psychotic entity." (Publisher's note)

Ronin. Frank Miller. DC Comics 2014 336 p. Color; Illustration
Grades: Adult   **741.5**
1. Fantasy graphic novels; 2. New York (NY); 3. Samurai
1401248950; 9781401248956, $29.99
LC 2014015203

In this graphic novel, by Frank Miller, "a legendary warrior, the Ronin, a dishonored, masterless 13th Century samurai, is mystically given a second chance to avenge his master's death. Suddenly finding himself reborn in a futuristic and corrupt 21st Century New York City, the samurai discovers he has one last chance to regain his honor: he must defeat the reincarnation of his master's killer, the ancient demon Agat." (Publisher's note)

"Before Miller redefined Batman with a dark, noir look and feel that influenced comics of the 1980s and beyond, his first series followed the adventures of a samurai warrior in a future dystopia. . . . The over-the-top violence is balanced against nimble and believable human anatomy and motion, and his technique of expressing emotion by showing a single face in multiple panels is especially effective." Pub Wkly

Original collected edition published 1987
Originally published in single magazine form as Ronin 1-6.

★ **Sin** City Vol. 1: The Hard Goodbye. Dark Horse Comics 2005 208p. Illustration
Grades: 11 12 Adult   **741.5; Fic**
1. Mystery graphic novels; 2. Graphic novels
1-59307-293-7, $17

Sin City is the place - tough as leather and dry as tinder. Love is the fuel, and Marv has the match ... not to mention a condition." He's gunning after Goldie's killer, so it's time to watch this town burn. Frank Miller is one of modern comic's first talents to publish a comic book that he created, crafted, and owned. That book is Sin City, which grew from the wellspring of Miller's passionate desire to create a comic book with two distinct qualities - it wouldn't be a superhero comic, and it had to be a crime comic. Enter Marv and Goldie. And a psychotic killer. And a crime-drenched town. And a corrupted diocese. The stark black and white art includes nudity and graphic violence, along with lots of harsh language.

Sin City Vol. 2: A Dame to Kill For. Dark Horse Comics 2005 208p. Illustration
Grades: 11 12 Adult   **741.5; Fic**
    1. Mystery graphic novels; 2. Graphic novels
    1-59307-294-5, $17
    It's one of those hot nights, dry and windless. The kind that makes people do sweaty, secret things. Dwight's thinking of all the ways he's screwed up and what he'd give for one clear chance to wipe the slate clean, to dig his way out of the numb gray hell that is his life. And he'd give anything. Just to cut loose. Just to feel the fire. One more time. And then Ava calls. Dwight thinks it's love, but Ava just needs him to kill her rich husband and she betrays him. No one does that to Dwight and gets away with it. This book includes lots of harsh language, graphic violence, nudity, and sexual situations.

Miller, John Jackson
    Star Wars: Knights of the Old Republic Volume One: Commencement. Script, John Jackson Miller ; art, Brian Ching and Travel Foreman, ; colors, Michael Atiyeh ; lettering, Michael Heisler ; cover art, Travis Charest. Dark Horse Comics 2006 Un Illustration
Grades: 8 9 10 11 12 Adult   **741.5; Fic**
    1. Adventure graphic novels; 2. Science fiction graphic novels; 3. Graphic novels
    978-1-59307-640-5, $18.95
    Thousands of years before Luke Skywalker would destroy the Death Star in that fateful battle above Yavin 4, one lone Padawan would become a fugitive hunted by his own Masters, charged with murdering every one of his fellow Jedi-in-training. From criminals hiding out in the treacherous under-city of the planet Taris, to a burly, mysterious droid recovered from the desolate landscape of a cratered moon, Padawan Zayne Carrick will find unexpected allies in his desperate race to clear his name before the unmerciful authorities enact swift retribution upon him.

Milligan, Peter
    Infinity Inc.: Luthor's monsters. Illustrated by Max Fiumara, Pete Woods ... [et al.]. DC Comics 2008 128p. Illustration
Grades: 10 11 12 Adult   **741.5; Fic**
    1. Mystery graphic novels; 2. Superhero graphic novels; 3. Graphic novels
    978-1-4012-1816-4, $14.99
    Infinity Inc. was a new superhero team, made up of young people who gained their super-powers thanks to Lex Luthor's metagene-manipulating Everyman Project. When they'd served their purpose, Luthor cut off their powers and abandoned them. More than a year later, the young ex-heroes

have undergone just about every kind of therapy, but something is starting to happen to them. Natasha, John Henry Steel's niece, was a member of Infinity Inc., and suddenly she turns to a gaseous form and disappears. He tries to track her down, but someone else, who also was part of Infinity Inc, is tracking down his former teammates with an entirely different agenda in mind. The book includes violence.

Millionaire, Tony
    Billy Hazelnuts. Fantagraphics Books 2005 111. Illustration
Grades: 9 10 11 12 Adult   **741.5; Fic**
    1. Adventure graphic novels; 2. Humorous graphic novels; 3. Graphic novels
    1-56097-701-9, $19.95
    This book transmutes nursery rhymes and the golem myth into a storybook about Becky, girl scientist, her friend Billy Hazelnuts (who was created from cooking ingredients by tailless mice), and their journey to find the missing moon while battling an evil steam-driven alligator with a seeing-eye skunk. Millionaire fuses the darker spirit of older fairy tales with an adventure story, throws gender politics into the mix, and uses his highly detailed, old-fashioned looking art to pull it all together.

    Sock Monkey: The Inches Incident. Dark Horse Comics 2007 88p. Illustration
Grades: 7 8 9 10 11 12 Adult   **741.5; Fic**
    1. Fantasy graphic novels; 2. Toys; 3. Graphic novels
    978-1-59307-842-3, $12.95
    Inches the doll was the cutest in the whole house. Loved by everyone, the world was Inches' oyster. Then one day something happened... The Sock Monkey and Mr. Crow became concerned for their diminutive friend, but by then it was too late. The truth sent the terrified Sock Monkey and Crow fleeing for their lives, for Inches had been invaded by a colony of evil ants. The sight of ants swarming over Inches and other things might be too creepy-crawly for some readers; the violence is aimed at toys rather than people, however, this is not a book for younger readers.

    Sock Monkey: Uncle Gabby. Dark Horse Comics 2004 Un Illustration
Grades: 8 9 10 11 12 Adult   **741.5; Fic**
    1. Adventure graphic novels; 2. Humorous graphic novels; 3. Graphic novels
    1-59307-026-8, $14.95
    Uncle Gabby, the Sock Monkey, and Drinky the crow set off on a journey to solve the mystery of unremembered memories. This looks like a children's book, but the underlying bitter sweetness of a lost past and longing is more suited to teens and adults.

Mills, Tarpé
    Miss Fury: Sensational Sundays 1944-1949. Tarpé Mills.. IDW Publishing 2011 229p Illustration
Grades: Adult   **741.5**
    1. Cartoons and caricatures; 2. Superheroes
    1600109055; 9781600109058, $49.99
    This book offers a collection of the Miss Fury Sunday newspaper adventure comic strip drawn by Tarpe Mills in the 1940s. The adventure comic strip includes "[c]atfights

and crossdressers, mad scientists and Gestapo agents with swastika branding irons - it's one . . . adventure after another in this . . . collection of the first female superhero created and drawn by a woman. Miss Fury was a sexy adventurer clad in a skin-tight panther costume. By day, she was socialite Marla Drake. By night, . . . Miss Fury." (Publisher's note)

Mina, Denise
   John Constantine: Hellblazer: Empathy is the Enemy. Leonardo Manco, artist; Jared K. Fletcher, letterer. DC Comics/Vertigo 2006 168p. Illustration
Grades: 11 12 Adult   **741.5; Fic**
   1. Horror graphic novels; 2. John Constantine (Fictional character); 3. Mystery graphic novels; 4. Graphic novels
   978-1-4012-1066-3, $14.99
   Beginning with a chance meeting in a London pub, occultist Constantine finds himself swept along on the road to Glasgow, Scotland, where the murder rate is soaring and the most popular diet consists of cigarettes, whiskey and sugar, in other words, a city where Constantine feels right at home. But things are different this time. Constantine has been cursed with the worst thing he can feel: empathy for his fellow human beings. He'll need to get over that before he confronts what awaits him in Glasgow: an angry ghost, an ancient cult, a magus as powerful as Constantine himself, and a horror beyond his imagination, and he's already seen the worst hell has to offer. The story has copious use of strong language, nudity, and considerable violence.

   John Constantine: Hellblazer: The Red Right Hand. DC Comics/Vertigo 2007 144p. Illustration
Grades: 11 12 Adult   **741.5; Fic**
   1. Horror graphic novels; 2. John Constantine (Fictional character); 3. Graphic novels
   978-1-4012-1342-8, $14.99
   When his friends and relatives are in trouble, the last person they'd dare turn to is John Constantine. But this time, there is no other option. As Praexis demons father around Glasgow, feasting on the bloody roil of emotions there, a larger threat looms. Soldiers and guns can't contain the deadly infection of empathy that has turned the Scottish city into a ghost town. Time is running out, and unless Constantine can pull a trick out of his trench coat sleeve, the whole world is going to succumb to the empathy plague. And the first to go will be Constantine's last few remaining intimates - who are already suffering from exposure to his horrific memories. The book includes lots of harsh language, violence, and horrific images.

Minekura, Kazuya
   Bus Gamer: 1999-2001 The Pilot Edition. Tokyopop 2006 240p. Illustration
Grades: 10 11 12 Adult   **741.5; Fic**
   1. Adventure graphic novels; 2. Games; 3. Manga; 4. Graphic novels
   1-59816-327-2, $9.99
   When Toki, Nobuto, and Kazuo are hired to play the "Biz" Game, company secrets and insane amounts of money collide in a frenzied competition that starts out as an innovative way to win some cash. But as the game goes on, the players are ushered into a world filled with mystery, deceit, and murder. Suddenly, they realize what is truly at

stake: their very lives. The book contains harsh language and violence.

   Wild Adapter Vol. 1. Tokyopop 2007 Un Illustration
Grades: 12 Adult   **741.5; Fic**
   1. Manga; 2. Mystery graphic novels; 3. Graphic novels
   978-1-59816-978-2, $9.99
   Makoto Kubota wandered through life, not taking things too seriously or looking too deep within himself. His job as the head of the Izumo Group's youth gang kept him pleasantly occupied with yakuza wars, mahjong and assassinations... Until the day he stumbled upon a strange drug called Wild Adapter that produces bizarre side-effects—including beast-like violent behavior and death. Forever changed, Kubota becomes entangled with a drifter named Minoru Tokito, and the two form an unlikely companionship that draws them deeper into the mystery of Wild Adapter... The book includes harsh language and graphic violence, later volumes will include some nudity as well.

Mitchell, C. Gaby
   The Black Diamond Detective Agency. First Second Books 2007 138p. Illustration
Grades: 10 11 12 Adult   **741.5; Fic**
   1. Mystery graphic novels; 2. Graphic novels
   978-1-59643-142-3, $16.95; 1-59643-142-3
   John Hardin is a desperate man. He is the sole suspect of the renowned Black Diamond Detective Agency, a private operation determined to solve the mystery of a deadly train bombing and bring its perpetrator to justice at any cost. Once a quiet Missouri corn farmer, Hardin now finds himself on the run in turn-of-the-century Chicago. Violence, harsh language, brief nudity, and an implied sexual encounter make this better for older teen and adult readers.

Mitsuki, Lay
   Yggdrasil vol. 1. Go! Comi 2008 Un Illustration
Grades: 9 10 11 12 Adult   **741.5; Fic**
   1. Fantasy graphic novels; 2. Manga; 3. Video games; 4. Graphic novels
   978-1-933617-91-6, $10.99
   It's the near-future, and online gaming is all the rage. Teenage gamer Ko has more of an edge than others, since his father works for the company that produces the biggest online game out there . . . at least, he had an edge, until someone hacks his account and starts playing his Phantom character that no one is supposed to know about. Ko is determined to find out who's been logging into his game, but he and his friends may have found more than they bargained for as they delve deeper into the fabulous world of Yggdrassil . . .

Miyabe, Miyuki
   Brave Story Volume 1. Art by Yoichiro Ono. Tokyopop 2007 198p. Illustration
Grades: 10 11 12 Adult   **741.5; Fic**
   1. Adventure graphic novels; 2. Fantasy graphic novels; 3. Manga; 4. Shonen manga; 5. Graphic novels
   978-1-4278-0489-1, $9.99
   Life couldn't be more average for junior high school student Wataru, whose only real skill is playing video games.

His parents' divorce is bad, but life is normal. That all changes in the blink of an eye when a mysterious transfer student comes to his school and drags him into a land of magic and monsters. Now, Wataru must face challenges he could not imagine in even his wildest dreams. There's some strong language and lots of monster fighting in this book, based on a novel which became a popular anime in Japan.

Miyamoto, Yuki

Cafe Kichijouji De Vol. 1. Digital Manga Publishing 2005 156p. Illustration
Grades: 9 10 11 12 Adult   741.5; Fic
1. Humorous graphic novels; 2. Manga; 3. Shojo manga; 4. Graphic novels
1-56970-949-1, $12.95
The staff at Cafe Kichijouji are a wacky bunch. When five guys of wildly different personalities get together, every day is a day full of raucous mayhem. They're the source of continual headaches for the poor cafe master who oversees them all. From disastrous shopping excursions to dealing with demonic scone batter, the wackiness at the cafe never ends. Even the most menial activities are fraught with disaster and weirdness when these five are around. This is a three-volume series.

Miyuki, Takahashi

Musashi #9, Vol. 1. [translation and adaptation by Tony Ogasawara]. CMX Manga 2005 206p. Illustration
Grades: 9 10 11 12 Adult   741.5; Fic
1. Adventure graphic novels; 2. Manga; 3. Spies; 4. Graphic novels
1-4012-0540-2, $9.95
Musashi #9 is the code name for one of the top operatives of ultimate Blue, a secret organization operating independently of any government, whose goal is to maintain world peace. A teenager who displays incredible martial arts skills, wields weapons with aplomb, moves with stealth, and uses disguises, Musashi #9 protects tough teen girl Yayoi when assassins come after her, helps an ex-FBI agent save his kidnapped sister, protects a Russian scientist and his son from spies, and helps two teen boys who stumble upon terrorists targeting the Russian president. The reader discovers, along with Yayoi, that Musashi #9 is actually a girl who usually disguises herself as a boy. This is the first volume of an ongoing manga series. There's lots of action, but minimal graphic depictions of violence and little in the way of harsh language or adult content.

Mizuki, Shigeru

NonNonBa. Shigeru Mizuki; translation by Jocelyne Allen. Drawn & Quarterly 2012 408 p. Illustration; Color
Grades: 7 8 9 10 11 12 Adult   741.5/952; 741.5
1. Autobiographical graphic novels; 2. Cartoonists — Japan — Biography; 3. Folklore — Japan; 4. Grandmothers; 5. Grandparent- grandchild relationship; 6. Mizuki, Shigeru, 1922-2015 — Childhood and youth; 7. Yokai (Japanese folklore)
1770460721; 9781770460720, $26.95
                                      LC 2012427667
This graphic novel, by Shigeru Mizuki, translated by Jocelyne Allen, is "a poetic memoir detailing his interest in yokai (spirit monsters). Mizuki's childhood experiences

with yokai influenced the course of his life and oeuvre; he is now known as the forefather of yokai manga. . . . Mizuki explores the legacy left him by his childhood explorations of the spirit world, explorations encouraged by his grandmother, a grumpy old woman named NonNonBa." (Publisher's note)
Includes bibliographical references

Onward towards our noble deaths. Translated by Jocelyne Allen. Drawn & Quarterly 2011 372p. Illustration
Grades: Adult   741.5; 818
1. Artists; 2. Authors; 3. Biographers; 4. Cartoonists; 5. Comic book writers; 6. Illustrators; 7. Memoirists; 8. Mizuki, Shigeru; 9. Soldiers; 10. World War, 1939-1945 — Campaigns — New Guinea; 11. World War, 1939-1945 — Japan
9781770460416; 978-1-77046-041-6, $24.95
This "English translation of legendary Japanese cartoonist Mizuki's 1973 antiwar screed is a lightly fictionalized account (90 percent fact, he claims in an afterword) of his time in the Imperial Army during WWII. Though some 30 soldiers are introduced in the opening character guide, no more than a few ever really differentiate themselves, a fitting reminder of the low premium that war puts on individual life. What comes through clearly is the litany of indignities the soldiers endure on a daily basis from slap-happy officers, perilously unforgiving conditions, and sudden outbursts of death on the receiving end of the enemy's bombs and bullets.—
This "English translation of legendary Japanese cartoonist Mizuki's 1973 antiwar screed is a lightly fictionalized account (90 percent fact, he claims in an afterword) of his time in the Imperial Army during WWII. Though some 30 soldiers are introduced in the opening character guide, no more than a few ever really differentiate themselves, a fitting reminder of the low premium that war puts on individual life. What comes through clearly is the litany of indignities the soldiers endure on a daily basis from slap-happy officers, perilously unforgiving conditions, and sudden outbursts of death on the receiving end of the enemy's bombs and bullets." Booklist

Shigeru Mizuki's Hitler. By Shigeru Mizuki (Author), Zack Davisson (Translator). Farrar, Straus & Giroux 2015 296 p. Illustration
Grades: Adult   943.086092; 741.5
1. Germany — History — 1933-1945; 2. Germany — Politics and government — 1933-1945; 3. Hitler, Adolf, 1889-1945; 4. World War, 1939-1945 — Biography
1770462104; 9781770462106, $24.95
This graphic novel, by Shigeru Mizuki, translated by Zack Davisson, delves deep into the history books to create an absorbing and eloquent portrait of [Adolf] Hitler's life. Beginning with Hitler's time in Austria as a starving art student and ending with a Germany in ruins, Shigeru Mizuki's Hitler retraces the path Hitler took in life, coolly examining his charismatic appeal and his calculated political maneuvering.ö (Publisher's note)

Showa 1944-1953: a history of Japan. Shigeru Mizuki; translated by Zack Davisson. Farrar, Straus & Giroux 2014 540 p. Illustration
Grades: Adult   952.03/3; 741.5

1. Japan — History — 1945-1952, Allied Occupation; 2. World War, 1939-1945 — Japan
1770461620; 9781770461628, $24.95

This graphic novel "continues the award-winning author Shigeru Mizuki's autobiographical and historical account of the Showa period in Japan. This volume recounts the events of the final years of the Pacific War, and the consequences of the war's devastation for Mizuki and the Japanese populace at large." (Publisher's note)

Showa 1953-1989: a history of Japan. Shigeru Mizuki; translation by Zack Davisson. Drawn & Quarterly 2013 552 p. Illustration
Grades: Adult   **952.03/3; 741.5**
1. Japan — History; 2. Japan — History — Showa period, 1926-1989; 3. Japan — Social life and customs; 4. Japan — Social life and customs; 5. Mizuki, Shigeru, 1922-2015 — Childhood and youth
9781770462014, $24.95; 1770462015
                                                LC 2013464735

This graphic novel, by Shigeru Mizuki, translated by Zack Davisson, illustrates Japan's utter defeat in World War II, as a country reduced to rubble struggles to rise again. The Korean War brings new opportunities to the nation searching for an identity. . . . Events like the Tokyo Olympiad and the World's Fair introduce a new, friendly Japan to the world, but this period of peace and plenty conceals a populace still struggling to come to terms with the devastation of World War II." (Publisher's note)

Translation of: Komikku Showa-shi.||Manga format; reads from back to front, right to left.
History of Japan

Showa, 1926-1939: a history of Japan. Shigeru Mizuki; translator, Zack Davisson. Drawn & Quarterly 2013 533 p. Illustration
Grades: Adult   **741.5; 952.03**
1. Great Depression, 1929-1939; 2. Japan — History — 1868-1945; 3. Japan — History — 1926-1945; 4. Japan — Social life and customs — 1912-1945
1770461353; 9781770461352, $24.95
                                                LC 2013464735

Translated by Zack Davisson, "'Showa 1926-1939: A History of Japan' is the first volume of Shigeru Mizuki's meticulously researched historical portrait of twentieth-century Japan. This volume deals with the period leading up to World War II, a time of high unemployment and . . . the Great Depression. Mizuki's photo-realist style effortlessly brings to life the Japan of the 1920s and 1930s, depicting bustling city streets and abandoned graveyards with equal ease." (Publisher's note)
Translation of: Komikku Showa-shi.

Showa, 1939-1944: a history of Japan. Shigeru Mizuki; translation, Zack Davisson. Drawn & Quarterly 2014 548 p. Illustration
Grades: Adult   **952.03; 741.5**
1. Japan — History — 1868-1945; 2. Japan — History — 1926-1945; 3. Japan — Social life and customs — 1912-1945; 4. Mizuki, Shigeru, 1922-2015 — Childhood and youth; 5. World War, 1939-1945
1770461515; 9781770461512, $24.95
                                                LC 2014407869

This book continues "author Shigeru Mizuki's autobiographical and historical account of Showa-era Japan. This volume covers the final moments of the lead-up to World War II and the first few years of the Pacific War, and is a chilling reminder of the harshness of life in Japan during this highly militarized epoch." (Publisher's note)

"As with the first volume, the narrative switches back and forth from a broad historical account of the war to a narrow view seen from the perspective of Mizuki and his family. This restricted view flattens world-changing events and highlights the mundane: the tedium of constant rationing and hunger and, once Mizuki is drafted, the hurry-up-and-wait uncertainty that comes with being a soldier." Booklist
Translation of: Komikku Showa-shi.

Mizuki, Shioko
Crossroad, Vol. 1. Go! Comi 2005 200p. Illustration
Grades: 10 11 12 Adult   **741.5; Fic**
1. Family life; 2. Manga; 3. Romance graphic novels; 4. Shojo manga; 5. Graphic novels
0-9768957-2-2, $10.99

Kajitsu has lived with her grandmother while her irresponsible mother, Rumiko, has flitted from one relationship to another. But now, her grandmother has died, and at fifteen Kajitsu is alone. Then her mother shows up, as well as Taro and Natsu, two of Kajitsu's stepbrothers. Before they know it Rumiko has run off again, but this time she has left behind a little girl, Satsuki. They have to make the best of the situation and live together as a sort of family, even though they have no blood connection to each other. Moments of broad comedy alternate with drama as the step-siblings try to settle into something resembling normal life.

Cy-believers. Go! Comi 2008 Un Illustration
Grades: 10 11 12 Adult   **741.5; Fic**
1. Humorous graphic novels; 2. Manga; 3. School stories; 4. Graphic novels
978-1-933617-76-3, $10.99

Rui has just transferred to a new high school in hope of finding some independence from a controlling family. Unfortunately, her fiance has been using his power as Public Safety Commissioner of the school to shut down many of the school's clubs. And Nijo seems to think he can control Rui's life at the school, which she doesn't like at all. With the help of a couple of cute computer nerds, Rui sets up a new club, the Cy-Believers. This volume includes some sexual situations.

Three in love, vol. 1. Go! Comi 2008 Un Illustration
Grades: 10 11 12 Adult   **741.5; Fic**
1. Humorous graphic novels; 2. Manga; 3. Romance graphic novels; 4. Graphic novels
978-1-60510-015-9, $10.99

Machiru has always been first-place in everything she has done, and she can't stand it when anyone else seems to do better than she can, so when Hanakago transfers into school and immediately makes a play for Machiru's childhood friend Suruga, Machiru can't let Hanakago have him as a boyfriend. They become a threesome, with the two girls constantly trying to outmaneuver each other. Complicating matters Ichiro has always tried to protect

Hanakago and has a crush on her, and Hiroo has been Machiru's friend for years. The book so far only shows some kissing, but there's a fair amount of talk about romance and sex.

Mizushiro, Setona
After School Nightmare Volume 1. Go! Comi 2006 200p. Illustration
Grades: 10 11 12 Adult   **741.5; Fic**
   1. Horror graphic novels; 2. Manga; 3. Shojo manga; 4. Supernatural graphic novels; 5. Graphic novels
   978-1-933617-16-9, $10.99
   You have just awakened to find your darkest, ugliest secret revealed to classmates who would do anything to destroy you. This is what's happened to Ichijou Mashiro, whose elite school education turns into the most horrifying experience of his life when he's enlisted by a mysterious school nurse to take an after-hours class. Only those who pass the class will graduate, and the only way for Mashiro to pass is to enter into a nightmare world... where his body and soul will be at the mercy of his worst enemies. Can Mashiro keep his life-long secret - that he is not truly a "he" nor entirely a "she" - or will he finally be "outed" in the most humiliating way possible? The book includes graphic violence, strong language, and sexual situations.

Mochizuki, Minetaro
Dragon Head Vol. 1. Tokyopop 2006 223p. Illustration
Grades: 11 12 Adult   **741.5; Fic**
   1. Apocalyptic fiction; 2. Manga; 3. Science fiction graphic novels; 4. Seinen manga; 5. Graphic novels
   1-59532-914-5, $9.99
   The end of everyone was just the beginning...Returning home by train after a class trip, Teru Aoki takes a most frightening ride inside a mountain tunnel. When the train derails, nearly everyone aboard is killed. Amidst the bloody carnage, Teru discovers two survivors—but salvation is far from their grasp. As they try to dig out from the wreck in order to come up with a plan to stay alive, the lack of light and food, combined with the stench of death and decay, will lead one member of the group down a dark and demented path. And with sudden, violent earthquakes shaking the tunnel, escaping to the outside world may lead them to an even greater danger... Violence, strong language, partial nudity, and sexual situations occur in the series.

Modan, Rutu
Exit Wounds. Drawn & Quarterly 2007 160p. Illustration
Grades: 12 Adult   **Fic; 741.5**
   1. Israelis; 2. Mystery graphic novels; 3. Graphic novels
   1-897299-06-0, $19.95
   Israeli taxi driver Koby Franco lives and works in Tel Aviv; he lives with his Aunt Ruby and Uncle Aryeh, and he hasn't seen his father in a long time. One evening he gets a fare; Numi is a soldier, and she tells Koby she thinks his father may have been killed in a terrorist bombing in Hadera. He reluctantly helps her, against the advice of his family, and he and Numi try to trace his father's last few months and see whether he died or not. As they do this, Koby must deal with his feelings about a father who never really connected with his own family. Angry with Numi because she'd had an

affair with his father, Koby eventually becomes her friend, and then her lover. The book includes one fairly graphic sex scene without any nudity.

★ The **Property**. By Rutu Modan and translated by Jessica Cohen. Farrar Straus & Giroux 2013 232 p. Color; Illustration
Grades: Adult   **741.5**
   1. Grandmothers; 2. Memory — Fiction
   1770461159; 9781770461154, $24.95
                  LC 2012517821
   Eisner Award: Best Graphic Album—New (2014)
   In this graphic novel written by Rutu Modan and translated by Jessica Cohen, "Regina Segal takes her granddaughter Mica to Warsaw, hoping to reclaim a family property lost during the Second World War. Regina is forced to recall difficult things about her past. Modan offers up a world populated by prickly seniors, smart-alecky public servants, and stubborn women—a world whose realism is expressed alternately in the absurdity of people's behavior and in the complex consequences of their sacrifices." (Publisher's note)
   "Nicely varied panel size and earth-tone coloration further distinguish this gratifying work of comics realism." Booklist

Moeller, Christopher
Iron Empires: Faith Conquers. Dark Horse Comics 2004 Un Illustration
Grades: 9 10 11 12 Adult   **741.5; Fic**
   1. Science fiction graphic novels; 2. Graphic novels
   1-59307-015-2, $17.95
   In the far future, eight weary nations are scattered among three million light years of the Milky Way Galaxy, all that is left of a once vast human civilization. The Vaylen Terror has ravaged humanity through the years, seizing a thousand worlds in a bloody rush, then pausing for decades of consolidation During these intervals of calm, the empires rebuild, rearm, then wage war on their neighbors. In this volume, readers will meet tough, uncompromising warrior-priest Trevor Faith, battling for his life and conscience on a border world. The book includes some strong language and lots of fighting violence.

Iron Empires: Sheva's War. Dark Horse Comics 2004 Un Illustration
Grades: 9 10 11 12 Adult   **741.5; Fic**
   1. Science fiction graphic novels; 2. Graphic novels
   1-59307-110-8, $17.95
   In the far future, eight weary nations are scattered among three million light years of the Milky Way Galaxy, all that is left of a once vast human civilization. The Vaylen Terror has ravaged humanity through the years, seizing a thousand worlds in a bloody rush, then pausing for decades of consolidation During these intervals of calm, the empires rebuild, rearm, then wage war on their neighbors. In this volume, readers will meet the beautiful Karsan noblewoman, Ahmi Sheva. As the planet she despises but is duty-bound to defend is caught up in an empire-wide catastrophe, Sheva finds herself fighting, not just for survival, but for her humanity. The book includes strong language and violence.

Molebash, Wes
    You'll Have That Vol. 1. Viper Comics 2006 64p.
Illustration
Grades: 9 10 11 12 Adult   **741.5; Fic**
    1. Humorous graphic novels; 2. Married people; 3.
    Graphic novels
    0-9777883-1-8, $4.95
                                                LC 2002-280685
    This book follows the lives of Andy and Katie, a
newlywed couple in their twenties, as they try to figure out
life together. In the first published volume of the webcomic
strip You'll Have That, newlyweds Andy and Katie battle
noisy neighbors, have an unpleasant restaurant visit, and
cope with the everyday struggles of married life. The book
includes some mildly strong language.

Momochi, Reiko
    Confidential Confessions: Deai Volume 1. Tokyopop
2006 216p. Illustration
Grades: 10 11 12 Adult   **741.5; Fic**
    1. Manga; 2. Mystery graphic novels; 3. Shojo manga; 4.
    Graphic novels
    1-59816-3868, $9.99
    Welcome to the seedy underbelly of the enormous
deai-kei industry, where men pay exorbitant fees to send
emails to various girls whom they hope one day to meet in
person. Rika is a young teen in need of a job. When the
opportunity to join a deai-kei site presents itself, she decides
to go for it—the money is good and the interaction seems
innocent enough. But the longer Rika works, the more her
inhibitions and boundaries are pushed to the limit—and she
begins heading down a path from which there is no return.
While this story is fictional, it's based on fact, and the
situation of high school girls dating older men for money has
been touched on in several other manga titles. This is the first
of two volumes. The book includes strong language, partial
nudity, sexual situations, and violence.

Moon, Fabio
    De: Tales: Stories from Urban Brazil. Dark Horse
Comics 2006 112p. Illustration
Grades: 10 11 12 Adult   **741.5; Fic**
    1. Graphic novels
    978-1-19307-485-2, $14.95
    This collection of short stories features Moon and Ba,
who are twins, working together, in tandem, or separately -
trading off on the roles of writing and illustrating, sharing
those roles or flying solo. Brimming with all the details of
human life, their tales move from the urban reality of their
home in Sao Paulo to the magical realism of their Latin
American background. Some stories feature brief partial
nudity and sexual situations and some mild harsh language.

    Two brothers. Fábio Moon, Gabriel Bá. Dark Horse
Books 2015 232 p. Illustration
Grades: Adult   **741.5/981; 741.5**
    1. Brazil; 2. Brazil — Fiction; 3. Brothers; 4. Brothers —
    Fiction; 5. Family secrets; 6. Twins — Fiction
    1616558563; 9781616558567, $24.99
                                                LC 2015018060
    In this novel by Gabriel Ba and Fabio Moon "twin
brothers Omar and Yaqub may share the same features, but

they could not be more different from one another. After a
brutally violent exchange between the young boys, Yaqub,
the good son, is sent from his home in Brazil to live with
relatives in Lebanon, only to return five years later as a
virtual stranger to the parents who bore him, his tensions
with Omar unchanged." (Publisher's note)

MOONSHOT: The Indigenous Comics Collection
    Edited by Hope Nicholson. Alternate History Comics
Inc 2015 176 p. Illustration
Grades: 6 7 8 9 10 11 12 Adult   **741.5**
    1. American literature — Native American authors; 2.
    Graphic novels
    0987715259; 9780987715258, $17.99
    This comic anthology, edited by Hope Nicholson, "from
traditional stories to exciting new visions of the future, . . .
presents some of the finest comic book and graphic novel
work in North America. The traditional stories presented in
the book are with the permission from the elders in their
respective communities, making this a truly genuine,
never-before-seen publication." (Publisher's note)
    "This collection of folklore from a powerhouse team of
Native authors, including Buffy Sainte-Marie and Richard
Van Camp, will wow readers with traditional and futuristic
tales based on tribal-specific cultural teachings. . . . The
full-page illustrations in some selections and the bright
colors in others add depth and understanding to the
narratives. The artwork is as diverse as the stories collected."
SLJ

Moorcock, Michael
    Michael Moorcock's Elric: The Making of a Sorcerer.
writer, Michael Moorcock; artist, Walter Simonson; colorist,
Steve Oliff; letterer, John Workman. DC Comics 2007 Un
Illustration
Grades: 9 10 11 12 Adult   **741.5; Fic**
    1. Adventure graphic novels; 2. Fantasy graphic novels; 3.
    Graphic novels
    978-1-4012-1334-3, $19.99
    This graphic novel reveals an untold chapter from the
novels starring the classic sword and sorcery character Elric.
Young Elric must first learn to protect his beloved homeland
from raiders. Then, he must learn the perils of making pacts
with the magical world in return for protection and power in
order to become a prince and ascend to the throne of
Melnibone. He'll have to learn to temper his youthful
enthusiasm with wisdom if he is going to rule the Bright
Empire. There is some incidental nudity, along with battles.

Moore, Alan
    Alan Moore's Complete WildC.A.T.S.. Art by various.
DC Comics/Wildstorm 2007 400p. Illustration
Grades: 10 11 12 Adult   **741.5; Fic**
    1. Superhero graphic novels; 2. Graphic novels
    978-1-4012-1545-3, $29.99
    Moore's defining run on the super-hero team known as
WildC.A.T.s is collected into a single volume, one in which
he is assisted by Travis Charest and other artists. He
envisioned a saga of honor, adventure, and betrayal that is
presented here in complete form. The book includes
violence and strong language.

★ **From** Hell. Top Shelf Productions 2000 Un Illustration
Grades: 11 12 Adult   **741.5; Fic**
1. Jack the Ripper murders, London (England), 1888; 2. Mystery graphic novels; 3. Graphic novels
0-9585783-4-6, $35

Legendary comics writer Alan Moore and artist Eddie Campbell have created a hallucinatory piece of crime fiction about Jack the Ripper. Detailing the events that led up to the Whitechapel murders and the cover-up that followed, Moore posits the theory that a Masonic conspiracy covered up the involvement of Queen Victoria's grandson. He tells the story from the viewpoint of the victims, of the police investigating the case, and of the killer. The book includes graphic violence and depiction of the murder victims, harsh language, and nudity.

★ The **League** of Extraordinary Gentlemen volume 1. Alan Moore, Kevin O'Neill. DC Comics 2012 192 p.
Grades: Adult   **741.5**
1. Historical fiction
1563898586; 9781563898587, $14.99
LC 2012027560

This book, by Alan Moore and Kevin O'Neill, "features a grand collection of signature 19th-century fictional adventurers, covertly brought together to defend the empire. The League of Extraordinary Gentlemen comprises such characters as Minna Murray (formerly Harker), from Bram Stoker's Dracula; Robert Louis Stevenson's Dr. Jekyll (and his monstrous alter ego, Mr. Hyde); and Jules Verne's Captain Nemo, restored to the dark, grim-visaged Sikh Verne originally intended." (Publisher's note)

Originally published in single magazine form as The League of Extraordinary Gentlemen Vol. 1 #1-6.
Volume 1 of 2

The **League** of Extraordinary Gentlemen: Black Dossier. DC Comics/America's Best Comics 2007 208p. Illustration
Grades: 12 Adult   **741.5**
1. Adventure graphic novels; 2. Spies; 3. Graphic novels
978-1-4012-0306-1, $29.99

Britain in 1958 is not the world we knew; the country is still at war with Germany (led by Hynkel). The League of Extraordinary Gentlemen had been disbanded after the last world war, and the members of the Murray Group" were labelled impersons." But now, the ever-youthful Mina Murray and a rejuvenated Allan Quatermain return to London and retrieve the Black Dossier, a legendary volume that details all the known facts about the league, going back centuries. Government spies pursue them, including one rather smarmy young agent called Jimmie (who likes his martinis stirred not shaken), Bulldog Drummond, and others. The book includes lots of full-frontal nudity, sexual situations, foul language, and violence.

★ **Miracleman**; Book 1: A dream of flying. By Mick Anglo; illustrated by Garry Leach, Alan Davis, Paul Neary, and Steve Dillon. Marvel Enterprises 2014 176 p. Color illustration
Grades: Adult   **741.5**
1. Reporters and reporting — Fiction; 2. Superhero graphic novels
0785154620; 9780785154624, $29.99

"Reporter Michael Moran always knew he was meant for something more-now, an unexpected series of events leads him to reclaim his destiny as Miracleman! After nearly two decades away, Miracleman uncovers his origins and their connection to the British military's 'Project Zarathustra'—while his alter ego, Michael Moran, must reconcile his life as the lesser half of a god." (Publisher's note)

"After two decades out of print, one of the seminal works of modern comics has finally been extricated from legal snarls of incredible complexity and made available again, beautifully recolored. Pre-Swamp Thing, pre-Watchmen, this was the first story by Alan Moore (pseudonymous here) to retool an existing series in a darker, more adult fashion." LJ

Contains material originally published in magazine form as Miracleman #1-4

★ **Miracleman:** Olympus Book three. By Alan Moore; illustrated by John Totleben. Marvel Enterprises 2015 328 p.
Grades: Adult   **741.5**
1. Superhero graphic novels
0785154663; 9780785154662, $39.99

In this graphic novel, by Alan Moore, illustrated by John Totleben, "Gods and monsters walk the earth, as the aliens whose technology created Miracleman seek to exterminate Project Zarathustra's survivors. And even as the future of humankind hangs in the balance on the far side of the galaxy, and the month-old baby Winter begins to speak, the price of godhood takes its toll on Johnny Bates. A single word is uttered, and hell on Earth is unleashed." (Publisher's note)

★ **Miracleman:** The Red King Syndrome Book two. By Alan Moore; illustrated by Chuck Austen, Rick Veitch, John Ridgway. Marvel Enterprises 2014 224 p.
Grades: Adult   **741.5**
1. Superhero graphic novels
0785154647; 9780785154648, $34.99

In this graphic novel, by Alan Moore, "Michael Moran has rediscovered the power of Miracleman, but unbeknownst to him, Dr. Emil Gargunza, the man behind Project Zarathustra, has set in motion plans decades in the making. . . . Gargunza's intentions for Miracleman's wife and unborn child set the stage for a confrontation between creator and creation. The origins of Gargunza and Zarathustra will be revealed, and life and death will be decided deep in the jungles of Paraguay." (Publisher's note)

Nemo: Heart of Ice. By Alan Moore and Kevin O'Neill. Top Shelf Productions 2013 56 p. Illustration
Grades: Adult   **Fic; 741**
1. Adventure graphic novels; 2. Arctic regions; 3. Superhero graphic novels
1603092749; 9781603092746, $14.95

This graphic novel, by Alan Moore and Kevin O'Neill, begins in "1925, fifteen years after the death of Captain Nemo, when his daughter Janni Dakkar launches a grand Antarctic expedition to lay the old man's burdensome legacy to rest. Accompanied by Nemo's shipmate Ishmael . . . and her father's log, Janni embarks on a perilous journey to the bottom of the world pursued by employees of an influential

publishing tycoon, who seek the return of plundered loot."
(Publisher's note)

Promethea Book Five. Alan Moore, writer; J.H.
Williams III, penciller & painter; Mick Gray, inker; Jose
Villarrubia, Jeromy Cox, coloring. DC Comics/America's
Best Comics 2005 160p. Illustration
Grades: 10 11 12 Adult   741.5; Fic
1. Adventure graphic novels; 2. Fantasy graphic novels; 3.
Graphic novels
1-4012-0620-4, $14.99

Sophie, the new personification of the goddess
Promethea, went into hiding after government agents
destroyed her world. As the years have passed, Sophie has
suppressed the goddess within her, but now, with the help of
Tom Strong, the government is closing in on her again, and
she has no choice but to release the mystic power of
Promethea, thereby unleashing an apocalypse upon the
world and everyone in it, both foe and friend. This is the final
volume of the series. The book includes nudity, sexual
situations, harsh language, and violence.

Promethea Book One. Alan Moore, J.H. Williams III,
Mick Gray. DC Comics/America's Best Comics 2001 160p.
Illustration
Grades: 10 11 12 Adult   Fic; 741.5
1. Adventure graphic novels; 2. Fantasy graphic novels; 3.
Graphic novels
1-56389-667-2, $14.99

Sophie Bangs was a just an ordinary college student in a
futuristic New York when a simple assignment changed her
life forever. While researching Promethea, a mythical
warrior woman, Sophie receives a cryptic warning to cease
her investigations. Ignoring the cautionary notice, she
continues her studies and is almost killed by a shadowy
creature when she learns the secret of Promethea. Surviving
the encounter, Sophie soon finds herself transformed into
Promethea, the living embodiment of the imagination. Her
trials have only begun as she must master the secrets of her
predecessors before she is destroyed by Promethea's ancient
enemy. The book includes some strong language, partial
nudity, and violence.
Volume 1 of 5

Saga of the Swamp Thing; Book one. Written by Alan
Moore; art by Stephen Bissette ... [et al.]; colored by Tatjana
Wood; lettered by John Costanza, Todd Klein. DC Comics
2012 205 p. Color illustration
Grades: Adult   741.5; 741.5/973
1. Swamp Thing (Fictional character)
1401220835; 9781401220839, $19.99
                                        LC 2012374624
This comic book collection, by Alan Moore, "begins
with the story "The Anatomy Lesson," a haunting origin
story that reshapes SWAMP THING mythology with
terrifying revelations that begin a journey of discovery and
adventure that will take him across the stars and beyond."
(Publisher's note)
Originally published in magazine form as The saga of
the Swamp Thing #20-27.
Volumes 2-6 also written by Moore

Smax Collected Edition. Alan Moore, writer; Zander
Cannon, artist; Andrew Currie, Richard Friend, inkers; Ben

Dimagmaliw, Wildstorm FX, coloring; Todd Klein,
lettering, logo and design. DC Comics/America's Best
Comics 2004 Un Illustration
Grades: 10 11 12 Adult   741.5; Fic
1. Adventure graphic novels; 2. Humorous graphic
novels; 3. Science fiction graphic novels; 4. Graphic
novels
1-4012-0290-X, $12.99

Jeff Smax, a major character in Alan Moore's Top 10
series, must return to his home world after many years on
Earth. Accompanied by his fellow Neopolis Precinct Ten
police officer Robin Toybox Slinger, he must face a myriad
of challenges ranging from cutting through mountainous red
tape to go on a quest, doing battle with the most monstrous of
all dragons, and adapting to a world where the laws of
physics are not only unheard of, they just plain don't work.
And then there's Jeff's sister ... While there's little in the way
of bad language and the violence is mostly against fantasy
monsters, the book does include some sexual
suggestiveness. And in Jeff's world, sex with one's sister is
normal.

Terra Obscura Vol. Two. Alan Moore and Peter Hogan,
co-plotters ; Peter Hogan, scripts ; Yanick Paquette, pencils ;
Karl Story, inks ; Jeremy Cox, colors. DC
Comics/Wildstorm 2005 Un Illustration
Grades: 8 9 10 11 12 Adult   741.5; Fic
1. Science fiction graphic novels; 2. Superhero graphic
novels; 3. Graphic novels
1-4012-0622-0, $14.99

Just as things have returned to normal for everyone on
Terra Obscura, including the members of S.M.A.S.H., a
mysterious object appears on the edge of their galaxy, and
it's on a collision course with the planet. Even more
distressing is that the object appears to be the spacecraft of
long-lost hero Captain Future. As the ship nears, time
anomalies crop up over the entire planet, wreaking terrible
havoc the closer the ship gets. Can Tom Strange and the
other heroes unravel this mystery before it spells doom for
the entire planet?

Tom Strong's Terrific Tales Book One. Alan Moore,
Steve Moore, Leah Moore, writers; Arthur Adams [and
others], artists. DC Comics/Wildstorm 2005 Un Illustration
Grades: 10 11 12 Adult   741.5; Fic
1. Adventure graphic novels; 2. Humorous graphic
novels; 3. Science fiction graphic novels; 4. Graphic
novels
1-4012-0029-X, $17.99
                                        LC Bd 05-068084
This anthology of stories features the science-fantasy
exploits of heroine Jonni Future, the escapades of young
Tom Strong in his early days on the exotic island of Attabar
Teru, stories starring Tom's daughter Tesla and the
intelligent ape King Solomon, and more. Moore works with
noted independent comics artists such as Peter Bagge, Peter
Kuper, Jaime Hernandez, and Sergio Aragones, among
many others. The book includes some nudity.

Top 10 Book Two. Alan Moore, writer; Gene Ha,
finishing artist; Zander Cannon, layout artist; Alex Sinclair,
Wildstorm FX, coloring; Todd Klein, lettering, logos and
design. DC Comics/Wildstorm 2002 Un Illustration
Grades: 10 11 12 Adult   741.5; Fic

1. Fantasy graphic novels; 2. Superhero graphic novels; 3. Graphic novels
1-56389-966-3, $14.95

Imagine a city where every citizen, from poorest slum-dweller to corporate honcho, has unusual powers and abilities - not to mention an alter ego and costume. How would you police such a city" Neopolis is the city of super powered citizens, and the police officers of Precinct Ten are also super powered. In this volume, they investigate the murder of an ex-sidekick rock star, deal with a murderous police commissioner who kills one of their own, and just try to get by each day. The book includes violence, nudity, and sexual situations.

Top 10: Book One. Alan Moore, writer; Gene Ha, finishing artist; Zander Cannon, layout artist; Wildstorm FX, colorin; Todd Klein, lettering, logos and design. DC Comics/America's Best Comics 2000 Un Illustration
Grades: 9 10 11 12 Adult   **741.5; Fic**
1. Mystery graphic novels; 2. Superhero graphic novels; 3. Graphic novels
1-56389-668-0, $17.95

Imagine a city where every citizen, from poorest slum-dweller to corporate honcho, has unusual powers and abilities, not to mention an alter ego and a costume. How does one police such a city? Rookie cop Robyn Singer is about to find out in her first day as part of Precinct 10 in Neopolis.

Top 10: The Forty-Niners. Alan Moore, writer; Gene Ha, artist; Art Lyon, colorist; Todd Klein, lettering, logos and design. DC Comics/America's Best Comics 2005 Un Illustration
Grades: 10 11 12 Adult   **741.5; Fic**
1. Superhero graphic novels; 2. Graphic novels
1-4012-0573-9, $17.99

This is the tale of Neopolis, a modern metropolis with a citizenry made up exclusively of super beings. In this city where everyone is blessed with powers, it takes a unique and powerful police force to protect and serve. The officers of Precinct 10 encounter all manner of the super powered and the supernatural on a routine basis. The TOP 10 team of writer Alan Moore and artist Gene Ha reunites for a graphic novel that delves into the past, revealing the origins of Neopolis and the first officers of Top Ten, from 1949. Discover the original Top 10 officers who blazed the trail and made Neopolis the city it is today. Some sexual situations and superhero violence occur in the book.

★ **V for vendetta.** Written by Alan Moore; art by David Lloyd; coloring by David Lloyd, Steve Whitaker, Siobhan Dodds; lettering by Jenny O'Connor, Steve Craddock, Elitta Fell. DC Comics 2008 288p. Illustration
Grades: 10 11 12 Adult   **741.5; Fic**
1. Science fiction graphic novels; 2. Graphic novels
978-1-4012-0841-7; 1-4012-0841-X, $19.99

The book is set in an alternate world in which England has embraced fascism after a devastating war has destroyed a lot of the world; it's 1997, and a young woman named Eve tries prostitution, only to be caught by the police on her first night. A man wearing a Guy Fawkes mask saves her, and thus begins his campaign to restore human spirit by rebelling

against the oppressive government. Known only as V, he uses terror tactics and murder to dismantle the government. Occasional nudity, some violence, and harsh language along with a complex plot make this a book for mature-minded readers.

Originally published in single magazine form in the United States as V for Vendetta 1-10—Title page

★ **Watchmen.** Alan Moore, writer; Dave Gibbons, illustrator/letterer; John Higgins, colorist. DC Comics 2005 Illustration
Grades: 11 12 Adult   **Fic; 741.5**
1. Superhero graphic novels; 2. Graphic novels
1-4012-0713-8; 978-0-930289-23-2 (pa)
1988 Eisner Award for Best Finite Series, Best Graphic Album, Best Writer, Best Writer/Artist; 1988 Hugo Award for Other Forms; 2005 listed in Time Magazine's 100 Greatest English Language Novels; 2006 Eisner Award to Watchmen Absolute Edition for Best Archival Collection, Comic Books

This graphic novel "begins with the paranoid delusions of a half-insane hero called Rorschach. But is Rorschach really insane or has he in fact uncovered a plot to murder super-heroes and, even worse, millions of innocent civilians? On the run from the law, Rorschach reunites with his former teammates in a desperate attempt to save the world and their lives." Publisher's note

"Nearly 20 years after the original publication, "Watchmen" shows an eerie prescience: the symmetry between current events and the conclusion of its story, concerning a villain who believes he can stave off real war by distracting the populace with a trumped-up one, and an act of mass murder perpetrated in the heart of New York City, is almost too fearful to bear." N Y Times Book Rev

Originally published in single magazine form as Watchmen 1-12; trade paperback edition still available Issued in slipcase. Awards: 1988 Eisner Award for Best Finite Series, Best Graphic Album, Best Writer, Best Writer/Artist; 1988 Hugo Award for Other Forms; 2005 listed in Time Magazine's 100 Greatest English Language Novels; 2006 Eisner Award to Watchmen Absolute Edition for Best Archival Collection, Comic Books

Wild Worlds. DC Comics/Wildstorm 2007 320p. Illustration
Grades: 12 Adult   **741.5; Fic**
1. Adventure graphic novels; 2. Horror graphic novels; 3. Superhero graphic novels; 4. Graphic novels
978-1-4012-1379-4, $24.99

Celebrated comics writer Alan Moore presents his take on some of Wildstorm's characters: WildC.A.T.s, Deathblow, Voodoo, and Majestic, and special guest star Spawn (from Image Comics), all of whom live in exotic, sometimes even outlandish, worlds: a stripper turned superhero turned private detective; a world populated by the clones of a secret agent; a time-twisted tale of a man who travels years into the future merely to find that even there, his past remains out of reach; and the last story of an immortal at the end of time. The book includes lots of violence, harsh language, and nudity.

Moore, B. Clay

Battle Hymn: Farewell to the First Golden Age. Drawn by Jeremy Haun. Image Comics 2006 Un Illustration
Grades: 10 11 12 Adult   **741.5; Fic**
1. Superhero graphic novels; 2. Graphic novels
1-58240-565-4, $14.99

It's 1944, and the first gathering of super-powered heroes may well be the last. In the waning days of World War II, at the dawn of the nuclear age, super-powered beings are emerging from the shadows of conflict, beginning with the arrival of the Artificial Man. Now the United States government has assembled this collection of genetic misfits, patriotic zealots, and half-human creatures to help with the war effort. At least, that's the official version of the story. Who lives" Who dies" And what exactly does the government have planned for the "heroes—" The book includes harsh language, violence, and brief sexual situations.

Casey Blue, beyond tomorrow. Writer, B. Clay Moore; pencils, Carlo Barberi; inks, Jacob Eguren. DC Comics/Wildstorm 2009 144p. Illustration
Grades: 10 11 12 Adult   **741.5; Fic**
1. Adventure graphic novels; 2. Science fiction graphic novels; 3. Graphic novels
978-1-4012-2208-6, $19.99

Casey Blue is an ordinary teenager, going to high school and playing on the volleyball team, living a nice, normal, suburban life. Then, one night it all goes weird. Leaving her brother Craig's downtown apartment after a visit, Casey feels a strange buzzing in her head, walks to another apartment building, goes up to one of the apartments, rings the doorbell, and when a man answers and opens the door, she brutally beats him to death. When she gets into her car afterwards, she can't remember how she got all that blood all over her. She also has nightmares about a future in which aliens have enslaved all humans. The news blares out the story of the murder of an industrialist who lived near Craig, and Casey starts to investigate on the Internet; this connects her to a young man in Brazil. An FBI agent comes after Casey and tries to kill her, then Craig's new neighbor Angela grabs Casey and tells her she is one of the few who will defend the world against aliens who are "Seeding" humans with a mind-controlling virus. Casey's nightmares are showing her the future. That strange buzzing in her head lets her know when a Seeded human is near, and her duty is to kill that person, no matter what. However, there are Seeded humans everywhere, hunting Casey and the other defenders being trained to fight. The story includes considerable bloody violence, and Casey seems to have a much curvier, busty body than most sixteen-year-olds.

Hawaiian Dick Volume 1: Byrd of Paradise. Written by B. Clay Moore; drawn by Steven Griffin, Nick Derington. Image Comics 2003 136p. Illustration
Grades: 10 11 12 Adult   **741.5; Fic**
1. Mystery graphic novels; 2. Supernatural graphic novels; 3. Graphic novels

978-1-58240-317-5, $14.95

In 1953 Hawaii, the supernatural manifestations of the islands' myths and legends lie just around every corner. Exiled stateside detective Byrd finds himself immersed in a dark paradise of exotic bar girls, murdered beauties, and high speed chases along the scenic Hawaiian coast, and the mysterious Night Marchers of the Pali Highway. The psychic Madame Chan, the eccentric but deadly Bishop Masaki and a restless corpse complete the mix in this slice of tropical noir. Violence and some strong language feature in the story in which Honolulu and its Chinatown of the time feature prominently (and accurately).

Hawaiian Dick Volume 2: The Last Resort. Written by B. Clay Moore; drawn by Steven Griffin, Nick Derington. Image Comics 2006 Un Illustration
Grades: 10 11 12 Adult   **741.5; Fic**
1. Mystery graphic novels; 2. Supernatural graphic novels; 3. Graphic novels
978-1-58240-664-0, $14.99

In Hawaii of the early 1950s, it's gangsters, guns and ghosts as Byrd is caught between warring gangs in a beautiful Hawaiian bay turned red with blood. Also, his Honolulu police detective friend Mo and Byrd's secretary Kahami decide to visit the Seaside Sands resort and get mixed up in trouble as well. The locals on the island know something bad is going to happen to all the haoles (white men), the gangs just don't know that yet. There's a lot of shooting and killing in this book.

The **Leading** Man. Written by B. Clay Moore; illustrated by Jeremy Haun; colored by Dave Bryant; lettered by Tom Bolton. Oni Press 2007 144p. Illustration
Grades: 10 11 12 Adult   **741.5; Fic**
1. Adventure graphic novels; 2. Mystery graphic novels; 3. Spies; 4. Graphic novels
978-1-932664-57-7, $14.95

There's more to the world's hottest actor than sexy starlets, tabloid gossip and primo parts, because Nick Walker isn't just a Hollywood hunk, he's also the world's greatest super spy. When a routine investigation off the coast of France turns up a terrorist training facility, Nick Walker must juggle espionage and screen time in this explosive and astonishing adventure. The book includes harsh language, violence, and sexual situations.

Moore, J. Stuart

Stuart Moore's Para. Penny-Farthing Press 2006 177p. Illustration
Grades: 9 10 11 12 Adult   **741.5; Fic**
1. Science — Experiments; 2. Science fiction graphic novels; 3. Graphic novels
0-9719012-4-4, $19.95

When Sara Eric was ten years old, her scientist father built a huge supercollider, but there was an accident that killed everyone. Nineteen years later, the supercollider has finally cooled off enough from the radiation for scientists to go in and investigate. Dr. Andersen, Dr. Eric's best friend, is leading the scientists, and Sara insists on going. However, the FBI has sent a Special Agent as well, and the team finds only more mysteries when they can't find any bodies. They do find the word "Para" scrawled all over the walls of the lab, and soon they discover a mysterious gateway that leads .

.. elsewhere. It will be up to Sara, the non-scientist, to figure out what happened nineteen years before.

Moore, Richard

Boneyard Volume 1. NBM 2005 96p. Illustration
Grades: 9 10 11 12 Adult   **741.5; Fic**
1. Humorous graphic novels; 2. Supernatural graphic novels; 3. Graphic novels
978-1-56163-427-9, $10.95

Michael Paris has inherited a plot in the remote town of Raven Hollow. As he arrives, he gets to find out what a doozie that is: he's inherited a cemetery that the villagers want razed. Why" It's haunted with apparently frightening creatures putting a curse on the whole town. But when Paris actually gets to meet some of the denizens of his inherited headache, it turns out they aren't all that bad (Abbey the vampire, in fact, is quite cute) and maybe the evil is not where it may seem... This book was originally published in black and white; this edition is in full color.

Boneyard Volume 2. NBM 2006 96p. Illustration
Grades: 9 10 11 12 Adult   **741.5; Fic**
1. Humorous graphic novels; 2. Supernatural graphic novels; 3. Graphic novels
978-1-56163-487-3, $11.95

Now that Beelzebub has been dealt a blow, it's the turn of the IRS to make Paris' life hell. But then, a certain beauteous Roxanna miraculously appears looking to solve all monetary problems. Paris resists as best he can, even putting on a monsters boxing contest to raise money, but the lures and the pressures... how strong can he stay" And as if that's not enough, Nessie the sexy gill girl (think of a female Creature from the Black Lagoon) and Abbey the vampire contend for Paris' affections. This book was originally published in black and white; this edition is in full color. The book includes some sexual innuendo.

Boneyard Volume 3. NBM 2008 96p. Illustration
Grades: 10 11 12 Adult   **741.5; Fic**
1. Humorous graphic novels; 2. Supernatural graphic novels; 3. Graphic novels
978-1-56163-515-3, $12.95

Glump devises a wondrous scheme to do a Monsters on the Beach special swimsuit issue to help the cash-strapped Michael Paris. Never mind that Glump is hiding a much worse scheme within the scheme. On a darker note, Roxanne shows her true powerful demonic self, resulting in a potentially deadly showdown with Abbey. With this volume, Moore kicks the sensual sexiness of the female characters up a notch. This is the color edition; the black and white edition, published in 2004, seems to be unavailable.

Boneyard Volume 4. NBM 2005 Un Illustration
Grades: 10 11 12 Adult   **741.5; Fic**
1. Humorous graphic novels; 2. Supernatural graphic novels; 3. Graphic novels
978-1-56163-424-8, $9.95

As Abbey recovers from her showdown with the much more powerful Lilith (who had disguised herself as Roxanne), swamp girl Nessie starts taking the upper hand in her pursuit of Michael (never mind she's married to Frankenstein monster-like Brutus). Meanwhile, Glump continues his schemes to rule the world, this time launching

the "Doomsday Frog.DD However, everyone comes together to face a new threat: zombies sprouting up from the cemetery. And Michael discovers that not all monsters are ... nice. The book includes some partial nudity and sexual situations, and violence. This is the original black and white edition.

Boneyard Volume 5. NBM 2006 Un Illustration
Grades: 10 11 12 Adult   **741.5; Fic**
1. Humorous graphic novels; 2. Supernatural graphic novels; 3. Graphic novels
978-1-56163-479-8, $9.95

After dealing with the zombie mess from the previous volume, Abbey, Michael and the Boneyard gang have to confront a two-pronged threat: a huge, masked,chainsaw-wielding serial killer in a girl's summer camp and the Pumpkinhead, whose very presence puts all in the 'yard into fevered sleep. Abbey barely survives the confrontation with the chainsaw brute, now it's up to Michael to face the worst threat, with Nodoze and a baseball bat. This book includes violence and some sexual innuendo.

Moore, Stuart

Lone. Dark Horse Comics 2004 Un Illustration
Grades: 9 10 11 12 Adult   **741.5; Fic**
1. Adventure graphic novels; 2. Science fiction graphic novels; 3. Western graphic novels; 4. Graphic novels
1-59307-265-1, $14.95

LC Bd 05-187024

Ravenous zombies have overrun the post-apocalyptic town of Desolation. Sharpshooter Luke and her older brother, Mark, are desperate. Their only hope is to track down and enlist the help of a gunman legendary in the western wasteland, a man known only as Lone. But if they find him, can they trust him" Cletus, a geezer who claims to know Lone, seems to know more than he's saying - especially after Luke mentions how the zombies are being controlled by a strange figure that bleeds yellow. And what are Gunfathers," anyway" After fighting off radiation-twisted mutants for two weeks, Luke and Mark are ready for answers. This is an example of the genre called weird Westerns." The book includes violence and some strong language.

Wolverine: Blood & Sorrow. Writer, Stuart Moore, Rob Williams, David Lapham; artist, C.P. Smith, Laurence Campbell, David Aja. Marvel Entertainment 2007 Un Illustration
Grades: 10 11 12 Adult   **741.5; Fic**
1. Superhero graphic novels; 2. Wolverine (Fictional character); 3. Graphic novels
978-0-7851-2607-2, $13.99

In "The Package," Logan must escape from an army of killers deep in the heart of war-torn Africa - with a baby strapped to his chest. In "Better to Give ...," a suicide cult dressed as elves has taken a Manhattan department store hostage on Christmas Eve. And Logan is one of the shoppers. In "The House of Blood and Sorrow," Wolverine lies at the edge of death in a Nebraska cornfield after crashing to Earth from the edge of the atmosphere where he'd been battling a giant robot. And then, things get bad. In "The Healing," Logan lies gutted in a Northwest forest, surrounded by wolves, as his body tries to heal. The book includes violence.

Moore, Terry

★ **Strangers** in Paradise Pocket Book 1. Abstract Studio 2003 360p. Illustration

Grades: 11 12 Adult   **741.5; Fic**
  1. Mystery graphic novels; 2. Graphic novels
  1-892597-26-8, $17.95

Katchoo is a beautiful young woman living a quiet life with everything going for her. She's smart, independent and very much in love with her best friend, Francine. Then Katchoo meets David, a gentle but persistent young man who is determined to win Katchoo's heart. The resulting love triangle is a touching comedy of romantic errors until Katchoo's former employer comes looking for her and $850,000 in missing mob money. As her idyllic life begins to fall apart, Katchoo discovers no one can be trusted and that the past she thought she left behind now threatens to destroy her and everything she loves, including Francine. This thick pocket book edition collects several of the original trade paperback volumes. The story includes strong language, sexual situations, nudity, and some violence.

★ **Strangers** in Paradise Pocket Book 2. Abstract Studio 2004 344p. Illustration

Grades: 10 11 12 Adult   **741.5; Fic**
  1. Friendship; 2. Graphic novels
  1-892597-29-8, $17.95

The second Strangers In Paradise pocket book finds Katchoo following David to California where she comes face to face with Darcy Parker. When Darcy makes Katchoo an offer she can't refuse, Katchoo transforms from prey to predator and begins to spin a web of her own. This book features 5 pages of Jim Lee art to open the story, hero-style. Also included is the most popular Strangers in Paradise short story ever—the Xena parody, "Warrior Princess." This volume collects several of the original trade paperback collections, including Vol. 6, High School. This volume includes violence, strong language, nudity, and sexual situations.

★ **Strangers** in Paradise Pocket Book 3. Abstract Studio 2004 372p. Illustration

Grades: 10 11 12 Adult   **741.5; Fic**
  1-892597-30-4, $17.95

In this third pocket book volume, Francine is stuck in a bad marriage and Katchoo is a successful artist but keeps everyone at a distance. David's mysterious past links him even closer to Katchoo, who still can't escape the Mafia life she had led with Darcy Parker. There are more friendships, breakups, makeups, and action. Readers should expect to find strong language, nudity, and sexual situations along with a little violence.

★ **Strangers** in Paradise Pocket Book 4. Abstract Studio 2005 360p. Illustration

Grades: 10 11 12 Adult   **741.5; Fic**
  1. Friendship; 2. Graphic novels
  1-892597-31-1, $17.95

Katchoo still loves Francine, but her wild past and dangerous enemies, such as Mafia types, prove to be more than Francine can handle. Meanwhile, David wants more

than friendship with Katchoo. And then Francine, on the verge of another marriage, calls it off and decides to return to Houston and see what will happen with Katchoo. This fourth pocket book volume collects three of the original trade paperback collections.

★ **Strangers** in Paradise Pocket Book 5. Abstract Studio 2005 376p. Illustration

Grades: 10 11 12 Adult   **741.5; Fic**
  1. Friendship; 2. Graphic novels
  1-892597-38-1, $17.95

While David finds solace with Katchoo, Francine can think of nothing but her past relationship with her former best friend and brings home a tattoo to prove it. It seems that Katchoo is destined to move on without Francine into the world of glitz, glamour, and art showings with her stunning display of 100 nudes. As Katchoo becomes the toast of the town, Francine finds herself looking for peace in the Caribbean. Our unlikely friends seem to be drifting apart until they are set on a collision course back to Houston. This pocket book volume also includes the Molly & Poo stories, which are illustrated prose stories set in Victorian England. Strong language, nudity, sexual situations, and violence punctuate the stories.

★ **Strangers** in Paradise Pocket Book 6. Abstract Studio 2007 272p. Illustration

Grades: 10 11 12 Adult   **741.5; Fic**
  1. Friendship; 2. Graphic novels
  1-892597-39-X, $17.95

Brad and Francine prepare to move to Houston, while free spirit Casey gets involved in the lives of her new roommates in Las Vegas and discovers a stalker. Back in Houston, Casey and David get Katchoo and Francine together again. Then David has to tell Casey and Katchoo his secret, a medical condition that may kill him. And in the final story, Francine leaves the cheating Brad and tries to reconnect with Katchoo, but she learns she's going to have to fight for her. This series lasted 90 issues and has ended the way Moore wanted it to. The stories include strong language, nudity, sexual situations, and violence.

Moore, Tony

The **Walking** Dead. Written by Robert Kirkman; Pencilled/inked by Tony Moore and Charlie Adlard. Image Comics 2006 Un Illustration

Grades: 10 11 12 Adult   **741.5; Fic**
  1. Horror graphic novels; 2. Graphic novels
  978-1-58240-619-0, $29.99

This hardcover features the first 12 issues of the hit series along with the covers for the issues in one oversized hardcover volume. An epidemic of apocalyptic proportions has swept the globe, causing the dead to rise and feed on the living. In a matter of months, society has crumbled. Rick Grimes finds himself one of the few survivors in this terrifying future. A couple months ago he was a small town cop who had never fired a shot and only ever saw one dead body. Separated from his family, he must now sort through all the death and confusion to try and find his wife and son. And when he finds them, along with a few other survivors, they must try to find a place of safety, for the walking dead are everywhere. The book includes lots of zombie violence, strong language, and some sexual situations.

Also available in trade paperback, omnibus, and compendium editions

Previously published as The Walking Dead issues #1-12.

Book 1 of an ongoing series

Mori, Kaoru
A **bride's** story, v1. Kaoru Mori. Yen Press 2011 192 p. Illustration

Grades: 11 12 Adult   **741.5**
1. Arranged marriage — Fiction; 2. Asia, Central — History — 19th century; 3. Man-woman relationships; 4. Silk Road; 5. Women — China
0316180998; 9780316180993, $17

LC 2012450076

In this graphic novel, author "Kaoru Mori brings the nineteenth-century Silk Road to lavish life, chronicling the story of Amir Halgal, a young woman from a nomadic tribe betrothed to a twelve-year-old boy eight years her junior. Coping with cultural differences, blossoming feelings for her new husband, and expectations from both her adoptive and birth families, Amir strives to find her role as she settles into a new life and a new home in a society quick to define that role for her." (Publisher's note)

"By the end of this first volume, the plot is only beginning to bloom, but there is ample enjoyment in watching the small, everyday activities that make up the family's life—laundry, hunting, raising children. Amir's cheerfulness is infectious, both to her new family and to readers." Booklist

Volume 1 of an ongoing series

Emma 1. Kaori Mori; translation, Sheldon Drzka; lettering, Abigail Blackman. Yen Press 2015 386 p. Illustration

Grades: 10 11 12 Adult   **741.5**
1. Great Britain — History — Victoria, 1837-1901 — Fiction; 2. Household employees; 3. Shojo manga
0316302236; 9780316302234, $35

In this manga by Kaoru Mori, translated by Sheldon Drzka, "calling upon his former governess, William Jones, gentleman, is startled when his knock is answered by an uncommonly beautiful servant, the soft-spoken Emma. Throughout his visit, William's eyes drift to the maid whenever she enters the room, and he contrives to meet Emma socially as she goes about her errands. But London society is a web of strict codes and divisions." (Publisher's note)

Originally published in Japan; Previously published in the U.S. by CMX

Volume 1 of 4

Emma, vol. 8. DC Comics/CMX 2009 208p. Illustration

Grades: 10 11 12 Adult   **741.5; Fic**
1. Great Britain — History — 19th century; 2. Manga; 3. Graphic novels
978-1-4012-2070-9, $9.99

This eighth volume collects short stories focusing on some of the supporting characters who have appeared throughout the course of the seven-volume series. One story features a young Kelly Stowner and her husband Doug, who

struggle to save up the two shillings needed for them to visit the Great Exhibition. Eleanor Campbell, whose engagement to William Jones has just ended, spends a vacation at Brighton trying to get over his rejection of her, and meets a surprising young man. One story is a series of vignettes of different characters reading the newspaper. And klutzy housemaid Natasha returns home for a visit. One of the story vignettes features a conversation between an older gentleman and his mistress, who is nude throughout the story.

Shirley volume 1. Del Rey Manga 2008 200p. Illustration

Grades: 8 9 10 11 12 Adult   **741.5; Fic**
1. Household employees; 2. Manga; 3. Graphic novels
978-1-4012-1777-8, $9.99

In Edwardian England, the independent Miss Bennett runs a cafe, but finds she has no time to take care of her house, so she advertises for a house maid. Young Shirley Madison answers the advertisement, and despite her very young age—she's only 13—she proves to be a competent maid and a good companion. In other stories, two maids take care of their young master, a five-year-old boy, but they don't know how to relieve his loneliness; and an experienced maid must deal with her bored master's pranks that have driven away most of the household help.

Morinaga, Ai
My Heavenly Hockey Club Vol. 1. Ballantine Books/Del Rey Manga 2007 212p. Illustration

Grades: 8 9 10 11 12 Adult   **741.5; Fic**
1. Hockey; 2. Humorous graphic novels; 3. Shojo manga; 4. Graphic novels
978-0-345-49904-2, $10.95

Hana Suzuki loves only two things in life: eating and sleeping. So when handsome classmate Izumi Oda asks Hana, his major crush, to join the school hockey club, persuading her proves to be a difficult task. True, the Grand Hockey Club is full of boys, and all the boys are super-cute, but given a choice, Hana prefers a sizzling steak to a hot date. Then Izumi mentions the field trips to fancy resorts. Now Hana can't wait for the first away game, with its promise of delicious food and luxurious linens. Of course there's also the getting up early, working hard, and playing well with others. How will Hana survive—

Morris, Steve
Blessed Thistle. Dark Horse Comics 2007 86p. Illustration

Grades: 11 12 Adult   **741.5; Fic**
1. Horror graphic novels; 2. Mystery graphic novels; 3. Graphic novels
978-1-59307-630-6, $9.95

Morris won Dark Horse's 2005 New Recruits Contest, resulting in publication of his first graphic novel.

Several stories come together: a desperate young man breaks into a house and finds the owner awake inside; a school teacher returns from a tropical vacation carrying a disturbing secret; a girl's playground bullying triggers a horrifying event. Some harsh language, violence, and ironic plot twists.

Morrison, Grant

All-Star Superman, Volume One. Written by Grant Morrison; pencilled by Frank Quitely. DC Comics 2007 160p. Illustration
Grades: 8 9 10 11 12 Adult   741.5; Fic
1. Superhero graphic novels; 2. Superman (Fictional character); 3. Graphic novels
978-1-4012-0914-8; 978-1-4012-1102-8 (pa), $12.99
Eisner Award: Best New Series (2006)
Writer Morrison and artist Quitely present several episodes in the life of the iconic superhero, Superman. When he saves a group of scientists from burning up in the sun, what no one realizes is that uber-villain Lex Luthor set up everything in order to kill Superman, who absorbed so much solar radiation that it is now slowly killing him. Once Superman learns that he is dying, he sets out to give Lois Lane a birthday she will never forget, by giving her his powers for one day. Then, when Jimmy Olsen takes charge of the science think tank P.R.O.J.E.C.T. for one day, they discover black kryptonite, which makes Superman turn evil. And, in his guise as Clark Kent, he interviews Lex Luthor in prison, but super-villain Parasite is taken from his shielded cell and begins to absorb Superman's powers, causing chaos.

Also available as a single volume collecting all 12 issues
Originally published as All-Star Superman issues #1-6
Volume 1 of 2

Batman and son. Grant Morrison, writer; Andy Kubert, penciller; Jesse Delperdang, inker ; Guy Major, Dave Stewart, colorists; Jared K. Fletcher, Rob Leigh, Nick J. Napolitano, letterers. DC Comics 2007 200p. Illustration
Grades: 9 10 11 12 Adult   Fic; 741.5
1. Batman (Fictional character); 2. Joker (Fictional character); 3. Superhero graphic novels; 4. Graphic novels
978-1-4012-1240-7, $24.99
Talia, daughter of archvillain Ra's al Ghul and Batman's onetime love, returns with a teenage boy she claims is Batman's son. She leaves Damian with Batman, but while the boy has Batman's skills, he was raised among the League of Assassins and doesn't share his father's morals. Soon, both Tim Drake, Bruce Wayne's newly adopted heir, and the faithful Alfred, become Damian's targets. The book also includes an interlude about the Joker, and a story set in the future, when Damian becomes Batman. The book includes some gory violence.

Batman: Arkham Asylum: A Serious House on Serious Earth. Written by Grant Morrison; illustrated by Dave McKean; lettered by Gaspar Saladino. DC Comics 2004 Un Illustration
Grades: 11 12 Adult   Fic; 741.5
1. Batman (Fictional character); 2. Horror graphic novels; 3. Joker (Fictional character); 4. Superhero graphic novels; 5. Graphic novels
1-4012-0425-2, $17.99
                    LC 2006-276659
In this painted graphic novel, the inmates of Arkham Asylum have taken over Gotham's detention center for the criminally insane on April Fools Day, demanding Batman in exchange for their hostages. Accepting their challenge, Batman is forced to live and endure the personal hells of the Joker, Scarecrow, Poison Ivy, Two-Face and many other

sworn enemies in order to save the innocents and retake the prison. During his run through this gauntlet, the Dark Knight's own sanity is placed in jeopardy. This edition also reproduces the original script with annotations by Morrison and editor Karen Berger. The book includes violence and some disturbing images.

Doom Patrol Book 5: Magic Bus. Writer, Grant Morrison; pencillers, Richard Case, Ken Stacey. DC Comics 2007 208p. Illustration
Grades: 11 12 Adult   741.5; Fic
1. Doom Patrol (Fictional character); 2. Superhero graphic novels; 3. Graphic novels
978-1-4012-1202-5, $19.99
This book reprints stories originally published in 1992; Morrison took a 1960s team and radically remade it, creating a weird team who fight utter weirdness. In this volume, Mr. Nobody and his new slate of Dadaists hit the presidential candidate trail. But when the team's members start going their own ways, they don't seem to see the danger growing in their midst, that threatens not only the Doom Patrol, but the world as well. The book includes some nudity, foul language, and violence, some of which might be disturbing.

Doom Patrol Volume 4: Musclebound. Written by Grant Morrison; artists, Richard Case and others. DC Comics 2006 256p. Illustration
Grades: 10 11 12 Adult   741.5
1. Doom Patrol (Fictional character); 2. Science fiction graphic novels; 3. Superhero graphic novels; 4. Graphic novels
978-1-4012-0999-5
Reality has always been flexible around the Doom Patrol, a bit too flexible if one is looking for some peace and quiet. But for the World's Strangest Heroes, staving off the annihilation of free will or the reformatting of the universe into an artistic statement is all in a day's work, not to mention the everyday assassination attempts and visits from Satan. From the sinister workings of the Ant Farm deep beneath the Pentagon to the inevitable return of the New New New Brotherhood of Dada, threats to the very structure of existence continue to bubble up. In these showdowns, only the weirdest will survive - fortunately, nobody out-weirds the Doom Patrol. Morrison has worked with a veritable host of artists on the stories collected in this volume. The stories include some strong language, partial nudity, sexual innuendo and situations, and some violence.

Doom Patrol; Volume 1: Crawling from the Wreckage. Written by Grant Morrison; pencillers, Richard Case, Doug Braithwaite; inkers, Scott Hanna, Carlos Garzon, John Nyberg; colorists, Daniel Vozza and Michele Wolfman; letterer, John Workman. DC Comics 2004 190 p. Color; Illustration
Grades: 10 11 12 Adult   Fic; 741.5
1. Superhero comic books, strips, etc
9781563890345, $19.99; 1563890348
"The new Doom Patrol puts itself back together after nearly being destroyed, and things start to get a lot weirder for everybody. The Chief leads Robotman, the recently formed Rebis and new member Crazy Jane against the Scissormen, part of a dangerous philosophical location that

has escaped into our world and is threatening to engulf reality itself." (Publisher's note)

Other Doom Patrol volumes by Morrison are: The Painting That Ate Paris; Down Paradise Way; Musclebound; Magic Bus; Planet Love

Flex Mentallo: man of muscle mystery. Grant Morrison, writer; Frank Quitely, artist; Peter Doherty, colorist; Ellie de Ville, letterer. Vertigo/DC Comics 2012 1 v. (unpaged) Color illustration
Grades: Adult   **Fic; 741.5; 741.5/9411**
1. Musicians; 2. Mystery fiction; 3. Superheroes
1401232213; 9781401232214, $22.99

LC 2012374596
Author Grant Morrison tells the story of Flex Mentallo, the "Hero of the Beach . . . and of the Doom Patrol. Now Flex Mentallo, the Man of Muscle Mystery, returns to investigate the sinister dealings of his former comrade, The Fact, and a mysterious rock star whose connection to Flex may hold the key to saving them both. . . . [The book is] an early collaboration between writer Grant Morrison and artist Frank Quitely." (Publisher's note)

Originally published in single magazine form as Flex Mentallo 1-4.

★ **Joe** the Barbarian. By Grant Morrison and illustrated by Sean Murphy. Vertigo 2013 224 p.
Grades: 10 11 12 Adult   **741.5/9411; 741.5**
1. Diabetes — Fiction; 2. Hallucinations and illusions — Fiction; 3. Graphic novels
1401237479; 9781401237479, $19.99

LC 2012047802
In this graphic novel by Grant Morrison "Joe is an imaginative young kid of 11 who happens to suffer from type 1 diabetes. Without supervision and insulin, he can easily slip into a delirious, disassociative state that presages coma and death. One fateful day, his condition causes him to believe he has entered a vivid fantasy world in which he is the lost savior — a fantastic land based on the layout and contents of his home." (Publisher's note)

Originally published in a single magazine form in Joe the Barbarian 1-8.

Kid Eternity. DC Comics/Vertigo 2006 Un Illustration
Grades: 10 11 12 Adult   **741.5; Fic**
1. Fantasy graphic novels; 2. Horror graphic novels; 3. Graphic novels
1-4012-0933-5, $14.99

Comics visionary Grant Morrison re-imagines the character of Kid Eternity, a young man who died before his true time and returns to Earth as a ghostly spirit, along with his guardian Mister Keeper. This book follows the terrifying night of aspiring stand-up comedian Jerry Sullivan as he joins Kid Eternity, who just escaped from Hell, on a quest back there to free Mister Keeper. Then the Kid learns he's been used as a pawn in the struggle between Order and Chaos. The book includes considerable violence and harsh language (f-bombs and s-bombs included).

The **Multiversity** deluxe edition. Grant Morrison, Frank Quitely, Ivan Reis. DC Comics 2015 448 p. Color; Illustration
Grades: 9 10 11 12 Adult   **741.5/973; 741.5**
1. Superhero comic books, strips, etc

1401256821; 9781401256821, $49.99

LC 2015014166
This comic book, by Grant Morrison, presents "a cast of unforgettable heroes from 52 alternative Earths of the DC Multiverse! Prepare to meet the Vampire League of Earth-43, the Justice Riders of Earth-18, Superdemon, Doc Fate, the super-sons of Superman and Batman, the rampaging Retaliators of Earth-8, the Atomic Knights of Justice, Dino-Cop, Sister Miracle, Lady Quark and the latest, greatest Super Hero of Earth-Prime: YOU!" (Publisher's note)

Supergods: what masked vigilantes, miraculous mutants, and a sun god from Smallville can teach us about being human. Spiegel & Grau 2011 444p. Illustration
Grades: 11 12 Adult   **741.5**
1. Comic books, strips, etc — United States; 2. Heroes; 3. Superheroes; 4. Superman (Fictional character); 5. Wolverine (Fictional character)
1-4000-6912-2; 978-1-4000-6912-5

LC 2010053712
A graphic novelist presents a history of the superhero in American comic books and movies. Index.

Includes bibliographical references

Superman - Action Comics; Volume 1. Grant Morrison, Rags Morales, Andy Kubert. DC Comics 2012 256 p.
Grades: 7 8 9 10 11 12 Adult   **Fic; 741.5/9411**
1. Adventure fiction; 2. Superhero comic books, strips, etc; 3. Superman (Fictional character)
1401235468; 9781401235468, $24.99

LC 2012010313
This comic book anthology, by Grant Morrison, illustrated by Rags Morales, presents volume one of "The New 52" re-launch of the DC Comics Superman series. This collection includes the first eight issues of the series, depicting "humanity's first encounters with Superman, before he became one of the world's greatest super heroes." (Publisher's note)

Vimanarama. DC Comics/Vertigo 2005 104p. Illustration
Grades: 9 10 11 12 Adult   **741.5; Fic**
1. Fantasy graphic novels; 2. Graphic novels
1-4012-0496-1, $12.99

Beneath the town of Bradford, England, a buried city of wonders holds an ancient evil; Ali and Sofia, two teenagers nervously anticipating their arranged marriage, accidentally awaken the evil. They must call upon the equally ancient Prince Ben Rama and his Ultrahadeen to drive the darkness back.

WE 3. DC Comics/Vertigo 2005 Un Illustration
Grades: 10 11 12 Adult   **741.5; Fic**
1. Animal experimentation; 2. Science fiction graphic novels; 3. Graphic novels
1-4012-0495-3, $12.99

2005 Eisner Award for Best Artist for Frank Quitely; this series was cited.

A top-secret research facility has taken a dog, a cat, and a rabbit and used cybernetics to transform the pets into armored smart weapons. The WE 3 are very successful; their enhanced intelligence allows them to communicate verbally with each other and adapt to any situation to carry out their mission. However, they're only prototypes, and when the project scientists advance to the next stage, the WE 3 are to be terminated. What the scientists and military brass haven't counted on is that their smart weapons possess enough reasoning to escape. Now Bandit the dog, Tinker the cat, and Pirate the rabbit are loose, and they want to find "Home." And they're ready to kill to find it.

Originally published as WE 3 issues #1-3.

Morrison, Robbie
White Death. AiT/Planet Lar 2002 Un Illustration
Grades: 11 12 Adult   **741.5; Fic**
1. War; 2. World War, 1914-1918; 3. Graphic novels
0-9709360-6-0, $12.95

It's 1916, and World War I, the Great War, is lurching across Europe. The Italian Front stretches across the Trentino mountain range, and Pietro Aquasanta has returned home only to find it a mass of trenches and death. If the enemy soldiers and their guns don't get you, the avalanches, the White Death, will. The men take comfort with the whores whenever they can to help them deal with the boredom and terror of the front. Harsh language, sexual situations, and the bloody violence of war permeate the story.

Wildcats: Nemesis. Pencilled by Talent Caldwell. DC Comics/Wildstorm 2006 208p. Illustration
Grades: 11 12 Adult   **741.5; Fic**
1. Mystery graphic novels; 2. Science fiction graphic novels; 3. Superhero graphic novels; 4. Graphic novels
978-1-4012-1105-90, $19.99; 978-1-4012-1105-9, $19.99

Zealot and her Coda sisters are the elite warrior-class on their homeworld of Khera, feared throughout the galaxy. A single name, however, strikes fear and hatred into their hearts: Nemesis. Frames for the betrayal and slaughter of Kheran military forces on Earth at the dawn of mankind, rogue warrior Charis Adrastea embarks on an epic quest. Hunted by former friends and foes alike, she is determined to clear her name and bring those responsible to justice. She'll soon discover a conspiracy that threatens the entire universe, but can one woman fight an entire war alone" The book includes lots of graphic violence, some nudity and sexual situations, and strong language.

Morrow, John
Kirby five-oh!: celebrating 50 years of the king of comics. [edited by John Morrow]. Twomorrows Publishing 2008 165p. Illustration
Grades: 7 8 9 10 11 12 Adult   **741.5**
1. Cartoonists; 2. Comic books, strips, etc — History and criticism; 3. Kirby, Jack, 1917-1994
978-1-893905-89-4, $19.95
                                        LC 2008-299709
In celebration of Jack Kirby's 50-year career in comics, this book features lists of such things as the best Kirby story published each year from 1938 through 1987, the best covers from each decade, Kirby's best 50 character designs, and more. The book includes a color section of photographs and art from his career.

Morse, Scott
Noble Boy. Adhouse Books/Red Window, Inc. 2006 Un Illustration
Grades: 9 10 11 12 Adult   **741.5; 92**
1. Animation; 2. Biographical graphic novels; 3. Noble, Maurice; 4. Noble, Maurice; 5. Graphic novels
0-9774715-0-0, $12.95

Using a board book design and a Dr. Seuss-style rhyming text, Morse creates a tribute to Maurice Noble, an animation designer whose works people know, even if they don't know his name. Noble worked for Walt Disney on such films as Fantasia, Snow White, Bambi, and other famous animated films. During World War II he met Theodore Geisel (better known as Dr. Seuss). After the war, Noble worked for Chuck Jones, and with Jones he worked on the cartoon version of How the Grinch Stole Christmas. In the later years with Jones, Morse came to work at the studio and Noble befriended and trained him. Morse uses full-color, full-page paintings that aren't so much representative as symbolic of the philosophy of desing Nobel taught him. One page, showing Noble gleefully and playfully peeing into a toilet across the room is the only image that could raise objections.

★ **Tiger!** Tiger! Tiger!. Adhouse Books/Red Window, Inc. 2008 48p. Illustration
Grades: 10 11 12 Adult   **741.5**
1. Courage; 2. Imagination; 3. Graphic novels
978-0-9774715-3-9, $14.95

Drawing himself and his family members as tigers, Morse ruminates on personal courage, keeping one's imagination strong, living in the same moment as his young son, and getting by day-today. He includes his day in downtown Oakland when he had to report for jury duty, and fills the pages with sketches of the people encountered in the jury pool and around the town. This is not a standard graphic novel with a regular story, but readers will be able to ask the same questions of themselves and perhaps come to their own conclusions about how to face life with courage from within and how to find joy in the little moments of life. While there is nothing here that should be objectionable, Morse's thoughts are best understood by older teens and adults.

Morvan, Jean David
★ **Classics** illustrated deluxe #6: the three Musketeers. [by] Alexandre Dumas; adapted by Jean David Morvan, Michel Dufranne, Rubèn, and Marie Galopin. Papercutz 2011 Un Illustration
Grades: 5 6 7 8 9 10 11 12 Adult   **741.5; Fic**
1. Adventure graphic novels; 2. Dumas, Alexandre, 1802-1870 — Adaptations; 3. France — History — 1589-1789, Bourbons; 4. Graphic novels
978-1-59707-253-3, $21.99; 978-1-59707-252-6 (pa), $16.99

In seventeenth-century France, young D'Artagnan initially quarrels with, then befriends, three musketeers and joins them in trying to outwit the enemies of the king and queen. This adaptation is suitable for many readers from age ten and up, but parents, teachers, and librarians might want to consider the visual depictions of sexual tensions and situations that might go over most young readers' heads in prose (there are some heaving bosoms, perspiring men, and a couple of scenes in bed), and the violence (most of it occurs off-panel). The book's endpapers include Dumas' introduction to his novel, an Epilogue, a brief biography of Dumas, and an illustrated character guide.

This book is a 70th Anniversary Edition of Classics Illustrated

Motter, Dean
★ **Electropolis:** the infernal machine. Dark Horse Books 2009 152p.
Grades: 10 11 12 Adult   **741.5; Fic**
1. Mystery graphic novels; 2. Robots; 3. Science fiction graphic novels; 4. Graphic novels
978-1-59582-363-2, $14.95

Menlo Park used to be a janitor robot in Electra City, but a private detective reprogrammed him to be his partner. Then, Jacob Ladder committed suicide by jumping off the Diogenes Tower, the tallest structure in the world. Sixteen years later, Menlo Park is still a private detective, complete with trench coat, fedora, and cigar and his new partner, Anesta. Femme fatale Tess LaCoyle comes to tell Park and Anesta that Jake didn't commit suicide, but was murdered. They reopen the investigation, which leads to a complicated situation full of twists and betrayals, and a mysterious object called the Astrolabe. Motter creates a future city that harkens back to the look of such films as the silent "Metropolis," and a noir mystery plot that could have come from the mind of Dashiell Hammett. The book includes some violence.

Mulligan, Brennan Lee
Strong Female Protagonist; Book one. Brennan Lee Mulligan and Molly Ostertag. Top Shelf Productions 2014 220 p. Illustration
Grades: 11 12 Adult
741.5
1. College students — Fiction; 2. Superheroes — Fiction
0692246185;
9780692246184, $19.95

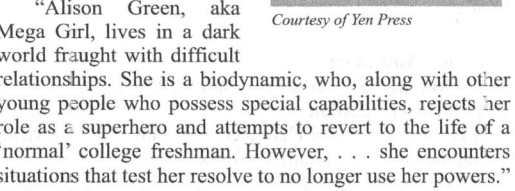
Courtesy of Yen Press

"Alison Green, aka Mega Girl, lives in a dark world fraught with difficult relationships. She is a biodynamic, who, along with other young people who possess special capabilities, rejects her role as a superhero and attempts to revert to the life of a 'normal' college freshman. However, . . . she encounters situations that test her resolve to no longer use her powers." (School Library Journal)

Originally appeared as a webcomic

Munroe, Kevin
El Zombo Fantasma. Dave Wilkins, Kevin Munroe, writers; Sean Galloway, Tony Washington, illustrators. Dark Horse Comics 2004 Un Illustration
Grades: 9 10 11 12 Adult   **741.5; Fic**
1. Mystery graphic novels; 2. Superhero graphic novels; 3. Graphic novels
1-59307-284-8, $9.95

El Zombo Fantasma was the most famous and notorious Mexican wrestler on the planet, up until he was murdered ... apparently for throwing a match. Now the luchador has fallen into a strange land of purgatory, and the only way to avoid an eternity of fiery damnation is to return to Los Angeles and guard the well-being of a struggling young spitfire, ten-year-old Belisa Montoya. However, this role as an undead guardian angel gives El Zombo the opportunity to hunt down his killer ... and unearth far more than he bargained for. The violence is very much like television's pro wrestling shows; the book does have some strong language.

Olympus Heights. IDW Publishing 2005 152p. Illustration
Grades: 9 10 11 12 Adult   **741.5; Fic**
1. Adventure graphic novels; 2. Fantasy graphic novels; 3. Graphic novels
1-932382-55-0, $19.99

Oliver Dobbs likes working for the local museum in Olympus Heights, Indiana. His run-ins with deity have been limited - so far - to statuary that turns up, without warning or explanation, at the museum's loading dock. Now, that's about to change. When he discovers that Zeus is his next door neighbor, and that he's suddenly become involved in an ancient feud, Oliver embarks on the adventure of his life. The book includes fantasy violence.

Murphy, Sean Gordon
Punk Rock Jesus. Sean Murphy. DC Comics 2013 224 p.
Grades: Adult   **745.1; 741.5/973**
1. Cloning — Fiction; 2. Reality television programs — Fiction
1401237681; 9781401237684, $16.99
      LC 2012048551

In this graphic novel by Sean Murphy "A reality TV show starring a clone of Jesus Christ causes chaos across the U.S. of the near future. When falling ratings force the network to cut Jesus's mother from the series the young star runs away, renounces his religious heritage and forms a punk rock band. Jesus goes to war against the corporate media complex that created him." (Publisher's note)

Originally published in single magazine form in Punk Rock Jesus 1-6.

Nadel, Dan
Art in time: unknown comic book adventures 1940-1980. Abrams ComicArts 2010 301p. Illustration
Grades: Adult   **741.5**
978-0-8109-8824-8; 0-8109-8824-0, $40
      LC 2009-31672

Nadel "rescues from oblivion an array of fascinatingly offbeat comics in a variety of genres (superhero, thriller, Western). In Art in Time, these meticulously reprinted full-length comic-book stories range from a terrifically sexy noir comic by Harry Lucey, 'The Cutie Killer Caper,' to Matt Fox's 'I Was a Vampire,' whose weirdly wooden art can be downright terrifying. Throughout, Nadel offers plenty of biographical details and brisk art criticism that make these riotous pages even more thrilling to rediscover." Entertainment Wkly

Naifeh, Ted

Courtney Crumrin and the fire thief's tale. Oni Press 2007 62p. Illustration

Grades: 7 8 9 10 11 12 Adult   **741.5; Fic**
1. Fantasy graphic novels; 2. Horror graphic novels; 3. Werewolves; 4. Graphic novels
978-1-932664-85-0, $5.95

Courtney travels with Uncle Aloysius to Romania, where they stay with Alexi Markovic, an old friend of Uncle Aloysius. Things aren't quite right there, though; the townspeople hunt wolves at night unnatural wolves, werewolves. Markovic's daughter has fallen in love with a Romany man even though her father has arranged her betrothal to an influential man in town. Courtney gets involved against Uncle Aloysius' wishes, and learns more than she wanted about werewolf origins and thwarted love.

Nakajo, Hisaya

Hana-Kimi: For You in Full Bloom Volume 1. Viz Media/Shojo 2004 184p. Illustration

Grades: 10 11 12 Adult   **741.5; Fic**
1. Humorous graphic novels; 2. Manga; 3. Romance graphic novels; 4. Shojo manga; 5. Graphic novels
1-59116-329-3, $9.95

Japanese-American track-and-field star Mizuki has transferred to a high school in Japan...but not just any school. To be close to her idol, high jumper Izumi Sano, she's going to an all-guys' high school...and disguising herself as a boy. But as fate would have it, they're more than classmates...they're roommates. Now, Mizuki must keep her secret in the classroom, the locker room, and her own bedroom. And her classmates—and the school nurse—must cope with a new transfer student who may make them question their own orientation... The book includes some strong language, brief nudity, and sexual situations.

Nakazawa, Keiji

Barefoot Gen: Hadashi no Gen : a cartoon story of Hiroshima. By Keiji Nakazawa; translated by Project Gen. New Society Publishers 1987 284 p. Illustration

Grades: 10 11 12 Adult   **741.5; 741.5/952**
1. Hiroshima (Japan) — Bombardment, 1945; 2. Hiroshima-shi (Japan) — History — Bombardment, 1945
0865710945; 0865710953; 0867196025; 9780867196023, $14.95

LC 88187202

This book, by Keiji Nakazawa, is "an all-new translation of the author's first-person experiences of Hiroshima and its aftermath. [It] is a reminder of the suffering war brings to innocent people. . . . Volume one of this ten-part series details the events leading up to and immediately following the atomic bombing of Hiroshima." (Publisher's note)

Volume 1 of 10

Nanatsuki, Kyoichi

Project Arms Volume 1. Viz Media 2003 216p. Illustration

Grades: 10 11 12 Adult   **741.5; Fic**
1. Manga; 2. Science fiction graphic novels; 3. Shonen manga; 4. Graphic novels
1-56931-889-1, $9.95

The future is a world of nano-machines, cybernetic assassins, powerful telekinetic opponents, and a secret organization dedicated to bringing forth the next evolution of humankind. Ryo Takatsuki thinks he's just a normal kid in high school, but strange things start happening—the new guy in school is trying to kill him; secret agents with high-powered weapons and modified limbs show up and start hunting him down; then his own body begins to transform into something grotesque and out of control. In order to find out what is going on, Ryo must come face to face with the underground world of secret organizations, fierce mercenary agents, and the secrets of his own mysterious past... The book includes graphic violence and harsh language.

Naraghi, Dara

Lifelike. IDW Publishing 2007 112p. Illustration

Grades: 10 11 12 Adult   **741.5; Fic**
1. Short stories; 2. Graphic novels
978-1-60010-122-9, $19.99

Abstract: Iranian-born writer Naraghi works with artists such as Marvin Mann, Tom Williams, and Adrian Barbu to illustrate this collection of slice-of-life stories. The stories range from crime noir to love stories to war memoirs to humorous conversation pieces, all populated by a multicultural, multiethnic cast of characters. Some stories include harsh language, violence, and partial nudity.

Narushima, Yuri

The **Young** Magician Volume 1. DC Comics/CMX 2005 240p. Illustration

Grades: 11 12 Adult   **741.5; Fic**
1. Fantasy graphic novels; 2. Manga; 3. Shojo manga; 4. Graphic novels
1-4012-0737-5, $9.99

A battle has broken out among rival sorcerers. The most nefarious group, the Necromancers, is killing young girls in Hong Kong to read the future in their entrails. Carno, a human youth raised by Aeromancers in a different dimension, is summoned back to his homeworld to join in the battle. Does Carno have what it takes to survive in a world of political alliances and emotional entanglements? The series includes graphic violence, harsh language, and nudity.

Natsume, Yoshinori

Batman: death mask. DC Comics 2008 Un Illustration

Grades: 10 11 12 Adult   **741.5; Fic**
1. Batman (Fictional character); 2. Manga; 3. Superhero graphic novels; 4. Graphic novels
978-1-4012-1924-6, $9.99

In this original manga story published in the manga format (with right-to-left orientation), Batman confronts a new killer whose arrival coincides with the arrival of a Japanese businessman with a new scheme for Gotham's rich. The killer slices off the faces of his victims; and in Bruce Wayne's nightmares, he confronts a shadowy figure who resembles Batman but with a different kind of mask. Bruce will have to delve into his past, to the time he trained in martial arts in Japan as a young man, to find the answer and identity of the killer. The book includes violence. Natsume's art is dynamic, his Batman is a muscular, athletic fighter, but his Bruce Wayne looks quite different from the regular DC comic art.

Togari Vol. 1. Viz Media 2007 192p. Illustration
Grades: 10 11 12 Adult   **741.5; Fic**
1. Fantasy graphic novels; 2. Horror graphic novels; 3. Manga; 4. Shonen manga; 5. Graphic novels
978-1-4215-1355-3, $9.99

Tobe is a ruthless killer from medieval Japan who's been suffering in Hell for 300 years. After what seems like an eternity, he's finally given a chance for redemption—armed with the magical wooden sword Togari, he's sent to modern-day Tokyo to destroy 108 malevolent demons in 108 days. However, these demons must be vanquished without causing harm to their possessed human hosts. Will the baffling ways of the modern world and his own criminal tendencies make Tobe's quest against evil an unwinnable war? Fast-paced action seasoned with a touch of moral philosophizing combines with considerable violence, and in this first volume, nudity.

Nauck, Todd
Wildguard Vol. 1: Casting Call. Image Comics 2005 Un Illustration
Grades: 9 10 11 12 Adult   **741.5; Fic**
1. Adventure graphic novels; 2. Superhero graphic novels; 3. Graphic novels
1-58240-470-4, $17.95

The cameras are rolling for the auditions of a new made-for-TV superteam: WildGuard. Hundreds of superheroes will try out, but only five will have what it takes to make the team... if they survive. Join a host of heroes through the agony of competition and unforeseen dangers, as they hope to be selected by a panel of judges, including the mysterious Producer X.

With Stan Lee's reality television series, "Who Wants to Be a Superhero?" airing its second season on the Sci-Fi Channel during the summer of 2007, this title is no longer so off the wall.

Nelson, Arvid
Hellgate London, vol. 1. Arvid Nelson, Lee Tae-Hang. Tokyopop 2008 Un Illustration
Grades: 10 11 12 Adult   **741.5; Fic**
1. Horror graphic novels; 2. Graphic novels
978-1-4278-0700-7, $10.99

Rugby scholarship college student John Fowler gets mixed up in his team members' prank which results in the awakening of an ancient evil to which he is related. They've uncovered the skeleton of a body which was buried in a fashion used for those who were witches or worshipped devils. John and his sister Lindsey fight a lot, but they find they must work together when they learn that their long-dead father was a Knight Templar, and that the body John accidentally dug up is that of their many times great-grandfather Isaac, who sided with evil, and that they now possess Isaac's pendant, which is a key to something they must prevent the awakened Isaac from possessing. This is a prequel to the video game of the same title, and includes considerable gory violence and British harsh language. The book is also in a global manga format.

Rex Mundi Book One: The Guardian of the Temple. Writer, Arvid Nelson; artist, Eric J. Dark Horse Comics 2006 Un Illustration
Grades: 10 11 12 Adult   **741.5; Fic**
1. Fantasy graphic novels; 2. Horror graphic novels; 3. Graphic novels
978-1-59307-652-8, $16.95

When a medieval scroll disappears from a Paris church, Doctor Julien Sauniere investigates, uncovering a series of horrific ritual murders and an ancient secret society. Julien cannot let these shadowy figures retreat into the darkness, lest they take up their killing once again. His investigation turns into a one-man quest into the bizarre secrets of the Catholic Church. The story is set in a world where the American Civil War ended in a stalemate, the Catholic Church controls Europe, and sorcery determines political power. Violent murders occur along with some incidental nudity. Older teen fans of The Da Vinci Code might like this story.

Neufeld, Josh
A.D.: New Orleans after the deluge. Pantheon Books 2009 193p. Illustration
Grades: Adult   **741.5; 976.3**
978-0-307-37814-9, $24.95; 0-307-37814-4
                                        LC 2008-55687

"Graphic artist Neufeld paints an emotive portrait of New Orleans during and after Hurricane Katrina, as seen through the eyes of seven of the city's citizens. The opening panels coalesce into a long cinematic pan, a thrumming setup for the disaster. The half-page and quarter-page panels—satellite views of weather patterns and close inspections of neighborhoods—are crisp, and the two-page spreads are softly focused. . . . Neufeld's words and images are commensurable and rhythmic, and the vernacular is sharp. Bristling with attitude and pungent with social awareness." Kirkus

Nicieza, Fabian
Civil War: Thunderbolts. Writer, Fabian Nicieza; pencilers, Tom Grummett, Dave Ross. Marvel Entertainment 2007 Un Illustration
Grades: 9 10 11 12 Adult   **741.5; Fic**
1. Superhero graphic novels; 2. Graphic novels
0-7851-1947-7, $13.99

The Super Human Registration Act has been signed into law, sides are being chosen, but what side do the former villains called the Thunderbolts fall on" Well, their identities are already public knowledge, and they sure can get good publicity by hunting down renegade heroes, so ... it's time for the Thunderbolts to, err, kick some spandex butt. Except, they also wear spandex, so ...

Civil War: X-Men Universe. Peter David, Fabian Nicieza; artists, Dennis Carlo, Barry Windsor-Smith. Marvel Entertainment 2007 Un Illustration
Grades: 9 10 11 12 Adult   **Fic; 741.5**
1. Deadpool (Fictional character); 2. Superhero graphic novels; 3. X-Men (Fictional characters); 4. Graphic novels
978-0-7851-2243-2, $13.99

The divisiveness of Civil War has spread to X-Factor: half of them want to cooperate with the government; the other half wants to take a stand against it. Quicksilver's return to the team may well decide whether X-Factor stays together or cracks apart. Plus: Cable and Deadpool find themselves on opposite sides of the fence, and both refuse to budge. It's going to lead to a fight, but this one may change both their lives.

Niffenegger, Audrey
   Raven girl. Audrey Niffenegger. Abrams Comicarts 2013 80 p.
Grades: Adult   **398.2; Fic**
   1. Fairy tales; 2. Fairy tales; 3. Raven (Legendary character)
   1419707264; 9781419707261, $19.95
                                                              LC 2012039266
   In this illustrated fairy tale, by Audrey Niffenegger, "a postman . . . encounters a fledgling raven while on the edge of his route and decides to bring her home. The unlikely couple falls in love and conceives a child—an extraordinary raven girl trapped in a human body. The raven girl feels imprisoned by her arms and legs and covets wings. . . . She reluctantly grows into a young woman, until one day she meets an unorthodox doctor who is willing to change her." (Publisher's note)

Nightow, Yasuhiro
   Trigun Maximum Volume 1: The Hero Returns. Dark Horse Comics 2004 192p. Illustration
Grades: 10 11 12 Adult   **741.5; Fic**
   1. Adventure graphic novels; 2. Manga; 3. Science fiction graphic novels; 4. Seinen manga; 5. Graphic novels
   1-59307-196-5, $9.95
   Vash the Stampede disappeared for two years after blasting a crater onto the moon orbiting the desert planet he saved from annihilation. But, with good and bad people alike trying to track him down he won't stay lost for long. He teams up again with Wolfwood, and learns of a new villain named Knives. As with the original manga series, humor combines with lots of fighting action; this time there's more violence, and some nudity and harsh language.

   Trigun Volume 1. Dark Horse Comics 2003 360p. Illustration
Grades: 9 10 11 12 Adult   **741.5; Fic**
   1. Adventure graphic novels; 2. Manga; 3. Science fiction graphic novels; 4. Shonen manga; 5. Graphic novels
   1-59307-052-7, $14.95
   Somehow, the past has placed a sixty billion double dollar bounty on Vash's head and the gunslinging pacifist can't seem to get away from money grubbing, itchy-trigger-finger citizenry. Find out why Vash is worth so much money dead. Feel the clumsy worry of the unfortunate citizens of the pulverose planet. Follow the follies of an unlikely hero in a forbidding world. Join Vash the Stampede " with his troubled past and uncanny ability to dodge a gazillion bullets " and a cavalcade of unlucky characters on a dusty, desert planet in the distant future. This series combines Old West action with high-tech weaponry and some crazy humor as bounty hunters and a couple of insurance investigators hunt for Vash. The series includes some harsh language, violence, partial nudity, and brief mild sexual innuendo.

Nihei, Tsutomu
   Blame! Volume 1. Tokyopop 2005 250p. Illustration
Grades: 10 11 12 Adult   **741.5; Fic**
   1. Manga; 2. Science fiction graphic novels; 3. Seinen manga; 4. Graphic novels
   1-59532-834-3, $9.99
   In a future world rife with decay and destruction, Killy is a man of few words who packs one very powerful gun. He wanders an endless labyrinth of cyberdungeons filled with concrete and steel, fighting off cyborgs and other bizarre silicate creatures. Everyone is searching for the Net Terminal Genes, but no one is quite certain what kind of power they contain. The answer may lie hidden among the scattered human settlements of this vast and desolate future world. The book includes graphic violence, some strong language, and some suggestive images.

Niles, Steve
   ★ **30** Days of Night. Steve Niles and Ben Templesmith. IDW Publishing 2003 104p. Illustration
Grades: 10 11 12 Adult   **741.5; Fic**
   1. Horror graphic novels; 2. Vampires; 3. Graphic novels
   0-9719775-5-0, $17.99
   The long night of winter is coming to Barrow, Alaska; it's normal, and the people living in this isolated town don't mind. However, this particular winter, a band of vampires has decided to come up to Barrow for the month-long night and play. Sheriff Eben Olemaun and his deputy, wife Stella, and the people of Barrow have no idea of the terror and death they face when vampires can roam freely all night, all thirty days of it.
   This is pure, raw horror with monstrous vampires; these are not the romantic, sexy vampires of so many supernatural romances, but nasty, ugly, blood-sucking monsters. Templesmith's art and the technique of setting his panels on black pages adds a claustrophobic element that adds to the horror.

   30 Days of Night: Dark Days. Written by Steve Niles; illustrated by Ben Templesmith. IDW Publishing 2004 144p. Illustration
Grades: 10 11 12 Adult   **741.5; Fic**
   1. Horror graphic novels; 2. Vampires; 3. Graphic novels
   1-932382-16-X, $19.99
   In this sequel, the action shifts from Barrow, Alaska to Los Angeles, as Stella Olemaun, her life forever altered by the vampires' assault and her husband's death, rededicates herself to wiping out vampires and alerting the world to their shadowed existence. Along the way, she meets new allies and new foes - lots and lots of enemies. The book includes lots of graphic violence and harsh language.

   30 Days of Night: Eben & Stella. IDW Publications 2007 104p. Illustration
Grades: 11 12 Adult   **741.5**
   1. Horror graphic novels; 2. Vampires; 3. Graphic novels
   978-1-60010-107-6, $17.99
   Stella Olemaun managed to bring back her vampire husband Eben back from beyond, but he came back hungry. Now, she's got a vampire baby the new would-be queen wants; the vampires have Eben; and vampire hunter Alice

and her husband want to destroy them all. The book includes lots of graphic bloody violence and foul language.

30 Days of Night: Return to Barrow. IDW Publishing 2004 144p. Illustration
Grades: 11 12 Adult   **741.5; Fic**
  1. Horror graphic novels; 2. Vampires; 3. Graphic novels
1-932382-36-4, $19.99
  Three years before, vampires came to Barrow, Alaska at the beginning of the long winter night and slaughtered most of the town's inhabitants. Sheriff Olemaun died saving the town and his deputy wife died fighting vampires elsewhere. Now a new sheriff has come to town four days before the winter night, and the vampires are returning to destroy Barrow for good. Monstrous, evil creatures who slaughter viciously with lots of bloodshed combine with Templesmith's art that promotes a claustrophobic feeling of terror in this sequel to 30 Days of Night.
  Originally published as 30 Days of Night: Return to Barrow issues #1-6.

Batman: Gotham County Line. DC Comics 2006 160p. Illustration
Grades: 10 11 12 Adult   **741.5; Fic**
  1. Batman (Fictional character); 2. Horror graphic novels; 3. Superhero graphic novels; 4. Graphic novels
978-1-4012-0905-6, $17.99
Batman investigates a series of murders in the suburbs, and faces an enemy he doesn't believe in. He faces the undead, and he must defeat them, or lose his sanity. The horror element and graphic violence in fighting the undead makes this for more mature readers than for most Batman titles.

Checkmate: Big Book of Horror. IDW Publishing 2006 Un Illustration
Grades: 6 7 8 9 10 11 12 Adult   **741.5; Fic**
  1. Horror graphic novels; 2. Shelley, Mary Wollstonecraft, 1797-1851 — Adaptations; 3. Stoker, Bram, 1847-1912 — Adaptations; 4. Wells, H G — Adaptations; 5. Graphic novels
978-1-600100-14-7, $19.99
Modern horror master Niles (30 Days of Night) retells three classic tales: Frankenstein, War of the Worlds, and Dracula. This book is not so much an adaptation of the stories as it is a telling inspired by the original novels. Scott Morse illustrates Frankenstein, Ted McKeever paints War of the Worlds, and Richard Sala does the honors for Dracula. Each artist paints full-page and double-page spreads in full color, with Niles' prose appearing on each page. Niles focuses on the main plot of each story; for example, in Dracula, the entire section dealing with Lucy Westenra and her suitors is omitted, so the reader only meets Jonathan Harker, Mina Murray, and Dr. Van Helsing. This book serves best as a brief introduction or as an accompaniment to the original novels.
  Originally published as three separate volumes under the series title Little Book of Horror.

The **Creeper:** welcome to Creepsville. DC Comics 2007 160p. Illustration
Grades: 10 11 12 Adult   **741.5**
  1. Batman (Fictional character); 2. Superhero graphic novels; 3. Graphic novels
978-1-4012-1554-5, $19.99
  The newest face in Gotham City is both a freak and a hero. When TV pundit Jack Ryder gets mixed up in a mob hit on a mad scientist, he finds himself transformed into the superstrong, super-agile, and quite possibly insane Creeper ... Or does the Creeper find himself transformed into Jack Ryder? The Creeper/Ryder try to find out what Dr. Yatz was really up to, with the help of Batman. While there is little in the way of foul language, the book includes fighting violence.

Freaks of the Heartland. Dark Horse Comics 2005 Un Illustration
Grades: 10 11 12 Adult   **741.5; Fic**
  1. Fantasy graphic novels; 2. Horror graphic novels; 3. Graphic novels
1-59307-029-2, $17.95
  Some folks would call Trevor's brother a monster. But to Trevor, Will is just another kid trapped in a dark reality he can't comprehend. When the situation moves from bad to worse, and their father threatens to do away with Will, Trevor learns that they're not alone - that "freak" children were born to other families in Gristlewood Valley. And just as they were all born at the same time, it seems their sad, frustrated, and emotionally spent parents seem to be hatching a plan to see that they disappear at the same time. Against all odds, and with nothing but love for his brother in his heart, Trevor is going to do whatever he can to get Will, and the other freak children, out of harm's way, if it's not already too late. The book includes fairly graphic violence and harsh language.

Fused Vol. 1: Canned Heat. Dark Horse Comics 2004 Un Illustration
Grades: 10 11 12 Adult   **741.5; Fic**
  1. Science fiction graphic novels; 2. Graphic novels
1-59307-192-2, $12.95
  Mark Haggerty was a promising young robotics engineer until his body became fused with an experimental robot suit during a routine testing session. Trapped inside a body that's not his own, and suddenly the unwilling pawn in a deadly struggle between obsessive egos and misguided military forces, Mark's life is forever changed. With his human body consumed more each day by the Cy-bot suit, his marriage suffering the consequences of his transformation, and the most dangerous elements in the world closing in around him, Mark's only recourse is to keep fighting - until he gets his life back. The book includes strong language and violence.

Fused Vol. 2: Think Like a Machine. Dark Horse Comics 2004 Un Illustration
Grades: 10 11 12 Adult   **741.5; Fic**
  1. Adventure graphic novels; 2. Fantasy graphic novels; 3. Horror graphic novels; 4. Graphic novels
1-59307-263-5, $12.95

In a world of subtle horrors, Elizabeth Mason is about to meet one monster she never counted on - herself. On the day of her 18th birthday Liz undergoes a strange metamorphosis which, for reasons unknown, causes her to transform into the monster called Crush whenever she bleeds. As if growing up isn't hard enough without that, Liz soon has to deal with a deadly, ruthless agent tailing her... with teenage werewolves. At least she has her best friend, Jen Tanaka, to count on. And what at first seems to be a curse may be the very thing that leads her to understand who she truly is. The book has some strong language and violence.

Last Train to Deadsville: A Cal McDonald Mystery. Dark Horse Comics 2005 Un Illustration
Grades: 10 11 12 Adult   **741.5; Fic**
1. Horror graphic novels; 2. Humorous graphic novels; 3. Mystery graphic novels; 4. Graphic novels
1-59307-107-8, $14.95

Detective of the weird Cal McDonald knows that the teen redneck on his porch isn't anything to worry about, but the sex-crazed succubus the kid summoned in a love spell gone wrong is a big problem. She's turned the entire male population of the kid's hometown into a throng of murderous monsters. But what's worse - dealing with the demon-possessed town, or with a girlfriend who's hinting at commitment? The book includes harsh language, violence, and sexual suggestiveness.

The Nail. Dark Horse Comics 2005 Un Illustration
Grades: 11 12 Adult   **741.5; Fic**
1. Horror graphic novels; 2. Graphic novels
1-59307-173-6, $14.95

Hunted in one of the most desolate regions of America, preyed upon by an evil that does not sleep, Rex Hauser is The Nail - and it's time he took a stand. A semi-pro wrestler, Hauser has been touring the country performing at small-time arenas until the fateful night he and his family run afoul of a bloodthirsty gang of Satanic bikers stalking the North Dakota Badlands. Now he's a lone man fighting for the survival of his loved ones in a no-holds-barred standoff against the forces of Hell itself. The book includes nudity, sexual situations, and lots of very harsh language and graphic violence. This book is co-written by rock star and horror film maker Rob Zombie.

Nilsen, Anders
Big questions, or, Asomatognosia. Anders Brekhus Nilsen.. Farrar, Straus and Giroux 2011 658p. Illustration
Grades: Adult   **741.5**
1. Fables; 2. Philosophy; 3. Graphic novels
9781770460447; 9781770460478; 1770460470
LC 2011488182
Ignatz Award: Outstanding Graphic Novel (2012)

This book is a collection of philosophical comic strips which "is the culmination of ten years and over 600 pages of work that details the metaphysical quandaries of the occupants of an endless plain, existing somewhere between a dream and a Russian steppe. A downed plane is thought to be a bird and the unexploded bomb that came from it is mistaken for a giant egg by the group of birds whose lives the story follows. The indifferent and stranded pilot is of great interest to the birds- some doggedly seek his approval, while others do quite the opposite, leading to tensions in the

group. . . . [The book] has roots in classic fable- the story's birds and snakes have more to say than their human counterparts and there are hints of the classic hero's journey, but the . . . moral that closes most fables is left here as open and ambiguous." (Publisher's note)

Dogs & Water. Drawn & Quarterly 2007 96p. Illustration
Grades: 10 11 12 Adult   **741.5**
1. Graphic novels
978-1-897299-08-1

A young man wandering a nameless path has only a stuffed bear as a companion, which inertly endures his desperation, anger, and musings along the way. The landscape is cold and bleak with few landmarks, and offers only precarious encounters with animals and armed men. These interactions are rife with instinct, the drive for survival, and human ethics concerning the killed and injured. He finds acceptance with a pack of dogs, though their nature is wild and their potential threat is as unsettling as the sudden presence of a massive pipeline on the horizon. The road disappears and only blind circumstance remains. All is uncertain and all can be lost, but he continues on regardless. This is for the thoughtful reader who doesn't mind a little bit of harsh language and some violence.

Don't Go Where I Can't Follow. By Anders Nilsen. Drawn & Quarterly 2012 90 p. Illustration; Color
Grades: Adult   **741.5**
1. Interpersonal relations; 2. Terminally ill
1770460918; 9781770460911, $19.95
Ignatz Award: Outstanding Graphic Novel (2007)

This book by Anders Nilsen is an "appreciation of the time the author shared with his fiancee, Cheryl Weaver. The story is told using artifacts of the couple's life together, including early love notes, simple and poetic postcards, tales of their travels in written and comics form, journal entries, and drawings done in the hospital in her final days. It concludes with a beautifully rendered account of Weaver's memorial." (Publisher's note)

Monologues for the Coming Plague. Fantagraphics Books 2006 260p. Illustration
Grades: 11 12 Adult   **741.5; Fic**
1. Humorous graphic novels; 2. Graphic novels
978-1-56097-718-6, $18.95

This book ranges from riffs on the gag cartoon to paranoid soliloquies of a surrealistic apocalypse, with references to contemporary politics, pop culture, religion, plays on language, and sequential abstractions. The "characters" (all unnamed) are abstract humans (one man's head is drawn as a big scribble), a bird, a dog, and a dinosaur. Nilsen uses a form of Automatic Writing, an aesthetic mode championed by Andre Breton at the beginning of the twentieth century that became the foundation of the Surrealist Movement. Some nudity, strong language, and violence occur, but the utter simplicity of Nilsen's art belies deep thought and sly humor.

Ninomiya, Tomoko
Nodame Cantabile, Vol. 1. Ballantine Books/Del Rey Manga 2005 188p. Illustration
Grades: 10 11 12 Adult   **741.5; Fic**

1. Manga; 2. Music; 3. Romance graphic novels; 4. Shojo manga; 5. Graphic novels
0-345-48172-0, $10.95
2004 Kodansha Manga Award for Shojo Manga.

Music student Shinichi Chiaki dreams of becoming a conductor, but his fear of flying and arrogant attitude hold him back. Then he meets Megumi Noda, who has a natural talent for piano, but she can't read a music score, she's a slovenly mess, and her apartment is a disaster area. Shinichi starts working with her, and Megumi falls for him. Romantic complications, new friendships, and music ensue. There are some mild sex scenes.

Nishimori, Hiroyuki

Cheeky Angel Vol. 1. Viz Media 2004 200p. Illustration

Grades: 10 11 12 Adult   **741.5; Fic**
1. Humorous graphic novels; 2. Manga; 3. Romance graphic novels; 4. Shonen manga; 5. Graphic novels
1-59116-397-8, $9.95

Megumi, a nine-year-old martial arts enthusiast and all around rapscallion always wanted to be, the manliest man on Earth." After saving a sorcerer from a group of local toughs, Megumi is presented with a magic genie which can grant any wish. Unfortunately, this genie misconstrues Megumi's desire as wanting to become the, womanliest woman on Earth," and in a flash, Megumi's Y chromosome is swapped for an X. Six years later...Megumi is the hottest girl in school, but has stayed true to his/her tough talkin', punk stompin' ways. If that's not enough, Genzo, the baddest dude in town, is smitten by Megumi's womanly wiles" ... The series includes some strong language and some violence, very little partial nudity.

Nishino, Jyutaroh

Steel fist Riku vol. 1. DC Comics/CMX 2008 162p. Illustration

Grades: 9 10 11 12 Adult   **741.5; Fic**
1. Humorous graphic novels; 2. Manga; 3. Martial arts; 4. Graphic novels
978-1-4012-1752-5, $9.99

Teenage Riku lives with Rocky, her gruff, adopted dad ("Call me Sensei!" he roars when she calls him Pops), who trained her in martial arts. In their world, semi-humans are common, such as a Pig Man, or the fact that Riku has a fist of steel. Rocky now runs a shop selling celebrity photos, but he used to be a professional martial artist. When the daughter of his old master ventures into the shop, Rocky kidnaps her in order to demand a rematch, 20 years after the fact, with his old rival Utsugizaki. This doesn't sit well with Riku, and she decides to take matters into her own hands. The book includes some raunchy humor and fan service (Riku's powers become even stronger when her breasts are unbound); Rocky is obsessed with women's breasts and suffers many nosebleeds (manga symbol for sexual arousal) while watching his DVDs, and characters declare that they're pissed off or that someone is a pain in the butt.

No, Yee-Jung

The **Visitor** Vol. 1. Tokyopop 2006 178p. Illustration
Grades: 9 10 11 12 Adult   **741.5; Fic**

1. Horror graphic novels; 2. Manwha; 3. Mystery graphic novels; 4. Graphic novels
1-59816-342-2, $9.99

Beautiful Hyo-Bin Na is the new girl in high school that everyone is dying to meet, but she is not a normal student. Hyo-Bin is cursed with supernatural abilities that she can't quite understand...or control. Every night she's haunted by disturbing dreams, while during the day she lives in fear—not of those around her, but of herself. Then she discovers another classmate, Mi-Soo, has the same dreams; what can this mean" The book includes some strong language and violence.

Noh, Mi Young

Threads of Time Volume 1. Tokyopop 2004 178p. Illustration

Grades: 9 10 11 12 Adult   **741.5; Fic**
1. Adventure graphic novels; 2. Fantasy graphic novels; 3. Manwha; 4. Graphic novels
1-59812-780-9, $9.99

The most frightening thing about Moon Bin Kim's nightmare is that he doesn't appear to be dreaming, this modern high school student lives a parallel life in the 13th century as the son of a prominent warrior family. When friends and family in his present-day existence assume roles in his historical life, Moon Bin struggles to learn exactly who he is and why his life spans hundreds of years across space, time, and consciousness. The book includes some nudity, strong language, and teen smoking.

Nolen-Weatherington, Eric

Modern Masters Volume Twelve: Michael Golden. Twomorrows Publishing 2007 120p. Illustration

Grades: Adult Professional   **741.5**
1. Doctor Strange (Fictional character); 2. Golden, Michael; 3. Graphic novels
978-1-893905-74-0, $14.95

Michael Golden is one of the most respected and influential artists working in the comic book industry today. From Bucky O'Hare" and Dr. Strange to his work for The 'Nam, he has shown the ability to adapt his unique style to any genre. Penciler, inker, colorist, writer - Michael Golden is the complete artist, and during his career has served as Art Director for Marvel Comics and Editor for DC Comics. Now, this first-ever look at the artist's life and career presents a cornucopia of rare and unseen art from Golden's files, as well as a career-spanning interview, and a deluxe color gallery of some of his finest work.

Modern masters volume sixteen: Mike Allred. Twomorrows Publishing 2008 120p. Illustration
Grades: 11 12 Adult   **741.5**
1. Allred, Mike; 2. Comic books, strips, etc — History and criticism; 3. Graphic novels — History and criticism
978-1-893905-86-3, $14.95

Mike Allred grew up in the 1960s and 1970s, then published his first comic in 1989. In 1991, he sprung his hip, Pop-inspired creation Madman upon the world. His first series of Madman comics won the Harvey Award for Best New Series. Allred is also an actor, filmmaker, and rock musician. This book features a long interview with Allred and includes lots of black and white reproductions of his art.

Nolen-Weathington, Eric
   Modern Masters volume fifteen: Mark Schutz. Twomorrows Publishing 2008 120p. Illustration
Grades: Adult   92; 741.5
   1. Cartoonists; 2. Comic books, strips, etc — History and criticism; 3. Schultz, Mark, 1955-
978-1893905-85-6, 14.95
   In the mid-1980s, independent comics flourished, and among the creators publishing new and different works, Mark Schultz created Xenozoic Tales, an adventure story set in a world full of dinosaurs. This book includes black and white illustrations from that title and from other works done by Schultz, along with a career-spanning interview that discusses his work on Superman, Aliens, and Predator comics among others. The art gallery includes some color artwork.

   ★ **Modern** Masters volume twenty-five: Jeff Smith. Twomorrows Publishing 2011 117p. Illustration
Grades: 6 7 8 9 10 11 12 Adult   741.5
   1. Artists; 2. Authors; 3. Cartoonists; 4. Comic books, strips, etc — History and criticism; 5. Graphic novels — History and criticism; 6. Smith, Jeff
978-1-60549-024-3, $15.95
   This volume in the Modern Masters series focuses on Jeff Smith, creator of Bone. In an interview that covers his childhood, college career, and early work before becoming a cartoonist, Smith talks about how he created Fone Bone when he was just five years old. The artwork in the book includes young Smith's hand-created comics from his childhood. Only a couple of "crap—s slip out. The book includes mostly black and white art and photographs, with a few color illustrations from the Bone comics.

Nonaka, Eiji
   Cromartie High School, Vol. 1. [translated by Brendan Frayne]. ADV Manga 2005 158p. Illustration
Grades: 10 11 12 Adult   741.5; Fic
   1. High school students; 2. Humorous graphic novels; 3. Manga; 4. School stories; 5. Graphic novels
1-4139-0257-X, $10.95
   Takashi Kamiyama enrolled at Cromartie High School, the worst high school in Tokyo, to help a friend, who then flunked the entrance exam. Now he's stuck in a school filled with juvenile delinquents, street toughs, and some very strange characters. They include a shirtless guy who looks like Freddy Mercury and never says anything, a gorilla who is smarter than everyone else, and Mechazawa, who looks like a canister-shaped robot. American readers may not be aware that, in Japan, students must pass entrance exams to get into the high school of their choice. It doesn't matter how rich your family is if you can't pass an entrance exam with a high enough score to get into a top school. This is the first volume of an ongoing manga full of wacky and sometimes deadpan humor.

North, Ryan
   ★ The **unbeatable** Squirrel Girl; Volume 1: Squirrel power!. Ryan North; illustrated by Erica Henderson. Marvel Enterprises 2015 136 p. Color; Illustration
Grades: 7 8 9 10 11 12 Adult   741.5

   1. Female superhero graphic novels; 2. Squirrel Girl (Fictional character); 3. Squirrels — Fiction; 4. Superheroes — Fiction
0785197028; 9780785197027, $15.99
   In this comic by Ryan North, illustrated by Erica Henderson, "supervillains and criminals meet their match . . . Squirrel Girl, aka Doreen Green, a college freshman with the appearance, speed, and agility of a squirrel. When Galactus threatens Earth, the heroine must rely on more than strength to defeat the Devourer of Worlds. She may have extraordinary strength . . . but it is her ability to form connections with people that proves to be her most powerful asset." (School Library Journal)
   Contains material originally published in magazine form as The Unbeatable Squirrel Girl #1-4 and Marvel Super-Heroes #8
   Volume 1 of an ongoing series

Nowak, Naomi
   Unholy kinship. NBM 2006 Un Illustration
Grades: 10 11 12 Adult   741.5; Fic
   1. Dreams; 2. Mental illness; 3. Sisters; 4. Graphic novels
1-56163-482-4, $9.95
   Young college student Luca has taken care of her mentally unstable older sister Gae ever since their single mother became a permanent resident of St. Mark's Asylum for the Demented. As the fall term starts, Luca starts having strange dreams as Gae begins to deteriorate emotionally. The doctors and nurses from St. Mark's Asylum claim they want to help Gae, but their drugs make things worse. And the dreams become stranger, until Luca can't be sure what is real. The cool tones of the artwork underscore the building sense of doom as the story progresses.

O'Barr, J.
   ★ The **Crow**. James O'Barr. Gallery Books 2011 272 p. Illustration; Color
Grades: Adult   741.5
   1. Angels; 2. Crow (Fictitious character); 3. Horror comic books, strips, etc; 4. Revenge
1451627254; 9781451627251, $18.99
                                            LC 2012374273
   This graphic novel, by James O'Barr, is the "cathartic story of Eric—who returns from the dead to avenge his and his fianc?e's murder at the hands of a street gang . . . re-released in an expanded version the author originally intended, complete at last with: thirty pages of never-before-seen artwork [and] a new Introduction by . . . O'Barr." (Publisher's note)
   "O'Barr's black-and-white artwork fluctuates wonderfully between brutal, inky darkness and picturesque beauty, mirroring a narrative torn between Eric's memories of his fianc?e and the bloody task at hand." LJ
   Originally published 1989

O'Malley, Bryan Lee
   Scott Pilgrim's Precious Little Life, Vol. 1. Oni Press 2004 Un Illustration
Grades: 10 11 12 Adult   Fic; 741.5
   1. Humorous graphic novels; 2. Martial arts; 3. Romance graphic novels; 4. Graphic novels
1-932664-08-4, $11.95

Twenty-three-year-old musician Scott Pilgrim is going steady with a Chinese high school girl (it's totally platonic), when he starts seeing a rollerblading girl in his dreams, at the library, at a party. . . She's Ramona Flowers, and Scott totally falls for her, just as Knives (his high school girl friend) wants to start heating up their relationship. Then, Scott discovers that he will have to fight Ramona's seven evil ex-boyfriends before he and Ramona can get together. It's wacky romance and martial arts action.

Also available in full-color hardcover editions

Other titles in this series are: Scott Pilgrim vs. the World (2005); Scott Pilgrim & the Infinite Sadness (2006); Scott Pilgrim Gets It Together (2007); Scott Pilgrim vs. the Universe (2009); Scott Pilgrim's Finest Hour (2010)

★ **Seconds**. Bryan Lee O'Malley. Ballantine Books 2014 336 p. Color; Illustration
Grades: 11 12 Adult   741.5
1. Restaurants — Fiction; 2. Graphic novels
0345529375; 9780345529374, $25
LC 2013456979
In this graphic novel by Bryan Lee O'Malley, "Katie's got it pretty good. She's a talented young chef, she runs a successful restaurant, and she has big plans to open an even better one. Then, all at once, progress on the new location bogs down, her charming ex-boyfriend pops up, her fling with another chef goes sour, and her best waitress gets badly hurt. And just like that, Katie's life goes from pretty good to not so much." (Publisher's note)

"O'Malley's engaging narrative voice hasn't diminished—üeven the self-absorbed Katie is likeable enough to root for, although it's obvious that she's making things worse for herself. O'Malley's sweet, nimble art, now in color, has acquired more confidence: the plot unfolds cinematically, and his character designs are more appealing than ever." Pub Wkly

O'Neil, Dennis
Batman unauthorized: vigilantes, jokers, and heroes in Gotham City. Edited by Dennis O'Neil. Benbella Books, Inc. 2008 219p. Illustration (Smart pop series)
Grades: 10 11 12 Adult   741.5
1. Batman (Fictional character); 2. Comic books, strips, etc — History and criticism; 3. Joker (Fictional character); 4. Robin (Fictional character); 5. Graphic novels
978-1-93377130-4, $17.95; 1-933771-30-5
LC 2007-46504
Former Batman comics editor and comic book writer O'Neil edits this collection of essays about Batman and his world, written by comics writers, magazine editors, and others. Topics include the cost of being Batman, calculated to the last dollar; why Batman is the most American of superheroes; whether Bruce Wayne might be mentally ill; why Batman needs Robin more than Robin needs Batman; why Arkham Asylum is doing more harm than good for Gotham City; why Batman works better when his world remains closer to reality; and more.
Includes bibliographical references

★ **Green** Lantern, Green Arrow. Dennis O'Neil, Elliot Maggin, writers; Neal Adams, penciller; Neal Adams, Dick Giordano, Frank Giacoia, Dan Adkins, Berni Wrightson, inkers; Cory Adams, Jack Adler, colorists; John Costanza,

Joe Letterese, letterers. DC Comics 2012 361 p. Color illustration
Grades: 10 11 12 Adult   741.5
1. Green Arrow (Fictional character); 2. Green Lantern (Fictional character); 3. Superheroes
1401235174; 9781401235178, $29.99
LC 2013363523
In this comic book collection, "Green Lantern Hal Jordan continued his usual cosmic-spanning adventures, as he used his amazing Power Ring to police Sector 2814 against universe-threatening menaces. Meanwhile, on Earth, Oliver Queen, the archer known as Green Arrow, was confronting menaces of a different kind: racism, poverty, drugs, and other social ills!" (Publisher's note)
Originally published in single magazine form in Green Lantern 76-87, 89; Flash 217-219, 226. Green Lantern/Green Arrow 1-7.

The **Question**: Zen and violence. Dennis O'Neil, writer; Denys Cowan, penciller. DC Comics 2007 174p. Illustration
Grades: 11 12 Adult   741.5; Fic
1. Crime; 2. Superhero graphic novels; 3. Graphic novels
978-1-4012-1579-8, $19.99
Investigative reporter Vic Sage, who is also the faceless, morally conflicted avenger known as The Question, works to bring down the politically corrupted mayor of Hub City and his advisers, but they have hired the mercenary Lady Shiva, who defeats him in combat and the henchmen of the crooked Rev. Hatch throw him into the river. But, Sage is not dead, he's rescued and healed, and told to find Richard Dragon. He stays with Dragon for a year, training in martial arts and disciplining himself. When he returns to Hub City, he now has the focus to go after the criminals and politicians mucking up the city. The book includes lots of violence and some harsh language.

O, Se-Yong
Buja's diary. NBM 2005 280p. Illustration
Grades: 11 12 Adult   741.5; Fic
1. Korea (South); 2. Graphic novels
1-56163-448-4; 978-1-56163-448-4, $19.95
LC 2005-50519
The thirteen "stories by this Korean "manwha" (comic book) author relate poignant tales of distressed humanity struggling with family, history, and culture. . . . Although O's eye is not unsympathetic, the world he depicts is unforgiving, sometimes graphically so. . . . Originally published in 1995, this book is a thoughtful examination of the human condition in the Korea of the recent past as well as universally." Voice Youth Advocates

Ochi, Yoshihiko
Atelier Marie and Elie: Zarlburg Alchemist Volume 1. Tokyopop 2007 162p. Illustration
Grades: 7 8 9 10 11 12 Adult   741.5; Fic
1. Fantasy graphic novels; 2. Manga
978-1-59816-525-8, $9.99
Welcome to the Zarlburg Royal Magic Academy" producers of the best alchemists in the world. When Marie, Zalburg's prodigal daughter and premier alchemist, returns to her alma mater after thrilling journeys in many foreign

lands, she suddenly realizes things are not too exciting at home. But all that changes after running into fellow alchemist Elie, who has plans to open an alchemy workshop and become famous. Now, adventure comes to them in all shapes and sizes—curious elves, flying broomsticks, giant monsters, and explosive bombs. It's all inside Yoshihiko Ochi's new manga series based on the popular video game franchise. There's lots of monster fighting action.

Oda, Eiichiro

★ **One** Piece Volume 1. Viz Media/Shonen Jump 2003 216p. Illustration

Grades: 8 9 10 11 12 Adult   **741.5; Fic**

1. Adventure graphic novels; 2. Fantasy graphic novels; 3. Manga; 4. Shonen manga; 5. Graphic novels

1-56931-901-4, $7.95

Monkey D. Luffy's main ambition is to become a pirate, inspired by listening to the tales of the buccaneer "Red-Haired" Shanks. When he accidentally eats the Gum-Gum Fruit, it gives him strange powers to stretch like rubber, but doing so also invokes the fruit's curse: anybody who consumes it can never learn to swim. Nevertheless, Monkey and his crewmate Roronoa Zoro, master of the three-sword fighting style, sail the Seven Seas of swashbuckling adventure in search of the elusive treasure "One Piece." As the series goes on, Luffy gains more crew and they encounter sea monsters, far away kingdoms, cloud island, and super powered pirates of every shape, size, and description - which means lots of epic and comical fight scenes.

Volume 1 of an ongoing series

Oeming, Michael Avon

Bastard Samurai Vol. 1, 2nd printing. Image Comics 2007 Un Illustration

Grades: 11 12 Adult   **741.5; Fic**

1. Adventure graphic novels; 2. Samurai

978-1-58240-746-3, $12.99

Jiro is a student of the KoZu Sword School, an underground training camp in midtown Manhattan that takes in orphans and twists and transforms them into Bushido warriors. The Yakuza use these kids in death matches staged across the city rooftops where Japanese businessmen gamble heavily on the always-fatal outcome. This killing life is all Jiro has ever known. But a rendezvous with fate is about to change all of that when he learns his latest kill is his own long-lost older brother. In one moment Jiro realizes that everything he has lived for is a lie. The Samurai live by the Bushido code, one of which is rectitude: the righting of wrongs. Now he sets out on a campaign of vengeance, determined to topple the entire organization. The story is full of foul language, some sexual situations, and lots of fighting action and violence, with plenty of beheadings.

Blood River. Written by Michael Avon Oeming and Daniel Berman; artwork by Brian Quinn; lettering by Adam Levine. Image Comics 2005 Un Illustration

Grades: 10 11 12 Adult   **741.5; Fic**

1. Graphic novels

1-58240-509-3, $7.99

Sex, Drugs and Zeppelin! In the 1970s, four life-long friends plan their escape from a small town in New Jersey.

They like to have drug parties out in the woods, but one night they find that fate, nature or some monstrous power has other plans for them... Based on a true story. Readers will find a recount of a true incident from the summer of 1916. Besides the use of drugs, readers will encounter considerable harsh language.

The **Cross** Bronx. Writers, Michael Avon Oeming and Ivan Brandon; artist, Michael Avon Oeming. Image Comics 2007 Un Illustration

Grades: 12 Adult   **741.5; Fic**

1. Mystery graphic novels; 2. Supernatural graphic novels; 3. Graphic novels

978-1-58240-690-9, $14.99

In New York City, veteran detective Rafael Aponte catches a homicide case that's not exactly a gang hit, but is definitely bloody and awful. Aponte finds a gun at the scene, and he learns it belonged to a beat cop who was killed on the job years before. When he visits the widow, he finds out their daughter is in the hospital, in a coma; she'd been repeatedly raped, beaten, then thrown out of a car. Soon Aponte realizes that the widow may be using dark arts to have her daughter's spirit take vengeance on those who hurt her, such as the men killed in the first homicide case.

This powerful story includes a lot of violence, harsh language, and some nudity.

Originally published as The Cross Bronx issues #1-4

Ogishima, Chiaki

Heat Guy J. Original story by Kazuki Akane and Satelight; character design by Nobuteru Yuki; art and story by Chiaki Ogishima. Tokyopop 2005 224p. Illustration

Grades: 10 11 12 Adult   **741.5; Fic**

1. Manga; 2. Mystery graphic novels; 3. Science fiction graphic novels; 4. Shonen manga; 5. Graphic novels

1-59182-777-9, $9.99

Daisuke Aurora works with the special division of peacekeepers in the city of Jewde, one of the largest cities on the planet. He and his android partner, Heat Guy J, team up to make sure that anything illegal stays off the streets and out of circulation. However, their presence doesn't sit too well with the local mob leader—a ruthless, unbalanced, well-armed son of the late Don, who is out to prove that he is not too young to take over the family business. In the city that never sleeps, will Daisuke and Heat Guy J sleep with the fishes? The book includes violence, strong language, partial nudity, and sexual situations.

Ogiwara, Noriko

The **Good** Witch of the West, Vol. 1. Tokyopop 2006 Un Illustration

Grades: 7 8 9 10 11 12 Adult   **741.5; Fic**

1. Fantasy graphic novels; 2. Shojo manga; 3. Graphic novels

1-59816-620-4, $9.99

Fifteen-year-old Firiel has grown up with her reclusive astronomer father, his devoted servants, and his apprentice, Rune. Life is basically good, until the night Firiel attends the Count's ball. She wears a necklace from her dead mother, and it turns out the necklace identifies her as one of the heirs to the throne of Graal. Her father, Professor Dee, has been branded a heretic, and now that people know Firiel is the daughter of Princess Edilene, events have been set into motion, bringing danger and death to the people she loves. This is the first volume of a manga series.

Oh! Great

Air Gear Vol. 1. Random House/Del Rey Manga 2006 Un Illustration
Grades: 10 11 12 Adult **741.5; Fic**
1. Adventure graphic novels; 2. Manga; 3. Shonen manga
978-0-345-49278-4, $10.95
LC Bd 06-250081
Itsuki Minami is the toughest kid at Higashi Junior High School, plus he lives with the mysterious and sexy Noyamano sisters. Life is never dull, but it becomes dangerous when Itsuki leads his school to victory over some vindictive Westside punks with gangster connections. Now he stands to lose his school, his friends, and everything he cares about. But in his darkest hour, the Noyamano girls come to Itsuki's aid. They can teach him a powerful skill that will save their school from the gangsters' siege-and introduce Itsuki to a thrilling and terrifying new world. The series includes crude humor, violence, partial nudity, sexual situations (including hints at sexual violence), and harsh language.

Okabayashi, Kensuke

Manga for dummies. Wiley Publishing, Inc. 2007 416p. Illustration (—For dummies)
Grades: 9 10 11 12 Adult **741.5**
1. Graphic novels — Drawing; 2. Manga
978-0-470-08025-2, $19.99
LC 2006-939589
This guide, written and illustrated by Okabayashi, who teaches art at the Educational Alliance Art School in New York City and who has interned with manga creators in Japan, shows aspiring manga artists how to create characters, how to draw weapons, cars, animals, and more, how to create plotlines and storyboards, how to convey motion and emotion, and more.

Okuda, Hitoshi

No Need for Tenchi! Vol. 1 (2nd edition). Viz Media 2004 184p. Illustration
Grades: 8 9 10 11 12 Adult **741.5; Fic**
1. Adventure graphic novels; 2. Humorous graphic novels; 3. Shonen manga; 4. Graphic novels
1-59116-610-1, $9.99
The trouble and fun began when ordinary teenager Tenchi Masaki inadvertently released the legendary demon Ryoko from his grandfather's shrine. Turned out Ryoko was actually a marooned space pirate; since then, she's become Tenchi's unwanted houseguest, attracting a host of other troublemaking alien women: Ayeka, a haughty alien pricess; Sasami, her mischievous little sister; and Washu, Ryoko's mad-scientist "mother." Add Ryo-oh-Ki, an adorable little carrot-eating spaceship, and you've got one full Shinto shrine. Now Tenchi's troubles double—in the form of Minagi, a dead-ringer for Ryoko who attacks our hapless friends and then conveniently develops amnesia. But Minagi is just a pawn of the alien warrior Yakage, who plans to steal Tenchi's miraculous sword and abduct Ayeka. And the only hero who has what it takes to rescue the kidnapped princess

is...Ryoko. The series includes some sexual innuendo, raunchy humor, comic violence, and a little strong language.

Oliver, Simon

The **Exterminators** Vol. 1: The Bug Brothers. Simon Oliver, writer; Tony Moore, artist; Brian Buccellato, colorist; Pat Brosseau, letter; Philip Bond, cover artist. DC Comics/Vertigo 2006 128p. Illustration
Grades: 11 12 Adult **741.5; Fic**
1. Horror graphic novels; 2. Graphic novels
978-1-4012-1064-9, $9.99
This book focuses on a dysfunctional group of bug killers prowling the barrios and bungalows of Los Angeles. Henry James, the newest exterminator, sees the job as a way to cleanse the sins of his dark past; he has a hard time getting his view across to his careerist girlfriend, sociopathic partner and the general bunch of freaks he calls co-workers. Meanwhile, what Henry and the "bug brothers" of Bug-Bee-Gone Co. don't understand is that human beings may be the true pests - and bugs could be the real exterminator. This book has graphic violence, some nudity and sexual situations, and lots and lots of nasty bugs, rats, and other pests.

One (Manga author)

★ **One-punch** man; Volume 1. Story by One; art by Yusuke Murata. Viz 2015 189 p. Illustration
Grades: 8 9 10 11 12 Adult **Fic; 741.5**
1. Manga; 2. Superheroes; 3. Graphic novels
1421585642; 9781421585642, $9.99
Eisner Nominee: Best U.S. Edition of International Material—Asia (2015)
"Nothing about Saitama passes the eyeball test when it comes to superheroes, from his lifeless expression to his bald head to his unimpressive physique. However, this average-looking guy has a not-so-average problem—he just can't seem to find an opponent strong enough to take on! Every time a promising villain appears, he beats the snot out of 'em with one punch!" (Publisher's note)
"The story is fast-paced, humorous, and entertaining in a way that looks and feels like an action movie." SLJ
Volume 1 of an ongoing series

Ono, Fuyumi

Ghost hunt, Vol. 1. Manga by Shiho Inada; story by Fuyumi Ono; translated by Akira Tsubasa; adapted by David Walsh; lettered by Foltz Design. Del Rey Manga 2005 216p. Illustration
Grades: 8 9 10 11 12 Adult **741.5; Fic**
1. Horror graphic novels; 2. Manga; 3. Shojo manga; 4. Graphic novels
0-345-48624-2, $10.95
A decrepit old building stands on the campus of Mai's high school; every time the school tries to demolish it, unexplained accidents occur. Finally, the school hires a psychic researcher, and when Mai accidentally injures his assistant and damages an expensive camera, Shibuya (the researcher) insists she work off her debt by helping him. A miko (Shinto priestess), a Buddhist monk, and a Roman Catholic exorcist also come—but none of their methods work to stop the strange occurrences. Despite herself, Mai gets drawn into the investigation. This is the first of an

ongoing manga series that provides some ghostly thrills without graphic violence, bad language, or sexual innuendo.

Ono, Natsume

★ **Gente:** the people of Ristorante Paradiso, volume 1. Story and art by Natsume Ono; translation Joe Yamazaki. Viz Signature 2010 Un Illustration

Grades: 10 11 12 Adult **741.5; Fic**
1. Family; 2. Josei manga; 3. Manga; 4. Restaurants; 5. Graphic novels
978-1-4215-3251-6, $12.99

In this companion and prequel to Ono's Ristorante Paradiso, readers meet the various handsome, mature, bespectacled men who staff Casetta dell'Orso, a popular restaurant in Rome. The stories in this volume include how Lorenzo, the owner, decides to choose the type of men that his wife Olga finds attractive; how cranky Luciano tries to hide his kind heart even as he babysits his young grandson; how playboy Vito meets a lonely college student at a health club; and more. Ono's somewhat sketchy art style is vastly different from the typical manga, more European than Japanese. While this is rated for Older Teens by the publisher, there is no content to raise any concerns, but its gentle, quiet stories focused on adults may appeal more to older teens and adults.

First volume of an ongoing series

Onote, Sora

Metamo Kiss, Volume 1. Tokyopop 2007 168p. Illustration

Grades: 9 10 11 12 Adult **741.5; Fic**
1. Humorous graphic novels; 2. Manga; 3. Romance graphic novels; 4. Shojo manga; 5. Graphic novels
978-1-59816-827-3, $9.99

Kohamaru has moved from the countryside to meet his family for the first time, when he literally runs into a girl at the train station, and they switch bodies. Nanao, the girl he ran into, wants to date Konatsu, who is Kohamaru's fraternal twin brother. The switched bodies, well, that's a family trait, and one generally can only switch with one's soul mate. Konatsu can't switch bodies, but somehow his kiss can cause Kohamaru and Nano to get back into their own bodies. Nanao will do what it takes to get close to Konatsu, who doesn't care about her; meanwhile, hapless Kohamaru is caught in the middle.

Oprisko, Kris

The **Complete** Metal Gear Solid. IDW Publishing 2006 Un Illustration

Grades: 10 11 12 Adult **741.5; Fic**
1. Adventure graphic novels; 2. Science fiction graphic novels; 3. Graphic novels
978-1-60010031-7, $55.00; 978-1-600100-17-1 (pa), $35.00

This graphic novel adapts the storyline from the popular console game. Infiltration expert Solid Snake attempts to save the world from a band of genetically enhanced terrorists who have overrun a secret weapons facility in Alaska. Metal Gear Solid is a shooting game, and this book is full of shooting and fighting sequences.

Orff, Joel

Thunderhead Underground Falls. Alternative Comics 2007 Un Illustration

Grades: 10 11 12 Adult **741.5**
1. Friendship; 2. Graphic novels
1-891867-88-1

Jack, a young army reservist, has one weekend left before shipping out for combat in the Middle East. He and a friend find themselves behind the wheel of his parent's car, driving farther and farther west into a snowy landscape. The book is an impressionistic exploration of Jack's flight from his future, as well as an exploration of this place that he's pledged his life to fight for. Jack and his friends want to experience the simple freedom of taking a drive, of seeing familiar things before his outlook is changed forever by the violence that he knows he will soon face. As the hours go by, Jack begins to consider desertion, but he knows that if he stays to hold onto the life that he knows, it will still be changed forever.

Oropeza, B. J.

The **Gospel** According to Superheroes: Religion and Popular Culture. Peter Lang Publishing 2005 295p. Illustration

Grades: Adult Professional **741.5**
1. Batman (Fictional character); 2. Fantastic Four (Fictional characters); 3. Graphic novels — Religious aspects; 4. Hulk (Fictional character); 5. Spider-Man (Fictional character); 6. Superman (Fictional character); 7. Wonder Woman (Fictional character); 8. X-Men (Fictional characters); 9. Graphic novels
0-8204-7422-3, $32.95

This book offers an intriguing look at superheroes in light of the spiritual and mythological roles they play in our lives. Editor B. J. Oropeza takes you through the adventuresome quest of three comic book eras as you read about the popular narratives of superheroes such as Batman, Superman, Spider-Man, X-Men, Hulk, Wonder Woman, the Fantastic Four, sci-fi film heroes, pulp heroes, antiheroes, and more. This book is a must-read for anyone interested in viewing the superheroes as both sinners and saints instead of mere good guys taking on the forces of evil.

Osada, Yuko

Toto! the wonderful adventure vol.2. Del Rey Manga 2008 202p. Illustration

Grades: 7 8 9 10 11 12 Adult **741.5; Fic**
1. Adventure graphic novels; 2. Manga; 3. Science fiction graphic novels; 4. Shonen manga; 5. Graphic novels
978-0-345-50555-2, $10.95

In this second volume, Dorothy and Kakashi have been trapped in a burning building by the Nassau Imperial Army, who are there to recover Toto, their "test subject." The cute little dog had turned into a gigantic monster, but Toto saves Dorothy and Kakashi. When the Army then tries to destroy Toto and Kakashi gets to him first, they merge, and the dog bracelet that had been around Toto's neck is now on Kakashi's right wrist. When danger threatens, Toto the monstrous weapon emerges from Kakashi's hand. The two kids flee to Dego City, hoping to catch a train to Emerald, but the Nassau Army has occupied the city and destroyed all the trains to use the metal for weapons. Kakashi and Dorothy meet Millica, an older girl who saves them, and the soldier Noil, who would much rather become a standup comedian. The book includes some violence and mild fan service.

Osborne, Rob

1000 Steps to World Domination. AiT/Planet Lar 2004 Un Illustration

Grades: 9 10 11 12 Adult   **741.5; Fic**
1. Humorous graphic novels; 2. Graphic novels
1-932051-26-0, $12.95
2003 Isotope Award for Excellence in Mini-Comics; 2004 Broken Frontier Paper Screen Gem Award for Humor.

Can one achieve world domination by writing comics" With a supportive spouse, one can do a lot. But what about talking chiimpanzees in plaid suits - or clown suits" The dog is not impressed.

Sunset City, For Active Senior Living. AiT/Planet Lar 2005 Un Illustration

Grades: 12 Adult   **741.5; Fic**
1. Retirement communities; 2. Graphic novels
1-932051-41-4, $9.95

Sunset City is a typical retirement community. Its residents enjoy golf and gossip and they all seem content to fritter away their golden years. Except Frank McDonald. A retired widower, he wrestles with the question: why am I here" Reading the newspaper, Frank keeps up on the minutia of the day; it provides a buzz to an otherwise humdrum life. One morning, Frank is overcome by a startling story, and he does something extraordinary: he takes life by the balls. The story includes some harsh language and violence, and the climactic scene may bother some readers.

Osborne, Wayne

FX. Art by John Byrne. IDW Publishing 2008 160p. Illustration

Grades: 7 8 9 10 11 12 Adult   **741.5; Fic**
1. Adventure graphic novels; 2. Humorous graphic novels; 3. Superhero graphic novels; 4. Graphic novels
978-1-60010-274-5, $19.99

Teenager Tom Talbot was playing with his best friend when Jack accidentally hit Tom so hard he went into a coma. When Tom recovers, he discovers that he's got the power to make what he imagines be real; he discovers this when they're playing around in an alley and Tom imagines he's got a bazooka and really destroys a dumpster. He cobbles together a masked costume, and finds himself fighting superpowered giant talking apes, nasty weapons-bearing lizards, and more. But someone notices him and decides he wants Tom's powers Lord Everos, the Father of Death. And it's not just Tom, either; Vicki, the class weirdo, does really talk with the dead, and Lord Everos wants her, too. And that's not the worst of it, for apparently Tom was never supposed to get the power of the thunderbolt, and a whole pantheon of heroes has just arrived to stop him. Oops again.

Ostrander, John

The **Legend** of Grimjack, Volume 1. Script, John Ostrander; art, Timothy Truman. IDW Publishing 2005 125p. Illustration

Grades: 10 11 12 Adult   **741.5; Fic**
1. Adventure graphic novels; 2. Fantasy graphic novels; 3. Graphic novels
1-932382-51-8, $19.99

Gathering all of the earliest GrimJack stories from the comic book series of the 1980s in one tome for the first time, The Legend of GrimJack, Volume One introduces the major characters and origin stories and also includes the GrimJack/Starslayer crossover saga. This volume also includes a brand new story and art as well as critical background information heretofore unrevealed. The book is full of grim, gritty action with considerable violence; the comics were originally published by First Comics in 1983 and 1984.

Star Wars: Clone Wars Volume 1: The Defense of Kamino. John Ostrander and Haden Blackman. Dark Horse Comics 2003 Un Illustration

Grades: 7 8 9 10 11 12 Adult   **Fic; 741.5**
1. Adventure graphic novels; 2. Science fiction graphic novels; 3. Star Wars; 4. Graphic novels
1-56971-962-4, $14.95

Two undercover Jedi discover a Separatist plan to destroy the cloning facility on the watery world of Kamino, thus crippling the Republic's ability to maintain their clone army. Obi-Wan Kenobi and Anakin Skywalker are part of a Jedi fighter squadron sent to protect the installation. Meanwhile, Mace Windu, the leader of the Jedi Council, must deal with a rift in the Jedi ranks—a matter that reveals a Jedi traitor and a new Dark Jedi working in league with Dooku. Mace is considered one of the best swordsmen in the galaxy, but can he stand up to the sword master who taught him everything he knows—including the mysterious technique known as Vaapad. The book includes battle violence.

Volume 1 of 9

Star Wars: Clone Wars Volume 2: Victories and Sacrifices. Written by Haden Blackman and John Ostrander ; Pencillers Tomás Giorello, Brian Ching, and Jan Duursema ; Inkers Dan Parsons, Joe Weems, Curtis Arnold. Dark Horse Comics 2003 Un Illustration

Grades: 7 8 9 10 11 12 Adult   **741.5; Fic**
1. Adventure graphic novels; 2. Science fiction graphic novels; 3. Star Wars; 4. Graphic novels
1-56971-969-1, $14.95

From one of the swamp moons of Naboo, to the war-torn cityscapes of Brentaal IV, the battles of the Clone Wars have thrown the galaxy into turmoil. New Separatist threats, ranging from deadly biological weapons, to dark Jedi, to unkillable alien bounty hunters, have the loyalist Jedi and their clone troops pushed to their limits. This graphic novel collection contains three separate, yet linked stories of heroism and sacrifice. The book includes battle violence.

Star Wars: Clone Wars Volume 3: Last Stand on Jabiim. Written by Haden Blackman and John Ostrander ; Pencillers Brian Ching and Jan Duursema ; Inkers Dan Parsons and Victor Llamas. Dark Horse Comics 2004 Un Illustration

Grades: 7 8 9 10 11 12 Adult   **741.5; Fic**
1. Adventure graphic novels; 2. Science fiction graphic novels; 3. Star Wars; 4. Graphic novels
1-59307-006-3, $14.95

General Obi-Wan Kenobi and his Padawan Anakin Skywalker find themselves in command of a regiment of

Clone Troopers on the muddy battlefields of the rain world of Jabiim. With their supply lines stretched thin and reinforcements unable to land due to the perpetual storms, the Jedi and their army have become easy targets for the rebel Alto Stratus and his elite Nimbus warriors. The situation goes from bad to worse when General Kenobi is listed missing in action, and Anakin is teamed with a group of other masterless young Jedi on a doomed mission to hold the last line in the Republic's defense.

Star Wars: Clone Wars Volume 6: On the Fields of Battle. Written by John Ostrander ; pencilled by Jan Duursema ; inked by Dan Parsons ; colored by Brad Anderson. Dark Horse Comics 2005 Un Illustration
Grades: 7 8 9 10 11 12 Adult   **741.5; Fic**
1. Adventure graphic novels; 2. Science fiction graphic novels; 3. Star Wars; 4. Graphic novels
1-59307-352-6, $17.95
Mace Windu leads an elite Jedi strike force against an army of trained killers in a demonstration of Jedi power and resolve... Aayla Secura must confront her former Master in an effort to retrieve the plans for a weapon that has already destroyedne world... Obi-Wan Kenobi and Anakin Skywalker must joins forces with a renegade Jedi to prevent a fleet of warships from falling into the hands of the enemy...

Star Wars: Clone Wars Volume 8: The Last Siege, the Final Truth. Written by John Ostrander ; pencilled by Jan Duursema ; inked by Dan Parsons ; colored by Brad Anderson. Dark Horse Comics 2006 Un Illustration
Grades: 7 8 9 10 11 12 Adult   **741.5; Fic**
1. Adventure graphic novels; 2. Science fiction graphic novels; 3. Star Wars; 4. Graphic novels
1-59307-482-4, $17.95
Beneath the surface of this Outer Rim planet, the Dark Jedi Sora Bulq has begun cloning an army of Morgukai assassins. Unwilling to leave this grave new threat unchecked, the Jedi and their armies soon find themselves entrenched in a five-month siege. Now, time and resources have run out, and it's up to a crack team of Jedi, led by Quinlan Vos and Aayla Secura, to infiltrate the Separatist base. The book includes battle violence.

Star Wars: Clone Wars Volume 9: Endgame. Written by John Ostrander and Welles Hartley ; art by Jan Duursema and Douglas Wheatley. Dark Horse Comics 2006 Un Illustration
Grades: 7 8 9 10 11 12 Adult   **741.5; Fic**
1. Adventure graphic novels; 2. Science fiction graphic novels; 3. Star Wars; 4. Graphic novels
978-1-59307-553-8, $17.95
Suddenly, clone troopers are turning on the Jedi and killing them; it's Order 66. In the jungles of the Wookiee homeworld Kashyyyk, Quinlan Vos wages a battle of impossible odds against his own troops to protect his loved ones. On the icy Outer Rim world of Toola, Jedi Master Kai Huddora takes a terrified Padawan into his charge after her own master falls to Order 66. Amidst the forests of New Plymto, Dass Jennir finds himself in league with a band of rebels he'd led attacks against only days before. And Darth Vader hunts for Obi Wan Kenobi.

Star Wars: Empire Volume One: Betrayal. Scott Allie and Ryan Benjamin. Dark Horse Comics 2003 Un Illustration
Grades: 7 8 9 10 11 12 Adult   **741.5; Fic**
1. Adventure graphic novels; 2. Science fiction graphic novels; 3. Star Wars; 4. Graphic novels
1-56971-964-0, $12.95
In the weeks before the events in Star Wars: A New Hope, as the Death Star is readied for its fateful first mission, a power-hungry cabal of Grand Moffs and Imperial Officers embark on a dangerous plan to kill Emperor Palpatine and Darth Vader and seize control of the Empire. When word that a Jedi has made an appearance on a backwater world lures Vader away from his master, the cabal makes its move. But even the galaxy isn't enough of a prize to sate the ambitions of some of the conspirators, and before long the would-be assassins are turning on one another. Their plans are further complicated by the actions of bounty hunter Boba Fett. And, of course, they may have fatally underestimated the cunning of their primary target: Emperor Palpatine.

Star Wars: Empire Volume Six: In the Shadows of Their Fathers. writers, Thomas Andrews, Scott Allie ; artists, Adriana Melo, Joe Corroney, Michel LaCombe. Dark Horse Comics 2006 Un Illustration
Grades: 7 8 9 10 11 12 Adult   **741.5; Fic**
1. Adventure graphic novels; 2. Science fiction graphic novels; 3. Star Wars; 4. Graphic novels
978-1-59307-627-6, $17.95
Luke Skywalker confronts the legacy of the Jedi father he never knew in an epic story involving Princess Leia, Darth Vader and the fate of an entire planet! When Luke and Leia travel to Jabiim recruiting allies for the fledgling Rebellion, they unwittingly set into motion events that will ignite one man's betrayal of his people, pit rebel hero against rebel hero and attract the attention of the Empire's deadliest enforcer - Darth Vader. The book includes battle violence.

Suicide Squad: from the ashes. DC Comics 2008 192p. Illustration
Grades: 11 12 Adult   **741.5; Fic**
1. Adventure graphic novels; 2. Science fiction graphic novels; 3. Superhero graphic novels; 4. Graphic novels
978-1-4012-1866-9, $19.99
Rick Flag commanded the Suicide Squad, a team of villains used to conduct covert operations missions in return for their freedom. He died in a nuclear blast while battling terrorism in Qurac " or did he" Years later, he has returned, and finds himself caught between two commanders: Amanda Waller, former coleader of Checkmate, and General Wade Eiling, who started the Suicide Squad. The new Suicide Squad, which includes old members Deadshot, Bronze Tiger, and Nightshade, goes on a mission to assassinate the Board members that run a huge conglomerate that has developed a deadly bioweapon; but Eiling has found a way to compromise the mission and take out his old enemies, especially Mrs. Waller. This book includes lots of graphic violence.

Otomo, Katsuhiro
★ **Akira;** Book five. Katsuhiro Otomo; [translation and English-language adaptation, Yoko Umezawa, Jo Duffy]. Kodansha Comics 2011 413 p.

Grades: Adult   **741.5**
1. Apocalyptic fiction; 2. Manga; 3. Supernatural —
Fiction; 4. Teenagers — Japan — Tokyo
1935429078; 9781935429074, $27.99
LC 2012371500

In this graphic novel, by Katsuhiro Otomo, "Neo-Tokyo lies in ruin, leveled in minutes by the infinite power of the child psychic Akira. From the flooded wasteland of rubble and anarchy rises the Great Tokyo Empire, populated by a ragtag army of zealots and crazies who worship and fear Akira and his mad prime minister, Tetsuo, an angry teen with immense powers of his ownû and equally immense, twisted ambitions. . . . The military strength of the planet is massing to take on the empire." (Publisher's note)

First published in Japan in 1990 by Kodansha Ltd., Tokyo—t.p. verso.

★ **Akira**; Book four. Katsuhiro Otomo; [translation and English language adaptation, Yoko Umezawa, Jo Duffy]. Kodansha Comics 2010 394 p.
Grades: Adult   **741.5**
1. Apocalyptic fiction; 2. Manga; 3. Parapsychology —
Comic books strips, etc; 4. Supernatural — Fiction; 5.
Teenagers — Japan — Tokyo
193542906X; 9781935429067, $27.99
LC 2011534775

In this graphic novel, by Katsuhiro Otomo, "Neo-Tokyo lies in ruin. Set off by the bullet of a would-be assassin, the godlike telekinetic fury of the superhuman child Akira has once again demolished [the city]. . . . Now cut off from the rest of the world, the Great Tokyo Empire rises, with Akira its king, the psychic juggernaut Tetsuo its mad prime minister, and a growing army of fanatic acolytes ready to go to any length to please their masters." (Publisher's note)"

Translated from the Japanese. First published in Japan in 1987 by Kodansha Ltd., Tokyo—t.p. verso.

★ **Akira**; Book one. Katsuhiro Otomo; translation and English-language adaptation by Yoko Umezawa, Linda M. York, Jo Duffy. Kodansha Comics 2009 363 p.
Grades: Adult   **Fic; 741.5**
1. Apocalyptic fiction; 2. Manga; 3. Supernatural —
Fiction; 4. Teenagers — Japan — Tokyo; 5. World War III
— Fiction
1935429000; 9781935429005, $24.99
LC 2010293135

This graphic novel, by Katsuhiro Otomo, is set in "Neo-Tokyo, built on the ashes of a Tokyo annihilated by a blast of unknown origin that triggered World War III. The lives of two streetwise teenage friends, Tetsuo and Kaneda, change forever when paranormal abilities begin to waken in Tetsuo, making him a target for a shadowy agency that will stop at nothing to prevent another catastrophe like the one that leveled Tokyo." (Publisher's note)

First published in Japan in 1984 Kodansha Ltd., Tokyo.

★ **Akira**; Book six. Katsuhiro Otomo; translation and English-language adaptation: Yoko Umezawa, Jo Duffy, Studio Proteus. Kodansha Comics 2011 434 p.
Grades: Adult   **741.5**
1. Apocalyptic fiction; 2. Manga; 3. Supernatural —
Fiction; 4. Teenagers — Japan — Tokyo
1935429086; 9781935429081, $29.99
LC 2011534774

In this graphic novel, by Katsuhiro Otomo, "the armed might of Earth is massed against the godlike powers of two psychic titans, the mute child Akira and the deranged youth Tetsuo. While Akira has unintentionally destoryed the city twice before, Tetsuo has ravaged the surface of the Moon for his sheer amusement, and his madness grows as his abilities expand. But he is gradually losing control of the limitless energies that rage within him." (Publisher's note)

First published in Japan in 1993 by Kodansha Ltd., Tokyo—t.p. verso.

★ **Akira**; Book three. Katsuhiro Otomo; [translation and English-language adaptation, Yoko Umezawa, Linda M. York, Jo Duffy]. Kodansha Comics 2010 282 p.
Grades: Adult   **741.5**
1. Apocalyptic fiction; 2. Manga; 3. Supernatural —
Fiction; 4. Teenagers — Japan — Tokyo
1935429043; 9781935429043, $24.99
LC 2011280454

In this graphic novel, by Katsuhiro Otomo, "Neo-Tokyo has risen from the rubble of a Tokyo destroyed by an apocalyptic telekinetic blast from a young boy called Akira—the subject of a covert government experiment gone wrong now imprisoned for three decades in frozen stasis. But Tetsuo, an unstable youth with immense paranormal abilities of his own, has done the unthinkable: He has released Akira and set into motion a chain of events that could once again destroy the city." (Publisher's note)

First published in 1986 by Kodansha Ltd., Tokyo—t.p. verso.

★ **Akira**; Book two. Katsuhiro Otomo; [translation and English-language adaptation, Yoko Umezawa, Linda M. York, Jo Duffy]. Kodansha Comics 2010 301 p.
Grades: Adult   **Fic; 741.5**
1. Apocalyptic fiction; 2. Manga; 3. Supernatural —
Fiction; 4. Teenagers — Japan — Tokyo
1935429027; 9781935429029, $24.99
LC 2010284394

In this graphic novel, by Katsuhiro Otomo, "Neo-Tokyo has risen from the ashes of a Tokyo obliterated by a monstrous psychokinetic power known only as Akira, a being who yet lives, secretly imprisoned in frozen stasis. Those who stand guard know that Akira's awakening is a terrifying inevitability. Tetsuo, an angry young man with immense—and rapidly growing—psychic abilities, may be their only hope to control Akira when he wakes." (Publisher's note)

First published in 1985 by Kodansha Ltd., Tokyo—t.p. verso.

Otsuka, Eiji
The **Kurosagi** Corpse Delivery Service Vol. 1. Dark Horse Comics 2006 202p. Illustration
Grades: 12 Adult   **741.5; Fic**
1. Horror graphic novels; 2. Manga; 3. Mystery graphic novels; 4. Shonen manga; 5. Graphic novels
978-1-59307-555-2, $10.95

Five young students at a Buddhist university, three guys and two girls, find little call for their job skills in today's Tokyo... among the living, that is. But all that stuff in college they were told would never pay off - channeling, dowsing, ESP - gives them a direct line to the dead... the dead who are still trapped in their corpses and can't move on to the next reincarnation. The five form the Kurosagi ("Black Heron" - their ominous bird logo) Corpse Delivery Service: whether suicide, murder, accident, or illness, they'll carry your body wherever it needs to go to free your soul! The kids from Kurosagi can smell a customer a mile away - it's a good thing one of the girls majored in embalming. Lots of violent murders, dismemberments, nudity, and strong language are present.

MPD-Psycho No. 1. Original story and script, Eiji Otsuka; art, Sho-u Tajima. Dark Horse Comics 2007 186p. Illustration

Grades: 12 Adult **741.5; Fic**
1. Horror graphic novels; 2. Manga; 3. Mystery graphic novels; 4. Graphic novels
978-1-59307-770-9, $10.95

Tokyo police detective Kobayashi Yousuke's life is changed forever after a serial killer notices something "special" about him. That same killer mutilates Kobayashi's girlfriend and kick-starts a "multiple personality battle" within Kobayashi that pushes him into a complex tempest of interconnected deviants and evil forces. After prison he works for a private detective organization, and the cases are all bloody and weird. The book shows lots of graphic violence and nudity, along with strong language. This series is very popular in Japan.

Ottaviani, Jim

Bone sharps, cowboys, and thunder lizards: a tale of Edwin Drinker Cope,Othniel Charles Marsh, and the gilded age ofpaleontology. By Jim Ottaviani & Big Time Attic. G.T. Labs 2005 165p. Illustration

Grades: 9 10 11 12 Adult **560**
1. Biographical graphic novels; 2. Cope, E D (Edward Drinker), 1840-1897; 3. Fossils; 4. Marsh, Othniel Charles, 1831-1899; 5. Paleontologists; 6. Zoologists; 7. Graphic novels
0-9660106-6-3; 978-0-9660106-6-4, $22.95

LC 2005-920326

"Ottaviani portrays the heyday of American dinosaur hunting with a ripsnorting Western feel. Rival scientist/dinosaur hunters Marsh and Cope play out their real-life drama in a mostly accurate historical telling. Copious notes at the back of the book point out where Ottaviani departs from the facts; science and history become fun in his hands." Voice Youth Advocates

Includes bibliographical references
Title from cover

Fallout. Jim Ottaviani et al. G.T. Labs 2001 239 p. Illustration

Grades: 11 12 Adult
1. Atomic bomb; 2. Nuclear energy; 3. Nuclear weapons
0966010639; 9780966010633, $24.95

LC 2001091068

In this nonfiction graphic novel about atomic bombs, by Jim Ottaviani, "the focus . . . is on the scientists themselves — in particular J. Robert Oppenheimer and Leo Szilard, whose lives offer a cautionary tale about the uneasy alliance between the military, the government, and the beginnings of 'big science.'" (Publisher's note)

★ **Feynman**. Written by Jim Ottaviani; art by Leland Myrick; coloring by Hilary Sycamore. First Second 2011 262 p. Illustration; Color

Grades: 9 10 11 12 Adult **B; 92; 530.092**
1. Atomic bomb; 2. Biography, Individual; 3. Feynman, Richard Phillips, 1918-1988; 4. Musicians — Biography; 5. Nobel Prizes; 6. Physicists
1596432594; 9781596432598, $29.99; 9781596438279, $19.99; 9781451722406, $33.99

LC 2010036260

Author Jim Ottaviani presents a "graphic novel biography . . . [of] Nobel-winning quantum physicist, adventurer, musician, world-class raconteur, and one of the greatest minds of the twentieth century: Richard Feynman . . . [The book] tells the story of the great man's life from his childhood in Long Island to his work on the Manhattan Project and the Challenger disaster." (Publisher's note)

This is a fascinating look at the life of an eccentric genius, a man who worked on the Manhattan Project, won a Nobel Prize, was the first great physicist to teach freshmen classes, and was the investigator into the cause of the Challenger explosion who discovered the problem was the 0-rings. This work was so entertaining it was difficult to put down. Voice Youth Advocates

The **Imitation** Game: Alan Turing Decoded. Jim Ottaviani; illustrated by Leland Purvis. Harry N Abrams Inc 2016 240 p. Illustration

Grades: 9 10 11 12 Adult **92; 741.5**
1. Mathematicians — Biography; 2. Turing, Alan Mathison, 1912-1954
1419718932; 9781419718939, $24.95

This graphic novel, by Jim Ottaviani and illustrated by Leland Purvis, "present[s] a historically accurate graphic novel biography of English mathematician and scientist Alan Turing. [It covers] Turing's life and groundbreaking research—as an unconventional genius who was arrested, tried, convicted, and punished for being openly gay, and whose innovative work still fuels the computing and communication systems that define our modern world." (Publisher's note)

Levitation: physics and psychology in the service of deception. [by] Jim Ottaviani and Janine Johnston; lettering by Tom Orzechowski. G. T. Labs 2007 71p. Illustration

Grades: 6 7 8 9 10 11 12 Adult **793.8; 741.5**
1. Magic tricks; 2. Graphic novels
978-0-9788037-0-4, $12.95

This book tells the story of how John Neville Maskelyne developed the stage magic trick of levitation, of the American Harry Kellar, who acquired the trick through devious means, of the old school engineer Guy Jarrett, who perfected the magicians' tricks, and of stage performer Howard Thurston, who inherited the levitation trick from Kellar and ruined it. Or did he" The book includes notes and reprints of old posters and other information on the magicians.

Includes bibliographical references
A General Tektronics Labs book

Primates: The Fearless Science of Jane Goodall, Dian Fossey, and Biruté Galdikas. Jim Ottaviani; illustrated by Maris Wicks. First Second 2013 133 p. Color; Illustration
Grades: 5 6 7 8 9 10 11 12 Adult **741.5; 599.8**

1. Fossey, Dian, 1932-1985; 2. Galdikas, Birute, 1946-; 3. Goodall, Jane, 1934-; 4. Primates
1596438657; 9781596438651, $19.99

LC 2013427678

This nonfiction graphic novel, by Jim Ottaviani, illustrated by Maris Wicks, presents an "account of the three greatestáprimatologists of the last century: Jane Goodall, Dian Fossey, and Birut? Galdikas. These three ground-breaking researchers were all students of the great Louis Leakey, and each made profound contributions to primatology—and to our own understanding of ourselves." (Publisher's note)

"More story than study, the book provides an accessible introduction to Goodall's, Fossey's and Galdikas' lives and work." Kirkus

Includes bibliographical references, page 138

Suspended in language: Niels Bohr's life, discoveries, and the century he shaped. Written by Jim Ottaviani; illustrated and lettered by Leland Purvis. G.T. Labs 2009 318p. Illustration

Grades: 10 11 12 Adult   92
1. Biographical graphic novels; 2. Bohr, Niels Henrik David, 1885-1962; 3. Nobel laureates for physics; 4. Physicists; 5. Physicists; 6. Quantum theory; 7. Graphic novels
978-0-9788037-2-8, $24.95

"Quantum physics gets an accessible yet substantive introduction through art that mixes fantasy and realism. Great for teens who like science." Booklist

Includes bibliographical references

First published 2004

Additional art by Jay Hosler, Roger Langridge, Steve Leialoha, Linda Medley, and Jeff Parker.

★ **T-Minus:** the race to the moon. [illustrated by] Zander Cannon, Kevin Cannon. Aladdin 2009 124p. Illustration

Grades: 4 5 6 7 8 9 10 11 12 Adult   629.45; 741.5
1. Apollo project; 2. Gemini project; 3. Space flight to the moon; 4. Graphic novels
978-1-4169-8682-9, $21.99; 1-4169-8682-0;
978-1-4169-4960-2 (pa), $12.99; 1-4169-4960-7 (pa)

LC 2009-920999

Ottaviani, Zander Cannon, and Kevin Cannon show what happened when the U.S. and the U.S.S.R. started the space race in the 1950s, and how it progressed to the NASA Apollo 11 mission which landed two men on the moon in July of 1969.

"Organized as a countdown, making the outcome seem inevitable, the frequent, prominent sidebars list a type of rocket, the duration of its flight, and whether the mission was a success or a failure. There are more than 30 attempts chronicled, and the shift between Soviet and U.S. successes creates an interesting balance in the narrative. . . . Ottaviani is particular with facts and eager to inspire readers with regard to the scientific process." SLJ

★ **Wire** mothers: Harry Harlow and the science of love. [by] Jim Ottaviani [and] Dylan Meconis. G. T. Labs 2007 84p. Illustration

Grades: 9 10 11 12 Adult   152.4; 741.5
1. Harlow, Harry F, 1905-1981; 2. Love; 3. Psychologists; 4. Graphic novels

978-0-9788037-1-1, $12.95; 0-9788037-1-X

LC 2007-900136

In the 1950s, psychologists warned parents about the dangers of too much love; in fact, they denied love was anything more than a base instinct based on the need for food. When scientist Harry Harlow began his experiments on mother love, was more than just an outsider trying to make his name. He was also an unhappy man who knew in his gut the truth about what love, and its absence, meant, and he set about to prove it. His experiments on monkeys and their stark results shocked the world. The emotional intensity of his experiments might be overwhelming for younger readers.

"This nonfiction graphic novel retelling psychologist Harry Harlow's famous experiments is as disturbing as it is excellent." Publ Wkly

Includes bibliographical references

A General Tektronics Labs book

Out of picture: art from the outside looking in volume 2.
Villard Books 2008 238p. Illustration
Grades: 10 11 12 Adult   741.5; Fic
1. Short stories; 2. Graphic novels
978-0-345-49873-1, $30

Animation production artists who have worked together at Blue Sky Studios have put together another volume of short stories in comics form. In one story, a giant of a man wants only to become a farmer, but the military has hunted him down because he was a biological weapon used by them to win a war; now, he can't be allowed to live. In another story, a young boy takes his first airplane ride and sees a strange being riding on the wing, fly-fishing in the sky. In another story, three friends " a cat, a pigeon, and a grumpy gargoyle " need to find a new home when their antique shop home is destroyed. None of the stories uses graphic violence or much in the way of harsh language, but the moods and intensity of emotion make the book more suitable for older teens and adults.

Pacheco, Carlos
  Green Lantern Vol. 2: Revenge of the Green Lanterns.
DC Comics 2006 Un Illustration
Grades: 9 10 11 12 Adult   741.5; Fic
1. Green Lantern (Fictional character); 2. Superhero graphic novels; 3. Graphic novels
1401209602; 9781401209605, $14.99

The Green Lantern Corps kept peace and order throughout the universe for millenia, until their greatest warrior, Hal Jordan of Earth, destroyed them. The Corps had been resurrected, and Jordan, freed of the alien entity that drove him to madness, had been fully reinstated as a Green Lantern of Earth. But now, after the events of the Infinite Crisis, Jordan is in trouble again, and a Green Lantern whom he thought he had killed years ago has returned with vengeance on his mind. Jordan and fellow Green Lantern Guy Gardner travel to the home world of the Corps' greatest enemies, the android Manhunters, to save the Lanterns.

Padua, Sydney

★ The **Thrilling** Adventures of Lovelace and Babbage: The (Mostly) True Story of the First Computer. Sydney Padua. Pantheon Books 2015 320 p. Illustration
Grades: Adult   **741.5**
1. Babbage, Charles, 1791-1871 — Fiction; 2. Inventions — Fiction; 3. Inventors — Fiction; 4. Lovelace, Ada King, Countess of, 1815-1852 — Fiction
0307908275; 9780307908278, $28.95
LC 2014004455

In this book, by Sydney Padua, "[m]eet Victorian London's most dynamic duo: Charles Babbage, the unrealized inventor of the computer, and his accomplice, Ada, Countess of Lovelace, the peculiar protoprogrammer and daughter of Lord Byron. . . . [This book] presents a rollicking alternate reality in which Lovelace and Babbage . . . build the Difference Engine and then use it to build runaway economic models, battle the scourge of spelling errors, [and] explore the wilder realms of mathematics." (Publisher's note)

"A prodigious feat of historically based fantasy that engages on a number of levels." Kirkus

Pak, Greg

X-Men: Phoenix: Endsong. Writer, Greg Pak; penciler, Greg Land. Marvel Entertainment 2005 Un Illustration
Grades: 9 10 11 12 Adult   **741.5; Fic**
1. Superhero graphic novels; 2. X-Men (Fictional characters); 3. Graphic novels
978-0-7851-1924-1, $14.99

The mysterious and powerful Phoenix Force is life incarnate, and yet it consumes whole worlds in a moment. Its long history with the X-Men is fraught with tragedy... especially concerning one of the most beloved of their number, Jean Grey. What will happen when the Phoenix returns to Earth in search of the one mortal who could ever contain its power... only to find her dead?

Palmiotti, Jimmy

21 Down: The Conduit. Jimmy Palmiotti, Justin Gray and Jesus Saiz. DC Comics/Wildstorm 2003 Un Illustration
Grades: 10 11 12 Adult   **741.5; Fic**
1. Mystery graphic novels; 2. Graphic novels
1-4012-0120-2, $19.95

Preston Kills is a 20-year-old tattoo artist from Coney Island who has the power to see the final moments before and after a person's death; no one with similar powers has lived past their 21st birthday, and his homicide cop brother Robert has exploited Preston's powers to advance his career. Enter FBI agent Mickey Rinaldi, who is investigating the situation of super-powered teens who die early. She and Preston meet at his tattoo shop, follow the trail of a serial killer, and try to come to terms with love, loss, and the hope of surviving 21 Down. The book includes violence, strong language, and partial nudity.

Hawkman: Rise of the Golden Eagle. Written by Justin Gray and Jimmy Palmiotti; pencilled by Christopher Moeller et al. DC Comics 2006 208p. Illustration
Grades: 10 11 12 Adult   **741.5; Fic**
1. Hawkman (Fictional character); 2. Superhero graphic novels; 3. Graphic novels

978-1-4012-1092-2, $17.99

In Ancient Egypt, he was known as Prince Khufu. Today he is called Carter Hall. Archaeologist. Winged Warrior. Hawkman. He's lived thousands of lives - his soul reincarnated again and again, destined forever to be reunited with his true love until now. Prince Khufu's "soul mate" has been reincarnated into the body of Kendra Saunders - also known as Hawkgirl, but with no memories of her past lives, Kendra has made it quite clear she wants nothing to do with Hawkman. Now the two heroes must figure out a way to work together as they unravel the mysteries within the enigmatic southern epicenter called St. Roch, travel to exotic lands, and battle an alliance of adversaries from the past. The book has some violence beyond superhero fighting.

The **Monolith**. Written & created by Jimmy Palmiotti & Justin Gray; artwork & cover by Phil Winslade; introduction by Jim Steranko; coloring by Chris Chuckry; lettering by Nick Napolitano & Phil Balsman; designed by Bill Tortolini; edited by Joey Cav. Image Comics 2012 96 p.
Grades: Adult   **Fic**
1. Monsters — Fiction; 2. Revenge — Fiction
1607065746; 9781607065746, $17.99

In this comic book collection, "we are introduced to Alice Cohen, a down-and-out ex-junkie who inherits a house in Brooklyn from her deceased grandmother. Alice discovers her diary and begins to read the tale of a lost love and revenge that begins in the factories of New York during the depression and shows the creation of a monster bent on revenge for the slaying of a good honest man." (Publisher's note)
Rated T: teen.

Uncle Sam and the Freedom Fighters. Written by Justin Gray and Jimmy Palmiotti; art by Daniel Acuna. DC Comics 2007 208p. Illustration
Grades: 10 11 12 Adult   **741.5; Fic**
1. Superhero graphic novels; 2. Graphic novels
978-1-4012-1336-7, $14.99

Meet the all-new Phantom Lady, Doll Man, Human Bomb and the Ray - members of the government task force known as SHADE, the country's first line of defense against super-powered threats and terrorists in the wake of the Infinite Crisis. When the resurrected Uncle Sam makes them realize that Father Time has used them to further his own interests that will harm the United States, they work with Uncle Sam as the new Freedom Fighters. There is considerable violence in this superhero title.

Papadatos, Alekos

Democracy. Concept, Alecos Papadatos; story, Alecos Papadatos & Abraham Kawa; script, Abraham Kawa; art direction & drawings, Alecos Papadatos; colouring, Annie Di Donna. Bloomsbury 2015 236 p. Color; Illustration
Grades: 11 12 Adult   **741.5**
1. Athens (Greece) — Fiction; 2. Democracy; 3. War stories
1608197190; 9781608197194, $27

This book by Alecos Papadatos, Abraham Kawa, and Annie Di Donna "opens in 490 B.C., with Athens at war. The hero of the story, Leander, is trying to rouse his comrades for the morrow's battle against a far mightier enemy, and begins to recount his own life, having borne direct witness to the evils of the old tyrannical regimes and to the emergence of a new political system. The tale that emerges is one of daring, danger, and big ideas, of the death of the gods and the tortuous birth of democracy." (Publisher's note)

"Papadatos's lively and energetic art illuminates battles, alliances, political machinations, and vivid personalities, and Di Donna's intense coloring is gloriously rich without a touch of gaudiness. For those interested in further background, the extensive back matter features useful commentary on both legendary and historical figures and concepts." Pub Wkly

Park, Eun Ah
   Bird Kiss Vol. 1. Tokyopop 2006 Un Illustration
Grades: 8 9 10 11 12 Adult   **741.5; Fic**
   1. Humorous graphic novels; 2. Manwha; 3. Romance graphic novels; 4. Graphic novels
   1-59816-491-0, $9.99
   Miyoul is a feisty, boy-crazed girl who is in love with Guelin, a talk, dark, and handsome high school boy. But Heerack—short, scrawny, and too dorky to be given the time of day—has the hots for Miyoul, and worships her every move. Of course, Miyoul is awfully embarrassed by him and tries to avoid him like the plague. And of course, it doesn't work. This Korean manwha is filled with the trials and tribulations of high school—and some wacky, slapstick moments.

Park, Hee Jung
   Hotel Africa volume one. Tokyopop 2008 Un Illustration
Grades: 10 11 12 Adult   **741.5; Fic**
   1. Graphic novels
   978-1-4278-0575-1, $12.99
   The narrator, a young man named Elvis, tells stories about the Hotel Africa, a small hotel run by his mother and grandmother, located in the middle of the Utah desert. To this place come a strange young Native American named Geo and a couple of young vagabonds. The book includes some harsh language. This is Korean manwha.

Park, Joong-Ki
   Shaman Warrior, Volume One. Dark Horse Comics 2006 214p. Illustration
Grades: 11 12 Adult   **741.5; Fic**
   1. Adventure graphic novels; 2. Fantasy graphic novels; 3. Manwha; 4. Graphic novels
   978-1-59307-638-2, $12.95
   Warrior Wizard Yarong and his faithful servant Batu travel to the desert wastelands of Kugai on a mission for their king. However, they find only an overwhelming force of fighters led by a warrior who seeks to kill Yarong. The two warriors face on attack after the other, until Yarong realizes he is going to die; he sends Batu away, to find Yarong's baby daughter Yaki. They have been betrayed by their General for political expediency. This was a top-selling manwha in Korea; the kinetic, violent story will appeal to older readers who enjoy Lone Wolf & Cub, Blade of the Immortal, and other warrior epics.

Park, Min-Seo
   Blazin' Barrels Volume 1. Tokyopop 2005 186p. Illustration
Grades: 8 9 10 11 12 Adult   **741.5; Fic**
   1. Adventure graphic novels; 2. Science fiction graphic novels; 3. Western graphic novels; 4. Graphic novels
   1-59532-559-X, $9.99
   Sting may look harmless and naive, but he's really an excellent fighter and a wannabe bounty hunter in the futuristic Wild West. When he comes across a notice that advertises a reward for the criminal outfit named Gold Romany, he decides that capturing the all-girl gang of bad guys is his ticket to fame and fortune. The book includes some strong language and sexual suggestiveness, along with some violence.

Park, Sang-Sun
   The **Tarot** Cafe Volume 1. Tokyopop 2005 176p. Illustration
Grades: 9 10 11 12 Adult   **741.5; Fic**
   1. Fantasy graphic novels; 2. Manwha; 3. Supernatural graphic novels; 4. Graphic novels
   1-59532-555-7, $9.99
   Pamela is a tarot card reader who helps supernatural beings living in the human world. She'll help anyone, whether they're a love-stricken cat, a vampire spending eternal life running from his one true love, an unattractive waitress looking for the man of her dreams, or even a magician who creates a humanoid doll to serve the woman he loves. Although Pamela is good-natured, she has a deep dark secret that she must deal with before she can move on to the next life. The book includes some violence and one bondage scene.

Parks, Ande
   Union Station. Written by Ande Parks; illustrated by Eduardo Barreto. Oni Press 2003 116p. Illustration
Grades: 11 12 Adult   **364.1; 741.5**
   1. Crimes — United States; 2. FBI; 3. Graphic novels
   1-929998-69-4, $11.95
   Kansas City, 1933. Frank Nash is a petty criminal who has been pinched by the Feds and is being brought back into town by train. When FBI agent Reed Vetterli heads down to Union Station to meet Nash and his uniformed escort, he has no reason to suspect that there will be any action. Neither does Charles Thompson, a reporter sent down to the station just to see what the fuss is for. Little do they know that Frank's buddy, Vern Miller, is going to bust him out. Nash may not be a big time player, but he's still earned some loyalty. The resulting clash ends in a massacre, with no one knowing who pulled the trigger first - or even who pulled it at all. Rumor has it that Pretty Boy Floyd was on the scene, but no one knows for sure, and J. Edgar Hoover doesn't particularly care. He just wants Floyd's butt in an electric chair, and when Vetterli, Miller, and Thompson find themselves in the way of Hoover's justice, they can't duck for cover fast enough. This graphic novel is based on a true incident. The book includes violence and strong language.

Patten, Fred
   Watching Anime, Reading Manga: 25 Years of Essays and Reviews. Stone Bridge Press 2004 384p. Illustration

Grades: Adult Professional   **741.5; 791.43**
1. Anime — History and criticism; 2. Manga — History
and criticism; 3. Graphic novels
9781880656921, $18.95; 1880656922
                                          LC 2004014856
Anime's influence can be found in every corner of
American media, from film and television to games and
graphic arts. And Fred Patten is largely responsible. He was
reading manga and watching anime before most of the
current generation of fans was born. In fact, it was his active
participation in fan clubs and his prolific magazine writing
that helped create a market and build American anime
fandom into the vibrant community it is today. This book
gathers together a quarter-century of Patten's observations
on the business of anime, fandom, artists, Japanese society
and the most influential titles. It's illustrated with original
fanzine covers and archival photos.

Will Eisner's Shop Talk. Dark Horse Comics 2001
335p. Illustration
Grades: Adult Professional   **741.5**
1. Graphic novels — History and criticism; 2. Graphic
novels
1-56971-536-X, $19.95
Will Eisner was a master of the comics medium, and
when he got together to chat with other masters of the
medium, what came of it was a collection of information
vital to everyone working in the industry, and indispensable
to anyone looking to get into it. Featuring interviews with
Jack Kirby, Joe Simon, Gil Kane, Joe Kubert, Jack Davis,
Neal Adams, C.C. Beck, Milton Caniff, Gill Fox, Harvey
Kurtzman, and distribution guru Phil Seuling, this book is
chock full of tidbits of comics knowledge.

Patton, Michael F.
The **cartoon** introduction to philosophy. Michael F.
Patton and Kevin Cannon; Illustrated by Kevin Cannon. Hill
& Wang 2015 176 p. Illustration
Grades: 11 12 Adult   **100; 741.5**
1. Cartoons and caricatures; 2. Philosophy; 3. Philosophy
— Introductions; 4. Graphic novels
0809033623; 9780809033621, $17.95
                                          LC 2014029343
In this book, authors "Michael F. Patton and Kevin
Cannon introduce us to the grand tradition of examined
living. With the wisecracking Heraclitus as our guide, we
travel down the winding river of philosophy, meeting
influential thinkers from nearly three millennia of Western
thought and witnessing great debates over everything from
ethics to the concept of the self to the nature of reality."
(Publisher's note)
"The dynamic, cartoony illustrations might lead some to
assume that this title is a little more accessible than it actually
is, but anyone with an interest in learning about the
philosophers and philosophical concepts that have shaped
21st-century life without having to plow their way through a
dry textbook will find this title a stimulating delight." LJ

Pedrosa, Cyril
Three shadows. Translated by Edward Gauvin. First
Second Books 2008 270p. Illustration
Grades: 10 11 12 Adult   **741.5; Fic**

1. Family life; 2. Graphic novels
978-1-59643-239-0, $15.95; 1-59643-239-X
                                          LC 2007-38499
Life is good for the family, mother, father, and son
Joachim. Then one night they find three shadows, figures on
horseback, watching them, and Joachim is frightened. The
parents dismiss his fears at first, but their presence every day,
every night, begins to wear on them. Finally, the father
decides to leave and take Joachim far away, from the
shadows. But wherever the two go, the shadows follow. The
book includes some nudity and violence.

Pekar, Harvey
9-11, emergency relief. By Harvey Pekar; illustrated by
James Kochalka, Dean Haspiel, Josh Neufeld, Graham
Annable. Alternative Comics 2002 208 p. Illustration
Grades: Adult
1. September 11 terrorist attacks, 2001
1891867121; 9781891867125, $14.95
This comic book, by Harvey Pekar, with illustrations by
James Kochalka, Dean Haspiel, Josh Neufeld, and Graham
Annable, focuses on the "terrorist attacks in New York,
Washington DC, and Pennsylvania on September 11, 2001. .
. . [It] benefit[s] the American Red Cross." (Publisher's note)

American splendor: the life and times of Harvey Pekar :
stories. By Harvey Pekar; introduction by R. Crumb; art by
Kevin Brown ... [et al.]. More American splendor : the life
and times of Harvey Pekar : stories / by Harvey Pekar; art by
Gregory Budgett ... [et al.].. Ballantine Books 2003 320 p.
Color; Illustration
Grades: Adult   **741.5/973; 741.5**
1. Everyday life
0345468309; 9780345468307, $24
                                          LC 2003545170
This book, by Harvey Pekar, "is the world's first literary
comic book. . . . Harvey chronicles the ordinary and
mundane in stories both funny and touching. His dead-on
eye for the frustrations and minutiae of the workaday world
mix in a delicate balance with his insight into personal
relationships." (Publisher's note)
Other American Splendor books are: More American
Splendor (1986); The New American Splendor
Anthology (1991); American Splendor Presents: Bob &
Harv's Comics (1996); American Splendor: Unsung
Hero (2003); Our Movie Year (2004); Best of American
Splendor (2005); Ego & Hubris: The Michael Malice
Story (2006); American Splendor: Another Day (2007);
American Splendor: Another Dollar (2009)

Harvey Pekar's Cleveland. By Harvey Pekar,
illustrated by Joseph Remnant. Top Shelf/Zip 2012 128p
Illustration
Grades: Adult   **977.132; 741.5**
1. Autobiographical graphic novels; 2. Cleveland (Ohio);
3. Pekar, Harvey, 1939-2010
1603090916; 9781603090919, $21.99
In this autobiographical graphic novel, by Harvey
Pekar, illustrated by Joseph Remnant, "a lifelong Cleveland
resident, . . . combines . . . autobiographical anecdotes with
key moments and characters in the city's history as relayed to

us by Our Man and meticulously researched and rendered by artist Joseph Remnant." (Publisher's note)

Macedonia: what does it take to stop a war?. [by] Harvey Pekar and Heather Robinson; illustrated by Ed Piskor. Villard Books 2007 163p. Illustration
Grades: 10 11 12 Adult   **979.7; 741.5**
   1. Eastern Europe; 2. Graphic novels
978-0-345-49899-1, $17.95
                            LC 2006-42106
For years Heather Roberson, a passionate peace activist, has argued that war can always be avoided. But she has repeatedly faced counterarguments that fighting is an inescapable consequence of world conflicts. Indeed, Heather finds proving her point to be a little tricky without examples to bolster her case. So she does something a little crazy: She sets out for far-off Macedonia, a landlocked country north of Greece and west of Bulgaria, to explore a region that has edged-repeatedly-close to the brink of violence, only to refrain. In the process, Heather is tangled in red tape, ripped off by cabdrivers and hotel clerks, hit on by creepy guys, secretly photographed, and mistaken for a spy. She also creates unlikely friendships, learns that getting lost means seeing something new, and makes some startling discoveries. War is hell and peace is difficult but conflict is always necessary. As written by Pekar and illustrated by Piskor, the book includes some harsh language and a few images of violence, but has no nudity or sexual situations.

Not the Israel my parents promised me. Harvey Pekar and JT Waldman. Hill and Wang 2012 172 p.
Grades: Adult   **956.94**
   1. Biographical graphic novels; 2. Jews — History; 3. Jews — History; 4. Jews — United States — Attitudes toward Israel; 5. Judaism — History; 6. Pekar, Harvey — Political and social views; 7. Zionism
0809094827; 9780809094820, $24.95
                            LC 2011047024
This "posthumous work by [Harvey] Pekar functions as a multipronged exploration of religious, political, and personal histories . . . . Pekar structures his narrative as a long-running bull session with his collaborator, artist [J.T.] Waldman . . . . [T]hey explore his parents' very passionate but unusual Zionism . . ., the history of the Jewish people and the creation of the state of Israel, and Pekar's own evolving feelings about that country." (Publishers Weekly)

Quitter. Harvey Pekar, writer; Dean Haspiel, artist; Lee Loughridge, gray tones; Pat Brosseau, letters. DC Comics/Vertigo 2005 Un Illustration
Grades: 10 11 12 Adult   **741.5; 92**
   1. Autobiographical graphic novels; 2. Monsters; 3. Pekar, Harvey; 4. Pekar, Harvey; 5. Graphic novels
1-4012-0399-X, $19.95
Harvey Pekar is now a famed independent comics creator, whose series American Splendor was adapted into a hit motion picture. In this book, he recounts his childhood, teen years, and early adulthood and examines the experiences that shaped his life. He gives an unflinchingly honest portrait of a boy who used fighting to get a tough reputation, who needed to excel in sports and academics and would quit if he felt he couldn't achieve what he wanted. He allows the reader to see into his soul.

Students for a Democratic Society: a graphic history. Written by Harvey Pekar; art by Gary Dumm; edited by Paul Buhle. Hill & Wang 2008 214p. Illustration
Grades: 10 11 12 Adult   **378.1; 741.5**
   1. College students — Political activity; 2. Students for a Democratic Society — History; 3. Graphic novels
978-0-8090-9539-1, $22; 978-0-8090-8939-0 (pa), $16
                            LC 2007-40641
Students for a Democratic Society formed as an organization in 1960, but had its roots as a New Left group in the League for Industrial Democracy, founded in 1905 with members such as Jack London and Upton Sinclair. The members in 1960 included Al Haber and Tom Hayden, and one of their most famous documents is the Port Huron Statement of 1962. By the late 1960s, with opposition to the Vietnam War in full swing, a radical subgroup called the Weathermen became more violent. Graphic novelist Pekar is joined by members of the SDS in telling the story of the organization, which dissolved soon after its 1969 convention. The book includes some harsh language and violence.
"The book acts like a sophisticated handbook on an often misunderstood organization. It's good comics and excellent history." Publ Wkly

Pendergast, Sara
   ★ **U-X-L** graphic novelists, 3v. [by] Tom Pendergast and Sara Pendergast; Sarah Hermsen, project editor. U-X-L/Thomson Gale 2007 Lxii, 634 Illustration
Grades: 9 10 11 12 Adult   **920.003**
   1. Cartoonists — Dictionaries; 2. Graphic novels — Dictionaries; 3. Reference books
1-4144-0440-9; 978-1-4144-0440-0, set $181
                            LC 2006-13711
The three volumes include 75 alphabetically-arranged articles that profile authors, illustrators, and author-illustrators, and include European, American, and

Japanese creators. The introduction provides some history of graphic novels, and there is a separate essay on manga.

"This accessible and readable survey of a timely topic should generate considerable attention in school library media center and public library collections. Well researched and documented, with subject and language appropriate for its intended audience, this set is highly recommended." Booklist

Includes bibliographical references

Perez, George

The **New** Teen Titans: Terra Incognito. DC Comics 2006 224p. Illustration
Grades: 7 8 9 10 11 12 Adult   741.5; Fic
1. Robin (Fictional character); 2. Superhero graphic novels; 3. Teen Titans (Fictional characters); 4. Graphic novels
978-1-4012-0972-8, $19.99

Tara Markov, the troubled teen princess of Markovia, is rescued from kidnappers by the Titans' green-skinned adventurer, Changeling. Thus begins her quest to use her powers over earth and gravity in the cause of justice. Does this obnoxious young powerhouse have what it takes to join the team" This is the original Teen Titans team, in which Dick Grayson is still Robin.

Wonder Woman Vol. 4: Destiny Calling. DC Comics 2006 176p. Illustration
Grades: 8 9 10 11 12 Adult   741.5; Fic
1. Superhero graphic novels; 2. Wonder Woman (Fictional character); 3. Graphic novels
978-1-4012-0943-8, $19.99

It's only been a short time since Diana, dubbed Wonder Woman by the media, came to Man's World with a message of peace, only to face countless foes and stop the advancement of a third world war. Now Diana must face her greatest challenge yet: a god among men. The Olympian god Hermes has decided to grace mankind with his presence, but along with him comes a world of new troubles for the Amazon. This volume reprints stories originally published in the 1980s, when Perez re-launched Wonder Woman.

Perry, Fred

Gold Digger Pocket Manga Vol. 1. Antarctic Press 1991 158p. Illustration
Grades: 10 11 12 Adult   741.5; Fic
1. Adventure graphic novels; 2. Fantasy graphic novels; 3. Humorous graphic novels; 4. Graphic novels
1-932453-00-8, $9.99

Gina "Gold Digger" Diggers—archaeologist, adventurer, and super-scientist—travels the world with her adopted were-cheetah sister, Britanny (called Cheetah), in search of knowledge, excitement, and treasure . . . as well as a cute guy, here and there. In this collection of the very first Gold Digger stories, Gina and Brit have to foil the dragon Dreadwing's attempt to control Merlin's Time Raft. Then, the pair are off on a wild journey to mythic places around the globe (and off it), including Shangri-La, Atlantis, and the Garden of Eden - all to stop the evil Atlantean wizard Gyphon from using his people's ancient artifacts to rule the world. The two sexy young women face a lot of action and get into a lot of martial arts fights. This series is one of the

early American manga, now more commonly called global manga.

Pet avengers classic

Marvel Entertainment 2009 208p. Illustration
Grades: 7 8 9 10 11 12 Adult   741.5; Fic
1. Adventure graphic novels; 2. Pets; 3. Superhero graphic novels; 4. Graphic novels
9780785139669, $24.99

This volume collects the various Marvel Pets stories, from 1960 to 2007, with each story featuring a different pet, from Lockjaw the teleporting dog to Kitty Pryde's dragon Lockheed to Brightwind the winged horse, and many more. Lockjaw, Lockheed, Redwing the falcon, the cat named Niels, and Zabu the saber tooth tiger all starred in th 2009 mini series titled Pet Avengers. Some of the stories in this collection include violence.

Petrou, Das

Ring of Roses. Written by Das Petrou; penciled and inked by John Watkiss. Image Comics 2005 142p. Illustration
Grades: 10 11 12 Adult   741.5; Fic
1. Mystery graphic novels; 2. Science fiction graphic novels; 3. Graphic novels
1-58240-425-9, $12.95

Ring of Roses is set in London in an alternate 21st century in which the Church rules England with an iron hand but has begun to lose its grip. Then six high-powered priests are brutally murdered on the Thames. Samuel Waterhouse, the flamboyant barrister hired to investigate, soon realizes he is out of his depth, so he hires a hardened criminal, William Barnett, to assist him. Barnett rams through a delicate web of conspiracy like an express train through a scout troop's tent. Meanwhile, the bubonic plague breaks out and thousands are dying. Throughout all this chaos, Waterhouse and Barnett are treading on the toes of the immensely powerful figures behind the scenes. This story was originally published years before The Da Vinci Code; readers will find some similarities. The book includes violence, strong language, and sexual situations.

Petrucci, Michele

Due. SLG Publishing 2005 Un Illustration
Grades: 11 12 Adult   741.5; Fic
1. Mystery graphic novels; 2. Graphic novels
1-59362-016-0, $12.95

Keires, in ancient Greek, means "hands" - the essence of creation. As a killer murders and mutilates his victims without any apparent logic, a misogynist detective, a university teacher searching for perfection, a sculptor trying to forget his awful past, and a group of students get involved in a tale of blood and suspicion. Everything revolves around a mysterious death that will lead the characters to a bitter end, where innocence and guilt mix together and truth proves herself to be just the last work created by the hands of man. With Silver Salts, it all begins when Bob Keller, photographer of the Los Angeles Herald, gets a call to cover a simple murder story. But Bob is used to looking at details through the lens of his camera, and knows the truth is not as it seems. Things hidden inside his own mind will slowly be revealed like a latent image developed with the help of the silver salts. The book includes some strong language, violence, and nudity. Translated from Italian; the title means "two."

Peyo

The **Smurfs** anthology; Vol. 1. Peyo. Papercutz 2013 190 p. Color illustration (The Smurfs graphic novels)
Grades: 4 5 6 7 8 9 10 11 12 Adult **741.5**
1597074179; 9781597074179, $19.99
1. Smurfs (Fictional characters)
"Newly remastered and presented in original publication order, along with a Smurfy collection of historical notes and photographs, the stories in this volume," by Belgian comics artist Peyo, "introduce us to Papa Smurf, Gargamel, Smurfette, and the rest of the village." (Publisher's note)

The **Smurfs** anthology; Vol. 2. Peyo. Papercutz 2013 192 p. Color illustration
Grades: 4 5 6 7 8 9 10 11 12 Adult **741.5**
1597074454; 9781597074452, $19.99
1. Smurfs (Fictional characters)
"Newly remastered and presented in original publication order, along with a Smurfy collection of historical notes and photographs, this volume," by Belgian comics artist Peyo, "introduces us to Smurfette and features a 'Johan and Peewit' story never before seen in the U.S." (Publisher's note)
"[A] delightful and instructive mix of Peyo's colorful tales. A series of essays interspersed throughout the collection provides social and historical context for the cartoons." Booklist
Translated from the French

Pfeifer, Will

Catwoman: It's Only a Movie. Will Pfeifer, writer; David Lopez, penciller; Alvaro Lopez, inker; Jeromy Cox, colorists; Jared K. Fletcher, letterer. DC Comics 2007 168p. Illustration
Grades: 10 11 12 Adult **741.5; Fic**
1. Catwoman (Fictional character); 2. Mystery graphic novels; 3. Superhero graphic novels; 4. Graphic novels
978-1-4012-1337-4, $19.99
Selina Kyle has prowled the skyline of Gotham City as Catwoman, the protector of the East End, for years. But one year ago, following the events of Infinite Crisis, she became pregnant and decided to leave the costumed world behind. In this volume, the father of Catwoman's baby is revealed. Learn the fallout from Catwoman's killing of Black Mask, including the horrible price she paid for vengeance and why she chose to bring a baby into the world. Plus, Selina pays a visit to Superman's home, Metropolis. There is some graphic violence.

Catwoman: The Replacements. Will Pfeifer, writer; David Lopez, penciller; Alvaro Lopez, inker; Jeromy Cox, Brad Anderson, colorists; Jared K. Fletcher, letterer. DC Comics 2006 144p. Illustration
Grades: 10 11 12 Adult **741.5; Fic**
1. Catwoman (Fictional character); 2. Superhero graphic novels; 3. Graphic novels
978-1-4012-1213-1, $14.99
Selina Kyle has prowled the skyline of Gotham City as Catwoman, the protector of the East End, for years. But one year ago, she became pregnant and decided to leave the costumed world behind. Now, a new inexperienced Catwoman continues Selina's trade cloaked in the shadows and tries to restore order in the streets, while the original feline fatale has her hands full with the baby who's become the most important person in her life. Will it be too late for Selina to return when she questions her decision to step away from her crimefighting life? The book includes more violence than in most superhero comics.

Captain Atom: Armageddon. DC Comics/Wildstorm 2007 224p. Illustration
Grades: 10 11 12 Adult **741.5; Fic**
1. Superhero graphic novels; 2. Graphic novels
978-1-4012-1106-6, $19.99
In the DC Universe, Captain Atom was saving the world by piloting a spaceship into a kryptonite asteroid that was headed for Earth. But at the point of impact, something happens and throws him into another world, a darker world, where superhumans are feared, even the "heroes." Atom first encounters Majestic, who immediately fights him. Then they discover that Atom's appearance in the Wildstorm Universe will end up destroying everything, unless he can find a way home. That's the problem, so far they can't find a way to get him back to where he belongs. This story has more violence than most superhero stories.

Phillipson, Phil

God the Dyslexic DoG. Bliss on Tap Publishing 2006 Un Illustration
Grades: 10 11 12 Adult **741.5; Fic**
1. Fantasy graphic novels; 2. Gods and goddesses; 3. Graphic novels
978-0-9763768-6-6, $19.95
An old poet writes words of wisdom and hides them in a box, christens his loyal dog God, and gives them both to Pandora with the warning that the box should never be opened. All the gods exist, the Greek gods, the Mayan gods, the Egyptians, and all others, but one of them, Dionysus, also known as Bacchus, wants to die. The only way he can is to get Pandora to open the box, which he does trick her into doing. He traps her in the box and carries it with him for a thousand years, during which doG lives but can't remember who and what he is. Eventually doG becomes one of Pavlov's experimental animals, and when his fellow dogs howl at the full moon, they release the Mayan gods from their limbo and set events into motion again. For what" They want the world to end in 2011. Bacchus wants the world to end period. And when doG does finally drool at Pavlov's signal, a new god is created: Darwin. And Darwin wants to destroy all humans; he decides to make all the gods deities of different animals, to turn on humans. The only one who can stop him is doG, and his new human master, Nez, the

dyslexic son of a psychic who talks to animals. The book includes some violence and alcohol consumption.

Pini, Richard
★ **Elfquest** Archives Vol. 3. By Wendy and Richard Pini. DC Comics 2005 224p. Illustration
Grades: 9 10 11 12 Adult   **741.5; Fic**
1. Adventure graphic novels; 2. Elves; 3. Fantasy graphic novels; 4. Graphic novels
1-4012-0412-0, $49.99
This third volume collects Elfquest #11-15. When Leetah and some of the others try to catch up to Cutter to warn him of danger, they are taken as slaves into the towering and mysterious Blue Mountain, stronghold of the ancient elves called the Gliders. There Cutter and the Wolfriders must face the evil Winnowill, who wields strong magic, to save family and friends. The book includes violence, partial nudity, and sexual situations.

Elfquest: The Searcher and the Sword. By Wendy and Richard Pini. DC Comics 2005 96p. Illustration
Grades: 9 10 11 12 Adult   **741.5; Fic**
1. Adventure graphic novels; 2. Elves; 3. Fantasy graphic novels; 4. Graphic novels
1-4012-0184-9, $14.99
                       LC 2004-304577
In this tale, the elves must adapt to a world without the Troll smiths, who forged their weapons and tools. They must seek the secret of ancient troll metallurgy. Painfully aware of her human heritage, Shuna leaves her adoptive family of Wolfriders and embarks on a quest to unite elves and humans in peace. The book includes some violence.

Pini, Wendy
★ **Elfquest** Archives Vol. 1. By Wendy and Richard Pini. DC Comics 2003 216p. Illustration
Grades: 9 10 11 12 Adult   **741.5; Fic**
1. Adventure graphic novels; 2. Elves; 3. Fantasy graphic novels; 4. Graphic novels
1-4012-0128-8, $49.99
Existing on a prehistoric world, the World of Two Moons, in which humans and elves are bitter enemies, the Wolfriders live a dangerous life of fatal battles, deadly hunts, and tribal traditions. Proud of their history but unaware of their origin, the Wolfriders are on an eternal quest to learn the mysteries of their past. This hardcover edition includes the Wolfriders' fateful battle with a band of humans, their surprising discovery of another clan of elves, and Cutter's first meeting with the enchanting healer, Leetah. The Pinis started publishing the Elfquest stories as black and white comics in the mid-1970s; this is a full-color deluxe hardcover edition of the first five issues. The book includes partial nudity, brief sexual situations, and violence.

★ **Elfquest** Archives Vol. 2. By Wendy and Richard Pini. DC Comics 2005 226p. Illustration
Grades: 9 10 11 12 Adult   **741.5; Fic**
1. Adventure graphic novels; 2. Elves; 3. Fantasy graphic novels; 4. Graphic novels
1-4012-0129-6, $49.99
The Wolfriders have found sanctuary, and Cutter and Leetah become lifemates. But their peace is threatened once more by men, and the trolls, and by the twin mysteries of the

Forbidden Grove and Blue Mountain. The book includes some violence and brief partial nudity.

Elfquest: The Discovery. Written by Wendy & Richard Pini ; script, art, letters, and colors by Wendy Pini. DC Comics 2006 128p. Illustration
Grades: 8 9 10 11 12 Adult   **741.5; Fic**
1. Adventure graphic novels; 2. Fantasy graphic novels; 3. Graphic novels
1-4012-0958-0, $14.99
Wonder and danger mount as the Wolfrider chief's son Sunstream finds romance in the form of the lovely sea elf Brill and fierce hostility whe he exposes her long-hidden tribe, the Wave Dancers. Rule by fear of the "Landers" who hunt and slay his folk, the mighty mer-chief Surge will do anything, even destroy Sunstream and Brill's happiness, to keep his tribe secret and safe. This full-color story is the first new Elfquest story in years.

Pins, Arthur de
Zombillenium: Gretchen. By Arthur de Pins. NBM Publishing 2013 48 p. (Zombillenium)
Grades: 10 11 12 Adult   **741.5; Fic**
1. Amusement parks; 2. Vampires
1561637343; 9781561637348, $14.99
                       LC 2013936651
In this graphic novel, by Arthur de Pins, "Francis von Bloodt, a vampire and good family man, operates the one-of-a-kind theme park Zombiellenium. But this unique amusement park doesn't just hire anyone: mere mortals need not apply—only genuine werewolves, vampires, zombies, and other citizens from the undead community are employed." (Publisher's note)

Piskor, Ed
★ **Hip** Hop Family Tree. By Ed Piskor. Fantagraphics Books 2013 112 p. Color; Illustration
Grades: Adult   **741.5; 782.421649**
1. Hip-hop — Encyclopedias; 2. Rap music — History and criticism; 3. Graphic novels
1606996908; 9781606996904, $24.99
Written and illustrated by Ed Piskor in a graphic novel format, "This encyclopedic comics history of the formative years of hip hop captures the vivid personalities and magnetic performances of old-school pioneers and early stars like DJ Kool Herc, Grandmaster Flash and the Furious Five, plus the charismatic players behind the scenes like Russell Simmons; Debbie Harry, Keith Haring and other luminaries make cameos." (Publisher's note)
"Piskor succeeds mightily in chronicling hip-hop's formative years with riveting detail." Pub Wkly
Includes bibliographical references (page 106), discography (page 106) and index.

★ **Hip** hop family tree; volume 2: 1981-1983. By Ed Piskor and Charlie Ahearn. Fantagraphics 2014 112 p. Color; Illustration
Grades: Adult   **741.5; 782.421649**
1. Hip-hop; 2. Hip-hop culture
1606997564; 9781606997567, $27.99
Eisner Award: Best Reality-Based Work (2015)
This graphic novel on the history of hip hop, by Ed Piskor, "covers the years 1981-1983. . . . Hip Hop has made a

big transition from the parks and rec rooms to downtown clubs and vinyl records. The performers make moves to separate themselves from the paying customers by dressing more and more flamboyant until a young group called RUN-DMC comes on the scene to take things back to the streets." (Publisher's note)

"The second collection of Piskor's hip-hop history in comics may be a better place to start reading it than the first. Several longer stories are embedded in it, whereas the first volume was primarily a succession of one-pagers. For instance, the making of the groundbreaking hip-hop movie, Wild Style, occupies several pages, which allows gratifyingly better acquaintance with a handful of players amid the blizzard of faces and names the chronicle throws at us." Booklist

Includes bibliographical references, discographies, and indexes

Hip hop family tree; Volume 3: 1983-1984. By Ed Piskor. W W Norton & Co Inc 2015 110 p. Color; Illustration
Grades: Adult   **782.421649; 741.5**
1. Hip-hop — History and criticism; 2. Rap music — History and criticism; 3. Rap musicians
160699848X; 9781606998489, $27.99

This book, by Ed Piskor, is "the third volume of the popular webcomic. . . . Book 3 highlights Run DMC's rise to fame and introduces unassailable acts like Whodini, The Fat Boys, Slick Rick, and Doug E Fresh. The Beastie Boys become a rap group. Rick Rubin meets Russell Simmons to form Def Jam." (Publisher's note)

Wizzywig. Ed Piskor. Top Shelf Productions 2012 288 p. Illustration
Grades: 11 12 Adult   **741.5**
1. Computer hackers — Fiction; 2. Telephones — Fiction
1603090975; 9781603090971, $19.95

This graphic novel, "inspired by tales of real-life hackers . . . follows the story of Kevin 'Boingthump' Phenicle, who gets his start tapping into telephone lines as a teenager and works his way up to infiltrating the phone company and its database. At his side is his best (and indeed only) friend, Winston, who goes from helping Kevin with his hacking to defending him on the radio when Kevin is eventually caught and incarcerated." (Publishers Weekly)

"With heavy technology content and social-issue relevance, plus hacker and comics industry in-jokes, this is a techie's dream read, enhanced by Piskor's thorough research and judiciously unpretty black-and-white art." LJ

Plaka, Christine
Yonen Buzz Volume 1. Tokyopop 2006 188p. Illustration
Grades: 9 10 11 12 Adult   **741.5; Fic**
1. Rock music; 2. Graphic novels
1-59816-403-1, $9.99

Four young musicians stand at a new threshold of their musical career. With Plastic Chew, the band they created in high school, set on a path to rock 'n' roll stardom, will the demands of jobs, schoolwork, and relationships get in the way? Can they be true to their artistic vision without becoming sellouts? No matter what happens, this band keeps on rockin' ... determined to not let anything derail their rock

odyssey. This is a global manga, originally published in German. The book includes some mildly harsh language.

PLUS
Hanami: International love story vol. 2. Art by Sung Jae Park. Dark Horse Comics 2007 204p. Illustration
Grades: 8 9 10 11 12 Adult   **741.5**
1. Humorous graphic novels; 2. Romance graphic novels; 3. Graphic novels
978-1-59307-738-9, $9.95

Joonho's first kiss came from Hanami, not Sae-un oops. Hanami still believes that Sae-un is just a friend, not a girlfriend, and things are going to get even more tangled if Joonho doesn't get over his guilt and act soon. But first he has to buy a cell phone, because Sae-un is fed up with his poor calling habits, and she makes him promise never to give the number to any other girl. In order to afford the thing, though, he has to get a job... at a fast-food restaurant... with David Bacon. At least his female coworkers are cute ... There's a brief instance of partial nudity and some fighting. This is a manwha (Korean comic) series.

Pond, Mimi
Over Easy. Mimi Pond. Farrar Straus & Giroux 2014 272 p. Illustration
Grades: Adult   **741.5**
1. Autobiographies; 2. Bildungsromans; 3. California
1770461531; 9781770461536, $24.95

This fictionalized memoir by Mimi Pond "is equal parts time capsule of late 1970s life in California . . . and bildungsroman of a young woman . . . from a na?ve, sexually inexperienced art-school dropout into a self-aware, self-confident artist. . . . At first she mimics these new and exotic grown-up friends. . . . Gradually she realizes that the adults she looks up to are a mess of contradictions, misplaced artistic ambitions, sexual confusion, dependencies, and addictions." (Publisher's note)

Pope, Paul
Batman: Year 100. By Paul Pope; colorist, Jose Villarrubia; letters, Jared K. Fletcher & John Workman. DC Comics 2007 232p. Illustration
Grades: 10 11 12 Adult   **741.5; Fic**
1. Batman (Fictional character); 2. Science fiction graphic novels; 3. Superhero graphic novels; 4. Graphic novels
978-1-4012-1192-9, $19.99

This is a futuristic mystery of epic proportions set in a dark, dystopian world devoid of privacy and filled with government conspiracies, psychic police, holographic caller ID and absolutely no room for "secret identities." In Gotham City, 2039, a federal agent is murdered and a contingent of Washington's top agents is hot on the suspect's trail. The Batman, a forgotten icon from the past, is wanted for the murder. Amid the chaos Gotham City Police Detective Gordon, grandson of the former commissioner, discovers that the man they are chasing shouldn't exist at all. The book has some bloody violence and some strong language.

The **one** trick rip-off + deep cuts. Paul Pope. Legendary Comics 2012 288 p.
Grades: Adult   **Fic; 741.5/973**
1. Short stories

1607067188; 9781607067184, $29.99

LC 2012934614

This book is a "collection of the earliest published works of [Paul] Pope." These short stories, "which were created between 1993 and 1996, . . . highlight the confidence that he employed in his work. The offerings range from gritty slacker crime drama to mysterious illustrated poetry, as well as the comedic, girlie grossness of 'Super Trouble.'" (Publishers Weekly)

Porcellino, John

The **Hospital** Suite. John Porcellino. Farrar Straus & Giroux 2014 250 p. Illustration

Grades: Adult   **92; 741.5**

1. Anxiety; 2. Obsessive-compulsive disorder; 3. Patients; 4. Porcellino, John

1770461647; 9781770461642, $22.95

Author John Porcellino presents "an autobiographical collection detailing his struggles with illness in the 1990s and early 2000s. In 1997, John began to have severe stomach pain. He soon found out he needed emergency surgery to remove a benign tumor. In the wake of the surgery, he had numerous health complications. The [book] is Porcellino's response to these experiences." (Publisher's note)

Porcellino's "simple, black lines and bare-bones drawings have a powerful economy that present the story cleanly, without flourish, detailing a frightening and inescapable spiral into dysfunction without hyperbole. The result is a clear-eyed, penetrating book about the helplessness of illness." Pub Wkly

King-Cat Classix. Drawn & Quarterly 2007 384p. Illustration

Grades: 10 11 12 Adult   **741.5**

1. Autobiographical graphic novels; 2. Graphic novels

978-1-894937-91-7, $29.95

This large collection focuses on the first fifty issues of Porcellino's autobiographical comics, with extensive endnotes and an index, along with selections of all the extra ephemera that makes an individual issue of King-Cat a unique experience-essays, articles, stories, and letters from friends. Included are more than two hundred and fifty pages of comics, ranging from Porcellino's earliest scrawls to his later, minimalist delineations. The comics range through all of his concerns-family, family pets, the natural world, work, music, romance. He uses some strong language and some sexual situations.

Perfect Example. Drawn & Quarterly 2005 Un Illustration

Grades: 10 11 12 Adult   **741.5; Fic**

1. Autobiographical graphic novels; 2. Graphic novels

1-896597-75-0, $16.95

A melancholic memoir of saying goodbye to the familiar road trips, drunken concerts, and late-night make-out sessions all swirl together in this coming-of-age graphic novel by King Cat cartoonist John Porcellino. Tackling the pain and uncertainty of the pivotal summer before college, Porcellino's story is drawn in his minimalist style. Perfect Example is a collection of Porcellino's self-published King Cat comics. Porcellino uses strong language throughout.

Thoreau at Walden. By John Porcellino, from the writings of Henry David Thoreau; introduction by D.B. Johnson. Hyperion 2008 Viii, 99 p. Illustration; Map (Center for Cartoon Studies presents)

Grades: 8 9 10 11 12 Adult   **818/.303; 741.5**

1. American authors; 2. Thoreau, Henry David, 1817-1862; 3. Walden Woods (Mass) — Social life and customs; 4. Graphic novels

1423100387; 1423100395; 9781423100386, $16.99; 9781423100393

LC 2007061358

This graphic novel, by John Porcellino, "introduces . . . Henry David Thoreau. . . . Thoreau's writings, excerpted out of chronological order, are recast into a narrative that moves from the philosopher's self-ostracism from society and his time at Walden and into the feeling of calm reverie he took from his experiences." (Booklist)

"Presents in graphic novel format an account of the two years that Thoreau spent at Walden Pond, excerpted from Thoreau's writings." Publisher's note

Includes bibliographical references (p. 99)

Postcards: True Stories That Never Happened.

Random House/Villard 2007 152p. Illustration

Grades: 10 11 12 Adult   **741.5**

1. Short stories; 2. Graphic novels

978-0-345-49850-2

Sixteen short stories inspired by antique postcards are in this anthology. Writers and artists include Tom Beland, Harvey Pekar, Stuart Moore, Neil Kleid, A. David Lewis, Ande Parks, and others. Stories range from the elegeiac (Beland's "Time") to ironic ("Best Side Out" by Antony Johnston) to dark horror ("Send Louis His Underwear" by Matt Dembicki) to heroic (Robert Tinnell's "The Midnight Caller's Holiday in Hades").

Powell, Eric

Billy the Kid's Old Timey Oddities. Writer, Eric Powell; artist, Kyle Hotz; colorist, Eric Powell; letterer, Michael Heisler. Dark Horse Comics 2006 Un Illustration

Grades: 10 11 12 Adult   **741.5; Fic**

1. Horror graphic novels; 2. Monsters; 3. Graphic novels

1-59307-448-4, $13.95

Notorious outlaw and gunslinger William Henry McCarty - known as Billy the Kid - faked his death and is alive and well when Fineas Sproule, the four-armed owner of a sideshow called Sproule's Biological Curiosities, identifies him and then makes an offer the Kid can't refuse. They seek a mystical gem called the Golem's Heart, and they must travel from the U.S. to Europe, to an isolated castle that is home to Victor Frankenstein. They need Billy's prowess with guns to protect them on their journey. When they arrive in the village near the castle, however, everyone is captured by the mad scientist, who plans to conduct horrible and nasty experiments on everyone. Billy has thought of his companions as freaks, but they're nothing like the pitiable monsters created by Frankenstein. This will appeal to horror movie fans who love monsters.

Originally published as Billy the Kid's Old Timey Oddities issues #1-4.

The **Goon** Vol. 1: Nothin' But Misery. By Eric Powell; colors by Eric and Robin Powell. Dark Horse Comics 2003 Un Illustration
Grades: 9 10 11 12 Adult   **741.5; Fic**
  1. Horror graphic novels; 2. Humorous graphic novels; 3. Graphic novels; 4. Goon (Fictional character)
  1-56971-998-5, $15.95
  Bones will be broken and heads will roll! An insane priest is building himself an army of the undead and filling the town with zombies, and there's only one man who can put them in their place: the man they call Goon. This volume collects The Goon series and The Goon Color Special, originally published by Albatross Exploding Funny Books, presented here for the first time in full color. Readers meet Goon, his pal Frankie, and lots of weird monsters in a story that mixes crime noir, horror, and slapstick comedy. The monsters and zombies look like they just came out of an old EC horror comic; they look icky but funny at the same time.

The **Goon:** Heaps of Ruination. By Eric Powell; color assists by Robin Powell [and others]; Hellboy sequence and dialogue by Mike Mignola; colors by Dave Stewart; letters by Clem Robins. Dark Horse Comics 2005 Un Illustration
Grades: 10 11 12 Adult   **Fic; 741.5**
  1. Fantasy graphic novels; 2. Hellboy (Fictional character); 3. Horror graphic novels; 4. Humorous graphic novels; 5. Graphic novels
  1-59307-292-9, $12.95
  All undead minions and other variegated doers of badness who rouse up trouble with the honest folks of Lonely Street answer to the Goon. Robot or alien, werewolf or vampire, zombie or gorilla (or zombie-gorilla), it makes no difference to the Goon - he'll serve them up a mouthful of broken teeth right quick, as evidenced by the tales collected in this third volume chronicling the triumphs and tragedies of the lone man brave enough to stand against the Zombie Priest and his ghoulish army. This volume also includes a very special guest appearance by Hellboy co-written and drawn by Hellboy creator, Mike Mignola. The book includes some strong language and comic horror violence.

The **Goon:** My Murderous Childhood (and Other Grievous Yarns). Dark Horse Comics 2004 Un Illustration
Grades: 10 11 12 Adult   **741.5; Fic**
  1. Fantasy graphic novels; 2. Horror graphic novels; 3. Humorous graphic novels; 4. Graphic novels; 5. Goon (Fictional character)
  1-59307-109-4, $13.95
  The Goon and Franky have been best friends ever since they were tykes. Find out how the two little ankle-biters became best pals and how they muscled their way into the rackets of big-time crime-boss, Labrazio - who, incidentally, nobody's seen in a while. Franky and the Goon are going to have to take on a horde of zombies, an army of hoboes, a couple of grave robbing freaks, a guy with a gold head and his killer robot, a pie-crazed skunk ape, one homely, man-crazy sea hag, and a whole lot of other things that smell just as bad, if not worse. The book includes some strong language and lots of comic horror violence.

The **Goon:** Rough Stuff. Dark Horse Comics 2004 Un Illustration
Grades: 10 11 12 Adult   **741.5; Fic**

1. Fantasy graphic novels; 2. Horror graphic novels; 3. Humorous graphic novels; 4. Graphic novels; 5. Goon (Fictional character)
  1-59307-086-1, $12.95
  This volume presents the origin of Eric Powell's The Goon, the earliest stories published for the first time. The Zombie Priest has just set up shop on Lonely Street and intends to build an undead army, and the Goon's the only man who can stop him. His early battles with the undead are mixed with stories of the Goon's youth, as the reader meets his circus-freak family and learns how he came to be the head of a notorious crime family. Also included in this volume is a look at the creation of the Goon and his world with a special "Evolution of The Goon" sketchbook section. The book includes some strong language and violence.

The **Goon:** Virtue and the Grim Consequences Thereof. Dark Horse Comics 2006 Un Illustration
Grades: 10 11 12 Adult   **741.5; Fic**
  1. Fantasy graphic novels; 2. Horror graphic novels; 3. Humorous graphic novels; 4. Graphic novels; 5. Goon (Fictional character)
  1-59307-456-5, $16.95
  2005 Eisner Awards for Best Continuing Series and for Best Humor Publication.
  Giant man-eating eyeballs from another dimension, mad scientists, rampaging killer robots and the Ghost of Christmas Past - no, there's nothing out of the ordinary in the world of The Goon. This volume collects five tales following the exploits of the man known only as The Goon as he fights his through a horde of killer robots and even creatures from another dimension to help save his sometimes friend and ally Dr. Hieronymous Alloy from a mysterious disease. But there are plenty of bumps along the way, ultimately landing the Goon in Cade's Island Penitentiary, proving once more that no good deed goes unpunished. The book includes comic horror violence and strong language.

The **Goon:** Wicked Inclinations. Dark Horse Comics 2006 Un Illustration
Grades: 10 11 12 Adult   **741.5; Fic**
  1. Fantasy graphic novels; 2. Horror graphic novels; 3. Humorous graphic novels; 4. The Goon (Fictional character); 5. Graphic novels
  978-1-59307-646-7, $14.95
  The tide has turned in Goon's war against the undead hordes of the Zombie Priest - or has it? With Buzzard now preventing the harvest of any fresh corpses from the cemetery, the Priest grows desperate. So desperate, that he unleashes incantations of previously unseen power to create a whole new breed of minion - one that may be beyond even the strength of the Goon to contain. But one pays a price for conjuring such evil into the world, and the Zombie Priest quickly discovers that the cost of such power may be far more than he bargained for. The book includes strong language and comic horror violence, lots of it.

Powell, Martin
  Sherlock Holmes Mysteries Volume Two. Art by Seppo Makinen. Moonstone 2004 Un Illustration
Grades: 9 10 11 12 Adult   **741.5; Fic**
  1. Mystery graphic novels; 2. Sherlock Holmes (Fictional character); 3. Graphic novels

0-9748501-4-4, $14.95

In Return of the Devil," the many drug addicts of London have fallen victim to a poisonous supply of cocaine, trapping Sherlock Holmes himself within its deadly grip. The Great Detective is submerged in a world of nightmares where the evil Professor Moriarty still lives, and Holmes' dream of love with Irene Adler, The Woman, seems to have become a reality. Holmes must do battle against his very soul, at last facing his most terrible enemy: himself. In The Loch Ness Horror," Holmes is lured out of retirement when the Vatican calls upon him to investigate the bizarre murder of a priest. He swiftly deduces that this is no ordinary crime, and that an immensely powerful holy relic has been stolen from the secret vaults. Aleister Crowley, the self proclaimed Most Wicked Man in the World," casts his evil designs against all humanity in a mad scheme to arouse Doomsday. Meanwhile, Dr. Watson returns to Baskerville Hall, where something demonic is once again haunting the fog-shrouded moors. The book includes some violence and some strong language.

Powell, Nate

★ **Swallow** me whole. Top Shelf Productions 2008 Un Illustration

Grades: 10 11 12 Adult   **741.5; Fic**
1. Mental illness; 2. Graphic novels
978-1-60309-033-9, $20.95

Stepsiblings Ruth and Perry share their secrets with each other; Ruth hears insects talking to her, and Perry has to deal with a tiny wizard who forces him to draw all the time. In high school, Ruth is diagnosed as an obsessive compulsive with schizophrenic tendencies, while Perry manages to hide his wizard. Ruth sees cicadas and other insects always surrounding her, to the point that she thinks she's completely covered with them and she can fly. Her Memaw (grandmother) warns her that what she sees can swallow her whole. This book includes considerable use of foul language, especially the f-bomb, and the story takes a very thoughtful, mature reader to comprehend what is happening.

Pratchett, Terry

The **Discworld** graphic novels: The colour of magic & The light fantasic. Adapted by Scott Rockwell; illustrated by Steven Ross. HarperCollins 2008 Un Illustration

Grades: 9 10 11 12 Adult   **741.5; Fic**
1. Fantasy graphic novels; 2. Humorous graphic novels; 3. Graphic novels
978-0-06-168596-5, $24.95

Discworld is a flat world, sitting on the backs of four elephants who hurtle through space balanced on a giant turtle. Terry Pratchett has been publishing his comic fantasy series for about 25 years; this volume collects the graphic novel adaptations of the first two novels in the series. Originally published in the U. K. in 1993, they are published for the first time in the U. S. The stories feature the spectacularly inept wizard Rincewind, who acts as a tour guide for the naive tourist named Twoflower—and for his sentient Luggage. The book includes some violence and sexual innuendo.

Priddy, Joel

The **gift** of the Magi. It Books/HarperCollins 2009 Un Illustration

Grades: 5 6 7 8 9 10 11 12 Adult   **741.5; Fic**
1. Christmas; 2. Gifts; 3. Henry, O, 1862-1910 — Adaptations; 4. Graphic novels
978-0-06-178239-8, $14.99

Della and Jim are a young married couple, struggling to make ends meet when Jim's pay has been cut. It's Christmas time, but despite squeezing every penny, Della has managed to save only a little bit of money, and it's not enough to buy Jim a good present. He owns a gold pocket watch, and Della wants to buy him a chain for it. She has only one thing of value that she can sell her beautiful, long, long hair. Out of her love for Jim, Della sacrifices her hair. And, of course, Jim has sacrificed his gold pocket watch in order to buy beautiful hair combs for Della's gorgeous hair. As O. Henry says, they "most unwisely sacrificed for each other the greatest treasures of their house," but also that "of all who give gifts these two were the wisest." Joel Priddy's adaptation of this classic story uses black and white illustrations except when Della lets down her hair to consider her one treasure. He preserves much of O. Henry's original prose, which means that younger readers will have to look up a lot of words to understand the story. This book is suitable for younger readers but will also appeal to teens and adults.

Prince, Liz

★ **Tomboy:** A Graphic Memoir. By Liz Prince. Zest Books 2014 256 p. Illustration

Grades: 7 8 9 10 11 12 Adult   **741.5; 305.309; 92**
1. Cartoonists — Caricatures and cartoons; 2. Cartoonists — United States — Biography; 3. Gender identity; 4. Gender role; 5. Prince, Liz; 6. Sex differences (Psychology); 7. Sex role; 8. Stereotype (Social psychology); 9. Graphic novels
1936976552; 9781936976553, $15.99

LC 2014034070

This memoir, by Liz Prince, "is a graphic novel about refusing gender boundaries, yet unwittingly embracing gender stereotypes at the same time, and realizing later in life that you can be just as much of a girl in jeans and a T-shirt as you can in a pink tutu." (Publisher's note)

"Prince's honest voice and self-deprecating humor help make young Liz a sympathetic and relatable character. The simply rendered black-and-white panel drawings have an unpretentious quality, in keeping with the narrative tone." Horn Book

Pruett, Joe

Kilroy Is Here. Image Comics 2006 Un Illustration

Grades: 11 12 Adult   **741.5; Fic**
1. Horror graphic novels; 2. Mystery graphic novels; 3. Graphic novels
1-58240-587-5, $24.99

A being of unknown origin and power who is drawn to scenes of human suffering, Kilroy is an avenger of the innocent and protector of the weak. In the stories collected here, he appears at such places as Tiananmen Square in 1989, Sarajevo, Mogadishu, anywhere people suffer unjustly and are unjustly killed, he's there to take vengeance.

The book includes some strong language, sexual situations, and graphic violence.

The Nameless: The Director's Cut. Writer, Joe Pruett; artists, Phil Hester, Bruce McCorkindale. ImageComics 2006 Un Illustration Grades: 10 11 12 Adult **741.5; Fic**
1. Fantasy graphic novels; 2. Horror graphic novels; 3. Graphic novels
1-58240-499-2, $15.99

He is a man without a past, without a future, and without a name. An evil hides in the shadows of modern day Mexico City, feeding on the thousands of abandoned and unwanted street children that plague the night. This "nameless" man finds himself drawn into the midst of a very real modern horror with its origins found in the mythical bloodthirsty rites of the extinct Aztec Empire. The violent rituals and gods of the sun worshipping tribe somehow hold a key to his past. The nameless man knows that if he survives and learns the ancient secrets, he will have to live with the answers. The book includes violence.

Untouchables. Writer, Joe Pruett; artist, John Kissee. Image Comics 2006 Un Illustration
Grades: 10 11 12 Adult **741.5; Fic**
1. Mystery graphic novels; 2. Graphic novels
978-1-58240-359-6, $16.99

Twenty years after the fall of Capone and the rise to fame of Ness comes a new group of Treasury agents code-named Untouchables. Prohibition never ended, and it now includes not only liquor, but tobacco and firearms. Joseph Tarpley comes to lead the new Untouchables in Chicago. Gun fights, car chases, gangsters, nightclubs and sexy dames galore can be found throughout this hard-boiled, alternate take on the days of the mob and the officers who hunted them.

The psychology of superheroes: an unauthorized exploration.
Edited by Robin S. Rosenberg with Jennifer Canzoneri. BenBella Books, Inc. 2008 259p. Bibliographic footnotes; Illustration (BenBella Books psychology of popular culture series)
Grades: 10 11 12 Adult **741.5**
1. Conduct of life; 2. Hulk (Fictional character); 3. Justice League (Fictional characters); 4. Spider-Man (Fictional character); 5. Superheroes (Fictional characters) — Psychology; 6. Superman (Fictional character); 7. Wonder Woman (Fictional character); 8. X-Men (Fictional characters)
1-933771-31-3; 978-1-933771-31-1, $17.95
LC 2007-41418

This book collects essays about superheroes from several psychological viewpoints, ranging from the positive moral aspects of superheroes to gender stereotypes, prejudice, anti-heroes, the place of Arkham Asylum (the notorious place where DC super villains get locked up), the role of rage in The Incredible Hulk, and more. Editor Rosenberg is a clinical psychologist, and many of the contributors hold degrees in psychology and have faculty positions at various universities.
Includes bibliographical references

Puckett, Kelly
Kinetic. Kelley Puckett, writer; Warren Pleece, artist. DC Comics 2005 Un Illustration
Grades: 9 10 11 12 Adult **741.5; Fic**
1. Teenagers; 2. Graphic novels
1-4012-0472-4, $9.99

Tom Morrell is a sickly and disabled ultra-loser facing the daily hell of high school. Worse yet, his sole means of emotional support is his loving but smothering mother who fears he'll drop dead at any moment. And the worst part is, she's right. Tom's only escape is the super-heroic exploits of Kinetic, his favorite comic-book hero. But unbeknownst to Tom, he's got some powers of his own, and they're going to change his life - assuming they manifest themselves before Tom reaches the end of his rope and decides that life isn't worth living. Foul language is represented by nonsense syllables.

Pyle, Kevin C.
Blindspot. Henry Holt & Company 2007 Un Illustration
Grades: 5 6 7 8 9 10 11 12 Adult **741.5; Fic**
1. Friendship; 2. Graphic novels
978-0-8050-7998-2 (pa), $13.95; 0-8050-7998-X (pa)
LC 2006041155

Dean and his friends have created an entire world in the woods behind their suburban housing development. In their army fantasy, they're at war, and Dean is the daring captain leading his troops through episodes of intrigue and danger. But no fantasy can last forever. A run-in with a homeless man in the woods snaps the boys back to reality, and little by little the real world pervades their imagined universe and drives them apart.

Quesada, Joe
NYX: Wannabe. writer, Joe Quesada; artists, Josh Middleton, Robert Teranishi. Marvel Entertainment 2006 Un Illustration
Grades: 10 11 12 Adult **Fic; 741.5**
1. Adventure graphic novels; 2. Superhero graphic novels; 3. X-Men (Fictional characters); 4. Graphic novels
0-7851-1243-X, $19.99

The X-Men's dream has always been one of creating hope from despair - in a young mutant's darkest hour Charles Xavier will always be just around the corner, ready with open arms and a helping hand. But Xavier can't be everywhere at once. What becomes of a group of young mutants that have to rely on themselves for everything from food to shelter to love? Wayward angels with dirty faces who, instead of preparing for Magneto's next big assault, must learn to survive in the cold, harsh world of the city that never sleeps. The world of the X-Men is brought to the streets, and the struggle for survival has never been more uncertain.

Quinn, Jason

Gandhi: My Life is My Message. By Jason Quinn; illustrated by Naresh Kumar. Random House Inc 2014 212 p. Color; Illustration

Grades: 8 9 10 11 12 Adult   **741.5; 92**
1. Gandhi, Mahatma, 1869-1948
9380741227; 9789380741222, $16.99

This book by Jason Quinn, illustrated by Naresh Kumar, focuses on the life of "Mohandas Karamchand Gandhi, better known as the Mahatma or Great Soul. . . . We discover the man behind the legend, following him from his birth in the Indian coastal town of Porbandar in 1869, to the moment of his tragic death at the hands of an assassin in January 1948, just months after the Independence of India." (Publisher's note)

"Just as the writing eloquently intertwines explication with reenactments of dramatic, poignant events, the panels are meticulously arranged to move the reader's attention from broad and busy scenes to intimate close-ups." Booklist

Steve Jobs: genius by design. By Jason Quinn; illustrated by Amit Tayal. Random House Inc 2012 104 p. Illustration; Color

Grades: 7 8 9 10 11 12 Adult   **741.5; 92**
1. Apple Inc — Officials & employees; 2. Biographical graphic novels; 3. Computer industry; 4. Jobs, Steve, 1955-2011
9380028768; 9789380028767, $12.99

This graphic novel, by Jason Quinn, illustrated by Amit Tayal, presents a biography of the 20th-century technology entrepreneur and Apple Inc. founder Steve Jobs. "Steve Jobs and his inventions changed the world we live in." The book ranges "from his birth and his adoption, through the advent of the computer age and on into the digital age. Forced out of the company he created, his indomitable vision allowed him to change the world of computers, movies, music and telecommunications." (Publisher's note)

"This cleverly designed volume provides a concise but well-balanced view of Steve Jobs the wunderkind, including his difficult personality and complex genius." Booklist

Rabagliati, Michel

Paul Has a Summer Job. Drawn & Quarterly 2003 Un Illustration

Grades: 10 11 12 Adult   **741.5; Fic**
1. Graphic novels
1-896597-54-8, $16.95

Paul is outraged that he is forced to stop his high school art training, but he's been asked to put art aside because his other grades are so terribly low. Defiant, he quits school and anticipates a summer of leisure. But instead Paul follows the path of so many Quebecois teenagers: he lands a job as a counselor at one of the many summer camps in the mountains outside the city. There he finds himself guiding a motley band of kids, misfits and troublemakers, much like himself. The book includes some nudity, sexual situations, and strong language.

Paul Moves Out. Drawn & Quarterly 2005 Un Illustration

Grades: 10 11 12 Adult   **741.5; Fic**
1. Graphic novels
1-896597-87-4, $19.95

Nineteen-year-old Paul takes another step into adulthood by moving out of his parents' house and into his first apartment with his girlfriend, enjoying life's pleasures as well as confronting its challenges. He attends art school in Montreal and must deal with the fact that a charismatic professor is gay. The book includes strong language and some sexual situations.

Ragawa, Marimo

Baby & Me, Vol. 1. Viz Media/Shojo Beat 2006 200p. Illustration

Grades: 6 7 8 9 10 11 12 Adult   **741.5; Fic**
1. Family; 2. Humorous graphic novels; 3. Manga; 4. Shojo manga
1-4215-0234-8, $8.99

Young Takuya has it tough. After his mother passed away it has been his job to take care of his baby brother, Minoru while their father, Harumi, works the long hours of a Japanese "salaryman." Takuya must sacrifice the playtime usually associated with childhood for the responsibilities of an adult. Cooking, cleaning, sewing and scolding are all now an integral part of the sixth-grader's life. "All work and no play" has Takuya incredibly frustrated and resentful of his little brother. Will Takuya find it in his heart to love the brother who is causing him so much grief? This isn't so much a soap opera drama as it is a comedy with dramatic moments.

Raicht, Mike

★ The **Stuff** of Legend; Omnibus one. By Mike Raicht and Brian Smith; illustrated by Charles Paul Wilson III. Th3rd World Studios 2014 284 p. Color illustration (The Stuff of Legend)

Grades: 8 9 10 11 12 Adult   **741.5**
1. Kidnapping; 2. Rescues; 3. Toys; 4. Graphic novels
9780983216193; 0989574482; 9780989574488, $29.99

"This hardcover collection brings together the first two volumes. . . . As Allied forces fight the enemy on Europe's war-torn beaches, another battle begins in a child's bedroom in Brooklyn when the nightmarish Boogeyman snatches a boy and takes him to the realm of the Dark. The child's playthings, led by the toy soldier known as the Colonel, band together to stage a daring rescue. On their perilous mission they will confront the boy's bitter and forgotten toys, as well as betrayal in their own ranks." (Publisher's note)

"Wilson renders the harrowing closet netherworld with full-fleshed detailing and sepia tones that nail both the 1940s time frame and the classicism of children's stories. But don't mistake this for a kids' comic: the violence is often explicit, and the Boogeyman creepy enough to slither his way right back onto grownups' most-terrifying lists." Booklist

★ The **stuff** of legend; Omnibus two. By Mike Raicht and Brian Smith; illustrated by Charles Paul Wilson III. Th3rd World Studios 2014 270 p. Color illustration (The Stuff of Legend)

Grades: 8 9 10 11 12 Adult   **741.5**
1. Horror comic books, strips, etc; 2. Kidnapping; 3. Toys; 4. Graphic novels
0989574490; 9780989574495, $34.99

The second omnibus edition "finds our toys at a crossroads. Unable to find their boy, our loyal toys' bonds have been tested and broken. Now scattered across The Dark, the toys must decide whether to continue their search or admit defeat and return home." (Publisher's note)

Raiku, Makoto
   Zatch Bell! Volume 1. Viz Media 2005 192p. Illustration
Grades: 9 10 11 12 Adult   **741.5; Fic**
   1. Fantasy graphic novels; 2. Humorous graphic novels; 3. Manga; 4. Shonen manga; 5. Graphic novels
   1-59116-586-5, $9.99
   Kiyo is a brilliant junior high student whose inflated ego (and tendency to blow the grading curve) has made him a major target for teasing at school. So his father sends him a bizarre birthday present - a strange boy named Zatch Bell - to help him make friends and reform his bad attitude. Zatch brings with him a mysterious red Volume of spells, and Kiyo discovers that Zatch has magic powers that are unleashed by reading from the book. But there are more surprises - Zatch is a Mamodo who must fight against the 99 other Mamodo who were sent to Earth in order to become the Mamodo King, and Kiyo is now along for the ride. There are lots of fight scenes.

Rall, Ted
   2024. NBM/ComicsLit 2001 96p. Illustration
Grades: 10 11 12 Adult   **741.5; Fic**
   1. Satire; 2. Science fiction graphic novels; 3. Graphic novels
   1-56163-279-1, $16.95
   Move forward two decades. The giant media moguls and software companies have become the new big brothers. They want the best for everyone. They know what's best for everyone. And society has chosen to be consumer heaven with no questions asked. A terrifying future where the past doesn't matter and no one cares. The motto to live by: "yes, no, whatever." Ted Rall updates and spoofs 1984 in a look at where the U.S. could be headed. Rall uses harsh language and some sexual situations.

   Silk road to ruin: is Central Asia the new Middle East?. NBM 2006 303p. Illustration; Map
Grades: 11 12 Adult   **958**
   1. Central Asia; 2. Graphic novels
   1-56163-454-9; 978-1-56163-454-5, $22.95
                                             LC 2006-42041
   "Moving between narrative and graphic novella interludes, . . . [the author] recounts several trips that he has made in the past decade to the five "Stans," those Central Asian nations that were so recently part of the USSR. . . . Rall takes readers on scary bus trips where armed guards threaten Westerners. . . . Diarrhea is a constant and bloody companion. Sports include a deadly horseback event in which opponents whip one another in the eyes." Voice Youth Advocates
   Rall's "awestruck descriptions of the region's natural beauty, crowded bazaars, and chaotic sporting tournaments will make adventurous readers want to see it all firsthand." SLJ
   Includes bibliographical references

Rauch, Mac
   Buckaroo Banzai: Return of the Screw. Story, Earl Mac Rauch; adaptation/new material, Joe Gentile; pencils, Steven Thompson; inks, Keith Williams; colors, Ken Wolak with Dave Alusik and Wally Lowe; letters, Erik Enervold. Moonstone 2007 120p. Illustration
Grades: 9 10 11 12 Adult   **741.5; Fic**
   1. Adventure graphic novels; 2. Mystery graphic novels; 3. Science fiction graphic novels; 4. Graphic novels
   978-1-933076-26-3, $16.95
   Everyone's favorite adventurer/surgeon/rock star is back again just in time to save the world. Along with his Hong Kong Cavaliers, Banzai must battle more than one surprise arch enemy, each with their own motives, but all acting in concert to bring Banzai (and the universe as we know it) to his knees. All this sandwiched between a couple of great rock and roll guitar solos, a few surgical procedures, a crazy gun battle on land and air, Buck's one chance for the ultimate revenge, his soul in turmoil, all the chicks digging him, engineering synchronicity, pretty toilets, a human pickle and a giant sombrero. The book includes some mildly strong language and some violence.

Raviv, Dan
   Comic Wars: Marvel's Battle for Survival. Marvel Comics 2004 352p. Illustration
Grades: Adult Professional   **741.5**
   1. Comic books, strips, etc — History and criticism; 2. Marvel Comics Group — History; 3. Graphic novels
   0-7851-1606-0, $13.99
   This is the true story of the business superheroes who rescued Marvel Comics from bankruptcy. In the mid-1990s, Marvel Entertainment became embroiled in a crisis as strange as one of its comic book stories. Locked in a battle for control of the half-century-old company were two Goliath-style corporate raiders and two virtually unknown Davids: Israeli immigrants with a passion for the toy business. This was a test of wills that led to a unique Wall Street showdown. The book takes readers behind the scenes of America's most bitter bankruptcy and captures the high-stakes twists and turns of this financial fiasco. The cast of characters ranges from tycoon Ron Perelman (who bankrupted Marvel through overexpansion) and Carl Icahn (who then launched a hostile takeover of Marvel) to Ike Perlmutter and Avi Arad, scrappy owners of Toy Biz and the duo who outmaneuvered the moguls.
   Previously published in hardcover in 2002 by Broadway Books under the title: Comic Wars: How Two Tycoons Battled Over the Marvel Comics Empire - And Both Lost.

Rawson, David
   Chiaroscuro: The Private Lives of Leonardo da Vinci. written by Pat McGreal and David Rawson; pencilled by Chaz Truog; inked by Rafael Kayanan; colored by Carla Feeny and Lovern Kindzierski; lettered by Clem Robins and John Costanza. DC Comics/Vertigo 2005 264p. Illustration
Grades: 11 12 Adult   **741.5; 92; Fic**
   1. Art; 2. Leonardo, da Vinci, 1452-1519; 3. Graphic novels
   1-4012-0498-8, $24.99

He was the ultimate Renaissance man, but what was Leonardo da Vinci really like? This historical drama follows the life of Leonardo as witnessed by his "Little Devil," Salai, a low-born youth whose beauty entranced da Vinci enough for the artist to adopt him, and whose quest for acceptance from the maestro led him to both love and betray the man. The creators conducted a lot of research, and this graphic novel has a full-page bibliography. The book contains harsh language, nudity, and sexual situations.

Raymond, Alex

★ **Flash** Gordon: On the Planet Mongo: Sundays 1934-37. Alex Raymond, Don Moore; restorations by Peter Maresca. Random House Inc 2012 192 p.
Grades: Adult   **Fic**
  1. Science fiction comic books, strips, etc
  0857681540; 9780857681546, $39.95

This anthology, by Alex Raymond, collects the comic strips featuring the science fiction hero Flash Gordon published from 1934 to 1937. "Volume One will spotlight the work of Alex Raymond, legendary for some of the finest storytelling of the 20th century. . . . Introducing Flash Gordon, Dale Arden, Dr. Hans Zarkov, and Ming the Merciless, this volume will catapult readers to the deadly planet Mongo." (Publisher's note)

Reaves, Michael

The **Irregulars** ... In the Service of Sherlock Holmes. Written by Steven-Elliot Altman & Michael Reaves; illustrated by Bong Dazo; lettered by Simon Bowland; cover by Ben Templesmith. Dark Horse Comics 2005 Un Illustration
Grades: 9 10 11 12 Adult   **741.5; Fic**
  1. Horror graphic novels; 2. Mystery graphic novels; 3. Graphic novels
  1-59307-303-8, $12.95

A madman stalks the streets of London's Whitechapel slum, leaving a trail of grisly murders in his wake. The police have only one suspect: a prominent and respected physician named John Watson. The master detective Sherlock Holmes, in order to solve the most fantastic mystery of his career and save his greatest friend from the gallows, employs a band of young street urchins to infiltrate the alleys of Whitechapel. They can go everywhere, see everything, overhear everyone. They are the Baker Street Irregulars, and this is the most fantastic and terrifying adventure of their lives, as they uncover an evil unlike anything Sherlock Holmes has ever faced, and end up in a nightmare future. Grisly murders and horrific sights along with some strong language occur.

Redniss, Lauren

Thunder & Lightning: Weather Past, Present, Future. Lauren Redniss. Random House Inc 2015 272 p. Color; Illustration
Grades: Adult   **551.6; 741.5**
  1. Meteorology; 2. Weather
  0812993179; 9780812993172, $35

This book, by Lauren Redniss, focuses on weather. It "roams from the driest desert on earth to a frigid island in the Arctic, from the Biblical flood to the defeat of the Spanish Armada. Redniss visits the headquarters of the National Weather Service, recounts top-secret rainmaking operations

during the Vietnam War, and examines the economic impact of disasters like Hurricane Katrina." (Publisher's note)

"This book is not simply a collection of oddments and odd fellows, but rather a genuine demonstration of weather as a phenomena and how it is fantastical on both the symbolic and systematized levels." Kirkus
Includes bibliographical references

Reed, Gary

The **Red** Diaries. Gary Reed; artists, Laurence Campbell, Chris Jones and Larry Shuput. Image Comics 2006 168p. Illustration
Grades: 10 11 12 Adult   **741.5; Fic**
  1. Mystery graphic novels; 2. Graphic novels
  978-1-58240-622-0, $16.95

Marilyn Monroe, John F. Kennedy, the Mob, Fidel Castro, J. Edgar Hoover, the CIA... It was a conspiracy of secrets, a conspiracy of murder. All was revealed in Marilyn's diaries, her Red Diaries, and it is about to blow everything out into the open more than thirty years later. Raven, Inc., a group used to investigating the paranormal, does a favor for someone and starts hunting for Marilyn Monroe's lost Red Diaries. There's some strong language and nudity, mostly from the notorious Playboy photographs of Marilyn Monroe.

Renfield: A Tale of Madness. Image Comics 2006 192p. Illustration
Grades: 9 10 11 12 Adult   **741.5; Fic**
  1. Horror graphic novels; 2. Vampires; 3. Graphic novels
  978-1-58240-674-9, $19.99

This book delves into the story of the bug-eating asylum inmate Renfield, from Bram Stoker's Dracula. Renfield foretold the coming of the vampire to England. Possessed by almost demonic forces and impassioned with the zeal of a religious fanatic, Renfield must struggle to grasp the overwhelming need to serve the darkness against his own humanity. There is some violence in this story that retells part of the story of Dracula, and particularly of Mina Harker, from Renfield's viewpoint.

Saint Germaine: Shadows Fall. Image Comics 2005 Un Illustration
Grades: 10 11 12 Adult   **741.5; Fic**
  1. Horror graphic novels; 2. Graphic novels
  1-58240-562-X, $14.99

An immortal being who has died 1,000 deaths, Saint Germaine has traversed the paths of mankind for untold years with his companion, Lilith. But Lilith's disappearance and the perils of the modern world direct him to undertake a new quest - to surrender his immortality. The book has some strong images of violence.

Regnaud, Jean

★ **My** mommy is in America and she met Buffalo Bill. Jean Regnaud & Émile Bravo (artist). Fanfare/Ponent Mon 2009 120p. Illustration
Grades: 6 7 8 9 10 11 12 Adult   **741.5; Fic**
  1. Family life; 2. Mother; 3. School life; 4. Graphic novels
  978-84-96427-85-3, $25

Essentials Award winner at the 35th Festival of Angouleme,n France, 2008; Tam Tam Literary Award

2009 from Salon du Livres et de la Presse Jeunesse, for Comic Album, age group eight to thirteen years old.

Narrator Jean has just started first grade and has a younger brother, Paul, in kindergarten. They live with their factory boss father and nanny Yvette; Jean says his mother is on a trip. As he talks about his first day at school, meeting a new friend, Alain, and fighting with Paul, he mentions his mother has been away so long he can't quite remember her. Next door neighbor Michelle claims to be receiving postcards from Jean's mother and reads them to him; they come from places such as Switzerland and the United States. As the reader sees Jean and Paul spend a day with their mother's parents and interact with their grandparents' friends, the reader understands what Jean does not: his mother is dead. This book, translated from its original French, won an award for best comic album for ages eight to thirteen; however, with the essential fact never stated and Jean deciding that he's getting to old to believe in his mother, just as he's too old to believe in Father Christmas, makes this more suitable for the upper age range, teens, and adults.

Reilly, Christopher P.
Punch and Judy: Twice Told Tales. SLG Publishing 2005 Un Illustration
Grades: 10 11 12 Adult   **741.5; Fic**
   1. Fantasy graphic novels; 2. Humorous graphic novels; 3. Graphic novels
   1-59362-015-2, $7.95

In The Comical Tragedy of Punch and Judy, Mr. Punch brandishes his infamous stick against all foes who threaten his precious and impressive nose, including his squalling baby, his quarrelsome wife Judy, Mr. Scaramouche and his dog Toby, the hangman and, finally, the Devil himself. In Punch and Judy: A Grand Guignol, Mr. Punch, not content with killing the Devil, taking over Hell and outlawing Goodness, sets his sight on the pinnacle of achievements: Getting on Santa's Nice List. Or if that doesn't work, ruining Christmas for the last two good children on Earth. The first story is a retelling of the traditional English puppet show (actually, there are versions all over Europe) that dates back at least to the mid-seventeenth century, with roots in the commedia dell'arte. The stories are full of shocking violence that seems much more sinister than in the puppet shows.

Remender, Rick
Fear Agent Volume One: Re-Ignition. Pencils, Tony Moore. Dark Horse Comics 2007 Un Illustration
Grades: 9 10 11 12 Adult   **741.5; Fic**
   1. Adventure graphic novels; 2. Science fiction graphic novels; 3. Graphic novels
   978-1-59307-764-8, $13.95

Heath Huston, an alien exterminator, stumbles upon a plot by a race called the Dressites to send feeders to Earth. The feeders are a life-form that consumes all organic matter until a planet is destroyed. When Huston and the human scientist, Mara, try to go in Huston's AI ship to Earth, they discover that the ship has taken on a type of hyper-fuel it can't handle, and they crashland on a planet in its distant past, whose dominant race invaded Earth. Huston is the last of the Fear Agents, elite soldiers of Earth, and he thinks he can prevent the invasion by changing the past.

Originally published by Image Comics as Fear Agent issues #1-4.

Fear Agent Volume Two: My Way. Art by Jerome Opeña. Dark Horse Comics 2007 Un Illustration
Grades: 11 12 Adult   **741.5; Fic**
   1. Adventure graphic novels; 2. Science fiction graphic novels; 3. Graphic novels
   978-1-59307-766-2, $14.95

Lost, beaten and trapped in the past, Heath Huston must face the demons of his inevitable future when he finds himself face to face with the automaton regime responsible for robbing him of all he loves. With the knowledge that the Feeders are progressing ever closer to Earth, will Heath be able to get payback from the automaton empire in time to save his home planet from the scourge of an alien infestation? This volume has nudity, sexual situations, harsh language, and violence.

Strange Girl Vol. 1: Girl Afraid. Image Comics 2005 Un Illustration
Grades: 11 12 Adult   **741.5; Fic**
   1. Horror graphic novels; 2. Supernatural graphic novels; 3. Graphic novels
   978-1-58240-543-8, $12.99

Ten years after the Rapture, beautiful occultist Bethany Black and her pet runt demon Bloato embark on a road trip to the last open gateway to heaven, in hopes of befriending God and escaping hell on earth. The book includes considerable graphic violence, harsh language, and some nudity.

Strange Girl Vol. 2: Heaven Knows I'm Miserable Now. Image Comics 2006 Un Illustration
Grades: 11 12 Adult   **741.5; Fic**
   1. Horror graphic novels; 2. Supernatural graphic novels; 3. Graphic novels
   978-1-58240-642-8, $14.99

There's a point in every journey where there seems to be no light - no hope. After returning to the human stronghold, Dead Western, Bethany Black learns there is little hope she'll ever find respite from hell on Earth. The book includes considerable graphic violence, harsh language, and some nudity.

Tales of the fear agent. Dark Horse Comics 2008 Un Illustration
Grades: 11 12 Adult   **741.5; Fic**

1. Horror graphic novels; 2. Humorous graphic novels; 3. Science fiction graphic novels; 4. Graphic novels
978-1-59307-959-8, $14.95

Heath Huston, the Fear Agent, lost his family and most of his life when invading aliens pretty much destroyed the Earth. This volume collects stories of his first ten years working as an alien exterminator. Huston spends much of his time as drunk as possible, and many of the stories include violence, harsh language, and partial nudity. The stories possess the style of 1950's science fiction and horror stories, with a lot of humor and action. Writers include Rick Remender, who created the Fear Agent, Kieron Dwyer, Steve Niles, Hilary Barta, Eric Nguyen, C. B. Cebulski, and more.

Uncanny Avengers: the red shadow. Rick Remender, illustrated by John Cassaday. Marvel Worldwide 2013 136 p.
Grades: 10 11 12 Adult   **Fic; 741.5**
1. Avengers (Fictional characters); 2. Captain America (Fictional character); 3. Thor (Fictional character); 4. Wolverine (Fictional character); 5. X-Men (Fictional characters)
0785168443; 9780785168447, $24.99

In this graphic novel by Rick Remender, "Captain America creates a sanctioned Avengers unit comprised of Avengers and X-Men, humans and mutants working together...so why is Professor Xavier's dream more at risk than ever" The Red Skull has returned - straight out of the 1940s and full of hatred - and his rebirth will alter the Marvel Universe forever!" (Publisher's note)

"[D]ense, intelligent writing that asks significant questions; a battle not only of arms but of ideologies; and a cast of characters that gives movie stars like Captain America, Thor, and Wolverine their due without ignoring the rich personalities of lesser-known players. . . . Cassaday's art, the most purely gorgeous in contemporary superhero comics [is] so clean and clear the pages practically glow with life." Booklist

Revel, Brahm
Guerillas Volume 2: Volume 2. Brahm Revel; [edited by] Charlie Chu. Oni Press, Inc 2012 120 p.
Grades: 11 12 Adult   **741; Fic**
1. Military personnel — United States; 2. Monkeys; 3. Vietnam War, 1961-1975
1934964999; 9781934964996, $17.99
LC 2012930679

In this book by Brahm revel "Private John Francis Clayton's strange tour of duty in Vietnam gets stranger as he struggles with the unbelievable facts he is faced with. The elite platoon of simian soldiers he's encountered don't make any more sense to him than the war he's been sent to fight, but is this squad of chain-smoking chimps the most dangerous force in the jungle, or are they merely a distraction from the larger evil growing in the wild?" (Publisher's note)

Rhoades, Shirrel
★ **Comic** books: how the industry works. Afterword by Stan Lee. Peter Lang Publishing, Inc. 2008 406p. Illustration
Grades: 11 12 Adult   **741.5**

1. Comic books, strips, etc — History and criticism; 2. Graphic novels — History and criticism; 3. Publishers and publishing
978-0-8204-8892-9, $32.95
LC 2007-32719

Rhoades, who was publisher of Marvel Comics after Stan Lee and has worked in publishing for more than forty years, gives an insider's look at how the comic book industry works. He discusses how superhero characters are created, how comic books are put together, how they're sold, how comics' intellectual property is licensed to other industries, adapting comics to television and movies, what manga is all about, and the move of graphic novels into bookstores. The chapters are broken down into subsections, and there are frequent sidebars with labels such as "speak up," "flashback," "comics trivia!" and others that provide even more tidbits of information in a highly readable format.

★ A **complete** history of American comic books. Afterword by Steve Geppi. Peter Lang Publishing Inc. 2008 353p. Illustration
Grades: 9 10 11 12 Adult   **741.5**
1. Comic books, strips, etc — History and criticism; 2. Graphic novels — History and criticism
978-1-4331-0110-6; 1-4331-0110-6, $119.95;
978-1-4331-0107-6 (pa); 1-4331-0107-6 (pa), $39.95
LC 2007-43460

Rhoades, former publisher of Marvel Comics (after Stan Lee stepped down to move to Hollywood and focus on Marvel Comics in the movies), dates the beginning of the American comic book to the 1930s, when the format was first used. He covers the history of comics from that time to the present, covering all the big names (Will Eisner, Jack Kirby, Stan Lee, etc.). The book is peppered with fun sidebars with such labels as "flashback," "comics trivia," "looking back," "true facts," and so one. These help to make the book fun to read. Rhoades doesn't employ a straight narrative, but includes interviews, the side bars, comics milestones, a list of fanboys who have and had careers in comics, and a comic book quiz.

Includes bibliographical references

Ricca, Brad
Super boys: the amazing adventures of Jerry Siegel and Joe Shuster: the creators of Superman. Brad Ricca. St Martins Pr 2013 432 p.
Grades: Adult   **741.5; 92**
1. Cartoonists — United States — Biography; 2. Comic books, strips, etc — United States — History and criticism; 3. Shuster, Joe, 1914-1992; 4. Siegel, Jerry, 1914-1996; 5. Superman (Fictional character); 6. Superman (Fictional character)
0312643802; 9780312643805, $27.99
LC 2013004046

This biography of Superman creators Jerry Siegel and Joe Shuster, by Brad Ricca, "reveals the real-life model for Lois Lane . . . and the model for Superman himself (Johnny Weissmuller, who played Tarzan). At the center of the story, of course, is Siegel and Shuster's decision to sell the Superman rights to Action Comics for a pittance—a choice they lamented the rest of their lives. The pair endured poverty, bad marriages, bad health, and a lack of recognition for their work." (Publishers Weekly)

"Ricca's comprehensive biography reveals the turmoil and creative genius that led to our most enduring superhero, the Man of Steel." Pub Wkly

Includes bibliographical references (pages 403-406) and index

Richardson, Mike

47 Ronin. Writer, Mike Richardson; artist, Stan Sakai. Dark Horse 2014 151 p. Color; Illustration
Grades: 11 12 Adult   **741.5**
1. Samurai
1595829547; 9781595829542, $19.99

Written by Mike Richardson and illustrated by Stan Sakai, "this collection of the acclaimed [comic book] mini-series recounts this sweeping saga of honor and violence in all its grandeur. Opening with the tragic incident that sealed the fate of Lord Asano, 47 Ronin follows a dedicated group of Asano's vassals on their years-long path of vengeance!" (Publisher's note)

"Richardson, founder of Dark Horse Comics, and Sakai, creator of the long-running and award-laden Usagi Yojimbo samurai series, combine talents to produce this terrific graphic interpretation of one of Japan's most important sagas. . . . The level of talent, the research, and the attention to both narrative and artistic detail shine through in this volume." LJ

Living with the dead. Artist, Ben Stenbeck. Dark Horse Comics 2008 Un Illustration
Grades: 11 12 Adult   **741.5; Fic**
1. Horror graphic novels; 2. Humorous graphic novels; 3. Zombies; 4. Graphic novels
978-1-59307-906-2, $9.95

A virus has doomed most of humanity to become zombies, but hard rockers Straw and Whip have managed to survive, going out disguised as zombies, pilfering what they need from deserted stores and malls. Then they meet Betty, saving her when there are too many zombies attacking for her to whack with a golf club. Her presence messes up the tight friendship and partnership the two guys have had, as they each get jealous about her. And their jealousy (and her need to kill zombies) makes them careless. The book includes lots of graphic violence.

The **secret**. Story by Mike Richardson; art and covers by Jason Shawn Alexander; letters by Clem Robbins. Dark Horse Comics 2007 112p. Illustration
Grades: 10 11 12 Adult   **741.5**
1. Horror graphic novels; 2. Mystery graphic novels; 3. Graphic novels
978-1-59307-821-8, $12.95

When outsider Tommy Morris gets invited to Pam's party, he finds she and her friends making prank phone calls to randomly punched numbers. When someone answers, they say "I know your secret." Then one of the calls gets weird when the person on the other end responds. When they go out to the park late at night, someone does show up, and his behavior scares them. And the next day, someone calls Pam on her cell phone and says How do you know my secret?" She disappears that afternoon, and her friends and the police think Tommy is involved. Now he can't stop until he finds Pam, to clear himself.

Ricketts, Mark

Night Trippers. Image Comics 2006 184p. Illustration
Grades: 10 11 12 Adult   **741.5; Fic**
1. Horror graphic novels; 2. Vampires; 3. Graphic novels
978-1-58240-606-0, $16.99

Once upon a time in swinging London, around 1966, there was a serial killer who loved Elvis, a fab foursome that worshiped Satan, trendy vampires looking for kicks, an ancient and hungry evil, young and hungry love... and there was revolution in the air. Get your trip together, baby. Tune in, turn on and fang out. The book includes some strong language and violence (especially vampire killing).

Ridley, John

The **American** Way. Written by John Ridley; penciled by Georges Jeanty. DC Comics/Wildstorm 2007 192p. Illustration
Grades: 10 11 12 Adult   **741.5; Fic**
1. Science fiction graphic novels; 2. Superhero graphic novels; 3. Graphic novels
978-1-4012-1256-8, $19.99

The 1960s were a decade of incredible change for America. It was a time of innocence. It was a time of optimism. It was a time of heroes. In the early '40s, the United States government hatched a plan to create the Civil Defense Corps: a group of "super-heroes" who could fight alien invasions, evil super-powered beings and communism, all in front of an adoring public, courtesy of television. But that dream was far from reality by the 60s, as new C.D.C. Marketing Director Wesley Catham is about to discover. How far will America go to protect its dream of a better tomorrow? White racists use the n-word, plus there's violence, and other foul language.

The **Authority:** Human on the Inside. Written by John Ridley; art by Ben Oliver. DC Comics/Wildstorm 2004 Un Illustration
Grades: 9 10 11 12 Adult   **741.5; Fic**
1. Superhero graphic novels; 2. Graphic novels
1-4012-0069-9, $17.99

The Authority, Earth's last defense, have performed godlike acts in defense of the planet, whether defeating ancient gods or fending off interdimensional invasion forces. But these brave acts haven't always endeared them to many in power.... particularly in the United States. The President, tired of being embarrassed by what he views as a bunch of costumed freaks, sets a plan in motion that could very well destroy the Authority from the inside, a plan so cunning it'll shake the Authority to their very core. With an unexpected threat from the future on Earth's doorstep, it could very well mean global extinction. The book has some violence and strong language.

Rieber, John Ney

The **Books** of Magic Book 4: Transformations. John Ney Rieber, writer; Peter Gross, artist; Sherilyn van Valkenburgh, Nathan Eyring, colorists; Richard Starkings & Comicraft, letterer. DC Comics/Vertigo 1998 128p. Illustration
Grades: 10 11 12 Adult   **741.5; Fic**
1. Fantasy graphic novels; 2. Magic; 3. Timothy Hunter (Fictional character); 4. Graphic novels

1-56389-417-3; 978-1-56389-417-6, $12.95

LC 99-229773

The son of a manipulative sorceress and a mystical falconer, Tim Hunter is destined to become the most powerful mage in the world. But as the young Londoner comes to terms with his abilities and future, he must deal with demons and wizards looking to claim his power. In the fourth volume of this enrapturing series, Tim's magical adventures continue as he has a remarkable encounter with Death, transforms himself into a cat, faces off against an ancient enchantress and "celebrates" his fourteenth birthday. The book includes some strong language and partial nudity.

The **Books** of Magic Book 5: Girl in the Box. John Ney Rieber, writer; Peter Gross, Peter Snejbjerg, artists. DC Comics/Vertigo 1999 192p. Illustration
Grades: 10 11 12 Adult   **741.5; Fic**
1. Fantasy graphic novels; 2. Magic; 3. Timothy Hunter (Fictional character); 4. Graphic novels
1-56389-539-0, $14.95

LC 2001-265347

Possessing infinite magical powers, Tim Hunter will become the Earth's greatest sorcerer. But as the fourteen-year-old boy begins his ascension to powerful mage, he must navigate the everyday travails of adolescence. Looking to escape his personal troubles, Tim runs away to America only to find his problems multiplying. Allying himself with a shape-shifting succubus in the form of a female model, the young wizard learns lessons of treachery and friendship as he contends with a seductive mermaid who is lost in the desert and Cupid and Psyche, two disillusioned gods looking to adapt to modern ways. The book includes strong language, partial nudity, and violence.

The **Books** of Magic Book 6: The Burning Girl. John Ney Rieber, Peter Gross, writers; Peter Snejbjerg, Peter Gross, artists; Nathan Eyring, Sherilyn Van Valkenburgh, colorists; Richard Starkings & Comicraft/LA, letter. DC Comics/Vertigo 2000 224p. Illustration
Grades: 10 11 12 Adult   **741.5; Fic**
1. Fantasy graphic novels; 2. Magic; 3. Timothy Hunter (Fictional character); 4. Graphic novels
1-56389-619-2, $17.95

LC 00-708603

An adolescent boy with unimaginable power, Tim Hunter is destined to become the greatest magic wielder of all time. But after a mystical adventure traps the young wizard in the mythical land of Faerie, he finds himself caught up in the alternate realm's war with Hell. Now in order to save himself and the inhabitants of Faerie from an impending holocaust, the reactionary sorcerer must free his girlfriend from his jealous mother's curse while simultaneously warding off the legions of the underworld. The book includes some strong language and violence.

The **Books** of Magic Book 7: Death After Death. DC Comics/Vertigo 2001 224p. Illustration
Grades: 10 11 12 Adult   **741.5; Fic**
1. Fantasy graphic novels; 2. Magic; 3. Timothy Hunter (Fictional character); 4. Graphic novels
1-56389-740-7, $19.95

Since learning that he would become a wizard of infinite power, young Tim Hunter has been cursed with a life of loss and death. Tired of the misery that has become his adolescence, the fourteen year-old mage releases all of his magic unto the universe. But as a war between Heaven and Hell erupts over the newly released power, Tim learns that his impulsive action may lead to the end of all Creation. Now the completely powerless sorcerer must find a way to outmaneuver and manipulate an assortment of angels, demons, and deities in order to regain his magic or watch as all of existence ceases to be. The book includes violence, some strong language, and nudity.

G. I. Joe Reloaded Vol. 1: In the Name of Patriotism. Devil's Due Publishing 2004 Un Illustration
Grades: 7 8 9 10 11 12 Adult   **741.5; Fic**
1. Adventure graphic novels; 2. G I Joe (Fictional character); 3. Graphic novels
1-932796-23-1, $12.95

The Threat: Unknown. The Mission: Critical. The Team: G.I. Joe. United by the twisted strategic genius of a madman, a deadly cabal of conspirators unleashes a savage assault on the very heart of America. The nation is defenseless against these faceless paramilitary hordes whose dread insignia is a striking cobra... Until a rogue Lieutenant Colonel forges a handful of hard-hitting soldiers into the ultimate elite fighting force: G.I. Joe. The book includes fighting action.

Robinson, Alex

Box office poison. By Alex Robinson. Top Shelf Productions 2001 602 p. Illustration
Grades: Adult   **741.5**
1. Authors; 2. Brooklyn (New York, NY) — Fiction
1891830198; 9781891830198, $29.95

LC 2009277811

Eisner Nominee: Best Graphic Album - Reprint (2002)

This graphic novel, by Alex Robinson, "is preoccupied with character. . . . The main personages include Sherman, a wannabe writer stuck in a dead-end bookstore job, and his college pal Ed, a budding comic book artist still looking to get laid for the first time. There are also Jane and Stephen, Sherman's negligent Brooklyn housemates; Dorothy, Sherman's hard-drinking, chain-smoking . . . girlfriend; and Irving Flavor, a . . . veteran graphic novelist." (Publishers Weekly)

Our Expanding Universe. Alex Robinson. Top Shelf Productions 2015 256 p. Illustration
Grades: Adult   **741.5; 741.5973**
1. Family; 2. New York (State); 3. Teenagers
160309377X; 9781603093774, $19.99

This book, written by Alex Robinson, "returns with a ôspiritual sequelö to his Eisner-winning debut Box Office Poison! It's been 15 years since the young cast . . . has graced the stage. Now, [this book] introduces another Robinson ensemble to explore how time can transform a group of friends. Marriage, children, affairs, divorce and that's just the beginning!" (Publisher's note)

Too cool to be forgotten. Top Shelf Productions 2008 128p. Illustration
Grades: 11 12 Adult   **741.5; Fic**
1. Humorous graphic novels; 2. School stories; 3. Time travel; 4. Graphic novels
978-1-891830-98-3, $14.95

Andy Wicks is in his forties and a longtime smoker who has tried just about everything to quit smoking. Now he's going to try hypnosis, what's the worst thing that could happen? Well, when he wakes up, he finds himself back in high school, in 1985, as his high school sophomore self. Is he doomed to relive all his mistakes, or can he use his return as a second chance to get things right? Things like asking out that girl from math class. . . . Then he finds himself reliving time with his father, who died of Lou Gehrig's disease in 1985 after a sudden decline. Is this, after all, what he really needs to do? The book includes quite a bit of harsh language and lots of drinking and smoking at a party."

Tricked. Top Shelf Productions 2005 350p. Illustration
Grades: 11 12 Adult   **741.5; Fic**
  1. Mystery graphic novels; 2. Rock music; 3. Graphic novels
1-891830-73-2, $19.95
Ignatz Award: Outstanding Graphic Novel (2006)
  The story follows the lives of six people: a reclusive rock legend, a heartbroken waitress, a counterfeiter, an obsessive crank, a lost daughter, and a backstabbing lover, whose lives are unconnected until an act of violence brings them spiraling in on each other. The story includes nudity and strong language.

Robinson, Dave
  Introducing Ethics. Dave Robinson, Chris Garratt. Totem Books 2005 176p. Illustration
Grades: 10 11 12 Adult   **170; 741.5**
  1. Ethics; 2. Graphic novels
1-84046-580-8, $12.95
  What are the acceptable limits of scientific investigation and genetic engineering, the rights and wrongs of animal rights, euthanasia and civil disobedience? This book confronts these dilemmas, tracing arguments of moral thinkers, including Socrates, Plato, Aristotle, and brings us up to date with postmodern critics. Using cartoons and a spare text, this book provides an introductory look at ethics; it includes a list of books for further reading.

  Introducing Kierkegaard, Rev. ed.. Dave Robinson and Oscar Zarate. Totem Books 2007 176p. Illustration
Grades: 10 11 12 Adult   **142; 741.5**
  1. Existentialism; 2. Kierkegaard, Soren, 1813-1855; 3. Philosophy; 4. Graphic novels
978-1-84046-758-1, $12.95
  Soren Kierkegaard is regarded as the founder of Existentialism and the first modern theologian. Philosophy, in Kierkegaard's radical view, was of no use unless it permanently changed people's lives. His distrust of grand abstract schemes, particularly Hegel's, and his insistence that philosophy is essentially writing also identify him as a forerunner of postmodernism. This book uses cartoons and a spare text to introduce readers to the ideas and life of Kierkegaard; it includes a list of books for further reading.

  Introducing Philosophy. Dave Robinson, Judy Groves. Totem Books 2004 176p. Illustration
Grades: 10 11 12 Adult   **100; 741.5**
  1. Philosophy; 2. Graphic novels
1-84046-576-X, $12.95

This volume uses cartoons and a spare text to provide an introductory guide to the thinking of all the significant philosophers of the Western world, from Heraclitus to Derrida. It examines and explains their key arguments and ideas. The book includes a list of books for further reading.

Robinson, James
  Batman: Face the Face. DC Comics 2006 192p. Illustration
Grades: 10 11 12 Adult   **741.5; Fic**
  1. Batman (Fictional character); 2. Mystery graphic novels; 3. Robin (Fictional character); 4. Superhero graphic novels; 5. Graphic novels
978-1-4012-0910-0, $14.99
  One year ago, Batman and Robin disappeared from Gotham City. Before his departure, Batman chose a guardian to protect Gotham's citizens from the city's usual predators. Now, the Dynamic Duo return to find that some of their most notorious foes are being brutally murdered, leaving Batman to wonder if the man he entrusted to carry on in his place has confused justice with vengeance. With James Gordon back as Commissioner and Harvey Bullock back on the Gotham police force, it's almost like old times. But Bruce Wayne also has a decision to make about Tim Drake. The book includes some graphic violence.

Robinson, James Dale
  ★ The **Shade**. James Robinson, Cully Hamner, Frazer Irving, Javier Pulido, Gene Ha, Darwyn Cooke, Jill Thompson. DC Comics 2013 280 p.
Grades: Adult   **741.5; 741.5/973**
  1. Adventure graphic novels; 2. Heroes and heroines — Fiction
1401237827; 9781401237820, $19.99
                                        LC 2012046875
  In this graphic novel, author James Robinson "returns to the world of his acclaimed Starman series in this new graphic novel starring the antihero known as The Shade! An attack at the Starman museum kicks off a globe-hopping, centuries spanning quest that will irrevocably change The Shade's life, and ultimately shed light on his true origin!" (Publisher's note)
  Originally published in single magazine form in The Shade 1-12.

Robinson, Jerry
  The **comics:** an illustrated history of comic strip art 1895-2010. Jerry Robinson; illustrated by Walt Kelly. Dark Horse Comics 2011 394 p.
Grades: Adult   **741.5**
  1. Comic books, strips, etc — History and criticism; 2. Drawing
1595826572; 9781595826572, $39.99
  This book by Jerry Robinson is a "reworked and updated edition of the 1974 classic that chronicles the origins and evolution of comic strips, from prior to The Yellow Kid through today, and highlights the game-changing contributions of such creative luminaries as Milton Caniff, Walt Kelly, Hal Foster, and Winsor McCay, among countless others." (Publisher's note)

Rogers, John
 Blue Beetle: Shellshocked. Writers, Keith Giffen & John Rogers; Cully Hamner . . . [et al], pencillers; Phil Balsman, Pat Brosseau, letterers; David Self, Guy Major, colorists; Cully Hamner, Phil Moy, Duncan Rouleau, Jack Purcell, inkers. DC Comics 2006 144p. Illustration
Grades: 8 9 10 11 12 Adult   **741.5; Fic**
 1. Adventure graphic novels; 2. Blue Beetle (Fictional character); 3. Superhero graphic novels; 4. Graphic novels
978-1-4012-0965-0, $12.99
 Ted Kord, the Blue Beetle, is dead; but the Blue Beetle scarab has chosen a new guardian, El Paso teenager Jaime Reyes. Supernatural powers can be a blessing or a curse, and when it comes to the powers of the Scarab, you don't get one without the other. The new hero will now have to deal with increasingly strange and dangerous days ahead, as he learns to handle his new skills while intergalactic trouble comes looking for him.

Romance Without Tears
 Edited by John Benson. Fantagraphics Books 2004 160p. Illustration
Grades: 8 9 10 11 12 Adult   **741.5; Fic**
 1. Romance graphic novels; 2. Graphic novels
1-56097-558-X, $22.95
 This revisionist collection of romance comics stories from the '50s challenges the clich? of the "tear-stained face" that later dominated the genre and became widely known and vilified as a tiresome icon of moral uplift. Editor Benson has picked stories that portray stron young women who learn from their mistakes and choose their guys, and get themselves out of trouble. The stories were all originally published by Archer St. John in the late-1940s to mid-1950s.

Root, Tom
 Writers on Comics Scriptwriting 2. Titan Books 2004 248p. Illustration
Grades: Adult Professional   **741.5**
 1. Batman (Fictional character); 2. Catwoman (Fictional character); 3. Flash (Fictional character); 4. Graphic novels — History and criticism; 5. Green Arrow (Fictional character); 6. Hellboy (Fictional character); 7. Hulk (Fictional character); 8. Spider-Man (Fictional character); 9. Superman (Fictional character); 10. X-Men (Fictional characters); 11. Graphic novels
1-84023-808-9, $16.95
 This book offers insider insight into every aspect of the creative process behind comics writing. With contributions from those responsible for some of the biggest-selling comics titles on shelves, this is packed with behind-the-scenes info and never-before-revealed anecdotes and stories. It features interviews with: Brian Azzarello (100 Bullets), Brian Michael Bendis (Ultimate Spider-Man), Ed Brubaker (Batman, Catwoman, Gotham Central), Mike Carey (Lucifer, Hellblazer), Andy Diggle (Losers, Swamp Thing), Paul Dini (Batman), Geoff Johns (Flash, JSA), Bruce Jones (Hulk), Mike Mignola (Hellboy), Mark Millar (Ultimate X-Men, Superman: Red Son), Peter Milligan (X-Men), Greg Rucka (Gotham Central), Dave Sim (Cerebus), Kevin Smith (Green Arrow and the director of Clerks and Jersey Girl), Craig Thompson (Blankets), Jill Thompson (Death: At Death's Door), Brian K. Vaughan (Y:

The Last Man, Pride of Baghdad), and Bill Willingham (Fables).

Rosa, Don
 Walt Disney's Uncle $crooge and Donald Duck: the Son of the sun. [written and drawn by Don Rosa; lettered by John Clark]. Fantagraphics Books 2014 207 p. Color; Illustration
Grades: 7 8 9 10 11 12 Adult   **741.5**
 1. Ducks — Fiction; 2. Fictional characters
1606997424; 9781606997420, $29.99
                                        LC 2012287668
 This collection by Don Rosa, featuring Disney's Donald Duck and Scrooge McDuck, is "filled with epic adventures, like hunting for buried treasure or recovering stolen money. . . . At the end of each volume are whole pages of reference notes, explaining each comic in depth and addressing Rosa's process and nods to previous works." (School Library Journal)
 "When Rosa began creating Uncle Scrooge comics in 1987, his work instilled childish wonder in readers. Disney comics had entirely disappeared from circulation, and those that had just preceded the fall had become completely hackneyedùrife with repeating storylines and drab artwork. But under Rosa's creative flair, a zippy, glamorous franchise suddenly appeared, with riveting stories and detailed yet kinetic artwork. While remaining totally true to Scrooge McDuck's ornery persona, Rosa turned the moody miser into a plucky adventurer worthy of Tintin." Pub Wkly
 Other titles in this series are: Return to plain awful (2014); Treasure under glass (2015)

Rosenkranz, Patrick
 ★ **Rebel** visions: the underground comix revolution, 1963-1975. Fantagraphics Books 2008 292p. Illustration
Grades: 11 12 Adult   **741.5**
 1. Cartoonists; 2. Comic books, strips, etc — History and criticism; 3. Graphic novels
978-1-56097-706-3, $34.99
 "The most lasting artistic legacy of the 1960s hippie movement, other than its music, is its eye-poppingly transgressive underground comics—black-and-white pamphlets that spread the counterculture message of sex, drugs, and rebellion to freak and straight alike. Rosencranz thoroughly documents the phenomenon, providing a year-by-year account of the underground scene, from 1968's Zap #1, which artist R. Crumb sold from a baby carriage on the streets of Haight Ashbury, to its crash in 1973 in the wake of obscenity rulings and a crackdown on head shops. . . . Rosencranz's writing may lack flair, but with personalities this colorful (the artists themselves provide fly-on-the-wall reminiscences) and art this outrageous (reprinted on nearly every page) to write about, who needs it?" Booklist

Ross, Steve
 Marked. Seabury Books 2005 Un Illustration
Grades: 9 10 11 12 Adult   **741.5; 225**
 1. Bible NT Mark — Adaptations; 2. Graphic novels
1-59627-002-0, $20
 An occupied country. A people infested with demons. A time of revolution. A liberator rises. One of the oldest stories in human history comes alive in this telling of the Gospel of

Mark. Join a carpenter as he changes the world. This is a human story of passion and murder. Of a compassionate man brutally killed and yet alive. Ross has set the story in a futuristic, urban world.

Rouleau, Duncan
  Metal Men. DC Comics 2008 Un Illustration
Grades: 9 10 11 12 Adult   **741.5; Fic**
  1. Robots; 2. Superhero graphic novels; 3. Graphic novels
  978-1-40112-1845-4, $24.99
  The Metal Men series was part of the Silver Age of comics. Now, they're back with a new origin story. Doc Will Magnus created androids from elements: Gold, Platinum, Mercury, Lead, Iron, Tin, and Copper; he used devices he calls responsometers to power them. However, the responsometers are also ancient weapons that that control the very fabric of the world, and things from the past hunt the "thief" who stole their weapons. Magnus and the Metal Men must also deal with his ex-mentor, T. O. Morrow, the toxic creature called Chemo, and Magnus' own brother. The book includes fighting, most of it machine against machine.

  The **Nightmarist.** Active Images 2006 Un Illustration
Grades: 11 12 Adult   **741.5; Fic**
  1. Horror graphic novels; 2. Graphic novels
  1-9766761-8-4, $14.99
  When an entity calling himself the Nightmarist appears in Beth Sorenson's dreams, claiming to protect her from forces plotting to twist her will, Beth's reality begins to crack. With horrors closing in around her, while awake and asleep, Beth must decide—has she gone crazy? Have her dreams become ground zero in a battle for the future of mankind? Can she trust The Nightmarist? Her choices may cost more than her soul. The book includes violence and some strong language.

Rowson, Martin
  Gulliver's travels. Adapted & updated by Martin Rowson. Atlantic 2012 128 p.
Grades: Adult   **Fic; 741.5**
  1. Gulliver, Lemuel (Fictitious character) — Fiction; 2. Literature — Adaptations; 3. Voyages and travels — Fiction; 4. Graphic novels
  1782390081; 9781782390084, $19.95; 9781848872820
                    LC 2012397583
  This graphic novel, by Martin Rowson, is an adaptation of Jonathan Swift's original story. "After a series of incidents, including being involved in a car crash and being dropped from a helicopter, a man named Gulliver finds himself washed ashore in a land full of tiny people called Lilliputians. This is not the Gulliver of old however; this is his descendant, and he's about to discover an unnerving world." (Publisher's Weekly)
  "Rowson revisits Jonathan Swift's classic caustic exploration of human nature in this visceral, contemporary graphic-novel sequel. . . . A filthy, fantastic and fitting continuation of a misanthropic classic." Kirkus

Rubio, Kevin
  Star Wars: Tag & Bink Were Here. Pencils by Lucas Marangon. Dark Horse Comics 2006 Un Illustration
Grades: 7 8 9 10 11 12 Adult   **741.5; Fic**

  1. Adventure graphic novels; 2. Humorous graphic novels; 3. Science fiction graphic novels; 4. Star Wars; 5. Graphic novels
  978-1-59307-641-2, $14.95
  Rebel officers Tag Greenley and Bink Otauna were minding their own business aboard a familiar, princess-harboring freighter when they suddenly found themselves under siege. Now under attack by the Empire, they will choose life over a noble death and "borrow" the armor off a pair of deceased stormtroopers. Their new disguises might get them off the freighter alive, but they'll also lead Tag and Bink on an adventure neither could have predicted. Chock-full of appearances by everyone's favorite Star Wars characters, Tag & Bink weaves the pair's misadventures into the movies themselves. No setting is safe as they traverse the galaxy from the Death Star to the Sarlacc pit to Cloud City to Endor.

Rucka, Greg
  Batwoman: elegy. Greg Rucka, writer; J.H. Williams III, artist; Dave Stewart, colorist; Todd Klein, letters.. DC Comics 2010 1 v. Color illustration
Grades: 11 12 Adult   **741.5**
  1. Batwoman (Fictional character); 2. Mentally ill — Fiction; 3. Superheroes — Fiction; 4. Graphic novels
  9781401226923, $24.99; 1401226922
                    LC 2010283560
  In this graphic novel, "Batwoman battles a madwoman known only as Alice, inspired by Alice in Wonderland, who sees her life as a fairy tale and everyone around her as expendable! Batwoman must stop Alice from unleashing a toxic death cloud over all of Gotham City—but Alice has more up her sleeve than just poison, and Batwoman's life will never ever be the same." (Publisher's note)
  "[A] nuanced, literary, and culturally charged story, but the real knockout element is Williams' art nouveau inspired compositions." Booklist

  Checkmate: A King's Game. Greg Rucka, Jesus Saiz, Cliff Richards. DC Comics 2007 166p. Illustration
Grades: 10 11 12 Adult   **Fic; 741.5**
  1. Green Lantern (Fictional character); 2. International security; 3. Superhero graphic novels; 4. Graphic novels
  978-1-4012-1220-9, $14.99
  After the events of Identity Crisis, Checkmate is re-chartered by the U.N. to deal with metahuman threats. It's a joint partnership between human and metahuman leaders, and they have titles based on chess. The White King is Alan Scott, the original Green Lantern, the White Queen is Doctor Amanda Waller, who used to work for Lex Luthor; the Black Queen in Sasha Bordeaux, a former super villain, and the Black King is Israeli Col. Taleb Beni Khalid. Checkmate is not immune to politics; the organization already faces dissolution that the leaders can stop only if they can learn which nation wants to dissolve Checkmate, even as they battle against terrorists Kobra and the Kali Yuga. Filled with action, politics, internal conflicts, and sexual tensions, this is a continuing comics series.
  Originally published as Checkmate issues #1-7.

  Lazarus; Book One. By Greg Rucka, illustrated by Michael Lark and Santiago Arcas. Image Comics 2013 96 p. Color; Illustration

Grades: Adult **741.5**
1. Dystopian fiction
1607068095; 9781607068099, $9.99

Written by Greg Rucka, illustrated by Santiago Arcas and Michael Lark, this comic book features "the first four issues of the Eisner-winning team of Rucka and Lark's critically acclaimed new series about Forever Carlyle, the Lazarus of the Carlyle Family. Included is the previously only-available-online, four-page short, 'Family: Prelude.' In a dystopian near-future, government is a quaint concept, resources are coveted, and possession is 100% of the law." (Publisher's note)

"Rucka crafts the story of a world shattered into fiefdoms and controlled by high-tech Mob families. Each family has their very own "Lazarus," a cybernetic warrior pledged to carry out the family's dirty work on their path to control their population. . . . Lark's sharp yet brooding art manages to be violent without becoming gratuitous, pulling back for the sake of tension and the movement of the story." Booklist

Originally published in single magazine format as Lazarus #1-4.
Volume 1 of an ongoing series

The **OMAC** Project: Countdown to Infinite Crisis. Art by Jesus Saiz and Cliff Richards. DC Comics 2005 Un Illustration
Grades: 9 10 11 12 Adult **Fic; 741.5**
1. Superhero graphic novels; 2. Superman (Fictional character); 3. Wonder Woman (Fictional character); 4. Graphic novels
1-4012-0837-1, $14.99

Originally designed by Batman, the Brother I satellite has been usurped by the government's Checkmate spy division, and Checkmate in its turn has been usurped by the insane Maxwell Lord, who reprograms the satellite and other technology to serve his twisted goals. Blue Beetle stumbled on the secret first, and paid for that knowledge with his life. Earth's super-heroes have to contend with OMACs, normal humans who can be turned into armored warriors with a single command. Now, Lord has taken possession of Superman's mind, forcing Wonder Woman to take action, an action that will forever change her relationship with her colleagues.

Queen & country: the definitive edition, volume 1. By Greg Rucka. Oni Press 2008 376 p. Illustration (Queen & country)
Grades: Adult **741.5**
1. Espionage; 2. Spy stories
1932664874; 9781932664874, $19.99
Eisner Award: Best New Series (2002)

In this graphic novel, by Greg Rucka, "readers are introduced to the . . . world of international espionage as SIS field agent Tara Chase is sent all over the world in service to her Queen & Country all the while Director of Operations Paul Crocker walks a narrow tightrope between his loyalty to his people and the political masters that must be served!" (Publisher's note)

"[T]he work offers the sense that espionage is just another job, exactly as grinding and tedious as any other

except that interoffice politics can get people killed. The action sequences are fast-paced and exciting." Pub Wkly
This collects issues 1-12 of the Oni Press comics series Queen & country as well as material from the Oni Press color special 2001—t.p. verso.

Queen & Country: the definitive edition, volume 4. By Greg Rucka; illustrated by Anthony Johnston, Brian Hurtt, Scott Morse, Rick Burchett, and Christopher J. Mitten. Oni Press 2009 320 p.
Grades: Adult **741.5**
1. Espionage; 2. Spy stories
1934964131; 9781934964132, $19.95

In this graphic novel by Greg Rucka, illustrated by Anthony Johnston, Brian Hurtt, Scott Morse, Rick Burchett, and Christopher J. Mitten, "readers are sucked into the . . . world of international espionage as SIS field agents are sent all over the world, often on their first mission, in service to Queen & Country." (Publisher's note)
This collects volumes 1-3 of the Oni Press comics series Queen & country : Declassified—t.p. verso.

Queen & country; Volume 02: the definitive edition, volume 2. By Greg Rucka; illustrated by Jason Alexander, Carla Speed McNeil, and Mike Hawthorne. Oni Press 2008 330 p. Illustration (Queen & country)
Grades: Adult **741.5**
1. Espionage; 2. Spy stories
9781932664898, $19.99; 1932664890
LC 2014378787

In this graphic novel by Greg Rucka, illustrated by Jason Alexander, Carla Speed McNeil, and Mike Hawthorne, "SIS field agent Tara Chase is put through the ringer as she must contend with espionage of the industrial kind, ghosts from her director's past, and politicians eager to use the service to their own ends!" (Publisher's note)
This collects issues 13-24 of the Oni Press comics series Queen & country—t.p. verso.

Queen & country; Volume 03: the definitive edition, volume 3. By Greg Rucka; illustrated by Mike Norton, Steve Rolston, and Chris Samnee. Oni Press 2008 395 p. Illustration (Queen & country)
Grades: Adult **741.5**
1. Espionage; 2. Spy stories
1932664963; 9781932664966, $19.99
LC 2014378005

In this graphic novel by Greg Rucka, illustrated by Mike Norton, Steve Rolston, and Chris Samnee, "readers are sucked into the . . . world of international espionage as SIS field agent Tara Chase is sent all over the world in service to her Queen & Country all the while Director of Operations Paul Crocker walks a narrow tightrope between his loyalty to his people and the political masters that must be served!" (Publisher's note)
This collects issues 25-32 of the Oni Press comics series Queen & country—t.p. verso.

Superman: Unconventional Warfare. Writer, Greg Rucka; pencillers, Matthew Clark, Renado Guedes, Paul Pelletier. DC Comics 2005 160p. Illustration
Grades: 9 10 11 12 Adult **741.5; Fic**
1. Superhero graphic novels; 2. Superman (Fictional character); 3. Graphic novels

1-4012-0449-X, $14.95

Superman has been away for a time, but now he's back in Metropolis and is putting his life in order. As Clark Kent, he finds himself assigned to ride along with the Metropolis Special Crimes Unit and is glad he did. A souped-up Replikon comes calling, the harbinger of a new, deadly threat to not only the Man of Steel but also all of Metropolis. Meanwhile, Lois Lane is an embedded reporter in Umec and her experiences are no less dangerous. Away from familiar turf, distanced from the man she loves, Lois witnesses a different kind of courage. The book includes some violence.

Whiteout Volume 1: The Definitive Edition. Written by Greg Rucka; illustrated & lettered by Steve Lieber. Oni Press 2007 128p. Illustration
Grades: 11 12 Adult   **741.5; Fic**
1. Mystery graphic novels; 2. Graphic novels
978-1-932664-70-6, $13.95

One of Oni Press' earliest and most acclaimed books returns in a brand new re-mastered and re-formatted edition. U.S. Marshal Carrie Stetko has made Antarctica her home. In the vastness of The Ice, she found peace ... Or at least that's what she thought, until someone commits a murder in her jurisdiction and the lawwoman is forced to use her detective skills once more or become another victim to this mysterious killer. The book includes violence and harsh language, including copious use of the f-bomb.

Whiteout Volume 2: Melt, The Definitive Edition. Written by Greg Rucka; illustrated & lettered by Steve Lieber. Oni Press 2007 120p. Illustration
Grades: 11 12 Adult   **741.5; Fic**
1. Mystery graphic novels; 2. Graphic novels
978-1-932664-71-3, $13.95
2000 Eisner Award for Best Finite Series/Limited Series.

One of Oni Press' earliest and most acclaimed books returns in a brand new re-mastered and re-formatted edition. U.S. Marshal Carrie Stetko investigates the explosion that destroyed a Russian science station that may have been a cache for weapons. The book includes violence, copious harsh language, nudity and sexual situations.

Wonder Woman: Eyes of the Gorgon. Greg Rucka, writer; Drew Johnson, James Raiz, Sean Phillips, pencillers; Ray Snyder, Sean Phillips, inkers; Richard & Tanya Horie, colorists; Todd Klein, letterer. DC Comics 2005 Un Illustration
Grades: 9 10 11 12 Adult   **741.5; Fic**
1. Justice League (Fictional characters); 2. Superhero graphic novels; 3. Wonder Woman (Fictional character); 4. Graphic novels
1-4012-0797-9, $19.99

As Diana tries to avert war at the White House, the deadly Medousa comes calling, and Wonder Woman's world is turned completely upside-down as she must face the Gorgon in a final confrontation that has tragic consequences for Diana and her loved ones. She must also prove herself once again to her comrades in the Justice League of America, and to the world. The book has superhero fighting action.

Wonder Woman: Land of the Dead. Greg Rucka, Geoff Johns, writers; Drew Johnson et al, pencillers. DC Comics 2006 128p. Illustration
Grades: 9 10 11 12 Adult   **Fic; 741.5**
1. Flash (Fictional character); 2. Superhero graphic novels; 3. Wonder Woman (Fictional character); 4. Graphic novels
1-4012-0938-6, $12.99

Just as Wonder Woman is starting to deal with her blindness (self-inflicted, in order to defeat Medusa), the Cheetah returns and teams up with another villain known for speed: The Reverse Flash. Wally West, the real Flash, joins forces with Wonder Woman to stop the villainous duo from causing untold havoc. Then, the goddess Athena sends Wonder Woman on a journey to retrieve Hermes from the Underworld. Joined by Wonder Girl and Ferdinand the Minotaur, Wonder Woman must face unimagined peril to complete her mission. But should she succeed, what will Diana ask in return from the all-seeing Goddess of Wisdom?

Wonder Woman: Mission's End. DC Comics 2006 Un Illustration
Grades: 10 11 12 Adult   **741.5; Fic**
1. Superhero graphic novels; 2. Superman (Fictional character); 3. Wonder Woman (Fictional character); 4. Graphic novels
978-1-4012-1093-9, $19.99

Wonder Woman had only recently regained her sight, when she was forced into battling against Superman, whose mind was being controlled by Max Lord. She could only stop Lord by crossing the line and doing something no superhero had done before, and her action forever changes her relationship with Superman, and the whole world. Then Infinite Crisis hits, and a swarm of OMAC robots descends upon her island home and she must fight even more.

Rudahl, Sharon

A **dangerous** woman: the graphic biography of Emma Goldman. The New Press 2007 115p. Illustration
Grades: 10 11 12 Adult   **335; 92; 741.5**
1. Anarchism and anarchists; 2. Anarchists; 3. Biographical graphic novels; 4. Essayists; 5. Family planning advocates; 6. Goldman, Emma, 1869-1940; 7. Memoirists; 8. Writers on politics; 9. Graphic novels
978-1-59558-064-1, $17.95

LC 2007-15415

Emma Goldman was a revolutionary activist, speaker, writer, and feminist and anarchist. An immigrant to the U.S., she spoke out against inhumane working conditions, taught contraception, and opposed conscription for World War I. She founded the Free Speech League (a precursor to the ACLU), and the magazine Mother Earth. When she was deported to Russia just after the Bolshevik Revolution, she became disillusioned with the authoritarianism she found there, and she ended up supporting the fight against fascism in the Spanish Civil War. Rudahl based her graphic novel on Goldman's autobiography. The book includes nudity, sexual situations, and some violence.

Rugg, Jim
   Street Angel. SLG Publishing 2005 208p. Illustration
Grades: 10 11 12 Adult   **741.5; Fic**
   1. Adventure graphic novels; 2. Homeless persons; 3.
   Graphic novels
   1-59362-012-8, $14.95
   Homeless, orphaned, rarely in school, twelve-year-old
skateboarder Jesse "Street Angel" Sanchez uses her board
skills and kung fu to fight crime on the streets of
Wilkesborough, the worst ghetto in Angel City. She has to
fight Dr. Pangaea and his ninja forces, deal with
time-warping pirates and Inca warriors, go dumpster-diving
to find food . . . Jesse does a lot of slicing and dicing with her
handy sword and knows how to handle automatic weapons
as well in the many graphically depicted fight scenes.
   Originally published as Street Angel issues #1-5.

Runton, Andy
   ★ **Owly** Vol. 2: Just a Little Blue. Top Shelf
Productions 2005 127p. Illustration
Grades: K 1 2 3 4 5 6 7 8 9 10 11 12 Adult   **741.5; Fic**
   1. Friendship; 2. Stories without words; 3. Graphic novels
   1-891830-64-3, $10
   Owly is a kind, yet lonely, little owl who's always on the
search for new friends and adventure. Owly learns that
sometimes you have to make sacrifices and work at things
that are important, especially friendship. He and Wormy try
to help a stubborn bluebird by building a new home, but the
bluebird rejects it and them.

   ★ **Owly** Vol. 3: Flying Lessons. Top Shelf Productions
2005 143p. Illustration
Grades: K 1 2 3 4 5 6 7 8 9 10 11 12 Adult   **741.5; Fic**
   1. Friendship; 2. Stories without words; 3. Graphic novels
   1-891830-76-7, $10
   Owly figures out why he can't fly (he failed his
childhood flying lessons), and helps another forest creature
with his own flying problems. The flying squirrel is
frightened by Owly, for he knows owls are hunters, but Owly
isn't like that. How can he convince the squirrel he just
wants to be friends?

   ★ **Owly** vol. 4: a time to be brave. Top Shelf
Productions 2007 132p. Illustration
Grades: K 1 2 3 4 5 6 7 8 9 10 11 12 Adult   **741.5; Fic**
   1. Fantasy graphic novels; 2. Friendship; 3. Owls; 4.
   Stories without words; 5. Graphic novels
   978-1-891830-89-1, $10
   A new visitor comes to the forest, but Wormy is scared
of him because Owly had just read stories about a scary
dragon, and the visitor seems to look scary. The visitor is just
as scared of Owly. Things aren't just as they seem, and
everyone soon finds out that a little bravery and a lot of
friendship can fix just about anything. This is the latest
volume in Runton's nearly wordless series about Owly and
his friends.

   ★ **Owly** volume five: tiny tales. Top Shelf Productions
2008 175p. Illustration
Grades: K 1 2 3 4 5 6 7 8 9 10 11 12 Adult   **741.5; Fic**
   1. Friendship; 2. Humorous graphic novels; 3. Graphic
   novels
   978-1-60309-019-3, $10

   This volume gathers short stories about Owly and his
friends, including stories originally published for Free
Comic Book Day issues from Top Shelf Productions, the
first Owly mini-comics, drawings of Owly before he met
Wormy, and more. Among the stories, Owly saves a friend
from drowning in the cold river when the ice cracks, only to
get caught in the hole himself; Owly finds a way to keep both
the bees and hummingbirds happy when they get into a
"turf" battle; Owly helps a friend when she falls and breaks
the fancy potted plant she bought for a present; and more.

Rushkoff, Douglas
   Testament: West of Eden. Writer, Douglas Rushkoff;
artist, Liam Sharp; Jim Devlin, colorist; Todd Klein, letterer.
DC Comics/Vertigo 2007 128p. Illustration
Grades: 11 12 Adult   **741.5; Fic**
   1. Fantasy graphic novels; 2. Graphic novels
   978-1-4012-1201-8, $12.99
   Rushkoff continues to retell stories from the Bible his
way in this second volume. Alan Stern creates a new kind of
life inside his laptop computer, but he and his wife Greta
discover that playing in the realm of the gods has
catastrophic consequences. Then their son Jake lives as a
fugitive from the police-state. His former classmate Alec
works to speed billionaire Pierre Fallow's push for a single,
global currency based solely on artificial intelligence. The
only way to stop them is for Jake to defy the gods and take
the story to places the Bible would never have dared to go.
The nudity, sexual situations, and language make this a book
for mature readers. It will also offend anyone who is a
devout Christian.

Russell, P. Craig
   The **P.** Craig Russell Library of Opera Adaptations;
Volume 1: The Magic Flute. Adaptation of Wolfgang
Amadeus Mozart, by P. Craig Russell. NBM 2003 138 p.
Color; Illustration
Grades: Adult   **741.5**
   1.   Opera;   2.   Mozart,   Wolfgang   Amadeus,
   1756-1791—Adaptations
   156163350X; 9781561633500, $24.95
                                LC 2003041218
   This book is an adaptation of Wolfgang Amadeus
Mozart's "The Magic Flute," by P. Craig Russell. "The story
begins as the Queen of the Night sets Prince Tamino on a
quest to rescue her daughter, Pamina from the evil Sarastro.
On the way, he meets the bird-catcher Papageno, who is
'persuaded' to help Tamino in his quest. Tamino's spiritual
quest is counterpoised with Papageno's own earthly search
for his one true love, Papagena." (Publisher's note)
   "Sure and confident, Russell's art switches from tense
action sequences to slapstick without missing a beat. His
sense of physical characterization is also impressive, helping
readers keep track of Mozart's often confusing cast of
characters. . . . Much of this graphic novel is told without
narration or dialogue (presumably to simulate the longer
musical passages Mozart included in the opera), and
Russell's selection of sequential images keeps the story
moving along without ever losing readers." Pub Wkly
   Other titles in this series are: Volume 2: Adaptations of
Paprsifal, Ariane and Bluebeard, I Pagliacci; Volume 3:

Adaptions of Pelleas & Melisande, Salome, Ein Heldentraum, Cavalleria Rusticana

Ruth, Greg
   Sudden Gravity (A Tale of the Panopticon). Dark Horse Comics 2006 168p. Illustration
Grades: 11 12 Adult   741.5; Fic
   1. Horror graphic novels; 2. Mystery graphic novels; 3. Graphic novels
   978-1-59307-565-1, $10.95
   Built on a site of great and forgotten power, the mammoth Bentham International Hospital was to be the very definition of modern medical science at its best. But over the years, the spectres and dark secrets of the Hospital began to bore away at its heart, leaving its foundations cracked and vulnerable to the oldest of horrors and nightmares. When a prominent Commissioner of the City's Housing and Urban Development Department is brought to the Panopticon for evaluation after murdering her family, the haunted secrets of the hospital begin to unravel, leaving no one untouched. Julius, the prosthetic boy in room 13 is waking up. The black eggs are found. The lines between the patients and the doctors are blurring. This is where the end begins. Every cure is paid with a curse and every sin is birthed anew as the once brilliant light of modern medicine forsakes the world for the shadows it can no longer hide. The book includes strong language, some violence, and disturbing scenes.

Ryall, Chris
   Beowulf. Based on the screenplay by Neil Gaiman & Roger Avery; written by Chris Ryall; art and cover by Gabriel Rodriguez. IDW Publishing 2007 104p. Illustration
Grades: 10 11 12 Adult   741.5; Fic
   1. Beowulf — Adaptations; 2. Fantasy graphic novels; 3. Graphic novels
   978-1-60010-128-1, $17.99
   This graphic novel adaptation of the motion picture screenplay written by Neil Gaiman and Roger Avary takes liberties with the original epic. In this version, the warrior Beowulf slays the monster Grendel who has slain many of King Hrothgar's warriors, but is seduced by Grendel's demon mother. This story states that Grendel is Hrothgar's son. It basically turns the epic saga upside down, showing that the heroes bring about the monsters. The book includes harsh language, nudity, and graphic violence.

Saavedra, Scott
   Dr. Radium Battles Phill, King of the Pill Bugs!. Amaze Ink/SLG Publishing 2004 112p. Illustration
Grades: 7 8 9 10 11 12 Adult   741.5; Fic
   1. Humorous graphic novels; 2. Science fiction graphic novels; 3. Graphic novels
   0-943151-84-8, $9.95
   Before "Dexter's Laboratory" and before "Jimmy Neutron," there was Dr. Radium, the last scientist left standing in the "perfect" world of tomorrow. Ignored by society and feared by his assistant, Dr. Radium pursues Science with happy disregard for knowledge, progress, or safety. Stuck with Penny, a girl from the present presently trapped in the future, Dr. Radium suffers distractions from giant scientist rats, screaming dinosaurs, and Phill, one very mad King of the Pill Bugs.

Sabin, Roger
   Comics, Comix & Graphic Novels: A History of Comic Art. Phaidon Press 1996 240p. Illustration
Grades: Adult Professional   741.5
   1. Comic books, strips, etc — History and criticism; 2. Graphic novels — History and criticism; 3. Hulk (Fictional character); 4. Superman (Fictional character); 5. Tintin (Fictional character); 6. Graphic novels
   0-7148-3993-0 (pa); 0-7148-3008-9, $59.95
   This fully documented study explores the graphic qualities of the comic book, and the development of the format into a sophisticated and culturally revealing popular art form. The book traces the history of the comic from early cartoon-like woodcuts through to the graphic strips of the nineteenth and twentieth centuries. Organized thematically it explores the various genres of the comic book, including humor, adventure, girls' comics, underground and alternative. The careers of the creators of the best-known characters - from Superman and Tintin to Tank Girl - are revealed, as are the stories behind the much-loved comics such as The Beano (a well-known British comic) and The Incredible Hulk.

Sable, Mark
   Grounded, Vol. 1: Powerless. Writer/creator, Mark Sable; artist, Paul Azaceta. Image Comics 2006 160p. Illustration
Grades: 10 11 12 Adult   741.5; Fic
   1. High school students; 2. School stories; 3. Superhero graphic novels; 4. Graphic novels
   978-1-58240-641-1, $14.99
   Ever since he was a little boy, Jonathan just knew that superheroes are real, and that he would eventually come into his power. Now he's in high school, and he has just discovered that he was right all along superheroes are real. In fact, his parents are two of the most famous heroes in the world. Disillusionment sets in when he catches his father in bed with another woman. He also has to face the fact that he has no powers at all, which doesn't help when his parents put him into a school for the children of heroes; he's the only one who doesn't have any. Even as he deals with bullying and nasty pranks, he learns that there's a dark side to the powers.
   Originally published as a comics miniseries

Sacco, Joe
   The **fixer:** a story from Sarajevo. Joe Sacco. Drawn and Quarterly 2003 105p. Illustration
Grades: 9 10 11 12 Adult   741; 741.5
   9781896597607, $24.95
   "Joe Sacco goes behind the scene of war correspondence to reveal the anatomy of the big scoop. He begins by returning us to the dying days of Balkan conflict and introduces us to his own fixer; a man looking to squeeze the last bit of profit from Bosnia before the reconstruction begins. Thanks to a complex relationship with the fixer Joe discovers the crimes of opportunistic warlords and gangsters who run the countryside in times of war. But the west is interested in a different spin on the stories coming out of Bosnia. Almost ten years later, Joe meets up with his fixer and sees how the new Bosnian government has 'dealt' with

these criminals and Joe ponders who is holding the reins of power these days." (Publisher's note)

Footnotes in Gaza. Metropolitan Books 2009 418p. Illustration
Grades: Adult   **956.04**
978-0-8050-7347-8; 0-8050-7347-7, $29.95
LC 2009-28433
1. Journalism
"Cartoonist and journalist Joe Sacco is the world's foremost creator of 'comics journalism'—a contemporary field he basically invented. . . . [This] book, whose 'footnotes' refer both to facts and metaphorically to history's forgotten people, is about two massacres of Palestinians in the Gaza Strip in November 1956. . . . Very little has been written about either event. Sacco conducted extensive research of U.N. documents and other materials, and additionally set out to interview as many eyewitnesses as he could track down. This is really the heart of this moving, precisely drawn work." Time Out N Y

Journalism. Joe Sacco. Metropolitan Books / Henry Holt and Co. 2012 Xiv, 191 p. Illustration; Color
Grades: Adult   **355.0209**
1. Journalism; 2. Military history; 3. Military history, Modern — 20th century; 4. Military history, Modern — 21st century; 5. Society and war; 6. War
0805094865; 9780805094862, $29.00
LC 2011052079
This book collects multiple short-form journalistic comics by Joe Sacco, depicting major military conflicts of the late 20th and early 21st centuries. Stories include descriptions of detention of Saharan refugees who have washed up on the shores of Malta; . . . the smuggling tunnels of Gaza; the trial of Milan Kovacevic, Bosnian warlord, in The Hague; and . . . [the U.S. war prison] Abu Ghraib. (Publisher's note)

Palestine. Joe Sacco; [edited by] Kim Thompson. Fantagraphics; Turnaround 2002 120p. Illustration
Grades: Adult   **741.5; 956.9405**
1. Israel-Arab conflicts; 2. Palestine
9781560974321, $24.99; 1-560-97432-X, £18.99 : CIP entry (Apr.)
LC 2015947334
This nonfiction graphic novel, by Joe Sacco, edited by Kim Thompson, relates journalism on the life and politics of Palestine under Israeli occupation in comic book form. The work is "based on several months of research and an extended visit to the West Bank and Gaza Strip in the early 1990s (where he conducted over 100 interviews with Palestinians and Jews)." (Publisher's note)

Safe area Gorazde. Fantagraphics Bks. 2000 227p. Illustration
Grades: 10 11 12 Adult   **949.7; 741.5; 949.702**
1-56097-392-7, $28.95; 1-56097-470-2 (pa), $19.95
Sacco "spent five months in Bosnia in 1996, immersing himself in the human side of life during wartime, researching stories that are rarely found in conventional news coverage. The book focuses on the Muslim-held enclave of Gorazde, which was besieged by Bosnian Serbs during the war. Sacco lived for a month in Gorazde, entering before the Muslims

trapped inside had access to the outside world, electricity or running water." (Publisher's note)

War's end: profiles from Bosnia 1995-96. Joe Sacco. Drawn & Quarterly 2005 65 p. Illustration
Grades: Adult   **949.74203**
1. Bosnia and Hercegovina; 2. Bosnia and Herzegovina — History — 1992-; 3. Karadzic, Radovan V, 1945-; 4. Seric-Shoba, Nebojsa; 5. Yugoslav War, 1991-1995; 6. Yugoslav War, 1991-1995 — Bosnia and Herzegovina
9781896597928, $14.95; 1896597920
LC 2005415443
This graphic novel, by Joe Sacco, presents two stories that "visit the Bosnian conflict. . . . In 'Soba,' Sacco captures the internal torment of the romanticized Sarajevo artist-warrior who captivated the Western media with his guitar and hard-partying ways. In 'Christmas with Karadzic,' Sacco gives the reader an inside peek at the darkly humorous news process that doesn't make the headlines back home as he chases after one of the most hated and sought-after Bosnian Serb leaders." (Publisher's note)
"These two stories by Sacco bookend his definitive works of comics journalism on the Bosnian War, The Fixer and Safe Area Gorazde. Like those books, these stories take readers with Sacco as he searches for some truth in all the conjecture and confronts his own fears and suspicions about the war." Pub Wkly

Said, Fehed
The **Clarence** Principle. writer, Fehed Said; artist, Shari Chankhamma. SLG Publishing 2007 Un Illustration
Grades: 11 12 Adult   **741.5; Fic**
1. Death; 2. Fantasy graphic novels; 3. Graphic novels
978-1-59362-064-6, $12.95
After Clarence commits suicide, he wakes up to find a message written on the bathroom mirror; he opens the door and finds himself in a bizarre afterlife where he meets whimsical and strange people. Some images may be disturbing for more sensitive readers (such as the people with vacant holes instead of eyes, complete with zippers, and some dismemberments).

Saijyo, Shinji
★ **Iron** Wok Jan! Volume 1. DRMaster Publications 2002 190p. Illustration
Grades: 9 10 11 12 Adult   **741.5; Fic**
1. Cooking; 2. Manga; 3. Shonen manga; 4. Graphic novels
1-58899-256-7, $9.95
Jan is a talented young chef at a top class restaurant in Tokyo called Gottancho. Jan is really arrogant and full of self-confidence regarding his cooking technique. He always challenges Kiriko—a talented chef of Gottancho. Both Jan and Kiriko have entered a cooking competition. Who will win? As the series progresses, Jan competes with every chef; he's actually more the villain with his maniacal approach to cooking. There's lots of cooking action, even recipes. Some female characters are drawn to emphasize certain physical attributes. There's also some violence; some of Jan's competitors use violence (such as breaking his hand or arm) to gain an advantage. The food competitions in the manga are like television's Iron Chef taken to the extreme.

Sakai, Stan

★ **Usagi** Yojimbo: Yokai. Created, written, and illustrated by Stan Sakai. Dark Horse Books 2009 62p. Illustration

Grades: 6 7 8 9 10 11 12 Adult   **741.5; Fic**
1. Adventure graphic novels; 2. Japan; 3. Monsters; 4. Samurai; 5. Usagi Yojimbo (Fictional character); 6. Graphic novels
978-1-59582-362-5, $14.95

LC 2009-20024

As he walks through a spooky forest at night, samurai rabbit Usagi Yojimbo encounters a woman who begs him to find her daughter, who was kidnapped and dragged into the forest. That night, the yokai—monsters, demons, and spirits from Japanese folklore—are amassing for a once-a-century attempt to take over the living world. Armed only with his swords and his wit, Usagi can't hope to win against so many supernatural beings, but luckily Sasuke the Demon Queller has come, knowing about the yokais' plan, and together they fight the gathered monsters. The fighting is not graphic or bloody, and the monsters and demons aren't too scary looking for most younger readers.

"Sakai's art deftly demonstrates that comics can be simultaneously cartoony and scary. . . . Usagi Yojimbo is a genuine pleasure for readers of all ages." Publ Wkly

Sakakibara, Mizuki

Tiger & Bunny 1; 1. By Mizuki Sakakibara and illustrated by Masakazu Katsura. Viz 2013 168 p.

Grades: Adult   **741.5**
1. Superheroes — Fiction; 2. Television programs — Fiction
1421555611; 9781421555614, $9.99

"Superpowered humans known as NEXT . . . fight crime . . . while promoting their corporate sponsors on the hit show 'HERO TV.' Hero Wild Tiger['s] . . . ratings have been slipping. Under orders from his new employer, Wild Tiger finds himself forced to team up with Barnaby Brooks Jr., a rookie with an attitude. Overcoming their differences will be at least as difficult for [them] as taking down . . . bad guys!" (Publisher's note)

Sakuishi, Harold

Beck: Mongolian Chop Squad, Vol. 1. Tokyopop 2005 214p. Illustration

Grades: 10 11 12 Adult   **741.5; Fic**
1. Humorous graphic novels; 2. Manga; 3. Rock music; 4. Shonen manga; 5. Graphic novels
1-59532-770-3, $9.99

Fourteen-year-old Yukio Tanaka is one heck of a boring guy. He has no hobbies, a weak taste in music, and only a small vestige of a personality. His shy and somewhat neurotic personality makes him his own worst enemy. Little does he know that his life will be forever changed when he meets rocker Ryusuke Minami, an unpredictable sixteen-year-old with a cool dog named Beck. Ryusuke has just returned to Japan from America, and when he inspires Yukio to get into music, the two begin a journey through the world of rock 'n' roll dreams. The series includes some fan service, harsh language, fight scenes and some sexual situations along with lots of music and raucous comedy.

Sakuragi, Yukiya

Inubaka: Crazy for Dogs, Vol. 1. Viz Media 2007 210p. Illustration

Grades: 10 11 12 Adult   **741.5; Fic**
1. Dogs; 2. Manga; 3. Seinen manga; 4. Graphic novels
978-1-4215-1149-8, $9.99

Naive Suguri wants to move to Tokyo and pursue a career now that she's finished high school. Teppei owns Woofles, a new pet store, and desperately needs someone to help take care of the dogs in his store. When Suguri's dog Lupin scores sexually with a purebred Labrador Retriever that Teppei wants to breed to get puppies to sell, Suguri ends up working at Woofles to make up for it. A fair amount of fan service (mostly panty shots), a little sexual innuendo, and lots of dog pee and poop make this title more appropriate for older teens who love dogs.

Sakurai, Ami

Made in Heaven Vol. 1. Written by Ami Sakurai; illustrated by Yukari Yashiki. Tokyopop 2006 204p. Illustration

Grades: 10 11 12 Adult   **741.5; Fic**
1. Josei manga; 2. Manga; 3. Romance graphic novels; 4. Science fiction graphic novels; 5. Graphic novels
1-59816-164-4, $9.99

After a near-fatal car accident, surgeons rebuilt Reiji with prosthetic parts and renamed him Himejima Kazemichi. It was a second chance at life, but there was no guarantee that his new body would last. As his artificial heart runs down, Kazemichi embarks on a journey to discover what his life really means, and live—and love—to the fullest. Along the way, he uncovers dark secrets about his past, including the organization that was responsible for resurrecting him... But the story is not always what it seems. The book includes some strong language, brief violence, nudity, and sexual situations.

Sakurakoji, Kanoko

Backstage Prince, Vol. 1. Viz Media/Shojo Beat 2007 188p. Illustration

Grades: 8 9 10 11 12 Adult   **741.5; Fic**
1. Kabuki; 2. Romance graphic novels; 3. Shojo manga; 4. Graphic novels
978-1-4215-1172-6, $8.99

High school freshman Akari stumbles into hottie Ryusei Horiuchi and hurts him with her school bag. That evening, she stumbles upon the kabuki theater where he, as famous kabuki actor Shonosuke Ichimura, is performing, and becomes his backstage assistant. Ryusei is very shy and aloof, and he's only opened up to his cat, Mr. Ken, and now to Akari; and she, despite herself, has fallen hard for Ryusei. Can an ordinary girl and a handsome, famous actor be together?

Sala, Richard

Delphine. Richard Sala. Fantagraphics Books 2013 126 p. Illustration

Grades: Adult   **741.5973**
1. Fairy tales; 2. Fantasy graphic novels
1606995901; 9781606995907, $24.99

LC 2012289882

This graphic novel, by Richard Sala, darkly retells the fairly tale of Snow White from the perspective of the Prince. "A mysterious traveler gets off the train in a small village surrounded by a thick, sinister forest. He is searching for Delphine, who vanished with only a scrawled-out address on a scrap of paper as a trace." (Publisher's note)

Mad Night. Fantagraphics Books 2005 231p. Illustration
Grades: 9 10 11 12 Adult   **741.5; Fic**
1. Humorous graphic novels; 2. Mystery graphic novels; 3. Graphic novels
1-56097-681-0, $18.95

Judy Drood, girl detective, along with her friend and reluctant aide, Kasper Keene, investigate a series of murders at Lone Mountain College. Imagine Nancy Drew in a noir mystery, mixed in with macabre and humorous elements from Lemony Snicket books and Charles Addams cartoons.

"Reading a Sala comic is a unique experience, both jarring and fun, good for a rainy day or a stormy night." (PW)

Salvatore, R. A.
DemonWars Vol. 1: The Demon Awakens. Art by Tim Seeley. Devil's Due Publishing 2007 Un Illustration
Grades: 8 9 10 11 12 Adult   **741.5; Fic**
1. Adventure graphic novels; 2. Fantasy graphic novels; 3. Graphic novels
978-1-932796-89-6, $18.99

A fearsome evil has awakened in the land of Corona. A demon determined to spread death and misery has unleashed his goblins and giants to ravage the settlements of the frontier. Two orphans, Pony and Elbryan, have survived the attacks. Taken in by elves, Elbryan grows up to be a formidable ranger. Meanwhile, on a far-off island, a shower of gemstones falls onto the black sand shores; these heaven-sent stones carry power for both good and evil. One young monk must liberate them from the corrupt monastery that harvests them. The book includes some violence.

The **Legend** of Drizzt Book 1: Homeland. R.A. Salvatore, writer; Andrew Dabb, script; Tim Seeley, pencils. Devil's Due Publishing 2005 Un Illustration
Grades: 9 10 11 12 Adult   **741.5; Fic**
1. Adventure graphic novels; 2. Fantasy graphic novels; 3. Graphic novels
1-932796-40-1, $14.95

Travel back to strange and exotic Menzoberranzan, the vast city of the drow and homeland to Icewind Dale hero Drizzt Do'Urden. The young prince of a royal house, Drizzt grows to maturity in the vile world of his dark kin. Possessing honor beyond the scope of his unprincipled society, young Drizzt faces an inevitable dilemma. Can he live in a world that rejects integrity? The story includes lots of fighting action.

Samura, Hiroaki
★ **Blade** of the Immortal Book 1: Blood of a Thousand. Dark Horse Manga 1997 136p. Illustration
Grades: 11 12 Adult   **Fic; 741.5**
1. Adventure graphic novels; 2. Manga; 3. Samurai; 4. Seinen manga; 5. Graphic novels
1-56971-239-5, $14.95
1998 winner of Japan's Media Arts Award; 2000 Eisner Award for Best U.S. Edition of Foreign Material

"To end his eternal suffering, he must slay one thousand enemies!" Manji, a ronin warrior of feudal Japan, has been cursed with immortality. To rid himself of this curse and end his life of misery, he must slay one thousand evil men. His quest begins when a young girl named Rin seeks his help in taking revenge on her parents' killers . . . and his quest won't end until the blood of a thousand has spilled. The problem comes in judging who is truly evil. This series includes lots of graphic violence, much harsh language, partial nudity, sexual situations, and anachronistic situations and dialog.

Volume 1 of 30

Ohikkoshi. Dark Horse Manga 2006 252p. Illustration
Grades: 10 11 12 Adult   **741.5**
1. Humorous graphic novels; 2. Manga; 3. Romance graphic novels; 4. Seinen manga; 5. Graphic novels
978-1-59307-622-1

"Ohikkoshi" follows the turbulent paths of several twenty-something art students as they fall in love, fall in lust, play in rock bands, ride motorbikes, eat, sleep (together) and try to avoid making life decisions while drunk. This romantic comedy is a "Japanese Art School Confidential" packed with absurd humor, obscure Death Metal references and some dramatic revelations. In "Luncheon of Tears Diary" Natsumi Funabashi, a virgin, is an aspiring manga creator on a quest for love and a fulfilling career. Along the way, she has to cope with overzealous men, gang warfare, a mahjong addiction and a lascivious manga editor. This collection is rounded off by Samura's "Kyoto Super Barhopping Journal: Bloodbath at Midorogaike," a rare, autobiographical travel piece. Samura is best known in the US for his manga series Blade of the Immortal. The book has some mildly strong language, brief violence, brief partial nudity, and sexual situations.

San Giacomo, Michael
Tales of the Starlight drive in. By Michael San Giacomo and twenty-three talented artists. Image Comics 2008 Un Illustration
Grades: 10 11 12 Adult   **741.5; Fic**
1. Motion picture theaters; 2. Graphic novels
978-1-58240-948-1, $19.99

The thirty-one stories in this book tell the tale of the Starlight Drive In movie theater, from 1955 to 2008. It's also the story of Adam Powell, who is a little boy whose family just moved into the house across the street from the theater in 1955. As the years go by, Adam sneaks into the theater, is befriended by Neil, who works there, becomes an assistant manager, and eventually owns the drive in. The stories are connected to the movies that were hits during the particular years and trace the declining fortunes of most drive ins. Some stories include harsh language, violence, and a rape scene.

Sanbe, Kei
   Testarotho Volume 1. DC Comics/CMX 2005 192p. Illustration
Grades: 11 12 Adult   **741.5; Fic**
   1. Fantasy graphic novels; 2. Manga; 3. Shonen manga; 4. Graphic novels
   1-4012-0742-1, $9.99
   In a dark future, rival warriors of warring sects persecute nonbelievers and die for their faith. But a disillusioned young novice and a deadly gun-toting priest may be about to change all that... Young Capria has completed her studies at the Arsenal School and has begun her internship with the Elysia Unification Council under Father Garrincha. But no lessons could prepare this sheltered novice for the outside world, where rebels battle against the dreaded Testarotho." Heretics are tried and burned at the stake, warring religious factions battle for power, and the common people live a miserable life in feudal servitude. Can she bring a spark of hope to a world filled with destruction and madness? Maybe if she lives long enough. The book includes nudity, harsh language, and graphic violence.

Sanders, Joe
   The **Sandman** Papers: An Exploration of the Sandman Mythology. Fantagraphics Books 2006 201p. Illustration
Grades: Adult Professional   **741.5**
   1. Gaiman, Neil, 1960-; 2. Graphic novels — History and criticism; 3. Graphic novels
   978-1-56097-748-3, $18.95
   Neil Gaiman's Sandman is a phenomenon-a mass-circulation comic book that caught and held the attention of serious readers. Besides its mass appeal, The Sandman has long interested students and teachers in myriad disciplines, and they have begun sharing their reactions by writing analytical essays. This book gathers some of the best of this criticism, mostly by young scholars. The book contains 12 wide-ranging essays of criticism, exploration, and appreciation. The first half of the book addresses aspects of Sandman more or less in order of publication and the individual essays discuss particular Sandman episodes or story arcs, such as "A Midsummer Night's Dream," "The Kindly Ones," and "Ramadan." The second half examines Gaiman's Sandman stories in relation to his other work and work by other writers-such as Jorge Luis Borges's interest in variable truths or Terry Pratchett's adaptations of ancient myths for modern audiences. Others examine how Gaiman's stories relate to other genres such as horror fiction and to social and cultural concerns about the roles of women. Each grapples with questions of how script and art combine to make The Sandman an especially complex, rewarding comic.

Sandoval, Tony
   Doomboy. Tony Sandoval; translated by Mike Kennedy. Magnetic Press 2014 136 p. Illustration
Grades: 10 11 12 Adult   **Fic; 741.5**
   1. Rock musicians — Fiction; 2. Teenagers — Fiction

0991332474; 9780991332472, $24.99
Eisner Nominee: Best Publication for Teens (2014)
   "Sandoval . . . places cartoon artwork—featuring a wan color palette and oddly large heads on slender bodies—and a well-detailed social scene replete with bands, friendships, breakups and jealousies against the familiar context of adolescent loss and longing to produce a story that is intimate in scale yet epic in emotional terms." LJ

Santiago, Wilfred
   21: the story of Roberto Clemente : a graphic novel. Wilfred Santiago.. Fantagraphics 2011 148p. Illustration
Grades: 11 12 Adult   **741.5; 92**
   1. Baseball; 2. Baseball players; 3. Clemente, Roberto, 1934-1972; 4. Graphic novels
   978-1-56097-892-3, $22.99
   This book "is an all-ages graphic biography of baseball star Roberto Clemente: No other baseball player dominated the 1960s like him and no other Latin American player achieved his numbers. '21' chronicles his early days growing up in rural Puerto Rico, the highlights of his career (including the 1960s World Series), the prejudice he faced, his private life and his humanitarian mission." (trplteens.wordpress.com)
   Includes bibliographic references.

Sardar, Ziauddin
   Introducing Cultural Studies, Third Ed.. Ziauddin Sardar and Borin Van Loon. Totem Books 2005 176p. Illustration
Grades: 10 11 12 Adult   **301; 741.5**
   1. Sociology; 2. Graphic novels
   978-1-84046-587-7, $12.95
   Cultural studies is a discipline that claims not to be a discipline, a radical critical approach for understanding racial, national, social, and gender identities. This book uses cartoons and a spare text to provide an introductory look, covering its origins in Great Britain and the U.S., examining the ideas of its leading exponents and providing a flavor of its use around the world. The book includes a list of books for further reading."

   Introducing Islam. Ziauddin Sardar, Zafar Abbas Malik; edited by Richard Appignanesi. Totem Books 2004 176p. Illustration
Grades: 10 11 12 Adult   **297; 741.5**
   1. Islam; 2. Graphic novels
   1-84046-582-4, $12.95
   This introductory guide recounts the history of Islam from the birth of the Prophet Muhammad to its status as a global culture and political force today, explaining the message of the Qur'ran and the features of Islamic law. Using cartoons and a spare text, this book shows how Muslims everywhere are trying to live their faith and are struggling to shape new Islamic ideas and ideals in a globalized world. It includes a list of books for further reading, and definitions of Islamic terms are defined in the index.

Sarkar, Sam
   Caliber: first canon of justice. Writer Sam Sarkar; artist Garrie Gastonny. Radical Books 2009 Un Illustration

Grades: 10 11 12 Adult   **741.5; Fic**
1. Adventure graphic novels; 2. Arthurian romances — Adaptations; 3. Western stories; 4. Graphic novels
978-1-935417-00-2, $14.95

Arthurian legend gets updated to the American West of the nineteenth century. In the town of Telacoma in the Pacific Northwest, certain men, led by Mr. Leary, run things the way they want, which includes getting the railroad to come through town and bring more business. Years before, these men caused Captain Pendergon and his men to die in a forced battle with the Native Americans on the reservation which was needed for the railroad. Now, Pendergon's son Arthur has returned to reclaim his birthright. Jean Michel Whitefeather is a shaman who once thought Arthur's father was the one to wield the gun forged from the metal of the sword Excalibur. Now he decides he must help Arthur fight against the corruption in Telacoma. They won't be alone; his old friend Gwen works in the saloon, a gunfighter named Lance comes to town, and Gwen's friend Sheng Yi helps them because she knows Arthur will help to free her father. Readers who know the stories of King Arthur and the Knights of the Round Table will find familiar story elements and characters, while those who don't know much about the old stories can enjoy a new Western adventure. The book includes violence and some partial nudity and mild sexual situations.

Satrapi, Marjane
Chicken with plums. Pantheon Books 2006 84p. Illustration
Grades: 11 12 Adult   **92; 741.5**
1. Biographical graphic novels; 2. Khan, Nasser Ali, d 1958; 3. Lute players; 4. Graphic novels
0-375-42415-6; 978-0-375-42415-1, $16.95
LC 2006-43156

In graphic novel format, the author chronicles "the life of her great-uncle Nasser Ali Khan. A revered musician, he takes to his bed and refuses sustenance after his frustrated wife breaks his tar—an Iranian lute—over her knee. It takes him eight days to die, and in that time Satrapi reveals the futures of his children and unearths his past. . . . Satrapi's deceptively simple, remarkably powerful drawings match the precise but flexible prose she employs in adapting to her multiple roles as educator, folklorist, and grand-niece." New Yorker

★ The **complete** Persepolis. Pantheon Books 2007 341p. Illustration
Grades: 11 12 Adult   **92; 741.5**
1. Artists; 2. Authors; 3. Autobiographical graphic novels; 4. Cartoonists; 5. Iran; 6. Memoirists; 7. Novelists; 8. Satrapi, Marjane, 1969-; 9. Graphic novels
978-0-375-71483-2, $24.95
LC 2007-60106
Ignatz Award: Outstanding Graphic Novel (2005)
Published in two separate volumes 2003-2004

"Persepolis is the story of Satrapi's unforgettable childhood and coming of age within a large and loving family in Tehran during the Islamic Revolution; of the contradictions between private life and public life in a country plagued by political upheaval; of her high school

years in Vienna facing the trials of adolescence far from her family; of her homecoming—both sweet and terrible; and, finally, of her self-imposed exile from her beloved homeland. It is the chronicle of a girlhood and adolescence at once outrageous and familiar, a young life entwined with the history of her country yet filled with the universal trials and joys of growing up." (Publisher's note)

Embroideries. Pantheon Books 2005 134p. Illustration
Grades: 11 12 Adult   **955; Fic**
1. Iran; 2. Women — Iran; 3. Graphic novels
0-375-42305-2, $16.95
LC 2004-58660

This book "explores the lives of Iranian women young and old. The book begins with Satrapi arriving for afternoon tea at her grandmother's house. There, her mother, aunt and their group of friends tell stories about their lives as women, and, more specifically, the men they've lived with and through." Publ Wkly

"Discussions of sex are frank and explicit and laced with high humor. . . . Satrapi's simple black-and-white cartooning style is tremendously effective, expertly portraying emotional nuances with just a few lines." Libr J

Satterlee, Chuck
Of Bitter Souls, Vol. 1: Saints & Sinners, Collected Edition. Created and written by Chuck Satterlee; art by Norm Breyfoble. Markosia Enterprises 2006 Un Illustration
Grades: 10 11 12 Adult   **741.5; Fic**
1. Superhero graphic novels; 2. Supernatural graphic novels; 3. Graphic novels
1-905692-07-2, $16.95

In New Orleans, a pastor named Secord chooses four very flawed individuals: a crooked cop, a prostitute, a drug addict, and an inveterate gambler, and grants them powers based on their character flaws. They use their powers against arcane enemies, such as vampires, ghosts, werewolves, demons, and other supernatural creatures, as they learn to trust each other and themselves. The book includes a pin-up gallery by other artists, and several prose stories.

Originally published as Of Bitter Souls issues #1-6.

Sattouf, Riad
★ The **Arab** of the Future: A Graphic Memoir. By Riad Sattouf. Henry Holt & Co. 2015 160 p. Illustration
Grades: Adult   **741.5; 92**
1. Arabs — Travel; 2. Libya — Social conditions; 3. Nomads; 4. Sattouf, Riad
1627793445; 9781627793445, $26
LC 2014041152
LA Times Book Prize Finalist: Graphic Novel/Comics (2015)

In this graphic memoir, author Riad Sattouf "recounts his nomadic childhood growing up in rural France, [Muammar] Gaddafi's Libya, and [Hafez] Assad's Syria—but always under the roof of his father, a Syrian

Pan-Arabist who drags his family along in his pursuit of grandiose dreams for the Arab nation." (Publisher's note)

"Caught between his parents, Sattouf makes the best of his situation by becoming a master observer and interpreter, his clean, cartoonish art making a social and personal document of wit and understanding." Pub Wkly

Sava, Scott Christian
The **Dreamland** Chronicles: Book One. Blue Dream Studios 2006 Un Illustration
Grades: 5 6 7 8 9 10 11 12 Adult   **741.5; Fic**
   1. Adventure graphic novels; 2. Fantasy graphic novels; 3. Graphic novels
978-0-9789168-0-0, $19.95

College student Alexander Carter has found a key that takes him back to the land of his childhood dreams. Every night he enters Dreamland, a magical world filled with dragons, fairies, and giants. Reunited with his childhood friends Paddington, Kiwi, and Nastajia, Alexander now embarks on a quest to save Dreamland from war with the Nightmare Realm. But, will his daytime life as a college student interfere" Colorful 3-D animated art makes the story look like a computer game.

Scalera, Buddy
Decoy: Storm of the Century. Buddy Scalera and Courtney Huddleston. Penny-Farthing Press 2003 151p. Illustration
Grades: 5 6 7 8 9 10 11 12 Adult   **741.5; Fic**
   1. Adventure graphic novels; 2. Friendship; 3. Science fiction graphic novels; 4. Graphic novels
0-9719012-0-1, $17.95

He's the champion of justice and fast one-liners, a green shape-shifting alien from the planet Nacrum whose primary purpose in life is to protect the innocent and to one-up his roommate in an ongoing battle of pranks and bad jokes. All goes well until a subterranean encounter with a long-forgotten threat changes Decoy's life and threatens the friendship with his only ally on the planet: his best friend. Faced with an identity crisis of cosmic proportions, loveable alien Decoy must team up with his buddy, rookie cop Bobby Luck, to battle meteorological and psychological disaster.

Schaffer, Dan
The **Scribbler:** Unzip Your Head. Image Comics 2006 Un Illustration
Grades: 11 12 Adult   **741.5; Fic**
   1. Multiple personality; 2. Mystery graphic novels; 3. Graphic novels
978-1-58240-700-5, $7.99

Suki has multiple personalities; she hears voices; she's nuts. But she's getting experimental treatment, the Siamese Burn Therapy, an experimental machine designed to eliminate multiple personalities. And it works. Suki is down to her last unwanted identity, but now she's losing time and the machine is changing into something that's going to turn her world inside out. And that unwanted identity... what do you do when it turns out to be you" The book includes violence, strong language, and some sexual situations.

Schelly, Bill
Alter ego: the best of the legenday comics fanzine. Twomorrows Press 2008 192p. Illustration
Grades: Adult Professional   **070.4; 741.5**
   1. Graphic novels — History and criticism; 2. Zines — History and criticism
978-1-893905-88-7, $21.95

Jerry Bails and Roy Thomas launched Alter Ego, the first fanzine devoted to comic books and their colorful history, in 1961. This volume collects the first eleven issues, published from 1961 to 1978. It provides readers a look at what comic book fandom was doing 40-50 years ago. Fans made costumes to dress like their favorite characters, they drew their own comics, they analyzed their favorite titles these are all activities carried on by fans young and old today, although they might appear as YouTube videos or in blogs and websites.

Schodt, Frederik L.
Dreamland Japan: Writings on Modern Manga. Stone Bridge Press 1996 360p. Illustration
Grades: Adult Professional   **741.5**
   1. Comic books, strips, etc — History and criticism; 2. Manga — History and criticism; 3. Graphic novels
0-880656-23-X, $19.95

                       LC 96-11375

Drawn in styles ranging from the crudely vulgar to the highly refined, and covering every genre from naive romance to high-tech cybervisions, manga (Japanese comics) are a sophisticated narrative art. In Japan, where manga were born, the art is actively evolving, with a whole new generation of younger artists making bold innovations in style and content. Dreamland Japan is a collection of thoughful essays on the state of the manga universe in the mid-1990s. Featured artists include Hinako Sugiura, King Terry, Yoshikazu Ebisu, Kazuichi Hanawa, Murasaki Yamada, Suehiro Maruo, Akira Narita, Shungicu Uchida, Shigeru Mizuki, Reiko Okano, Yuji Aoki, Yoshiharu Tsuge, Milk Morizono, Fujiko F. Fujio, Seiki Tsuchida. There are also discussions of the work of Osamu Tezuka and Hayao Miyazaki, plus features on important magazines of the time, like CoroCoro Comic, Jump, Big Comics, Morning, June, Yan Mama, and the avant-garde Garo, as well as the dojinshi (fan-produced work) phenomenon. Some of the illustrations come from adult titles and portray nudity and sexual situations.

Schrauwen, Olivier
Arsène Schrauwen. Drawn by O. Schrauwen. Fantagraphics Books 2014 257 p. Color; Illustration
Grades: Adult   **741.5**
   1. Colonists; 2. Comic books, strips, etc — Belgium — Translations into English; 3. Schrauwen, Arsene; 4. Utopias
1606997300; 9781606997307, $34.99

                  LC 2012285781

"In 1947, the author's grandfather, Arsene Schrauwen, traveled across the ocean to a mysterious, dangerous jungle colony at the behest of his cousin. Together they would build . . . a modern utopia in the wilderness—but not before Arsene falls in love with his cousin's wife, Marieke." (Publisher's note)

"Arsène's improbable trek through the jungle to achieve a mad dream recalls Fitzcarraldo, and the story's unsettling depiction of the madness underpinning European colonization evokes Conrad, but this is a stunningly unique work." Booklist

This story was first published as a three part series by the author himself — facing title page

The translation and production of this book are funded by the Flemish Literature Fund (Vlaams Fonds boor de Letteren) — end pages.

Schultz, Mark

The **stuff** of life: a graphic guide to genetics and DNA. Written by Mark Schultz; art by Zander Cannon and Kevin Cannon. Hill and Wang 2009 150p. Illustration

Grades: 9 10 11 12 Adult   **576.5; 741.5**

1. Genetics; 2. Graphic novels

978-0-8090-8946-8, $30; 978-0-8090-8947-5 (pa), $14.95

Eisner and Harvey Award winning writer Schultz uses the device of an alien writing a report to describe genetics and DNA in five chapters, from molecular structure of Earth organisms to sexual reproduction to genetic inheritance to genetic counseling and the genome Project and beyond. The black and white cartoons add some humor to the sound information, and the book includes a list of suggested reading ranging from magazines and books to websites, along with a glossary of terms.

Includes bibliographical references

Superman and Batman Versus Aliens and Predators. Writer, Mark Schultz; artist, Ariel Olivetti; letterer, Todd Klein. DC Comics/Dark Horse Comics 2007 Un Illustration

Grades: 9 10 11 12 Adult   **741.5; Fic**

1. Aliens (Fictional characters); 2. Batman (Fictional character); 3. Predators (Fictional characters); 4. Superhero graphic novels; 5. Superman (Fictional character); 6. Graphic novels

978-1-4012-1328-2, $12.99

DC's iconic heroes square off against two of the most popular movie aliens in a joint publishing venture. There's lots of fighting action, but not as intense as in the movies, and with little harsh language.

A lost colony of Predators has lived under a dormant volcano in the Andes mountains for centuries, but volcanic activity has begun, their home is unsafe, and they've come out, and started killing humans. Superman and Batman have fought them before and want to send them back to their home planet, but the Terrestrial Defense Initiative wants to destroy all the aliens and they're willing to kill Superman and Batman to do it.

Schulz, Charles M.

★ The **Complete** Peanuts: 1950-1952. Fantagraphics Books 2004 330p. Illustration

Grades: 2 3 4 5 6 7 8 9 10 11 12 Adult   **Fic; 741.5**

1. Humorous graphic novels; 2. Peanuts (Comic strip); 3. Graphic novels

1-56097-589-X, $28.95

This is the first volume of a project to collect all of Schulz's Peanuts comic strips from 1950 to 2000. This volume includes the strips published from October 2, 1950

through all of 1952. These early strips featured characters younger readers may not recognize: Patty (not Peppermint Patty), Violet, Shermy, and a Snoopy who behaves like a normal dog. Schroeder is a baby who's already a whiz at the toy piano; Lucy is a toddler who already causes trouble for Charlie Brown; Linus shows up as a baby in September 1952. Lucy pulls the football trick on Charlie Brown for the first time in November 1952. This volume also includes a biography of Schulz and a long interview with him.

Volume 1 of 26

Schwartz, David B.

Meltdown: The Definitive Collection. Image Comics 2007 Un Illustration

Grades: 10 11 12 Adult   **741.5; Fic**

1. Superhero graphic novels; 2. Graphic novels

978-1-58240-821-7, $14.99

Caliente, the Flare, is dying. His own super-powers are eating him alive, melting him down from within. During his final days, Cal must struggle with his volatile life and the questionable decisions he's made along the way, hoping to find redemption before time runs out. See the final moments that prove what a hero can - and should - be. The story has considerable violence.

Schwarzman, Mat

Beginner's Guide to Community-Based Arts. Keith Knight, Mat Schwarzman and many others. New Village Press 2005 171p. Illustration

Grades: 10 11 12 Adult   **741.5; 701**

1. Art and society; 2. Graphic novels

978-0-9766054-3-0

LC 2005929142

Ten transformative local arts projects come alive in this illustrated training manual for youth leaders and teachers. This energetic guidebook demonstrates the enormous power of art in grass-roots social change. It presents proven models of community-based arts programs, plus techniques, discussion questions, and plentiful resources.

Schweizer, Chris

★ **Crogan's** loyalty. Chris Schweizer; [edited by] James Lucas Jones. Oni Press, Inc. 2012 150 p. Color; Illustration

Grades: 8 9 10 11 12 Adult   **741.5**

1. Adventure graphic novels; 2. United States — History — 1775-1783, Revolution

9781934964408, $14.99; 1934964409

LC 2011943514

"Schweizer takes another bite out of history in this story of two brothers divided by the American Revolution. Charlie, the elder Crogan and a Loyalist ranger, is infuriated that his younger brother would turn rebel, stating 'There's a passion that makes most young men wanna tear society down because they ain't in charge of it.' Meanwhile, Will, a colonial scout, is no less incensed that his older brother would stand for a tyrant against his own country." (Booklist)

★ **Crogan's** march. Oni Press 2009 212p. Illustration

Grades: 8 9 10 11 12 Adult   **741.5; Fic**

1. Adventure graphic novels; 2. Imperialism; 3. North Africa — World history — 20th century; 4. Graphic novels
978-1-934964-24-8, $14.95

When brothers Eric and Cory squabble at the dinner table, their father tells them the story of Peter Crogan, one of their ancestors, who fought in the French Foreign Legion in 1912. Crogan's five-year term of service is one month from completion when he's asked to stay and become an officer. His unit is stationed in North Africa, where the French hold territory and depend on the French Foreign Legion to police the territory, putting down the rebellious attacks of the Tuaregs. He finds himself torn between the heroic Captain Poitelet (who tends to be the sole survivor of various battles) and the grizzled sergeant who actually cares about the people the Legion polices. When Crogan's unit escorts a caravan that endures an attack by Tuaregs, the captain's reckless actions endanger everyone, and Crogan must find help. Schweizer's story includes the kind of violence military actions cause, but very little in the way of bad language. Some may wince at the heavily French-accented English of some of the characters ("zee Daughters of France send zem out to all of zee units," etc.). This action-packed historical fiction graphic novel will appeal to teens, but adults who remember such novels as Beau Geste by Percival Christopher Wren (and the movies, of course) will also enjoy reading Schweizer's tale.

This book is part of The Crogan Adventures series
Sequel to: Crogan's vengeance (2008)

★ **Crogan's** vengeance. Book design by Keith Wood; edited by James Lucas Jones with Jill Beaton. Oni Press 2008 185p. Illustration
Grades: 8 9 10 11 12 Adult   **741.5; Fic**
1. Adventure graphic novels; 2. Pirates; 3. Graphic novels
978-1-934964-06-4, $14.95

Catfoot Crogan serves as an honest and honorable sailor on a ship commanded by an unjust captain when the ship is taken over by pirates. In order to save their lives, the sailors all take the oath to become pirates, but Crogan immediately runs afoul of D'Or, a brutal man who enjoys torturing others. Catfoot is a pirate, but he's determined to remain as honest and honorable as he can be, which continually puts him in danger. This swashbuckling tale shows a less romantic story than Rafael Sabatini's Captain Blood, with more violence, but it is more action-oriented than merely violent.

"Filled with mutiny, ferocious storms, shark-infested waters, commandeering of ships, and—of course—swashbuckling sword fights, this book has high teen appeal." SLJ

Part of the Crogan Adventures series

Scrambly, Crab
The **13th** of Never. SLG Publishing 2004 72p. Illustration
Grades: 9 10 11 12 Adult   **741.5; Fic**
1. Fantasy graphic novels; 2. Horror graphic novels; 3. Graphic novels
0-943151-90-2, $7.95

Cursed with bad luck and trapped in a monotonous life, an unfortunate young man named Zazil longs to escape from the drudgery of his waking life and the troubled thoughts that haunt him. A good luck charm that Zazil finds in a dusty curio shop proves to be his ticket away from the mundane, but it brings him everything but good luck. When soul-stealing creatures called Charnoks pursue Zazil through strange lands and ghost trains, he must use his wits and courage to escape them - and finally face his past. This illustrated novel has no bad language or real violence, but has a macabre feel.

Seagle, Steven T.
American Virgin: Head. Steven T. Seagle; art by Becky Cloonan. DC Comics/Vertigo 2006 112p. Illustration
Grades: 11 12 Adult   **741.5; Fic**
1. Mystery graphic novels; 2. Revenge; 3. Graphic novels
978-1-4012-1065-6, $9.99

Adam Chamberlain is a youth minister and author, head of a national virginity movement. When his fiancee, Cassie, is brutally murdered in Africa, Adam travels there with his black-sheep stepsister Cyndi, trying to discover meaning in Cassie's death.   Confronted by hit men, paparazzi, pornography, and even the voice of God, Adam finds himself lost in a vortex of spiritually uncharted territory. This series has nudity, strong language, and violence.

Genius. By Steven T. Seagle, illustrated by Teddy Kristiansen. First Second 2013 128 p.
Grades: Adult   **741; Fic**
1. Physicists; 2. Quantum theory
1596432632; 9781596432635, $17.99

In this graphic novel, by Steven T. Seagle, illustrated by Teddy Kristiansen, "Ted Marx works hard at his career as a quantum physicist. But . . . then Ted makes a startling discovery: his wife's father once knew Einstein and claims that Einstein entrusted to him a final, devastating secret. . . . If Ted can convince his father-in-law to tell him what Einstein had to say, his job will be safe. But does he dare reveal Einstein's most dangerous secret to those who might exploit it—" (Publisher's note)

Kafka. By Steven T. Seagle & Stefano Gaudiano; lettering by Richard Starkings. Active Images 2006 Un Illustration
Grades: 10 11 12 Adult   **741.5; Fic**
1. Adventure graphic novels; 2. Mystery graphic novels; 3. Graphic novels
0-9766761-5-X, $14.99

Dan Hutton lost everything ... his name, his past, his wife, his life. Having lived in a witness relocation program for years, Dan is told his new identity has been compromised, by two different groups who each claim to be CIA operatives. Unable to trust anyone, Dan runs back to the world that took everything he loved, hoping he can reclaim his past. The book is filled with suspense and action with very little violence.

Sandman Mystery Theatre: The Scorpion. Matt Wagner, Steven T. Seagle, writers; Guy Davis, artist; David Hornung, colorist; John Costanza, letterer. DC Comics 2006 104p. Illustration
Grades: 10 11 12 Adult   **741.5; Fic**
1. Mystery graphic novels; 2. Graphic novels
1-4012-1040-6, $12.99

This reimagination of the original Golden Age Sandman finds Wesley Dodds still driven by his dreams to fight injustice in the dark of night while trying to make sense of a world slipping into the madness of war. Taking on a twisted anti-capitalist vigilante wielding a poisoned whip who calls himself the Scorpion, Dodds finds himself closer than ever to death—and to revealing his secret life to his paramour, Dian Belmont. Readers will find some harsh language, including ethnic slurs uttered by villains, and some violence.

Secret identities: the Asian American superhero anthology.
New Press 2009 194p. Illustration
Grades: 9 10 11 12 Adult   **741.5; Fic**
1. Asian Americans; 2. Superhero graphic novels; 3. Graphic novels
978-1-59558-398-7, $21.95
LC 2009-1536

Yang, Shen, Chow, and coeditor Jerry Ma have put together a collection of twenty-six stories by Asian American creators about Asian American superheroes. The book is divided into sections: War and Remembrance, Many Masks, When Worlds Collide, Girl Power, Ordinary Heroes, and From Headline to Hero. The Preface, the Prologue, all section introductions, and the Epilogue, are all done in comic book format. Creators include Gene Luen Yang, Greg Pak, Dustin Nguyen, Kazu Kibuishi, Cliff Chiang, Christine Norrie, and many more. Some stories deal with the Nisei soldiers of the 100th Battalion/442nd Regimental Combat Team during World War II, others confront the idea that the Asian character can only be the sidekick, still others explore the stereotypical attitudes of some Americans toward Asian Americans. The book includes some violence and some harsh language.

Seino, Shizuru
Heaven!! Volume 1. Tokyopop 2007 Un Illustration
Grades: 9 10 11 12 Adult   **741.5; Fic**
1. Fantasy graphic novels; 2. Manga; 3. Romance graphic novels; 4. Shojo manga; 5. Graphic novels
978-1-59816-816-7, $9.99

Rinne is a girl who not only can see and exorcise ghosts with a paper fan (called a harisen). When she's saved from becoming a ghost by the school punk, he ends up in a coma. Fortunately, that doesn't stop their unique relationship from forging: Rinne and her rescuer's now-disembodied spirit must defend his prone body from being possessed by a muddled collection of local ghosts. When Rinne fails in her task, an ancient playboy god takes over the punk's body—leaving him to inhabit a pink stuffed monkey. There's some harsh language and quite a bit of mildly suggestive behavior.

Sen, Jai
★ **Garlands** of Moonlight. Written by Jai Sen; illustrated by Rizky Wasisto Edi. Shoto Press 2002 86p. Illustration
Grades: 9 10 11 12 Adult   **741.5; Fic**
1. Horror graphic novels; 2. Vampires; 3. Graphic novels
0-9717564-0-6, $4.59
LC 03-311055

Silent and merciless, a creature of darkness has come to prey on an island village. Babies vanish, mothers are murdered, and the threat of evil grows with each night. The village becomes a battleground as the onrush of the twentieth century clashes with tradition—and the restless spirits of the island's mythical past... Set in late colonial Indonesia, this book relates a Malay vampire legend in graphic novel format. Printed in a black and silver duotone, the book captures the feel of turn-of-the-century daguerreotype photographs. There is some violence.
Malay Mysteries Book 1

Serchay, David S.
The **librarian's** guide to graphic novels for children and tweens. Neal-Schuman Publishers 2008 272p.
Grades: Adult Professional   **025.2; 741.5**
1. Children — Books and reading; 2. Libraries — Special collections; 3. Graphic novels
978-1-55570-626-5 (pa), $55; 1-55570-626-5 (pa)
LC 2008-6487

This book provides a brief history of graphic novels, describes genres, discusses manga, gives librarians reasons to include graphic novels in library collections and in school curricula. It also discusses some of the major comic book publishers in the U.S., suggests how to purchase graphic novels, and how to process, catalog, and shelve them, and also how to use them in programming. Several lengthy appendices provide annotated lists of titles that are suitable for children and tween readers, online resources for purchasing, reviews, and news, and additional, comics-related books

"An insightful introduction to this format as well as an effective selection tool, this guide is highly recommended." Booklist

Includes bibliographical references

Seth
Clyde Fans Book 1. Drawn & Quarterly 2004 156p. Illustration
Grades: 11 12 Adult   **741.5; Fic**
1. Graphic novels
1-896597-84-X, $19.95

This book focuses on the lives of two brothers and their fan manufacturing company. After one more disastrous attempt at selling, Simon returns to the office defeated and unsure of what he'll do next. Even after studying manuals on the art of selling, he still can't seem to clinch that final deal. In the eyes of his brother Abraham, he is a failure. Simon's plight is reminiscent of Arthur Miller's play, "Death of a Salesman." Here, Seth explores the complex and fascinating relationship of the two brothers behind Clyde Fans. There's one brief scene of incidental nudity.

The **G.N.B.** Double C: the Great Northern Brotherhood of Canadian Cartoonists. Seth. Drawn and Quarterly 2011 133 p. Illustration; Color
Grades: Adult   **741.5/971; 741.5**
1. Cartoonists; 2. Cartoonists — Canada — History and criticism— Fiction; 3. Comic books, strips, etc — Canada — History — Fiction — Pictorial works; 4. Private clubs — Fiction
9781770460539, $24.95; 1770460535
LC 2011505786

This graphic novel, by Seth, is "a sort-of companion piece to 'Wimbledon Green' (2005), in which he limned a fictional history of comic-book collectors, Seth's latest effort postulates an alternate universe set in a Canada where lionized cartoonists were viewed as important cultural figures, with membership in a prestigious guild, the G. N. B. Double C. of the book's title." (Booklist)

Includes index.

Great Northern Brotherhood of Canadian Cartoonists

★ **George** Sprott: 1894-1975 : a picture novella. Seth. Drawn & Quarterly 2009 96p. Illustration
Grades: Adult   **741.5**
9781897299517, $24.95; 1897299516

"Seth weaves the fictional tale of George Sprott, the host of a long-running television program. The events forming the patchwork of George's life are pieced together from the tenuous memories of several informants, who often have contradictory impressions. His estranged daughter describes the man as an unforgivable lout, whereas his niece remembers him fondly. His former assistant recalls a trip to the Arctic during which George abandoned him for two months, while George himself remembers that trip as the time he began writing letters to a former love, from whom he never received replies." (Publisher's note)

It's a good life, if you don't weaken: A Picture Novella. By Seth. Drawn & Quarterly 2001 163, [20] p. Illustration
Grades: Adult   **741.5; 741.5/971**
1. Cartoonists; 2. Cartoonists — Canada; 3. Seth, 1962-
1896597319; 1896597327; 1896597335; 189659770X;
9781896597706, $24.95

LC 2005440925

In this picture novella, author Seth "pays homage to the wit and sophistication of the old-fashioned magazine cartoon. While trying to understand his dissatisfaction with the present, Seth discovers the life and work of Kalo, a forgotten New Yorker cartoonist from the 1940s. But his obsession blinds him to the needs of his lover and the quiet desperation of his family." (Publisher's note)

Originally serialized in issues four thru nine of the comic book series, Palookaville—t.p. verso.

It is a good life, if you do not weaken

Wimbledon Green: The Greatest Comic Book Collector in the World. Drawn & Quarterly 2005 Un Illustration
Grades: 11 12 Adult   **741.5; Fic**
1. Collectors and collecting; 2. Graphic novels
1-896597-93-9, $19.95

Meet Wimbledon Green, the self-proclaimed world's greatest comic-book collector who brokered the world's best comic-book deal in the history of collecting. Comic-book retailers, auctioneers, and conventioneers from around North America, as well as Green's collecting rivals, weigh in on the man and his vast collection of comic books. Are Green's intentions honorable? Does he truly love comics or is he driven by the need to conquer" Lastly, is he really even Wimbledon Green?

The Seven Soldiers of Victory Archives Volume 1
Edited by Dale Crain. DC Comics 2005 237p. Illustration
Grades: 6 7 8 9 10 11 12 Adult   **Fic; 741.5**

1. Green Arrow (Fictional character); 2. Superhero graphic novels; 3. Graphic novels
1-4012-0401-5, $49.95

Collecting Leading Comics #1-4, featuring the adventures of The Seven Soldiers of Victory: The Crimson Avenger, Green Arrow, the Shining Knight, The Vigilante, the Star-Spangled Kid, and their sidekicks Speedy, Stripesy, and Wing (yes, there were eight of them). In 1941, one year after DC Comics launched the Justice Society of America in All-Star Comics, sister company All-American Comics released Leading Comics #1 featuring its very own super-team; in these early stories they take on various criminals and villains who possess super-senses.

Sexy Chix: Anthology of Women Cartoonists.
Dark Horse Comics 2006 104p. Illustration
Grades: 10 11 12 Adult   **741.5; Fic**
1. Short stories; 2. Women; 3. Graphic novels
1-59307-238-4, $12.95

Don't let the title fool you - this isn't the average collection of comics featuring impossibly proportioned vixens in spandex. This time around the sexy chix in question are the writers and artists behind the comics, representing some of the best and brightest talent contributing to the medium of comics and graphic novels today. With stories ranging from mainstream adventures to comic shorts to autobiography, Sexy Chix is devoted to the under-recognized contingent of female cartoonists in an overwhelmingly male-oriented industry. It's about time these creators get to tell the stories they want to, and the result is a variety of artistic visions and styles. Among the sexy chicks are New York Times best-selling author Joyce Carol Oates, Eisner Award-winning illustrator Jill Thompson (Scary Godmother), A Distant Soil writer/artist Colleen Doran, Bitchy Bitch creator Roberta Gregory, DC Comics writer Gail Simone, novelist Sarah Grace McCandless (Grosse Pointe Girl) and many, many more. Some stories include nudity, sexual situations, harsh language, and violence.

Sfar, Joann
Dungeon: Parade Vol. 1: A Dungeon Too Many. By Joann Sfar, Lewis Trondheim & Manu Larcenet. NBM 2007 Un Illustration
Grades: 6 7 8 9 10 11 12 Adult   **741.5; Fic**
1. Adventure graphic novels; 2. Fantasy graphic novels; 3. Humorous graphic novels; 4. Graphic novels
978-1-56163-495-8, $9.95

Marvin the Vegetarian Dragon and Herbert the Duck do battle with the new, rival dungeon next door that is actually a theme park. Then, Herbert finds a magic lamp that has one wish left, and he and Marvin set out on a quest to find a dying sage to get advice on the best wish.

Klezmer, Book One: Tales of the Wild East. First Second Books 2006 140p. Illustration
Grades: 11 12 Adult   **741.5**
1. Jews; 2. Musicians; 3. Graphic novels
1-59643-198-9

Klezmer tells a tale of love, friendship, survival, and the joy of making music in pre-World War II Eastern Europe. Noah is perfectly content as the leader of a traveling klezmer band, until his bandmates are brutally murdered by rival musicians. He sets out for Odessa alone, but is joined by Chava, a beautiful girl with a voice like an angel. Meanwhile, Yaacov is expelled from his yeshiva for stealing; he too makes his way to Odessa along with Vincenzo, a violinist, and Tshokola, a gypsy entertainer. When these five misfits finally come together, they must set aside their differences and learn to work together (and rock a crowd) through their music. Some nudity and a fair amount of violence make this better for older readers.

The **professor's** daughter. [story by] Joann Sfar & [illustrated by] Emmanuel Guibert; translated by Alexis Siegel. First Second Books 2007 63p. Illustration
Grades: 7 8 9 10 11 12 Adult   741.5
1. Humorous graphic novels; 2. Mummies; 3. Romance graphic novels; 4. Graphic novels
978-1-59643-130-0; 1-59643-130-X, $16.95
LC 2006-22177
In Victorian London, Lillian, the daughter of a famed archeologist, has fallen in love with the mummy of Imhotep IV; he thinks that Lillian bears a strong resemblance to this long-dead wife. Their love faces many obstacles, from Lillian's father, the police, a pirate who is actually Imhotep III (yes, the father and another mummy), even Queen Victoria herself. Dainty Victorian manners mix with broad farce and black comedy in a beautifully illustrated book with muted colors and sepia tones.

The **rabbi's** cat. Pantheon Books 2005 142p. Illustration
Grades: 11 12 Adult   741.5; Fic
1. France — History — 1914-1940; 2. Jews; 3. North Africa; 4. Rabbis; 5. Graphic novels
0-375-42281-1, $21.95; 0-375-71464-2 (pa), $16.95
LC 2004-61406
"A slinky gray cat lives with a rabbi and his beautiful young daughter. One day, the feline eats their parrot, only to find that he has gained the bird's ability to talk. Witty and highly intelligent, the cat immediately decides that he wants to learn more about Judaism, from the Kabbalah to the Torah.... There is plenty for teens to like—humor, romance, and theological questioning combined with a folkloric quality to bring to life a multifaceted work." SLJ

Vampire loves. Color by Audré Jardel; translation by Alexis Siegel. First Second Books 2006 187p. Illustration
Grades: 9 10 11 12 Adult   741.5; Fic
1. Romance graphic novels; 2. Vampires; 3. Graphic novels
978-1-59643-093-8; 1-59643-093-1, $16.95
LC 2005-21498
When the vampire Ferdinand breaks up with Lani, his cheating girlfriend, he starts looking for love and romance. In the process he meets the vampire sisters Ritaline and Aspirine, tries his hand at detective work, goes on a cruise and meets the ghost, Sigh, and gets mixed up in a fight between mummy pirates and Professor Joseph Bell.
"Edgy and creepy but at the same time universal and normal, Vampire Loves is a unique study in contrasts that will be a pleasurable discovery for graphic novel enthusiasts." Voice Youth Advocates
First published in four volumes in France with title: Grand vampire

Shaffer, Neal
The **Awakening**. Written by Neal Shaffer; illustrated by Luca Genovese; lettering by Manfredi Toraldo. Oni Press 2004 104p. Illustration
Grades: 10 11 12 Adult   741.5; Fic
1. Horror graphic novels; 2. Mystery graphic novels; 3. Graphic novels
1-932664-00-9, $9.95
Francesca, the only child of an affluent family, is excited to be attending one of the most prestigious boarding schools in New England. Unfortunately, things go horribly wrong when, shortly after her arrival, she finds one of her classmates brutally murdered, sending her into a deep shock, putting her into a coma. Even worse, immediately following the tragic incident, Francesca begins to have visions of which girl will be slain next, and even though she has awakened, she's unable to tell anyone about it. Is this a new horror being visited on the longstanding institution, or is it something much more, going to the core of the school itself, to an evil that defies description" The book includes strong language, violence, and some nudity.

Shakespeare, William
William Shakespeare's King Lear. Illustrated by Ian Pollock. Black Dog & Leventhal/Workman Publishing 2006 148p. Illustration
Grades: 7 8 9 10 11 12 Adult   741.5; 822.3
1. Shakespeare, William, 1564-1616 — Adaptations; 5. Graphic novels
978-1-57912-617-9, $12.95
This graphic novel adaptation of King Lear, originally published in 1984, uses excerpted text from the play together with full-color illustrations to tell the story of the king whose ill-fated attempts to learn which of his daughters loves him best causes loss and madness.
Part of the Shakespeare Graphic Library.

William Shakespeare's Macbeth. Illustrated by Von. Black Dog & Leventhal/Workman Publishing 1982 92p. Illustration
Grades: 7 8 9 10 11 12 Adult   741.5; 822.3
1. Shakespeare, William, 1564-1616 — Adaptations; 5. Graphic novels
978-1-57912-621-6, $12.95
This graphic novel adaptation of Macbeth, originally published in 1982, uses excerpted text from the play together with full-color illustrations to tell the story of the Thane of Cawdor who listens to a trio of witches and slays the King of Scotland to take his throne.
Part of the Shakespeare Graphic Library

Shanower, Eric
Age of bronze volume 3A: Betrayal part one. Image Comics 2007 176p. Illustration
Grades: 10 11 12 Adult   741.5; Fic
1. Adventure graphic novels; 2. Greek mythology; 3. Troy (Extinct city)
978-1-58240-755-5, $17.99
The graphic novel retelling of the story of the Trojan War continues, as High King Agamemnon's army passes the island of Tenedos on its journey to conquer Troy. When a snake bites Philoktetes on the foot, his cries of pain bother

the army so much that Odysseus must find a solution. Then, the Achaeans send an embassy to Troy in hopes of preventing a war. This book includes some nudity and sexual situations as well as some violence. Shanower includes a lengthy bibliography of historical sources.

Sequel to Sacrifice (2004)

Age of Bronze: Betrayal part 2. By Eric Shanower. Image Comics 2013 176 p. Illustration
Grades: 10 11 12 Adult   741.5
1. Greece — Fiction; 2. Trojan War — Fiction; 3. Graphic novels
1607067579; 9781607067573

In this graphic novel, written and illustrated by Eric Shanower, "the Trojan plain fills with death as Achaean forces clash in blood with the Trojan army. In the city of Troy, Pandarus pulls the strings to put Troilus in Cressida's bed. But when Cressida is ripped away to the enemy camp, how far will Troilus fight" (Publisher's note)

"Shanower's graphic-novel retelling of the Trojan War is one of the great artistic visions of the comics medium. Where both mythology and heroic-adventure comics typically lean toward vast spectacle and archetypal characters, Shanower is uncompromising in his sharp, humanizing focus. Betrayal, Part 2, the second part of the third part of Shanower's projected seven-part series, begins with Achilles and his Myrmidons invading the beach of Troy and ends with Troilus' breakdown during a bloody skirmish with a squad of Achaeans. . . . Seldom has a work shined so brightly on every page." Booklist

Age of Bronze: Sacrifice. Image Comics 2004 223p. Illustration; Map (Age of bronze)
Grades: 10 11 12 Adult   741; 741.5; Fic
1. Greek mythology; 2. Trojan War; 3. Graphic novels
1-58240-360-0; 1-58240-399-6 (pa), $19.95

"Sacrifice begins by recapitulating the story thus far. Paris sails back to Troy, just as self-regarding and shortsighted as when he left. Thrilled with his own prize (Helen), he has no understanding of the political complications. Priam does, but he is swayed by the machinations of Helen and by Hecuba's generosity. Not only are the major characters (Achilles, Klytemnestra, Odysseus) complex, but even a minor player like Telephus is carefully developed." SLJ

Includes bibliographical references
Followed by Betrayal (2008)
This is the second book in the author's projected seven-volume graphic novel about the Trojan War. The first volume, A thousand ships, was published in 2001

Little Nemo: Return to Slumberland. Written by Eric Shanower; illustrated by Gabriel Rodriguez. IDW Publishing 2015 120 p. Color; Illustration
Grades: 10 11 12 Adult   741.5
1. Dreaming; 2. Friendship
1631400592; 9781631400599, $21.99
Eisner Award: Best Limited Series (2015)

This graphic novel, by Eric Shanower, illustrated by Gabriel Rodriguez, "sees King Morpheus' daughter, in the Royal Palace of Slumberland, selecting her

next-playmate—Nemo! Only Nemo has no interest in being anyone's playmate, dream or no dream!" (Publisher's note)

Originally published as: Little Nemo: Return to Slumberland, issues #1-4

Shaw, Dash
New School. By Dash Shaw. W W Norton & Co Inc 2013 340 p.
Grades: Adult   741.5
1. Amusement parks; 2. Brothers
1606996444; 9781606996447, $39.99

In this graphic novel by Dash Shaw "a boy mov[es] to an exotic country and his infatuation with an unfamiliar culture . . . quickly shifts to disillusionment. Danny's older brother, Luke, travels to a remote island, [employed by] ClockWorld, an ambitious new amusement park. Danny travels to ClockWorld to convince Luke to return to America. But Luke has made a new life . . . rendering him almost unrecognizable. Danny . . . explores the island, ClockWorld, and fights to bring his brother home." (Publisher's note)

Shazam!: the greatest stories ever told
DC Comics 2008 224p. Illustration
Grades: 4 5 6 7 8 9 10 11 12 Adult   741.5; Fic
1. Adventure graphic novels; 2. Captain Marvel (Fictional character); 3. Superhero graphic novels; 4. Graphic novels
978-1-4012-1674-0, $24.99

This book collects comics stories about Captain Marvel dating from 1940 to 1998. Captain Marvel predated Superman as a comic book superhero; young newsboy Billy Batson could transform into the flying superhero by shouting the magic word "Shazam!" This gave him the wisdom of Solomon, the strength of Hercules, the stamina of Atlas, the power of Zeus, the courage of Achilles, and the speed of Mercury. In these fourteen stories, he battles against such foes as Dr. Sivana, Mr. Mind, and the Monster Society of Evil.

Sheikman, Alex
Robotika. Archaia Studios Press 2006 128p. Illustration
Grades: 11 12 Adult   741.5; Fic
1. Adventure graphic novels; 2. Science fiction graphic novels; 3. Graphic novels
978-1-932386-21-9, $19.95

In a future world full of human/machine hybrids and organic technology, a samurai named Niko serves the Queen. When a new piece of technology that can revolutionize the world and render cyborgs obsolete is stolen and its inventor killed, the Queen sends Niko to retrieve it. He must fight and kill many warriors along the way and succeeds, only to see the Queen destroy the object to create a hair ornament. He gives up the sword, but still joins yojimbo (wandering masterless samurai bodyguards) Cherokee Geisha and Uri Bronski to protect a caravan of pilgrims seeking their god's temple.

Sheikman uses color, differing visual styles, even vertical lettering (for Cherokee Geisha's speech), and combines genre elements of the Western, samurai action, and science fiction to create a story set in a well-realized world.

Two short stories give background on Cherokee Geisha and Bronski.

Originally published as Robotika issues #1-4.

Sherman, M. Zachary

SOCOM: Seal Team Seven Vol. 1. Writer, M. Zachary Sherman; Roberto de la Torre, artist. Image Comics 2006 Un Illustration

Grades: 10 11 12 Adult   **741.5; Fic**
1. Adventure graphic novels; 2. Science fiction graphic novels; 3. Graphic novels
1-58240-586-7, $12.99

When a submarine is mysteriously downed in the Persian Gulf, CIA tactician Douglas Griffin is reactivated into his former SEAL team to investigate. Simultaneously, a string of mystifying attacks pits the U.S. Navy against the underwater Kingdom of Atlantis in a full-blown war against humanity's extinction. With the threat of global devastation imminent, twisting realities lead the SEALs from Atlantis' 5000 fathoms to the even deeper political waters of the U.S. government. The book includes lots of harsh language and violence.

Shiga, Jason

Bookhunter. Sparkplug Comics 2007 Un Illustration
Grades: 10 11 12 Adult   **741.5; Fic**
1. Humorous graphic novels; 2. Librarians; 3. Mystery graphic novels; 4. Graphic novels
978-0-9742715-6-9, $15

When a rare Caxton Bible is stolen from the Oakland Public Library in 1973, Agent Bay of the Library Police is on the case. Reading very much like a police procedural mystery, but set in the library, Bookhunter combines humor, library technology of the early 1970s, and lots of action movie tropes. The book includes a few harsh words and some violence.

Shigematsu, Takako

King of the lamp. Go! Comi 2007 208p. Illustration
Grades: 11 12 Adult   **741.5; Fic**
1. Manga; 2. Romance graphic novels; 3. Graphic novels
978-1-933617-46-6, $10.99

In this one-volume manga, teenage girls in the throes of unrequited love encounter a mysterious merchant who sells a magic lamp. This lamp hold a genie, who is actually a king from a far land who lived long ago; because he took one thousand beautiful girls for his harem, he was imprisoned in the lamp and must grant the wishes of one thousand girls who are looking for love. What each girl learns, however, is that he can exact a price from them for their wishes, and the price ranges from a kiss to sex. Hinata loves Togo, but her older sister has been dating him. When Togo gets into an accident and is blinded, Hinata wishes that she could sound like her unfaithful sister and comfort Togo. Enter the prince, who grants her wish. Pretending to be her sophisticated older sister isn't easy, but Hinata discovers the hardest part is she's falling more deeply in love with Togo. This is just one of several stories. Each of them ends with the characters having sex, although it's not graphically portrayed; but there is partial nudity.

Shigeno, Shuichi

Initial D Volume 1. Tokyopop 2002 229p. Illustration
Grades: 8 9 10 11 12 Adult   **741.5; Fic**
1. Automobile racing; 2. Seinen manga; 3. Graphic novels
1-931514-98-4, $9.99

Tak Fujiwara spends a lot of time behind the wheel, delivering tofu for his dad's shop. He races down the treacherous roads of Mount Akina all the time, and without even realizing it, he has mastered racing techniques that take most drivers a lifetime to learn. None of his friends realize this, because they're too busy watching the local street racing team. When the Red Suns, an outside team, shows up to challenge the Akina Speed Stars, it doesn't look good for the local team; then a mysterious Trueno Eight Six shows up and the driver exhibits great skill. Who is the driver" The book includes some strong language and some sexual situations (the girl Tak likes is dating older men for money).

Shiki, Satoshi

Kami-Kaze Volume 1. Tokyopop 2006 268p. Illustration
Grades: 12 Adult   **741.5; Fic**
1. Fantasy graphic novels; 2. Horror graphic novels; 3. Manga; 4. Seinen manga; 5. Graphic novels
1-59532-924-2, $9.99

Everyone is after the legendary Girl of Water, whose blood can unlock the trans-dimensional prison that holds the fabled 88 beasts...and unleash them unto our world. The only problem is that no one knows where the Girl of Water is, nor do they know if the power she wields has awakened in whatever body she has chosen to possess. Intent on tracking her down, a host of supernatural warriors descends upon Tokyo, all thirsting for the imminent destruction of mankind. All, that is, except one rogue swordsman, who is inexplicably duty-bound to protect the Girl of Water at all costs. The book is full of explicit, graphic violence and extremely harsh language, along with some nudity and sexual situations.

Shimabukuro, Mitsutoshi

Toriko, vol. 1. Viz Media/Shonen Jump 2010 208p. Illustration
Grades: 8 9 10 11 12 Adult   **741.5; Fic**
1. Adventure graphic novels; 2. Food; 3. Humorous graphic novels; 4. Hunting; 5. Manga; 6. Graphic novels
978-1-4215-3509-8, $9.99

Toriko is a Gourmet Hunter, who earns huge bounties for finding ferocious, delicious foods. We're not talking salmon fishing or deer hunting here, but eight-legged alligators and rare fruit guarded by four-armed, bloodthirsty gorilla-type creatures. Toriko himself has a huge appetite for the rare foods, and sometimes eats most of what he's supposed to bring to the fancy restaurants that hire him. Komatsu, the head chef at Igo, a restaurant that caters to those wealthy enough to afford the rare foods, tags along with Toriko, who is a muscular giant of a man. This odd couple forms a friendship born in their mutual love of fine foods. The book is full of crazy action, lots of bugeyed, drop-jawed, slapstick moments, and some potty humor.

Shimizu, Aki

Qwan Vol. 1. Tokyopop 2005 180p. Illustration

Grades: 9 10 11 12 Adult   **741.5; Fic**
1. Adventure graphic novels; 2. Fantasy graphic novels; 3. Manga; 4. Graphic novels
1-59532-534-4, $9.99

In the mystical lands of Han Dynasty China (206 B.C.-A.S. 220), where magical beings are a part of everyday life, Qwan is a strange amnesiac boy who can devour demons and absorb their power. However, he's looking for more than a quick bite. Qwan's quest is to find the sutra known as the Essential Arts of Peace, an ancient verse which will ultimately reveal the ultimate purpose of his existence. The book includes violence, mildly strong language, and mild sexual situations.

Shimizu, Reiko

Moon Child. DC Comics/CMX 2006 192p. Illustration
Grades: 10 11 12 Adult   **741.5; Fic**
1. Manga; 2. Romance graphic novels; 3. Science fiction graphic novels; 4. Shojo manga; 5. Graphic novels
1-4012-0825-8, $9.99

According to prophecy, a half-mermaid, half-human girl will either bring an end to the feud between humanity and the mer-people, or bring about the destruction of all life on Earth. When the mer-man named Shona returns to Earth to find the girl, he meets a young boy suffering from amnesia. The boy, Jimmy, joins Shona in his search. Will they be able to avert the prophecy, or will finding the secret of Jimmy's identity delay them and set Earth on the path to destruction" One of the secondary characters, an old black woman, is drawn in a stereotypical fashion. This series includes some partial nudity, sexual situations, and some mild violence.

Shimizu, Takashi

Ju-On 2. Story by Takashi Shimizu; Manga adaptation by Meimu. Dark Horse Manga 2006 Un Illustration
Grades: 10 11 12 Adult   **741.5; Fic**
1. Horror graphic novels; 2. Manga; 3. Graphic novels
978-1-59307-531-6, $9.95

When horror movie queen Kyoko Harase signs on to appear in a made-for-television special investigating a haunted house, she has no idea that her life has begun to resemble the films that made her an icon. Gruesome and eerie incidents soon plague the cast and crew as an ominous presence pervades their private affairs. What sits just below the surface, burning to manifest itself and satisfy a deep-seated rage" This standalone volume contains strong language and graphic violence.

Shimoku, Kio

Genshiken: The Society for the Study of Modern Visual Culture, Vol. 1. Ballantine Books/Del Rey Manga 2005 190p. Illustration
Grades: 10 11 12 Adult   **741.5; Fic**
1. College students; 2. Humorous graphic novels; 3. Manga; 4. Seinen manga; 5. Graphic novels
0-345-48169-0, $10.95

College freshmen Kenji Sasahara, Makoto Kousaka, and Saki Kasukabe must join a social circle (college clubs in Japan are important avenues of student social life); Sasahara and Kousaka end up joining Genshiken, which is the ultimate otaku club, combining anime, manga, games, doujinshi, and cosplay in one organization. Saki doesn't want Kousaka, whom she considers to be her boyfriend, to be with these people, but she gets sucked into the club despite herself. The doujinshi, which are manga fanzines, are filled with pornographic images (which the reader doesn't usually see); Kousaka has lots of pornographic video games, and there is some fan service. This series gives an insider's look at the otaku lifestyle even while satirizing it.

Shinjo, Mayu

Demon Love Spell. Story and art by Mayu Shinjo; translated and adapted by Tetsuchiro Miyaki; touch-up art & lettering by Inori Fukuda Trant. Viz 2012 155 p.
Grades: 10 11 12 Adult   **741.5/952; Fic**
1. Spirits — Fiction; 2. Supernatural — Fiction
142154945X; 9781421549453, $9.99

In this book by Mayu Shinjo "Miko is a shrine maiden who has never had much success at seeing or banishing spirits. Then she meets Kagura, a . . . demon who feeds off women—s feelings of passion and love. Kagura—s insatiable appetite has left many girls at school brokenhearted, so Miko casts a spell to seal his powers. Surprisingly the spell works—sort of—but now Kagura is after her!" (Publisher's note)

Translated from the Japanese.

Book reads right to left in the original Japanese format.

Shinkai, Makoto

★ **Hoshi** No Koe: The Voices of a Distant Star. Original concept by Makaoto Shinkai; manga adaptation by Mizu Sahara. Tokyopop 2006 232p. Illustration
Grades: 8 9 10 11 12 Adult   **741.5; Fic**
1. Manga; 2. Romance graphic novels; 3. Science fiction graphic novels; 4. Graphic novels
1-59816-529-1, $9.99

In the mid-twenty-first century, high school student Mikako joins a research team heading out to space on a U.N. ship, to explore recent contact with aliens called the Tarsians. Her friend Noboru stays behind on Earth. While he continues with school, he receives cell-phone text messages, his only contact with Mikako. As her ship travels farther away, the low-priority messages take longer to reach Noboru, and he grows older while Mikako remains a teenager. Even as he considers moving on with his life, Noboru learns that love will find a way. This one-volume manga adapts the anime film; however, it stands alone as a story.

Shiomi, Chika

Canon Vol. 1. DC Comics/CMX 2007 200p. Illustration
Grades: 8 9 10 11 12 Adult   **741.5; Fic**
1. Horror graphic novels; 2. Shojo manga; 3. Vampires; 4. Graphic novels
978-1-4012-1163-9, $9.99

Suspense and the supernatural collide in the tale of Canon—the only student to escape the bloody vampire attack that takes the lives of her fellow classmates. But she doesn't get very far before she is captured, bitten and turned into a vampire herself. Struggling against the terrible needs that compel the undead, Canon commits herself to using her powers for good. She'll do whatever she can to avenge the death of her friends and her own unfortunate fate. Joining forces with Fuui—a talking vampire crow—she begins her quest to find Rodd, Lord of the Vampires. There's some mildly harsh language and lots of fighting vampire attacks, but nothing more than has been seen in most Buffy the Vampire Slayer or Angel episodes on television.

Night of the Beasts Volume 1. Go! Comi 2006 200p. Illustration
Grades: 10 11 12 Adult   **741.5; Fic**
   1. Horror graphic novels; 2. Manga; 3. Shojo manga; 4. Supernatural graphic novels; 5. Graphic novels
978-1-933617-14-5, $10.99

   Aria's got a reputation as the toughest girl in school because she can't resist taking on bullies - especially guys who aggressively hit on innocent girls. Which is why she's taken by surprise when her first kiss is stolen by a complete stranger. Not only does he keep making moves on her, but it seems like every time they meet, it's at the latest crime scene of a murder spree that's plaguing Aria's neighborhood. How is it that he seems to know all about the supernatural murderer of these innocent girls? And how will Aria react to his claim only she can save him from a destiny so bloody that even the violent deeds of black demon slaughtering victims all over town will pale in comparison? The book includes mildly strong language, some bloody violence, and mild sexual situations.

Yurara, Vol. 1. Viz Media/Shojo Beat 2007 192p. Illustration
Grades: 10 11 12 Adult   **741.5; Fic**
   1. Fantasy graphic novels; 2. Ghosts; 3. Manga; 4. Shojo manga; 5. Graphic novels
978-1-4215-1350-8, $8.99

   Translated by JN Productions. First year high school student Yurara Tsukinowa is a quiet girl; she has seen ghosts most of her life, but has kept it a secret from anyone outside her family. Since she reacts emotionally in the presence of ghosts, she has a reputation for being weird. At school, she meets Mei Tendo and Yako Hoshino, two handsome boys who have powers to ward off vengeful spirits. When she's threatened by the ghost of a girl at her classroom desk, Yurara's guardian spirit manifests herself; this dark-haired, bold girl has the power to release souls. Yurara has to fend off Mei's teasing advances and her female classmates' jealousy while trying to figure out just what she can now do. The story features some supernatural violence and sexual innuendo.

Shirodaira, Kyo
   The **record** of a fallen vampire vol. 1. Story by Kyo Shirodaira; art by Yuri Kimura. Viz Media 2008 208p. Illustration
Grades: 9 10 11 12 Adult   **741.5; Fic**
   1. Fantasy graphic novels; 2. Manga; 3. Vampires; 4. Graphic novels
978-1-4215-1773-5, $9.99

   Long, long ago, Vampire King Akabara "Red Rose" Strauss lost both his kingdom and his queen, whose power went out of control when she tried to save her husband. Since humans were unable to kill the queen, they sealed her away then erected thousands of fake seals so that Akabara would never find her. For centuries, Akabara has hunted down seals

and destroyed them one by one, always pursued by dhampires, half human/half vampire beings determined to destroy all vampires, and by the Black Swan. The Black Swan possesses a young human girl every fifty years, giving her the power to destroy the Vampire King and his queen. Now Akabara faces the 49th Black Swan; each new incarnation is stronger than the last. The series includes graphic, bloody violence and some harsh language.

Shirow, Masamune
   The **ghost** in the shell. Story and art by Shirow Masamune; translation and English adaptation, Frederik L. Schodt and Toren Smith. Kodansha Comics 2009 348 p. Illustration; Color
Grades: 11 12 Adult   **741.5; 741.5/952**
   1. Androids — Fiction; 2. Cyborgs
9781935429012, $26.99
                    LC 2010292697

   In this book, by Shirow Masamune, "the line between man and machine has been inexorably blurred. . . . In this rapidly converging landscape, cyborg superagent Major Motoko Kusanagi is charged to track down the craftiest and most dangerous terrorists and cybercriminals. . . . When Major Kusanagi tracks the cybertrail of one such master hacker, the Puppeteer, her quest leads her into a world beyond information and technology." (Publisher's note)
   Translated and adapted from the Japanese.
   Other titles in this series are: Ghost in the Shell 2: Man-Machine Interface; Ghost in the Shell 1.5: Human-Error Processor

Shonen, Sasaki
   Lunar Legend Tsukihime Vol. 1. DrMaster Publications 2006 208p. Illustration
Grades: 10 11 12 Adult   **741.5; Fic**
   1. Horror graphic novels; 2. Manga; 3. Shonen manga; 4. Graphic novels
978-1-59796-075-5, $9.95

   A childhood accident has left young Shiki Tohno with the ability to see the hidden lines or weak points in all things - be they organic or inanimate. By striking or cutting along these lines Shiki can slice through anything. Unfortunately the giftomes packaged with a nearly irresistable urge to kill using his new ability. The story includes graphic violence and some sexual situations.

Showcase Presents The Flash, Volume One
   DC Comics 2007 509p. Illustration
Grades: 7 8 9 10 11 12 Adult   **741.5; Fic**
   1. Flash (Fictional character); 2. Superhero graphic novels; 3. Graphic novels
978-1-4012-1327-5, $16.99

   A freak accident gives Central City police scientist Barry Allen fantastic super-speed abilities. Inspired by his favorite childhood comic book hero, Allen uses the name the Flash and uses his powers to help humanity. He soon finds himself facing such villains as Captain Cold, Mirror Master, Gorilla Grodd, the Pied Piper, Weather Wizard, and more. This volume collects 39 stories from the 1950s and 1960s in black and white.

Showcase Presents: Jonah Hex Volume 1.
DC Comics 2005 528p. Illustration
Grades: 10 11 12 Adult   741.5; Fic
1. Jonah Hex (Fictional character); 2. Western graphic novels; 3. Graphic novels
1-4012-0760-X, $16.99
He was a hero to some, a villain to others; and wherever he rode, people spoke his name in whispers. He had no friends, this Jonah Hex, but he did have two companions: one was death itself, the other - the acrid smell of gun smoke. These are the earliest adventures of the gunslinger, which were first published in the early 1970s, at a time when the spaghetti westerns of Sergio Leone and others had introduced tough, violent antiheroes to the American fiction staple. The stories include a considerable amount of violence, but it's not too graphic, and very little strong language.

Showcase Presents Superman Family Volume One
Otto Binder [and others], writers ; C.C. Beck [and others], pencillers and inkers. DC Comics 2006 572p. Illustration
Grades: 6 7 8 9 10 11 12 Adult   741.5; Fic
1. Jimmy Olsen (Fictional character); 2. Lois Lane (Fictional character); 3. Superhero graphic novels; 4. Superman (Fictional character); 5. Graphic novels
978-1-4012-0787-8, $16.99
This volume spotlights Superman's girlfriend Lois Lane and his pal Jimmy Olsen. Learn more about these two dynamic personalities in their solo stories as each braves danger for the latest scoop. These stories from the 1950s also introduceing elements such as the Daily Planet's Flying Newsroom and Jimmy's penchant for disguises. The Showcase series reprints the older comics stories in black and white collections.

Showcase Presents The Unknown Soldier Volume 1
DC Comics 2006 552p. Illustration
Grades: 8 9 10 11 12 Adult   741.5; Fic
1. Adventure graphic novels; 2. Unknown Soldier (Fictional character); 3. Graphic novels
978-1-4012-1090-8, $16.99
His face hideously disfigured by a grenade explosion in the early days of World War II, the young man who would become the Unknown Soldier was determined to continue fighting for his country. His true identity kept top secret, he became the perfect covert operative, using a multitude of disguises to carry out his exploits against the Axis powers. The first 38 adventures of the Unknown Soldier are collected in this black and white reprint volume, with stories dating from 1970 through 1975.

Showcase Presents: Green Arrow Volume 1
Otto Binder [and others], writers ; C.C. Beck [and others], pencillers and inkers. DC Comics 2006 528p. Illustration
Grades: 7 8 9 10 11 12 Adult   741.5; Fic
1. Green Arrow (Fictional character); 2. Superhero graphic novels; 3. Graphic novels
1-4012-0785-5, $16.99
Millionaire Oliver Queen mastered the bow and arrow as a matter of survival when he was trapped on a desert island. Back home in Star City, he chose to use his newfound skills as the costumed champion Green Arrow. With his sidekick, Speedy, he tackled crooks and solved mysteries with energy, style, and the occasional boxing glove arrow. The stories collected in this black and white volume were originally published from 1958 through 1969

Showcase Presents: The House of Mystery Volume 1
DC Comics 2006 552p. Illustration
Grades: 7 8 9 10 11 12 Adult   741.5; Fic
1. Horror graphic novels; 2. Supernatural graphic novels; 3. Graphic novels
978-1-4012-0786-1, $16.99
Just beyond the door of the House of Mystery await spine-chilling (and some rib-tickling) stories of the supernatural, tales of ghosts and witches, ghouls and gargoyles, all hosted by Cain, the caretaker of the House. This black and white volume reprints House of Mystery issues 174-194, dating from 1968 through 1971. Some of the stories have a "Twilight Zone" feel, others are a little more gruesome.

Showcase Presents: Legion of Super-Heroes Volume 1
DC Comics 2007 552p. Illustration
Grades: 7 8 9 10 11 12 Adult   741.5; Fic
1. Legion of Super-Heroes (Fictional characters); 2. Superhero graphic novels; 3. Graphic novels
978-1-4012-1382-4, $16.99
The Legion of Super-Heroes, teenagers from across the cosmos, each with a unique ability, are the sworn protectors of the galaxy. Headquartered in their Super-Hero Club House, Lightning Lad, Saturn Girl, and Cosmic Boy have high standards for young hopeful champions wishing to join their ranks. With the largest roster of any super-team of the 2960s, they patrol all sectors of the universe to ensure peace and justice for all sentient beings. This volume collects black and white reprints of stories originally published from 1958 through 1964.

Showcase Presents: Martian Manhunter Volume 1
DC Comics 2007 544p. Illustration
Grades: 7 8 9 10 11 12 Adult   741.5; Fic
1. Martian Man hunter (Fictional character); 2. Superhero graphic novels; 3. Graphic novels
978-1-4012-1368-8, $16.99
After being accidentally teleported to Earth, Martian J'onn J'onzz finds himself stranded in a strange new world, with no way home. Using his powers to disguise his appearance, J'onn J'onzz adopts the name of deceased Denver police detective John Jones. With this new identity, he joins the Middleton Police force, secretly using his powers to help the inhabitants of Earth. Jack Miller and Joe Samachson were principal writers on the series in the early years, and artist Joe Certa did all the pencils; this black and white volume reprints stories originally published from 1953 through 1962.

Showcase Presents: Metamorpho, the Element Man Volume 1
DC Comics 2005 560p. Illustration
Grades: 7 8 9 10 11 12 Adult   741.5; Fic

1. Science fiction graphic novels; 2. Superhero graphic novels; 3. Graphic novels
1-4012-0762-6, $16.99

Adventurer Rex Mason would do almost anything for the right price, but he ended up paying with his own humanity for stealing the legendary Orb of Ra for millionaire industrialist Simon Stagg. The mysterious relic transformed Rex into a freakish "element" man, with the ability to transform his body into hundreds of different substances. Calling himself Metamorpho, Rex considered his life cursed and sought a way to reverse the Orb's powers. Along the way, Stagg used Metamorpho's unique skills for his own purposes, and the Element Man would go along, since it meant more time with Stagg's gorgeous daughter Sapphire. The stories in this black and white volume date from 1964 through 1966.

Showcase Presents: Sgt. Rock
DC Comics 2007 543p. Illustration
Grades: 8 9 10 11 12 Adult   **741.5**
1. Adventure graphic novels; 2. Sgt Rock (Fictional character); 3. World War, 1939-1945; 4. Graphic novels
978-1-4012-1713-6, $16.99

Sgt. Rock, created by Robert Kanigher, was an ordinary soldier fighting in World War II. The stories collected in this volume, published from 1959 through 1962, depict Rock and his Easy Company fighting against evil during the war. Even today, Sgt. Rock is a symbol of patriotism and of America's fighting spirit. The stories include battle action.

Showcase Presents: Superman Volume 1
Otto Binder [and others], writers ; C.C. Beck [and others], pencillers and inkers. DC Comics 2005 560p. Illustration
Grades: 6 7 8 9 10 11 12 Adult   **741.5; Fic**
1. Superhero graphic novels; 2. Superman (Fictional character); 3. Graphic novels
1-4012-0758-8, $9.99

This first volume in the Showcase Presents Library of Classics features stories about Superman dating from 1958 through 1959. The adventure collected here have influenced the history of Superman and his extended family. From the introduction of his first love, the mermaid Lori Lemaris, to the introduction of his cousin Supergirl, Superman faces his most dangerous opponents, including Bizarro, Metallo, and Brainiac.

Showcase Presents: Superman Volume 2
DC Comics 2006 576p. Illustration
Grades: 7 8 9 10 11 12 Adult   **741.5; Fic**
1. Superhero graphic novels; 2. Superman (Fictional character); 3. Graphic novels
978-1-4012-1041-0, $16.99

The beginning of the 1960s ushered in a new era for Superman. These Silver Age exploits see Superman confront a wide array of villains, explore the planet Krypton, and overcome Kryptonite exposure, become a Bizarro, and more. The stories, reprinted here in black and white, date from December 1959 through May 1961.

Showcase Presents: Teen Titans Volume 1
DC Comics 2006 528p. Illustration

Grades: 6 7 8 9 10 11 12 Adult   **Fic; 741.5**
1. Flash (Fictional character); 2. Robin (Fictional character); 3. Superhero graphic novels; 4. Teen Titans (Fictional characters); 5. Graphic novels
978-1-4012-0788-5, $16.99

The Teen Titans were all sidekicks to such heroes as Batman, Wonder Woman, Aquaman, and the Flash. When teen heroes Robin, Aqualad, and Kid Flash joined together, they became a forced to be reckoned with. Wonder Girl quickly joined them, and occasionally Speedy would come, and they all proved they were just as capable of defeating the bad guys and saving the world as their mentors, while still being teens and having fun. The black and white reprinted stories originally appeared from 1964 through 1968. Today's teens will get a kick out of what the writers thought was cool "teen speak" back then.

Showcase Presents: The War That Time Forgot
DC Comics 2007 560p. Illustration
Grades: 6 7 8 9 10 11 12 Adult   **741.5; Fic**
1. Adventure graphic novels; 2. Dinosaurs; 3. World War, 1939-1945; 4. Graphic novels
978-1-4012-1253-7, $16.99

On an unnamed, uncharted Pacific island, dinosaurs continued to thrive while World War II raged across the globe. It is on this island that members of the U.S. Armed Forces found themselves " armed only with standard issue weapons against the deadliest predators ever to roam the Earth. This volume collects Star Spangled War Stories issues #90-128, from 1960 through 1966. There's a lot of war action and dinosaur-fighting action. The stories here have been reprinted in black and white.

Siegel, Jerry
The **Superman** Chronicles Volume Three. Superman created by Jerry Siegel & Joe Shuster ; all stories written by Jerry Siegel and illustrated by Joe Shuster. DC Comics 2007 190p. Illustration
Grades: 6 7 8 9 10 11 12 Adult   **741.5; Fic**
1. Superhero graphic novels; 2. Superman (Fictional character); 3. Graphic novels
978-1-4012-1374-9, $14.99

In this third volume of the adventures of Superman presented in chronological order, the Man of Steel faces the villain who would plague him ever since: Lex Luthor. Clark Kent and Lois Lane become European war correspondents covering the conflicts that will eventually become World War II. And Superman maintains his reputation as the champion of the oppressed by battling jewel thieves, blackmailers, and predatory monsters.

The **Superman** Chronicles Volume Two. Superman created by Jerry Siegel & Joe Shuster ; all stories written by Jerry Siegel and illustrated by Joe Shuster. DC Comics 2007 192p. Illustration
Grades: 7 8 9 10 11 12 Adult   **741.5; Fic**
1. Superhero graphic novels; 2. Superman (Fictional character); 3. Graphic novels
978-1-4012-1215-5, $14.99

Experience the history of Superman with this series that reprints the early adventures of the Man of Tomorrow in chronological order. This volume features classic tales from

1939 and 1940 written and illustrated by Superman co-creators Jerry Siegel and Joe Shuster, in which the Man of Tomorrow battles crooked politicians and slumlords as he brings justice to the downtrodden masses.

Superman: The World's Finest Comics Archives Volume 1. Jerry Siegel & Joe Shuster. DC Comics 2004 240p. Illustration
Grades: 7 8 9 10 11 12 Adult   **741.5; Fic**
1. Superhero graphic novels; 2. Superman (Fictional character); 3. Graphic novels
1-4012-0151-2, $49.99

This Archives volume collects Superman stories from World's Finest Comics, dating from 1939 through 1944, with stories by the original creators, Siegel and Schuster. In these early adventures, Superman battled "regular" criminals, and his super powers were but a fraction of what they are in current Superman comics. These full-color reprints are bound in a sturdy hardcover edition.

Siegel, Mark
★ **Sailor** Twain: or, The mermaid in the Hudson. Mark Siegel. First Second 2012 399 p.
Grades: Adult   **741.59**
1. Fantasy graphic novels; 2. Love stories; 3. Mermaids and mermen — Fiction; 4. Sailors
1596436360; 9781596436367, $24.99
      LC 2012289260

This historical fantasy graphic novel, by Mark Siegel, is set "one hundred years ago. On the foggy Hudson River, a riverboat captain rescues an injured mermaid from the waters of the busiest port in the United States. A wildly popular—and notoriously reclusive—author makes a public debut. A French nobleman seeks a remedy for a curse. As three lives twine together and race to an unexpected collision, the mystery of the Mermaid of the Hudson deepens." (Publisher's note)

Sierra, Sergio A.
Frankenstein by Mary Shelley: a Dark graphic novel. Adaptation Sergio A. Sierra; illustration Meritxell Ribas. Enslow Publishers 2013 95 p.
Grades: 6 7 8 9 10 11 12 Adult   **741.5**
1. Horror stories; 2. Monsters — Fiction; 3. Graphic novels; 4. Frankenstein (Fictional character)
0766040844; 9780766040847, $25.26
      LC 2011035826

This book is a black-and-white graphic novel adaptation of Mary Shelley—s 19th-century gothic novel "Frankenstein." The plot tells the "tale of a monster, assembled by a scientist from parts of dead bodies, who develops a mind of his own as he learns to loathe himself and hate his creator." (WorldCat)
Includes bibliographical references.

Sievert, Tim
That salty air. Top Shelf Productions 2008 116p. Illustration
Grades: 10 11 12 Adult   **741.5; Fic**
1. Bereavement; 2. Fishing; 3. Ocean; 4. Graphic novels
978-1-60309-005-6, $10

Fisherman Hugh has treated the ocean and its inhabitants with respect and reverence, but when he receives word that his mother died by drowning at sea, he acts as though the ocean itself has betrayed him. His loyal wife MaryAnne has just learned that she's pregnant, and she tries to help her husband. But he returns to fishing with a vengeful attitude that nearly destroys him. A mystical giant squid figures in Hugh's struggles deal with his grief and with the world.

Silady, Matt
The **Homeless** Channel. AiT/Planet Lar 2007 162p. Illustration
Grades: 10 11 12 Adult   **741.5**
1. Homeless persons; 2. Graphic novels
978-1-932051-49-0

When Darcy Shaw starts a 24-hour cable network called The Homeless Channel, she thinks she's got everything figured out. But confronted with an unexpected romance, a sibling out on the streets and corporate sponsors who think they know what's best for her network, Darcy starts to wonder which is more important: saving the world or saving herself. The book includes some sexual situations and strong language.

Simmonds, Posy
Tamara Drewe. Posy Simmonds. Houghton Mifflin 2008 136 p. Color illustration
Grades: Adult   **741.5/942; 741.5**
1. Man-woman relationship — Fiction; 2. Man-woman relationships — Fiction; 3. Villages — Fiction; 4. Graphic novels
0547154127; 9780547154121, $16.95
      LC 2008010924

This graphic novel, by Posy Simmonds, "follows a year at Stonefield, a bucolic writer's retreat run by Beth and Nicholas Hardiman, where Dr. Glen Larson, an American professor and struggling novelist, is staying. The ambitious young Tamara Drewe, mourning the loss of her mother, has returned to her family home nearby. A bookish girl not so long ago, Tamara is now a gossipy columnist at a London paper and undeniably sexy." (Publisher's note)
Originally published: London : Random House, 2007.

Simmons, Josh
House. Fantagraphics Books 2007 Un Illustration
Grades: 11 12 Adult   **741.5; Fic**
1. Horror graphic novels; 2. Graphic novels
978-1-56097-855-8, $12.95

In the thick of a dense wood, a young man comes upon a decrepit house and two teen-aged girls, who quickly decide to explore the abandoned house together. Simmons captures the aloof ennui and deep curiosity of being a teenager-that is, until events force them to confront their own mortality. One of the girls takes a horrible fall, and her clothes are torn; for the rest of the book she is partially nude because of it.

Simone, Gail
Birds of Prey Vol. 4: The Battle Within. Gail Simone, writer; Joe Bennett [and others], pencillers. DC Comics 2006 240p. Illustration

Grades: 9 10 11 12 Adult 741.5
1. Adventure graphic novels; 2. Birds of Prey (Fictional characters); 3. Superhero graphic novels; 4. Graphic novels
978-1-4012-1096-0
Oracle and the others have left Gotham after their headquarters was destroyed but continue their work, stopping a young witch with a split personality, then taking on a met human vigilante who calls herself Harvest and kills unpunished killers. However, Oracle's controlling ways have caused Huntress to remove herself and go after Gotham mobsters on her own. Black Canary enlists the help of Wildcat in Singapore to go after drug dealers, while back home Oracle is overcome by the techno-virus left in her body after she had defeated Brainiac. There's lots of fighting action, but little graphic violence.

Birds of Prey Vol. 5: Perfect Pitch. Gail Simone, writer; Paulo Siqueira [and others], pencillers. DC Comics 2007 Illustration
Grades: 10 11 12 Adult Fic; 741.5
1. Batgirl (Fictional character); 2. Birds of Prey (Fictional characters); 3. Joker (Fictional character); 4. Superhero graphic novels; 5. Graphic novels
978-1-4012-1191-2, $17.99
After being paralyzed by the Joker, former Batgirl Barbara Gordon became Oracle and formed a crime-fighting team with other female heroes including the martial artist with a devastating sonic scream, Black Canary, the vigilante known as the Huntress and the mysterious Lady Blackhawk. In this collection, the team is shaken up as members depart and new teammates are added to the roster. Who will be asked to join Oracle in her all-new Birds Of Prey" Who will refuse, and who will fly the coop for good" There's lots of hand-to-hand fighting in this book.

Birds of Prey: Between Dark & Dawn. Gail Simone, writer; Ed Benes et al, pencillers. DC Comics 2006 Un Illustration
Grades: 9 10 11 12 Adult Fic; 741.5
1. Birds of Prey (Fictional characters); 2. Justice League (Fictional characters); 3. Superhero graphic novels; 4. Graphic novels
978-1-4012-0940-7, $14.99
Huntress goes undercover to infiltrate a religious cult with a dangerous secret and a hidden operative, while Black Canary and Oracle uncover the true nature of Sovereign Brusaw's organization. It all leads to the Huntress's battle against former Justice League member Vixen. Oracle wages a private, internal battle against Brainiac, who has infected her with a techno-organic virus. Finally, the Birds must face the aftermath of the Gotham Gang War, leading to a decision that changes the team's fate forever.

Birds of Prey: Of Like Minds. Gail Simone, writer; Ed Benes, penciller; Alex Lei with Rob Lea, inkers; Hi-Fi, colorist; John E. Workman, Rob Leigh, Jared K. Fletcher, letterers; Ed Benes, Alex Lei with Rob Lei, original series covers. DC Comics 2004 143 p. Color; Illustration
Grades: 9 10 11 12 Adult 741.5
1. Black Canary (Fictional character); 2. Catwoman (Fictional character); 3. Female superhero graphic novels
9781401201920, $14.99; 140120192X
LC 2005295809

"The wheelchair-bound Oracle (Barbara Gordon, formerly Batgirl) now fights crime as a superhacker and cyberspy. Her field agent, Dinah Lance, is the Black Canary, a tough martial artist. When a case goes wrong, and a blackmailer called Savant captures the Canary, he threatens to kill her unless Oracle can supply him with a choice piece of information: the secret identity of Batman." (Library Journal)
Originally published in single magazine form in Birds of prey #56-61

Birds of Prey: Sensei & Student. [Gail Simone, writer; Ed Benes ... [et al.], pencillers; Alex Lei ... [et al.], inkers; Hi-Fi, colorist; Jared K. Fletcher, Rob Leigh, Nick Napolitano, letterers]. DC Comics 2005 Un Color; Illustration
Grades: 9 10 11 12 Adult 741.5
1. Black Canary (Fictional character); 2. Female superhero comic books, strips, etc; 3. Huntress (Fictional character); 4. Oracle (Fictional character)
9781401204341, $17.99; 1401204341
"Black Canary goes to China on a mission of mercy and runs into the DC Universe's most deadly combatant; Lady Shiva! Shiva is acting with a hidden agenda, making Canary an offer that could change the course of her life. Meanwhile, Oracle's life is tearing at the seams as the information she feeds out to aid her various heroes starts going strangely and dangerously awry! Not to mention Huntress stumbling upon some of her secrets!" (Publisher's note)
Originally published in single magazine form in Birds of Prey #62-68—t.p. verso.

Gen 13: Best of a Bad Lot. Talent Caldwell, penciller. DC Comics/Wildstorm 2007 Un Illustration
Grades: 10 11 12 Adult 741.5; Fic
1. Gen 13 (Fictional characters); 2. Superhero graphic novels; 3. Graphic novels
978-1-4012-1323-7, $14.99
The life of a teenager can be a strange experience, but when super-powers are added to the mix things get a whole lot more confusing. Meet Caitlin, Sarah, Roxy, Bobby, and Eddie " outcast teenagers from different parts of the country who quickly learn they all have something in common: abilities far beyond those of their classmates. Discover the secret to their wonderful and scary powers and what role the nefarious Tabula Rasa and International Operations play in their lives as they learn to work as a team. Jim Lee and J. Scott Campbell created Gen 13 in the 1990s; this is a fresh start for the team. This book has a lot of violence in addition to the superhero action.

Killer Princesses. Written by Gail Simone; illustrated by Lea Hernandez; cover colors by Laura Martin. Oni Press 2002 96p. Illustration
Grades: 10 11 12 Adult 741.5; Fic
1. Humorous graphic novels; 2. Mystery graphic novels; 3. Graphic novels
978-1-929998-31-9, $9.95
Meet Charity, Faith, and Hope: the girls of the Tri-Omega Sorority. To some, they're the most popular girls on their campus, but to others, they're the most unstoppable, cruel, and dangerous (not to mention dumbest) assassins in the world! They might not have the highest IQ, but they sure do know how to kick the crap out of the bad guys. The girls

jump, skip, and river dance their way into a military base to bust the heads of evil villains and stop a nuclear weapon from being unleashed by a terrorist's spoiled son. Then they attend a splendid gala event which is hosted by someone from their sorority Mother's past who wants to kill her. They go up against some of the cutest Russian terrorists to hit this side of the Pacific, and deal with a new sorority sister. Danger, intrigue, and hilarity ensue as the girls race against the clock to save the day and get back home in time to look good for class. The story includes some strong language, violence, and sexual suggestiveness.

Secret Six: Six Degrees of Devastation. Gail Simone, writer; Brad Walker, penciller; Jimmy Palmiotti, inker. DC Comics 2007 128p. Illustration
Grades: 11 12 Adult   **741.5; Fic**
   1. Adventure graphic novels; 2. Superhero graphic novels; 3. Graphic novels
978-1-4012-1231-5, $14.99
The mysterious team of misfits walks the line between good and evil and takes on the dirtiest, craziest tasks in the DC Universe. Their first mission, to rescue one of their own from a North Korean prison before he's executed, leads them to the realization that someone is trying to have them all killed. The book includes lots of graphic violence, considerable nudity, sexual situations, and strong language.

Welcome to Tranquility volume 2. DC Comics/Wildstorm 2008 144p. Illustration
Grades: 10 11 12 Adult   **741.5; Fic**
   1. Horror graphic novels; 2. Superhero graphic novels; 3. Zombies; 4. Graphic novels
978-1-4012-1773-0, $19.99
Tranquility, the town where retired superheroes and villains live side-by-side, was rocked by violence and murders, but has been recovering. Now, zombies keep coming back from the dead. It's up to Sheriff Tommy Lindo to find out what's happening, but it's going to take all the retired heroes and villains, and some thought long dead, to fight the powerful demon who wants the human infestation gone from the city. The book includes some partial nudity and lots of violence, especially zombie fighting.

Superman: Strange Attractors. Written by Gail Simone; pencilled by John Byrne. DC Comics 2006 Un Illustration
Grades: 9 10 11 12 Adult   **Fic; 741.5**
   1. Superhero graphic novels; 2. Superman (Fictional character); 3. Graphic novels
1401209173; 9781401209179, $14.99
First, Superman must contend with Dr. Polaris, but something's just not right with the good doctor ... Then, Dr. Psycho comes to Metropolis to mess with Superman's head. And with his Secret Society comrade Black Adam not far behind, a throw down between Adam and Superman is a certainty. Plus, Satanus, the Queen of Fables, and Livewire make Superman's life a living nightmare.

Welcome to Tranquility, book one. DC Comics/Wildstorm 2007 144p. Illustration
Grades: 10 11 12 Adult   **741.5; Fic**
   1. Crime; 2. Superhero graphic novels; 3. Graphic novels
978-1-4012-1516-3, $19.99

Tranquility is like any other small town in America, except for one thing—it's the town where superpowered beings go when they want to retire and raise families. From the Golden Age to the Modern Age, heroes and villains alike live in Tranquility, and the unique blend of personalities and conflicts causes headaches for local law enforcement. When a camera crew comes with a reporter to film a news segment about the town, things get turned upside down by a murder, and it becomes clear Tranquility isn't . . . tranquil. The book includes violence and harsh language.

Sinclair, Alex
   Tom Strong Book Five. Written by Steve Aylett, Brian K. Vaughan, Mark Schultz, Peter Hogan, Ed Brubaker; Pencilled by Peter Snejbjerg, Shawn McManus, Pasqual Ferry, Duncan Fegredo, Chris Sprouse. DC Comics 2005 Un Illustration
Grades: 10 11 12 Adult   **741.5; Fic**
   1. Adventure graphic novels; 2. Science fiction graphic novels; 3. Superhero graphic novels; 4. Tom Strong (Fictional character); 5. Graphic novels
1-4012-0624-7, $24.99
In this volume, other writers have taken over from Alan Moore, who created Tom Strong and his world. Tom and his associates face an ancient menace in the sky; a young woman who distorts reality; and an unusual art thief who brings paintings to life. In a two-part story, Tom is an ordinary schlub who just dreams about being a science super hero; his psychiatrist keeps trying to make him understand that holding on to the dreams is holding him back from reality.

Sizer, Paul
   Moped army, Vol. 1. Cafe Digital Comics 2005 136p. Illustration
Grades: 10 11 12 Adult   **741.5; Fic**
   1. Science fiction graphic novels; 2. Graphic novels
0-9768565-4-9; 978-0-9768565-4-2, $12.95
This graphic novel is set in the same universe as Little White Mouse (2005). "Feeling unsatisfied with her circumscribed life and rich, cruel boyfriend, a privileged teenaged girl runs away to the lower city where the poor dwell, finding a home and a new "family" among the young rebels who call themselves the Moped Army. Even readers who don't like science fiction will enjoy this story that depends on strong characterization." Voice Youth Advocates

Slade, Christian
   ★ **Korgi,** Book 1: Sprouting Wings. Top Shelf Productions 2007 88p. Illustration
Grades: 2 3 4 5 6 7 8 9 10 11 12 Adult   **741.5; Fic**
   1. Dogs; 2. Fantasy graphic novels; 3. Stories without words; 4. Graphic novels
978-1-891830-90-7, $10
In this wordless book, a young Mollie (woodland people) named Ivy and her young Korgi companion named Sprout embark on adventures in Korgi Hollow, an enchanted place. When they wander from the Mollie village, the two fall through a hole in the ground and find nasty, monstrous creatures who want to eat them. As they deal with the danger and make their escape, Ivy and Sprout both discover new

talents. Slade's extensively cross-hatched yet delicate art is highly expressive, and readers young and old will have no trouble figuring out what is going on. The Korgi are based on Welsh corgi dogs, of which Slade and his wife have two.

Korgi, book 2. Top Shelf Productions 2008 Un Illustration
Grades: 3 4 5 6 7 8 9 10 11 12 Adult   **741.5; Fic**
1. Adventure graphic novels; 2. Fantasy graphic novels; 3. Stories without words; 4. Graphic novels
978-1-60309-010-0, $10

In this second wordless volume, the young Mollie named Ivy and her Korgi cub Sprout, experience a harrowing adventure. Someone has been hunting the Mollies and cutting off their wings. Ivy and Sprout rescue one older Mollie named Art and his Korgi when they fall into a deep trap in the woods; then as Ivy flies, a barbed arrow cuts one of her wings off. She and Sprout see a strange creature carrying her wing and they follow him to his place, where he hangs all the Mollie wings like trophies. Ivy decides she wants her wing back, but she and Sprout will have to fight the creature and his automated and nasty bots.

Small, David
★ **Stitches:** a memoir. W.W. Norton 2009 329p. Illustration
Grades: 10 11 12 Adult   **92; 741.5**
1. Art teachers; 2. Artists; 3. Authors; 4. Autobiographical graphic novels; 5. Cancer; 6. Children's authors; 7. Family life; 8. Illustrators; 9. Small, David, 1945-; 10. Graphic novels
978-0-393-06857-3, $23.95; 0-393-06857-9
LC 2009-22526

David Small grew up in a dysfunctional family, with a radiologist father who was distant, an angry mother who expressed her anger in eloquent silences, and an older brother who played drums a lot to express his frustrations. When he was eleven, he had a lump, a growth, on the side of his neck. Nothing was done until he was fourteen. He thought he was going in for a minor surgery to remove the cyst from his neck; instead, there were two surgeries, and when he woke up, he had no voice—a vocal cord was removed. He later learned he had cancer, something his parents refused to discuss. After he finds his mother in bed with another woman and his father confesses that he exposed him to x-rays when he was very young, Small leaves home at age sixteen, with little except his dreams that his art could be his life. In one early scene, Small shows the indignities wrought upon his body by his father, including an enema. In another scene, young Small and his older brother look at their father's medical books and see a woman's breast and a man's penis; towards the end of the book, Small draws his grandmother stripping all her clothes off and dancing wildly after setting her house on fire. Other than these few images, Small's depictions of his horrible childhood and teen years are quiet and low-key.

"Emotionally raw, artistically compelling and psychologically devastating graphic memoir of childhood trauma." Kirkus

Smith, Dwayne Alexander
Speed Racer. Art by Dwayne Alexander Smith. Seven Seas Entertainment 2007 Un Illustration

Grades: 8 9 10 11 12 Adult   **741.5; Fic**
1. Adventure graphic novels; 2. Automobile racing; 3. Racer, Speed (Fictional character); 4. Graphic novels
978-1-933164-33-5, $9.99

The popular cartoon character Speed Racer is back in an original global manga story. Speed comes from a family with racing in its blood; his older brother Rex presumably died in an accident. Speed drives the Mach 5 and, in this book, he's participating in a grueling three-day, 900 mile race. His main opponent, Adam Matic, determines to win at any cost and tries to sabotage the Mach 5, but on the second day of the race, he's the one who dies. His father, the mad scientist Otto Matic, takes Adam's heart and builds a cyborg version of his son to carry on; but Adam 2 also retains the original man's hatred and tries to kill Speed. Several publishers are bringing Speed Racer back to the U.S. in book form, and a new live-action movie is scheduled for a May 2008 release. This one has lots of action and some violence that makes it more suitable for teen readers.

Smith, Ian
Oddjob: The Collected Stories Volume 1. By Ian and Tyson Smith. Slave Labor Graphics 2002 Un Illustration
Grades: 9 10 11 12 Adult   **741.5; Fic**
1. Humorous graphic novels; 2. Mystery graphic novels; 3. Graphic novels
0-943151-63-5, $19.95

The odd has arrived. Moe is the Investigator of the Odd, the man called when the going gets too strange for the police, too askew for the FBI, too creepy for the CIA. His exploits with his unemployable sidekick clown Robin, and ball player Moose Mulligan span eight issues and five mad scientists, as well as living gummi men, sloths, Amish cyborgs, and exploding echidna. The collection comes complete with a newly unearthed story, commentary, and rare case files.

Smith, Jeff
★ **Bone** Book Seven: ghost circles. Scholastic/GRAPHIX 2008 152p. Illustration
Grades: 3 4 5 6 7 8 9 10 11 12 Adult   **741.5; Fic**
1. Adventure graphic novels; 2. Fantasy graphic novels; 3. Graphic novels
978-0-439-70629-2, $19.99; 978-0-439-70634-6 (pa), $9.99
LC 2007-9568403

The Bone cousins, Gran'ma Ben, Thorn, and their loyal rat creature cub Bartleby venture on a journey through the mysterious ghost circles to Atheia, the old city of the royal family. Meanwhile, the Barrelhaven villagers and the Veni Yan face enemy hordes. Steve Hamaker is the colorist for this full color version of Smith's comic epic.

★ **Bone** vol. 8: treasure hunters. Scholastic/Graphix 2008 138p. Illustration
Grades: 5 6 7 8 9 10 11 12 Adult   **741.5; Fic**
1. Adventure graphic novels; 2. Fantasy graphic novels; 3. Graphic novels
978-0-439-70630-8, $18.95; 978-0-439-70633-9 (pa), $9.99
LC 2008-9568403

The Bone cousins, Gran'ma Ben, and Thorn reach the city of Atheia, where they prepare to battle the Lord of the Locusts. Meanwhile, Thorn's visions are becoming more threatening and Phoney Bone is convinced Atheia is rich in gold, and he is determined to find it. But all is not well in Atheia, and Thorn is in great danger, not only from Briar and the Lord of the Locusts. This edition is in full color, done by Steve Hamaker.

RASL. Jeff Smith. Cartoon Books 2013 472 p. Illustration; Color

Grades: Adult   **741.5**
1. Adventure graphic novels; 2. Thieves
1888963379; 9781888963373, $39.95

LC 2011277280

In this graphic novel, by Jeff Smith, "when Rasl, a thief and ex-military engineer, discovers the lost journals of Nikola Tesla, he bridges the gap between modern physics and history's most notorious scientist. But his breakthrough comes at a price. In this twisting tale of violence, intrigue, and betrayal, Rasl finds himself in possession of humankind's greatest and most dangerous secret." (Publisher's note)

Also available in four individual volumes

Smith, Kevin
Spider-Man and the Black Cat: The Evil That Men Do. writer, Kevin Smith; artist, Terry Dodson. Marvel Entertainment 2007 Un Illustration

Grades: 10 11 12 Adult   **741.5; Fic**
1. Spider-Man (Fictional character); 2. Superhero graphic novels; 3. Graphic novels
978-0-7851-1079-8, $14.99

The mysterious disappearance of an old friend brings Felicia Hardy, the Black Cat, to New York in search of answers, and a certain web-slinging ex-lover of hers is following the same trail. How long will it take before they do some... catching up? This book is written by filmmaker and former comic store owner Kevin Smith (of Jay and Silent Bob fame). The book includes some sexually suggestive content.

Smith, Mark Andrew
The **amazing** Joy Buzzards volume 1: here come the spiders. Image Comics 2008 Un Illustration

Grades: 9 10 11 12 Adult   **741.5; Fic**
1. Fantasy graphic novels; 2. Humorous graphic novels; 3. Rock music; 4. Spies; 5. Graphic novels
978-1-58240-918-4, $19.99

Rockers Gabe, Biff, and Stevo are the Amazing Joy Buzzards, a hot rock band managed by Dalton, who works for the Creative International Artists Agency. Yes, its initials read "CIA." And yes, it is the covert government agency. The boys in the band have no idea that they're a front for intelligence agency covert operations. They get into enough trouble on their own, such as when Stevo becomes a giant monster, or when Gabe stars in a movie and movie star Brick Brannigan is nearly killed, or when the boys throw a free concert and the entire audience is turned into bloodthirsty zombies, ... This book collects the first two trade paperback volumes of the adventures of the Amazing Joy Buzzards, and Image Comics has been publishing a new ongoing

comic book series of more rocking, bopping, fantastical, super spy type stories. There is some violence and some brief moments of sexual innuendo.

Aqua Leung. Mark Andrew Smith; art by Paul Maybury. Image Comics 2008 Un Illustration

Grades: 9 10 11 12 Adult   **741.5; Fic**
1. Adventure graphic novels; 2. Fantasy graphic novels; 3. Ocean; 4. Graphic novels
978-1-58240-863-7, $17.99

Adam Leung has never quite fit in, especially at school. Then one day he comes home and finds his parents slaughtered and the murderer waiting for him. Atlantean warriors save him and take him under the ocean, where Adam finds he can breathe, and he learns that he is the son of the king. Taking back his true name of Aqua, he begins the process of learning everything about his true home so he can undertake the journey to take back his father's kingdom from the evil lords who rule over it. The book includes violence, bloodshed and military battles.

Popgun, volume one: a graphic mixtape. Image Comics 2007 448p. Illustration

Grades: 11 12 Adult   **741.5**
1. Short stories; 2. Graphic novels
978-1-58240-824-8, $29.99

This anthology of graphic short stories rams through the various genres with stories from comics veterans and newcomers, including Eric Larsen, Mike Allred, Dan Hipp, Rick Remender, Phil Yeh, Richard Starkings, Jamie S. Rich, Jim Mahfood, Leah Moore, and many more. Many of the stories include nudity, sexual situations, harsh language, and violence.

Sniegoski, Tom
Talent. Written by Christopher Golden & Tom Sniegoski; art by Paul Azaceta; colors by Ron Riley; letters by Marshall Dillon. Boom! Studios 2007 120p. Illustration

Grades: 10 11 12 Adult   **741.5**
1. Mystery graphic novels; 2. Graphic novels
978-1-934506-05-9, $14.99

When a plane crashes, sole survivor Nicholas Dane discovers he can channel his dead fellow passengers' talents. Chased by the killers who destroyed the plane, Dane stays one step ahead of death, while putting the pieces of the mystery together. Aided by a ... spirit ... Dane soon learns that some of the passengers on the ill-fated flight were killers working for the organization now hunting him. The book includes violence.

Snyder, Scott
American vampire; Volume 1. Scott Snyder, Stephen King, writers; Rafael Albuquerque, artist; Dave McCaig, colorist; Steve Wands, letterer. Vertigo 2010 Un Color; Illustration

Grades: Adult   **741.5**
1. Hollywood (Calif) — Fiction; 2. Horror graphic novels; 3. Vampires — Fiction
1401229743; 1401228305; 9781401229740, $19.99; 9781401228309, $24.99

LC 2011453896

Eisner Award: Best New Series (2011)

"This volume follows two stories: one written by Snyder and one written by King. Snyder's story is set in 1920's LA; we follow Pearl, a young woman who is turned into a vampire and sets out on a path of righteous revenge against the European Vampires who tortured and abused her. This story is paired with King's story, a western about Skinner Sweet, the original American Vampire—a stronger, faster creature than any vampire ever seen before, with rattlesnake fangs and powered by the sun." (Publisher's note)

Volume 1 of an ongoing series

Batman: night of the owls. By Scott Snyder and Greg Capullo. DC Comics 2013 368 p. Illustration; Color

Grades: Adult **741.5/973; Fic**

1. Batgirl (Fictional character); 2. Batman (Fictional character); 3. Catwoman (Fictional character); 4. Nightwing (Fictional character); 5. Robin (Fictional character); 6. Graphic novels

1401237738; 9781401237738, $29.99

LC 2012040574

This graphic novel, written by Scott Snyder and Greg Capullo, features the superhero Batman. "As evil spreads across Gotham City, Batman's allies, including Red Robin, Batwing, Robin, Batgirl, the Birds of Prey, Nightwing and even Catwoman find themselves in a battle coming from all sides. The Court of Owls have shown their hand, and it's up to the collective effort of these heroes, some more unlikely than others, in this sprawling tale of corruption and violence."

Originally published in single magazine form in Batman 8-11, Nightwing 8-9, All-Star Western 9, Catwoman 9, Batgirl 9, Batman: The Dark Knight 9, Batman and Robin 9, Batwing 9, Birds Of Prey 9, Red Hood and The Outlaws 9, Batman Annual 1.

Batman; Volume 1. Scott Snyder, Greg Capullo, Jonathan Glapion. DC Comics 2012 176 p.

Grades: Adult **741.5; 741.5/973**

1. Adventure fiction; 2. Batman (Fictional character); 3. Superhero comic books, strips, etc; 4. Graphic novels

1401235417; 9781401235413, $24.99

LC 2011051796

This collection begins a new era of The Dark Knight as with the relaunch of 'Batman,' as a part of DC Comics-The New 52! After a series of . . . murders rocks Gotham City, Batman begins to realize that . . . these crimes go far deeper than appearances suggest. . . . [Batman] discovers a conspiracy going back to his youth and beyond to the origins of the city he's sworn to protect. (Publisher's note)

Batman; Volume 1: The court of owls. Scott Snyder, writer; Greg Capullo, penciller; Jonathan Glapion, inker. DC Comics 2012 Un Color; Illustration (New 52)

Grades: 9 10 11 12 Adult **741.5**

1. Batman (Fictional character); 2. Superhero comic books, strips, etc

1401235425; 9781401235420, $16.99

"After a series of brutal murders rocks Gotham City, Batman begins to realize that perhaps these crimes go far deeper than appearances suggest. As the Caped Crusader begins to unravel this deadly mystery, he discovers a conspiracy going back to his youth and beyond to the origins of the city he's sworn to protect. Could the Court of Owls,

once thought to be nothing more than an urban legend, be behind the crime and corruption? Or is Bruce Wayne losing his grip on sanity and falling prey to the pressures of his war on crime?" (Publisher's note)

Batman; Volume 2: The City of Owls. Written by Scott Snyderr and James Tynion IV; illustrated by Greg Capullo, Jonathan Glapion, Rafael Albuquerque, Jason Fabok, Becky Cloonan, Andy Clarke, and Sandu Florea; colored by FCO Plascencia Dave McCaig, Peter Steigerwald, Nathan F. DC Comics 2013 208 p. Color illustration

Grades: Adult **Fic; 741.5/973**

1. Batman (Fictional character); 2. Graphic novels

1401237770; 9781401237776, $24.99; 9781401237783, $16.99

LC 2012045985

"Batman must stop the Talons that have breeched the Batcave in order to save an innocent life and Gotham City. In the backup story, [readers] learn more about the Pennyworth family and the secrets they've kept from the Wayne family." (Publisher's note)

Originally published in single magazine form in Batman 8-12, Batman Annual 1 — Title page verso.

Swamp thing volume 1: raise them bones. Scott Snyder, Yanick Paquette, Marco Rudy. DC Comics 2012 168 p. Color illustration

Grades: Adult **Fic; 741.5/973**

1. Monsters; 2. Superhero comic books, strips, etc; 3. Superhero graphic novels

1401234623; 9781401234621, $14.99

LC 2012015245

This collection, by Scott Snyder, illustrated by Yanick Paquette, presents volume one of "The New 52" re-launch of the DC Comics "Swamp Thing" series. "Alec Holland has his life back . . . but the 'Green' has plans for it. A monstrous evil is rising in the desert, and it'll take a monster of another kind to defend life as we know it!" (Publisher's note)

Originally published in single magazine form in SWAMP THING 1-7.

Other Swamp Thing volumes written by Snyder are: 2: Family tree; 3: Rotworld

The **Wake.** Scott Snyder, writer; Sean Murphy, artist. DC Comics/Vertigo 2014 256 p. Color; Illustration

Grades: Adult **741.5**

1. Mermaids and mermen — Fiction; 2. Science fiction graphic novels

1401245234; 9781401245238, $24.99

LC 2014026869

Eisner Award: Best Limited Series (2014)

In this graphic novel, by Scott Snyder and illustrated by Sean Murphy, "when marine biologist Lee Archer is approached by the Department of Homeland Security for help with a new threat, . . . soon she is plunging to the depths of the Arctic Circle to a[n] . . . underwater oilrig . . . on the brink of an incredible discovery. But when things go horribly wrong, this scientific safe haven will turn into a house of horrors at the bottom of the ocean." (Publisher's note)

"Snyder's story is a ripsnorter from start to finish, heavy on the action and quips." Pub Wkly

Collects The Wake #1-10

Wytches 1. Story, Scott Snyder; art, Jock; colors, Matt Hollingsworth; letters, Clem Robins; editor, David Brothers. Image Comics 2015 144 p. Color; Illustration
Grades: Adult **741.5**
1. Horror graphic novels; 2. Monsters — Fiction; 3. Witches — Fiction
1632153807; 9781632153807, $9.99

In this graphic novel by Scott Snyder, illustrated by Jock, "when the Rooks family moves to the remote town of Litchfield, NH to escape a haunting trauma, they're hopeful about starting over. But something evil is waiting for them in the woods just beyond town. Watching from the trees. 'Wytches' takes the mythology of witches to a far creepier, bone-chilling place than readers have dared venture before." (Publisher's note)

Snyder "uses familiar genre archetypes to create an easily accessible environment, with quick twists and unexpected reveals to put a fresh spin on a seemingly familiar story. His scares are as grotesque as they are originalùthe wytches trap their victims graphically in treesùbut what makes this book stand out is the chemistry between the Rooks." Booklist

Originally published in single magazine form as Wytches #1-6
Volume 1 of an ongoing series

Soda, Masahito
Firefighter! Daigo of Fire Company M Volume 1. Viz Media 2003 208p. Illustration
Grades: 9 10 11 12 Adult **741.5; Fic**
1. Adventure graphic novels; 2. Firefighters; 3. Manga; 4. Shonen manga; 5. Graphic novels
1-56931-955-3, $9.95

Fire, smoke, adrenaline, and fear—when everyone is running to escape from a fire, a few courageous people are running to jump right into the thick of it. Firefighters put their own lives on the line to protect others and Daigo Asahina has always dreamed of becoming one. He's eighteen years old, fresh out of the training academy, and has been newly assigned to Medaka-Ga-Hama fire station. Cocky and overconfident, Daigo responds to a few calls and is quickly humbled and put in his place—he's still got a lot to learn before he can call himself a true firefighter. There's some mildly bad language and mild violence in the stories that focus on Daigo and his fellow firefighters and their job.
Volume 1 of 20

Son, Hee-Joon
IDeNTITY Volume 1. Tokyopop 2005 192p. Illustration
Grades: 9 10 11 12 Adult **741.5; Fic**
1. Adventure graphic novels; 2. Fantasy graphic novels; 3. Manwha; 4. Graphic novels
1-59532-345-7, $9.99

In real life, Roto, Boromid and Ah-Dol are average kids with average problems, but in the virtual world of Lost Saga, they're heroes. They might even become legends...if they can stop bickering long enough to level up. Whether it's werewolves running rampant or a gorgeous pair of troublesome thieves, our boys must be ready for anything, because in Lost Saga nothing is what it seems and murder can happen with a click of a mouse. The book includes

fantasy gaming violence, some strong language, and some sexual suggestiveness.

Song, Ji-Hyung
XS Hybrid Vol. 1. Dark Horse Comics 2007 192p. Illustration
Grades: 11 12 Adult **741.5; Fic**
1. Manwha; 2. Science fiction graphic novels; 3. Graphic novels
978-1-59307-628-3, $10.95

In a strange future where gifted, "hybrid" humans police the planet, Mina is a likeable tomboy with growing psychic powers. When a young boy falls into a coma after gazing into her eyes, it's clear that there's more to Mina than her pretty looks. This young boy, Huin Chang, grows up to be quite a daredevil, and his awkward, secret love for Mina fuels his protective fire when mysterious men arrive, bringing the violence of the "hybrid" world with them. The book includes considerable graphic violence and use of foul language.

Sonic the Hedgehog: The Beginning
Archie Comics 2003 96p. Illustration
Grades: 3 4 5 6 7 8 9 10 11 12 Adult **741.5; Fic**
1. Adventure graphic novels; 2. Humorous graphic novels; 3. Sonic the Hedgehog (Fictional character); 4. Graphic novels
1-879794-12-8, $10.95

In 1993, Sonic the Hedgehog sped his way from video games to comic books, and has been going strong ever since. Now, readers can enjoy his earliest comic book adventures with this edition that reprints the first appearances of Tails, Princess Sally, Antoine, Rotor, Uncle Chuck, and Muttski. Fans can also marvel at Sonic's magic rings, the freedom emeralds, and King Acorn's magic crown; while booing and hissing at the villainous Robotnik, his evil Swat-Bots, and his myriad dastardly devices.

Sorachi, Hideaki
Gin Tama Vol. 1. Viz Media/Shonen Jump Advanced 2007 216p. Illustration
Grades: 10 11 12 Adult **741.5; Fic**
1. Humorous graphic novels; 2. Manga; 3. Shonen manga; 4. Graphic novels
978-1-4215-1358-4, $7.99

The samurai didn't stand a chance. First, the aliens invaded Japan. Next, they took all the jobs. And then they confiscated everyone's swords. So what does a hotheaded former samurai like Sakata "Gin" Gintoki do to make ends meet" Take any odd job that comes his way, even if it means losing his dignity. Sleazy alien moneylenders, monsters on the rampage, and a ticking time bomb may all be in a day's work for Gin, but a drop in his blood sugar level means trouble for everyone. Some harsh language and lots of fighting action fill this alternate history comedy.

Soria, Gabriel
★ **Life** sucks. [text by] Jessica Abel, Gabe Soria; [art by] Warren Pleece; coloring by Hilary Sycamore. First Second Books 2008 186p. Illustration
Grades: 10 11 12 Adult **741.5; Fic**

1. Horror graphic novels; 2. Humorous graphic novels; 3. Romance graphic novels; 4. Vampires; 5. Graphic novels
978-1-59643-107-2, $19.95; 1-59643-107-5

Anyone who thinks the vampire life is all romantic and ethereal better have another think. Dave can tell them, it sucks. He's the night manager for a convenience store, and he's a vampire, "made" by his boss (master), Radu. He's not the only one; in their neighborhood, most of the shops are owned by vampires who make their night managers vampires. Dave can't make himself drink from humans, so he drinks bottled blood. His roommate is human but tolerant. Then Dave sees the perfect girl, Rosa, one of the goth vampire groupies who hangs out in the neighborhood. However, surfer/slacker Wes, whom Dave replaced as the night manager, also has his eye on Rosa, and Wes isn't above killing to get his way. The book includes some violence (including the tearing off of one girl's head), and some harsh language.

"Warren Pleece's art marvelously captures the humor of the mundane that lends the book's crew of late-night wage-slave vamps believability and energy. A really fun read!" Booklist

Soule, Charles

She-Hulk 1: Law and Disorder. Charles Soule, illustrated by Javier Pulido, Ron Wemberly. Marvel Enterprises 2014 136 p. Color; Illustration
Grades: Adult   741.5
1. Female superhero graphic novels; 2. Superhero graphic novels
0785190198; 9780785190196, $15.99

"Jennifer Walters is . . . the She-Hulk! . . . She's also a killer attorney with a pile of degrees and professional respect. But juggling cases and kicking bad guy butt is a little more complicated than she anticipated. With a new practice, a new paralegal and a mounting number of super villains she's racking up as personal enemies, She- Hulk might have bitten off more than she can chew!" (Publisher's note)

"Similar in tone and look to Matt Fraction's lauded Hawkeye, Soule's story shows more of an everyday superhero, with emphasis on character development in more realistic settings. The artwork is equally impressive: Pulido's run evokes a slick, bright pop-art feel, while Wimberly takes slightly more risks with his signature blend of gritty 1980s comics and stylish manga." Booklist

Contains material originally published in magazine form as She-Hulk #1-6—Title page verso.

She-Hulk: disorderly conduct. Charles Soule; illustrated by Javier Pulido. Marvel Enterprises 2015 136 p. Color; Illustration
Grades: Adult   741.5
1. Adventure fiction; 2. Superheroes
0785190201; 9780785190202, $15.99

In this graphic novel by Charles Soule, illustrated by Javier Pulido, "She-Hulk, Hellcat and Giant-Man team up to save one of Jen's officemates...but what else does Hank Pym have at stake, and what isn't he telling them?" (Publisher's note)

Sowa, Marzena

★ **Marzi:** a memoir. DC Comics 2011 230p. Illustration

Grades: Adult   92; 741.5
1. Authors; 2. Autobiographical graphic novels; 3. Communism — Poland; 4. Novelists; 5. Sowa, Marzena, 1979-; 6. Graphic novels
978-1-4012-2959-7, $17.99

LC 2011011160

"Marzena Sowa ("Marzi") shows readers what life was like for her as a young girl growing up in what would soon become post-Communist Poland. While this book starts off with Marzi as a child, the broader political implications presented by the series of vignettes—such as her family's use of ration cards, waiting in long lines for food and petrol, and worrying about her father when he strikes from his factory—are more appropriate for older readers. Savoia's clean and expressive illustrations incorporate the extensive narration nicely and help move the story forward." Booklist

Spangler, Bill

Tom Corbett: space cadet. Art by John DaCosta and Wilson Ramos Jr.. Bluewater Productions 2010 96p. Illustration
Grades: 7 8 9 10 11 12 Adult   741.5; Fic
1. Adventure graphic novels; 2. Science fiction graphic novels; 3. Tom Corbett, Space Cadet (Television series); 4. Graphic novels
978-1-4507-0014-6, $15.95

In the year 2251 A.D., Solar Guard Cadets Tom Corbett, Roger Manning, and Astro Deaver come to Rescue Station RSA-4 to conduct routine maintenance, but instead they find big trouble when the fully automated station doesn't respond to their computers, and the robots attack them. When the cadets manage to stop an alien robot that had taken over the station, they take it back to the Academy, where Solar Guard scientists discover that it isn't alien, but based on the old designs of Dr. Sanderson Dale of Earth. Then robot-run ships attack every planet of the Solar System except Earth, with a demand that humans leave space and return to Earth or face destruction. The Solar Alliance's only hope is to find Dr. Dale's original software, in order to reboot the robots of the One State. This space adventure is an original story set in the universe created for the Tom Corbett, Space Cadet television series that aired in the 1950s, as well as the novels and comics that were spun off the series. Spangler wrote some of the comics published in the 1990s. DaCosta's full-color art uses a retro/epic look for the outer space architecture and ships. This book was originally published as a four-issue miniseries of comic books.

Spencer, Nick

Morning Glories 7: Honors. Nick Spencer, illustrated by Joe Eisma. Image Comics 2014 124 p. Color; Illustration
Grades: 10 11 12 Adult   741.5
1. School stories; 2. Graphic novels
1607069431; 9781607069430, $12.99

"The Truants are back in class, and that means new mysteries abound! And whatever happened to Abraham" The answer to that question and more as Season Two races on! Collects the suspense-filled arc 'Honors.'" (Publisher's note)

Originally published in single magazine form as Morning glories, #35-38

Morning glories: Vol. 2 All Will Be Free. Nick Spencer, illustrated by Joe Eisma and Rodin Esquejo. Image Comics 2011 168 p. Color; Illustration
Grades: 10 11 12 Adult   **Fic; 741.5**
1. Good and evil — Fiction; 2. School stories; 3. Graphic novels
1607064073; 9781607064077, $12.99
"It's the Glories' first day of school, and they've already landed themselves in detention! Now, anywhere else that might just mean the start of a bad year, but they're about to find out when you're enrolled at Morning Glory Academy, corporal punishment takes on a whole new-and deadly-meaning!" (Publisher's note)
"Zoe, Hunter, Jun, Jade, Ike, and Casey . . . continue to fight for survival while trying to figure out who they can trust among the staff and their fellow students. Meanwhile, snippets of their pasts are revealed in flashbacks but only serve to bring about more questions than answers." (Booklist)
Collects issues 7-12—P. [4] of cover

Morning Glories; 1: for a better future. Nick Spencer, words; Joe Eisma, art; Rodin Esquejo, covers; Alex Sollazzo, colors; Johnny Lowe, letters. Image 2011 192 p. Illustration
Grades: 9 10 11 12 Adult   **741.5**
1. Good and evil — Fiction; 2. School stories
1607063077; 9781607063070, $9.99
Originally published in single magazine form as Morning Glories #1-6
"Morning Glory Academy is one of the most prestigious prep schools in the country . . . but something sinister and deadly lurks behind its walls. When six gifted, but troubled, students arrive, they find themselves trapped and fighting for their lives as the secrets of the academy reveal themselves." (Publisher's note)
"[C]ompelling character studies, mind games, and action-packed sequences [feature] in this gorgeously inked mystery." Booklist
Volume 1 of an ongoing series

Morning glories; Volume 3: P.E.. Nick Spencer, illustrated by Joe Eisma and Rodin Esquejo. Image Comics 2012 240 p. Color; Illustration
Grades: 10 11 12 Adult   **741.5; Fic**
1. Good and evil — Fiction; 2. School stories; 3. Graphic novels
1607065584; 9781607065586, $14.99
"When the faculty cancels classes and sends the students on an outing in the nearby woods, all hell breaks loose, sending the Glories on a mysterious journey through time and space. Nothing is what it seems to be as Academy's hold on the kids collapses and new threats emerge!" (Publisher's note)
"Following an ensemble cast makes identifying with characters a challenge, but the momentum of the plot should carry readers along." LJ
Collects: Morning Glories issues 13-19

Morning glories; Volume five: Tests. Nick Spencer, illustrated by Joe Eisma. Image Comics 2013 136 p. Color; Illustration
Grades: 10 11 12 Adult   **741.5**
1. School stories; 2. Graphic novels

1607067749; 9781607067740, $12.99
"The Glories are scattered, The Faculty broken, and The Truants on the attack!" (Publisher's note)
Originally published in single magazine form Morning Glories, #26-29—T.p. verso

Morning glories; Volume four: Truants. Nick Spencer, illustrated by Joe Eisma. Image Comics 2013 216 p. Color; Illustration
Grades: 10 11 12 Adult   **741.5; Fic**
1. School stories; 2. Graphic novels
1607067277; 9781607067276, $14.99
"Still reeling from the climactic events of 'P.E.,' the Glories find themselves lost in time and space, confronted by a new group of students who might be even more dangerous than the faculty themselves—the truants!" (Publisher's note)
Originally published in single magazine form as Morning glories #20-25

Morning glories; Volume six: Demerits. Nick Spencer, illustrated by Joe Eisma. Image Comics 2013 144 p. Color; Illustration
Grades: 10 11 12 Adult   **741.5**
1. School stories; 2. Graphic novels
1607068230; 9781607068235, $14.99
"After the climactic events of the Season Two premiere, the Glories and the Truants find themselves more lost than ever before, haunted by the things they've seen and done" (Publisher's note)
Originally published in single magazine form Morning Glories, #30-34

Spider-Man: The Birth of Venom
Marvel Entertainment 2007 Un Illustration
Grades: 8 9 10 11 12 Adult   **Fic; 741.5**
1. Fantastic Four (Fictional characters); 2. Spider-Man (Fictional character); 3. Superhero graphic novels; 4. Graphic novels
978-0-7851-2498-6, $29.99
The Beyonder's Battleworld might seem a strange place to get new threads, but it's Spider-Man who becomes unraveled when his new symbiotic, shape-changing costume attempts to darken his life as well as his fashion sense. But ridding himself of his black costume proves an even greater mistake when its alien enmity bonds with mortal madness to form our hero's most dedicated enemy, Venom. Other stories include the first appearances of Puma and the Rose, Mary Jane Watson's startling secret, and the debut of the battling . . . Bag-Man." The Black Cat, the Fantastic Four and other Marvel characters appear.

Spider-Man: Saga of the Sandman
Marvel Entertainment 2007 176p. Illustration
Grades: 7 8 9 10 11 12 Adult   **Fic; 741.5**
1. Fantastic Four (Fictional characters); 2. Hulk (Fictional character); 3. Spider-Man (Fictional character); 4. Superhero graphic novels; 5. Graphic novels
978-0-7851-2497-9, $19.99
It was no day at the beach when criminal Flint Marko was mutated into one of Marveldom's most versatile villains. This book recounts his origins and some of the best battles between Sandman, Spider-Man, the Fantastic Four and the Hulk.

Spiegelman, Art

Breakdowns: portrait of the artist as a young @&*!.
Art Spiegelman. Pantheon Books 2008 96 p. Illustration;
Color
Grades: Adult   **741.5; 741.5/973**
1. Spiegelman, Art
0375423958; 9780375423956, $27.50
                                                            LC 200860695
This graphic novel, by Art Spiegelman, "traces the
artist's evolution from a MAD-comics obsessed boy in Rego
Park, Queens, to a neurotic adult examining the effect of his
parents' memories of Auschwitz on his own son. . . . Pulling
all this together is an illustrated essay that looks back at the
sixties as the artist pushes sixty, and explains the obsessions
that brought these works into being." (Publisher's note)

★ **Co-Mix:** A Retrospective of Comics, Graphics, and
Scraps. By Art Spiegelman. Farrar Straus & Giroux 2013
120 p.
Grades: Adult   **741.5**
1770461140; 9781770461147, $39.95
Harvey Nominee: Best Biographical, Historical, or
Journalistic Presentation (2014)
This book, "a companion piece to a retrospective
exhibition . . . collects some of [Art] Spiegelman's best work
spanning nearly six decades along with biographical
information and critical essays. The editors trace his career
from commercial work for Playboy to his underground,
experimental work, including the Raw anthology where he
first serialized 'Maus'. . . . The book also features many of
Spiegelman's controversial 1990's New Yorker covers and
autobiographical comics." (Publishers Weekly)
"Maus did much to 'legitimize' comics to the wider
world, but this thoughtfully curated, elegantly presented
volume is an even more convincing testament to the
potential of the medium." Booklist

★ **In** the shadow of no towers. Pantheon Books 2004
Illustration
Grades: 10 11 12 Adult   **741; 973.931; 741.5**
1. September 11 terrorist attacks, 2001; 2. Graphic novels
0-375-42307-9, $19.95
                                                            LC 2004-43870
This is a "memoir of the attacks on the World Trade
Center, which Spiegelman witnessed from close range, a
rant on their effects on the world at large and within the
author, and a monograph on the Sunday newspaper comic
strips of the early 20th century." N Y Times Book Rev
The author "provides a hair-raising and wry account of
his family's frantic efforts to locate one another on
September 11 as well as a morbidly funny survey of his
trademark sense of existential doom. . . . This is a powerful
and quirky work of visual storytelling by a master comics
artist." Publ Wkly

★ **Maus:** a survivor's tale, 2v in 1. Art Spiegelman..
Pantheon Bks. 1996 295 p. Illustration; Map; Color
Grades: 7 8 9 10 11 12 Adult   **741.5; 92; 940.53**
1. Biographical graphic novels; 2. Holocaust, 1933-1945;
3. Spiegelman, Vladek; 4. Graphic novels
0-679-40641-7, $35
                                                            LC 96-32796
Awards: 1992 Pulitzer Prize Special Award; Eisner
Award for Best Graphic Album: Reprint for Maus II;

Harvey Award for Best Graphic Album of Previously
Published Work (for Maus II); 1993 Los Angeles Times
Book Prize for Fiction (for Maus II)
"An undisputed classic and award-winning title
(including a Pulitzer Prize in 1992) in which renowned
cartoonist Spiegelman depicts his father's experiences as a
World War II Nazi concentration camp survivor. The memoir
is also a chronicle of Spiegelman's relationship with his
father as we witness their visits and disagreements. The
black-and-white drawings are straightforward, but with an
interesting twist: all of the Jews are depicted as mice and the
Nazis as cats." LJ
Also available: paperback boxed set edition $23.25
(ISBN 0141014083)
A combined edition of Maus I : My father bleeds history
(1986) and Maus II : And here my troubles began (1991)

★ **MetaMaus**. Pantheon Books 2011 299p. Illustration
Grades: 11 12 Adult   **92; 741.5**
1. Authors; 2. Autobiographical graphic novels; 3.
Cartoonists; 4. Cartoonists; 5. Holocaust survivors; 6.
Holocaust, 1933-1945; 7. Nonfiction writers; 8.
Spiegelman, Art; 9. Graphic novels
978-0-375-42394-9, $35
                                                            LC 2010052045
The New York cartoonist traces the creative process that
went into drawing his Pulitzer Prizewinning classic,
revealing the sources of his inspiration and describing his
parents' emotional struggles as Holocaust survivors after the
end of World War II.

Spotnitz, Frank
The **X-files**. Writers, Frank Spotnitz, Marv Wolfman,
Doug Moench; artist, Brina Denham; colors, Kelsey
Shannon and Carlos Badilla; letters, Ed Dukeshire. DC
Comics/Wildstorm 2009 176p. Illustration
Grades: 9 10 11 12 Adult   **741.5; Fic**
1. Supernatural graphic novels; 2. X-files (Television
program); 3. Graphic novels
978-1-4012-2527-8, $19.99
FBI agents Fox Mulder and Dana Scully investigate
several cases that involve possession, then a murder case that
involves a company conducting secret research for the U.S.
government. The Lone Gunmen help Mulder uncover the
company's wrongdoing. A murder investigation in San
Francisco sees Mulder and Scully go up against members of
the Tong underworld. Then, the two travel to the Badlands to
investigate a series of disappearances that leads them deep
underground, to a Netherworld inhabited by strange
creatures. Spotnitz worked as a producer and screenwriter
for the television series; Wolfman and Moench are veteran
DC Comics creators.

Squarzoni, Philippe
Climate changed: a personal journey through the
science. Philippe Squarzoni; translated by Ivanka
Hahnenberger. Abrams ComicArts 2014 480 p. Illustration
Grades: Adult   **551.6**
1. Climate change; 2. Climatic changes; 3. Graphic novels
1419712551; 9781419712555, $24.95
                                                            LC 2014000177

In this book, journalist Philippe Squarzoni "digs deep into the science, economics, politics, international policies, and ethics that together force cataclysmic climate change into our very near global future. While the experts he interviews throughout this volume present accessible yet technically specific details, . . . it is by inserting himself and his personal exploration of responsibilities and choices that Squarzoni makes the most demanding call to action." (Booklist)

"Squarzoni's text, skillfully translated by Hahnenberger, is supported by his detailed black-and-white art, which conveys the urgency of the situation without falling prey to despair or nihilism." Pub Wkly

Stanley, John
Little Lulu vol. 17: The Valentine. Writer, John Stanley ; artists, John Stanley, Irving Tripp. Dark Horse Comics 2007 228p. Illustration
Grades: 3 4 5 6 7 8 9 10 11 12 Adult   **741.5**
1. Friendship; 2. Humorous graphic novels; 3. Little Lulu (Fictional character); 4. Graphic novels
978-1-59307-686-3, $10.95

In this seventeenth volume, Lulu gets into more fun mischief, tricking Tubby into taking a sponge for a walk, rescuing a pair of pants from the tough west side gang, and defeating the clubhouse boys in a snowball war. She also tells neighborhood little terror Alvin more stories of Witch Hazel, and during a day at the beach, she tries to win a doll at the ball throwing booth where Tubby is working.

★ **Little** Lulu, vol. 1: My dinner with Lulu. [by] John Stanley and Irving Tripp. Dark Horse Comics 2005 200p. Illustration
Grades: 4 5 6 7 8 9 10 11 12 Adult   **741.5; Fic**
1. Friendship; 2. Humorous graphic novels; 3. Graphic novels
1-59307-318-6, $9.95

Lulu Moppet plays with best friend Tubby, except when he hangs out with the other neighborhood boys and tries to keep girls out of their clubhouse; she deals with terrible toddler Alvin by weaving extravagant tales featuring herself; and other everyday adventures. This is the first volume of a series that will eventually reprint every Little Lulu comic for new young readers.

Volume 1 of 29

Little Lulu, volume 21: Miss Feeny's folly and other stories. John Stanley & Irving Tripp. Dark Horse Comics 2009 200p. Illustration
Grades: 1 2 3 4 5 6 7 8 9 10 11 12 Adult   **741.5; Fic**
1. Friendship; 2. Humorous graphic novels; 3. Little Lulu (Fictional character); 4. Graphic novels
978-1-59582-365-6, $14.95

This volume collects the Little Lulu stories from issues #100 to 105 of the Dell Comics series. Lulu and Annie carry on their battle with the boys over the boys' clubhouse, Lulu tells little Alvin more stories of the poor little girl and the wicked Witch Hazel, Tubby goes to the dentist, all the neighbor kids have to attend Miss Feeny's dance party, Tubby and then Lulu each have to clean up parts of their houses and try to trick the other into helping, and more. These stories are mostly in full color, with just a few one-page stories in black and white.

Little Lulu: the alamo and other stories. John Stanley & Irving Tripp. Dark Horse Comics 2009 200p. Illustration
Grades: 1 2 3 4 5 6 7 8 9 10 11 12 Adult   **741.5; Fic**
1. Humorous graphic novels; 2. Little Lulu (Fictional character); 3. Graphic novels
978-1-59582-293-2, $14.95

With this nineteenth volume of Little Lulu reprints, the comics are in full color; this volume collects issues 88 through 93, originally published by Dell Comics in 1955 through 1956. Among the stories in this volume, Tubby and the boys try to trick Lulu and Annie into digging a well, Tubby's parents pay Lulu to keep him company while they go out, and Lulu and Annie get revenge on Tubby and the boys by dousing them with water bombs while the boys are wearing their Davy Crockett coonskin caps. These stories appeal to younger readers as well as adults who remember reading the original comic books.

★ **Nancy,** volume 1: the Johnny Stanley Library. From the comic strip by Ernie Bushmiller ; script and layout by John Stanley ; finished art by Dan Gormley. Drawn & Quarterly 2009 128p. Illustration
Grades: 2 3 4 5 6 7 8 9 10 11 12 Adult
741.5; Fic
1. Humorous graphic novels; 2. Nancy Drew (Fictional character); 3. Graphic novels
978-1-897299-77-7, $24.95

Courtesy of Drawn and Quarterly

LC C2009-901565-X

The comic book character Nancy was created by Ernie Bushmiller; Dell Comics published the comics scripted by John Stanley with art by Dan Gormley starting with issue 146 in 1957. In these stories, Nancy meets Oona Goosepimple, a spooky girl who lives in a haunted house, has an incredible run of bad luck because of what she thinks is a four-leaf clover, and has all kinds of everyday adventures and misadventures with her friend Sluggo, their nemesis Spike, neighborhood rich kid Rollo, and her Aunt Fritzi. Always short of money yet needing some to buy ice cream sodas and other treats, many of Nancy's adventures with Sluggo involve various moneymaking schemes to get the dime needed (those were the days ...). The kinds of adventures the kids have are somewhat similar to Stanley's other work on Little Lulu, but set in an urban environment rather than the suburban neighborhood of Lulu and her friends. The book, designed by Seth, retains the soft original coloring of the old comics, with the paper even looking like old comics (but much sturdier). This book should have the same all-ages appeal as Little Lulu; the 2009 Free Comic Book Day issue featuring Nancy was a big hit with readers five years old and up to adults who remembered reading Nancy comics when they were kids.

Star Trek the Manga Volume 1: Shinsei Shinsei
Tokyopop 2006 Un Illustration
Grades: 7 8 9 10 11 12 Adult   **741.5; Fic**

1. Adventure graphic novels; 2. Science fiction graphic novels; 3. Star Trek; 4. Graphic novels
1-59816-744-8, $9.99

Ten writers and artists deliver tales of triumph aboard the original NCC-1701, the starship Enterprise, featuring the characters from the original television series. These new stories venture into the terrain of social politics, personal reflection ... and bare-knuckled brawls between Captain Kirk and various alien creatures, Spock's unflappable logic, Dr. McCoy's flare for drama, Scotty's perpetual struggle to keep the engines running smoothly, and more. The stories are written and illustrated as global manga.

Star Trek the Manga: Uchu
Tokyopop 2008 Un Illustration
Grades: 7 8 9 10 11 12 Adult   **741.5; Fic**
1. Science fiction graphic novels; 2. Star trek (Television program); 3. Graphic novels
978-1-4278-0787-8, $10.99

This third collection of manga-style stories set in the original Star Trek universe includes "Art of War" by Star Trek: The Next Generation actor Wil Wheaton and artist E. J. Su, "Bandi" by The Trouble with Tribbles writer David Gerrold and artist Don Hudson, "Inalienable Rights" by Nathaniel Bowden and artist Heidi Arnhold, and "The Humanitarian" by Luis Reyes and artist Nate Watson. Kirk has an encounter with a Klingon that makes both men rethink their hatred; the Bandi is yet another alien creature that has invaded the Enterprise, this one is highly empathic and can influence peoples' emotions; Kirk and his command team visit a planet and find a society in which bureaucracy runs wild; and Spock has command of the Enterprise during a very difficult situation, when a huge explosion causes major casualties of the Enterprise crew. People who like Star Trek's original series and characters will find stories in keeping with the philosophy of that series.

Star Wars: Clone Wars Volume 5: The Best Blades
Dark Horse Comics 2004 Un Illustration
Grades: 7 8 9 10 11 12 Adult   **741.5; Fic**
1. Adventure graphic novels; 2. Science fiction graphic novels; 3. Star Wars; 4. Graphic novels
1-59307-273-2, $17.95

The darkest days of the Clone Wars have arrived, when even victories are cause for abiding sorrow; when the hopes for a brighter future are lost in the turmoil of a divided galaxy; and when friendships are tools of convenience and the reason for betrayals. From political intrigue within the Senate to bloody battlefields on exotic worlds, the war has left its mark on the bystanders as well as the combatants. Obi-Wan Kenobi and Anakin Skywalker battle for survival, Senator Bail Organa struggles to preserve freedom within the Republic, and Master Yoda strives to prevent an old friend from plunging a system into war in four stories from the Clone Wars. The book includes battle violence.

Star Wars: Empire Volume Five: Allies and Adversaries
Written by Jeremy Barlow and Ron Marz ; art by Brandon Badeaux, Jeff Johnson, et al. Dark Horse Comics 2006 Un Illustration
Grades: 7 8 9 10 11 12 Adult   **741.5; Fic**

1. Adventure graphic novels; 2. Science fiction graphic novels; 3. Star Wars; 4. Graphic novels
1-59307-466-2, $14.95

Luke Skywalker fights side-by-side with a shipwrecked veteran from the Clone Wars, Han Solo's flirtations with an old flame land him in the fire, and BoShek (the galaxy's second-coolest smuggler) attracts a whole lot of blaster fire from Rebels and Imperials alike in this collection featuring some of the most unexpected stories in the era of the Empire. Whether it's BoShek transporting an innocent-enough looking girl, Han making a supply run for the resource-strapped Alliance or Luke flying escort for a Rebel Intelligence team on a supposedly deserted planet, these adventures may start as routine missions, but their endings are anything but predictable. The book includes battle violence.

Star Wars: Empire Volume Four: The Heart of the Rebellion
Dark Horse Comics 2005 Un Illustration
Grades: 7 8 9 10 11 12 Adult   **741.5; Fic**
1. Adventure graphic novels; 2. Science fiction graphic novels; 3. Star Wars; 4. Graphic novels
1-59307-308-9, $17.95

She was the catalyst that helped to turn a rag-tag rebellion into the Rebel Alliance. She provided the impetus for the 'Heroes of Yavin' in their attack on the Death Star. And she was the spark that ignited the flames of passion in one of the galaxy's most notorious rogues. 'She,' of course, is Princess Leia, the leader—and heart—of the Rebellion against Palpatine's galactic Empire. The four stories in this volume follow Leia from the weeks just before the events in A New Hope, to the time just before The Empire Strikes Back—from her first transforming experience with armed rebellion, to facing the ramifications of consequences of the destruction of her home planet, to the beginnings of true love. The book includes some battle violence.

Star Wars: Empire Volume Three: The Imperial Perspective
Dark Horse Comics 2004 Un Illustration
Grades: 7 8 9 10 11 12 Adult   **741.5; Fic**
1. Adventure graphic novels; 2. Science fiction graphic novels; 3. Star Wars; 4. Graphic novels
1-59307-128-0, $17.95

A loyal Stormtrooper, thwarted by the very bureaucracy which he serves, struggles to track down a Rebel saboteur on board the Death Star in the days and hours before the fateful Rebel attack. Darth Vader, the sole survivor of the explosion of the Death Star, crash lands on a primitive world where savagery is the key to survival. A young Imperial lieutenant learns all service comes at a price when his small company of Stormtroopers is attacked by thousands of angry aliens. Assassins vow revenge on the man responsible for killing their families - the Dark Lord, Darth Vader. These four tales are all told from the point of view of the major villains of the Star Wars galaxy - the Imperials. But, as these stories show, even the bad guys are no strangers to loyalty, honor, and sacrifice. The book includes battle violence.

Star Wars: Tales Volume 6
Dark Horse Comics 2006 232p. Illustration

Grades: 7 8 9 10 11 12 Adult   **741.5; Fic**
1. Adventure graphic novels; 2. Science fiction graphic novels; 3. Star Wars; 4. Graphic novels
1-59307-447-6, $19.95

The vastness of the Star Wars galaxy hosts an ever-unfolding mythology, filled with character-driven stories of loss and tragedy, of heroism and redemption. Collected here are ten such tales - adventures that traverse and illuminate every era in the Star Wars mythos. From the life-affirming lessons of the Force to the moral and emotional fall-out that comes with giving oneself over to the ways of the Sith, these stories will change the way readers see that galaxy far, far away.

Starkings, Richard
★ **Elephantmen:** Wounded Animals. Image Comics 2007 Un Illustration
Grades: 10 11 12 Adult   **Fic; 741.5**
1. Mystery graphic novels; 2. Science fiction graphic novels; 3. Graphic novels
978-1-58240-691-6, $24.99

They were genetically engineered to be super-human weapons of mass destruction, but now they must walk amongst the people they were created to destroy and face hatred and fear every day. Ebony Hide is one of them, an Elephantman. Even when he is befriended by a small girl, Hide is still haunted by his past and is forced to recognize that suspicion and contempt will always be his constant companions. The book includes some violence and strong language.
Volume 1 of an ongoing series

Hip Flask: Concrete Jungle (The Big Here & the Long Now). Richard Starkings and Joe Casey; art by Ladronn. Image Comics 2007 96p. Illustration
Grades: 10 11 12 Adult   **741.5; Fic**
1. Mystery graphic novels; 2. Science fiction graphic novels; 3. Graphic novels
978-1-58240-679-4, $29.95

2162: They are the survivors of genetic engineering experiments and indoctrination by Doctor Kazushi Nikken and MAPPO, a sinister organization which sought to create superhuman weapons of mass destruction. Now, freed and rehabilitated by the United Nations Intelligence Taskforce, the ?nhumans" now live amongst men. Legitimized by the Elephantmen Act, they are nevertheless denied the right to bear arms and must survive on their wits alone... Business person Ebony's organization has been targeted by someone, while private investigator Hip Flask tries to find a mystery aircar. The book includes violence and strong language.

Tim Sale: black and white (revised and expanded). Brought to you by Richard Starkings & John 'JG' Roshell with Tim Sale. Image Comics 2008 272p. Illustration
Grades: 10 11 12 Adult   **741.5**
1. Artists; 2. Batman (Fictional character); 3. Catwoman (Fictional character); 4. Comic books, strips, etc — History and criticism; 5. Daredevil (Fictional character); 6. Graphic novels — History and criticism; 7. Hulk (Fictional character); 8. Illustrators; 9. Sale, Tim; 10. Superman (Fictional character)
978-1-58240-880-4, $39.99

Comics artist Tim Sale is well known because of the art he did for the television series "Heroes," but he's been in the comics business for a long time before that. This book collects a lot of his work, from his earliest years in the Buscema School in the 1970s, to his work on "Heroes." In between, Sale has worked on books for Marvel (Daredevil: Yellow and Hulk: Gray among others) and DC (Superman for All Seasons, Batman: The Long Halloween, Catwoman, and more) as well as independent work such as Thieves' World and Billi 99. The book includes interviews with Sale, a sketchbook section of his art, and more. Some images include partial nudity.

Starlin, Jim
Batman: a death in the family. Writers, Jim Starlin, Marv Wolfman; layouts and co-plotter, George Perez; pencillers, Jim Aparo, Tom Grummett; inkers, Mike DeCarlo, Bob McLeod; original series covers, Mike Mignola and George Perez. DC Comics 2011 269 p. (Batman)
Grades: Adult   **741.5**
1. Batman (Fictional character); 2. Good and evil; 3. Joker (Fictional character); 4. Robin (Fictional character); 5. Superheroes
1401232744; 9781401232740, $24.99
LC 2012376784

In this graphic novel, "Batman readers were allowed to vote on the outcome of the story and they decided that Robin should die! As the second person to assume the role of Batman's sidekick, Jason Todd had a completely different personality than the original Robin. Rash and prone to ignore Batman's instructions, Jason was always quick to act without regard to consequences. In this fatal instance, Robin ignores his mentor's warnings when he attempts to take on the Joker by himself." (Publisher's note)

Stassen, Jean-Philippe
Deogratias: a tale of Rwanda. [by] Stassen; translated by Alex Siegel. Roaring Brook 2006 79p. Illustration
Grades: 11 12 Adult   **741.5; Fic**
1. Genocide; 2. Rwanda; 3. Graphic novels
1-59643-103-2; 978-1-59643-103-4, $17.95
LC 2005-17576

In this "fictionalized account of the Rwandan genocide, readers meet Deogratias, a teenaged Hutu. His friends Benina and Apollinaria are Tutsi—a race that is being ethnically cleansed by Hutu extremists. As the conflict escalates, Deogratias witnesses murders and is forced to become involved in brutal acts of violence. He suffers a mental breakdown. The story is told through a series of flashbacks while he skates the line between rational and insane. Stassen spares his readers none of the brutality and visceral cruelties of this atrocity. Scenes of rape, harsh language, and some sexual content solidly designate this book for a mature audience. . . . A masterful work with vibrant, confident art, this book will stay with and haunt its readers." SLJ

Stavans, Ilan
Latino U.S.A.: a cartoon history. By Ilan Stavans; illustrated by Lalo Alcaraz. Basic Books 2012 Xxi, 217 p. Illustration

Grades: Adult   **741.5; 973/.0468**
1. Hispanic Americans; 2. Hispanic Americans —
History; 3. Latinos (US); 4. United States — History
0465082211; 0465082505; 9780465082216, $24.95;
9780465082506
                    LC 2012429058
    This book "represents the culmination of Ilan Stavans'
lifelong determination to meet the challenges of capturing
the joys, nuances, and multiple dimensions of Latino culture
within the context of the English language. In this cartoon
history of Latinos, Stavans also seeks to combine the
solemnity of so-called 'serious literature' and history with
the inherently theatrical and humorous nature of the
comics." (Publisher's note)
    Includes index.

Steig, William
    Cats, dogs, men, women, ninnies, & clowns: the lost art
of William Steig. With illustrations by William Steig.
Abrams 2011 Illustration
Grades: Adult   **741.5**
1. Steig, William, 1907-2003
978-0-8109-9577-2, $40; 0-8109-9577-8
                    LC 2010041853
    "A treasure trove of hundreds of previously
unpublished illustrations by children's book icon Steig, this
compendium is organized thematically (people, dogs, 'odd
ducks,' etc.); the late Steig's wife, Jeanne, introduces each
section with delightful, insightful anecdotes." Publ Wkly

Steinbach, Hans Hanzo
    Midnight Opera Vol. 1. Tokyopop 2005 Un Illustration
Grades: 8 9 10 11 12 Adult   **741.5; Fic**
1. Fantasy graphic novels; 2. Horror graphic novels; 3.
Graphic novels
1-59816-265-9, $9.99
    For nearly a millennium, undead creatures have blended
into a Europe driven by religious dogma... Ein DeLaLune is
an underground Goth metal sensation on the Paris music
scene, tragic and beautiful. He has the edge on other Goth
music powerhouses...he's undead, a fact he's kept hidden for
centuries. But his newfound fame might just bring out the
very phantoms of his past from whom he has been hiding for
centuries, including his powerful brother, Leroux. And if the
two don't reconcile, the entire undead nation could rise up
from the depths of modern society to lay waste to mankind.
There's fighting action between the two undead brothers.

Stephenson, Eric
    Nowhere men; Volume 1: Fates worse than death. Eric
Stephenson, Nate Bellegarde, and Jordie Bellaire. Image
Comics 2013 184 p. Color; Illustration (Nowhere Men)
Grades: Adult   **741.5**
1. Science; 2. Scientists
1607066912; 9781607066910, $9.99
Eisner Nomination: Best Continuing Series (2014)
    In this graphic novel, written by Eric Stephenson and
illustrated by Nate Bellegarde and Jordie Bellaire, "Dade
Ellis, Simon Grimshaw, Emerson Strange, and Thomas
Walker . . . became the most celebrated scientists of all time.
They changed the worldûand we loved them for it. But
where did it all go wrong" And when progress is made at any

and all cost, who ultimately pays the price?" (Publisher's
note)
    "Through nonlinear flashbacks and interspersed text
pieces, Stephenson expertly fills in fascinating details about
the group's rise and fall. Underscoring the series's tagline
'Science is the new rock 'n' roll,' he peppers the text with
music references." LJ

    Put the Book Back on the Shelf: A Belle & Sebastian
Anthology. Image Comics 2006 Un Illustration
Grades: 10 11 12 Adult   **741.5; Fic**
1. Short stories; 2. Graphic novels
1-58240-600-6, $19.99
    Belle and Sebastian is a Scottish indie pop band that has
gained critical acclaim for its music. In this anthology,
independent comic creators and cartoonists put their own
spins on a cross section of Belle and Sebastian's songs,
crafting narratives inspired by the band's music. Rick
Spears, Andi Watson, Jennifer de Guzman, Leela Corman,
Rick Remender, Ande Park, ad Mark Ricketts are just a few
of the creators who contributed to this collection. Nudity,
drug use, and violence occur in some of the stories.

Stern, Roger
    Captain America: War & Remembrance 2nd ed.. Artist,
John Byrne ; inker, Rubinstein, Joe. Marvel Entertainment
2007 207p. Illustration
Grades: 8 9 10 11 12 Adult   **Fic; 741.5**
1. Avengers (Fictional characters); 2. Captain America
(Fictional character); 3. Superhero graphic novels; 4.
Graphic novels
978-0-7851-2693-5, $24.99
    Captain America's endless war on crime and tyranny
sets him against new enemies and old, from an army of robot
replicas to the black deeds of Baron Blood. Plus: "Cap for
president." This book guest-stars the Avengers, S.H.I.E.L.D.
and Union Jack, and features Cobra, Mister Hyde and Batroc
the Leaper. This is the complete Stern/Byrne run,
culminating with the standard-setting version of Cap's
origin. Byrne co-scripted as well as pencilled the art.

    Spider-Man Visionaries: Roger Stern Vol. 1. Marvel
Entertainment 2007 256p. Illustration
Grades: 7 8 9 10 11 12 Adult   **741.5; Fic**
1. Spider-Man (Fictional character); 2. Superhero graphic
novels; 3. Graphic novels
978-0-7851-2710-9, $24.99
    Roger Stern sets his stamp on Spider-Man and his
supporting cast with a collection of costumed criminals,
would-be alien abductors, and gangsters both local and
imported. Spidey is up against Belladonna, the Vulture, the
Prowler, the Smuggler, Mysterio, a roomful of aliens, and an
abundance of gas. These stories were originally published in
the 1980s, and Stern worked with a number of different
artists, including Steve Leialoha and Marie Severin.

Stewart, Cameron
    The **Apocalipstix**. Oni Press 2008 Un Illustration
Grades: 9 10 11 12 Adult   **741.5; Fic**
1. Adventure graphic novels; 2. Humorous graphic
novels; 3. Rock music; 4. Science fiction graphic novels;
5. Graphic novels
978-1-932664-45-4, $11.95

Mandy, Megumi, and Dot were on track to be one of the greatest rock bands in the world until Armageddon hit and nuked most of it. The three survived and decided they would go on an "End of the World" tour with a group name like The Apocalipstix, it seemed appropriate. Riding an armored tour bus, the trio deals with road pirates who turn out to be major fans, giant ants just like in the old movies, and a rock contest with gasoline as the big prize. Megumi speaks mostly in Japanese, which is shown in the word balloons in Japanese text with English subtitles. All three can kick butt, and there's plenty of fistfights and giant ant fighting going on.

★ **Batgirl**; Volume 1: Batgirl of Burnside. Written by Cameron Stewart & Brenden Fletcher; art by Babs Tarr; breakdown art by Cameron Stewart. DC Comics 2015 176 p. Color; Illustration
Grades: 10 11 12 Adult   741.5
1. Batgirl (Fictional character)
9781401253325, $24.99
                                LC 2015006319
"Barbara Gordon's ready for a fresh start. She's packing her bags, crossing the bridge, and heading to Gotham's coolest neighborhood: Burnside. And when a freak fire burns up her costume and gear, Babs has the chance to become a whole new Batgirl! But she barely slips on her new DIY costume before Batgirl starts trending as Gotham's first viral vigilante—and attracting a new wave of enemies." (Publisher's note)
"While most attempts at updating an established character to tap into the youth culture zeitgeist feel phony and fall flat, this reinvigoration of Batgirl manages to be big fun and actually tuned in to Millennial culture. . . . The supporting cast is diverse and fully developed, and the action is intense, rendered in a bright, dynamic style that evokes animation with just a hint of Japanese influence." LJ

★ **Sin** titulo. By Cameron Stewart, edited by Sierra Hahn. Dark Horse Books 2013 166 p.
Grades: Adult   741.5; Fic
1. Dreams — Fiction; 2. Grandfathers — Fiction; 3. Life change events — Fiction
1616552484; 9781616552480, $19.99
In this Eisner Award-winning book, by Cameron Stewart, "Alex Mackay has no idea that he is letting important relationships slip away, until he drops in on his grandfather, Robert, at his nursing home, only to discover that the old man died a month before. Left pondering the small box of his grandfather's personal effects, . . . Alex sets out on a journey of discovery that only raises more questions and reveals that his recurring dream of a gnarled tree on a beach is far more important than he previously believed." (Publishers Weekly)

Stok, Barbara
Vincent. By Barbara Stok; translation by Laura Watkinson. SelfMadeHero 2014 144 p. Color; Illustration
Grades: 9 10 11 12 Adult   741.5; 92
1. Gogh, Vincent van, 1853-1890; 2. Gogh, Vincent van, 1853-1890 — Juvenile literature
1906838798; 9781906838799, $19.95
                                LC 2014431349
This biography, by Barbara Stok, "documents the brief and intense period of creativity Vincent van Gogh

(1853-1890) spent in Arles, Provence, in southern France. Here van Gogh dreams of setting up an artists' studioùa haven where he and his friends can paint together. But attacks of mental illness leave the painter confused and disoriented. . . . Throughout this period of intense emotion and hardship, Vincent's brother Theo stands by him." (Publisher's note)
"Stok doesn't try to reproduce van Gogh's visuals; instead, she uses heavy lines, solid colors, and minimal background details to focus attention on characters and history. When she breaks away from this pattern—in jagged panel lines showing van Gogh's slipping sanity, or the brilliance of his paintings exploding behind him—it's emotionally charged and made all the more immediate by the iconography." Pub Wkly
Text in English, translated from the Dutch

Stokoe, James
Won ton soup: a space trucker cooking opera, vol.1. Oni Press 2007 Un Illustration
Grades: 10 11 12 Adult   741.5
1. Cooking; 2. Humorous graphic novels; 3. Science fiction graphic novels; 4. Graphic novels
978-1-932664-60-7, $11.95
Space trucker Johnny Boyo used to be the best student at the Plaxos Cooking School, but he gave it all up to travel in space for a year. Now, he and his partner Deacon have returned to Plaxos for needed repairs after a space ninja attack. Johnny reconnects with his girlfriend Citrus and his old cooking master Mongolius Grahm, but a visit to the school results in a cooking challenge from the twins from Nebula 5; they have a psychic connection and absorb flavors through their pores. The book includes violence, some harsh language, and verbal sexual innuendo.

Stones, Tad
Hellboy Animated Volume 1: The Black Wedding. Jim Pasco and Tad Stones ; Pencils by Fabio Laguna and Rick Lacy. Dark Horse Comics 2007 Un Illustration
Grades: 7 8 9 10 11 12 Adult   741.5; Fic
1. Fantasy graphic novels; 2. Hellboy (Fictional character); 3. Horror graphic novels; 4. Graphic novels
978-1-59307-700-6, $6.95
In the lead feature, "The Black Wedding," written by Jim Pascoe and drawn by Rick Lacy, Liz Sherman is kidnapped by an ancient cult, dragging the entire Bureau for Paranormal Research and Defense into a horrifying tale of witchcraft and possession. Tad Stones and Fabio Laguna team up in "Pyramid of Death," in which radio hero Lobster Johnson inspires a young Hellboy to inflict some imaginary justice of his own, causing havoc on the military base where he lives. The art matches the style used in the Hellboy Animated features shown on Cartoon Network, and the horror is kept to a level suitable for younger teen readers.

Straczynski, J. Michael
Bullet Points. J Michael Straczynski and Tommy Lee Edwards. Marvel Entertainment 2007 Un Illustration
Grades: 9 10 11 12 Adult   Fic; 741.5
1. Hulk (Fictional character); 2. Iron Man (Fictional character); 3. Spider-Man (Fictional character); 4. Superhero graphic novels; 5. Graphic novels

978-0-7851-2010-0, $13.99

It's World War II, and America needs a super soldier. Only one man possesses the formula to create the perfect fighting machine from volunteer Steve Rogers. But when a deadly bullet kills Dr. Erskine along with his bodyguard, M.P. Ben Parker, Steve's destiny - and that of the Marvel Universe - is changed forever. Steve Rogers becomes Iron Man. Years after the war, a rebellious teenage Peter Parker gets lost on a testing field and accidentally irradiated with gamma rays, becoming the Hulk. Dr. Bruce Banner gets bitten by a spider exposed to gamma rays and becomes Spider-Man. All of them, and every other super powered hero, is needed when Galactus comes to devour the planet.

Civil War: Fantastic Four. Writers, J. Michael Straczynski & Dwayne McDuffie; penciller, Mike McKone; inkers, Andy Lanning, Kris Justice, & Cam Smith; colorist, Paul Mounts. Marvel Entertainment 2007 Un Illustration
Grades: 9 10 11 12 Adult　　　　　　**741.5; Fic**
1. Fantastic Four (Fictional characters); 2. Superhero graphic novels; 3. Graphic novels
0-7851-2227-3, $17.99

One member of the Fantastic Four lies hospitalized, a casualty of the Civil War that has fragmented the superhuman community. Another member of the team is secretly helping the opposition. Amid the tumult and tensions, the Fantastic Four is breaking up. Who will toe the line with the government, who will join the resistanace, and who will leave the battlefield altogether?

Civil War: The Amazing Spider-Man. Writer, J. Michael Straczynski; penciler, Ron Garney et al. Marvel Entertainment 2007 Un Illustration
Grades: 9 10 11 12 Adult　　　　　　**741.5; Fic**
1. Spider-Man (Fictional character); 2. Superhero graphic novels; 3. Graphic novels
0-7851-2237-0, $17.99

Life couldn't be more complicated - or more dangerous - for Peter Parker. After rushing to the aftermath of the Stamford Massacre to offer aid to its victims, Peter travels with Tony Stark to Washington, D.C. and the White House, where the enactment of the Super Human Registration Act appears imminent. As the world braces for the implications of legislation that will forever change the societal status of super heroes, Peter is forced to make an important personal decision, maybe the most important decision of his life. As Civil War tears apart the super hero community, will Spidey stay true to that decision?

Strip Search.
Dark Horse Comics 2004 128p. Illustration
Grades: 9 10 11 12 Adult　　　　　　**741.5; Fic**
1. Short stories; 2. Graphic novels
1-59307-099-3, $14.95

More than a dozen young artists and writers strut their stuff in this collection. These strips are culled from Dark Horse's on-line comics talent search/contest, Strip Search, and represent the best of the strips posted in 2002 and 2003. Some stories include harsh language and some violence.

Strokes, Johanna
Death Valley. Story by Andrew Cosby; written by Johanna Stokes; pencils and inks by Rhoald Marcellus;

colored by Arif Priyanto; lettered by Marshall Dillon. Boom! Studios 2007 Un Illustration
Grades: 9 10 11 12 Adult　　　　　　**741.5; Fic**
1. Horror graphic novels; 2. Zombies; 3. Graphic novels
978-1-934506-08-0, $14.99

Sam and some of her high school senior classmates hold an "End of the World" rave in their school's old bomb shelter, when the trap door closes and sticks, shutting them in over night. When they manage to open it, they find something has happened, and everyone they meet has become a bloodthirsty zombie. As they try to stay alive and to find shelter, Sam's knowledge of guns and self-defense (thanks to her military father) comes in handy, but the overwhelming numbers of zombies in San Fernando Valley means that the odds are against them; and the students fall, one by one ... Cosby (cocreator and head writer) and Stokes also write for Eureka, a fun television science fiction show that airs during the summers on SyFy, and the art by Marcellus doesn't go overboard with gory details just enough to satisfy readers who want some horror.

Sturm, James
James Sturm's America: God, gold, and golems. Drawn & Quarterly 2007 192p. Illustration
Grades: 10 11 12 Adult　　　　　　**741.5; Fic**
1. Baseball; 2. Gold mines and mining; 3. Revivals; 4. United States — History; 5. Graphic novels
978-1-897299-05-0, $24.95

This book compiles three of Sturm's stories that are set in quieter periods of American history, during relatively peaceful non-war and pre-Depression times. "The Revival," set around 1801, portrays frontier life and early religious revival movements as a couple makes their way from Ohio westward and stop off at a camp where people push themselves into religious frenzies. "Hundreds of Feet Below Daylight" examines the people who continue gold mining after the euphoria has died down and life becomes tough. Some readers may be shocked by the brutality exhibited by some of the miners who so desperately hunt for money. "The Golem's Mighty Swing" features a Jewish professional baseball team traveling the country just trying to get by in the 1920s. Facing racial and religious taunts and sometimes violence, they try a gimmick—disguising their African American player as a golem—in order to generate ticket sales."

"Social issues, including racial prejudice and intolerance, poverty, and family dynamics, are broached via both plot and character. . . . This [is] an easy crossover graphic novel for readers who enjoy American history made into well-told stories." Booklist

Suburbia, Liz
★ **Sacred** Heart. Liz Suburbia. Fantagraphics 2015 312 p. Illustration
Grades: 11 12 Adult　　　　　　**741.5; Fic**
1. Mystery fiction; 2. Teenagers
1606998412; 9781606998410, $24.99
　　　　　　　　　　　　LC 2015942121
Alex Award (2016)

In this graphic novel, by Liz Suburbia, "the children of . . . Alexandria are just trying to live like normal teens until their parents' promised return from a mysterious, four-year religious pilgrimage, and Ben Schiller is no exception. She's just trying to take care of her sister . . . and get through her teen years. But her relationship with her best friend is changing, her younger sister is hiding a dark secret, and a terrible tragedy is coming for them all." (Publisher's note)

Sun Tzu

The **art** of war. Sun Tzu; illustrated by Shane Clester; adapted by Cullen Bunn and Shane Clester. Roundtable Press 2011 Un Illustration

Grades: 9 10 11 12 Adult   741.5
1. Competition; 2. Philosophers; 3. Strategy; 4. Sun-tzu, 6th cent BC — Adaptations; 5. Writers on the military; 6. Graphic novels
978-1-61066-010-5, $12.95

Sun Tzu's classic book on strategy has now been adapted into a graphic novel. This adaptation is more a summary of the principles of strategy discussed in The Art of War, illustrated by Clester using modern situations to demonstrate the principles. For example, Sun Tzu's statement that "he who wishes to fight must first count the cost" is depicted with rival gangsters. This short book can't replace the original, but it provides a good summary of the main points and serves as an introduction for high school students and busy adults who may not have the time to read the whole original text.

Superman Archives Volume 7

Edited by Dale Crain. DC Comics 2006 237p. Illustration

Grades: 8 9 10 11 12 Adult   741.5; Fic
1. Superhero graphic novels; 2. Superman (Fictional character); 3. Graphic novels
978-1-4012-1051-9, $49.99

This volume of the Ring series collects three short stories that provide background clues about the evil Sadako and what makes her otherworldly scheme work so well. "Coffin in the Sky" relates Mai Takano's last days gestating the next Sadako; Lemon Heart" tells a story of Sadako's ill-fated young love; and Sakado" takes the reader to the icy depths of the tragic young psychic girl's creeping vengeance. The book includes nudity and harsh language."

Superman in the Eighties

Otto Binder [and others], writers ; C.C. Beck [and others], pencillers and inkers. DC Comics 2006 192p. Illustration

Grades: 8 9 10 11 12 Adult   741.5; Fic
1. Superhero graphic novels; 2. Superman (Fictional character); 3. Graphic novels
1-4012-0952-1, $19.99

The '80s were a decade that forever redefined the world's first super-hero. The first half of the decade brought the story of Superman to a close, while the latter half of the decade brought a revamped Man of Steel to an all-new audience. This volume includes ten stories by such creators as John Byrne, Curt Swan, Gil Kane, George Perez, Marv Wolfman, Jim Starlin, and Len Wein. Writer/artist Jerry Ordway provides historical and personal perspectives to these stories.

Superman in the Forties

Otto Binder [and others], writers ; C.C. Beck [and others], pencillers and inkers. DC Comics 2005 192p. Illustration

Grades: 6 7 8 9 10 11 12 Adult   741.5; Fic
1. Superhero graphic novels; 2. Superman (Fictional character); 3. Graphic novels
1-4012-0457-0, $19.99

At the end of the 1930s, comics saw a new breed of hero. The man could withstand bullets, leap over tall buildings in a single bound, and bend steel in his bare hands. Fighting for the oppressed, this man of steel captured the imagination of the readers. He was, of course, Superman. This volume reprints stories originally published from 1938 through 1949. The reader sees Superman first fighting "regular" criminals, but as the years go by, super-powered villains start to menace Metropolis, along with such villains as Lex Luthor and troublemakers such as the mischievous Mr. Mxyztplk.

Superman: Back in Action

DC Comics 2007 144p. Illustration

Grades: 8 9 10 11 12 Adult   741.5; Fic
1. Superhero graphic novels; 2. Superman (Fictional character); 3. Graphic novels
978-1-4012-1263-6, $14.99

This book collects several stories. When Superman returns after the events of Infinite Crisis, he faces skepticism from the people and then gets kidnapped and put up for an intergalactic auction. In stories from the past, he encounters the Metal Men, Firestorm, and Deadman.

Superman: The Greatest Stories Ever Told Volume Two

DC Comics 2006 192p. Illustration

Grades: 7 8 9 10 11 12 Adult   741.5; Fic
1. Superhero graphic novels; 2. Superman (Fictional character); 3. Graphic novels
978-1-4012-0956-8, $19.99

This volume includes nine stories from different times in Superman's career. Readers can experience Superman's first meeting with the other dimensional imp Mr. Mxyztplk, his return to Krypton, a deadly battle against the team of Lex Luthor and Brainiac, an after-life adventure with Pa Kent, his greatest secret revealed, and more.

Suzuki, Koji

The **Ring** Vol. 4: Birthday. Dark Horse Manga 2004 159p. Illustration

Grades: 10 11 12 Adult   741.5; Fic
1. Horror graphic novels; 2. Manga; 3. Graphic novels
1-59307-267-8, $12.95

This volume of the Ring series collects three short stories that provide background clues about the evil Sadako and what makes her otherworldly scheme work so well. "Coffin in the Sky" relates Mai Takano's last days gestating the next Sadako; "Lemon Heart" tells a story of Sadako's ill-fated young love; and "Sakado" takes the reader to the icy depths of the tragic young psychic girl's creeping vengeance. The book includes nudity and harsh language.

Suzuki, Yasushi

Purgatory Kabuki. DrMaster Publications Inc. 2008 150p. Illustration

Grades: 10 11 12 Adult   **741.5; Fic**
1. Manga; 2. Samurai; 3. Supernatural graphic novels; 4. Graphic novels
978-1-59796-070-0, $9.95

This is a samurai action story set in the underworld of the afterlife. For reasons unknown, former samurai Imanotsurugi is obsessed with leaving the afterlife. To die in battle is a samurai's greatest honor. Yet, he must claim 1,000 swords from the fallen warriors who now share residence in the dark underworld. By these means alone, this highly skilled blades master will be allowed admittance back into the living world. But to what end? Upon what purpose does he sharpen his edge? The story borrows heavily from various Japanese legends and myths, and the art is reminiscent of ukiyo-e. The book includes considerable violence with its many sword fights.

Takada, Rie

Happy Hustle High Volume 1. Viz Media/Shojo 2005 190p. Illustration

Grades: 10 11 12 Adult   **741.5; Fic**
1. Manga; 2. Romance graphic novels; 3. Shojo manga; 4. Graphic novels
1-59116-912-7, $9.99

Hanabi Ozora is a rambunctious 16-year-old tomboy who comes to the rescue of her less assertive friends—sometimes in exchange for food. So what does she do when, all of a sudden, her all-girls school is integrated with an all-boys school? She meets and falls in love—naturally—with one of the three most popular boys in the Student Council, Yasuaki Garaku. Unfortunately, Yasuaki doesn't care for girls... but when the girls' Student Council clashes head-on with the boys' Student Council, Hanabi steps in to become a member—hoping she'll change Yasuaki's mind. The book includes crude humor, sexual situations (in Vol. 5, the girls decide to attack sexual perverts who expose themselves to the girls), and some strong language. This is a 5-volume manga series.

Takagi, Ryo

The **Devil** Within Volume 1. Go! Comi 2007 Un Illustration

Grades: 10 11 12 Adult   **741.5; Fic**
1. Fantasy graphic novels; 2. Humorous graphic novels; 3. Manga; 4. Shojo manga; 5. Graphic novels
978-1-933617-22-0, $10.99

Rion's convinced that men are devils and only little boys are angels, that is, innocent. And just when she's found the boy of her dreams, she finds herself forced by her father into an engagement to a trio of suitors. While fighting off their advances and trying to win over the heart of her reluctant young love, Tenshi, she discovers the shocking secret of the handsome trio... and something sinister about herself. The book includes a lot of sexual innuendo but so far no graphic depictions and no nudity.

Takahashi, Kazuki

Yu-Gi-Oh! Duelist Volume 1. Viz Media/Shonen Jump 2005 216p. Illustration

Grades: 7 8 9 10 11 12 Adult   **741.5; Fic**
1. Adventure graphic novels; 2. Games; 3. Shonen manga; 4. Graphic novels
1-59116-614-4, $7.95

In the second saga of the Yu-Gi-Oh! epic, Duel Monsters is the world's most popular collectible card game-but to Yugi, it's the most dangerous game of all. Entering the Duel Monsters world championship, Yugi fights ruthless opponents like game designer Maximillion Pegasus and teenage multimillionaire Kaiba Seto, hoping to discover the origin of the game...and his own powers. When Yugi beat Kaiba, little did he know the consequences: a trip through Kaiba's "Death T" - a theme park of death - and a series of evil spells against Yugi's family. It doesn't help that Kaiba's little brother also has a score to settle. There's more gaming violence in the manga series compared to what has been shown on American television; this is not a book for younger children.

Yu-Gi-Oh! Millenium World Volume 1. Viz Media/Shonen Jump 2005 200p. Illustration

Grades: 7 8 9 10 11 12 Adult   **741.5; Fic**
1. Adventure graphic novels; 2. Games; 3. Shonen manga; 4. Graphic novels
1-59116-878-3, $7.95

This is the final Yu-Gi-Oh! story. After hundreds of battles, Yugi has finally gathered all the Egyptian God Cards... the key to unlocking his memories of his past life as an Egyptian pharaoh. When Ryo Bakura gives him the Millennium Eye, Yugi opens the door to the "world of memory," and his mind travels back in time to ancient Egypt, when the magic and monsters were real. Now Yugi and his friends must explore the world of Yugi's forgotten past...and fight an enemy who has been waiting for them for 3,000 years. The manga contains more action and violence in the gaming action than has been shown in the animated series that has aired on American television; this series is not for younger children.

Takahashi, Rumiko

One-pound gospel, vol. 1. Viz Media 2008 242p. Illustration

Grades: 10 11 12 Adult   **741.5; Fic**
1. Boxing; 2. Humorous graphic novels; 3. Manga; 4. Shonen manga; 5. Graphic novels
978-1-4215-2030-8, $9.99

Kosaku Hatanaka is a talented boxer, but he suffers from an insatiable appetite that makes it extremely difficult to make weight for his boxing matches (he's a featherweight who should weigh 126 pounds). He drives his poor coach crazy and tends to lose matches because he has to starve himself to lose weight, which saps his strength. Then he meets Sister Angela, a novice nun who tries to help him; she's so cute, Kosaku has a crush on her. Between his coach at Mukaida's Gym and Sister Angela's prayers, Kosaku starts to win his bouts—but usually with such bizarre circumstances and incredible luck that his opponents hate him. The boxing action is pretty well done and fairly graphic; this volume doesn't include much at all in the way of strong language, but Viz has put a warning about strong language and realistic violence on the title page. This series was originally published starting in 1989 and is now

released in Viz's now standard unflipped tankobon size book.
Volume 1 of 4

Ranma 1/2. Rumiko Takahashi, translated from Japanese by Gerard Jones & Matt Thorn. Viz Media 2014 359 p. Illustration
Grades: 10 11 12 Adult   **741.5**
1. Gender role — Fiction; 2. Manga
1421565943; 9781421565941, $14.99
"One day, teenaged martial artist Ranma Saotome went on a training mission with his father and ended up taking a dive into some cursed springs at a legendary training ground in China. Now, every time he's splashed with cold water, he changes into a girl. His father, Genma, changes into a panda! What's a half-guy, half-girl to do?" (Publisher's note)
"One of the bestselling manga from the early '90s, a gender-bending rom-com mixed with copious martial arts action, returns in this rerelease. World-class martial artist Ranma Saotome has been cursed with a special fate: when doused with cold water, he turns into a girl. This oddity is little more than an irritation to him until he becomes engaged to Akane Tendo, a prodigiously strong fighter who also happens to hate men." Pub Wkly
38 volumes originally released in Japan from 1987-1996

Takarai, Saori
Manga Moods: 40 Faces + 80 Phrases. Japanime Co. Ltd./Manga University 2006 96p. Illustration
Grades: 6 7 8 9 10 11 12 Adult   **741.5**
1. Manga; 2. Graphic novels
978-4-921205-13-3, $12.95
A raised eyebrow, a curled lip, a wink of the eye. All it takes is a single stroke of the pen to instantly change a manga character's mood from one extreme to the other: glad to sad, sassy to shy, angry to embarrassed. In addition, each of the facial expressions is labeled with the Japanese word for the mood being depicted, along with common Japanese conversational phrases and English translations, making this book fun for aspiring artists, language enthusiasts and manga fans. As a bonus, the 46 basic hiragana, as well as contracted hiragana and two-dash and one-circle hiragana characters are shown for those who want to start learning to write Japanese.

Takei, Hiroyuki
Shaman King Volume 1. Viz Media/Shonen Jump 2003 204p. Illustration
Grades: 8 9 10 11 12 Adult   **741.5; Fic**
1. Adventure graphic novels; 2. Shonen manga; 3. Supernatural graphic novels; 4. Graphic novels
1-56931-902-2, $7.95
When he takes a shortcut through a cemetery, Manta Oyamada meets a strange kid with headphones - surrounded by ghosts. The kid is the teenage shaman Yoh Asakura. Tapping the supernatural swordfighting powers of samurai ghost Admidamaru, Yoh fights Bokuto no Ryu, a sword-wielding gang member. But an even more dangerous opponent is stalking Yoh and Manta - a Chinese shaman who wants to possess Amidamaru.

Takemiya, Kiko
★ **To** Terra Volume One. Vertical, Inc. 2007 343p. Illustration
Grades: 9 10 11 12 Adult   **Fic; 741.5**
1. Manga; 2. Psychics; 3. Science fiction graphic novels; 4. Shojo manga; 5. Graphic novels
9781932234671, $13.95; 1932234675
The future. Having driven Terra to the brink of environmental collapse, humanity decides to reform itself by ushering in the age of Superior Domination (S.D.), a system of social control in which children are no longer the offspring of parents but progeny of a universal computer. The new social order, however, results in an unexpected byproduct: the Mu, a mutant race with extrasensory powers who are forced in exile by The System. The saga begins on educational planet Ataraxia, where Jomy Marcus Shin, a brash and unpredictable teenager, is nervously preparing to enter adult society. When his Maturity Check goes wrong, the Mu intervene in the great hope that Jomy, who possesses Mu telepathy and human physical strength, can lead them back home, to Terra...
Volume 1 of 3

Takemoto, Novala
Kamikaze Girls. Story by Novala Takemoto; art by Yukio Kanesada; English translation & adaptation, Tomo Kimura. Viz Media/Shojo Beat 2006 190p. Illustration
Grades: 10 11 12 Adult   **741.5; Fic**
1. Manga; 2. Shojo manga; 3. Graphic novels
978-1-4215-0268-7, $8.99
Momoko is a Lolita stranded in the boondocks of rural Ibaraki prefecture, although she'd much rather be living in the Palace of Versailles. Ichigo is a member of a girls-only biker gang who firmly believes in honor, loyalty, and fist fighting. Together this unlikely duo strikes out on a journey to find a legendary embroiderer who might just be able to make their dreams come true. The book includes some strong language, some violence, and teen smoking. This is a standalone one volume manga.

Takemura, Masaharu
The **manga** guide to biochemistry. Masaharu Takemura, Kikuyaro, Office Sawa. Oreilly & Associates Inc 2011 Xii, 253 p. Illustration
Grades: 11 12 Adult   **572**
1. Biochemistry
1593272766; 9781593272760, $24.95; 1593274211; 9781593274214, $24.95
LC 2011038517
In this work of graphic nonfiction, "Kumi explores the mysteries of her body's inner workings." Topics include "biopolymers like DNA and proteins, the metabolic processes that turn our food into energy, and the enzymes that fuel our bodies' chemical reactions." Also discussed are "the metabolism of substances like carbohydrates, lipids, proteins, and alcohol . . . mitochondria . . . DNA transcription . . . [and] enzyme kinetics." (Publisher's note)
Includes index.

Takeuchi, Mick
Her Majesty's Dog, Vol. 1. Go! Comi 2005 200p. Illustration

Grades: 10 11 12 Adult   **741.5; Fic**
1. Manga; 2. Romance graphic novels; 3. Shojo manga; 4. Supernatural graphic novels; 5. Graphic novels
0-9768957-3-0, $10.99

New students Amane and Hyoue cause a stir in their high school because they kiss so much. Amane is a psychic, Hyoue is actually her guardian demon-dog, and he feeds on her life force by their kisses. Together, they hunt demons, but in school they need to learn how to deal with everyday hazards such as bullies, jealousy, and making friends. This series combines teen romance with supernatural horror.

Takizaki, Mamiya
Element line vol.1. Tokyopop 2008 Un Illustration
Grades: 10 11 12 Adult   **741.5; Fic**
1. Adventure graphic novels; 2. Fantasy graphic novels; 3. Manga; 4. Graphic novels
978-1-4278-0527-0, $9.99

On a world devastated by monstrous Rizoms, humanity lives in the remaining cities, surrounded by huge walls called Shields and protected by soldiers of the Guild. Laolyth was a great hero among the Guild, but he disappeared fourteen years ago. Kam, an orphan boy brought to live in the city of Grisfynn, is preparing to become a Guild member, which would allow him to travel as a guard for merchant caravans going between the fortified cities. However, he also hides a dangerous secret: he is the son of Laolyth, and something is happening to his body, making him fear he will become a Rizom. Meanwhile, the heir to the Guild's grand master discovers that his mother has been a political manipulator and revealed some of the Guild's deepest secrets. The series includes considerable bloody violence.

Takizawa, Seiho
Who Fighter with Heart of Darkness. Dark Horse Manga 2006 208p. Illustration
Grades: 10 11 12 Adult   **741.5; Fic**
1. Manga; 2. Seinen manga; 3. War; 4. Graphic novels
978-1-59307-626-9, $11.95

The first story in this anthology, "Who Fighter," is a play on the legendary "Foo Fighters," the nickname given to the mysterious, UFO-like fireballs that were sighted by World War II pilots. An ace Japanese pilot manages to shoot one of the fireballs down... or does he? As ominous signs and visions begin to follow in his steps, the bewildered pilot wonders if he's lost not only his memory of the incident-but also his very mind. "Heart of Darkness" is Takizawa's take on the Joseph Conrad novel. A Japanese war hero, Colonel Kurutsu, has gone rogue, setting up his own private kingdom deep upriver in the jungles of Burma. A young captain, sent to execute Kurutsu, finds that the true reasons for the Colonel's "desertion" are very different from what he was told. Finally, a short piece, "Tanks," closes out the collection with a surreal voyage through one hundred years of armored vehicle battles. The book includes some violence and some mildly strong language.

Talbot, Bryan
★ **Alice** in Sunderland: An Entertainment. Dark Horse Comics 2007 324p. Illustration
Grades: 10 11 12 Adult   **741.5**
1. Fantasy graphic novels

978-1-59307-673-3

Sunderland was once the greatest center of learning in Christendom and the birthplace of English consciousness. In the time of Lewis Carroll it was the greatest shipbuilding port in the world, and here are buried the roots of Carroll's surreal masterpiece, Alice in Wonderland. Talbot mixes fact and fiction in his meditation on myth, history, storytelling. The book includes some strong language, particularly Briticisms.

★ The **tale** of one bad rat. Dark Horse 2010 Un Illustration
Grades: 9 10 11 12 Adult   **741.5; Fic**
1. Child sexual abuse; 2. Runaway teenagers; 3. Graphic novels
978-1-59582-493-6, $19.99

This book's "heroine is teenager Helen Potter, who has run away from an abusive father and whose path to recovery takes her from a squat in London to refuge at an inn in the British countryside. Along the way, she meets characters and situations that Talbot derives from the work of Helen's namesake, Beatrix Potter, whose life he symbolically links to Helen's. Talbot's vivid, realistic full-color illustration brilliantly evokes the story's settings, yet even more effective are his compassionate characterizations." Booklist
First published 1995
This volume collects issues one through four of the Dark Horse comic-book series Verso of title page

Talbot, Mary M.
Dotter of her father's eyes. Mary M. Talbot; art by Bryan Talbot. Diamond Comic Distributors 2012 96 p. Illustration; Color
Grades: 11 12 Adult   **741.5**
1. Atherton, James S; 2. Bildungsromans; 3. Joyce, James, 1882-1941
1595828508; 9781595828507, $14.99
Costa Biography Award Winner 2012

Author Mary M. Talbot's book "contrasts two coming of age narratives: that of Lucia, the daughter of James Joyce, and that of author Mary Talbot, daughter of the eminent Joycean scholar James S Atherton. Social expectations and gender politics, thwarted ambitions and personal tragedy are played out against two contrasting historical backgrounds." (mary-talbot.co.uk)
Includes bibliographical references.

Talon, Durwin S.
Comics Above Ground: How Sequential Art Affects Mainstream Media. Twomorrows Publishing 2004 168p. Illustration
Grades: Adult Professional   **741.5**
1. Comic books, strips, etc — History and criticism; 2. Popular culture — United States; 3. Graphic novels
1-893905-31-4, $19.95

Comics have had a tremendous effect on popular culture and are now being felt in other storytelling mediums. Top comics professionals talk about their inspirations and training from the comics profession and its effects in "Mainstream Media," including: Conceptual Illustration, Video Game Development, Children's Books, Novels, Design, Illustration, Video Game Animation, Motion

Pictures and other media. Bruce Timm, Bernie Wrightson, Adam Hughes, Louise Simonson, Dave Dorman, Greg Rucka and other creators share their perspectives and their work in both comics and their "other professions." This book also includes career overviews, never before seen art, and interviews, as well as featuring the creators' favorite works in comics.

Tamaki, Jillian
★ **SuperMutant** Magic Academy. Jillian Tamaki. Drawn & Quarterly 2015 274 p. Illustration
Grades: 10 11 12 Adult   **741.5**
1. Comic books, strips, etc — Canada; 2. Fantasy graphic novels; 3. Private schools; 4. School stories; 5. Teenagers; 6. Teenagers — Fiction
1770461981; 9781770461987, $22.95
                     LC 2015376543
In this graphic novel, author Jillian Tamaki "paints a teenaged world filled with just as much ennui and uncertainty, but also with a sharp dose of humor and irreverence.... The SuperMutant Magic Academy is a prep school for mutants and witches, but their paranormal abilities take a backseat to everyday teen concerns. Science experiments go awry, bake sales are upstaged, and the new kid at school is a cat who will determine the course of human destiny." (Publisher's note)
"There are flickering moments of transcendent wisdom and kindness, but the overall tone is one of insouciant, salty resignation to the mundane realities of existence. Simultaneously heartbreaking and hilarious." Booklist

Tamaki, Mariko
★ **This** One Summer. Mariko Tamaki, Jillian Tamaki. First Second 2014 320 p. Illustration
Grades: 7 8 9 10 11 12 Adult   **Fic; 741.5**
1. Friendship — Fiction; 2. Vacations — Fiction; 3. Graphic novels
159643774X, 17.99; 1626720940, 21.99; 9781626720947, $21.99; 9781596437746, 17.99
Caldecott Honor Book (2015)
Printz Honor Book (2015)
Eisner Award: Best Graphic Album—New (2015)
Ignatz Award: Outstanding Graphic Novel (2014)
Harvey Nominee: Best Artist (2015)
Harvey Nominee: Best Graphic Album of Original Work (2015)
Harvey Nominee: Best Original Graphic Publication For Young Readers (2015)
In this young adult graphic novel written by Mariko Tamaki and illustrated by Jillian Tamaki, "Every summer, Rose goes with her mom and dad to a lake house in Awago Beach.... Rosie's friend Windy is always there, too, like the little sister she never had. But this summer is different.... It's a summer of secrets, and sorrow, and growing up, and it's a good thing Rose and Windy have each other." (Publisher's note)
"This captivating graphic novel presents a fully realized picture of a particular time in a young girl's life, an in-between summer filled with yearning and a sense of ephemerality." SLJ

Tamura, Yumi
Basara Volume 1. Viz Media/Shojo 2003 200p. Illustration
Grades: 10 11 12 Adult   **741.5; Fic**
1. Adventure graphic novels; 2. Fantasy graphic novels; 3. Manga; 4. Romance graphic novels; 5. Shojo manga; 6. Graphic novels
1-53961-974-X, $9.99
Born under a prophecy that will liberate and unite a post-apocalyptic Japan, Sarasa has had to take her brother Tatara's place as the "Boy of Destiny." Fighting for the oppressed, Sarasa journeys across Japan to gain allies and defeat her enemies—all while keeping her identity a secret. Ironically, while she leads her people in rebellion against the Red King, she falls in love with him before realizing who he is. The series includes nudity, sexual situations, and violence.

Tanabe, Yellow
Kekkaishi, Vol. 1. Viz Action 2005 192p. Illustration
Grades: 9 10 11 12 Adult   **741.5; Fic**
1. Manga; 2. Shonen manga; 3. Supernatural graphic novels; 4. Graphic novels
1-59116-968-2, $9.99
Junior high student Yoshimori Sumimura is a kekkaishi, a demon hunter; it's the family business. The Yukimuras next door are also kekkaishi, rivals of the Sumimuras. Their daughter Tokine is also a demon hunter. Yoshimori would much rather become a pastry chef, but he can't let Tokine always get the demons. This is the first of an ongoing manga series that has lots of demon hunting action but not too much violence, and considerable humor.

Tanaka, Masashi
Gon vol.6. DC Comics/CMX 2008 Un Illustration
Grades: 6 7 8 9 10 11 12 Adult   **741.5; Fic**
1. Gon (Fictional character); 2. Manga; 3. Stories without words; 4. Graphic novels
978-1-4012-1278-0, $5.99
In this volume, Gon acquires headgear—a bird's nest with three orphaned chicks falls onto his head when he headbutts a tree, and the three young birds are in for the ride of their life as Gon goes his way. Then he and a band of ragtag creatures make their way through a forest and a fire. And he befriends an old elephant as they make their way to a goal only the old elephant knows. The book includes animal-on-animal violence.

Gon Volume 1. DC Comics/CMX 2007 Un Illustration
Grades: 6 7 8 9 10 11 12 Adult   **Fic; 741.5**
1. Humorous graphic novels; 2. Manga; 3. Stories without words; 4. Graphic novels
978-1-4012-1273-5, $5.99
Volume 1 of 7
A tiny dinosaur with a feisty attitude marches across the wilderness defending the friendly and furry from the mean and hungry. Told entirely without words, the stories highlight the detailed art and visual storytelling ability of creator Masashi Tanaka. This new edition from CMX restores the book to its original right-to-left orientation.

Gon volume 4. DC Comics/CMX 2008 Un Illustration
Grades: 7 8 9 10 11 12 Adult   **741.5; Fic**

1. Adventure graphic novels; 2. Dinosaurs; 3. Gon (Fictional character); 4. Manga; 5. Graphic novels
978-1-4012-1275-6, $5.99

Gon, the little dinosaur living in the time of mammals, is back for more wordless adventures. First, he finds a turtle shell and decides to try it on, only to find he can't get out of it. He ends up doing his best to protect the newly hatched sea turtles as they face a gauntlet of hungry predators in their journey to the sea. Then Gon finds himself in the desert with several savannah animals after a tornado dumps them there, and has to save them. The book includes predator/prey animal violence; some readers might get upset to see the baby turtles being eaten by so many other animals.

Gon volume 5. DC Comics/CMX 2008 Un Illustration
Grades: 7 8 9 10 11 12 Adult   **741.5; Fic**
1. Animals; 2. Gon (Fictional character); 3. Manga; 4. Graphic novels
978-1-4012-1277-3, $5.99

In this book-length episode, Gon starts out by exploring an anthill, then defending prairie dogs against a coyote. When an earthquake sends Gon, a prairie dog and the adult coyote and its pup underground, they unite against a giant spider that traps the pup. They must deal with various giant insects (ants, pillbugs, mayflies), bats, and the deadly huge spider. People who don't like to see so many creepy crawlies on the page may want to skip this book.

Tangent Comics, volume one.
DC Comics 2007 206p. Illustration
Grades: 9 10 11 12 Adult   **741.5**
1. Flash (Fictional character); 2. Green Lantern (Fictional character); 3. Superhero graphic novels; 4. Graphic novels
978-1-4012-1530-9, $19.99

In 1997, DC published a series of comics featuring familiar character names, but they were all ... different. The Atom had atomic powers, the Flash (a woman) was made of light, the Metal Men weren't robots but soldiers, the Green Lantern was a woman and used an artifact to raise the dead for one final mission, and so on. Now, DC has collected some of the stories into this trade paperback collection.

Taniguchi, Jiro
The **Ice** wanderer and other stories. Fanfare/Ponent Mon 2007 244p. Illustration
Grades: 10 11 12 Adult   **741.5; Fic**
1. Adventure graphic novels; 2. Manga; 3. Graphic novels
978-84-96427-33-4, $21.99

This volume collects six short stories by Taniguchi, which deal with the relationship of man to nature. Lost in the Great North, two men are saved by an old hunter who recounts a strange legend to them. Surrounded by wolves and fighting for their survival, two explorers head for Alaska to bury their companion. A marine biologist begins a quest to find the mythical graveyard of whales. An inexperienced young city boy goes abalone hunting with a young teenage girl and they get swept out to sea by sudden rough weather. Some stories include some violence.

Tardi, Jacques
The **Arctic** marauder. Written and illustrated by Jacques Tardi; translated from French by Kim Thompson.. Fantagraphics Books 2011 63p Illustration
Grades: Adult   **741.5**
1. Adventure fiction; 2. Arctic regions; 3. Graphic novels
9781606994351, $16.99

This graphic novel "follows a young man named Jerome Plumier and his search for clues to his uncle's death and the ... possible connection to the oddly large number of ships presently being sunk by icebergs in the Arctic. In his journey, Plumier will wander the streets of Paris, read a newspaper, ride a train upon which occurs a murder, discover a note from a secret ally, and receive a thorough tour of a villain's curiously inconvenient choice of hideouts. At . . . sixty-three pages, [author Jacques] Tardi . . . incorporat[es] . . . a variety of tropes, drawn mostly from his generic predecessor . . . Jules Verne. At one point, a vessel named the 'Jules Vernez' receives a sinking barrage of cannon fire from the titular, icy vessel known as the 'Arctic Marauder.'" (Strange Horizons)

★ **It** was the war of the trenches. Translated by Kim Thompson. Fantagraphics 2010 118 p. Illustration
Grades: Adult   **741.5/944**
1. Military art and science; 2. World War, 1914-1918; 3. World War, 1914-1918
1606993534; 9781606993538, $24.99
LC 2014501963

This book, by Jacques Tardi, on World War I "focuses on the day to day of the grunts in the trenches. He also delves deeply into the underlying causes of the war, the madness, the cynical political exploitation of patriotism. Tardi . . . itemizes the ghastly human cost of the war, and lays out the future 20th century conflicts." (Publisher's note)

"The third Fantagraphics volume bringing the work of eminent French comics creator Tardi to American readers is the first he wrote as well as drew, and it shows that he's as singular a writer as he is an artist. It's a relentlessly grim, ground-level depiction of WWI as seen through the eyes of French soldiers mired in the trenches." Booklist
Includes bibliographical references
World War I; World War One

New York mon amour. By Jacques Tardi; illustrated by Benjamin Legrand and Dominique Grange.. Fantagraphics Books 2012 82 p. Illustration; Color
Grades: Adult   **741.5/944; Fic; S C**
1. Crime; 2. Historical fiction; 3. New York (NY)
1606995243; 9781606995242, $19.99

This graphic novel was "[o]riginally published in the early 1980s" and "captures the then grungy urban sprawl [of New York City], told through four tales of its troubled inhabitants struggling to carve out something resembling a life. The main story [is] about a pitiful exterminator who inadvertently sees too much, thus attracting the worst kind of attention." (Publishers Weekly)
Translated from the French by Kim Thompson.

Tatsumi, Yoshihiro
Abandon the Old in Tokyo. Drawn & Quarterly 2006 Un Illustration
Grades: 12 Adult   **741.5; Fic**

1. City and town life — Japan; 2. Manga
1-894937-87-2, $19.95
Abandon the Old in Tokyo continues to delve into the urban underbelly of 1960s Tokyo, exposing not only the seedy dealings of the Japanese everyman but Tatsumi's maturation as a story writer. These stories were originally published in 1970, and most of them feature burned-out, defeated men in relationships with dissatisfied, shrewish women. His considerable use of strong language, sexual situations and nudity make his work most appropriate for older, mature-minded teens and adults.

Fallen words. Yoshihiro Tatsumi. Drawn & Quarterly Publications 2012 278 p.
Grades: Adult   741.5
1. Fables; 2. Rakugo; 3. Short stories; 4. Storytelling
1770460748; 9781770460744, $19.95
LC 2012397995
In this collection of short stories, "[Yoshihiro] Tatsumi . . . draws upon the storytelling tradition of rakugo—in which a live storyteller recounts both sides of a conversation—and provides a series of cautionary tales about day-to-day hopes, fears, and petty excesses." (Publishers Weekly)
Translated from the Japanese. Book reads from right to left in the traditional Japanese format.

★ The **Push** Man and Other Stories. Drawn & Quarterly 2005 208p. Illustration
Grades: 12 Adult   741.5; Fic
1. City and town life — Japan; 2. Manga; 3. Graphic novels
1-896597-85-8, $19.95
Tatsumi is considered the grandfather of alternate manga for the adult reader; the stories in this collection date back to the late 1960s and explore the darker aspects of Japanese urban life. The look of his art is very different from most manga, and his stories comment on the interplay between an overwhelming, bustling, crowded, modern society and the troubled emotional and sexual life of the individual. He invented the term "gekiga" (dramatic pictures) in 1957 to describe his manga Strong sexual overtones, violence, and strong language make Tatsumi's work more suitable for older, mature-minded teens and adults.

Taylor, R. G.
Growing up with comics. All illustrations by R. G. Taylor. Desperado Publishing 2008 Un Illustration
Grades: 10 11 12 Adult   741.5; 920
1. Biographical graphic novels; 2. Books and reading; 3. Hulk (Fictional character); 4. Spider-Man (Fictional character); 5. Spirit (Fictional character); 6. Graphic novels
978-1-935002-12-3, $16.99
This book collects stories about the writers' various experiences as comic book readers. Some of the writers own or work in comics shops, others are comic book creators, some just continued to be comic book readers into adulthood. Many of the stories center on a particular comic book that made an impression upon the writer. The art shows them as adults, but also depicts the comics they loved when they were kids. It gives a glimpse into childhoods of the past

and how one's love for a comic book, be it a Spider-Man or Hulk or The Spirit, could transform one's life.

Templeton, Ty
Howard the duck: media duckling. Writer, Ty Templeton; artist, Juan Bobillo. Marvel Entertainment 2008 Un Illustration
Grades: 9 10 11 12 Adult   741.5; Fic
1. Howard the Duck (Fictional character); 2. Humorous graphic novels; 3. Graphic novels
978-0-7851-2776-5, $11.99
Steve Gerber's creation, Howard the Duck, is back. The trouble starts when fraternal twin physicists who were unsuccessful on their duck hunt encounter cabbie Howard and decide he'll be their hunting trophy. When he beats them up with their own rifles, he's caught on video by his friend Beverly's play director, Serge, who puts the video online. Renegade science organization A.I.M.'s media-mad creature M.O.D.O.T. (Mental Organism Designed Only for Talking) decides to use the video to turn Howard into a media sensation and help him take over the world. The story includes cartoony violence and Beverly is often clad in her stage costume of fig leaves.

TenNapel, Doug
Black Cherry. Image Comics 2007 Un Illustration
Grades: 11 12 Adult   741.5; Fic
1. Horror graphic novels; 2. Mystery graphic novels; 3. Science fiction graphic novels; 4. Graphic novels
978-1-58240-830-9, $17.99
Down-on-his-luck Mafioso Eddie Paretti is so desperate for cash he's agreed to steal a dead body from his own mob boss. Things only get worse when he discovers the body isn't human. With few options and fewer people he can trust, Eddie calls on the man who raised him, Father McHugh. The priest tells Eddie that the body was stolen from his monastery by the Mafia. Father McHugh is accompanied by Mary, a beautiful woman Eddie swears looks just like a stripper he once fell in love with named Black Cherry. The book is full of very foul language (f-bombs and s-bombs galore), nudity, sexual situations, and graphic violence. It also has a deeply-felt religious core that may confuse some readers. TenNapel has written a foreword for readers that explains it.

Creature Tech. Top Shelf Productions 2002 208p. Illustration
Grades: 8 9 10 11 12 Adult   741.5; Fic
1. Science fiction graphic novels; 2. Graphic novels
978-1-891830-34-1, $17.95
Resurrected by the Shroud of Turin, the zombified Dr. Jameson intends to finish what he started 150 years ago—destroying the earth with a giant space eel. Standing in his way is Dr. Ong, a would-be pastor turned scientist who now works in a government research facility infamously known as "Creature Tech." Aided by an unlikely cast of rednecks, symbiotic aliens, and a CIA-trained mantid, Dr. Ong embarks on a journey of faith, love, and self-discovery. All in a day's work at Creature Tech. There's some mild violence and language.

Earthboy Jacobus. Image Comics 2005 272p. Illustration

Grades: 7 8 9 10 11 12 Adult   741.5; Fic
1. Science fiction graphic novels; 2. Graphic novels
1-58240-492-5, $17.95

"The alien settings are vivid, weird, and even bordering on goofy, but this story's very human characters provide a grounding that keeps the reader involved and believing. The heavily inked black-and-white panels serve well for quiet scenes as well as those bursting with action or bathroom jokes." (VOYA)

Ex-Marine and Chief of Police "Chief" Edwards hits a whale while driving home; he rescues a boy from the inside and becomes an "instant" father. Jacobus comes from a rather nasty parallel world, and Chief has to teach the boy to defend himself against the enemies who inevitably come. When they end up in Jacobus' world, the values "Chief" had instilled comprise the well from which Jacobus can draw strength.

Flink. Image Comics 2007 122p. Illustration
Grades: 6 7 8 9 10 11 12 Adult   741.5; Fic
1. Adventure graphic novels; 2. Sasquatch; 3. Graphic novels
978-1-58240-891-0, $13.99; 1-58240-891-2

Conrad is flying with his father on his first hunting trip when the plane crashes in the wilderness. When Conrad comes to after the crash, he's completely alone, with only the clothes on his back, a handheld game player, and a pocketknife his father had just given him. When he wakes up from a sleep, he finds a deerskin wrapped around him and follows a trail of berries; a Bigfoot named Flink has saved him. Now they have to deal with a rabid she-bear that injures Flink; he needs his brother's medicine to heal, but the Bigfoot community hates humans who hunt them. How can Flink convince them that Conrad is harmless? The book includes some violence and one scene where Conrad pees on a tree.

Iron West. Image Comics 2006 160p. Illustration
Grades: 8 9 10 11 12 Adult   741.5; Fic
1. Science fiction graphic novels; 2. Western stories; 3. Graphic novels
978-1-58240-630-5, $14.99

Preston Struck has worked as a con artist and crooked gambler, but when he encounters a horde of technological killers while escaping bounty hunters, he discovers an unfortunate streak of responsibility. Awakened by greedy miners, an alien artifact has begun manufacturing humanoid form robots to kill every human, starting with the town of Twain Harte. Aided by a wizened shaman, a Sasquatch, and the not-too-trusting sheriff, Struck reluctantly sets out to stop the killer robots.

TenNapel uses well-worn cliches of American Westerns and turns them on their heads, including Native American stereotypes, the saloon gal with a heart of gold. The level of violence is similar to that seen in any classic Western movie (think John Wayne films). "This finely balanced piece of work is polished with style." Voice Youth Advocates

Tezuka, Osamu
Apollo's Song. Vertical, Inc. 2007 541p. Illustration
Grades: 10 11 12 Adult   741.5; Fic
1. Love; 2. Manga; 3. Graphic novels
978-1-932234-66-4, $19.95

The gods, with their poetic justice, can be unrelenting. Just ask the young cynic Shogo, who sinned against love. Electroshock therapy was only meant to bring him face to face with his own violent misdeeds, but instead landed him in the court of a stern goddess. If the encounter was a hallucination, then it's a hallucination that starts to encroach on reality in this tale. Shogo is sentenced to fall in love with the same woman over and over again, through all time and many incarnations, beginning with him as a guard and the woman a young Jew being transported to a concentration camp during World War II. The book has strong language, lots of nudity and sexual situations.

Astro Boy books 1 and 2. Dark Horse Comics 2008 424p. Illustration
Grades: 3 4 5 6 7 8 9 10 11 12 Adult   741.5; Fic
1. Adventure graphic novels; 2. Astro Boy (Fictional character); 3. Robots; 4. Science fiction graphic novels; 5. Graphic novels
978-1-59582-153-9, $14.95

When a scientist loses his young son, he builds a robot to look exactly like the boy, but when he activates the robot, the scientist becomes repulsed and rejects him. Professor Ochanomizu (gotta love the name, it means tea water and is also a famous Tokyo neighborhood) rescues the boy robot from a circus and names him Astro Boy. He deals with aliens, with people who would use robots to commit crimes, and with adventures in outer space. This new edition collects the first two volumes of the Dark Horse manga editions.
Also available in omnibus editions
Volumes 1 and 2 of a 23 volume series

★ **Black** Jack, volume 1. Vertical, Inc. 2008 287p. Illustration
Grades: 9 10 11 12 Adult   741.5; Fic
1. Manga; 2. Medical practice; 3. Surgeons; 4. Graphic novels
978-1-934287-27-9, $16.95

Black Jack is the only known name for a mysterious, scarred surgeon from Japan who can perform surgical miracles but is considered to be a creepy mercenary. He will perform highly risky surgeries for an exorbitant price, and he's unlicensed. However, most people don't realize that he actually does a lot for more altruistic reasons as well. In this first volume that reprints the original stories by pioneer mangaka (manga creator) Tezuka, stories include one in which Black Jack operates on a crime boss's son using the body of an unjustly convicted man; and one where he removes a teratoid cystoma from a unidentified wealthy and famous woman, but he refuses to kill the cystoma, which contains the body parts of the woman's unborn twin. While there are some surgical scenes that might not be for the squeamish, the stories offer little in the way of graphic violence or bad language while providing action and some thought about ethics and morals.

"With genre-spanning stories—horror, sci-fi, romance—and Tezuka's signature blend of drama, bathos and extreme broad comedy jammed together on every page, Black Jack is a wild but extravagantly entertaining ride." Publ Wkly
Volume 1 of 17

★ **Buddha** Volume 1: Kapilavastu. Vertical, Inc. 2003 400p. Illustration

Grades: 10 11 12 Adult   **Fic; 741.5**
   1. Buddhism; 2. Manga; 3. Graphic novels
   1-932234-56-X (pa); 1-932234-43-8, $24.95;
   9781932234565, $14.95

     In this first of eight volumes, Tezuka starts the story of Buddha before the birth of the prince Siddhartha. His fictional characters, the slave Chapra, the pariah Tatta, the monk Naradatta, and many others, populate the story and will have an effect on the prince's life. The book includes sexual situations and considerable nudity; the pariahs never wore clothes. Tezuka also throws in a lot of humorous and anachronistic comments; but underlying everything is a profoundly deep understanding of Buddhism. The book also includes some violence.

     ★ **Ode** to Kirihito. Vertical, Inc. 2006 822p. Illustration
Grades: 10 11 12 Adult   **Fic; 741.5**
   1. Manga; 2. Seinen manga; 3. Graphic novels
   978-1-93-223464-0, $24.95

     It may or may not be contagious. There seems to be no cure for it. Yet, Monmow Disease, a life-threatening condition that transforms a person into a dog-like beast, is not the only villain in this shocking medical thriller. Young doctor Kirihito Osanai investigates the source of the disease, only to be infected himself. Then he discovers his betrayal by the medical community, the violent reactions of most of society because of the deformity of his facial features, and he sets out around the world to find a cure. The book includes violence, nudity, rape, and some strong language.

     Also available as two separate volumes

     Phoenix Vol. 10: Sun, Part One. Viz Media/Signature 2007 339p. Illustration
Grades: 10 11 12 Adult   **741.5; Fic**
   1. Manga; 2. Religion; 3. Science fiction graphic novels; 4. Graphic novels
   978-1-4215-0972-3, $15.99

     This volume in Tezuka's Phoenix series covers two vastly different time periods; in 663 A.D., a young soldier named Harima is punished by the enemy general by putting a wolf's head on him. Rescued by an old woman, he travels with her and a Japanese general to Japan. Harima suffers nightmares in which he sees visions of a future world; Bardo Suguru is a warrior in the twenty-first century, fighting on behalf of banished humans. In the seventh century, Harima battles against those who would force Buddhism upon the people; in the twenty-first century, Suguru battles against the Church of Light, which has forced "unbelievers" to hide underground. This volume has some partial nudity and such violence as beheadings.

     Phoenix Vol. 5: Resurrection. Viz Media/Editor's Choics 2004 324p. Illustration
Grades: 10 11 12 Adult   **741.5; Fic**
   1. Manga; 2. Science fiction graphic novels; 3. Graphic novels
   1-59116-593-8, $15.95

     In the year 3344, Prof. Saruta lands on the moon and meets and acquires Robita in his final form. On Earth, the Robita model robots, now sentient, rebel in the only way left open to robots programmed to obey. And Leon, miraculously brought back to life after dying in an accident, realizes he was murdered and tries to remember what he was

doing that would get him killed. There's some violence and some sexual suggestiveness.

     Phoenix Vol. 7: Civil War Part One. Viz Media/Signature 2006 424p. Illustration
Grades: 10 11 12 Adult   **741.5; Fic**
   1. Manga; 2. Graphic novels
   978-1-4215-0517-6, $15.95

     At the end of the Heian Period (12th century), a hunter named Benta comes to Kyoto in search of his abducted fiance, Obuu. Obuu is forced to become the attendant of a powerful man of the time, who wishes to cheat death and extend the life of his clan by obtaining the legendary phoenix. Meanwhile, dissent is brewing among a people fed up with their corrupt government. Kyoto is on the verge of a civil war. The book includes violence, strong language, and some sexual situations.

     Phoenix Volume 8: Civil War Part Two. Viz/Signature 2006 338p. Illustration
Grades: 10 11 12 Adult   **741.5; Fic**
   1. Manga; 2. Graphic novels
   978-1-4215-0518-3, $15.99

     This volume continues the story of the turbulent events of 12th century Japan, when the Taira and Minamoto clans fought each other; one of the stories about this was is called the Heike Monogatari. The everyman Benta has become an unwilling samurai, witness to senseless killings and the replacement of one brutal regime with another even more so. The book also includes Tezuka's retelling of the Japanese fable Hagoromo-densest, called here "Robe of Feathers," which he illustrates as though it's a play being enacted on stage. The book includes some sexual content, strong language, and violence.

Thomas, Roy
     The **Chronicles** of Conan Volume 1: Tower of the Elephant and Other Stories. Written by Roy Thomas; illustrated by Barry Windsor-Smith and others. Dark Horse Comics 2003 166p. Illustration
Grades: 9 10 11 12 Adult   **741.5; Fic**
   1. Adventure graphic novels; 2. Conan the Barbarian (Fictional character); 3. Fantasy graphic novels; 4. Graphic novels
   1-59307-016-0, $15.95

     In the early 1970s, Robert E. Howard's Conan the Barbarian exploded on to the comics scene. Writer Roy Thomas teamed with a young artist named Barry Smith, and together the two mapped out Conan adventures over the course of their 24-issue run together. Thomas and Smith defined Conan for a generation of comics readers, and now those stories are collected here in a series of trade paperbacks. This series features completely remastered color and text corrections, and contains material not available for nearly thirty years. Some of the stories are original, others adapt the original Howard stories; they all include action and violence and some suggestive scenes, as Conan fights warriors and monsters and encounters beautiful, sexy women.

     John Romita ... And All That Jazz!. Twomorrows Publishing 2007 189p. Illustration
Grades: Adult Professional   **741.5**

1. Romita, John Sr, 1930-; 2. Spider-Man (Fictional character); 3. Graphic novels
978-1-893905-75-7, $24.95

In this new book, Jazzy" John Romita - the artist who made The Amazing Spider-Man Marvel's #1-selling comic book in the 1960s - talks about his life, his art and his contemporaries. Authored by former Marvel Comics editor in chief and writer Roy Thomas and historian Jim Amash, it features the most definitive interview Romita's ever given, about working with such comics legends as Stan Lee and Jack Kirby, following Spider-Man co-creator Steve Ditko as artist on the strip, and more. Plus, Roy Thomas shares memories of working with Romita in the 1960s-70s, and Jim Amash examines the artistry of Ring-a-Ding Romita (the funny nicknames were bestowed on Romita by Stan Lee). Lavishly illustrated with Romita's art - original art and unseen masterpieces - as well as illustrations by some of Marvel's and DC's other artists, this is at once a career overview of a comics master, and a firsthand history of the industry by one of its leading artists.

Thompson, Craig

★ **Blankets:** an illustrated novel. Top Shelf 2003 582p. Illustration
Grades: 10 11 12 Adult   **Fic; 741; 92; 741.5**
1. Artists; 2. Autobiographical graphic novels; 3. Cartoonists; 4. Family life; 5. Illustrators; 6. Thompson, Craig, 1975-; 7. Graphic novels
1-891830-43-0, $29.95; 9781891830433
LC 2004-297892

This "memoir recreates the confusion, emotional pain and isolation of the author's rigidly fundamentalist Christian upbringing, along with the trepidation of growing into maturity. Skinny, naive and spiritually vulnerable, Thompson and his younger brother manage to survive their parents' overbearing discipline (the brothers are sometimes forced to sleep in "the cubbyhole," a forbidding and claustrophobic storage chamber) through flights of childhood fancy and a mutual love of drawing . . . Thompson manages to explore adolescent social yearnings, the power of young love and the complexities of sexual attraction with a rare combination of sincerity, pictorial lyricism and taste. His exceptional b&w drawings balance representational precision with a bold and wonderfully expressive line for pages of ingenious, inventively composed and poignant imagery." Publ Wkly

Carnet de Voyage: Travel Journal Volume One. Top Shelf Productions 2004 224p. Illustration
Grades: 10 11 12 Adult   **741.5; 910**
1. Autobiographical graphic novels; 2. Travel; 3. Graphic novels
1-891830-60-0, $14.95

Craig Thompson spent three months traveling through Barcelona, the Alps, and France, as well as Morocco, researching his next graphic novel, Habibi. Spontaneous sketches and a travelogue diary document his adventures and quiet moments, creating a portrait of countries, culture and the wandering artist. Very occasional partial nudity and mild harsh language punctuate Thompson's narrative.

★ **Habibi.** Pantheon Books 2011 655p. Illustration
Grades: Adult   **741.5; Fic**

1. Refugees; 2. Slavery; 3. Graphic novels
978-0-375-42414-4, $35
LC 2010050963

"Child bride Dolola is sold by her impoverished parents in the Middle East to a clumsy but well-meaning older man who teaches her to read and write. When slavers kill her husband and kidnap her, she manages to escape carrying the dark-skinned baby of another captive. She finds refuge in an abandoned ship stranded in the desert, where she raises little Zam to adolescence, telling him stories and teaching him literacy. Further adventures separate them but reunite them later. As escaped harem prostitute and escaped eunuch, they forge an intimate bond and move into the future." Libr J

"Though in the form of a comic book, Thompson's story is decidedly not for youngsters: Rape and murder figure in these pages, as does sex between minors. A mature—in all its meanings—glimpse into a world few Westerners are at home with, and Thompson is respectful throughout." Kirkus

Thompson, Jill

Death: At Death's Door. DC Comics/Vertigo 2003 204p. Illustration
Grades: 10 11 12 Adult   **741.5; Fic**
1. Adventure graphic novels; 2. Fantasy graphic novels; 3. Horror graphic novels; 4. Humorous graphic novels; 5. Graphic novels
1-56389-938-8, $9.95

A member of the Endless, a family of beings who have existed longer than the gods, Death enjoys manifesting herself in the persona of a Goth girl. Along with her siblings, she interacts and influences the lives of humans on a daily basis. In this shojo manga-style adventure, Death's little sisters, Delirium and Despair, have thrown a party at her apartment for hell's escapees. But as the festivities get out of control, it falls on Death's black-clad shoulders to regain order and save the afterlife - not to mention her carpet. Despair is always drawn as nude. The events in this book occur around the time of the Sandman volume, Season of Mists.

The **Little** Endless Storybook. DC Comics/Vertigo 2004 Un Illustration
Grades: 9 10 11 12 Adult   **741.5; Fic**
1. Adventure graphic novels; 2. Fantasy graphic novels; 3. Graphic novels
14012-0428-7, $15.95

Jill Thompson takes Neil Gaiman's the Endless and draws them as little children in this story. Puppy Barnabas has been entrusted with watching and protecting Delirium, who is always easily ... distracted. When he leaves her for just a minute or so, she gets lost. He searches the waking world but can't find her. Now, he must travel to the strange and unlikely realms of each of the Endless to see if Delirium's siblings have seen their missing sister. While the pictures are cute and the book resembles a child's picture book, the story has enough of an edge to make it more suitable for older teens. Despair is, as always, drawn as nude.

Thompson, Robbie

Silk: the life and times of Cindy Moon. By Robbie Thompson; illustrated by Stacey Lee. Marvel Enterprises 2015 160 p. Color; Illustration
Grades: 10 11 12 Adult

1. Women superheroes
0785197044; 9780785197041, $19.99

In this comic book, by Robbie Thompson, illustrated by Stacey Lee, "Cindy Moon . . . learned that she had been bitten by the same radioactive spider from the first arc of AMAZING SPIDER-MAN. She then went on to save Peter Parker's life (more than once!) and traverse the Spider-Verse alongside Spider-Woman. Now, as SILK, Cindy is on her own in New York City, searching for her past, defining her own future, and webbing up wrong-doers along the way!" (Publisher's note)

Volume 1 of an ongoing series

Thung, Diana
★ **Captain** Long Ears. SLG Publishing 2010 168p. Illustration
Grades: 5 6 7 8 9 10 11 12 Adult   741.5; Fic
1. Adventure graphic novels; 2. Amusement parks; 3. Death; 4. Graphic novels
978-1-59362-187-2, $12.95

Eight-year-old Michael, aka Captain Long Ears, goes on a mission to Headquarters (an amusement park) with Captain Jam, who is actually his purple toy stuffed gorilla. They're searching for Captain Big Nose, who is Michael's father; he's been gone "on a mission" for two years. In Headquarters, Captain Long Ears and Captain Jam encounter monsters (a preschool teacher and a park attendant), then they find a large crate in a locked enclosure. When they open the crate, they find a young elephant the boy calls "Little Big Nose." They decide they must save Little Big Nose, so they hide in the park overnight. Meanwhile, Michael's mother comes home late from work and doesn't realize her son is missing until the next day. Back in the park, Michael has several dreams of his father leaving him behind. He's so caught up in his fantasy of Captain Long Ears that he doesn't realize the dangers he faces in trying to save the young elephant from abusive handlers. Thung's art shows most of the action through Michael's imagination; readers soon realize that Michael hasn't accepted his father's death. The use of words such as "ass," "caca brain," and other childish epithets may cause more conservative schools to carefully consider their purchase. This imaginary adventure and exploration of the mourning process brings to mind such books as The Bridge to Terabithia and has a similar emotional impact. Despite Michael's young age, this book is more suited to upper elementary and middle school age readers on up.

Tiede, Dirk I.
Paradigm shift part one: equilibrium. Dirk Tiede Cartoons & Illustrations 2006 98p. Illustration
Grades: 10 11 12 Adult   741.5; Fic
1. Adventure graphic novels; 2. Mystery graphic novels; 3. Graphic novels
978-0-9789717-1-7, $9.95

Chicago cops and partners Kate and Mike stumble onto a major case when they shake down an informer for information that leads them to Chinatown and a pool hall brawl that leaves Kate shot. In the hospital, the emergency room staff tells her she's not seriously hurt, but she knows she lost a lot of blood, too much for it to be a minor injury. Meanwhile, she and Mike are pulled off that case and told to

investigate a mauling death that might be homicide. The victim looks as though he had been attacked by a monstrous animal. Can Kate's nightmare, in which she becomes the creature, be a clue to what's going on? This global manga story was originally published in 2003 and is still available online under that original ISBN (978-1591098690). The book includes one panel with partial nudity, some violence, and the occasional use of harsh language, including s-bomb and f-bomb.

Tieri, Frank
Civil War: War Crimes. Writer, Frank Tieri; artist, Staz Johnson. Marvel Entertainment 2007 Un Illustration
Grades: 10 11 12 Adult   Fic; 741.5
1. Captain America (Fictional character); 2. Iron Man (Fictional character); 3. Superhero graphic novels; 4. Graphic novels
0-7851-2652-X, $17.99

Wilson Fisk, the incarcerated ex-Kingpin of Crime, proposes a deal to Iron Man, to use his underworld connections to help track down Captain America and his anti-Registration underground in exchange for consideration on his sentence. But can the Kingpin be trusted, or is he playing a deeper game? In a Civil War prequel story, career criminal Jackie Dio, fresh out of prison, finds the New York underworld has changed, and he finds trouble. If he's going to have a shot at surviving, he may have to find the shadowy figure known only as "The Consultant" - that is, if he even exists. There is more graphic violence in this title, and some strong language.

Tillieux, Maurice
Murder by high tide. [by] M. Tillieux. Fantagraphics 2011 92p. Illustration
Grades: 11 12 Adult   741.5; Fic
1. Mystery graphic novels; 2. Graphic novels
978-1-60699-451-1, $18.99

"Dapper private detective Gil Jordan is the star of these funny adventure stories, aided by ex-burglar assistant Crackerjack, eccentric friend Inspector Crouton, and no-nonsense secretary Miss Midge. "Murder by High Tide" sets an antiques dealer's death at an irresistible location, on a tidal causeway leading to the decrepit Tower of the Merrie Knight. And in "Leap of Faith," escaped convict Joe the Syringe stays one leap ahead of the good guys as he seeks revenge on his attorney. Plausibility may not be the watchword here, but no matter: these are a ton of fun and the full-color art, beautifully produced and fairly bursting with sweat beads, stink lines, and other emanata, is an animated delight." Booklist

Translated from the French

Timony, Bobby
★ The **night** owls. Peter Timony and Bobby Timony. DC Comics/Zuda Comics 2010 Un Illustration
Grades: 9 10 11 12 Adult   741.5; Fic
1. Humorous graphic novels; 2. Mystery graphic novels; 3. Supernatural graphic novels; 4. Graphic novels
978-1-4012-2673-2, $14.99

Occult specialist Ernest Baxter, fighting flapper girl Mindy Markus, and Roscoe the Gargoyle are the Night Owls, a private detective agency specializing in supernatural cases involving such creatures as vampires, werewolves, ghosts, and other things that go bump in the night. Some of the cases in this volume include the murderous, faceless Mr. You, who steals people's faces, bootleggers with banshees, and a jealous ghost of an actor who haunts his old theater. Most of the book is illustrated in sepia tones, except for the stories set in the fairy tale kingdom that is Mindy's real home. It includes some on-page violence, including a strangulation. This book collects the Night Owls webcomic originally posted at www.zuda.com.

Tinnell, Robert

The **Black** Forest. Written by Todd Livingston & Robert Tinnell; illustrated by Neil Vokes; lettered by Anthony Schiavino & Adam Levine. Image Comics 2004 104p. Illustration
Grades: 10 11 12 Adult   **741.5; Fic**
1. Adventure graphic novels; 2. Fantasy graphic novels; 3. Horror graphic novels; 4. Graphic novels
1-58240-350-3, $9.95
During World War I, in the battle between good and evil, evil just got creative. The Germans are developing a mysterious weapon to break through the trenches. American pilot Jack Shannon and Archie Caldwell, Britain's greatest stage magician, are sent behind enemy lines, into the heart of the supernatural vortex that is the Black Forest. There, in a remote castle, they match wits with evil occultist Avery Dye, who aims to use Frankenstein's Monster as a template to create an army of unstoppable re-animated dead. In order to thwart the forces of evil, Jack and Archie will be forced to battle Nosferatu, werewolves, a sorcerer, and Frankenstein's Monster himself. The book includes violence.

The **Faceless**: A Terry Sharp Story. Written by Robert Tinnell; artist, Adrian Salmon. Image Comics 2005 64p. Illustration
Grades: 10 11 12 Adult   **741.5; Fic**
1. Fantasy graphic novels; 2. Horror graphic novels; 3. Humorous graphic novels; 4. Graphic novels
978-1-58240-516-2, $6.99
Once upon a time in England, 1962. By day, Terry Sharp is a successful director of horror films, consumer of cocktails, and chaser of skirts. By night, the horror is real as he battles tirelessly against a Satanic conspiracy that reaches the highest levels of government. Sharp's willing to go to hell... so you won't have to. The book includes mildly bad language and some violence as Sharp fights the Faceless.

Tinsley, Kevin

Stonehaven: Milk Cartons & Dog Biscuits. Kevin Tinsley, words & colors; Phil Singer, art. Stickman Graphics 2004 214p. Illustration
Grades: 10 11 12 Adult   **741.5; Fic**
1. Fantasy graphic novels; 2. Mystery graphic novels; 3. Graphic novels
0-9675423-3-2; 0-9675423-4-0 (pa)
Ranger Dan Parsons comes from the Far Reaches to the big city, Stonehaven, searching for his runaway teenage daughter. He's forced to ask half-elf private detective Victor Jardine for help, and they soon find out that Melody Parsons faces danger from her friends, including one young man who has dabbled in dark magic to transform into a werewolf. Can

Parsons and Jardine save Melody while also dealing with the police, the werewolf Wild Pack, and the Tong?
Tinsley combines hard-boiled crime noir with high fantasy and the supernatural in this story. Stonehaven bears some resemblance to New York City. Singer uses subdued, earthy tones for the art. Bloody murders that look like werewolf attacks make this more suitable for older readers.

Tipton, David

Star Trek: Alien spotlight volume 1. Written by Scott Tipton; Art by David Messina. IDW Publishing 2008 152p. Illustration
Grades: 6 7 8 9 10 11 12 Adult   **741.5; Fic**
1. Adventure graphic novels; 2. Science fiction graphic novels; 3. Star Trek; 4. Graphic novels
978-1-60010-179-3, $19.99
This volume collects a series of one-shots (standalone comics issues), each devoted to one of the alien races featured in the Star Trek series. Readers meet the Gorns, Vulcans, Andorians, Orions, the Borg, and the Romulans in stories that also give the aliens' point of view. The stories are set in the various time periods of the Star Trek universe; for example, Captain Clark Terrell and Pavel Chekov (before they were captured by Khan in "The Wrath of Khan") and their landing party encounter the Gorns on a planet designed to train Gorn warriors, while Captain Picard encounters the Borg.

Star Trek: miror images. David and Scott Tipton ; art by Sara Pichelli and David Messina. IDW Publishing 2010 128p. Illustration
Grades: 7 8 9 10 11 12 Adult   **741.5; Fic**
1. Adventure graphic novels; 2. Science fiction graphic novels; 3. Star Trek (Television series); 4. Graphic novels
978-1-60010-293-6, $19.99
In Star Trek, the original television series, the second-season episode called "Mirror, Mirror" put Captain Kirk, Dr. McCoy, Lieutenant Uhura, and Commander Scott into an alternate universe where the Federation had never been. In that universe, Captain Kirk commanded the I.S.S. Enterprise for the Terran Empire, where promotions occurred by assassination. That Mirror-Kirk was evil. This book shows how Mirror-Kirk seized command of the Enterprise from Captain Pike. One doesn't have to know the television episode in order to enjoy the story, but that knowledge will help readers know right away just what device Mirror-Kirk has Mirror-Scotty building for him. The book also includes an incident in a young Lieutenant Jean-Luc Picard's career; it's about seventy years since the "Mirror, Mirror" incident. At the end of the episode, Captain Kirk encouraged Mirror-Spock to seize command of the Mirror-Enterprise and find a way to gain control of the Empire so he can try to change the Empire to be more like the Federation. As far as Mirror-Picard is concerned, those changes made by Emperor Spock have weakened the Empire. Things come to a head when the I.S.S. Starbreaker encounters a force of Klingon-Cardassian Alliance ships. Captain Sorek, a Vulcan, refuses to fight back and is ready to surrender the ship, so Picard decides to take action. "Mirror, Mirror" ended with Kirk's hope that Mirror-Spock would bring about a change for the better; Mirror-Picard's story show that such change didn't do much good for the Terran Empire. Picard utters the word "merde" once, one will have

to know at least a little French to know he said a bad word. The book's cover is somewhat misleading, since it shows Spock and Mirror-Spock instead of Kirk and Mirror-Kirk.

Tipton, Scott
    Star Trek: Klingons: blood will tell. David and Scott Tipton ; art by David Messina. IDW Publishing 2007 168p. Illustration
Grades: 7 8 9 10 11 12 Adult   **741.5; Fic**
    1. Science fiction graphic novels; 2. Star Trek; 3. Graphic novels
    978-1-60010-108-3, $24.99
    In this volume, readers look back at some of the most famous encounters between the United Federation of Planets and the Klingon Empire, from the Klingon perspective. Kahnrah must decide if he will side with Gorkon and ask the Federation for aid in a time of crisis for all Klingons, and he seeks enlightenment from the actions of his relatives who encountered such Federation officers as Captain James T. Kirk of the starship Enterprise. The book includes the Klingon language variant of the first comic book issue.

Tiwary, Vivek J.
    The **Fifth** Beatle: The Brian Epstein Story. By Vivek Tiwary; edited by Philip Simon; illustrated by Andrew C. Robinson and Kyle Baker. Dark Horse 2013 144 p. Color; Illustration
Grades: Adult   **92; 741.5**
    1. Beatles; 2. Biographical graphic novels; 3. Epstein, Brian, 1934-1967
    1616552565; 9781616552565, $19.99
    LAMBDA Literary Award Finalist: Graphic Novel (2014)
    Eisner Award: Best Reality-Based Work (2014)
    Harvey Award: Best Graphic Album of Original Work (2014)
    Harvey Award: Best Biographical, Historical, or Journalistic Presentation (2014)
    This graphic novel, by Vivek Tiwary, edited by Philip Simon, and illustrated by Andrew C. Robinson and Kyle Baker, "is the untold true story of Brian Epstein, the visionary manager who discovered and guided the Beatles—from their gigs in a tiny cellar in Liverpool to unprecedented international stardom." (Publisher's note)
    "Robinson and Baker's artwork is colorful and fluid, and it avoids looking like copies of publicity stills (a cliché of biographical comics), with rich, deep color palettes capturing the mod energy of the '60s." Pub Wkly

Tobe, Keiko
    With the Light: Raising an Autistic Child (Hikari to Tomoni). Yen Press 2007 528p. Illustration
Grades: 8 9 10 11 12 Adult   **Fic; 741.5**
    1. Autism; 2. Manga; 3. Graphic novels
    978-0-7595-2356-2, $14.99
    Born during the sunrise - an auspicious beginning - the Azumas' newborn son is named Hikaru, which means "light." But during one play date, his mother notices that her son is slightly different from the other children. In this alternately heartwarming and bittersweet tale, a young mother tries to cope with both the overwhelming discovery of her child's autism and the trials of raising him while

keeping her family together. This fictional story is based on true accounts; and the book includes notes about how parents can deal with certain situations depicted in the story.
    Volume 1 of 8

Tobin, Paul
    Bandette: Presto!. By Paul Tobin, illustrated by Collen Coover, edited by Brendan Wright. Dark Horse Books 2013 144 p. (Bandette)

Courtesy of Yen Press

Grades: 7 8 9 10 11 12 Adult   **741.5**
    1. Burglars; 2. Organized crime — Fiction; 3. Paris (France); 4. Teenage girls — Fiction; 5. Thieves
    1616552794; 9781616552794, $14.99
    LC 2013024226
    Eisner Award: Best Digital Comic (2013)
    In this graphic novel by Paul Tobin and Colleen Coover, "the world's greatest thief is a costumed teen burglar in swinging Paris by the nome d'arte of Bandette! But it's not all breaking hearts and purloining masterpieces when a rival thief discovers that an international criminal organization wants Bandette dead!" (Publisher's note)
    "[O]ne of the brightest, and most fun, comics of the year." Pub Wkly
    Another title about Bandette is: Stealers keepers! (2015)

Toboso, Yana
    Black butler, vol. 1. [translation: Tomo Kimura; lettering: Tania Biswas].. Yen Press 2010 184p. Illustration
Grades: 10 11 12 Adult
741.5; Fic
    1. Fantasy graphic novels; 2. Household employees; 3. Manga; 4. Mystery graphic novels; 5. Graphic novels
    978-0-316-08084-2, $10.99

Courtesy of Yen Press

    In an alternate England, the young Earl Phantomhive, Ciel, lives just outside London; he's only twelve years old, but he runs a massive toy manufacturing company, aided by his butler Sebastian. In this world, magic coexists with science and technology, cars from the early twentieth century drive the roads and Ciel tests video games. Sebastian commands the other workers: Finnian the Gardener (who tends to kill plants), Mey-Rin the klutzy housemaid, and Baldroy the chef, who always has a cigarette dangling from the corner of his mouth. The dapper butler always finds a way to save the day, whether it's transforming a destroyed courtyard into a Japanese rock garden, teaching his young charge to dance the waltz, or saving him from gangsters. He is too good to be true; he is, as he says, "a devil of a butler." The book includes some graphic violence and occasional, mildly bad language ("bastard," "damned").

First volume in an ongoing series

Togashi, Yoshihiro
   YuYu Hakusho Vol. 1. Viz Media/Shonen Jump 2003 208p. Illustration
Grades: 8 9 10 11 12 Adult   741.5; Fic
   1. Fantasy graphic novels; 2. Shonen manga; 3. Supernatural graphic novels; 4. Graphic novels
   1-56931-904-9, $7.95

   Yusuke Urameshi was a tough teen delinquent until one selfless act changed his life...by ending it. When he died saving a little kid from a speeding car, the afterlife didn't know what to do with him, so it gave him a second chance at life. Now, Yusuke is a ghost with a mission, performing good deeds at the behest of Botan, the spirit guide of the dead, and Koenma, her pacifier-sucking boss from the other side. But what strange things await him on the borderline between life and death? It's going to include a lot of battles against supernatural creatures. The series includes some strong language, lots of supernatural martial arts fighting action, and some mildly suggestive humor.

Tomasi, Peter
   Batman and Robin; Volume 1. Peter J. Tomasi, writer; Patrick Gleason, penciller; Mick Gray, Guy Major, inkers; John Kalisz, colorist; Patrick Brosseau, letterer.. DC Comics 2012 192 p. Illustration; Color
Grades: Adult   Fic; 741.5/973
   1. Batman (Fictional character); 2. Fatherhood; 3. Robin (Fictional character); 4. Superhero graphic novels
   9781401238384, $16.99; 1401234879; 9781401234874, $24.99
                LC 2012010314
   This graphic novel features a "story arc [that] shows the master crime fighter learning to be a father. Damian Wayne, the latest Robin, spent the first 10 years of his life being trained as an assassin, so he doesn't understand Batman's refusal to kill." Batman has trouble explaining "his rigid code of morality," just as the villain Nobody arrives. He "simply erases the villains he encounters. He is, in short, a dangerously appealing father figure for Batman's alienated son." (Publishers Weekly)
   Originally published in single magazine form in BATMAN AND ROBIN 1-8—t.p. verso.

Tomasi, Peter J.
   Light Brigade. Peter J. Tomasi, story and words; Peter Snejbjerg, artist; Bjarne Hansen, colorist; Ken Lopez and Rob Leigh, letterers. DC Comics 2005 Un Illustration
Grades: 10 11 12 Adult   741.5; Fic
   1. Supernatural graphic novels; 2. World War, 1939-1945; 3. Graphic novels
   1-4012-0795-2, $19.99
   In the middle of World War II, American soldier Chris Staros just wants to survive so he can go home and raise his son after learning that his wife has died. He and his fellow soldiers soon learn that they have to worry about a lot more than surviving attacks by a superior Nazi force. Their captain is the immortal centurion who thrust his spear into

Jesus' side at the Crucifixion almost two millenia before; he's been tracking and killing grigori, the fallen angels and the nephillim, their half-angel/half-mortal children. Now, he and the small band of American soldiers under his command must find the Sword of God before the last grigori and his nephillim do and prevent them from storming Heaven's Gate.
   Originally published as a four-issue miniseries.

Tomine, Adrian
   ★ **Killing** and Dying. Adrian Tomine. Farrar Straus & Giroux 2015 128 p. Illustration
Grades: Adult   741.5
   1. Family; 2. Identity (Psychology)
   1770462090; 9781770462090, $22.95
   This graphic novel collection by Adrian Tomine is an "exploration of loss, creative ambition, identity, and family dynamics. 'Amber Sweet' shows the disastrous impact of mistaken identity in a hyper-connected world; 'A Brief History of the Art Form Known as 'Hortisculpture' details the invention and destruction of a vital new art form; the title story, 'Killing and Dying', centers on parenthood, mortality, and stand-up comedy." (Publisher's note)

   ★ **Shortcomings**. Drawn & Quarterly 2007 108p. Illustration
Grades: 10 11 12 Adult   Fic; 741.5
   1. Graphic novels
   978-1-897299-16-6, $19.95; 1-897299-16-8
   Ben Tanaka, a Japanese American in his late twenties, has trouble. His girlfriend, Miko, suspects that Ben's wandering eye is doing so in the direction of white women. This accusation, and its various implications, becomes the subject of heated, spiraling debate, setting in motion a story that pits California against New York (they both live in Berkeley), devotion against desire, and truth against truth. The book includes some strong language, nudity, and sexual situations.

Tooks, Lance
   Lucifer's Garden of Verses Volume Three: The Student (Or Nude Descending a Staircase ... Head First). NBM/ComicsLit 2004 80p. Illustration
Grades: 10 11 12 Adult   741.5; Fic
   1. Art; 2. Horror graphic novels; 3. Graphic novels
   1-56163-446-8, $15.95
   Inspired by the German silent film classic "The Student of Prague," this is the story of Andre Baldwin, a down-on-his-luck would-be Basquiat who enters into a Faustian bargain with a powerful art critic in exchange for status, riches and the love of a woman. Acquanetta Scapinelli is the critic in question, and she recounts this bitter tale with sardonic delight..." For what shall it profit a man if he gain the whole world and lose his own soul? This book includes harsh language, violence, and some sexual situations.

   Lucifer's Garden of Verses, Volume One: The Devil on Fever Street. NBM/ComicsLit 2005 Un Illustration
Grades: 11 12 Adult   Fic; 741.5
   1. Devil; 2. Romance graphic novels; 3. Graphic novels
   1-56163-409-3, $15.95

Satan awakens, after a hundred-year sleep, depressed and disillusioned. It is a mere seven days before he's expected to bring Armageddon to Earth and he is wracked with spiritual doubt and severe performance anxiety. He decides that and old-fashioned temptation will be just the thing to return him to form. His chosen temptee: Black Lily, the purest, most virtuous woman on Earth. Alas, he may have met his match or more... Nudity and sexual situations as Satan falls in love.

Volume 1 of 4

Toppi, Sergio
  Sharaz-de: Tales from the Arabian Nights. Sergio Toppi. Archaia Entertainment LLC 2012 224 p.
Grades: Adult   **741.5**
  1. Storytelling — Fiction; 2. Supernatural — Fiction
  1936393484; 9781936393480, $29.95
  This comic book by Sergio Toppi is "a set of tales inspired by the Arabian Nights . . ., exploring a barbaric society where the supernatural is the only remedy to injustice, as Sharaz-de, captive to a cruel and despotic king, must each night spin tales to entertain her master and save her head from the executioner." (Publisher's note)

Toriyama, Akira
  Dr. Slump Volume 1. Viz Media/Shonen Jump 2005 192p. Illustration
Grades: 9 10 11 12 Adult   **Fic; 741.5**
  1. Humorous graphic novels; 2. Manga; 3. Shonen manga; 4. Graphic novels
  1-59116-950-X, $7.99
  When goofy inventor Senbei Norimaki (his name means seaweed-wrapped rice cracker) creates a precocious robot named Arale, his masterpiece turns out to be more than he bargained for, for she is very strong; however, she's nearsighted. Senbei scrambles to get Arale in working order so the rest of Penguin Village won't have reason to suspect she's not really a girl. But first Senbei needs to find her a pair of glasses and some clothes... It doesn't help that Arale also talks to poop. The book includes some sexual innuendo, crude humor, and lots of silliness.
  Volume 1 of 18

Torres, Alissa
  ★ **American** widow. Illustrated by Sungyoon Choi. Villard Books 2008 209p. Illustration
Grades: 11 12 Adult   **92; 974.7; 741.5**
  1. Autobiographical graphic novels; 2. Educators; 3. Memoirists; 4. September 11 terrorist attacks, 2001; 5. Torres, Alissa; 6. Widows; 7. Graphic novels
  978-0-345-50069-4, $22
                                              LC 2008-08396
  Alissa Torres' husband Luis had just started his new job in the World Trade Center on September 10, 2001. The next day, he died in the terrorist attacks that destroyed the twin towers. Alissa was more than seven months pregnant. In this book, she recounts the personal struggles she suffered as a pregnant "terror widow," first heaped upon with sympathy, then publicly scorned. She describes the tragedies suffered by all the families who lost loved ones on September 11, 2001 and the frustrations they experienced dealing with

bureaucrats as they tried to get even the smallest physical trace of their loved ones.
  The author's "tragedy of errors inspires anger on her behalf, although the story is calmly and beautifully told. Choi's simple and attractive line art is set off by turquoise wash, yielding to a full-color photo at the end when Alissa embraces her life anew." Libr J

Torres, J.
  Blue Beetle: reach for the stars. John Rogers, J. Torres, Keith Giffen, writers ; Rafael Albuquerque, David Baldeon, Freddie Williams II, pencillers ; Rafael Albuquerque, Steve Bird, Dan Davis, inkers ; Guy Major, colorist ; Phil Balsman, Pat Brosseau, letterers. DC Comics 2008 168p. Illustration
Grades: 8 9 10 11 12 Adult   **Fic; 741.5**
  1. Adventure graphic novels; 2. Green Lantern (Fictional character); 3. Superhero graphic novels; 4. Teen Titans (Fictional characters); 5. Graphic novels
  978-1-4012-1642-9, $14.99
  In the previous volume, teenager Jaime Reyes discovered that the scarab fused to his spine that turns him into the Blue Beetle was created by aliens. Now he learns that those aliens are invading Earth, but they're doing it so insidiously that humans are welcoming the Reach and no one will believe one boy from Texas. It's up to Jaime, his friends, and some other superheroes, such as Green Lantern Guy Gardner and the Teen Titans, to try to stop them. The book includes some violence.

  Days Like This. Written by J. Torres ; illustrated by Scott Chantler. Oni Press 2003 Un Illustration
Grades: 6 7 8 9 10 11 12 Adult   **741.5; Fic**
  1. Rock music; 2. Graphic novels
  1-929998-48-1, $8.95
  It's the early 1960s, and rock'n'roll and r&b are ushering in a new golden age of pop music. Tina & the Tiaras, three teenage girl singers, songwriter Karen Prince, and new music mogul Anna Solomon team to create a new girl group sound and move up the charts.

  Ninja scroll. Writer, J. Torres; artist, Michael Chang Ting Yu. DC Comics/Wildstorm 2007 144p. Illustration
Grades: 10 11 12 Adult   **741.5; Fic**
  1. Ninja; 2. Supernatural graphic novels; 3. Graphic novels
  978-1-4012-1318-3, $19.99
  Jubei Kibagami was a ninja, now he's a wandering ronin who wants nothing more than a good night's sleep. One thing after another keeps him awake, though—demons, devils, bloodthirsty tengu—and he must fight over and over again. The book includes considerable violence and some partial nudity.

Towle, Ben
  Midnight sun. SLG Publishing 2007 Un Illustration
Grades: 10 11 12 Adult   **741.5; Fic**
  1. Arctic regions; 2. Graphic novels
  978-1-59362-088-2, $14.95
  In 1928, an Italian airship expedition to the North Pole disappears shortly after radioing that it has reached the North Pole. The stranded members of the airship crew prepare for a stay on the drifting icepack where they've crashed, hoping to survive until rescuers can find them. A newspaper reporter

who drinks too much in speakeasies is sent to the Arctic on board a Russian rescue ship to cover the story; there, he meets the Russian reporter whose boyfriend is a member of the airship crew. There are scenes of drinking.

Tran, G. B.
Vietnamerica: a family's journey. Written and illustrated by GB Tran.. Villard Books 2010 279 p. Color illustration
Grades: 11 12 Adult   **741.5**
1. Artists; 2. Illustrators; 3. Vietnamese Americans — Biography; 4. Graphic novels
0345508726; 9780345508720, $30

LC 2011283144

In this personal memoir, drawn in the style of a graphic novel, the author ôtries to make sense of a shattered family history. [G. B.] Tran was born in America shortly after his family fled Vietnam during the fall of Saigon. However, he sees how deeply his parents still feel connected to their homeland, even as they can't fully admit their dismay at being cut off from it. . . . By visiting Vietnam and exploring memories, Tran learns how his grandfather, a lifelong Vietminh supporter, was horrified at the brutal results of the Communist victory and how his father became a glum autocrat after his career as an artist was destroyed. He watches how his parents interact uneasily with the swarm of relatives and friends they left behind. (Publishers Weekly)

Trombetta, Jim
The **Horror!** The horror!: comic books the government didn't want you to read!. Selected, edited, and with commentary by Jim Trombetta; introduction by R. L. Stine. Abrams ComicArts 2010 304p. Illustration
Grades: Adult   **741.5**
1. Censorship — United States; 2. Horror comic books, strips, etc; 3. Graphic novels
0810955954; 9780810955950, $29.95

LC 2008-54346

The Horror! The Horror! examines the pre-Code horror comics of the 1950s. (Publisher's note) Index.
Includes bibliographical references (p. 302) and index.

Trondheim, Lewis
Approximate Continuum Comics. Lewis Trondheim.. Fantagraphics Books 2011 144 p. Illustration
Grades: Adult   **741.5/944; B**
1. Autobiographical graphic novels; 2. Cartoonists — France — Biography; 3. Trondheim, Lewis
1606994107; 9781606994108, $18.99

LC 2013363506

This autobiographical graphic novel, by Lewis Trondheim, depicts the author's life as a cartoon character and "contains the first three chapters serialized in the 'Nimrod' comic book, the last three (never-before-translated) chapters, and a hilarious 'rebuttal' section in which Trondheim's family and cartoonist friends (including Epileptic creator David B. and Trondheim's mom) dispute (or ruefully agree with) Trondheim's depictions." (Publisher's note)

Dungeon: Twilight Vol. 2: Armageddon. Joann Sfar, Lewis Trondheim, story. NBM 2006 Un Illustration

Grades: 10 11 12 Adult   **741.5; Fic**
1. Adventure graphic novels; 2. Fantasy graphic novels; 3. Graphic novels
978-1-56163-477-4, $14.95

Marvin, saved at the last minute from certain death in a duel by his young warrior admirer Marvin the Red, simply cannot be let to die like he wishes. Whatever he loses, he regains in different powers. He's even become invincible. It's to the point where he'd rather exchange body parts to get back his mortality. But then he is led to a discovery that may make continuing to live actually worth it. Unlike the first Dungeon series, this one includes more violence, some nudity, and sexual situations.

Li'l Santa. NBM Publishing 2002 Un Illustration
Grades: 3 4 5 6 7 8 9 10 11 12 Adult   **741.5; Fic**
1. Fantasy graphic novels; 2. Humorous graphic novels; 3. Santa Claus; 4. Stories without words; 5. Graphic novels
1-56163-335-6, $14.95

LC 2002-32131

You have no idea what Santa must go through, all the way up there at the North Pole, until you read this fully silent graphic novel. Besides the huge yearly job that faces him, the North Pole is no friendly place, what with Impies and a Snow Dragon and the like. Santa must use all his best cunning to make all the world's kids happy.

Little nothings: the curse of the umbrella. NBM Publishing 2008 126p. Illustration
Grades: 9 10 11 12 Adult   **92; 741.5**
1. Biographical graphic novels; 2. Humorous graphic novels; 3. Graphic novels
978-1-56163-523-8, $14.95

LC 2008-113013

French cartoonist Trondheim, creator of the Dungeon series, A.L.I.E.E.E.N., Mr. O, and many other comics, collects here little snippets of everyday life, covering everything from being the plant-killer of all time (nothing he tries to grow ever survives), getting kittens as pets, dealing with a wife who tells him that wearing a t-shirt under a short-sleeved shirt is ugly, realizing that his eleven-year-old son is too jaded by horror movies to be scared by "Alien," the inconvenience of having athletic shoes with hidden metal that set off airport security alarms, and more "little nothings."

Mister i. NBM 2007 32p. Illustration
Grades: 10 11 12 Adult   **741.5; Fic**
1. Humorous graphic novels; 2. Stories without words; 3. Graphic novels
978-1-56163-486-6, $13.95

This volume has page after page of goofy gags crammed with little frames showing the mishaps of Mr. i, who, no matter what he tries, whether getting a pie out of an oven or getting an apple, always ends up killed, poor fellah. The humor is full of cartoony violence, and although it's not gory, will be disturbing for younger readers.

The **Spiffy** Adventures of McConey: Harum Scarum. Fantagraphics Books 1998 48p. Illustration
Grades: 8 9 10 11 12 Adult   **741.5; Fic**
1. Humorous graphic novels; 2. Mystery graphic novels; 3. Science fiction graphic novels; 4. Graphic novels
1-56097-288-2, $10.95

This is a story about horrible monsters and science gone awry ... about kidnappings, murder, arson, and pitiless beatings ... about fairy dust, time machines, and the teleportation cap ... about sinister commies, double agents, and corrupt commissioners ... about the niceties of tipping and the precise location of the jugular vein. McConey the bunny and his friends blunder and wisecrack their way through a monstrous mystery.

Tiny tyrant. Lewis Trondheim; translated by Alexis Siegel; illustrated by Fabrice Parme. First Second 2007 124 p. Color illustration

Grades: 4 5 6 7 8 9 10 11 12 Adult   **741.5/944; Fic**
   1. Humorous graphic novels; 2. Kings and rulers — Fiction; 3. Graphic novels
   9781596430945, $12.95; 159643094X

                    LC 2006021479

Translations into English of eight French stories originally published by Delacourt, 2001-2004.

"In this illustrated collection of eight translated French stories, King Ethelbert rules as much by whim as by moral or regal standards; this lack of perspective can be excused, though, since he's only six. . . . Grades three to eight." (Bull Cent Child Books)

"Tiny child-king Ethelbert is spoiled and difficult, expecting to have his every whim fulfilled-or else. . . . In the end, though, he becomes a hero. The dynamic cartoons are filled with details and riddled with humor; most pages have between six and eight small pictures. . . . This title will have wide appeal. It's young and accessible enough for elementary-grade kids, but teens will also be charmed by the rascally king." SLJ

Tsutsui, Yasutaka

Telepathic Wanderers Volume 1. Story by Yasutaka Tsutsui; art by Sayaka Yamazaki. Tokyopop 2005 192p. Illustration

Grades: 11 12 Adult   **741.5; Fic**
   1. Manga; 2. Mystery graphic novels; 3. Seinen manga; 4. Graphic novels
   1-59532-938-2, $9.99

When Nanase, a beautiful young telepath, return to her hometown, she stumbles across others possessing telepathic powers, and her life suddenly turns to chaos. On a train she meets Tsuneo, a man with the power to tell the future, and dire predictions for the riders of the train! Will Nanase find her way to safety in time? The book includes nudity, sexual situations, very harsh language, and violence.

Tucci, Billy

★ **Sgt.** Rock: the lost battalion. DC Comics 2009 Un Illustration

Grades: 10 11 12 Adult   **741.5; Fic**
   1. Japanese Americans; 2. Sgt Rock (Fictional character); 3. Soldiers; 4. World War, 1939-1945; 5. Graphic novels
   978-1-4012-2533-9, $24.99

After the Allied force landing at Normandy in 1944, Sgt. Frank Rock and his Easy Company are attached to the 141st Infantry and march deep into the Vosges Mountains, their assignment to open an avenue straight into the heart of Germany. However, the German forces have dug in deeply with snipers, Tiger tanks, and elite infantry troops, ready to keep the Americans trapped until reinforcements come to help them destroy the Allies. As Sgt. Rock and his men, along with the rest of the Lost Battalion, try to hang on with dwindling ammunition and rations, American commanders keep trying to send help. Everyone fails, except for the "Little Iron Men" of the 442nd Regimental Combat Team. These Japanese American soldiers, many of whom have family forced to live in internment camps, are the only hope for the Lost Battalion; and Hitler has just ordered their execution. This story does portray the violence of war, but Tucci keeps his art fairly subdued and the language pretty clean (dang, nuts, etc.). He heavily researched this book so the facts are there, he just added the fictional Sgt. Rock and Easy Company to the real soldiers. Anyone who wants to get a feeling for what war was like for the everyday Army soldier will get it in this story, with no glorification of fighting or violence.

Tucci, William

Shi: Ju-Nen. Story and illustrations by Billy Tucci. Dark Horse Comics 2005 Un Illustration

Grades: 10 11 12 Adult   **741.5; Fic**
   1. Adventure graphic novels; 2. Ninja; 3. Graphic novels
   1-59307-451-4, $12.95

Ana Ishikawa returns to her native Japan where she desperately tries to avert an all out war between the secretive sects of the Kyoto and Nara Sohei. And with the Narans on the verge of annihilation, the Kyoto Sohei are about to rub it in - with the encouragement of the Yakuza and with potentially disastrous consequences. Once again, Ana in the guise of Death Incarnate, will take up the naginata and don her grandfather's Kabuki face paint in order to save both cities, even if it means turning to her father's murderer Masahiro Arashi to do so. The book includes lots of violence and some skimpy clothing on Tomoe and Shi.

Turner, James.

Rex Libris volume one: I, Librarian. [written and illustrated by James Turner]. Slave Labor Graphics 2007 Un Illustration

Grades: 10 11 12 Adult   **741.5; Fic**
   1. Fantasy graphic novels; 2. Humorous graphic novels; 3. Librarians; 4. Graphic novels
   978-1-59362-062-2, $14.95

Rex Libris is the head librarian at Middleton Public Library, the best public library ever, with a vast collection including many rare items. He also has to deal with demons, space aliens, and other odd library patrons. And when a book is overdue, he will go to whatever lengths it takes to get the book back. In this volume, Rex must travel to another planet to confront the powerful Space Warlord Vaglox, who has not returned the Principia Mathematica. Meanwhile, his fellow librarians (including Circe the witch from Homer's Odyssey) must fend off a manifestation of bloodthirsty Vandals set on burning the library. The book includes some harsh language, including the s-bomb.

Tyler, Carol

A **good** and decent man. Written and illustrated by C. Tyler. Fantagraphics Books 2009 Un Illustration

Grades: Adult   **92; 741.5**

9781606991442, $24.99; 1606991442
Followed by Collateral damage (2010) and Soldier's heart (2012)

Tyler tells the story of her father's time during WWII and her parents' early relationship, skillfully interweaving it with Tyler's own story. We see her as an adult artist and mother, creating the book even as she deals with tumult in her own life and marriage. This first volume in what will be a trilogy about her father's life, and her own, provides a moving, personal portrait of one member of what's become known as the greatest generation.

Tyler, Joe
   Grimm Fairy Tales Vol. 1. Joe Tyler and Ralph Tedesco. Zenescope Entertainment 2007 Un Illustration
Grades: 10 11 12 Adult   741.5; Fic
   1. Fairy tales; 2. Fantasy graphic novels; 3. Graphic novels
   978-0-9786874-0-3, $15.99
   For more than two hundred years the powerful stories of the Brothers Grimm have enchanted millions of readers around the world. This book explores the original darker side of these classic stories while updating the original works. In these stories, morality is tested and the results of one's actions have consequences. Red Riding Hood faces a werewolf; Cinderella seeks vengeance for the years of torture she suffered; Hansel and Gretel run away from horrors at home only to find worse in the woods; Sleeping Beauty learns that narcissism can be a gruesome trait; an envious sister marries the Robber Bridegroom before she realizes her danger; a desperate beauty strikes a deal with Rumpelstiltskin, but he triumphs after all. The book includes violence and reprints the very sexy and suggestive covers from the original issues.

Tynion, James, IV
   The **woods**; Volume 1: The arrow. James Tynion IV; illustrated by Michael Dialynas. Boom! Studios 2014 96 p. Color; Illustration
Grades: 11 12 Adult   741.5
   1. High school students — Fiction; 2. Missing persons; 3. Science fiction graphic novels
   1608864545; 9781608864546, $9.99
   "On October 16, 2013, 437 students, 52 teachers, and 24 additional staff from Bay Point Preparatory High School in suburban Milwaukee, WI vanished without a trace. Countless light years away, far outside the bounds of the charted universe, 513 people find themselves in the middle of an ancient, primordial wilderness. Where are they? The answers will prove stranger than anyone could possibly imagine." (Publisher's note)
   "Tynion pulls no punches as he puts these kids through hell, and in the few moments they are allowed to stop to take a breath, they reveal very unique and original personalities, making them less like horror stereotypes and more like real, breathing kids." Booklist
   Volume 1 of an ongoing series

Ubukata, Tou
   Le Chevalier D'Eon, Volume 1. Story by Tou Ubukata; manga by Kiriko Yumeji. Ballantine Books/Del Rey Manga 2007 Un Illustration
Grades: 11 12 Adult   741.5; Fic

1. France — History — 1589-1789, Bourbons; 2. Manga; 3. Supernatural graphic novels; 4. Graphic novels
0-345-59622-1, $10.95
   During the reign of King Louis XV of France, Paris experiences a series of horrific murders. Young virginal women are slowly drained of their blood, which serves as the "ink" for nefarious books of poetry written by men who want to transform themselves into superhuman monsters. Slacker police officer D'Eon de Beaumont, who is actually a secret operative working for the King, is the repository for his slain sister Lia's soul; when she possesses D'Eon's body, she wields a powerful, supernatural sword that she uses to destroy the killer poets. The black and white art helps to mitigate the bloody killings and the violence of the battles between Sphinx (Lia) and the monsters. This manga series is very loosely based on a historical character; D'Eon de Beaumont was a transvestite who served King Louis XV.

Uderzo, Albert
   Asterix and Obelix All at Sea. Orion/Sterling Publishing 2002 48p. Illustration
Grades: 4 5 6 7 8 9 10 11 12 Adult   741.5; Fic
   1. Asterix (Fictional character); 2. Humorous graphic novels
   0-75284-778-3, $9.95
                                          LC 2002-282560
   In ancient Rome the slaves are revolting ... and not only that, they've stolen Julius Caesar's own galley, the finest warship in the Roman navy. Under their heroic leader Spartakis, the former galley slaves make for the little Gaulish village where Julius Caesar's old enemies Asterix and Obelix live - only to find the place in crisis, for Obelix, after drinking the druid Getafix's magic potions on the sly, is first turned to stone and then reverts to childhood. In search of a cure for him Asterix, Getafix and their new friends the galley slaves sail to the wonderful continent of Atlantis, ruled by its high priest Absolutlifabulos - and the ensuing sea battles against the Roman navy are fast and furious ...

Ueda, Rinko
   Tail of the Moon Vol. 1. Viz Media/Shojo Beat 2006 196p. Illustration
Grades: 10 11 12 Adult   741.5; Fic
   1. Humorous graphic novels; 2. Manga; 3. Ninja; 4. Romance graphic novels; 5. Shojo manga; 6. Graphic novels
   978-1-4215-0764-4, $8.99
   Sometimes it seems like Usagi is hopeless. Sure, she's good with healing herbs, but she's the granddaughter of the leader of a prestigious ninja village and she's such a klutz that she's never made it out of the kiddie class. Finally frustrated with Usagi's lack of progress, her grandfather sends her to marry Hattori Hanzo, leader of the ninja clan's main branch, and have lots of ninja babies. But Hanzo has no interest in her or her child bearing potential. After years of goofing around, Usagi is finally determined to reach her goals—she's going to become a ninja and capture Hanzo's heart. This series combines ninja action with romance with lots of bare-chested men and some sexual situations.

Ugawa, Hiroki

Shrine of the Morning Mist Volume 1. Tokyopop 2006 192p. Illustration

Grades: 9 10 11 12 Adult   **741.5; Fic**
1. Fantasy graphic novels; 2. Manga; 3. Romance graphic novels; 4. Shojo manga; 5. Graphic novels
1-59816-343-4, $9.99

Sisters Kurako, Yuzu and Tama are miko, Shinto priestesses, entrusted with keeping an eye on the often volatile spirit world. But when you're a teenager like Yuzu, you want nothing more than to lead a normal life and deal with growing up and falling in love. Enter Tadahiro, the sisters' cousin, who has a mysterious connection to Yuzu's past—and a strained relationship with his other relatives. However, family drama may have to wait. The spirit world suddenly shifts out of balance, unleashing demons into the world who have set their sights on Tadahiro... There is some violence as the monsters try to get Tadahiro.

Umezu, Kazuo

The **Drifting** Classroom Vol. 1. Viz Media/Shojo 2006 194p. Illustration

Grades: 11 12 Adult   **741.5; Fic**
1. Horror graphic novels; 2. Manga; 3. Shonen manga; 4. Graphic novels
978-1-4215-0722-4, $9.99

In the aftermath of a strange earthquake, an entire elementary school vanishes, leaving nothing but a hole in the ground. While parents mourn and authorities investigate, the students and teachers of find themselves somewhere far away...somewhere cold and dark... a lifeless, nightmarish wasteland among which their school stands like a lone fortress. As panic turns to terror, as the rules start to fall apart, a 6th-grade boy named Sho and his friends must try to survive in a hostile new world... The book includes some brutal, graphic violence.

According to Jason Thompson in Manga: The Complete Guide (he also edited this manga series), this was originally published in Japan for younger readers; given the brutal nature of the violence depicted, here in the U.S. it's rated for older teen and adult readers.

Scary Book Volume 1: Reflections. Dark Horse Manga 2006 231p. Illustration

Grades: 10 11 12 Adult   **Fic; 741.5**
1. Horror graphic novels; 2. Manga; 3. Shojo manga; 4. Graphic novels
978-1-59307-476-0, $13.95

This book offers two tales: "Mirror," in which a narcissistic girl's reflection begins to take ruthless command of her life; and "Demon of Vengeance," where a sadistic warlord bent on seeking retribution for his selfish and reckless son's injuries finds the tables of revenge turned against him. Umezu is considered a master of horror manga; these stories were originally published in the 1960s and 1970s in Japan. This book includes some violence and some strong language.

Other titles in this series are: Volume 2: Insects; Volume 3: Faces

Umino, Chica

Honey and Clover vol. 1. Viz Media/Shojo Beat 2008 184p. Illustration

Grades: 10 11 12 Adult   **741.5; Fic**
1. Humorous graphic novels; 2. Manga; 3. Romance graphic novels; 4. Shojo manga; 5. Graphic novels
978-1-4215-1504-5, $8.99

College sophomore art student Takemoto thinks his greatest worries in life are finding ways to eat more meat and getting to class on time, but with his friends, life is not so tame. Morita has been a senior for years, because he keeps missing a crucial freshman class; he tends to disappear for days or weeks at a time and return with lots of cash. Yamada works part time for a woman on whom he has a major crush. Then Professor Hanamoto's cousin's daughter Hagumi starts attending college; she looks younger than 18 and she's an art prodigy. And Takemoto has fallen completely for her. The story includes some mild sexual innuendo.

Unita, Yumi

★ **Bunny** drop vol. 1. [translation, Kaori Inoue; lettering, Alexis Eckerman].. Yen Press 2010 196p. Illustration

Grades: 8 9 10 11 12 Adult
741.5; Fic
1. Josei manga; 2. Unmarried fathers; 3. Graphic novels
978-0-7595-3122-2, $12.99

Thirty-year-old bachelor Daikichi is a salaryman, a junior executive, living on his own in Tokyo. When he goes

Courtesy of Yen Press

home for his grandfather's funeral, he discovers that his grandfather had a younger lover who left him with a little girl, Rin (which makes her his aunt). The lover is nowhere to be found, and none of Daikichi's relatives will have anything to do with Rin, who won't talk to anyone but sticks close to Daikichi, who closely resembles his grandfather. When no one will step forward to take care of the six-year-old, Daikichi impulsively decides he will. Once he brings Rin home, the reality of his new situation finally dawns on him; Daikichi is now a single father and has to provide care for Rin. There's one scene with Rin and Daikichi together in their furo bath (a very typical Japanese family scene), and a few panels with Rin and Daikichi in their underwear. In one chapter, Daikichi has to deal with Rin's night time bedwetting, and Rin is shown changing her clothes.

"This sweet-natured manga shows the joys, frustrations, and quirks of family life; and while it is aimed at teens, it would also be more than welcome in the hands of adult readers." Booklist

First published 2006 in Japan

★ **Bunny** drop, vol. 2. Yen Press 2010 206p. Illustration

Grades: 8 9 10 11 12 Adult   **741.5; Fic**
1. Humorous graphic novels; 2. Single-parent families; 3. Graphic novels
978-0-7595-3119-2, $12.99

Thirty-year-old bachelor Daikichi Kawachi had impulsively decided to become the guardian of his dead grandfather's illegitimate child, six-year-old Rin, when all the other relatives refused to help her. The reality of the responsibilities he's taken on have hit, and he makes a risky job transfer in order to have more time for Rin. Now, he has to navigate the choices for school as he must enroll Rin in elementary school, and he continues to search for Rin's mother. Being a parent is not easy, and being a male single parent is even harder. And just how is he supposed to help when Rin says her classmates tell her she is not cute? Picture a bachelor trying to brush a little girl's hair into pigtails.

Courtesy of Yen Press

Urasawa, Naoki

Master Keaton 1. By Naoki Urasawa, Takashi Nagasaki, and Hokusei Katsushika. Viz 2014 316 p. Illustration

Grades: Adult   **741.5**
1. Adventure graphic novels; 2. Insurance investigators
1421575892; 9781421575896, $19.99

"Taichi Hiraga-Keaton, the son of a Japanese zoologist and a noble English woman, is an insurance investigator known for his successful and unorthodox methods of investigation. Educated in archaeology and a former member of the SAS, Master Keaton uses his knowledge and combat training to uncover buried secrets, thwart would-be villains, and pursue the truth." (Publisher's note)

"Though the exotic locales and murder mysteries endemic to this profession are entertaining enough on their own, Keaton's background as an archaeology lecturer and former member of the British Special Air Service is what takes the comic from good to great." Pub Wkly

Volume 1 of 12 (ongoing in U.S.)

★ **Monster;** Volume 1. Story & art by Naoki Urasawa; translation & English adaptation, Camellia Nieh; lettering, Steve Dutro; editor, Mike Montesa. Viz Media 2014 418 p. Illustration; Color

Grades: 10 11 12 Adult   **741.5**
1. Physicians — Fiction; 2. Serial killers — Fiction
142156906X; 9781421569062, $19.99

"Dr. Tenma is the third son in a family of doctors, who left Japan years ago to work under his idol in a hospital in Dusseldorf, Germany. . . . He's on the fast track to promotion and power, until he refuses the hospital director's order to leave the victim of a brutal crime on the table and go help the mayor instead. Suddenly he goes from the cusp of a bright future to a grunt. His fiance leaves him, his promotion is given away, and his patients are removed from his care. But when the men who took everything from Tenma wind up

suddenly dead, he's set down a path that will change his life forever." (School Library Journal)

Volume 1 of 9

★ **Naoki** Urasawa's 20th century boys, vol. 1. Viz Media 2009 216p.

Grades: 10 11 12 Adult   **741.5; Fic**
1. Manga; 2. Mystery graphic novels; 3. Graphic novels
978-1-59116-922-2, $12.99

In 1997, Kenji has given up his dream of being a rock musician and manages his family's convenience store. When one of his childhood friends, a science teacher, commits suicide, Kenji starts to think back to 1969, when he and his friends created a hideaway, swore to do what they could to save the world, and buried a time capsule with a symbol they designed drawn on top. In 1997, that symbol starts showing up as grafitti in Kenji's neighborhood. And a strange cult led by a man who calls himself "Friend" uses that symbol (an eye with a hand pointing upward). As Kenji reunites with his buddies, they talk about what they did in 1969, and they dig up the time capsule. Does it have anything to do with their friend Donkey's death? The book includes graphic violence and partial nudity.

Volume 1 of 22

★ **Pluto**: Urasawa x Tezuka, vol. 1. By Naoki Urasawa. Viz Media 2009 200 p. Illustration

Grades: 9 10 11 12 Adult   **741.5; Fic**
1. Astro Boy (Fictional character); 2. Manga; 3. Mystery graphic novels; 4. Robots; 5. Robots — Fiction; 6. Graphic novels
1421519186; 9781421519180, $12.99

"In a distant future where sentient humanoid robots pass for human, someone or some thing is out to destroy the seven great robots of the world. Europol's top detective Gesicht is assigned to investigate these mysterious robot serial murdersùthe only catch is that he himself is one of the seven targets." (Publisher's note)

Original Japanese edition, 2004

Volume 1 of 8

Urrea, Luis Alberto

★ **Mr.** Mendoza's paintbrush. Artwork by Christopher Cardinale; color masking and compositing, Anthony Cardinale; design, Anne M. Giangiulio. Cinco Puntos Press 2010 Un Illustration

Grades: 7 8 9 10 11 12 Adult   **741.5; Fic**
1. Artists; 2. Humorous graphic novels; 3. Mexico; 4. Young adult literature — Works; 5. Graphic novels
978-1-933693-23-1, $17.95

LC 2008-11636

Rosario is a small town in the Sinaloa region of Mexico, nestled into a wet, green, mango-sweet subtropical landscape. There, Mr. Mendoza wields his paintbrush to write graffiti with a purpose. When Mr. Mendoza catches the young narrator and his best friend Jaime spying on the girls who are swimming, he strips them, writes graffiti all over their bodies, and chases the naked boys down the street through town. He also appoints himself as the town's conscience and angers the authorities with his graffiti on the town's whorehouse, bridge, and other places. Then, one day, he takes his paint and paintbrush to the center square and paints steps into the sky and walks up until he disappears.

Women and girls are shown in their underwear, and the naked boys are shown only from the back. The talk of sex, the way the boys sneak peeks at the girls and one of the town's women, make this book suitable for teens even though the format resembles a picture book.

"Not only does the art perfectly capture the mood of the piece—from the blocky woodcuts to the muted earth tones—but it also reinforces the lucid dreamlike quality of its magical realism, serving as an enticing invitation to further explore the genre." Horn Book Guide

Urushibara, Yuki
  Mushishi 1. Random House/Del Rey Manga 2007 240p. Illustration
  Grades: 10 11 12 Adult   **741.5:; 741.5**
    1. Fantasy graphic novels; 2. Manga; 3. Seinen manga; 4. Graphic novels
  978-0-345-49621-8
  The mushi are a primitive life-form that has existed long before humans came to be. Some mushi can co-exist peacefully with mankind, but some are deadly to humans. Ginko is a mushi-shi, a master who has studied the mushi and knows how to control them, and to destroy them if need be. He travels the countryside of old Japan, ending infestations and helping people when he can. The publisher has rated this for older teens, but there's little in the way of overt violence, harsh language, or any other content issues in this first volume. As a seinen manga, this was published in Japan for adult men.
  Volume 1 of 10

Valentino, Serena
  Gloomcookie, Volume Five: The Final Curtain. Written by Serena Valentino; drawn by Ted Naifeh; art assistant: Tristan Crane; lettering assistants: Eric Russell & Nikki Coffman. SLG Publishing 2007 Un Illustration
  Grades: 9 10 11 12 Adult   **741.5; Fic**
    1. Fantasy graphic novels; 2. Supernatural graphic novels; 3. Graphic novels
  978-1-59362-066-0, $15.95
  In this volume of the Gloomcookie series, the Carnival Wars are over. Sebastien killed the evil Marguerite in the previous volume, but he feels guilty. The curse on Lex and Damion has been broken, but now Damion is overprotective of Lex. Meanwhile, Vermilion (a bad goth poet) thinks he has found his true love; but Moon Raven does not have the dark powers she has claimed. Can Sebastien and Lex help their friends, and themselves? There's enough information for first-time readers to piece together what has gone on before. Although the atmosphere is very gothic and dark, there's no violence or nudity, just lots of dark humor and some gentle drama.
  Originally published as Gloomcookie issues #24-28.

  Nightmares & Fairy Tales Volume Three: 1140 Rue Royale. Written by Serena Valentino; art by Crab Scrambly. SLG Publishing 2007 Un Illustration
  Grades: 10 11 12 Adult   **741.5; Fic**
    1. Horror graphic novels; 2. Graphic novels
  978-1-59362-065-3, $14.95
  In antebellum New Orleans, Delphine Lalaurie tortured and killed her slaves in the house at 1140 Rue Royale. Now,

decades later, elderly Victoria and her niece Rebecca have come to live in the house. Everyone tells them the house is haunted, and both Victoria and Rebecca see visions of the past. One of the spirits in the house possesses Rebecca and shows her the horrible, evil acts perpetrated upon the slaves and servants, and she realizes she must help the victims find peace.

This volume stands alone as a complete story. Older teens who enjoy moody, atmospheric, Gothic horror stories will like this.

Originally published as Nightmares & Fairy Tales issues #13-18.

Van Lente, Fred
  Action Philosophers Giant-Size Thing Vol. 2. By Fred Van Lente and Ryan Dunlavey. Evil Twin Comics 2007 94p. Illustration
  Grades: 9 10 11 12 Adult   **180; 741.5**
    1. Philosophers; 2. Graphic novels
  978-0-9778329-1-0, $8.95
  Karl Marx: The People's Hero! Jacques Derrida: The Deconstructonator! St. Thomas Aquinas: The Scholastic Spastic! Isaac ben-Luria: Rabbi of the Mystic Arts! They're not just great thinkers, ... They also make great comics. This book collects issues #4-6 of the Action Philosophers series, detailing the lives and thoughts of the men above, plus Machiavelli, Sartre, Descartes, Kierkegaard, Wittgenstein. There's just a little bit of strong language in this volume.

Van Meter, Jen
  Hopeless Savages. Art by Christine Norrie and Chynna Clugston-Major. Oni Press 2002 128p. Illustration
  Grades: 7 8 9 10 11 12 Adult   **741.5; Fic**
    1. Family; 2. Humorous graphic novels; 3. Rock music; 4. Graphic novels
  1-929998-24-4, $13.95
  Family ties are the earliest ties that bind, setting the tone for the paths we will take in our future. So what if your father is Dirk Hopeless and your mother Nikki Savage, a superstar couple from the days of punk rock? When you're born a rebel, what can you possibly do to make yourself stand apart? For Rat Hopeless-Savage, the answer is to leave home and become a normal citizen with a nine-to-five job.

  Hopeless Savages Vol. 2: Ground Zero. Art by Christine Norrie, Chynna Clugston-Major, Andi Watson, and Bryan Lee O'Malley. Oni Press 2004 128p. Illustration
  Grades: 7 8 9 10 11 12 Adult   **741.5; Fic**
    1. Family; 2. Humorous graphic novels; 3. Rock music; 4. Romance graphic novels; 5. Graphic novels
  1-929998-99-6, $11.95
  When you're sixteen, the world is a different place. When you're Zero Hopeless-Savage, the youngest daughter of rock stars Dirk Hopeless and Nikki Savage, the world is practically unrecognizable. Imagine you're in the midst of high school, you have your first band, and WHAMMO! Some boy comes along who doesn't think you're a total freak, and you think he's pretty swell, too. But before you can do anything about it, there's a TV crew outside your house that wants to chronicle the gossip and scandals of your parents' careers, and a massive misunderstanding has gotten

you grounded. How's a self-respecting young lady supposed to handle all that?

Hopeless Savages Vol. 3: Too Much Hopeless. Art, Christine Norrie and Ross Campbell. Oni Press 2004 Un Illustration

Grades: 7 8 9 10 11 12 Adult **741.5; Fic**
1. Family; 2. Humorous graphic novels; 3. Martial arts; 4. Romance graphic novels; 5. Graphic novels
1-929998-85-6, $11.95

This was supposed to be a leisurely vacation. Arsenal Hopeless-Savage has a rematch with an old high school rival in a kung-fu tournament in Hong Kong. She and her brother Twitch figured they could turn it into a nice jaunt with their boyfriends to meet their aging grandmother, a renowned Chinese fortune teller. Too bad Grandma Shi didn't phone ahead to tell them that it was going to be the trip from Hell. It begins at the airport when a shady character slips something into Arsenal's bag, putting the quartet on the radar of the local bad guys, the British secret service, and the Hong Kong police. It becomes even more complicated when the rest of the Hopeless-Savage clan decides to join the middle children in Asia, getting caught up in the international intrigue themselves. Arsenal is the only person that can get them all out of the jam they're in, and for her it's all too much. Twitch's gay relationship is treated matter-of-factly.

JSA Classified: Honor Among Thieves. Jen Van Meter, Peter J. Tomasi, writers; Patrick Olliffe, Don Kramer, pencillers; Ruy Jose, Drew Geraci, Keith Champagne, inkers; Nathan Eyring, John Kalisz, colorist: Rob Leigh, letterer. DC Comics 2007 128p. Illustration

Grades: 9 10 11 12 Adult **741.5; Fic**
1. Flash (Fictional character); 2. Justice Society of America (Fictional characters); 3. Superhero graphic novels; 4. Graphic novels
978-1-4012-1218-6, $14.99

The villainous Injustice Society re-forms with a new mission: break into the Justice Society of America's headquarters to steal the key of Prometheus. But a flurry of betrayals and the loss of a teammate might threaten any chance that the Injustice Society has. Plus, a mysterious figure has gained control of the Spear of Destiny and is using it to pit the Flash and Wildcat against each other.

Van Sciver, Noah
★ The **Hypo:** The Melancholic Young Lincoln. Noah Van Sciver. Fantagraphics 2012 192 p. Illustration

Grades: 11 12 Adult **92; 973.7092; 741.5**
1. Biographical graphic novels; 2. Depression (Psychology); 3. Lincoln, Abraham, 1809-1865
1606996193; 9781606996195, $24.99

This graphic novel, by Noah Van Sciver, "is based on [Abraham] Lincoln's battle with depression. . . . [It] follows the twenty-something Abraham Lincoln as . . . a rising Whig in the state's legislature as he arrives in Springfield, IL to practice law. . . . But, as time passes and uncertainty creeps in, young Lincoln is forced to battle a dark cloud of depression brought on by a chain of defeats and failures culminating into a nervous breakdown that threatens his life and sanity." (Publisher's note)

"A thoroughly engaging graphic novel that seamlessly balances investigation and imagination." Pub Wkly

Vance, James
Kings in disguise. James Vance and Dan Burr; introduction by Alan Moore.. W.W. Norton 2006 184 p. Illustration

Grades: Adult **741.5**
1. Great Depression, 1929-1939
0393328481(pbk.); 9780393328486(pbk.)
  LC 2005058549
Eisner Award: Best Single Issue/Story (1989)
Eisner Award: Best New Series (1989)
Harvey Award: Best New Series (1989)

"When 12-year-old Freddie's long-out-of-work father leaves home to look for a job, Freddie's older brother Al tries to fill his shoes. But when Al is arrested, Freddie leaves home to look for their father and quickly finds himself living the life of a hobo, riding the rails under the watchful eye of a drifter who calls himself the King of Spain. On his search, Freddie watches and helps as the jobless rally to demand a better life—or try to build that life themselves—all the while dogged by injustice and tragedy in a world that shuns and oppresses them." (Library Journal)

Vanistendael, Judith
When David lost his voice. Judith Vanistendael; [translated from the French edition by: Nora Mahony]. SelfMadeHero 2012 267 p. Color illustration

Grades: Adult **741; Fic**
1. Belgian fiction (French) — 21st century; 2. Cancer; 3. Cancer — Patients — Family relationships; 4. Cancer patients — Fiction; 5. Graphic novels — Belgium
1906838542; 9781906838546, $24.95
  LC 2012451584
In this graphic novel, by Judith Vanitendael, "David has cancer. . . . David's wife becomes progressively consumed by the looming shadow of death while his daughters struggle to be as helpful as possible. Meanwhile, David soldiers on, not wanting the tumor to rob him of everything, including the chance to see his granddaughter grow up." (Publisher's note)

Published in French as David les femmes et la mort, ? Editions du Lombard (Dargaud-Lombard S.A.) 2012, by Vanistendael (Judith)—t.p. verso.

Varon, Sara
Robot dreams. First Second 2007 205p. Illustration
Grades: 3 4 5 6 7 8 9 10 11 12 Adult **741; 741.5; Fic**
1. Dogs; 2. Robots; 3. Graphic novels
978-1-59643-108-9 (pa), $16.95; 1-59643-108-3 (pa)
  LC 2006-52640
The friendship between a dog and a robot is portrayed in this wordless graphic novel. (Bull Cent Child Books)

"Varon's drawing style is uncomplicated, and her colors are clean and refeshing. Although her story seems equally simple, it is invested with true emotion." Booklist

Vaughan, Brian K.
Batman: false faces. Pencilled by Scott McDaniel, Rick Burchett, Scott Kolins, Marcos Martin. DC Comics 2008 160p. Illustration
Grades: 10 11 12 Adult **741.5; Fic**

1. Batman (Fictional character); 2. Superhero graphic novels; 3. Wonder Woman (Fictional character); 4. Graphic novels
978-1-4012-1640-5, $19.99

Throughout his crimefighting career, the Dark Knight has managed to balance his double life as Batman and billionaire Bruce Wayne. But he has taken on other identities as well, including that of criminal Matches Malone. What happens when leading multiple lives becomes too much to handle" As Batman faces old enemies the Ventriloquist and the Mad Hatter, his greatest adversary may be his own secret lives. And Wonder Woman faces a crisis of her own, when Clayface steals part of the source of her power, and she must enlist the help of Donna Troy. The book includes some violence.

Buffy the Vampire Slayer season eight volume 2: No future for you. Writers, Brian K. Vaughan and Joss Whedon ; art by Georges Jeanty. Dark Horse Comics 2008 Un Illustration
Grades: 8 9 10 11 12 Adult   **741.5; Fic**
1. Buffy the Vampire Slayer (Fictional character); 2. Fantasy graphic novels; 3. Horror graphic novels; 4. Graphic novels
978-1-59307-963-5, $15.95

While Buffy is busy trying to uncover just who or what "Twilight" is, Giles recruits Faith to carry out an undercover mission. A Slayer in Great Britain has gone rogue, and she must be stopped. Since she's the daughter of a Peer, Faith has to make like Eliza Doolittle and learn how to become a "lady" in order to infiltrate into the upper crust world to carry out her mission. It's only when she's in the middle of the job that she learns this rogue Slayer is messing around with evil magic and wants to slay Buffy. The book includes brief partial nudity and some violence.

Doctor Strange: The Oath. Writer, Brian K. Vaughan; art, Marcos Martin. Marvel Enterprises 2007 Un Illustration
Grades: 9 10 11 12 Adult   **741.5; Fic**
1. Doctor Strange (Fictional character); 2. Superhero graphic novels; 3. Graphic novels
0-7851-2211-7, $13.99

Doctor Stephen Strange embarks on the most important paranormal investigation of his career, as he sets out to solve an attempted murder - his own. And with his most trusted friend, Wong, also at death's door, Strange turns to an unexpected corner of the Marvel Universe to recruit a new ally. The Night Nurse runs a clandestine clinic for superheroes, but she insists on accompanying Doctor Strange on his quest to find help for Wong.

★ The **Escapists**. Dark Horse Books 2009 176p. Illustration
Grades: 10 11 12 Adult   **741.5; Fic**
1. Adventure graphic novels; 2. Graphic novels
978-1-59582-361-8, $14.95

Inspired by Michael Chabon's Pulitzer Prizewinning novel, The Amazing Adventures of Kavalier and Clay, this story shows what it's like to start with nothing in Cleveland, Ohio, and end up with a comic so hot a major corporation wants to steal it from you. Maxwell Roth spends his inheritance to buy the rights to The Escapist, the comic book character created by Kavalier and Clay decades ago, and he and his high school friend Case Weaver set out to make new

comics of The Escapist. Artist Denny Jones joins them, and together the three create a new comic book series that makes a smash debut. Then, Omnigrip Corporation, which long ago sold the rights away, wants it back. When Roth says no, the corporation uses every dirty trick to force him to sell the rights back. The story of Roth, Weaver, and Jones is intermixed with adventures of the Escapist from the old comics. Artists Steve Rolston and Philip Bond illustrate the present-day story of the three independent comics creators, while Jason Shawn Alexander and Eduardo Barreto illustrate the classic Escapist stories. The book includes some violence and some harsh language.

★ **Ex** Machina Vol. 1: The First Hundred Days. Brian K Vaughan; art by Tony Harris. DC Comics/Wildstorm 2005 Un Illustration
Grades: 10 11 12 Adult   **741.5; Fic**
1. Politics; 2. Superhero graphic novels; 3. Graphic novels
978-1-4012-0612-3, $9.99

This book tells the story of civil engineer Mitchell Hundred, who becomes America's first living, breathing super-hero after a strange accident gives him amazing powers. Eventually Mitchell tires of risking his life merely to maintain the status quo, retires from masked crime fighting, and runs for mayor of New York City, winning by a landslide. But Mayor Hundred has to worry about more than just budget problems and an antagonistic governor, especially when a mysterious hooded figure begins assassinating plow drivers during the worst snowstorm in the city's history. Strong language and some violence figures into this political superhero story.

Volume 1 of 10

★ The **Private** Eye. Brian K. Vaughn; illustrated by Marcos Martin. Image Comics 2015 300 p. Illustration
Grades: Adult   **741.5**
1. Identity — Fiction; 2. Private investigators — Fiction; 3. Secrets — Fiction
1632155729; 9781632155726, $49.99
                    LC 2016001103
Eisner Award: Best Digital/Online Comic (2015)
Harvey Award: Best Online Comics Work (2015)

This graphic novel, by Brian K. Vaughn and illustrated by Marcos Martin, is "about an unlicensed private investigator who stumbles onto the most important case of his life. The series is set in 2076, a time after 'the cloud has burst', revealing everyone's secrets. As a result, there is no more Internet, and people are excessively guarded about their identity, to the point of appearing only masked in public." (Publisher's note)

"Vaughan and Martin's vision of the future is chilling in its realism, but fascinating in its hyperbole. Martin's art—accentuated beautifully by Vicente's colors—handles thrilling action and contemplative scenes equally well, allowing Vaughan's script to dig deep into identity, the balance between liberty and security, the role of technology in our lives, and the implicit trust we place in it." Pub Wkly

★ **Saga** 4. By Brian K. Vaughan; illustrated by Fiona Staples. Image Comics 2014 144 p. Color illustration
Grades: Adult   **741.5**
1. Adventure fiction; 2. Family — Fiction; 3. Outer space — Fiction; 4. Science fiction
1632150778; 9781632150776, $14.99

Eisner Award: Best Continuing Series (2015)
Harvey Award: Continuing or Limited Series (2014)
Harvey Award: Best Writer (2014)
Harvey Award: Best Artist (2014)
"Hazel becomes a toddler, while her family struggles to stay on their feet." (Publisher's note)
Originally published in single issues as Saga #19-24

★ **Saga** [Vol. 3]. Brian K. Vaughan, writer; Fiona Staples, artist. Image Comics 2014 144 p. Color; Illustration
Grades: Adult   **741.5; Fic**
1. Fantasy fiction; 2. Science fiction
1607069318; 9781607069317, $14.99
Eisner Award: Best Continuing Series (2014)
Harvey Award: Continuing or Limited Series (2014)
Harvey Award: Best Writer (2014
Harvey Award: Best Artist (2014)
In this fantasy comic book by Brian K. Vaughan, illustrated by Fiona Staples, part of a series, "When two soldiers from opposite sides of a never-ending galactic war fall in love, they risk everything to bring a fragile new life into a dangerous old universe. . . . In volume 3, as new parents Marko and Alana travel to an alien world to visit their hero, the family's pursuers finally close in on their targets." (Publisher's note)
Originally published in single magazine form as Saga #13-18

★ **Saga.** [Vol. 1]. Brian K. Vaughan, illustrated by Fiona Staples. Image Comics 2012 160 p.
Grades: Adult   **Fic; 741.5**
1. Adventure graphic novels; 2. Family life; 3. Fantasy graphic novels; 4. Monsters
1607066017; 9781607066019, $9.99
Hugo Award: Best Graphic Story (2013)
Eisner Award: Best New Series (2013)
Eisner Award: Best Continuing Series (2013)
Eisner Award: Best Writer (2013)
This fantasy graphic novel, by Brian K. Vaughan, illustrated by Fiona Staples, presents "the sweeping tale of one young family fighting to find their place in the worlds. . . . Two soldiers from opposite sides of a never-ending galactic war fall in love. . . [and] risk everything to bring a fragile new life into a dangerous old universe." (Publisher's note)
Rated M / mature.

★ **Saga.** [Vol. 2]. Brian K. Vaughan, illustrated by Fiona Staples. Image Comics 2013 144 p.
Grades: Adult   **Fic; 741.5**
1. Adventure graphic novels; 2. Family life; 3. Fantasy graphic novels; 4. Monsters
9781607066927, $14.99; 1607066920
TIME Top 10 Comics and Graphic Novels (2013)
Washington Post Top 10 Graphic Novels (2013)
Eisner Award: Best Continuing Series (2014)
Harvey Award: Continuing or Limited Series (2013)
Harvey Award: Best Writer (2013)
Harvey Award: Best Artist (2013)
"This smash hit continues to be a powerhouse: intergalactic intrigue, truly alien aliens, multifaceted characters, and a universe full of lush environments all wrapped around a compellingly told story of forbidden love in wartime." Booklist
Rated M / mature.

Saga: Voume Five. By Brian K. Vaughan; illustrated by Fiona Staples. Image Comics 2015 152 p. Color illustration
Grades: Adult   **741.5; 741.5973**
1. Outer space — Fiction; 2. Science fiction
1632154382; 9781632154385, $14.99
In this comic book, by Brian K. Vaughan, illustrated by Fiona Staples, "Multiple storylines collide. . . . While Gwendolyn and Lying Cat risk everything to find a cure for The Will, Marko makes an uneasy alliance with Prince Robot IV to find their missing children, who are trapped on a strange world with terrifying new enemies." (Publisher's note)

Y: The Last Man Vol. 1: Unmanned. Written by Brian K. Vaughan; art by Pia Guerra. DC Comics/Vertigo 2003 128p. Illustration
Grades: 10 11 12 Adult   **Fic; 741.5**
1. Science fiction graphic novels; 2. Graphic novels
978-1-56389-980-5, $12.99
Escape artist Yorick Brown and his male pet monkey are the only surviving males left on Earth after a plague instantaneously kills all the other males on the planet. As women take over ... everything ... latter-day Amazons declare all men must die, Yorick's congresswoman mother arranges protection for him, and mysterious Israeli soldiers seem highly amused. The story includes strong language, nudity, and violence.
Volume 1 of 10

Vehlmann, Fabien
Beautiful Darkness. By Fabien Vehlmann and Kerascoët and translated by Helge Dascher. Farrar Straus & Giroux 2013 96 p.
Grades: Adult   **741.5**
1. Allegories; 2. Good and evil — Fiction; 3. Princesses — Fiction
1770461299; 9781770461291, $22.95
In this book by Fabien Vehlmann and Kerascoët, readers "join princess Aurora and her friends as they journey to civilization's heart of darkness in a bleak allegory about surviving the human experience. The sweet faces and bright leaves of Kerascot's delicate watercolors serve to highlight the evil that dwells beneath Vehlmann's story as pettiness, greed, and jealousy take over." (Publisher's note)

Last Days of an Immortal. Fabien Vehlmann and Gwen de Bonneyal. Pgw 2012 149 p.
Grades: Adult   **Fic; 741.5/944**
1. Death; 2. Science fiction graphic novels
1936393441; 9781936393442, $24.95
In this science fiction graphic novel, by Fabien Vehlmann, illustrated by Gwen de Bonneyal, "Elijah is a member of the 'Philosophical Police,' who must solve conflicts that arise out of ignorance of the Other. Two species are fighting a war with roots in a crime committed centuries ago, and Elijah must solve the crime and bring peace between their species, while also confronting his own immortality in a world where science provides access to eternal life." (Publisher's note)

Veitch, Rick

Swamp Thing: Infernal Triangles. Steve Bissette, Artist. DC Comics/Vertigo 1988 Un Illustration
Grades: 10 11 12 Adult   **741.5; Fic**
1. Superhero graphic novels; 2. Swamp Thing (Fictional character); 3. Graphic novels
978-1-4012-1008-3, $19.99
After much trial and error, the elemental entity known as the Swamp Thing has succeeded in harnessing the life-force of his successor into the one form with which he can co-exist, a new human soul, to be born of his love Abby, with help from the sardonic magus John Constantine. But even as the couple begin preparing for their impending domesticity, forces far beyond their intimate world are conspiring to drive them apart once more. There's no nudity or graphic violence, little harsh language, but the themes are mature.

Swamp Thing Vol. 8: Spontaneous Generation. Rick Veitch, Alfredo Alcala; Tatjana Wood, colorist; John Costanza, letterer. DC Comics 2005 Un Illustration
Grades: 11 12 Adult   **741.5; Fic**
1. Superhero graphic novels; 2. Swamp Thing (Fictional character); 3. Graphic novels
1-4012-0793-6, $19.99
When the Swamp Thing returned to Earth from the endless void of space, he discovered that a replacement had been created to take his place as the avatar of Earth's plant life. He resolves to find a way to coexist with the new, as-yet unborn spirit, but each attempt he makes causes the embryonic elemental to become more corrupt. Swamp Thing can think of only one more way to try, and it needs John Constantine, the Hellblazer, to make it work. This book includes violence, some strong language, nudity, and sexual situations.

Venditti, Robert

The **homeland** directive. Illustrated by Mike Huddleston. Top Shelf Productions 2011 148p. Color illustration
Grades: 11 12 Adult
741.5
1. Bioterrorism — Fiction; 2. Mystery fiction; 3. Political corruption — Fiction; 4. Suspense fiction
9781803090247 (pa); 9781603090247
This book tells the story of Dr. Laura Regan, head of the U.S. National Center for Infectious Diseases. "When her research partner is murdered and Laura is blamed for the crime, she finds herself at the heart of a vast and deadly conspiracy." (Publisher's note). "A cabinet minister decides to persuade the public that more trackable behavior is in the service of antiterrorist surveillance. But since his incentive involves virally induced 'justified' death for thousands along the way, Regan throws in with the good feds to stop a developing plague and expose the minister. Not that she has much choice: the bad

Courtesy of Top Shelf Productions

fed operatives are out to kill her since she created the vaccine that could stop their plot cold." (Libr J)

The **Surrogates**. Created and written by Robert Venditti; illustrated and colored by Brett Weldele. Top Shelf Productions 2006 208p. Illustration
Grades: 10 11 12 Adult   **741.5; Fic**
1. Mystery graphic novels; 2. Science fiction graphic novels; 3. Graphic novels
1-891830-87-2, $19.95
The year is 2054, and life has been reduced to a data feed. The fusing of virtual reality and cybernetics has ushered in the era of the surrogate, a new technology that lets users interact with the world without ever leaving their homes. It's a perfect world, and it's up to Detectives Harvey Greer and Pete Ford of the Metro Police Department to keep it that way. But to do so they'll need to stop a techno-terrorist bent on returning society to a time when people lived their lives instead of merely experiencing them. There's some violence in the story.

Verheiden, Mark

Aliens Omnibus Volume 1. Art by various. Dark Horse Comics 2007 384p. Illustration
Grades: 10 11 12 Adult   **741.5; Fic**
1. Adventure graphic novels; 2. Science fiction graphic novels
978-1-59307-727-3, $24.95
The first three Dark Horse Aliens stories based on the movies are collected in this volume: Outbreak, Nightmare Asylum, and Female War. Outbreak starts thirteen years after the events of the movie Aliens; Billie is in a mental institution suffering from nightmares about what happened at the colony outpost of Rim, and Wilks is in prison. They're both offered a chance to return to Rim. In Female War, Ripley must go with another team of Marines to another planet for another "bug hunt." The stories use strong language and show violence as the humans fight the Aliens.

The **American**. Dark Horse Comics 2005 368p. Illustration
Grades: 11 12 Adult   **741.5; Fic**
1. Superhero graphic novels; 2. Graphic novels
1-59307-419-0, $14.95
He's the ultimate American hero. Since the fifties, he has been a symbol of hope and courage for the entire nation, an indestructible one-man army standing tall for freedom, justice, and the American way - but what about truth? When reporter Dennis Hough is assigned to cover a story about his boyhood hero, he begins to see the cracks in the legend. Does The American have feet of clay? Or is he himself a victim of a larger conspiracy?

Superman: Sacrifice: Countdown to Infinite Crisis. Greg Rucka, Mark Verheiden, Gail Simone, writers; Ed Benes [and others], pencillers. DC Comics 2005 Un Illustration
Grades: 10 11 12 Adult   **741.5; Fic**
1. Superhero graphic novels; 2. Superman (Fictional character); 3. Wonder Woman (Fictional character); 4. Graphic novels
1-4012-0919-X, $14.99

The pivotal story that forever alters the relationship between Superman and Wonder Woman is collected here for the first time. Max Lord has taken over Superman's mind and has him in his total thrall. With his peers and loved ones threatened, Superman is helpless. But not Wonder Woman, who must battle past the Man of Steel and decisively end the threat. Her actions, and the repercussions, are explored in this story that leads into Infinite Crisis. Some of the fighting in this book is brutal.

Superman: The Journey. Mark Verheiden, writer; Ed Benes ... et al., pencillers. DC Comics 2006 144p. Illustration
Grades: 9 10 11 12 Adult   **Fic; 741.5**
1. Flash (Fictional character); 2. Superhero graphic novels; 3. Superman (Fictional character); 4. Graphic novels
1-4012-0918-1, $14.99
Even the Man of Steel needs to get away from it all, and when he tries to relocate his Fortress of Solitude to South America, a chain of events begins that will test his bravery more than ever. After his first contact with an OMAC, a cybernetic being set to destroy all super-heroes, Superman then must contend with the arrival in Metropolis of Bizarro, as well as Zoom, the Reverse-Flash. Then Blackrock returns with more power than ever; and Lex Luthor seeks deadly vengeance, again.

Vernon, Ursula
★ **Digger:** the complete Omnibus edition. By Ursula Vernon. Sofawolf Press, Inc. 2013 850 p.
Grades: 9 10 11 12 Adult   **Fic; 741.5**
1. Adventure graphic novels; 2. Wombats
1936689324; 9781936689323, $29.44
Hugo Award: Best Graphic Story (2012)
This graphic novel, by Ursula Vernon, is "about a particularly no-nonsense wombat who finds herself stuck on the wrong end of a one-way tunnel in a strange land where nonsense seems to be the specialty. Now, with the help of a talking statue of a god, an outcast hyena, a shadow-being of indeterminate origin, and an oracular slug she seeks to find out where she is and how to go about getting back to her Warren." (Publisher's note)

Vess, Charles
The **Book** of Ballads. Tor 2004 192p. Illustration
Grades: 11 12 Adult   **741.5; 808.81**
1. Ballads; 2. Graphic novels
0-765-31214-X, $24.95
"Vess shows off his ability to use a wide variety of styles and formats. . . . The ballad from which each story is taken is written in its traditional form at the end of each tale." (VOYA)
Artist Vess works with authors such as Charles de Lint, Neil Gaiman, Jane Yolen, Jeff Smith, and others who adapt ballads from the English, Scottish, and Irish traditions. Moods range from comedic hilarity (such as in "Galtee Farmer") to the somber lover's test ("Sovay"). Many of the stories include nudity and some sexual content.

Vidaurri, S. M.
Iron: Or, The War After. Shane-Michael Vidaurri. Archaia Entertainment 2013 152 p. Illustration
Grades: Adult   **741; Fic**
1. Animals; 2. Resistance to government
193639328X; 9781936393282, $24.95
This graphic novel, by Shane-Michael Vidaurri, is set in "the aftermath of a long war, in a world of constant winter. An intelligence spy from the Resistance—the rabbit, Hardin—steals secret information from a military base of the Regime. His actions set off a chain of events that reverberates through the ranks of both sides. . . . When the snow finally settles, who will be the true patriot and who the true traitor?" (Publisher's note)

Vinton, Will
Jack Hightower. Created and written by Will Vinton and Andrew Wiese; art by Fabio Laguna; colors by Rain Beredo; letters by Nate Piekos. Dark Horse Comics 2006 Un Illustration
Grades: 10 11 12 Adult   **741.5; Fic**
1. Adventure graphic novels; 2. Humorous graphic novels; 3. Spies; 4. Graphic novels
978-1-59307-392-3, $14.95
Secret agent Jack Hightower was at the height of his career when something BIG happened. Now the world-class operative and infamous ladies man is seeing things from a whole new perspective... a very, very different perspective, to say the least. Tall, daring, and handsome, Jack had it all - a stellar career, beautiful women, and more power and influence than he could shake a supermodel at. But despite it all, Jack longed for one thing that eluded him - the capture of his long-time archnemesis, Dr. Litigious Savant. On the fateful night when Jack's dream of cornering the elusive Savant is realized, things go terribly, dreadfully wrong, and Jack gets cut down to size by one of the doctor's insidious inventions... the size of your average action figure, to be exact. Partial nudity, sexual situations, alcohol consumption and violence are all here, in a book that is a big departure from Claymation animator Vinton's usual work.

Voger, Mark
The **Dark** Age: Grim, Great & Gimmicky Post-Modern Comics. Twomorrows Publishing 2006 168p. Illustration
Grades: Adult Professional   **741.5**
1. Batman (Fictional character); 2. Comic books, strips, etc — History and criticism; 3. Daredevil (Fictional character); 4. Hellboy (Fictional character); 5. Superman (Fictional character); 6. X-Men (Fictional characters); 7. Graphic novels
1-893905-53-5, $19.95
Do you remember The Dark Knight Returns and Watchmen? The polybagged premium craze" The death of Superman? Renegade superheroes Spawn, Pitt, Bloodshot and Cyberforce? When vigilantes spilled blood by the gallon - and those were the good guys" Readers can read all about the sometimes glorious, sometimes gory era of comics known as The Dark Age, covering the years from the 1980s into the 2000s.
The book features interviews with Dark Age greats Todd McFarlane (Spawn), Dave Gibbons (Watchmen), Jim Lee (X-Men), Kevin Smith (Clerks), Alex Ross

(Kingdom Come), Mike Mignola (Hellboy), Erik Larsen (Savage Dragon), J. O'Barr (The Crow), David Lapham (Stray Bullets), Joe Quesada (Daredevil), Mike Allred (Madman), Dennis O'Neil (Batman: Knightfall) and others. It includes a color section spotlighting highlights - and lowlights - of The Dark Age.

Vollmar, Rob
   Bluesman. Rob Vollmar & Pablo Callejo. NBM Publishing/ComicsLit 2008 208p. Illustration
Grades: 10 11 12 Adult   **741.5; Fic**
   1. African Americans — Southern states; 2. Blues music; 3. Graphic novels
   978-1-56163-532-0, $24.95
   All Lem Taylor ever wanted was to play the blues. In Arkansas in the late 1920s, life isn't easy for African Americans, whatever their ambitions. When he and piano player Ironwood Malcott play at Shug's speakeasy out in the woods, they catch the attention of a man who says if they get to Memphis, he'll record their songs. However, while staying the night with a young woman, a young white man comes and kills Ironwood and the young woman. Taylor is wounded, and another woman comes and chases him out before she kills the white man. Taylor is trying to get to Memphis any way he can, but the white folk in town want revenge for the white man's murder (never mind the three dead blacks). The only white man who cares about justice is the sheriff. The story was originally published in three parts. It includes graphic violence, sexual situations, and harsh language.

Voloj, Julian
   Ghetto Brother: Warrior to Peacemaker. Julian Voloj; illustrated by Claudia Ahlering. NBM Publishing 2015 128 p. Illustration
Grades: 11 12 Adult   **741.5; 92**
   1. Gangs; 2. Melendez, Benjy; 3. Peace movements; 4. Puerto Ricans — New York (NY)
   1561639486; 9781561639489, $12.99
   This graphic novel by Julian Voloj, illustrated by Claudia Ahlering, "tells the true story of Benjy Melendez, a Bronx legend, son of Puerto-Rican immigrants, who founded, at the end of the 1960s, the notorious Ghetto Brothers gang. From the seemingly bombed-out ravages of his neighborhood, wracked by drugs, poverty, and violence, he managed to extract an incredibly positive energy from this riot ridden era: his multiracial gang promoted peace rather than violence." (Publisher's note)
   "Using Melendez as narrator-protagonist, Voloj places the seminal events of November and December 1971 in the contexts of post-WWII Puerto Rican immigration and difficult assimilation to New York, and of Melendez's personal development as he learned of and adopted his Jewish heritage. Ahlering bases her artwork partly on news and documentary photography, although she doesn't incorporate or copy photos but draws on them for detail, composition, and tonal variety." Booklist

Von Sholly, Pete
   Pete Von Sholly's Extremely Weird Stories. Dark Horse Comics 2006 96p. Illustration
Grades: 11 12 Adult   **741.5; Fic**

   1. Fantasy graphic novels; 2. Horror graphic novels; 3. Graphic novels
   978-1-59307-554-5, $14.95
   Von Sholly uses the European fumetti style of using photographs and combines them with special effects to illustrate his horror stories that seem to come right out of the monster movies of the 1950s and 1960s. There are some pretty gruesome, graphically violent and horrifying images, and some sexual situations.

   Pete Von Sholly's Morbid. Dark Horse Comics 2003 96p. Illustration
Grades: 10 11 12 Adult   **741.5; Fic**
   1. Fantasy graphic novels; 2. Horror graphic novels; 3. Satire; 4. Graphic novels
   1-59307-028-4, $14.95
   While employing the European "fumetti" format of using photographs instead of drawn art, this book goes beyond that simple approach; custom-sculpted models, costumed actors, and mind-boggling computer-generated "special effects" come together to create a visual storytelling format. The stories themselves run the gamut from tongue-in-cheek lampoons of '50s drive-in movies to horror in the Lovecraft tradition. The book includes strong language and some sexually suggestive scenes.

   Pete Von Sholly's Morbid 2: Dead But Not Out!. Dark Horse Comics 2005 96p. Illustration
Grades: 10 11 12 Adult   **741.5; Fic**
   1. Fantasy graphic novels; 2. Horror graphic novels; 3. Satire; 4. Graphic novels
   1-59307-289-9, $14.95
   Von Sholly takes the European "fumetti" method to its next level with custom-sculpted models, costumed actors, and computer-generated special effects. In this volume, stories include parodies of Lost World type stories with dinosaurs invading the modern world, to Lovecraftian monsters in the graveyard (and one brave young woman to fight them), to ghost stories, and more. The book includes harsh language, violence, and some sexually suggestive scenes.

Wada, Shinji
   Crown, vol. 1. Go! Comi 2008 Un Illustration
Grades: 10 11 12 Adult   **741.5; Fic**
   1. Adventure graphic novels; 2. Manga; 3. Graphic novels
   978-1-60510-005-0, $10.99
   Teenage orphan Mahiro has been living with the owners of a Chinese takeout restaurant while working several jobs to earn money after relatives took over her parents' house when they died. Suddenly two very handsome young men show up at her construction site job, sweep her into their car, drive to her parents' home and evict the bad relatives, then take her to a condominium. One of the men is Mahiro's long-lost brother, Ren, the other is his best friend Jake; they have worked as mercenaries but now have come to protect Mahiro. She is the rightful heir to the throne of a small island kingdom, she possesses the jewel called the Crown, and the current queen, her stepmother, wants Mahiro dead so she can take over the country. Ren and Jake are very good at what they do, and they have to be, because the queen of Regalia decides to send a small army to Tokyo to kill Mahiro. The

book includes violence and fan service (including partial nudity) to appeal to both male and female readers.

Wagner, John
A **History** of Violence. Written by John Wagner; art by Vince Locke; lettering by Bob Lappan. DC Comics/Vertigo 2004 286p. Illustration
Grades: 11 12 Adult   **741.5; Fic**
1. Mystery graphic novels; 2. Revenge; 3. Graphic novels
978-1-56389-367-4, $9.99
It was just another quiet day at McKenna's Diner—until a couple of wanted killers walked in looking for trouble. Instead, they got bullets, and Tom McKenna got to be an instant media celebrity. That got him a lot of attention from some people he thought he'd escaped long ago. The kind of people who never forget a face—even after twenty years... Now Tom must confront a group of cold-blooded mobsters intent on settling the score. As much as he tries to deny it, he's a man with a history of violence—and with the lives of his family hanging in the balance, he'll do anything to make sure his secret past stays buried...forever. This story has lots of graphic violence and strong language. This original graphic novel was originally published in 1997.

Wagner, Matt
Batman and the Monster Men: Dark Moon Rising. Matt Wagner, story and art; Dave Stewart, colors; Rob Leigh, letters; Matt Wagner, covers. DC Comics 2006 144p. Illustration
Grades: 10 11 12 Adult   **741.5; Fic**
1. Batman (Fictional character); 2. Mystery graphic novels; 3. Superhero graphic novels; 4. Graphic novels
978-1-4012-1091-5, $14.99
It has been one year since the mysterious Batman first appeared to protect the people of Gotham. In that time, he has waged war on the common criminals and members of organized crime who have plagued his city. But the brutal massacre of some of the city's most notorious gangsters reveals that a far more dangerous threat is emerging, one for which the young Bruce Wayne is woefully unprepared: genetically engineered, horribly mutated men who have developed a taste for human flesh. They are the stuff of nightmare. And as they wreak havoc on Gotham's criminal community, Batman soon discovers that even the woman he loves may be threatened. Can the Dark Knight stop the carnage, or will he become the next victim of the Monster Men? The book includes violence, some graphic.

Batman/Superman/Wonder Woman: Trinity. DC Comics 2003 208p. Illustration
Grades: 9 10 11 12 Adult   **741.5; Fic**
1. Batman (Fictional character); 2. Superhero graphic novels; 3. Superman (Fictional character); 4. Wonder Woman (Fictional character); 5. Graphic novels
1-4012-0187-3, $17.99
When Batman's greatest nemesis, Ra's al Ghul, recruits Bizarro and an Amazon warrior to aid him in his plan to create global chaos, the Dark Knight Detective suddenly finds himself working with the Man of Steel and the Amazon Princess, Wonder Woman. Looking to thwart the madman's plot to simultaneously destroy all satellite communications as well as all of the world's oil reserves, Earth's greatest

heroes reluctantly band together. But if Batman, Superman and Wonder Woman are to have any hope of stopping Ra's nuclear missile assault, they will first need to overcome their own biases and reconcile their differing philosophies. The book includes some violence.

Grendel: Devil's Legacy. creator-writer-cover artist: Matt Wagner; pencillers-inkers, Arnold & Jacob Pander; inkers Jay Geldhof, Rich Rankin; colorist: Jeromy Cox; letterer: Steve Haynie. Dark Horse Comics 2001 120p. Illustration
Grades: 10 11 12 Adult   **741.5; Fic**
1. Mystery graphic novels; 2. Science fiction graphic novels; 3. Supernatural graphic novels; 4. Graphic novels
1-56971-662-5, $29.95
The mind of a vigilante murderer is complex, wrought with anger and blood; it echoes through time in ancestral screams for revenge. And the cycle of death that comes from such a spirit is often endless and tragic. Such is the story of Christine Spar, adopted granddaughter of the terribly notorious, yet rich and graceful Hunter Rose, a.k.a. the original Grendel. It's the near future, and Spar takes her son, Anson, to see a kabuki show, not knowing what tragedy lies ahead. The mysterious leader of the troupe cuts a terrifying figure, cat-like and dangerous, with an odd fixation for Spar and her son. Soon Anson disappears, and Spar takes up the mantle of Grendel to hunt for him. So the cycle begins. The book includes violence and harsh language.

Madame Xanadu: disenchanted. Matt Wagner, writer; Amy Reeder Hadley, penciller. DC Comics/Vertigo 2009 Un Illustration
Grades: 10 11 12 Adult   **741.5; Fic**
1. Fantasy graphic novels; 2. Magic; 3. Graphic novels
978-1-4012-2291-8, $12.99
In the days of King Arthur and Camelot, Nimue used woodland magic. Despite her power, the warnings of a stranger with glowing eyes comes too late for her to save the land against the machinations of Merlin and her own sister, Morgana. Using her herb lore to maintain her youth, Nimue next shows up in the court of Kublai Khan, where she is known as the Western Seer. Again, the Phantom Stranger shows up, this time with the party of Marco Polo, who become targets of a plot to discredit the Westerners. Nimue helps, only to learn that it wasn't enough, and the Stranger abandons her in the middle of the Gobi Desert. Then she appears in France, known there as Madame Xanadu, a favorite of Queen Marie Antoinette. This time, Nimue reads the portents for herself and knows that the Revolution will topple the King; the Phantom Stranger appears again, but because she can't trust him, she ends up imprisoned, betrayed by the former Queen whom she believed to be a friend, and Nimue has to trick Death herself. In London of the 1880s, Madame Xanadu tries to help the prostitutes of Whitechapel, but the Phantom Stranger says the murders committed by Jack the Ripper serve a larger purpose and he thwarts her again. In New York City of the 1930s, Nimue has found another magician, John Zatara and they are lovers, but the Phantom Stranger comes again and this time Nimue decides to trap him. What consequences will her actions have upon the people around her, including a heroic policeman named James Corrigan? The book includes some gory violence, some harsh language, some sexual suggestiveness and one not-very-graphic rape scene. This

series, in its pamphlet comic issue form, was nominated for four Eisner Awards in 2009: Best Writer, Best Cover Artist, Best New Series, and Best Penciler Inker Team.

Volume 1 of 4

Sandman Mystery Theater: Dr. Death and The Night of the Butcher. Matt Wagner, Steven T. Seagle, writers; Guy Davis, Vince Locke, artists; David Hornung, colorist; John Costanza, Gaspar Saladino, letterers. DC Comics/Vertigo 2007 210p. Illustration

Grades: 10 11 12 Adult   **741.5; Fic**
1. Mystery graphic novels; 2. Sandman (Fictional character); 3. Supernatural graphic novels; 4. Graphic novels
978-1-4012-1237-7, $19.99

Wesley Dodds is driven by his dreams to fight injustice in the dark of night. Donning a gas mask, fedora, business suit and cape, Dodds goes after evildoers as the vigilante known only as The Sandman. Dr. Death and the Night of the Butcher follows Wesley Dodds through two new cases of serial murderers, each more grisly than the last. But the real challenge for The Sandman will be holding on to his paramour, Dian Belmont, once she finally uncovers his secret career. This volume includes strong language, some sexual situations, and some violence.

Wagner, Richard
Richard Wagner's The Ring of the Nibelung Volume One. Adapted for comics by P. Craig Russell; translated by Patrick Mason; colored by Lovern Kindzierski; lettered by Galen Showman. Dark Horse Comics 2002 Un Illustration

Grades: 9 10 11 12 Adult   **741.5; Fic**
1. Fantasy graphic novels; 2. Norse mythology; 3. Opera; 4. Graphic novels
1-56971-666-8, $21.95

2001 Eisner Award for Best Limited Series; 2001 Eisner Award to P. Craig Russell for Best Penciller/Inker of Penciller/Inker Team.

The Rhinegold and The Valkyrie comprise the first volume of Russell's adaptation of the Ring cycle by German composer Richard Wagner. Woton has exhausted himself and his godly resources to have a mighty fortress built with the labor of the giants, Fasolt and Fafnir. But in his bargaining with them, he has promised the fair Freia, keeper of the golden apple tree whose fruit gives power and immortality to the gods. The giants come to collect their pay, and only Log?, the trickster god, can find something to offer the giants in exchange: the Rhinegold. The only problem is, Woton doesn't have the Rhinegold yet.

Richard Wagner's The Ring of the Nibelung Volume Two. Dark Horse Comics 2002 Un Illustration

Grades: 9 10 11 12 Adult   **741.5; Fic**
1. Fantasy graphic novels; 2. Norse mythology; 3. Opera; 4. Graphic novels
1-56971-734-6, $21.95

2001 Eisner Award for Best Limited Series; 2001 Eisner Award to P. Craig Russell for Best Penciller/Inker of Penciller/Inker Team.

This volume adapts Wagner's Siegfried and Gotterdammerung: The Twilight of the Gods. Siegfried is separated from his love, the Valkyrie Brunhilde, and even the All-Father himself cannot make things right. In the

conclusion, all of creation hangs in the balance because of gods meddling in the affairs of man - all over the gold of the Rhinemaids.

Waid, Mark
Amazing Spider-Man: family business. By Mark Waid and James Robinson; illustrated by Gabriele Dell'Otto and Werther Dell'Edera. Marvel Enterprises 2014 112 p. Color; Illustration

Grades: 9 10 11 12 Adult   **741.5**
1. Spider-Man (Fictional character)
0785184406; 9780785184409, $24.99

In this graphic novel, by Mark Waid and James Robinson, "someone has Spider-Man in their crosshairs and the only person in the Marvel Universe who can save him is . . . Peter Parker's sister! As the web-slinger meets family he never knew, will she end up becoming his greatest ally . . . or the one who damns him? And what does the KINGPIN have to do with it?" (Publisher's note)

"Waid's story is perfectly blended, with all the one-liners and gags that fans have come to expect as well as a level of mystery and intrigue that's a welcome addition. And with four villains vying for the death of Spider-Man (one literally dug up from the past), this original graphic novel is certainly not short on action." Booklist

★ **Daredevil**. Writer, Mark Waid; artists, Paolo Rivera, Marcos Martin. Marvel 2013 Color illustration (Daredevil (2011))

Grades: 10 11 12 Adult   **741.5**
1. Daredevil (Fictional character); 2. Spider-Man (Fictional character); 3. Superhero comic books, strips, etc
0785168060; 9780785168065, $34.99

"Matt Murdock is back in New York and hoping to resuscitate his law practice, but not everyone is happy to see him. And Daredevil hits the streets as Klaw, master of sound, makes his deadly return! Then, a blind client holds the key to a global conspiracy perpetrated by some familiar foes. Can Daredevil protect him long enough to bring down an international criminal organization? And when a piece of cutting-edge technology goes missing, Daredevil and Punisher team up to track it down and clear the Black Cat of the crime. But is Black Cat really innocent? And after someone exhumes Battlin' Jack Murdock's grave, DD heads underground to find the villain responsible." (Publisher's note)

Collects Daredevil (2011) 1-10, 10.1; Amazing Spider-Man (1963) 677

Volume 1 of 2 (hardcover collection)

★ **Kingdom** come. Mark Waid, Alex Ross. DC Comics 2012 228 p. Color illustration

Grades: Adult   **741.5**
1. Batman (Fictional character); 2. Heroes; 3. Justice League (Fictional characters); 4. Superhero graphic novels; 5. Superman (Fictional character); 6. Wonder Woman (Fictional character)
1401220347; 9781401220341, $19.99
      LC 2012040863

Eisner Award: Best Limited Series (1997)

In this graphic novel, by Mark Waid and Alex Ross, "the DC Universe is spinning inexorably out of control. The new generation of heroes has lost their moral compass, becoming just as reckless and violent as the villains they fight. The previous regime of heroes—the Justice League—returns under the most dire of circumstances, setting up a battle of the old guard against these uncompromising protectors in a battle that will define what heroism truly is." (Publisher's note)

Originally published in single magazine form in Kingdom Come #1-4.

Legion of Super-Heroes Vol. 1: Teenage Revolution. Mark Waid, writer; Barry Kitson, penciller. DC Comics 2005 Un Illustration
Grades: 8 9 10 11 12 Adult   **741.5; Fic**
1. Science fiction graphic novels; 2. Superhero graphic novels; 3. Graphic novels
1-4012-0482-1, $14.99

Poverty, famine, war, and disease have been eliminated in the early days of the 31st century. The Dawning Millenium is utopian: shining, optimistic, hopeful ... and deadly dull. Dull, that is, until a team of bright, defiant, super-powered teenagers from different worlds assemble. The come together as activists and fierce dreamers, crusading to make a difference in a society that has forgotten how to change. Cosmic Boy, Lightning Lad, Saturn Girl, and the rest of the Legion of Super-Heroes fight for freedom and justice while learning from, and learning to tolerate, one another.

Legion of Super-Heroes Vol. 2: Death of a Dream. DC Comics 2006 Un Illustration
Grades: 9 10 11 12 Adult   **741.5; Fic**
1. Legion of Super-Heroes (Fictional characters); 2. Superhero graphic novels; 3. Graphic novels
978-1-4012-0971-1, $14.99

A bright, defiant, energized team of super-powered teenagers from different worlds joins forces to form a legion of passionate activists that crusade to leave their mark on a complacent society that has forgotten how to fight for change. A hidden mastermind plans the downfall of the United Planets, and only the Legion has the combined knowledge and power needed to stop him. But a struggle for control of the team has split the Legion into two clashing factions. Can the members put aside their personal differences in time to stop the intergalactic menace?

Supergirl and the Legion of Super-Heroes: Strange Visitor from Another Century. Mark Waid, writer; Barry Kitson [and others], pencillers; Mick Gray [and others], inkers. DC Comics 2006 144p. Illustration
Grades: 10 11 12 Adult   **741.5; Fic**
1. Mystery graphic novels; 2. Superhero graphic novels; 3. Graphic novels
978-1-4012-0916-2, $14.99

In the 31st century, the rebel teens of the Legion of Super-Heroes has ended the greatest threat to the peace and stability of the galaxy. The United Planets was to make the Legion an officially sanctioned peace-keeping force. Then, 21st-century hero Supergirl arrives in their time, with no memory of how she got there and no idea how to get back, so she applies for full-time Legionnaire membership. The story includes superhero action, and some violence in a locked-room mystery.

Superman: Birthright. Mark Waid, writer; Leinil Francis Yu, penciller; Gerry Alanguilan, inker; Dave McCaig, colorist; Comicraft, letterer. DC Comics 2004 304p. Illustration
Grades: 9 10 11 12 Adult   **741.5; Fic**
1. Superhero graphic novels; 2. Superman (Fictional character); 3. Graphic novels
1-4012-0252-7, $19.99
LC 2005-284647

The whole world knows that Superman fights for truth and justice ... but why does he? What drives a farm boy from Kansas to divide his life between posing as a mild-mannered reporter and embarking on a career as a super hero? This book retells the origin of Superman, from his infancy through his first appearance as Superman, and why Lex Luthor is so obsessed with destroying him.

Walker, Brian

The **comics** before 1945. Brian Walker. H.N. Abrams 2004 P. cm
Grades: Adult   **741**
0-8109-4970-9
LC 2004-9514

1. Comic books, strips, etc. — History and criticism
"Starting with the late 1800s, the book features informative introductions to US newspaper comic strips, broken down by decade, each placing the funnies in sociocultural/political context and highlighting the roles of important cartoonists and characters. Profiles of comic-strip masters are tucked in between the introductions, and many pages offer brilliant displays of color and black-and-white strips. In his introductory material, Walker does not take the usually cited date of 1895 as the start of comics but goes back to the roots in Europe." (Choice Reviews)

The **comics** since 1945. Brian Walker. H.N. Abrams 2002 P. cm Illustration; Color
Grades: Adult   **741.5**
1. Comic books, strips, etc — History and criticism
0-8109-3481-7; 9780810934818, $49.95
LC 2002-8375

"This volume completes Walker's profusely illustrated two-volume history of American newspaper comic strips.... Some 700 illustrations, many in brilliant color, are included. Particularly appealing among them are numerous strips spoofing societal foibles and personalities and others reminiscing about—or humorously reflecting on—their creators or cartooning itself. Walker organizes the content by decade. For each he provides an essay setting strips in historical context, a page each on two or three featured artists, and paragraph-long commentaries on other artists and on genres/themes—all interspersed with scores of images." (Choice)

Wallace, Daniel

★ The **DC** Comics encyclopedia: the definitive guide to the characters of the DC universe. Text by Scott Beatty ... [et al.]; updated text by Dan Wallace. DK Pub. 2008 399p. Illustration
Grades: 9 10 11 12 Adult   **741.5**
978-0-7566-4119-1; 0-7566-4119-5, $40
LC 2008-300609

The authors "meticulously profile 1000 DC heroes and villains created since DC's 1935 founding. The entries are organized alphabetically, by character name, while introductory insets consistently detail first appearance, hero/villain status, physical statistics, and special powers. A genuinely essential DC character reference." Libr J

Waltz, Tom
 Children of the grave. Illustrated by Casey Maloney. IDW Publishing 2007 122p. Illustration
 Grades: 11 12 Adult   741.5; Fic
  1. Atrocities; 2. War; 3. Graphic novels
  978-1-60010-166-3, $19.99
 Team Orphan, a three-man Special Forces team, have orders to assassinate Colonel Akbar Assan, a terrorist who is on a mission to massacre all the children of his enemies. When the squad locates a mass grave site, the men get a weird feeling when they see all the graves are empty. And as they continue on their mission, each man is haunted by the dead in his own past, while Lt. Michael Drake also sees the dead children. The book includes graphic violence, copious use of harsh language, and a rape scene.
 This book was published in 2006 in black and white.

 Finding peace. Tom Waltz; [artist], Nathan St. John; design and letters by Neil Uyetake. IDW Publishing 2008 Un Illustration
 Grades: 10 11 12 Adult   741.5; Fic
  1. War; 2. Graphic novels
  978-1-60010-218-9, $14.99
 Set in an unnamed country that could be anywhere in the Middle East or Latin America or Eastern Europe, three stories in reverse chronological order tell the tale of an unending civil war that destroys too many lives. The first story shows just how dangerous a "peacekeeping" tour of duty can be, as a young soldier recalls a violent riot and the death of a fellow peacekeeper from a sniper's bullet. In the second story, a soldier watches his female sergeant during a raid as they hunker in a bunker and realizes that her momentary vulnerability both humanizes her and makes her a stronger soldier in his eyes. A young civilian girl narrates the third story, as she watches her country torn apart by civil war and brutal violence and is forced to make a final stand herself. St. John's sketchy illustrations depict the violence in such a way that readers won't feel brutalized by blood and gore yet will feel the impact and horror of war.

Ware, Chris
 ★ **Building** stories. Chris Ware. Pantheon Books 2012 P. cm.
 Grades: Adult   741.5/973; 741.5
  1. Buildings; 2. City and town life
  9780375424335, $50.00
                                             LC 2012007946
 Harvey Nominee: Best Graphic Album of Original Work (2013)
 This graphic novel by Chris Ware, assembled as separate pieces in a box, "imagines the inhabitants of a three-story Chicago apartment building: a 30-something woman who has yet to find someone with whom to spend the rest of her life; a couple, possibly married, who wonder if they can bear each other's company another minute; and the

building's landlady, an elderly woman who has lived alone for decades. . . . 'Building Stories' is a book with no deliberate beginning nor end." (Publisher's note)

 ★ **Jimmy** Corrigan: the smartest kid on earth. Written by F.C. Ware. Pantheon Books 2002 380 p.
 Grades: Adult   741.5/973; 741.5
  1. Chicago (Ill) — Fiction; 2. Father-son relationship — Fiction; 3. Men — Fiction
  0375714545; 9780375714542, $19.95
                                             LC 2006272880
 Eisner Award: Best Graphic Album: Reprint (2001)
 This graphic novel, by F.C. Ware, "is a . . . view at a lonely and emotionally-impaired 'everyman' (Jimmy Corrigan: The Smartest Kid on Earth), who is provided, at age 36, the opportunity to meet his father for the first time. An improvisatory romance which gingerly deports itself between 1890's Chicago and 1980's small town Michigan, the reader is helped along by thousands of colored illustrations and diagrams." (Publisher's note)

Warren, Adam
 Livewires Vol. 1: Clockwork Thugs, Yo. Story & layouts: Adam Warren; penciler: Rick Mays. Marvel Entertainment 2005 Un Illustration
 Grades: 9 10 11 12 Adult   741.5; Fic
  1. Robots; 2. Science fiction graphic novels; 3. Graphic novels
  0-7851-1519-6, $7.99
 Hollowpoint Ninja. Gothic Lolita. Cornfed. Stem Cell. Social Butterfly. They're nanobuilt human form combat mecha, with "smartware" bodies specialized for covert ops and Artificially Intelligent minds programmed for suicidal loyalty. They're the superhuman products of a top-secret, quasi-governmental R&D program with a unique agenda: namely, to seek out and destroy other top-secret, quasi-governmental R&D programs. And in the ultra-tech underbelly of a Marvel Universe infested with mad super-geniuses, homebrewed WMDs, and bootlegged alien technologies, they have a lot of work to do...

Watanabe, Taeko
 Kaze Hikaru, Vol. 1. Viz Shojo Beat 2005 190p. Illustration
 Grades: 10 11 12 Adult   741.5; Fic
  1. Japan — History — 0-1868; 2. Shojo manga; 3. Graphic novels
  1-4125-0189-9, $8.99
 "The talk of catamites and homosexual sex among the young men of the Mibu-Roshi and the almost perpetually drunken state of their older members make this title more suited to older teens." (VOYA)
 In the waning years of the Tokugawa Shogunate, a band of young samurai called the Mibu-Roshi, gathers in Tokyo. They are loyal to the Shogun and will eventually become the Shinsengumi. Fifteen-year-old Seizaburo Kamiya, who has lost his father and brother to murderous supporters of the Emperor, joins the Mibu-Roshi, and young master swordsman Okita Soji befriends him. Soon, though, Soji learns Seizaburo's secret - he's actually a girl. He agrees to keep her secret and Sei becomes a mainstay in the group, but that doesn't end her danger.

Watase, Yuu

Absolute Boyfriends Volume 1. Viz Media/Shojo Beat 2006 208p. Illustration

Grades: 10 11 12 Adult   **741.5; Fic**
1. Humorous graphic novels; 2. Manga; 3. Romance graphic novels; 4. Shojo manga; 5. Graphic novels
978-1-4215-0016-4, $8.99

Shy high school student Riko Izawa aches for a boyfriend but guys just won't look her way. Then one day she signs up for a three-day trial of a mysterious "lover figurine," and the next thing she knows, a cute naked guy is delivered to her doorstep—and he wants to be her boyfriend. Has Riko died and gone to heaven? The cute naked guy (she names him Night) turns out to be smart, super nice, stylish and a gourmet chef. Plus, he looks like a million bucks ... Trouble is, that's about what he's going to cost Riko because she didn't return him in time. The book includes partial nudity, sexual innuendo, and some slightly strong language.

Ceres: Celestial Legend Vol. 1: Aya. Viz Media/Shojo 2003 208p. Illustration

Grades: 10 11 12 Adult   **741.5; Fic**
1. Horror graphic novels; 2. Romance graphic novels; 3. Science fiction graphic novels; 4. Shojo manga; 5. Graphic novels
1-56931-980-4, $9.95

Aya and her twin brother Aki thought they were going to a celebration of their sixteenth birthday at their grandfather's home, but the funeral-like atmosphere tips them off that something's not right. Their "birthday present" turns out to be a mummified hand—the power of which forces an awakening within Aya, and painful wounds all over Aki's body. Grandfather Mikage announces that Aki will be heir to the Mikage fortune, and Aya must die. Aya has allies in the athletic cook and martial artist Yûhi, and the attractive, mysterious Tôya. But can even two handsome and resourceful guys save Aya when it's her own power that's out of control? The series includes nudity, sexual situations, strong language, and violence.

Fushigi Yugi Genbu Kaiden Volume 1. Viz Media/Shojo Beat 2005 200p. Illustration

Grades: 10 11 12 Adult   **741.5; Fic**
1. Adventure graphic novels; 2. Fantasy graphic novels; 3. Shojo manga; 4. Graphic novels
1-59116-896-1, $8.99

When schoolgirl Takiko Okuda attempts to destroy her father's translation of "The Universe of the Four Gods," she is instead literally sucked into the story, becoming the Priestess of Genbu in an epic journey to find the seven Celestial Warriors. In her first encounter, she meets the mysterious Limdo, one of the Celestial Warriors who has a tattoo of the Chinese character for "woman" on his chest. As it turns out, it's there for a good reason: Limdo can not only summon the wind as one of his special powers, but also transform into a woman! Caught up in pursuit, because Limdo is regarded an outlaw, Takiko falls in with the bowman Chamka, who is hunting Limdo. Chamka regards Takiko an outlaw as well, but they eventually become traveling companions, for it seems Chamka is a one of the seven Celestial Warriors as well ... This prequel series to Fushigi Yugi is darker, more violent, and has more nudity than the original series.

Way, Daniel

Wolverine: Origins & Endings. Writer, Daniel Way; artists, Javier Saltares and Mark Texeira. Marvel Entertainment 2006 Un Illustration

Grades: 11 12 Adult   **741.5; Fic**
1. Superhero graphic novels; 2. Wolverine (Fictional character); 3. Graphic novels
978-0-7851-1979-1, $13.99

Left shaken at ground zero after the cataclysmic events of House M, Logan has no choice but to soldier on, as he's done so many times before - but has the burden now become too great" In his lifetime, Logan has been both a hero and a villain, a player and a pawn... but what is he now" This book includes some bloody violence.

Wolverine: Origins Vol. 1. Born in Blood. Writer, Daniel Way; artist, Steve Dillon. Marvel Entertainment 2007 Un Illustration

Grades: 11 12 Adult   **741.5; Fic**
1. Superhero graphic novels; 2. Wolverine (Fictional character); 3. Graphic novels
978-0-7851-2287-6, $13.99

Armed with the one thing that could kill him, as well as key clues to his very existence, Logan embarks on the first leg of a long and bloody quest for vengeance against those who once enslaved him. No longer feeling the need to play it quiet, Logan's first strike elicits a Condition Critical response from the U.S. government. With no other choice, they drop their bomb - when Logan hits D.C., someone's going to be waiting for him. This book includes considerable violence.

Wolverine: Origins Vol. 2: Savior. Writer, Daniel Way; artist, Steve Dillon. Marvel Entertainment 2007 Un Illustration

Grades: 10 11 12 Adult   **741.5; Fic**
1. Superhero graphic novels; 2. Wolverine (Fictional character); 3. Graphic novels
978-0-7851-2286-9, $19.99

Completely shattered by recent revelations, Logan must now ask himself some hard - almost impossible - questions, such as whether he can continue on his quest...or if he even should. Though he now remembers who he was, the more pressing question becomes who - and what - is he now" Answering these questions will take the help of one of Logan's closest friends, and one of his deadliest enemies: Omega Red. The book includes some violence.

Weiner, Stephen

101 outstanding graphic novels. Stephen Weiner; [edited by] Daniel J. Fingeroth. NBM Pub. 2015 80 p.

Grades: Adult Professional   **016.7415; 741.5**
1. Graphic novels
1561639443; 9781561639441, $15.99

LC 2014958652

"The popular primer on the best graphic novels, initially called The 101 Best Graphic Novels, is back in its third updated edition. Expert librarian Stephen Weiner—with the crowdsourcing help of professionals in the field, from artists to critics to leading comic store owners—has sifted through the bewildering thousands of graphic novels now available to come up with an outstanding, not-to-be-missed 101." (Publisher's note)

Previously called 101 Best Graphic Novels

Faster Than a Speeding Bullet: The Rise of the Graphic Novel. NBM 2004 64p. Illustration

Grades: Adult Professional **741.5**

1. Graphic novels — History and criticism; 2. Graphic novels

1-56163-368-2, $9.95

LC 2003058827

Weiner provides a brief history of graphic novels, from the first comic books in the 1930s to the explosion of publication and mainstream coverage in the early 2000s.

The **Will** Eisner companion: the pioneering spirit of the father of the graphic novel. [by] N.C. Christopher Couch and Stephen Weiner; introduction by Dennis O'Neil; afterword by Denis Kitchen. DC Comics 2004 174p. Illustration

Grades: 11 12 Adult **741.5**

1. Authors; 2. Cartoonists; 3. Comic book writers; 4. Eisner, Will, 1917-2005; 5. Publishing executives

1-4012-0422-8; 1-4012-0423-6 (pa), $12.99

"This book is part mini-biography and part summary of the major works of the man who invented and reinvented the art of the graphic novel." SLJ

"Wherever Eisner's books—either the Spirit collections that DC Comics is lavishly republishing, or the graphic novels—have proven popular, their fans will value this authoritative supplement to them." Booklist

Includes bibliographical references

Weinstein, Lauren

Girl stories. By Lauren R. Weinstein. Henry Holt 2006 237p. Illustration

Grades: 7 8 9 10 11 12 Adult **741.5; Fic**

1. Friendship; 2. Girls; 3. Humorous graphic novels; 4. Graphic novels

978-0-8050-7863-3, $16.95; 0-8050-7863-0

LC 2005-46205

"Smart, creative Lauren sheds her geeky rep in high school in Weinstein's collection of comic strips, which have to intimacy of a teen's diary. The color-washed sketches have an edgy quality." Booklist

Weinstein, Simcha

Up, up, and oy vey!: how Jewish history, culture, and values shaped the comic book superhero. 2006 143p. Illustration

Grades: Adult Professional **741.5**

1. Captain America (Fictional character); 2. Comic books, strips, etc — History — Jewish influences; 3. Hulk (Fictional character); 4. Spider-Man (Fictional character); 5. Superman (Fictional character); 6. X-Men (Fictional characters); 7. Graphic novels

978-1-881927-32-7, $19.95

From the birth of Krypton in Cleveland to the Caped Crusader, Captain America, the Incredible Hulk, Spider-Man, the X-Men, and more, this book chronicles the story behind the story about the origins of the planet's most famous superheroes. While the Jewish contribution to film, theater, music, and comedy has been well-documented, the Jewish role in the creation of the All-American superhero

has not been—until now. Rabbi Weinstein explores comics' roots in Jewish values, history, culture, and mysticism.

Weir, Christina

Amazing Agent Luna Volume 1. Nunzio Defilippis and Christina Weir ; artist, Shiei. Seven Seas Entertainment 2005 184p. Illustration

Grades: 8 9 10 11 12 Adult **741.5; Fic**

1. Adventure graphic novels; 2. Science fiction graphic novels

193316400X; 9781933164007, $10.99

This is the story of Luna, the perfect secret agent. A girl grown in a lab from the finest genetic material, she has been trained since her birth fifteen years ago to be the U.S. government's ultimate espionage weapon. But now she is given an assignment that will test her abilities to the utmost - high school. In order to uncover an evil plot, the government sends Luna to a prominent high school to pose as a student. But the one thing Luna has not been trained to handle is her own feelings. They are powerful and out of control, like your average teen, but without parents or the usual interaction with her peers to guide her. Putting her in high school is lighting the fuse on an emotional bomb of adolescent confusion, especially when she starts making friends, creating rivals, and having her first big crush on bad boy Jonah, the son of her arch-nemesis, Count Von Brucken.

Volume 1 of 11

Maria's Wedding. Nunzio Defilippis and Christina Weir ; art by Jose Garibaldi. Oni Press 2003 88p. Illustration

Grades: 8 9 10 11 12 Adult **741.5; Fic**

1. Family; 2. Weddings; 3. Graphic novels

1-929998-57-0, $10.95

Few events exude as much joy, happiness, and hope as a wedding, and for the Pirellis these ceremonies mean even more. Pirelli weddings are about tradition and family as much as they're about the happy couple, or at least they used to be. When Joseph Pirelli married Matthew it rocked the clan to its knees. Now a year later, the tension and downright animosity between different factions of the family have turned Maria's special day into a powder keg. And poor Frankie, Joseph's outspoken brother, is holding the match. But while some fear the fuse being lit, others in the family are ready for and secretly looking forward to the blow-up. Frankie, on the other hand, thinks his reputation for speaking his mind is undeserved. He just wants to see his favorite cousin get married and maybe rekindle his childhood romance with Maria's maid of honor, Brenna. Can Frankie balance the Pirellis expectations of him with his own or will the scales tip and bring the whole ceremony crashing down?

The **Tomb**. Written by Nunzio DeFilippis & Christina Weir; illustrated by Christopher Mitten; design by Keith Wood; cover by Christopher Mitten & Guy Major. Oni Press 2004 144p. Illustration

Grades: 9 10 11 12 Adult **741.5; Fic**

1. Adventure graphic novels; 2. Horror graphic novels; 3. Graphic novels

1-929998-95-3, $14.95

In 1922, Lord Earl Carnarvon financed the Egyptian expedition that unearthed King Tut's tomb. While the fact that the dig gained a reputation for being "cursed" is well known, Mathias Fowler slipped away into anonymity.

Fowler, an American on the team, had grown obsessed with the Ancient Egyptians and when he returned to the States it was with several stolen artifacts in tow. Fowler had become so consumed by the era that when he died, he killed all of his household staff and had them buried in his mansion with him - a modern day Pharaoh's Tomb. Almost 60 years after Fowler's death, Jessica Parrish, archeologist and would-be Indiana Jones, has been hired to assemble and lead a team into the house to take back the missing pieces and disable the booby traps that have already cost one unfortunate group their lives. Can Parrish and her comrades navigate the elaborate deathtraps with their persons intact or will the curse of Tut's tomb just add to its mounting body count? Strong language and violence pepper this horror story.

Weissman, Steven
    White flower day. Fantagraphics 2002 112p. Illustration
Grades: 5 6 7 8 9 10 11 12 Adult   **741.5; Fic**
    1. Humorous graphic novels
1-56097-514-8, $14.95
    This book will appeal to older children who enjoy such things as "The Grim Adventures of Billy and Mandy" on Cartoon Network, with its somewhat gross and twisted humor.
    "Scratch panels highlighted in ocher cast {a} jaundiced pall over three . . . twisted tales of rascaldom. They feature the Frankenstein-like Pullapart Boy, devilish L'il Bloody, and several equally weird young characters who venture forth to create mayhem, from innocent to morbid." Booklist
    Another 'Yikes' book

Wells, H. G.
    Classics illustrated #12: The Island of Dr. Moreau. Adapted by Steven Grant ; Illustrated by Eric Vincent. Papercutz 2011 Un Illustration
Grades: 7 8 9 10 11 12 Adult   **741.5; Fic**
    1. Authors; 2. Historians; 3. Horror graphic novels; 4. Novelists; 5. Science fiction writers; 6. Wells, H G (Herbert George), 1866-1946; 7. Wells, H G (Herbert George), 1866-1946 — Adaptations; 8. Writers on politics; 9. Writers on science; 10. Graphic novels
978-1-59707-235-9, $9.99
    Edward Prendick is the sole survivor of a shipwreck when a passing ship picks him up. It carries a strange cargo of animals, a doctor, who takes care of Prendick, and an odd man who looks more like an ape. Montgomery, the doctor, is taking the animals to a small island he won't name, and Prendick ends up with them when the drunken ship's captain casts him off. On that island, Prendick discovers half-human, half-beast creatures, all created by the arrogant Dr. Moreau. This book adapts Wells' classic story; it was originally published in 1990 as part of the Classics Illustrated line published by First Comics. This edition includes an interview with Steven Grant, who wrote the adaptation.

Wells, Zeb
    Civil War: Young Avengers & Runaways. Writer, Zeb Wells ; artist, Stefano Caseli ; color art, Daniele Rundoni ; letterer, Virtual Calligraphy's Cory Petit. Marvel Entertainment 2007 Un Illustration

Grades: 8 9 10 11 12 Adult   **741.5; Fic**
    1. Runaways (Fictional characters); 2. Superhero graphic novels; 3. Graphic novels
0-7851-2317-2, $11.99
    As the Civil War goes on between the two super hero camps, the public turns against their heroes, and the teen Runaways get caught up in the struggle despite their best efforts to stay out of the fight. When the Young Avengers offer their assistance, how can the Runaways believe they're on the same side?

    Fantastic Four/Iron Man: Big in Japan. Writer, Zeb Wells; artist, Steve Fisher. Marvel Entertainment 2006 Un Illustration
Grades: 9 10 11 12 Adult   **741.5; Fic**
    1. Fantastic Four (Fictional characters); 2. Humorous graphic novels; 3. Iron Man (Fictional character); 4. Superhero graphic novels; 5. Graphic novels
0-7851-1776-8, $12.99
    The Fantastic Four, the world's first super-hero big-monster battling squad, and playboy industrialist Tony Stark have descended on the Land of the Rising Sun to dedicate the opening of the Kaiju Museum and Celebration. It's an all-out romp with big monsters a-go-go as Droom, Giganto and Eerok, the giant ape - along with hundreds of manic '50s Marvel monsters - return to trample all over Tokyo and a Japanese worshipper of the kaiju (that means giant monster, by the way) warps reality.

    Shekhar Kapur's Snake Woman Vol. 1: A Snake in the Grass. Created by Shekhar Kapur; script, Zeb Wells; art, Michael Gaydos. Virgin Comics 2007 Un Illustration
Grades: 10 11 12 Adult   **741.5; Fic**
    1. Fantasy graphic novels; 2. Horror graphic novels; 3. Graphic novels
978-1-934413-01-2, $14.99
    Jessica Peterson is learning first-hand that the cycle of revenge cannot be broken. Without understanding why, she finds herself turning into a creature - a vicious Snakewoman. Her mission - to avenge a centuries old wrong that was conceived half a world away, deep in the jungles of India. Terrified by her true nature and hunted by a mysterious organization known only as "The 68," Jessica must confront the monster that lurks inside her before it is too late. The book includes strong language, violence, and sexual situations.

Wertz, Julia
    Drinking at the movies. By Julia Wertz; introduction by Janeane Garofalo. Koyama Press 2015 187 p. Illustration
Grades: Adult   **741.5; 741.5/973**
    1. Bildungsromans; 2. Cartoonists — United States — Biography; 3. Wertz, Julia
0307591832; 1927668263; 9780307591838; 9781927668269, $15
                                        LC 2010009234
    This book presents "Julia Wertz's critically acclaimed first graphic memoir in a new format, with a brand new sketchbook from Wertz, and an introduction by Janeane Garofalo. But don't worry; we haven't replaced any of the wrenching and ribald, whiskey-soaked coming-of-age tale." (Publisher's note)
    Originally published 2010 by Three Rivers Press

Whedon, Joss

★ **Astonishing** X-Men Vol. 1: Gifted. Writer, Joss Whedon; artist, John Cassaday; colorist, Laura Martin; letterer, Chris Eliopoulos. Marvel Entertainment 2004 Un Illustration

Grades: 9 10 11 12 Adult **Fic; 741.5**
1. Superhero graphic novels; 2. X-Men (Fictional characters); 3. Graphic novels
978-0-7851-1531-1, $14.99
Eisner Award: Best Continuing Series (2006)
Eisner Award: Best Penciller/Inker (2005)

Cyclops and Emma Frost re-form the X-Men with the express purpose of "astonishing" the world. But when breaking news regarding the mutant gene unexpectedly hits the airwaves, will it derail their new plans before they even get started" As demand for the mutant cure" reaches near-riot levels, the X-Men go head-to-head with the enigmatic Ord, with an unexpected ally - and some unexpected adversaries - tipping the scales.

Other Astonishing X-Men volumes by Whedon and Cassaday are: 2: Dangerous; 3: Torn; 4: Unstoppable

Buffy the Vampire Slayer Omnibus Volume 1. Dark Horse Comics 2007 318p. Illustration

Grades: 9 10 11 12 Adult **741.5; Fic**
1. Adventure graphic novels; 2. Horror graphic novels; 3. Vampires; 4. Graphic novels
978-1-59307-784-6, $24.95

This first omnibus volume begins at the beginning - The Origin, a faithful adaptation of creator Joss Whedon's original screenplay for the film that started it all. The newly-chosen slayer's road to Sunnydale continues in Viva Las Buffy and Slayer, Interrupted. Next, high school, the Scoobies and an English librarian lead the way into Season One continuity. Plus, The Goon creator Eric Powell provides pencils to "All's Fair," featuring Spike and Drusilla at the 1933 World's Fair. This omnibus project will publish the Buffy graphic novels in chronological order. There are scenes of violence in fighting vampires and other monsters.

Buffy the Vampire Slayer season eight, volume 1: the long way home. Writer, Joss Whedon ; artists, Georges Jeanty, Andy Owens, Jo Chen. Dark Horse Comics 2007 136p. Illustration

Grades: 8 9 10 11 12 Adult **741.5**
1. Adventure graphic novels; 2. Buffy the Vampire Slayer (Fictional character); 3. Horror graphic novels; 4. Graphic novels
978-1-59307-822-5, $15.95

The television series of Buffy the Vampire Slayer lasted seven seasons; this volume begins the comics-only eighth season. Buffy and her friends may have destroyed the Hellmouth, but all is not fun and games, as an old enemy returns, younger sister Dawn experiences some "growing pains," and a former decoy Slayer has her own troubles. There is a considerable amount of monster fighting.

Fray. Created and written by Joss Whedon; penciller, Karl Moline; inker, Andy Owens; colorists, Dave Stewart, Michelle Madsen; letterer, Michelle Madsen. Dark Horse Comics 2003 Un Illustration

Grades: 9 10 11 12 Adult **741.5; Fic**
1. Adventure graphic novels; 2. Monsters; 3. Graphic novels

1-56971-751-6, $19.95

Hundreds of years in the future, Manhattan has become a deadly slum, run by mutant crime-lords and disinterested cops. Stuck in the middle is a young girl who thought she had no future, but learns she has a great destiny. In a world so poisoned that it doesn't notice the monsters on its streets, how can a street kid like Fray unite a fallen city against a demonic plot to consume mankind? Creator Whedon set this story in the future of Buffy the Vampire Slayer's world, with Fray a new slayer, aided by a demonic Watcher. The story has some violence and mild harsh language.

Runaways: dead end kids. Writer, Joss Whedon ; artist, Michael Ryan. Marvel Entertainment 2008 Un Illustration

Grades: 7 8 9 10 11 12 Adult **741.5; Fic**
1. Adventure graphic novels; 2. Runaways (Fictional characters); 3. Superhero graphic novels; 4. Graphic novels
978-0-7851-2853-3, $19.99

When the team's Los Angeles hideout is compromised, they flee to New York, where they become mixed up with Kingpin, and he pressures them to pull a "minor" heist. When the Punisher shows up, with more killers behind him, the Runaways make a desperate escape and find themselves a hundred years in the past. They find that there are other "specials" in that time, too, and more danger, even as they try to find a way back home.

Wheeler, Shannon

Screw Heaven, When I Die I'm Going to Mars. Dark Horse Comics 2007 144p. Illustration

Grades: 9 10 11 12 Adult **741.5; Fic**
1. Humorous graphic novels; 2. Graphic novels
978-1-59307-820-1, $12.95

This new collection of Wheeler's comic strips blends the coffee-fueled cynicism of "Too Much Coffee Man" with the slightly more tender take on humor found in "How to Be Happy" and "Postage Stamp Funnies." He takes aim at lots of things that deserve to be made fun of, from the insipidity of coffee culture to the sad state of the American political system to the horrendous reality of dating. And all this without a single bad word (except what's in the title) or bit of violence.

Too Much Coffee Man: How to Be Happy. Dark Horse Books 2005 144p. Illustration

Grades: 10 11 12 Adult **741.5; Fic**
1. Humorous graphic novels; 2. Graphic novels
1-59307-353-4, $12.95

Too Much Coffee Man has been percolating in the comics underground for years now, and like everything else that was once "alternative," he's sold out, been used by the man (as an advertising tool for Hewlitt Packard and Converse, among others), and is now middle-aged, depressed, broke, and cynical. Who better to write a book, then, called How to be Happy? Political humor, some strong language, and some violence appear in the short comic strips collected here.

White, Shane

North Country. NBM/ComicsLit 2005 94p. Illustration

Grades: 10 11 12 Adult **741.5; Fic**
1. Autobiographical graphic novels; 2. Graphic novels

978-1-56163-435-4, $13.95

Sometimes, you have to escape your past to get to the truth. After years of being away from the northern New York town where he grew up and making a life for himself, Shane finally travels back home. On his way, his mind is flooded with the memories of his blue-collar family under tremendous pressure and pushed to the breaking point by alcoholism and abuse. For a kid growing up in this, the pain can be tremendous. As an adult, resentment battles reconciliation. There's some harsh language, but the scenes of physical abuse, while never truly graphically portrayed, could be disturbing.

Whitta, Gary

Death Jr. Vol. 1. Gary Whitta & Ted Naifeh. Image Comics 2005 Un Illustration

Grades: 8 9 10 11 12 Adult   **741.5; Fic**
1. Adventure graphic novels; 2. Fantasy graphic novels; 3. Horror graphic novels; 4. Graphic novels
1-58240-526-3, $14.99

When a school field trip to the local museum coincides with coming-of-age angst and an overly inquisitive friend (a cute goth girl named Pandora), Junior releases an ancient evil into the world... and it's up to him to fix it. He's helped by his friends Stigmartha, whose hands bleed when she gets nervous; Smith & Weston, two twins conjoined at the head and The Seep, a foul-mouthed, armless, legless fetus in a tube. He's your average, everyday, happy-go-lucky middle-school student... who just happens to be the son of the grim reaper.

The Wicked West II: Abomination & Other Tales.

Image Comics 2006 192p. Illustration

Grades: 10 11 12 Adult   **741.5; Fic**
1. Horror graphic novels; 2. Supernatural graphic novels; 3. Graphic novels
978-1-58240-661-8, $15.99

Cotton Coleridge is a cowboy who lives in an Old West out of a horror show nightmare. The "lightning rod for the supernatural" faces zombies, ghosts, resurrectionists, giant flies, carnivorous slugs, demons and lots of pure evil in this collection of 22 short stories by lots of different creators, including Todd Livingston, Robert Tinnell, Neil Vokes, Mike Baron, Chris Moreno, Michael Avon Oeming, Mark Ricketts, Filip Sablik, and many others. There's some harsh language and lots of fighting and monster killing.

Wiebe, Kurtis J.

Rat Queens; 1: Sass & Sorcery. By Kurtis J. Wiebe; edited by Laura Tavishati; illustrated by Roc Upchurch and Ed Brisson. Image Comics 2014 128 p. Color; Illustration (Rat Queens)

Grades: Adult   **741.5**
1. Fantasy fiction; 2. Gangs — Fiction; 3. Violence — Fiction; 4. Graphic novels
1607069458; 9781607069454, $9.99

"The Rat Queens are a tough, insouciant gang of ne'er-do-well girls . . . who love a good bar brawl. When they are assigned a mission as punishment for their latest recklessness by the mayor of Palisade and it turns out to be a trap, Hannah, Violet, Dee, and Betty come back to the town

to figure out who has it in for them and the other local fighting gangs." (Booklist)

"Possessed of very different body types, personalities, and idiosyncrasies, and not afraid to share exactly what they're feeling, the Rat Queens are refreshing characters whose story will leave readers thirsty for more." Pub Wkly

Originally published in single magazine form as RAT QUEENS #1-5.

Volume 1 of an ongoing series

Wight, Eric

My dead girlfriend, Vol. 1. Tokyopop 2007 Un Illustration

Grades: 8 9 10 11 12 Adult   **741.5; Fic**
1. High school students; 2. Romance graphic novels; 3. School stories; 4. Supernatural graphic novels; 5. Graphic novels
978-1-59816-996-6, $9.99

As a perfectly normal boy, Finney Bleak stands out among the monsters and ghosts of his town and in school, Mephisto Prep. He's the youngest in a family known for the many weird and wacky ways everyone has died. In school, Finney must deal with bullies such as Karl the Frankenstein-type monster, teen vampire Drake, and others. He had one memorable night at the carnival with the perfect girl, Jenny, months ago, but she never made it to the meeting they had arranged for the next day. Now, as he's chased in the woods by Karl and company, somebody comes to his aid—it's Jenny, who's now a ghost. So, nobody's ever perfect, right? This is another global manga title, the first of a projected series.

Williams, Aaron

PS 238, volume VI: senseless acts of tourism!. Do Gooder Press 2008 Un Illustration

Grades: 3 4 5 6 7 8 9 10 11 12 Adult   **741.5; Fic**
1. Humorous graphic novels; 2. Superhero graphic novels; 3. Graphic novels
978-1-933288-49-9, $15.99

After the town had been pretty much leveled by invading aliens and repair work begins, Miss Kyle takes a vacation to Las Vegas. However, Zodon has convinced Poly and Julie that Miss Kyle is leaving for good, so they hitch a ride on the plane. They don't know that others are following and trying to kidnap Zodon. Meanwhile, Flea has hitched a ride on the bad guys' jet. Once they all get to Las Vegas, they end up helping the Masquerade Casino catch the person who has been cheating and winning too much in the casino. Meanwhile, back at PS 238, Tyler is stuck in a stasis pod because he was infected with an alien virus that could destroy the world; then Tom comes and takes Tyler, or at least a part of his soul, to make a crucial decision about whether humanity should continue to gain super powers. And then Cecil, who still sees aliens everywhere, goes with mysterious millionaire Kent Allard to scout out possible aliens. There's lots of superhero action going on, all of it at kid-friendly level.

PS 238: To the Cafeteria . . . For Justice!. Henchman Publishing/Dork Storm Press 2005 Un Illustration

Grades: 4 5 6 7 8 9 10 11 12 Adult   **741.5; Fic**

1. Elementary schools; 2. Humorous graphic novels; 3. Superhero graphic novels; 4. Graphic novels
1-933288-13-2, $15.99

PS 238 is the only public school for metahuman children, where the students learn how to use their powers, socialize with normal as well as super-powered classmates, and have fun adventures. In this second volume, the students learn about the importance of primary sources for history research (time traveling Tom brings a girl to the present to give them straight information about her father). Also, Tyler, son of two superheroes who hasn't yet come into his powers, spends some time training with the vigilante hero, Revenant. And in shop class, the students make some super accessories. The first volume is not available, but readers can pick up on things from this volume. This is a continuing series.

PS238 Vol. III: No Child Left Behind!. Dork Storm Press/Henchman Publishing 2006 Un Illustration
Grades: 5 6 7 8 9 10 11 12 Adult   **741.5; Fic**
  1. Adventure graphic novels; 2. Humorous graphic novels; 3. Superhero graphic novels; 4. Graphic novels
1-933288-24-8, $15.99

In this third volume, readers meet Malphast, the child of divine and not-so-divine parents, who involves almost everyone in a cosmic game of four-square. Then Tom Davidson discovers an unusual castle floating outside of time and space. And Harold Nelson, after whom PS238's "Rainmaker Program" was named, has decided that a sizeable number of students need to be "rescued" from the school. Tyler works with the Revenant to save his friends from Nelson.

Williams, Ian (Physician)

The **bad** doctor: the troubled life and times of Dr. Iwan James. By Ian Williams. Pennsylvania State University Press 2015 224 p. Color; Illustration (Graphic medicine)
Grades: Adult   **741.5**
  1. Physicians — Fiction
0271067543; 9780271067544, $24.95
           LC 2015005728

In this graphic novel, by Ian Williams, readers meet "Dr. Iwan James: cyclist, doctor, would-be lover, former heavy metal fan, and, above all, human being. Weighed down by his responsibilities—from diagnosing personality disorders to deciding who can hold a gun license—he doubts his ability to make decisions about the lives of others when he may need more than a little help himself." (Publisher's note)

"The simple black-and-white panels augment the story well enough, but Williams' real strength is using everyday interactions between Dr. James and the people around him to reveal the motives of this complex but relatable character." Booklist

Williams, Rob

Star Wars: Rebellion Volume 1: My Brother, My Enemy. Script, Rob Williams ; "Crossroads" script, Thomas Andrews ; art, Brandon Badeaux and Michel Lacombe ; colors, Wil Glass ; lettering, Michael Heisler. Dark Horse Comics 2007 Un Illustration
Grades: 8 9 10 11 12 Adult   **Fic; 741.5**

1. Adventure graphic novels; 2. Science fiction graphic novels; 3. Graphic novels
9781593077112, $14.95; 1593077114

Having rescued Rebel strategist Jorin Sol from the Empire, Luke Skywalker now leads X-Wing attack runs on Imperial convoys to rustle up much needed supplies for the Rebel fleet. Little does he know that within Sol lies a secret that will put the entire Alliance in danger. What's worse, when Luke receives a coded message from Lt. Sunber, who wants to defect to the Rebel Alliance, he must decide whether to trust his old friend or obey the orders of Princess Leia who believes Tank may be part of an Imperial plot to capture the Rebellion's greatest hero.

Willingham, Bill

Day of Vengeance: Countdown to Infinite Crisis. Written by Bill Willingham and Judd Winick; pencilled by Ian Churchill, Justiano, Ron Wagner.. DC Comics 2005 Un Illustration
Grades: 9 10 11 12 Adult   **741.5; Fic**
  1. Adventure graphic novels; 2. Superhero graphic novels; 3. Superman (Fictional character); 4. Graphic novels
1-4012-0840-1, $12.99

Eclipso, the original spirit of vengeance, needs a new human host. The Spectre, the current spirit of vengeance, has just lost its human host and is vulnerable. When Eclipso seeks a new body, it first tries to control Superman; it takes Captain Marvel, the World's Mightiest Marvel, to stop him. Inhabiting the body of a familiar, tortured soul, Eclipso sets its sights on seducing the Spectre and destroying Earth's practitioners of magic. Seven heroes stand in their way. All very different. All with different goals at stake. And then they find an eighth, a girl who might be the most powerful teenager in the universe. Can this group, who call themselves Shadowpact, stop the angry spirits of vengeance?

Fables Vol 8: Wolves. Art by Mark Buckingham and Shawn McManus. DC Comics/Vertigo 2006 160p. Illustration
Grades: 10 11 12 Adult   **741.5; Fic**
  1. Adventure graphic novels; 2. Fantasy graphic novels; 3. Graphic novels
978-1-4012-1001-4, $17.99

Fabletown's ex-sheriff Bigby Wolf and ex-deputy mayor (and power behind King Cole's former mayoral throne) Snow White finally tie the knot in this arc from the series about the fairy-tale characters who walk among us (or, at least, New Yorkers). That can't happen before Mowgli finds missing, moping Bigby and the latter undertakes a reprisal mission against the Adversary. This eighth volume includes some violence, strong language, and nudity.

Fables Vol. 15: Rose Red. Bill Willingham, writer; Lan Medina, penciller; Steve Leialoha, Craig Hamilton, inkers; Sherilyn van Valkenburgh, colorist; Todd Klein, letterer.. Vertigo 2011 184p Color illustration
Grades: Adult   **741.5**
  1. Folklore; 2. Magic — Fiction; 3. Graphic novels
9781401230005
           LC 2004540381

In this graphic novel, "[t]he next volume in the New York Times best-selling series [written by Mark

Buckingham and William Willingham], . . . Rose Red, sister of Snow White, has finally hit rock bottom. Will she stay there, or is it time to start the long, tortuous climb back up" The Farm is in chaos, as many factions compete to fill the void of her missing leadership. And there's a big magical fight brewing down in the town square." (Publisher's note)

★ **Fables** Vol. 1: Legends in Exile. Art by Lan Medina. DC Comics/Vertigo 2002 128p. Illustration
Grades: 10 11 12 Adult   **Fic; 741.5**
1. Fantasy graphic novels; 2. Mystery graphic novels; 3. Graphic novels
1-56389-942-6, $9.99; 9781401237554
In Fabletown, where fairy tale legends live alongside regular New Yorkers, the question on everyone's mind is who killed Rose Red? But only the Big Bad Wolf can actually solve the case (since he's the Fabletown sheriff) - and, along with Rose's sister Snow White, keep the Fabletown community from coming apart at the seams. The book includes strong language, violence, nudity, and sexual situations.
Also available in deluxe hardcover editions
Volume 1 of a 22 volume series

Fables Vol. 2: Animal Farm. Written by Bill Willingham; art by Mark Buckingham. DC Comics/Vertigo 2003 128p. Illustration
Grades: 10 11 12 Adult   **741.5; Fic**
1. Fantasy graphic novels; 2. Graphic novels
1-4012-0077-X, $12.95
In upstate New York, the non-human Fable characters have lived for centuries on a farm, miles from mankind. But all is not well on the farm - and a conspiracy to free them from the shackles of their perceived imprisonment may lead to a war that could wrest control of the Fables community away from Snow White. Goldilocks and the Three Little Pigs inflame the farm's inhabitants with fiery revolutionary rhetoric, and both Snow White and her sister Rose Red face threats to their lives. The book includes violence and some strong language.

Fables Vol. 3: Storybook Love. Written by Bill Willingham; art by Mark Buckingham. DC Comics/Vertigo 2004 190p. Illustration
Grades: 10 11 12 Adult   **741.5; Fic**
1. Fantasy graphic novels; 2. Graphic novels
1-4012-0256-X, $14.99
In the Fables' world, there isn't a lot of happily-ever-after to go around. As refugees from the lands of make-believe, the Fables have been driven from their storybook realms and forced to blend into the mundane world. But that doesn't mean they don't have any room for romance, or the pain, betrayal, and jealous rage that go along with it. In fact, love may be blooming between two of the most hard-bitten, no-nonsense Fables around - Snow White and Bigby Wolf. Meanwhile, Bigby teams up with several other Fables to stop a reporter from publishing a story that exposes the Fables and the lives they've built in New York. The book includes violence.

Fables Vol. 5: The Mean Seasons. Written by Bill Willingham; art by Mark Buckingham. DC Comics/Vertigo 2005 168p. Illustration
Grades: 11 12 Adult   **741.5; Fic**

1. Adventure graphic novels; 2. Fantasy graphic novels; 3. Graphic novels
1-4012-0486-4, $14.99
With the Battle of Fabletown won, and the surrounding city of New York none the wiser, the Fables have gained a little time for rebuilding and reflection, in between the interrogation of the Adversary's agent and the anticipation of Snow White's impending motherhood. For Bigby Wolf, the father of the soon-to-be newborns, that means a visit with an old friend, and a reminiscence of another, even deadlier war. For the new Mayor of Fabletown, Prince Charming, it means a rude awakening to the harsh realities of civic administration, and its conflicting demands. And for Snow herself, it means a long, painful labor, and a series of joyful, heart wrenching surprises. The book includes some violence, brief sexual situations, and strong language.

Fables Vol. 6: Homelands. Written by Bill Willingham; art by Mark Buckingham. DC Comics/Vertigo 2005 192p. Illustration
Grades: 10 11 12 Adult   **741.5; Fic**
1. Adventure graphic novels; 2. Fantasy graphic novels; 3. Graphic novels
1-4012-0500-3, $14.99
The Fables have beaten back the Adversary's first advance into their world, but now they must prepare themselves for the war that is sure to follow. Jack decides to skip town and heads for Hollywood, where he becomes a sleazy movie mogul. Boy Blue appropriates some weapons and heads back to the Homelands, killing enemies as he makes his way to the heart of enemy territory. The story features some nudity and sexual situations, some strong language, and considerable violence.

Fables: Arabian Nights (And Days). Written by Bill Willingham; art by Mark Buckingham. DC Comics/Vertigo 2006 Un Illustration
Grades: 10 11 12 Adult   **741.5; Fic**
1. Fantasy graphic novels; 2. Graphic novels
978-1-4012-1000-7, $14.99
Now that the Adversary's identity has been revealed, it's time to begin making preparations in earnest for the defense of the Fabletown stronghold. That means forging new alliances with whoever remains unconquered by the Adversary's legions. But the arrival in Fabletown of a delegation from the Arabian Homelands shows just how tricky this kind of coalition-building can be ... especially when one side is concealing Weapons of Magical Destruction. This volume includes some strong language and violence.

Robin/Batgirl: Fresh Blood. DC Comics 2005 Un Illustration
Grades: 9 10 11 12 Adult   **741.5; Fic**
1. Batgirl (Fictional character); 2. Nightwing (Fictional character); 3. Robin (Fictional character); 4. Superhero graphic novels; 5. Graphic novels
1-4012-0433-3, $12.99
After the traumatic events of Batman: War Games, two of Gotham's youngest heroes, Robin and Batgirl, relocate to Bludhaven, where they must pick up the pieces of their lives and start anew. But before they can get fully settled in, they discover they have new threats to face, including Nightwing's enemy Shrike and their old friend the Penguin.

In order to save the day, the two heroes realize there's only one thing they can do: battle each other to the death.

Robin: Days of Fire and Madness. Bill Willingham, writer; Scott McDaniel, penciller; Andy Owens, inkers; Guy Major, colorist; Phil Balsam, letterer. DC Comics 2006 144p. Illustration
Grades: 9 10 11 12 Adult   **741.5; Fic**
1. Mystery graphic novels; 2. Robin (Fictional character); 3. Superhero graphic novels; 4. Graphic novels
978-1-4012-0911-7, $14.99

Recruited into a covert military team by the mysterious and powerful man known only as the Veteran, Robin realizes that he has entered an entirely new world of danger when his first assignment takes him to the Middle East where he and his new teammates engage an enemy of unimaginable horror, flesh-eating demons. Back home, the battle continues as the Teen Wonder comes face to face with the inexplicable resurrection of his former girlfriend - determined to kill Robin in order to stay with Tim Drake forever - even as the city of Bludhaven suffers an attack by the supremely powerful, supremely deadly OMACs. Can the mystical superheroes of Shadowpact save Robin and his newfound allies? Or will this be his final battle? Lots of superhero fighting and demon fighting.

Robin: To Kill a Bird. Bill Willingham, writer; Damion Scott, Giusseppe Camuncoli, Scott McDaniel, Pop Mhan, pencillers; Sandra Hope, Damion Scott, Andy Owens, inkers; Guy Major, colorist; Phil Balsam, Jared K. Fletcher, Rob Leigh, letterers. DC Comics 2006 Un Illustration
Grades: 8 9 10 11 12 Adult   **741.5; Fic**
1. Robin (Fictional character); 2. Superhero graphic novels; 3. Graphic novels
978-1-4012-0909-4, $14.99

It's a brand-new start for Batman's sidekick, Robin: a new town (Bludhaven), a new school, new adventures and new problems.Before our hero can fully recover from the recent deaths of his father and girlfriend Spoiler, he must come face to face with his enemies: the Penguin, the Dark Rider, the Veteran, and a mysterious archer who seems to want the Boy Wonder dead. There's lots of superhero fighting action.

The **Sandman** Presents: Thessaly, Witch for Hire. Written by Bill Willingham; illustrated by Shawn McManus; colored by Pamela Rambo. DC Comics/Vertigo 2005 96p. Illustration
Grades: 10 11 12 Adult   **741.5; Fic**
1. Supernatural graphic novels; 2. Witches; 3. Graphic novels
1-4012-0497-X, $12.99

She's the world's oldest and most powerful witch, but nothing has prepared Thessaly for the persistence of lovesick ghost Fetch, or the conniving, underhanded lengths he'll go to in order to win her heart. It's bad enough he attached her name to a monster-slaying business card, but now he's agreed to take on the universe's ultimate destructive force, and that's just plain stupid. Faced with this kind of courtship, it'll be a miracle if Thessaly can survive long enough to smack some sense into Fetch's intangible head ... never mind stopping the unstoppable doom he's unleashed. There's some nudity and some strong language, and lots of monster-killing violence.

Shadowpact: The Pentacle Plot. Written by Bill Willingham; art by Bill Willingham, Cory Walker, Steve Scott, Tom Derenick, Shawn McManus. DC Comics 2007 168p. Illustration
Grades: 9 10 11 12 Adult   **741.5; Fic**
1. Mystery graphic novels; 2. Superhero graphic novels; 3. Supernatural graphic novels; 4. Graphic novels
978-1-4012-1230-8, $14.99

Nightmaster, Ragman, Nightshade, Blue Devil, Enchantress, and Detective Chimp are Shadowpact, magical heroes who explore the darkest corners of the DC Universe, fighting the mystical villains that other heroes can't, or won't. In this volume, they must content with their evil counterparts known as the Pentacle, and deal with the fact that they've lost a whole year in their lives. There's supernatural monster fighting and some incidental partial nudity.

Teen Titans Vol. 5: Life and Death. Geoff Johns, Bill Willingham, Tony S. Daniel, Scott McDaniel. DC Comics 2006 210p. Illustration
Grades: 10 11 12 Adult   **741.5; Fic**
1. Robin (Fictional character); 2. Superhero graphic novels; 3. Teen Titans (Fictional characters); 4. Graphic novels
978-1-4012-0978-0, $14.99

The line between life and death is crossed as the Teen Titans must confront the deceased members of the team that have seemingly returned from the dead. As Donna Troy recruits the mightiest members of the team to battle in the Infinite Crisis, Robin is confronted by his predecessor, the bygone Boy Wonder, Jason Todd. The remaining Titans face the onslaught of Brother Blood and his army of followers which include the deceased Titans Aquagirl, Omen, Hawk, and Dove. As the Crisis hits, Superboy teams up with all of the reserve members of the team to battle his evil counterpart from another dimension. There is considerable violence in the personal battles.

Wilson, G. Willow

★ **Air**, vol. 1: letters from lost countries. G. Willow Wilson, writer; M.K. Perker, artist; Chris Chuckry, colorist; Jared K. Fletcher, letterer. DC Comics/Vertigo 2009 144p. Illustration
Grades: 11 12 Adult   **741.5; Fic**
1. Adventure graphic novels; 2. Fantasy graphic novels; 3. Graphic novels
978-1-4012-2153-9, $9.99

Blythe works as a stewardess on Clearfleet Airlines, an odd choice of career for someone suffering from acrophobia, but that's what she does. As she works on various flights, she keeps encountering a man who changes his appearance and name every time she sees him; she suspects he could be a terrorist, but he never actually does anything. Then one day a man approaches her on a flight to Amsterdam and tells her he's part of a group called the Etesians, and they fight terrorists. One of the Etesians asks Blythe to deliver a briefcase, but when the fellow with the ever-changing identity tells her to check inside, she finds plans to hijack one of the Clearfleet jets. This gets her into bad trouble, and things start to get very weird. Zayn finally tells her his real name when they start a sexual relationship, then one day after he's been gone on an assignment for too long, he sends Blythe a letter from a country that doesn't exist. Or does it" Along the way, Blythe starts to figure out that things aren't quite normal at the airline, and the Etesians are really bad people. The book includes some violence, including scenes of torture (that really aren't too graphic), some sexual situations, and the occasional s-bomb and f-bomb.

★ **Cairo.** Written by G. Willow Wilson; art by M.K. Perker; lettered by Travis Lanham. DC Comics/Vertigo 2007 160p. Illustration
Grades: 9 10 11 12 Adult   **741.5; Fic**
   1. Adventure graphic novels; 2. Fantasy graphic novels; 3. Graphic novels
   978-1-4012-1140-0, $24.99
   A stolen hookah, a spiritual underworld, and a genie on the run change the lives of five strangers in Cairo. A drug runner, a down-on-his-luck journalist, an American expatriate, a troubled young student, and a female Israeli soldier end up all working together to help the jinn that Lebanese American Shaheed calls Shams to recover a special box from the evil magic-wielding drug lord Nar. The book includes some violence.
   "Scripting and art complement each other well in an adventure with lots of appeal for readers willing to try a literary graphic novel and for those simply looking for the next good one." Booklist

★ **Ms.** Marvel 1: No Normal. Writer, G. Willow Wilson; artist, Adrian Alphona. Marvel Enterprises 2014 120 p. Color; Illustration
Grades: 9 10 11 12 Adult   **741.5**
   1. Female superhero comic books, strips, etc; 2. Muslim women — Fiction
   078519021X; 9780785190219, $15.99
   Hugo Award: Best Graphic Story (2015)
   In this comic, written by G. Willow Wilson and illustrated by Adrian Alphona, "Kamala Khan is an ordinary girl from Jersey City—until she is suddenly empowered with extraordinary gifts. But who truly is the all-new Ms. Marvel? Teenager? Muslim? Inhuman? Find out as . . . Kamala discovers the dangers of her newfound powers [and] she unlocks a secret behind them as well." (Publisher's note)
   "Wilson's story touches on many issues bubbling up around comics today—diversity, gender, culture, sexuality—though never with a heavy hand. The story is the focus here, and together with Alphona's playful and stylish artwork, Wilson offers a superhero comic full to bursting with heart and charm." Booklist
   Contains material originally published in magazine form as Ms. Marvel #1-5 and All-new Marvel now! point one #1—Title page

Ms. Marvel 2: Generation Why. By G. Willow Wilson; illustrated by Jacob Wyatt and Adrian Alphona. Marvel Enterprises 2015 136 p. Color; Illustration
Grades: 9 10 11 12 Adult   **741.5**
   1. Female superhero comic books, strips, etc; 2. Muslim women — Fiction; 3. Pakistani Americans — Fiction; 4. Teenage girls — Fiction; 5. Wolverine (Fictional character); 6. Women superheroes
   0785190228; 9780785190226, $15.99

"Who is the Inventor, and what does he want with the all-new Ms. Marvel and all her friends" Maybe Wolverine can help! Kamala may be fan-girling out when her favorite (okay maybe Top Five) super hero shows up, but that won't stop her from protecting her hometown." (Publisher's note)
   "Alphona's distinctive panels make great use of exaggerated angles and distorted figures, and his line work, more intricate than most comic-book artists', packs each page with captivating, tongue-in-cheek detail." Booklist
   Contains material originally published in magazine form as Ms. Marvel #6-11—Title page verso.

Ms. Marvel: Crushed. G. Willow Wilson; illustrated by Takeshi Miyazawa and Elmo Bondoc. Marvel Enterprises 2015 112 p. Color; Illustration
Grades: 9 10 11 12 Adult   **741.5**
   1. Female superhero graphic novels; 2. Pakistani Americans; 3. Superhero comic books, strips, etc; 4. Teenage girls; 5. Valentine's Day
   0785192271; 9780785192275, $15.99
   In this graphic novel by G. Willow Wilson, illustrated by Takeshi Miyazawa and Elmo Bondoc, "Love is in the air in Jersey City as Valentine's Day arrives! Kamala Khan may not be allowed to go to the school dance...but Ms. Marvel is! Well sort of - by crashing it attempting to capture Asgard's most annoying trickster! Yup, it's a special Valentine's Day story featuring Marvel's favorite charlatan, Loki!" (Publisher's note)
   "As always, Wilson's rollicking superhero action is sprinkled with both hilarity and meaningful cultural commentary, and Kamala herself is as appealing as ever." Booklist
   Contains material originally published in magazine form as Ms. Marvel #12-15 and S.H.I.E.L.D #2.

Wilson, Sean Michael
   The **book** of five rings: a graphic novel. From the book by Miyamoto Musashi; based on the translation by William Scott Wilson; adapted by Sean Michael Wilson; illustrated by Chie Kutsuwada; with an afterword by William Scott Wilson.. Shambhala 2012 160 p. Illustration
Grades: Adult   **355.5\47; 355.5**
   1. Martial arts; 2. Military art and science; 3. Military art and science — Early works to 1800; 4. Swordplay — Japan — Early works to 1800; 5. Graphic novels
   1611800129; 9781611800128, $14.95
                                      LC 2012023362
   This "graphic adaptation of [Miyamoto] Musashi's 17th-century treatise on the martial arts makes . . . use of imagery to emphasize both the narrative and instructional aspects of the original text. Musashi's work is divided into five books, which address each aspect of battle: 'Earth,' 'Fire,' 'Water,' 'Wind,' and 'Emptiness.' That structure is retained here." (Publishers Weekly)

A **Christmas** Carol: The graphic novel original text by Charles Dickens. Illustrated by Mike Collins. Classical Comics 2008 144p. Illustration
Grades: 6 7 8 9 10 11 12 Adult   **741.5; Fic**
   1. Christmas; 2. Dickens, Charles, 1812-1870 — Adaptations; 3. Ghosts; 4. Graphic novels
   978-1-906332-51-8, $16.95

Miserly Ebenezer Scrooge has pronounced "Bah, humbug!" against Christmas, but on this Christmas Eve night, the ghost of his dead partner Jacob Marley visits him and proclaims his only hope to escape Marley's fate is to endure the visits of the Ghosts of Christmas Past, Present, and Future. Scrooge sees his past as a hopeful young man who slowly becomes bitter and obsessed with money as a means to avoid poverty, sees how his relatives and employees view him in the present, and how his future death is a matter of joy. This graphic adaptation uses dialog and narration taken directly from Dickens' novel. Back matter includes a short biography of Dickens, a description of a typical Victorian period Christmas celebration, a description of the harsh poverty in London of the mid-nineteenth century, and more.

Also available quick text version $16.95 (ISBN: 978-1906332-52-5)

Parecomic: the story of Michael Albert and participatory economics. Sean Michael Wilson and Carl Thompson; introduction by Noam Chomsky. Seven Stories Press 2013 224 p.
Grades: Adult   **330.1**
    1. Albert, Michael, 1947-; 2. Capitalism; 3. Cooperation; 4. Distributive justice; 5. Economic policy — Citizen participation; 6. Economics; 7. Political activists — United States; 8. Graphic novels
    1609804562; 9781609804565, $18.95
                                             LC 2013001624
    This graphic novel by Sean Michael Wilson and illustrated by Carl Thompson is "about the system we live in—what's wrong with it, and how we might be able change it for the better. The recent upsurge in popular protest around the world shows that people are not happy with the state of capitalism. [It] is about Michael Albert—the visionary behind participatory economics—and his life's struggle as a left-wing activist in the US." (Publisher's note)

Winget, Larry
    Shut up, stop whining and get a life: a kick-butt approach to a better life. Larry Winget; illustrated by Shane Clester; adapted by Cullen Bunn. Smarter Comics 2011 80p. Illustration
Grades: 10 11 12 Adult
646.7; 741.5
    1. Self-help techniques; 2. Self-improvement; 3. Graphic novels
    978-1-61066-002-0, $12.95
    Larry   Winget's bestselling self-help book is now   a   graphic   novel. Self-described   "Pitbull of Personal   Development" Winget's approach takes aim at the usual advice found in most self-help books; he says that people need to take responsibility for their own lives, acknowledge their

Courtesy of Smarter Comics

mistakes, learn from them, and change what they need to change in order to achieve their goals, whatever they may be. Even if one doesn't agree with everything he says, his approach is refreshing and full of common sense advice. Comics writer Bunn adapts Winget's prose, and comics illustrator Clester uses a lot of humor in the art to make Winget's points. Older teens and college students may discover that this book can truly help them.

Winick, Judd
    Batman: Harley and Ivy. Writers, Paul Dini and Judd Winick; Art by Ronnie Del Carmen, Joe Chiodo, Bruce Timm, Shane Glines. DC Comics 2007 136p. Illustration
Grades: 10 11 12 Adult   **741.5; Fic**
    1. Batman (Fictional character); 2. Humorous graphic novels; 3. Superhero graphic novels; 4. Graphic novels
    978-1-4012-1333-6, $14.99
    The sexy, madcap super-villain duo of Harley Quinn and Poison Ivy plan to take down Batman once and for all in this volume that collects the miniseries Batman: Harley and Ivy, written and drawn by Paul Dini and Bruce Timm, who created Batman: The Animated Series. The book also includes Harley and Ivy: Love on the Lam, written by Judd Winick and painted by Joe Chiodo, and "The Bet," a newly colored short story. Partial nudity and some suggestive scenes occur throughout the stories.

    Batman: Under the Hood. Judd Winick, writer; Doug Mahnke, Paul Lee, pencillers; Tom Nguye, Cam Smith, inkers; Alex Sinclair, colorist. DC Comics 2005 Un Illustration
Grades: 10 11 12 Adult   **741.5; Fic**
    1. Batman (Fictional character); 2. Superhero graphic novels; 3. Graphic novels
    1-4012-0756-1, $9.99
    While battling new criminal chieftains brought in by new Gotham crime boss Black Mask, Batman is confronted with a hidden face from the past. The Red Hood seems to be fighting the Black Mask for territory, but who is wearing the mask, and what will he do to Batman" Revelations from the past start to haunt the Dark Knight. This book contains quite a bit of violent fighting action.

    Batman: Under the Hood Volume Two. Judd Winick, writer; Doug Mahnke, Shane Davis, Eric Battle, pencillers; Tom Nguyen [and others], inkers; Alex Sinclair, colorist; Pat Brosseau, Jarek K. Fletcher, Travis Lanham, letterers. DC Comics 2006 Un Illustration
Grades: 10 11 12 Adult   **Fic; 741.5**
    1. Batman (Fictional character); 2. Joker (Fictional character); 3. Robin (Fictional character); 4. Superhero graphic novels; 5. Graphic novels
    978-1-4012-0901-8, $9.99
    The Red Hood has been unmasked, and it's ... Jason Todd. Who was once Robin, successor to Dick Grayson, and killed by the Joker. He's changed, he wants revenge against the Joker, he wants power, he's angry at Batman. As the Red Hood, he's been taking over Black Mask's territory, and there will be a showdown. This book contains lots of violent fighting action.

    ★ The **big** book of Barry Ween, boy genius. Oni Press 2009 368p. Illustration
Grades: 10 11 12 Adult   **741.5; Fic**

1. Adventure graphic novels; 2. Humorous graphic novels; 3. Science fiction graphic novels; 4. Graphic novels

978-1-934964-02-6, $19.95

This volume collects all the Barry Ween comics published previously in three miniseries and then trade paperbacks, plus it includes a full-color one-shot story called "Barry Ween Ween Out Color Special." This last story, co-written with Greg Rucka, puts Barry into Antarctica U.S. Marshal Carrie Stetko's territory; Barry and best friend Jeremy blast into Antarctica instead of the movie theater, and Barry's terraforming procedure to keep them from freezing to death has gone way out of control, creating a tropical jungle environment that will keep growing unless Barry can stop it. Barry Ween is a ten-year-old super genius with an extremely foul mouth, his best friend Jeremy is a doofus who obsesses about sexual matters (a typical comment: "Will you look at the triceratops. Big lizard, tiny penis. No wonder they're extinct."). The stories include some violence, lots of f-bombs and s-bombs and other foul language, lots of sexual inferences and innuendo, and lots of hilarity. Teens who can handle the language and violence will enjoy this. The first trade paperback: The Adventures of Barry Ween, Boy Genius, was included in the 2002 YALSA Popular Paperbacks list, Graphic Novels: Superheroes and Beyond.

Green Arrow: Crawling Through the Wreckage. Judd Winick, writer; Scott McDaniel, penciller; Andy Owens, inker; Guy Major, colorist; Pat Brosseau, letterer. DC Comics 2007 144p. Illustration

Grades: 9 10 11 12 Adult   741.5; Fic

1. Green Arrow (Fictional character); 2. Superhero graphic novels; 3. Graphic novels

978-1-4012-1232-2, $12.99

After the Infinite Crisis has left Star City devastated and without resources, Oliver Queen - the Green Arrow - takes steps to save his home town ... by becoming the Mayor. The problem is that politics, executive powers, and his explosive arrows can't fix what's wrong with Star City. Someone is importing tainted drugs and causing the addicts to turn into mindless killers, corporate raiders want to take over the city and turn it into glitzy casinos and unaffordable housing, and on top of it all, someone has hired the world's deadliest assassin - Deathstroke - to kill Queen. The Mayor's plans include performing gay marriages, in order to attract people to come to Star City and spend money in its hotels and restaurants, and Green Arrow teams up with a former crime kingpin turned superhero to try to keep the ghettos safer until he can bring the walls down. There's some harsh language and lots of fighting.

Green Arrow: Straight Shooter. Judd Winick, writer; Phil Hester, penciller; Ande Parks, inker; Guy Major, colorist; Sean Konot, letterer. DC Comics 2004 144p. Illustration

Grades: 9 10 11 12 Adult   741.5; Fic

1. Green Arrow (Fictional characters); 2. Superhero graphic novels; 3. Graphic novels

1-4012-0200-4, $12.95

LC 2004-301698

When Green Arrow discovers corporate corruption in Star City, he goes after those responsible. The last thing he expects is a fight with a 3-ton ogre. And more than one of them. As he delves into this mystery, he also falls into an unexpected romance, with tragic results. The book includes violence, some strong language, and brief sexual situations.

Outsiders Volume 5: The Good Fight. Judd Winick, writer; Matthew Clark [and others], pencillers. DC Comics 2007 192p. Illustration

Grades: 9 10 11 12 Adult   741.5; Fic

1. Outsiders (Fictional characters); 2. Superhero graphic novels; 3. Graphic novels

978-1-4012-1195-0, $14.99

The Outsiders have been thought dead for months. Then, deep undercover in the African country of Mali, trying to save innocent lives and stop a civil war, they are discovered. With a new team consisting of members from teams past and one former super-villain, the team finds itself at odds with an entire nation, not to mention the super-hero community. Also, the Outsiders try to thwart the Brotherhood of Evil's plot to sell metahumans to the underworld.

Outsiders: Crisis Intervention. Judd Winick, Jen Van Meter, writers; Matthew Clark, Dietrich Smith, pencillers; Art Thibert, Steve Bird, inkers. DC Comics 2006 128p. Illustration

Grades: 9 10 11 12 Adult   741.5; Fic

1. Outsiders (Fictional characters); 2. Superhero graphic novels; 3. Graphic novels

1-4012-0973-4, $12.99

The Outsiders are left reeling after the revelation of one of their members' ultimate betrayal. Before they can pick up the pieces, they must face a rematch with the Fearsome Five and Sabbac, who now has the power of the Seven Deadly Sins. Plus, with Infinite Crisis looming, Donna Troy recruits half the team, along with other heroes, for an important mission in space, while the rest must contend with the villainous Secret Society.

Outsiders: Wanted. Judd Winick, writer; Tom Raney, ChrisCross, Ivan Reis, pencillers; Scott Hanna, Sean Parsons, Marc Campos, inkers; Gina Going, Sno-Cone, colorists; John Workman, Comicraft, Nick Napolitano, letterers; Tom Raney & Scott Hanna, Michael Golden, original series covers. DC Comics 2005 Un Illustration

Grades: 9 10 11 12 Adult   741.5; Fic

1. Outsiders (Fictional characters); 2. Superhero graphic novels; 3. Graphic novels

1-4012-0460-0, $14.99

In this third volume, the team works with John Walsh to take down a child abduction ring that had once had Grace before her powers kicked in. Then they find out just who has been funding the team, and the knowledge has Nightwing steamed. Things get worse when Roy, who thought he'd been getting intel for the Outsiders from Batman, discovers who really was doing it. Just as the team was starting to gel, the Outsiders become a team in crisis. The book includes strong language and violence, and alien sexual situations.

Superman/Shazam/First Thunder. Judd Winick, writer ; Joshua Middleton, artist ; Nick J. Napolitano, letterer. DC Comics 2006 128p. Illustration

Grades: 8 9 10 11 12 Adult   741.5; Fic

1. Shazam (Fictional character); 2. Superhero graphic novels; 3. Superman (Fictional character); 4. Graphic novels

978-1-4012-0923-0, $12.99

With one word, young orphan Billy Batson transforms into a man imbued with the powers of the gods, but even one gifted with the Wisdom of Solomon can learn from a Superman. While Superman must stop members of a cult from stealing ancient artifacts from the Metropolis Natural History Museum, Billy must battle giant robots rampaging through Fawcett City. These separate events lead the heroes to cross paths, and a mighty friendship is formed as Earth's most powerful defenders team up to stop such menaces as Lex Luthor, Dr. Sivana, Eclipso, and the monstrous Lord Sabbac. There's some violence, and the climax is heartbreaking.

The **Trials** of Shazam! Volume One. Judd Winick, writer; Howard Porter, artist; Rob Leigh, letterer. DC Comics 2007 Un Illustration
Grades: 9 10 11 12 Adult　　　　　　**741.5; Fic**
1. Captain Marvel (Fictional character); 2. Fantasy graphic novels; 3. Superhero graphic novels; 4. Graphic novels
978-1-4012-1331-2, $14.99

Given powers by an ancient and mysterious wizard, boy reporter Billy Batson need only say the word "Shazam!" and he is transformed into the powerful adult hero Captain Marvel. Magical turmoil in the aftermath of INFINITE CRISIS force Captain Marvel to give up his role as Earth's Mightiest Mortal to keep the supernatural under control. Freddie Freeman, also known as Captain Marvel Jr., has been left powerless by these events, but is given the opportunity to take over the mantle of his mentor if he can pass tests administered by the gods themselves. The only catch is that he has to earn each of his super-abilities from scratch.

Winshluss
Pinocchio. Winshluss; colored by Cizo, assisted by Frederic Boniaud, Thomas Bernard, Frederic Felder. Last Gasp 2011 187p Color illustration
Grades: Adult　　　　　　**741.5**
1. Pinocchio (Fictional character); 2. Robots; 3. Graphic novels
9780867197518; 9780861661725, $23.95

This "graphic novel, translated from the French, . . . begins with a shooting, and then flashes back to Pinocchio's creation (he is now a robot-like android) and adventures. Collodi's original story is also darker than Disney's version. [Author] Winshluss [whose name is Vincent Paronnaud] has injected politics into his story which also played a part in Collodi's original. Monstro the whale is replaced by a toxic, giant mutated fish, and there's even a subplot of a hard-boiled detective woven in. . . . Pinocchio was awarded the Fauve d'Or at the Festival International de la Bande Dessine in Angoulme 2009 and best foreign comic book in Germany 2010." (Publisher's note)

Wisna, Chris
Doris Danger, volume one: Giant monster adventures. SLG Publishing 2009 96p. Illustration
Grades: 8 9 10 11 12 Adult　　　　　　**741.5; Fic**
1. Humorous graphic novels; 2. Monsters; 3. Graphic novels

978-1-59362-180-3, $9.95

Intrepid ace photo-journalist Doris Danger seeks out the truth about giant alien monsters, and her quest takes her to isolated islands, jungles in Africa, rural Kansas, the Niagara Falls, and many other places where mysterious military officials cover up the existence of creatures such as Splazoo, Kockh, and Spoosh. Also, everywhere she goes in search of the giant alien monsters, the Monster Liberation Army shows up. The book reads like a collection of stories from a magazine, and Wisna's black and white art resembles the old Jack Kirby monster comics of the 1950s and 1960s.

Wolfman, Marv
★ **Crisis** on infinite earths. Marv Wolfman, writer; George Perez, penciller; Dick Giordano, Mike DeCarlo, Jerry Ordway, inkers; John Costanza, letterer; original covers by George Perez. DC Comics 2015 364 p. Color; Illustration
Grades: Adult　　　　　　**741.5**
1. Science fiction comic books, strips, etc; 2. Superheroes — Fiction; 3. Time — Fiction
1401258417; 9781401258412, $49.99; 9781563897504
　　　　　　　　　　　　　　LC 2012032625

This comic book, by Marv Wolfman, illustrated by George Perez, "is the story that changed the DC Universe forever. A mysterious being known as the Anti-Monitor has begun a crusade across time to bring about the end of all existence. As alternate earths are systematically destroyed, the Monitor quickly assembles a team of super-heroes from across time and space to battle his counterpart and stop the destruction." (Publisher's note)

Originally published in single magazine form as Crisis on Infinite Earths 1-12.

Homeland: The Illustrated History of the State of Israel. Marv Wolfman, writer; Mario Ruiz, illustrator and graphic designer; William J. Rubin, executive editor. Nachschon Press 2007 124p. Illustration
Grades: 9 10 11 12 Adult　　**305.892; 741.5; 956.94**
1. Israel — History; 2. Israelis; 3. Jews; 4. Palestine; 5. Graphic novels
978-0-9771507-0-0, $19.95

Using the conceit that a university professor is teaching a class, this book covers about 4,000 years of history in the Middle East, focused on Israel. It goes back to the Biblical narrative of Abram's journey from Mesopotamia, quickly progresses to the Middle Ages, explains the complicated circumstances surrounding the Zionist movement and efforts to establish the modern state of Israel, and covers the recent situations there. Readers may not be so familiar with the history of Israel and the Jews beyond the Old Testament narratives, the World War II Holocaust, and the current struggles. This book gives a concise explanation of the history which is valuable whether or not one supports Israel today.

The **New** Teen Titans: Terra Incognito. Marv Wolfman, writer ; George Pérez, penciller ; Romeo Tanghal, Pablo Markos, inkers ; Adrienne Roy, colorist. DC Comics 2006 224p. Illustration
Grades: 7 8 9 10 11 12 Adult　　　　　　**741.5; Fic**

1. Robin (Fictional character); 2. Superhero graphic novels; 3. Teen Titans (Fictional characters); 4. Graphic novels
978-1-4012-0972-8, $19.99

Tara Markov, the troubled teen princess of Markovia, is rescued from kidnappers by the Titans' green-skinned adventurer, Changeling. Thus begins her quest to use her powers over earth and gravity in the cause of justice. Does this obnoxious young powerhouse have what it takes to join the team? This is the original Teen Titans team, in which Dick Grayson is still Robin.

Wonder Woman Vol. 4: Destiny Calling. DC Comics 2006 176p. Illustration
Grades: 8 9 10 11 12 Adult   **741.5; Fic**
1. Superhero graphic novels; 2. Wonder Woman (Fictional character); 3. Graphic novels
978-1-4012-0943-8, $19.99

It's only been a short time since Diana, dubbed Wonder Woman by the media, came to Man's World with a message of peace, only to face countless foes and stop the advancement of a third world war. Now Diana must face her greatest challenge yet: a god among men. The Olympian god Hermes has decided to grace mankind with his presence, but along with him comes a world of new troubles for the Amazon. This volume reprints stories originally published in the 1980s, when Perez re-launched Wonder Woman.

Wolk, Douglas
★ **Reading** comics: how graphic novels work and what they mean. Da Capo Press 2007 405p. Illustration
Grades: Adult Professional   **741.5**
1. Graphic novels — History and criticism
978-0-306-81509-6; 0-306-81509-5
                                    LC 2007-05232
Suddenly, comics are everywhere: a newly matured art form, filling bookshelves with brilliant, innovative work and shaping the ideas and images of the rest of contemporary culture. In Reading Comics, critic Douglas Wolk shows us why this is and how it came to be. Wolk illuminates the most dazzling creators of modern comics—from Alan Moore to Alison Bechdel to Dave Sim to Chris Ware—and introduces a critical theory that explains where each fits into the pantheon of art. The book is accessible to the hardcore fan and the curious newcomer; it is the first book for people who want to know not just what comics are worth reading, but also the ways to think and talk and argue about them.

Wong, Tony
The **Four** Constables Vol. 1. Director, Tony Wong ; illustrator, Andy Seto ; original story, Rui-An Wen ; translator, Yun Zhao. ComicsOne/DrMaster Publications 2004 Un Illustration
Grades: 8 9 10 11 12 Adult   **Fic; 741.5**
1. Adventure graphic novels; 2. Martial arts; 3. Mystery graphic novels; 4. Graphic novels
1-58899-383-3, $13.95

Four of China's supremely skilled assassin/detectives serve only their Master Zhuge Zhen-Wo - The Little Flower, who in turn is head bodyguard and advisor for China's all powerful Emperor. . Yayu Sheng, "Emotionless," is a master of weapons and devices. Yuxia Tie, "Iron Hands," possesses

incredible chi and can stop the sharpest blades bare-handed. Lieshan Cui, "Life Snatcher," is highly skilled in light-foot, granting him undaunted legwork and kicks. Lingqi Len, "Cold Blooded," was raised by wolves and since learned to transfer his pain when fighting to strength, enabling him to defeat opponents much stronger than himself. Each of them is entrusted by the Emperor with the power to arrest and execute any corrupt officials or lawless criminals with the Chinese Empire. These Imperial Constables act as protectors. With their venerable skill they root out potential usurpers and discern the cause of many strange occurrences happening during the Sung Dynasty. This is a Chinese manhua series, published in full color and filled with martial arts action.
Volume 1 of 5

Wood, Brian
Channel zero: the complete collection. Brian Wood. Dark Horse Books 2012 295 p.
Grades: Adult   **741**
1. Dystopian graphic novels; 2. Manga; 3. Science fiction
1595829369; 9781595829368, $19.99

This graphic novel, by Brian Wood, illustrated by Becky Cloonan, collects the 1997 Channel Zero comic book series "that combined art, politics, and graphic design. . . . Hitting on themes of freedom of expression, hacking, cutting-edge media manipulation, and police surveillance, . . . [t]he Channel Zero collection contains the original series, the prequel graphic novel Jennie One . . . and almost fifteen years of extras, rarities, short stories, and unused art." (Publisher's note)

The **Couriers**. Brian Wood and Rob G. AiT/Planet Lar 2003 Un Illustration
Grades: 11 12 Adult   **741.5; Fic**
1. Adventure graphic novels; 2. Mystery graphic novels; 3. Graphic novels
1-932051-06-6, $12.95

The story is set in New York City, featuring Moustafa and Special: mercenary couriers. They do the work the normal couriers are only barely aware of: intelligence, large cash transfers, protection, assassinations, blockade-running ... you name it. But there is one job they always knew they would refuse, known as a biologic.? But when their latest package turns out to be a young deaf/mute girl from Nepal, with a gone-rogue Chinese Red Army Brigade hot on her heels, how can they NOT get involved? The book is full of action, with lots of harsh language (f-bombs and s-bombs all over the place) and graphic violence.

The **Couriers** 02: Dirtbike Manifesto. Brian Wood and Rob G. AiT/Planet Lar 2004 Un Illustration
Grades: 11 12 Adult   **741.5; Fic**
1. Adventure graphic novels; 2. Graphic novels
1-932051-18-X, $12.95

Sometimes Moustafa and Special, The Couriers, run guns. It's not the most admirable job in the world to take on, but they have rent to pay and ammo to buy, and M has acquired a rather expensive new hobby: building the ultimate motocross dirtbike from scratch. But their latest gig goes bad... all kinds of wrong... and it ticks them off. They head to upstate New York to track the guns to the source and to get a little vengeance and get P-A-I-D in the process. In those small New York towns, the slow economy has hit hard, the streets are dead on a weekend, and half the shops are boarded up. There are lots of angry people with too much time on their hands, and half of them own guns. They don't need two young arrogant punks from The City to roll into town like they own the place ... The book includes lots of harsh language with f-bombs and s-bombs flying all over, and lots of graphic violence.

The **Couriers** 03: The Ballad of Johnny Funwrecker. Brian Wood and Rob G. AiT/Planet Lar 2005 Un Illustration
Grades: 11 12 Adult   **741.5; Fic**
 1. Mystery graphic novels; 2. Graphic novels
 1932051-31-7, $12.95
Book Three in the Couriers saga hits the rewind button on the lives of everybody's two favorite urban mercenary couriers and goes back, way back, to 1993. Moustafa's a dirtbag grunge kid selling weed by the cube at Astor Place, and Special's a riot grrrl with a mean streak, looking to carve a place for herself in the criminal underworld. How do these two unlikely partners meet up and become the tight-knit team they are now? Meet Johnny Funwrecker, the hilarious larger-than-life Chinatown mob boss and role model for little street rat hooligans all over. The book contains lots of violence, drug dealing, very harsh language, and some nudity.

Couscous Express. AiT/Planet Lar 2001 Un Illustration
Grades: 10 11 12 Adult   **741.5; Fic**
 1. Mystery graphic novels; 2. Graphic novels
 1-9709360-2-8, $12.95
Scooter enthusiast and spoiled brat, Olive Yassin, delivers food for her parents' award-winning Middle Eastern restaurant, Couscous Express. She hates it. It's boring. She would much rather be hanging out with her courier-mercenary boyfriend, Moustafa. But when the local branch of the stylish and dangerous Turkish Scooter Mafia make a move against the restaurant, she knows she has to do something, anything, to protect her family. This book combines delicious food, automatic weapons fire, and scooter culture into an adrenaline-fueled story of love, family, war, and the best hummus recipe in New York City. Readers will find lots of harsh language and violence.

Demo, Second ed.. Written by Brian Wood; illustrated by Becky Cloonan; lettered by Ryan Yount. AiT/Planet Lar 2003 Un Illustration
Grades: 11 12 Adult   **741.5; Fic**
 1. Graphic novels
 1-932051-42-2, $19.95
This book collects the twelve issues of Demo, with twelve stories about young people coming to terms with particular powers they have. These are not necessarily superhero-type powers, but anyone who watched the television series Heroes, which debuted in 2006, will find these stories to be very much in line with what the series depicted. Strong language, some sexual situations, and violence will make this more appropriate for older readers.

DMZ. Brian Wood, Riccardo Burchielli. DC Comics 2012 137 p.
Grades: 11 12 Adult   **741.5**
 1. Manhattan (New York, NY) — Fiction; 2. Militia movements — Fiction; 3. Militia movements — United

States; 4. New York (NY) — Fiction; 5. Survival skills — Fiction
 1401234798; 9781401234799, $14.99
                                        LC 2012010317
This comic book by Brian Wood was a "New York Times" Bestseller. "As New York City starts the healing process, the political realities on the ground are impossible to ignore. Matty's seen to it that everyone's voice is being heard, but will the social order devolve into anarchy, or is there a new New York to be discovered somewhere underneath the rubble?" (Publisher's note)
Originally published in single magazine form in DMZ 67-72.

Supermarket. Written by Brian Wood; illustrated by Kristian. IDW Publishing 2006 102p. Illustration
Grades: 11 12 Adult   **741.5; Fic**
 1. Adventure graphic novels; 2. Organized crime; 3. Graphic novels
 978-1-600100-09-3, $17.99
In the future world of Supermarket, legitimate and black-market economies rule the City, overseen by the vying factions of the Yakuza and Porno Swede crime families. Convenience store clerk and sixteen-year old suburban wise-ass Pella Suzuki suddenly finds herself in the middle of it all, heir to an empire she couldn't possibly inherit, but hitmen on both sides aren't taking any chances. Pella's world is full of violence and harsh language.

Woodfin, Rupert
 Introducing Aristotle, New Edition. Rupert Woodfin & Judy Groves. Totem Books 2006 176p. Illustration
Grades: 10 11 12 Adult   **100; 741.5**
 1. Ancient philosophy; 2. Aristotle, 384-322 BC; 3. Graphic novels
 978-1-84046-759-8, $12.95
Aristotle was named the "master of those who know" He is a foundational thinker in every field of inquiry. He established logic as a systematic discipline, conceived the earliest rules of science, developed a rational psychology, a political science and an outline of sociology, and gave us a virtue theory of ethics that is still a model today. His contributions to metaphysics continue to permeate modern philosophy. He supplied the first theory of aesthetics, which still provides the basis of debates today. Aristotle's authority extended beyond his time to influence Islamic society and medieval scholasticism. For fifteen hundred years he remained the paradigm of knowledge itself, until scientific empiricism in the 17th century is said to have discredited his methods. Is this true" How 'scientific' is Aristotle? This volume uses cartoons and a spare text to introduce readers to Aristotle's philosophy; it includes a list of books for further reading.

Woodring, Jim
 Congress of the animals. Jim Woodring. Fantagraphics Books 2011 104 p. Illustration
Grades: Adult   **741.5**
 1. Adventure graphic novels; 2. Frank (Fictional character: Woodring); 3. Moving
 1606994379; 9781606994375, $19.99
                                        LC 2012289652

In this graphic novel, by Jim Woodring, "an act of casual rudeness sets into motion a chain of events which propels Frank into a world where he is on his own at last." The book depicts "Frank losing his house, taking a factory job, falling in with bad company, fleeing the results of sabotage, escaping the Unifactor in an amusement park ride, surviving a catastrophe at sea, traveling across hostile terrain toward a massive temple seemingly built in his image, . . . and intervening in an age-old battle." (Publisher's note)

Courtesy of Fantagraphics

Fran. Jim Woodring. Fantagraphics 2013 120 p. Illustration
Grades: Adult   **741.5**
  1. Animals; 2. Love stories
  1606996614;
  9781606996614, $19.99
  This graphic novel by Jim Woodring answers questions from its prequel, "Congress of the Animals" such as: "Would Frank become placid and domesticated" Would he be jilted? Would he turn out to be a dreadful cad? Would he become a downtrodden and exhausted paterfamilias staring vacantly into the dimming fire of life as obnoxious grandchildren pulled his peglike ears and stole his porridge?" (Publisher's note)

Courtesy of Fantagraphics

Wright, Edgar
  Shaun of the Dead. Adapted by Chris Ryall; penciled and inked by Zach Howard. Dark Horse Comics 2005 104p. Illustration
Grades: 10 11 12 Adult   **741.5; Fic**
  1. Graphic novels
  1-933239-43-3, $17.95
  This "director's cut" adaptation of the romantic zombie comedy - produced with the full participation of the movie's co-writer/director and co-writer/star, Edgar Wright and Simon Pegg - features deleted scenes and other never-before-seen material. This volume also contains movie storyboards, production stills, and additional bonus material courtesy of Edgar and Simon. The book features zombie violence and some strong language.

Yabuki, Kentaro
  Black Cat, Volume 1. Viz Media/Shonen Jump 2006 200p. Illustration

Grades: 10 11 12 Adult   **741.5; Fic**
  1. Adventure graphic novels; 2. Manga; 3. Shonen manga; 4. Graphic novels
  978-1-4215-0605-0, $7.99
  Translated by JN Productions. Train Heartnet, known as "Black Cat," worked as a top assassin for a secret organization called Chronos, but quit. Now he's a sweeper, a bounty hunter, partnered with the one-eyed Sven. Even as Train has to deal with assassins from his past, he and Sven go after wanted men for the bounties. Then beautiful thief Rinslet Walker proposes that they partner with her to take down a weapons smuggler who is developing dangerous new weapons. At first glance, Train's world is similar to ours, but science fictional elements such as nanotechnology and mystical elements of chi come into play as well. Sven seems to always have a cigarette in hand, and Train seems to always find someone he has to fight, but in the first four volumes there hasn't been any gratuitous cleavage or panty shots.

Yagami, Yu
  Hikkatsu! Strike a Blow to Vivify, vol. 1. Go! Comi 2007 196p. Illustration
Grades: 10 11 12 Adult   **741.5**
  1. Science fiction graphic novels; 2. Shonen manga; 3. Graphic novels
  978-1-933617-57-2, $10.99
  In the future, geomagnetic abnormalities make every day a struggle to survive. Static electricity storms are bad enough, but the human race faces its greatest threat from ordinary, everyday appliances that go on the blink. But Shota is mastering his Repair Blow technique so he can do more than just beat machines. The book includes some mild violence and harsh language.

Yagi, Norihiro
  Claymore Vol. 1. Viz Media/Shonen Jump Advanced 2006 188p. Illustration
Grades: 10 11 12 Adult   **741.5; Fic**
  1. Fantasy graphic novels; 2. Horror graphic novels; 3. Manga; 4. Shonen manga; 5. Graphic novels
  978-1-4215-0618-0, $7.99
  A Claymore - a female warrior named for the sword she carries - travels from medieval village to village to destroy Yoma, monsters who disguise themselves as humans and who are almost impossible to kill. Claymores are half-humans, half-demons who willingly transformed themselves by mixing their blood with monster's blood. Clare, nicknamed silver-eyed killer, is such a powerful Claymore, she can slay a Yoma using only one hand. But she must constantly struggle to keep from becoming a monster herself. The book includes a considerable amount of monster-slaying violence.

Yakin, Boaz
  ★ **Jerusalem:** A Family Portrait. Boaz Yakin; illustrated by Nick Beretozzi. First Second 2013 400 p.
Grades: Adult   **741.5**
  1. Brothers; 2. Jerusalem
  1596435755; 9781596435759, $24.99
  This comic "follows the families of two estranged Israeli brothersùfocusing primarily on the sons of those

brothersùas the many wars involving Jerusalem rage around them. They suffer life, death, and everything in between, all while searching for their own identities within a passionate love for the place they call home." (Publishers Weekly)

Yamashita, Matt

Ghostbusters: Ghost Busted. Stories by Nathan Johnson and Matt Yamashita ; art by Chrissy Delk et al. Tokyopop 2008 Un Illustration

Grades: 7 8 9 10 11 12 Adult   **741.5; Fic**

1. Fantasy graphic novels; 2. Ghosts; 3. Humorous graphic novels; 4. Graphic novels

978-1-4278-1459-3, $12.99

In the time since the Ghostbusters last saved New York City (as seen in the second film), the team finds itself pretty busy. A major producer hires Ray, Peter, and Egon to save his new lavish musical from destruction, which would ruin him. Then, the mayor's former right hand man returns, intent on getting revenge on all the Ghostbusters for ruining his reputation. Meanwhile, Peter, Ray, and Egon each disappear while out on individual calls, and now it's up to Winston to find and save them. This is a global manga and includes ghostly manifestations, ectoplasm, and ghostbusting action.

Yamazaki, Joe

Flame of Recca Volume 1. Viz Media 2003 184p. Illustration

Grades: 10 11 12 Adult   **Fic; 741.5**

1. Fantasy graphic novels; 2. Manga; 3. Martial arts; 4. Ninja; 5. Shonen manga; 6. Graphic novels

1-59116-066-9, $9.95

Teenager Recca Hanabishi is always up for a good-natured tussle with his friends. That's because he's famous at school and around town for being a super ninja geek. Armed with the power to control flame, Recca suddenly finds himself in an awkward situation. On the day he pledges his undying ninja allegiance to a pretty classmate named Yanagi Sakoshita, a mysterious older woman pops into his life. Is she good? Is she evil? What exactly does she want? And what's the deal with tomboy, Fuko Kirisawa? She's got the power of wind at her command. Does she want to smash Recca to smithereens, or does she simply want to kiss him? The series includes strong language, nudity, sexual innuendo, and graphic violence.

Volume 1 of 33

Yamazaki, Toru

Octopus Girl Vol. 1. Dark Horse Manga 2006 190p. Illustration

Grades: 12 Adult   **741.5; Fic**

1. Horror graphic novels; 2. Humorous graphic novels; 3. Manga; 4. Graphic novels

978-1-59307-540-8, $12.95

Good school girl Takako is horribly bullied by other students in school, including having her mouth stuffed with octopus (she's allergic). The next day, she wakes up to find she has mutated into a hybrid form, with a human head upon an octopus body; she decides to exact bloody revenge upon her tormenters. The book mixes sick, crass humor with gross-out violence and horror, nudity, and harsh language.

Yang, Gene Luen

★ Boxers. Gene Luen Yang; color by Lark Pien. First Second 2013 328 p.

Grades: 7 8 9 10 11 12 Adult   **741.5**

1. China — History — Boxer Rebellion, 1899-1901; 2. Historical fiction

1596433590; 9781596433595, $18.99

LC 2013947229

National Book Award for Young People's Literature: Finalist (2013)

Boston Globe-Horn Book Honor: Fiction (2014)

"Life in Little Bao's peaceful rural village is disrupted when . . . a priest and his phalanx of soldiers . . . arrive." They start "smashing the village god, appropriating property, and administering vicious beatings for no reason. Little Bao and his older brothers train in kung fu and swordplay." . . . Little Bao "becomes the leader of a peasant army, eventually marching to Beijing." (School Library Journal)

"China's Boxer Rebellion is the unlikely backdrop for this graphic treatment of young villagers on the opposite sides of history. Bao wants to drive out the white devils that poison his country with opium and Christianity. Four-Girl is an unwanted daughter who finds purpose in the missionary life. Their stories collide in a moment of grace that could only be penned by the Printz Award-winning author of 'American Born Chinese.'" LJ

★ Level up. First Second Books 2011 160p. Illustration

Grades: 10 11 12 Adult   **741.5; Fic**

1. Angels; 2. Bildungsromans; 3. Chinese Americans; 4. College students; 5. Graphic novels — Juvenile literature; 6. Young adult literature — Works; 7. Graphic novels

978-1-59643-235-2, $15.99

LC 2010-36257

"Pham's watercolor artwork, mostly in muted pallet, is a perfect match for Yang's story. This gentle tale of loss and redemption, family responsibility, and dreams might not be to all teens' tastes (especially by the end), but the mix of fantasy and realism will please the right crowd." Voice Youth Advocates

★ Saints. By Gene Luen Yang and Lark Pien. First Second 2013 170 p.

Grades: 7 8 9 10 11 12 Adult   **741.5**

1. China — History — Boxer Rebellion, 1899-1901; 2. Historical fiction

1596436891; 9781596436893, $15.99

LC 2013947228

National Book Award for Young People's Literature: Finalist (2013)

Boston Globe-Horn Book Honor: Fiction (2014)

This graphic novel, by Gene Luen Yang and Lark Pien, "follows a lonely girl . . . . Unwanted by her family, Four-Girl isn't even given a proper name until she converts to Catholicism and is baptized by the very same priest who bullies Little Bao's village. Four-Girl, now known as Vibiana, leaves home and finds fulfillment in service to the Church, while Little Bao roams the countryside committing acts of increasing violence as his army grows." (School Library Journal)

"Yang presents a 'diptych' of graphic novels set during China's Boxer Rebellion. Boxers follows Little Bao, who learns to harness the power of ancient gods to fight the spread of Christianity; Saints centers on Four-Girl, who sits squarely on the other side of the rebellion. Yang's characteristic infusions of magical realism, bursts of humor, and distinctively drawn characters make for a compelling read." (Horn Book)

Yazawa, Ai
 Nana, Volume One. Viz Media/Shojo Beat 2006 Un Illustration
Grades: 11 12 Adult   **741.5; Fic**
 1. Josei manga; 2. Manga; 3. Romance graphic novels; 4. Shojo manga; 5. Graphic novels
 978-1-4215-0108-6, $8.99
 Two young women, both named Nana, both the same age, but different in personalities, each want to move to Tokyo. Nana Komatsu is somewhat immature, and so far her life has revolved around men. Nana Osaki is a punk rock vocalist with an attitude to match; she wants to make her band a success. Nana K wants to be with her friends even if she failed all the college entrance exams; she also wants to become more self-reliant. The two Nanas meet on the train to Tokyo, then meet again when looking for an affordable apartment. The series includes considerable strong language and sexual situations.
 Volume 1 of 21

Yoon, Jae-ho
 In Dream World Vol. 1. Tokyopop 2005 198p. Illustration
Grades: 9 10 11 12 Adult   **741.5; Fic**
 1. Adventure graphic novels; 2. Fantasy graphic novels; 3. Manwha; 4. Graphic novels
 1-59532-516-6, $9.99
 Nightmares are bad enough when you are asleep, but in this land of dreams, Nightmares are real, physical monsters. Drake, Hanee and Kyle fight these Nightmares with "In Dream Cards," magical cards that have unusual and devastating powers. Those who wield the cards are masters of their elements. But just how did our heroes become entangled in this dream world? And what will it take to get home? The book includes violence and partial nudity.

Yoshida, Akira
 Conan and the Demons of Khitai. Writer, Akira Yoshida; artist, Paul Lee; letterers, Richard Starkings and Comicraft's Albert Deschesne; cover artist, Pat Lee and Dream Engine. Dark Horse Comics 2006 Un Illustration
Grades: 11 12 Adult   **741.5; Fic**
 1. Adventure graphic novels; 2. Conan the Barbarian (Fictional character); 3. Fantasy graphic novels; 4. Graphic novels
 978-1-59307-543-9, $12.95
 Set many years in the future from the ongoing series, this book marks Conan's first appearance as King in Dark Horse's comics revival of the legendary fantasy hero. When King Conan receives an invitation from the Eastern kingdom of Khitai to open trade in precious jewels and spices, he decides that he will travel into this long-mysterious land. Yet to do so is perilous, as those who have requested his company may have far more devious intentions, and beasts unseen by Western eyes lurk amidst the shadows. The book

contains graphic, bloody violence as men fight monstrous beasts.

 X-Men: Kitty Pryde - Shadow & Flame. Written by Akira Yoshida ; art by Paul Smith. Marvel Entertainment 2006 Un Illustration
Grades: 8 9 10 11 12 Adult   **741.5; Fic**
 1. Adventure graphic novels; 2. Superhero graphic novels; 3. X-Men (Fictional characters); 4. Graphic novels
 0-7851-1816-0, $14.99
 A deadly mystery draws Kitty Pryde and her fire-breathing friend Lockheed to the shores of Japan. Ninjas and dragons will be the least of their worries, however, as a long-forgotten villain from Kitty's past is about to finally make his move. There's lots of ninja fighting action.

Yoshida, Sunao
 Trinity Blood Vol. 1. Story by Sunao Yoshida; illustrated by Kiyo Kyujo. Tokyopop 2006 178p. Illustration
Grades: 10 11 12 Adult   **741.5; Fic**
 1. Fantasy graphic novels; 2. Horror graphic novels; 3. Manga; 4. Vampires; 5. Graphic novels
 1-59816-674-3, $9.99
 In a dark and distant future, Armageddon has giving rise to the fabled Second Moon—and a perpetual war between the vampires and the humans. Esther is a nun in the city of Istavan. When she crosses paths with Abel Nightroad, a priest sent from the Vatican to combat the local order of vampires, the two form a holy alliance to battle the most evil of threats: Gyula, the leader of the vampires. In this gothic-action series the very survival of the human race is at stake. The book includes some violence.

Yoshida, Tatsuo
 Speed Racer: Mach go go go vol. 1 & 2, 2v. Digital Manga Publishing 2008 Illustration
Grades: 7 8 9 10 11 12 Adult   **741.5; Fic**
 1. Adventure graphic novels; 2. Automobile racing; 3. Manga; 4. Graphic novels
 978-1-56970-731-9, set $39.95
 This two-volume set reprints the original Speed Racer manga in its entirety, released for the 40th anniversary of Speed Racer. All the characters are here: Speed, Pops, Sparky, Mom, Trixie, Spritle, Chim Chim, and the mysterious Racer X. Readers will learn how Pops had to set out on his own, how Speed became a professional racecar driver in order to help finance Pops design the special, 12 cylinder Mach 5 engine. In addition to racing, Speed has to deal with people who try to steal Pops' engine plans, rival racers who'll try any cheating tactic to win, and try to figure out who Racer X is. While the animated television series was fine for children to watch, this manga includes violent action that makes it more suitable for teen readers. A note about the title: in Japanese, "go" means "5."

Yoshinaga, Fumi
 Antique Bakery Vol. 1. Digital Manga Publishing 2005 192p. Illustration
Grades: 10 11 12 Adult   **Fic; 741.5**
 1. Humorous graphic novels; 2. Josei manga; 3. Manga; 4. Romance graphic novels; 5. Shojo manga; 6. Graphic novels

1-56970-946-7, $12.95

Three young men run a European style bakery and cafe in a former antique shop. Tachibana, the manager, and master pastry chef Ono are thirty-two years old and former high school classmates. Twenty-one-year-old Eiji is a boxer forced to retire because of eye injuries; he lives to eat fine pastries and has apprenticed himself to Ono. Ono is shy in the kitchen, but he's gay and seems to charm even straight men, except for Tachibana and Eiji. The stories revolve around their interactions in the bakery, and around some of their customers, in comedy that never degenerates into sitcom cliches. One scene showing Ono and a young man having sex doesn't show much graphically, yet it is perfectly clear what is happening. The books include lots of pointers about French pastries. This is a four-volume series.

★ **Ooku**: the inner chambers. Fumi Yoshinaga. Hakusensha 2005 205 p. Illustration
Grades: Adult   **741.5/952; 741.5**
1. Japan — History
1421527472; 9781421527475, $12.99
                                              LC 2009513893

This graphic novel, written and illustrated by Fumi Yoshinaga, is set "in Edo period Japan, [where] a strange new disease called the Red Pox has begun to prey on the country's men. . . . Women have taken on all the roles traditionally granted to men, even that of the Shogun. The men, precious providers of life, are carefully protected. And the most beautiful of the men are sent to serve in the Shogun's Inner Chamber." (Publisher's note)

Volume 1 of an ongoing series

What did you eat yesterday?; Volume 1. Fumi Yoshinaga. Vertical 2014 153 p. Illustration
Grades: Adult   **741.5**
1. Cooking, Japanese; 2. Dining — Fiction; 3. Gay men — Fiction; 4. Gay men — Japan — Tokyo; 5. Gourmets; 6. Manga; 7. Seinen manga; 8. Tokyo (Japan) — Fiction
1939130387; 9781939130389, $12.95
                                              LC 2012474656

"A hard-working middle-aged gay couple in Tokyo come to enjoy the finer moments of life through food. After long days at work, either in the law firm or the hair salon, Shiro and Kenji will always have down time together by the dinner table, where they can discuss their troubles, hash out their feelings and enjoy delicately prepared home cooked meals!" (Publisher's note)

"Yoshinaga draws characters with simple, clean realism, exaggerating faces amusingly for emotional moments. Yet the images of food are crafted in fine-line detail, making the ingredients and textures amazingly appetizing. Between episodes, the author provides brief recipes and cooking tips." LJ

Translated from the Japanese

Originally published as: Kinou nani tabeta? in Japan

Volume 1 of an ongoing series

Yoshizaki, Seimu
★ **Kingyo** used books, vol. 1. [translation, Adrienne Weber]. Viz Media/Viz Signature 2010 191p. Illustration
Grades: 9 10 11 12 Adult   **741.5; Fic**
1. Books and reading; 2. Manga; 3. Graphic novels
978-1-4215-3362-9, $12.99

Courtesy of VIZ Media LLC

This manga collects several stories based in or connected to Kingyo Used Books, a used manga store in Tokyo. An art student finds inspiration in a manga series based on the life of the famous artist Hokusai; a silly gag manga helps an archer regain his focus in time for a match; a young Japanese man raised in the U.S. uses an old detective manga series from the 1950s to model his life; the manga store owner's son tries to get away from manga by living in Europe, where he discovers that comics are everywhere; a busy housewife rekindles the passion in her life when she rediscovers a shojo manga featuring a dreamy male protagonist. While there is no violence or bad language, all the main characters are adults.

Young, Ethan
Nanjing: the burning city. By Ethan Young. Dark Horse Books 2015 216 p. Plate; Illustration
Grades: Adult   **741.5; 951.04/2**
1. Nanjing (Jiangsu Province, China) massacre, 1937; 2. Nanjing, Battle of, Nanjing, Jiangsu Sheng, China, 1937; 3. Nanjing, Battle of, Nanjing, Jiangsu Sheng, China, 1937 — Juvenile literature; 4. Sino-Japanese Conflict, 1937-1945; 5. Graphic novels
9781616557522, $24.99
                                              LC 2015008366

In this graphic novel, by Ethan Young, "After the bombs fell and shook the walls of Nanjing, the Imperial Japanese Army entered and seized the Chinese capital. Through the dust of the demolished buildings, screams echo off the rubble. Two abandoned Chinese soldiers are trapped and desperately out numbered inside the walled city. What they'll encounter will haunt them. But in the face of horror, they'll learn that resistance and bravery cannot be destroyed by the enemy." (Publisher's note)

Tails : Book 1. Ethan Young. Hermes Press 2012 160 p.
Grades: 10 11 12 Adult   **Fic; 741**
1. Artists; 2. Superhero comic books, strips, etc
161345015X; 9781613450154, $15.99
                                              LC 2012934894

Ethan may seem like your typical struggling cartoonist. The trouble is, Ethan's just too hapless to realize it yet. As his life gets weirder in the real world, it also does on the comic page. Before he knows it, Ethan gets in over his head when fantasy and reality combine—and then things get really weird.

Young, Larry
Astronauts in Trouble: Master Flight Plan. AiT/Planet Lar 2003 Un Illustration
Grades: 9 10 11 12 Adult   **741.5; Fic**
1. Science fiction graphic novels; 2. Graphic novels
1-932051-16-3, $16.95

"Live from the Moon" launches fifty years after Armstrong's one small step. The world's richest man claims the moon as his own personal property... and Channel Seven is there! "Space: 1959" is a period adventure featuring an earlier generation of the Channel Seven newshounds from "Live from the Moon." They uncover the story of Col. Lloyd Macadam's top-secret moon-shot program. Macadam's plans are accelerated when a Russian spy commandeers the rocket and the Colonel must choose between his country and his life. "One Shot, One Beer" picks up ten years after the events of "Live from the Moon" where space jockeys relate tales of life on Earth's desolate sister, far from home. The stories portray lots of action.

Young-Oh, Kim

Banya: The Explosive Delivery Man Vol. 1. Dark Horse Comics 2006 Un Illustration
Grades: 10 11 12 Adult   **741.5; Fic**
1. Adventure graphic novels; 2. Fantasy graphic novels; 3. Manwha; 4. Graphic novels
978-1-59307-614-6, $12.95

With a worldwide war raging between humans and monsters, the young delivery men of the Gaya Desert Post Office do not pledge allegiance to any country or king. They are banded together by a pledge to deliver. "Fast. Precise. Secure." Banya, the craziest and craftiest of the bunch, will stop at nothing to get a job done. Known as the "Explosive Delivery Man" for his risk taking, bold resolve, and impeccable record, Banya agrees to complete a wounded soldier's mission to transport a parcel of great importance - not knowing what dangers lie in store for him and his friends. As their arduous journey begins, Banya promises, "There isn't a delivery I can't make. I always deliver." Kim Young-Oh's fantastical world is filled with unique monsters, vicious swordplay, and a dash of hotfooted humor.

Yukimura, Makoto

Planetes Omnibus 1. By Makoto Yukimura. Random House Inc 2015 528 p.
Grades: 10 11 12 Adult
1. Outer space — Exploration — Fiction; 2. Science fiction graphic novels; 3. Space colonies — Fiction; 4. Space debris — Fiction
1616559217; 9781616559212, $19.99

In this book, by Makoto Yukimura, "It's the 2070s, and mankind has conquered space, making interplanetary travel possible and igniting the imaginations of the world. It's also vastly increased the amount of dangerous space debris, and someone has to clean it up. Hachimaki, Yuri, and Fee are a crew on that beat, each with their own goals, tendencies, and personal problems." (Publisher's note)
Originally published in the U.S. by Tokyopop in 4 volumes
Volume 1 of 2

Vinland Saga; Volume 1. Makoto Yukimura; translation, Stephen Paul; lettering, Scott O. Brown; editing, Ben Applegate. Kodansha 2013 467 p. Illustration; Map
Grades: Adult   **741.5; Fic**
1. Canute I, King of England, 995?-1035; 2. Great Britain — History — Anglo-Saxon period, 449-1066; 3. Historical fiction; 4. Revenge; 5. Seinen; 6. Þorfinnur

Karlsefni, active 10th-11th century; 7. Vikings; 8. Vikings — Fiction
9781612624204, $19.99; 1612624200
LC 2014430279

In this graphic novel, by Makoto Yukimura, "as a child, Thorfinn sat at the feet of the great Leif Ericson and thrilled to wild tales of a land far to the west. . . . Raised by the Vikings who murdered his family, Thorfinn became a terrifying warrior, forever seeking to kill the band's leader, Askeladd, and avenge his father." (Publisher's note)
Volume 1 of an ongoing series

Yun, Mi-Kyung

Bride of the water god, vol. 1. Dark Horse Comics 2007 186p. Illustration
Grades: 8 9 10 11 12 Adult   **741.5**
1. Fantasy graphic novels; 2. Romance graphic novels; 3. Graphic novels
978-1-59307-849-2, $9.95

Soah's impoverished, drought-stricken village sacrifices her to the Water God Habaek in hopes of getting rain. Instead of dying, Soah finds herself in the land of the gods, and she meets Habaek, who is a young boy. What she doesn't know (but the reader does) is that he takes the form of an adult man at night. She's supposed to be Habaek's bride, but so far she's just an outsider who doesn't belong anywhere. This is sunjeong manwha the Korean equivalent of shojo manga.

Yune, Tommy

Speed Racer & Racer X: the origins collection. Art by Jo Chen. IDW Publishing 2008 Un Illustration
Grades: 8 9 10 11 12 Adult   **741.5; Fic**
1. Adventure graphic novels; 2. Automobile racing; 3. Racer, Speed (Fictional character); 4. Speed Racer (Fictional character); 5. Graphic novels
978-1-60010-211-0, $19.99

In 1999, Wildstorm Productions relaunched Speed Racer with a three-part origins story; it was successful enough to launch another three-part story telling the origins of Speed's brother, Racer X (come on, it's not a spoiler, everyone but the Racer family knows this). IDW Publishing has collected the stories into this volume. Here is the story of how Speed becomes the driver of the Mach 5, designed by Pops Racer, and here is the story of why Rex Racer left the family, how he "died," and Racer X was born from the wreckage. There is a lot of racing action, some violence, and some mild fan service.

Yurkovich, David

Less Than Heroes. Top Shelf Productions 2004 152p. Illustration
Grades: 10 11 12 Adult   **741.5; Fic**
1. Superhero graphic novels; 2. Graphic novels
1-891830-51-1, $14.95

In the city of Philadelphia there is a tall building at 18th and Market Streets atop of which live four individuals. They are the official protectors of the city. Their job is to be around when traditional law enforcement fails. But are they really heroes" Meet Philadelphia's contracted super-hero team, Threshold. A quartet more interested in milk and cookies than crime and punishment. A team more concerned with battling indigestion than their arch enemies. Sure, they have super-powers. They can leap tall buildings, fly, and do all the stuff other heroes do. More than human? Probably. Less than heroes? Without a doubt. While there's little in the way of overt violence or strong language, the story itself has more appeal to mature readers.

Zahler, Thomas F.
★ **Love** and capes, vol. 1: do you want to know a secret?. Story and art by Thomas F. Zahler. IDW Publishing 2008 160p. Illustration
Grades: 8 9 10 11 12 Adult   **Fic; 741.5**
   1. Humorous graphic novels; 2. Romance graphic novels; 3. Superhero graphic novels; 4. Graphic novels
978-1-60010-275-2, $19.99
Independent bookseller Abby falls in love with her accountant, Mark; then he confesses to her that he's the superpowered crime-fighter, the Crusader. How does one have a romantic relationship with a superhero? Even without meaning to do it, Abby gives away Mark's secret to her sister Charlotte. Oops. So begins a "heroically super situation comedy" in which Abby feels she's competing against the beautiful Amazonia (Mark's superpowered ex-girlfriend), not to mention Mark's over-protective mother, and Mark has to deal with Abby's obnoxious brother Quincy, who thinks Mark is a wimp.
Volume 1 of 4

★ **Love** and capes, vol. 2: going to the chapel. IDW Publishing 2010 192p. Illustration
Grades: 8 9 10 11 12 Adult   **741.5; Fic**
   1. Humorous graphic novels; 2. Romance graphic novels; 3. Superhero graphic novels; 4. Graphic novels
978-1-60010-680-4, $19.99
Independent bookstore owner Abby and accountant Mark Spencer, who is also the superhero called the Crusader, have fallen deeply and completely in love. Which is wonderful, except Mark can't quite seem to figure out how to propose to Abby and almost blows it. When he gets over that hurdle, more problems crop up. For one thing, Abby wants the PERFECT wedding dress. Then, a super villain impersonates Mark and almost destroys their relationship. Abby has to find a new bookstore employee when her sister Charlotte gets the chance to go back to college in Paris. France. Abby decides she needs to understand what Mark goes through as a superhero, and she gets superpowers, and a new identity, only to learn that it's far more difficult, and tragic, than she ever imagined. And then, on the eve of the wedding, another super villain strikes, this time changing history, and only Abby has the power to put things right again, which she'll have to do if she wants to marry Mark. This story has superhero action, romance, comedy, drama, romance ... the only content that might bother some people happens when Abby and Amazonia, Mark's superhero ex-girlfriend, get drunk and bond together.

Zimmerman, Dwight Jon
   The **hammer** and the anvil: Frederick Douglass, Abraham Lincoln, and the end of slavery in America. Dwight Jon Zimmerman; illustrated by Wayne Vansant; foreword by James M. McPherson; editorial consultant, Craig Symonds. Hill and Wang 2012 Ix, 150 p. Color illustration; Color; Map

Grades: 10 11 12 Adult   **B; 973.7092/2; 973.7092**
   1. Abolitionists — Biography; 2. African American abolitionists — Biography; 3. Antislavery movements — United States — History — 19th century; 4. Douglass, Frederick, 1818-1895; 5. Lincoln, Abraham, 1809-1865; 6. Presidents — United States — Biography; 7. Presidents — United States — Biography
0809053586; 9780809053582, $24.95; 9780809053599, $15.95; 0809053594
                  LC 2011032361
   This book presents a "graphic biography" of "Abraham Lincoln and Frederick Douglass. For both men, the book . . . show[s] the challenges that they faced as children, their efforts to overcome difficult circumstances, and the very real impact both men had on shaping the social and political consciousness of their times. It draws parallels between the humble circumstances of their early years . . . [and] look[s] at the difficulties both men faced and what motivated them." (Publishers Weekly)
   Includes bibliographical references.
   A novel graphic from Hill and Wang.

Zinn, Howard
   A **people's** history of American empire: a graphic adaptation. By Howard Zinn, Mike Konopacki, and Paul Buhle. Henry Holt and Company/Metropolitan Books 2008 275p.
Grades: 10 11 12 Adult   **973; 741.5**
   1. College teachers; 2. Historians; 3. Nonfiction writers; 4. Social activists; 5. United States — Foreign relations; 6. United States — History; 7. United States — History; 8. United States — Territorial expansion; 9. Zinn, Howard, 1922-2010 — Adaptations; 10. Graphic novels
978-0-8050-7779-7, $30; 978-0-8050-8744-4 (pa), $17
                  LC 2007-31150
   First published in 1980, A People's History of the United States triggered a revolution in the way history is told, chronicling events as they were lived, from the bottom up. Now Howard Zinn, historian Paul Buhle, and cartoonist Mike Konopacki have collaborated to retell a chapter of A People's History: the centuries-long story of America's actions in the world. Narrated by Zinn, this version opens with the events of 9/11 and then jumps back to explore the cycles of U.S. expansionism from Wounded Knee to Iraq, stopping along the way at World War I, Central America, Vietnam, and the Iranian revolution. The book also follows the story of Zinn, the son of poor Jewish immigrants, from his childhood in the Brooklyn slums to his role as one of America's leading historians. The Civil Rights Movement is also included. The book includes images of violence, both in photographs and drawn art.

Zinsmeister, Karl
   Combat Zone: True Tales of GIs in Iraq. Marvel Entertainment 2005 Un Illustration
Grades: 9 10 11 12 Adult   **Fic; 741.5**
   1. Iraq War, 2003-; 2. Graphic novels
0-7851-1516-1, $19.99
   Longtime embedded journalist Karl Zinsmeister (Boots on the Ground: A Month with the 82nd Airborne in the Battle for Iraq) and penciler Dan Jurgens (Thor, Superman)

chronicle three months in the lives of the 82nd Airborne in the Battle for Iraq in this series. As Zinsmeister states in his introduction, the stories are all based on real-life accounts; he changed the names of the soldiers and in some cases combined some of the incidents. The book includes battlefield violence and some mildly strong language.

Zograf, Aleksandar

Regards from Serbia: A Cartoonist's Diary of a Crisis in Serbia. Top Shelf Productions 2007 Un Illustration
Grades: 10 11 12 Adult
741.5
1. Autobiographical graphic novels; 2. War; 3. Graphic novels
978-1-891830-42-6, $19.95

Courtesy of Top Shelf Productions

Serbian cartoonist Zograf used diary comics and email to reach out to other cartoonists when NATO bombs started falling on his town, Pancero, in 1999. This book collects those comics and emails, along with Zograf's earlier comics from the early 1990s, to give readers a local view of what to most Americans was a distant conflict.

Zub, Jim

★ **Skullkickers:** 1000 Opas and a dead body. Writer/creator, Jim Zub; line art, Edwin Huang and Chris Stevens; colors, Misty Coates and Chris Stevens. Image Comics 2011 Un Illustration
Grades: 9 10 11 12 Adult   Fic; 741.5
1. Adventure graphic novels; 2. Fantasy graphic novels; 3. Humorous graphic novels; 4. Graphic novels
978-1-60706-366-7, $9.99
First published in magazine form as Skullkickers #1-5
Volume 1 of 6

Author Index

Title Index

Subject Index

AESOP'S FABLES — ADAPTATIONS

AFRICA — FICTION

AFRICA — HISTORY

AFRICAN AMERICAN ABOLITIONISTS — BIOGRAPHY

AFRICAN AMERICAN AGRICULTURISTS — BIOGRAPHY — JUVENILE LITERATURE

AFRICAN AMERICAN ATHLETES

AFRICAN AMERICAN CIVIL RIGHTS WORKERS

AFRICAN AMERICAN EDUCATORS — BIOGRAPHY — JUVENILE LITERATURE

AFRICAN AMERICAN EXPLORERS — BIOGRAPHY

AFRICAN AMERICAN INVENTORS

AFRICAN AMERICAN LEGISLATORS

AFRICAN AMERICAN SCIENTISTS — BIOGRAPHY — JUVENILE LITERATURE

AFRICAN AMERICAN SOLDIERS

AFRICAN AMERICAN WOMEN

AFRICAN AMERICAN WOMEN — ALABAMA — MONTGOMERY — BIOGRAPHY

AFRICAN AMERICAN WOMEN — BIOGRAPHY

AFRICAN AMERICANS

AFRICAN AMERICANS — BIOGRAPHY

AFRICAN AMERICANS — BIOGRAPHY — JUVENILE LITERATURE

AFRICAN AMERICANS — CIVIL RIGHTS

AUTHORS — BIOGRAPHY

AUTHORSHIP

AUTHORSHIP — FICTION

AUTISM

AUTOBIOGRAPHICAL COMIC BOOKS, STRIPS, ETC

AUTOBIOGRAPHICAL GRAPHIC NOVELS

BATTLES — FICTION

BATWOMAN (FICTIONAL CHARACTER)

BAUM, L FRANK, 1856-1919

BEARDS — FICTION

BEARS

BEAST (FICTIONAL CHARACTER)

BEAT GENERATION

BEATLES

BEAUTY, PERSONAL — FICTION

BEAVERS — FICTION

BECHDEL, ALISON, 1960-

BEDTIME

Nordling, Lee. BirdCatDog: a graphic novel, 111
Pearson, Luke. Hilda and the Black Hound, 119, 347
Robbins, Trina. The big flush, 131

DOGS — JUVENILE FICTION
Weing, Drew. Flop to the Top!, 32

DOGS — WAR USE — FICTION
Keenan, Sheila. Dogs of war, 83, 293

DONALD DUCK (FICTIONAL CHARACTER)
Vitaliano, Fausto. Donald Duck and friends: double
duck, 167, 418

DONKEYS
Guibert, Emmanuel. Ariol: Happy as a pig, 59

DONNER PARTY
Hale, Nathan. Donner dinner party, 61, 260

DOOM PATROL (FICTIONAL CHARACTER)
Morrison, Grant. Doom Patrol Volume 4: Musclebound,
674, 1038
Morrison, Grant. Doom Patrol Book 5: Magic Bus, 673,
1038

DOORS — FICTION
Kibuishi, Kazu. Explorer: the hidden doors, 296

DOUGLASS, FREDERICK, 1818-1895
Zimmerman, Dwight Jon. The hammer and the anvil:
Frederick Douglass, Abraham Lincoln, and the end
of slavery in America, 837, 1167

DOYLE, ARTHUR CONAN SIR, 1859-1930
Cosson, M. J.. Sherlock Holmes and a scandal in
Bohemia, 27, 216
Goodwin, Vincent. Sir Arthur Conan Doyle's, The
adventure of the empty house, 53, 249, 550
Goodwin, Vincent. Sir Arthur Conan Doyle's The
adventure of the speckled band, 52, 248, 549
Goodwin, Vincent. Sir Arthur Conan Doyle's The
adventure of the Red-Headed League, 52, 248, 549
Goodwin, Vincent. Sir Arthur Conan Doyle's, The
adventure of the dancing men, 52, 248, 550
Goodwin, Vincent. Sir Arthur Conan Doyle's, The
adventure of the Abbey Grange, 52, 248, 549
Shaw, Murray. Sherlock Holmes and the adventure of
the blue gem, 141, 375

**DOYLE, ARTHUR CONAN SIR, 1859-1930 —
ADAPTATIONS**
Cosson, M. J.. Sherlock Holmes and a scandal in
Bohemia, 27, 216
Goodwin, Vincent. Sir Arthur Conan Doyle's, The
adventure of the empty house, 53, 249, 550
Goodwin, Vincent. Sir Arthur Conan Doyle's The
adventure of the speckled band, 52, 248, 549
Goodwin, Vincent. Sir Arthur Conan Doyle's The
adventure of the Red-Headed League, 52, 248, 549
Goodwin, Vincent. Sir Arthur Conan Doyle's, The
adventure of the dancing men, 52, 248, 550
Goodwin, Vincent. Sir Arthur Conan Doyle's, The
adventure of the Abbey Grange, 52, 248, 549

Shaw, Murray. Sherlock Holmes and the adventure of
the blue gem, 141, 375
Goodwin, Vincent. Sir Arthur Conan Doyle's The
adventure of the blue carbuncle, 51

DRACULA, COUNT (FICTIONAL CHARACTER)
Williamson, Joshua. Dear Dracula, 173
Bar-el, Dan. That one spooky night, 11
Gelev, Penko. Bram Stoker's Dracula, 151, 392, 768
Nickel, Scott. Buzz Beaker vs Dracula, 109, 332
Williamson, Joshua. Dear Dracula, 173

DRAGONS
Aguirre, Jorge. Dragons beware!, 3
Alice, A. (Alex). Siegfried 1; 1, 180, 439
Deutsch, Barry. Hereville: how Mirka got her sword, 35,
226
Thompson, Jill. Magic Trixie and the dragon, 159

DRAGONS — FICTION
Rioux, Jo-Anne. The golden twine; Book 1, 131, 361
Weigel, Jeff. Dragon Girl: The Secret Valley, 169, 420

DRAMA
Earle-Bridges, Michele. Picture This! Shakespeare:
Julius Caesar Teacher's Resource Book, 232, 518
Earle-Bridges, Michele. Picture This! Shakespeare:
Hamlet Teacher's Resource Book, 232, 517
Page, Philip. Picture This! Shakespeare: A Midsummer
Night's Dream, 345, 698
Page, Philip. Picture This! Shakespeare: Twelfth Night
Teacher's Resource Book, 345, 699

DRAMATISTS
Appignanesi, Richard. Picture This! Shakespeare:
Romeo and Juliet, 345, 699
Appignanesi, Richard. Hamlet, 185, 448, 849
Appignanesi, Richard. A midsummer night's dream,
185, 448
Appignanesi, Richard. The tempest, 185
Beaulieu, Jean Francios. The Wonderful Wizard of Oz,
4, 13, 181, 195, 859
Belanger, Andy. Kill Shakespeare, vol. 1: a sea of
troubles, 650, 1015
Carre, Lilli. The fir-tree, 23, 208, 882
Conner, Daniel. The graphic canon, volume 2: from
Kubla Khan to the Bronte sisters to The picture of
Dorian Gray, 553
Eisner, Will. The Last Knight: An Introduction to Don
Quixote, 41, 233, 519
Hinds, Gareth. The merchant of Venice: a play, 270,
576, 957
Maeda, Mahiro. Gankutsuou: the Count of Monte
Cristo, vol., 642, 1008
McDonald, John. Henry V: the graphic novel: original
text version, 320, 651, 1016
Morvan, Jean David. Classics illustrated deluxe #6: the
three Musketeers, 107, 328, 675, 1040
Robinson, Alex. A kidnapped Santa Claus, 132, 362,
724
Shakespeare, William. William Shakespeare's King
Lear, 140, 374, 744, 1094

GRAPHIC NOVELS — AUTHORSHIP

GRAPHIC NOVELS — BELGIUM

GRAPHIC NOVELS — BIBLIOGRAPHY

GRAPHIC NOVELS — COTE D'IVOIRE

GRAPHIC NOVELS — DICTIONARIES

GRAPHIC NOVELS — DRAWING

HUMOROUS STORIES

HUNDRED YEARS' WAR, 1339-1453

HUNTING

HUNTRESS (FICTIONAL CHARACTER)

HURRICANE KATRINA, 2005

HURRICANES

HURRICANES — JUVENILE LITERATURE

SCIENCE FICTION WRITERS

SHONEN MANGA

SHONEN-AI MANGA

SHOPLIFTING

SHORT STORIES

SUPERHEROES

SURFING

SURGEONS

SURVIVAL

SURVIVAL — FICTION

SURVIVAL AFTER AIRPLANE ACCIDENTS, SHIPWRECKS, ETC

SURVIVAL SKILLS — FICTION

SUSHI

SUSPENSE FICTION

SUSPENSE GRAPHIC NOVELS

ZOMBIES — FICTION